D0820596

HarperCollins

READER'S
ENCYCLOPEDIA
of
AMERICAN
LITERATURE

2ND EDITION

HarperCollins

READER'S ENCYCLOPEDIA

of

AMERICAN LITERATURE

2ND EDITION

(Previously published as *Benét's Reader's Encyclopedia® of American Literature*)

Edited by

GEORGE PERKINS, BARBARA PERKINS, AND PHILLIP LEININGER

HarperResource
An Imprint of HarperCollins*Publishers*

PORTIONS OF THIS BOOK APPEARED IN A SOMEWHAT MODIFIED FORM IN THE READER'S ENCYCLOPEDIA OF AMERICAN LITERATURE PUBLISHED BY T.Y. CROWELL IN 1962 AND IN BENÉT'S READER'S ENCYCLOPEDIA, THIRD EDITION, PUBLISHED BY HARPER & ROW IN 1987.

Originally published in hardcover by HarperCollins in 1991 under the title BENÉT'S READER'S ENCYCLOPEDIA® OF AMERICAN LITERATURE.

SECOND EDITION

Designed by Fritz Metsch

Library of Congress Cataloging-in-Publication Data has been applied for.

ISBN 006019815X

02   03   04   05   06   RRD   10   9   8   7   6   5   4   3   2   1

PREFACE

In this edition, we have aimed to continue the primacy of *The Reader's Encyclopedia of American Literature* among comprehensive single-volume reference books in its field. Most recently revised in 1991 by the present editors and Phillip Leininger as *Benét's Reader's Encyclopedia of American Literature*, the book first appeared in 1962 under the editorship of Max J. Herzberg. Bringing it up to date, we have reclaimed its original name and have thoroughly revised it to reflect the changes affecting American literature at the start of the 21st century.

The coverage is from the beginnings of European exploration and the earliest Native American oral records to the latest writers, books, and trends at the beginning of the new millennium. Emphasizing the United States and the English language, we have also paid attention to the literatures of Canada, Mexico, Central and South America and the Caribbean, and to writers in French, Spanish, and Portuguese.

Alphabetized under "H," a History of American Literature forms the skeletal framework fleshed out in the rest of the book. Similar broad overviews appear under the headings Canadian Literature in English, Canadian Literature in French, and Latin American Literature. Globalization of American Literature, an entry new to this edition, addresses a recent phenomenon that is changing radically the ways the literature of the United States can be construed. The general History entry concludes with a list of cross-references to supplementary essays ranging from Afro-American Literature and Asian-American Literature through Feminism, Humor, and Native American Literature to Science Fiction and The South.

The bulk of the book consists of entries on authors, titles, characters, literary genres, periodicals, groups and movements, and historical persons and events directly related to literature. The social, political, religious, and philosophical backgrounds of American literature are treated in entries on presidents, political figures, and military personnel who have figured prominently in literature or themselves contributed to it. Many American military actions are given separate entries, as are documents such as the Mayflower Compact, the Declaration of Independence, the Federalist Papers, and the Constitution. American Indian tribes receive coverage along with individual entries on Native American writers. There are entries on Puritanism, Congregationalism,

Methodism, and other religious groups, and on spiritual and philosophic topics such as Deism, the Great Awakening, and Transcendentalism. Entries on social experiments range from Brook Farm to the Federal Writers Project.

Topics have been selected and space allotted to give due respect to the past, to the changing critical attitudes of our time, to the increases in contributions by women and ethnic minorities in the years since the mid-20th century, and to the literature of a larger worldview brought to North America by the changing patterns of immigration as the century approached its close. Major writers and trends receive more space than those whose place in literary history seems less significant. As far as is possible, the entry for each author includes biographical information, discussion of major works, and lists of lesser writings. Many entries also list biographical and critical works.

All unsigned entries new to this edition are the work of George and Barbara Perkins, who have also checked for accuracy all unsigned entries from previous editions, revising where necessary. Signed entries were written by the more than 130 scholars listed as contributors. In instances where a signed entry has been updated by someone else, the name of the original writer is followed by either the name or the initials of the reviser—for example, for Hemingway, "Philip Young/GP."

American literary scholarship has been diminished by the recent passing of our friend and colleague Phillip Leininger. His contribution to this edition was limited to advice on its scope and shape, and the book continues to profit from his solid earlier work. Among many others who shared their thoughts with us, we are especially thankful to Henry Taylor, whose careful reading of the previous edition suggested many emendations and additions in this new one, and to Lisa Samuel, whose advice on poetry and poets proved especially valuable. We are grateful to Greg Chaput of Harper-Collins for shepherding the book through the press and to our agent, Michael Valentino of Cambridge Literary Associates, for his painstaking contract negotiations. We take final responsibility for the contents.

GEORGE PERKINS
BARBARA PERKINS

CONTRIBUTORS

Gay Wilson Allen
Quentin Anderson
George Warren Arms
Robert Atwan
Steven Gould Axelrod
Milton J. Bates
Harold Beaver
Bert Bender
John Bensko
Normand Berlin
Neil K. Besner
Jean Frantz Blackall
Mutlu Konuk Blasing
Cleanth Brooks
John Burt
Ronald Bush
Francelia Butler
Oscar Cargill
Dennis Carroll
Hayden Carruth
Neil Carson
Franklin D. Case
Robert L. Caserio
Jules Chametzky
King-Kok Cheung
Paul Christensen
Samuel Coale
Ruby Cohn
Marcel Cornis-Pope
Richard Crowder
Selwyn R. Cudjoe
Michael Davidson
Sharon L. Dean
George Dekker

Rachel Blau DuPlessis
Wallace B. Eberhard
Jim Elledge
Everett Emerson
Mark A. R. Facknitz
Ellen G. Friedman
Norman Friedman
John Gassner
David Geherin
Roger Gilbert
Lewis L. Gould
Donald J. Greiner
M. E. Grenander
John Edward Hardy
Charles B. Harris
William J. Harris
Ramon J. Hathorn
David Havird
Howard W. Hintz
Molly Hite
Alan Holder
Margaret Holly
M. Thomas Inge
Frederick R. Karl
W. J. Keith
Carl F. Klinck
Ira Konigsberg
John Kuehl
Linda Kuehl
Earle Labor
Lewis Leary
David Adams Leeming
Ernest E. Leisy
Naomi Lindstrom

Richard C. Lyon
Thomas O. Mabbott
Lucinda H. MacKethan
Paul Mariani
Frederick T. McGill, Jr.
Frank McHugh
Nellie Y. McKay
David Harry Miller
Charles Molesworth
Frank Luther Mott
Elsa Nettels
William Van O'Connor
Patrick O'Donnell
Thomas Parkinson
Donald E. Pease, Jr.
Suzanne Perkins-Hart
Alice Hall Petry
James Phelan
Ellen Pifer
Sanford Pinsker
Louise Pound
Nancy Sorkin Rabinowitz
Peter J. Rabinowitz
Arnold Rampersad
Paul W. Rea
John M. Reilly
Russell J. Reising
David S. Reynolds
David Henry Richter
Joseph W. Ridgely
Julie Rivkin
Karen E. Rowe
Glenn R. Ruihley
A. LaVonne Brown Ruoff

Robert Sattelmeyer
William W. Savage, Jr.
Daniel R. Schwarz
Philip A. Shelley
Alan Shucard
Sam Smiley
Annette Smith
Charlotte Spivack
R. W. Stallman
David Stouk
W. J. Stuckey
Guy Sylvestre
Leona Toker
Neal L. Tolchin
Kim Townsend
Thomas J. Travisano
David Van Leer
Linda Wagner-Martin
Charles C. Walcutt
Melissa Walker
Robyn R. Warhol
Regina Weinreich
Robert Weisbuch
Herbert Faulkner West
Ray B. West, Jr.
Alan Williamson
Raymond J. Wilson III
Sharon R. Wilson
Cynthia Griffin Wolff
James Woodress
Dudley Wynn
Philip Young
Robert Zaller

NOTES

Cross-references appear in SMALL CAPITALS.

Authors with pen names are listed under the name by which they are best known. Brackets set off parts of authors' names not commonly used.

Titles beginning with "The" are found under the first significant word (e.g., **Huckleberry Finn, The Adventures of**).

In the text of an entry, foreign language titles are generally given in the original form, followed by a translation if the work has been published in English.

Dates cited for nondramatic literary works are those of first publication, unless otherwise indicated. Dates of plays are those of first performance, when known; otherwise, the dates of first printing.

Common abbreviations include:

c. circa, about	**q.v.** quod vide, which see
ed. edited, editor, edition	**repr.** reprinted
eds. editors	**rev.** revised
fl. flourit, flourished	**tr.** translated, translation
prod. produced	**v.** volume
pub. published	

A

Abbey, Edward (1927–1989), novelist, nature writer, memoirist. Born in Indiana, Pennsylvania, Abbey grew up in nearby Home, served briefly in the military, attended several universities, and graduated from the University of New Mexico. He wrote of American desert and wilderness areas, extolling their beauty and lamenting the destruction wrought by humans. Early novels, including *The Brave Cowboy* (1956) and *Fire on the Mountain* (1962), stressed western themes, and he later gained great popularity with another novel, *The Monkey Wrench Gang* (1975), about a group that sabotages ecologically destructive industries. *Fool's Progress* (1988) continues the exploits of the Monkey Wrench Gang. He based *Desert Solitaire* (1968), nonfiction, on his work as a park ranger at Arches National Monument in Utah, and derived the bulk of his work thereafter from personal experience: books include *Appalachian Wilderness* (1970), about the western Pennsylvania of his youth; *Cactus Country* (1973), an illustrated coffee-table book; *The Journey Home* (1977); *Abbey's Road* (1979); and *Down the River with Henry David Thoreau and Friends* (1982). *Beyond the Wall* (1984) and *One Life at a Time, Please* (1988) are essay collections. See also *Slumgullion Stew: A Reader* (1985, reprinted as *The Best of Edward Abbey*, 1988) and *The Serpents of Paradise: A Reader* (1995).

Abbey, Henry (1842–1911), businessman, poet. Abbey wrote simple, mostly didactic verse. His first collection was *May Dreams* (1862); others are *Ballads of Good Deeds* (1872), *Poems* (1879), and *Dream of Love* (1910). His most memorable poem begins: "What do we plant when we plant a tree?"

Abbot, Willis J[ohn] (1863–1934), newspaperman, historian. Abbot wrote mainly for young people; his *Blue Jackets of '76* (1888) and *Battlefields and Campfires* (1890) were especially popular. He first applied the phrase "the Great Commoner" to WILLIAM JENNINGS BRYAN.

Abbott, Eleanor Hallowell [Mrs. Fordyce Coburn] (1872–1958), novelist, short-story writer. Granddaughter of JACOB ABBOTT and niece of LYMAN ABBOTT, she wrote *Molly Make Believe* (1910), her most celebrated book, as well as *Sick-a-Bed Lady and Other Stories* (1911), *Fairy Prince and Other Stories* (1922), and *Being Little in Cambridge When Everyone Else Was Big* (1936, autobiographical).

Abbott, George (1887–1995), actor, playwright, director, producer. Born in Forestville, New York, and educated at the University of Rochester and in GEORGE PIERCE BAKER's legendary theater workshop at Harvard, Abbott became one of the most successful theatrical men of his time, enthusiastically feted on his one-hundredth birthday in 1987. Primarily identified with Broadway, Abbott also acted on television and directed several films, including *All Quiet on the Western Front* (1930), *The Pajama Game* (1957), and *Damn Yankees* (1979).

Originally an actor, Abbott earned his greatest celebrity as a director of such plays as PAL JOEY (1940), *Call Me Madam* (1950), and *A Funny Thing Happened on the Way to the Forum* (1962). He collaborated with James Gleason on *The Fall Guy* (1925), with Phillip Dunning on BROADWAY (1926), with Ann Preston Bridgers on *Coquette* (1928), with JOHN CECIL HOLM on *Three Men on a Horse* (1935), with Richard Bissell on *The Pajama Game* (1954), with Douglas Wallop on *Damn Yankees* (1955), and with JEROME WEIDMAN on *Fiorello!* (1959). He wrote one novel, *Tryout* (1979), and a candid autobiography, *Mister Abbott* (1963), and directed his own new work, *Frankenstein*, at 101.

Abbott, Jack Henry (1944–   ), convict, writer. Born Rufus Henry Abbot in Oscoda, Michigan, Jack Abbott served sentences in state and federal prisons from the time he was a teenager until his late thirties. He was briefly celebrated for *In the Belly of the Beast: Letters from Prison* (1981), a description of prison life championed by NORMAN MAILER. He enjoyed his celebrity as a free man for only a year. He was convicted of manslaughter in the stabbing death of a waiter and was sentenced in 1982 to fifteen years' further imprisonment.

Abbott, Jacob (1803–1879), clergyman, teacher, author of books for children. His twenty-eight Rollo Books (begun in 1834), stories about a boy named Rollo whose experiences on a New England farm and out in the wide world (including Europe), were used by Abbott to teach lessons of self-improvement, honesty, and industry. These stories and his Franconia Stories, the Gay Family series, and others helped break down the puritanic prejudice of the times against allowing children to read fiction. In all, Abbott wrote more than two hundred books, some with his brother, JOHN S. ABBOTT.

Abbott, John S[tevens] (1805–1877), clergyman, teacher, historian. Abbott collaborated with his brother Jacob. His own best-known work was *The History of Napoleon Bonaparte* (1855).

Abbott, Lyman (1835–1922), clergyman, editor. This son of JACOB ABBOTT began by studying law, later became a Congregationalist minister, succeeding HENRY WARD BEECHER as pastor of the Plymouth Church in Brooklyn and as editor of a magazine originally called *The Christian Union* and later THE OUTLOOK. He was a liberal in both theology and politics. He wrote *The Theology of an Evolutionist* (1897), *Life of Henry Ward Beecher* (1903) and *Reminiscences* (1915). Ira V. Brown wrote *Lyman Abbott, Christian Evolutionist* (1953).

Abe Lincoln in Illinois (1938), a play by ROBERT E. SHERWOOD. In this Pulitzer Prize-winning (1939) drama Sherwood shows Lincoln from his beginnings in New Salem until his departure for Washington as President. Lincoln grows in the play, becomes more certain of himself, yet remains humble. He frequently speaks actual words Sherwood selected from Lincoln's speeches and writings. One feels throughout the intensity of Sherwood's devotion to democracy, his belief in America. He prepared a movie version of the play (1939) and also a radio play that provided a sequel to it, *Abe Lincoln in Washington* (1948).

Abe Martin, a character in humorous newspaper columns and books by KIN HUBBARD.

Abie's Irish Rose (produced 1922, published 1924), a comedy by Anne Nichols. A Jewish boy and an Irish girl fall in love. Fearing to tell their fathers about the affair, they are married by a Methodist minister. Their further attempts at concealment stirred laughter and tears in audiences for a record-breaking run on Broadway—2,327 performances over a period of five years. Later it formed the basis for a novel (1927), a radio program (1942), and a movie (1946).

Abish, Walter (1931–), novelist, poet. Born in Vienna, Austria, and raised in China, Abish became a U.S. citizen in 1960 and taught for a decade at Columbia University. A MacArthur Prize Fellow, Abish is chiefly known for his experimental fiction, which includes *Alphabetical Africa* (1974), a novel in which every word of the first chapter begins with the letter A; the second with A or B; the third with A, B, or C; and so on. At Z the process is reversed, and the final chapter consists of words beginning with the letter A. *How German Is It* (1980), also a novel, has a more conventional surface masking further linguistic and formal experiments. For *How German Is It*, Abish received the PEN Faulkner Award (1981). *Duel Site* (1970) is a volume of poetry, and his short stories are collected in *Minds Meet* (1975) and *In the Future Perfect* (1977). His latest fictions are *99: The New Meaning* (1990) and *Eclipse Fever* (1993), a novel set in Mexico.

Absalom, Absalom! (1936), a novel by WILLIAM FAULKNER. Three narrators reveal their personalities and concerns as each tells the story of Thomas Sutpen, the central character. Miss Rosa Coldfield, Sutpen's sister-in-law, first tells the story to Quentin Compson shortly before his departure for Harvard. Her story is supplemented by that of Quentin's father. Quentin in turn relates the stories of the first two narrators, in addition to giving his own interpretation to his Harvard roommate, Shreve McCannon.

The story centers on Thomas Sutpen and his attempts to fulfill his grand design to become accepted as a southern aristocrat and the founder of a wealthy family. The son of a West Virginia poor white, he raises himself to social eminence in Jefferson, Mississippi, and at the climax of his career is elected Colonel of Jefferson's regiment in the Civil War. Returning to his estate, Sutpen's Hundred, after the war, he finds his daughter confirmed in spinsterhood, his son disappeared, and his plantation half ruined. He attempts to have another son to continue his name, but the poor-white girl with whom he has an affair bears a daughter, and Sutpen is murdered by her grandfather. As the Sutpen saga comes to an end in 1910, all that is left of his dream is an idiot black man, Jim Bond, Sutpen's only living descendant, howling in the ashes of the burned house. Having accepted the social code of the Old South as a part of his grand design, Sutpen had repudiated his first partly black wife and their son; the consequences of this act pursue him through life and triumph over his dream after his death.

Accent. A LITTLE MAGAZINE published at the University of Illinois. Founded in 1940 and appearing quarterly until 1960, it published the fiction of Thomas Mann, Katherine Anne Porter, Irwin Shaw, and Kay Boyle; the poetry of Horace Gregory, Wallace Stevens, Conrad Aiken, and E. E. Cummings; and critical pieces by David Daiches, Kenneth Burke, and Edwin Berry Burgum. Two editors of *Accent*, Kerker Quinn and Charles Shattuck, prepared an *Accent Anthology* (1946).

Aciman André (1950–), memoirist. Born in Alexandria, Egypt, where he spent his boyhood, Aciman emigrated to New York as a young man in 1968. He writes about "exile, remembrance and the passage of time" concerning the Jewish, Italian, and Turkish heritage that was his in Alexandria, and his family's exilic life in Rome and Paris. Educated at Harvard, he has lived mostly in Manhattan and has taught at Bard College. Books include OUT OF EGYPT: A MEMOIR (1994), treating three generations of his family in Alexandria, as members rise to political and social prominence before changes force them away in the 1960s; and FALSE PAPERS (2000), more memories of a Europeanized Alexandria and the rise of the nationalism and Islamic fundamentalism that caused most European Jews to leave.

Acker, Kathy (1948–1997), novelist. Educated at Brandeis University and the University of California, Acker has gained attention for novels approaching pornography—she has been compared with HENRY MILLER and WILLIAM S. BURROUGHS—and for her practice of lifting long passages and situations directly from earlier novelists, including Proust and Dickens. Her novels include *The Childlike Life of the Black Tarantula* (published as by The Black Tarantula, 1973), *I Dreamt I Was a Nymphomaniac* (1974), *Kathy Goes to Haiti* (1978), *Great Expectations* (1982), *Blood and Guts in High*

School (1984), *Don Quixote* (1986), *Empire of the Senseless* (1988), *In Memoriam to Identity* (1990), *My Mother: Demonology* (1995), and *Pussy, King of the Pirates* (1996).

Acorn, Milton (1923–1986),   poet, writer. Born and raised in Charlottetown, Prince Edward Island, Acorn returned there in 1981 after a number of years in Toronto. Successfully combining poetry and leftist politics, and drawing his images and themes from Prince Edward Island and from Canada generally, as well as from personal experience, he has written an essentially working-class poetry and has been called "the People's Poet." *Dig Up My Heart: Selected Poems 1952–1983* (1983) presents much of his best work. *I've Tasted My Blood: Poems 1956–1968* is an earlier collection. In 1970 he was presented the Canadian Poets' Award and in 1975 the Governor General's Award. *The Uncollected Acorn* (1987) is one of several posthumous publications.

Acosta, Oscar Zeta (1935–?),   novelist. Author of *The Autobiography of a Brown Buffalo* (1972) and *The Revolt of the Cockroach People* (1973), Acosta was a Chicano defense lawyer in the 1960s. His life is reflected in the poverty, drugs, and violence of his Chicano characters and in HUNTER THOMPSON's portrayal of Gonzo (based on Acosta) in *Fear and Loathing in Las Vegas*. In the 1970s he vanished in Mexico.

Across the Plains (1892),   a travel book by ROBERT LOUIS STEVENSON. It continues the account of Stevenson's adventures in the United States begun in *The Amateur Emigrant* (1883), describing a railroad trip from New York to San Francisco.

Across the Wide Missouri (1947),   a history by BERNARD DE VOTO. This Pulitzer Prize volume tells the story of the mountain men who from 1832 to 1838 penetrated the unknown land between the Missouri River and the Rocky Mountains, stripped the territory of furs, destroyed its isolation, and unwittingly welded two coastlines into a continent and a nation. The text is supplemented by on-the-spot drawings and paintings by Alfred Jacob Miller, Charles Bodmer, and GEORGE CATLIN, many reproduced for the first time in De Voto's book.

Active Service (1899),   a minor novel by STEPHEN CRANE. The hero is a newspaper man covering the Greek War who rescues his sweetheart and her father.

Actress of Padua, The (1836),   a tragedy by RICHARD PENN SMITH. This play was based on one by Victor Hugo, and no copy survives. But its story is included in *The Actress of Padua and Other Tales* (published anonymously, 2 v. 1836).

Adair, James (c.1709–c.1783),   trader, pioneer. Born in Ireland, Adair for many years after his arrival in America in 1735 lived with Chickasaw and Cherokee Indians. In 1775 he published *History of the American Indians*, which describes Indian customs and maintains that the Indians are descendants of the ancient Jews.

Adamic, Louis (1899–1951),   novelist, social critic. Born in Yugoslavia, Adamic emigrated to the U.S. when he was fifteen. He described his life as an immigrant in *Laughing in the Jungle* (1932), his impressions when he revisited Yugoslavia

in *The Native's Return* (1934). *Dynamite: The Story of Class Violence in America* (1931) is a study of labor. *Grandsons* (1935) relates the saga of a Slovenian family that emigrates to America. In later years Adamic was greatly concerned with America as a melting pot that was melting too slowly. He spoke of American society as being in a state of "psychological civil war." *My America* (1938) shows his beliefs. *From Many Lands* (1940) illustrates the contributions made by immigrants to the greatness of the United States. Adamic in 1940 became first editor of *Common Ground*, a magazine devoted to bringing together the country's diverse elements. In *Two-Way Passage* (1941), he proposed that Americans from Europe return home to help disseminate democracy. Always a caustic critic, Adamic in *Dinner at the White House* (1946) gave his account of conversations with President Roosevelt and Prime Minister Churchill, along with comments on each. His other books are *Cradle of Life* (1936), *What's Your Name?* (1942), *My Native Land* (1943), and *The Eagle and the Roots* (1952), a biography of Marshal Tito.

Adams, Abigail [Smith] (1744–1818),   wife of JOHN ADAMS [2]. Her literary fame is based on her letters, first printed by her grandson, Charles Francis Adams, Sr., in 1840. A second collection, edited by Stewart Mitchell, appeared as *New Letters, 1788–1801* (1947). Lyman H. Butterfield edited *Adams Family Correspondence* (2 v. 1963), and, with others, *The Book of Abigail and John: Selected Letters of the Adams Family, 1762–1784* (1975). With no formal education, Adams might have been thinking of herself when she wrote, "If we mean to have heroes, statesmen, and philosophers, we should have learned women"; in her letters, among the liveliest ever written by an American, she mixed laughter with learning. A biography is Lynne Withey's *Dearest Friend* (1981).

Adams, Alice (1926–1999),   novelist, short-story writer. Born in Virginia, raised outside Chapel Hill, North Carolina (where her father taught at the University of North Carolina), and educated at Radcliffe, Adams after that lived mostly in the San Francisco area. Her fiction evokes the worlds of her North Carolina childhood, of academics, and of women searching for independence and success, frequently in California. *Careless Love* (1966, in England *The Fall of Daisy Duke*, 1967), her first novel, tells of a woman finding a small measure of independence through part-time jobs. *Families and Survivors* (1974) was based in part on North Carolina memories. In *Listening to Billie* (1978), a woman's memories of Billie Holiday play against the events of her later life. In *Rich Rewards* (1980) a woman supports herself as an interior designer. *Superior Women* (1984), much longer than the earlier novels, gained more attention, partly because critics compared it with Mary McCarthy's *The Group* (1963). In the Adams novel, four Radcliffe women of the author's class of 1946 are traced from their freshman year into their late fifties. Other novels include *Second Chances* (1988); *Almost Perfect* (1993); *Medicine Men* (1997), a "medical" comedy; and *A Southern Exposure* (1995) and its sequel, *After the War* (2000), set in a southern college town. Collections of stories include *Beautiful Girl* (1979), *To*

ADAMS FAMILY

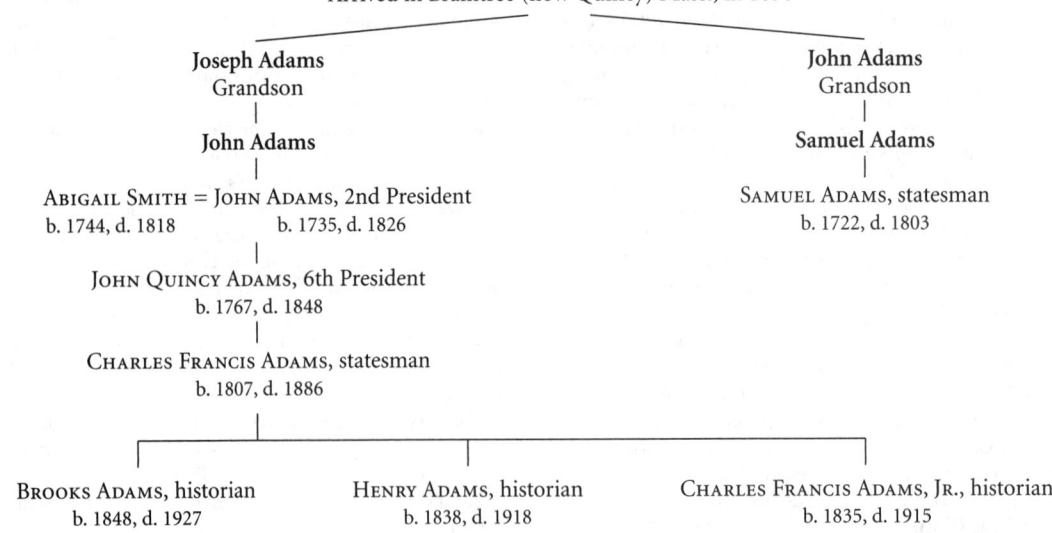

Henry Adams
Arrived in Braintree (now Quincy) Mass., in 1636

Joseph Adams
Grandson

John Adams

Abigail Smith = John Adams, 2nd President
b. 1744, d. 1818   b. 1735, d. 1826

John Quincy Adams, 6th President
b. 1767, d. 1848

Charles Francis Adams, statesman
b. 1807, d. 1886

John Adams
Grandson

Samuel Adams

Samuel Adams, statesman
b. 1722, d. 1803

Brooks Adams, historian
b. 1848, d. 1927

Henry Adams, historian
b. 1838, d. 1918

Charles Francis Adams, Jr., historian
b. 1835, d. 1915

See You Again (1982), *Return Trips* (1985), *After You've Gone* (1989), *Caroline's Daughters* (1991) and *The Last Lovely City* (2000).

Adams, Andy (1859–1935),   author. Born in Whitley County, Indiana, Adams came to know cowboy life at first hand, and his best-known book, LOG OF A COWBOY (1903), includes many autobiographical episodes. *The Outlet* (1905) describes the methods of railroad companies and politicians; *Cattle Brands* (1906) is a book of short stories; *Reed Anthony, Cowman* (1907) is a novel about post–Civil War ranching in Texas.

Adams, Bill (1870–?),   writer of sea stories. Born in England, Bertram Martin Adams went to sea at seventeen and left a few years later to settle in the San Francisco Bay area. His early sea stories were collected in *Fenceless Meadows* (1923); others, including some prize winners, remain uncollected. *Wind in the Topsails* (1931) is verse; an autobiography of his sea years is *Ships and Women* (1937).

Adams, Brooks (1848–1927),   historian, lawyer. The great-grandson of JOHN ADAMS [2], Brooks Adams was a lawyer who wrote sardonically on the prejudices and venalities of judges, a descendant of Puritans who examined with skepticism the annals of their early rule in Massachusetts, and an aristocrat who analyzed history as a mere ebb and flow of greed and fear, centralization and decentralization. He developed elaborate theories of civilization, mostly based on a mechanistic analogy, and expounded them in several volumes: *The Law of Civilization and Decay* (1895); *Theory of Social Revolution* (1913); and a lengthy preface to *The Degradation of the*

Democratic Dogma (1919), the rest of the volume being a letter by his brother HENRY ADAMS. Brooks Adams was a reactionary nonconformist who saw in religion and capitalism the twin enemies of human progress and who felt that the modern world is plunging into degradation and destruction.

Adams, Charles Follen (1842–1918),   writer of humorous verse. Born in Dorchester, Massachusetts, Adams made his reputation by writing poems in the so-called scrapple English spoken by the Pennsylvania Dutch and by the German immigrants he encountered while serving in the army during the Civil War. His favorite character appeared frequently in *Leedle Yawcob Strauss and Other Poems* (1878, reissued as *Yawcob Strauss and Other Poems*, 1910).

Adams, Charles Francis (1807–1886),   congressman, statesman. Son of JOHN QUINCY ADAMS and father of HENRY, BROOKS, and CHARLES FRANCIS ADAMS, JR., Adams was minister to Great Britain during the Civil War, serving the Union cause with great effectiveness. Founder of the Boston *Whig*, he ran for vice president as a Free-Soil candidate in 1848. He edited the *Works* (10 v. 1850–56) of his grandfather JOHN ADAMS, the *Memoirs* (12 v. 1874–77) of his father, and the *Letters* (2 v. 1840) of his grandmother, ABIGAIL ADAMS.

Adams, Charles Francis, Jr. (1835–1915),   lawyer, railroad expert, historian. This brother of HENRY and BROOKS ADAMS was a successful businessman, president of the Union Pacific Railroad (1884–1890), who became disgusted with money-getting and turned to writing history. He was chiefly interested in the history of Massachusetts and wrote *Three Episodes of Massachusetts History* (1892) and *Massachusetts: Its*

History and Historians (1893). Earlier he had exposed conditions of the railroads in *Chapters of Erie and Other Essays* (1871) and *Railroads: Their Origins and Problems* (1878). He published lives of RICHARD HENRY DANA, JR. (1891) and of his father (1900), as well as an *Autobiography* (1916).

Adams, Frank R[amsay] (1883–1963), playwright, novelist, screenwriter. Adams wrote musical comedies while still at college, in collaboration with Will M. Hough. Thirteen of these were produced, including *The Prince of Tonight* (1909). From this came the lyric (written to music by J. E. Howard) "I Wonder Who's Kissing Her Now." Among Adams's novels are *The Long Night* (1929), *Gunsight Ranch* (1939), *Arizona Feud* (1941), *When I Come Back* (1943), *The Hearse at the Wedding* (1945), *Nothing to Lose* (1946), and *Thirteen Lucky Guys* (1951). He also collaborated on nineteen motion pictures.

Adams, Franklin P[ierce] [F.P.A.] (1881–1960), columnist, poet, translator, editor. Adams was a newspaper columnist for the Chicago *Tribune*, the New York *Evening Mail*, the New York *Tribune* (his column was called THE CONNING TOWER), the New York *World*, the renamed *Herald Tribune*, and the New York *Post*. He also appeared on the radio program "Information, Please," contributing a mixture of dry wit and esoteric data relating to Gilbert & Sullivan, baseball, and barber-shop singing. Adams was a versifier, a diarist (in the Pepysian style he often parodied), a connoisseur of typographical and grammatical errors, and a gifted translator from the Latin of Horace, Propertius, and others. In his "Conning Tower" appeared some of the earliest work of a long line of celebrated authors, including Edna St. Vincent Millay, Dorothy Parker, Christopher Morley, Ring Lardner, and George S. Kaufman.

Among Adams's books are *Tobogganing on Parnassus* (1911), *The Conning Tower Book* (1926), *The Second Conning Tower Book* (1927), *The Diary of Our Own Samuel Pepys* (1935), and *Nods and Becks* (1944). In 1947 he wrote a new version of GEORGE M. COHAN's *Forty-five Minutes from Broadway*, a 1906 musical comedy success. He also compiled a *Book of Quotations* (1952).

Adams, George Matthew (1878–1962), newsman. Through the George Matthew Adams Service, Adams originated or took over numerous features widely syndicated in newspapers all over the world. His own feature, "Today's Talk," had wide circulation for more than twenty years. Adams wrote *You Can* (1913), *Just Among Friends* (1928), *Better Than Gold* (1949), and *The Great Little Things* (1953).

Adams, Hannah (1755–1831), historian. Sometimes called the first professional woman author in America, she was born in Medfield, Massachusetts. She compiled an *Alphabetical Compendium of the Various Sects . . . from the Beginning of the Christian Era to the Present Day* (1784) and wrote *A Summary History of New England* (1799), *The Truth and Excellency of the Christian Religion Exhibited* (1804), and *The History of the Jews* (1812). Her *Memoirs* appeared in 1832.

Adams, Henry [Brooks] (1838–1918), historian, novelist, memoirist. Adams was born in Boston, the son of CHARLES FRANCIS ADAMS. Although he was a descendant of pres-

idents and a part of a family long used to taking an active part in the shaping of the nation, Adams's temperamental variations from the family norm led him first to become a special correspondent from Washington to the Boston *Daily Advertiser*. Later, while accompanying his father, who was Minister to England, he sent dispatches to the Boston *Courier* and the New York *Times*. In 1870 he became editor of the *North American Review*, to which he had contributed, and an assistant professor of history at Harvard. He taught medieval, European, and American history for seven years, and thus laid the foundation for his later original work in the philosophy of history. His biography of Albert Gallatin (4 v. 1879) led him to study the Jefferson and Madison papers and directed him toward his nine-volume *History of the United States of America During the Administrations of Thomas Jefferson and James Madison* (1889–91). This work presented a segment of history at the point of transition between European domination and American expansion. It seemed to Adams most fit to illustrate his naturalistic and deterministic theories, which argue that man and his acts, no matter how noble, are incapable of changing or even directing the course of the world.

In 1872 Adams married Marian Hooper of Boston; from that time until her suicide in 1885 little is known of Adams's life, for the years between 1872 and 1892 are omitted from his autobiographical writings. He wrote two anonymously published novels, DEMOCRACY (1880) and ESTHER (1884). Although not of great literary value, the novels reflect Adams's concerns during those years and deal respectively with the two major problems of the day: the corruption in government resulting from a capitalistic economy and the inroads made on religious faith by new discoveries in science.

After the death of his wife Adams made several trips to the Orient with his friend, the artist JOHN LA FARGE, gaining a knowledge of Asiatic religion, and to the high Sierras with the geologist CLARENCE KING, who furthered Adams's interest in science. He traveled to Europe and found in Mont-Saint-Michel and the cathedral at Chartres the symbols he needed to express both his theory of history and of man's inner need and struggle for unity. Accordingly, MONT-SAINT-MICHEL AND CHARTRES (privately printed 1904, published 1913) was subtitled *A Study in Thirteenth-Century Unity*, and THE EDUCATION OF HENRY ADAMS, subtitled *A Study in Twentieth-Century Multiplicity* (privately printed 1907, published 1918). The forces that governed the 13th century, in which Adams found man's need for inner unity most fully realized, were symbolized by the Virgin; the dynamo was his symbol for the 20th century, with its emphasis on science and reasoning and in which nature and not man was the center of the universe. Taken together, the books present the ideological conflict between man and nature, forming an aesthetic whole expressive of man's inner need to create unity out of the chaos of multiplicity.

Adams's other writings include a biography of JOHN RANDOLPH (1882), *Historical Essays* (1891), and *Memoirs of Marau Taaroa, Last Queen of Tahiti* (1893). His "A Letter to American Teachers of History" succinctly expressed his ideas for historians and was reprinted by his brother Brooks Adams in *The*

Degradation of the Democratic Dogma (1919). *The Letters of Henry Adams* (6 v. 1982–87) was edited by J. C. Levenson and others. *The Selected Letters of Henry Adams* (1951) was edited by Newton Arvin. Ernest Samuels wrote a biography in three volumes (1948–64). Elizabeth Stevenson wrote a one-volume biography (1955). Earl N. Harbert wrote *The Force So Much Closer to Home: Henry Adams and the Adams Family* (1977).

Adams, J[ames] Donald (1891–1968), editor, author. Adams was best known for his weekly column, "Speaking of Books," which began to appear in the *New York Times Book Review* in 1943, when he became a contributing editor. His books include *The Shape of Books to Come* (1944), *The Treasure Chest: An Anthology of Contemplative Prose* (1946), *Literary Frontiers* (1950), *The New Treasure Chest: An Anthology of Reflective Prose* (1953), *Triumph over Odds: An Anthology of Man's Unconquerable Spirit* (1957), and *Copey of Harvard: A Biography of Charles Townsend Copeland* (1960).

Adams, James Truslow (1878–1949), historian. Adams was a successful businessman and in World War I served on the so-called House Commission to prepare data for the Peace Conference. On his return from France in 1919, he began writing history. His interests expanded from New England history (his *The Founding of New England*, 1921, won a Pulitzer Prize) to the general history of the United States, then to the history of the British Empire: *Revolutionary New England* (1923), *New England in the Republic* (1926), *The March of Democracy* (2 v. 1932–33), *Building the British Empire* (1938), and *Empire on the Seven Seas: The British Empire, 1784–1939* (1940). In addition, although himself not a Boston Adams, he wrote an account of *The Adams Family* (1930) and of *Henry Adams* (1933), as well as analyses of Hamilton and Jefferson (1938). He was general editor of the *Dictionary of American History* (6 v. 1940), *Atlas of American History* (1943), and *Album of American History* (4 v. 1944–48). His *Epic of America* (1931) has been translated into nine foreign languages. *The American* (1943) surveys American history to demonstrate "the making of a new man," with a presentation of the geographical, historical, and social forces that have made Americans different from citizens of any other nation. In *Big Business in a Democracy* (1945) he depicted our huge industrial and commercial concerns much more favorably than other historians have. He saw big business as "a function of American democracy" and as the most characteristic of our folkways. His thesis throughout was that Americans love property but hate privilege.

Adams, John [1] (1704?–1740), clergyman, poet. Probably Nova Scotian by birth, Adams attended Harvard, and served as a minister in several New England towns. His *Poems on Several Occasions* (1745) includes translations from Horace and devotional poems, many in heroic couplets.

Adams, John [2] (1735–1826), pamphleteer, lawyer, statesman, second President. Born in Braintree, Massachusetts, in the section that later became the town of Quincy, Adams was graduated from Harvard (1755), was admitted to the bar in 1758, and married ABIGAIL ADAMS in 1764. He was carrying on a successful practice of law when the Stamp Act of 1765 drew him into politics. He wrote a series of articles, later collected as *A Dissertation on the Canon and Feudal Law*, in which he argued that the Stamp Act was contrary to the "inherent rights of mankind." He was a delegate to the first Continental Congress, in 1774. His *Thoughts on Government* (1776) included a plan for the government of the colonies that is particularly notable for its insistence on a second body to act as a "mediator" between the representatives of the people and the executive. He was instrumental in the choice of Thomas Jefferson as the author of the DECLARATION OF INDEPENDENCE, and he himself defended the Declaration when it was presented to Congress.

In 1785, after several years' service as minister to France, Britain, and Holland, he began to write his *Defence of the Constitutions of Government of the United States of America* (3 v. 1787–88), in which he discussed the history of republican government. Elected vice president under Washington, he became president in 1796. He quarreled with Hamilton over a treaty with France in 1800, and the resulting split in the Federalist party contributed to his loss to Jefferson in the election of 1800.

John Adams's essentially conservative political philosophy placed him between the extreme Federalism of Hamilton and the agrarianism of Jefferson. His concept of Republicanism was based on a "balance" of power that would prevent the power-hungry from gaining control, and his awareness of the weaknesses and vices of mankind led him to put his faith in the "natural aristocracy" of a few men, who, like himself, would use the power vested in them for the good of the people rather than for their private ends.

His *Works* (10 v. 1850–56) was edited by CHARLES F. ADAMS. *Adams Family Correspondence* (2 v. 1963) was edited by Lyman H. Butterfield. Page Smith wrote a biography (2 v. 1963). See DANIEL LEONARD.

Adams, John Quincy (1767–1848), lawyer, diplomat, sixth President. John Quincy Adams was born in Braintree, Mass., in the section that later became Quincy. An extraordinarily bright child, young Adams accompanied his father JOHN ADAMS [2], a diplomat, to Europe, and studied in Paris and at the University of Leiden; he graduated from Harvard in 1787 and began to practice law in Boston in 1790.

In 1791 Adams replied to Thomas Paine's RIGHTS OF MAN in a series of articles signed PUBLICOLA, stressing the rights of the minority as opposed to Paine's doctrine that the will of the majority must prevail. The Publicola papers were considered the best defense of the Federalist position holding that the violation of the "immutable laws of justice" was not within the rights of majority rule. Adams wrote two other series of articles, signed Marcellus and Columbus respectively, defending President Washington's position regarding the war between England and France, and attacking Edmond Genêt, who sought American support for France in the war.

Adams's writings brought him to the attention of Washington, and in 1794 he was made minister to Holland, and served as Minister to Portugal and Prussia before returning to America in 1801. He was elected to the Senate in 1803, but often voted independently of his party, finally breaking with the Federalists and resigning from his post in 1808. He held several other diplomatic positions until 1817, when he was appointed Secretary of State under Monroe; Adams was largely responsible for the establishment of the MONROE DOCTRINE.

Although Andrew Jackson received more electoral votes than Adams (99 to 84) in the election of 1824, the election was given to the House of Representatives, no candidate having a majority. Henry Clay, the candidate who had received the smallest number of electoral votes, gave his support to Adams, and Adams was elected. When he appointed Clay Secretary of State, the followers of Jackson cried "corrupt bargain" (although it is doubtful that a bargain between Adams and Clay had been made), and the Republican party split.

In 1830, after one term as president, Adams was elected to the House of Representatives, where he served for seventeen years. He fought for free speech when a motion was made to restrict the petitions of the Abolitionists from the floor of the House and argued for the right of the government to free slaves in time of war.

Adams's diary, covering more than sixty years, edited and published by his son, CHARLES FRANCIS ADAMS, was entitled *The Memoirs of John Quincy Adams* (12 v. 1874–77); a selection of the *Memoirs* was made by Allan Nevins in 1929. Adams made a capable translation (first published in 1940) of the German poet Martin Wieland's romance *Oberon*, and wrote verse in the 18th-century fashion, including *Poems* (1848) and *Poems of Religions and Society* (1859). He wrote the classic treatise *On Weights and Measures* (1821) and published his *Harvard Lectures on Rhetoric and Oratory* (delivered 1806, published 1810). Samuel F. Bemis wrote *John Quincy Adams and the Foundations of American Foreign Policy* (1949) and *John Quincy Adams and the Union* (1956).

Adams, John Turvill (1805–1882),   novelist. Adams's *The White Chief Among the Red Men, or, Knight of the Golden Melice* (1859) was one of several 19th-century accounts of the life of SIR CHRISTOPHER GARDINER. Among his other novels was *The Lost Hunter* (1856), set in Connecticut.

Adams, Léonie [Fuller] (1899–1988),   New York poet, teacher of English at New York University, Bennington College, and Columbia University. Her poems are marked by a deeply mystical view of nature, vigorous metrics, and a sense of song that lends delicacy to her so-called tough lines. Her books include *Those Not Elect* (1925); *High Falcon* (1929); *This Measure* (1933); *Poems: A Selection* (1954).

Adams, Oscar Fay (1855–1919),   historian, storyteller. His books include *Through the Years with the Poets* (12 v. 1886), *A Dictionary of American Authors* (1897), *The Archbishop's Unguarded Moment and Other Stories* (1899), and *Sicut Patribus and Other Verse* (1906).

Adams, Ramon F. (1889–1976),   businessman, collector of folklore. A resident of Dallas, Adams assembled the folklore, special language, and history of cattlemen. His books

include *Cowboy Lingo* (1936), *Western Words: A Dictionary of the Range, Cow Camp, and Trail* (1944), *Six-Guns and Saddle Leather: A Bibliography of Books and Pamphlets on Western Outlaws and Gunmen* (1954), and *Rampaging Herds* (1959).

Adams, Samuel (1722–1803),   orator, pamphleteer, political leader. Born in Boston, a second cousin of JOHN ADAMS and a graduate of Harvard (1740), Adams was a leading figure in the events leading to the American Revolution and a signer of the Declaration of Independence. Governor THOMAS HUTCHINSON summarized much of his activity as "for near twenty years a writer against government in the public newspapers." In these writings Adams gave voice to many ideas later doctrinal for Americans, as when he said in 1772: "Among the natural rights of the colonists are these: First, a right to life; secondly, to liberty; thirdly, to property; together with the right to defend them in the best manner they can." He protested against the Stamp Act in 1765, helped organize resistance to British imports, helped bring on the Boston Massacre, with John Hancock helped organize the Sons of Liberty, and organized the Boston Tea Party. General THOMAS GAGE issued a warrant for the arrest of Adams and Hancock in 1775, but they escaped. Adams was a member of the Continental Congress (1774–81) and governor of Massachusetts (1794–97). *Writings* (4 v. 1904–08) was edited by H. A. Cushing.

Adams, Samuel Hopkins (1871–1958),   journalist, novelist, historian, biographer. While on the staffs of *McClure's* and *Collier's*, Adams was active in exposing frauds, especially in the field of medicine, and helped to bring about enactment of the Pure Food and Drug Act. His *The Great American Fraud* (1906) deals with patent medicines. A long series of novels and short-story collections deal with the fictional recollection of American life, among them THE CLARION (1914), *Success* (1921), *The Gorgeous Hussy* (1934), *Canal Town* (1944), *Banner by the Wayside* (1947), *Sunrise to Sunset* (1950), *Grandfather Stories* (1955), and *Tenderloin* (1959). The Harding era engaged him in *Revelry* (1926), in which he depicted Harding as a suicide, and in *The Incredible Era: The Life and Times of Warren Harding* (1939). In 1930 Adams did a biography of Daniel Webster called *The Godlike Daniel*; a later biography, *A. Woollcott: His Life and His World* (1945), reads like a novel. *Average Jones* (1911) is a book of detective stories, and *Plunder* (1948) depicts post–World War II Washington. *The Harvey Girls* (1942) became a successful motion picture musical.

Adams, William Taylor ["Oliver Optic"] (1822–1897), teacher, author of books for boys. Adams wrote more than a thousand short stories and more than a hundred books, all arranged in series. He was in his day the chief rival of HORATIO ALGER, but his books laid stress on character rather than on mere success. In 1865 he gave up his work as principal of the Bowditch School in Boston to devote his entire time to writing; two years later he founded *Oliver Optic's Magazine for Boys and Girls*, which continued publication for eight years. He later edited *Our Little Ones* and *Student and Schoolmate*. His books, including *The Boat Club Series* (1854), *Army and Navy Series* (1865 onward), *Onward and Upward Series* (1870),

Yacht Club Series (1872 onward), and Great Western Series (1875–82) took his young characters through exciting and educational experiences, at home and abroad.

Addams, Charles [Samuel] (1912–1988), cartoonist. Born in Westfield, New Jersey, Addams attended Colgate University, the University of Pennsylvania, and Grand Central School of Art in New York. He published most of his work in THE NEW YORKER, beginning with a first sale in 1935 and becoming a regular contributor in 1940. His cartoons were celebrated examples of the macabre, featuring ghosts and ghouls, coffins and tombstones. Exhibited in galleries and museums, they also inspired a popular television series of the 1960s, "The Addams Family." They were collected in twelve books by Addams, the last being Creature Comforts (1982), and in various collections from The New Yorker featuring other artists as well.

Addams, Jane (1860–1935), settlement worker, sociologist, author. The nature of Addams's remarkable work and influential viewpoint, together with many of her significant experiences, are related in her TWENTY YEARS AT HULL HOUSE (1910) and The Second Twenty Years at Hull House (1930). Addams's early dedication to the cause of the poor and oppressed was followed by a lifetime of beneficent activity, so that Hull House became a center of civic activity in Chicago. Also a determined worker for international peace, she published Democracy and Social Ethics (1902) and Peace and Bread in Time of War (1922), among other writings, and shared a Nobel Peace Prize in 1931.

Adding Machine, The (1923), a play by ELMER RICE. This satiric attack on the half-men produced by the machine age tells how Mr. Zero, discharged when adding machines are introduced into his office, kills his employer in a fit of insanity and is joined in suicide by a middle-aged worker in the same office, Daisy Diana Dorothea Devore. Finding his company in heaven too indecent (Swift and Rabelais, for instance), although he enjoys operating a celestial adding machine, he is consigned back to earth to become the perfect industrial slave. A fine example of expressionistic drama in America, the play uses fantasy to depict inner states usually hidden by surface appearances.

Addams, Mozis. See GEORGE WILLIAM BAGBY.

Ade, George (1866–1944), newspaperman, fabulist, playwright. Indiana born, and educated at Purdue, Ade joined (1890) the old Chicago Morning News (later the Record), where he wrote realistic but amusing "Stories of the Street and the Town," collected in Artie (1896). Later Ade gathered stories of a bootblack in Pink Marsh (1897) and of a gentlemanly liar in Doc' Horne (1899).

In 1898 Ade wrote his first fable in slang, The Blond Girl Who Married a Bucket Shop Man, establishing a formula of colloquial expressions, irregular capitalizations, characters out of everyday life, and a moral frequently seasoned with impertinence. For ten years he continued to write his tales, about one a week, gathered in FABLES IN SLANG (1900), More Fables (1900), Forty Modern Fables (1901), and others.

His career as a playwright began with the successful musical comedy, The Sultan of Sulu (produced 1902, published 1903). His nonmusical plays, The County Chairman (produced 1903), The College Widow (produced 1904), and Father and the Boys (produced 1908) were equally popular. The College Widow was made into a musical comedy, Leave It to Jane, with music by Jerome Kern.

Adeler, Max. See CHARLES HEBERT CLARK.

Adler, Felix (1851–1933), philosopher, teacher, founder of the Ethical Culture movement. Born in Germany, Adler came to America at sixteen and attended Columbia University. While teaching at Cornell in 1876 he founded the Society for Ethical Culture, which emphasized the need for a stronger morality to meet the problems of the time, advocated the moral education of children and various social and labor reforms. Adler established the first free kindergarten for the children of the poor in New York; this soon grew into a vocational school, the first to include manual training and ethical instruction in its curriculum. He was instrumental in the establishment of the Tenement House Commission of 1884, arranged for trained nurses to visit the poor, argued for parks and playgrounds in poor areas, and opposed child labor. Ethical Culture Societies soon appeared in several other large American cities and in Europe. Adler wrote a number of books, including The Ethics of the Political Situation (1884), The Moral Instruction of Children (1892), Marriage and Divorce (1905), What the Ethical Culture School Stands For (1910), An Ethical Philosophy of Life (1918), and The Reconstruction of the Spiritual Ideal (1923).

Adler, Mortimer J[erome] (1902–2001), philosopher, writer, lecturer. Born in New York City, Adler dropped out of high school, but later attended Columbia and began teaching there without completing his degree. In 1927 he taught psychology at the City College of New York, lectured at the People's Institute, and gave a Great Books course in the basement of a church. After receiving his Ph.D. from Columbia, he joined the faculty of the University of Chicago in 1930, where he taught philosophy until 1952. During this period he wrote Crime, Law and Social Science (1933, with J. Michael); What Man Has Made of Man (1937); St. Thomas and the Gentiles (1938); and Problems for Thomists (1940). These books develop his opposition to PRAGMATISM, relativism, and subjectivism and his affirmation of absolute values and of the moral and intellectual order he found in Aristotle and St. Thomas Aquinas. How to Read a Book (1940) and How to Think About War and Peace (1944) were best sellers, indictments of the modern inability to read or think properly. The Great Books Program, which he organized with Robert M. Hutchins in Chicago in 1946, led to Great Books of the Western World (1952), a monumental anthology of 54 volumes containing 443 works by 76 authors from Homer to Freud. Its two-volume master-key, called the Syntopicon (a new word coinage meaning "collection of topics"), is an index of ideas, covering 102 general topics, referring the reader to the passages in the books where the ideas are discussed, and to related topics. As a direct outgrowth of his work on the *Syntopicon*, in 1952 Dr. Adler became director of the newly founded Institute for Philosophical Research. There he wrote *The Idea of Freedom* (1958), the first volume of the Institute's analyses of philosophical literature from ancient Greece to the present. The second volume came out in 1961. Other books by Mortimer Adler are *The Capitalist Manifesto* (1958, with Louis O. Kelso); *The Revolution in Education* (1958, with Milton Mayer); *Aristotle for Everybody*, (1978); *Six Great Ideas* (1981); *Ten Philosophical Mistakes* (1985); and *The Great Ideas: A Lexicon of Western Thought* (1992). Memoirs include *Philosopher at Large* (1977) and *A Second Look in the Rearview Mirror* (1992).

Adler, Renata (1938–   ), journalist, novelist, memoirist. Born in Italy and educated at Bryn Mawr, the Sorbonne, Harvard, and Yale Law School, Adler contributed reviews and articles to THE NEW YORKER for a quarter century (1963–1989). Later, in the memoir *Gone: The Last Days of The New Yorker* (2000), she wrote a gossipy and scathing indictment of that journal's decline. Her brief stint as an acclaimed movie reviewer for the *New York Times*, is recorded in *A Year in the Dark: Journal of a Film Critic 1968–69* (1970). Other nonfiction includes *Toward a Radical Middle* (1970), and *Reckless Disregard* (1986), a study of libel accusations arising from reporting by CBS and *Time* in Vietnam and Lebanon. Her novels closely reflect her life and opinions. In *Pitch Dark* (1983) a woman journalist has an affair with a married man. The earlier *Speedboat* (1976) follows a journalist's initiation, with the young woman voicing what some would see as a foreshadowing of Adler's own career: "I think when you are truly stuck, when you have stood still in the same spot for too long, you throw a grenade in exactly the spot you were standing in, and jump, and pray."

Adrea (1904), a romantic melodrama by DAVID BELASCO and JOHN LUTHER LONG. It is laid in the fifth century, on an island in the Adriatic Sea, and depicts a conflict between two sisters, royal princesses. It ran in New York for two seasons.

Adulateur, The: A Tragedy (1773), a satirical play by MERCY OTIS WARREN. Supposedly laid in Serbia, the play deals with the Boston Massacre and other events preceding the Revolution. It attacks the loyalist THOMAS HUTCHINSON and introduces many figures of the time in disguise, including the author's brother, JAMES OTIS, who is called Brutus. The play was probably never performed.

Adventures. For narratives where this is the first principal word in the title, see the proper name instead, for example, *The Adventures of Tom Sawyer*: see *Tom Sawyer*.

Adventures of a Young Man (1939), a novel by JOHN DOS PASSOS.

Advertisements for the Unexperienced Planters of New England, or Any Where (1631), by CAPT. JOHN SMITH. In a subtitle Smith calls his book "the Pathway to Erect a Plantation." It gives advice based on much experience and is addressed primarily to John Winthrop and the settlers of Massachusetts.

Aesop, G. Washington. See GEORGE T. LANIGAN.

Afloat and Ashore, or, The Adventures of Miles Wallingford (1844), a novel by JAMES FENIMORE COOPER. Two boys and a Negro slave run off to sea, fight Malay pirates, are shipwrecked on Madagascar, and manage to reach their home in New York again. Later one of them ships again with the slave, helps to capture French privateers, sails for the Pacific, and has adventures on the coast of South America and in China. Cooper includes some strong passages on the evils of the impressment of sailors.

Afro-American Literature. Although a once widely held belief, Afro-Americans did not entirely lose their African roots as a result of the brutality of slavery. Contemporary scholarship reveals that while whites had enormous influence on the lives of Africans, affecting later patterns in black America's social development, significant African survivals remain in Afro-American life and culture. Some of the most easily recognizable are those in Afro-American music and folklore. Until recently, these were ignored in white social and literary treatments of blacks. In the early years, black people were interpreted by whites in ways to justify the beliefs and actions of their oppressors. The result was the institution of negative stereotypes that showed up in white American literature (the buffoon, mammy, whore, tragic mulatto, black beast, happy darky, for instance) by such important writers as James Fenimore Cooper, John Pendleton Kennedy, Dion Boucicault, and Joel Chandler Harris. Meanwhile, black writers struggled to create images of the group that presented individuals as human beings.

The first literature by blacks in America was not in written form, but in the oral tradition—a rich body of folklore and stories (many from African origins), and songs. From the words of thousands of black American folktales and secular and religious songs, we know how Afro-Americans viewed themselves and others, and how they amused and sustained themselves in a hostile white society. There are exaggerated humorous tales; stories of experiences in heaven and hell; biblical stories; stories of natural catastrophes, of good and bad people, of inordinately wise or foolish people; tales of exaggeration (the flying African, for instance); and a wealth of animal stories. Joel Chandler Harris's UNCLE REMUS: HIS SONGS AND HIS SAYINGS (1880), the first of his nine books on black folklore, is the earliest attempt to collect this oral literature. Other white writers followed suit into the twentieth century, recording the tales from their Anglo Saxon perspectives. When later black writers such as Arna Bontemps, Langston Hughes, and Zora Neale Hurston recorded the same tales, their emphases were different. The blues, spirituals, and work songs—their lyrics speaking to suffering and hope, oppression and elation, lost loves, pain, and religious faith—are an integral part of the early literature of black people in America.

The earliest extant written literature by a black person in America was poetry, Lucy Terry's "Bars Fight," the twenty-eight line verse of a young New England slave in 1746 (not published until 1893), describing an Indian raid on the village of Deerfield, Massachusetts. Eighteenth-century black poets include JUPITER HAMMON, a New York slave who wrote religious poetry and urged African Americans to resign themselves to slavery. Hammon's "An Evening Thought: Salvation by Christ with Penetential Cries" (1760) made him the first black person to appear in print in this country. George Moses Horton was a North Carolina slave who wrote love poems to order for the students at the University of North Carolina, Chapel Hill, in the late 18th century. His first book appeared in 1829. The first African American to publish a book in America, *Poems on Various Subjects, Religious and Moral* (London, 1773; Philadelphia, 1786) was PHILLIS WHEATLEY. Wheatley had been brought to America from Senegal at about age nine and sold to a wealthy Boston family. In the home of the Wheatleys she learned to read and write, and achieved competency not only in English, but in Greek and Latin as well. Her poetic model was Alexander Pope. Eighteenth-century black poets were slaves, dependent on the generosity of their owners to publish their works. Thus, almost no sentiments related to slavery and black life in the country appear in their writings.

Four autobiographies, the earliest texts in the slave narrative tradition (personal stories of former slaves), constitute the extant of black prose narrative of the 18th century: BRITON HAMMON's *A Narrative of the Uncommon Suffering and Surprising Deliverance of Briton Hammon* (1760); James Albert Ukawsaw Gronniosaw's *A Narrative of the Most Remarkable Particulars in the Life of James Albert Ukawsaw Gronniosaw, An African Prince* (1770); John Marrant's *A Journal of the Rev. John Marrant, from August the 18th, 1785 to the 16th of March 1790. To Which Are Added Two Sermons* (1790), and OLAUDAH EQUIANO's *The Interesting Narrative of the Life of Olaudah Equiano, or Gustavus Vassa, the African. Written by Himself* (1789).

The SLAVE NARRATIVE tradition flowered fully in the 19th century, as did the spiritual narrative written by former slaves and free-born blacks. Primary among these are FREDERICK DOUGLASS's *Narrative of the Life of Frederick Douglass, An American Slave, Written by Himself* (1845) and his *My Bondage and My Freedom* (1855); WILLIAM WELLS BROWN's *Narrative of William Wells Brown, a Fugitive Slave. Written by Himself* (1847); Jarena Lee's *The Life and Religious Experience of Mrs. Jarena Lee, a Colored Lady, Giving an Account of Her Call to Preach the Gospel. Revised and Corrected From the Original manuscript. Written by Herself* (1836); and HARRIET JACOBS's *Incidents in the Life of a Slave Girl* (1861). Eighteenth- and 19th-century slave and religious narratives represent complementary black journeys to freedom through language. The first was the search for release from physical bondage; the second, the quest for black authority and power through the word of the *scriptures*.

A number of Afro-Americans in the 19th century adopted the essay as a tool to fight against slavery. Chief among such still-extant documents are David Walker's *Appeal in Four Articles; Together with a Preamble, to the Colored Citizens of the World, but in Particular, and Very Expressly, to Those of the*

United States of America (1729); Maria Stewart's *Religion and the Pure Principles of Morality, the Sure Foundation on Which We Build* (1831), and miscellaneous essays by Frances Watkins Harper that appeared in Abolitionist newspapers.

Black poetry also flourished in the 19th century, when the writings of more than three dozen poets found their way into print. Frances Watkins Harper published at least eight volumes. The most memorable of these poets was PAUL LAURENCE DUNBAR, the first in his race to achieve national acclaim by winning high praise from William Dean Howells. Between 1893 and 1905 he published eight volumes of poetry and eight novels and collections of stories. BOOKER T. WASHINGTON called him the "Poet Laureate of the Negro Race." Although Dunbar considered himself a lyricist, his fame rests mostly on his dialect poetry, which Howells called the best contribution that Afro-American poetry could make to American poetry. Anthologies of Afro-American poetry from the middle of the 1700s to the end of the 1920s, which include early oral poetry, are *The Book of American Negro Poetry* (1922, revised 1931), JAMES WELDON JOHNSON: *The Negro Caravan* (1941), eds. STERLING A. BROWN, Arthur P. Davis, and Ulysses Lee; *Caroling Dusk: An Anthology of Verse by Negro Poets* (1927), COUNTEE CULLEN; and *Negro Poets and Their Poems* (1923), Robert Thomas Kerlin. Erlene Stetson's *Black Sister: Poetry by Black American Women*, 1746–1980, contains the most comprehensive listing of black women poets.

The first black character in drama appeared on the New York stage in 1769 as a slave in a comic opera. In early American plays, blacks on stage were buffoons who danced, joked, and made uncouth remarks, or they were docile and self-effacing. Through the 19th century until emancipation, plays by white writers featured black characters in such roles. Slavery was a favorite topic. The most influential play by a white on that subject was GEORGE AIKEN's adaptation of Harriet Beecher Stowe's UNCLE TOM's CABIN.

King Shotaway (script no longer extant), a drama of a slave insurrection in the island of St. Vincent, staged at the African Grove Theatre in New York, 1820–1821, is probably the first play written and performed by Afro-Americans. Historical records indicate that the African Grove Theatre, America's first black professional theater, was so popular that special arrangements were made to enable whites to attend. Disorderly conduct by white vandals forced its closing in 1822. William Wells Brown, who published a slave narrative (see above) and the first novel written by an Afro-American (see below), wrote dramas that he read to enthusiastic audiences during his Abolitionist lecture tours in America and Europe. One that survives is *The Escape, or a Leap For Freedom. A Drama in Five Acts* (1858). Other Afro-American dramatists (including IRA ALDRIDGE, Elizabeth Taylor Greenfield, and Victor Sejour), without serious outlets for their talents or writing in this country, were successful abroad. In post-Emancipation America, Afro-Americans, with cork-blackened faces, performed in minstrel shows in bawdy song, dance, joke, and impersonation routines. By the end of the 19th century the musical revue with its chorus line of beautiful and talented young women and elaborately costumed male and female dancers replaced minstrelsy. John W. Isham, a black producer, helped bring this about in the 1890s.

Afro-American fiction begins with WILLIAM WELLS BROWN's *Clotel, or the President's Daughter*, a protest against slavery (London, 1853; America, 1864). In 1958, in *The Negro Novel in America*, literary historian Robert Bone identified eight novels written by blacks between 1853 and 1899. Scholars now account for more than three dozen during that period. The Afro-American Novel Project, a computer-generated research venture based at the University of Mississippi, spearheads efforts to recover the names of authors and titles otherwise unknown. The Black Periodical Fiction Project at Cornell University makes available (on microfiche) 150,000 pieces of fiction, poetry, book reviews, and literary notices published between 1827 and 1940 in nine hundred 19th-century black periodicals and newspapers. The thirty-one volume *Schomburg Library of Nineteenth Century Black Women Writers*, published in 1988, contains all known extant texts of the writings of 19th-century black women. The best-known 19th-century fiction writers include Frank J. Webb, *The Garies and Their Friends* (1857); MARTIN R. DELANY, *Blake; or the Huts of America* (1859); HARRIET WILSON, *Our Nig* (1859), FRANCES WATKINS HARPER, *Iola Leroy, or Shadows Uplifted* (1892); Victoria Earle, *Aunt Lindy: A Story Founded Upon Real Life* (1893); Alice Dunbar Nelson, *Violet and Other Tales* (1895) and *The Goodness of St. Rocque and Other Stories* (1899); PAUL LAURENCE DUNBAR, *The Uncalled* (1898), and *Folks From Dixie* (1898); CHARLES CHESNUTT, *The Conjure Woman* (1899) and *The Wife of His Youth and Other Stories* (1899); and Sutton Griggs, *Imperium in Imperio* (1899). Griggs published four additional novels: *Overshadowed* (1901), *Unfettered* (1902), *The Hindered Hand* (1905), and *Pointing the Way* (1908).

Autobiography dominated Afro-American literature in the nineteenth century while fiction does so in the twentieth century. The writer to bridge the two centuries most successfully was Charles W. Chesnutt, America's first black man of letters. He began publishing short fiction in newspapers in the mid-1880s, and in the *Atlantic Monthly* in 1887. His first two books appeared in 1899 (see above). Chesnutt's 20th-century fiction includes *The House Behind the Cedars* (1900), *The Marrow of Tradition* (1901), and *The Colonel's Dream* (1905). Chesnutt consciously sought to write fiction and not sociology, but aimed to persuade white readers of the worth and equality of Afro-Americans. He was a pioneer of the "New Literature" of the early 1900s, and the first black novelist to be taken seriously by the white literary establishment. Born in the South, where he lived for most of his life, he considered himself an Afro-American native son and identified with traditions of southern writing, appropriating or rejecting them to reveal the South through the eyes of a black man. Of approximately two dozen black novelists who published between 1900 and 1920, the most important books other than Chesnutt's are W. E. B. DuBois's *The Quest of the Silver Fleece* (1911), and JAMES WELDON JOHNSON's *The Autobiography of an Ex-Colored Man* (1912).

The 1920s ushered in the decade of the HARLEM RENAISSANCE, when Afro-American art and culture flourished more than ever before. The acknowledged parents of the movement were W. E. B. DuBois (1868–1963), the Harvard- and Berlin-trained sociologist and historian widely considered to have been one of America's most significant thinkers of the 20th century; ALAIN LOCKE, a Harvard-trained philosopher and America's first Rhodes Scholar; CHARLES S. JOHNSON, a sociologist, editor, and educational statesman; and James Weldon Johnson, writer, lyricist, editor, and civil rights activist. This was the era of the "New Negro" (a phrase coined by Locke). New Negroes unequivocally discredited negative stereotypes of blacks in white American literature in favor of proud black slaves. Literary and cultural historians disagree on time boundaries surrounding the Harlem Renaissance. It began, some believe, with either of CLAUDE MCKAY's poems. "The Harlem Dancer" (1917), or "If We Must Die" (1919), or with LANGSTON HUGHES's poem "The Negro Speaks of Rivers" (1921), and although the stock market crash of 1929 had a major impact on its demise, works as late as those published in 1934 are sometimes included within the movement's history. What is clear is that toward the end of the second decade of this century, as large numbers of Afro-Americans from the South, fleeing poverty and racism, began to settle in Harlem, New York was the magnet for black people from other parts of the country, the West Indies, and Africa. The energy this blending produced effected a collective consciousness of a black identity, and attracted whites with money and/or access to such advantages as publishing possibilities to promote the art and culture of black America. Writers, artists, entertainers, and other culture makers and bearers enjoyed a period of unprecedented success that causes the period to be known as the time "when Harlem was in vogue." Much of the discourse on the Renaissance focuses on happenings in New York City, because most of its most visible participants lived there, but other cities like Los Angeles, Chicago, and Washington, D.C. experienced an increase in artistic and cultural vitality during this time.

The first full-length book by a black writer to come out of the period, *Cane* (1923), by JEAN TOOMER, combines fiction, poetry, and drama into an impressionistic rendering that celebrates the Afro-American experience. Unlike the black writers who preceded him, Toomer, whose literary colleagues were the writers of the Lost Generation, broke with traditional black literature by rejecting realism to experiment with more abstract forms of literary representation. His text was hailed as the harbinger of new developments in Afro-American writing.

The most notable fiction of the Renaissance includes JESSIE FAUSET's *There is Confusion* (1924), *Plum Bun* (1928), *The Chinaberry Tree* (1931), and *Comedy American Style* (1933); WALTER WHITE's *The Fire in the Flint* (1924) and *Flight* (1926); Eric Walrond's *Tropic Death* (1926); W. E. B. DuBois's *Dark Princess* (1928), Rudolph Fisher's *The Walls of Jericho* (1928), and *The Conjure Man Dies* (1932); NELLA LARSEN's *Quicksand* (1928) and *Passing* (1929); Claude McKay's *Home to Harlem* (1928), *Banjo* (1929), *Gingertown* (1932), and *Banana Bottom*

(1933); WALLACE THURMAN's *The Blacker the Berry* (1929) and *Infants of the Spring* (1932); and Langston Hughes's *Not Without Laughter* (1930).

Between the end of the century and the beginning of the Harlem Renaissance, the major black poets were WILLIAM STANLEY BRAITHWAITE, Fenton Johnson, and James Weldon Johnson. Much of the poetry of the Harlem Renaissance appeared in periodicals and anthologies. CRISIS and *Opportunity*, journals of the NAACP and the Urban League respectively, were the principal outlets for these writers. Each month they printed the works of young writers, and each year they awarded prizes for the best poetry, short fiction, and drama that appeared in their pages. The primary poets of the period, who also published multiple volumes of their own works, include Langston Hughes, Countee Cullen, Claude McKay, James Weldon Johnson, and Georgia Douglass Johnson. Maureen Honey's *Shadowed Dreams: Women's Poetry of the Harlem Renaissance* contains the writings of fourteen women of that time. Of these, only Georgia Douglass Johnson and Mae V. Cowdery brought out independent volumes of their works.

The years before the Renaissance saw little in terms of serious black drama. In 1900, for instance, BERT WILLIAMS, the foremost black actor of his time, and George Walker produced their first musical, *The Sons of Ham*, in blackface on Broadway. One important event was the 1918 *Crisis* publication of Alice Dunbar Nelson's *Mine Eyes Have Seen*, a one-act play that questions the responsibility of black men to serve in the military in the face of racial oppression in America. In 1920, Angelina Grimke published *Rachael*, an angry, bitter, and satirical play responding to lynching. Many dramas, comic and serious, ranging from folk to problem plays, were written by blacks in the 1920s. Few were produced and those that were printed appeared largely in black periodicals or anthologies of black plays.

At the same time, between 1917 and 1930 no less than fifteen white playwrights, many of their works appearing on Broadway, were making use of black themes in drama. These included Eugene O'Neill's THE EMPEROR JONES (1920); Paul Green's IN ABRAHAM's BOSOM (1926), a Pulitzer Prize winner; and DuBose and Dorothy Heyward's PORGY (1926). For black playwrights there were few opportunities to produce plays of black life. Like the poetry, much of what was written appeared in the pages of the *Crisis* and *Opportunity*. Willis Richardson, with eleven plays to his credit, was the most prolific of the group. Important anthologies of plays of the period are Alain Locke and Montgomery Gregory's *Plays of Negro Life* (1926); Willis Richardson and May Miller's *Negro History in Thirteen Plays* (1935) and *Pageants from the Life of the Negro* (1930); and Randolph Edmond's *Six Plays for a Negro Theatre* (1934).

Harlem Renaissance writers in all areas, intellectuals from the growing black middle class, wrote to define their culture and facilitate pride in racial heritage. In spite of philosophical differences between the older and younger generations, they shared a conviction that through their exemplary talents they could use literature and art to make things better for themselves and all black people.

The outpouring of Afro-American literature during the 1920s came almost to a standstill in the 1930s, the years of the GREAT DEPRESSION. In poetry, Langston Hughes did the most in individual volumes: *Dear Lovely Death* (1931); *Scottsboro Limited: Four Poems and a Play in Verse* (1932); and *A New Song* (1938). Countee Cullen published *The Media and Other Poems* (1938); Georgia Douglass Johnson. *An Autumn Love Cycle* (1938); and STERLING BROWN, *A Southern Road* (1932), perhaps the most significant book of poems to come from the period. James Weldon Johnson's *Along This Way*, Angelo Herndon's *Let Me Live*, and Claude McKay's *A Long Way from Home* are autobiographies of note. In drama, black playwrights continued to publish one-act plays as they had in the 1920s. Langston Hughes, May Miller, Hall Johnson, Owen Dodson, Theodore White, and Willis Richardson are writers who continued to contribute to the tradition.

Fiction fared better than the other genres in the 1930s. ZORA NEALE HURSTON published four of her five novels in the decade: *Jonah's Gourd Vine* (1934), *Mules and Men* (1935), *Their Eyes Were Watching God* (1937), and *Moses Man of the Mountain* (1939). RICHARD WRIGHT's journal stories were published as *Uncle Tom's Children* (1938); as was Langston Hughes's *The Ways of White Folks* (1934). There were also Wallace Thurman's *Infants of the Spring* (1932); ARNA BONTEMPS's *God Sends Sunday* (1931), *Black Thunder* (1936), and *Drums at Dusk* (1939); George Schuyler's *Black No More* (1931) and *Slaves Today* (1931); Countee Cullen's only novel, *One Way to Heaven* (1932); and WILLIAM ATTAWAY's *Let Me Breathe Thunder* (1939).

In the 1940s, black fictional energy exploded with Richard Wright's *Native Son*. This was the decade that saw CHESTER HIMES's *If He Hollers Let Him Go* (1945) and *Lonely Crusade* (1947); ANN PETRY's *The Street* (1946) and *Country Place* (1947); DOROTHY WEST's *The Living Is Easy* (1948); William Gardener Smith's *Last of the Conquerors* (1948); FRANK YERBY's *The Foxes of Harrow* (1946), *The Vixens* (1947), *The Golden Hawk* (1948), and *Pride's Castle* (1949); and Zora Neale Hurston's *Seraph on the Suwanee* (1948). Wright and Himes, in particular, wrote in the naturalistic tradition. Petry and West were the first novelists to openly explore the oppression of black women against the background of race and sex.

Published drama of the 1940s increased from the previous decade, but not significantly. Langston Hughes, Loften Mitchell, Countee Cullen, OSSIE DAVIS, and Arna Bontemps wrote plays that were sometimes performed in Harlem, but no significant breakthroughs into the larger world of theater and drama occurred. In autobiography, W. E. B. DuBois's *Dusk of Dawn* (1940), Langston Hughes's *The Big Sea* (1940), and Mary Church Terrell's *A Colored Woman in the White World* (1940) launched the decade. These were followed by Zora Neale Hurston's *Dust Tracks on a Road* (1942), J. SAUNDERS REDDING's *No Day of Triumph* (1942), Richard Wright's *Black Boy* (1945), Era Bell Thompson's *American Daughter* (1946), and Walter White's *A Man Called White* (1948). Autobiography of the 1940s embodied the psychological search for the individual self within the context of the black communal identity.

Several of the most significant black poets of the century emerged in the 1940s. Langston Hughes, who began publishing in the 1920s, continued to do so through the 1960s, publishing four volumes in the 1940s; *Shakespeare in Harlem* (1942); In *Freedom's Plow* (1943), *Fields of Wonder* (1947), and *One Way Ticket* (1949).

New poets and new volumes continually appeared, and most of the writers had careers that continued for decades beyond the 1940s. Most notable were ROBERT HAYDEN, *Heart Shape in the Dust* (1940), *Figure of Time* (1955), *A Ballad of Remembrance* (1962), *Selected Poems* (1966), and *Words in the Mourning Time* (1970); NAOMI LONG MADGETT, *Songs to a Phantom Nightingale* (1941), *One and Many* (1961), and *Star by Star* (1965); MARGARET WALKER, *For My People* (1942) and *Prophets for a New Day* (1970); MELVIN B. TOLSON, *Rendezvous with America* (1944), *Libretto for the Republic of Liberia* (1953), and *Harlem Gallery Book I* (1965); GWENDOLYN BROOKS, *A Street in Bronzeville* (1945), *Annie Allen* (1949), *Bronzeville Boys and Girls* (1956), *The Bean Eaters* (1960) (for which she became the first African-American Pulitzer Prize winner), *Selected Poems* (1963), and *In the Mecca* (1968); and Owen Dodson, *Powerful Long Ladder* (1946) and *The Confession of Stone* (1960).

Autobiography in the 1950s was not distinguished, but in drama, important developments were in the making. The new generation of playwrights included Alice Childress, *Florence* (1950), *Just a Little Simple* (1950), *Gold Through the Trees* (1952), and *Trouble in Mind* (1955); Ted Shine, *Cold Day in August* (1950), *The Bats out of Hell* (1955), *Epigraph for a Bluebird* (1958), and *A Rat's Revolt* (1959); William Branch, *A Medal for Willie* (1951), *In Splendid Error* (1954), *Light in the Southern Sky* (1958), and *Fifty Steps Toward Freedom* (1949); Julian Mayfield, *The Other Foot* (1952) and *A World Full of Men* (1952); and Louis S. Peterson, *Take a Giant Step* (1954). It was LORRAINE HANSBERRY's prize-winning drama *A Raisin in the Sun* (1959), however, that opened the doors of the larger theater world for black playwrights.

During the Harlem Renaissance, black artists subscribed to the positive qualities of the American heritage and shaped an art embedded in black pride. During the 1930s and 1940s the swing was toward an art that highlighted the brutal effects of racial oppression on all Afro-Americans: they understood their worth and value to the nation and wanted to be treated fairly and justly. Like the writers of slave narratives in the 19th century, modern black writers appealed to the consciences of whites toward this end. But events after World War II took a different turn. The civil rights movement, beginning in the 1950s, irrevocably changed the nature of Afro-American and American culture that emerged in the second half of the 20th century. In life and literature, black people no longer were content to seek redress for past oppression against them passively: freedom and equality "by any means necessary" became the slogan governing the words and deeds of large numbers of Afro-Americans. Furthermore, as the movement gained momentum in the 1960s, it gave rise to the Black Arts Movement, which in all areas of literature and arts excoriated Amer-

ican racism and promoted black independence and nationalism even at the cost of physical violence.

In this time, in addition to Hansberry, who saw only one other of her plays on stage before her untimely death, and other playwrights of the 1940s and 1950s, including Hughes, Dodson, Ward, Davis, Mitchell, Childress, and Shine, the Black Arts era of the 1960s and 1970s produced a militant black theater with dozens of plays that spoke directly to black people of their relations with white America. Architects of this drama include ADRIENNE KENNEDY, JAMES BALDWIN, IMAMU AMIRI BARAKA (LeRoi Jones), ED BULLINS, Douglas Turner Ward, Ron Milner, and SONIA SANCHEZ. Black art had a message, a rallying cry for black people to throw off the shackles of white oppression and take control of their lives and destinies. Among later dramatists, AUGUST WILSON had secured special praise by the end of the century.

Fiction also flourished and adopted similar harsh racial tones in the 1950s and 1960s. From Europe, self-exiled Richard Wright published novels with such titles as *The Outsider* (1953) and *Savage Holiday* (1954). Among dozens of new novelists to emerge or continue to write between 1950 and 1969, ANN PETRY wrote of interracial sex and lynching northern style in *The Narrows* (1953); James Baldwin rocketed to fame with *Go Tell It on the Mountain* (1953), *Giovanni's Room* (1956), and *Another Country* (1962), and with his fiery essays on race in America; PAULE MARSHALL initiated the novel of the West Indian immigrant in the United States into American literature in *Brown Girl, Brown Stones* (1959), and of Western exploitation of the islands in *The Chosen Place, the Timeless People* (1969); and RALPH ELLISON's *Invisible Man* (1962) raised black literature to theretofore unknown respect among white critics.

Similarly, the new poetry, rejecting loyalties to western forms and choosing instead to work with the rhythms and language of the black working classes, was as powerful as the new fiction and drama. Many dramatists were also poets, and the message was the same in both genres. Haki Madabuhti (Don L. Lee), Mari Evans, SONIA SANCHEZ, JUNE JORDAN, NIKKI GIOVANNI, MICHAEL HARPER, and Larry Neale were among the vanguard in the movement for a distinctive black art that experimented with the limits of language in these areas. They encouraged a functional, communal art that often led to writing collectives and cultural organizations for the purpose of educating the black community. Meanwhile, JAY WRIGHT emerged as an important poet rejecting boundaries.

Autobiography, although fewer works were published than in earlier decades, followed the patterns of drama, fiction, and poetry in its experimentation and primary commitment to the black community. For example, the 1960s gave us the AUTOBIOGRAPHY OF MALCOLM X (1964), Claude Brown's MANCHILD IN THE PROMISED LAND (1965), Gordon Parks's *A Choice of Weapons* (1965), ANNE MOODY's *Coming of Age in Mississippi* (1968), H. Rap Brown's *Die Nigger Die!* (1969), and Julius Lester's *To Be A Slave* (1970). These are radical political documents that define their authors as survivors of an oppression that sought to destroy them and all black people. In the combination of the personal and political embedded in these texts, the survivors of the 1960s declare their identities within the larger black community.

Although black women have written since Lucy Terry's 18th-century "Bars Fight," for more than a hundred years their voices generally failed to gain currency similar to that achieved by black male writers. By the early 1970s, at the intersection of the black and women's liberation movements, this began to change. Although black men such as CHARLES JOHNSON, WALTER MOSLEY, and August Wilson produced literary works of high merit, in the last two decades of the twentieth century the works of black women poets, essayists, dramatists, and fiction writers took the spotlight in Afro-American literature. The most significant contribution of this literature is its exploration of the themes of black women's experiences against the background of race and sex. These writers force readers toward new understandings of the meanings of good and evil, strength and weakness, oppression and survival.

Fiction writers TONI MORRISON and ALICE WALKER are among the best known. Often acknowledged as one of the finest American writers of this century, Morrison has seen five of her novels become American classics. Her fifth, *Beloved*, won her a Pulitzer Prize, and in 1993 she became the first black woman to win a Nobel Prize for literature. Walker, who works in multiple genres, is the author of four novels, four volumes of poems, two volumes of short stories, and a collection of essays. She won a Pulitzer for her third novel, *The Color Purple* (1983). Other notable black women novelists include GLORIA NAYLOR; TONI CADE BAMBARA; GAYL JONES; Octavia Butler, a science fiction writer; Paule Marshall; Louise Meriwether: Sherley Anne Williams; NTOZAKE SHANGE; JAMAICA KINCAID; and TERRY MCMILLAN.

Equally impressive in number and talents are black women poets, dramatists, and essayists of the 1980s and 1990s, many of whom were leaders in the fight for change in the 1960s. Many also work successfully in various media. Among these, Mari Evans, Nikki Giovanni, AUDRE LORDE, Carolyn Rodgers, JUNE JORDAN, SONIA SANCHEZ, and Sherley Anne Williams have influenced a generation of dozens of women writing in all genres. While the group mentioned above publish with major houses, black periodicals and journals still provide the most reliable outlets for the work of the younger generation. The recent establishment of a number of women's and Third World small presses is helping them become more visible.

No longer bound by the restrictions of realism or other literary traditions, black women writers of the 1980s stretch their art to meet the demands of their imaginations. Although grounded in the entire black community, they are mostly concerned with the interior landscape of women's lives and express themselves in a variety of creative ways. For instance, poets RITA DOVE, named Poet Laureate of the United States in 1994; Audre Lorde, in *The Cancer Journals* (1980) and *Sister Outsider* (1984); June Jordan in *Civil Wars* (1981) and *On Call, Political Essays* (1985); and Alice Walker in *In Search of Our Mother's Gardens* (1983) integrate their personal experiences and political goals to create multidimensional but unified selves. Autobiography takes new shape in their handling of the essay, especially in the autobiographic books of MAYA ANGELOU, who read a poem at President Clinton's inauguration in 1993. In this and other ways, black women writers have come into their own in the last two decades of the twentieth century, claiming space and voice within the literary tradition from which they were excluded for many generations, and making Afro-American literature richer than ever before.

NELLIE MCKAY/GP

After the Ball (1891),   a lyric by CHARLES K. HARRIS. One of the most popular songs ever written in America, this was first sung in a Milwaukee production of Charles H. Hoyt's farce *A Trip to Chinatown*. John Philip Sousa played it regularly at the Chicago World's Fair.

After the Fall (1964),   a play by ARTHUR MILLER. In this deeply personal play, Miller presents the action as a dramatization of the "mind, thought, and memory" of Quentin, a man of about 50. Quentin's situation resembles that of Miller. Key events include two suicides: one of a friend who is a former Communist feeling the pressures of MCCARTHYISM, the other that of a man with a well-known wife.

Agar, Herbert [Sebastian] (1897–1980),   journalist. Although he was born in New Rochelle, New York, and died in England, Agar was at first associated with the southern AGRARIANS. With Allen Tate he edited *Who Owns America?* (1936). He lived in England as correspondent for the *Louisville Courier-Journal*, working there in publishing and television, and served as American ambassador. His best-known book was *The People's Choice* (1933), a harsh dissection of the American presidency, which won a Pulitzer Prize. Other books include *Bread and Circuses* (1930), *Land of the Free* (1935), *Pursuit of Happiness* (1938), *A Time for Greatness* (1942), *The Price of Union* (1950), *A Declaration of Faith* (1952), *Abraham Lincoln* (1952), and *The Price of Power: America Since Nineteen Forty-Five* (1957).

Agassiz, [Jean] Louis [Rodolphe] (1807–1873), naturalist, educator, author. Born in Switzerland, Agassiz had already won a notable reputation for his study of glaciers and his work on fish when, in 1846, he came to the United States as a lecturer and decided to remain permanently. He became widely known as a professor at Harvard and curator of the noted Agassiz Museum at Cambridge; he also founded the Marine Biological Laboratory (1872) at Woods Hole, Massachusetts. Chief among his writings is *Contributions to the Natural History of the United States of America* (4 v. 1857–62), which includes his "Essay on Classification." He was an influential teacher of laymen as well as students, and he epitomized his teaching in the directive: "Go to Nature; take the facts in your own hands; look, and see for yourself!" Although he opposed the Darwinian theory of evolution, he did much to arouse interest in the natural sciences and to establish methods of study and classification. His wife Elizabeth Cary Agassiz, a founder and president of Radcliffe College, wrote his biography (2 v. 1885); Jules Marcou prepared *The Life, Letters, and Works* (2 v. 1896); and J. D. Teller wrote, *Louis Agassiz, Scientist and Teacher* (1947).

Agee, James (1909–1955),   poet, critic, film writer, novelist. Agee was born in Knoxville, Tennessee. His father was raised on a farm, his mother in a family with strong interests in business, religion, and the arts. The values of both his parents profoundly influenced him. He was educated at Saint Andrew's, Exeter, and Harvard. In 1932 he joined the staff of *Fortune* magazine, remaining until 1939. His first book, *Permit Me Voyage* (1934), published in the Yale Younger Poet series, reflects his concern for craftmanship, his affection for the Tennessee countryside, and his religious temperament. No other volume of his poetry appeared until the posthumous *The Collected Poems of James Agee* (1968), edited by Robert Fitzgerald. Agee's masterpiece, *Let Us Now Praise Famous Men* (1941), with photographs by Walker Evans, documented the ways of life of three Alabama tenant-farming families. The book originated in 1936, when *Fortune* sent Agee and Evans to study the southern sharecroppers. Subsequently, the magazine declined to publish their work. *Let Us Now Praise Famous Men* is a unique and complex book, deeply honest and compassionate, and remarkable for its extraordinary descriptive, lyric, and meditative prose. In 1939 Agee moved from *Fortune* to *Time* magazine, working as a book reviewer until 1941 and thereafter, until 1948, as a film critic. He also reviewed films for the *Nation* from 1942 to 1948. In his film criticism he maintained a high standard. All his reviews for the *Nation* and some of his reviews for *Time, Life, Partisan Review,* and *Sight and Sound* were published in the first volume of *Agee on Film* (1958). From 1948 on, Agee wrote for motion pictures and television and completed two autobiographical novels. Five film scripts, including adaptations of Stephen Crane's *The Bride Comes to Yellow Sky* (1948) and C. S. Forester's *The African Queen* (1951), were published in the second volume of *Agee on Film* (1960). Agee also wrote a successful five-part television series, *Abraham Lincoln: The Early* Years (1951). His first novel, *The Morning Watch* (1951), a brief, intense, elaborately written work, concentrates on one crucial day in a boy's life at a monastery boarding school. His second novel, *A Death in the Family,* published posthumously in 1957, is a fictional account of Agee's father's death; it is a poised and brilliantly detailed study of relationships within a family. It won a Pulitzer Prize in 1958 and, under the title *All the Way Home,* was adapted for the stage in 1960 and for the screen in 1963. Agee's best work, including *A Death in the Family* and *Let Us Now Praise Famous Men,* puts him among the best prose stylists of his time, and his movie reviews helped establish film criticism in the United States as a serious discipline. Laurence Bergreen's *James Agee: A Life* (1984) is the best biography of Agee. The reminiscences of his friends in *Remembering James Agee,* edited by David Madden (1974), provide much insight into Agee's character and writings.
FRANK K. McHUGH

Age of Anxiety, The (1947),   a poem by W. H. AUDEN.
Age of Chivalry and Age of Fable.   See THOMAS BULFINCH.
Age of Innocence, The (1920),   a novel by EDITH WHARTON that won a Pulitzer Prize. A satirical picture of social life in New York during the 1870s, it describes the marriage of Newland Archer to May Welland, bound by the tribal code of the elite, and his attraction to her unconventional cousin, Ellen Olenska, from which he can never derive satisfaction because they are both too obedient to the code.
Age of Reason, The (Part I, 1794; Part II, 1796),   an attack on traditional religion by THOMAS PAINE. Paine wrote the first part while he was helping the cause of the French Revolution in Paris, the second part after his imprisonment for opposing the execution of Louis XVI. An affirmation of DEISM, not of atheism, as many thought, it asserts "I believe in one God" and contains the admirable sentence: "The world is my country, all mankind are my brethren, and to do good is my religion."
Agrarians.   A name given to a group of writers known best for I'LL TAKE MY STAND (1930), twelve essays and a manifesto that championed traditional virtues of the agrarian South as solutions to the problems of the 20th century's rampant industrialism. Prominent among the Agrarians were the poets ALLEN TATE, JOHN CROWE RANSOM, ROBERT PENN WARREN, and DONALD DAVIDSON, all of whom had earlier been leaders of the FUGITIVES. Others of the remaining eight were JOHN GOULD FLETCHER, ANDREW NELSON LYTLE, and STARK YOUNG. Their association lasted from about 1928 to 1935, with their program for reform conducted primarily through letters and essays.
Ahab, Captain.   The monomaniac one-legged ship captain in Herman Melville's MOBY-DICK (1851).
Ahkoond of Swat, Threnody for the (1878),   a humorous poem by GEORGE THOMAS LANIGAN.
Ah Sin.   The innocent-seeming Chinese card player in BRET HARTE's PLAIN LANGUAGE FROM TRUTHFUL JAMES (1870). The popularity of the poem led Harte to collaborate with Mark Twain on a play, *Ah Sin,* which ran for five weeks in 1877.
Ah, Wilderness! (1933),   a play by EUGENE O'NEILL.
Aiken, Albert W. (dates unknown),   writer of DIME NOVELS, about one a week over a long period of years. One of his earliest was *The Brigand Captain* (1871); later he wrote *Sol Ginger, the Giant Trapper* (1879) and *Lone Hand, the Shadow* (1889). (Dates of issue are all uncertain.)
Aiken, Conrad [Potter] (1889–1973),   poet, novelist, critic. Born in Savannah, Georgia, Aiken carried with him for life the psychic wounds received at age ten, when he heard two pistol shots and discovered that his father had killed his mother and then committed suicide. He was sent to live with relatives in New Bedford, Massachusetts, and was educated at Middlesex School in Concord and Harvard University. He married the first of his three wives in 1912, traveled to Europe, and embarked on a career as a man of letters, living at first near London and in later years in and near Boston and in Brewster, on Cape Cod. Influenced early by the work of EDGAR ALLAN POE, he modeled his first poetic efforts also on the

French Symbolists and the Imagists (see IMAGISM). He was deeply influenced by Freud, Havelock Ellis, WILLIAM JAMES, and Henri Bergson, as he tried to understand the ways of the human mind and reproduce something of its indirections in his creative work.

Aiken's *Collected Poems 1916–1970* (1971) draws from over thirty books, omitting poems from his first volume, *Earth Triumphant* (1914). His second book, *The Jig of Forslin: A Symphony* (1916), declared in its title Aiken's continual concern for extended musical structures. *The Charnel Rose, Senlin: A Biography, and Other Poems* (1917), features in Senlin a "little old man" questioning his identity who reappears in Aiken's poems as late as *The Divine Pilgrim* (1949). Among other significant verse collections are *Preludes for Memnon* (1931), meditations on love and death; *Time in the Rock: Preludes to Definition* (1936); *Brownstone Eclogues and Other Poems* (1942); and *The Kid* (1947), on American historical myths.

Aiken's finest prose work is perhaps *Ushant: An Essay* (1952), which is autobiographical as well as fictional. Besides explorations of his life as he struggled forward from early tragedy, Ushant includes portraits of EZRA POUND, T. S. ELIOT, JOHN GOULD FLETCHER, MALCOLM LOWRY, and others of his acquaintance, all presented under pseudonyms, but with a key provided. His novels, experimental works steeped in Freudian psychology, include *Blue Voyage* (1927), concerned with a trip to Europe that is also a quest for self; *Great Circle* (1933), a second voyage and search; *King Coffin* (1935), a psychoanalytic thriller; *A Heart for the Gods of Mexico* (1939); and *Conversation: or, Pilgrim's Progress* (1940). A *Collected Novels* appeared in 1964. *The Collected Short Stories* (1960) includes some fine works, among them the classic "Silent Snow, Secret Snow." *A Reviewer's ABC* (1958) collects criticism; it was later issued as *Collected Criticism* (1968). Clarissa M. Lorenz wrote *Lorelei Two: My Life with Conrad Aiken* (1983), illuminating from another perspective some of the material of *Ushant*. Edward Butscher's *Conrad Aiken: Poet of White House Vale* (1988) is the first volume of a two-volume biography.

Aiken, George L. (1830–1876), actor, playwright. He is remembered chiefly for his dramatization of UNCLE TOM'S CABIN, first produced in 1852. Though not the first stage version of Mrs. Stowe's novel, it soon surpassed all its predecessors in popularity. Aiken incorporated minstrel songs and banjo music into the play, as well as the memorable scene of Eliza crossing the ice. The unprecedented success of the play made drama respectable in many communities that had previously shunned it. By the 1890s perhaps 500 companies, many of school children, were performing versions of the play.

Aitken, Robert (1734–1802), publisher. Born in Scotland, Aitken settled in America in 1771 and published the PENNSYLVANIA MAGAZINE. His Aitken Bible (1777–82) was the first complete version in English printed in America—England had maintained a monopoly prior to the Revolution.

Akers, Elizabeth [Chase] ["Florence Percy"] (1832–1911), poet, novelist, newspaper editor. Mrs. Akers did editorial work for the Portland *Transcript* and the Port-

land *Daily Advertiser*, and contributed verse to the *Atlantic Monthly* and other magazines. She became renowned for the poem *Rock Me to Sleep, Mother*, the most memorable lines of which are: "Backward, turn backward, O Time, in your flight; / Make me a child again just for tonight." The verses first appeared in the *Saturday Evening Post* (June 9, 1860), later in her collections *Poems* (1899) and *Sunset Song and Other Verses* (1902).

Akins, Zoë (1886–1958), poet, dramatist, screenwriter. Born in Missouri, Akins began in newspaper work, then turned to writing plays in New York for the Washington Square Players. She won a Pulitzer Prize for her dramatization of Edith Wharton's THE OLD MAID, produced in 1935. An intelligent, sincere observer of the American scene, Akins had her first success with *Déclassée* (1919), which depicts the decline of an English peeress from a secure position in England to a dubious one in America. Next was *Daddy's Gone A-Hunting* (1921), in which a man leaves his wife for a career in painting. Later she turned to light romantic comedy and did some of her best work in such plays as *The Varying Shore* (1921), *The Texas Nightingale* (1922; also called *Greatness)*, *A Royal Fandango* (produced, 1923), *The Greeks Had a Word for It* (1930), *O Evening Star* (1936), *Another Darling* (1950), and *The Swallow's Nest* (1950). In later years Akins devoted herself mainly to writing screenplays, among them that of Edna Ferber's SHOW BOAT. She also wrote verse and a novel, *Forever Young* (1941).

Al Aaraaf (1829), a poem by EDGAR ALLAN POE. Al Aaraaf is a region placed by Arabian poets between heaven and hell; the presiding spirit is Nesace, a beautiful maiden. As Poe conceives it, Al Aaraaf is a wondrous star, lolling on the golden air near four bright suns. Thither is brought Angelo, a passionate youth hoping to enter this realm of an ideal beauty, but an earthly love prevents him from hearing Nesace call him.

Albee, Edward (1928–), playwright. Albee was born in Virginia and was adopted in infancy by Reed and Frances Albee, part-owners of the Keith-Albee Theater Circuit. Educated at Trinity College, in Hartford, Albee grew up in Larchmont, New York, in a household whose appointments included servants, tutors, horses, his maternal grandmother, and frequent visits from theater personalities. He left home in 1950 for Greenwich Village, where he supplemented the income from his trust fund with jobs as office boy, record salesman, and Western Union messenger boy and wrote his first play, *The Zoo Story*, in 1958.

The enthusiastic reception following the play's first American performance in the Provincetown Playhouse on January 14, 1960, led to acclaim of Albee as long-awaited successor to Tennessee Williams as America's preeminent playwright. In scenes that allude to events of Albee's life, *The Zoo Story* and the five plays that followed it in the next two years—*The Death of Bessie Smith* (1960), *The Sandbox* (1960), *Fam and Yam* (1960), *The American Dream* (1961), and *Who's Afraid of Virginia Woolf* (1962)—Albee dramatizes his characters' conflicting loyalties to their stereotypical family identities of the past and the mysteries of their present existence. Before Albee's characters can become truly responsive to one another, they are compelled to sacrifice the sources of familiarity within themselves, no matter whether these derive from the family album or from the stereotypes of popular culture.

Insofar as *The Zoo Story* entails a passing stranger's sacrifice of his life as the cost of another person's genuine care, it exemplifies the power of Albee's confrontational drama. As Jerry, an itinerant New York artist, escalates his friendship with Peter, a Madison Avenue executive he meets on a park bench, from a casual encounter to a life-and-death confrontation, the narratives with which they explain their presence to one another undergo transformation. Because Jerry understands that Peter's stories are a defensive reaction, he tells a story that robs Peter of his complacency. In this story of "Jerry and the Dog," Jerry changes his persona from familiar narrator to the violent agency within a mysterious drama he improvises at the play's conclusion: After Jerry impales himself on the knife with which Peter has defended himself, Peter has to acknowledge extraordinary involvement with another person.

In Albee's next four plays, he further explores the dramatic potential in allegorical confrontations he constructs between representatives of the archetypical American family and a sacrificial victim who undermines its structures. All these plays deal with people struggling to remove themselves from environments that isolate them from one another. In *The Sandbox, Fam and Tam,* and *The American Dream,* Albee experiments with surrealistic techniques and distorts the family scenario into infantile fantasies structured in unresolved oedipal crises. Having redesignated Mommy, Daddy, and Child as spurious roles responsible for social estrangement, he associates these family identifications as the basis for racism in *The Death of Bessie Smith.* Bessie did not want to die. Her death in 1937 was the result of a whites-only policy in a Memphis hospital. As Albee examines the motives of the characters who witness the death, he substitutes realistic for surrealistic representations and associates his dramatic themes with a larger politics of representation.

The beneficiary of Albee's developing dramatic gifts over this two-year period was *Who's Afraid of Virginia Woolf,* his greatest dramatic achievement. The characters are realistic rather than archetypal, and the relationships are believable as well as allegorical. The play's principal characters, George and Martha, are not strangers, but a married couple whose marriage begins to fall apart following a late-evening visit by a younger couple, Nick and Honey, within a college community where both George and Nick are professors. By dramatizing the subtle ways in which the characters are estranged from one another within the family structure, Albee reveals the mystery and intrigue informing otherwise forgettable structures of everyday life. The agency of George and Martha's transformation into characters who care about one another, is George's symbolic sacrifice of the imaginary child they long have used to preserve their marriage. In the final act of the play, after George reports the child's death, he ritualistically strips himself and Martha of their roles as father and mother and turns them toward the profound mystery of their status as separate persons.

In 1963, Albee received two Tony Awards and the New York Drama Critics' Circle Award for *Virginia Woolf.* With the exception of *A Delicate Balance,* performed in 1966, the plays that followed *Virginia Woolf—The Ballad of the Sad Cafe* (1963), *Tiny Alice* (1965), *Malcolm* (1966), *Everything in the Garden* (1967), *Box and Quotations from Chairman Mao Tse-Tung* (1968), *All Over* (1971), *Seascape* (1975), *Listening and Counting the Ways* (1977), and *The Lady from Dubuque* (1980)—failed to measure up to the achievement of *Virginia Woolf.* These later plays refer to the disintegration of Albee's dramatic medium. In *Tiny Alice,* for example, Albee questions his characters' motives not within a social milieu but within the context of the more inclusive allegory that their lives represent. In the play, Brother Julian becomes a sacrificial victim to the requirements of an allegory whose mystery does not arouse the interest of the audience. By the end of the play, its narrative plot has been completely dissociated from its dramatized actions, and its characters from any meaningful context whatsoever.

Box and *Quotations from Mao Tse-Tung* further explore the separation between the demands of Albee's dramatic medium and larger social imperatives. *Box* is devoid of characters and plot altogether. The audience sees a large cube and hears a voice delivering an incomprehensible monologue. And while *Quotations* refers to Maoism, it too is disconnected both from any other referential context and comprehension by the audience. When, in *Seascape,* Albee returned to the dramatic topic that established his reputation as a serious dramatist, he indicated his inability to take it seriously by representing it as a confrontation between a married couple and a pair of sea serpents.

The allegory to which these plays are answerable refers to Albee's increasing alienation from his public. As if to acknowledge the distance between his plays and any public for them, Albee in his later plays of the 1970s transformed the wish of his dramatic art to become self-referential rather than comprehensible, making self-reference the sole performative motive. Insofar as *The Lady from Dubuque* named the figure who would be unresponsive to it, that play completed the separation of Albee's drama from any public whatsoever. *Three Tall Women,* which won the Pulitzer Prize in 1994, put him in touch once more with the public, in an autobiographical study featuring his adoptive mother. *The Play About the Baby* (London, 1998; New York, 2001) returns to abstracted self-reference in a masterful late summation. Mel Gussow's *Edward Albee: A Singular Journey* (1999) is a solid biography.

DONALD PEASE/GP

Alcott, [Amos] Bronson (1799–1888),   educator, reformer. Born near Wolcott, Connecticut, Alcott received little formal education and worked as a peddler in the South before taking up teaching. In his Temple School (1834–39), in Boston, he put into practice liberal theories of education, with an emphasis on tapping through free expression the intuitive perceptions of children. The experiment was described in his *Conversations with Children on the Gospels* (1835) and in *Record of a School* (1835) by ELIZABETH PALMER PEABODY, his assistant. After some notoriety the school failed and Alcott moved to Concord. There he became a leading figure in TRANSCENDENTALISM. He published his ORPHIC SAYINGS in the DIAL and was associated with BROOK FARM, although he did not live there. He ran his own farm without success and organized the short-lived FRUITLANDS experiment. In 1859 he became superintendent of schools in Concord, but remained poor until income from the writings of his daughter LOUISA MAY ALCOTT relieved the family's financial stress. Later he established the Concord School of Philosophy (1879–88). In his theories of education he stressed the unity of all souls with God, the innate abilities of children, the importance of emphasizing and integrating mental, physical, and spiritual development of a child's entire being.

Among his writings are *Observations on the Principles and Methods of Infant Instruction* (1830); *Tablets* (1868), a miscellany in prose and verse; *Concord Days* (1872), a memoir based on his journals; *Table Talk* (1877); *New Connecticut* (1881), about his youth; *Sonnets and Canzonets* (1882), a memorial to his wife; and *Ralph Waldo Emerson* (1882). Odell Shepard edited his *Journals* (1938) and wrote *Pedlar's Progress, The Life of Bronson Alcott* (1937). R.L. Herrinstadt edited *Letters* (1969).

Alcott, Louisa May (1832–1888),   novelist. Louisa May Alcott was born in Germantown, Pennsylvania. The Alcott family, memorialized as the Marches in *Little Women*, moved in 1834 to Boston, where Louisa's father, BRONSON ALCOTT, founded the Temple School to practice his theories of childhood education. When the experiment failed six years later, the family moved to Concord, becoming neighbors and friends of the Emersons, Thoreaus, and Hawthornes. After Bronson Alcott's unsuccessful attempt in 1834 to found a utopian community, FRUITLANDS, described by Louisa in "Transcendental Wild Oats" (1874), the burden of supporting the family passed to his wife, who did social work in Boston, and then to Louisa, whose writing eventually became the family's main source of income.

Alcott published her first book, *Flower Fables*, a collection of fairy tales, in 1854. Several years later she began writing Gothic stories under the pseudonym A. M. Barnard, and in the next thirty years published more than 150 short stories. She established her reputation with the widely praised *Hospital Sketches* (1863), a fictionalized account of her six weeks as a volunteer nurse in a military hospital in Washington, an ordeal culminating in typhoid fever, which permanently undermined her health. Her first adult novel, *Moods* (1864), a psychological study of a failed marriage, was unfavorably reviewed, but she won international renown when *Little Women* (1868) and its sequel, *Good Wives* (1869), became best sellers destined to sell millions of copies. Alcott, in the trials and triumphs of the March sisters, Meg, Jo, Beth, and Amy, idealized the family life she and her sisters Anna, Elizabeth, and May had known,

blending humor and pathos in vivid characterizations that made her books unique in juvenile fiction. She continued the story of the Marches in *Little Men* (1871), in which Jo and her husband successfully run a school for boys on the educational principles of Bronson Alcott, and in *Jo's Boys* (1886) depicting the careers and marriages of the sisters' children and their schoolmates. The immense popularity of the March books ensured a wide readership for Alcott's other juvenile novels: *An Old-Fashioned Girl* (1870), *Eight Cousins* (1875), *Rose in Bloom* (1876). *Under the Lilacs* (1878), and *Jack and Jill* (1881). An ardent supporter of women's rights, Alcott affirmed the values of the single woman's life and portrayed women who succeed in such careers as medicine, acting, and painting. But her feminism never undermined her celebration of the virtues of True Womanhood—self-sacrifice, moral purity, and selfless devotion to husband and children.

Renewed interest in Alcott has accompanied the reprinting of her lesser works, including several volumes of the Gothic tales, edited by Madeleine B. Stern; *A Modern Mephistopheles* (1877), a Gothic novel about a failed poet and his tempter, inspired by Goethe's *Faust; Diana and Persis*, an unfinished novel about two women artists; and the novel *Work: A Story of Experience* (1873), portraying the struggles of a poor girl to earn her living by a succession of jobs that Alcott herself held: domestic servant, governess, seamstress, and companion. Madeleine Stern, Joel Myerson, and Daniel Shealy have edited Alcott's letters (1987) and her journals (1989). Martha Saxton's feminist biography *Louisa May* (1977) supplements earlier biographies by Katherine Anthony, Cornelia Meigs, and Madeleine Stern. A century after Alcott's death, all her juvenile novels were still in print, *Little Women* in more than twenty-five editions.

ELSA NETTELS

Alcuin (1797),   a tract in dialogue by CHARLES BROCKDEN BROWN in which Brown pleaded for the legal, political, economic, and cultural freedom of women.

Alden, John (1599?–1687),   one of the settlers of Plymouth, a founder of Duxbury, and a leading character in Longfellow's THE COURTSHIP OF MILES STANDISH (1858). He signed the MAYFLOWER COMPACT, and in Longfellow's poem Priscilla Mullens speaks to him the celebrated words: "Why don't you speak for yourself, John?"—words founded on an oral tradition in the family of Longfellow, himself a descendant of the Plymouth pair.

Aldrich, Bess Streeter (1881–1954),   teacher, novelist. Born in Iowa, Aldrich taught school for a number of years, and wrote some of her best books about pioneer life. A LANTERN IN HER HAND (1928) is laid in Nebraska, and *Song of Years* (1939) in Iowa. She was particularly interested in the character of pioneer mothers and wrote of them with admiration and humor. *The Man Who Caught the Weather* (1936) collects short stories. *The Lieutenant's Lady* (1942) is a novel of 19th-century white and Indian relations. Among her other books: *A White Bird Flying* (1931), *Miss Bishop* (1933), *Journey Into Christmas* (1949), and *The Bess Streeter Aldrich Reader* (1950).

Aldrich, Thomas Bailey (1836–1907),   editor, poet, novelist, dramatist, essayist. Born in Portsmouth, New Hampshire, Aldrich took a job in business at sixteen, when his father died, but he soon turned to writing verse and found editorial work on a New York magazine. When the Civil War broke out, he went to the front as a correspondent but resumed magazine work after the war. In 1881 he succeeded William Dean Howells as editor of the ATLANTIC MONTHLY, and continued in that position until 1890, when he retired to give all his time to writing.

Aldrich was a man of brilliant wit, with a wide circle of friends. As a poet he had technical skill in the so-called genteel tradition. His stories are ingeniously plotted, some of them memorable for their originality and humor. Best known is MAJORIE DAW, but Aldrich's best book is probably THE STORY OF A BAD BOY (1870), a novel that draws heavily on his early memories of Portsmouth. Other fiction includes *Marjorie Daw and Other People* (short stories, 1873); *Prudence Palfrey* (1874); *The Stillwater Tragedy* (1880); and *Two Bites at a Cherry, with Other Tales* (1894). His collections of verse include *The Bells* (1855); *Cloth of Gold* (1874); *Friar Jerome's Beautiful Book* (1881); *Mercedes and Later Lyrics* (1884); *Judith and Holofernes* (1896). He dramatized *Mercedes* (1894) and *Judith and Holofernes* (produced as *Judith of Bethulia*, 1904). *From Ponkapog to Pesth* (1883) and *Ponkapog Papers* (1903) are collections of essays and travel sketches. His *Writings* appeared in eight volumes (1897) and in nine volumes (1907). Ferris Greenslet wrote a biography of Aldrich (1908).

Algría, Ciro (1909–1967),   Peruvian novelist. Son of a small landowner, Alegría wrote mostly of the problems of the Indians. An opponent of the Peruvian regime, and imprisoned in 1931, he went into exile in Chile in 1934, lived in the U.S. during World War II, and later in Cuba. His novels are *La serpente de oro* (1935; tr. *The Golden Serpent*, 1943), about village raftsmen on the Marañón river; *Los perros hambrientos* (1938; tr. *The Hungry Dogs),* about Indians suffering from a drought; *El mundo es ancho y ajeno* (1941; tr. *Broad and Alien Is the World*, 1941, 1983), about the expulsion of a group of Indians from their traditional lands.

Aleichem, Shalom [pen name of **Solomon J. Rabinowitz**] (1859–1916),   short-story writer. Born in Russia, Aleichem became a rabbi at the age of seventeen. He was forced to flee Russia in the pogrom of 1905. He came to America briefly in 1906, but went back to Europe until the outbreak of World War I, when he again had to flee to the U.S. In New York he contributed sketches to Lower East Side journals and had two plays produced in the Yiddish theater.

His pen name means "Peace be with you" in Hebrew. Aleichem wrote in Hebrew, Russian, and Yiddish, but was particularly insistent on the potential of Yiddish as a literary medium. His collected writings in Yiddish fill 23 volumes. Numerous English translations of story collections have appeared: *Stempenyu* (1913), *Jewish Children* (1920), *The Old Country* (1946), *Inside Kasrilevke* (1948), *Tevye's Daughters* (1949), *Wandering Star* (1952), and *The Adventures of Mottel,*

The Cantor's Son (1953). *The Great Fair: My Childhood and Youth* (1950) is an autobiographical novel. A play, *The World of Shalom Aleichem* (1953), dramatized his stories. The musical *Fiddler on the Roof* (1964), based on some of his sketches, played on Broadway and elsewhere and was made into a film.

Alencar, José Martiniano de (1829–1877),   novelist, politician. Born in Ceará, Alencar was educated at São Paulo University and became a journalist. He wrote on Brazilian politics and served as Minister of Justice (1868–70) before turning full-time to literature. Influenced by Chateaubriand, Scott, and JAMES FENMORE COOPER, he earned his greatest fame for idealized, poetic treatments of Brazil's Indians and the country's natural landscape. Among these are two romantic novels, *O Guarani* (1857), depicting the love of an Indian chief for the daughter of a Portuguese nobleman; and *Iracema* (1865; trans. *Iracema, The Honey Lips: A Legend of Brazil*, 1886), reversing the interracial theme in a story of love between an Indian princess and a Portuguese officer. An Indian novel is *Ubirajara* (1874). Plays include *Mãe* (1862), dealing with blacks; and *O Jesuita* (1875), a historical drama. *Obra completa* appeared in 3 volumes in 1958–59.

Alexander's Bridge (1912),   a novel by WILLA CATHER. Bartley Alexander, an American engineer, encounters an actress, a dangerous flame of his youth, on a visit to London. The conflict between his attraction to her and his loyalty to his wife is still unresolved when a bridge on which he is working crashes and he is killed.

Alexie, Sherman (1966–   ),   novelist, short-story writer, poet. A Spokane/Coeur d'Alene Indian, born and raised on the reservation in Wellpinit, Washington, he survived early alcoholism to graduate from Washington State University and become a prolific novelist, poet, short-story writer, musician, and film writer and director. The award-winning first novel *Reservation Blues* (1995) draws on experiences on and off the reservation, and includes songs written with Jim Boyd, recorded by Alexie and Boyd in an album of the same name. *The Lone Ranger and Tonto Fistfight in Heaven* (1994), short stories, won the PEN/Hemingway Award for a first book of fiction; one of its stories formed the basis for the movie *Smoke Signals*. A second novel, *Indian Killer* (1996), set in Seattle, depicts current and past violence, including rape, murder, and scalping, to highlight continuing patterns entwined in a history as ambiguous as the novel's title. Poetry collections include *The Business of Fancydancing* (1992), *Old Shirts & New Skins* (1993), *First Indian on the Moon* (1993), and *The Summer of the Black Widow* (1996).

Alger, Horatio, Jr. (1832–1899),   writer of stories for boys. Alger, oldest child of a Massachusetts Unitarian minister, attended Harvard College and Harvard Divinity School, but fled to Paris as a rebellious bohemian. He was finally persuaded to come back to the U.S. and become a minister. In 1866 he was made chaplain of a Newsboys' Lodging House, to which he devoted his time, money, and affection for the rest of his life.

Alger's fame resulted from his boys' books. Herbert R. Mayes, in *Alger: A Biography Without a Hero* (1928), lists 119 titles. Alger's fictive heroes were bootblacks and newsboys who were smugly good and as a result (so Alger implied) they became rich and successful. Perhaps 20,000,000 copies of his books have been sold. Among the most popular were the RAGGED DICK series (1867), the *Luck and Pluck* series (1869), and the *Tattered Tom* series (1871). He also wrote juvenile biographies of famous men.

Algerine Captive, The (2 v. 1797), a novel by ROYALL TYLER. The book, whose title derives from the difficulties America was then having in Tripoli, had a preface urging the production of a distinctively native fiction in response to an increasing domestic demand for novels. The narrator, Dr. Updike Underhill, satirizes college education in New England, quack medicine in the backwoods, and slavery in the southern United States and in Africa. While on his travels, he is taken into captivity as a slave in Algiers, but returns to denounce the miserable condition of all such prisoners.

Algerine War. The last in a series of American military encounters with Barbary states that lasted from 1800 to 1815, known collectively as the Tripolitan War or BARBARY WARS.

Algic Researchers (1839), a book by H.R. SCHOOLCRAFT. This collection of Indian tales and legends was of great assistance to Henry Wadsworth Longfellow when he came to write HIAWATHA.

Algonquin Hotel. See THE ROUND TABLE.

Algonquin [or Algonkin] Indians. Tribes of North American Indians sharing a common linguistic stock, the Algonquian branch of the Algonquian-Wakashan languages. With their territories stretching from Virginia north to the St. Lawrence and westward to the Mississippi, these were the Indians who first met the English, Dutch, and French explorers and settlers, the first to resist the Europeans' westward march from the Atlantic colonies. They were mostly forest Indians, travelers by means of the famed birch-bark canoe, though some lived on the western plains. There were perhaps a hundred separate tribes, some loosely organized into confederacies. They included on the coast from Virginia to New York, the DELAWARE; in New England, the MASSACHUSET, WAMPANOAG, PEQUOT, NARRAGANSETT, MAHICAN, and MOHEGAN; farther west, the Algonquin of Canada—the tribe from which the whole group derived its name—the SHAWNEE, POTAWATOMI, SAUK and Fox OJIBWAY (or Chippewa), and OTTAWA. Still farther west were the BLACKFEET and CHEYENNE. Well-known individuals included POCAHONTAS, POWHATAN, MASSASOIT, SQUANTO, KING PHILIP, PONTIAC, TECUMSEH, and BLACK HAWK. Vast though their territories were, they had begun to lose them, even before the coming of the Europeans, to the warlike IROQUOIS. The history of their acquaintance with immigrant Europeans is long and complicated, beginning often in friendship and ending in bloodshed, as in the peaceful relationships in New England that preceded KING PHILIP'S WAR.

Algren, Nelson (1909–1981), novelist and short-story writer. Born in Detroit, Algren lived a long time in Chicago, and the slums of that city's west side provided the background for most of his novels and short stories. His first novel, *Somebody in Boots* (1935), was a bitter portrayal of depression youth. *Never Come Morning* followed in 1942. This story of poverty and crime among the Poles of Chicago's west side brought Algren recognition as a writer of importance; he was compared with JAMES T. FARRELL and RICHARD WRIGHT, both acknowledged masters of the Chicago school of realism. Algren's most important work, THE MAN WITH THE GOLDEN ARM (1949), about a morphine addict called Frankie Machine, won the National Book Award and was made into a motion picture. Algren also published *The Neon Wilderness* (short stories, 1947), *Chicago: City on the Make* (1951), and *A Walk on the Wild Side* (1956).

Alhambra, The (1832), a collection of tales and sketches by WASHINGTON IRVING. The book took its title and its inspiration from the Moorish castle in Granada, Spain, where Irving lived in 1829. A great citadel of the Moorish kings and a monument to their occupation of Spain until their expulsion in the late 15th-century, it savored of the romance of conflicting cultures and lost causes.

Alias Jimmy Valentine (1909), a play by PAUL ARMSTRONG. It was based on O. Henry's A RETRIEVED REFORMATION, included in *Roads of Destiny* (1903). See WILSON MIZNER.

Alice Adams (1921), a novel by BOOTH TARKINGTON that was awarded a Pulitzer Prize and by some critics regarded as Tarkington's best. It deals with the disintegration of the middle-class Adams family in a small midwestern town. Virgil Adams has a minor position in a drug company, a nagging wife with overweening ambitions, a shiftless son, and a daughter, Alice, who does her best to be pretty, vivacious, popular. The failure of her pathetic efforts makes the story. A wallflower at dances, she lies to win admiration and does her best to conceal the truth about her family. At the end of the book she is seen entering the stairway that leads to Frincke's Business College. It is the end of her hopes, but she enters bravely.

Alice of Old Vincennes (1900), a historical novel by JAMES MAURICE THOMPSON. In this story of frontier days in Indiana the central figure is a girl abducted in her childhood and brought up by a French trader. She becomes strong, reliant, beautiful, expert in the use of gun and sword. She wins the love of Lieutenant Beverley, an officer in GEORGE ROGERS CLARK's famous expedition against British-held Vincennes during the Revolutionary War. See SIMON KENTON.

Alison's House (1930), a play by SUSAN GLASPELL that won a Pulitzer Prize. It is based on the life of Emily Dickinson and depicts a poet whose love poems are preserved against her wishes by her sister. The scene is an Iowa village, and the action takes place many years after the death of the poet. Glaspell stresses the contrast between two generations and their attitude toward the love of a man already married.

Allatoona (1874), a play by Major General Judson Kilpatrick and J. Owen Moore. One of the earliest plays to deal with the Civil War, *Allatoona* is a chronicle in which two classmates at West Point fight on opposite sides in the great struggle.

Allen, Donald M[erriam] (1912–   ),   editor. An editor at Grove Press, Allen coedited the influential EVERGREEN REVIEW (1957–60) and then served as its West Coast editor (1960–70). His anthology *The New American Poetry, 1945–60* (1960) gave Black Mountain and Beat poets their first wide audience. Allen also edited works by Robert Creeley, Edward Dorn, Allen Ginsberg, Jack Kerouac, and Frank O'Hara, as well as (with Warren Tallman) *The Poetics of the New American Poetry* (1973), and (with George F. Butterick) *The Postmoderns: New American Poetry Revised* (1984). See BEAT GENERATION; BLACK MOUNTAIN POETS.

Allen, Ethan (1738–1789),   leader of the GREEN MOUNTAIN BOYS, philosopher, author. Born in Litchfield, Connecticut, Allen led a force of Vermont and Connecticut volunteers against Fort Ticonderoga during the American Revolution. Later he was captured by the British and held prisoner for two years. Before the war he had been prominent in the territorial controversy between Vermont and New York; his exacerbated Vermont patriotism led afterward to what some have regarded as treasonable correspondence with the British. He wrote a vigorous *Narrative of Colonel Ethan Allen's Captivity* (1774) and an exposition of his religious views, REASON THE ONLY ORACLE OF MAN (1789). (See DEISM.) Allen appears in Daniel Pierce Thompson's *The Green Mountain Boys* (1840), Melville's *Israel Potter* (1855), F. F. Van de Water's *Reluctant Rebel* (1948), and other novels. C. A. Jellison wrote a life of Ethan Allen (1969).

Allen, Fred (1894–1956),   comedian. Allen's real name was John Florence Sullivan. Born in Cambridge, Massachusetts, he began as a juggler in vaudeville, appeared in several musical comedies, but earned his greatest fame in radio. Some of his sayings were widely quoted, as when he summed up a celebrity who went to church wearing sun glasses: "He is afraid God might recognize him and ask him for an autograph." Allen's own story of his career, *Treadmill to Oblivion* (1954), was continued in *Much Ado About Me* (1956).

Allen, Frederick Lewis (1890–1954),   editor, teacher, historian. Born in Boston and educated at Harvard, where he taught for a time, Allen was on the editorial staffs of ATLANTIC MONTHLY (1914–16), CENTURY MAGAZINE (1916–17), and HARPER'S MAGAZINE (1923–53). Observing the "tremendous trifles" of the 1920s, he wrote a best seller, *Only Yesterday* (1931), followed by *Since Yesterday* (1940), *I Remember Distinctly* (with his wife Agnes Rogers, 1947), and *The Big Change* (1952), all social chronicles. He also prepared two collections of photographs with commentaries, *American Procession* (1933) and *Metropolis* (1934), and wrote *The Lords of Creation* (1935), an account of America's financial expansion, and a life of J. Pierpont Morgan (1949).

Allen, Gay Wilson (1903–1995),   biographer, critic. Born in North Carolina and educated at Duke and the University of Wisconsin, Allen taught at Bowling Green University and at New York University. He is best known for his work on Whitman, beginning with the valuable *Walt Whitman Handbook* (1946). *The Solitary Singer: A Critical Biography of Walt Whitman* (1955) was a model of scholarship. His other books include *William James: A Biography* (1967), *A Reader's Guide to Walt Whitman* (1970), *The New Walt Whitman Handbook* (1975), *Aspects of Walt Whitman* (1977), and *Waldo Emerson, A Biography* (1981). With Sculley Bradley he served as general editor of the multivolume *Collected Writings of Walt Whitman* (1961–   ).

Allen, Henry W. [Will Henry, Clay Fisher] (1912–1991),   novelist, short-story writer. Born and educated in Kansas, Henry Allen was a journalist and writer for MGM in Hollywood before beginning his career as a novelist with *No Survivors* (1950), by "Will Henry," a widely admired account of Custer's last stand. Over fifty books have followed, all by either Henry or "Clay Fisher"; most are, at least in part, historical. His book sales have been in the millions.

From Where the Sun Now Stands (1960), by Will Henry, has been called his best work. Taking its title from CHIEF JOSEPH's stirring declaration "From where the sun now stands, I will fight no more forever," and narrated by the chief's nephew, it presents the Indian side of the struggle against the white man. Others written as Will Henry and especially admired include *The Gates of the Mountains* (1963), on the Lewis and Clark expedition; *Alias Butch Cassidy* (1967); *One More River to Cross* (1967); *Chiricahua* (1972), involving an 1833 Indian uprising; and *I, Tom Horn* (1975), a fictional autobiography of a man who lived with Apaches and became a Pinkerton detective. Among the best of the Clay Fisher books is *Red Blizzard* (1951), fictionalizing a massacre by Red Cloud and the Oglala Sioux. See Robert L. Gale, *Will Henry/Clay Fisher* (1984).

Allen, [William] Hervey (1889–1949),   poet, novelist, biographer. Allen's first books were in verse and included *Carolina Chansons* (1922), written with DUBOSE HEYWARD. *Towards the Flame* (1926) is an autobiographical novel of his war service. His biggest success was *Anthony Adverse* (1933), a best-selling romance of the Napoleonic era. *Action at Aquila* (1938) is a Civil War novel. *The City in the Dawn* (1950) collects three novels and an unfinished sequel, all dealing with prerevolutionary Pennsylvania and New York: *The Forest and the Fort* (1943), *Bedford Village* (1944), and *Toward the Morning* (1948). His biography of Edgar Allan Poe, *Israfel* (1926), is readable, though outdated.

Allen, James Lane (1849–1925),   teacher, essayist, novelist. Born in the bluegrass region of Kentucky, Allen used that setting as the background for novels widely read at the turn of the century, particularly A KENTUCKY CARDINAL (1894), its sequel *Aftermath* (1896), and *The Choir Invisible* (1897), a tale of misdirected love. Allen had begun in the 1880s with *Harper's Magazine* sketches collected as *The Blue-Grass Region of Kentucky* (1892). Other novels are *A Summer in Arcady* (1896), *The Reign of Law* (1900), *The Mettle of the Pasture* (1903), *The Bride of the Mistletoe* (1909), *The Doctor's Christmas Eve* (1910), *The Sword of Youth* (1915), and *The Alabaster Box* (1923). *The Landmark* (1925) is a collection of short stories. Studies are by Grant C. Knight (1935) and W. K. Borrtorff (1964).

Allen, Paul (1775–1826), poet, historian, editor. A Philadelphia writer, born in Providence, Rhode Island, and educated at what now is Brown University, Allen published *Original Poems, Serious and Entertaining* (1801). Under various pen names he contributed to magazines. With JOHN NEAL he wrote a *History of the American Revolution* (2 v. 1819); with Nicholas Biddle he edited *The History of the Expedition Under the Command of Captains Lewis and Clark* (1814).

Allen, Paula Gunn (1939–), poet, scholar. Born in Cubers, New Mexico, Paula Gunn Allen is of Laguna Pueblo, Sioux, and Lebanese-Jewish ancestry and grew up in a multilingual family. She was educated at the University of New Mexico and became chair of Native American Studies at San Francisco State University. In poetry and prose she portrays the heritage of Native Americans in uneasy confrontation with changing times and the pressures of cultural assimilation. Volumes of verse include *Shadow Country* (1982) and *Skins and Bones: Poems 1979–87* (1988). A novel is *The Woman Who Owned the Shadows: The Autobiography of Ephanie Atencio* (1983). A scholarly work is *The Sacred Hoop: Recovering the Feminine in American Indian Tradition* (1986). She has edited *Spider Woman's Granddaughters: Traditional Tales and Contemporary Writing by Native American Women* (1989).

Allen, Steve [Stephen Valentine Patrick William] (1921–2000), television personality, composer, musician, author. Born in New York City and educated in journalism, he began his career as radio announcer, comedian, and disc jockey. In 1950 he achieved national recognition in television with *The Steve Allen Show*, a forerunner of later comedy and variety shows. He played leading roles in a number of films, including *The Benny Goodman Story* and *College Confidential*. He wrote more than three thousand songs, among them the title songs for such film successes as *Picnic; Houseboat; Sleeping Beauty*; and *Bell, Book and Candle. Steve Allen's Songs* (1999) prints 100 lyrics with commentary. His books include: *Fourteen for Tonight* (1955); *Bop Fables* (1955); *The Funny Men* (1956); *Wry on the Rocks* (verse, 1956); *The Girls on the Tenth Floor* (1958); *Mark It and Strike It: an Autobiography* (1960); *Not All of Your Laughter, Not All of Your Tears* (1962), a novel; *The Wake* (1972), an autobiographical novel; *The Talk Show Murders* (1982), a novel; *Funny People* (1982); *How to Make a Speech* (1985); *Hi-Ho, Steverino! My Adventure in the Wonderful Wacky World of TV* (1992); and comic detective novels featuring Allen and his wife Jayne Meadow.

Allen, Woody (1935–), actor, director, writer. Born Allen Stewart Konigsberg in Brooklyn, New York, Allen started his career as a gagwriter, writing jokes for others, turned to delivering his own material in clubs and on talk shows, and launched his film career as writer and actor in *What's New, Pussycat?* (1965). A master of neurotic, self-deprecating humor who has published in THE NEW YORKER and has written plays, Allen has had his greatest acclaim for directing, acting in, and writing (or cowriting) such films as *Bananas* (1971); *Everything You Always Wanted to Know About Sex but Were Afraid to Ask* (1972); *Sleeper* (1973); *Love and Death* (1975); *Annie Hall* (1977); and *Manhattan* (1979). Among other screenplays are *Stardust Memories* (1980); *A Midsummer Night's Sex Comedy* (1982); *Zelig* (1983); *Broadway Danny Rose* (1984); *The Purple Rose of Cairo* (1985); *Hannah and Her Sisters* (1986); *Radio Days* (1987); *September* (1988); *Crimes and Misdemeanors* (1989); *Husbands and Wives* (1992); *Mighty Aphrodite* (1995); and *Small Time Crooks* (2000). Books include *Getting Even* (1971); *Without Feathers* (1975); *Side Effects* (1980); and *The Floating Light Bulb* (1982).

Allende, Isabel (1942–), Chilean novelist. Born in Lima, Peru, niece of Salvador Allende, Chilean president assassinated in 1973, Allende turned to fiction to deal with the horrors of Chilean political life. *La casa de los espiritus* (1982, tr. *The House of the Spirits*, 1985), was a popular as well as critical success. Frequently compared with GARCIA MARQUEZ's *One Hundred Years of Solitude*, her novel follows four generations of women in Chile, uniting personal with national history, and suggesting hope even though it culminates in the bloodshed and torture of the military coup that ended her uncle's regime. More recent are *De amor y de sombra* (1984, tr. *Of Love and Shadows*, 1987) *Eva Luna* (1987, tr. 1988), and *The Stories of Eva Luna* (tr. 1991). In 1988 she moved to California, where she has lived since. In her next novel, *The Infinite Plan* (1993), she developed themes of poverty, material success, and spiritual anguish in Los Angeles, Berkeley, Hollywood, and Vietnam. *Daughter of Fortune* (1999), a historical romance, revises the North American view of the California Gold Rush, viewing those times from the perspective of a female adventurer from Chile and her Chinese friend and protector. *Paula* (tr. 1995), a memoir, treats the death of her daughter after a long coma. See THE GLOBALIZATION OF AMERICAN LITERATURE.

All God's Chillun Got Wings (1924), a play by EUGENE O'NEILL. White Ella Downey marries Jim Harris, an African-American who is struggling to become a lawyer. The tragic consequences of her mental inferiority are intensified by racial prejudice as she tries to gain superiority before lapsing into insanity and a regression to childhood.

All My Sons (1947), a play by ARTHUR MILLER.

All Quiet Along the Potomac, a poem by ETHEL LYNN BEERS.

Allston, Joseph Blythe (1833–1904), South Carolina lawyer, soldier, poet. An officer in the Civil War, he won fame with "Stack Arms," written while a prisoner at Fort Delaware.

Allston, Washington (1779–1843), painter, poet, novelist. Born in South Carolina and educated at Harvard, Allston studied painting in Europe and was an intimate of some of the great writers and artists of the day. One of his best works was a portrait of Samuel Taylor Coleridge; another was *Dead Man Revived by Touching the Bones of the Prophet Elisha*. In 1818 he returned to America and began a huge allegorical canvas, *Belshazzar's Feast*, unfinished at his death. He published a volume of sentimental and satiric poems, *The Sylphs of the Seasons* (1813), and a novel with a painter hero, *Monaldi* (1841). His brother-in-law Richard Henry Dana edited his *Lectures on Art and Poems* (1850).

All the King's Men (1946),   a novel by ROBERT PENN WARREN. Jack Burden, a young intellectual, narrates the story of the rise and fall of Willie Stark, a southern demagogue modeled on Huey Long. Willie starts off as a popular reformer, but degenerates into an unprincipled power-seeker. Even at his worst, however, Stark accomplishes some good things, such as building a clinic. This forces Burden to confront the problem of identifying good and evil, and leads him to a new self-understanding at the end of the book, after Stark has been assassinated. Warren adapted the Pulitzer Prize–winning novel into a motion picture that received an Academy Award, and into a stage play.

All the Pretty Horses (1992),   novel. First in *The Border Trilogy*, by CORMAC MCCARTHY.

almanacs.   Two books were almost sure to be found in every early American home, a Bible and an almanac. It is believed that the first American-printed production in English, apart from broadsides, was *An Almanac Calculated for New England*, issued at Cambridge (1639) by WILLIAM PEIRCE [or Pierce]. The first humorous almanac is said to have been compiled by JOHN TULLEY, of Saybrook, Connecticut (1687). Boston became a center of almanac-making, but numerous almanacs also appeared in New York and Philadelphia, and one in Virginia. Among these were Samuel Danforth's *An Almanac for the Year of our Lord 1649*; Josiah Flint's *Almanac* (1666); and John Richardson's *Almanac* (1670), which anticipated BENJAMIN FRANKLIN with its humorous hard sense. By 1720 at least five almanac series were running concurrently; by 1765 there were thirty-one series running. Among the chief almanac-makers were Franklin, DANIEL LEEDS and his son Titan Leeds, and NATHANIEL AMES, father and son. In the 19th century almanacs became more specialized, representing not merely farmers but groups like the Free Masons, temperance enthusiasts, and religious sects. Especially popular were the many *Crockett Almanacs*, which capitalized on the fame of DAVY CROCKETT. Most memorable of all almanacs was Franklin's POOR RICHARD'S ALMANAC (begun 1733). Longest continued was THE OLD FARMER'S ALMANAC, first issued in 1792 and still going strong. Most widely circulated today is the *World Almanac*, founded in 1868. See also BENJAMIN WEST; COMIC ALMANACS.

Alonzo and Melissa, or, The Unfeeling Father (1811).   See ASYLUM, THE.

Alsop, George (1638?–?),   traveler, writer. Alsop came to this country in 1658 and wrote in 1666 *A Character of the Province of Mary-Land*. It is written in mingled verse and prose, with alternate seriousness and jocularity.

Alsop, Joseph [Wright, Jr.] (1910–1989), and **Stewart [Johonnot Oliver]** (1914–1974),   journalists. Born in Connecticut, the two brothers wrote the syndicated column "Matter of Fact," which originated with the New York *Herald Tribune*, from 1946 to 1958. The column was distinguished for its fact-finding, clear thoughts, and strong opinions, and was continued by Joseph alone (1958–74) after Stewart went on to other writing, including a bimonthly column for *Newsweek*.

Their books together include *We Accuse* (1954), on the allegations against nuclear scientist J. Robert Oppenheimer (1904–1967); and *The Reporter's Trade* (1958). Stewart described his struggles with a rare blood disease in *Stay of Execution* (1973). *I've Seen the Best of It* (1992), a memoir, was written by Joseph, with Adam Platt.

Alsop, Richard (1761–1815),   poet, satirist. Educated at Yale, Alsop was a member of the HARTFORD (or Connecticut) WITS. He wrote a good deal of verse, but not so exclusively as to prevent his acquiring a fortune in trade. With LEMUEL HOPKINS and THEODORE DWIGHT he published THE POLITICAL GREENHOUSE FOR THE YEAR 1798, a sometimes witty blast against Jacobins and their American sympathizers. He also collaborated with others of the Hartford Wits. A long poem in heroic couplets, *The Charms of Fancy*, was not published in book form until 1856. See THE ECHO.

Altamirano, Ignacio Manuel (1834–1893),   novelist, poet. Altamirano was a full-blooded Indian, brought up in a small Indian village in Mexico. When he completed his education, he joined Benito Juárez, another Indian, in his resistance to French attempts to establish a Mexican empire (1864–67). Altamirano then became important in the movement to create a national consciousness in the Mexican republic under the presidency of Juárez, editing the newspaper *Correo de México* (1867) and founding *Renacimiento*, a literary review, in 1869. His best-known novels are *Clemencia* (1869), set during the war against the French; and *La navidad en las montañas* (1870), a story of Christmas in a village that includes criticism of the clergy, the educational system, and the army. *El Zarco* (1901), published posthumously, resists nineteenth-century stereotypes as it elicits sympathy for a dark-skinned villager opposed to a blue-eyed bandit in their love for the same woman. His poetry, noted for its descriptions of the Mexican landscape, was collected in *Rimas* (1880).

Altgeld, John Peter (1847–1942),   lawyer, public official. Born in Germany and brought to Ohio by immigrant parents as a child, Altgeld received little formal schooling. After service in the Union Army during the Civil War, he read law and became an attorney. In *Our Penal Machinery and Its Victims* (1884) he argued that our system discriminates against the poor. As governor of Illinois (1892–1896), he pardoned three anarchists convicted in connection with the HAYMARKET RIOT. This, together with his activity in support of labor and his early support of WILLIAM JENNINGS BRYAN, earned him a reputation as a radical that cost him reelection as governor in 1896. VACHEL LINDSAY praised him in a poem, THE EAGLE THAT IS FORGOTTEN (1913), and HOWARD FAST made him the hero of a novel, *The American* (1946).

Alther, Lisa [Reed] (1944–   ),   novelist. Alther was born in Tennessee and educated at Wellesley College. Her first novel, *Kinflicks* (1976), won wide admiration for its frank and witty exploration of a woman's psyche as she contemplates her growth toward a personal freedom traditionally denied women in the small town of her birth. *Original Sins* (1981) is another novel of growth, following five children whose lives become separated by social forces, including sex, class, and race. *Other Women* (1985) portrays a friendship between a lesbian mother and her therapist, displaying once again the difficulties of breaking free. *Bedrock* (1990) is another novel of personal and sexual exploration. *Five Minutes in Heaven* (1995) treats sexual awakening in the 1960s, with lesbianism and ambiguous sexual relations.

Alvarez, Julia (1950–   ),   novelist, poet. Born in New York City, raised until age ten in the Dominican Republic, she returned to the United States in 1960 when her family fled the Rafael Trujillo regime after an aborted coup. She attended Connecticut College, graduated from Middlebury College (B.A. 1971) and Syracuse University (M.F.A., 1975), and attended the Breadloaf School of English. In 1988 she began teaching at Middlebury. Quoting CZESLAW MILOSZ's observation that "Language is the only homeland," she has used her writing to help bridge the gap between her Dominican childhood and her bicultural identity in the United States. Personal experience informs her novels: *How the Garcia Girls Lost Their Accents* (1991), fifteen related stories about life before and after immigration from the Dominican Republic to New York City; *In the Time of the Butterflies* (1994), a fictionalized account of the 1960 killing of three sisters, activists in opposition to Trujillo; and *Yo!* (1996), the Garcia girls again, with one of them now a successful novelist, portrayed in the voices of sixteen people who have known them. Poetry is collected in *Homecoming: New and Selected Poems* (1995), with a sequence of forty-one autobiographical sonnets among its other poems; and *The Other Side/El Otro Lado* (1995), including a long poem about her residence in a Dominican artist's colony. *Something to Declare* (1998), nonfiction, consists of reminiscences and autobiographical essays.

Amado, Jorge (1912–2001),   novelist. Brazil's best-known writer, Amado has published some thirty novels over the last sixty years and has been translated into more than forty languages. His early fiction, often overtly political, espoused his strongly socialist vision; novels from this period include *O paiz do carnaval* (1932); *Cacau* (1933); *Suor* (1934); *Jubiabá* (1935, tr. 1984); *Mar morto* (1936, tr. *Sea of Death*, 1984); and *Capitaes de areia* (1937, tr. *Captains of the Sand*, 1988). His writing has been most celebrated, however, for its exploration of the lives of simple characters who find love, joy, and magic in the midst of the poverty and hardships of their everyday lives. Most often set on the northeast coast of Brazil, his novels chart the violent history of this region's development: this is the theme of *Tocaia grande* (1984, tr. *Showdown*, 1988). The first novel to win him a wide North American readership was *Gabriela, Cravoe canela* (1958, tr. *Gabriela, Clove and Cinnamon*, 1962). Set in Ilheus, the coastal city of Amado's birth, the novel unfolds the development of a love story within the struggles of Ilheus between its adherence to traditional codes of conduct—central among them, the unwritten law that a cuckold must avenge his honor by killing the adulterous wife and her lover—and the forces of progress, which bring with them calls for social change. The temperate response of Nacib to the infidelity of Gabriela dramatizes the transformation of Ilheus in the face of the tyrannical

landowning "colonels" and their armed men. Bridging the gap between serious and popular fiction, Amado's novels passionately evoke many of the paradoxically modern and primitive tones and textures of 20th-century Brazil. Other novels include *Terras do sem-fim* (1942, tr. *The Violent Land*, 1945); *Sao Jorge dos Ilheus* (1944); *Os Velhos Marinheiros* (1961, tr. *Home Is the Sailor*, 1964); *Os Pastores da Noite* (1966, tr. *Shepherds of the Night*, 1966); *Dona Flor e seus dois maridos* (1966, tr. *Dona Flor and Her Two Husbands*, 1969), *Tiêta do agreste* (1979, tr. *Tieta*, 1979), and *O Sumiço da Santa* (1988, tr. *The War of the Saints*, 1993).

NEIL BESNER

Ambassadors, The (1903),   a novel by HENRY JAMES. James makes an ironic study of the deteriorating influence of Europe's wickedness on Americans. Chad Newsome refuses to come back from Paris to Massachusetts to take care of his legitimate business; his widowed mother, a woman of wealth and social position, suspects the worst. She sends two ambassadors to find out what's wrong and bring her son home. The first, Lambert Strether, who is about to marry Mrs. Newsome, is himself seduced by the charm of France and is convinced that Chad's relationship with Mme. de Vionnet is entirely virtuous. Then Mrs. Newsome sends her daughter Sarah, who sees through it all, demands that her brother return at once, and tells Strether that all is over between him and her mother. Although Strether, by accident, then learns that everything charged against Chad and his friend is true, he still believes Chad should stay, but goes back to America himself. The entire action is skillfully and slowly revealed through Strether's mind. James considered *The Ambassadors* his best book, its essence being summed in a remark by Strether, "Live all you can; it's a mistake not to." When Strether makes the remark, however, he does not understand its full import. Later, when he does, he has come to believe that classifying Chad's relationship with Mme. de Vionnet as a "virtuous attachment" was after all only "a technical lie."

Ambitious Guest, The   (published in *The Token* 1835; in TWICE-TOLD TALES, 1837), a story by NATHANIEL HAWTHORNE. Hawthorne depicts a young man stopping for the night in a lonely cottage in the White Mountains. There he and the members of the household discuss their ambitions and wishes. The youth himself speaks freely of his yearning for fame and fortune. Then, during the night, a great landslide destroys them all.

Ambrose, Stephen E[dward] (1936–   ),   historian, biographer. Author of numerous military histories of World War II as well as biographies of Presidents Nixon and Eisenhower, Ambrose received his widest popular audience for *Undaunted Courage; Meriwether Lewis, Thomas Jefferson, and the Opening of the American West* (1996). Ambrose was born in Decatur, Illinois, and educated at the University of Wisconsin (B.S., 1957, Ph.D., 1963) and Louisiana State University (M.A.). He has taught at the University of New Orleans and Johns Hopkins, but the bulk of his career has been devoted to writing multivolume biographies of Eisenhower and Nixon.

He received the Freedom Foundations's National Book Award for *Eisenhower: Soldier, General of the Army, President-Elect 1890–1950* (1983). In addition to his writing on General Eisenhower's role during the war, Ambrose has written other histories of World War II, including *Band of Brothers* (1993), *D-Day June 6, 1944* (1995), *Citizen Soldier* (1997), and *The Victors* (1998).

SUZANNE PERKINS-HART

America. The name honors the explorations of AMERIGO VESPUCCI. It was first applied to the New World when Martin Waldseemüller, a German geographer, placed it across the new lands on his 1507 world map. In 1538 the Flemish cartographer Gerardus Mercator applied it to both North and South America on his first map of the world. Others resisted, with the Spanish and Portuguese referring to the "Indies" for the next two centuries.

America (1831), a patriotic hymn by the Rev. Samuel Francis Smith (1808–1895). It was first sung at a Fourth-of-July meeting in Boston in 1831, and was published in 1832. The tune was originally English and is the music also of "God Save the Queen."

American, The (1877), a novel by HENRY JAMES, dramatized by James in 1891. Christopher Newman, a wealthy self-made American in France, falls in love with and loses the daughter of French aristocrats. Despite the snobbishness he finds in high places, he is deeply impressed by French culture. The French aristocrats, on the other hand, are taken aback by Newman's brisk and energetic self-confidence. The story is based on one of James's favorite themes—the contrast between two ways of life, forthright simplicity and subtle sophistication.

American Academy and Institute of Arts and Letters. The National Institute of Arts and Letters, founded in 1898, created the separate American Academy of Arts and Letters in 1904; the first seven men elected to membership were William Dean Howells, Augustus Saint-Gaudens, Edmund Clarence Stedman, John La Farge, Samuel L. Clemens, John Hay, and Edward MacDowell. The Institute and Academy were combined in 1976. Membership is limited to 250 U.S. citizens and 75 foreign honorary members. It awards medals and prizes for distinguished work, and holds almost continuous art exhibits in its building, Broadway at 155th Street, New York City. *A Century of Arts & Letters*, R. W. Lewis and John Updike (1998), recounts the first hundred years.

American Academy of Arts and Sciences. A society founded in 1780 to encompass all areas of scholarship. With about 3,700 members, it has its headquarters in Cambridge, Massachusetts, and publishes *Daedalus*.

American Anthology, the Spirit of the Public Journals; or, Beauties of the American Newspapers for 1805 (1806). This is believed to be the first collection of extracts from American newspapers.

American Antiquarian Society. Founded by ISAIAH THOMAS in Worcester, Massachusetts, in 1812, its collection of Americana is in some areas unequaled for the period up to the late 19th century and is made available to visiting scholars, some supported by fellowships.

American Caravan, The (1927–36), an annual volume edited by VAN WYCK BROOKS in the first year, thereafter by ALFRED KREYMBORG, LEWIS MUMFORD, and PAUL ROSENFELD. It published many writers of note, including Sherwood Anderson, Hart Crane, Robert Frost, Ernest Hemingway, Katherine Anne Porter, Robert Penn Warren, and William Carlos Williams.

American Claimant, The (1892), a novel by Mark Twain, derived in part from *Colonel Sellers as a Scientist*, a play by Twain and William Dean Howells. Produced in 1887, this play developed further a character from Twain's earlier play *Colonel Sellers* (produced 1874; as *The Gilded Age*, 1880), which was derived in turn from the novel *The Gilded Age* (1873), by Twain and Charles Dudley Warner. In *The American Claimant* Twain showed Sellers aspiring to an English earldom. Sellers' perennially comic schemes for advancement were based in part on the claims on one of Twain's distant cousins, Jesse Madison Leathers, to be rightful Earl of Durham. (See COLONEL BERIAH SELLERS.)

American Commonwealth, The (1888, rev. 1910, 50th anniversary edition, 1939), by James Bryce (1838–1922). A classic by an English statesman and historian of the structure of American government and the character of American society. Bryce, later an ambassador to the U.S., visited America five times before writing his two-volume work, the most important study of this nation since DE TOCQUEVILLE's *Democracy in America*. He dealt with the Federal government, the state and municipal government, political machinery and the party system, the workings of public opinion, the strength and weakness of democratic government, and the social, intellectual, and spiritual forces operating in American life. Bryce was an enthusiastic believer in America but not blind to American faults and weaknesses. A supplementary chapter on the Tweed Ring in New York City caused the entire first edition to be suppressed.

American Crisis, The (December 19, 1776–April 19, 1783), sixteen pamphlets by THOMAS PAINE. The first, published in *The Pennsylvania Journal*, was begun while Washington was retreating across New Jersey and opens with a famous sentence: "These are the times that try men's souls." Washington had it read to his downhearted troops, and it had a great effect in arousing new zeal for the American cause. In succeeding years Paine continued to comment on the course of events, to inspire the colonists to continue their struggle against England, and to oppose compromise. The last pamphlet is called *Thoughts on the Peace and the Probable Advantages Thereof*, and begins: "The times that tried men's souls are over."

American Democrat, The, or Hints on the Social and Civic Relations of the United States of America (1838). JAMES FENIMORE COOPER wrote this diatribe against his countrymen on his return from a seven-year stay in Europe. Brought up in the aristocratic Federalist tradition, Cooper abroad had become an ardent defender of democracy. Returning home, he was repelled by much that he saw in the

Jacksonian era, He repudiated as vicious a system of government founded on property, but refused to believe that a majority could do no wrong, or that special intelligence dwelt under a coonskin cap or in a log cabin. Other books that Cooper wrote in his attempt to reform the vulgarity and crudity of his country include A LETTER TO HIS COUNTRYMEN (1834); THE MONIKINS (1835); HOMEWARD BOUND (1838); and *Home as Found* (1838). They brought upon him such epithets in the press of the time as "spotted caitiff" and "leprous wretch." Cooper brought libel suits against several American newspapers, acted as his own lawyer, and for the most part not merely won verdicts but helped to establish legal remedies against the kinds of attacks he had suffered, but he lost a fortune to win his point.

American Dictionary of the English Language (1828), the original title given to his monumental work by NOAH WEBSTER. He spent twenty years on the compilation of this volume, the most ambitious publication issued up to that time in America and a great scholarly achievement. Webster favored usage rather than purity as his guide, and insisted that America had its own language.

American Dream, An (1965), a novel by NORMAN MAILER.

American Dream, The (1961), a play by EDWARD ALBEE.

American Folklore Society. A scholarly society founded in 1888 for "the study of folklore in general and, in particular, the collection and publication of the folklore of North America." In addition to the rich material published in *Journal of American Folklore*, the Society has published since 1894 a series of valuable monographs.

American Guide Series. See WORKS PROGRESS ADMINISTRATION.

American Heritage. A magazine first issued in 1949 by the American Association for State and Local History. Enlarged and revised under BRUCE CATTON, who edited it from 1954 to 1959, it became a hardbound, colorful monthly associated with the Society of American Historians, with a circulation by 2000 of over 300,000.

American Humor: A Study of the National Character (1931), a historical and critical study by CONSTANCE ROURKE. Rourke assembles oral and written expression in a pattern to demonstrate how "the popular arts—humor is one of them—have much to say as to underlying forces in American life."

American-Indian Literature. See NATIVE AMERICAN LITERATURE.

Americanization of Edward Bok, The (1920). See EDWARD BOK.

American Jest-Book, The (1796). Published at Boston, this was perhaps the earliest American imitation of the English "Joe Miller" collections. Another collection with the same title was published in Philadelphia, 1833.

American Language, The (1919, 1921, 1923, 1936; *Supplement One*, 1945; *Supplement Two*, 1948), a treatise by H. L. MENCKEN. Mencken first began writing on the American language in the Baltimore *Evening Sun* in 1910. He felt that American English was departing from the parent stem, and it seemed likely that the differences between American and English would increase. But from 1923 on, he judged that the pull of American had become so powerful that it was beginning to drag English with it, and in consequence some of the differences once visible had begun to disappear. Mencken, with infinite detail, treated the two streams of English, the beginnings of American, the period of growth, the language of his time, the differences between American and English, the pronunciation of American, American spelling, the common speech, proper names in America, American slang, the future of the language, and non-English dialects in America.

American Literature (1929–), scholarly journal published quarterly by the Duke University Press for the American Literature Group of the Modern Language Association of America. The journal features historical and critical essays, book reviews, and bibliographies.

American Magazine, The. Several periodicals have borne this title, the most notable of which were:

1. *The American Magazine, or, A Monthly View of the Political State of the British Colonies* was the first magazine to be issued in America. It appeared on February 13, 1741 (dated "January, 1740–41"), from the press of Andrew Bradford in Philadelphia. Half its pages were occupied by the proceedings of colonial assemblies. The only belles-lettres consisted of an excerpt of "characters" from the *London Magazine*. The venture lasted only three months.

2. NOAH WEBSTER's *American Magazine*, which had only twelve issues, showed a variety and spirit unusual for its time. It was New York's first monthly magazine, and was issued by the printer-bookseller Samuel Loudon in December 1787. Webster, a strong Federalist, printed much about the newly written Constitution; he was also an educational leader and made schools and teaching a favorite subject. Women's interests received more attention than in any previous American magazine. Extracts from American books and some new fiction and poetry were included.

3. NATHANIEL PARKER WILLIS's *American Monthly Magazine* was founded in Boston in April 1829, and lasted through twenty-seven numbers; it was one of the most entertaining magazines yet published in America. Modeled on Thomas Campbell's *New Monthly Magazine* in London, it was filled with essays, tales, criticism, and humor, a large part of which was written by the editor. Other contributors included Richard Hildreth, John L. Motley, Lydia Sigourney, Albert Pike, and Park Benjamin. The magazine's satirical bent and disregard of Boston mores offended many, and in 1831 Willis turned his subscription list over to the *New York Mirror*, of which he became associate editor.

4. HENRY WILLIAM HERBERT, better known as "Frank Forester," founded the *American Monthly Magazine* in 1833 in New York as a competitor of the new KNICKER-

BOCKER in the magazine's second year, Herbert took CHARLES FENNO HOFFMAN as his partner. The two editor-publishers wrote much of the *American's* contents, but also included the work of James K. Paulding, Gulian C. Verplanck, and James Hall. The magazine had variety, and Herbert's commentary on New York theaters, music, and art was notable. Herbert yielded his place at the end of 1835 to Park Benjamin, who made an unsuccessful effort to make a tri-city publication of the *American* through the interest of Boston and Philadelphia publishers. Each number now had an engraved plate, and special interest articles on the new West, the Indians, Latin America, German literature, and the American Lyceum. In its last year or two the magazine became more a political review, and its Whig tendencies were emphasized by the contributions of Horace Greeley. In 1838 its subscription list was turned over to Greeley's *New-Yorker*.

5. *Frank Leslie's Popular Monthly* (see FRANK LESLIE) was begun in New York in January 1876 as a $2.50 general magazine in competition with the $4 monthlies. Its contributors included Joaquin Miller, Amelia E. Barr, Harriet Prescott Spofford, and Brander Matthews. Mrs. Frank Leslie, who managed the magazine after her husband's death in 1880, leased it to others in 1895 but had to take it back after three years of decline; she changed format, lowered the price to ten cents, and made it a success again. Ellery Sedgwick, formerly of the *Youth's Companion* and later of the *Atlantic Monthly*, brought current public affairs into *Leslie's Magazine*, as it came to be called in 1904, and recruited such contributors as Stephen Crane, Frank R. Stockton, and Stewart Edward White. Ellis Parker Butler's *Pigs Is Pigs* was a hit of 1905. After 1906 the magazine was taken over by a staff deserting from *McClure's*, headed by JOHN S. PHILLIPS as publisher and including Ida M. Tarbell, Lincoln Steffens, Ray Stannard Baker, Finley Peter Dunne, and William Allen White. The monthly, renamed the *American Magazine*, stressed serious MUCKRAKING and human-interest articles and sketches. The Crowell-Collier Publishing Company bought the *American* in 1915 and made John M. Siddall editor, and the magazine began to stress success stories, S. S. Van Dine's detective stories, and Clarence Budington Kelland's endless Scatter-good Baines serials. The 2,500,000 circulation, which the magazine reached in the 1920s, did not attract advertisers, who were disinclined to pay high rates for so generalized a mass medium, and after some floundering in policy the *American Magazine* was discontinued by the Crowell-Collier Company in 1956.

American Men of Letters Series. [1] A series of biographical and critical studies of American authors edited by Charles Dudley Warner and published by Houghton Mifflin. It began with Warner's own *Washington Irving* in 1881 and continued through 22 volumes to 1904. [2] A similar series of 11 volumes published by William Sloane from 1948 to 1951, including books by Mark Van Doren, Joseph Wood

Krutch, and Newton Arvin on, respectively, *Hawthorne*, *Thoreau*, and *Melville*.

American Mercury, The. William D'Alton Mann founded the SMART SET (1900–1930) as a monthly magazine of general literature with much the same kind of snob appeal that characterized his more scandalous weekly, *Town Topics* (1879–1937). The *Smart Set* was distinguished under later ownerships by the work of a number of brilliant writers. In 1908 HENRY L. MENCKEN became its book-review editor, and the next year GEORGE JEAN NATHAN its theater editor. When Nathan and Mencken became editors and part-owners in 1914, they introduced such contributors as F. Scott Fitzgerald, Maxwell Anderson, Eugene O'Neill, and Ruth Suckow, and supplied their own pungent social, literary, and dramatic criticism. By 1923 Mencken and Nathan had tired of the *Smart Set* and readily accepted Alfred A. Knopf's offer to provide them with a more impressive and dignified forum in a new monthly in which they would have a one-third interest as working editors. It was the *American Mercury*, founded in 1924. Nathan retired as coeditor after one year, but remained five years longer as a departmental editor. In the new magazine Mencken found it "an agreeable duty to track down some of the worst nonsense prevailing and do execution upon it." Some of the *Mercury's* departments were continued from the *Smart Set*, such as the always entertaining "Americana," a collection of current absurdities in popular culture and cults, arranged geographically by states. Not all of the *Mercury* was negative. There were able articles on folk literature, anthropology, the American Negro, newspapers, major literary figures, philology (with emphasis on examples of American usage), picturesque personalities and events, and unswept corners of American history. Among its contributors were Margaret Mead, Lewis Mumford, Louis Adamic, William E. Dodd, and Fred Lewis Pattee. Notable writers of fiction were Sinclair Lewis, James Stevens, and William Faulkner; among the poets were Vachel Lindsay, Edgar Lee Masters, Carl Sandburg, Countee Cullen, James Weldon Johnson, and George Sterling. The beginning of the Depression of the 1930s coincided with a recession in Mencken's popularity, and he retired in 1933. Lawrence E. Spivak came into control for the next fifteen years, and the magazine soon became a pocket-size miscellany with strongly conservative tendencies in politics and economics. It ceased publication in 1980.

American Notes for General Circulation (1842), Charles Dickens's account of his tour of the United States in 1842. He visited New York and Boston, got as far west as St. Louis, admired some of what he saw, but was so severe on American manners and so scathing on the subject of American piracy of English books that his book was most unfavorably received in the United States. See MARTIN CHUZZLEWIT.

American Renaissance: Art and Expression in the Age of Emerson and Whitman (1941), F.O. MATTHIESSEN's masterful study of the first great period in American literature.

American Revolution. Literature written during the American Revolution was almost without exception political.

It played on patriot pride, ridiculed the enemy at home and abroad, or addressed itself in sober argument to the task of persuasion. No masterworks appeared, except for the DECLARATION OF INDEPENDENCE, its authorship probably multiple and still disputed; but much of the writing of this period is remembered with pride because it provided substantial ideological foundations on which later generations have built. It was a time for plain speaking and the reduction of thought to essentials. Literary style was often sacrificed to achieve simplicity and guarantee understanding.

As the war years approached, men with literary aspirations put them aside for practical application of their talents to current events. By 1776 patriots like William Livingston, who was to become wartime governor of New Jersey, and who as a younger man had written polite prose and verse in the manner of Alexander Pope and the London essayists, turned to the rough-and-tumble of pamphlet warfare. In Philadelphia the little literary group which, under the leadership of the Reverend WILLIAM SMITH, provost of the college there, had made that city merry with songs and masques and even serious drama written by FRANCIS HOPKINSON, NATHANIEL EVANS, THOMAS GODFREY, Thomas Coombe, and others, was dispersed by death or divided loyalties. Of those prominent among them only Hopkinson remained, to create in prose A PRETTY STORY (1774) and in verse THE BATTLE OF THE KEGS (1777), small, bright, patriotic pieces now remembered more affectionately than Hopkinson's serious or more heavily satirical contributions to patriotic newspapers.

PHILIP FRENEAU and HUGH HENRY BRACKENRIDGE, recently graduated from Princeton, both turned from purely literary ambition to become ardent propagandists. TIMOTHY DWIGHT and JOEL BARLOW, from Yale, shelved plans for epic poems in order to dedicate their talents to war. Young ALEXANDER HAMILTON left college to become a pamphleteer, then a soldier. BENJAMIN FRANKLIN, who had been writing for fifty years and who in 1771 had begun quietly to record his AUTOBIOGRAPHY proved his pen was still sharp in such essays as EDICT BY THE KING OF PRUSSIA (1773) and "Rules by Which a Great Empire Might Be Reduced to a Small One." (1773). In Connecticut JOHN TRUMBULL, whose wit had been directed against collegiate follies in *The Progress of Dulness* (1772–73), pointed it now toward Tories and mob-directed rebels in the deft octosyllables of M'FINGAL (1772–82), which became, perhaps after the ubiquitous YANKEE DOODLE (c. 1778), the most popular native poem of its time.

Most consistently active among the verse-makers was Freneau, remembered with some justification as "the poet of the American Revolution." Between 1775 and 1783 he anathematized the British or celebrated patriot triumphs in scores of partisan rhymes, many of which were collected after the war in his *Poems* (1786). Best remembered among them are THE HOUSE OF NIGHT (1779), which speaks less of war than of turmoil within the poet's mind; THE BRITISH PRISON-SHIP (1781), a long hate-filled diatribe based on its author's own experience as a captive; and "To the Memory of the Brave Americans"

(1781). In "The Political Balance" (1782) Freneau hurls ridicule against defeated redcoats in anapestic lines that show better control of meter and imagery than of an uneven temper. When the war was over, Freneau turned to poetry of a less raucous kind, producing such deft and distinctive lyrics as THE WILD HONEY SUCKLE (1786) and "Neversink" (1791), until caught up again by politics as an ardent but ultimately disillusioned republican.

Freneau's wartime prose, which was never completely collected although much of it was reprinted in his *Miscellaneous Works* (1788), is less adroit and forceful than his verse. More persuasive in his prose was the urbane JOHN DICKINSON. Until his hesitation in 1776 over the question of whether complete independence was really desirable, Dickinson seemed luminously to sum up colonial grievances in such writings as LETTERS FROM A PENNSYLVANIA FARMER (1768). After the Declaration of Independence, THOMAS PAINE's pamphlet signed COMMON SENSE (1776), and the sixteen issues of *The Crisis* (1776–83) (see THE AMERICAN CRISIS) caught and held public attention. Cogent yet passionate, these works expressed confidence that in those times when men's souls were tried, American freemen would prevail, aided by divine power and by the resolute strength of their arms and convictions. Only in later years, with THE RIGHTS OF MAN (1791–92) and THE AGE OF REASON (1794–95), did Paine, even more than Freneau, seem to conservative countrymen to carry notions of human freedom to extremes. These two voices rose, often stridently, above the clamor of other men who from press or pulpit pelted laggard neighbors or haughty foes with emotion-packed phrases. Hundreds of others contributed squibs, verses, and columns of polemic, satirical, sincere, and enthusiastic prose. Although their cumulative influence was large, they are now forgotten. They wrote, it has been said, wisely but not often well.

The most polished and continuingly attractive prose came from the pen of HECTOR ST. JEAN DE CRÈVECOEUR, a French settler in upper New York, an observant noncombatant who was suspected and harried by both sides. During the last year of the war he made his way to London, where he published LETTERS FROM AN AMERICAN FARMER (1782), a work later translated and expanded in French. It presented idyllic descriptions but also forthright, realistic accounts of the customs and labors and pleasures of life on the American frontier, and posed and answered the tantalizing question: "What then is the American, this strange man?" More than a century later further materials, earlier suppressed by Crèvecoeur or his publisher, were discovered and printed as *Sketches of Eighteenth Century America* (1925). Here tales of privation were told, of marauding attacks by patriots and loyalists alike, of house burnings and terror and slaughter, similar to those revealed in the letters of ANN ELIZA BLEECKER in her *Posthumous Works* (1792), or in Hilliard d'Auberteuil's *Mis Mac Rea* (1784).

Accounts of atrocities and captivity like Freneau's *The British Prison-Ship* played a quickening role in sustaining patriot resolution. A NARRATIVE OF COLONEL ETHAN ALLEN'S CAPTIVITY (1779), which Melville was later to use in ISRAEL POTTER, went through many hastily printed editions. *A Narrative of the Captivity and Treatment of John Dodge by the English at Detroit* (1779) and *The Old Jersey Captive* (1781) realistically reinforced contemporary convictions of the cruel barbarism of the enemy. Though not printed until 1857, the autobiographical *Narrative of the Capture of Henry Laurens, of His Confinement in the Tower of London, and So Forth, 1780, 1781, 1782* contains, it has been said, an "unsurpassed embodiment of the proudest, finest, wittiest, most efficient, and most chivalrous Americanism" of that time. Colonials who chose the other side, daring patriot wrath by remaining loyal to England, endured their share of hardship more silently, except in letters, journals, and petitions for reimbursement submitted to the Parliament in London, many of which are heartrending and authentic personal documents, not intended as literature.

Loyalist poets and propagandists, however, were not silent. Joseph Stansbury, socially prominent in Philadelphia, filled the newspapers of that city with witty verse and playful, satirical prose until he shipped off to Nova Scotia for the duration. JONATHAN ODELL, a clergyman from New Jersey, became a chaplain in the British army, under the protection of which in occupied New York he peppered his patriot neighbors with polished verses done after the satirical model of Pope, Dryden, and Juvenal. After Freneau's, his was the clearest poetic voice of those times. His *The Congratulation* (1779) and *The American Times* (1780) speak valiantly of the colonial rebellion as an uprising of unthinking men against tradition and authority. SAMUEL PETERS, an Anglican clergyman from New England who fled from the wrath of his patriot countrymen, published in London a grotesquely fabricated *General History of Connecticut* (1781), which branded all Yankees as bland hypocrites, misguided in morality and politics. The former colonial governor of Massachusetts, THOMAS HUTCHINSON, a man of greater breadth and probity, completed in England the third volume of his monumental *History of the Colony and Province of Massachusetts Bay* (1764–1828).

Patriot historians were also active. William Henry Drayton, a member of the Continental Congress from South Carolina, worked in Charleston and Philadelphia over his *Memoirs of the American Revolution* (1821), printed long after his death; and DAVID RAMSAY, also of Charleston, collected materials there for his later *History of the War in South Carolina* (1791). MERCY OTIS WARREN, better remembered for her patriotic dramas, who as a woman could not participate in war, spent these years gathering materials for her *History of the Rise, Progress and Termination of the American Revolution* (1805). Opposed to conflict of any kind, Quaker Robert Proud spent the war-torn years writing his precise and ponderous *History of Pennsylvania* (1797).

Several patriot authors turned their hands to drama (see DRAMA IN THE U.S.), most of it meant to be read as propaganda or to be played by amateur groups as ardent as they. Mercy Otis Warren in Massachusetts wrote THE ADULATEUR (1773), described as "A Tragedy, as it is now Acted in Upper Servia," but which was in reality a satire directed against Tory activity in Boston. Like her later THE GROUP (1775), it is more interesting

for what it reveals of dissension among colonials than for its excellence as literature. Most ambitious of the patriot dramas was THE FALL OF BRITISH TYRANNY (1776), usually ascribed to John (or Joseph) Leacock of Philadelphia. A tragicomedy in five acts, in which farce and melodrama are relieved by pastoral interludes offering shepherds commenting innocently on passing events, it vigorously details supposed evil intentions abroad and braveries at home. Its final scene introduces General Washington in his first appearance as a character on the stage.

Bombastic but better were the two short plays in verse written by HUGH HENRY BRACKENRIDGE for production by students in his Maryland academy. THE BATTLE OF BUNKERS HILL (1776) celebrates the courage of patriot volunteers; *The Death of General Montgomery* (1777) denounces the cowardice and treachery of the enemy. Attributed to Thomas Paine is *A Dialogue between the Ghost of General Montgomery, Just Arrived from the Elysian Fields, and an American Delegate in a Wood near Philadelphia* (1776), which is hardly dramatic at all, but an argument cogently and forcefully reasoned. Best plotted and most finished of the dramas of these times was THE PATRIOTS (1776), by Colonel Robert Munford of Virginia, who found subjects for quiet satire among both patriots and loyalists. *The Motley Assembly* (1779), which reviles social-climbing collaborators, is sometimes attributed to Mrs. Warren, but it is a coarse, indignant, slapstick affair, hardly the kind to be expected of a lady from Boston.

Tories turned to drama also. The anonymous *A Dialogue Between a Southern Delegate and His Spouse on His Return from the Grand Continental Congress* (1774) is slight but amusing: how much better, it suggests, would affairs have turned out if women had been allowed to manage them. JONATHAN SEWALL, once attorney-general of Massachusetts, wrote a sharp criticism of his countrymen in *The Americans Roused in a Cure for the Spleen* (1775), which pretended to record "the substance of a conversation on the times over a friendly tankard and a pipe" between colonials met in a tavern; the patriots among them were bumpkins of little sense or knowledge, while the loyalists included better men, like the parson and the justice of the peace. After General Burgoyne's farce, THE BLOCKADE (1776), was performed by British troops in Boston, it was countered by a scurrilous patriot reply called *The Blockheads* (1776), another topical satire sometimes said (though probably wrongly) to have been written by Mrs. Warren. Other British plays were performed, perhaps written or adapted for jubilant occasions, by officers of His Majesty's army stationed in New York or Boston. Among them was another *The Blockheads*, an opera in two acts, performed and printed in the former city, probably late in the war, and republished in London in 1782. But most writers, patriot or Tory or among the British occupation forces, were busy with other things than drama. Many, like Freneau, who left unfinished *The Spy*, a play based on the capture of Major André, must have begun to write or wanted to write dialogues or dramatic sketches to celebrate these exciting, liberating times. College students, for example,

John Smith of Dartmouth, who produced "Dialogue between an Englishman and an Indian" (1779), tried their hands hurriedly, but then quickly turned to other things.

Almost all the writing done in America during the war years was copied or adapted, sometimes parodied, from English models. Much of it was brief, written for an occasion, hurriedly or in the heat of controversy. Colonel DAVID HUMPHREYS, an aide-de-camp to General Washington, composed ponderous poems in praise of patriot victories. JOHN PARKE, also a patriot officer, composed odes about battles and American heroes that were collected after the war as *The Lyric Works of Horace, Translated into English Verse* (1786). James McClurg, a physician and collegemate of Thomas Jefferson, wrote martial songs, as did ST. GEORGE TUCKER of Williamsburg and BENJAMIN YOUNG PRIME, long known as a minor part-time poet in New York. But few of their songs have survived, nor have the battle songs and hymns of Joel Barlow and Timothy Dwight, who wrote with no less patriotic fervor.

It might almost be said that not until after the war did the literature of the American Revolution begin to appear. Then Freneau was able to collect his poems, Parke, his *Lyric Works*, and Humphreys, volume after volume of patriotic lines. Then Dwight could complete his *The Conquest of Canaan* (1785), a Biblical epic which, in spite of its author's protests, most readers thought was about Washington emblemized as Joshua, who led loyal hosts to the promised land of freedom, Joel Barlow completed and published *The Vision of Columbus* (1787), which stumbled earnestly through versified anticipations of the new country's great future. Then GEORGE WASHINGTON began to emerge as a national hero in plays, poems, novels, and biographies, to reign supreme for seventy-five years, until Abraham Lincoln took his place. MASON LOCKE WEEMS, in his *Life of Washington* (1800), fixed forever the story of young George and the cherry tree, an incident that outlasts any detailed in the better lives by John Marshall (1804–07), James Kirke Paulding (1835), or Washington Irving (1855–59).

In drama, PETER MARKOE celebrated Washington in *The Patriot Chief* (1784). WILLIAM DUNLAP in his tragedy *André* (1789) provided a prominent role for the former commander. But of the scores of plays written about Washington or the American Revolution, none really survives, nor have poems on these subjects been conspicuously successful. Almost every native poet, from Bryant through Holmes and Lowell to Stephen Vincent Benét, has touched on the subject, but perhaps only RALPH WALDO EMERSON's "Concord Hymn" (1837), which speaks of the "rude bridge which arched the flood" and the "shot heard round the world," convincingly combines patriotism and poetry.

In fiction, however, the situation has been quite different. Hundreds of novels and tales have been written about the Revolutionary conflict. Perhaps best known of them are James Fenimore Cooper's THE SPY (1821) and his tales of maritime adventures, such as THE PILOT (1823) and THE RED ROVER (1827). William Gilmore Simms' seven Revolutionary novels include THE PARTISAN (1834), *Woodcraft* (1835), and *The Forayers* (1855). John Pendleton Kennedy wrote of skirmishes on the Southern frontier in HORSE-SHOE ROBINSON (1835); Lydia Maria Child combined war and romance in *The Rebels* (1825), as did Catherine M. Sedgwick in *The Linwoods* (1835); JAMES KIRKE PAULDING's *The Old Continental* (1846) may seem dull beside Herman Melville's ISRAEL POTTER (1855), which tells of battles at sea and captivity on land, but both will admit precedence to S. Weir Mitchell's HUGH WYNNE, FREE QUAKER (1897), which has been called the best novel of the American Revolution, or to SARAH ORNE JEWETT's *The Tory Lover* (1901), which combines sentiment with controlled sensibility. Most popular of recent novels of the Revolution are Kenneth Roberts' ARUNDEL (1930), RABBLE IN ARMS (1933), and OLIVER WISWELL (1940); Walter D. Edmonds' DRUMS ALONG THE MOHAWK (1936); Inglis Fletcher's several novels, from *Raleigh's Eden* (1940) to *Roanoke Hundred* (1948); HOWARD FAST's *The Unvanquished* (1943); and JOHN JAKES's best-sellers of the 1970s.

Helpful studies include MOSES COIT TYLER, *The Literary History of the American Revolution* (1897); Bruce I. Granger, *Political Satire in the American Revolution* (1960); Perry Miller, *The Life of the Mind in America: From the Revolution to the Civil War* (1965); Kenneth Silverman, *A Cultural History of the American Revolution* (1976); Lawrence Buell, *New England Literary Culture: From Revolution through Renaissance* (1986). LEWIS LEARY/GP

American Scene, The (1907), a descriptive and analytical travel book by HENRY JAMES, reflecting the impressions of his 1904 visit. Although he visited Baltimore, Washington, Charleston, and Florida, his best passages reflect the changes in New York and New England form his memories of a generation earlier. Concerned for the future of culture and the arts in America, James is attracted and repelled by the empowering wealth, the generative power of industry, and the attendant and pervasive vulgarity. A vision of New York harbor, for example, leaves him admiring and apprehensive as "the breezy brightness of the Bay puts on the semblance of the vast white page that awaits beyond any other perhaps the black overscoring of science."

American Scholar, The (August 31, 1837), an address by RALPH WALDO EMERSON delivered before the Phi Beta Kappa Society of Harvard. It was published separately in 1837, and reprinted in *Nature, Addresses, and Lectures* (1849). Oliver Wendell Holmes called it "our intellectual Declaration of Independence." Emerson exhorted his listeners, and America generally, to mental independence and self-confidence. He called on scholars to "defer never to the popular cry" and "to cheer, to raise, and to guide men by showing them facts amidst appearances."

American Songbag, The (1927), a collection of folk songs and ballads made by CARL SANDBURG.

American Spectator, The (1932–1937), monthly literary newspaper founded by George Jean Nathan, Sherwood Anderson, Ernest Boyd, James Branch Cabell, Theodore Dreiser, and Eugene O'Neill, but sold by its founders in 1935. Soon after going bimonthly, it went out of business.

American Speller, The (1783), by NOAH WEBSTER. This textbook originally formed part of Webster's GRAMMATI-

CAL INSTITUTE OF THE ENGLISH LANGUAGE, COMPRISING AN EASY, CONCISE, AND SYSTEMATIC METHOD OF EDUCATION DESIGNED FOR THE USE OF ENGLISH SCHOOLS IN AMERICA. This consisted of three parts: a spelling book, a grammar, and a reader, in all of which Webster emphasized his patriotic as well as educational ideas. The speller soon took on an independent existence, and was the first American schoolbook. It continued in use throughout the 19th and into the 20th century, reaching a sale ultimately of more than 75,000,000 copies. The book helped standardize American spelling and pronunciation.

American Tragedy, An (1925),   a novel by THEODORE DREISER, based on an actual case, that of Chester Gillette, who murdered Grace Brown at Big Moose Lake in the Adirondacks in July 1906. Dreiser selected this case after considering sixteen similar ones in which a poor boy murdered his pregnant girlfriend so that he could marry a rich girl, a tragic occurrence Dreiser thought peculiarly American. The book shows Dreiser sometimes following the facts of the Gillette-Brown case, at other times altering them to suit his purpose. Clyde Griffiths—and presumably his real life counterparts—are shown to be victims of a destructive American dream.

After becoming a bellboy in a luxurious Kansas City hotel, Clyde turns his back on the piety and poverty of his parents. When he is involved in an automobile accident in which a girl is killed, he runs away, first to Chicago, then to upstate New York, where he does menial work in a collar factory owned by his rich uncle. Alone and neglected by his uncle's family, Clyde seduces Roberta Alden, one of the factory girls. Later, he is taken up by a local socialite, whom he dreams of marrying. After failing to terminate Roberta's pregnancy, Clyde plots to drown her. Dreiser arranges matters so that Clyde's nerve fails him at the last moment, but the boat overturns and Roberta is drowned. Technically, then, Clyde is not guilty of murder, but he is tried and convicted, partly because of public outrage but also and mainly because of the political ambitions of the district attorney. In Dreiser's view, Clyde is a victim of his own weak nature and of a society that encourages him to dream of acquiring wealth and luxury by marrying a rich girl, then kills him for trying to do so.

Early humanist critics condemned the novel's naturalism and Dreiser's alleged lack of feeling for Roberta. More recently critics have praised the book's artistry, particularly the power of the narrative and the artful structuring of the novel. *An American Tragedy*, despite its sometimes awkward style, is now regarded as one of the important American novels of the 20th century.

W. J. STUCKEY

America's Lost Plays (1940, rpr. 1963–1965),   a collection in 20 volumes edited by Barrett Clark (with supplement, 1969, edited by Walter J. Meserve and William R. Reardon) of over 100 American plays surviving in manuscript from the 18th century onward.

America the Beautiful (1895, rev. 1904, 1911),   by KATHARINE LEE BATES. The poem has been set to music many times, but the tune with which it is most frequently associated is "Materna," by Samuel A. Ward. It has often been suggested that the poem should replace *The Star-Spangled Banner* as the American national anthem.

Amerika (1927, tr. 1938),   a fragment of a novel by Franz Kafka (1883–1924), published posthumously. The story relates a fantastic, often comic adventure in America, a land Kafka had never seen. It developed from a short story called "The Stoker" (*Der Heizer*), published in 1913.

Ames, Fisher (1758–1808),   statesman, essayist. Born in Dedham, Massachusetts, the son of NATHANIEL AMES, this leading representative of New England Federalism argued that "the quintessence of good government is to protect property and its rights," and referred to "the dangerous mass of the poor and vicious." As a member of Congress, he was a supporter of Hamilton and an opponent of Jefferson. As an orator on many public occasions, Ames won a wide reputation: he was offered the presidency of Harvard, but declined. His *Works* appeared in 1809, an enlarged edition in 1854.

Ames, Nathaniel (1708–1764),   physician, compiler of almanacs. Ames issued his first almanac when he was seventeen, eight years before Franklin's POOR RICHARD'S ALMANACK. It was called *Astronomical Diary and Almanack*, and was continued until 1775 by his son, Dr. Nathaniel Ames. The younger Ames was as ardent a Republican as his brother Fisher was a Federalist. In 1891 appeared *The Essays, Humor, and Poems of Nathaniel Ames, Father and Son, of Dedham, Mass., from Their Almanacks, 1726–1775*, edited with notes and comments by Samuel Briggs.

Ammons, A[rchie] R[andolph] (1926–2001),   poet. Ammons was born and brought up on a family farm near Whiteville, North Carolina, in a house that had but a single book, the Bible. He recalled that in his childhood he substituted "for normal human experience, which was unavailable to me much of the time, [a] sense of identity with the things around me." Not long after graduating from high school he joined the navy—World War II was then in progress—and served aboard a destroyer escort. He began writing poetry during the long intervals between watches. Leaving the navy in 1946, he continued writing while attending Wake Forest on the G.I. Bill. He kept his poetry a secret for almost all his years in college and majored not in literature, but in science. After graduation, Ammons did some teaching, married, and served as a principal in a tiny school on Cape Hatteras in North Carolina. He attended graduate school for a year at Berkeley and in 1952, moved to New Jersey, where he lived for twelve years, working as a business executive.

His first volume, *Ommateum* (1955), attracted no notice, but in the 1960s Ammons's career took a quantum leap. During the course of that period he began teaching at Cornell (where he became Goldwin Smith professor of poetry), published five volumes of poetry, including *Tape for the Turn of the Year* (1965), and received a Traveling Fellowship from the American Academy of Arts and Letters, as well as a Guggenheim Fellowship. In the next two decades he produced many more volumes of verse, including *Uplands* (1970), *Briefings* (1971), *Collected Poems* (1951–1971) (1972), *Sphere: The Form of a Motion* (1974), *A Coast of Trees* (1981), *Lake Effect Country*

(1983), and *Sumerian Vistas* (1987), and he was the recipient of a National Book Award, the Bollingen Prize and a MacArthur Prize Fellow Award.

In his long poem "The Ridge Farm," Ammons names some persons accompanying him on a trip to the place designated in the title, but immediately drops any further reference to them, going on to tell us he would "buy a whole 130-acre farm for one hermit lark, his song. . . ." This dispensing with his human companions and embracing of the hermit lark (in an interview he identified himself with that bird) points up an often noted feature of the Ammons canon. His poems largely lack a focus on people other than himself, although his father appears at times to be forcing a partial entry. So, for the most part, we find Ammons failing to attend to love, sex (except in a curious form, at once bawdy and abstract), or past or present personal relationships. ("Easter Morning" is a notable exception.) He is more likely to engage in a conversation with the wind or a mountain than with another human being. Other materials virtually banished from his oeuvre, or at least marginalized, include history, politics, race, class, work (apart from the work of making poems), art (apart from the art of poetry), physical interiors, the city. Even Ammons's own feelings are admitted into view in a selective way, and sometimes simply named without being elaborated on or contextualized—no confessional poet he, or if so, only fitfully and qualifiedly. All these exclusions help make Ammons, in his own phrase for himself, an "abstract poet."

With so much left out, what is left for this human hermit lark to sing about? Nothing less than the physical cosmos (Ammons might be taken as a modern day Lucretius), and the biological processes operating within it, even though his vantage point on a given occasion may be only that of his backyard. With the exception of his first volume, he has repeatedly situated himself in a universe whose physics and biophysics enthrall him. Materials that might be thought of as the jumping off place for scientists' mullings have been appropriated by him and subjected to a strenuous play of consciousness and of language. He is the singer of stasis and movement, the passage from liquid states to solid ones or vice versa, weightings and unweightings, the interplay of matter and energy, structure and flow.

At the center of Ammons's physical world is the element of "motion" (the word itself is one of the most frequently used by him), an element so pervasive as to be virtually indistinguishable from reality. Fused with form, motion becomes ordered process, and a series of such processes are reverently regarded by him as maintaining our individual and collective existences, though such processes also undo us: "nature that roots under us . . . flows through assembling us but eventually . . . flows through/taking us apart, returning fine knots/to recycling's fuzzy frays."

If the universe flows, if it is permeated by motion, so too is the poet's consciousness. (Those epitomes of flowing, brooks, may be said to function as his totemic models.) The honoring of flow is reflected in his restricting the use of periods to the ends of his poems, however long, and his habitual employment of the colon, though its presence is much reduced in *Sumerian Vistas*. For even as it marks a pause, the colon may be said to look forward, to keep things going.

Ammons's work has been linked to Emerson, Whitman, Dickinson, Wallace Stevens (perhaps the list of American forebears might be extended to include Edward Taylor), as well as to the English Romantics. As far as his preoccupation with motion goes, perhaps the predecessor text most relevant may be the passage in Wordsworth's "Tintern Abbey" that, itself using a colon, speaks of something whose dwelling is "the blue sky, and in the mind of man:/A motion and a spirit, that impels/All thinking things . . . /And rolls through all things." Many of Ammons's shorter poems are narrowly focused, but the longer ones show his mind constantly embodying a motion of thought, a relentless, widely ranging rumination on the motions of the physical and biological world, his diction roving with a matching freedom through the wide spaces of the English language.

For all its engagement with movement, Ammons's poetry is also preoccupied with structure, the presence and operations of patterning. A formal reflection of this can be seen in the fact that most of the long poems, while eschewing, like many of the short ones, rhyme, syllable count, meter, and stanzaic closure, commit themselves to a stanza of a set number of lines. Motion and structure constitute one of several polarities permeating Ammons's work, the ultimate one being that generated by the classical philosophical question of the One and the Many, the problem of formulating some sort of encompassing order that will be seen to synthesize the multiple particulars of existence. Associated with the One in Ammons's poetry are ascents, heights, the notion of a center, unity, silence, abstraction; associated with the Many are, correspondingly, descents, low places, the notion of periphery, diversity, speech, concreteness. (For Ammons had not only called himself an "abstract poet" but also "the exact/poet of the concrete *par excellence*.") He is continually engaged in an epistemological dialectic that involves back and forth movements between the One and the Many, and between the elements respectively associated with them.

Ammons's poetry celebrates not only our world, both in its marvelous particulars and grand processes, but also the mind, at once doomed to extinction and grand in its reaches, able to employ the gift of language to contemplate the cosmos and itself in the act of contemplation. He has significantly extended and placed his own stamp on the Romantic concern with the natural world and the consciousness that mediates on it.

Works in addition to those named above include *Selected Longer Poems* (1980), and *The Selected Poems Expanded Edition* (1987). Studies include Alan Holder, *A. R. Ammons* (1978), and Steven P. Scheider, *A. R. Ammons and the Poetics of Widening Scope* (1994).

ALAN HOLDER

Amory, Cleveland (1917–1998),   social historian, journalist, novelist, and animal rights activist. Born in Nahant,

Massachusetts, and educated at Harvard, Amory earned his primary reputation for his sharp, humorous sketches of American society. He won early fame with *The Proper Bostonians* (1947), a dissection of Boston's first families from colonial times onward. *The Last Resorts* (1952) followed, a study of the great society resorts of the late 19th and early 20th centuries. *The Proper Bostonians Revisited* (1972) brought him back to his first subject from the perspective of another quarter century. Other works include the novel *Home Town* (1950), a satire on book publishing; *Who Killed Society?* (1960); *Man Kind? Our Incredible War on Wildlife* (1974); *Animal* (1976); *The Trouble with Nowadays,* (1979); *The Cat Who Came for Christmas* (1987); *The Cat and the Curmudgeon* (1990); *The Best Cat Ever* (1993); and *Ranch of Dreams* (1997).

Amos Judd (1895),   a novel by JOHN AMES MITCHELL. A young rajah, in a time of civil war, is smuggled out of India to Connecticut, where he is brought up as Amos Judd, in ignorance of his origin. Mitchell depicts skillfully the development of traits that make it clear how far the young Hindu's character is from that of the practical Yankees around him.

Anahareo.   See GREY OWL.

Anarchiad, The: A Poem on the Restoration of Chaos and Substantial Night (Oct. 26, 1786–Sept. 13, 1787).   This mock-heroic poem, by several of the HARTFORD WITS, appeared originally in the *New Haven Gazette and Connecticut Magazine,* was widely reprinted in newspapers, and first published as a whole in 1861. The authors chiefly concerned were DR. LEMUEL HOPKINS, DAVID HUMPHREYS (who probably originated the idea), JOHN TRUMBULL, and JOEL BARLOW. In its 1,200 lines, the poem strongly supported the Federalist point of view. It attacked SHAYS' REBELLION, paper money in Rhode Island, and the delay in ratifying the Constitution and setting up a strong central government.

Anaya, Rudolfo A. (1937–   ),   novelist, short-story writer, essayist. Born in Pastura, New Mexico, of Mexican-American parents, Anaya was educated at the University of New Mexico and taught in Albuquerque public schools, at the University of Albuquerque, and at the University of New Mexico. After his first novel, *Bless Me, Ultima* (1972), won a QUINTO SOL literary award, he became recognized as one of the foremost Chicano writers, although unlike some of the other Quinto Sol writers his chosen language has been English rather than Spanish. In *Bless Me, Ultima,* the 1945 atomic explosion at White Sands, New Mexico, heralds great changes in the surrounding area. What has been shattered is in part restored as the young hero creates a new identity out of Spanish, Indian, and Anglo ingredients, which are magically unified with the help of a folk healer. In *Heart of Aztlan* (1976), *Tortuga* (1979), and *Lord of The Dawn: The Legend of Quetzalcoatl* (1987), Anaya continued his fictional quest for unification. Short stories, collected in *Cuentos: Tales from the Hispanic Southwest* (1980) and *The Silence of the Llano* (1982), and a travel account, *A Chicano in China* (1986), provided a break from novels, which he returned to in *Alburquerque* (1992), an ambitious work that returns the "r" to Albuquerque, a letter

lost, according to legend, by an Anglo mistake. In this novel, "a child of the line that separated white from brown" searches for a father in a land where political struggles over water and real estate serve as emblems of continuing divisions between races and times. Murder mysteries include *Zia Summer* (1995) and *Rio Grande Fall* (1996).

Ancona, Vincenzo (1915–2000),   poet, folk singer, sculptor. Born in Sicily, Ancona emigrated to New York in 1956. Writing in Sicilian, and following Sicilian meters and rhyme schemes, he found a following in Sicilian communities in the United States and Canada for his celebrations of American life and recapitulations of Sicilian folk tales. *Malidittu la Lingua* ("Damned Language," 1990) is bilingual; an accompaying cassette includes readings by the author. He was also a folk singer and folk artist whose work was shown at the Museum of American Folk Art.

Anderson, Laurie (1947–   ),   performance artist, writer, composer. Born in Wayne, Illinois, and educated at Barnard College (B.A., 1969) and Columbia University (M.F.A., 1972), Anderson has taught art history at the City University of New York and written criticism for art journals, but has achieved her fame as a recording artist and stage performer. Success with early recordings, including "It's Not the Bullet that Kills You—It's the Hole" (1977), "O Superman" (1981), and "You're the Guy I Want to Share My Money With" (1983), led to multimedia shows that included the six-hour Brooklyn Academy of Music presentation *United States* (1983) and the film *Home of the Brave* (1986), which she wrote, directed, and acted in, reworking some of the material from the earlier presentation. *Stories from the Nerve Bible* (1993) was a successful touring presentation. With Hsin-Chien Huang, she created an interactive CD-ROM, *Puppet Motel* (1995). For many, her most ambitious project to date was her touring presentation *Songs and Stories from Moby Dick* (1999). *United States* (1984) and *Stories from the Nerve Bible, A Retrospective 1972–1992* (1994) are book versions of the stage presentations. Many of her works are available online, in video form, or as CDs.

Anderson, Maxwell (1888–1959),   playwright. Born in Atlantic, Pennsylvania, and educated at the University of North Dakota and Stanford, Anderson taught in colleges and wrote for newspapers in San Francisco and New York. He met LAURENCE STALLINGS, with whom he collaborated on three plays, when they both wrote for the New York *World.* Their WHAT PRICE GLORY? (1924), a play about World War I that did not romanticize combat, attracted considerable attention. Other Anderson-Stallings productions are *First Flight* (1925), on the youth of ANDREW JACKSON, and *The Buccaneer* (1925), on SIR HENRY MORGAN. Anderson also collaborated with Harold Hickerson on *Gods of Lightning* (produced 1928), about the Sacco-Vanzetti case. Anderson's *Saturday's Children* (1927) is a domestic comedy centering on an immature couple hampered by poverty and in-laws. His other early plays are *White Desert* (1923) and *Outside Looking In* (1925), based on an autobiography by JIM TULLY.

In his first verse drama, ELIZABETH THE QUEEN (1930), Anderson managed to combine the serious message that drama was obliged to convey with his intellectual conviction that poetry was a viable medium for 20th-century theater. The experiment was a financial success. The conflict of two historical characters, Queen Elizabeth and Essex, is vital and compelling though the text contains few memorable lines of verse. His next historical play, *Night Over Taos* (1932), centering on the New Mexico Indian leader Montoya, is less successful.

Both Your Houses (1933), a political satire about an idealistic Congressman's failed fight against corruption, won the Pulitzer Prize. Returning again to history in *Mary of Scotland* (1933), Anderson depicted Mary as a noble protagonist tragically betrayed and defeated by her scheming cousin, Elizabeth. His attempt to define George Washington as a tragic figure in *Valley Forge* (1934) was less compelling.

In *The Essence of Tragedy* (1939), Anderson set forth his notions of the serious mission of the modern theater, which he thought of as a force for democratic education. Updating Aristotle's definitions of tragedy, Anderson decreed that plays must illuminate the inner life of a character struggling with questions of good and evil. The protagonist, representing the forces of good, must triumph and, though imperfect, be a clearly better person by the end of the drama. He attempted to demonstrate these ideals in his own work, particularly those dealing with historical figures.

Anderson was more successful in using the Sacco-Vanzetti case for a background in a second attempt. *Winterset* (1935), a verse play, is widely regarded as his best work. The central figure is the son of a man executed for a crime he did not commit. Seeking to clear his father's name and avenge him, he falls in love with the sister of one of the criminals he hopes to expose and finds that the ennobling effect of love is more powerful than the desire for revenge. His verse, using modern diction, proved an effective medium for the stage.

Anderson achieved some success with comic material, particularly in HIGH TOR (1937) and in KNICKERBOCKER HOLIDAY (1938), based on Washington Irving's accounts of early Dutch settlements, with music by KURT WEILL. *Lost in the Stars* (1949), another musical with Weill, is based on Alan Paton's *Cry, the Beloved Country*. With the rise of fascism in Europe, Anderson turned again to serious material with *Key Largo* (1939), about a returned American volunteer in the Spanish Civil War who finds courage to stand up to gangsterism in Florida, and with *Candle in the Wind* (1941), a story of Nazi cruelty in France. *The Eve of St. Mark* (1942) and *Storm Operation* (1944) are also about World War II.

Joan of Lorraine (1946), centering on the life of another historical woman, uses the device of a play in rehearsal. *Anne of the Thousand Days* (1948) presents Henry VIII as a sympathetic figure. *Barefoot in Athens* (1951) treats the life of Socrates. Anderson's last play, *The Bad Seed* (1955), based on a novel by WILLIAM MARCH, is a tense psychological drama of an innately evil child. Anderson was a prolific writer who produced twenty other plays in addition to those mentioned here.

One volume of Anderson's lyric poetry, *You Who Have Dreams* (1925), was published during his lifetime; *Notes on a Dream* (1971) appeared posthumously. *The Bases of Artistic Creation* (1942), with Rhys Carpenter and Roy Harris, and *Off Broadway* (1947) are essay collections.

Anderson, Patrick (1917–1979), poet, travel writer, editor. Born in Surrey, England, Anderson studied at Oxford and Columbia University, and in 1940 moved to Montreal. There he edited the leftist magazine *Preview* (1942–46) and published in *A Tent for April* (1945) his first adult poems. *The White Centre* (1946) was widely admired, especially for "Poem on Canada" and "The Country Still Unpossessed." Briefly a professor at McGill (1948–1950), he left Canada to teach at the University of Malaya and did not return until 1971. In spite of his years of absence, however, critics have credited him with a major impact on the substance and style of Canadian poetry.

During his years abroad, Anderson published nine prose works of travel and autobiography, including *Snake Wine: A Singapore Episode* (1955); *Search Me, Autobiography—The Black Country, Canada and Spain* (1957); and *The Character Ball: Chapters of Autobiography* (1963). With Alistair Sutherland, he edited *Eros* (1961), an anthology collecting prose and poetry on love between men. After his return to Canada, he revised some of his early poems, wrote some new ones, and collected much of the best of his work in *Return to Canada: Selected Poems* (1977).

Anderson, Robert Woodruff (1917–   ), playwright, teacher, film writer. Robert Anderson was born in New York City and sudied at Harvard. Anderson married Phyllis Stohl in 1940 and remained married to her until her death in 1956. From 1942 to 1946, Anderson served as a lieutenant and worked in naval intelligence in the Pacific war zone. His play *Come Marching Home* (1945) was written aboard ship and later was awarded the National Theater Conference Prize. In 1946 he taught playwrighting at the American Theater Wing as a recipient of a Rockefeller playwrighting fellowship. He married Teresa Wright in 1959 and became President of the New Dramatists Guild.

Although known best for his plays *Tea and Sympathy* (1953), which presents the problem confronting a lonely youth accused of homosexuality, and *I Never Sang for My Father* (1968), about alienation between a father and son, Anderson's major works also include *The Eden Rose* (1948), about the roles of sex and love in marriage; *All Summer Long* (1951), an adaptation of Donald Wetzel's novel *A Curse and a Wreath*, about the rites of passage; *The Days Between* (1965), about midlife crisis in a man whose marriage has grown stale; *You Know I Can't Hear You When the Water's Running* (1967), four short comedies that attack notions of American maleness; and *Solitaire/Double Solitaire* (1971), two short works produced together concerning aloneness and estrangement in marriage.

Anderson also wrote a number of film scripts. Noteworthy among them are *Tea and Sympathy* (1956), *The Nun's Story* (1959), *The Sand Pebbles* (1966), and *I Never Sang for My*

Father (1970). His one novel, *After* (1973), further expresses his major dramatic themes of loneliness and alienation.

Anderson's plays are significant for their bold treatment of sensitive sexual matters between men and women. His themes of loneliness and alienation in sexual relationships, particularly in marriage, clearly place him in the mainstream of 20th-century American drama.

FRANKLIN D. CASE

Anderson, Sherwood (1876–1941), novelist, short-story writer, essayist. Born in Camden, Ohio, the third of seven children, Sherwood Anderson was the son of an itinerant, wayward harness maker and house painter and a long-suffering mother whom he credited with awakening his "hunger to see beneath the surface of lives." He spent most of his youth in Clyde, Ohio, the town that would provide the backdrop for his most memorable work, *Winesburg, Ohio.* Because of his efforts to help support the family, Anderson completed less than one year of high school. Shortly after his mother died, in 1895, he left Clyde to seek his fortune in Chicago.

Failing to do so, he enlisted to fight in the Spanish-American War. Arriving in Cuba after the armistice had been signed, he came back, finished high school in a year (at age 23), and returned to Chicago as an advertising solicitor and copywriter. In 1904 he married. From advertising he moved on to the mail-order business; by 1907 he headed his own business, The Anderson Manufacturing Company, specializing in Roof-Fix, in Elyria, Ohio, and in that year the first of his three children was born. In 1912 he went through a midlife crisis that was to become legendary. In late November he wandered away from his office in a "fugue state" and four days later came to his senses in a Cleveland hospital. For several years he had been trying to write, to imagine a less material existence for himself in writing, and he did not abandon the world of advertising until he could afford to, but he devoted his new life to expressing what he thought was America's promise, often as it was embodied in himself.

Leaving his family behind, he returned once again to Chicago, this time to participate in its literary renaissance. Young critics like VAN WYCK BROOKS and WALDO FRANK saw proof in his stories that America was coming of age. In 1921 he received the first *Dial* award for service rendered to American letters; by 1925 he was, in H. L. Mencken's words, "America's most distinctive novelist." In the intervening years he went to Europe, he lived in Alabama, in New Orleans, and in New York, and he remarried, divorced, and married again. From the profits of his one commercially successful work, *Dark Laughter,* he built a home in southwestern Virginia, and there, in the late twenties, realizing that his powers as a fiction writer were failing, he bought and edited two newspapers. During the Depression he toured the mills and factories of the South and in his writing celebrated the perseverance of the people whom he saw and Roosevelt's efforts to meet their needs. His work was inspired by Eleanor Copenhaver, a young Y.W.C.A. executive, with whom he entered a final, and happy, marriage in 1933. In 1941 Anderson sought to extend his travels and his

interest in the potentials of small communities to South America, but he died of peritonitis on the way, his intestines having been perforated by a broken toothpick.

In his first novel, WINDY MCPHERSON'S SON (1916), Anderson recreated his own experiences growing up in a small midwestern town and his own misguided attempts to realize the American dream in material terms; he explored the implications of such failures for male-female relationships and expressed his desire for a truly richer, more imaginative life. His personal visions would always be implicitly political, but as is the case in his next novel, *Marching Men* (1917), whose hero leads workers in protest against the life imposed upon them by industrial America but offers them no program of their own, Anderson was more inclined to exhort men to realize the ideals of a democracy within themselves than to suggest how they might go about it together. In the *Mid-American Chants* (1918) that followed, he was no more convincing exhorting in the manner of Whitman and the King James Bible. Beginning in 1915 he wrote the stories, or tales, that would become WINESBURG, OHIO (1919). Each focused on a "grotesque," a figure whose life had become misshapen through devotion to one truth, one idea or passion, that passion being (for the times) often startlingly sexual. The "grotesques" form a whole, given the pervasive presences of the young reporter to whom they often confess and of the older narrator intent on evoking our sympathetic understanding of them. They inhabit a small Ohio town but Anderson modeled them after people he saw in Chicago, where he wrote the tales, and meant them to express the condition of contemporary American culture generally.

Drawing again on his midwestern heritage, on his memories of small towns and, this time, of Mark Twain, in *Poor White* (1920), Anderson successfully rendered the interconnections between a man's drives toward material success and his failures as a mate, and once again envisioned salvation in the creative life. The tales he collected in THE TRIUMPH OF THE EGG (1921) and *Horses and Men* (1923) tended to focus on young men's emergence into manhood; *Many Marriages* (1923) and DARK LAUGHTER (1925), his next novels, were poetic in their celebration of men's liberation from societal conventions, the latter (as the title indicates) coinciding with a particularly intense period of cultural exploitation of African Americans for that purpose. The first of Anderson's explicitly autobiographical works was *A Story Teller's Story* (1924), followed by *Tar: A Midwest Childhood* (1926) and *Sherwood Anderson's Memoirs* (1942). *Hello Towns!* (1929) contains the results of his efforts as a newspaperman. Out of his explorations of the Depression years came two novels, *Beyond Desire* (1932) and *Kit Brandon* (1936), and two volumes of nonfictional prose, *Perhaps Women* (1931) and *Puzzled America* (1935).

Anderson's is a colloquial style, often reminiscent of Twain's. It is seemingly simple, the diction and syntax consciously unliterary, but with it Anderson was capable of exploring unusual pscyhological depths in the realms of gender and sexual relationships. A scorner of neatly plotted stories, he was most at home in works controlled by the rhythms and voice of the teller of tales. Not without justification he claimed originality for the way he created the loose unity of *Winesburg, Ohio*. He was generous in his support of the greater writers who were to succeed him, WILLIAM FAULKNER and ERNEST HEMINGWAY in particular, and he had some influence on their literary manners and choice of subject matter. ERSKINE CALDWELL, JAMES T. FARRELL, WILLIAM SAROYAN, JOHN STEINBECK, THOMAS WOLFE and, more recently, RAYMOND CARVER are among those who have also been inspired by his commitment to the craft of writing as a means of exploring common men's lives openly and clearly.

The Complete Works of Sherwood Anderson was edited by Kichinosuke Ohashi (21 v. Kyoto, 1982). Studies include Irving Howe, *Sherwood Anderson* (1951), and Kim Townsend, *Sherwood Anderson: A Biography* (1987).

KIM TOWNSEND

Andersonville (1955), a novel by MACKINLAY KANTOR. This best seller, which won a Pulitzer Prize, depicts with grim realism the horrors of the infamous military prison during the Civil War.

Andrade, Carlos Drummond de (1902–1987), Brazilian poet. Born in Itabira and brought up on a ranch, Andrade was a pharmacist, language teacher, and journalist who became one of Latin America's best-known modernist poets. A resident of Rio de Janeiro from his early thirties onward, he published a series of collections in which he attempted to deal with his personal anxieties and with his strong sense of the world's problems. In *Marsh of Souls* (1934), his second book, private anguish dominates; by the time of his third, *A Feeling for the World* (1940), he enlarged his themes to embrace human solidarity. *The People's Rose* (1945) is strongly political. Other titles are *Poetry* (1942), *Poetry until Now* (1948), *Clear Enigma* (1951), *Pocketguitar* (1952), *Lessons in Things* (1962). *Confessions of Minas* (1944) is prose. One of his translators is Elizabeth Bishop, long a resident of Brazil; seven of her translations appear in her *Complete Poems 1927–1979* (1983).

Andrade, Mario [Raul] de [Morais] (1893–1945), Brazilian poet and novelist. Born in São Paulo and educated at the Conservatory of Music and Drama, Andrade was an ethnomusicologist whose knowledge of folklore, anthropology, and myth provided important sources for his most important creative work. His first book of verse, *Há uma gôta de sangue em cada poema* (1917) was self-conscious and derivative. In his second, *Paulicéia desvairada* (1922; tr. *Hallucinated City* 1968), Andrade built on his European models to create visionary images of his native city. This work is credited with giving major impetus to Brazilian modernism. His long association with his contemporary Brazilian modernists, Oswald de Andrade and MANUEL BANDEIRA, began at this time.

Andrade's novel *Macunaíma* (1928; tr. 1984) unites native and immigrant folk myths to relate the adventures of an Amazon folk hero who reaches an apotheosis in a transformation into the constellation Ursa Major. The narrative's rich and difficult vocabulary combines native words and dialects with contemporary slang. Andrade's critical work O *moviemento*

modernisto (1942) is a milestone in Brazilian criticism. His verse is collected in *Poésias completas* (1955).

Andrade, Oswald de (1890–1954), Brazilian poet and novelist. Influential in the rise of Brazilian modernism, Andrade was born in São Paulo and owed to coffee the wealth that permitted him to take the trips to Europe, beginning in 1912, that exposed him to the avant-garde ideas he successfully promoted in Brazil in the 1920s. In 1922 he helped organize Modern Art Week in São Paulo; two years later, in his manifesto *Pau Brasil* he called for a new Brazilian poetry strong enough to take a leading place in world literature. His efforts gave impetus to the work, among others, of Mario de Andrade and Carlos Drummond de Andrade (the three were not related). *Memórias Sentimentales de João Miramar* (1923), his first important novel, is a witty and discontinuous narration employing mixed levels of diction, including slang, obscenities, and regional idioms. A polemic, *Anthropophagical Manifesto* (1928), preaches the elevation of native materials and methods over imported ones in literature.

By the time of the publication of the novel *Serafim Ponte Grande* (1933), Andrade had become a Marxist, and his later work was committed to advancing the proletariat. Poetry is collected in *Poesias Reunidas* (1966). Other novels include *Os Condenados* (1922) and the trilogy *Marco Zero* (1943).

André, John (1751–1780), British major in the Revolutionary War. He was hanged as a spy by Washington, despite British protests, for his negotiations with Benedict Arnold over a plot to betray West Point. He figures in William Dunlap's blank verse tragedy *André* (1798).

Andrews, Jane (1833–1887), writer of juvenile stories. Among her books were *The Seven Little Sisters Who Live on the Round Ball That Floats in the Air* (1861), *Ten Boys Who Lived on the Road from Long Ago to Now* (1886), and *Stories Mother Nature Told Her Children* (1889).

Andrews, Mary Raymond Shipman (1865?–1936), novelist, short-story writer. Her fictional description of the circumstances of Lincoln's Gettysburg Address, *The Perfect Tribute* (1906), sold many hundreds of thousands of copies through the years. Among Andrews' other books were two collections of short stories, *The Eternal Masculine* (1913) and *The Eternal Feminine* (1916), and A *Lost Commander: Florence Nightingale* (1929).

Andrews, Roy Chapman (1884–1960), zoologist, explorer, author, radio commentator. His voyages were in both space and time. Andrews first hunted whales in the East Indies and near Alaska. He then explored remote regions in Tibet, China, and Burma; his discoveries in the Gobi Desert and elsewhere threw important light on prehistoric man and extinct mammalia. He was director of the Museum of Natural History from 1935 to 1941. His experiences supplied material for many books of lively interest, among them *Whale Hunting with Gun and Camera* (1916); *Camps and Trails in China* (1918); *Across Mongolian Plains* (1921); *On the Trail of Ancient Man* (1926); *The New Conquest of Central Asia* (1932); *This Business of Exploring* (1935); and *Meet Your Ancestors* (1945).

Under a Lucky Star (1943) and *An Explorer Comes Home* (1947) together provide an entertaining autobiography.

Andrews, Stephen Pearl (1812–1886), social reformer, linguist. A Massachusetts lawyer and freethinker, Andrews was an Abolitionist before the war, and afterward an advocate of a social organization he called Pantarchy, described in his *The Science of Society* (1851). From his knowledge of thirty-two languages he developed a forerunner of Esperanto that he called Alwato, publishing a *Primary Synopsis* in 1871. Other books include *Cost, the Limit of Price* (1851) and *Basic Outline of Universology* (1872).

Androboros (1714), a satirical farce by Robert Hunter (?–1734), governor of New York and New Jersey (1709–19). The first American play of which a printed copy exists, it mocks an English administrator, Sir Francis Nicholson (1655–1728), the Androboros (man-eater) of the title, as well as members of the colonial Assembly and clergy. The title page says it was printed at Moropolis (fools' town) and it employs both invective and physical comedy in its attacks on Nicholson and other identifiable people of the time. It was perhaps not publicly performed and it is printed in AMERICA'S LOST PLAYS, Volume 21 (1969).

Andros, Sir Edmund (1637–1714), first appointed governor of New York (1674) by the Duke of York, later becoming governor of the Dominion of New England when the colonies were consolidated by James II. His style of governance was bitterly criticized in New York and in New England. When the residents of Boston learned in 1688 that James II had been overthrown, they rebelled (1689), seized the governor and other officials, and sent them to England as prisoners. Andros was soon released and served as governor of Virginia (1692–1697) before being recalled in response to colonist complaints.

Angelou, Maya (1928–   ), singer, dancer, actress, writer. Born Marguerite Johnson in St. Louis, educated in Arkansas and California, Angelou began a theatrical career in a touring *Porgy and Bess* (1954–55) and in Off-Broadway shows, including Jean Genet's *The Blacks* (1960) and *Cabaret for Freedom*, which she wrote with Godfrey Cambridge. She has written short plays and films and television documentaries, served as Northern Coordinator of the Southern Christian Leadership Conference (1959–1960), worked as a newspaper editor in Egypt, held an administrative position at the University of Ghana, lectured at various American universities, and read her verse at the inauguration of President Clinton. Her celebrated autobiography *I Know Why the Caged Bird Sings* (1970) tells of her life up to age sixteen, ending with the birth of a child, and includes her rape at age eight. She continues her story in other volumes: *Gather Together in My Name* (1974) and *Singin' and Swingin' and Gettin' Merry Like Christmas* (1976), about her late adolescence, which included periods of prostitution and drug addiction; *The Heart of a Woman* (1981), on her activity in the civil rights movement in the 1960s; and *All God's Children Need Traveling Shoes* (1987), covering her four years in Ghana. A later autobiography is *Wouldn't Take Nothing for My Journey Now* (1993). The *Com-*

plete Collected Poems appeared in 1994. Earlier poetry titles include *Just Give Me a Cool Drink of Water 'fore I Diiie* (1971), *Oh Pray My Wings Are Gonna Fit Me Well* (1975), *And Still I Rise* (1978), and *Shaker, Why Don't You Sing?* (1983).

Angoff, Charles (1902–1979), journalist, novelist. Born in Russia, Angoff grew up in Massachusetts, graduated from Harvard, and worked with Mencken on the *American Mercury*. Among his works are many novels of Jewish-American life, including *Journey to the Dawn* (1951), *In the Morning Light* (1951), *The Sun at Noon* (1953), *Between Day and Dark* (1959), and *Bitter Spring* (1961).

Annabel Lee (October 9, 1849), a poem by EDGAR ALLAN POE. The poem appeared in the New York *Tribune* two days after Poe's death. Usually believed to be in memory of his wife, it is another poem on one of Poe's favorite themes—the death of a beautiful woman.

Anna Christie (1922), a play by EUGENE O'NEILL. Anna's father, Chris Christopherson, a crusty old captain of a coal barge, hopes to save his daughter from "dat old davil sea." She lives on a farm, but suddenly appears on the barge, on which the captain lives with an old drab named Marthy. Marthy immediately realizes that Anna is "no good," and Anna readily admits her sins. Father and daughter leave New York on the barge and pick up a boatload of shipwrecked sailors; one of them, Mat Burke, falls in love with Anna. When she tells him of her past, he leaves her and gets drunk. But the play closes on the possibility that Anna may still be saved. The play is a slice of life but has overtones of mysticism and symbolism. O'Neill had earlier written, and unsuccessfully produced, *Chris Christopherson* (1920), from which considerable portions of the later play were taken.

Anne of Green Gables (1908), a novel by L[UCY] M[AUD] MONTGOMERY. Montgomery based her plot on a simple suggestion she found in her notes: "Elderly couple apply to an orphan asylum for a boy. By mistake a girl is sent to them."

Annie Kilburn (1888), a novel by WILLIAM DEAN HOWELLS. This sociological novel calls for justice, not alms, for the poor. In it a New England lady goes crusading indiscriminately, but learns discretion as she gains experience. Howells depicts the disintegrating effects of the new industrial order upon the simple and narrow-minded inhabitants of a New England community.

annuals and gift books. The American annuals and gift books were patterned on the European literary almanac, a cross between the practical almanac, an annual repository of useful information, and the literary anthology, a retrospective collection of belles-lettres. The first had appeared in France in 1765, *L'Almanach des Muses, contenant unchoix des meilleures Pièces de Poësies fugitives, qui ont paru en 1764*. The species spread successively to Germany, England, and the United States. The earliest American example was *Le Souvenir, or Picturesque Pocket Diary; containing an Almanac, Ruled Pages for Memoranda, Literary Selections, and a Variety of Useful Information for 1825*, which was published in 1824 at Philadelphia. A year later there appeared in the same city a second volume with a similar title and also a competing publication, *The Philadelphia Souvenir; A Collection of Fugitive Pieces from the Philadelphia Press, With Biographical and Explanatory Notes, By J. E. Hall*. Both of these were more in the nature of anthologies than of original annuals. The first legitimate literary almanac to appear in the United States was *The Atlantic Souvenir*, published annually at Philadelphia for the years 1826 to 1832, and thereafter transplanted to Boston and combined with a competitor as *The Token and Atlantic Souvenir* (for 1833 to 1842). *The Token* itself had first been published for 1828. The first literary almanac in New York, THE TALISMAN, was published in three annual volumes (for 1828 to 1830) and then reissued in 1833 as *Miscellanies First Published under the Name of The Talisman, by G. E. Verplanck, W. C. Bryant, and Robert C. Sands*.

Annuals and gift books flourished throughout the eastern seaboard, and they appeared sporadically even in the West and South, for example, *The Western Souvenir, A Christmas and New Year's Gift for 1829* (Cincinnati); *The Souvenir of the Lakes for 1831* (Detroit); *The Charleston Book of 1845*; and *The New-Orleans Book of 1851*. Although Philadelphia retained preeminence in the field, most other Eastern cities produced specimens of their own, many with the name of the city in the title. More than a thousand American representatives of the species, including entire series as well as single publications, are estimated to have appeared, with the annual harvest increasing gradually down to the mid-forties. The number soared to an average of sixty each for the years 1846 to 1852. The size of editions of individual volumes ran as high as 10,000 copies. Most annuals were quartos, but miniature 24mos and 32mos were also issued. Many were embellished with leather bindings, tooled or embossed, and some even sported bindings of varnished papier-mâché, mounted with medallions and inlaid with mother-of-pearl. The gift books were, in fact, characteristic table decorations of the ormolu age, bought as much for their bindings and their richly engraved illustrations as for their contents.

Contributors to the annuals and gift books ranged from the lesser literary lights to the great luminaries of the period. Some of the favorites were N. P. Willis, William Leete Stone, William Gilmore Simms, Willis Gaylord Clark, Charles West Thomson, Lydia Sigourney, Hannah Flagg Gould, Sarah Josepha Hale, and Harriet Beecher Stowe. The general level of achievement was low, but the most eminent authors of the day welcomed the opportunities offered by the gift books. Emerson had contributed his first published writings, anonymously, to *The Offering*, for 1829, and later he acknowledge others in *The Gift and The Diadem. The Gift* also published five of Poe's tales, four of them for the first time. In *The Token* appeared at least twenty-seven of Nathaniel Hawthorne's stories, some of which upon reprinting were appropriately entitled TWICE-TOLD TALES. Longfellow, Lowell, Holmes, together with Irving, Bryant, Whittier, and many other writers of reputation contributed to the annuals. Indeed, of all major American writers who reached maturity by 1845, probably only Melville, Thoreau, and Whitman did not appear in the annuals and gift books.

The annuals performed a valuable service to American letters. At a time when the writings of established English authors, unprotected by copyright, were pirated and reprinted without cost in current American publications, the annuals and gift books published and paid for contributions by native authors. Thus, they fostered the native literature at a time when professionalism in American arts was scarcely possible. They performed other services as well. They assisted in the dissemination of foreign literature by printing translations from German, French, Spanish, Russian, and Scandinavian authors. They supported social progress and reform, notably the Abolitionist and Temperance movements, and they fostered fraternal and religious life. Among those devoted to religion may be mentioned *The Religious Souvenir* for the years 1833 to 1839, *The Christian Keepsake and Missionary Annual* for the years 1838 to 1840 and 1847 to 1849, *The Opal: A Pure Gift for the Holy Days* of 1844 to 1849, and, the longest-lived of all the annuals, *The Rose of Sharon: A Religious Souvenir* for the years 1840 to 1857. Fraternal publications included *The Odd-Fellows' Offering for 1843* and for the following years to 1854. Reform was represented by, among others, *The Fountain: A Temperance Gift* of 1847 and *The Temperance Offering for 1853*, both of which were reissued a number of times, even under different titles. Abolition was the subject of several volumes and series, chief among them *The Liberty Bell, By Friends of Freedom*, issued annually and sponsored by Mana Weston Chapman, with four exceptions, from 1839 to 1857. It contained contributions by many prominent supporters of abolition, both American and European, among them Lowell, Emerson, Wendell Phillips, Harriet Beecher Stowe, Elizabeth Barrett Browning, Harriet Martineau, Giuseppi Mazzini, Nicholas Turgenev, and Fredrika Bremer. See ALMANACS.

PHILIP ALLISON SHELLEY/GP

Another Country (1962),   novel by JAMES BALDWIN. The theme is self-discovery amidst interracial and sexual tension in Harlem and elsewhere in Manhattan as Baldwin depicts the failures of love between Rufus Scott, an angry, unemployed black jazz musician, his white mistress, his sister, and their white friends. After Rufus dies by jumping from the George Washington Bridge, his sister Ida becomes the lover of Rufus's white novelist friend Vivaldo Moore, with almost equally unsatisfying results.

Anspacher, Louis [Kaufman] (1878–1947),   dramatist, lecturer. His plays include *The Unchastened Woman* (1915), *That Day* (1917), *All the King's Horses*(1920), *Dagmar* (1923), and *The Jazz Clown* (1933). Posthumously published was *Challenge of the Unknown: Exploring the Psychic World* (1947).

Antheil, George (1900–1959),   composer, author. Antheil, a concert pianist, had a successful musical career abroad and after his return to the United States in 1933 became active in Hollywood. His Carnegie Hall production of his *Ballet Mécanique*, which makes use of sound-producing instruments not generally considered musical, won him a reputation for eccentricity he found hard to throw off. Antheil wrote an amusing account of his career in *Bad Boy of Music* (1945). His musical compositions are many, including operas, chamber works, and several movie scores.

Anthology Club or **Society.**   This informal organization of "gentlemen of literary interests" was founded in Boston on Oct. 3, 1805, and was dissolved on July 2, 1811. Two years before the founding of the club appeared a magazine called *Monthly Anthology, or Magazine of Polite Literature*, and one purpose of the club was to finance this magazine and supply it with material. George Ticknor, Bryant, Allston, Webster, and Joseph Story were among those involved in the club. Four years after both magazine and club died, the same group promoted publication of the NORTH AMERICAN REVIEW. The Anthology Club also founded a library in Boston, known as the Anthology Reading Room but incorporated in 1807 as the BOSTON ATHENAEUM.

Anthony, Susan B[rownell] (1820–1906),   reformer. Born in Adams, Massachusetts, daughter of a Quaker abolitionist, Anthony began her campaign for women's rights at seventeen, when she began teaching in rural New York. She sought equal pay, coeducation, and college training for women, and abolition of Negro slavery. Barred by men from their organization, she organized the first women's temperance association. From 1851 on she was a lifelong friend and associate of ELIZABETH CADY STANTON; together, they spearheaded the women's movement in the 19th century. With Stanton and Matilda Joslyn Cage she compiled volumes 1–3 of the *History of Women Suffrage* (1881–86) and she contributed to volume 4 of the series completed by Ida Husted Harper (volumes 4–6, 1900–1922). She is *The Mother of Us All* in the Gertrude Stein/Virgil Thomson opera (1947).

Antigonish (1922),   a once popular quatrain by Hughes Mearns (1875–1965), which was inspired by a ghost in a haunted house that always was absent when reporters called:

I met a man upon the stair,
The little man who wasn't there.
He wasn't there again today,
Oh, how I wish he'd go away.

Antin, Mary (1881–1949),   autobiographer, lecturer. Born in Russia, Antin came to the United States at fourteen. At eighteen she published her first book, *From Plotzk to Boston* (1899), a collection of letters she had written to an uncle in Russia describing her American experience; for the book she translated the Yiddish to English. Her next book, *The Promised Land* (1912), expanded the story and it became one of the most popular immigrant autobiographies of all time. In *They Who Knock at Our Gates: A Complete Gospel of Immigration* (1914) she argued for an open door policy to "accord with the loftiest interpretation of our duty as Americans." For much of the rest of her life she suffered from nervous ailments, sought spiritual and mental health, and produced little writing.

Antinomianism.   From the Greek *anti nomos* (literally, against the law). Antinomianism was one of the two extreme extensions (heresies) that threatened the orthodox middle way of 17th-century Calvinism in and around Massachusetts Bay. According to antinomian thinking, a Christian's relationship with God was entirely a private, inner matter, and a product exclusively of God's arbitrarily given grace rather than of any good works "earning" salvation. While extreme forms of subjectivism were common problems, especially as they appeared in organized sects, like that of the QUAKERS, antinomianism as a social and theological movement reached a crescendo during the trial and subsequent expulsion of ANNE HUTCHINSON. Primary among Hutchinson's challenges to the stability of the Puritan status quo—a patriarchal status quo according to many recent critics and historians—was her assertion, in the words of JOHN WINTHROP's *Journal* (October 21, 1636):

1. That person of the Holy Ghost dwells in a justified person. [and] 2. That no sanctification can help to evidence to us our justification.

It was feared that these two "dangerous errors" threatened the delicate existence of the colony with the rampant subjectivism and potential lawlessness that would follow the belief that a saved Christian was literally inhabited by the Holy Spirit and that, as a result, everything the justified person thought, said, or did was divinely mandated and, therefore, beyond the understanding and jurisdiction of earthly social and religious organization and enforcement.

In its more general sense, antinomianism has come to represent nearly any form of subjectivism that frees the individual from communal sanctions. Cultural manifestations of this privileged inner voice are as varied as Hutchinson's challenge to Puritan orthodoxy, THOMAS PAINES's claim in THE AGE OF REASON that "my own mind is my own church," to the acts and beliefs of early literary characters such as Theodore Wieland in WIELAND (who murders his family at the prompting of divine voices he believes he hears), Hester Prynne's claim in THE SCARLET LETTER that what she and Dimmesdale did had "a sanctification of its own," to the critical commonplace that American literature itself is antinomian. See ARMINIANISM.

RUSSELL J. REISING

Anti-Rent Laws.   The Dutch PATROONS from 1839 to 1846 experienced difficulties in collecting rent from their New York tenants. Soon a revolt broke out against the entire patroon system, a revolt that Governor William H. Seward used the militia to suppress. But as a consequence of the disorder, so-called anti-rent laws were passed in the New York legislature, of a kind to prevent serious hardships to tenants. The revolt and its causes were used by James Fenimore Cooper as the background of his novels SATANSTOE (1845), THE CHAINBEARER (1846), and THE REDSKINS (1846)—a trilogy called the *Littlepage Manuscripts*.

Antoninus, Brother.   See EVERSON, WILLIAM.

Antrim, Donald (1959?–   ),   novelist, short-story writer. After graduation from Brown University in 1981, with a concentration in English and American literature, Antrim spent a year in theater with a professional repertory company before settling into publishing in New York City. With his first novel, *Elect Mr. Robinson for a Better World* (1993), he won critical praise but no great readership for his satiric dissection of small town pieties and violence. With the two novels that followed he increased his technical grasp of a disquieting narrative perspective where everyday realities move inexorably toward the utterly fantastic. The result forms a kind of trilogy of neurotic and paranoic displacement, conveyed with a sometimes astonishing precision of language and insight. In *The Hundred Brothers* (1996), a family of literally one hundred brothers comes together for an evening by the fireplace in the vast library of the family estate. Although they never leave the room, it is not inconsequential that beyond the borders of the estate they can see the fires where the neighborhood homeless huddle against the cold. The evening ends in various kinds of unhinged lunacy, though "there is nothing like a blaze in the hearth to soothe the nerves and restore order to a house." The whole, Antrim has suggested, is in some ways a picture of academic life at Brown, but it radiates as well into many other closed societal situations. In *The Verificationist* (2000), Antrim continues and enlarges his methods and themes: a first-person narrator of high intelligence and acute sensibilities, haunted by neuroses, driven to fantasy, confined to the company of others for whom he feels both a bond and an antipathy throughout the space of an evening in a pancake house. This time, however, there are not just brothers and good male horseplay, but also women and sex, both possible and hallucinatory, and the final verification, chillingly revealed, is incipient insanity.

Anza, Juan Bautista de (1735–1788),   Spanish-American official. Born in Mexico, in 1776 he founded the mission and presidio of San Francisco and later served as governor of New Mexico (1777–88). He wrote extensively on his experiences. H. E. Bolton edited Anza's *California Expeditions* (5 v. 1930).

Apache Indians.   Nomad tribes found in the arid deserts of the Southwest, but allied to the Athapascan peoples otherwise localized in northern sections of the continent. Like the NAVAJOS, the Apaches were for centuries the foes of the more peaceful village Indians of this section. They were also enemies of the white man, and the last of our Indian "wars" was waged against these fierce nomads, whose name became a synonym for the red man at his most bloodthirsty and vindictive. Yet these deadly fighters were also expert weavers and basket makers, and developed complex religious ceremonies and dances. The most famous of their chieftains was GERONIMO, who led bloody attacks on the whites but was finally defeated by General George Crook in 1885–86. Arizona, sometimes called the Apache State, contains the present reservations of this tribe, where the Apaches now are ranchers and farmers. Apaches appear in frequently in novels, including PAUL WELLMAN's *Broncho Apache* (1932); Elliott Arnold's *Blood Brother* (1947); Ed Newsom's *Wagons to Tucson* (1954) and *Ride to High Places* (1955); HENRY W. ALLEN's *Chiracahua* (1972, as Will Henry); and OAKLEY HALL's *Apaches* (1986).

Apes, William (1798–?),   author. A PEQUOT INDIAN of partial white ancestry, Apes (or Apess) fought for the Americans in the War of 1812. In 1829 he became a Methodist missionary and actively sought to correct abuses from which the Indians of Massachusetts suffered. He was a descendant of the Indian leader about whom he wrote his *Eulogy of King Philip* (1836). He related his own story in *A Son of the Forest* (1829) and also wrote *The Experiences of Five Christian Indians* (1833). See NATIVE AMERICAN PROSE AND POETRY.

Apley, George.   See THE LATE GEORGE APLEY.

Apostle to the Indians.   See JOHN ELIOT.

Appleseed, Johnny.   His real name was either John or Jonathan Chapman. He was born in Springfield, Massachusetts, in 1774 or 1775. As a young man he wandered westward, first to Pittsburgh, later to Marietta, Ohio, where he became an orchardist and a Swedenborgian. Presumably because of a disappointment in love, he began a nomadic existence, preaching to all he met for fifty years and distributing apple seeds everywhere. According to legend, it was to these seeds that the apple orchards of Pennsylvania, Ohio, Illinois, and Indiana owe their origin. He died in Fort Wayne, Indiana, in 1847. A carefully documented biography is Robert Price's *Johnny Appleseed: Man and Myth* (1954).

Johnny Appleseed has become a folk hero, and has been celebrated in many stories and poems. VACHEL LINDSAY devoted to him a long poem, *In Praise of Johnny Appleseed* (1923). Monuments to Johnny Appleseed have been erected in Indiana and Ohio.

Araucana, La (1569–1590),   an epic poem by Alfonso de Ercilla y Zúñiga (1533–94), a Spanish soldier and poet who went to Chile after the conquest and fought against the indomitable Araucanian Indians. The stubborn resistance of the Araucanians against Spanish rule is the theme of the poem. Ercilla stresses the nobility and valor of the Indians and of their leaders Lautaro and Caupolicán, who are drawn in Homeric proportions.

Arbella,   flagship of the fleet of four that brought the first settlers to the MASSACHUSETTS BAY colony. It arrived at Salem on June 12, 1630, and among its passengers were JOHN WINTHROP, ANNE BRADSTREET and her husband Simon, and Thomas Dudley (Anne Bradstreet's father). Winthrop's sermon "A Model of Christian Charity" was preached on board and his *Journal* records the journey.

Archer, Isabel.   See PORTRAIT OF A LADY.

archy and mehitabel.   archy is the cockroach and mehitabel is the cat in what some regard as DON MARQUIS's most original and amusing works. The two appeared frequently in the columns that Marquis wrote after 1916 in the New York *Sun* and later in the *Herald Tribune*. The sketches were collected in *archy and mehitabel* (1927), *archy does his part* (1935), and *the life and times of archy and mehitabel* (1940). archy, who suffered from literary ambitions but was unable to work the shift key on the typewriter, of necessity wrote without capital letters when he did his writing in the newspaper office after the less literary denizens had gone home. mehitabel, about whom archy writes with gentle deprecation, took as her motto "toujours gai." Between them they afforded Marquis many opportunities for satirizing American life between the two World Wars. *archy and mehitabel*, a short jazz opera by George Kleinsinger and Joe Darion, was first produced on Dec. 6, 1954.

Archy Moore (1836),   a novel by RICHARD HILDRETH. See THE SLAVE.

Arcturus (1841–1842),   a critical magazine founded by E. A. Duyckinck and Cornelius Mathews. See BOSTON MISCELLANY.

Arenas, Reinaldo (1943–1990),   novelist. Born and raised in Cuba's Oriente province, Reinaldo was a "wild boy," who once claimed 5,000 sexual encounters by the age of twenty-five. Persecuted for his writings and open homosexuality in Castro's Cuba, he lived in exile in New York from 1980 until his death (suffering from AIDS, he committed suicide). *El mundo alucinante* (1969, tr. *Hallucinations*, 1971), based on the life of an eighteenth-century Mexican priest, brought early fame. More ambitious is his cycle of five novels depicting the Cuba of his childhood and the years after the revolution: *Celestino antes del alba* (1967, tr. *Singing from the Well*, 1988); *El palaciode las blanquisimas mofitas* (1975, tr. *The Palace of the Very White Skunks*, 1980); *Otra vez el mar* (1982, tr. *Farewell to the Sea*, 1986); *El color del verano* (*The Color of Summer*, 1991); and *El asalto* (1991, tr. *The Assault*, 1993). *El central* (1984) is a poem about forced labor in the sugar industry. *La vieja rosa* (1980, tr. *Old Rosa*, 1989) depicts a woman's aging in a changed society. *Arturo, the Shining Star* (1984, tr. 1992) tells of the experiences of a homosexual in a Cuban concentration camp. *Adios a mama* (*Goodbye to Mama*, 1994) is a memoir of childhood. *Antes que anochezca* (1992, tr. *Before Night Falls*, 1993; movie version, 2000) is a more complete autobiography. Delores Koch edited *Mona and Other Tales* (2001).

Arendt, Hannah (1906–1975),   political theorist. Born in Germany, Arendt emigrated to the U.S. in 1941 and taught at Princeton, the University of Chicago, and the New School for Social Research. Her books include *Origins of Totalitarianism* (1951), *The Human Condition* (1958), *Eichmann in Jerusalem* (1963), and *On Violence* (1970). She analyzed the mass horrors of the 20th century, observing that in the bureaucracies of recent governments the result is often "rule by nobody," and contributing to the language the phrase "banality of evil."

Arguedas, Alcides (1879–1946),   Bolivian novelist, historian, diplomat. Arguedas lived for years in Europe and was Bolivian consul in France. His major writing, however, is of Bolivia. *Pueblo enfermo* (1909) is a pioneering study calling attention to racial and environmental influences on Bolivian society. *Raza de bronce* (1919) is a novel protesting the oppression by landlords of the Lake Titicaca Indians and shows something of the native culture; it is a revision of the author's earlier *Wata-Wara* (1904). Two other novels are *Pisagua* (1903) and *Vida criolla* (1912). Arguedas's five-volume *Historia de Bolivia* (1920–1929) is a standard work covering the years 1809 to 1872. *Obras completas* was published in 1959–1960.

Arguedas, José Maria (1911–1969),   Peruvian novelist, scholar, poet. Although Arguedas was not an Indian, he grew up in Indian villages and spoke Quechua before he spoke Spanish. Later, as a Professor of Quechua and Anthropology at San Marcos University, he used his unique background to capture through his writings the flavor of the vanishing Indian culture, its folklore, songs, and language. In his first novel, *Agua* (1935), he was already mixing Indian words with Spanish to try to create an appropriate medium for presenting things Peruvian. His second, *Yawar Fiesta* (1941; tr. 1984) treats the plight of Indians expelled from their hereditary lands. *Los rios profundos* (1958; tr. *Deep Rivers*, 1978), usually considered his major novel, is rooted in autobiography. In it an adolescent is torn between loyalty to the Indians with whom he has been raised and the pressures put on him at Catholic boarding school to renounce that heritage. The novel *El sexto* (1961), also autobiographical, treats political imprisonment. *Todas las sangres* (1964) explores the gulf between white landowners and Indians. Other works include a novel, *Diamantes y Pedernales* (1954); a collection of short stories, *Amor mundo* (1967); and a volume of translations from Quechua, *Canto Kechwa* (1938; tr. *The Singing Mountains*, 1971).

Aria da Capo,   a play by EDNA ST. VINCENT MILLAY.

Ariel (1965),   the posthumous collection of the poetry of SYLVIA PLATH that catapulted her into fame. Among the poems included were "The Applicant," "Daddy," and "Lady Lazarus."

Arikara Indians,   sometimes called **Ricarees** or **Rees**, a tribal group of PLAINS INDIANS related to others of the Caddoan linguistic stock. They lived along the upper Missouri River from at least the 14th century, building lodges of timber and earth, and cultivating corn and hunting buffalo. The first French traders visited them as early as 1700, Lewis and Clark in 1804. To their north were the Mandans, whose last survivors joined the Arikawas after their separate existence as a tribe ended in the early 19th century. Together with the Hidatsas they were finally settled on the Fort Barthold Reservation in North Dakota. JOHN G. NEIHARDT treats them in *Song of Hugh Glass* and *Song of the Indian Wars*.

Arkansas Traveler, The.   One of the most memorable tunes and tales of American folklore. The tune and the accompanying dialogue have been ascribed to José Tasso, a renowned fiddler in the Ohio Valley region; the dialogue is attributed by others to Col. Sandford Faulkner.

Armies of the Night, The (1968),   NORMAN MAILER's autobiographical report of the Peace March on the Pentagon in October, 1967. Subtitled *History as a Novel, the Novel as History*, the work is an impressive example of NEW JOURNALISM. It reports not only on the public event, but on the personal reactions of Mailer and other prominent participants, including Robert Lowell.

Arminianism,   doctrines originated by Jacobus Arminius (1560–1609), Dutch theologian who challenged Calvinistic teachings of predestination. Arminius taught that although God is omnipotent, He has left humans free to seek salvation through good works. Arminianism was a heresy to 17th- and 18th-century Puritans, but salvation through works became a doctrine of the Methodists (see METHODISM) as Americans began to embrace more liberal religious ideas. JONATHAN EDWARDS (1703–1758) was a late, brilliant defender of Puritan orthodoxy. See ANTINOMIANISM.

Armour, Richard [Willard] (1906–1989), teacher, poet, humorist. Born in Pomona, California, Armour earned a Ph.D. from Harvard, served in the army in World War II, and taught at Scripps College, in California. He was best known for whimsical doggerel published widely in magazines and collected in books, including *Yours for the Asking* (1942), *Golf Bawls* (1946), *Light Armour* (1954), and *Nights with Armour* (1958); and for humorous accounts of history and literature, including *It All Started with Columbus* (1953), *Twisted Tales from Shakespeare* (1957), *It All Started with Eve* (1956), and *It All Started with Stones and Clubs* (1967).

Arnold, Benedict (1741–1801), Revolutionary general and traitor. After service in the colonial militia in the FRENCH AND INDIAN WARS, Arnold prospered in the fur trade. In the Revolution, he led an expedition against the British at Fort Ticonderoga, taking the fort jointly with forces commanded by ETHAN ALLEN. In the Quebec campaign, he invaded Canada by way of the forests of Maine. Later his leadership was important in the American victory at Saratoga. His career was marred by controversy, however, as he was passed over for promotion in 1777 and, in another incident, court-martialed in 1779. When Washington gave him command of West Point in 1780, he was already planning to betray the fort to the British. After the arrest of Major André, he escaped and subsequently led raids for the British in Virginia and Connecticut before passing into exile in England and Canada.

He has been portrayed in plays by Hugh Henry Brackenridge, Delia Bacon, Samuel Woodworth, W. W. Lord, Clyde Fitch, John Jay Chapman, and others. Novelistic treatments include Daniel Pierce Thompson's *The Green Mountain Boys* (1839), Harold Sinclair's *Westward the Tide* (1840), F. J. Stimson's *My Story* (1917), and Kenneth Roberts' ARUNDEL (1930) and RABBLE IN ARMS (1933).

Arnold, George (1834–1865), newspaperman, humorist, poet. Arnold became a member of the celebrated group that gathered at PFAFF'S BEER CELLAR, in New York City. He adopted several pen names—McArone, Graham Allen, and Pierrot. The MCARONE PAPERS began in *Vanity Fair* (November 24, 1860), continued in the *Leader*, and reached their close in the *Weekly Review* (October 14, 1865). After Arnold's death his poems were edited by WILLIAM WINTER to make two collections, *Drift* (1866) and *Poems Grave and Gay* (1867); these were combined in one volume in 1870.

Arnold, Matthew (1822–1888), British poet, essayist. Arnold crossed the Atlantic in 1883 to see what the United States was like and to deliver lectures here, and again in 1886 to visit his daughter, who had married an American. His impressions were conveyed in DISCOURSES IN AMERICA (1885) and *Civilization in the United States* (1888).

Arnow, Harriette Simpson (1908–1986), novelist. In her masterpiece, *The Dollmaker* (1954), Arnow traces dislocations in the lives of Kentucky people transplanted to Michi-

gan to work in the Willow Run bomber plant during World War II. *Hunter's Horn* (1949) and *Between the Flowers* (1999), the latter published posthumously, also portray mountain people in the stress of changing times.

Arp, Bill, a pseudonym of CHARLES H. SMITH.

Arrington, Alfred W. (1810–1867), lawyer, writer. Born in North Carolina, Arrington spent most of his life on the western frontier. Under the pseudonym Charles Summerfield he wrote *The Desperadoes of the Southwest* (1847) and *The Rangers and Regulators of the Tanaha* (1856). His *Poems* appeared in 1869.

Arrow and the Song, The. A poem by HENRY WADSWORTH LONGFELLOW. It appeared originally in *The Belfry of Bruges and Other Poems* (1845).

Arrowmaker, The (1910), a play by MARY AUSTIN.

Arrowsmith (1925), a novel by SINCLAIR LEWIS. This satiric picture of the scientist in the midst of industrialists, newspapermen, and rich women stirred up a great controversy. Lewis follows the career of Dr. Martin Arrowsmith from a small-town practice, through the health department of a small city, an institute sponsored by a rich man and his wife, to an isolated West Indian island, to an equally isolated Vermont farm. Arrowsmith encounters meanness, corruption, misunderstanding, willful obstruction, jealousy, sensationalism, race prejudice, also a modicum of nobility and idealism. Arrowsmith's quest is in a measure a religious one—the truth of pure science. He is often frustrated, and his greatest failure comes when he himself refuses to carry to the logical extreme his test of a new serum because it means some people will die whom he might otherwise have saved. But there is frequent satire, too, as in BABBITT. By general agreement, moreover, Arrowsmith's first wife, Leora, is the only likable woman character Lewis created.

Some of the medical lore for *Arrowsmith* came from Lewis's observation of his own father, a physician, and perhaps from his mother, the daughter of a physician. But he depended for many of the technical details on PAUL DE KRUIF, whose *Microbe Hunters* appeared the year after *Arrowsmith* was published. Jacques Loeb (1859–1924), a biologist, suggested the character of Max Gottlieb in *Arrowsmith*.

Arsenal at Springfield, The (1845), a poem by HENRY WADSWORTH LONGFELLOW. The opening lines—"This is the Arsenal. From floor to ceiling, / Like a huge organ, rise the burnished arms"—were suggested to the poet by his wife when they were on their wedding journey and visited the Springfield Arsenal. In a letter she said, "We grow quite warlike against war, and I urged H. to write a peace poem."

Arsenic and Old Lace (1941), a comedy by Joseph Kesselring (1902–1967). It concerns two apparently gentle old ladies who poison derelicts for their own good.

Arthur, Timothy Shay (1809–1885), editor, author, reformer. Arthur began as a watchmaker but gradually drifted into writing. He contributed to GODEY'S LADY'S BOOK and then founded several imitations, one of which, ultimately called *Arthur's Home Magazine* (1853), had a considerable circulation; he was still editing it at his death. He also edited the Baltimore *Saturday Visiter* [sic] for a while and contributed to other magazines. Meanwhile he was writing novels—against gambling, about domestic virtues, in favor of temperance. He was himself neither a teetotaler nor a prohibitionist. Finally one of his stories gained a vogue that made it a minor classic of American literature—TEN NIGHTS IN A BARROOM AND WHAT I SAW THERE (1854), the tale of a drunkard who ruins his family. It was made into a play, produced seriously at first, then as a burlesque.

Arthur Mervyn (Part I, 1799; Part II, 1800),   a novel by CHARLES BROCKDEN BROWN. It is a strange mixture of violent deeds and emotions, showing the strong influence of William Godwin's *Caleb Williams*. Arthur is a young man who becomes entangled with a criminal named Welbeck and is accused of being his accomplice. He clears himself and finds friends. The most vivid portion of the novel is the firsthand description of the yellow fever epidemic in Philadelphia in 1793. The book indicates Brown's great interest in abnormal psychology, but it is a confused work, impressive only in spots.

Artist of the Beautiful, The,   tale by NATHANIEL HAWTHORNE, collected in his MOSSES FROM AN OLD MANSE (1846). It is an allegory in which a watchmaker, Owen Warland, makes a marvelous mechanical butterfly but cannot impress the woman he loves, who marries a hearty blacksmith. In the end, the butterfly is destroyed by the couple's child. The story is one of a number of expressions of Hawthorne's fear that his own work was unpopular and ephemeral. After Owen's creation is crumpled, however, the reader is told that "He had caught a far other butterfly than this. When the artist rose high enough to achieve the beautiful, the symbol by which he made it perceptible to mortal senses became of little value in his eyes while his spirit possessed itself in the enjoyment of the reality."

Arundel (1930),   historical novel by KENNETH ROBERTS. The first of a series on Arundel (an older name for Kennebunk, Maine), this one tells of the expedition against Quebec led by BENEDICT ARNOLD.

Asbury, Francis (1745–1816),   clergyman. Born in England, Asbury reached America in 1771 and in 1772 was made John Wesley's superintendent in this country. Friction with other religious leaders led to his recall (1775), but he refused to return and became an American citizen, aligning himself with the movement for separation from England. He became prominent in the organization of the Methodist Episcopal Church, was consecrated as superintendent, assumed the title of bishop (1785), and ruled the church till his death. His *Journals* (3 v.) were published in 1852.

Asbury, Herbert (1891–1963),   newspaperman, historian. A descendant of FRANCIS ASBURY. Asbury early revolted against his religious upbringing, although one of his books is *A Methodist Saint* (1927), a life of his grandfather. His first book, however, was *Up from Methodism* (1926). His special field of writing was the portrayal of the shadier side of the past of great American cities. Asbury first gained fame with a story called "Hatrack," which appeared in the AMERICAN MERCURY, and drew the wrath of the censors. Among his books were *The*

Gangs of New York (1928), *Life of Carry Nation* (1929), *The Barbary Coast* (1933), *The French Quarter* (1936), *Sucker's Progress* (1938), and *The Great Illusion: an Informal History of Prohibition* (1950).

Asch, Nathan (1902–1964),   novelist. Born in Poland, Asch came to the U.S. at the age of thirteen; his father was the novelist SHOLEM ASCH. His book *The Road* (1937) is a search for America, a report on the way Americans think and feel. His fiction is marked by realism, so extreme in the case of *Pay Day* (1930) that the book was suppressed. He also wrote *The Office* (1925) and *The Valley* (1935), as well as scripts for Hollywood.

Asch, Sholem (1880–1957),   novelist, dramatist. Asch was the chief Yiddish novelist of the first half of the 20th century. Born in Poland, he lived in various European countries until 1910, then came to America and was naturalized in 1920. By 1924 his short stories, novelettes, novels, plays, and poems had become so numerous that they were published in a collected edition of eighteen volumes in Warsaw, all in Yiddish. Several of his books appeared in English between 1917 and 1933; in the latter year his *Three Cities* (St. Petersburg, Warsaw, Moscow) became a best seller. More sensational still was the success of *The Nazarene* (1939), a faithful, friendly portrayal of Jesus, followed by *The Apostle* (1943) and *Mary* (1949). *East River* (1946), a novel laid in New York City, presents a section of the metropolis in which men and women of many races and creeds struggle, love, hate, and merge to some degree to form the complex character that we call American. Asch's later writings tend toward a mingling of the realistic and the sentimental. A more sordid realism was found in his play *The God of Vengeance*, produced by Max Reinhardt in Berlin in 1910 and closed by the police in New York in 1922. Asch's later works include *Moses* (1951), *A Passage in the Night* (1953), and *The Prophet* (1955).

Ashbery, John (1927–   ),   poet. Born in Rochester, New York, Ashbery grew up on a farm in nearby Sodus. He was educated at Deerfield Academy, Harvard, Columbia University, and New York University. He spent 1955 to 1966 in France, first as a Fulbright fellow and later as an art critic for the *Herald Tribune* and *Art News*. Returning from Paris, he was Executive Editor of *Art News* for seven years before joining the creative writing faculty at Brooklyn College. His involvement with avant-garde movements in art, his association with experimental poets in New York, his work on modern French writers, and his interest in contemporary music all contributed to Ashbery's distinctive style, along with the more predictable influences of Wallace Stevens and W. H. Auden.

Chosen by Auden for the Yale Series of Younger Poets, Ashbery's first book, *Some Trees* (1956), contains a number of more or less inscrutable poems in traditional forms—accomplished "accents" that "seem their own defense." His second book, *The Tennis Court Oath* (1962), counters the lyric preciosity of *Some Trees*; here, Ashbery tests the limits of incoherence in programmatically disjunctive experiments. These early books are exaggerated examples of the two poles between which his subsequent work veers. He experiments with traditional forms, alluding to, yet refusing to meet, the expectations of clarity and coherence inscribed within canonical forms. Nor does he have a naive faith that open forms can capture presence and process. He questions whatever form he employs, characteristically violating any consistency the moment it becomes recognizable and never allowing the medium to become transparent. A series of such self-questioning self-revisions also defines the shape of his career. Since by now the avant-garde is itself a tradition, "there is no point in looking to imaginative new methods": "all of them are in constant use." When the possibility of any efficacious revolt disappears, there is "no intrinsic value in doing one thing or the other," and Ashbery's career seems to "amble" on by "doing the recalcitrant thing," working against any idiom that threatens to become responsive and therefore rhetorical.

Rivers and Mountains (1966) and *The Double Dream of Spring* (1970) represent what Ashbery calls his "synthetic period" after his "analytic period," as he rebounds toward greater coherency and formal control and a more self-consciously critical and discursive idiom. He deploys an increasingly flexible diction, remarkable verbal and tonal resources, and a wide-ranging allusiveness in addressing the postmodern problem of authorship without authority. His "characteristic devices" include "ellipses" and "frequent changes of tone, voice, . . . point of view," as he tries to "put together as many different kinds of language and tone as possible, and to shift them abruptly, to overlap them all." In his attempt to dispel the illusion of a single, authoritative speaker, he abandons even pronominal consistency. Only such a relentlessly unauthorized voice can tell us how it feels when "personality," as well as a historically solid "space or time in which it was lived," has eroded unrecognizably.

Three Poems (1972), Ashbery's experiment in exploiting "the ugliness of prose" for poetic uses, resulted in prosier rhythms in his later work. He attributes the success of *Self-Portrait in a Convex Mirror* (1975), which won the National Book Award, the National Book Critics Circle Award, and the Pulitzer Prize, to the "essayistic thrust" of its title poem. Since then, he has published *Houseboat Days* (1977), *As We Know* (1979), *Shadow Train* (1981), *A Wave* (1984), *Selected Poems* (1985), *April Galleons* (1987), *Flow Chart* (1991), *Hotel Lautremont* (1992), *And the Stars Were Shining* (1994), *Can You Hear, Bird?* (1995), and *Girls on the Run: A Poem* (1999). Formally, he has continued to do "the recalcitrant thing," and his experiments include prose poems, a volume of fifty poems of four quatrains each, a 68-page poem in two columns, and one-line poems. Thematically, he has been increasingly concerned with the "awareness of time and regret and nostalgia," the "feel" of time as it passes, the "movement" of thought "from one point to another rather than the destination or the origin," and the "difficulty of living, the everchanging, minute adjustments that go on around us and which we respond to from moment to moment." He is also interested in exploring the similar difficulties of communication, the poignant "inaccuracies and anomalies of common speech," the "pathos and liveliness of ordinary human communication," and the "sor-

row" of "producing automatically as an apple tree produces apples this thing there is no name for."

The much-lamented difficulty of Ashbery's work is in part a mannerism, a willful jumbling of the various codes of articulation. In part, however, it is generic to writing in the postmodern era, when the poet no longer has "any metaphysical reasons" for "doing the things I do." Ashbery keeps describing his work as "romantic poetry"; but in his romantic poetry, "nature" is a palimpsest of simulacra and the subject a "polyphony" of any number of private and public discourses.

Ashbery's work is seductive precisely because it alludes to shared traditions and assumptions about poetry. His poems attract us with their gestures of "meaningful" discourse, the meditative pace of their syntax and the memories and expectations of meaningfulness that it evokes, the careful use of qualifiers, and the precisions and surprises of his diction. But Ashbery's violations of consistencies preclude the emergence of a "pattern that may carry the sense." This ascetic project of achieving "the extreme austerity of an almost empty mind" yields a language of "anti-referential sensuousness," which luxuriates in a full range of elegiac tones—from various shades of parodic nostalgia—for a "collective past," a future, "central" truths, or "roots" connecting private and public experience—to the "pathos" of the "lush, Rousseau-like foliage" of a "desire to communicate/Something between breaths."

"Poetry," Ashbery remarks, "seems to involve failure—a celebration of a failed state of affairs," and he gives us a writing immersed in the "detritus" of the past without the sense of an authoritative and usable past. His poems move forward with a "You can't say it that way any more" at each step, projecting themselves into a possibly nonexistent collective future. For all its insistence on the present, where "we must stay, in motion," Ashbery's work is really an extended elegy for the humanist tradition: it glances backward, "always invoking the echo," as it resolutely moves forward, weaving "cold pockets/ Of remembrance" in the face of "the outlook for continued cold."

Ashbery's other books include a novel, *A Nest of Ninnies* (with JAMES SCHUYLER, 1969); *The Vermont Notebook* (1975); *Three Plays* (1978); a volume of art criticism, *Reported Sightings* (1989); and *Other Traditions* (2000), on six writers important to his work. Useful criticism includes *Beyond Amazement*, edited by David Lehman (1980); *On the Outside Looking Out: John Ashbery's Poetry* (1994), by John Shoptaw; and *John Ashbery and American Poetry*, by David Herd (2000).

MUTLU KONUK BLASING/G.P.

Ashbridge, Elizabeth (1713–1755),   memoirist. An immigrant, she wrote of her life as an indentured servant and her conversion to Quakerism in *Some Account of the Fore-Part of the Life of Elizabeth Ashbridge* (1774).

Ashe, Thomas (1770–?),   adventurer, writer. Born in Ireland, Ashe was employed in government service under Jefferson. His *Travels in America, Performed in 1806, for the Purpose of Exploring the Rivers Allegheny, Monongahela, Ohio, and Mississippi* (1808) presents a generally unflattering view of the United States.

Ashley, Lady Brett, the neurotic heroine of THE SUN ALSO RISES (1926) by Ernest Hemingway.

Ash Wednesday (1930), poem by T.S. Eliot. The poem is a religious meditation on spiritual regeneration; it plays variations on the idea of turning announced in the first line, "Because I do not hope to turn again." Humans must face the necessity of turning away from earthly considerations in anticipation of the turning to dust that awaits the body as the soul seeks a different level of existence.

Asian-American Literature. Early Asian immigrants arrived in the U.S. in successive waves: Chinese (1850–1882), Japanese (1885–1924), Korean (1903–1905), South Asians (1904–1924), Filipino (1907–1930). Generally each wave began as a response to labor shortage and ended in legislative exclusion. The Chinese Exclusion Act of 1882 banned the further immigration of Chinese laborers; those who stayed could not send for their wives in China. The Gentleman's Agreement in 1907 likewise curtailed Japanese and Korean laborers, but immigrants could arrange to have their wives or "picture brides" come to the U.S. Other laws included the 1917 Immigration Act, which prohibited Asian Indian immigration; the 1924 Immigration Quota Act, which halted all immigration from mainland Asia; and the 1934 Tydings-McDuffie Act which restricted Filipino immigration. Immediate concern with survival and the problem of language barriers confined writings by most early Chinese and Japanese immigrants to native languages and literary forms. (Exotics such as Yone Noguchi, Shiesei Tsuneishi, and Sadakichi Hartmann were exceptions.) Much of this literature has been collected only recently in anthologies such as *Wooden-Fish Books: Critical Essays & an Annotated Catalog Based on the Collections in the University of Hong Kong*, ed. Leung Pui-Chee (1978); *Island: Poetry and History of Chinese Immigrants on Angel Island, 1910–1940*, ed. Him Mark Lai, Genny Lim, and Judy Yung (1980); *Ayumi: A Japanese American Anthology*, ed. Janice Mirikitani et al. (1980); *Songs of Gold Mountain: Cantonese Rhymes from San Francisco Chinatown*, ed. and tr. by Marlon Horn (1987).

Early writings in English consisted mostly of autobiography and autobiographical novels, such as Lee Yan Phou's *When I Was a Boy in China* (1887), Yung Wing's *My Life in China and America* (1909), Etsu Sugimoto's *Daughter of the Samurai* (1925), New Il-Han's *When I Was a Boy in Korea* (1928), and YOUNGHILL KANG's *Grass Roof* (1931) and *East Goes West* (1937). Most of these books focus on the author's ancestral lands, a trend that seemed to reflect the taste of the American public. The publications of nisei such as Taro Katayama, Iwao Kawakami, and Toyo Suyemoto, were mostly restricted to the English sections of bilingual newspapers and literary magazines. Two writers devoted to portraying Chinese- and Japanese-Americans, however, were read outside of their ethnic communities. Sui Sin Far, pseudonym of Edith Eaton, an Eurasian whose tales are collected in *Mrs. Spring Fragrance* (1912), sketches characters that populated the Chinatowns of San Francisco, Seattle, and Los Angeles. TOSHIO MORI excels in capturing Japanese-American life in Seattle; his collection of short stories, *Yokohama, California*, was slated for publication in 1942, but because of the war did not appear until 1949.

World War II had a mixed impact on Asian-American literature. Because China and the Philippines were American allies in the Pacific, Americans of Chinese and Filipino descent were suddenly looked upon favorably. Publishers responded to the changes in public attitudes, and works by two American-born Chinese and two Filipino immigrants appeared during or shortly after the war. Pardee Lowe's *Father and Glorious Descendant* (1943) and JADE SNOW WONG's *Fifth Chinese Daughter* (1945), both autobiographies, center on the interaction and conflicts between immigrant parents and American-born children. CARLOS BULOSAN's *America Is in the Heart* (1946), an autobiographical novel, describes the harsh working conditions for Filipino farm laborers and the racial prejudices they encountered; poet Jose Garcia Villa, whose work reflects metaphysical rather than ethnic concerns, received international acclaim for *Have Come, Am Here* (1942). These books depicting life in the U.S. were followed by Lin Yutang's *A Chinatown Family* (1948), C.Y. Lee's *Flower Drum Song* (1957), LOUIS CHU's *Eat a Bowl of Tea* (1961), Virginia Lee's *The House that Tai Ming Built* (1963), and Chuang Hua's *Crossings* (1968). Diana Chang's *Frontiers of Love* (1956), though set in Shanghai, is presented from the perspective of a Eurasian born and raised in the U.S.

By contrast, anti-Japanese sentiment prevented most Japanese-American writers from gaining national recognition till almost a decade after the end of the war. An exception was Hisaye Yamamoto, who published five stories in national journals between 1949 and 1952. Recently collected in *Seventeen Syllables* (1988), her fiction frequently explores the relationship between issei and nisei. Also devoted to this theme are Monica Sone's *Nisei Daughter* (1953) and Milton Murayama's *All I Asking for Is My Body* (1959). The bombing of Pearl Harbor and the subsequent internment of people of Japanese ancestry left indelible marks on their creative work and continue to be reprised in literature to this day. The bombing is recalled in *Lucky Come Hawaii* (1965) by Jon Shirota and in *Journey to Washington* (1967) by Daniel Inouye with Lawrence Elliot. Works that evoke life in camps include JOY KOGAWA's *Obasan* (Japanese-Canadian novel, 1981); Edward Miyakawa's *Tule Lake* (1979); Mine Okubo's *Citizen 13660* (1946); and Daisuke Kitagawa's *Issei and Nisei* (1967), JEANNE HOUSTON and James Houston's *Farewell to Manzanar* (1973), YOSHIKO UCHIDA's *Desert Exile* (1982), and Mitsuye Yamada's *Desert Run* (1988). JOHN OKADA's *No-No Boy* (1957) delineates the trauma of a nisei who refuses the draft.

The civil rights movement of the 1960s, when the term "Asian-American" gained currency, fostered a collective identity among Americans of Asian descent and encouraged them to define themselves against externally imposed stereotypes. Furthermore, it led to the development of ethnic studies programs throughout the nation, thereby providing forums for discussing works written by and about Asian-Americans. The resulting bloom in creativity has been accompanied by growing political consciousness. Writers who emerged after the movement are concerned not only with exposing racial and sexual inequities but also with affirming Asian-American heritage. These concerns are evident in fiction such as Jeffery Paul Chan's "Jackrabbit" (1974), Frank Chin's *The Chinaman Pacific and Frisco R. R. Co.* (1988), Ruthanne Lum McCunn's *Thousand Pieces of Gold* (1981), David Masumoto's *Silent Strength* (1984), Shawn Wong's *Homebase* (1979), and Lawrence Yep's *Dragonwings* (1975); in plays such as R. A. Shiomi's *Yellow Fever* (1982), Philip Gotanda's *Fish Head Soup* (1986), DAVID HWANG's *FOB* (1979), and Wakako Yamauchi's *And the Soul Shall Dance* (1982). Interaction between generations remains a popular subject among Asian-American writers, as evident in drama such as Frank Chin's *Year of the Dragon* (1981), Momoko Iko's *The Gold Watch* (1974), Paul Stephen Lim's *Mother Tongue* [n.d.], Darrell Lum's *Oranges Are Lucky* (1978); in prose works such as Cynthia Kadohata's *The Floating World* (1989), Ronyoung Kim's *Clay Walls* (1986), MAXINE HONG KINGSTON's *The Woman Warrior* (1976) and *China Men* (1980), AMY TAN's *The Joy Luck Club* (1989), and Yoshiko Uchida's *Picture Bride* (1987). Increasingly, writers have also begun to explore interethnic and interracial themes in fiction such as Cecilia Brainard's *Woman with Horns* (1988), Jeffery Chan's "The Chinese in Haifa" (1974), Paulino Lim's *Passion Summer* (1988), Maxine Hong Kingston's *Tripmaster Monkey* (1989), Susan Nunes's *A Small Obligation*, and in David Hwang's play *M Butterfly* (1989).

Asian-American literature since the late 1960s has been equally rich in poetry, where eastern and western allusions, Asian expressions, and Americanisms often merge. Images of Asia inform Marilyn Chin's *Dwarf Bamboo* (1987), Alex Kuo's *Changing the River* (1986), Stephen Liu's *Dream Journeys to China* (1982), Al Robles's *Kayaomunggi Vision of a Wandering Carabao* (1983), and Arthur Sze's *Two Ravens*. Vernacular idiom or local color is registered in Fay Chiang's *In the City of Contradictions* (1979), Eric Chock's *Ten Thousand Wishes* (1978) and *Last Days Here* (1990), Sesshu Foster's *Angry Days* (1987), Juliet Kono's *Hilo Rains* (1988), Alan Lau's *Songs for Jardina* (1980), Genny Lim's *Winter Place* (1988), James Mitsui's *After the Long Train* (1985), Jeff Tagami's *October Light* (1987), and Ronald Tanaka's *Shino Suite* (1981). Familial and communal portraits abound in GARRETT HONGO's *Yellow Light* (1982) and *The River of Heaven* (1988), Kimiko Hahn's *Air Pocket* (1989), Chungmi Kim's *Selected Poems* (1982), Li-Young Lee's *Rose* (1986), Amy Ling's *Chinamerica Reflections* (1984), and Wing Tek Lum's *Expounding the Doubtful Points* (1987). Cadences and images from music and visual arts animate Mei-Mei Berssenbrugge's *Heat Bird* (1983), Diana Chang's *What Matisse Is After* (1984), Jessica Hagedorn's *Dangerous Music* (1975), Lawson Inada's *Before the War* (1971), David Mura's *After We Lost Our Way* (1989), CATHY SONG's *Picture Bride* (1983) and *Frameless Windows, Squares of Light*, and JOHN YAU's *Corpse and Mirror* (1983). Third World and feminist concerns converge in Theresa Cha's *Dictee* (prose poem, 1982), Geraldine Kudaka's *Numerous Avalanches at the Point of*

Intersection (1978), JANICE MIRIKITANI's *Awake in the River* (1978) and *Shedding Silence* (1987), Kitty Tsui's *The Words of a Woman Who Breathes Fire* (1983), Nellie Wong's *The Death of a Long Steam Lady* (1986), and Wanwadee Larsen's *Confessions of a Mail Order Bride: American Life Through Thai Eyes* (1989).

With the passage of the Immigration and Naturalization Act of 1965, which abolished the quota system of selecting immigrants by race or national origin, and with the end of the Vietnam War, came a huge number of new Asian immigrants and Southeast Asian refugees. Unlike the early immigrants, who were mostly laborers and farmers, many of the newcomers are professionals and intellectuals from urban areas. Writers such as Meena Alexander, G. S. Sharat Chandra, Zulfikar Ghose, N.V.M. Gonzalez, Kim Yong Ik, Ko Won, Shirley Lim, Nguyen Mong Giac, Raja Rao, Ninotchka Rosca, Thich Nhat-Hanh, Tran Van Dinh, and Linda Ty-Casper had already achieved literary fame in their native countries. Among the works set in Asia the most widely read has been RICHARD KIM's *The Martyred* (1964), an award-winning novel of the Korean War. More recently, other works set in Asia have received a wide readership, including GAIL TSUKIYAMA's *The Samurai's Garden* (1994) and HA JIN's *Waiting* (1999). Works depicting recent immigrant experiences include Wendy Law-Yone's *The Coffin Tree* (1983), VED MEHTA's *Sound-Shadows of the New World* (1985), BHARATI MUKHERJEE's *Darkness* (1985) and *The Middleman* (1988), Hualing Nieh's *Mulberry and Peach* (1981), Bienvenido N. Santos's *The Scent of Apples* (1979), and Ty Pak's *Guilt Payment* (1983). The themes of exile, loneliness, alienation, and cultural conflict run through many of these works.

Asian-American literature continued to proliferate in the 1990s. While generational differences remained a persistent theme, the decade also witnessed bolder depictions of interracial, gay and lesbian, and transnational encounters. Intergenerational and interracial dynamics can be found in Peter Bacho's *Cebu* (1991) and *Dark Blue Suit and Other Stories* (1997); Lan Chao's *Monkey Bridge* (1998); Frank Chin's *Gunga Din Highway* (1994); Chitra Banerjee Divakaruni's *Arranged Marriage* (1995) and *The Mistress of Spices* (1997); GISH JEN's *Typical American* (1991) and *Mona in the Promised Land* (1996); CHANG-RAE LEE's *Native Speaker* (1995) and *A Gesture Life* (1999); Gus Lee's *China Boy* (1991) and *Honor and Duty* (1994); LI-YOUNG LEE's *The Winged Seed: A Remembrance* (1995); David Wong Louie's *Pangs of Love* (1991) and *The Barbarians Are Coming* (2000); Fae Myenne Ng's *Bone* (1993); Gary Pak's *The Watcher of Waipuna and Other Stories* (1992) and *A Ricepaper Airplane* (1998); Lisa See's *On Gold Mountain* (1995); Amy Uyematsu's *30 Miles from J-Town* (1992) and *Nights of Fire, Nights of Rain* (1998); Shawn Wong's *American Knees* (1995); Lois-Ann Yamanaka's *Saturday Night at the Pahala Theatre* (1993) and *Wild Meat and the Bully Burgers* (1996); Mako Yoshikawa's *One Hundred and One Ways* (1999).

The intersections of race, gender, and sexuality are explored in Jessica Hagedorn's *Dogeaters* (1990) and *Gangster of Love* (1996); Wanwadee Larsen's *Confessions of a Mail Order Bride: American Life through Thai Eyes* (1989); Russell Leong's *The*

Country of Dream and Dust (1993) and *Phoenix Eyes and Other Stories* (2000); R. Zamora Linmark's *Rolling the R's* (1995); Timothy Liu's *Vox Angelica* (1992); Nina Revoyr's *The Necessary Hunger* (1997); Kitty Tsui's *Breathless* (1996); Norman Wong's *Cultural Revolution* (1994).

Exilic or diasporic sensibilities are expressed in Meena Alexander's *Fault Lines* (1993) and *River and Bridge* (1995); Shauna Singh Baldwin's *English Lessons and Other Stories* (1996); Lan Samantha Chang's *Hunger* (1998); Susan Choi's *The Foreign Student* (1999); Le Ly Hayslip's *When Heaven and Earth Changed Places* (1989) and *Child of War, Woman of Peace* (1993); Jade Ngoc Quang Huynh's *South Wind Changing* (1994); Myung Mi Kim's *Under Flag* (1991) and *Dura* (1998); JHUMPA LAHIRI's *Interpreter of Maladies* (1999); Wendy Law-Yone's *Irrawaddy Tango* (1993); Shirley Geok-lin Lim's *Among the Half-Moon Faces: An Asian-American Memoir of Homelands* (1996); Rohintin Mistry's *Such a Long Journey* (1991) and *A Fine Balance* (1995); David Mura's *Turning Japanese* (1991); Ruth L. Ozeki's *My Year of Meats* (1988); Qui Duc Nguyen's *Where the Ashes Are* (1994); S. P. Somtow's *Jasmine Nights* (1994); Karen Tei Yamashita's *Brazil Maru* (1992) and *Tropic of Orange* (1997).

Helpful secondary sources include King-Kok Cheung and Stan Yogi, comp., *Asian American Literature: An Annotated Bibliography* (1988), and King-Kok Cheung, ed., *An Interethnic Companion to Asian American Literature* (1997).

KING-KOK CHEUNG

As I Lay Dying (1930), a novel by WILLIAM FAULKNER. Written in only six weeks, *As I Lay Dying* is one of Faulkner's finest novels. The story unfolds in some sixty short sections, each labeled with the name of the character who narrates his thoughts and perceptions through direct interior monologue.

As the story opens, a Mississippi farm woman, Addie Bundren, is dying. The members of her family—her husband, Anse; four sons, Cash, Darl, Jewel, and Vardaman; and a daughter, Dewey Dell—as well as some of her neighbors, individually reveal their relationship to Addie in words and actions. Addie has made Anse promise to take her to Jefferson to be buried, and the major part of the book concerns the Bundrens' journey with the coffin to the burying ground. Various mishaps beset the family en route: in crossing a flooding river, the mules are drowned, Cash's leg is broken, and the coffin is upset and rescued by Jewel at the risk of his life. On the other side the family rests at a farmhouse, where Darl sets fire to the barn in an attempt to destroy the by-then-putrescent corpse; the coffin is rescued again by Jewel, who is badly burned. The family finally reaches Jefferson, where Addie is buried, Darl is taken without warning to the insane asylum, and Anse acquires a new wife, "duck-shaped" and popeyed.

In the course of the narrative it is revealed that Jewel was born of Addie's affair with Whitfield, a local preacher. Her relationship with Anse had been spiritually and emotionally barren, based on words that were just "shape[s] to fill a lack." Jewel, the child of Addie's relationship in which no words were necessary, is significantly silent; a passionate, active man, he lives intuitively and impulsively. Darl, the extreme opposite of

Jewel, is extraordinarily sensitive and perceptive, but lives in the private world of his mind, several removes from reality and from human contact. Cash is concerned with balance—both in terms of his trade as a carpenter and in his growing ability to balance thought and action, word and fact.

As I Like It, a department conducted by WILLIAM LYON PHELPS in *Scribner's Magazine* from 1922 to 1936. Phelps wrote about books, plays, and people in a way that won him a large audience; very frequently his judgment of a book or play secured its success. Selections from these essays appeared under the same title in three books (1923, 1924, 1926).

Asimov, Isaac (1920–1992), novelist, writer on many subjects, especially science. Born in Russia, Asimov earned his Ph.D. at Columbia University in 1948 and taught biochemistry at the Boston University School of Medicine. In 1957 he won the Thomas Alva Edison Foundation award for *Building Blocks of the Universe* and in 1960 the Howard W. Blakeslee award from the American Heart Association for *The Living River* (1959), in which he analyzed the chemical composition of blood and related it to other aspects of the universe.

Asimov was a remarkably prolific writer, publishing over 425 books on a wide variety of subjects. For young people there are the Lucky Starr series of adventure stories beginning with *David Starr, Space Ranger* (1952) and various simple explanations of scientific phenomena. Novels range from *I Robot* (1950)—which introduced his famous Three Laws of Robotics: robots may not injure a human, or by inaction allow a human to be harmed; robots must obey human orders unless doing so conflicts with the first law; robots must protect their own existence except when doing so will conflict with the first two laws—to *The Robots of Dawn* (1983). Among story collections is *Best Science Fiction of Isaac Asimov* (1986). Nonfiction includes *The Human Brain: Its Capabilities and Functions* (1964); *Asimov's Biographical Encyclopedia of Science and Technology* (1964; rev. 1974); *To the Ends of the Universe* (1967; rev. 1975); *Asimov's Guide to the Bible: Old Testament* (Volume I, 1968); *New Testament* (Volume II, 1969); *Asimov's Guide to Shakespeare* (2 v. 1970); *Possible Tomorrows: Science Fiction* (1972); *The Best of Isaac Asimov: 1939–1972* (1973); *Birth and Death of the Universe* (1975); *Asimov's Guide to Science* (2 v. 1975); *Asimov on Science Fiction* (1981); *The Dangers of Intelligence* (1986); *Did Comets Kill the Dinosaurs?* (1987); *Unidentified Flying Objects* (1988); and *Asimov's Chronology of Science and Discovery* (1989). Among his autobiographical volumes are *In Memory Yet Green* (1979) and *In Joy Still Felt* (1980).

Aspern Papers, The (1888), a short novel by HENRY JAMES. According to passages in his notebook; James based *The Aspern Papers* on a story he had heard concerning the mistress of Byron, then living, who was in possession of several unpublished papers and letters of both Byron and Shelley. The narrator of *The Aspern Papers* learns that the former mistress of the romantic poet Jeffrey Aspern is still living in Italy and has in her possession a collection of the poet's papers, which she will not permit to be published. In hope of somehow gaining access to the papers, the narrator rents a room from the old lady and her middle-aged niece, but his plans are frustrated when, at the old lady's death, the niece demands marriage as the price of the papers.

Assignation, The (*Godey's Lady's Book*, 1834; TALES OF THE GROTESQUE AND THE ARABESQUE, 1840), a story by EDGAR ALLAN POE. A wealthy young man rescues the young child of the Marchesa Aphrodite from drowning while her aged husband looks on indifferently. She makes an assignation with the young man for one hour after sunrise. The narrator accompanies the hero to his magnificent home. At the hour set a messenger arrives with word that the marchesa is dead; and the narrator discovers that his host, apparently asleep after taking a glass of wine, is dead too. Both had taken the same poison; the assignation had been kept.

Assiniboin Indians, northern Plains tribe located after the 17th century near Lake Winnipeg and still later around the upper Saskatchewan and Missouri rivers. They fought with the Cree against the Blackfeet Indians. Many now live on a reservation in Montana, others in Canada. They appear in JOHN G. NEIHARDT's *Song of Three Friends*.

Assistant, The (1957), a novel by BERNARD MALAMUD. Set in a poor neighborhood in New York, the novel deals with Morris Bober, his wife, Ida, and his daughter, Helen, who own a grocery store. It is held up by a thug and his crony, Frank Alpine. After the robbery Alpine is drawn back inexplicably to the store, takes to living in the basement, and finally tries to help Morris. The book is the story of Frank's gradual implication in Morris's problems and his final understanding of that implication. Though oppressed with guilt for the robbery, he continues to steal money from Morris and is fired. Later he reveals his love for Helen and is rebuffed. When all fails in the store, Morris makes an abortive attempt at suicide; Frank saves him and runs the store during Morris's recovery. Frank finally confesses that he was one of the thieves. His changing attitude toward himself and his crimes is mirrored in his attitude toward the Jews. Finally, he himself becomes a Jew.

Aston, Anthony (?–?), English actor. He arrived in Charleston, S.C., in 1703 or thereabouts and became the first professional actor, so far as is known, in American history. He also wrote plays, of which only one, *The Fool's Opera* (c. 1730), survives. It is a parody of John Gay's *The Beggar's Opera*.

Astoria, or, Anecdotes of an Enterprise Beyond the Rocky Mountains (1836), a descriptive and historical work by WASHINGTON IRVING. The book recounts the history of JOHN JACOB ASTOR's fur trade. Astoria itself, once called Fort Clatsop, was a town in Oregon near the mouth of the Columbia River. In 1811 Astor established a fur trading post at this point, but sold his interest in it to British traders during the War of 1812; Astoria later was returned to the United States in the Treaty of Ghent (1814).

Asturias, Miguel Angel (1899–1974), Guatemalan novelist, short-story writer, poet. Born into a well-to-do family of mixed ancestry (he was proud of his Mayan features), Asturias grew up in Guatemala, but spent much of his life in exile because of his opposition to dictatorships. When he was sympathetic to his country's leadership, he served as ambassa-

dor to El Salvador and later to France. After taking a law degree (1923) in Guatamala, he went to London to study economics but became fascinated with the Mayan materials in the British Museum. Soon he was in Paris, studying anthropology at the Sorbonne. He translated the sacred Mayan text *Popol Voh* into Spanish in 1925, developing a deep concern for the Mayan culture that was to weave its myth and history into everything he wrote, though never to the exclusion of his social and political statements. His greatest novel is *El señor presidente* (1946; tr. *The President*, 1963), a phantasmagoric satire on Latin American military dictators, based largely on the regime of Manuel Estrada Cabrera, president of Guatamela (1898–1920) during his youth. In his second novel, *Hombres de maiz* (1949, tr. *Men of Maize*, 1975), he tried to show the transformation of the Indian way of life from a native perspective, shaped in myth. Prominent among later works is a trilogy attacking the exploitation of Guatamalan banana plantations by U.S. owned companies: *Viento fuerte* (1950, tr. *Strong Wind*, 1969); *El papa verde* (1954, tr. *The Green Pope*, 1971); and *Los ojos de los enterrados* (1960, tr. *The Eyes of the Interred*, 1972). Other novels include *El Al-hajadito* (1961, tr. *The Bejeweled Boy*, 1971) and *Mulata de tal* (1963, tr. *Mulata*, 1967). *Week-end en Guatemala* (1956) is a collection of stories about the CIA-directed overthrow of the government of Jacobo Arbenz, whom Asturias had supported. After Arbenz was ousted, Asturias went into exile, returning to Guatemala in 1966. In 1967 he was appointed ambassador to France, the same year in which he was awarded the Nobel Prize in Literature.

Asylum, or, Alonzo and Melissa, The (1811), a novel, probably written by Isaac Mitchell, a New York newspaper editor. A plagiarism, ascribed to Daniel Jackson, appeared the same year under the title *Alonzo and Melissa, or, The Unfeeling Father*. Set in the era of Revolution, *The Asylum*, a story in the Gothic manner, relates how the father of Melissa parts her from Alonzo because he is poor; she escapes to Charleston, whence comes a false report of her death, while Alonzo enlists in the navy and is captured by the British. When Benjamin Franklin helps him escape, he goes to Charleston and meets a mysterious lady who turns out to be Melissa. There is also a castle haunted by ghosts who are really smugglers working for the British.

Atala (1801, American translation, 1802), a novel by FRANÇOIS RENÉ CHATEAUBRIAND. Later incorporated in his *Génie du Christianisme*, this romance was originally intended to form part of a trilogy with *Les Natchez* and *René*. All three stories were suggested by a trip Chateaubriand made to America in 1791, during which he spent part of the time residing with an Indian tribe. Deeply under the influence of Rousseau, Chateaubriand for the most part paints the noble savage, although the number of homicides, suicides, and massacres in the tale does not support his thesis materially.

Atall, Peter. See ROBERT WALN.

Atherton, Gertrude [Franklin] (1857–1948), novelist, biographer, historian. Born in San Francisco, Atherton began writing very early, but did not really start on a literary career until the late 1880s—and continued producing books of all kinds until she was almost ninety. *My San Francisco*, a book of mingled history and reminiscence, appeared in her 90th year. Her work, which was uneven in quality but rich in variety of theme and background, included *The Californians* (1898), *Senator North* (1900), *The Conqueror* (1902), *Rezánov* (1906), *California: An Intimate History* (1914), *Black Oxen* (1923), *The Immortal Marriage* (1927), and *Adventures of a Novelist* (1932). *The Conqueror* is a fictional biography of Alexander Hamilton, and she edited *A Few of Hamilton's Letters* (1903). *Black Oxen*, with glandular rejuvenation as its theme, joined JURGEN, THE SUN ALSO RISES, and similar books in defying the raised eyebrows of the puritanical. See THE EROTIC SCHOOL.

Atkinson, [Justin] Brooks (1894–1984), newspaperman, drama critic, writer. Born in Melrose, Massachusetts, and educated at Harvard, Atkinson began as a reporter on Springfield, Massachusetts, and Boston newspapers, in 1922 joined the New York *Times* staff as editor of the book review section, then in 1925 turned drama critic, a position he held until his retirement after the 1959–60 season. From 1942 to 1946 he was a war correspondent for the *Times* in China and Russia, then returned to reviewing plays. The vivid dispatches he wrote from China won a Pulitzer Prize. The variety of Atkinson's interests is shown in his books: *Henry Thoreau, The Cosmic Yankee* (1927); *East of the Hudson*, rural wanderings (1931); *The Cingalese Prince*, an account of a round-the-world trip on a freighter (1934); *Broadway Scrapbook* (1947); and *Once Around the Sun*, essays (1951). Collections of articles are *Tuesdays and Fridays* (1963) and *Brief Chronicles* (1966). *Broadway* (1970) is a theater history. Retiring as drama critic, Atkinson continued to write for the *Times* on general subjects in an irregularly appearing column called "Critic at Large." His wife, Oriana, wrote *Over at Uncle Joe's: Moscow and Me* (1947), *Manhattan and Me* (1954), *The South and West of It: Ireland and Me* (1956), and several books of fiction.

Atlantic Monthly, The. Founded in Boston in November 1857 by Moses Dresser Phillips of the publishing firm of Phillips, Sampson & Company, the *Atlantic Monthly* was purchased two years later by Ticknor & Fields for $10,000. H. O. Houghton (later Houghton, Mifflin & Company) bought it in 1874, and the Atlantic Monthly Company, a stock concern, has owned it since 1908. The magazine enjoyed the editorship of a distinguished series of men of letters: JAMES RUSSELL LOWELL (1857–1861), JAMES T. FIELDS (1861–1871), WILLIAM DEAN HOWELLS (1871–1881), THOMAS BAILEY ALDRICH (1881–1890), HORACE E. SCUDDER (1890–1898), WALTER HINES PAGE (1898–1899), BLISS PERRY (1899–1909), Ellery Sedgwick (1909–1938), and Edward A. Weeks (1938–1966). It was for many years regarded as the preeminent literary magazine of the country; though points of emphasis have shifted, the *Atlantic* and *Harper's* remained in the late 20th century the sole survivors of the traditional quality magazine of the 19th century.

Through its first 15 years, the *Atlantic* relied mainly on New England writers, and the volumes of those early years, filled with the work of Emerson, Longfellow, Whittier, Lowell, Holmes,

Hawthorne, and Harriet Beecher Stowe, set a high literary standard. A change came over the magazine with Howells's editorship, when it came to recognize southern, midwestern, and far-western writers, publishing the work of Mark Twain, Bret Harte, Mary N. Murfree, John Hay, Maurice Thompson, and Paul Hamilton Hayne. Another break came with the advent of Ellery Sedgwick, who introduced lively articles on the economic, political, social, and scientific changes in the American scene. Circulation passed 100,000 in 1921 and increased to over 260,000 by 1961, and 470,000 in 2000. The Weeks editorship was notable for a greater breadth of international outlook and increased interest in current problems. Among leading authors published in the first half of the twentieth century were Stephen Vincent Benét, Robert Frost, Howard Mumford Jones, Van Wyck Brooks, Bernard De Voto, Gertrude Stein, Rebecca West, and Virginia Woolf. Still more recent authors include Bernard Malamud, Raymond Carver, and Louise Erdrich. Ellery Sedgwick included selections from forty-six authors in *Atlantic Harvest* (1947). Helen McMahon wrote *Criticism of Fiction: A Study of Trends in the Atlantic Monthly, 1857–98* (1952). Edward Weeks and Emily Flint edited a selection from the *Atlantic's* first hundred years in *Jubilee* (1957).

Attaché, or, Sam Slick in England, The (4 v. 1843–1844), by T. C. HALIBURTON. In these sketches Haliburton continued to write with sardonic humor observations supposedly made by the Yankee clockmaker whom he had made famous. But Haliburton, a Canadian, here chose to poke fun at some of his own countrymen. The book was popular in Canada and England.

Attaway, William (1911–1986), novelist. Born in Mississippi, Attaway was raised in Chicago, graduated from the University of Illinois and became one of the African-American writers supported by the FEDERAL WRITERS' PROJECT. His two novels soon followed: *Let Me Breathe Thunder* (1939), about young white hoboes, and *Blood on the Forge* (1941), about southern blacks competing for northern steel-mill jobs. His *Hear America Singing* (1967) is a children's book.

Atwood, Margaret [Eleanor] (1939–   ), novelist, poet, short-story writer, critic. Born in Ottawa, Atwood was educated at the University of Toronto and Radcliffe College. She lived in the Quebec bush when she was young and has since traveled widely, currently residing in Toronto with the writer Graeme Gibson and their daughter Jess. Her numerous literary prizes include the Governor General's Medal for *The Circle Game* (1966) and *The Handmaid's Tale* (1985), and the Booker Prize for *The Blind Assassin* (2000).

The Circle Game, Atwood's first major volume of poetry, introduces two important themes running throughout Atwood's work: game playing—between males and females or different dimensions of the self, within the artist, with language—and, consequently, fragmentation of identity. Here and elsewhere, her unreliable narrators, characteristically good at double solitaire, are either trapped in or afraid to enter the "rooms" of relationships. They are symbolic photographers, trying to freeze reality and one another while perfecting disguises to escape the "glass eye" of camera, mirror, self, or other.

As Atwood emphasizes, however, in her cover design—a spiral maze rather than a circle—and her narrator's words, "I want the circle / broken" (title poem), one can break the mirror of narcissism. Metamorphosis is possible: in the final poem, "The Settlers, "our bones grew flesh again, / came up trees and / grass." The poems of *Power Politics* (1971) brilliantly dramatize the menace of the room: not only the assumption or projection of monster/victim roles but literal and figurative dismemberment. "Hesitations Outside the Door," like many Atwood visual and literary works, embeds fairy tales: the Grimms' "The Robber Bridegroom" and "Fitcher's Bird." Characters of this poem and volume, wearing and projecting Bluebeard/victim false skins, again both desire and fear "love without mirrors" and its adjacent horrors: amputation or nothingness. "If we make stories for each other / about what is in the room / we will never have to go in." Still, it is just possible that "In the room we will find each other." *The Journals of Susanna Moodie* (1970) is a poetic sequence based on the life of a 19th-century Canadian pioneer. *Surfacing* (1972) is a novel about a search for a father in northern Quebec. Her volume of literary criticism, *Survival: A Thematic Guide to Canadian Literature* (1972), broad in focus, includes issues of personal identity as well as Canadian literary issues.

Bluebeardian sexual politics and fragmented personal or national identity receive comic and parodic treatment in several prose fictions, including *The Edible Woman* (1969), where Marian fears cannibalistic consummation: *Lady Oracle* (1976), where Joan traps herself in mazes of multiple identities and in her own gothic romance plots; and the title story of *Bluebeard's Egg* (1983), where Sally, writing a contemporary "Fitcher's Bird" story, begins to see her philandering husband as a "Bluebeard."

Themes of game playing, fragmentation, and metamorphosis and related—often gothic—images continue in subsequent work, becoming increasingly political in the novel *Bodily Harm* and the poems of *True Stories* (both 1981); *Second Words: Selected Critical Prose* (1984); and *The Handmaid's Tale* (1985), a futuristic story involving enslavement of women. In "An End to Audience" (*Second Words*), Atwood delineates the artist's eyewitness function: "to speak the forbidden . . . especially in times of political repression. . . . the writer testifies."

Bodily Harm's Rennie, initially another camera-carrying creator of tourist-brochure reality, assumes this responsibility. Discovering that "there is no longer a *here* and a *there*," Rennie becomes a cell in the "world body." Like her author and the voice of *True Stories*, she sees and testifies. One of North America's finest artists, Margaret Atwood is also one of its most humane.

Other novels include *Life Before Man* (1979), about fragmented characters in a love triangle; *Cat's Eye* (1988), about the childhood of a woman painter in northern Canada and Toronto (Atwood has painted watercolors as illustrations or covers for her books); *The Robber Bride* (1993), a revisioning of the Grimms' fairy tale "The Robber Bridegroom," Great Goddess myth, and vampire legend to present a female "robber" who disrupts the lives of her "friends"; *Alias Grace* (1996),

using illustrations and names of quilt patterns in its postmodern and postcolonial questioning about a real 19th-century Canadian crime and the nature of identity and reality. *The Blind Assassin* (2000), a Booker Prize winner, mixes narratives and narrative genres, including a story within a story and elements of lurid pulp and science fiction, to explore the melodramatic lives of an eccentric Canadian family through the generations from World War I. Additional volumes of verse are *The Animals in that Country* (1968); *Procedures for Underground* (1970); *You Are Happy* (1974); *Two-Headed Poems* (1978); *Interlunar* (1984); and *Morning in the Burned House* (1995). *Murder in the Dark* (1983) contains short fiction and prose poems. Other volumes of short fiction are *Dancing Girls and Other Stories* (1977) and *Wilderness Tips* (1991). Atwood's children's literature includes *For the Birds* (1990) and *Princess Prunella and the Purple Peanut* (1995). A volume of essays, *Strange Things: The Malevolent North in Canadian Literature* (1995), follows up on ideas first presented in *Survival*.

Criticism includes Coral Ann Howells, *Margaret Atwood* (1995), and Karen F. Stein, *Margaret Atwood Revisited* (1999).
SHARON R. WILSON

Aubert de Gaspé, Phillippe (1786–1871),   lawyer, novelist, historian. A native of Quebec, Aubert de Gaspé studied law at the Quebec seminary and was high sheriff of the district of Quebec for many years until forced to withdraw from public life because of business difficulties and debts. At the age of seventy-six, he brought out his first book, *Les anciens canadiens* (1863). This historical romance, a classic of French Canadian literature, has been translated into English as *The Canadians of Old* (1864, Georgiana M. Penee; 1890, Charles G. D. Roberts). His *Mémoires* (1886) is a collection of notes and hints for historians. A son, Alfred Aubert de Gaspé, published a posthumous collection of essays and sketches, *Divers* (1893).

Auchincloss, Louis [Stanton] (1917–   ),   lawyer, novelist, short-story writer. Born in Lawrence, New York, Auchincloss was educated at Groton, Yale, and the University of Virginia. He was admitted to the New York bar in 1941, served in the U.S. Navy during World War II, and has been a member of New York law firms, as well as president of the Museum of the City of New York. Like Edith Wharton, whom he much admires, Auchincloss is a chronicler of New York aristocracy, a close observer of monied and privileged people with backgrounds similar to his own. In their stories he occasionally finds comedy, but also the more serious effects of lives lived only to get money, to enjoy the benefits of wealth without engaging directly in the tainted world of commerce, or, in the case of his lawyers, to manage the money of others. In his first novel, *The Indifferent Children* (1947), published under the pseudonym Andrew Lee, he introduced some of his themes by portraying social dilletantism during World War II. His novels, mostly with a contemporary New York background, include *Sybil* (1952), *The Great World of Timothy Colt* (1956), *Venus in Sparta* (1958), *Pursuit of the Prodigal* (1959), *The House of Five Talents* (1960), *Portrait in Brownstone* (1962), *The Embezzler* (1966), *A World of Profit* (1968), *The*

Dark Lady (1977), *The Country Cousin* (1978), *The House of the Prophet* (1980), *Exit Lady Masham* (1983), *Fellow Passengers* (1989), *The Lady of Situations* (1990), *The Education of Oscar Fairfax* (1995), and *Her Infinite Variety* (2000). *Watchfires* (1982) treats a New York lawyer during the time of the Civil War. *The Rector of Justin* (1964) portrays the headmaster of a boys' school in New England.

Collections of short stories by Auchincloss, frequently on themes similar to those of his novels, include *The Injustice Collectors* (1950), *The Romantic Egoists* (1954), *Powers of Attorney* (1963), *Second Chance* (1970), *The Partners* (1974), *Narcissa and Other Fables* (1983), and *Three Lives* (1993). *The Collected Stories* appeared in 1994. Books on literary subjects include *Reflections of a Jacobite* (1961); *Ellen Glasgow* (1964); *Pioneers and Caretakers: A Study of Nine American Women Novelists* (1965); *Motiveless Malignity* (1969), on Shakespeare; *Henry Adams* (1971); *Edith Wharton: A Woman in Her Time* (1971); *Reading Henry James* (1975); and *The Style's the Man: Reflections on Proust, Fitzgerald, Wharton, Vidal, and Others* (1994). *Life, Law and Letters* (1979) is a prose miscellany. Auchincloss edited *The Hone & Strong Diaries of Old Manhattan* (1989), a picture of the city from 1830 to 1875, illustrated with prints and engravings. *A Writer's Capital* (1974) is autobiographical. In *The Vanderbilt Era: Profiles of a Gilded Age* (1989), Auchincloss sketched the period from the 1880s to World War I. *Woodrow Wilson* (2000) is a brief life of the president.

Auden, W[ystan] H[ugh] (1907–1973), poet, dramatist, critic, and librettist. The third of three sons, Auden was born into an educated middle-class family in Birmingham, England. (His father was a medical officer and professor of public health at the University of Birmingham, his mother a nurse.) He studied at Christ Church, Oxford, originally on a science scholarship and later read English literature. While a student, he formed close ties with many of the artists and writers who dominated the thirties, notably C. Day Lewis and Louis MacNeice. Stephen Spender recalls him from student days as a young man who was a "confident and conscious . . . master of his situation," even imperious at an early age, though Spender was eager to publish Auden's first collection, *Poems* (1928), in a handpress edition of forty-five copies.

After a sojourn in Berlin, where he began his long association with CHRISTOPHER ISHERWOOD, Auden returned to England and began teaching school. At the urging of T. S. Eliot, then a reader at Faber and Faber, the firm published a revised edition of *Poems* (1930), and the collection's positive reception launched Auden's public career. In 1932 Auden published a second book of poems, *The Orators*, and began a long association with Rupert Donne's Group Theatre, which produced his first play, *The Dance of Death* (1933). There followed three plays written in collaboration with Isherwood, *The Dog Beneath the Skin* (1935), *The Ascent of F6* (1936), and *On the Frontier* (1938), in which typically Auden provided verse passages and Isherwood prose, and all of which dealt with the theme of the isolated individual and the growing threat of fascism.

In 1935 Auden began work with the GPO Film Unit and married Erika Mann, the daughter of Thomas Mann, in order to provide her with a passport out of Nazi Germany. While in Germany Auden was influenced by the thinking of Homer Lane, an American psychologist who, like Rousseau, maintained that civilization corrupted humanity's natural nobility. In the late thirties, Auden traveled extensively, going to Iceland with MacNeice, a trip that resulted in their collaborative effort, *Letters from Iceland* (1937), and to Spain during the Civil War with ambivalent intentions. The result was *Spain* (1937), expressive of the despair provoked by the desecration of Roman Catholic churches and the slaughter of priests, and the moment marks the beginning of Auden's migration away from left-wing politics toward a distinctly Anglo-Catholic religiosity that marks the second half of his career.

A trip to China with Isherwood led to their collaboration on *Journey to a War* (1939). Together the two men emigrated to New York in January 1939, a move that Cyril Connolly characterized as "the most important literary event of the decade." Visiting Auden in Greenwich Village, Spender took particular notice of the crucifix on Auden's mantel and found that while before Auden "had fitted the world around him into a Freudian or a Marxist pattern, now he fitted it into a Christian one." Naturalized in 1946, Auden made his living by lecturing and teaching in American colleges, such as Swarthmore, Bryn Mawr, and Bennington, and during his residence in America produced many of his most important collections. *Another Time* (1940) includes several of his most celebrated poems, notably "Lullaby" and "September 1939," an important poem Auden would later try to expunge from the canon. *The Double Man* followed in 1941 and contains revisions of earlier poems that reflect the increasingly Christian tone of his work. In the same year his mother died, and to her, a devout Anglo-Catholic, Auden dedicated *For the Time Being: A Christmas Oratorio* (1946), published with *The Sea and the Mirror*, a series of dramatic monologues inspired by *The Tempest*. Other volumes from the American period include *Nones* (1951) and *The Shield of Achilles* (1955), which won the National Book Award for Poetry and is regarded by many as his best single collection. It contains Auden's personal favorite, "In Praise of Limestone."

In Britain Auden's emigration was seen as defection; nevertheless, he was elected to a five-year tenure as Professor of Poetry at Oxford in 1956. Though he continued to publish for the rest of his life, the great works were mostly in the past. He would publish *Homage to Clio* (1960), containing much light verse, and *About the House* (1967) and *City Without Walls* (1970), works that are personal and informal while continuing to manifest his technical skill at versification, the constant feature of Auden's poetry. Increasingly dependent on friends and the often fickle love of his companion, Chester Kallman, Auden divided his time between the intellectual bower of Oxford—where he was made a Fellow of Christ Church in 1972—and his country house in the small town of Kirchstetten in Lower Austria. He died suddenly in a Viennese hotel in 1973.

Though Auden is clearly the most important poet of his generation, he accomplished much besides poetry. An active anthologist, editor of *The Oxford Book of Light Verse* (orig. pub. 1938) and *The Living Thoughts of Kierkegaard* (1952), he also worked as a librettist and practical critic. Benjamin Britten, who had set to music Auden's *On this Island* and several love poems which Auden addressed to him in 1937, collaborated with the poet on the opera *Paul Bunyan* while both were in New York in 1941. Though the opera was a failure (Britten suppressed it for many years), Stravinsky's invitation to Auden to do a libretto based on Hogarth's *The Rake's Progress* produced a far happier result (1947). He made a fresh English translation of Mozart's *The Magic Flute* in 1956. Auden's intelligent and lucid occasional criticism is collected in *The Enchafèd Flood* (1950), *The Dyer's Hand* (1962), *Secondary Worlds* (1968), and *Forewords and Afterwords* (1973).

Edward Mendelson's *Collected Poems* (1976) is the comprehensive edition of the poetry and represents the poems in the final revisions that Auden preferred. Among many studies are Monroe K. Spears, *The Poetry of W. H. Auden* (1963); Samuel Hynes, *The Auden Generation* (1977); Humphrey Carpenter, *W. H. Auden: A Biography* (1981); Edward Mendelson, *Early Auden* (1981) and *Later Auden* (1999); and John Fuller, *W. H. Auden: A Commentary* (1998).

MARK A. R. FACKNITZ/GP

Audubon, John James (1785–1851),   naturalist, artist, author. Born in Les Cayes, Santo Domingo (now Haiti), the son of a French naval officer and a Creole woman, Audubon was educated in France. At eighteen he came to the family estate near Philadelphia, where he began his bird-banding experiments and met and married Lucy Bakewell (in 1808), his supportive, self-sacrificing wife. She bore two sons, raised them, and ran a private school for a while in Louisiana to help with the family finances. From 1808 to 1820, home was mostly in Kentucky; in the 1820s in Louisiana, where Audubon taught briefly in his wife's school. During these years, he worked at a variety of trades, but put his energy into traveling on the American frontier, observing, painting, and writing, as he compiled the materials for his great work. His two sons assisted; one of them, John Woodhouse Audubon, journeyed in 1849–50 to California, a trip described in his *Western Journal* (1906). After his initial success, Audubon lived in his later years in Manhattan.

A visit to England in 1826 found Audubon a publisher for THE BIRDS OF NORTH AMERICA (1827–38), published first as an elephant folio in parts and later in octavo form (1840–44). The accompanying text, written in collaboration with the Scottish naturalist William MacGillivray, was separately published as *Ornithological Biography* (1831–39). *The Viviparous Quadrupeds of North America* (plates, 1842–45; text, 1846–54) followed; this work was done in collaboration with John Bachman and with the help of his sons.

Although others of his time were better scientists, Audubon displayed his genius in the scope of his work, his splendid paintings, and his lively narrative accounts of the American frontier. Editions of his journals and other writings include *Delineations of American Scenery and Character*, ed. Francis Hobart Herrick (1926) and *Journal of John James Audubon, Made During a Trip to New Orleans in 1820–21* (1929) and *Letters* (1930), both edited by Howard Corning.

Augie March, The Adventures of,   a novel by SAUL BELLOW (1953). This modern picaresque novel about a youth who grows up in Chicago during the depression catapulted its author into national recognition. The book was a best seller and received the National Book Award. Because Augie will not accept any defining role in life, he finds himself being swept along in a current of alternately hilarious and tragic adventures; he works in a saddle shop, steals, attempts to smuggle immigrants into the United States from Canada, becomes a union organizer, tries to train a bald eagle to hunt iguanas in Mexico, and makes an unfortunate marriage with an actress. Unlike his brother Simon, who marries the daughter of a wealthy Chicago coal dealer in order to rise from his lower-class Jewish slum environment, Augie refuses every opportunity for a settled existence that comes his way. He suffers some hard knocks, but as he says, there is an "*animal ridens* in me, the laughing creature, forever rising up." His ability to laugh at himself as he tells his story makes Augie a memorable hero. In sharp contrast to the economy of style popular in American writing after Hemingway, Augie's prose is endlessly rich, varied, and complex. Through him the author speaks at once in the pithy language of the streets and the inversions of a University of Chicago intellectual.

Aunt Polly.   A character in MARK TWAIN'S TOM SAWYER and its sequels. She is Tom's aunt and guardian, and was drawn from Twain's mother.

Auslander, Joseph (1897–1965),   poet, literary historian. Popular without displaying undue sentimentality, Auslander employed conventional forms with varied themes and appeals. Among his collections are *Sunrise Trumpets* (1924), *Cyclops' Eye* (1926), *Letters to Women* (1930), *Riders at the Gate* (1938), and *The Unconquerables* (1943). In collaboration with Frank Ernest Hill, Auslander prepared a history of poetry for young people, *The Winged Horse* (1927), followed by *The Winged Horse Anthology* (1928). He published translations of La Fontaine (1930) and Petrarch (1931). Auslander and his wife, AUDREY WURDEMANN, collaborated on *My Uncle Jan* (1948), reminiscences in the form of a novel, and *Islanders* (1951).

Auster, Paul (1947–   ),   novelist, poet, memoirist. Born in Newark, New Jersey, and raised in South Orange and Maplewood, Auster majored in English at Columbia University (B.A. 1969, M.A. 1970). Best known for his New York Trilogy of novels (*City of Glass*, 1985; *Ghosts*, 1986; and *The Locked Room*, 1987), postmodern dark comedy thrillers involving loneliness, obsession, and literature, he has also been a prolific poet, translator, editor, and playwright, whose works reflect his interest in Beckett and other avant-garde and Euopean writers. Other novels are *In the Country of Last Things* (1987), focused on dystopian horrors in the twentieth century; *Moon Palace* (1989), with thematic links between the life of its protagonist and significant events in American history; *The Music of Chance* (1990), about men building a wall; and *Timbuktu* (1999). *Disappearances*, selected poems, appeared in 1988. *The Art of Hunger: Essays, Prefaces, Interviews* (1992) includes autobiographical essays and meditations. *Hand to Mouth: A Chronicle of Early Failure* (1997) recounts an adventuresome youth.

Austin, Jane Goodwin (1831–1894),   writer of stories for girls. Austin wrote mainly of life in her native New England, especially of the Pilgrim past. The best-known of these tales were *Standish of Standish* (1889) and *Betty Alden* (1891).

Austin, Mary [Hunter] (1868–1934),   poet, critic, novelist, playwright. Born in Carlinville, Illinois, Mary Hunter, one of six children of George Hunter, talked to God under a walnut tree when she was five years old and never thereafter relinquished the conviction that she had special intuitive powers. In 1888 the Hunters moved to California, first as homesteaders, later as storekeepers; Mary learned much of western lore and became attached to Spanish California. In 1891 she married Stafford W. Austin, a homesteader in the Panamint district. Failing as winegrowers, the Austins moved to San Francisco, where Mary Austin sold her first story to the OVERLAND MONTHLY. They moved later to various locations in the Owens River valley, where she had her first close acquaintance with Indian life and the ways of the desert.

Mary Austin's life during this period was lonely and frustrated; her marriage was not a success and her only child, a daughter, suffered from mental illness. In 1905 she and her husband separated permanently. She went to live in Carmel and there met JACK LONDON, GEORGE STERLING, and other literary figures of the West Coast. Her novel *Outland* (1910) is probably an account of Sterling's unhappy marriage. A few years later, believing herself ill with cancer, she journeyed to Italy, where she entered into mystical exercises. When her health improved, she stayed in Paris and London. Her Italian experiences confirmed her mystical mode of thought. She returned to New York in 1910 to assist in the production of THE ARROW MAKER, her most popular play.

From 1910 to 1924, Austin's life shifted between New York and Carmel; she lectured widely and wrote many books and essays. She was active in the feminist movement, alert to social and political affairs, interested in all signs of artistic awakening in the United States. She liked the role of *chisera* (Indian prophetess), and her pronouncements were frequently based on what she chose to call her insight into aboriginal life. In 1924 she took up residence in Santa Fe, New Mexico, where her attention was concentrated more and more on regionalism and the folk arts. She plunged into a campaign for the preservation of Indian and Spanish handicrafts, became an amateur folklorist, and represented New Mexico at the Boulder Dam Conference in 1927, fighting for the regional autonomy of the mountain and desert states. Her adobe house in Santa Fe, named Casa Querida (beloved house), became a stopping-off place for literary friends and a center of local cultural activities. As self-appointed champion of the Indians and Spanish-Americans she was supreme.

Austin produced thirty-two books and more than two hundred essays, as well as poems, reviews, introductions, etc. Some of her themes are virtually obsessive. The difficulties of marriage, considered from a feminist point of view, run through much of her work: *Santa Lucia, A Common Story* (1908), a novel; *Lost Borders* (1909), a collection of desert stories; *The Arrow Maker* (1911); *Love and the Soul Maker* (1914), a treatise; and *No. 26 Jayne Street* (1920), a novel. In some of her work social problems become dominant, as in *The Ford* (1917), a novel about the struggle of California farmers against inevitable urban growth. Her mystical experiences afforded the background for other works: *Christ in Italy* (1912); *The Man Jesus* (1915; reissued as *A Small Town Man*, 1925); *Everyman's Genius* (1925); *Experiences Facing Death* (1931); and *Can Prayer Be Answered?* (1934). Her historical romance *Isidro* (1905) is set in Spanish California. But her most enduring work was that of an amateur naturalist. Her nature writing is strongly evocative, done in the Transcendental manner and manifesting a sometimes pantheistic ecstasy. Indeed, Austin boasted that she had done for the desert what Thoreau had done for New England—and with a much more difficult subject. She wrote THE LAND OF LITTLE RAIN (1903), *The Flock* (1906), *California: The Land of the Sun* (1914), and *The Land of Journey's Ending* (1924). Her novel *Starry Adventure* (1931) is notable for the way in which the New Mexican landscape is made to serve as, so to speak, the chief character of the story.

The American Rhythm (1923) is a treatise on poetry containing her own reexpressions of Indian verse. It is a strong plea for freedom of form and language as the proper techniques for an indigenous American lyricism. She noted that the Indians, working in a wholly American culture, had discovered free verse as their natural mode. In *One-Smoke Stories* (1934) she attempted to extend her folk theories into the practice of fiction. Her autobiography, *Earth Horizon* (1932), throws much light on her work and reveals her as in some respects a rather pathetic and frustrated woman who nevertheless sought for herself a genuinely independent philosophy in the spirit of her illustrious New England predecessors. A critical biography is Esther Lanigan Stineman's *Mary Austin: Song of a Maverick* (1989).

DUDLEY WYNN/GP

Austin, William (1778–1841),   lawyer, legislator, short-story writer. Austin was identified with Boston and its environs throughout his life, aside from a period spent in London studying law. This residence abroad led to Austin's *Letters from London* (1804), which American lawyers enjoyed for its bright pictures of London legal lights and statesmen. It had been preceded by *Strictures on Harvard University* (1798), in which Austin applied the ideas and standards of Rousseau to his *alma mater*. Austin's best-known story is PETER RUGG, THE MISSING MAN.

Authors' League of America.   Founded in 1911 to safeguard the rights of authors. It includes the Authors' Guild and represents authors and playwrights. A similar group, the Writers' Guild of America, represents motion picture, broadcast, cable, and news writers.

Autobiography of Alice B. Toklas, The (1933), by GERTRUDE STEIN. The book is really Stein's autobiography, presented as though written by her secretary, Alice Toklas. The book provoked a rejoinder from various Parisian artists and writers, *Testimony Against Gertrude Stein* (1935). In it Georges Braque wrote: "For one who poses as an authority on the epoch it is safe to say she never went beyond the stage of the tourist." For the average reader, however, Stein's book holds much fascination in its views of Parisian life and personalities, and the whole is offered in a genuinely witty style.

Autobiography of an Ex-Colored Man, The, novel by JAMES WELDON JOHNSON.

Autobiography of Benjamin Franklin, The, Franklin's account of his life, written for his son William. At sixty-five, Franklin described his first twenty-four years for his son, then colonial governor of New Jersey. During the Revolutionary War, the manuscript was put aside (and Franklin's relations with his son broken off as William chose the British side in the conflict). Franklin later more than doubled the length (writing in 1783, 1784, 1788), but still took the story only to 1757–1759, ending before the period of his greatest public service. Still, the book remains the first undisputed classic of American literature and one of the most interesting autobiographies in English.

Various unauthorized and inaccurate editions appeared in the 18th and 19th centuries, beginning with *Mémoires de la Vie Privée de Benjamin Franklin* (1791). The first American edition appeared in 1818, but more accurate editions date from 1868, after the discovery of Franklin's manuscript in France. A modern scholarly edition is *The Autobiography of Benjamin Franklin*, ed. L. W. Labaree et al. (1964).

Autobiography of Malcolm X, story of MALCOLM X ghostwritten by ALEX HALEY.

Autocrat of the Breakfast Table, The (*Atlantic Monthly*, beginning November 1857; in book form, 1858), a prose work by OLIVER WENDELL HOLMES. A great conversationalist, Holmes found in this series of dialogues a congenial and inspiring medium. They are conducted at a boardinghouse breakfast table, and a variety of characters participate; the autocrat does not always get the best of it. Interspersed are a number of Holmes's most lasting poems among them THE DEACON'S MASTERPIECE and THE CHAMBERED NAUTILUS. The book has kept its freshness, despite its now obscure contemporary allusions. The brilliant and witty talk ranges over many topics, including science, theology, and the nature of American society. Striking, too, are many of Holmes's epigrams: "Put not your trust in money, but put your money in trust." "Sin has many tools, but a lie is the handle which fits them all." Holmes continued the series in *The Professor at the Breakfast Table* (1859), *The Poet at the Breakfast Table* (1872), and *Over the Tea Cups* (1890). See BREAKFAST TABLE SERIES.

Avison, Margaret (1918–), poet. Born in Galt, Ontario, Avison was educated at the University of Toronto, Indiana University, and the University of Chicago. She has since been employed as a librarian, university teacher, and social worker in Ontario. While on a Guggenheim Fellowship, she wrote some of the poems later collected in *Winter Sun* (1960), which won the Governor General's Award for poetry in Canada. This and *The Dumbfounding* (1966) were collected as *Winter Sun/The Dumbfounding: Poems 1940–1966* (1982). More recent poems are in *Sunblue* (1978). Her work is generally intricate and imagistic, grounded in a search within the natural world for spiritual enlightenment. A *Selected Poems* appeared in 1991.

Avon's Harvest (1921), a narrative in verse by EDWIN ARLINGTON ROBINSON. Avon is a New York lawyer, a fear-haunted man, who encounters again and again the same enemy. He learns of the man's death, but is not relieved of his psychosis, and dies of what the doctor calls an "aneurism" but admits that it may have been "the devil." In writing this poem Robinson turned from medieval to modern themes. He was interested less in the story than in the analysis of subtle states of mind.

Awake and Sing! (1935), a play by CLIFFORD ODETS. Regarded as Odets' best play, *Awake and Sing!* tells of a poverty-stricken Jewish family in the Bronx—mingled idealists and practical persons. Among the latter is the mother, who—with the best intentions—browbeats her husband, forces her daughter to marry a man she doesn't love, and opposes her son's romance with a poor orphan. The results are disastrous, but they lead the idealistic son to devote his life to the betterment of humanity. The action is often melodramatic, but the dialogue is richly human and the characters are viewed with compassionate humor.

Awakening, The (1899), novel by KATE CHOPIN. Edna Pontellier, born and raised in protestant Kentucky, has married into a French-Creole family in New Orleans. Confused by her awakening sexuality and by the expectations of an alien culture, she flirts with a young Creole, Robert Lebrun, has an affair with another, Alcée Arobin, and moves out of her husband's house to begin an independent life. In the end, she swims into the ocean to drown. The novel's brief, powerful, and heavily symbolic scenes were too frank for most reviewers in her time. Chopin, disappointed with its reception, wrote and published little thereafter. Today, many critics consider it a classic.

Awakening, The Great. See GREAT AWAKENING.

Awkward Age, The (1899), a novel by HENRY JAMES. James tells, with endless subtlety, the story of a girl's emergence out of "the awkward age" into modernity and understanding. Nanda and her mother are in love with the same man; the mother wants her to marry Mitchett, but the Duchess, her friend, wants Mitchett to marry her niece, Aggie. The result is a social battle complicated by the appearance of the wealthy Mr. Longdon, who sees in Nanda a close resemblance to her grandmother, with whom he had once been in love. However, Nanda is at last freed from subservience to social conventions she does not like.

Axelrod, George (1922–), playwright, novelist, screenwriter, director. Born in New York City, Axelrod wrote for radio, television, and the movies, winning his greatest success with two Broadway comedies: *The Seven Year Itch* (1952), which ran for three years, and *Will Success Spoil Rock Hunter?* (1955). Both were made into movies.

Axel's Castle (1931),   a volume of critical essays by EDMUND WILSON. These deal largely with symbolism as it appears in the works of various French, Irish, and American writers. The title refers to a poetic drama, *Axel* (1890, English translation, 1925), by Villiers de l'Isle Adam. Other authors of whom Wilson writes are Yeats, Valéry, T. S. Eliot, Gertrude Stein, Rimbaud, Joyce, and Proust.

Ax-Helve, The,   blank verse narrative by ROBERT FROST. First published in *The Atlantic Monthly* (September 1917) and collected in *New Hampshire* (1923), the poem depicts the cultural differences between the Yankee narrator and his French-Canadian neighbor, a woodsman who loves his work. As he shows the narrator "the lines of a good helve," Baptiste explains that they are "native to the grain." Just so, Baptiste keeps his children from school to help them achieve their natural potential. In 1916, Frost read the poem at the Phi Beta Kappa exercises at Harvard.

Azevedo, Aluízio de (1857–1913),   Brazilian novelist. In Azevedo's second novel, *O Mulato* (1881), he introduced NATURALISM to Brazil with a melodramatic tale of illegitimacy and miscegenation in which a young man discovers the secret of his birth. Other novels include *Casa de Pensao* (1884), about a Rio de Janeiro boarding house; *O Homen* (1887), on sexual frustration; and *O Cortiço* (1890, tr. *A Brazilian Tenement*, 1928), on a slum landlord in Rio de Janeiro. Translated as *The Slum*, most recently in 2000, this is generally considered his masterpiece. *Obras Completas* was published in 14 volumes (1939–41).

Aztec Indians.   These inhabitants of Mexico at the time of the conquest by CORTEZ (1519–21) had reached an extraordinarily high stage of civilization. Their society embodied advanced artistic and commercial practices, together with an excellent system of laws and courts. Their religion, however, remained barbaric though complex. The Spaniards suppressed the Aztecs brutally, though Aztec stock remains strong in Mexico to the present day. The Aztecs are believed to have come from the north at the end of the 12th century, and their language is related to that of tribes in Arizona and other parts of the United States. William Hickling Prescott's *History of the Conquest of Mexico* (1843), a masterpiece of historical writing, tells of the arrival of the Spaniards, the fall of the Aztec capital Tenochtitlan (now Mexico City), and the capture of the emperor MONTEZUMA. A major Spanish source for Prescott was Bernal Diaz del Castillo, whose work has been translated as *The Discovery and Conquest of Mexico* (1928). Among many other writings inspired by the Aztecs is WILLIAM CARLOS WILLIAMS's fine chapter on Tenochtitlan in *In The American Grain* (1925).

Azuela, Mariano (1873–1952),   Mexican novelist. Author of forty-one novels, Mariano began writing while still a medical student at Guadalajara and he continued to combine the careers of doctor and writer. In *Mala yerba* (1909, tr. *Marcela*, 1932), he attacked the Mexican landowners. In 1915 he joined Villa's revolution as a surgeon, and from that experience came one of his finest novels, LOS DE ABAJO (1915, tr. *The Underdogs*, 1929). *Los caciques* (1917, tr. *The Bosses*, 1956) treats economic oppression before the revolution; *Las moscas* (1918, tr. *The Flies*, 1956) tells of the flight of members of the ruling class as the revolutionaries enter Mexico City. Later works, less directly political, include *La malhora* (1923); *La luciérnaga* (1932, tr. *The Firefly*, 1963); and *Las tribulaciones de una familia decente* (1938, tr. *The Trials of a Respectable Family*, 1963).

B

Babbitt (1922), satirical novel by SINCLAIR LEWIS. In Zenith, the Zip City, George Babbitt—realtor, booster, joiner, self-styled typical American—holds forth. Middle-aged and hopelessly middle-class, he ultimately realizes that being a prosperous family man and all-around good fellow is not enough. He tries to revolt, seeks a woman who will understand him, but finds he cannot escape. When his son elopes, however, he has the courage to turn against the conventional clichés of his own life, and tells his son: "I've never done a single thing I've wanted to. . . . Don't be scared of the family. No, nor all of Zenith. Nor of yourself, the way I've been."

The novel, perhaps Lewis's best, made a tremendous sensation when it appeared. Although businessmen and boosters' clubs denounced it bitterly, Babbitt undoubtedly helped turn some of the latters' meetings away from silly antics and toward something more adult. Lewis' observation of details in the American social landscape is superb, his dialogue and descriptions magnificently satiric. The name of the book identified an American type and gave a new word to the language.

Babbitt, Irving (1865–1933), teacher, critic, essayist. Babbitt, born in Ohio and educated at Harvard and later in Paris, became a professor of Romance languages, first at Williams in 1893, then at Harvard, from 1894 to his death. His first book, *Literature and the American College*, appeared in 1908. It was followed by *The New Laokoön* (1910), *Masters of Modern French Criticism* (1912), ROUSSEAU AND ROMANTICISM (1919), *Democracy and Leadership* (1924), and *On Being Creative* (1932). *Spanish Character* (1940) appeared posthumously.

Along with PAUL ELMER MORE, NORMAN FOERSTER, and T. S. ELIOT, Babbitt expounded the New Humanism. See HUMANISM.

Bacheller, Irving [Addison] (1859–1950), newspaperman, novelist. Bacheller, born in Pierpont, New York, became a newspaperman in his early twenties, eventually joining the staff of *The New York World*. Soon he began writing fiction. His first two novels were *The Master of Silence* (1890) and *The Still House of O'Darrow* (1894). EBEN HOLDEN (1900) was a great success, especially in its depiction of the northern New York types with whom Bacheller was familiar, and more than a million copies were sold. Other novels included D'RI AND I (1901), *Keeping Up with Lizzie* (1911), *A Man for the Ages* (1919), and *A Candle in the Wilderness* (1930). He wrote auto-

biographical reminiscences in *Coming Up the Road* (1928) and *From Stores of Memory* (1938).

Back Bay. A once-genteel section of Boston, on the south bank of the Charles River, created on a landfill that reclaimed an earlier bay near Beacon Hill. Its name became a symbol for the social élite of Boston and the scene of many novels laid in that city, including William Dean Howells' THE RISE OF SILAS LAPHAM (1885).

Backus, Isaac (1724–1806), preacher, historian, author of *History of New England, with Particular Reference to the Denomination of Christians Called Baptists* (3 v. 1777–96).

Backward Glance o'er Travel'd Roads, A (1888), a prose piece by WALT WHITMAN. The preface and perhaps the most significant piece in NOVEMBER BOUGHS, a miscellaneous collection of prose and poetry, it was included in LEAVES OF GRASS (1889), of which it is both an explanation and a defense. He remarks, "I abandon'd the conventional themes, none of which appear in it," although he adds that "I have put on record elsewhere my reverence and eulogy for those never-to-be-excell'd poetic bequests" from the Old World.

Backwoodsman, The (1818), an idyllic tale in verse by JAMES KIRKE PAULDING. It tells of the pioneer West and its freedom from convention.

Bacon, Delia [Salter] (1811–1859), critic, novelist, dramatist. Bacon, born in Ohio, was a supporter of the so-called Baconian theory. At first a teacher, she became a lecturer on literature and history and wrote *Tales of the Puritans* (1831) and a play. In 1852, led to the notion perhaps by the similarity of names, she became "the first Baconian." She was convinced that a group of Elizabethans, all the great men of that age, had gathered around Sir Walter Raleigh to compose the plays that went under Shakespeare's name. Principal among them was Sir Francis Bacon, but Edmund Spenser helped. Moreover, the plays were more than plays, she argued. Within them a system of ciphers concealed a great system of thought, wisdom the world was waiting for. She also contended that opening Shakespeare's grave would reveal the entire grim story.

Bacon went to England, hovered around the tomb, but lost courage. Emerson for a while encouraged her; Carlyle listened to her but demanded proofs; and Hawthorne, then consul at Liverpool, befriended her and even wrote an introduction for her book, *The Philosophy of the Plays of Shakespeare Unfolded* (1857). Hawthorne describes the insanity that preceded Bacon's death in *Our Old Home* (1863). Among Bacon's fanatical followers was IGNATIUS DONNELLY, who wrote *The Great Cryptogram* (1888) and *The Cypher in the Plays and on the Tombstone* (1899).

Bacon, Frank (1864–1922),   actor, playwright. One of the best-loved American actors, his greatest role was the amusing inveterate liar Lightnin' Bill Jones of LIGHTNIN', written in collaboration with WINCHELL SMITH. It began its run on August 26, 1918, and continued for 1,291 performances.

Bacon, Josephine Dodge [Daskam] (1876–1961), novelist. Josephine Daskam, as she was then known, made her first hit with *Smith College Stories* (1900), published two years after her graduation from Smith. Best known of her amusing satires on Americans, especially young Americans, are *The Madness of Philip* (1902), *Memoirs of a Baby* (1904), *Square Peggy* (1919), *Luck of Lowry* (1934), and *The Root and the Flower* (1939).

Bacon, Leonard (1887–1954),   teacher, poet, critic. Bacon (Delia Bacon was his great-aunt) began teaching English at the University of California in 1910 but left in 1923 to devote full time to writing. He made his reputation with many volumes of verse, becoming known as one of the most intellectual, satiric, adroit, and melodious poets of the day. He won the Pulitzer Prize for poetry with his *Sunderland Capture* (1940). Among his other volumes of verse are *Ulug Beg* (1923), *Ph.D's* (1925), *Animula Vagula* (1926), *The Legend of Quincibald* (1928), *The Furioso* (1932), *The Goose on the Capital* (1936), *Rhyme and Punishment* (1936), and *Day of Fire* (1944). *Semi-Centennial* (1939) is his autobiography.

Bacon, Nathaniel (1647–1676),   leader of Bacon's Rebellion, the first popular revolt in America. Born in England, educated at Cambridge, and fashionably married, Bacon emigrated to Virginia in 1673 and built himself a mansion on the James River. At that time Sir William Berkeley (1606–1677) was governor of the colony. He made Bacon a member of his council, but Bacon was disgusted by conditions in the colony, remarking, "The poverty of the country is such that all the power and sway is got into the hands of the rich, who by extortious advantages, having the common people in their debt, have always curbed and oppressed them in all manner of ways." When Berkeley, in addition to his other negligences, also refused to help the settlers in their conflicts with the Indians, Bacon organized a troop of frontiersmen. Berkeley ordered him arrested as a rebel, whereupon Bacon marched his followers on Jamestown, burned the town (1676), and required citizens to take an oath of allegiance to himself. He died shortly after, whereupon Berkeley took terrible vengeance on his foes, hanging many of them. It is said that King Charles II exclaimed: "That old fool has put to death more people in that naked country than I did here for the murder of my father." He recalled him to London, and while the English for a time paid more attention to the complaints of the colonists, power remained in the hands of the aristocracy.

An account of the rebellion was put together in a manuscript that was found after the American Revolution among the papers of Captain Nathaniel Burwell of Virginia. It is believed that either JOHN COTTON or his wife Ann "of Acquia Creek," contemporaries of Bacon, was the author of the manuscript, which also includes two poems, "Bacon's Epitaph, Made by His Man" and "Upon the Death of G. B." [General Bacon].

Many novelists have been fascinated by the strange figure of Bacon, who appears in W. A. Carruther, *The Cavaliers of Virginia* (1835); George Tucker, *Hansford* (1857); Maude Wilder Goodwin, *White Aprons* (1896); Clifford Sublette, *Bright Face of Danger* (1926); Nathan Schachner, *The King's Passenger* (1942); P. L. Scruggs, *Man Cannot Tell* (1942); Roy Flanagan, *The Forest Cavalier* (1952); and Charles B. Judah, *Christopher Humble* (1956). Bacon also appears in Aphra Behn's play *The Widow Ranter* (produced in 1690) and in Ebenezer Cooke's burlesque poem *The History of Colonel Nathaniel Bacon's Rebellion* (in *The Maryland Muse*, 1731).

Bacon, Peggy [Mrs. Alexander Brook] (1895–1987), caricaturist, illustrator, writer. Bacon, born in Connecticut, wrote and illustrated many children's books, including *The Lion-Hearted Kitten* (1927) and *Mercy and the Mouse* (1928). Among her collections of caricatures are *Off with Their Heads* (1934), *Cat-Calls* (1935), and *Starting from Scratch* (1945). *The Inward Eye* (1952) is a mystery novel. In 1957 she published *The Good American Witch*.

Bacon's Rebellion.   See NATHANIEL BACON.

Bad Boy, The Story of a.   See STORY OF A BAD BOY, THE.

Bagby, George William (1828–1883),   Southern humorist. A Virginia journalist, editor of the *Southern Literary Messenger* (1860–64), Bagby wrote newspaper sketches using the character Mozis Addums that exploited the fad of the time for humor from misspellings, dialect, and local color. (See works by ARTEMUS WARD, JOSH BILLINGS, and others.) A collection, edited by Thomas Nelson Page, is *The Old Virginia Gentleman and Other Sketches* (1910).

Bagdad-on-the-Subway,   O. HENRY's name for Manhattan.

Bailey, Francis (c. 1735–1815),   publisher, almanac maker. Bailey founded *The United States Magazine* in 1779, *The Freeman's Journal, or, North American Intelligencer* in 1781. Appealing to the large German-speaking population in his native state of Pennsylvania, he issued a *Nord Americanische Kalender* (1779) at Lancaster. In this appears for the first time in print, so far as is known, a designation of Washington as Father of his Country—in a caption, "Des Landes Vater," under his portrait. The first appearance in English of the phrase seems to have occurred in an editorial in *The Pennsylvania Packet*, July 9, 1789; the same periodical had used "the Father of His People" on April 21, 1789. Juvenal had employed the phrase, *pater patriae*, to designate Cicero, and it has been given to others in the course of European history. Bailey was official printer to the Continental Congress.

Bailey, James M[ontgomery] (1841–1894),   newspaperman, humorist. Bailey, born in Albany, New York, bought the Danbury (Connecticut) *Times* in 1878 and became known as the Danbury News Man for his humorous column of domestic and public sketches, sometimes regarded as the first true newspaper column. His books were also popular: *Life in Danbury* (1870), *They All Do It* (1877), *England from a Back Window* (1878), *Mr. Phillips' Goneness* (1879), and *The Danbury Boom* (1880).

Bailey, [Irene] Temple (early 1870s–1953), novelist. Bailey, born in Virginia, found wide audiences for her work, which included *Contrary Mary* (1915), *The Tin Soldier* (1919), *The Trumpeter Swan* (1920), *The Gay Cockade* (1921), *Peacock Feathers* (1924), *Silver Slippers* (1928), *Enchanted Ground* (1933), *Fair as the Moon* (1935), *The Blue Cloak* (1941), and *Red Fruit* (1945). She began her literary career with *Judy* (1907), a book for girls, and continued to write for girls and women. In 1953 it was estimated that three million copies of her books had been sold.

Bailyn, Bernard (1922–), historian, editor. Bailyn is best known for his analysis of the personalities and events of Colonial and Revolutionary America. He was born in Hartford, Connecticut, and educated at Williams College (A.B., 1945) and Harvard University (M.A., 1947 and Ph.D., 1953), where he has taught since. He won the Pulitzer Prize for *Ideological Origins of the American Revolution* (1967) and *Voyagers to the West: A Passage in the Peopling of America on the Eve of the Revolution* (1986). Other books include *The Ordeal of Thomas Hutchison* (1974), *Faces of Revolution: Personalities and Themes in the Struggle for American Independence* (1990), and *The Debate on the Constitution: Federalist and Anti-Federalist Speeches, Articles and Letters* (ed., 2 vols. 1993).

SUZANNE PERKINS-HART

Baines, Scattergood. See CLARENCE BUDINGTON KELLAND.

Baker, George Pierce (1866–1935), teacher, editor, author. Baker, born in Providence, Rhode Island, was one of the most successful and creative of modern teachers. He was educated at Harvard and went on to teach English and rhetoric there. In 1895 he published a textbook called *The Principles of Argumentation* and in 1907 *The Development of Shakespeare as a Dramatist.*

But Baker's interest turned more and more to the living theater, and in 1905 he opened his celebrated 47 Workshop, in which aspiring students were taught the art of playwriting and given the opportunity of seeing their plays performed, at first by their fellow students in the theater at Agassiz House. Baker's successful alumni included Eugene O'Neill, George Abbott, Philip Barry, S. N. Behrman, Sidney Howard, Robert Edmond Jones, John Dos Passos, John Mason Brown, John V. A. Weaver, Rachel Field, and Thomas Wolfe, the last of whom portrayed Baker as Professor Hatcher in *Of Time and the River* (1935). In 1925 Baker moved to Yale, where every facility was provided for him, including a theater donated by Edward S. Harkness. The Workshop here developed into the Yale graduate school of drama, and Baker continued to give courses in playwriting, stage designing, costuming, lighting,

and dramatic criticism. He edited *Plays of the 47 Workshop, I–IV* (1918–25) and *Yale One-Act Plays* (1930).

Baker, Ray Stannard ["David Grayson"] (1870–1946), essayist, biographer, editor. Born in Michigan, Baker began writing as a reporter on the Chicago *Record* (1892–97). His short stories in the *Century Magazine* and *Youth's Companion* brought him an offer from *McClure's Magazine* and the McClure Syndicate in New York; he remained with this group from 1897 to 1905, contributing essays on railways, mine strikes, and lynching that were seen as part of the MUCKRAKING LITERATURE of the time.

From 1906 to 1915 he edited the *American Magazine*, beginning there under the name David Grayson the series of familiar essays collected in book form as ADVENTURES IN CONTENTMENT (1907), *Adventures in Friendship* (1910), *Adventures in Understanding* (1925), *Under My Elm* (1942), and other titles. In 1910 Baker met WOODROW WILSON and thereafter devoted much energy to Wilson's ideals, so much so that Wilson named him press director at Paris in 1919. Baker and W. E. Dodd edited *The Public Papers of Woodrow Wilson* (6 v. 1925–26), then wrote an authorized biography, *Woodrow Wilson—Life and Letters* (8 v. 1927–39), which received the 1940 Pulitzer Prize for biography. Baker closed his literary career with *Native American* (1941), dealing with his youth in a frontier region, and *American Chronicle* (1945), continuing the story into the 1920s.

Baker's Blue-Jay Yarn. One of Mark Twain's best tall tales, about a blue jay that tries to fill up a house with acorns, told in A TRAMP ABROAD (1880).

Baldwin, Faith [Cuthrell] (1893–1978), novelist. Born in New Rochelle, New York, Baldwin published her first novel, *Mavis of Green Hill*, in 1921 and followed with a stream of popular romances for women that sold, in total, well over ten million copies. Her titles include *Those Difficult Years* (1925), *Three Women* (1926), *Office Wife* (1930), *White Collar Girl* (1933), *Men Are Such Fools!* (1936), *American Family* (1935), *Station Wagon* (1939), *Medical Center* (1940), *Temporary Address: Reno* (1941), *He Married a Doctor* (1943), *Woman on Her Way* (1946), *Many Windows* (1958), *Blaze of Sunlight* (1959), and *The Lonely Man* 1964). *Widow's Walk* (1954) collects poems. *Testament of Trust* (1960) is an autobiography.

Baldwin, James (1924–1987), essayist, novelist, short-story writer, playwright, poet, social activist. Baldwin was born in Harlem, where he was raised by his mother, Berdis, and his stepfather, David, a storefront preacher. Baldwin remembered his early childhood as "the usual bleak fantasy," marked by poverty and his stepfather's hostility. He was a withdrawn child who internalized his pain and turned for relief to books and a natural talent for writing. In grade school and DeWitt Clinton High School, from which he was graduated in 1942, several exceptional teachers encouraged him in his reading and in his writing.

At age fourteen, suddenly overwhelmed by what he perceived as his sexual depravity, he turned to the church for help and was saved through Mother Horn, a preacher at Mount Calvary of the Pentecostal Faith Church. Soon he became a young minister himself, gaining a certain fame as a preaching prodigy in various Harlem churches.

In 1942, Baldwin left home and the church for Greenwich Village, thus resolving an inner struggle between his religion and his writing. During the Village years, he kept himself alive with odd jobs, developed a circle of friends who shared his concerns about racism, attempted to confront his sexual ambiguity, and wrote when he could.

Some success came in 1947 and 1948. He sold his first short story, "Previous Condition," about the difficulties of a young black man attempting to live in the white world of Greenwich Village, and several New York journals solicited book reviews and even a few essays. A number of these articles and others written during the next few years were collected in NOTES OF A NATIVE SON (1955), a work through which Baldwin emerged as an articulate African-American spokesman. The voice that speaks in *Notes* and in the works that would follow is simultaneously prophetic, objective, and sharply ironic, reflecting at once the Old Testament rhetoric learned in the storefront pulpit, the skepticism and the anger that were the legacy of a deprived childhood and denied birthright, and extensive reading in such writers as Charles Dickens and Henry James. Most of all, in *Notes* Baldwin establishes the theme that was to color his work for the next thirty-two years: The "Negro Problem," was, in fact, a "white problem"—"I'm only black if you think you're white."

Baldwin had left America for Paris in 1948. There, before returning home briefly for the first time in 1952, he completed his first novel, GO TELL IT ON THE MOUNTAIN (1953), an autobiographical story of a Harlem child's relationship with his father against the background of his being saved in the pentecostal church.

In the early Paris years Baldwin began to openly accept his homosexuality, a fact that, with his experience in the atmosphere of bohemian expatriate Paris, would make possible his second novel, *Giovanni's Room* (1956). It was Baldwin's attempt to come to grips with his own sexuality in fictional form. It is also the novel in which he most articulately expresses his belief that to deny love and the demands of love for social reasons is to do irreparable damage to one's soul. Baldwin, as he often said, left the pulpit to "preach the gospel." In the tragedy of Giovanni and his sometime lover, David, we experience the power of Baldwin's gospel.

In 1953, Baldwin began work on a play, which he completed in New York in 1954 with the help of a Guggenheim Fellowship. *The Amen Corner*, produced at Howard University in 1955 and on Broadway in 1965, is concerned with a family torn between the requirements of religion and those of art and love. The main character, Sister Margaret, is based on the instrument of Baldwin's childhood salvation, Mother Horn.

Baldwin returned to Paris in 1955 and completed *Giovanni's Room*. By 1957 the two novels and *Notes of a Native Son* had brought a certain celebrity and notoriety to their author. He felt that he must use some of that fame to further the cause of civil rights in his own country, and he returned to Greenwich Village only to leave almost immediately for his first trip

to the South. That trip would provide the basis for the title essay of NOBODY KNOWS MY NAME (1961), a collection of essays written between 1954 and 1961 that are powerful statements of the psychological and spiritual damage done to white Americans by their denial of love and their oppression of African-Americans. An important essay in the collection is "Alas, Poor Richard," in which Baldwin attempts to explain his controversial criticism of RICHARD WRIGHT in the earlier *Notes* essay, "Everybody's Protest Novel" (1949).

In the late fifties Baldwin began work on ANOTHER COUNTRY (1962), a novel he wrote with great difficulty on both sides of the Atlantic and finally finished in Turkey, a country he visited frequently in the 1960s. *Another Country* examines the question of the demands of love in a bisexual, biracial context and depicts a bohemian Greenwich Village life that Baldwin knew well.

With THE FIRE NEXT TIME (1963) James Baldwin became a national celebrity and major civil rights spokesman. Through a study of the emergent Black Muslims and a remembrance of his own experience as a preacher, he prophesies to the white world: wake up or be destroyed; "God gave Noah the rainbow sign, no more water, the fire next time." For the next two years Baldwin traveled extensively, preaching his gospel in the context of civil rights. In 1964 his play *Blues for Mr. Charlie* opened on Broadway. The play was a metaphorical representation of the struggle between the Bible and the gun, between the approaches to civil rights taken at the time by Martin Luther King and Malcolm X.

In the 1960s Baldwin also wrote *Nothing Personal* (1964), a photographic essay on America done with the photographer Richard Avedon, and published his collected short stories, *Going to Meet the Man* (1965), the title story of which is a brilliant study of the relationship between sexual myths and the curse of racism. In 1965 he joined the world tour of his early play *The Amen Corner* and eventually settled in Istanbul to complete a new autobiographical novel. *Tell Me How Long the Train's Been Gone* (1968) follows the career of a black actor who longs for the love that his success has made it difficult for him to find. Baldwin lived in Hollywood in 1968 and wrote a screenplay for ALEX HALEY's *Autobiography of Malcolm X*. The scenario, published as *One Day, When I Was Lost* (1971), was never produced, and Baldwin moved to the south of France, where he was to live for at least half of every year for the rest of his life.

Although Baldwin's fame decreased in the 1970s, he remained a sought-after speaker and interviewee, and he continued to write. There were dialogues, *A Rap on Race* (1971) with MARGARET MEAD, and *A Dialogue* (1973) with the African American poet NIKKI GIOVANNI that, along with the long autobiographical essay *No Name in the Street* (1972), revealed Baldwin's disillusionment with the failure of America to heed the gospel he and others—many of them eventually assassinated—had preached for so long. A novel, *If Beale Street Could Talk* (1974), in which the love of a young Harlem couple must struggle against the powers of racism, is a fictional reflection of that disillusionment.

The 1970s found Baldwin returning to an old love, the cinema, in *The Devil Finds Work* (1976), a book-length essay about American movies as seen through the eyes of an American black growing up. Growing up black is also the theme of his children's book, *Little Man, Little Man: A Story of Childhood* (1976).

The last Baldwin novel, *Just Above My Head* (1979), is an ambitious work with strong autobiographical overtones about the struggles of an African-American musician and his family to cope with his homosexuality and the demands of his art in the face of ever present racism. Plagued by ill health, Baldwin managed in the 1980s to teach on a regular basis at several American colleges; research and write *Evidence of Things Not Seen* (1985), a book on racism as it applied to a series of child murders in Atlanta; and collect a book of poetry, *Jimmy's Blues* (1985). A significant work of that period is *The Price of the Ticket* (1985), a collection of his nonfiction, including autobiographical essays of great interest not collected elsewhere.

James Baldwin died in France of cancer. As an essayist, he occupies a large area in territory inhabited by such figures as Ralph Waldo Emerson, Henry David Thoreau, and Frederick Douglass. Like other poet-prophets, he forces us to look through our myths to see what we really are. But Baldwin's contribution as a writer of fiction and drama is also significant. Few minority writers have so articulately and successfully touched the conscience of an entire nation.

Fred Standley and Louis H. Pratt compiled *Conversations with James Baldwin* (1989). A biography is William J. Weatherby, *James Baldwin: Artist on Fire* (1989). Studies include Louis H. Pratt, *James Baldwin* (1978), Horace A. Porter, *Stealing the Fire: The Art and Protest of James Baldwin* (1989), and James Campbell, *Talking at the Gates: A Life of James Baldwin* (1991).

DAVID LEEMING

Baldwin, Joseph Glover (1815–1864),   lawyer, jurist, humorist. Largely self-educated, Baldwin prepared himself to practice law in Virginia, then decided to try the fresh fields of Mississippi and Alabama. Riding the circuit in these sparsely inhabited regions and later moving to California—he became an associate judge of the Supreme Court there—he published his best work, THE FLUSH TIMES OF ALABAMA AND MISSISSIPPI (1853). He later wrote *Party Leaders* (1855), sober portraits of contemporary political figures, including Henry Clay, Thomas Jefferson, and Andrew Jackson.

Balestier, [Charles] Wolcott (1861–1891),   novelist, publisher. Balestier, born in Rochester, New York, became a reporter on the Rochester *Post-Express*, later contributed to *The Atlantic Monthly*, and then began writing novels, including *A Potent Philtre* (1884), and *Benefits Forgot* (1892), set in Colorado mining camps. But his fame is chiefly due to his collaboration on a novel, *The Naulakha* (1892), with his brother-in-law Rudyard Kipling. Kipling dedicated *Barrack-Room Ballads* (1892) to him.

Ballad of the Sad Café, The (1951),   a collection of stories by CARSON MCCULLERS. In the title novella, dramatized by EDWARD ALBEE for Broadway in 1963, a grotesquely tall woman runs a café that becomes a magnet for other grotesques, including the hateful dwarf she falls in love with.

Ballads, American.   See FOLKSONGS AND BALLADS.

Ballads and Other Poems (1842),   a collection by HENRY WADSWORTH LONGFELLOW. Among longtime favorites included are THE SKELETON IN ARMOR, THE WRECK OF THE HESPERUS, THE VILLAGE BLACKSMITH, and EXCELSIOR. There is also a section of "Poems on Slavery."

Balloon Hoax, The   (New York *Sun*, April 13, 1844), a fiction by EDGAR ALLAN POE based on an actual flight made in 1836 by Monck Mason and others. Poe proved that a hoax can be printed twice in the same paper. On April 13, 1834, the *Sun* had perpetrated the Moon Hoax and had thereby increased its circulation to the largest in the world (19,360—the editor proudly announced). The hoax consisted in reprinting a series of articles from a nonexistent Edinburgh *Journal of Science*, in which were described the marvelous bat-men (along with other wonders) that Sir John Herschel had discovered on the moon through his new telescope. The articles were written by a *Sun* reporter, Richard Adams Locke—or, possibly, by a French scientist, Joseph Nicholas Nicollet, then in the United States. In 1844 Poe, who had followed the *Sun* articles with interest, tried it again. He told how a Mr. Monck Mason and eight passengers, starting from Wales, had crossed the Atlantic in a balloon inflated with coal gas, making the trip in 75 hours and landing at Sullivan's Island, Charleston. There was excitement for several days, and the *Sun* and Poe were greatly pleased.

Introducing the piece in his *Tales* (1845), Poe wrote that "if (as some assert) the *Victoria did* not absolutely accomplish the voyage recorded, it will be difficult to assign a reason why she *should* not have accomplished it."

Ballou, Adin (1803–1890),   clergyman, author. Ballou, born in Rhode Island, helped form the Hopedale Community in Milford, Massachusetts, in 1841, the avowed object of which was to practice "brotherly love and the Gospel of Jesus Christ," and which carried on numerous economic and community enterprises, including farming, building, and publishing. Ballou was for a time president of the community, which after 1856 disintegrated into a commercial organization that turned the town into a manufacturing center. Ballou published *The Independent Messenger* from 1831 to 1839 at a time when he was preaching Unitarian and Universalist doctrines. At Hopedale he edited *The Practical Christian* as an organ of the community and wrote *Practical Christian Socialism* (1854), in which he outlined plans for a "Practical Christian Republic." Later he wrote *Primitive Christianity and Its Corruptions* (1870), and his *Autobiography* appeared in 1896. To Ballou has sometimes been attributed an influence on Tolstoy, who mentions in *The Kingdom of God Is Within You* Ballou's doctrines of nonresistance, and on Mohandas K. Gandhi, who read Tolstoy's book and put the doctrines momentously into practice.

Bambara, Toni Cade (1939–1995),   short-story writer, novelist. Born Toni Cade (she added Bambara in 1970), she was educated at Queens College and City College of New York and studied acting and mime in Florence and Paris. She has taught, lectured, given public readings, written screenplays, and taken an active role in raising African-American consciousness. Her fiction has been praised for lyrical capture of black American English, for keen observation of character, and for a sometimes dreamlike mixture of myth and reality. Short stories are collected in *Gorilla, My Love* (1972) and *The Sea Birds Are Still Alive* (1977). Novels are *The Salt Eaters* (1980) and *If Blessing Comes* (1987). She has edited *The Black Woman* (as Toni Cade, 1970), and *Tales and Stories for Black Folks* (1971).

Writings posthumously published are *Deep Sightings and Rescue Missions: Fiction, Essays, and Conversations* (1996) and a novel, *Those Bones Are Not My Child* (1999), both edited by Toni Morrison.

Bancroft, George (1800–1891),   historian, public official. An infant prodigy, Bancroft was born in Worcester, Massachusetts, and was educated at home and abroad. After teaching briefly at Harvard, he went to Northampton and founded what may well have been the first progressive school. Among its principles were the elimination of classroom discipline and the adaptation of classes to "individual variability." After eight years at the Round Hill School, however, he retired from teaching to turn to politics and writing.

Bancroft the politician adhered to what was for Massachusetts of that day the unpopular side; he became a Jeffersonian, a Jacksonian, in later days a follower of Lincoln. He believed sincerely and flamboyantly in "the common mind." As almost the only Democrat of prominence in Massachusetts, it was inevitable that as the Jacksonians gained power, Bancroft should rise with them—as he did, to become collector of the Port of Boston, then Polk's secretary of the navy and later minister to England and Germany.

But Bancroft did not neglect his writing. Aside from orations and essays, and a collection of *Poems* (1823), he began in the 1830s a gigantic task—the writing of a *History of the United States*, really of the people of the United States, that would present democratic rather than Federalist ideas and ideals. The first volume appeared in 1834. As he went on to the remaining nine volumes—the last was published in 1874—it became more and more obvious that, as contemporaries said, "every line in the *History* is a vote for Jackson." Bancroft collected facts indefatigably, carried on a vast correspondence, and worked endless hours every day. His notes were spread on the pages with scholarly prodigality, but his purpose remained. He saw America as humanity's noblest experiment. He loved and extolled the energy of the American people in their westward course and in their establishment of a great republic. Indeed, his volumes were a gigantic Fourth of July oration.

Bancroft did not, however, fail to listen to criticism, and he made efforts to improve his style as well as to tighten up the facts. He cut the ten volumes down to six in 1876. He added two volumes on the *History of the Formation of the Constitution* (1882), an important pioneer work. There was a final revision to six volumes (1883–85).

Bancroft, Hubert Howe (1832–1918),   publisher, historian. Born in Ohio, Bancroft became a bookseller in San Francisco and eventually proprietor of the largest book and stationery firm in the West. A passionate collector of the literature of the American West, including North and South America, he conceived the idea of a mammoth history that grew eventually to 39 volumes (1874–90). Individual portions included *Native Races of the Pacific States* (5 v. 1874), and histories of states and sections (Central America, Mexico, Texas, Arizona, California, Nevada, Utah, etc.). The whole was issued as *The Works of Hubert Howe Bancroft* (1882–90). *Literary Industries* (1890), the last volume, includes autobiographical material and an account of the project. Although Bancroft was attacked for his methods (much of the writing was hired out to others in a kind of history factory), the work remains useful. In 1905, he presented his library of 60,000 items to the University of California. It became the foundation of the Bancroft Library at Berkeley, a major repository of Western Americana.

Bancroft Library.   See BANCROFT, HUBERT HOWE.

Bandeira [Filho], Manuel [Carnerode Sousa] (1886–1968),   Brazilian poet, essayist. Born in Recife, Bandeira studied architecture in São Paulo but gave up that career because of his tuberculosis. In 1913 he left Brazil to enter a Swiss sanitorium, where he met the French poet Paul Eluard (1895–1952), later involved in French dadism and surrealism. Returning to Brazil in 1914, Bandeira began to develop a poetic style that by the 1920s made him a leading figure in the Brazilian avant-garde. In 1940 he was elected to the Brazilian Academy of Letters, and in 1943 became a professor of literature at the University of São Paulo. Early poems were collected in *A Cinza das Horas* (1917) and *Carnaval* (1919). The titles of *O Ritmo Dissoluto* (*The Dissolute Rhythm*, 1924) and *Libertinagem* (*Libertinism*, 1930) proclaimed his modernist aesthetic. His poems were characteristically ironic about the present, nostalgic toward childhood, witty and colloquial, open in form. He advocated the use of "all the words, especially barbarisms; and all the rhythms, especially those beyond metrics." In a later volume, *Estrela da Manhã* (1936), he turned for subject matter to the black folklore of his native Recife. *Poesia e Prosa* (2 v. 1958) includes essays and an autobiography as well as verse.

Bandelier, Adolph Francis Alphonse (1840–1914), archaeologist, author. One of the earliest American archaeologists, Bandelier was born in Switzerland, came to the United States as a boy, and later explored various parts of the Western Hemisphere. His most fruitful researches were among the Pueblo Indians of New Mexico, whom he treated in a novel, *The Delight Makers* (1890), a vivid account of prehistoric Indian life in the Southwest. A later book was *The Gilded Man* (1893), concerning the legend of EL DORADO. Bandelier became in 1903 a member of the staff of the American Museum of Natural History in New York. He published many learned works, among them one on the art of war in ancient Mexico.

Bangs, John Kendrick (1862–1922),   editor, humorist, lecturer. Bangs spent most of his life in Yonkers, New York, when he wasn't away from home delivering lectures or down in New York City, where he edited PUCK (1904–05) and other magazines. In *A Houseboat on the Styx* (1895) Bangs assembles celebrated characters of history—from Diogenes down to Sam Johnson, Napoleon, and George Washington—for comic and satiric purposes. There was a sequel, *The Pursuit of the Houseboat* (1897), which keeps up the fun. Among the forty or so books he wrote, there were some that were almost as good, among them *Methuselah* (1888), *Coffee and Repartee* (1893), *Mr. Bonaparte of Corsica* (1895), *The Idiot* (1895), *The Enchanted Typewriter* (1899), *Autobiography of Methuselah* (1909), and *Half Hours with the Idiot* (1917). He was on the staff of *Harper's Monthly* from 1888 to 1899, and later on other Harper periodicals. Before joining *Harper's* he was with *Life* for four years.

Banker's Daughter, The (1878),   a play by BRONSON HOWARD, one of the first plays to appeal to an American audience as an American comedy. It was a rewrite of an earlier play, *Lillian's Last Love* (1873). Howard described the revision in *Autobiography of a Play* (1910).

Banks, Russell (1940–   ),   novelist, short-story writer. Born in Newton, Massachusetts, and educated at Colgate and the University of North Carolina, Banks writes of the consequences of economic decline in his native New England. The title character of *Hamilton Stark* (1978) is an angry and abusive pipefitter. The separate but interlocking stories of a New Hampshire oil-burner repairman and a Haitian woman who wants to emigrate to the U.S. with her infant son are woven together in *Continental Drift* (1985). *Cloudsplitter* (1998) is a fictional rendition of the life of John Brown, the abolitionist who led the 1859 raid on the arsenal at Harpers Ferry. Other novels include *Family Life* (1975), *The Book of Jamaica* (1980), *Affliction* (1989), and *The Sweet Hereafter* (1991). *Trailerpark* (1981) is a story collection dealing with residents of mobile homes. *The New World* (1978) and *Success Stories* (1986) are also story collections. *The Angel on the Roof* (2000) collects thirty-one earlier and new stories set mostly in or around Catamount, New Hampshire, the fictional mill town of *Trailerpark* and others of his earlier works.

Banning, Margaret Culkin (1891–1982),   novelist. Born in Minnesota, Banning was educated at Vassar. She wrote essays and stories on contemporary domestic problems for most major magazines, and was elected a member of the Commission on Education of Women of the American Council of Education. Her more than thirty-five novels reflect her extensive travels and civic interests. They include *This Marrying* (1920), *Half Loaves* (1921), *Country Club People* (1923), *The Women of the Family* (1926), *Money of Her Own* (1928), *Mixed Marriage* (1930), *Letters to Susan* (1936), *Out in Society* (1940), *The Clever Sister* (1947), *Give Us Our Years* (1950), *Fallen Away* (1951), *The Dowry* (1955), *The Convert* (1957), *Echo Answers* (1960), *The Vine and the Olive* (1964), *Mesabi* (1969), *The Spendid Torments* (1976), and *Such Interesting People* (1979). Other titles are *Women for Defense* (1942), on women in both world wars, and *Letters from England, Summer 1942* (1943).

Baptists.   Various Protestant Christian denominations that reject infant baptism, postponing that ceremony to the age of discretion in accordance with their doctrine that baptism should be administered only to believers. In Europe some earlier groups, including Anabaptists and Mennonites, held similar doctrines; the first English Baptists came together among Separatists in Holland *c.* 1608. Their history in the United States began in Rhode Island in 1639, when ROGER WILLIAMS and others established a church founded on individual professions of faith, rejecting infant baptism. The Baptists' tenets, however, were generally considered heretical in New England, and in the late 17th and early 18th century, groups from New England brought their beliefs to the Carolinas, maintaining there the New England congregational way of church governance. In the Southeast they flourished, and they brought their religion westward into the mountains after the Revolution.

Historically, Baptists were either General Baptists (believing Christ's atonement was not only for the elect, but was general) or Particular Baptists (believing atonement to be individual). American Baptists in New England were Particular. The split between the two types in the South led to the designations Hard Shell Baptists or Primitive Baptists for the Particular, more Calvinistic, Baptists who settled in the Southern mountains; these were also called Anti-Mission Baptists for their opposition to the worldwide missionary activity begun by General Baptists in 1814. In time, Baptists subdivided into numerous organizations, such the Southern Baptist Convention and the Northern Baptist Convention (differing on the question of slavery), the National Baptist Convention of America (largely African American), and the National Primitive Baptist Convention.

Baraka, Amiri (1934–   ),   poet, essayist, music critic, novelist, short-story writer. Baraka was born to black American middle-class parents as Everett LeRoy Jones in Newark, New Jersey. He attended Howard University, where he studied with such outstanding black scholars as Nathan A. Scott, Jr., Sterling A. Brown, and E. Franklin Frazier, all of whom made a lasting impact on Baraka's intellectual and artistic development. Shortly before entering college, he began spelling his first name in its Frenchified form, LeRoi.

In 1957, after being dishonorably discharged from the U.S. Air Force, Baraka moved to Greenwich Village, where he came under the influence of such Beat and avant-garde figures as Allen Ginsberg and Frank O'Hara. During this period he founded and coedited two influential avant-garde magazines, *Yugen* (1958–1962) and *The Floating Bear* (1961–1963). In 1960 he visited Cuba, where he encountered Third World intellectuals, who forced him to reexamine his bourgeois poetics and initiate his journey toward a radically engaged art. With the 1965 assassination of Malcolm X, Baraka left Greenwich Village and the white world. He became a Black Cultural Nationalist committed to the creation of a black culture and values through art. At the end of 1966, after an explosive period in Harlem, he returned to Newark and in 1967 changed his name to Amiri Baraka (tr. blessed prince). In 1974 he rejected Cultural Nationalism and became a Third World

Marxist-Leninist. In 1979 he joined the African Studies Department at SUNY, Stony Brook, was promoted to professor in 1984, and retired in 1999.

During Baraka's Beat period, he produced his first collection of poetry, *Preface to a Twenty-Volume Suicide Note* (1961), detailing his alienation from the square world and his lack of moral certainty. Significantly, this volume manifests little ethnicity. The persona thinks of himself "as any other sad man here / american." However, in *The Dead Lecturer* (1964), the poet desperately wants to escape the white wasteland to gain a world of authentic black action. In the Obie-winning play *Dutchman* (1964), which catapulted Baraka into national prominence, he explores the revolutionary potential of the educated black middle-class intellectual, represented by the protagonist, Clay, a would-be poet. When Clay is exposed as dangerous—that is, as a latent killer—by white society, seductively imaged as a beautiful white woman named Lula, he is summarily executed by that society. *The Slave* (1964), a fable set in a future of war between the races, continues the theme of black revolutionary militancy. The protagonist, Walker Vessels, is a former poet who has become a black revolutionary, that is, a Clay at a later stage in his development. As a revolutionary Walker substitutes black actions for ineffectual white words.

Baraka's only short-story collection, *Tales* (1967), lyrically documents his sojourn in Harlem and his desire to reunite with his people in the language of his tribe. His Cultural Nationalist collection of poetry, *Black Magic* (1967), shows the failure of liberalism and the need for revolutionary violence. The poet simply asks, "Will the machinegunners please step forward?" After an inauspicious beginning, Baraka has produced substantial Marxist writings, including "In the Tradition" (1980), a long poem celebrating the heroes of the black tradition and the inherent revolutionary nature of African-American music. *Wise, Why's, Y's* (1995), an epic poem, traces the meaning of freedom and slavery throughout African-American history. *Funk Lore* (1996) collects recent poems, and *Eulogies* (1996) commemorates deceased African-American cultural and political leaders.

Baraka has demonstrated that great art can be both politically engaged and ethnically centered. Moreover, not only as an artist but also as a theoretician, he has made a lasting contribution to American literature. In addition to those mentioned above, his works include *Blues People* (1963), *Home: Social Essays* (1966), and *The Autobiography of LeRoi Jones/Amiri Baraka* (1984, restored ed., 1997), *Transbluesency: Selected Poems* (1995), and *The Fiction of LeRoi Jones/Amiri Baraka* (2000). Hettie Jones's *How I Became Hettie Jones* (1990) is his wife's memoir. Critical books include Werner Sollors, *Amiri Baraka/LeRoi Jones: The Quest for a "Populist Modernism"* (1978) and William J. Harris, *The Poetry and Poetics of Amiri Baraka: The Jazz Aesthetic* (1985).

WILLIAM J. HARRIS

Barbara Frietchie (1863), a poem by JOHN GREENLEAF WHITTIER. On September 6, 1862, when Frederick, Maryland, was occupied by Confederate troops under the leadership of Stonewall Jackson, Mrs. Frietchie, then in her nineties, is said to have flaunted the American flag in the face of the soldiers marching by. General Jackson forbade any interference with her. The poem's most frequently quoted lines are "Shoot if you must, this old gray head, / But spare your country's flag, she said."

Later CLYDE FITCH wrote *Barbara Frietchie* (1899), a play in which Barbara is a young girl in love with a Union officer.

Barbary Wars [also called **Tripolitan War**]. From the 15th to the early 19th centuries, Barbary corsairs infested the Mediterranean, inflicting great damage on commerce and taking many Christians as slaves. England, France, later the United States, and other nations bore these attacks without more than sporadic attempts to resist, even paying the pirates annual tribute. At the close of the War of 1812, American naval units under Commodores Stephen Decatur and Bainbridge attacked the marauders in their home ports, captured their warships, and exacted submission from the dey of Algiers, the bey of Tunis, and the bashaw of Tripoli. The Americans thereby put an end to the piratical raids on American commerce. England and France took similar action, and in 1830 France occupied and annexed Algeria. The Barbary pirates were treated in Susanna Rowson's *Slaves in Algiers* (1794), Royall Tyler's ALGERINE CAPTIVE (1797) and James Fenimore Cooper's HOMEWARD BOUND (1838). Kenneth Roberts made use of the setting in *Lydia Bailey* (1946), as did H. L. Davis in *Harp of a Thousand Strings* (1947). Other novels set in this period include John Jennings' *The Salem Frigate* (1946), Elisabeth Meg's *Plenty of Pirates* (1953), Edison Marshall's *American Captain* (1954), Alexander Laing's *Jonathan Eagle* (1955), and John Jennings' *The Wind in His Fists* (1956). See JOEL BARLOW.

Barbour, Ralph Henry (1870–1944), novelist. Barbour's *The Half-Back* (1899) was the first of more than a hundred books, most of them for boys. Among his other titles are *For the Honor of the School* (1900), *Behind the Line* (1902), and *The Crimson Sweater* (1906).

Barbour, Thomas (1884–1946), naturalist, author. A Harvard professor of zoology, Barbour wrote of his work in a number of books, including *Naturalist at Large* (1943), *That Vanishing Eden: A Naturalist's Florida* (1944), and *A Naturalist in Cuba* (1945).

Barefoot Boy, The (originally published in the juvenile magazine *The Little Pilgrim*, January, 1855; later collected in *The Panorama*, 1856), a tribute to the joys of childhood in the country, by JOHN GREENLEAF WHITTIER.

Barker, James Nelson (1784–1858), politician, dramatist, essayist, biographer. Born in Philadelphia, Barker served as an assistant adjutant-general during the War of 1812, then as an alderman in Philadelphia, and in 1819 as mayor. A Jacksonian in politics, he was appointed collector of the Port of Philadelphia, then comptroller of the Treasury, but resigned from the latter to become a clerk in the Treasury Department until his death. Meanwhile, he wrote steadily, and his plays reflect his ardent Americanism and interest in politics. *Tears* *and Smiles* (1807) studied Philadelphia manners. THE INDIAN PRINCESS (1808) was the first play on an Indian subject—also the first American play, produced in America, to be performed in England. MARMION (1812) was a version of Scott's poem. The theme of SUPERSTITION (1824), considered his best play, was principally the witchcraft madness in Salem. *The Court of Love* (produced, 1836; written in 1817 as *How to Try a Lover*) was based on a French novel.

Barlow, Joel (1754–1812),   teacher, lawyer, diplomat, poet, humorist. Born in Connecticut and educated at Yale, Barlow served in the Revolutionary Army. Later, after teaching school and becoming a lawyer, he went abroad as an agent for land companies promoting western settlement and investment. When this project failed, he became a political journalist, associated with THOMAS PAINE in his activities on the side of the French Revolutionaries. He prospered in his career of businessman and diplomat and returned to America a man of wealth and reputation. In 1795, as consul to Algiers, he secured an excellent treaty with the Barbary states. Sent to negotiate a treaty with Napoleon in 1811, he was caught in the retreat from Moscow and suffered hardships so severe that he died from the effects and was buried in Poland.

V. L. PARRINGTON said that Barlow's "admirable prose writings have been forgotten, and THE COLUMBIAD (1807) returns always to plague him." Ambitiously conceived as "the great American epic," this poem had begun with *The Vision of Columbus* (1787), an earlier attempt to hail America's greatness. When it grew to *The Columbiad*, its dull and almost endless succession of heroic couplets presented past, present, and future glories. Reverently presented in a handsome printing and binding, it was attacked by English reviewers for such Americanisms as *utilize, millenial,* and *crass:* "as utterly foreign as if they had been adopted from the Hebrew or Chinese." As a poet, Barlow survives best in THE HASTY-PUDDING (1706), a mock pastoral written in praise of his native cornmeal while abroad, and in "Advice to a Raven in Russia" (written in 1812 and first published in 1843 in the *Erie Chronicle*), on Napoleon's carnage. Among his prose works are *A Letter to the National Convention of France on the Defects of the Constitution of 1791* (1792) and *Advice to the Privileged Orders* (1792), a reply to Edmund Burke's *Reflections on the Revolution in France.* The former won him honorary citizenship in France, while the latter was suppressed in England by Pitt. He also edited *The American Mercury* with Elisha Babcock (1784–1785) and contributed to the ANARCHIAD (1786–1787), a publication of the HARTFORD WITS. He is the subject of *A Yankee's Odyssey* (1958), a biography by James Woodress.

Barlowe, Arthur (fl. 1580s),   English explorer. Barlowe wrote "The First Voyage Made to the Coasts of America," an enthusiastic account of his travels along the shore of what is now North Carolina in a expedition lead by Philip Amadas. Barlowe had served in the military under Sir Walter Raleigh in Ireland in 1580–81, and Raleigh was the probable sponsor of the Carolina trip. Barlowe commanded the smaller of two vessels. John White, the sketch artist, and Thomas Harriot, the

naturalist, may also have been on this ship. Barlowe described the landscape, as well as its native inhabitants, who welcomed the explorers ashore.

Barnes, Charlotte Mary Sanford (1818–1863), dramatist. She is remembered for *Octavia Brigaldi* (1837), a rendering in blank verse of the Kentucky Tragedy (see BEAUCHAMPE) set in 15th-century Milan, and for *The Forest Princess* (1848), on Pocahontas.

Barnes, Djuna [Chappell] (1892–1982),   journalist, novelist, playwright, poet. Born in Cornwall-on-Hudson, New York, Barnes was privately educated and studied at the Art Students' League in New York. From 1913 to 1931 she worked as a journalist and illustrator, after 1931 devoting full time to her writing. Associated with avant-garde groups from her twenties, she was an original member of the Theater Guild. She acted and had three experimental plays produced in 1919 by the Provincetown Players (*Three from the Earth, Kurzy of the Sea, An Irish Triangle*). The publication of *Nightwood*, (1936) with an introduction by T. S. Eliot, brought her fame. It is an account of the tangled sexual and psychological relationships between various expatriates in Paris and Berlin. Narrated in part through an alcoholic haze of stream of consciousness, it owes its reputation as an avant-garde work partially to its frank treatment of lesbianism. Other writings display similar interests. *Ladies Almanack* (1928), published anonymously in Paris, is a *roman à clef*, with contemporary lesbians, including Radcliffe Hall, masked under such names as Lady Buck-and-Balk. *Ryder* (1928), a novel, is a satiric family history expurgated in the American edition. *The Antiphon* (1958) is a blank-verse tragedy set in England in World War II. *The Book of Repulsive Women* (1915) included poems and drawings. Stories, verse, and short plays were variously collected as *A Book* (1923), *A Night Among the Horses* (1929), and *Spillway* (1962). *Vagaries Malicieux* (1974) includes two stories of Paris. *Selected Works* appeared in 1962.

Barnes, Margaret Ayer (1886–1967),   novelist and short-story writer. Barnes grew up in Chicago and was educated at Bryn Mawr. She championed women's education and, as Alumna Director, instituted Bryn Mawr's Working Woman's College. After a serious accident (1925), she began to write, encouraged by EDWARD SHELDON, her collaborator on two theater productions (*Jenny* and *Dishonored Lady*). Her early work also included a staging of EDITH WHARTON's *Age of Innocence* as well as several short stories, collected as *Prevailing Winds* (1928). She is known best for her novels. *Years of Grace* (1930) won the Pulitzer Prize in 1931. Her other novels, *Westward Passage (1931), Within This Present (1933), Edna His Wife* (1935), and *Wisdom's Gate* (1938) were all popular even though they failed to match the success of her first effort.

Barnes has generally been dismissed as a conventional domestic novelist whose narrow focus on the social history of Chicago's upper middle class justifies her neglect. Read from a feminist perspective, however, her fiction details how economic structures support male dominance, revealing the ways in which women are forced to bear a disproportionate burden in attaining and maintaining precisely that middle-class social status. Her novels thus turn out to be not complacent chronicles of gentility, but incisive indictments of the sexual politics of 20th-century American capitalism. A study is Lloyd C. Taylor, *Margaret Ayer Barnes* (1974).

NANCY SORKIN RABINOWITZ, PETER J. RABINOWITZ

Barnum, P[hineas] T[aylor] (1810–1891), showman, author. Born in Connecticut, Barnum began his career as showman in 1835 when he bought and exhibited a slave who claimed to be 161 years old and the nurse of George Washington. Seven years later he opened his American Museum, in New York City, exhibiting the Fiji Mermaid (half monkey, half fish), General Tom Thumb (a midget less than three feet tall), and the original Siamese Twins, Chang and Eng. He also arranged the American tour of Jenny Lind, known as the Swedish Nightingale. After serving as mayor of Bridgeport and as a member of the Connecticut legislature, he organized "The Greatest Show on Earth," a circus that opened in Brooklyn, New York, in 1871. A merger in 1881 created Barnum and Bailey's. Its star attraction was Jumbo, a six and one-half ton African elephant. Barnum's books include a *Life of P. T. Barnum, Written by Himself* (1855, frequently revised), *The Humbugs of the World* (1865), *Struggles and Triumphs (1869), and Money Getting* (1883). A.H. Saxon wrote a biography, *P. T. Barnum: The Legend and the Man* (1990).

Barr, Amelia E[dith Huddleston] (1831–1919), novelist, poet. Born in England, Barr lived in Texas and in New York, where she wrote for Henry Ward Beecher's newspapers. She earned a modest income from verse, but is remembered chiefly for her popular, sentimental novels, which are usually historical. They include *Romance and Reality* (1872; *Jan Vedder's Wife* (1885); *The Bow of Orange Ribbon* (1886), set in New York City when it was still called New Amsterdam; *Remember the Alamo* (1888); *The Belle of Bowling Green* (1904); *The House on Cherry Street* (1909); and *The Paper Cap* (1918). Her autobiography is *All the Days of My Life* (1913).

Barr, Stringfellow (1897–1982), educator, author. Born in Virginia, Barr was a professor of history and president of St. John's College (1937–46). His works include *Three Fables* (1932); *Mazzini: Portrait of an Exile* (1935), a biography of the Italian patriot; *Pilgrimage of Western Man* (1949); *Citizens of the World* (1952), a proposal for aid to underdeveloped countries (expanded from *Let's Join the Human Race*, 1950); *Copydog in India* (1955); *Purely Academic* (1958), a novel drawing on his experience as professor and administrator; *The Will of Zeus* (1961), on ancient Greek culture; and *Voices that Endured* (1971), on great books.

Barras, Charles M. (1826–1873), playwright, author of THE BLACK CROOK.

Barrell, Sarah Sayward. See WOOD, SARAH SAYWARD [BARRELL] KEATING.

Barren Ground (1925), a novel by ELLEN GLASGOW. As is the case in a number of Glasgow's other novels, the subject is woman's independence. Dorinda Oakley, a Virginia farm girl, disappointed in love for young Jason Greylock, matures into a strong-willed, effective, and self-sustaining woman. She finds work in New York, rejects the hand of a young doctor, and returns to the family farm after her father's death. With her energy and managerial skill, and with little help from an invalid mother and lazy brother, she turns the barren ground into a successful dairy farm. Later, she weds a storekeeper in a sexless marriage of convenience and still later takes in her first love, Jason, by then a penniless drunkard. Jason soon dies. The antithesis of the conventional romance of the South, the novel was advertised by its publisher with the phrase "Realism crosses the Potomac."

Barrett, William Edmund (1900–1986), popular novelist. Barrett was born in New York City. After his first published work, the biography *Woman on Horseback* (1938), he concentrated almost exclusively on fiction: *Flight from Youth* (1939); *To the Last Man* (1948); *The Evil Heart* (1946); *The Number of My Days* (1946); *The Left Hand of God* (1951, made into a motion picture in 1955; *The Shadows of the Images* (1953); *The Sudden Strangers* (1956); *The Empty Shrine* (1958); and *The Edge of Things* (1960). He has also published a work of historical nonfiction, *The First War Planes* (1960). He began to demonstrate a religious preoccupation in his later works, notably *The Left Hand of God* and *The Empty Shrine*, both of which deal with the search for faith.

Barrios, Eduardo (1884–1963), Chilean novelist, short-story writer. Educated in Lima, Eduardo rejected an army career and broke with his widowed Peruvian mother. After wandering throughout Latin America and working at a variety of jobs, he settled in Santiago, where he served in the 1920s as minister of education and director of the national library. Mastery of the psychological tale is especially evident in his portrayal of hypersensitive personalities. Such is the ten-year-old protagonist of the novelette *El niño que enloqueció de amor* (1915), who falls in love with one of his mother's friends. The hero of *Un perdido* (1917) is an overwrought weakling unable to cope with reality, who finds refuge in alcohol. Barrios's best work is probably *El hermano asno* (1922, tr. *Brother Ass*, 1942), which deals with the inner conflicts of Brother Lázaro and Brother Rufino, two Franciscan monks. *Gran señor y rajadiablos* (1948) follows José Pedro Valverde, a strongly drawn character, through a life centered mostly about a large *fundo* (ranch). Barrios's last novel, *Los hombres del hombre* (1950), is a lyrical story of sexual jealousy and insecurity in family life. His *Obras completas* appeared in two volumes in 1962.

Barry, Dave (1947–   ), humorist, newspaper columnist, novelist. Born in Armonk, New York, and educated at Haverford College, Barry has written a humor column about everyday experiences for the *Miami Herald* since 1983, and has had a television sitcom based on his life. His first book, *The Taming of the Screw: Several Million Homeowners' Problems Sidestepped* (1983), inaugurated a series of column gatherings including *Dave Barry's Greatest Hits* (1988), *Dave Barry Slept Here: A Sort of History of the United States* (1989), *Dave Barry Turns Forty* (1990), *Dave Barry Is from Mars and*

Venus (1997), and *Dave Barry Turns Fifty* (1998). *Big Trouble* (1999) is a comic mystery novel set in south Florida.

Barry, Philip (1896–1949), playwright. Born in Rochester, New York, Barry was graduated from Yale and then studied with GEORGE PIERCE BAKER in the 47 Workshop at Harvard. There he wrote his first published plays, *A Punch for Judy* (1921) and *You and I*, the latter produced in New York in 1922. Most of Barry's plays, including the most successful ones, are high comedies of domestic crises among people of wealth and social standing, but there is also a more serious turn to many of them. Typically, his protagonists seek to define a personal place in the world apart from the conventional boundaries imposed by family or society. His more than twenty titles include *The Youngest* (1924); *In a Garden* (1925); *White Wings* (1926); *Paris Bound* (1927); *Holiday* (1929); *Hotel Universe* (1930); *The Animal Kingdom* (1932); *Here Come the Clowns* (1938), a version of Barry's novel *War in Heaven* (1938); *The Philadelphia Story* (1939); *Liberty Jones* (1941); *Without Love* (1943); and *Foolish Notions* (1945). Of these, *Holiday* and *The Philadelphia Story* have proven most popular and most enduring.

Barrymores, The. First family of the American theater, beginning with Maurice Barrymore and his wife. Barrymore's real name was Herbert Blythe (1847–1905), and he was born in India. His wife was Georgiana Drew (1856–1893), daughter of the actor John Drew (1827–1862). Their children were Lionel (1878–1954), Ethel (1879–1959), and John (1882–1942), all of whom scored many great stage and motion-picture successes. *The Royal Family* (1927), by GEORGE S. KAUFMAN and EDNA FERBER, satirizes the foibles of a family of actors not dissimilar to the Barrymores. Gene Fowler's *Good Night, Sweet Prince* (1943), is mainly about John Barrymore, but tells much about the others. So do Lionel's own (ghosted) book, *We Barrymores*, (1951) and Ethel's *Memories* (1955).

Bart, Lily. Chief character in Edith Wharton's THE HOUSE OF MIRTH (1905). Lily is a beautiful orphan, of good social connections but little money, whose fortunes sink from bad to worse and who finally commits suicide.

Barth, John [Simmons] (1930–), novelist, short-story writer. Barth was born in Cambridge, on Maryland's Eastern Shore. He was educated at Juilliard, where he spent the summer after high school graduation studying orchestration, and Johns Hopkins University, where he earned two degrees. He has held academic appointments at Pennsylvania State University, SUNY-Buffalo, Boston University, and Johns Hopkins, where he has been the Alumni Centennial Professor of English and Creative Writing since 1973.

Despite his reputation as a writer of metafiction, Barth's concerns are more than merely formal. Ideas abound in his fiction. But Barth, an opposite-sex twin whose novels also tend to come in pairs, almost always contradicts in the second novel of the pair whatever philosophical position he seems to have arrived at in the first. *The Floating Opera* (1956) apparently makes a case for ethical subjectivism, as Todd Andrews concludes that in the absence of absolutes, relative values are in no way inferior. In *The End of the Road* (1958), on the other hand,

Barth first attributes Todd's conclusion to Joe Morgan and then has Jake Horner undo that position. Similarly, *The Sot-Weed Factor* (1960), the first of Barth's pair of "gigantic," purposely inflated, novels, apparently rejects the possibility of attaining the transcendental unity represented by Eben's quixotic quest for ideal beauty and Henry's desire for coalescence. But in *Giles Goat-Boy* (1966), George does transcend categories, perceiving at once universal unity.

By refuting in one book a position he seems to have upheld in a prior book, Barth achieves the overall effect of a constant grasping for meaning, on the one hand, balanced by the realization that all meaning is projected, on the other. The world we perceive, and in the act of perceiving help to create, is therefore no more ontologically secure than the world contained in works of fiction. To reinforce this idea, Barth's work draws attention to its own artificiality in a variety of ways. In *Lost in the Funhouse* (1968), self-reflexive fictions such as "Title," "Autobiography," and "Life-Story" are primarily about their own processes. In *Chimera* (1971), on the other hand, self-reflexiveness is absorbed into the work's narrative flow. Since its ground situation involves protagonists acutely aware of the problems they are having in composing the work confronting the reader, the writing process forms a central element in the fictional plot.

Letters (1979), an encyclopedic reorchestration of characters and themes from his first six books, is—among other things—a history of the novel from its origins through postmodernism. Barth's later works, *Sabbatical* (1982), *The Tidewater Tales: A Novel* (1987), and *The Last Voyage of Somebody the Sailor* (1991), extend Barth's novelistic investigation into the relationship between narrative and reality. *The Friday Book: Essays and Other Nonfiction* (1984), a collection of essays and lectures Barth wrote on Fridays, the other four days of the week having been reserved for fiction, casts valuable light on the Barthian aesthetic, especially such essays as "The Literature of Exhaustion" and "The Literature of Replenishment." *Further Fridays: Essays, Lectures and Nonfiction 1984–1994* appeared in 1995. Stories are collected in *On with the Story* (1996). *Once upon a Time: A Floating Opera* (1994) is autobiographical fiction centering on a sailing trip of Barth and his second wife. *Coming Soon!!!* (2001) is a self-referential novel of a student and his professor.

Despite his celebrated virtuosity, form for Barth is always a metaphor for other concerns, never an end in itself. In his own phrase, he strives to attain "passionate virtuosity," a combination of formal dexterity and thematic "aboutness." Informing this aesthetic ideal is a belief that the world is a *worded* world after all, and language, properly understood, is the mythic ligature connecting human beings, time, and world in a dynamic unity. Barth has come to understand that the world does not exist *in* so much as *through* the word, a notion that informs as it explains his virtuosity. Studies include Charles B. Harris, *Passionate Virtuosity: The Fiction of John Barth* (1983); Max F. Schulz, *The Muses of John Barth* (1990), and Patricia Tobin, *John Barth and the Anxiety of Continuance* (1992).

CHARLES B. HARRIS/BP

Barthelme, Donald (1931–1989), short-fiction writer and novelist. Barthelme was born in Philadelphia but raised outside Houston, where his architect-father had built the family a modern house that attracted much local attention. The writer served in his early thirties as director of the Museum of Contemporary Art in Houston, where he introduced many avant-garde artists and trends. He moved to New York City in the 1960s and became known best for his frequent appearances in *The New Yorker*. The style of this extremely polished magazine combined a culture of highly acquisitive capitalism with knowing and facile wit. For many readers, Barthelme's fiction seemed a perfect match for such a publishing outlet. Barthelme himself mocked how often his aesthetic had been linked to the modernist fascination with fragmentation and collage. Known as a practitioner of "metafiction," he often focused attention on the machinery of fiction itself, but never lost sight of how storytelling functions to show us "the way we live now." Indeed, he could often weave together an astonishing amount of mundane information, thematic development, and surprisingly perceptive characterology in stories that seldom exceeded a length of four or five pages. His treatment of his material was sprightly, brash and irreverent—he had learned much from the oddball juxtapositions of S. J. Perelman and the laconic alienation of Hemingway. But increasingly the stories pursued their experimental purposes, and certain themes began to recur.

Chief among the themes were the agony of divorce (Barthelme himself went through a divorce but eventually remarried and had a daughter with his second wife) and the persistence of what he called "double consciousness." This consciousness was heavily indebted to the irony of modernist literature, but Barthelme carried it into areas resembling those explored by the so-called black humorists, such as Samuel Beckett, while also applying it more frequently to all areas of everyday life. The Barthelmean hero is seldom in control and almost always mired in a crippling self-consciousness. The stories constitute a compendium of what is called popular culture: widely circulated images from the media, the random feeling of urban life, and the skittish pace of human relationships.

His first collection, *Come Back Dr. Caligari* (1964), alludes in its title to the world of silent movies and a feeling of loss and nostalgia. Several more collections followed regularly, including *Unspeakable Practices, Unnatural Acts* (1968), *City Life* (1970), *Sadness* (1972), *Amateurs* (1976), and *Great Days* (1979) as well as a group of essays and experimental nonfiction prose pieces, *Guilty Pleasures* (1974). There were also two novels, rather short and in texture and structure much like the stories: *Snow White* (1967) and *The Dead Father* (1975). *Sixty Stories* appeared in 1981 and showed how various were his subjects. Another novel, *The King* (1990), transfers the legendary world of King Arthur to the days of World War II. His death was widely mourned, especially by those who kept faith with experimental art.

CHARLES MOLESWORTH

Barthelme, Frederick (1943–   ), novelist, short-story writer. Born in Houston, the younger brother of Donald Barthelme, Frederick studied art and architecture at Tulane, the University of Houston, and the Museum of Fine Art in Houston. After two books mixing experimental prose and graphic arts, *Rangoon* (1970) and *War and War* (1971), he turned more seriously to fiction, studying for an M.A. (1977) with John Barth at Johns Hopkins. A few years later he produced a collection of short stories, *Moon Deluxe* (1983). This was followed by the novels *Second Marriage* (1970), *Tracer* (1985), *Two Against One* (1988), and *Natural Selection* (1990); all have been praised for their minimalist rendition of the details of housekeeping, junk food, and shopping malls that surround his bored, self-absorbed characters. With his brother, Steven Barthelme, he wrote *Double Down: Reflections on Gambling and Loss* (1999), an account of the gambling addiction that caused them to lose their entire inheritance in Gulf Coast riverboat casinos. *The Law of Averages: New and Selected Stories* appeared in 2000.

Bartleby the Scrivener (1853), a long short story by HERMAN MELVILLE. Immediately successful in *Putnam's Magazine, Bartleby* has since been recognized as one of the great American short stories. It was collected in *Piazza Tales* (1856). The narrator, who operates a law office on Wall Street, employs a young scrivener named Bartleby, who, like the two other employees, is told to copy and proofread legal documents. He eventually rejects these menial chores; his eyes glazed, he prefers to stare endlessly at a stone wall, rejecting all entreaties to work with, "I would prefer not to." Unable to persuade Bartleby either to work or to leave the office in which he seems to have taken up permanent residence, the narrator moves his business elsewhere. Bartleby is finally taken to prison, and the narrator, feeling vaguely responsible for him, visits him and arranges for him to receive special privileges. But Bartleby does not accept the privileges. He refuses to eat and finally dies. Bartleby is something of a comic hero, but his fate is haunting rather than amusing.

Bartleby's story is an allegory of withdrawal suggesting more than one level of interpretation. Among them. Bartleby may be seen as a writer (like Melville), who chooses no longer to write; or as a human walled off from society by his employment on Wall Street, by the walls of his building, by the barriers of his office nook within the building, by the brick surface he faces out his window, and by the walls of the prison where he dies. Bartleby's employer, the narrator of the story, has several walls of his own to break out of. In his final grasp at communication, the narrator invites the reading that Bartleby's life, and the story that presents it, are like dead letters that will never reach those that would profit from them. He leaves us with the words, "Ah, Bartleby! Ah, humanity!"

Bartlett, John (1820–1905), bookseller, editor, publisher. Bartlett's famous book is his *Familiar Quotations*, compiled while he worked in his college bookstore in Cambridge, Massachusetts. First published in 1855, it went through nine editions in his lifetime and has been revised a number of times in the 20th century under other editors. His other books include *A New Method of Chess Notation* (1857), *A Shakespeare Phrase Book* (1882), and *A New and Complete Concordance to Shakespeare* (1894). After the Civil War, he went to work for the publisher Little, Brown & Company, becoming a senior partner in 1878.

Barton, Clara [Harlowe] (1821–1912),   humanitarian. Barton was first a teacher, then showed executive ability as a clerk in the Patent Office. At the outset of the Civil War she volunteered for hospital service, won the confidence of Lincoln, and became an organizer of aid to war casualties. After the war she induced the United States to become a member of the Red Cross and headed the American branch. Hers was the innovation by which the Red Cross gives help in any time of distress, during peace and war. She wrote *An Official History of the Red Cross* (1882) and *The Story of My Childhood* (1907).

Barton, William E[leazar] (1861–1930),   clergyman, author. Barton first wrote *A Tale of the Cumberland Mountains* (1887), republished in 1890, with additions as *Life in the Hills of Kentucky*. Later Barton made himself an authority on the life of Lincoln, writing *The Paternity of Abraham Lincoln* and *The Soul of Abraham Lincoln* (both 1920), *The Life of Abraham Lincoln* (1925), *The Lineage of Lincoln* (1929), and *Lincoln at Gettysburg* (1930). His *Autobiography* appeared in 1932.

Bartram, John (1699–1777),   botanist, explorer, author. Born in Pennsylvania, orphaned early, and self-educated, Bartram became, according to Linnaeus, "the greatest natural botanist in the world." On land purchased in 1728 on the banks of the Schuylkill River, near Philadelphia, he established the first botanical garden in the United States. His *Observations* (1761) described his travels "from Pennsylvania to Onondaga, Oswego, and Lake Ontario." Appointed by George III as Royal Botanist of the Floridas, he traveled to that newly won British possession in 1765–66, publishing a journal of that trip, illustrated by his son William Bartram, as *A Description of East Florida* (1769).

Bartram, William (1739–1833),   botanist, explorer, author. Son of John Bartram, raised in the Quaker faith on the grounds of his father's botanic garden, he eventually outstripped the fame of the elder Bartram on the strength of one book, his *Travels Through North and South Carolina, Georgia, East and West Florida* (1791). William had traveled with his father in his youth to rural Pennsylvania and New York. When the chance for the Florida trip of 1765–66 came, with that territory opening up to the English as a result of the Peace of Paris of 1763, he took it, accompanying his father and drawing the sketches that illustrated his father's journal. Later he set out on an expedition that lasted four years (1773–77) and took him into Florida and west to the Mississippi, providing the material for his *Travels*.

Although William, like his father, listed the flora and fauna of his travels (his list of 215 native birds was the most comprehensive of his time), his fame derived more from his descriptive and narrative powers than from his achievement as a naturalist. Published in England almost immediately after its first appearance in the United States, the *Travels* supported many Europeans in their romantic sense of the beauties, dangers, and natural sublimity of the American frontier. Writers such as Coleridge, Wordsworth, Southey, and Chateaubriand admired him and sometimes mined his work for their own primitive or pastoral images. Bartram's genuine love of the wilderness still shines through his best set pieces: his descriptions of the lush and fruitful forests and savannahs, the roaring of the alligators, the menace of the rattlesnakes, the bountiful waters, the Indian maids joyful in strawberry fields.

See *The Travels*, ed. Francis Harper (1958); N. Bryllion Fagin, *William Bartram* (1933); and Ernest Earnest, *John and William Bartram* (1940).

Baruch, Bernard [Mannes] (1870–1965),   financier, government advisor. Born in South Carolina, Baruch was educated City College of New York. He served the federal government in many capacities, including membership in the commission in charge of all purchases for the Allies during World War I. He became adviser to James F. Byrnes, war mobilization director, in 1943, and was made U.S. representative to the United Nations Atomic Energy Commission in 1946. He wrote *American Industry in the War* (1941), *A Philosophy for our Time* (1954), *Baruch: My Own Story* (1957), and *Baruch, the Public Years* (1960).

Barzun, Jacques [Martin] (1907–   ),   teacher, critic. Born in Paris, Barzun came to the U.S. in 1919. After completing his studies at Columbia University, he remained there as a professor of history, dean, and eventually provost. Among his books are *The French Race* (1932), *Race! A Study in Modern Superstition* (1937), *Romanticism and the Modern Ego* (1943), *Teacher in America* (1945), *Berlioz and the Romantic Century* (1950), *God's Country and Mine* (1954), and *The House of Intellect* (1959). The last is an attack on the pseudointellectual world of modern society. In *Science: The Glorious Entertainment* (1964) he deflates scientists' view of their calling. Other titles include *The American University* (1968); *The Use and Abuse of Art* (1974); and *A Word or Two Before You Go* (1986), essays. *From Dawn to Decadence* (2000) is a survey of 500 years of cultural history.

Bassett, John Spencer (1867–1928),   historian, biographer, editor. Bassett taught history at Trinity College (now Duke University) and nearly lost his position when he spoke out boldly on the Negro question in the October 1903 issue of the *South Atlantic Quarterly*, which he had founded in 1902. From 1906 on he taught at Smith College and inaugurated the *Smith College Studies in History*. Among his more important writings are *Anti-Slavery Leaders of North Carolina* (1898), *The Writings of Colonel William Byrd* (1901), *The Federalist System* (1906), *The Life of Andrew Jackson* (1911), *A Short History of the United States* (1913), *The Middle Group of American Historians* (1917), *The Southern Plantation Overseer as Revealed in His Letters* (1925), and *Expansion and Reform* (1926).

Basso, [Joseph] Hamilton (1904–1964),   novelist. Born in New Orleans, Basso began writing for newspapers, including the *Times-Picayune*, and from 1944 on was a frequent contributor to *The New Yorker*. His novels include *Relics and Angels* (1929); *Cinnamon Seed* (1934); *In Their Own Image* (1935); *Courthouse Square* (1936); *Days Before Lent* (1939); *Sun in Capricorn* (1942), about a politician much like HUEY LONG; *The View from Pompey's Head* (1942), concerning a man returning to the South after living in New York; *The Light Infantry Ball* (1959); and *A Touch of the Dragon* (1964). *Beauregard: The Great Creole* (1933) is a biography of the Confederate general. *Mainstream* (1943) concerns great Americans from colonial days to Franklin Roosevelt. *A Quota of Seaweed* (1960) collects travel sketches.

Bat, The (1920), a mystery play by MARY ROBERTS RINEHART and AVERY HOPWOOD. This play, which ran on Broadway for 867 performances, was based on Mrs. Rinehart's equally successful novel, THE CIRCULAR STAIRCASE (1908).

Bateman, Sidney Frances [Cowell] (1823–1881), actress, playwright. Cowell appeared on the stage in New Orleans in 1837, and in 1839 married Hezekiah Linthicum Bateman, a theatrical manager. At the latter's St. Louis theater she produced *Self* (1856) and *The Golden Calf* (1857), satires on society in New York and in Europe. In New York she followed with *Geraldine* or *Love's Victory* (1859). In 1860 she dramatized Longfellow's EVANGELINE, with her daughter Kate (1843–1917) in the leading role. Kate toured England with such success that her family followed her, and Mrs. Bateman became a prosperous manager of several London theaters. In 1880 she produced JOAQUIN MILLER's *The Danites*, the first all-American company in an American play given in London.

Bates, Arlo (1850–1918), novelist, poet, English professor. Born in Maine, Bates was educated at Bowdoin, worked on a newspaper in Boston, and taught at MIT. His volumes of verse include *Sonnets in Shadow* (1887). His novels are *Mr. Jacobs* (1883); *The Pagans* (1884); *A Wheel of Fire* (1885); *The Philistines* (1889), about a painter who marries into Boston society; and *The Puritans* (1898). *The Intoxicated Ghost* (1908) collects stories. His textbooks include *Talks on the Study of Literature* (1895) and *Talks on Writing English* (1896; second series 1901).

Bates, Ernest Sutherland (1879–1939), teacher, author. Bates's best-known book is *The Bible Designed to Be Read as Living Literature* (1936), a skillful and reverent rearrangement of the King James Version. He likewise dealt with the Bible in *The Friend of Jesus* (1928), an account of Judas Iscariot, and wrote *A Biography of the Bible* (1937). Bates became intensely interested in America, its creed and its great figures; his last book, published posthumously, was *The American Faith* (1940).

Bates, Katharine Lee (1850–1929), teacher, poet, editor. Bates spent the greater part of her adult life as a professor of English at Wellesley. She wrote short stories and books for children, but her reputation rests on the widespread acceptance of AMERICA THE BEAUTIFUL (1895).

Bathtub Hoax, The. This incident represents H.L. MENCKEN's fulfillment of the notion that you can fool all of the people some of the time. On Dec. 28, 1917, Mencken published in the New York *Evening Mail* an article entitled "A Neglected Anniversary." It presented a series of preposterous statements regarding the origin of bathtub bathing in the United States in the 1840s, all of them invented by the Baltimore humorist. But his so-called facts were promptly accepted as gospel and found their way into innumerable newspaper and magazine articles, lectures by self-styled authorities, and even government publications and history texts. Curtis D. MacDougall, in his book on *Hoaxes* (1940), winds up with Mencken's masterpiece as a grand finale. Robert McHugh edited *The Bathtub Hoax, and Other Blasts and Bravos; from the Chicago Tribune* (1958).

Battle Hymn of the Republic, The (published in the *Atlantic Monthly*, Feb. 1862, and in *Later Lyrics*, 1866), a poem by JULIA WARD HOWE. Late in 1861 she and her husband, Samuel Gridley Howe, both deeply interested in philanthropic causes and the success of the Union, visited Washington. It was after Bull Run, and the capital was a gloomy place. On their way back they sang a song popular with the soldiers of the Northern Army—*John Brown's Body*. A member of the party named J.F. Clarke urged Mrs. Howe, who had already published two volumes of verse, to write words to the music of this song—"good words for a stirring tune." That night, toward the dawn, Mrs. Howe awakened and found the words of a poem in her head, ready to march with the tune. With a sudden effort, she relates, she sprang out of bed, and in order not to awaken a baby who slept near her, she wrote, without a light, *The Battle Hymn*.

Battle of Bunkers Hill, The (1776), a play in blank verse by HUGH HENRY BRACKENRIDGE, written for performance by his students at Somerset Academy in Maryland. American and British officers discuss successively the question of American courage.

Battle of the Kegs, The (1778), a satirical poem by FRANCIS HOPKINSON. This ballad tells the story of an actual incident. Kegs charged with gunpowder were sent in January 1778 down the Delaware River from Bordentown, in a manner designed to harass the British fleet anchored at Philadelphia. Only one of the kegs exploded, killing four men and creating a panic among the British. These mechanical kegs had been built in the cooperage of Col. Joseph Borden, Hopkinson's father-in-law. Hopkinson's verses spread rapidly through the colonies and annoyed the British deeply. Angered as much by the poem as by the kegs themselves, they razed the home and store of Col. Borden. The poem is still amusing. It is sung to the tune of *Yankee Doodle*. See SIR WILLIAM HOWE.

Battle-Pieces and Aspects of the War (1866), a book of poems by HERMAN MELVILLE. Comprising seventy-two poems, this collection of verses on the Civil War shows the wrack of the country as something to be mourned and pitied. In *Battle-Pieces* there is a sense of the tragedy of early death, and a renewed passion for human suffering, and the best poems reflect a deeply elegiac temper.

Baum, L[yman] Frank (1856–1919), newspaperman, editor, dramatist, writer for juveniles. Born in Chittenango, New York, and educated at Peekskill Military Academy,

Baum tried many trades, including poultry farmer and salesman, before he began writing children's books and won popular success with *Father Goose* (1899). A year later his reputation was firmly established with THE WONDERFUL WIZARD OF OZ. Baum continued to the end of his life to write about misadventures in Oz, fourteen books in all. It was a land of great happiness and strange creatures—the Tin Woodman, the Cowardly Lion, the Wizard, the Scarecrow. In 1901 a musical extravaganza called *The Wizard of Oz*, starring Montgomery and Stone, packed the theaters; in 1939 a motion picture of the same name, starring Judy Garland, was equally successful and became a classic. Baum also wrote books for boys under the pen names Captain Hugh Fitzgerald and Floyd Akers; for girls under the pen name Mrs. Edith Van Dyne. Three adventure tales were signed Schuyler Stanton.

Baxter, Charles (1947–   ),   novelist, short-story writer, poet. Born in Minneapolis, Baxter was educated at Macalester College and earned a Ph.D. at the State University of New York at Buffalo; he teaches at the University of Michigan. *Chameleon* (1970), his first publication, is a collection of poetry, as is *Imaginary Paintings and Other Poems* (1990). Critics have been most interested in Baxter's fiction, characterized by the inclusion of realistic details of life in the Middle West. *Harmony of the World* (1984), with its award-winning title story, was followed the next year by *Through the Safety Net* (1985). In the stories of *A Relative Stranger* (1990), characters are jolted out of their stolid lives by people they meet. *Believers* (1997) includes a novella and stories set in Michigan.

First Light (1987), Baxter's first novel, is written in reverse chronological order, prefaced by a quote from Kierkegaard ". . . life can only be understood backwards." Hugh Welch and his sister Dorsey are reunited on the 4th of July; as the novel proceeds we find out the reasons for their strained relationship. Wyatt Palmer of *Shadow Play* (1993) is emotionally paralyzed due to his distressing childhood, which included an unstable foster brother for whom he feels responsible. *The Feast of Love* (2000) treats the blemished loves of ordinary people in a town geographically reminiscent of Ann Arbor, Michigan, where Baxter now lives.

Burning Down the House: Essays on Fiction appeared in 1997.

Bayou Folk (1894),   a collection of twenty-three stories by KATE CHOPIN. They are varied tales of the Creoles and Acadians of the Louisiana bayous—delicate, humorous, tragic, and sympathetic.

Bay Psalm Book, The (1640),   full title *The Whole Booke of Psalms Faithfully Translated into English Metre*. The translators were RICHARD MATHER, Thomas Weld, and JOHN ELIOT, along with other ministers; and they used the King James Version as the basis for their translations. The book—the first bound book printed in the colonies—was published in Cambridge in an edition of 1,700 copies by Stephen Daye, a locksmith who had come to Massachusetts two years before. It sold for one shilling eightpence a copy. To facilitate church use, only six metrical forms were used and most of the psalms appeared in common meter, short meter, or long meter; suggestions for appropriate tunes appeared at the end of the book.

Beach, Rex (1877–1949),   novelist. Born in Michigan, Beach is remembered chiefly for novels of Alaska. Among these are *Pardners* (1905); *The Spoilers* (1906), on gold mining; *The Silver Horde* (1909), on salmon fishing; and *The Iron Trail* (1913), about a woman journalist in the Yukon. Other titles include *The Ne'er-do-well* (1911), *The Auction Block* (1914), *Wild Pastures* (1935), and *The World in His Arms* (1945). His autobiography is *Personal Exposures* (1941).

Beach, Sylvia (1887–1962),   bookseller. An expatriate who kept a bookshop at No. 12 Rue de l'Odéon, Paris, commercially known as Shakespeare & Co., Beach did much to encourage new and young writers of all nationalities during the late 1920s. She told the story of this venture in *Shakespeare & Co.* (1959). She published James Joyce's *Ulysses* (1922) in France, using French typesetters, and shared with him the literary and legal assaults that the book provoked. In 1950 she received the Clairovin Memorial Award for her translation of Henri Michaux's *A Barbarian in Asia*.

Beadle, Erastus F[lavel] (1821–1894),   editor, author, publisher. In 1858 Beadle, with his brother Irwin P. Beadle and with Robert Adams, formed the New York City firm of Beadle and Adams. Orville J. Victor became their editor, and during the next thirty years he selected for the firm the thousands of tales that they published. The firm's slogan was "a dollar book for a dime," and they enormously increased the reading public of the day. They began with song books and joke books. In 1860 the first dime novel was issued. This was MALEASKA, THE INDIAN WIFE OF THE WHITE HUNTER, by ANN S. STEPHENS. Another early success was EDWARD S. ELLIS's SETH JONES, OR THE CAPTIVE OF THE FRONTIER (1860), of which 600,000 copies were sold in half a dozen languages. Others who wrote for the firm were Captain Mayne Reid, Ned Buntline, Edward L. Wheeler and Colonel Prentiss Ingraham. See DIME NOVEL.

Bear, The,   novella by WILLIAM FAULKNER, published in its final form in 1942 as part of a group of related stories entitled *Go Down, Moses*. The book deals with the saga of the McCaslin family's plantation in Yoknapatawpha County as representative of the South's history and destiny. Like *Go Down* itself, "The Bear" unfolds, in modernist style, out of chronological sequence and is divided into five sections.

The first takes place in 1883 when Isaac ("Ike") McCaslin, grandson of the founder, is 16 and begins by mentioning the wild dog, Lion, which was trained to help hunt down Old Ben, the great mythical bear that the men of the county pursue every year, without any real intention of killing him, but as a kind of ritual—until the time comes when Old Ben doesn't want to live anymore. This section also contains flashbacks to Ike's 10th and 11th years when he was first permitted, under the tutelage of Sam Fathers, the half-Indian-half-black chief hunter, to see the bear.

The second shows Ike between the ages of 12 and 15, when he witnesses the capture and training of Lion, and the approach of the time when Old Ben will finally be killed.

The third brings us back to Ike at 16 and the climax of the hunt: the bear and Lion are killed, and Sam dies mysteriously—his time coterminous with Old Ben's.

Section four, itself as long as the rest of the story and much more complex, flashes forward to when Ike is 21 and discussing the tragedy of his family's history—miscegenation, incest, slavery—with his older cousin Cass. Having decided to relinquish his inheritance, he explains that he views the South's history as part of God's plan to redeem man's inhumanity to man by a kind of homeopathic purging of evil by evil, until it reaches a point where people see they must stop. It began in Europe and was transplanted and repeated here by the European settlers, who took the land from the Indians (themselves participating in the evil by sometimes selling the land to the settlers) and brought slaves from Africa to build their plantations. The South's suffering in the Civil War was also part of the divine blue-print, and now (1888) the descendants of the slaveholders must find ways of breaking the chain of guilt.

Furthermore, Ike sees that what he learned in the wilderness as a hunter motivates this repudiation of his history: compassion, humility, harmony with natural process, and the communal anonymity of brotherhood, as opposed to the possessiveness, aggrandizement, and subjugation of fellow human beings represented by the tamed land of the plantation. Cass, who agrees with Ike on the diagnosis, cannot accept his prescription for the cure. Representing history, in contradistinction to Ike's myth, he argues in turn that they can't fulfill their responsibility simply by running away from it—in effect, they must stay with their burden and actually do something practical to destroy the bondage of the African-American, even as Uncle Buck and Uncle Buddy tried; and even as Ike himself, when younger, tried—searching out Tennie's Jim in 1885—to give him his legacy.

Section five flashes back to when Ike was 18, the time-shift seeming to emphasize the effect of timelessness. Returning to the scene of the hunt, Ike realizes that the glory of the wilderness is giving way before the encroachments of civilization (in this case a railroad and a sawmill), and paradoxically achieves a kind of mystic acceptance of the endless cycles of time and knowledge of immortality—symbolized by his encountering a snake and saluting it, as Sam Fathers had done, as a totemic animal.

"The Bear," when read as a separate story, seems to endorse Ike's myth, but "Delta Autumn," which is the penultimate story in *Go Down*, shows Ike as a lonely, lost, and bitter old man who cannot accept history. Faulkner probably intended the reader to see truth in both views and falsehood in either when taken alone.

NORMAN FRIEDMAN

Beard, Charles A[ustin] (1874–1948),   historian. Born in Indiana, Beard was educated at DePauw University, Oxford, Cornell, and Columbia. After teaching at Columbia (1904–17), he resigned as a protest over the university's treatment of pacifist professors and helped found the New School for Social Research, which he directed from 1917 to 1922. His textbooks helped shape the teaching of history to encompass economics, intellectual and cultural life, and politics. Among them is the classic *The Development of Modern Europe* (1907), written with JAMES HARVEY ROBINSON. Much of his best work, however, was on the United States. In *An Economic Interpreta-*

tion of the Constitution (1913) and *Economic Origins of Jeffersonian Democracy* (1915), he described the influence of conservative thought and economic self-interest on the men of property among the country's founding fathers. Other early books included *American Government and Politics* (1910), *American City Government* (1912), and *The Economic Basis of Politics* (1922, revised 1945).

Beard's long collaboration with his wife, MARY R. BEARD, bore early fruit with *American Citizenship* (1913). Together they earned fame with graceful, panoramic histories for the general public, including *The Rise of American Civilization* (2 v. 1927), *America in Mid-Passage* (1939), and *The American Spirit* (1943). Their *Basic History of the United States* appeared in 1944 (revised, 1960). Charles Beard's other works on his own include *A Charter for the Social Sciences* (1932), *Public Policy and the General Welfare* (1941), *American Foreign Policy in the Making: 1932–1940* (1946), and *President Roosevelt and the Coming of the War: 1941* (1948). Criticized in his early career as a radical, he was in later life sometimes seen as an arch-conservative, particularly for his opposition to F.D.R. and his policies.

Beard, Daniel C[arter] (1850–1941),   naturalist, author, artist, Boy Scout leader. Born in Ohio, Beard became a founder of the Boy Scout movement in the United States and its constant mentor in woodcraft and nature lore. Among his books are *American Boys' Handy Book* (1882), *Boy Pioneers and Sons of Daniel Boone* (1909), *Do It Yourself* (1925), *The Wisdom of the Woods* (1927), and his autobiography, *Hardly a Man Is Now Alive* (1939).

Beard, Mary R[itter] (1876–1958),   historian. Remembered especially for histories written in collaboration with her husband CHARLES A. BEARD, Mary Beard was born in Indiana and married her husband in 1900. On her own, she was interested in women and labor, writing *A Short History of the American Labor Movement* (1920, revised 1925), *On Understanding Women* (1931), *America through Women's Eyes* (1934), *Woman: Co-Maker of History* (1940), *Women as a Force in History* (1946), and *The Making of Charles A. Beard* (1955). With Martha Bensley Bruère she edited an anthology, *Laughing Their Way: Women's Humor in America* (1934).

Beare and Ye Club [or Cubb], Ye (1665),   a play, the first in English known to have been performed in the colonies. The authors, all Virginians, were Cornelius Watkinson, Philip Howard, and William Darby. The play was accused of licentiousness, but the playwrights were acquitted after it was performed in court. The text has disappeared.

Beat Generation.   The Beat movement emerged into public attention in 1956 with the publication of Allen Ginsberg's HOWL AND OTHER POEMS and Jack Kerouac's ON THE ROAD. The movement was not purely literary but expressed a state of mind embodied in the Bohemian atmosphere of New York City's Greenwich Village and San Francisco's North Beach, and was well underway by the end of World War II. It later spread to Venice West, where Lawrence Lipton memorialized it in *The Holy Barbarians* (1959). The social atmosphere of the Beat movement produced a rebellious tone of disaffiliation from society and a devotion to the concept of voluntary poverty.

Socially speaking, the main tone was negative, and the movement was primarily an evasion rather than an attempt to improve the conditions it protested against. An anarchic individualism was the primary motivating force—although a remarkable sameness of dress, a ritual use of hip language and jazz argot, and a tendency to cluster together in espresso bars and party pads created the image of a community with a relaxed tone and common rites.

Many of the patterns of this community were agreeable to the Beat writers, who found in its milieu an audience and an atmosphere for their work. In the term *beat* they retained the common meaning of worn-out, tired, and pooped but saw in this depressed condition a possible way of escaping from the strictures and what they saw as false values of conventional society. Hence *beat* took on connotations of blessedness: beatific, beatitude, beatified. To the Beat writers, the way down was the way out, and through voluntary poverty, conscientious disaffiliation from the blandishments of an adjusted life, and complete annihilation of the motives of an acquisitive society, they sought illumination and joy. The concept of illumination was central to their view of life. It might result from simple surrender to the process of experience, from sexual ecstasy, from drunkenness and abandon, from such hallucinogenic drugs as peyote and LSD, from the disciplines of Buddhism, from anything that increased the illusion of receptivity to life. Their main aim was release—from the confines of social and moral judgment, from the conventions of literature.

Among the chief writers are ALLEN GINSBERG, JACK KEROUAC, GREGORY CORSO, WILLIAM BURROUGHS, LAWRENCE FERLINGHETTI, JOHN CLELLON HOLMES, MICHAEL MCCLURE, GARY SNYDER, and PHIL WHALEN. Numerous other writers shared their preoccupations in one way or another, and certain older and more established writers supported them, notably Norman Mailer, Henry Miller, Kenneth Rexroth (briefly), and William Carlos Williams. With the exceptions of Kerouac, Burroughs, and Holmes, the Beat writers are best known as poets, and their work is often symbolized by Allen Ginsberg's *Howl*, a prophetic poem, a form of jeremiad written in a long line derived from the Bible, Whitman, Blake, and Christopher Smart. The poem treats a world in which all values have become dehumanized; it is a diatribe against a military and commercial society. The first section of the poem describes the fate of "the best minds of my generation." Their lives are disorderly, self-destructive, criminal, and insane. Their experience is chaotic and their suffering unredeemed. Life offers neither security nor stability, and the measures of society create a false and vulnerable order. These judgments are presented in a blend of jazz argot, surrealist imagery, and violent action.

The second section of the poem ascribes to Moloch the immediate cause of these conditions. This generation ". . . broke their backs lifting Moloch to heaven!" The veneration of false values is the betrayal of the American dream, and the sensitive and percipient person is driven into outlawry. The third section addresses Carl Solomon (to whom the poem is dedicated) with the refrain "I am with you in Rockland" (a mental hospital), to express the author's identification with suffering human life. The footnote to *Howl*, which is a coda to the poem, declares the absolute holiness of all existence, however stultified and depraved.

Between *Howl and Other Poems* (1956) and *Kaddish* (1961), Ginsberg published various poems in magazines and attained a certain notoriety in the mass media. He traveled widely in Europe and in the United States and read his poems at various colleges, as did Gregory Corso and other Beat writers. His work remained concerned with the same basic subjects. *Kaddish* is a long prophetic poem, overtly personal and focused on the life and death of the poet's mother. It is permeated with a tone of deep sadness, is less hortatory and satiric than *Howl*, and suggests a greater variety and range. Ginsberg's work displays many of the interests of the Beats: drugs, hallucinogenic and addictive; sexual disorder; voluntary poverty; rejection of the society; quest for illumination; jazz rhythms and hip language; and rootless wandering.

In Kerouac's Beat novels (especially *On the Road, The Subterraneans*, and *The Dharma Bums*), he presents a quasi-fictional view of the Beat milieu. The Beat novels form only a relatively small part of Kerouac's total work. His aim as a writer was to create a comprehensive image of his experience, beginning with his childhood in Lowell, Massachusetts. In this respect his work resembles that of Thomas Wolfe and Henry Miller, and like them he is extremely uneven. His obsession with the details of his own life often overloads his stories with irrelevancies, and he has no clear sense of fictional form. His works tend to be either prolonged portraits of individuals who have a special importance to him or picaresque delineations of casual events, or of experience as one thing after another.

On the Road is picaresque in structure and episodic. Its characteristic action is either hitchhiking across country for no purpose or driving cars at outrageous speeds from New Orleans to New York to Denver to San Francisco with no particular aim in mind. The book reflects an existence without coherent structure. There is no reason for the actions of the novel, and the total effect is to suggest a group of people in constant flux, with no enduring loyalties to place or person. The characters seek sensation, and their few efforts to reach some condition that gives sensation context and meaning are fumbling and doomed. *The Subterraneans* is less episodic and more concentrated, largely because it centers on an attempt between a man and woman to establish a valid sexual relation. The milieu is also more tightly fixed, in San Francisco's North Beach, and the result is a sharpening of effect. *The Dharma Bums* treats the same basic milieu, with extensive side trips into the mountains of California and the Pacific Northwest. The character of Japhy in this book, like most of Kerouac's figures, is modeled on a particular figure who attracts his prolonged interest. The original of the highly distorted portrait, Gary Snyder, is one of the most highly regarded Beat poets.

Of the Beat writers, Gary Snyder has the most extensive genuine knowledge of Buddhism. He has a scholar's knowledge of Chinese and Japanese and has spent much time in the Orient. Snyder's poetry reflects a childhood experience in the great forests of the Pacific Northwest, intensive studies of

Amerindian legend, studies in Oriental philosophy and religion, and travels as a logger in the United States and as a seaman on the oceans of the world. His first book, *Riprap* (1959), is essentially a selection from early poems that grew out of experience gained in working in various areas. His early work sounds a great deal like the nature poems of Kenneth Rexroth, from whom Snyder takes much of his poetic discipline. His second book, *Myths and Texts* (1960), is a highly organized presentation of life on the Pacific Coast, divided into three sections. Section 1, "Logging," shows the destruction of the natural landscape in the interests of commerce. Section 2, "Hunting," shows the destruction of the fauna. Section 3, "Fire," treats the irrational desires of men and thus clarifies the motives that led to the actions of the first two sections. He uses Amerindian legends and Buddhist myths to frame the several actions of the book, and he employs many of the verse techniques of Ezra Pound's cantos. Like Pound and Rexroth, Snyder also translates from Chinese and Japanese poetry, and he writes extremely observant and percipient prose.

Phil Whalen has been associated with Snyder since their years together at Reed College. He is also a student of Buddhism. He is an extremely beguiling writer, and of the Beat poets the most consistently humorous. Some of his most amusing poems treat his plight as an uninspired poet. His observation of the natural world shows his affinity with Rexroth and William Carlos Williams. *Like I Say* (1960) is a collection of his early poems. *Memoirs of an Interglacial Age* (1960) shows his development toward a more fluent and introspective verse.

Michael McClure, who accompanied Whalen on his first reading tour of American colleges, has been associated with the Beat writers from their first emergence. His *Hymns to Saint Geryon* contains many finely shaped poems, including a long analysis of his state of mind during an experiment with peyote. His following book, *Dark Brown* (1961), is an exploration of the concept of complete physical abandon. His work is tightly conceived and ordered, with an extremely physical sense of the weight and impact of the poetic line.

Lawrence Ferlinghetti, who at one time was the most popular of the Beat poets, is also a publisher (City Lights Books). He has provided an outlet for Ginsberg and Corso, and has printed some of his own work and the work of writers not necessarily associated with the Beat movement. His poetry resembles the work of Jacques Prévert, which Ferlinghetti has translated. His *Pictures of the Gone World* (1955) shows the influence not only of Prévert, but also of Apollinaire and Cummings. *A Coney Island of the Mind* (1958) includes some poems from the earlier book and many new poems. He is a gifted public reader and has read some of his poems to jazz accompaniment, as have Whalen and Kerouac. His work is good-tempered and witty, but it has considerable bite. Unlike most of the Beat writers, he is seriously concerned with political issues, and his popularity is at least partly due to his sense of the public relevance of poetry.

Gregory Corso, like Ferlinghetti, has a winning impudence and ready wit. His first book, *The Vestal Lady of Brattle* (1955),

shows his natural irreverence, but his best work appears in *Gasoline* (1958) and *The Happy Birthday of Death* (1960). His chief poetic method seems to be to allow one image to suggest another, until the highest level of logical irrelevancy is attained. He intends to be provocative and annoying; one of his favorite devices is to choose a word—*bomb, power, army, marriage*—and play variations of the several themes suggested by it. In his effort to be impudent he is sometimes dangerously frivolous, as in "Bomb," but when he controls and plays with his subject to establish a fitting tone, he can be remarkably effective, as in "Marriage." Even when he is most frivolous, there is a deep undercurrent of sadness in his work, and an abiding seriousness.

W. S. Burroughs stands apart from the other Beat writers because of the relative isolation of his life and the savagery of his work. He enjoyed a considerable subterranean reputation before *The Naked Lunch* (Paris, 1959) appeared as a whole. The typescript had been circulating for some years, and parts of the book had appeared in magazines of limited circulation. It is a long, nightmarish book, designed as the expression and revelation of a sick mind in a sick world. In it depravity reaches levels normally reserved to the wildest dreams of the criminally insane. No limit is prescribed to the imagination, and physiological processes are described with callous iteration of detail. By Burroughs' own testimony, he intends to shock the mind past complacency to a full understanding of the horror of existence. He represents a world toward which other Beat writers move only tentatively—a world of absolute need and absolute moral emptiness that his characters experience and that he symbolizes in the helpless condition of the dope addict. When moral emptiness is attained, depravity rushes to fill the void, so that in the later sections of *The Naked Lunch* a hideous inversion of morality becomes the norm. Burroughs, in spite of his avowed intentions, is the only true nihilist among the Beat writers.

The Beat movement had two separable elements. The first was a social group, the Beatniks, as they were derisively dubbed. After a period of faddish notoriety that lasted until about 1960, the Beatniks left public attention and, in effect, ceased to exist as a coherent group. In this social sense, the Beat movement hardly represented a generation. American Bohemia had merely taken a special and relatively transitory form that was symptomatic and clarifying but had no enduring power as a social force. In literary terms, however, the Beat movement brought to public attention the works of several writers who remained productive and who developed toward increasing maturity of perception.

The emergence of the Beat writers called attention to other experimental writers—notably of the SAN FRANCISCO RENAISSANCE and BLACK MOUNTAIN COLLEGE groups who had until that time been relatively ignored. The example of Burroughs, Kerouac, and Ginsberg had some influence on other writers of prose and verse. The accomplishments of Beat writers are largely the introduction of special tones and personal qualities. Ginsberg's work has tone—personality—and is very carefully structured and designed. It opens out on the international tradition of literature that stems in large part from Whitman, and it brings vividly into English many of the designs of Appollinaire, Cendrars, Desnos, Breton, and other Europeans. Snyder's translations from Oriental languages are widely admired by competent Orientalists, and his original poetry has the density and force that suggest a distinguished and enduring poetic legacy. Kerouac's novels, conceding their unevenness in texture and flaws of structure, have intermittent scenes of brilliance and persuasiveness. Numerous individual poems by Corso, Ferlinghetti, McClure, and Whalen are also compelling and successful.

The New American Poetry (1960), edited by Donald M. Allen, included Beat and other experimental poets, with extensive bibliography. It was revised as *The Postmoderns: The New American Poetry Revised* (1982). Other books on the beats are *The Beat Generation and the Angry Young Men* (1958), G. Feldman and M. Gartenberg, eds.; *The Beats* (1960), Seymour Krim, ed.; and *The Beat Scene* (1960), Elias Wilentz, ed. Francis Rigney's *The Real Bohemia* (1961) made a sociological study of the Beatniks of San Francisco's North Beach. Lawrence Lipton's *The Holy Barbarians* (1959) used the Venice West colony to comment on the social importance of the Beat movement. *The Beat Hotel: Ginsberg, Burroughs and Corso in Paris, 1958–1963* (2000) was written by Barry Miles.

THOMAS PARKINSON/CP

Beath, Paul R. See FEBOLD FEBOLDSON.

Beattie, Ann (1947–), novelist, short-story writer. Born in Washington, D.C., Beattie was educated at American University and the University of Connecticut. She has taught at Harvard and the University of Virginia. A child of the sixties, she came into the tranquil seventies in a sophisticated East Coast environment no longer pulsing with social activism. Her characters are of that same generation, young, educated, middle class, bored by the anomie of their existence. Alienated from loved ones and society, some hold jobs well below the level of their education, or remain unemployed; all lack satisfactory personal goals. In spare and lucid prose, Beattie defines them by indirection, seeing them through others, through the mirror of their self-reflections, and in significant part by the light of the headlines, television shows, consumer products, and popular songs that situate them in time. Her novels are *Chilly Scenes of Winter* (1976), about a man who yearns for the wife who left him; *Falling in Place* (1980), where the falling of Skylab provides a metaphor for characters falling in their lives; *Love Always* (1985), about characters writing for or acting in the soap opera that serves as central metaphor; and *Picturing Will* (1990), a record of a boy in his sixth year, abandoned by his father and tied to a mother whose primary concern seems to be her career as photographer. *My Life, Starring Dara Falcon* (1997) details the effect of a glamorous newcomer on the life and expectations of Jean Warner, a young, traditional wife.

Beattie's short stories are among the best in a rich period for the American short story. Gems of precise and witty observation, many published first in THE NEW YORKER, they treat the same materials as her novels. Collections are *Distortions* (1976), *Secrets and Surprises* (1978), *The Burning House* (1982), *Where You'll Find Me* (1986), *Park City: New and Selected Stories* (1998), and *Perfect Recall* (2001).

Beauchamp, Lucas, a character created by WILLIAM FAULKNER. Lucas, the son of ex-slaves and grandson of Carothers McCaslin, the founder of the McCaslin family, is a dignified and independent man who lives on the borderline between the white and African-American worlds, thus causing a great deal of consternation to those white people who consider him arrogant and disrespectful. He is a main character in INTRUDER IN THE DUST and in "The Fire and the Hearth," a short story in GO DOWN, MOSES.

Beauchampe, or, The Kentucky Tragedy (1842), a novel by WILLIAM GILMORE SIMMS. Simms used as the basis of his novel an astonishing crime that had won nationwide attention. Anna Cook, a Kentucky girl who had been seduced by Col. Solomon P. Sharp, married an attorney, Jeroboam O. Beauchamp, in 1825 and made him take an oath to kill her seducer. He tried several times and finally succeeded in stabbing Sharp to death (Nov. 5, 1825) in Frankfort. Put on trial, Beauchamp denied his guilt but was convicted. The evening before the execution, Anna joined him, and both took an overdose of laudanum. Anna died, but Beauchamp survived to be hanged the next day. Beauchamp's own *Confession* (1826) was widely circulated; it included some verse by his wife. Thomas Holley Chivers treated the theme in his verse drama *Conrad and Eudora* (1834), Edgar Allan Poe in the tragedy POLITIAN (parts published, 1835–36; complete text, 1923). Charlotte Mary Barnes employed the plot in the blank-verse tragedy *Octavia Bragaldi, or, The Confession* (1837), as did Mary E. MacMichael in *The Kentucky Tragedy* (1838) and Charles Fenno Hoffman in the romance GREYSLAER (1849), dramatized by an anonymous author in the same year. Simms then wrote *Beauchampe, or, The Kentucky Tragedy, A Tale of Passion* (1842) and in 1856 expanded the first part of the book into a new novel, CHARLEMONT, OR, THE PRIDE OF THE VILLAGE, A TALE OF KENTUCKY. *Beauchampe* was revised to make the second part. After more than a century of obscurity, the plot came to life again in Robert Penn Warren's romantic novel WORLD ENOUGH AND TIME (1950), and in Joseph Shearing's *To Bed at Noon* (1951). See BORDER ROMANCES.

Beauties of Poetry, British and American, The (1791), a publication of MATHEW CAREY in Philadelphia believed to be the first anthology in book form published in this country.

Beauties of Santa Cruz, The (1776, published 1786), a poem by PHILIP FRENEAU. Freneau resided on Santa Cruz or St. Croix, in the Virgin Islands, for more than two years, apparently in an escape from the revolutionary troubles at home; he felt, on his return to the mainland, "as Adam did after he was banished from the bowers of Eden." The poem reveals Freneau as an early romantic poet.

Beautiful and Damned, The (1922), a novel by F. SCOTT FITZGERALD satirizing the younger generation. In the novel Fitzgerald defines the pervading goal of his day as "the final polish of the shoe, the ultimate dab of the clothes-brush, a sort of intellectual There!"

Beautiful Snow (*Harper's Weekly*, Nov. 27, 1858), an anonymously published poem that quickly became a folk classic. Now attributed to John Whitaker Watson (1824–1890), who reprinted it in a collection called *Beautiful Snow and Other Poems* (1869).

Beaver, Tony, a folk hero of West Virginia lumberjacks. His exploits took place in the Cumberland Mountains and have been related by Margaret Prescott Montague in *Up Eel River* (1928). Among other deeds, Tony invented peanut brittle when he threw surplus molasses and peanuts into the river to stop a dangerous flood.

Bech: A Book (1970) and **Bech Is Back** (1982), collections of stories by JOHN UPDIKE. The linked stories provide a wry and humorous commentary on a contemporary literary career through an examination of the life of the character Henry Bech, whom Updike distances from his own identity by making Bech Jewish.

Becker, Carl [Lotus] (1873–1945), teacher, historian. Becker became a disciple of FREDERICK JACKSON TURNER at the University of Wisconsin and spent the major part of his academic career at Cornell. Among his most important books, aside from textbooks, were *The Declaration of Independence; A Study in the History of Political Ideas* (1922), *The Heavenly City of the 18th-Century Philosophers* (1932), and *How New Will the Better World Be?* (1944).

Becknell, William (1790?–1832?), explorer, author. He traced the Santa Fe Trail in 1822; his *Journal* was published in the *Collections* (July, 1906) of the Missouri Historical Society.

Beckwourth, James P. (1798–1867?), hunter, explorer. Beckwourth, born in Virginia, wandered over many parts of the West and became well acquainted with Indian life. In his autobiography, *The Life and Adventures of James P. Beckwourth* (1856; reedited by Charles G. Leland, 1892), taken down by T. D. Bonner, he relates how he became a chief of the Crow Indians and adopted their habits and their dress, and took an Indian wife.

Bedott, Widow. See FRANCES M. WHITCHER.

Bedouin Song (1855), a lyric by BAYARD TAYLOR. Regarded by his age as a great writer, Taylor is known today chiefly for his poem, which achieved popularity in a musical setting as the *Bedouin Love Song*.

bedtime story. See THORNTON W. BURGESS and HOWARD R. GARIS.

Beebe, [Charles] William (1877–1962), naturalist, author. Beebe early found his vocation as a worker in science, and gained worldwide renown in 1934 with a record-breaking descent into the ocean depths near Bermuda in a bathysphere. He made numerous field expeditions and recorded his observations and experiences in scientific papers and in books for the general public. Among them are *Jungle Peace* (1918), *Galapagos, World's End* (1923), *Jungle Days* (1925), *Beneath Tropic Seas* (1928), *Nonsuch, Land of Water* (1932), *Half Mile Down* (1934), *Book of Naturalists* (1944), *High Jungle* (1949), and *Adventuring with Beebe* (selections from his writings, 1955).

Beecher, Catherine E[sther] (1800–1878), teacher, reformer, author. Beecher was the daughter of the Rev. LYMAN BEECHER; two of her brothers—EDWARD and HENRY WARD—and a sister—HARRIET BEECHER STOWE—became famous. She was among the first who sought to provide proper education for young women and helped organize schools and colleges for them in Hartford, Cincinnati, Milwaukee, and elsewhere. Her writings deal mainly with social and political problems; slavery, wrongs suffered by women and children, evils in education, woman suffrage. Her titles include *An Essay on Slavery and Abolitionism* (1837), *The Evils Suffered by American Women and . . . Children* (1846), *Physiology and Calisthenics for Schools and Families* (1856), *Women Suffrage* (1871), and *Educational Reminiscences and Suggestions* (1874).

Beecher, Edward (1803–1895), clergyman, editor, author. Another of LYMAN BEECHER's distinguished children; cofounder of *The Congregationalist* and editor-in-chief (1849–53). He published *The Conflict of Ages* (1853) and *The Concord of Ages* (1860).

Beecher, Henry Ward (1813–1887), clergyman, editor, author, lecturer. Born in Connecticut, Beecher was brought up by his father, LYMAN BEECHER, "to put my hand to anything"; and he was indeed adept at "anything" in the preaching, lecturing, and writing line. He was the only boy in the school for children conducted by his sister CATHERINE, was graduated from Amherst (1834) and the Lane Theological Seminary in Cincinnati; he was licensed to preach in 1837. He had various churches in western cities, was invited to a Boston church, and finally at his wife's insistence accepted a call (1847) to Plymouth Church in Brooklyn.

There he achieved his renown. He liked to illustrate his sermons with parables from everyday life, and displayed in many of them a sense of humor that might have made him an equally celebrated newspaper columnist. There were few references in his preaching to lakes of boiling pitch and eternal damnation or to the fore-ordination and election his father had preached. His philosophical trend, though somewhat vague, was taken from Emerson. He discarded reason as a guide and preferred the "secret chords of feeling." Parrington calls him "the high priest of emotional liberalism," who "swept his thousands of idolizing followers along the path of Utopian emotionalism." He praised liberty and love, man and a manlike God, with lyric enthusiasm; and Thoreau saw him as a "magnificent pagan." He preached extemporaneously, but his sermons were taken down, printed, and widely circulated. He declared against slavery and in favor of woman suffrage. He was not friendly to Lincoln and received a cold reception when he toured in some English cities mainly because of this fact. In 1874 THEODORE TILTON charged him with adultery with Mrs. Tilton. In a trial the following year the jury disagreed and Beecher, whom Plymouth Church had supported loyally, on his return there was given an ovation by the crowded and enthusiastic congregation. His reputation never recovered, but it is said that 40,000 persons attended his funeral.

Beecher edited THE INDEPENDENT from 1861 to 1864, *The Christian Union* from 1870 to 1881. *Seven Lectures to Young Men* (1844) was addressed to clerks, mechanics, and salesmen and has a flavor of Poor Richard. It was his most popular work. The book came after long and apparently prayerful study of Darwin, leading Beecher finally to an acceptance of the new science as a kind of religion *Evolution and Religion* was published in 1885. Between work on the two books, Beecher wrote lively, sensible essays on many topics, including *Plain and Pleasant Talk about Fruits, Flowers, and Farming* (1859); also a novel, *Norwood, or, Village Life in New England* (1868), containing good descriptions of New England landscape. His style in general was homely and racy, his details concrete; he was definitely an orator, even in print.

Beecher, Lyman (1775–1863),   preacher, author. Born in Connecticut, Beecher became one of the notable preachers of the day and the father of a large family, four of whom— CATHERINE, EDWARD, HENRY WARD, and HARRIET BEECHER STOWE—became celebrated. Beecher held pastorates at Easthampton, Long Island; Litchfield, Connecticut; Boston; and Cincinnati; he was president of the Lane Theological Seminary in Cincinnati (1832–52). He had studied theology under TIMOTHY DWIGHT at Yale and strongly supported traditional Calvinism, fighting what he called the "icy system" of Unitarianism. His household agonized and wept over the salvation of their souls, and regarded God as a stern detective watching children from above. So drastic was the domestic discipline that Henry Ward Beecher revolted from it and moved toward his liberal views of religion. Lyman Beecher was accused of heresy by more conservative groups, but was acquitted by the synod. Paxton Hibben describes him going up and down the country "rallying the forces against toleration, against innovation and democracy, against the separation of church and state." He denounced the use of liquor and was strongly anti-Catholic. The Beecher household probably provided the details for Harriet Beecher Stowe's OLDTOWN FOLKS (1869). Lyman Beecher's sermons and articles were gathered in his *Works* (1852) and in his *Autobiography*, which appeared in 1864.

Beer, Thomas (1889–1940),   novelist, short-story writer, biographer. Born in Iowa and a Yale graduate, Beer wrote three novels: *The Fair Rewards* (1922), *Sandoval* (1924), and *The Road to Heaven* (1928); also short stories, some collected as *Mrs. Egg and Other Barbarians* (1933, reprinted with additional stories in 1947), others as *The Agreeable Finish* (1941). His *Stephen Crane* (1923) did much to establish Crane's later reputation, though it depended on doubtful sources, some perhaps invented by Beer. Later Beer wrote *The Mauve Decade* (1926; reprinted, 1941) and *Hanna* (1929), both dealing with the 1890s.

Beers, Clifford [Whittingham]   (1876–1943), humanitarian. In *A Mind That Found Itself* (1908), Beers, who had been taken ill three years after his graduation from Yale, told of his experiences in various mental institutions and his

final recovery in the home of a kindly hospital attendant. His report made America aware that basic reforms were required if adequate care was to be given to its mentally ill. He established the National Commission for Mental Hygiene (1909) and was the founder of the International Foundation for Mental Hygiene (1931). Together with a number of assistants he published a quarterly, *Mental Hygiene*, and put out numerous pamphlets to combat the general lethargy on this subject. His revolutionary spirit inspired great social changes, and he was fortunate in seeing some of them in his lifetime.

Beers, Ethel Lynn   [pen name of **Ethelinda Eliot Beers**] (1827–1879), poet and short-story writer. Beers became known chiefly for her poem *The Picket Guard*, later called ALL QUIET ALONG THE POTOMAC, about an unknown soldier killed in the Civil War, published in *Harper's Weekly* in 1861. In 1879 appeared *All Quiet Along the Potomac and Other Poems*.

Before Adam (1906),   a novel by JACK LONDON. The story recounts the experiences of mankind in the far-distant past, with information supposedly taken from the narrator's dreams, in which he lives again the life of Big Tooth, a primitive ancestor. The dream technique somewhat resembles that employed later by London in THE STAR ROVERS (1914).

Beggar on Horseback (1924),   a comedy by GEORGE S. KAUFMAN and MARC CONNELLY, with music by Deems Taylor. This remarkably agile satire on big business and its ways with the artist takes its title from the proverbial phrase, and the idea of using a dream to express satire from a German play, Paul Apel's *Hans Sonnenstoessers Hoellenfahrt*. A poverty-stricken composer, Neil McRae, is persuaded to propose marriage to Gladys Cady, a rich girl. In a dream he learns the horrid consequences, as he is set to work in the Cady factory—it manufactures widgets—and sees the stupidity of so-called business efficiency. In desperation he murders the Cady family and is put on trial; he is sentenced to a prison cell where he manufactures endless inane lyrics. He finally finds release from prison and, on awakening, from his engagement. A movie based on the play was directed by James Cruze in 1925.

Beggars of Life (1924),   an autobiography by JIM TULLY. The book won Tully his first recognition. MAXWELL ANDERSON dramatized the book in *Outside Looking In* (1925).

Behrman, S[amuel] N[athaniel]   (1893–1973), playwright, short-story writer, screenwriter. Born in Massachusetts, Behrman came under the influence of G. STANLEY HALL at Clark University, GEORGE PIERCE BAKER at Harvard, and BRANDER MATTHEWS and JOHN ERSKINE at Columbia. After the success of *The Second Man* (1927), a comedy of manners, other comedies followed, mostly in the same vein: *Serena Blandish* (1928), a dramatization of a novel by the English novelist Enid Bagnold (1925); *Meteor* (1929); *Brief Moment* (1931); *Biography* (1932), about a woman portrait painter and a journalist; *Rain from Heaven* (1934), one of the earliest anti-Nazi plays; *End of Summer* (1936), a comedy on the use of wealth; *Amphitryon 38* (1937), an adaptation from the French and, ultimately, from the ancients; *Wine of Choice* (1938), on liberalism and its difficulties; *No Time For Comedy* (1939), with a dramatist as protagonist; *The Talley Method* (1941); *The Pirate* (1942); *I Know My Love* (1949); *Lord Pengo* (1962); and *But for Whom Charlie* (1964). With Franz Werfel he wrote *Jacobowsky and the Colonel* (1944), with Joshua Logan *Fanny* (1954). An autobiographical book, *The Worcester Account* (1954), was dramatized as *The Cold Wind and the Warm* (1958). Behrman turned to biography with two books, *Duveen* (1952), a work on the career of the art dealer, and *Portrait of Max* (1960), a profile of Max Beerbohm, the fin de siècle English satirist. *The Burning Glass* (1968) is a novel about a young playwright. A memoir is *People in a Diary* (1972). Behrman also wrote film scripts in Hollywood, including *Queen Christina* (1933) for Greta Garbo.

Bei Dao [Zhao Zhenkai] (1949–   ),   poet, short-story writer. Born in Beijing, China, and since the early 1990s a resident of the United States, Bei Dao lost his formal education to the Cultural Revolution in 1966. First a Red Guard, and then a manual laborer in Hebei Province from 1970 to 1977, he began writing under the names "Bei Dao" ("North Island") and "Shi Mo" instead of his given name, Zhao Zhenkai. As Bei Dao, he helped originate the Chinese movement of "melongshi" ("shadows poetry"), verse in which political or social content lies hidden in obscure images or clouds of metaphor. From the 1970s on, he found acceptance in official Chinese publications and achieved some fame as part of a new wave of Chinese thought and culture. *Bodong*, stories, was published in Hong Kong in 1985 and translated as *Waves* in London in 1987 and New York in 1990. *Shi xuan*, "Collected Poems," appeared in Guangzhao [Canton], China, in 1986 and in translation as *The August Sleepwalker* in London in 1988 and New York in 1990. In Tiananmen Square in June 1989, his poems were used as chants by the dissident students; he was abroad and has continued to live in exile, writing in Chinese. His poems have been translated into over a dozen languages. Recent volumes include *Old Snow* (1991), with three sections—"Berlin," "Oslo," "Stockholm"—suggestive of his alienation from home; *Forms of Distance* (1995); *Landscape Over Zero* (1996); and *Unlock* (2000).

Belany, Archibald Stansfeld.   See GREY OWL.

Belasco, David (1859–1931),   actor, theatrical producer, playwright. Born in San Francisco, Belasco followed a theatrical career that included many years on Broadway as a successful manager, producer, and playwright. He developed the talents of Mrs. Leslie Carter, David Warfield, Minnie Maddern Fiske, Blanche Bates, Lenore Ulric, Ina Claire, Helen Gahagan, Lionel Atwill, Fanny Brice, and others. As a writer Belasco won great success with THE HEART OF MARYLAND (1895), ZAZA (1898), *DuBarry* (1901), THE GIRL OF THE GOLDEN WEST (1905), THE RETURN OF PETER GRIMM (1911), and *Van Der Decken* (1915). In collaboration with other playwrights he wrote HEARTS OF OAK (with JAMES A. HERNE, 1879), *The Charity Ball* (with Henry C. De Mille, 1889), THE GIRL I LEFT BEHIND ME (with FRANKLIN FYLES, 1893), MADAME BUTTERFLY (with JOHN LUTHER LONG, 1900), THE DARLING OF THE GODS (with Long, 1902), and ADREA (with Long, 1904).

Belasco took over the Stuyvesant Theater on West 44th Street, New York City, and renamed it the Belasco; it was associated with some of his most notable hits. He produced nearly four hundred plays and greatly influenced the American theater in the direction of greater emotionalism and more realistic stage properties and in developing the star system.

Belknap, Jeremy (1744–1798),   clergyman, historian. Born in Boston, Belknap wrote a *History of New Hampshire* (published in parts, 1784, 1791, 1792), which William Cullen Bryant said was the first historical work "to make American history attractive." He wrote a satirical allegory, *The Foresters* (1792), and began a pioneer work, *American Biography* (1794–1798) on early explorers and leaders. With others Belknap founded the Massachusetts Historical Society.

Bell, Alexander Graham (1847–1922), and **Bell, Alexander Melville** (1819–1905),   speech experts, inventors. Father, Alexander Melville, and son, Alexander Graham, were born, educated, and began their careers in Scotland, continuing their work in London and, from the 1870s onward, in the United States. The elder Bell, a teacher of the science of correct speech, wrote *Visible Speech* (1867) to demonstrate an alphabet visually showing the articulating position of the vocal organs for each sound. He also wrote books on elocution. His son developed a system for teaching speech to the deaf, but is principally known as the inventor of mechanical devices, above all the telephone (1876, 1877).

Bell for Adano, A,   novel by JOHN HERSEY.

Bell Jar, The,   novel by SYLVIA PLATH. First published in England in 1963 under the pseudonym Victoria Lucas, the novel appeared only later under Plath's name (England, 1966; U.S., 1971). It is a semiautobiographical exploration of neurosis and potential suicide, focusing on Esther Greenwood, a Smith College student who spends a summer as an intern on a women's magazine in New York.

Bell, Madison Smartt (1957–   ),   novelist, short-story writer. Born in Nashville, Tennessee, Bell was educated at Princeton and Hollins College. By the time he was 35 years old, he had published six novels. *The Washington Square Ensemble* (1983), *Waiting for the End of the World* (1985), *Straight Cut* (1986), *The Year of Silence* (1987), *Soldier's Joy* (1989), and *Doctor Sleep* (1991) established the reputation of their author as a postmodern minimalist writing about the outcasts of late 20th-century society. *Save Me, Joe Louis* (1993) deals with the crime spree of a fringe couple, Macrae and Charlie, whose misalliance ends in violence. *All Souls' Rising* (1995) is set in the bloody 17th-century uprising against the French in Haiti. Highly praised, it was followed by a sequel, *Master of the Crossroads* (2000), and a third novel of a developing trilogy has been promised. *Ten Indians* (1996) is also a novel. Story collections include *Zero db* (1987) and *Barking Man and Other Stories* (1990). *Narrative Design: A Writer's Guide to Structure* appeared in 1997.

Bell, Thomas (1903–1961),   novelist, short-story writer. Bell had an extremely varied background before he turned writer, holding jobs that ranged from electrician to merchant seaman. He wrote *All Brides Are Beautiful* (1936), a novel; *Till I Come Back to You* (1953), a play; and *In the Midst of Life* (1961), a poignant journal of the twenty months preceding his death from cancer.

Bellah, James Warner (1899–1976),   novelist, short-story writer. He was educated at Columbia University and taught English there for several years. From 1927 to 1928 he was a news correspondent in China. A pilot in World War I, he served also in World War II. In 1929 he was commissioned as a special reporter by the *Saturday Evening Post* on all initial flights by Pan American Airways through the West Indies and Central America. Among his novels are *These Frantic Years* (1927); *Dancing Lady* (1932); *South by East and Half East* (1936); *Ward 20* (1945); *Irregular Gentleman* (1948), which is autobiographical; *The Apache* (1951); *The Valiant Virginians* (1955); *Blood River* (1959); and *A Thunder of Drums* (1961).

Bellamann, Henry (1882–1945),   musician, author. Born in Missouri, Bellamann at first devoted himself exclusively to music, but in 1926 turned novelist with *Petenera's Daughter*, and went on to success with *Kings Row* (1940), *Victoria Grandolet* (1943), and *Doctor Mitchell of Kings Row* (1945). His widow, Katherine Bellamann, completed his unfinished novel *Paris Mitchell of Kings Row* (1948).

Bellamy, Edward (1850–1898),   novelist, reformer. Bellamy came from a long line of New England ministers, and although he espoused no particular creed, his essentially religious nature continually expressed itself in his ethical, anti-materialistic bent. His text was: "If we love one another, God dwelleth in us"; and his love for his fellow man turned him into an impassioned and beloved social reformer. He was educated at Union College and in Germany, returned to the United States to study law, but never practiced. He joined the staff of the New York *Evening Post*, then edited the Springfield (Massachusetts) *Union*, and founded the Springfield *Daily News* (1880). Meanwhile, he was writing fiction of originality and stylistic distinction. *The Duke of Stockbridge*, a novel about SHAYS' REBELLION, was published serially in 1879 (and completed and published in book form by a cousin in 1900). *Six to One: A Nantucket Idyl* (1878) reflects his voyage to Hawaii in the previous year. *Dr. Heidenhoff's Process* (1880) and *Miss Ludington's Sister* (1884) are powerful psychological studies reminiscent of Hawthorne. His imaginative short stories were published in *The Blind Man's World and Other Stories* (1898).

Fame came with publication of LOOKING BACKWARD: 2000–1887 (1888). This "Utopia of collectivism," advocating state capitalism as a step to state socialism through nonviolent means, was immensely popular and influential. It sold nearly a million copies in ten years; it was imitated by a host of lesser utopian novels and led to the founding of a Nationalist Party advocating Bellamy's principles. Although familiar with Marx's work, taking over what he liked about it, Bellamy advocated quite different techniques for achieving a new world. He turned an idealistic deaf ear to many opportunities to capitalize on his success, entering instead upon a ten-year period of controversy and campaigning. He founded the *New Nation* in

1891. *Equality* (1897), a sequel to *Looking Backward*, was less popular, being more of a theoretical tract, but it exhibits bolder economic criticism in its attack on the profit system and its preaching of economic equality as "the corner-stone of our state." Bellamy's health broke while writing *Equality*, and he died shortly of tuberculosis.

Bellamy, Joseph (1719–1790),   clergyman. Born in Connecticut, Bellamy was a follower of Jonathan Edwards. His *True Religion Delineated* (1750) was an attempt to clarify the issues of the GREAT AWAKENING. Among his pamphlets and sermons, *The Millennium* (1758) presented a vision of a militant Church actively propagating the Kingdom of God.

Belli, Carlos Germán (1927–   ),   Peruvian poet. Belli writes ironically about modern man's sense of himself as a miscast figure in nature. In Belli's verse, peculiar combinations of archaic conceits, hyperbole, and everyday language make man appear as a sad, unintended error, ambulating in the midst of nebulous technology, language, and desire. His sense of this imperfect and nostalgic beast is recorded in *¡O hada cibernetica!* (1961), the work that established Belli as one of the most significant contemporary Spanish-American poets. He also published *El pie sobre el cuelo* (1967), *Sextinas y otros poemas* (1970), and *Antologia personal* (1988).

Bello, Andrés (1781–1865),   Venezuelan scholar and poet. As a promising young man in Caracas, Bello studied classical literature, law, and philosophy. His interest in the natural sciences was stimulated by meeting Alexander von Humboldt, who greatly influenced him. In 1810 Bello was sent to England to seek support for the revolutionary junta of Caracas, as part of a three-man delegation that also included Simón Bolívar. In England, where he remained for nearly twenty years, he began his edition of the *Poema del Cid*, based on the 12th-century text, and wrote his best-known poems: *Alocución a la poesía* (1823), a declaration of literary independence, in which he exhorts the Muse to abandon Europe for America, and *La agricultura de la zona tórrida* (1826), notable for its description of the plants of America, in which realistic detail is combined with classical allusions. From 1829 until his death, Bello resided in Chile, where he held important government posts, was a founder and first president of the University of Chile, and was chief architect of the Chilean civil code. During this period, he published *La oración por todos* (1843), an adaptation of Hugo's *La Prière pour tous* (1830) that is sometimes considered better than the original. His most enduring achievement, however, is probably his *Gramática de la lengua castellana* (1847), still the outstanding authority on Spanish grammar. See SARMENTO, DOMINGO FAUSTINO.

Bellow, Saul (1915–   ),   novelist, short-story writer, essayist. The child of Russian Jews who emigrated from St. Petersburg to Canada in 1913, Bellow was born in Montreal and raised in Chicago. He was educated at the University of Chicago and Northwestern University. Supporting himself at the beginning of his writing career by occasional teaching and odd jobs, Bellow won a Guggenheim fellowship in 1948, and traveled to Europe, setting up residence in Paris, where he lived and wrote for two years. Returning to the United States in 1950, he lived for the next decade in New York.

Bellow has taught at the University of Minnesota, New York University, Princeton, Bard College, and Boston University. From 1962 until 1994, he lived and worked in Chicago, where he served on the University of Chicago's Committee on Social Thought. Among the many awards and prizes the novelist has received are three National Book Awards (1953, for THE ADVENTURES OF AUGIE MARCH; 1964, for HERZOG; 1971, for *Mr. Sammler's Planet*); the Jewish Heritage Award (1968); the French *Croix de Chevalier des Arts et Lettres* (1968); the Pulitzer Prize (1975); the Nobel Prize for Literature (1976); and the 1990 National Book Foundation Medal for distinguished contribution to American letters.

Bellow's prolific career as a novelist spans over half a century. Although he most often writes about Jewish-American immigrants or their children, the scope of his fiction is universal. Through the central consciousness of a protagonist who is often an intellectual, his novels give voice to the dilemmas and contradictions of 20th-century life. In Bellow's first novel, *Dangling Man* (1944), his main character, Joseph, poses the question, "How should a good man live; what might he do?" This question reverberates throughout Bellow's novels, as the protagonists embark on quests to discover the meaning and purpose of their existence—searching for the ground of moral and intellectual truth upon which to base their conduct in the world.

Like the predecessor he admired, Dostoevsky, Bellow perceives the modern individual as deeply conflicted. Dispossessed of traditional religious values and ethical codes, he is torn between reason and faith, idealism and nihilism, love and contempt for his fellow human beings. Joseph, in *Dangling Man*, suffers such intense inner strife that he, like so many of Bellow's subsequent protagonists, spends days alone in his room, trying to resolve his dilemma. Failing in the attempt, Joseph enlists in the Army before he is drafted to fight in World War II. Physically on the move at last, the "dangling man" remains at a psychic impasse—having failed to discover any sense of purpose, commitment, or belief.

Bellow's second novel, *The Victim* (1947), is the study of a man who has given up, before trying, the quest for inner knowledge and thereby placed his humanity at risk. Convinced that he has barely skirted the abyss of personal and professional failure, Asa Leventhal warily navigates through life, hoping he can avoid its fathomless depths. The catalyst for Leventhal's eventual release from wooden impassivity is a man named Kirby Allbee, a former colleague who accuses Leventhal, a Jew, of responsibility for his (Allbee's) suffering. Goaded by Allbee's anti-Semitic jibes, Leventhal is thrown into a turmoil of doubt, insecurity, and guilt. Paradoxically, the painful confrontation of Jew and anti-Semite leads both men to acknowledge their mutual bond.

In order to resolve their personal dilemmas, Bellow's characters are increasingly driven to ponder the human condition. Are human beings free moral agents capable of real choice, or merely products of the conditioning forces of biology, culture, and history? This is the question that Augie March puts to himself in *The Adventures of Augie March* (1953). While the nature of Augie's quest grows out of Bellow's earlier fiction, the shape of his third novel is a marked departure from the tight formal construction of *Dangling Man* and *The Victim*. Having employed the Flaubertian model in his first two novels, he found that it did not give him scope to express his intimate knowledge of immigrant life in America.

Exploiting the freedom of the picaresque form in *Augie March*, Bellow created an expansive narrative style new to American fiction in the 1950s. Augie narrates his adventures in a voice at once spontaneous and allusive, colloquial and lyrical. Employing both Yiddish and biblical intonations to evoke the immigrant neighborhoods of his youth, Augie's voice also registers the influence of Whitman, Blake, and Dickens. Vividly rendering the sights, sounds, and smells of Chicago, Bellow does more than paint a realistic urban landscape. He draws on the visionary language of poet and prophet to dig beneath appearances, exploring a theme that persists throughout his fiction: the modern metropolis as a New World Babylon.

Growing up and out of his native Chicago, Augie March embarks on adventures that take him to Mexico and Europe as well as through "the length and breadth of America." Reminiscent of that other American picaro, Twain's Huckleberry Finn, Augie is driven by restlessness and curiosity, eager to "light out" for new territory. By keeping on the move, moreover, he can elude the snares of countless "reality instructors" he meets. Each of these "Machiavellis" would like, Augie notes, to enlist him in his particular "version" of reality. Resisting their instruction, Augie persists in his quest to discover, as he says, "what I was meant to be." By the end of the novel he has not arrived at his goal, but the quest continues. Although married and living in Europe, Augie remains, in all senses of the term, a "traveling man."

Bellow's subsequent protagonist, Wilhelm Adler in *Seize the Day* (1956), bears more resemblance to Asa Leventhal than to Augie March. Fear or spiritual sloth has led Wilhelm, like Leventhal, to abandon the search for a significant fate. Like *The Victim, Seize the Day* focuses on the urban pressures of New York City life; in this novella, Bellow also returns to the formal strictures and compressed style of his earlier fiction. On the "day of reckoning" during which the action of *Seize the Day* unfolds, Wilhelm—who has already lost his job, home, and family—is in the process of losing his last few dollars on the commodities market. This day of drastic losses proves a spiritual turning point. The unlikely catalyst for Wilhelm's revelation of the true "business of his life" is a desperate charlatan, Dr. Tamkin. By pressuring Wilhelm into a bad investment, Tamkin not only divests Wilhelm of his money but, in the process, deprives him of false hope and illusion.

In the novels published since *Seize the Day*, Bellow has abandoned the compressed, economical style of his early fiction for the more expansive form of *Augie March*. He has continued, however, to publish shorter works of fiction in various magazines and journals, and these have been collected into two volumes, *Mosby's Memoirs and Other Stories* (1968) and *Him with His Foot in His Mouth and Other Stories* (1984). In addition to publishing numerous essays, interviews, and speeches, Bellow has written several plays, most notably his full-length comedy, *The Last Analysis* (1965), which opened on Broadway in 1964. He has also published a vivid memoir of his 1975 trip to Israel, *To Jerusalem and Back: A Personal Account* (1976).

According to Bellow, in order to write his next two novels he "had to tame and restrain the style I developed in *Augie March*." In both HENDERSON THE RAIN KING (1959) and *Herzog* (1964), the novelist interweaves his characters' comic highjinks with a deep thread of spiritual contemplation. In *Henderson*, the Gentile protagonist is a Connecticut millionaire, whose quest for meaning leads him into the *terra incognita* of both a continent and his own inner life. Overwhelmed by a doom-laden sense of mortality, Henderson sets out for Africa because, as he later says, "I wouldn't agree to the death of my soul."

Rendered suggestively rather than factually, Bellow's Africa is actually located, as Henderson puts it, "beyond geography." Henderson's trials among the Arnewi and Wariri tribes, his friendship with King Dahfu, and his ordeal with the lion Atti bring him into direct confrontation with death. Having confronted and survived this ultimate terror, Henderson discovers his vital connection to life. From the African wilderness he emerges at the end of the novel, like Lazarus, a man reborn.

Whereas Henderson embarks on a series of strenuous physical ordeals, the struggles of Bellow's subsequent protagonist, Moses Herzog, occur mainly in his head. The protagonist of *Herzog* spends a great deal of time lying down, either in his New York apartment or at his country retreat. This physical inertness only serves to underscore the turmoil of Herzog's hyperactive mind. The novel's action occurs mainly in flashbacks and is interspersed with lengthy monologues and unsent letters that Herzog addresses, in his head, to public figures as well as to personal enemies and friends. On one level, *Herzog* rehearses the myriad arguments, theories, and explanations that the modern mind has brought to bear on human experience.

An author and academic, Herzog has, with the failure of his second marriage, suffered a personal crisis. Triggered by the discovery of his wife's infidelity, Herzog's state of confusion derives ultimately from his loss of faith in systematic ideas. Seeking answers to critical questions concerning the nature and meaning of human existence, he finds his education and academic training to be of no avail. Gradually he discovers that "he, Herzog, had committed a sin of some kind against his own heart, while in pursuit of a grand synthesis." The quest for meaning, Bellow suggests here and throughout his fiction, demands an open heart as well as an open mind.

In *Mr. Sammler's Planet* (1970), Bellow's protagonist is an octogenarian wearied by the pressing demands that life makes on the human heart. A Polish Jew, Artur Sammler is the sur-

vivor of two World Wars, a man stripped bare by history. In the Holocaust he "lost his wife, lost an eye" and lost the underlying sense of being grounded in human existence. As he paces the streets of New York City in the late 1960s, Sammler grows ever more heartsick at the spectacle of moral disorder and social decay. The chaos and menace of urban life recall to him the cataclysmic history of Europe and, beyond that, the "barbarous" corruption of the ancient world.

Longing to escape this New World Babylon, with its "Byzantine luxury" and "degradation," Sammler attempts to disengage himself mentally from the claims of human existence. Through his encounters with an African-American pickpocket, who physically threatens him, Sammler is caught up in a series of incidents that implicate him in the very conditions from which he seeks refuge. Mourning the death of a beloved nephew, Sammler affirms, in the novel's closing lines, the "contract" that binds each human being to this troubled "planet."

In HUMBOLDT'S GIFT (1975), Bellow explores the relationship of the artist to urban America in all its "Babylonishness"— calling attention to the burden of "collective abstractions" weighing down modern consciousness. His protagonist, a writer named Charlie Citrine, is attempting to realign his relationship to the "reality instructors," in order to pursue "a different kind of life." Convinced that contemporary culture has abandoned true reality for the merely material—"the plastered idols of the Appearances"—Citrine is in quest of a deeper, "personal connection with the external world."

Turning to the writings of "the famous but misunderstood Dr. Rudolf Steiner," an Austrian philosopher and the founder of anthroposophy, Citrine undertakes certain spiritual exercises that begin to transform his view of reality. At the same time, Citrine reviews his early friendship with, and subsequent estrangement from, Von Humboldt Fleisher—a gifted poet who has died some years before the novel opens. (This character is modeled after Bellow's own former friend, the American poet and fiction writer, Delmore Schwartz.)

In Citrine's view, Humboldt was silenced as a poet and finally destroyed as a man by the massive pressures of a materialistic society, "the American dollar-drive." As Citrine begins to disentangle himself from these massive pressures, however, he gains new insight into Humboldt's life and career. His discovery, at the end of the novel, of a posthumous letter and "gift" from Humboldt bolsters this insight. (Meanwhile, in striking contrast to his dead friend's posthumous "gift" and "act of love," Citrine's mistress, Renata Koffritz, abandons him for a prosperous undertaker.) By acting on Citrine's consciousness "from the grave," Humboldt validates the message he wrote to Citrine in his final letter: "remember, we are not natural beings but supernatural beings."

Like *Humboldt's Gift*, Bellow's subsequent novel, *The Dean's December* (1982), takes place in Chicago. In the latter novel, however, Bellow expands the urban setting to include the Rumanian capital of Bucharest. When Albert Corde, the dean of a Chicago college, accompanies his wife to Bucharest to visit her dying mother, he is in a special position to compare the societies of East and West, communism and capitalism. Weighing the "cast-iron gloom" of totalitarian bureaucracy against the degradation of America's inner-city slums, Corde discovers similarities emblemized by the freezing weather.

In both these far-flung cities, December heralds more than the end of a year. In Bucharest and Chicago, culture itself is dying—replaced by mechanical forms of organization indifferent to the highest ideals and achievements of humanity. Attempting to free himself from this bitter vision of global frost and inevitable doom, Corde spends most of his time, like Citrine, trying to adjust his insight, correct his vision of reality. At the end of the novel, Corde travels to California with his astronomer-wife. There, at the Mt. Palomar observatory, he registers "the atmospheric distortions" governing all human perceptions of material phenomena. To discover essential reality, he perceives, one must delve deeper—going down, as Bellow puts it, "to the very blood and crystal forms inside your bones."

The Bellovian character's need to penetrate appearances and discover saving reality is a predominant theme in virtually all of his fiction. In *More Die of Heartbreak* (1987), this visionary enterprise serves as the focus of the novel's action. Kenneth Trachtenberg, the novel's narrator, takes a job teaching at a midwestern American university in order to be near his uncle, an internationally renowned botanist. According to Kenneth, Benn Crader is not merely a great scientist but a "plant clairvoyant." Benn, says his nephew, "saw into or looked through plants." From his uncle, Ken hopes to learn to see beneath appearances and beyond the local disturbances of a troubled life. Ironically, however, Ken's narrative records his account of Benn Crader's fall from vision into moral blindness.

Through a disastrous love affair and marriage, Uncle Benn gets involved with an ambitious family that wants to use him as a pawn in a money-making scheme. In the end, Benn escapes to the Arctic, to join a team of research scientists. There, pursuing a comparative study of lichens, he hopes to recover his former self and vision. Dismayed by this turn of events, his nephew appears, nonetheless, to have progressed to a turning point in his own life. Some of Benn's "powers of seeing," Ken avows, "*had* been transmitted to me." He resolves to continue his "quest for a revelation."

For most of his writing career, Bellow, like his protagonist Moses Herzog, has wrestled long and hard with the "demon" of "modern ideas." In the late 1980s, he announced a turning point in his career. "I think I've done all the thinking that I'm going to do," Bellow remarked in an interview. "All my life long I have been seriously pondering certain problems and I'll probably continue to do that, but I'm now in a position to use this pondering as a background for the story, and not intrude it so much into the narrative." Evincing this shift in attitude is the series of four novellas Bellow began publishing in 1989, at the age of seventy-five. In his foreword to *Something to Remember Me By*, the 1991 volume in which the first three novellas were collected, Bellow declares his loss of interest in writing "fat" books—and pays homage to Anton Chekhov, the

Russian playwright and short-story writer who had a "mania for shortness." According to Bellow, the "modern taste for brevity and condensation" is a reaction to the relentless demands on our attention by advertising and the media. If the modern writer wants to be heard, he must "write as short as he can." Underscoring Bellow's new approach to narrative, the heroine of his 1989 novella, *A Theft*, does not share Herzog's obsession with "thinking"; nor does she "take much stock in the collapsing culture bit."

Clara Velde—four times married, thrice divorced—clearly has other things to worry about. Convinced, however, that one cannot "separate love from being," Clara is far more sanguine about human life and relationships than her male predecessors. And although she loses heart at several points in the story, Clara is not ultimately disappointed. At the end of *A Theft*, she recovers both her faith in the power of love and the stolen ring that is its symbol.

The narrator of the second novella, *The Bellarosa Connection*, is an elderly gentleman, the retired founder of "the Mnemosyne Institute in Philadelphia," but here too Bellow celebrates the warmth, intelligence, and wit of a central female character. Unlike Clara Velde, a fashionable New York executive decked out in designer clothes, Sorella Fonstein is a New Jersey housewife, a woman so fat that "she made you look twice at a doorway. When she came to it, she filled the space like a freighter in a canal lock." But Sorella is larger than life in a more telling sense. "Greatness," avows the narrator, is the only word for Sorella's special "candor." He adds, "in this world of liars and cowards, there *are* people like Sorella. One waits for them in the blind faith that they *do* exist."

The narrator pays homage to Sorella's existence by recounting events that transpired thirty years earlier—when, for the sake of her husband, Harry, she administered a dose of her "candor" to the Broadway producer Billy Rose. Three decades later, Sorella and Harry Fonstein die in a collision on the New Jersey Turnpike, erased from existence before the narrator can accomplish his hoped-for reunion with them. He reconnects with the past in the only way he can, "with a Mnemosyne flourish," paying homage to the human powers of memory and the rescue operation it performs against death and oblivion.

In the novella that lends its title to the collection, *Something to Remember Me By*, the narrator is also an elderly man—one who glimpses, like so many Bellow protagonists before him, a new and liberating vision of reality. Sounding like Albert Corde at the end of *The Dean's December*, the narrator penetrates beneath appearances, finding "that the truth of the universe was inscribed into our very bones. That the human skeleton was itself a hieroglyph." The protagonist of Bellow's latest novella, *The Actual*, published in 1997, is also preoccupied with ultimate things. Returning to his hometown, Chicago, with a fortune acquired in the Far East, Harry Trellman is a "mystery" not only to others but to himself. Although still in his fifties, Trellman, like Artur Sammler, feels estranged from existence, suspended "somewhere between a shadow and a shade of one of the departed." In quest of the real or "the actual," he discovers it in the woman he has loved, mostly at a distance, for forty years.

The year 2000 marked yet another shift in Bellow's long career. After devoting more than a decade to shorter narratives, he published a novel that, like *Humboldt's Gift*, pays homage to a dead friend. *Ravelstein's* eponymous hero is a thinly disguised version of Bellow's close friend and colleague at the University of Chicago, Alan Bloom. A scholar and teacher of philosophy, Professor Bloom came to widespread public attention with the appearance of his controversial book, *The Closing of the American Mind*, which was violently attacked by the academic establishment at the same time that it rose high on best-seller lists. Detailing, as he expands upon, the facts of Bellow's friendship with Bloom, the novel's narrator, Chick, recounts Abe Ravelstein's sudden rise to wealth and notoriety and chronicles the painful history of his illness and death. To Chick, Ravelstein is a magnificent creature, larger than life even when on the brink of death. Taking visceral delight in "broad comedy, old routines, wounding remarks, brashness and raw fun," Ravelstein is also a thinker of the first order—a man who lives his ideas in emulation of his heroes, Plato and Socrates. Years younger than Chick, Ravelstein is dying from Guillain-Barré disease, to which he falls prey after contracting AIDS. Homosexual adventures suggest only one aspect of Ravelstein's risk-prone character; his chain-smoking, his passion for Paris and politics, his love of high living and straight-talking all get him into trouble. Loathed by his enemies, adored by his friends and followers, Ravelstein has bold views on every subject from Michael Jackson to Celine to the fate of the Jews. He shares them unstintingly with Chick as the two friends talk and talk, often for hours, reflecting on their century and its genius for death. The presence of death is everywhere in this novel—but death staved off by a fierce desire to live to the last, and to laugh at the foibles of humankind. Like Socrates, Ravelstein occupies himself with society, not nature, which pales before "the human drama." As if taking revenge, nature concocts the virus that kills him, as it produces the toxin that nearly kills Chick. Escaping to the "tropical paradise" of Saint Martin island after Ravelstein's death, Chick dines on red snapper infected by the deadly "cigua toxin," which attacks his nervous system. Deathly ill, he is saved by his young wife, Rosamund—a former doctoral student of Ravelstein's—who rushes Chick home to the hospital. In the novel's final pages Chick's close encounter with the mystery of death opens a spiritual terrain that restores him to the "laughing" presence of his dead friend. As Chick says in the novel's closing line, "You don't easily give up a creature like Ravelstein to death." Fortified by this understanding, Chick is able to discharge, six years after Ravelstein's death, his promise to write his friend's life. Contemplating his own demise in this late novel, Bellow evokes the paradoxical riches of life and its possible aftermath.

From the postwar years to the era of postmodernism, Bellow has continued to honor, in his work as a novelist, the traditional forms and techniques of literary realism. In his view,

"the development of realism in the 19th century" is still "the major event of modern literature." At the same time, however, Bellow is aware of the potential dangers or excesses to which realism lends itself. With its emphasis on the facts of ordinary life, "the realistic tendency," he points out, "is to challenge the human significance of things."

As the world becomes glutted with more and more things, their human significance proves increasingly difficult for the writer to render. Confronting the dire facts of 20th-century life—facts to which Bellow's novels amply attest—his protagonists are understandably tempted by theories of decline, visions of apocalyptic doom. In the end, however, they resist this negative vision of human history and fate as one more formulation, or dubious version, of reality.

Bellow is, as John Updike has said, "one of the rare writers" who take "mimesis a layer or two deeper than it has gone before." Only by shedding systematic formulations of reality can the individual discover, he suggests, a personal connection to the creative mystery underlying appearances. As the novelist, now in his mid-eighties, continues to search for "human significance" in a seemingly senseless, chaotic world, his distinguished body of fiction has made one thing, at least, clear. Bellow is not only the most significant writer of his generation; he is one of America's—and the 20th century's—finest.

See studies by Malcolm Bradbury (1982), Daniel Fuchs (1984), and Ellen Pifer (1990) and James Atlas's biography of Bellow (2000).

ELLEN PIFER

Bells, The (1849),   a poem by EDGAR ALLAN POE. This is probably the most sustained exercise in onomatopoeia in poetry. Poe was visiting a friend, Mrs. Marie Louise Shew, at 47 Bond St. in New York, late in the spring of 1848. Mentally and emotionally exhausted, he was, says Mrs. Shew, much annoyed by church bells, of which there were several nearby, including the silver bell of the old Middle Dutch Church. At the same time he said he had to write a poem for immediate publication—"I have no feeling, no sentiment, no inspiration." Then, after tea in the conservatory, Mrs. Shew took a piece of paper, wrote at the top "The Bells, by E. A. Poe," and gave him a further hint by adding the words "the little silver bells." Poe began to write, and soon stopped. Then Mrs. Shew gave him another inspirational shove: she wrote the words "the heavy iron bells." Poe resumed but composed only seventeen lines. The manuscript survives. At first Poe called it "Mrs. Shew's poem," but he soon took it over. He revised it three times; the second and last appeared in Sartain's UNION MAGAZINE, edited by John Sartain, in 1849. The poem has been called a jingle, but it follows an exact pattern in its succession of silver, golden, brass, and iron sounds, suggesting the cycle of life. Sound echoes sense in a technical tour de force.

Bemelmans, Ludwig (1898–1962),   painter, writer. Born in Austria, Bemelmans came to the U.S. in 1914 and was naturalized in 1918. His early years here were spent working in a hotel, an experience that greatly influenced his writings. At one time he ran a restaurant of his own. He wrote and illustrated children's books; he did settings for a Broadway play; he worked in Hollywood (uncomplimentary result: his novel *Dirty Eddie*, 1947); and he contributed to *The New Yorker, Vogue, Town and Country*, and *Stage* articles and stories highly individual in style and content. Among his books are *Hansi* (1934); *Golden Basket* (1936); *Castle Number Nine* (1937); *Quito Express* (1938); *My War with the United States* (an account of his experiences in the Army, 1937); *Hotel Splendide* (1941); *Small Beer* (1940); *I Love You, I Love You, I Love You* (1942); *Now I Lay Me Down to Sleep* (1944, made into a successful play in 1950); *The Blue Danube* (1945); *The Eye of God* (1949); *Father, Dear Father* (1953); an omnibus collection, *The World of Bemelmans* (1955); *The Woman of My Life* (1957); *My Life in Art* (1958); *Are You Hungry Are You Cold* (1960); and *Bemelmans' Italian Holiday*, a collection of articles (1961).

Bemis, Samuel Flagg (1891–1973),   historian. Bemis was a leading authority on the history of American foreign policy and Sterling Professor of Diplomatic History and Inter-American Relations at Yale University, where he taught from 1935 to 1960. He twice received the Pulitzer Prize: in 1926 for *Pinckney's Treaty, A Study of America's Advantage from Europe's Distress*; and in 1950 for *John Quincy Adams and the Foundations of American Foreign Policy*. His *Diplomatic History* (1955) was revised to give greater emphasis to 20th-century problems and was retitled *A Short History of American Foreign Policy and Diplomacy* (1959). Bemis is coauthor of *Guide to the Diplomatic History of the United States, 1776–1921* (1935) and editor and contributor to *The American Secretaries of State and Their Diplomacy*, 10 volumes (1927–29).

Ben Bolt (published in *The New Mirror*, Sept. 2, 1843), a sentimental ballad by THOMAS DUNN ENGLISH. Set to saccharine music, it was widely popular in its day, and was revived when George du Maurier used it effectively in *Trilby* (1894).

Benbow family,   characters in Faulkner's SARTORIS and SANCTUARY, mentioned also in ABSALOM, ABSALOM! and THE UNVANQUISHED. Horace and Narcissa Benbow, brother and sister, become involved in the history of the Sartoris family through Narcissa's marriage to the youngest Bayard Sartoris.

Benchley, Nathaniel (1915–1981),   humorist. Son of ROBERT and father of PETER BENCHLEY, Nathaniel wrote novels, film scripts, and plays as well as biographies of his father and of Humphrey Bogart (1975).

Benchley, Peter [Bradford] (1940–   ),   writer. The son of NATHANIEL and grandson of ROBERT BENCHLEY, Peter had huge success with the novel *Jaws* (1974), later a motion picture. Other books include *The Deep* (1976), *The Island* (1979), *The Girl of the Sea of Cortez* (1982), and *Rummies* (1989).

Benchley, Robert [Charles] (1889–1945),   essayist, humorist, actor. Born in Worcester, Massachusetts, and educated at Harvard, Benchley began by writing advertising copy for the Curtis Publishing Company, went on to editorial work in New York City, wrote for the *New York World, Life* in its pre-Luce stage, *The Bookman*, and *The New Yorker*. He made movie shorts in Hollywood, appeared in several motion pictures

there and later in radio programs, and came back to Scarsdale, New York, to live.

Benchley was primarily a writer, yet he won great success on the air and in some of his absurdly funny shorts, such as *How to Sleep* (which won an Academy Award in 1935), and he continued to win applause with repetitions of his sketch *The Treasurer's Report*. In his essays Benchley portrayed his life as a series of humiliations and frustrations. *My Ten Years in a Quandary* (1936) reveals him at his most frustrated. He wrote, among other books, *Of All Things* (1921), *Love Conquers All* (1922), *Pluck and Luck* (1925), *20,000 Leagues Under the Sea, or, David Copperfield* (1928), *The Treasurer's Report* (1930), *From Bed to Worse* (1934), *Inside Benchley* (1942), and *Benchley Beside Himself* (1943). Posthumously published was a collection called *Chips Off the Old Benchley* (1949); also *The "Reel" Benchley* (1950), a collection of six scripts of the movie shorts he had written and produced. His son Nathaniel wrote an appealing biography of Benchley (1955). Benchley had the ideal illustrator in Gluyas Williams.

Benedict, Leopold.   See MORRIS WINCHEVSKY.

Benedict, Ruth F[ulton] (1887–1948),   anthropologist, poet, teacher. Benedict early won a reputation as one of the world's leading anthropologists with her studies of various Indian tribes of the West and Southwest. From 1923 until her death she taught at Columbia University. For general readers she wrote two notable books, *Patterns of Culture* (1934) and *Race, Science, and Politics* (1940). Her last book, *The Chrysanthemum and the Sword* (1946), deals with Japan. Early in her career Dr. Benedict wrote verse under the name Anne Singleton; her poems appeared in *Poetry*, the *Nation*, and other magazines.

Benefield, [John] Barry (1877–1956),   newspaperman, short-story writer, novelist. Born in Texas, Benefield worked first on the Dallas *Morning News*, later on the *New York Times*. Some of his short stories appeared in the collection *Short Turns* (1926). Among his novels are *The Chicken-Wagon Family* (1925), *A Little Clown Lost* (1928), *Valiant Is the Word for Carrie* (1935), *April Was When It Began* (1939), *Eddie and the Archangel Mike* (1943), and *Texas, Brooklyn and Heaven* (1948).

Benét, Laura (1884–1979),   poet, biographer. Born in Fort Hamilton, New York, Benét was trained as a social settlement worker but, like her brothers WILLIAM ROSE and STEPHEN VINCENT BENÉT, soon turned to writing. She published several collections of verse: *Fairy Bread* (1921), *Basket for a Fair* (1934), *Is Morning Sure?* (1947), *In Love with Time* (1959), and *Bridge of a Single Hair* (1974). She also wrote a series of biographies for young people, including *Young Edgar Allan Poe* (1941) and *Thackeray* (1947). Among her later books are *Coleridge, Poet of Wild Enchantment* (1952), *Famous American Humorists* (1959), and *The Mystery of Emily Dickinson* (1974). *Come Slowly, Eden* (1942) is a novel. A memoir is *When William Rose, Stephen Vincent, and I Were Young* (1976).

Benét, Stephen Vincent (1898–1943),   poet, short-story writer, dramatist. Born in Pennsylvania and a graduate of Yale (1919), Benét was the brother of WILLIAM ROSE BENÉT. He began his career with several modestly successful collections of verse: *Five Men and Pompey* (1915), *Young Adventure* (1918), *Heavens and Earth* (1920), *The Ballad of William Sycamore* (1923), and *Tiger Joy* (1925). On a Guggenheim fellowship, he went to Paris to complete JOHN BROWN'S BODY (1928), which won a Pulitzer Prize for its realistic, profoundly sympathetic picture of the Civil War. A dramatized version opened in New York City in 1953 and has been performed frequently since. A collection of his *Ballads and Poems* (1931) was followed by *Burning City* (1936), *The Ballad of Duke's Mercy* (1939), *Nightmare at Noon* (1940), and *Western Star* (1943). The last book is the first part of another epic of America left incomplete at Benét's death. In 1933 he had written for young people *A Book of Americans* with his wife, Rosemary Benét.

Meanwhile Benét had turned to prose fiction. His stories are collected in *Thirteen O'Clock* (1937), *Johnny Pye and the Fool-Killer* (1938), *Tales Before Midnight* (1939), and *The Last Circle: Stories and Poems* (1946). His best remembered stories include "Sobbin Women" (1926), the basis for the musical comedy *Seven Brides for Seven Brothers*, and THE DEVIL AND DANIEL WEBSTER (1937), one of the most memorable of its time, later an opera and a movie. His novels, generally less admired, include *Spanish Bayonet* (1926) and *James Shore's Daughter* (1934). He is remembered also for radio scripts, including *They Burned the Books* (1942).

Benét, William Rose (1886–1950), poet, editor. Educated at Yale, Benét wrote seriously from the time he was twenty-one. He was the elder brother of STEPEN VINCENT BENÉT, and ELINOR WYLIE was his second wife. A long line of collections of verse made him widely known: *Merchants from Cathay* (1913), *The Falconer of God* (1914), *The Burglar of the Zodiac* (1918), *Moons of Grandeur* (1920), *Man Possessed* (1927), *Starry Harness* (1933), *Golden Fleece* (1935), *Day of Deliverance* (1944), *The Stairway of Surprise* (1947), and *The Spirit of the Scene* (1951). *Rip Tide* (1932) and *The Dust Which Is God* (1941) were presented as novels in verse; the second is autobiographical. His *Reader's Encyclopedia* (1948), covering world literature, was published in a fourth edition in 1996.

Benezet, Anthony (1713–1784), teacher, humanitarian. Born in France, Benezet came to Pennsylvania and became a Quaker and associate of JOHN WOOLMAN. He published his observations on slavery, alcoholism, Quakers, and Indians in A *Caution to Great Britain and Her Colonies* (1766), *An Historical Account of Guinea* (1771), *The Mighty Destroyer Displayed* (1774), *A Short Account of the People Called Quakers* (1780), and *Some Observations . . . on the Indian Natives of This Continent (1784).*

Ben-Hur: A Tale of the Christ (1880), a novel by LEW WALLACE. An aristocratic young Jew, Judah Ben-Hur, falsely accused by a friend of seeking to murder the Roman governor of Palestine, is sent to the galleys, and his mother and sister are imprisoned. He escapes, becomes a Roman officer; engages in a chariot race with his false friend Messala, and eventually is converted, with his mother and sister, to a belief in Christ. An immense success and translated into many languages, the book had sold at least a million copies before Sears, Roebuck issued a thirty-nine cent edition (1913) and sold

another million. *Ben-Hur* was also hugely successful in a stage production first performed in 1899 and featuring a treadmill and real horses in the chariot race; this was played 6,000 times in various cities in the next twenty-one years. MGM spent $4,000,000 on a silent film starring Francis X. Bushman (1925, re-released, with sound effects, 1931) and $15,000,000 on a mammoth remake (1959).

Benito Cereno, a story by HERMAN MELVILLE. See PLAZZA TALES, THE.

Benjamin, Park (1809–1864), journalist, editor. Born in British Guiana, Benjamin became owner of the *New England Magazine*, which he merged (1835) with the New York *American Monthly Magazine*. He is most remembered for his weekly *New World* (1839–1845), which published American authors such as Longfellow, but also exploited the copyright laws by reprinting British authors without payment.

Bennett, Emerson (1822–1905), novelist. Born in Monson, Massachusetts, Bennett brought out some poems, *The Brigand* (1842), at age twenty, and wrote a novelette, *The Unknown Countess*, in the following year. He wrote over 50 novels and several hundred short stories, mostly on pioneer days in the West. His books include *The League of the Miami* (1845), *The Bandits of the Osage* (1847), MIKE FINK (1848), and *The Prairie Flower* and *Leni-Lioti* (both 1849).

Bennett, James Gordon (1795–1872), newspaper editor. Born in Scotland, Bennett came to America in 1819 and settled finally in New York City. He wrote for two New York newspapers, *The Enquirer* and *The Courier,* and founded and edited the *New York Herald* (1835–67). It was an aggressive, widely read paper that often attacked and was itself attacked. His ostensible aim was exposure of fraud and hypocrisy, but he reveled in scandalous details. His son, James Gordon Bennett (1841–1918), succeeded him as editor in 1867. The younger Bennett sent Stanley to Africa to find Livingstone and supported other expeditions to Africa and the Arctic. He also was the founder of the Paris edition of the *Herald* (1887), now the *International Herald-Tribune.*

Bennett, John (1865–1956), illustrator, writer of children's books. Bennett is remembered chiefly for *Master Skylark* (1897), set in Shakespeare's time, and for *Barnaby Lee* (1902).

Benson, Sally (1900–1972), writer. Benson's best-known book, *Junior Miss* (1941), became a successful play (1941), movie, and radio series. *People Are Fascinating* (1936) and *Emily* (1938) collect stories. *Meet Me in St. Louis* (1942) drew on memories of her St. Louis childhood and provided the basis for a 1944 film. *Women and Children First* (1944) followed.

Bentley, Eric (1916–), dramatic critic, translator, editor. Born in England, Bentley was educated at Oxford and Yale. He was drama critic for the *New Republic* (1952–56) and taught at Columbia (1953–69). His translations and productions of the plays of Bertolt Brecht and Luigi Pirandello helped bring them to the attention of Americans. Among his books are *A Century of Hero-Worship* (1944), a study of hero-worship in modern literature; *The Playwright as Thinker* (1946); *Bernard Shaw* (1947); *In Search of Theatre* (1953);

What Is Theatre? (1956); *The Life of the Drama* (1964); *The Theatre of Commitment* (1967); and *Theatre of War* (1972). He edited *The Importance of Scrutiny* (1948); *From the Modern Repertoire*, 3 series (1949, 1952, 1956); *The Modern Theatre* (6 v. 1955–60); *The Classic Theatre* (4 v. 1958–61); *The Great Playwrights* (2 v. 1970).

Benton, Thomas Hart [1] (1782–1858),   statesman, orator, author. Born in North Carolina, Benton was senator from Missouri from 1812 to 1851. He strongly represented the interests of the West, was a vigorous supporter of President Jackson, and was finally defeated for reelection because he supported the Union against the South. He wrote his autobiography in *Thirty Years' View* (2 v. 1854, 1856) and edited *An Abridgment of the Debates of Congress* (15 v. 1857–61). Benton appears vividly in Irving Stone's biographical novel *Immortal Wife* (1944).

Benton, Thomas Hart [2] (1889–1975),   painter. Born in Missouri, Benton was a grandnephew of the senator with the same name. Benton's best-known murals are found at the New School for Social Research, the library of the Whitney Museum of American Art, the state capitol at Jefferson City, Missouri, and the Truman Library in Independence, Missouri. He wrote two volumes of autobiography, *An Artist in America* (1937, revised 1951) and *An American in Art* (1969).

Bercovici, Konrad (1882–1961),   author. Born in Rumania, Bercovici came to the U.S. in 1916 and began writing for newspapers. In 1917 he published his first book, *Crimes of Charity*. His books cover a wide range of subjects and forms: sociological and historical studies, novels, short stories, and plays. Among them are *Dust of New York* (1918), *Ghitza and Other Romances of Gypsy Blood* (1919), *Around the World in New York* (1924), *The Story of the Gypsies* (1928), *Alexander: A Romantic Biography* (1929), *The Incredible Balkans* (1933), *It's the Gypsy in Me* (1941), and *Savage Prodigal* (1948). *This is Only the Beginning* (1941) is autobiographical.

Berenice   (*Southern Literary Messenger*, 1835; in TALES OF THE GROTESQUE AND ARABESQUE, 1840), a story by EDGAR ALLAN POE. Berenice is an epileptic whose white teeth fascinate the narrator, her cousin. While she has a seizure and appears to be dead, he pulls out her teeth, whereupon her death proves to be merely a trance.

Berenson, Bernard [**Bernhard**, in later years] (1865–1959),   art critic. Born in Lithuania, Berenson was brought to the United States as a boy and was educated at Harvard. He later took up residence in England and from 1900 until his death lived in Italy. He became acknowledged leader among critics of Italian Renaissance painting and was known particularly for his painstaking studies of style and his skill in resolving doubtful attributions. Berenson published many important works, among them *Venetian Painters of the Renaissance* (1894), *Florentine Painters of the Renaissance* (1896), *The Drawings of the Florentine Painters* (1903, revised 1938), and *Three Essays in Method* (1937). His writing is known for its clarity and unhurried elegance. Among his later writings are *Seeing and Knowing* (1954), *Essays in Appreciation* (1959), *Passionate Sightseer* (1960), and *One Year's Reading For Fun*

(selections from a 1942 diary, 1960). Nicky Mariano edited his *Diaries 1947–1958* (1963).

Berger, Thomas [**Louis**] (1924–   ),   novelist. Born in Cincinnati and educated at the University of Cincinnati and Columbia University, Berger gained respect with his first novel, *Crazy in Berlin* (1958), which follows the comic antihero Carlo Reinhart from adolescence through adventures as a soldier in occupied Berlin into his bumbling attempts to fashion a life back home in America. Reinhart's adventures continue in *Reinhart in Love* (1961), *Vital Parts* (1970), and *Reinhart's Women* (1981). Berger's comedy is grounded often in parody of genres taken seriously by other writers. Among his best is *Little Big Man* (1964), a tale of the old West as seen by Jack Crabb, a 111-year-old survivor of the battle of Little Big Horn. Other works, all more or less parodic, include *Killing Time* (1967), about a mass murderer; *Regiment of Women* (1973), showing a futuristic society dominated by women; *Sneaky People* (1975), midwestern life in the 1930s; *Who Is Teddy Villanova?* (1977), a detective novel; *Arthur Rex* (1978), the Arthurian legend; *Neighbors* (1980), community life turned violent; *The Feud* (1983), set in the South in the 1930s; *The Houseguest* (1988); *Changing the Past* (1990), a fable about a man granted the opportunity to change his past; and *Orrie's Story* (1990), echoing the *Oresteia* in the U.S. at the end of World War II. Other novels include *Meeting Evil* 1992, *Robert Crews* (1994), *Suspects* (1996), and *The Return of Little Big Man* (1999).

Berkeley, George (1685–1783),   Anglo-Irish philosopher and clergyman. Bishop Berkeley's philosophical works include *Essay Towards a New Theory of Vision* (1709), *A Treatise Concerning the Principles of Human Knowledge* (1710), and *Three Dialogues Between Hylas and Philonus* (1713). In them, he argued the case for a subjective idealism allowing material things no existence independent of human perception, which itself depends on the empowerment of the mind of God. Later he turned his vision toward the New World, imagining a college in Bermuda to convert Indians. His "Verses on Planting Arts and Learning in America," once much-quoted, contains these lines: "There shall be sung another golden age, / The rise of empire and of arts; / . . . Westward the star of empire takes its way." Pursuing this vision, he went to Rhode Island in 1728, but stayed only three years.

Berkeley, Sir William (1606–1677),   colonial governor. See NATHANIEL BACON.

Berlin, Ellin Mackay (1903–1988).   Novelist, short-story writer, and society heiress, whose multimillionaire Catholic father threatened to disinherit her because she intended to marry IRVING BERLIN, an Orthodox Jew. The marriage caused a sensation in the 1920s, but lasted until her death 62 years later (his songs "Always" and "The Song Is Ended" were written for her). In her career as an author, she wrote short stories for *The Saturday Evening Post* and other magazines, articles for the *New Yorker*, and four novels: *The Land I Have Chosen* (1944), on Nazi Germany; *Lace Curtain* (1948); *Silver Platter* (1957), based on the lives of her pioneer ancestors in Nevada; and *The Best of Families* (1970).

Berlin, Irving (1888–1989),   songwriter. Born in Russia as Israel Baline, Berlin came to the United States in 1893. His first great hit was "Alexander's Ragtime Band" (1911). This was followed by such great successes as "Everybody's Doin' It," "Oh, How I Hate to Get Up in the Morning" (written for *Yip, Yip, Yaphank*, a World War I Army Show), "All Alone," "Remember," "Always," "White Christmas," and "Cheek to Cheek." Some formed part of the popular *Music Box Revues* (1921, 1922, 1923, 1925) and the Ziegfeld Follies. His other Broadway shows include *As Thousands Cheer* (1933), *Louisiana Purchase* (1940), *Annie Get Your Gun* (1946), *Miss Liberty* (1949), *Call Me Madam* (1950), and *Mr. President* (1962).

Bernard, John (1756–1828),   actor, autobiographer. One of the first touring stars, Bernard acted in New York, Philadelphia, and Boston from 1797 to 1819. A portion of his lively autobiography, *Retrospections of America, 1797–1811*, was published in 1887.

Bernard, William Bayle (1807–1875),   dramatist. Bernard, the son of JOHN BERNARD, appeared for a while on the stage before turning to writing. His dramas of rural American and allegedly western characters were among the earliest of their kind. Both Easterners and the English obtained their main impressions of life in America from such plays as his *The Kentuckian* (1833). Bernard also dramatized RIP VAN WINKLE (1832), among the first of numerous versions. He edited his father's papers, *Retrospections of the Stage* (1830).

Bernstein, Charles (1950–   ),   poet. Born and raised in New York City, Bernstein emerged in the 1980s as a leader of the LANGUAGE POETS, co-editing the journal *L-A-N-G-U-A-G-E* and a book of essays with the same name (1984). Verse is collected in *Poetic Justice* (1979), *Controlling Interests* (1980), *Islets/Irritations* (1983), *The Sophist* (1987), *Rough Trades* (1991), and *My Way: Speeches and Poems* (1999). Critical books include *Content's Dream: Essays 1975–1984* (1986) and *A Poetics* (1992). He is the editor of *Close Listening: Poetry and the Performed Word* (1998) and *99 Poets/1999: An International Poetics Symposium* (1999), with contributors from many nations.

Bernstein, Leonard (1918–1990),   conductor, composer, pianist, lecturer. Bernstein's extraordinarily varied career includes the following jobs: assistant to Serge Koussevitzky at Berkshire Music Center in 1942; conductor of the New York City Symphony, 1945–1948; musical adviser to the Israel Philharmonic Orchestra, 1948–1949 season; head of conducting department of the Berkshire Music Center, 1951–1956; professor of music at Brandeis University, 1951–1956; assistant conductor of the New York Philharmonic during the 1943–1944 season, and again for the Philharmonic, coconductor and then musical director, 1958–1970. His book *The Joy of Music* (1959) contains essays and scripts from seven of his extraordinarily popular "Omnibus" lectures on TV. Another book is *The Infinite Variety of Music* (1966). His musical compositions include *Symphony No. One, "Jeremiah"* (1942); *Hashkivenu* (a setting of part of text from Friday evening synagogue service, 1945); *Trouble in Tahiti* (1952), a one-act

opera; scores for the Broadway musicals *On the Town* (1944), *Wonderful Town* (1953), *Candide* (1956), and *West Side Story* (1957); the score for the film *On the Waterfront* (1954); and incidental music for Christopher Fry's play, *The Lark* (1957). *The Unanswered Question* (1976) collects lectures delivered at Harvard; *Findings* (1982) includes a variety of essays written throughout his life.

Berriault, Gina (1926–1999),   short-story writer, novelist. Born Arline Shandling in Long Beach, California, she lived in Los Angeles and, after marriage to John Berriault, in San Francisco. She was an award-winning short-story writer when her first novel, *The Descent* appeared in 1960. Other novels are *Conference of Victims* (1962, revised and published as *Afterwards* in 1988), *The Son* (1966), and *The Lights of Earth* (1984). Short-story collections are *The Mistress* (1965), *The Infinite Passion of Expectation* (1982), and the critically acclaimed *Women in Their Beds* (1996). She adapted her short story "The Stone Boy" for a 1984 film.

Berrigan, Daniel (1921–   ),   priest, social activist, writer. A Catholic priest, brother of PHILIP BERRIGAN, he gained fame for his involvement in civil rights and antiwar activities in the 1960s; these led to indictment, life as a fugitive, and imprisonment for destroying selective service files in Catonsville, Maryland. He has written several volumes of poetry, including *Selected and New Poems* (1973) and *Prison Poems* (1974); *The Trial of the Catonsville Nine* (1970), a play; *The Dark Night of Resistance* (1971); *Lights on in the House of the Dead* (1974), prison memoirs; and *To Dwell in Peace: An Autobiography* (1988). *Daniel Berrigan: Poetry, Drama, Prose*, edited by Michael True, appeared the same year.

Berrigan, Philip Francis (1923–   ),   priest, social activist, writer. Known with his brother DANIEL BERRIGAN for social activism in the 1960s, he founded the Catholic Peace Fellowship. Like his brother, he served time in prison for destroying selective service files. The experience spawned *Prison Journals of a Revolutionary Priest* (1970) and *Widen the Prison Gates* (1973).

Berry, Frances Miriam.   See FRANCES MIRIAM WHITCHER.

Berry, Wendell (1934–   ),   poet, novelist, essayist, environmentalist. Born in Henry County, Kentucky, where he has continued to live and farm, Berry was educated and taught until his early forties at the University of Kentucky. His books are mostly pastoral, rising from the ground and people of rural Kentucky, but they also display his social and environmental concerns. His poetry is gathered in *Collected Poems, 1957–1982* (1985) and *The Selected Poems of Wendell Berry* (1998). Individual poetry titles include *The Broken Ground* (1964), *Openings* (1968), *Findings* (1969), *Farming: A Handbook* (1970), *The Country of Marriage* (1973), *Clearing* (1977), *A Part* (1980), *The Wheel* (1982), *The Farm* (1995), and *A Timbered Choir: The Sabbath Poems 1979–1977* (1998). His novels are *Nathan Coulter* (1960), *A Place on Earth* (1967; revised, 1983), which has been called his masterpiece, set in a small Kentucky town in 1945; *The Memory of Old Jack* (1974);

Remembering (1988); and *Jayber Crow* (2000). His essays are collected in *The Long-Legged Horse* (1969), *The Unforeseen Wilderness* (1971), *A Continuous Harmony* (1972), *The Unsettling of America: Culture and Agriculture* (1977), *Standing by Words* (1983), *What Are People For?* (1990), *Sex, Economy, Freedom and Community: Eight Essays* (1993), and *A World Lost* (1996). *The Hidden Wound* (1970) is a memoir of racism observed in childhood.

Berryman, John (1914–1972),   poet, critic, teacher. Born in Oklahoma, Berryman moved with his family to Florida in 1926. Berryman's father, John Allyn Smith, committed suicide later that year, and his widow then married John Angus Berryman, who adopted the poet-to-be and moved the family to New York City. The effect of the suicide of Berryman's father on his son is reflected throughout his poetry. Berryman was educated at Columbia University, where he established lifelong friendships with Mark Van Doren, his most brilliant teacher, and with Allen Tate and R. P. Blackmur. Berryman also spent two years as a Kellett fellow at Cambridge.

Returning to the U.S. in 1938, Berryman taught at Wayne State, Harvard, Princeton, and Iowa, before joining the Humanities Department of the University of Minnesota in 1955, where he taught until his death. At the same time, he was pursuing a career as poet, critic, Shakespearean scholar, and story writer, a career that brought him gradually increasing acclaim, culminating in the Pulitzer Prize in 1965 and the National Book Award and the Bollingen Prize in 1969 for *The Dream Songs*. Three times married and twice divorced, an alcoholic who could never control his drinking for more than a few months, he was charismatic but often erratic in his social and professional dealings. His busy, difficult life ended in suicide at the age of 57, an act his poems had often contemplated.

Berryman's impersonal and derivative early poems were first published in book form in *Five Young American Poets* (1940), which also included RANDALL JARRELL. His next book, *Poems* (1942), continued to display an awkward dependence on such models as Yeats and Auden. In *The Dispossessed* (1948) Berryman began to escape his stiff early style. His critical biography *Stephen Crane* (1950) is a probing analysis of a writer with whom Berryman felt important affinities. *Berryman's Sonnets*, not published until 1967, were written in 1947; they explore the emotional highs and lows of an illicit love affair.

Homage to Mistress Bradstreet, published in the *Partisan Review* in 1953 and in book form three years later, marks a breakthrough to a new and more personal style, a style characterized by jagged syntax, multilevel diction, an oblique approach to narrative, and vivid, often dreamlike imagery.

Berryman began composing his major work, *The Dream Songs*, in 1955. A few of the Dream Songs, which exploited his new style with desperate verve, appeared along with other poems in *His Thought Made Pockets & The Plane Buckt* (1958). There followed *77 Dream Songs* (1964) and *His Toy, His Dream, His Rest* (1968), which completed the poem. The combined 385 poems were issued as *The Dream Songs* in 1969.

Berryman turned to a more straightforwardly autobiographical style in *Love and Fame* (1970), which was followed by the involuted *Delusions, Etc.* (1972), published just after his death. His production was rounded out with three other posthumous publications: *Recovery* (1976), a novel based on his attempt to overcome alcoholism; *The Freedom of the Poet* (1976), a brilliant essay and story collection; and a collection of previously unpublished poems, *Henry's Fate* (1977). Two lifelong projects, a biographical study of Shakespeare and a critical edition of *King Lear*, were never completed.

Berryman's poetry is notable for its often startling combination of bleak introspection and giddy comedy. He was labeled a confessional poet by his contemporaries, but Berryman rejected the term, perhaps in order to stress that Henry, the antihero of *Dream Songs*, was an imaginative creation, whatever his parallels with Berryman's own life. Berryman is often paired with ROBERT LOWELL as masters of a new kind of poetry that blended self-examination with exploration of public wrongs, but his voice and vision are unique.

The Collected Poems of John Berryman was published in 1989. Biographies are John Haffenden, *The Life of John Berryman* (1982), and Paul Mariani, *Dream Song: The Life of John Berryman* (1990).

THOMAS J. TRAVISANO

Best American Short Stories, The.   A series of annual anthologies begun in 1915 by EDWARD J. O'BRIEN and continued by him until his death in 1941; later edited by MARTHA FOLEY, it has since 1978 been edited first by Shannon Ravenel and then by Katrina Kenison with a distinguished guest editor each year. Small-circulation and so-called little magazines frequently furnish the bulk of the material. *Prize Stories: The O. Henry Awards* is a rival annual collection. See O. HENRY PRIZE STORIES.

Beston, Henry [Sheahan] (1888–1968),   writer. Beston's parents were a New England physician and a Frenchwoman. After studying at Harvard in 1911, he taught for a year at the University of Lyons. Later he taught at Harvard, edited *Living Age* for several years, and was on the editorial board of *The Atlantic*. In 1930 he married the poet ELIZABETH COATSWORTH. His best-known book, *The Outermost House* (1928), is a journal of Beston's yearlong residence in Thoreau-like solitude in a house on the outer dunes of Cape Cod in Eastham. The work is a classic of its kind. His quiet life on a northern New England farm and his extensive travels in Europe found their way into his work. His books include *Full Speed Ahead* (1919); *The Book of Gallant Vagabonds* (1924); *Herbs and the Earth* (1935); *American Memory* (1937); *The Lawrence River* (in THE RIVERS OF AMERICA SERIES, 1942); *Northern Farm* (1948); *White Pine and Blue Water* (a regional reader of the state of Maine, 1950); and *Henry Beston's Fairy Tales* (1952).

best sellers.   When THE BOOKMAN was started in February 1895, the editor, HARRY THURSTON PECK, began publishing a list of "Books in Demand" in the bookstores of various selected cities, changing the heading to "The Six Best Sellers" in 1903. The term was soon adopted by other publications, and such lists are now a standard feature of many literary magazines and newspaper book sections. After World War II, and the advent of paperback books, sales of books increased greatly, and the former best sellers (exclusive of the Bible)— Shakespeare's *Plays, Ivanhoe*, UNCLE TOM'S CABIN, BEN-HUR— were outdistanced by more recent works. By the 1950s, Charles Monroe Sheldon's IN HIS STEPS (1897) was estimated to have sold approximately eight million copies since its publication. Other blockbusters were Benjamin Spock's *The Common Sense Book of Baby and Child Care* (1946) with 7,850,000 copies; Erskine Caldwell's GOD'S LITTLE ACRE (1933), nearly 6,600,000; *Better Homes and Gardens Cook Book* (1930), about 5,800,000; Margaret Mitchell's GONE WITH THE WIND (1937), 5,000,000; Dale Carnegie's *How to Win Friends and Influence People* (1937), almost 4,900,000; and Mickey Spillane's *I, the Jury* (1947), nearly 4,450,000. Toward the end of the 20th century, the best-selling phenomenon was often attached to writers whose fans turned each of their books into best sellers, frequently followed by movies. Among the most successful have been PAULO COELHO, MICHAEL CRICHTON, JOHN GRISHAM, and ROBERT LUDLUM.

The term *best seller* is relative, and sales records should be considered in relation to increasing population. THE BAY PSALM BOOK went to nearly every colonial American family, a level of readership few books since have attained. Similarly, MICHAEL WIGGLESWORTH's *The Day of Doom*, a best seller in the 17th century, continued to be popular for 150 years. Later, the poems of LONGFELLOW were best sellers on both sides of the Atlantic, and another kind of literature, the DIME NOVEL, sometimes sold hundreds of thousands of copies per title. Textbooks have often been among the best sellers of any period; Noah Webster's *Speller*, for example, reached sales of some 75,000,000. Overall, the most enduring themes among best sellers have included religion, adventure, romance, education, self help, controversial issues, sexual sensationalism, and murder.

Bettelheim, Bruno (1903–1990),   psychologist, educator, and author. Born in Vienna, Bettelheim came to the U.S. in 1939 as a survivor of Dachau and Buchenwald Nazi concentration camps. Drawing from this experience, he wrote the widely read and influential study *Individual and Mass Behavior in Extreme Situations* (1943). He is known best, however, for his psychiatric work with severely disturbed children and its application to the study and education of normal children. *Love Is Not Enough* (1950), addressed to parents and general readership, describes his work in his Orthogenic School at the University of Chicago for emotionally disturbed children. It also outlines means for meeting children's and parents' needs in the modern family situation. Among his many other books are *The Children of the Dream* (1969), about communal childrearing in a kibbutz; *A Home for the Heart* (1974); and *The Uses of Enchantment* (1976), in which he discusses the psychosocial importance of fairy tales. *Surviving and Other Essays* (1979) treats problems in American society, surviving under extreme duress, and childhood schizophrenia. *Freud and Man's Soul* was published in 1983, and *A Good Enough Parent* was a final summing up, in 1987.

Beverley, Robert (c. 1673–1722),   traveler, historian. Beverley's family came from Yorkshire to Virginia, where Robert was born on his father's plantation. He served in the General Court, the Council, and the General Assembly. A man of shrewd insight, he gathered his observations of the world around him into an account of *The History and Present State of Virginia* (1705, edited by Louis B. Wright, 1947).

Beyond the Horizon (1920),   a play by EUGENE O'NEILL. Two brothers on the Mayo farm love the same girl; she marries one, the other goes to sea. Then the girl thinks she is in love with the one she didn't marry, but on his return is disillusioned. He leaves once more to go to the Argentine; where he makes and loses a fortune in grain. Returning, he finds that matters have gone from bad to worse on the farm. His brother tells him they have all been failures. As he dies he is, however, happy at last, "with the right of release—beyond the horizon."

Bibelot, The.   A magazine of reprints published by Thomas B. Mosher at Portland, Maine, 1895–1915. Mosher was a lover of fine literature and a creator of beautiful books, and his little magazine was an example of both enthusiasms. It contained chiefly poetry and short stories reprinted from European authors; it is a collector's item today.

Bible in the United States, the.   The impact of the Bible on America's development and culture is undeniable and makes Bible study valuable to the student of American literature. To Jews and Christians alike the Bible represents the inspired word of God. The people of these faiths have painstakingly translated numerous versions of the Bible with the hope that others could share in its riches. Yet many readers admire the Bible not only for its religious value but also for its literary virtures. Regardless of individual religious interpretation, the Bible has influenced the prose, poetry, and drama of the United States most dramatically. Since the country's beginnings, the Judeo-Christian values of the Bible have permeated its culture and have had widespread influence throughout the history of American literature.

The Bible's grandeur and strength have helped make it the most widely distributed book in the history of the United States. The *King James Version* (1611) was the first translation brought to America by immigrants and remains one of the most popular versions today. The Catholic *Rheims-Douay Version* (New Testament 1582, Old Testament 1609) arrived soon after the KJV, but scholars consider it an unsatisfactory translation. The KJV was compiled in part from previous English translations at the request of King James I of England and has long been praised for its beauty and elegance of translation. The stated purpose of nearly every version since the *King James Version* has been to render the Bible into the modern language of the day. Despite the wide acceptance of some of these newer translations among religious groups, the *King James Version* remains dear to those who study the Bible as literature.

The KJV remained unchallenged by other translations for nearly 300 years, but by the late 19th century, biblical scholars felt the need for a new translation. Equipped with a better knowledge of the original Greek and Hebrew manuscripts, these scholars corrected many errors in the KJV, publishing the New Testament in 1881, the Old Testament in 1885, and the Apocrypha in 1895. Though the resulting new translation, the *Revised Version*, met with early success, the KJV has maintained its popularity.

American Bible translators published little before the 20th century, but many of their contributions in the past ninety years are highly regarded by biblical and literary scholars. Americans originally worked in cooperation with the English on the *Revised Version*, but numerous differences separated the parties. The Americans published the *American Standard Revised Version* in 1901, a translation immediately considered superior to its English predecessor.

In 1923 Edgar J. Goodspeed and his associates at the University of Chicago published the next important American translation, *The New Testament: An American Translation*, and *The Bible: An American Translation*, which followed in 1935, was widely read until the late 1950s. In 1946 the International Council of Religious Education published a revision of the *American Standard Version* of 1901 under the title *The New Testament Revised Version*. That organization later published the complete Bible under the title *The Revised Standard Version* (1952). Liberal scholars translated these texts, and their work met with mixed acceptance. Their translation is unreliable in many critical passages, and among conservatives that version has not succeeded in replacing the *King James, Revised Version* or *American Standard Version*. A second edition of the *Revised Standard Version* appeared in 1971 and contains substantial revision of the New Testament. The Jewish Publication Society of America published the Old Testament as *The Holy Scriptures According to the Masoretic Text* in 1914, but this version has had little acceptance outside the Jewish community.

Two paraphrased versions of the Bible have met with widespread success. In 1966 Dr. Robert G. Bratcher and others published *Good News for Modern Man*. Since many evangelists used this translation, its popularity grew quickly. Kenneth N. Taylor translated a version and called it *The Living Bible* (1971). He based his work on the *American Standard Version* of 1901, but he also consulted Greek and Hebrew experts who referred to the most respected original manuscripts.

Roman Catholic translations of the recent past include the *Jerusalem Bible* (England, 1966) and the *New American Bible* (1970). The latter is the first completely American Roman Catholic translation and is considered one of the best translations of this century. Over fifty Catholic, Protestant, and Jewish scholars worked on it for twenty-six years. Prior to this version Catholics could consult only the Latin Vulgate for translation.

Currently, two of the most widely used translations are the *New American Standard Bible* (1971) and the *New International Version* (1978). The first is an update of the *American Standard Version* of 1901. The translators of the *New American Standard* aimed to provide an accurate translation in clear English with adequate notes, three characteristics for which it is highly praised. Many literature teachers and students use this version because it avoids the paraphrasing common in most translations of this century. The *New International Version* is more freely translated than the *American Standard Version* but is popular for its fluent modern English. Recognized by Christians for its conservative theology, this version misrepresents some of the original texts through excessive paraphrasing.

Because the Bible is the major theological resource for Christianity and Judaism and because those religions have been significant influences on the cultural life of the United States, the power of the Bible in American literature has been both widespread and incalculable.

In Colonial times, the Puritans drew from the Bible the spirit and often the letter of their law. John Cotton, Nathaniel Ward, John Eliot, and Cotton Mather were early Puritan leaders who wrote under the influence of the Bible. Jonathan Edwards combined his study of Locke and Berkeley with study of the Bible and became one of the leading authors of the 18th century.

Although the literary forms and styles, genres, and movements of 19th-century America multiplied, biblical influence remained strong. Such major American authors as Emerson, Thoreau, Hawthorne, Longfellow, and Whittier drew inspiration and subject matter from the Bible, but by comparison with the Puritans, the works of these men exhibited far more independent thought. The Bible provided ideas to such 19th-century essayists as Edward Everett Hale and Henry Ward Beecher; poets Sidney Lanier, Julia Ward Howe, and Edward Arlington Robinson; and novelists Lew Wallace, Harriet Beecher Stowe, and Henry James. And one of the nation's most beloved presidents, Abraham Lincoln, drew much of his wisdom from the Bible.

During the 20th century, the influence of the Bible in the United States has persisted in the work of many authors. Published in 1904, J. L. Hurlbut's *Story of the Bible* sold three million copies by mid-century. Mary Ellen Chase's *Life and Language in the Old Testament* (1955) and Edmund Wilson's *The Dead Sea Scrolls* (1955) helped renew literary interest in biblical matters. Although the inspirational value of the Bible is difficult to assess, many authors drew material directly from it, for example, poets Archibald MacLeish, Robinson Jeffers, and Stephen Vincent Benét; playwrights Maxwell Anderson, Marc Connelly, Barry Stavis, and Arthur Miller; short-story writers Flannery O'Connor, John Cheever, and Eudora Welty; and novelists Sholem Asch, Howard Fast, and Lloyd C. Douglas.

In all its editions and nearly 500 million copies with its more than 50 types of literature—poems, stories, hymns, riddles, essays, history, proverbs, and dramatic scenes—the Bible remains a significant inspirational force in American literature.
SAM SMILEY

Bibliography of American Literature. A compilation by Jacob Blanck (1906–1974) sponsored by the American Bibliographical Society, it contains information about first editions by authors from the Federal period to 1930. Published in nine volumes, it is also available on computer disk.

Bickerstaff, Isaac. Pen name of BENJAMIN WEST.

Bidart, Frank (1939–   ),   poet. Bidart was born in California, educated at the University of California, studied poetry under ROBERT LOWELL at Harvard, and has taught at Brandeis, Berkeley, and Wellesley. His poems are sometimes monologues, sometimes auditory montages, his cutting technique learned in part from his early fascination with the movies. His books include *Golden State* (1973), *The Book of the Body* (1977), *The Sacrifice* (1983), *In the Western Night: Collected Poems 1965 to 1990* (1990), and *Desire* (1997).

Bierce, Ambrose [Gwinnett] (1842–1914),   short-story writer, aphorist, newspaperman, essayist, versifier. Not only the United States—the Midwest and both coasts—but England as well can lay claim to having been the home of Ambrose Bierce. Born in Ohio, he grew up in Indiana. In 1861, when the Civil War erupted, he enlisted at the age of eighteen as a volunteer in the Ninth Indiana Infantry Regiment. A brave and disciplined soldier who served in some of the war's most celebrated battles, he was promoted to first lieutenant before he was mustered out in 1865; two years later he was brevetted to major. He settled in San Francisco in 1867, where he began training himself to become a writer, publishing poems, essays, sketches, and his first story. In March 1872, however, he and his wife, Mollie Day, sailed for England, where their sons, Day and Leigh, were both born, and where Bierce wrote for the British humorous weekly *Fun*, as well as for other periodicals. Despite admiration for England, he returned to California in September 1875 to join his pregnant wife, who had preceded him a few months earlier. Their only daughter, Helen, was born in San Francisco. Except for a brief foray into mining in 1880, most of his professional time was spent in editorial work for *The Argonaut* and *The Wasp* until 1887. He was then hired by WILLIAM RANDOLPH HEARST's *San Francisco Examiner*, where he continued a well-known column, "Prattle," which he had started in *The Argonaut*. His association with Hearst lasted almost to the end of his career. His personal life, however, was not stable. In 1888 he and Mollie separated, although they were not divorced until 1905; in 1889, their first son, Day, was killed in an adolescent shootout over a girl.

In 1896 Hearst sent Bierce to Washington to head the lobby opposing passage of a funding bill that would have mulcted taxpayers of millions of dollars for the benefit of the Central and Southern Pacific railroads. After the bill's defeat, Bierce returned to San Francisco, but in 1899 he left again for the East, taking up permanent residence in Washington, D.C., where he lived until his departure for Mexico in 1913. He wrote for the *New York Journal, New York American*, and *Cosmopolitan* magazine as well as the *San Francisco Examiner* until his final resignation from Hearst's service in 1909, the year he began preparing his twelve-volume *Collected Works*, completed in 1912. In October 1913, after a preliminary trip through his old Civil War battlefields, he made his way southwest to Texas and in November crossed the border into Mexico to join Villa's forces as an observer. His last letter, dated December 26, was from Chihuahua. Almost certainly, he was killed in the battle of Ojinaga on January 11, 1914.

Bierce's first three books appeared under the pseudonym "Dod Grile" during his stay in England: *The Fiend's Delight* (1873), *Nuggets and Dust Panned Out in California* (1873), and *Cobwebs from an Empty Skull* (1874). All were sketches, epigrams, and fables taken from his periodical writings. After his return to the United States, he published two collections of short stories, *Tales of Soldiers and Civilians* (1892), later given the title of its first English edition, *In the Midst of Life* (from the Anglican Book of Common Prayer, "In the midst of life we are in death"), and *Can Such Things Be?* (1893), a title derived from *Macbeth*. He also published two volumes of satirical verse, *Black Beetles in Amber* (1892) and *Shapes of Clay* (1903). His *Fantastic Fables* (1899), which turn received wisdom upside down, are exemplified by "The Thoughtful Warden":

> The Warden of a Penitentiary was one day putting locks on the doors of all the cells when a mechanic said to him:
> "Those locks can all be opened from the inside—you are very imprudent."
> The Warden did not look up from his work, but said;
> "If that is called imprudence I wonder what would be called a thoughtful provision against the vicissitudes of fortune."

One of Bierce's books, known today as *The Devil's Dictionary*, was years in the making. Its definitions began appearing in his newspaper columns as early as 1877, and in 1906 a number of them appeared in book form as *The Cynic's Word Book*. His pithy definitions have been and are frequently quoted. The following samples convey the flavor of the book:

> EDUCATION, n. That which discloses to the wise and disguises from the foolish their lack of understanding.
> IMPUNITY, n. Wealth.
> TRUST, n. In American politics, a large corporation composed in greater part of thrifty working men, widows of small means, orphans in the care of guardians and the courts, with many similar malefactors and public enemies.

Many of Bierce's most thoughtful works are essays. A Texas admirer, Silas Orrin Howes, published a collection of them as *The Shadow on the Dial and Other Essays* (1909).

The serious student, however, would be well advised not to search for these books, but to concentrate on *The Collected Works of Ambrose Bierce* (1909–12), prepared by the author himself from the enormous amount of writing he had done over a lifetime of journalism. *The Collected Works* includes everything he thought worth preserving, with the exception of a useful little stylebook, *Write It Right* (1909), which has gone through numerous editions and is still valuable.

Bierce has always been a problem for literary historians,

who have had great difficulty fitting him under the rubric of realism and naturalism that is conventionally assigned to his contemporaries. More useful in understanding Bierce is impressionism. According to this tradition, external reality does not exist independently of the awareness of a perceiver; moreover, space and time are not inflexible categories of knowledge, but expand and contract according to an individual's perceptions. These ideas bore their remarkable fruit in his story "An Occurrence at Owl Creek Bridge," in which a condemned spy, at the very moment of being hanged, believes himself to be executing a daring escape to the arms of his beloved wife. The epiphany, or sudden flash of insight, is another impressionistic technique Bierce used. In "Chickamauga" a deaf-mute boy playing merrily with gruesomely wounded soldiers whose condition he fails to comprehend suddenly recognizes the dead body of his mother in the blazing ruins of his ravaged home.

Still another facet of Bierce's writing setting him apart from contemporaries like Mark Twain was his preference for wit over humor. Wit, he wrote, does not make us laugh; it makes us wince. It is "not altogether true, and therefore not altogether dull, with just enough of audacity to startle and just enough of paradox to charm, profoundly wise, as bleak as steel." Bierce used wit in his acerbic definitions, fables, aphorisms, and essays to reevaluate unexamined clichés in politics, law, science, philosophy, and society. Many of his positions have been difficult for commentators to deal with, however, because the analytical tools necessary to cope with them did not exist until recently.

For example, as a social and political critic he has never received his just due. Although he was out of sympathy with the doctrinaire socialism of such acquaintances as JACK LONDON, he actually saw the dangers posed by America's greedy plutocrats more clearly than they. But until economic theory devoted to public choice had been developed, it was difficult to locate Bierce's position with any exactitude. Now, however, it is possible to recognize him as a keen analyst of what we have learned to call the "rent-seeking society": special interest groups who tried to seize the levers of political power in order, through legislative maneuvering, to choke off free entry into the marketplace, with competition throttled by restrictive state-imposed barriers. Bierce fought long and successfully against the rent-seekers of his day—notably San Francisco's "Big Four": Mark Hopkins, Leland Stanford, Charles Crocker, and Collis Huntington—not only in Sacramento, but also in Washington. His most celebrated foray against them was his Hearst-financed battle against Collis Huntington and the railway Funding Bill.

Many examples of Bierce's attacks on the rent-seeking society could be adduced from his writings, but the satirical fable "Ants and Grasshopper" is typical:

Some Members of a Legislature were making schedules of their wealth at the end of the session, when an Honest Miner came along and asked them to divide with him. The members of the Legislature inquired:

"Why did you not acquire property of your own?"

"Because," replied the Honest Miner, "I was so busy digging out gold that I had no leisure to lay up something worth while."

Then the Members of the Legislature derided him, saying:

"If you waste your time in profitless amusement you cannot, of course, expect to share the rewards of industry."

In moral philosophy, Bierce repeatedly attacked the position called "consequentialism," that is, judging the wisdom of a course of action by its outcome. As he pointed out, this criterion is useless except in retrospect, since no one can foretell the future. Instead, the individual who acts must proceed in the light of the best knowledge available to him, even though his decision may prove disastrous. Bierce satirized consequentialism in his first book, The Fiend's Delight, and continued to deride it in satirical verse and essays. Thus, in attacking the vices and follies of Columbus, whom he regarded as a knavish pirate, he says that "the wisdom of an act is not to be determined by the outcome, but by the performer's reasonable expectation of success." Perhaps his most chilling evocation of the problems with consequentialism, however, is to be found in "The Coup de Grâce." In this story a Federal officer, unable to stand the torment of his hideously wounded comrade, whose trailing intestines are evidence of his disembowelment by rooting swine, puts the mutilated soldier out of his misery with a sword-thrust just before a rescue party arrives, accompanied by the officer's worst enemy, the victim's brother.

Bierce has never been popular with mass audiences. But those readers who have been willing to cope with the demands he makes on their intelligence have found him stimulating and provocative. Even in his own day, he had an international following, which has continued to spread. His influence on H. L. MENCKEN, STEPHEN CRANE, and ERNEST HEMINGWAY is well known. However, postmodern writers have also recognized him as their spiritual godfather: JORGE LUIS BORGES, JULIO CORTÁZAR, CARLOS FUENTES, and Ryunosuke Akutagawa. The British critic Brigid Brophy has commented that a century ago Bierce had done—and done better—the things that writers like these are being hailed for doing today as if they were startling innovations.

See biographical and critical studies by Carey McWilliams (1929), Paul Fatout (1951, 1956), M. E. Grenander (1971), and Cathy N. Davidson (1984).

M. E. GRENANDER

Big Bear of Arkansas, The, a story by T. B. THORPE. An early representative of the colloquial humor and tall-tale tradition later exploited more skillfully by writers such as Twain and Faulkner, the story appeared first in 1839 in WILLIAM T. PORTER's Spirit of the Times and was reprinted in his The Big Bear of Arkansas and Other Sketches (1845). Thorpe included a more readable text in his The Hive of "The Bee-Hunter" (1854).

Big Clock, The (1946), a novel by KENNETH FEARING. An ingenious tale of a manhunt in which the quarry must track himself down, it was made into a movie (1948) by Jonathan Latimer.

Bigelow, John (1817–1911),   editor, author, diplomat. Bigelow traveled extensively and wrote entertainingly about his experiences, served as American consul-general at Paris and later as minister to France, worked with WILLIAM CULLEN BRYANT on the New York *Evening Post*, was secretary of state to Samuel J. Tilden during the latter's service as governor of New York. Out of his experiences grew two biographies, *William Cullen Bryant* (1893) and *Samuel J. Tilden* (1895), as well as an autobiography, *Retrospections of an Active Life* (5 v. 1909–13). In addition, he wrote many historical works on Franklin, Frémont, Beaumarchais, and others. Margaret Clapp wrote a fine biography, *Forgotten First Citizen, John Bigelow* (1947).

Big-Foot Wallace, The Adventures of (1870),   by John C. Duval (1816–1897). The story of W. A. A. WALLACE (1817–1899). Wallace was a Virginian ranger and hunter who became embroiled in the troubles between the Texans and the Mexicans in the 1830s and acquired his nickname because it was difficult to find shoes big enough to fit him when he was a prisoner in Mexico. His adventures are related autobiographically with old-style graphic American humor. Walter Stanley Campbell wrote a biography, *Big-Foot Wallace* (1942), in which he attempted to separate fact from legend.

Biggers, Earl Derr (1884–1933),   playwright, novelist. Biggers was a Boston journalist, born in Ohio and educated at Harvard. His successful mystery novel, *Seven Keys to Baldpate* (1913), was made into a play by GEORGE M. COHAN and was also filmed. He wrote other novels, but is chiefly known for his series about the Chinese detective CHARLIE CHAN. These include *The House Without a Key* (1925), *The Chinese Parrot* (1926), *Behind That Curtain* (1928), *The Black Camel* (1929), *Charlie Chan Carries On* (1930), and *Keeper of the Keys* (1932).

Biglow Papers, The,   poems and prose sketches by JAMES RUSSELL LOWELL. The first poem appeared in the Boston *Courier*, June 17, 1846, and was followed by eight others. Together with four published in the NATIONAL ANTI-SLAVERY STANDARD, the poems were collected in *The Biglow Papers* (1848). A second series ran during the Civil War in *The Atlantic Monthly* and was collected in 1867. Together, they made two series of satiric poems, prose sketches, and critical miscellanea.

The Biglow Papers marked Lowell's true start as a widely known publicist of antislavery causes, and as an ardent defender of things American. They helped win acceptance for American speechways in the best literary circles. The first series centered on the war with Mexico, the second on the slavery issue. The verses were written in Yankee dialect, while the accompanying prose was mostly straight English. There were three chief characters: Hosea Biglow, a forth-right commentator on current issues; his friend Birdofredom Sawin, something of a scoundrel; and the Rev. Homer Wilbur, used as a foil. With bludgeonlike blows Lowell satirized the politicians of his day and the doctrines they preached, the way in which war was made, the cowardice of editors, and the folly of men of wealth and alleged statesmen North and South. One impor-

tant poem avoids political issues—THE COURTIN', reckoned among Lowell's masterpieces. It inspired a best-selling novel, *Quincy Adams Sawyer* (1900), by Charles Felton Pidgin.

Sometimes overlooked is the significance of Lowell's use of Americanisms, especially Yankeeisms. For many American readers through several generations it provided the first literary introduction to the American language. Mencken felt that in the critical material that accompanied *The Biglow Papers* Lowell "did a great service to the common tongue of the country, and must be numbered among its true friends." See YANKEE IN AMERICAN LANGUAGE AND LITERATURE.

Big Money, The (1936),   a novel by JOHN DOS PASSOS. With THE 42ND PARALLEL, and *1919* (q.v), it forms the trilogy U.S.A. (1938). Completing the chronological sweep of the trilogy, *The Big Money* focuses on the pursuit of big money in the 1920s that ends in the stock market crash and the GREAT DEPRESSION. Society is in flux in its pursuit of the American dream of riches and fame. Charley Anderson, a returned war hero, seeks his fortune in the aircraft industry and marries an heiress, has an affair with Margo Dowling, on her way to a career in Hollywood, becomes involved in land fraud, and dies in an accident. Other characters move in and out of the events and employments of the times. Sketches of real people intrude: Henry Ford, Isadora Duncan, the Wright Brothers, Rudolph Valentino, and William Randolph Hearst. Newspaper headlines scream, "Sacco and Vanzetti Must Die." The novel and trilogy conclude with the magnificent sketch of the generic "Vag," as a young man hitchhikes across America, still seeking the place where the promises will be fulfilled.

Big Sky, The (1947),   a novel by A. B. GUTHRIE, JR. A story of the mountain men who followed after Lewis and Clark, it follows the adventures of Boone Caudill, a young man who quits Kentucky and travels up the Missouri River in the 1830s. He meets other mountain men, lives with Indians, takes an Indian as wife, and kills a friend he thinks has fathered his wife's baby. The novel has been especially praised for its grounding in accurately reported details of time and place.

Big Sleep, The (1939),   the novel in which RAYMOND CHANDLER introduced his celebrated detective, Philip Marlowe. In 1946 it was made into a popular film.

Billings, Josh   [pen name of **Henry Wheeler Shaw (Uncle Esek)**] (1818–1885),   auctioneer, real-estate agent, humorist. Born in Massachusetts, Shaw was professedly a Yankee, who in his essays and lectures created for his Josh Billings an amusing family of Yankee characters. He went to college, but as he himself testified: "Hamilton College has turned out a good many fine men—it turned me out." He became an explorer, a coal operator, farmer, steamboat captain, and finally an auctioneer and real-estate dealer. Then he took to writing humorous essays as an avocation. When they attracted no attention, Billings discovered the contemporaneous key to success by studying ARTEMUS WARD and adopting misspelling as the cap-and-bells to his wit and wisdom. He was widely quoted and misquoted, and his fame led him on to lecturing, in which he also was highly successful. He published volumes of *Sayings* (1865, 1866) and a series of *Allminax* (1869–79) in one volume (1902). Among his other publications were *Josh Billings on Ice and Other Things* (1868), *Everybody's Friend, or Josh Billings' Encyclopedia and Proverbial Philosophy of Wit and Humor* (1876), *Complete Comical Writings of Josh Billings* (1876, 1877), *Josh Billings' Struggling with Things* (1881), *Josh Billings' Spice Box* (1881, 1882), and *Josh Billings, His Works Complete* (4 v. 1888).

Billy Budd, Sailor (posthumously published, 1924), a novel by HERMAN MELVILLE. Like much of the poetry and prose written in the last decade of Melville's life, *Billy Budd* offers final, if finite, statements on issues Melville had pondered for a lifetime. He had dealt with the problem of the collision of good and evil even in REDBURN (1849), developed the theme in most of the subsequent novels, and given it poetic resolution in CLAREL (1876). In *Billy Budd* it is presented in its starkest form, with Billy and Claggart, the villainous master-at-arms, representing almost allegorically abstract opposites. Their interaction admits of no ambiguity. Innocence and its obverse are inadequate for survival; the man of extreme polarity inevitably destroys himself or is destroyed, whereas the men who reconcile the opposites—Ishmael of MOBY-DICK and Jack Chase of WHITE JACKET—survive.

Billy Budd is the last flowering of Melville as symbolist. Captain Vere's decision to hang Billy for slaying the evil Claggart represents the triumph of law. Vere, allegorically the just God of the Old Testament, realizes his first obligation is to preserve society, not self, so he must condemn Billy to death despite his paternalistic feelings for him. Billy, the representative of the New Dispensation, willingly accepts martyrdom, crying at the end, "God bless Captain Vere!" As the Christ-like Billy mounts the yardarm, the golden sun penetrates the fleecy clouds, signifying the hero's resurrection into eternal life.

Billy the Kid (1859–1881), sobriquet of William H. Bonney, frontier outlaw. Born in New York City, Bonney was brought to Kansas City at the age of three and at age twelve killed his first man, in Silver City, New Mexico, for insulting his mother. After many crimes in various parts of the Southwest he joined a gang in the Lincoln County cattle war in New Mexico, and while visiting his sweetheart at Fort Sumner was killed by a former friend, Sheriff Pat Garrett. Old-timers, journalists, dime-novelists, and balladists built him into a folk hero, and he has been a favorite subject for biographies and novels, including LARRY MCMURTRY's *Anything for Billy* (1988).

Bingham, Caleb (1757–1817), textbook author. Bingham was one of the first to provide schoolbooks for Americans, including *The Young Lady's Accidence, or, A Short and Easy Introduction to English Grammar* (1785); *The Child's Companion* (1792); *The American Preceptor* (1794); and *The Columbian Orator* (1797). He also translated Chateaubriand's *Atala* (1802).

Bingham, George Caleb (1811–1879), painter, politician. Born in Virginia, Bingham grew up in Missouri and studied art in Pennsylvania and Europe. He was a member of the state legislature and held other political posts in Missouri. His paintings, which record some of the most familiar images of frontier life, include *Fur Traders Descending the Missouri, Daniel Boone Coming Through the Cumberland Gap, Raftsmen Playing Cards*, and *Stump Speaking*.

Bingham, Hiram (1789–1869); **Bingham, Hiram** (1831–1908); **Bingham, Hiram** (1875–1956). The first Hiram Bingham was a Congregationalist missionary from Vermont who with his wife, Sybil Moseley, became a missionary to Hawaii, created a written form of the native language, published a textbook, *Elementary Lessons in Hawaiian* (1822), and with associates translated the Bible into Hawaiian. The second Hiram Bingham became a missionary with his wife, Clarissa Brewster, to the Gilbert Islands. There he followed his father's example by adapting the local language to writing, preparing a dictionary, and translating the Bible and hymns. The third Hiram Bingham, son of the second, became a noted archeologist, historian, and politician. Educated at Yale, the University of California, and Harvard, he headed expeditions of exploration in South America, discovering the Inca cities of Vitcos and Machu Picchu. He headed an Allied flying school in France during World War I and later was lieutenant governor and governor of Connecticut, and U.S. senator. His books include *Journal of an Expedition across Venezuela and Columbia* (1909), *Across South America* (1911), *In the Wonderland of Peru* (1913), *The Monroe Doctrine, An Obsolete Shibboleth* (1913), *Inca Land* (1922), *Machu Picchu, a Citadel of the Incas* (1930), *Elihu Yale—The American Nabob of Queen Square* (1939), and *Lost City of the Incas* (1948).

Binns, Archie (1899–1971), novelist, biographer. Born in Washington, he wrote excellent novels of the sea and of the Northwest, including *Lightship* (1934), *The Laurels Are Cut Down* (1937), *The Land Is Bright* (1939), *The Timber Beast* (1944), and *You Rolling River* (1947). *Mrs. Fiske and the American Theatre* (1955), written with Olive Kooken, is a biography of Minnie Maddern Fiske. He also wrote *Enchanted Islands* (a juvenile, 1956) and *Headwaters* (1957).

Birches (1915), one of ROBERT FROST's best-known poems. It describes the trees bent to the ground by ice storms. The poet imagines they have been bent by a boy swinging on them. Published first in *The Atlantic Monthly*, August 1915, it was collected in *Mountain Interval* (1916).

Bird, Robert Montgomery (1806–1854), physician, dramatist, novelist. Born in Delaware, Bird received an M.D. from the University of Pennsylvania in 1827 but gave up his practice because of his reluctance to collect fees. EDWIN FORREST helped him out by buying several of his plays: *Pelopidas* (1830), THE GLADIATOR (1831), ORALLOOSA (1832), and THE BROKER OF BOGOTA (1834). For these Bird received a tiny fraction of the profits and Forrest refused to let Bird publish them. The American copyright laws did not adequately protect the playwright at that time, so Bird decided to try his hand at novel writing.

His novels proved considerably more profitable for the author than had his plays. His dramatic talent and experience infused the novels with excitement and suspense. The characters are carefully molded of conflicting passions, which in NICK OF THE WOODS (1837) produce a hero with a split personality. *Sheppard Lee* (1836), published anonymously, is a colorful satire in which the hero, a New Jersey farmer, indulges in metempsychosis to explore the follies of contemporary life at all social levels. Bird's other books include CALAVAR (1834), THE INFIDEL (1835), THE HAWKS OF HAWK HOLLOW (1835), *Peter Pilgrim* (1838), and *The Adventures of Robin Day* (1839). *The Broker of Bogota* was finally published in *Representative American Plays* by A. H. Quinn in 1917. Of the remaining plays, some are in Clement E. Foust's *Life and Dramatic Works of Robert Montgomery Bird* (1919), and some in AMERICA'S LOST PLAYS.

Birdofredom Sawin. See BIGLOW PAPERS.

Birds of Killingsworth, The (1863), a narrative poem by HENRY WADSWORTH LONGFELLOW, included in TALES OF A WAYSIDE INN. Some Connecticut farmers kill the birds, whom they blame for destroying their crops. But when the birds are gone, caterpillars do even more damage.

Birds of North America, The (1827–1838), a treatise by JOHN JAMES AUDUBON. The volume contains more than a thousand illustrations in color and identifies more than five hundred species of birds. First printed in England, these huge folios have become rare and expensive collectors' items. William MacGillivray assisted Audubon considerably in the preparation of the text.

Birkbeck, Morris (1764–1825), traveler, farmer, founder of Wanborough and Albion, Illinois. He was the center of a controversy in England on the advisability of British farmers settling in this country. He was a successful farmer on his own account when he came to America in 1817 to look into the arguments for emigrating. His *Notes on a Journey in America from the Coast of Virginia to the Territory of Illinois* (1818) and *Letters from Illinois* (1818) called frontier Americans lazy and unenterprising, but suggested that opportunities for more industrious settlers were great. With Robert Flower and Flower's brother, Birkbeck purchased land and started a settlement that eventually attracted four hundred other British and seven hundred American settlers.

Birney, [Alfred] Earle [or Earl] (1904–1995), Canadian poet, professor. Born in Calgary, Alberta, Birney was a member of one of the pioneer families of Alberta. He was educated at the University of British Columbia, the University of California at Berkeley, and the University of Toronto and began his career teaching English at the University of Utah. He lived later in Canada and held professorships at the University of Toronto and the University of British Columbia. He also worked for Radio Canada and served as an editor for *Canadian Forum* (1936–40), *Canadian Poetry Magazine* (1946–48), and *Prism International* (1964–65).

Birney won recognition as a poet with his first two books, *David and Other Poems* (1942) and *Now Is the Time* (1945). He published four other books before his *Selected Poems 1940–1966* (1966) served as a capstone to his early work. He had established himself as a leading interpreter of Canadian landscapes and people, with a reputation for leftwing moralizing. The books kept coming, however, and his commentary gave way to a more concrete presentation, suggesting an acceptance of a world not always perfect. Later collections especially admired include *Rag and Bone Shop* (1971), *Bear on the Delhi Road* (1973), and *What's So Big About Green?* (1973). *Collected Poems* (2 v. 1974) was followed by more books of verse, including *Ghost in the Wheels* (1977) and *Fall by Fury* (1978). *Last Makings* (1991) contains new and selected poetry. He has also written radio plays and two novels: *Turvey: A Military Picaresque* (1949), a humorous account of World War II; and *Down the Long Table* (1955), a satiric thrust at 1930s leftists.

Birthmark, The, story by NATHANIEL HAWTHORNE. First published in *The Pioneer* (March 1843), it was collected in MOSSES FROM AN OLD MANSE (1846). It tells how a scientist, Aylmer, seeks to remove a birthmark from the cheek of his beautiful wife, Georgiana. He succeeds, but she dies.

Birth of a Nation, The (1915), motion picture. Based on *The Clansman*, by THOMAS DIXON, this film of the Civil War and its aftermath established motion pictures as an art form of tremendous power and D. W. GRIFFITH as a master director. It provoked race riots in many cities, however, and brought charges of racism against Griffith for his portrayal of African-Americans and of the Ku Klux Klan.

Bishop, Elizabeth (1911–1979), poet, memoirist. Born in Worcester, Massachusetts, she suffered the death of her father when she was eight months old. Bishop's mother was permanently institutionalized when her child was five years old, an event later remembered in the luminous story "In the Village." Bishop was raised by various relatives, chiefly in Boston and Great Village, Nova Scotia. As a child she was isolated by serious illnesses, and in adulthood she often struggled with shyness, yet her interest in books, nature, and people was strong. Bishop's mature writing is marked by lively curiosity and an intense inwardness. She was educated at home and then at Walnut Hill School, where she developed an interest in poetry and published profusely in the school literary magazine.

Later Bishop attended Vassar College, where her friends included MARY MCCARTHY and MURIEL RUKEYSER. Shortly before graduation in 1934, she met the older poet MARIANNE MOORE, who became her mentor and friend. Moore wrote an introduction to the first poems Bishop published in book form, those appearing in the anthology *Trial Balances* (1935). She later developed strong friendships with ROBERT LOWELL and RANDALL JARRELL.

After 1939, much of Bishop's life was spent in the tropics, first in Key West and then, from 1951 until 1973, in Brazil. She won the Pulitzer Prize in 1955 and the National Book Award in 1969. From 1970 until 1973, she alternated fall terms teaching at Harvard with seasons in Ouro Preto, Brazil, and in 1974 she moved permanently to Boston and began teaching at Harvard full time. She died of a stroke in her Boston home in 1979.

Bishop's first book of poetry, *North & South*, was published in 1946. It is remarkable for the contrast between her earlier poems, set in the North, which are curious fables, both witty and intense, about the rewards and limitations of a life of introspection, and a later group, set in the South, which explore the sensuous richness of tropical experience. Her second book, *A Cold Spring*, was collected with *North & South* under the title *Poems* in 1955. It contains several poems of remarkable richness, particularly "Over 2,000 Illustrations and a Complete Concordance" and "At the Fishhouses." The former is one of her most powerful considerations of the rewards and frustrations of travel, the latter one of the best of her many poems, balanced between sea and shore.

Her move to Brazil was dramatized in her next book, *Questions of Travel* (1965). In a subtly orchestrated sequence of poems, she explores a transition in consciousness from the superficial awareness of the tourist confronting a strange culture to the more penetrating insight of a foreign observer who has come to know native customs and traditions from the inside. A second group, which returns to the Nova Scotia of the poet's childhood, conveys a poignant but delicately controlled sense of loss. In 1962 Bishop published a prose work, *Brazil*, for Life World Library, and with Emanuel Brasil she edited *An Anthology of Twentieth Century Brazilian Poetry* (1972), which contains many of her own translations.

Geography III (1976), the final book published in Bishop's lifetime, is considered her best. In a series of extraordinary poetic meditations, such as "In the Waiting Room," "Crusoe in England," "One Art," "The End of March," and "The Moose," Bishop explores the themes treated throughout her work with a new directness, flexibility, and power, but with no loss in subtlety or control. As readers have absorbed this book, the sense that she must have all along been a major poet has gained wider acceptance. Two posthumous publications, *The Complete Poems: 1927–1979* (1983) and *The Collected Prose* (1984), have brought together nearly all her published work and much that had never previously been published or collected in book form, and have helped to solidify her reputation. Her prose works take the form of funny and touching memoirs of past experience, and these have helped to mitigate the impression of Bishop as a coolly impersonal poet.

Bishop's poems are notable for their freshness and precision of observation, their conversational tone, their subtle, apparently casual organization, and their quiet, sometimes mysterious movement toward symbolic resolution. Her work deals repeatedly with the movement from one realm of experience to another. Many poems dramatize the shift from a northern to a southern awareness, or the transition from childhood to adulthood, from dreaming to waking, from imprisonment to freedom, from civilization to nature, or from fact to imagination. Her poems hardly ever generalize. Instead, they accumulate details in a quietly narrative form that gradually drifts toward a convincing resolution. This approach had an important influence on the form of Robert Lowell's groundbreaking book *Life Studies*, as he gratefully acknowledged in their extensive correspondence.

The vividly observed detail in her poetry attests to the influence of the Imagist movement and, more specifically, of Marianne Moore. One feels Bishop's equally important response to the work of WALLACE STEVENS in her persistent questioning of the scope and limits of imagination. Her absorption in meditational religious poetry, particularly that by George Herbert and Gerard Manley Hopkins, was also crucial. The tension between observation and meditation is unusually well resolved in her work; one of its mysterious achievements is that the reader often finds it impossible to say just where observation ends and meditation begins. Bishop's influence is felt in the work of a wide range of living poets. JOHN ASHBERY, JAMES MERRILL, FRANK BIDART, ROBERT PINSKY, AMY CLAMPITT, and SANDRA MCPHERSON, among others, have been drawn to her work because she successfully resolves the paradoxical current demand for a casual linguistic surface overlying a unified symbolic foundation, and because she successfully joins the texture of ordinary experience with the texture of dreams. She has taken her place alongside Herbert, Hopkins, and Emily Dickinson as one of the distinctive lyric voices in the language.

See critical studies by Robert Dale Parker (1988) and Thomas J. Travisano (1988). A critical biography is Brett C. Miller, *Elizabeth Bishop: Life and the Memory of It* (1993).

THOMAS J. TRAVISANO

Bishop, John Peale (1892–1944), poet, fiction writer, essayist. Bishop was born in West Virginia and educated at Princeton. After World War I, he became managing editor of *Vanity Fair* and in 1922 joined a group of expatriates in Paris, among them FITZGERALD, HEMINGWAY, and MACLEISH. His books include *Green Fruit* (poems, 1917); *The Undertaker's Garland* (poems in collaboration with EDMUND WILSON, 1922); *Many Thousands Gone* (short stories, 1913); *Now with His Love* (poems, 1933); *Act of Darkness* (novel, 1935); *Minute Particulars* (poems, 1936); *Selected Poems* (1941); *Collected Essays* (1948); and *Collected Poems* (1948). In 1943 he was made consultant in comparative literature at the Library of Congress. After his death a John Peale Bishop Memorial Literary Prize Contest was conducted in 1945 by *The Sewanee Review* and Prentice-Hall, and the prize essays, stories, and poems were collected in *A Southern Vanguard* (1947), edited by Allen Tate, who spoke of Bishop's awareness of the tensions between the South today and the outside world. Bishop has been compared to Keats, but also owes a debt to the 17th-century metaphysical poets. His letters to and from Tate were edited in *The Republic of Letters in America* (1981).

Bishop, Morris [Gilbert] (1893–1973), teacher, versifier, translator, biographer. Bishop, a teacher at Cornell University from 1921, was known particularly for his excellent light verse. He wrote *A Gallery of Eccentrics* (1928), *Paramount Poems* (1929), *Love Rimes of Petrarch* (1931), *Ronsard, Prince of Poets* (1940), *Spilt Milk* (1942), *A Treasury of British Humor* (1942), *The Life and Adventures of La Rochefoucauld* (1951), and *A Bowl of Bishop* (1954). His *Limericks Long After Lear* have appeared in *The New Yorker*. He wrote *The Widening Stain* (1942), a mystery novel, under the pseudonym W. Bolingbroke Johnson.

Bishop, Thomas Brigham (1835–1905), song writer. Bishop wrote songs for minstrel shows. To him are attributed WHEN JOHNNY COMES MARCHING HOME; "Shoo, Fly, Don't Bodder Me"; and the original JOHN BROWN'S BODY.

Bissell, Richard (1913–1977),   novelist, playwright. Born in Iowa, Bissell contributed to such outstanding Broadway hits as *The Pajama Game*, in collaboration with GEORGE ABBOTT (1954), and *Say Darling* (1959), in collaboration with his wife Marian Bissell and Abe Burrows. The first was adapted from his novel *7½ Cents* (1952), and *Say Darling* is about an author making a musical from a novel. His short stories appeared in *Collier's, Esquire,* and *Holiday.* His books include *A Stretch on the River* (1950); *The Monongahela* (1951); *High Water* (1955); *Goodbye Ava* (1960), a novel; *Still Circling Moose Jaw* (1965), a novel; *Julia Harrington* (1969), a novel; and *My Life on the Mississippi* (1973).

Bitter-Sweet (1858),   a poem by J. G. HOLLAND. Set in a New England homestead, this melodramatic poem seeks to prove that there is nothing inconsistent in the simultaneous existence of good and evil. It was immensely popular in its day.

Bixby's Hotel.   This 19th-century hostelry was located at the southeast corner of Broadway and Park Place in New York City and was conducted by Daniel Bixby, at one time a bookseller in Lowell, Massachusetts, who welcomed authors and publishers to his hotel. It was the first New York home of Alice and Phoebe Cary, and James Fenimore Cooper and Washington Irving often lodged there in their later years. Others frequently seen in the hotel were Fitz-Greene Halleck, N. P. Willis, Nathaniel Hawthorne, Oliver Wendell Holmes, Bayard Taylor, and Ralph Waldo Emerson.

Black, Alexander (1859–1940),   novelist, editor, photographer. His novels include *Miss Jerry* (1891), *The Seventh Angel* (1921), and *Jo Ellen* (1923). He wrote an autobiography, *Time and Chance* (1937).

Black April (1927),   a novel by JULIA PETERKIN. Its powerful, realistic depiction of life on an isolated South Carolina plantation excited both admiration and disapproval on its publication. The plot centers around Black April and his complete domination of the plantation workers. No white characters appear in the book.

Blackbeard [Teach, Edward] (died 1718),   pirate. He obtained letters of marque from England during the War of the Spanish Succession, and after the peace continued to rove the seas in search of prey. He made the Spanish Main and the Atlantic his chosen territory as far north as the coast of the Carolinas. Notorious for his ferocity in battle and for his cruelty, he was killed in a battle at Ocracoke Inlet, North Carolina, and most of his crew members were hanged. A comic opera, written under the pseudonym Andrew Barton by THOMAS FORREST, called *The Disappointment; or the Force of Credulity* (1767), poked fun at the search for Blackbeard's treasure.

Black Boy (1945),   autobiography by RICHARD WRIGHT. Selecting a generic title for the first volume of his autobiography, Richard Wright deliberately associated his personal 20th-century story with the line of 19th-century slave narratives that form the originating prose tradition of Afro-American written literature. As the authors of texts conceived in the service of the abolition movement recounted the physical beatings, material deprivation, and exploitive labor conditions that characterized slavery, so did Wright illustrate the continuing legacy of slavery in the practices of Jim Crow. For Wright, as with the authors of the previous century, the social theme of his writing was the systematic attempt by slaveholders and then by segregationists to exclude blacks from the circle of human culture and, by rendering them beasts, to justify the supremacy of the white caste over mere slaves and black boys.

Dramatic and effective counterstrategy inheres in the writing of a life story. A book expressing by its creation the accomplishment of reason and literacy testifies at the same time to the existence of distinctive personality. Latent in the precedent slave stories, this principle of subjectivity becomes in *Black Boy* the visible source of incident and narrative shape, accounting on the one hand for a protagonist at odds with the white society but alienated as well from the Afro-American community and, on the other hand, fixing autobiographical memory on the emergence of the artist's sensibility.

After submission for publication, Wright's manuscript was divided, the first part—the section we know as *Black Boy*—concluding with the young man newly arrived in Chicago in 1927 as a fugitive from the white South that never knew him. This part relates his nomadic life in Tennessee, Arkansas, and Mississippi, abandoned by his father and with his mother working at menial jobs or incapacitated by illness. The second part, relating what he found after he repeated the flight of the slaves who reached the North, was issued in 1977 under the title *American Hunger.*

JOHN M. REILLY

Blackburn, Paul (1926–1971),   poet, translator. Born in Vermont, Blackburn was educated at the University of Wisconsin. He spent time in France and Spain and translated *The Cid* (1966), French troubadours, and other poets. In his own poetry, he was influenced by the open forms of William Carlos Williams and was associated particularly with ROBERT CREELEY, CHARLES OLSON, and other BLACK MOUNTAIN COLLEGE poets. He taught at the City College of New York and at the State College at Cortland. Among his books are *The Dissolving Fabric* (1955), *Brooklyn-Manhattan Transit* (1960), *The Cities* (1967), and *In. On. Or About the Premises* (1968). Robert Kelly edited *The Journals* (1975).

Black Cat, The   (published in the *U.S. Saturday Post*, Aug. 19, 1843; in *Tales*, 1845), one of EDGAR ALLAN POE's greatest horror tales. A murderer places the dead body of his wife in a cellar vault that he conceals with cement. He immures in the vault at the same time a cat that he hates, and the cries of the cat bring the crime to light.

Black Crook, The (1866),   a play by CHARLES M. BARRAS, with music and ballet, that took five hours to perform. It was revived by CHRISTOPHER MORLEY in burlesque style in Hoboken (1929) and is called the first American musical.

Black Elk (1863–1950),   Oglala SIOUX warrior and priest. An active defender of the rights and culture of his people, he survived Little Big Horn and Wounded Knee to continue to propagate the old ways of the Sioux. His memoirs, *Black Elk Speaks* (1932), were recorded by JOHN G. NEIHARDT. His account of Sioux religious rites appears in *The Sacred Pipe* (1953), edited by John Epes Brown.

Blackfeet [or Blackfoot] Indians.   Native American people occupying territory on the upper Missouri and north into Canada. The farthest west of the Algonquian tribes, they had acquired horses by 1750, when they first came into contact with white fur traders. Their PLAINS INDIANS culture depended on nomadic pursuit of buffalo, and after the coming of the white man they prospered by the sale of beaver pelts. In their early trading with the Hudson's Bay Company and the North West Company on the Saskatchewan, they acquired guns they used to terrify Shoshonis and other neighboring tribes. Although they were never formally at war with the white men, their encounter with Lewis and Clark, in which two Indians were killed in a horse-stealing attempt, left them enemies of the mountain men and, later, pioneers. About 1830 the Blackfeet reached the height of their power. Smallpox devastated them in 1836 and returned in 1870. Their decline was also attributable to the depletion of buffalo herds, which left them starving by the late 19th century. At present, they inhabit reservations in Montana and Alberta. They appeared in literature early in Washington Irving's A TOUR ON THE PRAIRIES (1835), ASTORIA (1836), and THE ADVENTURES OF CAPTAIN BONNEVILLE (1836). More recently, JAMES WELCH drew on his Blackfeet heritage for *Fool's Crow*, a fine novel of tribal life in the Montana Territory in 1870.

Black Hawk (1767–1838),   leader of the SAUK INDIANS. Born near the present Rock Island, Illinois, Black Hawk supported the efforts of TECUMSEH to organize an Indian confederacy and fought on the British side in the WAR OF 1812. His continued opposition to U.S. encroachments culminated in the Black Hawk War of 1832. He retreated to Wisconsin, where most of his tribe, including women and children, were massacred on the Bad Axe River by troops under General Henry Atkinson (1782–1842), assisted by SIOUX warriors. Black Hawk surrendered, was imprisoned and taken to Washington, New York, and other eastern cities, where he received an enthusiastic welcome. He was released in 1833 to join the remnants of his tribe in Iowa. Black Hawk dictated an *Autobiography* (1833), edited by Donald Jackson (1955). Accounts include Cyranus Cole's *I Am a Man: The Indian Black Hawk* (1938). He appears as a character in Iola Fuller's *The Loon Feather* (1940), LOUIS ZARA's *This Land Is Ours* (1940), and Charlton G. Laird's *Thunder on the River* (1949).

Black Hills,   a group of mountains in western South Dakota and northeastern Wyoming, occupying an area of about 6,000 square miles. Aside from such attractions as an astonishing petrified forest and many caves, the Black Hills draw thousands of tourists each year to view the tremendous sculptures of GUTZON BORGLUM on Mount Rushmore—a peak 6,040 feet high, on the face of which Borglum carved (1927–41) the faces of Washington, Jefferson, Lincoln, and Theodore Roosevelt. Washington's stone nose is longer than the entire face of Egypt's Great Sphinx, and Lincoln's face is

about sixty feet from chin to forehead. Albert Williams described the *Black Hills* (1953), and Paul Fatout wrote *Ambrose Bierce and the Black Hills* (1956). Hoffman Birney's novel, *The Dice of God*, has its setting in the Black Hills.

Black Horse Tavern,   Hartford, Connecticut. Meeting place of the HARTFORD WITS in the late 18th century.

Black Mask,   a monthly magazine, founded in 1919 and edited by Joseph T. Shaw. The stories Shaw published showed crime unsentimentally, and many of his authors became well known, notably DASHIELL HAMMETT. Shaw edited *The Hard-Boiled Omnibus: Early Stories from Black Mask* (1946). In 1953 *Black Mask* was taken over by the *Ellery Queen Mystery Magazine*. See HARD-BOILED FICTION.

Black Mountain College,   experimental liberal arts college. Founded near Asheville, North Carolina, in 1933, Black Mountain became important to literature during 1951 to 1956, the years when CHARLES OLSON was rector. It supported ROBERT CREELEY's journal, THE BLACK MOUNTAIN REVIEW. Students and faculty included Creeley, ROBERT DUNCAN, and EDWARD DORN. See BLACK MOUNTAIN POETS.

Black Mountain Poets.   Both a movement and a group of poets, the term "Black Mountain" has been a problematic designation for identifying one of the major innovative forces in postmodern writing. Essentially, the term refers to poets who made common cause with or were influenced by CHARLES OLSON (1910–1970), whose essays of the 1950s set forth a critique of orthodox, or "closed," verse he sought to replace with "open," or "projective" verse. Olson's quarrel with orthodoxy in American writing had mainly to do with its emphasis on the personality of the individual, the "lyrical interference of the ego," as he spoke of it in his 1950 essay "Projective Verse." Closed or formal verse employed artificial conventions of language such as regular meters and intricate rhyme schemes that ornamented discourse but obscured actual perceptions and responses of the imagination. The open verse forms Olson promoted called attention to intricacies of thought and emotion, and called into relation the role of the body in the act of verse composition. Where ego is central to closed verse, Olson reasoned, breath was central to open verse, the rhythms of which determine line lengths and stanzaic structure. Even more basic are the functions of sound in open poetry, the units with which a line of verse is constructed and which precede any consideration of meaning. Olson's key essays, "Projective Verse," "The Gate and the Center," "Human Universe," and "Equal, That Is, to the Real Itself" emphasize the collaborative relation of mind and body in the making of a work of art. The purpose of art, these essays assert, is not the elaboration of an artist's individuality or a social concept, but an exploration of nature and reality as perceived by an alert mind.

The Black Mountain poets were first identified as a group by DONALD ALLEN in his groundbreaking anthology *The New American Poets: 1945–1960* (1960), where he featured ten poets in the opening section and described them in his preface as being associated with two avant-garde quarterlies, *The Black Mountain Review* and *Origin*. The basis of this designation has been questioned by critics, who have applied the term variously ever since. Only some of the group published their work in these journals, while others were directly associated as teachers or students with BLACK MOUNTAIN COLLEGE in North Carolina, where *The Black Mountain Review* was produced during its seven-issue span from 1954 to 1957. Charles Olson was the leading figure of the group and a featured writer of both journals.

Other leading figures in the group were ROBERT CREELEY, whom Olson brought to Black Mountain in 1954 to edit *The Black Mountain Review*, and to teach and study, and ROBERT DUNCAN, whom Olson appointed playwright-in-residence for 1956. Both writers felt strong allegiance to Olson's critical and philosophical principles and declared their sympathies with him in early poems. In 1953, Creeley published Olson's first book of poems, *In Cold Hell, In Thicket* while living in Majorca, Spain, prior to joining Olson at the college. In 1966, he edited Olson's *Selected Writings* and has written many insightful essays on Olson's work. Duncan's relation to Olson was less intimate, and occasionally complicated by disagreements on aesthetic issues. In his essay "Against Wisdom as Such," Olson criticized Duncan's self-aggrandizements in the role of poet as an indulgence in egotism, to which Duncan made several replies in defense of his view of the poet as a visionary or seer of special imaginative powers.

Despite occasional friction, Olson, Creeley, and Duncan widened the boundaries of poetic content and varied the poem's formal structure with new strategies of composition. Creeley's short, intense lyrics focus on the intricacy of thought itself, the peculiar redundancies, puns, and riddlesome ambiguities that exist in a moment's attention. Creeley's dissections of awareness led him to increasingly minimal statements that his critics mistook as mere fragments of language. But even these bits and pieces of lyric statement convey the inexhaustible ambiguity of simple, unadorned language and helped to undermine the presumed certainties of thought in more orthodox modes of discourse. Duncan's ardently romantic poetry features a lush texture of eloquent formulations and rich, musical phrasing. Whereas Creeley engages in minute particulars and their ambivalent properties, Duncan's poetry mingled allegory and dreams in its commentaries. Gifted with insight into the workings of his own imagination, some of Duncan's poems reenact with uncanny understanding the processes by which imagination draws on rational and irrational faculties in the making of verse. In the poems "Poetry, A Natural Thing" and "An Owl Is an Only Bird of Poetry," Duncan makes rapturous expositions of the poetic Olson had formulated and which Duncan now extended and applied. But all three poets of the Black Mountain movement succeeded in shifting the focus of American poetry away from declarations of individuality to explorations of human identity and the complexities of consciousness.

DENISE LEVERTOV, PAUL BLACKBURN, Larry Eigner, and Paul Carroll, whom Allen also identified as Black Mountain poets, had no affiliation with the college but appeared frequently in the

journals of the movement. Each has expressed interest in the work of the leading figures of the movement or has contributed to the fund of ideas and themes that represent the movement. Levertov, an English-born writer, emigrated to the U.S. in 1948 and began publishing poems in *Origin*; her friendships with Creeley and Duncan drew her into the group. With Duncan's encouragement, Levertov began exploring the nature of womanhood at a time when feminist causes were converging into a national movement for women's liberation. Her verses probed the subtleties of a female mythology in tersely worded, carefully crafted lyric poems. Her public quarrel with Ginsberg over the informalities of spontaneous verse, as in Peter Orlovsky's "Second Poem," published in the Allen anthology with numerous typographical and spelling errors, hastened her separation from avant-garde circles, though her friendship with Duncan deepened over the years. During the Vietnam War, Levertov was a prominent voice of protest in anti-war groups. Paul Blackburn, a New York poet, formed close friendships with CID CORMAN and Robert Creeley, whose styles of brief, concise lyric influenced the limpid notational mode of Blackburn's poetry. Blackburn distinguished himself as a translator of troubadour and Spanish poetry, and his style of pithy observation proved a suitable medium for recording his life in New York and for the verse journals he kept of his travels and later years. Blackburn's imagery frequently depicts a realm of things and natural settings animated by their own will and independence from human agency, another aspect of postmodern vision.

Paul Carroll's association with the Black Mountain poets was limited to a friendship with Creeley and to occasional appearances in *The Black Mountain Review*. As coeditor of *Big Table* (1959–1960), a Chicago quarterly, Carroll brought the work of the San Francisco Renaissance to the Midwest, where its influences spread quickly to the region's poets. In his critical study, *The Poem in Its Skin* (1968), Carroll helped explain the new poetry to the common reader. Larry Eigner, a minimalist in the tradition of Corman and Creeley, and their predecessors among the earlier Objectivists, was only marginally associated with the Black Mountain poets.

A younger generation of writers also appeared in Allen's anthology, which featured the early work of Ed Dorn, Joel Oppenheimer, Jonathan Williams, and John Weiners, who studied writing under Olson at the college and came to prominence in the late 1960s. Dorn's *Gunslinger* (1975), widely regarded as a postmodern classic, satirizes Western civilization and its principal vulgarities in the cultures of Las Vegas and California. It was to Dorn that Olson addressed his remarks in "A Bibliography on America for Ed Dorn," which counseled the beginning writer to pick a subject and master it over a sustained period, as Olson had done with the history of Gloucester, Massachusetts. Dorn's subject was the western U.S. and its history of bitter conflict between white settlers and indigenous Indian tribes. Dorn's book *The Shoshoneans* (1966) joins other sensitive portrayals of Indian life by postmodern writers.

The Black Mountain poets, though not as well defined or organized as were other contemporary groups such as the BEAT

GENERATION, the poets of the SAN FRANCISCO RENAISSANCE, and the poets of the NEW YORK SCHOOL, were nonetheless influential and formed the leading edge in the making of innovative poetry at midcentury. Olson's ideas filtered down into the work of diverse poets and prompted many to question the primacy of the individual in American writing, and to reconsider the importance of a multitude of intervening stages in the process of expressing one's feelings and thoughts in a poem. Olson and the Black Mountain poets championed the "open" mode of verse, which attempted to record the precise steps by which mind grappled with its content of dreams, myths, and facts in verse language. See Martin Duberman, *Black Mountain: An Exploration in Community* (1973).

PAUL CHRISTENSEN

Black Mountain Review, The (1954–57), little magazine. Founded by ROBERT CREELEY on Majorca, the journal was associated with BLACK MOUNTAIN COLLEGE and served as an outlet for the group that came to be known as the BLACK MOUNTAIN POETS.

Blackmur, Richard [Palmer] (1904–1965), poet, critic. Though Blackmur had no formal education beyond high school, early in life he became editor of the *Hound and Horn*, a periodical on arts and letters published in Cambridge, Massachusetts. He became known as a leading American critic. His criticism, though not prolific, is tough, vigorous, and honest—enduring qualities. Perhaps because of its quiet tone it is, however, less widely known than that of other literary critics whose stature does not match Blackmur's. He was a Guggenheim Fellow and a member of the National Institute of Arts and Letters. Among his books are *Double Agent* (1935), *The Expense of Greatness* (1940), *The Second World* (1942), *Language and Gesture* (1952), *The Lion and the Honeycomb* (1955), *Anni-Mirabiles, 1921–25* (1956), and *Form and Value in Modern Poetry* (1957).

Black Riders and Other Lines, The (1895), a collection of poems by STEPHEN CRANE. With the poems of EMILY DICKINSON, this was one of the few lasting books by a new poet of the 1890s. The poems are brief parables in free verse, similar in rhythm to the cadences of the Bible, Whitman, and Dickinson. Harland Garland saw a source in Olive Schreiner's *Dreams*; others have perceived likenesses to the parables of Ambrose Bierce.

Black Thunder (1935), a novel by ARNA BONTEMPS. The hero, Gabriel Prosser, is a slave in the days of the French Revolution who participates in several rebellions.

Blair, James (1655–1743), clergyman, university president, author. Blair, a deputy to the Bishop of London, in whose diocese Virginia was included, founded the College of William and Mary and was named its president "during his natural life." His many sermons brought him wide praise, in particular his 117 discourses on *Our Saviour's Divine Sermon on the Mount* (5 v. 1722). With Henry Hartwell and Edward Chilton, he wrote *The Present State of Virginia and the College* (1727).

Blair, Walter (1900–1992), professor, author, editor. Blair, who taught at the University of Chicago, wrote widely in American literature, particularly American humor and folk themes: *Two Phases of American Humor* (1931); *Mike Fink, King of Mississippi Keelboatmen* (with F. J. Meine, 1933), the first of their two books about this folk hero's exploits; NATIVE AMERICAN HUMOR, 1800–1900 (1937, rev. 1960); *Horse Sense in American Humor* (1942); *Tall Tale America: a Legendary History of our Humorous Heroes* (1944); *Davy Crockett: Truth and Legend* (1955); *Half Horse, Half Alligator: The Growth of the Mike Fink Legend* (with F. J. Meine, 1956); and *Mark Twain and "Huck Finn"* (1960).

Blais, Marie-Claire (1939–), novelist, poet. Born in Quebec City, Blais left convent school at seventeen and by twenty-one had published two novels: *La Belle Bête* (1959; tr. *Mad Shadows*, 1960) and *Tête blanche* (1960; tr. 1961). *La Belle Bête* was hailed as a work of genius, a lyric and surrealist portrayal of the stifling world in which children grow up in Quebec. *Tête blanche* is a smaller picture of rebellious youth. Sponsored by EDMUND WILSON, she was granted a Guggenheim Fellowship in 1962 and spent a year in France and time on Cape Cod and in Brittany before returning to Canada. *Parcours d'un ecrivain: notes américaines* (1993) is a collection of articles printed in *Devoir* during that time; it was translated as *American Notebooks: a Writer's Journey* in 1996. Two volumes of poetry, *Pays voilés* (1963) and *Existences* (1964), stemmed in part from her French and U.S. experience; together they were translated as *Veiled Countries/Lives* (1984). From the 1960s onward she has been a major figure in the literature of French Canada, a private but prolific author of personal, anguished, and existential fiction. *Une saison dans la vie d'Emmanuel* (1965, tr. *A Season in the Life of Emmanuel*, 1966) describes the bleak, brutish life, including tuberculosis and prostitution, of a family of an illiterate Quebec farmer with sixteen children. Three novels follow the life of Pauline Archange, a semiautobiographical figure growing up in a world of brutal parents and evil priests: *Manuscrits de Pauline Archange* (1968) and *Vivre! Vivre!* (1969), these two translated as *The Manuscripts of Pauline Archange* (1970); and *Les Apparences* (1970), translated as *Dürer's Angel* (1976). She draws on her lesbian experience in portraying a young man's homosexuality in *Le Loup* (1972, tr. *The Wolf*, 1974), and the lives of the patrons of a lesbian bar in *Les Nuits d'underground* (1978; tr. *Nights in the Underground*, 1979). Other novels include *Un Joualonais, sa joualonie* (1973, tr. *St. Lawrence Blues*, 1974), a satiric thrust at the use of dialect by Québécois writers; and *Le Sourd dans la ville* (1979, tr. *Deaf to the City*, 1980), set in a dilapidated hotel in Montreal. The novellas *Le jour est noire* (1967) and *Les voyageurs sacrés* (1969) have been translated together as *The Day Is Dark and Three Travelers* (1967, 1985). *L'ange de la solitude* (1989, tr. *The Angel of Solitude*, 1993) concerns eight lesbians trying to form a perfect society. *Soifs* (1995) won Blais her third Governor General's Award. *L'île* (1989, tr. *The Island*, 1991) is a drama.

Blaise, Clark (1940–), novelist, short-story writer, essayist. Born in North Dakota, Blaise is French-Canadian by descent. He was educated at Denison University, Harvard, and the University of Iowa, and has taught in Canada and the

United States. Questions of identity inform his work: "Sociologically," he has written, "I am an American. Psychologically, a Canadian. Sentimentally, a Québécois. By marriage, part of the Third World." His stories are collected in *A North American Education* (1973) and *Tribal Justice* (1974). His novels include *Lunar Attractions* (1979), about a boy who discovers his French-Canadian ancestry; and *Lusts* (1983), of marriage and suicide. *Days and Nights in Calcutta* (1977), written with his wife BHARATI MUKHERJEE, presents divergent views of India. *Resident Alien* (1986) combines fiction and nonfiction.

Blanco Fombona, Rufino (1874–1944),   Venezuelan novelist, short-story writer, poet, and essayist. Blanco Fombona was an exile during the long dictatorship of Juan Vincente Gómez, returning to Venezuela after the latter's death in 1935. His writing reflects his angry dismay at the stupidity, iniquity, and sordidness he seemed to find everywhere. Accordingly, his novels are weakened by heavy-handed social satire and political propaganda. They include *El hombre de hierro* (1907), which depicts the triumph of evil over virtue; *El hombre de oro* ("The Man of Gold," 1916), which exposes the venality and incompetence of Venezuelan politicians; and *La mitra en la mano* (1927), the story of an ambitious priest, a character that has been called a Venezuelan Elmer Gantry. *Cuentos americanos* (1904) and *Dramas mínimos* (1920) are his best-known collections of short stories. His poetry, which includes the collections *Pequeña ópera lírica* (1904) and *Cantos de la prisión y del destierro* (1911), shows the influence of MODERNISMO. Among his other works are *Letras y letrados de Hispano-América* (1908) and *Grandes escritores de América* (1917), literary criticism; *La lámpara de Aladino* (1915), autobiographical sketches; and *El conquistador español en el siglo XVI* (1922), a study of the Spanish conquerors. Blanco Fombona also edited the letters of Simon Bolivar and edited and published several series of great American books. *Camino de imperfección; diario de mi vida* (1906–13) recounts his early life.

Bland, James A. (1854–1911),   minstrel, songwriter. Bland wrote Virginia's state song, "Carry Me Back to Old Virginny" (1875), and about seven hundred other ditties, including "O Dem Golden Slippers" and "In the Evening by the Moonlight." J. J. Daly wrote his biography, *A Song in His Heart* (1951).

Blavatsky, Helena Petrovna (1831–1891),   Russian spiritualist. Madame Blavatsky traveled widely in Europe, the Near East, and Asia, and claimed to have learned occult secrets in Tibet. During her stay in the United States (1873–78), she founded the Theosophical Society and later moved its headquarters to India. Followers thought her capable of miracles; others claimed fraud. Her works include *Isis Unveiled* (1877) and *The Secret Doctrine* (2 v. 1888), on THEOSOPHY.

Bleecker, Ann Eliza (1752–1783),   poet, novelist. Bleecker's hardships during the Revolutionary War were reflected in poems collected in *The Posthumous Works of Ann Eliza Bleecker* (1793). She also composed a novel in letter form, *The History of Maria Kittle* (1797), about an American woman captured by Indians during the French and Indian War.

Blennerhassett, Harman (1765–1831),   associate of Aaron Burr in his alleged conspiracy to invade Mexico.

Blennerhassett left England after marriage with his niece, which then was illegal. In 1805 he became Burr's associate, was arrested, and was released without trial; he returned to England financially ruined. *The Blennerhassett Papers* were edited by William H. Safford in 1864. Blennerhassett appears prominently in Charles Felton Pidgin's novel, *Blennerhassett, or, The Decrees of Fate* (1901).

Blest Gana, Alberto (1830–1920),   Chilean novelist, One of the outstanding realists of Latin-American fiction, Blest Gana, who spent many years in France, sought to be the Balzac of Chile. His best-known novel is *Martín Rivas* (1862). Dealing with the experiences of an impoverished provincial youth who falls in love with a girl of the aristocracy, the work gives an incisive, satirical view of Chilean society in the 1850s. Other works by Blest Gana include *Durante la reconquista* (1897), an epic of Chile's struggle for independence; *Los trasplantados* (1904), which depicts decadent Chilean émigrés in Paris; and *El loco estero* (1909), portraying the Santiago of his childhood.

Blish, James [Benjamin] (1921–1975),   American science-fiction author. Blish wrote many short stories, including "Surface Tension" (1952), which is about life in the microcosm. His best work appears in two tetralogies: *Cities in Flight* (1955–62), in which Earth's cities roam the universe looking for work, and *After Such Knowledge*, concerned with the relationship between religious and scientific knowledge. The latter series includes the much-admired *A Case of Conscience* (1958) and a fine historical novel about Roger Bacon, *Doctor Mirabilis* (1964). Blish also wrote a number of children's books and novelizations of the television series *Star Trek*. Under the name William Atheling, Jr., he produced two important early works of science-fiction criticism: *The Issue at Hand* (1964) and *More Issues at Hand* (1970). *The Best of James Blish* was published in 1979.

Blithedale Romance, The,   NATHANIEL HAWTHORNE'S third novel (1852) and his only one to deal closely and explicitly with issues and concerns of his own era and place. Set primarily in Blithedale, a fictional utopian community with important resonances from his own life at Brook Farm. *The Blithedale Romance* suggests Hawthorne's skepticism concerning utopian socialist living experiments by exposing the contradictions, hypocrisies, and paradoxes—emotional, ideological, economic, and otherwise—of the various individuals endeavoring to create an ideal community immune to the social and market pressures of New England culture. Hawthorne's skepticism toward the project is partly deflected through the aloof, ironic, and to many critics self-incriminating narrative by Miles Coverdale, whose account of the Blithedale experiment reveals the flaws and the renewed force of classist and sexist oppression permeating the utopian group. Hollingsworth, an idealistic but egotistical reformer; Zenobia, an ardent feminist and exotic beauty, Priscilla, her frail and mysterious sister; Old Moody, their manipulative father; Westervelt, a demonic mesmerist; and Miles Coverdale, an aesthete, people this account of the frailties, betrayals, and inherent moral weaknesses that shatter family bonds and vio-

late all forms of social organization, from the marketplace and prison system of the dominant culture to the utopian communities dedicated to eradicating social injustices. Compare Hawthorne's assault on Transcendental hopes with Melville's equally withering critiques in PIERRE and THE CONFIDENCE-MAN.
RUSSELL J. REISING

Blitzstein, Marc (1905–1964),   playwright, composer, pianist. As musician and writer Blitzstein has experimented widely with formal techniques and has frequently dealt with proletarian themes. His works include *I've Got the Tune* (radio song-play, 1937); parts of THE CRADLE WILL ROCK (opera, 1937); *No for an Answer* (opera, 1941); *Reuben, Reuben* (1951); and an adaptation of Kurt Weill's *Threepenny Opera* (1952).

Blix (1899),   a novel by FRANK NORRIS. A partly autobiographical work, *Blix* is the love story of Condy Rivers, a struggling newspaperman, and Blix Bessemer, a rich girl. Their marriage becomes possible only when Condy is offered a job with an eastern magazine (actually *McClure's*).

Blockade, The (performed 1775),   a play by SIR JOHN BURGOYNE. Burgoyne wrote the play to amuse his fellow-Britishers in Boston. He made fun of the rebels and played down the British peril. A performance on Jan. 8, 1776, was broken up by word that the Americans were attacking at Bunker's Hill. Later, an anonymous playwright (not MERCY OTIS WARREN, to whom it was once attributed) retorted with another farce, *The Blockheads* (1776), satirizing Sir William Howe's unsuccessful attempt to take Dorchester Heights.

Blood, Benjamin Paul (1832–1919),   poet, philosopher. Born in Amsterdam, New York, Blood early began composing long philosophical poems. A mystical experience resulting from inhaling nitrous oxide (laughing gas) in a dentist's chair started him on strange lines of thought that led him to repudiate monism and adopt pluralism. WILLIAM JAMES called Blood's book *The Anaesthetic Revelation and the Gist of Philosophy* (1874) one of the "stepping-stones" of his own thinking, and wrote *A Pluralistic Mystic* in his praise. Blood's *Pluriverse* was published posthumously (1920). Blood's verse includes the long poems *The Bride of the Iconoclast* (1854) and *The Colonnades* (1868). His unusual religious opinions appear in *The Philosophy of Justice* (1851) and *Optimism* (1860). See PLURALISM.

Bloom, Harold (1930–   ),   critic. Born in New York City, Bloom was educated at Cornell and Yale. A longtime member of the Yale faculty and a proponent of Romanticism, he began his challenges to the New Critical stance with *Shelley's Mythmaking* (1959) and *The Visionary Company* (1961). *The Anxiety of Influence* (1973), *A Map of Misreading* (1975), *Kabbalah and Criticism* (1975), and *Poetry and Repression* (1976) examine the ways in which poets build their careers in conflict with their intellectual predecessors. Bloom has written studies of Blake (1963, 1965), Yeats (1970), and Freud (1984) and has been influential in forming the reputation of Wallace Stevens with *Wallace Stevens: The Poems of Our Climate* (1977), as well as such poetic heirs of Stevens as JOHN ASHBERY and A. R. AMMONS. His other titles include *Deconstruction and Criticism* (1979), *Agon: Towards a Theory of Revisionism* (1981), *Poetics*

of Influence: New and Selected Criticism (1984), *Ruin the Sacred Truths: Poetry and Belief from the Bible to the Present* (1989), *The Book of J* (1990), *The Western Canon* (1994), and *Shakespeare: The Invention of the Human* (1998). See NEW CRITICISM.

Bloomer, Amelia [Jenks] (1818–1894),   reformer, editor. Born in Homer, New York, Bloomer wrote articles advocating reforms in education, marriage laws, suffrage, and dress. She wore loose trousers that came to be called "bloomers." She founded *The Lily*, a feminist and temperance magazine (1848–54), first published in Seneca Falls, New York.

Bloomsgrove Family, Memoirs of the (1790),   an epistolary novel by ENOS HITCHCOCK. The second American novel published in book form, it has a meager plot. Hitchcock's main aim was to set up a model for domestic education and promote "the dignity and importance of the female character."

Bloudy Tenet of Persecution for Cause of Conscience, The (1644),   a tract by ROGER WILLIAMS attacking the ideas of JOHN COTTON, who replied in *The Bloudy Tenet Washed and Made White in the Bloud of the Lamb* (1647). Williams counterattacked in *The Bloudy Tenet Yet More Bloudy* (1652). Williams carries the argument for religious freedom far beyond other writers of his times. He urges that just as magistrates have no right to interfere in church government, so the clergy have no call to meddle with the magistracy.

Blount, Roy [Alton], Jr. (1941–   ),   humorist, novelist. Born in Indiana, Blount has been a columnist and reporter for several southern newspapers as well as a performer on such programs as "A Prairie Home Companion." *About Three Bricks Shy of a Load* (1974, rev. 1989) is a humorous treatment of professional football, especially the Pittsburgh Steelers. *One Fell Soup; or, I'm Just a Bug on the Windshield of Life* (1982), *What Men Don't Tell Women* (1984), *Not Exactly What I Had in Mind* (1985), and *Now, Where Were We?* (1989) are among gatherings of newspaper columns. Other titles include *Roy Blount's Book of Southern Humor* (1994) and *The Great Rock 'N' Roll Joke Book* (1997, with D. Marsh, K. Glodmark, and G. Shields).

Blue and the Gray, The (*Atlantic Monthly*, September 1867), a poem by FRANCIS MILES FINCH. These sentimental verses immortalizing Civil War uniforms were presumably occasioned when women of Columbus, Mississippi, strewed flowers over the graves of both Union and Confederate dead. A play of the same title was written for Harrigan (see EDWARD HARRIGAN) and Hart (1875); it was also the title of a song by PAUL DRESSER.

Blue-Backed Speller, Webster's.   See NOAH WEBSTER.

Blue Hotel, The (1899),   a short story by STEPHEN CRANE. A Swede comes to a Nebraska hotel, expects to meet wild life in the West, himself creates a brawl, and is killed. Who is to blame, the Swede himself or the men he quarreled with? One of the characters remarks, "Every sin is the result of a collaboration." This story appears in the collection THE MONSTER AND OTHER STORIES.

Blues: A Magazine of New Rhythms,   a monthly published from February 1929 to autumn 1930 at Columbus,

Mississippi. It was edited by Charles Henri Ford, who was only sixteen at the time. *Blues* published the first magazine work of James T. Farrell, Erskine Caldwell, Kay Boyle, and others.

Blue Voyage, The (1927), a novel by CONRAD AIKEN. It effectively describes the people and incidents of a transatlantic voyage, largely in the stream-of-consciousness technique.

Blume, Judy (1938–), writer of fiction for children and adolescents. Born in New Jersey, Blume was educated at New York University. A mother of two and married to a lawyer, she became in the 1970s one of the most widely read American authors, as young people turned eagerly to a succession of stories reflecting their innermost concerns. By the late 1980s her sales had passed thirty million books. Her first book, *The One in the Middle Is the Green Kangaroo* (1969) established the pattern by treating the problems of the middle child in a family. Her skill and popularity grew with other books, including *Iggie's House* (1970), about racial integration; *Are You There God? It's Me, Margaret* (1970), on questions of belief; *Tales of a Fourth Grade Nothing* (1972) and its sequel *Superfudge* (1980), hugely popular accounts of sibling rivalry; *Otherwise Known as Sheila the Great* (1972), about a girl's compulsion to be perceived as extraordinary; *Deenie* (1973), about a girl suffering from scoliosis; *Blubber* (1974), on obesity; *Forever . . .* (1975), a story of teenage sex, frequently attacked in some quarters as too explicit; *Starring Sally J. Freedman as Herself* (1977), semiautobiographical; and *Tiger Eyes* (1981), about childrens' grief after the murder of their father. Her novels for adults are *Wifey* (1978), about a woman diminished by marriage, *Smart Women* (1984), and *Summer Sisters* (1998).

Blumenthal, Michael (1949–), poet. Raised in Manhattan by German-speaking parents, Blumenthal was educated at the State University of New York at Binghamton and, in law, at Cornell. He practiced law briefly, but soon became an editor, administrator for the National Endowment for the Arts, director of documentary films, and Director of Creative Writing at Harvard. Meanwhile, much of his energy went into poems that are verbally inventive, witty, humorous, and sometimes poignant. His collections include *Sympathetic Magic* (1980), *Days We Would Rather Know* (1984), *Laps* (1984), *Against Romance* (1987), *Wages of Goodness* (1992), and *Dusty Angel* (1999). *Weinstock Among the Dying* (1993) is a comic academic novel. *When History Enters the House* (1997) includes essays on central Europe prompted by a Fulbright lectureship in Hungary.

Bly, Nellie [pen name of **Elizabeth Cochrane Seaman**] (1867–1922), journalist. Elizabeth Cochrane, born in Pennsylvania, took the name "Nellie Bly" from a Stephen Foster song when she began writing for the *Pittsburgh Dispatch*. Moving to New York, she became by twenty-two one of the most famous journalists of her day, a celebrity for her exploits and a pioneer of investigative reporting. In a stunt to convince Joseph Pulitzer of her skills, she began writing for the New York *World* after feigning madness to get herself committed to Blackwell's Island, the city's insane asylum for women,

and then writing of the terrible conditions there; as a result three million dollars was appropriated for improvements. Other targets were lobbyists, prisons, factories, and nursing homes, as her name became not merely a byline, but part of the headlines by which papers were sold. In 1889, she became briefly the most famous woman in the world as readers followed in the papers her attempt to beat the record set by Jules Verne's fictional Phileas Fogg in *Around the World in Eighty Days* (1873); she completed the trip in 72 days, 6 hours, and 11 minutes. Her books include *Ten Days in a Mad-House* (1887), *Six Months in Mexico* (1888), *The Mystery of Central Park* (1889), and *Nellie Bly's Book: Around the World in Seventy-Two Days* (1890).

Bly, Robert [Elwood] (1926–), poet, translator, critic. Bly was born in Minnesota to a farming family. After serving in the navy, he was educated at Saint Olaf College in Minnesota, Harvard, and after several years in solitary study, at the University of Iowa, which by then had a renowned writing program. After traveling in Norway on a Fulbright grant, Bly returned to Minnesota, where he now lives with his wife, the writer Carol Bly.

Bly is called by some our foremost living poet-teacher, a fact belied by his apparent lack of interest in academic appointments. Bly has instead chosen to become a wandering troubador *cum* lecturer, giving well-attended poetry readings, complete with dulcimer accompaniment, that often include disquisitions on topics ranging from Jung to the bicameral brain to the nature of maleness. In addition, his work as editor and commentator (under the pseudonym "Crunk") in the influential series of magazines he founded, *The Fifties*, *The Sixties*, *The Seventies*, and *The Eighties*; as a translator of such poets as Kabir, Rilke, Neruda, Machado, and Tomas Transtromer; and as an anthologist and essayist have made him one of the most influential presences in contemporary poetry. He has consistently espoused the values of the primitive, the instinctive, and the unconscious over the artifice and terrors of modern civilization.

Bly's major impact, of course, has been as a poet. Broadly speaking, his poetry can be divided into three parts, though these do not correspond to any strict chronological sequence. The works for which he continues to be best known are the hushed landscape poems gathered in the volumes *Silence in the Snowy Fields* (1962) and *This Tree Will Be Here for a Thousand Years* (1979). It is this work that has placed Bly, together with his friend, the late JAMES WRIGHT, at the forefront of the Deep Image group, less a school than a loose alliance of poets working with a strong belief in the mystical resonance of natural images unsupplemented by abstract commentary. Deeply affected by Spanish surrealism, Bly's most characteristic Deep Image poems feature mysterious "leaps" among seemingly discrete perceptions and thoughts, a quasipantheistic sense of the "consciousness in things," a muted tone, plain diction, and almost austerely simplified syntax. In their delicacy of perception and boldness of metaphor, these poems hauntingly evoke the silences that unite nature and the self.

Another group of poems, written primarily in reaction to the Vietnam War, and published in *The Light Around the Body* (1967) and *Sleepers Joining Hands* (1973), employ a longer, more flexible line and a more intensely rhetorical style. While these poems were effective editorials in their day, they have not held up well, in part because of their topical character, but also because Bly lacks real talent for humor, irony, or satire, arguably a serious handicap for a political poet.

The third major division of Bly's work consists of his prose poems, published in *The Morning Glory* (1975) and *This Body Is Made of Camphor and Gopherwood* (1977). These share many of the qualities of the Deep Image poems—their concern with natural objects, whether landscapes or the human body, their leaps of intuition and perception—but they seem less willfully restrained. The greater informality of the prose setting gives them an appealingly idiomatic flavor.

Bly's most recent work combines elements of all these modes. The poems in *The Man in the Black Coat Turns* (1981) extend the themes of his earlier poetry, but with more variety of form and a new willingness to experiment with narrative and meditative structures. The love poems gathered in *Loving a Woman in Two Worlds* (1985) are particularly moving and sensuous lyrics that bring a more intimate tone to his consecrations of body, earth, and spirit. The best introduction to Bly's work is his *Selected Poems* (1986), which includes a valuable commentary by the poet. *American Poetry: Wilderness and Domesticity* (1990) collects essays. *Iron John: A Book About Men* (1990) is a prose work on the importance to men of myth and ritual. *Eating the Honey of Words: New and Selected Poems* appeared in 1999.

ROGER GILBERT

Bobbsey Twins, The.   The two leading characters in a series of sentimental and highly popular books for children by Laura Lee Hope (pseudonym for EDWARD STRATEMEYER).

Bodenheim, Maxwell (1893–1954),   poet, novelist, playwright. Born in Mississippi, Bodenheim came to New York City in his early twenties. Celebrated as an avant-garde writer in the 1920s, he led a Greenwich Village bohemian life that turned in the end to alcoholism and poverty; he and his third wife were found murdered in a dingy furnished room. His writing, often cynical and iconoclastic, was multifaceted. His verse ranged from exercises in imagism to espousal of social causes. His collections are *Minna and Myself* (1918); *Advice* (1920); *Introducing Irony* (1922), including "poetic short stories"; *The Sardonic Arm* (1923); *Returning to Emotion* (1927); *The King of Spain* (1928); *Bringing Jazz!* (1930); *Lights in the Valley* (1942); and *Selected Poems 1914–1944* (1946). His novels, often brutal and sometimes funny, include *Blackguard* (1923), a partly autobiographical portrait of a young artist; *Crazy Man* (1924); *Replenishing Jessica* (1925); *Ninth Avenue* (1926), with a character based on BEN HECHT; *Georgie May* (1928), the story of a prostitute's decline; *Sixty Seconds* (1929); *Naked on Roller Skates* (1930); and *Slow Vision* (1934), on the Depression. He collaborated with Hecht on a novel, *Cutie* (1924), and a play, *The Master-Poisoner* (1918), published in *Minna and Myself*.

Bodsworth, [Charles] Fred[erick] (1918–   ), Canadian novelist, journalist. Born in Port Burwall, Ontario, Bodsworth rose from Depression jobs to newspaper work to immediate success with his first novel, *Last of the Curlews* (1955). In it, he combines ornithological accuracy and narrative skill in a fictional account of the life of probably the last male of the species, extrapolated from a sighting in Texas in 1945. Other novels are similar moral fables arising out of a concern for nature. In *The Strange One* (1959), he connects the story of a lost barnacle goose with a tale of love between a white ornithologist and a Cree woman. *The Atonement of Ashley Morden* (1964) ranges from World War II bombings to postwar bacteriology. *The Sparrow's Fall* (1967) is a man-against-wilderness story of Arctic natives. *The Pacific Coast* (1970) is a history of British Columbia.

Body of Liberties.   Code of laws drawn up by NATHANIEL WARD and adopted by the General Court of Massachusetts in December 1641, as the first written laws of the colony.

Bogan, Louise (1897–1970),   poet, critic. Louise Bogan was born in Maine and educated at Girls' Latin School in Boston and Boston University. Influenced by the English metaphysical poets, Bogan's poetry is subtle, restrained, and intellectual. She received two prizes from *Poetry*, and many critics have praised her warmly. She published several collections: *Body of This Death* (1923); *Dark Summer* (1929); *The Sleeping Fury* (1937); *Poems and New Poems* (1941); and *Collected Poems* (cowinner of the Bollingen Prize in 1954). Her final collection was *The Blue Estuaries: Poems 1923–1968* (1968). She wrote much criticism of a high order, especially her poetry reviews for *The New Yorker*. Her historical review of *Achievement in American Poetry, 1900–1950* appeared in 1951, and *A Poet's Alphabet*, containing criticism, in 1970.

Bojer, Johan.   Author of THE EMIGRANTS [1].

Bok, Edward W[illiam] (1863–1930),   editor, essayist, autobiographer. Born in the Netherlands, Bok was brought to the United States at the age of six, and began working for the Brooklyn *Eagle* when he was thirteen. Experience in the magazine field and with a syndicate service he founded brought him an offer in 1889 to edit THE LADIES' HOME JOURNAL. He married the publisher's daughter, Mary Louise Curtis, became one of the most successful magazine editors in the world, and retired in 1919.

His autobiography, *The Americanization of Edward Bok* (1920), reports his achievements memorably in the third person. As editor of *The Ladies' Home Journal* Bok practically revolutionized the American home. He offered a huge variety of services to his readers, particularly in connection with baby care and the appearance of houses. His suggested architectural plans were so extensively used that the architect Stanford White proclaimed Bok the greatest single influence for good in the architectural profession. He was also deeply interested in music and in movements for world peace, tried to communicate these interests to his readers, and provided liberal endowments for both causes. He did not like the women's clubs of his day, and ultimately persuaded clubwomen to devote more time to cultural interests and civic affairs. He campaigned against venereal disease, billboards, and the common drinking cup. Bok also published volumes of inspirational and platitudinous essays, such as *Successward* (1890) and *Dollars Only* (1926).

Boker, George Henry (1823–1890),   poet, playwright. Boker wrote many plays in verse, but only FRANCESCA DA RIMINI (produced, 1855; published, 1856) won much critical success. He also wrote excellent sonnets and other lyrics. He showed great ability as minister to Turkey (1871–75) and Russia (1875–79). A native of Philadelphia, he helped edit LIPPINCOTT'S MAGAZINE and did much to encourage young writers and restore the city to literary eminence.

Bollingen Prize.   Beginning in 1949 the Library of Congress instituted an annual series of awards in the arts with money provided by the Bollingen Foundation, a philanthropic trust created by Paul Mellon, Yale Class of 1929. A distinguished panel of Fellows in American Letters of the Library of Congress awarded the prize to EZRA POUND, "the author of the book of verse which, in the opinion of the jury of selection, represents the highest achievement of American poetry in the year for which the award is made" (in this case 1948) for *The Pisan Cantos, Cantos* 74–84 of his long work. The jury comprised Conrad Aiken, W. H. Auden, Louise Bogan, Katherine Garrison Chapin, T. S. Eliot, Paul Green, Robert Lowell, Katherine Anne Porter, Karl Shapiro, Allen Tate, Willard Thorp, Robert Penn Warren, Leonie Adams, and Theodore Spencer. The poems had been written after the war in Pisa, Italy, where Pound was incarcerated before being transported to the United States to stand trial for treason. (He had been indicted on July 26, 1943, as a result of his propaganda broadcasts for Mussolini.) A controversy ensued over the advisability of honoring Pound with an award. As a result the Bollingen Foundation canceled further prizes in any field of the arts. Debate raged in the newspapers, in magazines big and little, and throughout the world of letters.

The debate has continued and been absorbed into the wider discussion concerning the relationship between literature and society. In 1950 it was announced that the annual Bollingen Prize for Poetry would be administered by the Yale University Library. The recipients in ensuing years have included some of America's most distinguished poets. Since 1964 the award has been biennial.

Bombal, María Luisa (1910–1980),   Chilean novelist. In Bombal's *La última niebla* (1935. tr. *The House of Mist*, 1947) and *La amortajada* (1938, tr. *The Shrouded Woman*, 1948), an irrational world breaks into the otherwise traditional realism of the Chilean novel. Bombal's characters, especially the women, inhabit an emotional zone closer to dream, fantasy, and death than to everyday life, although they are grounded in particular historical settings. In *La amortajada* a dead woman relives, in a series of impressionistic takes, the hopelessness of her family relations and the futility of romantic love.

Bombeck, Erma (1927–1996),   newspaper columnist, humorist. Born in Ohio, she was educated at the University of

Dayton and wrote for the *Dayton Journal-Herald*. After a twelve-year hiatus to raise three children, she returned to writing. Since 1965, her syndicated column has appeared in newspapers throughout the country. In the column and in her books and television commentaries, she satirizes domestic crises and family relationships from the stance of a suburban housewife. Her pieces are collected in books with titles such as *The Grass Is Always Greener over the Septic Tank* (1976); *Motherhood: The Second Oldest Profession* (1983); *Family: The Ties that Bind . . . and Gag* (1987); *When You Look Like Your Passport Photo, It's Time To Go Home* (1991); *A Marriage Made in Heaven . . . , or, Too Tired for an Affair* (1993) and *Forever, Erma: Best-Loved Writings from America's Favorite* (1996).

Bond, Carrie Jacobs (1862–1946),   story writer, essayist, poet, songwriter. Born in Wisconsin, Bond published numerous collections, among them *Path o' Life* (1909), *Tales of Little Cats* (1918), *Tales of Little Dogs* (1921), *Little Monkey with a Sad Face* (1930), and *The End of the Road* (1941). She compiled *Old Melodies of the South* (1918) and wrote an autobiography, *Roads of Melody* (1927). She also contributed syndicated articles to newspapers, under the heading "Friendly Preachments," but Mrs. Bond became known best for her songs set to her own music, particularly "A Perfect Day" and I LOVE YOU TRULY.

Bonifacius (1710),   essays by COTTON MATHER, later known as "Essays to Do Good." They influenced Benjamin Franklin in his own public-spirited attempts, as Franklin reports in his *Autobiography*. Franklin echoed the title in his "Dogood Papers."

Bonner, Sherwood.   Pen name of KATHERINE MACDOWELL.

Bonneville, Benjamin Louis Eulalie de (1769–1878), U.S. army officer. Taking a leave from his frontier posting, he led the expedition in the Rocky Mountains chronicled by Washington Irving in *Adventures of Captain Bonneville* (1837).

Bonney, William H.   See BILLY THE KID.

Bonnin, Gertrude Simmons [Zitkala-Sa] (1876–1938),   author and activist. Born on the Yankton Sioux reservation in North Dakota, Zitkala-Sa was deserted by her white father, brought up by her Sioux mother, and given her stepfather's name, Simmons. As an adult she chose Zitkala-Sa (Red Bird) for her name, and it is under that name that her writing was published.

At the age of eight she went to White's Manual Institute, a Quaker boarding school for Indians in Wabash, Indiana. Her experiences there are described in "The School Days of an Indian Girl," part of a series of autobiographical essays published in *The Atlantic Monthly* (1900). She later attended Earlham College and the New England Conservatory of Music.

In addition to the essays in the *Atlantic*, memoirs and fiction were published in *Harper's* and *Everybody's* magazines and brought together in *American Indian Stories* (1921). Joseph T. Keiley's photographs of her in Indian dress were exhibited and became part of the Alfred Stieglitz collection.

Old Indian Legends, another collection, appeared in 1901. "Sun Dance," an opera written with William Hanson, premiered in Utah in 1913 and was performed by the New York Light Opera Guild in 1937. As secretary of the Society for the American Indian, and later founder of the National Council of American Indians, Gertrude Bonnin was an influential advocate.

Bontemps, Arna [Wendell] (1902–1973), teacher, writer. Born in Louisiana, Bontemps was educated at the University of Chicago and became a librarian at Fisk University. His writing identified him with a movement often called the Harlem Renaissance. Among his books are *God Sends Sunday* (1931), BLACK THUNDER (1935), *Drums at Dusk* (1939), *Story of the Negro* (1948), and *One Hundred Years of Negro Freedom* (1961). In collaboration with COUNTEE CULLEN he dramatized *God Sends Sunday* as a musical called *St. Louis Woman* (1946), which was produced on Broadway. He edited *Golden Slippers: An Anthology* (1941) and *Father of the Blues* (W. C. Handy's compositions, 1941). In collaboration with Langston Hughes he wrote *The Poetry of the Negro* (1949) and *The Book of Negro Folklore* (1958).

book clubs. Book clubs already existed in Germany when Harry Scherman hit on the idea of the Book-of-the-Month Club in 1926. The German clubs sold their own low-priced reprints of the classics. Scherman's venture, organized for distribution only, was to be a clearinghouse between publisher and reader. Since it was selected by a distinguished board of literary judges, the book of the month was bound to be one of the most worthwhile recent publications. The club was and has continued to be highly successful. It started with 4,750 members and within twenty years had grown to nearly a million. The Literary Guild, founded in 1927, has also had a huge success.

At first, American booksellers often charged book clubs with unfair competition. The clubs answered the charge with the claim that selling books to thousands by mail stimulated a market for books in areas where there was a limited number of retail booksellers. It has been estimated that by the mid–20th century, book clubs accounted for 30% of total book sales in the United States. Because of their widespread memberships, they have been a dominant influence in the making of a best seller. In the 1990s, Oprah Winfrey's television book club has created enormous sales for many writers who might otherwise have been less noticed.

Aside from book clubs that fall into the category of mass distributors, there are many small, select clubs catering to the interests of special groups, such as farmers, yachtsmen, and religious denominations.

Bookman, The. A magazine whose first issue was published in February 1895, with Professor HARRY THURSTON PECK of Columbia University as editor. It ceased publication in 1933, after Seward Collins had made it an organ for NEW HUMANISM. Among other editors of *The Bookman* were Robert Cortes Holliday, JOHN FARRAR, and BURTON RASCOE. Lively controversies were conducted in its columns, as when Hugh Walpole replied vigorously to H. L. Mencken's charge that American books were not sufficiently appreciated in England,

and when Heywood Broun debated censorship with John S. Summer, secretary of the New York Society for the Suppression of Vice. During Farrar's tenure, Broun was a frequent reviewer for the magazine, and other contributors included Robert Benchley, Sidney Howard, Laurence Stallings, Donald Ogden Stewart, Corey Ford, and Herschel Brickell. See R. S. BAKER, BEST SELLERS.

Book of Annandale, The (1902), a story in blank verse by EDWIN ARLINGTON ROBINSON, part of the collection called CAPTAIN CRAIG. A man has promised his dying wife never to marry again, and a woman has given the same assurance to her dying husband. The two survivors fight a spiritual battle with their consciences, but life wins out. Robinson also wrote a sonnet, "How Annandale Went Out" (1910), that tells how a physician, tending a friend and finding him "a wreck, with hell between him and the end," employs "a slight kind of machine," apparently a hypodermic, to put him out of his misery.

Book of Mormon (1830), sacred text of the Church of Latter-Day Saints, or MORMONS. JOSEPH SMITH claimed to have translated it from golden tablets revealed to him in Palmyra, New York, in 1827.

Boomerang, The. A daily newspaper founded by EDGAR WILSON NYE at Laramie, Wyoming. Many of Nye's pieces (signed Bill Nye) first appeared in *The Boomerang* and established his reputation as a humorist. His first book was called *Bill Nye and Boomerang* (1881).

Boone, Daniel (1734–1820), frontiersman. Boone was born in Pennsylvania and grew up near the Yadkin River in North Carolina, where he learned to love hunting and exploring and became an expert marksman. In 1760 he made his way through the wilderness to what later became Tennessee. He heard glowing talk of "the dark and bloody wilderness," soon to be called Kentucky, and with five companions explored that country for two years. Returning home, he persuaded his family to move to Kentucky, and a party set out to make a settlement. Some were killed, but the others reached their destination and founded Boonesborough on the magnificent Kentucky River. During the Revolutionary War Boone helped the colonists, and at one time was captured by the British and carried to their post at Detroit, from which he escaped to help his people when he heard that an Indian attack on Kentucky was imminent. Like the old Puritans and many of the frontiersmen Boone despised lawyers and the law, and as a consequence twice forfeited great land possessions, once by failing to register his holdings in Kentucky. In disgust he moved to Spanish territory near St. Louis and later was again evicted from his holdings. But this time they were restored to him by Congress (1814), in view of his great services in opening up the wilderness. There, in Missouri, he died surrounded by his descendants to the fifth generation.

Boone, the mild-mannered, courageous pioneer, became legendary even in his lifetime. He seems to have dictated an account of his exploits to John Filson, who inserted it in his *Discovery, Settlement, and Present State of Kentucky* (1784). Soon after Boone's death Byron celebrated him in *Don Juan* (1823) as a kindly child of nature, loving the wilderness and fleeing civilization. In the same year, Cooper found in him the prototype of his NATTY BUMPPO, and he has appeared in many stories, including Winston Churchill's THE CROSSING (1904) and Stewart Edward White's *The Long Rifle* (1932).

Booster, The.   A magazine, in French and English, originally published in Paris under the supervision of the American Country Club as an aid to tourists. A good part of the magazine consisted of travel advertisements. In September 1937 HENRY MILLER and a group of his friends took over the magazine and made it a vehicle for their advanced literary, social, and biological views. Protests from the former owners brought about a hasty withdrawal of advertising. In April 1938 the name was changed to *Delta*, and with the Christmas issue the magazine expired.

Booth, Edwin [Thomas] (1833–1893),   actor, son of JUNIUS BRUTUS BOOTH. He was acclaimed as an actor in the United States and abroad. His frequent playing of tragic roles was matched by the tragedy of his own career, particularly his brother's killing of President Lincoln. Eleanor Ruggles wrote an excellent biography of him called *Prince of Players* (1953). The Players Club in New York City, where Booth made his home in his last years, is rich in Booth memorabilia.

Booth, General William, Enters Heaven.   See GENERAL WILLIAM BOOTH ENTERS HEAVEN.

Booth, John Wilkes (1838–1865),   actor, son of JUNIUS BRUTUS BOOTH and brother of EDWIN BOOTH. He had been successful in Shakespearean roles when he conceived his insane intention to assassinate President Lincoln. Booth was either killed or committed suicide.

Booth, Junius Brutus (1769–1852),   a member of a celebrated family of American actors. Born in London, he came to the United States in 1821 and made many tours of the country, usually in romantic dramas of violence and bloodshed.

Booth, Philip (1925–   ),   poet. Born in New Hampshire and educated at Dartmouth, Booth has taught for many years at Syracuse University. His poems, mostly traditional, are generally about New England, often the Maine coast. His books include *Letter from a Distant Land* (1957), looking back in blank verse to Thoreau; *The Islanders* (1961); *Weathers and Edges* (1966); *North by East* (1967); *Beyond Our Fears* (1968); *Margins* (1970); *Available Light* (1976); and *Before Sleep* (1980).

Booth, Wayne C[layson] (1921–   ),   teacher, critic. Born in Utah, Booth was educated at Brigham Young University and the University of Chicago. Trained as a neo-Aristotelian critic under R. S. Crane (see CHICAGO CRITICS), Booth has become one of the most influential rhetorical critics in America. His first book, *The Rhetoric of Fiction* (1961), exemplifies the power of the Aristotelian principle that techniques cannot be properly evaluated apart from their contribution to a larger purpose, and it sketches an approach to fiction as rhetoric. In accomplishing the first task, Booth overturned such dogmas about narration as "showing is better than telling" and "true art ignores the audience." In accomplishing the second, he showed that every choice an author

makes has consequences for how the audience will respond to the work's developing representation and, more generally, for the kind of meeting of minds that can occur between author and reader. Booth's concern for the way minds can meet through language and literature unites his otherwise very different 1974 books, *A Rhetoric of Irony* and *Modern Dogma and the Rhetoric of Assent*. In *Irony*, he investigates the special nature of communications in which authors covertly ask audiences to reject the literal meaning of their utterances and reconstruct their indirectly expressed meanings. He demonstrates the possibility and pleasures of sharing stable ironies—communications whose reconstructions are not themselves undercut—and conducts a fascinating, if less conclusive, examination of unstable ironies—communications in which no reconstruction is secure. In *Modern Dogma*, he seeks to establish appropriate warrants for giving assent to another's argument, and ends by suggesting that giving assent is a more fundamental human act than expressing denial. In *Critical Understanding* (1979), Booth applies the rhetoric of assent to the domain of criticism. He proposes a pluralism that rejects the notion that all critical statements are equally meritorious even as it insists on the validity and importance of multiple questions about literature. Above all, the pluralism proposes that our critical discourse honor three enduring values—vitality, justice, and understanding—because serving them will best enable critics to engage in productive communal discourse. Booth's rhetorical analysis of literary and critical discourse is extended in *The Company We Keep: Ethical Criticism and the Ethics of Reading* (1988) and *The Vocation of a Teacher: Occasions for Rhetoric 1967–88* (1989). *For the Love of It: Amateuring and Its Rivals* (1999) reports on the author's love of music.

JAMES PHELAN

Boothe, [Ann] Clare.   See LUCE, CLARE BOOTHE.

Borden, Lizzie (1860–1927),   indicted as a murderess. She was charged with the axe-murder (August 4, 1892) of her father and stepmother in Fall River, Massachusetts, and her trial was followed closely all over the country. She was acquitted, but the murder became the theme of several ballads and poems that rejected the verdict, also of an anonymous but widely quoted quatrain: "Lizzie Borden took an axe/ And gave her mother forty whacks;/ When she saw what she had done,/ She gave her father forty-one." Three full-length plays—Donald Blackwell's *Lizzie* (1930), John Colton's *Nine Pine Street* (1933), and Reginald Lawrence's *The Legend of Lizzie* (1959)—as well as a one-act play, *Goodbye, Miss Lizzie Borden*, (1947) by Lillian de la Torre, were based on the case, as were two novels, Mark E. Wilkins Freeman's *The Long Arm* (1895) and Lily Dougall's *The Summit House Mystery* (1905). Charles and Louise Samuels' *The Girl in the House of Hate* (1953) and Edward D. Radin's *Lizzie Borden: The Untold Story* (1961) are nonfiction. *Fall River Legend* (1948) is a ballet by Agnes de Mille.

Border Romances.   Novels by WILLIAM GILMORE SIMMS, giving a sensational, mainly unrealistic picture of life on the southern border. Among them were: GUY RIVERS (1834), a successful story of a fiendish Georgia bandit; *Richard Hurdis* (1838) and its sequel, *Border Beagles* (1840); BEAUCHAMPE, OR, THE KENTUCKY TRAGEDY (1842); and the highly sensational *Charlemano* (1856).

Borges, Jorge Luis (1899–1986),   short-story writer, essayist, poet. Late in life, Borges was recognized as the foremost writer in Latin America, a man of letters whose international reputation placed him in the company of such 20th-century masters of the bizarre as Franz Kafka, VLADIMIR NABOKOV, and Samuel Beckett. Born in Buenos Aires, he counted as ancestors some who had fought for Argentinian independence as well as a maternal grandmother from England, who read to him in English before he had learned to read for himself in Spanish. English, and the world of literature generally, came to him also from his father, a psychology teacher who attempted poetry and fiction. The fact that the elder Borges translated FitzGerald's *Rubaiyat*, itself a translation from an Arabic original, is suggestive of the cross-cultural threads important to the son's later fiction. Borges's multilingual education continued in Geneva, where from 1914 to 1918 he attended a French school, learned German, and discovered German expressionism. From 1918 to 1921 he lived in Spain, becoming part of the international literary circle that included the Chilean VINCENTE HUIDOBRO. When he returned to Argentina, he brought with him some of the ideas of the *ultraismo* movement, an attempt to develop a pure poetry of magical metaphors and images unrestricted by considerations of reality. In Buenos Aires, he helped found avant-garde literary journals, wrote poetry, worked as a librarian, and lectured on Anglo-Saxon literature at the University of Buenos Aires. Under the anti-intellectual Perón regime, he suffered the indignity of an appointment as chicken inspector in 1946, but after the fall of that regime he became director of the National Library. He was in his thirties before he began to write the short stories that came to be seen as his major contribution to literature. International fame came in the 1960s, following his sharing of the Formenter Prize with Samuel Beckett in 1961 and the translation into English in 1962 of his *Ficciones* (1944).

Borges developed the distinctive art of his fictions from a number of sources, many within himself. Hints came from his familiarity with the attempts of avant-garde poets to break free of mimetic constraints, from his reading in the fabulous literature of earlier times, from his acquaintance with the work of such a 19th-century antirealist as AMBROSE BIERCE, and from his awareness of the fountains of cultural diversity in Latin America that gave rise to MAGICAL REALISM.

A major concern of Borges's fiction is the nearly invisible line that separates reality and illusion. In *Historia universal de la infamia* (1935, tr. *A Universal History of Infamy*, 1972), he presents fiction as though it were real biography. More important are the tales of his next two collections, *Ficciones* (1944, tr. *Fictions*, 1962), and *El Aleph* (1948, tr. 1970), including such masterpieces as "Pierre Menard, Author of the *Quixote*," which presents fiction as though it were an essay. *El informe de Brodie* (1970, tr. *Dr. Brodie's Report*, 1972) includes the chilling "The Gospel According to Mark," wherein brutish farm laborers confuse the message of the gospel and prepare a crucifixion. *Labyrinths* (1962) presents a selection of writings in translation, reminding the reader in its title of the labyrinthine nature of much of his work. As in a labyrinth, the reader turns down paths that seem to promise enlightenment, only to discover one dead end after another as the ways that seem to lead to truth turn instead into other fictional alleys. From his fifties onward, Borges's eyesight deteriorated rapidly until, by age seventy, he was approaching blindness. Some of his later work suggests that the labyrinth of life does not give up its secrets easily to the fully sighted, that surface illusions are more readily penetrated with the mind than with the eyes.

In *El hacedor* (1960, tr. *Dreamtigers*, 1964), Borges mixed poetry and prose, including an account of Homer's blindness. His verse is generally lyrical and metaphysical and is often inspired by Argentine life or history. His collections include *Fervor de Buenos Aires* (1923), *Luna de enfrente* (1925), and *Cuaderno San Martin* (1954). His poems appear in translation in *Selected Poems: 1923–1967* (1972); and *In Praise of Darkness* (1974). Essays on philosophy and literature are collected in *Inquisiciones* (1925); *Otras inquisiciones* (1952, tr. *Other Inquisitions*, 1964); and *Nuevo essayos dantescos* (*Nine Dantesque Essays*, 1982). *The Craft of Verse* (2000) is a series of lectures given at Harvard in 1967. Among his other works are *Antologia personal* (1961, tr. *A Personal Anthology*, 1967); *The Book of Imaginary Beings* (1967, tr. 1969), including revisions of well-known myths and inventions of new ones; *El Libro de arena* (1975, tr. *The Book of Sand*, 1977); *Sietas noches* (1980, tr. *Seven Nights*, 1984); and *Los conjurados* (*The Conspirators*, 1985). *Selected Nonfictions*, edited by Eliot Weinberger, appeared in 1999.

Borglum, [John] Gutzon [De La Mothe] (1870–1941), sculptor. Borglum studied art in San Francisco and Paris. In 1904 he won a gold medal at the Louisiana Purchase Exposition with a bronze group, *The Mares of Diomedes*, now in the Metropolitan Museum, New York. His sculptures are found in such places as the Capitol in Washington and the Cathedral of St. John the Divine in New York City, but he is chiefly known for his massive group of four great American leaders on Mount Rushmore, South Dakota. (See BLACK HILLS.) He was responsible for the Confederate memorial carved on Stone Mountain, Georgia. Robert J. Casey and Mary Borglum wrote *Give the Man Room: The Story of Gutzon Borglum* (1952).

Borland, Hal [Harold Glen] (1900–1978),   nature writer, autobiographer, novelist. Born in Sterling, Nebraska, Borland grew up on a Colorado ranch and was noted as a nature and conservation writer with books that include *American Year: Country Life and Landscapes through the Seasons* (1946), *Beyond Your Door: A Handbook to the Country* (1962), *Sundial of the Seasons* (1964), *Hill Country Harvest* (1967), *Countryman: A Summary of Belief* (1965), *Homeland: A Report from the Country* (1969), *Seasons* (1973), *The History of Wildlife in America* (1975), and *A Place to Begin: The New England Experience* (1976). His novels and juvenile fiction, some published as Ward West, often focus on nature or western Americana and include *Rocky Mountain Tipi Tales* (1924);

Trouble Valley (1934); *Halfway to Timberline* (1935); *When the Legends Die* (1963), about an aging rodeo cowboy, widely translated, and filmed in 1972; and *The King of Squaw Mountain* (1964). His autobiographical books are *High, Wide and Lonesome* (1956), *This Hill, This Valley* (1957), and *Country Editor's Boy* (1970).

Boss, The (produced 1911, published 1917),   a play by EDWARD SHELDON. Sheldon mingles the story of Michael Regan, a corrupt contractor and politician, with what ultimately turns out to be a love affair between Regan and the daughter of a fine family; she eventually marries him to save her father.

Boston (1928),   a novel by UPTON SINCLAIR. An elderly woman, one of the Boston BRAHMINS, suffers pangs of social conscience and goes to work in a factory, where she becomes acquainted with Sacco and Vanzetti. (See SACCO-VANZETTI CASE.) As the battle between industry and labor increases in intensity, she observes at close range the world-shaking events following the arrest of the two men for murder and their trial, appeal, and execution. The book, which partially follows the trail transcript, seethes with indignation.

Boston Athenaeum.   Founded 1805 as a reading room by the ANTHOLOGY CLUB, the Athenaeum has become a Boston institution. The building, constructed in 1845, houses a large and excellent library available to scholars and others.

Boston Gazette, The.   Two newspapers by this name appeared during the 18th century in New England. The first ran from 1719 to 1741, and was either the second or third newspaper to appear in the colonies; the second was published from 1755 to 1798. The earlier *Gazette* was printed by JAMES FRANKLIN, but he lost the contract in 1721 and founded THE NEW ENGLAND COURANT, as radical and outspoken as the *Gazette* was conservative and reserved. The later *Gazette* was an advocate of American independence, publishing letters of John Adams ("Novanglus") and others.

Bostonians, The (1886),   a novel by HENRY JAMES. Satirically, James portrays a strong-minded Boston woman, Olive Chancellor, representing a new generation of do-gooders, who takes life hard and is interested above all in the emancipation of women. She finds or thinks she finds a kindred soul in a beautiful and impressionable girl, Verena Tarrant, and the plot turns on the domination of one woman by the other. Verena is converted to feminism and primed for a career as a lecturer, but she is also courted by Basil Ransom, a lawyer from Mississippi, who wins her over in the end for home and family. The memorable Miss Birdseye has suggested ELIZABETH PEABODY to some readers.

Boston Miscellany of Literature and Fashion (1842–1843).   Founded apparently as an offshoot of *Arcturus*, a critical magazine, the *Miscellany's* contributors included Poe and Lowell.

Boston News-Letter.   JOHN CAMPBELL, Boston postmaster, was actively interested in conservative politics. On April 24, 1704, he founded a news sheet, at first handwritten, called *Boston News-Letter*, credited with being the first newspaper in America. John Draper became its editor and publisher in 1733, his son Richard its publisher in 1762. News of

events abroad was garnered somewhat belatedly from English newspapers as they arrived in Boston. Young Draper changed the name first to *Boston Weekly News-Letter*, later to *The Massachusetts Gazette and Boston News-Letter*. Two years after Draper's death the newspaper ceased publication (February 22, 1776); for a time it was the only paper published during the British occupation of Boston and espoused the Tory side.

Boston Quarterly Review (1838–1842).   A personal organ for ORESTES BROWNSON, who filled its pages mainly with his own writings. If reflected his chameleon changes of opinion in religion and politics. In 1842 he merged the magazine with the *Democratic Review*. In 1844, when this magazine declined to print any more of his contributions, he founded *Brownson's Quarterly Review*, which he edited until 1875.

Both Your Houses (1933),   a play by MAXWELL ANDERSON. An exposé of corruption among congressmen, as revealed in an attempt to pass a large appropriations bill laden with graft. An idealistic young congressman gets evidence to make the corruption clear, but finds that the father of the young woman he is in love with is among the congressmen involved, even if unintentionally. The play won a Pulitzer Prize.

Botkin, B[enjamin] A[lbert] (1901–1975),   teacher, editor. Botkin, a writer in the field of American folklore, has said: "I like to think of myself as a Bostonian by birth, an Oklahoman by adoption, and a New Yorker by preference; a teacher and researcher by temperament, and a popularizer by persuasion." He published *The Southwest Scene* (1931); *A Treasury of American Folklore* (1940); *A Treasury of New England Folklore* (1947); *A Treasury of American Anecdotes* (1957); *The Illustrated Book of American Folklore*, with Carl Withers (1958); and *A Civil War Treasury of Tales, Legends and Folklore* (1960). From 1925 to 1935 he edited the annual *Folk-Say: A Regional Miscellany*.

Boucher, Jonathan (1738–1804),   clergyman, lexicographer. Born in England, Boucher came to Virginia as rector of a parish and to conduct a private school. As rector at Annapolis he founded the Homony Club, a genteel literary organization. He was frank to express his loyalist sentiments in sermons as well as in conversation. In 1775 he returned to England and there published thirteen sermons as *A View of the Causes and Consequences of the American Revolution*; he held that a good Christian would necessarily be a good subject of the British monarch. The book was dedicated to his old neighbor, General Washington.

After Boucher's death his friends published (1807) *A Glossary of Archaic and Provincial Words*, intended to supplement Samuel Johnson's *Dictionary*; he had worked on this book for thirty years. This covered part of "A"; in 1832 material up to "Bl" was published, and then the work stopped. In the latter volume is a list of thirty-eight Americanisms gathered by Boucher, also a pastoral, *Absence*. Boucher predicted that Americans would break away in speech as in government from England.

Boucicault, Dion (1820–1890),   actor, playwright. Born in Ireland, Boucicault (originally Dionysius Lardner Boursiquot) had already established his reputation in England as a skillful playwright when he came to the United States in 1853. Although he returned to London later (1862–72), most of his 132 plays were produced in New York. His first play, *London Assurance*, was produced when he was only nineteen and was a great success. His first important production in this country was *Grimaldi, or, The Life of an Actress* (New Orleans, 1855), in which he and his wife appeared, as did later E. A. Sothern and Julia Marlowe. He dramatized French stories and two stories by Dickens, based another play, THE OCTOROON (1859), on Mayne Rejd's novel, *The Quadroon* (1856), and collaborated with JOSEPH JEFFERSON on RIP VAN WINKLE (1865). But his specialty in time became plays with Irish settings: *The Colleen Bawn* (1860); *Arrah-na-Pogue* (1864); *The Shaughraun* (1874); and others. In *Arrah-na-Pogue* Boucicault took an old tune, *The Wearing of the Green*, and wrote new words to it. It led to the universal use in Ireland of a sprig of shamrock as a symbol of love of Erin. In 1860 Boucicault inaugurated the first touring company to appear on the road in a single play.

Boudinot, Elias [1] (1740–1821),   public official, author. Born in Philadelphia, Boudinot became active in New Jersey politics, served in the Continental Congress, was elected its president in 1782, proclaimed a Day of Thanksgiving (1783), became a representative in Congress (1789–1805), was Director of the Mint (1805–1821). He founded the American Bible Society (1816) and was active in the education of Indians and deaf-mutes. He wrote several books on religion, including *The Age of Revelation* (1801), a refutation of Tom Paine's THE AGE OF REASON (1794). George Adams Boyd wrote *Elias Boudinot, Patriot and Statesman* (1952).

Boudinot, Elias [2] (1803?–1839),   editor. A Cherokee, called Galagina (buck deer) in his own tongue. Boudinot was born in Georgia and educated at a mission school in Cornwall, Connecticut; he adopted the name of Elias Boudinot as an act of gratitude to the school's patron. In 1823 he helped translate the New Testament into Cherokee and in 1828 became editor of *The Cherokee Phoenix*, the first newspaper printed for an Indian tribe, and suppressed in 1835 because it criticized the official Washington attitude toward the Cherokees. In 1833 he published a novel, *Poor Sarah, or, The Indian Woman*. Meanwhile the Cherokees continued to suffer one grave injustice after another from the federal government and from the state of Georgia, and in 1838 were driven off their lands, on which gold had been discovered. Boudinot, under unfortunate influence, signed a treaty which agreed to this removal, and was assassinated soon after his arrival in Indian Territory, now Oklahoma.

Bound East for Cardiff (1916),   one-act play by EUGENE O'NEILL. This play, presented by the PROVINCETOWN PLAYERS at the Wharf Theater, was the first production of O'Neill's to reach the stage. It gives the last moments in the life of the seaman Yank, who is dying from a fall on the British tramp steamer *Glencairn*.

Bourjaily, Vance [Nye] (1922–   ),   novelist, editor. Born in Ohio and educated at Bowdoin College, Bourjaily

began his career as a chronicler of his times with *The End of My Life* (1947), a semiautobiographical novel following an ambulance driver in World War II in the Middle East and Italy. In his next novel, *The Hound of Earth* (1955), a scientist flees from his involvement in the development of the atomic bomb. *The Violated* (1958) depicts lives, including those of children, disrupted by the effects of war. *Confessions of a Spent Youth* (1960), semiautobiographical, is a fine evocation of the ambience that led to the emergence of the Beat Generation. *The Man Who Knew Kennedy* (1967) and *Brill Among the Ruins* (1971) are novels of the sixties. *Now Playing at Canterbury* (1976) and *A Game Men Play* (1980), both novels, are further examinations of contemporary society. *Old Soldier* (1990) is a novel about fishing in Maine. His nonfiction works include *The Unnatural Enemy* (1963), on hunting, and *Country Matters* (1973). Bourjaily was an editor of DISCOVERY (1953–1955), a teacher of writing at the University of Iowa (1957–1980) and other Universities: With his son Philip, he wrote *Fishing by Mail: The Outdoor Life of a Father and Son* (1993).

Bourke-White, Margaret (1906–1971),   photographer. Industrial and news photography, from 1927, took her to thirty-four countries and won her the American Woman of Achievement Award in 1951. She is known for the books done in collaboration with writer ERSKINE CALDWELL, her former husband: *You Have Seen Their Faces* (1937), one of the first books successfully to combine the techniques of journalism and photography; *North of the Danube* (1939); and *Say! Is This the U.S.A.?* (1941). Her own work, text as well as pictures, includes *Eyes on Russia* (1931); *U.S.S.R.: A Portfolio of Photographs* (1934); *Shooting the Russian War* (1942); *Purple Heart Valley* (1944); *Halfway to Freedom, A Study of the New India* (1949); and *Portrait of Myself* (1963). She was associated with *Fortune* and *Life* magazines as editor and war correspondent.

Bourne, Randolph [Silliman] (1886–1918),   essayist. An early accident made Bourne helplessly handicapped for the rest of his life. After an unhappy childhood he entered Columbia University on a scholarship and later, on another scholarship, traveled and studied in Europe. He became a radical in education and politics, hating war and detesting the society around him. For a time Bourne wrote for *The New Republic*, but his articles expressed his views so acidly that he was forced out and thereafter found it difficult to earn a living. Among his books are *Youth and Life* (1913), *The Gary Schools* (1916), *Education and Living* (1917), and *Untimely Papers* (1919). Van Wyck Brooks, an intimate of Bourne's, edited *The History of a Literary Radical* (1920, reprinted 1956).

Bowditch, Nathaniel (1773–1838),   mathematician, authority on navigation. Born in Salem, Massachusetts, and self-educated, Bowditch discovered an error in Newton's *Principia Mathematica* (1686, 1687) and translated the first four volumes of Laplace's *Traité de Mécanique Céleste* (1799–1825). He made five sea voyages and set out to revise J. Hamilton Moore's *Practical Navigator*, which led to his own *The New American Practical Navigator* (1802, frequently revised). This book helped make possible the astounding achievements of the Yankee clippers and is still in use.

Bowen, Catherine Drinker (1897–1973), writer. Bowen wrote first about music, later a history of Lehigh University (1924), finally a series of biographies and histories—of Tchaikovsky (*Beloved Friend*, 1937); of Anton Rubinstein (*Free Artist*, 1939); of Justice Oliver Wendell Holmes (*Yankee from Olympus*, 1944), a great popular success; *John Adams and the American Revolution* (1950); *The Lion and the Throne* (1956), of Sir Edward Coke; and *Francis Bacon: The Temper of the Man* (1963). She also wrote *Adventures of a Biographer* (1959), autobiographical.

Bower, B[ertha] M[uzzy] (1871–1940), writer of western stories. Writing merely under initials, Mrs. Bower managed to attract countless male readers who believed she was a man and probably a cowboy. Her first book, *Chip of the Flying U* (1904), was one of her best. She continued to publish two books a year for many years, including *The Lonesome Trail* (1909), *Casey Ryan* (1921), and *The Flying U Strikes* (1934).

Bowering, George (1935–), Canadian poet and fiction writer. Bowering's editing in the 1960s of the avant-garde newsletter *Tish* set off a new wave of Canadian poetry inspired, like Bowering's own, by the work of WILLIAM CARLOS WILLIAMS and the BLACK MOUNTAIN POETS. In his verse, he aims at precision and integrity in rendering felt experience, employing the language and cadence of common speech. His collections include *Points on the Grid* (1964), *The Man in Yellow Boots* (1965), *Sitting in Mexico* (1970), *Particular Accidents: Selected Poems* (1981), *Kerrisdale Elegies* (1984), and *Delayed Mercies* (1986). Among his numerous publications are several novels, including *A Mirror on the Floor* (1967), *Burning Water* (1980), and *Caprice* (1987). *A Place to Die* (1973), *Fly-catcher* (1974), and *Protective Footwear* (1978) are collections of short stories.

Bowers, Claude [Gernade] (1878–1958), ambassador, historian. Bowers, always deeply interested in American politics, frankly espoused the Democratic party in many of his activities. He was ambassador to Spain (1933–39) and to Chile (1939–53). Among his best-known books are *The Party Battles of the Jackson Period* (1922), *Jefferson and Hamilton* (1925), *The Tragic Era: The Revolution after Lincoln* (1929), *Jefferson in Power: The Death Struggle of the Federalists* (1936), *The Young Jefferson* (1945), *My Mission to Spain* (1954), and *Chile Through Embassy Windows* (1958). The last two are autobiographical and there is a memoir, *My Life* (1962).

Bowers, Edgar (1924–2000), poet. Bowers was born in Rome, Georgia, and served in the U.S. Army's Counterintelligence Corps during World War II. After the war he attended the University of North Carolina and later earned a Ph.D. at Stanford University. He taught at the University of California at Santa Barbara most of his life. Bowers used traditional forms in his work writing rhymed poems at first and blank verse later. His collections include *The Form of Loss* (1956), *The Astronomer* (1965), *Living Together* (1973), *Witnesses* (1981), and *Thirteen Views of Santa Barbara* (1989). He

was awarded the Bolligen Prize in 1989. His last collection was *For Louis Pasteur* (1990).

Bowery, The. An old and wide street in lower Manhattan, extending northward from Chatham Square to the junction of Third and Fourth Avenues at Cooper Union. It ran originally through part of Peter Stuyvesant's farm—the Dutch *bouwerij* (farmstead) is from *bouwer* (farmer). During the 19th century it became a street of dance halls, beer gardens, dives, and cheap theaters. The inhabitants of the Bowery were believed to be impudent rascals of the lower classes with a remarkable dialect of their own. Aside from an early play, *A Glance at New York* (1848), which depicted Bowery characters, the street first became literature in Stephen Crane's MAGGIE, A GIRL OF THE STREETS (1893) and in his novelette, GEORGE'S MOTHER (1893). In 1900 they were published as *Bowery Tales*. A little later Edward W. Townsend, a friend of Crane, gave a more popular and less literary picture of the district in a series of stories that began with *Chimmie Fadden, Major Max, and Other Stories* (1895). (See CHIMMIE FADDEN.) Charles Hoyt's A TRIP TO CHINATOWN (produced, 1891) made the Bowery famous, both as a street and as a song. The song tells of the various scrapes a yokel gets into when he hits the Bowery and includes the line "The Bowery! the Bowery! I'll never go there any more!"

Bowles, Jane [Sydney Auer] (1917–1973), novelist, playwright. Born in New York City and educated privately in Switzerland, Bowles married PAUL BOWLES in 1938, moved with him to Tangier in 1952, and remained there for the rest of her life. Her one novel, *Two Serious Ladies* (1943), is a surrealistic tale of women who pursue opposite goals of sainthood and self-fulfillment. *Plain Pleasures* (1966) collects short stories. *In the Summer House* (1954) is a play. Her small following during her life has been augmented since her death by readers who respond to her unconventionality and to the issues raised in the conflicts between sensuality and independence, strong women and weak men, that mark her work. *Collected Works* (1996) was expanded as *My Sister's Hand in Mine* (1978).

Bowles, Paul [Frederick] (1910–1999), composer, novelist. Born in New York City, Bowles studied at the University of Virginia (1928–29) and with Aaron Copland and Virgil Thomson in New York, Berlin, and Paris. Married to JANE BOWLES, he lived after 1952 mostly in Tangier. His many works as a composer include songs, ballets, music for plays and films, and the opera *The Wind Remains* (1941). His novels, mostly set in Morocco, are unsettling, absurdist visions of life freed from traditional Western constraints. They include *The Sheltering Sky* (1949), *Let It Come Down* (1952), *The Spider's House* (1955), and *Up Above the World* (1966). His short-story collections began with *The Delicate Prey* (1950) and went for a number of volumes, later appearing as *Collected Stories* (1979). His volumes of poetry are *Scenes* (1968) and *The Thicket of Spring* (1971) and *Next to Nothing: Collected Poems, 1926–1977*. His travel books are *Yallah* (1956) and *Their Heads Are Green* (1963). He has translated Sartre's *No Exit* (1946) and translated and edited Moroccan works, including *Love with a Few Hairs* (1967) and *A Life Full of Holes* (1964). His autobiography is *Without Stopping* (1972). Other titles include: *Days: Tangier Journal 1987–1989* (1991), and *Too Far from Home: The Selected Writings of Paul Bowles* (1995). Correspondence is collected in *In Touch: The Letters of Paul Bowles*, edited by Jeffrey Miller (1993).

Bowles, Samuel (1797–1851), and **Bowles, Samuel** (1826–1878), newspaper editors. The elder Bowles founded the influential Springfield, Massachusetts, *Republican*. His son published several travel books based on letters printed in The *Republican*, among them *Across the Continent* (1865) and *The Switzerland of America* (1869), later combined as *Our New West* (1869).

Boyd, Ernest [Augustus] (1887–1946), critic. Boyd's international ancestry and background—born in Ireland, he first came to the U.S. as a member of the British consular service—along with his strong enthusiasms and prejudices are reflected in his books, including: *Ireland's Literary Renaissance* (1922), *Studies in Ten Literatures* (1925), H. L. Mencken (1925), *Literary Blasphemies* (1927), and *The Pretty Lady* (1934). His wife, Madeleine Boyd, wrote a novel about him, *Life Makes Advances* (1939).

Boyd, James (1888–1944), novelist. Boyd was born in Pennsylvania, grew up in North Carolina, and was educated at Princeton. His spirited and authentic novels of American history include DRUMS (1925), MARCHING ON (1927), *Long Hunt* (1930), *Roll River* (1935), and *Bitter Creek* (1939). He also wrote *Eighteen Poems* (1944) and the posthumous *Old Pines and Other Stories* (1952).

Boyd, Nancy. A pseudonym of EDNA ST. VINCENT MILLAY, used on the title page of a series of sketches, *Distressing Dialogues* (1924).

Boyd, Thomas Alexander (1898–1935), newspaperman, novelist, biographer. Boyd fought as a marine in World War I and chronicled his experiences in a novel, *Through the Wheat* (1923). *In Time of Peace* (1928) depicted a hard-drinking ex-sergeant working after the war as a newspaper reporter. He also wrote biographies of the renegade SIMON GIRTY (1928), Anthony Wayne (1929), and Light-Horse Harry Lee (1931).

Boyesen, Hjalmar Hjorth (1848–1895), teacher, philologist, novelist. Norwegian born, Boyesen visited the United States in 1869, intending to stay only a little while, but the interest William Dean Howells showed in Boyesen's story about Norwegian life, *Gunnar*, and its serial publication in the *Atlantic Monthly* (published in book form, 1874) caused him to take up permanent residence. He taught at Cornell and Columbia and published several scholarly books, among them *Essays on Scandinavian Literature* (1895). His books for young people were widely read and are still readable, particularly *Boyhood in Norway* (1892). Toward the end of his life he turned to realistic fiction: *The Mammon of Unrighteousness* (1891), *The Golden Calf* (1892), and *The Social Strugglers* (1893).

Boyle, Kay (1902–1992), novelist, short-story writer, poet. Born in Minnesota, Boyle lived for over thirty years in Europe before and after World War II. In the 1960s, she taught at various American universities. Earlier, she contributed to little magazines, particularly *Broom* and *Transition*, and earned a reputation for subtle, almost poetic explorations of the relationships between Europeans and Americans in novels and short stories set mainly in Europe. Her novels include *Plagued by the Nightingale* (1931), about a close-knit French family; *Year Before Last* (1932), about a young poet dying of tuberculosis; *Gentlemen, I Address You Privately* (1933), on sexual perversion; *My Next Bride* (1934), about an artist who steals to emulate success; and *Death of a Man* (1936), in which an American woman rejects a Nazi doctor. Several of her novels deal specifically with Europe during or just after World War II: *Primer for Combat* (1942), *Avalanche* (1944), *A Frenchman Must Die* (1946), and *Generation Without Farewell* (1960). In *The Underground Woman* (1975) a woman is jailed for anti-Vietnam War protest. Her stories appeared first in *Short Stories* (1929), in several subsequent collections, and then in *Fifty Stories* (1980). Her verse collections include *A Glad Day* (1938), *American Citizen* (1944), *Collected Poems* (1962), and *Testament for My Students* (1970). For the 1968 edition of ROBERT MCALMON's *Being Geniuses Together* she added her own reminiscences of the 1920s and 1930s abroad. Her last publication was *Words That Must Somehow Be Said: Selected Essays of Kay Boyle* (1985).

Boyle, T. Coraghessan (1948–) novelist, short-story writer. Born in Peekskill, New York, Boyle studied music before turning to literature under the spell of absurdist, anti-heroic, and black-comedic writers such as Eugene Ionesco, JEAN GENET, JOHN BARTH, and THOMAS PYNCHON. He studied at the University of Iowa with VANCE BOURJAILY and JOHN IRVING, earned a Ph.D. (1977), and two years later published the first of three early collections of stories: *Descent of Man* (1979), *Greasy Lake* (1985), and *If the River Was Whiskey* (1989). *The Collected Stories of T. Coraghessan Boyle* appeared in 1993. Many are zany exercises in hyperbole and parody, enriched with startling metaphors and general linguistic exuberance as they tell of Idi Amin at a Dada fair, Eisenhower in love with Mrs. Khrushchev, and a daredevil riding the axle of a truck cross-country. More recent is *After the Plague and Other Stories* (2001). His novels are similarly fantastic. *Water Music* (1981) is based in part on the Scottish explorer Mungo Park's adventures in 18th-century Africa. *Budding Prospects* (1984) involves marijuana cultivation in northern California. *World's End* (1987) brings the author back to his native Peekskill in his most accomplished work thus far. In it he spins a story of three hundred years of Hudson River fact and fable, with the actors of the earliest events still capable of haunting their descendants in the 20th century. *East is East* (1990) follows a Japanese seaman, Hiro Tanaka, after he jumps ship off the coast of Georgia. *The Road to Wellville*, a tale of breakfast cereal innovator John Harvey Kellogg, was followed by *The Tortilla Curtain* (1995), *River Rock* (1998), and *A Friend of the Earth* (2000).

Boynton, Henry W[alcott] (1869–1947), teacher, critic, editor. Boynton ably edited many classics for use in schools, and in collaboration with THOMAS WENTWORTH HIGGINSON prepared *A Reader's History of American Literature*

(1903). He published *Literature and Journalism, and Other Essays* (1904) and *Annals of American Book-Selling* (1932).

Boynton, Percy H[olmes] (1875–1946), teacher, critic. Long associated with the University of Chicago, Boynton wrote several books, including *Some Contemporary Americans* (1924), *More Contemporary Americans* (1927), *The Rediscovery of the Frontier* (1931), *Literature and American Life* (1936), *The American Scene in Contemporary Fiction* (1940).

Boys, The (published in *The Atlantic Monthly*, February 1859), an anniversary poem by OLIVER WENDELL HOLMES celebrating a reunion of his 1829 class at Harvard.

Boy's Will, A (1913), poems by ROBERT FROST. This was Frost's first book, first published in England (an American edition appeared in 1915). The collection established the poet's reputation immediately. The title comes from Longfellow's line in *My Lost Youth:* "A boy's will is the wind's will."

Brace, Gerald Warner (1901–1978), novelist, teacher. Brace studied architecture but turned to writing and teaching English at Williams, Dartmouth, Harvard, and Boston University, among other institutions. His novels, all set in New England, include *The Islands* (1936), *The Wayward Pilgrims* (1938), *Light on a Mountain* (1941), *The Garretson Chronicle* (1947), *A Summer's Tale* (1949), *The Spire* (1952), *The World of Carrick's Cove* (1957), *Winter Solstice* (1960), *The Wind's Will* (1964), *Between Wind and Water* (1966), and *The Department* (1968), in which a professor looks back at his teaching career. *Days That Were* (1976) is a memoir of Brace's youth, and his critical works include *The Age of the Novel* (1957) and *The Stuff of Fiction* (1969).

Bracebridge Hall, or, The Humorists (1822), forty-nine tales and sketches by WASHINGTON IRVING. The book is a continuation of THE SKETCH BOOK, with more gently romantic or Gothically melancholic narratives. Their background is sometimes American, sometimes French or Spanish, frequently English. Irving gives a pleasing but highly idealized picture of English rural scenes and rural existence.

Brackenridge, Hugh Henry (1748–1816), clergyman, lawyer, editor, writer. Brackenridge was born in Scotland and was five when his family emigrated to America. At Princeton he met JAMES MADISON and collaborated with PHILIP FRENEAU on a commencement poem, *The Rising Glory of America* (1772). During the war he was a chaplain and an ardent advocate of the revolutionary cause. After the war religious doubts caused him to abandon the ministry and become a lawyer. In the frontier town of Pittsburgh he helped found its first newspaper, *The Pittsburgh Gazette* (1786), and also established its first bookstore and first school. He spoke ardently for the adoption of the Constitution and favored the rebels in the Whiskey Rebellion of 1793. He became a leader in the Republican (later Democratic) Party, and during his last years was a justice of the Pennsylvania Supreme Court. His best-known work is a remarkable comic novel, MODERN CHIVALRY (1792–1815). In this, as in his political and legal activities, he shows himself a believer in balance, against aristocratic pretensions and democratic shams alike. In his earlier school-

teaching days he wrote two plays: THE BATTLE OF BUNKERS HILL (1776) and *The Death of General Montgomery* (1777).

Brackenridge's son Henry Marie (1786–1871), editor and writer of travel books, was a pioneer in the discussion of United States-South American relations. His views in *South America* (1817) helped to mold the Monroe Doctrine. A lawyer by vocation, he practiced as far west as St. Louis, keeping a journal that helped Washington Irving when he wrote ASTORIA (1836). Byron first heard of Daniel Boone when he read Brackenridge's *Views of Louisiana* (1814).

Brackett, Charles (1892–1969), screenwriter, director, producer. Much of Brackett's successful Hollywood career was carried out in collaboration with Billy Wilder. Often they directed and produced, as well as wrote, their screenplays, which include *Bluebeard's Eighth Wife* (1938); *Ninotchka* (1939); *Ball of Fire* (1942); *The Major and the Minor* (1942); *Five Graves to Cairo* (1943); *The Lost Weekend* (1945), for which he and Wilder received awards for the best screenplay of the year from the Motion Picture Academy; *A Foreign Affair* (1948); *Sunset Boulevard* (1950), judged Best Story and Screenplay for 1950; *Titanic* (1953), for which they again shared a similar award; and *Journey to the Center of the Earth* (1959). Brackett was drama critic of *The New Yorker* for three years and also wrote a number of novels, among them *The Counsel of the Ungodly* (1920); *Week-end* (1925); and *Entirely Surrounded* (1934), a *roman à clef* about Alexander Woollcott and his island colony on Lake Bomoseen, Vermont.

Bradbury, Ray [Douglas] (1920–   ), fiction writer. Born in Illinois, Bradbury attended Los Angeles High School and became a writer in 1943. His short stories, novels, plays, film, radio, and television scripts and other writings, mostly counted as science fiction or fantasy, number in the hundreds. They range from light humor through satire to gothic extravagance. His novels are *Fahrenheit 451* (1953), set in a totalitarian future that prohibits all forms of writing or individual thought, *Something Wicked This Way Comes* (1962), of a boyhood in the Midwest, and *A Graveyard for Lunatics* (1990), loosely autobiographical. A tireless writer of short stories, he has published many collections, including *Dark Carnival* (1947), *The Martian Chronicles* (1950), *The Illustrated Man* (1951), *The Golden Apples of the Sun* (1953), *The October Country* (1955), *Dandelion Wine* (1957), *A Medicine for Melancholy* (1959), *The Machineries of Joy* (1964), *I Sing the Body Electric!* (1969), *The Last Circus and the Electrocution* (1980), *A Memory of Murder* (1984), and *The Toynbee Convector* (1988). *Ahmed and the Oblivion Machines* appeared in 1998. Animal poetry is contained in *Poems: With Cat for Comforter* and *Dogs Think that Every Day is Christmas*, both appearing in 1997.

Bradford, Gamaliel (1863–1932), biographer, poet, dramatist. Born in Massachusetts, Bradford was a descendant of Governor William Bradford and inherited frail health and financial competence from his mother. He composed about two thousand poems (some gathered in three volumes), wrote fifteen plays (only one printed and none produced), kept a journal running to 1,400,000 words, one-seventh of which appeared after his death as *The Journal of Gamaliel Bradford* (edited by Van Wyck Brooks, 1933). To these should be added his "spiritual autobiography," *Life and I* (1928) and a selection from his thousands of letters, *Letters, 1918–1931* (1934).

In a score of volumes he collected 114 character sketches that he called "psychographs"—his major works. This term had been used by H. A. Taine (1828–1893) to describe the verbal portraits of the great French critic Sainte-Beuve (1804–1869). These books include: *Types of American Character* (1895); *Lee the American* (1912); *Confederate Portraits* (1914); *Union Portraits* (1916); *Portraits of Women* (1916); *A Naturalist of Souls* (1919); *American Portraits* (1922); *Damaged Souls*, his most popular work (1923); *Bare Souls* (1924); *Soul of Samuel Pepys* (1924); *Wives* (1925); *The Quick and the Dead* (1931); and *Elizabethan Women* (1936).

Bradford, John (1749–1830), printer. Bradford's *Kentucke Gazette*, begun in 1787, was the first newspaper in the territory, his *Kentucke Almanac* (1788) the first pamphlet. His "Notes of Kentucky" appeared in the *Gazette* (1826–29).

Bradford, Roark ["Whitney Wickliffe"] (1896–1948), newspaperman, short-story writer, playwright. Born in Tennessee, Bradford served in World War I, then became a newspaperman in Atlanta and New Orleans. A series of stories about African Americans provided material for his first book, *Ol' Man Adam an' His Chillun* (1928), which was the basis of a very successful play, THE GREEN PASTURES, written for the stage by MARC CONNELLY, 1930. *John Henry* (1931) was dramatized in 1940 with music by Jacques Wolfe. Other books by Bradford include *Ol' King David an' the Philistine Boys* (1930), *The Three-Headed Angel* (1937), and *The Green Roller* (1949).

Bradford, William [1] (1590–1657), colonial governor and historian. Born in Austerfield, in south Yorkshire, England, he became while still in his teens a member of a Separatist church in nearby Scrooby. To practice their variety of Puritanism, Bradford and the other church members moved in 1608 to Holland, where he followed the trade of weaver. In 1620 he and many of these Separatists sailed to the New World on the *Mayflower*, along with a group of "strangers." Bradford was to write a vivid account of their arrival in Plymouth, Massachusetts. In 1621 he was unanimously elected governor and served as governor for thirty-three years. Perhaps in this capacity he participated in the writing of *A Relation . . . of the beginning and proceedings of the English Plantation at Plymouth*, published in 1622 and generally known as *Mourt's Relation*. (The introduction is signed "G. Mourt.")

In 1630 Bradford began *Of Plimmoth Plantation*, an account of the origins and history of the colony beginning with the English Reformation. In the part written at this time, Bradford explains why his people had chosen to come to America and describes the difficulties of their undertaking. He concludes this part with a description of the erection of the first house at Plymouth. In 1646, when the colony was in obvious decline, he returned to his task and carried his account to 1646, then stopped writing. Since his aim was to encourage future generations to emulate the founders of the colony, he then began a series of poems and dialogues concerning their religious ideals and intentions. Bradford's dedication to his religious principles is suggested by the fact that he began the study of Hebrew at an advanced age "to see," he explained, "with my owne eyes something of that . . . language . . . in which the Law and Oracles of God were writ." After a long life, Bradford died in 1657.

In his great history *Of Plimmoth Plantation*, written in the third person, Bradford utilized the historical books of the Old Testament as model. His first book is a celebration of God's providence in leading the "pilgrims," as he calls them, to safety in the New World and of the heroic faith of the colony's founders. In deliberate, sober, rhythmical prose, he tells his story in the context of a complex and sophisticated providential philosophy of history. The result is one of the great achievements of American historiography, especially useful for an understanding of the piety that motivated these people. In the second book Bradford was writing from a different perspective: now he was attempting to reach an understanding of why the colony was suffering divisions and backslidings. In the end this is not a success story but one of disillusionment. He could only call up nostalgia for comfort, as he read the words he had written in 1630: "May not & ought not the children of these fathers [the colony's founders] rightly say: *Our fathers were Englishmen which came over this great ocean and were ready to perish in this wilderness, but they cried unto the Lord, and he heard their voice and looked on their adversite*." Vivid passages, such as the account of THOMAS MORTON and the hedonistic settlement at nearby Merrymount, continue to make the second book of the history engaging. Throughout, one's sense of the attractive and modest creator of this authoritative account is deeply appealing. Frequently consulted by later historians, Bradford's history was not published until 1856.

EVERETT EMERSON

Bradford, William [2] (1663–1752), printer. Born in England, Bradford became the first printer in Philadelphia (1685) and, in 1693, royal printer for New York. He printed the first American Book of Common Prayer (1710); the first printed American play, *Androboros*. (1714); and New York's first newspaper, the Royalist *New York Gazette* (1725–44).

Bradford, William [3] (1722–1791), printer. Grandson of WILLIAM BRADFORD [2], he established in Philadelphia the anti-British *Pennsylvania Journal and Weekly Advertiser* (1743–97), which competed with Franklin's Gazette; and published *The American Magazine and Monthly Chronicle* (1757–58). An opponent of the Stamp Act and a leader of the Sons of Liberty, he became official printer to the First Continental Congress.

Bradley, David [Henry, Jr.] (1950–), novelist. Born in Pennsylvania and educated at the University of Pennsylvania and King's College, London, Bradley has received high praise for his novels *South Street* (1957), set in a Philadelphia black ghetto, and *The Chaneysville Incident* (1981), an UNDERGROUND RAILROAD novel with its roots in a story from the author's childhood of thirteen escaped slaves who die rather than face recapture and return.

Bradley, Marion Zimmer (1930–1999), novelist. Born in Albany, New York, Bradley began to write science fiction in her teens. The Darkover novels, twenty-one books beginning with *The Planet Savers* (1985), concern a planet colonized by earthlings in the 21st century. Her best-known novel is a version of the Arthurian myths from a feminist perspective, *The Mists of Avalon* (1983). *The Firebrand* (1987) recounts the events of the Trojan War from the perspective of Cassandra. She found and edited *Fantasy Magazine* from 1988 to her death.

Bradstreet, Anne [Dudley] (1612?–1672), the first American poet of note, born in Northampton, England, to a nonconformist family. She was tutored by her father, Thomas Dudley, and was allowed to use the extensive library at Sempringham Castle where her father was steward to the Earl of Lincoln. She describes herself as a studious child who, at the age of six or seven, "found much comfort in reading the Scriptures."

She married SIMON BRADSTREET in 1628 and two years later she and her husband and her parents sailed for the Massachusetts Bay Colony on the same ship with Governor JOHN WINTHROP and other noted Puritans. Both her father and her husband held major offices in the colony, and her family was quite prominent. Mrs. Bradstreet lived in several settlements before making her permanent home in North Andover. There she gave birth to eight children: four girls and four boys. All but one survived her. Though colonial living conditions were very harsh and she was plagued with ill health, Mrs. Bradford had a large family and held a prominent place in the community besides finding time for her writing. The manuscripts of poems printed in the first collection of her work date from 1632 to 1643.

Her brother-in-law had this first collection printed in London in 1650, apparently without her permission. *The Tenth Muse Lately Sprung Up in America . . . By a Gentlewoman in those Parts* consists chiefly of rhymed discourses and chronicles using a form the author called "quaternions," or groups of four: the four elements, the four humors, the four ages of man, the four seasons. Bradstreet consciously imitated the 16th-century French Protestant poet, Guillaume de Bartas, and shows in this work the influence of reading Sir Walter Raleigh's *History of the World* and the writings of Bishop Ussher.

In 1664, at the request of her son Simon, Mrs. Bradstreet collected her prose devotional writing under the name *Meditations*. She regarded these writings as a legacy for her children and vouched for their originality, noting, "I would leave you nothing but myne owne." They are simple in style and draw from her daily life and observations of the way the earliest New Englanders lived.

About 1666 she revised all her poems for an authorized edition; these poems along with a dozen poems found among her papers after her death were printed in a second collection (1678). A third edition in 1758 attests to the popularity of Mrs. Bradstreet's work among her fellow colonists. Bradstreet's more lyrical poems show her reading of Sidney, Spencer,

Donne, Quarles, and Herbert. Those poems deal with religious feeling, nature, her family, and everyday life and are delicate and charming. "Contemplations," thought by many to be her best poem, describes the natural beauty to be seen in an autumn walk along the Merrimack River near her home.

Her collections are *The Works of Anne Bradstreet in Prose and Verse*, edited by J. H. Ellis (1867) and *The Complete Works of Anne Bradstreet*, edited by Joseph R. McElrath, Jr. and Allan P. Robb (1981). Biographies and critical works include Samuel Eliot Morison, *Builders of the Bay Colony* (1930) and Ann Stanford, *Anne Bradstreet: The Worldly Puritan* (1974).

Bradstreet, Simon (1603–1697), governor of Massachusetts Bay Colony. Born in Lincolnshire, England, he married ANNE BRADSTREET and emigrated to America in 1630. He held a number of positions in the colony, represented its interests in England, and was twice governor (1679–86 and 1689–92). His wife addressed some of her most affecting poems to him, and Hawthorne pictured him in "Howe's Masquerade," "The Grey Champion," and *The Dolliver Romance* (1876).

Brady, Cyrus Townsend (1861–1920), clergyman, novelist. First a graduate of Annapolis and a navy officer, Brady resigned to become a railroad worker in the West, then a minister in various parts of the Middle West and the East. He wrote many historical novels, stories for boys, biographies, and histories. Among his books are *For Love of Country* (1898); *Stephen Decatur* (1900), *Border Fights and Fighters* (1902), *Indian Fights and Fighters* (1904), and *Britton of the Seventh* (1914).

Brady, Mathew B. (1823?–1896), photographic historian. Brady, born in upstate New York, published *Gallery of Illustrious Americans* (1850) but is especially known for his *National Photographic Collection of [Civil] War Views* (1870) and his portraits of Lincoln.

Bragdon, Claude Fayette (1866–1946), architect, poet, philosopher. Bragdon designed railroad stations and other public buildings, also stage sets. Deeply interested in mysticism, he helped translate and publish P.D. Ouspensky's *Tertium Organum* (1920). His own books include *Architecture and Democracy* (1918), *Old Lamps for New* (1925), *The Eternal Poles* (1930), and *More Lives Than One* (autobiography, 1938).

Brahma (1857), a poem by RALPH WALDO EMERSON. In terms of Hindu philosophy Emerson expresses pantheistic doctrine—that God is everywhere, that in seeking God you have found God in the very act of seeking.

Brahmins. Appropriating the name of the highest Hindu caste, Oliver Wendell Holmes applied it to "The Brahmin Caste of New England" in Chapter I of *Elsie Venner* (1861), where he described at length "the harmless, inoffensive, untitled aristocracy."

Brainard, John Gardiner Calkins (1796–1828), editor, poet. Born in New London, Connecticut, Brainard edited the *Connecticut Mirror*, publishing there poems collected as *Occasional Pieces of Poetry* (1825). His "Niagara" is well known in his time. He wrote a historical romance, *Letters Found in the Ruins of Fort Bradford* (1824), and *Fugitive Tales*

(1830), collected after his early death. Whittier wrote a brief biography to introduce his *Literary Remains* (1832).

Brainerd, David (1718–1747), missionary, diarist. Born in Haddam, Connecticut, Brainerd was expelled from Yale and became a missionary to Indians along the Hudson Valley. He was a follower of JONATHAN EDWARDS and his doctrines and was betrothed to Edwards' daughter. In 1747 he died at Edwards' home of tuberculosis. Portions of his diary were published as *Mirabilia Dei inter Indicos* (1746), other sections in *Divine Grace Displayed* (1746). In 1749 Edwards printed additional portions in *An Account of the life of the late Reverend Mr. David Brainerd* (1749); in 1768 John Wesley published an abridgment. The diary appeared in full in 1822, again in 1884. It was long regarded as a guide for missionaries. Richard Ellsworth Day told Brainerd's story in *Flagellant on Horseback* (1950).

Braithwaite, William Stanley [Beaumont] (1878–1962), poet, editor. Born in Boston, the son of West Indian parents, Braithwaite attended Boston Latin School and became a poet through his love of Keats. He was editor of *Colored American Magazine* (1901–02), then for many years, beginning in 1905, literary editor and columnist for the *Boston Evening Transcript*. Still later, he taught at Atlanta University (1935–45). His conviction that poetry should stress beauty, not political or social content, seemed narrow to many later African-American poets and critics, and his partiality for traditional verse forms left him outside the developing poetics of modernism. Nevertheless, he had a large following through his essays and reviews in popular magazines and through his many anthologies, including his annual *Anthology of Magazine Verse and Year-book of American Poetry* (1913–29). His other anthologies include *The Golden Treasury of Magazine Verse* (1918) and *The Book of Modern British Verse* (1919). His own poetry was collected in *Lyrics of Life and Love* (1904), *The House of Falling Leaves* (1908), and *Selected Poems* (1948). His novels are *The Canadian* (1901) and *Going Over Tindal: A Fragment Wrenched from the Life of Titus Jabson* (1924). *Frost on the Green Tree* (1928) collects stories. *The Bewitched Parsonage* (1950) is a study of the Brontes. *The House Under Arcturus* (1941) is an autobiography. Philip Butcher edited *The William Stanley Braithwaite Reader* (1972).

Branch, Anna Hempstead (1875–1937), poet. Born in Connecticut, Branch published *The Heart of the Road, and Other Poems* (1901), *The Shoes that Danced, and Other Poems* (1905), *Rose of the Wind, Nimrod, and Other Poems* (1910), and *Sonnets from a Lock Box and Other Poems* (1929). *Last Poems* appeared in 1944. Her lyric gift tends to become complicated and is often subdued by moral or social preoccupations.

Branch, Taylor (1947–), novelist, historian, journalist. Branch is most highly regarded for his biographical histories of civil rights leader Martin Luther King, Jr. Born in Atlanta, Georgia, Branch was educated at the University of North Carolina at Chapel Hill (A.B., 1968) and Princeton University (1968–70). He worked as a reporter for *Washington Monthly*, *Harper's* and *Esquire* during the 1970s. He received both the Pulitzer Prize and the National Book Critics Circle Award for *Parting the Waters: America in the King Years 1954–1963* (1988). He is the author of *Second Wind: The Memoirs of an Opinionated Man* (with basketball player Bill Russell, 1979); *The Empire Blues* (1981), a novel; *Labyrinth* (with Eugene M. Popper, 1982) and *Pillar of Fire: America in the King Years 1963–1965* (1997).

SUZANNE PERKINS-HART

Brand, Ethan.   See ETHAN BRAND.

Brand, Max.   Pseudonym of FREDERICK FAUST.

Brandeis, Louis D[embitz] (1856–1941), lawyer, jurist, writer. Born in Kentucky, and educated at Harvard, Brandeis practiced law in Boston, acted as counsel without fee for many popular causes, was named for the Supreme Court by Woodrow Wilson and thereafter was a supporter of Justice Oliver Wendell Holmes in developing legal machinery to ensure preservation of traditional American ideals. He wrote *Other People's Money* (1914), *Business, A Profession* (1914), and *The Curse of Bigness* (1934). Solomon Goldman compiled *The Words of Justice Brandeis* (1953) and Alpheus T. Mason wrote *Brandeis, A Free Man's Life* (1946, 1956). Brandeis University, founded in Waltham, Massachusetts, in 1948, was named in his honor.

Brann, William Cowper (1855–1898), newspaperman. After following a varied career, Brann turned to newspaper work, first on the St. Louis *Globe-Democrat*; later in Texas. His vituperative editorials resulted in his losing a position with the Houston *Post*, and in July 1891 he founded a monthly, *The Iconoclast*, at Austin: he became widely known as "Brann the Iconoclast." The magazine was sold in 1894, together with a printing press, to W. S. Porter (O. Henry), who changed the name to THE ROLLING STONE. For a while Brann wrote articles for newspapers, then bought back his press and started *The Iconoclast* again, this time at Waco. There he engaged in a bitter controversy with a newspaper editor and with Baylor University. When the newspaper editor and his brother were killed in a pistol battle, Brann was blamed; and on April 1, 1898, a Capt. T. E. Davis opened fire on him; Brann retaliated and both men were fatally wounded.

In his lifetime were published his *Speeches and Lectures* (1895?), *Potiphar's Wife* (1897), *Brann's Scrap-Book* (1898); after his death *Brann, the Iconoclast* (2 v. 1898–1903) and his *Complete Works* (1919) appeared.

Brant, Joseph [Native American name: **Thayendanegea**] (1742–1807). Born in what is now Ohio, Brant was among the greatest of MOHAWK chiefs. He fought for the English under SIR WILLIAM JOHNSON in the FRENCH AND INDIAN WAR and Johnson sent him to Eleazar Wheelock's Indian school in Lebanon, Connecticut (1761). He served again under Johnson (1763) in Pontiac's Rebellion. In the Revolution, he and his warriors fought with the British at Oriskany (1777). Disappointed in the disastrous outcome of that battle, he turned to leading his own raids on the settlers on the Mohawk over the next six years. After the war, he led his people into Canada, and settled around the present Brantsford,

Ontario. He visited England in 1775 and 1785, where he is reported to have refused to bend his knee to the king, though he kissed the hand of the queen. A devout Christian, he translated into the Mohawk language the Book of Common Prayer and the Gospel of Mark. Among the many artists who painted his portrait are George Romney, Charles Wilson Peale, George Catlin, and Wilhelm Berezy.

Brass Check, The (1919),   a treatise by UPTON SINCLAIR. Much of this study of American journalism is autobiographical and relates Sinclair's experiences, usually unfavorable at that date, with newspapers.

Brathwaite, [Edward] Kaman (1930–   ),   Barbadian poet, cultural critic. Since 1991 a professor of comparative literature at New York University, Brathwaite's most important poetic work is a trilogy *The Arrivants: A New World Trilogy*(1973) incorporating the earlier *Rights of Passage* (1967), *Masks* (1968), and *Islands* (1969). In it Brathwaite uses African and Caribbean languages, rhythms and themes to survey the involuntary migration of slaves and to trace the historical and psychological results. A second poetic triad is composed of *Mother Poem* (1977), *Sun Poem* (1982), and *X-Self* (1987), exploring the possibility of creating unity out of the diverse strands of island culture. His most important cultural study is *The Development of Creole Society in Jamaica: 1770–1820* (1971). *History of the Voice: The Development of Nation Language in Anglophone Caribbean Poetry*(1984) is literary criticism. Other poetry titles include: *Middle Passages* (1992), *Roots* (1993), and *Black + Blues* (1995). *The Zea Mexican Diary: 7 Sept. 1926–7 Sept. 1986* (?) contains excerpts from his diary after he learned that his wife was dying of cancer.

Brattle, Thomas (1658–1713),   New England merchant. He organized the Brattle Street Church in Cambridge and was treasurer of Harvard from 1693 to 1713. He was a foe of the Mathers, condemned the Salem witchcraft trials, and wrote *A Full and Candid Account of the Delusion Called Witchcraft* (published 1798).

Brautigan, Richard (1935–1984),   fiction writer, humorist. Born in Tacoma, Washington, Brautigan earned fame in the 1960s for his whimsical espousals of alternative lifestyles, freed from the restraints of traditional America. *Trout Fishing in America* (1967) became a cult classic, selling over two million copies; it tells of the narrator's cross-country search for the perfect trout stream (among other revelations, he discovers that the Cleveland Wrecking Yard sells them for $6.50 a foot). His verse is collected in a number of volumes, including *The Pill Versus the Springhill Mine Disaster* (1968). Other fictions include *In Watermelon Sugar* (1964), set in a commune; *A Confederate General from Big Sur* (1965); *The Abortion: An Historical Romance* (1971); *The Hawkline Monster: A Gothic Western* (1974); *Willard and His Bowling Trophies: A Perverse Mystery* (1974); *Sombrero Fallout: A Japanese Novel* (1976); *Dreaming of Babylon: A Private Eye Novel* (1977); *The Tokyo-Montana Express* (1980); and *So the Wind Won't Blow It All Away* (1982). In the latter books, sadness mingled with the humor. Brautigan died a suicide by gunshot. *The Edna Webster Collection of Undiscovered Writings*, juvenilia entrusted to a friend's mother, was published in 1999.

Bravo, The (1831),   a novel by JAMES FENIMORE COOPER. An Italian in the period of the Renaissance attempts to fight the Venetian Senate. He pretends to be a bravo, or hired assassin, and accomplishes some good, but in the end is falsely accused of murder and executed. Cooper seeks to show the superiority of democracy over aristocracy. See THE HEADSMAN; HEIDENMAUER.

Brawley, Benjamin [Griffith] (1882–1939),   clergyman, teacher, historian. Brawley taught English at several universities, particularly Howard. He wrote on literature, especially on the contributions of African-Americans, as in *The Negro in Literature and Art in the U.S.* (1918), *A Social History of the American Negro* (1921), *Paul Laurence Dunbar* (1936), and *The Negro Genius* (1937). He edited *Early Negro American Writers* (1935).

Bread and Cheese Club.   A club founded about 1822 by JAMES FENIMORE COOPER. It was limited to thirty-five members, met at first in Washington Hall, New York City (north of City Hall on Broadway), at times in the City Hotel (at Broadway and Thames Street). Among its other members were Chancellor James Kent, Bryant, Halleck, G. C. Verplanck, and S. F. B. Morse. In 1827 some of the members seceded and formed the Sketch Club, later (1847) the CENTURY ASSOCIATION.

Bread Loaf Writers' School and Conference. Under the sponsorship of Middlebury College, in Vermont, the school for writers was founded in 1920, the annual conference in 1925. The conference has been outstandingly successful. From the beginning ROBERT FROST took a warm interest in the conference and helped to make it both friendly and practical.

Bread-winners, The   (published as a serial in *The Century Magazine*, August 1883—January 1884; as a novel, 1884, both times anonymously), by JOHN HAY, whose authorship was first acknowledged after Hay's death, in an edition issued in 1915. The book defended the economic status quo against the increasing demands of labor, largely by portraying capitalists as virtuous men, labor leaders as villains. Its publication created a sensation and provoked fictional replies by other writers. Best remembered of these is H. F. Keenan's *The Money-Makers* (1885), which depicts the economic struggle as one between greedy plutocrats and humanity-saving liberals.

Breakfast at Tiffany's (1958),   short novel by TRUMAN CAPOTE, celebrated for its free-spirited heroine, Holly Golightly. The novel was later made into a successful movie.

Breakfast Table Series,   by OLIVER WENDELL HOLMES. A series of volumes in which Holmes gave free play to his wit, learning, and experience of life, and sometimes told a story. The framework is a conversation, usually dominated by one person—frequently Holmes himself in easily penetrated disguise. The atmosphere is natural, and the discussion shifts readily from one topic to another. Always the group of personalities includes someone who blurts the rude truth; generally among those present is a pleasant feminine figure; often the ideas expressed are much more. Startling than one would expect from a Brahmin of BRAHMINS. The series began in germ with two papers that Holmes published in *The New England Magazine* for November 1831 and February 1832. Then, in the opening issue of *The Atlantic Monthly*, November 1857, began THE AUTOCRAT OF THE BREAKFAST TABLE, which was published in book form from the following year. Later volumes in the series, in which there was increasing stress on the story element, were *The Professor at the Breakfast Table* (1860), THE POET AT THE BREAKFAST TABLE (1872), and *Over the Teacups* (1891).

Breitmann, Hans. The hero of a series of ballads written in GERMAN-AMERICAN DIALECT and pen name of the author, Charles Godfrey Leland. They began with what became the most famous of them: *Hans Breitmann's Barty*, published May 1857 in *Graham's Magazine*, of which Leland was then editor. He had experimented earlier with German dialect in *Meister Karl's Sketch-Book* (1855). The verses he wrote about Breitmann were very popular, and a collection of them was published as *The Breitmann Ballads* (1871). Later came *Hans Breitmann in Tyrol* (1894) and a posthumous collection, *Hans Breitmann's Ballads* (1914).

Bremer, Frederika (1801–1865), Swedish novelist, poet. Bremer's travels in the U.S. between 1849 and 1861 resulted in *The Homes of the New World* (1853) and a series of letters later published as *America of the Fifties* (1924).

Brentano, Lowell (1895–1950), dramatist, novelist, editor. Brentano, born in New York City, wrote successful plays: *The Spider* (in collaboration with FULTON OURSLER, 1926) and *Great Lady* (1937) and novels, *The Melody Lingers On* (1934) and *Bride of a Thousand Cedars* (with Bruce Lancaster, 1939). He edited magazines, anthologies, and (with Ralph Hancock) a series of books, *Invitation to Travel* (1947 and later), describing countries in this hemisphere. He assisted his wife, Frances Isabella Brentano, in compiling an anthology, *The Questing Spirit* (1947), in the field of religious literature.

Brereton, John. See JOHN BRIERTON.

Brer Rabbit. Character in UNCLE REMUS stories.

Brewster, Elizabeth (1922–   ), poet, novelist. Born in Chipman, New Brunswick, Brewster was educated at the University of New Brunswick, Radcliffe, the University of Toronto, and Indiana University. She has worked as a librarian and taught at a number of Canadian universities. *Selected Poems 1944–1977* (1985) and *Selected Poems 1977–1984* (1985) draw from earlier volumes to display her as a poet of rural, nostalgic, everyday themes. Other poetry collections are *Wheel of Change* (1993) and *Footnote to the Book of Job* (1995). Novels are *The Sisters* (1974), of a girl growing up in conditions much like her own, and *Junction* (1983), also set in New Brunswick. Stories are collected in *It's Easy to Fall on the Ice* (1977), *A House Full of Women* (1983), and *Visitations* (1987). *The Invention of Truth* (1991) is a memoir.

Brewster's Millions (1902), a novel by GEORGE BARR MCCUTCHEON. A farcical account of what Brewster did with an unexpectedly inherited fortune, it was capably dramatized by WINCHELL SMITH and Byron Ongley in 1906; stock companies found it a surefire hit for many years.

Bricks Without Straw (1880), a novel by A. W. TOURGÉE. One of the earliest works to deal with racial problems in the South in the post–Civil War period, this novel has as its protagonist a New England schoolteacher in the South who sympathizes with the African-Americans.

Bride Comes to Yellow Sky, The. See STEPHEN CRANE and OPEN BOAT AND OTHER TALES OF ADVENTURE.

Bridge, Horatio (1806–1893), Bowdoin College classmate and lifelong friend of Hawthorne. He wrote *Journal of an African Cruiser* (1845) and *Personal Recollections of Nathaniel Hawthorne* (1893).

Bridge, The [1], poem by HENRY WADSWORTH LONGFELLOW, collected in *The Belfry of Bruges and Other Poems* (1845). The speaker visits the bridge in happiness at midnight, but remembers other visits made in unhappiness. The ebb and flow of the tidal river suggests earthly transience, but the moon returns unchanged. He concludes that "The moon and its broken reflection / And its shadows shall appear, / As the symbol of love in heaven, / And its wavering image here."

Bridge, The [2] (1930), poem by HART CRANE, an attempt to create a unity out of the disparate elements of American experience. The bridge of the title is first of all the Brooklyn Bridge, but it is also an imagined bridge spanning the country in all its diversity from the East Coast to the West Coast, and, yet again, it is a bridge of time, stretching from the first explorations into the 20th century. It is also other bridges, as suggested below. Beneath the Brooklyn Bridge, the flow of the East River suggests the flux of eternity, so too for the verbal bridge across the continent, with the Mississippi River draining the land north to south, as seen most insistently in one of the most successful sections of the poem, "The River." The ends of these rivers of time are, of course, the oceans of eternity into which they flow, "Meeting the Gulf, hosannas silently below."

Crane intended other connections as well. He felt that he was "really building a bridge between the so-called classic experience and many divergent realities of our seething confused chaos of today." Figures in the poem, including Columbus, Pizarro, Pocahontas, Priscilla, Rip Van Winkle, and Whitman, may all be seen as part of the bridge structure, or as ends that the bridge reaches toward. Columbus, for example, forms a bridge between the old world and the new. Rip Van Winkle suggests the passing of time unseen. The poet's personal life enters the poem also as he tries to build a bridge between the child and the adult poet. There are bridges intended between the pastoral past of America, or the present rural and small-town America, and the America of fast trains, radio waves, and subway tunnels.

Bridge of San Luis Rey, The (1927), a novel by THORNTON WILDER. "On Friday noon, July the twentieth, 1714, the finest bridge in all Peru broke and precipitated five travelers into the gulf below." So begins Wilder's best-known novel, a brilliantly written fable that became a best seller, won the

Pulitzer Prize, and was made into a movie. Brother Juniper, a Franciscan friar and Wilder's mouthpiece, witnesses the accident and wonders whether it really was an accident or a deliberate plan of the Almighty. His investigation of the victims' lives, to prove that their sudden deaths were justified, forms the core of the book. The five characters are the Marquesa de Montemayor (based on Mme. de Sévigné); the little girl Pepita, dominated by the Marquesa; Esteban, rival of his twin brother Manuel for the favors of the actress Camilla Périchole (heroine of the Offenbach operetta); Uncle Pio, a lovable adventurer; and Camilla's young son Jaimé.

Bridger, James (1804–1881), fur trader, scout, frontiersman. Born in Virginia, Bridger was a guide for early Western expeditions. He accompanied the William Ashley expedition up the Missouri to the Yellowstone (1822–23); later, while with Jedediah Smith, Bridger earned fame as the first white man to see the Great Salt Lake (c. 1824). He visited the Grand Canyon (1830), established Fort Bridger (1843), discovered the route through Bridger's Pass (1856), served as a guide for Captain Bonneville, and passed into folk legend. See BERNARD DE VOTO, ACROSS THE WIDE MISSOURI (1947).

Brierton [sometimes Brereton], John (1572?–1619?), clergyman, explorer. He accompanied the expedition along the New England coast led by Bartholomew Gosnold in 1602. In that year he published *A Brief and True Relation of the Discoverie of the North Part of Virginia*.

Brigadoon (1947), a musical fantasy by ALAN JAY LERNER with music by FREDERICK LOEWE. Its plot, centered in a vanished and occasionally reappearing Scotch village, is similar to that of a German classic, *Germelshausen*, by Friedrich Wilhelm Gerstaecker.

Briggs, Charles Frederick (1804–1877), editor, novelist. Briggs in 1839 published a novel, *The Adventures of Harry Franco*, based on his experiences at sea. In 1845 he founded the *Broadway Journal*, to which Poe contributed and of which he became editor and owner. Briggs went on to do editorial work for *Putnam's Magazine*, the New York *Times*, and the Brooklyn *Union*, and he also wrote other autobiographical novels under the name of Harry Franco.

Brill, A[braham] A[rden] (1874–1948), psychiatrist, author. Born in Austria and educated at New York University and Columbia, Brill became internationally known as an authority on psychiatry, especially the doctrines of Sigmund Freud and Carl Jung. He familiarized Americans with Freudian terminology and interpreted Freudian doctrine. Among his writings, aside from direct translations from Freud and Jung, are *Psychoanalysis, Its Theories and Practical Application* (1912), *Freud's Contribution to Psychiatry* (1944), *Lectures on Psychoanalytic Psychiatry* (1946), and *Basic Principles of Psychoanalysis* (1949).

Bring 'Em Back Alive (1930), an account of FRANK BUCK's adventures in capturing wild animals, told in collaboration with EDWARD ANTHONY. *Wild Cargo* (1932) is a sequel by the same authors.

Brinig, Myron (1901–1991), novelist. Born in Minneapolis, Brinig gave sustained treatment to life in Montana.

Among novels he set there are *Singermann* (1929), about a Jewish family; *This Man is My Brother* (1932), its sequel; *Wide Open Town* (1931), about mining at the turn of the century; *Sun Sets in the West* (1935), about mining during the Depression; *The Sisters* (1937), about a druggist's daughters; *The Gambler Takes a Wife* (1943), set in the 1880s; and *Footsteps on the Stair* (1950), about Jewish and Irish families.

Brink, Carol [Ryrie] (1895–1981), editor, writer. Her first book for children, *Anything Can Happen on the River!* (1934), is a story of France. Brink's *Caddie Woodlawn* won the John Newbery Medal for 1935, and she dramatized it in 1945. Later juveniles include *Mademoiselle Misfortune* (1936), *Lad with a Whistle* (1941), *Buffalo Coat* (1944), *Family Grandstand* (1952), *Family Sabbatical* (1956), *Andy Buckram's Tin Men* (1966), and *Winter Cottage* (1968). She also wrote a biography about the singing Hutchinson family, *Harps in the Wind* (1947). Her other works for adults include *The Headland* (1955); and *Snow in the River* (1964).

Brinnin, John Malcolm (1916–1998), poet, editor, teacher. Born in Nova Scotia, Brinnin rebelled against his strict Catholic upbringing and embarked on a program of self-education, simultaneously editing various avant-garde periodicals. Later, he entered the University of Michigan and supported himself by opening a bookshop. His volumes of poetry include *The Garden Is Political* (1942), which deals with the atmosphere of World War II; *The Lincoln Lyrics* (1942), *No Arch, No Triumph* (1945), *The Sorrows of Cold Stone* (1951), and *Skin Diving in the Virgins* (1970).

As director of the Poetry Center at the YMHA in New York, he invited Dylan Thomas to give readings in the United States. This visit provided Brinnin with much of the material for his *Dylan Thomas in America* (1955). Besides teaching and lecturing at various universities, he is author of *The Third Rose; Gertrude Stein and Her World* (1959), *Sextet: T. S. Eliot and Truman Capote and Others* (1981), and *Truman Capote: A Memoir* (1986).

Brinton, [Clarence] Crane (1898–1968), teacher, historian. A teacher at Harvard from 1923, Brinton wrote with sound scholarship and a rare vivacity and gift of phrase. Among his books are *The Political Ideas of the English Romanticists* (1926), *The Jacobins* (1930), *English Political Thought in the 19th Century* (1933), *The Lives of Talleyrand* (1936), *The Anatomy of Revolution* (1938), *Nietzsche* (1941), *Ideas and Men: The Story of Western Thought* (1950), *The Shaping of the Modern Mind* (1953), and *A History of Western Morals* (1959). He also edited the *Portable Age of Reason Reader* (1956) and *Society of Fellows* (1960).

Brinton, Daniel Garrison (1837–1899), anthropologist. A Philadelphia physician who taught after 1886 at the University of Pennsylvania, Brinton published treatises on Native American race and culture, including *The Lenape and Their Legends, With the Complete Text and Symbols of the Walam Olum* (1885), an extended *Library of Aboriginal Literature* (8 v: 1882–90), and *The American Race* (1891).

Brisbane, Albert (1809–1890), a social crusader. Born in Batavia, New York, Brisbane was seized early with a messianic compulsion to eliminate squalor from the world. He discovered his method in the doctrines of Charles Fourier (1772–1837), with whom he studied in Paris, and whose *Traité de l'association domestique et agricole* (1822) advocated a cooperative organization of society into phalansteries, or phalanxes. In 1834 Brisbane began to form Fourierist groups in New York and Philadelphia, and in 1840 published *The Social Destiny of Man*, a mixture of passages from Fourier with his own interpretations and additions. The book made a deep impression, won an eminent convert in HORACE GREELEY, and led about 8,000 Americans to invest their goods and their future in phalanxes from Massachusetts to Green Bay, Wisconsin. Among the phalanxes was the celebrated experiment at BROOK FARM, described in Hawthorne's THE BLITHEDALE ROMANCE (1852), in which Brisbane was the model for one of the least complimentary portraits. In these phalanxes the family was regarded as an outmoded institution and even the very young were trained in masses for productive labor. All the phalanxes failed, and only that at Green Bay Showed a profit—its land rose in value through no effort of the phalanx. See NORTH AMERICAN PHALANX.

In 1876 he published a *General Introduction to Social Sciences*, a recapitulation of the theories of association. His autobiography, *Albert Brisbane: A Mental Biography* (1893), was edited, with an introduction, by his wife Redelia Brisbane.

Bristow, Gwen (1903–1980),   reporter, novelist. Born in South Carolina, Bristow began her career as a reporter on the staff of the New Orleans *Times-Picayune* in 1925. *The Invisible Host*, a mystery written in collaboration with her husband, Bruce Manning, was dramatized and presented in New York in 1930 under the title of *The Ninth Guest. Deep Summer* (1937), *The Handsome Road* (1938), and *This Side of Glory* (1940) constitute her *Plantation Trilogy* (1962). Among her other books are *Tomorrow Is Forever* (1943), *Jubilee Trail* (1950), *Celia Garth* (1959), *Calico Palace* (1970), and *Golden Dreams* (1980).

British Prison Ship, The (1781),   a poem by PHILIP FRENEAU. On his way to the West Indies in 1780, Freneau was captured by the British and confined for six weeks, first on a prison ship, later on a hospital ship. On his release Freneau in this poem described with vivid bitterness the horror of his experiences.

British Spy, Letters of the (1803),   by WILLIAM WIRT. See LETTERS OF THE BRITISH SPY.

Broadhurst, George H[owells] (1866–1952), newspaperman, playwright. Born in England, he came to America and produced Broadway hits in *The Man of the Hour* (1907), which dealt with political corruption, and *Bought and Paid For* (1913), later a popular movie. He made a considerable fortune from his plays, returned to England to live, but died in Santa Barbara, California.

Broadside Press.   See DUDLEY RANDALL.

Broadway.   One of the world's famous streets. It starts at Bowling Green, near the Battery in New York City, and runs northward to 242nd Street. At its southern tip it still derives somewhat of a maritime character from the shipping district nearby. Shortly it becomes the country's chief financial district, with Wall Street as its main tributary. Passing City Hall and Park Row, once the heart of newspaper publication in the city, Broadway becomes a mercantile district. Then it heads into a region of theaters and restaurants, centered at Times Square. Continuing north, it skirts Central Park, runs between rows of hotels and apartment houses, crosses the grounds of Columbia Univeristy, and goes on to the city line.

The term "Great White Way" supposedly comes from the play, *The Great White Way* (1901), by ALBERT BIGELOW PAINE. The bright lights of Broadway with their spectacular advertising signs have always attracted much attention. G. K. Chesterton, seeing them for the first time, remarked, "How beautiful it would be for someone who couldn't read!" One of the best-known American popular songs continues to be George M. Cohan's *"Give My Regards to Broadway."*

Broadway (1926),   a play by Philip Dunning and GEORGE ABBOTT. Cabaret performers and bootleggers are the chief characters in this melodramatic comedy of the prohibition era.

Broadway Jones (1912),   a play by GEORGE M. COHAN. A young spendthrift discovers his responsibilities for the business he has inherited—responsibilities he cannot evade merely by selling it. Cohan also made it into a musical, *Billie* (1929).

Brodkey, Harold (1930–1996),   novelist, short-story writer. Born in Illinois, Brodkey was adopted by paternal relatives after the death of his mother before he was two years old. He studied at Harvard with the poet Archibald MacLeish. His association with *The New Yorker* magazine, where he was a staff writer, began in 1953 with the publication of his short story, "State of Grace," later included in *First Love and Other Sorrows* (1958). *Women and Angels* (1985) and *Stories in an Almost Classical Mode* (1988) are also story collections. Sexual activity was Brodkey's major theme; in fact a short story titled "Innocence" (*American Review*, 1973) was a 31-page description of a single sexual act.

His novel *The Runaway Soul* was finally published in 1991, after having been announced as forthcoming in Farrar, Straus & Giroux catalogues for several years. Told in the first-person by the protagonist, Wiley Silenowicz, it describes his life with his cousins, S. L. and Lila, who adopted him, and Nonie, his older adoptive sister. A second novel, *Profane Friendship*, about a homosexual love affair, appeared in 1994.

In 1993, Brodkey announced in the pages of *The New Yorker* that he was infected with the AIDS virus as a result of his bisexuality. He wrote a diary of his illness and treatment for the same magazine. His death, three years later, was attributed to the disease.

Brodsky, Joseph [Iosif Alexandrovich] (1940–1996), poet, essayist. Born to a Jewish family in Saint Petersburg, formerly Leningrad, Russia, Brodsky was receiving encouragement for his writing from such older poets as Anna Akhmatova by the time he was 18. After a government crackdown on "social parasites," he was convicted and sent to a forced-labor camp in the Arctic. His growing international reputation caused him to be stripped of his Soviet citizenship and exiled. Assisted by W.H. Auden, he came to the United States in 1972, was welcomed as poet-in-residence at the University of Michigan, and soon became an American citizen. After seven years in Ann Arbor, he headed east, where he taught at various colleges: Queens, Smith, Hampshire, and Mount Holyoke. In 1981 he was named a MacArthur Foundation Fellow, a decade later United States Poet Laureate. In the interim, in 1987, he won the Nobel Prize for Literature.

Brodsky's allegiance to his adopted country and its literature was enthusiastic. He said he had always read American poetry and had been "an American long before I arrived on these shores." Though, at first, he continued to write in Russian, his involvement in translation was intense, and soon he began to translate his own work. Finally, in his 1977 "Elegy for Robert Lowell," and many of the poems in his posthumously published *So Forth* (1996), he composed directly in English. As Poet Laureate, he worked hard to make poetry widely available, campaigning to have soft bound books placed in hotel rooms and sold in supermarket checkout lanes. As an American he developed a colloquial voice and described American vistas, ideas, and the disjunctions between his earlier and later life in poems such as "Lullaby of Cape Cod," "A Song [I wish you were here, dear]," and "To My Daughter."

Collected Poems in English appeared in 2000. An earlier gathering in English is *To Urania: Selected Poems 1965–1985* (1988). Other translations include *Poems by Joseph Brodsky* (1972), *Selected Poems* (1973), and *A Part of Speech* (1980). *Less Than One: Selected Essays* (1986) and *Watermark* (1992) are prose; *Marbles* (1989) is a three-act play.

Broker of Bogota, The (1834), a play by R. M. BIRD. It is a melodrama noted for being one of the earliest writings from the United States to be set in a Latin-American country.

Brom Bones. The character in Washington Irving's LEGEND OF SLEEPY HOLLOW who frightens ICHABOD CRANE into flight by pretending to be the "Headless Horseman."

Bromfield, Louis (1896–1956), novelist, playwright, essayist. Bromfield was born in Ohio and educated at Cornell and Columbia. After service in World War I, he worked as a journalist in New York before settling with his wife and daughters in France (1925–38). His early novels—THE GREEN BAY TREE (1924), *Possession* (1925), EARLY AUTUMN (1926), and *A Good Woman* (1927)—formed a tetralogy on the theme of escaping from family and tradition. These were well received, but later novels did not fare as well with critics until *The Rains Came* (1937), set in India, restored some of his reputation. *Night in Bombay* (1940) also has an Indian setting. In 1939 he settled near his birthplace in Ohio on a thousand-acre farm, to which he gave the name Malabar, from India. He farmed, as his ancestors had, and continued to write. Among his many other novels, some of the most noteworthy are *Twenty-Four Hours* (1930); *The Farm* (1933), following an Ohio family through one hundred years; *Mrs. Parkington* (1943); and *The Wild Country* (1948), showing midwestern change from frontier to civilization. His stories and short novels are collected in

Awake and Rehearse (1929), *Here Today and Gone Tomorrow* (1934), and *The World We Live In* (1944). His plays are *The House of Women* (1927, from *The Green Bay Tree*); *DeLuxe* (with John Gearnon, 1934); and *Times Have Changed* (1935). Of his nonfiction books, a number center on farm life at Malabar, including *Pleasant Valley* (1945), *A Few Brass Tacks* (1946), *Malabar Farm* (1948), *Out of the Earth* (1950), and *From My Experience* (1955). *Animals and Other People* (1955) collects pieces on nature and folklore.

Brooke, Frances [Moore] (1724–1789), English-born Canadian novelist. The wife of a clergyman, Brooke followed her husband to Canada, where he was chaplain to the garrison at Quebec. Her four-volume *History of Emily Montague* (1769) is an epistolary novel set mostly in Canada in the 1760s. It describes the Québécois, the Indians, and the Canadian scenery and is often considered the first Canadian novel. She stayed in Canada only about five years before returning to England in 1768 with her family.

Brook Farm. The official name of this experiment in transcendentalism, communism, and "association" was the Brook Farm Institute of Agriculture and Education. It was established on a 200-acre farm at West Roxbury, Massachusetts, on April 1, 1841; it collapsed in 1846. GEORGE RIPLEY was a leader in the founding of the community, and numerous persons of note were from time to time associated with it—Theodore Parker, William Henry Channing, NATHANIEL HAWTHORNE, MARGARET FULLER, Charles A. Dana, and ALBERT BRISBANE, who brought to the community the influence of Fourierism. When this doctrine was accepted, the name of the farm was changed to Brook Farm Phalanx, and the end came when the uninsured Central Phalanstery burned down. Channing has referred to it as a "great college of social students." Emerson apparently felt that to live in Brook Farm would merely mean exchanging one prison for another, and he held shrewdly that "in the arrangements at Brook Farm, as out of them, it is the person, not the communist, that avails." It was he who called Brook Farm "the Age of Reason in a patty-pan." Hawthorne made use of his experiences on the farm in his BLITHEDALE ROMANCE (1852).

Brooklyn Eagle, The. Founded in 1841 by Edward C. Murphy, this daily newspaper had a distinguished career. Among noted writers who served on its staff are Walt Whitman, Edward W. Bok, H. V. Kaltenborn. The *Eagle* suspended publication on March 16, 1955.

Brooks, Cleanth (1906–1994) educator, critic. Born in Kentucky, Brooks was educated at Vanderbilt, Tulane, and Oxford, where he was a Rhodes Scholar. He taught English at Louisiana State University from 1932 to 1947, later at Yale. He was associated with NEW CRITICISM. He coedited the journal SOUTHERN REVIEW with ROBERT PENN WARREN (1935–42) and produced *Understanding Poetry* (1938); *Understanding Fiction* (1943) in collaboration with Warren; and *Understanding Drama* (with Robert Heilman, 1945). These textbooks, along with his own *Modern Poetry and the Tradition* (1939) and *The Well-Wrought Urn* (1947), had a major impact on methods of teaching literature, emphasizing close reading and structural analysis, and urging treatment of the poem as poem apart from its place in the author's life or literary history.

Brooks, Elbridge S[treeter] (1846–1902), newspaperman, editor, author of juveniles. Among his many books for young people are *Historic Boys* (1875), *Historic Girls* (1877), *The Century Book for Young Americans* (1894), *A Boy of the First Empire* (1895), and *Chivalric Days* (1898).

Brooks, Gwendolyn (1917–2000), poet, novelist. Born in Topeka, Brooks has lived for many years in Chicago. She achieved recognition with her first poetry collection, *A Street in Bronzeville* (1945), and *Annie Allen* (1949) was awarded the Pulitzer Prize. The subject of this poetry is the lives of African-American residents of northern urban ghettos, particularly women, and Brooks has been praised for her depiction of that experience in forms ranging from terza rima to blues meter.

In *Maud Martha* (1950), a novel, she presents segments from the life of a woman who stands up for her dignity against a racist store clerk. Her *Selected Poems* appeared in 1963. The title poem of *In the Mecca* (1968) is a long narrative about a child lost in a tenement. Poetry from this book and later collections shows an increased political expression, which Brooks has traced to a gathering of African-American writers at Fisk University in 1967. As an expression of political concern, she left Harper and Row and chose to have her poetry published by Dudley Randall's Broadside Press, which published *Riot* (1969), *Family Pictures* (1970), *Aloneness* (1971), *Aurora* (1972), two anthologies, and *Report from Part One* (1972), an autobiography. She served as Poetry Consultant to the Library of Congress in 1985–86, the first African-American woman to fill that post. *The World of Gwendolyn Brooks* (1971) and *Blacks* (1987, 1991) are collections of poetry and prose.

Brooks, Maria [Gowen] (1794?–1845), poet, novelist. Born in Massachusetts, Brooks was extravagantly praised by the English Lake poets. She lived for a year near Grasmere, in the Lake District, and virtually became a member of the group. Charles Lamb said of her *Zophiël* (1833) that she couldn't possibly have composed it—"as if there ever had been a woman capable of anything so great!" Even so, her passionate and melodramatic poetry was received without favor at home. Brooks married her elderly brother-in-law after her sister died; she later became estranged from him and fell in love with a young Canadian officer. In 1823 her husband died, but her match with the officer did not come off. She twice attempted suicide and wrote of the affair in her autobiographical novel *Idomen, or, The Vale of Yumuri* (1843). While living on an inherited Cuban estate, Brooks and her two stepsons died of fever.

Brooks, Noah (1830–1903), newspaperman, government official, author. Born in Maine, Brooks worked as a journalist in California, Washington, and New York. He knew Lincoln and wrote some careful historical works, for example, *Abraham Lincoln and the Downfall of American Slavery* (1984) and *Short Studies in American Party Politics* (1896). But his

books for boys have survived longer than his other writings. Among them are *The Boy Emigrants* (1876), *The Fairport Nine* (1880), and *The Boy Settlers* (1891).

Brooks, Phillips (1835–1893), clergyman, orator, author. Born in Boston, he became a preacher and eventually a bishop in the Protestant Episcopal Church. Brooks was a chief voice of the new thought and the new criticism that were remolding Protestantism. He wrote *Yale Lectures on Preaching* (1877), *Essays and Addresses* (1892), and the hymn "O Little Town of Bethlehem" and appears as a character in Arlo Bates's novel *The Puritans* (1898).

Brooks, Van Wyck (1886–1963), critic, biographer. Born in New Jersey and educated at Harvard, Brooks for a time worked as a journalist and traveled in Europe, where his first book was published, *The Wine of the Puritans* (London, 1908; New York, 1909). In pointing out shortcomings of the Puritan heritage, *The Wine of the Puritans* approached contemporary American culture from both historical and psychological points of view. In *America's Coming of Age* (1915) Brooks continues his analysis of the American literary past, finding that the Puritan duality of isolated idealism and practical materialism resulted in a literature that had become artificially separated from life and identified with the "thin moral earnestness" of the New England highbrow. Seeking a valid tradition for American literature in which life and art were not divorced, he found in Walt Whitman a synthesis of literature and the vital aspects of life.

Brooks then turned to critical biography liberally supplied with psychological interpretations to illustrate the crippling effect of the Puritan dualism on the American writer; *The Ordeal of Mark Twain* (1920, rev. ed. 1933) found Twain's Calvinistic background and his provincial Missouri home responsible for his failure to fulfill his genius. In the same vein Brooks analyzed another so-called American failure, Henry James, who fled to Europe rather than face the conflicting demands of life and art in America. After *The Pilgrimage of Henry James* (1925) came *The Life of Emerson* (1932).

Brooks next turned to the creative task of hewing a valid tradition out of America's literary history. In the five volumes comprising the "Finders and Makers" series, Brooks used his earlier technique of critical biography to establish the relationship between the writer and his society, between the work and the cultural milieu out of which it emerged. THE FLOWERING OF NEW ENGLAND, *1815–1865* (1936), the first in order of publication but second in the series, was a best seller for more than a year, and was awarded the Pulitzer Prize. The other volumes (in the order of the series) are *The World of Washington Irving* (1944), *The Times of Melville and Whitman* (1947), NEW ENGLAND: INDIAN SUMMER, *1865–1915* (1940), and *The Confident Years: 1885–1915* (1952). In 1956 Brooks and Otto L. Bettman made an abridgment of the series that was published as *Our Literary Heritage*, a pictorial history of the writer in America from 1800 to 1915.

Brooks also wrote *Letters and Leadership* (1918), *The Literary Life in America* (1921), *Opinions of Oliver Allston* (1941), *The*

Writer in America (1953), the autobiographical *Scenes and Portraits* (1954), *Helen Keller: Sketch for a Portrait* (1955), *John Sloan: A Painter's Life* (1955), *Days of the Phoenix: The 1920's I Remember* (1957), *The Dream of Arcadia: American Writers and Artists in Italy, 1760–1915* (1958), *From a Writer's Notebook* (1958), *Howells: His Life and World* (1959), *From the Shadow of the Mountain* (1961), and *Fenollosa and His Circle* (1962).

Broom (November 1921–January 1924), one of the best-known LITTLE MAGAZINES. Originally edited by Harold A. Loeb and ALFRED KREYMBORG, it published work by European and American writers.

Brossard, Chandler (1922–1993), novelist, magazine editor. Brossard, born in Idaho and self-educated after age 11, worked as a journalist in Washington and New York. His uneven novels include *Who Walk in Darkness* (1952), an evocation of squalid Bohemian (or BEAT GENERATION) life in New York City; and *The Bold Saboteurs* (1953), a memorable, if disjointed, picture of childhood delinquency. He also wrote plays and nonfiction.

Brossard, Nicole (1943–), novelist, poet. Born in Montreal and educated at *l'Université de Montréal*, Brossard is noted for avant-garde poetry and fiction, combined in her later work with feminist and lesbian content. Her novels include *Un livre* (1970); *Sold Out: étreintel illustration* (1973); and *French Kiss: étreinte/exploration* (1974); her verse is collected in *Le Centre blanc: poèmes 1965–1975* (1978); *Mécanique jongleuse suivi de masculin grammaticale* (1974), which won a Governor General's Award; *Amantes* (1980); and *Le sens apparent* (1980). *Picture Theory* (1982) combines fiction and theory. *Installations (avec et sans pronoms)* (1989) and *Langues obscures* (1992) are concerned with the nature of subjectivity in language. *Le désert mauve* (1987) and *Baroque d'aube* (1995) are novels.

Brother Jonathan. Early in Yankee folk tradition, Jonathan became a typical name for any Yankee, especially the country bumpkin who is smarter than he seems to be. Richard M. Dorson, in *Jonathan Draws the Long Bow* (1946), on New England popular tales and legends, relates a number of stories in which Jonathan appears as a character. The name was early given to a personification of the United States, and was explained by a sort of folk etymology as being due to the fact that General Washington greatly relied on the advice of his aide, Jonathan Trumbull, of whom he sometimes said, "We must consult Brother Jonathan." A weekly called *Brother Jonathan* was founded by Park Benjamin, 1839–43. One of its editors, JOHN NEAL, wrote a novel called *Brother Jonathan* (1825). Oliver Wendell Holmes used "Brother Jonathan" to designate the Union or the North in his poem *Brother Jonathan's Lament for Sister Caroline*, written after South Carolina's secession in 1861.

Brother to Dragons (1953), narrative poem by ROBERT PENN WARREN. It tells of the axe-murder of a slave by nephews of Thomas Jefferson.

Brougham, John (1810–1880), actor, playwright. Born in Ireland, Brougham came to the United States as a suc-

cessful comedian, but was best known as the author of several burlesques, including two with Indian characters, *Metamora, Or, The Last of the Pollywoags* (1847) and *Po-ca-hon-tas!* (1855). He adapted novels by Dickens and Harriet Beecher Stowe for the stage, presented a *Dramatic Review for 1868* that anticipated the annual revues of a later day. In the 1860s, he and DION BOUCICAULT were the most popular dramatists in America.

Broun, Heywood [Campbell] (1888–1939), journalist. Born in New York City, Broun earned fame as a lively and witty columnist and a crusader against injustice in New York papers, including the *Morning Telegraph, Tribune, World,* and *Telegram,* and in *The Nation* and *The New Republic.* His books include *The A.E.F.* (1918), on his experiences as a correspondent in wartime France; *The Boy Grew Older* (1922), a novel about a journalist; *Pieces of Hate* (1922); *Sitting on the World* (1924); *It Seems to Me* (1935); and *A Collected Edition* (1941), gathering from newspaper columns, which appeared under the title "It Seems to Me."

Brown, Alice (1857–1948), novelist, short-story writer, dramatist, poet. Born in New Hampshire, Brown followed in SARAH ORNE JEWETT's literary footsteps. She wrote *Meadow-Grass* (1895), *Tiverton Tales* (1899), *Country Neighbors* (1910), *Vanishing Points* (1913), and a play, *Children of Earth* (1915).

Brown, Charles Brockden (1771–1810), novelist, editor. Brown was born in Philadelphia. His father, a prosperous conveyancer, was an enthusiastic reader of Godwin and Wollstonecraft. After attending the Friends' Latin School under the tutelage of Robert Proud (1781–86), Brown took up his father's enthusiasms, sketching utopian architectural plans and plotting epics on the adventures of Columbus, Cortez, and Pizarro. Finding himself bored with the study and practice of law, which he had undertaken in the office of Alexander Willcocks (1787–92), Brown persuaded his reluctant family to accept his decision to support himself by his pen. (Brown is widely considered the first American to attempt to do so.) His first productions, a series of periodical essays under the title "The Rhapsodist," appeared in the *Columbian Magazine* in 1789.

During the 1790s, Brown moved back and forth between Philadelphia and New York, where he joined the Friendly Club, a literary circle gathered by Brown's friend Elihu Hubbard Smith, the publisher of the *Medical Repository.* Smith had been a student of Timothy Dwight, and through Smith Brown met his later biographer, William Dunlap; Noah Webster and the HARTFORD WITS; and Charles Adams, the son of John Adams. Brown's acquaintances in New York also included Albert Gallatin, later President Jefferson's Secretary of the Treasury, and Jedidiah Morse, whose paranoid conspiracy theories would influence Brown's *Ormond* (1799) and the unfinished *Carwin the Biloquist* (1822). During the few years in which he wrote most of his best fiction, his political convictions shifted from the romantic utopianism evident in his early sketches and in his dialogue favoring education and property rights for women, *Alcuin*—the first two parts of which appeared in the *Philadelphia Weekly Magazine* in 1798—to the stubborn Federalism of his later writings. In 1804 he married Elizabeth Linn, with whom he had four children. After giving up his attempt to support himself by his pen alone, he worked in his family's importing business until its failure in 1806, and was an independent trader afterward until his death.

Brown's output was prodigious. Like Poe after him, but with even less success, he devoted much effort to establishing and editing literary magazines, such as *The Monthly Magazine and American Review* (1799–1800), *The Literary Magazine and American Register* (1803–1807), and *The American Register* (1807–1810). Frequently, lack of submissions required that he write entire issues himself. Brown's first novel, *Sky-Walk, or, The Man Unknown to Himself*, was lost when the printer died of yellow fever, but the promise of its prospectus to depict "soaring passions and intellectual energy" was fulfilled in his later novels, all six of which appeared between 1798 and 1801.

Brown's major novels stand in two different fictional worlds. WIELAND (1798), considered his most important work, is a Gothic novel that more often looks forward to Hawthorne and Melville than back to Lewis and Walpole. Its protagonist, who thinks himself called to murder by the voice of God, embodies for Brown the cruxes in which the mind discovers itself when it faces ultimate questions, such as the nature of divinity and of faith. As a work of ideas it anticipates Kierkegaard's *Fear and Trembling* and stands in the direct line of descent of such more recent works as Flannery O'Connor's *The Violent Bear it Away*. In EDGAR HUNTLY (1799), the nightmare wanderings of a well-meaning but obsessive and destructive protagonist in a bizarre landscape of forests, caves, and cliffs (through which he trails a sleepwalking acquaintance whom he mistakenly believes has murdered his best friend) chillingly portray the darker aspects of a human mind at war with itself and unaware of its own motivations. ORMOND, although in many ways a conventional novel of attempted seduction, is also a Bildungsroman of female development, and an interesting treatment of the conspiracy theme, which Brown seems to have introduced to American literature. In ARTHUR MERVYN (2 v. 1799–1800), Brown combines the misadventures of a misunderstood and professedly innocent protagonist who resembles Godwin's Caleb Williams with a depiction of his self-interested maneuvers and speculations, which seem to owe something to the *Autobiography of Benjamin Franklin*. So dense is the web of misapprehensions and mixed appearances in *Arthur Mervin* that there is still no consensus about whether its hero is an abused naif or a devious scoundrel. Two other novels, *Clara Howard* and *Jane Talbut* (both 1801), are of less interest. Although all his works are deeply flawed by a headlong prose style, and sometimes by confused plots, Brown was unequaled among American writers before Hawthorne at depicting the manic intensity of a mind possessed by metaphysical questions, and Hawthorne and Poe (as well as Shelley) mention him with respect.

Brown also wrote a considerable amount of nonfiction. Enraged by the Spanish retrocession of Louisiana to France in 1802, Brown wrote his most influential political tract, the pamphlet "An Address to the Government of the United States on the Cession of Louisiana to the French" (1803). Ostensibly authored by a French Counselor of State, the pamphlet so plausibly laid out the course by which Napoleon could control the Mississippi and suborn the whole South and West into his interest that it contributed to the pressures on President Jefferson that led him to enter into the Louisiana Purchase in 1803. Brown was the author of several other influential political tracts, all of a Federalist persuasion, such as "The British Treaty of Commerce and Navigation" and "An Address on the Utility and Justice of Restrictions upon Foreign Commerce," in which he defended British conduct in the *Chesapeake* affair and denounced Jefferson's embargo. Brown also translated C. F. Volney's massive *A View of the Soil and Climate of the United States of America* and was engaged in a work on world geography at his death.

See studies by David Lee Clark (1952), Donald A. Ringe (1966), Alan Axelrad (1983), Bill Christopherson (1993), and Steven Watts (1999).

JOHN BURT

Brown, Claude (1937–   ),   autobiographer, novelist. Born in New York City and educated at Howard University, Stanford, and Rutgers, Brown earned immediate fame with *Manchild in the Promised Land* (1965), an autobiography. It tells of his youth in Harlem—gangs, reformatories, shootings, drugs, pimps, prostitutes, numbers runners; it is perhaps the first book to present in vivid and convincing detail the plight of young African-Americans in the inner city. In a novel, *The Children of Ham* (1975), he continues the study in a tale of Harlem teenagers trying to survive in an environment dominated by heroin.

Brown, Goold (1791–1857),   grammarian. Brown, born in Providence, Rhode Island, was a prescriptive grammarian. He held that usage is not a safe guide and that to speak and write correctly it is necessary to rely on rules committed to memory. Language, he said, has no change or growth, except toward impurity; the grammarian must be a bulwark against these alterations. In his gigantic *Grammar of English Grammars* (1851) he provided rules, exercises, and quotations from authors who had violated these rules and whose English was therefore to be "corrected."

Brown, Harry [**Peter McNab, Jr.**]   (1917–1986), poet, novelist, humorist, playwright, screenwriter. Born in Maine, Brown worked before World War II for *Time* and *The New Yorker*; during the war he was on the staff of YANK and wrote the ARTIE GREENGROIN sketches, collected in a book in 1945. Artie, a Brooklynite talking Brooklynese in England, makes shrewd and unconventional comments on English and American life. Brown had previously written a fine novel, *A Walk in the Sun* (1944), and went on to a play, *A Sound of Hunting* (1946). He also wrote successful screenplays and the novels *Wake of the Red Witch* (1949); *Thunder on the Mountain* (1954); *Stars in Their Courses* (1960), a story of the West in the 1870s; *The Wild Hunt* (1973); and *The Gathering* (1977). His poetry collections include *The End of a Decade* (1941), *The Violent* (1943), and *The Beast in His Hunger* (1949).

Brown, John (1800–1859), crusader against slavery. Brown was born in Connecticut and grew up in Ohio. So fanatical was he in his attitude toward slavery that when he moved with his five sons to Osawatomie, Kansas, and discovered that some of his neighbors took the southern point of view, he murdered five of them—taking the view that he was an instrument of God. He also operated an underground railroad from his home. He had long planned an invasion of the South to free slaves from their owners. On October 16, 1859, he entered Harper's Ferry, Virginia, with twenty-one men, and by daybreak was in complete control of the federal arsenal and the town. Soldiers under the command of Col. Robert E. Lee crushed the venture ruthlessly, and Brown and the other survivors were arrested. Brown was tried and conducted himself with great dignity and eloquence, but he was condemned to die and was hanged on December 2, 1859.

The invasion, its tragic outcome, and the speeches and letters of Brown resulted in a reaction in his favor. His activities dramatized the coming conflict and probably made it more difficult to settle peaceably. Brown has become a favorite theme in song, story, and biography. His name was immortalized in the Union marching song, JOHN BROWN'S BODY LIES A-MOULDERING IN THE GRAVE. Thoreau, Bronson Alcott, and others mourned his passing and proclaimed his greatness. Studies include those by W. E. B. Du Bois (1909); Oswald Garrison Villard (1910); Robert Penn Warren (*John Brown: The Making of a Martyr*, 1929); James C. Malin (1942); and R. O. Boyer (1973). Laurence Green wrote an account of Brown in *The Raid* (1953) from the point of view of the villagers of Harper's Ferry. Leonard Ehrlich made him the hero of his novel *God's Angry Man* (1932). Many poets have written about Brown, and the greatest of all is the epic poem JOHN BROWN'S BODY (1928), by Stephen Vincent Benét.

Brown, John Mason (1900–1969), drama critic, journalist, essayist, lecturer. Brown, a graduate of Harvard, began as a reporter for the Louisville *Courier-Journal*, and taught history of drama at the University of Montana. During World War II he served in the navy and participated in the invasions of Sicily and Normandy. His accounts of what was happening, broadcast to the crews of the invading fleet, were collected in *To All Hands* (1943) and *Many a Watchful Night* (1944). Among his collected essays in criticism are *The Modern Theater in Revolt* (1929), *Two on the Aisle* (1938), *Broadway in Review* (1940), *Seeing Things* (1946), *Seeing More Things* (1948), and *As They Appear* (1952). He also wrote *Morning Faces* (1949), a charming book about his two sons; *Through These Men* (1956), a brilliant gallery of biographical sketches; and *Daniel Boone* (1952), a biography for young people.

Brown, Margaret Wise (1910–1952), writer of children's books. Brown employed several pseudonyms, including Golden MacDonald, Timothy Hay, and Juniper Sage in writing *Little Lost Lamb* (1945); *The Little Island* (1946); *Horses* (1944); and *The Man in the Manhole and the Fix-It Men* (1946), with Edith Thacher Hurd. Books under her own name include *The Streamlined Pig, Bumble-Bugs and Elephants*, and *The Little Fireman* (all 1938). Her two most successful books,

The Runaway Bunny (1942) and the classic *Goodnight Moon,* were illustrated by Clement Hurd. Forty-eight years after her death, manuscripts found in the barn of her Maine house yielded two titles: *Mouse of My Heart* and *A Child Is Born* (2000).

Brown, Rita Mae (1944–), novelist, poet. Born in Pennsylvania, Brown was educated in Florida and at the New York School of Visual Arts. She was awarded a Ph.D. by the Institute for Policy Studies in 1976. Her first novel, *Rubyfruit Jungle* (1973), earned her a following for its celebration of the joys of lesbian sexuality. Her other novels are *In Her Day* (1976), *Six of One* (1978), *Southern Discomfort* (1982), and *Sudden Death* (1983). Her verse is collected in *The Hand that Cradles the Rock* (1971) and *Songs to a Handsome Woman* (1973). *Plain Brown Wrapper* (1976) collects essays. With *Wish You Were Here* (1990) Brown began writing mystery novels, allegedly with the assistance of her cat Sneaky Pie. These include *Rest in Pieces* (1992) and *Outfoxed* (2000).

Brown, Sterling A[llen] (1901–1989), poet, teacher. Born in Washington, D.C., the son of a Howard University professor, Brown was educated at Williams College and Harvard. He taught English at Virginia Seminary, Lincoln University, and Fisk University, and then for forty years (1929–69) at Howard University, where he counted among his students the writers AMIRI BARAKA and TONI MORRISON and the actor OSSIE DAVIS. His honors include a Guggenheim Fellowship and a dozen honorary doctorates. As a pioneer in African-American studies, he wrote a landmark essay, "Negro Characters as Seen by White Authors" (1931), and the books *The Negro in American Fiction* (1937) and *Negro Poetry and Drama* (1937, rev. ed. 1969). With Arthur P. Davis and Ulysses Lee he edited *The Negro Caravan* (1941, rev. ed. 1970), the first large-scale anthology of African-American writing. Brown's first collection of poetry, *Southern Road* (1932), earned praise for replacing traditional dialect with the living speech of contemporary African-Americans. After his publisher rejected a second volume, he fell silent as a poet until DUDLEY RANDALL published *The Last Ride of Wild Bill* (1975) in his Broadside Press. With *The Collected Poems* (1980), selected by MICHAEL HARPER, his reputation rose again.

Brown, William Hill (1765–1793), poet, dramatist, novelist. In Boston in 1789 appeared a novel THE POWER OF SYMPATHY, a thinly disguised account of a scandal of the time, the supposed seduction of a young woman by her brother-in-law and her subsequent suicide. The actual incident occurred in the family of the poet SARAH WENTWORTH MORTON, whose husband was the alleged seducer. The Morton family bought up all copies they could lay hands on and destroyed them, but a few survived. In 1895 the novel was reprinted serially in *The Bostonian Magazine*, and the more plausible theory was aired that William Brown, a neighbor of the Mortons, was the author. He also wrote dramas, including a tragedy about Major André, *West Point Preserved* (1797); essays, verses, and a short novel, *Ira and Isabella* (1807), a variation on *The Power of Sympathy*.

Brown, William Wells (1816–1884), abolitionist, autobiographer, novelist, poet. Born into slavery in Kentucky and raised in St. Louis, where he worked for the Abolitionist printer ELIJAH LOVEJOY, Wells moved to Ohio and assisted the underground railway there. His *Narrative of William Wells Brown, a Fugitive Slave* (1847), published two years after FREDERICK DOUGLASS's *Narrative*, thrust him into prominence in the Abolitionist movement. Brown successfully dramatized his *Narrative as The Escape; or, A Leap to Freedom* (1856); a successor, *Experience; or How to Give a Northern Man a Backbone* (1856), apparently not produced, was given as a reading. A novel, *Clotel; or, The President's Daughter* (1853), perhaps the first by an African-American, told of Thomas Jefferson's daughter by one of his slaves. First published in England, it was brought out in the United States without reference to the president as *Clotel: A Tale of the Southern States* (1864). Brown's other works include *The Anti-Slavery Harp* (1848), poems; *Three Years In Europe* (1852); and *The Black Man: His Antecedents, His Genius, and His Achievements* (1863; expanded as *The Rising Sun*, 1874).

Browne, Charles Farrar. See ARTEMUS WARD.

Browne, J[ohn] Ross (1821–1875), travel writer, diplomat. Born in Ireland, Browne lived in Kentucky before shipping on a whaler from New Bedford and gathering material for *Etchings of a Whaling Cruise* (1826), one of the many sources Melville drew on for *Moby Dick*. His later books include *Yusef, or, A Journey of the Frangi: A Crusade in the East* (1853); *Crusoe's Island, with Sketches of Adventures in California and Washoe* (1864), a description of a trip around Cape Horn; and in some ways an anticipation of Twain's western sketches; *Adventures in Apache Country* (1869); *An American Family in Germany* (1866). Browne held government posts in the West, and was for a time U.S. Minister to China.

Brownell, Henry Howard (1820–1872), lawyer, poet. A Connecticut lawyer and newspaper lyricist, Brownell became secretary to Admiral David Farragut during the Civil War. He published *Lyrics of a Day* (1864) and *War Lyrics and Other Poems* (1866).

Brownell, W[illiam] C[rary] (1851–1928), editor, critic. For many years Brownell was an editor for Charles Scribner's Sons. He issued volumes of criticism, among them *French Traits* (1889), *Victorian Prose Masters* (1901), *American Prose Masters* (1909), *Criticism* (1914), *Standards* (1917), and *Democratic Distinction in America* (1927). In 1933 Gertrude Hall Brownell prepared an anthology of Brownell's work.

Brownlow, William Gannaway (1805–1877), preacher, editor, politician. Born in Virginia, Brownlow became known as the Fighting Parson in East Tennessee, where he was an itinerant preacher and editor of pro-Union newspapers. Jailed by Confederates (1861–62), he later served as Governor of Tennessee (1867–69) and U.S. Senator (1869–73). He wrote *Sketches of the Rise, Progress, and Decline of Secession* (1862).

Brownson, Orestes Augustus (1803–1876), editor, writer on philosophy and theology, novelist. Brownson was born in Vermont and received no formal education, but became a New Englander so thoroughly individualistic that he could not agree long with anybody—even with himself. He was brought up as a strict Puritan, in 1822 formally joined the Presbyterian church, became a Universalist in 1824 and was later ordained a Universalist minister, was rejected because of his too-liberal views by the Universalists, came under WILLIAM ELLERY CHANNING's [1] influence, became a Unitarian minister, in 1836 founded his own church, and in 1844 was converted to Roman Catholicism but was branded as a heretic and severely condemned when he tried to found an American form of Catholicism. He was at first a Socialist, in league with Robert Owen; helped organize a Workingmen's Party; sent his son to BROOK FARM; established an organ of the Democratic party; and then renounced democracy and rule of the people and became an advocate of a form of republicanism that showed his loss of faith in the intelligence and integrity of the common people. He cherished the conviction that there was a Divine Order, with leaders who would pursue the general welfare *of* the people but would have little or nothing done *by* the people. To spread his views Brownson established the BOSTON QUARTERLY REVIEW (January 1838), which in 1842 was merged with the *United States Democratic Review* and in 1844 became *Brownson's Quarterly Review*, continued till January 1865, was revived in 1872, and died in 1875. His writings include *New Views of Christianity, Society, and the Church* (1836), an attack on organized Christianity; *Charles Elwood, or, The Infidel Converted* (1840), an autobiographical novel of conversion to Unitarianism; *The Mediatorial Life of Jesus* (1842), on Roman Catholicism; *The Spirit-Rapper* (1854), a fictive account of the Satanic element in spiritualism; *The Convert, or Leaves from My Experience* (1857), an autobiographical report of conversion to Catholicism; *The American Republic* (1865); and *Conversation on Liberalism and the Church* (1870). A *Complete Works* was published in twenty volumes (1882–87).

Bruce, Charles (1906–1971), newspaperman, poet, fiction writer. Bruce was born in Nova Scotia and worked most of his life for the Canadian Press news agency in Toronto. His writing is often traditional, narrative (though there are lyrics, as well), and evocative of Nova Scotia. His collections of verse include *Tomorrow's Tide* (1932); *Personal Note* (1941), a wartime narrative; *Grey Ship Moving* (1945), with the title poem telling of a troopship out of Halifax; *The Flowing Summer* (1947), the story of a boy's return home to the seashore. *The Mulgrave Road* (1951), a prize-winning collection of verse, gave its title to a later sampling, *The Mulgrave Road: Selected Poems* (1985). *The Channel Shore* (1954), a novel, and *The Township of Time* (1959), linked stories, tell of Nova Scotia coastal life over several generations.

Bruising Bill (1845), a novel by JOSEPH HOLT INGRAHAM. This is one of two tales that appeared in a single paperbound book, the other being *Alice May*. *Bruising Bill* is one of the earliest works of fiction about Harvard. The incidents—a row between Town and Gown—may have been based on some actual incidents in 1840.

Brush, Katharine [Ingham] (1902–1952), novelist, short-story writer, columnist. Katherine Brush's first fiction was contributed to *College Humor* and later she became a favorite in many magazines, particularly *Cosmopolitan*, *Good Housekeeping*, and *The American Magazine*. She was a frank, sometimes acidulous annalist of the jazz age. Among her books were *Glitter* (1926), *Young Man of Manhattan* (1930),

The Red-Headed Woman (1931), and *Don't Ever Leave Me* (1935). One collection of her short stories, *Night Club* (1929), contains some of her best work, and there is another entitled *Other Women* (1932). She collected contributions from her syndicated column, "Out of My Mind," in a 1943 book by that title. In her autobiography, *This Is on Me* (1940), she discusses her problems as an author candidly. She also wrote many movie scripts.

Brutus, or, The Fall of Tarquin (London, 1818; New York, 1819), a tragedy in verse by JOHN HOWARD PAYNE. When this play, based on the old Roman story that told how Brutus condemned his own son to death for treason, was produced in London, it brought back Edmund Kean to popular favor and made Payne a celebrated figure. JUNIUS BRUTUS BOOTH toured the West with the play in the 1820s and made hatred of tyrants popular west of the Mississippi.

Bryan, William Jennings (1860–1925), political orator, editor. "Crusading is my business," the "Great Commoner" once said; "early in life God revealed to me my power over men." Bryan was born in Illinois. In 1890 he went to Congress from a Nebraska district and in 1892 was reelected. In 1896 he electrified the Democratic presidential convention with the speech that ended, "You shall not press down upon the brow of labor this crown of thorns, you shall not crucify mankind upon a cross of gold." He was nominated for president on a platform demanding that gold's value as against silver be reduced to a ratio of sixteen to one. After a hectic campaign that thoroughly terrified the gold-standard East, he was defeated. He was nominated again in 1900 and 1908, and again defeated. When WOODROW WILSON became president in 1913, he made Bryan his secretary of state. In 1915 Bryan resigned on the peace-and-war issue. In 1925 he sided with legislators intent on preventing the teaching of evolution in American schools. The issue was joined when a Tennessee instructor in biology, John T. Scopes (1900–1970), was brought to trial at Dayton, Tennessee, in July 1925. CLARENCE DARROW defended him, and Bryan led the opposition. The press of the United States, Canada, and England assembled in unprecedented numbers to report a remarkable trial that came to be called the "monkey trial." Bryan, who took the stand and faced Darrow's merciless cross-examination, was more like a defendant than a prosecutor. Scopes was convicted and paid a fine, but by his courage made clear, as he had intended, the stupidity of the whole proceeding. Bryan died five days after the trial closed. (See SCOPES TRIAL.) In 1955 a play, *Inherit the Wind*, by Jerome Lawrence and Robert E. Lee, presented a vivid portrayal of the trial.

Bryan played a considerable role in the great CHAUTAUQUA movement. Best-loved of all his talks was one on "The Prince of Peace," repeated innumerable times in every state of the union until 1924. His *Speeches* (2 v.) were collected in 1909. His *Memoirs* appeared in 1925. He edited a weekly called *The Commoner* at Lincoln, Nebraska, from 1901 to 1923, and it had a wide circulation for a while. Vachel Lindsay paid tribute to Bryan in his poem *Bryan, Bryan, Bryan, Bryan: The Campaign of 1896, as Viewed at the Time by a 16-Year-Old* (1919), but it is likely that

Bryan will be remembered longer because of Mencken's vituperative *In Memoriam: W. J. B.* (*Prejudices*, 5th Series, 1926).

Bryant, Edwin (1805–1869), travel writer. Bryant was a Kentuckian who became an official of the San Francisco district of California. He described his 1846 trip from Missouri westward in *What I Saw of California* (1848), reprinted sometimes as *Rocky Mountain Adventures.*

Bryant, William Cullen (1794–1878), poet, editor, critic. Bryant was born in Cummington, Massachusetts, and learned his love of nature early by accompanying his father, a doctor, on rambles through the surrounding woods. His earliest desire was to be a poet, and he was writing poems by the time he was nine. When he was fourteen, his father sent his first collection, *The Embargo* (1808), to a Boston publisher. This, a Federalist satire against Jefferson's restrictions on trade, was followed in the next year by a second volume, *The Embargo and Other Poems* (1809). He then spent a year at Williams College before going on to study law. He was admitted to the bar in 1814. From 1816 to 1825 he practiced law in Great Barrington, Massachusetts, married, and wrote some of his finest poems. The first draft of "Thanatopsis" was written in 1811. Published in *The North American Review* (September 1817), it drew immediate attention. Meanwhile he had also written "The Yellow Violet," "Inscription for the Entrance to a Wood," and "To a Waterfowl." With the publication of his first collected *Poems* (1821), he began to turn more definitely toward a life of letters. In 1825 he moved to New York City and in the following year became an editor of the New York *Evening Post*. For half a century, from 1829 until his death, he was part owner and editor-in-chief.

Many of Bryant's early poems are reflective of the English poets he admired as a boy. These include neoclassic poets such as Alexander Pope; the "graveyard school" of Robert Blair, James Thomson, Edward Young, and Thomas Gray; and the romantics Sir Walter Scott, Robert Burns, Samuel Taylor Coleridge, and William Wordsworth. When he read the *Lyrical Ballads* at sixteen, he later remembered, "a thousand springs seemed to gush up at once into my heart, and the face of nature, of a sudden, to change into a strange freshness."

After his move to New York, he remained a poet of nature and the people, but his imagination deepened and his voice became more clearly his own. As a member of the KNICKERBOCKER SCHOOL, he helped make New York a center for the rising tide of American literature. As a leading citizen of the city and editor of a major periodical, he championed liberal causes in articles and editorials. In politics he turned away from his youthful Federalism and became a liberal Democrat, supporting free trade, freedom of speech and religion, movements toward collective bargaining, and, in a crucial issue that divided the Democratic party, free soil and freedom for slaves. In 1855–56, he became an active organizer of the Republican party, the party of Lincoln. His interest in humanitarian causes continued, and at eighty-four, just a few days before he died, he delivered the address at the unveiling of the Statue of Liberty. Over the years, his religious stance changed as well. "Thanatopsis" was in part a rejection of the Calvinism of his New England forefathers. Later, he passed through a stage of Deism to become a prominent leader of Unitarianism. In a very late poem, THE FLOOD OF YEARS (1876), he expressed something of his final attitude as he considered the flood of time that engulfs all things past and then looked forward to a future existence "in whose reign the eternal Change / That waits on growth and action shall proceed / With everlasting Concord hand in hand."

In Bryant's later poems, he continued the concern for nature and religion that informs his youthful work and added more insistent humanitarian concerns. As one of the long-lived New England sages whose pictures once graced school-rooms throughout the United States, he expressed a practical idealism that later came to appear old-fashioned. Among his best poems, in addition to those already mentioned, there are THE AGES (1821), "Oh Fairest of the Rural Maids" (1832), A FOREST HYMN (1832), "The Two Graves" (1832), "To the Fringed Gentian" (1832), "Song of Marion's Men" (1832), and "The Prairies" (1834). A notch below his best are his graceful occasional poems such as the sonnet, "To Cole, the Painter, Departing for Europe," or his stanzas in long meter on "The Death of Lincoln." His humanitarianism, if not his strongest poetry, appears in such poems as "The African Chief" and "An Indian at the Burial Place of His Fathers." Throughout his long life he remained popular. A dozen separate volumes and editions followed the 1821 *Poems* before the final collection, *The Political Works of William Cullen Bryant*, Household Edition (1876). In addition to his own poems, he produced fine translations of the *Iliad* (1870) and the *Odyssey* (1871–72). Among his collections of prose are *Letters of a Traveller, or, Notes of Things Seen in Europe and America* (1850; second series, 1859), and *Orations and Addresses* (1873). He also edited *A Library of Poetry and Song* (1871), one of the best American anthologies of the nineteenth century. See biographies by Parke Godwin (1883), Albert F. McLean (1964), Charles H. Brown (1971).

Bryce, James. See THE AMERICAN COMMONWEALTH.

Bryson, Bill [William] (1951?–), essayist, travel writer. Born in Iowa, Bryson attended Drake University and moved to Britain in 1977, where he lived for twenty years, working on various newspapers and writing books on travel and language such as *The Lost Continent: Travels in Small-Town America* (1989), a humorous account of driving in thirty-eight states, and *The Mother Tongue: English and How It Got That Way* (1990). In the mid-1990s he moved back to the U.S., settling in New Hampshire. *A Walk in the Woods: Rediscovering America on the Appalachian Trail* (1998) was a best seller. Other titles include: *Neither Here nor There: Travels in Europe* (1992), *Made in America: An Informal History of the English Language in the United States* (1994), *Notes from a Small Island: An Affectionate Portrait of Britain* (1995), and *In a Sunburned Country* (2000), on Australia.

Buck, Frank (1884–1950), explorer, motion-picture producer, writer. From his boyhood in Texas, Buck was interested in animals. His first expedition to study them was made to South America; later he traveled all over the world collect-

ing animals for zoos and circuses. He was fortunate in finding a good collaborator, Edward Anthony, who wrote with him BRING 'EM BACK ALIVE (1930) and *Wild Cargo* (1932). Other books are *Fang and Claw* (with Carol Weld, 1935) and *Animals Are Like That* (1939). His autobiography, *All in a Lifetime*, appeared in 1941. Among his motion-picture productions were versions of several of his books.

Buck, Pearl [Sydenstricker] (1892–1973), novelist, translator. Pearl Buck was born in West Virginia. Her missionary parents took her to China when she was five months old, and she spent many years in that country, although she returned home to attend Randolph-Macon College and Cornell. Many of her books have a Chinese background. The best of those not directly or entirely laid in China, *Fighting Angel* (1936) and *The Exile* (1936), brought together as *The Spirit and the Flesh*, are portraits of her mother and father. She taught in Nanking from 1921 to 1931. In later years she became active in the East and West Association (president after 1941), in world peace movements, and in advocating for the mixed race children she called Amerasians. She was awarded a Pulitzer Prize in 1932, the William Dean Howells medal in 1935, and the Nobel Prize in literature in 1938.

Among Mrs. Buck's books are *East Wind—West Wind* (1930); THE GOOD EARTH (1931); *Sons* (1932); *The First Wife and Other Stories* (1933); *The Mother* (1934); *The Patriot* (1939); DRAGON SEED (1942); *What America Means to Me* (1943); PAVILION OF WOMEN (1946); *Far and Near* (stories, 1948); PEONY (1948); *Kinfolk* (1949); *Come, My Beloved* (1953); *My Several Worlds: A Personal Record* (1954); *Letter from Peking* (1957); *Command the Morning* (1959); *A Bridge for Passing* (autobiographical, 1962); *Hearts Come Home* (stories, 1962); *Stories of China* (1964); *The Good Deed and Other Stories of Asia* (1969); *Mandala* (1970); *East and West* (stories, 1975); and *The Lovers and Other Stories* (1977). She translated *All Men Are Brothers* (2 v. 1933) from the Chinese of Shui Hu Chan. *Imperial Woman* (1956) is a fictional biography of China's last empress. Her works include many plays and juvenile books.

Bucke, Richard Maurice (1837–1902), physician, author. Born in England, Bucke came to Canada in 1838 to study and practice medicine, and later specialized in care of the insane. His main connection with literature was through his friendship with WALT WHITMAN out of which grew two studies, *Walt Whitman, a Contemporary Study* (1883) and *Walt Whitman, Man and Poet* (1897), as well as two works based on the poet's pantheistic philosophy, *Man's Moral Nature* (1879) and *Cosmic Consciousness* (1901). He was one of Whitman's literary executors and edited many of his letters and papers.

Buckler, Ernest (1908–1984), novelist, memoirist. Born in Nova Scotia, Buckler was educated at Dalhousie University and the University of Toronto. He worked for a while in insurance in Toronto before returning to Nova Scotia's Annapolis Valley for a life of farming and writing. His first novel, *The Mountain and the Valley* (1952), remains his most celebrated. Set in the Annapolis Valley, it is a lyrical, complex, and richly textured history of the growth of a sensitive young man, David Canaan, toward adulthood as a writer. In a second novel, *The Cruelest Month* (1963), talented people face personal crises in a Nova Scotia guest house. *Ox Bells and Fireflies* (1968) is a memoir of Buckler's boyhood in Nova Scotia, a lyrical recording of pastoral ways now rapidly disappearing. His other books are *Nova Scotia: Window on the Sea* (1973), with photographs by Hans Weber; *The Rebellion of Young David and Other Stories* (1975), collecting earlier work; and *Whirligig: Selected Prose and Verse* (1977).

Buckley, William F[rank], Jr. (1925–   ), editor, author. Born in New York and educated at Yale, he became a leading conservative spokesman as a television commentator, editor of *The National Review* (1955–90), and author of books such as *Up from Liberalism* (1959) and *Right Reason* (1985). He has also written mystery and spy novels, including *Saving the Queen* (1976), and books on sailing such as *Atlantic High: A Celebration* (1983) and *Windfall: The End of the Affair* (1992). *Happy Days Were Here Again: Reflections of a Libertarian Journalist* (1993) collects articles from 1985 to 1993.

Buckminster, Joseph Stevens (1784–1812), clergyman. Born in New Hampshire, Buckminster was a leader of the "liberal Christians," who in the first decade of the 19th century were to move toward Unitarianism. In 1805 he became minister of the fashionable Brattle Street Church and there delivered cultured, highly intelligent addresses, collected after his death in *Sermons* (1839). He organized the ANTHOLOGY CLUB and helped produce the *Monthly Anthology*, one of the earliest of American literary magazines. In 1806 he traveled for a year in Europe and brought back a collection of 3,000 volumes, which became the nucleus of the Athenaeum Library.

Budd, Lanny. Hero of a long series of novels by UPTON SINCLAIR, beginning with *World's End* (1940). The illegitimate son of a Connecticut munitions millionaire, Budd becomes a latter-day questing spirit who, in the course of the novels, becomes intimate with many of the world's most prominent figures and witnesses many of modern history's most important events. Through Budd, Sinclair voices his convictions concerning modern political and social developments, beginning with World War I.

Budd, Thomas (?–1698), historian. Budd came to New Jersey in 1678 and settled there long enough to have a town—Buddtown—named after him. On his return to England he published *Good Order Established in Pennsylvania and New Jersey* (1685).

Buechner, [Karl] Frederick (1926–   ), novelist, clergyman. Born in New York City, Buechner served in the army in World War II before graduating from Princeton. After teaching at the Lawrenceville School in New Jersey and working in an employment office in Harlem, he took a degree at Union Theological Seminary and became a Presbyterian minister and head of the Religion Department of Phillips Academy in Exeter, New Hampshire (1958–1967). His early novels, Jamesian psychological studies, were *A Long Day's Dying* (1949), a complex analysis of the relationships between a mother, her son, and the son's college instructor caught in a

tangle of lies and sexuality; *The Season's Difference* (1951), on children, their tutor, and adults; and *The Return of Ansel Gibbs* (1948), about a man appointed to a cabinet post. In the novels since his ordination, religion has been at the forefront. These include *The Final Beast* (1965), about a minister whose actions are misinterpreted; *The Entrance to Porlock* (1970), about a family's Oz-like search for a mystic happiness; *Lion Country* (1971), in part a parody of contemporary Christianity; and *Open Heart* (1972), *Love Feast* (1974), and *Treasure Hunt* (1977), all on religious themes. The four novels from the 70s were printed in one volume called *The Book of Bebb* (1979). Later fiction includes *The Son of Laughter* (1993), *On the Road with The Archangel* (1997) and *The Storm* (1998). His nonfiction includes *The Magnificent Defeat* (1966), sermons; *The Hungering Dark* (1969); *The Alphabet of Grace* (1970); *Wishful Thinking* (1973); *The Faces of Jesus* (1974); and *Telling the Truth* (1977). *The Sacred Journey* (1982) is a memoir as is *The Longing for Home: Recollection and Reflections* (1996).

Building of the Ship, The (1849), a poem by HENRY WADSWORTH LONGFELLOW, collected in *The Seaside and the Fireside* (1849). In the opinion of his northern contemporaries, Longfellow attained his poetic peak in the concluding lines of this poem, beginning "Thou, too, sail on, O Ship of State!" Longfellow describes the building of a ship, interweaving the details with those of an approaching marriage between the builder's daughter and the owner's son, with a constant symbolism in which the ship is life itself and becomes, at the close, a metaphor of the Union. It was Longfellow's most powerful contribution to Union sentiment in the face of the crises leading to the Civil War.

Bukowski, Charles (1920–1994), poet, fiction writer. Bukowski was born in Germany, the son of a U.S. soldier and a German woman, and grew up in Los Angeles. He writes prolifically of the world of society's dropouts, of sex, drugs, and street violence. Poetry came first—the volumes include *Flower, Fist and Bestial Wail* (1960), *It Catches My Heart in Its Hands* (1963), *Burning in Water, Drowning in Flame* (1974), *Love Is a Dog From Hell* (1977), *Dangling in Tournefortia* (1980); and *War All the Time; Poems 1981–84* (1984). *Notes of a Dirty Old Man* (1969) is a fictionalized memoir. His novels include *Post Office* (1971), *Factotum* (1975), *Women* (1978), and *Ham on Rye* (1982). Among his short-story collections are *Life and Death in the Charity Ward* (1973), *South of No North* (1973), and *The Day It Snowed in L.A.* (1987). *Septuagenarian Stew* (1990) collects stories and poems. *Confessions of a Man Insane Enough to Live with Beasts* (1965) and *Shakespeare Never Did This* (1979) are autobiographical. *What Matters Most Is How Well You Walk Through the Fire* (1999) is among several posthumously published collections.

Bulfinch, Thomas (1796–1867), clerk, teacher, writer. A son of the architect CHARLES BULFINCH (1763–1844), Thomas spent his life in a humble business post and devoted his leisure to writing. His *Age of Fable* (1855) is still useful as an introduction to Greek, Roman, Scandinavian, and Celtic mythology. Less popular is *The Age of Chivalry* (1858). These expurgated versions of ancient myths have awakened in many young readers a love of the great tales and have served as a guide to mythological references in literature.

Bullins, Ed (1935–   ),   playwright, fiction writer. Bullins was born in Philadelphia, served in the navy (1952–55), and was educated at William Penn Business Institute, Los Angeles City College, and San Francisco State College. By the mid-sixties, he was involved with African-American drama in San Francisco and was serving also as a cultural director for the local Black Panthers. When he moved to New York, his one-act plays began to appear regularly at the American Place Theatre and other Off-Broadway theaters as he established himself as an extraordinarily prolific playwright. *Five Plays* (1969) collected some of his best early work: *Clara's Old Man* (1965), which first established his reputation; *In Wine Time* (1968); *A Son, Come Home* (1968), frequently anthologized; *The Electronic Nigger* (1968); and *Goin' a Buffalo: A Tragifantasy* (1968). *Four Dynamite Plays* (1971) collected angry political plays: *It Bees Dat Way* (1970), *The Pig Pen* (1970), *Death List* (1970), and *Night of the Beast* (a screenplay, 1971). Another collection, with a number of titles, is *The Theme Is Blackness* (1972). *New/Lost Plays by Ed Bullins: An Anthology* appeared in 1993. *The Hungered One* (1971) is a collection of short fiction. *The Reluctant Rapist* (1973) is a novel. Bullins served as editor of *Black Theatre* (1968–73) and has edited and contributed to other books, including *The New Lafayette Theatre Presents* (1974).

Bulosan, Carlos (1913–1956),   migrant worker. Bulosan was born in the Philippines and self-educated. His *American Is in the Heart* (1946) is based on his experiences as a migrant worker in fields and canneries on the west coast of America in the 1930s.

Bumppo, Natty.   A character in James Fenimore Cooper's LEATHER-STOCKING TALES (1823–1841). He is called Bumppo or Deerslayer in THE DEERSLAYER, Hawkeye in THE LAST OF THE MOHICANS, Pathfinder in THE PATHFINDER, Natty Bumppo or Leatherstocking in THE PIONEERS, and the trapper in THE PRAIRIE. Cooper found suggestions for Bumppo in a leatherstockinged hunter named Shipman whom he knew when he was a boy, and Daniel Boone contributed some elements. The sequence of publication of the five novels was not the same as the chronology of Bumppo's career, and Cooper's treatment of him varies. He sometimes sees Bumppo realistically, sometimes romantically; sometimes Bumppo speaks an illiterate vernacular, sometimes with impressive poetic fervor. At Cooperstown, New York, stands a shaft of Italian marble topped by a figure of Bumppo, with his hound Hector at his feet.

Bunce, Oliver Bell (1828–1890),   publisher, playwright, editor. Born in New York City, Bunce began life as a playwright, went on to establish a publishing firm, and later joined Harper's and finally Appleton as an editor. Among his plays are MARCO BOZZARIS (1850), *Fate* (1856), and *Love in '76* (1857). He helped William Cullen Bryant edit a successful series of travel books: *Picturesque America* (1872–74), *Picturesque Europe* (1875–79), and *Picturesque Palestine*

(1881–84). His *Opinions and Disputations of Bachelor Bluff* (1881) was widely read.

Bundren.   Family name of central characters in Faulkner's AS I LAY DYING.

Bunker Hill.   [more properly, Bunker's Hill] The Battle of Bunker Hill was really fought for the most part at nearby Breed's Hill, where American soldiers on the night of June 16, 1775, erected fortifications. The battle between them and the British, whom the Americans had been holding within Boston, began on the following day. As the British advanced, General Putnam gave the command "Don't fire until you can see the whites of their eyes." The British charged again and again, finally driving the Americans toward Bunker Hill, but with heavier British losses. (General Greene said, "I wish we could sell them another hill at the same price.") General Joseph Warren was killed in the battle, and John Pierpont commemorated his heroism in *Warren's Address to the American Soldiers*. In 1825 the cornerstone of a monument at Bunker Hill was laid by Lafayette, and Daniel Webster delivered an oration on the occasion. In 1843 the monument was completed, and again Webster delivered an oration. Bunker Hill plays a part in James Fenimore Cooper's LIONEL LINCOLN (1825), and in H. H. Brackenridge's verse drama, THE BATTLE OF BUNKERS HILL (1776).

Bunner, H[enry] C[uyler] (1855–1896),   poet, short-story writer, novelist, editor. Born in Oswego, New York, Bunner turned early to a literary career and for the greater part of his short life did not leave it. He became editor of PUCK within a year of its foundation in 1877, remained with it till his death, and wrote mainly for its columns. Although Bunner wrote novels—*The Midge* (1886), about a bachelor and his orphan ward, is the best—he was above all a writer of short short stories, tailored to fit the pages of a magazine determined not to be boring. As such he practically founded a new genre in the United States, the anecdotal tale. The most celebrated of his books is *Short Sixes: Stories to be Read While the Candle Burns* (1891), which contains such classics as "The Love Letters of Smith," "The Nine Cent-Girls," and "Zenobia's Infidelity." Later came *Made in France: French Tales with a United States Twists* (1893), ten stories transmuted rather than translated into American idiom and folkways—including one story by Bunner himself, hidden among the rest and undetected by most contemporary critics. He also published *More Short Sixes* (1894) and *Love in Old Cloathes* (1896) and wrote *vers de société* and poetic parodies.

The best of his poems appeared in *Airs from Arcady and Elsewhere* (1884), later in a collected edition of his poems (1896).

Buntline, Ned.   Pen name of E. Z. C. JUDSON.

Bunyan, Paul.   The mighty lumberjack of the American forests recalls Hercules, Thor, and Samson in his tremendous strength and preternatural exploits, but he especially resembles Baron Münchausen. Unlike the mythological figures of Greece and Rome, Paul is a comic figure who seems to have been created largely by individual writers, rather than by the folk imagination. Around him have gathered a host of other fabulous characters: TONY BEAVER, MORGAN KEMP, FEBOLD FEBOLDSON, JOHN HENRY, and others. The stories told about him and his friends are tall tales, narratives in which the storyteller tries to surpass other storytellers.

He first appeared in print, so far as can be discovered, in an advertising pamphlet, *Paul Bunyan and His Big Blue Ox*, published in 1914 by the Red River Lumber Company, originally located in Minnesota. The booklet became popular immediately and was issued in larger and larger editions. Both the text and the amusing illustrations were done by W. B. Laughead, who stated: "The student of folklore will easily distinguish the material derived from original sources from that written for the purposes of this book. It should be stated that the names of the supporting characters, including the animals, are inventions by the writer of this version. The oral chroniclers did not, in his hearing, which goes back to 1900, call any of the characters by name except Paul Bunyan himself." In 1914 Douglas Malloch wrote a poem about Bunyan, "The Round River Drive," which appeared in *The American Lumberman* (April 25, 1914). Carl Sandburg included a patterned narrative, "Who Made Paul Bunyan?" in THE PEOPLE, YES (1936). Many storytellers have retold the Bunyan stories.

Burdette, Robert J[ones] (1844–1914),   newspaperman, columnist, clergyman, lecturer. One of the earliest professional columnists, Burdette also became a professional humorist who enlarged his income greatly by lecturing. His most popular piece, "The Rise and Fall of the Moustache," was delivered, it is said, more than 5,000 times and appeared in book form in 1877. His column was called "Hawkeyetems of Roaming Robert" and appeared in the Burlington (Iowa) *Daily Hawk Eye*. His books include *Hawkeyes* (1879) and *Chimes from a Jester's Bells* (1897).

Burgess, [Frank] Gelett (1866–1951),   humorist. Born in Boston, Burgess became part of the 1890s attempt to make San Francisco a literary center, editing the little magazine *The Lark* (1895–97) there. In the first issue, he published his quatrain, endlessly repeated: "I've never seen a purple cow,/ I never hope to see one,/ But I can tell you anyhow,/ I'd rather see than be one." Later he went to New York and continued his career with many books of light verse, drawings, and stories. His books include *Goops and How to Be Them* (1900); *Are You a Bromide?* (1907); *The Heart Line* (1907, a novel of San Francisco); *The Maxims of Methuselah* (1907); *The Maxims of Noah* (1913); *Burgess Unabridged* (1914); and *Look Eleven Years Younger* (1937).

Burgess, Thornton W[aldo] ["W. B. Thornton"] (1874–1965),   editor, author. Born in Massachusetts, Burgess earned fame as a writer of books and newspaper stories for children, most of which were animal tales, with an emphasis on nature lore. His first book, *Mother West Wind's Children* (1910), began a series that reached eight volumes by 1918. In 1912 he began his syndicated newspaper feature "Little Stories for Bedtime," collected as *The Adventures of Reddy Fox* (1913), first of twenty in the *Bedtime Story Series* (1913–1919). The newspaper column continued in syndication as "Burgess Bedtime Stories" for many years, eventually

offering over 10,000 stories. Among his other books and series are the *Boy Scouts* series (1912–1915), *Green Meadow* series (1918–1920), *Burgess Bird Book for Children* (1919), *Tales from the Story-Teller's House* (1937), and *The Old Briar Patch* (1947).

Burgoyne, John (1722–1792),   general, playwright. Born in England, Burgoyne was sent to America in 1775 with reinforcements for General Gage in Boston, witnessed the battle of BUNKER HILL, and returned home in disgust at the British failure. He was sent back twice to Canada, the second time to lead the ill-fated Saratoga Campaign, which resulted in his surrender at Saratoga (October 17, 1777). In Boston he wrote and saw performed *The Blockade* (1775), an unpublished play satirizing the colonials. The rebels answered with an anonymous farce, *The Blockheads* (1776), at one time attributed to Mercy Otis Warren. Other plays by Burgoyne, written in England, are *The Maid of the Oaks* (1774) and *The Heiress* (1786), both comedies. Burgoyne figures prominently in Bernard Shaw's *The Devil's Disciple* (1900) and in Kenneth Roberts' *Rabble in Arms* (1933).

Burke, John Daly (1775?–1808),   editor, playwright. A political refugee from Ireland, Burke reached the United States in 1796. His best-known production was *Bunker Hill, or The Death of General Warren* (performed in 1797). He also wrote a play called *Female Patriotism, or The Death of Joan d'Arc* (performed in 1798). He founded a paper called *The Polar Star and Boston Daily Advertiser* (October 6, 1796), which expired after six months, and another paper, *The Time Piece*, which also failed.

Burke, Kenneth [Duva] (1897–1993),   critic, philosopher. Born in Pittsburgh, Burke was educated at Ohio State and Columbia. In his early years he was involved with little magazines such as BROOM and Secession. At times he was a music critic for *The Dial* (1927–29) and *The Nation* (1934–36). His fame has come, however, as a difficult and influential literary critic, interested in the philosophy of language and creativity. His books include *Counter-Statement* (1931); *Permanence and Change: An Anatomy of Purpose* (1935); *Attitudes Toward History* (2 v. 1937); *The Philosophy of Literary Form: Studies in Symbolic Action* (1941); *A Grammar of Motives* (1945): *A Rhetoric of Motives* (1950); *The Rhetoric of Religion* (1961); *Language as Symbolic Action* (1966); and *Dramatism and Development* (1972). *Towards a Better Life* (1932, revised 1966) is an experimental novel. His short fiction is collected in *The White Oxen* (1924) and *The Complete White Oxen* (1968), and his poems in *Book of Moments* (1955) and *Collected Poems* (1968). *The Selected Correspondence of Kenneth Burke and* MALCOLM COWLEY appeared in 1988.

Burlin, Natalie Curtis (1875–1921),   a collector of Native American and African-American folk songs and music, among the first to bring this material to popular attention. Among her books are *The Indians' Book* (1907) and *Hampton Series of Negro Folk Songs* (4 v. 1918–19).

Burlingame, [William] Roger (1889–1967),   editor, writer. Born in New York City, Burlingame worked for Charles Scribner's Sons, 1914–1926, then turned to writing verse, stories, and magazine articles. His novel *You Too* (1924) satirized advertising, and among his other novels are *High Thursday* (1928) and *Three Bags Full* (1936). Interested in the history of technology in the United States, Burlingame wrote *March of the Iron Men* (1938); *Engines of Democracy* (1940); *Whittling Boy* (a biography of Eli Whitney, 1941); *Of Making Many Books* (1946), a history of the first hundred years of Charles Scribner's; *Inventors Behind the Inventor* (1947); *Machines that Built America* (1953); *Henry Ford* (1955); *The American Conscience* (1957), a history of moral attitudes through three centuries, 1600 to 1900; and *Scientists Behind the Inventors* (1960). Burlingame, a veteran of World War I, was a correspondent in World War II.

Burman, Ben Lucien (1896–1984),   war correspondent, novelist. Born in Kentucky, Burman was educated at Harvard. *Miracle on the Congo* (1942) and *Rooster Crows for Day* (1945) describe his wartime experiences in Africa. The latter won for him the Thomas Jefferson Memorial Prize in 1945. These years of wartime activity interrupted Burman's series of novels on the Mississippi region, which began with *Mississippi* (1929); *Steamboat Round the Bend* (1933, filmed in 1935 with Will Rogers); *Blow for a Landing* (1938); and *Big River to Cross* (1940). After the war came *Everywhere I Roam* (1949); *The Four Lives of Mundy Tolliver* (1953); a series of animal fables: *High Water at Catfish Bend* (1952); *Seven Stars for Catfish Bend* (1956); *The Owl Hoots Twice at Catfish Bend* (1961); *The Strange Invasion of Catfish Bend* (1980); *The Street of the Laughing Camel* (1959), of a *Texan in Africa*; *It's a Big Continent* (1961); and *Look Down that Winding River* (1973).

Burnett, Frances [Eliza] Hodgson (1849–1924), novelist, writer of children's stories, playwright. Born in England, Frances Hodgson came with her parents to Tennessee in 1865. A writer from age seventeen on, she published her books under her first married name, and lived variously in Europe, England, Washington, D.C., and Long Island. Of her approximately fifty books, she is chiefly remembered for two: LITTLE LORD FAUNTLEROY (1886), an enormously popular story of an American-born boy who inherits an English estate, and *The Secret Garden* (1911), a children's classic telling how a spoiled orphan, Mary, and her sickly cousin, Colin, find health and happiness in restoring a walled and forgotten garden. A third perennial favorite among her children's books is *A Little Princess* (1905). Little Lord Fauntleroy's curls and his velvet suit, lace collar, cuffs, and sash created a fashion long imposed on reluctant children by their mothers. Her dramatization of *Little Lord Fauntleroy* (1888) became important to English copyright history when she won a lawsuit against an English dramatist who was attempting to produce an unauthorized version. Mrs. Burnett's first literary success had been a novel for adults, *That Lass o' Lowrie's* (1877), set in Lancashire coal-mining country. *Haworth's* (1879) was another Lancashire novel. Among her other novels are *A Fair Barbarian* (1881); *Through One Administration* (1883), a realistic portrayal of Washington lobbying; *A Woman's Will* (1887); *Sara Crewe* (1887); *Editha's Burgler* (1888); *A Lady of Quality* (1896); *The Making of a Marchioness* (1901); *The Shuttle*

(1908); and *The White People* (1917), dealing with the supernatural. Alone and with collaborators, she wrote and saw produced a dozen plays (1878–1912), many adapted from her novels. *The One I Knew Best of All: A Memory of the Mind of a Child* (1893) is an autobiography.

Burnett, Whit[ney Ewing] (1899–1973),   newspaperman, editor, short-story writer. With his wife MARTHA FOLEY, he founded and edited the magazine STORY. He also edited anthologies of short stories and wrote *The Maker of Signs* (1934), stories; and *The Literary Life and the Hell with It* (1939).

Burnett, W[illiam] R[iley] (1899–1982),   novelist, short-story writer. Born in Ohio, Burnett became a leading writer of HARD-BOILED FICTION with the publication of *Little Caesar* (1929), a best-selling novel of racketeering. As a film (1931) starring Edward G. Robinson, it established a pattern for Hollywood gangster movies. His later novels, often similarly tough-minded, include *Iron Man* (1930), *The Silver Eagle* (1931), *The Giant Swing* (1932), *Dark Hazard* (1933), *Goodbye to the Past* (1934), *King Cole* (1936), *High Sierra* (1940); *Nobody Lives Forever* (1943), *Tomorrow's Another Day* (1945), *The Asphalt Jungle* (1956), *Captain Lightfoot* (1954), *Pale Moon* (1956), and *Underdog* (1957). His Civil War novels are *The Goodhues of Sinking Creek* (1934) and *The Dark Command* (1938). His novels of the West are *Abode Walls* (1953), about an Apache uprising, and *Mi Amigo* (1953), on BILLY THE KID.

Burns, John Horne (1916–1953),   novelist. Born in Massachusetts and educated at Phillips Academy, Andover, and at Harvard, Burns served in the army in World War II. His *The Gallery* (1947), a vivid fiction drawing on his war experiences in North Africa and Italy, ranks high in the literature of that war. He wrote two more novels before his early death: *Lucifer with a Book* (1949), portraying a boy's boarding school, and *A Cry of Children* (1952).

Burr, Aaron (1756–1836),   lawyer, diarist, third Vice-President of the United States. Born in Newark, New Jersey, and educated at Princeton, Burr studied law and fought in the Revolutionary War. After the war he gained success in law and politics, organizing Tammany Hall into a strong political machine in New York. He became Vice-President under Jefferson (1801–05). His longstanding enmity with ALEXANDER HAMILTON reached a climax in a duel in which Hamilton was killed (July 11, 1804). The duel, which ruined Burr personally and politically, made a martyr of Hamilton. Burr wandered to the West and South (see HARMAN BLENNERHASSETT), was tried and acquitted for treason, lived abroad, again practiced law in New York, unsuccessfully married "that elegant strumpet" Madame Jumel, died on Staten Island. Burr as a writer appears chiefly in a two-volume work, *The Private Journal of Aaron Burr* (1838 and 1903), consisting of nearly a thousand pages of Burr's intimate diary entries for the years 1808–12; and in his correspondence with his daughter Theodosia, edited by Mark Van Doren (1929). Few American historical figures have appeared so frequently in novels. To name only a few, consider Harriet Beecher Stowe's THE MINISTER'S WOOING (1859), Gertrude Atherton's *The Conqueror* (1902), Kenneth Roberts'

ARUNDEL (1930), Elizabeth Page's *The Tree of Liberty* (1939), and Anya Seton's *My Theodosia* (1941). Gore Vidal wrote a fictionalized biography, *Burr* (1973).

Burritt, Elihu (1810–1879), "the Learned Blacksmith." Born in Connecticut, the son of a cobbler, Burritt became a blacksmith but had a passion for learning and for helping humanity. An astounding linguist who mastered more than forty languages, Burritt published a Sanskrit handbook and grammars of Arabic, Persian, Hindustani, and Turkish. Later in life Burritt became deeply devoted to the cause of pacifism, issuing a weekly newspaper, *The Christian Citizen* (1844–51), advocating his cause, and lectured widely on the same theme. He published *Sparks from the Anvil* (1846) and *Lectures and Speeches* (1866).

Burroughs, Edgar Rice (1875–1950), novelist. Born in Chicago and educated at Phillips Academy, Burroughs served in the United States Cavalry and tried many jobs before turning to writing. His first sale, "Under the Moons of Mars," serialized in *All-Story Magazine* (1912), was a fantasy of extraterrestrial life, later published as the novel *A Princess of Mars* (1917). Meanwhile, in his first book, *Tarzan of the Apes* (1914), he created his most enduring character. Over 70 titles followed, more than a dozen of them posthumous. They include many fantasies of life on Mars, Venus, and the moon, and 25 more Tarzan books (see TARZAN). His few more realistic novels, set in Chicago and Hollywood, were less successful. Over 36 million copies of his works have been sold thus far and some have been translated into 30 or more languages.

Burroughs, John (1837–1921), naturalist, essayist, critic, poet. Burroughs was affectionately called Uncle John of Woodchuck and The Sage of Slabsides. (Slabsides was a rustic cabin he built for himself on his farm at Riverby on the Hudson River). It was not Thoreau but RALPH WALDO EMERSON who most deeply influenced Burroughs. His first published contribution in *The Atlantic Monthly* in 1860 was mistaken by Lowell himself for a piece by Emerson and was so listed later in Poole's *Index to Periodical Literature*. In addition to Emerson, Walt Whitman greatly impressed him, and in later years Henri Bergson was a potent influence.

Burroughs was a farmboy who deeply loved nature, though not the wild life of the forest. Birds were his special love, and his first view of Audubon's pictures made him resolve to become a naturalist. For a time he was a clerk in the Treasury in Washington, where he became acquainted with WALT WHITMAN. Later he was a bank examiner. Finally he settled down at Riverby, and the fame he acquired by his numerous essays on nature and his natural history collections attracted many visitors. He became a national figure, with his snowy white beard and his broad forehead and benign expression. Universities gave him honorary degrees, he received a gold medal from the National Academy of Arts and Letters (1916), and celebrated men sought him out—he was a particular friend of Theodore Roosevelt. In his honor was established the John Burroughs Medal, given for books on natural history.

Most intimate of his friends was Whitman, a frequent visitor to his home. Burroughs wrote the first biographical study of Whitman, *Notes on Walt Whitman as Poet and Person* (1867), later expanded into *Walt Whitman: A Study* (1896). Among his books are *Wake-Robin* (1871); *Locusts and Wild Honey* (1879); *Fresh Fields* (1884), a travel book; *Signs and Seasons* (1886); *Bird and Bough* (1906), poems; *Time and Change* (1912); *The Breath of Life* (1915); and *Accepting the Universe* (1922). As he wrote in *The Summit of the Years* (1913): "I got to books and nature as a bee goes to a flower, for a nectar that I can make into my own honey." *My Boyhood* (1922) is autobiographical.

Burroughs, William S[eward] (1914–1997), novelist. Born into a socially prominent family in St. Louis, Burroughs was educated at Harvard, lived on a family allowance, was quickly discharged on psychiatric grounds from service in the Army during World War II, and drifted from job to job. For fifteen years (1944–57) he was a drug addict. During those years he was also a member of the BEAT GENERATION, an example to such younger Beats as JACK KEROUAC and ALLEN GINSBERG. He lived many years in Tangier and Paris, then in New York, California, and Kansas.

In his first book, *Junkie: Confessions of an Unredeemed Drug Addict* (1953), Burroughs adopted the name "William Lee" to report some of his drug years, which were not yet past. Published in paperback as an Ace Double Book, it was bound back to back with a reprint of Maurice Helbrant's *Narcotic Agent* (first published in 1941), the story of a man "responsible for the arrest of more than 500 sellers of narcotics." In *Junkie*, Burroughs disguised names and omitted or changed facts in a terse, unrepentant record, in which the junkie by the end has tried "junk and weed and coke" and is about to go to Colombia in search of yage, perhaps "the final fix." His next and most celebrated book, *Naked Lunch* (Paris 1959; New York 1962), is an autobiographical novel that discards the conventional narrative prose of *Junkie* to present a surrealistic vision of a liberated, hallucinatory counterculture set in opposition to a mass-produced, technological society bent on self-destruction. In this and the books of the next few years, Burroughs relied on such techniques as random cutting and pasting to create an extreme montage effect. Surviving obscenity trials in the U.S., *Naked Lunch* became an icon of the emancipated sixties. Pages left over from *Naked Lunch* became the basis for three more experimental fictions presenting the same general messages: *The Soft Machine* (1961), *The Ticket that Exploded* (1962), and *Nova Express* (1964). His other fictions with similar materials and techniques include *The Wild Boys: A Book of the Dead* (1971), about homosexuality; *Port of Saints* (1973), semiautobiographical; and *Exterminator!* (1974).

After his return to the U.S. in 1974, Burroughs began to write more conventional narratives. *Cities of the Red Night* (1981) won praise for its mixture of stories set in the 18th and 20th centuries and a mythic city of 100,000 years ago. In it Burroughs expands his longtime interest in such subjects as telepathy, cosmic struggle, and time travel. *The Place of the Dead Roads* (1984) is a time- and space-travel novel moving from contemporary Greenwich Village to the gunfighting West to the planet Venus. *The Western Lands* (1987) extends these themes again, as the characters set out to arrive at immortality by reaching the ancient Egyptian land of the dead.

Queer (1985) belongs to an earlier period. It is another William Lee account; written 33 years before its publication, it evolved out of Burroughs' accidental shooting of his wife in 1951. Lee seeks escape and forgetfulness in homosexual pursuits in Latin America. His movie scripts include *The Last Words of Dutch Schultz* (1970) and *Blade Runner* (1979). With Allen Ginsberg he wrote *The Yage Letters* (1963). *Letters to Allen Ginsberg 1953–1957* appeared in 1982. *Last Words: The Final Journals of William S. Burroughs* was published posthumously in 2000. A biography is Ted Morgan's *Literary Outlaw: The Life and Times of William S. Burroughs* (1988).

Burt, [Maxwell] Struthers (1882–1954),   newspaperman, teacher, rancher, writer. Burt, a dyed-in-the-wool Philadelphian who was born by accident in Baltimore, started out in newspaper work in Philadelphia. He went west and served as president of the company running the Bar B.C. Ranch in Wyoming. Later he and his wife, Katharine Newlin Burt, lived on a smaller ranch in the same state. He began his writing career with a collection of verse, *In the High Hills* (1914). He went on to publish short stories and novels: *John O'May and Other Stories* (1918), *The Interpreter's House* (1924), *The Delectable Mountains* (1927), and *Festival* (1931). *The Delectable Mountains* makes good use of the author's special knowledge of Philadelphia society and Wyoming ranches. He continued to publish verse: *Songs and Portraits* (1920) and *War Songs* (1942), and wrote a lively account of Wyoming's *Powder River* (1938) and two slightly irreverent accounts of Philadelphia: *Along These Streets* (1942) and *Philadelphia: Holy Experiment* (1945).

Burton, Richard [Eugene] (1861–1940),   teacher, poet, critic, lecturer. Burton was born in Connecticut and for most of his life taught at the University of Minnesota. In 1925 he moved to New Jersey, where he became a popular lecturer and critic. He published many books: collections of poems, from *Dumb in June* (1895; 10th ed., 1927) to *Collected Poems* (1931); biographies; discussions of plays and novels; and essays.

Burton, William Evans (1804–1860),   actor, editor, dramatist, humorous essayist. A comic actor of considerable ability, Burton came to the United States in 1834 from England and remained here for the rest of his life. He wrote a play, *Ellen Wareham* (1833), short stories and sketches collected as *Waggeries and Vagaries* (1848), and edited *Burton's Comic Songster* (1837) and *The Cyclopedia of Wit and Humor* (1858). He published *The Gentleman's Magazine* (1837–40), giving EDGAR ALLAN POE a position as his assistant. Poe's moodiness and critical severity eventually led to a break, but Poe meanwhile contributed many reviews and essays to the magazine, reprinted several of his poems in its pages, and gave it one of his greatest stories, THE FALL OF THE HOUSE OF USHER (September 1839).

Burton's Gentleman's Magazine.   See GRAHAM'S MAGAZINE.

Burwell Papers, The.   A collection of papers in the custody of Nathaniel Burwell of Virginia, written about 1676 and now usually attributed to JOHN COTTON or his wife Ann. They contain an account of BACON'S REBELLION. The papers were first published in the Massachusetts Historical Society *Collections* (1814), then reprinted with fewer errors in 1866 and placed in the care of the Virginia Historical Society.

Bury the Dead (1936),   a one-act play by IRWIN SHAW. In this powerful pacifist fantasy, six men killed in World War I refuse to be buried and at last persuade their fellow soldiers to join them in a revolt against war.

Busch, Frederick (1941–   ),   novelist, short-story writer. Born in Brooklyn, Busch was educated at Muhlenberg College and Columbia University (1967). He is a teacher at Colgate and winner of several awards, including a Guggenheim Fellowship. Busch's novels focus on family relations; *I Wanted a Year Without Fall* (1971) is a story passed from father to son. *Manual Labor* (1974) concerns a couple's struggle to deal with their baby's death, and *Rounds* (1980) also focuses on children, birth, and death. *The Mutual Friend* (1978) is a study of three years in Dicken's life. *Take This Man* (1981) details a boy's relations with his two fathers, and *Invisible Mending* (1984) traces the tensions of a marriage between a man and woman of different religions. In *Sometimes I Live in the Country* (1986), *Harry and Catherine* (1990) *Closing Arguments* (1991), *Long Way from Home* (1993) and *Girls* (1997), he continues his novelistic exploration of love and family. *War Babies* (1989) is a novella. His short-story collections include *Breathing Trouble* (1974), *Domestic Particulars: A Family Chronicle* (1976), *Hardwater Country* (1979), *Too Late American Boyhood Blues* (1984), and *Absent Friends* (1989). *The Children in the Woods: New and Selected Stories* appeared in 1994. *When People Publish* (1986) is a collection of essays. Busch has also written a critical study of JOHN HAWKES (1973).

Busch, Niven (1903–1991),   novelist, short-story writer, screenwriter. Born in New York City, Busch became a prolific writer of popular fiction ranging in setting from the Old West to 20th-century Europe and California. His books, many of them best sellers, include *The Carrington Incident* (1941), *Duel in the Sun* (1944), *They Dream of Home* (1944), *Day of the Conquerors* (1946), *The Furies* (1948), *The Hate Merchant* (1953), *The Actor* (1955), and *California Street* (1959). Busch's stories and articles have appeared in many magazines, and there is a collection of some of his early *New Yorker* pieces, *Twenty-One Americans* (1930).

Bushnell, Horace (1802–1876),   clergyman, theologian. Born in Connecticut, Bushnell became a Congregational minister, pastor of the North Church, Hartford (1833–59). His widely influential books on liberal Protestant thought include *Christian Nurture* (1847); *God in Christ* (1849), for which he was attacked for heresy; *Christ in Theology* (1851); *The Age of Homespun* (1851), on the New England of his youth; *Nature and the Supernatural* (1858), a response to transcendentalism; *The Vicarious Sacrifice* (1866), presenting his "moral influence" theory of atonement; *Sermons on Living Subjects* (1872); and *Forgiveness and the Law* (1874). His daughter, M.B. Cheney, edited a *Life and Letters* (1880, 1903).

Busy-Body Papers. "Busy-Body" was a pseudonym adopted by the author of thirty-two papers contributed in 1729 to Andrew Bradford's Philadelphia magazine *The American Weekly Mercury*. They were written in imitation of Addison and were intended to tease Bradford and BENJAMIN FRANKLIN's business rival, SAMUEL KEIMER. Six were written by Franklin. It is probable that some of Franklin's friends contributed a few of the papers.

Butler, Ellis Parker (1869–1937), humorist, editor. Born in Iowa, Butler was a prolific writer whose fame rests on one story, "Pigs Is Pigs," written at the suggestion of Ellery Sedgwick, then editor of *The American Magazine*, and published in that magazine in 1905. It swept the country and went into innumerable printings. It tells of an express agent to whom is brought a consignment of guinea pigs. He contends that "pigs is pigs" and hence to be charged express rates as livestock, not as pets. In the long ensuing dispute with the consignee, the guinea pigs increase so rapidly that they overrun the entire express company office.

Butler, Frances ["Fanny"] Anne. See FRANCES KEMBLE.

Butler, Nicholas Murray (1862–1947), teacher, university president, political figure, lecturer, author. His career at Columbia University spanned sixty-seven years—at twenty-eight he became professor of philosophy, at thirty-nine president of the university. Active as a lecturer and in politics, he ran as vice-presidential candidate with Taft in the 1912 election and over a long period kept nine secretaries busy with his thousands of articles, speeches, and books. Among his works are *The Meaning of Education* (1898, revised 1915); *A World in Ferment* (1918); *The Faith of a Liberal* (1924); *Across the Busy Years* (autobiography, 1939); and *The World Today* (1946).

Butler, Robert Olen [Jr.] (1945–   ), novelist and short-story writer. Born in Granite City, Illinois, Butler was educated at Northwestern University and the University of Iowa writing program, and teaches at McNeese State University in Louisiana. His service in Army intelligence during the Vietnam War brought him into contact with Vietnamese culture and folklore, materials used in his critically acclaimed story collection, *A Good Scent from a Strange Mountain* (1992), where he writes in the voices of Vietnamese who have come to Louisiana, and other books. *The Alleys of Eden* (1981), his first published novel, is the story of Cliff, an Army deserter, and his life in the back alleys of Saigon and the U.S. with his lover, a Vietnamese prostitute. *Sun Dogs* (1982) concerns a former prisoner of war. *On Distant Ground* (1985) centers on an intelligence officer obsessed with finding and releasing a prisoner whose cell-wall graffiti has touched him. Other novels include *Countrymen of Bones* (1983), in which an archeologist must finish work in the desert near Los Alamos in the short time before the site will be used to test the first atom bomb; *Wabash* (1987), set in Illinois during the Depression; *The Deuce* (1989), about homelessness; *They Whisper* (1994), about the sexual explorations of a man of thirty-five; and *The Deep Green Sea* (1998), about the return to Vietnam of an American veteran. *Tabloid Dreams* (1996) collects stories unified by their origins in the wild headlines of supermarket tabloids. "Help Me Find My Spaceman Lover," from that book, is the basis for the comedy *Mr. Spaceman* (2000). The novel features Desi, from outer space, who has learned to speak English from watching television and is married to Edna, a beautician he met at a Wal-Mart. Assigned to learn about life on earth, Desi abducts a busload of tourists and interviews them on his spaceship.

Butler, William Allen (1825–1902), lawyer, poet, humorist. Born in Albany, New York, Butler was active in political and social causes and became a well-known speaker. He wrote a biography of Martin Van Buren (1862), but his reputation rests chiefly on the satirical poem "Nothing to Wear" (published anonymously in *Harper's Weekly*, 1857, and in book form in the same year without the author's consent). It tells the story of Miss Flora M'Flimsey, who spent six weeks in Paris on a shopping spree and yet was in utter despair because she had nothing to wear. Butler attacks the "spoiled children of fashion" for overlooking the plight of the wretched and the starving. The poem was widely read and imitated.

By Blue Ontario's Shore (1856), a poem by WALT WHITMAN. The form and the title of this lengthy poem underwent many changes and became in the end the most extensively revised of all Whitman's poems. Originally, the thought appeared in the prose preface of the 1855 edition of *Leaves of Grass*. It was called *Poem of Many in One* in the 1856 edition; in 1860 it was included in *Chants Democratic*; it appeared again in 1867 under the title *As I Sat Alone by Blue Ontario's Shore* and finally was given its present title in 1881. It is a poem of striking, deliberately extravagant individualism in behalf of the United States and of the poet as one of its citizens; "It is who I am great or to be great, it is You up there, or any one."

Byles, Mather (1707–1788), clergyman, poet, humorist. Byles was a member of the Mather family, and it was he who inherited COTTON MATHER's great library. Byles was strongly pro-British in his sympathies during the Revolutionary War and was dismissed by his Boston congregation and spent his last years in retirement. For a time he was under military guard. An inveterate punster, he described his anomalous situation during the war as follows: "I have been guarded, reguarded, and now, disreguarded." It is said the old wag finally marched up and down the street, guarding himself. He had his study painted brown so that people visiting him could find him "in a brown study." He imitated and corresponded with Alexander Pope, and wrote in the style of Isaac Watts; to some extent he substituted aesthetic for purely moralistic standards in poetry. He was author of a collection, *Poems on Several Occasions* (1744); a long poem, *The Conflagration* (1755); and a number of theological works. He appears briefly in Hawthorne's *Howe's Masquerade* (in *Twice-Told Tales*, 1842).

Bynner, Edwin Lassetter (1842–1893), Brooklyn-born novelist who mainly wrote historical romances, including *Agnes Surriage* (1886), *The Begum's Daughter* (1890), and *Zachary Phips* (1892).

Bynner, [Harold] Witter (1881–1968), poet, playwright, translator. EDWIN LASSETTER BYNNER was his uncle. Born in Brooklyn, Bynner maintained a high level of excellence in his many collections of verse, beginning with *An Ode to Harvard* (1907), later changed to *Young Harvard* (1925). After his graduation from Harvard, Bynner went on to editoral work with *McClure's* magazine, but after 1907 moved to New Hampshire and spent the next ten years almost entirely absorbed in writing. During these years he wrote three one-act plays later published in *A Book of Plays* (1922).

Bynner was influenced by the art and literature of both China and India, and traveled extensively in the Orient. *The Jade Mountain* (1929, 5th ed. 1939) is the English translation (in collaboration with Kiang Kang-hu) of *Three Hundred Pearls of the T'ang Dynasty*. Other books by Bynner are *Indian Earth* (1929, verse); *Eden Tree* (1931, verse); *Selected Poems* (1936); *The Way of Life According to Laotzu* (1944); *Take Away the Darkness* (1947); and *Journey With Genius* (1951), an account of the time he spent with D. H. Lawrence and his wife in New Mexico in 1922 and 1923. During the latter part of the 1950s and the beginning of the 1960s, despite failing sight, Bynner brought out *New Poems* (1960) and appeared in a new creative phase. Neither experimental nor avant-garde, these poems express some qualities of both these attitudes, with lines of rapid insight and immediate brightness. Among his other books are *Greenstone Poems* (1917), *A Book of Plays* (1922), *Book of Lyrics* (1955), and *New Poems* (1960). He is said to appear as a character in D. H. Lawrence's *The Plumed Serpent* (1926). See SPECTRA AND THE SPECTRIST SCHOOL.

Byrd, Richard E[velyn] (1888–1957), naval officer, explorer, author. Byrd, a descendant of WILLIAM BYRD, engaged in numerous remarkable explorations, many of them by airplane. He flew over both the North and the South Poles (1926, 1929), and took part in three important expeditions to Antarctica (1928–30, 1933–35, 1939). He wrote accounts of his flights and expeditions in *Skyward* (1928), *Little America* (1930), *Discovery* (1935), and *Alone* (1938).

Byrd, William (1674–1744), planter, lawyer, public official, writer. Born in Virginia, Byrd was one of the state's great gentlemen. He was a writer just as he was a scientist, merely as a hobby. His writings were not published until nearly a century after his death, in *The Westover Manuscripts* (1841). A modern edition was edited by Mark Van Doren as *A Journey to the Land of Eden* (1928). In it may be found A HISTORY OF THE DIVIDING LINE RUN IN THE YEAR 1728 [between Virginia and North Carolina], A JOURNEY TO THE LAND OF EDEN, A.D. 1733 (Eden was ironically Carolina), and A PROGRESS TO THE MINES, IN THE YEAR 1732. In addition, volumes of extracts from Byrd's diaries are available (1941, 1942, 1958), edited by Louis B. Wright, Maude H. Woodfin, and Marion Tinling. These explain much about the social history of the day. Byrd was also the author of a tract published anonymously in London in 1721—*A Discourse Concerning the Plague, with Preservatives Against it. By a Lover of Mankind* (republished as *Another Secret Diary by William Byrd*, 1942.) The tract is a clever piece of propaganda in favor of tobacco as a deterrent of the plague. So engaging is Byrd's style and so effective his satire that he has justifiably been claimed as one of our first humorists. An aristocrat, he observed with disdain the inhabitants of "Lubberland," or Carolina, when he visited there. The independence and lawlessness of the people seemed to him dangerous. About his own sometimes difficult and risky experiences he wrote with unfailing good humor. L. B. Wright edited *The Prose Works of William Byrd* (1966). Marion Tinling edited *The Correspondence of the Three William Byrds* 1684–1776 (1977). See also Pierre Marambaud, *William Byrd of Westover* (1971).

Byrne, Donn. See BRIAN DONN-BYRNE.

C

Cabbages and Kings (1904), a novel by O. HENRY (William Sydney Porter). In 1896 Porter was indicted for embezzlement and fled to Central and South America for a year before being sentenced to the penitentiary. Out of his adventures during that year he built the episodes of *Cabbages and Kings*, taking his title from the ballad on the Walrus and the Carpenter in Lewis Carroll's *Alice in Wonderland*. Nineteen loosely connected narratives are laid in a Central American country called Coralio, and the same characters frequently reappear.

Cabell, James Branch (1879–1958), novelist, essayist, poet, historian. Born in Richmond, Virginia and educated at the College of William and Mary, Cabell belonged by birth and training to the First Families of Virginia. Some of his writings are concerned with the genealogy of his own and other Virginia families, and he held offices in several genealogical societies. His first book, *The Eagle's Shadow*, appeared in 1904. In the following year, while writing *Gallantry* (1907), Cabell was irritated by problems of local geography raised by the fact that the scene was laid in Tunbridge Wells, England, which he had never visited. Thereafter, his stories would be laid in a land of his own, the history, scenery, customs, and morals of which he would himself contrive. Thus was born the medieval French province of Poictesme, probably compounded from Poitiers and Angoulême. Poictesme became a real country to Cabell and his readers. Its history from 1234 to 1750 was carefully described, its laws and legends wrought into the fabric of Cabell's stories. The diction of the country was an odd mixture of irony and circumlocution. Its manners were courtly, its sexual morality free and easy. Cabell's escapism was curious, since it led to an existence that seemed romantic enough but was really futile, disillusioned, bitter. The trappings were splendid, the result boredom. In philosophy Cabell was a skeptic, a sort of American Anatole France. His heroes make love with endless women and contribute a potent ancestry to most of the European dynasties, but the women turn out to be singularly alike, and in the end all is vanity.

The books had more success with the critics than with the public, at least until the appearance of JURGEN (1919). The attempt to suppress *Jurgen* for immorality led naturally to a large increase in Cabell's income. He continued meanwhile to live a life of orthodox sobriety in Richmond and brought together the huge epic of POICTESME in the *Storisende Edition* (18 v. 1927–30). In this edition appear all the novels dealing with Dom Manuel and his descendants, arranged in genealogical order rather than in the order in which the books were published. The books form a complicated concatenated narrative—*Beyond Life* (1919); *Domnei* (1920—originally *The Soul of Melicent*, 1913); *Chivalry* (1909); *Jurgen* (1919); *The Line of Love* (1905); *Gallantry* (1907); *The Certain Hour* (1916); *The Cords of Vanity* (1909); *The Rivet in Grandfather's Neck* (1915); *The Eagle's Shadow* (1904); THE CREAM OF THE JEST (1917); *Figures of Earth* (1921); *The High Place* (1923); *The Silver Stallion* (1926); *Something about Eve* (1927); and others. The series has been described as "the most ambitiously planned literary work which has ever come out of America." Later Cabell wrote a group of three stories, *Smirt* (1934), *Smith* (1935), and *Smire* (1937), which failed to create any excitement. There also were *There Were Two Pirates* (1946); *Let Me Lie*, essays on Virginia (1947); and *The Devil's Own Dear Son* (1949). *Quiet, Please* (1952) is mainly autobiographical. *I Remember It* (1955) is subtitled "Some Epilogues in Recollection."

When American sexual folkways changed after World War I, Cabell's popularity collapsed. Yet, at the height of his fame, he was praised almost ecstatically by many leading critics, including H. L. Mencken. On the question of pronouncing his name, Cabell rhymed, "Tell the rabble my name is Cabell."

Cabet, Étienne (1788–1856), utopian socialist. A member of the chamber of deputies in France, Cabet fled to Great Britain in 1834 to escape charges of treason. There, influenced by ROBERT OWEN, he developed ideas for a communistic society. Returning to France, he published *Voyage en Icarie* (1840), a best-selling book that is said to have gained him 400,000 followers by 1847. He sent French settlers to an Icarian community in Texas (1848) that soon failed, and himself headed a second settlement (1849–1856) at the old Mormon town of Nauvoo, Illinois; later settlements were made, briefly, at Cheltenham, Missouri, and, more successfully, near Corning, Iowa (1860–1898).

Cabeza de Vaca, Alvar Núñez (1490?–1559), Spanish explorer. Cabeza de Vaca (sometimes called simply Alvar Núñez) reached Florida with the expedition of Pánfilo de

Narváez in 1528, which had left Spain with six hundred men. When the expeditionary forces were destroyed by hardship, disease, Apalachee Indians, and shipwreck, Cabeza de Vaca was one of four survivors (three Spaniards and a Moroccan slave) to reach an island (probably Galveston Island) on what is now the Texas coast. During eight years of wandering, they were captives and slaves of various tribes, but were also venerated for their shamanistic powers, including faith healing. They traveled to West Texas, probably New Mexico and Arizona, and possibly California, before reaching the Spanish outpost at Culiacán, Mexico (1536). They were probably the first white men to see buffalo, and their stories of the Pueblo Indians fed legends of the Seven Cities of Cibola and El Dorado. Cabeza de Vaca's account, written in 1536 and published in 1542 as *Los naufragios* (*The Shipwrecked Men*) is the first North American captivity narrative. It was translated into English by Thomas Buckingham Smith as *The Narrative of Alvar Núñez Cabeça de Vaca* (1851) and reprinted in F. W. Hodge's *Spanish Explorers in the Southern United States* (1907) and I. R. Blacker and H. M. Rosen's *The Golden Conquistadores* (1960). Cabeza de Vaca also spent time in Brazil, explored the Paraná River to Bolivia, was imprisoned, and wrote of his South American adventures in *Commentarios* (1555). See Morris Bishop, *The Odyssey of Cabeza de Vaca* (1933) and Haniel Long, *The Marvelous Adventures of Cabeza de Vaca* (1973).

Cable, George Washington (1844–1925),   short-story writer, novelist, historian. Cable was born in New Orleans. With the death of his father and the failure of the family business, he left school at age fourteen and went to work to support his mother and sisters. He joined the Confederate Army in the spring of 1862 and served until the end of the war, recounting his experiences during this period in *The Cavalier* (1901). After the war he worked for a cotton wholesaler and tried his hand at surveying with an engineering expedition, but contracted malaria and was unable to work for almost two years. During his illness he contributed a weekly column of humorous sketches and poems to the New Orleans *Picayune*, using the pseudonym "Drop Shot." The column became popular and was soon appearing daily, and Cable was offered a job as reporter. However, as a Calvinist, he refused to write theatrical criticism and was dropped from the paper. He became an accountant for a firm of cotton factors, married, and pursued a rigorous course of self-education. He learned French and studied the New Orleans archives, fascinated by the city's colorful history.

Cable's first literary success was OLD CREOLE DAYS (1879), a collection of seven stories previously published in *Scribner's Monthly*. They included four of Cable's best short works: "Jean Ah Poquelin," a weird tale of a former slave trader; "Tite Poulette," a story dealing with miscegenation; "Café des Exilés," a story of a smuggling plot; and "Belles Demoiselles Plantation," a pathetic story of a proud father's loss. THE GRANDISSIMES, Cable's first novel, appeared in 1880. It was a study of the Louisiana Creoles, descendants of original French and Spanish settlers in the South and in Latin America. The novel

deals with a feud between two aristocratic Creole families, the Grandissimes and the De Grapions. Like much of Cable's other work, it is chiefly valuable for its descriptions of locale and treatment of Creole and slave dialects.

His next book, MADAME DELPHINE (1881), which was included in later editions of *Old Creole Days*, is a long short story dealing with the unhappy place of the quadroon in New Orleans society. *The Creoles of Louisiana* (1884), a historical work, angered the Creoles because of Cable's version of their ancestry. He claimed they were descendants of men who had come to America for commercial reasons and had married Indian and African women, "and the inmates of French houses of correction."

Always an enemy of slavery, Cable became a zealous reformer and began to write articles, later collected in *The Silent South* (1885), arguing for prison reform, the abolition of contract labor, and better treatment of African-Americans. His writings found small favor in the South as a whole, and the Creoles particularly resented his stories about them, charging that his characters from the uneducated lower-class Creoles did not represent the group as a whole. Partially as a result of his unpopularity in the South, Cable moved to Massachusetts, where he was active as a reformer and philanthropist and continued to write on social problems, as in *The Negro Question* (1888) and *The Southern Struggle for Pure Government* (1890).

At the turn of the century he again turned to fiction, but this work was without his early richness and color. He is chiefly remembered as an important figure in the beginning of the local-color movement who depicted New Orleans society with exotic brilliance and charm. In his treatment of race relations and violence he foreshadowed such modern writers as ROBERT PENN WARREN and WILLIAM FAULKNER.

Other books by Cable include DR. SEVIER (1884), *Bonaventure* (1888), *Strange True Stories of Louisiana* (1889), *John March, Southerner* (1894), *Strong Hearts* (1899), *Bylow Hill* (1902), *Kincaid's Battery* (1908), "*Posson Jone*" *and Père Raphaël* (1909), *Gideon's Band* (1914), *The Amateur Garden* (1914), *The Flower of the Chapdelaines* (1918), and *Lovers of Louisiana* (1918). See Arlin Turner, *George W. Cable* (1956) and Louis D. Rubin, *George W. Cable* (1969).

Cabral de Melo Neto, João (1920–1999),   Brazilian poet and diplomat. Born in Recief, a member of a distinguished family that included his cousin Manuel Bandeira, a leading poet of the Brazilian avant-garde in the 1920s, Cabral moved to Rio de Janeiro in 1940 and published his first book of verse, *Pedra do sono* (*Stone of Slumber*), two years later. From 1945 through 1990, apart from a brief period in the early 1950s when he was suspended from duty as a suspected Communist sympathizer, he served as a diplomat on four continents and was finally an ambassador to Senegal, Ecuador, and Honduras. Meanwhile, he earned a reputation as a cerebral poet whose concrete language, cinematic materials, and traditional structures were frequently those of the northeast region of Brazil where he was born and raised. "Morte e vida Severina" (1955), his most popular poem, tells of a peasant's bleak existence in lines that are known at least in part to millions of Brazilians. It became a play, a film, and a television drama. Although not widely known outside of Brazil, his poetry earned the praise of poets in English, including Elizabeth Bishop, a longtime resident of Brazil and translator of some of his verse, who praised him as Brazil's "most important poet of the postwar generation" in *An Anthology of Twentieth-Century Brazilian Poetry*, which she edited with Emanuel Brasil. *Selected Poetry, 1937–1990* (1995) is a collection in English.

Cabrera Infante, Guillermo (1929–   ),   Cuban novelist and short-story writer. Until 1965, Cabrera Infante played an important role in Cuban literary affairs under Castro, but he then severed his connections with the Castro government and with Cuba. His best work is *Tres tristes tigres* (1965, tr. *Three Trapped Tigers*, 1971), a funny, dark novel of disoriented characters who continually seek a significance they never find. Verbally extravagant, the story is set against the backdrop of nightlife in the last days of Batista's Havana. His other books include *Vista del amanecer en el tropico* (1974, tr. *View of Dawn in the Tropics,* 1979), consisting of vignettes of violence and deception throughout Cuba's history; *Exorcismos de estilo* (1976); and *La Habana para un infante difunto* (1979, tr. *Infante's Inferno,* 1984). *Holy Smoke* (1986), a novel, was written originally in English. Other works are *Mea Cuba* (1992; tr. 1994) and an earlier book, *Así en la paz como en la guerra* (1971), translated as *Writes of Passage* (1993).

Caddo Indians.   Native American tribes sharing the languages of the Caddoan linguistic stock. These loosely federated tribes include the Caddos, the ARIKARAS, the PAWNEES, and the Wichitaws. The Caddos themselves lived along the Red River in northwestern Louisiana, southwestern Arkansas, northwestern Texas, and nearby Oklahoma; the others lived westward to the Brazos River and north into Kansas and Nebraska. The Caddos lived in beehive-shaped thatched houses, of the kind now on display at Anardarko, Oklahoma. They planted corn and hunted buffalo. The remnants of the Caddo tribe live mostly in Oklahoma.

Cadman, Charles Wakefield (1881–1946), composer, critic, lecturer, editor. Cadman was among the first American composers to become interested in Indian songs and customs. His works range from songs ("From the Land of the Sky-Blue Water") to symphonic and operatic creations. Two of his operas, *The Garden of Mystery* (1925) and *The Witch of Salem* (1926), had New England connections; the former was based on Hawthorne's short story RAPPACINI'S DAUGHTER (*Mosses from an Old Manse*, 1846). *Shanewis* (1918) was an opera with an Indian story, libretto by Nelle Richmond Eberhardt. *The Willow Tree* was the first radio opera and was produced by NBC on October 4, 1932.

Cage, John (1912–1992),   composer. Born in Los Angeles, Cage attended Pomona College, studied with Arnold Schoenberg and other musicians, and began to earn fame with his unorthodox music in New York in the 1940s. His theories, first, of "total soundspace," which allows for all sounds and non-sounds (or silence) to be used in music, and, second, of composition by chance, for example, with notes determined by rolling dice, have influenced not only his own works and those of other musicians, but the works of avant-garde poets and prose writers as well. Among Cage's compositions influential on writers are *Williams Mix* (1952), mingling prerecorded country sounds, city sounds, conventional music, and so on; and *Empty Words* (1973), a mixed-media presentation combining the sounds of phrases, words, syllables, and letters with projected images. The point that the sounds of language do not have to combine syntactically to produce meaning has influenced a number of writers, including FRANK O'HARA, JOHN ASHBERY, the poet-performer LAURIE ANDERSON, and the LANGUAGE POETS. Cage's books include *Silence* (1961), *A Year from Monday* (1967), *M: Writings '67–'72* (1973), *Empty Words: Writings '73–'78* (1979), *Themes and Variations* (1982), *A. John Cage Reader* (1982), *X. Writings '79–82* (1983), and *I–VI* (1990), lectures delivered at Harvard, accompanied with cassette recordings.

Cahan, Abraham (1860–1951),   journalist, editor, novelist. Born in Russia, Cahan came to the United States in 1882. In 1897 he helped found the Yiddish *Forverts* (the *Jewish Daily Forward*); he became editor-in-chief in 1902. Under his guidance, the *Forward* gained a wide circulation (up to 245,000 a day), put up its own building in New York and a printing plant in Chicago, and acquired a radio station. Cahan was a committed socialist who took a strong stand against the Soviet government, maintaining that "communism is despotism without any rights for anyone at all." He also wrote fiction: *The Imported Bridegroom and Other Stories of the New York Ghetto* (1898), *Yekl, a Tale of the New York Ghetto* (1896), and THE RISE OF DAVID LEVINSKY (1917), besides much writing in Yiddish that was not translated. William Dean Howells was one of the first critics to review Cahan's fiction favorably.

Cain, James M[allahan] (1892–1977),   newspaperman, novelist, playwright. Born in Annapolis and educated at Washington College, Maryland, Cain was a reporter on the Baltimore *American*, worked on the Baltimore *Sun*, taught journalism at St. John's College in Annapolis, and became an editorial writer on the New York *World*. Later he did magazine, syndicate, and motion-picture work, publishing his first novel, THE POSTMAN ALWAYS RINGS TWICE, in 1934. His other novels include *Serenade* (1937); *Mildred Pierce* (1941); *Love's Lovely Counterfeit* (1942); *Three of a Kind* (1943); *Past All Dishonor* (1946), set in Nevada during the Civil War; *The Butterfly* (1947); *The Moth* (1948); *Galatea* (1953); *Mignon* (1962), a novel of post–Civil War New Orleans; *The Magician's Wife* (1965); *Rainbow's End* (1975); and *The Institute* (1976). His stories are collected in *The Baby in the Icebox* (1981). His first novel made him a foremost exemplar of the hard-boiled school of writers, and the influence of Ernest Hemingway was obvious. The novel tells what happens when a young hobo saunters into a roadside sandwich stand run by a Greek immigrant and his American wife; the hobo takes one look at the wife and decides to settle down to work at the stand. The violence and passion that ensue move at breathless speed. The novel has been dramatized, filmed, and made into an opera.

Caine Mutiny, The (1951),   a novel by HERMAN WOUK. A college boy begins his service in World War II on the mine sweeper *Caine*. He takes part in a desperate mutiny of the officers against their inefficient and cowardly commander, and the episode turns the boy into a real fighter. The novel has remarkable and sustained narrative power, with humor as well as grim suspense and terror. It became an immediate best seller and later a successful play and a movie.

Cajun.   The word, a corruption of *Acadian*, refers to the French settlers deported by the British from Acadia (now Nova Scotia) in 1755. Henry Wadsworth Longfellow used the episode in his narrative poem EVANGELINE (1847). A number of the exiles settled in French-speaking Louisiana in the bayou regions, where they have maintained their unity to this day and have continued to speak their own kind of French.

Calamity Jane   [nickname of Martha Jane (Canary) Burke] (1852?–1903). Reared in a Montana mining community, Calamity Jane learned to ride and gained a reputation for marksmanship. She was probably a scout with General George Custer and a circuit rider on the pony express. At her death she asked to be buried next to her friend JAMES B. [WILD BILL] HICKOK. She was the heroine of *Deadwood Dick on Deck, or Calamity Jane the Heroine of Whoop Up*, one of a series of dime novels by EDWARD L. WHEELER that began to appear in 1884.

Calamus [1] (1860),   a section of poems in WALT WHITMAN's LEAVES OF GRASS that was included in the third edition and intended as a complementary section to CHILDREN OF ADAM. There are thirty-nine poems in the group, among them "Whoever You Are Holding Me Now in Hand," "The Base of All Metaphysics," "I Saw in Louisiana a Live-Oak Growing," I HEAR IT WAS CHARGED AGAINST ME, and "Full of Life Now." In general, the poems celebrate "the manly love of comrades" and have been cited as evidence that Whitman was a homosexual. The name *Calamus* is derived from that of a plant (sometimes called "sweet flag") which "symbolizes with its close-knit leaves the mutual support gained from comradeship." See CALAMUS [2].

Calamus [2] (1897),   a series of letters from WALT WHITMAN to Peter Doyle, 1868–1880. Doyle was an unschooled Confederate soldier who became a streetcar conductor in Washington, D.C., during the period of Whitman's residence there. These letters were published after the poet's death, with the appropriate title taken from *Leaves of Grass*. See CALAMUS [1].

Calavar (1834),   a novel by ROBERT MONTGOMERY BIRD. A follower of James Fenimore Cooper, Bird found in the early history of Mexico material for this historical romance. The exploits of Cortez are described in detail. A sequel, THE INFIDEL, appeared in 1835.

Calaveras County, Celebrated Jumping Frog of. See CELEBRATED JUMPING FROG.

Caldecott Medal.   An award, first made in 1938, given to the illustrator of the most distinguished picture book for children published during the preceding year. It was established in honor of the distinguished British artist Randolph Caldecott (1846–1886), remembered best for his illustrations for children's books.

Caldwell, Erskine [Preston] (1903–1987),   novelist, short-story writer, screenwriter. Born in Moreland, Georgia, Caldwell studied at Erskine College in South Carolina, the University of Virginia, and the University of Pennsylvania. He was briefly a reporter on the *Atlanta Journal* (1925), later a Hollywood screenwriter, and from 1938 to 1941 a foreign correspondent with assignments from Mexico to Russia and China. He first won recognition with TOBACCO ROAD (1932), a novel that shocked contemporary sensibilities with its portrayal of southern poor whites and was turned in the next year into a play that ran seven years on Broadway. GOD'S LITTLE ACRE (1933) followed. With their bawdiness and earthy humor, the two works continued at the forefront of Caldwell's huge success over the years.

Caldwell's reputation with critics paled beside the rising reputation of WILLIAM FAULKNER and the appearance of later southern Gothic writers, such as FLANNERY O'CONNOR and EUDORA WELTY. Caldwell had begun with two short novels, *The Bastard* (1930) and *The Fool* (1930), and had published a collection of stories, *American Earth* (1931), before attaining fame. In all, Caldwell published over forty books of fiction, and his sales ran rapidly into the tens of millions. Among his other novels are *Trouble in July* (1940), concerning southern racial hatred; *All Night Long* (1942), of guerrilla warfare in Russia; *Tragic Ground* (1944), of a Georgia farmer facing the effects of a wartime boom; *A House in the Uplands* (1946); *The Sure Hand of God* (1947); *This Very Earth* (1948); *A Place Called Estherville* (1949), of southern relations between blacks and whites; *Episode in Palmetto* (1950); *A Lamp for Nightfall* (1952), a Maine novel; *Love and Money* (1954), a satire of a best-selling writer; *Gretta* (1955), of nymphomania; *Claudelle Inglish* (1958); *Jenny by Nature* (1961); *Summertime Island* (1968); *The Weather Shelter* (1969); and *Annette* (1973). Some of his best work is in his collections of short stories. In addition to *American Earth*, these include *We Are the Living* (1933), *Kneel to the Rising Sun* (1935), *Jackpot* (1940), *Georgia Boy* (1943), *The Courting of Susie Brown* (1952), *Gulf Coast Stories* (1956), *When You Think of Me* (1959), and *Men and Women* (1961). His *Complete Stories* appeared in 1953. Among the memorable individual stories are "Country Full of Swedes," "Kneel to the Rising Sun," and "Candy-Man Beechum."

With the photographer MARGARET BOURKE-WHITE, to whom Caldwell was married at the time, he collaborated on four books: *You Have Seen Their Faces* (1937), about southern sharecroppers; *North of the Danube* (1939), on Czechoslovakia; *Say! Is This the U.S.A.?*; and *Russia at War* (1942). His other books of nonfiction include *Tenant Farmer* (1935), *Some American People* (1935), *All-Out on the Road to Smolensk* (1942), *Around About America* (1964), *Deep South* (1968), and *Afternoons in Mid-America* (1976). *Call It Experience: The*

Years of Learning How to Write (1951) is a literary autobiography. *In Search of Bisco* (1965) is an account of his search for an African-American man who had been his boyhood friend.

Caldwell, [Janet Miriam] Taylor (1900–1985), novelist. Caldwell came to this country from England at the age of seven. Her literary career, an extraordinary succession of best sellers, began with *Dynasty of Death* (1938), a story of two great families in control of a huge munitions trust. This story was continued in *The Eagles Gather* (1940) and *The Final Hour* (1944). *The Earth Is the Lord's* (1941) is a romance about Genghis Khan. *The Turnbulls* (1943) describes the private life and destiny of a cotton industrialist in England. *The Wide House* (1945) lays emphasis on the racial and religious storms preceding the Civil War. *This Side of Innocence* (1946) is laid in New York in the decades after the Civil War, the plot again concerning families of wealth and power, internecine battling among relatives, details of high finance and industrial backgrounds, and providing careful historical data. Her later books include *There Was a Time* (1947); *Melissa* (1948); *The Devil's Advocate* (1952); *Never Victorious, Never Defeated* (1954); *The Sound of Thunder* (1957); *Dear and Glorious Physician* (1959); *The Listener* (1960); *Your Sins and Mine* (1961); *A Pillar of Iron* (1965), a fictional life of Cicero; *The Captain and the Kings* (1972); and *Answer as a Man* (1981). She used the pseudonym Max Reiner for her *Time No Longer* (1941), about Nazi Germany. *Dialogues with the Devil* (1967) is nonfiction.

Calef, Robert (1648–1719), merchant, writer. Born in England, Calef came to Boston in 1688 and became an opponent of the Salem witchcraft trials (1692). In 1693 COTTON MATHER published WONDERS OF THE INVISIBLE WORLD, with numerous observations on devils and their activities in Salem and nearby points. Calef commented freely on the book, on Mather and his father Increase Mather. Cotton Mather brought a suit for slander against Calef, but the case was dropped. Calef wrote a book on the trials, MORE WONDERS OF THE INVISIBLE WORLD. When no Boston printer would take it, Calef sent it off to London to be published. It appeared in 1700 and made a great stir in the colony. According to one story, INCREASE MATHER caused the book to be burned in Harvard Yard; he was then president of the college. Cotton Mather called Calef "a very wicked sort of Sadducee."

California and Oregon Trail, The (1849), a narrative of travel by FRANCIS PARKMAN. See OREGON TRAIL.

Calisher, Hortense (1911–), novelist, short-story writer. Born in New York City and educated at Barnard College, Calisher has achieved a reputation for complex and subtle fictions covering a wide range of situations. Some of her works are novellas, including the title story of *Extreme Magic* (1964) and *The Railway Police, and The Last Trolly Ride* (1966). Seven novellas are collected in *The Novellas of Hortense Calisher* (1997). Her novels include *False Entry* (1962) and *The New Yorkers* (1969, loosely connected); *Textures of Life* (1963); *Journal from Ellipsia* (1965), unconventional science fiction involving interplanetary travel; *Queenie* (1971), about a female sexual adventurer who becomes a financial success; *Eagle Eye* (1973); *On Keeping Women* (1977); *The Bobby-Soxer* (1986);

Age (1987), a Manhattan marriage story; *In the Palace of the Movie King* (1994), about a Bergman-like director; and *In the Slammer with Carol Smith* (1997). Her story collections include *In The Absence of Angels* (1952), *Tale for the Mirror* (1963), and *Collected Stories* (1975). *Herself* (1972) and *Kissing Cousins* (1988) are memoirs.

Callaghan, Morley [Edward] (1903–1990), novelist, short-story writer. Born in Toronto, Callaghan was encouraged in fiction by ERNEST HEMINGWAY, whom he met while working summers for the *Toronto Star*. Educated at the University of Toronto (1925), he gave up a legal career after his stories began to appear in the little magazines in Paris to which Hemingway carried them, and then found favor with F. SCOTT FITZGERALD and with MAXWELL PERKINS of Scribner's. After Scribner's published his first novel, *Strange Fugitive* (1928), and a collection of short stories, *A Native Argosy* (1929), he left for Paris, later recording his stay there in one of the most engaging memoirs of the LOST GENERATION, *That Summer in Paris* (1963). Mostly, however, he lived and worked in Toronto, establishing an international reputation as one of the foremost Canadian novelists.

After two more apprentice novels, *It's Never Over* (1930) and *A Broken Journey* (1932), Callaghan wrote some of the strongest Canadian novels of the 1930s, displaying in each a moral commitment derived from a strong Catholicism. In *Such Is My Beloved* (1934), a priest, Father Dowling, encounters the disapproval of his parishioners when he sets out to reform two prostitutes. *They Shall Inherit the Earth* (1935) recounts a tragedy surrounding the return of a modern prodigal son. *More Joy in Heaven* (1937) fictionalizes the career of the bank robber Red Ryan, turning it into a parable of a reformed criminal in a violent and cynical society. Some years passed before Callaghan turned to novels again with *The Loved and the Lost* (1951), a strong, best-selling story of relations between blacks and whites in Montreal. His later novels are *The Many Colored Coat* (1960), set in the world of corporate power; *A Passion in Rome* (1961), a love story set in a Rome engaged in electing a new pope after the death of Pius XII; *A Fine and Private Place* (1975), a roman à clef, including characters drawn from Callaghan himself and his long-time admirer EDMUND WILSON; *Close to the Sun Again* (1977), a novella about a successful man injured in a car accident; *A Time for Judas* (1983), a rewriting of the crucifixion story; and *Our Lady of the Snows* (1985), an expansion of the earlier *The Enchanted Pimp* (1978).

Compared from the beginning with Hemingway and Fitzgerald (and for a time celebrated for a boxing match with Hemingway), Callaghan far outstripped them in literary output. Among his best works, and among the best of their time, are his short stories. Collections after the first include *Now That April's Here* (1936), *Morley Callaghan's Stories* (1959), and *The Lost and Found Stories of Morley Callaghan* (1985). A biography is Patricia Morley's *Morley Callaghan* (1978).

Call It Sleep (1934), a novel by HENRY ROTH.

Call of the Wild, The (1903), a novel by JACK LONDON. The background is a cruel Alaska winter during the

KLONDIKE GOLD RUSH. Buck, part St. Bernard, stolen from a California home, becomes a loyal sled dog in the Klondike. After the death of his master, he joins a wolf pack. London works out in the course of the story his ideas on the need for adaptation to survive and on the influence of heredity.

Calvert, George Henry (1803–1889), poet, dramatist, novelist, essayist. Calvert came from good Maryland stock, was educated at Harvard and in Germany, and lived after 1840 in Newport, Rhode Island. He made Benedict Arnold and Major André the subjects of a tragedy in 1864, published *Poems* (1847) and *Comedies* (1852), discussed *Goethe: His Life and Works* (1872), and issued a final collection, *Threescore and Other Poems* (1883).

Calverton, V[ictor] F[rancis] [formerly George Goetz] (1900–1940), critic and editor. He was the author of a number of books that interpreted American literature, history, and culture from a Marxist and sociological point of view. Among these are *The Newer Spirit* (1925), *Sex Expression in Literature* (1926), *The Bankruptcy of Marriage* (1928), *The New Grounds of Criticism* (1930), *American Literature at the Crossroads* (1931), *For Revolution* (1932), *The Passing of the Gods* (1934), *The Making of America* (1938), and *The Awakening of America* (1939). He was also the author of a history of early utopian experiments in America, *Where Angels Dared to Tread* (1941); a collection of short stories, *Three Strange Lovers* (1929); and a novel, *The Man Inside* (1935).

Cambridge History of American Literature, The (4 v. 1917, 1918, 1921), edited by William Peterfield Trent, JOHN ERSKINE, STUART P. SHERMAN, and CARL VAN DOREN. This scholarly account of the progress of American literature is on a larger scale than any previous history and the first composed with the collaboration of scholars from all parts of the United States and Canada. It provides an extensive bibliography and aims to furnish "a survey of the life of the American people as expressed in their writings rather than a history of *belles-lettres* alone."

Campbell, Bartley (1843–1888), journalist, playwright, producer. Campbell was born in Pittsburgh, self-educated, and became a newspaperman and drama critic in Pittsburgh before producing his first play, *Through Fire*, in 1871. Later he wrote and produced melodramas and comedies in Philadelphia, Boston, New York, Chicago, and San Francisco, where he met and became a friend of Mark Twain's. At the height of his success, in the early 1880s, he had as many as six road companies producing his plays across the United States, and some were performed in England, Scotland, and on the continent. Although some critics considered him America's leading dramatist, only a few of his many plays have been preserved. AMERICA'S LOST PLAYS prints texts of *The Virginian* (1874), a post–Civil War domestic drama once popular in the South; *My Partner* (1879), generally judged his best, modeled in part on Bret Harte's California tales and depicting a woman who survives her sins to marry happily; *The Galley Slave* (1879), set in Italy and France; *Fairfax* (1879), of slaves and masters in pre–Civil War Louisiana and Florida; and *The White Slaves* (1882). The last mentioned, his most popular

work, was derived from Dion Boucicault's THE OCTOROON. It was playing somewhere in the United States, virtually continuously, from 1882 to 1918.

Campbell, John (1653–1728), newspaperman. A Scottish emigrant to Massachusetts in about 1695, Campbell founded the BOSTON NEWS-LETTER.

Campbell, John Charles (1867–1919), educator. Campbell taught in Southern mountain schools for many years and wrote *The Southern Highlander and His Homeland* (1921). His wife, Olive (Dame Campbell), born in 1822, founded with Margaret Butler the John C. Campbell Folk School in Brasstown, North Carolina, modeled after the Danish Folk Schools, to supplement the public education of young adults with a "community living" curriculum that includes recreational, cultural, economic, and educational features. With Cecil Sharp, she compiled *English Folk Songs from the Southern Appalachians* (1928).

Campbell, Joseph (1904–1987), mythologist. Born in New York City, Campbell made extensive studies in Europe and America in literature, mythology, philology, and art history. He became a member of the literature department of Sarah Lawrence College in 1934, teaching a course in comparative mythology. Campbell did not begin publishing until *Where the Two Come to Their Father: A Navaho War Ceremonial* (1934, with J. King and M. Oakes). The next year saw the appearance of *A Skeleton Key to Finnegans Wake*, written with Henry Morton Robinson. The book remains a helpful adjunct to Joyce's cryptic masterpiece. Throughout his studies, his books, and his several editions of foreign works, Campbell consistently finds the same mythological archetypes. In *The Hero With a Thousand Faces* (1949) he describes a single story, or monomyth, which he believes all myths recapitulate in whole or in part. Using Freudian and Jungian concepts along with his own erudition, Campbell retells myths of many times from many parts of the world—Indian, Greek, Christian, Eskimo, Tibetan, Chinese, Japanese, Australian—and shows that each contains the story of a hero's departure, initiation, and return. The book has importance in anthropology, mythology, and literary criticism. His four-volume study *Mask of God* was published in 1969. Among his other books are *Grimm's Fairy Tales: Folkloristic Commentary* (1944); *The Portable Arabian Nights* (1952); *Mask of God*: V. I, *Primitive Mythology* (1959); V. II, *Oriental Mythology* (1962); V. III, *Occidental Mythology* (1964); V. IV, *Creative Mythology* (1968); *The Flight of the Wild Gander* (1969); *The Portable Jung* (1971); *Myths to Live By* (1972); and *The Mythic Image* (1974).

Campbell, Thomas. Author of GERTRUDE OF WYOMING.

Campbell, Walter Stanley ["Stanley Vestal"] (1887–1957), teacher, biographer, historian, poet. Born in Kansas, Campbell under his pen name wrote many books dealing with the Old West, among them *Fandango, Ballads of the Old West* (1927), *Kit Carson* (1928), *Sitting Bull* (1932), *Mountain Men* (1937), *Big-Foot Wallace* (1942), *The Missouri* (1945), *Jim Bridger* (1946), *War Path and Council Fire* (1948), *Dodge City* (1952), and *Joe Meek* (1952). Under his own name he edited documents and books relating to Indians and explorations and compiled *The Book Lover's Southwest: A Guide to Good Reading* (1955).

Campbell, [William] Wilfred (1861–1918), poet, novelist. Born in Ontario, Campbell was educated at Wycliffe College, the University of Toronto, and the Episcopal Divinity School at Cambridge, Massachusetts. During his residence there he was encouraged in his poetical career by Oliver Wendell Holmes. He was ordained in 1885 and assigned the parish of West Claremont, Massachusetts, but resigned from his church offices in 1891, feeling that their formality and dogmas restricted him. He returned to Canada and held a Civil Service position in Ottawa.

Campbell is associated with a school of poets known as The Group of the Sixties, so-called because the birth dates of each of the poets fell close to the year 1860. Among others of this group were Archibald Lampman, Duncan Campbell Scott, Archdeacon Frederick George Scott, and Bliss Carman. Campbell's poetry began to receive attention during the 1880s. In addition to contributions to periodicals, he wrote the following books of poems: *Snowflakes and Sunbeams* (1888), *Lake Lyrics* (1889), *The Dread Voyage and Other Poems* (1893), *Mordred and Hildebrand* (1895), and *Beyond the Hills of Dream* (1899). Collections of Campbell's poems include *Poems of Wilfred Campbell* (1905), *Poetical Tragedies* (1908), *Sagas of Vaster Britain* (1914), and *Poetical Works of Wilfred Campbell* (1922). Campbell edited two anthologies, *Poems of Loyalty* (1913) and *The Oxford Book of Canadian Verse* (1914).

Campbell is also noted for his historical novels, especially *Ian of the Orcades* (1906), a Scottish romance; and *A Beautiful Rebel* (1909), a novel of the War of 1812. His historical and descriptive sketches of Canada include *The Beauty, History, Romance and Mystery of the Canadian Lake Region* (1910) and the first volume of *The Scotsman in Canada* (1912).

Campbell, William Edward March. See WILLIAM MARCH.

Canadian Literature in English: Before 1960. The name *Canada* originally signified the French colony along the St. Lawrence River. After General Wolfe took Quebec for the British in 1759, it stood for the same area and people, but under British rule. In 1791 Upper Canada (now Ontario) was separated from Lower Canada (now Quebec). In 1867 the British North America Act established Canada as a confederation of four provinces north of the United States border; later these were joined by six others, so that the new nation stretched from sea to sea. *Canadian* as a historical term may thus include retrospectively a province like Nova Scotia, which had a proud and independent existence as a British colony early in the 18th century, and Newfoundland, which dates from the very beginning of Britain's colonial expansion. As a term applied to literary history of all periods, *Canadian* should include *la littérature canadienne*—CANADIAN LITERATURE IN FRENCH. This essay, however, will be limited to what has been written in English.

Canada is an environment for literary works produced by *sojourners* from the time of Jacques Cartier (about 1534) to the present day; by *settlers* mainly since the introduction of printing at Halifax in 1752, Quebec City in 1764, Montreal in 1776, and Niagara in 1792; and by the *native-born* since about 1800. Major writings of intellectual or artistic quality by the settlers or by the native-born are claimed for this country's literature, as are also those books by sojourners that have their principal reference here. In practice this formula arouses little controversy regarding claims for works written in early or in recent years, from the *Jesuit Relations* of the 17th century to the posthumous *Hear Us O Lord From Heaven Thy Dwelling Place* (1961) by MALCOLM LOWRY. It registers properly the depth and breadth of the Canadian cultural heritage—including the background of literature in the British Isles and France, the fruitful interaction of English and French literatures on the other side of the Atlantic and in Quebec, and the contribution made by the United States in colonial and later times.

The English, for example, ultimately appropriated the results of French exploration and discovery, but they had even earlier shared the French narratives, in the original or in translation, concerning voyagers and travelers like Jacques Cartier, Samuel de Champlain, Father Louis Hennepin, Baron de Lahontan, and the Jesuit P. F. X. Charlevoix. Knowledge about settlement in the American colonies and the associated Canadian areas was circulated abroad in the works of the New England Puritans, some of whose Loyalist descendants came to Nova Scotia and New Brunswick, and in historical-descriptive books like *The History of the Five Indian Nations of Canada* (London, 1750) by CADWALLADER COLDEN, a resident of New York State, the home of other Loyalists who fled to Upper Canada after the American War of Independence.

The dates given for the introduction of printing apply also to the beginnings of journalism—to the official gazettes of the various colonies and newspapers developed from these toward the end of the 18th century. Canadian-printed books lagged behind, appearing a generation or two later. But one important literary work, published in England, came out of the former French colony in the interval between Wolfe's conquest and the arrival of the Loyalists. It was *The History of Emily Montague* (1769) by FRANCES BROOKE, who lived in Quebec City with her husband, the chaplain of the garrison, in the mid-1760s. Her novel, in the epistolary fashion of Samuel Richardson, whom she had known in England, was devoted to a lively analysis of love as an "intellectual pleasure." It is notable for its wit, elegance, common sense, and a reflection of contemporary society, all nicely fitted into the romantic scenery and New World conditions of Quebec. The early date, 1769, leaves only CHARLOTTE LENNOX as a rival of Brooke for the title of first North American novelist.

The Loyalists—known in the United States as Tories—came in the 1780s to the Maritime Provinces and to the areas now known as Quebec and Ontario. They brought with them ready-made American culture on various social levels, the literary stratum in Nova Scotia and New Brunswick being represented chiefly by Tory satire and, in Upper Canada, by gazettes and newspapers reflecting internal politics. In the city of Quebec, where the Loyalist migration was not keenly felt, the

Gazette (established 1764) continued to record events for the official and military capital of British North America. Montreal, with its own *Gazette* (established in 1778), was the center for the fur trade and other business with the West and the South (that is, the United States). Canada's first distinctive North American period lasted until after the War of 1812 against the United States, when greatly increased British immigration, especially after 1830, gave rise to a new era.

The pattern of early publications may be discovered in the following representative facts. In John Lambert's *Travels Through Lower Canada, and The United States* (1810), half the space was given to Quebec City; histories of Canada were published by George Heriot (in England, 1804) and by the Loyalist William Smith (in Quebec, 1815); and the Earl of Dalhousie sponsored a Literary and Historical Society, founded in 1824. More appropriate to Montreal were remarkable accounts of the fur trade, SIR ALEXANDER MACKENZIE's *Voyages from Montreal* (London and Edinburgh, 1801) and Alexander Henry, the Elder's *Travels and Adventures* (New York, 1809). A former employee of the North West Company in Montreal founded and edited a literary journal, *The Scribbler* (1821–27), soon to be followed by the *Canadian Magazine* (1823–25) and *The Canadian Review* (1824–26), edited by two Scots, David Chisholme and Dr. A. J. Christie. Poetical works were published by Margaret Blennerhasset, wife of the expatriate Irish-American HARMAN BLENNERHASSET (*The Widow of the Rock*, Montreal, 1824) and by the Canadian-born Levi Adams (*Jean Baptiste*, Montreal, 1825, and *Tales of Chivalry and Romance*, Edinburgh, 1826). Adam Hood Burwell of Colonel Thomas Talbot's settlement in Upper Canada published poems in the Montreal *Scribbler* in the early 1820s. British-born firebrands Robert Gourlay (1778–1863) and William Lyon Mackenzie (1795–1861) rocked Upper Canada by their political journalism after they arrived in 1817 and 1820 respectively.

With certain local differences, the pattern of literary activity was similar in the Maritime Provinces. In Halifax John Howe edited a *Nova Scotia Magazine* as early as 1789–91, a parallel to the *Quebec Magazine* in English and French (1792–94). John Howe's son, JOSEPH HOWE, later a Canadian statesman, conducted the *Nova Scotian* after 1828. In this newspaper, literary influences of Washington Irving and *Blackwood's Magazine* were discernible as a series of papers called "The Club" led to *The Clockmaker* (1836) of THOMAS CHANDLER HALIBURTON (1796–1865). When they were published in a series of books, these humorous essays about Sam Slick and the Squire made Haliburton internationally known and gave him a secure place in the development of American humor. Thomas McCulloch (1776–1843) deserves mention beside his better-known compatriot; the author of *Letters of Mephibosheth Stepsure* (1821–23) is now being hailed as "the founder of genuine Canadian humor." A New World poet named Oliver Goldsmith (1787–1861) published *The Rising Village* in London in 1825.

Howe, Haliburton, and Goldsmith were born in Nova Scotia. Their emergence in literature coincides with that of a native-born Upper Canadian, Major JOHN RICHARDSON, whose *War of 1812* is the principal record of that American-British-Canadian-Indian struggle along the borders of the yet undeveloped West. Richardson had fought beside Tecumseh and had been on the field of Moraviantown when the celebrated Shawnee died. His best novel, *Wacousta* (1832), was based on family love concerning Pontiac, dating back to the days of Major ROBERT ROGERS, known to Americans as the author of PONTEACH. Richardson ended a career that included residence in London, Paris, Spain, and the West Indies as an author of paperback novels in New York.

In the 1820s, partly because Upper Canada came to the attention of the British through publicity given to the American War of 1812, a wave of immigration began, chiefly from England, Ireland, and Scotland, and reached flood level after 1830. The proportion of Americans in the population dropped considerably as thousands of half-pay British officers, adventurous gentlemen, journalists, tradesmen, and poor people took up land near lakes Ontario, Erie, and Huron. Travel literature of the period was written by John Howison, E. A. Talbot, John Mactaggart, Sir George Head, Francis Hall, John McGregor, Thomas Magrath, Patrick Shirreff, Francis Marryat, Samuel Strickland, William Kingston, and others.

JOHN GALT (1779–1839), the Scottish novelist, acted as a superintendent of the Canada Company (a colonization project), and published two books of North American fiction, *Lawrie Todd* (1830) and *Bogle Corbet* (1831). His friend William "Tiger" Dunlop (1792–1848), a veteran of *Blackwood's* literary revels, came out to settle and wrote amusing variations on the themes of American campaigns and emigrant handbooks. Two sisters of Agnes Strickland (the biographer of queens of England), namely CATHERINE PARR TRAILL (1802–1899) and SUSANNA MOODIE (1803–1885), refined travel and emigrant literature in *The Backwoods of Canada* (1836) and *Roughing It in the Bush* (1852), respectively. The gentility of these ladies, fostered in their English home, matched the American gentility, probably also English in inspiration, found in the mid-century ladies' magazines published in the United States. Their writings helped sustain the reputation of *The Literary Garland* (1838–51), a Montreal journal edited at first by John Gibson and later by E. L. Cushing and Harriet V. Cheney. They were both daughters of HANNAH FOSTER, author of one of the earliest novels in the United States, THE COQUETTE (1797). The lyrics of CHARLES SANGSTER (1822–1893), published in 1856 and 1860, and an anthology, *Selections from Canadian Poets*, edited by Edward Hartley Dewart in 1864, stand as examples of the verse of a period when the feminine and social aspects of colonialism appeared to prevail.

CHARLES HEAVYSEGE (1816–1876), a Montreal cabinetmaker who produced belated Shakespearean poetic dramas, and ALEXANDER MCLACHLAN (1820–1896), a voice from the farm, ignored or scorned the so-called cultural movement. Canadian interest in the country's history remained strong. The journalists were only half bookish; domestic politics was their chief concern, both before and after the rebellion of 1837–38 in the Canadas. Systematic exploration, farther and farther west, yielded scientific papers by geologists such as Sir John

William Dawson (a Nova Scotian), Sir William Logan, and Henry Youle Hind. The influence of Britain on its emigrant sons and daughters was generally beneficent and nourishing while it was tempered by distance, as the American influence was also tempered by great Canadian distrust of the political intentions of the United States. In spite of this, Canadians kept on borrowing from American culture, but even those of non-British origin, borrowed like Britons. Such was the "spirit of Canada" as it was exhibited by THOMAS D'ARCY MCGEE (1825–1868), an exile from Erin who became a Father of Canadian Confederation, teaching Canadians what he had learned in the Young Ireland movement of the 1840s—how to employ ballads, orations, and histories in the making of a nation.

After four provinces joined in a dominion in 1867, the Canadian spirit was exhibited chiefly in a vigorous thrust westward, described, for example, in the works of CHARLES MAIR (1838–1927), and symbolized by the Riel uprisings of 1870 and 1885, as well as by completion of the first Canadian transcontinental railway, the Canadian Pacific, in 1885. ISABELLA VALANCY CRAWFORD (1850–1887) wrote strong, imaginative poems about pioneers, city folk, and cowboys. PAULINE JOHNSON (1861–1913), an Ontario Indian girl who recited her poems everywhere, eventually resided on the Pacific Coast. ROBERT W. SERVICE (1876–1958), author of *Songs of a Sourdough* (1907), went far north to create world-famous images of the Yukon, where there was gold before the old Canadian dream of a Northwest Passage was realized. Sir GILBERT PARKER (1862–1932), whose novels ranged over the Empire, conceived his Canadian prose tales—*Pierre and His People* (1892), for example—with all the poetry that was in him. Fiction of the West seemed romantic even when it was close to accurate reporting. CHARLES W. GORDON—better known as Ralph Connor—(1860–1937) moved from nostalgia for Glengarry, a county in Ontario, to excitement about the Great West and his hopes for strong religious adventure. Millions of people read his books, as they did those of his American contemporary, JAMES OLIVER CURWOOD.

Such literature was not calculated to give the reading world a proper impression of growing villages, towns, cities, and industrial centers in the East. Until the First World War, indeed, the agricultural nature of the home bases for expansion is apparent. Small-town piety provided material for much popular fiction and verse, until the acme was reached in the gentle burlesque of *Sunshine Sketches of a Little Town* (1912), by STEPHEN LEACOCK (1869–1944). This brilliant economics professor from McGill spent his writing career in a vast number of similar efforts to entertain by sane displays of incongruity—the typically Canadian substitute for, and equivalent of, a muckraking school (see MUCKRAKING LITERATURE). The rural life of Quebec was sentimentally and amusingly interpreted in the verses of WILLIAM HENRY DRUMMOND (1854–1907), the "habitant poet" (see HABITANT). Domestic fiction of high quality was provided for the young in two notable and popular works: *Beautiful Joe: The Autobiography of a Dog* (1894), by Marshall Saunders (1861–1947), a native of

Nova Scotia, and ANNE OF GREEN GABLES (1908), by L. M. MONTGOMERY (1877–1942), who was born in Prince Edward Island. The perennial interest in history of the Old Regime in Quebec brought forth THE GOLDEN DOG (1877), by WILLIAM KIRBY (1817–1906) of Niagara, a book long regarded as Canada's principal contribution to historical romance.

Recalling the small town can also serve to explain why regionalism was strong in the East, and also why it was not stronger, that is to say, why some writers cultivated literature close to home and others simply had to seek opportunities elsewhere. A young woman from Brantford, Ontario, could become a journalist, travel around the world, and pay her way by writing articles, not to speak of marrying an Englishman in India. This was true of Sara Jeanette Duncan (Mrs. Everard Cotes, 1862–1922), author of *The Imperialist* (1904) and many other novels. The United States also, in the 1890s, provided richer financial returns for periodical verse and prose than Canadians had known before or have known since. Sir CHARLES G. D. ROBERTS (1860–1943), a native of New Brunswick, gave up school and college teaching to pursue writing in the United States and Britain, certainly outside of Canada, from 1896 to 1925. Although Roberts was sensitive to many fashions in these years, he wrote his most memorable poems on themes suggested by his New Brunswick home and the Nova Scotian land of Evangeline. His meticulously accurate, poetic short stories of animal life are noteworthy literary adaptations of popular ideas about evolution. BLISS CARMAN (1861–1929), his cousin, lived in the United States from 1890 to 1929; his sensitivity made him an unusually interesting poet of the post-Emersonian-Victorian period, which led not so much to the Georgians as to the Montreal School of the late 1920s and thereafter. He was most popular for *Low Tide on Grand Pré* (1893) and for *Songs from Vagabondia* (published jointly with Richard Hovey, 1894), written while his mythology of Mother Earth was taking a distinctively Canadian turn.

In this respect he was joined by one of the stay-at-home poets, WILFRED CAMPBELL (1862–1918), whose imperialist "Laureate poems" fade badly in comparison with his works built on primitive religion, nature myths, and the spell of the Lake Huron–Georgian Bay region. Campbell was soon drawn to the civil service at Ottawa and literary companionship with ARCHIBALD LAMPMAN (1861–1899) and DUNCAN CAMPBELL SCOTT (1862–1947). Lampman wrote of the woods and fields of Ontario, while Scott won from the wilderness and the Indian people a poetic imagery happily blending man and nature. They belonged in their own way to the generation in which RICHARD MAURICE BUCKE (1837–1902) of London, Ontario, could detect the prophet in Walt Whitman and make a religion of cosmic consciousness.

MARJORIE PICKTHALL (1883–1922), English-Canadian in origin but Celtic in imagination and craftsmanship, won admirers during and after the First World War for her devotion to beauty in its richest aspects. WILSON MACDONALD (1880–1967) displayed a gift for the "lyric cry" and offered "flagons of beauty" to a bitter postwar era. JOHN MCCRAE (1872–1918), a Canadian doctor, wrote "In Flanders' Fields," the most frequently mentioned poem about World War I, in which he perished.

A major new poetic voice was that of E. J. PRATT (1882–1964), a rugged and amiable Newfoundlander. With a fine sweeping style, great love of words, delight in people and things, and command of allegory, Pratt used the powers of sea and majestic land to acknowledge the savagery and honor the compassion of men. His most characteristic narratives are *The Witches' Brew* (1925), *The Roosevelt and the Antinoe* (1930), *The Titanic* (1935), *Brébeuf and His Brethren* (1940), and *Towards the Last Spike* (1952), concerned, respectively, with prohibition of liquor, a rescue at sea, the shipwreck of a great liner, the Jesuit martyrs of Fort Ste. Marie, and construction of Canada's first transcontinental railway. With Pratt, poetry in Canada turned academic, but he did not lose the common touch.

A. J. M. Smith and soon A. M. KLEIN were more explicit than Pratt in their attack on problems of economic depression and European fascism, and they were ready in the 1920s to go along with their young contemporaries in England and America who were beneficiaries of the symbolists, the imagists, Frazer's *The Golden Bough*, Donne, Yeats, Edith Sitwell, and T. S. ELIOT. These McGill writers brought Canadian poetry into an academic and cosmopolitan phase, nourished by literary criticism in the universities and by international movements. Scott was the most persistent advocate of social reform, but he wrote with a mature sense of humor and a desire to retain the best things, like art, in the planned amelioration of all men's lives. DOROTHY LIVESAY swung far to the left before she mingled her hopes for social reconstruction with more personal views of human needs. A. M. Klein, trained in Jewish lore, was absorbed in anger about Nazi horrors and in zeal for the building of a new Israel. His studies of Joyce and his experimentation with striking language mark his Montreal poems as well as the modern pentateuch and the psalms for the Jewish people found in his highly original book, *The Second Scroll* (1951). A. J. M. Smith, leader of the group in the early years, was always more moderate with regard to special causes, except the cause of pure poetry. In *News of the Phoenix* (1943) and *A Sort of Ecstasy* (1954) his purpose is plainly spiritual, and his meanings reside in subtly contrived forms.

The response of the intellectuals to the depression years of the 1930s may be seen also in EARLE BIRNEY's *Down the Long Table* (1955), and in HUGH MACLENNAN's *The Watch That Ends the Night* (1959). FREDERICK PHILIP GROVE (1879–1948) recorded the plight of the prairie farmers and his own struggle for adjustment. The titles of his novels are unusually revealing: *A Search for America* (1927), *Our Daily Bread* (1928), *Fruits of the Earth* (1933), and *In Search of Myself* (1946), a fictional autobiography. Grove always wrote in a mood of high seriousness and with a desire to transcend naturalism. His work is uneven, and his narratives fall short of his excellent essays in *Over Prairie Trails* (1922) and *The Turn of the Year* (1923). The troubles of industry in Ontario, where he later made his home, moved him to write an ambitious but unwieldy novel, *The Master of the Mill* (1944).

JALNA (1927) by MAZO DE LA ROCHE (1879–1961) is delightfully different. The author shows passionate concern for her characters, although the setting seems to most Canadians a kind of inspired contrivance. Her Jalna world could exist—and has indeed existed—near Toronto and Hamilton, unknown to all except a special class of gentlemen farmers until she described it in her immensely popular novels.

The historical romance proceeded along lines laid down by Kirby and his contemporaries, but with evidences of improving craftsmanship and stronger realism. *The Viking Heart* (1923) of Laura Goodman Salverson (1890–1970) and the prairie novels of FREDERICK NIVEN (1878–1944) are examples from the West, as *His Majesty's Yankees* (1942) and *Pride's Fancy* (1946) by THOMAS H. RADDALL (1903–1994) are from the East. THOMAS B. COSTAIN (1885–1965), a United States author, has devoted himself to historical works, such as *High Towers* (1949) and *Son of a Hundred Kings* (1957), set in Canada, the land of his birth. But novels more strictly realistic in purpose, especially those of MORLEY CALLAGHAN (1903–1990) and Hugh MacLennan (1907–1990), have won a popular as well as a critical audience. After meeting Hemingway in Toronto in the early 1920s, Callaghan went abroad to become acquainted with brilliant expatriate American writers in Paris and brought home an understanding of the aims and techniques of REALISM as it was practiced between the great wars. Callaghan's individuality in tone and style won widespread acclaim. His short stories were among the best of his time, and his many novels include *Such Is My Beloved* (1934), *The Loved and the Lost* (1951), and *The Many Colored Coat* (1960). Callaghan shuns the spectacular as well as the doctrinaire in social theory and avoids revelation of character as a kind of extension of environment. He plays on personal relationships that become symbolic by unemphatic suggestion, and ironical because irony is built into human affairs.

MacLennan tries to cope with life in a broader way. A Cape Breton man with a strong conscience, he has an affinity for the problem novel. *Barometer Rising* (1941), set in Halifax at the time of the great 1917 explosion, shows him at his best in style and structure. He portrayed in *Two Solitudes* (1945) the social and personal dilemmas of French and English in Quebec. *The Precipice* (1948) and *Each Man's Son* (1951) were followed by a great popular success, *The Watch That Ends the Night* (1959), the story of three people who come through depression and war, still face to face with life and death. MacLennan writes competently, at times eloquently, with genuine narrative skill, while he falters before self-imposed lines of inquiry that seem to call for indirection of expression. In *The Village of Souls* (1933), *God's Sparrows* (1937), *Day of Wrath* (1945), and *Mr. Ames Against Time* (1949), PHILIP CHILD (1898–1978) shows an inclination to employ parable and psychological study but, no less than MacLennan, a conscious desire to regulate the reader's ideas about good and evil.

Both these authors may have helped to prepare the way for the recent immigrant and racial novels that concentrate on the new Canadians who have poured into Canada since Hitler began to shake Europe. Some examples are *The Rich Man*

(1948), by Henry Kreisel (1922–1991); *The Sacrifice* (1956), by Adele Wiseman (1928–1992); *Under the Ribs of Death* (1957), by John Marlyn (1912–　); and, among other novels by MORDECAI RICHLER (1931–2001), *Son of a Smaller Hero* (1955) and *The Apprenticeship of Duddy Kravitz* (1959). An immigrant in the Irish tradition is the central figure in *The Luck of Ginger Coffey* (1960) by BRIAN MOORE (1921–　), himself a newcomer from Ireland who had previously published *Judith Hearne* (1955) and *The Feast of Lupercal* (1957). Any resemblance to MacLennan is accidental if one moves from Moore's problem novels into those of the apprenticeship kind. DAVID WALKER (1911–　) became widely known for a half-dozen novels, especially for the Highland story *Geordie* (1950) and *Where the High Winds Blow* (1960), set in the Canadian north.

Realism of an intense psychological kind is successfully handled in *As for Me and My House* (1941), by Sinclair Ross (1908–1996), his study of a man and wife in a prairie setting that shatters both of them. There is also realism of the all-seeing eye. ROBERTSON DAVIES (1913–1995), essayist, dramatist, and novelist, is one of the chief exponents. His *Diary of Samuel Marchbanks* (1947) and other books of essays urbanely expose to ridicule a wide range of his neighbors' cultural pretensions. Davies shows no desire to be a spiritual guide; he enjoys exploding firecrackers. The fun continues in his Salterton novels, *Tempest Tost* (1951) and *Leaven of Malice* (1953). Many of the plays that make him a leading dramatist carry on this salutary battle of sophistication with provincialism. ETHEL WILSON (1888–1980) wrote a book entitled *The Innocent Traveller* (1949), but it is generally conceded that her own innocence is related to the deep experience informing works such as *Swamp Angel* (1954). RODERICK HAIG-BROWN (1908–1976), a nature essayist of the West Coast, composed masterworks of sporting literature. And, along the same coast, on the Queen Charlotte Islands, EMILY CARR (1891–1945), a strong individualist among Canadian painters, repeated her totem-pole art in the superb prose sketches of *Klee Wyck* (1941) and *The Book of Small* (1942).

Not far from these authors, in a suburb of Vancouver, is where Malcolm Lowry lived during his most productive period, 1939–1954. The Canadian background is important to the short stories of *Hear Us O Lord From Heaven Thy Dwelling Place* (1961). In *Under the Volcano* (1947), a major modernistic novel, he employed symbols derived from visits to Mexico to describe the last days of an alcoholic. Lowry's level of linguistic brilliance is absent from other Canadian novels of the time, but *The Mountain and the Valley* (1952) by ERNEST BUCKLER (1908–1984) displays considerable power over symbols and imagery, and a strange richness of suggestion pervades *The Double Hook* (1959), by SHEILA WATSON.

Poets and critics emerging from World War II to 1960 were found chiefly in the cities, in or near universities. Two prominent in Vancouver were GEORGE WOODCOCK (1912–1995), travel writer, critic, and editor of the journal *Canadian Literature* from 1959 to 1977; and EARLE BIRNEY (1904–1995). Birney's desire to experiment became evident in this period in his unusual poetic diction; in his tour de force of good-natured satire about Van-

couver, *Trial of a City* (1952); and in a picaresque war story, *Turvey* (1949). In Edmonton appeared ELI MANDEL (1922–1992), whose *Fuseli Poems* were published in 1960. London, Ontario fostered the poetry of JAMES REANEY (1926–　), whose *The Red Heart* (1949) and *A Suit of Nettles* (1958) established him as a leading myth-maker. The group to which Reaney and Mandel belong grew out of critical movements at the University of Toronto, particularly at Victoria College, where NORTHROP FRYE (1912–1991), the internationally acclaimed author of *Fearful Symmetry* (1947), a study of Blake, and *Anatomy of Criticism* (1957), exerted a profound influence on Canadian intellectuals. Others who displayed a similar interest in myth, fantasy, and song are MARGARET AVISON (1918–　), PHYLLIS WEBB (1927–　), and DARYL HINE (1936–　).

Among other poets, CHARLES BRUCE (1906–　) is generally identified with the Maritime Provinces. RAYMOND SOUSTER (1921–　) attracted notice with several books, including *Go to Sleep World* (1947), writing often about Toronto. In the 1940s PATRICK ANDERSON (1915–1979) led the short-lived *Preview* (1942) movement, which brought into prominence PATRICIA K. PAGE (1916–　); her ironic social studies in vivid psychological imagery were to be found in *As Ten, As Twenty* (1946) and *The Metal and the Flower* (1954). After her came Miriam Waddington (1917–　) and LOUIS DUDEK (1918–　). More important is IRVING LAYTON (1912–　), whose volumes in the period include *The Bull Calf and Other Poems* (1956), *Red Carpet for the Sun* (1959), and *The Swinging Flesh* (1961). Layton boasts about his lust for life; the learning and skill with which he can release and control this zest make him a major Canadian poet. Among other poets less celebrated are DOUGLAS LEPAN (1914–　), who dealt with the war in Italy in *The Wounded Prince* (1949) and *The Net and the Sword* (1953); GEORGE JOHNSTON (1913–　), who wrote the casual, witty poems of *The Cruising Auk* (1959); RALPH GUSTAFSON (1909–1995); Fred Cogswell (1917–　); and ELIZABETH BREWSTER (1922–　).

CARL F. KLINCK/G.P.

Canadian Literature in English: Since 1960.

A number of factors combined in the late 1950s and 1960s to encourage a flowering of Canadian literature. These included establishment of the Canada Council in 1957, initiating a system of state support for the arts; launching of McClelland and Stewart's New Canadian Library in the same year, guaranteeing the availability of significant texts in cheap format; founding of *Canadian Literature* in 1959, providing a forum for advanced literary-critical discussion; proliferation of universities in the 1960s; technological developments that encouraged the founding of small presses and little magazines; and above all, perhaps, the wave of nationalism that centered on the centenary celebrations of 1967. Fortunately, a generation of remarkably gifted writers succeeded in taking advantage of these developments.

In poetry, the importance of an earlier generation of verse writers became recognized, and publication of their work in collected editions revealed both the quantity and quality of their achievements. E. J. Pratt's edition appeared in 1958 (augmented in 1989), followed by A. J. M. Smith's in 1967, Irving Layton's in a series between 1971 and 1992, Louis Dudek's in 1971, Dorothy Livesay and James Reaney's in 1972, A. M. Klein's in 1974, Earle Birney's in 1975, the first volume of Raymond Souster's in 1980, F. R. Scott's in 1981, and a generous P. K. Page selected edition in 1985.

The heady atmosphere of the late 1960s encouraged an extraordinary burst of poetic activity. Much of this was ephemeral, but it also produced a remarkable number of continuing poets, only some of whom can be mentioned here. ALFRED PURDY (1918–2000), who came to prominence in the early 1960s, evolved a garrulous, colloquial, ruminative kind of verse in which the cadence of a contemporary Canadian speaking voice could express itself on all subjects from the philosophical to the sexual, from the national and international to the intimately personal. His *Collected Poems* appeared in 1986 and a more complete *Beyond Remembering: The Collected Poems of Al Purdy* in 2000. At another extreme, MARGARET ATWOOD (1939–   ), from *The Circle Game* (1966) onward, has perfected a cool, laconic, acerbic, tight-lipped, deadpan poetry in which meaning reveals itself as much between the lines as within them. LEONARD COHEN (1934–   ) caught the restless mood of the sixties with his adaptation of a late Romantic consciousness to the pop world of guitars and protest, while MICHAEL ONDAATJE (1943–   ) has drawn on the aesthetics of film and the mass media to create in poetic form a disturbing, multifaceted picture of the combination of order and disorder, violence and tenderness, that haunts contemporary experience. On the West Coast, the *Tish* poets have been especially interested in technical experimentation and have tried to break away from the Europe-derived traditions supposedly current in eastern Canada. Ironically, however, the most substantial achievement of the group to date has been GEORGE BOWERING's *Kerrsdale Elegies* (1984), an impressive translation/appropriation of Rilke's Duino poems.

In fiction, the most conspicuous developments have been the prominent achievement of women writers and the remarkable revival and extension of the short-story form. MAVIS GALLANT (1922–   ) and ALICE MUNRO (1931–   ) qualify in both categories. Gallant has been a regular contributor to *The New Yorker* since the 1950s and has lived most of her life in Europe. Her stories are not conspicuously Canadian, since she writes of expatriates and displaced persons of varied origins, but her sharp but sympathetic analyses of the traumas and challenges of post–World War II Europe benefit from a North American detachment. The confidence, intelligence, and exquisite fictional craft of her stories are unparalleled. Munro, by contrast, began by concentrating on stories about the small towns of southwestern Ontario in which she grew up. They frequently portray half-amusing, half-painful experiences in the growth from girlhood to womanhood—*Lives of Girls and Women* (1971) is an example—though in recent years she has branched out to treat adult experience and explore the perilous but promising gray areas between fiction and nonfiction, between truths and inventions.

MARGARET LAURENCE and MARGARET ATWOOD, though both writers of short stories, have concentrated on full-length fiction. Laurence began by writing of her years in Africa, but is best known for her series of novels set in the fictional prairie town of Manawaka and remarkable for their compassionate and perceptive presentation of women from restrictive origins who are feeling their way painfully toward a larger world. Atwood's novels range from the Gothic to the political and even to the farcical, but are united by an essentially satiric vision that, while equally critical of the old-fashioned and the excessively trendy, focuses on the frustrations and psychological pressures of modern urban living.

Of the male novelists, ROBERTSON DAVIES (1913–1995) inaugurated a new development with the publication of *Fifth Business* in 1970, and has since written two trilogies of novels combining psychological probing with generally good-humored irony and the discussion of erudite and often bizarre intellectual subjects. Undoubtedly Canada's foremost novelist of ideas, he is remarkable for the wit and elegance of his prose and his talent for combining the deft puncturing of sacred cows with a serious defense of traditional cultural values. MICHAEL ONDAATJE (1943–   ) won worldwide celebrity with *The English Patient* (1992), famously filmed. HUGH HOOD (1928–   ) is often credited with production of the first truly significant collection of Canadian short stories with *Flying a Red Kite* (1962) and has gone on to write short fiction and novels of distinction, including the beginnings of an ambitious twelve-novel series, *The New Age*, scheduled for completion at the turn of the century and designed to illustrate the development of eastern Canada in the 20th century.

Other fiction writers include RUDY WIEBE (1934–   ), who writes long, rugged, historically conscious novels about his own Mennonite people and the fortunes of Indian and Métis groups on the Canadian prairies; ROBERT KROETSCH (1927–   ), perhaps the most successful and articulate champion of postmodernism in Canadian fiction (and poetry); MORDECAI RICHLER (1931–2001), with his lively and iconoclastic presentations of Jewish experience; TIMOTHY FINDLAY (1930–   ), whose work conveys an almost paranoiac distaste for and fascination with the violence and politicizing of contemporary life; and JACK HODGINS (1938–   ), whose refreshingly vigorous and zany fiction about Vancouver Island combines humor and seriousness with amazing verve and zest.

While poetry and fiction have enjoyed an extraordinary advance since 1960, Canadian drama has been more noticeable for activity than for lasting achievement. Many communities built theaters and established drama companies during the expansive and nationalistic mood of the sixties, and there has certainly been an outburst of dramatic writing compared with the modest attempts of the past. Canadian dramatists have not yet been able, however, to break through to international recognition. The most substantial achievements have been a series of plays by David French (1939–   ) that trace the fortunes of a Newfoundland family that moves to Toronto, the poet JAMES REANEY's *Donnellys* trilogy about a murder feud in

19th-century Ontario, and the varied dramas of Michael Cook (1933–   ) that concentrate on Newfoundland or historical subjects. Other frequently performed plays include *The Ecstasy of Rita Joe* by GEORGE RYGA (1932–1987), *Blood Relations* by Sharon Pollock (1936–   ), *Billy Bishop Goes to War* by John Gray (1946–   ), and *Creeps* by David Freeman (1947–   ). These plays indicate the breadth of contemporary Canadian theatrical activity and are building a foundation, one hopes, for a more substantial dramatic future.

The major sources of information on Canadian literature are Carl F. Klinck, ed. *Literary History of Canada* (1965, 2nd ed. 3 v. 1976); Eugene Benson and William Toye, eds. *The Oxford Companion to Canadian Literature*, 2nd ed. (1997); David Stouck, *Major Canadian Authors: A Critical Introduction* (1984); W. J. Keith, *Canadian Literature in English* (1985); and W. H. New, *A History of Canadian Literature* (1989).

W. J. KEITH/GP

Canadian Literature in French: Before 1960

French-Canadian literature dates back to the middle of the 19th century. The first major literary achievement by a French-Canadian author was FRANÇOIS-XAVIER GARNEAU's *Histoire du Canada*, a four-volume survey of the first 300 years of Canada's history. The first volume came out in 1845 and the series was completed in 1852. In 1848 the first Canadian government responsible to the elected assembly was established. Both events, the literary and the political, were the culmination of a long development from colonial dependency to nationhood, and both marked the end of an era and the beginning of a new age. Garneau's work was hailed as the "national Bible" of the French-Canadians, and its influence, both literary and political, was considerable and lasting.

Some writing was done in New France, but the pioneer authors were all Frenchmen born and educated in France, and the significance of their work was more historical than literary. These early chronicles are among the main sources of Canada's early history, and while they are an important part of the nation's cultural heritage, they do not constitute a national literature. Achievement of this goal began to be realized in the second half of the 19th century. The most important of the early documents are the memoirs of Cartier and Champlain; the historical narratives of Lescarbot, Sagard, Leclercq, La Potherie, Hennepin, Charlevoix, and Lahontan; the correspondence and spiritual writings of Marie de l'Incarnation; and the *Relations des Jésuites*. There was also published in Paris in 1664 the *Histoire naturelle et véritable des moeurs et productions de la Nouvelle-France* by Pierre Boucher. The first work by a Canadian-born author was the *Annales de l'Hôtel-Dieu de Montréal* by the nun Marie Morin (1649–1717). Thus, when New France fell under British rule in 1763, there was no French-Canadian literature worthy of the name.

Nor was this literature produced in the first seventy-five years that followed the British conquest. Introduction of printing in 1764 led to publication of newspapers, magazines, pamphlets, and a few books, but most of this early production could boast little, if any, literary merit. The most influential literary and political newspaper of the early 19th century was *Le Canadien*, the organ of the French-Canadian patriots fighting for survival of the French-speaking majority that was ruled and exploited by a small group of British colonists.

The first book of verse came out in 1830, *Epîtres, satires, chansons et autres pièces de vers* by Michel Bibaud. The first novel was *L'Influence d'un livre* by Philippe Aubert de Gaspé, Jr., published in 1837, and the first play was Antoine Gérin-Lajoie's *Le Jeune Latour* (1844). Among the books published at that time were such novels as *Les Fiancés de 1812* by Joseph Doutre, and *Charles Guérin* by Pierre Chauveau; historical books such as Michel Bibaud's *Histoire du Canada* in three volumes; and books of law, agriculture, medicine, and religion.

Most of the best prose and verse published in newspapers and magazines in the first half of the 19th century was collected by James Huston in a four-volume anthology entitled *Répertoire national* (1848–1850). All this is of limited literary value. When Lord Durham wrote that the French-Canadians had "no literature and no history," he was right as far as literature went, but wrong with respect to history—as Garneau immediately set out to demonstrate. In revealing the basic characters and aspirations of the French-Canadian people as he recorded their past history, Garneau provided his contemporaries with a major reference book from which writers could draw their subjects and inspiration.

The development of a native literature reflected the growth of the French-Canadian community. The foundation of colleges, libraries, literary clubs, bookstores, and magazines contributed to improvement in the literary quality of the production, and the first books still readable today appeared between 1845 and 1866. Most writers of the first generation quite naturally were men of action, militant writers rather than artists. Most of the literature of the time was historical, sociological, political, and religious, and it was provincial in scope, light in substance, and deficient in technique. Of local interest were the works of those who wrote mainly to assist the French-Canadians in their struggle for survival. Such are the recorded speeches of public men like Papineau, La Fontaine, Morin, and Cartier; and the writings of religious leaders such as Louis-François Laflèche, as well as of the better journalists, Jean-Charles Taché and Etienne Parent.

Quebec City was then the metropolis of Lower Canada, and most writers of the first generation lived and worked in this capital city of the colony. There was established in 1852 the first Canadian university in which French was the language of instruction. Also established in Quebec City were the first newspapers, magazines, and bookstores. There Garneau wrote his *Histoire du Canada*, and there lived most of the other historical writers of the time, including Jean-Baptiste Antoine Ferland, whose *Cours d'historie du Canada* remains a basic reference book for the history of New France; and Henri-Raymond Casgrain, author of many monographs, including biographies of Marie de l'Incarnation, Montcalm, Lévis, and others.

The works of many versifiers are included in Huston's *Répertoire national*, such as those of the historian Garneau, of Joseph Lenoir, and of Louis-Joseph Fiset, but the first poet worthy of the name was Octave Crémazie, whose inspiration was mainly historical and patriotic and whose influence was much greater than his literary talent justified. Poetry remained mainly historical in inspiration and romantic in style for some forty years. The major poet of the time was LOUIS-HONORÉ FRÉCHETTE, whose most important work was his *Légende d'un peuple*, a series of epics inspired by the leading men and main events of French Canada's history. Other poets of the first generation were Pamphyle Lemay, the poet of rural life; William Chapman, Fréchette's rival in oratorical developments; and Alfred Garneau, who opened a new era in turning his back on historical subjects to express the intimate feelings of his soul.

Similarly, most early Canadian novels were historical. The best work of fiction of that period was *Les Anciens Canadiens* by PHILIPPE AUBERT DE GASPÉ, a chronicle of the life of the *seigneur* and *habitant* under the old regime. Gaspé also wrote very interesting *Mémoires*; he is, with Garneau, the best prose writer of his generation. The most popular historical novels of the time were *Une de perdue, deux de trouvées* by Georges Boucher de Boucherville; *Jacques et Marie* by Napoléon Bourassa; and those of Joseph Marmette and Laure Conan. *Angéline de Montbrun* by Conan was the first psychological novel to be published in Canada. Short stories, tales, and legends were also written at the time, and the best collections of such works of fiction were *Forestiers et voyageurs* by Joseph-Charles Taché, and those of Casgrain, Faucher de Saint-Maurice, and Louis Fréchette.

Worthy of mention also are such journalists as Hector Fabre, Napoléon Legendre and, foremost, Arthur Buies; and such orators as Wilfrid Laurier and Honoré Mercier. By the end of the 19th century, there had appeared a few books of verse, three or four novels, and as many collections of short stories, but most of the writing was still militant literature dedicated to the religious and ethnic survival of a small community separated from the rest of the continent by the language barrier.

At the turn of the century, new trends developed in French-Canadian letters. Without completely turning their backs on historical subjects, most writers began to look at the contemporary scene and to pay more attention to an inner life. Montreal became a more active literary center than Quebec City, and smaller centers began to contribute authors to the nation. The leading writers were poets, historians, or journalists; strangely enough, few novels were published during that period, and none of them is remarkable. The better works of fiction were collections of folksy tales and sketches such as Adjutor Rivard's *Chez nous*, Marie-Victorin's *Croquis laurentiens*, and Lionel Groulx's *Rapaillages*.

Poetry, on the other hand, flourished throughout the period. Fréchette, Lemay, and Chapman were still writing at the turn of the century, and historical subjects were still in fashion. The regional school grouped many poets, such as Blanche Lamontagne, the poetess of Gaspé, and rustic poets such as Jules Tremblay, Adolphe Poisson, Louis-Joseph Doucet, and Gonzalve Desaulniers. Nérée Beauchemin was the outstanding poet of the group, as demonstrated in *Floraisons matutinales* and *Patrie, intime*; Albert Ferland, the poet

of the Canadian forests, was the most original of the group. Traditions of the 19th century were thus maintained well into the 20th century, and the romantic school still had several adepts.

New trends, new themes, and new techniques were introduced, however, mainly by poets of the École littéraire de Montréal and by a few independent poets. Baudelaire's influence superseded that of Hugo, and Verlaine, Rollinat, Rodenbach, Régnier, and other French poets also had their Canadian disciples. Poetry became more personal than historical, more lyrical than narrative; the general evolution was from the outer world to the inner life. Romanticism still prevailed in the works of a few members of the École littéraire, such as in Charles Gill's epic *Le Cap Éternité* or in the sentimental poems of Albert Lozeau. Other poets, such as Jean Charbonneau and Alphonse Beauregard, were more attracted to philosophical themes, while Louis Dantin and Lucien Rainier in the main were religious poets. The most accomplished artist of that generation was ÉMILE NELLIGAN, who produced some of the best poems ever written in Canada before going out of his mind in his early twenties. Thanks to him and to Beauchemin, Lozeau, and Delahaye, by the time of World War I French-Canadian poetry had attained a standard never reached in the 19th century—it was more diversified in inspiration and more accomplished in craftsmanship than ever before.

The best prose throughout the period was written by men of action or by scholars. Journalists of the nationalist school had a deep influence on many intellectuals, and there appeared some gifted writers. The leader of the nationalist movement was Henri Bourassa, a sharp journalist and a great debater; he was supported by men like Olivar Asselin, Jules Fournier, and Paul-Émile Lamarche. Economists such as Errol Bouchette and Edmond de Nevers are worthy of mention here, and one of the best prose writers of the time was Léon Gérin, whose essays on sociology were collected in *Le Type économique et social du Canadien* and in *Aux Sources de notre histoire*.

Many historical works appeared during that period, mainly as biography. Narcisse-Eutrope Dionne, Alfred De Celles, Ernest Gagnon, Auguste Gosselin, and Laurent-Olivier David popularized important figures of the past as well as living personages. The two leading historians of the time, however, were Thomas Chapais and Joseph-Edmond Roy. The latter wrote many monographs and two larger works, *Histoire du notariat* and *Histoire de la seigneurie de Lauzon*, which throw much light on the daily life and customs of Canadians of the past. Chapais, for his part, in addition to writing biographies of Talon and Montcalm, completed Garneau's survey by writing a general history of Canada covering the period 1763–1867; his *Cours d'histoire du Canada* is a detailed study of British colonial policy in Canada and of the constitutional development of the colony into an independent nation.

Finally, during that period, Adjutor Rivard, Camille Roy, Henri d'Arles, Louis Dantin, and others contributed to make French-Canadian letters better known by reviewing the better books as they were published.

Progress was achieved in most fields of literary activity between the two world wars. Louis Hémon's *Maria Chapdelaine* clearly showed that, with a Canadian theme, a gifted writer could achieve a book of universal appeal. It was an achievement local authors could endeavor to emulate. When World War I made rural Quebec a highly industrialized province, the resulting social transformations were soon reflected in local literature, mainly in the novels of the '20s and '30s. Traditional, folksy subjects still attracted some novelists, such as Damase Potvin (*La Robe noire*), as did historical subjects, as may be seen with Lionel Groulx (*Au Cap Blomidon*), Robert de Roquebrune (*Les Habits rouges* and *La Seigneuresse*), and Léo-Paul Desrosiers, Canada's best historical novelist (*Les Engagés du grand portage, Les Opiniâtres*).

Other novelists, however, showed their concern for economic, social, and religious problems resulting from the deep changes then going on in traditionally rural French Canada. Most significant among those are *Marcel Faure* and *Les demi-civilisés* by Jean-Charles Harvey; *André Laurence* by Pierre Dupuy; and *La Chesnaie* by Rex Desmarchais. The best novels of the '30s, however, were portrayals of rural manners and customs, such as *Un Homme et son péché* by Claude-Henri Grignon and, particularly, *30 arpents* by Ringuet (Philippe Panneton). Remarkable also was a poetical epic by Félix-Antoine Savard, *Menaud, maître-draveur*. All these authors showed more skill in the art of writing and a deeper insight into the human soul and into social problems than had their predecessors.

In poetry, the romantic trend was still alive, thanks to ROBERT CHOQUETTE and to a group of women poets that included Simone Routier, Eva Sénécal, and Jovette Bernier. More influenced by the French *Parnasse* were PAUL MORIN, whose *Paon d'émail* is one of the most polished books of verse published in Canada, and Alfred Desrochers, the poet of *Á l'Ombre de l'Orford*. In 1937, there appeared *Regards et jeux dans l'espace* by Saint-Denys-Garneau, a small book that influenced many younger poets and is now considered a turning point in the history of Canadian poetry.

More literary essays and book reviews were collected in book form between the two wars than before or after. The best critics of the time were Albert Pelletier, Marcel Dugas, Louis Dantin, Claude-Henri Grignon, Maurice Hébert, Victor Barbeau, and Séraphin Marion. History remained the favored field of literary activity during that period. The most active historians were Pierre-Georges Roy, Gustave Lanctôt, and Jean Bruchési. The leading historian of the period was Lionel Groulx, whose nationalistic interpretation of Canada's historical development was much discussed. By the time World War II broke out, French-Canadian literature had reached a standard never attained before.

Several authors had already broken away from the provincial traditions of the past generations and grappled with more universal themes, as they had experimented with new techniques. Their example was to be followed by most of the younger writers, and French-Canadian literature became more cosmopolitan, more individualistic, and more diversified than ever before.

The novel reached new peaks with GABRIELLE ROY, Germaine Guévremont, Roger Lemelin, Yves Thériault, and André Langevin. Gabrielle Roy is the dominant figure here with *Bonheur d'occasion*, which portrays a poverty-stricken family during the depression of the '30s; *La Petite poule d'eau*, two poetical narrations of her youth in her native Manitoba; the portrait of a common man, *Alexandre Chenevert*; and the largely autobiographical stories of *Rue Deschambault*. Germaine Guévremont's *Le Survenant* is a highly poetical novel of a rural family, while ROGER LEMELIN's novels, such as *Au Pied de la pente douce* and *Les Plouffe*, are fine satires of parochial customs in Quebec City. The prolific YVES THÉRIAULT has achieved at least two very good novels, *Agaguk*, about Eskimo life, and *Ashini*, about Indian life. *Poussiére sur la ville* is considered to be André Langevin's best novel.

Other novelists of distinction are Robert Charbonneau (*Ils Posséderont la terre*), Robert Elie (*La Fin des songes*), André Giroux (*Le Gouffre a toujours soif*), all writers of psychological novels.

A few authors wrote successfully for the stage during this period: Gratien Gélinas (*Tit-Coq* and *Bousille et les justes*); Marcel Dubé (*Zone, Florence*, and *Un Simple soldat*); Jacques Languirand (*Le Gibet* and *Les Insolites*); and Paul Toupin (*Brutus* and *Le Mensonge*).

Traditional poetry was maintained by poets such as Clément Marchand (*Les Soirs rouges*) and Sylvain Garneau (*Objêts trouvés*). Most of this poetry is, however, rather esoteric and shows the dominant influence of the French surrealists. Its leading poet is ALAIN GRANDBOIS (*Les îles de la nuit; Rivages de l'homme*). Two other major contemporaries are ANNE HÉBERT (*Poèmes*) and Rina Lasnier (*Présence de l'absence*).

GUY SYLVESTRE/RH

Canadian Literature in French: Since 1960.

During Quebec's Quiet Revolution in the 1960s, artists, poets, singers, and novelists in their works urged social, religious, and political changes. In the 1970s women writers produced a rich literature expounding feminist perspectives, while in the 1980s and 1990s much emphasis was placed by writers on literary theory and experimental form. At the same time such aesthetic concerns were tempered by a series of lengthy novels or sagas exploring various facets of life prior to the 1960s. Québécois literature, the term now used to describe contemporary writing in French, has become a rich, vibrant, socially relevant literature.

In the 1960s, traditional approaches to the novel gave way to psychological introspection and abandonment of linear plot lines. Frequently, the normative French of Paris gave way to *joual*, the French spoken by Montrealers. *Le libraire* (1960, *Not for Every Eye*) by Gérard Bessette (1920–) shockingly criticized clerical censorship and religious hypocrisy, while *Le poids de dieu* (1962, *The Burden of God*) by Gilles Marcotte (1925–) analyzed the taboo topic of a French-Canadian priest's crisis of faith. Anticlericalism and political revolt characterize many novels of the period. *Le couteau sur la table* (1965, *The Knife on the Table*) by Jacques Godbout (1933–) uses cinematic techniques to depict federalist-separatist conflict in Quebec. *Ethel et le terrorist* (1964) by Claude Jasmin (1930–), written after terrorist bombings in Montreal, analyzed the suppressed alienation simmering below the surface of the counter-culture in French Canada.

In the second half of this decade, the publication of several nouveaux romans (new novels) confirmed the weaning of Québécois fiction from traditional forms, while retaining their social relevance. In haunting surrealistic prose, MARIE-CLAIRE BLAIS (1939–) probed the ugliness of poverty and sexual abuse of children in *Une saison dans la vie d'Emmanuel* (1965). The exquisite lyrical prose of *Prochain Episode* (1965) by Hubert Aquin (1929–1970) depicts the flight from justice of a Montreal terrorist seeking independence for his people. Aquin continues his effort to turn the novel into an art form created by both author and reader in two other important novels: *Trou de mémoire* (1960) and *L'antiphonaire* (1969, *The Antiphonary*). In the next two decades Blais continued to probe the under-belly of Montreal society, exploring the brutal world of the homosexual in *Un Joualonais, sa joualonie* (1974, *St. Lawrence Blues*) and the world of the lesbian in *Les nuits de l'undergound* (1978, *Nights in the Underground*).

Parody, burlesque, and satire in literature reflect new trends and a rapidly changing society. The carnivalesque *La Guerre yes sir!* (1968) by Roch Carrier (1937–) reinterprets pre-war village life in Quebec with biting black humor; *Le jardin des délices* (1978, *The Garden of Delights*) revisits the same community a generation later. The influence of the oral tradition and nationalism is seen also in the numerous works of Jacques Ferron (1921–1985); *L'amélanchier* (1970, *The Juneberry Tree*) recaptures a vision of childhood. In *Volkswagen Blues* (1984) by Jacques Poulin (1937–), realism is tempered with tenderness and compassion.

Three women writers have attracted international fame. In addition to key novels, for example, *Bonheur d'occasion* (1945, *The Tin Flute*), GABRIELLE ROY (1909–1983) has left us many essays and short stories, including *Ces enfants de ma vie* (1977; *Children of My Heart*), and a moving autobiography, *La détresse et l'enchantement* (1984, *Enchantment and Sorrow*). ANNE HÉBERT (1916–) excels in psychological dramas marked by violence, dramatic tension, and poetic prose. Two of her best are *Kamouraska* (1970) and *Les fous de Bassan* (1982, *In the Shadow of the Wind*). ANTONINE MAILLET (1929–) has become the literary voice of Canada's Acadian French minority, in 1979 receiving the Prix Goncourt for *Pélagie la charrette* (1979, *Pelagie, the Return to a Homeland*), a picaresque epic of the return of deported Acadians from the United States to their homeland.

Feminist writers such as Louky Bersianik (*L'Euguélionne*, 1976), Yolande Villemaire (*La vie en prose*, 1982), and France Théoret (*Nous parlerons comme on écrit*, 1982) reflect the vitality of Québécois literature by trying to create a non-patriarchal language in new fictional forms. *Triptyque lesbien*

(1980) by Jovette Marchessault (1938–) expresses lesbian solidarity, and *Amantes* (1980) represents the most avant-garde work of NICOLE BROSSARD (1943–). A return to traditional novels recreating recent Quebec life is seen more recently in the novels of Victor-Lévy Beaulieu (1945–); the five-novel social chronicle of Montreal's Plateau Mont-Royal district by Michel Tremblay (1942–), equally popular, have all been translated into English. *Le Matou* (1981, *The Alley Cat*) of Yves Beauchemin (1941–) with its sale of one million copies in many languages and a film adaptation, inaugurated the era of *le best-seller in Quebec*.

From 1953 to 1963 the Hexagone Press, dedicated to "action through publishing," provided poets with access to the marketplace. Influenced heavily by ALAIN GRANDBOIS (1900–1975), surrealism, and the revolutionary *Refus global* (1948) of the painter Paul-Emile Borduas, automatist writers such as ROLAND GIGUÈRE (1929–) and PAUL-MARIE LAPOINTE (1929–) invented new forms and rhythms. The group's charismatic founder, GASTON MIRON (1928–1996), preaches political independence in *L'homme rapaíllé* (1970, *The Agonized Life*). Fernand Ouellette (1930–) in *Ici, ailleurs, la lumière* (1977) and Jacques Brault (1933–) in *L'en-dessous admirable* (1975) argue for the importance of humanistic values in a disordered, modern world.

In the 1960s Quebec's social upheaval was reflected in such committed and popular works as *L'afficheur hurle* (1965) by Paul Chamberland (1939–) and his political manifesto, *Terre Québec* (1964). Gérald Godin (1938–1994) denounced the War Measures Act of 1970 and his own arrest as a separatist in *Libertés surveillées* (1975), while Michèle Lalonde (1937–) expressed the resentment of many Quebecers in *Speak White* (1974), a bitter denunciation of English and American cultural domination.

Avant-garde approaches to poetry are associated with *Les Herbes rouges*, which published over 100 titles in ten years. The modernism of this school has produced a large body of feminist writings such as *Bloody Mary* (1977) by France Théoret. Its most important theoretician is Nicole Brossard (1943–), whose attempt to renew poetic language is seen in *Le Centre blanc* (1970) and *Amantes* (1980).

The first performance of *Tit-Coq* in 1948 marked the birth of contemporary Québécois drama for its author, Gratien Gélinas (1909–), and brought to the Montreal stage authentic working-class French-Canadians who spoke North American rather than European French. Best known for his contribution to the training of professional actors, Gélinas produced only four plays, including *Hier les enfants dansaient* (1966, *Yesterday the Children Were Dancing*). Influenced by the theater of the absurd, Jacques Languirand (1931–) posed the dilemma of Quebecers affirming their cultural identity in *Les grands départs* (1958, *The Departures*). The prolific Marcel Dubé (1930–) dominated the Montreal stage during the 1960s, delving into the Québécois psyche in *Florence* (1966) and *Les beaux dimanches* (1968); *Au retour des oies blanches* (1969), considered to be his best play, resembles *Oedipus Rex* in plot and form but is firmly planted in a Quebec setting. Françoise Loranger (1913–1995), like Dubé, stresses middle-class family relationships but with violent undertones, as in *Une maison . . . un jour* (1965). Political and social problems dominate her later work: *Médium saignant* (1970), reflecting the bitterness of the conflict in Montreal, opened just days prior to election of Quebec's first separatist government.

The major dramatic figure of the 1970s is Michel Tremblay (1942–   ), whose plays have been translated into English and other languages and have been produced internationally. *Les belles-soeurs* (1968) changed the course of theater in Quebec by Tremblay's firm rejection of international French as the standard for the stage and his innovative use of *joual*, the curious but colorful French of urban Montreal. Almost all his plays deal with characters living in the Plateau Mont-Royal district of Montreal. One of his best is *A toi pour toujours, ta Marie-Lou* (1973, *Forever Yours, Marie-Lou).* *La duchesse de Langeais* (1970) and *Hosanna* (1973) present homosexual protagonists who, according to Tremblay, resemble French Quebecers constantly in search of their national identity.

Social satire marks the plays of Robert Gurik (1932–   ). *Hamlet, prince du Québec* (1969) uses a Shakespeare plot to illustrate separatist tensions in Canada, while Jean-Claude Germain (1939–   ) and Jean Barbeau (1945–   ) both opt firmly for *joual*. Germain tempers social satire with humor in *Un pays dont la devise est je m'oublie* (1976), as does Barbeau in *Joualez-moi d'amour* (1972). *Citrouille* (1974), however, with its brutal depiction of violence to women, underscores female alienation. Antonine Maillet (1929–   ) has chosen for her heroes and heroines the poor of New Brunswick who speak Acadian French. In one of her many plays, *La Sagouine* (1971), a charwoman 72 years old tells stories of her past, unaware that she is using the coarse language of 16th-century France still spoken in the Maritimes.

The 1970s mark the advent of a vigorous feminist theater. Collective creations such as *La nef des sorcières* (1976, *A Clash of Symbols*) counterbalance individual works by Denise Boucher, Elizabeth Bourget, and Marie Laberge; *La Saga des poules mouillées* (1981; *The Saga of the Wet Hens*), by Jovette Marchessault (1938–   ) proposes the creation of a female culture within a patriarchal society. Exciting new directions emerged in the 1980s and 1990s in the work of Robert Lepage (1958–   ), a Montreal dramatist who attracted international attention by his adaptation of cinematic and television techniques to the stage and his use of surrealistic decors, as in *Trilogie des dragons* (1985–1987) and *Les sept branches de la rivière Ota* (1994–1996).

The major sources of information on Québécois literature are Caroline Bayard, *The New Poetics in Canada and Quebec: From Concretism to Postmodernism* (1989); Eugene Benson and Leonard Conolly, eds. *The Oxford Companion to Canadian Theatre* (1989); Maurice Lemire, ed. *Dictionnaire des oeuvres littéraires de Québec*, Volumes 4 and 5 (1960–1975); Clément Moisan, *A Poetry of Frontièrs: Comparative Studies in Quebec-Canadian Literature* (1983); Ben-Zion Shek, *Social Realism in the French-Canadian Novel* (1977); Larry Shouldice, ed. *Contemporary Quebec Criticism* (1979); Eugene Benson and William Toye, eds. *The Oxford Companion to Canadian Literature*, 2nd edition (1997); Paul Wyczynski, ed. *Archives des lettres canadiennes*, Vol. 5: and *Le Théâtre canadien-français* (1976).

RAMON HATHORN/GP

Canby, Henry Seidel (1878–1961),   teacher, editor, literary critic, biographer. Canby, born in Delaware and educated at Yale, taught at Yale for more than two decades. For some years following World War I, he served as literary editor of the *New York Post*. In 1924 he helped found and became the first editor of the *Saturday Review of Literature*. In 1926, Canby was named chairman of the editorial board of the newly formed Book-of-the-Month Club and served for twenty-eight years. Among Canby's many books are *The Short Story* (1902), a standard text for many years; *Walt Whitman: An American* (1943); and *Turn West, Turn East: Mark Twain and Henry James* (1951). In the 1930s he began writing a series of volumes in which his autobiography is skillfully interwoven with reflections on American education, literature, and culture: *The Age of Confidence* (1934); *Alma Mater: The Gothic Age of the American College* (1936); and AMERICAN MEMOIR (1947).

Candelaria, Nash (1928–   ),   novelist, short-story writer. Born in Los Angeles and educated at the University of California, Los Angeles, Candelaria considers himself "a New Mexican by heritage and sympathy," noting that his ancestors include "one of the founding families of Albuquerque" and the author of a history of New Mexico published in 1776. In his writings he has emphasized that heritage in four novels following the history of the Rafa family: *Memories of the Alhambra* (1977), in which Jose Rafa pursues his genealogical ties to Spanish conquistadors and a European background in an attempt to escape his sense of an inferior mestizo and Indian heritage; *Not by the Sword* (1982), examining the Mexican War as seen by New Mexicans who became Americans through conquest; *Inheritance of Strangers* (1984), on problems of assimilation forty years after the war; and *Leonar Park* (1991), set in New Mexico during the Depression. A theme of understanding and necessary adaptation to change runs through the series. Stories are collected in *The Day the Cisco Kid Shot John Wayne* (1988) and *Uncivil Rights and Other Stories* (1998).

Candidates, The (1770),   a play by ROBERT MUNFORD. Local elections are satirized in this play, which introduced an African American on the American stage, perhaps for the first time.

Cane (1923),   a miscellany of prose sketches and poems by JEAN TOOMER. Unified by an impressionistic style and by settings in rural Georgia and in Washington, D.C., the pieces combine to make one of the most influential books of the HARLEM RENAISSANCE.

Cane, Melville [Henry] (1879–1980),   lawyer, poet. Cane was born in Plattsburgh, New York, became a lawyer, and began contributing verse to magazines in the early 1900s. His collections include *January Gardens* (1926), *Behind Dark Spaces* (1930), *A Wider Arc* (1947), *And Pastures New* (1956),

Bullet-Hunting (1960), and *Snow Toward Evening* (1974). *All and Sundry* (1968) is autobiographical.

Canfield, Dorothy. See DOROTHY CANFIELD FISHER.

Caniff, Milton A[rthur] (1907–1988), cartoonist. Caniff was born in Ohio and educated at Ohio State. At thirteen he began contributing cartoons to newspapers. After a brief attempt at acting, he continued as a cartoonist, drawing *Dickie Dare* and *The Gay Thirties* for the Associated Press. He found fame and 30 million readers with *Terry and the Pirates* (1934–1946), a strip drawn for the Chicago *Tribune*–New York *Daily News* Syndicate and remembered especially for Terry's encounters with the Dragon Lady, beautiful, seductively cunning, and Chinese. In 1946, Caniff quit drawing *Terry and the Pirates*, which he did not own, and launched *Steve Canyon*, an adventure strip about an Air Force colonel, for the Chicago *Sun* Syndicate. *Terry and the Pirates* was continued by George Wunder until its demise in 1973.

Canin, Ethan (1960–   ), short-story writer, novelist. Born in Ann Arbor, Michigan, raised in California, Canin impressed others with his talents from an early age. Danielle Steele, his teacher in a private secondary school, wrote of his "extraordinary gift for writing" when he was seventeen and he published his first story when he was nineteen. At Stanford he majored in physics before turning to English (A.B., 1982), which led to an M.F.A. in 1984 from the Iowa Writers Workshop. At this point he was publishing every story that he wrote, but unsure of his vocation and needing "to feel useful in some ways" he entered medical school at Harvard, emerged with an M.D. in 1992, and began practice as a physician. Meanwhile, his critically acclaimed first book, *Emperor of the Air* (1988), a collection of short stories exploring family tensions, became a best seller, and *Blue River* (1991), a novel of two brothers, one successful, the other not, was also highly praised. His books since, *The Palace Thief* (1994), collecting four longer stories, and *For Kings and Planets* (1998), a novel, have continued to display great strengths of style, character development, and psychological penetration.

Cannery Row (1945), a novel by JOHN STEINBECK. In this episodic work Steinbeck returned to the manner of TORTILLA FLAT (1935) to produce a rambling account of the adventures and misadventures of workers in a California cannery and their friends. One character, Doc, was reportedly modeled on the marine biologist Edward F. Ricketts.

Cannon, Charles James (1800–1860), poet, playwright, short-story writer. A New Yorker by birth, Cannon had his greatest success with a tragedy set in Ireland, *The Oath of Office* (1850). His other works include fiction in *Mora Carmody; or, Woman's Influence* (1844) and *Ravellings from the Web of Life* (1855); and verse in *Poems: Dramatic and Miscellaneous* (1851).

Cannon, LeGrand, Jr. (1899–1979), novelist. His works include three New Hampshire novels—*A Mighty Fortress* (1937), *The Kents* (1938), and *Look to the Mountain* (1942).

Canonchet, chief of the NARRAGANSETT INDIANS, who led them into defeat against the whites in KING PHILIP'S WAR

and was killed in 1676. He appears in William Hubbard's NARRATIVE OF THE TROUBLES WITH THE INDIANS IN NEW ENGLAND (1677) and is central to Cooper's *The Wept of Wish-ton-Wish* (1829).

Can Such Things Be? (1893), twenty-four stories by AMBROSE BIERCE.

Cantos, The, long poem by EZRA POUND. He worked on *The Cantos*, his masterwork, for over fifty years, beginning in earnest in 1915 and publishing a *Drafts and Fragments of Cantos CX–CXVII* in 1969. The first three cantos appeared in *Poetry: A Magazine of Verse* in three issues (June, July, August 1917) and then together as "Three Cantos" in Pound's *Lustra* (1917). In between came numerous publications of various portions. *The Cantos* (1970) brought most together, and a third printing in 1972 added one more.

The Cantos begins with a loose translation, with omissions, of the first 100 lines of Book XI of Homer's *Odyssey*, the descent to the underworld. In later passages, Pound ranges in his allusions through world literature and philosophy, quotes from foreign languages, prints Chinese ideograms, rails against usury, and comments on his own life (famously in *The Pisan Cantos*, LXXIV–LXXXIV, 1948, written while Pound was imprisoned and awaiting trial for treason against the United States; with some regret in Canto CXVI). Although critics are divided on the success of the work, both as a whole and in its parts, it remains one of the most influential poems of the 20th century and contains some fine passages.

Cantwell, Mary (1930?–2000), journalist, memoirist. Born in Providence, Cantwell grew up in Bristol, Rhode Island. After graduating from Connecticut College in 1953, she worked for *Mademoiselle* magazine for two decades as a copywriter and editor. In 1980 she joined the staff of the *New York Times*, where she wrote a "Hers" column and served on the editorial board until not long before her death. Her concerns in her column and her essays were often for the lives of women, who in her generation were largely shut out, she felt, from what was still a man's world. "It took a brave woman," she wrote, "braver than I, to write books." She did write them, however, but late in life. *American Girl: Scenes from a Small Town Childhood* (1992) is a memoir of growing up Irish-American and Catholic in a Protestant town, a time and place she remembered with affection. She followed *American Girl* with two more memoirs, *Manhattan, When I was Young* (1995), about her early years as a journalist, and *Speaking With Strangers* (1998), about her life after the breakup of her marriage to the literary agent Robert Lescher and her affair with the poet James Dickey. The three are collected as *Manhattan Memoir* (2000).

Cantwell, Robert E[mmett] (1908–1978), journalist, novelist. Born in Little Falls, Washington, Cantwell attended the University of Washington, served in the Coast Guard, worked in a lumber mill, and began a literary career in the early 1930s. Eventually he became an editor of *Time* and *Newsweek*, and published biographies of Hawthorne (1948) and the ornithologist Alexander Wilson (1961). His first novel, *Laugh and Lie Down* (1931), drew on his mill experiences. *The*

Land of Plenty (1934), about factory work, has won particular praise as a strong proletarian novel. *The Hidden Northwest* (1972) is a historical study.

Cape Cod (chapters appeared in *Putnam's Magazine*, 1855, and the *Atlantic Monthly*, 1864; the whole was published posthumously, 1865),   sketches by HENRY DAVID THOREAU. Thoreau visited the Cape and nearby Nantucket in 1849, 1850, and 1855.

Capote, Truman (1924–1984),   novelist, short-story writer, journalist. Born in New Orleans and educated in private schools in New York and Connecticut, Capote worked as a young man on *The New Yorker*. He won early fame with *Other Voices, Other Rooms* (1948), a tale of youthful innocence in decadent surroundings, told in a polished, lyrical style that announced the arrival of a distinctive new voice in American literature. It was followed by *A Tree of Night and Other Stories* (1949) and *The Grass Harp* (1951; as a Broadway play, 1952), further lyric contributions to the postwar literature of the gothic South. Of later fictions, BREAKFAST AT TIFFANY's (1958) was widely admired for its witty portrayal of life in New York City, and for its central character, Holly Golightly. *A Christmas Memory* (1966) is a short return to the world of the author's youth.

After Capote's astonishing debut as a writer, his later reputation owed much to his life as a New York celebrity, numerous gossipy accounts of his substance abuse, mental illness, lawsuits, and broken friendships. But he continued also as sometimes brilliant writer, more of nonfiction than fiction. *In Cold Blood* (1965), his account of two psychopaths who murdered a Kansas family, helped inaugurate the vogue for the nonfiction novel. His other works include *Local Color* (1950), travel sketches; *The Muses Are Heard* (1956), a description of his visit to Russia with a touring company of *Porgy and Bess; The Dogs Bark; Public People and Private Places* (1966); and *Music for Chameleons* (1980), a prose miscellany. He wrote the book for the Broadway musical *House of Flowers* (1964, music by Harold Arlen); a play, *The Thanksgiving Visitor* (1968); and with John Huston, the screenplay for the film *Beat the Devil* (1954). *Answered Prayers: The Unfinished Novel* (1987) is a gossipy posthumous publication.

Capp, Al[fred Gerald] (1909–1979),   cartoonist. Born in Connecticut as Alfred Gerald Caplin, Capp won fame with his comic strip *Li'l Abner*, which entertained millions and was one of the most successful in the history of its genre, timelessly funny, and sometimes topically satiric. Set in the hillbilly town of Dogpatch, the strip featured a large number of brilliantly conceived and memorably drawn characters and situations, including Li'l Abner's parents, Ma and Pa Yokum; his girl friend, Daisy Mae; the dirty but beautiful Moonbeam McSwine; and the Sadie Hawkins Day race, with women in pursuit of the town's eligible bachelors. The strip first appeared in 1934 and remained popular into the '60s. It inspired a movie (1940) and a musical comedy (1956).

Capps, Benjamin [Franklin] (1922–   ),   western writer. Born in Dundee, Texas, Capps served in the armed forces in World War II, returned to graduate from the Univer-

sity of Texas (B.A. 1948, M.A. 1949) and work a variety of jobs before becoming a novelist with *The Hanging at Comanche Wells* (1962). In this and later novels, he chronicles the life of southwestern cattlemen toward the end of the nineteenth century, winning praise for the accuracy of his portrayals. Among the best are *The Trail to Ogallala* (1964) about a cattle drive; *Sam Chance* (1965), the life of a Texas cattleman from the end of the Civil War to the 1920s; *A Woman of the People* (1966), of white girls kidnapped and raised by Comanches; *The White Man's Road* (1969), about a Comanche boy's restlessness on the reservation; and *Woman Chief* (1978), a fact-based story of Sweet Thunder Woman, a slave from a neighboring tribe who becomes a warrior chief of the Crows.

Capra, Frank (1897–1991),   film director and producer. Capra came to the United States from Italy at the age of six and studied at the California Institute of Technology. He entered the motion-picture business in 1921 and distinguished himself by directing or producing many notable pictures, including *Platinum Blonde* (1931); *It Happened One Night* (1934); *Mr. Deeds Goes to Town* (1936); *Lost Horizon* (1937); YOU CAN'T TAKE IT WITH YOU (1938); and STATE OF THE UNION (1948). His films during his most successful period were notable for their sentimental comedy and idealistic belief in the triumph of the common man in a world riddled with deceit and hypocrisy. From 1934 through 1938, he won three of the five Academy Awards given for direction. During World War II, Capra directed the documentary series *Why We Fight*, the first of which, *Prelude to War* (1942), won the Academy Award for best documentary in its year. His autobiography is *Frank Capra: The Name Above the Title* (1971).

Captain Bonneville, The Adventures of (1837),   a narrative prepared by WASHINGTON IRVING from the papers of Captain Benjamin Louis Eulalie de Bonneville (1796–1878). Bonneville, educated at West Point, explored northwestern sections of the United States in 1832–35 and served in the Mexican and Civil Wars. While writing ASTORIA (1836), Irving met this soldier-explorer, bought his maps and papers, and rewrote his story, which forms a sequel to *Astoria*.

Captain Craig (1902),   a narrative poem by EDWIN ARLINGTON ROBINSON. One of Robinson's longest poems, it describes a talkative old vagabond who preaches the doctrine that "God's humor is the music of the spheres" and that one must "laugh with God."

Captain Jinks of the Horse Marines (1901, revived 1925),   a comedy by CLYDE FITCH. An American-born opera singer who has assumed an Italian name (Mme. Trentini) and made a fortune abroad comes back to New York. She is met at the dock by three men who have made an arrangement among themselves that each of them will try to win her. Whoever succeeds will share her fortune with the remaining two. Jinks is successful, but the others betray him and the opera singer indignantly throws him over. He makes his peace with her, and all is well. Ethel Barrymore made her stage debut in this play.

Captains Courageous (1897),   a novel by Rudyard Kipling. A product of Kipling's residence in Vermont (1892–96), the story tells how a pampered, wealthy boy, lost overboard from a luxury liner, learns manhood on the Grand Banks with the fishermen of the Gloucester fleet.

Captain Stormfield's Visit to Heaven (1909), MARK TWAIN's satire on conventional notions of heaven and religion. Inspired by a popular sentimental novel, THE GATES AJAR, it was written in 1868, but held back from publication because Twain thought it would shock the public.

Captivity and Restauration of Mrs. Mary Rowlandson, Narrative of the (1682).   This was the first of the many INDIAN CAPTIVITY NARRATIVES. Its full title was *The Soveraignty and Goodness of God: Together with the Faithfulness of His Promises Displayed; Being a Narrative of the Captivity and Restauration of Mrs. Mary Rowlandson.* Immensely popular, it was reissued at least thirty times, including C. H. Lincoln's edition of *Narratives of the Indian Wars, 1675–1699* (1913). Mary White Rowlandson (c. 1635–c. 1678), the wife of a Massachusetts minister, was taken captive with her young daughter Sarah during King Philip's War. She was held for seven weeks and five days, and was transported to twenty different sites; her child died in her arms during the ordeal. Mrs. Rowlandson was released after a ransom had been paid and she retained enough self-possession to write her narrative of the attack and her subsequent tribulations with realism, dignity, and cheerfulness. She made accurate observations on the habits of her captors and commented shrewdly on their characters, though the only positive merit she could ascribe to her abductors was that "not one of them ever offered the least abuse of chastity to me, in word or action."

Caputo, Philip (1941–   ),   memoirist, novelist. Born in Chicago, Caputo graduated from Loyola University (B.A., 1964) and served in Vietnam as a lieutenant in the Marines. From that experience and his work for the *Chicago Tribune* as a correspondent in Rome, Beirut, Saigon, Moscow, Afghanistan, and Africa came two memoirs: *A Rumor of War* (1977), a powerful indictment of the transformative evil of war for American soldiers and for their country in Vietnam, and *Means of Escape* (1991), a less celebrated work of "imaginative autobiography" mixing "memory and imagination" in a dark vision of the world witnessed by a foreign correspondent in a deeply troubled time. Novels that focus on war and its aftermath include *Horn of Africa* (1980), on civil war in Ethiopia; *DelCorso's Gallery* (1983), of a photojournalist obsessed with the horror, not the heroism, in Vietnam and Lebanon; and *Indian Country* (1987), healing from the wounds of Vietnam found in the woods and the Indian heritage of Michigan's Upper Peninsula. Another novel, *Equation for Evil* (1996), portrays white supremacists, Cambodian refugees, and mass murder in the San Joaquin valley of California. *The Voyage* (1999) represents a departure for Caputo, a sea story of young men sent from Maine on a mysterious cruise for reasons known only to their father, told by a great-granddaughter in hopes of recovering some long-lost truth.

Carew, Jan [Rynveld] (1925–   )   Guyanan novelist. Educated in Guyana, the U.S., and Prague, Carew has also lived in London, where he was variously actor, journalist, editor, and radio playwright. Guyana is usually the setting of his novels, which contrast the simplicity and beauty of village life with the destructive effects of civilization. He often employs the parable form, as in *Black Midas* (1958), and acknowledges the influence of the modern primitive painters Gauguin and Rousseau. Among his other works are *The Last Barbarian* (1960); *Moscow Is Not My Mecca* (1964); a volume of poetry, *Sea Drums in My Blood* (1981); *Dark Night, Deep Water* (1981); *Death Comes to the Circus* (1983); *Grenada: The Hour Will Strike Again* (1985); an essay collection, *Fulcrums of Change* (1988); and *The Rape of Paradise: Columbus and the Birth of Racism in the Americas* (1994).

Carey, Mathew (1760–1839),   publisher, editor, essayist, poet, economist. Forced to flee Ireland because of his violent attacks on English rule, Carey came to America in 1784 and began a long journalistic and publishing career. He edited many magazines, in particular *The American Museum* (1787–92), which he founded. He attacked William Cobbett in *The Porcupiniad* (1796). Some of his best work is collected in *Autobiographic Sketches* (1829) and *Miscellaneous Essays* (1830): See BEAUTIES OF POETRY: COLUMBIAN MAGAZINE.

Carey, Peter (1943–   ),   novelist, short-story writer. One of Australia's most distinguished writers, Peter Carey was born in Bacchus Marsh, Victoria, and educated at Monash University. He lived in Melbourne, London, and Sydney before moving to New York in the late 1980s. Supporting himself at first as an advertising writer, he earned an Australian following with the stories in *The Fat Man in History* (1974), and *War Crimes* (1979), some of the best of which were combined under the first title for publication in the United States in 1993, after his move to that country. Among these, "A Windmill in the West" and "American Dreams," both from the 1974 volume, present casebook studies of the Australian fascination with things American. Other collections include *Exotic Pleasures* (1990) and *Collected Stories* (1994). Carey's greatest achievements, however, are his novels, the best of which place him among the major writers in English in the closing decades of the twentieth century. *Bliss* (1981), the story of an advertising man who experiences an out-of-body recognition of the Hell of his life, was the first of three of his novels to win Australia's Miles Franklin Award. *Illywhacker* (1985), with its 139-year-old narrator providing a wild, mythic history of Australia, won awards for fantasy and science fiction in Australia and was short-listed for the Booker Prize in Great Britain. The following year, the Booker went to Carey's *Oscar & Lucinda* (1988), a novel that sweeps in epic fashion from Victorian England through the Australian Outback. Novels subsequent to his move to New York include *The Tax Inspector* (1991), about a tax visitation to a G.M. dealership in Sydney controlled by a demented matriarch; *The Unusual Life of Tristan Smith* (1994), a satire in which a deformed child in an imaginary country searches for a father; *Jack Maggs* (1997), a novel that is also a meditation on the responsibilities of the author, with *Great Expectations* revised as though seen through the eyes of the convict, and the hapless Dickensian writer confused and bullied by his subject; and *True History of the Kelly Gang* (2000), a major accomplishment, in which Australia's great folk hero Ned Kelly, who died on the gallows with the famous last words "Such is life," writes for his unseen and unknown daughter in California an aggressively demotic justification for his life as a bushranger.

Carib Indians. A tribe inhabiting the Lesser Antilles, in the West Indies, at the time of the arrival of Columbus. Known at first to the Spaniards as Galibi, their name was soon corrupted to Canibal, in English, Cannibal. Not many Caribs survived European colonization, but some mixed with escaped slaves on St. Vincent, and after various removals found their way to the coast of Guatemala. A few remain on a reservation on the island of Dominica.

About a century before the arrival of Columbus, they arrived in the Caribbean area, perhaps from Central or South America, bringing their Carib language. They drove out the the Arawak natives of the area, taking their women; the result was an unusual culture in which the men spoke one language, the women another. JEAN BAPTISTE LABAT gives an account of them in his *Nouveau voyage aux isles de l'Amerique* (8 v. 1724–42).

Carleton, Henry Guy (1856–1910), engineer, playwright, editor, humorist. Carleton wrote and produced numerous plays, including *Memnon* (1881), *The Gilded Fool* (1892), *The Butterflies* (1893), and *Ambition* (1894). *The Butterflies*, written for John Drew and Maude Adams, established the reputation of the actress. Carleton also contributed humorous material to *Life* magazine, of which he became managing editor in 1893. His best-known sketches were collected as *The Thompson Street Poker Club* (1884) and *Lectures Before the Thompson Street Poker Club* (1889).

Carleton, Will[iam McKendree] (1845–1912), poet, newspaperman, short-story writer, lecturer. Carleton, born on a farm in Michigan, wrote sentimental ballads that won wide popularity. FARM BALLADS (1873) includes his poem OVER THE HILL TO THE POORHOUSE. Other collections are *City Ballads* (1885), *City Legends* (1889), and *City Festivals* (1892). He became a popular lecturer and recited his own verses widely.

Carman, [William] Bliss (1861–1929), poet, essayist, lecturer. Born in Fredericton, New Brunswick, Carman was educated at the University of New Brunswick, the University of Edinburgh, and Harvard, where he met RICHARD HOVEY. He and Hovey collaborated on SONGS FROM VAGABONDIA (1894), *More Songs from Vagabondia* (1896), and *Last Songs from Vagabondia* (1901).

Carman finally settled down as a member of the editorial staff of THE INDEPENDENT and other magazines, but continued to write poetry profusely and published over fifty volumes; among them are *Low Tide on Grand Pré* (1893); *Behind the Arras* (1895); *Pipes of Pan* (5 v. 1902–05); *The Rough Rider and Other Poems* (1909); and *April Airs* (1916). From 1886 on, he lived in the United States but continued to make frequent visits to Canada. His reputation was for many years solid and international.

Carmer, Carl [Lamson] (1893–1976), teacher, writer, editor, broadcaster. Carmer spent several years teaching

at Syracuse, Rochester, Hamilton (his alma mater), and Alabama. In 1927 he became a columnist on the New Orleans *Morning Tribune*, and later assistant editor of *Vanity Fair* and of *Theatre Arts Monthly*. In 1928 he printed privately a collection of verse, *Frenchtown*; another verse gathering, *Deep South*, appeared in 1930. While in Alabama Carmer had gone up and down the state studying its folklore and legends, observing the ways of the people, listening to their casual talk. His collection of material took shape in *Stars Fell on Alabama* (1934), a best seller. Carmer wrote a similar book about New York, *Listen for a Lonesome Drum* (1936), then a book of folk tales for younger readers, *The Hurricane's Children* (1937), and a book, *The Hudson* (1939), in The Rivers of America series; later he became editor of the series. He also undertook a radio program, "Your Neck o' the Woods," in which the treasures of folk tale and folk song were explored on the air. With Carl Van Doren he prepared *The American Scriptures* (1946). Among his books are *Windfall Fiddle* (1950), which won the Herald Tribune Children's Book Award; *The Susquehanna* (1955); *The Screaming Ghost* (1955); and *Pets at the White House* (1959).

Carnegie, Andrew (1835–1919), industrialist, philanthropist, writer on economic topics. The descendant of a family of weavers, Carnegie came from his native Scotland to the United States in 1848 and worked his way up to a commanding position in the steel industry. In 1901 he retired and devoted the rest of his life to planning the disposal of his fortune. He provided the funds for numerous Carnegie Library buildings all over the country, for public education, and for international peace. He endowed the Carnegie Corporation of America with $125,000,000 to continue his donations after his death. He wrote *Triumphant Democracy* (1886), a sincere panegyric; THE GOSPEL OF WEALTH AND OTHER TIMELY ESSAYS (1900); an *Autobiography* (1920); and *The Empire of Business* (1933).

Carnegie, Dale (1888–1955), lecturer, author, broadcaster, teacher of public speaking. Born in Missouri, Carnegie taught thousands of people to speak in public with greater confidence. *How to Win Friends and Influence People* (1936), translated into dozens of languages, has sold millions of copies. His other books include *Public Speaking and Influencing Men in Business* (1926), *Lincoln the Unknown* (1932), and *How to Stop Worrying and Start Living* (1948).

Carolina Folk Plays. On March 14, 1919, under the inspiration of Frederick H. Koch, at that time a member of the faculty of the University of North Carolina, a group called the Carolina Playmakers began to produce short plays in a theater improvised in Gerrard Hall. "The little homespun plays found an eager and lusty welcome," records Koch. According to him, the phrase "folk play" was used for the first time in the Carolina project, although he had earlier experimented with such drama at the University of North Dakota. The plays, taken on tour, revived interest in the theater in a region that had seemed barren soil. Beginning in March 1928, Koch edited and published *The Carolina Play-Book*, an illustrated quarterly of native plays and articles. In 1922 he issued the first of a series of *Carolina Folk-Plays*; others followed in 1924 and 1928 and were collected in a single volume (1941). Here may be found plays by authors who later went on to national fame, especially PAUL GREEN and THOMAS WOLFE; others who made important contributions include Elizabeth A. Lay, Erma Green, and Wilbur Stout.

Carpenter, Don (1931–1995), novelist, screenwriter. Born in Berkeley, California, a veteran of the Korean War and a graduate of Portland State University in Oregon, with an M.A. from San Francisco State College, Carpenter became identified with Bay Area writers such as EVAN S. CONNELL, JR. and RICHARD BRAUTIGAN. His first novel, *Hard Rain Falling* (1966), launched a career that included much screenwriting and several novels about Hollywood, including *The True Life Story of Jody McKeegan* (1975), *Turnaround* (1981), and *A Couple of Comedians* (1979), the last of which he considered his best work. Other titles are *Class of Forty-Nine* (1985), *Dispossessed* (1986), and *From a Distant Place* (1988). After a severe bout with tuberculosis, he died from a self-inflicted gunshot wound.

Carpenter, Edward Childs (1872–1950), newspaperman, playwright, novelist. Carpenter became financial editor of the Philadelphia *Inquirer* (1905–16) and while in that position wrote several successful novels, among them *Captain Courtesy* (1906), *The Code of Victor Jallot* (1907), and *The Easy Mark* (1912). He had even more success with his plays: *The Challenge* (1911), *The Cinderella Man* (1916), *The Pipes of Pan* (1917), *The Bachelor Father* (1928), *Order, Please* (1934), and others.

Carpentier [y Valmont], Alejo (1904–1980), Cuban novelist, essayist, musicologist. Born in Havana of a French father and Russian mother, Carpentier moved to Europe with his parents in 1914, returning to Cuba in the early 1920s. From 1928 to 1939 he lived in Paris. He returned to Cuba at the outbreak of World War II; at other times, he lived and worked in the United States and Venezuela and other countries and served under Castro as Cuban cultural attaché in Paris. As a young man a student of architecture, later a professor of musicology who wrote the first history of Cuban music, and active in avant-garde literary circles, he brought an international perspective to his writing, combining diverse elements like surrealism, Afro-Cuban folklore, and—in the early *Ecue-Yamba-O!* (1933)—socialist realism. In the preface to *El Reino de este Mundo* (1949, tr. *The Kingdom of This World*, 1957), he introduced the concept of MAGICAL REALISM, mixing dream with reality and ignoring conventional chronology. The novel tells of an 18th-century slave rebellion in Haiti. A later work, *Los pasos perdidos* (1953, tr. *The Lost Steps*, 1957), is considered by some to be his best novel. Set in Venezuela it describes a musicologist's search for early instruments, and for a better life than the modern, among primitive people and utopian adventurers on the upper reaches of the Orinoco. His other works include *El acoso* (1956, tr. *Manhunt, Noon III*, 1959), about the pursuit of a political informer; *La guerra del tiempo* (1958, tr. *The War of Time*, 1969), experimental stories; *El siglo de las luces* (1962, tr. *Explosion in a Cathedral*, 1963), a

historical novel of Cuba, Jamaica, Guadalupe, and Guiana in the time of the French Revolution; *El recurso del método* (1974, tr. *Reasons of State*, 1976), a satire directed at a Latin American dictator.

Carpet-Bag, The. A humorous weekly published in Boston (March 29, 1851–March 26, 1853), under the editorship of BENJAMIN PENHALLOW SHILLABER, whose sketches of Mrs. Partington appeared in the magazine. Other well-known contributors were Charles F. Browne (Artemus Ward). G. H. Derby (John Phoenix), John T. Trowbridge, Sylvanus Cobb, and Elizabeth Akers. Most prominent was Samuel L. Clemens, whose first published piece, *The Yankee Frightening the Squatter*, appeared in *The Carpet-Bag* anonymously on May 1, 1852.

Carr, Emily (1871–1945), painter, memoirist. Born in Victoria, British Columbia, Carr studied art in San Francisco, England, and France and then returned to Victoria. Summers on Queen Charlotte Island gave her the Native American and coastal landscape subjects that finally, when she was in her fifties, began to earn her recognition as one of Canada's most accomplished painters. Late in life she began a distinguished series of memoirs, including *Klee Wyck* (1941), about her early encounters with Native Americans; *The Book of Small* (1942), on her childhood in Victoria; *The House of All Sorts* (1944), describing a period when she kept a boardinghouse and bred dogs; and *Growing Pains* (1946), the most substantial of the group, covering her entire life. *Hundreds and Thousands: The Journals of Emily Carr* (1966) is a posthumous collection, valuable for insights into her artistic development. Other posthumous gatherings are *The Heart of a Peacock* (1953), stories and sketches, mostly of animals; and *Pause: A Sketch Book* (1953), about her time in a sanitorium in England in 1903–1904.

Carr, John Dickson ["Carr Dickson," "Carter Dickson"] (1906–1977), mystery writer. A popular writer of mystery stories in the literate English tradition, often with overtones of the macabre, Carr wrote books that reflect his enthusiasm for Sir Arthur Conan Doyle's Sherlock Holmes and his long residence in England (1931–1948). While there, he worked for the B.B.C. and collaborated with Adrian Conan Doyle on *The Life of Sir Arthur Conan Doyle* (1949). His books, which stress the intellectual or puzzle element in the solution of crimes and frequently have a historical setting, include *The Bride of Newgate* (1950); *Behind the Crimson Blind* (1952); *Poison in Jest* (1952); *Eight of Swords* (1953); *Cut-Throat* (1955); *The Dead Man's Knock* (1958); *The Witch of the Low Tide: An Edwardian Melodrama* (1961); *The Man Who Explained Miracles* (1963), short stories; *Panic in Box C* (1966); *The Ghosts' High Noon* (1970); *The Hungry Goblin: A Victorian Detective Novel* (1972); and *The Door to Doom* (1980).

Carrera Andrade, Jorge (1903–1978), Ecuadoran poet, diplomat, anthropologist. As a student, Andrade helped found the Ecuadoran Socialist Party. He lived at times in Germany, France, and Spain and once was secretary to GABRIELA MISTRAL. He evokes images of his native land and his Indian forebears in impressionistic poems sometimes imitative of haiku. His books of verse include *Estanque inefable* (1922),

Boletines de mar y tierra (1930), *Registro del mundo* (1940), *Lugar de Origen* (1945), and *Edades poeticas* (1958). A collected edition is *Obra poetica completa* (1976). His essays appear in *Latitudes* (1940) and *Rostros y climas* (1948). *Selected Poems*, translated by R. H. Hays, was published in 1972.

Carroll, Gladys Hasty (1904–1989), novelist, short-story writer, author of books for children. Born in New Hampshire and educated at Bates College, Carroll has written regional fiction presenting the people of New England, especially Maine, as members of a still living and growing community. Carrying on the work of such earlier novelists as SARAH ORNE JEWETT and MARY E. WILKINS FREEMAN, she wrote *As the Earth Turns* (1933), a best seller about longtime Maine residents and Polish immigrant neighbors. A movie, and then a folk play performed in South Berwick for many years, it became the subject of *The Book That Came Alive* (1979). Other books are *A Few Foolish Ones* (1935); *Neighbor to the Sky* (1937); and a short-story collection, *Head of the Line* (1942). *Dunnybrook* (1944) is a fictional narrative based on fact, the study of a Maine community and of one of its families through ten generations. Among her later novels are *While the Angels Sing* (1947), *West of the Hill* (1949), *Christmas Without Johnny* (1950), *One White Star* (1954), *Sing Out the Glory* (1957), *Come with Me Home* (1961), *Man on the Mountain* (1969), and *Next of Kin* (1974). *Only Fifty Years Ago* (1962) and *Years Away from Home* (1972) are memoirs.

Carroll, John (1735–1815), clergyman. Born in Maryland, Carroll was educated in Europe and ordained as a Jesuit priest in 1769. Returning to America, he became a friend of Benjamin Franklin, an ardent supporter of the Revolution, founder of Georgetown University (1789), bishop of Baltimore and, in 1808, an archbishop. His controversial pamphlet on Catholic loyalties, *An Address to the Roman Catholics of the United States of America*, appeared in 1784.

Carruth, Hayden (1921–) poet, editor. Born in Connecticut, Carruth has established a reputation as a New England poet with a voice that in its varied modulations has been compared with those of Frost, Yeats, Stevens, and Eliot. His poetry is concrete, sometimes bitter, often elegiac. His books include *The Crow and the Heart* (1959); *Journey to a Known Place* (1961); *Nothing for Tigers* (1965); *For You* (1970); *From Snow and Rock, for Chaos* (1973); *The Bloomingdale Papers* (1975), written during hospitalization for a mental breakdown; *Asphalt Georgics* (1985), depicting the world of shopping malls; *Collected Shorter Poems* (1992); *Collected Longer Poems* (1993); *Scrambled Eggs and Whiskey: Poems 1991–1995* (1996); and *Summer with Tu Fu* (1996). *Appendix A* (1963) is a novel. *Working Papers* (1982) is a prose miscellany. Carruth edited a highly praised anthology, *The Voice That Is Great Within Us: American Poetry of the Twentieth Century* (1970). Recent prose includes *Selected Essays and Reviews* (1996); *Reluctantly: Autobiographical Essays* (1998); and *Beside the Shadblow Tree: A Memoir of James Laughlin* (1999).

Carryl, Charles Edward (1841–1920), stockbroker, writer of books for children. Carryl began his literary career by issuing a *Stock Exchange Primer* (1882), but this was followed by books of a totally different character—the classic *Davy and the Goblin* (1885); *The Admiral's Caravan* (1892); *The River Syndicate and Other Stories* (1899, for older readers); *Charades by an Idle Man* (1911). The children's books, written in a style reminiscent of Lewis Carroll, contain some brilliant nonsense verse.

Carryl, Guy Wetmore (1873–1904), poet, novelist, humorist, writer for children. Guy Wetmore was the son of CHARLES CARRYL. His parodies of Aesop, Mother Goose, and the Grimm fairy stories were collected in *Fables for the Frivolous* (1898), *Mother Goose for Grown-Ups* (1900), and *Grimm Tales Made Gay* (1902).

Carson, Anne (1950–) poet, scholar, essayist. Born in Toronto, Carson grew up in small towns in northern Ontario. She was educated through the Ph.D. (1980) at the University of Toronto before entering on a distinguished career as classical scholar, essayist, and poet at the University of Calgary, Princeton, Emory, and McGill (where she has been director of graduate studies) and as a visiting scholar and poet at the University of Michigan and Berkeley. Widely published in major journals, she is one of two Canadians (ALICE MUNRO is the other) to be honored by the Lannan Literary Award, a $50,000 prize given by a Los Angeles foundation; that, in 1996, was followed two years later by a Guggenheim Fellowship. Her work mixes forms and contents as traditional essay and poetic expectations spill into one another. Influences range from the ancient Greeks of her professorial specialty through Gertrude Stein, European surrealists, Virginia Woolf, and Christian and Eastern mysticism. Among her books are *Eros: The Bittersweet: An Essay* (1986), with a focus on the poetry of Sappho; *Short Talks* (1992), prose poems later included in *Plainwater: Essays and Poetry* (1995); *Glass, Irony and God: Essays and Poetry* (1995); and *Autobiography of Red: A Novel in Verse* (1998), bringing the Greek mythic hero Geryon into a modern world of teenagers, T-shirts, and confused sexuality. In *Men in the Off Hours* (2000) she writes from within the minds of people as diverse as Lazarus and Tolstoy, Freud and Emily Dickinson; included is the prose poem "Irony Is Not Enough: Essay on My Life as Catherine Deneuve," where French actress and classics professor merge in a manner suggestive of the connection between the personal and cultural made also in earlier poems such as "The Fall of Rome: A Traveller's Guide." In all of her work, including recent mixed media experiments, she continues to consider herself a classicist, "conserving the past—it's what classicists do" in ways appropriate to the present.

Carson, Kit [Christopher] (1809–1868). American trapper and guide. Born in Kentucky, Carson crossed the Mohave desert in 1830 and served as a guide in Frémont's first expedition in 1842. As an Indian fighter and later as a lieutenant-colonel in the Civil War, he became the hero of numerous dime novels, He dictated a brief autobiography to an army surgeon, De Witt Peters, which appeared as *The Life and Adventures of Kit Carson, The Nestor of the Rocky Mts.*

(1858). Joaquin Miller's poem, KIT CARSON'S RIDE, describes the scout's wedding day and his frenzied gallop with his bride through a prairie fire. He appears also in Willa Cather's *Death Comes for the Archbishop.*

Carson, Rachel [Louise] (1904–1964), marine biologist, writer. Born in Pennsylvania, Carson earned fame for the precise observations and lucid style of her books on marine life, including *Under the Sea Wind* (1941), *The Sea Around Us* (1951), and *The Edge of the Sea* (1954). Her *Silent Spring* (1962) played an important role in awakening Americans to the dangers to the ecosystem attendant on widespread use of insecticides.

Carter, Jimmy [James Earl, Jr.] (1924–   ), 39th president of the U.S. (1977–81). Carter was born in Plains, Georgia, grew up there, and returned there after his presidency. He was educated at the Naval Academy at Annapolis and at Union College. After serving in the Navy's nuclear submarine program, he returned to Plains to run the family peanut warehouse, then was elected as Georgia state senator and as governor (1970–74). In 1976, he caught the country's imagination as representing a fresh and moral force outside the Washington corruption highlighted by the Watergate Scandal that ended the Nixon administration. He won the Democratic nomination and defeated Gerald Ford in the election. During his presidency, he distinguished himself in his battle for worldwide human rights and in the personal diplomacy that led to the Camp David Accords bringing peace between Israel and Egypt. His bid for reelection fell under the cloud of severe inflation and the Iranian hostage situation which he had been unable to solve, and he lost to Ronald Reagan. In retirement, he has continued his humanitarian efforts, particularly with respect to low-cost housing for the poor, and in his sponsorship of a research institute at Emory University with a special focus on meeting the needs of third-world countries. Among his writings are *Why Not the Best?* (1975), *A Government as Good as Its People* (1977); *Keeping Faith: Memoirs of a President* (1982); *Negotiations: The Alternative to Hostility* (1984); *The Blood of Abraham: Insights into the Middle East* (1985); with his wife, Rosalynn Carter, *Everything to Gain: Making the Most of the Rest of Your Life* (1987); *An Outdoor Journal* (1988); *Talking Peace: A Vision for the Next Generation* (1993); and *The Virtues of Aging* (1998). His religion is discussed in *Living Faith* (1996), a spiritual autobiography, and *Sources of Strength: Meditations on Scripture for a Living Faith* (1997). *Always a Reckoning* (1995) is a verse collection. His affecting memoir, *An Hour Before Daylight: Memories of My Rural Boyhood* (2001), sheds light on the man and president he became.

Carter, Nick. Carter was a fictional detective apparently created by JOHN R. CORYELL, who seems to have worked in a writing team with THOMAS CHALMERS HARBAUGH (1849–1924) and Frederick Van Rensselaer Dey (1861?–1922), writing numerous Nick Carter stories. Nick apparently made his first appearance in *The Old Detective's Pupil* (1886). Among others who used Nick Carter in their stories were Frederick William

Davis, GEORGE CHARLES JENKS, and Eugene Taylor Sawyer. More than a thousand Nick Carter stories were written altogether, and the character also was used in the movies and for radio mystery plays.

Cartwright, Peter (1785–1872), clergyman, memoirist. An itinerant Methodist preacher in Kentucky and Illinois, Cartwright is remembered as the unsuccessful opposition candidate to Lincoln when he ran for Congress. Cartwright wrote about his experiences in his *Autobiography of Peter Cartwright, the Backwoods Preacher* (1856), and *Fifty Years as a Presiding Elder* (1871).

Caruthers, William Alexander (1800–1846), novelist. Caruthers was born in Virginia and is thought to have attended Washington (later Washington and Lee) College. He published three novels: *The Kentuckian in New York, or, The Adventures of Three Southerners* (1834); *The Cavaliers of Virginia* (1835), a story of Bacon's Rebellion; and *The Knights of the Horseshoe, a Traditionary Tale of the Cocked Hat Gentry in the Old Dominion* (1845), a historical romance about the colonial governor Alexander Spotswood.

Carvel, Richard. See RICHARD CARVEL.

Carver, Jonathan (1710–1780), explorer, travel writer. Born in Weymouth, Massachusetts, Carver served in the French and Indian War; in 1766–77, hired by Major Robert Rogers to explore the west, he followed the Mississippi nearly to the site of Minneapolis. On a second trip, he reached Lake Superior. His account, the first description in English of the area, was published in London as *Travels Through the Interior Parts of North America in the Years 1766, 1767, and 1768* (1778). Widely popular, and admired by such writers as Wordsworth, Coleridge, CHATEAUBRIAND, and Schiller, it went through over 30 editions.

Carver, Raymond (1938–1988), short-story writer, poet. Born in Oregon, Carver grew up in Yakima, Washington. Married at nineteen and a father of two by twenty, he moved with his family to California, worked nights, and attended Chico State College and then Humboldt State College. At Chico State he studied under JOHN GARDNER, who influenced his care for detail and for the moral dimension of fiction. After a brief time in the Iowa Writers Workshop in 1963, he dropped out to return to California and work in unskilled jobs, as a textbook editor, and later as a university teacher. Alcoholism led to hospitalization, smoking to the cancer from which he died. From 1977 onward, however, he managed a more stable life with the poet Tess Gallagher (1943–   ).

Widely acclaimed as the most significant short-story writer of his generation, Carver depicted the frustrations, deprivations, and loneliness of blue-collar Americans living on a West Coast where sunshine, glamor, and affluence seemed to belong to someone else's world. His is a fiction of MINIMALISM: minimal events rendered in spare prose. If the experience of his characters is restricted, however, his interest in them is not. His minute observations accumulate to create an empathy, more powerful in his later work, that convinces readers that these lives matter. He was already a master in his first major collection, *Will You Please Be Quiet, Please?* (1976), a gathering of stories that had been appearing in little magazines for a dozen years. Three more collections followed: *What We Talk About When We Talk About Love* (1981), *Cathedral* (1983), and *Where I'm Calling From* (1988), thirty stories from earlier books and seven new ones. A high point in his growth was achieved in two of the stories of *Cathedral*: the title story, in which a jealous husband reaches out to a blind man; and "A Small, Good Thing," in which the death of a child brings strangers together over the bread of communion. His verse collections include *Where Water Comes Together with Other Water* (1985) and *Ultramarine* (1987). *No Heroics, Please: Uncollected Writings* (1992) includes a foreword by Tess Gallagher. *All of Us: The Collected Poems* appeared in 1998. *Call If You Need Me* (2000) is a miscellany, with five previously unpublished stories.

Cary, Alice (1820–1871),   poet, prose writer. Born near Cincinnati, Alice was the sister of PHOEBE CARY; the two overcame poverty and Ohio frontier hardships to establish a a small reputation with a first collection, *Poems of Alice and Phoebe Cary* (1850); later, in New York City, the sisters became a part of the cultural and intellectual life there, dedicated to abolitionist and suffragist causes. Alice's *Lyra and Other Poems* appeared in 1852. Her collection of prose sketches, *Clovernook* (1852), is an early account of the difficulties of frontier life from a woman's perspective. Whittier wrote "The Singer" about her.

Cary, Phoebe (1824–1871),   poet. Sister of ALICE CARY, she wrote some of the *Poems* (1850), and also *Poems and Parodies* (1854); and *Poems of Faith, Hope, and Love* (1868).

Casey, John [Dudley] (1939–   ),   novelist, educator. Born in Worcester, Massachusetts, Casey was educated at Harvard and the University of Iowa, and has taught at the University of Virginia. His first novel, *An American Romance* (1977), drew praise for its warmly satiric view of love among American intellectuals. *Spartina* (1989), a novel about the love of a Narragansett Bay fisherman for his boat, won a National Book Award. His other titles are *Testimony and Demeanor* (1979), short fiction; *South Country* (1988), a novel; and *The Half-Life of Happiness* (1998), a novel set in Charlottesville, involving politics and the dissolution of a marriage.

Casey, Robert J[oseph] (1890–1962),   editor, writer. Casey worked on the Des Moines *Register and Leader*, the Houston *Post*, and the Chicago *Daily News*. Among his books are *The Land of Haunted Castles* (1921), *The Cannoneers Have Hairy Ears* (1927), *Baghdad and Points East* (1928), *Cambodian Quest* (1931), *I Can't Forget* (1941), *Torpedo Junction* (1942), *Such Interesting People* (1943), *This Is Where I Came In* (1945), *Battle Below: The War of the Submarines* (1945), *More Interesting People* (1947), *The Black Hills and Their Incredible Characters* (1949), *The Texas Border and Some Borderliners* (1950), *Chicago Medium Rare* (1952), and *Give the Man Room* (a life of Gutzon Borglum, 1952, with Mary Borglum).

Casey at the Bat   (published under the pseudonym "Phin" in the San Francisco *Examiner*, June 3, 1888), a humor-

ous poem by Ernest Lawrence Thayer (1863–1940). The verses relate how the mighty Casey, hero of the Mudville baseball team, strikes out and loses the game. The poem became famous when DeWolf Hopper, a well-known entertainer, made it part of his between-the-acts repertoire.

Casey Jones,   a ballad. One of the memorable railroad songs, "Casey Jones" tells of a train wreck and the death of an engineer who was trying to make up time. Authorship of the song is disputed. Casey was perhaps John Luther Jones, born in or near Cayce, Kentucky, and killed in a wreck in 1900; his widow, described sometimes as "Mrs. Casey Jones," died in 1958 at age 92.

Casket, The.   See GRAHAM'S MAGAZINE.

Cask of Amontillado, The (1846),   story by EDGAR ALLAN POE. The story was first published in *Godey's Lady's Book*, November 1846, and first collected in Griswold's edition of Poe's *Works* (1850). Montresor relentlessly leads Fortunato to his death in carnival time, tempting him on with a tale of a choice amontillado, and walling him into an underground vault. The story is distinguished by its many ironies, sardonic humor, and unrepentant narration by Montresor, fifty years after the deed.

Caspary, Vera (1904–1987),   novelist, screenwriter. Caspary first came into prominence as a writer of good, tight mystery fiction with the publication of *Laura* (1942), later a major film (1944). One of her earliest novels was *The White Girl* (1929). Her work includes *Thicker Than Water* (1932), *Bedelia* (1945), *The Weeping and the Laughter* (1950), *The Husband* (1957), *Evvie* (1960), *A Chosen Sparrow* (1964), and *The Rosecrest Cell* (1967). An autobiography is *The Secrets of Grown-Ups* (1979).

Cassady, Neal (1926–1968),   friend of JACK KEROUAC, and the model for Dean Moriarty of ON THE ROAD and Cody Pomeray of Kerouac's *Visions of Cody*.

Cassandra Southwick (1843),   a poem by JOHN GREENLEAF WHITTIER. Lawrence Southwick of Salem received Quakers as guests in his home, and his young son and daughter refused to attend church services. The Southwicks were fined and were unable or unwilling to pay. The children were condemned by John Endicott (1589?–1665), governor of the colony, to be sold as slaves in Virginia or the Barbados. But no sea captain could be found who was willing to convey them to the slave market, and they were freed. Whittier's stirring ballad about this incident is put into the mouth of Cassandra Southwick. The poem is an attack on the harsher manifestations of Puritanism, and it contains a powerful denunciation of slavery.

Cassidy, Hopalong.   A cowboy character who first appeared in *Bar 20* (1907), a novel by CLARENCE E. MULFORD, and in many subsequent Mulford books. In the movies, he was played by William Boyd, who starred in 66 films involving Cassidy, beginning with *Hop-A-Long Cassidy* (1935) and extending to 1948; these were also extraordinarily popular on television into the fifties. The Hopalong of the books, a crusty Westerner with a bad leg, was a far cry from the romanticized hero of the movies.

Cassill, R[onald] V[erlin] (1919–), fiction writer, teacher. Born in Iowa and educated at the University of Iowa, Cassill served in the army in World War II and has taught at a number of universities. His first novel, *The Eagle on the Coin* (1950), described race relations in the Midwest. His other novels include *Clem Anderson* (1961), on the death of a young author; *Pretty Leslie* (1963), set in Iowa; *The President* (1964), about academic politics; *La Vie Passionée of Rodney Buckthorne* (1968), of Greenwich Village bohemian life; *Dr. Cobb's Game* (1970), based on England's Profumo scandal of 1963; *The Goss Woman* (1974); *Hoyt's Child* (1976); and *Labors of Love* (1980), about an author's failures in life. His short-story collections include *The Father* (1965) and *The Happy Marriage* (1970). Among his other fictions are *Labors of Love* (1980), *Flame* (1980), *Three Stories* (1982), *After Goliath* (1985), and *Collected Stories* (1989). He has also published popular fiction as Owen Aherne.

Cassique of Kiawah (1859),   a novel of colonial life in Charleston by WILLIAM GILMORE SIMMS.

Castaneda, Carlos (1923–1998),   anthropologist. Born in Peru, Castaneda claimed to have spent five years in Mexico as a spiritual apprentice to the Yaqui Indian he calls Don Juan, but whose person and teachings he invented, at least in part. His first book, *The Teachings of Don Juan: A Yaqui Way of Knowledge* (1968), describes Don Juan's teaching that all humans are born with a finite quantity of energy, regulating the way they perceive reality. In human history the mode of perception has evolved from spiritual intuition to reason; Castaneda preaches a return to the more direct "silent knowledge." Associated with the New Age movement, he has sold 8 million books in 17 languages; they include *A Separate Reality: The Phenomenology of Special Consensus* (1971), *Journey to Ixtlan* (1974), *Tales of Power* (1975), *The Second Ring of Power* (1977), *The Eagle's Gift* (1982), *The Fire From Within* (1984), and *The Power of Silence: Further Lessons of Don Juan* (1987).

Casting Away of Mrs. Lecks and Mrs. Aleshine, The (1886),   a comic novel by FRANK R. STOCKTON. Two widows decide to leave their New England village and see the world. On their voyage across the Pacific they are shipwrecked. Together with a Mr. Craig, they make their way to a desert island, where they find a deserted but comfortable house to live in. Each week they conscientiously deposit a sum in a ginger jar to pay for board. Soon they are joined by a missionary, his daughter, and others, and Craig marries the daughter. Rescued, they make their way back to the United States, are caught in a blizzard, and finally land in Pennsylvania, where there is more marrying. The more improbable the tale grows, the more realistic Stockton makes the details. He also wrote a sequel, *The Dusantes* (1888).

Castlemon, Harry.   Pen name of C. A. FOSDICK.

Catcher in the Rye, The (1951),   a novel by J. D. SALINGER. This short work captured the imagination of a generation of young people. The adolescent narrator, Holden Caulfield, speaks a colloquial prose that uniquely conveys contemporary youth's dissatisfaction with adult society. The book is an extended monologue by Holden that begins:

"If you really want to hear about it, the first thing you'll probably want to know is where I was born, and what my lousy childhood was like, and how my parents were occupied and all before they had me, and all that David Copperfield kind of crap, but I don't feel like going into it, if you want to know the truth."

Holden tells the story as one recovering from a nervous breakdown. For him it is "this madman stuff that happened to me around last Christmas just before I got pretty rundown and had to come out here and take it easy." There is an edge to his voice as he tells of the "phoniness" of his surroundings at a boarding school, Pencey Prep, and his running away for two aimless, adventurous days in New York City. He meets a prostitute, visits his little sister Phoebe, flees from the homosexual advances of his former English teacher, takes Phoebe to the Central Park Zoo and for a ride on the carousel. But Holden seems now to have have his malaise under control, and he will "go home next month maybe."

The image that gave the book its title has been imprinted on the minds of millions of readers. Asked by his sister to name something he would like to be, Holden imagines himself as the older protector of small children. He stands in a field of rye, while they run about and play. "I have to catch everybody," he says, "if they start to go over the cliff . . . I'd just be the catcher in the rye and all. I know it's crazy, but that's the only thing I'd really like to be."

Catch-22 (1961).   JOSEPH HELLER's free-wheeling novel is at once a darkly comic account of American aviators during the final months of World War II's European campaign and a commentary on bureaucratic absurdities endemic to modern warfare. Survival dominates the thoughts of those forced to fly missions in a war that is effectively over, while political jockeying, public relations, and visions of power dance through the heads of their officers. In a world where Yossarian, the novel's protagonist, is determined to "live forever or die in the attempt," the consequences of "catch-22" are everywhere. One observes its black humor in the Great Loyalty Oath Campaign, in the burgeoning capitalist empire of Milo Minderbinder, in the outrageousness of the rumors about German Le Page anti-aircraft guns that glue formations together and, of course, in the rule that effectively sends both the sane and the crazy into battle.

Despite the high jinks and parodic humor, *Catch-22* is a death-haunted novel. An enormous number of minor characters die: some (like Clevinger) simply fly into a cloud and never return; others (like Doc Daneeka) suffer bureaucratic terminations, removed from the rolls of the living with the stroke of a pen as they stand there insisting otherwise. Most haunting of all is the description, foreshadowed, but its full impact delayed until the end, of Snowden bleeding to death and literally freezing in Yossarian's arms.

"Catch-22" has become part of our language. Moreover, after nearly thirty years, Heller's novel retains its position not only as the most distinctive fiction of World War II, but also as the most wildly imaginative and telling account ever of the ongoing battle between modern bureaucracy and the resisting individual.

SANFORD PINSKER

Catesby, Mark (1679?–1749), English naturalist, explorer, author. *The Natural History of Carolina, Florida, and the Bahamas Islands* (1731–1743) was illustrated with the author's own paintings. Another, more technical book was *Hortus Britanno-Americanus, or a Collection of 85 Curious Trees and Shrubs, the Production of North America Adapted to the Climate and Soil of Great Britain* (1737).

Cathedral, The (1869), a poem by JAMES RUSSELL LOWELL. The poem, originally called "A Day at Chartres," describes a day at the French city and in the cathedral. Written in blank verse, it deals primarily with the conflicting values of science and religion and the troubles that conflict has brought to souls in search of God. It is, at the same time, an attempt to reconcile the present of America with the past of Europe, the Yankee with the classicist. The location and theme prefigure a later work, Henry Adams's MONT SAINT-MICHEL AND CHARTRES (1905).

Cather, Willa [Sibert] (1873–1947), novelist, short-story writer. Cather is generally acknowledged today to be one of the major fiction writers of the 20th century. Although she enjoyed both a popular and critical success during her lifetime, in the sociological 1930s she was attacked as a purveyor of nostalgia and escapism, and by her death in 1947 her reputation had undergone a partial eclipse. In the past generation, however, the academic community rediscovered her and her star is still in the ascendancy. She is the author of twelve novels and fifty-eight stories, all kept in print by her publishers, and she annually is the subject of a large number of critical essays as well as frequent books and dissertations.

Born in Virginia, Cather moved to Nebraska with her family when she was nine. She spent her first months there on a prairie farm, then moved to the village of Red Cloud. She went to Lincoln to attend the state university, from which she was graduated in 1895. Her first job was that of editor of a home magazine in Pittsburgh, for which she had prepared by working as a drama critic and columnist during college for the *Nebraska State Journal*. From the magazine she moved to the Pittsburgh *Leader*, mostly as drama and music critic. Weary of the daily grind of journalism, she became a high school teacher of English. In 1906, however, S. S. McClure lured her to New York to become an editor and two years later managing editor of his remarkable magazine, a job she held through 1911. At that point she resigned and became a writer.

Cather had been publishing stories since her undergraduate years in Nebraska, and this activity had culminated in the publication of *The Troll Garden* (1905), which contains two of her best-known stories, "The Sculptor's Funeral" and "Paul's Case." But this was not her first book, as she had published a volume of poems, *April Twilights*, in 1903. Her first novel, ALEXANDER'S BRIDGE (1912), came out soon after she left *McClure's Magazine*, and while she herself later disparaged it (the story of a bridge-builder torn between love for his Boston wife and a London actress), it is a competent piece of fiction and contains a number of themes and situations she later developed more powerfully in her best novels.

The novel she liked to consider her first was *O Pioneers!* (1913), the book in which, as she put it, she hit the home pasture. After living in Pittsburgh and New York for seventeen years, she discovered Nebraska as a prime subject for fiction, and her memories of her youth there came flooding back. She always maintained that a writer's most important material was acquired before the age of fifteen, and in *O Pioneers!* she drew on the pioneer families she had known as a child. It is the story of Swedish immigrants who tame the wild land, the protagonist being Alexandra Bergson, a strong-willed, capable woman of mythic proportions. The novel evokes memorably the spirit of the pioneers and contrasts it with the materialism of the next generation, a theme that figures prominently in Cather's later fiction. The novel ends in a tragic love affair between Alexandra's younger brother and the wife of a neighboring Czech farmer.

After publishing *O Pioneers!* Cather next combined her use of Nebraska in pioneer times with music, another of Cather's consuming interests. This resulted in THE SONG OF THE LARK (1915), a bildungsroman of the career of a celebrated singer. The prototype for the singer as child and adolescent was Cather herself growing up in Red Cloud, and the model for the adult singer was Olive Fremstad, then the leading Wagnerian soprano at the Metropolitan Opera. Cather's fourth novel, MY ÁNTONIA (1918), is one of her two most celebrated works, a novel that captures poignantly the life of Czech immigrants, most notably the title character, Ántonia Shimerda, who in real life was a close friend of Cather's. This novel fashions a narrator, Jim Burden, whose life parallels Cather's own and through whose eyes the reader sees Ántonia. It is a superb drama of memory. Again Cather creates a character rooted in actuality but infused with mythic overtones. Ántonia is a madonna of the wheat fields, described by the author as the mother of races. Here also is the story of the farming frontier symbolized by a vivid image of the plough against the sun as it is seen by Jim, Ántonia, and two other immigrant girls, who picnic by the river just before Jim goes off to college.

My Ántonia was followed by a collection of stories, YOUTH AND THE BRIGHT MEDUSA (1920), containing four stories reprinted from *The Troll Garden* and several new ones dealing with the lives of singers. Cather's fifth novel, *One of Ours* (1921), takes place during World War I and was inspired by the death of Cather's cousin on the Western Front in France in 1918. Claude Wheeler in this novel is an idealistic Nebraska farm boy who enlists in the army after an unhappy life on the farm and a failed marriage. He dies thinking he is helping save the world for democracy. The Nebraska scenes in the novel are vintage Cather, but the battle sequences had to be written from secondhand experience, a method alien to Cather's best work. Even so, the novel won the Pulitzer Prize, but writing it cost Cather four years of effort, and it drew a fair amount of hostile criticism. The novel is inferior only when compared with Cather's best work, and critics who panned it missed the satire and irony.

Cather came back from her disappointment with the reception of *One of Ours* to write A LOST LADY (1923), which the critics acclaimed as a minor masterpiece. It is the story of a woman Cather had known when she was growing up in Red Cloud, Mrs. Silas Garber, wife of a former governor of Nebraska, pioneer, and railroad-builder. Again Cather created a triangular situation in Marian Forester's affair with Frank Ellinger, and again she told the story through the eyes of a boy, as she had with Jim Burden in *My Ántonia*, but this time she used a third-person point of view. Again Cather contrasted the pioneers with the next generation of moneygrubbers by juxtaposing Captain Forrester and shyster lawyer Ivy Peters. Marian Forrester is a lost lady only in the eyes of Niel Herbert, the point-of-view character, for she rides out the death of her husband and his loss of fortune, survives the era, and at the end makes a new life for herself. This novel well illustrates the narrative principles Cather spelled out in her essay "The Novel Démeublé," in which she argues for elimination of excess furniture in the novel and quotes the elder Dumas to the effect that "to make a drama, a man needed one passion, and four walls."

After *A Lost Lady* Cather went on to write a novel that is becoming increasingly popular with critics, *The Professor's House* (1925). Here Cather creates a professor of history who has just won an important prize for his history of the Spanish in North America, but he is dissatisfied with life. The novel, which reflects the professor's mildlife crisis, is in many ways autobiographical—Cather herself was experiencing a similar malaise. After nearly dying of asphyxiation at the end of the novel, the professor, as Cather did, comes to terms with life as a diminished thing. Also in this novel as a long insert is the story told retrospectively of Tom Outland, the one really remarkable student of the professor's career. Tom grew up in the Southwest, where he was a cowboy and a discoverer of the cliff-dwellings at Mesa Verde, but after the frustration of being unable to interest the Smithsonian Institution in the Indian artifacts and the disappointment of having his partner sell the artifacts to a collector, he goes north and enters the professor's university. When the novel takes place, Tom has long since died in World War I, but his influence shapes the events of the story.

"Tom Outland's Story" is a product of Cather's growing passion for the Southwest, which she began to visit when she left *McClure's Magazine* in 1912. She first made use of this material in *The Song of the Lark*, returned to it in *The Professor's House*, and made full use of it in DEATH COMES FOR THE ARCHBISHOP (1927). But before writing *Archbishop*, she had one more short novel to get out of her system, *My Mortal Enemy* (1926). Cather said in the preface to an essay collection she published in 1936 that the world had broken in two about 1922, but despite this attitude she produced some of her most important fiction in the next five years. Yet the 1920s were a dispiriting time for her. The critical hostility toward *One of Ours*, her midlife crisis, the Prohibition she hated, the materialism of the Jazz Age—all these factors seem to have contributed to a sense of alienation. *My Mortal Enemy* is a bitter

book that drained the last bit of gall from her. It is the story of Myra Driscoll, who elopes with Oswald Henshawe from a Midwest town and is disinherited by her great-uncle, a rich, bigoted Irish Catholic who hates the Protestant Henshawe. Myra lives to regret bitterly marrying for love, and the story ends in a West Coast city with Myra and Oswald in poverty and Myra alone with her mortal enemy. Myra returns to her Catholic faith just before dying of an incurable disease.

From *My Mortal Enemy* Cather went on to write *Death Comes for the Archbishop*, which she and many critics considered her best book. This was the first of three historical novels produced during a period of thirteen years. It is an experimental modernist novel, loosely episodic, with no conventional plot, and laced with inset stories. Cather said she was trying to write a novel that was like a series of frescoes she had seen in Paris in 1902 by Puvis de Chavannes depicting the life of Ste. Geneviève. Also she said she was trying to do something like the lives of the saints in *The Golden Legend*, in which their martyrdoms are no more dwelt upon than the trivial events of their lives. The immediate inspiration for the book, however, came from Cather's finding on a visit to Santa Fe the biography of the priest who had been vicar to the first bishop, later archbishop, of New Mexico. The two men were missionary priests from France, Jean Baptiste Lamy and Joseph Machebeuf, and the biography contains a vivid account of their mission organizing the new diocese of New Mexico after its acquisition by the United States from Mexico. The book gave Cather the idea of how to handle her subject. She always had thought that the history of the Catholic missions in the Southwest was one of the region's most interesting stories. The novel that followed creates the fictional bishop Jean Marie Latour and his vicar Joseph Vaillant, who together bring order out of chaos and years of neglect in the Church's affairs in the New Mexico territory. It is a noble story, beautifully told in Cather's simple but eloquent prose style, a book that is universally today regarded as a classic of American literature.

Soon after Cather finished *Death Comes for the Archbishop*, her father died, her mother had a stroke, and Cather had to move from the Greenwich Village apartment she had lived in for fifteen years. Life seemed to be falling apart. During the three years when her mother was paralyzed and living in California with her brother, Cather camped out in the Grosvenor Hotel on lower Fifth Avenue and made annual trips to California. Her salvation in this period was the writing of SHADOWS ON THE ROCK (1931), a novel laid in 17th-century Quebec. This is the story of one year in the life of the French colony perched on its rock in the St. Lawrence River and centers on the life of the apothecary Euclide Auclair and his daughter Cécile. Count Frontenac and Bishop Laval, historical figures, are characters in the novel, and the book is remarkable for its descriptions of Quebec at various times of the year, a fine example of writing analogous to impressionistic painting. While the novel is not in the same class as Cather's best fiction, no novel she wrote is less than beautifully written. In all her works Cather carries out the principle she learned from her role model, Sarah Orne Jewett, whom she knew briefly during her years at McClure: "If he [the writer] achieves anything enduring, it must be by giving himself absolutely to his material. And this gift of sympathy is his great gift."

After Cather's mother died in 1931, Cather returned to Red Cloud for a Christmas reunion with her brothers and sisters, following which she never went back to Nebraska but lived on in her new New York apartment on Park Avenue, summered on Grand Manan Island in the Bay of Fundy, and spent part of most autumns at Jaffrey, New Hampshire, where she is buried. The death of Cather's father in 1928 and her mother's long illness turned her mind back to Nebraska and Red Cloud, and the result was a collection of three stories published as *Obscure Destinies* (1932), her final major work using the Midwest setting for which she is known. "Neighbor Rosicky" is a story of a Czech farmer and his family and in some ways is a sequel to *My Ántonia*, as the characters of husband and wife are again patterned after the heroine of the former novel and her husband. "Old Mrs. Harris," the finest of all Cather's stories, creates in fiction Cather's grandmother, who is the title character; Victoria, drawn from Cather's mother; and Cather herself as Vickie, a teenager getting ready to go to college. "Two Friends" is a lesser tale, which was inspired by Cather's memory of listening as an adolescent to two Red Cloud businessmen talk on summer evenings outside James Miner's store. The Miner family were the neighbors who sat for the portrait of the Harlings in *My Ántonia*.

Two more novels complete the Cather canon, *Lucy Gayheart* (1935) and SAPPHIRA AND THE SLAVE GIRL (1940). *Gayheart*, another of Cather's lesser works, returns to the story of a musician who goes to Chicago to study, as did Thea Kronborg in *The Song of the Lark*. Lucy is not the artist that Thea is, and her story ends in defeat and tragedy. She falls in love with a famous singer, for whom she plays accompaniments, and when he dies in a drowning accident, she returns to her home town—another avatar of Red Cloud—lonely and unhappy. Later she also drowns when she goes skating alone at a place in the river that, unbeknownst to her, had become treacherous in her absence. Cather's last novel, *Sapphira and the Slave Girl*, is one of her half-dozen best novels and the only one in which she used her native Virginia as setting. It is a historical novel laid in the village of her birth in the decade before the Civil War. The story involves the conflict between Sapphira's efforts to sell her servant Nancy and her husband's refusal to consent to the transaction. There is a great deal of Cather family history in this novel, as Sapphira and Henry Colbert are patterned after Cather's maternal great-grandparents, and the character of Mrs. Blake is a fictional representation of Cather's Grandmother Boak, "Mrs. Harris" in the previously mentioned story. In the climactic scene Mrs. Blake helps Nancy escape to Canada via the Underground Railroad, an act that Mrs. Boak had accomplished in real life. Plot, setting, and characterization are handled with exceptional skill in this novel, even though Cather was at the end of her career and her health was breaking down.

After publishing *Sapphira and the Slave Girl*, Cather wrote only a few more stories and an unfinished novel that was destroyed after her death by her longtime companion, Edith Lewis. She died of a cerebral hemorrhage in her New York apartment on April 24, 1947, her reputation secure. She had gotten out of life what she most had wanted, which was to live an untrammeled life as a writer. Few writers have been so dedicated to their art as Cather. She had maintained from the time she was a college freshman that an artist had to sacrifice everything for art. In her case this included matrimony and children, for though she had proposals of marriage during her Pittsburgh years, she remained single throughout her life. In recent years she has been called a lesbian because all her close relationships outside of her father and brothers, her former boss McClure, and her publisher Alfred Knopf were with women, but all the evidence points to a celibate writer married only to her work.

The original biography of Cather by E. K. Brown (1953) has been superseded by a work by James Woodress, *Willa Cather: A Literary Life* (1987). Two good critical studies of Cather's work are David Stouck's *Willa Cather's Imagination* (1975) and Susan Rosowski's *The Voyage Perilous: Willa Cather's Romanticism* (1986). Criticism is collected in John Murphy, ed., *Critical Essays on Willa Cather* (1983), and two useful reference books are Marilyn Arnold, ed., *Willa Cather: A Reference Guide* (1986), which is an annotated list of secondary comment, and Joan Crane's comprehensive *Willa Cather: A Bibliography* (1982). Sharon O'Brien's *Willa Cather: The Emerging Voice* (1987) is an important psychological study down to 1912, and the University of Nebraska Press makes available all the stories Cather did not collect herself and much of her journalism, interviews, and speeches: *Collected Short Fiction, Uncle Valentine and Others*; Bernice Slote, ed., *The Kingdom of Art*; William Curtin, ed., *The World and the Parish*; and Brent Bohlke, ed., *Willa Cather in Person*.

JAMES WOODRESS

Catherwood, Mary [Hartwell] (1847–1902), teacher, novelist. Born in Ohio, Catherwood made a specialty of life in old-time French America and the Old West and won the commendation of FRANCIS PARKMAN for her fidelity to history. The first of her novels to win wide popular success was THE ROMANCE OF DOLLARD (1889); others were *The Story of Tonty* (1890), *The Lady of Fort St. John* (1891), and *Lazarre* (1901), a romance of the lost Dauphin.

Catlin, George (1796–1872), explorer, artist, writer. Catlin was born in Pennsylvania. Although his mother had as a child been captured by Indians in the Wyoming Massacre, Catlin felt no strong resentment toward Native Americans and devoted his life to making a pictorial and verbal record of Indian customs. He went to live among Indians in Florida and the West, studied their languages, painted them, exhibited his pictures, and wrote books about his observations and experiences. Late in life he also undertook explorations of South America. Many of his paintings are now in the Smithsonian Institution. Among his books are *Letters and Notes on the Manners, Customs, and Conditions of the North American Indians* (1841), *North American Indian Portfolio* (1844), *Life Among the Indians* (1867), *Okeepa, A Religious Ceremony, and*

Other Customs of the Mandans (1867), and *Last Rambles Amongst the Indians of the Rocky Mountains and the Andes* (1868).

Cat on a Hot Tin Roof (1955),   a play by TENNESSEE WILLIAMS. Set on a plantation in the Mississippi Delta country, the play centers on the wealthy Pollitt family. It opens just after the other members of the family have discovered that Big Daddy Pollitt is suffering from incurable cancer. Gooper, the oldest son, and his wife, Mae, plot to ensure that Big Daddy's money and property go to them and their brood of children rather than to Brick, the younger son, who is an alcoholic ex-football star. Brick's wife Maggie, the cat, is childless and is growing bitter and frustrated because Brick blames her for driving his friend Skipper to his death by convincing him that the friendship between the two men was latently homosexual. In a scene with Big Daddy, Brick accuses the world in general and the family in particular of "mendacity," although Brick himself is living a lie in his inability to face the implications of his relationship with Skipper, his rejection of Maggie, and his escape into alcohol. Forced by Big Daddy into admitting his failings, Brick strikes back by telling Big Daddy he is dying of cancer. Finally, knowing that Big Daddy favors Brick and would like Brick to have a child, Maggie announces, to the consternation of all, that she is pregnant. Although Brick knows she is lying, he does not contradict her, and the play ends with a hope of reconciliation between them. The play was made into a memorable film in 1958.

Cat's Cradle (1963),   a novel by KURT VONNEGUT. In it, Vonnegut's first novel to receive serious critical attention, the narrator tells of an eccentric inventor of an atom bomb and a crystal called ice-nine, which freezes anything it touches. Mixing that story with an account of a Latin American dictatorship and its religion of untruth, the narrator brings the two together in a frozen apocalyptic end.

Catton, Bruce (1899–1978),   journalist, Civil War historian. Born in Michigan, Catton was educated at Oberlin College and worked for newspapers in Cleveland, Boston, and Washington. His service during World War II as Director of Information for the War Production Board led to *The War Lords of Washington* (1948), his first major book. Celebrity followed publication of his trilogy of studies of the Union Army of the Potomac: *Mr. Lincoln's Army* (1951), *Glory Road* (1952), and *A Stillness at Appomattox* (1953), the last a Pulitzer Prize winner. In 1954 Catton became an editor of *American Heritage* magazine. His other Civil War histories include *U.S. Grant and the American Military Tradition* (1954), *This Hallowed Ground* (1956), *Grant Moves South* (1960), *The Centennial History of the Civil War* (3 v. 1961–1965), and *Grant Takes Command* (1969). With his son William, he wrote biographies of Lincoln and Jefferson Davis, *Two Roads to Sumter* (1963). His other books include *Michigan: A Bicentennial History* (1976) and a memoir of his youth, *Waiting for the Morning Train* (1972).

Caulfield, Holden.   The protagonist and narrator of THE CATCHER IN THE RYE, by J. D. SALINGER.

Cavender's House (1929),   a narrative poem by Edwin Arlington Robinson. It tells how Cavender, who had pushed his wife off a cliff because he suspected her of infidelity, is still uncertain twelve years later, and describes the thoughts that torment him as he wanders to the edge of the cliff again.

Cawdor   (in *Cawdor and Other Poems*, 1928), a narrative poem by ROBINSON JEFFERS. Based on the story of Phaedra and Hippolytus, *Cawdor* deals with the desire of Fera Cawdor for her stepson Hood, who rejects her advances. Cawdor, suspecting the boy has seduced Fera, kills him. Cawdor, learning later that Hood was innocent, is unable to expiate his guilt—there can be no future life and no punishment on earth to cleanse him.

Cawein, Madison [Julius] (1865–1914),   poet, called the Keats of Kentucky. Born in Kentucky, Cawein wrote more than thirty books, beginning with *Blooms of the Berry* (1887) and closing with *The Cup of Comus* (1915). His poems were collected in five volumes in 1907, and in 1902 a selection made by Edmund Gosse was issued in England as *Kentucky Poems.*

Celebrated Jumping Frog of Calaveras County, The (1865),   a tall tale by MARK TWAIN. In this, Twain's first famous story, the miner Jim Smiley makes a bet that his frog Dan'l Webster can jump farther than the frog casually selected by a stranger. While Jim's attention is distracted, the stranger loads Dan'l down with quail shot—a fact Jim doesn't discover until the stranger departs. Mark Twain did not invent the story. It was a folk tale current in mining camps during the early years of the gold rush era, and versions have been found in print in the Sonora *Herald* of June 11, 1853, and the San Andreas *Independent* of December 11, 1858. Twain's version first appeared in *The Saturday Press* of New York on November 18, 1865, under the title "Jim Smiley and His Jumping Frog." It was reprinted in Beadle's *Dime Book of Fun* in 1866. Then it appeared, with other sketches, as Twain's first book, *The Celebrated Jumping Frog* (1867).

Celestial Railroad, The (1843),   a short story by NATHANIEL HAWTHORNE, later included in MOSSES FROM AN OLD MANSE. It is a modern treatment of *Pilgrim's Progress*, in which the traveler uses up-to-date facilities for his journey but finds himself beset by age-old pitfalls.

Centaur, The (1963),   a novel by JOHN UPDIKE. Updike focuses on three days in the life of a high school teacher, George Caldwell, and his son Peter. The town, Olinger, Pennsylvania, is a fictionalized Shillington, where Updike grew up, and father and son are based on the author and his father. Like other Olinger stories, the details are realistic for their time and place; for this one, Updike added another dimension by creating parallels with Greek myth. George Caldwell is Charon, Peter Caldwell is Prometheus, and other characters have similar correspondences. At the suggestion of Updike's wife, he listed over 50 names and terms in a "Mythological Index" at the end of the book.

Center for Editions of American Authors.   An organization created in 1963 by the Modern Language Association of America to oversee publication of dependable editions of the writings of American authors.

Century Association, The   [The Century Club], New York City. An association composed of "authors, artists, and amateurs of letters and the fine arts," founded in 1846. Among its presidents were George Bancroft, William Cullen Bryant, and Elihu Root.

Century Illustrated Monthly Magazine, The. *Scribner's Monthly*, subtitled "An Illustrated Magazine for the People," was founded by Roswell Smith, who conceived the original idea; JOSIAH G. HOLLAND, popular essayist and poet; and Charles Scribner, of the book publishing house. Holland became editor, Smith business manager and later president of the company that took it over and renamed it the *Century*. It entered the field as a strong competitor of *Harper's New Monthly* in November 1870. It was copiously illustrated with fineline woodcuts by Timothy Cole, George Kruell, Francis G. Attwood, and others; and it was unusually well printed (1874–1914) by Theodore Low DeVinne.

Though *Scribner's* began by using some serials by foreign writers, as *Harper's* was doing, it soon was filling its fiction pages with the work of Holland, Rebecca Harding Davis, H. H. Boyesen, Frances Hodgson Burnett, Bret Harte, George W. Cable, Henry James, Frank R. Stockton, and Saxe Holm (Helen Hunt). Greatest of the nonfiction serials was Edward King's copiously illustrated *The Great South*. This was followed by a number of short stories and serials of Southern life by Cable, Joel Chandler Harris, Thomas Nelson Page, James Lane Allen, and others. Departments of comment and miscellany conducted by RICHARD WATSON GILDER and Richard Henry Stoddard were important in the magazine, as were Charles Dudley Warner's *Back-Log Studies* (1871–1872), nature essays by John Burroughs and John Muir, and art criticism by W. C. Brownell and Clarence Cook.

Management differences caused a split in the Scribner house in 1881, and the magazine's name was changed to *Century Illustrated Monthly Magazine* by the new ownership. Gilder was the new editor. The magazine's policy changed but little, except for increased emphasis on public affairs. In the 1880s the magazine featured a series on the Civil War, including the recollections of Generals Grant, McClellan, Eads, Johnston, Hill, Longstreet, Beauregard, and many others. Even unmilitary Mark Twain told of his war experiences. Other important nonfiction serials were George Kennan's *Russia and the Exile System*—an international sensation—and an 1890 feature on the California gold miners.

Important fiction serials came from Howells, Mrs. Humphry Ward, Jack London, and Mark Twain, who provided a slightly bowdlerized version of *Huckleberry Finn*. The *Century* exploited the new craze for historical fiction with S. Weir Mitchell's *Hugh Wynne* and F. Marion Crawford's *Via Crucis*.

The magazine's highest circulation of 200,000 was reached shortly before 1890. Roswell Smith died in 1892, and Gilder carried on as editor until 1909, when ROBERT UNDERWOOD JOHNSON, long an associate editor, took over for a few years.

But the *Century* was losing its audience. After 1913 it had a journalistic emphasis, but under Glenn Frank's editorship

(1921–1925) it was again more literary, with many distinguished contributors. In 1930 it merged with *The Forum*.

Century of Dishonor, A   (1881),   an account by HELEN HUNT JACKSON of governmental mistreatment of Native Americans. The book was based on careful investigation and was followed by the widely read romance RAMONA (1884), on the same theme. See MISSION INDIANS.

Cervantes, Lorna Dee   (1954–   ),   poet. Born in San Francisco and educated at San Jose State University and University of California–Santa Cruz, Cervantes was part of the 70s' second wave of Hispanic-American publishing, the first wave having been dominated by men. She founded her own press and a poetry magazine called *Mango*. The influence of the mystic CARLOS CASTANEDA is apparent in her work, which defines life as a struggle to free the spiritual forces of nature to counter class and culture dualities and tensions between the sexes. Often she sprinkles Spanish words and phrases in her verse. In *Emplumada* (1981), for instance, she uses the metaphor of the pen, playing on the fact that in Spanish *pluma* means both pen and feather, so to be "emplumed" may mean either covered by feathers like a bird, or an Indian in ceremonial dress, or using a quill, or pen, like a writer. *From the Cables of Genocide: Poems of Love and Hunger* appeared in 1991.

Césaire, Aimé   (1913–   ),   poet, dramatist, essayist. Césaire was born in 1913 in Martinique, into a poor black family. In Paris from 1931 to 1939, he and his fellow black students—among them Léopold Senghor of Senegal—were somewhat influenced by contemporary African-American writers. As a result, they launched and publicized the concept of *negritude*, seeking to end the alienation of their race through a rediscovery of its positive qualities. Back in Martinique during the war, Césaire became involved with leftist politics and anticolonialist movements. Elected mayor of Fort-de-France and deputy to the French Assembly in 1945, Césaire worked at writing, administering his constituency, and fighting colonialism in its various global manifestations. He chose, however, not to lead his own island to a separation from France, instead promoting the cultural autonomy he considers a step toward political autonomy.

Césaire's best-known work is a book-length poem, *Cahier d'un retour au pays natal* (Notebook of a Return to the Native Land, 1939), in which the narrator confronts his blackness, descending to the depth of despair and self-contempt before finding pride and joy in his negritude. The powerful three-movement free verse lyrical journey evokes centuries of servitude while finding reasons for blacks to transcend or even forgive their oppressors. The *Notebook* became a seminal text not only for blacks of various nations but for men of good will in general. His other verse collections include *Les Armes miraculeuses* (Miraculous Weapons, 1946); *Soleil cou coupé* (Solar Throat Slashed, 1948); *Corps perdu* (Lost Body, 1950); *Ferrements* (1960); *Noria* (1976); and *Moi laminaire* (1982). They show a decreasing influence of Surrealism on Césaire's style, becoming more and more elegiac and personal as they became more topical. Nevertheless, Césaire had harnessed Surrealism to the service of negritude and made it a potent instrument of liberation from the forms of traditional French poetry.

Césaire's plays, *La Tragédie du roi Christophe* (1963), *Une Saison au Congo* (1967), and *Une Tempête* (1969) are as skillful and profound as his poetry. They also address the topics of colonialism and negritude, in historical form in the case of the first two and in symbolic form (freely adapted from Shakespeare) in the case of the third. Césaire has also published a three act "oratorio," *Et les chiens se taisaient* (And the Dogs Were Silent, 1956) and several poetic and philosophical essays: *Póesie et connaissance* (Poetry and Knowledge, 1944); *Discours sur le colonialisme* (1951); and *Toussaint L'Ouverture* (1960).

Oeuvres complètes appeared in 1976. Translations include *The Collected Poetry* (1983); *Aimé Césaire: Lyric and Dramatic Poems 1964–1982* (1990); *King Christopher* (1970); and *A Season in the Congo* (1971). See A. J. Arnold, *Modernism and Negritude* (1981) and R. L. Scharfman, *Engagement and the Language of the Subject in the Poetry of Aimé Césaire* (1987).
ANNETTE SMITH

Chabon, Michael (1963–), novelist, short-story writer. Born in Washington, D.C., Chabon graduated from the University of Pittsburgh (1984) and earned an M.F.A. at the University of California, Irvine. He won attention with his first novel, *The Mysteries of Pittsburgh* (1988), about a summer of exhilarating and confusing possibilities faced by a young college graduate. A second novel, *Wonder Boys* (1995), finds humor in a writer's inability to write his great novel. *A Model World* (1991) and *Werewolves in Their Youth* (1998) collect stories mostly of the wry disfunctions of family life. *The Amazing Adventures of Kavalier and Clay* (2000) won the Pulitzer Prize.

Chainbearer, The (1845), a novel by JAMES FENIMORE COOPER. The second in the trilogy *The Littlepage Manuscripts*, it expresses Cooper's detestation of frontier leveling and of self-government carried to extremes. Mordaunt Littlepage seeks to improve the family patent and comes into conflict with squatters. See ANTI-RENT LAWS. REDSKINS, and SATANSTOE.

Chakley, Thomas (1675–1741), sea captain, preacher, author. Chalkley was a Quaker preacher in England and at times in the colonies. In SNOW-BOUND (1866) Whittier calls him "gentlest of skippers, rare seasaint" and retells an exciting episode from his journal (1747), a widely admired account of religion and adventure.

Chambered Nautilus, The (1858), a poem by OLIVER WENDELL HOLMES. It first appeared in *The Atlantic Monthly* (February 1858) as part of THE AUTOCRAT OF THE BREAKFAST-TABLE series and in *The Autocrat* volume later that year. The nautilus, a sea creature that enlarges its shell as it grows, becomes a symbol for the soul, which can build itself more and more stately mansions as the swift seasons roll, leaving its "low-vaulted past." Holmes was especially proud of its verse pattern and said he had written it in "the highest state of mental exaltation and crystalline clairvoyance" that had ever been granted him.

Chamberlain, George Agnew (1879–1966), novelist. Born in Brazil, Chamberlain studied at Princeton, became a consular official in various parts of Latin America, wrote well-told and spirited romances, and in later years lived in New Jersey. Among his books are *Through Stained Glass* (1915); *John Bogardus* (1916); *The Lantern on the Plow* (1924); *In Defense of Mrs. Maxon* (1938); *Knoll Island* (1943); *Scudda-Hoo! Scudda-Hay!* (1946, movie version 1948); and *Lord Buff and the Silver Star* (1955).

Chambers, Robert W[illiam] (1865–1933), painter, novelist, short-story writer. Born in Brooklyn, Chambers was a painter and illustrator who turned to writing with *In the Quarter* (1894), a novel; *The Red Republic* (1895), a historical romance about the Franco-Prussian War; and *The King in Yellow* (1895), short stories. His other novels include *A King and a Few Dukes* (1896); *Lorraine* (1898); *Ashes of Empire* (1898); *Cardigan* (1901), about the American Revolution; *Iole* (1905), about the poet; and *The Tracer of Lost Persons* (1906), about a Mr. Keen, who later became the central figure of a successful radio serial; *The Firing Line* (1908); *Police!!!* (1915); *The Restless Sex* (1918); *The Hi-Jackers* (1923); and *The Drums of Aulone* (1927).

Champlain, Samuel de (1567?–1635), French explorer. He first made himself familiar with the lands of the Caribbean Sea, later accompanied fur-trading expeditions to the Gulf of St. Lawrence, and ascended the St. Lawrence River to the Lachine Rapids (1603). He also explored portions of Nova Scotia, founded Quebec (1608), went down the New York lake that bears his name (1609), and visited the Great Lakes (1615). The British captured Quebec and took Champlain to England as a prisoner. Subsequently, he became governor of the French colony (1633–35). He wrote several books recording his journeys and observations, summing them up in his *Voyages de la Nouvelle France* (1632).

Chan, Charlie. The pudgy, wise, smiling Chinese detective living in Hawaii who appears in a number of mystery novels by EARL DERR BIGGERS.

Chance Acquaintance, A (1873), a novel by WILLIAM DEAN HOWELLS. A New York girl, Kitty Ellison, on a trip along the St. Lawrence and into Quebec, falls in love with a proper Bostonian, Miles Arbuton. They become engaged, but Miles, meeting some fashionable and snobbish acquaintances, ignores Kitty and she breaks the engagement, knowing she can never be happy with a Brahmin. The novel draws its background from the honeymoon trip in the same region that Howells described in THEIR WEDDING JOURNEY (1871).

Chancellorville, Battle of (May 2–4, 1863), the culmination of a campaign led by General Joseph Hooker in which the Northern army attempted to flank General Lee's position around Fredericksburg and cut his communication with Richmond. Lee didn't wait, and Hooker, slow to deal with a surprise attack, was defeated and forced to withdraw. According to family tradition, STEPHEN CRANE heard much about the Battle of Chancellorsville from his uncle Edmund Crane, who had taken part in it, and this information provided background for the battle described in THE RED BADGE OF COURAGE (1895).

Chandler, Raymond (1888–1959),   mystery writer, scriptwriter. Born in Chicago, but raised and educated in England, France and Germany, Chandler at first wrote verse, essays, book reviews, and special articles for British newspapers. After World War I, in which he served in the Canadian and British forces, he returned to the U.S., entered business, and became an officer in various oil companies. In the early 1930s he began to write for the pulps, and in 1933 *Black Mask* bought a story of his called "Blackmailers Don't Shoot." Thereafter, his success was steady. In 1939 appeared THE BIG SLEEP, followed by *Farewell, My Lovely* (1940), *The High Window* (1942), *The Lady in the Lake* (1943), *Red Wind* (1946), *Spanish Blood* (1946), *The Little Sister* (1949), *The Long Goodbye* (1954), and *Playback* (1958). His collections of short stories include *Five Murderers* (1944); *Five Sinister Characters* (1945); *Finger Man* (1946); *The Simple Art of Murder* (1950), with commentary by the author; and *Killer in the Rain* (1964). His HARD-BOILED FICTION has won admiration for his ability to depict Los Angeles low life and for his creation of private eye Philip Marlowe. Several of his novels became popular films. Tom Hiney and Frank MacShane edited *The Raymond Chandler Papers: Selected Letters and Non-Fiction*, 1909–1959, (2001).

Chang, Eileen [Chang Ai-ling] (1920–1995),   novelist, short-story writer. A native of Shanghai, daughter of a wealthy family, Chang suffered emotional and physical abuse as a child. When her education at the University of Hong Kong was aborted in 1942 by the Japanese invasion Chang returned to Shanghai, where she earned early popular success during the Japanese occupation as a writer of romances. She gained serious attention with *The Golden Cangue* (1943), a novel named for a stock-like restraint, telling of family tyrannies and unhappy love; adapting it in English as *The Rouge of the North* (1967), Chang cut some of the most distressing scenes. After immigrating in 1955, she lived the last forty years of her life in the United States, writing or translating her works into English. She met her American husband at the MACDOWELL COLONY (he died in 1967), spent time as a scholar or writer-in-residence at Miami University in Ohio, Radcliffe, and Berkeley, and although she lived much of her later life as a recluse, she continued as one of the most respected Chinese authors in Taiwan, Hong Kong, and other Chinese communities worldwide. *The Rice Sprout Song* (1955) and *The Naked Earth* (1956), published in both Chinese and English, display an intense antipathy toward Communism that caused the long-time suppression of her works in mainland China. Less political works treat especially women, isolation, and loneliness. Hailed by some as a potential Nobel Prize winner, had it not been for her anomalous political situation, she has been compared to Western writers such as Flannery O'Connor and Franz Kafka. Even in age and isolation, her reputation continued to grow among Chinese readers, as the films *Love in a Fallen City* (1990), *The Rouge of the North* (1991), and *Red Rose, White Rose* (1995) kept her in the public eye. See GLOBALIZATION OF AMERICAN LITERATURE.

Changing Light at Sandover, The (1982),   volume of poetry by JAMES MERRILL. In this book, Merrill collected three earlier works—"The Book of Ephraim," from *Divine Comedies* (1976); *Mirabell: Books of Number* (1978); and *Scripts for the Pageant* (1980)—and added a coda, "The Higher Keys." The whole is presented as a sequence of conversations, frequently in blank verse, with spirits reached through a Ouija board. The world envisioned includes angelic and demonic characters from religion, folklore, and fantasy fiction, as well as real people with whom the poet feels a particular identification, including his mother, W. H. AUDEN, and Einstein.

Channing, Edward Tyrrell (1790–1856),   editor, teacher. A younger brother of WILLIAM ELLERY CHANNING [1], Edward Channing practiced law, helped found and edit THE NORTH AMERICAN REVIEW, and finally was appointed Boylston Professor of Rhetoric at Harvard. Many important writers of the day came under his guidance, including Emerson, Thoreau, Holmes, Lowell, Edward Everett Hale, and R. H. Dana, Jr. Dana edited Channing's *Lectures* (1856).

Channing, William Ellery [1] (1780–1842),   clergyman, propagandist. Born in Newport, Rhode Island, Channing became a teacher and then was ordained as Congregational minister in 1803 and became pastor of the Federal Street Church in Boston, remaining there until his death. Two great causes engaged him all his life, Unitarianism and Abolitionism, although by temperament he hated controversy. He early became convinced that Calvinism was not for him, and at the ordination of JARED SPARKS in 1819 preached a sermon that resulted in the establishment of Unitarianism. In 1821 he helped found and edit a magazine, *The Christian Register*, which advocated Unitarian doctrines, and in 1825 he founded the American Unitarian Association. In the interests of Abolitionism, he wrote *Slavery* (1835), *The Abolitionist* (1836), *Emancipation* (1840), and *The Duty of the Free States* (1842). His essay *On National Literature* (1830) insisted that American writing and writers deserved more encouragement.

Channing, William Ellery [2] (1818–1901),   poet, essayist. Born in Boston, Channing was the nephew of WILLIAM ELLERY CHANNING [1]. He studied at Harvard for three months, tried farming in Illinois, and practiced journalism in Cincinnati, where he married Ellen Fuller, the younger sister of MARGARET FULLER. In 1842, he settled in Concord, Massachusetts, near Ralph Waldo Emerson, who published Channing's verses and essays in *The Dial*. He wrote for Horace Greeley's *New York Tribune* and edited *New Bedford Mercury* (1856–59). He published nine volumes of poetry and prose, besides countless contributions to newspapers and magazines. Most significant among them are *The Spider*, a sprightly verse which appeared in the *New England Magazine* (1835) and probably suggested Emerson's THE HUMBLE-BEE; *Poems* (1843) and *Poems, Second Series* (1847), the 1843 volume provoking one of Poe's most scathing reviews; and *Thoreau, the Poet-Naturalist* (1873), the first biography of his closest friend. F. B. SANBORN republished this work (1902) with some additions and in the same year edited what he considered the best of Channing's verses, *Poems of Sixty-Five Years.*

Channing is remembered especially for his contribution to the life and work of the Concord writers, all good friends of his. He was the most constant of Thoreau's walking companions and encouraged him in his nonconformity. See TRANSCENDENTALISM.

Channing, William Henry (1810–1884), clergyman, propagandist, editor. Born in Boston a nephew of WILLIAM ELLERY CHANNING [1] and cousin of WILLIAM ELLERY CHANNING [2], he was interested in helping humanity and took part in BROOK FARM and the Fourierist movement. He was a Unitarian leader, but with doubts. Channing wrote *The Gospel of Today* (1847), *The Civil War in America* (1861), and a biography of his celebrated uncle (1848). See ODE INSCRIBED TO W. H. CHANNING.

Chanteys.   SAILORS' SONGS.

Chanting the Square Deific (1865),   a poem by WALT WHITMAN in which he sums up his religious ideas. He names as four sides of the square, Jehovah representing inexorable natural law, Christ representing consolation and love, Satan representing individual will, and Santa Spirita a feminine soul including everything—all life on earth, God, Savior, Satan.

Chap-Book, The.   A semimonthly magazine founded at Cambridge (1893) and moved to Chicago in 1894 along with the publishing firm of Stone & Kimball. It earned a high reputation because of the rigid literary standard it set. Both American and foreign authors contributed freely to its pages, including Henry James, Eugene Field, Max Beerbohm, William Ernest Henley, Bliss Carman, and H. G. Wells. In its design it imitated the English periodical *The Yellow Book*. In turn it was itself imitated by *The Lark* and other American little magazines. In 1898 it merged with *The Dial.*

chapbooks.   During the early 19th century, reading of all kinds of literature—good, bad, and indifferent—was greatly encouraged by the wide sale of what were called *chapbooks*—small books sold at a low price. (The word *chap* is a cognate of *cheap*.) Their vogue recalls that experienced in the later 20th century by paperback books. Chapbooks were usually sold by peddlers (*chapmen*) on foot or on horseback. ISAIAH THOMAS, a Worcester, Massachusetts, printer, was the best-known publisher of chapbooks. His publications contained stories, orations, collections of jests, moral tales, ballads, biographical sketches, fables, and reprintings of well-known writings.

Chaplin, Charlie [Charles Spencer] (1889–1977), actor, producer, Born in England, this extraordinary pantomimist made his screen debut in the United States with the Keystone Film Co., and became famous all over the world for his creation of the little tramp, with his derby, mustache, baggy trousers, oversize shoes, and cane. In such movies as *The Tramp* (1915), *The Vagabond* (1916), *Shoulder Arms* (1918), *The Kid* (1921), *The Gold Rush* (1925), *City Lights* (1931), and *Modern Times* (1936), Chaplin showed his unique mixture of

satire, pathos, and fantasy. Later he appeared in a powerful attack on the pre–World War II totalitarian madness, THE GREAT DICTATOR (1940); in a tragicomic psychological study, *Monsieur Verdoux* (1947); *in Limelight* (1952); and in a satire on American society, *King of New York* (1958). He always took an active part in preparing his scripts and, frequently, his background music; some later scripts, such as *Monsieur Verdoux*, he wrote himself. He never became a citizen; in 1952 he was refused reentry to the United States because of his alleged Communist sympathies. He lived in Vevey, Switzerland, with his wife, Oona O'Neill, and their eight children, returning to the U.S. in 1972 to receive a special Academy Award. In 1975 he was knighted by Queen Elizabeth II. His *My Autobiography* appeared in 1964.

Chapman, John [or Jonathan].   See JOHNNY APPLESEED.

Chapman, John Jay (1862–1933),   critic, essayist, poet, playwright. Born in New York City and educated at Harvard, Chapman practiced law before becoming a writer. A friend of William James and other Boston intellectuals, he earned a reputation for vigorous individualism—Emersonian but also aristocratic. His books include *Emerson and Other Essays* (1898), *Causes and Consequences* (1898), *Learning and Other Essays* (1910), *William Lloyd Garrison* (1913), *Memories and Milestones* (1915), *Greek Genius and Other Essays* (1915), *Songs and Poems* (1919), *Letters and Religion* (1924), and *New Horizons in American Life* (1932). He also wrote a number of plays, including *The Treason and Death of Benedict Arnold* (1910).

Chapman, Maria Weston (1806–1865),   editor, writer. Born in Weymouth, Massachusetts, Chapman was associated with WILLIAM LLOYD GARRISON in the Massachusetts Anti-Slavery Society and as an editor of *The Liberator*. She sponsored *The Liberty Bell* (1839–58), an Abolitionist annual, and edited *The Life of Harriet Martineau* (1877).

Character and Opinion in the United States (1920), essays by GEORGE SANTAYANA. Santayana discusses the nature of American civilization and the traits of Americans. He includes memories of his fellow professors at Harvard, WILLIAM JAMES and JOSIAH ROYCE. The essays were written some years after Santayana had gone to live abroad.

Charlemont, or, The Pride of the Village (1846), a novel by WILLIAM GILMORE SIMMS. In 1842 Simms had published BEAUCHAMPE, his account of the so-called Kentucky Tragedy, which attracted widespread attention in his day. In *Charlemont* he expanded the first part of the story, describing the seduction and desertion of Margaret Cooper.

Charlotte Temple (1794),   a novel by SUSANNA ROWSON. This was the American title of a novel first published in England as *Charlotte: A Tale of Truth* (1791). Widely read on both sides of the Atlantic, it was the most popular early American novel and has been printed in over 200 editions. The story begins in Great Britain and ends in New York City during the Revolution. Charlotte is seduced and betrayed by an officer of the King's army, gives birth to a daughter, and dies in poverty.

A sequel is *Charlotte's Daughter; or, The Three Orphans* (1828), later reprinted as *Lucy Temple*.

Chase, Edna Woolman. See ILKA CHASE, also VOGUE.

Chase, Ilka (1905–1978), actress, novelist, autobiographer. Her mother, Edna Woolman Chase (1877–1957), was editor-in-chief of VOGUE. Ilka was born in New York City and introduced to society at an early age. Beginning at age eighteen, she appeared in numerous plays, movies, and radio programs. Her first autobiographical volume, *Past Imperfect* (1942), had a great success for its frankness and wit. Its successor, *Free Admission* (1948), did not do as well. She also wrote fiction: *In Bed We Cry* (1944), *I Love Miss Tilli Bean* (1946), and *New York 22* (1951). Chase's background is brightly depicted in her mother's self-portrait, *Always in Vogue* (1954).

Chase, Mary Coyle (1907–1981), playwright, author. Chase was born in Denver. *Now You've Done It* (1937) and other early plays achieved little success, but in 1944 her play HARVEY won the Pulitzer Prize. *Harvey's* success lay in its highly imaginative escapist plot involving an invisible rabbit six feet tall. Her next two plays, *Mrs. McThing* (1952) and *Bernadine* (1952), were also well received on Broadway. *Midgie Purvis* opened on Broadway in 1961 to considerably less enthusiasm. Her other plays are *Mickey* (1969) and *Cocktails with Mimi* (1974). Chase also wrote a children's book, *Loretta Mason Potts* (1958).

Chase, Mary Ellen (1887–1973), novelist, essayist. Brought up in Maine and classically educated, Chase taught first in country schools and in several private schools. She taught English at the University of Minnesota, and from 1926 on at Smith College.

Chase was one of the leading regional writers of her time, interpreting Maine past and present at its best and most characteristic. Her vigorous, clean-cut prose and her subtle portrayals, especially of her female characters, give her novels a depth and solidity sometimes lacking in regional writers. She wrote first several stories for young people, including the popular *Mary Christmas* (1926), followed by *Uplands* (1927) and *Gay Highway* (1933). *Mary Peters* (1934) and *Silas Crockett* (1935), two chronicle novels, are probably her most enduring works. *Dawn in Lyonesse* (1938), for once not set in Maine, is an interesting modern parallel of the Tristan and Isolde story. Her later novels are *Windswept* (1941), *The Plum Tree* (1949), *The Edge of Darkness* (1957), *Sailing the Seven Seas* (1958), and *Lovely Ambition* (1960).

Her frequent summers in England led to a book of humorous essays, *This England* (1936). Her autobiography, *A Goodly Heritage* (1932), deals mainly with her teaching experiences; its sequel is *A Goodly Fellowship* (1939). A later autobiographical work, *The White Gate* (1954), is subtitled "Adventures in the Imagination of a Child." She also wrote *The Bible and the Common Reader* (1944) and *Life and Language in the Old Testament* (1955), and two biographies, *Jonathan Fisher: Maine Parson, 1768–1847* (1948) and *Abby Aldrich Rockefeller* (1950).

Chase, Richard V[olney], Jr. (1914–1962), teacher, critic. Chase was professor of literature at Columbia University. His *The American Novel and Its Tradition* (1957) was widely influential in shaping a view of the American novel as descendant of the European, but differing from it in its characteristic employment of "romance" rather than "REALISM." Through the form of "romance," which deals less with character than with action and is not bound to realistic detail, the great American novels have embraced the violent contrarieties of our native culture. His other books: *Emily Dickinson* (1953) and *Walt Whitman Reconsidered* (1955), both in the AMERICAN MEN OF LETTERS SERIES; *Quest For Myth* (1949); *Herman Melville* (1949); and *The Democratic Vista* (1959), a book of conversation about American culture dramatized like Platonic dialogues.

Chastellux, Marquis François Jean de (1734–1788), French soldier. This major-general in Rochambeau's army served from 1780 to 1782 and published an account of his observations, *Travels in North America, in the Years 1780, 1781, and 1782* (2 v., 1786). An English translation appeared in London the following year.

Chateaubriand, François René, Vicomte de (1768–1848), French author. Chateaubriand spent five months in America in 1791, visiting Baltimore, Niagara Falls, and places between. His fictions ATALA (1801), *René* (1802), and LES NATCHEZ (1826) helped spread romantic conceptions of American Indians and the American landscape. His account of his travels, *Voyage en Amérique* (1827), dependent on other sources and partly imaginary, was also widely influential.

Chauncy, Charles (1705–1787), clergyman. Chauncy's great-grandfather Charles Chauncy (1592–1672), also a clergyman, had been the second president of Harvard, where the younger Chauncy was graduated in 1724. In 1727 he became pastor of the First Church (Congregational) of Boston and remained there for the rest of his life. His great mission was to overthrow the harsher doctrines of Calvinism. He began by opposing the revivals of the GREAT AWAKENING, which had become a feature of religion in New England under the leadership of JONATHAN EDWARDS (1703–1758) and George Whitefield (1714–1770). Chauncy fought the battle of rationality and optimism, coming to believe that God would ultimately save all sinners from damnation. In 1782 he published anonymously a book that created a sensation as he allied himself with UNIVERSALISM in New England—*The Salvation of All Men: The Grand Thing Aimed at in the Scheme of God*. Earlier he had published a *Sermon on Enthusiasm* (1742) and *Letters to Whitefield* (1744, 1745) and later issued *The Benevolence of the Deity* (1784). He fought the British attempt to force bishops on the American church, and as an ardent patriot before and during the Revolution wrote a number of political tracts.

Chautauqua. An adult education movement, combined with publications and summer-school activities. The movement grew out of an intelligent young minister's desire for better-trained Sunday school teachers. John H. Vincent (1832–1920) undertook to train teachers by gathering them in groups each summer for all-day study. Then he decided to start a summer school on a more ambitious scale, took over a defunct camp site at Lake Chautauqua, New York, and named the institution the Sunday-School Teachers' Assembly. Forty students attended in the summer of 1874, and the idea of Chautauqua was born. It eventually spread to all parts of the world; millions of people attended Chautauqua lectures and enjoyed planned recreation in great tents all over the United States. In 1878 Chautauqua started a Literary and Scientific Circle. Among books published by Chautauqua Press was *An Outline Sketch of American Literature* by Henry A. Beers of Yale, an introduction to authors many of whom are still considered canonical. The list of contributors to Chautauqua lecture platforms and book publications was virtually a Who's Who of the times.

By 1924 the movement was beginning to decline, although it has continued in a restricted area and with many changes. At its height it was an immensely powerful cultural force and gave the public reliable information on such subjects as suffrage, soil conservation, child welfare, and the humanities.

Chavez, Denise (1948–   ),   short-story writer, novelist. Born in Las Cruces, New Mexico, she was educated in drama and creative writing. Chavez has encouraged the writing of other women by editing, with Linda Feyder, a collection of six plays: *Shattering the Myth: Plays by Hispanic Women* (1994) and a poetry anthology featuring the verse of inmates of the Radium Springs Center for Women. *The Last of the Menu Girls* (1986) is a collection of seven related stories depicting the experience of seventeen-year-old Rocio Esquibel at Altavista Memorial Hospital, where she distributes menus to the patients. Her first novel, *Face of an Angel* (1994), is narrated by a waitress, once divorced and later widowed by suicide, who has worked in a Mexican restaurant for 30 years, all the while working on "The Book of Service," a manual for waitresses and advice book for young women.

Chayefsky, Paddy (1923–1981),   playwright, producer. Born Sidney Chayefsky in New York City and educated at the City College of New York, Chayefsky served in the army in World War II. He began his dramatic writing on television, depicting lives of some of the ordinary people he had known while growing up during Depression years. *Marty* (1953) told sympathetically the love story of a plain Bronx butcher and a plain old-maid schoolteacher. The movie version (1955) won an Academy Award. Two other television plays, *The Bachelor Party* (1953) and *The Catered Affair* (1955), were made into movies, as was the stage play *The Middle of the Night* (1954), with which Chayefsky turned from television to the theater.

Both praised and criticized for his adherence to naturalistic dialogue in the tape-recording school of dramatic style, Chayefsky began to feel while working with the two inarticulate protagonists of *The Middle of the Night* that realism is confining and unimportant. In his play *The Tenth Man* (prod. 1959, pub. 1960) he combined a shabby realistic setting with a fantastic East European legend of the Dybbuk. In 1960, turning to the Bible for his story, to stylization for his method, and occasionally to poetry for his language, he wrote *Gideon* (1961), an ironic story of man's refusal to accept God's assurance even after a series of miracles. Other works include *The Goddess* (1958), a film; *The Passion of Josef D.* (1964), a play

about the Russian Revolution; *The Latent Heterosexual* (1968), a play; *The Hospital* (1971) and *Network* (1975), Academy Award–winning films; and *Altered States* (1978), a science fiction novel and film (1979).

Cheaper by the Dozen (1948),   a family saga by Frank B. Gilbreth, Jr., and Ernestine Gilbreth Carey. Next to Clarence Day, Jr.'s *Life with Father*, this was in its time perhaps the most widely read of the many sprightly accounts of life in an American home. The book was turned into a movie in 1950.

Cheetham, James (1772–1810),   newspaper editor, biographer. Cheetham's connection with liberal movements in England forced him to leave that country for the United States in 1798. He joined De Witt Clinton in buying an interest in the New York *Argus*, changed the name to *American Citizen*, and became a spokesman of the Republicans (later called Democrats). He wrote a savage attack on Aaron Burr for his methods in seeking to win the presidency in 1800; in 1809 he published a vindictive biography of Thomas Paine.

Cheever, John (1912–1982),   short-story writer, novelist. Born in Quincy, Massachusetts, John Cheever grew up in the Yankee formality of a socially conscious, if impecunious, household. His father, Frederick (1863–1945), a shoe salesman and manufacturer, lost his job in the 1920s, and his mother, Mary Liley (1873–1956), an energetic and dominating Englishwoman, began to support her family in 1926, when she opened a gift shop. Cheever developed a strong emotional bond with his brother Fred (1905–1976), which Cheever described as a "Siamese situation." Images of weak and eccentric fathers, strong, domineering mothers and wives, and dark querulous brothers appear throughout his fiction.

After expulsion from Thayer Academy, Cheever turned to writing. For seventeen years he lived in New York City and, because of his poverty, often stayed and wrote at Yaddo, the artists' colony in Saratoga. He wrote stories about middle-class people living in reduced circumstances in the city. In 1950 he joined the millions of Americans who had moved from the city to suburbia after World War II and made suburban life the focus and setting of his fiction. With *The Housebreaker of Shady Hill and Other Stories* (1958), Cheever became known as a chronicler of suburbia. He contrasted the genteel, comfortable facade of suburban living with his characters' grapplings with lust, morality, mortality, and disappointment. His ambivalent attitudes toward suburban life can be seen in the names he gave his towns: Gory Brook, Proxmire Manor, and Bullet Park. His best-known stories include "The Enormous Radio" (1947), "Goodbye, My Brother" (1951), "The Country Husband," (1954), "The Death of Justina" (1961), and "The Swimmer" (1964).

Despite Cheever's guise as the landed patrician, his problems with alcoholism, homosexuality, and depression hounded him for years. In 1975 he made a recovery from alcohol abuse, but homosexuality continued to plague him, particularly in the last decade of his life. In his journals Cheever confronted his themes and his vision: "There is no home, there is no surety or permanence in this world." He also saw clearly the fragility of his own writing: "That bridge of language, metaphor, anecdote and imagination that I build each morning to cross the incongruities in my life seems very frail indeed." Cheever began to accumulate both literary prizes and public recognition, and with publication of his fourth novel, *Falconer* (1977), he became wealthy as well. *The Wapshot Chronicle* (1957), his first novel, won the National Book Award. He won the William Dean Howells Medal from the American Academy of Arts and Letters in 1965 for the best fiction written during a five-year period. His triumph came in 1978 with *The Stories of John Cheever*, which contained 61 of his stories, earned him a $500,000 advance from his publishers, and went on to win both the National Book Critics' Circle Award and the Pulitzer Prize.

Cheever took nearly twenty years to write *The Wapshot Chronicle*, which followed the rise and fall of the New England Wapshots, based loosely on his own family background, and contrasted a lyric celebration of family rituals and customs with a darker look at the rootless, nomadic ways of contemporary American life. His style both celebrated a nostalgic recreation of memory and hope in his characters' vision of the world and ironically undercut that nostalgia in their false reliance on it. This basically dualistic approach in his fiction never deserted him.

The Wapshot Scandal (1964) presented a darker and more disruptive picture of contemporary mores. It was followed by his most experimental and dualistic work, *Bullet Park* (1960), in which the main characters, Hammer and Nailles, battle the suburban facade of gentility and decorum in their different ways, the former withdrawing into a drug-induced stupor in order to coast through daily existence, the latter attempting to commit murder as a way of destroying what he took to be the spiritual complacency of his neighbors. Both seem to be symmetrically opposing sides of one badly splintered psyche. It may be Cheever's masterpiece.

Falconer surprised readers, since Cheever dispensed with suburbia to write about life in prison. He maintained that all his work was about confinement, and that Ezekiel Farragut's final escape from prison was a symbol of the kind of redemption and renewed spiritual liberation Cheever had celebrated throughout his fiction.

At first Cheever was viewed as a *New Yorker* writer of glib and superficial tales of good manners and the smug upper classes. The mistaken appraisal came from his association with *The New Yorker*, in which, beginning in 1935, he published 121 stories. But as a moralist, Cheever was soon drawn to more prophetic visions of contemporary life, made resonant and suggestive by his use of myth and fantasy. *Time*'s 1964 cover story, describing him as the Ovid of Ossining, comes closer to what Cheever was up to. His inclusion of myth within the boundaries of social realism opened up new fictional strategies for such contemporary fabulists as JOHN BARTH, THOMAS PYNCHON, and JOHN GARDNER.

Cheever's fiction was built on the contradictory opposites and polarities of such American romancers as Hawthorne, Melville, and Scott Fitzgerald. His light and decorous style revealed the bizarre and often cruel misdeeds and yearnings of his characters. In the Wapshot novels he juxtaposed the more lyric Coverly Wapshot with his more demonic brother Moses. The apotheosis of these dualities culminated in *Bullet Park* and in Ezekiel Farragut's murder of his brother in *Falconer*.

At the same time Cheever's characters' dreams and phobias constantly invaded and undermined the comfortably suburban patina of their lives, causing confusion and anxiety. Apocalypse always seemed right around the corner, as if some cataclysm were about to erupt and destroy whatever vestige of morality and decency Cheever's characters tried to cling to. This unrelenting and unresolved dialectic places Cheever among the best American writers.

Yet, Cheever's method was essentially comic. The characters perform in a specific social setting and are shaped by it. The reader is distanced from them by this setting, however darkened and anxious, and can often laugh, if painfully, at the situations that engulf them. It is this essential graceful and comic form of Cheever's style that shapes our lasting impressions of his art, and it is that balanced, decorous and lyric style for which Cheever may be most celebrated.

Cheever's daughter, Susan Cheever, portrayed her father in a memoir, *Home Before Dark* (1984). Scott Donaldson's *John Cheever* (1988) is a biography.

SAMUEL COALE

Cheney, John Vance (1848–1922), librarian, poet, essayist. Cheney, an associate of Edwin Markham, Joaquin Miller, and other literary lights of California, won a moderate reputation with his collections of lyrics, including *Thistle-Drift* (1887) and *Poems* (1905).

Cherokee Indians. The Cherokees occupied the Piedmont and Appalachian regions in what are now North and South Carolina, Georgia, Alabama, and Tennessee, speaking an Iroquoian language. By the 16th century, when Hernando de Soto visited them, they had established an agricultural economy. Frequently at war with the New York Iroquois, they generally sided with the British against the French, but they also went to war with the colonists in 1760. Treaties with the United States after the Revolution led to an era of immense progress. By 1820, Cherokees had established a republican form of government and in 1827 they adopted a constitution and formed the Cherokee Nation. The Cherokee chieftain SEQUOYA performed the prodigious feat of creating an alphabet. Cherokees quickly became literate, publishing books and newspapers (*The Cherokee Phoenix*, founded in 1828, suppressed in 1835; *The Cherokee Advocate*, founded in 1844). Discovery of gold in their territory, however, increased the pressures against them, resulting in the infamous Trail of Tears, the forced removals, beginning in 1835, of 18,000 Cherokees to the Indian Territory (now Oklahoma) in the West. An estimated 4,000 died en route. Descendants of the few who escaped removal or returned have continued to live in western North Carolina. In Oklahoma they established a capital at Tahlequah, founded schools, and published newspapers. In 1906, they disbanded as a tribe and became U.S. citizens.

Primary and secondary literature on the Cherokees is extensive. WILLIAM BARTRAM's *Travels* (1791) includes descriptions of Cherokee culture observed at first hand in the 1770s around the upper reaches of the Little Tennessee River. Elias Boudinot, Cherokee editor of *The Cherokee Phoenix*, in 1833 published a novel, *Poor Sarah, or The Indian Woman*. Cherokees of the early frontier appear also in stories by WILLIAM GILMORE SIMMS; MARY NOAILLES MURFREE's *The Amulet* (1906); and CAROLINE GORDON's *Green Centuries* (1941). See JOHN M. OSKISON, JOHN RIDGE, LYNN RIGGS, and WILL ROGERS.

Chesnut, Mary Boykin (1823–1886), diarist. Chesnut, daughter of a U.S. senator from South Carolina, and wife of an ardent secessionist, had a ringside seat at the events leading to the Civil War, and recorded her observations with humor and understanding in a diary running to some 400,000 words. It was published in 1905 with certain passages omitted. Ben Ames Williams reissued it as A DIARY FROM DIXIE (1949), and C. Vann Woodward edited the complete text as *Mary Chesnut's Civil War* (1982).

Chesnutt, Charles W[addell] (1858–1932), novelist, short-story writer. Born in Cleveland, Chesnutt became a teacher, newspaperman, and lawyer. In August 1887, his first story, "The Goophered Grapevine," was published in the *Atlantic*, and a series of such stories made up his first book, *The Conjure Woman* (1899), centering around Uncle Julius McAdoo. Chesnutt's later books considered race prejudice frankly: *The Wife of His Youth and Other Stories of the Color Line* (1899), *The House Behind the Cedars* (1900), and *The Colonel's Dream* (1905). In 1928 he received the Spingarn gold medal award for "pioneer work as a literary artist depicting the life and struggle of Americans of Negro descent." Helen N. Chesnutt's *Charles W. Chesnutt, Pioneer of the Color Line* (1952) describes him as "a pioneer Negro author, the first to exploit in fiction the complex lives of men and women of mixed blood." *The Journals of Charles W. Chesnutt* (1993) and *To Be an Author: Letters of Charles W. Chesnutt, 1889–1905* (1997) are recent scholarly compilations.

Chester, George Randolph (1869–1924), novelist, short-story writer, critic. Born in Ohio, Chester wrote stories that won great popularity, particularly in *The Saturday Evening Post*. The best-known told of GET-RICH-QUICK WALLINGFORD, who managed to make money by means barely legal but generally amusing. A play by GEORGE M. COHAN was based on the stories (1910).

Cheyenne Indians. Tribe of Native Americans who spoke an Algonquian language. In the 17th century they left their Minnesota home to the hostile Sioux and Ojibwa and settled to the southwest, along the Missouri River. There they build earth-lodge houses and continued as a corn-growing society until the acquisition of horses turned them, about 1800, into nomadic PLAINS INDIANS. Early in the 19th century they split into the Southern Cheyenne, around the upper Arkansas River, and the Northern Cheyenne, between the North Platte and the Yellowstone. Conflict with whites passing through Southern Cheyenne territories resulted in a treaty placing them on a reservation in Colorado in 1861. Soon starving, they made raids that brought on an 1864 massacre of Indians at Sand Creek, Colorado, Indian warfare, and defeat of

the Cheyenne by General GEORGE CUSTER in 1868. The Northern Cheyenne then joined with the Sioux in the massacre of Custer and his men at Little Bighorn in 1876. A year later, the Cheyenne were finally defeated, and placed first on a reservation in Colorado, later in Montana.

The Cheyenne appear frequently in literature, including HAMLIN GARLAND's novel *The Captain of the Gray-Horse Troop* (1902) and in his *The Book of the American Indian* (1923); HOWARD FAST's *The Last Frontier* (1941); and THOMAS BERGER's *Little Big Man* (1964). Books by writers of Cheyenne descent include John Stands in Timber's *Cheyenne Memories* (1967), an as-told-to autobiography, and Hyemeyohsts Storm's *Seven Arrows* (1972) and *Song of Heyoehkah* (1981).

Chicago (1913), a poem, and *Chicago Poems* (1916), a collection, by CARL SANDBURG.

Chicago Critics. In the 1940s and '50s a number of philosophers and critics at the University of Chicago—most notably Richard McKeon, R. S. Crane, Elder Olson, and W. R. Keast—developed a system of interpretation derived from the method of Aristotle's *Poetics*, and a view of criticism as a discipline derived from Aristotle's general philosophical method. They defined the literary text as the representation of some human action, thought, or feeling designed either to produce a specific emotional effect or to inculcate some belief or intellectual attitude in its audience. They adopted the method of reasoning back from the effects of a work to the causes of those effects in the work itself. Thus, for them interpretation became an inquiry into the way in which the parts of a given text—the objects imitated (character, setting, and action), the manner of imitation (the poetic, narrative, or dramatic technique), and the means of imitation (language)—are synthesized into an organic whole with the power to move an audience in a particular way.

Their broader view of criticism can be called methodological pluralism: just as Aristotle acknowledged the different kinds of knowledge sought by poetic, rhetorical, ethical, and metaphysical inquiries, the Chicago critics argued that different kinds of questions about literature could offer different kinds of worthwhile knowledge. Thus, rather than privileging their concern with constructed form they also welcomed inquiries focusing primarily on authors, audiences, culture, history, and many other issues.

Though never the dominant movement of American criticism, Chicago Aristotelianism has been an active and influential school. Many of the ideas and principles of the original group have been extended and revised over the past forty years, and the influence of this work has been felt most strongly in the criticism of the novel and in discussions of critical methodologies and their interrelations.

JAMES PHELAN

Chicana and Chicano Literature. See HISPANIC-AMERICAN LITERATURE.

Chickasaw Indians. Tribe of Native Americans who spoke a Muskhogean language and were located in what is now northern Mississippi and western Tennessee. They were an aggressive people, enemies of the Choctaw, Creek, Cherokee, and Shawnee tribes. When De Soto visited and made unwelcome demands, they killed eleven of his men and most of his horses. In conflicts between the English and French, they sided with the English. By 1820 they had adopted a number of white frontier ways, building schools, cultivating crops, holding black slaves, and raising livestock. In 1837–38 they moved by treaty to Oklahoma; later they joined with the Cherokee, Choctaw, Creek, and Seminole Indians in the confederation known as the Five Civilized Tribes. Faulkner treats them in a number of works, including the stories "Red Leaves," "A Justice," and "A Courtship." His IKKEMOTUBBE is a Chickasaw chief; SAM FATHERS is part Chickasaw, part African-American. LINDA HOGAN is of Chickasaw descent.

Child, Francis J[ames] (1825–1896), teacher, philologist, ballad collector. Born in Boston and educated at Harvard and in Germany, Child became a Harvard professor specializing in Middle English. His great work, however, the product of many years of collecting, was the eight volumes of ENGLISH AND SCOTTISH POPULAR BALLADS (1857–58), which appeared in revised form in 1883–98 (10 v.). The work immediately became the most authoritative publication on the subject and has not been superseded. It printed 305 distinct English and Scottish ballads, as many as possible from manuscript sources, and usually with all the known versions, in addition to an exhaustive critical apparatus and notes on distribution. Few important additions have been made to the collection. Child had numerous disciples. His teaching and his great collection gave stimulus to the gathering of other ballads in the United States and elsewhere.

Child, Lydia Maria [Francis] (1802–1880), novelist, crusader. Born in Medford, Massachusetts, Child established the *Juvenile Miscellany* (1826), the first monthly for children in the United States, She wrote an early anti-slavery book, *Appeal in Favor of That Class of Americans Called Africans* (1833), and edited HARRIET JACOBS's *Incidents in the Life of a Slave Girl* (1861). She also wrote books helping women in their household problems, *The Frugal Housewife* (1829) and *The Mother's Book* (1831). She was a pioneer in advocating women's suffrage and sex education and wrote *A History of the Condition of Women in Various Ages and Nations* (1835). Child also wrote fiction: HOBOMOK (1824), in which a Native American marries a white girl; *The Rebels* (1825), picturing Boston before the Revolution; *Philothea* (1836), set in ancient Greece; and *A Romance of the Republic* (1867), which deals with Abolitionism. She probably is most frequently remembered for a poem she wrote on *Thanksgiving Day* (1857), one stanza of which begins:

Over the river and through the wood,
To grandfather's house we'll go.

H. W. Sewall collected some of her correspondence in a volume of *Letters* (1883).

Child, Philip (1898–1978), novelist, poet. Born in Hamilton, Ontario, and educated at the University of Toronto, Cambridge, and Harvard. He served in the army in World War I, worked as a journalist, and taught English in universities in the United States and Canada. In 1942 he became a professor at Trinity College, University of Toronto. His first novel, *The Village of Souls* (1933), has been highly praised. This historical novel, mythic in scope, tells of a voyageur torn between love for a Native American and a French woman. A Christian humanism informs most of his work, including the novels *God's Sparrows* (1937), anti-war; *Day of Wrath* (1945), set in wartime Germany; and *Mr. Ames Against Time* (1949), about urban problems. The title piece of *The Victorian House and Other Poems* (1951) is a narrative celebrating the value of continuity. *The Wood of the Nightingale* (1965) is another narrative poem.

Children of Adam. A group of poems in WALT WHITMAN's LEAVES OF GRASS. They first appeared in the 1860 edition of *Leaves of Grass* as fifteen poems entitled *Enfans d'Adam*. Whitman deleted one poem, added two others, and translated the title into English in the edition of 1867. The section created a great deal of controversy because of its forthright praise of physical love, procreation, and the beauty of the human body. Whitman intended that *Children of Adam* be a companion section to CALAMUS [1] (1860), in which he celebrated the love of comrades.

Children of the Night, The (1897, reprinted 1905), a collection of poems by EDWIN ARLINGTON ROBINSON. In it are included some poems from Robinson's earlier collection, *The Torrent and the Night Before* (privately printed, 1896). President Theodore Roosevelt liked the volume and gave Robinson a sinecure as clerk in the New York Custom House. The book includes such admired pieces as "Luke Havergal," RICHARD CORY, and "Two Men" and reveals Robinson's mastery of psychological portraiture.

Children's Hour, The [1] (1860), poem by HENRY WADSWORTH LONGFELLOW. It is devoted to those "blue-eyed banditti," his three daughters—"grave Alice and laughing Allegra and Edith with golden hair." They come down "between the dark and the daylight" and overwhelm him with their kisses. The three girls described were children of his second marriage, to Frances Appleton.

Children's Hour, The [2] (1934), play by LILLIAN HELLMAN, based on an actual case in Edinburgh. A child at a boarding school maliciously starts a rumor that the two heads of the school are lesbians, and the result is tragic. An attempt was made to suppress the play. It was filmed successfully in 1936 without the lesbian theme; in 1962, less well, with it. Hellman acknowledged her debt to the late William Roughead's essay "Closed Doors, or the Great Drumsheugh Case" in his book *Bad Companions* (1931).

children's literature. American children's literature stems from all countries and all literature: ancient fables, folktales, epics and legends, poetry and other writings, including religious writings shared by children and adults. Indeed, the best literature for children has always been that which children and adults enjoy sharing. An important source was England, since many early colonists brought their literature from England when they came to the new land of America. Besides the Bible, the main book for family reading that the colonists brought with them, a separate strain of literature appeared in the 17th century—didactic literature aimed primarily at improving the moral nature of children.

However, lessons for children had been written down in fable and proverb form from the time of the Sumerians. There also had been courtesy books from the early Renaissance to teach proper conduct, horn books (wooden tablets covered with horn) from the 16th century in Europe and England, and comparable lesson books in ancient Rome. The most notable early book in this category insofar as Americans were concerned was *The Token for Children*, an account of the conversion, exemplary lives, and joyful deaths of several young children (1672) by the English preacher James Janeway (1636?–74). This was imitated by many colonial writers, most notably COTTON MATHER (1662?–1728?), who added *A Token for the Children of New-England*. (A unique copy is held by the American Antiquarian Society, Worcester, Massachusetts.) One American offshoot of Janeway's book even described the deaths of holy Native American children. It was called *Triumphant Deaths of Pious Children, In the Choctaw Language*, by Missionaries of the American Board of Commissioners of Foreign Missions (1835).

Also derived from English sources and popular in the early through the mid-19th century were the books stemming from the Sunday School movement, particularly those published by the American Tract Society. The movement was started in England in 1780 by a businessman in Gloucester, Robert Raikes, and was initially designed to use religion as a tool to cut down on vandalism through threats of divine punishment. Factory children, at loose ends on Sunday, were kept off the streets. But it also had a benevolent function, for it taught poor children, otherwise uneducated, to read the Bible. The first Sunday School in the United States is believed to have been organized by William Elliott in Acomac County, Virginia in 1785.

Of enormous influence in America was THE NEW ENGLAND PRIMER, with many editions between 1687 and the mid-19th century, which in some editions published excerpts from Isaac Watts's *Divine and Moral Songs for Children* (1715). *The New England Primer* stemmed from an English publication, *The Protestant Tutor for Youth*, published by Benjamin Harris, who later migrated to Massachusetts. The *Primer* contained rhyming alphabets, syllables, the Lord's Prayer, the Ten Commandments, and approximately the same material as its English predecessor.

Much children's literature of the early and mid-19th century was more concerned with teaching morality than it was with literary excellence. In this category, and of enormous influence with children and adults alike, were the *McGuffey Eclectic Readers*, written by WILLIAM HOLMES MCGUFFEY in the course of a succession of academic positions at the University of Miami, Cincinnati College, Ohio University, Woodward College, and the University of Virginia. Beginning in 1836 and going on through 1857, these *Readers* sold 122 million copies and were used by two generations of students. Their importance waned, but they were still published in reprints through the 20th century and did much to establish norms for social conduct.

Again, of minor literary importance but with great social impact, were the *Elsie Dinsmore* books by MARTHA FARQUHARSON FINLEY (1828–1909). The first of the twenty-eight volumes was published in 1868. The books chronicled the life of an abused child long before child abuse was accepted as a reality by most adults. As late as 1927, Ruth Suckow wrote in *The American Bookman* (October 27, 1927) that the Dinsmore books "still have outsold any other juveniles except Louisa May Alcott's." The author spent her life in the Midwest and in her incestuous erotic stories shows no discernible influence from English sources. The power of her work lies in its intensity. She appears to have been impelled by her own masochistic ideas about how life should be lived to write these stories for children.

John Bunyan's *Pilgrim's Progress* (1675) was popular both with adults and children and appeared in American editions, including one of *Pilgrim's Progress in Words of One Syllable* (1885). It was influential throughout the 19th century, as one can see in LITTLE WOMEN (1867) by LOUISA MAY ALCOTT. Alcott's first chapter is devoted to a description of children play-acting the plot of *Pilgrim's Progress*.

In general, the history of children's literature followed the history of English literature, moving in the 17th century from folk literature to religious tracts to a return of the classics and then other fiction and folk literature. The folktales collected by Perrault in France, later by the Grimm Brothers in Germany, and subsequently the color fairy books of Andrew Lang were popular both in England and America and led to a uniquely American type of folk literature, the tall tale, characterized by exaggeration and exuberance.

As the country began to develop its own identity, a number of local works appeared, often of uneven quality, but nevertheless, puckish, fresh, and typically American. Among them is the simplistic *Life and Memorable Acts of George Washington* (1800) by the Reverend MASON LOCKE WEEMS (1759–1825), which contains the well-known account of little George Washington chopping down the cherry tree, fabricated by Weems to teach a moral. *The Remarkable Story of Chicken Little* (1840), published with other juvenile books by John Greene Chandler, possibly satirized the fear of the Millerites, a religious group, that the world might be coming to an end.

Christmas was never quite the same again after the publication in 1823 in the Troy (New York) *Sentinel* of "A Visit from St. Nicholas," by CLEMENT CLARKE MOORE (1779–1863). Another unforgettable American poem for children and adults came along later in the century when Ernest Lawrence Thayer (1863–1940) wrote CASEY AT THE BAT (1888), which is still a popular recitation, especially when accompanied by audience participation. It first appeared in the *San Francisco Examiner*, and immortalized not only its antihero, Casey, but America's love for its favorite sport.

More uniquely American and less didactic than *Peter Parley's Tales* by SAMUEL GOODRICH (1793–1860) were the *Franconia Stories* of JACOB ABBOTT (1803–1879), which were told against a New England setting; Goodrich unfortunately was a man of his time, who wrote nearly two hundred dull and didactic books for children, the best of which were his accounts of nature, as in *Peter Parley's Farewell* (1839). Abbott's *Franconia Stories*, in contrast, are charming, natural tales of the lives of children in pastoral settings. His stories might be grouped with the amusing PETERKIN PAPERS (1880) by LUCRETIA P. HALE.

A brief but unforgettable poem of American origin is MARY HAD A LITTLE LAMB (1830) by SARAH J. HALE (1788–1879) editor of *Godey's Lady Book*, a fashion magazine popular among women and girls. JOHN GREENLEAF WHITTIER wrote a number of charming poems with popular appeal. His sentimental poem "In School Days" (1870), about an incident in a one-room schoolhouse, is perhaps best remembered. Another New Englander, HENRY WADSWORTH LONGFELLOW (1807–1892) wrote "The Song of Hiawatha" (1855) and "Paul Revere's Ride" (1861), long dramatic poems still enjoyed by children and adults.

Because of the beauty of the American wilderness, there was a trend along with the anthropomorphism of so many children's stories toward books shared by children and adults that described nature realistically, for example, the bird books of Audubon (1827–38). Interest in his books was lasting. A century later, Constance Rourke wrote *Audubon* (1936), a biography for children of this colorful man. Naturalist ERNEST THOMPSON SETON (1860–1946) accurately described *Wild Animals I Have Known* (1898), which was very popular with children and adults.

JAMES FENIMORE COOPER (1785–1851) wrote absorbing books about frontier life, particularly the confrontations between frontiersmen and Native Americans. Best known are his *Leather-Stocking Tales*, notably *The Last of the Mohicans* (1857), in which a noble savage tries to save his identity and that of his tribe.

Far more realistic in characterization are the stories by MARK TWAIN, whose *Tom Sawyer* (1876) and *Huckleberry Finn* (1884) are warm and realistic depictions of real boys with real vices and virtues, and other people as well.

In the United States, New England was the largest but not the only source for early American children's books. Certain books printed in the South were geared to particular interests, such as the *Plain and Easy Catechism Designed for the Benefit of Coloured Children* (1833), in which a slave child is instructed:

Q. How should you act to your master and mistress?
A. I should love and honour them, obey / And strictly attend to all they say.
Q. What advice does St. Peter give to servants?
A. Servants, be subject to your masters with all fear / Not only to the good and gentle, but also to the froward ones.

The Greek classics were introduced to children in a rather wordy way by NATHANIEL HAWTHORNE (1804–1864), the first edition of whose *Wonder-Book for Children* appeared in 1852 and was very popular.

The 19th century saw poverty and periodic depressions, which were mirrored in some publications of the time. Notable among the writers for children on the subject was HORATIO ALGER, JR. (1832–1899), who wrote 135 books with a total sale of 200 million copies. In them he depicted the struggles of poor boys to become successful. The first was *Ragged Dick*, initially serialized in *Student and Schoolmate* and then published in book form (1867). Undistinguished in style and content, these books nevertheless influenced the behavior of many future American businessmen. Like all Alger's heroes, as Russel Crouse writes in the Crown edition of *Struggling Upward*, another Alger success: "Dick is poor, honest, cheerful, manly, and ambitious. He starts at the bottom and ends at the top." Better written is another story of struggle in the 20th century, Watty Piper's *The Little Engine That Could* (1930). A small engine pulls a heavy load up a hill that the larger engines had refused to try to pull. The little engine accomplishes the feat by repeating, "I think I can, I think I can."

Both in the 19th and 20th centuries, most animal stories depicted animals as human. This is true of the cowardly lion, for instance, in the classic *The Wonderful Wizard of Oz* (1900) by L. FRANK BAUM (1856–1919), the quality of whose work was not appreciated by many academic critics for several decades. The film *The Wizard of Oz* (1938) and the critical works of Martin Gardner and Russell B. Nye (1957) and Michael Patrick Hearn (1973) helped draw deserved attention to Baum's work.

Shortly after the appearance of Oz came *Rebecca of Sunnybrook Farm* (1903), by KATE DOUGLAS WIGGIN (1856–1923), a romantic story of the struggle of a young girl to grow up. Mark Twain called it "beautiful and moving and satisfying," a flattering comment which one suspects is somewhat on the level of the blurbs to encourage the sale of modern novels. The book had an enormous sale and was made into a movie (1917) starring Mary Pickford.

Born in Manchester, England, FRANCES HODGSON BURNETT (1849–1914) became a naturalized American citizen and wrote her two best-known books, *Little Lord Fauntleroy* (1886) and *The Secret Garden* (1911), after emigrating to the United States in 1865. A superb storyteller, Burnett created work that is highly pictorial, and both her books have successfully been made into films. The books have to do with reversal of fortune, but *The Secret Garden* goes far beyond this theme to show how two children who have been psychologically abused are restored to health, as are other principal characters. Nature plays an important role in the restoration. The book has great psychological subtlety and depth, and remains a perennial favorite. Another English-born author was HUGH LOFTING (1886–1947), who wrote most of the *Doctor Dolittle* books in the United States.

Of less literary interest are the anthropomorphic tales of THORNTON BURGESS (1874–1965), notably *Reddy Fox* (1915). The tales were syndicated in many newspapers and thus reached a large number of American children. They are dated now by such things as the African-American accent assigned to the turkey buzzard.

CARL SANDBURG (1878–1967) wrote about the Huckabuck family in *Rootabaga Pigeons* (1923), homespun humorous tales set in the Midwest. His *Rootabaga Stories* (1922) are accurately described by Ruth Hill Viguers in *A Critical History of Children's Literature* as "the folklore of America." Among the tales, "The White Horse Girl and the Blue Wind Boy" has become a favorite for storytellers because of its romantic and poetic quality.

With increasing frequency, children's stories in the 20th century began to deal with social issues, such as the destructiveness of war, and ways of coping with the problem. A tale of lasting memory is *The Story of Ferdinand the Bull* (1936) by MUNRO LEAF (1905–1976), illustrated by Robert Lawson. Such a story was subtle enough in its message of passivity to be accepted by a society in which educating children on achievement of peace was regarded as too controversial. Later, *The Search for Delicious* (1969) by Natalie Babbitt (1932–   ) was a beautiful symbolic treatment of the problem of war. More explicit and less popular was *Tiger Eyes* (1981) by JUDY BLUME (1938–   ), which dealt with the lack of moral fiber of some of those engaged in the military profession. By the 1980s, many books began to treat war and its horrors explicitly. Perhaps the most powerful was *The Butter-Battle Book* (1984) by DR. SEUSS (1904–1991), which confronts the ultimate result of an arms build-up so dramatically that it often is relegated to adult collections by cautious librarians.

From the 1920s through the early 1970s, LOIS LENSKI (1893–1974), a Midwesterner, wrote quiet books principally about poor families and illustrated them herself. A prolific writer, her books were mainly designed for children through the middle grades. Less prolific because she began writing in her sixties was LAURA INGALLS WILDER (1867–1967), who wrote nostalgic stories about her childhood in the Midwest. The first was *Little House in the Big Woods* (1956), and these stories of her childhood, written in third person, became so popular that they were developed into a long-running television series. The stories of yet another Midwesterner, Elizabeth Enright (1909–1968), were noted for the author's skill at characterization. Her tales of *The Melendy Family* (1947) were pleasing to many children of the postwar generation.

An Easterner, ELEANOR ESTES (1906–1988), is known for her keen memory of how life appears to children. *The Moffats* (1941), written from the perspective of a ten-year-old, has been especially well received by children as has *Rufus M.* (1943), a charming and believable story about the problems a little boy meets in trying to get a library card.

Born a Virginian but widely traveled because of her husband's assignments as an navy admiral, Natalie Savage Carlson was a prolific children's writer for four decades. One of her notable books is *The Talking Cat and Other Stories* (1952), a collection of tales told to her mother by a French relative. Perhaps her most successful work is *The Family Under the Bridge* (1969), illustrated by Garth Williams. The story developed out of an extended stay in Paris. A French tramp living under a bridge feeds on the smells from expensive restaurants. In *The Empty Schoolhouse* (1965), she adapts her talent to a story of the effects of segregation on children.

Also belonging to the baby boom period after World War II is E. B. WHITE's *Charlotte's Web* (1952), a seemingly simple, actually deep philosophical contemplation of the meaning of life and death. The book has immortalized Wilbur the pig and Charlotte the spider.

To return to the history of poetry for children, the folksy Hoosier poet, JAMES WHITCOMB RILEY (1848–1916), will be remembered for such poems as "Little Orphant Annie" (1891) and EUGENE FIELD (1850–95) for his sentimental "Little Boy Blue." Indeed, sentimentality seems to be a trait that Americans have time for, whether they be children or children and adults who watch 20th-century soap operas. A better poem in Field's *Poems of Childhood* (1896) is "The Duel," about a gingham dog and calico cat who fight until they eat each other up. It is still pertinent to peace efforts.

Early feminists had little influence on children's literature in the 19th century except indirectly. A notable exception was the novelist Caroline Gilmore, who edited a magazine for children, known first as *The Rosebud*, later as *The Rose* in Charleston, South Carolina (1832–39). In one story, for instance, she describes boys flying kites on the battery in Charleston, and comments that it would be nice if girls could be up there flying them too. Some feminists have seen streaks of independence in Jo's character in *Little Women*, but others feel she is not independent enough to be a heroine to exponents of women's rights. The independent streaks in the character of *Anne of Green Gables*, a Canadian tale published in 1904 by L. M. MONTGOMERY (1874–1942), are still refreshing. Louise Fitzhugh's *Harriet the Spy* (1964) portrays a little girl with a mind of her own who acts independently and boldly. In the 20th century, the Nancy Drew stories, written for the Stratemeyer Syndicate (see EDWARD STRATEMEYER), portray a reasonably independent young woman pursuing life on her own terms. The trend is toward more stories of this nature. By 1989, the pseudostories of *Dick and Jane*, used as reading tools for young children and giving a passive view of girls, finally went out of print. *William's Doll* (1972) by Charlotte Zolotow deals with the universal conditioning of male children in sexist ways. The book became part of a musical compilation, *Free to Be You and Me*, by Marlo Thomas.

Beginning in the late 1920s, talented artists interpreted texts in beautiful books for children, but with cut-backs in color choices, particularly after World War II, their work was made increasingly difficult. One of the early artists of great talent was WANDA GAG (1893–1946), who wrote and illustrated *Millions of Cats* (1928). A charming picture book written and illustrated by the author was *Madeline* (1939), by LUDWIG BEMELMANS (1898–1962). Most notable among 20th-century artists—again admired both by children and adults—is MAURICE SENDAK (1928–   ). Known best for his text and illustrations to *Where the Wild Things Are* (1967), he does spunky and unconventional drawings, taking infinite care to coordinate them with the mood and content of the text. *Where the Wild Things Are* is the first of an autobiographical trilogy that continues with *In the Night Kitchen* (1970), a book recounting Sendak's New York experiences and offering many bits and pieces of his observations, including the WINSOR MCCAY drawings of *Little Nemo* and even a reference in "Hosmer's Sugar" to an old friend, Henry Hosmer, who ran a children's museum in Lancaster, Massachusetts, as well as a puppet theater. The protagonist falls out of a dream into the story, which is one of the first children's books to depict male nudity. The third book in the trilogy is *Outside Over There* (1981), which takes place within an 18th-century world and includes the music of Mozart, folklore such as the Juniper Tree, and, quixotically, five goblins that may be the Dionne quintuplets. Ida with her billowing cape might reflect a girl Sendak knew as a child.

James Marshall (1942–   ) is known for his wit, especially in his drawings for the Stupid books and the text and illustrations for the George and Martha series (1970s). He has also done clever illustrations for *The Night Before Christmas, Red Riding Hood,* and *Goldilocks and The Three Bears* and has made subtle changes in the folk texts of these stories. An artist with an odd way of looking at life and a bizarre and amusing approach to his subjects is Chris Van Allsburg. His *Polar Express* (1985) received a Caldecott Award. It takes a boy to the North Pole to receive a gift from Santa Claus. The artist's drawings and writings carry a sense of mystery.

These 20th-century artists succeed the lively and dramatic predecessors of the previous century, including Randolph Caldecott—claimed both by the United States and by England—and HOWARD PYLE, illustrator of *Robin Hood* (1883) and other exciting adventure stories.

Magazines of great influence for children in the 19th century include THE YOUTH'S COMPANION (1827–1929) and ST. NICHOLAS (1873–1943). The latter was edited by MARY MAPES DODGE (1831–1905), who also wrote *Hans Brinker and the Silver Skates* (1865). Many of the superb stories for children by FRANK M. STOCKTON (1834–1902) were originally published in *St. Nicholas*. In fact, through these magazines, excellent storytellers for children found a voice, among them, Louisa May Alcott. *Cricket* (1937) is notable among children's magazines of the 20th century.

As America became more affluent and more aware of life beyond its boundaries, books about children in other lands became popular—such as the Hans Brinker book, and also such books as those by LUCY FITCH PERKINS (1865–1937), about twins in various countries. *The Dutch Twins* (1911) was one of the most popular. Through such books, children could learn in an entertaining way about life outside their own provincial setting.

Biographies of people in whom children could take pride took on increasing importance. James Daugherty (1887–1974) contributed distinguished books, including *Daniel Boone* (1939), *Poor Richard* (1941) (on Benjamin Franklin), *Abraham Lincoln* (1943), *Walt Whitman's America* (1964), and *Henry*

David Thoreau, a Man for Our Time (1967). Feenie Ziner wrote a biography of *Squanto* (reprinted, 1989), and Jim Haskins wrote a number of biographies of African-American leaders, including *The Life and Death of Martin Luther King Jr.* (1977), *Diana Ross: Star Supreme* (1985), and *Ralphe Bunche: A Most Reluctant Hero* (1974). The striking picture biographies done by Ingrid and Edgar Parin d'Aulaire include those of *Abraham Lincoln* (1939), *Benjamin Franklin* (1950), *Leif the Lucky* (1951), *Columbus* (1955), *Pocahontas* (1946), and *Buffalo Bill* (1952), as well as *The Book of Greek Myths* (1962) and *Norse Gods* (1967).

Literary fantasy has long been popular. It includes the whimsical fantasies of JAMES THURBER, for example, *Many Moons* (1943). A moving story in this category is one by RUSSELL HOBAN (1925–   ), *The Mouse and His Child* (1967), illustrated by Lillian Hoban, about a discarded toy and a tramp who go looking for love. Later, the many fantasies of Jane Yolen (1939–   ), such as *The Girl Who Cried Flowers* (1974), contributed to this genre. *The Giving Tree* (1964) by the poet Shel Silverstein (1932–   ) is a portrait of a life of beauty and pathos. *Sylvester and the Magic Pebble* (1969), another memorable fantasy, was written and illustrated by WILLIAM STEIG (1907–   ). The delicate fantasy *Rabbit Hill* (1944), written and illustrated by Robert Lawson (1892–1957), suggests that there can be peaceful coexistence between people and nature.

Poetry of quality sometimes appeared. One of the most notable poets was Hilda Conkling, a child genius who wrote *Poems by a Little Girl* (1920). Some critics might argue that her poetry was more for adults than for children, but this seems an unfair criticism, particularly since she began writing poetry at four. Here is an excerpt of a poem she chanted at six:

Tree-toad is a small gray person
With a silver voice.
Tree-toad is a leaf-gray shadow
That sings.
Tree-toad is never seen
Unless a star squeezes through the leaves,
Or a moth looks sharply at a gray branch.
How would it be, I wonder,
To sing patiently all night,
Never thinking that people are asleep?

Conkling appeared in Harriet Monroe's *Poetry Magazine*, which also published the work of such poets as Ezra Pound and T. S. Eliot. Better known is *The Bat-Poet* (1964) by RANDALL JARRELL (1914–1965). This poem, which Jarrell said he wrote "half for children, half for grownups," depicts the loneliness of the artist in society.

In all countries the poetry written by children themselves, particularly their skip-rope rhymes, are often quite beautiful. Within the invisible world of the turning rope, they skip out their concerns in chants that are evidently rituals, for if they stumble, they start in again from the beginning, so as not to break the spell.

For instance, the writer heard this rhyme in 1949 chanted by a mentally retarded boy in Cherrydale, Virginia. He had composed it himself:

There was a little boy and his name was Tommy
He ran through the meadows where the frogs croaked clear
He ran through the meadows with a song on his tongue
And he picked a few flowers for his mother.

Picking the flowers was the least—and the most—that he could do.

A number of the best children's writers and illustrators have no children of their own. Their work seems to be triggered by an inner loneliness that best finds expression through conveying meaning to children. They themselves have retained their childlike quality and can best communicate through the child within.

One of the most philosophical writers and illustrators of the late 20th century was ARNOLD LOBEL (1933–1986). A noted expert on the philosophy of fantasy, Gareth Mathews, was especially impressed with how Lobel conveyed the meaning of certain concepts, for example, fear to children in his *Frog and Toad* books.

With the landing of the first man on the moon, interest in science fiction increased both for children and adults. In 1988, Superman, popular both in comics and in film, celebrated his fiftieth birthday, and vied with Batman for popularity. A science-fiction book of quality enjoyed both by children and adults is *A Wrinkle in Time* (1962) by Madeleine L'Engle, one of the best writers for children of our time. Also in the field of science fiction are the distinguished children's books of URSULA LE GUIN (1929–   ), particularly *The Earthsea Trilogy*, comprising *The Wizard of Earthsea* (1967), *The Tombs of Atuan* (1972), and *The Farthest Shore* (1973), which received the National Book Award. She makes brilliant use of Jungian psychology in her trilogy; like Lewis, Tolkien, and Lloyd Alexander, creates an imaginary world; and is particularly adroit in the use of language appropriate to that world. Unlike Lloyd Alexander's Prydain series, imitative of Tolkien, her style is unique.

Because many African-Americans had little opportunity to read during the 19th century and were subsequently still limited in education, few works of quality were turned out by African-Americans during the 19th century. *The Uncle Remus Tales*, turned out by a white writer on the *Atlanta Constitution*, JOEL CHANDLER HARRIS, are based on the Anansi tales that slaves had brought with them from Africa. They mainly have to do with how a clever rabbit (slave?) could outwit power. Later, ANN PETRY (1908–1997) wrote two books on the plight of an African-American child; *Tituba of Salem Village* (1964), a story set in colonial America; and *Harriet Tubman, Conductor on the Underground Railroad* (1955).

Virginia Hamilton (1936–   ) wrote a number of books about African-American children popular with all children.

Several of these appeared in the late 1960s and 1970s. The haunting tale "How Jahdu Ran Through Darkness in No Time At All" is an example of her skill as a storyteller (see *Time-Ago Lost: More Tales of Jahdu*, 1973). John Steptoe (1950–1989) wrote *Stevie* (1969), which brought contemporary idiom to picture books.

Many of the best of African-American stories—as well as Native American stories, such as the Abenaki stories recorded by Joseph Bruchac—are folklore. Hugh Morgan Hill (Brother Blue) is a soul storyteller noted for such stories as "Muddy Duddy," which has surface fascination and philosophical depth. Original with Brother Blue, "Muddy Duddy" nevertheless has a folk quality combined with profound impact on the hearer, as do "Miss Wunderlich" and "Once I Had a Brother." Beginning as seemingly simple tales, they turn out to be something quite different from what the auditor expects. One that has been written down and recorded is "Muddy Duddy," which can be found in *The Wide World All Around* (1987).

Some books of the Nobel Prize–winning author I. B. SINGER 1904–1991) qualify as children's literature, including *Zlateh the Goat and Other Stories* (1975), illustrated by Maurice Sendak, and *The Fools of Chelm and Their History* (1973), illustrated by Uri Shulevitz.

In the 1970s, sexuality was a favorite theme of children's books. Books by Judy Blume (1928–   ) take up many facets of the subject from menstruation to pregnancy to abortion. A few books deal with homosexuality, the best known of which is probably John Donovan's *"I'll Get There. It Better Be Worth the Trip"* (1969).

Bitter and bleak stories like *The Chocolate War* (1974) by Robert Cormier (1925–   ) might be classified as belonging to the trend toward realism, or the fictional nonfiction of much biography.

The durable Dr. Seuss (Theodor Seuss Geisel, 1904–1991) continued to write books of seeming simplicity but often of considerable depth, which he illustrated with outlandish animals. Though written by a known author, the books have the quality of folklore or folkrhymes—they deal with universal concerns and are easily remembered. His imaginative *And to Think That I Saw It on Mulberry Street* (1939) was followed by *The 500 Hats of Bartholomew Cubbins* (1940) and a book of human devotion, *Horton Hatches the Egg* (1942), which is often considered his best, though it has competition in his sequel, *Horton Hears a Who!* (1954), which extolls the importance of the voice of the common man. Perhaps his most popular book is *The Cat in the Hat* (1957), in which the Jungian shadow of the children dominates the mask for a while. *How the Grinch Stole Christmas* (1957) has been translated to film and become a Christmas classic. *Yertle the Turtle* (1961) shows what happens to a Hitler figure. The strange story *I Had Trouble in Getting to Solla Sollew* (1965) is a shamanistic *Pilgrim's Progress*, a haunting reminder of Alice's voyage through Wonderland. Of great social import is *The Lorax* (1971), which Seuss is said to regard as his finest and which prophesies concern over the destruction of rain forests.

Among prolific and long-lasting writers, E. L. Konigsburg achieved a special place when she won the 1997 Newbery Award for *The View from Saturday*, self-illustrated, nearly three decades after her first Newbery Award, in 1968, for *From the Mixed-up Files of Mrs. Basil E. Frankweiler.*

Critical interest in children's literature was initiated primarily by librarians. In 1921, the American Library Association established the Newbery Awards for the best children's books, named after John Newbery, an 18th-century publisher of children's books. In 1937, the Caldecott awards were established and awarded annually for the best illustrations in a children's book. In 1969, the National Book Awards were established. In 1924, *The Horn Book* began publication of criticism of children's literature. The popular anthologies of May Hill Arbuthnot, begun in 1958, stimulated the teaching of children's literature in schools of education and library science. The humanities were slow in entering the field. Though established in 1883, the Modern Language Association held its first national seminar in children's literature in 1969. After that, seminars were held for several years, and finally a national permanent division was established at the Houston convention of 1980. The Children's Literature Association, designed for those in the humanities, education, and library science, was established in Storrs, Connecticut, by Anne Devereaux Jordan in 1973. The year before, also in Storrs, *Children's Literature*, a scholarly annual journal, was established. It was published by the Parousia Press, then by Temple University, and in 1980 went to Yale University Press. Other journals of importance include *Children's Literature in Education, The ChLA Quarterly, The Lion and Unicorn, School Library Journal*, and the *Advocate.*

The National Endowment for the Humanities funded the first Institute for Children's Literature in the Humanities in 1983. Teachers of children's literature came from throughout the United States and have continued to attend subsequent institutes at various universities, the purpose being to develop critical standards for the field.

Although strong programs, primarily from the point of view of library science or education, now exist at Simmons College and Columbia University Teachers College, important graduate programs have not developed in English departments, although many distinguished scholars have taught or are teaching in the field, including ALISON LURIE, Pulitzer Prize novelist, in the English Department at Cornell, who was an editor of *The Garland Library of Children's Classics*, as well as of a book in which she collected old folktales that initially were nonsexist. U. C. Knoepfelmacher, holder of the Paton Foundation Professorship of Ancient & Modern Literature at Princeton, not only teaches in the field of children's literature but has conducted several national institutes. LESLIE FIEDLER taught in the field and appeared on a panel on children's literature at a national forum of the Modern Language Association.

The history of American children's literature seems to be on an upward developmental curve, with education, the humanities, and library science all working to encourage writers with ability and imagination to enter the field, and to set higher critical standards, but much progress still remains to be made.

Reference works include Zena Sutherland, *Children and Books*, 9th ed. (1996); Donna and Saundra Norton, *Through the Eyes of a Child: An Introduction to Children's Literature*, 5th ed. (1998); and Rebecca Lukens, *A Critical Handbook to Children's Literature*, 6th edition (1999).

FRANCELIA BUTTER/GP

Chillingworth, Roger. In Hawthorne's THE SCARLET LETTER, the vengeful husband of HESTER PRYNNE.

Chimmie Fadden. See FADDEN, CHIMMIE.

Chin, Frank (1940–   ),   essayist, playwright, novelist. Born in Berkeley, Chin attended the University of California there, as well as the University of Iowa Writer's Workshop and the University of California at Santa Barbara. He has been an outspoken critic of such writers as MAXINE HONG KINGSTON, AMY TAN, and DAVID HENRY HWANG. In a long essay "Come All Ye Asian American Writers," printed in *The Big Aiiieeeee! An Anthology of Chinese American and Japanese American Literature* (1991), edited by Chin with Jeffrey Paul Chan, Lawson Fusao Inada, and Shawn Wong, Chin complains that the three well-known writers have counterfeited "all of Asian American history and literature." The language of his plays, stories, and novels is similarly provocative. *The Chickencoop Chinaman*, the first play by a Chinese-American to be produced on the New York stage, and *The Year of the Dragon* were both produced at the American Place Theater and printed in one volume in 1981. *The Chinaman Pacific & Frisco R.R. Co.*, a collection of stories, appeared in 1988. *Donald Duk* (1991), his first novel, is about a 12-year-old boy who hates his name, given in tribute to an uncle who is a star of the Chinese opera, and hates looking Chinese. *Gunga Din Highway* (1994) concerns Longman Kwan, a struggling actor who dreams of playing Charlie Chan, but is only given minor roles. Chin was also a co-editor of the earlier *Aiiieeeee! An Anthology of Asian American Writers* (1974).

Chinese Nightingale, The (1915),   a poem by VACHEL LINDSAY. Lindsay called it "A song in Chinese tapestries" in a subtitle. He contrasts the sordid slum surroundings of Chang, the Chinese laundryman in San Francisco, with something romantic and beautiful that might have happened to Chang in ages long ago.

Chingachgook. An Indian chieftain in Cooper's LEATHER-STOCKING TALES (1823–1841). Cooper may have had a real Indian in mind when he first presented Chingachgook in THE PIONEERS, but gradually the figure, intimate friend of NATTY BUMPPO, was more and more idealized. He is grave, silent, courageous, self-sacrificing, and wise, in short, the epitome of the noble savage.

Chinook Indians. Native-American tribe of the Penutian linguistic stock. Twelve tribes, including the Chinook themselves, spoke the Chinook language, and all lived along the lower Columbia River. They lived in villages, fished, and gathered roots and berries. The *Potlach*, a gift-giving feast, was a famed ceremony among them. They encountered white traders by the late 18th century, and Lewis and Clark visited them in 1805–06. Franz Boas collected *Chinook Songs* (1888).

Chippewa Indians. See OJIBWAY INDIANS.

Chisholm Trail. Trail used for cattle drives from Texas to the railways in Kansas after the Civil War. Named for Jesse Chisholm, half-Cherokee, it began with the ruts left by his wagon in 1866 as he brought buffalo hides through the Oklahoma Indian territory to his trading post near Wichita, Kansas. After about twenty years, the trail fell into disuse as lands became fenced and railroads more extensive. It is celebrated in cowboy ballads and western novels.

Chita: A Memory of Last Island (1889), LAFCADIO HEARN's beautifully written story of the destruction by a tidal wave in 1856 of an island in the Gulf of Mexico off the Louisiana coast.

Chivers, Thomas Holley (1809–1858), poet. Born in Georgia, the son of a wealthy plantation owner, Chivers was educated as a physician, but gave up medicine for poetry. His works include *The Path of Sorrow* (1832), poems on his first marriage; *Conrad and Eudora* (1834), a verse drama (see BEAUCHAMPE); *The Lost Pleiad and Other Poems* (1845), containing an elegy for his daughter; and *Eonchs of Ruby, a Gift of Love* (1845). His charges and countercharges of plagiarism involving Poe, his sometime friend, caused a stir at one time. A prose work is *Search After Truth; or, A New Revelation of the Psycho-Physiological Nature of Man* (1848).

Choctaw Indians. A Native American tribe that spoke a Muskhogean language and lived in southern Mississippi. They were visited by De Soto in 1540 and fought a battle with the Spaniards, killing many of them. They later sided with the French against the English and their allies, the Chickasaw. The Choctaw were successful farmers, generally peaceful, and among the first to move (1832) to the Indian Territory, later Oklahoma, where they joined in the confederation of the FIVE CIVILIZED TRIBES. They appear in works by FRANÇOIS DOMINIQUE and ADRIEN ROUQUETTE, brothers who lived among them in the early 19th century.

Chopin, Kate [Katherine O'Flaherty] (1851–1904), short-story writer, novelist. Born in St. Louis, she was raised in the French-speaking household of her Creole mother after the death of her Irish immigrant father. Married to Oscar Chopin, a Louisiana cotton trader, she came to know Creole and Cajun life in New Orleans and in Natchitoches Parish before her husband died and she returned with her six children to St. Louis in 1884. Her stories of Louisiana began appearing in magazines in 1889 and were collected in *Bayou Folk* (1894) and *A Night in Acadie* (1897). Novels include *At Fault* (1890) and THE AWAKENING (1899), the latter a powerful account of a married woman's growing awareness of her sexuality, independent worth, and restricted horizons. Impatient with the conventions of 19th-century realism in the United States, she modelled her work in part on that of continental writers like Maupassant, though she also admired SARAH ORNE JEWETT and MARY E. WILKINS FREEMAN and was influenced by WHITMAN. Praised in her own time for her realistic portraits of black and white residents of the city and the bayou, she shocked critics at the turn of the century with her strong evocations of the emotional lives of women, especially in *The Awakening*, now considered her masterpiece. *The Complete Works*, ed. Per Seyerstad (1969), includes material unpublished in her lifetime. A biography is Emily Toth, *Kate Chopin* (1990). Among studies are Per Seyerstad, *Kate Chopin: A Critical Biography* (1969); and Barbara C. Elwell, *Kate Chopin* (1986).

Choquette, Adrienne (1915–1973), novelist, journalist. Born in Shawnigan Falls, Quebec, Choquette, a cousin of ROBERT CHOQUETTE, became an acclaimed Québecois writer largely on the basis of her novel *Laure Clouet* (1961). It depicts old traditions in Quebec by recounting the story of a spinster whose life begins to expand after her mother's death. An earlier novel is *La Coupe vide* (1948). Her stories are collected in *La Nuit ne dort pas* (1954) and *Le Temps des villages* (1975).

Choquette, Robert (1905–). Born in New Hampshire, Choquette grew up in Montreal and was educated at Loyola College there. In addition to his career as a novelist, poet, and writer for radio and television, he served as Canadian ambassador to Argentina, Uruguay, and Paraguay, and as director-general of Information Canada in Quebec. Two long poems won special praise: *Metropolitan Museum* (1931), a depiction of civilization—past, present, and future—inspired by a visit to the Metropolitan Museum in New York; and *Suite marine* (1953), a meditation on nature and beauty in 6,000 alexandrine lines. His other collections of verse include *A Travers les vents* (1925), lyrics; and *Poésies nouvelles* (1933). A collected edition is *Oeuvres poétiques* (1956, revised 1967). Novels derived from Choquette's radio series include *Le Curé de village* (1936, also a film, 1949); *Les Velder* (1941); and *Elise Velder* (1958).

Chrisman, Arthur Bowie (1889–1953), teacher, farmer, lecturer, writer. While he was working on a story that involved a Chinese character, Chrisman turned to a study of China and produced *Shen of the Sea* (1925), a book for children that won the Newbery Medal. Later came *The Wind That Wouldn't Blow* (1927) and *Treasures Long Hidden* (1941).

Christian Disciple, The. See THE CHRISTIAN EXAMINER.

Christian Examiner, The. A bimonthly Unitarian magazine founded in January 1824. It was originally called *The Christian Disciple*, founded in 1813 by WILLIAM ELLERY CHANNING [1] and others. It ceased publication in 1869.

Christian Herald, The. A Protestant magazine originally founded in 1878 as a New York edition of a London magazine of the same name. T. DE WITT TALMAGE was one of its early editors; Daniel A. Poling was later its editor for many years. An anniversary anthology was published to mark its 75th year of publication: *Golden Moments of Religious Inspiration: A Treasury of Faith from the Christian Herald.*

Christian Philosopher, The (1721), essays by COTTON MATHER. In this early attempt to reconcile science and religion, Mather wrote: "The essays now before us will demonstrate that [natural] philosophy is no enemy, but a mighty and wondrous incentive to religion. . . . The works of the glorious God in the creation of the world are what I now propose to exhibit. . . . Glorious God, I give thanks to thee for the benefits and improvements of the sciences, granted by Thee unto these our later ages." Mather gives an outline of recent developments in science and concludes that God can interfere in human affairs.

Christian Science.   See MARY BAKER EDDY.

Christian Science Monitor, The.   A daily newspaper published by the Christian Science Publishing Society. MARY BAKER EDDY instructed Archibald McLellan to direct the paper's first issue (1908) and assume its editorship. Since that time it increased its circulation, became read worldwide, and was acclaimed as one of America's most distinguished newspapers.

Christie, Anna.   See ANNA CHRISTIE.

Christmas, Joe,   the protagonist of LIGHT IN AUGUST, by William Faulkner. The illegitimate child of Milly Hines and a man supposed to be Mexican, Joe is placed in an orphanage by his fanatically religious grandfather, who believes him to be part African-American. He is adopted by a strict Calvinist couple, who know nothing of his origins, although Joe himself occasionally claims that he is a "nigger." After wandering over the Southwest for several years, Joe arrives in Jefferson, Mississippi, where he has an affair with a white woman, kills her, and becomes the object of a manhunt.

Christowe, Stoyan (1898–   ),   journalist, memoirist. Born in Greek Macedonia, Stoyan tells of his hardships as an immigrant in search of the good life in *My American Pilgrimage* (1947). He was a reporter for the *Chicago Daily News* and the North American Newspaper Alliance and a writer of articles and books about the Balkans and the United States, including *Heroes and Assassins* (1935); *Mara* (1937); *This is My Country* (1938); *The Lion of Yanina* (1941), about Ali Pasha; and *The Eagle and the Stork* (1976).

Christus, A Mystery (1872,   a single volume containing THE GOLDEN LEGEND, 1851; THE NEW ENGLAND TRAGEDIES, 1868; and *The Divine Tragedy*, 1871), a trilogy of dramatic poems by HENRY WADSWORTH LONGFELLOW.

Christy, Edwin P. (1815–1862),   actor, singer. Christy was the founder and leader of the troupe called Christy's Minstrels and is generally regarded today as the originator of blackface minstrelsy. He was the first to seat his performers in a semicircle on stage with an interlocutor in the middle and with comic end men.

Chu, Louis (1915–1970),   novelist. Born in Canton, China, Chu came with his family to Newark, New Jersey when he was nine. Educated at New York University, he served with the U.S. Army in World War II, later owned a record shop, and was a disk jockey in New York City. In his novel *Eat a Bowl of Tea* (1961) he provides a realistic portrayal of life in New York's Chinatown, portraying well the colloquial speech and the tensions of a world in which all the characters are Chinese.

Church, Benjamin (1639–1718),   and his son Thomas Church (1673–1748). The father took a leading part in King Philip's War (1675–76) and wrote *The History of King Philip's War*, published in 1865. His son published *Entertaining Passages Relating to King Philip's War* (1716) from his father's notes.

Church, Benjamin III (1734–1776?),   physician, poet, pamphleteer. A grandson of Benjamin Church, the Indian fighter, the later Church pretended loyalty to the Revolutionary cause while serving British interests. He was accused of writing essays defending the patriots and preparing the Tory responses to his own arguments. In October 1775, he was tried by court martial, found guilty, and imprisoned. On parole, he was allowed to sail from Boston in May 1776; his ship was apparently lost at sea. His verse closely imitates British models, as in *The Choice: A Poem After the Manner of Pomfret* (1802).

Churchill, Winston (1871–1947),   novelist. Churchill was a graduate of Annapolis but never served in the navy. After writing a moderately successful novel, *The Celebrity* (1898), supposedly a satire on RICHARD HARDING DAVIS, he went on to bestsellerdom with RICHARD CARVEL (1899), a story of the American Revolution, and the novels that succeeded it. At first, Churchill composed mainly historical romances: THE CRISIS (1901), a vivid novel of the Civil War; THE CROSSING (1904), a romance of the settlement of inland Empire; *Coniston* (1906), a study of a political boss in New Hampshire; and *Mr. Crewe's Career* (1908), a story about state politics controlled by a railroad. Becoming interested in contemporary social conditions and in religion, he also wrote *The Inside of the Cup* (1913), dealing with the relations of religion and modern society; *A Far Country* (1915), a story of a modern prodigal son; and *The Dwelling Place of Light* (1917), in which the restless modern world is contrasted with eternal truths. In 1913 Churchill ran for governor of New Hampshire on the Progressive Party (Theodore Roosevelt) ticket. Among his last writings was *The Uncharted Way: The Psychology of the Gospel Doctrine* (1940).

Chute, Carolyn (1947–   ),   novelist, short-story writer. A Maine native, born in Portland, Chute attended the University of Southern Maine and has worked variously in the minimally skilled jobs of the Maine underemployed—restaurant, hospital, chicken factory, potato farm, school bus driver—as well as in the more elevated positions of teacher, journalist, creative writing instructor. *The Beans of Egypt, Maine* (1985), a novel, made her famous as a chronicler who could portray the backwoods with humor, sympathy, and understanding, and earned her comparison with William Faulkner and Erskine Caldwell. About it she proclaimed on the cover, "This book was involuntarily researched. I have lived poverty. I didn't CHOOSE it." Egypt, Maine continues central in two more novels, *Letourneau's Used Auto Parts* (1988) and *Merry Men* (1994), neither as celebrated as the first novel, although Madison Smartt Bell ranks the latter as among the most important fictions of our time, "a monument to all the people the Reagan years destroyed." Radical in her politics, in *Snow Man* (1999) she writes of a Maine right winger who assassinates a U.S. senator.

Chuzzlewit, Martin. See MARTIN CHUZZLEWIT.

Ciardi, John (1916–1986),   poet, translator. Born in Boston, Ciardi was educated at Bates and Tufts, taught at Harvard and Rutgers, and was poetry editor (1956–72) of *The Saturday Review*. His colloquial, witty, often ironic poems were collected in *Homeward to America* (1940), *Other Skies* (1947), *Live Another Day* (1949), *From Time to Time* (1951), *As if, Poems New and Selected* (1955), *I Marry You* (1958), *In Fact* (1963), *Person to Person* (1964), *Lives of X* (1971), and *For Instance* (1979). His translation of Dante's *Inferno* (1954) was much admired for its rendering of idiomatic English in terza rima; his translations *Purgatorio* (1961) and *Paradiso* (1970) followed. His books for children include *I Met a Man* (1961) and *Fast and Slow* (1974). His fascination with words and their origins led to his *A Browser's Dictionary* (1980) and *A Second Browser's Dictionary* (1983).

Cibola, The Seven Cities of.   The land of the Zunis, who in the 16th century occupied seven pueblos in what is now western New Mexico. The Spaniards believed that these pueblos concealed fabulous wealth, supposedly collected by a kinsman of Montezuma who had fled from Mexico and established a kingdom of his own. There, the Spaniards said, ships from China came and landed their rich cargoes. On the plains nearby, wandered huge herds of cattle of deformed shape and frightening aspect—the white men later called them buffalos. Gold and silver were so abundant that everyone used them in making tableware. The Spanish explorer CABEZA DE VACA (1490?–1557) first started the legend. Then FRANCISCO VASQUEZ CORONADO (1510–1554) sought to verify the stories by sending out a Franciscan friar, Fray Marcos, to visit the region; he brought back a report of so many marvels that Coronado went to see for himself. The reality disgusted him, and he wrote to the viceroy in Mexico: "I can assure your honor that the friar told the truth in nothing that he reported."

Cimarron (1930)   a novel by EDNA FERBER. It deals with the spectacular land rush of 1889 in Oklahoma, beginning when the country was still Indian Territory and continuing through the oil boom and thereafter. The book depicts the degeneration of Yancey Cravat, a brilliant editor, lawyer, and wanderer, and the accompanying evolution of his wife, Sabra, into a practical and tenacious businesswoman, ultimately a congresswoman. It was made into a movie in 1960.

Circuit Rider, The (1874),   a novel by EDWARD EGGLESTON. In it, Eggleston provides a study of the frontier and its crudities, at the same time describing the impact of Methodism. (Eggleston was himself a Methodist minister.) Its hero is Morton Goodwin, a young Methodist preacher who suffers from a rejection in love but finally rescues himself through religion, becomes a circuit rider, and experiences the joys and perils that accompany preaching in the wilderness. Eggleston presents both sides, shows the contrast between the refined Methodism of the East and the nerve-racking ecstasies of the frontier. Other treatments of these frontier preachers include John L. Dyer's *The Snow-Shoe Itinerant* (1889), Corra Harris's *A Circuit Rider's Wife* (1910), and Sidney and Marjorie Green-

bie's *Hoof-Beats to Heaven* (1955), a biography of PETER CARTWRIGHT.

Circular Staircase, The (1908),   a mystery story by MARY ROBERTS RINEHART. It established her reputation as a writer of crime stories that display a sense of humor as well as ingenuity. The story became a play called THE BAT, in which the plot—altered by the author and Avery Hopwood—made the supposed detective the criminal. This device became a favorite with detective-story writers.

Circus in the Attic, The (1948),   a collection of two novelettes and twelve short stories by ROBERT PENN WARREN, including the masterful "Blackberry Winter."

Cisneros, Sandra (1954–   ),   short-story writer, poet. Born in Chicago, daughter of a Mexican father and Mexican-American mother, Cisneros spent part of her early life shuttling between her father's family home in Mexico City and various communities in the United States. A graduate of Chicago's Loyola University and the Writer's Workshop of the University of Iowa, she has lived much of the time since in Texas, teaching and associating herself with the social, artistic, and cultural bilingualism of the Mexican-American border region. A Chicana feminist, she is concerned with ethnicity and sexual identification within individuals and communities. In *The House on Mango Street* (1984), an adolescent narrator weaves together sketches about growing up among Mexican-Americans in Chicago. *Woman Hollering Creek and Other Stories* (1991) brings together stories and sketches from Texas and Mexico. *My Wicked Wicked Ways* (1987), poetry, includes some verse published earlier in the chapbook *Bad Boys* (1980). *Loose Woman* (1994) presents poems in celebration of love from a feminine perspective.

City in the Sea, The   (earliest version, 1831, in *Poems*, under the title "The Doomed City"; printed as "The City of Sin" in the *Southern Literary Messenger*, August 1836; called "The City in the Sea" in *The Raven and Other Poems*, 1845), a poem by EDGAR ALLAN POE.

City Lights Bookstore.   Center for avant-garde writing in San Francisco, important from the 1950s on for its encouragement of BEAT and San Francisco Renaissance writers. LAWRENCE FERLINGHETTI, the proprietor, also inaugurated City Lights Books, publishing Ginsberg's *Howl* (1956) and books by many other authors, American and foreign, including Paul Bowles, William Burroughs, Frank O'Hara, Jack Kerouac, Charles Olson, and Ferlinghetti himself.

Civil Disobedience (1849),   an essay by HENRY DAVID THOREAU. Prompted by Thoreau's night in jail in July 1846, the essay was first delivered as a lecture called "The Relation of the Individual to the State" in Concord on January 26, 1848. It was first printed in ELIZABETH PALMER PEARBOY's periodical *Aesthetic Papers* (May 1849) as "Resistance to Civil Government." The title "Civil Disobedience" came from posthumous printings; it appeared in *A Yankee in Canada* (1866) and *Miscellanies* (1893).

Neglected for many years, the essay has had far-reaching consequences in its effects on political thought and on the practical application of its principles by Mahatma Gandhi, MARTIN LUTHER KING, and other leaders of freedom movements of various kinds in a number of places. For Thoreau, the catalyst was the Mexican War. His refusal to support it with his poll tax led to jailing, and he was freed only when the tax was paid by someone else.

He began the essay on an understanding of personal liberty consonant with ideas of Paine and Jefferson: "I heartily accept the motto,—That government is best which governs least." Prompted also by a transcendental view of individual value— "We must be men first and subjects afterwards"—he questioned the principle of majority rule: "a government in which the majority rule in all cases cannot be based on justice, even as far as men understand it." The individual in the right has the duty to resist unwise laws not merely by casting a vote, but by taking action in civil disobedience against the tyranny of the majority. That his argument is not a prescription for anarchy is suggested toward the end: "They who know of no purer sources of truth . . . stand, and wisely stand, by the Bible and the Constitution, and drink at it there with reverence and humility." But the world is not yet perfect, and people of vision must continue the struggle toward universal betterment.

Civil War in literature, the.   War between the North and South, a "second American Revolution" in the words of historians Charles and Mary Beard, seemed imminent when South Carolina and other slaveholding states seceded from the Union shortly after the election of ABRAHAM LINCOLN to the presidency in 1860. With the Confederate attack on the Federal arsenal at Fort Sumter, South Carolina, on April 12, 1861, the Civil War began.

To the North, the primary objective of the war was the restoration of the Union; after 1862, freeing of the slaves became a second aim. Though the Northern states had superior numbers, a balanced economy, and naval supremacy, the secessionists, who had only to defend successfully to win, were confident of victory. They doubted Northern willingness to fight for preservation of the Union and were confident that England and France, dependent on cotton, would recognize the independence of the Confederacy and give material aid as well. Lincoln maintained that the secessionists were merely rebels defying their government, but by proclaiming a blockade of Southern ports and by banning trade with the seceded states he in fact recognized the existence of a state of war.

The Union rout at Bull Run (July 21, 1861) led Lincoln to name GEORGE B. MCCLELLAN commander-in-chief of the Northern forces. Dismissed after the Seven Days' Battle (June 26–July 2, 1862), McClellan was reinstated and repulsed the Confederate troops under ROBERT E. LEE at Antietam, Maryland (Sept. 17, 1862), in what was the bloodiest day of the war. Though McClellan was again removed for failing to pursue the Southerners, the technical victory at Antietam enabled Lincoln to issue a preliminary Emancipation Proclamation (September 22, 1862), which stated that the slaves would be freed if the South did not surrender before January 1, 1863, the date on which the final proclamation was made.

Defeated at Vicksburg (July 4, 1863) after a long and costly campaign led by ULYSSES S. GRANT, and at Gettysburg (July 1–3, 1863) by George B. Meade, the Confederates found themselves surrounded on the west and north by Union soldiers and on the east and south by the Union navy. In March 1864, Grant was made supreme commander of the Union forces and turned to an assault on Richmond, the Confederate capital. In May his successor in the western theater, WILLIAM T. SHERMAN, began his march through Georgia, while PHILIP SHERIDAN devastated the Shenandoah Valley. After a gallant defense, Lee was forced to evacuate Richmond (April 2, 1865), and was prevented by Sheridan's forces from escaping with his battered army. On April 9, 1865, Lee surrendered to Grant at Appomattox, Virginia.

With the possible exception of the Napoleonic Wars, no other conflict has produced more books. It has been estimated that more than a hundred thousand volumes have been written on the Civil War.

CARL SANDBURG's *Lincoln* and MARGARET MITCHELL's GONE WITH THE WIND gave impetus to a continuing flood. A Civil War Book Club was established in 1955. A currently published journal is *Civil War Times Illustrated*.

Civil War writing falls under several headings:

1. *Oratory and polemics*. Never was formal oratory more noble and effective than in the decades preceding the attack on Fort Sumter. Webster, Clay. Calhoun, Hahne, Everett, Douglas, and Lincoln spoke well on the issues of slavery, states' rights, and compromise. A good summary is Merrill Peterson's *The Great Triumvirate: Webster, Clay and Calhoun* (1987).

   The spirit of polemic was also carried into print. Most writers of the time contributed to the heated discussion of the problems that led to the war. During the conflict itself Lincoln rose to the heights. His addresses, state papers, and letters are among the best examples of American prose.

2. *Biography, history, and memoirs*. The War Between the States produced memoirs in profusion. Grant, Sherman, Sheridan, and McClellan all published important recollections of the war, as did the Southern generals Jubal Early, Joseph E. Johnston, JAMES LONGSTREET, John B. Hood, and Richard Taylor. Unfortunately, Robert E. Lee left no memoirs. For a critique of Lee's strategy, see Thomas L. Connelly, *The Marble Man* (1977). The best biography of Jackson and his campaigns is still G. F. R. Henderson, *Stonewall Jackson and the American Civil War*, 2 v. (1898). Grant's *Personal Memoirs* (1884) has been called by EDMUND WILSON the "best American autobiography." The best biography of Grant is Bruce Catton's two volumes: *Grant Moves South* (1960) and *Grant Takes Command* (1969).

   A prodigious literature has gathered around Lincoln, becoming year by year the largest devoted to any man in history. His apparent simplicity contrasted with the real complexities of his character has provoked commentator after commentator to write at length about him and his times. Carl Sandburg and Lord Charnwood are particularly memorable in this endeavor. History, biography, poetry, drama, motion pictures, and radio and television plays have all contributed to the apotheosis of Lincoln. Historians, notably JAMES FORD RHODES and James Garfield Randall, have written at great length about the war. Perhaps the best single-volume life is *With Malice Towards None* (1977) by Stephen B. Oates. A Southern viewpoint informs Hudson Strode's biography, *Jefferson Davis* (3 v. 1955–1964).

The atmosphere of the capital city is vividly conveyed in MARGARET LEECH's Pulitzer Prize book, *Reveille in Washington, 1860–65* (1941). Another Pulitzer Prize Winner is DOUGLAS S. FREEMAN's *Robert E. Lee* (4 v. 1942–44).

Other significant books include *The Private Mary Chestnut: The Unpublished Civil War Diaries*, ed. C. V. Woodward (1984); Kenneth P. Williams, *Lincoln Finds a General* (1952); ALLAN NEVINS, *Statesmanship of the Civil War* (1953); Clifford Dowdey, *The Land They Fought For* (1955); Fletcher Pratt, *Civil War in Pictures* (1955); Ned Bradford, *Battles and Leaders of the Civil War* (1888, reprint 1982); JEFFERSON DAVIS, *The Rise and Fall of the Confederate Government* (1881); Earl Schenck Miers, *The Great Rebellion: The Emergence of the American Conscience* (1958); Richard Ernest Dupuy, *The Compact History of the Civil War* (1960); Otto Eisenschiml, *The Hidden Face of the Civil War* (1961); Archer Jones, *Confederate Strategy from Shiloh to Vicksburg* (1961); and Edwin Charles Rozwenc, *The Causes of the American Civil War* (1961). Bruce Catton became the leading authority on the Army of the Potomac with such books as *Mr. Lincoln's Army* (1951), *Glory Road* (1952), *A Stillness at Appomattox* (1953), and *This Hallowed Ground* (1956), and he wrote a good three-volume *The Centennial History of the Civil War* (1961–1965).

In the area of biography two works are of use: John F. C. Fuller's *Grant and Lee: A Study in Personality and Generalship* (1957) and Ezra J. Warner's *Generals in Gray: Lives of the Confederate Commanders* (1959). Particularly valuable as an anthology is HENRY S. COMMAGER's *The Blue and the Gray* (1950).

Shelby Foote's three-volume *The Civil War, A Narrative* (1958–1974) sees the conflict brilliantly from both sides, as does James McPherson's superb one-volume *Battle Cry of Freedom* (1988), which treats history as "contingencies."

3. *Poetry*. Events of the Civil War provided much material for occasional poets on both sides of the conflict. The history of John Brown's raids gave rise to E. C. Stedman's "How Old Brown Took Harper's Ferry"; Henry Howard Brownell's "The Battle of Charleston"; John Greenleaf Whittier's "Brown of Osawatomie"; and, in the 20th century, to Stephen Vincent Benét's epic poem JOHN BROWN's BODY [2]. Bayard Taylor, A. J. H. Duganne, Thomas William Parsons, T. B. Read, and Thomas Dunn English treated such topics as the battle of the *Merrimac* and the *Cumberland*, emancipation, and Sherman's march to the sea. As would be expected, Lincoln's death stimulated the greatest contemporary poetical reaction. R. H. Stoddard's "Abraham Lincoln"; James Russell Lowell's "Ode Recited at the Harvard Commemoration"; and Walt Whitman's "When Lilacs Last in the Dooryard Bloom'd" and "O Captain! My Captain!" all mourn the great leader. Edwin Markham later eulogized Lincoln in "Lincoln, the Man of the People." Any list of Civil War poems should also include William Cullen Bryant's "The Past" and "The Death of Slavery," Lowell's "The Biglow Papers," Whittier's "Ichabod" and "Barbara Frietchie," and Oliver Wendell Holmes's "Brother Jonathan's Lament for Sister Caroline."

Poets who published books of their own Civil War poems include HENRY HOWARD BROWNELL, *Lyrics of a Day* (1864) and *War Lyrics* (1866); George Henry Baker, *Poems of the War* (1864); Walt Whitman, DRUM TAPS (1865); and Herman Melville, BATTLE-PIECES AND ASPECTS OF THE WAR (1866). From the South came the work of Henry Timrod, PAUL HAMILTON HAYNE, and ABRAM JOSEPH RYAN. Two songs rallied the North and South, respectively: Julia Ward Howe's "Battle Hymn of the Republic" and Dan Emmett's "Dixie."

Collections were made, North and South, of some of the poems connected with the war. They include: Frank Moore, ed., *Rebel Rhymes and Rhapsodies* (1864); Richard Grant White, ed., *Poetry, Lyrical, Narrative, and Satirical of the Civil War* (1866), WILLIAM GILMORE SIMMS, ed., *War Poetry of the South* (1866); William Gordon McCabe, ed., *Ballads of Battles and Bravery* (1879); Francis F. Browne, ed., *Bugle Echoes, Northern and Southern* (1886); and H. M. Wharton, ed., *War Songs and Poems of the Southern Confederacy* (1904).

The best-known modern poems are Robert Lowell's "For the Union Dead" (1960) and Allen Tate's "Ode to the Confederate Dead" (1959) with its line "inscrutable infantry rising/ Demons out of the earth."

4. *Fiction*. More novelists have written about the Civil War than any other single national event. Mainly, they have depended on such staple themes as the struggle between brothers, the personality of Lincoln, the maturation of young men at war, and the nostalgic dream of the antebellum South. Among the earliest novels concerned with the war were Henry Morford, *Shoulder Straps* (1863), *The Coward* (1863), and *In the Days of Shoddy* (1864); John Esten Cooke, *Surry of Eagle's Nest* (1866); Jeremiah Clemens, *Tobias Wilson: A Tale of the Great Rebellion* (1867); Sidney Lanier, TIGER-LILIES (1867); John W. De Forest, MISS RAVENEL'S CONVERSION (1867); E. D. E. N. Southworth, *How He Won Her* (1869); Edward P. Roe,

His Sombre Rivals (1883); S. Weir Mitchell, *Roger Blake* (1886); and Thomas Nelson Page, *Two Little Confederates* (1888) and *Red Rock* (1898). Edward Eggleston, in THE GRAYSONS (1888), was one of the first to introduce Lincoln as a character in a fictional work. The most faithfully remembered and intensely studied book of the war is Stephen Crane's fine psychological study, THE RED BADGE OF COURAGE (1895).

Other noteworthy fiction on diverse aspects of the war is seen in Ambrose Bierce, *Tales of Soldiers and Civilians* (1891) and *Can Such Things Be?* (1893); Irving Bacheller, EBEN HOLDEN (1900); Winston Churchill, THE CRISIS (1901); Ellen Glasgow, *The Battleground* (1902); Mary Raymond Shipman Andrews, THE PERFECT TRIBUTE (1906); Mary Johnston, THE LONG ROLL (1911) and *Cease Firing* (1912); Upton Sinclair, *Manassas, A Novel of the War* (1923); and James Boyd, MARCHING ON (1927).

In the 1930s, Civil War fiction became increasingly serious and attempted to throw light on present-day parallels. The analogies were tailor-made. The problems of Reconstruction paralleled those of the Great Depression; Lincoln became a symbol of the strong, honest leader the country desperately needed; and the plight of the plantation slave made an ironic juxtaposition with the continuing problems of the 20th-century African-American. In the South, historical authenticity was carefully maintained, but realistic substance was often beclouded by a romantic loyalty to a lost cause. Among the important novels of this period are Joseph Hergesheimer, *The Limestone Tree* (1931); John Peale Bishop, *Many Thousands Gone* (1931); DuBose Heyward, *Peter Ashley* (1932); Stark Young, *So Red the Rose* (1934); MacKinlay Kantor, *Long Remember* (1934), *Arouse and Beware* (1936), and ANDERSONVILLE (1955); Margaret Mitchell, *Gone with the Wind* (1936); Caroline Gordon, *None Shall Look Back* (1937); Edgar Lee Masters, *The Tide of Time* (1937); Hervey Allen, *Action at Aquila* (1938); and WILLIAM FAULKNER, *The Unvanquished* (1938). Among the best fictions of the two decades after the thirties are William James Blech, *The Copperheads* (1941); Louis Bromfield, *Wild Is the River* (1941); James Street, *Tap Roots* (1942); Joseph S. Pennell, *The History of Rome Hanks* (1944); Ben Ames Williams, HOUSE DIVIDED (1947) and *The Unconquered* (1953); ROSS LOCKRIDGE, *Raintree County* (1948); Bruce Lancaster, *No Bugles Tonight* (1948) and *Roll Shenandoah* (1956); SHELBY FOOTE, *Shiloh* (1952); Jere Wheelright, *The Gray Captain* (1954); IRVING STONE, *Love Is Eternal* (1954); ROBERT PENN WARREN, *Band of Angels* (1955); John Brick, *Jubilee* (1956); Harold Sinclair, *The Horse Soldiers* (1956); Upton Sinclair, *Theirs Be the Guilt* (1959); and Henry Allen, *Journey to Shiloh* (1960). More recent testimonials to the continued fascination with the period include GORE VIDAL, LINCOLN (1984); Michael Shaara, *The Killer Angels* (Pulitzer Prize, 1974); JOHN JAKES, *North and South* (1982), *Love and War*

(1984), and *Heaven and Hell* (1987); Bernard Cornwell, *Rebel* (1993), *Copperhead* (1994), *Battleflag* (1995), and *The Bloody Ground* (1996); and Charles Frazier, *Cold Mountain* (1997).

Rebecca W. Smith covered part of the fictional output in *The Civil War and Its Aftermath in American Fiction, 1861–99* (1932). Robert A. Lively wrote *Fiction Fights the Civil War* (1956), a survey of over five hundred Civil War novels with an extensive bibliography. A major study is Daniel Aaron, *The Unwritten War: American Verities and the Civil War* (1973).

5. *Drama.* Both fiction and drama of the Civil War began their course with the publication of Harriet Beecher Stowe's UNCLE TOM's CABIN (1852) and its prompt dramatization nearly eight years before the outbreak of war. But the speed with which the theater made use of contemporary materials during the war was extraordinary. As early as January 16, 1861, an anonymous play, *Our Union Saved*, was produced in New York. In the following month, George H. Miles inserted a patriotic tableau into a spectacle called *The Seven Sisters* that drew audiences for 177 nights. Bull Run was fought on July 21, 1861, and on August 15th *Bull Run*, by Charles Gayler, was on the boards. Occurrences such as this were numerous, but the plays so hastily put together proved to have little artistic value. In the 1870s Dion Boucicault dominated the theatrical scene. Although several of his plays and adaptations are concerned with the South, only *Belle Lamar* (1874) is directly concerned with the Civil War. J. Culver wrote an action-packed melodrama, *Loyal Mountaineers: or The Guerrilla's Doom* (1889), after Cyrenus Osborne Ward had earlier offered the ambitious five-act play *The Great Rebellion: Reminiscences of the Struggle That Cost a Million Lives* (1881). Later dramas dealing with the Civil War include Sinclair Lewis, *Jayhawker* (1935); Paul Green, *Wilderness Road* (1956); and Robert D. Hock, *Borak* (1961).

Television and the movies continue to validate the dramatic content of the war, with the John Jakes *North and South* series, the 1990 Public Broadcasting series *The Civil War*, written by Geoffrey Ward and others and filmed by Ken Burns, and the historically sound *Glory* (1989).

Clampitt, Amy (1920–1994),   poet. Born in Iowa and educated at Grinnell College and Columbia, Clampitt worked in New York City for Oxford University Press, the National Audubon Society, and E. P. Dutton. She later won acclaim for her poetry, beginning with *The Kingfisher* (1983). Her poems are dense, allusive, and specific in imagery as they portray nature, the author's travels, or the passing of time. Other collections include *What the Light Was Like* (1985), *Archaic Figure* (1987), *Westward* (1990), and *A Silence Opens* (1994). An essay collection is *Predecessors, et Cetera* (1991).

Clancy, Tom (1947–   ),   novelist. A Baltimore native, Clancy was educated there at Loyola College. He worked as an insurance agent before turning to the best-selling novels that quickly made him wealthy. His books are marked by complex plots, details of technology, and strong narrative pull. His first was *The Hunt for Red October* (1984), a thriller dealing with espionage and nuclear submarines. The hero, Jack Ryan, is a professor of naval history at Annapolis who also works for the CIA. Ryan continues his exploits in *Red Storm Rising* (1986), on naval engagements in the North Atlantic in a third world war; *Patriot Games* (1987), in which Ryan seeks to revenge the harming of his daughter by an IRA terrorist; *The Cardinal of the Kremlin* (1988), on espionage and antimissile systems; *Clear and Present Danger* (1989), about the war on drugs in Colombia; and *The Sum of All Fears* (1991), with a nuclear warhead missing in the Mideast. Another hero, the ex-Navy SEAL John Clark, is central to *Without Remorse* (1993), concerning drugs in Baltimore and POWs in Vietnam; *Debt of Honor* (1994) and *Executive Orders* (1996), connected stories of espionage and conflict with Japan wherein Ryan succeeds to the presidency of the U.S.; and *Rainbow Six* (1998), with terrorists and the potential end of the world at issue. Like some other contemporary popular writers, including Robert Ludlum and Clive Cussler, Clancy now runs a kind of production company, franchising his name for movies and television, as well as for a line of mass-market paperbacks called "Tom Clancy's Op-Center," written by Steve R. Pieczenik.

Clansman, The (1905),   the novel by THOMAS DIXON that was turned into the movie BIRTH OF A NATION.

Clappe, Louise Amelia Knapp Smith (1819–1906), writer. Clappe came from Massachusetts to California with her husband in 1849 and wrote letters giving a woman's view of the gold rush. Published in San Francisco's *Pioneer Magazine* (1854–55) as letters from a Dame Shirley to her sister, they appeared later in the book *The Shirley Letters* (1922).

Clare, Ada.   See MCELHENEY, JANE.

Clarel (1876),   a long poem by HERMAN MELVILLE. Set in and around Jerusalem and based on Melville's own trip to the Holy Land in the late 1850s, *Clarel* is both a guided tour to sacred spots and a symposium on major philosophical problems of the day. The central figure of the poem, the questor, is Clarel, a young and relatively innocent theological student who is oscillating between faith and doubt. In Jerusalem he falls in love with Ruth, a young Jewish girl, and leaves her to join a heterogeneous group of pilgrims journeying from Jerusalem to Gethsemane, to the Dead Sea, to Bethlehem, and back to Jerusalem. The pilgrims talk continually, and most of the talk is directed to Clarel, a willing listener. Taken collectively, the pilgrims represent virtually every religious and social persuasion possible: Nehemiah, a saintly old man knows the time of the Second Coming but not the time of day; Vine, the seclusive aesthete resembles Melville's old friend NATHANIEL HAWTHORNE; Derwent, an Emersonian apostle of an optimistic Christianity; Mortmain and Ungar, bitter and cynical pessimists; Margoth, a geologist and materialist who is held in general contempt; a Dominican friar who defends Catholicism; and others in profusion—prodigals, revolutionaries, Arabian guides, monks—representing the full panorama of

desert society. Ruth dies just as Clarel returns to Jerusalem, and at the end of the poem Clarel is alone to face a new reality with a new wisdom.

Clarel is not a poem of ideas, and the final question it raises is broadly cultural: Is Western civilization, having lost its traditional faith through the incursions of science, doomed to an ultimate sterility? Technically, the poem suffers from constant inversions, ellipses, and lack of action and narrative flow; at best it is a masterly presentation of place in verse that is replete with a hard intellectual resonance.

Clarion, The   (1914),   a novel by SAMUEL HOPKINS ADAMS. An attack on quackery and dishonest journalism, the novel relates the story of Hal Surtaine, a young man of high principles who purchases a newspaper with money his father has made from a patent medicine concern. Hal must decide whether or not to publish the truth about the concoction to which he owes his fortune.

Clark, [Charles] Badger (1883–1957),   poet. Clark specialized in cowboy life and western lore. One of his poems, "The Glory Trail" (in his collection *Sun and Saddle Leather*, 1915), has been sung by cowboys under the title "High Chin Bob." His poems are also collected in *Grass-Grown Trails* (1917) and *Sky Lines and Wood Smoke* (1935). *Spike* (1923) is a collection of short stories.

Clark, Charles Heber ["Max Adeler"] (1847–1915), newspaperman, humorist. As Max Adeler he indulged in wild, fantastic humor, particularly in a book of suburbanite sketches called OUT OF THE HURLY-BURLY, OR LIFE IN AN ODD CORNER (1874), very popular in its day. Other novels include *Elbow-Room* (1876) and *The Quakeress* (1905). *By the Bend in the River* (1914) collects short stories.

Clark, Eleanor [Mrs. Eleanor C. Warren] (1913–1996),   novelist, essayist. Clark was educated at Vassar. Her first novel, *The Bitter Box* (1946), was well received. *Rome and a Villa* (1952) is a series of impressionistic essays on the Eternal City. Her other books include *The Oysters of Locmariaquer* (1964), local color sketches of Brittany; *Eyes, Etc.* (1977), about her loss of sight; *Baldur's Gate* (1971), *Gloria Mundi* (1979), and *Camping Out* (1986), novels; and a translation of Ramón Sender's *Dark Wedding* (1945). In 1952 she married ROBERT PENN WARREN.

Clark, George Rogers   (1752–1818),   surveyor, Indian fighter, soldier. Clark was born in Virginia and served (1774) in Lord Dunmore's War. During the Revolution he obtained authority from Patrick Henry, governor of Virginia, to raise a force for the conquest of the Northwest. With only 150 riflemen, he took town after town as far away as the Mississippi, and although the British recaptured Vincennes, the chief posts were all in the hands of Clark at the time of the Revolution. This fact resulted in cession of the region to the United States. Clark's story is told by himself in M. M. Quaife's *The Capture of Old Vincennes* (1927); *Background to Glory* (1956), by John Bakeless, is a biography of Clark. He and his Rangers appear in much fiction, including R. M. Bird's *Nick of the Woods* (1837); Daniel Pierce Thompson's *The Rangers*

(1851); Maurice Thompson's ALICE OF OLD VINCENNES (1900); Winston Churchill's THE CROSSING (1904); Louis Zara's *This Land of Ours* (1940); and Harold Sinclair's *Westward the Tide* (1940); Clark's brother WILLIAM participated in the Lewis and Clark Expedition.

Clark, Lewis Gaylord (1808–1873) and Willis Gaylord Clark (his twin brother, d. 1841), editors, humorists. The Clarks together edited the KNICKERBOCKER MAGAZINE and made it the leading periodical of the antebellum period. Both had a gift for humorous and fanciful writing, and Willis in addition wrote religious verse, which was praised by Poe. His death from tuberculosis cut short a promising literary career. Willis published a volume of verse, *The Spirit of Life* (1833), and his brother edited his *Literary Remains* (1844). Lewis Clark also wrote a volume of memoirs, *Knick-Knacks from an Editor's Table* (1852). See KNICKERBOCKER SCHOOL.

Clark, Mary Higgins (1928?–), mystery writer, novelist. Born in New York City as Mary Higgins, she was educated at Villa Maria Academy, Ward Secretarial School, NYU, and Fordham. Left with five children when her husband, Warren Clark, died in 1964, she turned to writing and after *Aspire to the Heavens: A Biography of George Washington* (1969), produced a best seller with her first novel, *Where Are the Children?* (1975), a thriller with the action limited to one day. Since that time her work has steadily grown in popularity to the point where in 2000 she signed a contract for $64 million for five books. A number of her works have been filmed for movies and TV. Readers praise her swift-paced mastery of suspense found in everyday situations when the bizarre, frightening, or insane suddenly intrudes. *A Stranger Is Watching* (1978) covers just three days. *Stillwatch* (1984) starts with a home break-in. *Loves Music, Loves to Dance* (1991) and *All Around the Town* (1992) explore mental illness. In *I'll be Seeing You* (1993) and *Moonlight Becomes You* (1996) the medical profession turns threatening, in the first with in-vitro fertilization and in the second with mysterious deaths in a nursing home. In *Pretend You Don't See Her* (1997) the federal witness program proves not fully protective. *All Through the Night* (1998) is a a gentle Christmas holiday story featuring her popular amateur sleuths, Alvirah and Willy. *Before I Say Goodbye* (2000) tells of politics, a boat explosion, and psychic powers. Stories, many first published in *The Saturday Evening Post, Redbook, McCall's,* and other magazines, are collected in *The Anastasia Syndrome* (1989), *The Lottery Winner: Alvirah and Willy Stories* (1994), and *My Gal Sunday* (1996).

Clark, Walter van Tilburg (1909–1971), short-story writer, novelist. Born in Maine, Clark grew up in Nevada and was educated at the University of Nevada and the University of Vermont. After writing verse and short stories, he won acclaim with his first novel, THE OX-BOW INCIDENT (1940), made into an unusually powerful and thoughtful movie in 1942. *The City of Trembling Leaves* (1945) Clark described as "a token biography of Reno, a city of adolescence"; *The Track of the Cat* (1949) features a sinister and symbolic black panther; and *The Watchful Gods* (1950) is a collection of short stories.

Clark, William (1770–1838),   soldier, explorer. Like his brother, GEORGE ROGERS CLARK. William penetrated the wilderness in action against the Native Americans. He was invited in 1803 by his friend Captain MERIWETHER LEWIS to join him in an expedition sponsored by Jefferson, with the goal of finding a route to the Pacific. This became the great Lewis and Clark Expedition (1804–06). Clark was made governor of the Missouri Territory, remained governor until 1821, then became Superintendent of Indian Affairs for the rest of his life.

Clarke, Austin C[hesterfield] (1934–), novelist, short-story writer, autobiographer. Born and educated in Barbados, Clarke came to Canada in 1955 to study at the University of Toronto. He has worked for the Canadian Broadcasting Company, taught writing at Yale and other universities, and served as cultural attaché at the Barbados Embassy in Washington. His first novel, *The Survivors of the Crossing* (1964), and his first collection of short stories, *Amongst Thistles and Thorns* (1965), depict Barbadian poverty and despair. His fiction depicting the struggles of West Indian immigrants in Toronto includes a trilogy: *The Meeting Point* (1967), *Storm of Fortune* (1973), and *The Bigger Light* (1975), as well as a second collection of short stories, *When He Was Free and Young and He Used to Wear Silks* (1971). *The Prime Minister* (1977) is a novel of political corruption in an unidentified tropical nation. Always, his concern is with blacks and whites in Barbados and the need to universalize experience and acceptance. A spokesman for blacks and for Black Power, he speaks of the need for Canadians to recognize the central fact of people of color: "We live here. I live here. I ain't going nowhere." His autobiographical works are *Growing Up Stupid Under the Union Jack* (1980), *Colonial Innocency* (1982), *Astounding Days: A Science Fictional Autobiography* (1990), and *A Passage Back Home* (1994). His other works include *When Women Rule* (1985), stories; *Nine Men Who Laughed* (1986), stories; and *Proud Empires* (1986) and *The Origin of Waves* (1997), both novels.

Clarke, George Herbert (1873–1953), poet. Clarke came from England to Canada as a boy, taught in U.S. colleges for a while (he edited THE SEWANEE REVIEW at the University of the South, 1920–25), and was head of the Department of English in Queen's University, 1925–1943. In that year he was awarded the Lorne Pierce Medal of the Royal Society of Canada for distinction in Canadian literature. Three collections of his verses are *At the Shrine and Other Poems* (1914), *The Hasting Day* (1930), and *Parley and Other Poems* (1934). He wrote numerous patriotic odes and described natural backgrounds with skill and insight.

Clarke, James Freeman (1810–1888), preacher, editor, biographer, historian. Born in New Hampshire and educated at Harvard Divinity School, Clarke joined a number of other Harvard men in a movement to the West. In 1835 they established a Unitarian magazine, WESTERN MESSENGER, in Cincinnati, and Clarke worked as an editor until 1839. In 1841 he returned to Boston to establish the Church of the Disciples and became a militant leader in the TRANSCENDENTALIST movement. He published numerous books, among them *Ten Great Religions* (two parts, 1871, 1883); *Memorial and Biographical Sketches* (1878); *Self-Culture* (1880); and *Autobiography* (1891). In a collection called *The Disciples' Hymn Book* (1884) he included some original pieces of his own.

Clarke, John (1609–1676),   clergyman. A Baptist, Clarke along with Obadiah Holmes and John Crandall came from Newport, Rhode Island, to Lynn, Massachusetts, in 1651 and there raised publicly certain theological questions that infuriated the other ministers and their followers—when they kept their hats on in the meeting-house, they were removed from their heads by force. The three men were tried and fined. Clarke eventually returned to Rhode Island, where he had been one of the founders of Newport, serving both as physician and minister. He wrote *Ill News from New England* (1652), an attack on the intolerance of the Massachusetts ministers.

Clarke, MacDonald (1798–1842),   poet. Born in Maine, Clarke became a member of the bohemian set of his day. Called "the mad poet of Broadway," he died in the asylum for the insane on Blackwell's Island, New York City. In his own lifetime a collection was published called *Elixir of Moonshine by the Mad Poet* (1822), and his *Poems* were collected in 1836. In an *Epigram* he wrote:

'Tis vain for present fame to wish—
Our persons first must be forgotten;
For poets are like stinking fish—
They never shine until they're rotten.

Clavell, James [duMaresq] (1925–1994),   novelist, screenplay writer. Born in Australia, Clavell fought with the Royal Artillery during World War II and survived three and half years in the notorious Changi prison camp, near Singapore. Afterwards, he studied briefly at the University of Birmingham (1946–1947), emigrated to the United States in 1953, and became a citizen in 1963. From the 1950s onward he was a Hollywood screenwriter, director, and producer, occupying all three roles in films that included *The Great Escape* (1963), which won the Writers Guild Best Screenplay Award, and *To Sir with Love* (1969). *King Rat* (1962), his bestselling first novel, follows a British soldier and his American comrade as they struggle to survive the brutish conditions at Changi, where 140,000 out of 150,000 prisoners died; adapted as a movie, it set the pattern for the extraordinary success of his later and more famous works. *Tai-Pan* (1966), set in 1841, tells of the founding of Hong Kong in a novel characterized by one critic as "gaudy and flamboyant with blood and sin, treachery and conspiracy, sex and murder." A gigantic bestseller, it, too, became a movie. The next book, *Shogun: A Novel of Japan* (1975), considered by many his best, is a thoroughly researched account of a 17th-century British sailor who becomes a Samurai. In *Noble House: A Novel of Contemporary Hong Kong* (1981), Clavell takes up the story of the Far East trading company founded in *Tai-Pan*, which is also featured in

Gai-Jin: A Novel of Japan (1993), an account based on late-19th-century history. *Whirlwind* (1986) is a fictional account of helicopter pilots caught in the chaotic events surrounding the fall of the Shah of Iran. His mammoth books, familiar to hundreds of millions in print or in screen adaptations, have given him one of the largest audiences of any 20th-century writer. Critics have compared him to Dickens for the intricacy of his plotting, the relentless pull of his narratives, and the social and political implications frequent in his work.

Clavers, Mary.   Pen name of CAROLINE KIRKLAND.

Clay, Henry (1777–1852),   statesman, orator. Born in Virginia, Clay was almost constantly in public service. He became a member of the Virginia state legislature in 1803, reached the United States Senate in 1806. He was speaker of the House or senator almost continuously during his later lifetime and was John Quincy Adams's secretary of state. A perpetual candidate for the presidency, he wittingly jeopardized his chances several times by voting for measures unpopular in the North. (It was he who said in a speech in 1850, "I would rather be right than president.") He did everything possible, along with his great colleagues Webster and Calhoun, to prevent a split that would lead to war, and his name is closely connected with the COMPROMISE OF 1850.

He is believed to have been the model for the satiric portrait of a politician in J. K. Paulding's novel, KONINGSMARKE (1823). He appears in Mary Dillon's romance *The Patience of John Morland* (1909) and in Alfred Leland Crabb's *Home to Kentucky* (1953).

Clean, Well-Lighted Place, A,   a story by ERNEST HEMINGWAY collected in *Winner Take Nothing* (1933). An old man sits in drunken loneliness at a table on the terrace of a Spanish cafe, discussed by two waiters. The older of the two sympathizes with the man; loneliness is everywhere, and perhaps all comes to *nada*, nothing.

Cleaver, [Leroy] Eldridge (1935–   ),   political activist, writer. Born in Arkansas, Cleaver when a young man spent nine years in prison for drug dealing and rape. His book *Soul on Ice* (1968), written in prison, depicts the forces that create anger and criminality in young African-Americans. Later, while he was active with the Black Panthers, Cleaver advocated armed resistance to the political system, became involved in a gun fight with police, and had his parole revoked. He fled the country and lived from 1968 to 1975 in Cuba, Algeria, and France. When visits to Communist countries left him disenchanted, he returned to the U.S. *Soul on Fire* (1978) relates his religious conversion. His other books include *Eldridge Cleaver: Post-Prison Writings and Speeches* (1969) and *Eldridge Cleaver's Black Papers* (1969).

Cleghorn, Sarah N[orthcliffe] (1876–1959),   poet, novelist. Born in Virginia but raised in Vermont, Cleghorn was a social activist, a pacifist working for prison reform and against capital punishment and running a school for workers' children. Robert Frost called her "a saint, a poet and a reformer" in his introduction to her autobiography, *Threescore* (1936). Among her writings is the biting quatrain:

The golf links lie so near the mill
That almost every day
The laboring children can look out
And see the men at play.

Her first novel, *The Turnpike Lady* (1907), tells of rural life in Vermont. A second, *The Spinster* (1916), is more autobiographical. Her poems were collected in *Portraits and Protests* (1917) and *Poems of Peace and Freedom*. She published two collections of essays with her friend DOROTHY CANFIELD FISHER, *Fellow Captains* (1916) and *Nothing Ever Happens and How It Does* (1940).

Clemens, Jeremiah (1814–1865), lawyer, soldier, statesman, novelist. Clemens had a distinguished political career in Alabama and was elected to the Senate in 1849. His support of Millard Fillmore for president alienated his constituents, and he retired from political activity to write novels, including *Bernard Lile* (1856), about the Mexican War; *The Rivals* (1860), about Burr and Hamilton; and *Tobias Wilson* (1865), about the Civil War.

Clemens, Samuel Langhorne. See TWAIN, MARK.

Clements, Colin [Campbell] (1894–1948), playwright, novelist. Clements collaborated with his wife, Florence Ryerson, on many plays, stories for children, and mystery novels. Their most popular play was *Harriet* (1943), starring Helen Hayes in the role of Harriet Beecher Stowe. Another was *Strange Bedfellows* (1948), a drama of women's suffrage.

Clemm, Virginia (1822–1847), EDGAR ALLAN POE's child wife, whose tragic death from consumption inspired ANNABEL LEE (1849). He married her on May 16, 1836.

Cliff Dwellers, The (1893), a novel by HENRY B. FULLER.

Clifton, [Thelma] Lucille (1936–), poet. Born in DePew, New York, Clifton was educated at Howard University and Fredonia State Teachers College and has taught poetry at a number of universities. "I am a Black woman poet," she has said, "and I sound like one." Her tough, vernacular, passionate verse includes "The Lost Baby Poem," about determination and tenderness learned from experiencing an abortion, and "I Once Knew a Man," about a man who "had wild horses killed" and "they rode him to the grave." Among her collections are *Good Times* (1969), *Good News About the Earth* (1972), *An Ordinary Woman* (1974), *Two-Headed Woman* (1980), and *Next* (1987). Her other works include *Generations* (1976), a memoir; *Good Woman: Poems and a Memoir: 1969–1980* (1987); *Quilting: Poems 1987–1990* (1991); *Terrible Stories: Poems* (1996); *Blessing the Boats: New and Selected Poems, 1988–2000* (2000), and many children's books.

Clinton, George (1739–1812), first governor of New York. In his opposition to the adoption of the Constitution, he carried on a controversy with ALEXANDER HAMILTON in the columns of the New York *Journal*, where Clinton published seven letters under the pen name "Cato." Hamilton replied in the *Daily Advertiser* under the name "Caesar." Clinton became vice-president in 1804 and later sought unsuccessfully election

as president. His *Public Papers* were gathered in ten volumes (1889–1911).

Clockmaker, or, The Sayings and Doings of Samuel Slick, of Slickville, The (in three series, 1836, 1838, 1840), sketches by T. C. HALIBURTON. Slick is an itinerant Yankee clockmaker, slangy, ill-bred, energetic, shrewd, and funny. The Canadian humorist's account of Slick's adventures and remarks won wide popularity in Canada, the United States, and England and exerted a great influence on the development of humor in the United States.

Clurman, Harold (1901–1980), critic, stage director, author. In his years in the theater, Clurman directed over fifty plays. His *The Fervent Years* (1945) is the story of the Group Theatre. He also wrote *Lies Like Truth* in 1959, a collection of theater criticism.

Coal Dust on the Fiddle (1943), songs and stories of the bituminous coal industry, collected by George Korson. This is an expansion of an earlier volume by Korson, *Minstrels of the Mine Patch* (1938), which dealt with Pennsylvania only. In the later collection Korson describes new surveys made in Ohio, Illinois, Indiana, West Virginia, Kentucky, Tennessee, Alabama, and Nova Scotia. He collected songs, ballads, stories, legends, folk remedies, sayings, and unwritten history. His book informally describes the social aspects of the bituminous industry.

Coates, Robert M[yron] (1897–1973), novelist, short-story writer. After World War I Coates began writing for the LITTLE MAGAZINES and then turned to art criticism for *The New Yorker* and to writing short stories and novels. His novel *The Eater of Darkness* was published in 1929 and reissued in 1960. Coates followed this novel with *Yesterday's Burdens* (1933); *The Bitter Season* (1933); *Wisteria Cottage* (1948), based on an actual murder case; and *The Farther Shore* (1957), another study in criminal psychology. He collected his short stories in *All the Year Round* (1943), *The Further Shore* (1955), and *The View from Here* (1960).

Coatsworth, Elizabeth [Jane] (1893–1986), poet, novelist, children's writer. Born in Buffalo, New York, and long resident in Massachusetts and Maine, Coatsworth wrote over forty books for children. *The Cat Who Went to Heaven* (1930) won the Newbery Award. Her verses are collected in *Fox Footprints* (1923), *Compass Rose* (1929), *Country Poems* (1942), and *The Creaking Stair* (1949). Her novels include *Here I Stay* (1938), *The Trunk* (1941), and *Silky* (1953). Two books about Maine, *Country Neighborhood* (1944) and *Maine Ways* (1947), won much praise. In 1958 she had three publications: *The White Room*, a novel; *Poems*, a collection; and *The Cave*, a juvenile. *Pika and the Roses*, a juvenile, and *Peaceable Kingdom*, a collection of poems, came out in 1959. *Personal Geography* (1976) is a memoir.

Cobb, Irvin S[hrewsbury] (1876–1944), humorist, writer, actor. Cobb was a descendant of a Vermont governor and a Virginia governor, and a representative of American humor at its most characteristic, a direct follower of BILL NYE, ARTEMUS WARD, and MARK TWAIN.

Cobb was a successful journalist for the New York *Evening Sun* and *The Saturday Evening Post*. His first book, *Back Home* (1912), was followed by a long series of volumes, many of them collections of material that had appeared earlier in magazines. Most popular were the Judge Priest stories, laid in the Southern background Cobb knew so well: *Old Judge Priest* (1915); *Judge Priest Turns Detective* (1937); and Cobb's first novel, *J. Poindexter, Colored* (1922), about the judge's servant, Jeff. Other stories are collected in *The Escape of Mr. Trimm* (1913) and other volumes. One of his most popular pieces was *Speaking of Operations* (1916), an account of a personal experience. He wrote lively travel books, such as *Europe Revised* (1914), and many humorous skits.

In 1932, when the movies took up the Judge Priest stories, Cobb settled in Hollywood as a scriptwriter. He made his acting debut in 1934 as a river captain along with Will Rogers in the movie based on Burman's *Steamboat Round the Bend*, and played successfully in other pictures. Cobb's autobiography is *Exit Laughing* (1941). His daughter's life of him is *My Wayward Parent* (1945).

Cobb, Joseph B[eckham] (1819–1858),   essayist, critic, novelist. Born in Georgia, Cobb wrote a romance, *The Creole* (1850), in which the pirate Lafitte appears. His sketches appeared in *Mississippi Scenes* (1851). His essays, *Leisure Labors* (1858), contain frank criticisms of contemporary writers.

Cobb, Sylvanus, Jr. (1821–1887),   short-story writer, novelist. Cobb was a favorite and voluminous storyteller for the New York weekly *Ledger*. Some of his tales were later printed in book form, among them *The Golden Eagle* (1850), *The Privateer of the Delaware* (1855), *The Patriot Cruiser* (1863), and THE GUNMAKER OF MOSCOW (1888). (See THE NEW YORK LEDGER.)

Cobbett, William (1763–1835),   British journalist. Cobbett's stays in Canada and the United States were marked by controversies generated by his journalism, as was his career in England. In the United States he published Federalist political attacks, including *A Bone to Gnaw for the Democrats* (1795), *A Kick for the Bite* (1795), and *The Scare-Crow* (1796). Personal attacks he wrote include a *Life of Tom Paine* (1796) and *Observations on the Emigration of Dr. Priestley* (1794). His short-lived *Porcupine's Gazette* (1797–99) was a daily newspaper in Philadelphia, his *Life and Adventures of Peter Porcupine* (1796) a summary of the times. Product of a later stay was his *A Year's Residence in the United States* (1818–19), which included observations by another visiting Englishman, Thomas Hulme.

Cocktail Party, The (1949, pub. 1950),   a play in verse by T. S. ELIOT. This often witty and sometimes powerful play begins and ends at a cocktail party. Its principal characters suffer from loneliness and a lack of self-knowledge. Through the mediation of an uninvited guest, ostensibly a psychoanalyst but also a sort of mysterious father-confessor, three of the guests attain salvation. A married couple achieve a modest degree of enlightenment, enough to enable them to save their marriage. A young woman becomes a nursing sister and is

martyred in Africa. The verse of the play is generally colloquial and unobtrusive, preserving the cadences and vocabulary of ordinary cultured speech, but it has moments of intensity and eloquence.

Codrescu, Andrei (1946–   ),   poet, novelist, social commentator. Born in Sibiu, Romania, Codrescu came to the United States in 1966 after his expulsion from the University of Bucharest for anti-Communist sympathies. Four years later, *License to Carry a Gun* (1970) established him as a promising American poet, reformed from his Romanian past under the influence of Whitman and William Carlos Williams and their descendants. Much of his work, including the poems of *Comrade Past and Mister Present* (1986) and the prose of *The Disappearance of the Outside: A Manifesto for Escape* (1990), addresses concerns common to many recent American writers displaced by choice or otherwise from significantly different pasts (see GLOBALIZATION OF AMERICAN LITERATURE). The title of *Alien Candor: Selected Poems, 1970–1995* (1996) reiterates the theme as it applies to a quarter century of verse. Prolific under his own name and pseudonyms that include Betty Laredo, Urmuz, and Marie Parfeni, he has become a National Public Radio personality with commentary on *All Things Considered*; an actor in the award-winning documentary *Road Scholar* (1993), which took him cross-country in a red Cadillac with a camera crew, and was adapted as the book *Road Scholar: Coast to Coast Late in the Century* (1994); a tireless translator and anthologist; and a professor of English at Louisiana State University. Novels include *The Blood Countess* (1995), linking 20th-century events in Hungary with the story of a 16th-century countess who bathed in the blood of murdered girls, and *Messiah* (1999), on millennial religious fervor. Essay collections include *The Muse Is Always Half-Dressed in New Orleans* (1993), *Zombification* (1994), *The Dog with a Chip in His Neck* (1996), *Hail Babylon! In Search of the American City at the End of the Millennium* (1998), and *The Devil Never Sleeps* (2000). *The Life and Times of an Involuntary Genius* (1975) and *In America's Shoes* (1975) are autobiographical. *The Hole in the Flag: A Romanian Exile's Story of Return and Revolution* (1994) reports disappointment with a country in flux.

Cody,   William   Frederick   ["Buffalo   Bill"] (1846–1917),   scout, showman, folk hero. Born in Iowa, and a man of limited formal education, Cody early acquired all the tricks of horsemanship and marksmanship. He became a gold prospector, Pony Express rider, hunter of horse thieves and hostile Indians, member of Kansas guerrilla bands, soldier in the Union army, and a hunter of bison. E. Z. C. Judson, who as "Ned Buntline" became the father of the dime novel, asserted—and this still is disputed—that he gave Cody the name Buffalo Bill because of the hunter's skill in killing bison. (Cody said he killed 4,861 of the animals in a single season.) Judson wrote a series of novels about Cody's career and produced a play, *The Scout of the Plains* (1872), in which Buffalo Bill himself appeared. After this, love of the limelight conquered the scout. In 1883 he organized a group of hunters and rough-riders who appeared at the Omaha fair grounds and made a great hit. Later, Cody found an astute manager, Nate Salsbury, who created *Buffalo Bill's Wild West Show*, which toured for twenty years. In time they acquired for the show ANNIE OAKLEY, whose fame soon equaled Buffalo Bill's. A great success, the show went east and, finally, abroad. After the death of Salsbury, Cody's recklessness with money caused him to lose control of his show and end his life in poverty.

Being a hero became Cody's prime vocation. For almost fifty years, in more than a thousand novels, in melodramas, and in his own shows, Cody remained "the finest figure of a man that ever sat on a steed." Wyoming named a town after him and made his birthday a holiday. Colonel Prentiss Ingraham, who constituted himself Cody's official biographer, made him the hero of more than two hundred dime novels. Cody himself is the author of *The Life of Hon. William F. Cody* (1879), *The Story of the Wild West and Campfire Chats* (1888), and *True Tales of the Plains* (1908).

Coelho, Paulo (1947   ),   Brazilian novelist. Born in Rio de Janeiro, and in his early career a pop lyricist, Coelho became an international phenomenon after the publication in English of his second novel, *The Alchemist* (1993; *O Alquimista*, 1987). "In the publishing world outside of the United States, nobody reads Spanish, much less Portuguese," he has said. By the year 2000 his works had been translated into 43 languages and sold over 26 million copies in over 100 countries, making him by one count the second most popular author in the world (after JOHN GRISHAM). *The Alchemist* is a brief fable in which a Spanish shepherd boy travels through the deserts of North Africa seeking to find fulfillment somewhere among the pyramids, and finds that what he most needed was after all closer to home. Spiritual searches lie at the center of most of his books, few of which have found as much as favor with critics as with readers. Other titles include *The Pilgrimage* (1987), about a personal journey along Spain's Road to Santiago; *Brida* (1990), about an Irish enchantress; *The Valkyries* (1992), forty days Coelho spent with his wife in the Mojave Desert; *By the River Piedra I Sat Down and Wept* (1994), a woman's spiritual adventure; *The Fifth Mountain* (1996), on the prophet Elijah; and *Veronika Decides to Die* (2000), set in a Slovenian mental hospital.

Coffin, Charles Carleton (1823–1896),   civil engineer, writer, lecturer. Coffin, a self-taught civil engineer and surveyor, went on to reporting the battles of the Civil War for a Boston paper. After the war he began writing manly stories for boys: *The Boys of '61* (1881, published originally as *Four Years of Fighting*, 1866); *The Boys of '76* (1876); *The Story of Liberty* (1879); *Life of Lincoln* (1892); and others. In his last years he lectured widely and often served in the Massachusetts legislature.

Coffin, Long Tom.   A character in James Fenimore Cooper's sea story THE PILOT (1823). Long Tom may be called a Leatherstocking with a harpoon instead of a rifle, a pea-jacket instead of a hunting shirt. During the Revolutionary War he takes part in some daring actions in the course of which American vessels, under the guidance of the mysterious

"Pilot," raid the British coast and do a little kidnapping as a way of repaying the British for their habit of impressing American sailors.

Coffin, Robert P[eter] Tristram (1892–1955), poet, teacher, essayist, editor. Coffin grew up on a Maine saltwater farm and was educated at Bowdoin, Princeton, and Oxford. He taught at Wells College, then at Bowdoin. He lectured all over the country on many topics, and in the midst of all his other activities, he ran two farms and frequently made drawings for his books. His books of verse are *Golden Falcon* (1929); *Ballads of Square-Toed Americans* (1933); *Strange Holiness* (1936, Pulitzer Prize); *Saltwater Farm* (1937); *Maine Ballads* (1938); *Primer for America* (1943); *Poems for a Son with Wings* (1945); *People Are Like Ballads* (1946); *Collected Poems* (1948); and *Selected Poems* (1955). In prose he wrote *The Kennebec* (in RIVERS OF AMERICA SERIES, 1937); *Book of Uncles* (1942); *Mainstays of Maine* (1944); *One-Horse Farm* (1949); *Coast Calender* (1949); and *Maine Doings* (1950).

Coggleshall, William Turner (1824–1867),   writer. An Ohio journalist and novelist, Coggleshall made early attempts to boost the literature of the West, writing in favor of a regional literature in *The Protective Policy in Literature* (1859) and editing an anthology of *The Poets and Poetry of the West* (1860).

Cohan, George M[ichael] (1878–1942),   actor, songwriter, playwright, director, producer. Cohan began acting while still a child as a member of a theatrical troupe, "The Four Cohans," starring his parents, his sister Josephine, and himself. Before he was 21 Cohan had written 150 vaudeville sketches, most of them for other performers. His first legitimate stage production was *The Governor's Son* (1901). Then came an expanded vaudeville sketch, *Running for Office* (1903). In 1904 he produced *Little Johnny Jones*, in which he played a role always thereafter associated with him, "the Yankee Doodle Boy." He wrote more than forty dramas and musical comedies, appearing in many of them himself. Among them are *Forty-Five Minutes from Broadway* (1906), GET-RICH-QUICK WALLINGFORD (1910), BROADWAY JONES (1912), *Seven Keys to Baldpate* (1913), *The Miracle Man* (1914), *The Song and Dance Man* (1923), and *Gambling* (1929). His "Over There," the American song still associated with World War I, brought him a Congressional Medal two decades after the war. "Give My Regards to Broadway" is another Cohan song of the war. Among his other songs that attained wide popularity are "I'm a Yankee Doodle Dandy," "Grand Old Flag," and "Mary Is a Grand Old Name." In 1937 Cohn came out of retirement to play Franklin D. Roosevelt in *I'd Rather Be Right*, a satire by George S. Kaufman and Moss Hart.

Cohen, Leonard (1934–   ),   poet, novelist, popular singer. Born in Montreal and educated at McGill, Cohen has lived in England, on a Greek island, in California and New York, and in Montreal. He won popular success in the 1960s, especially with the young people. Collections of his poems include *Let Us Compare Mythologies* (1956), *Flowers for Hitler* (1964), *Selected Poems* (1968), *The Energy of Slaves* (1972), and

Death of a Lady's Man (1978). *The Best of Leonard Cohen* (1975) is a selection of songs. His novels are *The Favorite Game* (1963) and *Beautiful Losers* (1966).

Cohen, Octavus Roy (1891–1959),   newspaperman, short-story writer, novelist. Born in Charleston, Cohen wrote for various newspapers in the South, then for *The Saturday Evening Post* and other magazines. His stories dealt humorously—in the style of his time—with a group of African-Americans in Birmingham. Later he wrote mystery stories with much ingenuity of plot and action. Among his books are *Polished Ebony* (1919), *Highly Colored* (1921), *Assorted Chocolates* (1922), *Florian Slappey Goes Abroad* (1928), *Epic Peters, Pullman Porter* (1930), *Florian Slappey* (1938), *Kid Tinsel* (1941), *Dangerous Lady* (1946), *More Beautiful Than Murder* (1948), and *Love Can Be Dangerous* (1955).

Colcord, Lincoln [Ross] (1883–1947),   nautical authority, poet, novelist. A descendant of five generations of seafarers, Colcord was born at sea off Cape Horn, but he always thought of himself as a Maine man. Between studies at the University of Maine, he spent many months at sea. At first a civil engineer, Colcord soon began writing for newspapers and magazines. In 1936 he became secretary of the Penobscot Marine Museum, and in 1941 was associate editor of *The American Neptune* (published at Salem, Massachusetts). His publications include *Vision of War* (1915), a book-length poem; *The Game of Life and Death* (1914), his best known book of sea fiction; and *An Instrument of the Gods* (1922), also fiction. His sister, Joanna Colcord (1882–1953), was a prominent social worker and author of *Songs of the American Sailorman* (1938) and *Sea Language Comes Ashore* (1945).

Colden, Cadwallader (1688–1776),   historian, physician, scientist. Colden emigrated to America from Scotland in 1708 or 1710, and settled in Philadelphia, later in New York. He knew Franklin well and corresponded with Samuel Johnson and with the great Swedish botanist Linnaeus, whose system he introduced into American botany. He was an ardent loyalist, burned in effigy because he defended the Stamp Act. His interest in Indians produced *The History of the Five Indian Nations* (1727; reprinted, 1866, 1902). His *Letters and Papers* were collected by the New York Historical Society (1918–37).

Cole, Thomas (1801–1848),   painter, poet. Born in England, Cole came with his family to Ohio in 1818. He studied painting in Philadelphia at the Pennsylvania Academy and moved in 1826 to New York, where he founded the National Academy of Design. He was a prominent member of the HUDSON RIVER SCHOOL, famed for its depictions of scenic grandeur. Among his best works are *The Oxbow, Catskill Mountains,* and two series of symbolic paintings, *The Course of Empire* and *The Voyage of Life.* The last mentioned was viewed by more than 100,000 people when it was displayed in New York after Cole's death.

Coles, Robert (1929–   ),   psychiatrist, biographer. Coles is best known for his five-volume series, *Children in Crisis,* which chronicles the lives of children, often in their own words. Born in Boston and educated at Harvard University (1950), Coles earned a medical degree in 1954 from Columbia University, with a concentration in child psychiatry. *Courage and Fear* (1967), the first volume in the series, chronicles the lives of African-American children during the volatile early years of forced school integration in the South. *Migrants, Sharecroppers and Mountaineers* was published in 1971, followed by *The South Goes North,* focusing on uprooted Appalachian children, in the same year. *Eskimos, Chicanos, Indians* and *Privileged Ones: The Well-Off and the Rich in America* both appeared in 1978. Coles received a MacArthur Foundation Fellowship in 1981 and wrote three other works which he considered to be part of the Children in Crisis series. These works, *The Moral Life of Children* (1986), *The Political Life of Children* (1986), and *The Spiritual Life of Children* (1990), take an international approach to analyzing the reactions of children to their environments. A prolific writer, Coles's numerous other books include biographies of Catholic activists Dorothy Day and Simone Weil.

SUZANNE PERKINS-HART

Coliseum, The (1833),   a poem by EDGAR ALLAN POE. It was later incorporated in the text of his blank-verse drama *Politian,* published in part in the *Southern Literary Messenger* (1835–36).

Collins, Billy (1941–   ),   poet. Born in New York City, educated at Holy Cross (B.A. 1963) and Berkeley (Ph.D., 1971) and for thirty years a professor of English at Lehman College in the Bronx, Collins became in the 1990s a best seller among poets, admired by critics and professional poets as well as by general readers, with publishers vying for the rights to his poems. Praised for a colloquial voice that is aware both of audience and the possibilities of verse in our time, he has attained his popularity in part through National Public Radio appearances. *Questions About Angels* (1991), winner of the National Poetry Series Competition, first brought him widespread attention as a witty poet, jazzy and funny, with a flair for turning the common into the metaphoric. *The Art of Drowning* (1995), *Picnic, Lightning* (1998), and *Sailing Alone Around the Room* (2001) added to his reputation as a poet whose playful conversational tone works for subjects as diverse as Emily Dickinson and a Victoria's Secret model. In 2001 he was named Poet Laureate.

Colman, Benjamin (1673–1747),   clergyman. Born in Boston and educated at Harvard, Colman visited and preached in England for four years before returning to become minister of the Brattle Street Church in Boston (1699–1747). A liberal Congregationalist, he played a minor part in the GREAT AWAKENING and published over ninety works, mostly sermons. They include *The Government and Improvement of Mirth* (1707); *God Deals with Us as Rational Creatures* (1723); and *Elijah's Translation* (1707), poetry. His son-in-law Ebenezer Turrell published *The Life and Character of the Reverend Benjamin Colman* (1749).

Colon and Spondee.   One of the earliest columns in American literature, conducted in collaboration by ROYALL

TYLER (Spondee) and JOSEPH DENNIE (Colon) in *The Farmers' Museum* and other periodicals during 1794 and later years. Tyler wrote the verse, Dennie the prose.

Colonel Carter of Cartersville (1891), a novel by F. Hopkinson Smith. In this story of the misadventures of a Virginian stranded in New York City, Carter has no money, but lives on loans; he has a wild scheme for building a railroad; he is kindly, chivalrous, and likable even at his most comic. Augustus Thomas dramatized the story in a play of the same title (1892). *Colonel Carter's Christmas* (1903) was a sequel.

Colonel Sellers. See SELLERS, COLONEL BERIAH.

Color Purple, The (1982), a novel by ALICE WALKER.

Colton, John (1889?–1946), dramatist. Colton's most successful plays include *Rain* (in collaboration with Clemence Randolph, 1922), based on W. Somerset Maugham's short story "Miss Thompson," and *The Shanghai Gesture* (1926), in which Mother Goddam, keeper of a Shanghai brothel, takes a fiendish revenge on an Englishman who had deserted her twenty years earlier. Other plays are *Nine Pine Street* (1933), based on the Lizzie Borden case, and *Saint Wrench* (1933).

Colton, Walter (1797–1851), navy chaplain, newspaperman, historian. Colton described a number of his sea journeys in books, his best remembered being *Deck and Port* (1850), the story of a voyage to California. Along with Robert Semple, he founded California's first newspaper, *The Californian* (1846), and wrote an important historical work, *Three Years in California* (1850).

Colum, Mary [Gunning Maguire] (1880?–1957) and **Padraic Colum** (1881–1972), writers, both born in Ireland, later becoming U.S. citizens. The Colums, married in 1912, came to the United States in 1914. Mrs. Colum set forth some of her ideas on literature in *From These Roots* (1937) and told her life and her many friendships in *Life and the Dream* (1947). Padraic Colum at an early age became a part of the Irish literary revival. He wrote a peasant drama, *Broken Soil*, at the age of twenty; it was later rewritten and published as *The Fiddler's House*. Many collections of excellent poetry, many books for children, books of personal reminiscence, and other volumes have come from his pen. Among them are *A Boy in Eirinn* (1913); *Dramatic Legends* (1922); *The Voyagers* (1925); *Poems* (1932); *A Half-Day's Ride* (1932); *The Frenzied Prince* (1947); *Collected Poems* (1953); *The Flying Swan* (1956); *Our Friend James Joyce* (with Mary Colum, 1958); *Ten Poems* (1958); and *Ourselves Alone!* (1959).

Columbia (1777), a patriotic song by TIMOTHY DWIGHT, composed while Dwight was serving as chaplain to the American army in the campaign against Burgoyne. The refrain became well known:

Columbia, Columbia, to glory arise—
The queen of the world and the child of the skies.

Columbia, the Gem of the Ocean (1843?). This American patriotic song may originally have been entitled *Britannia, the Pride of the Ocean*, for British consumption. It is said that Thomas à Becket, a young English actor, wrote it while playing at a Philadelphia theater for an English actor named David Taylor Shaw, to be sung at a benefit performance for Shaw. Shaw published it as "written, composed, and sung by David T. Shaw, and arranged by Thomas à Becket, Esq." Becket later published it as "written and composed by T. à Becket, and sung by D. T. Shaw." According to other accounts, the poem was written by Stephen Joseph Meany in England in 1842, with music by Thomas F. Williams and with the British title. Or it may have been taken later to London by an American actor named Edward Loomis Davenport (1815–77) and sung there under its British title.

Columbiad, The (1807), a poem by JOEL BARLOW. This expansion of Barlow's *The Vision of Columbus* (1787) in an epic of America in heroic couplets. Columbus, in chains, has a vision in which he sees the future glory of America, including events that occurred before the poem was written—such as the Revolutionary War—and events still to come, for example, including the building of the Panama Canal, airplanes, submarines, and a united nations and world language. According to his preface, Barlow wrote "to inculcate the love of rational liberty and to discountenance the deleterious passion for violence and war; and to show that on the basis of republican principle all good morals, as well as good government and hopes for permanent peace, must be founded." Handsomely printed and bound, the poem has often been ridiculed, and readers have generally found it far more dull than inspiring.

Columbian Lady's and Gentleman's Magazine, The. Founded in New York City in 1844, expired in 1849. John Inman, the editor, secured as contributors some of the important writers of the day, including Poe and J. K. Paulding. The magazine, featuring engravings and color plates, proved unsuccessful as a rival to GRAHAM's.

Columbian Magazine, The. Founded by MATHEW CAREY in Philadelphia, September 1786, it expired in 1792. FRANCIS HOPKINSON and C. B. BROWN were among the contributors. The magazine was interested in general knowledge, especially scientific developments, and in literature. After it merged in 1790 with the *Philadelphia Magazine and General Asylum* (the two were then called *University Asylum* and *Columbian Magazine*), BENJAMIN RUSH became the chief contributor. In the *Columbian* appeared much of the work of JEREMY BELKNAP, particularly a series of satirical letters on the early history of New England that were collected as *The Foresters* (1792).

Columbus, The Life and Voyages of (3 v. 1828), a biography by WASHINGTON IRVING. While an attaché in the American Legation at Madrid, Irving gathered materials for this massive work. He had access to many treasures of source material, including some made available to him by the Duke of Veraguas, a descendant of Columbus. His view of the discoverer is an exalted one and has been questioned, but he produced a clear, well-written biography. Later he added an account of *The Companions of Columbus* (1831).

Columbus, The Vision of (1787), a poem by Joel Barlow. See COLUMBIAD.

Colwin, Laurie [E.] (1944–1992), novelist, short-story writer. Born in New York City, educated at Bard and Columbia, Colwin worked for New York publishers and literary agents and wrote about middle- and upper-class Manhattanites in a manner that earned her comparison with John Cheever and John Updike. Often she finds gentle humor in characters whose search for romantic love runs up against their desire for personal careers, marital fidelity, and individual privacy. Novels include *Shine On, Bright and Dangerous Object* (1975); *Happy All the Time* (1978), in the words of one critic, "a Manhattan Pastoral" that is "at least as much fun to read as *Sense and Sensibility*"; *Family Happiness* (1982), with an affair threatening the peace of the title; *Goodbye Without Leaving* (1990); and *A Big Storm Knocked It Over* (1993), with friendship proving more lasting than marriage. Short stories are collected in *Passion and Affect* (1974); *The Lone Pilgrim* (1981), especially celebrated; and *Another Marvelous Thing* (1986), linked stories about marital infidelity and ultimate faithfulness. A food columnist for *Gourmet Magazine*, she also wrote *Home Cooking: A Writer in the Kitchen* (1988) and *More Home Cooking: A Writer Returns to the Kitchen* (1993).

Come Up from the Fields, Father (1865), a poem by WALT WHITMAN. An affecting picture of the receipt of bad news at a home in Ohio, from which a boy had gone to join the Union army. Perhaps the lines represent Whitman's imaginative reconstruction of a scene that must many times have resulted from the hundreds of letters that he himself wrote for soldiers when he worked as a volunteer in hospitals in Washington. It is one of his few poems that attempt something by way of drama and character portrayal.

Comfort, Will Levington (1878–1932), newspaperman, fiction writer. His novel *Routledge Rides Alone* (1910), based on his experience in the Russo-Japanese War, is so graphic that peace societies circulated it as propaganda. Comfort told the story of his life with candor in *Midstream* (1914).

comic almanacs. From the beginning almanacs popular with colonial readers and their successors emphasized humor. The Yankee was a constant figure in the almanacs, and in Franklin's portrait of Poor Richard a wry smile may be perceived. Often the compiler of early almanacs did no more than perform the feat modern comedians call a "switch," taking an old joke and giving it contemporary details and coloring. In time, some almanacs became deliberately and primarily comic, at least in intent. Apparently there was a growing public for almanacs free of the agricultural, meteorological, statistical data, and moralizing that formed the staple of earlier almanacs. The first of this special type is believed to have been *The American Comic Almanac*, published at Boston by Charles Ellms in 1831. It contained crude jokes and crude pictures, but caught the popular fancy and had many imitators, among them *Comic Token* and *Broad Grins* (both 1832), *American Comic Annual* (1833), Elton's *Comic All-My-Neck* (1834), and Finn's *Comic Almanac* (1835).

Most famous of the comic almanacs was Davy Crockett's *Almanac of Wild Sports of the West and Life in the Backwoods* (1835). Crockett died in the next year, but his heirs continued to publish Crockett almanacs. Later, one Ben Hardin or Harding—possibly mythical—took them over. In 1839 the firm of Turner & Fisher of New York began to publish the Crockett almanacs and continued to do so until 1856. The anecdotes and tall tales were in Yankee dialect; the text was accompanied by crude woodcuts. Other comic almanacs appeared up to the outbreak of the Civil War: *The Rip Snorter, Whim Whams, The Merry Elephant*, and *The Devil's Comical Texas Oldmanick*. William Murrell, writing *The History of American Graphic Humor* (v. 1, 1934; v. 2, 1938), found "the illustrations in many instances much more humorous than the texts."

comics. The comic strip is an open-ended humorous or dramatic narrative about a recurring number of primary and secondary characters, told in pictures and words, with the dialogue supplied in balloons, and published on a daily basis in newspapers, usually in color on Sundays. The comic book has some of the same characteristics, except that the visual narratives are published in a small magazine, traditionally in color, and issued monthly. In the beginning, the comic book was intended to reprint the newspaper comics before publishers began to develop original material for its pages and a distinct market. While the roots of the comics are found in European graphic satire, narrative art, the pictorial broadsheet, illustrated novels and children's books, and cartoons in humorous periodicals, the comics in the form we know have been an American creation. Figures such as Mickey Mouse, Superman, and Charlie Brown have become part of modern folklore and are recognized as American symbols in most parts of the world. While circulation figures change and reader interests vary, the comics have become a permanent part of the American cultural landscape and have matured into a form of creative expression intended more often for adults rather than for children. Only television appears to reach more people of all ages and economic and social levels in this country.

The comic strip took its present form under the hand of cartoonist RICHARD FELTON OUTCAULT, who began in 1895 to draw a series of single-panel features about Hogan's Alley, a fictional back-street immigrant section of New York where children engaged in a variety of riotous activities and games. Among the children was a short character, part Oriental and part Irish in appearance, dressed in a yellow shift on which dialect words were written. This urchin would become wildly popular and the star of his own comic strip feature, known as *The Yellow Kid* and the center of a newspaper war over ownership of the character. Outcault would eventually leave the Kid to create another popular feature, *Buster-Brown*.

In the wake of his success, other cartoonists began to contribute humorous and comic features to the pages of the newspaper supplements, now published in color and eventually to become known as the "funny papers." These included *The Katzenjammer Kids* by Rudolph Dirks; *Happy Hooligan* and *Maude the Mule* by FREDERICK BURR OPPER; *Mutt and Jeff* by

Bud Fisher (the first regularly published daily comic strip); *Bringing Up Father* (with Maggie and Jiggs) by GEORGE MCMANUS; *Barney Google* (and eventually *Snuffy Smith*) by Billy De Beck; *Polly and Her Pals* by Cliff Sterret; *Thimble Theater* (starring Popeye after 1929) by Elzie C. Segar; and *Moon Mullins* by Frank Willard. The two masterpieces of this period were WINSOR MCCAY's *Little Nemo in Slumberland*, the most beautifully drawn and aesthetically pleasing page ever to grace the Sunday papers, and GEORGE HERRIMAN's *Krazy Kat*, a whimsical fantasy of the absurd that lyrically celebrated unrequited love between Krazy Kat, Ignatz the Mouse, and Offisa Pup.

Adventure entered the comic strips with the swashbuckling escapades of a soldier of fortune, Roy Crane's *Captain Easy*, and the picaresque story of a young right-wing busybody named *Little Orphan Annie*, by HAROLD GRAY, both in 1924. It wasn't until the appearance of an adaptation of EDGAR RICE BURROUGHS's *Tarzan* and *Buck Rogers* by Richard W. Calkins and Phil Nowlan in 1929, however, that adventure became a staple of the comics. Among the most popular in this genre were *Dick Tracy* by Chester Gould, *Terry and the Pirates* and the postwar *Steve Canyon* by MILTON CANIFF, *Flash Gordon* by Alex Raymond, *Mandrake the Magician* and *The Phantom* by Lee Falk, *Prince Valiant* by Harold Foster, *Buzz Sawyer* by Roy Crane, and Will Eisner's *The Spirit*, in a masterfully drawn newspaper comic book supplement.

Sidney Smith's *The Gumps* in 1917 and Frank King's *Gasoline Alley* in 1918 introduced melodrama to the comics. The soap-opera strips that have survived include Allen Saunders's *Mary Worth* and writer Nicholas Dallis's three creations, *Rex Morgan, M.D.*, *Judge Parker*, and *Apartment 3-G*. Middle-class family values have been celebrated in *Blondie* by Chic Young and *Hi and Lois* by Mort Walker and Dik Browne.

AL CAPP's 1934 hillbilly comedy *Li'l Abner* gradually evolved into a vehicle for satire, a mode that began to flourish and has remained dominant since the 1950s. WALT KELLY's animal fable *Pogo* and CHARLES SCHULZ's strip about worldly wise children, *Peanuts*, are considered the highwater marks, but other popular titles are *Beetle Bailey* by Mort Walker, *B.C.* by Johnny Hart, *The Wizard of Id* by Hart and Brant Parker, *Cathy* by Cathy Guisewite, *Garfield* by Jim Davis, *Shoe* by Jeff MacNelly, *Kudzu* by Doug Marlette, and *Mutts* by Patrick McDonnell. The four most recent masters of satire are considered to be Garry Trudeau in *Doonesbury*, deftly keyed to immediate political events; Gary Larson in *The Far Side*, bizarre in its style and content; Berke Breathed in *Bloom County*, an outrageous combination of humans and animals involved in potent commentary; and Bill Watterson in *Calvin and Hobbes*, an incisive use of child psychology and imagination to reflect on the human condition.

The first comic books, beginning in 1933 with *Funnies on Parade* and *Famous Funnies*, were only as popular as the comic strips they reprinted, but Jerry Siegel and Joe Shuster changed that when they created Superman, who debuted in the first issue of *Action Comics* in 1938. So compelling was his example that the superhero with a secret origin and unusual mental and physical powers became the standard fare in comic books,

including figures like Batman, Captain Marvel, Wonder Woman, Captain America, and Plastic Man. As the comic book gained strength among its readers (one billion copies sold annually during the best years), it branched out into other areas, including funny animals, westerns, romance, war, teenage humor, detectives, and science fiction.

By 1950, crime and horror had become extremely popular among comic book readers, as represented by some of the best titles in the history of the medium from William Gaines's EC firm—*Tales from the Crypt*, *The Vault of Horror*, and *The Haunt of Fear* among them. Unable to see beyond the explicit violence to the moral values underlying the formulaic stories, a crusade developed against all horror and crime comic books. It was led by Dr. Fredric Wertham, whose book *Seduction of the Innocent* tried to link juvenile delinquency with comic book reading, and Estes Kefauver, who conducted a Senate investigation that resulted in the Comics Code Authority, an industry self-regulation code. Gaines responded by closing down his comic book business and developing one of his titles, *Mad*, into America's most popular satiric magazine.

In the 1960s interest in comic books revived when Stan Lee helped create a new stable of heroes who experienced the normal insecurities and frustrations of ordinary people, such as *The Fantastic Four* and *Spider-Man*. Another creative boost was provided by Robert Crumb, Gilbert Shelton, S. Clay Wilson, Trina Robbins, and numerous others in the Underground Comix movement who set out to violate all the principles of the Comics Code and produced some of the most innovative and influential work in comics since the 1940s. Out of this ferment has come a series of full-length novels in comic book form, called "graphic novels," in the 1980s, the most notable of which include *A Contract with God* by Will Eisner, *The First Kingdom* by Jack Katz, *The Dark Knight Returns* (a reinterpretation of Batman) by Frank Miller, *Watchman* by Alan Moore and Dave Gibbons, Harvey Pekar's autobiographical meditations on life in *American Splendor*, and Art Spiegelman's retelling of the Holocaust in animal fable form, *Maus*, which was nominated for a National Book Critics Circle Award in biography and received a Pulitzer Prize. The controversial material with which comic books now deal is a sign of their artistic maturity and the fact that the readers have largely become adult. More than ever before, it shows promise of becoming a significant literary/art form of the future.

The following books about comics can be used with profit: Coulton Waugh, *The Comics* (1947); Stephen Becker, *Comic Art in America* (1959); Pierre Couperie and others, *A History of the Comics* (1968); Jerry Robinson, *The Comics: An Illustrated History of the Comic Strip* (1974); Will Eisner, *Comics & Sequential Art* (1985); Joseph Witek, *Comic Books as History* (1989); M. Thomas Inge, *Comics as Culture* (1990); Scott McCloud, *Understanding Comics* (1993); Trina Robbins, *A Century of Women Cartoonists* (1993); and Robert C. Harvey, *The Art of the Funnies: An Aesthetic History* (1994) and *The Art of the Comic Book* (1996).

M. THOMAS INGE

Coming of Age in Samoa (1928), by MARGARET MEAD. The celebrated anthropologist describes her book in a subtitle as "a psychological study of primitive youth for Western civilization." She sets out to answer the question: Are the disturbances that vex our adolescents due to the nature of adolescence itself or to the civilization in which they live? The chief lesson she learned from her examination of Samoan culture was this: "Adolescence is not necessarily a time of stress and strain, but cultural conditions make it so." In Samoa the young girls pass through the same physical changes as elsewhere, but little attention is paid to them and there is no emotional tension. Accompanying this placidity is, however, a degree of freedom in sex relations before marriage that is foreign to Western notions. In a foreword Franz Boas says of her book that it "confirms the suspicion long held by anthropologists, that much of what we ascribe to human nature is no more than a reaction to the restraints put upon us by our civilization."

Commager, Henry Steele (1902–1998), historian, biographer, editor, essayist, teacher. Born in Pittsburgh, Commager explored the tenets of democracy and the legacy of the Constitution, becoming one of the most respected historians of the 20th century. He devoted sixty-five years to teaching history, joining the faculty of New York University in 1926, Columbia University in 1939, and Amherst College in 1956. Known for his accessible and detailed narrative style, Commager enjoyed both critical acclaim and popular success. Among his most influential books are *The Growth of the American Republic* (with Samuel Eliot Morison, 1931, 1942); *Majority Rule and Minority Rights* (1943); *The American Mind* (1950); *The Empire of Reason* (1977); and *Commager on Tocqueville* (1993), described by the New York Times as "his most brilliant work." He edited some excellent anthologies: *Documents of American History* (1934), which he considered one of his most significant contributions to historical study; *The St. Nicholas Anthology* (2 v. 1948, 1950); and *The Blue and the Gray* (2 v. 1950). Commager was vocal in his opposition to McCarthyism and the American involvement in Vietnam; he supported both stances with arguments based on the U.S. Constitution. In 1972, he was named Simpson Lecturer at Amherst, the school's most prestigious appointment, and was also awarded the Gold Medal for History from the National Academy of Arts and Letters. Some of his other books include *Theodore Parker* (1936); *The Heritage of America* (with Allen Nevins, 1939); *Freedom, Loyalty, Dissent* (1954); and *Atlas of the Civil War* (1958).

SUZANNE PERKINS-HART

Commentary (1945–), monthly journal. Founded by the American Jewish Committee as a forum for "significant thought and opinion on Jewish affairs and contemporary issues," *Commentary* has been edited by Elliot E. Cohen (1945–59) and Norman Podhoretz (1960–). Generally conservative in its views, *Commentary* has published many influential writers, including Hannah Arendt, James Baldwin, Saul Bellow, Leslie Fiedler, Paul Goodman, Sidney Hook, Irving Hook, Norman Mailer, Lionel Trilling, and Edmund Wilson.

Common Lot, The (1904), a novel by ROBERT HERRICK. It depicts a young Chicago architect who succumbs to commercialism and builds houses that later are destroyed in a fire with loss of life. His wife helps regenerate and save him.

Common Sense (published January 10, 1776), a pamphlet by THOMAS PAINE. This is possibly the most influential writing of its kind ever published. Paine landed in America in November 1774, obtained some small literary jobs, and became deeply interested in the cause of American independence. Dr. BENJAMIN RUSH met Paine in a Philadelphia bookshop in February 1775 and suggested that he write an appeal for independence under the title *Common Sense*. After some difficulty in finding a publisher, the pamphlet was issued and in three months sold 100,000 copies. It cast aside all theoretical considerations and based its appeal on the economic advantages that would come if the colonists cut their ties with England. It attacked the monarchical principle and the Tory assumption that the English constitution was divine. Americans were won over; the Declaration of Independence was formulated within six months.

Commonweal, The. A magazine published in New York City by Roman Catholic laymen. It was founded on November 12, 1924, and throughout its course has followed an independent line.

Compensation (1841), an essay by RALPH WALDO EMERSON, first published in his *Essays* (1841). It is among the most famous and influential of Emerson's writings, rich in his characteristic paradoxes and offering his combination of Platonic wisdom and Yankee horse sense. The central thought is repeated under various guises and in brilliant epigrams. Perhaps it is most simply stated in the often quoted sentence that "every sweet hath its sour; every evil its good." Again he says, "Every act rewards itself" and "For everything you have missed you have gained something else; and for everything you gain, you lose something." It follows, says Emerson, that "it is as impossible for a man to be cheated by anyone but himself, as for a thing to be and not to be at the same time."

Compromise of 1850. At the close of the Mexican War (1846–48), violent debate broke out in Congress on whether the newly annexed territories would be slave or free. HENRY CLAY and DANIEL WEBSTER, who wished to see the Union preserved at all costs, supported compromise measures rather than the pro-slavery measures advocated by JOHN C. CALHOUN in his address of March 4, 1850. Webster replied to Calhoun in his "Seventh of March Speech." JOHN GREENLEAF WHITTIER subsequently composed his poem, ICHABOD (1850), with its magnificent invective directed against Webster for having supported the compromise. The bill nevertheless passed. In later years Whittier somewhat regretted the lashing he had given Webster, and in THE LOST OCCASION (1881) paid tribute to the greatness of Webster's character and oratory.

Compson family, the. A group of characters in THE SOUND AND THE FURY and other works by WILLIAM FAULKNER.

COMPSON GENEALOGY

Quentin MacLachan Compson
b. 1699, d. 1783

|

Charles Stuart Compson

|

JASON LYCURGUS COMPSON

|

Quentin MacLachan Compson II

|

JASON LYCURGUS COMPSON II
d. 1900

|

Caroline Bascomb = JASON COMPSON III
d. 1933   d. 1912

Sydney Herbert Head = CANDACE,   QUENTIN III   BENJY, b. 1895   JASON IV
b. 1892   d. 1910   (first called Maury)

|

QUENTIN (daughter by Dalton Ames)
b. 1911?

One of the old, aristocratic families of YOKNAPATAWPHA COUNTY, the Compsons trace their American ancestry back to the early 18th century, but by the early 20th century the family is decaying. In the 1930s the family property is sold and the last male Compson is a childless bachelor. Members of the family are the following:

Benjamin Compson. Christened Maury, after his mother's only brother, and renamed when it is apparent he is an idiot, Benjy narrates the opening section of *The Sound and the Fury.*

Candace Compson [Caddy]. After having been seduced by Dalton Ames, Caddy is hastily married to Sydney Herbert Head, a northern banker. Ames is the father of Quentin, whom Caddy brings back to Jefferson to be raised by her family. Caddy disappears, divorces Head, marries a "minor moving picture magnate" in Hollywood, divorces him, and is last heard of in Paris during the German occupation. She appears as a child in "That Evening Sun."

Jason Lycurgus Compson I. The first Compson to settle in Mississippi, Jason bought Compson's Mile from Ikkemotubbe, a Chickasaw chief, and built the Compson house with the help of the French architect who built Thomas Sutpen's mansion (see THE SUTPEN FAMILY).

Jason Lycurgus Compson II. A brigadier general during the Civil War, Jason II was the only friend of Thomas Sutpen and the character to whom Sutpen tells part of the story of his life, as related in ABSALOM, ABSALOM!

Jason Compson III. Originally a lawyer, Jason III drifts toward dipsomania and spends his time reading and writing satiric Latin verses. He sells part of the family property to pay for Caddy's wedding and for Quentin III's education at Harvard.

Jason Compson IV. A shrewd, practical, selfish man, Jason IV becomes a storekeeper. After the other members of the family have died or disappeared, Jason sells what is left of the property and goes to live in town. Since he does not marry, the Compson name ends with him. He appears as a child in "That Evening Sun."

Quentin Compson. The daughter of Caddy and Dalton Ames, Quentin is named before her birth for her uncle Quentin III. At seventeen she steals money sent to her uncle Jason for her support. Hidden by him, she runs away with a carnival pitchman and is never heard of again.

Quentin MacLachan Compson III. A hypersensitive, introspective young man, Quentin narrates the second part of *The Sound and the Fury* and the short story "That Evening Sun" and is one of the narrators of *Absalom, Absalom!* Because of his inability to reconcile his conception of honor with the realities of the world in which he lives, Quentin commits suicide while a student at Harvard in 1910.

Compton, Francis Snow. A pen name used by HENRY ADAMS on the title page of his novel *Esther* (1884).

Comstock, Anthony (1844–1915), censor of literature and art. He founded the Society for the Suppression of Vice and became its secretary for life. He conducted relentless campaigns against what he regarded as obscenity, secured the passage of an act (1873) excluding immoral matter from the mails, caused the conviction of countless persons, and destroyed 160 tons of obscene literature and nearly 4 million pictures.

Comstock Lode. In the early 1850s prospectors had searched the valleys on the eastern side of the Sierras and found small quantities of placer gold. Not till 1859, however, were the surface outcroppings of the Comstock Lode discovered in Nevada—one of the world's mineral treasure stores, which at its best yielded $20,000,000 worth of mingled gold and silver annually, and over time produced a total of $400,000,000 worth of precious ore. The shaft ultimately went down 2300 feet, but stifling gases at this depth prevented further penetration of the mine, which ceased to be worked after the middle 1870s. The discovery brought a great influx of prospectors. MARK TWAIN, who had accompanied his brother Orion to Nevada when Orion was appointed acting governor of the territory in 1861, soon drifted to Virginia City, at the site of the Comstock Lode. He staked claims without much success but gained the experience that led to his ROUGHING IT (1872). He also wrote letters (some of them reprinted in *Mark Twain of the Enterprise*, ed. by Henry Nash Smith, 1957) to the *Territorial Enterprise* of Virginia City, then in 1862 joined the paper's staff. It was then that he took "Mark Twain" as his pseudonym. Among novels treating the Cornstock Lode is Vardis Fisher's *City of Illusion* (1941).

Concord, Massachusetts. Concord—seventeen miles northwest of Boston—was settled in 1635. It was a center of patriotic feeling during the pre-Revolutionary period. Here the first Provincial Congress met in 1774, with JOHN HANCOCK presiding, and here the Minutemen were organized and supplies stored. Early on April 19, 1775, the British sent a force of eight hundred men to seize these supplies, but the Americans had been warned in time by PAUL REVERE and his helpers. The Battle of Concord was fought over a bridge that spanned the Concord River. The battle was celebrated in Emerson's poem the *Concord Hymn* (1837), with its line about the embattled farmers who "fired the shot heard round the world." Among famous residents of the town were Emerson, Hawthorne, Thoreau, the Alcotts, William Ellery Channing, and F. B. Sanburn. BRONSON ALCOTT established here a Concord School of Philosophy (1879), which became a center of transcendental thought.

Condensed Novels and Other Papers (1867), by BRET HARTE. This, the first of Harte's books, includes fourteen "Condensed Novels," twelve "Civic Sketches," and seven "Legends and Tales." Among authors parodied or imitated are Cooper, Dickens, Dumas, Hawthorne, Hugo, Irving, and N. P. Willis.

Condon, Richard [Thomas] (1915–1996), novelist. Born in New York City, Condon had been a film publicist for most of his life when he published his first novel, *The Oldest Confession* (1958). More than twenty others have followed, many of them best sellers. Considering himself primarily an entertainer, he has written fast-paced novels reflecting contemporary concerns. Typically they are thrillers, often satiric, with their premises extended to extremes of black comedy.

Early fame came from *The Manchurian Candidate* (1959, filmed in 1962), a story of an American soldier, brainwashed by the Chinese, who becomes a pawn in a political murder plot. Among the targets of satire are communism and MCCARTHYISM. His other novels include *Some Angry Angel* 1960), about a newspaper columnist; *An Infinity of Mirrors* (1964), about the marriage between a French Jew and a Prussian officer caught up in the evil of Hitler's Germany; *Winter Kills* (1974, filmed 1979), about the assassination of a Kennedy-like president; *Prizzi's Honor* (1982, filmed 1985), first in a trilogy about a Mafia family from Brooklyn; and *Emperor of America* (1990), about a six-star general who takes over the country.

Conduct of Life, The, a series of lectures given first at Pittsburgh, 1851; later in Boston; published in 1860, by RALPH WALDO EMERSON. In these nine lectures Emerson brilliantly restates some of his doctrines on fate, power, wealth, culture, behavior, worship, "considerations by the way," beauty, and illusions. They are sometimes transcendental, sometimes shrewdly practical. Among his epigrams and sayings are these: "Coal is a portable climate." "Solitude, the safeguard of mediocrity, is to genius the stern friend." "One of the benefits of a college education is to show the boy its little avail." "Shallow men believe in luck."

confessional poetry, a term that should be used with the awareness that almost all the poets to whom it is applied were uncomfortable with it, fearing implications of artlessness or sensationalism. It has, nevertheless, become the conventional designation for a group of poets who, in the late 1950s and the 1960s, brought many of the resources of the novel into poetry and broke the quiet of the Eisenhower years with overt discussion of mental illness, conflict between parents and children, the "woe that is in marriage."

Perhaps the most surprising thing about this directly autobiographical poetry is that it should have seemed so surprising. The Roman poets Catullus and Propertius had written about tormented love affairs; Coleridge had written about depression, Clare and Nerval about schizophrenia; and William Carlos Williams and Hart Crane had included candid sketches of their parents in their work. But in the 1940s and 1950s, these were forgotten precedents. The New Criticism—with its emphasis on the necessary distance between the actual poet and the "speaker" in the poem—had created among university-trained poets a vogue of self-consciously symbolic, impersonal poems, against which autobiographical poetry seemed both shocking and, as ROBERT LOWELL (1917–1977) put it, a "breakthrough back into life."

Lowell's *Life Studies* (1959) is usually considered the watershed volume, although in fact two of Lowell's students, W. D. SNODGRASS (1926–) and ANNE SEXTON (1928–1974), had written careful, courageous personal poems, eventually collected in *Heart's Needle* (1959) and *To Bedlam and Part Way Back* (1960), respectively, before Lowell did. Lowell had achieved early fame as a high-style poet and a visionary, radical Roman Catholic convert. Chastened by several bouts of manic-depressive illness, he virtually gave up poetry and began a prose autobiography, hoping to find the roots of vision and illness in the family romance and the legacy of Puritan Boston. The challenging examples of the Beat poets, and of William Carlos Williams's late poem "Asphodel, That Greeny Flower," led Lowell to feel that his prose could be made over into a new kind of poetry. The resulting volume, *Life Studies*, was an explosive mixture of form and conversational wryness, of harrowing disclosures and cool, precise novelistic objectification, that polarized literary judgments for years to come.

Confessional poetry, despite its apparent privacy, had a close affinity with political poetry from the very start, as shown in Lowell's subsequent volumes, *For the Union Dead* (1964) and *Near the Ocean* (1967). In an age whose public events—the Holocaust, Stalin's purges, the nuclear arms race—often seemed literally mad, the mechanisms of madness—paranoia, projection and scapegoating, manic intoxication—might offer a better way of understanding them than conventional pragmatism. To Lowell, whose illness involved visitations from heaven and identifications with Hitler and other men of power, these metaphors came particularly readily. They became an increasingly conscious element in his work, culminating in the scathing yet compassionate comparison of President Johnson's motives with his own in "Waking Early Sunday Morning" (1965). This psychopolitical analogy has been attacked by recent critics, notably Paul Breslin, but it was certainly the dominant mode of protest poetry during the Vietnam War, embracing poets as different otherwise as Allen Ginsberg, Denise Levertov, Adrienne Rich, Robert Bly, and W. S. Merwin.

Two other major confessional poets emerged in the years after 1959. JOHN BERRYMAN (1914–1972), a brilliant teacher and helpless alcoholic, dramatized his lack of control over his own life in a tragicomic psychomachia, *The Dream Songs*, published in two volumes in 1964 and 1968. The title gives a good sense of the atmosphere, in which the poet's impulses, self-dramatizations, punishing superego—and an embattled tolerant ego that appears in minstrel show blackface—chase each other through shifting voices, personae, and spectacularly funny, fantastic situations.

SYLVIA PLATH (1932–1963), once a student of Lowell's, received almost instant posthumous fame for *Ariel* (1965), a dazzling volume written in the six months before her suicide at age thirty. With Plath, personal poetry turns away from the novelistic toward a lyrical, if ferocious, inner landscape—darkly numinous mental atmospheres, a fascination with death, an aggrandizement of parents, lovers, the self into ambivalent Jungian archetypes. Like Lowell, Plath combines the public and the private in controversial ways, applying images from the Nazi death camps to inward experiences of depersonalization like those recorded in R. D. Laing's *The Divided Self*. As more became known about Plath's struggle with her attachment to conventional feminine roles, and about her marriage and separation, she attracted considerable feminist interest. These issues have sometimes obscured her genius for sound-values and the texture of language—the best, perhaps, in the confessional group.

Several other poets are sometimes considered confessional on the strength of a few poems, or one period of their work. THEODORE ROETHKE (1908–1963), like Lowell a manic-depressive, used nursery-rhyme language to explore the childhood psyche and its reemergence in moments of crisis, in *Praise to the End* (1951). Roethke had a considerable influence on Plath, but his later work turns more toward mystical affirmation in the manner of Yeats. RANDALL JARRELL (1914–1965) shares the confessional poets' interest in psychoanalysis, and he gives a more tender—from some points of view, a more normal—rendition of childhood in his last volume, *The Lost World*. Finally, Allen Ginsberg (1926–1997), though usually contrasted, as a Beat poet, to Lowell and Berryman, who had university affiliations and liked traditional forms, is certainly confessional in his long poem about his mother's insanity, *Kaddish*, which Lowell called "a terrible masterpiece."

In one sense, the confessional movement has never ended, but literary fashion turned somewhat against it during the 1970s. Many readers considered the later work of Berryman, Sexton, and even Lowell self-indulgent, feeling along with Mark Strand that these poets had "lost . . . in the fervor of this inner debate, the idea of poetry." Nevertheless, the legacy of self-exploration and anecdotal freedom within lyric poetry can be seen in poets as different as ADRIENNE RICH (1929–   ) and JAMES MERRILL (1926–1995), and perhaps less fortunately in the hundreds of parent- and grandparent-poems that spill out of writing programs and little magazines. Perhaps the purest example of a latter-day confessional poet is FRANK BIDART (1939–   ). His spare, ascetic poems, like Lowell's—though there is almost no stylistic resemblance—move back and forth between personal trauma and the universal human issues of which they are the magnified instance, showing once again the moral largeness of the confessional project at its best.

ALAN WILLIAMSON

Confessions of Nat Turner, The (1967),   a novel dealing with a slave rebellion, by WILLIAM STYRON.

Confidence-Man, The: His Masquerade (1857),   a novel by HERMAN MELVILLE set aboard a Mississippi riverboat on April Fools' Day. It is a satire, but unfortunately almost completely lacking in plot and filled with dialogues in which the characters are not clearly defined or even, at times, distinguishable. The Confidence Man, whose disguise changes as the book proceeds, is a smiling, intelligent hypocrite whose single pleasure in life is in the exercise of his evil spells. If he succeeds, it is because he knows what men want and fear most. He knows that among the desperate there is always a market for false hope, and among the unwary, a market for false pity. He sells patent medicine for incurable diseases and solicits funds for nonexistent charities, capitalizing on mankind's gullibility. The "gimlet-eyed" realist who tries ineffectually to expose the Confidence Man fails because in a world without principle the Confidence Man is king and evil generally triumphs.

Congo, The: A Study of the Negro Race (1914),   a poem by VACHEL LINDSAY. It is in three sections: "Their Basic Savagery," "Their Irrepressible High Spirits," and "The Hope of

Their Religion." *The Congo* is memorable for its skillful rhythm and refrains.

Congregationalism. A form of Protestant church organization in which each congregation controls its own affairs. Essentially, the congregation is a gathering of church members responsible to no higher church authority. Its only link to other congregations stems from the fellowship of common belief. Congregationalism had its roots in England late in the 16th century as a reaction against the Church of England's systems of worship as controlled by bishops and linked to the state. By the early 17th century, congregations seeking to dissolve the link had earned the name SEPARATISTS and included a group at Scrooby that settled in Holland to escape persecution and then, in 1620, became the PILGRIMS of Plymouth Colony. Other congregationalists, less determined separatists, included the Puritans that ten years later began to settle the Massachusetts Bay Colony (see MASSACHUSETTS BAY COMPANY, PURITANS AND PURITANISM). In 1648 the Cambridge Platform, signed at Cambridge, Massachusetts, established the principles of church government for Congregationalism. As later colonists followed, Congregationalism became the dominant form of church organization in New England. From there it spread south and west to play an important part in American Protestantism generally. Congregationalism's emphasis on self-government played an important role in the development of the New England town meeting system and in establishing principles of independence and individualism underlying such later developments as the American Revolution and New England TRANSCENDENTALISM. Congregationalists have also strongly supported non-sectarian education, founding, among other colleges, Harvard, Yale, Williams, Amherst, and Oberlin.

Congressional Record, The. Records of the proceedings of the nation's legislative body have been kept from the start. But the *Journals of the Continental Congress* were not collected till the 20th century (in 34 volumes, 1904–37). The *Annals of Congress* (1789–1824) began with the first meeting of the Congress of the United States. The name was changed to *Register of Debates* (1824–37), then *Congressional Globe* (1837–72), and finally *Congressional Record* (1872–   ).

Conkling, Grace [Walcott] Hazard (1878–1958), poet, teacher, lecturer. Conkling became a member of the faculty of Smith College in 1914. Her published collections of verse include *Afternoons of April* (1915), *Wilderness Songs* (1920), *Flying Fish* (1926), and *Witch and Other Poems* (1929).

Connecticut Wits. See HARTFORD WITS.

Connecticut Yankee in King Arthur's Court, A (1889),   a novel by MARK TWAIN. A blow on the head during a quarrel conveys the superintendent of a Hartford arms factory back to the days of King Arthur, with all his Yankee ingenuity and know-how intact. Twain uses the opportunity to satirize the Old World, medieval chivalry, kings, and the church. Many of the characters made famous in various renderings of the Arthurian saga appear, but are seen with the Yankee's practical, unimpressed eye. He introduces some modern inventions, and knows some things not discovered

until centuries later—he has foreknowledge of an eclipse, for example—so he can surprise King Arthur and his court. In one scene he transfers five hundred knights from horseback to bicycles. The Yankee's knowledge proves a doubtful blessing, however, and the satire becomes two-edged. The reader is brought to question the idea of 19th-century progress, for example, as gunpowder proves more effective at killing than swords.

Connell, Evan S[helby], Jr. (1924–   ),   novelist, short-story writer. Born in Kansas City, Missouri, Connell attended Dartmouth, served in the naval air force (1943–45), and graduated from the University of Kansas. Two novels, *Mrs. Bridge* (1959) and *Mr. Bridge* (1969), provide episodic portrayals of a suburban couple between the two world wars. *The Patriot* (1960) tells of a young man's naval flying experience, his postwar study, and his relations with his militaristic father. His other novels include *The Diary of a Rapist* (1966); *The Connoisseur* (1974), about a man's interest in Mayan art; *Double Honeymoon* (1976); *Son of the Morning Star* (1984), about Custer's Last Stand; *The Alchymist's Journal* (1991); and *Deus Lo Volt! A Chronicle of the Crusades* (2000). His collections of stories include *The Anatomy Lesson* (1957), *At the Crossroads* (1965), *St. Augustine's Pigeon* (1980), and *Collected Stories* (1995). His miscellaneous works include *Notes from a Bottle Found on the Beach at Carmel* (1963), *Points for a Compass Rose* (1973), *A Long Desire* (1979), and *The White Lantern* (1980).

Connell, Richard [Edward] (1893–1949),   novelist, short-story writer. Connell first worked on newspapers and in the advertising business. In 1919 he began to write fiction, also occasional scripts in Hollywood. His collections of shorter fiction include *The Sin of Monsieur Petipon* (1922), *Apes and Angels* (1924), and *Ironies* (1930). Among his novels are *Mad Lover* (1927), *Playboy* (1936), and *What Ho!* (1937).

Connelly, Marc[us Cook] (1890–1980),   newspaperman, versifier, dramatist. Born in Pennsylvania, Connelly worked on Pittsburgh papers before moving to New York, where he wrote lyrics for plays and articles for newspapers, and became fascinated with the theater. A friendship with GEORGE S. KAUFMAN resulted in collaboration on several successful plays. DULCY (1921) is a clever comedy taking its central character from a stupid but well-meaning young woman who had originally appeared in FRANKLIN P. ADAMS's column in the New York *Tribune*. *To the Ladies* (1922) is a study in illusions. MERTON OF THE MOVIES (1922) is a dramatization of HARRY LEON WILSON's satiric novel about Hollywood in its early days. BEGGAR ON HORSEBACK (1924) is a dream play, perhaps the finest success of the collaboration. Later, by himself, Connelly wrote *The Wisdom Tooth* (1926), a clerk's futile but pleasant dream of how he defies his employer; THE GREEN PASTURES (1929), based on ROARK BRADFORD's African-American stories and considered Connelly's best play; *The Farmer Takes a Wife* (1934), with characters taken from WALTER D. EDMONDS's *Rome Haul* (1929); and *A Story for Strangers* (1948), a parable about a talking horse. In 1947 Connelly became a professor of playwriting at Yale. His works also include a novel, *A Souvenir from Qam*

(1965), satirizing spy stories, and a memoir, *Voices Offstage* (1968).

Connolly, James B[rendan Bennet] (1868?–1957), war correspondent, writer of sea stories. Born in Boston, Connolly early won celebrity as an Olympic champion and later reported Mexican incidents and World War I for *Collier's*. His sea stories are mainly of Gloucester fishermen. Among his books are *Out of Gloucester* (1902); *The Seiners* (1904); *Open Water* (1910); *Book of the Gloucester Fishermen* (1927); and an autobiography, *Sea-Borne: Thirty Years A-Voyaging* (1944).

Connor, Ralph. The pen name of CHARLES WILLIAM GORDON.

Conqueror Worm, The (*Graham's Magazine*, Jan. 1843), a poem by EDGAR ALLAN POE. It was included in his collection of 1845, *The Raven and Other Poems*, and was also interwoven with the story called LIGEIA, originally published without it in 1838.

Conquest of Canaan, The (1785), epic poem by TIMOTHY DWIGHT. The poem is an allegory in which Dwight equates the conquest of Canaan, as narrated in the Old Testament, with the taking of Connecticut from the British. In eleven books and 10,000 lines, all in heroic couplets, Dwight made the first attempt to write an epic poem of America.

Conquest of Granada, A Chronicle of the (1829, rev. 1850), an account of the winning of Granada from the Moors by WASHINGTON IRVING. Irving's sympathies are with the civilized, heroic Moors, not the barbarous Christian conquerors of the 15th century. The work was grounded in Irving's careful research in Spain and has been praised for its accuracy, but it is presented in the form of tales based on the work of a fictional Fray Antonio Agapida, supposedly a monk of the time.

Conquest of Mexico, History of the (3 v. 1843), by WILLIAM H. PRESCOTT. This is the brilliantly told story of the conquest of Mexico by Cortez and a handful of Spanish soldiers who invaded the empire of Montezuma contrary to the orders of Cortez's superior officer. Prescott's painstaking research—conducted stubbornly despite constant and serious eye trouble—made the book a model of accuracy in its account of Aztec civilization and the Spanish conquest.

Conquest of Peru, History of the (1847), a historical narrative by W. H. PRESCOTT. The great success of THE CONQUEST OF MEXICO led Prescott to go on to a similar volume on the overrunning of Peru by Pizarro and his marauders. The work falls into five sections: the civilization of the Incas, the discovery of Peru, the conquests, the civil wars among the conquerors, and the settlement of the country.

Conquistador (1932), epic poem by ARCHIBALD MACLEISH. This long narrative in modified terza rima is adapted from the account of the conquest of Mexico written by Bernal Díaz del Castillo, with scenic impressions based on MacLeish's own trip through Mexico by foot and muleback in the winter of 1929. Seen through the eyes of this conqueror, the conquest was not made to carry out the expansion plans of the Spanish governors, mercenaries, or missionaries, but rather was done against their advice through the love of individual men for

adventure, challenge, even bloodshed. When the conquest is actually completed and the civilizers follow, there is no more use for the conqueror, and he mourns that "the west is gone now." The poem won a Pulitzer Prize.

Conrad, Barnaby (1922–), painter, writer. After graduating from Yale in 1944, Conrad spent much of his time in and near Spanish bullrings. Like another aficionado, TOM LEA, Conrad regarded himself as a painter who could write. His work is a product of his own experience in the bullring as well as that of celebrated *toreros* he has known. *Matador* (1952) communicates much of the tension and brutality of the bullring. Other books include *The Innocent Villa* (1949); *La Fiesta Brava* (1953); *My Life as a Matador* (1954); *Gates of Fear* (1955); *The Death of Manolete* (1957); *San Francisco* (1959); *Dangerfield* (1961), the story of a famous (unspecified) novelist, probably suggested by Sinclair Lewis, who once employed Conrad as a secretary; two translations, *Wounds of Hunger* (1958) and *The Second Life of Captain Contreras* (1960); *Hemingway's Spain* (1989); and *Name Dropping: Tales from My Barbary Coast Saloon* (1994), a memoir.

Conrad, Robert Taylor (1810–1858), lawyer, newspaperman, poet, playwright. Conrad practiced law in his native city, became judge of the court of criminal sessions and mayor of Philadelphia. In 1843 he was chairman of the committee that awarded $100 to Poe for *The Gold Bug*. He wrote several plays, including *Jack Cade* (1835).

Conroy, Jack (1899–1980), novelist, editor. Born in Missouri, the son of a coal miner, Conroy grew up in a company town, briefly attended the University of Missouri, married, and worked in mills, factories, and mines in the 1920s. His autobiographical novel *The Disinherited* (1933) has been seen as a classic of proletarian literature. From Moberly, Missouri, he edited a leftist magazine, *The Anvil* (1933–37), following it with a Chicago magazine edited with NELSON ALGREN, *The New Anvil* (1939–41); contributors included Erskine Caldwell, James T. Farrell, Langston Hughes, Michael Gold, Richard Wright, and Frank Yerby. His books include a second novel, *A World to Win* (1935), and an *Anvil* anthology, *Writers in Revolt* (1973). With ARNA BONTEMPS he wrote *They Seek a City: A Study of Negro Migration* (1945, revised as *Anyplace But Here*, 1966) and children's books, including *The Fast Sooner Hound* (1942), *Slappy Hooper* (1946), and *Sam Patch* (1951).

Conroy, [Donald] Pat[rick] (1945–), novelist. Born in Atlanta, the son of a military officer, educated at a military college, The Citadel, Conroy has drawn on his and his family's experiences for the bizarre events, the eccentrics and misfits, and the warring fathers and sons that inhabit his bestselling novels of the South. After a book about The Citadel, *The Boo* (1970) and the openly autobiographical *The Water Is Wide* (1972), about teaching in a black community on a South Carolina island, he turned to fiction in *The Great Santini* (1976), about a son's coming of age in a family ruled by a tough Marine. *The Lords of Discipline* (1980) narrates the tensions, the loyalties, and final betrayal and death that arise when the first black student enrolls at a military academy like The Citadel. *The Prince of Tides* (1986), the most celebrated of his works, brings a high school English teacher and football coach from South Carolina to New York to assist his sister, a suicidal poet, escape the family's history of rape and death. *Beach Music* (1995) is an ambitious novel reaching out from South Carolina to Rome, Venice, and Vietnam to examine some of the illnesses of our time.

Conspiracy of Pontiac, History of the (1851),   the first of a series of books by FRANCIS PARKMAN intended to describe the struggle between the British and the French for control of North America. Parkman pays constant attention to the role of Native Americans in this struggle, and his opening volume tells about the Ottawa chief who led a rebellion against the English in the Ohio Valley and regions farther east (1763–65).

Constitution of the United States.   On May 25, 1787, a convention was organized in the Philadelphia State House to revise the Articles of Confederation. The convention continued to meet until September 17, 1787, when the Constitution was formally adopted and signed; it was ratified by September 28. The original is now in the National Archives Building in Washington, in a bronze and marble shrine.

The Constitution, after a brief preamble, is divided into seven *Articles*. These deal with (1) legislative organization and powers, (2) the presidency and its functions, (3) judicial powers and certain legal restrictions, (4) powers of the states and restrictions on them, (5) amendment of the Constitution, (6) supremacy of the Constitution and prohibition of religious tests for office, and (7) machinery of ratification for the Constitution. Some states refused to ratify until immediate addition of a Bill of Rights. This was accomplished by December 15, 1791, when the First Congress secured adoption of the first ten amendments.

Compromise was the procedure of the Constitutional Convention. No matter what their reservations were on individual points, the delegates were convinced that a strong central government had to be set up at once, and that it would be better to agree on compromises rather than deadlock the convention. The Constitution represents a compromise between centralization and local autonomy. It shows as strong a dependence on British political philosophy, particularly John Locke.

The Records of the Federal Convention are usefully available in the four-volume edition (1911–37) edited by Max Farrand. The *Debates* that preceded ratification of the Constitution were collected in five volumes (1836–45) by Jonathan Elliot. The most famous of the arguments for ratification were papers called THE FEDERALIST, printed in the form of letters to newspapers in 1787–88; the authors were principally ALEXANDER HAMILTON and JAMES MADISON. An immense body of writings has gathered around the origin and making of the Constitution and around the background and philosophy of the makers. Exceedingly important has been the interpretation of the Constitution by the courts, especially the Supreme Court.

Constitutional Courant, The.   A single issue of this paper appeared on September 21, 1765. It attacked the Stamp Act and reproduced a *Pennsylvania Gazette* cartoon represent-

ing a snake in eight sections that symbolized the colonies and bore the motto, "Join, or Die." The editor was James Parker, who from 1758 to 1760 had printed THE AMERICAN MAGAZINE at Woodbridge, New Jersey.

Contemplations (1678),   a poem by ANNE BRADSTREET, published in the second edition of her TENTH MUSE (1650). It is a meditative and descriptive poem and includes some of Bradstreet's best lines.

Continental Congress, The.   In 1774 the Continental Congress met in Philadelphia with delegates from all the colonies except Georgia, its chief purpose being that of offering more determined resistance to British measures. It governed the country, with varying degrees of efficiency, until the establishment of the Union in 1789. The first Congress addressed the British king in a statement of grievances, and its members later adopted the DECLARATION OF INDEPENDENCE. They appointed Washington commander-in-chief, sent representatives abroad, set up the ARTICLES OF CONFEDERATION (which gave them written powers as the Congress of the Confederation), and prepared the way for the CONSTITUTION. *The Journals of the Continental Congress* were collected in thirty-four volumes (1904–37).

Contrast, The (1787),   a play by ROYALL TYLER, marking the true beginning of American drama. Tyler, a Bostonian of good family who was active as a patriot during the Revolutionary War, had considerable literary ability, particularly as a comic writer. Serving as a major in the Army in the course of Shays' Rebellion (1786–87), he was sent as an observer to New York City in March 1787. There he visited the theater and became acquainted with Thomas Wignell, the leading American comedian of the day. Hardly a month later, on April 16, *The Contrast* was given at the JOHN STREET THEATER, in New York City, the first native comedy to be produced by a company of professional actors. Wignell himself played the role of Jonathan, first of the innumerable stage Yankees of American and foreign drama. Tyler presented Wignell with the copyright, and Wignell published the play in 1790 by subscription.

The plot involves a complicated series of courtships and philanderings, centering mostly around Billy Dimple, a wealthy Anglophile who is affianced to the clever Maria but pays attention carelessly to other women. He finally loses his wealth and also Maria, who marries the staid but attractive Colonel Manly, a Revolutionary officer. Dimple has a manservant, Jessamy, who tries to educate Jonathan, Manly's attendant, in the ways of the world, but Jonathan remains truly rural.

It is largely because of Jonathan that the play has retained so vigorous a life. He is presented in decided contrast to Jessamy, who is proud to be the servitor of wealthy and fashionable men. He expects to marry Tabitha Wyman, the deacon's daughter, and when he fails to make any headway with a fashionable maid he exclaims, "If this is the way with your city ladies, give me the twenty acres of rock, the Bible, the cow, and Tabitha, and a little peaceable bundling." This stage Yankee became a symbol of American defiance to British criticism of America. Within a few years many imitations of Jonathan held the stage, in William Dunlap's *The Modest Soldier* (1787) and THE FATHER (1788), Samuel Low's *The Politician Outwitted* (1788), the anonymous *The Better Sort* (1789), SUSANNA ROWSON's *Americans in England* (1796), and the anonymous *The Traveler Returned* (1798).

Conway, Moncure D[aniel] (1832–1907), clergyman, editor, reformer, biographer. A descendant of slaveholding Southerners, Conway became an ardent Abolitionist. A Methodist by upbringing, he turned to Unitarianism and became president of the New York Freethinkers' Society. He wrote books about Carlyle (1881), Emerson (1882), and Hawthorne (1890), but his most celebrated works are his life of Thomas Paine (1892) and his edition of Paine's writings (1894–96). He also wrote a novel about the Civil War, *Pine and Palm* (1887), and an *Autobiography* (1904).

Conwell, Russell H[erman] (1843–1925), clergyman, lecturer, author. Born in Maine, Conwell followed many pursuits before he became minister of a church in Lexington, Massachusetts, and then one of the most celebrated lecturers in the country, first on the Redpath, later on the Chautauqua circuit. Best known of his lectures was *Acres of Diamonds* (1888), delivered more than 6,000 times. Conwell influenced millions of listeners with his doctrine that wealth and power lay within the grasp of everyone, that no one had the "right to be poor," and that "love is the grandest thing on God's earth, but fortunate is the lover who has plenty of money." Conwell amassed a large fortune, using it mainly to help poor youths get an education and then founding Temple University.

Cook, Ebenezer (c. 1672–1732), poet, satirist. According to one of his poems, THE SOT-WEED FACTOR; OR A VOYAGE TO MARYLAND (London, 1708), Cook was an Englishman who visited America and on his return gave his unfavorable and contemptuous observations of colonial life in verse that imitated Butler's *Hudibras*. He may actually have been an American who was given the title "Laureate" by Lord Baltimore. He may also have been the author of several elegies and may have written *Sotweed Redivivus* (1730), a serious treatise in verse on tobacco and its overproduction. He may likewise have composed a burlesque poem on the rebellion of NATHANIEL BACON. Whoever he was, he became the hero of *The Sot-Weed Factor* (1960), a comic novel by John Barth.

Cook, Fannie (1893–1949), teacher, civic worker, lecturer, novelist. Born in Missouri, Cook won various awards for her work among sharecroppers and for her contributions to interracial welfare. Her novel *Mrs. Palmer's Money* in 1946 won the first George Washington Carver Memorial Award of $2,500 for making, among the year's publications, "the most effective literary contribution to the Negro's place in American life." She also wrote *The Hill Grows Steeper* (1938), *Boot-Heel Doctor* (1941), and *Storm Against the Wall* (1948).

Cook, George Cram (1873–1924), teacher, novelist, playwright, actor, poet. Born in Iowa, Cook became a key figure in the American LITTLE THEATER. In 1903 he published *Roderick Taliaferro*, a story of Montezuma's empire, and in 1911 *The Chasm*, a socialist novel.

In 1913 Cook married SUSAN GLASPELL—his third marriage—and his career took a new turn. They went to Provincetown, Massachusetts, and there in 1915 organized the PROVINCETOWN PLAYERS. The theater was an old fish house on a wharf owned by Mary Heaton Vorse; it had been used by Mrs. Wilbur Daniel Steele as a studio. There were produced the first plays of EUGENE O'NEILL, often in outdoor settings that repeated the scenes of the plays. "Jig" Cook himself took the role of Yank in the first production of BOUND EAST FOR CARDIFF. A one-act comedy on a Freudian theme, SUPPRESSED DESIRES (1915), by Cook and his wife, actually inspired the undertaking. It was first given in a private home at Provincetown. The success of the venture encouraged the group to undertake operations in New York City (1916–29). Various buildings were employed, two of them on Macdougal Street in Greenwich Village. In 1920 the Players produced O'Neill's THE EMPEROR JONES, so successfully that it had to be moved to an uptown theater. They also gave Cook's *The Spring* (1921), Glaspell's *The Verge* (1922), and O'Neill's *Diff'rent* (1921) and *The Hairy Ape* (1922).

Having fulfilled his purpose of giving new impetus to American drama, and not wishing to compete with the commercial theater, Cook lost interest in the project. In 1921 he sailed for Greece, where he settled down, grew a prophet's beard, fraternized with the peasants and local poets, and won general esteem. On his death his grave was marked by a stone taken from the ruins of Apollo's temple at Delphi. His widow wrote an affectionate account of him in *The Road to the Temple* (1926).

cookbooks, American. The first cookbooks printed in America appeared in the middle of the 18th century and were reprints of English cookbooks. The first cookbook written by an American woman was Amelia Simmons's *American Cookery* (1796), with more than 170 recipes. Other books followed: *The Family Receipt Book* (1819); the novelist Eliza Leslie's *Seventy-Five Receipts for Pastry, Cakes, and Sweetmeats* (1828); and the antislavery leader Lydia Maria Child's *The Frugal Housewife* (1829), which went through twenty-six editions in twenty-one years. Sarah Josepha Hale, editor of *Godey's Lady's Book*, turned out a *Receipt Book* (1846) that was in great demand. Mary Virginia Hawes Terhune, who wrote stories under the penname Marion Harland and whose son was ALBERT PAYSON TERHUNE, compiled a popular volume called *Common Sense in the Household* (1871). Cooking schools produced their own cookbooks. Accurate measurements came in with Fannie Farmer's fabulously popular *Boston Cooking-School Cookbook* (1896), still widely sold.

Cooke, [Alfred] Alistair (1908–   ), journalist, broadcaster, author. Born in England, Cooke attained celebrity in England and the United States as a versatile and sympathetic commentator on current affairs and popular culture in the United States. In 1934, after a two-year stay in United States as a Commonwealth Fellow at Yale and Harvard, he became film critic for the British Broadcasting Company (1934–37), and his interest in this field ultimately expressed itself in two books: *Garbo and the Night Watchmen* (1937) and *Douglas Fairbanks* (1940). He was the NBC London correspondent in 1936–37, a commentator on American affairs for the British Broadcasting Company from 1938, and a reporter on American affairs for the *London Times*, the *London Daily Herald*, and the *Manchester Guardian*. He became the *Guardian's* chief American correspondent in 1948. In 1952, Cooke became the host of the award-winning television series *Omnibus* and more recently host of TV's *Masterpiece Theater*. His books include *A Generation on Trial* (1950), an account of the Alger Hiss trials; *One Man's America* (1952), a collection of informal essays on life and manners in America originally designed for the British radio audience; *Christmas Eve* (1952); *A Commencement Address* (1954); *Talk About America* (1968), taken from his BBC broadcasts; and *Alistair Cooke's America* (1973), based on a television series. A biography is Nick Clarke, *Alistair Cooke* (2000)

Cooke, John Esten (1830–1886), novelist, biographer, historian. Cooke was a member of the First Families of Virginia, by birth and in spirit. His older brother, PHILIP PENDLETON COOKE, and a cousin, JOHN PENDLETON KENNEDY, were also authors. General J. E. B. Stuart was his nephew by marriage. Cooke wrote historical novels, with JAMES FENIMORE COOPER as a literary model. After serving in the Confederate ranks, he wrote other novels with the Civil War as a background. The three generally considered his best are THE VIRGINIA COMEDIANS (1854), a romantic account of the love affairs of a Virginia gentleman; its sequel, HENRY ST. JOHN, GENTLEMAN (1859), laid in the period preceding the Revolution; and *Surry of Eagle's-Nest* (1866), in which the life of the hero parallels the career of Stonewall Jackson. Cooke also wrote biographies of Jefferson (1854), Stonewall Jackson (1863), Lee (1871), and Samuel J. Tilden (1876). One of his best books is *Virginia: A History of the People* (1883).)

Cooke, Philip Pendleton (1816–1850), lawyer, author. This older brother of JOHN ESTEN COOKE died in his early thirties of tuberculosis. He published only one volume, *Froissart Ballads and Other Poems* (1847). His best-known piece was "Florence Vane," published in *Burton's Magazine* in 1840. It was a sentimental ballad, set to music and widely translated.

Cooke, Philip St. George (1809–1895), soldier, memoirist. The uncle of JOHN ESTEN COOKE and PHILIP PENDLETON COOKE, Cooke served in the army in the West and the Mexican War and fought for the Union in the Civil War, becoming a major general. He wrote *Scenes and Adventures in the Army* (1857) and *Conquest of New Mexico and California* (1878).

Cooke, Rose Terry (1827–1892), short-story writer, poet. Born in Connecticut, Cooke became a social historian of a fading New England culture; with HARRIET BEECHER STOWE she established the ground for later writers like MARY E. WILKINS FREEDMAN and SARAH ORNE JEWETT. Her tales range from genre sketches to realistic portraits of mill town and village life. Her collections include *Somebody's Neighbors* (1881), *Root-Bound*

and Other Sketches (1885), *The Sphinx's Children* (1886), and *Huckleberries Gathered from New England Hills* (1891).

Coolbrith, Ina Donna (1842–1928), teacher, librarian, poet. Born in Illinois, Coolbrith went to California as a child in 1852 in a prairie schooner and thereafter was closely identified with the literary history of that state. She was a coeditor of the OVERLAND MONTHLY and with BRET HARTE and CHARLES WARREN STODDARD formed the Golden Gate Trinity, nucleus of San Francisco's flourishing literary colony. She became the librarian of the Bohemian Club, the only woman admitted, and at the Panama-Pacific Exposition in 1915 organized a World Congress of Authors. She was made Poet Laureate of California by the legislature. Her poetry appeared in *A Perfect Day* (1881), *The Singer of the Sea* (1894), and *Songs from the Golden Gate* (1895).

Coolidge, [John] Calvin (1872–1933), thirtieth president of the United States. Coolidge was born in Plymouth Corners, Vermont. After graduation from Amherst, he studied law and practiced in Northampton, Massachusetts. He became successively city councilman, city solicitor, mayor, state representative, state senator, court clerk, lieutenant governor, governor, and vice president. His political creed was uncompromisingly Republican. He became president on Harding's death, August 2, 1923, and was elected for a full term in 1924. At a time of overwhelming national prosperity—before the 1929 depression—he constantly praised and practiced frugality, both public and private. After Hoover's election, Coolidge retired and wrote an *Autobiography* (1929).

Some 82,000 pieces of Coolidge correspondence were presented to the Library of Congress (1929, 1954). In 1950 enough material to make eleven bound volumes of transcripts recording Coolidge's press conferences was unearthed in the Forbes Library at Northampton, Massachusetts.

Coolidge, Clark (1939–   ), poet. Born in Providence, Rhode Island, Coolidge attended Brown University (1956–1958), where his father taught music. A jazz and rock musician since high school, influenced by Jack Kerouac's ON THE ROAD, he writes fluid, disconnected verse that has earned him a place among the LANGUAGE POETS. Books include *Space* (1970); *Solution Passage: Poems, 1978–1981* (1986); *Sound as Thought: Poems, 1982–1984* (1990); *Own Face* (1993); *Now It's Jazz: Writings on Kerouac and the Sounds* (1999); and *On the Nameways* (2000).

Coolidge, Susan. Pen name of SARAH CHAUNCEY WOOLSEY.

Cool Tombs (1915; published in *Cornhuskers*, 1918), a poem on death by CARL SANDBURG. It is written in free verse and makes effective use of the phrase "in the dust, in the cool tombs" to establish a pattern.

Cooper, Courtney Ryley (1886–1940), press agent, newspaperman, novelist, feature writer. Cooper worked first with the circus, and some of his best books are about life under the big tent. He wrote *Memories of Buffalo Bill* (with L. F. Cody, 1918); *Under the Big Top* (1923); *Lions 'n' Tigers 'n' Everything* (1924); *Annie Oakley* (1927); and *Circus Day*

(1931). Cooper led a sensational career with theatrical people, on the battlefront in World War I, and in association with Secret Service men, leading to his *The Eagle's Eye*, written in collaboration with W. J. Flynn, 1918. In Hollywood he wrote and directed several crime movies and spent his last days investigating fifth-column activities in Mexico.

Cooper, Frank.   Pen name of W. G. SIMMS.

Cooper, James Fenimore (1789–1851),   novelist, travel writer, social commentator. Cooper was born in Burlington, New Jersey, but grew up in Cooperstown, New York, a frontier settlement established by his father, Judge William Cooper (1754–1809). The elder Cooper was not only a rags-to-riches success story in his business enterprises but also an influential Federalist politician who served two terms as a U.S. Representative and formed connections with eminent state and national figures, notably John Jay, who would prove important to his son. Much evidence, including his ambivalent portrait of the frontier patriarch Judge Temple in THE PIONEERS (1823), points to Fenimore Cooper's deeply conflicted feelings about his father's powerful personality and his need to find avenues for rivaling Judge Cooper's imposing public achievements. Thus, after expulsion from Yale for a dangerous prank, he went to sea as a sailor before the mast and then as a midshipman in the U.S. Navy, gaining experience he would draw on later in a dozen novels involving adventure at sea. His naval career was cut short by two events: the death of William Cooper, which promised a life of genteel leisure for his heirs, and Fenimore Cooper's betrothal to Susan De Lancey, whose condition for marrying him was that he leave the Navy. It was then that he joined Fenimore, his mother's family name, to his patronymic, henceforth usually signing himself J. Fenimore Cooper.

Through his marriage he allied himself not only with the woman he loved but also with a patrician New York family that had supported the British side during the War of Independence. So encumbered with legal claims had his father's estate proved that he found himself unable to live up to his social position and was financially dependent on the De Lanceys—a situation intolerable to one not only proud but distinctly touchy about being, and being seen to be, his own man. At this point, allegedly in response to Susan's friendly challenge to bear out his boast that he could write a better book than one he had been reading, Cooper discovered a way to get the better of both his father and his father-in-law. *Precaution* (1820) was probably modeled on the moralistic courtship fiction of the English novelist Amelia Opie, but in its elaborate play with problems of perception and judgment may show the influence of Jane Austen.

If the anonymously published *Precaution* persuaded even British reviewers that its author was female and English, Cooper's next novel, THE SPY (1821), showed that he could do even better using the emphatically masculine and American voice that was to characterize all his subsequent writings. In this and most of his subsequent fictions, Cooper's chosen form was the historical romance, the novelistic subgenre Sir Walter Scott was then popularizing in a series of works beginning with *Waverley* (1814). Many writers before Scott, especially the gothic novelists, had set their stories in the past, but Scott was the first to strive for historical authenticity not only in details of action, dress, and physical setting but especially in the psychology of his characters. In the Waverley novels, novelistic plot was designed to reveal the emerging shape—what may be called the master plot—of national history. The novels were called romances not principally because they included a love story—they invariably did—but because the term connoted out-of-the-ordinary actions set in remote times or places. Scott had many important imitators besides Cooper, but none came as close to matching his unprecedented popularity.

A tale of military conflict and intrigue during the War of Independence, *The Spy* had a great and immediate success, partly because it had a compelling main character in the double agent Harvey Birch, partly because it was an exciting adventure narrative, and partly because it answered a widely articulated patriotic demand for historical romances employing American scenes, character types, and historical settings. Yet although the novel—especially in its hagiographical portrait of George Washington—reflects and caters to the nationalistic spirit of the era, Cooper achieves a degree of moral complexity by offering a partly sympathetic view of the side chosen by his wife's ancestors. The impressive strengths of *The Spy* were to reappear in most of his subsequent novels. And so were its weaknesses: a sometimes prolix and clumsy style; stereotypical delineations of minor, especially female, characters; actions excessively dependent on coincidence and disguise; and moralistic narratorial intrusions. Some of these weaknesses might have been avoided if he had written more concisely and trusted less to inspiration. But, like Scott, he did not conceive of the novel as an art form that demanded as much meticulous attention to design and execution as a work of history or epic poetry. It would be wrong to suggest that he wrote only to make money or to influence public opinion, but it would be equally wrong to think of Cooper as possessing and failing to live up to the dictates of an exacting artistic conscience like that of Hawthorne or Flaubert.

The Spy launched Cooper's career as a professional writer. He moved from rural Westchester County to New York City, the regional center of literary activity, and went rapidly ahead with a series of brilliant successes: *The Pioneers* (1823), THE PILOT (1824), THE LAST OF THE MOHICANS (1826), THE PRAIRIE (1827), and THE RED ROVER (1827). In *The Pilot* and especially in *The Red Rover* he invented the modern sea novel by making ships and the ocean major protagonists in the action. In the other novels produced during this extraordinarily creative period, he wrote three of the books, eventually five in number, in which the life story of his greatest character, the illiterate wilderness scout Leatherstocking, is traced from adolescence to old age as he is gradually driven from the forest wilderness of mid-18th-century York Colony to the bleak plains country recently acquired by President Jefferson as part of the Louisiana Purchase. What Cooper was doing without quite realizing it at first was writing the epic of the American westward movement. His hero NATTY BUMPPO—also called Leather-stocking, Hawkeye, Pathfinder, Deerslayer—was a character whose simple integrity, cool courage, and almost incredible prowess made him the perfect central figure of an epic action. Now, too, Cooper's genius as a descriptive writer flowered. Nobody before him had pictured the grandeur of American nature and the high seas as he did, and partly because of their novelty and partly because of their enduring power, his scenes soon captivated the imaginations of readers not only throughout the U.S. but wherever English or translations into the main European languages could reach.

Within six years, Cooper had traveled from dependence and obscurity to fortune and international fame as *"le grand écrivain américain."* When he took his family to Europe in 1826 for an extended educational visit, he had no way of knowing that he would remain away from home for nearly seven years or that he was already nearing the end of his greatest vogue and earning power as an author.

Basing himself in Paris at a time of revolutionary ferment throughout Europe, Cooper became involved in partisan politics as a result of his acquaintance with the Marquis de Lafayette, the venerable soldier-statesman who had fought for American independence and was now the recognized leader of the liberal party in France. At Lafayette's prompting, Cooper wrote NOTIONS OF THE AMERICANS (1828), a glowing account of the democratic experiment in the U.S. that struck conservative reviewers as more fictional than his novels. The same political sympathies inspired a series of European historical novels that explore the evils of aristocratic and oligarchic forms of government. The most powerful of these novels, THE BRAVO (1830), is set in early-18th-century Venice but can be read as an oblique commentary on oligarchic institutions in contemporary England and Russia as well as on the subversive designs of reactionary political factions in the U.S. These books offended conservative readers and bored others, who wanted Cooper to stick to tales of frontier and maritime adventure. Hurt by hostile reviews and declining sales at home, he announced in 1834 that his career as a novelist was over. Settling in Cooperstown when he returned to America in 1836, he channeled his literary energies into five volumes of European travels (1836–38) and began research for his *History of the Navy of the United States* (1839).

An outspoken champion of democratic government during his stay in Europe, Cooper no sooner returned to America than he began to act and speak in ways that allowed critics, particularly the editors of Whig party newspapers, to pillory him as a Europeanized aristocrat. Had Cooper changed or was it, as he began to think, that his country had changed from a democratic republic to a mobocracy? Something of both had doubtless occurred, but it is important to recognize not only that the political identities of individuals, parties, and nations do not remain static but also that they invariably and bewilderingly combine contradictory elements. In *The Pioneers*, Cooper himself was among the first observers to call attention to the democratizing effects of frontier life, and in doing so he was writing out of his own early experience. On the other hand, as the son of Judge Cooper he was educated to become a member and ideological adherent of a ruling class which, especially in the formerly patroon-dominated State of New York, had markedly different tastes and political-economic interests than the majority of citizens. During his heyday as a popular and widely appreciated author, years coinciding with the so-called Era of Good Feeling in national politics and his own absence from the U.S., he was able to subscribe to the Jeffersonian thesis that the interests of the leisure and laboring classes were not inimical and that the democratic system would work admirably so long as men of education and standing were active in it and ready to respond to the call of the electorate. Accordingly, while maintaining friendships with many leading Federalists and Whigs, he became and remained a lifelong supporter of the party of Jefferson and Jackson.

But the advent of modern political campaigning at this time, coupled with what seemed the increasingly intrusive and unscrupulous practices of newspaper editors, persuaded an already depressed Cooper that American democracy was in a state of crisis. At this juncture, too, tenants on the great Hudson River estates began refusing to pay rents on the grounds that the ancient tenant-farming system of New York was unjust and contrary to American principles. When Cooper was publicly denounced for placing a no-trespassing sign on a piece of family land vandalized by picnickers, he concluded that it was time to speak out about the rights and wrongs of contemporary American society. And so in 1838 he published several books maintaining that while the majority certainly had its rights, the rights that needed defending at the moment were those of property, individuals, and minorities—by which he primarily meant refined gentlefolk. The most of important of these books were THE AMERICAN DEMOCRAT (1838), a trenchant treatise on American institutions intended for use in schools, and the satirical novel of manners *Home as Found* (1838). The latter, which contained a thinly fictionalized account of recent episodes in his own life, exposed him to partisan attacks by Whig reviewers and editors. Cooper countered the attacks with libel suits he conducted himself with remarkable success, but at a high price in terms of time and psychic energy.

Extremely uneven in quality, the fiction he wrote after 1838 can be divided into three main groups: forgettable novels like WING-AND-WING (1842) and *Jack Tier* (1846–48), apparently written just to make money, which tend to cannibalize the plots and characters of his earlier fiction: politically inspired novels like WYANDOTTE (1843), THE REDSKINS (1846), and *The Ways of the Hour* (1850), which contain powerful scenes but are generally too crochety and polemical to sustain the interest of anybody except a Cooper scholar; and a handful of wonderful novels in which, given the opportunity to create scenes and societies remote in time or place, Cooper's imagination becomes rich and expansive again. Such novels are the last two Leather-Stocking Tales, THE PATHFINDER (1840) and THE DEERSLAYER (1841); SATANSTOE (1845), a nostalgic portrait of a mid-18th-century English colony; THE CRATER (1847), a Crusoe-like narrative of island discovery and development which turns into a dystopia; and THE SEA LIONS (1849), a *Doppelgänger* tale of adventure in the Antarctic seas that features some of Cooper's best descriptive writing.

When a commemorative meeting was held in New York in 1852, the year after his death, the meeting was called to order by America's most eminent surviving man of letters, Washington Irving, who turned the chair over to the Whig orator Daniel Webster. The main address was delivered by William Cullen Bryant, a Democrat and America's most honored poet. It was a national event that transcended literary and political factionalism, and virtually every notable American writer contributed a statement praising the first American fictionalist to achieve a major international reputation. Yet, as Herman Melville said in one of the letters read out to the meeting, "He was a great, robust-souled man, all whose merits are not seen, yet fully appreciated." Melville may well have been one of the few contemporary readers who appreciated the artistry and moral substance of Cooper's best work. That several speakers stressed the wholesome "moral purity" of his novels pointed to what would be their fate for almost a century after Cooper's death: the Leather-Stocking Tales, *The Spy*, and a few of the early sea novels would survive as classics of American, indeed world, literature for children.

Regarded as novels for adolescent readers, Cooper's are inferior to those of, say, Mark Twain and Robert Louis Stevenson, authors whose moral sentiments are no less pure, whose plots are equally exciting, whose styles are more economical and clear, and who wrote, at least in some of their novels, specifically for children. Like other leading British and American novelists of the early 19th century, Cooper wrote for a family audience and, therefore also like them, he aimed to supply something that catered to the special interests of each sector of the family circle, and to include nothing that would break the circle. Thus, nearly all his thirty-one novels provide love interest in the form of a courtship plot, and while the possibility of rape is often implicitly—never explicitly—entertained, sexual passion is closely disguised, and adultery or illegitimate birth is excluded from the range of novelizable events. Again, the great majority of his novels combine the courtship plot with, and often subordinate it to, an action-packed flight-and-pursuit narrative in which not infrequently absurd situations and events are somehow made convincing for the moment. In addition to amusing the young and young at heart of both sexes with adventure and romantic love, however, Cooper's novels also draw emphatic moral conclusions for their benefit, sometimes through the speeches of wise characters who obviously have the author's approval and often, too often, through direct narratorial interventions.

If there were no more to Cooper's novels than has just been described, they would not have commanded the serious interest of such readers as Melville, Balzac, Joseph Conrad, and D. H. Lawrence. That Cooper had not only adolescents but also thoughtful adult readers in mind is indicated by his willingness, against all commercial counsels, to end many novels unhappily. This is true of such important works as *The Last of the Mohicans, The Bravo, The Deerslayer*, and a novel not previously mentioned, THE WEPT OF WISH-TON-WISH (1829), which

exhibits many of Cooper's characteristic strengths and can be taken here as an exemplary text.

The Wept is a romance of the 17th-century New England frontier in which one of the historical protagonists of KING PHILIP'S WAR, the Narragansett chieftain Conanchet, plays a central part. The action concludes tragically with an actual event, Conanchet's execution by Native American auxiliaries of the colonial government, but the conflict between the two peoples is given a complexity unimaginable by the old Puritan chroniclers when Cooper invents a marriage between Conanchet and the captive daughter of an English family. This is the only instance in the Cooper *oeuvre* of an interracial marriage being consummated, and it can be argued that the death of Conanchet and his white wife is his way of punishing transgression of the American taboo against miscegenation. But whatever his unconscious motives may have been, he is explicit in condemning racial prejudice and in approving characters of both races who seek to bridge cultures and bond peoples through various forms of surrogate kinship. The heroic Puritan leader Mark Heathcote's extended family includes not only blood relatives but white orphans and even Conanchet when as a boy he is a captive of the settlers. Indeed, in terms of moral character, Mark's true son is obviously Conanchet, not the well-meaning but weak man who bears Mark's name. Mark's relationship with Conanchet cuts across generations as well as races and cultures, and is part of an intricate binary pattern which, after the fashion of Scott's Waverley novels, organizes the work as a whole.

Although he was willing to simplify the historical record and supplement it with plausible invented incidents, Cooper was as serious as Scott about the general accuracy of his historical pictures and interpretations, and as keen to base them on a wide range of reading among early documents and more recent synthetic accounts. For, like Scott, he understood the various forms of human behavior—for example, methods of warfare, styles of revolution, and institutions of worship—as products of historical circumstances, especially modes of subsistence. Thus, in this novel as in the Leather-Stocking Tales, the Native Americans view forests differently than white settlers not because they are of different races but because the former are hunters and the latter are herdsmen or farmers. By the same same token, the Native Americans conduct warfare differently because when they fight they employ the methods appropriate to a wilderness context and proven successful in hunting. Believing that human values and behavior were historically determined and culturally blinkered, Cooper tended to be pessimistic about short-term solutions to communication problems between peoples, and inclined to expect life to go hard for the bridging figures—like Mark Heathcote, Conanchet, and of course Leatherstocking—who are the principal heroes of his fiction.

After all allowances are made for the contributions of Charles Brockden Brown and others, it is clear that Cooper was the foundational figure for the American novel tradition. More than anybody else's, his descriptions created the 19th-century European image of American character, nature, and society. Adapting Scott's model to New World conditions, he led the way in creating a popular interest in American history and a more informed awareness of the roots of American culture and institutions. (The great historian Francis Parkman said that Cooper's writings had helped determine the course of his own career.) As the inventor of the frontier novel and sea novel, he exerted an influence on the characteristic themes, character types, and symbolism of these novelistic subgenres that extends into the 20th century, for example, in the works of Joseph Conrad and William Faulkner. Cooper himself anticipated that he would be remembered chiefly for the Leather-Stocking Tales, and it is true that the Leatherstocking and his life story have proven as central to American literary culture and mythology as the characters and stories of Hester Prynne, Huckleberry Finn, and Jay Gatsby. Over the past fifty years, however, critics have come to admire a number of novels—notably *Satanstoe, The Bravo,* and *The Wept of Wish-ton-Wish*—largely neglected by 19th-century readers. The task of reassessing Cooper's achievement is far from complete.

The standard edition is *The Writings of James Fenimore Cooper,* ed. James Franklin Beard and others (1980–   ). Biographical and critical sources include James Grossman, *James Fenimore Cooper* (1949, repr. 1967); *Letters and Journals of James Fenimore Cooper,* ed. James Franklin Beard (1960–68); and George Dekker, *James Fenimore Cooper the Novelist* (1967). See A LETTER TO HIS COUNTRYMEN; THE MONIKINS.

GEORGE DEKKER

Cooper, Myles (1735–1785),   clergyman, educational administrator, loyalist. Cooper served as the second president of King's [Columbia] College, from 1763 to 1775, then fled to England. There he wrote *National Humiliation and Repentance Recommended* (1777). His earlier loyalist writing include *The American Querist* (1774) and *A Friendly Address to All Reasonable Americans* (1774).

Cooper, Peter (1791–1883),   inventor, industrialist, philanthropist, author. Born in New York City, Cooper had many important inventions, built several large factories, founded Cooper Union, and attacked some of the evils of the day in his *Autobiography* (1877) and *Ideas for a Science of Good Government* (1883).

Cooper, Susan Fenimore (1813–1894),   writer, editor, biographer. Cooper devoted herself to the study of nature and to writing about it, also to the preparation of material about her father, JAMES FENIMORE COOPER. Her best-known work, sketches of Cooperstown life, was called *Rural Hours* (1850). *Pages and Pictures* (1861) contains selections from her father's books along with comments on them; she also wrote prefaces for the volumes of an edition (1876–84) of his writings.

Cooper, Thomas (1759–1839),   scientist, writer. An English liberal who favored the cause of the French Revolution, Cooper sought a more sympathetic environment in the United States. He joined the Jeffersonians and began writing political pamphlets attacking the Federalists; these were collected later in *Political Essays* (1799). In *Some Information Respecting America* (1795), Cooper for the first time used a famous phrase: "The government is a government *of* the people and *for* the people." He became an American citizen, taught at Dickinson College, later becoming professor of chemistry at South Carolina College and eventually its president.

Cooper, William (1754–1809),   author, father of JAMES FENIMORE COOPER. Originally a resident of Burlington, New Jersey, Cooper removed to a large estate at Cooperstown, New York, with land holdings that at one time amounted to 750,000 acres. He published in Dublin *A Guide to the Wilderness* (1810), a book on the settlements in western New York. He appears as Judge Temple in his son's *The Pioneers* (1823).

Cooperstown, New York.   When JAMES FENIMORE COOPER was about a year old his father moved the family into the wilderness at the outlet of Lake Otsego, where in 1788 he had founded Cooperstown. Here young Cooper spent his boyhood, and here he spent his last years. In 1838 he published *Chronicles of Cooperstown.* THE DEERSLAYER (1841) takes place on Otsego Lake (the Glimmerglass of Cooper's stories) and along its borders. Otsego Hall, built by WILLIAM COOPER, is made the residence of Marmaduke Temple in THE PIONEERS (1823), and Judge Temple in the same book is the novelist's father. NATTY BUMPPO's original was possibly an old hunter named Shipman who used to offer his game at Judge Cooper's door. Since 1940 Cooperstown has undergone a restoration, and numerous mementoes of Cooper and his family can be found there. It also contains the National Baseball Museum and Hall of Fame, in honor of Abner Doubleday, who lived there when, it long was said, he invented the game in 1839, and the Farmer's Museum, including buildings representative of a 19th-century New York village.

Cooper Union   (also called **Cooper Institute**), New York City. It was founded by PETER COOPER in 1857–59 for the "advancement of science and art," since then giving free courses in science, chemistry, engineering, and art. Here Lincoln delivered on February 27, 1860, his *Cooper Institute Address,* which helped him win the Republican nomination.

Coover, Robert [Lowell] (1932–   ),   novelist, short-story writer, playwright, essayist. Born in Iowa, Coover drifted with his family through the Midwest and was educated at Indiana University and the University of Chicago. After a few years in the United States Naval Reserve, he began writing innovative, nonconventional stories later collected in *Pricksongs and Descants* (1969). His first novel, *The Origin of the Brunists* (1966), loosely based on occurrences in Herrin, Illinois, where his father edited a newspaper, probes man's need to construct explanatory myths around catastrophic events. *The Universal Baseball Association, Inc., J. Henry Waugh, Prop.* (1968) continued this exploration, using a lonely accountant's obsession with a tabletop baseball game as occasion for a critique of system building and narrative control. Together with *The Origin of the Brunists,* which won the Faulkner Award, this novel established Coover's reputation as a postmodern writer.

Through the early seventies, Coover published stories and plays (*Theological Position,* 1972), but his main attention was devoted to a major political-experimental novel, *The Public Burning,* whose publication was delayed until 1977 because of

Coover's iconoclastic use of historical figures (including Richard Nixon as narrator). Since 1976 Coover has lived in Providence, Rhode Island, teaching at Brown University and publishing complex, innovative fictions: *After Lazarus* (1980), *Charlie in the House of Rue* (1980), *A Political Fable* (1980), *Spanking the Maid* (1981), *In Bed One Night* (1983), *Gerald's Party* (1986), *Night at the Movies* (1987), *Pinocchio in Venice* (1991), *John's Wife* (1996), *Briar Rose* (1997), and *Ghost Town* (1998). In turn hyperrealistic and antirealistic, Coover's narratives examine the relation between reality and fiction, imagination and control, highlighting the cultural process that constructs symbolic systems and ideological worlds.

Critical studies include Lois Gordon, *Robert Coover: The Universal Fictionmaking Process* (1984), Jackson I. Cope, *Robert Coover's Fictions* (1986), and Paul Maltby, *Dissident Postmodernists* (1991).

MARCEL CORNIS-POPE

Copland, Aaron (1900–1990), composer, author. One of America's most illustrious and popular contemporary composers, Copland agitated vigorously on behalf of 20th-century music and taught and lectured extensively at Harvard and elsewhere. Among his many musical productions are *El Salón México* (1934), *Billy the Kid* (a ballet, 1938), *Lincoln Portrait* (1942), *Rodeo* (a ballet, 1942), *Appalachian Spring* (a ballet, 1944), and *The Tender Land* (1954). He also composed film scores, including one for *Our Town* (1940). His writings include *Our New Music* (1941), *Music and Imagination* (1952), *What to Listen for in Music* (1939, revised 1957), *Copland on Music* (1960), and *The New Music: 1900–1960* (revised 1968).

Copperheads. Northerners (mainly Democrats) who during the Civil War favored the cause of the South and advocated a negotiated peace. They were made the subject of Bret Harte's poem, *The Copperhead* (1868), of Harold Frederic's novel, *The Copperhead* (1893), of Augustus Thomas's play, *The Copperhead* (1918), and of Bernard Cornwell's Starbuck trilogy, *Rebel* (1993), *Copperhead* (1994), and *The Bloody Ground* (1996).

Copway, George [Kah-ge-ga-gah-bowh] (1818–1869), preacher, writer. An Ojibwa, born and raised in Canada, Copway converted to Christianity at twelve and from 1834 to 1836 assisted in missionary work among the Ojibwa in Wisconsin before continuing his education in Illinois. Married to a white woman, he continued missionary work among the Sioux and Ojibwa in the Upper Mississippi, became a Methodist preacher in Canada, and earned celebrity with *The Life, History, and Travels of Kah-ge-ga-gah-bowh (George Copway), a Young Indian Chief of the Ojibwa Nation, a Convert to the Christian Faith, and Missionary to His People for Twelve Years* (1847). Revised as *The Life, Letters, and Speeches of Kah-ge-ga-gah-bowh* (1850), the book went through several printings, appearing also as *Recollections of a Forest Life* (1851). Copway toured the United States, lectured on Native American rights, proposed the establishment of a country for Indians, Kahgega (Ever to Be) on the Upper Missouri, and established a newspaper, *Copway's American Indian*, in sup-

port of the program. *The Traditional History and Characteristic Sketches of the Ojibwa Nation* (1850; reprinted as *Indian Life and Indian History by an Indian Author*, 1860) won international fame and an invitation to address a peace conference in Germany. *Running Sketches of Men and Places in England, France, Germany, Belgium and Scotland* (1851) followed. A controversial figure, he received praise and friendship from Longfellow, Parkman, and others, but some supporters turned against him and he spent his last years attempting to scratch out a living. After Copway's death, his epic poem, *The Objibway Conquest* (1850), was claimed, without much evidence, by a Kansas writer, Julius Taylor Clark.

Coquette, The (1797), an epistolary novel by Hannah Webster Foster, published anonymously. It purported to give an account of the seduction of the author's cousin, Elizabeth Whitman, supposedly by Pierpont Edwards, son of Jonathan Edwards, and of her death in childbirth. (Another contemporary account makes the seducer Aaron Burr.)

Corbett, Elizabeth Frances (1887–1981), novelist, biographer. More than forty-five books flowed from the pen of this popular author of unaffectedly homey, familiar, escapist fiction. Her family audience especially delighted in "the Graper girls" and "Mrs. Meigs" series. Among her works are *Cecily and the Wide World* (1916); *Mr. and Mrs. Meigs* (1940); *Out at the Soldiers' Home* (semiautobiographical, 1941); and *Hidden Island* (1961).

Corbin, Alice. See ALICE HENDERSON.

Corey, Giles. One of the victims of the SALEM WITCHCRAFT TRIALS, Corey became an admired figure in New England legend and poetry. A man of eighty, he died unflinchingly pressed under heavy weights in 1692; his wife was hanged at the same time. An account of his martyrdom appeared in Robert Calef's MORE WONDERS OF THE INVISIBLE WORLD (1700), a contemporary ballad was written about him, Longfellow made him the subject of the second of his NEW ENGLAND TRAGEDIES (*Giles Corey of the Salem Farms*, 1868), Mary E. Wilkins Freeman wrote a six-act play about him (*Giles Corey, Yeoman*, 1893), and he appears in Arthur Miller's play *The Crucible* (1953).

Corey, Paul [Frederick] (1903–), editor, novelist, writer on economic and political affairs. Educated at the University of Iowa, Corey worked for several years on *The Economist* and the staff of the *Encyclopedia Britannica*, traveled abroad, and devoted himself more and more to the study of farm conditions in the United States. *Buy an Acre* (1944) and *Homemade Homes* (1950) are nonfiction. Among his novels are a trilogy with a Midwestern setting, *Three Miles Square* (1939), *The Road Returns* (1940), and *County Seat* (1941); *Acres of Antaeus* (1946); and *Milk Flood* (1956).

Corle, Edwin (1906–1956), novelist, nonfiction writer. Born in New Jersey, Corle wrote mostly of the West and Southwest. His books include *Mojave* (1934), desert stories; *Fig Tree John* (1935), about relations between an Apache and whites in the 19th century; *People on the Earth* (1938); *Burro Alley* (1938), set in Santa Fe; *Listen, Bright Angel* (1946); *In*

Winter Light (1949), about Navajo life; and *Billy the Kid* (1953). *Three Ways to Mecca* (1947) is satire. *Desert Country* (1941) and *The Gila: River of the Southwest* (1951) are nonfiction.

Corman, Cid [Sidney Corman] (1924–   ), writer, editor. Born in Boston, Corman was educated at Tufts University. His journal *Origin* (1951–56) was important in its time in advancing the work of avant-garde poets, including those associated with Black Mountain College. (See BLACK MOUNTAIN POETS.) His own poetry has been collected in many volumes, including *Thanksgiving Eclogue* (1954), *Sun Rock Man* (1962), *Words for Each Other* (1967), and *Livingdying* (1970). For many years he lived in Japan, conducting his Origin Press there. *Aegis* (1984) and *And the Word* (1987) are selections of his poems. *One Man's Moon* (1984) contains haiku translations and is one of a number of volumes of translations. *Nothing Doing* (2000) presents a number of his own poems, marked by a Zen-like precision and brevity.

Corn, Alfred (1943–   ), poet. Born in Georgia and educated at Emory University and Columbia, Corn has taught at Columbia University. His poetry is collected in *All Roads at Once* (1976); *A Call in the Midst of the Crowd* (1978); *The Various Light* (1980); *Notes from a Child of Paradise* (1984), a long autobiographical poem; *The West Door* (1988); *Autobiographies* (1992); and *Stake: Poems 1972–1992* (1999). *Part of His Story* (1997) is a meditative novel about a writer who loses his lover to AIDS. *The Metamorphoses of Metaphor* (1987) collects criticism.

Cornplanter. See SENECA INDIANS.

Cornwell, Bernard (1944–   ), writer of romantic and historical fictions. Born in London, Cornwell was working for the British Broadcasting Company before his marriage to an American brought him to the United States, where he became a prolific and popular novelist, living on Cape Cod. He credits his teenage love of C. S. Forester's Horatio Hornblower books as providing the inspiration for his own frankly imitative Sharpe's series on a British officer in Wellington's army in the Napoleonic Peninsular War of 1808–1814, "Hornblower-on-Land" as he once described the idea. *Sharpe's Eagle: Richard Sharpe and the Talavera Campaign* (1981) was the first of sixteen Sharpe's books in print by 2000. A second series, following the adventures of Nate Starbuck, Northern born, as he fights on the Southern side in the American Civil War, includes *Rebel* (1993), *Copperhead* (1994), and *The Bloody Ground* (1996). The series he has said is his best to date, however, is a trilogy on King Arthur (portrayed with significant differences from the tales known to readers of Malory): *The Winter King* (1996), *Enemy of God* (1997), and *Excalibur* (1998). *Stonehenge: A Novel of 2000 B.C.* appeared in 2000. *Wildtrack* (1988) and *Killer's Wake* (1989) are contemporary adventure stories. Historical novels written as "Susannah Kells" are *A Crowning Mercy* (1983), *The Fallen Angels* (1984), and *Coat of Arms* (1986).

Cornwell, Patricia [Daniels] (1956–   ), writer of murder mysteries. Patricia Daniels was born in Miami, Florida and educated at Davidson College. From 1979 to 1981

she was a prize-winning police reporter in Charlotte, North Carolina, she gave that up to move to Richmond, Virginia with her husband and publish her first book, *A Time for Remembering: The Story of Ruth Bell Graham* (1983), a biography of the wife of evangelist Billy Graham, a personal friend. Wanting to write crime novels, she apprenticed herself to a medical examiner in Richmond, doing computer analysis and studying forensic pathology. In *Postmortem* (1990), she introduced Dr. Kay Scarpetta, a medical examiner and sleuth who overcomes sexist expectations of inadequacy and through extensive forensic knowledge and keen intellect discovers the identity of a serial rapist and murderer. Scarpetta continues her successful and critically praised work in *Body of Evidence* (1991), where a writer is murdered, apparently after allowing the murderer into her home; *All That Remains* (1992), with couples killed in their cars; *Cruel and Unusual* (1993), introducing a criminal genius, Temple Gault, serial killer of children, who escapes capture in what becomes a personal contest with Scarpetta; *The Body Farm* (1994), Gault as killer of an eleven-year-old girl; *From Potter's Field* (1995), Gault murders a homeless woman on Christmas Eve in New York's Central Park; *Cause of Death* (1996), a neo-fascist cult and the murder of a reporter; *Unnatural Exposure* (1997), e-mailed photos and serial murders in Ireland and Virginia; *Point of Origin* (1998), less favorably reviewed than others; *Black Notice* (1999), a string of international killings, with Scarpetta's identity stolen by an Internet thief; and *The Last Precinct* (2000), ruminative and retrospective, continuing some of the themes of *Point of Origin* and *Black Notice*. Police novels without Scarpetta include *Hornet's Nest* (1997) and *Southern Cross* (1998). *Scarpetta's Winter Table* (1998), a gift to fans, brings the heroine together with friends to cook and supply recipes for the winter holidays.

Corso, [Nunzio] Gregory (1930–2001), poet. Born in New York City, Corso was raised by foster parents and in institutions and spent three years in jail, beginning at age 17. Encouraged by ALLEN GINSBERG and others he became a BEAT GENERATION poet. Collections of his sometimes witty, sometimes angry poems include *The Vestal Lady on Brattle* (1955), *Gasoline* (1958), *Bomb* (1958), *The Happy Birthday of Death* (1960), *Long Live Man* (1962), *Elegiac Feelings American* (1970), *The Herald of the Autochthonic Spirit* (1981), and *Mindfield: New and Selected Poems* (1989). *The American Express* (1961) is a novel.

Corsons Inlet, poem by A. R. AMMONS, collected in the book of the same name (1965). As the speaker recounts "a walk over the dunes" at Corsons Inlet in New Jersey, he describes the ever-changing natural scenery he encounters, and creates from the experience a metaphor for writing and for life. He concludes "that tomorrow a new walk is a new walk."

Cortázar, Julio (1914–1984), novelist, short-story writer. Born in Brussels to Argentinian parents, Cortázar was raised in Argentina and began as an author there with a book of poems published as *Julio Denis* in 1938. Turning to short stories he published a first collection, heavily influenced by

JORGE LUIS BORGES, in 1951. In that same year, in opposition to the regime of Juan Perón, he left for France, where he worked as a translator for UNESCO and pursued his literary ambitions. He never again lived in Argentina, and in 1981 he became a French citizen.

Like Borges, Cortázar is concerned with metaphysical themes and questions of identity expressed in vivid, original imagery, grotesque characterization, and labyrinthine plots. His best-known novel, RAYUELA (1963, tr. *Hopscotch*, 1966), Joycean, Borgesian, and surrealistic, was one of the most influential Latin American novels of its time. His other novels include *Los premios* (1960, tr. *The Winners*, 1965), an allegorical tale of passengers on a cruise liner going nowhere; *62: modelo para armar* (1968, tr. *62: A Model Kit*, 1972); *Libro de Manuel* (1973, tr. *A Manual for Manuel*, 1979); and *Un tal Lucas* (1979, tr. *A Certain Lucas*, 1984). Much of his best work is in his short stories. Three early volumes—*Bestario*, 1951; *Final del juego*, 1956; and *Las armas secretas*, 1959—were translated as *End of the Game* (1967). His other collections are *Historias de cronopios y famas* (1962, tr. *Cronopios and Famas*, 1969); *Todos los fuegos el fuego* (1966, tr. *All Fires the Fire*, 1971); *Alguien que anda por ahii* (1977, tr. *A Change of Light*, 1980); and *Queremos tanto a Glenda* (1981, tr. *We Love Glenda So Much*, 1983*).*

Cortez [or Cortes], Hernando (1485–1547), Spanish conqueror of Mexico. He sailed from Cuba in 1518, coasted along the Yucatan and Mexico, landed and founded Vera Cruz, and then destroyed his fleet so his men would have no thoughts of returning. He conquered the Aztec armies as he marched inland, and entered Mexico City on November 8, 1519. He took Montezuma as a hostage, but Montezuma later died of wounds received while he was addressing an Aztec army in revolt against the Spaniards. Cortez for a time was driven back, but finally made himself master of Mexico. He was deposed (1526), then recalled to Spain and received with honors (1528); in a return to Mexico he discovered Lower California (1536). He returned to Spain to die on his estate at Seville.

Some letters of his on the conquest of Mexico have been preserved, but the details of the expedition were best given in Bernal Díaz's *True History of the Conquest of Mexico* (3 v. 1632). W. H. Prescott wrote a HISTORY OF THE CONQUEST OF MEXICO (3 v. 1843), and Archibald MacLeish used Diaz's account as the basis of his powerful poem *Conquistador* (1932).

Coryell, John Russell (1848?[52]–1924), a dime novelist who wrote under many pen names, particularly NICK CARTER. He formed one of a group of writers who wrote on demand sensational, romantic, and sentimental fiction of all kinds, including such titles as *The American Marquis, The Old Detective's Pupil, Among the Nihilists, Nick Carter Down East,* and *Wife or Stenographer—Which?*

Cosmopolitan. A magazine founded in Rochester, New York, in 1886 by Joseph N. Hallock. In 1887 its editorial offices were moved to New York City, and when John Brisben Walker became the owner and editor in 1889, it became one of the most popular magazines of the day. Walker sold the magazine to WILLIAM RANDOLPH HEARST in 1905. Hearst merged it in 1925 with *Hearst's International*, but kept the name and the volume numbering of *The Cosmopolitan*. It has published some of the most distinguished writers of several generations, especially in fiction, and at one time also published books.

Costain, Thomas [Bertram] (1885–1965), editor, novelist. Costain was born in Brantford, Ontario, and came to the United States in 1920, after editing *Maclean's*, a Canadian magazine. He was fiction editor of THE SATURDAY EVENING POST and worked for Doubleday & Co., Twentieth Century-Fox Film Corp., and others. Costain was known best for his historical romances, which include *For My Great Folly* (1942), on 17th-century piracy; *Ride with Me* (1943), about an Englishman in China during the time of Kublai Khan; *The Moneyman* (1947), set in 17th-century France; *High Towers* (1949), of 18th-century Montreal; *The Silver Chalice* (1952), on the quest for the grail; *The Tontine* (1955), a 19th-century family novel; *Below the Salt* (1957), England in the time of King John; *The Darkness and the Dawn* (1959), of the time of Attila; and *The Last Love* (1963), Napoleon on St. Helena. He also wrote a history of pre-Dominion Canada, *The White and the Gold* (1954); a popular history, *Pageant of England*, in four volumes—*The Conqueror* (1949), *The Magnificent Century* (1951), *The Three Edwards* (1958), and *The Last Plantagenets* (1962); and an account of Alexander Graham Bell's Brantford years, *The Chord of Steel* (1960).

Cotton, John (1584–1652), clergyman, writer. Born in Derbyshire, England, and educated at Cambridge, Cotton served for twenty years as vicar of St. Botolph's Church in Boston, Lincolnshire. He arrived at Massachusetts Bay in 1633 and became immediately one of the most important men of the colony. Autocratic in his approach to church matters, he worked to build a Massachusetts theocracy. He was a leader in the charges of heresy brought against ANNE HUTCHINSON and in the banishment of ROGER WILLIAMS. When Williams wrote his BLOUDY TENET OF PERSECUTION FOR CAUSE OF CONSCIENCE (1644), Cotton replied with *The Bloudy Tenet Washed and Made White in the Bloud of the Lamb* (1647). A strong force in early Congregationalism, he wrote *The Keys of the Kingdom of Heaven* (1644), *The Way of the Churches of Christ in New England* (1645), and *The Way of the Congregational Churches Cleared* (1648). His *Milk for Babes, Drawn out of the Breasts of Both Testaments* (1646) is a book of religious instruction for children. His other works include *God's Promise to His Plantation* (1630). His daughter married INCREASE MATHER and became the mother of COTTON MATHER.

Coulter, John (1888–1980), playwright. Born in Belfast, Ireland, Coulter worked in the theater and as a journalist in Ireland and England before coming to Canada and settling in Toronto in 1936. He wrote prolifically for radio, television, and the theater. Among plays with Irish settings are *Father Brady's New Pig* (1937), *The House in the Quiet Glen* (1937), *The Family Portrait* (1938), and *The Drums Are Out* (1948). His plays with Canadian settings include *Riel* (1962) and *The Trial of Louis Riel* (1968), about the leader of a 19th-century rebellion in Manitoba. Among his other works are librettos for radio operas; a book of verse, *The Blossoming Thorn* (1946); a novel, *Turf Smoke* (1945); and a book of memoirs, *In My Day* (1980).

Country of the Pointed Firs, The (1896),   sketches by SARAH ORNE JEWETT. Thinly bound together by a faint thread of plot, these sketches describe an isolated Maine seaport town. Local color is deftly applied, and humor mingles with sentiment in descriptions of characters who are resolutely themselves. Willa Cather thought so well of the book that she placed it alongside *Huckleberry Finn* and *The Scarlet Letter*.

Cournos, John (1881–1966),   novelist, critic, poet, translator. Born in Russia, Cournos was brought to the United States in 1891 and held many jobs before turning to newspaper work and writing. His first three stories—*The Mask* (1919), *The Wall* (1921), and *Babel* (1922)—form a trilogy based largely on his own experiences. *The New Candide* (1924) satirizes American customs. He published his *Autobiography* in 1935. His later books are primarily biographical and historical studies for young people, among them *Famous Modern American Novelists* (1952) and lives of Roger Williams (1953) and John Adams (1954).

Courtin', The (1867),   a poem in Yankee dialect by JAMES RUSSELL LOWELL, published in the *Second Series* of THE BIGLOW PAPERS.

Courtship of Miles Standish, The (1858),   a long narrative poem by HENRY WADSWORTH LONGFELLOW. Like many 19th-century American writers, Longfellow was concerned with investing the American scene with a useful native mythology, especially in his three long narrative poems— EVANGELINE (1847), HIAWATHA (1855), and *The Courtship of Miles Standish*.

The story concerns the early days of the settlement at Plymouth. The captain of the colony, Miles Standish, sends his friend and emissary, John Alden, to woo Priscilla. She prefers John to the older man, despite the honest pleas John offers on Miles's behalf. When Miles is reported killed in the war, the lovers are left free to plan marriage. Miles returns on the eve of the wedding and gives the young lovers his blessing.

Cousins, Norman (1915–1990),   writer, editor. Born in New Jersey, Cousins earned celebrity as editor of *The Saturday Review* (1940–78), which he made into a leading journal of humanitarian concerns. Among his books are *The Good Inheritance: The Democratic Chance* (1942); *Modern Man Is Obsolete* (1945); *Who Speaks for Man?* (1952); *The Last Defense in a Nuclear Age* (1960); *The Celebration of Life* (1974); *Anatomy of an Illness* (1979), an inspirational account of his self-cure; *Human Options* (1982), on world unity; *The Healing Heart: Antidotes to Panic and Helplessness* (1983); and *Head First: The Biology of Hope* (1989), on the effect of emotions on bodily resistance to disease. *Present Tense* (1967) is an account of his work on *The Saturday Review*.

Covenant Theology.   Covenant theology was a central and far-reaching tenet for English and American Puritans. According to covenant thinking, God entered into an agreement with his chosen people—originally Adam and Eve under a covenant of works, later the Puritans under a covenant of grace. Both parties in this agreement were bound by the terms of their covenant, people agreeing to abide individually and communally by the laws of God, and God by supporting their missions and by operating in ways that more or less conform to the terms of human understanding. The sense of a favored status and the corresponding sense of duty suggested by the logic of covenant thinking permeated all areas of Puritan experience. For example, American Puritans justified their emigration on the grounds that England had broken its covenant; hence, they believed they were legally permitted (obligated) to form a new culture to carry on God's work. The covenant also provided a framework binding the individual to God—the individual was bound to the religious and civil rulers, and those rulers, ultimately, to God. In this respect, covenant theology was the foundation of Puritan theocratic social and political organization. Viewed by some historians as a legalistic strategy to render comprehensible an otherwise inscrutable God who ruled by absolute decree, the covenant represented the rationality and priorities of the middle-class and legal backgrounds of those attracted to Puritanism.

Perhaps the best articulation of covenant thinking is JOHN WINTHROP's lay sermon delivered aboard the *Arbella*. Concluding his carefully reasoned plea for social cooperation, Winthrop offers the following theological rationale for their work:

> Thus stands the cause between God and us. We are entered into covenant with him for this work. We have taken out a commission, the Lord hath given us leave to draw our own articles. We have professed to enterprise these actions, upon these and those ends, we have hereupon besought him of favor and blessing. Now if the Lord shall please to hear us, and bring us in peace to the place we desire, then hath he ratified this covenant and sealed our commission, [and] will expect a strict performance of the articles contained in it. But if we shall neglect the observation of these articles which are the ends we have propounded and, dissembling with our God, shall fall to embrace this present world and prosecute our carnal intentions, seeking great things for ourselves and our posterity, the Lord will surely break out in wrath against such a perjured people, and make us know the price of the breach of such a covenant.

Other representative texts include JOHN COTTON's "A Treatise of the Covenant of Grace" (1636); THOMAS SHEPARD's "The Gospel-Covenant; or the Covenant of Grace" (1651); Peter Bulkeley's "The Gospel-Covenant" (1651); and the introductory remarks from COTTON MATHER's *The Wonders of the Invisible World* (1962).

RUSSELL J. REISING

Cowley, Malcolm (1898–1989),   poet, editor, critic, translator. Born in Pennsylvania, Cowley was educated at Harvard and drove an ambulance in Europe in World War I. A member of the American expatriate colony in Paris in the 1920s, Cowley helped publish two expatriate magazines, *Secession* and *Broom*, and made a study of expatriate psychology in

EXILE'S RETURN (1934, rev. ed., 1951). His collections of verse are *Blue Juniata* (1929) and *Dry Season* (1942). His criticism, *After the Genteel Tradition; American Writers Since 1910* (1937, reissued in 1959) and *The Literary Situation* (1954), was well received. Cowley edited a number of books, among them *The Portable Hemingway* (1944), *The Portable Faulkner* (1946), *The Complete Walt Whitman* (1948), *The Portable Hawthorne* (1948), and *The Stories of F. Scott Fitzgerald* (1950). His later works include *Think Back on Us* (1967), on the 1930s; *A Many-Windowed House* (1970); *A Second Flowering* (1973), on recent American literature; and *And I Worked at the Writer's Trade* (1978), essays. *In The Dream of the Golden Mountains* (1980), he remembers the 1930s; and *The View from 80* (1981) is a memoir.

Cowperwood, Frank.   Chief character in Theodore Dreiser's trilogy—THE FINANCIER (1912), THE TITAN (1914), and THE STOIC (1947). Dreiser had the financier Charles T. Yerkes in mind when he depicted Cowperwood and his career. He appeared also in *The Bulwark* (posthumous, 1946).

Cox, Palmer (1840–1924),   writer, illustrator. Born in Quebec, Palmer came to the United States in 1876. He earned fame as the creator of a popular series of books on the adventures of brownies, beginning with *The Brownies: Their Book* (1887).

Coxe, Louis O[sborne] (1918–1993),   poet. Born in New Hampshire, Coxe was educated at Princeton (1940), served in the Navy in World War II, and taught at Bowdoin and other colleges. His books of verse include *The Sea Faring* (1947); *The Second Man* (1955); *The Wilderness* (1958); *The Middle Passage* (1960), a blank verse narrative on the slave trade; *The Last Hero* (1965); *Nikal Seyn and Decoration Day* (1966); and *The North Well* (1985). With Robert H. Blanchard he turned Melville's celebrated novella into a successful drama, *Billy Budd* (1951). *Enabling Acts* (1976) collects criticism.

Cozzens, Frederick S[wartwout] (1818–1869), wine merchant, essayist, humorist. Cozzens followed in his father's footsteps as a food wholesaler, but was an enthusiastic amateur in the literary field. He edited (1854–61) a trade magazine, *The Wine Press*. His collections of writings include *Yankee Doodle* (1847) and his most popular work, *The Sparrowgrass Papers* (1856), a humorous account of a city man's experiences in the country.

Cozzens, James Gould (1903–1978),   novelist. Born in Chicago and educated at Harvard, Cozzens wrote his first novel, *Confusion* (1924), while he was an undergraduate. Three others soon followed: *Michael Scarlett* (1925), *Cock Pit* (1928), and *The Son of Perdition* (1929). With his fifth, *S.S. San Pedro: A Tale of the Sea* (1931), based on a mysterious ship sinking, he began to attain the level of craftsmanship critics have taken most seriously. His most praised novels, however, are studies of privileged Americans. These include *The Just and the Unjust* (1942), about a murder trial; *Guard of Honor* (1948), set on an Air Force base in World War II; and *By Love Possessed* (1957), a best seller about the loves of a lawyer. His other novels are *The Last Adam* (1933, in England *A Cure of Flesh*); *Castaway* (1934); *Men and Brethren* (1936); *Ask Me*

Tomorrow (1940); and *Morning, Noon, and Night* (1968). His stories are collected in *Children and Others* (1968) and *A Flower in Her Hair* (1975).

Cracker.   A disparaging term for a poor white inhabitant of the southeastern United States. Georgia crackers have appeared frequently in fiction, for example, in the works of A. B. LONGSTREET and ERSKINE CALDWELL.

cracker-barrel [or cracker-box] philosophers and humor.   The cracker barrel or box in the general store common in New England and other American communities was a gathering place for those who came to enjoy a little gossip and exchange of anecdotes. Traditionally, much rustic wit was generated in these exchanges; traditionally, too, such rustic talk was far superior in ultimate wisdom to the sophisticated but unsound conversation of city folk.

Thus, it early became a custom among American humorists to disguise their epigrams and characterizations in some form of nonstandard English, such as Yankee speech. The traditional homespun philosopher was given to the deliberate manufacture of malapropisms and solecisms. Sometimes the disguise took the form of misspelling, mispronunciation, or learned word-mangling; everywhere was the homely simile, the down-to-earth metaphor. Writers of high literary standard did not hesitate to join the ranks of the rustic philosophers—James Russell Lowell, for example, in the BIGLOW PAPERS. Other writers who early exploited cracker-barrel humor include SEBA SMITH and THOMAS CHANDLER HALIBURTON.

Craddock, Charles Egbert.   Pen name of MARY NOAILLES MURFREE.

Cradle Will Rock, The (1937),   a musical drama by MARC BLITZSTEIN. Originally sponsored by the WPA Theater, the play was canceled on opening night because of its attack on capitalism. Actors and audience moved to a nearby theater, and the play was put on without scenery, costumes, or properties. The author played the score on a paino and provided a running commentary on the action. This arrangement proved so successful that it was retained when ORSON WELLES produced the play on Broadway shortly after.

Crafts, William (1787–1826),   lawyer, public official, essayist, poet. Born in South Carolina and educated at Harvard, he wrote for the Charleston *Courier* and collected his poems in *The Raciad and Other Occasional Poems* (1810) and *Sullivan's Island and Other Poems* (1820).

Cranch, Christopher Pearse (1813–1892),   clergyman, essayist, poet, painter. A Virginian by birth, Cranch had a talent for humor, evidenced in his two juveniles—*The Last of the Huggermuggers*, 1856, and *Kobboltozo*, 1857—and in some of his drawings and caricatures. He had ample means and lived for many years in Rome and Paris. His best-known work was an able translation of the *Aeneid* (1872). His verses were published in *The Dial, The Western Messenger*, and other journals and collected in *The Bird and the Bell* (1875).

Crane, Frank (1861–1928),   clergyman, columnist. At the height of his career, Crane was the most widely syndicated of American columnists. His mixture of quotations, truisms, and good sense won him an enormous following. Some of his writings were collected in *Adventures in Common Sense* (1916); *Four-Minute Essays* (10 v. 1919); and *The Crane Classics* (10 v. 1920).

Crane, [Harold] Hart (1899–1932),   poet. Born in Ohio, Crane was a poet from the age of thirteen on. Little understood by his unsympathetic father, a well-to-do Cleveland candy manufacturer who sought to make a man out of him, or by his doting mother, who alternately indulged and denied him, Hart Crane had his full quota of misery in adolescence and merely compounded it in manhood. The Cranes quarreled violently over their son. Education stopped for him with the public schools, but at seventeen, after six months at his maternal grandfather's fruit ranch on the Isle of Pines, he came to New York City to write and to prepare for college. His talents and his precocity, however, recommended him to the bohemian literati, and his education was permanently postponed. This may have been his salvation as a poet, for Crane could pick up what he wanted as he ran. His mind had none of the trammels that the college man unconsciously acquires. A deficient substance, a want of allusiveness, is not Crane's limitation. He knew Donne, Marlowe, Poe, Melville, Whitman, Dickinson, Laforgue, Rimbaud, Dostoevski, Eliot, and Sandburg better than casually and reflected them in his verse. Irregularly employed, Crane forged ahead as a poet.

From *Bruno's Bohemian* he moved on to the *Little Review*, *Pagan*, *Poetry*, and *The Dial*. In 1926 appeared WHITE BUILDINGS, his first volume of verse. He appealed to Otto Kahn for financial aid, and it was through the largesse of that modern Maecenas that THE BRIDGE (a limited edition inscribed to Kahn, 1929; general edition, 1930) was written. A Guggenheim Fellowship carried him to Mexico and work on a poem on Montezuma, and it was on his return from Vera Cruz, on the steamship *Orizaba*, that he took his life by leaping overboard.

In 1933 appeared Crane's *Collected Verse*. Incorporated in this, the earlier *White Buildings* signalizes at once both his debt to T. S. ELIOT and his revolt against that Missouri Oxonian. Crane looked upon *For the Marriage of Faustus and Helen*, the major piece in this first volume, as "an answer to the cultural pessimism" of Eliot. The Fausti of the world—its poets—are bidden to enjoy the evanescent yet perdurable beauty of its Helens. Bathing in the "gleaming tides" cleanses one of pessimism and makes one newly generative, as it did Erasmus. There is a "world dimensional for those untwisted by the love of things irreconcilable. . . ." Passionate perception rather than intellectual scrutiny is the proper character for the vision of the poet. This idea is central in Crane and is his meaning when elsewhere he writes that "wine redeems the sight." Crane's own clear vision found its most loved object in this first volume— "that great wink of eternity," the sea. His best pieces all have to do with it: "Emblems of Conduct," "North Labrador," "At Melville's Tomb," and "Voyages."

Loving the sea, Hart Crane was drawn to Rimbaud and his *Le Bateau ivre* rather than to Coleridge, for the former immerses himself whereas the latter merely floats. Rimbaud's methods and his effects were closely studied by the Ameri-

can—in technique Rimbaud was Hart Crane's master. But this should be observed: Crane struggled to fuse more disparate impressions than Rimbaud ever brought together, and he sought to reach the ultimate in aesthetic economy, as a letter to Harriet Monroe elucidating one of his poems makes clear. Crane's incoherence comes from this physical effort, but so too do some of his grandest effects—as when he describes Brooklyn Bridge as "harp and altar of the fury fused." He is at his best, however, when from inspiration drawn from love, the economy of expression is natural and not forced:

> The sun beats lightning on the waves,
> The waves fold thunder on the sand.

The element ever invited him: he is the Palinurus of American poets.

Hart Crane has his monument in the Brooklyn Bridge, the structure that inspired his greatest poem and a poem which, after all its faults have been enumerated, is still one of the best of modern times. In his letters to Otto Kahn, since published in *Hound and Horn*, Crane makes clear not only the symphonic structure of his masterpiece but also states the "movements" of the composition with considerable explicitness.

Yet the wrong emphasis must not be put upon his declaration, "What I am really handling, you see, is the Myth of America." Allen Tate, for all his devotion to Crane, did his friend an unwitting disservice in asserting that "if we subtract from Crane's idea its periphery of sensation, we have left only the dead abstraction, the Greatness of America. . . ." Why this operation should ever be performed upon *The Bridge* is a mystery; it is comparable to saying that if we subtract the music from Dvořák's *New World Symphony*, all we have left is a dead abstraction, the Greatness of America. The truth is that what Tate describes as sensation—the imagery, the symbolism—is the poem itself, whereas the "Myth of America" (not quite the same thing as "the Greatness of America") is peripheral. As Crane carefully explains to Otto Kahn, one can get "the chronological historical angle" from "any history primer." He meant, and he succeeded in getting, his music and his imagery to suggest great passages out of the American Myth to a meditative mind partially narcotized by the symphonic flood. We should inquire not whether he presents a plausible legend, like Homer, but whether the total experience is plausible, whether the myth is introduced naturally or is forced.

Though Crane wrote Allen Tate that his poem is not perfectly "realized," its realization is closer than he allowed. Of all the poems by moderns that have the analogy of musical composition for their design, *The Bridge* is the most satisfactory. Crane has carried nearest to perfection the idea that teased Whitman, Lanier, Mallarmé, Pound, Eliot, and Wallace Stevens. Though a measure of his greatness, the total composition is not his chief triumph; it is the fusing of fire and water in his scintillating imagery, fire of the poet's passionate heart and water, not merely of the aqueous humor but of the tidal depths and shallows, such as lovingly laved the Parsee, Starbuck, Ahab—and the White Whale. *Hart Crane: Complete Poems*

(Centennial Edition, 2000) was edited by Marc Simon. Paul Mariani, *The Broken Tower* (1999) is a biography.

Oscar Cargill/GP

Crane, Nathalia [Clara Ruth Abarbanel]

(1913–   ),   novelist, poet. Some of her poems were submitted for publication when she was nine and were accepted as adult productions. *The Janitor's Boy* (1924), her first collection, created a sensation; later collections—*The Singing Crow* (1926), *Pocahontas* (1930), and *Swear by the Night* (1936)—puzzled and pleased readers. There was much naiveté, but also an astonishing command of poetic technique, the obvious influence of Emily Dickinson, and some philosophizing. Her later books include a dramatic poem, *Death of Poetry* (1941). *The Sunken Garden* (1926) tells of the Children's Crusade, and *An Alien from Heaven* (1929) is a novel.

Crane, Stephen [Townley]

(1871–1900),   war correspondent, novelist, short-story writer, poet. The fourteenth child of the Reverend J. T. Crane, presiding elder of the Newark district in New Jersey, and Mary Helen Peck Crane, Stephen started life with printer's ink in his veins, as both his parents were writers and two of his brothers were newspapermen. He wrote stories when he was but eight; at sixteen he did ghost writing for his New York *Tribune* correspondent brothers and reporting for his mother's column in that paper.

Crane grew up in full rebellion against the Methodist strain in his family tradition and engaged in the vices that his father—a learned divine, a manuscript preacher, and a noted wit—preached against and wrote about: baseball, which Stephen preferred to books; the theater, to which he aspired by writing plays; and novels, which he not only read but wrote. Nor would his father have approved of Stephen's having love affairs with a woman who was already betrothed (Helen Trent), with a woman who was already married and who later obtained a divorce (Lily Brandon Munroe), with an actress (Amy Leslie), and with the twice-married hostess and proprietress of a nightclub brothel (Cora Howorth, also known as Cora Taylor).

A woman of broad culture, Stephen's mother was the daughter of the Reverend George Peck, an eloquent Methodist minister and at one time the editor of the *Christian Advocate*, official organ of the Methodist Episcopal Church. A niece of Bishop Jesse Peck, one of the founders of Syracuse University, she was much concerned in the cause for temperance. She died when Stephen was beginning his twenty-first year, and his father had died eleven years before. As for the soldier strand in Crane's heritage, the Cranes during the American Revolution, to quote Stephen Crane: "were pretty hot people. The old man Stephen served in the Continental Congress (for New Jersey) while all four sons were in the army . . . the family is founded deep in Jersey soil (since the birth of Newark), and I am about as much of a Jerseyman as you can find."

Schooled in Asbury Park and then at the Pennington Seminary (New Jersey), Crane attended Claverack College and the Hudson River Institute (1888 to 1890). After a semester at Lafayette College, where he joined Delta Upsilon, he spent one semester at Syracuse University (spring, 1891), and there, in the Delta Upsilon house, he wrote the first draft of Maggie: A

Girl of the Streets. Knowing then little about the Bowery, slum life, and prostitution, Crane invented the plot of his story about a girl turned streetwalker—trapped by her environment. His literary source was Flaubert's *Madame Bovary*, Crane's *Maggie* being *Madame Bovary* recast in Bowery style. He published *Maggie* at his own expense in 1893. The *Tribune* published five of his Sullivan County sketches and *Cosmopolitan* magazine published "A Tent in Agony" in 1892. In the latter part of his twenty-first year he began writing The Red Badge of Courage, completing the first draft early in 1893, and in his twenty-third year he spouted off the verses of The Black Riders, which was published in 1895. *The Red Badge* (1895) first appeared in a short newspaper version in the Philadelphia *Press* from December 3 to December 8, 1894. His third novel, George's Mother, begun in 1893 and completed late in 1894, was not published until 1896, when *Maggie* was reissued in revised form and in hard covers. The London edition (1896) had the variant title *Maggie: A Child of the Streets*. In that year he also issued a collection of short stories, The Little Regiment and Other Episodes of the American Civil War, and in 1897 published his fourth novel, *The Third Violet*, which he had completed at the end of 1895. Crane described it as the story "of life among the younger and poorer artists in New York."

Crane spent the early part of his twenty-third year out in the Far West and in Mexico, traveling for the Bacheller and Johnson syndicate to gather material for sketches and short stories. The main thing he wrote out West, apart from newspaper sketches such as "Mexican Sights and Street Scenes," was a war tale, "A Mystery of Heroism." His only western tale in that year (1895) was "Horses—One Dash!" which he wrote in Philadelphia while trying to hire himself out to the Philadelphia *Press* as drama critic. His best western tales were written much later. The single perfect bead on his string of western tales is "The Bride Comes to Yellow Sky," which he wrote in England in 1897. The Blue Hotel also was written in England in 1898.

In 1896—he was then celebrated on both sides of the Atlantic as the author of *The Red Badge of Courage*—two articles about him pointed out the important fact that Crane's ancestry included several clergymen and soldiers. "It is an interesting study in heredity," said the *Monthly Illustrator*, "to note the influence of these two professions in Mr. Crane's literary work, the one furnishing the basis of style, the other of incident." Crane got from his parents not only a natural bent for writing but also a marked predilection for frequently casting his ideas, incidents, and even his style in biblical form or fashion.

Irving Bacheller sent Crane to Jacksonville, Florida, to cover a filibustering expedition to Cuba, and en route there on the *Commodore* he was shipwrecked on New Year's Day of 1897. He recreated his experiences after the *Commodore* disaster in The Open Boat, which has been called one of the finest short stories in the English language. Meanwhile, he had fallen in love with Cora Taylor at her Hotel de Dream, in Jacksonville. During his final three years in England she lived with him as his wife. Unable to get to Cuba, Crane went to Greece as war correspondent for the New York *Journal*. Writing under the pseudonym "Imogene Carter," Cora was with Stephen in

Greece—the first woman war correspondent. When the Greco-Turkish war ended, they went to London, and in July 1897, rented a house at Oxted, Surrey. There Stephen soon began his close friendship with Joseph Conrad. In April 1898, Crane left England for Cuba to report on the Spanish-American War, leaving Cora behind to manage somehow. In New York City he tried to enlist in the Navy, but was turned down. He accepted an offer of the New York *World* and submitted twenty dispatches from Cuba, including "Stephen Crane's Vivid Story of the Battle of San Juan" (the *World*, July 14, 1898). On being refused an advance by Pulitzer's paper, he switched to the New York *Journal* and sent it twenty dispatches between August 5 and November 9. The war was over by mid-August, but Crane stayed on in Havana to write story after story, article after article. There he also wrote the first draft of ACTIVE SERVICE (1899), a novel of the Greek war, which he reworked when he finally returned to Cora and England nine months after his departure. He and Cora settled at Brede Place, a 14th-century manor house in Sussex, and the pair bled themselves financially by entertaining a constant stream of guests, some of them uninvited—"Indians," Crane called them.

No sooner had he landed in England than creditors leaped at him, and financial troubles and ill health plagued Crane during his stay at Brede Place, the last full year of his short life. Threatened with bankruptcy, he tried desperately to write himself out of debt, but never succeeded. He began writing three types of stories: tales of western American life similar to "Twelve O'Clock"; the Whilomville tales of childhood (published posthumously as WHILOMVILLE STORIES, 1900); and more war tales, two of them short masterpieces: "Upturned Face," published in *Ainslee's Magazine* (March, 1900) and "An Episode of War," which was first printed in the posthumous collection *Last Words* (1902). After *The Open Boat and Other Tales of Adventure and Pictures at War*, which duplicates *The Little Regiment* collection but adds to it *The Red Badge of Courage*, Crane published the next year (1899) WAR IS KIND, his second volume of poetry; *Active Service* and THE MONSTER AND OTHER STORIES, its title story having appeared in 1898 in *Harper's Magazine*. That concludes Crane's book list except for posthumous publications such as *Bowery Tales, Whilomville Stories*, and WOUNDS IN THE RAIN (1900); *Great Battles of the World* (1901); *Last Words* (1902); and *The O'Ruddy* (1903), a romance left unfinished by Crane and completed by Robert Barr.

The panic of his snarled finances and his hopeless prospects for survival is evoked in the letters Stephen and Cora wrote James B. Pinker, Crane's literary agent and financial godfather in London, particularly during Crane's last months in 1900. (See R. W. Stallman and Lillian Gilkes, eds., *Stephen Crane: Letters*, 1960.) Suffering from tuberculosis, Crane collapsed early in April 1900, and on the advice of medical specialists, he left Dover—Conrad, H. G. Wells, and Robert Barr seeing him off—for the Black Forest in Germany, where at Badenweiler he died on June 5. Cora sailed on the *Bremen* from Southampton with Crane's body and, after a service at the Metropolitan Temple in New York City, Stephen was buried in the Crane family plot at Hillside, New Jersey. Cora returned to Jack-

sonville, Florida, in 1902 and built a new house on the Row called the Court, which she operated until her death at forty-five in 1910. (See Lillian Gilkes, *Cora Crane: A Biography of Mrs. Stephen Crane*, 1960.)

Seeing Crane for the last time, H. G. Wells wrote in the *North American Review* (August 1900): "If you would figure him as I saw him, you must think of him as a face of a type very typically American, long and spare, with very straight hair and straight features and long, quiet hands and hollow eyes, moving slowly, smiling and speaking slowly, with that deliberate New Jersey manner he had, and lapsing from speech again into a quiet contemplation of his ancient enemy. For it was the sea that had taken his strength, the same sea that now shone . . . warm and tranquil beneath the tranquil evening sky."

The notion that Crane died "tragically young," "a boy spiritually killed by neglect," is contradicted by the fact that no man of his generation was more admired and loved or received greater critical recognition. What killed him was not literary neglect but his own will to burn himself out, his Byronic craving to make of his body "a testing ground for all the sensations of life." "I decided that the nearer a writer gets to life, the greater he becomes as an artist," said Crane, whose training as a newspaper reporter accounts in part for his theory. He subscribed to Hamlin Garland's veritism, the theory that art is founded on personal experience and copies reality, and to W. D. Howells's critical standard of "realism," which meant truth and fidelity to the facts of experience; almost everything Crane wrote was motivated by this principle. Yet his art was at its greatest when he wrote at some distance from the reality he had experienced, or when, on the other hand, he wrote out of no personal experience—as in *The Red Badge of Courage*. As artist he transcended the realities which as journalist he felt committed to know at first hand. In a frenzied search for experiences, he needlessly expended himself, exhausted his health, and thus wasted his genius. He produced too much, he kept repeating himself, and too often the artist succumbed to the journalist, especially in *Active Service, Great Battles of the World*, and in *The O'Ruddy*.

Although his works were published in the 19th century, he and Henry James, particularly, mark the beginning of modern American fiction. Crane's writings look backward to Twain and forward to Hemingway, who praised *The Red Badge of Courage* as "one of the finest books of our literature . . . it is all as much of one piece as a great poem is." While Crane's influence can be documented by a formidable catalogue of specific echoes in later American fiction, it persists more significantly in less subtilized form: his naturalistic outlook is found in modern novels of slum life, and his concept of the soldier as Everyman, in modern novels of war. Maggie's brother is a forebear of Studs Lonigan, and Crane in several of his stories ("An Episode of War" is one example) foreshadows Hemingway. *A Farewell to Arms* is an inverted *Red Badge of Courage*: the one deals with disenchantment and withdrawal, the other with quest and ironic triumph. Crane in his use of dialect and in his stories of childhood is linked to Kipling and Twain, and his best-known follower is Booth Tarkington. Crane's Tom Sawyer is Jimmie Trescott in "Making an Orator," and his SULLIVAN COUNTY SKETCHES (collected by Melvin Schoberlin in 1949) and *Whilomville Stories* had their inspirational source in Twain's *Roughing It* and *Life on the Mississippi* (Crane's favorite book). More important is the kinship Twain and Crane establish in the history of American literature: they each brought new subject matter into fiction. *The Red Badge* has the same form as *Huckleberry Finn* in its repetitions of ironic episodes; both works deal with heroes in quest of selfhood.

Crane's importance is less, however, that he brought new subject matter into fiction, than that he was an innovator in technique and a unique stylist. *The Red Badge of Courage* is a literary exercise in language, in the patterning of words and the counterpointing of themes, tropes, and colors; it is far more than a war novel to be praised for its realism. It is a symbolic construct. No work of art is what it appears to be. Crane's style is prose pointillism. It is composed of disconnected images that coalesce like the blobs of color in French impressionist paintings, every word group having a cross-reference relationship, every seemingly disconnected detail being interrelated to the configured whole. There is a striking analogy between Crane's use of colors and the painting method of the French impressionists; it is as though he had known about their theory of contrasts and had composed his own prose paintings by the same principle. "Impressionism was his faith," said his painter friend R. G. Vosburgh. As H. G. Wells concluded: "There is Whistler even more than there is Tolstoy in *The Red Badge of Courage*."

Like *The Red Badge*, *Maggie* and *The Open Boat* are constructed by a concatenation of striking contrasts, alternations of contradictory moods. Crane's fiction at its best probes the thought and actions of trapped or baited men fighting the destructive forces in nature, in other men, or in themselves. Crane is always dealing with the paradox of man's plight. Paradox patterns his best stories and defines their kinship—for example, "The Bride Comes to Yellow Sky" and "The Upturned Face." Every Crane story worth mentioning is designed on a single ironic incident, and they are all concerned with virtually the same problem: the moral problem of conduct. It is the same with the works of Joseph Conrad. Technically, Crane's affinities are with Chekhov, whose stories build up to a crucial moment of impasse and collapse—nothing happens. Crane, like Chekhov, is a master of the contradictory effect. All Crane stories end in irony; *Maggie* and *George's Mother* end not with a bang, but with a whimper.

In *Maggie* Crane broke new ground. The then seemingly sordid realism of that story of the demiworld of New York City initiated the subsequent literary trend of the next generation. *Maggie* anticipated the sociological realism of Frank Norris, Theodore Dreiser, and James T. Farrell (see NATURALISM). *Maggie*, however, is not a realistic photograph of slum life. Not copyistic of reality, *Maggie* is rather a tone painting like *The Red Badge* and "The Open Boat." They are all exemplars of the art novel—a category to which all Crane's best works belong. A great stylist, Crane uses language poetically, that is, reflex-

ively and symbolically. The works that employ this reflexive and symbolic language constitute what is permanent of Crane.

Collected editions are *The Virginia Edition of the Works of Stephen Crane* (10 v. 1969–1976) and *The Works of Stephen Crane* (12 v. 1925–1927). Stanley Wertheim and Paul Sorrentino edited *The Correspondence of Stephen Crane* (2 v. 1988). Biographies include those by Christopher Benfey (1992), James B. Colvert (1984), and R. W. Stallman (1968), and, earlier, by Thomas Beer (1923) and John Berryman (1950).

R. W. STALLMAN/G.P.

Crapsey, Adelaide (1878–1914), poet. Daughter of a noted heterodox minister, Adelaide Crapsey was born in Brooklyn and raised in Rochester, New York. She attended school at Kemper Hall, Wisconsin, and Vassar College, later studying archaeology in Rome. During most of her brief life she was a teacher of literature at private girls' schools and at Smith College. Most of her poetry was composed in her last year, when she was dying of tuberculosis at Saranac. Delicacy, firmness, and concentration are the principal characteristics of her verse, and its most typical form is the "cinquain," an innovation of Crapsey's (derived from Japanese lyric forms, the *tonka* and *haiku*), a five-line, unrhymed stanza, with successive lines of two, four, six, eight, and two feet. A collection of poetry, *Verse* (1915), and an unfinished technical study, *Analysis of English Metrics* (1918), were published posthumously.

Crater, The, or, Vulcan's Peak (1847), a novel by JAMES FENIMORE COOPER. On an island in the Pacific is created a Utopia, happy and successful until several clergymen, a lawyer, and an editor sow seeds of dissension. At the end the island and its people sink into the sea. The book expresses Cooper's disillusionment with democratic procedures.

Crawford, F[rancis] Marion (1854–1909), novelist, short-story writer. The nephew of JULIA WARD HOWE and son of Thomas Crawford (1813–1857), the sculptor whose circle is portrayed in Hawthorne's *The Marble Faun*, Crawford was born in Bagni di Lucca, Tuscany, Italy. He was educated by private tutors in Rome and at Trinity College, Cambridge; the Technische Hochschule in Karlsruhe, Germany; the University of Heidelberg; and Harvard. A world traveler with a reported command of 16 languages, he became one of the most successful American novelists of his time. In three decades, he wrote over forty novels; in the best he combined detailed observations of countries he knew well with a skillful command of narrative. From 1885 to the end of his life he lived in Sorrento, Italy.

Crawford's first novel, *Mr. Isaacs: A Tale of Modern India* (1882), earned him immediate fame. It is a story of a diamond merchant, based on a man Crawford had met when he lived in India and edited the *Indian Herald* in Allahabad (1879–80). The novel anticipated Kipling in portraying Indian life for Western readers. His next, also based on fact, was *Doctor Claudius: A True Story* (1883); it told of a Swedish-born Ph.D from Heidelberg with an American fortune who weds a Russian countess. Among his best is a trilogy on a powerful Roman family at the end of the 19th century: *Saracinesca*

(1887), *Sant' Ilario* (1889), and *Don Orsino* (1892). His other novels set in Italy include *A Roman Singer* (1884), based in part on Crawford's own ambition to be an opera singer; *To Leeward* (1884) and *Pietro Ghisleri* (1893), of marriage and love between English girls and Italian men; *Marzio's Crucifix* (1887); *Casa Braccio* (1895), of the love of an Italian nun for a Scot; *Corleone: A Tale of Sicily* (1897); and *The White Sister* (1909), of another nun torn by love. His novels set in Germany include *Greifenstein* (1889), on university life, and *A Cigarette-Maker's Romance* (1890). Among his American novels are *An American Politician* (1884), a Gilded Age novel; *The Three Fates* (1892) of a young author's loves; and *Katherine Lauderdale* (1894) and *The Ralstons* (1895), studies of New York society. Among his historical romances, *In the Palace of the King* (1900) won particular praise for its portrayal of Philip II's Spain; others include *Zoroaster* (1885), set in ancient Persia; *Via Crucis* (1898), about the second crusade; *Marietta* (1901), set in 15th-century Venice; and *Arethusa* (1907), set in 14th-century Constantinople. Among his other novels, *A Tale of a Lonely Parish* (1886) has been praised for its portrayal of English country life. His short-story collections include *The Upper Berth* (1894) and *Wandering Ghosts* (1911, published also as *Uncanny Tales*). Crawford also wrote a play, *Francesca Da Rimini* (1901), and collaborated on dramatic versions of *Doctor Claudius* and *The White Sister*. In *The Novel: What It Is* (1893) he details his theories of fiction as a popular art of entertainment. His works also include three histories of Italy.

Crawford, Isabella Valaney (1850–1887),   Canadian poet. After emigrating from Ireland, Crawford spent her short life mainly in Ontario. In 1884 she published a collection of her verses, *Old Spookses' Pass*, many Canadian in setting. In 1905 a selection from her writings, *Collected Poems*, was edited by John W. Garvin.

Crawford, John Wallace [Jack]   (1847–1917), miner, soldier, Indian fighter, Indian agent, poet known as the "Poet Scout." Born in Ireland, Crawford was at first a miner, then a fighter in the Civil War, later chief of scouts for the Black Hill Rangers, and finally a rancher on the Rio Grande. He published *The Poet Scout* (1879) and other volumes in verse and prose, including *The Broncho Book* (1908).

Crayon, Geoffrey.   The pseudonym under which WASHINGTON IRVING published *The Sketch Book* (1819). The name later appeared in *The Crayon Miscellany* (1835), including *A Tour of the Prairies*, *Legends of the Conquest of Spain*, and *Abbotsford and Newstead Abbey*.

Crazy Horse (1849?–1877).   A Sioux chieftain who, with Sitting Bull, led his tribe in an uprising (1875) against the white invasion of the Black Hills. In the course of the conflict, General Custer was killed (1876) at the Battle of the Little Big Horn. Crazy Horse plays an important role in John G. Neihardt's *Song of the Indian Wars* (1925). His Native American name was Tashunca-uitco. He was killed while resisting imprisonment. Mari Sandoz published a biography (1942).

Cream of the Jest, The (1917, rev. 1920),   a novel by JAMES BRANCH CABELL. This comedy of evasions is the story of

an author, Felix Kennaston, who by means of a hieroglyphic disk escapes into a dream world where he pursues a changing yet always similar image of his loved one. She turns out to be his wife.

Creek Indians.   A confederacy covering about fifty towns in Alabama and Georgia, most of whose members spoke a Muskhogean language. They were a settled, agricultural people who were named by whites who observed their settlements along creeks and rivers. De Soto visited them in 1540. In colonial days, they befriended the English against the Spanish and sold their coastal lands to Oglethorpe for his Georgia colony. Later, pressed by white settlers, they followed the lead of the SHAWNEE chief TECUMSEH in opposing white advances; the result was the Creek War of 1813–14 in which they were defeated by Andrew Jackson at Horseshoe Bend, in Alabama. In subsequent treaties they ceded their lands to the United States and in the 1830s they were removed to Oklahoma, where they became one of the FIVE CIVILIZED TRIBES. WILLIAM GILMORE SIMMS, whose father served in Jackson's army, visited the Creeks and they appear in his verse and fiction. They appear also in WASHINGTON IRVING's *A Tour of the Prairies* (1835) and in the works of Chateaubriand. Creek writers include ALEXANDER POSEY and JOY HARJO.

Creekmore, Hubert (1907–1966),   poet, novelist, critic. Creekmore was born in Mississippi, and his novels reflect the depth of his feelings for the South, where his family lived since the 18th century. *The Chain in the Heart* (1953) is the story of three generations of an African-American family, from just after the Civil War to 1930. Creekmore's poetry invades his prose to its advantage. Among his books are *Personal Sun* (1940), *The Stone Ants* (1943), *The Fingers of Night* (1946), *The Long Reprieve* (1946), *Formula* (1947), *The Welcome* (1948), and *No Harm to Lovers* (1950). *A Little Treasury of World Poetry* (1952) includes translations from Egyptian, Babylonian, and Chinese, as well as European and South American verse. His *Lyrics of the Middle Ages* appeared in 1959.

Creeley, Robert (1926–   ),   poet. Born in Arlington, Massachusetts, Creeley drove an ambulance in World War II, dropped out of Harvard, helped CID CORMAN establish *Origin*, and pursued a career as a poet in France and on Majorca before returning to the United States. Identified with the BLACK MOUNTAIN POETS, he established THE BLACK MOUNTAIN REVIEW and taught briefly at BLACK MOUNTAIN COLLEGE, where he was an associate of CHARLES OLSON, ROBERT DUNCAN, and EDWARD DORN. In the 1950s he also visited San Francisco and met such BEAT GENERATION writers as ALLEN GINSBERG, JACK KEROUAC, and GARY SNYDER. In the ensuing years, in addition to some time spent in Latin America, he taught at a number of American colleges. His poetics is open, derived from Pound and Williams, inspired by jazz and abstract art. Distrusting metaphor, he seeks a plain speech in which each word will represent itself only, often expressed in short lines. *The Collected Poems of Robert Creeley, 1945–75* was published in 1982, and *So There: Poems 1976–83* in 1998. Other collections include *For Love, Poems 1950–1960* (1960); *Words* (1967); *The Charm:*

Early and Uncollected Poems (1969); *Selected Poems* (1976); and *Memory Gardens* (1986). *A Day Book* (1972) combines prose and poetry. *The Collected Prose of Robert Creeley* (1984) includes *The Island* (1963), a novel, and *The Gold Diggers* (1954), stories. *The Collected Essays* appeared in 1989 and *Tales Out of School: Selected Interviews* in 1993.

Creole. A term used in the United States to designate the descendants of early French settlers in Louisiana, especially New Orleans, as distinguished from the exiled Acadians, known as Cajuns, who arrived later. Early Creole society was aristocratic in culture and manners, and its members prided themselves on the purity of their French. Later, the term was applied to a class of comparatively well-to-do French-speaking persons of mixed African-American and white ancestry who were among the chief artisans and petty tradesmen of New Orleans toward the end of the 19th century. In the West Indies, the term signified a person of European, usually Spanish ancestry; in Haiti, at one time, an African-American born in the New World rather than one brought from Africa. Creole life in Louisiana in the 19th century is depicted in fiction by GEORGE WASHINGTON CABLE, GRACE KING, and KATE CHOPIN.

Crespi, Juan (1721–1782), a Spanish explorer and missionary who accompanied Gaspar de Portola (1723?–1784) in his thousand-mile march north from Mexico that resulted in discovery of San Francisco Bay. His diaries have survived and appear in H. E. Bolton's *Fray Juan Crespi, Missionary and Explorer* (1927).

Crèvecoeur, St. John de (1735–1813), writer of descriptions of America. Born Michel Guillaume Jean de Crèvecoeur in France, Crèvecoeur came to the New World in 1755 as a surveyor for the French colonial army. After discharge in 1759 he explored the Atlantic seaboard from Maine to Virginia, then westward to the present St. Louis, Chicago, and Detroit. In 1765 he became a citizen of New York under the name of J. Hector St. John. In 1769 he married and settled in Orange County, New York, where he became a substantial landholder and farmer. He celebrated his experiences as a farmer and interpreted the new nation developing in America in a series of charming and keenly observant essays written in a disarmingly unpretentious style. A lover of peace, he regretted the American Revolution and its division of neighbors into patriots and tories. In 1779, leaving his wife and two children at home, he began a journey to France with his older son to secure his children's inheritance. After detention in New York City by the occupying British forces and wartime transportation delays, he reached London in 1781. There he sold to an English publisher a collection of his sketches, presented as letters to an English friend, and they were published as LETTERS FROM AN AMERICAN FARMER in 1782.

In France he translated, revamped, and augmented the sketches into *Lettres d'un cultivateur Américain*, published in France in 1784. He was lionized in French circles as the typical settler of the new American nation. He became a friend of Jefferson and corresponded with Franklin and Washington. He returned to America in 1783 as French consul to New York, New Jersey, and Connecticut. On arrival he found that his wife

was dead and that their house had been destroyed during the war but that the children had survived. During sick leave in France he enlarged his French *Lettres*, published in 1787 in three volumes.

In 1790 Crèvecoeur retired from his position and returned to Europe, where he lived his later years with his daughter and her husband. In 1801 his *Voyage dans la Haute Pensylvanie et dans l'état de New-York* was published in Paris. In 1813 he died at his son-in-law's home in Sarcelles.

Letters from an American Farmer is now a recognized classic. It describes life in America as an idyll. Purportedly written by Farmer James, a native-born Pennsylvanian, its sketches tell of the opportunities available to immigrants in America. Several essays eulogize the pleasures of an independent farmer. The celebration of the possibilities of life in America includes essays on Nantucket, which its inhabitants have made into a deeply rewarding culture despite its physical limitations. The most famous essay poses the question, What is an American? and then answers, in the earliest expressions of America as a melting pot, that he is an immigrant who has become a new man because of the new context in which he lives. A charming chapter tells of a visit to the Pennsylvania botanist JOHN BARTRAM; a contrasting one describes the horrors of slavery in South Carolina. The final chapter reports the coming of the Revolution, when the bucolic idyll is destroyed and the Native Americans seem to offer the only rational way of life in peace.

In 1925 a volume of previously unpublished Crèvecoeur essays was located among the family papers and published as *Sketches of Eighteenth Century America*. The supplement the *Letters*, and several describe aspects of the Revolution from a loyalist perspective. These manuscripts, those of the 1782 *Letters*, and additional unpublished sketches in English were obtained by the Library of Congress in 1986. A biographical and critical study is Thomas Philbrick, *St. John de Crèvecoeur* (1970).

EVERETT EMERSON

Crews, Harry [Eugene] (1935–), novelist and journalist. Crews, a Southerner, writes with sardonic humor about obsessed, decadent, or grotesque characters in bizarre situations. He first gained recognition with *The Gospel Singer* (1968), which was followed by such novels as *The Hawk Is Dying* (1973), *The Gypsy's Curse* (1974), *A Feast of Snakes* (1976), and *All We Need of Hell* (1987). *A Childhood: A Biography of a Place* (1978) is a vivid evocation of the Georgia of his youth. Selections from his column in *Esquire* magazine were published in *Blood and Grits* (1979). Other works dealing with his generally redneck world include *Florida Frenzy* (1982); a story collection, *Two* (1984); *The Knockout Artist* (1988); *Body* (1990); *Scar Lover* (1992); *The Mulching of America* (1995); and *Celebration* (1998), a black comedy about aging in a Florida trailer park. *Classic Crews: A Harry Crews Reader* appeared in 1993.

Crichton, Kyle [Samuel] (1896–1960), author, editor. Educated at Lehigh, Crichton worked in coal mines and steel mills and was an associate editor of *Scribner's Magazine* and *Collier's Weekly*. Under the pen name Robert Forsythe, he wrote for the *Daily Worker* and the *New Masses* the biting articles on American celebrities collected in *Redder Than the Rose* (1935) and *Reading From Left to Right* (1936). Under his own name he wrote illustrated interviews for *Collier's Weekly* and published a number of biographies, including *The Marx Brothers* (1950), and two novels: *Proud People* (1944), a story of a Spanish family in New Mexico, and *The History of the Adventures of George Whigham and His Friend Mr. Clancey Hobson* (1951), a farce on New York society.

Crichton, [John] Michael (1942–   ),   novelist, screenwriter. Born in Chicago, educated at Harvard (A.B., summa cum laude, 1964; M.D., 1969), Crichton helped finance medical school with pseudonymous paperback thrillers by "John Lange" and "Jeffrey Hudson"; one of these, *A Case of Need* (1968), found unexpected success with its account of a Chinese-American physician accused of an abortion performed on the daughter of a prominent surgeon. The next year, while he was still a student, the first of his major books, *The Andromeda Strain* (1969), about a deadly microorganism from outer space threatening life on earth, confirmed a career as a writer of thrillers set most frequently in the zone where science merges with extrapolations of fantasy to produce immensely popular novels and films. By 2000, *Newsweek* had proclaimed him "the most financially successful novelist of the day." Not especially adept at characterization, he pulls the reader forward with well-researched illuminations of esoteric subject matters combined with inventive, life-threatening plots. Novels include *The Terminal Man* (1972), in which a brain is implanted with misfiring electrodes; *The Great Train Robbery* (1975), a 19th-century thriller largely divorced from science; *Congo* (1980), scientists, diamonds, voice recognition software, and killer apes; *Sphere* (1987), a submerged spacecraft, black holes, submarine technology, and a killer squid; *Jurassic Park* (1990), one of his most acclaimed novels and a blockbuster Steven Spielberg film, with rampaging dinosaurs, DNA replication, and chaos theory; *Rising Sun* (1992), politics, but no science; *Disclosure* (1994), computers and sexual harassment; *The Lost World* (1995), *Jurassic Park* revisited; *Airframe* (1996), aerodynamics and Bernoulli's principle; and *Timeline* (1999), an absorbing, carefully researched time-travel adventure, bringing scientists from contemporary Arizona to 14th-century France. Nonfiction includes *Five Patients: The Hospital Explained* (1970), *Electronic Life: How to Think about Computers* (1983), and the autobiographical *Travels* (1988).

Cries of New York, The (1814).   This was described as "printed and sold by Samuel Wood in the Juvenile Book-Store." It is perhaps the most important of the little books of "Cries" prepared toward the beginning of the 19th century as vocational guides for children who expected to engage in peddling or other occupations. Vocational advice was accompanied by short homilies encouraging the small peddlers to industry. The books often expressed indignation at the plight of chimney sweeps exposed to cold and hardship.

Crisis (1910–34),   a journal of the NAACP, edited by W. E. B. DU BOIS.

Crisis, The (1901),   a historical novel by WINSTON CHURCHILL. The action centers in St. Louis during the controversy over free and slave states; the hero, Stephen Brice, is a Yankee; the heroine, Virginia Carvel, a Southerner. The novel shows the inevitability of war, yet stresses that neither side wanted it and includes a notable portrait of Lincoln.

Crisis, The American,   a series of sixteen pamphlets by THOMAS PAINE. The first appeared in the *Pennsylvania Journal* on December 19, 1776, and within the week was issued also in three pamphlet editions. The last appeared on December 9, 1783. The first, signed "Common Sense," has remained most famous. It begins "These are the times that try men's souls. The summer soldier and the sunshine patriot will in this crisis, shrink from the service of his country; but he that stands it Now, deserves the love and thanks of man and woman." Written, according to tradition, on a drumhead, it inspired the army at a time when defeat seemed nearly certain. Washington had it read to each regiment and, within days, struck successfully across the Delaware and won victories at Trenton and Princeton, with Paine participating in both battles. Others in the series continued the call for determination in the struggle.

Crisp, Quentin [Denis Pratt] (1908–1999),   writer, actor. Denis Pratt, born in a London suburb, adopted the name Quentin Crisp after an unhappy childhood, gay in a straight world. Beginning as a prostitute, book illustrator, and nude model in the 1930s, he became famous with *The Naked Civil Servant* (1968), an account of his openly gay life in London. He had decided early, he wrote, to dedicate his life to "making the existence of homosexuality abundantly clear to the world's aborigines." A dramatized version shown on American television in 1976, starring John Hurt, brought him American attention, and from 1977 on he lived in Manhattan's East Village, celebrated for his feminine manner and flamboyant appearance, sometimes in women's dresses and makeup. *An Evening with Quentin Crisp* played Off Off Broaway in 1978. Books include *How to Have a Lifestyle* (1979), *How to Become a Virgin* (1984), and *Resident Alien* (1997).

Critical Fable, A (1922),   an imitation of James Russell Lowell's FABLE FOR CRITICS (1848) from the pen of his kinswoman AMY LOWELL, who discusses a score of the poets of her time.

Criticism and Fiction (1891),   collection of critical essays by WILLIAM DEAN HOWELLS, first published in Howells's column "The Editor's Study" in *Harper's Magazine* (1886–91). In these, Howells presents his views of REALISM AND NATURALISM and of the relationships between literature, national life, and morality.

Croaker Papers, The.   A series of humorous verses that appeared from March 10 to July 24, 1819, in the New York *Evening Post* under the pseudonym Croaker & Company. Croaker was the name of a doleful character in Oliver Goldsmith's *The Good-Natured Man* (1768). In the *Post* verses Croaker was JOSEPH RODMAN DRAKE. Croaker, Jr. was his intimate friend, FRITZ-GREENE HALLECK; the authorship was never admitted. A pirated edition appeared in 1819; a collected edition, called *The Croakers*, in 1860.

Crockett Almanacs. See DAVY CROCKETT.

Crockett, Davy (1786–1836), frontiersman, public official, soldier, autobiographer. Crockett's father was a veteran of the Revolutionary War and an Indian fighter. Crockett was born in Tennessee, went to school for a while, and married at eighteen. The Crocketts moved to a new settlement on the Mulberry Fork of the Elk River. There, says Crockett, "I began to distinguish myself as a hunter and to lay the foundation for all my future greatness." He became a tremendous killer of "b'ars," engaged in the Creek War under General Jackson and won his commendation, decided he could collect votes as easily as he killed "b'ar," and became a politician. He dispensed rough justice as a magistrate, was elected first to the Tennessee legislature and then to Congress, and became known as the coonskin Congressman.

Long an outspoken admirer of Andrew Jackson, Crockett changed sides in January 1829. Immediately the newspapers and pamphlets of the time reversed themselves, and he suddenly became the hero of the Whig faction, the villain of the Jacksonians. In either case, Crockett's experiences became grist for the humor of the period, and he became legendary during his own lifetime. To set people straight, Crockett wrote his own *Narrative of the Life of David Crockett* (1834), possibly with assistance. In 1835 there appeared *An Account of Col. Crockett's Tour to the North and Down East*, perhaps rewritten by someone else from Crockett's notes. He opposed Jackson on the issue of a national bank and, greatly to his credit, he was against the president's orders to break the treaty with the Creeks. Finally defeated, he made up his mind to help the Texans win their independence, and died fighting at the Alamo. He was speedily made a major demigod of American folklore who could talk the language of animals, ride the lightning, lie with extravagant grandeur, and whip his weight in wildcats. *Colonel Crockett's Exploits and Adventures in Texas* (1836) appeared shortly after his death. The three Crockett volumes were combined as *The Life of Davy Crockett* in 1899.

To Americans of his day, Crockett was the supreme exponent of mother-wit and one of the earliest to show disdain, largely assumed, for mere book-larnin'. Actually, he took some care to become educated himself and to give his children proper schooling; one of his sons became a teacher. Constance Rourke calls his *Narrative* "a classic in our literature because it was one of the first to use the American language with fullness and assurance, and because it reveals a way of life in a distinctive style." Even before Crockett's death the almanac makers, perhaps with his approval, began to turn to him for subject matter, and from 1835 to 1856 the almanacs continued to appear. About fifty issues of *Crockett Almanacs* have been discovered. They gave meteorological and astronomical data in addition to information on natural history and sometimes introduced Daniel Boone, Mike Fink, the sea serpent, and other figures in folklore. But, says Constance Rourke, "Crockett remained the dominating figure—the mythical, comical Crockett."

He has appeared in many short stories, novels, plays, ballads, and folklore collections. J. K. Paulding probably had Crockett in mind when he drew the character of Col. Nimrod Wildfire in THE LION OF THE WEST (1831). In 1933 the Carolina Playmakers produced John Philip Milhous's folkplay *Davy Crockett, Half Horse, Half Alligator*. A "ballet ballad" called *The Eccentricities of Davy Crockett* was produced in New York in 1948. Constance Rourke's *Davy Crockett* (1934) is an important biographical study, and Richard M. Dorson wrote the authoritative *Davy Crockett, American Comic Legend* (1939). J. A. Shackford's *David Crockett: The Man and the Legend* (1955) chiefly presents the historical Crockett. The Nashville Series of the *Crockett Almanacs* was reprinted in 1955.

Crosby, Frances Jane ["Fanny"] (1820–1915), hymn writer. Although blind from infancy, Crosby began composing hymns in 1864, and completed some six thousand, it is believed. The most famous was "Safe in the Arms of Jesus." She published several collections of verse, also *Fanny Crosby's Life Story, by Herself* (1903). John Hawthorne wrote her biography (1931).

Crossing, The (1904), a novel by WINSTON CHURCHILL that depicts the settlement of the Inland Empire. It begins in North Carolina, continues to the unsettled West, and closes in New Orleans. George Rogers Clark, Simon Kenton, and Daniel Boone appear in the novel.

Crossing, The (1994), volume two of CORMAC MCCARTHY's *Border Trilogy*.

Crossing Brooklyn Ferry (1856 in LEAVES OF GRASS, where it was called *Sun-Down Poem*; somewhat revised in 1881), a poem by WALT WHITMAN. Whitman loved to sit in the pilothouse of the picturesque vessels that carried crowds of passengers and many horse-drawn vehicles between Manhattan and Brooklyn. The poet expresses his intense feeling of identification with "the great tides of humanity" and praises physical objects, the "dumb, beautiful ministers."

Cross of Gold speech. See W. J. BRYAN.

Cross of Snow, The, poem by HENRY WADSWORTH LONGFELLOW. In an Italian sonnet, Longfellow laments the death of his second wife, Frances Appleton, burned to death in their home in 1861. Written in 1879, the poem remained unpublished during the poet's lifetime and was first printed by Samuel Longfellow in his *Life* of his brother (1886).

Crothers, Rachel (1878–1958), playwright. Born in Illinois, and educated at Illinois State Normal School, Crothers studied acting in New York and became for many years the most successful woman playwright in America. Generally she was in complete control of her plays, writing, directing, and sometimes acting in them, and earned a reputation especially for witty social satire. Her dominant theme—woman's attempt to escape social oppression and find her own place in the world—informed many of her more than thirty plays from 1903 to 1937. They include *The Three of Us* (1906); *A Man's World* (1909), in which a woman writer raises the illegitimate son of a deceased friend, but refuses on moral grounds to marry the father, whom she loves; *He and She* (originally *The Herfords*, 1912), on a woman's choice between her career and family responsibility; *Young Wisdom* (1914); *Nice People* (1921), on liberated women; *Mary the Third* (1923); *Expressing*

Willie (1924); *Let Us Be Gay* (1929), on divorce; *As Husbands Go* (1931); *When Ladies Meet* (1932), on adultery; and *Susan and God* (1937), on a marriage threatened by a woman's religious fervor. With KATE DOUGLAS WIGGIN she collaborated on *Mother Cary's Chickens* (1917), from the Wiggins novel.

Crothers, Samuel McChord (1857–1927),   clergyman, essayist. Born in Illinois, at first a Presbyterian then a Unitarian minister, Crothers became a center of liberal faith in the Midwest. He was later a preacher in Boston and Cambridge. As an essayist of mellow wisdom and humor, Crothers first won fame with *The Gentle Reader* (1903). Other books are *The Pardoner's Wallet* (1905), *By the Christmas Fire* (1908), and *The Cheerful Giver* (1923).

Crouse, Russel (1893–1966),   newspaperman, historian, playwright, producer. Born in Ohio, Crouse worked for nearly twenty years on various newspapers in the Midwest and in New York before he entered the theater. In 1931 he wrote the libretto for the musical comedy *The Gang's All Here*. He established himself as an author with two books on 19th-century American life, *Mr. Currier and Mr. Ives* (1930) and *It Seems Like Yesterday* (1931). In 1934 he met HOWARD LINDSAY and began work on the book for the musical *Anything Goes*; their partnership became one of the most successful in American theater. Their collaboration produced LIFE WITH FATHER (1939), based on the books by Clarence Day, which ran for eight years; STATE OF THE UNION (1945), a satire on American politics which won the Pulitzer Prize; *Life with Mother* (1948), based on other stories by Clarence Day; *Call Me Madam* (1950); *The Great Sebastians* (1956); and *Tall Story* (1959). Crouse also wrote the book on which *The Sound of Music* (1960) was based. With Lindsay he produced Joseph Kesselring's ARSENIC AND OLD LACE (1940).

Crow Indians.   Native American people speaking a Siouan language. Counted among the PLAINS INDIANS, they inhabited the area around the Yellowstone River and its tributaries. They cultivated tobacco and were traditional enemies of the BLACKFEET and the SIOUX, fighting beside the U.S. Army against the latter. JAMES P. BECKWOURTH described his life among them in *Life and Adventures* (1856). Another early portrait is in WASHINGTON IRVING's *Adventures of Captain Bonneville* (1837). They are viewed from a Blackfeet perspective in JAMES WELCH's *Fools Crow* (1986).

Croy, Homer (1883–1965),   newspaperman, novelist. Croy began his career by writing for country, and later city, newspapers. He was the first person to travel around the world taking motion pictures. Although his novels are mainly humorous, *West of the Water Tower* (1923) is a serious, realistic story that reflects the influence of Dreiser and Hardy. Croy wrote many books on American folklore and frontier history, among them *Wheels West, the Story of the Donner Party* (1955) and *Last of the Great Outlaws, the Story of Cole Younger* (1956). *Our Will Rogers* (1953) is a biography of the humorist. Croy's other works include *How Motion Pictures Are Made* (1918); *They Had to See Paris* (1926), which became Will Rogers's first talking picture; *Mr. Meek Marches On* (1941); *Family Honeymoon* (1942); *Jesse James Was My Neighbor* (1949); *Lady from

Colorado (1957); *Trigger Marshall* (1958); *The Star Maker: TV Story of D. W. Griffith* (1959).

Crucible, The (1953),   a play by ARTHUR MILLER. This play about the SALEM WITCHCRAFT TRIALS opened at New York in 1953. Its first audiences saw parallels between the search for satanic conspirators in 17th-century Salem and for Communist conspirators in the America of Senator Joseph McCarthy. Later audiences, however, have concentrated on the Salem drama itself and its moral issues. *The Crucible* powerfully dramatizes the hysteria that swept through Salem in the form of a fear that Satan was possessing the town. The play explains this upheaval as an entirely natural happening. It presents the instigators of the panic as people unwilling to accept their shortcomings, people who blame the devil and his helpers for their own lust, greed, or ambition. They spread confusion and suspicion as well as terror. The counterforce in *The Crucible*, and the protagonist of the play, is the farmer John Proctor, one of many accused of witchcraft. Proctor is clearheaded, sensible, and responsible. Unlike his accusers he has brought himself to acknowledge his faults, especially his infidelity to his wife, and has been strengthened by this self-knowledge. At the climax of the play he confesses his sinfulness but will not permit Danforth, the cunning prosecutor, to exploit his guilt. He refuses to sign the confession that would misrepresent his sin, destroy innocent friends, and justify the witch trials. His death on the gallows affirms his humane values in an inhumane time.

FRANK McHUGH

Cruz, Sor Juana Inés de la (1648–1695),   Mexico's first major poet and playwright. Of illegitimate birth, she was early recognized as a prodigy and spent time at the viceroy's court before deciding on the life of a nun. In the convent, she incurred the displeasure of her superiors by filling her cell with books, scientific paraphernalia, maps, and musical instruments, and by continually writing poetry and plays. Criticized for her activities and for neglecting her religious duties, she wrote a celebrated defense of intellectual freedom for women as well as men, her *Respuesta a Sor Filotea de la Cruz* (1691). Nevertheless, she gave up her studies and writing at age forty, sold her library of 4,000 volumes, and turned to care of the poor. Ministering to others in a plague, she contracted the disease and died.

Her early poems were somewhat conventionally erotic, Gongorist in style. In "Primer sueno," she turned her Gongorism to the support of metaphysics as she described a soul's struggle toward knowledge. Other poems were more clearly Mexican in tone, marking the beginning of a Spanish poetic tradition in Mexico separate from that of Spain. Alan S. Trueblood translated some of her poems in *A Sor Juana Anthology* (1988). OCTAVIO PAZ wrote a critical biography, *Sor Juana: Her Life and Her World* (1982, tr. 1988).

Crying of Lot 49, The (1966),   a novel by THOMAS PYNCHON.

Cudjo's Cave (1864),   a novel by J. T. TROWBRIDGE. It describes conditions in Tennessee during the early years of the Civil War, particularly relations between Confederate and

Union sympathizers. The cave of the title serves as a refuge for runaway slaves and Union supporters.

Cullen, Countee (1903–1946), poet, teacher. Born in New York City, the adopted son of a Harlem minister, Cullen was educated at New York University and Harvard. An African-American poet of widely acknowledged genius, Cullen became widely known with his first book, *Color* (1925). Thereafter he won many awards, particularly for poems on racial themes. He wrote one novel, *One Way to Heaven* (1932), and edited *Caroling Dusk: An Anthology of Verse by Negro Poets* (1927). Later collections of his own verse are *Copper Sun* (1927), *The Ballad of the Brown Girl* (1928), *The Black Christ and Other Poems* (1929), and *The Medea and Some Poems* (1935). A selection of his best verse is *On These I Stand* (1947). After 1934 he taught junior high school in New York and published stories for children: *The Lost Zoo* (1940) and *My Lives and How I Lost Them* (1942).

Cumberland, The. An American frigate that was sunk on March 8, 1862, in an encounter with the Confederate ironclad *Virginia* (originally, when under Union control, called the *Merrimac*). Its sinking meant the end of the wooden warship era, and a day later the *Virginia* was itself defeated by the *Monitor*. The sinking of the *Cumberland* inspired Thomas Buchanan Read's *The Attack*, Longfellow's *The Cumberland*, G. H. Boker's *On Board the Cumberland*, and Melville's *The Cumberland*.

Cummings, E[dward] E[stlin] (1894–1962), poet, playwright, essayist, painter. The chief formative influences on Cummings's career were three, beginning with family and education. Born in Cambridge, Massachusetts, he occupied himself with drawing pictures and writing poems from childhood on. His family was warm and close, and he attended the Cambridge Latin School. He then took degrees at Harvard, where he received a thorough grounding in classical, European, and English languages and literature. It is important to specify his scholarly background, for during the first half of his career he was regarded as an iconoclast and experimentalist, while during its second half he was revealed as a traditionalist in modernist dress. This should have surprised no one. Cummings was an authentic and original innovator who was, despite his characteristic pose as the innocent child, a meticulous craftsman and profoundly cognizant and respectful of the art of the past.

The second formative influence follows upon his move to New York City to pursue his career. The pressures of World War I were making themselves felt, however, and he enlisted in the Norton-Harjes Ambulance Corps in 1917. This move gave him his first view of Paris, and from there he was sent to the front. Soon, he and a friend aroused the suspicion of the nervous French censors by writing letters home that were critical of the conduct of the war. They were interrogated and sent to the detention center at La Ferté-Macé in Normandy to await the decision of the judicial commission that visited the center at three-month intervals.

Thus culminated Cummings's induction into the world at large. He was 23 years old and living in a big room with other prisoners under miserable conditions, where he experienced firsthand and early in the century what it means to be a political prisoner under concentration camp conditions. Released after three months, he returned to New York early in 1918 in a somewhat sadder state than when he had left. He was then drafted into the U.S. Army and spent the remaining time until shortly after the Armistice at Fort Devens, not far from Cambridge. Free again, he returned to New York to spend the rest of his life writing and painting.

The third influence has to do with Cummings's several marriages. The first was to Elaine Orr, with whom he had a relationship before their marriage in 1924. Their daughter Nancy had been born in 1919, but the marriage foundered and Cummings lost any legal rights to the child, who was raised entirely apart from him after her mother remarried. In the late 1920s he married Anne Barton, but their relationship ended soon after, and in the early 30s he met and married Marion Morehouse, a fashion model, actress, and photographer, who remained with him for the rest of his life.

Cummings traveled abroad frequently and in 1931 spent about a month in Russia, visiting writers and artists and touring the landmarks. Most of his summers were spent at Joy Farm in New Hampshire, which he inherited from his family, and it was there that he died, suffering a stroke after coming in to rest after splitting wood. He had not quite completed his 68th year.

Although the manuscript from which his first books of poems were drawn was ready by 1922, Cummings's first published book was THE ENORMOUS ROOM of that year, an idiosyncratic journal of his stay at La Ferté-Macé in which he celebrated the persecuted individual over the persecuting state. His first book of poems, *Tulips and Chimneys*, came out in the following year. Several more volumes, drawn from the original manuscript, were published in 1925—beginning Cummings's habit of unique titles—*&* and *XLI Poems*. The fourth book of poems, published in 1926, was called *is 5*, meaning two-times-two is a miraculous five rather than a sensible four. The prolific productivity of the first decade of his professional work was capped in 1927 by publication of a play called *HIM*, which is the name he gives to the protagonist, and so he calls the heroine Me.

From these titles alone it readily can be seen why Cummings came into prominence as an avant-gardist, and the volumes themselves confirm the reputation he earned of mixing lyric and satire, of sensuousness, sensuality, and an amazing openness to the physical world, both urban and rural. It is *Him*, however, that embodies, albeit in surrealist-poetic fashion, the painful struggle Cummings actually had with the potentially conflicting claims of marriage, art, and parenthood. Interestingly, the title page bears an ecstatic epigraph attributed to Anne Barton.

The 1930s saw the appearance of his next two volumes of poetry—*W* (ViVa) in 1931 and *No Thanks* in 1935—and of his *Collected Poems* (actually a selection) in 1938, that, along with *The Enormous Room*, became Cummings's most popular works. During this decade his capacity for experimentation was stretched to its utmost, and he began to find the limits of his life and art. *EIMI* (Greek for I am), published in 1933, is a journal—even more idiosyncratic than *The Enormous Room*—

of his trip to Russia, where he found, contrary to the opinion of many artists and intellectuals of the time, that the Soviet Union was, as he put it, another "enormous room" and not the socialist paradise it claimed to be.

Cummings brought out *50 Poems* in 1940 and *1 × 1* (One Times One) in 1944. These volumes reveal a somewhat more regularized use of poetic forms and a somewhat less sensual approach to life and love, accompanied by a deepening seriousness about love itself. *Santa Claus* appeared in 1946, a play in verse about a young daughter looking for her lost father—unquestionably a reflection of his broken relationship with Nancy, who in fact was reappearing in his life at just about this time. (*Fairy Tales*, although not published in book form until 1965, was probably written during the 1920s for Nancy when she was a little girl.) Two additional books of poems were published in the 1950s—*Xaipe* (Greek for Greetings! or Rejoice!) in 1950, and *95 Poems* in 1958—and *73 Poems* appeared posthumously in 1963.

Cummings's theory of art, which he inherited from the Romantics and Transcendentalists, was based on the attempt to catch the aliveness of the moment in poetic form, so his at-first startling array of experimental techniques must be seen in the service of that end. The aim is to counteract the bad habit language has of coming between us and the very reality we are trying to grasp and express by its means. Thus, to surprise us out of our habits, Cummings manipulates typography, imagery, structure, diction, punctuation, grammar, syntax, and the various forms of rhyme, meter, and free verse.

The ultimate goal, however, is not simply to collect "moments" à la Walter Pater. Cummings has sometimes been accused of not developing and maturing, and this charge is in part due to a lack of appreciation of that visionary core out of which his experiments come and which in turn give to these moments their artistic significance and value: To be truly in touch with the aliveness of the present moment is to make contact with Unity of Being itself and thus to find the polarities of matter and spirit, time and timelessness "annihilated," as Cummings put it.

His career was further distinguished by the many awards he received—a *Dial* award, several Guggenheims, an American Academy of Poets Fellowship, the Charles Eliot Norton Professorship at Harvard, a National Book Award, the Bollingen Prize, and the Boston Arts Festival Award. He was also in great demand to give readings of his poems.

E. E. Cummings: Complete Poems: 1904–1962 (1994), edited by George J. Firmage, supersedes earlier collections. His other works include a book with no title (1930), which is a collection of dadaesque satirical tales with accompanying drawings; *Anthropos* (1930), a playlet exemplum about the Artist vs. the State; *CIOPW* [charcoal, ink, oils, pencil, watercolor] (1931), a collection of art works; *Tom* (1935), a scenario for a ballet based on *Uncle Tom's Cabin*; *i:SIX NONLECTURES* (1953), autobiographical talks given at Harvard; *E. E. Cummings: A Miscellany* (1958, 1965), essays by the poet edited by George J. Firmage; *Adventures in Value* (1962), a book of photographs by Marion Morehouse, with captions by the poet; *Selected Let-*

ters (1969) edited by F. W. Dupee and George Stade; and *Etcetera: The Unpublished Poems of E. E. Cummings* (1983) edited by Firmage and Richard S. Kennedy. The definitive biography is Kennedy's *Dreams in the Mirror* (1980). Chief critical works are *E. E. Cummings: The Art of His Poetry* (1960) and *E. E. Cummings: The Growth of a Writer* (1964) by Norman Friedman; *E. E. Cummings: An Introduction to the Poetry* (1979) by Rushworth M. Kidder; and *Poet and Painter: The Aesthetics of E. E. Cummings's Early Work* (1987) by Milton A. Cohen.

NORMAN FRIEDMAN

Cummins, Maria Susanna (1827–1866), novelist. Cummins had her greatest success with THE LAMPLIGHTER (1854), the story of a Boston orphan girl, which was for many years a best seller. In another popular novel, *Mabel Vaughan* (1857), she portrayed a rich city girl from the East who conquers poverty and becomes a Midwestern pioneer. Her other novels include *El Fureidis* (1860) and *Haunted Hearts* (1864).

Cunningham, J[ames] V[incent] (1911–1985), poet, teacher. Born in Maryland, Cunningham was raised in Montana and educated at Stanford University. Most of his teaching career was spent at Brandeis University. A highly skilled poet of spare, satiric verse in traditional forms, he published his first book, *The Helmsman*, in 1942. Five more slim volumes preceded *The Collected Poems and Epigrams of J. V. Cunningham* (1971). *The Collected Essays* appeared in 1971. Timothy Steele, ed. *The Poems of J. V. Cunningham* (1997) is a gathering of all his verse.

Cuppy, Will[iam Jacob] (1884–1949), humorist, critic. Cuppy as a humorist made a specialty of burlesque books: *How to Be a Hermit* (1929), *How to Tell Your Friends from the Apes* (1931), and *How to Become Extinct* (1941). *The Decline and Fall of Practically Everybody* (1950), a book of unconventional history, became a best seller. Also a specialist on crime tales, he reviewed nearly four thousand detective and western novels for the New York *Herald Tribune Weekly Book Review*. *How to Attract the Wombat* (1949) contains a miscellany of pieces.

Curfew Must Not Ring Tonight! (1867), a poem by ROSE HARTWICK THORPE. It appeared in a Detroit newspaper and won immediate popularity with its sentimental tale of an English lord condemned to death for spying and saved by his sweetheart—she clings to the clapper of the bell that is supposed to announce curfew, the hour of his death. David Belasco drew on the ballad in his Civil War play, THE HEART OF MARYLAND (1895), which has a famous bell-clapper scene. Reprinted in *The New Yorker* magazine (1939), the poem was illustrated—and demolished—by JAMES THURBER.

Curtis, George Ticknor (1812–1894), lawyer, biographer, historian, author of legal treatises. Born in Watertown, Massachusetts, Curtis defended DRED SCOTT. He was a Whig and opposed to abolition, but during the war supported the Union cause. He published many books, including biographies of Daniel Webster (1870) and James Buchanan (1883), a constitutional history of the United States (1854–1858), and a treatise on copyright (1847). His *John Charakes* (1889) is a Civil War novel.

Curtis, George William (1824–1892), essayist, editor, orator. Born in Rhode Island, Curtis lived two years at Brook Farm as a youth and was influenced by Emerson and other transcendentalists. His travels in the Near East as a correspondent for the New York *Tribune* resulted in sketches collected as *Nile Notes of a Howadji* (1851), *The Howadji in Syria* (1852), and *Lotus-Eating* (1852). These were followed by THE POTIPHAR PAPERS (1853) and PRUE AND I (1856), New York sketches. *Trumps* (1861) is a novel of society and politics. Curtis edited *Harper's Weekly* (1863–92) and also earned a reputation as a lecturer and reformer. He supported antislavery, women's rights, and other liberal causes and served as president of the National Civil Service Reform League (1881–1892).

Curwood, James Oliver (1878–1927), novelist, writer of outdoor stories. Born in Michigan, Curwood wrote many books of wilderness adventure, especially in the Hudson's Bay area. Best known was *The Valley of Silent Men* (1920). Others include *The Courage of Captain Plum* (1908), *The Grizzly King* (1916), and *Nomads of the North* (1919). *Son of the Forest* (1930) is an autobiography.

Cushing, Frank Hamilton (1857–1900), ethnologist, explorer. Born in Pennsylvania, Cushing was always interested in Native American culture, and in later life made himself a great authority on the Zuñis. They adopted him as a member of their tribe and helped him with his researches. He discovered the so-called SEVEN CITIES OF CIBOLA and wrote treatises on *Zuñi Fetiches* (1881), *Myths of Creation* (1882), *Adventures in Zuñi* (1883), and *Zuñi Folk Tales* (1901).

Custer, Elizabeth Bacon (1842–1933), biographer, writer on frontier life. Born in Michigan, Custer accompanied her husband, General GEORGE ARMSTRONG CUSTER, throughout his army career. Her books include *Boots and Saddles, or, Life in Dakota with General Custer* (1885), *Tenting on the Plains* (1887), *Following the Guidon* (1890), and *The Boy General* (1901).

Custer, George Armstrong (1839–1876), army officer. Custer was born in Ohio and educated at West Point. Raised to the rank of brigadier general of volunteers (1863), Custer became the youngest general in the Union army. He fought at Gettysburg and in the Shenandoah Valley and was present at Lee's surrender at Appomattox. Later he served in the West as a lieutenant colonel with the 7th Cavalry, where he fought against the CHEYENNE at Washita (1868), and commanded an expedition into the Black Hills (1874) that led to renewed hostilities with the SIOUX. He died along with over 200 of his men at the Battle of Little Bighorn (1876), defeated by Sioux warriors led by SITTING BULL and CRAZY HORSE. He wrote *My Life on the Plains* (1874). See ELIZABETH BACON CUSTER.

Custis, George Washington Parke (1781–1857), playwright. Born in Maryland, Custis was the grandson of Martha Washington through her first marriage. Washington adopted him and his sister after the death of their father. Custis wrote several plays, including one on *Pocahontas* (1830), as well as *Recollections and Private Memories of Washington* (1860).

Custom of the Country, The (1913), a novel by EDITH WHARTON. The heroine is a beautiful but ruthless social climber named Undine Spragg who, through several marriages and divorces, samples the pleasures of money and aristocratic titles. Wharton satirizes the vulgarity of Midwesterners and the customs of the nouveaux riches.

Cynic's Word Book, The (1906), by AMBROSE BIERCE. See THE DEVIL'S DICTIONARY.

D

dada or **dadaism.**   A revolutionary movement in the arts begun in Switzerland in 1915 by students protesting the meaningless destruction of war; their most prominent figure was the poet Tristan Tzara. Their method consisted to a large degree of reducing sense to nonsense in poetry, drama, painting, and the dance. Its influence in Europe was short lived, in the United States brief. In New York it was introduced by Marcel Duchamp, Francis Picabia, and Arthur Cravan (a nephew of Oscar Wilde) and by an art exhibit at Grand Central Gallery in 1917. (This exhibit was revived in part at the Museum of Modern Art in 1961.) Duchamp's contribution to the exhibit was entitled "La Fontaine," a urinal. Though the sponsors of the exhibit managed to hide it behind a partition, it caused a sensation nonetheless, as did a speech filled with four-letter words delivered by Cravan. In 1929 Duchamp and Man Ray assembled a single number of a publication they called *New York Dada*. A few Americans in Paris momentarily were influenced by the dadaist creed: E. E. Cummings, Matthew Josephson, and especially Margaret Anderson, who published some dadaist work in the LITTLE REVIEW.

Daddy,   poem by SYLVIA PLATH. Written in 1962 and collected in Plath's posthumous ARIEL (1965), the poem is addressed to the poet's dead father, who is likened to a Nazi. Touching on suicide and on the speaker's relation to her husband, it is a good example of the revelation of personal pain that earned Plath recognition as a CONFESSIONAL POET.

Daedalus (1955–   ),   quarterly journal of the American Academy of Arts and Sciences.

Dahlberg, Edward (1900–1977),   novelist, essayist, poet. Born to a single mother in Boston, Dahlberg was raised in an orphanage and educated at the University of California, Berkeley, and Columbia. He won praise first as a novelist of social realism in *Bottom Dogs* (1929), about childhood in slums and an orphanage; *From Flushing to Calvary* (1932), set in New York City; and *Those Who Perish* (1934), about Nazism and American Jews. His short stories were collected in *Kentucky Blue Grass Henry Smith* (1932). Later Dahlberg became widely praised as an essayist with a wide range and learned style, mixing criticism, mysticism, satire, and comedy. His literary criticism and essays on modern society appear in *Do These Bones Live?* (1941, revised as *Can These Bones Live?* 1960); *The Flea of Sodom* (1950); *Truth Is More Sacred* (1961);

and *Alms for Oblivion* (1964). His classical studies include *The Sorrows of Priapus* (1957) and *The Carnal Myth* (1968). *Truth Is More Sacred: A Critical Exchange on Modern Literature* (1961) was written with Herbert Read. *The Confessions of Edward Dahlberg* (1971) is peopled with characters with names like Logic, Pity, and Dr. However Pointless. Dahlberg's poems are collected in *Cipango's Hinder Door* (1965). *The Olive of Minerva* (1976) is a comic novel. His letters are collected in *Epitaphs of Our Time* (1967). *Because I Was Flesh* (1964), counted one of his best books, is autobiographical.

Daisy Miller (1878),   a novelette by HENRY JAMES. James takes what he regards as a typically American girl and contrasts her to the sophisticated society of Europe. The book became one of the most popular of James's writings.

Daly, [John] Augustin (1838–1899),   drama critic, producer, playwright. Born in North Carolina, Daly was at first a writer about the stage for several New York papers and in 1862 produced his first play, *Leah the Forsaken*, an adaptation of a German work. He went on to write numerous plays, many of them adaptations. Some of his work was produced under his own direction—he made his first great success with the melodrama UNDER THE GASLIGHT (1867). He won success with plays of his own, plays by other authors, and revivals. On the stages of the various theaters he owned, including one in London, appeared many of the best actors of the day. HORIZON (1871) helped define the American West for theatergoers. *Divorce* (1871) and *Pique* (1875) were early approaches to the social problem play.

Daly, Elizabeth (1878–1967),   poet, mystery writer. Educated at Bryn Mawr and Columbia University, Elizabeth Daly went on to produce amateur plays and pageants. It was not until 1940 that her first book, *Unexpected Night*, appeared. Following on the creation of her urbane, bookish detective, Henry Gamadge, in *Unexpected Night*, Daly continued to publish a number of well-plotted whodunits. *Deadly Nightshade* came out in 1940; *Murder in Volume 2* in 1941; and *Wrong Way Down* in 1946.

Daly, Thomas A[ugustine] (1871–1948),   newspaperman, editor, columnist, poet. Born in Philadelphia, Daly won celebrity with a dialect poem, "Mia Carlotta," followed by others of the same kind, which were collected in *Canzoni* (1906), *Carmina* (1909), *Madrigali* (1912), *McAroni Ballads*

(1919), *McAroni Medleys* (1931), *Selected Poems of T. A. Daly* (1936), and *Late Lark Singing* (1946). Daly was an adept versifier who did Irish dialect as well as Italian. Poetry was his avocation; his newspaper column appeared first in the Philadelphia *Evening Ledger* in 1891, later in the *Evening Bulletin*.

Damnation of Theron Ware, The (1896),   a novel by HAROLD FREDERIC. It portrays a clergyman and the disintegration of religious orthodoxy toward the end of the 19th century in upstate New York.

Damon, S[amuel] Foster (1893–1971),   teacher, poet, critic, biographer. Damon mingled with literary figures and became an authority on Amy Lowell. His verses, collected in *Astrolabe* (1927) and *Titled Moons* (1929), are often humorous. His biographies of William Blake (1924) and Thomas Holley Chivers (1930); his orchestral suite, *Crazy Theater Music* (1938); his *Seven Songs* (1951); and other works show his versatility. He also wrote plays, among them *Witch of Dogtown* (1954) and *Punch and Judy* (1957).

Damrosch, Walter [Johannes] (1862–1950),   conductor, composer, broadcaster. Damrosch, who was born in Germany and came to the United States when he was nine years old, often found inspiration in American themes and books, as in the opera *The Scarlet Letter* (1894); *An Abraham Lincoln Song* (1936); *Death and General Putnam* (based on ARTHUR GUITERMAN's ballad, 1936); and THE MAN WITHOUT A COUNTRY (1937). During the 1930s his educational radio broadcasts for children formed the chief musical fare in many American schools. His father, Leopold Damrosch (1832–1885), was a noted conductor, the founder of the New York Oratorio Society (1873) and the New York Symphony Society (1878).

Dana, Charles A[nderson] (1819–1897),   newspaperman, reformer, editor, government official. Born in New Hampshire, Dana began as an ardent reformer who sought to cure the obvious ills of society with ideas put into practice in the BROOK FARM experiment. When that failed, Dana turned to newspaper work, first as editor of the Boston *Daily Chronotype*, then as city editor and later managing editor on the New York *Tribune*. But then he disagreed with HORACE GREELEY on the policies governing the Civil War and was fired. For a while he was connected with the War Department, finally becoming assistant secretary under Stanton.

After the war he bought the New York *Sun*, which he made the leading newspaper in the United States. He took as the motto of the paper: "If you see it in the *Sun*, it's so." H. L. Mencken said of Dana that he "produced the first newspaper on earth that was decently written." Dana wrote one book, *The Art of Newspaper Making* (1895).

Dana, Henry Wadsworth Longfellow (1881–1950), teacher, lecturer, editor, biographer. A descendant of RICHARD HENRY DANA, JR. and of Longfellow, Dana devoted several of his writings to them: *The Craigie House—The Coming of Longfellow* (1939), *The Dana Saga* (1941), *Longfellow and Dickens* (1943), and an edition of *Two Years Before the Mast* (1946).

Dana was also an authority on European drama, especially that of Russia, and the author of *A Handbook of Soviet Drama* (1938), *Drama In Wartime Russia* (1943), and *Seven Soviet Plays* (1948).

Dana, James Dwight (1813–1895),   geologist, zoologist. After participation in an expedition to the South Seas, Dana became professor of natural history at Yale. In 1837, when he was only twenty-four years old, he published his *System of Mineralogy*, which became a classic in its field. Dana, as he made clear in his *Manual of Geology* (1862), looked upon geology as a historical science. Other books of his are *Crustacea* (1852–54), *Corals and Coral Islands* (1872), and *Characteristics of Volcanoes* (1890).

Dana, Richard Henry, Sr. (1787–1879),   poet, editor, lecturer. Born in Cambridge, Massachusetts, Dana was trained as a lawyer but was mainly interested in writing. As associate editor of the *North American Review*, he accepted Bryant's *Thanatopsis* in 1817. He also contributed to numerous newspapers and magazines, gave lectures on literary subjects, and published *The Buccaneer and Other Poems* (1827) and *Poems and Prose Writings* (1833).

Dana, Richard Henry, Jr. (1815–1882),   writer, lawyer. Born in Cambridge, Massachusetts, Dana studied at Harvard under EDWARD TYRRELL CHANNING, who taught him—along with other famous pupils like Emerson, Holmes, Motley, and Parkman—something of the art of writing. In later years Dana edited Channing's brilliant lectures (1856). His sight suffered during his student days at Harvard, and rather than take a conventional pleasure voyage, he shipped out from Boston as a common sailor on the vessel *Pilgrim* in 1834. Gold had not yet been discovered, and the *Pilgrim* was heading for California to purchase hides. Dana returned home on the *Alert* in 1836, his health much improved. From the notes he kept in his journal he wrote what has become a classic of American literature, TWO YEARS BEFORE THE MAST (1840). His description of Cape Horn, the storms at sea, the little-known land which is now the state of California, in addition to his accounts of the abuses he and his mates suffered found attentive reception, and a number of maritime reforms came about because of Dana's accurate chronicle.

In the meantime Dana had reentered Harvard (1836) and a year later was graduated at the head of his class. For a while he taught at Harvard, but in 1840 was admitted to the bar. The oppression of sailors that he had witnessed gave him a fervent interest in seamen and he became known as the sailors' lawyer; his office, it is said, smelled like a forecastle, so crowded was it with men of the sea. He battled for them and their rights and compiled a manual, *The Seaman's Friend* (1841), that became an authority frequently consulted in the United States and in England. He was also an Abolitionist and was deeply interested in international law.

Dangling Man (1944),   a novel by SAUL BELLOW.

Daniels, Jonathan [Worth] (1902–1981),   newspaperman, writer, public official. The son of JOSEPHUS DANIELS followed in his father's footsteps, and after working for the

Louisville *Times* became a reporter for the Raleigh *News and Observer*, which his father owned. In 1948, on his father's death, Jonathan Daniels became its editor officially, though he had held that post unofficially in his father's lifetime. From 1943 to 1945 Daniels was administrative assistant to President Franklin D. Roosevelt. *Frontier on the Potomac*, which he published in 1946, describes the lively Washington scene of these years. He began his career as an author with a novel, *Clash of Angels* (1930), but he is best known for his candid depictions of conditions in North Carolina and elsewhere in the South, and in Washington. Among his books are *A Southerner Discovers the South* (1938); *A Southerner Discovers New England* (1940); *Tar Heels: A Portrait of North Carolina* (1941); *The Man of Independence* (1950, a life of President Truman); and *The End of Innocence* (1954), a rich store of Washington lore in the days of Woodrow Wilson, culled from the diaries of Daniels's father, Josephus, when he was secretary of the navy and ambassador to Mexico. *Prince of Carpetbaggers* (1958) was followed by *Stonewall Jackson* (1959); *Robert E. Lee* (1960); *The Time Between the Wars* (1966), covering the Harding through Roosevelt years; *The Randolphs of Virginia* (1972); and *White House Witness, 1942–45* (1975), about his years in various Washington posts.

Daniels, Josephus (1862–1948),   newspaperman, cabinet official, ambassador. Born in North Carolina, Daniels became a newspaper reporter when he was eighteen. He became editor of the Raleigh *News* in 1884 and continued as editor for the rest of his life. He became secretary of the navy under Wilson and was a capable administrator, but was widely attacked and caricatured for his attacks on privilege in the navy and for his insistence on making the navy "dry." In 1933 Roosevelt appointed Daniels ambassador to Mexico, and he did much to build friendly relations and close cooperation with that nation. He wrote a series of autobiographical volumes of historical value: *Editor: In Politics* (1940); *The Wilson Era* (2 v. 1944, 1945); and *Shirt Sleeve Diplomat* (1947).

Danites in the Sierras, The (produced, 1877; published, 1882),   a play by JOAQUIN MILLER. The plot revolves around an attempt of the Danites, a secret association of Mormons, to take revenge on Nancy Williams, a young girl who disguises herself in male costume and lives alone in a cabin in the Sierras to avoid their pursuit. The play, which shows the influence of BRET HARTE, was one of the most popular of frontier dramas and was equally popular in London when it played there in 1880.

Dannay, Frederic.   See ELLERY QUEEN.

Danticat, Edwidge (1969–   )   novelist, short-story writer. Born in Haiti, Danticat was left behind with an aunt and uncle while her parents sought economic advantage in the United States. Living with an extended family for the first twelve years of her life, she absorbed the folktales and history of her native island, as well as reading widely in French literature. After joining her parents in New York, she earned a degree in French literature at Barnard College and an M.F.A. in writing at Brown University.

Breath, Eyes, Memory (1994), her first novel, centers on Sophie's childhood in Haiti, her adolescence in New York, and eventual return to Haiti, where she is reunited with her mother. It was a selection of Oprah Winfrey's television book club. *Kric? Krak!*, a 1995 story collection, was nominated for the National Book Award. In it Danticat first dealt with the 1937 massacre of thousands of cane workers which is the background for her second novel, *The Farming of Bones* (1998). Amabelle Desir and Sebastien Onius, the Haitian lovers of the novel, are doomed by the terrible events surrounding them on the Dominican side of the island the two countries share. As a child, Danticat had heard family members' concerns about whether a repetition of history might endanger her relatives who had gone to work in the Dominican cane fields. From these overheard conversations and historical reading, she pieced together the facts of the brutal murders of ten to fifteen thousand Haitians, whose lives and deaths had almost completely disappeared from historical record.

Dao, Bei.   See BEI DAO.

D'Arcy, Hugh Antoine.   See THE FACE ON THE BARROOM FLOOR.

Dare, Virginia (1587–?),   first child of English parents born in America. Her parents were members of SIR WALTER RALEIGH's so-called lost colony on Roanoke Island.

Dargan, Olive [Tilford] ["Fielding Burke"] (1869–1968),   dramatist, novelist. Dargan wrote melodious verse, also several plays in verse. Among her collections are *Semiramis and Other Plays* (1904), *Lords and Lovers and Other Dramas* (1906), *Path Flowers and Other Poems* (1914), and *Lute and Furrow* (1922). As Fielding Burke she wrote two proletarian novels, *Call Home the Heart* (1932) and a sequel, *A Stone Came Rolling* (1935). Among her other books are *From My Highest Hill* (1941), *Sons of the Stranger* (1947), and *Spotted Hawk* (1958).

Daring Young Man on the Flying Trapeze, The (published in *Story*, 1934, and in the same year as the title work in a collection), a short story by WILLIAM SAROYAN. A mingling of fantasy and realism, this early work did much to establish its author's reputation.

Darío, Rubén [pen name of **Félix Rubén García Sarmiento**] (1867–1916),   Nicaraguan poet and essayist, famed as the high priest of MODERNISMO. Born in San Pedro de Metapa, Darío was raised by an aunt in León. He wrote verse as a child and was known in Central America as the boy poet. He visited Paris at twelve, then in Managua read widely in the National Library. In 1886 he went to Chile, where he published his first major work, *Azul* (1888), a collection of verse and prose sketches that bore the imprint of the French Parnassians and revealed the fondness for lush, exotic imagery that was to characterize his work. In 1890 he returned to Central America and the first of his two unhappy marriages. After a short visit to Spain in 1892, he moved to Buenos Aires. The appearance of *Prosas profanas* (1896, tr. 1922), in which the influence of the French SYMBOLISTS is fused with that of the Parnassians, marked the highpoint of the modernist movement. In 1898 Darío went again to Spain, now as a correspondent for a Buenos Aires newspaper. Much of the rest of his life was spent abroad. He was acclaimed by the intellectuals of Spain's *generación del 98*, who, like Darío, were profoundly affected by the outcome of the Spanish-American War. *Cantos de vida y esperanza*, generally regarded as his best work, appeared in 1905. It shows the technical excellence and lyric beauty of his earlier poetry as well as greater freedom and a new feeling for the native themes, which he had previously rejected. Darío's concern for "our America" is also evident in "A Roosevelt," a poetic diatribe against the U.S., motivated by the seizure of Panama in 1903, and in *Canto a la Argentina* (1910). Darío's later work reveals a growing disillusionment and despair. Although he was named Nicaraguan minister to Spain in 1908, his last years were marred by financial difficulties and poor health, due in part to heavy drinking. In 1915, after an unsuccessful lecture tour of the U.S., he was stricken by pneumonia in New York and died soon after his return to Nicaragua. Darío's influence on Spanish poetry can be measured by the statement of Pedro Henríquez Ureña that "of any poem written in Spanish, it can be told with certainty whether it was written before or after him." *The Selected Poems of Rubén Darío* appeared in English translation in 1965.

Darius Green and His Flying Machine (OUR YOUNG FOLKS, March 1867; in the collection *The Vagabonds and Other Poems*, 1869), a humorous poem by JOHN TOWNSEND TROWBRIDGE about a man who believed firmly that "the air is also man's dominion."

Dark Laughter (1925), a novel by SHERWOOD ANDERSON. The chief character, John Stockton, becomes weary of the shoddy newspaper work he is doing, drifts in an open boat down the Illinois and Mississippi Rivers, under the name Bruce Dudley starts working in a factory in his native town, is involved in an affair with his employer's wife, Aline Grey, and runs away with her. The white man, Anderson seeks to show, has been corrupted by civilization; and today only the African-American, with his "dark laughter," has escaped, showing scorn for the white man's lack of moral scruples.

Darling of the Gods, The (1902), a romantic tragedy by DAVID BELASCO and JOHN LUTHER LONG. The Princess Yo-San, betrothed to a man she does not love, sets him an impossible task—capture of a notorious outlaw, Prince Kara. Kara had once saved the life of Yo-San, but without revealing himself; now she tries to save him and does so by betraying the hiding place of his followers. But he returns to his men and dies with honor, surrounded by the dead bodies of the samurai. Long based the play on an incident in Japanese history. The play, lavishly produced, ran for two years and was also successfully presented in London, Berlin, and elsewhere.

Darley, Felix Octavius Carr (1822–1888), illustrator, lithographer, painter. Born in Philadelphia, Darley was best known for pen-and-ink illustrations for books, including works of Cooper, Hawthorne, Irving, Longfellow, Parkman, Simms, and other authors, American and English. He illustrated *The Library of Humorous American Works* (29 v. 1846–53). Among his other books are *Scenes in Indian Life* (1843) and *Sketches Abroad with Pen and Pencil* (1869).

Darrow, Clarence S[eward] (1857–1938), lawyer, lecturer, reformer, writer. Born in Kinsman, Ohio, Darrow had only a meager education, supplemented by books in his father's library but became the best-known lawyer and nonpolitical figure of his times. He practiced at first in Ohio, later went to Chicago and rose rapidly in his profession, becoming a highly paid railroad lawyer. But he was irked at the type of cases he had to defend, and his sympathy often lay with the lowly people who were suing the railroads. In the EUGENE DEBS case he resigned his position and won an acquittal for Debs; later he defended Nathan Leopold and Richard Loeb, murderers of young Bobby Franks in 1924, and saved them from being sentenced to death. He was chief counsel for J. T. Scopes, who was accused of violating Tennessee law by teaching evolution in a public school; in the resulting "monkey trial," Darrow lost his case but succeeded in destroying the reputation of the aging WILLIAM JENNINGS BRYAN, who argued in court on the side of the prosecution. (See SCOPES TRIAL.)

Irving Stone, in *Clarence Darrow for the Defense* (1941), speaks of the "amazing mixture of cynicism, compassion, and incredibly brilliant intelligence that made up Darrow's character." Darrow himself wrote two novels, *Farmington* (1904) and *An Eye for an Eye* (1905). He wrote *Crime: Its Cause and Its Treatment* (1922) and with Wallace Rice edited an anthology, *Infidels and Heretics* (1929). He told *The Story of My Life* (1932), in large part a continuation and expansion of *Farmington*. Paul Muni played him superbly in Jerome Lawrence and Robert E. Lee's *Inherit the Wind* (1955), a play based on the Scopes trial, later made into a movie (1960), and Darrow also figures largely in Meyer Levin's *Compulsion* (1956, a book, a play, and a movie), based on the Loeb-Leopold case. *Attorney for the Damned* (edited by Arthur Weinberg, 1957) contains nine of Darrow's summations and four speeches made outside the courtroom.

Daughter of the Middle Border, A (1921), HAMLIN GARLAND's sequel to his autobiographical narrative SON OF THE MIDDLE BORDER (1917). It deals with his marriage and later career.

Davenport, Guy [Mattison, Jr.] (1927–), essayist, poet, short-story writer, translator. Born in South Carolina, he was educated at Duke University, attended Oxford as a Rhodes scholar, and earned a Ph.D. at Harvard. Davenport's highly allusive fiction, including *Tatlin!* (1974), *DaVinci's Bicycle* (1979), *Eclogues* (1981), *Trois Caprices* (1982), *Apples and Pears* (1984), *The Jules Verne Steam Balloon* (1987), *The Drummer of the Eleventh North Devonshire Fusiliers* (1990), *A Table of Green Fields: Ten Stories* (1993), *The Cardiff Team: Ten Stories* (1996), and *Twelve Stories* (1997), aims to weave together elements of cultural experience from ancient to modern times. The introduction of historical figures, philosophical musings, dream sequences, and the juxtaposition of literary references from ancient Egypt to the 20th century produce a unique fictive style. Poetry is collected in *Flowers and Leaves: Poema vel sonata, carmina autumni primaeque veris transformationum* (1966), *The Resurrection in Cookham Churchyard* (1982), *Goldfinch Thistle Star* (1983), and *Thasos and Ohio: Poems and Translations, 1950–1980* (1986). An accomplished scholar, Davenport has translated the poetry of Sappho and others, written literary criticism, including *Cities on Hills: A Study of I–XXX of Ezra Pound's Cantos* (1983), as well as art and music criticism and libretti. *The Geography of the Imagination* (1981) and *Every Force Evolves a Form* (1987) are collections of literary criticism.

Davenport, James (1716–1757),   clergyman. The grandson of JOHN DAVENPORT, James Davenport wrote *Confessions and Retractions* (1744), an account of his activities as an itinerant preacher during the GREAT AWAKENING.

Davenport, John (1597–1670),   clergyman. Born in England and educated at Oxford, Davenport came to New England with Theophilus Eaton in 1637. In 1638 he helped found the New Haven colony, which he served as pastor until, after a dispute over the union of the New Haven and Connecticut colonies, he moved to Boston in 1667. Among his works is *A Discourse About Civil Government in a New Plantation Whose Design Is Religion* (1663).

Davenport, Marcia (1903–1996),   editor, music critic, biographer, radio commentator, novelist. As the daughter of the singer Alma Gluck, Davenport was born into the world of music, and her vivacious fiction frequently reflects this background. Her first book was a life of Mozart (1932, revised 1956); she followed this with a number of novels, including *Of Lena Geyer* (1936), about a musician; *The Valley of Decision* (1942), about Pittsburgh steel mills; *East Side, West Side* (1947); *My Brother's Keeper* (1954); and *Constant Image* (1960). A memoir is *Too Strong for Fantasy* (1967).

David Harum (1899),   a novel by EDWARD N. WESTCOTT. Published after the author's death, it met with instantaneous success and continued to sell steadily for many years; its total sale is well in the millions. In 1900 a stage version was presented, with William H. Crane as David, and later a film adaptation with Will Rogers. Subtitled *A Story of American Life*, the book tells the story of an upstate New York country banker, quaint and unlettered, shrewd but kindly, and given to homely sayings: "Do unto the other fellow the way he'd like to do unto you an' do it fust."

Davidson, Donald [Grady] (1893–1968),   critic, poet. Born in Tennessee, Davidson was a member of the FUGITIVE group of poets at Vanderbilt University, and one of the founders and editors of *The Fugitive* magazine. His Southern conservatism exerted a strong influence on younger Southern writers and intellectuals. He was a prominent member of the group that published I'LL TAKE MY STAND (1930), a collection of essays that served, in a sense, as the manifesto of recrudescent Southern agrarianism. In *The Attack on Leviathan* (1938) he made a critical analysis of economic centralization in the North. His poetry appeared in three volumes: *The Piper* (1924), *The Tall Men* (1927), and *Lee in the Mountains* (1938). He

taught at Vanderbilt University for many years. *Southern Writers in the Modern World*, a group of essays, appeared in 1958.

Davidson, Jo[seph] (1883–1952),   sculptor. After giving up his premedical studies at Yale, Davidson went to New York and then to Paris to study sculpture. He first attained prominence as the sculptor of many of the important figures at the Versailles Conference in 1918, including Woodrow Wilson, Marshall Foch, General Pershing, and Clemenceau. Later, he did busts of such literary figures as Anatole France and Walt Whitman and portrait busts of such eminent contemporaries as Franklin D. Roosevelt, Robert La Follette, Winston Churchill, Will Rogers, and Rabindranath Tagore. Davidson's autobiography, *Between Sittings*, was published in 1951.

Davidson, Thomas (1840–1900),   teacher, philosopher. Born in Scotland, Davidson came to Canada in 1866 and shortly thereafter began teaching in the St. Louis public schools. He founded several schools at which his own doctrines were taught, many of them representing a reaction against Hegelianism and a return to Plato and Aristotle. His Fellowship of the New Life (one of his English activities) is regarded as a forerunner of the Fabian Society, but Davidson himself was greatly opposed to socialism. Another of his schools was the Bread-Winner's College in New York, conducted for workers. In his biography of Davidson (1907) William Knight calls him "the wandering scholar"; William James's memorial article (1905) described him as "a knighterrant of the intellectual life." He wrote *Aristotle and Ancient Educational Ideals* (1892), *Education of the Greek People* (1894), and *The Education of the Wage-Earner* (1905). (See IDEALISM.)

Davies, [William] Robertson (1913–1995),   editor, essayist, dramatist, novelist. A senator's son, Robertson Davies attended Queen's University, Ontario, as a special student, and afterward Balliol College, Oxford. His thesis, *Shakespeare's Boy Actors*, appeared in 1939, by which time he was acting minor roles with the Old Vic Company in London. In 1940 he married Brenda Mathews, a girl he met at Oxford, and returned that same year to Canada as literary editor of *Saturday Night* magazine. Two years later he became editor and eventually publisher of the Peterborough *Examiner*, an association lasting twenty years. During that period Davies wrote a number of award-winning plays including *Overlaid* (1948), five one-act pieces published as *Eros at Breakfast and Other Plays* (1949), *Fortune, My Foe* (1949), and *A Jig for the Gypsy* (1954). *At My Heart's Core* (1950) is a three-act play based on the lives of the pioneering Strickland family (Susanna Moodie and Catharine Parr Traill). Meanwhile, Davies was also writing humorous essays under the name Samuel Marchbanks, an irascible Johnsonian eccentric living in Skunk's Misery, Ontario. These essays, offering scathing opinions on humankind in general and on Canadians in particular, were collected from the *Examiner* in *The Diary of Samuel Marchbanks* (1947), *The Table Talk of Samuel Marchbanks* (1949), and *Samuel Marchbank's Almanack* (1967).

But Davies's real metier was the novel, and he published three trilogies that comprise some of the best novels written in Canada. The first three, known as the Salterton trilogy, explore the problems of promoting culture in Canada. *Tempest-Tost* (1951) describes the misadventures of a group of amateurs involved in mounting a production of *The Tempest. Leaven of Malice* (1954) continues to make fun of Canadian provincialism with a plot that turns deftly on the repercussions ensuing from a false engagement announcement. This novel won the Stephen Leacock Medal for Humour and in dramatized form (titled *Love and Libel*) had a brief New York run in 1960. *A Mixture of Frailties* (1958) traces the unlikely development of a Salterton girl into a famous opera singer.

Davies did not achieve international fame as a writer until publication in 1970 of *Fifth Business*, the novel regarded as his masterwork. This first volume of the Deptford trilogy draws heavily on Jungian psychology, with characters that correspond to Jungian archetypes and a hero whose search for self-knowledge follows Jung's process of individuation. Dunstan Ramsay, the protagonist, loses a leg in World War I and becomes a history teacher in a private boys' school. His involvement with a madwoman and with a boy from his home town inform his lifetime pursuit to understand the relation of history to myth. Two sequels concern some of the same characters from the town of Deptford: *The Manticore* (1972), cast in the form of Jungian psychoanalysis, won the Governor General's Award for fiction; *World of Wonders* (1975), the story of a magician, completes the trilogy in which Davies argues that the concerns of the spirit are more important than worldly matters. Davies wrote the Deptford trilogy after assuming the post of master of University of Toronto's Massey College. A third trilogy, built around the life of eccentric art historian, Francis Cornish, satirizes academic life and probes the nature of good and evil as experienced by an artist. This trilogy consists of *Rebel Angels* (1981); *What's Bred in the Bone* (1985), for which Davies was nominated for a Booker Prize; and *The Lyre of Orpheus* (1988). *Murther and Walking Spirits* (1991) and *The Cunning Man* (1994) are his last.

Davies was also a prolific essay writer. Some of his best pieces appear in *A Voice from the Attic* (1960), *One Half of Robertson Davies* (1978), *The Enthusiasms of Robertson Davies* (1979), and *The Well Tempered Critic* (1981). Michael Peterman's *Robertson Davies* (1986) surveys the author's life and art.

DAVID STOUCK

Davis, Andrew Jackson (1826–1910),   lecturer, spiritualist. Known as the Poughkeepsie Seer, Davis delivered his lectures on mysticism and the occult from a hypnotic trance and collected them in *Principles of Nature, Her Divine Revelations, and a Voice to Mankind* (1847). His many other books include *The Great Harmonia* (1850), on spiritualism.

Davis, Angela (1944–   ),   political activist, writer. Born in Alabama and educated at the Sorbonne and Brandeis University, Davis earned celebrity in California as a professor of philosophy, communist, and Black Panther. Her writings include *If They Come in the Morning: Voices of Resistance* (written with others, 1971); *Angela Davis: An Autobiography* (1974); and *Women, Race and Class* (1981).

Davis, Charles Augustus (1795–1867),   merchant, newspaperman, humorist. During the great attack of humorists on Andrew Jackson's administration, the most widely read satires were those of SEBA SMITH, who in 1830 began to publish in the Portland *Courier* a series of letters, supposedly written by one Major Jack Downing and composed in homespun Down East speech. Then, in June 1833, the New York *Daily Advertiser* ran a series of letters, allegedly from the same J. Downing but really written by Davis, a member of the New York circle of literati. Davis was a staunch conservative, hostile to Jackson. The Davis letters became, according to Walter Blair, even better known than those of Smith, and "many historians mention Davis and not Smith as Downing's creator." The Davis letters were collected as *Letters of J. Downing, Major, Downingville Militia* (1834).

Davis, Clyde Brion (1894–1962),   newsman, novelist. Born in Nebraska, Davis worked on newspapers from coast to coast. One of the best of his novels is THE GREAT AMERICAN NOVEL (1938), the story of a newspaperman whose roving life is spent in dreaming about the great American novel he expects to write; meanwhile, his life is that novel. His books include *The Anointed* (1937), an ironical story of a sailor who thinks he is divinely inspired; *Nebraska Coast* (1939), a tale of pioneer life based in part on the experiences of Davis's family; *Follow the Leader* (1944), about a war hero; *The Rebellion of Leo McGuire* (1944), about a "good" burglar; *The Stars Incline* (1946), another newspaper story; *Temper the Wind* (1948), which tells of a garage mechanic who becomes a prize fighter; *Thudbury* (1952); *The Newcomer* (1954); and *The Big Pink Kite* (1960). He also wrote *The Arkansas* (1940), in the RIVERS OF AMERICA SERIES, and some amusing memoirs, *The Age of Indiscretion* (1950).

Davis, Elmer [Holmes] (1890–1958),   newspaperman, writer, news analyst. Indiana-born, Davis wrote *A History of the New York Times* (1921) after ten years on the paper's staff. He joined CBS in 1939, interrupted his work there to serve as director of the Office of War Information (1942–45), then returned to radio work. He also wrote novels and short stories, including *I'll Show You the Town* (1924); *Friends of Mr. Sweeney* (1925); *Strange Woman* (1927); and "Giant-Killer" (1928), a story of King David, with David taking credit for great deeds performed by others. A book of essays, *Not to Mention the War* (1940), was followed by *But We Were Born Free* (1954) and *Two Minutes Till Midnight* (1955), on nuclear arms. Roger Burlingame wrote a biography of Davis called *Don't Let Them Scare You* (1961).

Davis, Gussie L.   Composer of IN THE BAGGAGE CAR AHEAD.

Davis, H[arold] L[enoir] (1896–1960),   cattle herder, surveyor, sheriff, poet, novelist. Born in Oregon, Davis won a prize from *Poetry* (1919) and a Guggenheim Fellowship (1932). His HONEY IN THE HORN (1935), a story of frontier life in Oregon, took the $7,500 Harper Prize and the Pulitzer award for fiction. Later he wrote *Harp of a Thousand Strings* (1947), a narrative ranging from the western prairies to the French Revolution; *Beulah Land* (1949) and *Winds of Morning*

(1951), both frontier novels; *Team Bells Woke Me* (1953), a sheaf of fine short stories; and *Distant Music* (1957), a family chronicle set in southeastern Oregon. His poetry dealt with outdoor life.

Davis, Jefferson (1808–1889), soldier, statesman, author. Born in Kentucky and educated at West Point, Davis served in the Indian wars and in the war with Mexico; later he was a member of the House of Representatives, the Senate, and secretary of war under President Pierce. When the Civil War broke out, he was chosen as president of the Confederacy. Imprisoned at the end of the war, he was released after two years and spent his last years peacefully on his estate near Biloxi, Mississippi. He closed his *Rise and Fall of the Confederate Government* (2 v. 1881) with a call for an end to recrimination and held that "on the basis of fraternity and faithful regard for the rights of the states, there may be written on the arch of the Union, *Esto perpetua*."

Davis, John (1774–1854), English traveler, novelist. Among his books with American settings are *The Farmer of New Jersey* (1800); a sequel, *The Wanderings of William* (1801); THE FIRST SETTLERS OF VIRGINIA (1805); and *Walter Kennedy* (1805). Davis also published his *Travels in America* (1803). He says he traveled mainly on foot, and "entered, with equal interest, the mud-hut of the Negro and the log-house of the planter."

Davis, Ossie (1917–   ), actor, playwright, director. Born in Georgia, Davis was educated at Howard University and Columbia and served in the army from 1942 to 1945. In 1961 his comedy *Purlie Victorious* won major Broadway success; he played the black preacher who attempts to claim an inheritance from a white landowner. He has acted in numerous other stage productions, radio and TV plays, and films. With his wife, the actress Ruby Dee, he has been active in civil rights and other humanitarian causes. Films he has directed include *Cotton Comes to Harlem* (1970).

Davis, Owen (1874–1956), mining engineer, playwright, movie and radio scriptwriter. Born in Maine, Davis was educated at Harvard. As a writer, he began with a serious verse tragedy and, discouraged by its failure, went on to write innumerable melodramas. His plays include westerns, society plays, and plays with sexual themes. The best-known were *Nellie, the Beautiful Cloak Model* (1906) and *The Nervous Wreck* (1923). More literary are *The Detour* (1921) and *Icebound* (1923), which won a Pulitzer Prize. In his later years Davis collaborated with his son, Owen Davis, Jr. He successfully dramatized numerous novels, especially *Ethan Frome* (1936). Davis wrote his autobiography in *I'd Like to Do It Again* (1931) and added to it in *My First 50 Years in the Theatre* (1950).

Davis, Rebecca [Blaine] Harding (1831–1910), novelist, short-story writer. Born in Pennsylvania, Rebecca Harding lived as a child in Alabama and in Wheeling, Virginia (later West Virginia), and was educated in a seminary in Pennsylvania. Her "Life in the Iron Mills" was based on personal observation in Wheeling; published in the *Atlantic Monthly* (April, 1861), it earned her a reputation as one of the earliest American realists. She warned her readers "I want you to hide your disgust, take no heed to your clean clothes, and come right down with me—here into the thickest fog and mud and effluvia." *Margaret Howth* (1862) followed. Married to L. Clarke Davis, an editor, she lived most of her later life in Philadelphia, where some of her work is set. Her other novels include *Waiting for the Verdict* (1868), an ambitious study of the problems awaiting the country after the abolition of slavery, and *John Andross* (1874), about political corruption. Her later reputation was overshadowed by that of her son, RICHARD HARDING DAVIS.

Davis, Richard Harding (1864–1916), newspaperman, war correspondent, short-story writer, novelist, playwright. Called the Beau Brummell of the Press, Davis was nevertheless a reporter of great ability, undoubted courage, and wide information; and he was a master storyteller. Born in Philadelphia, the son of REBECCA HARDING DAVIS, he established himself in New York on the *Sun*, then went on to other newspapers. He covered assignments all over the world, reported many wars, major and minor, and talked to generals as an equal. Although forbidden by the rules of war, he took part in the Battle of San Juan Hill and was offered a commission by Theodore Roosevelt, which he declined. In World War I he was so eager to get to the battle line that he was almost shot by the Germans as a spy. When he reported the English boat races he wore a boating costume, and at the yacht-club races he was faultless as a yachtsman. He announced his engagement to the world by sending his fiancée a ring by a messenger boy who traveled 8,000 miles against all sorts of difficulties, with bulletins on his progress given daily to the press.

Davis's fiction is laid in countries all over the world, his characters of all varieties, but all highly theatrical. His style is the rapid communication of a reporter, and the plots are what Davis might have imagined as occurring in his own sensational life. One of his characters, Van Bibber is a socialite who is kind to the poor and gets mixed up in amusing adventures (*Van Bibber and Others*, 1892); young Gallegher is in the newspaper business (*Gallegher and Other Stories*, 1891); excitement is in the blood of Captain Macklin and others like him (*Captain Macklin*, 1902; *Soldiers of Fortune*, 1879); and suspense and danger can be found in London (*In the Fog*, 1901) or South America (*The Exiles*, 1894; *The Dictator*, 1904). Inevitably, Davis's stories found their way to the stage; he himself wrote more than twenty plays, some based on his own stories.

Davis surely was not a notable stylist, but he knew how to spin a yarn. Moreover, he well represented his age, the mauve decade. Out of a combination of his and CHARLES DANA GIBSON's talents emerged in the literature and popular art of the period a conception of an ideal American male: tall, handsome, constantly on the go, chivalrous, good to the poor and downtrodden, courageous, a keeper of the code of good manners and noble conduct. This ideal male did not long survive the events of the 20th century.

Davison, Peter [Hubert] (1928–   ), poet, editor. Born in New York City and educated at Harvard, Davison has written poems of New England and his family, often traditional in form, narrative in content. These include *Dark Hours* (1971), a biography of his father, and *Half Remembered* (1973), an autobiography. His other titles are *The Breaking of the Day* (1964), *The City and the Island* (1966), *Pretending to Be Asleep* (1970), *Walking the Boundaries* (1974), *A Voice in the Mountain* (1977), *Barn Fever* (1981), *Praying Wrong: New and Selective Poems 1959–1984* (1984), and *The Great Ledge* (1989). In 1972 he became poetry editor of the *Atlantic Monthly*. *Collected Poems* appeared in 1994 and *The Poems of Peter Davison, 1957–1995* in 1995. Davison has written essays and memoirs on the writing of other poets including *The Fading Smile: Poets in Boston 1955–1960, from Robert Frost to Robert Lowell to Sylvia Plath* (1994).

Daw, Marjorie. See MARJORIE DAW.

Dawson, Coningsby [William] (1883–1959), newspaper correspondent, novelist, poet. Born in England, Dawson came to the United States in 1905, became a specialist in Canadian affairs for English newspapers, lived in New Jersey, and later in California. He first won an audience with his novels *The Garden Without Walls* (1913) and *The Raft* (1914). Among his other novels are *The Kingdom Round the Corner* (1921), *The Coast of Folly* (1924), and *The Moon Through Glass* (1934). A remarkable novelette of his, *The Unknown Soldier* (1929), tells of the return of Jesus to earth during World War I. He also published a collection of poems, *Florence on a Certain Night* (1914).

Day, Clarence [Shepard], Jr. (1874–1935), essayist, artist. From 1920 to 1935 Day published seven books. Six of them, all marked by unorthodox humor, attracted little attention from the general public: *This Simian World* (1920); *The Crow's Nest* (1921); *Thoughts Without Words* (1928); *God and My Father* (1932); *In the Green Mountain Country* (1934), an impressive description of former President Coolidge's funeral; and *Scenes from the Mesozoic* (1935). But in 1935 also appeared LIFE WITH FATHER, followed by the posthumous *Life with Mother* (1936), and Day achieved prominence. The two books sold widely and they provided the basis for two excellent plays, later made into movies; in dramatic form *Life with Father* (which opened in 1939) established a record for longevity with 3,224 performances. Born in New York City and an invalid for the greater part of his life, Day composed his later books with great physical difficulty. Day was a constant contributor to *The New Yorker* magazine, whose humorous moods and modes he helped to form.

Day, Holman [Francis] (1865–1935), poet, novelist. Born in Maine, Day was educated at Colby College and wrote for Maine newspapers and magazines. After 1900, when he published *Up in Maine*, his first collection of poems, he became for his time one of Maine's chief literary interpreters. *Pine Tree Ballads* (1902) was especially popular, as were the novels *Squire Phin* (1905), *King Spruce* (1908), *The Ramrodders* (1910), and *The Rider of the King Log* (1919). His material is humorous and folksy, and rooted in oral tradition. It includes tales of the supernatural and legends of witches and haunts.

Daye, Stephen (c. 1594–1668), printer. Born in England, he came to Massachusetts Bay in 1638 with Joseph Glover, who was bringing the first printing press. When Glover died on the voyage, Daye set up the Cambridge Press and printed THE OATH OF A FREE MAN (1639), a broadside that was the first printing done in the colonies. The first book, THE BAY PSALM BOOK (1640), quickly followed.

Day Is Done, The (1844), a poem by HENRY WADSWORTH LONGFELLOW. It appeared as an introduction to a collection of minor poems, *The Waif*, edited by Longfellow.

Day of Doom, The (1662), a narrative in double stanzas of common meter (hymns and ballads) picturing the Last Judgment, by MICHAEL WIGGLESWORTH. Frank Luther Mott calls this "the first American best seller." It appeared in an edition of 1,800 copies, nearly all sold within a year, and was constantly reprinted. It was familiar to every New Englander. Children were required to memorize it, and as late as the 19th century some elderly New Englanders could still recite all 1,792 lines. James Russell Lowell wrote sardonically that it was "the solace of every fireside, the flicker of the pine knots by which it was conned perhaps adding a livelier relish to its premonitions of eternal combustion." In the poem's 224 stanzas doom breaks upon a peaceful world, Christ takes his place as an inexorable judge, the dead arise, and saints are separated from sinners. Babes who died before being baptized are charitably assigned "the easiest room in hell." Then the fire is lighted, the sulfurous fumes ascend, and the sinners are dragged away. "Christ pities not your cry," the poet exults. "Depart to hell, there may you yell and roar eternally."

Day of the Locust, The (1939), the last novel by NATHANAEL WEST, written after he went to Hollywood as a scriptwriter. It is not so much a story of Hollywood as a parable of the failure of the American dream. Homer Simpson, the central character, finds himself in the midst of people who have been brought up on the movies and are bored with life as they find it. He is typical of the thousands of middle-aged middle-class folk who save their money and go to California in search of sunshine and glamour, only to find monotony and tinsel, and finally to die. Other characters include Faye Greener, a stage-struck, empty-headed blonde; her father Harry, a former music-hall performer; Tod Hackett, an idealist who came to Hollywood to learn scenery design and gave up his attempts at art; a Mexican who owns fighting cocks; a man who dresses in gaudy cowboy outfits; and a bookmaking dwarf. The novel's underlying motif is the falsity of American values: everything in the book is phony—the language, the buildings, the actors, and finally, life itself.

Days (composed in 1852, published in *The Atlantic Monthly*, November, 1857, then in *May-Day and Other Pieces*, 1867), one of the most characteristic of RALPH WALDO EMERSON's poems. It repeats the thought expressed in his essay *Works and Days*: "He only is rich who owns the day. . . . [The days] come and go like muffled and veiled figures, sent from a distant friendly party; but they say nothing, and if we do not use the gifts they bring, they carry them as silently away."

Dazey, Charles Turner. Author of IN OLD KENTUCKY.

Deacon's Masterpiece, The, or, The Wonderful "One-Hoss Shay" (published in *The Atlantic Monthly*, September, 1858, in an installment of THE AUTOCRAT OF THE BREAKFAST TABLE), a poem by OLIVER WENDELL HOLMES. Holmes in a subtitle describes this poem as "a logical story." It can be read as a humorous tale of a New England deacon who built a chaise that would last forever. But Holmes meant the "shay" to be a symbol of Calvinism, and its breakdown to mean the decay and disintegration of that hard creed. This theme he treated elsewhere in his writings, especially in his comments on Jonathan Edwards.

Dead End (produced, 1935; published, 1936), a play by SIDNEY KINGSLEY. On a dead-end street leading to the East River in New York City, a region where luxurious apartments overlook the slums, live five children whose environment produces in them a hatred of people and of law. A young woman of the neighborhood does her best to improve conditions but has little success. There is constant contrast between the better classes above and the slum people below. The play was turned into an effective movie (1937), played by the same young actors who had appeared in the stage version; they became known as the Dead End Kids and went on to make several other motion pictures.

Deadwood Dick. A favorite character in the dime novels written by EDWARD L. WHEELER and his imitators, among them *Deadwood Dick on Deck, or, Calamity Jane, the Heroine of Whoop Up; The Double Dagger, or, Deadwood Dick's Defiance*; and *Deadwood Dick in Denver*. Deadwood Dick may have been based on Robert Dickey (1840–1912), who served as a scout under General George Crook and was also a trapper and fur merchant, or Richard W. Clarke (1845–1930), an Indian fighter and express guard who took part in Deadwood, South Dakota, historical celebrations.

Deal, Borden (1922–1985), novelist, short-story writer. Born in Mississippi and educated at the University of Alabama, Deal focused his writing on the new South, from 1890 on. He won acclaim with his second book, *Dunbar's Cove* (1957), a novel of a Tennessee farm family faced with the changes accompanying the Tennessee Valley Authority's dam-building in the 1930s. Widely translated, it was also the basis for the movie *Wild River* (1960). Some of his later novels formed his New South Saga: *The Loser* (1964), *The Advocate* (1968), and *The Winner* (1973). Others told of olden times: *The Least One* (1967) and *The Other Room* (1974). His other titles include *Walk Through the Valley* (1957), *The Insolent Breed* (1959), *Dragon's Wine* (1960), *The Spangled Road* (1962), *Bluegrass* (1976), and *Adventure* (1978). He also wrote novels under the pseudonyms Lee Borden and Leigh Borden.

Dean's December, The (1982), a novel by SAUL BELLOW. Albert Corde, dean of a Chicago college and married to a Hungarian wife, serves as the central figure in a study of capitalistic and communist dissolution in American academia, urban Chicago, and Bucharest, Romania.

Death Comes for the Archbishop (1927), a novel by WILLA CATHER. Often regarded as Cather's masterpiece, this narrative is closely based on the lives of two eminent French clerics, Bishop Jean Baptiste Lamy (1814–1888) and his vicar-general, Father Joseph Machebeuf. In the book the men are called Fathers Latour and Vaillant. They brave all adversities to attain their end, to build a cathedral in the wilderness. The story is told as the archbishop waits for death; an old man, he looks back on a lifetime of hardship and accomplishment.

Death in the Afternoon (1932), a loosely organized book on bullfighting in Spain by ERNEST HEMINGWAY. Hemingway depicts the bullfight as an emblematic tragedy, a test of courage, with a bloody and not entirely predictable end. Throughout, he digresses to philosophize on life and death in exchanges with a character he calls the Old Lady.

Death in the Deep South (1936), a powerful novel by WARD GREENE based on the trial and lynching of Leo Frank in 1915. It was filmed as *They Won't Forget* (1937).

Death in the Family, A (1957), JAMES AGEE's fictional account of his father's death.

Death of Artemio Cruz, The (*La muerte de Artemio Cruz*, 1962; tr. 1964), a novel by CARLOS FUENTES. Fuentes takes a deep plunge into the dying body and the sharply aware conscience of Artemio Cruz, a political boss of contemporary Mexico. As Cruz's life passes before him, his personality unfolds into an adversary I/Thou relationship. A third voice sets the events recalled by the accusatory "Thou" and the defensive "I" into objective historical frames. The story of the agonizing Cruz amounts to a tale of survival by betrayal of friends, ideals, and country. When the accusatory voice forces Cruz into shame for his cynicism and immorality, his ego protests that at least he survived, while all the idealists are dead. The power of the story is heightened by the brilliant use of STREAM OF CONSCIOUSNESS technique, which provides a multileveled depiction of life in Mexico during and after the revolution of 1910.

Death of a Salesman (1949). ARTHUR MILLER's tragedy about the American Dream in general and about the Loman family in particular has become one of America's most honored plays. It received, among other distinctions, the New York Drama Critics' Circle Award and a Pulitzer Prize. *Death of a Salesman* questions a wide range of cultural assumptions about business ethics, about the meaning of Success, about the claims of family.

Willy Loman (his last name suggesting a low man) begins the play at the end of his economic and psychic tether. He is cracking up, and it is his breakdown—and the efforts he mounts against its inevitability—that we watch as the play progresses. Willy is a believer in the gospel of being well liked, but neither he nor his sons, Biff and Happy, have made good on his great expectations. What they lack is the capacity for hard work that Willy's catechism of good looks and likability leaves out. Moreover, as a seventeen-year-old, Biff had seen his formerly godlike father utterly compromised, and what was once an object of love now becomes an occasion for contempt.

As the nets around Willy close, he rationalizes that his one chance to help his boys, to breathe life back into the old dream, is to give them the gift of his life insurance policy. Thus misguided, he drives off to a suicidal death by car, and the play ends with the mourners divided among Happy's insistence that he will lick the business world for Pop's sake, Charley's eloquent eulogy about a salesman's need to dream, and Biff's tragic recognition that Willy "never knew who he was," and that, at long last, Biff does.

SANFORD PINSKER

Death of the Hired Man, The (1914), a narrative poem by ROBERT FROST. One of Frost's best pieces—deft in character revelation, well done as poetry, dramatic—it has been successfully performed as a one-act play. Two characters appear, a farmer and his wife; another character is discussed, the hired man, once proud and respected, lately broken in health and spirit. He has been in the habit of going off and leaving them for other employment, then coming back in time of need; and now he has returned again. The farmer does not want to keep him, but the wife pleads for him. When the farmer seeks him out, he is dead. Justifiably well-remembered are the lines in which the husband and wife exchange definitions of home. Home, says the farmer, "is the place where, when you have to go there, they have to take you in." Home, says his wife, is "something you, somehow, haven't to deserve."

Deathsong of a Cherokee Indian, The. See next entry.

death songs, Indian. How widespread the custom was has not yet been determined, but certainly Indians in many parts of America were practitioners of the death song—sung when the end was near, sometimes given the form of a dream. These songs greatly impressed white men and came to constitute a poetic genre. It has been studied by Frank E. Farley in *The Dying Indian* (*Kittredge Anniversary Papers*, 1913). One such song appeared in Sarah W. A. Morton's *Ouabi, or, The Virtues of Nature* (1790), but the best-known is *The Deathsong of a Cherokee Indian*, attributed variously to PHILIP FRENEAU, a Mrs. John Hunter, and ROYALL TYLER, in whose play THE CONTRAST it was sung. One version of the poem may be found in Joseph Ritson's *Origin and Progress of Natural Song* (1783), another in Mathew Carey's *American Museum* (January 1, 1787), where it was assigned to Freneau, but it does not appear in Freneau's collected works. Definitely Freneau's are two other death songs, THE DYING INDIAN and *The Prophecy of King Tammany*.

Debo, Angie (1890–1988), historian. Educated at the University of Oklahoma, Debo devoted her life to Native American history. Working as an independent scholar from her home in Oklahoma, she added immeasurably to our understanding. Her books include *The Rise and Fall of the Choctaw Republic* (1934, 1967), *And Still the Waters Run* (1940), *The Road to Disappearance: A History of the Creek Indians* (1941), *The Five Civilized Tribes of Oklahoma* (1951), *A History of the Indians of the United States* (1970), and *Geronimo: The Man, His Time, His Place* (1976).

Debs, Eugene V[ictor] (1855–1926), American socialist leader, orator. Founder of the Social Democratic Party and its leader during the period of its greatest influence (1897–1916), Debs was five times an unsuccessful candidate for the presidency and was renowned for his campaign oratory: "While there is a soul in prison, I am not free." Born in Indiana, Debs first came to prominence as a leader of the notorious Pullman strike in Chicago in 1894, as a result of which he went to prison. Debs was for a time a powerful figure in American politics, always insisting on the primacy of democratic procedures, and he made a deep impression on many American writers and public men. His *Writings and Speeches* were collected (1948) by Arthur M. Schlesinger, Jr.

de Camp, L[yon] Sprague (1907–2000), science-fiction and fantasy writer. Born in New York City, de Camp was educated at California Institute of Technology and Stevens Institute of Technology. His over one hundred books, by himself and with others, include popularizations of science and technology, juveniles, and *The Great Monkey Trial* (1968), on the Scopes case; *Great Cities of The Ancient World* (1972), on thirteen ancient sites; and *The Bronze God of Rhodes* (1960), a historical novel. He is known best, however, for his tales of time or space travel. These include *Lest Darkness Fall* (1941), with a time-traveler considering changing history in ancient Rome; *The Wheels of If* (1948), stories; *Rogue Queen* (1951), about insect-like creatures on a planet visited by humans; *Cosmic Manhunt* (1954), an interplanetary detective story; *The Glory That Was* (1960), mixing space travel, ancient Greece, and mind control; and *The Great Fetish* (1978), sword-and-sorcery adventure on a planet somewhat like earth. With Robert E. Howard, his wife Catherine Crook de Camp, and others he wrote over a dozen books, beginning with *Tales of Conan* (1955), that inspired the films *Conan the Barbarian* (1982) and *Conan the Destroyer* (1984). *The Conan Chronicles* (1989) and *The Conan Chronicles 2* (1990) are omnibus collections.

Decatur, Stephen (1779–1820), American naval officer. (See BARBARY WARS.)

Declaration of Independence, The. One of the most potent and influential political documents in the history of mankind, the Declaration of Independence was mainly the work of THOMAS JEFFERSON. On June 7, 1776, RICHARD HENRY LEE of Virginia laid before the Continental Congress, in session at Philadelphia, a resolution that "these United Colonies are, and of right ought to be, free and independent states," bringing the issue of freedom from Great Britain to the point of action. On June 10 a committee was appointed to draft a Declaration: THOMAS JEFFERSON, JOHN ADAMS [2], BENJAMIN FRANKLIN, Roger Sherman, and Robert R. Livingston. The committee itself chose Jefferson as chairman and authorized him to write the draft of the Declaration. With a few changes by Adams and Franklin, this draft was presented by the Committee of Five to Congress on June 28.

The purpose of the Declaration is set forth in the Preamble: "When in the course of human events, it becomes necessary for one people to dissolve the political bands which have connected them with another . . . they should declare the causes which impel them to the separation." The Declaration was not designed to declare independence, but rather to explain to the world the colonists' reasons for declaring independence. In the second main part of the Declaration, Jefferson formulated a political philosophy affirming the right of a people to establish and to overthrow its own government: ". . . that to secure these rights, Governments are instituted among Men, deriving their just powers from the consent of the governed,—that whenever any Form of Government becomes destructive of these ends, it is the Right of the People to alter or to abolish it. . . ."

Jefferson goes on to state that those certain conditions which will justify revolution prevail in the colonies, and that the people have submitted to them as long as it is possible: "Prudence, indeed, will dictate, that governments long established should not be changed for light and transient causes. . . . But when a long train of abuses and usurpations . . . evinces a design to reduce them under absolute despotism, it is their right . . . to throw off such government. . . ." Jefferson then lists the oppressive measures of the king. The Declaration asserts that the prevalence of these conditions is due to the tyranny of the king and not to any act the colonists have committed or left undone: "In every stage of these oppressions we have petitioned for redress. . . ." The colonists must therefore either throw off the yoke or submit to being slaves. The conclusion of the Declaration asserts their choice of freedom over slavery.

Jefferson's formulation of a political philosophy justifying revolution attests the continuing influence of Locke, and the theories of natural law and right, social compact, sovereignty of the people, and derivative authority of government. Locke had argued that, in his original state of nature, man was governed by the law of nature; then, in the interest of survival, he joined in society with others. By means of the social compact, a government was established. But the granting of powers to the government did not divest individuals of all their "natural rights." The government had agreed to protect these, and its violation of them entitled men to revolt.

On July 1, Congress sat as a committee to debate the Lee resolution for independence. On July 2, Congress, sitting in formal session, took the final, unanimous vote for independence. Adams thought that the adoption of this resolution should be celebrated "from one end of this continent to the other, from this time forward, forevermore."

Congress next debated the form and content of the Declaration prepared by Jefferson, making several changes. On July 4, the amended Declaration of Independence was approved and its publication authorized. The Committee of Five was ordered to "superintend and correct the press." All through the night the printers worked. On July 19, Congress ordered the Declaration engrossed on parchment, with the title changed to "The Unanimous Declaration of the 13 United States of America." On August 2 it was signed by the members of Congress then present.

The concepts of equality, of the right to revolt, of the functions of government expressed in the Declaration were the final fruit of a growth of centuries. Jefferson was particularly indebted to John Locke, whose *Two Treatises of Civil Government* (1690) and *Letters Concerning Toleration* (1689, 1690, 1692) deeply influenced American thought and made him "America's philosopher." In his list of human rights Locke included "property," for which Jefferson substituted "the pursuit of happiness"; but as far back as 1651 John Hall, a friend of Thomas Hobbes, had urged that the liberty to make one's life "happy and advantageous" was a "privilege stemming from God and nature."

The most warmly discussed phrase in the Declaration has been that which reads, "All men are created equal." Obviously the rest of the thought is that men are equal in certain "unalienable rights"; among them, "life, liberty, and the pursuit of happiness." Lincoln said that nobody ever misunderstood Jefferson's statement on equality "except a fool or a knave."

Deephaven (1877), sketches of a New England town woven into a story by SARAH ORNE JEWETT. Two young women pass a summer in a deserted seaport and meet many of the kindhearted, eccentric, lively, or forlorn characters of the place, all of them well described. The book was one of the earliest works of regional American fiction. The town itself—said to be South Berwick, Maine—is as real as any character in the book.

Deep Image Poetry. See ROBERT BLY.

Deerslayer, The (1841), a novel by JAMES FENIMORE COOPER. In the series of LEATHER-STOCKING TALES, this is the first in the fictitious chronology of NATTY BUMPPO's life, the last in actual order of publication. The action occurs on, in, and near Lake Otsego, called Glimmer-glass in the story. Nat is shown as a young hunter living among the Delaware Indians and joining with them in fighting the Hurons, who are at last driven off with the help of the British. Judith Hutter, a soiled enchantress whose family Deerslayer helps to defend, falls in love with him, but he resists her advances because she has too much of the settlement about her. The Delaware chieftain Chingachgook is an important personage in the book, which is one of Cooper's most lyrical.

De Forest, John W[illiam] (1826–1906), novelist, memoirist, travel writer. Born in Connecticut and educated in local schools, De Forest lived in Syria, Florence, and Paris as a young man. His early books include *History of the Indians of Connecticut* (1851), *Oriental Acquaintance* (1856), and *European Acquaintance* (1858). At the outbreak of the Civil War he entered the Union army and served for three years. After the war he was head of the Freedmen's Bureau in South Carolina. His reputation rests chiefly on the novel MISS RAVENEL'S CONVERSION FROM SECESSION TO LOYALTY (1867), based largely on his own experiences and observations and notable for a realistic treatment of war that anticipated STEPHEN CRANE. De Forest also wrote a historical novel, *Witching Times* (1856); a novel of social conflict, *Seacliff* (1859); a novel of Western adventure, *Overland* (1871); a satire on political corruption, HONEST JOHN VANE (1875); and a realistic romance, *Playing the Mischief* (1875). *A Volunteer's Adventures*, memoirs of the war, was posthumously published in 1946. Later came a sequel, *A Union Officer in the Reconstruction* (1948). De Forest influenced and was praised by HOWELLS.

deism.   A system of religious thought postulating a Supreme Being that created the world, runs it by established laws, and judges man, but rejecting the divinity of Jesus and the divine inspiration and miracles of the Bible. Deism has been called natural religion; it is based on reason and hence opposed to revealed religion. Deism sprang up with the spread of scientific knowledge during the Renaissance and reached its height during the 18th century. In England its followers included Lord Herbert of Cherbury (1583–1648), the third Earl of Shaftsbury (1671–1713), and Lord Bolingbroke (1678–1751); in France, Voltaire (1694–1778) and the Encyclopedists. Their ideas affected literature—for example, Pope's *Essay on Man* (1733–34) and the views of nature entertained by Wordsworth, Shelley, and others—and these in turn influenced American writers such as JOEL BARLOW and THOMAS PAINE. IN THE AGE OF REASON (1794–96), the latter wrote: "I do not believe in the creed professed by the Jewish church, by the Roman church, by the Greek church, nor by any church that I know of. My mind is my own church." Leading American writers and statesmen were avowed deists, among them Franklin, Washington, and Jefferson; a belligerent deist was ETHAN ALLEN (REASON THE ONLY ORACLE OF MAN, 1784).

De Jong, David Cornel ["Tjalmar Breola"] (1905–1967),   short-story writer, novelist. Born in the Netherlands, De Jong came to the United States when he was thirteen. He wrote novels of his native land and his adopted land. *Belly Fulla Straw* (1934) tells the story of a Dutch immigrant family. It was followed by many other books, among them *Old Haven* (1938); *Day of the Trumpet* (1941); *Domination of June* (1944), a volume of poetry; *With a Dutch Accent* (1944), which describes his experiences; *Somewhat Angels* (1945); *Snow-on-the Mountain* (1946) and *The Unfairness of Easter* (1959), which contain some of his numerous short stories; *The Desperate Children* (1949); *Two Sofas in the Parlor* (1952); and *Outside of Four Walls* (1961).

de Kruif, Paul (1890–1971),   popular writer on science and medicine. De Kruif (whose name is pronounced to rhyme with *knife*) studied bacteriology at the University of Michigan and the Rockefeller Institute. He supplied Sinclair Lewis with much of the technical background for ARROWSMITH (1925). De Kruif wrote *Our Medicine Men* (1922); *Microbe Hunters* (1926); *Hunger Fighters* (1928); *Men Against Death* (1932); *Yellow Jack* (1934, a play with Sidney Howard); *Health Is Wealth* (1940); *Life Among the Doctors* (1949); and *A Man Against Insanity* (1957). *The Sweeping Wind* (1962) is an autobiography.

de la Guard, Theodore.   Pen name of NATHANIEL WARD.

Deland, Margaret [Wade Campbell] (1857–1945), novelist, short-story writer. Born in Allegheny, Pennsylvania, she grew up near Pittsburgh in a small town called Manchester (the "Old Chester" of her stories). *John Ward, Preacher* (1888), her first novel, is set in Ashurst, a town that "rather prided itself on being half asleep." Ward, a Calvinist, marries Helen Jeffrey, a woman with freethinking tendencies. He suffers keenly as a result of the conflict between his love for his wife and his strict faith. His public prayer for her salvation causes a furor in the community, but in the end he dies without getting his wish to hear her confess that she has seen the light.

The Awaking of Helena Richie (1906) and its sequel, *The Iron Woman* (1911), portray a selfish and forceful woman who gradually learns to accept societal values in place of personal ones. *The Rising Tide* (1916) is a sociological novel dealing with women's suffrage. *The Vehement Flame* (1922) is the story of a romance between a youth and an older woman. *The Kays* (1926) and *Captain Archer's Daughter* (1932) are novels of New England life. OLD CHESTER TALES (1898) is probably her most enduring collection of short stories. Other books derived from early memories include *Doctor Lavendar's People* (1903), *Around Old Chester* (1915), *New Friends in Old Chester* (1924), and *Old Chester Days* (1935). *If This Be I (As I Suppose It Be)* (1935) and *Golden Yesterdays* (1941) are autobiographical.

Delaney, Martin Robinson (1812–1885),   editor, writer. A free-born African-American, Delaney published *Mystery*, a Pittsburgh newspaper, and then assisted FREDERICK DOUGLASS with the *North Star*. Briefly a student of medicine at Harvard, he published the tract *The Condition, Elevation, Emigration, and Destiny of the Colored People of the United States* (1852). A novel, *Blake; or, The Huts of America*, was serialized in the *Afro-American Magazine* (1859–60). During the Civil War he served as the first African-American major. His *Principia of Ethnology* (1878) is a defense of African-American achievements and potential.

Delano, Alonzo (1802?–1874).   humorist, historian. Born in Aurora, New York, Delano was an early practitioner of the type of comic writing associated with pioneering days in California. He set out for California on April 19, 1849, arrived there by mid-September after suffering considerable hardship on the way. He earned more money by his pen than as a merchant or miner, and his sketches (signed The Old Block) were published in various newspapers. Many of them were collected in *Pen-Knife Sketches* (1853) and *Old Block's Sketch-Book* (1856). *His Life on the Plains and Among the Diggings* (1854) has historical value and was reprinted in 1936. *Alonzo Delano's California Correspondence* was published in 1952.

Delano, Amasa (1763–1823),   sea captain, memoirist. Delano's *Narrative of Voyages and Travels: Comprising Three Voyages Round the World* (1817) furnished material for Melville's *Benito Cereno* (1856). The book also contains a long account of the mutiny on the *Bounty* and the colony of mutineers on Pitcairn's Island.

Delany, Samuel R[ay, Jr.] (1942–   ),   writer of science fiction. Born in New York City, Delany was educated at

City College and began his prolific career at twenty, with *The Jewels of Aptor* (1962, expanded 1976). He has earned a reputation for opening new fields of writing for African-American authors and for innovations of structure, theme, and style that expanded science fiction beyond its traditional generic limitations. Novels include *Babel-17* (1966), an exploration of how language structures reality; *The Einstein Intersection* (1967), about problems of creating a culture in a post-apocalyptic world; *Nova* (1968), a space opera about worlds in conflict over scarce fuel; *Dhalgren* (1975), a long and complex work in which an amnesiac becomes the focus for questions about bisexuality and the nature of reality; *Triton* (1976), about a sexual utopia; and *Stars in My Pocket Like Grains of Sand* (1984), a futuristic, interstellar story. Autobiography, straight or thinly disguised, informs books that include *The Motion of Light in Water; Sex and Science Fiction Writing in the East Village 1957–1965* (1989); *Atlantis, Three Tales* (1995); *Bread and Wine: An Erotic Tale of New York City* (1998); and *Times Square Red, Times Square Blue* (1999), about sex, homosexuality, and social life. Delany has also written swords-and-dragons fiction, the Neveryon series, set in a magic past and theoretical works on the nature of science fiction. *1984: Selected Letters* appeared in 2000.

De la Roche, Mazo (1879–1961),   novelist. Born in Toronto and educated at the University of Toronto, De la Roche had a huge success with her Jalna saga, sixteen novels that by the mid-1960s had sold 11 million copies worldwide. *Jalna* (1927) was followed by *Whiteoaks of Jalna* (1929), *Finch's Fortune* (1931), *The Master of Jalna* (1933), *Young Rennie* (1935), *Whiteoak Harvest* (1936), *Whiteoak Heritage* (1940), *Wakefield's Course* (1941), *The Building of Jalna* (1944), *Return to Jalna* (1946), *Mary Wakefield* (1949), *Renny's Daughter* (1951), *Whiteoak Brothers* (1953), *Variable Winds at Jalna* (1954), *Centenary at Jalna* (1958), and *Morning at Jalna* (1960). The series centers on the fortunes of the Whiteoaks family, genteel farmers and horse-traders, whose house "Jalna" is in Clarkson, Ontario. Its picture of rural Ontario—humane, English, colonial—has defined an idealized Canada for generations of readers abroad.

Jalna came late in De la Roche's writing career, which began with a story in the *Atlantic Monthly* in 1915. Her collections of stories include *Explorers of the Dawn* (1922), *The Sacred Bullock and Other Stories of Animals* (1939), and *A Boy in the House* (1952). Her other novels, some less romanticized than the Jalna books, include *Possession* (1923); *Delight* (1926), the story of an immigrant girl; *Lark Ascending* (1932), a Sicilian romance; *Growth of a Man* (1938); and *The Two Saplings* (1942). *Ringing the Changes* (1957) is an autobiography.

Delaware Indians.   A name given by white men to the tribes that inhabited the Delaware River Valley. They were of Algonquin stock, and in Delaware and neighboring states called themselves the Leni-Lenape ("the men of our nation" or "the original people"). They were a friendly people with whom the settlers had few difficulties. Henry Hudson, who first met them in 1609, called them a "loving people." They frequently made treaties, like that with William Penn in 1682. They lived by agriculture, hunting, and fishing. JOHN HECKEWELDER (1743–1824) gave an authentic and copious account of them in his *History, Manners and Customs of the Indian Nations Who Once Inhabited Pennsylvania and the Neighboring States* (1819). JAMES FENIMORE COOPER, when he came to describe them in the LEATHER-STOCKING TALES, made good use of the material in the Heckewelder book, which saw the Native American as a noble savage. An early picture of them is also found in James Kirke Paulding's novel KONINGSMARKE (1823); Paulding lays his scene among the Swedish settlers of Delaware and the Native Americans of Pennsylvania. The Delaware Indians after 1720 moved into Ohio, where they sided with the French against the English and with the English against the Americans. An attack on one of their settlements in 1782 led some of them to flee to Ontario; others migrated farther west, to Missouri, Kansas and, by the 1880s, to the Indian Territory of Oklahoma. Their experiences in Kansas are reported fairly accurately in the novel *Both Banks of the River* by Argye M. Briggs. One of their chieftains, Tamend, who appears in LAST OF THE MOHICANS, gave rise to the name *Tammany*. (See also WALAM OLUM.)

De La Warr, Thomas West, Baron (1577–1618),   a British administrator. He became governor and captain general of the colony of Virginia (1610) and managed to prevent disruption of the colony. He returned to England for aid in 1611 and died on a second voyage to Virginia, in 1618. Delaware was named for him. He wrote *a Relation of the Colony of Virginia* (1611).

Delbanco, Nicholas [Franklin] (1942–   ),   novelist, short-story writer. Born in London, Delbanco came to the United States as a child of six. He was educated at Harvard and Columbia and has taught creative writing at a number of colleges and universities, including the University of Michigan. His novels include *The Martlet's Tale* (1966), set in Greece and based on the biblical tale of the prodigal son; *Consider Sappho Burning* (1969); *Small Rain* (1975); the Sherbrooke trilogy: *Possession* (1977), *Sherbrookes* (1978), and *Stillness* (1980), on the history of a troubled New England family; *In the Name of Mercy* (1995), concerning unexplained deaths in a hospice; *Old Scores* (1997), an academic love story set twenty-five years later, when professor and student meet again; and *What Remains* (2000), a generational, memoir-like novel about German Jews, the Holocaust, and life in England and the United States. *About My Table, and Other Stories* (1983) and *The Writer's Trade, and Other Stories* (1990) are gatherings of short fiction. *Running in Place: Scenes from the South of France* (1989) is a travel book. Nonfiction includes *Group Portrait: Joseph Conrad, Stephen Crane, Ford Madox Ford, Henry James, and H. G. Wells* (1982) and *The Beaux Arts Trio* (1985). *The Lost Suitcase: Reflections on the Literary Life* (2000) collects essays on writing and a novella based on the young Hemingway's loss of the manuscript of his first novel.

De Leon, Thomas Cooper (1839–1914),   novelist, playwright, memoirist. In addition to two novels, *Creole and*

Puritan (1889) and *Crag-Nest* (1897), De Leon, who was born in South Carolina, wrote memoirs of life under the Confederacy, *Four Years in Rebel Capitals* (1890), and of the South after the war, *Belles, Beaux, and Brains of the '60s* (1907). But he was chiefly renowned for a burlesque, *Hamlet Ye Dismal Prince* (1870), which struck contemporary critics as very funny when it was produced on the same night as Edwin Booth's production of *Hamlet*.

De Lillo, Don (1936–   ),   novelist. De Lillo was born in New York City, grew up in the South Bronx, and was educated at Fordham University. He worked as an advertising copywriter and began writing fiction whose bizarre subject matter and offbeat style appealed initially to a specialized reading public.

Although De Lillo had already published eight novels before *Libra* (1988), the popular success of that book changed his identity from cult figure to serious American novelist. In the eight previous novels, De Lillo associated the occupational paranoia of his protagonists with the more inclusive third person identity he provided in the coda to his first novel, *Americana* (1971): "In this country there is a universal third person, the man we all want to be. Advertising has discovered this man. It uses him to express the possibilities open to the consumer. To consume in America is not to buy, it is to dream. Advertising is the suggestion that the dream of entering the third person singular might possibly be fulfilled." All De Lillo's characters respond to the absence of fulfillment in the false promises of consumerism with varying degrees of frustration and despair. David Bell, the protagonist of *Americana*, buries himself in a sacramental journey in quest of the spiritual meaning of the Navahos, but ends up filming misfits in Fort Curtis. In the seven subsequent novels, De Lillo's protagonists aspire to identify with representative third persons in American literature. In *End Zone* (1972), Gary Harkness unsuccessfully tries to redeem his life through identification with the archetypical football hero at Logos College. Bucky Wunderlick in *Great Jones Street* (1973) aspires to become a rock and roll star. Billy Twillig is a 14-year-old mathematical genius trying to decode a message from outer space in *Ratner's Star* (1976). Lyle becomes an astronaut intent on attaining absolute weightlessness in *Players* (1977), and *Running Dog* (1978) treats of espionage. In *The Names* (1982), a prototypical father searches the mistakes and misspellings of his child for the meaning of the universe. Jack Gladney, the protagonist of *White Noise* (1985), looks in a supermarket for the deepest clues to the meanings of American culture.

None of the bizarre schemes in which these third persons from De Lillo's earlier novels involve themselves coincide with the larger official narratives out of which the American public construct their personae. But in *Libra* De Lillo intuits the correlation between the characters in his previous novels and Lee Harvey Oswald, whose plot to assassinate President Kennedy seemed an expression of their collective rage. As he conjoins materials from Oswald's diaries with the larger concerns of the Kennedy conspiracy, De Lillo draws on his other characters' obsessive drives and successfully transforms this complex

event within the shared national allegory into a vision of *Americana* continuous with his own. The themes of *Libra* continue in *Mao II* (1992), as a reclusive novelist disappears while trying to assist a hostage trapped in a Beirut basement. *Underworld* (1997) begins a tour of the Cold War period with the baseball game between the Giants and the Dodgers that decided the 1951 National League pennant race. Bobby Thompson's winning home run, coinciding with the test explosion of a Russian nuclear device in Kazakhstan, sets the tone for the period of fear and distrust, from 1951 to 1992, covered by the novel. *The Body Artist* (2001) is a brief fictional meditation on identity, perception, and death.

DONALD PEASE/BP

Delineator, The.   A magazine edited 1907–1910 by THEODORE DREISER. Founded in 1873 by Ebenezer Butterick, a tailor of Fitchburg, Massachusetts, as a magazine for women containing tissue-paper dress patterns and fashion plates, it moved to New York and in 1894 began publishing fiction of a type likely to appeal to women. It attained in time a circulation of over two million. In May 1937, it merged with the *Pictorial Review*. Another editor of note was HONORÉ WILLSIE MORROW (1914–1920).

De Lisser, Herbert G[eorge] (1878–1944)   Jamaican novelist. Of Portuguese, Jewish, and African ancestry, De Lisser worked as a journalist, serving as editor of the *Jamaica Daily Gleaner* for about forty years. A central figure in the development of modern West Indian writing, De Lisser introduced the first black West Indian heroine, in *Jane's Career* (1913). His other novels, which have elements of the metaphysical as well as social realism, include *Susan Proudleigh* (1915); *The White Witch of Rosehall* (1929), his best-known work, a story of witchcraft and a slave revolt on an early 19th-century plantation; and *Arawak Girl*, published posthumously in 1958.

Dell, Floyd (1887–1969),   journalist, novelist, playwright. Born in Illinois, Dell worked briefly on a Davenport, Iowa, newspaper in 1905 before going to Chicago, where he worked on various newspapers and became associated with the new group of young Midwestern writers known as the Chicago School. In 1914 he moved to New York and became an associate editor of the MASSES and its successor, the LIBERATOR. During this period Dell began to write plays, and with the publication of his novels MOONCALF (1920), its sequel *The Briary-Bush* (1921), *Janet March* (1923), and others, became known as a spokesman for the jazz age and life and love in Greenwich Village. His most successful play was the comedy *Little Accident* (1928), based on his novel *The Unmarried Father* (1927). He has also written *Love in the Machine Age* (1930), a reasoned statement of his attitudes toward sex and a contribution to the change in American sexual mores after World War I. His autobiography *Homecoming* appeared in 1933, and indicates that much of the material in his first two novels was a sifting of his own experience.

Della Cruscanism.   An English school of poetry, started by young Englishmen in Florence, Italy, among them Robert Merry (1755–98): *Della Crusca* means "of chaff," and the group adopted its name from the *Accademia della Crusca*, founded in 1582 to winnow the chaff from the Italian language. Their style was silly, sentimental, and pretentious, but very popular for a time. They were attacked scathingly by William Gifford in the satirical poems *Baeviad* (1794) and *Maeviad* (1795). Their affected style seems to have been anticipated by the American versifier Joseph Brown Ladd (1764–86). His *Poems of Arouet* (1786) appeared almost simultaneously with the rise of the English school in Florence. A few years later the movement had gained a great hold in the U.S., chiefly in the writings of SARAH WENTWORTH MORTON, who was called the American Sappho by her admirers and who eulogized the Della Cruscan manner in an address prefixed to her narrative poem *Ouabi, or The Virtues of Nature* (1790). The style also appeared in the verses of ROBERT TREAT PAINE, JR.

Delmar, Viña [Croter] (1905–1990), novelist, playwright, short-story writer. Delmar's first novel, *Bad Girl*, a realistic narrative about the loves of a young typist, was a best seller in 1928 and was dramatized in 1930. Its success was followed up with *Loose Ladies* (1929), *Kept Woman* (1929), *Women Live Too Long* (1932), and *The Marriage Racket* (1933)—books considered rather sensational and even censorable in their time. Then, for almost two decades, aside from occasional short stories in popular magazines, she published no new work. In 1950 appeared *About Mrs. Leslie*, then *The Marcaboth Women* (1951), *The Laughing Stranger* (1953), *Beloved* (1956), *Breeze From Camelot* (1959), *The Big Family* (1961), and *A Time for Titans* (1974), several of them on historical subjects. *McKeever*, her last novel, appeared in 1976. *The Becker Scandal* (1968) is a memoir. She is also the author of two plays produced in New York, *The Rich Full Life* (1945) and *Midsummer* (1953).

Deloria, Vine, Jr. (1933–   ), writer. Born and raised on a South Dakota reservation, Deloria is a Standing Rock SIOUX who studied theology and law and has become a leading spokesman for Native Americans, an advocate of political separatism. His works include *Custer Died for Your Sins: An Indian Manifesto* (1969); *We Talk, You Listen: New Tribes, New Turf* (1970); *God Is Red* (1973); *Behind the Trail of Broken Treaties: An Indian Declaration of Independence* (1974), an account of events underlying the 1973 encounter at Wounded Knee; *Indians of the Pacific Northwest* (1977); *The Metaphysics of Modern Existence* (1979); *Indian Education in America: Eight Essays* (1991); and *Red Earth, White Lies: Native Americans and the Myth of Scientific Fact* (1995).

Delphian Club. A Baltimore literary association, founded August 31, 1816. Its members included John Pierpont, H. M. Brackenridge, Francis Scott Key, William Wirt, John Howard Paine, Rembrandt Peale, John Neal, Samuel Woodworth, and John P. Kennedy. Under Neal's editorship they issued a periodical, *The Portico*, from 1816 to 1818, when the club expired. The magazine, like the members, expressed a nationalistic and antiforeign viewpoint. JOHN NEAL told about the club in his *Wandering Recollections* (1869).

del Rey, Lester (1915–1993), science-fiction writer, editor. Born in Minnesota, del Rey became a prolific author under his own name, some ghostwritten or in collaboration

with others, and several pseudonyms, including Philip St. John, Erik van Lhin, Philip James, Kenneth Wright, and Wade Kaempfert. Among his novels are *Day of the Giants* (1959), a fantasy based on Norse mythology, and *The Eleventh Commandment* (1962, revised 1970), a post–atomic holocaust story in which famine and human fertility threaten worldwide disaster. His short stories, frequently on the conflict between humans and their machines, are collected in *Robots and Changelings* (1958), *Gods and Golems* (1973), *Early del Rey* (2 v. 1978), and *The Best of Lester del Rey* (1978).

de Man, Paul (1919–1983), literary critic. Born in Antwerp, de Man attended the University of Brussels (1939–42) and worked as a journalist and translator before coming to the U.S. in 1947. After taking a Ph.D. at Harvard (1960), he taught at Cornell and Johns Hopkins before becoming, at Yale between 1970 and 1983, a key figure in the movement known as deconstruction. Texts are for him elusive, words slippery, meaning illusory. Reading is a process of deconstructing apparent connections between words and the world outside the page. Traditional literary criticism fails in its attempts to define traditions and periods or to discuss genres because it assigns meanings and coherence that can be immediately challenged. Controversies surrounding de Man and deconstruction—which critics have seen as nihilistic, antihistorical, and anti-humanistic—flared in 1988 and after, with particular attention to de Man's many 1940–41 writings for *Le Soir*, an anti-Semitic, pro-Nazi Belgian newspaper. His books include *Blindness and Insight: Essays in the Rhetoric of Contemporary Criticism* (1971, 1983); *Allegories of Reading: Figural Language in Rousseau, Nietzsche, Rilke, and Proust* (1979); and *The Rhetoric of Romanticism* (1984). Posthumous collections include *The Resistance to Theory* (1986) and *Aesthetic Ideology* (1988). (See YALE CRITICS.)

Demby, William (1922–   ), novelist. Born in Pittsburgh and educated at West Virginia State College and Fisk, Demby worked as a jazz musician and wrote screenplays in Rome and taught at the College of Staten Island and the City University of New York. His first novel, *Beetlecreek* (1950), tells of race relations in West Virginia. *The Catacombs* (1965) tells of an African-American writer named William Demby working in Rome. His other novels are *Love Story Black* (1978) and *Blueboy* (1979).

De Mille, Agnes (1905–1993), dancer, choreographer, author. De Mille is particularly well known for choreographic productions in such musical plays as OKLAHOMA!, *Carousel*, and *Brigadoon*. She has written her autobiography in two books: *Dance to the Piper* (1952) and *And Promenade Home* (1958). REPRIEVE (1981) is a memoir written in collaboration with her doctor, Fred Plum, on her rehabilitation from a cerebral hemorrhage she suffered in 1975.

De Mille, Cecil B[lount] (1881–1959), playwright, movie director. With his brother William, De Mille wrote and produced two plays, *The Genius* (1906) and *The Royal Mounted* (1908), and is credited with help on David Belasco's THE RETURN OF PETER GRIMM (1911). When he went to Hollywood in 1913, his real career began, and he left a deep impress on movie production and the viewpoints of the industry. He developed the use of crowd scenes and spectacle movies. Among his major works are THE SQUAW MAN (1913 and 1918); *The King of Kings* (1927); *The Sign of the Cross* (1931); *Reap the Wild Wind* (1942); *The Unconquered* (1947); *Samson and Delilah* (1949); and *The Ten Commandments* (1957). He also collaborated with his brother, **William Churchill De Mille** (1878–1955), on a number of stage productions. William De Mille, who in his later years taught drama at the University of Southern California, was also a playwright and lecturer. His best-known play was *Strongheart* (1905).

Deming, Philander (1829–1915),   lawyer, writer of fictional sketches. Born in Carlisle, New York, Deming knew the Adirondacks well and wrote about them realistically in *Adirondack Stories* (1880), *Tompkins and Other Folks* (1885), and *The Story of a Pathfinder* (1907).

Democracy (1880),   a novel by HENRY ADAMS. It was published anonymously and can only loosely be described as a novel, but it gives an effective satirical picture of social and political Washington as seen by a disillusioned man. Among those pictured are President Rutherford B. Hayes and James G. Blaine. Another character, Representative Gore, may be Adams himself. The story is told in terms of a young New York widow who seeks power through political intrigue in Washington, becomes disillusioned, and leaves for Europe.

Democratic Vistas,   a philosophical tract by WALT WHITMAN, written in 1867–68 and published as a book in 1871. Whitman started out to reply to Carlyle's dour view of democracy in "Shooting Niagara: And After?" but as he worked on his reply he reluctantly came to agree with much of Carlyle's indictment. He admitted the "depravity of the business classes of our country," and that "Society, in these States, is canker'd, crude, superstitious, and rotten. . . ." But he held on to his belief in the innate honesty and perfectibility of the common people and argued that "Political democracy . . . with all its threatened evils, supplies a training-school for making first-class men." This pragmatic approach to social philosophy anticipated the PRAGMATISM of William James and John Dewey. Despite the extremely awkward style and diction, this essay is an important contribution to American social thought. G. W. A.

Demon of the Absolute, The (1928),   a book of literary criticism by PAUL ELMER MORE. Considered by some critics the best statement of More's critical method, *The Demon of the Absolute* presents an argument against "rationalism, or reason run amuck" which sets up its own absolutes in nature. More finds that "certain standards of taste exist, which approximate, more or less, to universality" and upholds these tastes as standards of value for literary critics. Like IRVING BABBITT, the humanist critic with whom he is often associated, More holds Rousseau responsible for romanticism, sentimental humanitarianism, illusions of progress, and a belief in the innate goodness of man, which More considers fallacious because of man's dual nature. *The Demon of the Absolute* advocates standards of taste based on tradition, classicism as opposed to

romanticism, and the application of ethical criteria to the examination and evaluation of literature.

Demos and Dionysus (published in 1925 in the collection DIONYSUS IN DOUBT),   a dialogue in verse by EDWIN ARLINGTON ROBINSON. In this lively and forceful poem Robinson expresses more than passing doubts about democracy. The poem becomes a violent attack on the extent to which democracy suppresses the individual and reduces mankind to a mediocre level. Humanitarian efforts, however well-meaning, may help bring about this sad result, although the few must save the many or the many will fall—a personal extension of the Calvinistic doctrine familiar to Robinson as part of his heredity and environment. In the poem Dionysus calls democracy a "faith in something somewhere out of nothing," and he denies that reason can save the world—it will only make "a dislocated and unlovely mess for undertakers." He identifies equality with uniformity and monotony.

Dennie, Joseph (1768–1812),   lawyer, editor, essayist. Born in Boston, and educated at Harvard, Dennie came to be regarded as an American Addison. As an editor he attracted to his periodicals many notable English and American writers—among them Thomas Moore (an intimate friend), Leigh Hunt, Thomas Campbell, and "Monk" Lewis. At the beginning of his career he formed an alliance with ROYALL TYLER and together they published satirical pieces under the pseudonym COLON (Dennie) AND SPONDEE (Tyler). At this stage Dennie acquired the wild bohemian habits that distinguished him for the rest of his life. His greatest success was obtained, nevertheless, under the pen name "The Lay Preacher," his byline for inspirational essays, practically sermons, that made him one of the most widely read authors of his day. At another time he employed the pen name "Oliver Oldschool, Esq." for essays that for a time influenced Washington Irving. He was an embittered Federalist who often regretted that he had not been born in England and hated things characteristically American, like Noah Webster's dictionary. Among the magazines he edited were *The Tablet* (1795), *The Farmer's Weekly Museum* (1796–99), and THE PORT FOLIO (1801–27). Some of his essays from the magazines were collected in book form, including *The Lay Preacher, or, Short Sermons for Idle Readers* (1796, 1817).

Dennis, Patrick [pseudonym of **Edward Everett Tanner III**] (1921–1976),   novelist. A New Yorker from Evanston, Illinois, Tanner won little acclaim with his first two novels, *Oh, What a Wonderful Wedding!* (1953) and *House Party* (1954), both written under the pseudonym Virginia Rowans. His third, *Auntie Mame* (1955), a hilarious account of a boy's attachment to his eccentric aunt, written as Patrick Dennis, made him famous and wealthy and continued its success as a play, a movie, and a Broadway musical. Others of his books, though often bestsellers, never matched that success. Those written as Patrick Dennis include *Around the World with Auntie Mame* (1958), *Little Me* (1961), *Genius* (1962), *The Joyous Season* (1964), *Tony* (1966), *How Firm a Foundation* (1968), *Paradise* (1971), and *3-D* (1972). Later Virginia Rowans books are *The Loving Couple* (1956) and *Love and Mrs. Sargent* (1961). He spent his millions lavishly, and when his talent ran out lived as a wealthy man's butler. A biography is Eric Myers, *Uncle Mame: The Life of Patrick Dennis* (2000).

Densmore, Frances (1867–1957), ethnomusicologist. Born in Minnesota, Densmore began her career as a piano teacher and lecturer on Wagnerian music. She was attracted by Alice Cunningham Fletcher's pioneer work on the music of the Omahas (1911), and her *Chippewa Music* (1910–13) was the first of a long series of studies on Native American music and tribal customs. An epitome of her writings was made in *The American Indians and Their Music* (1926). More than any other person she helped preserve the music and poetry of Native Americans; she made detailed analyses of the music and the circumstances under which it was created and sung, at the same time providing graceful English translations. Among the achievements of her later years was work on the Smithsonian-Densmore Collection of sound recordings of the music. She remained active until well into the 1950s, publishing in 1953 *The Belief of the Indian in a Connection Between Song and the Supernatural*.

Denton, Daniel (*fl.* 1656–1696), landowner, politician. Born in Connecticut, Denton settled in New York soon after the English took possession from the Dutch. His *A Brief Description of New York* (1670) extolls this "terrestrial Canaan . . . where the land floweth with milk and honey." Denton's is the first English description of the area and is carefully limited to the things he personally observed, but it is clearly intended to encourage settlement.

De Quille, Dan [pen name of **William Wright**] (1829–1898), newspaperman, humorist. Born in Ohio, De Quille went west as a prospector and became editor of *The Territorial Enterprise* of Virginia City, Nevada, and a friend of MARK TWAIN. His *History of the Big Bonanza* (1877) tells of the COMSTOCK LODE. His *The Fighting Horse of the Stanislaus: Stories and Essays* (1990) was edited by Lawrence I. Berkove.

Derby, George Horatio ["Squibob," "John Phoenix"] (1823–1861), engineer, humorist. Derby was born in Dedham, Massachusetts, and educated at West Point. Sent to the West Coast as a surveyor, he began contributing to newspapers under pseudonyms, indulging his natural love of fun. His writings show the influence of tall-tale humor, and he was a master of the anecdote that recounts an impossible incident with the most solemn of faces. Both MARK TWAIN and BRET HARTE owed much to his technique. Irreverence was also one of his most characteristic traits and was similarly imitated by the Western humorists. He extracted humor from weird figures of speech, big words, and high-sounding expressions, but often delivered himself of shrewd aphorisms, and in this respect was again a model for Mark Twain.

His contributions appeared in various newspapers from 1849 to 1856. He wrote the first PIKE COUNTY BALLAD, in the *Vallectos Sentinal* (June 31, 1854). A collection called *Phoenixiana, or, Sketches and Burlesques* (1856) went into edition after edition and brought him national recognition. This was followed by THE SQUIBOB PAPERS (1865).

Derleth, August [**William**] (1909–1971), writer. Derleth's fiction derives mainly from his native region. He was born in Sauk City, Wisconsin, and made it the locale of his Sac Prairie Saga, a series of novels depicting life in a Midwestern community from the early 1800s until the present. A smaller group of novels, his Wisconsin Saga, includes *Bright Journey* (1940) and *The Hills Stand Watch* (1960). Among his other novels are *Still Is the Summer Night* (1937), *Wind Over Wisconsin* (1938), *Restless Is the River* (1939), and *The Shield of the Valiant* (1945). *Sac Prairie People* (1948) and *Wisconsin Earth* (1948) are collections of stories. His *Village Year* (1941) and *Village Daybook* (1947) give passages from his *Journal*—descriptions, anecdotes, reflections. *Walden West* (1961) and *Return to Walden West* (1970) combine journals and autobiographical material and have been called classics of their kind. Derleth also wrote detective stories. (His detective is Solar Pons, an echo of Sherlock Holmes; he also has a "Judge Peck" series.) *Still Small Voice* (1940) is a biography of Zona Gale, and there are several volumes of verse. He edited numerous anthologies, among them science-fiction collections. He published over 100 books of his own, edited many others and, as owner of the publishing firm Arkham House, was especially active in keeping alive the reputation of H. P. LOVECRAFT.

Derrida, Jacques (1930–), philosopher, critic, essayist. Born in Algiers in a Jewish family, Derrida left for Paris in 1950 to study philosophy at the École Normale Supérieure. He emerged as a major poststructuralist thinker in 1967, when he published *Speech and Phenomena* (tr. into English 1973), a deconstructive discussion of Husserl's phenomenology; *Of Grammatology* (tr. 1976), a critique of Saussure's logocentric linguistics, valorizing writing and the play of language instead of referential speech; and *Writing and Difference* (tr. 1978), essays developing Derrida's views on meaning as infinitely expandable and dependent on linguistic and interpretive operations.

In the 1970s Derrida collaborated with GREPH, a group researching philosophic education in France. In 1972 he published three more books: *Dissemination* (tr. 1981), a critical demonstration that writing plays a major role in Plato's ontometaphysics; *Margins of Philosophy* (tr. 1981), essays highlighting the pervasiveness of metaphor in philosophy; and *Positions* (tr. 1981), interviews clarifying Derrida's poststructuralist stand. These were followed by *Glas* (1974, tr. 1987), Derrida's most experimental writing exploring multiplicity of meaning and discourse.

Introduced in America by rhetorical critics such as PAUL DE MAN, Geoffrey Hartman, and J. Hillis Miller, Derrida's ideas have been rehashed into a method of close reading that seeks the blind spots of texts and their disseminating force. More radical aspects of Derrida's thought have sometimes been overlooked. For example, *Spurs: Nietzsche's Styles* (bilingual, 1976); *The Postal Card: From Socrates to Freud and Beyond* (1980, tr. 1988); and *Otobiographies* (1984) focus on the politics of reception, exposing the institutional perversion of philosophic projects, including his own. More recently Derrida's work has become more interested in an applied critique of cultural institutions and norms, as in *The Gift of Death* (1992, tr. 1996). Critical studies include Rodolphe Gasché, *The*

Tain of the Mirror: Derrida and the Philosophy of Refection (1986) and Christopher Norris, *Derrida* (1987).

MARCEL CORNIS-POPE

Desai, Anita (1937–   ),   novelist, short-story writer, children's fiction. Born in Mussoorie, India and educated at Delhi University, Desai came to the United States in 1987. She has taught at several American colleges, including the Massachusetts Institute of Technology. Desai's novels center on the problems of contemporary life in post-colonial India. *Cry, the Peacock* (1963) and *Where Shall We Go This Summer?* concern women attempting to assert individuality in a closed society. *Voices in the City* (1965), *Bye-Bye, Blackbird* (1968), and *Fire on the Mountain* (1977) deal with intercultural and intergenerational conflicts. *Baumgartner's Bombay* (1989) treats the experience of a German refugee in India. The 1995 novel *Journey to Ithaca* centers on a European couple traveling to India to seek spiritual enlightenment. Children's books include *The Peacock Garden* (1974), *Cat on a Houseboat* (1976), and *The Village by the Sea* (1982).

Descent into the Maelstrom, A,   a story by EDGAR ALLAN POE, published in *Graham's Magazine*, 1841; included in *Tales*, 1845. Poe tells how during a storm two Norwegian fishermen are drawn into a maelstrom. The men are brothers; one goes insane, and the other lashes himself to a cask and comes to the surface with his hair whitened from fear and his expression altered. The survivor tells the story.

Desire Under the Elms (1924),   a tragedy by EUGENE O'NEILL. Set in New England, the play deals with an elderly farmer and his three sons. The elder sons decide to leave home for California just as Ephraim, the father, returns home with Abbie, a woman of 35, his new wife. Abbie seduces Eben, the youngest son, hoping she can bear a son by him and claim that the child is Ephraim's. When it appears to Eben that Abbie has used him only for her own ends, he threatens to expose her infidelity, and to prove her love for him she smothers the child. The play exemplifies O'Neill's deep interest in Freudian psychology and is considered one of his best works.

De Smet, Pierre-Jean.   See SMET, PIERRE-JEAN DE.

De Soto, Hernando [also, **Fernando da Soto**] (1500?–1542),   Spanish explorer. De Soto visited regions in Central America and Peru and then led an expedition to conquer Florida (1539–42). His expedition went far beyond the boundaries of present-day Florida. He ventured as far as the west bank of the Mississippi River (1541) and was often in conflict with hostile Indian tribes. Unable to find the gold he was seeking, De Soto started to turn back, died on the banks of the great river he had discovered, and was buried in its waters by his followers.

De Spain, Major Cassius, and **de Spain, Major Manfred,**   characters in works by FAULKNER. Cassius, a former Confederate cavalry officer, figures prominently in *Absalom, Absalom!* and the stories "Barn Burning" and "The Bear." Manfred, his son, a West Point graduate, veteran of the Spanish-American War and mayor of Jefferson, is outwitted by Flem Snopes in the Snopes Trilogy.

detective fiction.   Also mystery story, thriller, whodunit, crime novel. A form of narrative fiction that focuses on crime and its solution. The agent of detection is usually a gifted amateur or a professional detective, either a member of the official police force or a private investigator.

An early example was William Godwin's *Adventures of Caleb Williams* (1794), which was immensely popular in England and the United States. In the 19th century, a number of circumstances, from Sir Robert Peel's 1829 founding of the London Police, headquartered in Scotland Yard, to the publication of the memoirs of the Parisian police detective Francois Eugene Vidocq (1775–1857), whose work inspired Dumas, Victor Hugo, and Charles Dickens, influenced the public interest in crime and detection. Cooper's characters in the LEATHER-STOCKING TALES (1823–1841), both white and Indian, exhibited exceptional abilities in reading clues in natural settings. In Frank Luther Mott's calculation of best sellers from colonial times to 1945, he reported that eighteen murder mysteries were among the books attaining widest popularity.

EDGAR ALLAN POE is widely credited with inventing the modern detective story with "The Murders in the Rue Morgue," which appeared in *Graham's Magazine* in 1841. Poe's detective hero, C. Auguste Dupin, is a Frenchman who possesses remarkable powers of deduction. Though he appeared in only two additional stories, "The Mystery of Marie Rogêt" (1842–1843) and "The Purloined Letter" (1845), Dupin established the model for all the intellectual detectives who followed. ANNA KATHERINE GREEN's *The Leavenworth Case* (1878) is cited as the first crime novel by an American woman.

The most famous of Dupin's successors is Arthur Conan Doyle's Sherlock Holmes, introduced in *A Study in Scarlet* in 1887. Holmes was a firm believer in the value of careful observation and logical deduction as a method of solving puzzling crimes. "From a drop of water," he insisted, "a logician could infer the possibility of an Atlantic and a Niagara without having seen or heard of one or the other."

Holmes became so popular with readers that when Doyle, tired of his detective hero, killed him off in 1893 in "The Final Problem," the public was outraged. Eight years later, bowing to public pressure, Doyle resurrected him and the Holmes stories continued to appear until 1927.

The brilliant but eccentric Holmes became the prototype for scores of detective geniuses, and the Holmesian tale became the model for the whodunit. Among those who created successful American versions of the intellectual detective are Jacques Futrelle, who introduced Professor S. F. X. Van Dusen (known as the Thinking Machine) in 1907; Arthur B. Reeve, whose Professor Craig Kennedy (known as the American Sherlock Holmes) made his debut in 1914; and S. S. Van Dine (pseudonym of WILLARD HUNTINGTON WRIGHT), whose Philo Vance made his debut in 1926.

Though Poe was an American writer, his detective was French and Dupin's successors were largely English gentlemen or American versions of the same figure. Creation of the first truly American detective hero can be credited to Carroll John

Daly, who in 1923 introduced a private detective named Race Williams in BLACK MASK, a pulp magazine originally begun by H. L. Mencken and George Jean Nathan. Williams is a tough-talking professional private detective who relies on guns rather than brains in solving criminal cases.

Four months later, DASHIELL HAMMETT, an ex-Pinkerton private detective, introduced in *Black Mask* an unnamed detective employed by the Continental Detective Agency in San Francisco. Known as the Continental Op, Hammett's private eye, together with another of his creations named Sam Spade, who appeared in *The Maltese Falcon* in 1929, established the prototype for the hard-boiled, or tough-guy, American private detective hero.

Hammett was a contemporary of Ernest Hemingway's and his influence on the detective novel can be compared with Hemingway's impact on American fiction. Both writers created tough, laconic heroes who are frequently bruised but seldom defeated by unpleasant and often violent experiences. Hammett's hard-boiled hero traced his ancestry back not to Poe's intellectual Dupin but rather to such American frontier heroes as JAMES FENIMORE COOPER's NATTY BUMPPO. And Hammett's use of colorful first-person narration, a distinctive blend of slang, wisecracks, and colloquial humor that has become a standard feature of the genre, owes much to Mark Twain's discovery of the music that resides in the American vernacular.

RAYMOND CHANDLER, a fellow *Black Mask* writer, praised Hammett for introducing realism into detective fiction: "Hammett gave murder back to the kind of people that commit it for reasons, not just to provide a corpse." Furthermore, he added, "he made them talk and think in the language they customarily used for these purposes."

Chandler's own contribution to the genre was every bit as important as Hammett's. Beginning with *The Big Sleep* in 1939, he produced a series of detective novels featuring private eye Philip Marlowe that are notable for their wit, colorful style, and acute sense of character and place (Southern California in the 1940s). Chandler proved that in the hands of a gifted artist like himself, the mystery story could be taken seriously as literature.

Chandler had many imitators. Some, like MICKEY SPILLANE, a writer of enormous popularity and small talent, capitalized on the attitudes of the post–World War II period and the rise of the new cheap paperback industry to turn out feverish revenge fantasies. His Mike Hammer books are among the most violent in the genre.

More talented writers, heartened by Chandler's example, further explored the literary potential of the genre. ROSS MACDONALD (pseudonym of Kenneth Millar) brought a poet's touch and a psychologist's concern to the depiction of crime in a series of novels featuring Southern California private eye Lew Archer. Macdonald's interest was less in whodunit and more on how lives are affected by crime, often one that occurred several years in the past. JOHN D. MACDONALD created a different sort of hero in Travis McGee, a self-styled tin-horn

Gawain who regularly risks his life to solve crime and right wrongs in sunny Florida. In 1937 crime-story writers formed the Mystery Writers of America, an association which awards annual "Edgars."

Among contemporary writers who are continuing to explore the literary possibilities of the private-eye genre are Robert B. Parker, Arthur Lyons, Stephen Greenleaf, Joseph Hansen, Jonathan Valin, and Loren Estleman. A recent development is crime fiction featuring female or minority detectives. PATRICIA CORNWELL's Kay Scarpetta is a medical examiner, actively working on solving crimes. SUE GRAFTON's Kinsey Millhone solves mysteries in alphabetical order; Marcia Muller, Sara Paretsky, and others use female detectives. The Navajo detectives Joe Leaphorn and Jim Chee, in the novels of TONY HILLERMAN, do their work against the background of the Four Corners area of the Southwest.

Though the hard-boiled detective novel came to dominate the mystery genre in America, a number of writers found success by more closely following the British whodunit tradition. Among the most popular were ELLERY QUEEN (pseudonym of cousins Frederick Dannay and Manfred B. Lee), also important as editor and anthologizer of mysteries; REX STOUT, creator of Nero Wolfe; JOHN DICKSON CARR, a master of the locked-room mystery; and ERLE STANLEY GARDNER, creator of Perry Mason, a lawyer who solves crimes in the courtroom.

Detective fiction enjoys widespread popularity today. One reason for this is the success of writers like GEORGE V. HIGGINS and Elmore Leonard, whose novels blur the distinction between the simple mystery story and serious fiction. Mystery readers continue to be attracted to the genre by the pleasures inherent in the detective story, but increasing numbers of readers are finding in the works of the best of these writers the rewards of good fiction.

DAVID GEHERIN/BP

De Tocqueville, Alexis.   See TOCQUEVILLE.

Deutsch, Babette (1895–1982),   poet, critic. Born in New York City, Deutsch not only wrote much excellent poetry but was noted for her sensitive and acute criticism. She was also a translator of Russian and German verse, usually in collaboration with her husband, Avrahm Yarmolinsky. Her collections of verse include *Banners* (1919), *Honey out of the Rock* (1925), *Fire for the Night* (1930), *Epistle to Prometheus* (1931), *One Part Love* (1939), *Take Them, Stranger* (1944), *Animal, Vegetable, Mineral* (1954), and *Coming of Age: New and Selected Poems* (1959). Her criticism includes *Potable Gold* (1929); *This Modern Poetry* (1935 and enlarged as *Poetry in Our Time*, 1952, 1956, 1962). Deutsch's prose works include *Heroes of the Kalevala, Finland's Saga* (1940); *Walt Whitman, Builder for America* (1941); *The Reader's Shakespeare* (1946); and *Poetry Handbook* (1957), a useful compilation revised through several succeeding editions.

Devil and Daniel Webster, The (1937),   a story by STEPHEN VINCENT BENÉT. The tale became a classic of American literature as soon as it was published in the *Saturday Evening Post*. It tells the story of Jabez Stone, a New Hampshire farmer who sells his soul to the devil and then, when Mr. Scratch comes to collect, retains the great lawyer and orator to save him. By his eloquence before a jury of remarkably depraved characters, Webster manages to secure Stone's acquittal. Benét made a superb adaptation of an ancient folklore theme to American folkways. Douglas Stuart Moore based an opera on the story (1938). A movie version was called *All That Money Can Buy.*

Devil in Manuscript, The (1851),   a story by NATHANIEL HAWTHORNE. Part of the collection called THE SNOW IMAGE AND OTHER TWICE-TOLD TALES, the story tells of a visit to a lawyer who is trying to turn novelist and is writing the narrative of "a fiend as represented in our traditions and the written records of witchcraft." But a devil is in the papers; moreover, seventeen publishers have already turned down his book. He throws his manuscript into the fire, and the fiend leaps up in one bright blaze—and sets the town on fire!

Devil-Puzzlers (1871),   a story by FREDERICK BEECHER PERKINS. The hero of this tale of a frustrated devil has the cleverness to insert an escape clause in the contract he makes with his Infernal Majesty. He stipulates that at the expiration of the period mentioned in the contract, he will be left unharmed in body and soul, provided that the devil proves unable to answer three questions. Satan manages to reply to the first question, on predestination and free will, and even to the second, on the immortality of the soul in the light of modern science. At this moment the hero's wife comes in, and she puts the third question: Which is the front end of *this?*—and she hands him her bonnet. He is unable to reply and in a blast of thunder angrily makes his exit by the window.

Devil's Dictionary, The   (called *The Cynic's Word Book*, 1906; retitled, 1911), a collection of about two thousand original epigrams and brief essays by AMBROSE BIERCE. He addresses his definitions to those "who prefer dry wines to sweet, sense to sentiment, wit to humor, and clean English to slang." In the definitions he expresses caustically his aversion to democracy, socialism, communism, and labor unions, but also to people with money, writers of the day as such, the human mind, and human beings. He describes *plan* as a way of bothering "about the best method of accomplishing an accidental result," *wit* as "the salt with which the American humorist spoils his intellectual cookery by leaving it out," *alone* as "in bad company," *impunity* as "wealth," *once* as "enough," and *adage* as "boned wisdom for weak teeth."

De Vinne, Theodore L[ow] (1828–1914),   printer, historian. Born in Connecticut, De Vinne founded and managed Theo. L. De Vinne & Co., later the De Vinne Press, and became widely known for the excellence and artistry of his printing and engravings. He printed such noted magazines as *St. Nicholas, Scribner's, The Century*, and also the earlier books of the Grolier Club, of which he was a founder and sixth president. Among his books are *The Invention of Printing* (1876), *Historic Printing Types* (1886), and *The Practice of Typography* (4 v. 1900–04).

De Voto, Bernard A[ugustine] (1897–1955), teacher, editor, author. Born in Utah and early in his career a professor of English at Northwestern University (1922–27) and Harvard (1929–36), De Voto was a voluminous writer with widely varying interests. His writings appeared in many kinds of periodicals, from the journals of learned societies to *College Humor.* He edited the *Saturday Review of Literature* from 1936 to 1938 and became the third occupant of *The Easy Chair* in HARPER'S MAGAZINE (1935–1955).

His books fall into at least four categories. He first won fame when he replied vigorously in *Mark Twain's America* (1932) to *The Ordeal of Mark Twain,* VAN WYCK BROOKS's disparaging book on Clemens. This was followed by *Mark Twain at Work* (1942). He also edited selections from Clemens's *Autobiography*, calling it *Mark Twain in Eruption* (1940). He wrote many controversial essays on literature, education, and social history, some of them collected in *Forays and Rebuttals* (1936), *Minority Report* (1940), *The Literary Fallacy* (1944), *The World of Fiction* (1950), and *The Easy Chair* (1955). The work he regarded as his most important was his historical writing, principally *The Year of Decision* (1943); ACROSS THE WIDE MISSOURI (1947), which won a Pulitzer Prize; and *The Course of Empire* (1952). He edited *The Journals of Lewis and Clark* (1953). Finally, his novels and short stories must be mentioned: *The Crooked Mile* (1924), *Mountain Time* (1947), and others, as well as several written under the pen name John August.

De Voto was the center of many controversies, in some of which he became involved because of his anger at American authors who knew little of American history or American life in the large and who neglected American themes.

De Vries, Peter (1910–1993),   novelist, humorist. Born in Chicago and educated at Calvin College and Northwestern, De Vries operated vending machines and acted on the radio in the 1930s, then was an editor for *Poetry* magazine (1938–44). His career as a novelist began with *But Who Wakes the Bugler?* (1940), with illustrations by the cartoonist CHARLES ADDAMS. Long associated with *The New Yorker*, De Vries published much of his short fiction there. Frequently, his targets are affluent suburbanites in places not unlike Westport, Connecticut, his home for many years. These inhabit especially the novels that by end of the 1950s had established him as one of the most distinguished comic writers of his time: *The Tunnel of Love* (1954), *Comfort Me With Apples* (1956), and *The Tents of Wickedness* (1959). His aim is varied, however, and his humor overlies a solid moral core. *The Tents of Wickedness* is in part a parody of other writers, including Faulkner, Erskine Caldwell, and Graham Greene. *The Blood of the Lamb* (1962) tells of faith confronted with incurable disease. *Let Me Count the Ways* (1965) deals with religious conversion. *The Vale of Laughter* (1967) focuses on sex and behavioral psychology. *Into Your Tent I'll Creep* (1971) satirizes women's liberation. *I Hear America Swinging* (1976) comments on the sexual revolution. His other novels include *Through the Fields of Clover* (1961); *Reuben, Reuben* (1964); *Madder Music* (1977), concerning a writer who thinks of himself as Groucho Marx; *Consenting Adults* (1980); *Slouching towards Kalamazoo* (1983); and *Peckham's Marbles* (1986), about a novelist addicted to word play. His stories are collected in *No, But I Saw the Movie* (1952) and *Without a Stitch in Time* (1972).

Dewey, John (1859–1952),   teacher, philosopher, educational reformer. Born in Vermont and educated at the University of Vermont and Johns Hopkins, Dewey taught at several universities before moving to Columbia University (1904–1930). Through his teaching, leadership, and books he became the chief influence on American education in the first half of the 20th century. A follower of WILLIAM JAMES, he turned PRAGMATISM to the cause of education, emphasizing the need to turn theory and knowledge to practical applications in the classroom. "Philosophy is of account only if it affords guidance to action," he wrote, rejecting authoritarian modes of teaching and emphasizing "learning by doing." A strong believer in democratic principles, he was an advocate of social welfare, academic freedom, and political reform. Among his books are *Psychology* (1887), *The School and Society* (1899). *Democracy and Education* (1916), *Reconstruction in Philosophy* (1920), *Human Nature and Conduct* (1922), *Experience and Nature* (1925), *The Quest for Certainty* (1929), *Art as Experience* (1934), *Logic: The Theory of Inquiry* (1938), *Freedom and Culture* (1939), and *Problems of Men* (1946).

Dewey, Melvil (1851–1931),   librarian. Dewey became known as the inventor of the Dewey Decimal System, extensively used as a readily remembered way of classifying books, although large libraries more often use the Library of Congress classification. Dewey devised his system while he was a student librarian at Amherst College. He later became librarian at Columbia University, where he founded the first library school (1887). He was also an advocate of simplified spelling.

Dexter, Timothy (1747–1806),   merchant, humorist. Born in Malden, Massachusetts, Dexter made a fortune through unusual business deals that included buying up apparently worthless Continental currency (later redeemed), selling warming pans in the West Indies, and trading in whalebone. Describing himself as First in the East, First in the West, and Greatest Philosopher of All the Known World, he built an eccentric mansion in Newburyport and left a charity bequest to the city. Much of his story he tells in *A Pickle for the Knowing Ones, or Plain Truths in a Homespun Dress* (1802) in a style enlivened by idiosyncratic spelling and without punctuation. In a second edition (1805) he includes a page of stops—periods, commas, etc.—for those who love punctuation and tells them to "peper and solt as they plese." John P. Marquand wrote a life of Dexter (1925) and revised it in 1960.

Dharma Bums, The,   novel by JACK KEROUAC.

Dial, The.   Four magazines with this name have appeared since 1840. The first was an organ of the Transcendentalist movement and was founded by THEODORE PARKER, BRONSON ALCOTT, ORESTES BROWNSON, MARGARET FULLER, JAMES FREEMAN CLARKE, and RALPH WALDO EMERSON. Fuller was the editor for the first two years, and Emerson took over until 1844, when the magazine died. In its short life it exerted great influence and gave an audience to Thoreau, the two Channings, Jones Very, and other Transcendentalist writers. The second *Dial* was founded by MONCURE CONWAY in Cincinnati in

1860. Conway, a young Congregationalist minister who had defended Tom Paine's writings, abolition, and other unorthodox creeds, envisioned it as "a legitimation of the Spirit of the Age, which aspires to be free in thought, doubt, utterance, love and knowledge." Among other contributions during its first—and last—year of existence, the magazine published poems by Emerson and the young W. D. Howells, and O. B. Frothingham's *The Christianity of Christ*, a series that sought to rescue the basic teachings of Christ from the distortions of dogma. In 1880 Francis F. Browne founded the third *Dial* in Chicago as a conservative literary journal. In 1898 the CHAPBOOK was incorporated into *The Dial*. Later editors were RICHARD HENRY STODDARD and William Henry Smith. In its conservative Chicago days, it acclaimed ELSIE VENNER but condemned THE RED BADGE OF COURAGE, LEAVES OF GRASS, and the dramas of Ibsen. In 1916 *The Dial* moved to New York City. There, under the editorship of C. J. Masseck, it began to publish the works of new writers. During this period CONRAD AIKEN, John Massey, PADRAIC COLUM, RANDOLPHY BOURNE, and VAN WYCK BROOKS were listed as editors. Scofield Thayer became editor in 1919, and *The Dial* began to publish works of well-known authors the world over: T. S. Eliot, Thomas Mann, Anatole France, George Santayana, D. H. Lawrence, Sherwood Anderson, Jules Romains, Edna St. Vincent Millay, William Butler Yeats, Edward Arlington Robinson, Ezra Pound, E. E. Cummings, and Gertrude Stein. MARIANNE MOORE became editor in 1925. The magazine ceased publication in 1929. In 1959 a new *Dial* magazine appeared under the editorship of James Silberman. A literary quarterly, it printed the work of Bernard Wolfe, Herbert Gold, and R. V. Cassill.

dialect in American literature.   Naturally enough, it is in humorous writing that dialect plays its major role. The pioneers of American humor introduced it early in the 19th century and it soon became a stock element in the stuff of comedy. The 20th century has seen the older types challenged, even superseded, by the cult of informality and slang. Historically it was the *Waverley* novels of Sir Walter Scott, very popular in America, that influenced the use of dialect. Along with the localization of characters and the suggestion of their backgrounds, the portrayal of peculiarities of their speech seemed essential.

The term *dialect* usually refers to substandard language, primarily to local or regional peculiarities that diverge from the accepted usage of the educated. The peculiarities may be of vocabulary, grammar, pronunciation, spelling, or syntax. Slang hardly deserves classification as dialect, though it is sometimes hard to create a demarcation. Dialect is relatively static, slang is transient; but slang terms sometimes are stabilized into dialect and sometimes, when there is a liking for them or they fill a need, they may make their way into the standard language. In this discussion an endeavor is made to indicate in broad lines the types of dialect appearing as our national literature has developed.

In colonial writing, dialect plays a negligible part, if any. The pioneer dialect-speaking character of significance was Jonathan, the Down East Yankee of Royall Tyler's play THE

CONTRAST (1787). Jonathan speaks colloquially, not the usual book English of the other characters, and he knows some of the slang of the day ("I'll swamp it," and "I vow"). Following Tyler's hit, Yankee plays began to appear all over the country. During the 1830s they were the most popular type of drama. Of importance, too, in the wake of Benjamin Franklin's POOR RICHARD were the almanacs, which enlivened themselves by using the New England vernacular. It began to appear in jest books and newspapers and travel books. Various other characters alongside the Yankee rustic and the Yankee peddler (originated in T.C. HAILBURTON's *Sam Slick* of 1836) speak it. It became stock, with its serving up of such expressions as "do tell," "I want to know," "tarnal," and its devotion to illiterate spellings. In the 1840s and 1850s there was wide contribution to newspapers of letters composed in rural dialect. The use of Down East talk to make characters more lifelike, vivid, and folksy flourished from about 1825 onward and reached its heyday about 1830–70. The popular humorists of the midcentury, such as Benjamin Shillaber (1814–1890), who created MRS. PARTINGTON, and FRANCES WHITCHER (1811–1852) of GODEY'S LADY'S BOOK, who created the Widow Bedott, belong to the Down East dialect writers.

On the whole the dialect of the New England region appears at its best in Lowell's BIGLOW PAPERS (1848, 1861–62). In the later *Papers* Lowell strove confessedly for scientific accuracy in presenting the rural speech he knew. His language, marked as it was by amusing turns of speech, peculiar vocabulary, homely metaphors and similes, and unlettered spellings, appealed to his readers no less than did his political and social satire and entertaining sayings. It was Lowell who inaugurated the popularity in verse of rustic speech. Among his ultimate followers were WILL CARLETON (1845–1912), JAMES WHITCOMB RILEY (1849–1916), EUGENE FIELD (1850–1895), SAM WALTER FOSS (1858–1911), and other interpreters of their widely scattered regions.

Contemporary with the Down East rustic and running parallel with him for a time was the Kentuckian. Other frontier characters, huntsmen, boatmen, and local figures followed. Their habitat was the old Southwest, Tennessee, Georgia, Louisiana, Mississippi, and Arkansas. They were celebrated in a rollicking literature chronicling their boasting and tall tales. The "ring-tailed roarer, half horse and half alligator" was one of their products. This era may be dated from SEBA SMITH's *Jack Downing Letters* of 1830, and it extended beyond the Civil War. Conspicuous figures, played up in the almanacs and other publications, were the historical DAVY CROCKETT, who gained legendary stature, and MIKE FINK, "last of the Keelboatmen." George W. Harris's yarn-telling hero in SUT LOVINGOOD (1867), whose spicy American vernacular was far from that of the Yankee, was especially influential. In this region the tall tale, told with gusto and exuberance, flourished. Strange words appeared and were given diffusion (*absquatulate, cahoots, cattawampus, flabbergasted, rambunctious, sockdolager*). Newspaper hoaxes and contributions from illiterate letter-writers retained popularity. Accounts of local manners, customs, and amusements are given with the boisterous humor supposed to appertain to the Southwest. The contrast is strong with the highly mannered narration and talk prevailing in contemporary fiction and short stories. On the whole, Seba Smith (1792–1868) is the best writer of dialect for backwoods and frontier portrayals, as Lowell was for the Down East.

In any chronological survey of dialect in American literature, a group of newspaper humorists of the Civil War period looms large. These preceded and influenced MARK TWAIN. Chief among them were Charles Farrar Browne (1834–1867), who called himself ARTEMUS WARD; David Ross Locke (1833–1888), who assumed the name of PETROLEUM VESUVIUS NASBY; ROBERT H. NEWELL (1836–1901), who wrote as Orpheus C. Kerr; and Henry Wheeler Shaw (1818–1885), whose pseudonym was JOSH BILLINGS. A younger group of these newspaper humorists included MELVILLE B. LANDON (1839–1910), who called himself Eli Perkins; ROBERT BURDETTE (1844–1914); and EDGAR WILSON (Bill) NYE (1850–1896). FINLEY PETER DUNNE (1867–1936) launched his popular Irish commentator, Mr. Dooley, in 1898. These men wanted new methods and unlocalized comedy. They sought and achieved nationwide appeal, and their humor, which lay chiefly in verbal expression, was not that of one region. Mainly they relied more and more on eccentricities of language, on the handling of sentences, grammar, quotations, and metaphors and smiles, than on creating characters and background. Sometimes, too, their devices in verbal form were pretty crude. One of Artemus Ward's specialties was deliberately unlettered spellings ("enahow," "snaik," "goaks," "yooth," "Sylvanus Kobb's last tail"). And there was liking among the group for pseudo-Shakespearean and romantic archaisms of the "Dost thou?" "I dost" type. Sometimes the humor lay in the verb forms, "I asked her if we could glide in the merry dance . . . and we glode." Culmination came with Mark Twain, whose HUCKLEBERRY FINN appeared in 1884. Twain did not limit himself to a single locality or to one type of device but exhibited all the linguistic whimsicalities of his predecessors, that is malapropisms, puns, misquotations, understatement, exaggeration, incongruities, illiteracies, and absurd spellings. The humor, the poetry too, of all types of folk speech became grist for his mill.

In fiction, dialect reached major importance with the arrival of the local color school. Earlier novelists had made some use of it. H. H. BRACKENRIDGE's MODERN CHIVALRY (1792) had an Irish clown, Teague O'Regan, but he was a transplantation from the English stage. WASHINGTON IRVING had Yankees in his *Knickerbocker History* and his ICHABOD CRANE is a Yankee, but they talk little and that little lacks the flavor of America. Cooper's LEATHERSTOCKING speaks a quaint language sprinkled with archaisms of vocabulary and pronunciation and lapsing into poetical rhapsody when his topic is nature. Cooper's David Gamut is also a Yankee and some of his characters from other lands, in his various books, speak brands of English colored by their mother tongues. J. P. KENNEDY and WILLIAM GILMORE SIMMS also try dialect at times. Hawthorne did not. Even his children speak pure English, though his skilled handling makes their talk seem natural. On the whole the advent of the local color school in the last half of the century marks a new period. These writers continue the tradition of regional portrayal, with attention to realistic detail. The Yankee reappears in the group of New England novels of Harriet Beecher Stowe, *Oldtown Folks* (1869) in particular. Edward Eggleston's THE HOOSIER SCHOOLMASTER (1871) sets forth the speech of the country folk of Indiana. BRET HARTE from 1868 onward depicted California, MARY N. MURFREE reproduced the dialect of the Tennessee mountains, 1884–97, G. W. CABLE wrote of New Orleans and Louisiana in the 1870s, notably in OLD CREOLE DAYS (1879), and JOEL CHANDLER HARRIS's Uncle Remus (1880–1910) told his animal tales in the folk speech of the Georgia African-Americans of his region. The high tide of local dialect lasted till the end of the century. The New York novel DAVID HARUM (1898) is a salient example, some say, of the B' Gosh School of fiction.

WALT WHITMAN is hardly to be described as a dialect writer but he cannot be excluded from a discussion of the American vernacular. He was a rebel against literary English. He championed the vigor of colloquialisms, even of vulgarisms and slang. He was ready to accept such terms as *skedaddle, shebang, yap, out with the bhoys, souse, yawp* in his prose and at times in his verse, and he did not mind manipulating standard words in his verse (*civilizee, imperturbe, philosoph*). He did much to influence oncoming writers toward the freer and more colloquial, more uncouth if you will, use of language.

African-American dialect in our literature has been an artificial product having little relation to real speech. Its popularity followed the success of DAN EMMETT's "Jim Crow" melodies and dances (1830 or 1831), and of the succeeding minstrelsy. A traditional dialect became established: "debbil," "trabble," "gwine," "massa," "honey," "de Lawd." Really there is as much regional and individual divergence among African-Americans as among whites. Addison Hubbard in *American Speech* (I, 1926) brought together, transcribed by competent persons, a passage from Aesop's *Fables* as it might be spoken by African-Americans from Harlem, East North Carolina, South Carolina, Georgia, Mississippi, and Louisiana. The dialect in these and in O'Neill's EMPEROR JONES and DuBose Heyward's PORGY is a far cry from the slapstick minstrelsy type or the strange Gullahesque bits in Poe's THE GOLD BUG.

The comedy German was also handed a stock dialect stemming from the popular *Hans Breitmann Ballads* (see under BREITMANN) of the 1860s and 1870s by Charles Godfrey Leland ("Dey vented to dis berson's house/To see some furnidure"). For a time the Irishman with his *begorry, bhoys, mavourneen,* and *shillelagh* had a place in journalism and song, culminating in the philosophical MR. DOOLEY (1898–1910). The Dooley dialect is marked by strong *r*'s, aspirated *d*'s and *t*'s, and archaic vowels ("wurruld," "ye could niver be a rale pathrite"). Pennsylvania German, often called Pennsylvania Dutch, entered dialect writing, and we have had served up to us the broken English of Italians, of Mexicans in the Southwest, and of Scandinavians from Minnesota and the Dakotas. WALLACE IRWIN's Schoolboy (*Letters from a Japanese Schoolboy,* 1909) had a picturesque dialect of English, and New York City Yiddish has had many popular successes, such as the POTASH AND PERLMUTTER

stories of Montague Glass (1910) and the *Nize Bebe* of MILT GROSS (1925). A Native American brand of English has been little heard from. Monosyllables, truncated sentences, and grunts ("Ugh!") mostly make it up. Or, educated in schools, these characters speak standard English.

Efforts in the 20th century have been directed more and more in plays, novels, and short stories toward "giving talk as it is talked." SINCLAIR LEWIS, for instance, had a sensitive ear for various types of American speech. The hardboiled school of fiction (DAMON RUNYON was influential here) strives to reproduce the language of the underworld and of the criminal classes, a sort of tough-guyese. (See HARDBOILED FICTION.) RING LARDNER brilliantly captured the speech of athletes and other semieducated persons. Some ultrarealists use words hitherto taboo, often seemingly to arrest attention or perhaps to shock. Rural mispronunciations and unlettered spelling still appear. But with the coming of interest in phonetic analysis closer representation of consecutive utterance is sought. Sentence fragments such as "How come?" and "You been away?" and amalgams such as *gotta, dincha, attaboy* and multilations such as *ittybitty,* and wordplays of many types are frequent. The clever ventures of O. Henry ("Broadway is New York's Yappian Way," "The Statue of the Dinkus Thrower in the Vatican"), which perhaps deserve literary recognition, have been succeeded by the violent perpetrations of *Billboard* and *Variety,* from which derive the verbal acrobatics of certain columnists. The ingenious concoctions of *Time* (*intelligentsiacs, ballyhooligans*) are now volunteered less frequently. If for rural dialect the lid is off much of the last century, the lid is off now, for better or worse, in other areas as well. Witness the grotesqueries of the advertisements of films and other publicity (*colossapendous, stupeficient*), or the uninhibited coinages of trade names (*Quink, Socony, Vegamato*). But these ventures are outside the literary field.

LOUISE POUND

Diamond Dick. A favorite character in dime novels. He was a creation of GEORGE CHARLES JENKS (1850–1929), who wrote under the pen name W. B. Lawson.

Diamond Lens, The (*Atlantic Monthly,* January, 1858), a tale by FITZ-JAMES O'BRIEN. One of the best-known stories of the mid-19th century, this tale relates how the inventor of a new microscope was suddenly able to see a charming sylph in a drop of water; when she died he went insane.

Diamond Lil (1928), a play by Mae West (1892–1980), who took the main role. The heroine is the mistress of Gus Jordan, a Bowery saloonkeeper who is also a pimp. Diamond Lil is so called because of the large amount of "ice" Gus has lavished on her, and she is generous with her favors. The resulting complications include a murder and several shootings and arrests. At the close Lil chooses as her favorite an alleged Salvation Army captain, in reality a prominent member of the vice squad. The play made Mae West famous; it included the line "Come up and see me some time."

Diary from Dixie, A (pub. 1905, 1949, 1982), by MARY BOYKIN CHESTNUT. A diary (from February 12, 1861, to August 2, 1865) of a woman in the South during the days of the Civil War. Mrs. Chestnut was the wife of James Chestnut, Jr., the first Southerner who resigned from the U.S. Senate, the man sent to demand the surrender of Fort Sumter, a general in the Confederate Army, and a member of the Confederate Senate. Mrs. Chestnut followed him everywhere in his missions, heard about everything, knew everyone, and in her diary expressed herself freely.

Diary of a Public Man, The   (*North American Review*, August–November 1879, 1946 in book form). When this alleged diary first appeared, it created a sensation with its vivid description of events preceding the election of Lincoln, his inauguration, and the fateful days that followed. The diary gave the first account of how Stephen A. Douglas held Lincoln's hat during the inauguration exercises—an incident now part of the Lincoln legend. The anonymous diarist reported talking to Lincoln as president-elect twice and as president once. Yet no one knew who he was or could vouch for the diary's authenticity. SAMUEL WARD has been suggested as author.

Diary of George Templeton Strong, The (4 v. 1952). This remarkable journal was the production of a New York City resident, educated at Columbia University and one of its trustees, a Trinity Church vestryman, one of the founders of the Philharmonic Society and of the School of Mines at Columbia, a lawyer of note, and a businessman. He knew the notable men of the city and the nation and spoke about them with frankness. He made his first entry on October 5, 1835, and continued the diary for forty years. It contains about 5 million words, from which Allan Nevins made a selection for publication. Strong liked men who worked for themselves and distrusted both Southern slave owners and Northern capitalists; neither, he thought, could quite be gentlemen. He was prejudiced against the races and creeds with which New York City began to fill up in his day, and he sneered at the unwashed democracy. But he had a mind for the graphic and described vividly celebrated crimes, P. T. Barnum's publicity stunts, the laying of the Atlantic cable, the ravages of cholera, and the fire at the Academy of Music.

Díaz del Castillo, Bernal (1496?–1584).   Spanish soldier and historian. Díaz was one of the soldiers who took part in the Spanish conquest of Mexico; he later settled down on an estate in Guatemala. As an octogenarian he read Francisco López de Gómara's *Conquest of Mexico* (1552), an official account that gave the credit to Cortez and scanted the contributions of his companions. To correct the record he wrote his *Historia verdadera de la conquista de la Nueva España (True History of the Conquest of New Spain)*. It remained in manuscript until 1632, when it was heavily edited by a priest for its first printing; a reasonably accurate edition did not appear until 1904. Showing the conquest from the view of the common soldier, the book is a classic among popular accounts of history. It is a lively, detailed report, sharpened perhaps by years of oral recounting by a master storyteller. Cortez is presented as a fallible human being, Montezuma is a worthy and princely opponent, Tenochtitlan more splendid than the cities of Europe. William H. Prescott used the *True History* as a

source for his *History of the Conquest of Mexico,* as did Archibald MacLeish for his CONQUISTADOR.

Diaz, Junot (1968–   ),   short-story writer, novelist. Born in the Dominican Republic, he came to the United States as a child and is a naturalized citizen. Educated at Rutgers and Cornell, Diaz has been published in prize story collections and been selected by *Newsweek* (1996) and *The New Yorker* (1999) as a promising young fiction writer. *Drown* (1996), a short-story collection, with stories narrated by teenagers from the Dominican Republic, met with favorable reviews. *Negocios* (1997) and *A Cheater's Guide to Love* (2000) are novels.

Dick, Philip K[indred] (1928–1982),   science-fiction writer. Born in Chicago, Dick was a prolific writer of novels and short stories in which he used traditional science-fiction materials to emphasize the dilemmas of characters who are generally not heroes and barely manage to survive. His work includes *The Man in the High Castle* (1962), in which a man manages to postpone a genocidal massacre; *Do Androids Dream of Electric Sheep?* (1968); *Galactic Pot-Healer* (1969); and *A Scanner Darkly* (1977).

Dickey, James (1923–1997),   poet, novelist, critic, teacher. Born in Atlanta, Dickey played football for a semester at Clemson College before enlisting in the Army Air Forces. After World War II, during which he flew with a night fighter squadron in the Pacific, he enrolled at Vanderbilt University, where he studied under DONALD DAVIDSON, one of the Southern Agrarians, who reinforced Dickey's regional piety.

After earning an M.A. from Vanderbilt in 1950, Dickey began a restless career in teaching, interrupted by military service during the Korean War (1951–52); a short-lived though successful career in advertising in New York and Atlanta (1956–61); fellowships from the *Sewanee Review* (1954) and the Guggenheim Foundation (1961), which took him to Europe; and two terms as poetry consultant to the Library of Congress (1966–68). After brief stints at Rice Institute (now University), the University of Florida, Reed College, San Fernando Valley State College (now California State University, Northridge), and other institutions, Dickey in 1969 became poet-in-residence at the University of South Carolina.

Dickey's most enduring work belongs to a single, prolific decade, which began with the appearance of *Into the Stone* in Scribner's *Poets of Today* VII (1960) and culminated in the publication of his *Poems 1957–1967* (1967), a major retrospective collection; *Babel to Byzantium* (1968), a lively compendium of essays and reviews: *Deliverance* (1970), a best-selling novel; and *Self-Interviews* (ed. Barbara and James Reiss, 1970), a spoken autobiography of the poet's creative life and an indispensable commentary on his *Poems 1957–1967*. This collection, the basis of Dickey's critical esteem, brings together most of the poems from his first four volumes—*Into the Stone; Drowning with Others* (1962); *Helmets* (1964); *Buckdancer's Choice* (1965), recipient of the National Book Award—and an additional twenty-five new poems, since published separately as *Falling, May Day Sermon, and Other Poems* (1981).

Dickey's characteristic poem derives from the demonic strain of English Romanticism. Well made, with a strong anapestic beat, it is wedded to incident and narrated in present tense and first person by a "middle-aged softening man" ("Springer Mountain"). Once an athlete ("The Bee") and a soldier ("Drinking from a Helmet," "The Firebombing"), he revitalized himself through contact with animals, whether at home ("A Dog Sleeping on My Feet"), in zoos ("Encounter in the Cage Country"), or in the wild ("The Summons"); through an immersion in nature ("Inside the River," "In the Mountain Tent"); through sexual fantasy ("In the Lupanar at Pompeii," "Slave Quarters"); and through illicit sexual activity ("Adultery," "Sustainment").

Dickey's later work includes *Sorties: Journal and New Essays* (1971); *Jericho: The South Beheld* (with Hubert Shuptrine, 1974), a coffee-table book; *The Central Motion: Poems 1968–1979* (1983), which comprises *The Eye-Beaters, Blood, Victory, Madness, Buckhead and Mercy* (1970), *The Zodiac* (1976), and *The Strength of Fields* (1979); *Puella* (1982) and *The Eagle's Mile* (1990), books of poems; and *Alnilam* (1987) and *To the White Sea* (1993), novels. *The Whole Motion: Collected Poems, 1949–1992* appeared in 1992 and *The Selected Poems* in 1998. *Understanding James Dickey* (1985) by Richard Baughman provides a coherent overview of the poetry and fiction, while Neal Bowers, in *James Dickey: The Poet as Pitchman* (1985), considers the relationship between Dickey's work and his flamboyant public persona. Christopher Dickey wrote *Summer of Deliverance: A Memoir of Father and Son* (1998). Matthew J. Bruccoli edited *Crux: The Letters of James Dickey* (1999).

David Havird/GP

Dickinson, Emily [Elizabeth] (1830–1886), poet. Certainly America's greatest woman author and possibly its greatest poet of either gender, Emily Dickinson chose a life of unbroken privacy. Perhaps the most remarkable fact about this artist is that she found a way to transform the elements of a completely private life into poetry of power and timeless diversity—poetry that has become centrally important to generations of readers. Dickinson journeyed away from her native Amherst, Massachusetts, fewer than a dozen times, yet her work has gone everywhere. It has been translated into scores of languages and is esteemed by millions of readers. Paradoxically, this distinguished author, whose external life was so devoid of noteworthy events that any factual account of it is necessarily brief and lacking in drama, was born into a family containing ambitious, cosmopolitan men who pursued active, sometimes flamboyant public careers. Ironically, these public men would scarcely be remembered today except for the extraordinary productions of their quiet kinswoman.

Emily Dickinson's grandfather, Samuel Fowler Dickinson, played a crucial role in the founding of Amherst College, and her father, his oldest son Edward, served for thirty-seven years as its treasurer. Both were successful lawyers, but Edward enjoyed far more sustained success than his father—becoming one of the wealthiest men in Amherst, serving many times in the Massachusetts Legislature, and even spending two years in Washington as a member of the House of Representatives. Although the oldest of Edward's children, Austin, was

expected to follow in his father's footsteps as a businessman and public servant (and to some extent did so), neither Emily nor her younger sister, Lavinia, was encouraged to seek any goals beyond those of house and home. All three of the Dickinson children were superbly educated: Emily completed her secondary school education at the Amherst Academy, where she received advanced instruction not only in languages and literature, but in mathematics and science as well; she went on to the newly created Mt. Holyoke Seminary, where she stayed for only one year, probably because the work was no more advanced than that which she had already completed at the academy. By the time her schooling was finished, she had received all the formal education any would-be writer male or female might require. Indeed, though she was a great deal more fully schooled than most young men at that time, she was expected to return to her father's house and help keep house until such time as she might leave to keep house for a husband.

It was not merely the case that no public role was expected of her; her entire family would have been horrified at the suggestion. It is no small irony that the father of this great poet ventured into print on only one subject, the necessity of keeping women in their proper place. As a young man of twenty-five, he published a series of essays in the local newspaper asking, "What duties were females designed to perform? Were they intended for Rulers, or Legislators, or Soldiers? Were they intended for the learned professions. . . . Should you like to dispute daily upon politics and religion, in your family—and above all, to be edified, at every interval of leisure, when you retire from the bustle of business. . . . By all means make sure of a *literary* wife. . . . Literature will . . . fill and warm and clothe you—Twill make your beds and sweep your rooms—wash and mend and cook for you." Nor did his views ever change: years later he scorned the woman suffragists in language equally vehement, and although he lived in close proximity to his gifted daughter for nearly half a century, he never seems to have had the slightest intimation of her genius or any interest at all in her intellect.

The attitude of Emily Dickinson's family toward her expected role was not unusual in mid-19th-century America: nice women were never expected to pursue a career, and few jobs of any kind were open to women. Women did sometimes write both fiction and poetry, and sometimes they published it, but it was clearly understood that women authors always wrote for a *popular audience*. *Men* might become serious writers—artists—but *women* were absolutely prohibited from such aspirations. Nothing displeased Emily Dickinson more than the prospect of becoming a popular writer of this sort: "If fame belonged to me," she wrote to her acquaintance THOMAS WENTWORTH HIGGINSON, an essayist and proponent of abolition and woman's suffrage, "I could not escape her—if she did not, the longest day would pass me on the chase—and the approbation of my Dog would forsake me." Moreover, the burden of such literary celebrity could be onerous for women: if an author's work became sufficiently popular, she might be obliged to undertake a lecture tour, thereby to endure the unwanted attentions of admirers and to experience the kind of notoriety that today's television performers confront. Any sensitive woman might shrink from such a prospect. Thus, although there is good reason to believe that Emily Dickinson would have liked to see her work in print—*provided that the circumstances were appropriate*—during her lifetime fewer than a dozen poems were actually published.

After Emily died, her sister, Lavinia, found almost two thousand poems among her papers: all were short lyrics, virtually none bore a title, and many hundreds of them bespoke the meticulous craftsmanship and power of genius. It was an unparalleled American literary discovery.

The fact that virtually none of Dickinson's work was published during her lifetime has presented readers with a number of problems. There were so many poems that they could not all be published immediately after her death; consequently, over a period of many years, a series of volumes were issued (by family and friends, some of whom undertook to correct the verse by "smoothing out" its rhythms, rhymes, and punctuation). Thus, publication was haphazard, and a complete, reliable edition of the work was not available until 1955. Even then, however, problems remained. Other than tracing the slow changes in handwriting, there has been no way to date any given poem's composition. In addition, more than half of the poems exist with variants—sometimes single words, sometimes as much as a line, sometimes entire stanzas—and there is no reliable way of determining the author's preferred choice. But perhaps the most damaging problems were introduced by readers' enthusiastic imaginations.

Despite the absence of colorful events in Dickinson's life, generations have presumed that there must have been *some* incident whose significance could account for the power of the verse. A number of different scenarios have been proposed. Emily Dickinson was not physically strong, and she had serious trouble with her vision, twice going to Boston so that her eyes might be treated by a specialist. Some of her readers have supposed that she must have had some mysterious ailment— perhaps that she even suffered a dramatic nervous breakdown. Emily Dickinson wrote passionate love poetry, but never married, so some of her readers have postulated that she loved in vain and turned to writing as compensation. Any number of figures have been identified as the man in her life—among them the Reverend Charles Wadsworth of Philadelphia, and Samuel Bowles, editor of the Springfield *Daily Republican*. As an adolescent Emily Dickinson wrote gushy, affectionate letters to her female friends, and she maintained a lifelong attachment to her brother's wife, who lived right next door, so some readers assert that Dickinson was America's first great lesbian poet.

Whatever may have been the secondary influences on Emily Dickinson's creativity, the primary influence could not have been more authentically American. Emily Dickinson's life coincided with the last great age of Puritanism in New England; during her young womanhood, Amherst still had public seasons of religious revival, when all were urged to submit to the will of God and undergo a religious conversion experience. It was a harrowing, humbling process. Emily Dickinson was pious enough to take the issue of conversion very seriously, but in the end she was too proud and too independent of mind for such renunciation of free will. She thought that an invisible God who had condemned all mankind to death and who demanded blind faith as the prerequisite for salvation while giving no assurances beyond the vague promises of the New Testament was not worthy of such obeisance. Thus, she rejected the Puritan inheritance of her forebears, but did so neither easily nor unambivalently.

Much of the poetry is an intense examination of the existential dilemmas raised by such religious issues as faith, mortality, and eternity. Sometimes, Dickinson captures human tragedy with a uniquely comic tone: "Of course—I prayed— / And did God Care? / He cared as much as on the Air / A Bird— had stamped her foot—." At other times, however, the underlying brutality of the Christian myth is dissected with ruthless clarity, and God's importunate quest for followers seems a form of Divine rape: "He fumbles at your spirit / As players at the keys / Before they drop full music on; / He stuns you by degrees." Many times, Dickinson dares contemplate the isolated terror of death itself in poems like "I heard a fly buzz when I died" or "Because I could not stop for Death— / He kindly stopped for me—."

Yet the range of Dickinson's poetry is not limited to these explicitly religious themes. She wrote many haunting poems that capture the strange, spare beauty of nature in New England. She wrote love poems of immense passion such as "Wild Nights—Wild Nights! / Were I with thee / Wild Nights should be / Our luxury!" She wrote poems that celebrate the simple virtues of a well-run home, for she knew the domestic realm with incomparable intimacy and appreciated humanity's need for the kindness and generosity so often associated with the merely private world. Far from condemning the country housewife, Emily Dickinson wrote movingly about the exhaustion, loneliness, and unheralded tragedies of such a life. And she wrote any number of eloquent threnodies to commemorate the lives of anonymous New Englanders.

Always averse to hypocrisy and pretentiousness, Dickinson could compose scathing satire. Perhaps no one has left so pungent a portrait of the prim, self-righteous Victorian matron: "What Soft—Cherubic Creatures— / These Gentlewomen are— / One would as soon assault a Plush— / Or violate a Star—." Her rendering of the saccharine 19th-century clergyman is equally devastating: "He preached upon 'Breadth' till it argued him narrow— / . . . What confusion would cover the innocent Jesus / To meet so enabled a Man!"

Perhaps no American poet has demonstrated greater range, and the final paradox of Dickinson's work may be that despite her geographical seclusion, she fulfilled Emerson's call for a Representative American Voice at least as well as her contemporary, the cosmopolitan Walt Whitman.

Because of the unsystematic way in which Dickinson's poetry came to public knowledge, many things are impossible to ascertain. No one knows exactly when she began to write seriously; the best estimate is sometime between 1850, when she was nineteen, and 1855. Furthermore, readers of Dickinson must be alert to the fact that the many corrupt versions of the poetry that were issued before the 1955 publication of the three-volume *Poems of Emily Dickinson*, edited by Thomas H. Johnson, have left a lingering confusion. Poems from these early volumes are not accurate, but they are nonetheless sometimes quoted because the copyright for them has expired. The situation has been complicated by the publication of *The Poems of Emily Dickinson: Variorum Edition* (1998), edited by R. W. Franklin, which supersedes the Johnson edition. Franklin has also published *The Poems of Emily Dickinson: Reading Edition* (1999), a one-volume distillation of the three-volume *Variorum*. Franklin earlier edited *The Manuscript Books of Emily Dickinson* (1981). Dickinson's *Letters* have also been published, edited by Thomas H. Johnson and Theodora Ward in 1958. There are two extended biographies of the poet: Richard B. Sewall's Pulitzer Prize–winning *Emily Dickinson* (1974) and Cynthia Griffin Wolff's more recent *Emily Dickinson* (1986). A number of plays have been based on the poet's life, most notably *The Belle of Amherst* by William Luce (1976), which has also been shown on television and is available on video cassette.

CYNTHIA GRIFFIN WOLFF/GP

Dickinson, John ["Fabius"] (1732–1808),   lawyer, merchant, landowner, pamphleteer. Born in Maryland, Dickinson studied law in England and became a rich man and a conservative who believed that a sound government should be founded on moderation, justice, and fair dealing together with respect for property rights. He never wanted to see the colonies severed from England, but his numerous pamphlets on taxation and other problems and his LETTERS FROM A FARMER IN PENNSYLVANIA TO THE INHABITANTS OF THE BRITISH COLONIES (1767–1768) increased in intensity of tone and exerted a profound influence both in the colonies and abroad. Dickinson refused to sign the Declaration of Independence, hoping that conciliation would still win the day. He wrote many of the state papers of the Continental Congress, participated in the Constitutional Convention, wrote his *Letters of Fabius* (1788) urging ratification, and composed in 1797 a second series of *Letters of Fabius* eloquently recommending the French cause. Dickinson wrote a song that became widely known. *A Song for American Freedom*, called the LIBERTY SONG (Boston *Gazette*, 1768). He was one of the founders of Dickinson College, which is named for him.

Dickinson, Jonathan.   A Quaker merchant known only for his diary, GOD'S PROTECTING PROVIDENCE.

Dictionaries.   See WEBSTER, NOAH; and WORCESTER, JOSEPH.

Dictionary of American Biography, The (20 v. 1928–36),   published under the auspices of the American Council of Learned Societies and edited first by ALLEN JOHNSON, then by DUMAS MALONE. Supplements have been issued periodically. The whole contains over 14,000 sketches by more

than 2,000 contributors. The DAB presents a vast panorama of the men and women who made America in all its varying eras. Living persons are excluded.

Dictionary of American English, A (4 v. 1938–44), edited by Sir William A. Craigie and James R. Hulbert, with a large staff of contributing specialists. It was twenty-five years in the making. The end of the 19th century was selected as a suitable stopping place, leaving for later collection an immense body of words produced during the years since 1900.

Dictionary of American History, The (6 v. 1940; 8 v. 1976),   edited by JAMES TRUSLOW ADAMS. A valuable compilation prepared by more than a thousand scholars.

Dictionary of Americanisms, A (1848),   edited by John R. Bartlett. This work went through four editions by 1877 and was reprinted in 1896. Described as a "Glossary of Words and Phrases Regarded as Peculiar to the United States," it contains about 3,725 terms, arranged in six, then (in the 1859 ed.) in nine categories.

Didion, Joan (1934–   ),   novelist, essayist. Didion's reputation has been based largely on her insights into the culture of her native California, which she presents as emblematic of the lost American Dream. The heroines of her novels *Run River* (1963), *Play It As It Lays* (1970), and *A Book of Common Prayer* (1977) drift numbly through lives illustrative of the cultural disintegration of their times. Two collections of essays, *Slouching Towards Bethlehem* (1968) and *The White Album* (1979), examine similar materials. Her other works include *Salvador* (1983), a report on conditions in El Salvador, and *Democracy*, a novel (1984). After twelve years, Didion returned to fiction with *The Last Thing He Wanted* (1996), about shady arms deals in Central America, following up on interests already treated in *Salvador* and *Democracy*. She is married to JOHN GREGORY DUNNE. *Essays and Interviews* appeared in 1984 and *Miami* in 1987. *After Henry* (1992), published as *Sentimental Journeys* in Britain, collects twelve essays on events in Washington, D.C., New York, and California.

Di Donato, Pietro (1911–1992),   writer, biographer. *Esquire* first published Di Donato's "Christ in Concrete." Almost entirely autobiographical, it tells the story of a family of Italian immigrants, including the memorable scene of the father's death in the collapse of a building when the boy was twelve years of age. From this story Di Donato developed his full-length novel of the same name (1939). For nearly twenty years thereafter, he published little significant writing. *Three Circles of Light* (1960) again deals with his family. His other books include *This Woman* (1958), *Immigrant Saint: The Life of Mother Cabrini* (1960), and *The Penitent* (1962). *Naked Author* (1970) is a miscellany of stories and excerpts from longer works.

Dietz, Howard (1896–1983),   press agent, librettist, writer of lyrics. Born in New York City and educated at Columbia, Dietz wrote some of the most popular stage and movie hits of his day, often in collaboration with noted composers or with other librettists. Among them were *Dear Sir* (with JEROME KERN, 1924); *Merry-Go-Round* (with Morrie

Ryskind, 1927); *The Little Show* (1929); *Second Little Show* (1930); *Revenge with Music* (1934); *Jackpot* (1944); *Inside U.S.A.* (1948); and *Jennie* (1963). Among song hits for which Dietz supplied the words are "Something to Remember You By," "Dancing in the Dark," and "You and the Night and the Music." In 1950 he adapted *Fledermaus* in English for the Metropolitan Opera Company. He also made an adaptation of Puccini's *La Bohème.* His autobiography is *Dancing in the Dark* (1975).

Digges, Thomas Atwood (1742–1822),   an American patriot friendly with many leaders, including Washington, Jefferson, Franklin, and Madison, who was in Portugal during the Revolution. To Digges has been attributed a novel entitled *The Adventures of Alonso, Containing Some Striking Anecdotes of the Present Prime Minister of Portugal.* It was published in London anonymously in 1775 and was described as being "by a native of Maryland, some years resident in Lisbon." It tells of the adventures of a young merchant and has some passages on government. If by Digges or another American of his time, it is the first American novel. Digges's *Letters* appeared in 1982.

Dillard, Annie (1945–   ),   essayist. Born in Pennsylvania and educated at Hollins College, in Virginia, Dillard has earned praise as one of the premier prose stylists of her day, particularly in *Pilgrim at Tinker Creek* (1974), which won a Pulitzer Prize, and in *Teaching a Stone to Talk* (1982). Her subject is specifically nature, more generally the world around her. Her prose is lucid, grounded in specificity, sometimes lyrical and metaphorical. *An American Childhood* (1987) is an outstanding autobiography, tracing the author's development from preschool through her teenage years. Her other titles include *Tickets for a Prayer Wheel* (1974), poetry; *Holy the Firm* (1977); *Living By Fiction* (1978), about contemporary fiction; *Encounters with Chinese Writers* (1984); and *The Writing Life* (1989). Dillard's first novel, *The Living* (1992), is a historical fiction set in the Pacific Northwest. *The Annie Dillard Reader*, a collection of poems, stories, and essays appeared in 1994, and *Mornings Like This: Found Poems* in 1995.

Dillon, George (1906–1968),   poet, editor. Born in Jacksonville, Florida, Dillon published *Boy in the Wind* (1927); *The Flowering Stone* (1931), which was awarded a Pulitzer Prize; and in collaboration with EDNA ST. VINCENT MILLAY a translation of Baudelaire's *Les Fleurs du Mal* (1935). He was the editor of POETRY from 1937 until 1950.

Dilsey,   a character in Faulkner's THE SOUND AND THE FURY.

dime novel, the.   A literary genre that owed its origin to ERASTUS F. BEADLE (1821–1894), who attained an amazing success when he published a *Dime Song Book* in Buffalo. In 1858 he moved to New York City, and together with his brother Irwin—and, later on, Robert Adams—began publication of yellow-backed dime novels, dealing chiefly with pioneer life, the Revolution, Indian fighting, and similar episodes in early American history. The Civil War helped Beadle & Adams attain a huge success, since easy and inexpensive reading matter in dime novels was exactly what the soldiers

wanted. By the middle of 1865 the firm had sold more than 4 million dime novels, some items selling as many as 80,000 copies. The two best sellers were an Indian story, MALAESKA (1860), by Ann S. Stephens (1813–1886), and SETH JONES, OR THE CAPTIVE OF THE FRONTIER (1860). Beadle & Adams ran many series of dime novels simultaneously, exploiting the market as much as possible, and other firms soon offered strong competition. NICK CARTER was one favorite character, Old Cap Collier another. The more sensational dime novels were close relatives of the penny dreadfuls popular in England during this same period.

At the beginning only original stories were printed, but the idea soon occurred to publishers that they might also put out cheap reprints of full-length novels, especially British novels unprotected by copyright. Even old-line houses entered into the ensuing fray, usually at prices above a dime.

An immediate predecessor of Beadle's shockers was the fiction of EDWARD Z. C. JUDSON (1820–86), who wrote western stories and plays, also sea stories, under the pen name Ned Buntline.

Dimmesdale, Arthur.   The minister in Nathaniel Hawthorne's THE SCARLET LETTER (1850) who is the unrevealed father of HESTER PRYNNE'S illegitimate child.

Dinner at Eight (1932),   a play by GEORGE S. KAUFMAN and EDNA FERBER, later a Hollywood film (1933).

Dinsmore, Elsie.   A character in twenty-eight novels by MARTHA FINLEY.

Dionysus in Doubt (1925),   title poem of a collection by EDWIN ARLINGTON ROBINSON, which also includes DEMOS AND DIONYSUS. The poem is another expression of the poet's fear and doubt of modern political developments, as set forth in a conversation with the Greek god. He denounces the hope of an "ultimate uniformity," which some will call "freedom and efficiency," whereas others will "rather call it hell."

Disappointment, The, or, The Force of Credulity (1767),   a play by Colonel Thomas Forrest ("Andrew Barton"). This satire came close to being the first play produced professionally in an American theater. It satirized the contemporary mania for seeking pirate treasure and made personal references to some residents of Philadelphia. As a result it was withdrawn from production, and *The Prince of Parthia* was played instead (April 24, 1767).

Discourses in America.   Three lectures delivered by MATTHEW ARNOLD on his tour of the United States in 1883 and published in 1885.

Discovery.   A magazine in paperback form that appeared in 1953 after the success of *New World Writing* had demonstrated the feasibility of publishing a paperback literary periodical aimed at a large audience. The magazine concentrated on American writing, mostly fiction and poetry, and offered a few essays. The first number, edited by John W. Aldrich and Vance Bourjaily, contained work by Hortense Calisher, Chandler Brossard, Kenneth Fearing, Norman Mailer, and Herbert Gold as well as William Styron's novella *The Long March*. Unfortunately, only six issues in all were to appear—

the last in July 1955. Though not a financial success, the magazine had a steady readership of 150,000 and could boast of having published some of the best young American authors of the 1950s. The second issue contained a manifesto by Bourjaily, by then sole editor, called "No More Apologies—A Critical Note." He contrasted the work of his contemporaries with that being produced by the older giants of American writing: Dos Passos, Hemingway, Faulkner. He named the new writers who, though they had not "yet produced as fine an individual work as the very best of what the older men have done . . . yet . . . the promise of masterpieces may be seen in them." These were Norman Mailer, J. D. Salinger, John Horne Burns, Carson McCullers, William Styron, Hortense Calisher, Nelson Algren, and Calder Willingham.

Disenchanted, The (1950),   a novel by BUDD SCHULBERG. The central character is Manley Halliday, a famous novelist of the 1920s, who is obviously intended as a portrait of F. SCOTT FITZGERALD.

Dismal Swamp, The.   A marsh approximately thirty by ten miles, extending from Norfolk, Virginia, south into North Carolina. It is described in William Byrd's *History of the Dividing Line*. Here lived DRED, the runaway slave who is the chief character in Harriet Beecher Stowe's novel by that name (1856). Longfellow wrote *The Slave in the Dismal Swamp* (1842).

Disney, Walt[er Elias] (1901–1966),   cartoonist, producer of animated sound cartoons, pictures combining cartoons and live actors, and natural history films. Disney's career began with his production of the *Alice Comedies*, a mingling of a live girl with animated cartoons, in 1923–26. Then he went on to *Oswald, the Rabbit* (1926–28), finally to the continuing and immensely popular *Mickey Mouse* and *Silly Symphony* series (since 1928). Mickey Mouse and Donald Duck, who made his first appearance in 1934, have become characters known all over the world. Two of Disney's most-admired short cartoons are *The Three Little Pigs* (1933) and *Ferdinand the Bull* (1939). In 1938 he dared produce the first feature-length cartoon, *Snow White and the Seven Dwarfs*, despite skeptical warnings of failure. It promptly broke attendance records throughout the country. Other full-length cartoons include *Pinocchio* (1940); *Fantasia* (with Deems Taylor, a cartoon interpretation of classical music, 1940); *Dumbo* (1941); *Bambi* (1942); *Alice in Wonderland* (1951); *The Lady and the Tramp* (1955); and *The Sleeping Beauty* (1959). Disney also produced live film versions of children's classics, such as *Treasure Island* (1950), *Swiss Family Robinson* (1961), and *Mary Poppins* (1964). One of his most interesting experiments was the production of full-length color films of animal life in various parts of the world: *Beaver Valley* (1950), *Water Birds* (1952), *The Living Desert* (1953), and *The Vanishing Prairie* (1954).

In 1955, Walt Disney Productions opened Disneyland, an amusement park in Anaheim, California, the first of an empire that by 2000 included parks in Florida, Japan, and France. In the 1960s, the company began to offer live-action films,

including *The Absent-Minded Professor* (1961) and *Mary Poppins* (1964), and remade the feature-length animated cartoon *101 Dalmations* (1961) as a live action film featuring Glenn Close (1966). Other live-action films followed, including, by the Touchstone Films division, *Splash* (1984) and *Pretty Woman* (1990). In the 1990s the Walt Disney Company (its name after 1986) returned to cartoons in a big way, with films that became mega-hits on the screen, as videos, and sometimes as Broadway musicals. These include *The Little Mermaid* (1989); *Beauty and the Beast* (1991); *Aladdin* (1992); *The Lion King* (1994) and *The Lion King II* (1998); *Pocahontas* (1995); *Toy Story* (1995), the first full-length film with computer animation, and *Toy Story II* (2000); and *The Hunchback of Notre Dame* (1996). A computer-animated *Fantasia 2000* was released in 2000.

Dispatches (1976),   a personal account of the Vietnam War by MICHAEL HERR.

Divina Commedia,   sonnet sequence by HENRY WADSWORTH LONGFELLOW. Published first in the *Atlantic Monthly* for December 1864 and November 1866, these six sonnets appeared in book form as introductions to Longfellow's translation of Dante's *Divine Comedy* (1865–67), a work undertaken to help the poet find relief after his second wife was burned to death in their home. The poems compare Longfellow's labors with Dante's masterpiece to the religious exaltation experienced on entering a great cathedral. They first appeared together as a sonnet sequence in *Flower-de-Luce* (1867).

Diving into the Wreck,   title poem of a collection (1973) by ADRIENNE RICH.

Divinity School Address, The (July 15, 1838),   a lecture by RALPH WALDO EMERSON. Invited by the students to address the Harvard Senior Class in Divinity, Emerson shocked conservatives with his views, especially his depiction of Jesus Christ as expressing in himself the divine Being incarnate in all men: "Alone in all history, he estimated the greatness of man. One man was true to what is in you and me." He enjoined the future ministers to be true to the divinity within them, to break with tradition and "speak the very truth" as it comes to them from "life and conscience." The resulting controversy Emerson referred to as "a storm in a washbowl." The essay was printed later that year and collected in *Nature, Addresses, and Lectures* (1849).

Dix, Dorothy.   See ELIZABETH MERIWETHER GILMER.

Dixie.   A patriotic song composed in 1859 by minstrel DANIEL DECATUR EMMETT (1815–1904). Sung that year in Bryant's Minstrel Show and published the following year, it became an immediate hit, especially in the South.

The origin of the word *Dixie* is obscure. It has been suggested that it has some connection with the Mason-Dixon Line. Others claim that a Louisiana bank, printing its pre–Civil War bills in French with a big "DIX" (ten) in the middle of the ten-dollar notes, made the South the land of the "dixies."

Dixon, Thomas (1864–1946),   Baptist clergyman, lawyer, legislator, novelist, dramatist. An unreconstructed

Southerner, born in North Carolina, Dixon in *The Clansman* (1905) wrote a novel that became the first million-dollar movie, *The Birth of a Nation* (1914), and led to the revival of the KU KLUX KLAN. Dixon was devoted to upholding "racial purity"; *The Clansman* formed part of a trilogy with THE LEOPARD'S SPOTS (1902) and *The Traitor* (1907). He wrote other novels, some exceedingly popular, and also several plays and motion pictures. Calling himself a "reactionary individualist," Dixon strongly opposed communism and the New Deal.

Dobie, Charles Caldwell (1881–1943), novelist, short-story writer, playwright. Dobie was an inveterate lover of his native city, which is the scene of many of his books, whether fact or fiction. Among them are *San Francisco: A Pageant* (1933), *San Francisco Tales* (1935), *San Francisco's Chinatown* (1936), and *San Francisco Adventures* (1937).

Dobie, J[ames] Frank (1888–1964), historian, folklorist. Dobie was born in Texas. After managing a 200,000-acre ranch (1920–21), he became the leading authority on Texas history and folklore, teaching at the University of Texas (1933–47) and briefly at Cambridge University, an experience described in *A Texan in England* (1945). Among his books are *Coronado's Children* (1931); *Tales of the Mustangs* (1936); *The Flavor of Texas* (1936); *Apache Gold and Yaqui Silver* (1939); *Guide to Life and Literature in the Southwest* (1943, rev. and enlarged, 1952); *The Voice of the Coyote* (1949); *The Mustangs* (1952); *Tales of Old-Time Texas* (1955); *I'll Tell You a Tale* (1960); and *Cow People* (1964).

Dobyns, Stephen (1941–), poet, novelist, essayist. Born in Orange, New Jersey, Dobyns was educated at Shimer College (1959–60), Wayne State University (B.A., 1964), and the University of Iowa (M.F.A., 1967). His poetry moves from realistic narratives to imaginative lyricism. *Concurring Beasts* (1972), *The Balthus Poems* (1982), and *Black Dog, Red Dog* (1984) were all critically well received. *Velocities: New and Selected Poems, 1966–1992* appeared in 1994. More recent collections include *Common Carnage* (1996) and *Pallbearers Envying the One Who Died* (1999). *Best Words, Best Order: Essays on Poetry* was published in 1996. Dobyns has also written detective novels and thrillers, including *Dancer with One Leg* (1983), *Cold Dog Soup* (1985), *The Church of Dead Girls* (1997), *Saratoga Strongbox* (1998), and *Boy in the Water* (1999). *Eating Naked* (2000) is a collection of short stories.

Doctor Grimshawe's Secret (1882), a novel by NATHANIEL HAWTHORNE. Left unfinished at his death and edited by his son Julian, *Doctor Grimshawe's Secret* tells of an American and his sister who, after being separated for years, find themselves at their ancestral home, which had been abandoned by their forefather in the days of Cromwell and to which the American is still the heir.

Doctor Heidegger's Experiment (*Salem Gazette*, March 1837; in *Twice-Told Tales*, 1837), a story by NATHANIEL HAWTHORNE. Three elderly men and an aged widow agree to drink a magic potion that a medical friend of theirs has prepared. They are restored to youth, and the three men, in wooing the widow whose beauty has been regained, display all the foolishness they had shown when young. Their youth fades again, but they have learned nothing from the experiment and resolve to go to Florida to look for the Fountain of Youth.

Doctorow, E. L. (1931–), novelist, dramatist, short-story writer. Edgar Laurence Doctorow was born in New York City, studied philosophy at Kenyon College and drama at Columbia University. He served in the United States Army from 1953 to 1955, was a manuscript reader at Columbia Pictures for several years, an editor at the New American Library from 1959 to 1964, and editor-in-chief at Dial Press from 1964 to 1969. His editorial experience improved his own narrative skills and acquainted him with the whole range of modern fiction, popular and sophisticated. His first two works were novels of ideas written in the manner of popular fiction. *Welcome to Hard Times* (1960), a Western novel, portrays the forces on the Dakota frontier that kill the well-meaning narrator and his American dream of community and prosperity. *Big as Life* (1966), a science fiction novel, satirizes governing elites for their resistance to new ideas, however valid, which threaten the status quo. Doctorow won his first critical acclaim with *The Book of Daniel* (1971), a novel suggested by the execution of Ethel and Julius Rosenberg on charges of espionage. Narrated as the meditation of Daniel Isaacson, whose parents have been executed, the novel probes the Cold War repression of the 1950s and 1960s, the radical political movements that opposed it, and the terrible fate of people caught between such powerful forces. Doctorow's first popular success was his fourth novel, *Ragtime* (1975), a massively documented but witty and entertaining depiction of America at the beginning of the 20th century. The narrator mixes fact and invention, historical and imaginary characters, somewhat as John Dos Passos had done in *U.S.A.*, in order to get at the truth of his era—its impressive accomplishments and its grave social problems. *Loon Lake* (1980) is set in the American 1930s. At its center is the all-powerful capitalist, F. W. Bennett, who destroys or appropriates every person who represents a vital alternative to his materialistic values. *World's Fair* (1985) takes a kindlier, though not uncritical, view of the 1930s. Written as a fictional memoir, it reconstructs in vivid, minute detail and on a monumental scale, the life and times of a boy growing up in the Bronx. *Billy Bathgate* (1989), a more chilling account of a Bronx boyhood, is narrated by a boy assistant to the gangster Dutch Schultz. *The Waterworks* (1994) is a historical fiction, set in nineteenth-century New York. *City of God* (2000), with its title reference to St. Augustine is a meditative novel, set at the end of the twentieth century, that explores the present, the Holocaust, and our time's "wrecked romance with God." Doctorow has published one play, *Drinks Before Dinner* (1979), which was first performed at the New York Shakespeare Festival's Public Theater in 1978. It considers, in Doctorow's words, "the corruption of human identity" in affluent contemporary America. His collection of short fiction, *Lives of the Poets* (1984), examines the condition of the modern writer. Three of his novels have been made into films: *Welcome to Hard Times* (1967), *The Book of Daniel* (1983), and *Ragtime* (1981). *Jack*

London, Hemingway, and the Constitution: Selected Essays 1977–1992 appeared in 1993.

FRANK K. McHUGH/GP

Doctor Sevier (1882), a novel by GEORGE W. CABLE. This is one of Cable's New Orleans stories. It is less about Dr. Sevier, a kindly and laconic physician, than about his young protégé, John Richling, and the development of Richling's character. The corruption of New Orleans in the era before the Civil War is attacked.

Doddridge, Joseph (1769–1826), author of *Notes on the Settlement and Indian Wars of the Western Parts of Virginia and Pennsylvania from 1763 to 1783* (1824) and a play, *Logan, The Last of the Race of Shikellemus* (1821), on the celebrated Native American chief JAMES LOGAN.

Dodge, Mary [Elizabeth] Mapes (1831–1905), editor, author of children's books. Dodge's reputation rests on two achievements: children's classic, *Hans Brinker, or, The Silver Skates* (1865); and her editorship of the children's magazine ST. NICHOLAS (1873–1905). The story was translated into many languages and was honored by the French Academy. To the magazine she attracted most of the noted writers of the day, including Kipling and Mark Twain, and made her name and the magazine's name household words. She wrote other books besides *Hans Brinker*, such as *Donald and Dorothy* (1883), but none attained the great success of *Hans Brinker*.

Dodsworth (1929), a novel by SINCLAIR LEWIS. Dodsworth, a captain of industry from Babbitt's metropolis of Zenith, is persuaded by his frivolous wife Fran to make a tour of Europe. She has several love affairs and at last breaks off with Dodsworth. He, after months of loneliness, falls in love with the widowed Mrs. Cortright, who persuades him to take a more social view of industry and inspires him with plans to build a truly American suburb in Zenith. Fran is cast off by her lover's family, and she induces Dodsworth to take her back home. But their reconciliation comes too late. The playwright Sidney Howard made a strong play out of the novel (1934), and the play was successfully transferred to the screen (1936).

Doesticks, Q. K. See MORTIMER THOMSON.

Dogood Papers, The (*New England Courant*, April–October 1722), essays by BENJAMIN FRANKLIN. Franklin was sixteen when he began contributing these essays (signed "Silence Dogood") to his brother James's newspaper. He was under two strong influences: COTTON MATHER (who had written *Essays to Do Good*, 1710) and Addison and Steele's *Spectator Papers* (1711–12). It was not until 1864 that James Parton, in his biography of Franklin, revealed that the papers had been written by him. His chief character is a woman with cheerful common sense who expresses the views of the poor and lowly, is not always elegant in her speech, and is fond of homely sayings and proverbs. Already one may catch the atmosphere of the coming Revolution, as when Franklin writes: "Without freedom of thought there can be no such thing as wisdom; and no such thing as liberty without freedom of speech."

Dog Soldiers (1974), Vietnam War novel by ROBERT STONE.

Dole, Nathan Haskell (1852–1935), teacher, newspaperman, novelist, translator, critic, editor. Born in Chelsea, Massachusetts, Dole taught school in Massachusetts, worked on newspapers in several parts of the country, was an editor at the Thomas Y. Crowell Company. His novels are *Not Angels Quite* (1893), a romantic comedy, and *Omar the Tent-Maker* (1899). He edited anthologies and the 10th edition of Bartlett's *Familiar Quotations*, and translated from Russian, Spanish, Italian, and French texts.

Dolittle, Doctor. In 1920 Hugh Lofting, Anglo-American writer, published *The Story of Dr. Dolittle*, and thereafter his juvenile admirers kept him busy writing further accounts of the eccentric country doctor whose love for animals leads him to learn their languages and devote himself to taking care of them rather than of human beings. Originally the story was sent home from the front in World War I in letters to Lofting's children, with illustrations. It was Mrs. Lofting who suggested putting them into book form. Among the sequels are *The Voyages of Dr. Dolittle* (1922, awarded Newbery Prize); *Dr. Dolittle's Garden* (1927); and *Dr. Dolittle's Return* (1933).

Dolliver Romance, The, a fragment by NATHANIEL HAWTHORNE. This romance was originally scheduled to be published in serial form, starting with the January 1864 issue of *The Atlantic Monthly*. It was the first time that Hawthorne attempted serial publication, but due to his increasing illness, the scheme was never carried out. Two chapters of the three-chapter manuscript were finally published posthumously in the magazine, and the entire manuscript appeared in 1876.

The theme of the fragment is the elixir of life and its promise of immortality. What exists of the plot concerns attempts of Dr. Dolliver to create an elixir, not for selfish reasons but that he might live to take care of his granddaughter Pansie. What little appears of Pansie in the fragment indicates the development of another of the author's fascinating young girls, such as Pearl in THE SCARLET LETTER and Phoebe in THE HOUSE OF THE SEVEN GABLES.

The story develops the contrast between Dr. Dolliver's selflessness and Colonel Dabney's demands for the elixir; Dabney dies of an overdose, and Hawthorne is ambiguous as to whether the Colonel did restore his youth before he died.

Domain of Arnheim, The (published in the *Columbian Magazine*, March, 1847), a story by EDGAR ALLAN POE. This was an expansion of *The Landscape Garden* (*Ladies' Companion*, October 1842) and is allied in theme to LANDOR'S COTTAGE (*Flag of Our Union*, June 9, 1849). Poe describes how Ellison, who has become fabulously wealthy, is able to indulge his ideas of landscape gardening and architecture on a vast scale. *Landscape Garden* gave Ellison's plans; *The Domain of Arnheim* tells how he carried them out. In a letter to Sarah Helen Whitman, October 18, 1848, Poe said that *The Domain of Arnheim* "expresses *much of my soul.*"

Domestic Manners of the Americans, The (1832). See FRANCES TROLLOPE.

Doña Bárbara (1929), a novel by RÓMULO GALLEGOS. The central character, Doña Bárbara, as her name implies, symbolizes barbarism. Believing herself possessed of super-natural powers, she rules a vast domain in Venezuela and bends men to her will through bribery, intimidation, and murder. Some saw in Doña Bárbara's rapacity and ruthlessness a resemblance to the practices of Juan Vicente Gómez, Venezuelan dictator when the book was published. As the dictator was among those who saw the resemblance, Gallegos went into exile. The novel was translated into English in 1931 (reprinted in 1948) by Robert Malloy.

Donatello, Count. A character in Hawthorne's THE MARBLE FAUN (1980). He is the Italian admirer of Miriam and bears a resemblance to the Faun of Praxiteles. Hawthorne leaves unsettled whether his ears, if his concealing locks should be lifted, would be revealed as human or animal. He is depicted as amoral, a human being corresponding to Adam before the fall, not knowing sin or suffering.

Donleavy, J[ames] P[atrick] (1926–), novelist. Born in Brooklyn and educated at Trinity College, Dublin, Donleavy has lived mostly in Ireland and became an Irish citizen in 1967. He won a wide following with his bawdy and comic first novel, *The Ginger Man* (Paris, 1955; London, 1956; New York, 1958), which remains his most celebrated book and was turned into a play produced in London and New York. An unexpurgated edition of the novel did not appear in the U.S. until 1965. The novel's hero, Sebastian Dangerfield, is an American law student at Trinity College, Dublin. He is charming, witty, endowed with a Joycean lyricism, amoral, and a formidable seducer of women. Later novels have generally continued to demonstrate Donleavy's manic sense of humor and verbal exuberance. They include *A Singular Man* (1963), *The Saddest Summer of Samuel S.* (1966), *The Beastly Beatitudes of Balthazar B.* (1968), *The Onion Eaters* (1971), *The Destinies of Darcy Dancer, Gentlemen* (1977). *Schultz* (1979), *Leila* (1983), *De Alfonce Tennis, the Superlative Game of Creative Champions* (1984), *Are You Listening Rabbi Loew* (1987), a sequel to *Schultz*, and *That Darcy, That Dancer, That Gentleman* (1990), a sequel to *Leila*. In the 1990s he began a series of short novels about odd characters in and around New York City. These include *The Lady Who Liked Clean Rest Rooms* (1997) and *Wrong Information Is Being Given Out at Princeton* (1998). His stories are collected in *Meet My Maker, the Mad Molecule* (1964).

Donn-Byrne, Brian Oswald (1889–1928), novelist, short-story writer. Born in Brooklyn and educated in Dublin, Donn-Byrne (also known as Donn Byrne) returned to New York in 1911 to begin his literary career. His most popular book was MESSER MARCO POLO (1921). Among his others are *The Stranger's Banquet* (1919), a problem novel on industrialism; *The Foolish Matrons* (1920), studies of four women; *The Wind Bloweth* (1922), about an Irish sailor; *Blind Raftery* (1924), a romance about the 19th-century Gaelic poet; *Hangman's House* (1926), set in 19th-century Ireland; *Brother Saul* (1927), about the apostle Paul; *Crusade* (1928), of an Irish crusader's love for a Saracen woman; and *Field of Honor* (1929), a tale of Napoleonic times. His story collections include *The*

Changeling (1923), *Destiny Bay* (1928), *Rivers of Damascus* (1931), and *The Woman of the Shee* (1932).

Donnelly, Ignatius (1831–1901), orator, public official, editor, novelist, historian. Born in Philadelphia, Donnelly first became a lawyer, then went west to found an ideal community called Nininger City in Minnesota. To help build the town, Donnelly began to publish *The Emigrant Aid Journal*. When the panic of 1857 hit, Nininger City collapsed. Donnelly blamed "the bankers" and ever afterward inveighed furiously against them. He was elected to some state offices and to the House of Representatives. He was a great orator and used his powers as a speaker in debates over conduct of the Civil War.

In 1882 appeared his most popular book, ATLANTIS: THE ANTEDILUVIAN WORLD, a serious attempt to prove that the world's original civilization had developed on the lost continent that Plato first mentioned. *Ragnarok* (1883) explains certain geological facts as being due to the earth's contact with a great comet ages ago. The novel *Caesar's Column* (1891) resembles Bellamy's *Looking Backward* (1888); it foretells many political changes, not all for the better, and also inventions actually made since his time. In the meantime Donnelly helped form the National People's Party (the Populists), which by 1892 had become a great force in the country. Its ideas for reforming political, economic, and social conditions were mainly Donnelly's, and in 1900 he was the vice-presidential candidate of his party.

Donnelly later became a devotee of DELIA BACON's theory that Francis Bacon had written the plays of Shakespeare. In *The Great Cryptogram* (1888) and again in *The Cypher in the Plays and on the Tombstone* (1899), Donnelly sought to establish the truth of this theory by unraveling a cipher, supposedly devised by Bacon, to be found in the plays and elsewhere. He also offered evidence that Bacon had written Marlowe's plays, Montaigne's essays, and Burton's *Anatomy of Melancholy*.

Donner party, the. A group including the Donner family from Illinois that camped at a lake in the Sierra Nevada Mountains while on their way to California in October 1846. When early and heavy snow blocked the passes, they were obliged to remain where they were all winter. Of eighty-seven persons caught in the winter trap, only forty-seven survived—partly, it was said, by practicing cannibalism. They were finally rescued by settlers from California. George Stewart in *Ordeal by Hunger* (1936) and Homer Croy in *Wheels West* (1955) tell the story of the Donner party. The episode is also part of the plot in Bret Harte's GABRIEL CONROY (1876), in Vardis Fisher's *The Mothers* (1943), and in Norah Lofts's *Winter Harvest* (1955).

Donoso, José (1924–1996), Chilean novelist and short-story writer. Born into a professional family, Donoso studied at an English school in Santiago, studied English literature at Princeton for two years, and wrote his first stories in English. His career, however, has been as a writer of Spanish exploring the culture of Chile in fiction that begins in realism but ranges into dreamlike allegory. He won acclaim with his first novel, *Coronación* (1957, tr. *Coronation*, 1965), a study of the decline of the Chilean aristocracy; its focus is on a half-mad matron, her retarded grandson, and their retinue of servants. Later novels are *Este domingo* (1965, tr. *This Sunday*, 1967), with similar themes depicted through adult conflicts and the mirror-images seen in the games of children; *El lugar sin limites* (1966, tr. *Hell Has No Limits*, 1972), set in a small town and involving prostitution, transvestitism, and the remnants of feudal power; *El obsceno pájaro de la noche* (1970, tr. *The Obscene Bird of Night*, 1973), with a nightmarish doubling of character and place; *La misteriosa desparación de la marquesita de Loria* (1980); and *Casa de Campo* (1978, tr. *A House in the Country*, 1983). His short stories are collected in *Cuentos* (1971, tr. *Charleston and Other Stories*, 1977). *Tres novelitas burguesas* (1973, tr. *Sacred Families*, 1977) contains three novellas. *Historia personal del "boom"* (1972, tr. *The Boom in Spanish-American Literature*, 1977) combines personal and literary history. His last works were *Where Elephants go to Die* (1995), concerning a visiting professor from Chile teaching in the United States, and *Conjectures About the Memory of My Tribe* (1996).

Don Segundo Sombra (1926, tr. *Shadows in the Pampas*, 1935), a novel by RICARDO GÜIRALDES. Güiraldes was a wealthy cosmopolite who traveled widely, but in this novel he draws on his childhood experiences at La Porteña, his family's ranch in Buenos Aires province. The narrator of the novel is a boy who runs away from the aunts who have raised him and attaches himself to Don Segundo Sombra, an itinerant ranch worker. During their five-year odyssey, the boy learns from his teacher not only how to be an expert cowboy and horseman but also how to live with courage and honor, that is, according to the gaucho code. After discovering that he is the illegitimate son of a wealthy rancher, who has left him his estate, the young man accepts his legacy and acquires a measure of formal culture. Don Segundo, feeling there is no longer need for his tutelage, goes on his lonely way. Considered the outstanding prose fictional example of GAUCHO LITERATURE, the novel captures the essence of the gaucho myth in the scenes of life on the pampas and, above all, in the idealized figure of Don Segundo.

Dooley, Mr. The hero of FINLEY PETER DUNNE's popular sketches. He is described as "the traveler, archaeologist, historian, social observer, saloonkeeper, economist, and philosopher, who has not been out of the ward for 25 years but twict." See HENNESSY.

Doolittle, Hilda [H. D.] (1886–1961), poet, novelist, memoirist, translator. Born in Pennsylvania, H.D. was educated at Bryn Mawr. Her friends included Ezra Pound and William Carlos Williams. In 1911, she went to Europe, traveled, and joined the literary circle around Pound. Her early poems, published in *Poetry* (1913), were taken by Pound and the English writer Richard Aldington as exemplary of Imagist tenets of clarity, precision, free rhythm, and passionate restraint. She married Aldington in 1913. Her earliest volumes *Sea Garden* (1916). *Hymen* (1921), *Heliodora and Other Poems* (1924), and *Collected Poems* (1925) combine the sharpness

and clarity of Imagist technique with themes from classical antiquity, including textual examinations of gender undertaken to situate herself as a woman writer. She continued her inventions and adaptations from the classical Greek in *Hippolytus Temporizes: A Play* (1927) and in a translation of Euripides' *Ion* (1937). In 1919, her marriage to Aldington essentially over, she gave birth to Frances Perdita, whose father was Cecil Gray, and began a lifelong bond of love and companionship with the English writer Bryher (Annie Winifred Ellerman MacPherson). In the mid-twenties, H. D. wrote a number of experimental novels, in two groups. One centered on classical antiquity—often in relation to modernist issues—such as *Palimpsest* (1926) and *Hedylus* (1928). The other centered on a construction and representation of her own biography and the struggles of a woman artist, such as *Asphodel* and *HER [HERmione]*, both published in 1981, and *Paint It Today* (1992). Her strong interest in cinema during the late twenties and early thirties was expressed in many articles in the early film journal *Close Up*, and in her roles in several experimental silent films, including *Borderline* (1930), which featured Paul Robeson. In 1933 and 1934, H. D. undertook psychoanalysis with Sigmund Freud. Her *Tribute to Freud* (1956) used free association over personal and cultural memories to represent the processes of spiritual quest via analysis. In 1939, she wrote the novel *Bid Me to Live* (1960), summarizing many of the autobiographical forces in the World War I period, and in 1941–43 produced an important memoir called *The Gift*, treating her Moravian childhood and family and regional history in relation to the political and spiritual issues raised by World War II (published in full in 1999). The magisterial long poem *Trilogy* (1942–44), written during the war and during the bombing of London, was published in 1944–46. The poem makes a prophetic or revisionary claim through myths of regeneration and resurrection especially involved with goddess figures. Other late-career longer poems included "Winter Love" and "Hermetic Definition," which were included in the volume *Hermetic Definition* (1972). H. D. also wrote a memoir of her relationship with Ezra Pound, *End to Torment* (1979). Her other memoirs remain unpublished. A book-length epic poem, *Helen in Egypt* (1961), treats the Helen story and the Trojan War in revisionary fashion. H. D.'s *Collected Poems, 1912–1944* was published in 1983, edited by Louis Martz.

RACHEL BLAU DUPLESSIS

Dorn, Edward [Merton] (1929–1999), poet. Born in Illinois, Dorn attended the University of Illinois before having his education "somewhat corrected" at BLACK MOUNTAIN COLLEGE. His first book, *What I See in the Maximus Poems* (1960), paid tribute to his mentor CHARLES OLSON. His own poems, sometimes lyric, usually open in form, are gathered in a number of books, including *Gunslinger* (1975, 1989). His earlier books appeared in 1968, 1969, and 1972. *Gunslinger* is his major work. Other titles include his first slim volume, *The Newly Fallen* (1961), *Twenty-four Love Songs* (1969), *Collected Poems* (1982), and *Abhorrences* (1989).

Dorris, Michael (1945–1997), novelist, memoirist, short-story writer, children's writer. Dorris was born in Louisville to a mother of Irish and French heritage and a father of the Modoc tribe. His father died when Dorris was two, and he was raised by his mother and a large extended family of women. Educated at Georgetown University and Yale, Dorris founded the Native American Studies Program at Dartmouth College in 1972. *Native Americans: Five Hundred Years After* (1975) was his first attempt to treat the Indian half of his heritage. With Arlene B. Hirschfelder and Mary Gloyne Byler, he edited *A Guide to Research on North American Indians* (1983). *A Yellow Raft in Blue Water* (1987), his first novel, tells the story of three generations of mixed-race women on a Montana Indian reservation. *Cloud Chamber* (1997), a sequel to the earlier novel, traces the backgrounds of the families beginning a hundred years earlier in Ireland. Dorris's most noted publication was the nonfiction *A Broken Cord* (1989), about his adopted son, Abel, a Sioux who was born with fetal alcohol syndrome. The book, also dramatized on television, helped bring national attention to the dangers of drinking during pregnancy. Abel Dorris was struck and killed by a car in 1992.

In 1981 he married the novelist Louise Erdrich, who is also of mixed racial stock but regards herself as Native American. After their marriage, they worked closely together, both in writing and in raising a large family of adopted and biological children. They published several short stories under the pseudonym Milou North, with the first name made up of portions their first names and the last for the part of the county they lived in. By their own account, writing always included joint consultation about plot and characters, even when the finished product might contain only the name of the primary author. *The Crown of Columbus* (1991), a novel on which both names appeared, deals with the theme of first encounters between Europeans and Native Americans. Dorris and Erdrich also wrote *Route Two and Back* (1991), a travel narrative. Other Dorris titles include *Rooms in the House of Stone* (1993); *Paper Trail* (1994), a collection of essays; *Working Men* (1993), a gathering of fourteen stories; and several children's books including *Morning Girl* (1992), *Guests* (1996) and *The Window* (1997). Estranged from his wife and children, who had moved to Minnesota expecting that he would follow, Dorris committed suicide in a New Hampshire motel.

Dorsey, George A[mos] (1868–1931), teacher, museum curator, anthropologist. Born in Ohio, Dorsey wrote books on Native Americans—*Traditions of the Arikara* (1904), *The Mythology of the Wichita* (1904), and *Pawnee Mythology* (1906)—that gave him a solid reputation among scholars. For popular consumption, he wrote *Why We Behave Like Human Beings* (1925), a best seller, and *Man's Own Show: Civilization* (1931).

Dos Passos, John [Roderigo] (1896–1970), novelist, poet, playwright, essayist. Grandson of a Portuguese immigrant, Dos Passos was born in Chicago and educated at Harvard. As a child and known as John Roderigo Madison, he lived a rootless life, traveling much in Europe. His mother,

Lucy Addison Sprigg Madison, a widow, could not marry his father, John Roderigo Dos Passos, until his first wife died. The couple finally married in 1910, when their son was fourteen, and in 1912 the boy took his father's name. Any happiness young John had was short-lived because his mother died in 1915. The secrecy surrounding his boyhood and the mixture of admiration and fear Dos Passos felt toward his powerful father—an important corporate lawyer and the author of standard books on trusts and the stock market—and his dependence on his beautiful, often unhappy mother left their marks on the adolescent. A comparatively timid boy, Dos Passos found his excitement in the art of the time, and his greatest joy in his writing. His early poems, along with those of E. E. Cummings and others, appeared in 1917 in the collection *Eight Harvard Poets*. This was shortly after Dos Passos was graduated from Harvard.

From what he saw as his distance from mainstream—and elite—American culture, Dos Passos was able to write tellingly about it. As the "Ishmael" among his Harvard friends, he tried to portray what he saw as the reasons for dissatisfaction with the American dream, ranging from the bitter anti-war sentiment of *One Man's Initiation: 1917* (1919) and THREE SOLDIERS (1921) to the bewilderment of college students in *Streets of Night* (1923) and of city dwellers in MANHATTAN TRANSFER (1925).

Dos Passos had served with the Norton-Harjes Ambulance Service in Italy and knew firsthand the destruction wrought by World War I. He also thought he understood the implicit inhumanity of capitalism and during the 1920s was much attracted by the Russian experiment. Like others of his generation, he was saddened and embittered by the SACCO-VANZETTI affair, and in 1927 published his defense of the men in *Facing the Chair: Story of the Americanization of Two Foreignborn Workmen*. Partly because of his anger at the American system of justice, and partly because of his aesthetic fascination with Expressionist drama and film, he visited Russia in 1928, but returned to America only moderately enthusiastic.

During the 1920s, Dos Passos lived by his writing—publishing a collection of poems, travel essays and collections, and two of his three plays that proved important to the development of American theater: *The Garbage Man: A Parade with Shouting* (1926, produced as *The Moon Is a Gong*) and *Airways, Inc.* (1928). *Fortune Heights* followed in 1933. Strongly influenced by the work of John Howard Lawson and by Cummings's play *Him*, Dos Passos drew into his plays elements from the real world and created remarkable pastiches of popular culture. His most important work was to begin shortly after his involvement in theater, however, when he used the dramatic montage technique in his fiction.

The first of his *U.S.A.* volumes, THE 42ND PARALLEL, appeared in 1930, engendering enthusiasm with his innovative Modernist techniques and his biting criticism of various American ways. The many characters that were to wind through the three volumes of *U.S.A.* represented all walks of American attitude and life, from women who had become interior decorators to avoid the boredom of more traditional women's lives to public relations men, pilots, factory workers, secretaries, and the politically involved. Juxtaposed with these stories about fictional characters were three other kinds of narrative: (1) the prose-poem "biographies," which portrayed Thomas Edison, Henry Ford, Isadora Duncan, and others Dos Passos felt represented American culture in important ways; (2) the "newsreels," collages of news headlines, lines from popular songs, and catch phrases of the time, which he built into ironic commentaries on the beliefs and events of the day; and (3) the impressionistic "Camera Eye" sections, haunting prose poems that drew largely from Dos Passos's own life and created his consciousness as the narrative observer of the trilogy. The blended and interrupted story lines created mock-confusion, similar to the narrative effect of his earlier *Manhattan Transfer*, but much more intense. By the time the other two volumes of the trilogy appeared—*1919* in 1932 (see under NINETEEN-NINETEEN) and THE BIG MONEY in 1936—many readers had abandoned the fiction because of its difficulty, but the work became a landmark of American Modernism, and led John Paul Sartre and other writers worldwide to consider Dos Passos as important an artist as Ernest Hemingway or William Faulkner.

The Dos Passos *U.S.A.* trilogy also placed him firmly within the camp of Marxist and Communist critics and readers, and his work was consistently praised by *New Masses* and other Marxist journals. Because he had criticized much of the American capitalistic way, Dos Passos was seen as a Communist—which he never was. Dos Passos was intent on justice, not on political affiliation. In his later writing, he was as critical of the injustices of labor unions as he had been earlier of the abuses of the capitalistic system. His chief sympathy was with individual persons trying to live respectable lives and trying to make it in a competitive system, regardless of their skills and ambitions.

For all the importance of his fiction, Dos Passos earned much of his living through travel writing and journalism. In 1934 he published *In All Countries*, in 1937, *The Villagers Are the Heart of Spain*, and in 1938, *Journeys Between Wars*. As the world political situation intensified, he became more involved in its currents, and spent time in Spain during the Spanish Civil War. His disillusion at the time of a Spanish friend's execution led to a rupture in his friendship with Hemingway, even though he had in 1929 married Katharine (Katy) Smith, one of Hemingway's Michigan friends. (Dos Passos settles his score with Hemingway in his portrayal of George Elbert Warner in his 1951 novel *Chosen Country*.) For Dos Passos, the primary motivation of his life was his art: most of his good friends were other writers and painters, and most of the events of his life were grounded in his writing. His wife was also a writer, and his comparatively late marriage allowed him to continue the primacy of his identity as writer.

Political events as the world moved toward Fascism disturbed Dos Passos enough that he turned in his writing to somewhat utopian subjects. He began the series of writings on American political figures that would dominate his late years—most notably his many books on Thomas Jefferson but also, in 1940, Tom Paine and, in 1941, various other American political philosophers. He also began what would become another trilogy of novels, publishing *Adventures of a Young Man* in 1939. In this story of a disillusioned young American Communist in Spain, Dos Passos was able to vent his anger at the blindness of some political enthusiasms. The two other volumes of this *District of Columbia* trilogy, as it came to be called—*Number One* (1943) and *The Grand Design* (1949)—were poorly received, and from then until his death in 1970, Dos Passos's writing received less attention than his earlier work had. The magic of technique and subject matter that had come together in *Manhattan Transfer* and the *U.S.A.* trilogy was not repeated, and the great quantity of writing Dos Passos did in the last twenty years of his life is now almost entirely out of print.

Dos Passos had always called himself a chronicler of American life, and his turn to outright history late in his career is a legitimate part of that definition. In his probing studies of historical figures like *The Men Who Made the Nation* (1957), his biographies of Jefferson, and his historical studies—*Mr. Wilson's War* (1962), *The Shackles of Power, Three Jeffersonian Decades* (1966), and others—Dos Passos presented the qualities that he thought made America a viable and promising experiment. While it might not have lived up to its exceptional promise in all ways, it still deserved the approbation Dos Passos gave it. In fact, some of the power of his earlier fiction came back into his last novel, *Century's Ebb: The Thirteenth Chronicle* (1975). Here, in this posthumously published book, the luminous image of American promise is the moon shot, the utopian glimpse of a promise of new worlds to explore and inhabit—locations for new experimentation and hope.

Dos Passos's writing career seems to have expressed the kind of spirit his own life represented: indefatigable promise. When his beloved wife, Katy, was killed in the same 1947 car accident in which Dos Passos lost an eye, and in spite of intense depression, he kept writing. In 1949 he married Elizabeth Holdridge, and the next year their child, Lucy, was born. For the next twenty years, he lived a happy and stable family life in Virginia, enjoying his life as both writer and family man. A solid biography is Townsend Ludington's *John Dos Passos: A Twentieth Century Odyssey* (1980).

LINDA WAGNER-MARTIN

Doty, Mark (1953–   ),   poet, memoirist. Married at eighteen and divorced soon after, Doty's sexual preference found expression in a long-term commitment to Wally Roberts, who died of AIDS in 1994. Doty is the author of poetry collections including *Turtle, Swan* (1987), *Bethlehem in Broad Daylight* (1991), *My Alexandria* (1993), *Atlantis* (1995), and *Sweet Machine* (1998). *Poetry Island Sheaf* appeared in 1998. Two books of memoirs, *Heaven's Coast* (1996) and *Firebird* (1999), detail the perpetual disorientation of his youth as the son of an Army engineer who was transferred to nuclear missile sites all over the country.

Doubleday, Abner (1819–1893), Union general. Born in Saratoga County, New York, and educated at West Point, Doubleday served in the Mexican War and the Civil War. He has been credited with inventing the game of baseball in 1839 at Cooperstown, New York. He wrote important accounts of Civil War battles, *Reminiscences of Forts Sumter and Moultrie in 1860–61* (1876) and *Chancellorsville and Gettysburg* (1882).

Douglas, Lloyd C[assel] (1877–1951), Lutheran, later Congregational clergyman, novelist. Douglas was born in Indiana. After serving as a pastor for more than a quarter of a century, he turned to writing novels and published his first, *The Magnificent Obsession* (1929), when he was over fifty. It was a great success, and he went on to writing other novels, including *Precious Jeopardy* (1933), *Green Light* (1935), *White Banners* (1936), *Disputed Passage* (1939), THE ROBE (1942), and *The Big Fisherman* (1948). These made him one of the most widely read authors of all time. All are inspirational, with at least a muted message of selflessness. *The Robe* and *The Big Fisherman*, historical novels of the time of Christ, have been especially popular. His autobiography, *Time to Remember* (1951), was continued by his daughters, Betty Douglas Wilson and Virginia Douglas Dawson, in *The Shape of Sunday* (1952). In 1955 a collection of his sermons, *The Living Faith*, was published.

Douglas, Stephen A[rnold] (1813–1861), lawyer, statesman, orator, public official. Born in Vermont, Douglas served as judge, congressman, senator. His fame rests chiefly on his debates with Lincoln (1858) in a senatorial contest, resulting in his reelection to the Senate, but Lincoln became a national figure and in 1860 defeated Douglas for the presidency. Douglas, as short as Lincoln was tall, was admiringly called the Little Giant. When the call to arms came, he declared firmly for the Union, offered Lincoln his complete support, and shattered Southern hopes of a divided North.

Douglas, William O[rville] (1898–1980), teacher, lawyer, Supreme Court justice, author. Born in Minnesota, Douglas began his distinguished career as a high-school teacher in Yakima, Washington. He then turned to law, was admitted to the bar in New York, practiced in New York City, and taught law at Columbia and Yale. He went into government service in 1929 and was named to the Supreme Court ten years later by President Roosevelt. Always an outdoorsman and a lover of nature, he began exploring foreign regions, and on his return from several trips wrote three books that were expert reports on political conditions abroad as well as vivid and accurate depictions of foreign scenes. He began with *Strange Lands and Friendly People* (1951), about the Middle East and India, and went on to *Beyond the High Himalayas* (1952) and *North from Malaya* (1953). He compiled *An Almanac of Liberty* (1954). His other books include *Democracy and Finance* (1940), *Of Men and Mountains* (1950), *We the Judges* (1955), *Russian Journey* (1956), *The Right of the People* (1958), *My Wilderness: The Pacific West* (1960), *A Living Bill of Rights* (1961), *Mr. Lincoln and the Negroes* (1963), *A Wilderness Bill of Rights* (1965), *Towards a*

Global Federation (1968), and *Holocaust or Hemispheric Cooperation* (1970). His autobiographical works are *Go East Young Man* (1974), on his life to his Supreme Court appointment; and *The Court Years* (1980).

Douglass, Frederick (1818–1895), abolitionist, autobiographer, journalist, statesman. Most of the available biographical information concerning the youth and early manhood of Douglass comes from his three autobiographies. Born a slave in Maryland, Douglass struggled intellectually and physically against slavery, finally escaping to freedom in the North. There, Douglass became known for his eloquence and, after meeting WILLIAM LLOYD GARRISON in 1841, was hired by the Massachusetts Anti-Slavery Society, for which he traveled throughout the North and East (as far west as Indiana) delivering anti-slavery lectures. (Douglass later traveled to England, Ireland, and Scotland to deliver his abolitionist message to receptive British audiences.) His success as a orator was immense, and he would often speak for almost two hours, punctuating his discourse with dramatic and often humorous stories and asides.

Desirous of a wider audience, of a format capable of accommodating greater and more complex detail, and of greater rhetorical freedom, Douglass produced the first of his autobiographies, *Narrative of the Life of Frederick Douglass, An American Slave: Written by Himself* (1845). His *Narrative* was the most popular of the hundred or so contemporary SLAVE NARRATIVES, primarily because it had been written by Douglass himself rather than by white abolitionists who would shape oral narratives to fit their needs, but also because of its powerful and complex representation of his personal struggle for literacy, identity, and freedom. The Douglass narrative documents vividly and often brutally his early life and his experience of domestic confusion and personal and communal oppression. It also provides insights into the contradictions that vexed slave owners, the many and various strategies for maintaining slavery and for deflecting criticisms of it, and the religious hypocrisy essential to its continuation. In short, it offers a thorough anatomy of slavery both as ideology and as institution.

Narrative was followed by two expansions, *My Bondage and My Freedom* (1855) and *Life and Times of Frederick Douglass* (1881, 1892), but the 1845 text was the most influential, selling over 11,000 copies in its first three years plus substantial sales in England, France, and the Netherlands—in English and in French and Dutch translations. *Narrative* is still the most frequently reprinted and anthologized of all slave narratives, often being situated centrally in African-American literary histories.

Douglass also wrote *The Heroic Slave* (1853), a fictional story of a mutiny aboard a slave ship and the continuing struggle for freedom by the slaves. While maintaining his abolitionist activities, Douglass also struggled for women's rights throughout the mid- to late-nineteenth century. In his later life, he distinguished himself as a journalist, as the first African-American to own a publishing house in America, as a banker, and as a statesman. He served as minister and consul-general to the Republic of Haiti and as chargé d'affaires for Santo Domingo. Douglass died of a heart attack in Washington, D.C. and is buried in Rochester, New York. Studies include Waldo E. Martin's *The Mind of Frederick Douglass* (1984), and William S. McFreely's *Frederick Douglass* (1991).

RUSSELL J. REISING

Douglass, William (1691–1752),   physician, historian. Born in Scotland, Douglas studied medicine at Edinburgh, Leyden, and Paris, toured the West Indies, and then settled (1718) in Boston. He combined papers mingling his interests in medicine, economics, politics, and humanity in a two-volume *Summary, Historical and Political, of the British Settlements in America* (published in London, 1735)

Dove, Rita (1952–   ),   poet, novelist, short-story writer, playwright. Born in Akron and educated at the Miami University, the University of Tübingen, and the University of Iowa, Dove has taught at several universities, including the University of Virginia. She has earned praise for plain-spoken poems reflecting her life and the experiences of African-Americans. Her first full collection was *The Yellow House on the Corner* (1980), followed by *Museum* (1983). *Thomas and Beulah* (1986), a Pulitzer Prize winner, follows the title characters from their birth in the South to lives in 1960s Akron. *Selected Poems* (1993) incorporates the first three books. *Grace Notes* (1989), *Mother Love* (1995), and *On the Bus with Rosa Parks* (1999) are also poetry collections. Dove served as American Poet Laureate in 1993 and 1994. *Fifth Sunday* (1985) is a short-story gathering. *Through the Ivory Gate* (1992) is a novel. *The Darker Face of the Earth* (1994), a verse play, retells the Oedipus myth against the background of Southern slavery.

Dowell, Coleman (1925–1985),   novelist. Born in Kentucky, Dowell in 1950 moved to New York City, where he pursued a theatrical career, producing two unsuccessful plays, an adaptation of Carl Van Vechten's *The Tattooed Countess* and *The Eve of the Green Grass*. Subsequently, five conceptually and formally intricate novels emerged over a period of fifteen years: *One of the Children Is Crying* (1968), *Mrs. October Was Here* (1974), *Island People* (1976), *Too Much Flesh and Jabez* (1977), and *White on Black or White* (1983). Dowell's collected stories, many of which are surrealistic, were published posthumously as *The Houses of Children* (1987). An experimental writer, called by Tennessee Williams "too good to succeed," Dowell focused on contemporary fragmentation and combined passionate subjectivity and dispassionate artistry. Some critics believe that *Island People* will rank among postmodern American masterworks. He committed suicide on August 3, 1985, three years after *The Review of Contemporary Fiction* had devoted a special issue to him.

JOHN KUEHL

down east.   New England, especially Maine (and also Nova Scotia). The natives of down east are Yankees, and they early made their way into literature, especially into American humor, in the writings of SEBA SMITH, for example. Generally the down-easter was portrayed as a stupid and awkward char-

acter, speaking a nasal dialect. (See YANKEE and AMERICAN LANGUAGE AND LITERATURE.)

Down Easters, The (1833),   a novel by JOHN NEAL. A melodramatic story in which two men are rivals for the hand of a widow. She elopes with one of them, but soon dies, and her husband is revealed as having been involved with another woman, who commits suicide.

Downing, Jack.   Supposed author of satirical papers which began to appear in the Portland (Maine) *Courier* in 1830 and turned in time to criticism of Andrew Jackson and his policies. The original papers were composed by SEBA SMITH, but many imitators sprang up in various parts of the country and shamelessly used Jack Downing as a pen name. The best of them was CHARLES A. DAVIS. Smith always signed the papers "Major (or as Captain) Jack Downing"; Davis signed his "J. Downing, Major."

Dragon Seed (1942),   a novel by PEARL BUCK, it tells of how the wisdom of old people is acquired by the young through experience. Old Ling Tan knows that as long as some have too much land and others too little, wars will continue. His children have to learn this for themselves, in the end realizing that the great wisdom is to live out their lives on the land and hold it till the enemy has gone.

Drake, Daniel (1785–1852),   physician, teacher, scientist. At an early age Drake was taken by his family to the region that ultimately became Kentucky. In his career he was active both there and in Ohio, where he founded the Ohio Medical College (1819). His chief scientific writing was *Treatise on the Principal Disease of the Interior Valley of North America* (2 v. 1850–54). His letters were collected in *Pioneer Life in Kentucky* (1870), edited by his son, and in *Dr. Daniel Drake's Letters on Slavery* (1940). He was called the Benjamin Franklin of the West, and in his writings shows a deep interest in humanity as well as in scientific matters.

Drake, Joseph Rodman (1795–1820),   poet, satirist. Drake's early death from tuberculosis may have prevented full development of his powers as a poet, but his verses reveal technical skill, graceful fancy, and genuine interest in the American scene. Born in New York City, he studied medicine, but preferred to conduct a pharmacy, on Park Row, in New York City. With his friend FITZ-GREENE HALLECK he composed the CROAKER PAPERS, clever skits on men and manners contributed (1819) to the New York *Evening Post. The Culprit Fay* (posthumously published, 1835) is a story of a fay, or fairy, who loves a mortal maiden. The scene is the banks of the Hudson. His best-known poem is "The American Flag" (New York *Evening Post*, May 29, 1819), once a popular recitation piece. Halleck wrote a beautiful tribute *On the Death of Joseph Rodman Drake*, and a New York City park, where Drake was buried, carries his name. See KNICKERBOCKER SCHOOL.

Drake, Temple,   a character in SANCTUARY and REQUIEM FOR A NUN, by William Faulkner. A seventeen-year-old college student in SANCTUARY, Temple is a provocative and irresponsible girl who is raped and confined in a brothel by POPEYE. She perjures herself at the murder trial of an innocent man, less out of malice toward the accused than out of indifference. In *Requiem for a Nun* she persists in her former attitudes by refusing until the very end to see herself as anything but the victim, a respectable woman wronged by circumstance.

Drama in the United States: Before 1960.   American drama was launched with numerous disadvantages, the greatest being the unfavorable view of the stage held in the colonies north of Virginia. Although the Pilgrims landed in New England in 1620, more than a century passed before the English colonists began writing plays of even minor consequence. The theater, it is true, found some amateur support at Harvard, Yale, and William and Mary. At Harvard in 1690, a historical play was produced, GUSTAVUS VASA, by the young Reverend Benjamin Colman. In September 1736, students at William and Mary presented a succession of British plays, including Joseph Addison's classic tragedy *Cato* and George Farquhar's *The Recruiting Officer* and *The Beaux' Stratagem*. But the impetus to write drama of some length and substance depended on the growth of interest in professional theater, first observable in Virginia and the Carolinas as a result of the arrival of the Hallams, a British acting company. At Williamsburg in September 1752, they presented *The Merchant of Venice* and Jonson's *The Alchemist*. Leaving Virginia the following year, the company went to New York City and performed later in Philadelphia and in Charleston. In 1763 the players, by then calling themselves the American Company, presented *The Prince of Parthia*, the first American play to receive a professional stage production.

The Prince of Parthia was written by THOMAS GODFREY (1736–1763), who had probably seen the American Company perform in Philadelphia. It was posthumously published by a friend in 1765, and was produced at the Southwark Theatre in Philadelphia on April 24, 1767—there appears to have been only one performance. This early work was not revived until March 1915, when it was staged at the University of Pennsylvania. As was likely to be the case with an 18th-century tragedy, it was written in blank verse, employed soliloquies, and had its share of familiar romantic ingredients.

Although the play looked to the Old World for style and theme, only three years later an American turned to a thoroughly American subject: Indian warfare. PONTEACH, OR THE SAVAGES OF AMERICA, was written by Major ROBERT ROGERS, an adventurer who had fought both Pontiac and the Cherokee. An undistinguished play in blank verse, it was published in London in 1766 but never performed.

The privately performed ANDROBOROS, written in 1714 by Robert Hunter, the governor of New York, is believed to be the first play written and printed in America. It was a political satire aimed at the governor's opponents, including the leaders of Trinity Church in New York City. During the Revolutionary War both sides wrote satires against each other. Noteworthy was the satire on the royalists—called "a swarm of court sycophants, hungry harpies, and unprincipled danglers"—in THE GROUP (1775), a burlesque written by General Warren's sharp-tongued wife, Mercy Otis Warren, and printed a day before the Battle of Lexington. Mrs. Warren also badgered the British

shortly after Bunker Hill with a dramatic exercise called *The Blockheads, or The Affrighted Officers.*

Comedy had been in vogue throughout the century, but it was not until the appearance of THE CONTRAST that American theater produced its first genuine comedy of manners. The second play by an American to receive professional production, *The Contrast* was a lively affair spiced, in the 18th-century manner, with some witty dialogue, vivid character sketches, and neat turns of plot. It opened at the John Street Theatre in New York on April 16, 1787. The play was written by ROYALL TYLER (1757–1826), a Harvard graduate who became aide-de-camp to General Benjamin Lincoln during the Revolutionary War and later attained distinction as a lawyer. Despite a resemblance to Sheridan's *The School for Scandal*, Tyler's play is essentially American in spirit, owing to its author's partiality for the native virtues of honest dealing and unaffected conduct. Tyler also wrote a farce, *May Day in Town*, which was produced about a month after *The Contrast*. A third play, *A Georgia Spec, or Land in the Moon*, dealing with land speculation, was shown in Boston and New York City in 1797. Although Tyler wrote genial comedy in *The Contrast*, he included considerable social satire in his portrait of Dimple, an Anglophile dandy who courts two coquettes simultaneously. Opposed to the foppish Dimple is the bluff and honest Colonel Manly, who is rewarded with the hand of the fair heroine Maria.

Manly's servant, Jonathan, is another homespun character, his plain practicality made him the prototype of the popular country figure known as the stage Yankee. An entire species of Yankee comedy came into vogue, with rustic characters bearing such names as Nathan Yank, in James Nelson Barker's comedy of manners *Tears and Smiles* (1807), a play suggested by *The Contrast*, and Jonathan Ploughboy in the otherwise conventional operatic play THE FOREST ROSE, OR AMERICAN FARMERS, by Samuel Woodworth, first produced in New York in 1825. Similar Yankee characters, Lot Sap Sago and Deuteronomy Dutiful, appeared in C. A. Logan's *Yankee Land* (1834) and *The Vermont Wool Dealer,* respectively; and Jebedia Homebred and SOLON SHINGLE in Joseph S. Jones's *The Green Mountain Boy* (1833) and *The People's Lawyer* (1839), respectively. The early American plays were as undistinguished as they were imitative.

A rash of Indian plays glorifying "the noble savage," romantic in sentiment, did not materially alter the conventional course of playwriting. One such play, METAMORA, OR THE LAST OF THE WAMPANOAGS, by John Augustus Stone, did make an impression, and won a prize offered by the popular American actor EDWIN FORREST for the best play dealing with an American subject. Forrest played the noble chieftain betrayed by unscrupulous English colonists and toured in the play for years. A reaction against this type of drama began in 1846 but by then, numerous Indian plays, including a *Pocahontas* (1830) and a *Last of the Mohicans* (1831), had already demonstrated that no great advance toward American theater could be registered so long as the sentiment in the plays with American themes remained conventionally romantic.

A national style of theater, except for frontier theatricals, minstrel shows, and other nonliterary ventures, was simply not in accord with the strivings of a nation that looked abroad for cultivated art and literature. The young Walt Whitman could dream of a truly democratic American drama, but the plays written by Americans were steeped in a theater that was indeed popular but not significantly democratic. It reflected the main trends of the English and European stage—the vogue of Shakespeare sustained by star actors, native or British, who toured extensively; the popularity of historical drama, and the growth of melodrama. These tendencies, along with a diminishing taste for high comedy and a growing taste for farce, account for the character of the American plays. Even those that carried a social message or reflected American problems, such as Dion Boucicault's play about race problems, *The Octoroon* (1859), were shaped as melodrama.

America's first professional playwright, WILLIAM DUNLAP (1766–1839), became one of the most prolific adapters of German and French types of romantic comedy, drama, and melodrama, especially as developed by the popular German playwright Kotzebue. Dunlap adapted more than a dozen of Kotzebue's plays, starting with *The Stranger*, produced in 1798. The Shakespearean influence appeared in Dunlap's Elizabethan domestic tragedy *Leicester* (1807), previously produced, in 1794, under the title *The Fatal Deception*. His *André* (1774, revived in 1803 as *The Glory of Columbia*), dealing with the ill-fated British spy Major André, was a historical play in turgid blank verse. Dunlap also wrote several lengthy volumes, including *History of the American Theatre* (1832), the first American chronicle of the stage.

Among other early historical dramas, SUPERSTITION (produced in Philadelphia in 1824) is worth noting for its attack on New England's religious fanaticism and witch-hunting. The author was JAMES NELSON BARKER (1784–1858), mayor of Philadelphia in 1819 and comptroller of the United States Treasury during the last twenty years of his life. *Superstition* was the climax of his career as a playwright, which began with his comedy of manners *Tears and Smiles*, performed in Philadelphia in 1807. Barker also wrote an opera, the first dramatic treatment of the Pocahontas story, entitled THE INDIAN PRINCESS, OR LA BELLE SAUVAGE, produced in Philadelphia in 1808. He also turned Sir Walter Scott's narrative poem *Marmion* into a play in 1812.

ROBERT MONTGOMERY BIRD (1806–54) made a strong impression with THE GLADIATOR, a tragedy in verse about the revolt of the Roman gladiators led by Spartacus. Edwin Forrest produced the play in New York and Philadelphia in 1831. Another tragedy, ORALLOOSSA, dealing with the conquest of Peru by the Spaniards, was successfully produced in 1832. Two years later he won even greater success with THE BROKER OF BOGOTA, first produced in New York in 1832 by Forrest, who appeared in the play from time to time for some thirty years: This domestic tragedy is noteworthy because Bird had the action revolve around middle-class characters.

Most successful among the early dramatists was JOHN HOWARD PAYNE (1791–1852), who had his first play, *Julia, or the Wanderer*, produced in 1806 at the Park Theatre, New York City, when he was not quite fifteen years old. Payne was a versatile playwright, author of some sixty plays, many of them adapted from English and French drama of his time. He succeeded with historical tragedy, as in BRUTUS, by his own admission compounded of seven earlier treatments of the subject; with historical comedy, as in *Charles the Second, or The Merry Monarch*—both plays were first produced in London, in 1818 and 1824, respectively; and especially with melodrama, as in *Therese, the Orphan of Geneva*. His *Clari, or the Maid of Milan*, first presented in 1823, brought him great popularity when its heroine's sentimental song HOME, SWEET HOME swept the country. The song, set to a Sicilian air by Sir Henry Rowley Bishop, expressed Clari's longings for her rustic home, which made her leave the duke whose mistress she was. Payne had another great success with his domestic tragedy *Richelieu*, in which the French statesman seduces a merchant's wife; the play was first produced in London in 1829 under the title of *The French Libertine*. Although Payne's plays had little intrinsic merit, they made him a public figure on both sides of the Atlantic. He was in love with Shelley's wife, Mary Wollstonecraft; collaborated with Washington Irving on two plays (one of these was *Richelieu*); and counted among his English friends Coleridge, Lamb, and the actor-manager Charles Kemble.

Romantic comedy, of which Payne's *Charles II* was representative, continued to be in favor with American playwrights during the first half of the 19th century. A popular work in this vein was TORTESA, THE USURER, a verse play by NATHANIEL PARKER WILLIS (1806–1867).

Romantic tragedy attained some literary and dramatic distinction in FRANCESCA DA RIMINI, by GEORGE HENRY BOKER (1823–1890), based on the familiar medieval tragedy of love that Dante recounted in the *Inferno*.

Francesca da Rimini must be regarded as a terminal point in the development of one type of American drama, for there was no place for romantic tragedy in the American theater until some three-quarters of a century later, when Maxwell Anderson began writing successful verse plays with ELIZABETH THE QUEEN (1930). A richer prospect remained open for comedy of manners, successfully represented in 1845 with Anna Cora Mowatt's FASHION, OR LIFE IN NEW YORK, which moved toward its conventional conclusion with satiric vivacity. Both Mrs. Tiffany, a newly rich society woman, and her daughter Seraphina become infatuated with a fortune-hunting impostor, Count Jolimaitre, who is ultimately exposed as a fraud. Seraphina is saved from an ill-advised elopement, and her father is freed from blackmail, by the father's homespun friend Adam Trueman, who scorns pretense and is unimpressed by titled foreigners. Mowatt (1819–1870) also had a successful career as an actress. Her experiences with the theater gave her the material for her *Autobiography of an Actress* (1854) and two works of fiction, *Mimetic Life* (1856) and *Twin Roses* (1857).

It was to be some time, however, before Mowatt's *Fashion* was equaled in quality or success by another American comedy. Melodrama ruled the theatrical world, although by 1850 its range began to widen to include problem plays, dramas of social tension, and even some rudimentary treatments of psychological conflict. A prolific and successful playwright was the Irish-born dramatist and actor-manager DION BOUCICAULT (1820–1890), who came to the United States in 1853 and ground out a variety of plays, among them adaptations from the French, dramatizations of novels by Dickens and Sir Walter Scott, comedies of Irish life (the most successful was *The Colleen Bawn* in 1860), and melodramas. He also wrote an extremely popular dramatization of Washington Irving's story RIP VAN WINKLE (1865), on which he collaborated with the popular stage star JOSEPH JEFFERSON, and one problem play, THE OCTOROON, OR LIFE IN LOUISIANA. Based on Mayne Reid's novel *the Quadroon* (1856), this suspense-laden melodrama created a sensation when it opened in New York City at the Winter Garden on December 5, 1859. For a play written shortly before the outbreak of the Civil War. *The Octoroon* was a singularly pacifying drama, placating the South with sympathetic portraits of Southern gentry. It differed in this respect from another melodrama devoted to the race problem, UNCLE TOM'S CABIN (1853), George L. Aiken's dramatization of the Harriet Beecher Stowe novel. Designed to expose the evils of slavery, this play helped whip up antislavery sentiment.

Melodrama in the United States, however, degenerated into undistinguished thrillers even in the hands of such an efficient practitioner as OWEN DAVIS, who wrote some three hundred plays after his entry into the theater with *Through the Breakers* (1898). In the latter half of the 19th century, plays seemed more and more to have been designed for spectacular stage effects, such as the scene in AUGUSTIN DALY's play UNDER THE GASLIGHT (1867), the high point of which was the rescue of its unfortunate heroine from an oncoming locomotive. Daly (1838–1899), an important stage producer in New York, became known as a prolific adapter and playwright to whom over ninety plays were credited.

The succession of melodramatists, whose sole object was to provide thrills and entertainment, extended well into the 20th century and had some able practitioners. Among these it is worth mentioning the popular actor, playwright, and producer GEORGE M. COHAN (1878–1942), and BAYARD VEILLER (1871–1943). Elmer Rice, who later became better known as a writer of social drama, started his stage career by introducing movie flashback technique into his melodrama ON TRIAL (1914). A variant form of murder mystery also gained popularity, the most popular being William Gillette's *Sherlock Holmes* (1899), which the actor played constantly until 1932, and THE BAT (1920), by Mary Roberts Rinehart and Avery Hopwood.

A psychological variant of melodrama that won considerable popularity was *The Witching Hour* (1908), by Augustus Thomas (1859–1934). In this play a character employs mental telepathy to clear a friend condemned to the electric chair for a crime actually committed by the district attorney. New dimensions of social- or problem-play playwriting also appeared. Social drama began to be written rather frequently after 1880 in response to growing industrialization, financial speculation,

monopolistic business, and friction between capital and labor. BRONSON HOWARD (1842–1908), who started out as a newspaper reporter and won attention as a serious playwright in 1870, is especially remembered for *Baron Randolph* (1881), his drama of class conflict, and for *The Henrietta* (1887), his satire on Wall Street speculation. STEELE MACKAYE (1824–1894), best known for developing stage machinery and overhead lighting, contributed a provocative labor play, *Paul Kauvar*, or *Anarchy*, in 1887. CHARLES KLEIN (1867–1915), who won success with his sentimental dramas *The Auctioneer* (1901) and *The Music Master* (1904), in which the popular actor David Warfield played leading roles, made exciting melodrama out of the struggle of a young man against a "malefactor of great wealth" in *The Lion and the Mouse* (1905), and paid tribute to the working-class girl in *Maggie Pepper* (1911). EDWARD SHELDON (1886–1946) advanced somewhat beyond these simple plays—though without forgoing melodramatic contrivance—with his racial problem play THE NIGGER (1910), in which a politically ambitious Southerner discovers he is partly African-American, and with THE BOSS (1911), the story of an unscrupulous politician. Theodore Roosevelt's clashes with big business and the excitement of muckraking journalism, which exposed scandals in city government, proved so contagious that even the urbane CLYDE FITCH (1865–1909), whose reputation rested on light comedies such as *The Climbers* (1901) and CAPTAIN JINKS OF THE HORSE MARINES (1902), began firing away at political corruption in his last play, *The City* (1909).

The main limitation of these and other treatments of the social scene was the artificiality of the characters and the plot. The dialogue reflected these faults and added to them the banal sentimentality and moral reformation then current in popular literature. Whatever realism the plays possessed lay on the surface. No matter how much later they reached the stage than Ibsen's *Ghosts* and *An Enemy of the People*, the plays were pre-Ibsenite or pseudo-Ibsenite in sentiment and opinion. The realism of the type of American playwriting that remained in vogue until 1920 was, with few exceptions, on a par with the so-called naturalism of DAVID BELASCO (1859–1931) and little more than a passion for putting the actual thing on the stage. For example, Belasco duplicated a Childs' Restaurant on stage in 1912, but he could not bring himself to renounce the plot contrivances and sentimentalities that proved so profitable in the plays he produced and often partially wrote. His showman's taste led him to the romanticized Orient with *Madame Butterfly* (1900) and to the occult with THE RETURN OF PETER GRIMM (1912). Even when he produced a relatively realistic character study, *The Easiest Way* (1909), he apparently considered that the essence of realism was the theatrical boardinghouse he reproduced as the set.

Mechanical means such as Belasco employed could make the theater spectacular, but they could not make it genuinely realistic; mere pictorialism could only prove a deception to those who equated realism, however superficial, with progress. A new outlook, ensuring penetration into individual character and social reality, was needed. Realism had to be developed in depth, and this required above all an unconventional spirit and a keen intellect. The alternative to genuine realism was genuine imagination, which entailed inventiveness rather than literalness, and creative selectivity rather than imitation, no matter how spectacular. But effective inventiveness and selectivity also required a penetrating mind and lively intelligence.

The necessary new ideals and principles of theater came from many quarters—from influential literary figures, such as Zola in Europe and William Dean Howells in America; from theoreticians and visionaries of the theater; from the experiments of European stage directors, such as Reinhardt and Stanislavsky; above all from the strivings of European and American playwrights. It is not extravagant to say that progress came in large part from a transfer of power and influence from actor-managers to playwrights; an actor's theater became a playwright's theater.

While the American drama was a feeble commodity throughout the 19th century and the first two decades of the 20th, the theater itself had been a thriving, if not an exciting, institution due to the talent of star actors who played in New York City and toured the country extensively, bringing their own companies with them or drawing on resident stock companies for a supporting cast. The star personalities awed or entranced the public, and their names carried a prestige that relatively few performers possessed after 1920.

The roster of stars available at one time or another to the American stage before World War I included Edmund Kean, JUNIUS BRUTUS BOOTH, William Charles Macready, FANNY KEMBLE, Sarah Bernhardt, Sir Henry Irving, Edward A. Sothern, Tommaso Salvini, Helena Modjeska, and Eleonora Duse in the foreign contingent; and EDWIN FORREST, Joseph Jefferson, Anna Cora Mowatt, JAMES H. HACKETT, Charlotte Cushman, Julia Marlowe, EDWIN BOOTH, RICHARD MANSFIELD, Ada Rehan, Lillian Russell, John Drew, Maude Adams, and Mrs. Fiske among the natives. None of the American playwrights contemporary with these actors achieved comparable reputations. The situation changed radically only after 1920, when progressive theater groups and critics aimed at ensemble performance and set themselves sternly against the star system. Although there were many excellent actors on the American stage after 1920, none of them—not even Katharine Cornell, Helen Hayes, and the Lunts—overshadowed Eugene O'Neill and Tennessee Williams or, for brief periods, Philip Barry, Maxwell Anderson, Clifford Odets, Arthur Miller, Rodgers and Hammerstein, and perhaps a few other playwrights. After 1914 the theater became increasingly dependent on the talents of the playwrights, a situation that remained unchanged until the writers began to lose their influence by default in the 1950s, when, with the rise of such powerful personalities as Joshua Logan and ELIA KAZAN, it seemed as if a so-called director's, rather than playwright's, theater had come into being.

Progress in drama, however, could not come from playwrights without the support of forward-looking individual managers such as ARTHUR HOPKINS (1878–1950) and aggressive art-theater or little-theater groups. These sprang up in profusion throughout the country after 1914, giving rise to a folk-theater movement and to many so-called regional plays produced locally.

Especially important was the little-theater movement that gained momentum in New York City, the center of the professional theater. The two most influential groups were the PROVINCETOWN PLAYERS, founded in 1915, from which Eugene O'Neill emerged as the leading American playwright, and the Washington Square Players, established at about the same time. The latter organization gave birth to the THEATRE GUILD, which rapidly became the leading American theatrical company after 1919. A dozen years later, a Guild splinter group, led by HAROLD CLURMAN and Lee Strasberg, became the Group Theatre (see THE GROUP), which first produced the plays of CLIFFORD ODETS, SIDNEY KINGSLEY, and WILLIAM SAROYAN. These progressive groups and a few courageous individual producers ensured the rise of modern drama in America.

Undoubtedly strong European influences were operative in the development of the American drama in the principal modern directions. The example of Ibsen, Hauptmann, Chekhov, Gorki, Galsworthy, and Shaw helped move American theater toward a realistic orientation in choice and treatment of subject matter. The example of Strindberg (for whose post-realistic plays O'Neill expressed admiration), Maeterlinck, Molnar, Pirandello, Andreyev, Brecht, and the sociological German expressionists Kaiser and Toller inspired opposite leanings toward imaginative and theatricalist theater. But there also were some early stirrings of modern theater on the American scene itself.

The most important as well as the earliest of the new realists was the actor, manager, and playwright JAMES A. HERNE (1839–1901). After adapting as well as helping to stage many run-of-the-mill plays, he wrote MARGARET FLEMING, which had three tryout performances, beginning on July 4, 1890. The first truly realistic play of American life, it gave an unconventional treatment of a moral problem in closing with a woman's willingness to care for her husband's illegitimate child and to reconcile with her wayward mate. The puritanical opposition of Boston's theater managers forced Herne to present the play privately in 1891 in a small Boston playhouse, where it had a critical success (Hamlin Garland and Thomas Bailey Aldrich were among the eminent authors of the time who praised it), and Herne sank his own money, earned with an earlier and conventional melodrama, into the production. The play was presented in New York on December 9, 1891, at Palmer's Theater; in Chicago in 1892; in New York again in 1894; and in Chicago again with Herne's daughters Chrystal and Julie Herne playing the title role in 1907 and 1915, respectively. Herne wavered between realism and popular Victorian playwriting, but tried to adhere to the principles he propounded in his essay "Art for Truth's Sake in the Drama" (Arena, February 1897). Herne wrote a second—and successful—realistic drama, SHORE ACRES, in 1892, giving a vivid picture of life in New England, but it is Margaret Fleming that made him a precursor of modern American realists in the theater, a position already granted him in the 1890s by WILLIAM DEAN HOWELLS, the leading American realistic novelist of the time.

Some advance was also achieved by the scholar and poet WILLIAM VAUGHN MOODY (1869–1910), who, after writing philosophical verse dramas, developed a realistic conflict between a puritanical young woman and a rough individualist in a play first entitled *A Sabine Woman* (1906) and then THE GREAT DIVIDE when produced in 1909. This work was a widely recognized contribution to the rising tide of critical realism in the American theater; it played successfully in New York and then on tour with Henry Miller and Margaret Anglin in 1906. Perhaps the most remarkable feature of *The Great Divide*, in which Moody predicated a great divide between conscience-burdened New England and the free American frontier, was the idea that the heroine of the play could fall in love with a man who had virtually violated her in the Wild West. Realism was also sustained, although less successfully, in Moody's next prose play, *The Faith Healer* (1909), which deals with the psychological crisis of a man of occult powers whose power to heal vanishes when he loses self-confidence in an unbelieving world. Another thrust in the modern direction was made by EUGENE WALTER (1874–1941) with one of his melodramatic plays, *The Easiest Way* (1908), in which a wealthy man's mistress makes an effort to leave him but is unable to reconcile herself to a life of poverty after having enjoyed leisure and luxury.

Even society comedy began to reflect a trend toward a keener realism, particularly observable in Langdon Mitchell's comedy of divorce in fashionable circles, *The New York Idea*, presented in 1906 by the progressive actress-manager Mrs. Fiske (Minnie Maddern Fiske, 1865–1932). More frequently the playwrights turned out farce-comedies such as Winchell Smith and Frank Bacon's folksy play LIGHTNIN' (1918) and, after 1920, briskly urban and broadly satirical, so-called wisecracking, plays. Most successful were the farces and comedies of GEORGE S. KAUFMAN (1889–1961) and BEN HECHT (1894–1964). These playwrights and their collaborators accounted for such deflationary entertainments as MERTON OF THE MOVIES (1922), *June Moon* (1929), THE MAN WHO CAME TO DINNER (1939), THE FRONT PAGE (1928), and *Twentieth Century* (1932). Noteworthy among other American authors who made satire their province was GEORGE KELLY, a glum satirist who won success with THE SHOW-OFF (1924) and with CRAIG'S WIFE (1925), a bleak indictment of self-centered middle-class American women. Deflationary tactics became so prevalent in the New York theater that they even infiltrated the world of musical comedy, especially in the case of PAL JOEY, a relentless exposé of egotism by John O'Hara, Richard Rodgers, and Lorenz Hart in 1940.

A neoromantic movement begun at the turn of the century had relatively meager results. There was little advance in poetic drama except for Percy MacKaye's THE SCARECROW (1908), a tragic fantasy in prose based on Hawthorne's tale FEATHERTOP. MacKaye had a strong vein of poetry in his many plays, masques, and operas, but he never again achieved the dramatic power of *The Scarecrow*. Other playwrights made little impression with their poetic plays on the Broadway stage until

the successful production of MAXWELL ANDERSON's blank-verse tragedy *Elizabeth the Queen* in 1930. A poetic renaissance was promised for a time by the popular success of other historical plays by Anderson, especially *Mary of Scotland* (1933) and *Anne of the Thousand Days* (1948), as well as his two verse plays that deal with contemporary life, *Winterset* (1935) and HIGH TOR (1936). But verse drama remained a relatively exotic genre in the American theater, despite the success of these plays and of T. S. Eliot's THE COCKTAIL PARTY (1949) and Christopher Fry's *The Lady's Not for Burning* (1948), both imported to Broadway from the British stage. Among American playwrights of the 1950s, only ARCHIBALD MACLEISH won popular success with poetry when his drama *J. B.* reached Broadway in the 1959–60 season after a production at Yale by F. Curtis Canfield.

However, even prose dramas were apt to convey poetic atmosphere and feeling. Several of the playwrights wrote flavorsome dialect and evinced a poetic feeling for nature and local color. Several writers also resorted to imaginative formal devices. So-called dream technique or fantastic distortion combined with abrupt telegraphic dialogue produced eerie effects of EXPRESSIONISM in plays by O'Neill, Elmer Rice, John Howard Lawson, and others after 1920. Expressionist extravaganza even found its way into comedy and into musical comedy. Imaginative theater also appeared in the documentary dramas, on topical matters such as the TVA and slum clearance (*Power and One-third of a Nation*), produced during the same period (1935–39) by the FEDERAL THEATER PROJECT. These so-called Living Newspapers arrestingly combined social fact with inventive theatricality, direct address to the audience, vaudeville skits, and symbolism. In *Power*, for example, the justices of the United States Supreme Court are represented by nine masks placed on a table.

There can be no doubt that despite strong leanings toward realism, the American theater was anything but indifferent to imaginative drama. Even specialists in social realism, urbane comedy, and lusty farce were likely to attempt fantasy or to employ nonrealistic techniques from time to time. Thus, PHILIP BARRY (1896–1949), the suave author of many a society comedy of the caliber of HOLIDAY (1928) and THE PHILADELPHIA STORY (1939), made attempts to write morality plays for the times, such as *Hotel Universe* (1930), a cross-section of modern life abounding in symbolism, and *Here Come the Clowns* (1938), an allegory of good and evil. The same partiality for departures from realistic style and technique was shown by O'Neill, Williams, Arthur Miller, and THORNTON WILDER, all of whom also manifested considerable talent for observing everyday reality.

Wilder, distinguished both as a playwright and novelist, was especially adept as well as consistent in his endeavor to achieve stylization and a high degree of theatricality, as demonstrated in his full-length plays OUR TOWN (1938), THE SKIN OF OUR TEETH (1942), and *The Matchmaker* (1956), and in many fugitive one-act pieces. *Our Town*, in which Wilder blended Chinese theatricalist stylization with simple realism, proved an exceptionally appealing feat of creative sympathy and imagination. Proceeding more self-consciously in *The Skin of Our Teeth*, Wilder nevertheless rooted this play too in human reality—in the splendors and miseries of the human race, specifically the anguish of people once more facing a world crisis in the early 1940s, from which escape even "by the skin of our teeth" seems dubious.

The attractions of imaginative drama affected even so determined a social realist as ARTHUR MILLER after his Ibsenist problem play *All My Sons* (1947). He employed expressionistic structure in DEATH OF A SALESMAN (1949), in which the salesman-hero's memories and fantasies developed Miller's theme of the failure of materialism and success worship. Miller also sought to achieve imaginative form and tone in THE CRUCIBLE (1953), a historical tragedy dealing with the Salem witchcraft trials, and in *A View from the Bridge* (1955), a drama of passion and lost honor set on the New York waterfront and distinctly patterned after Greek tragedy.

The career of EUGENE O'NEILL (1888–1953) is virtually a summary of all but one of the most important aspects of the modern drama, the exception being social drama—the direct treatment of contemporary political, social, and economic conflicts. O'Neill combined vigor with imagination, toughness with sensitivity, and realistic detail with atmospherics or symbols. He dealt with authentic American types and backgrounds, but often shifted his emphasis from commonplace reality to religious questioning, cosmic longing, and spiritual struggle. He also conducted numerous experiments in modern dramatic styles, ranging from realism to expressionism, and from the one-act play form, of which he achieved mastery with half a dozen sea pieces early in his career (1914–18), to oversized plays, running to as many as nine acts in the case of STRANGE INTERLUDE (1928), and constituting a trilogy in the case of MOURNING BECOMES ELECTRA (1931). O'Neill's partly naturalistic one-act plays, especially those dealing with the sea, are suffused with ironic circumstances, oppressive moods, and symbolic atmosphere suggestive of the lostness of humanity and the malignity of fate. The same qualities distinguish his early, more or less naturalistic, full-length dramas BEYOND THE HORIZON (1920), ANNA CHRISTIE (1921), and DESIRE UNDER THE ELMS (1924), in all of which family relationships and the duel between the sexes produce intense conflicts and attained symbolic significance.

At the same time, feeling drawn to the dramatic techniques favorable to subjective and philosophical drama, O'Neill turned to expressionism, under the avowed influence of Strindberg's experiments. O'Neill's early experiments in subjective dramaturgy, *The Emperor Jones* (1920) and *The Hairy Ape* (1922), were impressive. THE EMPEROR JONES, in which a fleeing dictator is overwhelmed by ancestral memories and atavistic fears while losing his way in a Caribbean jungle, is completely successful; and THE HAIRY APE, dealing with the symbolic search of a burly stoker for a place in the world as a human, rather than subhuman, being constitutes provocative and powerful drama despite a somewhat confusing shift of

focus. In ALL GOD'S CHILLUN GOT WINGS (1924) O'Neill treats racial tension in a largely metaphysical vein with the aid of expressionistic stylization. He also conveys the alienation of the artist and the spiritual bankruptcy of the seemingly adjusted philistine in American society by means of the interchangeable masks of THE GREAT GOD BROWN (1926). His concern with the divided nature of modern men and women in *Strange Interlude* (1928) produced a multileveled account of an emotionally shattered woman's life with the help of the Joycean interior monologue. In this intentionally novelistic work he endeavors to sustain psychological drama with extravagant recourse to the Elizabethan convention of the aside, in which a character expresses his secret thoughts without being overheard by any of the characters who share the stage with him.

In his next major effort, *Mourning Becomes Electra* (1931), O'Neill domesticated Greek tragedy by stating the Orestean theme in Freudian terms and giving the action a New England setting. O'Neill returned to primarily realistic dramaturgy in this work, but also used symbolic elements and masklike effects. A renewed reliance on realism appeared especially in his genial comedy of turn-of-the-century American life, *Ah, Wilderness!* (1933), and in the plays he wrote during his long retirement: THE ICEMAN COMETH (1946), *A Moon for the Misbegotten* (1947), the autobiographical LONG DAY'S JOURNEY INTO NIGHT (1956), and *A Touch of the Poet* (1958). Recurrent themes in these latter-day works, as well as in the long one-act play *Hughie*, are man's lostness and dependence on sustaining illusions. O'Neill's pessimism, temporarily in abeyance when he wrote *Ah, Wilderness!*, returned in full force in his last plays. O'Neill's career had two great periods, an early one and a late one, separated by a hiatus of a dozen years, but his viewpoint was consistent and was given urgency by his dramatic talent whether he favored its realistic or expressionistic aspect. In favoring the former in the late plays, moreover, he was able to write with renewed power and enriched sympathy, strengthening his position as the playwright to whom the American theater owed a large measure of its claim to international importance. This was especially evident when O'Neill received the Nobel Prize for literature in 1936. He became an international figure in the 1920s, and he remained one after his death, chiefly as a result of posthumous productions in Sweden, where several of his late plays first appeared on the stage.

In the first decade after World War I several of O'Neill's contemporaries, notably ELMER RICE and SIDNEY HOWARD (1891–1939), acquired impressive reputations, the former with *Street Scene* (1929) and *Counsellor-at-Law* (1931), the latter with his folk comedy THEY KNEW WHAT THEY WANTED (1924), the medical drama *Yellow Jack* (1934), and numerous competent dramatizations of novels (especially *Dodsworth*, 1934) and adaptations from the French (especially *The Late Christopher Bean*, 1934). In the second decade Maxwell Anderson was sometimes considered O'Neill's rival on the strength of his poetic plays, from *Elizabeth the Queen* to *Winterset*, although his versification was usually flabby and his tragic sense largely derivative. CLIFFORD ODETS was acclaimed as the new hope of the theater on the basis of his vitality as a social dramatist in WAITING FOR LEFTY (1935), AWAKE AND SING (1935), and GOLDEN BOY (1937). During the 1940s Tennessee Williams and Arthur Miller arrived on Broadway with *The Glass Menagerie* and *All My Sons,* respectively, then acquired worldwide reputations with the psychological and social dramas A STREETCAR NAMED DESIRE (1947) and *Death of a Salesman* (1949), and strengthened their position with later plays, such as *Cat on a Hot Tin Roof* (1955) and *The Crucible.*

It was evident before 1960 that the American drama, regardless of its limitations and in spite of increasingly unfavorable conditions of theatrical production, had achieved an impressive record and was highly regarded abroad, especially in England, Central Europe, and Scandinavia. No other American playwright actually came within hailing distance of O'Neill, but the aforementioned authors accounted for a good deal of the vitality and vigor of the American stage after 1920, and their labors were supplemented by the work of Paul Green, Lillian Hellman, Robert Sherwood, S. N. Behrman, Sidney Kingsley, William Saroyan, William Inge, and others.

Author of the moving chronicle IN ABRAHAM'S BOSOM (1927), the Southern family drama *The House of Connelly* (1932), and the antiwar satire *Johnny Johnson* (1937), among other works, PAUL GREEN brought deep sympathies, a fine sense of justice, rich regional flavor, and technical innovation to his plays. He also worked with fervor and skill in the special art of pageant writing, most notably in his first so-called symphonic drama, *The Lost Colony* (1937). He gained undisputed mastery of the one-act play with such powerful pieces as *White Dresses* (1928) and *Hymn to the Rising Sun* (1936). Thornton Wilder cultivated a rich vein of fantasy and Yankee shrewdness in a manner that was at once philosophical and theatrical in *Our Town, The Skin of Our Teeth,* and even in the lighthearted farce *The Matchmaker.*

LILLIAN HELLMAN revealed a strong talent for blending social realities, moral judgment, and realistic portraiture in hard-driving and penetrating plays, such as THE CHILDREN'S HOUR (1934), THE LITTLE FOXES (1939), WATCH ON THE RHINE (1941), and *The Autumn Garden* (1951).

ROBERT SHERWOOD's talent for showmanship was abundantly evident in his urbane romantic comedies *The Road to Rome* (1926) and *Reunion in Vienna* (1931). His concern with the state of the world deepening, he dramatized failure of the nerve among intellectuals in his Western melodrama THE PETRIFIED FOREST (1935) and a recovery of nerve in THERE SHALL BE NO NIGHT (1940). He also produced a brilliantly theatrical antiwar protest in IDIOT'S DELIGHT (1936), and turned his political idealism into a moving tribute to human greatness in ABE LINCOLN IN ILLINOIS (1938).

S. N. BEHRMAN developed an individual style of thoughtful comedy with *The Second Man* (1927), *Biography* (1932), *End of Summer* (1936), and *No Time for Comedy* (1939), in which he expressed a growing concern with the state of the world. Sidney Kingsley specialized successfully in social realism with the

hospital-drama MEN IN WHITE (1933), the naturalistic study of slum life DEAD END (1935), and the moral analysis of *Detective Story* (1949), a warning against inflexible righteousness. He also enriched political drama with his historical play *The Patriots* (1943), deriving a lesson in national unity from the early years of the American republic, and with his antitotalitarian *Darkness at Noon,* a deft dramatization of Arthur Koestler's novel.

WILLIAM SAROYAN delighted playgoers with his improvisatory playwriting in such half-fanciful plays as *My Heart's in the Highlands* and THE TIME OF YOUR LIFE (both 1939).

WILLIAM INGE attained a rueful type of small-town realism, at once penetrative and compassionate, in *Come Back, Little Sheba* (1950), *Picnic* (1953), *Bus Stop* (1955), and *Dark at the Top of the Stairs* (1957).

With additional contributions after 1920 from numerous reliable writers, such as Paul Osborn, ZOE AKINS, RACHEL CROTHERS, Philip Barry, George Kelly, SAM and BELLA SPEWACK, JOHN VAN DRUTEN, Robert Anderson, HOWARD LINDSAY, and RUSSELL CROUSE and from mavericks such as Edwin Justus Mayer, John Balderson (*Berkeley Square*), John Howard Lawson, Lynn Riggs, the poet ROBINSON JEFFERS, and Edward Albee, American dramatic output of the 1920–60 period looked like a bumper harvest.

In the creation of realistic drama, American playwrights were unsurpassed after World War I, and in the writing of social drama Rice, Lawson, Kingsley, Odets, Hellman, and Miller were surpassed only by the German playwright Bertolt Brecht (1898–1956). In the art of cultivated high comedy or comedy of manners, American playwrights fell below British and French standards, but exceptions may be noted in the case of Barry, Behrman, and the London-born John Van Druten (1901–1957), who first established himself as a playwright in England. In low comedy and farce American writers, led by George S. Kaufman, cut a wide swath with their gusto and lively irreverence. Only in the areas of distinctly fanciful playwriting did American playwrights of the 1920–60 period reap a meager harvest, but exceptions could be noted in the development of folk drama by Paul Green and Lynn Riggs, in the creation of music drama by George Gershwin and Gian-Carlo Menotti, and of MUSICAL COMEDY, where American supremacy was established by Jerome Kern, Irving Berlin, Oscar Hammerstein II, Moss Hart, Richard Rodgers, Frank Loesser, Alan Jay Lerner, Frederick Loewe, Abe Burrows, and others with such productions as *Porgy and Bess, Oklahoma!, South Pacific, Guys and Dolls, West Side Story,* and *My Fair Lady.*

It would be misleading, however, to conclude a review of American drama after World War I on an optimistic note without also observing signs of deterioration and distress. Granting the obvious superiority of the plays and the productions to most prewar achievements in the American theater, it must be said that the improvement in quality was accompanied by a continual decrease in quantity. By 1960 the professional American theater had shrunk to a fraction of its former size, and it had become an unprofitable enterprise on the whole except in the specialized area of popular musical enter- tainment. The compensating developments were the impres- sive growth of amateur production on numerous campuses and in relatively small communities, and the rise in New York City of the Off Broadway movement, consisting of scaled- down production in smaller theaters, often on some sort of stock-company basis. The Off Broadway movement, in addi- tion to producing provocative European plays and reviving prominent foreign and native works, introduced such avant- garde American writers in the late 1950s and the 1960s as EDWARD ALBEE (*The Zoo Story* and *The American Dream*), JACK GELBER (*The Connection*), and JACK RICHARDSON (*The Prodigal* and *Gallows' Humor*). But by 1960 the Off Broadway theater was also threatened by inflationary production costs. It was evident, moreover, that a diminution had occurred in the resources of playwriting along with a narrowing of interests— in the case of the new avant-garde, to a cult of nihilism and abstraction. A general decline in creative energy was apparent, beginning by the end of the 1930s and halted from time to time only by the fortunate emergence of some talented play- wright, such as Williams, Miller, or Inge.

In the 1920s the theater's resources were greatly enriched by the rise of sophistication, skepticism, and candor, and by the growth of social criticism and psychological analysis. Assimi- lating European advances in realism and expressionism, adopting an open mind toward sex, and conducting a vigorous campaign against puritanism and philistinism, the young dramatists of the 1920s devoted themselves to artistic experi- ment and social rebellion. The results were most apparent in the early work of O'Neill and in the breezily skeptical Kauf- man farce-comedies, but they could be seen invigorating a great variety of dramatic effort, ranging from the folksy com- edy of Sidney Howard's *They Knew What They Wanted* to the fashionable high comedy of Philip Barry's *Holiday* and Behrman's *The Second Man*; and from the vivacious expres- sionistic satire of Kaufman and Connelly's *Beggar on Horse- back* (1924) and Lawson's *Processional* (1925) to sultry protests against materialism and arid existence devoid of beauty or romance, such as Lawson's expressionistic drama of disori- ented youth *Roger Bloomer* (1923), and Sophie Treadwell's expressionistic murder melodrama *Machinal* (1928). The American theater of the 1920s was alive with intelligence, scorn, and protest, and it was bent on making provocative dis- coveries in dramatic style that would serve its interests. Long after the conditions favorable to theater of the period had van- ished, one could still find its spirit alive in the work of play- wrights who had survived from the period.

The depression decade of the 1930s manifested noteworthy vitality despite the domestic tensions and international upheavals of the period, the threat of fascism, and the coming of a second world war. The creative energy of the 1920s spilled over into the next decade, bringing with it such weighty work as O'Neill's *Mourning Becomes Electra* and Maxwell Ander- son's verse tragedies. Augmented or transformed vitality appeared in the work of other established writers, such as

Sherwood (*The Petrified Forest, Idiot's Delight,* and *Abe Lincoln in Illinois*), and Paul Green (*Johnny Johnson*), who responded as far as temperament and talent would allow to the challenge of the decade. Moreover, fresh creative energies appeared in a new generation that included Odets, Hellman, Kingsley, John Wexley, Robert Ardrey, E. P. Conkle, Irwin Shaw, John Stein- beck, and Saroyan. Masterpieces were few in that period, but energy was abundant. American social drama was at its peak in the 1930s, and its influence was felt by the generation that entered the theater at the conclusion of World War II—it is well to remember that both Williams and Miller had been Depression-period writers in their youth.

The first half of the 1940s was a relatively sterile period in the American theater. Its playwrights were, in the main, inca- pable of rising to the occasion of World War II sufficiently to write heroic drama, and at the same time they maintained a self-imposed moratorium on the sophistication that had flourished in the 1920s and on the social criticism that had sparked the theater of the 1930s. With the end of the war in 1945 a new burst of creativity appeared. The theater of the sec- ond half of the decade was galvanized into some semblance of life by Williams, Inge, and Miller, ARTHUR LAURENTS (*Home of the Brave*), John Patrick (*The Hasty Heart*), Mary Chase (*Har- vey*), GARSON KANIN (*Born Yesterday*), and Lindsay and Crouse (*State of the Union*).

But the promised renascence of the American drama failed to materialize after 1950. A combination of social and political circumstances, including cold war jitters and MCCARTHYISM, resulting in a reduction of intellectual ferment and a diminu- tion of idealistic fervor, left the new decade of the 1950s limp and diffident except for an occasional explosion of protest, such as Arthur Miller's *The Crucible* and Williams's symbolist *Camino Real*. Among the new writers who appeared on Broad- way, only ROBERT ANDERSON (*Tea and Sympathy*) rose distinctly above the average. Some new plays of the decade, many of them adaptations (adaptations multiplied as playwriting lost personal passion), achieved various degrees of distinction— Hellman's *Toys in the Attic*, Patrick's *Teahouse of the August Moon*, Van Druten's *I Am a Camera*, PADDY CHAYEFSKY's *The Tenth Man*, MacLeish's verse drama *J.B.*, William Gibson's *Two for the Seesaw* and *The Miracle Worker*, Lorraine Hansberry's drama of urban African-American life *Raisin in the Sun*, and KETTI FRINGS's dramatization of Thomas Wolfe's novel LOOK HOMEWARD ANGEL. In addition to introducing Gelber, Richard- son, and Albee, Off Broadway enterprise also gave a new lease on life to previously unsuccessful plays, such as Williams's chronicle of frustration *Summer and Smoke*, and O'Neill's pow- erful drama *The Iceman Cometh*.

The harvest of original new drama was meager, however, for a period of some dozen years. Not the least disturbing, more- over, was the absence of proof that the promising playwrights of the previous decade, including Williams, Miller, and Inge, were moving toward enriched artistry and augmented signifi- cance. There was more evidence of stalemate than of progress in the drama after the American theater had rounded out its fourth post-Victorian, or modern, decade. Perhaps a new dispensation would reach the stage before long, but in 1962 it was not at all clear what this dispensation would be, where it would originate, and what course it would follow. It was apparent only that the economic foundations of the theater would have to be strengthened, possibly with the aid of federal as well as local subsidy, and that the condition of the stage would depend, to a considerable degree, on the condition of American society and the increasingly precarious state of the world.

Important historical and critical works on American drama to 1960 include T. Allston Brown, *History of the American Stage* (3 v. 1903); Arthur Hornblow, *A History of the Theatre in America* (2 v. 1919); Helen Deutsch and Stella Hanau, *The Provincetown* (1931); Eleanor Flexner, *American Playwrights: 1918–1938* (1938); Burns Mantle, *Contemporary American Playwright* (1938); Arthur Hobson Quinn, *A History of the American Drama* (2 v. 1945); Glenn Hughes, *A History of the American Theatre, 1700–1950* (1951); John Gassner, *The Theatre in Our Times* (1954); Eric Bentley, *The Dramatic Event: An American Chronicle* (1954); Alan Downer, *Fifty Years of American Drama, 1900–1950* (1957); Joseph Wood Krutch, *The American Drama Since 1918* (rev. ed. 1957); Barnard Hewitt, *Theatre U.S.A., 1668–1957* (1959); Elmer Rice, *The Living Theatre* (1959); John Gassner, *Theatre at the Crossroads* (1960); and Alan Downer, *Recent American Drama* (1961).

Important collections of plays include Burns Mantle and Garrison P. Sherwood, eds., *The Best Plays of 1919–1920 to 1923–1924* (annual volumes, 1920–24); *The Best Plays of 1924–25 to 1958* (annual volumes since 1924); *The Best Plays of 1909–1919* (1933); *The Best Plays of 1899–1909* (1944); Barrett H. Clark and Kenyon Nicholson, eds., *The American Scene* (1930), which contains thirty-four one-act plays; Margaret Mayorga, ed., *One-Act Plays by American Authors* (1937); Pierre De Rohan, ed., *Federal Theatre Plays* (2 v. 1938); Eugene O'Neill, *The Plays of Eugene O'Neill* (3 v. 1948); John Gassner, ed., *A Treasury of the Theatre*, v. 2 (1951) and *Library of Best American Plays* (6 v. 1939–1961); Arthur Hobson Quinn, ed., *Representative American Plays. From 1767 to the Present Day* (7th ed., 1953); and Jack Gaver, ed., *Critics' Choice: New York Drama Critics' Circle Prize Plays, 1933–1955* (1955).

JOHN GASSNER/D.C.

Drama in the United States: Since 1960.

Revitalization of American drama in the mid-1960s came from the Off Off Broadway movement—an explosion of informal theaters converted from cafes, churches, and garages and spiraling out from the Greenwich Village area from 1964. This movement was partly a response to the increasing failure of Off Broadway to remain a viable alternative to Broadway. Almost all of the noteworthy playwrights to emerge in the late 1960s had their first stagings in venues such as Joe Cino's Cafe Cino, Ellen Stewart's Cafe La Mama, and Al Carmine's Judson Poets' Theatre. The movement's participants regarded the political and theatrical establishment of the time as hypocritical, antediluvian, and spiritually bankrupt—and their spirit of rebellion was cross-fertilized by an excitement in theatrical experimentation unparalleled since the 1920s.

The influence of this movement on the drama of the time was seminal—not only in its vigor and irreverent tone, but in technique. Emphasis on free-wheeling and nonlinear action, disdain for traditional realism, and reliance on bizarre and surreal imagery, nonverbal sound, and ritualized movement together determined the style and tone of a vigorous New Wave of American drama from 1965 to 1975.

The most important playwright who emerged at this time was SAM SHEPARD (1943–   ), whose early short plays included *Chicago* (1965), *Icarus' Mother* (1965), *Red Cross* (1966), and *Cowboys #2* (1967). His signature style employs paradoxical images of escape and entrapment; mythic motifs from the Old West, science fiction, and the rock culture; and aria-like verbal explorations of his characters' minds. He capped the bracing experiments of this first period of his work with *The Tooth of Crime* (1972), a stylistically dazzling duel to the death between two rock-star archetypes.

Other important playwrights who emerged from the same time and context include Jean-Claude Van Itallie (1936–   ), whose spare, corrosive myths of depersonalized existence include *America Hurrah* (1965) and *The Serpent* (1967), co-authored with the Open Theatre; JOHN GUARE (1938–   ), more expansively comic but equally savage, in such plays as *Muzeeka* (1967) and *The House of Blue Leaves* (1970); and the lyrical LANFORD WILSON (1937–   ), whose *Balm in Gilead* (1965) may be the first full-length play presented Off Off Broadway, and whose early work includes *The Rimers of Eldritch* (1967) and *The Hot L Baltimore* (1973). Other—but not all—new playwrights, including MEGAN TERRY, Maria Irene Fornes, Terence McNally, Murray Mednick, Leonard Melfi, and Robert Patrick, owe their initial success to Off Off Broadway. Two exceptions are Arthur Kopit (1938–   ) and Michael Weller (1942–   ). Another is DAVID RABE (1940–   ). Producer JOSEPH PAPP (1921–1991) staged the acclaimed first two plays of Rabe's so-called Vietnam trilogy—*Sticks and Bones* (1971) and *The Basic Training of Pavlo Hummel* (1971).

Of the older playwrights who had risen to prominence on Broadway in the 1940s and 1950s, it was only ARTHUR MILLER who consolidated his reputation. After a silence of eight years, he produced *After the Fall* (1964), *Incident at Vichy* (1965), and *The Price* (1968). A disappointment to many was the failure of Tennessee Williams to strike out in new directions. EDWARD ALBEE, however, emerged from Off Broadway success to become a golden boy for a time with the success of *Who's Afraid of Virginia Woolf* (1962), in which a ferociously articulate faculty couple spend all night demolishing the fantasy that has sustained their marriage. But Albee's later Broadway plays, including *Tiny Alice* (1964) and *A Delicate Balance* (1966), became increasingly stylized and allegorical. The most popular Broadway playwright between 1960 and 1980 was NEIL SIMON (1927–   ), who in his 18 hits of those years sometimes poked gingerly at disturbing issues but always provided reassuring closure.

At the end of the 1960s, several important African-American theaters were established, including the Negro Ensemble Company, the New Lafayette Theatre, and the Spirit

House, and there were strong advances in African-American drama. In *Dutchman* (1964), Le Roi Jones (IMAMU AMIRI BARAKA, 1934–   ) combined a militant political thrust with the cruelty of Artaudian myth; he followed this arresting debut with *The Toilet* (1965), *Baptism* and *The Slave* (1966), and *Slave Ship* (1969). Other important African-American playwrights who made their mark at much the same time include ED BULLINS, Lonnie Elder III, JOSEPH A. WALKER, ADRIENNE KENNEDY, Charles Gordone, and Douglas Turner Ward.

In the mid-1970s, the alternative theater movement ebbed as its political basis changed with the withdrawal from Vietnam and the onset of less clearly defined imperatives in foreign policy. Much alternative theater energy was absorbed into a mainstream consumer theater, which included a network of professional regional organizations. This broad-based theater diversified more than ever the sources from which new plays came, and it was strengthened by increased public and private funding for theater following establishment of the National Endowment for the Arts in 1965.

At the same time, a divergence grew stronger between theater based on scripted drama and theater based on images, movement, and *mise en scène*. The latter includes the hypnotic, slow-motion spectacle-plays of Robert Wilson and the work of Richard Foreman's Ontological Hysteric Theatre, Lee Breuer and Joanne Akalaitis's Mabou Mines, and Elizabeth Le Compte's Wooster Group. The scripted-drama category was marked by a return to the realist tradition, the mainstay of American drama and theater from the 1930s through the 1950s, but it was a return with a difference.

This new, or renovated, realism was profoundly affected by the antirealist innovations of the immediately preceding period. The style of realism was often used in deconstructive or self-reflexive ways. The kind of structure most often used was not that of the older, linear, well-made plays—their action often seemed static or redundant, and dialogue often did not define or reveal character but was deflective weaponry to prevent communication rather than facilitate it.

Foremost among the new realists is DAVID MAMET (1947–   ), and typical in that his talent was not forged in New York but outside it, in Chicago. Mamet's characteristic early work included *Sexual Perversity in Chicago* (1975) and *American Buffalo* (1977), and his most impressive achievement so far is *Glengarry Glen Ross* (1983), which exposes the desperate tactics of a Chicago salesman to remain competitive in the rat race of off-color real estate. Mamet limns the will to communion—often failed, but never extinguished—while clearly deploring the moral emptiness of characters betrayed by a national mythology out of step with the times.

The other most interesting newcomers are those who have used the new realism most idiosyncratically, often with an ironic overlay. They include Christopher Durang, with his black satires of authoritarianism and the Catholic Church, *Sister Mary Ignatius Explains It All for You* (1979) and *The Marriage of Bette and Boo* (1985); Wallace Shawn, with *Marie and Bruce* (1979) and *Aunt Dan and Lemon* (1985), the latter a deceptively deadpan and neo-Shavian examination of totali-

tarianism; BETH HENLEY, with her tart portrayals of Southern Gothic womanhood in *Crimes of the Heart* (1979) and *The Miss Firecracker Contest* (1981); and Tina Howe, performing clinical dissections of WASP mores and milieu, in *Painting Churches* (1983) and *Coastal Disturbances* (1987). Somewhat more traditional but powerful contributions have been made by African-American playwright AUGUST WILSON, with *Ma Rainey's Black Bottom* (1981); *Fences* and *The Piano Lesson* (1987); MARSHA NORMAN, with *Getting Out* (1977) and *'night, Mother* (1983); and Emily Mann, with *Still Life* (1980) and *Execution of Justice* (1984).

Other playwrights, both men and women, have more actively promulgated feminist theater and the agendas of social and sexual minorities. For example, NTOZAKE SHANGE's *For colored girls who have considered suicide/when the rainbow is enuf* (1976) is a heady fusion of feminist and African-American theater in a nonlinear, quasimusical theatrical mode; several plays by Joan Holden have been a mainstay of the San Francisco Mime Troupe, with which she has worked for twenty years. Gay theater has offered not only the parodic work of Charles Ludlam and Ronald Tavel, but also the more conventional dramaturgy of plays like HARVEY FIERSTEIN's *Torch Song Trilogy* (1982). TONY KUSHNER's trilogy *Angels in America*, opening on Broadway in 1993, treated the effects of the AIDS epidemic on the gay community. PAULA VOGEL, though interested in gay subjects, treated a variety of sexual situations in *How I Learned to Drive* (1997) and other plays. Chicano, Amerasian, and other minority playwrights have also made an impact on regional and New York theater in recent years.

The playwrights who came to prominence in the late 1960s have successfully negotiated various degrees of compromise with the new realism. For example, David Rabe developed from the surreal and episodic dramaturgy of the Vietnam Trilogy to the more unbroken realist patterning of *Streamers* (1976) and *Hurlyburly* (1983). Sam Shepard revealed a similar tendency, without entirely abandoning his surreal-flecked idiosyncrasies, in *Curse of the Starving Class* (1978), *Buried Child* (1979), *True West* (1980), *Fool for Love* (1982), and *A Lie of the Mind* (1986). Lanford Wilson and John Guare have negotiated a similar development. Of the older generation of playwrights, Edward Albee, Arthur Miller, and Neil Simon are still active, Simon especially so.

The musical is no longer the uniquely American form it had become by the 1950s. The plot-centered form popularized by Rodgers and Hammerstein has given way to the so-called concept musical controlled by a directorial as much as an authorial vision, pioneered with *Company* (1970) by STEPHEN SONDHEIM and George Furth and directed by Harold Prince. This development reached its most commercially successful embodiment in *A Chorus Line* (1975), by Hamlisch, Kirkwood, Dante, Kleban, and Michael Bennett.

In the last decades of the twentieth century, few important new plays appeared. TINA HOWE's *Coastal Disturbances* came to Broadway in 1986, while RICHARD NELSON made a name for himself with London's Royal Shakespeare Company. EMILY MANN brought the story of centenarian twin sisters to the stage in *Having Our Say* (1997). Large cast musicals, including such imports as *Cats* and *Ragtime*, were staged, along with revivals such as *Chicago* and *Annie Get Your Gun*. Stage translations of movies included a musical called *Titanic* and an elaborately staged version of Disney Studios' *The Lion King*.

At the beginning of the twenty-first century, it appears that American theater has a diversity and a national (as distinct from Broadway-based) support that ensures its future health. While there are a number of fine working directors, several associated with the emergence of specific playwrights, it is evident that no single director or teacher has shaped American performance and playwriting of the last thirty years to the extent that Lee Strasberg and Elia Kazan did in an earlier period. But the claim of new playwrights has been addressed as never before, with theaters such as the Louisville Theater and workshops such as the O'Neill Theater Center giving unprecedented opportunities for the discovery and development of new playwriting talents.

Significant historical and critical books on American drama that emphasize the more recent period include the three-volume study by C. W. E. Bigsby, *A Critical Introduction to Twentieth Century American Drama* (1980–85); Gerald M. Berkowitz, *New Broadways* (1982); Travis Bogard, Richard Moody, and Walter J. Meserve, *The 'Revels' History of Drama in English, v. 8: American Drama* (1977); Ruby Cohn, *New American Dramatists 1960–1980* (1982); James Haskins, *Black Theater in America* (1982); David Savran, *In Their Own Words: Contemporary American Playwrights* (1988); Theodore Shank, *American Alternative Theatre* (1982); Gerald Weales, *The Jumping Off Place: American Drama in the 1960s* (1969); and *Contemporary American Playwrights* (1999) by Christopher Bigsby.

Important anthologies of plays include William M. Hoffman, ed. *New American Plays* (1967–71); John Lahr and Jonathan Price, eds., *The Great American Life Show: Nine Plays of the Avant-Garde* (1972); Bonnie Marranca and Gautam Dasgupta eds., *Wordplays 1–5* (1980–88); Brooks McNamara, ed., *Plays From the Contemporary American Theater* (1988); and Albert Poland and Bruce Mailman, eds., *The Off Off Broadway Book: The Plays, People, Theatre* (1972).

DENNIS CARROLL/BP

Dramatists' Guild [originally, **Association of Dramatists**].   An association formed in 1926 by 131 playwrights in New York City, under the leadership of GEORGE MIDDLETON, for their protection in making contracts with producers. It is part of the Authors' League of America. A subsidiary organization is the Dramatists' Play Service, founded by Barrett H. Clark, to provide plays and make royalty arrangements with amateur players.

Draper, Ruth (1884–1956),   actress. A granddaughter of CHARLES A. DANA, Draper won international reputation as a satiric monologist. She wrote her own sketches, among the most popular of which were *Opening a Bazaar* and *Three Women and Mr. Clifford*.

Dream Songs, The (1969),   poems by JOHN BERRYMAN.

dream songs, Indian.   This type of music was treated in FRANCES DENSMORE's paper, "The Belief of the Indian in a Connection between Song and the Supernatural" (Bureau of American Ethnology, *Bulletin* 151). A dream song may come in natural sleep, but the first important song of this kind is likely to come during a fasting vigil or as a result of taking jimson weed, a drug. "The silence becomes vibrant, it becomes rhythmic, and a melody comes to mind." It is a highly individual song, which no one sings except the warrior to whom it has come, although the dream songs of the warriors of former days are sometimes sung in war dances as an honor to their memory. Generally, some bird or other animal may then become part of one's name, as in the case of Brave Buffalo, a Sioux who had his first dream, about a buffalo, when he was ten years old. Or the warrior may wear a symbol that recalls the dream. Through his dream song the Indian maintains contacts with supernal powers, who can give him aid in every undertaking. One Pawnee heard thunder in his dream, learned the song that recorded the fact, and sang it when he went to war: "Beloved, it is good./ He, the thunder is saying quietly,/ It is good." Margot Astrov gives several examples of dream songs in her anthology *The Winged Serpent* (1946).

Dred: A Tale of the Great Dismal Swamp (1856), novel by HARRIET BEECHER STOWE. In this novel she continued the description of slavery begun in *Uncle Tom's Cabin* (1852). Dred is a runaway slave living in the Dismal Swamp. The story reveals the deteriorating influence of slavery on white masters and suggests that the solution is a system of paternalistic emancipation. In the story, however, the problem is resolved by removing the fugitives to Canada.

Dreiser, Theodore [Herman Albert] (1871–1945), novelist. Born in Indiana, the son of a crippled mill superintendent only intermittently employed and a doting mother who did her best to encourage her boy's yearning for knowledge, Dreiser learned the facts of poverty at an early age. All his life he remained sensitive to manifestations of hardship and oppression. When he was fifteen, a priest who heard his confession one day told the boy not to read science and philosophy, on threat of being forbidden to attend Communion. He chose to continue his reading, but he did not abandon the Church without a struggle; in the end he became extremely bitter toward organized religion. With his mother's help he finished high school, then at seventeen worked as a janitor in Chicago until a former teacher, Mildred Fielding, insisted on paying his expenses for a year at Indiana University.

Dreiser became a newspaperman and worked in St. Louis, Chicago, Pittsburgh, and New York. He was encouraged in his attempts to write fiction by his editors and fellow workers and especially by his brother Paul, a successful songwriter, who lent him money, invented jobs for him, and helped him through his devastating spells of depression. In *Twelve Men* (1919) Dreiser writes of his brother in a way that reveals the deep affection between the two. (See PAUL DRESSER.)

Dreiser finished SISTER CARRIE, his first novel, in 1900 and sent it to Doubleday, Page & Co., where FRANK NORRIS read it and accepted it with enthusiasm. A contract was signed during the absence of Doubleday, the head of the firm, who returned from Europe and expressed horror when he read the manuscript. He called a conference with Dreiser to discuss cancellation of the contract, but Dreiser, upon the advice of Norris, refused to release the publishers. Doubleday fulfilled the letter of the contract. A thousand cheap copies of *Sister Carrie* were printed but not advertised, displayed, or distributed. Norris sent out many review copies, but the press echoed the publisher's disgust. Despondent and embittered, Dreiser contemplated suicide until he was again rescued by his brother Paul, who got him a job with Butterick Publications. (See THE DELINEATOR.) Dreiser succeeded so well that in a few years he was head of the firm, with the enormous salary of $25,000. The history of *Sister Carrie* had not ended. The reputation of the book grew with Dreiser's later emergence as a major writer. In 1981 the University of Pennsylvania published an unexpurgated edition, restoring thirty-six thousand words that had been cut from the edition of 1900 in order to make it more palatable to readers of the time.

Encouraged by Paul and a few discriminating critics, Dreiser published JENNIE GERHARDT in 1911. Though that novel, like *Sister Carrie*, is a sympathetic portrait of a sinful woman, it had a better reception and Dreiser began to acquire the recognition he deserved. In 1912 came THE FINANCIER, the first of his Trilogy of Desire presenting the life of FRANK COWPERWOOD; the second in the trilogy was THE TITAN (1914). Cowperwood, a superman, claws his way up from poverty to a position of wealth and power, experiencing many erotic adventures on the way. The stories, based on the career of Charles T. Yerkes, traction magnate of Philadelphia and Chicago, were thoroughly documented by Dreiser in the best tradition of literary NATURALISM. In light of Dreiser's later belief in socialism, it is a temptation to read the Cowperwood novels as satires, but this was almost certainly not Dreiser's intention at the time. Cowperwood is presented as the hero, a Nietzschean figure whose struggle for success somehow promotes the evolutionary aspirations of all mankind.

THE "GENIUS" (1915) concerns another superman, this time the artist Eugene Witla, modeled on the painter Everett Shinn, who fascinated Dreiser; on a young art editor of Butterick Publications who committed suicide; and on Dreiser himself. It is by far the most personal of Dreiser's novels, and Witla's complex and turbulent love life is close to Dreiser's own: the author had been divorced from his first wife and was living with the actress Helen Patges, whom he later married, and at the same time was engaged in several other affairs. Dreiser told Helen later that he liked to carry on two or more affairs simultaneously, finding that he was stimulated by the tension he felt in the competition of women for his love, and that he wrote the better for it.

From 1921 to 1924 Dreiser lived in California in the midst of the movie colony, but then went to upper New York State to collect material for AN AMERICAN TRAGEDY, a novel based on the celebrated Chester Gillette–Grace Brown murder case of 1906. The book, packed with meticulous documentation that constituted an indictment of American social and business values, appeared in two volumes in 1925. Not Clyde Griffiths, the weak hero convicted for the murder of his pregnant sweetheart, but society is made responsible for the tragedy, a society that has fascinated the youth with its glitter while failing to provide him with moral restraint. Nevertheless, the novel seems more hopeful and positive than Dreiser's earlier works and furnishes in the idea of social reform a change from the sense of purposelessness of the earlier novels.

Dreiser's popularity in Europe, particularly in Russia, increased rapidly during the 1920s; in October 1927, he was invited by the Soviet government to visit Russia as a guest. By-products of this trip *were Dreiser Looks at Russia* (1928) and *Tragic America* (1931), expressing his faith in socialism as opposed to his former groping, despairing fatalism. Returning to the United States, he became active in left-wing organizations. In 1931, with Dos Passos and others, he formed the Dreiser Committee to investigate conditions among coal miners in Bell and Harlan counties in Kentucky. Feeling ran so high that the Bell County grand jury indicted the committee for criminal syndicalism, but after wide publicity and national indignation the charges against the committee were dropped.

The Stoic, last of the Cowperwood trilogy, was published posthumously in 1947, although Dreiser had written most of it many years before. It is not a good novel. By the time he came to write it, he had outgrown the attitudes that prevail in the earlier Cowperwood stories. Nevertheless, it is interesting to the student for its discussion of Hinduism, to which the book's heroine turns in her final despair. Rather surprisingly, Dreiser apparently also turned to Oriental mysticism; at least he studied it seriously and he seems to have found in the leap to pure Spirit a usable antidote to his purposeless wandering in the materialistic flux. Nor is Brahminism so far, perhaps, from the concept of life's aimlessness that dominated Dreiser's early gropings. At any rate he found in it an expression of his love for man, and ideal expression far superior to anything he could find in institutionalized society.

The Bulwark (1946), begun as early as 1910, is an awkward story that seemed quite unsatisfactory when it was published. Dreiser's great contribution to naturalism had been completed in his small group of major novels. Indeed, he often expressed his naturalistic theories and his philosophy of life more directly in his autobiographical works: *A Traveler at Forty* (1913); *A Hoosier Holiday* (1916); *A Book About Myself* (1922, later republished as *Newspaper Days*, the title Dreiser originally gave it); and particularly *Hey-Rub-a-Dub-Dub: A Book of the Mystery and Terror and Wonder of Life* (1919). By the time he died, the tide of naturalism had turned and a new conservatism was on the way. The crusading novelists were dead or silent, with perhaps the exception of JAMES T. FARRELL, to whom Dreiser in his old age turned for criticism and encouragement.

The most formidable obstacle to an appreciation of Dreiser's work has been his style—so frequently described as elephantine as to have won a proprietary right to the adjective. While there are many passages of forceful and passionate writing in his novels, his style is often dull, awkward, and banal. Nevertheless, with all his faults, Dreiser created an image of American life that has had a wide and enduring relevance. He indicated the tragic possibilities inherent in the conflict between the individual driven by a desire for self-realization and a society characterized by repressive and narrow moral and social conventions, on the one hand, and the glorification of material success, on the other. There is in his work an integrity, a compassion, a dedication to the task of finally making moral and metaphysical sense out of his vast apparatus of realistic detail, which places it among the best of modern American fiction.

No collected edition of Dreiser's works exists. Full-length studies are *Theodore Dreiser: Apostle of Nature* (1949), by Robert H. Elias; and *Dreiser* (1965), by W. A. Swanberg. Critical works include *Theodore Dreiser* (1951), by F. O. Matthiessen; *Two Dreisers* (1969), by Ellen Moers; *The Novels of Theodore Dreiser* (1976), by Donald Pizer, and *Theodore Dreiser* (2 vols.; 1986, 1990), by Richard Lingeman. His *Letters* (3 v. 1959) were edited by Robert H. Elias.

CHARLES CHILD WALCUTT/GP

Dresbach, Glenn [Ward] (1889–1968),   poet. Born in Illinois, Dresbach received many awards and prizes for his poetry, much of it vividly descriptive of Southern and Southwestern scenes. Among his collections are *The Road to Everywhere* (1916), *In Colors of the West* (1922), *Cliff Dwellings and Other Poems* (1926), *Star-Dust and Stone* (1928), *The Wind in the Cedars* (1930), *Selected Poems* (1931), and *Collected Poems* (1948, enlarged ed., 1950).

Dresser, Paul (1857–1906),   songwriter. Dresser's name was originally Dreiser; he was the brother of THEODORE DREISER. Born in Indiana, Dresser earned fame in New York with such widely popular songs as "On the Banks of the Wabash, Far Away" (1899), "The Blue and the Gray, or, A Mother's Gift to Her Country" (1900), and "My Gal Sal" (1905). The Wabash song (Theodore Dreiser said he had helped compose it) became Indiana's official state song.

D'ri and I (1901),   a novel of the War of 1812 by IRVING BACHELLER. The leading character is Darius Olen, a stalwart woodsman, who watches over the son of his employer in many stirring adventures.

Dring, Thomas (1758–1825),   author of *Recollections of the Jersey Prison-Ship* (1829), a vivid description of conditions aboard a British prison ship during the Revolutionary War.

Drummond, William Henry (1854–1907),   Irish-born Canadian poet, physician, teacher, storyteller. Drummond's busy life as medical man, teacher of medical jurisprudence, and (in his later years) operator of a silver mine was refreshed at regular intervals by composing poems in the dialect of French Canada. These poems are a mingling of humor and sentiment, at times slightly satirical. The *habitant* on his little farm, the *voyageur* journeying on dangerous rivers, and the woodsman are depicted in their humor, pathos, and picturesqueness. Drummond's recitation of his own poems was very effective. He published several collections: *The Habitant and Other French-Canadian Poems* (1905); *Johnnie Courteau and Other Poems* (1901); and *The Voyageur and Other Poems* (1905). A collected edition of his verse and other writings appeared in 1912.

Drums (1925),   a historical novel by JAMES BOYD. Boyd writes realistically of his hero Johnny Fraser's service in the Revolutionary War with Paul Jones and General Morgan. (See JOHN BEAUCHAMP JONES.)

Drums Along the Mohawk (1936),   a historical novel by WALTER D. EDMONDS. The bitter struggle in the Mohawk Valley between the rebels of the Revolution and their British foes is vividly portrayed. Stress is laid on the destructiveness of the Tories and their Indian allies. The novel was based on careful research, described in *How You Begin a Novel* (*Atlantic Monthly*, August 1936).

Drum-Taps (1865),   poems by WALT WHITMAN. To this was added in 1866 a *Sequel to Drum-Taps*, which contains some of Whitman's most famous poems, including O CAPTAIN! MY CAPTAIN! and WHEN LILACS LAST IN THE DOORYARD BLOOM'D. The collection was gathered into a new edition of LEAVES OF GRASS in 1867.

Drunkard, The, or, The Fallen Saved (1844),   a play by William H[enry] Smith (1806–72). This was a sentimental and melodramatic plea for temperance, occasionally revived in the 20th century, including in Hollywood, where the play opened on July 6, 1923, at the Theatre Mart and closed on October 10, 1959, having run for twenty-six consecutive years. It is estimated that over three million people saw the play. W. C. Fields, notoriously antitemperance, saw it thirty times. Beer was served at the performances.

Drury, Allen [Stuart] (1918–1998),   novelist, journalist. Born in Houston and educated at Stanford, Drury served in the army, then on the staff of the U.S. Senate and as a reporter for various journals. His experiences provided material for *Advise and Consent* (1959), a sprawling chronicle of a battle for Senate confirmation of a nominee for Secretary of State. The novel won a Pulitzer Prize, became a stage play (1960), and a movie (1962). His other political novels are *A Shade of Difference* (1962), about emerging African nations, U.S. policies, and the United Nations; *Capable of Honor* (1966); *Preserve and Protect* (1968); *The Throne of Saturn* (1971); *The Promise of Joy* (1975); and *The Hill of Summer* (1981). *A God Against the Gods* (1976) and *Return to Thebes* (1976) concern ancient Egypt. *That Summer* (1965) is set in a resort in the Sierras.

Dubie, Norman (1945–   ),   poet, teacher. Born in Maine, Dubie was educated at Goddard College and the University of Iowa and has taught at Iowa, Ohio University, and Arizona State University. His poems, some developing the voices of historical characters and some more immediately personal, are gathered in a number of books, beginning with *The Horsehair Sofa* (1968) and including *The City of Olesha Fruit* (1979), *The Everlastings* (1980), *Selected and New Poems* (1983), *The Springhouse* (1986), *Radio Sky* (1991), and *The Clouds of Magellan* (1992).

DuBois, Blanche.   Character in Tennessee Williams's A STREETCAR NAMED DESIRE (1947).

Du Bois, W[illiam] E[dward] B[urghardt] (1868–1963),   educator, author. Born in Massachusetts and of French and African descent, Du Bois was educated at Fisk, Harvard, and the University of Berlin. He taught at Wilberforce and edited CRISIS (1910–34). With other leaders of the Niagara Movement (1905–09), he sought to abolish distinctions based on race. Active with the NAACP, which he helped found but later thought too conservative, he was a crusader for social betterment and in later life a leader of the peace movement. (He was awarded the Lenin International Peace Prize in 1958.) Shortly before his death he joined the Communist Party, emigrated to Ghana, and became a citizen of that country.

THE SOULS OF BLACK FOLK (1903), not well received at first, has more recently seemed an important seminal work. His other books on African-American history and sociology include *The Suppression of the African Slave-Trade to the United States of America, 1638–1870* (1896); *The Philadelphia Negro* (1899); *John Brown* (1909), a biography; *The Negro* (1915); *Darkwater: Voices from Within the Veil* (1920); *Black Reconstruction, 1860–1880* (1935); *Black Folk, Then and Now* (1939), a history of blacks in Africa and America; *Dusk of Dawn* (1940), on the concept of race; *Color and Democracy* (1945), against imperialism; and *The World and Africa* (1947), on Africa in world history. His novels include *Dark Princess: A Romance* (1928) and a trilogy—*The Ordeal of Mansart* (1957), *Mansart Builds a School* (1959), and *Worlds of Color* (1961), collected as *The Black Flame* (1976). *In Battle for Peace* (1952) and *The Autobiography of W. E. B. Du Bois* (1968) are autobiographical; *Darkwater* and *Dusk of Dawn* are partly autobiographical. David Levering Lewis's two-volume biography (1993, 2000) is standard.

Dubus, Andre [Jr.] (1936–1999),   short-story writer. Born in Louisiana, Dubus was educated at McNeese State College and the University of Iowa. He taught for eighteen years at Bradford College in Massachusetts and published a novel and seven story collections before an automobile accident in 1986 forced his retirement. Many of his *Selected Stories* (1988) take place in or around Haverhill, Massachusetts. They involve hard moral choices in violent situations and are often tinged with Roman Catholicism. Dubus continued writing though confined to a wheelchair and in constant pain. *The Cage Keeper and Other Stories* (1989) and *Dancing after Hours* (1996) are story collections. *Voices from the Moon* (1998) is a novella; *Meditations from a Movable Chair* (1998) are essays. His son, **Andre Dubus III**, is also a writer, author of *House of Sand and Fog* (1999), a novel.

Du Chaillu, Paul B[elloni] (1835–1903),   explorer, writer of travel books. Du Chaillu's earlier years are thought to have been spent on the African coast, where his father was a trader. He came to the United States, probably in 1852, and managed in 1856 to secure funds for exploring Africa under the sponsorship of the Philadelphia Academy of Natural Sciences. After four years he returned with what sounded like wild tales of chimpanzees and gorillas (*Explorations and Adventures in Equatorial Africa*, 1861) and was attacked as a fabricator. He was in Africa again from 1863 to 1865 and

emerged with material for *Journey to Ashangoland* (1867), *Stories of the Gorilla Country* (1868), *Wild Life Under the Equator* (1869), *Lost in the Jungle* (1869), *My Apingi Kingdom* (1870), and *The Country of the Dwarfs* (1871). Again he was attacked, this time particularly for his stories of African pygmies. Yet, later explorers largely confirmed Du Chaillu's observations. In later years Du Chaillu visited Scandinavia and wrote two books on his travels. *The Land of the Midnight Sun* (1881) and *The Viking Age* (1889). He died in Russia while gathering material for still another volume.

Dudek, Louis (1918–   ),   poet, teacher. Born in Montreal, Dudek was educated at McGill and Columbia University. During his years of teaching at McGill (1951–82) he encouraged young poets through his association with the journals *First Statement Contact* and *Delta*, his own journal; through the McGill Poetry Series; and through his founding, with IRVING LAYTON and RAYMOND SOUSTER, of *Contact Press*. His books include collections of lyrics, such as *East of the City* (1946) and *Twenty-four Poems* (1952); and the longer, meditative poems *Europe* (1955), *En Mexico* (1958), *Atlantis* (1980), *Continuation I* (1981), *Infinite Worlds* (1988), and *Continuation II* (1990). *Collected Poetry* was published in 1971, *Selected Poems* in 1979.

Duffus, R[obert] L[uther] (1888–1972),   journalist, novelist. Two of Duffus's most important publications are *Books: Their Place in a Democracy* (1930) and *Our Starving Libraries* (1933). In 1937 he joined the staff of *The New York Times*, writing frequently for its Sunday sections. His first volume of reminiscences, *The Innocents at Cedro* (1944), is particularly good in its memories of Thorstein Veblen. A novel, *Non-Scheduled Flight* (1950), portrays a flight from New Orleans to Guatemala. *Williamstown Branch* (1958) describes his boyhood.

Dugan, Alan (1923–   ),   poet. Born in Brooklyn, Dugan was educated at Mexico City College. His *Poems* (1961) won the National Book Award and the Pulitzer Prize. These and later poems reveal strong feeling and an original point of view expressed in sometimes unpoetic language. His other volumes include *Collected Poems* (1969) and *New and Collected Poems* (1983). *Poems Six* appeared in 1989.

Duganne, Augustine Joseph Hickey (1823?–1884), soldier, author. Born in Boston, Duganne wrote a play, *The Lydian Queen* (1848), and novels. When the Civil War broke out, he joined the Union army as a lieutenant colonel. His experiences in Southern prison camps resulted in his most important book, *Camps and Prisons* (1865). His *Poetical Works* appeared in 1855.

du Jardin, Rosamond Neal (1902–1963),   novelist, poet, short-story writer. Born in Illinois, du Jardin wrote more than a hundred short stories, many published in such magazines as *Cosmopolitan, Redbook*, and *Good Housekeeping*. Her adult novels are *All Is Not Gold* (1935), *Only Love Lasts* (1937), and *Tomorrow Will Be Fair* (1946). Her novels for teenagers are *Practically Seventeen* (1949), *Double Date* (1951), *Boy Trouble* (1953), *A Man for Marcy* (1954), *Senior Prom* (1957), *Wedding in the Family* (1958), and *Double Wedding* (1959).

Dukesborough Tales (1871), short stories by RICHARD MALCOLM JOHNSTON. These are revisions of stories originally published as *Georgia Sketches* (1864). The scene of the stories, the imaginary Dukesborough, was Powelton, near which stood Johnston's plantation birthplace "Oak Grove." He wrote about school life, family feuds, red-letter days in the village, always sympathetically and humorously.

Dulcy (1921), a comedy by GEORGE S. KAUFMAN and MARC CONNELLY. The leading character, a master at the art of bromides and platitudes, was transferred from a column by Franklin P. Adams. In the play she is in addition a blunderer who almost ruins a business deal for her husband. But her efforts unexpectedly turn out all right.

Dunbar, Paul Laurence (1872–1906), poet, novelist. The poet's predecessors in the use of African-American dialect were white writers, such as Irwin Russell, Stephen Collins Foster, Joel Chandler Harris, and Thomas Nelson Page, but they were unable to portray African-American life with Dunbar's personal insights. He lived in a time when literary regionalism and the use of dialect were the vogue; he was especially under Page's influence and was an admirer of Robert Burns and James Whitcomb Riley. As an Ohioan, born in Dayton, he did not know the Deep South, and more bitter portrayals of black life in a white culture were still to come. His mother had been a slave. He listened to her stories and knew many small black communities in various parts of the country. He regretted the neglect of his poems not in dialect, which he thought some of his best. His early verse collections, *Oak and Ivy* (1893) and *Majors and Minors* (1895), were brought together in *Lyrics of Lowly Life* (1896). Later came *Lyrics of the Hearthside* (1899), *Lyrics of Love and Laughter* (1903), and *Lyrics of Sunshine and Shadow* (1905). His novels—including *The Uncalled* (1898) and *The Sport of the Gods* (1902)—were less admired.

Duncan, Isadora (1878–1927), dancer, writer. Born in San Francisco, Duncan became one of the first exponents of modern dance, creating a sensation in Europe with her interpretive programs on naturalistic and classical Greek themes. She established dance schools in several European capitals with considerable success, and also one in the United States, but her popularity in this country never equaled her reputation abroad. She was widely acclaimed by the young American expatriate writers of the early 1920s, who admired her break with the conventions of her art and with conventions in general. She married the celebrated Russian lyric poet Sergei Esenin in 1922. Duncan wrote *The Art of the Dance* (1928) and spoke in frank terms of her career in *My Life* (1927). She died in a freak automobile accident.

Duncan, Norman (1871–1916), Canadian newspaperman, storyteller, teacher. Duncan went to Newfoundland to gather material for a volume of sea stories and from then on was deeply attracted to sea life. His best books have the ocean as their background: *Doctor Luke of the Labrador* (1904), *The Adventures of Billy Topsail* (1906), *The Cruise of the Shining Light* (1907), and *Australian Byways* (1915).

Duncan, Robert (1919–1988), poet. In his early years, Robert Duncan retained the name of his adopted parents, Symmes, reverting to his birth name in 1940. The young Robert Edward Symmes absorbed his adopted family's theosophical and hermetic beliefs, a fact that features prominently in his poetry. Born in Oakland, Duncan spent his early years in California and was educated at the University of California, Berkeley. He left in the late 1930s for the East, where he participated in literary circles surrounding Henry Miller and Anaïs Nin. In 1944 he published "The Homosexual in Society," an important early statement of his own sexual orientation and a pioneering polemic against homophobia. In 1945, Duncan moved back to the Bay Area, where he became close to Kenneth Rexroth, Mary Fabilli, William Everson, Jack Spicer, Robin Blaser, and other writers who would become central to the San Francisco Renaissance of the 1950s.

Duncan's first book, *Heavenly City, Earthly City* (1947), and the long sequences, "Medieval Scenes" and "The Venice Poem", announce Duncan's retrieval of the romance tradition out of medieval and Renaissance art and philosophy. In 1950, Duncan met the painter and collagist Jess (Collins) who was to become his lifelong companion. Their relationship resulted in text-art collaborations, such as *Caesar's Gate* (1955), *A Book of Resemblances* (1966), *Names of People* (1968), and *Letters Poems MCMLIII–MCMLVI* (1958), which reflect both artists' interest in literary modernism (Joyce, Pound, and Stein are central literary figures) as well as in the nonsense rhymes of Edith Sitwell and Edward Lear.

The pair moved to Mallorca in 1955, returning in 1956 for a brief stay at BLACK MOUNTAIN COLLEGE, where Duncan taught courses in theater. Returning to the Bay Area the same year, Duncan participated in the San Francisco poetry renaissance of the late 1950s, writing the poems that appeared in 1960 as *The Opening of the Field*. This book announces Duncan's strong adherence to Charles Olson's theories of projective verse, but adds his own interests in myth and occult science. His subsequent books, *Roots and Branches* (1964) and *Bending the Bow* (1968), continue this commitment to field verse, best illustrated by the long sequence "Passages," inaugurated in the latter volume. Throughout the 1970s and early 1980s, Duncan exerted a commanding influence on American experimental poetry, although he never received the national recognition of many of his peers. In the late 1970s, he began to suffer from kidney failure, which ultimately caused his death, in 1988. His last books, *Groundwork I: Before the War* (1984) and *Groundwork II: In the Dark* (1987), conclude his career.

Heraclitean in his belief in biological and cosmic change, Duncan created poems whose rhythms were as open and variable as the natural world; Augustan in his faith in the orderliness of nature, he sought to establish measure and balance as an organic principle. Other books by and about Duncan include *Fictive Certainties: Essays by Robert Duncan* (1985) and Ekbert Faas, *Young Robert Duncan: Portrait of the Poet as Homosexual in Society* (1983).

MICHAEL DAVIDSON

Duncan, Sara Jeannette (1861–1922), journalist, travel writer, novelist. Born in Brantford, Ontario, Duncan attended Toronto Normal School and wrote for a few years for the Washington *Post*, Toronto *Globe*, and *Montreal Star*. From 1888 on, she lived mostly in India and England. Her early works were loose travel narratives focused on independent women: *A Social Departure: How Orthodocia and I Went Round the World by Ourselves* (1890); *An American Girl in London* (1891); and *A Voyage of Consolation* (1898). Among her best works are the novels *The Imperialist* (1904), set in her native Brantford, and *Cousin Cinderella* (1908), about a Canadian girl in London. Her other novels are Anglo-Indian, including *The Simple Adventure of a Memsahib* (1893); *His Honour, and a Lady* (1896); *Hilda: A Story of Calcutta* (1899); *Set in Authority* (1906); and *The Burnt Offering* (1909).

Dunlap, William (1766–1839), artist, dramatist. Born in New Jersey, Dunlap was a portrait painter whose subjects included George and Martha Washington. He studied for three years under Benjamin West in London, but on his return to New York he turned to playwriting. His first play to be produced, THE FATHER (1789), was a successful follow-up to Royall Tyler's *The Contrast*. He wrote sixty-five plays in all, including thirty original plays and many adaptations of French and German plays; for a time he had at least one new play a year on stage in New York. In 1798 he became owner of New York's Old American Company and produced his own plays until his theater went bankrupt in 1805. He continued as a theater manager; attempted to publish a magazine, *The Monthly Recorder* (1813); and then returned to his career as a painter. In later years, he taught at the National Academy of Design, which he helped to found in 1826.

Among the best of his plays are ANDRÉ (1798) and THE ITALIAN FATHER (1799). His other works include a *History of the American Theater* (1832) and a *History of the Rise and Progress of the Arts of Design in the United States* (2 v. 1834); a *Life of Charles Brockden Brown* (1815); a *History of the New Netherlands, Province of New York, and State of New York* (2 v. 1839–40); and a temperance novel, *Thirty Years Ago; or, The History of a Water Drinker* (1836). Dorothy C. Barck edited *The Diary of William Dunlap* (3 v. 1930).

Dunne, Finley Peter (1867–1936), newspaperman, editor, humorist. Born in Chicago, Dunne earned his fame from his Mr. Dooley, created for the Chicago *Post*. Dooley is a Chicago Irishman with a heavy brogue who presides over a small saloon. From behind his bar of justice, Mr. Dooley reviews events, social institutions, and leaders of the world with a wit and wisdom his era found irresistible. He makes his remarks to his friend Malachi Hennessey, whom Dooley describes as "a post to hitch ye'er silences to."

Dunne wrote more than seven hundred pieces about Mr. Dooley. His books include *Mr. Dooley in Peace and War* (1898); *Mr. Dooley in the Hearts of His Countrymen* (1898); *What Mr. Dooley Says* (1899); *Mr. Dooley's Philosophy* (1900); *Mr. Dooley's Opinions* (1901); and several other collections down to 1919, when Dooley at last fell silent with *Mr. Dooley on Making a Will*.

Dunne, John Gregory (1932–   ), writer. Born in Connecticut, Dunne has earned praise for his crime novels, such as *True Confessions* (1977) and *Dutch Shea, Jr.* (1982),

and his nonfiction, including *Delano* (1967), about attempts to organize farm workers in California; *The Studio* (1969), about the movie industry; and *Vegas* (1974), on gambling. *Quintana and Friends* (1978) collects miscellaneous prose pieces. *The Red White and Blue* appeared in 1987, *Harp* in 1989, and *Playland* in 1994. He is married to JOAN DIDION.

Dunton, John (1659–1733), an English bookseller who traveled in New England for several months in 1686 and published impressions of his visit in *The Life and Errors of John Dunton* (1705). His fictional *Letters from New England* were not printed until 1867.

Dupin, C. Auguste. An amateur detective in three stories of Edgar Allan Poe, THE MURDERS IN THE RUE MORGUE (1841), THE MYSTERY OF MARIE ROGÊT (three parts, 1842–43), and THE PURLOINED LETTER (1845). His personality, his unofficial status, his bewildered friend and admirer who narrates the stories, his use of clues, his dextrous employment of unjust suspicions, his logic in unveiling the criminal—all these traits have become characteristic of many later fictional detectives.

Du Ponceau, Pierre [Peter] Étienne [Stephen] (1760–1844), historian, philologist, lawyer. Born in France, Du Ponceau came to America as Baron Steuben's secretary and served him as aide-de-camp, with the rank of captain. Forced to leave because of illness, he became an American citizen in 1781, was admitted to the bar in 1785, and became an authority on international law. He was elected president of the American Philosophical Society in 1828. In addition to writing on law and philology—including treatises on the Chinese system of writing and on the grammar of some of the Indian tribes—he wrote *A Discourse on the Necessity and the Means of Making Our National Literature Independent of That of Great Britain* (1834).

Dupuy, Eliza Ann (1814–1881), novelist. Dupuy was born in Virginia. In addition to numerous short stories written for the New York *Ledger* under the pen name Annie Young, she wrote several historical novels, the best-known of which were *The Conspirator* (1850), with AARON BURR as the central figure, and *The Huguenot Exiles* (1856), based in part on her family history.

Durant, Ariel K[aufman] (1898–1981), historian; coauthor of works with her husband WILL DURANT.

Durant, Will[iam James] (1885–1981), teacher, philosopher, historian. Born in North Adams, Massachusetts, Durant became a well-known popularizer of philosophic ideas. He wrote *The Story of Philosophy* first as a lecture series, then as a series for THE LITTLE BLUE BOOKS of Haldeman-Julius. When the lectures were printed as a book in 1926, they had a phenomenal success. The grand total of copies sold soon passed the million mark, and the book was translated into a dozen languages. His great work, the last four volumes written with his wife, ARIEL DURANT, is *The Story of Civilization* in ten volumes: *Our Oriental Heritage* (1935), *The Life of Greece* (1939), *Caesar and Christ* (1944), *The Age of Faith* (1950), *The Renaissance* (1953), *The Reformation* (1957), *The Age of Reason Begins* (1961), *The Age of Louis XIV* (1963), *The Age of Voltaire* (1965), and *Rousseau and Revolution* (1967). His novel *Transition* (1927) was largely autobiographical. His late works with his wife include *The Lessons of History* (1968), *Interpretations of Life* (1970), and *A Dual Autobiography* (1977).

Duranty, Walter (1884–1957)   journalist, novelist. Born in England and educated at Harrow and Cambridge, Duranty wandered for some years through England, France, and America as a tutor and free-lance writer. In 1913 he joined the Paris bureau of the *New York Times*, serving in World War I as a correspondent. In 1921 he was sent to Russia, where he won a reputation as one of the ablest foreign correspondents. Although his fiction—*One Life, One Kopeck* (1937), *The Gold Train* (1938), and *Return to the Vineyard* (1945, with Mary Loos)— was not highly praised, his books on Russia received warm reviews. Among the latter are *Moscow Trials* (1929), *Duranty Reports Russia* (1934), *I Write as I Please* (1935), *The Kremlin and the People* (1941), *USSR* (1944), and *Stalin & Co.: The Politburo—the Men Who Run Russia* (1949). *Search for a Key* (1943) is a fictional account of a European correspondent between two world wars.

Dutchman (1964).   A play by AMIRI BARAKA.

Dutchman's Fireside, The (1831),   a novel by JAMES KIRKE PAULDING. Sybrandt Nestbrook, a rural lad in the period of the French and Indian Wars, woos a fashionable girl whose hand is sought by many suitors. The hero has adventures on the frontier and is reported killed, but returns in time to win the hand of his Catalina Vancour. Westbrook seems to have been modeled in part on Paulding himself. The book has been praised for the faithfulness with which it depicts old Dutch life. See SIR WILLIAM JOHNSON.

Duval, John C.   See THE ADVENTURES OF BIG-FOOT WALLACE.

Duyckinck, Evert Augustus (1816–1878),   and George Long Duyckinck (1823–1863), editors, literary historians, biographers, encyclopedists. These brothers, both born in New York City, were active in the literary life of the city and the nation during the middle years of the 19th century and exerted a beneficent influence in helping new and young authors and in writing sound literary information and criticism. They often worked together, for example, in editing the New York LITERARY WORLD [1] (1847–53) and in compiling their monumental and still valuable two-volume *Cyclopaedia of American Literature* (1855). In the encyclopedia they discussed all the important authors up to and including their own times, and provided liberal selections from these authors' writings. It ran to 1,470 pages. In 1886 Evert Duyckinck prepared a *Supplement* of 160 pages. In 1875 Michael Laird Simons brought the book down to 1873, with the two volumes running to 2,080 pages. The elder Duyckinck edited *Arcturus* (1840–42). He left his extensive library to the New York Public Library, together with his correspondence and notebooks. The younger brother wrote biographies of George Herbert (1858), Jeremy Taylor (1860), and others.

Lowell gave Evert Duyckinck a place in *A Fable for Critics* (1848), calling him a ripe scholar and a neat critic, "who through Grub Street the soul of a gentleman carries." His house was a rendezvous for men of letters in his day, and he encouraged Melville at a time when he particularly needed help. Hawthorne, Bryant, Irving, Lowell, Simms, and many others were his intimate friends.

Dvořák, Anton (1841–1904),   Czech composer and music director. In a prolonged visit to the United States, this great musician directed the National Conservatory of Music in New York (1892–95) and was impressed with the musical possibilities of the New World's folksongs. His *New World Symphony* (1893) includes fragments and echoes of some of these folksongs, for example, "Swing Low, Sweet Chariot," "Yankee Doodle," and "Peter Gray." According to Sigmund Spaeth (*A History of Popular Music in America*, 1948), William Arms Fisher turned the Largo of the symphony into a song called "Goin' Home" (1922), "now widely accepted as an authentic Negro spiritual, even though entirely the work of two white men." Then in 1934, Billy Hill and Peter De Rose built a song hit, "Wagon Wheels," on "Goin' Home" and "Swing Low." Dvořák's popular HUMORESQUE, written for the violin, was used by Fannie Hurst as the title of her short story by that name (1919), and the story later was made into a movie (1920).

Dwight, John S[ullivan] (1813–1893),   clergyman, music critic, editor. One of the earliest and most influential of the transcendentalists. Born in Boston, Dwight was active at BROOK FARM, wrote for THE DIAL and became music editor of a Brook Farm periodical called *The Harbinger* (1845–49), which continued to be published after the colony passed out of existence. In 1852 he founded *Dwight's Journal of Music*, organized music groups in Boston and nearby, and became a leading authority in the field. He was attracted to German romanticism and was influential in introducing German philosophical ideas in America. His sister, **Marianne Dwight Orvis** (1816–1901), was also a transcendentalist and wrote *Letters from Brook Farm, 1844–47* (1928). (See TRANSCENDENTALISM.)

Dwight, Theodore (1764–1846),   lawyer, editor, poet. Dwight, born in Northampton, Massachusetts, like his brother Timothy, was one of the Hartford Wits, and in THE ECHO and THE POLITICAL GREENHOUSE wrote passable verse. He was a staunch Federalist, attacking the anti-Federalists in his *History of the Hartford Convention* (1833) and in *The Character of Thomas Jefferson* (1839). His son, **Theodore Dwight, Jr.** (1796–1866), was an editor (*Dwight's American Magazine*, 1845–52) and the author of travel books and biographies. He also wrote *The Father's Book, or, Suggestions for the Government and Instruction of Young Children* (1834). (See CONNECTICUT WITS, THE ECHO.)

Dwight, Timothy [1] (1752–1817),   clergyman, teacher, poet. Born in Northampton, Massachusetts, he entered Yale at thirteen and was graduated with full honors. After a career as teacher, chaplain in the Continental army, minister, and literary man, he came back to Yale as president in 1795 and as professor of theology, holding both positions until his death. Prominent among the HARTFORD WITS, Dwight owed his literary reputation primarily to three poems: THE CONQUEST OF CANAAN (1785), a Biblical epic; *The Triumph of Infidelity* (1788), an anonymous defense of Calvinism and satiric attack on holders of other beliefs; and GREENFIELD HILL (1794), describing the Connecticut village where he served for years as pastor. Among his other poems are visions of American glory: "America; or, A Poem on the Settlement of the British Colonies" (1772?), and "Columbia, Columbia, to Glory Arise" (1777). His religious convictions and strong Federalism inform his prose works, including *The True Means of Establishing Public Happiness* (1795), *The Nature, and Danger, of Infidel Philosophy* (1798), and *The Duty of Americans at the Present Crisis* (1798). After the duel between his cousin Aaron Burr and Alexander Hamilton, he wrote *Folly, Guilt, and Mischiefs of Dueling* (1805). Sermons he delivered at Yale were collected in *Theology, Explained and Defended* (5 v. 1818–19). His *Travels in New England and New York* (4 v. 1821–22) records the scenes, social, and religious conditions of the times.

Dwight, Timothy [2] (1828–1916), grandson of TIMOTHY DWIGHT [1], and like him a president of Yale (1886–98).

Dying Cowboy, The. An American folk song, also known as *The Cowboy's Lament*, it is related to *The Unfortunate Rake*, current in Ireland as early as 1790, and also to "The Saint James Infirmary Blues."

Dying Indian, The. (1784), a poem by PHILIP FRENEAU. One of the earliest American writings to set forth a picture of "the noble red man," as a counterpoise to the more popular notion of "the ferocious savage."

Dylan, Bob (1941–), singer, songwriter. The most important songwriter of his generation, Dylan has had a powerful influence on the evolution of popular music. The lyrics of many of his songs, beginning with modern classics from the early and mid-1960s like "Blowin' in the Wind" (1962) and "The Times They Are A-Changin'" (1963), have become cultural watchwords for several generations. Born Robert Zimmerman in Hibbing, Minnesota, Dylan left home as a teenager, changing his name from Zimmerman to Dillon, to follow in the footsteps of WOODY GUTHRIE, one of his heroes. Accompanying himself on guitar and harmonica, his voice harsh and abrasive, Dylan sang caustic, street-smart, cryptically allusive songs that transformed mainstream popular music into a vehicle for political and social commentary. Although Dylan's first album, *Bob Dylan*, was released in 1962, it was with his appearance at the Newport Folk Festival in July 1963 that his legend really began. To date, Dylan has recorded well over five hundred of his own songs and released some forty-five albums. The directions of his career have been as diverse as the masks of his persona: outcast poet with a searing social conscience; folksinger who grafted his own idiom onto the traditional forms; rebel; religious convert; blues singer; self-styled song and dance man; and always consummate writer of long narrative songs that trace relationships and states of mind along complex political, moral, and mythical pathways. Recent notable albums include *Good as I Been to You* (1992), *World Gone Wrong* (1993), and *Time Out of Mind* (1997). In Dylan's several voices, many hear the most compelling renditions of the discords of their time.

NEIL BESNER

E

Each and All (*Western Messenger*, February 1839), a poem by RALPH WALDO EMERSON included in the *Poems* of 1847. Expressing Emerson's intense faith in the oneness of the universe, the poem praises "the perfect whole" in which all parts depend on one another: "Nothing is fair or good alone." The poem was inspired by a walk along the seashore, described in the poet's *Journals*.

Each in His Own Tongue (1906; in a collection by the same title, 1909), verses by William Herbert Carruth (1859–1924). Reprinted several times since its original publication, the poem was sometimes called "Evolution," from its best-known line, "Some call it Evolution, others call it God."

Eagle, The. A newspaper, also called *The Dartmouth Centinel*, published from 1793 to 1799 in New Hampshire. It was especially notable for the contributions of JOSEPH DENNIE and ROYALL TYLER.

Eagle That Is Forgotten, The (published in *General William Booth Enters into Heaven and Other Poems*, 1913), a poem by VACHEL LINDSAY. It is an elegy dedicated to the memory of the liberal and courageous governor of Illinois, JOHN PETER ALTGELD (1847–1902).

Eames, Wilberforce (1855–1937), librarian, bibliographer. Born in New Jersey, Eames joined the staff of the Lenox Library in 1885 and in 1895 became chief bibliographer of the New York Public Library. His specialty was Americana, and he continued Sabin's *Dictionary of Books Relating to America* (1885–92). Among his books are *John Eliot and the Indians* (1915) and *The First Year of Printing in New York* (1928).

Earl of Pawtucket, The (1903), a comedy by AUGUSTUS THOMAS. Against the background of the old Waldorf-Astoria Hotel in New York City, a British nobleman pretends to be an American named Montgomery Putnam in order to win the hand of an American girl. She turns out to be the divorced wife of the man whose name he has taken. He blunders on to a happy ending.

Early Autumn: A Story of a Lady (1926), a novel by LOUIS BROMFIELD. A bleak story of the effect of Puritanic views on a woman who seeks in vain to escape. Her marriage to a wealthy New Englander puts her in a prison of tradition with unhappy people all around her. She is ready to get away when she is trapped into staying even while knowing a drab existence will be hers in the future. One of Bromfield's portraits is of the rising New England Irishman—Michael O'Hara, self-made man and politician, who is denied entrance into the high society. The novel won a Pulitzer Prize.

Eastburn, James W[allis] (1797–1819), clergyman, hymn writer, poet. Born in England, Eastburn came to New York when he was six, and became an Episcopal clergyman in Virginia. He was one of the first American writers to depict Native Americans in a friendly light. In collaboration with ROBERT C. SANDS, a New York editor (1799–1832), he wrote an epic in six cantos entitled *Yamoyden: A Tale of the Wars of King Philip* (1820), taking some of the material from William Hubbard's NARRATIVE OF THE TROUBLES WITH THE INDIANS IN NEW ENGLAND (1677).

Eastlake, William (1917–1997), novelist, short-story writer. Born in New York City, Eastlake attended the Alliance Française in Paris. After his return to the United States, he moved to a cattle ranch in New Mexico, the background for his novels *Go in Beauty* (1956), *Bronc People* (1958), and *Pilgrims to the Wake* (1961). Among his other novels are *Portrait of an Artist with Twenty-Six Horses* (1963), *Castle Keep* (1964), *The Bamboo Bed* (1970), *Dancers in the Scalp House* (1975), *The Long Naked Descent into Boston* (1977), and *Pretty Fields*, a novella (1987). *Jack Armstrong in Tangier* (1984) is a story collection, and *A Child's Garden of Verses for the Revolution* (1971) contains poetry and essays.

East Lynne (1861), a novel by Mrs. Henry Wood. This English novel of intrigue among characters of high social rank was a best seller in the United States and equally popular as a play. Lady Isabel Vane mistakenly accuses her husband of infidelity and runs off with another man. Later, disguised as a nurse, she is hired by her remarried husband to care for her own children. Disclosure of the pretense and their reconciliation occur at her deathbed.

Eastman, Charles A[lexander] [Native American name, **Ohiyesa**] (1858–1939), physician, historian, autobiographer. Born in Minnesota, of Sioux descent, Eastman devoted his writings to accounts of his own life and to the history and glorification of Native Americans. Among his books are *An Indian Boyhood* (1902); *Red Hunters and the Animal People* (1904); *Old Indian Days* (1907); *Wigwam Evenings* (with his wife, Elaine Goodale Eastman, 1909); *The Soul of the Indian* (1911); *From the Deep Woods to Civilization* (1916); and *Indian Heroes and Great Chieftains* (1918).

Eastman, Charles Gamage (1816–1860), newspaperman, poet. His verses, collected in *Poems* (1848), won him a wide popular reputation. Born in Maine, Eastman was called the Burns of New England. He established two periodicals, *Spirit of the Age* (1840) and *Vermont Patriot* (1846).

Eastman, Mary H[enderson] (1818–1880), historian, writer on Indian legends, storyteller. Born in Virginia, Eastman in her *Dahcotah, or, Life and Legends of the Sioux Around Fort Snelling* (1849) is believed to have inspired Longfellow to write HIAWATHA (1855). She also compiled *The American Aboriginal Portfolio* (1853). Her *Aunt Phillis's Cabin; or, Southern Life As It Is* (1852) was a rejoinder to Stowe's *Uncle Tom's Cabin* (1852). Her husband, **Seth Eastman** (1808–1875), an artist and army officer born in Maine, became familiar with Indian tribes in the course of his service and illustrated several books dealing with Native Americans. Among them were Henry R. Schoolcraft's *Information Concerning the History, Condition, and Prospects of the Indian Tribes of the U.S.* (published by order of Congress, 1851–57) and some books by his wife, among them *Dahcotah*.

Eastman, Max [Forrester] (1883–1969), poet, critic, teacher, essayist, historian, editor. Eastman, born in Canandaigua, New York, began his career as a teacher of philosophy and psychology at Columbia University. He was then primarily interested in aesthetics, and some of his best books were in this field, particularly *The Enjoyment of Poetry* (1913) and *The Enjoyment of Laughter* (1936). World War I drew him into political and economic controversy. He became a Marxist, but was subsequently a bitter opponent of the Stalinist development of Marxism. He edited works of Karl Marx and translated some of Pushkin and Trotsky. He helped found and edit two important magazines, THE MASSES (1911) and THE LIBERATOR (1917), and was tried for sedition when the former was suppressed for antiwar writings in 1917. His first book, *The Enjoyment of Poetry*, went into over twenty editions. Other books by Eastman are *Marxism: Is It Science?* (1940); *Heroes I Have Known* (1942); *Lot's Wife*, a narrative poem (1942); *Enjoyment of Living* (1948); *Poems of Five Decades* (1954); *Reflections on the Failure of Socialism* (1955); and *Great Companions—Critical Memoirs of Some Famous Friends* (1959). *Love and Revolution* (1965) is an autobiography.

Eastman, Seth   See MARY H. EASTMAN.

East of Eden (1952), a novel by JOHN STEINBECK. The most ambitious of Steinbeck's novels, *East of Eden* is based on a reconstruction of the biblical story of Cain and Abel. It centers around the lives of Adam Trask and his two sons, Cal and Aron. Adam Trask fights with his brother Charles for the love of their father, then sets out from their New England farm on a series of journeys that finally bring him and his new wife, Cathy, to the Salinas Valley in California. Cathy bears Adam twin sons and then deserts him to become a prostitute, leaving Adam emotionally crippled. Thanks to the intervention of

Lee, the Chinese servant, and the fatherly wisdom of Sam Hamilton, Adam partially recovers and is able to raise the children, but as the boys grow older it is apparent that they are reenacting the Cain and Abel drama in themselves. Adam favors Aron at the expense of Cal and is unable to forgive Cal when he drives Aron to his death by telling him that their mother is a prostitute. The moral and philosophical import of the book lies in its long central section in which Lee and Adam discuss God's admonition to Adam after the Fall, and the implications of the Hebrew word *timshel*, which Steinbeck interprets to mean "thou mayest" (rather than "thou shalt") conquer over sin. Given a choice, man is free and can decide for himself; Adam's final realization of this enables him to forgive Cal at the close of the book.

Eaton, Edith Maud (1865–1914) short-story writer. Born in England, the daughter of an English father and Chinese mother, she immigrated to Montreal, Canada with her family when she was seven. Though her facial features did not identify her as Asian, she considered herself so, and always made her home in Chinese settlements. After 1900 she moved to the West Coast and from there traveled to Asian enclaves throughout North America. Using the pseudonym Sui Sin Far—Chinese for water lily—she advocated for an end to racial bigotry and better treatment of immigrants. Her realistic fiction, describing the hardships endured by Asians, was published in *Overland, Century, The Chautauquan, Good Housekeeping*, and *The New England Magazine* in the late 1880s. She was the first writer of Chinese ancestry to call attention to the harsh effects of U.S. immigration policies, especially the Chinese Exclusion Act of 1882. Her fiction was collected in *Mrs. Spring Fragrance* (1912). "Leaves from the Mental Portfolio of an Eurasian" is an autobiographical essay. Her tombstone in the Protestant cemetery in Montreal bears a Chinese inscription meaning "the righteous one does not forget her country."

Eaton, Walter Prichard (1878–1957), teacher, critic, author of books for boys. Eaton worked on Boston and New York newspapers, became professor of playwriting at Yale (1933–47), and wrote extensively on the theater. Among his books are *The American Stage of Today* (1908); *The Idyl of Twin Fires* (1915), a novel; *The Actor's Heritage* (1924); *The Theater Guild* (1929); and *New England Vista* (1930).

Eben Holden (1900), a novel by IRVING BACHELLER. One of the most popular books of the day, it is laid in the middle years of the 19th century and tells about an orphan lad who is befriended by a hired man, later gets a job on the New York *Tribune* with Horace Greeley, and fights for the North in the Civil War.

Eberhart, Mignon [Good] (1899–1996), writer of detective fiction. In many of the stories that made her reputation, the sleuth is a nurse, particularly the popular Sarah Keate. First of her approximately 70 books was *The Patient in Room 18* (1929). More widely read were *While the Patient Slept* (1930) and *From This Dark Stairway* (1931). Her other novels include *The Dark Garden* (1933), *The Glass Slipper* (1938), *The*

Sisters (1944), *Five Passengers from Lisbon* (1946), *Never Look Back* (1951), *Unknown Quantity* (1953), *Man Missing* (1954), *Melora* (1959), *Jury of One* (1960), *Run Scared* (1963), *Witness at Large* (1966), *Murder in Waiting* (1973), *The Patient in Cabin C* (1983), and *A Fighting Chance* (1986).

Eberhart, Nelle Richmond (1871–1944), teacher, poet, librettist. Eberhart collaborated frequently with the composer Charles Wakefield Cadman and for him wrote the lyrics of two enduring songs, "At Dawning" (1906) and "From the Land of the Sky-Blue Water" (1909). She supplied Cadman with lyrics for other Indian songs and with him wrote an opera, *A Witch of Salem* (1920), and the first radio opera, *The Willow Tree* (produced by NBC, October 4, 1932).

Eberhart, Richard (1904–   ), teacher, poet, lecturer. Born in Minnesota, Eberhart was educated at the University of Minnesota, Dartmouth, Cambridge University, and Harvard. He taught at St. Mark's School, in Massachusetts, was a lieutenant commander in the Naval Reserve during World War II, and then taught at several colleges and universities before settling in at Dartmouth (1956–70). His many honors include an appointment as consultant in poetry (1959–61) at the Library of Congress and the Bollingen Prize (1962), Pulitzer Prize (1966), and National Book Award (1977). He was elected to the National Institute of Arts and Letters (1960) and the American Academy of Arts and Sciences (1967).

Eberhart's *Collected Poems: 1930–1986* (1986) gathers the poet's best works from many previous volumes published over half a century, beginning with *A Bravery of Earth* (1930). As is suggested by that first title and some others—*Burr Oaks* (1947), *An Herb Basket* (1950), and *Fishing for Snakes* (1965)—he turns frequently to images drawn from nature. One of his best-known poems, "The Groundhog," combines that interest and a recurring concern with change and death. Others, such as "The Fury of Aerial Bombardment," speak to man's inhumanity to man. Generally, his vision is affirmative, as the things of transient nature signify a transcendent permanence captured in verse. *New and Selected Poems 1930–1990* appeared in 1990. Works in addition to poems include *Collected Verse Plays* (1962), *Selected Prose* (1978), and *Of Poetry and Poets* (1979).

Echeverría, Esteban (1805–1851), Argentine poet. During a five-year stay in Paris, Echeverría absorbed the tenets of French romanticism, which permeate his works of poetry, especially *Elvira, o la novia del Plata* (1832), *Consuelos* (1834), and *La cautiva* (1837), notable for its depiction of the Argentine pampas and the people who live there. Echeverría's opposition to dictator Juan Manuel de Rosas led him and other idealistic youths to form the Asociación de Mayo, a revolutionary group dedicated to liberal, democratic principles. His hatred for Rosas also inspired him to write *El Matadero* (*The Slaughterhouse*, 1871), the work for which he is probably best known today. Written during the 1830s, *El Matadero* is the unfinished draft of a novel denouncing the brutality of the dictatorship of Juan Manuel de Rosas. Its crude realism stands in sharp contrast to the romanticism that characterizes Eche-

verría's poetry. The story is set in a Buenos Aires slaughterhouse, where henchmen of Rosas murder a member of the opposition who passes by.

Echo, The. A composite work of several of the Hartford Wits, but mainly of THEODORE DWIGHT and RICHARD ALSOP. A verse satire, it appeared in twenty sections in the *American Mercury* (1791–1805) and then as a collection (1807). The poem is vehemently and dogmatically Federalist in tone. Jefferson and others who revealed democratic tendencies were particular victims of the often effective ridicule.

Eddy, Mary [Morse] Baker [Glover Patterson] (1821–1910), religious leader, editor, author. The founder of Christian Science, Eddy published SCIENCE AND HEALTH (1875) as an exposition of her ideas and as the official statement of the organization she headed. In this book and others of her *Miscellaneous Writings* (1896) she taught that pain, disease, old age, and death were what she called errors. Born in New Hampshire, she founded the Church of Christ, Scientist, in Boston (1879) and THE CHRISTIAN SCIENCE MONITOR. She wrote under the influence of Phineas P. Quimby (1802–1866) and the transcendentalists, particularly Emerson, who had once said, "Never name sickness." Toward the end of her career she was subjected to attacks by the New York *World*, *McClure's Magazine*, and Mark Twain, who wrote a book on *Christian Science* (1907) ridiculing her doctrines.

Eddy, Sherwood (1871–1963), social worker. As a YMCA executive, Eddy did much of his work in various Asian countries, and he wrote books to help Americans understand these lands. Among his books are *India Awakening* (1911), *The New Era in Asia* (1913), *The Students of Asia* (1915), and *The Challenge of Russia* (1930). He also wrote *God in History* (1947) and told the story of his life in *Eighty Adventurous Years* (1955) and *Why I Believe* (1957).

Edel, [Joseph] Leon (1907–1997), biographer, editor, literary critic. Born in Pittsburgh, Edel was educated at McGill University, the University of Montreal, and the University of Paris. He worked as a journalist before beginning his long academic career at New York University in 1950. His major focus was Henry James. He edited James's novels, tales, plays, essays, and letters and wrote the definitive biography, *Henry James: A Life* (5 v. 1953–72; one-volume version, 1985). His other books include *James Joyce* (1947), *The Modern Psychological Novel* (1955), *Literary Biography* (1957), *Bloomsbury, A House of Lions* (1979), and *Stuff of Sleep and Dreams* (1982). He also edited Edmund Wilson's *Notebooks and Diaries* (3 v. 1972).

Edgar Huntly, or Memoirs of a Sleep-Walker (1799), a novel by CHARLES BROCKDEN BROWN. The plot involves strange occurrences in frontier Pennsylvania. In a memorable sequence, the narrator, Edgar Huntly, finds himself in a cave, where he must kill a panther and several Indians before he can escape. In the preface, Brown prided himself on introducing "incidents of Indian hostility, and the perils of the Western wilderness" to American literature. The novel includes murders, real and supposed; a mad Irishman, Clithero Edny; and a heroine, Mary Waldegrave, recipient of the narrator's letters.

Edgars. Awards given annually in several categories since 1946 by the Mystery Writers of America. They are named for Edgar Allan Poe.

Edict by the King of Prussia (Philadelphia *Public Advertiser*, September 1773), a satire by BENJAMIN FRANKLIN, reprinted in Volume VI of his *Writings*. The piece, which was read by Franklin in England to a group of friends, was a circumstantial account of a claim to English territory supposedly presented by Frederick the Great. He based his claim on the fact that England itself had been settled by colonists from Germany, had never been emancipated, and had hitherto rendered little revenue to "our august house." It went on with straight-faced logic to strengthen Franklin's case with numerous details, set forth in addition what Englishmen would be permitted to do in the future by way of manufacturing goods, and noted that thereafter he intended to send all German criminals to settle in England.

Edison, Thomas A[lva] (1847–1931), inventor, industrialist. Born in Ohio, Edison influenced the craft of writing by his inventions in various fields, for example, the telegraph, the typewriter, the motion-picture camera, and the phonograph. *The Diary and Sundry Observations of Thomas Alva Edison* (edited by Dagobert D. Runes, 1948) showed him as a whimsical person with something of a poet's imagination. He is credited with the definition of *genius* as 2% inspiration and 98% perspiration.

Editor's Drawer, The, and **The Editor's Easy Chair.** Two departments in HARPER'S MAGAZINE. The former was started in 1852, the latter in 1851. The Drawer had many humorous contributions, and its editors included Charles Dudley Warner and John Kendrick Bangs. The Chair was more definitely associated with persons who spoke their views on many matters, significant or whimsical. Among its occupants were D. G. Mitchell, George William Curtis, William Dean Howells, E. S. Martin, Bernard De Voto, and John Fischer.

Edmonds, Walter D[umaux] (1903–1998), novelist. Edmonds made his native region of northern New York his own literary property. Practically all his life he lived in Boonville, the attractive village in which he was born, with its many historic memories; and the Black River, the Black River Canal, and the Erie Canal dominated his imagination. His stories are historical in setting, lively in manner. Among them are *Rome Haul* (1929), *Erie Water* (1933), DRUMS ALONG THE MOHAWK (1936), *Chad Hanna* (1940), *In the Hands of the Senecas* (1947), and *The Wedding Journey* (1947). He has also written a number of juveniles, including *Tom Whipple* (1942) and *Uncle Ben's Whale* (1955), and two books of history: *The First Hundred Years* (1948) and *They Fought With What They Had* (1951), about the U.S. Air Force in the Pacific in World War II.

Education of Henry Adams, The (privately printed, 1907; published, 1918), an autobiography by HENRY ADAMS. It is an informal history of the times rather than a complete account of Adams's life. Referring to himself in the third person and always with irony, Adams describes his attempts at understanding his world in hopes of adapting to it and living a useful life. Despite his accomplishments as scholar and writer, Adams insists he has failed to educate himself. But, he implies, so has everyone else. This is because enormous increases in mechanical power, symbolized by the locomotive and the dynamo, have complicated the world beyond anyone's understanding. Adams finds confusion in science, diplomacy, politics, journalism, and education. His chapter entitled "Chaos" is a vision of anarchy. His chapter "The Dynamo and the Virgin" contrasts the unity of 13th-century Europe (the subject of his MONT-SAINT-MICHEL and CHARTRES) with the baffling multiplicity of the modern *multiverse*. Near the end of his book, however, and writing out of his old age, Adams offers an elaborate theory of history—evidence of his continuing determination to master the forces unleashed by modern science. If the Henry Adams of this book is pessimistic he is also a model of intelligence and integrity.

FRANK MCHUGH

Education of H*y*m*a*n K*a*p*l*a*n, The (1937), a collection of humorous sketches by Leonard Ross (pen name of LEO CALVIN ROSTEN). Mr. Parkhill, who conducts the beginners' class in the American Night Preparatory School for Adults, regards the school not merely as a place where foreigners may learn the English language—"It [is] an incubator of Americans, a kind of intellectual Ellis Island." The account of what takes place, published originally in *The New Yorker*, still makes hilarious reading. A sequel, *The Return of H*y*m*a*n K*a*p*l*a*n*, appeared in 1959.

Edwards, Gus (1879–1945), singer, actor, producer, songwriter. Born in Germany, Edwards went on the American stage at an early age, won renown as a singer, and wrote popular songs. His earliest hit was "I Couldn't Stand to See My Baby Lose" (1899). The best known of his songs are "School Days" (1907), which made him well known and led him to establish a music publishing firm, and "By the Light of the Silvery Moon" (1909). He made a specialty of encouraging new talent, including Eddie Cantor, Joe Cook, Groucho Marx, Lila Lee, Mae Murray, and Helen Menken. A motion picture, *The Star Maker* (1939), presented incidents of his career and revived some of his songs.

Edwards, Harry Stillwell (1855–1938), lawyer, editor, public official, storyteller. Born in Georgia, Edwards won a $10,000 prize for his novel *Sons and Fathers* (1896) and published other volumes, but it was not until he was sixty-four that he wrote the little book that made his name—*Eneas Africanus* (1919). It is the story of a former slave who in 1865 becomes separated from his master and then for eight years wanders through the South. The master tries to find him, and they are finally reunited. Edwards also wrote *Eneas Africanus, Defendant* (1921).

Edwards, Jonathan (1703–1758), theologian, philosopher. One of the most extraordinary men produced on the American continent, Edwards was a precocious child with a deep interest in nature, science, philosophy, and theology. Born in Connecticut, he entered Yale at thirteen, and at seventeen experienced a mystic conversion which he described twenty years after in his "Personal Narrative." The pattern of

Edwards's philosophical thought had begun to take shape while he was still a student, and he wrote his "Notes on Natural Science" and "Notes on the Mind." He lived in an age of scientific discovery; the works of Newton and Locke, just published at the end of the previous century, stimulated him to see the world, like Locke, in terms of sense impressions from which ideas are derived, and in terms of natural and immutable laws that reflect the perfection and absolute sovereignty of the Creator. Edwards thus came to a philosophically idealistic and mystic view that all natural manifestations are shadows of a divine reality, and that as ideas are a result of sense impressions, so is moral grace acquired through the senses, not through will or reason.

In the "Treatise on Grace" (published posthumously in 1865) Edwards differentiates between "common grace" and the regenerative "supernatural grace," which accompanies conversion and grants the individual a new sense of spiritual awareness. This doctrine contained two concepts radically new in Puritan thought: conversion was an unmistakable occurrence, and it involved the emotions even more than reason. The Puritan church in the latter part of the 17th century had admitted to church membership and to communion all who wished to join, reflecting the belief that communion might be a means of grace for the unregenerate. Edwards insisted that communion was a sacrament only for those who had already experienced conversion. This seemed intolerable to his parish, accustomed to more lax standards, and he was asked to resign his leadership of the Church at Northampton in 1750. His beliefs on the place of the emotions in religious experience led him to champion the GREAT AWAKENING (c. 1734–40) in which he saw dramatic conversions to be evidence of the "peculiar and immediate" manifestation of God.

Edwards's theology was more basically Calvinistic than that of some earlier Puritan divines, who emphasized the covenantal relation between man and God, rather than the absolute supremacy of a God not bound by contract. Edwards also followed Calvinistic thought in his assertions on the reality of sin; he felt sin to be a "property of the species" that justified God's punishment of man and made possible mercy and redemption. His sermon on SINNERS IN THE HANDS OF AN ANGRY GOD (1741), so horrifying to later readers, was an exhortation on the necessity of salvation as well as a reminder of the torments that awaited the unregenerate. He believed "that the essence of all religion lies in holy love," that all virtue is disinterested benevolence that springs from "love to Being" and finally from God as the summation of Being, and all sin from a defect or distortion of that love.

The last eight years of Edwards's life were spent in the frontier settlement of Stockbridge, where he was a missionary to the Indians and composed his most important writings. Upon the death of his son-in-law, Aaron Burr, Sr., who had been president of the College of New Jersey (later Princeton), Edwards became president of the college, but died almost immediately after taking office. His most important works include *God Glorified in the Work of Redemption* (1731); *A Divine and Supernatural Light* (1734); *A Faithful Narrative of the Surprising Work of God in the Conversion of Many Hundred Souls* (1737; see NARRATIVE OF SURPRISING CONVERSIONS); *Some Thoughts Concerning the Present Revival of Religion in New England* (1742); *A Treatise Concerning Religious Affections* (1746); *A Farewell Sermon* (1751); *Charity and Its Fruits* (1851); and *A Careful and Strict Enquiry into . . . Freedom of Will* (1754; see FREEDOM OF THE WILL). Other, posthumous writings are *The Great Christian Doctrine of Original Sin Defended* (1758); IMAGES OR SHADOWS OF DIVINE THINGS (1948, taken from Edwards's notebooks now in the Yale University Library); *The Nature of True Virtue* (1765); and *Concerning the End for Which God Created the World* (1765).

Eggleston, Edward (1837–1902), clergyman, novelist, editor, historian. A Hoosier, Eggleston in his novels contributed to the development of regional fiction. He was an ardent reformer, campaigned against religious denominationalism, advocated kindergartens for young children, and vigorously advocated copyright reform. Best-known of his novels are THE HOOSIER SCHOOLMASTER (1871), *The End of the World* (1872), THE CIRCUIT RIDER (1874), ROXY (1878), *The Hoosier Schoolboy* (1883), and THE GRAYSONS (1888).

Eggleston, George Cary (1839–1911), teacher, newspaperman, author of books for boys, historian. The younger brother of EDWARD EGGLESTON, he began teaching in a country school at the age of sixteen, and his experiences helped provide his brother with information for THE HOOSIER SCHOOLMASTER. Later he studied law, fought in the Confederate army, and became a newspaperman in New York. Perhaps his best book is his memoir, *A Rebel's Recollections* (1874). He also wrote *Strange Stories from History* (1886) and the romantic novels *Dorothy South* (1902) and *Evelyn Byrd* (1904).

Eguren, José María (1882–1942). Peruvian poet. Originally identified with MODERNISMO and particularly the symbolist influence associated with that movement, Eguren's work represents a renovation of technique. His major volumes, *Simbólicas* (1911), *La canción de las figuras* (1916), and *Poesías* (1929), evoke a personal, dreamlike, quizzical, often mysteriously wounded vision of the world. Before CÉSAR VALLEJO, Eguren was considered the greatest Peruvian poet. His *Poesías completas*, which first appeared in 1955, was reprinted and supplemented in 1961 and 1970.

Eighth of January, The (1829), a play by RICHARD PENN SMITH. This play celebrated the victory of Andrew Jackson in the Battle of New Orleans in 1815, and his election as president, viewed as the triumph of democracy over the "Adams dynasty."

Eimi (1933, reprinted 1948), a narrative of travel in Russia by E. E. CUMMINGS. This book, like the author's poetry, includes puns, parodies, and typographical innovations. The title is Greek and means "I am." Cummings tells what he himself saw, heard, and felt.

Einstein, Albert (1879–1955), theoretical physicist. Einstein taught in various German, Czech, and Swiss universities, and announced in 1905 his special theory of relativity and in 1915 his general theory of relativity. In 1933 he was teaching in Germany when the Nazis came to power; he left for the

United States and became an American citizen in 1940. In 1933 he became a life member of the Institute for Advanced Study at Princeton. A shy, kindly little man whose pastimes were sailing and playing the violin, he was a beloved member of the community until his death. He was exceptionally modest: at a Hollywood reception where he was greeted with fantastically eulogistic speeches he replied, "Thank you, but I'd be crazy to believe what you say about me." He is rumored to have said, "I can't explain my equation to you, but I'll gladly play it on the fiddle."

In the general conception, Einstein has been considered to have abolished the meaning of absolute time and absolute space: time acquires dimensions similar to length, breadth, and thickness. Among Einstein's books are *Meaning of Relativity* (1923, revised 1945); *Investigations on the Theory of the Brownian Movement* (1926); *About Zionism* (1931); *On the Method of Theoretical Physics* (1933); *The World as I See It* (1934); and *The Evolution of Physics* (with Leopold Infled, 1938). He won the Nobel Prize for Physics in 1921. In 1939 he signed a historic letter to President Roosevelt explaining the potentialities of atomic energy. Some of his best miscellaneous essays are collected in *Out of My Later Years* (1950).

Eiseley, Loren [Corey] (1907–1977),   poet, essayist, teacher. Professor of anthropology and provost of the University of Pennsylvania, Eisley was the author of *The Immense Journey* (1957), a work on physical anthropology and archaeology. His other books include *Darwin's Century* (1958), *The Firmament of Time* (1960), *The Man Who Saw Through Mirrors* (1973), and *The Unexpected Universe* (1969). *All the Strange Hours* (1975) is autobiographical.

Eisenhower, Dwight D[avid] (1890–1969),   soldier, 34th president of the United States. Eisenhower was born in Denison, Texas, and educated at West Point. In 1942 he was made commander of the Allied forces landing in North Africa and became a general in February 1943. Appointed supreme commander of the Allied Expeditionary Forces in Europe, he led the Normandy invasion and directed the defeat of the Nazis in 1944–45. Eisenhower told his own story in *Crusade in Europe* (1948).

In July 1952, Eisenhower resigned from the army. He had been eyed for nomination as president by Republican and Democratic leaders. He accepted the Republican bid and defeated Adlai E. Stevenson, the Democratic candidate.

His other books include the two-volume *The White House Years*, including *Mandate for Change* (1963) and *Waging Peace* (1965). *At Ease* (1967) is a memoir.

El Dorado.   (Spanish for "the gilded man.") It is said that Chibcha Indians near what is now Bogotá used to inaugurate new chieftains in an elaborate ceremony that included daubing them with oil and sprinkling gold dust all over their bodies. In time the ceremony disappeared, but the legend persisted, and has been associated with other tribes as well. It met the Spaniards on their conquest of South America. Everywhere they heard of El Dorado and they dreamed of a land where everything was made of gold and jewels. Many expeditions set out in search of El Dorado. Two were led by Sir Wal-

ter Raleigh, in 1595 and in 1616. He told the story in *The Discovery of the Large, Rich, and Beautiful Empire of Guiana, with a Relation of the Great and Golden City of Manoa, Which the Spaniards Call El Dorado* (1596).

Both Milton, in *Paradise Lost*, and Voltaire, in *Candide*, mention El Dorado. In 1849 the name was attached to California during the Gold Rush, and BAYARD TAYLOR wrote *Eldorado* (1850) to describe a visit to this land of gold. But Edgar Allan Poe wrote his poem of the same name (printed in *Flag of Our Union*, April 21, 1849) to describe a quest for supernal beauty rather than a quest for gold.

Eleonora   (published in *The Gift*, 1842), a story by EDGAR ALLAN POE. As much a prose poem as a story, "Eleonora" tells of a youth who weds his beautiful cousin and resides in the Valley of the Many-Colored Grass. When she dies, he lives for a while with her mother, then remarries—but learns in a dream that he has not been untrue to the memory of Eleonora.

Eliot, Charles W[illiam] (1834–1926),   teacher, educator, chemist. Born in Boston, Eliot served as president of Harvard from 1869 to 1909 and helped make the university one of the greatest and best known in the world. He also helped establish Radcliffe College (1894).

Eliot once remarked, in protest against the idea that education needs elaborate physical equipment: "All the books needed for a real education could be set on a shelf five feet long." An important publisher of books bought on subscription, P. F. Collier & Son, took him up on his remark and induced him to edit the "Harvard Classics" (1909–10), a fifty-volume set occupying five feet of shelf space. He wrote *The Happy Life* (1896), *Educational Reform* (1898), *The Durable Satisfactions of Life* (1910), *A Late Harvest* (1924), and other books.

Eliot, John   (1604–1690),   teacher, missionary, linguist. Eliot, educated at Cambridge, taught for a while in England, then emigrated in 1631 with the Winthrop family to New England. He settled finally at Roxbury and became a teacher and later pastor in the church there; he also helped found the Roxbury Latin School. His chief interest became the conversion of Native Americans to Christianity, to teach them, he said, "original sin and the damned state of man." He published a translation of the New Testament into the dialect of the Naticks, a Massachusetts branch of the Algonquins (1661), and a version of the entire Bible two years later. Eliot popularized the word MUGWUMP (originally spelled *mugquomp*), a term for *chief* that he used in place of *duke* as it appears in the Authorized Version of Genesis, xxxvi. Eliot helped Native Americans set up independent communities, the oldest and best-known of which was at Natick, in addition to schools and seminaries, but all these were swept away in King Philip's War (1675–76), when the PRAYING INDIANS were caught between the unconverted ones and the whites.

He had long meditated the outlines of a Christian Utopia founded strictly on the Bible. In 1659 he published *The Christian Commonwealth*. In this he rejected all ideas of natural rights—insisting that there were only duties—in complete obedience to the Scriptures. Society was to be organized in a hierarchy of magistrates; the rebel would be a social outcast to be silenced at all costs. Earlier in his career, Eliot had voted to banish ANNE HUTCHINSON, who was accused of heresy. Now Eliot was condemned. In a session of the General Court held at Boston on May 22, 1661, the book was ordered suppressed for fear of angering the restored monarchy in England. Eliot had to make a public retraction. (See BAY PSALM BOOK.)

He wrote several books in Indian language as well as English: *Up-Bookum Psalmes* (1663), *Communion of Churches* (1665), *The Indian Primer* (1669), and *The Harmony of the Gospels* (1678).

Eliot, T[homas] S[tearns] (1888–1965),   poet, critic, editor. Born in St. Louis, Eliot studied at Smith Academy and Milton Academy, and in 1906 entered Harvard, where his attendance in the classes of IRVING BABBITT, the New Humanist critic of Romanticism, became an important factor in determining his development as a poet and critic. (See HUMANISM.) He then attended the Sorbonne for a year, before returning to Harvard for further study. In 1913, however, he went abroad on a Sheldon traveling fellowship, studying at Oxford and in Germany, and the outbreak of World War I prevented his return to Harvard for his final doctoral examinations. In England Eliot taught school and worked for Lloyd's Bank, dealing in prewar enemy debts and foreign exchanges. When the United States entered the war, he was rejected for naval service. In 1917 he became an assistant editor of *The Egoist*, and in 1922 he founded and edited *The Criterion*, a quarterly review which continued until 1939. In 1935 he joined Faber & Faber, the British publishing firm, having become a British subject in 1927. He married twice, in 1915 to Vivien Haigh-Wood, who died in 1947, and in 1957 to Esmé Valerie Fletcher.

As a boy Eliot had published verse and prose sketches in school publications, notably a comic poem in the manner of Byron, and at Harvard he became an editor of the *Advocate*, to which he contributed a number of poems revealing an early acquaintance with modern verse techniques and a growing disaffection with certain aspects of American culture. An important early influence was the poetry of Jules Laforgue, which Eliot had encountered through Arthur Symons's essays on the French *Symbolistes*. First drafts of some of Eliot's later poems were composed while he was still at Harvard. In London he made the acquaintance of EZRA POUND, who arranged for publication of his first mature work, including THE LOVE SONG OF J. ALFRED PRUFROCK in *Poetry* (June 1915), and who wrote enthusiastically in America and in England about Eliot's accomplishments. To what extent Pound influenced Eliot and to what extent the two came to similar points of view by independent routes cannot be determined now with much certainty, but at least Pound's enterprise and stubborn insistence on a thoroughly professional discipline must have furnished an important example to the younger poet. In fact, Eliot's first separately published critical work was *Ezra Pound, His Metric and Poetry* (1917), and elsewhere he recorded his debt to Pound for the latter's assistance in revising and shortening the final draft of *The Waste Land*.

Eliot's first book of poems, *Prufrock and Other Observations*, was published in London in 1917. It was followed by *Poems* (1920); THE WASTE LAND (1922); THE HOLLOW MEN (1925); *Poems, 1909–1925* (1925); ASH WEDNESDAY (1930); *Sweeney Agonistes; Fragments of an Aristophanic Melodrama* (1932, see SWEENEY); *The Rock* (1934); *Collected Poems* (1936); *East Coker* (1940); *Burnt Norton* (1941); *The Dry Salvages* (1941); the latter three, with *Little Gidding*, were collected in FOUR QUARTETS (1943). (See also GERONTION.) The importance of Eliot's poetry in shaping the development of 20th-century Anglo-American literature can scarcely be exaggerated, especially the importance of *The Waste Land*, which is thought by many critics to be Eliot's best poem. His influence spread quickly in the 1920s but began to diminish in the 1950s. His poems were for over two decades the chief instruments in popularizing among writers the techniques of symbolism, the desiderata of control and precision in the use of language, and the notion of poetic form as a dynamically mobile structure. Even Eliot's personal style—a concise diction, a dry irony, the use of descending cadences—was widely imitated and occasionally parodied. The early poems, including *The Waste Land* and *The Hollow Men*, may be broadly characterized as negative, that is, as deriving their chief motifs from a critical and sharply ironic appraisal of the positivistic elements in modern Western culture, although this is countered by a steadily deepening emphasis on the values to be sought in tradition, spiritual awareness, conservatism, and responsibility to history. Beginning with *Ash Wednesday*, Eliot's poetry was more pointedly affirmative and appears to have been intended as a conscious contribution to the Anglo-Catholic literature of faith. Throughout all the poetry, certain recurrent symbolic themes are apparent: sexuality, childhood, the rose and other tokens of Christianity, and—rather surprisingly in a poetry whose total impression is of an almost exclusive urbanity—images of nature, especially birds. One other book of verse should be noted, *Old Possum's Book of Practical Cats* (1939), a collection of light verse. Possum is a nickname acknowledged by Eliot—possibly in part as a euphemism for Parson, a name applied half maliciously by some of his critics—and it appears in a number of Ezra Pound's *Cantos*.

Eliot's criticism is an indispensable adjunct to his poetry, and neither can be fully appreciated without the other. From the literary point of view, his most valuable essays have been those in which he calls attention to the merits and techniques of the minor Elizabethan dramatists and the 17th-century metaphysical poets, as well as a small group of essays in which he discusses his methods of composition and literary analysis. Among the latter the essay called "Tradition and the Individual Talent" acquired particular prominence. Widely quoted, praised, and attacked, the essay became standard fare in many university courses. But Eliot also wrote important essays on classical literature, on Dante, on the symbolist poetry of France, and on 20th-century literature. In his historical, philosophical, and religious essays, he argued brilliantly for the conservative tradition and for the restoration of the unified religion-aesthetic society which he believed to have existed in

Europe before the advent of the rationalistic delusions. Eliot's first important volume of criticism was THE SACRED WOOD (1920). Others are *Homage to John Dryden* (1924), *Shakespeare and the Stoicism of Seneca* (1928), *For Lancelot Andrewes* (1928), *Dante* (1929), *Thoughts After Lambeth* (1931), *Selected Essays* (1932), *The Use of Poetry and the Use of Criticism* (1933), *After Strange Gods* (1934), *Elizabethan Essays* (1934), *Essays Ancient and Modern* (1936), *The Idea of a Christian Society* (1939), *Poetry and Drama* (1951), *The Three Voices of Poetry* (1954), *On Poetry and Poets* (1957), and *The Elder Statesman* (1959).

Eliot's interest in the theater was active and lifelong, and proceeded chiefly in the direction of restoring the verse drama to a position of practical esteem in the modern stage repertoire. His early efforts were the fragmentary *Sweeney Agonistes* and *The Rock*, never successfully performed. MURDER IN THE CATHEDRAL (1935), on the other hand, achieved a great success and has been frequently performed in England and America since its first production by the Friends of Canterbury Cathedral. Based on the martyrdom of Thomas à Becket, the drama is a work of symbolism written in alternating lyrical and prosaic passages and employing devices common to classical and medieval drama, for example, a verse chorus. Eliot said, however, that he believed the chief problem of the verse drama in his time was the proper adaptation of verse technique to the modern naturalistic stage: verse drama must acquire the same realism as prose drama in the presentation of scenes from ordinary life. His later plays moved progressively in this direction, retaining a loosely metrical verse pattern but venturing into essentially Ibsenian modes of dealing with contemporary society. Eliot's other plays are THE FAMILY REUNION (1939); THE COCKTAIL PARTY (1950); and *The Confidential Clerk* (1954). *The Complete Poems and Plays* of Eliot appeared in 1952.

Although Eliot's poems and critical theories were among the foremost instruments in discrediting the shallow gentility of post-Victorianism, Eliot himself, in his writing and in his public character, affected an older and perhaps in some respects sterner gentility that deeply colored intellectual life in the 20th century. In his public appearances Eliot often presented himself as a mildly clerical English man of leisure, devoted to punctilious and circumscribed entertainments and to a rather exacting decorum. That this was a pose, at least in part consciously assumed, was shown by Eliot himself in his occasional recourse to an equally calculated comic vulgarity—like other leaders of the poetic revolution he knew the value of shock—but his genuine artistic seriousness, when dealing with matters of importance, belies any ultimate frivolity. Nevertheless, this aspect of Eliot's artistic personality, prissiness not devoid of mock-humility and dogmatism, sometimes aroused his antagonists to a pitch far exceeding polite controversy. Actually, although in general Eliot was the most admired Anglo-American writer of his time, from the beginning he provoked strong opposition, and historians may eventually conclude that the most important responses to his work were the counteractions—not only of the men of his own generation, for example, WILLIAM CARLOS WILLIAMS, who chose differ-

ent paths, but also of leading poets in succeeding generations who have sought to reverse the force of his influence. For most of his lifetime, however, Eliot remained the dean of English letters and had extraordinary power in the literary world. He used his power wisely on the whole, writing many reviews and introductions to help worthy young authors and to right imbalances in the reputations of the past. He was given degrees by scores of European and American universities and was awarded the Nobel Prize for literature in 1948.

Finally, readers should note that Eliot's public character was by no means entirely superficial or unmeaningful. His career was a programmatic search for sources, a backtracking through time and distance in pursuit of origins and the tradition stemming from them. A descendant of Sir Thomas Elyot (1490?–1546, English author, diplomat, etc.), T. S. Eliot removed by stages from Missouri to his ancestral England and to a certain extent from the 20th century to the 16th, thereby seeking the specifics of cultural continuity upon which his beliefs depend. In his poem *East Coker* he celebrates his descent, and in his last major poem, *Little Gidding*, he places the bombing of London in World War II firmly within this self-created matrix of history and religious affirmation. His whole work was a poetic fiction with deep historical roots, devoted to establishing a poetic character, a *persona*, of great but definable complexity—the man of spirit in an antagonistic world.

Biographical studies include Lyndall Gordon, *Eliot's Early Years* (1977) and *Eliot's New Life* (1988). Critical studies include Elizabeth Drew, *T. S. Eliot: The Design of His Poetry* (1949); Helen Gardner, *The Art of T. S. Eliot* (1950); F.O. Matthiessen, *The Achievements of T. S. Eliot* (third edition, 1958); Bernard Bergonzi, *T. S. Eliot* (1971); Derek Traversi, *T. S. Eliot: A Study in Character and Style* (1983); Grover Smith, *The Waste Land by T. S. Eliot* (1983); Calvin Bedient, *He Do the Police in Different Voices: "The Waste Land" and Its Protagonist* (1987); Christopher Ricks, *T. S. Eliot and Prejudice* (1989); and Anthony Julius, *T. S. Eliot, Anti-Semitism, and Literary Form* (1995).

HAYDEN CARRUTH/G.P.

Eliza. A character in Harriet Beecher Stowe's UNCLE TOM'S CABIN (1852). She is a daughter of Cassy, once Legree's favorite, later a "wreck of beauty" who is finally reunited with her daughter; Eliza also is rejoined by her husband, George Harris, who follows her by the Underground Railway after she makes her escape across the Ohio River on the ice, carrying her boy Harry.

Elizabeth the Queen (1930), a historical drama by MAXWELL ANDERSON. Anderson employs blank verse, including lines from Shakespeare, in this account of the love story of the Earl of Essex and the Queen of England, whom "a kingdom kept apart." Essex seeks power and war; Elizabeth, setting her country above her lover, prefers peace. Essex threatens the throne and is tried and condemned. In the end Essex realizes Elizabeth is right and goes off to his execution stoically.

Elkin, Stanley [Lawrence] (1930–1995), novelist, short-fiction writer. Elkin was born in New York City and raised in Chicago. His father, a traveling salesman and raconteur, was an early inspiration for Elkin as storyteller. In 1955, Elkin married Joan Marion Jacobson and began service in the Army. After his two-year stint, Elkin completed his education at the University of Illinois, writing his dissertation on William Faulkner. He began writing stories during graduate school, and in 1960 joined the English Department at Washington University in St. Louis. Elkin wrote a dozen novels and short-fiction collections that explore the extremities of life and culture in middle-class, contemporary America. From his first novel, *Boswell: A Modern Comedy* (1964), to the *The Rabbi of Lud* (1987), Elkin evolved a tragicomic vision of existence as the attempted fulfillment of fantasy and desire contending against the constraints imposed by the impoverishments of contemporary culture and the limitations of the human body. *Criers and Kibitzers, Kibitzers and Criers* (1966) and *Searches and Seizures* (1973) are collections of short fiction exhibiting the variety of Elkin's fictive universe, where salesmen, bums, knights, and grave robbers talk out their dreams and griefs while living in dire conditions. *A Bad Man* (1967) tells the story of a department store owner gone wrong; *The Dick Gibson Show* (1971) is a transcription of confessions over the airwaves to a late-night radio talk show host; *The Franchiser* (1976), Elkin's finest novel, recounts the adventures of a man dying of multiple sclerosis—Elkin himself suffered from it—while attempting to amalgamate his financial empire. In *The Living End* (1979), Elkin explores the hereafter and finds it to be a comic, mirror-version of the here and now. *George Mills* (1982) compares the life of a medieval peasant to that of a modern-day furniture mover living in St. Louis. *The Magic Kingdom* (1985) and *The Rabbi of Lud* (1987), companion novels, contain further explorations of Elkin's fascination with death as the termination of life's indeterminacies in the very young and the very old. In all these works, Elkin continued—always through his own peculiar combination of bravado and humor—to discover mystery in everyday life, and to confront the banal terrors of the mundane with endless talk and conversation. Other titles are *The Coffee Room* (1988); *The MacGuffin* (1991); *Pieces of Soap* (1992); *Van Gogh's Room at Arles: Three Novellas* (1992); and *Mrs. Ted Bliss* (1995). A study is Peter Bailey, *Reading Stanley Elkin* (1995).

PATRICK O'DONNELL

Ellery Queen. See QUEEN, ELLERY.

Elliot, Sarah Barnwell (1848–1928), novelist. Georgia-born, Elliot lived and wrote in Tennessee. Her works include *Jerry* (1891), *The Felmeres* (1879), *A Simple Heart* (1887), *John Paget* (1893), and *The Dark Sperret* (1898).

Elliott, George P[aul] (1918–1980), novelist, short-story writer. Born in Indiana, Elliott was educated at the University of California, Berkeley and taught writing at Cornell, Barnard, Syracuse, and other schools. His novels are *Parktilden Village* (1958), dealing with a sociologist and a California housing development; *David Knudsen* (1962), about the son of a scientist who worked on the atomic bomb; *In the World* (1965), about a dissatisfied law professor; and *Muriel* (1972). His short stories are collected in *Among the Dangs* (1961),

whose title story is his most acclaimed single work, and *An Hour of Last Things* (1968). His other titles include *From the Berkeley Hills* (1969), poems; and two collections of essays, *A Piece of Lettuce* (1964) and *Conversions* (1971).

Elliott, Maud Howe (1854–1948), historian, biographer, author of travel books. Born in Boston, the youngest of Julia Ward Howe's daughters was a social and civic leader in Newport, Rhode Island, where she lived for many years. She met the notables of several generations, married an English painter, and devoted several of her books to chronicling her times. She campaigned for women's rights and for Theodore Roosevelt. Her best-known book is a biography of her mother, *The Life and Letters of Julia Ward Howe* (2 v. 1916), written in collaboration with her sisters LAURA ELIZABETH RICHARDS and FLORENCE HOWE HALL. It received a Pulitzer Prize. Among her other books are *A Newport Aquarelle* (1883); *Laura Bridgman* (with Mrs. Hall, 1902); *Three Generations* (1923); *Uncle Sam Ward and His Circle* (1938); and *This Was My Newport* (1944).

Ellis, Bret Easton (1964–   ), novelist. Born in Los Angeles, Ellis was educated at Bennington College in Vermont. *Less Than Zero* (1985), his first novel, concerns the rich youth of L.A. coming back from Eastern colleges to the parties, cars, and drugs they left behind. Though its publication caused considerable stir, his third novel was even more controversial. When pre-publication publicity indicated that Patrick Bateman, the first-person narrator of *American Psycho*, was a Wall Street broker by day and serial rapist, murderer, and cannibal by night, Simon and Schuster, who had given the author a large advance, cancelled the project. Vintage published it in 1991. Other titles are *The Rules of Attraction* (1987), set in a small liberal arts college; *The Informers* (1994), again set in L.A.; and *Glamarama* (1999), a satirical look at the dark side of the fashion industry.

Ellis, Edward S[ylvester] (1840–1916), teacher, novelist, historian. Ellis was one of the most successful of the dime novelists (see DIME NOVELS). His SETH JONES (1860) sold 450,000 copies on its original publication, thereafter became a standard in various dime and half-dime libraries. Later Ellis wrote a six-volume illustrated *History of the United States* (1896) that was sold by subscription all over the country. He wrote his dime novels under seven pseudonyms.

Ellis Island. In 1892 Ellis Island replaced Castle Garden as a receiving station for immigrants. Two more islands were created, in 1898 and 1905, by filling in nearby places; all three are now connected by causeways and are virtually one island. In earlier days the Dutch used the island (then called Oyster Island) as a picnic ground; later it was called Gibbet Island after the pirate Anderson was hanged there in 1765. Still later it was bought by a New Jersey merchant, who gave it its present name. For many years it was the headquarters of the Immigration and Naturalization District of southern New York and northern New Jersey, through which many hundreds of thousands of European immigrants passed between 1892 and 1943. In 1965 it became a part of the Statue of Liberty National Monument.

Ellison, Harlan (1934–   ),   short-story writer, novelist. Born in Cleveland, Ellison left Ohio State University for a career as a writer, employing many pseudonyms for his hundreds of short stories, novels, and television and movie scripts. Early classified as a science fiction writer, he has preferred the term "magic realism" as more accurate for fantasies sometimes reminiscent of Poe, sometimes of John Barth or Kurt Vonnegut. Among his numerous collections of short stories are the *Deadly Streets* (1958), *Gentleman Junkie* (1961), *Paingod, and Other Delusions* (1965), *I Have No Mouth and I Must Scream* (1967), *The Beast That Shouted Love at the Heart of the World* (1969), *Alone Against Tomorrow* (1971), *Deathbird Stories* (1975), *Strange Wine* (1978), *Shatterday* (1980), *Angry Candy* (1989), *Slippage* (1994), and *"Repent, Harlequin!" Said the Ticktockman: The Classic Story*, illus. by Rick Berry (1997). His novels include *Rumble* (1958, as *Web of the City* 1975); *Rockabilly* (1961, as *Spider Kiss* 1975); *Demon with a Glass Hand* (1967); *All the Lies That Are My Life* (1980); and *Mefisto in Onyx* (1993).

Ellison, Ralph [Waldo] (1914–1994),   novelist, essayist. Replying to questions of interviewers and drafting his own impressive essays on the sources of his work. Ralph Ellison characteristically emphasized the creative potential of cultural pluralism. In "The Little Man at Chehaw Station," for example, he tells of his meeting with coal heavers who spoke in the idiom of formally uneducated Afro-American working men, but who employed their vernacular to discuss operatic technique with an expertise gained from years of experience as extras at the Metropolitan Opera. The experience remains fresh for Ellison, illuminating as though in a great American joke "the incongruities of race, economic status, and culture" that must lead one to appreciate "the arcane ways of American cultural possibility." Besides indicating Ellison's conviction that Americans must acknowledge that their culture is an amalgam, the anecdote also confirmed his sense that he led a representative American life.

Born in Oklahoma City a few years after the territory became a state, Ellison was reared in social circumstances nearer to the fluid arrangements of the frontier than to the rigid caste system the sizable population of black migrants had left behind in the Old South. Among the role models available, it was the outlaw jazz musicians who impressed him most, their improvisational art expressing both idealized individualism and the collectivity of the musicians in a jam session repeating the past history and revising the present performance of a tune. Not surprisingly, when he entered Tuskeegee Institute in 1933 he intended to study classical music, conceived by Ellison then as the means to a creative state of being in which he would be another Richard Wagner composing a major symphony before he was twenty-six.

A continuing need for money and the chance to study sculpture soon took him to New York City, another opportunity for the play of imagination on the theme of potentiality. In 1937 he met RICHARD WRIGHT, who asked him to write a review and then some fiction for *New Challenge* magazine. Probably it was Wright who guided Ellison into left-wing pol-

itics, which permitted an apprenticeship in such publications as NEW MASSES. Some of Ellison's stories in *New Masses* suggest in their portrayal of young protagonists the education theme of INVISIBLE MAN, but the gestation of the novel continued through the wartime years, when Ellison abandoned a book-length project and worked at the conception of invisibility and the writing of antiheroic episodes. Near the end of this period he published two of his best stories, "Flying Home" and "King of the Bingo Game," before turning in earnest to the novel in 1945 and struggling with it for the years remaining until its appearance in 1952. Soon after publication, *Invisible Man* entered the canon of most frequently taught and cited American novels. It has been the cause also of a continuing flow of critical discussion, reflecting changes in Ellison's reputation, but confirming its importance.

Although portions of a second novel appeared in periodicals, the whole has not been published. Ellison's stories were collected after his death in *Flying Home and Other Stories* (1996), edited by John F. Callahan. The essays in *Shadow and Act* (1964) and *Going to the Territory* (1986) kept before his audience Ellison's irrepressible interest in the materials of America's diverse culture that he believed provided the sources of identity, art, and democracy itself.

JOHN M. REILLY/BP

Elmer Gantry (1927),   a novel by SINCLAIR LEWIS. The novel deals with a brazen ex-football player, Elmer Gantry, who enters the ministry and, through half-plagiarized sermons, physical attractiveness, and an unerring instinct for promotion, becomes a successful evangelist and later the leader of a large Midwestern church. A film based on the book appeared in 1960.

Elsie Dinsmore.   See DINSMORE, ELSIE.

Elsie Venner: A Romance of Destiny (1861),   a novel by OLIVER WENDELL HOLMES. It was originally published, like so much else of Holmes's work, in *The Atlantic Monthly* as a serial (beginning December 1859), and was called *The Professor's Story*. Although subtitled "a romance," the story is in reality a strange but effective mixture: a series of discursive descriptions and characters, an analysis of New England traits and ideas, an allegory illustrating Holmes's views on predestination and free will, and an anticipation of modern mental hygiene and psychiatry. The heroine's mother was bitten by a snake, so Elsie is born with a strong serpent complex—half-snake, half-woman. Whether Holmes had any confidence in this sort of superstition or not is immaterial. He posits it as a condition of his story: to what extent can Elsie overcome the condition into which she was born? She falls in love with Bernard Langdon, who does not care for her, even after she saves his life when he is bitten by a rattlesnake. When Bernard rejects her, she becomes ill and dies.

Emancipation Proclamation, The.   As early as July 22, 1862, Lincoln submitted to his cabinet the draft of a proclamation freeing the slaves as a military measure. The cabinet members all concurred in the necessity for such a measure, but Seward urged that it be withheld until the North had won some kind of victory. Then came the victory at Antietam on September 17, and on September 22 the Emancipation Proclamation appeared, announcing to the three million slaves in the country that if their masters were still in rebellion on January 1, 1863, they should regard themselves as free. Slaves in the border states or parts of them that were not in rebellion were not freed by the proclamation. But as Northern armies captured a region, the slaves were manumitted. The slaves in Confederate territory were not greatly affected by the proclamation—there were no rebellions and perhaps Lincoln neither contemplated nor desired any such result. The London *Spectator* commented: "The principle is not that a human being cannot justly own another, but that he cannot own him unless he is loyal to the United States." Only with the Thirteenth Amendment to the Constitution, ratified December 18, 1865, were slaves in all parts of the United States freed.

Emerson, Ralph Waldo (1803–1882),   essayist, poet, philosopher. Most literary historians acknowledge Ralph Waldo Emerson as a seminal figure in American literature. Those attracted to Emerson's style see in his loosely structured prose and poetry the inauguration of an American tradition of prophesy, leading from the exuberant affirmations of Walt Whitman to the measured meditations of such modern masters as Wallace Stevens and John Ashbery. Those less impressed have identified in his moral philosophy—especially his individualistic doctrine of self-reliance—the beginning of American commercialism and political isolationism. Yet, in their haste to lay at Emerson's feet the praise (or blame) for contemporary society, critics often undervalue the meaning of Emerson's work in its own time and culture.

Emerson was born in Boston on May 25, 1803, the fourth child of an old and respected, though not wealthy, New England family. His father, William, was minister at the prestigious First Church in Boston, the sixth generation of Emersons to serve as ministers. William preached a soothing doctrine of liberal Christian humanism and literary sophistication similar to that which others of his generation would later formulate as UNITARIANISM. At home William and his wife, Ruth Haskins Emerson, provided a stable though frugal and strict home life for their eight children, of whom three died in infancy. The family's financial situation was aggravated by the father's declining health after 1808, ending in his death three years later. During those years Emerson's relation to his father seems to have been troubled, though perhaps not more so than might be expected from any boy in his situation.

The central figure of these early years was Emerson's paternal aunt, Mary Moody Emerson, who after the father's death moved in with the family to help Ruth raise the children and run the boardinghouse that supplemented their meager income. Aunt Mary was intellectually more aggressive than her older brother William. Theologically she rejected the blandness of liberal Christianity for the greater rigor of New Light Calvinism. More generally she identified with the new views of the Romantic age, particularly those of Mary Wollstonecraft, Madame de Staël, and the Scottish Common Sense philosophers. Aunt Mary's relations with her nephew were not always

even. His theology occasionally struck her as heretical, and in his later characterizations Emerson tended to emphasize her personal quirks more than her intellectual influence. But in both the inquisitiveness of her mind and the intensity of her beliefs she clearly stood as Emerson's chief mentor throughout his adolescence and college days.

Emerson's schooling was traditional for someone of his social standing. In 1812 he began to prepare for college at the Boston Public Latin School. Five years later, at fourteen, he entered Harvard, the youngest member of his class. Although his older brother William had a distinguished record at the college—as would his younger brothers Edward and Charles— Emerson's own performance was more commonplace. He twice won a second place in the Bowdoin essay competition and was named class poet—after six classmates had refused the honor. He was graduated in the middle of his class, thirtieth out of a total of fifty-nine.

More important than any specific academic achievements was the informal education, both intellectual and emotional, that would occupy him throughout the rest of his life. During his junior year he began to keep the journals that supplied material for many of his publications. In his last two years at Harvard, he was introduced to new European thought in the classes of EDWARD EVERETT and GEORGE TICKNOR. These were supplemented in his senior year by Professor Levi Frisbie's course in moral philosophy, which served as his formal introduction to, among others, Dugald Stewart and Richard Price (both prized by Aunt Mary) and formed the basis of his second Bowdoin essay. Finally, during these college years Emerson experienced the first of many intense and unsuccessful friendships, a two-year infatuation with a younger student, Martin Gay. The two men seem rarely to have spoken, and the homosexual dimension of this undergraduate crush should not be overstated. But the uncertainty and sexual ambivalence of Emerson's response to Gay would reappear in his personal relationships throughout his adult life.

Although ambivalent about his education at Harvard, in 1825 Emerson gave up teaching at a girls' school to return there, this time to the Divinity School to prepare for a career in the ministry. Various illnesses interrupted this training, but he was approbated to preach in 1826 and served widely as a guest minister until called to the pulpit of the Second Church in Boston in 1829. During this same period, while serving as a visiting preacher in New Hampshire, he fell in love with Ellen Tucker. Although nervous about Ellen's ill health, Emerson became engaged to her a year later and they were married in the fall of 1829.

This early happiness was relatively brief. Never strong, Ellen became seriously ill after six months of marriage and died early in 1831. The emotional strain on Emerson was great and long-lasting, so much so that a year after her death he reopened Ellen's coffin in an attempt to deal with his grief. Moreover, he found his religious duties increasingly onerous. Although he enjoyed the literary activities of writing and delivering sermons, his pastoral duties were more taxing. Especially unpleasant were the formalized aspects of the service. This difficulty came to a head when Emerson asked to be relieved of celebrating the sacrament of the Lord's Supper, a ritual with which he found little sympathy. In 1832 the elders voted regretfully to sever Emerson's relation to the church, although continuing to pay his salary through the end of the year. With that remaining salary, he sailed to Europe on Christmas morning for a nine-month stay.

Emerson's European tour is often read as the start of his new career as philosopher and bard. Unimpressed by some of the writers he met—especially Walter Savage Landor, Coleridge, and Wordsworth—Emerson became instant friends with the iconoclastic Thomas Carlyle, whose masterwork *Sartor Resartus* Emerson would publish three years later. More invigorating even than the Germanic spiritualism taught by Carlyle was the occult interrelation between man and the natural world Emerson saw illustrated on his visits to the Musée Nationale d'Histoire Naturelle and the Jardin des Plantes in Paris.

On his return to America in October 1833, Emerson began to forge a new career as lecturer, essayist, and poet. The settlement of Ellen's estate in 1834 ensured him an annual income about two-thirds of his former salary at the Second Church. Emerson supplemented this inheritance with fees from his guest sermons, preaching almost every Sunday after his return. In late 1833, he began to deliver informational lectures on natural history (based on his discoveries in the Jardin des Plantes), and by early 1835 was offering lecture series—first on "Biography" and later on such topics as "The Philosophy of History," "The Times," and "The Conduct of Life." This lecturing career became sufficiently lucrative that in 1839 Emerson delivered his last (recorded) sermon.

During these years Emerson also began to associate with the Boston and Concord intellectuals with whom he would be historically linked in the "Transcendentalist" movement. In 1835 he married Lydia ("Lidian") Jackson and moved to a house in Concord. Among the most eccentric of the many guests the newlyweds received was BRONSON ALCOTT, a self-taught Platonist whose pedagogic methods caused a scandal in the following year at his Temple School in Boston. Also a frequent visitor was ELIZABETH PALMER PEABODY, another educator, and soon to become Alcott's amanuensis (and Nathaniel Hawthorne's sister-in-law) and whose Boston bookstore would be a clearing house for the "new views." Later, in 1836, Emerson met MARGARET FULLER, the feminist and journalist with whom he had a long and tempestuous relationship both professional and personal. Finally, sometime in 1837, there appeared HENRY DAVID THOREAU, a Concord neighbor who in this early stage of his career was Emerson's chief disciple. These friends, along with Emerson's more orthodox Harvard classmates, constituted the core of what came to be called the TRANSCENDENTAL CLUB, a group that met irregularly at Emerson's home and elsewhere to discuss topics of general interest, primarily in philosophy, literature, and moral theology.

In September 1836, a few weeks before the first meeting of the Transcendental Club, Emerson published his first work—the brief book NATURE. Rejecting the retrospective quality of his tradition-bound culture, Emerson encouraged readers to build their own worlds, arguing that the natural world itself taught this need for spiritual reformation. Although not commercially successful, the book became notorious, arousing the contempt of conservatives, who read its enthusiasm as a sign of the degeneracy of youth, and the admiration of the rebels, who embraced it as a credo, albeit a flawed one. It is still a matter of debate whether Emerson adequately represented the interests of all the Transcendentalists, or even how coherent TRANSCENDENTALISM as a movement was. Whatever the relation of *Nature* to Transcendentalism, the book was a forceful individual statement. In it Emerson dealt indirectly with a host of family tragedies: the deaths of his brother Edward in 1834 and especially of Charles in 1836; the continuing institutionalization of a third brother, Bulkeley and, more generally, the sense of personal inadequacy that had plagued him since his school years. Intellectually the book was Emerson's demonstration of his philosophical maturity, the entering wedge with which he introduced his characteristic concerns. And critical debates about Emerson's idiosyncratic mix of literary styles and voices commence with the divisions of this perplexing text—whose overelaborate analytic core is surrounded by a rhapsodic preface and epilogue.

Throughout the late 1830s Emerson continued to find himself at the center of controversy in Boston, largely because of his reputation as chief spokesman for the Transcendentalists. While still recovering from the numerous attacks on himself and his friend Alcott in 1836, Emerson was in 1837 invited back to Harvard to address Phi Beta Kappa, an academic society to which he had not been elected in college. His lecture—later published as THE AMERICAN SCHOLAR—announced America's independence from the outworn literary modes of Europe and suggested as a model the scholar Emanuel Swedenborg, an 18th-century religious mystic who had figured prominently in *Nature*. Although the lecture's exhortations to "self-trust" were as antiestablishment as the prophecies of the earlier book, the apparent nationalism of Emerson's literary vision spoke to a cultural climate dominated economically by the Panic of 1837 and politically by the expansionist rhetoric of manifest destiny. Dr. Oliver Wendell Holmes declared the essay "our intellectual Declaration of Independence," and the published version sold well.

In the following year Emerson was invited by the Harvard Divinity students to speak (unofficially) on the eve of their graduation. The resulting DIVINITY SCHOOL ADDRESS in July 1838 caused the greatest scandal of his career. Emerson stepped precipitately into the middle of an acrimonious debate about the importance of Christ's miracles—whether Christ's extraordinary acts were essential evidence of His divinity (as older Unitarians like Professor Andrews Norton taught) or whether no historical event could prove the inner truth of spirituality (as argued the younger ministers such as Emerson's friend GEORGE RIPLEY). Emerson dismissed the subtleties of the controversy by attacking established Christianity as merely historical. Expanding on his earlier rejection of the Lord's Supper, he insisted that a preoccupation with the biographical details of Christ's life was a form of superstitiousness, even idolatry. Christ should be worshiped not as the unique Son of God but merely as an example of the divinity attainable to all men and women.

Emerson's attacks on tradition in *Nature*, "The American Scholar," and the Divinity School "Address" were of a piece with the individualistic spirit of the age. His philosophical emphasis on the meaning of perception was more fully his own. Drawing upon Plato, Plotinus, and the Scottish Common Sense philosophers, Emerson judged contemporary models of the mind too mechanical, unable to explain the existence of human feelings. In the transcendental idealism of the German philosopher Immanuel Kant (whose work he probably knew only indirectly), Emerson found proof that the mind (or Me) was superior to the material world (or Not Me), which was known only through the filter of that mind. For Kant, the mind was not enslaved to the tyranny of sensation, as it had been for previous philosophers like Locke and Hume; instead, our experience of things (as perceptions) was determined by the structure of the mind. Far from being a passive tablet on which nature wrote, mind, or self, actively recorded and organized sensory data; and this shaping and processing of sensation made experiences perceivable in the first place.

From Kant's demonstration of the priority of mind, Emerson evolved an argument for the divinity of thought. *Nature* examined the spiritual implications of the Kantian argument that no external reality was experienced apart from the mind without first being thought or structured by that mind. Any experience (for example, "there is a tree in the courtyard") assumed the presence of an experiencer (an unstated "I think"). This omnipresence of the perceiving Me carried with it both great power and a moral imperative. Not only could man, if he wished, assert his supremacy over the material world and make disagreeable appearances vanish, but the redemption of modern society required that we align our perceptual axis of vision with reality, conforming our lives to the pure idea in our minds.

The two later essays considered the literary and moral implications of the supremacy of the Me over the Not Me. In "The American Scholar," thought was itself an activity, self-trust a necessary prelude to thought, and all deeds approximations of a former ideal state where thoughts and actions had been unified in a cosmic unity called the One Man. In the Divinity School "Address," rejecting the suggestion of the Common Sense philosophers that morality was a kind of sixth sense, Emerson concluded (again following Kant) that virtue was an absolute obligation. People were not good for any reason; if they were, that very reasonableness would make their goodness merely prudent. Instead virtue was something that had to be done for its own sake: an imperative "I ought" implicitly accompanied every virtuous idea just as the subjective "I think" implicitly accompanied every experience.

The youthful muscularity of these intellectual essays of the 1830s gave way in the 1840s to the more free-form meditative character of the works that Emerson collected in his two series of ESSAYS. In part his new tone and subject matter reflected the

growing political consciousness of Transcendentalism. The broad cultural overviews of the 1830s were superseded in the 1840s by more precise critiques of specific social injustices, for example, Fuller's campaigns for women's equality or Thoreau's for abolition. Ripley withdrew from theological debate and the church to found a communitarian reform movement at BROOK FARM, a 19th-century precursor of the 20th century's communes and kibbutzim. And in 1840, the Transcendentalists decided to make their own private conversations more public with the publication of a journal, THE DIAL.

Emerson was less involved in political movements than some Transcendentalists. Although Brook Farm was intended in part to answer his call for spiritual reform in "The American Scholar," Emerson refused Ripley's invitation to live at the commune. While continuing to promote Thoreau's writing, Emerson was less supportive of his political activities and (reputedly) displeased by Thoreau's night in jail. Similarly Fuller's feminist activity, along with her unwelcome emotional demands, led Emerson to distance himself from her after 1840. Emerson did participate actively in the *Dial*, which he edited with Fuller from 1840 to 1842, and then alone for two more years. Yet his need to distinguish his own focus from that of the others became increasingly apparent, especially in his lecture on the Transcendentalists in his series on "The Times" (1841–42).

In the 1840s Emerson moved in different directions than his friends; however, his work like theirs responded to the changes in the political climate. In such lecture series as "The Present Age" (1839–40) and "The Times," Emerson showed an explicit desire to address directly the condition of contemporary culture. His general essays also evidenced his growing discomfort with his earlier abstract formulations. Most obvious was the change in style. The early pieces were exhortative and, especially in the case of *Nature*, elaborately structured as logical arguments. The new essays were less oracular in tone, ruminative rather than assertive, and more likely to make their points through paradox and ironic juxtaposition than through proof or prophecy. It was this new, more characteristic style that would lead some auditors and readers to describe Emerson's work as "pure tone" and others to claim wrongly that though able to write sentences, Emerson had difficulty organizing his thoughts into paragraphs or arguments.

His themes changed as well, becoming less optimistic and more personal. In his *Essays: First Series* (1841), he continued to argue for the presence of a Universal Mind underwriting man's relation to nature, and some pieces, like the bombastic THE OVER-SOUL, recycled earlier enthusiasms with less conviction. More characteristic of the series, however, was his desire to situate universal truths within social reality. In works like "History," "Love," and "Friendship," Emerson discussed political and interpersonal relationships, though too abstractly for the tastes of some readers. More immediate was his account in "Circles," where the abstract metaphor of concentric circles introduced a pessimistic vision of universal flux—especially in terms of Emerson's personal experiences of the inconstancy of temperament and infrequency of inspiration.

But the real center of this first series was SELF-RELIANCE,

Emerson's most famous essay and his most criticized. The essay seemed to revive the earlier optimism about the invincibility of the soul while at the same time denying the importance of social cooperation, which it rejected as a conspiracy against the manhood of the individual. In fact the essay reconsidered that earlier faith in self-trust with great skepticism. Emerson, of course, continued to question the value of conformity to society's rules and even consistency to one's own self-image. Yet self-reliance as a form of nonconformity or inconsistency was less a goal to be pursued than an inevitable result of what it meant to be a self. No man could violate his own nature, for the common excuse that "I was not myself when I did that" made no precise sense. "Self" was simply the name for all one's thoughts and activities, and self-reliance was not some special thing one should do, but by definition whatever one did.

Essays: Second Series (1844) continued this concern with the social implications of subjectivity, focusing on issues of variety and otherness—finally of "world"—as they related to the unifying tendency of the perceiving self. In the relatively early essay on "The Poet" (perhaps intended for the first series), Emerson repeated the familiar Romantic trope that the poet was a bard, recapturing the poetic origin of language by reattaching words to things, much as did Adam in the Garden of Eden. The other essays of the series, however, were less optimistic about man's ability to know absolute truth. "Politics," "Gifts," "Character," and the second "Nature" all treated from different angles the inadequacy of universal categories or generalizing principles. And even the light-hearted "Nominalist and Realist" rejected the universalizing tendency of the mind as one of the sillier forms of human egotism: "Nature will not be Buddhist. . . . Nick Bottom cannot play all the parts, work it how he may: there will be somebody else, and the world will be round."

But Emerson's most extended criticism of his former abstractions was the grim masterpiece "Experience." Growing out of the personal trauma Emerson had suffered two years earlier at the death of his five-year-old son, the essay reconsidered the subjectivism of the first *Nature*. The power of the Me, which then had seemed deifying, now felt like the fall of man. The discovery that everything was perceived through the possibly distorting lenses of human subjectivity made it impossible to believe in the absolute reality of any truth—even so bleak a truth as the undeniable grief felt at the death of one's child. The world of the Not Me, which earlier had seemed uninteresting compared with the subjective Me, he now acknowledged contained much—like beliefs and emotions—that one valued. Yet these valuable experiences were liable to "vanish" or "tumble in" to an omnivorous Self, which seemed as empty and uninteresting as it was powerful, "great and crescive."

The solemn conclusions of "Experience" marked a turning point in Emerson's philosophical career. Throughout his early years he had celebrated the divine potential of the human mind. Truth had appeared axiomatic or self-evident, less a measure of the accuracy of man's representations and deductions than the mark of his mind's direct access to the universal and ideal. Now, however, the unifying potential of the Me

seemed to shut people off from reality, locking them in the very solipsistic "labyrinth of the mind" that Emerson had feared in *Nature*. His solution was to admit defeat honestly. Having tried, like Kant, to deduce something about absolute truth from the structure of the mind, Emerson in "Experience" accepted that his conclusions, however correct logically, could not tell him the kinds of things he wanted to know. Epistemology, or the theory of knowledge, which had been his main focus throughout these most productive years of his career, had led him to a dead end of "bleak rocks." And with the intellectual courage that characterized his work throughout, Emerson began to look elsewhere.

After about 1845, Emerson's career took a number of new turns. Professionally he became more successful. The publication of his *Poems* in 1846 yielded a small income, and both REPRESENTATIVE MEN (1850) and ENGLISH TRAITS (1856) sold better than the volumes of essays. More important, his lectures were increasingly profitable. After a triumphant visit to Europe in 1847–48, Emerson on his return to America augmented both the number and scope of his lecturing engagements. In 1850 and the winter of 1852–53, he undertook extensive Western tours to great acclaim. Perhaps the best mark of Emerson's established reputation, however, was Walt Whitman's decision in 1856 to print Emerson's praise (in gold) on the cover of his second edition of *Leaves of Grass*.

With growing fame Emerson seemed more willing to engage in political debate. He had never been as apolitical as some of his otherworldly statements suggested. In 1838, he had protested the confiscation of Cherokee lands in a public letter to President Martin Van Buren. Yet, in the early years Emerson tended to argue that the pursuit of specific political goals distracted from his more important project of personal self-reformation. Political aloofness became less possible after 1850, however, when the Fugitive Slave Law institutionalized Northern cooperation with slavery by requiring all states to return escaped slaves to their Southern masters. Emerson spoke against the law twice, at Concord in 1851 and more publicly at New York in 1854. He also spoke in favor of women's equality and against the execution of the radical abolitionist JOHN BROWN.

Yet with the success of middle age came a loss in literary vitality. Emerson's poems, collected in 1846 but written through his life, were uneven. His innovative use of rhyme and meter startled his contemporaries, who were accustomed to the more regular cadences of Bryant and Longfellow. Some—like "Uriel," the ODE INSCRIBED TO W. H. CHANNING, and THRENODY—were compelling poetic renderings of ideas familiar from the essays. And some—like "Hamatreya," "Bacchus," and MERLIN—experimented with a kind of prophetic poetry that became more familiar and better controlled in later works by Whitman and Stevens. Yet critics continue to feel that Emerson fulfilled his poetic principles more consistently in his prose style and theoretical statements than in his actual poems.

A similar falling off could be seen in the later essays. Emerson never wrote less than beautifully, and much prose published after 1845 was compelling and engaging. The tension that made the early pieces so vibrant, however, was less in evidence. *English Traits*, the account of his second trip to Europe, was perhaps his most polished work. As a travel narrative, however, it displayed little of Emerson's characteristic intellectual and moral intensity. Even *Representative Men*, his 1850 version of lectures delivered over the preceding five years, seemed less conclusive than earlier pieces. Surprisingly, Emerson now found a "use" for the kind of greatness in others that he felt in "Self-Reliance" conspired against our own greatness. Exactly what that use was remained unclear. The individual character sketches were often highly critical, especially of Emerson's former idol Swedenborg. And the most successful essay, "Montaigne; or, the Skeptic," celebrated a man who distrusted the very notions of greatness and representativeness the series pretended to affirm.

Only in the collection THE CONDUCT OF LIFE (1860), and especially its grim introductory essay on "Fate," did Emerson recapture his earlier intellectual intensity. His question was no longer the epistemological one of "how do I know?" but the practical one of "how shall I live?" To counteract America's "bad name for superficialness" (and his own), Emerson admitted the sentimentality of his earlier descriptions of nature and presented as apology an almost gleeful catalogue of natural savagery. Yet this brave admission turned in the essay's final pages into one more celebration of blessed unity and beautiful necessity. Just as "self" meant merely "whoever one is," so "fate" or "conduct" meant simply "whatever is done." And to the question of how man shall live, he answered, "As he can." There was no more a standard for conduct than there was for perception. Without any external absolute against which to measure the accuracy of our acts (or perceptions), "fate" (or "experience") became simply the name for the whole system, in which man had to continue as best he could.

In Emerson's final years, he was honored widely as the Sage of Concord, the most original American philosopher of the 19th century. In the late 1860s he was awarded an honorary degree by Harvard and elected to its Board of Overseers. In 1867 he once again delivered a Phi Beta Kappa address, thirty years after "The American Scholar." And in 1870 he was invited to offer a series of sixteen (non-credit) lectures in philosophy—"Natural History of Intellect"—at the same Harvard that had formerly declared him a mediocre intellect and a rebel. He traveled widely: in 1871 to California, where he lectured successfully and met the future naturalist JOHN MUIR; and to Europe and Egypt in 1872–73. Yet his publications after 1860—*Society and Solitude* (1870), *Letters and Social Aims* (1975), and the posthumous *Miscellanies and Natural History of Intellect*—were largely compilations of earlier work, sometimes heavily edited by James Elliot Cabot. In his final years Emerson suffered increasingly from aphasia, poignantly unable to remember Longfellow's name at the poet's funeral. He himself died on April 27, 1882.

The controversies surrounding Emerson question his tone, his style, his depth, and his politics. Closer examination of the late pessimistic essays, like "Experience," "Montaigne," and "Fate," and fuller consideration of the emotional turmoil of his early years have largely overturned objections to what was once felt to be Emerson's excessive optimism. Attacks on his epigrammatic style have also abated, as readers became more aware of the structures of his paragraphs and even essays.

In another sense, however, the apparent discontinuity of Emerson's prose no longer even counts as a stylistic or intellectual weakness. Since Nietzsche, himself deeply indebted to Emerson, philosophers have avoided the ponderous system-building of the German idealists in favor of a fragmented playful prose strongly reminiscent of Emerson's own. Recent philosophers like Wittgenstein and Derrida have taught us to question the very possibility of consistency. So too have modern poets and fiction writers made a stylistic virtue of discontinuity. This postmodern fascination with contradiction and incongruity has resulted in a reevaluation of Emerson's supposed deficiencies. Some critics have even gone so far as to celebrate Emerson's unpublished journals as a deconstructive masterpiece, the great *roman-fleuve* of American romanticism, comparable to the artistic autobiographies of Wordsworth, Joyce, and Proust.

Only in terms of the political implications of his philosophy is Emerson still occasionally criticized. The canonization of Emerson did celebrate his most traditional beliefs, values that today can seem isolationist and even elitist. And it is true that his doctrine of self-reliance was used after his death to support a conservative policy of laissez-faire economics. The man who became an American institution, the Sage of Concord whose name still graces the hall at Harvard, this mythic Emerson may have unwittingly lent his prestige to these misreadings. But the real man—the tortured, mercurial mind of the early essays—represented the best in American antitraditionalism. And if Emerson has subsequently been tamed and sentimentalized, we need only return to the original texts and the historical contexts in which they were generated to appreciate the power of a truly creative and rebellious intellect.

The Collected Works (1971–), in progress under the editorship of Robert Spiller, Alfred Ferguson, et al., will supersede *The Complete Works* (12 v. 1903–04), ed. Edward Waldo Emerson. *The Journals and Miscellaneous Notebooks* (16 v. 1960–82) was edited by William Gilman et al. *The Letters* (6 v. 1939) was edited by Ralph L. Rusk. Also of interest are *Young Emerson Speaks: Unpublished Discourses on Many Subjects* (1938), sermons edited by Arthur Cushman McGiffert, Jr.; and *The Early Lectures* (3 v. 1959–72), edited by Stephen Whicher et al. Biographies are Ralph L. Rusk, *The Life of Ralph Waldo Emerson* (1957); Gay Wilson Allen, *Waldo Emerson* (1981); Evelyn Barish, *Emerson: The Roots of Prophecy* (1989); and Robert D. Richardson, Jr., *Emerson: The Mind on Fire* (1995). Studies include Stephen Whicher, *Freedom and Fate: An Inner Life of Ralph Waldo Emerson* (1953); Jonathan Bishop, *Emerson on the Soul* (1964); David Porter, *Emerson and Literary Change* (1978); Joel Porte, *Representative Man: Ralph Waldo Emerson in His Time* (1979); Julie Ellison, *Emerson's Romantic Style* (1984); David Van Leer, *Emerson's Episto-*

mology: *The Argument of the Essays* (1986); Lawrence Rosenwald, *Emerson and the Art of the Diary* (1988). See BRAHMA, COMPENSATION, DAYS, EACH AND ALL, THE HUMBLE-BEE, THE RHODORA, SAADI, and VOLUNTARIES.

DAVID VAN LEER

Emigrants, The [1] (translated from the Norwegian, 1925),   a novel by Johan Bojer (1872–1959). Bojer's story relates the trials and eventual triumphs of a group of Norwegian immigrants in the Dakota Territory.

Emigrants, The [2] (1951),   a novel by Vilhelm Moberg (1898–1973). In this story, the Swedish novelist recounts the adventures of a group of migrants who find in America a land free of masters. It was followed by *Unto a Good Land* (1954) and *The Last Letter Home* (1961).

Emigrants, The, or, The History of an Expatriated Family (1793),   a novel by Captain GILBERT IMLAY. This story of an English family removed to the Pennsylvania border is a highly romanticized account of frontier life and a glorification of the Indian.

Emma and Eginhard (1872, published in TALES OF A WAYSIDE INN, Part Three, 1873),   a narrative poem by Henry Wadsworth Longfellow. A king's daughter outwits her father's supervision but is forgiven by him. Longfellow took the story from an old chronicle, *De Factis Caroli Magni*, as it was repeated in a lecture by Charles Perkins (Longfellow's *Diary*, May 12, 1872).

Emmett, Daniel Decatur (1815–1904),   minstrel, songwriter. Emmett wrote the song DIXIE (1860) and both the words and music of the popular songs "Old Dan Tucker" (1843) and "My Old Aunt Sally" (1843). Other songs generally attributed to him are "Jordan Is a Hard Road to Travel" (1853) and "The Blue-Tail Fly" (also called "Jimmy Crack Corn" 1846). After working with a circus he organized the Virginia Minstrels in 1842, a new type of vaudeville that survived for many decades. (See MINSTREL SHOWS.) In 1857 he joined the Bryant Minstrels, for whom he wrote "Dixie." After the war he again organized a troupe of his own.

Emperor Jones, The (produced, 1920; published, 1921), a play by EUGENE O'NEILL. O'Neill lays the scene of the play "on an island in the West Indies [presumably Haiti] as yet un-self-determined by white marines." On this island a former Pullman car porter, Brutus Jones, has made himself emperor. He is wanted in the States on two murder charges. But on the island he is a contemptuous monarch, looting the blacks and secure in his confidence that he can be killed only by a silver bullet. At last the natives rebel and Jones is obliged to flee to the jungle. He encounters phantoms from the past, circles the jungle, and is finally killed by his subjects—with silver bullets as he had predicted. In this play O'Neill began to create new techniques or to revive old ones he found useful. The chief character is a twisted, warped, and lost soul; the movement of the play is a cunning and subtle interweaving of the physical and the psychological. The steady beat of tomtoms throughout the jungle scenes has as powerful an effect on the audience as it has on Jones.

According to an interview in the *New York World* (November 9, 1924), O'Neill got the idea for the play from an old circus man who told him a story about a former president of Haiti who predicted no one would ever kill him with a lead bullet—he'd get himself first with a silver one. A year later he read something about a religious dance in the Congo, and the play was born. O'Neill was also influenced by Henri Christophe, the slave-born general who helped free Haiti from the French in 1811 and who called himself King Henry I. The play took New York by storm and had to be moved from a small theater on Macdougal Street (the Provincetown Theatre) to an uptown theater. The play was made into an opera (1933) by Louis Gruenberg (libretto by Kathleen de Jaffa) and produced a sensation at the Metropolitan with Lawrence Tibbett as Jones. It became a movie in the same year, the title role played by Paul Robeson.

Emporia Gazette, The.   A newspaper published and edited at Emporia, Kansas, by WILLIAM ALLEN WHITE from 1895 until his death. His son, William L. White, carried on the paper thereafter.

Encantadas, The, or, The Enchanted Isles   (first published serially in *Putnam's Monthly* in 1854 under the pen name Salvator R. Tarnmoor; later included in PIAZZA TALES, 1856), ten sketches by HERMAN MELVILLE. These sketches are laid in the Galapagos Islands off Ecuador. Melville, age twenty-one and a first-class seaman on the whaler *Acushnet*, visited the islands in the autumn of 1841. How long he stayed is not known, but the islands remained deeply imprinted on his memory. Perhaps his use of a pseudonym was dictated by the sharp decline of his fame that came with publication of MOBY-DICK (1851) and PIERRE (1852). The giant tortoises on the islands fascinated him. He called them "these mystic creatures, suddenly translated by night from unutterable solitudes to our peopled deck." Seven of the sketches are descriptive, the remaining three introduce human characters; one, especially powerful, the tale of a half-breed woman, contributes to Melville's somber examination of good and evil.

Encyclopaedia Britannica.   A major reference work. The first edition appeared in Edinburgh in 1768; it consisted of three volumes put out by a "society of gentlemen." Other editions, constantly increasing in size and authority, appeared in England, and American scholars were sometimes called on for contributions, the first such being Edward Everett, president of Harvard. The *Encyclopaedia* became a popular work of reference in the United States, so much so that in 1901 it was bought by two Americans, for a time became the property of Sears, Roebuck & Co., and in 1943 became affiliated with the University of Chicago. The editors still seek to maintain the *Encyclopaedia*'s international scope and character. In 2000 the encyclopedia posted its contents online as Britannica.com on a site that is also a search engine.

Endicott or **Endecott, John** (1589?–1665),   colonial administrator. He came to America in 1628, was acting governor of the Massachusetts Bay Colony until 1630, when Governor JOHN WINTHROP arrived. Thereafter he was assistant governor from time to time, and served as governor in 1644, 1649, 1651–53, 1655–64. Though competent as an administrator, he was cruel and intolerant in character and extremist in doctrine. Under his administration Quakers were severely persecuted and four were executed. In "Endicott and Red Cross" (TWICE-TOLD TALES 1837) Hawthorne tells how Endicott cut the sign of the cross from the British ensign because he regarded it as a sign of popery. The first of Longfellow's NEW ENGLAND TRAGEDIES (1868) is called *John Endicott* and tells how the governor persecuted the Quakers in Boston and condemned his own son when he attempted to aid the daughter of one of them.

Endymion   (*Atlantic Monthly*, February 1888; included in *Heartsease and Rue*, 1888), a poem by JAMES RUSSELL LOWELL. To make his poem Lowell gathered a "heap of fragments" from his notebooks and wove them together into what became, as he subtitled it, "A Mystical Comment on Titian's 'Sacred and Profane Love.' "

Engle, Paul [Hamilton] (1908–1991),   teacher, poet, novelist. Born in Iowa, Engle was a Rhodes Scholar who taught at the University of Iowa and there was instrumental in developing the famed creative writing program. His poems, Whitmanesque at first, and generally celebrating the Midwest, are collected in *American Song* (1934); *Break the Heart's Anger* (1936); *Corn* (1939); *West of Midnight* (1941); *American Child* (1945, 1956), a sonnet sequence; *The World of Love* (1951); *Poems in Praise* (1959); *A Prairie Christmas* (1960); *A Woman Unashamed* (1965); and *Embraced* (1969). A novel, *Always the Land* (1941), is set in Iowa.

English, Thomas Dunn (1819–1902),   physician, lawyer, public official, author. Born in Philadelphia, English practiced medicine in Newark, New Jersey, and served in the New Jersey Assembly and then in Congress. Among his writings were more than twenty plays, only one of which, *The Mormons, or, Life at Salt Lake City* (1858), won much success. Similarly only one of his several novels, *Jacob Schuyler's Millions* (1886), won more than mild applause. He wrote for newspapers, edited and published a humorous magazine, *John Donkey*, and composed *Fairy Stories and Wonder Tales* (1897).

At one time English was a friend of Poe's, but later became a bitter enemy. Poe sued the publisher of the New York *Evening Mirror* for printing a statement by English accusing him of forgery, and damages of $225 were assessed against the publisher. In addition, Poe, according to a letter he wrote Henry Beck Hirst (June 27, 1846), gave English "a flogging which he will remember to the day of his death—and, luckily, in the presence of witnesses." In an earlier letter (September 8, 1844) Poe called English "a bullet-headed and malicious villain." He also ridiculed him as "Thomas Dunn Brown" in "The Literati of New York City" (1846).

English gained his most lasting literary fame with the poem BEN BOLT, which appeared in the *Mirror* (September 2, 1843), was set to music by Nelson Kneass, and was sung in a play, *The Battle of Buena Vista*. In 1894 *The Select Poems of Dr. Thomas Dunn English* appeared in a private edition issued by his daughter, Alice English. In the same year George Du Maurier

revived the song "Ben Bolt" by having Trilby sing it in his novel *Trilby*; and again it swept America and England.

English and Scottish Popular Ballads (1882–98), edited by FRANCIS JAMES CHILD. A monument of American scholarship and an early contribution to the comparative study of literature.

English Notebooks, Passages from the (2 v. 1870), by NATHANIEL HAWTHORNE. These were published posthumously by Hawthorne's widow, who omitted passages. An edition from manuscript sources was published by Randall Stewart (1941). A considerable portion of the material was used by Hawthorne in OUR OLD HOME (1863). The *Notebooks* tell the story of his busy life in England as an American consul. They also mention literary projects he was unable to carry out, and give the germ ideas of some that did materialize. He makes keen observations on English life and writes some memorable passages of description.

English Traits (1856),   an analysis of the English people by RALPH WALDO EMERSON. After two visits to England, Emerson in 1848 delivered a series of lectures describing his impressions, published eight years later as *English Traits*. He tells of his visits to Coleridge, Carlyle, and Wordsworth, then discusses "Race," "Ability," "Character," "Aristocracy," "Wealth," "Religion," "The Times," and other subjects. He finds himself amused by English ceremonials and bewigged officials, is deeply impressed by English writers (especially Carlyle), lauds the English, but with eyes open to their defects.

Enormous Room, The (1922),   an autobiographical narrative by E. E. CUMMINGS. On a false charge of treason, Cummings was imprisoned in a French military camp (1917–18). He describes his experiences and tells how his companions in the camp reacted to their harsh treatment.

Enough Rope (1926),   a collection of poems by DOROTHY PARKER. The book established Parker's fame as a poet of technical skill and striking content whom readers ordinarily averse to poetry greatly enjoyed. As Edmund Wilson put it, "Dorothy Parker's unprecedented feat has been to raise to the dignity of poetry the 'wise-cracking' humor of New York." The book went through eleven printings by 1928, then was included in *Not So Deep as a Well* (1936). Two poems in the volume continue to be quoted: "Résumé," on suicide, and "News Item," about girls who wear glasses.

Enters, Angna (1907–1989),   dancer, artist, author. Calling herself a "dance mime," a term she originated, Enters from 1926 on presented over one hundred Episodes and Compositions in Dance Form in the United States and abroad. Among her books are *First Person Plural* (1937); *Love Possessed Juana* (1939); *Silly Girl* (1944), personal memories, self-illustrated; and *Among the Daughters* (1955). *Artist's Life* (1958) is a continuation of *Silly Girl* and a chronicle of self-education.

Entropy (1960),   a short story by THOMAS PYNCHON. First published in *Kenyon Review*, Spring 1960, "Entropy" was collected in *Slow Learner* (1984), where Pynchon wrote of it: "The story is a fine example of a procedural error beginning writers are always being cautioned against. It is simply wrong to begin with a theme, symbol or other abstract unifying agent, and then try to force characters and events to conform to it." The story unites a narrative of a lease-breaking party in one apartment and another of an attempt to keep a bird alive in an apartment above by passing to it the warmth of human hands. Together, the narratives comment in different ways on the dissipation of energy in, emblematically, Washington, D.C., in 1957.

Equiano, Olaudah [Gustavas Vassa] (1745?–1797?), memoirist. Equiano was born what is now eastern Nigeria and was captured by slave traders at 10. Eventually he accepted the name Gustavas Vassa. He served several masters, including a Philadelphia Quaker; was released from slavery in 1766; and continued his travels, which by the end had taken him to the West Indies, Canada, Central America, England (his home in later life), Ireland, the Arctic, and the Mediterranean. He was active in the antislavery movement in England and served as Commissary for Stores for the Black Poor, freed slaves leaving for Sierra Leone. *The Interesting Narrative of the Life of Olaudah Equiano, or Gustavus Vassa the African, Written by Himself* (1789) remains, with the poems of PHILLIS WHEATLEY, among the most memorable works in English by native Africans of the 18th century. Celebrated in its time, it appeared in about a dozen editions in England and the United States between 1789 and 1827. Passages tell of Equiano's American experience, serving his master in the trade to the West Indies.

Erdrich, Louise (1954–   ),   novelist, short-story writer, poet. The poetry collection *Jacklight* (1984) and the novels *Love Medicine* (1984), *The Beet Queen* (1986), and *Tracks* (1988), part of a projected tetralogy set between 1912–84, quickly established Erdrich as a major American writer. Of Native American (French and Chippewa on her mother's side) and German descent, Erdrich focuses her work on the complex cultural identity that emerges from her mixed heritages. She grew up in North Dakota and sets her work in and around the North Dakota and Minnesota Indian reservations of her childhood. Her work is characterized both by wonderfully comedic touches and the poignancy of cultural fragmentation and loss. Erdrich said that she and her late husband, the Native American scholar and novelist MICHAEL DORRIS (1946–1997), collaborated closely on their work.

Love Medicine comprises fourteen linked stories, which are narrated in Faulknerian style by seven members of three generations of the Lamartine and Kashpaw families of the Turtle Mountain Chippewas. In *The Beet Queen*, set between 1930 and 1970, Karl and Mary Adare are abandoned when their mother, Mary, flies away with a carnival barnstormer. Mary winds up in Argus, North Dakota, with her mother's sister and takes over her butcher shop with the part-Indian Celestine, who later bears Karl's child, Dot, a minor character in *Love Medicine*. Wallace Pfef introduces sugar beet agriculture to Argus and also becomes involved with Karl. *Tracks*, set between 1912 and 1924, celebrates the life of the half-blood Fleur Pillager, a powerful yet destructive woman with magical powers, who is an ancestor of characters in *Love Medicine*. The

novel, set in the time when the Chippewas were being destroyed by starvation and illnesses contracted from the white man, concerns Fleur's romance with Eli Kashpaw and their relationship with Nanapush, a Chippewa elder and father-figure.

With her late husband, Michael Dorris, Erdrich collaborated on the novel *The Crown of Columbus* (1991), in which two scholars try to find the diary of Columbus's voyage. *Baptism of Desire* (1991) is a poetry collection. Characters from the Pillager, Lamartine, and Kaspaw families featured in earlier novels continue to appear in Erdrich's fiction. Lyman Lamartine, for instance, is the focal point of *The Bingo Palace* (1994), where his efforts to better the lives of reservation residents through founding a bingo hall lead to both comic and sad consequences. Lyman also plays a minor role in *Tales of Burning Love* (1997) in which the four ex-wives of a man believed to have burned to death meet to share stories of their lives with him. *The Antelope Wife* (1998) is a dreamlike combination of traditional animal transformation myths and contemporary experiences among urban Native Americans. Father Damien, the central figure in *The Last Report on the Miracles at Little No Horse* (2001), is really a former nun named Agnes, who has taken on the identity of a flood victim who died en route to the reservation and who has spent a lifetime ministering to people suffering from starvation and illness and being cheated out of their patrimony. An emissary is sent to the region to investigate the miracles attributed to Sister Leopolda, who, like many characters in this novel, has appeared in other Erdrich fictions. *The Blue Jay's Dance: A Birth Year* (1996) is a childbirth journal. *Grandmother's Pigeon* (1999) and *The Birchbark House* (1999) are books for young readers.

NEAL L. TOLCHIN/BP

Ericson, Leif (*fl.* 999–1003),   Norse navigator and explorer. This famous sailor is believed to have landed on the shores of America in about the year 1000. A son of Eric the Red (who colonized Greenland, 986), Leif may have been born in Iceland but seems to have been reared in Greenland. He heard from Norse mariners that they had occasionally sighted land far to the west. He bought a ship, hired a crew of thirty-five, and apparently reached the American continent. He named three places—Helluland, Markland, and Vinland, sometimes identified as Labrador or Newfoundland, Nova Scotia, and New England at Cape Cod. He is believed to have landed at Vinland, where grapes grew in profusion, but the evidence is dubious. There are also tales that two of Leif's brothers made expeditions inland, and that one was killed by the native inhabitants. The information regarding Leif's voyages comes from the *Saga of Eric the Red* and the *Saga of Olaf Tryggvason*. Longfellow had these old legends in mind when he wrote THE SKELETON IN ARMOR (1840).

Erie Canal.   A waterway connecting the Hudson River with Lake Erie. It extended 363 miles from Albany to Buffalo, and was often called Clinton's Big Ditch, after Governor De Witt Clinton, under whose administration the work was carried out. Completed in 1825, the canal drastically reduced the cost of freight and opened up great markets to the merchants of New York City. A great wave of settlers from New England traveled to the Midwest via the canal.

Erotic School, The. A name given to a group of writers c. 1888 by newspaper critics, who decried the extremes to which these writers, among them Amélie Rives (see PRINCESS TROUBETZKOY), EDGAR SALTUS, GERTRUDE ATHERTON, and ELLA WHEELER WILCOX, went in rebelling against the prevailing rules of propriety. These writers anticipated to a certain extent the revolt that came after World War I. They acted chiefly under the influence of the art-for-art's-sake movement in England.

Erskine, John (1879–1951), teacher, novelist, editor, essayist, musician. Born in New York City, Erskine was at the beginning a scholar and teacher specializing in Elizabethan poetry, but with the publication of *The Private Life of Helen of Troy* (1925), which attained an extraordinary popular success, he began a new career. The book dealt irreverently with ancient Greek figures and helped confirm the trend of the 1920s toward idol-breaking. Erskine followed up this book with others of similar character, including *Galahad* (1926), ADAM AND EVE (1927), *Penelope's Man* (1928), and *Tristan and Isolde* (1932). *The Start of the Road* (1938) is about Whitman as a young man, *Give Me Liberty* (1940) about Patrick Henry. Music became one of Erskine's chief interests, and in later years he began telling the story of his life—entertainingly, sometimes a little maliciously—in *The Memory of Certain Persons* (1947), *My Life as a Teacher* (1948), *My Life in Music* (1950), and *My Life as a Writer* (1951).

Eshleman, Clayton (1935–), poet, translator, editor, teacher. Born in Indianapolis, Eshleman was educated at Indiana University and has lived in Japan, Korea, Peru, and France. He has taught at California Institute of Technology and Eastern Michigan University. As founder and editor of two avant-garde magazines, *Caterpillar* (1967–73) and *Sulfur* (1981–2000), he has propagated a cross-cultural poetics rooted in his admiration for CESAR VALLEJO and other modern, mostly non-English masters. A recipient of Guggenheim, National Endowment for the Arts, and National Endowment for the Humanities fellowships, he has published translations that include (with Jose Rubia Barcia) *Cesar Vallejo: The Complete Posthumous Poetry* (1978) and (with Annette Smith) *Aime Cesaire: The Collected Poetry* (1983). Poems from his first book, *Mexico & North* (1962), and many that followed, are collected in *The Name Encanyoned River: Selected Poems 1960–1985* (1986). *Juniper Fuse: Upper Paleolithic Imagination and the Construction of the Underworld* appeared in 1999.

Eskimos. People of Asian origin inhabiting northeastern Siberia and the North American coast from the Bering Sea to Greenland. Their languages are classified as Eskimo-Aleut (the latter for the inhabitants of the Aleutian Islands). For many, Inuit, signifying "the people" and comprising Eskimos speaking a number of dialects, is preferred over Eskimo (and will be used here). Long in contact with European explorers and settlers, they have generally been friendly in their relations and have maintained a traditional way of life until relatively recently. A written language, Inuktitut, was introduced by Europeans in the 18th century as a way of spreading Christianity. Major collections of traditional songs and legends came much later, generally in the reports of explorers; still later came works like Maurice Metayer's *Tales from the Igloo* (1972) and John Robert Colombo's *Poems of the Inuit* (1981). In recent times, Inuit writers have published in Inuktitut and in English in periodicals and books. Among literary depictions by outsiders are JACK LONDON's "The Law of Life," and LESLIE MARMON SILKO's "Storyteller."

Esquivel, Laura (1950–), novelist. Born in Mexico City, Esquivel has been a schoolteacher, children's book writer, and screenwriter; she now lives in her native city with her second husband. *Like Water for Chocolate* (1992, tr. 1993) was translated into thirty languages and made into a highly successful movie, directed by her first husband, Alfonso Arau. Described as "a novel in monthly installments with recipes, romances and home remedies," it is a tale of thwarted and fulfilled love, set in revolutionary and post-revolutionary Mexico. Interspersed throughout are recipes and Mexican food and folk lore. As the youngest daughter in a traditional rural family, Tita is slated to eschew marriage and live only to care for her mother, but her love for Pedro, her childhood sweetheart, cannot be denied and the resulting marriage is incandescent. *The Law of Love* (English tr. 1996) is a multimedia novel set in the 23rd century. Acuzena, an astroanalyst, helps patients recall memories from past lives. The book is accompanied by a CD of dance music and selections from Puccini and includes illustrations from Miguelanxo Prado.

Essay for the Recording of Illustrious Providences (1684), a treatise by INCREASE MATHER, republished twice in the 19th century as *Remarkable Providences*. A collection of reports involving supernatural incidents in early New England history, the book claims to examine these cases scientifically, sometimes attacking popular superstition in order to prove and illustrate the direct intervention of God in human affairs. In spite of its less-than-scientific approach, the book contributed to the fanaticism that resulted in the Salem witchcraft trials. Mather repudiated the extremity of the trials in his *Cases of Conscience Concerning Evil Spirits* (1693).

Essays, First and Second Series (1841, 1844), by RALPH WALDO EMERSON. In the *First Series* Emerson wrote on history, self-reliance, compensation, spiritual laws, love, friendship, prudence, heroism, the over-soul, circles, intellect, and art. In the *Second Series* he wrote on the poet, experience, character, manners, gifts, nature, politics, nominalism and realism, and New England reformers. The essays were frequently delivered first as lectures, the sources for which included Emerson's copious *Journals*.

Estes, Eleanor (1906–1988), writer of juvenile fiction. The Moffat family and their pets are Estes's best-known creation. In 1951, she won the Herald Tribune spring Book Festival Award for *Ginger Pye*, and the Newbery Medal for the most distinguished contribution to American literature for children in the same year. Among Estes's many books, often illustrated by the writer, are *The Moffats* (1941), *The Witch Family* (1960), and *The Hundred Dresses* (1944).

Esther (1884), a novel by HENRY ADAMS published under the pseudonym Frances Snow Compton. It relates under a thin veil something of the story of Adams's own marriage. The heroine, who resembles Marian Adams, falls in love with the clergyman Stephen Hazard, but they separate because of incompatibility of their religious views. Adams in the book makes clear his own loss of religious faith. Another prominent character is the artist Wharton, recalling in many ways the sculptor AUGUSTUS SAINT-GAUDENS, who created the impressive memorial to Mrs. Adams in the Rock Creek Cemetery in Washington. The letters gathered in *Henry Adams and His Friends* (1947) include some to Adams's publisher, Henry Holt. They express Adams's view that the novel was merely an experiment in publishing—to see how well a novel could sell without advertising. Oscar Cargill noted parallels between the clergyman in the book and Adams himself, and advanced the theory that the suggestion of suicide made to Esther in the novel may have seemed to Adams in later years not unconnected with his wife's suicide.

Ethan Brand (published in the *Dollar Magazine*, Philadelphia, May 1851, under the title "The Unpardonable Sin," later included in THE SNOW IMAGE, 1851), a story by NATHANIEL HAWTHORNE. Ethan, who has tended a limekiln in his native village, returns to it convinced he has committed "the unpardonable sin"—intellectual pride, or, as Hawthorne expressed it in *The American Notebooks*, "the separation of the intellect from the heart." Ethan destroys himself in the kiln; his successor finds a whitened human skeleton with a marble heart.

Ethan Frome (1911), a novel by EDITH WHARTON. This is sometimes considered Wharton's masterpiece, though she herself did not think so. It is an ironic tragedy of love, frustration, jealousy, and sacrifice. The scene is a New England village, where Ethan barely makes a living out of a stony farm and is at odds with his wife, Zeena (short for Zenobia), a whining hypochondriac. Mattie, a cousin of Zeena's, comes to live with them, and love develops between her and Ethan. They try to end their impossible lives by steering a bobsled into a tree, instead ending up crippled and tied for the rest of their unhappy time on earth to Zeena and the barren farm. Zeena, however, is transformed into a devoted nurse and Mattie becomes the nagging invalid.

Ethnogenesis (1861), a poem by HENRY TIMROD. Filled with enthusiasm for the newborn Confederacy, Timrod prophesied its victory in war and its greatness in peace. The poem was included in his *Poems* (1873).

Ethnopoetics. A branch of postmodern poetry dealing with oral cultures and their rituals, healing songs, myths, and other literature previously little known in the West except to anthropologists and other cultural specialists. The first anthology to collect the literary traditions of remote, primitive, and oral cultures was Jerome Rothenberg's *Technicians of the Sacred* (1967, 1985), whose original 1967 preface noted a contemporary "yearning to create a meaningful spiritual life . . . the oldest, most universal of human traditions." With the collapse of European and English empires after World War II, numerous American poets began expressing their interest in the mythology, history, and folk traditions of former Western colonies, now the developing countries of the Third World. CHARLES OLSON (1910–1970), a prominent writer at midcentury, proclaimed in his essays and poems the importance of archaic and primitive culture to contemporary poetry. The poet GARY SNYDER (1930–   ) also became a leading spokesman of the importance of primitive communal values for modern society. By the mid-1960s, Rothenberg, David Antin, Armand Schwerner, Rochelle Owens, and other poets in New York began performing works based on primitive chants and ritual songs, sometimes with musical accompaniment on simple instruments. The term *ethnopoetics*, coined by Rothenberg, was derived from similar terms in other disciplines, such as ethnomusicology, the study of music in other cultures, and ethnology, the study of economic and cultural systems of primitive societies. Though ethnopoetics grew directly out of postmodern poetics, it coincided with other social trends in the U.S. of the period that revived interest in folk culture and native traditions, abroad and domestically, and played its part in the ideological upheavals of the civil rights era (1954–1968). Other anthologies on ethnopoetic themes include Rothenberg's *A Big Jewish Book* (1968), *Symposium of the Whole* (1983), a prose sequel to *Technicians* coedited with his wife, the anthropologist Diane Rothenberg, and *Shaking the Pumpkin* (1972, 1986), a collection of North American Indian poetry. The movement has attracted social scientists as well as poets to contribute to its broad coverage of cultural diversity outside the modern West and among native groups within it.

PAUL CHRISTENSEN

etiquette, books on. A mirror, even if somewhat distorted, of the development of American culture may be found in the books on etiquette that have from age to age molded our manners. Religion and law at first laid down rules for American manners. Many of the colonies legally punished scandal-mongering, cursing, lying, flirting, even making faces. Modes of dress were also governed, mainly to prevent the lower classes from imitating the finery of the aristocrats. Young children were taught, first of all, to pay implicit respect to their elders. Silence in the meetinghouse and at meals was enjoined upon them; they were not to go "singing, whistling, nor hollowing along the street." Girls were expected to maintain "a retiring delicacy." Idleness was severely denounced. As early as 1754 *The School of Good Manners* was published for the benefit of young people. British manuals became popular as wealth grew in the colonies; from these or native imitations Americans sought to learn what to wear, how to arrange a dinner, how to converse in company.

The birth of the Republic brought about few changes until the era of Jackson, when a new conception arose, that anybody might become a lady or gentleman by exhibiting proper manners. Arthur Schlesinger, in his study of American etiquette books called *Learning How to Behave* (1946), estimates that, aside from revisions and new editions, twenty-eight different manuals appeared in the 1830s, thirty-six in the 1840s, and thirty-eight more in the 1850s. Then came the Civil War and the economic boom that followed it. Profiteers and parvenus, a sham aristocracy, were in a hurry to learn manners, especially transatlantic manners, and magazines and books did all they could to help them. Entertaining details are given in Dixon Wecter's *The Saga of American Society* (1937). Journalism leaped to the rescue, and EDWARD BOK relates (*The Americanization of Edward Bok*, 1922) that when he engaged Isabel A. Mallon to conduct, under the pen name of Ruth Ashmore, a department on social proprieties and problems for *The Ladies' Home Journal*, her "Side Talks with Girls" brought her 158,000 letters in sixteen years.

After World War I a new crop of millionaires appeared, more ruthless than the post–Civil War ones. Prohibition produced strange crudities of manners, with the bootlegger as the arbiter of elegance, and the younger generation concluded it was smarter to be rowdy or smart-alecky than to be gracious. A more informal spirit of fellowship developed between the sexes, and movies brought into vogue Hollywood's notion of good manners. Yet more books on etiquette were sold than ever before. Two in particular became popular and sold by the hundreds of thousands: Lillian Eichler (Mrs. T. M. Watson) published her *Book of Etiquette* in 1921, and EMILY POST her *Etiquette, the Blue Book of Usage* in 1922. Many other persons, sometimes socialites with the help of ghost writers, offered their advice, for example, Amy Vanderbilt in *Everyday Etiquette* (1956). More recently, Judith Martin, writing as *Miss Manners*, has brought a sometimes acerbic wit to the field in her newspaper columns and books.

Eureka (1848),   an "essay on the material and spiritual universe" by EDGAR ALLAN POE. Under the influence of Newton and Laplace, Poe presented a view of the universe as a mystic and material unity, with all parts interdependent and all equally cause and effect. In this way he sought to solve problems both major and minor: the problem of good and evil, for example, and the problem of composing a fictional story. The result is, as H. H. Clark expressed it, a "magnificent vision of a universe of ordered harmony." Poe's piece is a contribution to scientific and philosophical thought and at the same time a prose poem. This essay had a great influence on some French writers, particularly on Paul Valéry, who claimed that the essay was "the intuitive progenitor of Einstein's relativity."

Europeans, The (1878),   a novel by HENRY JAMES. Two expatriates, the Baroness Muenster and her brother Felix Young, come to Boston to visit some relatives they have never seen. The baroness futilely tries to make a wealthy marriage, and Felix seeks to paint portraits of the Bostonians he meets. A contrast is drawn between the sophistication of the pair and the strict New Englanders. Felix marries one of his kinswomen, who is eager to escape from her bleak environment.

Eutaw Springs.   Scene of the important battle, September 8, 1781, in South Carolina at which General Nathanael Greene and his American forces finally compelled the British to withdraw northward. Military historians regard the battle as a turning point of the Revolution. Concerning the battle PHILIP FRENEAU wrote his beautiful elegy, *To the Memory of the Brave Americans* (1781), which Sir Walter Scott is said to have learned by heart. On the same theme WILLIAM IOOR wrote a play, *The Battle of Eutaw Springs* (1807, produced 1813), and WILLIAM GILMORE SIMMS a romance, *Eutaw* (1856), a sequel to his earlier *The Forayers* (1855).

Eva St. Clare.   See LITTLE EVA.

Evangeline, A Tale of Acadie (1847),   a narrative poem by HENRY WADSWORTH LONGFELLOW. As early as 1829 Longfellow was interested in the Acadians, and planned to write a sketch, *Down East: The Missionary of Acadie*, to be included in a series of New England Sketches. In 1838 an Episcopal clergyman, Horace Lorenzo Connolly, told Nathaniel Hawthorne the story of a young couple who had been separated by the British order expelling about 6,000 inhabitants from Acadie, a region in Nova Scotia. The bride set off in search of her husband, and at last found him on his deathbed. Connolly urged Hawthorne to write a novel based on this incident, and Hawthorne considered it carefully for a long time. But in 1840, at a dinner in Longfellow's home the story was retold in the poet's hearing. Hawthorne said, "The story is not in my vein," and Longfellow, with Hawthorne's consent, took it over. He conducted minute researches for several years, but was held up by other tasks; he finally began to write the poem on November 28, 1845 and completed it on February 27, 1847. It appeared that year, and won an immediate success.

The poem was written in dactylic hexameters, and was influenced by Goethe's *Hermann und Dorothea* (1797). It tells how the bridegroom Gabriel Lajeunesse is carried to Louisiana, and the bride Evangeline Bellefontaine to New England. She follows him, and after years of fruitless wandering comes, an old woman, to Philadelphia, where as a Sister of Mercy she cares for the poor and sick. There, during an epidemic, she at last finds Gabriel dying in the almshouse. Her own death follows, and both are buried in the Catholic cemetery. There have been numerous dramatizations, musical settings, and film versions. Statues suggested by the poem have been erected at Grand Pré, Nova Scotia, and St. Martinville, Louisiana.

Evans, Augusta J[ane] (1835–1909),   novelist. Born in Georgia, in later life she wrote under her married name, Wilson. Evans's sentimental tales were popular in her own day, particularly her ST. ELMO (1866). Its heroine is a pious orphan who makes it her business to reform a worldly sophisticate and in the end marries him. The banality of the story is only partially concealed by a display of erudition that deeply impressed its readers. Evans also wrote *Inez: A Tale of the Alamo* (1855), *Beulah* (1859), *Macaria; or, The Altars of Sacrifice* (1864), and *Devota* (1907).

Evans, Donald (1884–1921),   poet. Evans, who died by his own hand, was a hero of Greenwich Village and the sophisticated set for a decade. His volumes of verse—*Discords* (1912), *Sonnets from the Patagonian* (1914), *Two Deaths in the Bronx* (1916), *Nine Poems from a Valetudinarian* (1916), and *Ironica* (1919)—contain many striking lines and influenced some of his contemporaries, including Wallace Stevens and E. E. Cummings.

Evans, George.   See IN THE GOOD OLD SUMMER TIME.

Evans, Nathaniel (1742–1767), clergyman, poet. Evans was born in Philadelphia. His early death prevented development of his poetic talent, but he was highly regarded by his contemporaries. He was a member of the group headed by FRANCIS HOPKINSON and like others of the group imitated the English poets of his day. Some of his poems were suggested by events in the French and Indian War. Elsewhere he paid tribute to Franklin as a scientist, and his most ambitious effort was his *Ode on the Prospect of Peace*. His *Poems on Several Occasions, with Some Other Compositions* was published posthumously (1772).

Evarts, Hal George (1887–1934), trapper, guide, writer of western stories. Evarts, a lover of the outdoors who was born in Kansas, became an authority on hunting and fishing in the undeveloped West of the early 19th century, especially the old Indian Territory and Wyoming. His best-known book is *Tumbleweeds* (1923), about riders of the cattle ranges in the Cherokee Strip. Others include *The Cross Pull* (1920), *Passing of the Old West* (1921), *Spanish Acres* (1925), and *Shortgrass* (1932).

Everett, Alexander Hill (1790–1847), diplomat, poet, essayist, editor. Everett was born in Boston. Perhaps his greatest literary service was that, as minister to Spain, he appointed WASHINGTON IRVING as an attaché to the legation at Madrid, thus shaping Irving's future career. From 1830 to 1835 he edited the NORTH AMERICAN REVIEW. He was a learned, witty man who wrote excellent books and papers on matters political and literary, translated Theocritus and Goethe, and was among the first Americans to give attention to Oriental studies. His volumes on *Europe* (1822) and *America* (1827) were translated into German, French, and Spanish. He also wrote *Essays, Critical and Miscellaneous* (1845–46).

Everett, Edward (1794–1865), clergyman, teacher, statesman, diplomat, orator, biographer. Born in Dorchester, Mass., Edward was the younger brother of ALEXANDER EVERETT and an even more accomplished man. His personal attractiveness and charm caused him to be called Apollo and Cicero, and Emerson referred to his "precise and perfect eloquence." He began as a Unitarian minister, went on to become a distinguished professor of Greek at Harvard, edited the NORTH AMERICAN REVIEW (1820–23), and finally began what was to be his true lifework by running for Congress, where he served for ten years (1825–35). Thereafter, he was governor of Massachusetts (1836–39), minister to England (1841–45), president of Harvard (1846–49), secretary of state (1852–53), and United States senator (1853–54). Until the outbreak of the Civil War he was inclined toward compromise on the slavery question, but from then on spoke vigorously for the Union.

Posterity remembers Everett because he delivered a two-hour oration at Gettysburg, Lincoln following him with his three brief paragraphs. Lincoln himself had no thought but that Everett would overshadow him, but there is evidence that Everett realized the greatness of Lincoln's address. Everett's style was artificial and grandiose, but his addresses were immensely popular, and his *Orations and Speeches on Various Occasions* (1853–68) reached a ninth edition in 1878.

Evergreen Review. From 1957 to 1973, *Evergreen Review* was a major force in shaping the literary tone of the avant-garde in the United States. Edited as a quarterly (1957–59) and then as a bimonthly by Barney Rosset in New York City, it attained a circulation far beyond that of the other little magazines it in some ways resembled. Publishing poetry, fiction, criticism, and essays, it helped spread the influence of such European writers as Sartre, Camus, Jean Genet, Beckett, Robbe-Grillet, and Ionesco. The American writers favored were experimental and iconoclastic, many of them identified with the BEAT GENERATION and the SAN FRANCISCO RENAISSANCE. Among its authors were Kenneth Rexroth, Henry Miller, Charles Olson, William S. Burroughs, Lawrence Ferlinghetti, Allen Ginsberg, Jack Kerouac, Gregory Corso, Robert Creeley, and Denise Levertov. It aspired to leadership in graphic arts, music, and social commentary, publishing reproductions and studies of abstract expressionists, reviews of jazz, and essays on civil rights, the American counterculture, and liberal politics.

Everson, William (1912–1994), poet. Born in California, Everson was raised as a Christian Scientist, attended Fresno State College, and during World War II was a conscientious objector. After the war he was associated with the poets of the SAN FRANCISCO RENAISSANCE and from 1951 to 1969 was a lay brother in the Dominican Order, writing as Brother Antoninus. His poems—anti-war, religious, mystic, and sometimes erotic—have been compared in both imagery and rhythm to those of Robinson Jeffers, whom he has admired. Some of his best work is drawn together in *The Residual Years: Poems 1934–1948* (1968) and *The Veritable Years: 1949–1966* (1978). His other titles include *The Rose of Solitude* (1967); *Man-Fate: The Swan Song of Brother Antoninus* (1974), a farewell to his religious order; *The Masks of Drought: Poems 1972–1979* (1980), *Naked Heart: Talking on Poetry, Mysticism, and The Erotic* (1992); and *The Blood of the Poet* (1993).

Eve's Diary (1906), the supposed diary of the first woman, by MARK TWAIN. It was a humorous skit written as a companion piece to *Extracts from Adam's Diary* (1904). Its last line, supposedly composed by Adam after Eve's death, became Olivia Clemens's epitaph: "Wheresoever she was, *there* was Eden."

Excelsior (1841), a poem by HENRY WADSWORTH LONGFELLOW. The poem is believed to have been suggested to the poet by the motto on the New York state shield. It became immensely popular in its own day as a fervent exhortation toward the seeking of higher goals; it has been frequently parodied.

Exile's Return (1934), a memoir of the so-called lost generation by MALCOLM COWLEY. This is a vivid and persuasive account of what happened to the young Americans who flocked to Europe, especially Paris, in the 1920s. In it appear some of the notable figures of the time—Faulkner, Dos Passos, Fitzgerald, Hart Crane, Pound, Hemingway, and others. Cowley himself had a large share in their literary and bohemian adventures. The book was revised and augmented in 1951.

existentialism. The term represents a diverse European philosophic movement that became so influential in the

20th century that it grew to represent a cultural attitude. Such diverse philosophers as Nietzsche (1844–1900), Edmund Husserl (1859–1938), and Kierkegaard (1813–1855) identified problems of existence, established intellectual methodologies, and suggested phenomenological solutions.

Nietzsche perceived such problems as the decline of religious dogma, the search for new behavioral sanctions, and the radical feeling of human finitude. Husserl furnished an intellectual method called phenomenology—a return to sources or "things themselves" and an insistence on self-reflexive psychological analysis. Kierkegaard asserted that each person can encounter the self not by means of detached thought or reason, but only through the involvement and pathos of choice.

Early in the 20th century, existential thought first appeared as an influence in the work of such major American authors as William James, Eugene O'Neill, and Ernest Hemingway.

At mid-century Sartre and Camus brought the movement of existentialism to world renown. Sartre denied an abstract human nature and insisted that because existence comes before essence the individual is the source of all value; therefore, each person is free to choose his or her own character. Camus joined Sartre in the exploration of the absurd dilemmas of modern life, especially the recognition of each individual's fragility, the awful freedom within the abiding walls of nothingness. Alienation and anxiety became important concepts. The absurdist writers Beckett and Ionesco established situational literature. In many guises later existential thought appeared in the works of even more American authors—such as Edward Albee, Joseph Heller, Saul Bellow, William Styron, and John Berryman.

SAM SMILEY

expressionism.   This early-20th-century movement in art and literature was in part a reaction against realism and naturalism, in part a revision of impressionism. It turned the artist's gaze inward, giving priority to thoughts and images rooted within the mind over those that more precisely reflect the world outside. The result seems distorted, dreamlike, nightmarish. The origins were European, in work by painters like Wassily Kandinsky (1866–1944) and Oskar Kokoschka (1886–1980) and in plays like August Strindberg's *A Dream Play* (1902). In American literature, expressionism came first in most memorable form to the stage. Examples include EUGENE O'NEILL, *The Emperor Jones* (1920) and *The Hairy Ape* (1922); ELMER RICE, *The Adding Machine* (1923); and TENNESSEE WILLIAMS, *Camino Real* (1953). The abstract expressionism of Jackson Pollock (1912–1956) was a later development, influential on literature especially in the poetry of the NEW YORK SCHOOL.

F

Fable, A (1954), a novel by WILLIAM FAULKNER. Set in France a few months before the end of World War I, *A Fable* is both an allegory of the passion of Christ and a study of a world that has chosen submission to authority and the secular values of power and chauvinism instead of individuality and the exercise of free will. The novel centers on the fate of a young corporal, born in a cowshed and raised by his two half-sisters, Marya and Marthe; he enlists in the French army and, with the aid of twelve companions, incites a mutiny in the trenches that results in a temporary armistice. Betrayed by a member of his own regiment, the corporal is executed for cowardice along with two other military criminals, becoming a martyr to his principles and his belief in humanity. When the gravesite is struck by an enemy shell, his body disappears. Most of the characters in the novel are nameless personifications of abstractions, and most of the named characters—Marya, Marthe, Magda—are intended to represent the figures their names suggest.

Fable for Critics, A (1848), a verse satire by JAMES RUSSELL LOWELL. Published anonymously, it was soon recognized as Lowell's. The poem employs the god of poetry, Apollo, and a contemporary American critic as the main characters. The chief writers of the day are described in rapid satiric profiles, written in what are often rough and uneven anapestic tetrameters that frequently close with startling rhymes. The wit and turbulent humor anticipate his great BIGLOW PAPERS. Among those he characterized in his poem are Emerson, Longfellow, Holmes, Whittier, Hawthorne, Cooper, Poe, Halleck, Griswold, Willis, Alcott, Bryant, Margaret Fuller, Theodore Parker, John Neal, Harry Franco, Lydia Maria Child, and—himself. Frequently Lowell mingled eulogies with depreciations. Many of his verdicts have been sustained by the judgment of posterity; others seem less than just.

In writing the *Fable*, Lowell had as models such poems as Pope's *Dunciad* (1728), Leigh Hunt's *The Feast of the Poets* (1814), and Byron's *English Bards and Scotch Reviewers* (1809). He repeated the devices of the *Fable* in *The Origin of Didactic Poetry* (1857), and his kinswoman AMY LOWELL imitated him in A CRITICAL FABLE (1922), but far less brilliantly.

Lowell's personal likes and dislikes are apparent in the *Fable*. This is shown most emphatically in the passages on MARGARET FULLER, who had belittled him in her essay *American Literature*. WILLIAM CULLEN BRYANT had once accused Lowell of plagiarism—hence the remarks on his icy coldness, which Lowell later regretted. EDGAR ALLAN POE received mixed praise and blame. Poe replied by assailing Lowell's confused metrics. He also attacked Lowell for his lack of appreciation of Southern writers; he was himself the only Southern writer given any space in the *Fable*. He attributed this defect to Lowell's overly ardent abolitionism. But the poem is notable for its sturdy insistence that literary America had come of age; it is in general a noteworthy and pioneering endeavor to summarize and appraise American literature up to its time.

Fables for Our Time and Famous Poems Illustrated (1940), by JAMES THURBER. A collection of twenty-eight modern fables by Thurber and nine famous poems by others, illustrated with Thurber's line drawings. Among the fables are "The Rabbits Who Caused All the Trouble"; "The Owl Who Was God," with the moral "You can fool too many of the people too much of the time"; and "The Unicorn in the Garden." The best were reprinted in *The Thurber Carnival* (1945) along with much other Thurber. *Further Fables for Our Time* appeared in 1956.

Fables in Slang (1899), stories by GEORGE ADE. The first of Ade's fables in modern language, the story of Luella and her sister Mae, appeared on September 17, 1897. There was little actual slang; the Americanisms were those of Indiana. Further *Fables*, appearing first in the *Record*, later in other newspapers, made a great hit. A collection of the stories appeared in December 1899. More than 69,000 copies were sold in 1900, and Ade became well known. Years later, when Franklin D. Roosevelt needed to make a point with his cabinet, he would read one of Ade's *Fables* to them—just as Lincoln had read Artemus Ward in similar circumstances.

Face on the Barroom Floor, The (1872 or 1887), a much-recited poem claimed both by John Henry Titus and Hugh Antoine D'Arcy. One version was published by Titus (1853?–1947) in the Ashtabula (Ohio) *Sentinel* (1872). Another version, called simply *The Face upon the Floor*, appeared in the New York *Dispatch* (August 7, 1887), with an actor named D'Arcy credited as author. In 1934 Titus brought legal action to prevent a song publisher from using his title for the song. Titus is said to have written 1,800 poems, but the only one to attain fame was his saloon piece. According to tradition D'Arcy took as the setting for his poem a now extinct barroom on Union Square, New York City, called "Joe's."

Facundo (1845), the popular title of a book by DOMINGO FAUSTINO SARMIENTO. Its full title is *Civilización y barbarie, Vida de Juan Facundo Quiroga*. A classic of Hispanic-American literature, the book is partly an attack on the dictatorship of Juan Manuel de Rosas (1793–1877), who controlled Argentina from 1829 until 1852. To get at Rosas, Sarmiento combined a fanciful biography of Facundo, an actual gaucho leader whose death was probably ordered by Rosas, with a sociological analysis of Argentine society. Sarmiento believed that Argentina's troubles stemmed from the conflict between the civilization of the Europeanized urban classes and the barbarism of the ignorant, untamed gauchos, exemplified by Rosas and Facundo. Written in a vigorous, spontaneous style, the book is also acclaimed for its descriptions of the Argentine pampas and of gaucho types such as the outlaw and the tracker. *Facundo* was first translated into English as *Life in the Argentine Republic in the Days of the Tyrants* (1868) by HORACE MANN's wife, Mary Tyler Peabody Mann (1806–1887), whom Sarmiento had met in the United States.

Fadden, Chimmie. A Bowery character in stories by Edward W. Townsend, based on one "Chuck" Connors. Many of them appeared in the New York *Sun* at the turn of the century, later in books: *Chimmie Fadden, Major Max, and Other Stories* (1895) and *Chimmie Fadden Explains* (1895). (See THE BOWERY.)

Fairbank, Janet Ayer (1879–1951), novelist. Fairbank was the elder sister of the more renowned MARGARET AYER BARNES. Her novels include *The Cortlands of Washington Square* (1923); *The Smiths* (1925); *The Lion's Den* (1930); *The Bright Land* (1932), following a 19th-century woman from childhood in New Hampshire to the Illinois frontier; and *Rich Man, Poor Man* (1936), about suffragettes. Her short stories are collected in *Idle Hands* (1927).

Fairfax, Beatrice. The pen name under which Marie Manning (1878?–1945) and others wrote the column "Advice to the Lovelorn" in the New York *Journal*, beginning on July 20, 1898. Sometimes eliciting 1,400 letters a day, it was syndicated by King Features. Manning avoided the vapid sentimentality of some of her competitors and counseled, "Dry your eyes, roll up your sleeves, and dig for a practical solution." She wrote stories and several books under her own name.

Fairfield, Sumner Lincoln (1803–1844), poet, teacher, actor, editor. Born in Massachusetts, Fairfield wrote and published many poems, collected in his *Poems and Prose Writings* (1841). He is chiefly remembered for *The Last Night of Pompeii* (1832). He accused Bulwer-Lytton of plagiarizing it in his novel *The Last Days of Pompeii* (1834).

Fair God, The (1873), a historical novel by LEW WALLACE. A story of the conquest of Mexico by CORTEZ, the tale centers on Montezuma's futile efforts to resist the Spanish invader. The fair god is Quetzalcoatl, Aztec god of the air. Wal-

lace began working on the story in 1843 and wove into it much careful research. The book became immediately popular and went through twenty editions in ten years.

Faithful Narrative of the Surprising Work of God, The. See NARRATIVE OF SURPRISING CONVERSIONS.

Falkner, William C[lark] (1825–1889), soldier, railroad builder, politician, writer. Falkner, great-grandfather of WILLIAM FAULKNER, provided the model for the latter's Colonel Sartoris. Born in Tennessee, he lived in Mississippi a legendary life for his grandson to build on, turning also at times to writing. His novel *The White Rose of Memphis* (1880) was a popular melodrama, *The Little Brick Church* (1882) a historical romance ranging back and forth in time between the Revolutionary War and 1850. He also wrote travel sketches, *Rapid Ramblings in Europe* (1884).

Fall of British Tyranny, The, or American Liberty Triumphant (1776), a play by John (Joseph?) Leacock. Never produced, the play portrays events in the opening year of the Revolution, with the scenes laid first in England and then in America, where the Battle of Lexington and succeeding events are shown. The characters have assumed names: Lord North is Lord Catspaw, Pitt is Lord Wisdom, General Howe is Elbow Room, and General Burgoyne is Caper.

Fall of the City, The (1937), a radio drama in verse by ARCHIBALD MACLEISH. The play is a dramatic application of President Franklin Roosevelt's "the only thing we have to fear is fear itself." The people of the city are demoralized by the enemy's propaganda and bow down before his approach. But the one man who looks upon their conqueror at close range finds inside his glittering armor no face, no substance: nothingness. "The people invent their oppressors," he declares.

Fall of the House of Usher, The (1839, in *Tales of the Grotesque and Arabesque*, 1840), a story by EDGAR ALLAN POE. A fantastic but powerful tale, practically a prose poem, it contains the poem THE HAUNTED PALACE. A friend comes to visit Roderick Usher in his gloomy, decayed mansion. They read together, and Roderick plays curious musical pieces of his own composition. Roderick's twin sister, Madeline, has been placed in the family vault for dead, but he is convinced she still lives, and when she appears suddenly in her shroud to Roderick and his friend, brother and sister die simultaneously. As the friend leaves the house and looks back in the moonlight, he sees it suddenly split asunder and fall into the tarn. The story is one in which atmosphere is evoked to a superb degree, without neglect of plot or characterization.

Family Reunion, The (1939), a verse play by T. S. ELIOT. This is the story of Lord Monchensey, who murders his wife and returns home to his mother, Amy, eight years later, pursued by Furies and hoping to find peace.

Faneuil Hall. A meeting place in Boston, built as the result of a donation by a Boston merchant, Peter Faneuil (1700–1743). It was designed by John Smibert in 1740 and in 1806 was enlarged by CHARLES BULFINCH. During the Revolution many important meetings took place there, and in later days all the best orators of America spoke within its walls. It has been called the Cradle of Liberty.

Fanning, Nathaniel (1755–1805),   author of *Narrative of the Adventures of an American Navy Officer* (1806). Fanning, a Connecticut man, narrates the adventures he had when serving under John Paul Jones on the *Bon Homme Richard*, in command of his own ships, as well as ashore in Europe.

Fanshawe (1828),   a first novel by NATHANIEL HAWTHORNE. Hawthorne made every effort to recall the book and had all the copies destroyed that he could locate, even those of his sisters. After his death, his wife had no knowledge of the work's existence. The plot and many of the characters are derived from the novels of Scott, and much of the detail is adapted from the Gothic novel, popular in England at the end of the 18th century. Set in Harley College, an obvious sketch of Bowdoin, Hawthorne's alma mater, the novel concerns itself with the attempted seduction of Ellen Langdon, the ward of Dr. Melmoth, Harley's president, and her rescue by the hero, Fanshawe, a scholar whose studies have isolated him from the world.

Farewell Address   of GEORGE WASHINGTON. In this influential document, first published in *Claypoole's American Daily Advertiser*, September 17, 1796, Washington addressed the American people and gave them his counsel on conducting the future course of the American government and on their own attitude toward public affairs. National unity and the best means of preserving it were the theme of his address, and he warned against sectional jealousy and party factions. He stressed the need for religion, morality, and education, urged that public credit be sustained, advised that impartial good faith be practiced toward all nations, and admonished against permanent entangling alliances with foreign nations. Washington had long meditated on the contents of such an address and had sought counsel from Alexander Hamilton and James Madison before writing it.

Farewell to Arms, A (1929),   a novel by ERNEST HEMINGWAY. A story of World War I, in which the fortunes of an American lieutenant, Frederic Henry, and an English nurse, Catherine Barkley, become remorselessly interwoven with the fortunes of war. When the lieutenant is wounded, the nurse takes care of him at Milan. They live happily together through the summer months, but even though she is pregnant she refuses to marry him, fearing that this will lead to her being sent back to England. The American goes back to the battlefront and witnesses the retreat of the Italian army from Caporetto. The lieutenant deserts, rejoins the nurse, and is with her when her child is born at Lausanne, where both mother and child die. The novel was dramatized by LAURENCE STALLINGS (1930), and film versions were made in 1932 and 1958.

Fariña, Richard (1936–1966),   novelist. Fariña, a folksinger as well as writer, studied at Cornell University and Reed College and wrote a comic novel of life at Cornell in 1958: *Been Down So Long It Looks Like Up to Me* (1966).

Farley, Harriet (1817–1907),   editor, essayist. Farley was a pioneer in the idea that workingmen and workingwomen are entitled to culture as well as better wages and living conditions. Born in New Hampshire in comfortable circumstances, she became a mill hand. The owners of the Lowell, Massachusetts, mill where she worked encouraged the formation of self-improvement clubs. One enterprise was a magazine, *The Lowell Offering, Written and Edited by Female Operatives*, to which Farley began to contribute, in time becoming editor (1842–45). It ceased publication for a while, then in 1847 began to appear again as the *New England Offering* (1847–50). The magazine attained celebrity in the United States and England. Some of Farley's essays and other material from the *Offering* were collected in *Mind Among the Spindles* (1844), *Shells from the Strand of Genius* (1847), and *Happy Nights at Hazel Nook* (1852).

Farm Ballads (1873),   sentimental poems by WILL CARLETON. They depict farm life in Michigan. The collection contains Carleton's best-known poem, OVER THE HILL TO THE POOR HOUSE.

Farmer, Fannie [Merritt] (1857–1915).   See BOSTON COOKING-SCHOOL COOKBOOK.

Farmer, Letters from an American.   See LETTERS FROM AN AMERICAN FARMER.

Farmer's Almanack.   See OLD FARMER'S ALMANAC.

Farrar, John [Chipman] (1896–1974),   publisher. After working for the New York *Sunday World*, Farrar became an editor of THE BOOKMAN, later an editor with Doubleday, Doran & Co. In 1929 he formed with Stanley Rinehart the publishing firm of Farrar & Rinehart. He withdrew in 1944 and in 1946 established with Roger W. Straus, Jr., the firm of Farrar, Straus & Co., which became Farrar, Straus, & Cudahy shortly thereafter. Throughout his career as a book publisher Farrar was known for his willingness to promote young, sometimes experimental authors within the context of commercial publishing. Farrar published several volumes of his own verse, including *Songs for Parents* (1921) and a collection of plays, *Indoor and Outdoor Plays for Children* (1933). In collaboration with STEPHEN VINCENT BENÉT he wrote a play, *That Awful Mrs. Eaton* (produced in 1925), set in the era of Jackson's squabbles with the ladies of his cabinet. *For the Record* appeared in 1943. Farrar is believed to be the Johnny Chipman who appears in two of Benét novels, *The Beginning of Wisdom* (1921) and *Young People's Pride* (1922), and the Johnny Chapman of CYRIL HUMES's *Wife of the Centaur* (1923).

Farrell, James T[homas] (1904–1979),   novelist, short-story writer. Born in Chicago, Farrell attended DePaul University and the University of Chicago but received no degree. Much of his education was obtained instead from his many jobs—in a shoe store, an express office, a gas station, a cigar store, a newspaper office, and so on. His earliest and most enduring subject was the South Side of Chicago, the world of Studs Lonigan and Danny O'Neill. The story "Studs" appeared first in *This Quarter* in 1930; from it grew *Young Lonigan: A Boyhood on the Chicago Streets* (1932), *The Young Manhood of Studs Lonigan* (1934), and *Judgment Day* (1935), published together as *Studs Lonigan: A Trilogy* (1935). In these and other works Farrell showed the continuing power of an unrelenting NATURALISM more common in American fiction a generation earlier. Danny O'Neill appeared in *Young Lonigan* and *Gas-House McGinty* (1933) before becoming the protagonist of his own series in *A World I Never Made* (1936), *No Star Is Lost* (1938), *Father and Son* (1940), *My Days of Anger* (1943), and *The Face of Time* (1953). *Bernard Clare* (1946) introduced a character, also known as Bernard Carr, who serves as protagonist in that novel and in *The Road Between* (1949) and *Yet Other Waters* (1952). These cycle novels, most dealing with Chicago but in the Bernard Clare books moving to other scenes, constitute an accomplishment rare in American literature as Farrell's heroes grow beyond the neat encapsulation of one or two stories. Few American authors have maintained so successfully the point of view of boyhood and young manhood, and few have matched the sustained treatment of a milieu that he gave to the world of the Irish Catholics of Chicago's South Side.

Although most attention has been paid to the works already mentioned, Farrell wrote many others. Another cycle of novels, *A Universe in Time*, focuses on a Chicago writer, Eddie Ryan, who in some ways resembles Farrell; it includes *The Silence of History* (1963), *What Time Collects* (1964), *When Time Was Born* (1966), *Lonely for the Future* (1966), *A Brand New Life* (1968), *Judith* (1969), *Invisible Swords* (1970), *The Dunne Family* (1976), and *The Death of Nora Ryan* (1978). Among his noncycle novels are *Ellen Rogers* (1941), praised by Thomas Mann as "the best modern love story"; *This Man and This Woman* (1951); *Boarding House Blues* (1961); and *New Year's Eve, 1929* (1967). Many collections of short stories interact with and stand separately from the novels. They include *Fellow Countrymen: Collected Stories* (1937), *An American Dream Girl* (1950), *An Omnibus of Short Stories* (1956), *Childhood Is Not Forever* (1969), and *Judith and Other Stories* (1973).

Farrell's criticism was collected in *A Note on Literary Criticism* (1936), important for its expression of 1930s Marxism; *The League of Frightened Philistines* (1945); *Literature and Morality* (1947); and *Reflections at Fifty* (1954). *My Baseball Diary* (1957) contributes personal reflections to the literature of the game. *The Collected Poems* appeared in 1965.

Fashion, or, Life in New York (1845),   a play by Anna Mowatt (1819–1870). This play has a somewhat confused plot, in the course of which a rich couple's daughter wishes to marry a fake count, but is urged by her father to wed a clerk who has discovered that the father has been indulging in forgery. A friend of the father finally saves her from both. The play, with its satiric thrusts at the mother, Mrs. Tiffany, who seeks to break into society, was a great success.

Fast, Howard (1914–   ),   novelist, short-story writer. Born in New York City, Fast early devoted himself to writing historical novels, some of them offering new interpretations of American history. Among them are *The Last Frontier* (1941), *The Unvanquished* (1942), and *Patrick Henry and the Frigate's Keel*, short stories (1945). From the beginning of his career, Fast showed a tendency to mingle propaganda with storytelling, and such works as *Citizen Tom Paine* (1943) and *Freedom Road* (1944) grew out of his association with the Communist Party. Similarly, *The American* (1946) espoused a radical cause in its praise of Governor Peter Altgeld of Illinois.

Fast later he broke with communism, though retaining his radical convictions, and described his disillusionment with the party in *The Naked God* (1957). His *Spartacus* (1958), a sympathetic portrayal of a Roman slave revolt, became a spectacular movie (1960). His other novels include *Moses, Prince of Egypt* (1958); *The Winston Affair* (1959), set in World War II; *Power* (1963), a labor novel; *Agrippa's Daughter* (1964); and *Max* (1982), about Hollywood. The Lavell family saga includes *The Immigrants* (1977), *Second Generation* (1978), *The Establishment* (1979), *The Legacy* (1981), *The Immigrant's Daughter* (1985), and *An Independent Woman* (1997). *Redemption* appeared in 1999. Fast's other works include children's books, detective stories written under the name E. V. Cunningham, plays, and short stories. His efforts on behalf of communism won him the Stalin International Peace Prize (1953), and for years Fast was blacklisted by the film industry. In *Being Red* (1990), he tells of the American Communist Party from the perspective of his long association with it.

Father, The, or, American Shandyism (1789),   a play by WILLIAM DUNLAP. This play, the second American comedy, depicts the rescue of two young women from an impostor, Captain Haller's servant Ranter, who pretends to be a British officer and who woos a neglected wife while he really intends to marry her wealthy young sister. The guardian of the two women appears in time to rescue them. The play, revised in 1806, was then called *The Father of an Only Child*.

Fathers, Sam.   A character in works by WILLIAM FAULKNER. Son of an Indian man and a slave woman, Fathers is a major figure in "A Justice," which tells how he earned his name, originally Had-Two-Fathers; "The Old People," and "The Bear."

Faulkner, William (1897–1962),   short-story writer, novelist. Born in New Albany, Mississippi, Faulkner came from a family long settled in northern Mississippi. His great-grandfather, William C. Falkner, was a plantation owner, a colonel in the Confederate army, a railroad builder, and, significantly, a novelist. His THE WHITE ROSE OF MEMPHIS was published in 1880 and enjoyed a considerable measure of popular success. Whenever the younger Faulkner's third-grade teacher asked the children what they meant to be, the future Nobel Prize winner would answer: "I want to be a writer like my great-granddaddy."

The crowded and exciting life of Colonel William Falkner ended violently in 1889 when a former business partner and political rival shot him down on the streets of his home town, Ripley, Mississippi. This and other episodes from Colonel Falkner's life were to furnish the raw material for such novels as SARTORIS and THE UNVANQUISHED, where Colonel Falkner is obviously the prototype of COLONEL JOHN SARTORIS. Faulkner's grandfather, John Wesley Thompson Falkner, also provided suggestions for the novels, and he would seem to be the model for Bayard Sartoris ("Old Bayard"), who is the young hero of *The Unvanquished*, and who is also seen as the aging banker of *Sartoris, The Town*, and some of Faulkner's short stories.

Murry Falkner, the father of the novelist, married an Oxford girl, Maud Butler, and though William was born at

New Albany, the Falkners moved to Oxford a few years later in 1902. As the family line descended to William Faulkner, there was a concomitant recession from Sartoris-like violence to the humdrum life of the small town. Murry Falkner ran a livery stable and then a hardware store before becoming business manager of the University of Mississippi, in Oxford.

William Faulkner attended the University of Mississippi for little more than a year. He was not an eager student and cared little for formal education—he dropped out of high school at the end of the tenth grade and had to be admitted to the university as a special student, a status he could claim as a World War veteran. Having been turned down in his attempt to enter the American Air Force because of insufficient height, Faulkner enlisted in the Royal Canadian Air Force in 1918 and during this period adopted Faulkner as the spelling of his name. The war ended before he could receive his commission or see service on the western front. He was made an honorary second lieutenant on December 22, 1918, after being mustered out.

In the years that followed, Faulkner was in and out of Oxford and in and out of one job after another—house-painter, store clerk, dishwasher, even a rumrunner during Prohibition—as he tried to find himself and establish himself as a writer. But Faulkner did not postpone marriage until he had established himself as a novelist. His boyhood sweetheart, Estelle Oldham, had returned to Oxford with her children, a boy and a girl, after divorcing her first husband. In 1929 Faulkner married her. Two children were born to this marriage, a boy who died in infancy and a girl.

Unlike many American writers who took up residence in New York or just outside it, Faulkner continued to live in his hometown, close to his chosen material. Beginning in 1936, he went to Hollywood from time to time to work as a writer on various movies. Later he undertook cultural missions for the State Department to France, Brazil, and Japan. But until 1957, except for occasional sojourns in New York, Oxford remained his home base. In 1957–1958, however, Faulkner was writer in residence at the University of Virginia. His daughter lived in Charlottesville, Virginia, and in his last few years the Faulkners divided their time between Oxford and Charlottesville. Faulkner held an honorary post in the University of Virginia Library until the time of his death in 1962.

An important element in Faulkner's education and in his preparation for a literary career came from his friendship with a fellow townsman, Phil Stone. Stone, educated at Yale, made Faulkner's acquaintance in 1914. He suggested authors for Faulkner to read, tried to put him in touch with the literary movements of the day, and helped finance Faulkner's book of poems The Marble Faun (1924.)

Faulkner accompanied Stone to New Haven in 1918 and lived there for a few months, working in the Winchester arms factory. Later on, Stone suggested that Faulkner try to get to New York, in the hope that in this great center of the publishing business he might meet other writers and editors. In 1923 Faulkner did go to New York and stayed with STARK YOUNG, the drama critic, who had formerly taught at the University of

Mississippi. Among other jobs in New York Faulkner clerked in a bookstore managed by Elizabeth Prall, a friend of Young's, but soon he was back in Oxford as university postmaster. It was scarcely a job calculated to hold the imagination of a restless young genius, and Faulkner finally retired from it with the now celebrated comment, variously reported: ". . . thank God I won't ever again have to be at the beck and call of every son of a bitch who's got two cents to buy a stamp." Early the next year, 1925, Faulkner went to New Orleans and there became acquainted with SHERWOOD ANDERSON, who had shortly before married Faulkner's friend, Elizabeth Prall.

It was through his association with Anderson that Faulkner produced his first novel. According to Faulkner, when Sherwood Anderson found that Faulkner had written a book, he promised to persuade his publisher to accept it provided that he himself would not have to read it. So, in 1926, Boni and Liveright published Soldier's Pay, a World War I novel. Though it received some favorable notices as an experimental novel by an unknown author, it did not sell. But it inaugurated Faulkner's long and brilliant career as a writer of fiction.

In the latter part of 1925 Faulkner and a friend shipped on a freighter to Europe for a walking trip through France and Germany. The trip supplied material for later stories. Faulkner returned to New York early in 1926, in time for the publication of Soldier's Pay, and returned to the Mississippi Gulf coast to write his second novel, Mosquitoes, about the New Orleans artistic colony.

It was only with his third novel, Sartoris (1929), that Faulkner turned to the locale he was to make celebrated in literature. Sherwood Anderson had said to Faulkner: "You're a country boy; all you know is that little patch up there in Mississippi where you started from. But that's all right too." In Satoris Faulkner began to write about this little patch of northern Mississippi. He created YOKNAPATAWPHA COUNTY and its county seat, Jefferson, a composite of several of the Mississippi towns he knew. (Jefferson is derived primarily from Oxford, but there are also touches of Ripley, New Albany, and Holly Springs.) He peopled his county with the human beings he knew and, as already remarked, with characters drawn from his own family history.

In Sartoris Faulkner also began to develop the themes that run through his greatest work. True, the style of his novel is still mannered in something of the fin-de-siècle fashion of his two early novels, and its world somewhat resembles that of Eliot's THE WASTE LAND. The protagonist is a restless young man, burnt out with his experiences in the war, returning to a life emptied of meaning, and craving violence as a kind of substitute for meaning. But this particular world-weary soldier, "young Bayard," is returning to a stable community. The deracinated young Southerner, in his fury and despair, is thus silhouetted against the traditional order of the old South.

In 1929 also appeared Faulkner's first great novel, THE SOUND AND THE FURY, a work still regarded by many critics as his finest. Like Sartoris, this novel is laid in Yoknapatawpha County, but it is centered within one household. Though some episodes occur as far away as Cambridge, Massachusetts, the focus remains almost obsessively with one family and with the relationships within their house. The Compsons, formerly one of the aristocratic families of the county, have fallen on evil days. The mother, a weak and whining hypochondriac, has poisoned the whole family relationship; the husband has taken to drink and cynicism; the daughter, Candace, has become a wanton and has finally left home. The three sons are Benjy, an idiot; Quentin, an obsessed young intellectual; and Jason, an embittered "practical" man.

Because of the audacity of its technique, the book became a critical sensation. Faulkner said that he began to tell the story entirely "through the eyes of the idiot child since I felt that it would be more effective as told by someone capable only of knowing what happened, but not why. I saw that I had not told the story that time. I tried to tell it again, the same story through the eyes of another brother [Quentin]. That was still not it. I told it for the third time through the eyes of the third brother [Jason]. That was still not it. I tried to gather the pieces together and fill in the gaps by making myself the spokesman."

The Sound and the Fury is a difficult work, though the idiot's section actually causes less trouble to the attentive reader than might be supposed. It is also probably Faulkner's most lyrical book, and many people feel it is his most despairing book. But it has its positive elements: there is the Negro servant Dilsey, with her powerful religious faith and her competence and her compassion, and there is the total perspective in which the author has placed all the events.

One year later Faulkner published his short novel AS I LAY DYING. In some ways it is Faulkner's most brilliant work. Like *The Sound and the Fury*, this novel deals with a Southern family, though this time a poor white family living in the hills. The story is at once comic, horrifying, and heroic, but Faulkner maintains complete control of his tone throughout the novel, and only the imperceptive reader will feel that the story is merely comic or merely horrifying or that it represents some uneasy mixture of the two.

In spite of the brilliance of *The Sound and the Fury* and of *As I Lay Dying*, it was not until 1931 that any of Faulkner's books achieved wide sales. In that year he published SANCTUARY. Faulkner once wrote that he decided, after his first two novels had failed to sell, to invent "the most horrific tale I could imagine" and that he wrote it in about three weeks. This he sent in the summer of 1929 to his publisher, who wrote back to him at once that he couldn't publish it: "We'd both be in jail." Faulkner was working on the night shift at the power plant of the university and by about eleven o'clock, when most people had gone to bed and the requirements for steam had reduced, he had time to write. So "on these nights, between 12 and 4, I wrote *As I Lay Dying* in six weeks, without changing a word." He sent it off to his publisher and more or less forgot about *Sanctuary* until suddenly, after *As I Lay Dying* had been published, he received the galley proofs. "Then I saw that [*Sanctuary*] was so terrible that there were but two things to do: tear it up or rewrite it. . . . So I tore the galleys down and rewrote the book. It had been already set up once, so I had to pay for the privilege of rewriting it, trying to make out of it

something which would not shame *The Sound and the Fury* and *As I Lay Dying* too much. . . ."

Faulkner did do a thorough revision, as the galley proofs, which have been preserved, show. Indeed, *Sanctuary* has been too much maligned. It is bitter and terrible, but it is not merely titillating, nor is it irresponsible in its vision of evil. Whether the public sensed its deeper virtues or was merely pleasurably shocked by the nature of the plot, Faulkner's name became a drawing card and from then on he was able to place stories in the better-paying magazines. It is significant that collections of his stories, *These Thirteen* and *Doctor Martino and Other Stories*, appeared in 1931 and 1934. Faulkner was a master of the short story—some of those printed in these collections are the finest of our time.

The succession of great novels continued in a brilliant display of power. One of the finest, LIGHT IN AUGUST, appeared in 1932. It is another story of Yoknapatawpha County, though the older and aristocratic families of the town hardly appear in it, nor for that matter do the blacks. It is a story of white men, yeomen, and poor whites.

Light in August exhibits one of Faulkner's most crowded canvases. It is packed with interesting characters and has a plot far too complicated to be summarized, but one can risk a single generalization: it is one of Faulkner's many books about the importance of community, and surely a basic theme is the Puritan's alienation from nature and his fear of the feminine principle. Its Puritan characters strive to hold themselves in rigid stance above the relaxed female world. Faulkner finds the spectacle—as with *As I Lay Dying*—sometimes monstrous, sometimes comic, sometimes heroic.

ABSALOM, ABSALOM! is perhaps Faulkner's masterpiece. In it we again meet Quentin Compson, the sensitive brother who commits suicide in *The Sound and the Fury*. Just before leaving Mississippi to enter Harvard, he becomes involved in the story of Thomas Sutpen, who had appeared out of nowhere seventy-six years before to erect a great plantation house, intending to found a dynasty of plantation owners. The decaying mansion still remains, but Sutpen's daughter Judith has long been dead, and his son Henry has never been heard of since he killed his sister's fiancé at the very gates of Sutpen's Hundred just after the Civil War. In the novel Quentin and his Canadian roommate at Harvard sift the meager evidence in an attempt to account for the ancient events.

Absalom, Absalom! also is in some sense Faulkner's most difficult novel. In reviewing the tiny sheaf of facts as interpreted by different personalities there is so much subjective interpretation, so much conjecture and speculation, that the indolent reader may give up in despair. But *Absalom, Absalom!* is much more than a virtuoso display of eerie Gothicism and much more than a somber commentary on the black problem. It raises profound questions about the meaning of the past and its availability to man, and considers the loyalties that are rooted in the deeper, irrational layers of man which, though they often seem absurd when examined under the glare of pure reason, nevertheless make man human, not a calculating monster.

Absalom, Absalom! was followed in 1938 by the most seriously underrated of Faulkner's novels, *The Unvanquished*. This book returns us to the fortunes of the Sartorises and ends with one of Faulkner's finest triumphs, his account of the coming to manhood of Bayard Sartoris.

In 1940 Faulkner published *The Hamlet*, the story of how the poor-white Flem Snopes, who represents sheer rapacity, takes over a little farming community some miles out from Jefferson and finally, having beaten down all opposition, marries the beautiful Eula Varner. Eula is already with child by another man and Flem is impotent, but he wants the marriage as a kind of badge of triumph. *The Hamlet* contains some of Faulkner's richest humor, including the celebrated tale of the spotted horses. Seventeen years later Faulkner brought Flem Snopes into Jefferson in *The Town* (1957). *The Mansion* (1959) completes this trilogy of novels on the SNOPES FAMILY. (See THE HAMLET for the trilogy.)

GO DOWN, MOSES AND OTHER STORIES (1942) has to do with the fortunes of the McCaslin family. It contains "The Bear," the most celebrated of all Faulkner's short stories, and perhaps his finest, though another story in this volume, "The Fire and the Hearth," is in its own way magnificent too. Lucas Beauchamp, Faulkner's great black character, first seen in "The Fire and the Hearth," is saved from a lynching in INTRUDER IN THE DUST (1948), a novel that deals with the modern South. It is this South also that is portrayed in REQUIEM FOR A NUN (1951), a sequel to *Sanctuary*.

A FABLE (1954) retells the story of Christ's passion as reenacted in the life of a corporal in the French Army in World War I. *A Fable* is probably Faulkner's most ambitious work, but many critics have felt that desertion of Yoknapatawpha County was a mistake and have deplored the tendency of this novel to turn into a kind of allegory.

Critics of Faulkner's early work had considerable difficulty in deciding what to make of it. Perhaps the first serious consideration came in 1939 with George Marion O'Donnell's article "Faulkner's Mythology." O'Donnell quite rightly saw Faulkner as a traditional writer and called him a traditional moralist. In *Sanctuary*, for example, O'Donnell found no meaningless display of horrors, but a kind of allegory in which the heroine stood for "Southern Womanhood Corrupted but Undefiled," whose drunken escort could be called "Corrupted Tradition" and who, in her encounter with POPEYE, falls into "the clutches of amoral Modernism . . . which is itself impotent, but which with the aid of its strong ally Natural Lust ('Red') rapes Southern Womanhood unnaturally and then seduces her so satisfactorily that her corruption is total, and she becomes the tacit ally of Modernism." O'Donnell overemphasized the allegorical import and portioned out the symbolism almost too neatly. But his essay pointed in the right direction in its insistence that Faulkner was an artist dealing responsibly with a traditional society.

Malcolm Cowley's introduction to *The Portable Faulkner* in 1946 has exercised a powerful influence on subsequent criticism. The essay stressed the continuity and consistency of Faulkner's work and pointed up Faulkner's concern with "the

tragic fable of Southern history." Indeed, Cowley set a whole generation of reviewers and critics talking about Faulkner's work as a "myth or legend of the South." In this legend the planters established a society that lived by a single-minded code but sanctioned slavery, something that put a curse on the land and brought about the Civil War. After the war had been lost, they freed their land from the carpetbaggers but found that they had enemies at home, "the unscrupulous tribe of Snopes." As "a price of victory . . . the Snopeses had to serve the mechanized civilization of the North, which [is] morally impotent in itself, but which, with the aid of its Southern retainers, ended by corrupting the Southern nation."

Cowley's essay thus cut the grooves in which Faulkner criticism has tended to run ever since. The excesses of much of this later criticism come from oversimplifications of the thesis set forth briefly in Cowley's useful essay. Later writers, knowing little of the rich diversity of Southern social structure, tend to turn all poor Southerners into Snopeses and all of Faulkner's gentlefolk into decadent aristocrats. Or, because of the intensity of interest in the race problem and in civil rights, critics bear down on certain moral issues almost independently of the fictional context: Faulkner is exposing the cruelty of the South and showing that Southern society was rotten to the core—or perhaps he is scolded because he is not severe enough in so exposing it.

When Faulkner is not the victim of moralizing literary sociologists, he is frequently kidnapped by the symbol-mongers, who tirelessly improve upon hints found in the fiction, hints of allegorical and symbolical meanings—but which the symbol-monger tends to abstract from the imaginative structure and to develop irresponsibly and out of context: Every character who dies at thirty-three is a "Christ-figure," horses are symbols of destruction, rain signifies death.

Like every other great artist, Faulkner used symbols. His best work is rooted in the experience of Southern history, but the significance of his use of the Southern heritage must be understood. As a novelist, Faulkner dealt not only with the problems of 20th-century man, but with the universal problems of mankind. In order to write about human beings, he naturally made use of the human beings he knew best in the setting he knew best. This setting provided him with a very important resource, for the background of a traditional society permitted the novelist to give a special focus to modern problems. Man's loss of community, his alienation, and his loneliness are common themes in 20th-century fiction, but the loneliness of Hightower and the alienation of Joe Christmas and the general break with the community made by half a dozen other characters in *Light in August* take on a special urgency and significance when seen against the background of Yoknapatawpha County, in which a living community exists—whether it be regarded as baleful in its paralyzing inertia or nourishing in its vitality.

Again, because in the South moral problems tend to be concrete, with good and bad polarized and not often shading off into a neutral gray penumbra, the entire problem of values can be put with dramatic force and conviction. Faulkner's concern with the larger issues of our time is plain in *A Fable*; but he has been more successful in dealing with these problems in the novels of Yoknapatawpha County, where they arise from a concrete context and are dramatized within that context.

Faulkner, a man of slight build, graying hair, and fine dark eyes, was quiet, even self-effacing. In spite of his essential shyness and old-fashioned courtliness, all kinds of legends have grown up about him, including stories about his bohemian behavior. But the quality and quantity of Faulkner's work make it quite clear he was a dedicated and energetic craftsman who could not often take a holiday from the world of responsible endeavor. The sheer quantity is impressive, and it is not work that was casually dashed off: Faulkner was very much the conscious artist. There is plenty of evidence—in terms of drafts and revisions—to show that he was careful to write and rewrite until his own artistic conscience had been satisfied.

Some of the more amusing Faulkner stories have to do with his Hollywood experiences, including the saga of cross-purposes in which the studio that had been paying him for six months couldn't find him in Hollywood and, in response to frantic telegrams, finally discovered that he was sitting quietly at home in Mississippi. But it should be said that Faulkner had taken his movie script work seriously, though he apparently had sealed it off in a separate compartment from the work on his novels and stories. Perhaps his ability to write without embarrassment or condescension for the audience of *The Saturday Evening Post* as well as for the intellectual shows a healthy lack of self-consciousness. It is hard to think of another American writer who could do so.

Faulkner is clearly one of the greatest American novelists. His Nobel Prize in 1949 was merely a special recognition of what most serious critics of fiction had already come to agree upon. Some of Faulkner's later novels were disappointing and those of the last twenty years scarcely came up to those of the great period from 1929 to 1942, but it is a measure of the vitality of Faulkner's creative urge that it never occurred to him to rest on his laurels, and he was still capable of magnificent writing in the latter part of his life—witness portions of *A Fable* and *The Mansion*.

His major works include *Soldier's Pay* (1926); *Mosquitoes* (1927); *Sartoris* (1929); *The Sound and the Fury* (1929); *As I Lay Dying* (1930); *Sanctuary* (1931); THESE THIRTEEN (short stories, 1931); *Light in August* (1931); *A Green Bough* (verse, 1933); *Doctor Martino and Other Stories* (1934); *Pylon* (1935); *Absalom, Absalom!* (1936); *The Unvanquished* (1938); THE WILD PALMS (1939); *The Hamlet* (1940); *Go Down, Moses and Other Stories* (1942); *Intruder in the Dust* (1948); KNIGHT'S GAMBIT (stories, 1949); *Collected Stories of William Faulkner* (1950); *Requiem for a Nun* (1951); *A Fable* (1954); *Big Woods* (stories, 1955); *The Town* (1957); *The Mansion* (1959); and *The Reivers* (1962).

Discussions and interviews appear in *Faulkner at Nagano* (1956), *Faulkner in the University* (1959), *Faulkner at West Point* (1964), and *The Lion in the Garden: Interviews 1926–1962* (1968). Faulkner's other titles include *Essays, Speeches, and Public Letters* (1965); *Flags in the Dust* (1973, a longer version of

Sartoris); *Selected Letters* (1977); *Uncollected Stories* (1979); and *Faulkner's Manuscripts* (44 volumes projected, 1986–   ).

Among biographies, Frederick R. Karl, *William Faulkner: American Writer* (1989) is recent, comprehensive, and authoritative. See also the authorized biography by Joseph Blotner, *Faulkner: A Biography* (2 v. 1974; revised in one volume, 1984). Among other biographical and critical works see especially Cleanth Brooks, *William Faulkner: The Yoknapatawpha Country* (1963), *William Faulkner: Toward Yoknapatawpha and Beyond* (1978), and *William Faulkner: First Encounters* (1983); David Minter, *William Faulkner: His Life and Work* (1981); and Stephen B. Oates, *Faulkner: The Man and the Artist* (1987).

CLEANTH BROOKS/GP

Fauset, Jessie Redmon (1884?–1961),   novelist, editor. Born in New Jersey, Fauset was educated at Cornell University (she was perhaps the first black woman graduate, 1905), the University of Pennsylvania, and the Sorbonne. She taught French in high school in Washington, D.C., then became literary editor of CRISIS (1919–26), encouraging the writers of the HARLEM RENAISSANCE, and wrote and edited *Brownie's Book* (1920–21), a magazine for African-American children. She portrayed mostly middle-class African-Americans, often striving for white acceptance, in four novels: *There Is Confusion* (1924), *Plum Bun: A Novel Without a Moral* (1928), *The Chinaberry Tree: A Novel of American Life* (1931), and *Comedy, American Style* (1933).

Faust, Frederick ["Max Brand"] (1892–1944) novelist, short-story writer, movie scriptwriter. Born in Seattle, Faust wrote mostly as Max Brand. He was a prolific writer of westerns, including *The Untamed* (1918) and *Destry Rides Again* (1930), perhaps his best known, and wrote the Dr. Kildare stories for films and in books. Under his own name he published poetry in *The Village Street* (1922) and *Dionysus in Hades* (1931).

Faust, Irvin (1924–   ),   novelist, short-story writer. Born in New York City and educated at City College and Columbia, Faust became a teacher and high school guidance counselor. *Roar Lion Roar* (1965) presents stories of ethnic diversity, with madness dominant. *The Steagle* (1966), a novel, depicts the descent into psychosis of an English professor in a New York City college. In *The File on Stanley Patton Bucha* (1970) a Vietnam veteran goes underground to spy on political extremists. *Willy Remembers* (1971), one of his best, is history with fact and fantasy mixed in the remembrance of a 93-year-old man. *Foreign Devils* (1973), a novel within a novel, was inspired by Nixon's trip to China; it deals with the Boxer Rebellion. *A Star in the Family* (1975) is about the reminiscences of an aging vaudevillian. *Newsreel* (1980) contrasts the sense of purpose of World War II with the deterioration of the 1950s and 1960s; the Kennedy assassination is seen through the eyes of a veteran army officer. *Jim Daudy* (1994) is set during the Italian conquest of Ethiopia.

Fawcett, Edgar (1847–1904),   novelist, poet, playwright, essayist. Fawcett devoted most of his novels to mild ridicule of New York society. Among his best are *Purple and*

Fine Linen (1873), *An Ambitious Woman* (1884), and *Social Silhouettes* (1885). His plays, especially *Americans Abroad* (1881), also indulged in social satire.

Fay, Theodore [Sedgwick] (1807–1898), writer, editor, diplomat, lawyer. Fay succeeded his father as editor of the New York *Mirror* and as the author of a column called "The Little Genius," and some of his contributions were later collected in *Dreams and Reveries of a Quiet Man* (2 v. 1832). After 1833 he traveled abroad, supplying the *Mirror* with travel sketches. *Norman Leslie* (1835) was his first and best novel. The plot was apparently based on an actual murder case. A girl disappears and a murder is suspected; Norman is tried and acquitted; later the girl reappears in Paris. His later novels, among them *Hoboken: A Romance of New York* (1843), did not do as well. He spent the latter part of his life in diplomatic posts. He also wrote *The Three Germanys* (2 v. 1889).

Fearing, Kenneth [Flexner] (1902–1961), editor, poet, novelist. Born in Illinois, Fearing was educated at the University of Wisconsin. He became a writer in New York, often using pseudonyms (including Donald F. Bedford). His verse, often satiric, was collected in *Angel Arms* (1929), *Poems* (1935), *Dead Reckoning* (1938), *Afternoon of a Pawnbroker* (1943), *Stranger at Coney Island* (1949), and *New and Selected Poems* (1956). Among his novels, the best known is THE BIG CLOCK (1946). Others are *The Hospital* (1939), *Clark Gifford's Body* (1942), *The Loneliest Girl in the World* (1951), *The Generous Heart* (1954), and *The Crozart Story* (1960).

Fear of Flying (1973), a novel by ERICA JONG.

Feathertop (*The International Magazine*, 1852), a story by NATHANIEL HAWTHORNE. It tells about a scarecrow that comes to life in 17th-century New England. On this story Percy MacKaye based his play THE SCARECROW (1908), which was later turned into an impressive silent movie, *Puritan Passions*. The story was included in later editions of MOSSES FROM AN OLD MANSE.

Feboldson, Febold. A legendary character closely resembling PAUL BUNYAN. Chief relator of the Feboldson activities was Paul R. Beath, a native of Illinois who came to live in Gothenburg, Nebraska, at an early age. In 1927 or 1928 he was attracted by stories about Feboldson that were appearing in the Gothenburg *Times* from the pen of Don Holmes. Holmes attributed creation of the character to Wayne T. Carroll, a local lumber dealer who wrote in the Gothenburg *Independent* tales about Feboldson under the pen name "Watt Tell." Later Carroll used Feboldson in advertising for his lumber company—an origin exactly like Bunyan's. He owes his continued existence mainly to Beath, who in 1937 prepared for the Federal Writers' Project in Nebraska a pamphlet entitled *Legends of Febold Feboldson* and later (1948) published *Febold Feboldson: Tall Tales from the Great Plains.*

Federalist, The (1787–88). A series of eighty-five papers by ALEXANDER HAMILTON, JAMES MADISON, and JOHN JAY written to bring about ratification of the CONSTITUTION. Seventy-seven were published originally under the pen name PUBLIUS in several New York City newspapers. They appeared from October 27, 1787 to April 2, 1788. These were collected in book form in 1788, with eight additional essays. In sober, convincing style they discussed dangers from foreign influence and from dissensions among the states, union as a safeguard against domestic faction and as a means of securing economy, the defects of the Confederation, military power, taxation, republican principles, powers conferred by the Constitution, the architecture of the new government, the character of the House of Representatives and the Senate, the Executive Department and the Judiciary, and other problems raised by the Constitution. So authoritative was this treatment by men who had themselves played a principal role in framing the great document that the *Federalist* papers have been taken into account by our courts in deciding Constitutional questions. Taking a place with Aristotle's *Politics*, Machiavelli's *Prince*, Hobbes's *Leviathan*, and Marx and Engels's *Communist Manifesto* among the most outstanding studies in the practical application of political theory, they have exerted an enormous influence in many lands. They appeared in French in 1792, later were translated into Portuguese, Spanish, German, and Italian, and were often reprinted when Latin American revolutions occurred. Carl Van Doren noted "the remarkable parallel between the arguments in favor of the United Nations." Jefferson's praise, bestowed in 1788, still is widely echoed: "The best commentary on the principles of government which ever was written."

The authorship has remained unclear. A copy of the two-volume edition of 1788 was specially bound by Hamilton, who had corrected the text, for presentation to General Washington; in it Madison made extensive autograph annotations indicating the authorship of each paper. Yet in an 1802 edition the names of the individual writers were still a secret. In 1804, however, Hamilton, about to fight the duel with Burr that—as he seemed to have anticipated—cost him his life, set down a memorandum giving the authorships, some incorrectly ascribed. His chief mistake was to deny Madison credit for twelve essays he had written and for a major part in three more; the existence of the manuscripts for some of these makes the mistake clear. Hamilton undoubtedly wrote a good majority of the essays, probably at least fifty-one. Madison wrote at least fourteen, and Jay five. The remaining fifteen were probably written primarily by Hamilton and Madison. Important among early editions are the first (1788); the George F. Hopkins edition, with alterations approved by Hamilton (1802); and the Jacob Gideon edition, with corrections by Madison (1818). Modern scholarly editions are those by Jacob E. Cooke (1961) and Benjamin F. Wright (1961).

Federal Theater Project. When the depression that began in 1929 was still being fought vigorously, an essential part of the battle was undertaken by the WORKS PROGRESS ADMINISTRATION (WPA), which sought among other things to provide a modest livelihood for artists of all types without hampering their creative freedom. On August 27, 1935, Hallie Flanagan, a former student of GEORGE PIERCE BAKER and for ten years director of the Vassar Experimental Theater, became director of the Federal Theater Project. She organized five regional theaters: the Living Newspaper, a dramatic discussion of social and economic problems; the popular price theater, for original plays by new authors; the experimental theater; the Negro theater; and the tryout theater. These theaters were established all over the country, and in four years put on thousands of productions. These included revivals, including Marlowe's *Dr. Faustus* and Elmer Rice's *Adding Machine*; new plays like the documentaries *Triple-A Plowed Under* (1936), *Injunction Granted* (1936), and Arthur Arent's *One-Third of a Nation* (1938) on the housing problem. Two series of *Federal Theater Plays* were issued in 1938.

By that year strong opposition to the Project made itself felt in Congress, as Flanagan later related in *Arena: The Story of the Federal Theater* (1940). The case against it was tried behind closed doors "with no adequate presentation of the evidence," comments Edmond M. Gagey in *Revolution in American Drama*, 1947. "The highlight in this Congressional farce-tragedy came," he says, "with the question by Representative Joe Starnes as to whether 'this Marlowe—author of *Dr. Faustus* [1588]—was a Communist.'" The Project was closed by Congress on June 30, 1939.

Federal Writers' Project. Established (1934) under Henry G. Alsberg as part of the WORKS PROGRESS ADMINISTRATION (WPA), the Federal Writers' Project was most active from 1935 to 1939, when it produced its massive series of American Guides to the various states; the series closed in 1941. The project also produced almanacs, historical leaflets, compilations of folklore, etc. In addition to forty-eight state directors, who enlisted local sponsorship and cooperation, the project at one time included 6,600 workers in state and local branches. It came to an end because of the general opposition to the idea of supporting people of artistic and literary ability as a special group, yet while it lasted it was a unique and in many ways excellent program of government sponsorship in the arts. Among writers given employment were James Agee, Conrad Aiken, Saul Bellow, Erskine Caldwell, John Cheever, Ralph Ellison, Archibald MacLeish, Edmund Wilson, Richard Wright, and Frank Yerby. Jerre Mangione wrote a history, *The Dream and the Deal: Federal Writers' Project, 1935–1943* (1971).

Federman, Raymond (1928–   ), novelist, critic, poet. Author of critical books on Samuel Beckett, Federman emerged in the 1970s as a proponent of an experimental fictional aesthetic he called Surfiction. Akin to earlier movements, like Dadaism and Surrealism, Surfiction borrows from film, television, and other sources to create deliberate fractures of coherence and logic in the verbal text. His novels include *Double or Nothing* (1971), *Take It or Leave It* (1976), *The Voice in the Closet* (1979), *The Twofold Vibration* (1982), *Smiles on Washington Square* (1986), winner of an American Book Award, *To Whom It May Concern* (1990), and *A Version of My Life* (1993).

Feeley, Mrs. A beer-drinking woman who, with various friends, conducts a series of comic escapades in novels by Mary Lasswell. The first was called *Suds in Your Eye* (1942).

Feibleman, Peter S[teiman] (1930–   ), novelist. Born in New York City, Feibleman studied in the drama department of the Carnegie Institute of Technology and at Columbia University, and worked as an actor in Spanish, French, and Italian films for eight years. His first novel, *A Place Without Twilight* (1958), won critical acclaim. Set in New Orleans, it deals with a "twilight" girl, not quite African-American yet not quite white, and with her search for self-realization. It was dramatized as *Tiger Tiger Burning Bright* (1963). *Daughters of Necessity* (1959), also set in the South, treats symbolically the relationships between a man and the five women in his family. *The Columbus Tree* (1972) is a novel of Americans in Spain, the author's home for seven years. *Charlie Bay*, a novel, appeared in 1980. *Strangers and Graves* (1966) collects four novellas.

Female American, The, or, The Adventures of Unca Eliza Winkfield (London, 1767; Newburyport, Massachusetts, 1790),   an adventure story. The book claims to present the actual experiences, often fantastic, of the person named in the title. It shows the settlers of Virginia, the marriage of Unca's father to an Indian princess, Unca's education in England, adventures on shipboard and on a desert island, and Unca's work as a missionary.

Female Poets of America, The. See RUFUS W. GRISWOLD.

Female Quixotism: Exhibited in the Romantic Opinions and Extravagant Adventures of Dorcasina Sheldon (1801),   a novel by TABITHA TENNEY (1762–1837). Tenney, an effective satirist, made it her purpose to check the excesses of novel reading on the part of romantically minded women like her thirty-four-year-old heroine. The novelist herself had obviously done much reading, not merely in the sentimental and Gothic romances of her day, but in Shakespeare, Richardson, Fielding, Smollett, and Sheridan. She had particularly in mind CHARLOTTE LENNOX's widely read parody, *The Female Quixote* (1752). Tenney's Dorcasina has a practical maid, Betty, who does her best to restrain her. At moments of crisis her father steps in, so she never suffers deeply for her indiscretions as she seeks a lover. Twice she rejects offers of marriage as not sufficiently romantic, and at the end she is still unwed and turns to a quiet spinsterhood and good deeds.

Feminism in Literary Studies. Before the 1970s, everyone knew what the classics of American literature were supposed to be. The names of the greats were household words—Hawthorne, Melville, Whitman, Dickinson, Hemingway, Fitzgerald, Faulkner—and only one of these names was that of a woman. With the entry of feminism into the American academy, questions arose: Why were there so few so-called great American women writers? Why were women portrayed so negatively in American classics? Who set the standards for quality in literature, and whose interests did those standards serve? Such questions resulted in a feminist reevaluation of the canon, the unofficial list of works deemed worthy of literary study.

Feminist critics began in the early 1970s to argue that the aesthetic criteria for works considered to be classics are not, as scholars had assumed, timeless and fixed, but are arbitrary and self-perpetuating. Established within academic institutions populated mainly by white upper-class and middle-class heterosexual men, the criteria for greatness served to exclude from the canon most writers whose sex, race, or class diverged from the mainstream. Great literature was supposed to have universal significance, but feminist critics point out that matters of universal interest to the dominant culture may hold little value for groups relegated to the margins of that culture. As a result, alternative American traditions began to emerge in the late 1970s and 1980s, for instance, the African-American women's traditions uncovered by such critics as Barbara Christian, Claudia Tate, Hortense Spillers, Valerie Smith, Nellie McKay, and Susan Wills; the lesbian traditions proposed by Catherine Stimpson, Bonnie Zimmerman, and Barbara Smith; and the traditions sketched out by practitioners of gynocriticism—Elaine Showalter's term for the study of women's writing.

Just as there are many traditions and canons in contemporary U.S. literary study, there are many feminisms. No single voice can speak for them all. Feminist criticism usually combines attention to women with various approaches based on contemporary literary theory, resulting in methodologies as diverse as historical-materialist or Marxian feminisms, psychoanalytic or Lacanian feminisms (especially strong in film studies), and poststructuralist feminisms drawing on the insights of Bakhtinian dialogics, Derridean deconstruction, narrative poetics, and reader-response theory. As the purpose of this essay is to explain the relationship of feminist criticism to the study of American literature, however, it will concentrate on the impact of influential U.S. feminist critics on that field. This impact has been felt in three broad stages, adapted here from an essay by Elaine Showalter, "A Criticism of Our Own": (1) a critique of the dominant, male tradition; (2) the construction of women's traditions; and (3) the consideration of how gender operates in culture at large and in the institution of literature more specifically.

Diverse as feminist critics may be, they share certain fundamental beliefs. They hold that the oppression of women is a fact of past and present lived experience, that sex leaves its marks in literary texts and in literary history, and that feminist literary criticism can serve as part of the effort to end oppression in the world outside of texts. Most American feminist critics in the early 1990s agree that oppressions based on race, social class, and sexual preference are inseparable from misogyny in Western culture, and that the so-called others in America—members of ethnic minorities, gay men and lesbians, working-class men and women, and women in general—merit more attention than they have traditionally received from literary critics. Feminist criticism is, then, a frankly political enterprise aimed at changing power structures in the academy and in the world.

Not all contemporary American women writers or critics are feminists; some, such as novelist GAIL GODWIN and critic Helen Vendler, argue for an androgynous ideal in art, averring that sex should make no significant difference in a writer's perspective, influences, or productions. Indeed, before the women's studies movement that began about 1960, the pro-androgyny stance operated as a form of feminism, in that it called for equal rights for women authors and academics. The critique of male-dominated culture growing out of the second wave of feminism in the 1970s, however, insisted that gender-based oppression was so endemic in all American institutions, including literature, that gender differences could no longer be overlooked.

Negative stereotyping of women in American men's classics is one kind of evidence feminists have gathered for textual oppression of women. KATE MILLETT's *Sexual Politics* (1969) initiated a sequence of feminist projects seeking to expose the derogatory portrayal of women in men's books, arguing that these portraits operate to reinforce the prejudices they seem to reflect. Judith Fetterley's *The Resisting Reader* (1977) took a different approach to the same problem, explaining that classic fiction by American men typically requires readers to identify with male protagonists against female adversaries. This results, Fetterley said, in what she termed the "immasculation" and alienation of women readers, who can nevertheless learn through feminist reading to resist that process. Such critiques have resulted in an awareness that so-called great works are of only relative value, and that one's pleasure in reading Melville or Hemingway may be mediated by one's sexual identification.

A parallel effort through the 1970s was the construction of American women's literary traditions. The major works of gynocriticism—Showalter's *A Literature of Their Own* (1977) and SANDRA GILBERT and Susan Gubar's *The Madwoman in the Attic* (1979)—focused mainly on British women writers, but several critics have traced American women's writing through the 19th century, including Nina Baym, Ann Douglas Wood, and ANNETTE KOLODNY, Gilbert and Gubar's *The Norton Anthology of Literature by Women* (1985)—controversial for its exclusive focus on feminist themes in women's literature and for its neglect of some marginalized groups, such as Chicana writers—places American authors alongside British contemporaries, emphasizing 19th- and 20th-century figures. Two anthologies of 19th-century American women's writing—*Provisions* (1985), edited by Judith Fetterley, and *Hidden Hands* (1985), edited by Lucy Freibert and Barbara White—bring forward the names of authors honored in their times but obscured by modern literary history.

The women's anthologies suggest a diversity among literary genres that has not been represented in traditional study of the American canon. Some of these fictional genres and their most often cited authors include the following: late 18th-century novels of sensibility and moral instruction—SUSANNA HASWELL ROWSON, HANNAH WEBSTER FORSTER; melodramatic fiction—E. D. E. N. SOUTHWORTH; frontier romance—LYDIA MARIA CHILD, CATHERINE MARIA SEDGWICK; realist domestic fiction—SARAH JOSEPHA BUELL HALE, CAROLINE KIRKLAND, HARRIET BEECHER STOWE, LOUISA MAY ALCOTT, ELIZABETH STUART PHELPS; regional realism—ROSE TERRY COOKE, SARAH ORNE JEWETT, MARY E. WILKINS FREEMAN, ALICE BROWN; didactic fiction—SUSAN WARNER, MARIA CUMMINS, MARTHA FINLEY; slave narratives—HARRIET JACOBS, Jarena Lee; and polemical or political fiction—SARA WILLIS PARTON (Fanny Fern), REBECCA HARDING DAVIS,

CHARLOTTE PERKINS GILMAN. Feminist criticism generally resists the idea that women's genres are minor, and has worked toward reducing the negative connotations of such terms as "sentimental," "didactic," and "regional," which are applied to 19th-century women's writing. As JOANNA RUSS has argued in *How to Suppress Women's Writing* (1983), placing women's writing into minor literary categories is one way that the academy has avoided taking women's texts altogether seriously. Although some feminists have held sentimental novels, for example, up to traditional aesthetic standards and found them wanting, Myra Jehlen, Nina Baym, Jane Tompkins, and others argue that these genres have standards and conventions of their own and should be read and evaluated in accordance with the tastes and expectations of their original audience.

Feminist scholarship has brought nonfictional genres into the foreground as well, looking at the work of diarists such as ALICE JAMES, lecturers—including such African-American speakers as SOJOURNER TRUTH and Maria W. Stewart, and such early feminists as ELIZABETH CADY STANTON—and essayists, MARGARET FULLER, Charlotte Forten Grimké. The poetry of EMILY DICKINSON has found new contexts for study in the work of other individual poets—PHILLIS WHEATLEY, LYDIA SIGOURNEY—and of women who collaborated on keepsake books and memorial poetry to be written and read within families.

The notion of women's traditions has encouraged critics of American feminists to regard women writers as answering, developing, and responding to one another's work. To do so is to see women's literary production in a context different from that of men. In the study of American literature, this separation did not arise by chance. Rather, it reflects the historical situation of women in 19th-century America. As historians such as Carroll Smith-Rosenberg, Mary Ryan, and Mary Kelley have shown, middle-class American social and cultural life depended on the so-called "ideology of separate spheres," the notion that men belong in the public world of economics and jobs, and women belong in the domestic sphere of childbearing and housekeeping. This division both fed on and perpetuated differences between the sexes in terms of attitudes, values, and experience. Such historically minded feminist critics as Mary Kelley, Annette Kolodny, and Jane Tompkins have argued that the division of the sphere is evident in the differences of content and aesthetics that separate 19th-century American women's writing from the work of their male contemporaries. Such generalizations can, of course, apply only to the middle- and upper-class women writers whose experience was governed by separate-spheres ideology. Historical circumstances contingent on the experiences of the working class come up in the work of such feminist critics as Lillian Robinson and Paul Lauter; racial and ethnic histories figure in the work of, for instance, PAULA GUNN ALLEN, who studies Native American genres; Amy Ling, Asian-American writing; Cherríe Moraga and Gloria Anzaldua, Chicana literature; and the critics mentioned above who are working on African-American women's literature.

In that it necessarily involves history, the construction of women's traditions in American literature overlaps with the study of how gender differences operate in American culture at large. "Gender studies," the most recent wave of U.S. feminist criticism, make a distinction between biologically determined *sex* (male/female) and culturally constructed *gender* (masculine/feminine). Whereas most people see sex as binary and absolute, gender is seen as existing on a continuum. Men and women place themselves or are placed at unfixed points along the spectrum of masculinity and femininity. Gender studies complicate the questions feminist criticism has raised, in that this approach sees no inevitable link between the sexes of authors and their ways of writing, or between the sexes and readers and their ways of responding to a text. Therefore, this kind of feminist criticism does not limit itself to studying the works of women writers or the experiences of women readers per se, but concentrates instead on the impact of gender on literary history, and on the signs of gender in texts and the role of gender in such institutions as the media or the university.

Jane Tompkins's *Sensational Designs: The Cultural Work of American Fiction, 1790–1860* (1985) is one influential application of this method to literary history, looking at the part gender has played in the formation of the American literary canon. Feminist gender studies have also begun concentrating on representations of masculinity in texts, as in the work of Eve Sedgwick, Joseph Boone, and Susan Jeffords, who specializes in film. Gender studies participate in breaking down the traditional boundaries of subject matter taught in English departments, extending their purview beyond literary genres and into mass-market forms. Feminist critics have been especially interested in products of popular culture aimed at female audiences, such as soap opera, women's films, and Harlequin-type romances. Feminists participating in American cultural studies include Mary Ann Doane, who studies Hollywood movies; Janice Radway and Leslie Rabine, who have published studies of mass-market romances; and Tania Modleski, whose work combines attention to both these genres with an interest in soap opera.

Feminist criticism, then, has contributed to the diversification of the American canon. In practical terms, this has meant inclusion of more women writers in anthologies and in course syllabi, as well as positive reassessment of female authors whose names had long been familiar but whose reputations were unsteady. In addition to Emily Dickinson, the women writers whose critical stock has risen since the feminist academic reevaluation of the 1970s and 1980s include Harriet Beecher Stowe, Louisa May Alcott, KATE CHOPIN—her novel *The Awakening* (1899) was one of the first discoveries of the women's studies movement in the 1970s—EDITH WHARTON, GERTRUDE STEIN, H. D. (Hilda Doolittle), MARIANNE MOORE, LILLIAN HELLMAN, EUDORA WELTY, GWENDOLYN BROOKS, and ADRIENNE RICH. These writers, among others, have been occupying increasingly secure ground in textbooks and classes, as academics try to achieve a more balanced representation of what American literature has been.

Feminist critics debate whether some women writers should be granted classic status, while others—too many of them representing cultures other than the white, middle-class, heterosexual mainstream—are excluded. Judging by how often certain texts are mentioned or analyzed by feminist critics and theorists, however, one could contend that a new feminist canon has emerged. Students of literature wishing to follow the debates within American feminist criticism would do well to know these works, which are the core of many literature curricula based on women's studies. Among others, the most frequently mentioned works by American women include Dickinson's poems, *Uncle Tom's Cabin* (1851–52), *Little Women* (1869), Charlotte Perkins Gilman's "The Yellow Wallpaper" (1892), Rebecca Harding Davis's "Life in the Iron Mills" (1861), *The Awakening* (1899), Edith Wharton's novels, ZORA NEALE HURSTON's *Their Eyes Were Watching God* (1937), Adrienne Rich's poems, MAXINE HONG KINGSTON's *The Woman Warrior* (1976), TONI MORRISON's novels, and ALICE WALKER's *The Color Purple* (1982). Arguably, all these works can be read as representing feminist perspectives on their subject matter, and all have provided fruitful ground for feminist criticism from many different approaches.

Some of the more radical approaches within feminism have affected the form of the literary critical essay itself. Contemporary feminist essays can be found in most major literary journals today, but they appear more consistently in U.S. periodicals specializing in women's literature and interdisciplinary gender studies, including *Feminist Studies, Women's Studies, Signs, Tulsa Studies in Women's Literature, Genders,* and *The NWSA* [National Women's Studies Association] *Journal*. In writing critical essays, some feminists have followed the lead of such French theorists as Julia Kristeva, Hélène Cixous, and Luce Irigaray, who experiment with *l'écriture feminine*, an attempt to "write [with/from/about] the body" of woman. These experiments result in a kind of writing that eschews traditional notions of thesis, evidence, and transitions. Reading them requires practice.

Collaboration among feminist critics—a direct political reaction against masculine ideas of individual achievement within a profession—has also led to new forms of essays. Some collaborators write in dialogue to highlight their differences and agreements; others try to write from the position of a unified "we." Personal pronouns are an especially complicated matter in feminist criticism of the 1990s. The genre is partial to autobiographical irruptions in the form of anecdotes and personal expressions of taste or feeling: these moments permit essayists to use "I" in a more directly referential manner than expository prose traditionally has encouraged. Because feminists are sensitive to the subjective nature of all (gendered) experience and of all utterances, feminist essayists are careful about the use of "we" and "they" in expounding feminist theory. If I say "we," the critic must ask, Am I speaking for all forms of feminism? For all women? For the academy? Because so many divisions and debates exist within academic feminism, no one can be certain who "we" are.

The status of the subject—the entity that speaks or writes—is the center of one major debate within feminist criticism in the 1990s. Depending on their theoretical framework, feminists may argue that the subject is a construction born of economic realities, a Marxist-feminist position; of an individual's childhood process of differentiating herself from her primary caretakers, a psychoanalytic perspective; of the circulation of power and control in a given society, a new-historicist approach; or of the vagaries of language itself, a poststructuralist position. How the subject gets gendered, as it were, is a question open to the insights of all such approaches.

A related current question in the early 1990s is the so-called gaze, the way written and visual texts direct the mind's eye at representations of the body, especially the female form. Feminists are asking whether the gaze operates differently in literature, film, advertising, and hardcore pornography; whether the gaze is the same when its object is male; and whether the gaze reflects a culture's collective desires or constitutes them. Other questions are more overtly political: Do mainstream feminists perpetuate the oppression of marginal groups when they concentrate on white, middle-class, heterosexual authors, or indeed when they use such terms as "marginal" and "mainstream"? Do they repeat the offenses of imperialism and colonialism when they write about minority or third-world literature? Do men have any warrant for writing feminist criticism? Has feminism been absorbed into the academy, making it just another piece of the power structure that keeps the status quo of institutions running? For clarity's sake, I have worded these questions in such a way that they appear to be answerable with a simple "yes" or "no." But contemporary feminism generally resists binary thinking. In practice, the questions and their answers are far more complex than this account can make them out to be.

While feminism has had a measurable impact on the study of American literature, feminist criticism is still too dynamic to be pinned down as a unified entity. In current literary studies, there is no feminism; there are instead feminisms, engaged in continuing conversations with the academic mainstream, with other oppositional movements such as ethnic studies and cultural studies, and with one another. See LITERARY CRITICISM.

ROBYN R. WARHOL

Fenimore Cooper's Literary Offenses (1895),   an essay by MARK TWAIN, first published in *North American Review*, July 1895. The essay was collected in *How to Tell a Story and Other Essays* (1897). In this burlesque of literary criticism, Twain writes, "There are nineteen rules governing literary art in the domain of romantic fiction—some say twenty-two. In *Deerslayer* Cooper violated eighteen of them." Underlying the humor are clear suggestions of the aims of the kind of fiction Twain approved.

Fenollosa, Ernest F[rancisco] (1853–1908),   poet, art critic, Orientalist. Fenollosa was born in Salem, Massachusetts. After living in Japan and teaching for twelve years at the University of Tokyo, he returned to the United States, where he became curator of the Boston Museum of Fine Arts and a widely received lecturer. Eventually he returned to Japan, then went to England; he died in London. His collected poems appeared as *East and West* (1893); his greatest art book was posthumous, *Epochs of Chinese and Japanese Art* (2 v. 1912). Fenollosa was one of the great Western authorities on Oriental art and literature. During a time of frantic Westernization and modernization in Japan, Fenollosa saved many ancient Japanese art treasures from mishandling and destruction. His private collection formed the nucleus of the Fenollosa-Weld Collection in the Boston Museum.

Many know him best for his influence on EZRA POUND, who became Fenollosa's literary executor. From his papers, Pound produced the celebrated poems from Li Po and others in *Cathay: Translations* (1915). *"Noh" or Accomplishment: A Study of the Classical Stage of Japan* (1916, reprinted as *The Classical Noh Theatre of Japan* 1959); and *Certain Noble Plays of Japan* (translations, 1916) were published as by Pound with Fenollosa.

Ferber, Edna (1887–1968), novelist, short-story writer, playwright. Born in Michigan, Ferber worked as a journalist in Wisconsin and Illinois before moving to New York. An adroit student of character, she began her career in fiction by studying an attractive member of a new social type, the woman in the business world, devoting to her several collections of short stories: *Roast Beef Medium* (1913), *Personality Plus* (1914), and *Emma McChesney & Co.* (1915). She continued to write excellent stories based on keen observation of life in America, went on to a series of successful novels: *The Girls* (1921); the Pulitzer Prize winner SO BIG (1924), later made into a movie; SHOW BOAT (1926); and CIMARRON (1930). *Show Boat* was made into a highly successful operetta (1927), with lyrics by OSCAR HAMMERSTEIN II and music by JEROME KERN. In collaboration with GEORGE S. KAUFMAN, Ferber wrote several plays: *Minick* (1924), based on one of the best of her short stories; *The Royal Family* (1927), which exhibited the BARRYMORES in humorous vein; DINNER AT EIGHT (1932); and *Stage Door* (1936). *Saratoga Trunk* (1941), a novel, was presented on Broadway as *Saratoga* (1960). Late novels that received considerable attention are *Giant* (1952), set in Texas, which became a major movie (1956); and *Ice Palace* (1958), set in Alaska. Autobiographies are *A Peculiar Treasure* (1939) and *A Kind of Magic* (1963).

Fergusson, Harvey (1890–1971), editor, novelist. Born in Albuquerque, Fergusson lived later in California. His earliest novel, *The Blood of the Conquerors* (1921), is the first of a trilogy on the development of the Southwest from the time of the Spanish landowners to the present; the later stories are called *Wolf Song* (1927) and *In Those Days* (1929). *Home in the West* (1945) is autobiographical. *Grant of Kingdom* (1950) and *The Conquest of Don Pedro* (1954) are historical novels of the West.

Ferlinghetti, Lawrence (1919–), publisher, poet. Born in Yonkers, New York, Ferlinghetti became owner of San Francisco's City Lights Bookshop and publisher of City Lights Books. He was an important figure in the SAN FRANCISCO RENAISSANCE even before his own poetry began to appear. He

encouraged young writers by giving them a place in his bookshop where they could meet and read their poetry, and by publishing their work in his Pocket Poets series of small paperbacks. His many volumes of poetry include *Pictures of the Gone World* (1955, enlarged edition 1995), *A Coney Island of the Mind* (1958), *Starting from San Francisco* (1967), *Back Roads to Far Places* (1971), *Who Are We Now?* (1976), *Landscapes of Living & Dying* (1979), *Endless Life: The Selected Poems* (1981), *A Trip to Italy & France* (1981), and *A Far Rockaway of the Heart* (1997). His novels are *Her* (1960) and *Love in the Days of Rage* (1988), set in Paris during the student uprising of 1968. See BEAT GENERATION.

Fern, Fanny. The pen name of SARA PAYSON WILLIS.

Fernald, Chester Bailey (1869–1938), story writer, playwright. Born in Boston, Fernald went to San Francisco when he was twenty and became an authority on that city's Chinatown, about which he wrote his two best-known books, *The Cat and the Cherub and Other Stories* (1896) and *Chinatown Stories* (1899). He traveled extensively, writing stories of the sea, collected in *Under the Jack-Staff* (1903), and of the Spanish-American War. In 1907 Fernald went to live in London, where he devoted himself chiefly to the theater.

Fernández de Lizardi, José Joaquín (1776–1827), Mexican satirist, frequently writing under the pen name *El Pensador Mexicano*. Lizardi turned to fiction when his anticlerical and antigovernment poems, pamphlets, and newspaper articles were censored by colonial authorities. A reformist and an outspoken critic of abuses, but not a revolutionary, he is best remembered for *El periquillo sarniento* (1816, tr. *The Itching Parrot* by Katherine Anne Porter, 1942), the first novel written in Latin America. Combining elements of the Spanish picaresque tradition and the 18th-century sentimental novel, Lizardi disguised his criticism of middle-class Mexican life as an adventure novel. He followed this with two more novels, *Noches tristes y día alegre* (1818) and *La quijotita y su prima* (1819), the latter about the education of women. The censors prevented publication of another novel, *Don Catrín de la Fachenda* (1832), which was published posthumously. His complete works, *Obras*, were published in two volumes in 1963 and 1969.

Ferré, Rosario (1938–), novelist, short-story writer, essayist. Born in Ponce, Puerto Rico, Ferré was educated at Manhattanville College, the University of Puerto Rico, and the University of Maryland, where she wrote her Ph.D. dissertation on JULIO CORTÁZAR. Although she has lived large portions of her life on the mainland, teaching at Berkeley, Rutgers, Harvard, and Johns Hopkins, as well as at the University of Puerto Rico, she insists on her Puerto Rican identity as a writer. In 1972, while enrolled as a graduate student in Puerto Rico, she founded a literary journal, *Zona carga y descarga*, where she first published the feminist stories collected in *Papeles de Pandora* (1976; revised and enlarged ed. 1979; tr. *The Youngest Doll*, 1991). In the essays of *Sitios a Eros* (1980, expanded ed. 1986), she pursued similar themes, especially in the widely translated "La cocina de la escritura." Her novels include *Maldito amor* (1987; tr. *Sweet Diamond Dust*, 1988), *La* *batalla de las virgenes* (1993), and the two books most celebrated to date: *The House on the Lagoon* (1995), her first published originally in English, exploring sexual differences and attitudes, as a wealthy American-educated woman decides to write a novel on her Puerto Rican family, but the text is interrupted by her Puerto Rican husband's interjections of his radically different understanding; and *Eccentric Neighborhoods* (1997), a family saga of connected stories that explore the political and social history of Puerto Rico. A more direct view into the past is her biography of her father, *Luis A. Ferré: Memories de Ponce* (1992). Children's stories from three earlier books, generally on her dominant themes of political and social reform, are collected in *Sonatinas* (1989).

Ferril, Thomas Hornsby ["Childe Herald"] (1896–1988),   poet, essayist, newspaperman, columnist. Born in Denver, Ferril became an authority on the literature of the ROCKY MOUNTAIN REGION and himself contributed to it. Beginning in 1939, he and his wife, Helen, published and edited the *Rocky Mountain Herald*, a pioneer weekly. His poems were collected in *High Passage* (1926), *Trial by Time* (1944), and *New and Selected Poems* (1953, 1960). A number of his prose contributions to the *Herald*, together with several essays contributed to *Harper's Magazine*, were collected in *I Hate Thursday* (1946). *And Perhaps Happiness*, a play in verse, appeared in 1957.

Ferry, David (1924–   ),   poet and translator. Born in Orange, New Jersey and educated at Amherst and Harvard, Ferry served in the Army Air Force during World War II. He is the Sophie Chantal Hart Professor Emeritus of Poetry at Wellesley College. *The Limits of Mortality: An Essay on Wordsworth's Major Poems* (1959) announced his interest in the craft of verse. His own collections began with *On the Way to the Island* (1960); other titles include *Strangers: A Book of Poems* (1984), *Painting Without a Brush* (1991), and *Dwelling Places: Poems and Translations* (1993). Throughout his writing and teaching career, Ferry worked on translations. His translation of the Babylonian epic *Gilgamesh* appeared in 1992. He has also translated from Latin, including *The Odes of Horace* (1998) and *The Eclogues of Virgil* (1999), and is working on Horace's letters. His *Of No Country I Know: New and Selected Poems and Translations* (1999) won several prizes, including the Rebekah Johnson Bobbitt National Prize, presented at the Library of Congress in December, 2000.

Fessenden, Thomas Green ["Dr. Caustic," "Christopher Caustic," "Peter Pepper Box"] (1771–1837),   lawyer, inventor, agricultural editor, satirist, poet, essayist. Fessenden was born in New Hampshire and edited newspapers in New York City, Brattleboro, and Boston. One of his best satiric pieces was written in his Dartmouth College days. In composition classes, students wrote solemn pieces modeled slavishly on English originals. But on one occasion Fessenden turned in "The Country Lovers, or, Mr. Jon Jolthead's Courtship with Miss Sally Snapper." The poem perhaps influenced Lowell's THE COURTIN'. Among Fessenden's publications were, in verse, *Terrible Tractoration!!* (1803), on Elisha Perkins's healing by "metallic tractors"; *Original Poems*

(1804), including "The Country Lovers"; and *Democracy Unveiled* (1805), attacking Jefferson and other anti-Federalists. In prose he wrote *Essay on the Law of Patents* (1810) and *The Ladies Monitor* (1818). In 1822 he founded *New England Farmer* and edited it until his death. Porter G. Perrin wrote *The Life and Works of T. G. Fessenden* (1925).

Few Figs from Thistles, A (1920),   a collection of poems by EDNA ST. VINCENT MILLAY, her second collection. It differed considerably in tone from the verses collected in RENASCENCE (1917). Where the latter was lyrical and romantic, *A Few Figs* was sophisticated, bored, and cynical—but brilliant in phrasing and rhythm. The poems had the atmosphere of Greenwich Village and were endlessly quoted by Villagers and their imitators. Among them are "First Fig," beginning, "My candle burns at both ends," and the lyrics "Recuerdo" and "The Philosopher."

Ficke, Arthur Davison (1883–1945),   poet, critic, novelist. Born in Iowa, Ficke developed interests divided between art, especially Japanese, and poetry. In the former field he published *Twelve Japanese Painters* (1913) and *Chats on Japanese Prints* (1915). As a poet he was especially notable for his sonnets; his two interests combined in *Sonnets of a Portrait Painter* (1914). He contributed a group of poems to the first issue of *Poetry*. Along with Witter Bynner he wrote the burlesque poems called SPECTRA (1917), parodying some of the excesses of poets in his day.

Fiedler, Leslie A[aron] (1917–   ),   critic, novelist, short-story writer. Born in Newark, New Jersey, Fiedler was educated at New York University and the University of Wisconsin. Beginning in 1941, apart from World War II service and fellowships and visiting appointments, he spent his teaching career at the University of Montana (until 1964) and the State University of New York at Buffalo. His fame came from his literary criticism, beginning with *An End to Innocence* (1955). In this book, along with studies of Whittaker Chambers, Alger Hiss, and Senator Joseph McCarthy, he included the controversial "Come Back to the Raft Again, Huck Honey!" suggesting buried homoerotic themes in Cooper, Hawthorne, Twain, and other American writers, as they portray a nation in which men flee to the wilderness or the high seas, seeking adolescent adventure and escaping complications of adult heterosexual society. Often the male bonding is between races, as whites try to assuage the guilt of their country's treatment of nonwhites. These views are expanded in *Love and Death in the American Novel* (1959), *Waiting for the End* (1964), and *The Return of the Vanishing American* (1968).

The Collected Essays of Leslie Fiedler (2 v. 1971) gathers the essays of *An End to Innocence; No! In Thunder* (1960), *To the Gentiles* (1972), *Unfinished Business* (1972), and *Cross the Border—Close the Gap* (1972). *Fiedler on the Roof: Essays on Literature and Jewish Identity* appeared in 1991. Other criticism he has written includes *The Stranger in Shakespeare* (1972), on women, Jews, and African-Americans; and *What Was Literature?* (1982), on popular American literature. His novels are *The Second Stone* (1963), *Back to China* (1965), and *The Messengers Will Come No More* (1974). His stories are collected in

Pull Down Vanity (1962), *The Last Jew in America* (1966), and *Nude Croquet* (1969).

Field, Eugene (1850–1895), newspaperman, columnist, poet, humorist, translator. Born in St. Louis, Field worked on newspapers in St. Joseph, St. Louis, Kansas City, and Denver, but finally settled in Chicago in 1883 and remained there for the rest of his life, working on the *Daily News*. He was one of the earliest of the columnists who became a feature of American newspaperdom. From his newspaper writing he gathered material for his numerous books. Among them are *The Tribune Primer* (1882), a parody; *A Little Book of Western Verse* (1889); *Echoes from the Sabine Farm* (with his brother, Roswell Field, 1891); *With Trumpet and Drum* (1892); *Love Affairs of a Bibliomaniac* (1896); and *Collected Works* (10 v. 1896). His favorite themes were book-collecting and Horace (he translated the latter freely), Chicago's cultural taste or lack of it, local feuds, and visiting notables. He wrote some of his best poems about and for children, among them "Little Boy Blue," about a child who died, but whose dust-covered toys awaited his return.

Field, Joseph M. (1810–1856), actor, newspaperman, humorist. Born in Ireland, Field went to St. Louis in its early days and wrote newspaper and magazine sketches that were collected in *Three Years in Texas* (1836), *The Drama in Pokerville and Other Stories* (1847), and other volumes. He also wrote plays. In the St. Louis *Reveille* from 1844 to 1847, he told MIKE FINK stories; Walter Blair calls these "the best early compilation of Mike Fink tales." Mark Twain, in such pieces as *Dandy Frightening the Squatter*, may have been specifically indebted to Field's stories and quips.

Field, Rachel [Lyman] (1894–1942), poet, novelist. Born in New York City, Field wrote several novels with New England settings that attained wide popularity, among them *Time Out of Mind* (1935), *All This, and Heaven Too* (1938) and *And Now Tomorrow* (1942). Equally well known are some of her books for children: *Polly Patchwork* (1928), *Hitty, Her First Hundred Years* (1929), and *Hepatica Hawks* (1932). *Points East* (1930) collects poetry.

Fields, James T[homas] (1817–1881), publisher, editor, poet, memoirist. Born in New Hampshire, Fields became in Boston the leading publisher of the United States, the confidant and adviser of many authors. He headed the firm of Ticknor & Fields, which was absorbed by Houghton, Mifflin & Co. in 1878, and was editor of *Atlantic Monthly* (1861–1871). The OLD CORNER BOOKSTORE in Boston, where Fields sat behind his green curtain, was a gathering place for authors. He was an active poet, and some of his verse long survived in popular memory—the amusing poem called "The Owl-Critic," for example, and the lines in "The Ballad of the Tempest," " 'We are lost!' the captain shouted, as he staggered down the stairs." He devoted two volumes to memories of Hawthorne and Dickens, but his best book is *Yesterdays with Authors* (1872), a miscellany of recollections, conversation, letters, and portraits. His wife, **Annie Adams Fields** (1834–1915), kept a journal and on it based her book *James T. Fields: Biographical Notes and Personal Sketches* (1881). She

wrote several other books—collections of verse, essays and criticisms, and biographies of authors she knew well, including Stowe, Hawthorne, C. D. Warner, and Sarah Orne Jewett. J. C. Austin wrote *Fields of the Atlantic Monthly* (1954).

Fields, Lewis ["Lew"] Maurice (1867–1941), American comedian. See JOSEPH M. WEBER.

Fierstein, Harvey (1954–   ), dramatist. Fierstein's *Torch Song Trilogy* (1981), one of the first commercially successful plays about homosexuality, was made into a movie in 1988 in which the playwright acted. He also wrote the book, from a French original, for the Broadway success *La Cage Aux Folles* (1983), which was filmed and spawned two film sequels. His other plays include *Safe Sex* (1987), *Spook House* (1987), and *Kaddish and Old Men*, a 1987 television script.

Fifth Column and First Forty-Nine Stories, The (1938), a play and short stories by ERNEST HEMINGWAY. *The Fifth Column* was produced, in an adaptation by Benjamin Glazer, in 1940. It describes the interaction of Fascist and Communist intrigue in Madrid during the Spanish Civil War. In his preface Hemingway wrote: "It will take many plays and novels to present the nobility and dignity of the cause of the Spanish people." The title was apparently taken from a radio address by a Franco general, Emilio Mola, after the fall of Toledo: "We have four columns advancing upon Madrid. The fifth column [sympathizers within the city] will rise at the proper time."

Fifty-Four Forty or Fight! (1909), a novel by EMERSON HOUGH. It deals with the controversy over the boundary line between Oregon and Canada. The phrase was first used by William Allen in 1844 and it was adopted as a slogan in the presidential candidacy of JAMES K. POLK in that year. On his election, however, Polk effected a compromise by which the disputed territory was split in two at the 49th parallel, and war was avoided.

Fifty Grand (in MEN WITHOUT WOMEN, 1928), a short story by ERNEST HEMINGWAY. It is about a prize fighter who is bribed to allow himself to be defeated.

Figure in the Carpet, The, a story by HENRY JAMES, collected in *Embarrassments* (1896). In a parable of literary art and criticism, James tells of an author, Hugh Vereker, whose works conceal a secret his young friend (the narrator) and a critic try in vain to discover. The critic tells the friend he has it, but he dies before he can publish it. The friend gets nowhere in his continued efforts, first with the critic's widow and later with her second husband, who has survived her, and is yet another critic.

Filson, John (1747?–1788), explorer, historian. Born in Pennsylvania, Filson wrote the first history of Kentucky, *The Discovery, Settlement and Present State of Kentucke* (1784). The book is notable for an appendix giving the first account of Daniel Boone (based apparently on conversations with the scout) and for a map of Kentucky that is surprisingly accurate. Filson continued his explorations and was killed by an Indian.

Financier, The (1912), a novel by THEODORE DREISER. This story was the beginning of a trilogy, and was followed by THE TITAN (1914) and *The Stoic* (1947). All three deal in epic detail with a typical industrial and financial magnate of the early 20th century. Dreiser based his central character, Frank Algernon Cowperwood, on the figure of Charles T. Yerkes (1837–1905), who had gained control of the Chicago street-railway system. The book begins in Philadelphia (where Yerkes was born) and goes on to Chicago. It gives in immense and ruthlessly realistic detail portraits of Cowperwood, his associates and enemies (sometimes the same people), and his numerous women.

Finch, Francis Miles (1827–1907),   jurist, poet, teacher. Born in Ithaca, New York, Finch was an associate judge of the New York Court of Appeals, then taught law at Cornell. He wrote pleasing, melodious verse. Two of his patriotic poems, "Nathan Hale" (1853) and THE BLUE AND THE GRAY (1867), were once frequent recitation pieces. His poems were collected in *The Blue and the Gray and Other Poems* (1909).

Findley, Timothy (1930–   ),   actor, playwright, novelist. Born in Toronto, Findley toured as an actor in Canada, Europe, and the United States, before turning to writing in Canada. Among his novels, *The Wars* (1977), winner of a Governor General's Award, has been most celebrated. It depicts the horrors of World War I, and ultimately of all wars, as seen through a narrator who attempts to reconstruct the past from newspaper clippings, photographs, letters, and interviews. His other novels include *The Last of the Crazy People* (1967), about tensions within an Ontario family; *The Butterfly Plague* (1969, revised 1986), on Hollywood, with parallels to Nazi Germany; and *Famous Last Words* (1981), weaving together Ezra Pound's character Hugh Selwyn Mauberley, quotations from Pound, and a story of spies at the end of World War II to create a commentary on civilization's decadence. *Can You See Me Yet?* (1977), a play, takes place in an insane asylum. *Headhunter* (1993) and *The Piano Man's Daughter* (1995) are novels on the theme of madness. *You Went Away* (1996) is a novella. *Inside Memory: Pages from a Writer's Notebook* (1990) is a memoir. He has also written scripts for radio and television.

Finger, Charles J[oseph] (1869–1941),   sailor, musician, railroad man, author, editor. After many adventures in Latin America Finger, who was born in England, came to the United States and was naturalized in 1896. His *Tales from Silver Lands* (1924) won a Newbery Medal; his romance *Courageous Companions* (1929) won a Longmans, Green juvenile fiction prize. Among his other books are *Ozark Fantasia* (1927), the autobiography *Seven Horizons* (1930), *Footloose in the West* (1932), and *Golden Tales from Far Away* (1940). For a time he helped edit *Reedy's Mirror*, which he took over and renamed *All's Well, or the Mirror Repolished* (1920–1935). See THE MIRROR [2].

Fink, Mike (1770?–1823?),   folk hero. Born on the frontier in Fort Pitt, Pennsylvania, Fink was at first an Indian scout and soon became renowned for his accuracy as a marksman. As the Indian tribes disappeared across the Mississippi, Fink and the other scouts became boatmen. He soon became known as King of the Keelboatmen and The Snapping Turtle of the Ohio. The battle waged by the boatmen against the river made them wild and reckless, and some of the stories told of Fink show that he had a strong sadistic strain. He was one of the humorists who believe that no joke's a joke unless it's carried too far. The first recorded account of Fink was made by Morgan Neville in the *Western Souvenir* (1829), where he wrote of him as "The Last of the Boatmen." One of the *Crockett Almanacs* tells of an encounter in marksmanship between Crockett and the boatmen in which Crockett loses. JOSEPH M. FIELD gave one of the ten or eleven versions of Fink's death in *The Drama in Pokerville* (1847). The Fink legend was also used in T. B. THORPE's *The Mysteries of the Backwoods* (1846), Emerson Bennett's *Mike Fink* (1848), JOHN G. NEIHARDT's *The River and I* (1910), and elsewhere. The legend is historically and impressively surveyed in Walter Blair and Franklin J. Meine's *Mike Fink, King of Mississippi Keelboatmen* (1933). Julian Lee Rayford wrote a novel called *Child of the Snapping Turtle* (1951).

Finley, John.   See HOOSIER.

Finley, Martha Farquharson (1828–1909),   teacher, novelist. Born in Ohio, Finley wrote under the name Martha Farquharson. Although some of her books were intended for adult readers, her fame was gained as a writer of Sunday-school stories for girls, notably her ELSIE DINSMORE tales (1868–1905) which ran to twenty-eight volumes, each in a blue or red cover with a pansy imprinted on it. She also wrote stories about "Mildred" (7 v. 1878–94). For a long time enormously popular, the "Elsie" books finally began to go out of print in the middle 1940s.

Finney, Jack (1911–1995),   novelist and short-story writer. Born in Milwaukee, **Walter Braden "Jack" Finney** was educated at Knox College. *Five Against the House* (1954), his first novel, concerns the attempt by college students to rob a casino. His best known popular thriller was *The Body Snatchers* (1955), filmed three times (1956, 1979, 1993) as *Invasion of the Body Snatchers*. His two time travel books, *Time and Again* (1970) and its sequel, *From Time to Time* (1995), involve a secret government project to reproduce the past. Simon Morley, an advertising artist, projects himself back to the 1880s in the first book and 1912 in the second, each time determined to alter history. Other novels include *Good Neighbor Sam* (1963), *The Woodrow Wilson Dime* (1968), *Marion's Wall* (1973), and *The Night People* (1977). *The Third Level* (1957) is a story collection.

Fire Next Time, The (1963),   an essay by JAMES BALDWIN.

First Settlers of Virginia, The (1802),   a novel by JOHN DAVIS. Davis, an Englishman, set this first idealistic treatment of the American Indian in Virginia and followed closely the facts and legends that had gathered around Capt. JOHN SMITH.

Fisher, Clay.   Pseudonym of HENRY W. ALLEN.

Fisher, Dorothy Canfield [formerly **Dorothy Canfield**] (1879–1958), novelist, short-story writer, critic, translator. Born in Kansas, Dorothy Canfield lived and wrote in Vermont after 1907, at first using her maiden name and later her married name. She was a discriminating interpreter of

American life, especially in New England, from the beginning of her career. Among her novels are *The Squirrel Cage* (1912), *The Bent Twig* (1915), *The Brimming Cup* (1921), *Rough Hewn* (1922), *The Home-Maker* (1924), *Her Son's Wife* (1926), *The Deepening Stream* (1930), *Bonfire* (1933), and *Seasoned Timber* (1939). In *Four-Square* (1949) seventeen of her short stories were collected. The best of her nonfiction work is *Vermont Tradition; The Biography of an Outlook on Life* (1953).

Fisher, M[ary] F[rances] K[ennedy] (1908–1992), memoirist, food writer. Born in California, Fisher spent many years in Europe in the 1930s and 1940s before returning to her home state. Beginning with *Serve It Forth* (1937), a combination cook book and narrative, Fisher described her cooking and entertaining. *The Art of Eating* (1954) is gleaned from her first five books. Written during the Second World War, when food shortages were common, it offers suggestions on how to make do with limited rations. Although she co-wrote a novel, *Touch and Go* (1939), with her second husband, Dillwyn Parrish, and wrote one on her own, *Not Now But Now* (1947), her real subject was autobiography with gourmet and travel details interspersed. *As They Were* (1983) treats boarding school memories and cooking in southern France. *Sister Age* (1983) confronts growing old. *The Gastronomical Me* (1943), written under the name Mary Frances Parrish, is considered by many to be her best book. It accumulates cooking narratives from 1912 to 1941 against the background of rising tensions in Europe between the world wars. Fisher ended her long life in the northern California wine country where she continued to write even after becoming bedridden. Other titles include *How to Cook a Wolf* (1951), *Long Ago in France: The Years in Dijon* (1991), *To Begin Again: Stories and Memoirs, 1908–1929* (1992), and *Stay Me, Oh Comfort Me: Journals and Stories, 1933–1945* (1993).

Fisher, Vardis [Alvero] (1895–1968), novelist. Fisher was born into a Mormon family in Idaho and grew up in an isolated area on the Snake River. He was perhaps the last novelist in the United States with a truly frontier upbringing and the first to write significantly of the Rocky Mountains. He was educated at the University of Utah and the University of Chicago. He taught at the University of Utah and New York University before turning to writing full time.

Fisher's first two novels, *Toilers of the Hills* (1928) and *Dark Bridwell* (1931), evoke a strong sense of place as they present the difficulties of pioneering in Idaho. The second introduces Vridar Hunter, an autobiographical figure who becomes the center of a tetrology: *In Tragic Life* (1932; published also as *I See No Sin*, 1934, and *The Wild Ones*, 1938); *Passions Spin the Plot* (1934); *We Are Betrayed* (1935); and *No Villain Need Be* (1936). From the present he turned to the past, with *Children of God* (1939), in which he told the story of Joseph Smith, Brigham Young, and other early Mormons and won his greatest acclaim. This was followed by other historical novels: *City of Illusion* (1941), about the COMSTOCK LODE; *The Mothers: An American Saga of Courage* (1943), about the DONNER PARTY; *Pemmican* (1956), about the HUDSON'S BAY COMPANY; *Tale of*

Valor (1958), about the LEWIS AND CLARK EXPEDITION; and *Mountain Men* (1965), about the western fur trade.

In the meantime, he had begun *Testament of Man*, twelve volumes telling man's history from the ape-like beginnings to the time of Vridar Hunter. This includes *Darkness and the Deep* (1943); *Golden Rooms* (1944), about Neanderthal man; *Intimations of Eve* (1946), about early hunters; *Adam and the Serpent* (1947); *The Divine Passion* (1948); *The Valley of Vision* (1951); *The Island of the Innocent* (1952); *A Goat for Azazel* (1956); *Jesus Came Again* (1956); *Peace Like a River* (1957); *My Holy Satan* (1958); and *Orphans in Gethsemane* (1960).

During WPA days, Fisher directed the FEDERAL WRITERS' PROJECT for Idaho (1935–39) and edited *Idaho: A Guide* (1937), *The Idaho Encyclopedia* (1938), and *Idaho Lore* (1939). Among his other books are *Love and Death: The Complete Stories* (1959), *Suicide or Murder: The Strange Death of Meriwether Lewis* (1961), and *Thomas Wolfe as I Knew Him and Other Essays* (1963).

Fiske, John (1842–1901), historian, philosopher. Born in Connecticut, Fiske became a lecturer on philosophy at Harvard, then a professor of history at Washington University (St. Louis). He was a popular lecturer on the ideas of Herbert Spencer and Auguste Comte. Among his books are *The Outline of Cosmic Philosophy* (1874), *Darwinism and Other Essays* (1879), *The Destiny of Man Viewed in the Light of His Origin* (1884), *The Critical Period of American History, 1783–1789* (1888), *The Beginnings of New England* (1889), *Civil Government in the United States* (1890), *The American Revolution* (1891), *The Mississippi Valley in the Civil War* (1900), and *New France and New England* (1902).

Fiske, Nathan (1733–1799), clergyman. A native of Brookfield, Massachusetts, he wrote of that town's past in *Historical Discourse* (1776). *The Moral Monitor* (1801) collects his essays.

Fitch, [William] Clyde (1865–1909), playwright. Born in Elmira, New York, Fitch began his career as author of over 30 plays by writing *Beau Brummell* (1890). Further dramatic triumphs were *Nathan Hale* (1899); *The Cowboy and the Lady* (1899); BARBARA FRIETCHIE (1899), which was later made into a musical comedy, *My Maryland* (1927), with music by Sigmund Romberg; and CAPTAIN JINKS OF THE HORSE MARINES (1901). Although Fitch's earlier plays are primarily romantic melodramas of the type that dominated the stage during the period, they are redeemed by his wit and by the appeal of his characters. His later plays constitute his more important contribution to the American stage. His mastery of social comedy and satire is shown in such plays as *The Climbers* (1901), THE GIRL WITH THE GREEN EYES (1902), *The Woman in the Case* (1905), *The Truth* (1906), *The Straight Road* (1906), and *The City* (1909).

Fitch, George (1877–1915), newspaperman, humorist. Although Fitch wrote other stories, those that centered around old Siwash College, believed to be Knox College in Illinois, won him his widest fame. Hilarious tales of a carefree generation, they were collected in *The Big Strike at Siwash* (1909) and *At Good Old Siwash* (1911).

Fitts, Dudley (1903–1968),   editor, translator, teacher. Born in Boston, Fitts taught English at Phillips Academy in Andover. He became a leading translator of the poetry and drama of the ancient Greeks. His own verse appeared in *Two Poems* (1932) and *Poems 1929–36* (1937). In collaboration with Robert Fitzgerald he translated Sophocles' *Oedipus Rex* (1949) and the *Alcestis* of Euripides (1936); he edited *Greek Plays in Modern Translation* (1948) and translated four plays of Aristophanes: *Lysistrata* (1954), *The Frogs* (1955), *The Birds* (1957), and *Ladies' Day* (1959). In his *Anthology of Contemporary Latin-American Poetry* (1942), translations (by various hands) appear on pages facing the Spanish or Portuguese originals. He edited the Yale Series of Younger Poets (1960–68).

Fitzgerald, Frances (1940–   ),   journalist. A graduate of Radcliffe, Fitzgerald won a National Book Award, a Pulitzer Prize, and a Bancroft Prize for *Fire in the Lake: The Vietnamese and the Americans in Vietnam* (1972). Her other works include *America Revised* (1979) and *Cities on a Hill* (1986).

Fitzgerald, F[rancis] Scott [Key]   (1896–1940), novelist, short-story writer. Though his own brief life was marked by dramatic highs and lows, Fitzgerald's posthumous literary reputation has remained consistently strong. His best-known novel, THE GREAT GATSBY (1925), continues to enjoy popularity among general readers and critical acclaim, while somewhat less attention is paid to what many consider his best novel, TENDER IS THE NIGHT (1934). In addition, perhaps a dozen of his 180 short stories are mainstays of college anthologies and continuing sources of interest to scholars of American fiction, including "Babylon Revisited," "The Rich Boy," "May Day," "The Diamond as Big as the Ritz," "Bernice Bobs Her Hair," "Winter Dreams," and "The Last of the Belles." Fitzgerald is still regarded as one of the most important American fiction writers of the 20th century despite the fact that he made neither technical nor theoretical contributions to the field. Rather, he is remembered for recording the American *Zeitgeist* between the two world wars and for being one of the few serious authors to achieve celebrity status even among ordinary readers.

As Fitzgerald himself was acutely aware, his life and career uncannily paralleled events on the national scene. Born in St. Paul, Minnesota, he came of age during World War I, when the United States established itself firmly as an international power and a nation of enormous promise. Fitzgerald was beginning to realize his own promise while an undergraduate at Princeton University, where his writings on behalf of the Triangle Club dramatic society and his efforts to produce one of the earliest college novels quickly bore fruit. Having left Princeton before graduation and enlisted in the U.S. Army, Fitzgerald worked on the manuscript of "The Romantic Egotist" while waiting to be shipped overseas. When the armistice was declared, he devoted himself even more fully to his novel, in hope that its publication would lead to marriage with Zelda Sayre, whom he had met

while stationed near her home in Montgomery, Alabama, in 1918. Eventually "The Romantic Egotist" was transformed into his first novel, THIS SIDE OF PARADISE (1920). Considered daring and intellectual in its day, the novel now seems naive and formless, but its enormous popularity established young Fitzgerald instantly as a major writer. He wed Zelda Sayre in New York City eight days after its publication.

Fitzgerald's life in the 1920s was a mirror to events occurring nationally during that decade. It was a time of challenge to the established order, of personal indulgence and even self-destructive excess, and Fitzgerald was its self-proclaimed spokesman and symbol. Spending his enormous story fees as quickly as they were received, drinking publicly during this era of Prohibition, and pursuing an unstable existence in a series of temporary homes in the United States and Europe, Fitzgerald somehow was able to produce the high-paying short stories that maintained his glitzy lifestyle, along with a badly overwritten and overlong second novel entitled *The Beautiful and Damned* (1922). Tracing the self-indulgence and mutual destruction of Anthony and Gloria Patch, this novel was transparently based on the lives of Scott and Zelda ,who, along with daughter Scottie, became celebrities for their unsettled and glamorous lives as much as for anything Fitzgerald wrote.

Two collections of stories were published to cash in on the popularity of the novels that immediately preceded them. *Flappers and Philosophers* (1920), containing eight stories produced during the burst of creativity from May 1919 to February 1920 that had followed acceptance of his first novel for publication, is an excellent collection. Much less successful was the second collection, *Tales of the Jazz Age* (1922), which essentially recycles old college sketches and two meager playlets, in addition to what is regarded as one of his better experimental efforts, the novella "May Day." *Tales of the Jazz Age* is marred in particular by the inclusion of a flippant table of contents, which essentially denigrates every story in the book, including "May Day." Most critics, unfortunately, used Fitzgerald's remarks as justification for their negative appraisals.

At this point there occurred a major redirecting of Fitzgerald's efforts. Evidently stung by the harsh words of critics and the failure as well of his presidential farce *The Vegetable* (1923), Fitzgerald made a conscious effort to concentrate on creating serious, even tragic works that addressed broad historical and social issues. Fitzgerald's new-found sense of vocation, his greater personal maturity, his increasingly complex sense of his era's place in world history, and his growing awareness of the technical and stylistic capabilities of the modern novel to convey these elements resulted in *The Great Gatsby*. Fitzgerald seems to have surprised himself in this story of the American dream gone wrong. What with his Long Island mansion, flashy roadster, and immense fortune derived from bootlegging, Jay Gatsby—the public persona of humble James Gatz—is indeed the self-made American businessman. But that success does not bring him love (in the form of Daisy Buchanan) or personal happiness. Worse, it ultimately costs him his life. Fitzgerald had found the quintessential story not only of the 1920s but also of the American experience, and he probed it in a novel written with unprecedented grace and power.

The collection of stories *All the Sad Young Men* (1926), published by Scribners on the strength of *Gatsby*, likewise reflects that novel's broader scope, greater maturity, and technical expertise. Several of Fitzgerald's best-known stories of early middle age, including "The Rich Boy" and "Winter Dreams," appear in this collection, as do several other excellent tales that have been overlooked by critics, such as "The Baby Party" and "Absolution."

As the Jazz Age drew to its traumatic close with the stock market crash of 1929, so did much of Fitzgerald's life and career. His wife, Zelda, exhibited increasingly erratic behavior after the appearance of *Gatsby*, as her own careers as writer and ballerina failed to provide her with the public attention, financial independence, and creative outlets she needed while overshadowed by her husband. A familial tendency toward mental illness finally manifested itself, and in early 1930 Zelda suffered the first of several complete breakdowns. Her mental instability, ultimately diagnosed as schizophrenia, required that she spend most of the last eighteen years of her life in a series of private sanatoriums in Europe and the United States. To pay the high medical bills, Fitzgerald focused on writing short stories for popular magazines, for example, *Saturday Evening Post* and *Esquire*. Though they were a source of ready income, the stories brought less and less money as the Depression continued, and Fitzgerald found himself producing them at ever greater speed. Such a situation is not conducive to high quality, and many of his worst stories—including his self-admitted trash—date from this period. Some indeed are so poor that they remain only in typescript to this day.

Not all of the stories of the 1930s, however, were dreadful. From this era came the "Basil and Josephine" stories, which many count among Fitzgerald's most memorable efforts. The tales about Basil Duke Lee cast a nostalgic glance back at his own childhood and young manhood, while those devoted to Josephine Perry probe the Fitzgeraldian notion of emotional bankruptcy. Worn out by too much fame too soon, by his temperamental inability to establish a stable home with financial and psychological security, and by his fear that he might have contributed to his wife's insanity through his own excesses, including alcoholism, Fitzgerald felt by the early 1930s that he was emotionally bankrupt, unable to regroup his resources to fulfill his roles as professional writer, husband, and father. He recorded this personal nadir in three essays for *Esquire* magazine in 1935: "The Crack-Up," "Pasting It Together," and "Handle with Care."

These confessional pieces, which many regard as statements not only of Fitzgerald's shattered emotional state but also of the national temper during the 1930s, are counted among his best work. Another unanticipated positive result of this terrible time in Fitzgerald's life was his fourth novel, *Tender Is the Night*. He had been attempting to find his footing with this new novel ever since the release of *Gatsby*, but not until Zelda's descent into madness did Fitzgerald find his theme. *Tender Is*

the Night essentially dramatizes the story of the Fitzgeralds, with Scott depicted in the brilliant young American psychiatrist Dick Diver, whose promising career and personal equanimity are compromised and then shattered by his marriage. Dick's wife is the American Dream: Nicole is beautiful, charming, wealthy—but insane. Transparently basing Nicole on Zelda, even to the point of including Zelda's letters and medical records in the novel, Fitzgerald had once again located a theme on a grand American scale while using the process of writing as catharsis for personal woes. Released in the midst of the Depression, *Tender Is the Night* did not sell well, though it had appreciative reviews. Likewise a poor seller was the novel's companion volume of stories *Taps at Reveille* (1935). It includes the best of the Basil and Josephine stories, along with a series of tales that are autobiographical in sentiment if not in fact. These include "Babylon Revisited," "The Last of the Belles," and "Crazy Sunday," the last his best-known Hollywood story.

By the mid-1930s Fitzgerald had come to the conviction that working as a screenwriter in Hollywood was a more lucrative source of income than writing stories or novels. He enjoyed a substantial salary working on a variety of projects, including *A Yank at Oxford*, *The Women*, *Three Comrades*, and (briefly) *Gone with the Wind*, and the income enabled him to pay off his enormous debts plus Zelda's huge medical bills. Fitzgerald also enjoyed one of the more fulfilling relationships in his life, a long affair with gossip columnist Sheilah Graham. The Hollywood interlude also gave him the inspiration to begin work on a fifth novel, *The Last Tycoon*. The tragic story of a Hollywood motion picture mogul reportedly based on Irving Thalberg, *The Last Tycoon* was still unfinished when Fitzgerald died of a heart attack in Hollywood on December 21, 1940. Though it is largely a series of unrevised chapters and notes, *The Last Tycoon*, published posthumously in 1941, probably would have been one of Fitzgerald's best novels.

Although Fitzgerald's four collections of short stories have long been out of print, the best tales are included in *The Stories of F. Scott Fitzgerald*, edited by Malcolm Cowley, and *The Short Stories of F. Scott Fitzgerald*, edited by Matthew J. Bruccoli. A large number of previously uncollected stories appear in *Bits of Paradise* (1973) and *The Price Was High* (1979), both edited by Matthew J. Bruccoli. Also of interest are two collections of Fitzgerald's miscellaneous writings: *Afternoon of an Author*, edited by Arthur Mizener (1958), and *The Crack-Up*, edited by Edmund Wilson (1956).

Most of Fitzgerald's papers are in the Firestone Library at Princeton University. His voluminous personal and business correspondence is collected in several books: *The Correspondence of F. Scott Fitzgerald*, edited by Bruccoli and Margaret M. Duggan, with the assistance of Susan Walker (1980); *The Letters of F. Scott Fitzgerald*, edited by Andrew Turnbull (1963); *As Ever, Scott Fitz—: Letters Between F. Scott Fitzgerald and His Literary Agent, Harold Ober, 1919–1940*, edited by Bruccoli (1972); and *Dear Scott/Dear Max: The Fitzgerald-Perkins Correspondence*, edited by John Kuehl and Jackson Bryer (1971).

The best biography is *Some Sort of Epic Grandeur: The Life of F. Scott Fitzgerald*, by Bruccoli (1981). Bruccoli's *F. Scott Fitzgerald: A Life in Letters* appeared in 1994. Other important biographical information may be found in *Zelda* by Nancy Milford (1970) and *Invented Lives: F. Scott Fitzgerald* by James R. Mellow (1984). Two valuable specialized studies are *Crazy Sundays: F. Scott Fitzgerald in Hollywood* by Aaron Latham (1971) and the psychoanalytical *Scott Fitzgerald: Crisis in an American Identity* by Thomas J. Stavola (1979).

Critical studies of Fitzgerald's work include *F. Scott Fitzgerald: The Last Laocoön*, by Robert Sklar (1967); *F. Scott Fitzgerald and the Craft of Fiction*, by Richard D. Lehan (1966); *The Golden Moment: The Novels of F. Scott Fitzgerald*, by Milton R. Stern (1970); and *Fitzgerald's Craft of Short Fiction: The Collected Stories, 1920–1935*, by Alice Hall Petry (1989).

ALICE HALL PETRY

Fitzgerald, Robert S[tuart] (1910–1985), poet, critic, translator. Fitzgerald was educated at Trinity College, Cambridge, and at Harvard. He became a reporter for the New York *Herald Tribune*, then a staff writer for *Time*. In 1946 he turned to teaching, at Sarah Lawrence, Princeton, Indiana, Notre Dame, Washington University, and Harvard. His poetry is collected in *A Wreath for the Sea* (1943), *In the Rose of Time* (1956), and *Spring Shade* (1971). He translated *Oedipus Cycle of Sophocles* in collaboration with Dudley Fitts (1939; reprinted in 1941 and 1949) and, on his own, *The Odyssey* (1961); *The Iliad* (1974); and *The Aeneid* (1983).

Fitzgerald, Zelda [Sayre] (1899–1948), novelist. Wife of F. SCOTT FITZGERALD, she told some of her side of their story in her novel *Save Me the Waltz* (1932).

Five Civilized Tribes, The. A name given to tribes that in response to changing situations in 1859 formed a loose federation: CHEROKEE, CHOCTAW, CHICKASAW, CREEK, and SEMINOLE.

Five-Foot Shelf. See CHARLES W. ELIOT.

Five Little Peppers and How They Grew (1881), a story for children by HARRIET LOTHROP, who wrote under the name Margaret Sidney. The story appeared originally in *Wide Awake* (1880), a magazine for young readers. In book form the story was a great success; it is said that in 50 years more than 2 million copies were sold. The story was one of a struggle against poverty, and Lothrop accompanied the plot with numerous moral lessons. There were several sequels: *The Five Little Peppers Midway*, *The Five Little Peppers Grown Up*, and others. The original story remained the most popular. Frank Ray Felder wrote a successful dramatization, *The Five Little Peppers* (1952).

Five Nations. See IROQUOIS.

Flaccus. Pen name of THOMAS WARD.

Flagg, James Montgomery (1877–1960), illustrator, author. Born in Pelham Manor, New York, Flagg is best remembered for a World War I recruiting poster of Uncle Sam pointing a finger, with the caption "Uncle Sam Wants You!" Among his books are *Yankee Girls Abroad* (1900), *Tomfoolery* (1904), *All in the Same Boat* (1908), and *City People* (1909). *Roses and Buckshot* (1946) is an autobiography.

Flaherty, Robert J. (1884–1951), film director. Born in Michigan, Flaherty was educated at the Michigan College of Mines. Expeditions among the Eskimos at Hudson's Bay led to his *Nanook of the North* (1922), a seminal work of the movie industry that helped earn him the title Father of the Documentary. Most celebrated of his later documentaries is *Man of Aran* (1934), about the life of an Irish fisherman. His other films include *Moana* (1926); *White Shadows of the South Seas* (1928); *Tabu* (codirected with F. W. Murnau, 1993); *Elephant Boy* (codirected with Zoltan Korda, 1937); *The Land* (1942); and *Louisiana Story* (1948). His wife Frances Flaherty collaborated on *Moana, Man of Aran, Louisiana Story*, and others.

Flammonde (1915), a poem by EDWIN ARLINGTON ROBINSON. One of Robinson's poems of Tilbury Town, this is a penetrating study of a character who is the Prince of Castaways, a man who lives by borrowing. But Flammonde is remembered by the poet because he somehow manages to understand the people of the town better than others and help them through his deep sympathy.

Flanagan, Thomas (1923–), novelist. Born in Connecticut, Flanagan earned recognition with *The Year of the French* (1979), a novel set in 1798 and chronicling an Irish uprising that attempted to use French assistance to drive the British from Ireland. He followed that with *The Tenants of Time* (1988), also well received, a novel that centers on a small Irish town, but ranges also to Dublin, London, Venice, New York, and Chicago. It encapsulates Irish history from the Fenian Rising of 1867 to the death of Parnell in 1891. Both are meticulously researched and employ multiple viewpoints to capture the wide rush of history. *The End of the Hunt* (1994) treats Irish history in the twentieth century. Other titles are *Louis David Riel: Prophet of the New World* (1996) and *Dangerous Edge of the Thing* (1999).

Flandrau, Charles Macomb (1871–1938), newspaperman, writer. Born in Minnesota, Flandrau wrote memoirs of college days embodied in a series of satiric stories: *Harvard Episodes* (1897); *The Diary of a Freshman* (1901); and *Sophomores Abroad* (not collected in book form till 1935). A visit south of the border resulted in a travel book, *Viva Mexico* (1908). His essays were collected in *Prejudices* (1911) and *Loquacities* (1935).

Flanner, Janet (1892–1978), writer. Born in Indiana, Flanner became Paris correspondent of *The New Yorker* magazine, under the name Genêt, and was one of the few women awarded the French Legion of Honor. She wrote profiles and articles on art for *The New Yorker*. She also wrote a novel, *The Cubical City* (1926), and *American in Paris* (1940), and translated Colette's *Claudine à l'école* (1930) and other works. *Men and Monuments* (1957) is about modern French artists. *Paris Journal* appeared in two volumes (1965, 1971).

Flavin, Martin [Archer] (1883–1967), novelist, playwright. Born in San Francisco, Flavin had a number of successes on Broadway, including *Children of the Moon* (1923), *The Criminal* (1929), and *Amaco* (1933). Flavin's novel *Journey in the Dark* (1943) won a Pulitzer Prize as well as the Harper Novel award. Later came *The Enchanted* (1947), the story of a group of children who seek to escape from the adult world. In a travel book, *Black and White: From the Cafe to the Congo* (1950), Flavin revealed himself as an honest, searching investigator. *Cameron Hill* (1957) is a story of a murderer.

Fletcher, John Gould (1886–1950),   poet. Born in Little Rock, Fletcher was educated at Harvard. In 1908 he traveled to Europe. Associating with Pound and Amy Lowell, and greatly influenced by the Orient, he was for a while an imagist and a writer of polyphonic prose. His best-known works were mood poems with color themes and such titles as "Blue Symphony." Although he lived mostly in England until 1933, when he returned to Little Rock, he aligned himself with the Southern AGRARIANS, contributing to I'LL TAKE MY STAND (1930). In his later years, he was considered a regional poet. *A Selected Poems* appeared in 1938 and won a Pulitzer Prize.

His other poetry titles include *Irradiations: Sand and Spray* (1915); *Goblins and Pagodas* (1916); *Japanese Prints* (1918); *Breakers and Granite* (1921); *Preludes and Symphonies* (1922); *Branches of Adam* (1926); *The Black Rock* (1928); *XXIV Elegies* (1935); *South Star* (1941), which includes a verse history of Arkansas; and *The Burning Mountain* (1946). Among his prose works are *Paul Gauguin; His Life and Art* (1921); *John Smith— Also Pocahontas* (1928); *The Two Frontiers* (1930), on Russia and America; and *Arkansas* (1947), history. An autobiography is *Life Is My Song* (1937).

Flexner, Anne Crawford (1874–1955),   playwright. Born in Kentucky, Flexner wrote several plays among them a dramatization of MRS. WIGGS OF THE CABBAGE PATCH (1903), *A Lucky Star* (1909), *The Marriage Game* (1916), and *Aged 26* (1937), based on the life of John Keats.

Flint, Timothy (1780–1840),   missionary, novelist, editor. Born in Massachusetts, Flint traveled as a missionary as far as Arkansas and Missouri, recounting his experiences in *Recollections of the Last Ten Years* (1826). His novels include *Francis Berrian; or, The Mexican Patriot* (1826), of a New Englander in the Mexican revolution of 1822; *The Life and Adventures of Arthur Clenning* (1828), ranging from the South Seas to the Illinois frontier; *George Mason, the Young Backwoodsman* (1829); *The Lost Child, a Romance* (1830); and *The Shoshonee Valley* (1830), of a New England seaman and his Chinese wife who go to live with the Indians. He published *The Western Monthly Review* (1827–30) and edited and perhaps largely wrote *The Personal Narrative of* JAMES OHIO PATTIE (1831), as well as a *Memoir of Daniel Boone* (1833).

Flood of Years, The (1876),   a poem by WILLIAM CULLEN BRYANT. This is a reconsideration of ideas on death and immorality the poet had expressed in THANATOPSIS more than six decades earlier. In resonant blank verse, he expresses deep sympathy with mankind and a hesitant belief in personal immortality.

Florida of the Inca, The (1605),   historical narrative by GARCILASO DE LA VEGA.

Florit, Eugenio (1903–1999),   Cuban poet and literary critic. In the late 1920s the Cuban literary world saw the emergence of two distinct groups of young poets: the socially

engagé poetry of NICOLÁS GUILLÉN; and the pure, meditative poetry of Florit. An elegiac and serene writer, Florit conveys in his verse a mystical fascination with his native landscape and his highly personal musings. *Hábito de esperanza, 1936–1964* (1965) is the most complete collection of his poems. Florit moved to the U.S. after the fall of the Batista regime. Poetry collections include *Castillo interior y otros versos* (1987) and *Tercero sueno y otros versos* (1989). The first five volumes of his complete works have been published as *Obres completas* (1983–1991).

Flowering Judas (1930, 1935),   collections of stories by KATHERINE ANNE PORTER. The first includes the title story and five others, the second a total of ten.

Flowering of New England, The (1936),   a literary history by VAN WYCK BROOKS. The book, a critical recounting of the years of literary preeminence in Boston and Concord, eventually took its place in Brooks's five-volume literary history of the United States. It won a Pulitzer Prize.

Flush Times of Alabama and Mississippi, The (1853),   humorous sketches of the frontier by JOSEPH G. BALDWIN. These stories are descriptions of the crooks, boasters, sharpers, and orators who found flush times awaiting their schemes among the naive settlers. The realism of the sketches and their rollicking wit in many ways presage the Mississippi tales of Mark Twain.

Flynt, Josiah.   See J. F. WILLARD.

Foerster, Norman (1887–1972),   teacher, critic, editor. A professor of English at the University of North Carolina (1914–30) and the University of Iowa (1930–44), Foerster became a leader in the movement known as the NEW HUMANISM and greatly influenced literary criticism in the United States. He was also a pioneer in scholarship and teaching in the field of American literature, and led the movement at Iowa for creative instead of scholarly Ph.D. dissertations. Among his writings are *Nature in American Literature* (1923), *American Criticism* (1928), *The Reinterpretation of American Literature* (1928), *The American Scholar* (1929), *Toward Standards* (1931), *The Humanities After the War* (1944), and *The Humanities and the Common Man* (1946).

Fogo Morto (1943, tr. 1944),   a novel by JOSÉ LINS DO RÊGO. In this, the sixth and culminating novel of Lins de Rêgo's cycle about plantation life in northeastern Brazil, he portrays the decadence of a dying aristocracy, intertwining lives of characters from the five previous novels. A central figure is Vittorino, whose fancies of quixotic honor and respect are treated with irony and compassion. As the characters watch society unravel, a tension builds between their individual perspectives and the reality around them, while the author loads his narrative with a heavy consciousness of time's passing.

Foley, Martha (1897?–1977),   newspaperwoman, editor, short-story writer, lecturer. Foley worked for various newspapers in the United States and Europe before she and her husband, WHIT BURNETT, founded the magazine STORY in Vienna in 1931. She continued with the magazine when it moved to New York City in 1933 and helped make it one of the most influential organs of advanced writing in the country. At the death of Edward J. O'Brien in 1941, she took over editorship of the annual BEST AMERICAN SHORT STORIES, and held that position from 1942 to 1977. Comprehensive collections she edited include *The Best of the Best Short Stories, 1915 to 1950* (1952), with her son, David Burnett, and *Two Hundred Years of Great American Short Stories* (1975).

Folger, Henry Clay (1857–1930),   lawyer, oil magnate, collector of Shakespeareana. For his great library of Shakespeare materials Folger erected a $2,500,000 building in Washington, D.C., the cornerstone of which was laid on May 28, 1930, two weeks before his death. It was opened to the public on April 23, 1932. He left it an endowment of $7 million and gave its management to the trustees of his alma mater, Amherst College.

Folger, Peter (1617?–1690?),   teacher, surveyor, missionary, interpreter, artisan, verse writer. Folger, the maternal grandfather of Benjamin Franklin, came to Massachusetts from England in 1635. In 1644 he purchased Mary Morrell (or Morrils), who was an indentured servant, and married her. In 1659 he went to Nantucket and worked there for Tristram Coffin and his associates. At one time he participated in a rebellion against the proprietors and spent some time in jail. His long poem, *A Looking Glass for the Times, or, The Former Spirit of New England Revived in This Generation* (1676), suggested that KING PHILIP's attacks were a punishment sent by God because of Puritan intolerance of Baptists, Quakers, and other proponents of dissident views.

Folger Shakespeare Library.   See HENRY CLAY FOLGER.

folklore in American literature.   Critics and literary historians have frequently emphasized the dependence of American literature on European models and traditions, but no literature can long survive without a root in native culture and from the end of the 18th century American authors turned more and more often to the lore of their own people. WASHINGTON IRVING gathered much native material for his Knickerbocker comedy and his legends of the Hudson valley. Even before him, authors such as H. H. BRACKENRIDGE and ROYALL TYLER had introduced native characters, and PHILIP FRENEAU, by romanticizing the Native American in his elegiac poems, prepared the way for JAMES FENIMORE COOPER. WILLIAM CULLEN BRYANT turned to folklore for some of his themes, as did EDGAR ALLAN POE, but neither made systematic use of native materials.

Cooper was the first to use folk themes extensively, especially in his LEATHER-STOCKING TALES, where he employed the lore of the IROQUOIS as he found it in Heckewelder and elsewhere. Leatherstocking was our first folk hero, enlarged from the legend of Daniel Boone and made somewhat more tractable than his prototype, but still acceptable at home and abroad. "Here," said Lowell, "was our new Adam of the wilderness, a figure as poetic as that of Achilles, as ideally representative as that of Don Quixote. . . ."

HAWTHORNE's preoccupation with folklore is apparent in his *Notebooks*, which contain the germs of many of his tales: a

mantle, the plague, a veil, mesmerism, plants with mystical potency, strange omens, and other folk themes that suggested to Hawthorne the symbols for his deeply moral narratives. THE GREAT STONE FACE, for example, is a genuine rural legend, as is YOUNG GOODMAN BROWN, and THE SCARLET LETTER draws on the folk tradition of Puritanism. THE HOUSE OF THE SEVEN GABLES he regarded as "a legend . . . from an epoch now gray in the distance . . . bringing with it some of its legendary mist."

Minor novelists drew heavily on popular lore. JAMES K. PAULDING related in KONINGSMARKE the amusing story of the long Finn. In his play THE LION OF THE WEST, he pictured the comic backwoodsman Davy Crockett as Colonel Nimrod Wildfire, and in WESTWARD HO! he burlesqued Natty Bumppo as Ambrose Bushfield. WILLIAM GILMORE SIMMS wove his fiction around the legends of Marion and the tales of Murrell and his gang. JOHN PENDLETON KENNEDY, WILLIAM ALEXANDER CARUTHERS, and JOHN ESTEN COOKE glamorized their beloved South with Cavalier myth. SYLVESTER JUDD in MARGARET and HARRIET BEECHER STOWE in her yarns of Sam Lawson converted their books into rich storehouses of New England custom and tradition. ROBERT M. BIRD introduced to literature in NICK OF THE WOODS that phantom of terror, the Jibbenainosay, and that curious creature of the "dark and bloody ground" of Kentucky: the ring-tailed roarer, half-horse, half-alligator.

The Transcendentalists were not much interested in folklore, but none of our writers has made more extensive use of it than HENRY WADSWORTH LONGFELLOW. His gift for folk expression displayed itself in ballad and metrical romance, beginning with such pieces as THE BATTLE OF LOVELL'S POND and "Lover's Rock" and continuing with THE WRECK OF THE HESPERUS, THE SKELETON IN ARMOR, EVANGELINE, THE SONG OF HIAWATHA, and THE COURTSHIP OF MILES STANDISH. In TALES OF A WAYSIDE INN he used many folk themes, especially the popular tale of Paul Revere's ride and the Norse saga of King Olaf.

JOHN GREENLEAF WHITTIER shared Longfellow's love of balladry and was interested even more in New England legend. "Mogg Megone" illustrates his extended handling of Indian legend, and "The Witch of Wenham" and "The Wreck of Rivermouth" embody local superstition. Much early lore is packed in LEAVES FROM MARGARET SMITH'S JOURNAL. Among the ballads, BARBARA FRIETCHIE, MAUD MULLER, and especially SKIPPER IRESON'S RIDE are noteworthy, and TELLING THE BEES is a touching use of old custom that is also referred to in HUCKLEBERRY FINN.

JAMES RUSSELL LOWELL, turning to the tradition of SAM SLICK and JACK DOWNING, made his great contribution to the literature of folklore in his BIGLOW PAPERS, where he recorded native speech with considerable accuracy and in the person of Birdofredom Sawin uttered much folk wisdom. THE COURTIN', in which the poet let himself go, is as "hahnsome as a girl in a gingham apron."

OLIVER WENDELL HOLMES was little interested in folklore, but HERMAN MELVILLE, like Hawthorne, sought many of his themes among the legends of the people, especially that of the huge white whale, as fabulous as the big bear of Arkansas and a great deal more significant. MOBY-DICK is truly "one of the first great mythologies created in the modern world."

WALT WHITMAN came nearest to Homer in his folk attitudes. He nourished his imagination on the great myths of the Greeks, then drifted into the carefree camaraderie of the open road in America, looking on everything with the eyes of a prophet. Near the close of his career he addressed in Platte Canyon the "Spirit that Form'd this Scene" with the stirring animism that had characterized his awareness of "these States" as a whole. Into the SONG OF MYSELF he swept such folk references as the murder of the young men at Goliad, the western turkey shoot, coon-hunters going through the regions of the Red River, slaves hoeing in the sugar field, the Missourian crossing the plains with his wares and cattle, and many more. His prototypical American possessed far more than human stature. Although Whitman lacked the ear for folk rhythm and phrase, his art, with its incremental repetition, parallelism, and catalogues, is close to natural lyricism and constitutes the marshland between folklore and literature.

During the second half of the 19th century the local color movement opened the way for a more realistic use of folk materials. Ironically, however, when BRET HARTE tried to prove that whatever the frontiersman lacked in culture he made up in innate moral virtue, he established a school of romantic hokum that has not only set the pattern for all westerns but has survived even the hard-boiled naturalism of JOHN STEINBECK. Other local colorists were somewhat more successful. EDWARD EGGLESTON used the Cinderella motif to portray the folkways of poor whites in Indiana. MARY NOAILLES MURFREE sought out the superstitions of the Smoky Mountains but did not go to the roots of life there as have ELIZABETH MADOX ROBERTS and JESSE STUART in Kentucky. GEORGE W. CABLE used voodooism and other exotic customs in his Creole tales. JOEL CHANDLER HARRIS embellished the animal symbolism of African-Americans and gave literary form to tales in the slave tradition, transported from Africa. Later, FINLEY P. DUNNE created in Mr. Dooley a great mythological figure of Irish-America, and Charles Godfrey Leland wrote amusingly of German-American ways in *Hans Breitmann's Ballads*. (See HANS BREITMANN.)

When MARK TWAIN leaped to fame astride a jumping frog, he used a yarn known not only in the West but often told by African-Americans along the levees of the Mississippi. ROUGHING IT contains such folk elements as the story of the buffalo hunt, a characteristic tall tale; the story of the old ram, well known in ballad lore; and the story of Dick Baker and his cat, which fits into the Uncle Remus type of bestiary. Baker's blue-jay yarn belongs here by right but somehow got into A TRAMP ABROAD. As for Colonel Sellers, he may have been modeled on the rascally Simon Suggs, according to Constance Rourke, who adds, "If he was not the fabulous single figure toward which the national types had tended to merge, his stride was great; he was accepted throughout the nation as its own." In LIFE ON THE MISSISSIPPI Twain recalled the tall talk of the keelboatmen as the Child of Calamity discourses on the nutritiousness of Mississippi water or goes through the extravagant ritual of

"Whoooop! bow your neck and spread, for the Pet Child of Calamity's a-coming!" And in TOM SAWYER and HUCKLEBERRY FINN the author used enough African-American superstition and backcountry lore to make the reputation of a lesser artist. Twain's art had the garrulity of native storytellers as well as their incongruity and their irreverence, but he lifted the poetry of folk speech to new heights of splendor.

Later came the folk literature of capitalism, drawing on and helping to create American popular myths of material success—THE GILDED AGE, THE RISE OF SILAS LAPHAM, THE OCTOPUS, THE PIT, THE FINANCIER, MAIN STREET, and a host of others. Realism and naturalism marked the works of such writers as THEODORE DREISER, SINCLAIR LEWIS, JOHN DOS PASSOS, and JAMES T. FARRELL. To a certain extent, these writers countered the rosy glow left by the local colorists, but they did so by turning to new urban themes, and others had to retrieve the still-untapped resources of the country folk. More and more 20th-century writers turned to a realistic treatment of the pioneer, the mountain man, and the farmer. JOHN A. LOMAX gathered cowboy songs and frontier ballads, helping to rectify the inaccuracies of OWEN WISTER's Western novels. ROARK BRADFORD gave us OL' MAN AN' HIS CHILLUN and such works as GREEN PASTURES, PORGY, and SCARLET SISTER MARY present authentic folk materials. VACHEL LINDSAY sang of the Chinese laundryman, the black, and the Salvation Army. WILLA CATHER treated sympathetically the folkways of Bohemians, Germans, and Scandinavians, and O.E. RÖLVAAG brought out the Viking strain in his characters as they adjusted to a new land and a new society. CARL SANDBURG found native symbols in innumerable acts and traditions of the people.

ROBERT FROST's poetry is close to daily living, to the comedies and tragedies of hard-handed New Englanders. STEPHEN VINCENT BENÉT in THE DEVIL AND DANIEL WEBSTER transformed pseudofolklore into a modern classic and in *Johnny Pye and the Fool-Killer* treated expertly a myth that had previously fascinated O. Henry. H. L. DAVIS in HONEY IN THE HORN told a lusty folk tale of the Oregon frontier. More recently John Steinbeck gave us the lore of the *paisano* in TORTILLA FLAT and of the Okies in THE GRAPES OF WRATH. Many other such genre studies, written in unaffected prose, add distinctly to the veracity of literature in America.

By the late 20th century, American folklore had become so interwoven with the country's literary traditions that the threads could be found everywhere. A few examples will have to serve. WILLIAM CARLOS WILLIAMS answered the European challenge of Eliot's *Waste Land* with PATERSON, heavily infused with the folklore of New Jersey. ARTHUR MILLER reviewed once more the American dream of success in DEATH OF A SALESMAN. TONI MORRISON invited comparison with Faulkner and his use of folk sources in novels like *Song of Solomon*, drawing on the African-American legend of a man who can fly, and *Beloved*, set in a misty, folklore-filled Ohio just after the Civil War. JOHN UPDIKE revised the vision of *The Scarlet Letter*, commenting on it and our own time in *Roger's Version* and S. To the strain of Jewish folklore incorporated in works from the earlier 20th century, must now be added the folktale elements in the work of ISAAC BASHEVIS SINGER. To earlier infusions of Asian folklore, must be added the tales incorporated in MAXINE HONG KINGSTON's *The Woman Warrior*. ALICE WALKER provides attractive metaphors for much of this activity with her emphasis on patchwork quilts and gardens in works that include the story "Everyday Use" and the novel *The Color Purple*.

For Native Americans and African-Americans, the folklore tradition was for a long time heavily oral. For both groups, large proportions of the tradition were at first captured in the writings of white authors with varying degrees of authenticity. Writers from both backgrounds appeared early—African-Americans by the late 18th, Native Americans by the early 19th centuries—and before long they had begun to record their own folklore. In the 20th century, particularly in the latter half, folklore has served as a major source of strength for writers identifying themselves with Native American and African-American backgrounds. The relationship between folklore and literature, however, is a neglected field. Richard Dorson's *Handbook of American Folklore* (1983) is a good general introduction to folklore considered mostly apart from literature.

ERNEST E. LEISY/GP

folksongs and ballads.   The earliest American folksongs were those of the Native Americans (see NATIVE AMERICAN LITERATURE). American folksongs in the European tradition were at first the songs carried here by immigrants. A large number of these are found in FRANCIS J. CHILD's *The English and Scottish Popular Ballads*. About 100 of the 305 ballads printed by Child have been collected in the United States and Canada, with the Southern Appalachians a fertile ground that kept some ballads alive after they had passed out of living tradition in Great Britain. Although they were not collected on this side of the Atlantic in the 17th or 18th centuries, we can assume that at least some were known to Americans from the days of earliest settlement. Songs in oral tradition here, in addition to those collected by Child, include about 275 that originated as British broadsides in the 18th and 19th centuries.

The native tradition of American folksong grew out of the English, adopting the dominant meters of the traditional English and Scottish ballads. The subject matter, however, was more akin to that of the British broadside. The stories tended to be the news of the day—murders, mine disasters, strikes—and the majority of the perhaps 250 that are native to North America were created between 1870 and 1900. The heroes are not the lords of the traditional British ballads, but the romantic figures of the later 19th century—cowboys, lumberjacks, sailors, and railroad men. Although the songs are often tragic, the tragedy frequently takes a peculiarly American turn as the events are undercut by humor or sentimentality.

Early in the 19th century, the British tradition of folksong in America began to be invaded by the traditions of African-American folksong. Although songs in predominantly white sections of the Appalachians continued to develop without the influence of other traditions until well into the 20th century, elsewhere the effects of spirituals and blues shaped a new tradition, distinctly American, with a strong emphasis on creative spontaneity and nonlinear development.

With the advent of records and radio, the conditions that shaped folksong changed dramatically, but remained evident in the work of WOODY GUTHRIE and in American blues, jazz, and popular music.

Alan Lomax, *The Folksongs of North America* in *the English Language* (1960), is a good general collection. Good regional collections include H. M. Belden, *Ballads and Songs Collected by the Missouri Folk Song Society* (1940); Vance Randolph, *Ozark Folksongs* (4 v. 1946–50); Cecil J. Sharp, *English Folk Songs from the Southern Appalachians* (2 v. 1932); and Newman Ivey White, ed., *The Frank C. Brown Collection of North American Folklore* (7 v. 1925–1964). Studies and collections of types of folksongs include Tristram P. Coffin, *The British Traditional Ballad in North America* (1963); G. Malcolm Laws, Jr., *Native American Balladry* (1964); John Lomax, *Cowboy Songs and Other Frontier Ballads* (1910, enlarged in later editions); N. Howard Thorp, *Songs of the Cowboys* (1966); Howard W. Odum and Guy B. Johnson, *The Negro and His Songs* (1925), and *Negro Workaday Songs* (1926); Newman I. White, *American Negro Folk-Songs* (1928); Franz Rickaby, *Ballads and Songs of the Shantey Boy* (1926), lumberjack songs; William Main Doerflinger, *Shanteymen and Shanteyboys* (1951), sea chanties; John Greenway, *American Folksongs of Protest* (1953); and Olive Wooley Burt, *American Murder Ballads* (1958).

Following the Equator (1897),   a travel book by MARK TWAIN describing a lecture tour he made around the world. It contains lengthy passages on Australia, India, and South Africa. Twain was not well when he undertook this tour to pay off debts incurred in his business enterprises, and the book shows signs of the author's weariness. Yet it is sprinkled with striking epigrams, mainly the fruit of Twain's bitterness at this period.

Fool's Errand, A (1879),   a novel "by One of the Fools" (ALBION W. TOURGÉE). A great popular success in its day, this anonymously published novel was hailed by some critics as the great American novel. The fool's errand is the attempt to remold the South in the image of the North after the Civil War. The novel reaches the conclusion that reconstruction has failed. Tourgée was a Northerner by birth but had long lived in the South, working as a journalist. The novel often becomes autobiographical. The hero is represented as a Union colonel who moves from Michigan to a Southern plantation after peace is declared and there tries to carry out ideas for helping the South. Later Tourgée documented his story in a signed publication called *The Invisible Empire* (1883) and wrote a sequel, BRICKS WITHOUT STRAW (1880), with a Southern hero and a Northern heroine. Steele MacKaye made a faithful dramatization of *A Fool's Errand* (1881).

Foote, John Taintor (1881–1950),   novelist, short-story writer, playwright, screen producer. Perhaps Foote will be best remembered for his stories of dogs, for example, *Dumb-Bell of Brookfield* (1917), and horses and other animals. He wrote about an outdoorsman in *Blister Jones* (1913), who reappeared in some of his later tales, among them *A Fowl Disaster* (1941). Foote also wrote *The Look of Eagles* (1916) and *Pocono Shot* (1925).

Foote, Mary Hallock (1847–1938), novelist. Born in New York City, Foote gained some attention as one of the first novelists to write realistically of the West, as she attempted to record in Howellsian fashion the life she observed while living there. Her novels of this period include THE LED-HORSE CLAIM (1883), about Colorado mines; *John Bodewin's Testimony* (1886); *The Chosen Valley* (1892); and *Coeur d'Alene* (1894), about unions in the mines in Colorado. Among her other works of fiction are *The Last Assembly Ball and The Fate of a Voice* (1889), with brief comments on the difficulties of portraying Western manners; *Edith Bonham* (1917); and *Groundswell* (1919). *A Victorian Gentlewoman in the Far West* (1972), memoirs, was edited by Rodman Paul. Wallace Stegner fictionized her life in *Angle of Repose* (1971).

Foote, Shelby (1916–), novelist, historian. Born in Mississippi, Foote was educated at the University of North Carolina and served in the Army and Marine Corps in World War II. He first gained notice with three novels linked, like Faulkner's, to portray a small area in Mississippi: *Tournament* (1949), *Follow Me Down* (1950), and *Love in a Dry Season* (1951). *Jordan County: A Landscape in Narrative* (1954) presents the same territory in seven connected stories. *Shiloh* (1952) is a historical novel centered on the Civil War battle. He received greater praise, however, for his three-volume history *The Civil War: A Narrative*, which includes *Fort Sumter to Perryville* (1958), *Fredericksburg to Meridian* (1963), and *Red River to Appomattox* (1974). Foote received significant public exposure as a commentator in the 1990 PBS documentary *The Civil War*. Renewed interest in his work was followed by the publication of two novels, *Child by Fever* (1995) and *Ride Out* (1996) and two Modern Library editions culled from his Civil War history, *Stars in Their Courses: The Gettysburg Campaign* (1994) and *The Beleaguered City: The Vicksburg Campaign* (1995). Other books include the novel *September September* (1977), about the kidnapping of an African-American boy by whites; *The Novelist's View of History* (1981); and *The Correspondence of Shelby Foote and Walker Percy* (1996).
SUZANNE PERKINS-HART

Forayers, The (1855), a novel by W. G. SIMMS. See EUTAW SPRINGS.

Forbes, Esther [Mrs. A. L. Hoskins] (1891–1967), novelist, biographer. Born in Massachusetts, Forbes wrote mostly of the history of her native state. Her biography *Paul Revere and the World He Lived in* (1942) won a Pulitzer Prize. Her historical novels include *O Genteel Lady!* (1926), set in 19th-century Boston; *A Mirror for Witches* (1928), about the Salem hysteria; *Paradise* (1937), about the time of KING PHILIP; *The General's Lady* (1938), a Revolutionary War story; *The Running of the Tide* (1948), about the era of clipper ships; and *Rainbow on the Road* (1954), about an itinerant painter. *Johnny Tremaine* (1943) is a children's book about the Revolution.

Forbes, Kathryn (1909–1966), writer. Forbes was the pen name of Kathryn Anderson McLean. Stories of her Norwegian immigrant grandmother were collected as *Mama's Bank Account* (1943) and dramatized by JOHN VAN DRUTEN as *I Remember Mama* (1948), later a television series. Other titles are *Transfer Point* (1947) and *The Dog Who Spoke to Santa Claus* (1956).

Force, Peter (1790–1868), printer, publisher, archivist, historian. Born in New Jersey, Force became a printer in Washington, D.C., and served as mayor (1836–40). In 1820–24 and 1828–36 he issued the *National Calendar and Annals of the U.S.* He also published *Historical Tracts* on early American history, from 1836 to 1846, and *American Archives* between 1837 and 1853. In 1867 his great collection of books and papers was acquired by the Library of Congress.

Forché, Carolyn (1950–) poet, journalist. Born in Michigan and educated at Michigan State University and Bowling Green State University, Forché has been a human rights activist as well as a writer. She was a correspondent for National Public Radio and a member of the Commission on U.S.–Central American Relations and has written two books on El Salvador: *Women and War in El Salvador* (1980) and *El Salvador: The Work of Thirty Photographers* (1983). She has also translated the work of Salvadoran poets. Her first book of poetry, *Gathering the Tribes* (1976), recounting experiences of her adolescence and youth, won the 1975 Yale Series of Younger Poets Award, and her second, *The Country Between Us*, was given the 1981 Lamont Poetry prize. Joyce Carol Oates praised Forché's ability to blend the personal with the political as placing her in the company of writers such as Pablo Neruda and Denise Levertov. Forché's images of political repression, such as the army officer (*The Colonel*, 1978) who, while making light of human rights offenses in his country, empties a bag of human ears in front of the poet, have the immediacy of television coverage of atrocities. *The Angel of History* (1994), winner of the *Los Angeles Times* book award, takes its name from a figure—imagined by German philosopher Walter Benjamin—who can record the suffering of humanity but is powerless to stop them. *Colors Come from God—Just Like Me!* appeared in 1995. Forché also edited *Against Forgetting: Twentieth-Century Poetry of Witness* (1993), an anthology of anti-war and anti-torture writing by 144 poets beginning with the Armenian genocide through the conflicts in Latin America, Africa, and the Middle East at century's end.

Ford, Corey ["John Riddell"] (1902–1969), humorist, playwright. In addition to the books and articles published under his own name, Ford wrote parodies under the pen name John Riddell. Among his books are *Three Rousing Cheers for the Rollo Boys* (1925); *Salt Water Taffy* (1929); *Short Cut to Tokyo* (1943); *Cloak and Dagger* (1946, with Alastair MacBain); *How to Guess Your Age* (1950); *Office Party* (1951); *The Day Nothing Happened* (1959); and, under his pseudonym, *Meaning No Offense* (1928) and *The John Riddell Murder Case* (1930). His other works of humor and parody include *In the Worst Possible Taste* (1932), *Guide to Thinking* (1961), and *What Every Bachelor Knows* (1961).

Ford, Gerald R[udolph] (1913–), 38th president of the U.S. (1974–77). Born in Omaha, Nebraska, to a mother soon divorced, Ford was raised in Grand Rapids, Michigan, where he assumed the name of his stepfather, Gerald R. Ford, who adopted him. He was educated at the University of Michigan and Yale Law School and was admitted to the Michigan bar in 1941. After service in the Navy he was elected to the U.S. House of Representatives and was Republican minority leader from 1965 to 1973, when he became vice president, appointed to succeed Spiro T. Agnew under the procedures of the 25th Amendment. When President RICHARD NIXON resigned on August 9, 1974, eight months after Ford had become vice president, he succeeded to the presidency. A month later he pardoned Nixon for all crimes committed while president. He was defeated in the next presidential election by JIMMY CARTER. His writings include a book of memoirs, *A Time to Heal* (1979). His papers are stored in the Gerald R. Ford Presidential Library at the University of Michigan.

Ford, Jesse Hill [Jr.] (1928–1996),   novelist. Born in Troy, Alabama, Ford was educated at Vanderbilt University and the University of Florida. He served in the Navy and worked in journalism and public relations before winning praise as a regional writer for fictions set in Tennessee. These include the novels *Mountains of Gilead* (1961) and *The Liberation of Lord Byron Jones* (1965) as well as the stories in *Fishes, Birds, and Sons of Men* (1967). The South remains central to other work, including the novels *The Feast of Saint Barnabas* (1969), about a race riot; and *The Raider* (1975), set in the pre–Civil War era. *Mr. Potter and His Bank* is a biography of a Nashville businessman. In 1971 Ford was found not guilty in the shooting of a black soldier who had pulled into Ford's private drive. In the aftermath of the trial his writing production declined. Despondent over his health, Ford committed suicide.

Ford, John (1895–1973),   film director, producer. Ford was born Sean Aloysius O'Feeney in Cape Elizabeth, Maine, and raised in Portland, Maine. In 1913 he went to Hollywood to join his brother Francis Ford (1882–1953), an actor and film director. A director as early as 1917, John Ford made important silent films—*The Iron Horse* (1924) and *Four Sons* (1928)—but achieved prominence in the sound era.

His finest films include *The Lost Patrol* (1934), *The Informer* (1935), *The Plough and the Stars* (1936), *Stagecoach* (1939), *Drums Along the Mohawk* (1939), *The Grapes of Wrath* (1940), *The Long Voyage Home* (1940), and *How Green Was My Valley* (1941). During World War II he made documentaries for the Navy, including *The Battle of Midway* (1942) and *December 7th* (1943). His films after the war include *My Darling Clementine* (1946), *Fort Apache* (1948), *She Wore a Yellow Ribbon* (1949), *Rio Grande* (1950), *The Quiet Man* (1952), *The Horse Soldiers* (1959), and *The Man Who Shot Liberty Valance* (1962).

Ford, Paul Leicester (1865–1902),   novelist, bibliographer, historian. With his father, Gordon Lester Ford, and his brother, Worthington Ford, he issued some important bibliographies, *Winnowings in American History* (15 v. 1890–91). He wrote various historical and biographical works, among them *The True George Washington* (1896) and *The Many-Sided Franklin* (1899). But his literary fame rests chiefly on two novels: the story of a politician, THE HONORABLE PETER STIRLING AND WHAT PEOPLE THOUGHT OF HIM (1894) and JANICE MEREDITH: A STORY OF THE AMERICAN REVOLUTION (1899). The former was

generally taken to be a portrait of Grover Cleveland. The latter became an immediate best seller, was dramatized, and had a long run.

Ford, Richard (1944–   ),   novelist, short-story writer. Born in Mississippi, Ford was educated at Michigan State University and the University of Michigan. His third novel, *The Sportswriter* (1986), won special praise. Ranging in setting from New Jersey to Michigan and Florida, it is a first-person narrative by Frank Bascombe, a man whose decision to give up his novel for sports writing is emblematic of other life choices, all made "to deflect the pain of terrible regret." His other novels are *A Piece of My Heart* (1976), a novel of Mexico, prison, and drugs; and *The Ultimate Good Luck* (1981). *Rock Springs* (1987) collects short stories. *Wildlife* (1990) is a brief novel about the dissolution of a family as seen through the eyes of a 16-year-old son. When the father is accused of theft, the mother has a brief affair with an older man and leaves. Set in Montana, it resembles the setting and circumstances of Ford short stories, with families caught in the moment when change and ruin begin. *Independence Day* (1995), a sequel to *The Sportswriter*, takes up Frank Bascombe's life as a New Jersey real estate salesman during the Fourth of July weekend in 1988. *Women with Men* (1997) is a collection of three stories.

Ford, Sewell (1868–1946),   short-story writer, novelist. Ford was chiefly noted for the tales he wrote about two comic characters, Torchy and Shorty McCabe. Among his collections are *Shorty McCabe* (1906), *Cherub Divine* (1909), *Just Horses* (1910), *Torchy* (1911), and *Inez and Trilby May* (1921).

Forester, Frank.   Pen name of HENRY WILLIAM HERBERT.

Forest Hymn, A (1825),   a poem by WILLIAM CULLEN BRYANT. Written in resonant blank verse, it begins with the line "The groves were God's first temples" and goes on to express views of the universe similar to those in Wordsworth's early poems. The feeling is markedly pantheistic, despite the fact that Bryant expresses a belief in a personal creator, a God of wrath as well as of love.

Forest Rose, The; or, American Farmers (1825),   a play by SAMUEL WOODWORTH. The type of stage Yankee created by Royall Tyler in THE CONTRAST (produced 1790) evoked many imitations; among the most popular was Jonathan Ploughboy in Woodworth's melodrama.

Forever Amber (1944),   a historical novel by KATHLEEN WINSOR. *Life* described the book as "about a beauty who went from mattress to mattress across Restoration London." Attempts were made in Massachusetts to have it legally suppressed, and it sold more than a million copies in a year.

Forrest, Edwin (1806–1872),   actor. Born in Philadelphia, Forrest, who was noted for his Shakespearean roles, first became celebrated when he played Othello in New York (1826). He encouraged American writers, several of whom wrote plays for him, but sometimes quarrels resulted. A feud with the English actor William Charles Macready led to a riot when the latter appeared in the Astor Place Theatre (May 10, 1849). Forrest in his will left his estate to found the Forrest Home for aged actors in Philadelphia.

Forrest, Col. Thomas, author of THE DISAPPOINT-MENT OR, THE FORCE OF CREDULITY. See ROBERT MONTGOMERY BIRD; THE GLADIATOR.

Fort, Charles [Hoy] (1874–1932), newspaperman. Fort gathered stories of strange and apparently inexplicable happenings in an endeavor to show that science was still limited in its ability to explain certain phenomena. He wrote *The Book of the Damned* (1919), *New Lands* (1923), *Lo!* (1931), and *Wild Talents* (1932). *The Books of Charles Fort* (1941) collected these in an omnibus volume edited by Tiffany Thayer. A group of Fort's admirers, including Thayer, Booth Tarkington, Theodore Dreiser, and Alexander Woollcott, founded the Fortean Society (1931) and issued a magazine called *Doubt* (1937). The society was dedicated to "the frustration of science."

For the Union Dead (1960), a poem by ROBERT LOW-ELL. Lowell printed the poem at the end of *Life Studies* (1960), where in an early printing it bore the title "Colonel Shaw and the Massachusetts 54th." Later it became the title poem of *For the Union Dead* (1964). The poem moves from memories of the South Boston Aquarium, long closed by the 1960s, to images of the Boston Common torn up for a municipal garage, while the "tingling Statehouse" faces the Robert Gould Shaw memorial, propped by planks to support it during the excavations. Meanwhile, "the drained faces of Negro school-children" confront us on our TV sets to remind us how little progress has been made in one hundred years to advance a cause for which blacks and whites once fought and died together.

Forty-niners. A name given to those who emigrated to California during the gold rush of 1849. About a hundred thousand in number, the prospectors came by way of the sea (around Cape Horn or across Panama) or overland, usually experiencing considerable hardship on either route. Many were adventurers, misfits, or criminals, but there were also a good number of business and professional men, including some eminent journalists—BRET HARTE, for example—who found in the new life as rich a source of fame and income as others found in the gold fields. The gold rush gave a great impetus to immigration and consequently to ethnic diversity in California as immigrants came not only from the eastern United States, but from many European nations and from Mexico, Australia, China, and elsewhere.

Forty-Second Parallel, The (1930), a novel by JOHN DOS PASSOS, the first of a trilogy collected in 1938 as *U.S.A.* The individual episodes and the characterization, the setting and the commentaries, are in themselves less important than the effectiveness of the entire book and the trilogy. Dos Passos employs with skill the modernist techniques that were coming into fashion during the first decades of the century. There is no definite plot; the book flows in a stream of time and is designed to portray the United States rather than to narrate the lives of the various—almost innumerable—individuals who figure in it. The method of narration was a bold innovation. Dos Passos uses systematically the "News-Reel," describing the social background; "Biographies," profiles of prominent per-

sonalities; "Novels," which deal with the more ordinary characters of the time; "the Camera Eye," by means of which the author himself can supply an impressionistic personal commentary on what is happening. The result is sometimes confusing, more often a powerful presentation of a vast panorama of human nature and of history.

Forty-Seven Workshop. See GEORGE PIERCE BAKER.

For Whom the Bell Tolls (1940), a novel by ERNEST HEMINGWAY. Laid in the time of the Spanish Civil War (1936–39), the story follows the fortunes of Robert Jordan, an American volunteer fighting on the side of the Loyalist forces. He is sent to join a guerrilla band whose mission is to blow up a bridge, and the narrative recounts his experiences during the three days, in the course of which he comes to doubt the enterprise, falls passionately in love with Maria, a girl who has been tragically wronged by the Falangists, seeks to have the order to blow the bridge countermanded, and finally carries it out but is fatally wounded as he does so. The novel introduces a host of well-drawn characters, in particular that of a dominating woman named Pilar, fanatically devoted to the Republic. The title of the book is taken from one of John Donne's *Devotions*: "No man is an island, entire of itself; every man is a piece of the continent . . . therefore never seek to know for whom the bell tolls; it tolls for thee."

Fosdick, Charles Austin ["Harry Castlemon"] (1842–1915), author of books for boys. Fosdick's experiences as a volunteer in the Civil War and his childhood experiences in Buffalo and in a small town in New York provided him with material for his fifty-eight volumes. They are straightforward narratives, teaching manliness and other virtues, and they rivaled the stories of Alger and Henty in popularity. Among his series are *The Gunboat Series* (1864–68), *The Rocky Mountain Series* (1867–71), and *The Rod and Gun Series* (1883–84). Fosdick's first book was *Frank, the Young Naturalist* (1864), which tells about Fosdick's childhood.

Fosdick, Harry Emerson (1878–1969), clergyman. Nephew of Charles Austin Fosdick, he was born in Buffalo, ordained a Baptist minister, and won a wide reputation for his reconciliation of older theological views with the demands of modern life. He became the pastor of Riverside Church in New York City and a teacher at the Union Theological Seminary. In addition to frequent radio addresses, Fosdick wrote a number of books that attained wide circulation, among them *The Manhood of the Master* (1913), *The Meaning of Prayer* (1915), *As I See Religion* (1932), *Successful Christian Living* (1937), *Living Under Tension* (1941), *On Being a Real Person* (1943), *The Man From Nazareth* (1949), *A Faith for Tough Times* (1952), *John D. Rockefeller, Jr.* (1956), *The Living of These Days* (1956, autobiography), *Jesus of Nazareth* (1957), *A Book of Public Prayers* (1959), and *Dear Mr. Brown* (1961).

Foss, Sam Walter (1858–1911), poet, editor, columnist, librarian. Born in New Hampshire, Foss, who owned the *Saturday Union* in Lynn, Massachusetts, discovered he had a facility for humorous verse. He became a contributor to *Puck* and *Judge*, and in 1894 began writing a daily poem for a syndicate. Often he wrote in dialect and generally expressed a creed of unshatterable and cheerful optimism. His verses were collected in *Back Country Poems* (1892); *Dreams in Homespun* (1897, which includes his best-known poem, THE HOUSE BY THE SIDE OF THE ROAD); *Songs of the Average Man* (1907, with additions 1911); and other volumes.

Foster, Hannah Webster.   See THE COQUETTE.

Foster, Stephen [Collins] (1826–1864),   song writer, composer. Foster was born in Pennsylvania. Although his first job was as a bookkeeper for his brother, he apparently had little head for figures; later, he was frequently victimized by dishonest music publishers, and he never won financial success. His short life was a combination of song, neurotic illness, alcoholism, and extreme poverty. At one point he was found nearly dead from starvation in a Bowery hotel. Among his most celebrated songs are "Old Folks at Home"; "Jeannie with the Light Brown Hair"; "Oh, Susanna"; "Old Black Joe"; "Come Where My Love Lies Dreaming"; "Camptown Races"; "Nelly Bly"; "My Old Kentucky Home"; "Beautiful Dreamer"; and Massa's in de Cold, Cold Ground." Although Foster seems to have had little contact with African-Americans, many of his songs attempt to mirror their speech and express a somewhat sentimentalized version of the slave's view of life. Foster was unmatched by song writers of his time for sustained popularity, and his songs became as much a part of the American musical consciousness as any folk melodies.

Fountain, The (1926),   a play by EUGENE O'NEILL dealing with Ponce de Leon. The dramatist has him fall in love with a woman much younger than himself and then seek the FOUNTAIN OF YOUTH in Florida in order to content his mistress. He fails tragically, but dies at peace as the result of a vision of eternal life. The play, produced in 1925, had a short run.

Fountainhead, The (1943),   a novel by AYN RAND. The hero, supposedly patterned after FRANK LLOYD WRIGHT, is an architect of enormous self-conceit who nevertheless succeeds in justifying his faith in the permanent values of honest design. The book was a best seller.

Fountain of Youth, The.   Early Spanish explorers of America believed and hoped that somewhere in the New World there would be found a bubbling fountain of the *elixir vitae* for which alchemists had been searching through the centuries. Among others, Ponce de Leon, governor of Puerto Rico, made up his mind to find the Fountain of Youth. He set out in 1513 with three ships, discovered Florida, coasted along its east and west shores, visited the Bahamas, but failed to find the fabled Bimini. On a second expedition to Florida he engaged in a battle with hostile Native Americans and died from a wound by a poisoned arrow. One island, which was named Bimini by the explorers, later became a convenient stopping-place for buccaneers, and during the prohibition era it was a busy haunt of bootleggers. Eugene O'Neill's THE FOUNTAIN (1926) deals with Ponce de Leon and his search.

Fourier, Charles (1772–1837),   French sociologist whose ideas exerted a strong influence in the United States, especially on Transcendentalists and on experiments with utopian colonies. Fourier advocated the creation of phalansteries, units of 1,600 persons of varying but complementary ability, who would live together as one family. The leading American Fourierist was PARKE GODWIN (1816–1904), of the New York *Post*, who wrote *A Popular-View of the Doctrine of Charles Fourier* (1844). When ALBERT BRISBANE became influential at Brook Farm, it was turned into a phalanstery and the Fourierist organ *The Phalanx* and its successor *The Harbinger* were published there. Brisbane's *Social Destiny* (1840) was one of the earliest discussions of Fourierism. BRONSON ALCOTT'S FRUITLANDS, in Massachusetts, was another well-known Fourierist colony, and others were located at Red Bank, New Jersey, and near Ripon, Wisconsin. Emerson scorned the movement as unidealistic, saying in a striking passage from his *Journals*: "Fourier learned from Owen all the truth he had, and the rest of his system was imagination, and the imagination of a banker, The Owen and Fourier plans bring no *a priori* convictions. They are come at merely by counting and arithmetic. . . . The Spartan broth, the hermit's cell, the lonely farmer's life are poetic; but the phalanstery, the 'self-supporting village' are culinary and mean."

Fourierism.   See CHARLES FOURIER.

Four in America (1947),   essays by GERTRUDE STEIN on George Washington, Ulysses S. Grant, Wilbur Wright, and Henry James. Stein imagines what would have happened had Grant become a religious leader, Wright a painter, James a general, and Washington a novelist.

Four Million, The (1906),   a collection of twenty-five stories by O. HENRY. The title refers to the population of New York City at the time and is in contrast to Ward McAllister's remark (1888) that "there are only about four hundred people in New York society." It contains one of O. Henry's best stories, THE GIFT OF THE MAGI. O. Henry's favorite characters—shop girls, tramps, humble folk in general—people these tales in abundance and give utterance to the author's uniquely humorous sentimentality. The book became a best seller.

Four Quartets (1943),   four related poems by T. S. ELIOT. Said to have been modeled on the late quartets of Beethoven, each poem is structurally analogous to the classical sonata form, progressing through five movements in which themes and variations are introduced, developed, and finally resolved. The *Quartets*, considered by some critics to be Eliot's finest work, are both the record of a journey from skepticism to faith and an attempt to communicate a religious experience in an age lacking traditional religious belief.

Each poem has as its primary image one of the four elements—air, earth, water, fire—and each is located by its title at a specific place: "Burnt Norton" refers to a 17th-century manor house; "East Coker" to the Somersetshire village from which Eliot's ancestor set out for the New World; "The Dry Salvages" to a group of rocks off the coast of Massachusetts, a landscape familiar to Eliot from childhood; and "Little Gidding" to the English village to which Nicholas Ferrar retired in the 17th century to lead a life of devotion, a place Eliot himself visited. The progression of the poems is from abstraction and deeply personal experience to universal experience; thus, the first poem is much more obscure and dependent on the rest of the group for its explication than the last poem, which can be understood without reference to the preceding three. The subject of Burnt Norton is the unexpected and unsought moment of joy at the "still point" out of time where the pattern of life and of past, present, and future can be apprehended. East Coker deals with the passage of time and the cyclic nature of human life and history. The Dry Salvages contrasts the time of the river, which is human time, with that of the sea, which is eternity. Little Gidding celebrates a visit to the chapel "where prayer has been valid" for a moment of dedication that has transcended time and space and in which the themes and images of the preceding poems find their resolution. Published in 1942, with some of its images drawn from the German bombing of London, Little Gidding is not only Eliot's last major poem, but also one of the finest poetic treatments of World War II.

Four Saints in Three Acts (1934),   a libretto by GERTRUDE STEIN, for an opera composed by Virgil Thomson. The Four Saints are St. Theresa, St. Ignatius, and the unhistorical St. Settlement and St. Chavez. Thomson added two characters to represent the laity. Largely plotless, the opera concerns imaginary incidents in 16th-century Spain. It was given its premiere at Hartford, Connecticut, in 1934.

Fowler, Gene [Eugene Devlan] (1890–1960), newspaperman, editor, writer. Although Fowler turned early from newspaper work and scriptwriting, he continued a journalistic concern with facts in his fictions. In Hollywood he wrote at least twenty-five scripts, among them *Union Depot* (1932), *Call of the Wild* (1935), and *Jesse James* (1939). But he hit his stride writing biographies, particularly accounts of contemporaries whom he knew personally. First of these books was *The Great Mouthpiece* (1931), about a New York lawyer of not-unblemished renown. It was followed by *Timberline* (1933), the account of two Denver editors; *Good-Night, Sweet Prince* (1943), a biography of John Barrymore and Fowler's best book; *Beau James* (1949), which describes the life and times of Jimmy Walker, once mayor of New York; *Schnozzola: The Story of Jimmy Durante* (1951); and *Minutes of the Last Meeting* (1954), sketches of celebrated theater people woven around a biography of Sadakichi Hartmann. *A Solo in Tom-Toms* (1933 in a private printing, 1946 for general circulation) and *Salute to Yesterday* (1937) deal with Fowler's earlier years. *Skyline* appeared posthumously in 1961.

Fox, John [William], Jr. (1863–1919),   novelist, short-story writer. Born in Kentucky, Fox won celebrity chiefly with two novels that became best sellers: THE LITTLE SHEPHERD OF KINGDOM COME (1903) and THE TRAIL OF THE LONESOME PINE (1908). Both were successfully dramatized by EUGENE WALTER (1912 and 1916). Earlier there had been other stories and novels by Fox, mainly laid in Kentucky and nearby, and they were followed by *The Heart of the Hills* (1913) and a historical novel, *Erskine Dale: Pioneer* (1920). Fox's short stories and sketches are collected in *A Cumberland Vendetta* (1895), *Hell fer Sartain* (1897), *Blue Grass and Rhododendron* (1901), and *Christmas Eve on Lonesome, and Other Stories* (1904). (See THE KENTUCKIANS.)

Foxes of Harrow, The (1946),   a popular historical romance by FRANK YERBY. Stephen Fox, a gambler, becomes an important plantation owner in Louisiana, tries to establish a respectable family, and is ruined by the Civil War.

Fra Elbertus.   See ELBERT HUBBARD.

Francesca da Rimini (produced 1855, published 1856), a play by GEORGE HENRY BOKER. Considered by some the best 19th-century American play, this verse drama, based on an episode in Dante's *Inferno*, is Boker's masterpiece. Another play by the same title was written by F. MARION CRAWFORD (1902), originally for production by Sarah Bernhardt.

Francis, Robert [Churchill] (1901–1987),   poet, novelist, essayist. Educated at Harvard, Francis settled in Amherst, Massachusetts, and devoted himself primarily to writing, receiving the Shelley Memorial Award (1939), an American Academy in Rome Fellowship (1957), and the Brandeis University Creative Arts Award (1974) among others.

Francis was a poet of the middle range; although his style and vision were fresh and interesting, his poems were often overly structured and explicit. The opening section of *The Orb Weaver* (1980), for example, one of his best books, is largely about skill—athletic as well as poetic—and its general concern is with the tension of balance. The second section of the book is mainly about Nature and her fullness and is somewhat more impressive, while the third is largely taken up with the relation of people to Nature.

"The Revelers," for example, is reminiscent of Wallace Stevens's "Credences of Summer." Dwelling more on night and winter, the fourth section becomes more somber, and "Three Darks Come Down Together" is memorable. The final section is still more somber: the title poem is about a ghastly spider reminiscent of the one in Frost's "Design." "Cold," which depicts a freeze, concludes "I huddle, hoard, hold out, hold on, hold on."

Collected Poems 1936–1976 (1976) reprints all his earlier volumes, including *The Orb Weaver*, as well as *Come Out into the Sun* (1965) and *Like Ghosts of Eagles* (1974). Francis's later style became more diverse, experimenting with word count, fragmented surface, and fused syntax. Although the later poems reveal signs of variations in mood, style, and structure, he remained largely impersonal and objective—not in the classical modernist way of absorbing the subject into the object, but rather in the way of being simply a disinterested observer.

He published his autobiography, *The Trouble with Francis*, in 1971, and several additional volumes of poetry, among them *Butter Hill and Other Poems* (1984). His other titles include *Traveling in Amherst: A Poet's Journal, 1931–1954* (1986) and collections of satirical sketches. *We Fly Away* (1948) is a novella.

NORMAN FRIEDMAN/BP

Franck, Harry A[lverson] (1881–1962),   teacher, lecturer, author of travel books. Franck, who was born in Michigan, traveled through many countries, often on foot. Among his books are *A Vagabond Journey Around the World*

(1910), *Four Months Afoot in Spain* (1911), *Roaming Through the West Indies* (1920), *Roving Through Southern China* (1925), *Foot-Loose in the British Isles* (1933), and *Rediscovering South America* (1943). His wife, Rachel Latta Franck, wrote *I Married a Vagabond* (1939).

Franco, Harry.   Pen name of CHARLES FREDERICK BRIGGS.

François, The Adventures of (1898),   a novel by S. WEIR MITCHELL. This is a historical novel laid in the period of the French Revolution and devoted to the career of a "foundling, thief, juggler, and fencing master." The hero was an actual person. *The Red City* (1907) was a sequel. Mitchell's son, the playwright Langdon Mitchell, dramatized the story in 1900.

Frank, Waldo [David] (1889–1967),   novelist, social critic. Born in New Jersey, Frank was educated at Yale, lived abroad for a while, and returned to New York City, where he helped edit *The Seven Arts* (1916–17). In novels and books of nonfiction he examined the United States and the world, frequently from a leftist perspective. His novels include *The Unwelcome Man* (1917); *Rahab* (1922), about prostitution; *Holiday* (1923), on race problems; *The Dark Mother* (1923); *The Death and Birth of David Markand* (1934), about the regeneration of an American businessman; *The Bridegroom Cometh* (1938); *Summer Never Ends* (1941); *The Invaders* (1948); and *Not Heaven* (1953). His works of observation and social criticism include *Our America* (1919); *Salvoe* (1924); *Virgin Spain* (1926, revised 1942); *The Re-Discovery of America* (1928); *America Hispana* (1931); *Dawn in Russia* (1932); *In the American Jungle* (1937); *Chart for Rough Water* (1940); *South American Journey* (1943); *The Jew in Our Day* (1944); *Bridgehead: The Drama of Israel* (1957); and *Cuba: Prophetic Island* (1961).

Franken, Rose [Lewin] (1895–1988),   playwright, novelist, short-story writer, scriptwriter. Rose Lewin was born in Texas, but was raised from age twelve in New York City. After high school she married and lived in New York, where most of her work is set. A first novel, *Patterns* (1925), of a young woman's growth and marriage and in part autobiographical, won praise but not many readers. Her later short stories and novels generally won less praise but were hugely popular and placed her among the most highly paid writers of her time. Most popular of all were the Claudia novels, eight books following the fortunes of Claudia and David Naughton, their relatives, and their maid. The series begins with *Claudia: The Story of a Marriage* (1939), and all eight volumes are gathered in *The Complete Book of Claudia* (1962).

Franken's greatest critical success came from her plays. As a play, *Claudia* (1941) was selected best of its season and was made into a movie (1943). Earlier, *Another Language* (1932), a satirical thrust at middle-class values and the place of women in the American family, won much praise, had a long run on Broadway, and was also made into a movie (1933). Franken's other plays include *Outrageous Fortune* (1943) and *Soldier's Wife* (1944), both successful; and *Doctors Disagree* (1943) and

The Hallams (1948), less so. *When All Is Said and Done* (1962) is an autobiography.

Frankie and Johnnie.   Perhaps the most famous American folk ballad. No one knows who wrote the words or the music, or when it was first sung in the United States. It relates the story of Frankie, who had many lovers but only one "man," who "done her wrong." Sigmund Spaeth traced its possible ancestry back to 1840, and it may be even older; innumerable versions exist.

Frank Leslie's Illustrated News.   See FRANK LESLIE.

Franklin, Ann (1696–1763),   America's first woman printer. Her husband, JAMES FRANKLIN (1697–1735), was the older brother of Benjamin Franklin. At the death of James, she took over his Boston business and conducted it until 1748, when their son James became its manager. When he died in 1762, she and a printer named Samuel Hall ran it in partnership. Ann and James founded the Newbury *Mercury* in 1758.

Franklin, Benjamin (1706–1790),   printer, philosopher, scientist, statesman, writer. Franklin sums up in his activities and ideas so much of his time that he may be considered an epitome of the 18th century. Born in Boston, he was the tenth and youngest son of Josiah Franklin, a tallow chandler and soapmaker. After some two years of schooling, he went to work for his father at the age of ten. Two years later he was apprenticed to his brother James, a printer who later (1721) established the NEW-ENGLAND COURANT, in which appeared young Benjamin's first literary productions, THE DOGOOD PAPERS (1722). During this period, Franklin tells us, he began the lifelong habit of concentrated reading that made him a self-educated man.

In 1723, as a result of quarrels with his brother, he left Boston for Philadelphia and found employment in a printing shop. He attracted the attention of Governor Keith, who recommended that the young man set up in business for himself and offered to help him financially if he would go to England for equipment. In London, finding that promised letters of credit from the governor had not arrived, Franklin again went to work as a printer, meanwhile continuing his writing. In answer to William Wollaston's *The Religion of Nature Delineated*, he wrote and printed *A Dissertation on Liberty and Necessity, Pleasure and Pain* (1725), a liberal exposition of ideas on necessity, as well as a pamphlet he later pretended to disavow.

Returning to Philadelphia in 1726, Franklin worked as a clerk for a Quaker merchant, then as a printer in the employ of SAMUEL KEIMER, and finally established his own printing business in 1728. Keimer having anticipated him in the publication of a newspaper, Franklin collaborated with Joseph Brientnal in contributing to Andrew Bradford's *American Weekly Mercury* a series of essays called "The Busy Body" (see BUSY-BODY PAPERS) in which he demonstrated by contrast the dullness of Keimer's competing weekly. The result was that in 1729 Keimer sold Franklin the PENNSYLVANIA GAZETTE, in the columns of which the new owner made his name and notions well known throughout the city. As a man of business he worked hard, but made it a point to appear to work even harder than he did. He won friends with ease, inspired confidence, and soon was recognized as a leader in local affairs. In 1727 he established the Junto, a debating society for young men who met to argue moral and political questions. Not long afterward he initiated projects for establishing a city police, for improving city fire companies, and for paving, better lighting, and better cleaning city streets. In 1731 he was influential in establishing a circulating library in Philadelphia, the first of its kind in America. Later he helped establish the American Philosophical Society, a municipal hospital, and an academy that grew to become the University of Pennsylvania. From 1726 to 1751 he was clerk of the Pennsylvania Assembly, and from 1737 to 1753 he was deputy postmaster for Philadelphia. For a few months he conducted THE GENERAL MAGAZINE (1741), the second monthly ever projected in America.

Perhaps best-remembered of his activities during these years was the annual publication from 1732 to 1757 of POOR RICHARD'S ALMANACK with its scores of proverbs. It made Franklin's name a byword throughout the colonies. Other occasional writings included essays on such practical matters as Indian affairs, paper currency, and local reform, and were characterized by sagacity and homely humor. His *Advice to a Young Man on the Choice of a Mistress* (1745), *Reflections on Courtship and Marriage* (1746), and *The Speech of Polly Baker* (1747), often reprinted, have become classics in the application of common sense to morality.

By the age of forty-two, Franklin had acquired enough wealth to entrust his business to a partner and look forward to a life of retirement. For some time he had been interested in scientific experiments. As early as 1737 he had written a study of earthquakes and had investigated the movements of windstorms. He had invented a fireplace (see his *Account of the New Invented Pennsylvania Fireplace*, 1744), perfected a clock, and was drawn toward experiments in electricity. These last established his reputation as a scientist. He corresponded with scientists in England and described his own findings in *Experiments and Observations in Electricity* (1751; reprinted with additions, 1753, 1760–62). But colonial affairs in America did not allow Franklin to remain in retirement long. In 1751 he became a member of the Pennsylvania Assembly. Two years later he was sent to represent that body at the Albany Congress, called to unite the colonists in war against the French. In the same year he was appointed deputy postmaster-general for the colonies. Finally, in 1757, he was sent by the Assembly to England to appeal directly to Parliament for settlement of a dispute with the proprietors of Pennsylvania. He visited with Collinson, Fothergill, Priestley, and other scientists, and corresponded with Lord Kames, David Hume, and Samuel Johnson. He was awarded an LL.D. by St. Andrews (1759) and a D.L.C. by Oxford (1762), and he published papers on scientific and political subjects, including *An Historical Review of the Constitution and Government of Pennsylvania* (1759) and *The Interest of Great Britain Considered with Regard to Her Colonies* (1760). He returned to Philadelphia in 1762, but was almost immediately sent off to England again, this time to obtain a recall of the Pennsylvania charter. As it turned out, he did not return to America until 1775, thirteen years later.

The events that led up to the American Revolution required Franklin to shoulder new responsibilities. His *Cool Thoughts on the Present Situation of Affairs* (1764); his forthright *Preface to the Speech of Joseph Galloway* (1764), in which he demanded that American colonials be granted the same right as British subjects at home; his statements before the House of Commons on the Stamp Act; and his plainspoken opposition to the Townshend Act (see his EDICT BY THE KING OF PRUSSIA, 1773, and *Rules by Which a Great Empire May Be Reduced to a Small One*, 1773) increased his prestige and reputation, with the result that he was named colonial agent for Georgia (1768), New Jersey (1769), and Massachusetts (1770), and became practically an ambassador from the New World to the Old. Until the coercive acts of 1775, Franklin worked strenuously for reconciliation between England and America, only gradually becoming convinced that separation from the mother country was inevitable. In the spring of that year, certain that Lord North was forcing the colonies into revolt, he returned to Philadelphia, where he was chosen a member of the second Continental Congress and became the first U.S. postmaster-general. He served on commissions to induce Canada to join the colonies in rebellion, to advise with Washington on defense, to treat with Lord Howe on proposals for peace, and to work with Jefferson in drafting the DECLARATION OF INDEPENDENCE. (See also THOMAS PAINE.) In September 1776, he was appointed, with Silas Deane and ARTHUR LEE, to a commission to negotiate a treaty with France. Late that year he sailed again for Europe.

In France the seventy-year-old Franklin was greeted by the people as a sage and a Rousseauistic philosopher, though the French government did not at once officially recognize him or his mission. His simple dress, his shrewd but benign countenance, and his wit and homely wisdom made him seem a symbol of the Age of Enlightenment and of the promise of America. He lived for nine years at Passy, near Paris, in constant familiar correspondence with men of science, in more frivolous epistolary exchanges with Mme. Helvetius and Mme. Brillon, and amusing himself and his friends by running off on his private press such bagatelles as *The Ephemera* (1778), *The Morals of Chess* (1779), *The Whistle* (1779), and *The Dialogue Between Franklin and the Gout* (1780). He did not neglect his public duties. Early in 1778, when Burgoyne's defeat inspired French confidence in American success, he succeeded in securing a treaty of commerce and defensive alliance and, when later in the same year he was appointed plenipotentiary to the French court, obtained repeated loans and negotiated commercial treaties with Sweden and Prussia. In 1783, with John Jay and John Adams, he was one of the commissioners who signed the Treaty of Paris, but it was not until two years later that he was finally recalled by Congress.

In his eightieth year, Franklin was prepared to lay aside all public responsibilities. But soon after his arrival in Philadelphia he was chosen president of the Executive Council of Pennsylvania and served in this position for three years. In 1787 he was a member of the Constitutional Convention where, when his own ideas were not adopted, he argued for effective and democratic compromise. During the last five years of his life, Franklin lived with his daughter on Market Street, Philadelphia. There he puttered with inventions—a device for lifting books from high shelves, as easy chair completely equipped for an old man's comfort—and he enjoyed to the last his "agreeable and instructive" correspondence with friends abroad. His *Autobiography*, begun in 1771 and never completed, recounts his life until 1757, with some random remarks that carry it to 1759. It is perhaps the most lasting monument to his wisdom and to his peculiar combination of common sense and optimistic assurance that all men may better themselves. His plain style, his practicality, and his honest pragmatism—touched now with humor, now with a hint of Shandyesque sentimentality—made him a truly representative man of his age. The *Autobiography* has been called the first American book that belongs permanently to literature.

Franklin's works are collected in Yale University's multivolume edition of *The Papers of Benjamin Franklin* (1959–   ); earlier editions include *The Complete Works* (10 v. 1887–88), edited by JOHN BIGELOW; and *The Writings of Benjamin Franklin* (10 v. 1905–07), edited by A. H. Smyth. L. W. Labaree and others edited a modern scholarly edition of *The Autobiography* (1964). Modern critical and biographical works on Franklin include Carl Van Doren, *Benjamin Franklin* (1938); Bruce I. Granger, *Benjamin Franklin: An American Man of Letters* (1964); Alfred O. Aldridge, *Benjamin Franklin: Philosopher and Man* (1965); Ralph Ketcham, *Benjamin Franklin* (1965); Claude-Anne Lopez and E. W. Herbert, *The Private Franklin: The Man and His Family* (1975); and Ronald W. Clark, *Benjamin Franklin: A Biography* (1983). Earlier studies, still useful, include James Parton, *The Life and Times of Benjamin Franklin* (2 v. 1864); J. B. McMaster, *Benjamin Franklin as a Man of Letters* (1887); and P. L. Ford, *The Many-Sided Franklin* (1899). See AUTOBIOGRAPHY OF BENJAMIN FRANKLIN.

LEWIS LEARY/GP

Franklin, James (1697–1735),   printer, editor. The half brother of the famous Benjamin initiated Benjamin Franklin into the business of being a printer and editor. He founded the NEW-ENGLAND COURANT (1721) and the *Rhode Island Gazette* (1732). (See BOSTON GAZETTE, ANN FRANKLIN.)

Franklin, William (1730?–1813),   son of Benjamin Franklin. William Franklin served in the post office, as a clerk of the provincial assembly, and as his father's secretary in England before becoming royal governor of New Jersey (1763–76). During the Revolution he sided with the Tories, and afterward lived in England. Benjamin Franklin began his *Autobiography* for William in 1771, when the son was governor, and one of the father's most memorable letters was addressed to the son from Passy, August 16, 1784, after the war.

Franklin Evans (1842),   a novel by WALT WHITMAN. A conventional liquor reform novel of the time, this is the story of a country boy who in New York City and elsewhere suffers torment and degradations as a result of his addiction to alcohol, but finally reforms and settles down to an honorable life. Four years after publication—it appears to have sold about two thousand copies—Whitman reprinted it as a serial in the Brooklyn *Eagle*, of which he was then editor.

Franny and Zooey (1961),   stories by J. D. SALINGER. Both appeared first in *The New Yorker*, "Franny" in 1955, "Zooey" in 1957. They form part of Salinger's series about the Glass family.

Frazier, Charles (1950–   ),   travel writer, novelist. Born in Asheville, North Carolina, Frazier was educated at the University of North Carolina and taught in his native state before becoming a full-time writer in 1990. His travels in South America became the basis for *Adventuring in the Andes: The Sierra Club Travel Guide to Ecuador, Peru, Bolivia, The Amazon Basin and the Galapagos Islands* (1985), written with Donald Secreast. His extensive experience hiking the mountains of his home region, combined with family stories about his great-great uncle, W. P. Inman, who deserted from the Confederate Army, form the backbone for his National Book Award–winning first novel, *Cold Mountain* (1997). Inman, recovering from a wound, deserts and sets out to walk the three hundred miles that separate him from his mountain home and Ada, his genteel city-born sweetheart. Frazier has described his novel as an attempt to explain how rural non-slaveowners got caught up "by a kind of war-fever hysteria" to the detriment of their personal lives and relationships.

Fréchette, Louis [Honoré], (1839–1908),   lawyer, poet, journalist, translator. Generally considered the best French-Canadian poet of the 19th century, Fréchette was born in Lévis, Quebec, and educated at Laval University. His first volume of poems was *Mes loisirs* (1863). He contributed articles to *Le Journal* and other newspapers. In 1867 he moved to Chicago, and worked as a foreign correspondent until 1871. There he wrote *La Voix d'un exile* (1871), an attack in verse on Canadian politicians. On his return to Canada he became involved with politics and was elected to the federal parliament. His poetic works include *Pêle Mêle* (1876), *Les fleurs boréales* (1879), *Les oiseaux de neige* (1880), *La légende d'un peuple* (1887), and *Les feuilles volantes* (1891). In 1880 the French Academy honored *Les fleurs* and *Les oiseaux* and Fréchette became Canada's first poet laureate. His prose includes *Lettres à Basile* (1872), *Originaux et détraqués* (1892), and *La Nöel au Canada* (1900). He was author of several plays and translated Cable's OLD CREOLE DAYS and Howells's A CHANCE ACQUAINTANCE into French.

Frederic, Harold (1856–1898),   novelist, short-story writer. Frederic was born and attended school in Utica, New York, the "Octavius" of his New York fictions. Apprentice work as a photographer's assistant in Utica and Boston (1871–74) and a subsequent career in journalism (1875–98) nurtured the observation and reportorial skills that distinguish his realist fiction. Laid in the Mohawk Valley region, these include two contemporary works, *Seth's Brother's Wife* (1887) and its sequel, *The Lawton Girl* (1890). *In the Valley* (1890) is a historical romance of the Revolutionary era. His most distinguished realist works, and those on which his reputation depends, are stories of the Civil War era treated from a civilian perspective—including *The Copperhead* (1893), *Marsena* (1894), and *In the Sixties* (1897)—and his contemporary masterpiece, *The Damnation of Theron Ware* (1896). Published in England as *The Illumination of Theron Ware*, this novel scrutinizes the ambiguous character of the awakening of a young Methodist minister to the Higher Criticism of the Bible, Pre-Raphaelite aestheticism, and the New Science. In 1884 Frederic left the editorship of the Albany *Evening Journal* and became a *New York Times* correspondent in London, where he wrote distinguished journalistic volumes, social satire, and all of his fictions. In five volumes set in Ireland and England, he began to develop new themes. The best of these "English" works are *March Hares* (1896), a frothy comic romance, perhaps with autobiographical overtones; *Gloria Mundi* (1898), which examines the British aristocracy; and *The Market-Place* (1899), a drama of the London stock exchange. A definitive edition in progress is Stanton Garner, ed., *The Harold Frederic Edition* (1985–   ). Thomas F. O'Donnell edited *Stories of York State* (1966). Studies include Thomas F. O'Donnell and Hoyt C. Franchere, *Harold Frederic* (1961); and Austin Briggs, Jr., *The Novels of Harold Frederic* (1969).

JEAN FRANTZ BLACKALL

Freedom of the Will, The (1754), a theological treatise by JONATHAN EDWARDS. Less frequently read today than other works by Edwards, this stands nevertheless as his most important contribution to theology. In it he attempted to defend a New England Calvinism by his time already outmoded, presenting a carefully reasoned argument for a deterministic view of the universe and man's place in it. The work was in part a response to theological doubts occasioned by the rise of science. Employing the tools of rationalistic inquiry to buttress the faith of an earlier age, Edwards established himself as America's first systematic philosopher.

Freeman, Douglas Southall (1886–1953), editor, historian, teacher, broadcaster. Freeman won the Pulitzer Prize for his exhaustive and distinguished *Robert E. Lee* (4 v. 1934), continued in *Lee's Lieutenants* (3 v. 1942–44), then went further back in American history with a six-volume life of Washington (1948–1954). He wrote these biographies during a busy career as editor of the influential Richmond *News Leader* and as a daily broadcaster. Volume 7 of the life of Washington was completed by J. A. Carroll and M. W. Ashworth (1957).

Freeman, Joseph (1897–1965), critic, novelist. Noted for Marxist works that include *Voices of October: Soviet Literature and Art* (1930) and *The Soviet Worker* (1932), Freeman also wrote an autobiography, *An American Testament* (1936), and two novels: *Never Call Retreat* (1943), about an Austrian refugee; and *The Long Pursuit* (1947), a World War II story.

Freeman, Mary E[leanor] Wilkins (1852–1930), novelist, short-story writer. Born in Randolph, Massachusetts, Mary Wilkins moved with her family to Brattleboro, Vermont, when she was fifteen and was educated at Mount Holyoke

Female Seminary and the Glenwood Seminary in West Brattleboro. After the death of her parents, she returned to Randolph in 1884 and lived there for the next fifteen years. In 1902 she married Dr. Charles M. Freeman, and moved with him to Metuchen, New Jersey, where she remained for the rest of her life.

Her best work was published as by Mary E. Wilkins, before she married, and dealt with the New England village life she observed in Massachusetts and Vermont. It was a culture in decay in some ways toward the end of the 19th century, but still strongly under the influence of New England Puritanism. As she expressed her aims in the preface to the Edinburgh edition of her first volume, A HUMBLE ROMANCE AND OTHER STORIES (1887), "These little stories . . . are studies of the descendants of the Massachusetts Bay colonists, in whom can still be seen traces of those features of will and conscience, so strong as to be almost exaggerations and deformities, which characterised their ancestors." A close student of character, with a fine sense for the psychology of humans in straitened emotional circumstances, she published over thirty books, but has been remembered primarily for her first two collections of stories and the two novels that immediately followed. A NEW ENGLAND NUN AND OTHER STORIES (1891) contains the title story, about a woman's fifteen-year wait for her lover to return from Australia, only to discover he loves another woman. The book also includes "The Revolt of 'Mother,'" about a farm wife who moves into the new barn when her husband fails to build them a new house. *Jane Field* (1892) and *Pembroke* (1894) are novels of New England, the latter characterized by a contemporary reviewer as a "treatise on the Divine Will manifested as the New England Won't." Her later novels include *The Heart's Highway* (1900), set in colonial Virginia, and *The Portion of Labor* (1901), about a strike in a shoe factory. Her other collections of short stories include *The Wind in the Rose-Bush and Other Stories of the Supernatural* (1903) and *Edgewater People* (1918). *Giles Corey, Yeoman* (1893) is a play about the Salem witchcraft trials. Henry W. Lanier edited *The Best Stories of Mary E. Wilkins* (1927).

free verse. Free verse (*vers libre*) designates various kinds of verse freed from the restrictions of conventional meter and rhyme. For most poets, the freedom granted has not been total, but involves instead an attempt to order language in patterns different from those dominant in English verse from the 14th into the beginning of the 20th century. T. S. Eliot expressed his sense of limitations by suggesting that "no verse is free for the man who wants to do a good job." William Carlos Williams, in other ways almost diametrically opposed to Eliot, echoed and elaborated, "No verse can be free, it must be governed by some measure, but not by the old measure." Both showed the way to many who followed, as did Ezra Pound, for some even more influential.

Free verse had begun earlier, however. In the United States, strivings to break free of traditional models can be seen in the poems of Emerson, who was impatient with all forms of received wisdom. When he saw the first edition of Walt Whitman's *Leaves of Grass* (1855), he wrote enthusiastically to the author, "I greet you at the beginning of a great new career," and it was Whitman who proved the great prototype in English for the verse freedoms of the 20th century. His parallelism—rooted in the rhythms of the King James Bible—catalogs, end-stopped lines, and simple repetitions of phrases, sounds, and images, have been echoed in poets down to the present. They are especially apparent, for example, in the earlier verse of Allen Ginsberg. Emily Dickinson also influenced many, with her hymn-based metrics and slant rhymes, as did Stephen Crane, with his colloquial voice.

In the 20th century, freedom from tradition has been explored in a variety of ways, as the strict metrics of the past have seemed at times to be entirely disappearing, only to be revived again in skillful use by master poets who have often written free verse and traditional metric verse side by side. Early, IMAGISM gave significant impetus to free verse forms. The so-called polyphonic prose of Amy Lowell and John Gould Fletcher was an attempt to erase the boundaries between verse and prose. E. E. Cummings, writing more than was immediately apparent to the eye in traditional meters and rhymes, nevertheless influenced much that followed with his scattering of lines on the page, demonstrating the possibilities of composition by typewriter. William Carlos Williams's life-long search for the "variable foot" culminated in the great poems of his late books. Charles Olson influenced many younger poets with his "Projective Verse," as poetry in open forms became a goal especially in the 1950s.

Frémont, Jessie Benton.   See next entry.

Frémont, John C[harles] (1813–1890),   soldier, explorer, memoirist. Frémont, the son of a French refugee, turned to exploration and then to writing lively, accurate accounts of what he had discovered. Much of the land he visited was beyond the Missouri and the Mississippi. His *Report of the Exploring Expedition to the Rocky Mountains and to Oregon and Northern California* (1845) was widely read for its literary skill—due in part to the help of his wife—and the practical suggestions it gave later travelers. In 1956 Allan Nevins edited Frémont's *Narratives of Exploration and Adventure*. When attempts were made to seize California from the Mexicans and also to prevent its falling into the hands of the British, Frémont played an active role in winning California for the United States. For a brief period he was senator from California and in 1856 became the first Republican presidential candidate. During the Civil War, he held several military commands, but Lincoln forced him to rescind a proclamation freeing slaves that he had issued as commander of the Department of the West.

Frémont was at times wealthy, but after the war sank into poverty. His wife, **Jessie Benton Frémont,** managed to support him and their family by writing. She helped him with his *Memoirs* (1887), and herself wrote *The Story of the Guard: A Chronicle of the War* (1863), *A Year of American Travel* (1878), *Souvenirs of My Time* (1887), *Far West Sketches* (1890), and *The Will and the Way Stories* (1891). Frémont was finally granted a pension as a retired major general, but died soon after. Jessie Frémont died in 1902. Allan Nevins wrote a biog-

raphy of Frémont, *Pathfinder of the West* (1928). Irving Stone wove the story of the Frémonts into a novel, *Immortal Wife* (1944). William Brandon wrote an account, *The Men, and the Mountains: Frémont's Expedition* (1955). *Exploring with Frémont: The Private Diaries of Charles Preuss, Cartographer for John C. Frémont on His First, Second and Fourth Expeditions to the Far West* (1958) was translated and edited by Erwin G. and Elizabeth K. Gudde.

French, Alice ["Octave Thanet"] (1850–1934), novelist, short-story writer. Born in Massachusetts, French lived for years in Iowa and Arkansas. Her well-told stories are placed in the local color school (see REGIONALISM) and are laid mostly in the villages of rural Arkansas. She had a special interest in the labor problems of her day—espousing cooperatives rather than labor unions. In *The Man of the Hour* (1905) she told the story of John Winslow's economic education, defending old-fashioned individual enterprise. Other books of hers are *Knitters in the Sun* (1887), *We All* (1888), *Stories of a Western Town* (1893), *The Heart of Toil* (1898), *A Slave to Duty and Other Women* (1898), and *Stories That End Well* (1911).

French and Indian War.   Last of a series of conflicts, known as the FRENCH AND INDIAN WARS, between England and France over control of colonies and resources in North America, it began in 1754 and ended in 1763, with the Treaty of Paris. The war spread from North America to Europe in 1756, and that phase is known as the Seven Years' War, a name sometimes applied erroneously to the nine-year struggle in the Western Hemisphere. After five years of ebb and flow, the war turned in favor of the British following the Battle of Quebec, in which General James Wolfe led a British force of 9,000 against half as many French troops under the command of Louis Joseph, MARQUIS DE MONTCALM, in September 1759. Both Wolfe and Montcalm died in the battle, and Quebec fell to the British. Within a year, the British forced surrender of all of Canada. During 1760 and 1761, Major ROBERT ROGERS, leader of the famed Rogers's Rangers, conducted mopping-up operations against French outposts in the northern Great Lakes region.

Spain, which had avoided taking sides in either theater of the war, concluded at last that a British victory would not be in its best interests. It joined the conflict on the side of France, suffered extensive losses of territory to the British almost immediately, and was compensated for those losses by being given all French territory west of the Mississippi. The Treaty of Paris resulted in cession to England of all other significant French holdings in North America.

The French and Indian War proved to the British that the North American colonies were incapable of defending themselves. Colonial militias had grown complacent and were ineffectual in the field, necessitating the posting of large numbers of British regular troops to North America during the war. Afterwards, it was decided that British troops should remain. In addition, Great Britain incurred an enormous debt in consequence of the war, and Whitehall believed that colonists could reasonably be expected to share the burden, inasmuch as they had received British protection. There followed a cycle of heavy taxation and sometimes heavy-handed tax collection, facilitated by the presence of British troops, who came to be viewed as minions of royal oppression. Thus, the French and Indian War and the circumstances it created were important contributing factors to the coming of the American Revolution.

The principal historian of the struggle for control of colonial North America was FRANCIS PARKMAN, whose great narratives were *Montcalm and Wolfe* (1884) and *A Half-Century of Conflict* (1892). James Fenimore Cooper, in THE LAST OF THE MOHICANS (1826), THE PATHFINDER (1840), THE DEERSLAYER (1841), and SATANSTOE (1845), used the setting of the wars in his continuing effort to create a distinctively American literature. The romance of his vision contrasts sharply with the work of later historical novelists, foremost among them Kenneth Roberts's NORTHWEST PASSAGE (1937), a solid and realistic examination of the career of Robert Rogers.

WILLIAM W. SAVAGE, JR.

French and Indian Wars.   A series of conflicts between the British and French in North America. They corresponded to more general wars in Europe: the War of the Grand Alliance, the War of the Spanish Succession, the War of the Austrian Succession, and the Seven Years' War. In North America they were known as King William's War (1689–97), Queen Anne's War (1701–13), King George's War (1744–48), and THE FRENCH AND INDIAN WAR (1754–63), discussed in the previous entry.

These wars decided whether England or France would rule the continent. The prize was the West—especially the Ohio Valley—and Canada. In King William's War, the British captured some important territory, failed to take Quebec, and finally gave back all they had won. In Queen Anne's War, the French invaded New England, but at the end ceded important Canadian territory to England, including Acadia. In King George's War, the British won some territory, but restored it to France by treaty. Finally, in the French and Indian War, the fortunes of the combatants wavered to and fro, but the Battle of Quebec (1759) decided the war in favor of the British. France gave up its empire in North America (1763).

French influence in America.   The first report of the new empire that France sought to carve for itself came from the pen of Champlain, who has been compared, both as a soldier and as a writer, to Caesar. Even more important were the reports of the Jesuit missionaries, known as *The Jesuit Relations and Allied Documents: Travels and Explorations of the Jesuit Missionaries in New France* (1610–1791), translated into English under the editorship of Reuben Gold Thwaites (73 v. 1896–1901). Some of the volumes had appeared in France as early as 1632, and some of the writers showed distinguished command of language. Other accounts were written by members of the Franciscan order. Best known of these was Father Louis Hennepin's *Description de la Louisiane* (1683), which ran to thirty-five editions in five languages.

From Louis-Armand de Lorn d'Arce, Baron de Lahontan, came a remarkable and influential work, *Nouveaux Voyages* (2 v. 1703), which was translated into English in the year of its publication and has been reissued in more than fifty editions

in five languages. Lahontan observed the Native Americans and proceeded to philosophize about their nobility in a fashion that is still popular. French critics have pointed out that Montesquieu and Rousseau drew inspiration from Lahontan's "noble savage," Adario, and from the Jesuit observers. The history of the French struggle with the British has been told best in books by FRANCIS PARKMAN. He wrote of the attempts by the Jesuits to convert the Indians and the vast contributions of French priests in the discovery and exploration of the West, the establishment of a regime in Canada, the half-century of conflict with the British.

The French lost their North American empire in 1763, but there remained to them in the New World, besides the small possessions of French Guiana and the French West Indies, two large areas of influence: French Canada and Louisiana. French Canada remained inveterately French. Similarly, Louisiana continues to offer examples of French folkways and language survivals. The French element of the population, calling itself Creole, was welded into self-conscious unity by the increasing incursion of other peoples from the North. During the first half of the 19th century, the most important Creole writers appeared: CHARLES ETIENNE ARTHUR GAYARRÉ (1805–1895), who wrote histories, among them *Histoire de la Louisiane* (1846–47); the two brothers FRANÇOIS-DOMINIQUE ROUQUETTE (1810–1890) and ADRIEN-EMMANUEL ROUQUETTE (1813–1887), who wrote lyrics idealizing nearby Choctaw Indians; and CHARLES TESTUT (1819?–1892?), who wrote historical novels. The Louisiana Cajuns, French people transported from Acadia, were more slow to develop a literature, but were early represented in the writings of others, for example, GEORGE WASHINGTON CABLE.

There has been a constant flow of intelligent observers from France whose reports on the United States have sometimes exerted marked influence in this country. Pierre François Xavier de Charlevoix included such observations in his *Histoire de la Nouvelle France* (1744), and this section of his book appeared in an English translation (2 v. 1761) as *Journal of a Voyage to North America*. Jacques Pierre Brissot de Warville published a sympathetic account of his *Nouveau Voyage dans les États-Unis de l'Amérique* (3 v. 1791), two volumes of which were translated by Joel Barlow (1792); and Ferdinand M. Bayard wrote *Voyage dans l'Interieur des États-Unis* (1797). CHATEAUBRIAND visited the United States in 1791 and recorded his impressions in several romantic novels: *Atala* (1801), *René* (1802), and *Les Natchez* (1826). Michel Chevalier published (1834) a book of his observations that were rendered into English (1839) as *Society, Manners, and Politics in the U.S.* Guillaume Tell Poussin wrote *De La Puissance Américaine* (2 v. 1843), and Louis Xavier Eyma wrote *Excentricités Américaines* (1860). Philarète Chasles published in 1851 a collection of his essays taken mainly from the *Revue des Deux Mondes*—*Études sur la Littérature et les Moeurs des Anglo-Américians au XIXᵉ Siècle*. To these books should be added the writings of the French-born St. Jean de Crèvecoeur. Most important is, of course, DE TOCQUEVILLE's *De la Démocratie en Amérique* (2 v. 1835; 2 supplemental v. 1840); the best English translation is

Phillips Bradley's (2 v. 1945). De Tocqueville showed an astonishing insight into American history and destiny; a century later, his prescience seemed unique.

Many other French writings influenced American thought, even though their authors never visited America. Montesquieu (1689–1755) unquestionably affected the thought of the American patriots; later, the ideas of Rousseau played a greater role. Subsequent French reformers who were influential in the United States include François Fourier, Étienne Cabet, and Auguste Comte.

Beginning in the 1890s, French naturalism found an echo in the writings of Kate Chopin, of French descent, and of Stephen Crane, Garland, Frank Norris, Dreiser, and others. In poetry the Parnassians (for example, Leconte de Lisle, Sully Prudhomme, Verlaine) and a little later the Symbolists (Mallarmé, Baudelaire, Arthur Rimbaud, Valéry) exerted a powerful influence in all the Americas, especially on modernist poetry. French culture affected Latin America from the very beginning, and the influence is still felt there. The intellectuals of Spanish and Portuguese descent have found France more of a spiritual home than the lands from which their ancestors had come.

More recently, French literature had great influence in America after World War II, especially in the writings of the existentialists (Sartre and Camus), of the new wave of experimental dramatists (Genet, Ionesco, and Beckett, an Irishman living in France), and of the *nouveau roman* novelists (Nathalie Sarraute, Robbe-Grillet, Michel Butor).

French, Marilyn (1929–   ),   novelist. Born in New York City, French was educated at Hofstra and Harvard. After a scholarly first book, *The Book as World—James Joyce's "Ulysses"* (1976), she achieved success with a novel, *The Woman's Room* (1977), which became a touchstone for feminists. *The War against Women* (1992) is a worldwide survey of oppression. Her other works include *The Bleeding Heart* (1980), a novel set in England; *Shakespeare's Division of Experience* (1981); *Beyond Power: On Women, Men and Morals* (1985); *Her Mother's Daughter* (1987); and the novel *Our Father* (1994), concerning the reunion of a troubled family of women around their father's sickbed. *My Summer with George* (1996) and *A Season in Hell* (1998) are memoirs.

Freneau, Philip [Morin] (1752–1832),   poet. Born in New York City, Freneau was the son of Pierre Fresneau, of Huguenot ancestry, and Agnes Watson Fresneau, of a Scottish family long settled in New Jersey. His boyhood was spent in New Jersey, where he was educated first at home and in private schools, later at the College of New Jersey (now Princeton). He entered as a sophomore in the same class with JAMES MADISON and HUGH HENRY BRACKENRIDGE. The three collaborated in literary exercises, producing a collection of versified *Satires Against the Tories*, and Brackenridge joined Freneau in composing both an embryonic novel, *Father Bombo's Pilgrimage*, and a longer, more serious commencement poem, *The Rising Glory of America* (1771), published anonymously a year later. After graduation, Freneau turned briefly to teaching and the study of theology. He published a volume of poems called *The*

American Village (1772), which "was damn'd by all good and judicious judges," the poet said, lamenting that "my name was on the title page." He signed his name to no other writing for fourteen years.

At the outbreak of revolutionary activities. Freneau was in New York turning out caustic satirical poems, such as *General Gage's Soliloquy* (1775) and *General Gage's Confession* (1775). Then, after involvement in a bitter exchange of versified insults, he left America in 1776 for two idyllic years in the Caribbean, chiefly on the island of St. Croix. There he wove the tropic splendors he saw into a romantic, descriptive poem, THE BEAUTIES OF SANTA CRUZ (1776), while at the same time he fumbled through a funereal philosophic poem called THE HOUSE OF NIGHT (1776), which may have been an attempt to rationalize his flight from revolutionary activities. In 1778 he returned to his homeland, probably in response to the news of intense fighting there, but was captured en route by the British. He was released just in time to find his native fields devastated by the Battle of Monmouth.

Touched now by the reality of war, Freneau devoted himself wholeheartedly to the Revolution. He became a militiaman, a privateer who ran supplies through the British blockade, and a writer of patriotic verse for Brackenridge's short-lived *United States Magazine* (1779). When captured again, in May 1780, and held on a prison ship in New York harbor, he was horrified at the treatment given prisoners of war. Released in July, he vowed to keep his satirical arrows flint-sharp against the British "hellhounds." He dashed off his denunciatory THE BRITISH PRISON-SHIP (1780), as vitriolic a poem of hate as was ever produced in America. He went to Philadelphia, where he worked for a while as a clerk in the post office, then became an editor of the patriotic *Freeman's Journal*, the columns of which he filled with sustained invective against the enemy, earning his sobriquet Poet of the American Revolution.

The war over, Freneau found himself increasingly involved in petty political bickering in Pennsylvania, and in 1785 he threw up his pen in disgust and turned, as he had ten years before, to the sea. For six years he was a sea captain of coastal vessels, plying between New York, Philadelphia, and Charleston, and becoming increasingly popular for the lightly satirical poems he contributed to newspapers in whatever port he visited. "The Jug of Rum," "The Virtue of Tobacco," and "The Pilot of Hatteras" were among his best-known works of this period and were reprinted in papers up and down the coast. The verse was flippant, humorous, critical, always good-humored. His most noteworthy poems, however, were works of romantic fancy that were less popular in his own time.

After his marriage in 1790 to Eleanor Forman, Freneau abandoned the sea to become editor of the New York *Daily Advertiser*. In the autumn of 1791, after and perhaps as a result of his appointment by Jefferson to a post as translator in the State Department, he established the NATIONAL GAZETTE in Philadelphia. Encouraged by Jefferson and helped by Madison and other prominent Republicans, he launched into bitter attacks on the policies of Federalists, for example, Alexander Hamilton and John Adams, becoming such an irritation to the administration that Washington called him "that rascal Freneau," though Jefferson loyally maintained that he had saved our constitution "when it was galloping fast into monarchy."

The yellow fever epidemic of 1793, together with the effective opposition of the Hamilton-supported GAZETTE OF THE UNITED STATES, put an end to Freneau's activities as a liberal journalist in the national capital. He returned to Monmouth to found the *Jersey Chronicle* (1795–96), in which he continued advocacy of Republican principles. That paper failing, he settled again in New York as editor of the *Time-Piece and Literary Companion* (1797–98) until the Sedition Law, in its turn, put a stop to his freely expressed attacks and forced him again to his family home in New Jersey. In retirement there, he contributed a series of essays to the Philadelphia *Aurora* over the signature of "Robert Slender" (1799–1801), a simple countryman who knew nothing of politics except what he read in his newspaper. With the election of Jefferson in 1800, Freneau apparently felt that his contribution to independence in America was complete. His advocacy of the rights of the common man had made enemies and interfered time and again with his literary career. Somewhat embittered, he retired to private life and rejected offers of political appointment. He discouraged a movement among his farmer neighbors who wished to send him to Congress. After 1803 he again became a sea captain, now venturing as far as Madeira and the Azores. His last years were spent on the family acres in Monmouth, under a darkening cloud of poverty. He published new verses during the War of 1812 and again in 1822 as he gathered materials for a hoped-for last volume. He died of exposure at the age of eighty as he made his way homeward across the fields in a snowstorm.

Freneau's accomplishment, increasingly apparent, nevertheless fell far short of his early intention. As a young man he had dreamed of triumphs in the tradition of the great literary masters on whom he had been bred. The Virgilian, Horatian, and Miltonic qualities of much of his college verse and his verbal and metrical debts to Pope, Thomson, Gray, and others show him as an apprentice advancing along well-worn paths, but the almost Keatsian imagery of THE POWER OF FANCY (1770) and the unresolved philosophical questioning of *The House of Night* (1779; enlarged for *Poems*, 1786) have led some critics to judge him a genuine poet in the old-world manner, thwarted in his career by the events of his lifetime. Freneau early demonstrated a quick sensitivity to criticism and an irrepressible tendency to chasten and reprove his critics, qualities that led him abruptly to satire and to a deep hatred of all things English. His best mature writing was done when the Revolution was over, in a simple, native idiom that sang almost self-consciously of American men and manners or developed the natural philosophies of politics and religion that might guide rational freemen. As in his later life Freneau would wear no clothing or eat no food that was not of native origin, so in his verse he became nationalistic almost to the point of parochialism.

But for all this, and to some extent because of it, Freneau developed not only as the outstanding poet in America who represented the transition from 18th-century traditionalism

to the free-soaring romanticism of the 19th century, but also as America's first full-blown Romantic poet. *The Wild Honey Suckle* (1786) and THE INDIAN BURYING GROUND (1788) break bravely from formalized poetic tradition to forecast, twelve years before Wordsworth's *Lyrical Ballads*, the renaissance of wonder that characterized the Romantic movement. As a patriotic satirist and a writer of rousing war songs, Freneau was unexcelled in his lifetime. As a comment on the foibles of Freneau's countrymen struggling toward personal and corporate freedom, his newspaper verse is of major historical importance, and his prose also deserves attention, especially such essay series as *The Pilgrim* (1782–84), *Tomo Cheeki: The Creek Indian in Philadelphia* (1791–97), the letters of "Robert Slender" (1799–1801), and his occasional humorous accounts of the misadventures of "Hezekiah Salem" (1788–97), a defrocked New England deacon. As editor and contributor, Freneau was among the first of the truly professional American journalists. (See THE DYING INDIAN; THE INDIAN STUDENT.)

In spite of his innovations in form and style, however, and in spite of his foreshadowing of Whitman's exuberant Americanism and his Emerson-like insistence on individualism, Freneau belonged essentially to the 18th century. His humanitarianism, his faith in the natural goodness of man, his primitivism and perfectionism—bound together by his belief that Nature, including man, is a revelation of God—were strains transplanted to America from the rich yield of the Enlightenment. His skepticism, his prejudices, his tendency to descend precipitately in argument from principle to personality, and the confused stimulation of changing standards under which he developed kept Freneau from making a synthesis that ever was satisfactory even to himself. He had few literary followers, for his lifelong quest to discover how free men could most effectively justify their right to freedom led him often to stubborn convictions that ill fitted with the prevailing notions of culturally ambitious and imitative early-19th-century America. He was consistent, crotchety, and contentious, even to the point of standing obstinately still while the democratic world to which he had sacrificed so much labor and talent advanced beyond him. His chief contributions as a man of letters were a dogged insistence on fundamental philosophical and political principles, an occasional lyricism involving the use of fresh tropes and the employment of native themes, and the development of an easy colloquialism that gave the appearance, if indeed it was not, of being unmistakably American.

The standard edition is *The Poems of Philip Freneau* (3 v. 1902–07), edited by F. L. Pattee. Lewis Leary edited *The Lost Poems of Philip Freneau* (1946). Philip M. Marsh edited *The Prose of Philip Freneau* (1955). Biographies are Lewis Leary, *That Rascal Freneau* (1941), and Jacob Axelrod, *Philip Freneau: Champion of Democracy* (1967).

LEWIS LEARY/ G.P.

Frescoes for Mr. Rockefeller's City (1933), poems by ARCHIBALD MACLEISH. In these free-verse celebrations MacLeish expresses his deep but unconventional patriotism. He examines the American landscape, considers the arrival and the helpfulness of the immigrants, describes empire-building in the West by explorers and then by venal financiers, and expresses the belief that Americans will cure their social ailments without doctrinaire ideology. The poems supposedly are panels to replace six murals that had been removed from Rockefeller Center because the artist Diego Rivera had been too outspoken in his pictorial comments on modern capitalist civilization.

Fresh the American (1881),   a comedy by ARCHIBALD CLAVERING GUNTER. F.N. Fresh is an American millionaire who travels abroad and in the spirit of Mark Twain deliberately shows his defiance of European and Oriental toadyism and snobbery. His mood is mainly humorous, but he is angry when the helpless are oppressed.

Friedan, Betty (1921–   ),   writer. Born in Illinois, Friedan was educated at Smith. Her *The Feminine Mystique* (1963), a polemic on the inferior position of women, gave great impetus to American feminism. Other titles are *It Changed My Life: Writings on the Women's Movement* (1976); *The Second Stage* (1981); *The Fountain of Age* (1993); and *Beyond Gender: The New Politics of Work and Family* (1997). *Life So Far* (2000) is a memoir.

Friedman, Bruce Jay (1930–   ),   novelist. Born in New York City, Friedman was educated at the University of Missouri and has worked in publishing in New York City. *Stern* (1962), his first novel, earned praise for its comic account of Jewish neuroticism. Later novels, generally mining the same vein to find offbeat humor in the lives of American Jews, include *A Mother's Kisses* (1964), on Jewish mothers; *The Dick* (1971); and *About Harry Towns* (1974). His short stories are collected in *Far from the City of Class* (1963), *Black Angels* (1966), and *Let's Hear It for a Beautiful Guy* (1984). His plays include *Scuba Duba: A Tense Comedy* (1968), *Steambath* (1970), and *Foot in the Door* (1979). *Tokyo Woes* appeared in 1985, and *The Current Climate*, novels, in 1989. *The Collected Short Fiction of Bruce Jay Friedman* and the nonfiction *The Slightly Older Guy* came out in 1995; *Even the Rhinos Were Nymphs*, a collection of magazine pieces, in 2000.

Friendly Club.   Two literary clubs had this name. One was founded c. 1785 in Hartford and included in its membership the writers known as the HARTFORD WITS. It went out of existence in 1807. The other was a continuation of the Philological Society of New York and took the new name in 1789. Among its members were William Dunlap, Noah Webster, Charles Brockden Brown, James Kent, and Richard Alsop. ELIHU HUBBARD SMITH seems to have moved in both groups.

Friendship Village (1908),   stories by ZONA GALE. The narrator is a woman who goes from a large city to a small community in the Midwest, like Portage, Wisconsin, which was Gale's home, and finds the people there more truly representative of America than those she had known. Often the plot problems are small social difficulties, which are treated with humor and realism. The book had several sequels.

Frings, Ketti (1915–1981),   novelist, screenwriter. Born Katherine Hartley in Ohio, Frings wrote two novels, *Hold Back the Dawn* (1942) and *God's Front Porch* (1945), but she is best known as a playwright and movie scriptwriter. She

wrote the scenarios for *Come Back Little Sheba* (1952), *About Mr. Leslie* (1954), *Fox Fire* (1955), *The Shrike* (1955), and *By Love Possessed* (1961). Her dramatic version of Thomas Wolfe's *Look Homeward, Angel* (1957) won the Pulitzer Prize and the Drama Critics' Circle Award.

Frohman, Charles (1860–1915), and **Daniel Frohman** (1851–1940),   theatrical producers. Born in Ohio, the two brothers were among the most active producers of their time, and Charles was as successful in London as in New York. Charles Frohman went down with the *Luisitania*. Daniel Frohman managed many New York theaters and introduced DAVID BELASCO as a playwright.

From Here to Eternity (1951),   a novel and later a movie by JAMES JONES. This long, violent book made a great sensation and became an immediate best seller. It is a story of life in the regular army before the Japanese attack at Pearl Harbor in 1941. The title is from a poem by Kipling, whose *Gentlemen Rankers* are "damned from here to eternity."

Fromm, Erich (1900–1980),   psychoanalyst, philosopher. Born in Germany, Fromm was educated at the Universities of Heidelberg and Munich and at the Psychoanalytic Institute in Berlin. Until 1932 he worked in Frankfurt's Psychoanalytic Institute and at the Institute for Social Research at the University of Frankfurt. In 1934 he came to the United States, where he taught at several institutes and universities. He wrote *Escape From Freedom* (1941), an inquiry into the meaning of freedom and the social and cultural conditions that have disposed modern man to seek escape from freedom into authoritarianism. *Man for Himself: An Inquiry into the Psychology of Ethics* (1947) is a continuation of the former work and develops the theory that man is for himself and must determine his own standards. His later books include *The Forgotten Language: An Introduction to the Understanding of Dreams, Fairy Tales and Myths* (1951); *The Sane Society* (1955); *The Art of Loving* (1956); *Sigmund Freud's Mission* (1959); *Zen Buddhism and Psychoanalysis* (1960); *May Man Prevail?* (1961); *The Crisis of Psychoanalysis* (1970); *The Anatomy of Human Destructiveness* (1973); and *The Greatness and Limitations of Freud's Thought* (1980).

Frontenac, Louis de Baude, Comte de (1620–1698). French governor of New France (1672–82, 1689–98). In conflict with the French government over his policies, which included greater political independence for Canada, he was recalled in 1682, but returned when successors were unable to solve problems. During his term of office, he aided the explorations of Louis Jolliet, Jacques Marquette, and the sieur de La Salle; established forts; and defeated the Iroquois (1696). Under him, during the first French and Indian War, Quebec was defended against the British, Sir William Phips's fleet was driven from Canada, and the French made raids on Boston and other targets on the New England coast. He is treated in FRANCIS PARKMAN's *Count Frontenac and New France Under Louis XIV* (1877).

frontier, the.   In the mind of an American, "the frontier" always means the American frontier. This placid assumption of uniqueness is an enduring feature of American culture and indicates the nature of the role the frontier plays in the national consciousness. American popular mentalities are little concerned with the frontier as a historical phenomenon; rather, the frontier is important to Americans mainly as the pseudohistorical matrix of the myths by which they define who they, as a people, think they are. As its crudest level, frontier mythology furnishes political oratory with some of its most cherished stock phrases and images, which continually and successfully appeal to American nationalism. That such an appeal implicitly lays stress on the predominantly English and northern European elements of the national community as being the *real* Americans is not accidental. While this stress may be declining, and while the refurbishing of Ellis Island and its designation as a national historical site may be seen as laying a compensatory stress on the role of the melting pot in American development, the implicit bias is probably still there. The national mythology stresses the pioneer, who bequeathed to posterity the honorable condition of being free men on their own land, upright, and self-reliant. As the frontier moved farther west, the stock character changes and the forest-clearing pioneer gives way to the equally admirable cowboy. The major themes of indomitable energy, courage, and nobility never change.

The Native American naturally plays a major role in the national mythology, both as noble savage and as villain, depending on whether or not the land he occupied at any given moment was in demand, and on whether he was regarded as likely or unlikely to resist (see William W. Savage, Jr., *Indian Life: Transforming an American Myth*, 1977). The role of racism in American attitudes toward Native Americans is investigated in H. Peckham and C. Gibson, *Attitudes of Colonial Powers Toward the American Indian* (1969).

The experiences of African-Americans on the frontier, although in fact many and varied, have usually been ignored in the mythology of the frontier. In recent years, ALEX HALEY's *Roots* (1977) suggested that an epic experience equivalent to frontiering has molded the culture of African-Americans. In addition, historians have pointed out the important role of African-American cowboys (E. L. Jones, *The Negro Cowboys*, 1965) and the gallant history of the black cavalry involved in the Indian wars of the trans-Mississippi west. (This is described in W. H. Leckie, *The Buffalo Soldiers*, 1967.) The average American, however, whether black or white, remains largely unaware of African-American participation in the great American saga, and it seems odd that no one has yet pondered the effect of this exclusion from the dominant national mythology on the evolution of African-American culture and consciousness in America. The same absence of information exists concerning the role of Asian-Americans, while the image of frontiering Hispanic-Americans is usually derogatory.

American writers have produced a considerable literary output dedicated to the mythology of the frontier. Indeed, the molding of the conventional image of both the frontiersman and the Indian began very early, with the novels of JAMES FENI-MORE COOPER. Such literature still enjoys a reliable market, as the continuing popularity of the Western as a genre suggests.

Although the variety and volume of pulp fiction on these familiar themes are large enough to defy summary in the space available, it should be observed that the movies and TV are now of far greater importance in the perpetuation of the myth.

As J. M. Marshall, *Land Fever: Dispossession and the Frontier Myth* (1986), has shown, the pioneer was often a man whose need for land arose primarily from the fact that the upper classes in settled areas had taken most of the good land, creating a relative overpopulation that westward expansion was supposed to relieve. Having moved without adequate capital into a new region, and having cleared and planted a small plot, the homesteader often failed to hold it for more than a few years before losing his stake to creditors, whereupon he often moved farther west to repeat the dismal process. Equally, as William W. Savage, Jr., in *Cowboy Life* (1979), has shown, the life of the cowboy was often that of an exploited menial. To be sure, biographers and fiction writers have produced many works concerning the harsher realities of life on the frontier, particularly for women, to cite only those of LAURA INGALLS WILDER, WILLA CATHER, and E. O. ROLVAAG. Nonetheless, as Savage's *The Cowboy Hero* (1982) suggests, America cherishes its heroes and the frontier myth will go on providing them.

Scholars, moreover, have generally assisted in the mythologizing of the American frontier. Among the scholarly myths is the notion of the frontier recapitulating the evolution of culture from primitivism to civilization, with the frontiersman being stripped of civilized habits and graces, and the repeated acting out of the scenario in one area after another as the frontier moved farther west. The most important of the scholarly frontier myths is that associated with FREDERICK JACKSON TURNER, which attributes the nation's democratic spirit, its inventiveness and practicality, to the availability of free land to the west. Revealingly, a 1941 questionnaire asking historians to comment on the Turner theory showed that significant numbers felt that it ought not to be investigated or too explicitly defined. These scholarly myths have been continuing features of what is still the predominant text in American frontier history. (See Ray Allen Billington, *Westward Expansion: A History of the American Frontier*, 5th edition, with Martin Ridge, 1982.) Attempts have been made in recent years to raise American writing about the history of the frontier above the romantic notion that has generally characterized it. Consider R. L. Nichols, *American Frontier and Western Issues: A Historiographical Review* (1986); J. O. Steffens, *The American West: New Perspectives, New Dimensions* (1979); and J. A. Carroll, *Reflections of Western Historians* (1969). These works have attempted to stimulate renewed discussion among historians concerning the meaning of the American frontier experience. There have been attempts to envision the American frontier experience in the wider context of world history and of other peoples' experiences, notably Walter Prescott Webb, *The Great Frontier* (1952). Nonetheless, the frontier, in the American imagination, remains a powerful symbol of America's self-image—regardless of where the truth lies.

DAVID HARRY MILLER

frontier fiction. The first great figure to write fiction about the frontier was JAMES FENIMORE COOPER, whose own early days were spent on a disappearing frontier, for which he shows a sentimental nostalgia. Several of JAMES KIRKE PAULD- ING's novels portray frontier life. Among other books, occa- sionally autobiographical, that deal with frontier life are Timothy Flint, *George Mason, the Young Backwoodsman* (1829); Robert Montgomery Bird, NICK OF THE WOODS (1837); Emerson Bennett, *The Bandits of the Osage* (1847) and *Forest and Prairie, or, Life on the Frontier* (1860); Joseph G. Baldwin, FLUSH TIMES OF ALABAMA AND MISSISSIPPI (1853); Edward Eggle- ston, THE HOOSIER SCHOOLMASTER (1871); Ralph Connor, *The Sky Pilot* (1899); Winston Churchill, THE CROSSING (1904); Willa Cather, O PIONEERS (1913), MY ANTONIA (1918), and DEATH COMES FOR THE ARCHBISHOP (1927); Hamlin Garland, *They of the High Trails* (1916); Emerson Hough, *The Covered Wagon* (1922); Johan Bojer, *The Emigrants* (1925); Ole Röl- vaag, GIANTS IN THE EARTH (1924) and PEDER VICTORIOUS (1932); ZANE GREY, *The Thundering Herd* (1925); Thomas Boyd, *Shadow of the Long Knives* (1928); Vardis Fisher, *Toilers of the Hills* (1928) and *Dark Bridwell* (1931); Maud Hart Lovelace, *Early Candlelight* (1929); James Boyd, *The Long Hunt* (1930); Edna Ferber, *Cimarron* (1930); Elizabeth Madox Roberts, THE GREAT MEADOW (1930); Stewart Edward White, *The Long Rifle* (1932); Rose Wilder Lane, *The Hurricane* (1933); Stephen Vincent Benét, *James Shore's Daughter* (1934); Harold L. Davis, HONEY IN THE HORN (1935) and *Beulah Land* (1949); Conrad Richter, *Early Americana* (1936) and *The Fields* (1946); Walter Van Tilburg Clark, *The Ox-Bow Incident* (1940); A. B. Guthrie, Jr., *The Big Sky* (1947); Felix Holt, *The Gabriel Horn* (1951); H. M. Drummond, *Hoot Owls and Orchids* (1956); Oakley Hall, *Warlock* (1958), *The Bad Lands* (1978), and *Apaches* (1986); and Larry McMurtry, *Lonesome Dove* (1985). The foregoing are representative of some of the best. From the DIME NOVEL to the modern Western, the titles are far too numerous for comprehensive listing. Direct per- sonal experience bulks large as well, including as one of the classics Mark Twain's *Roughing It* (1872). The distinctive humor of the frontier has been studied by such specialists as Walter Blair, Franklin J. Meine, and Constance Rourke. (See WESTERNS and POETS AND POETRY OF THE WEST.)

Frontier in American History, The (1920).   Essays by FREDERICK JACKSON TURNER, the most important of which is "The Significance of the Frontier in American History," a paper originally presented at the American Historical Association in July 1893, and published in the proceedings of the association in 1894. Turner claimed that the frontier expansion caused the development of a unique and fundamentally democratic cul- ture as the availability of free land emancipated men from the restrictions of more conventional society in long-settled areas. The main theme, on the function of free land, was borrowed without citation from the Italian scholar Achille Loria, but free land was subsidiary to the real thrust of the piece, a vague state- ment of the need for a nationalistic American historiography. American historians adopted this "frontier hypothesis" of

Turner without question—Turner advanced it at a time when American historians were desperate to find meaning in the American past. The frontier hypothesis is not an explanatory paradigm so much as it is a means of lending the appearance of intellectual substance to a tradition of nationalism. It has been highly influential and was one of the foundation pieces of the emerging so-called New History of American scholars of the early 20th century. The status of the frontier hypothesis as the reigning theory of American historiography has been chal- lenged in works that include J. G. Leyburn, *Frontier Folkways* (1935); L. B. Wright, *Culture on the Moving Frontier* (1955); D. H. Miller and W. W. Savage, Jr., in their introduction to Turner's *The Character and Influence of the Indian Trade in Wis- consin* (1977); Miller and J. O. Steffen, in the introduction to *The Frontier: Comparative Studies* (1977); and J. M. Marshall, *Land Fever: Dispossession and the Frontier Myth* (1986). Most American historians appear to skirt the issue of the meaning of Turner's ideas, paying lip service to Turner as a founder of American historiography. A few still enthusiastically boost the frontier hypothesis, including the late Ray Allen Billington, *Frederick Jackson Turner* (1973).

DAVID HARRY MILLER

Frontier Index, The.   A "press on wheels," founded in May 1866, at Kearney City, Nebraska, by Frederick Kemper Freeman (1841–1928) and operated by him and his brother Lewis. It moved westward with the steady advance of the Union Pacific Railroad, appearing triweekly in various towns in Nebraska, Wyoming, and Utah. In Corinne, Utah, it was renamed *Freeman's Farmer* and halted its westward progress.

Front Page, The (1928),   a comedy of newspaper life by BEN HECHT and CHARLES MACARTHUR. Both Hecht and MacArthur were alumni of Chicago journalism and are believed to have taken Walter Howey of the *Chicago City Press* as the model for the play's trumpet-toned managing editor, Walter Burns. Critics agree generally that the play was realistic in its profanity and many of its details, but was essentially a romantic presentation of the newspaper world.

Frost, A[rthur] B[urdett] (1851–1928),   illustrator, cartoonist. Born in Philadelphia, Frost was a successful maga- zine and book illustrator. He produced several collections of his own, including *Stuff & Nonsense* (1884), *The Bull Calf and Other Tales* (1892), and *Carlo* (1913), but he was known best for his humorous contributions to *Life* and for his illustrations for books by Twain, H. C. Bunner, John Kendrick Bangs, and, above all, Joel Chandler Harris.

Frost, Frances [Mary] (1905–1959),   poet, novelist, newspaper writer, teacher. Born in Vermont, Frost became a frequent contributor to magazines and newspapers and won a reputation particularly for her graceful poems of New Eng- land scenery and life. Among her collections of verse are *Hem- lock Wall* (1929), *Blue Harvest* (1931), *These Acres* (1932), *Pool in the Meadow* (1933), *Road to America* (1937), *Christmas in the Woods* (1942), *Mid-Century* (1946), *This Star of Wonder* (1953), and *This Rowdy Heart* (1954). Among her novels are *Innocent Summer* (1936) and *Uncle Snowball* (1940). She was also known for her children's books, such as the series about Windy Foot.

Frost, Robert [Lee] (1874–1963),   poet. Remembered first for his rural New England subject matter and perhaps only second for the poetic skill that placed him among the major American poets of the 20th century, Frost was born in San Francisco. His father was a journalist with Southern sympathies who left New Hampshire during the Civil War. After his death from tuberculosis in 1885, Frost's mother returned to her people and raised her children in New Hampshire and Massachusetts. A Swedenborgian and a schoolteacher, she introduced her son to the poetry of Wordsworth, Emerson, and Bryant, all of whom derived much of their power from the spoken voice stretched across a metrical line, and something more from mystic insights discovered in contemplation of nature.

Frost was graduated from high school in Lawrence, Massachusetts, in 1892 as covaledictorian with Elinor White, whom he married three years later. In the fall of 1892, he entered Dartmouth College, but failed to complete a semester. Instead, he worked in a textile mill in Lawrence and taught school. Two years after his marriage, he entered Harvard as a special student (1897–99), acquiring a further grounding in Latin that enhanced his developing word sense. After discontinuing this second experiment in higher education, he briefly tried poultry farming, then in 1900 moved to a farm in Derry, New Hampshire, purchased with money from his grandfather. For the next twelve years, the Frosts lived in Derry. Frost farmed without signal success and taught English at Pinkerton Academy in Derry (1905–11). In 1912 he sold the farm and at thirty-eight sailed from Boston to Glasgow with his wife and four children, intent on making his reputation in England as a poet. He settled near London, published *A Boy's Will* (1913) and *North of Boston* (1914). Three years after leaving Boston, with England embroiled in World War I, he returned home, his reputation assured.

Frost's first poem to be sold, and the earliest to be retained in his collected work, was "My Butterfly," which appeared in *The Independent* for November 8, 1894. In the same year Frost had published that poem and four others in *Twilight*, a small book privately printed in two copies, one for Elinor White and another for himself. Other poems appeared in various periodicals over the next two decades, but when his first book appeared in England, it included only nine more among those earlier published that Frost was to retain later. In his second book, there were only three. Under these circumstances, Frost's sailing to England represented an extraordinary act of faith, tinged perhaps with the desperation of a poet approaching middle age who saw his chance slipping away if he did not firmly grasp it while he was still able. With confidence born of his first acceptance into English literary circles, he wrote in 1913 in an exuberant Fourth of July letter to a former student of his from Pinkerton Academy, "To be perfectly frank with you I am one of the most notable craftsmen of my time. That will transpire presently."

In England, Frost met Ezra Pound, who reviewed *A Boy's Will* and *North of Boston*, and became particularly close to Edward Thomas, who died in the war in 1917, encouraging him as a poet. The Frosts returned home in 1915, settling on a farm near Franconia, New Hampshire, the locale that suggested the title for his next book, *Mountain Interval* (1916). In the year after his return, he read THE AX-HELVE as the Phi Beta Kappa poem at Harvard, delivering within it a sly commentary on educational and cultural systems that fail to allow for the individual bent that, like the lines of a good ax handle, is "native to the grain." In 1917, he began his long association with Amherst College, teaching there until 1920, when he left for a farm in Vermont and helped found the Bread Loaf School of English at Middlebury College. Later teaching appointments took him to Wesleyan, the University of Michigan, Dartmouth, Yale, and Harvard, and he became a frequent lecturer at many other schools. Among his many honors were his appointment as poetry consultant to the Library of Congress (1958), election to the American Academy of Arts and Letters, and honorary doctorates from Cambridge and Oxford. His reading of "The Gift Outright" at the inauguration of President John F. Kennedy remains a high point for poetry in the 20th century.

The kindly poet with the twinkle in his eye remembered by so many from his personal appearances and his poetry had also a darker side. His private life was marred by tragedy. His first child died of cholera in 1900; his younger sister first, and a daughter, later, were committed to mental hospitals; another daughter died of puerperal fever after childbirth; and the sudden death of his wife in 1938 left him bereft of her support not long before the suicide of their son. He suffered from severe depressions, and the portrait of the man given in Lawrence Thompson's biography is not an entirely attractive one. His poetry has the dark side that RANDALL JARRELL was one of the first critics to stress in his essay in *Poetry and the Age*.

He was, as he boasted, "one of the most notable craftsmen" of his time. In the same letter that carried that statement, he explored the implications of what he called "the sound of sense." It is, he said, "the abstract vitality of our speech. It is pure sound—pure form. One who concerns himself with it more than the subject is an artist." You can get at it, he suggested, by listening to voices behind a door, where you can hear the sounds, but cannot distinguish the words. "But if one is to be a poet he must learn to get cadences by skillfully breaking the sounds of sense with all their irregularity of accent across the regular beat of the meter." For English, of course, the regular beat is iambic, and more often pentameter or tetrameter than otherwise. What Frost accomplishes in this respect, better than almost any other poet of this century, is to bridge the gap between sense and meter, carefully matching the tunes of both. In the voices of his mostly rural New Englanders, and in his own voice in the poems that seem not far from his persona as poet, the lines rarely diverge so far from ordinary speech as to seem unrealistically elevated; at the same time, the meter rarely diverges so far from regularity as to seem broken or undisciplined.

In the craft of Frost, sound must be accompanied by sense. In "The Figure a Poem Makes," published as an introduction to his *Collected Poems* (1939), he conceded, "Granted no one but a humanist much cares how sound a poem is if it is only *a* sound. The sound is the gold in the ore." Still, Frost comes down on the side of the humanist. The poem must be about things that matter. "It begins in delight and ends in wisdom." Both the writing and the reading of poetry must give rise to emotional and intellectual change: "No tears in the writer, no tears in the reader. No surprise for the writer, no surprise for the reader."

For Frost, the chief vehicle of sense was the metaphor, but just as the sound of his lines was the sound of what we might by the addition of a word call common sense, so the metaphor he most prized was the common object or event seen in the light of a surprising relation. Even in the names of some of his most memorable poems he memorialized this idea of commonplace surprise: "The Road Not Taken," "Birches," "The Ax-Helve," "Nothing Gold Can Stay," "Stopping by Woods on a Snowy Evening," "West-Running Brook," "The Silken Tent," and "Take Something Like a Star." Particularly instructive is the metaphor at the center of "Home Burial" that the man unwittingly grasps in his desperate avoidance of the plain facts of his child's death. "Three foggy mornings and one rainy day," he says, "Will rot the best birch fence a man can build." But though the man's wife has repeated the lines, she has not attended to the meaning, and the poem ends as a tragedy of failed communication. Words, Frost tells us, are important, metaphors elevate their usefulness, and poetry lodges them in our consciousness.

Frost took the title of *A Boy's Will* from Longfellow's "My Lost Youth": "A boy's will is the wind's will, / And the thoughts of youth are long, long thoughts." Apart from "The Tuft of Flowers," it contained few of his more lasting poems. The mostly narrative *North of Boston* included some of his best-known works: MENDING WALL, THE DEATH OF THE HIRED MAN, HOME BURIAL, "Blueberries," "After Apple-Picking," and "The Wood-Pile." *Mountain Interval* included THE ROAD NOT TAKEN, BIRCHES, "The Hill Wife," and "Out, Out." Among the poems in *New Hampshire* (1923) were "The Ax-Helve," "The Witch of Coös," "Fire and Ice," "Stopping by Woods on a Snowy Evening," and "Two Look at Two." After his late start, in the space of eleven years, Frost had published four books containing more than half of his eventual poetic production, apart from his two short plays. In 1922, two years before Frost celebrated his fiftieth birthday, the appearance of Eliot's THE WASTE LAND had given poetry in English a modernist thrust that for many made Frost's verse appear old-fashioned. His major books thereafter came less frequently: *West-Running Brook* (1928), containing the title poem, "Once by the Pacific," and "Tree at My Window"; *A Further Range* (1936), containing "Two Tramps at Mud Time," "Departmental," "Desert Places," and "Design"; *A Witness Tree* (1942), containing "The Silken Tent," "Come In," and "The Gift Outright"; *Steeple Bush* (1947), containing "Directive," one of his last major poems; and *In the Clearing* (1962).

Frost's public persona and his celebrated wry humor made his achievement difficult for critics to assess. Taking issue in "Design" with the conventional argument of design as proof of God's existence, he could present a solemn vision of a white flower, white moth, and white spider as a "design of darkness to appall," then immediately and typically undercut the effect with the humorously wicked qualification "If design govern in a thing so small." Playfulness was at the heart of his poetics: play with sound, play with sense, play with rhythm, play with metaphor. But the play was serious, and out of it he built verses that last.

Books not mentioned above include the brief dramatic works A MASQUE OF REASON (1945) and A MASQUE OF MERCY (1947). The most complete edition is the Library of America's *Collected Poems, Prose, and Plays* (1995). *The Poetry of Robert Frost*, edited by Edward Connery Lathem, appeared in 1969. Lawrence Thompson edited *Selected Letters* (1964). Lathem edited *Interviews with Robert Frost* (1966). A full biography is Lawrence Thompson, *Robert Frost* (3 v. 1966–1977, the last with R. H. Winnick); it was abridged in one volume by Lathem (1981). Other biographies are Elizabeth S. Sergeant, *Robert Frost: The Trial by Existence* (1960) and William H. Pritchard, *Frost: A Literary Life Reconsidered* (1984). Other books of criticism and biography include Richard Poirier, *Robert Frost: The Work of Knowing* (1977); John Evangelist Walsh, *Into My Own: The English Years of Robert Frost* (1988); and Joseph Brodsky, Seamus Heaney, and Derek Walcott, *Homage to Robert Frost* (1996).

Fruitlands.   A utopian society founded by AMOS BRONSON ALCOTT at Cambridge, Massachusetts. It lasted only a few months, spring to autumn of 1843. Alcott envisaged a society in which all family life would disappear in a communal physical, mental, and spiritual development. The members were to live on a vegetarian diet, live in a manner that did not exploit animals, do all manual tasks in common, and dwell in sweetness and light. Louisa May Alcott pictured the colony with gentle humor in "Transcendental Wild Oats," a fictional sketch in *Silver Pitchers* (1876).

Frye, Northrop (1912–1991),   literary critic, educator. Frye was born in Sherbrooke, Quebec, and moved to Moncton, New Brunswick, when he was five. After graduating from Victoria College, University of Toronto, in 1933, Frye studied theology at Emmanuel College and spent the summer of 1934 as a student preacher for the United Church in Saskatchewan. After graduating from Emmanuel College in 1936 he left his theological studies and went to Merton College, Oxford, to study literature. Frye in 1940 joined the faculty of the University of Toronto, where he remained for the rest of his career, becoming chancellor of Victoria College in 1979.

Frye's career as one of the preeminent literary critics of his time began with his first major work, *Fearful Symmetry: A Study of William Blake* (1947). Although Frye wrote some thirty books and edited many others—on Blake, Milton, Shakespeare, T. S. Eliot, Romanticism, literary criticism, and Canadian literature, among other subjects—he is most widely known for his 1957 study *The Anatomy of Criticism: Four Essays*—the most frequently cited work by a 20th-century critic—and *The Great Code: The Bible and Literature* (1982), the first of a projected two-volume study of the influence of the Bible on Western literature. His longstanding interest in Canadian literature was reflected in such works as *The Modern Century* (1967), *The Bush Garden: Essays on the Canadian Imagination* (1971), and *Divisions in a Ground: Essays on Canadian Culture* (1982). Some of Frye's theories about the development of Canadian culture—that its tradition has evolved in large part from what Frye calls a "garrison mentality," for example—have been a major influence on Canadian literary criticism. Frye was deeply interested not only in the study of literature but also in teaching. His collection of lectures *Northrop Frye on Shakespeare* (1986) won the Governor-General's Award for nonfiction in Canada.

The importance of *The Anatomy of Criticism* lies in its detailed and systematic explication of Frye's central propositions concerning the centrifugal and centripetal nature of all literature, which in Frye's view is a coherent and autonomous order of words that finds its shape primarily in the patterns of the imagination rather than in the historical world. The four essays of the *Anatomy* establish the order and relations of literary works in terms of their modes, symbols, archetypes and myths, and genres. This view of the provenance of literature and of its ways of meaning has been as controversial as it has been influential in modern literary theory. Although Frye has been widely celebrated for his complex syntheses, some scholars have seen his criticism as an idealized system that denies the implications of history in literary meaning. In the two main parts of *The Great Code*, "The Order of Words" and "The Order of Types," Frye develops his theory that the major influence on Western literature has been the imagery and narrative of the Bible, which have provided a framework for our literature that Frye calls a "mythological universe." By 1990, Frye had been awarded thirty-six honorary degrees from universities in North America and Europe.

Neil Besner

Fuchs, Daniel (1909–), novelist, short-story writer. Born in New York City, Fuchs wrote *Summer in Williamsburg* (1934), *Homage to Blenholt* (1936), and *Low Company* (1937), portraits of Jewish slum life on New York's Lower East Side gathered as *Three Novels* (1961). *West of the Rockies* (1971), a later novel, grew out of his experience as a Hollywood scriptwriter. His short fiction is collected in *The Apathetic Bookie Joint* (1979).

Fuentes, Carlos (1928–), novelist and short-story writer. Born in Mexico City to a wealthy family, he was educated in Chile, Argentina, Washington, D.C., and Geneva, Switzerland, where he earned a degree in law. Like his father, he has been a diplomat, living in the United States and Europe, most recently as Mexican ambassador in Paris.

His native Mexico is the setting and subject for his fiction. His first novel, ironically titled *La región más transparente* (1958, tr. *Where the Air Is Clear*, 1960), is a complex and panoramic vision of Mexico City in the years after the Revolution, showing how reform has been thwarted by the dominance of a new bourgeoisie. *Las buenas conciencias* (1959, tr. *The Good Conscience*, 1971) is a realistic treatment of a wealthy young man's transition from rebellion to retreat into his privileged social position.

Fuentes gained international attention with *La muerte de Artemio Cruz* (1962, tr. *The Death of Artemio Cruz*, 1964), again set in the postrevolutionary period. The title character has turned from patriot to exploiter and, on his deathbed, narrates from three perspectives (I, you, and he) a fragmented and nonchronological vision of his life. *Cambio de piel* (1967, tr. *A Change of Skin*, 1968) revolves around a trip by two couples to Cholula; it mixes Aztec myths with the present and shifts focus from Mexico to Nazi concentration camps. *Terra Nostra* (1975, tr. 1976), a historical novel, concerns the 16th-century monarch Philip II of Spain. His other novels include *Una familia lejana* (1980, tr. *Distant Relations*, 1982); *El gringo viejo* (1986, tr. *The Old Gringo*, 1986), a fictional account of AMBROSE BIERCE's last days in Mexico; and *Christopher Unborn* (1989), in which an unborn child narrates an apocalyptic vision of Mexico's imminent future. His stories are collected in *Blindman's Song* (1964), *Burnt Water* (1980), and *Constancia and Other Stories for Virgins* (1990). *Myself with Others* (1988) is a collection of essays translated into English. *La campaña* (1990, tr. *Campaign: A Novel*, 1991) and *Nuevo Tiempo Mexicano* (1994, tr. *A New Time for Mexico*, 1996) treat the chaotic politics of his native country at the end of the 20th century. *The Years with Laura Diaz* (2000) traces the life of the title character through Mexico's 20th-century history.

Fugitives, The. A group of poets who came together in Nashville not long after World War I at Vanderbilt University and included townspeople. Fugitives from contemporary poetry as they perceived it in their time and from Victorian sentimentalism, they sought new directions for their journal *The Fugitive* (1922–1925), publishing in it their own poetry and the work of then new poets elsewhere, such as Robert Graves, LAURA RIDING, and HART CRANE. JOHN CROWE RANSOM and DONALD DAVIDSON were Vanderbilt English instructors. ALLEN TATE and ROBERT PENN WARREN began as their students. Others in the group included Ridley Wills, a novelist, and MERRILL MOORE, physician and sonneteer, as well as several people more peripheral to literature. Although poetry was their main concern, they were also interested in social, philosophical, religious, and cultural questions. Ransom, Davidson, Tate, and Warren were later prominent among the AGRARIANS, who emerged as a distinct group in 1928.

Although the Fugitives did not survive the 1920s as a formal group, the central quartet exerted an enormous influence on American literature through their poetry and criticism; through later journals like *The Southern Review* (1935–1942), edited by Warren and CLEANTH BROOKS, and THE KENYON REVIEW, founded by Ransom in 1939; and through books like Brooks and Warren's *Understanding Poetry* (1938), a phenomenally successful textbook, and Ransom's THE NEW CRITICISM

(1941), which named a critical movement begun earlier in England and dominant in the United States for many years thereafter.

Fuller, Charles [H., Jr.] (1939–   ),   playwright. Born in Philadelphia and educated at Villanova and La Salle College, Fuller was codirector of the Afro-American Arts Theatre in Philadelphia (1967–71) and, with *A Soldier's Play* (1981), became the second African-American to win a Pulitzer Prize for drama. *A Soldier's Play* centers on the investigation following the murder of an African-American army sergeant. Fuller also wrote the screenplay for the film version, *A Soldier's Story* (1984). His other plays include *The Village: A Party* (1968), on racial integration; *The Brownsville Raid* (1976), based on an actual event—the dismissal of 167 African-American soldiers in Brownsville, Texas, in 1906; and *Zooman and the Sign* (1979), about the aftermath of the shooting of a child. *Sally, Prince, Jonquil,* and *Burner's Frolic* are a series of plays produced from 1988 to 1990 that treat the lives of black Americans at the end of the 19th century.

Fuller, Henry B[lake] ["Stanton Page"] (1857–1929), novelist, poet, critic. Born in Chicago, Fuller turned early to novel writing and was successful from the start with a story laid in Italy, *The Chevalier of Pensieri-Vani* (1890). His best-known book was *The Cliff Dwellers* (1893), a novel about Chicago, considered the first notable American city novel. Among his other novels are *The Chatelaine de la Trinité* (1892), *With the Procession* (1895), *From the Other Side* (1898), *A Sicilian Romance* (1900), *Under the Skylights* (1901), *Waldo Trench and Others* (1908), and the posthumous *Not on the Screen* (1930). Fuller, a book critic for Chicago newspapers, was active in Chicago's literary circles, especially those engaged in making *Poetry* the most important magazine of its kind in the country. Fuller himself issued two collections of verse, *The New Flag* (1899) and *Lines Long and Short* (1917). He was one of the forerunners of naturalism in the United States, particularly in *The Cliff-Dwellers*, which portrays the greed and futility of a materialistic civilization.

Fuller, [Sarah] Margaret, Marchesa Ossoli (1810–1850),   teacher, translator, poet, transcendentalist, editor, critic, writer on social questions. Born in Massachusetts and educated by her father, Fuller surpassed in scholarship and in critical acumen most of the men of her day—many disliked her intensely. She had a gift for languages and knew many well. She taught school for a while and held forth every Saturday afternoon in "conversations" that would spellbind Boston intellectuals. She translated vigorously from the German, and her admiration of Goethe was infectious. With Emerson she started THE DIAL (July 1840–April 1844) as a medium for the transcendentalists; it was vigorous only as long as she was editor. She became a powerful critic of literature on the New York *Tribune*. Her unfavorable remarks on Lowell and Longfellow especially enraged some of the Boston Brahmins. Yet Poe praised her ability as a critic and admired her freedom from adulation, although he censured her grammatical and stylistic carelessness.

In 1846, fulfilling an ardent desire, she went to Europe, where she mingled with the leading authors of the day. She showed deep interest in Italy's endeavors to win freedom, meeting Giovanni Angelo, Marquis Ossoli, who was ten years younger than she, and becoming his mistress. They had a son and found family life difficult, but they later married, the exact date of the marriage being unknown. She became active in the hospitals once fighting began in Italy, and began to write a book on Guiseppe Mazzini (1805–1872) and the war of liberation. In May 1850, the family set sail for New York. They were shipwrecked off Fire Island, and the body of the infant son was washed ashore. The other bodies were never recovered.

During her lifetime Fuller published a perceptive travel book on the Midwest, *Summer on the Lakes* (1844); a volume attesting to her keen interest in feminism, *Woman in the 19th Century* (1845); and *Papers on Literature and Art* (1846). Posthumous works were *At Home and Abroad* (1856) and memoirs called *Life Without and Life Within* (1859). Horace Greeley published her complete works in 1869.

Lowell gave considerable space to her in A FABLE FOR CRITICS, stressing her spitefulness and egotism. During the BROOK FARM experiment, Hawthorne knew her well and portrayed her in THE BLITHEDALE ROMANCE, in which some of her traits appear in the character of Zenobia. Carlyle made some puzzled references to her. In his *Journal* he relates: "Yesternight there came a bevy of Americans from Emerson, one Margaret Fuller the chief figure of them—a strange, lilting, lean old maid, not nearly such a bore as I expected." To him is attributed a comment on Fuller's sublime announcement, "I accept the universe!" Carlyle said, "By God! She'd better!" Yet Carlyle also thought her courage "high and clear" and called her "a truly heroic mind, altogether unique, so far as I know, among the writing women of this generation." Emerson both respected and feared her. He said about her in his *Journal*: "Strange, cold-warm, attractive-repelling conversation with Margaret, whom I always admire, and sometimes love; yet whom I freeze and who prevents me to silence when we promise to come nearest." V. L. Parrington later spoke for many: "Her tragic life, despite its lack of solid accomplishment, was an epitome of the great revolt of the New England mind against Puritan asceticism and Yankee materialism."

Fulton, Alice (1952–   ),   poet. Born in Troy, New York and educated at the State University of New York and Cornell University, Fulton has taught at the University of Michigan since 1983. Her vividly imagistic poetry concerns itself with the tensions between faith and technology and the seductions of popular culture. Among her gatherings are *Anchors of Light* (1979), *Dance Script with Electric Ballerina* (1983), *Palladium* (1986), and *Powers of Congress* (1990). In 1991, Fulton was awarded the prestigious five-year John D. and Catherine T. MacArthur Foundation Fellowship. Critics were enthusiastic about *Sensual Math* (1995), a wide-ranging view of modern life and technology. *Feeling as a Foreign Language: The Good Strangeness of Poetry* (1999) collects essays. In *Felt* (2001), Fulton uses the unwoven cloth as a metaphor for the tangled mat of interdependence made up of humans and animals on our planet.

Furness, Horace Howard (1833–1912),   lawyer, scholar, editor. Beginning in 1866 Furness devoted himself to the *Variorum Shakespeare*, a monumental series that opened with the publication of *Romeo and Juliet* (1871). Numerous volumes appeared until the death of Furness, and the work was then continued, but not completed, by his son **Horace Howard Furness, Jr**. (1865–1930). The series was originally a project of the Shakespearean Society of Philadelphia (founded 1851).

Further Range, A (1936),   a collection of poems by ROBERT FROST. The verses include a large number of humorous and satirical pieces, also a group of epigrams called "Ten Mills." The politics of the day greatly interested the poet. The longest poem in the book, "Build Soil," has a note by the poet saying that it was "delivered at Columbia, May 31, 1932, before the national party conventions of that year."

Fyles, Franklin (1847–1911),   drama critic, playwright. Fyles, who covered the theater in New York for the *Sun* from 1885 to 1903, wrote a book on *The Theater and Its People* (1900) as well as three plays: THE GIRL I LEFT BEHIND ME (with DAVID BELASCO, 1893), *Cumberland '61* (1897), and *Kit Carson* (1901).

G

Gabriel Conroy (1876),　a novel by BRET HARTE. The longest of Harte's fictional writings, it vividly depicts mining conditions during the early days of the gold rush. Among the characters is Harte's gambler, JACK HAMLIN.

Gaddis, William [Thomas] (1922–1998),　novelist. Born in New York City, Gaddis entered Harvard in 1941, and subsequently became president of the *Lampoon*, which published his diverse early writings. Because of a fracas in his senior year, he left Harvard without a degree. He worked as a checker on *The New Yorker* and, beginning in 1947, traveled widely in Central America and Europe, notably Spain. His travels are reflected in his first novel, *The Recognitions*. The father of two, Gaddis supported himself during his long career mainly through industrial, corporate, and other professional writing.

Gaddis was the author of four remarkable novels: *The Recognitions* (1955), *JR* (1975), *Carpenter's Gothic* (1985), and *A Frolic of His Own* (1994). *The Recognitions* has been called an encyclopedic novel and *JR* an acoustical novel. The former is crammed with abstruse information and literary, historical, and religious allusions, while the latter, which proceeds by nearly undifferentiated dialogue, is even more difficult to read. Much shorter and less experimental, *Carpenter's Gothic* nonetheless extends Gaddis's interrelated principal motifs of "the separating of things today without love" and entropy. Previous influences, for example, Empedocles, Willard Gibbs, and especially Norbert Wiener, are once again discernible. In *Carpenter's Gothic*, as in *The Recognitions* and *JR*, disorder and disinformation prevail. The author, whose protagonists are failed artists, opposes this chaos through linguistic and formal coherence, thus challenging the "bad books and bad everything" that characterize our civilization.

A Frolic of His Own treats the abuses and absurdities of the law. Oscar Crease, a college professor and writer, is caught up in a suit against a Hollywood producer who has stolen the play he wrote about his grandfather's Civil War experiences. The opening line . . . "You get justice in the next world, in this world you have the law" sums up the litigation trap. For this novel, Gaddis won his second National Book Award.

Public recognition was very long in coming for Gaddis, though his brilliant novels won awards from the National Institute of Arts and Letters (1963), the National Endowment for the Arts (1966, 1974), the John Simon Guggenheim Foundation (1981), and the John D. and Catherine T. MacArthur Foundation (1982). After winning the National Book Award for *JR*, Gaddis emphasized *l'oeuvre* over *l'homme* in his 1976 acceptance speech: "I feel like part of the vanishing breed that thinks a writer should be read and not heard, let alone seen. I think this is because there seems so often today to be a tendency to put the person in place of his or her work, to turn the creative artist into a performing one, to find what a writer says about writing somehow more valid, or more real, than the writing itself." The years 1982 to 1984 were particularly gratifying. In 1982, besides becoming a MacArthur Fellow, he was the subject of a special issue of *The Review of Contemporary Fiction* and Steven Moore's *A Reader's Guide to William Gaddis's "The Recognitions."* During 1983, Gaddis was the focus of a special session at the Modern Language Association convention; during 1984, *In Recognition of William Gaddis*, a collection of critical essays, appeared, and he was inducted into the American Academy and Institute of Arts and Letters. Before his death, Gaddis was said to have finished his fifth novel, to be entitled *Agape Agape*; in his second novel, *JR*, the writer Jack Gibbs is trying to finish a book by that title.

JOHN KUEHL/BP

Gág, Wanda (1893–1946),　artist, illustrator, translator, author of books for children. Gág (pronounced GOG), of Czech descent, was born in Minnesota and made her way from an environment of extreme poverty into a position of leadership among American artists. Her work found permanent exhibition in the Metropolitan Museum of Art and other collections. In 1928 she published her first book for children, *Millions of Cats*, which immediately became a children's classic. Making use of her own translations from Grimm, she illustrated *Tales from Grimm* (1936), *Snow White and the Seven Dwarfs* (1938), and *Three Gay Tales from Grimm* (1943). She also did pictures for *The Funny Thing* (1929), *Snippy and Snappy* (1931), and *Gone Is Gone* (1935). In *Growing Pains* (1940) she depicted in diary form her life from the age of fifteen to twenty-four, a book described by one reviewer as "a unique record of the evolution of an artist."

Gage, Frances Dana [Barker] ["Aunt Fanny"] (1808–1884),　reformer, lecturer, editor, author of children's stories. Born in Ohio, Gage spoke and wrote freely on slavery, women's rights, the temperance movement, and other causes. In her later years she began writing sketches and poems for children. Her best-known work was *Elsie Magoon, or, The Old Still-House in the Hollow* (1867). She also wrote *Gertie's Sacrifice* (1869) and *Steps Upward* (1870).

Gage, Thomas (1596?–1656), clergyman, traveler. Although he was English by birth, Gage went to Spain, became a Dominican and then a Spanish missionary in Central America (1625–37). Later he returned to England and became an Anglican clergyman; he died in Jamaica while accompanying a military expedition to the West Indies. He wrote of his experiences in *The English-American: His Travail by Sea and Land* (1684).

Gaine, Hugh (1727–1807), bookseller, printer, publisher. Born in Ireland, Gaine founded one of New York City's early newspapers, the weekly *Mercury*, which began publication in 1752. His bookshop, The Bible and Crown, was a center of literary activity. In 1768 he became the official printer of the Province of New York. Paul Leicester Ford edited his *Journals* (2 v. 1902).

Gaines, Ernest J[ames] (1933–   ), novelist, teacher. Born in Louisiana, Gaines grew up from age 15 in Vallejo, California and was educated at Vallejo Junior College, San Francisco State College, and Stanford. He has taught at several colleges, including Denison, Stanford, and the University of Southwestern Louisiana. His fiction stems largely from his experience among African-Americans in the Louisiana bayou region (his father was a plantation worker) and is set often in an imagined area he calls Bayonne. Among his honors are Rockefeller and Guggenheim grants. His most-praised novel, *The Autobiography of Miss Jane Pittman* (1971), recounts a history spanning 100 years from the Civil War to the 1960s. His other novels are *Catherine Carmier* (1964), *Of Love and Dust* (1967), *In My Father's House* (1978), *A Gathering of Old Men* (1983), and *A Lesson Before Dying* (1993). His stories are collected in *Bloodline* (1968, 1997).

Galaxy, The (1866–1878), New York literary monthly. It published distinguished contributors, including Rebecca Harding Davis, J. W. De Forest, Henry James, Mark Twain, and Walt Whitman.

Galbraith, John Kenneth (1908–   ), economist, author. An influential economist, Galbraith has had a distinguished career in education and government. He was born in Ontario, Canada. After attending the Universities of Toronto, California, and Cambridge, he taught at Princeton and Harvard, served in the National Defense Advisory Commission and the Office of Price Administration during World War II, and was director of the Strategic Bombing Survey (1946) and the Office of Economic Security Policy (1946). In succeeding years he resumed teaching at Harvard, was a member of the board of editors of *Fortune* magazine (1943–48), served as American ambassador to India (1961–63) under President Kennedy, and was national chairman (1967–69) of Americans for Democratic Action. As an economic theorist he has advocated greater government spending in support of public services and to fight inflation, presenting his case in polished, lucid prose. Among his books are *American Capitalism* (1952), *The Great Crash: 1929* (1955), *The Affluent Society* (1958), *The Liberal Hour* (1960), *Ambassador's Journal* (1969), *The New Industrial State* (revised 1971), *Economics and the Public Purpose* (1973), *The World Economy Since the Wars: An Eyewitness Account* (1994), and *The Good Society: The Humane Dimension* (1996). His novels include *A Tenured Professor* (1990), a witty satire of the workings of the American economy. He has also written accounts of his travels. *Name-Dropping: From FDR On* (1999) is a highly informative and amusing account of well-known 20th-century figures.

Gale, Zona (1874–1938), novelist, short-story writer, dramatist, poet. Gale was born and raised in Portage, Wisconsin, the small Midwestern city that was to dominate her life and work. After graduating from the University of Wisconsin in 1895, she worked as a reporter for several Milwaukee newspapers. In 1901 she joined the staff of the New York *World*, but resigned eighteen months later to devote her time to free-lance writing. Undismayed by rejection slips, she finally sold a short story to *Success* in 1903. Her stories began to appear in leading magazines, and her first novel, *Romance Island*, was published in 1906.

During World War I her pacifist views brought her the enmity of some of her Portage neighbors, who suspected her of being a German sympathizer. This experience greatly altered her conception of village life, which she had been unable to see as a mixture of virtues and defects in her popular early stories set in a mythical and sentimental *Friendship Village* (1908). This change in attitude is reflected in BIRTH (1918), in which she depicted a small town with affection but with unwavering realism. Her short novel MISS LULU BETT (1920) was an immediate success. Published in the same year that Sinclair Lewis published *Main Street*, it tells the bittersweet story of a middle-aged drudge, exploited by her dull, selfish relatives. Her dramatization of the novel won the Pulitzer Prize in 1921 and, as the *Nation* later said, "belongs among the very earliest of plays which broke away from theatrical convention to establish upon the stage a new American literature." In the same realistic vein are *Faint Perfume* (1923), which pits the sensitivity of her heroine against the crassness of middle-class life, and two collections of short stories, *Yellow Gentians and Blue* (1927) and *Bridal Pond* (1930). A strain of mysticism, hinted in earlier work, is apparent in *Preface to a Life* (1926) and in much of her subsequent writing. Her other novels include *Borgia* (1929) and *Papa La Fleur* (1933).

Her last novel, *Magna*, was published posthumously in 1939. Her autobiographical works are *When I Was a Little Girl* (1913) and *Portage, Wisconsin* (1928). A book of verse is *The Secret Way* (1921).

Gallagher, Tess (1943–   ), short-story writer, poet. Born in Port Angeles, Washington, Gallagher was educated at the University of Washington and the University of Iowa. Her first publications were poetry collections including *Under Stars* (1978), praised by Hayden Carruth for its "feminine" language and depth of perception; *Willingly* (1984), with its theme of the influence of the writer's father; *Amplitude:*

New and Selected Poems (1987); and *My Black Horse: New and Selected Poems* (1995). The latter book incorporates the sixty poems from *Moon Crossing Bridge* (1992) on the death of her third husband, RAYMOND CARVER. *The Lover of Horses* (1986), *Across the Bridge* (1994), and *At the Owl Woman Saloon* (1997) are story collections.

Gallagher, William Davis (1808–1894),   poet, editor, public official. In his early years Gallagher moved to Ohio, recording his observations on the beauties of the western wilderness in conventional but effective verse—three collections called *Erato* (two published in 1835, the third in 1837), and *Miami Woods and Other Poems* (1881). In addition he issued *Selections from the Poetical Literature of the West* (1841), one of the first anthologies of regional literature. He worked on newspapers in Louisville, Cincinnati, and elsewhere, and his political activities won him an appointment from Lincoln as special collector of the customs.

Gallant, Mavis (1922–   ),   novelist, short-story writer. Although Gallant has published two novels, a play, and a fine collection of nonfiction, the short story has been her major form. To date, nine highly acclaimed books of stories have appeared, most of them originally published in *The New Yorker* over the last fifty years. Born in Montreal, Gallant was educated at a series of boarding-schools; her father died when Gallant was a girl, and she spent her teenage years living in New York City with a foster family. She returned to Montreal at eighteen and wrote for the *Montreal Standard* from 1944 to 1950, when she left for Europe. Gallant eventually settled in Paris, where she has lived since 1950. Gallant's stories are celebrated as much for their highly finished style as for their incisive portrayals of North American and local characters adrift in postwar Europe, where the fragmentation of recent history is seen to haunt individual and cultural memories. Other stories offer powerful evocations of tenuous marriages and of strained relations between parents and children. In all her fiction, Gallant's ability to pattern luminous details into moments of revelation is complemented by her sharp comic wit. Among her best books are *The Other Paris* (1956), *My Heart Is Broken: Eight Stories and a Short Novel* (1964), *The Pegnitz Junction: A Novella and Five Short Stories* (1973), *From the Fifteenth District: A Novella and Eight Short Stories* (1979), and *Overhead in a Balloon: Stories of Paris* (1985). Her other works include *The End of the World and Other Stories* (1974), *Home Truths: Selected Canadian Stories* (1981), *In Transit: Twenty Stories* (1989), and *Across the Bridge* (1993). Her widely praised *Collected Stories* appeared in 1996.

NEIL K. BESNER

Gallatin, [Abraham Alphonse] Albert (1761–1849), statesman, diplomat, ethnologist. Born in Switzerland, Gallatin came to America in 1780, helped American troops in the war, taught French at Harvard, and in 1783 moved to Virginia. There he bought an extensive tract, became acquainted with Washington, and entered politics; in 1793 he was elected United States senator, but held that office only two months, being disqualified because of the date of his citizenship. In later years he became a prominent financier, representing what

was then called the Republican Party and opposing the Federalists. He served three terms in Congress, was appointed secretary of the Treasury by Jefferson and instituted many important reforms, but was blamed for the weakness of our military defenses in the War of 1812. He was one of the negotiators of the Treaty of Ghent, which ended that war. He served later as minister to France and to Great Britain. He was greatly interested in America's aborigines, and his book called *Synopsis of the Indian Tribes within the United States, East of the Rocky Mountains and in the British and Russian Possessions in North America* (1836) won him a reputation as the father of American ethnology. He helped found an ethnological society and issued a pamphlet on *The Oregon Question* (1846). His *Writings* were edited by Henry Adams (3 v. 1879), who also published a biography (1879).

Gallegos [Freire], Rómulo (1884–1969),   Venezuelan novelist, educator, political leader. When lack of funds forced Gallegos to abandon his legal studies, he turned to teaching and served as director of various educational institutions from 1912 to 1930. Publication of DOÑA BÁRBARA (1929, tr. 1948), Gallegos's best-known novel, aroused the hostility of Juan Vicente Gómez, Venezuela's dictator, who tried to silence the author by offering him a seat in the senate. Gallegos chose voluntary exile instead, returning to Venezuela only after the death of Gómez in 1935. After a liberal coup in 1945, he was elected president of Venezuela for the term 1948–52. Late in 1948, however, Gallegos was deposed by a military junta and remained in exile until the overthrow of Marcos Pérez Jiménez, in 1958.

As a novelist, Gallegos is known for his interpretation of the people and customs of the Venezuelan *llanos*, or tropical prairies, in a realistic style touched by impressionism. Besides *Doña Bárbara*, his most popular novels are *Cantaclaro* (1934) and *Canaima* (1935, tr. 1984).

Gallery, The (1947),   a novel by JOHN HORNE BURNS.

Gallico, Paul [William] (1897–1976),   writer of short stories, novellas, novels, screenplays. Born in New York City, Gallico was educated at Columbia University and became a reporter and columnist for the *New York Daily News* before turning to fiction. A successful sports-writer and writer of slick fiction for *The Saturday Evening Post, Collier's, Cosmopolitan*, and other magazines, he published no books until *Farewell to Sport* (1938), nonfiction. Forty titles followed in the next three decades, with some of the best classed as novellas, fantasy, or juveniles, including *The Snow Goose* (1941), *The Small Miracle* (1951), *Scruffy: A Diversion* (1962), and *The Man Who Was Magic* (1966). His other fictions include *Mrs. 'Arris Goes to Paris* (1958), whimsical adventures of a London charwoman; two sequels, *Mrs. 'Arris Goes to New York* (1960) and *Mrs. 'Arris Goes to Parliament* (1965); and *The Poseidon Adventure* (1969). His stories and reflections on writing are collected in *Confessions of a Story Writer* (1946) and *Further Confessions of a Story Writer* (1961).

Galt, John (1779–1839),   novelist. A popular Scottish writer, Galt came to Canada as a representative of the Canada Company and founded the town of Guelph, Ontario, in 1827.

While in North America, he accumulated material for the frontier scenes in two novels: *Lawne Todd, or, The Settlers in the Woods* (1830), about upstate New York, and *Bogle Corbet, or, The Emigrants* (1831), set mainly in Canada. North American material appears also in his *Autobiography* (1833) and *Literary Life and Miscellanies* (1834).

Gálvez, Manuel (1882–1962),   Argentine novelist. Educated as a lawyer, Galvez had a lifelong interest in social problems that was often reflected in his novels. His first and greatest success came with *La maestra normal* (1914), a naturalistic novel depicting the hard life of a country schoolmistress. Among his other novels are *El mal metafisico* (1917), about a writer in Buenos Aires; *Nacha Regules* (1919), about prostitution; a trilogy set in the 19th century, *Escenas de la Guerra del Paraguay* (1928–29); and *Miércoles santo* (1930), about a parish priest.

Game, The (1905),   a novelette by JACK LONDON. A young fighter engaged to be married is begged by his fiancée to abandon boxing, but insists on fighting one last fight. An accidental slip on the canvas leads to a blow that causes his death.

Gamesters, The, or, Ruins of Innocence (1805), a novel by Caroline Matilda Warren. This sentimental, moralistic novel was intended to paint the evil consequences of gambling and to offer a characteristic example in the person of its leading character, an orphan who is corrupted by bad company and finally ends in suicide. The book was reprinted several times.

Gann, Ernest K[ellogg] (1910–1991),   novelist. Born in Nebraska, Gann flew transport planes in World War II and later wrote of flying in a novel, *The High and the Mighty* (1953), and a memoir, *Fate Is the Hunter* (1961). Other novels include *In the Company of Eagles* (1966) and *The Aviator* (1981).

Gant, Eugene.   Gant is the name under which THOMAS WOLFE usually appears in his autobiographical novels, LOOK HOMEWARD, ANGEL (1929) and of TIME AND THE RIVER (1935). In THE WEB AND THE ROCK (1939) and YOU CAN'T GO HOME AGAIN (1940), Gant becomes George Webber. Other characters of the same family name are also drawn from life—Oliver Gant, Eugene's father; Eliza Gant, his mother; Ben Gant, his older brother; and others.

Garcés, Francisco Tomás Hermenegildo (1738–1781),   Spanish missionary, explorer. Father Garces accompanied Juan Bautista de Anza (1735–1788) on his expedition overland from New Mexico to California in 1774. Elliott Coues published Garcés's diaries in *On the Trail of a Spanish Pioneer* (2 v. 1900).

García Márquez, Gabriel (1928–   ),   novelist, short-story writer. A Colombian, García Márquez stands at the head of the group of Latin American writers celebrated for the new life they have given to the novel by redefining the traditional claims of realism on the form. *One Hundred Years of Solitude* (1967, tr. 1970), the most widely read and admired Latin American novel of its time, has had a major influence on writers and critics, bridging traditional gaps between highbrow and lowbrow, serious and popular, fiction. It also is one of the finest exemplars of MAGICAL REALISM, a fictional mode often associated with contemporary Latin American writing.

García Márquez was born in Aracataca, a small town near the Caribbean coast of Colombia. Until he was eight, he lived in Aracataca with his grandparents. García Márquez believes he learned everything he knows by the time he was eight: his grandfather was a masterful storyteller, and García Márquez grew up fascinated by the tales and myths about the region and its people that his grandfather loved to tell him. Shortly after completing high school near Bogotá in 1946, he began studying law and published his first story in 1947 in a Bogotá newspaper. The assassination in 1948 of Jorge Eliécer Gaitán, the Liberal presidential candidate, initiated the ten years of civil war in Colombia known as *la violencia* and precipitated García Márquez's moves to Cartagena, where he continued to study law and to work as a journalist, and then to Barranquilla in 1950, where he strengthened his contact with the writers known as the Group of Barranquilla and gave up his law studies. His first novel, *La hojarasca* (1955, tr. *Leaf Storm*, 1972), was published in Bogotá during this period; in 1955 he traveled to Europe and settled in Paris, where he devoted himself to writing fiction and worked on two novels, *El coronel no tiene quien le escriba* (1961, tr. *No One Writes to the Colonel*, 1968) and *La mala hora* (1962, tr. *In Evil Hour*, 1980). Attracted to the ideals of the Cuban revolution, in 1959 he wrote for Cuba's *Prensa Latina* in Bogotá, Cuba, and New York, and he remains a friend and supporter of Fidel Castro to this day.

García Márquez began to write *Cien años de soladad (One Hundred Years of Solitude)* in 1965; its publication two years later, and its translation into English in 1970, marked García Márquez's real arrival on the international scene. *One Hundred Years of Solitude*, like much of García Márquez's fiction, is distinguished by its intricate and epic distortions of time, particularly by its extension of characters' lives beyond plausible expectation, conferring on them the haunting burden of solitude suggested in the title and typical of the experience of many García Márquez characters—most notably, of Colonel Aureliano Buendía in this novel and of the tyrannical general in *Elotoño del patriarca* (1975, tr. *The Autumn of the Patriarch*, 1976). The expanded time frame explores the haunting reaches of individual memories, alloyed with chimerical fantasies and with reflections of Colombian history. The Buendía family becomes the focus of Márquez's elaboration of the inturning cycles that the successive generations of the family—many of them named after each other—seem fated to repeat for at least a hundred years. Colombian history figures in several ways in the novel: the fictional military record of Colonel Aureliano Buendía, for example, recalls the historical record of General Rafael Uribe Uribe, who allegedly fought and lost thirty-six battles in the infamous civil war between Liberals and Conservatives (1899–1902), and who was the subject of many of García Márquez's grandfather's tales. Just as important as the various magical distortions of time and probability in García Márquez's fiction is his creation of place. This novel's setting in the small town of Macondo, which first appeared in *Leaf Storm*, established it as a fictional territory that resonates as powerfully as Faulkner's Yoknapatawpha County for many readers.

Following *Innocent Eréndira and Other Stories* (1972, tr. 1978), García Márquez published his next major work, *The Autumn of the Patriarch*, in 1975 (tr. 1976). This novel, with its elaborate sentences often running for pages, shows most clearly the considerable influence of Faulkner on García Márquez's style and subject matter. More intensely than *One Hundred Years of Solitude, The Autumn of the Patriarch* focuses on the monstrous solitude of a single character, in this case an all-powerful general, sole ruler of his country, afflicted with a series of physical deformities and a spiritual, psychological, and sexual depravity as he tyrannizes his people over the course of an impossibly long life, lived largely in the seclusion and baroque dissolution of his labyrinthine palace. The distortions of time are intensified in this novel by its narrative structure: we hear of all of the events, spanning several lifetimes, from an unnamed and many-voiced narrator who relates each episode as a strand of story emanating from the recurring moment of the discovery of the general's body being pecked at by vultures in the palace.

Although not as well known as his major novels, *Cronica de una muerte anunciada* (1981, tr. *Chronicle of a Death Foretold*, 1982) is a masterful novella that ranks with the finest works in any language in this difficult form. Based on an actual murder in defense of a family's honor—and thus a somber interrogation of this code, among other things—the novella is narrated by a reporter who tells the story from the perspective he shapes after the murder has taken place. The telling of the story seems to confirm the melancholy inevitability of the killing's coming to pass, and the fates of the characters become at once social and narrative imperatives. Beautifully constructed and strikingly vivid, *Chronicle of a Death Foretold* embeds a condemnatory anatomy of social mores in its seemingly pieced-together chronicle of the events leading to the killing of Santiago Nasar by the Vicario brothers.

In 1982, García Márquez was awarded the Nobel Prize for literature. Seven years earlier, he had declared he would henceforth prefer to devote himself to journalism, although the appearance of *Chronicle of a Death Foretold* had already belied that wish. But with the appearance of *El amor en los tiempos del cólera* (1985, tr. *Love in the Time of Cholera*, 1988) García Márquez showed that his powers as a novelist had not waned. More than any other of his fictions, *Love in the Time of Cholera* evokes the world of romance and unrequited love that so often appears in García Márquez's fiction, but that world is usually defeated by the operations of class and power or by the depredations of time. García Márquez has explained that he drew on the story of his father's courtship of his mother, and, to a lesser degree, his own courtship of Mercedes Barcha—his wife—for the shape of this story, in which the undying love of Florentino Ariza for Fermina Daza survives the long course of her marriage to Dr. Juvenal Urbino. After Urbino's death and fifty-three years of impassioned courtship, Ariza is finally united with Fermina during a ceremonial boat trip on which the passengers are stranded due to the cholera that has infected them and that has taken on literal and metaphorical dimensions throughout the novel. While indulging unashamedly in the languors of sentiment and nostalgia, this novel is the sweetest and most sustained exploration of romantic love in all of García Márquez's fiction to date.

Where García Márquez's imagination will venture next is difficult to predict. But the constellation of his fictions that illuminate one sector of our literary universe has already established him as a great fabulist, a masterful chronicler and conjurer of all the dimensions of the past, and above all as a writer who, for readers in many languages, has expanded and extended our apprehension of the real. His other works include *Big Mama's Funeral* (1962, tr. 1971); *The Story of a Shipwrecked Sailor* (1985, tr. 1986); *Clandestine in Chile: The Adventures of Miguel Littin* (1987); *The General in His Labyrinth* (1990), a novel about Simón Bolívar; *Doce cuentos peregrinos* (1992, tr. *Strange Pilgrims: Twelve Stories*, 1993). *Collected Stories* appeared in 1984 and 1999, *Collected Novellas* in 1990 and 1999. A study is Raymond L. Williams, *Gabriel García Márquez* (1984).

NEIL BESNER

Garcilaso de la Vega (1539–1616).   Peruvian historian. Known as El Inca and born in Cuzco, Garcilaso has been called the first writer of distinction born in America. He was the illegitimate son of a conquistador and a native princess; his grandfather was a brother of one of the last Inca rulers. Educated from age nineteen in Spain and for thirty years a soldier in European wars, he finally settled in Spain as a priest and historian. In his masterpiece, *Comentarios reals* (*Royal Commentaries*; two volumes, 1609, 1617), he portrayed the Inca empire and its conquest by Spain. An earlier book, *Florida del Inca* (*Florida of the Inca*, 1605), describes De Soto's explorations in Florida and the Southwest.

Gardiner, Sir Christopher.   A mysterious character who appeared in New England in the early 1630s and who turned out to be an agent of FERDINANDO GORGES in his attempts to win control over New England. He lived in Maine for a while, then disappeared, to turn up in England as a witness for Gorges before the Privy Council. His strange irruption into New England affairs attracted the attention of several writers. The first to make use of him was CATHERINE MARIA SEDGWICK, who introduced him under the name Sir Philip Gardiner as the villain of her novel HOPE LESLIE (1827), in which he attempts to kidnap the heroine. Then JOHN LOTHROP MOTLEY, the historian, included him as a character in his romance called *Merry-Mount* (1849). JOHN T. ADAMS, author of several historical novels, made him a character in his *The White Chief Among the Red Men* (1859). But he won greatest prominence when Longfellow wrote the *Rhyme of Sir Christopher Gardiner* (1873) as the last of his *Tales of a Wayside Inn*.

Gardner, Erle Stanley (1889–1970),   lawyer, detective-story writer. Born in Massachusetts and educated as a lawyer, Gardner became one of the most successful writers of crime fiction in the history of publishing, with sales of his books reaching well over 100,000,000 copies in his lifetime. For the most part, Gardner employed two detectives, Perry Mason and

Douglas Selby. The lawyer Perry Mason is hero of a long series—*The Case of the Velvet Claws* (1933, Gardner's first book), *The Case of the Lucky Legs* (1933), *The Case of the Perjured Parrot* (1939), *The Case of the Borrowed Brunette* (1946), and many others. Douglas Selby appears in a number of other volumes, also with standardized titles—*The D.A. Calls It Murder* (1944), *The D.A. Holds a Candle* (1945), *The D.A. Breaks an Egg* (1949), and many others. In addition Gardner wrote under pseudonyms—A. A. Fair, Charles J. Kenny, and Carleton Kendrake. As A. A. Fair he wrote over twenty books. Gardner wrote with incredible facility. His first book was completed in three and a half days. In that same month he wrote eleven novelettes and a 27,000-word feature story.

Most of Gardner's stories were written to a formula, at first in the hardboiled tradition. Later, with Perry Mason, he became gentler and more cerebral, seeming to aim at a mass market typified by *The Saturday Evening Post*. Gardner's success with the gentler Perry Mason is amply demonstrated in a long-running television series starring the lawyer-detective.

Gardner, Isabella (1915–1981),   poet. Born in Newton, Massachusetts, to a prominent family, Gardner studied acting in New York and London, and was married four times, the last time (1959–66) to ALLEN TATE. Her verse appeared first in *Birthdays from the Ocean* (1955), later in *The Looking Glass* (1961) and *West of Childhood: Poems 1950–1965* (1965); in it she displays a careful touch with rhythms and sound patterns as she writes of small, personal matters. Roland Flint edited *The Complete Poems* (1985).

Gardner, John (1933–1982),   novelist, teacher. Gardner was born in Batavia, New York and raised on the family farm. He was educated at DePauw University, Washington University in St. Louis, and Iowa State University. Committed to literature as a moral force, and believing it necessary not only to write but to teach, he held positions at various universities throughout his life, completing his career at the State University of New York at Binghamton. He died in a motorcycle accident.

Gardner's last years were embroiled in controversy aroused by his *On Moral Fiction* (1978), an essay asserting the primacy of high moral purpose in literature and judging his contemporaries deficient in that quality. Roundly attacked by other writers, he fought back in writings and interviews. His own commitment had been clear from the first, however; for the most part he had avoided the tendency toward self-reflexivity divorced from immediate social relevance that marked the work of some other writers of his generation. Nevertheless, his fiction ranged widely in subject and method. A first novel, *Resurrection* (1966), about a dying philosophy professor, introduced his common theme of rebirth in the upstate New York locale of many of his later fictions. In *The Wreckage of Agathon* (1970), he turned to ancient Greece for a story centered on freedom and civilization. In *Grendel* (1971), he retold the Anglo-Saxon classic *Beowulf* from the monster's point of view. In his next three novels Gardner turned to settings in upstate New York to raise in times closer to the present various questions concerning human responsibility. In *The Sunlight Dia-*

logues (1972), set in Batavia, New York, the major conflict is between the existential freedom of a strange magician and the rule of law represented by his nemesis, the police chief. In *Nickel Mountain* (1973) the owner of a diner attempts to find life through helping a young waitress. In *October Light* (1976), an aging brother and sister seek resolution of their longstanding conflicts. In *Mickelsson's Ghosts* (1982) the setting is in similar country in the mountains of Pennsylvania, where a professor of philosophy has returned to try to reassemble his life. In *Freddy's Book* (1980), a novel within a novel, a reclusive, deformed 20th-century author spins a tale of 16th-century Scandinavia. Another novel is *In the Suicide Mountains* (1977). His short stories are collected in *The King's Indian* (1974) and *The Art of Living* (1981). *Stillness and Shadows* (1986), edited by Nicholas Delbanco, collects two unfinished novels, both autobiographical. His volumes of verse are *Jason and Medea* (1973) and *Poems* (1978). His scholarly works are *The Complete Works of the Gawain Poet* (1965) and *The Life and Times of Chaucer* (1977), and his children's books include *Dragon, Dragon* (1975) and *A Child's Bestiary* (1977).

Garfield, James A[bram] (1831–1881),   soldier, congressman, 20th president of the United States. Born in Orange, Ohio, Garfield worked his way through Western Reserve Eclectic Institute in Hiram, Ohio, and was graduated from Williams College. He became president of Western Reserve at the age of twenty-six, took part in the Civil War, rose to be a major-general, and then, after being chosen as a dark horse candidate, was elected president in 1880. A disappointed seeker of federal office shot him on July 2, 1881, and Garfield died a few months later in a private cottage at Elberon, New Jersey. His writings were collected in *The Works of James A. Garfield* (2 v. 1882–83). The career of the hero of Albion W. Tourgée's *Figs and Thistles* (1879) is based on that of Garfield.

Garis, Howard R[oger] (1873–1962),   newspaperman, children's book writer. Born in Binghamton, New York, Garis joined the staff of the Newark (New Jersey) *Evening News* in 1896 and continued with it for the rest of his career. Some of his stories about a lovable rabbit named Uncle Wiggily were first written (1910) for the *News*, and Garis used for them the term "bedtime stories," apparently the first time the term was employed. He wrote for this series steadily, and the tales were widely syndicated. Some appeared in book collections, amounting in the course of the years to more than thirty-five volumes. All told, there are perhaps twelve thousand Uncle Wiggily stories. In addition Garis wrote the *Curlytop Series* (10 v.), the *Daddy Series* (10 v.), and the *Teddy Series* (7 v.) as well as many others. Altogether Garis published more than three hundred volumes.

Garland, [Hannibal] Hamlin (1860–1940),   short-story writer, novelist. Born in western Wisconsin, Garland moved with his family to Iowa in 1869. When they moved to a homestead in the Dakota territory in 1881, he worked in Illinois and Wisconsin before he homesteaded in what is now South Dakota in 1883. These experiences formed the basis for his harsh, realistic fiction and memorable autobiographies and family histories. A graduate of the Cedar Valley Seminary in

Osage, Iowa, in 1884 he went east and taught at the Boston School of Oratory. After a visit home in 1887, and influenced by the social doctrines of HENRY GEORGE and the realism of WILLIAM DEAN HOWELLS, he began to write the six stories collected as MAIN-TRAVELLED ROADS (1891; five more were added in later editions). In these Garland gave memorable expression to a personal anger derived from observation of the hardships of farm life on the Middle Border. Other stories written in this period, first published as *Prairie Folks* (1892) and *Wayside Courtships* (1897), were later collected as *Other Main-Travelled Roads* (1910). Taken together, the *Main-Travelled Roads* stories, thirty in all, constitute his most enduring fiction. In his only serious critical work, *Crumbling Idols* (1894), he expressed his theory of veritism, a kind of Howellsian realism, built on careful observation and detailed representation, but differing from Howells in emphasizing the value of passionate attachment to local verities, the truths that give each region its distinction.

Frequently, his novels suffer from the burden of political messages attached to them. In *Jason Edwards: An Average Man* (1892) he attempted to explain the benefits of Henry George's single tax. In *A Spoil of Office* (1892) he dealt with the Populist movement. In *A Member of the Third House* (1892) he explored the legislative power of the railroads. More successful as fiction are *A Little Norsk* (1892), a story of the bleak farm life of an orphaned Norwegian girl, and ROSE OF DUTCHER'S COOLLY (1895), telling of a Wisconsin farm girl's struggle to gain a college education and become a writer in Chicago. For the next dozen years, Garland turned from realism and social comment to write mostly popular novels of Indians and the West, achieving his first significant financial success with *The Captain of the Gray Horse Troop* (1902). This was followed by *Hesper* (1903), about labor problems among miners; *Money Magic* (1907), about a gambler; *Cavanaugh, Forest Ranger* (1910), about western cattlemen; and *The Forester's Daughter* (1914), set in Colorado.

Some of his best works were fully or partly autobiographical. *Boy Life on the Prairie* (1899, revised 1908) foreshadowed four later works, of which the first two are most interesting: A SON OF THE MIDDLE BORDER (1917), A DAUGHTER OF THE MIDDLE BORDER (1921), *Trail-Makers of the Middle Border* (1926), and *Back-Trailers from the Middle Border* (1928). Another kind of interest sustains *The Book of the American Indian* (1923), containing tales and legends. Later books include literary reminiscences—*Roadside Meetings* (1930), *Companions on the Trail* (1931), *My Friendly Contemporaries* (1932), and *Afternoon Neighbors* (1934)—and two works on spiritualism, *Forty Years of Psychic Research* (1936) and *The Mystery of the Buried Crosses* (1939). Studies include Jean Holloway, *Hamlin Garland: A Biography* (1960) and Joseph B. McCollough, *Hamlin Garland* (1978).

Garneau, François-Xavier (1809–1866), historian, poet. Garneau was born in Montreal, where he worked as a notary and accountant. In 1828, he made a brief trip to the United States. The periodical *Le Canadien* published his first poem in 1831, and in the same year he traveled to Europe. Two years in England and France and acquaintance with their institutions and historians inspired his monumental history of Canada. After his return to Canada in 1833, he continued his literary activities, contributing poetry to various magazines and founding two periodicals. The first volume of *Histoire du Canada* appeared in 1845 (v. 2, 1846; v. 3, 1848; v. 4, 1852); it was later translated into English by A. Bell. *Voyage en Angleterre et en France* (1855) recounts his trip abroad.

Garner, Hugh (1913–1979), novelist, journalist. Born in Yorkshire and raised from age six in Toronto, Garner led an itinerant life in Canada and the United States during the Depression and served in the Abraham Lincoln Brigade in the Spanish Civil War and in the Canadian navy during World War II. In *The Storm Below* (1949), a novel, he portrays six days at sea in 1943. *Cabbagetown*, a novel set in the 1930s in the slum area of his boyhood was published next in an abbreviated version (1950); in its complete text (1968) it was praised as one of Canada's major social novels. A later novel, *The Intruders* (1976), shows the same area in the throes of gentrification. His other novels include *The Silence on the Shore* (1962), set in a Toronto rooming house; *A Nice Place to Visit* (1970), about a crime in a small town; and three police novels about Inspector Walter McDumont: *The Sin Sniper* (1970), *Death in Don Mills* (1975), and *Murder Has Your Number* (1978). His short fiction was collected in *Hugh Garner's Best Stories* (1963). *One Damn Thing After Another* (1974) is an autobiography.

Garrard, Lewis II. (1829–1887), explorer, travel writer. Garrard was born in Cincinnati. When he was still in his teens he went with a trade caravan to Bent's Fort on the Arkansas River and observed keenly the manners, language, and characters of the traders, trappers, Native Americans, and settlers with whom he came in contact. He recorded his experiences in *Wah-to-yah and the Taos Trail* (1850).

Garreau, Louis-Armand (1817–1865), novelist. Born in New Orleans, Garreau is remembered chiefly for *Louisiana: Épisode emprunté à la Domination Française en Amérique* (1862). This is a tale of the anti-Spanish conspiracy of 1768, a favorite theme of Creole authors; it drew upon some of the historical narratives of Garreau's predecessor, CHARLES ÉTIENNE ARTHUR GAYARRÉ.

Garrett, George [Palmer, Jr.] (1929–   ), novelist, short-story writer, poet, editor. Born in Florida, Garrett took his B.A. at Princeton, served in the army (1953–55), and returned to Princeton for his M.A. He has taught at various places, including Wesleyan University, Hollins College, the University of South Carolina, and the University of Virginia. Three historical novels set in Renaissance England have earned him praise as one of the few contemporary masters of the genre. *Death of the Fox* (1971) centers on the last days of Sir Walter Raleigh. *The Succession: A Novel of Elizabeth and James* (1983) centers on the dying Elizabeth and her cousin, godson, and successor, James VI of Scotland. *Entered from the Sun* (1990) depicts the life of Christopher Marlowe. His other novels include *The Finished Man* (1959), about modern Florida politics; *Which Ones Are the Enemy?* (1961), set in Trieste under American occupation after World War II; and *Do, Lord, Remember Me* (1965), concerning the visit of an evangelist to a Southern town. *The Old Army Game* containing a novel and stories appeared in 1994. *The King of Babylon Shall Not Come Against You* (1996) is a novel. His short stories are collected in *King of the Mountain* (1958), *In the Briar Patch* (1961), *Cold Ground Was My Bed Last Night* (1964), *A Wreath for Garibaldi* (1969), *The Magic Striptease* (1973) and *An Evening Performance* (1985). Garrett has also written screenplays and several volumes of verse, including *Collected Poems* (1984) and *Days in Our Lives Lie in Fragments: New and Old Poems 1957–1997* (1998).

Garrigue, Jean (1914–1972),   poet. Born in Indiana, Garrigue was educated at the University of Chicago and taught at the University of Iowa, Bard College, and Queens College. Her first work appeared in collection in *Five Young American Poets* (1944) and was followed by *The Ego and the Centaur* (1947), *The Monument Rose* (1953), *A Water Walk by the Villa D'Este* (1959), *Country Without Maps* (1964), *New and Selected Poems* (1967), and *Studies for an Actress* (1973). Her poems combine lyric celebration of nature with a delicate self-scrutiny. Richard Eberhart spoke of the "cool, free play and deep sincerity" of her verse, and other critics have praised her poetry for its inventiveness and vitality of language, richness of detail, and intricate and personal music. *The Animal Hotel* (1966) is a novel.

Garrison, William Lloyd (1805–1879),   cobbler, carpenter, printer, editor, poet, abolitionist. Born in Newburyport, Massachusetts, and brought up in poverty and privation, Garrison became, as V. L. Parrington called him, "the flintiest character amongst the New England militants." When he had found what he believed to be the truth or when he saw an evil that should be corrected, he spoke with a courage that seemed to others foolhardiness and that made him one of the most hated and also one of the most respected men of his time. Slavery in particular aroused his bitter hatred, and on January 1, 1831, he published the first issue of a little weekly newspaper, THE LIBERATOR, the salutatory of which contains these defiant words: "I will be heard!" Immediately underneath the title of the weekly appears: "Our country is the world—our countrymen are all mankind." The violent sentiments he expressed led to equally violent attacks on him; in 1835 a mob dragged him through the streets of Boston with a rope around his body.

He organized an Anti-Slavery Society, the first of its kind, and gradually gained the attention of a brilliant group of orators and writers. In 1865, the 13th Amendment to the Constitution, abolishing slavery, became law and *The Liberator* ceased publication that year. During the last years of his life Garrison supported women's suffrage, temperance, and world peace.

His works include *Thoughts on African Colonization* (1832). Henry Mayer wrote a solid biography, *All on Fire: William Lloyd Garrison and the Abolition of American Slavery* (1998).

Gaspé, Philippe Aubert de (1786–1871),   novelist. Gaspé served as high sheriff of the district of Quebec for many years, until business difficulties and debts impelled him to withdraw from public life. At age seventy-six he published *Les Anciens Canadiens* (*The Canadians of Old,* 1863), a historical romance ranking among the best French-Canadian works of the period. His *Mémoires* (1866) is a collection of notes and hints for historians.

Gass, William H[oward] (1924–   ),   novelist, critic. Gass, the son of an alcoholic mother and an invalid father, was born in North Dakota. Early in the son's childhood, the entire family moved to Ohio. Gass attended Kenyon College and, briefly, Ohio Wesleyan before serving in the Navy during World War II. He returned to Kenyon to complete his undergraduate studies and went on to do graduate work at Cornell. In 1969, after teaching briefly at the College of Wooster and for a longer time at Purdue, he became professor of English and philosophy at Washington University, in St. Louis.

Gass writes prose that with few exceptions blurs the conventional boundaries of fiction, autobiographical meditation, essay, and philosophical treatise. He is singularly interested in the explosive and sensual possibilities of language play. To date, Gass has contributed a series of controversial, fascinating, and idiosyncratic works to contemporary American letters. The magazine *Accent* was the first to recognize his talent. The bulk of its Winter 1958 issue was devoted to his work. Wider acclaim came in 1966 with the publication of *Omensetter's Luck*, a novel rejected by many publishers before the New American Library brought it out and so established Gass as a major voice. *Omensetter's Luck* is a novel of several voices and perspectives, and Gass gives his love of language free rein. It was followed by a similarly varied and audacious collection of stories, *In the Heart of the Heart of the Country* (1968), and by *Willie Master's Lonesome Wife* (1971), a novella/essay on an erotic theme that mixes photography, prose, and typographical eccentricity on pages of various colors and textures. *The Tunnel* (1994) received a PEN/Faulkner and an American Book Award.

Nowhere does Gass allow his readers to forget that fiction is a supremely artificial medium, though one that can provoke real pleasure, and the erotics of the imagination at play with language are the principal subject of four major works of criticism: *Fiction and the Figures of Life* (1970); *On Being Blue* (1976), a rhapsodic meditation on everything blue from blue movies to the Platonic ideal of blueness; *The World Within the Word* (1978), which includes the quintessential statement of his aesthetic in the essay "The Ontology of the Sentence, Or How to Make a World of Words"; and, most recently, *Habitations of the Word* (1985). *The First Winter of My Married Life* (1979) and *Culp* (1985) are story collections. *Cartesian Sonata* (1998) is a gathering of four novellas. Criticism includes Arthur Saltzman's *The Fiction of William Gass: The Consolation of Language* (1986).

MARK A. R. FACKNITZ

Gassner, John W[aldhorn] (1903–1967),   editor, lecturer, writer on drama. Born in Hungary, Gassner came to the United States in 1911 and became a citizen in 1929. He was active in the theater, edited several anthologies of plays—among them, *A Treasury of the Theater* (4 v. 1935–1951), *Best*

Plays of the Modern American Theater (1939), *Best American Plays* (5 v. 1939–1958) with *Supplement* (1961)—some collections of best film plays, and a *Library of Drama and Music*, which began publication in 1945. He wrote a learned and useful survey of dramatic literature, *Masters of the Drama* (1940); and his *Theater in Our Times* (1954) covers modern drama to the post–World War II theater in France. With Edward Quinn, he edited the *Reader's Encyclopedia of World Drama* (1969).

Gastonia strike.   Gastonia, a city in North Carolina, is a center of textile manufacturing. In 1929 it was the scene of an unsuccessful strike that culminated in violence. The incident shocked the conscience of the country, and on it were based two novels, Mary Heaton Vorse's *Strike!* (1930) and Grace Lumpkin's *To Make My Bread* (1932).

Gates, Eleanor (1875–1951),   novelist, playwright. Gates was born in Shakopee, Minnesota. Among her writings are *The Biography of a Prairie Girl* (1902); *The Poor Little Rich Girl* (first a novel, then a play, 1913); *We Are Seven* (produced, 1913); and *The Rich Little Poor Boy* (1921).

Gates, Henry Louis, Jr. (1950–   ),   critic and scholar. Born in Keyser, West Virginia, Gates was educated at Yale and Cambridge. He has taught at Cornell, Duke, and Harvard universities. Gate's editing of several significant African-American texts, especially the thirty volumes from the Schomburg collection, *The Oxford-Schomburg Library of Nineteenth-Century Black Women Writers* (1988), has kept them available for scholarly use. Important works of criticism include *The Signifying Monkey: Towards a Theory of Afro-American Criticism* (1988), *Loose Canons: Notes on the Culture Wars* (1992), and *Thirteen Ways of Looking at a Black Man* (1997). *Colored People* (1994) is a memoir of growing up as his hometown was becoming integrated. He is editor, with Nellie McKay and others, of *The Norton Anthology of African American Literature* (1997). *Wonders of the African World* (1999) and *Africana* (1999), edited with Kwame Anthony Appiah, are reference books on the history and geography of the African continent and its influences on world culture.

Gates, Horatio (1727?–1806),   soldier. Born in England, Gates served in the British army under Braddock, returned to England, and then at Washington's urging came to America to live. During the Revolution he fought on the American side, received a high command, and was given credit for repulsing Burgoyne at Saratoga (1777). Out of the reputation thus won rose the Conway Cabal—an attempt to replace Washington with Gates. This failed, and when Gates was disastrously defeated in the Battle of Camden (1780), he was retired in disgrace. In 1782 he was ordered back into service under Washington, whom he served loyally to the end of the war. Gates appears often in historical novels laid in the Revolutionary period. Examples include J. P. Kennedy's HORSE-SHOE ROBINSON (1835), William Gilmore Simms's *The Partisan* (1835) and *Eutaw* (1856), and Kenneth Roberts's *Rabble in Arms* (1933).

Gates, Lewis E[dwards] (1860–1924),   teacher, critic. Gates was celebrated as a teacher at Harvard. Among his students was Frank Norris, who wrote portions of MCTEAGUE

(1899) while he was a student of Gates. Gates's lectures and essays were collected in *Three Studies in Literature* (1899) and *Studies and Appreciations* (1900). He made it his role to reconcile NATURALISM with academic criticism and to define the significance of IMPRESSIONISM; he also stressed the importance of scholarship in criticism.

Gates Ajar, The (1868),   a novel by ELIZABETH STUART PHELPS WARD. There were three sequels: *Beyond the Gates* (1883), *The Gates Between* (1887), and *Within the Gates* (1901). The first of these novels was written with the purpose of consoling those who had lost relatives or friends in the Civil War. It centers around a young woman who had lost her brother. She is at first inconsolable, but her aunt brings her at last to a belief in the immortality of the soul. The other stories follow a similar pattern. *The Gates Ajar* was the best seller of its day.

Gatsby, Jay.   See THE GREAT GATSBY.

gaucho literature.   Literature concerned with gauchos—cowboys of the South American pampas. Like the literature of the American West, the life depicted is free-ranging, sometimes outlaw. Often the gaucho emerges as a romantic symbol of an uncomplicated life now gone or passing. In other works the treatment is realistic; far from admiring the gaucho, some writers employ him as an exemplar of the national ills of Argentina and Uruguay, for example, DOMINGO FAUSTINO SARMIENTO in his FACUNDO (1845). Among other early writers to depict the gaucho in fiction was Eduardo Gutiérrez (1853–1890), whose *Juan Moreira* (1880) was dramatized (1884) and helped make the gaucho a familiar character on stage, notably in the plays of FLORENCIO SÁNCHEZ. Later gaucho novels include *Soledad* (1894) by Eduardo Acevedo Díaz; *Gaucha* (1899) by Javier de Viana (1872–1926); *Romance de un gaucho* (1930) by Benito Lynch (1885?–1951); and DON SEGUNDO SOMBRA (1926), perhaps the best of all, by RICARDO GÜIRALDES.

Gaucho folklore and folksong have had a strong influence on poetry. One of the early works in verse was *Santos Vega* (1851, 1872) by Hilario Ascasubi (1807–1875); the title character and narrator is legendary among *payadors* (gaucho minstrels). In *Fausto* (1866) by Estanislao del Campo (1834–1880), a gaucho narrates in his own vernacular his impressions of a performance of *Faust*. The masterpiece of narrative poetry in this genre is MARTÍN FIERRO (1872), by JOSÉ HERNÁNDEZ.

Gauvreau, Émile [Henry] (1891–1956),   newspaperman, editor, columnist. Born in Connecticut, Gauvreau won a national reputation through his pioneer work with tabloid newspapers. He was the editor and publisher of the New York *Evening Graphic* (1924–29), then became managing editor of the New York *Daily and Sunday Mirror* (1929–35). Later he became a news columnist and edited a rotogravure section for the Philadelphia *Inquirer* and *Click*, a picture monthly. His most important book is his autobiography, *My Last Million Readers* (1941), an account of his experiences with noted men and with the newspaper reading public. Among his other books are *Hot News* (1931); *The Scandal Monger* (1932); and a book on Russia, *What So Proudly We Hailed* (1935).

Gayarré, Charles Étienne Arthur (1805–1895), lawyer, public official, historian, novelist, playwright. Born near New Orleans, Gayarré held several public offices and was elected to the United States Senate (1835). Always deeply interested in the history of his native state, he translated an English work on the subject into a French abridgement (1830), some years later wrote *Histoire de la Louisiana* (2 v. 1846, 1847), and then his most important work, a four-volume *History of Louisiana* (1851–66), which began with a separate work, *Romance of the History of Louisiana* (1848). In this Gayarré wrote under the influence of Sir Walter Scott, and the complete work is soundly historical. He was also active in writing imaginative works: *The School for Politics* (1854); *Fernando de Lemos—Truth and Fiction* (1872), which was in part autobiographical; a sequel called *Aubert Dubayet* (1882); and a play, *Dr. Bluff in Russia* (1865).

Gayler, Charles (1820–1892), newspaperman, dramatist. Born in New York City, Gayler worked for newspapers in Cincinnati and New York City, but from the time when he studied law as a young man he was interested in the stage; his first play, *The Heir of Glen Avon*, was produced in 1839. From then until 1888 he continued to write for the stage, producing numerous hits. Disappointed with the responses of critics, he produced *The Magic Marriage* (1861) under a different name, won unanimous praise in the press, and then revealed his authorship. Both his industry and his speed were immense. Bull Run was fought on July 21, 1861; on August 15 Gayler's *Bull Run* was on the stage of the New Bowery Theater. His *Hatteras Inlet, or Our Naval Victories* was produced in the same year, three months after the event. Others of his better known plays are *The Buckeye Gold Hunters* (1849), *Out of the Streets* (1868), *Fritz: Our Cousin-German* (1870), and *Lights and Shadows of New York* (1888).

Gazette of the United States. A New York weekly founded in 1789 by John Fenno (1751–1798) and financed by ALEXANDER HAMILTON as an organ of the Federalists. To combat this paper "of pure Toryism, disseminating the doctrines of monarchy, aristocracy, and the exclusion of the people," as Jefferson expressed it, Philip Freneau, who at that time was editor of *The Daily Advertiser* in New York, was asked to set up a competing periodical, the NATIONAL GAZETTE (1791), to "go through the states and furnish a Whig vehicle of intelligence." The two papers engaged in lively battles, printing virulent news stories, editorials, poems, and skits, some of them directed against the highest figures in the new republic. In the Federalist *Gazette* appeared *Discourses on Davila* (1790), by John Adams. In 1973 the paper became a daily. After Fenno's death his son became editor. In 1804 the name was changed to *United States Gazette*; later it merged with other papers and survived until 1847.

Geddes, Virgil (1897–?), dramatist, poet. Born in Nebraska, Geddes aroused interest and controversy with two of his plays, laid in the Midwest, *The Earth Between* (1929) and *Native Ground* (1932). He also has written *The Frog* (1927)

and later produced *Pocahontas and the Elders* (1933) and *Four Comedies from the Life of George Emery Blum* (1934). His two best-known plays deal with the theme of incest. In 1941 Geddes was appointed postmaster in Brookfield, Connecticut. He told of his experiences in *Country Postmaster* (1952).

Geisel, Theodor Seuss. See DR. SEUSS.

Geismar, Maxwell [David] (1909–1979), short-story writer, critic, teacher. Born in New York City, Geismar became the author of a distinguished series on the American novel after 1890: *Writers in Crisis: The American Novel, 1925–1940* (1942); *The Last of the Provincials: The American Novel, 1915–1925* (1947); *Rebels and Ancestors: The American Novel, 1890–1915* (1953); and *American Moderns: From Rebellion to Conformity* (1958).

Gelber, Jack (1932–), playwright. Born in Chicago, Gelber was educated at the University of Illinois. His play *The Connection* (1959) received high praise and gave great impetus to the development of significant Off Broadway theater in the 1960s and after. An innovative production, it employs improvisational techniques, jazz, and other devices to destroy the distance that traditionally separates audience and players as a few heroin addicts await the connection that will supply their need. Gelber also wrote the screenplay for the film version (1962). In later plays, less acclaimed, he has experimented further with relationships between actors and audience. These include *The Apple* (1961), *Square in the Eye* (1965), *The Cuban Thing* (1968), *Sleep* (1972), and *Rehearsal* (1976). A novel is *On Ice* (1964).

Gellhorn, Martha (1906–1998), journalist, novelist. As a war correspondent for *Collier's* from 1938 to 1945 Gellhorn experienced some of the most exciting and horrifying events of the time. She reported on the Spanish Civil War in 1937–38, Russia's attack on Finland in 1939, Japan's attack on China in 1940–41, and the European war from England, Italy, France, and Germany until 1945. She met ERNEST HEMINGWAY during the Spanish Civil War, was married to him in 1940, and divorced in 1945. She is said to be the original of the woman in Hemingway's play THE FIFTH COLUMN. FOR WHOM THE BELL TOLLS was dedicated to her. Gellhorn's fiction derives mostly from actual events she reported on and has been praised for its immediacy and journalistic excellence. *The Trouble I've Seen* (1936) is the fictionalized result of a report for Harry Hopkins's Federal Emergency Relief agency on the living conditions of people on welfare in industrial areas. Her articles as war correspondent are collected in *The Face of War* (1959). Some other books are *The Honeyed Peace* (1954); *Two by Two* (1958), stories about marriage; *His Own Man* (1961), a novel; *Pretty Tales for Tired People* (1965); *The Lowest Trees Have Tops* (1969), a Mexican novel; *The Weather in Africa* (1988); and *Travels with Myself and Another* (1979), an autobiography. *The Novellas of Martha Gellhorn* appeared in 1993.

General History of Virginia, New England, and the Summer Isles, The (1624), the most important of several reports and tracts by JOHN SMITH.

General Magazine and Historical Chronicle, for all the British Plantations in America, The (January–June

1741). This magazine, issued by BENJAMIN FRANKLIN, just missed being the first magazine published in the English colonies. John Webbe, whom Franklin had engaged as editor, left him for a rival publisher, Andrew Bradford, who anticipated Franklin by three days with *The American Magazine.* The latter was published, however, for only three months. Franklin's magazine closely imitated English models and was largely devoted to discussion of foreign affairs.

General William Booth Enters into Heaven (1913), a poem by VACHEL LINDSAY. This poem was the first of Lindsay's to attract wide attention. It was written in 1912, following the death of the leader of the Salvation Army, and was published in the next year in the magazine *Poetry* and in a collection of Lindsay's poems. The poem successfully catches the rhythm of Salvation Army chants, and it goes well with an accompaniment of banjos and tambourines. Lindsay himself often recited the poem effectively. Many of the lines are skillful examples of onomatopoeia.

"Genius," The (1915), a novel by THEODORE DREISER. The hero is a Midwestern artist, Eugene Witla, who becomes the art director of a large magazine corporation, has numerous love affairs, attains financial and social success, and marries Angela, who dies in childbirth. Witla suffers a breakdown, but recovers his health and devotes himself thereafter to painting and caring for his daughter. According to Helen Dreiser, in her book *My Life with Dreiser* (1951), Witla is a composite of the artist Everett Shinn, an art editor Dreiser knew, and Dreiser himself.

Genteel Tradition at Bay, The (1931), an essay by GEORGE SANTAYANA. The term "genteel tradition" was applied at the close of the 19th century to a group of American writers who had set up a standard—literary, social, and moral—that emphasized correctness and conventionality. These writers avoided reporting the American scene with any degree of realism. Santayana defined this tradition as a "New England disease," which sought austerity and rigid mental discipline and was opposed to pagan conceptions that tended to release the emotions. Santayana also attacked the New Humanism of IRVING BABBITT and PAUL ELMER MORE because of their desire to reinstate a "settled belief" in a supernatural human soul and in a precise divine revelation. (See HUMANISM.) Santayana argued rather in favor of a rational and uninhibited quest for truth. He continued his attack on New England ideals in his novel THE LAST PURITAN (1935).

Gentle Boy, The (1837, in TWICE-TOLD TALES, *First Series*), a story by Nathaniel Hawthorne. Hawthorne imagines what would happen if a young Quaker child had been left helpless among the Puritans. Every man is against him, his timid kindness is rewarded with treachery, and he dies inevitably. The five-year-old Ilbrahim is made an instance of innocence suffering in a world of evil.

Gentleman from Indiana, The (1899), a novel by BOOTH TARKINGTON. In this first novel, Tarkington anticipated the muckraking school of a few years later. He tells the story of John Harkless, a promising young college graduate who buys and edits a newspaper in a small Hoosier town. Harkless discovers many things that are wrong, especially in local politics, and he attacks with particular vigor a gang of "White Caps." They assault him, and his disappearance leads to the belief that he has been murdered. The girl he has fallen in love with takes over his paper and carries it on with equal vigor. Young John returns, secures a nomination to the House of Representatives, and is elected. He sees his enemies punished and the community purified.

Gentleman Johnny. See SIR JOHN BURGOYNE.

Gentleman's Agreement (1947), a novel by LAURA HOBSON. Phil Green, a member of the editorial staff of *Smith's Weekly*, is assigned to write a series of articles about anti-Semitism in America. He decides to pose as a Jew for six months, and he has some extraordinary experiences. The novel was made into a successful movie (1946).

Gentlemen Prefer Blondes (1925), a novel by ANITA LOOS. This story of Lorelei Lee, good-looking but empty-headed, is subtitled "The Illuminating Diary of a Professional Lady." The author had been working in Hollywood, where she discovered models for Lorelei and Lorelei's Mr. Gus Eisman, the Button King. In 1926 a successful stage version was produced, in 1928 a movie, in 1949 a musical comedy. Loos wrote a less successful follow-up, *But Gentlemen Marry Brunettes* (1926), which also became a film (1955).

Gentle People, The (1939), a comedy by IRWIN SHAW. This play is subtitled "A Brooklyn Fable." It tells how two harmless middle-aged men, who have bought a boat to take them to the Gulf of Mexico for some fishing, are molested by a gangster. They lure him into their boat, row out to Sheepshead Bay and drown him, then continue with their trip. The play was intended as a parable showing what to do about fascists, a burning problem in the year of its production.

George, Elizabeth (1949–), crime novelist. Born in Warren, Ohio, George was educated at the University of California, Riverside and California State University. Her novels, largely set in England, are so accurate in their detail that many readers have assumed she is British. George maintains a London apartment and visits to research each location in preparation for writing, but continues to live and write in the United States. *A Great Deliverance* (1988) introduced her odd-couple pair of detectives—Thomas Lynley, the eighth Lord Asherton, and his working-class assistant, Detective Sergeant Barbara Havers—investigating a wealthy man's beheading. Forensic pathologist Simon St. James, a friend who was crippled in an accident when Lynley was driving, assists in this and later cases. *Payment in Blood* (1989) has a playwright pierced through the neck by a dagger; *Well-Schooled in Murder* (1990) opens with the nude body of a schoolboy found in a churchyard. Similar mayhem occurs in *A Suitable Vengeance* (1991), *For the Sake of Elena* (1992), *Missing Joseph* (1993), *Playing for the Ashes* (1994), *In the Presence of the Enemy* (1996), and *Deception of His Mind* (1997). A case of double murder on the moors of Derbyshire is the subject of *In Pursuit of a Proper Sinner* (1999). Shakespearean quotations and themes are often present in the George books, reflecting the writer's lifelong interest in the playwright.

George, Henry (1839–1897),   editor, lecturer, econo-mist. Born in Philadelphia, George spent a year at sea when he was sixteen, then entered a printing office to learn typesetting, and acquired the rudiments of printing and publishing, with which he was associated in one way or another for the rest of his life. He left the printing office after nine months and again went to sea, this time en route for California, where he spent more than five years in and out of work and in poverty. In October 1868, the *Overland Monthly* printed the first of his articles, which anticipated his later thesis. Written just before completion of the transcontinental railroad, "What the Rail-road Will Bring Us" argued that increased population and business would bring greater wealth for a few and greater poverty for many. George traveled to New York and was again struck that the most cosmopolitan and civilized of American cities should present a "shocking contrast between monstrous wealth and debasing want."

Upon his return to California he became editor of the *Oakland Transcript*, a newly established democratic paper. During this time he came to the conclusion that land increases in value as the population grows, and the men who work the land are obliged to pay more for the privilege. This was the germ of PROGRESS AND POVERTY (1879), in which George argued that every man has a right to work the land and enjoy the products of his labor, but when land is in private ownership he must pay a rent and thus loses some of his labor. Since the increased value of the land in populated communities is due less to the owner of the land than to the community as a whole, the land-lord is robbing both the worker and the community by exact-ing rent. To combat this, George proposed a single tax on the land, to give back to the community the part of the land's value the community had created. This tax—on the land and on nothing else—would relieve industry and labor from taxes, since it would be sufficient for the functioning of the state. Although initially published at George's expense, *Progress and Poverty* went through over a hundred editions and reached a wide circulation. Its indictment of ownership by absentee landlords, monopolies, and land speculation was echoed by thousands of workers, farmers, and tenants, as well as by writ-ers. HAMLIN GARLAND and WILLIAM DEAN HOWELLS, among oth-ers, were greatly influenced by George's ideas.

After publication of *Progress and Poverty* George moved to New York, where he wrote *The Irish Land Question* (1881). He wrote a series of articles for *Frank Leslie's Illustrated Newspaper* later published as *Social Problems* (1883), and made two tours to Great Britain. In 1886, he was an unsuccessful candidate for mayor of New York City, and was called a dangerous fanatic by Tammany Hall because of his social-welfare campaign. In 1897 he again ran for mayor, in spite of ill health, but died shortly before the election. His other works include *Protection and Free Trade* (1886) and *The Science of Political Economy* (1897). His ideas have been kept alive by Henry George Schools of social science in New York City and elsewhere, and by the Robert Schalkenbach Foundation. Among his noted converts were Tolstoy, Sun Yat-sen, and Ramsay MacDonald. As late as 1947 a party calling itself the Georgeists won several

seats in the Danish parliament. His son Henry (1862–1916) wrote his biography, *The Life of Henry George* (1900), and Anna George de Mille, daughter of the younger George, wrote *Henry George, Citizen of the World* (1950).

George's Mother (1896),   a novel by STEPHEN CRANE. It is a tale of George Kelsey, who is his mother's ideal, but she is deluded. (It is significant that Crane at first called this novel "A Woman Without Weapons.") Her whole life sacrificed to his well-being, she anticipates that her son will become "a white and looming king among men." She worships him with the intensity of a sweetheart and, with the blind devotion of a reli-gious fanatic, dies still believing in him.

The New York *World* complained that this tale of eastside life in New York City can hardly be called a novel, for it is barely a novelette and there is no plot and no action. Howells praised Crane's social realism: the pathos of the underprivi-leged "rendered without one maudlin touch."

George Washington Slept Here (1940),   a farce by GEORGE S. KAUFMAN and MOSS HART. The authors satirize the city dweller's urge to buy and completely renovate a house in the country.

Georgia Scenes, Characters, Incidents, &c., in the First Half Century of the Republic (1835),   eighteen humorous sketches by AUGUSTUS BALDWIN LONGSTREET. The sketches appeared originally in the *Southern Recorder* (of Milledgeville, Georgia) and the *Augusta State Rights Sentinel* in 1827. In book form they attained great popularity and went through many editions. Longstreet was an admirer of Addi-son, and some of his pieces follow that writer's style. In others he becomes a pioneer regionalist, reproducing the folkways and the language of Georgia and the Southeast in early days with faithfulness and humor.

German American dialect.   Since the German word for "German" is *Deutsch*, it was easy for Americans to speak of Germans as "Dutch." The first center of German dialect in the United States was Pennsylvania, and both the descendants of Germans in that state and their special form of speech are still called Pennsylvania Dutch.

The dialect received its first literary recognition when Charles Godfrey Leland in 1856 contributed the first of his *Hans Breitmann Ballads* (see under BREITMANN) to *Graham's Magazine*. He was imitated by CHARLES FOLLEN ADAMS in a *Lee-dle Yawcob Strauss* series (1877–1910). In 1913 Kurt M. Stein began contributing verses in a modified German-American dialect to Bert Leston Taylor's column in the Chicago *Tribune*. In 1925 appeared the collection *Die Schoenste Lengevitch*, fol-lowed by *Gemixte Pickles* (1927) and *Limburger Lyrics* (1932).

German influence in America.   German migration to North America began in the late 17th century with the arrival in Pennsylvania of Mennonite colonists, the forerun-ners of many groups of German Protestants—Amish, Dunkards, Moravians, and Schwenkfelders—who came to the New World during the next 150 years. New waves of immi-grants, many of them political refugees, continued to arrive during the 19th and 20th centuries, including among them many prominent artists, writers, scholars, and scientists. Eventually, the German element in the American population became second in size only to the British, and many sections of the country, for example, parts of Pennsylvania, Milwaukee, St. Louis, and others, retain a distinctly German character. The influence of German culture on American thought and institutions has been exerted through these immigrants, through American travelers in Germany, and of course also through the introduction and translation of much German literature in the United States. The chief influences have been those of the German idealists and romanticists of the late 18th and early 19th centuries, notably the influence of Kant on American TRANSCENDENTALISM and that of Goethe and his successors on a series of American writers, including Irving, Hawthorne, Poe, Longfellow, and Whitman. In the early 19th century, German, especially Prussian, theories of education began to exert a profound influence on American education, both in public schools and in universities. Indeed, the concept of American graduate education is German in origin. In the 20th century, German EXPRESSIONISM found admirers among American writers and artists, particularly American Abstract Expressionists.

Gernsback, Hugo (1884–1967),   publisher, editor, author. Born in Luxembourg, Gernsback founded America's first science-fiction magazine, *Amazing Stories*, in 1926. In his earlier *Modern Electrics* he serialized in 1911 his *Ralph 124C 41 + : A Romance of the Year 2660*, a tale of technological predictions. In honor of his pioneering efforts in the field, the awards for achievement in science fiction given annually since 1953 by the World Science Fiction Convention are called Hugos.

Geronimo (c. 1829–1909),   APACHE chieftain. Born in Arizona, Geronimo was a Chiricahua Apache who accompanied Cochise on forays against the U.S. army. After the Chiricahua Reservation was abolished (1876), Geronimo led his followers to Mexico. Captured and returned to a reservation in New Mexico, he escaped again in 1881 and led raids in Arizona and Mexico until his capture in 1883 by forces under General George Crook (1829–1890). Returned to the reservation, he left again in 1885 and finally surrendered in 1886 to Crook's successor, General Nelson A. Miles (1839–1925). Imprisoned first in Florida, then in Alabama, he was sent in time to Fort Sill, Oklahoma, where he became a farmer and member of the Dutch Reformed Church. His appearance at the St. Louis World's Fair and in Theodore Roosevelt's inaugural procession confirmed his status as a national celebrity. *Geronimo's Story of His Life* (1906) is an autobiography dictated to Stephen M. Barrett. ANGIE DEBO wrote *Geronimo: The Man, His Time, His Place* (1976). Jason Betzinez, an Apache, dictated an autobiography, *I Fought with Geronimo* to Wilbur S. Nye, printed in 1959.

Geronimo Rex (1972),   a novel by BARRY HANNAH.

Gerontion,   a poem by T. S. ELIOT, first collected in his *Poems* (1920). The title is derived from the Greek *geron* (an old man). A meditation of an old man uncertain of spiritual rebirth, it presents "thoughts of a dry brain in a dry season," it was considered by Eliot at one time as a prelude to THE WASTE LAND.

Gerould, Gordon Hall (1877–1953),   scholar, novelist. Born in New Hampshire, Gerould taught English at Princeton (1905–46). His scholarly works include *The Ballad of Tradition* (1932). Among his novels are *Peter Saunders, Retired* (1917); *Youth in Harley* (1920), set in Vermont; and *A Midsummer Mystery* (1925). He was married to KATHERINE FULLER GEROULD.

Gerould, Katherine Fuller (1879–1944),   novelist, short-story writer. Born in Brockton, Massachusetts, she taught English at Bryn Mawr, married GORDON HALL GEROULD, and earned a reputation as a writer of fiction modeled on the work of Henry James and Edith Wharton, in which desire for personal freedom conflicts with societal expectations. In the title story of *Vain Oblations and Other Stories* (1914), a New England woman captured by African savages decides that she prefers to remain with them. In *The Great Tradition* (1915), stories of family problems include one about a woman who sacrifices her happiness for her daughter, another about an artist who comes into money and leaves his family. Another collection is *Valiant Dust* (1922). Her novels are *A Change of Air* (1917); *Lost Valley* (1922); *Conquistador* (1923), set in Mexico during the revolutionary times of Pancho Villa; and *The Light That Never Was* (1931). Her essays are collected in *Modes and Morals* (1919) and *Ringside Seats* (1937).

Gershwin, George (1898–1937),   composer. Born in Brooklyn, Gershwin sold his first song at eighteen; two years later he wrote the classic song "Swanee" for Al Jolson, and the score for a complete musical comedy, *La, La, Lucille*. Beginning in 1920 he composed the music for five successive *George White Scandals* and in the same period wrote many popular songs, including "Somebody Loves Me" (1924). Part of one performance of the 1923 *Scandals* was a one-act opera, *135th Street*, later performed independently at Carnegie Hall. It was serious in tone, even though it employed the idiom of jazz; as a result, Paul Whiteman commissioned Gershwin to write the enduring *Rhapsody in Blue* (1923). Gershwin went on to other great successes, including music for *An American in Paris* (1928), *Strike Up the Band* (1930), OF THEE I SING (1931), and *Let 'Em Eat Cake* (1933). Finally came his masterpiece, *Porgy and Bess* (1935), a folk opera based on the book by DUBOSE HEYWARD, with lyrics by Heyward and by IRA GERSHWIN. (See PORGY.) Gershwin's *Jazz Piano Preludes* was composed in 1936.

Gershwin, Ira (1896–1983),   lyricist. Born in New York City, Ira Gershwin wrote the words for his brother George's earliest compositions and continued to write lyrics after George's death in 1937. A book of his personal experiences, *Lyrics on Several Occasions*, came out in 1959. Among the Broadway shows for which he wrote the lyrics are *Lady Be Good* (1924); *Oh, Kay!* (1926); *Funny Face* (1927); *Strike Up the Band* (1930); OF THEE I SING (1931); *Let 'Em Eat Cake* (1933); *Porgy and Bess* (1935), with DUBOSE HEYWARD; *Lady in the Dark* (1941); *An American in Paris* (a movie, 1951, with music by GEORGE GERSHWIN); and *A Star Is Born* and *The Country Girl* (both movies, 1954).

Gerstäcker, Friedrich (1816–1872),   German traveler, writer. Gerstäcker traveled widely, visiting the United

States in 1837. He also visited South America, California (in 1849), the Sandwich Islands, Mexico, Central America, and the West Indies, and wrote of his travels when he returned to his native Germany. His translations include *The Wanderings and Fortunes of Some German Immigrants* (1848), *The Daughter of the Riccarees* (1851), *Narrative of a Journey Round the World* (1853), *The Regulators of Arkansas* (1857), and *The Young Gold-Digger* (1860).

Gertrude of Wyoming (1809),   a narrative poem by Thomas Campbell. The British poet (1777–1844) was one of the earliest European writers to take an American setting for a work of imagination. In skillful but uninspired Spenserian stanzas, he described the devastation wrought by an Indian attack in 1778 on the quiet valley of Wyoming in Pennsylvania, and on the marriage of Henry Waldegrave and Gertrude, daughter of the patriarch Albert.

Get-Rich-Quick Wallingford (1908),   a group of related stories by GEORGE RANDOLPH CHESTER. Wallingford, whose name has become part of American folklore, is a company promoter. With his satellite Blackie Daw, he engages in many dubious enterprises and manages to escape the hand of the law. Chester continued his adventures in several other books: *Young Wallingford* (1910), *Wallingford and Blackie Daw* (1913), and *Wallingford in His Prime* (1913). GEORGE M. COHAN made a successful dramatization of the stories (1910), which concluded piously with Wallingford saying: "What a fool a man is to be a crook!"

Gettysburg, Battle of,   and the **Gettysburg Address,** an address delivered at the dedication of a national cemetery on November 19, 1863, by Abraham Lincoln. Only four months before Lincoln's "few remarks," Robert E. Lee with the full Army of Northern Virginia, 70,000 men, invaded Pennsylvania with the aim of winning a decisive battle on northern soil that would lead to Southern independence. He joined in battle the Army of the Potomac, led by General George Meade, in command only three days, on July 1 at Gettysburg, about 10 miles north of the Maryland line. A titanic three-day battle cost 6000 deaths and upwards of 40,000 wounded and was climaxed by perhaps the last Napoleonic charge in the history of warfare, led by George Pickett with 12,000 men. The charge, sometimes called "the high water mark of the Confederacy," was repulsed, ending the battle. To Lincoln's disappointment, Meade was hesitant in pursuit of the retreating Lee, who led his army safely back to Virginia. The Union dead were buried on Cemetery Hill, where Lincoln spoke after a two-hour address by EDWARD EVERETT. Lee's defeat at Gettysburg, coming on the same day Ulysses Grant took Vicksburg, a thousand miles to the southwest, cutting the Confederacy in two, spelled the end of the South's realistic chances for world recognition as an independent country, ensured the preservation of the union, and guaranteed the final abolition of slavery. These prospects notwithstanding, the war was to continue for nearly another two years.

Five versions of the Gettysburg Address exist. Lincoln wrote one in the White House, revised it en route or in Gettysburg, and delivered a still somewhat different version. Another version was written at Everett's request, and was sold in a fair held for the benefit of Union survivors. Two more versions were written by Lincoln for a similar occasion. C. B. Strozier, in *Lincoln's Quest for Union* (1982), notes that Lincoln during the war moved steadily to take away powers of the states and to build a nation. He reached a climax in the Gettysburg Address, a speech about a nation, spoken to a nation, not to a league of states.

The battle immediately inspired Northern verses: Bayard Taylor's "Gettysburg Ode," Clarence Stedman's "Gettysburg," and Bret Harte's "John Burns at Gettysburg." The battle is also treated in many novels, including Michael Shaara's *The Killer Angels* (1974), which depicts the battle as experienced by key officers of both armies. Historical literature on the battle is vast. A good account is Edwin B. Coddington, *The Gettysburg Campaign, a Study in Command* (1963). A brief, accurate summary is given by Bruce Catton in *Gettysburg, the Final Fury* (1974).

Giants in the Earth: A Saga of the Prairie   (published in Norwegian, 1924–25; in English, 1927), a novel by OLE E. RÖLVAAG. In this powerful depiction of the life of an immigrant family on the plains of South Dakota, Rölvaag tells how Per Hansa, whose early days were spent on the sea, brings his family in 1873 to a farm far from any neighbors, and becomes passionately devoted to the land. But his wife continues to long for the civilized comforts of Norway and is reconciled only when a minister visits them and gives her the comforts of religion; in fact, she becomes a religious fanatic. When a friend lies dying, she insists that her husband go out and bring back a minister; he leaves in a blizzard and never returns. The narrative describes endless struggles with harsh nature in a new land. The English version was made by the author in collaboration with Lincoln Colcord; a stage version of the book by Thomas Job appeared in 1928. Rölvaag wrote two sequels: PEDER VICTORIOUS (1927) and THEIR FATHER'S GOD (1931).

Gibbons, James Cardinal (1834–1921),   religious leader, author, memoirist. Ordained a priest in 1861, Gibbons rose steadily until he was made a cardinal in 1886. He helped established the Catholic University of Washington. Among his writings are *The Faith of Our Fathers* (1877), *Our Christian Heritage* (1889), and *A Retrospect of 50 Years* (2 v. 1916).

Gibbs, Emily.   Young heroine of OUR TOWN, play by Thornton Wilder. She dies in childbirth and returns as a grieving spirit to her New Hampshire village. What she sees and learns there in a poignant realization of life reconciles her to her eternal future.

Gibbs, Josiah Willard (1839–1903),   physicist, philosopher. Born in New Haven, Connecticut, Gibbs was educated at Yale and became a professor there (1871–1903), winning fame especially for his work on thermodynamics. Albert Einstein called him "the greatest mind in American history." His most important work was *On the Equilibrium of Heterogeneous Substances*. This was first published in installments in the *Transactions of the Connecticut Academy* (October 1875, May 1876, May 1877), then in the *American Journal of*

Science (December 1878). P.S. Epstein, in *A Commentary on the Scientific Writings of J. Willard Gibbs* (1936), wrote: "We see here a phenomenon almost unparalleled in the history of science. A young investigator, having discovered an entirely new branch of science, gave in a single contribution an exhaustive treatment of it which foreshadowed the development of theoretical chemistry for a quarter of a century." Among Gibbs's other writings are *Elementary Principles in Statistical Mechanics* (1902); *Scientific Papers* (collected in 1906); and *Collected Works*, edited by W. R. Longley and R. G. Van Name (2 v. 1928). In *Willard Gibbs* (1942) Muriel Rukeyser explores some of the philosophical and mystical implications of Gibbs's ideas.

Gibbs, Wolcott (1902–1958), critic, short-story writer, parodist. Born in New York City, Gibbs was closely associated with THE NEW YORKER throughout his professional career, as editor, reporter, fiction writer, and drama critic. Gibbs did much to shape *The New Yorker's* early iconoclastic attitudes. He wrote *Bed of Neuroses* (1937), part of which was republished in *More in Sorrow* (1958), his last book. His one play, *Season in the Sun* (1950), was moderately successful, and one of its leading characters was modeled on Harold Ross of *The New Yorker*.

Gibson, Charles Dana (1867–1944), illustrator, author. Born in Roxbury, Massachusetts, Gibson won success in his teens and held it to the end of his life. The greater part of his career was spent working for *Life*. He illustrated many books and articles, notably the stories of RICHARD HARDING DAVIS, but his greatest triumph was the creation (1896) of the "Gibson Girl," who appeared in innumerable drawings. (His model was his wife, the former Irene Langhorne.) She was beautiful, dignified, and fashionable—the last because everybody from the "400" to the shopgirl immediately began imitating her looks, clothes, and manners. Gibson published collections of his drawings and his travel observations, among them, *Drawings* (1894), *Pictures of People* (1896), *Sketches and Cartoons* (1898), *The Education of Mr. Pipp* (1899), *Sketches in Egypt* (1899), *The Americans* (1900), *A Widow and Her Friends* (1901), *Social Ladder* (1902), and *Our Neighbors* (1905).

Gibson, William (1914–), author, playwright. Born in New York City, Gibson attended the City College of New York. He wrote for years with little success prior to his comedy *Two for the Seesaw* (1959). A bright success on Broadway, it tells the story of a Bronx gamine, with ulcers and heavy emotional problems, who is involved with a Midwestern lawyer. *Dinny and the Witches*, a fantasy, was produced Off Broadway in 1959. *The Miracle Worker* became a great success in 1960, after its adaptation from the original television play. It is the story of HELEN KELLER as a child, and of the heroic efforts of her tutor, Anne Sullivan, to break through the seemingly insurmountable barrier of Helen's deafness and blindness and communicate to her the basic concepts of learning. *Monday, After the Miracle* (1982), shows the characters twenty years later. His other plays are *Golda* (1977), about Golda Meir; a musical version of *Golden Boy* (1965), by Clifford Odets; and *Raggedy Ann* with music by Joe Raposo (1984). *The Seesaw Log* (1959) records the adventures and misadventures of *Two for*

the Seesaw on the road. *A Mass for the Dead* (1968) is a book of memoirs.

Gideons, Society of the. See BIBLE IN THE U.S.

gift books. See ANNUALS and LADY'S BOOKS.

Gift of the Magi, The (1906), a story by O. HENRY. Containing the best of O. Henry's trick endings, this Christmas narrative tells how an impoverished young husband and wife try to buy one another suitable Christmas presents. He sells his watch to buy her a set of combs; she has her beautiful hair cut off and sells it to buy him a watch-fob. The tale is included in THE FOUR MILLION.

Giguère, Roland (1929–), poet, printer, publisher. Born in Montreal, Giguère studied printing there and in Paris. With Editions Erta, which he founded in Montreal in 1949, he became a publisher of books of poems and artwork by Québécois artists. From the beginning he has been devoted to SURREALISM, counting on the intuitive, elemental, and erotic to provide an imaginative power to art and rebellion in Quebec's struggle toward independent intellectual and social identity. During visits to France in the late 1950s and early 1960s he was especially influenced by the work of André Breton. His collected volumes of verse include *L'âge de la parole: poèmes 1949–1960* (1965); *La main au feu, 1949–1968* (1973); and *Forêt vierge folle* (1978), a major collection. *Temps et lieux* (1988) presents both poetry and art. A collection in translation is *Mirror and Letters to an Escapee* (1977), by Sheila Fischman. Giguère's work as a printer has been widely exhibited, and drawings appear in *A l'orée de l'oeil* (1981). *Les sorciers de l'île d'Orleans* appeared in 1985.

Gilbert, Humphrey (1539?–1583), English navigator and soldier. The half-brother of Sir WALTER RALEIGH, Gilbert served in various European military expeditions and finally set out on an expedition to settle colonists in the New World (1578–79). The attempt failed. In a second try (1583) he established the first British colony in North America at St. John's, Newfoundland. His voyage was described in Edward Haies's contemporary narrative, *Sir Humphrey Gilbert and His Enterprise of Colonization in America* (printed, 1903). Longfellow wrote the ballad "Sir Humphrey Gilbert."

Gilbert, Sandra M[ortola] (1936–), critic, poet. Born in New York City, she was educated at Cornell, New York University, and Columbia. Author of critical studies of Shakespeare, Forster, Lawrence, Yeats, and Woolf, Gilbert is best known for feminist work done in collaboration with Susan Gubar (1944– : *Madwoman in the Attic* (1979), an influential study of 19th-century woman writers; *Shakespeare's Sister* (1979); *Norton Anthology of Literature by Women* (1985); *No Man's Land*, analyzing 20th-century authors; and *Masterpiece Theater: An Academic Melodrama* (1995). Her poetry collections are *In the Fourth World* (1978), *The Summer Kitchen* (1983), *Emily's Bread* (1984), and *Blood Pressure* (1988). *Wrongful Death* (1995) concerns the death of her husband Elliot.

Gilchrist, Ellen (1935–), novelist, short-story writer, poet. Born in Mississippi, she was educated at Vanderbilt and Millsaps College and has attended the University of

Arkansas. She has worked as a journalist and a broadcaster for National Public Radio. Her accomplished short stories commonly use little narrative comment but depend on dialogue to present the scene. Many are set in New Orleans or small towns in the states bordering the Mississippi River. *In the Land of Dreamy Dreams* (1981) was her first collection, followed by *Victory Over Japan* (1984), which won a National Book Award, *Drunk with Love* (1986), *Light Can Be Both Wave and Particle* (1989), *The Age of Miracles* (1995), *Rhoda: A Life in Stories* (1995), *The Courts of Love* (1996), *Flights of Angels* (1998), *Cabal* (2000), and *Collected Stories* (2000). *The Land Surveyor's Daughter* (1979) is a poetry collection. Her novels are *The Annunciation* (1984), *The Anna Papers* (1989), *Net of Jewels* (1992), and *Sarah Conley* (1997). Three novellas are collected in *I Cannot Get You Close Enough* (1990). *Falling Through Space* (1988) is a collection of journal entries.

Gilded Age, The (1873), a novel by MARK TWAIN and CHARLES DUDLEY WARNER. The plot is a sensational affair, involving seduction, murder, political corruption, the destruction of a steamboat by fire, wild financial speculation, and more. The book's mixture of satire, romance, and exposure became a success, perhaps chiefly owing to the central character, Colonel Beriah Sellers (see under COLONEL SELLERS, who strongly recalls Dickens's Micawber in his optimistic schemes for getting rich and his invariable failures. Sellers persuades his friend Squire "Si" Hawkins to join him in the development of some lands in Missouri; the project ends in a fiasco. The squire's adopted daughter Laura is seduced by Colonel Selby; later, in Washington, she murders him, is tried, and acquitted. One or two incidental love affairs develop more happily but might just as well have been omitted. Much of the tale is based on reminiscence; Colonel Sellers is Twain's kinsman James Lampton, and Laura Hawkins was suggested by Mrs. Laura Fair of California, who had recently been acquitted of murder on the ground of emotional insanity. Senator Dilworthy, a corrupt politician, was modeled on Senator Pomeroy of Kansas; William M. Weed and his associates closely resemble the Tweed Ring of New York. In the dramatic version of the novel (1874) Seller's first name was changed to Mulberry, and that name was also employed in THE AMERICAN CLAIMANT (1892), a sequel to the novel. The term "Gilded Age" has become a common description of the hectic post–Civil War period of which Twain and Warner wrote; and the novel itself was a forerunner of many similar attacks on political corruption and financial juggling.

Gilder, Richard Watson (1844–1909), newspaper and magazine editor, poet. Born in New Jersey, Gilder headed an important literary circle in the final decades of the 19th century—first in Newark, later in New York City. He served as a newspaper editor in Newark, later conducting SCRIBNER'S MONTHLY (1870–81), and *The Century Magazine* (1881–1909). He wrote poetry, including *The New Day* (1876) and *Five Books of Songs* (1900); his *Letters* appeared in 1916. His sister, Jeanette Gilder (1849–1916), helped make the news of authors a literary commodity and wrote entertainingly about her encounters with writers in *The Autobiography of a Tomboy* (1900) and *The*

Tomboy at Work (1904). She and her brother Joseph founded and edited *The Critic* (1881–1906), and they collaborated on *Essays from "The Critic"* (1883) and *Authors at Home* (1888).

Gildersleeve, Basil L[anneau] (1831–1924), teacher, classicist, editor. Born in Charleston, Gildersleeve became an authority on Greek and Latin, as in his *Essays and Studies* (1890) and *Hellas and Hesperia* (1909), but also a writer of vigor on *The Creed of the Old South, 1865–1915* (1915). He founded and edited the *American Journal of Philology* (1876–1915).

Giles Corey. See COREY, GILES.

Giles Goat-Boy (1966), a novel by JOHN BARTH.

Gillette, William [Hooker] (1855–1937), actor, playwright. Born in Hartford, Connecticut, Gillette became a popular actor, especially in his own plays. The best of them was his four-act dramatization of Arthur Conan Doyle's famous stories, under the title *Sherlock Holmes* (1899). Almost equally popular were *Esmeralda* (1881), based on a novel by FRANCES HODGSON BURNETT; and HELD BY THE ENEMY (1886) and *Secret Service* (1895), both about the Civil War. He also played many Shakespearean roles.

Gilligan, Edmund (1899–1973), novelist. Gilligan was born in Waltham, Massachusetts. Many of his novels of the sea were depictions of Gloucester fishermen in which realistic details gave plausibility to romantic plots. Among them are *White Sails Crowding* (1939), *The Gaunt Woman* (1943), *Voyage of the Golden Hind* (1945), *I Name Thee Mara* (1946), *Storm at Sable Island* (1948), and *My Earth, My Sea* (1959).

Gillilan, Strickland (1869–1954), newspaperman, editor, comic writer. Although Gillilan wrote much else, he is remembered mainly for a poem about an Irish railroad foreman who had been told to "make it brief" when reporting wrecks. The telegram the foreman sent on one occasion was turned into a poem by Gillilan. Its refrain is, "Off agin, on agin, gone agin, FINNIGIN." This became the leading poem of Gillilan's collection *Including Finnigin* (1910). In 1940 he calculated that he had recited the poem more than 11,000 times. In 1894 Gillilan published in the Baltimore *American* another widely quoted poem. It is called *Microbes* and reads: "Madam,/Adam/Had 'em." Gillilan collected his writings in *You and Me* (1917), *A Sample Case of Humor* (1918), *Laugh It Off* (1924), and *Gillilan, Finnigin, & Co.* (1940).

Gilliss, Walter (1855–1925), printer, poet, memoirist. Born in Lexington, Kentucky, Gilliss founded the Gilliss Press in New York City in 1871, and it became noted for the beauty and excellence of its volumes. He wrote *A Printer's Sun Dial* (1913), *Verses and Songs* (1916), and *Recollections of the Gilliss Press* (1926).

Gilman, Arthur (1837–1909), editor, historian. Gilman edited *Chaucer* (3 v. 1879); *Lothrop's Library of Entertaining History* (6 v. 1880–85); *A Library of Religious Poetry* (1887); and other works, including *Boston, Past and Present* (1873). He is chiefly remembered as a champion of higher education for women. He proposed the Harvard Annex (founded 1878), which extended Harvard College instruction to women. When this became Radcliffe College in 1893, he was promoted from executive secretary to regent of the college.

Gilman, Caroline Howard (1794–1888),   poet, editor, memoirist. Born and brought up in Boston, she became the wife of a Unitarian minister in the South and wrote of the life in both regions in *Recollections of a New England Housekeeper* (1834), *The Poetry of Traveling in the United States* (1838), and *Recollections of a Southern Matron* (1838). Her verse was collected in *Tales and Ballads* (1839) and *Verses of a Lifetime* (1849). In 1832 she commenced publication of *The Rose Bud*, a weekly juvenile publication, one of the earliest, if not the first, of its kind in the country.

Gilman, Charlotte Perkins (1860–1935),   novelist, short-story writer, feminist, reformer. She was born Charlotte Anna Perkins in Hartford, Connecticut. Her father, FREDERICK BEECHER PERKINS—the grandson of LYMAN BEECHER and the nephew of HENRY WARD BEECHER and HARRIET BEECHER STOWE—deserted his family shortly after her birth. During her lonely childhood, she tried to establish a relationship with him, but he took little interest in his daughter beyond suggesting readings for her. After home tutoring and a brief stint at the Rhode Island School of Design, she took a job designing greeting cards and began to write, publishing a short newspaper article in 1883. Her first poem, beginning "In duty bound, a life hemmed in . . ." was printed in 1884, the same year in which she married Charles Stetson, an artist.

Suffering from postnatal depression, she was treated by DR. S. WEIR MITCHELL, the neurologist, an experience she used in her masterpiece "The Yellow Wallpaper" (written 1890; published in *New England Magazine*, January 1892). He prescribed "as domestic a life as possible" and "never to touch pen, brush or pencil again." To escape this intellectual imprisonment, she and her daughter moved to California in 1887. Her divorce and her relinquishing of child custody to her ex-husband and his second wife generated unfavorable publicity.

From 1889 to 1891, she edited the *Pacific Monthly* in Los Angeles, and during the 1890s she toured the nation lecturing on women's rights. With *Women and Economics* (1898) she became celebrated for her conclusion that women's economic dependence on men stunts the growth of all of humanity. In later works such as *Concerning Children* (1900) and *The Home* (1904), she advocated for changes in the family and domestic work to free women for a more productive life. *Man-Made World* (1911) and *His Religion and Hers* (1923) predicted that a larger role for women in international life and theology would lead to fewer wars and a more positive public policy.

In 1900 she married her first cousin, George Houghton Gilman, who shared many of her progressive attitudes. The Gilmans lived happily in New York and Connecticut; writing under the name Charlotte Perkins Gilman, she continued her feminist work. From 1909 to 1916 she published and edited *The Forerunner*, a monthly magazine. When George Gilman died suddenly in 1934, she went to live with her daughter in Pasadena. Ill with cancer and fearing that her productive life was over, she committed suicide in 1935. *The Living of Char-*

lotte Perkins Gilman, An Autobiography was published in the same year.

Gilman turned to novels late in life. *What Diana Did* (1910) and *The Crux* (1911) were published in *The Forerunner*. Her utopian novels, such as *Moving the Mountain* (1911), *Herland* (1915), and *With Her in Ourland* (1916), dramatize social ills and propose feminist solutions. A selection of writings is *The Charlotte Perkins Gilman Reader*, edited by Ann Lane (1980). Studies include Ann Lane, *The Herland and Beyond: The Life and Work of Charlotte Perkins Gilman* (1990).

Gilmer, Elizabeth Meriwether ["Dorothy Dix"] (1870–1951),   newspaperwoman, columnist. After her marriage Gilmer became a reporter and feature writer on the New Orleans *Picayune*, adopting a pen name which in time became well known throughout the country. Her column "Dorothy Dix Talks" reached perhaps sixty million readers all over the world. Three days a week there was a sermonette, usually sensible advice and exhortation. On the other three days, letters from readers appeared together with comments. She published *How to Win and Hold a Husband* (1939) and other collections. Harnett T. Kane wrote a biography, *Dear Dorothy Dix* (1952).

Gilpatric, Guy (1896–1950),   aviator, advertising copywriter, short-story writer, novelist. Born in New York City, Gilpatrick became a test pilot and flying instructor before World War I and served during the war in the A.E.F. He began to write in 1918, especially stories dealing with a rough-and-ready character, such as "Muster Colin Glencannon," chief engineer of the *S.S. Inchcliffe Castle*. Gilpatric's books include *Scotch and Water* (1931), *Half Seas Over* (1932), *Mr. Glencannon* (1935), *Three Sheets in the Wind* (1936), *The Glencannon Omnibus* (1937), *The Gentleman with the Walrus Mustache* (1938), *Glencannon Afloat* (1941), *Second Glencannon Omnibus* (1942), *Action in the North Atlantic* (1943), *Guy Gilpatric's Flying Stories* (1945), *The Canny Mr. Glencannon* (1947), and *The Last Glencannon Omnibus* (1953).

Gilpin, William (1813?–1894),   soldier, public official. Born in a Quaker family in Pennsylvania, Gilpin nevertheless entered West Point, but left shortly to study law. However, adventure in the West and army life attracted him strongly. He joined Frémont in his Pacific explorations, served in the war with Mexico, made himself thoroughly acquainted with the West. When Lincoln became president, Gilpin was appointed first territorial governor of Colorado, which he helped save for the Union cause. He settled permanently in Denver and began to write books of visionary theory. Within what he called "the Isothermal Zodiac" all great civilizations develop, Gilpin stated. The United States lay within that belt and would in time become the great world example of unity, peace, and prosperity. He urged methods of uniting the nations, for example, intercontinental railroads at the Bering Strait and Gibraltar. These ideas were set forth in *The Central Gold Region* (1860, reissued 1873 as *The Mission of the North American People*) and *The Cosmopolitan Railway Compacting and Fusing Together All the World's Continents* (1890).

Gilroy, Frank D[aniel] (1925–   ),   playwright. Born in the Bronx, Gilroy attended Dartmouth and the Yale School of Drama. He first gained a wide audience with *The Subject Was Roses* (1964), a Pulitzer Prize play about an Irish family in the Bronx. His other plays include *Who'll Save the Playboy?* (1962), *That Summer—That Fall* (1967), *The Only Game in Town* (1968), *The Next Contestant* (1978), *Dreams of Glory* (1979), and *Last Licks* (1979). *Present Tense* (1972) is a dramatization of one of his novels. Several short plays including *Dreams of Glory* (1980), *Real to Reel* (1993) and *Getting In* (1997) were produced at the Off Broadway Ensemble Theater.

Ginger Man, The (1955),   a novel by J. P. DONLEAVY.

Gingrich, Arnold (1903–1976),   advertising copywriter, editor. Gingrich became editor of a trade magazine, *Apparel Arts*, and in 1933 became editor of *Esquire*, which he made into a successful combination of risqué humor and some of the best serious writing done in the United States. From 1952, he was the publisher of *Esquire*. He also edited *Coronet*.

Ginsberg, Allen (1926–1997),   poet. Born in Newark, New Jersey, Ginsberg was educated at Columbia University. Ginsberg decided early on a career as a poet, corresponding with WILLIAM CARLOS WILLIAMS in nearby Rutherford (some of his letters were incorporated into Williams's PATERSON at a time when his ambitions were as yet unrealized). In the late 1940s and early 1950s he also began to associate with JACK KEROUAC and others of the BEAT GENERATION in New York City, accumulating a reputation that made him a character in the literature of others while Ginsberg was still young. He is said to have provided the model for the strangely disconnected student in LIONEL TRILLING's story "Of This Time, of That Place" as well as for characters in JACK KEROUAC's *The Town and the City* (1950) and JOHN CLELLON HOLMES's *Go* (1952). Meanwhile, he worked as a dishwasher, as a welder in the Brooklyn Navy Yard, and served in the Merchant Marine. Ginsberg also reviewed for *Newsweek*. He was hospitalized for a nervous breakdown and experimented with drugs and wrote poems modeled on the works of Blake and Whitman.

Celebrity came with the publication of *Howl and Other Poems* (1956) in the Pocket Poets Series of LAWRENCE FERLINGHETT's City Lights Books. The title poem offended many, and attempts were made to suppress the publication. At the same time the notoriety thrust Ginsberg into the public consciousness with Kerouac and WILLIAM S. BURROUGHS as a leader of the Beats. "Howl" has remained his best-known poem and a central statement of Beat attitudes. The 1956 volume includes three more of Ginsberg's most admired poems—"A Supermarket in California," "Sunflower Sutra," and "America." After 1956, Ginsberg traveled widely, living in the Far East in 1962 and 1963. His verse became more and more a performance poetry with a musical or drumbeat background, its verbal rhythms based not only on the catalogs, repetitions, and parallelism of Whitman, but on various incantatory models such as Indian mantras. He became a public poet, popular at readings, and also a prominent figure in civil rights campaigns, war resistance movements, and antiestablishment rallies. An advocate of alternative lifestyles, he became associated with the rise of interest in America in Zen Buddhism, hallucinatory drugs, and gay liberation.

Among Ginsberg's poems after the early ones, most celebrated has been "Kaddish," a long and touching poem on the death of his mother, Naomi Ginsberg. It was collected in *Kaddish and Other Poems, 1958–1960* (1961). *Collected Poems 1957–1980* (1980) is authoritative to that date. Later volumes are *White Shroud: Poems 1980–1985* (1986), and *Cosmopolitan Greetings* (1994). *Selected Poems 1947–1995* appeared in 1996. *Spontaneous Mind: Selected Interviews, 1958–1996* (2001) was edited by David Carter. Barry Miles wrote *Ginsberg: A Biography* (1989) and Michael Schumaker's *Dharma Lion: A Critical Biography of Allen Ginsberg* appeared in 1992.

Ginsberg, Louis (1896–1976),   poet. Father of ALLEN GINSBERG. A teacher of English in the Paterson (New Jersey) Central High School for many years, Ginsberg contributed verse to magazines and newspapers. His poems were collected in *The Attic of the Past and Other Poems* (1921) and *The Everlasting Minute and Other Poems* (1937).

Giovanni, Nikki (1943–   ),   poet. Born Yolande Cornelia Giovanni, Jr. in Knoxville, she was educated at Fisk University, the University of Pennsylvania, and Columbia University. She became prominent as a spokesperson for African-American militancy with ideas expressed especially in the verse of her early books, all first published by DUDLEY RANDALL's Broadside Press: *Black Feeling, Black Talk* (1968), *Black Judgment* (1968), *Re: Creation* (1970), and *Ego Tripping and Other Poems for Young People* (1974). Later volumes, generally less militant and broader in their concerns for family and living, include *My House* (1972), *The Women and the Men* (1975), *Cotton Candy on a Rainy Day* (1978), and *Those Who Ride the Night Winds* (1983). She has also written a number of books of verse for children. *Gemini: An Extended Autobiographical Statement of My First Twenty-Five Years of Being a Black Poet* appeared in 1971.

Giovanni's Room (1956),   a novel by JAMES BALDWIN.

Giovannitti, Arturo (1884–1959),   teacher, preacher, poet. When Giovannitti came to the United States from his native Italy, he became a crusader for economic and social changes. He worked for a time in religious missions, then as a labor organizer. He participated in strikes, and his experiences in jail during a textile strike in Lawrence, Massachusetts, furnished material for several impressive prose poems. Occasionally he wrote in meter and rhyme. His principal poems were collected in *Arrows in the Gale* (1914). The lynching of labor leader Frank Little inspired the poem "When the Cock Crows" (1917).

Girl I Left Behind Me, The (1893),   a melodrama by DAVID BELASCO and FRANKLIN FYLES. This play is laid in an army post in the Sioux country. An Indian attack is about to succeed, and the commander of the post is about to kill his daughter Kate to save her from the Sioux, when suddenly the clear bugle notes of rescuing cavalry are heard.

Girl of the Golden West, The (1905),   a play by
DAVID BELASCO. "The Girl," heroine of this play, runs a saloon in
a mining camp of the Old West. The sheriff and an outlaw fall
in love with her, and she with the outlaw; she gambles with the
sheriff for the outlaw's life, cheats, and wins. But he is captured
anyway. When the miners realize how deep her love for the
outlaw is, they release him, and the lovers set out for another
part of the country. Giacomo Puccini, the Italian composer
(1858–1924) based *La Fanciulla del West* (1910) on Belasco's
play—the first grand opera written on an American theme.

Girl of the Limberlost, A (1909),   a novel by Gene
Stratton-Porter (see under PORTER). A continuation of Mrs.
Porter's popular novel *Freckles* (1904), it tells of a girl who
hunts moths in Indiana swamplands in order to earn money
for an education.

Girl with the Green Eyes, The (produced, 1902; published, 1905),   a play by CLYDE FITCH. This play is a study of
a pathologically jealous woman. After revelations of several
kinds have convinced her how wrong she has been, she tries to
commit suicide. Fitch manages, however, to give the play a
happy, albeit somewhat artificial ending.

Girty, Simon (1741–1818),   known as the Great Renegade. A Pennsylvanian by birth, Girty deserted from the Continental army in 1778 and fought with Indians and British
against the colonists. He fled to Canada when the British gave
up Detroit in 1796. He has been the subject of several books:
Uriah James Jones's *Simon Girty, the Outlaw* (1846); Charles
McKnight's *Simon Girty, "The White Savage"* (1880); C. W.
Butterfield's *History of the Girtys* (1880); and Thomas Boyd's
Simon Girty (1928).

Gist, Christopher (1706?–1759),   explorer, soldier.
Even earlier than Daniel Boone, Gist had explored regions of
Ohio and Kentucky for the Ohio Company. He was with
George Washington on his trip to Fort Duquesne (1753–54)
and is credited with saving Washington's life. Later he guided
Braddock's expedition (1755). He kept *Journals*, which were
published in 1893.

Give me liberty, or give me death!   Speaking in the
Virginia House of Delegates, March 23, 1775, PATRICK HENRY
made a speech in defiance of the British, concluding with the
words: "I know not what course others may take, but as for me,
give me liberty, or give me death!" This is according to the
report of William Wirt in his *Sketches of the Life and Character
of Patrick Henry* (1817).

Gladiator, The (1831),   a play by ROBERT MONTGOMERY
BIRD. Written in blank verse, this drama furnished a vehicle for
EDWIN FORREST, who appeared in it more than a thousand
times. It was persistently revived till the 1890s. It tells the rousing story of Spartacus, the Thracian slave who led a revolt
against Rome and was killed in battle (71 B.C.). The subject
was remarkably opportune in consideration of the slavery
question. Walt Whitman said it was "as full of 'abolitionism' as
an egg is of meat."

Glancy, Diane (1941–   ),   poet, novelist, short-
story writer. Born in Kansas City, Glancy was educated at the

University of Missouri and Central State University in Oklahoma. Glancy's Native American identification, through her
Cherokee grandmother, has helped define her as a writer.
Known first as a poet with such titles as *Traveling On* (1982),
Brown Wolf Leaves the Res and Other Poems (1984), and *Iron
Woman* (1990), Glancy began to attract more critical attention
with *Firesticks* (1993), a story collection blending poetry and
prose and emphasizing mixed-race characters and their search
for spiritual meaning in contemporary urban settings. *Pushing
the Bear* (1996), her first novel, concerns the 19th-century
forced march of the Cherokee, often called "the Trail of Tears"
because so many died along the way to Oklahoma. *The Only
Piece of Furniture in the House* (1996), *Flutie* (1998), and *The
Fuller Man* (1999) are novels dealing with the spiritual struggles of young women in deprived circumstances. *Claiming
Breath* (1992) and *The Cold and Hunger Dance* (1998) are collections of short, related autobiographical pieces inspired by
her work traveling across Oklahoma as artist-in-residence for
the state Arts Council. Glancy has also taught at Macalester
College in Minnesota. *War Cries* (1997) is a collection of plays
written in the 1980s and 1990s. *The Voice That Was in Travel*
(1999) is a story gathering.

Glasgow, Ellen [Anderson Gholson] (1873–1945),
novelist, short-story writer, memoirist. Glasgow was born in
Virginia and became one of the best regional writers of her
time. She chose to remain within a limited area that she knew
very well—not merely the South but rather the Old Dominion. Born at a time when the harsh conditions of the Reconstruction were at last being accepted grimly by the defeated
South, she saw the defects of the South, but she has a character
in *The Sheltered Life* (1932) say, "It is all nonsense to talk as if
Southerners were a special breed, all wanting the same things
and thinking after the same pattern." There is no doubt about
the total effect of her writings. In the words of Henry Seidel
Canby: "She was a major historian of our times, who, almost
singlehandedly, rescued Southern fiction from the glamorous
sentimentality of the Lost Cause." Alfred Kazin has said Glasgow was born "imprisoned in a social and physical tradition
not of her making, and made her career by satirizing it." In her
own words, however, she merely "tilled the fertile soil of man's
vanity."

After two books set in New York—*The Descendant* (1897)
and *Phases of an Inferior Planet* (1898)—she turned to a series
of novels that amount to a social history of Virginia from the
Civil War to World War I, a record of the passing of economic
and political power from a ruling aristocracy to a rising middle class. These include *The Voice of the People* (1900), *The
Battle-Ground* (1902), *The Deliverance* (1904), *The Romance of
a Plain Man* (1909), *The Miller of Old Church* (1911), *Virginia*
(1913), and *Life and Gabriella* (1916). Fine as this accomplishment was, in a sense it only prepared the ground for works yet
to come. The 1920s and the early 1930s constituted her greatest period, producing such books as BARREN GROUND (1925),
perhaps her best novel; the Queenborough trilogy, set in a fictional Richmond and consisting of THE ROMANTIC COMEDIANS

(1926), *They Stooped to Folly* (1929), and *The Sheltered Life* (1932); and VEIN OF IRON (1935).

For her novel *In This Our Life* (1941) she belatedly won a Pulitzer Prize. She published a collection of stories, *The Shadowy Third and Other Stories* (1923), some of them—like "The Past," a tale of a ghost exorcised—of lasting merit. Her last book was *A Certain Measure: An Interpretation of Prose Fiction* (1943). Her books appeared in two collected editions: the Old Dominion Edition (8 v. 1929–33), revised and with prefaces by Glasgow; and the Virginia Edition (12 v. 1938). Posthumously published were *The Woman Within* (1954), her autobiography; a selection of *Letters of Ellen Glasgow* (1958), edited by Blair Rouse; and *Collected Stories* (1963).

Glaspell, Susan (1876?–1948),   novelist, dramatist, memoirist. Born in Davenport, Iowa, Glaspell worked for Des Moines papers, began writing short stories, and went on to write a novel, *The Glory of the Conquered* (1909). In 1913 she married GEORGE CRAM COOK, a fellow writer, and went to live at Provincetown, CAPE COD. There in 1915 she and her husband organized the PROVINCETOWN PLAYERS, an experimental theater formed to combat Broadway commercialism and to introduce serious new playwrights. In collaboration with her husband she wrote for the first bill a satirical one-act play, SUPPRESSED DESIRES (1915, published 1920), which was produced on a ramshackle wharf. TRIFLES (produced 1916; published 1920), dealing with the death of a man and the arrest of his wife on suspicion, has been, like the earlier play, a continuing favorite with little theaters and amateur groups. The Cooks ardently sponsored these theaters, encouraged young dramatists like EUGENE O'NEILL, and continued to prepare plays strikingly different from the stereotyped material of the time. Glaspell wrote several works of fiction: *The Visioning* (1911), *Lifted Masks* (1912), *Fidelity* (1915), *Brook Evans* (1928), *Judd Rankin's Daughter* (1945), and others. Among her plays are *The People* (1917), *Bernice* (1919), *The Inheritors* (1921), *The Verge* (1921), and ALISON'S HOUSE (1930). The last, a play based on the life of EMILY DICKINSON, was awarded a Pulitzer Prize. Cook, an authority on the Greek drama, emigrated to Greece, lived there for several years, and died there in 1924. *The Road to the Temple* (1926) is Glaspell's biography of her husband. Barbara Ozieblo, *Susan Glaspell* (2001), is a critical biography.

Glass, Hugh (?–1833?),   trapper. On one occasion he was attacked by a grizzly bear, left for dead, but later revived. On this legend John G. Neihardt built his narrative poem, *The Song of Hugh Glass* (1915). F. F. Manfred's novel *Lord Grizzly* (1954) gives a vivid account of this scout and mountain man.

Glass, Montague [Marsden] (1877–1934),   lawyer, short-story writer. A man of many talents, Glass was forced by popular demand to specialize in the humor of New York City's garment manufacturers. So successful were his tales that in 1909 he abandoned his law practice. His collections include POTASH AND PERLMUTTER (1910), *Abe and Mawruss* (1911), *Potash and Perlmutter Settle Things* (1919), *The Truth about Potash and Perlmutter and Five Other Stories* (1924), and other books. Several of the stories found their way to Broadway, in

successful collaboration with CHARLES KLEIN, R. C. Megrue, and other playwrights.

Glassco, John (1909–1981),   poet, novelist, translator. Born and educated in Montreal, Glassco left McGill University before graduating and went to Paris in 1928, an experience he described in *Memoirs of Montparnasse* (1970), considered by some one of the finest Canadian autobiographies. He returned to Quebec in 1935, choosing a rural life, which provided the tone and imagery for much of his poetry in *The Deficit Made Flesh* (1958), *A Point of Sky* (1964), and *Selected Poems* (1971). Using various pseudonyms, he also wrote fiction, notably as Miles Underwood, and under that name wrote *The English Governess* (1960, reprinted as *Harriet Marwood, Governess*, 1976), an attempt to recreate the Victorian novel of masochistic education.

Glass Key, The (1931),   a detective novel by DASHIELL HAMMETT. One of the best-known in the hard-boiled school of detective fiction and Hammett's own favorite among his books. A bootlegging gang is involved in the murder of a public official's son. Ned Beaumont gets himself appointed a special investigator, succeeds in running down the murderer, and takes the girl of the town's political boss away from him.

Glass Menagerie, The (1944),   a play by TENNESSEE WILLIAMS. His first successful play, and one of his best lyric dramas, opened in Chicago in December 1944 and in New York in March 1945. It narrates and dramatizes the memories of Tom Wingfield, using episodic movement, music, and special lighting effects to suggest the quality of memory. The impoverished Wingfields are out of place in the urban tenement life of the Depression. Tom haunts the movie houses to escape that life and scribbles poetry in the warehouse where he works. Amanda, the mother, yearns for the imagined South of her girlhood, with its belles and gentleman callers. The morbidly shy, delicate Laura lives for her collection of fragile glass animals. In the principal action of the play, contrived by Amanda, Tom brings Laura a gentleman caller, an acquaintance from the warehouse. At the climax of his visit, in a moving, candlelit scene, Jim O'Connor awakens Laura's expectations but dashes them when he tells her he is soon to be married. What is a minor incident for Jim is catastrophe for the Wingfields, the end of their hopes. It sends Laura into reclusion and Tom far from home and the problems he cannot solve. The musical and often elegiac language of this play conveys the full pathos of the Wingfields' story.

FRANK MCHUGH

Glencarn, or, The Disappointments of Youth (1810),   a novel by GEORGE WATTERSTON. Watterston was a follower of CHARLES BROCKDEN BROWN in the Gothic tradition. Misfortune follows Glencarn from the time when he is laid as a foundling on someone's doorstep; at the end, however, he is rescued from his various griefs and even discovers his parents.

Glick, Carl (1890–1971),   actor, director, playwright, teacher, author of books on China. Born in Iowa, Glick began an active career in the theater in 1909, especially in the community theaters of Waterloo, Iowa; San Pedro and San Antonio, Texas; York, Pennsylvania; Columbia, South Carolina; and Schenectady, New York. Among his plays are *It Isn't Done* (1928), *The Devil's Host* (1934), and *The Laughing Buddha* (1937). Among his books on Chinese subjects are *Shake Hands with the Dragon* (1941), *Three Times I Bow* (1943), *The Secret of Serenity* (1951), and *Death Sits In* (1954). His autobiography is *I'm a Busybody* (1949). Glick wrote numerous children's books and edited *A Treasury of Masonic Thought* (1953).

Glidden, Frederick D[illey].   See LUKE SHORT.

Glimpses of Unfamiliar Japan (1894),   by LAFCADIO HEARN. Hearn arrived in Japan in 1890, obtained a position as a teacher in a small town still ruled by feudal customs, and with the help of interpreters and his keen sympathy obtained an intelligent view of Japanese life and character. His observations during two years appear in this book.

Globalization of American Literature.   The late-20th-century infusion of works written by authors born abroad into the mainstream of American literature, a phenomenon magnified by the simultaneous increase in writing by second-generation immigrants. First defined and given wide currency in George and Barbara Perkins's textbook anthology *The American Tradition in Literature* (9th edition, 1998), globalization is represented there by selections from ISABEL ALLENDE, SAUL BELLOW, JOSEPH BRODSKY, JAMAICA KINCAID, DENISE LEVERTOV, CZESLAW MILOSZ, BHARATI MUKHERJEE, VLADIMIR NABOKOV, CHARLES SIMIC, and ISAAC BASHEVIS SINGER. Rapidly gaining force as the century approached its close, by the year 2000 the globalization of American literature was playing a large part in shaping the ways that residents of the United States viewed their lives and their literature, and, in turn, the ways the lives and literature of Americans are viewed abroad.

At the level of highest achievement, the history of the Nobel Prize for Literature bears stark witness to the change. From 1930 to 1962 the list of American winners was short and unequivocal: SINCLAIR LEWIS, EUGENE O'NEILL, PEARL BUCK, T. S. ELIOT, WILLIAM FAULKNER, ERNEST HEMINGWAY, and JOHN STEINBECK were all native born. Except for TONI MORRISON, however, the list from 1962 through 2000 contains no native-born Americans. Instead, there are a number who by naturalization, long residence, or significant achievement within the United States can in some sense be designated "American": ALEXANDER SOLZHENITSYN, SAUL BELLOW, ISAAC BASHEVIS SINGER, CZESLAW MILOSZ, JOSEPH BRODSKY, and DEREK WALCOTT. Another indicator of trends comes from the Library of Congress, where two of the six poets laureate of the United States appointed in the 1990s, MARK STRAND and JOSEPH BRODSKY, were born abroad.

For the nearly two centuries between the Declaration of Independence and the Second World War, the central figures of American literature were native born. From WASHINGTON IRVING through COOPER, EMERSON, THOREAU, LONGFELLOW, POE, HAWTHORNE, STOWE, DOUGLASS, MELVILLE, and on to WHITMAN, DICKINSON, TWAIN, and JAMES, and into the twentieth century with DREISER, CATHER, FROST, WHARTON, ELIOT, FITZGERALD, HEMINGWAY, DOS PASSOS, and STEINBECK, the roll call of major authors contains none born abroad. Immigrants made valuable contributions before and during the American Revolution, but afterwards patriotic fervor and enthusiastic encouragement favored the native writer. After the Revolution, the names of immigrant writers appear in histories only in specialized lists of the foreign born, or in very lengthy general listings of American writers that run into the hundreds rather than the dozens of those who have been most read and admired. Only recently has the trickle of non-native writing turned into a stream of accomplishment that is changing the character of the nation's literature.

In the 19th century and the beginning of the 20th, LAFCADIO HEARN, ABRAHAM CAHAN, OLE RÖLVAAG, MARY ANTIN, and other immigrants won attention beside the hordes of the native born, standing as literary exemplars of America's long-standing commitment to immigration and multiculturalism, apart from, rather than central to, the American literary tradition. In recent years, however, the few have turned into the many. "The tired," the "poor" and the "huddled masses yearning to be free" of the lines from EMMA LAZARUS inscribed at the base of the Statue of Liberty have continued to flock to the United States, typically needing a generation or two to become settled, earn livelihoods, educate their children and grandchildren, and produce writers of merit, who then, of course, are native born. Since World War II, however, the ranks of American immigrants have been swelled not only by the tired, poor, and huddled, but also by the energetic, economically stable, and fiercely independent.

The Immigration and Naturalization Act of 1965 proved crucial in opening the doors to new waves of immigrants, especially from Asia (see ASIAN-AMERICAN LITERATURE). As result of more welcoming immigration policies since then, the demographic face of America has changed: in the year 2000 nearly one in ten of the 281 million inhabitants of the United States was born abroad, a number and a percentage unmatched earlier in the nation's history. A surprising number of these new Americans are writers. Many have become writers after their arrival, and many others arrived with literary reputations already established. They have come for a variety of reasons, including exile and estrangement from their homes, desire for political or economic freedom, and recognition that with the spread of English as a world language and the United States remaining as the last global power, the United States stands highest among places on the globe where literary reputations are made, maintained, and solidified.

Many of these new immigrants assert their Americanness directly. Writing in English in Switzerland, long after his abandonment of his native Russia and Russian language, VLADIMIR NABOKOV defined himself as "an American writer who has once been a Russian one." JOSEPH BRODSKY claimed to be "an American long before I arrived on these shores." BHARATI MUKHERJEE posed in a cornfield wrapped in an American flag, asserting the power of the immigrant's claim on the new country: "I am a voluntary immigrant. I became a citizen by choice, not by the simple accident of birth." Like some other immigrants, Mukherjee and ISABEL ALLENDE have attempted to reshape the history of their new country in images drawn from their personal heritages, Mukherjee in *The Holder of the World* (1993), ranging from Puritan New England to Mughal India, and Allende in *Daughter of Fortune* (1999), bringing together Argentina, China, and the California gold rush. Others write of the pervasive influence of American culture. In his stories "A Windmill in the West" and "American Dreams," PETER CAREY demonstrated his fascination with the United States over two decades before he left Australia for New York. CHARLES SIMIC, born in Yugoslavia, raised in Chicago, has noted, "Jazz made me an American and a poet."

In addition to those named above, foreign-born authors who have contributed to the literature of the United States in the 20th century, mostly since World War II, include ANDRÉ ACIMAN, VINCENZO ANCOMA, REINALDO ARENAS, W. H. AUDEN, JACQUES BARZUN, BEI DAO, CARLOS BULOSAN, EILEEN CHANG, LOUIS CHU, JAMES CLAVELL, ANDREI CODRESCU, MARY AND PADRIAC COLUM, ALISTAIR COOKE, BERNARD CORNWELL, QUENTIN CRISP, EDWIDGE DANTICAT, NICHOLAS DELBANCO, ANITA DESAI, JUNOT DIAZ, THOM GUNN, SHIRLEY HAZZARD, JAMES HILTON, ROBERT HUGHES, RUTH PRAWA JHABVALA, HA JIN, YOUNGHILL KANG, THOMAS KENEALLY, RICHARD KIM, HANS KONING, JHUMPA LAHIRI, CHANG-RAE LEE, LI-YOUNG LEE, JAIME MANRIQUE, VED MEHTA, ORLANDO PATTERSON, MANUEL PUIG, JONATHAN RABAN, EDWARD SAID, BIENVENIDO SANTOS, NATALIE ANDERSON SCOTT, ELIZABETH SEWELL, WILFRED SHEED, MANIL SURI, NICCOLÒ TUCCI, LUISA VALENZUELA, PAUL WEST, ELIE WIESEI, P. G. WODEHOUSE, ANZIA YEZIERSKA, and MARGUERITE YOURCENAR.

Children of immigrants have continued to write of the confrontations and acculturation that accompany the immigrant experience, just as in years past, but their works have recently taken on additional meaning within the context of literary globalization. Among the most visible in the 20th century have been: JULIA ALVAREZ, SANDRA CISNEROS, PIETRO DIDONATO, HERBERT GOLD, DAVID HWANG, GARRETT HONGO, GISH JEN, MAXINE HONG KINGSTON, JERRE MANGIONE, JOHN OKADA, WILLIAM SAROYAN, AMY TAN, GAIL TSUKIYAMA, YOSHIKO UCHIDA, and JOHN YAU.

Gloucester, Massachusetts.   A town, founded in 1623 on Cape Ann, was noted for its fishing industry and more recently as a resort. While Gloucester fishermen range up and down the seas from the capes of Greenland to Virginia, they have especially sought the Grand Banks. Several novelists, particularly JAMES B. CONNOLLY and EDMUND GILLIGAN, have written stories about these fishermen. WILLIAM VAUGHN MOODY wrote *Gloucester Moors* (1901), a stirring poem in behalf of the economic underdog. A well-known juvenile story, Kirk Munroe's *Dorymates* (1890), describes the life of Gloucester fishermen. Other books on Gloucester include James Babson's *History of the Town of Gloucester* (1860), C. B. Hawes's *Gloucester: By the Sea* (1923), and James B. Connolly's *The Port of Gloucester* (1940). Probably the greatest of all stories based on Gloucester, however, is Rudyard Kipling's *Captains Courageous* (1897). CHARLES OLSON made Gloucester the setting for *The Maximus Poems* (1983).

Glück, Louise (1943–   ),   poet. Born on Long Island, Glück was educated at Sarah Lawrence College and Columbia University and has taught in writing programs in various colleges. In her verse she has been concerned especially with youthful anxieties, especially those of women, expressed often through references to myth and symbol. Her volumes include *Firstborn* (1968), *The House on the Marshland* (1975), *Descending Figure* (1980), *The Triumph of Achilles* (1985), *Ararat* (1990), *The Wild Iris* (1992), *The First Four Books of Poems* (1995), and *Meadowlands* (1996). *Proofs and Theories: Essays on Poetry* appeared in 1994.

Goddard, Charles William (1880–1951),   newspaperman, playwright, scriptwriter. See PERILS OF PAULINE.

Goddard, Pliny Earle (1869–1928),   ethnologist, authority on Native Americans. Born in Maine, he became curator of the department of ethnology of the American Museum of Natural History in 1909 and continued in that office until his death. He was editor of *The American Anthropologist* (1915–20) and wrote many monographs on tribal life, including *Life and Culture of the Hupa* (1903), *Indians of the Southwest* (1913), and *Indians of the Northwest Coast* (1922).

Godey's Lady's Book.   Louis A. Godey (1804–1878) combined hard business sense with soft sentiment to make his *Lady's Book* the most successful of all American magazines before the mid-19th century; by that time it was bringing delight to 40,000 homes and had made its publisher a millionaire. It was highly regarded for its hand-colored fashion plates and its art reproductions made through the medium of excellent steel and copper engravings. It published leading American authors (at good contributors' rates), such as Poe, Longfellow, Emerson, Hawthorne, W. G. Simms, N. P. Willis, and Harriet Beecher Stowe, as well as endless sentimental stories and verses by popular writers. Godey founded the magazine in Philadelphia in 1830 and was sole editor for its first six years; he brought in SARAH JOSEPHA HALE when he bought her Boston *Ladies' Magazine*. Godey, however, always shared in the editorship of his magazine. In 1877 Mrs. Hale retired, and in the next year Godey died. The magazine soon was outstripped by its Philadelphia rival, *Peterson's Magazine* (1842–1898). It was moved to New York in 1892 and there expired six years later.

Godfrey, Thomas (1736–1763),   poet, playwright. Born in Philadelphia, Godfrey wrote verse published in *The Court of Fancy* (1752), *Victory* (1753), as well as *Ode on Friendship, The Invitation,* and *Ode to Wine* (all 1758). He also wrote a play in blank verse, *The Prince of Parthia*, published two years after his death along with *Juvenile Poems on Various Subjects*; there is no direct evidence that it was actually performed.

Godkin, E[dwin] L[awrence] (1831–1902),   newspaperman, editor, author. Godkin was born in Ireland, but after service on several British newspapers came to the United States in 1856 and became a lawyer here. During the Civil War, he went back to newspaper work as correspondent for the London *Daily News*. In 1865 he became the first editor of THE NATION, of which he was one of the founders, and continued in that post till 1881. In that year the magazine became the weekly edition of the New York *Post*, with Godkin as associate editor of the newspaper; in 1883 he became editor and continued as such till 1900. He then retired to England, where he died two years later. Godkin was noted for keen intellect, liberalism, wide range of information, remarkable powers of expression, and unswerving integrity. He was an unsparing critic of the Gilded Age and established new standards in book reviewing, scorning panegyric. Some of his best writings are collected in *Reflections and Comments, 1865–95* (1895), *Problems of Democracy* (1896), and *Unforeseen Tendencies of Democracy* (1898). He also wrote *The History of Hungary and the Magyars* (1853). Rollo Ogden prepared a *Life and Letters* (2 v. 1907), and Godkin appears prominently in Allan Nevins's *The Evening Post* (1922).

Go Down, Moses, a group of seven interrelated stories by WILLIAM FAULKNER, published in book form in 1942. The title derives from a spiritual in which Moses is enjoined to persuade old Pharaoh to let his people go out from slavery. The book deals primarily with the history of the McCaslin family as representative of the tangled race relations in the South from the early days of the settlers to the present (1940). Two of these stories—"The Fire and the Hearth" and "The Bear"—are actually of novella length, and "The Bear" is the most striking, complex, central, and well-known of the group.

In modernist style, the stories are arranged in the book in achronological order. "Was" takes place in 1859 and relates how Uncle Buck, along with his great nephew Cass (nine years old at the time), goes to Hubert Beauchamp's neighboring plantation to retrieve Tomey's Turl, son of Old Carothers and his slave Eunice, who is in love with the Beauchamps' slave, Tennie. Buck mistakenly falls into Hubert's sister Sophonsiba's bed at night and so he must marry her.

"The Fire and the Hearth," set in 1940, deals primarily with Lucas, a great-grandson of Old Carothers and Eunice and son of Turl and Tennie, and his obsession as an old man with a machine that is said to find gold. He is later a principal character in Faulkner's *Intruder in the Dust* (1948).

"Pantaloon in Black" also takes place in 1940 and is the one story in the group not directly connected to the McCaslin saga. Rider, a giant of a black man, goes wild with grief at the lumbermill where he works over the death of his wife, Mannie. Rider deliberately gets into trouble gambling, kills a white man, and is lynched.

"The Old People" shows Isaac "Ike" McCaslin, son of Buck and Sophonsiba, accomplishing his initiation ritual as a hunter at age 12 (1879) under the tutelage of Sam Fathers, who is of Indian and black parentage.

"The Bear" covers the period 1880–88 and presents Ike as learning the lesson of compassion and brotherhood as a hunter, which motivates him, along with his discovery of the chain of miscegenation set in motion by Old Carothers, to repudiate his inheritance when he comes of age.

"Delta Autumn" returns once again to 1940, as does the next and and final story, and reveals Ike as an old man out of

tune with the times, despite his gesture of acceptance that concludes "The Bear," and refusing to tolerate the idea of interracial marriage.

"Go Down, Moses" shows Molly, wife of Lucas, arranging with lawyer Gavin Stevens for the burial of her grandson Samuel's body. Samuel has been executed for murder.

NORMAN FRIEDMAN

God's Little Acre (1933), a novel by ERSKINE CALDWELL, a depiction of shiftless and amoral Georgia mountaineers. The protagonist has set aside one acre of his land, the income of which is to go to the church, but the acre shifts in location according to his needs at the moment.

God's Protecting Providence (1699), a diary by Jonathan Dickinson, a Quaker merchant who often traveled in the West Indies. This narrative tells how on one trip his ship goes down off the coast of Florida. He, his wife, and their infant child, along with nine sailors, reach the shore, fall among hostile Indians, suffer many hardships, and lose five of the party before they reach St. Augustine—naked, emaciated, half-frozen. The book was reprinted in England and translated into Dutch and German. American printers kept on reissuing it. It was reprinted as *Jonathan Dickinson's Journal* (1945) under the editorship of Evangeline Walker Andrews and Charles McLean Andrews.

God's Trombones: Seven Negro Sermons in Verse (1927), poetry by JAMES WELDON JOHNSON. Johnson took sentiments common to rural black folk sermons and removed the dialect in order to show in rhythmical standard English the power of the ideas and of the African-American preacher's rhetorical devices.

Godwin, Gail (1937–), novelist, short-story writer. Born in Birmingham, Alabama, and raised in Asheville, North Carolina, Godwin was educated at the University of North Carolina, worked at the United States embassy in London (1962–65), and returned for graduate study at the University of Iowa. In novels and short stories, she has explored especially the conflicts faced by women seeking both self-realization and fulfillment in traditional feminine roles. Her novels include *The Perfectionists* (1970), about a marriage between an American woman and British man; *Glass People* (1972), in which a wife leaves her husband, but returns; *The Odd Woman* (1974), about a female scholar; *Violet Clay* (1975), about an illustrator of romance novels; *A Mother and Two Daughters* (1982); *The Finishing School* (1985), in which a young woman learns from an older one; *A Southern Family* (1987), her richest work with a murder and suicide at its center; *Father Melancholy's Daughter* (1991); and *The Good Husband* (1994). Her stories are collected in *Dream Children* (1976) and *Mr. Bedford and the Muses* (1983). *Heart: A Personal Journey through Its Myths and Meanings* (2001) is nonfiction.

Godwin, Parke (1816–1904), newspaperman, editor, biographer. Born in Paterson, New Jersey, Godwin took a position on the New York *Post* with WILLIAM CULLEN BRYANT, later his father-in-law. He was a transcendentalist and a political radical, expressing his views not only in the *Post* but in other media, among them a short-lived journal, *The Pathfinder*, which he founded in 1843, and THE HARBINGER, which he edited briefly. His pamphlet *Democracy, Constructive and Pacific* (1844) was called by Horace Greeley the best of the contemporary studies of collectivism. In that same year he published *A Popular View of the Doctrines of Charles Fourier*. He translated books from the German, including a version of Goethe's autobiography (1846–47). In 1860 he became part owner of the *Evening Post*. In 1878, on Bryant's death, he became editor-in-chief, but in 1881 left the paper to become editor of the *Commercial Advertiser*. He prepared a *Cyclopedia of Biography* (1866), also *A Biography of William Cullen Bryant* (2 v. 1883) and *A New Study of the Sonnets of Shakespeare* (1900).

Goetz, Ruth and Augustus.   See THE HEIRESS.

Goffe, William (1605?–1679?),   English regicide. One of the judges at the trial of Charles I, Goffe fled to New England with his father-in-law, Edward Whalley, when it became certain that Charles II would be restored to the throne. The two men were received in a friendly manner by the officials of Massachusetts and Connecticut, and were concealed from royalist investigators in various homes until their deaths. Goffe, the more prominent of the pair, appears in many stories and novels, among them Cooper's THE WEPT OF WISH-TON-WISH (1829), Delia Bacon's *Tales of The Puritans* (1831), Hawthorne's "The Grey Champion" (1837), and J. K. Paulding's THE PURITAN AND HIS DAUGHTER (1849). He was likewise the subject of a play, SUPERSTITION (1824), by James Nelson Barker. Sir Walter Scott introduced him as a character in *Peveril of the Peak* (1823).

Going After Cacciato (1978),   a novel by TIM O'BRIEN. One of the finest novels of the Vietnam War, *Going After Cacciato* is essentially two stories woven together, united by their presence in Paul Berlin's mind as he stands guard on an observation tower on a November night in 1968. The first story tells of the events Paul witnesses between his arrival in Vietnam in June 1968 and his November night on guard. In the second, he imagines an alternative reality, a pursuit of the deserter Cacciato overland to Paris. Beginning with facts, the surrounding of Cacciato on a hilltop in Vietnam in October, Paul imagines a trip that takes him, significantly, well beyond the present November into the following spring, April in Paris. The first story is jumbled in Paul's mind, as he has difficulty confronting the facts of the past, some of which he cannot at first remember at all. The second forges chronologically ahead as Paul gets closer to constructing a happy ending. As his imagined journey reflects off and illuminates the facts of his past, however, Paul begins to discover lasting truths concerning human limitations, including the limitations of imagination in its power to confront and order the facts of the real world we live in.

Gold, Herbert (1924–   ),   novelist, short-story writer. Born in Cleveland, Gold served in the army, was educated at Columbia University and the Sorbonne (1949–51),

and has taught at a number of universities. His *The Fathers: A Novel in the Form of a Memoir* (1967), rooted in Gold's family life, was praised for its picture of a Russian Jewish immigrant who rises from pushcart vendor to family grocer. Similarly close to the author's experience is *Therefore Be Bold* (1960), about a Jewish adolescence in the Midwest in the 1930s. *Family* (1981) is another novel of immigration experience. His other novels include *Birth of a Hero* (1951), about self-discovery; *The Prospect Before Us* (1954) and *The Great American Jackpot* (1970), treating black-white relations; *The Man Who Was Not With It* (1956), about carnival life and drugs; *The Optimist* (1959); *Salt* (1963), a New York City novel; *Swiftie the Magician* (1974); *Waiting for Cordelia* (1977), set in Berkeley in the 1960s; *He/She* (1980); *True Love* (1982); *Mister White Eyes* (1984), *A Girl of Forty* (1986); *Dreaming* (1988); and *She Took My Arm as If She Loved Me* (1997). His stories are collected in *Love and Like* (1960), *Stories of Misbegotten Love* (1985), and *Lovers and Cohorts* (1986). *The Magic Will* (1971) and *A Walk on the West Side: California on the Brink* (1981) contain stories and essays. *The Age of Happy Problems* (1962) contains essays. *My Last Two Thousand Years* (1972) is autobiographical.

Gold, Michael [pen name of **Irving Granich**] (1894–1967),   novelist, critic, editor. From the time of his editorship of THE MASSES and *The New Masses*, Gold was one of the most important figures in American "proletarian literature." The term had its first clear definition in Gold's article "Towards Proletarian Art" in the *Liberator* magazine (February 1921). His novel *Jews Without Money* (1930) became a model for any aspiring proletarian novelist. This series of sketches based on Gold's impoverished childhood on New York's Lower East Side is intensely emotional, often sentimental. His earlier fiction was collected in *The Damned Agitator and Other Stories* (1926), and some of Gold's articles are collected in *Change the World!* (1937). His plays include *Hoboken Blues* (1928); *Fiesta* (1925), set in Mexico; and *Battle Hymn* (1936), with Michael Blankfort, about John Brown. Among his books are *The Hollow Men* (1941), essays on literature; *The Mike Gold Reader* (1954); and *Mike Gold: A Literary Anthology* (1972). See PROLETARIAN LITERATURE.

Goldbarth, Albert (1948–   ),   poet. Born in Chicago and educated at the University of Illinois and the University of Iowa, Goldbarth has taught at various schools, including the University of Texas and Wichita State University. Wide-ranging and prolific, he is given especially to exploring the borderlines between poetry and prose. His works include the long poem *Opticks* (1974); *Original Light: New and Selected Poems, 1973–1983* (1983); *Arts and Sciences* (1986); *Popular Culture* (1990); *Across the Layers: Poems Old and New* (1945); and *Adventurers in Ancient Egypt: Poems* (1996). *A Sympathy of Souls* (1990) and *Great Topics of the World* (1996) are essay collections.

Gold Bug, The (in *The Dollar Newspaper*, June 21–28, 1843; later in *Tales*, 1845), a story by EDGAR ALLAN POE. This was one of the earliest serious tales to use the search for buried treasure as a theme and to introduce a message in cipher. The scene is Sullivan's Island, near Charleston, South Carolina; the treasure is one left by Captain Kidd; and its discovery, after much difficulty, restores the fortunes of an impoverished Southern gentleman who is the chief character. Suspense is skillfully maintained, and Poe shows dextrously how ratiocination leads to the solution of the problem. Poe was probably partly inspired by Irving's comic *Wolfert Webber*, in which a similar team of a somewhat mysterious wonder-worker, a stolid man, and an old free African-American search for treasure on Manhattan Island.

Golden, Harry [Lewis] (1902–1981),   editor, essayist, biographer. Born of Jewish immigrant parents and brought up on New York's LOWER EAST SIDE, Golden later adopted Charlotte, North Carolina, as his home. These strikingly different environments provide the background for his humorous essays, which appeared in his newspaper *The Carolina Israelite* and were collected in three best-selling volumes: *Only in America* (1958), later adapted for Broadway (1959); *For 2¢ Plain* (1959); and *Enjoy, Enjoy!* (1960).

Golden, John (1874–1955),   actor, playwright, songwriter, producer. Golden's was one of Broadway's most impressive careers. He wrote or had a hand in writing many plays, produced scores of others, wrote hundreds of songs, composed the librettos for at least a dozen musical shows, took a deep interest in encouraging new talent for the theater—especially through the John Golden Foundation, established in 1944—and helped set up the City Center of Music and Drama in New York. Perhaps his greatest producing success was Winchell Smith and Frank Bacon's LIGHTNIN' (1918), which played for 1,291 consecutive performances. His productions displayed his genius for stagecraft. His most popular song was "Poor Butterfly" (1916).

Golden Bowl, The (1904),   a novel by HENRY JAMES. Maggie Verver, daughter of a millionaire, marries an Italian prince who has had a love affair with Maggie's closest friend, Charlotte Stant. Charlotte visits the pair and continues her intimacy. Then she marries Maggie's father. Everybody tries to keep secret from the others that he or she ultimately knows all that has happened or is happening. The complications are solved when Maggie's father goes back to America with Charlotte. James depicts with all the subtlety of his late style the cultural and moral involvements that follow on international marriage and irregular sex relationships.

Golden Boy (1937),   a play by CLIFFORD ODETS. Odets portrays a young Italian-American who should have become a violinist but thinks it will be easier to win fame and fortune in the boxing ring. He has an affair with his manager's mistress, becomes arrogant and conceited, and kills an opponent in the ring. In a wild flight, he and the girl take a furious ride in his new automobile and are killed in a crash. This is the most successful of Odets's works.

Golden Day, The (1926),   a "study in American experience and culture" by LEWIS MUMFORD. Mumford examines New England from 1830 to 1860, with special reference to Emerson, Thoreau, and Hawthorne and with an analysis of

Whitman and Melville. The Civil War brought on what seems to Mumford a crisis in the competition between slave and machine, from which the machine emerged victorious.

Golden Dog, The (unauthorized, 1877; auth. ed., 1896), a novel by WILLIAM KIRBY. This was the first Canadian novel to achieve widespread popularity. The story, set in old French Quebec, served as a model for numerous Canadian historical romances in the 19th century and later.

Golden Era, The (1852–93),   San Francisco journal noted, especially in its early days, for publishing works of Bret Harte, Mark Twain, Joaquin Miller, and other writers of the Far West.

Golden Legend, The (1872),   the second part of a loosely connected trilogy called *Christus: a Mystery*, by HENRY WADSWORTH LONGFELLOW. This poem is essentially the Faust legend in its reflection of the attitudes of the Middle Ages toward Christian truths.

Golden Multitudes: The Story of Best-Sellers in the United States (1947),   a historical study by FRANK LUTHER MOTT. Mott surveys his field with painstaking thoroughness. He deals with religion and sensationalism in the days of the Puritans, books for children, the pensive poets, politics in the Revolutionary era, Shakespeare and the Bible as perennial best sellers, the pirated European novelists and poets, the coming into popularity of American writers from Cooper and Irving on, the cheap "libraries" of 1875–93, the crusaders, the literary fevers of the 1890s, family novels, the amazing popularity of writers like CHARLES M. SHELDON and HAROLD BELL WRIGHT, Westerns, juvenile stories, and war books. He analyzes the secrets of best-sellerdom insofar as they can be discovered. The result is a fascinating history of popular taste and social change.

Goldman, Emma (1869–1940),   anarchist. Born in Russia, Goldman came to the United States in 1886, became known as an agitator, and in 1893 was sentenced to prison for a year. She published *Anarchism and Other Essays* (1910) and *The Social Significance of the Modern Drama* (1914). In 1919 she visited Russia, became disgusted with the Soviet regime, and wrote *My Disillusionment in Russia* (1925) on leaving that country. She published her autobiography, *Living My Life*, in 1931. An important figure in the heyday of American radicalism, Goldman commanded not only the respect but the affection of her fellow workers.

gold rush.   See FORTY-NINERS.

Goldwyn, Samuel (1882–1974),   producer. Goldwyn came from his native Poland to the United States in 1896. An astute judge of what a movie audience would like, he helped found the film company of Metro-Goldwyn-Mayer, and was associated with other Hollywood enterprises. He was influential in bringing eminent writers and actors into the motion picture field. He wrote his memoirs, *Behind the Screen*, in 1923; Alva Johnston wrote an amusing book, *The Great Goldwyn* (1937), about him.

Gollomb, Joseph (1881–1950),   novelist, historian, teacher, writer of boys' books. Born in Russia, Gollomb taught

English in De Witt Clinton High School in New York City and later made this school the scene of several of his stories, where it is called Lincoln High School. The best known of these was *That Year at Lincoln High* (1918). His narratives combine storytelling skill and a sense of social values, shown also in his book *What's Democracy to You?* (1940).

Gompers, Samuel (1850–1924),   labor leader, economist, memoirist. Born in England, Gompers came to the United States in his teens, worked as a cigar maker, rose to leadership in the feeble Cigarmaker's Union, reorganized it, was president of the American Federation of Labor from 1886 to 1924 (except in 1895), and was active in international labor organizations. He wrote *Labor in Europe and America* (1910); *Labor and the Common Welfare* (1919); and an autobiography, *Seventy Years of Life and Labor* (1925).

Gonçalves Dias, António (1823–1864),   Brazilian poet. Born in Maranhao, he studied law, became a teacher, studied education in Europe (1854–1858), and participated in exploring the Amazon (1859–1861). Meanwhile, he had begun his career as a romantic, patriotic poet with *Primeiros Cantos* (1847). His other volumes include a later *Cantos* (1857) and a narrative poem, *Os Tambiras* (1857). Frequent subjects included Indian courage in defeat by the Portuguese and celebrations of the tropical landscape of Brazil. His poem "Cançao do exilio" ("Song of Exile," 1846) begins with lines familiar to all literate Brazilians: "There are palm trees in my homeland, / Where the sabiá sings." He also compiled a dictionary of one of the Indian languages.

Gone with the Wind (1936),   a novel by Margaret Mitchell (1900–1949). Mitchell wrote only one novel, a stupendous success. By the time of her death in an accident (1949), it had won a Pulitzer Prize and sold more than 8,000,000 copies in thirty languages and forty countries; the movie version (1939) was equally successful. *Gone with the Wind* shows considerable literary skill and social insight. The heroine, Scarlett O'Hara, is an embodiment of the indomitable spirit of the South. She wants to marry Ashley Wilkes, but he marries Melanie Hamilton instead, and in a pique Scarlett marries Charles Hamilton. Later she marries another man for his money, and then finally marries Rhett Butler, a dashing and outspoken Byronic hero. Around her surges the tumult of the Civil War, the despair of Reconstruction days, and the collapse of the old social order. Scarlett's dogged determination to restore Tara, the family estate, after Sherman destroys Atlanta, attains its goal, but at the cost of the realization that she has sacrificed everything else for money and security.

Gonzales, Ambrose Elliot (1857–1926),   editor, authority on the Gullah dialect. Editor of *The State* at Charleston from 1891 to 1926, Gonzalez became much interested in the Gullahs. All his books deal with this group—*The Black Border* (1922), which has a glossary; *With Aesop Along the Black Border* (1924); *The Captain* (1924); and *Laguerre, a Gascon of the Black Border* (1924).

Gonzo Journalism.   See HUNTER S. THOMPSON

Goodbye, Columbus and Five Short Stories (1959), fiction by PHILIP ROTH. In addition to the title work, the book includes "The Conversion of the Jews," "Defender of the Faith," "Epstein," "You Can't Tell a Man by the Song He Sings," and "Eli, the Fanatic."

Good Earth, The (1931),   a novel by PEARL BUCK. It is a story of northern China, many of the details taken from Buck's observations while she was living in China as a child and later. It follows birth, marriage, and death in a Chinese peasant family. The story, generally regarded as Buck's masterpiece, won universal praise for its narrative power and for its sympathetic and realistic picture of life in China. It won the Pulitzer Prize in 1932 and the William Dean Howells Medal in 1935; it also was largely responsible for the award to Buck of the Noble Prize in 1938. A movie was made of the novel (1937).

Good Gray Poet, The (1866),   an apology by WILLIAM DOUGLAS O'CONNOR. In 1865 WALT WHITMAN was dismissed from his position in the Interior Department, ostensibly for including certain poems on sex in *Leaves of Grass*. His friend O'Connor wrote in warm indignation on Whitman's behalf, and the phrase he used as a title stuck thereafter to Whitman. In a posthumous collection, *Three Tales* (1892), O'Connor presented a Christlike picture of Whitman.

Goodman, Jules Eckert (1876–1962),   playwright. After working as an editor on several magazines, Goodman began writing plays, a number of them successfully produced. Among them are *The Test* (1908), *The Silent Voice* (1914), *The Man Who Came Back* (1916), and *Chains* (1923). He collaborated with MONTAGUE GLASS on several plays in which Potash and Perlmutter were the leading characters.

Goodman, Paul (1911–1972),   writer. Born in New York City, Goodman began publishing in *New Directions* in the early 1940s and continued doing distinguished writing in many fields. *Communitas* (1947), written with his brother, Percival Goodman, dealt with city planning; *Gestalt Therapy* (1951) drew on the author's experience as a psychoanalyst; and *Growing Up Absurd* (1960) was a brilliant analysis of the contradictions that face contemporary American youth. Goodman worked throughout his career on *The Empire City* (1959), a panoramic novel about the 1930s to 1950s. His other novels are *The Grand Piano* (1949), *The Dead of Spring* (1950), and *Making Do* (1963). In *Growing Up Absurd* he argued that young people are cut off from nature in a society that no longer offers them honest work. He proposed work camps for youths where they could be in contact with nature. Goodman's plays include *Faustina* (1949); *The Young Disciple* (1955); *The Cave at Machpelah* (1959); and a one-act play, *The Theory of Comedy* (1960). Among his other works are *Art and Social Nature* (1946); *Kafka's Prayer* (1947); *The Structure of Literature* (1954); *The Break-Up of Our Camp*, short stories (1949); *A Visit to Niagara* (1961); and *Collected Poems* (1974)

Good News from New England (1624),   an account by EDWARD WINSLOW (1595–1655), one of the Pilgrims who came over on the *Mayflower*. He kept a journal and so did WILLIAM BRADFORD [1]; their accounts were first used in the volume known, because of its publishers, as *Mourt's Relation* (1622). *Good News* continued the latter narrative. See GEORGE MORTON.

Goodrich, Arthur [Frederick] (1878–1941), novelist, playwright. Goodrich's best-known production was his dramatization of Browning's *The Ring and the Book*, called CAPONSACCHI (1926). He also wrote *So This Is London* (1922), *The Perfect Marriage* (1932), *A Journey by Night* (1935), and *I Can't Help It* (1938). *Caponsacchi* was made into an opera, *Tragedy in Arezzo* (1932), with music by Richard Hagerman.

Goodrich, Frank Bott. See SAMUEL GRISWOLD GOODRICH.

Goodrich, Marcus [Aurelius] (1897–1991), newspaperman, advertising copywriter, screenwriter, novelist. During World War I Goodrich served on a destroyer with the Asiatic Fleet, the basis for the novel *Delilah* (1941). This won applause for its depiction of warfare at sea.

Goodrich, Samuel Griswold ["Peter Parley"] (1793–1860), publisher, editor, author of children's books, memoirist. Born in Connecticut, Goodrich published the annual gift book THE TOKEN (1828–1842). In it he introduced NATHANIEL HAWTHORNE to the public, and some of the finest of the TWICE-TOLD TALES first appeared in its pages. He initiated the modern period of juvenile publishing in the United States when he started his series of Peter Parley books with *The Tales of Peter Parley About America* (1827). For about thirty years he devoted himself to writing volumes of history, geography, science, and travel for children with the help of collaborators, including Hawthorne. In *Recollections of a Lifetime* (1856), he enumerated his books in six closely printed pages. His PARLEY'S MAGAZINE (1833–1844) had some distinguished contributors. It was taken over by *Merry's Museum* (1841–1872); this in turn was merged with YOUTH'S COMPANION (1827–1929). Goodrich's son, **Frank Bott Goodrich** (1826–1894), was a newspaperman and playwright. He wrote *Tri-Colored Sketches of Paris* (1855) and *Man Upon the Sea* (1858, republished as *Ocean's Story*, 1873). He wrote plays in collaboration with DION BOUCICAULT, *The Poor of New York* (1858) and others. See NURSERY RHYMES.

Goodspeed, Edgar Johnson (1871–1962), scholar, translator. Goodspeed's career, spent mainly at the University of Chicago, won him many scholarly honors. In Paris in 1928 he made an important discovery, the so-called Codex 2400 of the Greek New Testament. Years later Goodspeed wrote a mystery story, *The Curse in the Colophon* (1935), which reflected the manuscript adventures that led to this discovery. The work that gave Goodspeed popular recognition was *The New Testament—An American Translation* (1923). It was followed by the *Bible, an American Translation*, written with J. M. P. Smith, (1931); *The Apocrypha, an American Translation* (1938); and *The Complete Bible—An American Translation*, written with J. M. P. Smith and others (1939). He also wrote books intended to help American readers understand the Bible—*The Story of the New Testament* (1916), *The Story of the Old Testament* (1934), *The Story of the Bible* (1936), *How Came the Bible?* (1940), *How to Read the Bible* (1946), *A Life of Jesus* (1950), *Key to Ephesians* (1956), and *Matthew, Apostle and Evangelist* (1959). Goodspeed's translations discard the alluring archaisms of the King James Version for contemporary readability, and they also make use of recent commentaries, especially in Hebrew scholarship. *As I Remember* (1953) is Goodspeed's autobiography.

Goodwin, Doris Kearns (1943–   ), historian, biographer, television commentator. Born in Rockville, New York, Doris Kearns was educated at Colby College and Harvard University (Ph.D., 1968). She is married to Richard Goodwin, a speechwriter and advisor to John and Robert Kennedy and Lyndon Johnson. As a White House Fellow, she wrote a piece for the *New Republic* critical of the Johnson administration's foreign policy. Subsequently, Johnson brought her onto his staff as a critic of his administration, and later asked her to write his biography. *Lyndon Johnson and the American Dream* (1976) was acclaimed both for its style and objectivity. Introduced to Rose Kennedy, the president's mother, Goodwin gained access to family papers, including those of Ambassador Joseph Kennedy. *The Fitzgeralds and the Kennedys: An American Saga* (1987) drew on these resources and garnered much critical acclaim. Goodwin won the Pulitzer Prize for her biography of Franklin and Eleanor Roosevelt entitled *No Ordinary Time* (1994). *Wait Til Next Year* (1997) is a memoir of her childhood and love of baseball. She has appeared as a political commentator on National Public Television's *News Hour* and other programs.

SUZANNE PERKINS-HART

Goodwin, Maud Wilder (1856–1935), novelist, historian. Born in Ballston Spa, New York, Goodwin wrote *The Colonial Cavalier* (1894), *White Aprons* (1896), *Dolly Madison* (1896), *Veronica Playfair* (1909), and other books based on history. See NATHANIEL BACON.

Gookin, Daniel (1612–1687), colonial administrator, writer on New England Indians. Born in England or Ireland, Gookin settled first in Virginia, then emigrated to New England, where he held various civil offices. At Roxbury, Massachusetts, he helped found a free grammar school. He was greatly interested in the welfare of the Indians and in 1656 was appointed superintendent of all the Indians who acknowledged the government of Massachusetts. He wrote *Historical Collections of the Indians in New England* (published 1792) and *An Historical Account of the Doings and Sufferings of the Christian Indians of New England* (completed 1674, published 1836). See KING PHILIP.

Goops and How to Be Them (1900), by GELETT BURGESS. The Goops were strange creatures designed for the entertainment of young readers. Burgess continued his account of them in *More Goops and How Not to Be Them* (1903), *Goop Tales* (1904), *The Goop Directory* (1913), and *The Goop Encyclopedia* (1916).

Gopher Prairie. The name given to the Minnesota pictured in Sinclair Lewis's MAIN STREET (1920), with its typical narrow-mindedness and prejudices. Many readers assumed that Lewis really had in mind his birthplace, Sauk Center, Minnesota.

Gordin, Jacob (1853–1909),   journalist, critic, novelist, translator, dramatist. Born in Russia, Gordin emigrated to the United States in 1892. In Russia he had written novels and articles; in New York, working as a contributor to Yiddish newspapers and magazines, he was gradually drawn to the Yiddish theater, for which he wrote and produced many serious plays, beginning with one called *Siberia*. Altogether, about seventy pieces came from his pen, the best of which were *Mirele Efros, Gott Mensch un Teufel*, and *Der Unbekannter*. His adaptation of Tolstoy's *The Kreutzer Sonata* was translated into English by Langdon Mitchell and successfully produced (1907). His *Collected Works* appeared in Yiddish in 1910. While in Russia, Gordin had founded a brotherhood to combine Christian and Jewish ethics; in New York he founded a similar organization, the Educational League.

Gordon, Caroline (1895–1981),   author, teacher. Born in Kentucky and educated at Bethany College, Gordon married ALLEN TATE in 1924. She lectured on creative writing and the novel at Columbia University, and the universities of North Carolina, Washington, Virginia, Utah, and Kansas. Her first novel, *Penhally* (1931), told the story of three generations on a Kentucky plantation and suggested the milieu and scope of her later work. Her other novels include *Aleck Maury, Sportsman* (1934); *None Shall Look Back* (1937), featuring a Confederate general, Nathan Bedford Forrest; *The Garden of Adonis* (1937), set on a Southern plantation in the Depression; *Green Centuries* (1941), about pioneer times in Kentucky; *The Women on the Porch* (1944), about a poet's reconciliation with his wife; *The Strange Children* (1951); The *Malefactors* (1956); and *The Glory of Hera* (1972). Her short stories are collected in *The Forest of the South* (1945), *Old Red and Other Stories* (1963), and *Collected Stories* (1981). Her theory of fiction is explained in *How to Read a Novel* (1957).

Gordon, Charles William ["Ralph Connor"] (1860–1937),   clergyman, novelist. A missionary, Gordon combined preaching and storytelling in his novels about Glengarry, his birthplace in Ontario, and the Canadian West in general. His books include *Black Rock* (1898), *The Sky Pilot* (1899), *The Man from Glengarry* (1901), *The Doctor* (1906), *The Rock and the River* (1931), and *The Girl from Glengarry* (1933). *Postscript to Adventure* (1938) is his autobiography.

Gordon, Mary [Catherine] (1949–   ),   novelist, short-story writer. Born on Long Island, Gordon was educated at Barnard College and Syracuse University. Her first novel, *Final Payments* (1978), focuses on Isabel Moore's painful reentry into the world after more than a decade of caring for her invalid father, a conservative and overbearing Catholic intellectual. *The Company of Women* (1981) deals with five single females and the priest who dominates them. In *Men and Angels* (1985) Ann Foster, struggling for greater self-determination, hires Laura to care for her children only to find that the smiling, unobtrusive young woman is religiously obsessed to the point of madness. *The Other Side* (1990) expands on the plot of an earlier short story, "Mrs. Cassidy's

Last Year," to explore relations between parents and offspring in three generations of Irish-Americans. Gordon's seventh book, *The Rest of Life* (1993), is a gathering of three novellas about women. *The Shadow Man* (1996) is a memoir about her father. *Joan of Arc* (2000) is labeled a "biographical meditation" on the personal appeal the saint had on the young Mary Gordon.

Gordon, Noah (1926–   ),   novelist. Born in Worcester, Massachusetts, Gordon was educated at Boston University. After Army service in World War II, Gordon became a journalist in the Boston area. Often his novels deal with subjects, such as medicine or history, he has treated as a reporter. *The Rabbi* (1965), his first novel, focuses on Michael Kind, a rabbi who must balance his relationship with a hypercritical Orthodox grandfather, an intolerant congregation, and his wife who has converted from Christianity. *The Death Committee* (1969) concerns members of the hospital group before whom a doctor who has lost a patient must defend his course of treatment. *The Jerusalem Diamond* (1979) follows Harry Hopeman, a New York diamond dealer, asked to represent the state of Israel in trying to buy a gem believed to have come from Solomon's temple. Gordon went back to medicine in the trilogy comprised of *The Physician* (1986), set in the 11th century; *Shaman* (1992), taking place in the 19th century; and *Matters of Choice* (1996), a 20th-century tale. The medieval story concerns Rob Cole, an orphan apprenticed to a barber-surgeon; in the second book, Dr. Robert Cole reads and comes to terms with his dead father's diary; the third finds a female doctor, R. J. Cole, dealing with a failing marriage, a teenage daughter, and abortion controversy.

Gordone, Charles (1925–1995),   playwright, actor, director. Born in Cleveland, Gordone won praise with *No Place to Be Somebody: A Black Comedy* (1967), which won the Pulitzer Prize for drama for its 1969 Broadway production. His later dramatic works include a group of monologues, *Gordone Is a Muthah* (1970); and *The Last Chord* (1977).

Gorey, Edward [St. John] (1925–2000),   writer, illustrator. Gorey, educated at Harvard, made a career of writing and publishing small, morbidly humorous books, with enigmatic texts and starkly detailed pen-and-ink illustrations. Eighteen of Gorey's works were presented as a musical review called *Gorey's Stories* (1978). *Amphigorey* (1972) collected a number of them. His other titles include *The Unstrung Harp* (1953), *The Hapless Child* (1961), *The Broken Spoke* (1976), *The Doubtful Guest* (1978), and (under the pseudonym **Ogred Weary**) *The Curious Sofa* (1997). For years an animated film by Gorey has served as the opening for PBS's "Mystery" series. After his death hundred of stories and sketches were found in his Cape Cod house. Material from that treasure trove was made into a theatrical presentation titled *Gorey Details* (2000).

Gorges, Sir Ferdinando (1566?–1647),   English soldier, mariner, and landowner in American colonial territory. Gorges sought to set up in the new crown territories a government that would be aristocratic, with Anglican doctrine prevailing, but the success of the Puritan colonies in Massachusetts prevented him from carrying out his designs. He received, along with John Mason (1600?–1672), grants of land in New England, in particular one section between the Piscataqua and Kennebec Rivers under the title of the Province of Maine (1622, 1639). He wrote *The Brief Narration of the Original Undertakings of the Advancement of Plantations into Parts of America* (1647), but failed to gain needed financial support. His grandson, of the same name (1630–1718), eventually sold his title to Massachusetts, which then changed the name to District of Maine and continued to govern it until Maine was admitted into the Union (1820). The younger Gorges wrote *America Painted to the Life* (1658), an account that made use of EDWARD JOHNSON's *Wonder-Working Providence* (1654).

Gorman, Herbert S[herman] (1893–1954), biographer, critic, novelist, poet. Born in Springfield, Massachusetts, Gorman worked for newspapers in Springfield and New York and then turned to writing biography and novels. His novels include *The Fool of Love* (1920), *Gold by Gold* (1925), *Jonathan Bishop* (1933), *The Mountain and the Plain* (1936), *The Wine of San Lorenzo* (1945), *The Cry of Dolores* (1947), and *The Breast of the Dove* (1950). He wrote lives of Longfellow (1926), Hawthorne (1927), Dumas the Elder (1929), Mary of Scotland (1932), and James Joyce (1940).

Gorton, Samuel (1592?–1677), theological controversialist. Gorton came to Boston in 1636, moved to Plymouth and later to Rhode Island; he suffered because of his religious views, breaking with Roger Williams and setting up his own colony in Rhode Island. He was exiled for four years to England, but returned to the town he named Warwick. He wrote *Simplicity's Defence against Seven-Headed Policy* (1646), *Saltmarsh Returned from the Dead* (1655), and *An Antidote Against the Common Plague of the World* (1657), and founded a sect called the Gortonites.

Gospel of Wealth, The. This was a general doctrine held by ANDREW CARNEGIE and first expressed in the article "Wealth" (*North American Review*, June 1900). He declared that the individual who by skill had amassed great wealth must do for the average man that which mediocrity prevented him from doing for himself. This doctrine of stewardship was expressed by Carnegie and many others in vast endowments to libraries, hospitals, museums, etc. *The Gospel of Wealth*, a collection of essays, appeared in 1901.

Go Tell It on the Mountain (1953), a novel by JAMES BALDWIN. *Mountain* is Baldwin's first, and aesthetically his best, novel, tightly structured, ironic, and brilliant in style. It develops autobiographical materials in the frame story of John Grimes, a Harlem adolescent, on his fourteenth birthday in March 1935. Its plot and principal theme coalesce in John's search for identity, which is at once his search for love and for acceptance in a hostile world. The middle section reveals the histories and inmost thoughts of the other principals—John's stepfather Gabriel Grimes; Gabriel's sister Florence; and his second wife Elizabeth, John's mother—while they are present at a storefront church "tarry" service. By this flashback technique Baldwin incorporates African-American social history from the time of slavery through the years of the Great Migra-

tion. Thus, the individual stories of these characters, and those with whom they interact, reiterate with different emphases the traumatic experience of being black in America and the conflicting emotions that attend blackness. Because all the other principals are perceived in relation to Gabriel and are subject to his Old Testament, patriarchal willfulness, he may be seen as the protagonist. Driven by lust and pride, which he subsumes into an eloquent pietism as a born-again Christian preacher, he hypocritically abuses both his wives and rejects his own and Elizabeth's bastard sons (the first Roy and John). Gabriel Grimes is God's sullied messenger, epitomizing the forces John must resist to attain selfhood. This John does provisionally through a conversion experience at the end of the tarry service.

JEAN FRANTZ BLACKALL

Gotham. A name originally applied to a town in Nottinghamshire in England, the inhabitants of which deliberately played the fool in order to discourage King John from building a castle there, with its attendant taxes. Washington Irving in the SALMAGUNDI PAPERS (1807) transferred the term to New York City.

Gothic fiction. In *The Castle of Otranto: A Gothic Story* (1764), Horace Walpole introduced and named a new genre in English literature, often called the Gothic romance. He wanted to turn away from the "common life" of Samuel Richardson and chose medieval Italy, a locale that became common in later works and offered haunted castles, abbeys, mysterious monks, family secrets, and ancient curses as convenient subject matter. Among famous English examples of the genre are William Beckford's *Vathek, an Arabian Tale* (1786), introducing the mysteries of the East; Ann Radcliffe's *The Mysteries of Udolpho* (1794); William Godwin's *Caleb Williams* (1794); and Mary Shelley's *Frankenstein* (1818), deriving terror from science.

CHARLES BROCKDEN BROWN introduced the gothic element to American fiction in *Wieland* (1798), where he discovered the necessary ingredients on the fringes of the wilderness. Poe was heavily influenced, as was Hawthorne, as the gothic supplied in early American literature sometimes a more interesting quality than did examinations of common life in the tradition of Richardson or, later, Jane Austen. Later novels and short stories often display a gothic influence. In the mid-20th century the term became popular once again in the phrase "southern Gothic," descriptive of qualities shared by many writers of the American South, including WILLIAM FAULKNER, CARSON MCCULLERS, FLANNERY O'CONNOR, EUDORA WELTY, TRUMAN CAPOTE, TENNESSEE WILLIAMS.

Goudy, Frederic William (1865–1947), printer, designer of printing types, founder of the Village Press. Goudy became the most famous of American type designers. More than one hundred type faces originated in his imagination and artistic skill. He printed many beautiful books, one of the earliest in honor of his master, the English poet and printer William Morris. He wrote *The Alphabet* (1918), *Elements of Lettering* (1921), *The Capitals of the Trajan Column at Rome* (1936), and *Typologia: Studies in Type Design and Type Making* (1940).

Gould, John [Thomas] (1908–   ), farmer, humorist, historian, memoirist. Born in Brighton, Massachusetts, Gould has written of New England, especially Maine. He composed a weekly "Dispatch from the Farm" to the *Christian Science Monitor*. He wrote an excellent historical account of the *New England Town Meeting* (1940), later went on to the first of his humorous writings, *Pre-Natal Care for Fathers* (1941), and described his marriage and experiences on his Maine farm in *The Farmer Takes a Wife* (1945); *Neither Hay nor Grass* (1951); and *The Fastest Hound Dog in the State of Maine* (1953). He edited *The Enterprise*, a weekly paper for all of Maine, and often contributed to *The Christian Science Monitor*, *The Baltimore Sun*, and the *New York Times Magazine*.

Goulding, Francis Robert (1810–1881), clergyman, writer of books for young people. His long series of juveniles extended from *Little Josephine* (1844) to *Nacoochee* (1871). The best were those that dealt with the life of boys on the southern seaboard. Particularly well-received was *The Young Marooners* (1852).

Gover, Robert (1929–   ), novelist. Born in Philadelphia, Gover was educated at the University of Pittsburgh (B.A. 1953). He won attention with a trilogy about the relationship between a black prostitute and her white middle-class lover: *One Hundred Dollar Misunderstanding* (1962), *Here Goes Kitten* (1964), and *J. C. Saves* (1968). His talents as a graphic recorder of extremes of sex and violence are perhaps more memorably displayed in *The Maniac Responsible* (1963), a novel that is also a commentary on the collective guilt Americans must share for their creation of a moral climate that engenders rape and murder. Other novels include *Poorboy at the Party* (1966); *Going for Mr. Big* (1973). *Bring Me the Head of Rona Barrett* (1981) is a story collection. Gover sometimes writes under the pen name "O. Gori." *To Morrow Now Occurs Again* (1975) and *Getting Pretty on the Table* (1975) both appeared under that name.

Governor-General's Literary Awards, Canadian. These were first established by the author John Buchan when, as Lord Tweedsmuir and governor-general of Canada in 1937, he set them up as a permanent system of recognition of literary merit. The rules and regulations are under the control of the Canadian Authors' Association, which selects the judges and frames the rules. The awards are presented to the authors of the best books in four classes—fiction, nonfiction, poetry, British Empire prizes. The authors must be residents of Canada. STEPHEN LEACOCK received an award (1938) for *My Discovery of the West*. Among others honored early are Gwethalyn Graham, Hugh MacLennan, E. J. Pratt, Arthur S. Bourinot, and Earle Birney. In addition a Stephen Leacock Medal for Humor was established by the Leacock Memorial Committee in 1946 and placed under the control of the Authors' Association.

"Go west, young man." This exhortation, which became emblematic of the pioneering and expansive spirit of America in the 19th century, seems to have been first used by John L. B. Soule (1815–1891) in an editorial or article in the Terre Haute *Express* in 1851. HORACE GREELEY used it often, particularly in a New York *Tribune* editorial (July 13, 1865) which gained wide currency, and it is usually attributed to Greeley. He himself, however, reprinted Soule's article to show the source of the phrase.

Goyen, [Charles] William (1915–1983), novelist, playwright. Born in Texas and educated at Rice University, Goyen served in the Navy (1940–45), taught at the New School for Social Research and Columbia University, and was an editor for McGraw-Hill in New York. Sometimes seen, especially in his early work, as a southern Gothic writer, he aimed beyond that label, creating fictions in which the events are internalized and the focus turns to fundamental questions of appearance and reality. His writing is lyrical, mystical, and dominated by the perceptions of the characters. Novels include *The House of Breath* (1950), about a boy in Texas; *In a Farther Country* (1955), about a Hispanic woman in New York City; *The Fair Sister* (1963), about religion and race; and *Come the Restorer* (1974). Collections of fiction include *Ghosts and Flesh: Stories and Tales* (1952); *The Faces of Blood Kindred: A Novella and 10 Stories* (1960); and *The Collected Stories* (1972). Plays are a dramatization of *The House of Breath* (1956); *The Diamond Rattler* (1960); *Christy* (1964); and *The House of Breath Black/White* (1971).

Grady, Henry W[oodfin] (1850–1889), newspaper publisher, editor, orator. A fervent spokesman for the South, Grady became its most famous orator. He won national renown when on Dec. 21, 1886, he delivered a speech before the New England Society in New York City entitled "The New South." Another famous speech of his was "The Race Problem in the South" (1889). Although Grady was ardent in his devotion to the South, he pleaded constantly for fairer treatment of African-Americans, since he recognized that the fate of the region depended upon establishing better racial conditions. In 1879 he bought a quarter interest in the Atlanta *Constitution*, with which paper his name was connected for the rest of his life. A posthumous collection of articles published in a New York newspaper was issued as *The New South* (1890). Edwin Du Bois Shurter edited his *Complete Orations and Speeches* (1910).

Grafton, Sue (1940–   ) crime novelist. Born in Kentucky, Grafton has shared her time between Santa Barbara, California and Louisville for many years. Her first published book *Keziah Dane* (1967), written under the tutelage of her father, C. W. Grafton, a bond attorney who wrote mystery stories at night, led to a series of crime novels built around the persona of Kinsey Milhous, an ex-cop in her thirties. The books are organized alphabetically from *A Is for Alibi* (1982) to *P Is for Peril* (2001). Detective Kinsey Milhous, with a cast of minor characters including Henry Pitts, her landlord, and Rose, who runs a favorite restaurant, solve crimes often connected to Kinsey's past or the Santa Teresa neighborhood where she lives. Grafton projects a schedule that will bring out a new book every eighteen months. The series-beginning "A" novel was set in the year of its publication; every two and a half books, the detective ages one year, so *Z Is for Zero* is planned to be set in the year 1990 when Kinsey Milhous is celebrating her fortieth birthday.

Graham, George Rex (1813–1894),   lawyer, editor, publisher. See GRAHAM'S MAGAZINE.

Graham, Gwethalyn (1913–1965),   novelist. Born in Toronto and educated there, in Switzerland, and at Smith College, she wrote *Swiss Sonata* (1938), then *Earth and High Heaven* (1944). In Canada the Governor-General's Award for Fiction was given to each of these books; the latter in addition received the Anisfield-Wolf Award because of its contribution to a better understanding of race relations. It deals with Jews and Gentiles in Montreal during World War II and was a huge success, translated into ten languages.

Graham, Jorie (1951–   ),   poet, American-born, Graham was raised in Italy, studied at the Sorbonne, and returned to graduate from New York University and the University of Iowa. Her concern for the visual in poetry may be traced to her growing up with a mother who was a painter and to her work in television; a musical presentation of images tending toward abstraction and mystery may be ascribed to her early reading in French symbolists. She has been praised for her philosophical examination of questions of creativity. Among her books of verse are *Hybrids of Plants and of Ghosts* (1980), *Erosion* (1983), *The End of Beauty* (1987), *Region of Unlikeness* (1991), *Materialism* (1993), *The Dream of the Unified Field: Selected Poems, 1974–1994* (1995), *The Errancy* (1997), and *Swarm* (2000).

Graham's Magazine.   In 1826 Samuel C. Atkinson and Charles Alexander, founders of the *Saturday Evening Post*, began an attractive little monthly called the *Casket*; it was largely eclectic, with puzzles and jokes, a "School of Flora," and articles taken over from the weekly *Post*. It carried an engraved plate in each number, and later some colored fashions in competition with *Godey's*. But it was not until George Rex Graham, an aggressive young editor-publisher, bought the *Casket* and merged it with *Burton's Gentleman's Magazine* (1837–1840) that the magazine became one of the foremost American monthlies. When Graham took over in 1839, he set out to secure the country's leading authors as contributors. He became the best paymaster in the business, and in the magazine's golden decade of the 1840s published the work of Lowell, Poe, Bryant, Longfellow, Cooper, N. P. Willis, R. H. Dana, and J. K. Paulding. Poe was literary editor for 15 months (1841–1842) and was succeeded by R. W. GRISWOLD (1842–1843). Popular writers of romance were Emma C. Embury, E. F. Ellett, and Ann S. Stephens. Sartain's mezzotints and various style designs from woodcuts, as well as hand-colored fashion plates, embellished the magazine. C. H. Bodmer and other engravers contributed western scenes as well as domestic and sentimental pictures. After 1850 the competition of *Harper's New Monthly Magazine* was difficult to meet, and the 40,000 circulation claimed in 1843 dropped off. The last editor was Charles Godfrey Leland, 1857–1858.

Grammatical Institute of the English Language, Comprising an Easy, Concise, and Systematic Method of Education, Designed for the Use of English Schools in America (1783),   by NOAH WEBSTER. This was a combination speller, reader, and grammar, designed to teach patriotism as well as English. Ultimately it became Webster's AMERICAN SPELLER, which sold in enormous numbers.

Grandbois, Alain (1900–1975),   poet. Born in Quebec, Grandbois was a world traveler from 1918 to 1938, based in Paris, before his return to Canada. His first poems were published in China in 1934; these, with others, became *Les îles de la nuit* (1944), a volume influential on the generation of poets then rising. His poems are elegiac and exotic, the expressions of a spiritual traveler observant of the fleeting nature of things of this world. Later collections of verse are *Rivages de l'homme* (1948); *L'étoile pourpre* (1957); and a collected *Poèmes* (1963, expanded 1979). *Selected Poems* (1965) is bilingual, with translations by Peter Miller. Short stories are collected in *Avant le Chaos* (1945, 1964). He also wrote prose works on explorers: *Né á Québec: Louis Jolliet* (1933; *Born in Quebec*, 1964); and *Les Voyages de Marco Polo* (1942).

Grand Canyon of Arizona.   A tremendous gorge cut by the Colorado River over millions of years. Many writers have attempted to convey some sense of the awesomeness and beauty of the canyon, including such poets as Henry van Dyke in *The Grand Canyon and Other Poems* (1914), and William H. Simpson in *Along the Old Trail* (1929). JOHN WESLEY POWELL (1834–1902) explored the Colorado River and reported his observations in *Exploration of the Colorado River* (1875), reprinted under the editorship of Horace Kephart as *First Through the Grand Canyon, 1869–70* (1915).

Grandissimes, The: A Story of Creole Life (1880), a historical romance by GEORGE W. CABLE. Many episodes are laid in New Orleans of 1803, beginning with Jefferson's purchase of Louisiana from the French. The conflicts of New Orleans society are depicted, mostly through the eyes of an American youth of German origin, Frowenfeld, who gradually learns some of the dark secrets of the lives of his aristocratic acquaintances, secrets in which he himself is ultimately involved: family feuds, race feuds, the struggle between the old order and the new "American" order, and complex love affairs. The Creole mother and daughter Nancanou and the African-American ex-prince Bras-Coupé are especially vivid characters.

Grandmothers, The (1927),   a novel by GLENWAY WESCOTT. This is described by the author as "a family portrait." The grandmothers (three, since Alwyn Tower's paternal grandfather married twice) are fully portrayed, as are Alwyn's parents and innumerable other relatives, many of whom live tragic, frustrated lives.

Granich, Irving.   See MICHAEL GOLD.

Grant, Anne McVickar ["Mrs. Grant of Laggan"] (1755–1838),   memoirist. Mrs. Grant as a girl lived near Albany, New York, where her father was stationed at a post of the British army. Many years later she wrote anonymously published recollections of her experiences, *Memoirs of an American Lady* (1808).

Grant, George Monro (1835–1902),   memoirist. Later a president of Queen's University, Ontario, Grant is remembered today for his *Ocean to Ocean: Sandford Fleming's Expedition through Canada in 1872* (1873), a narrative account of the trip based on diaries the author kept as secretary to Fleming.

Grant, Percy Stickney (1860–1927), clergyman, poet, essayist. An Episcopalian minister, Grant was outspoken in his views on social conditions and on theological controversies. He resigned his pastorate in a dispute with his bishop. Among his books are *Ad Matrem and Other Poems* (1905); *Essays* (1922); and *A Fifth Avenue Parade and Other Poems* (1922).

Grant, Robert (1852–1940), lawyer, judge, novelist, essayist, poet. Boston-born, as a lawyer and jurist Grant was a liberal, although he approved of a report that led to the execution of Sacco and Vanzetti. His experience as a lawyer was reflected in his novels, including *The Average Man* (1883), *Unleavened Bread* (1900), *The Undercurrent* (1904), *The Orchid* (1905), *The Chippendales* (1909), and *The Bishop's Granddaughter* (1925). *The Chippendales* has been praised as a classic picture of the futilities and foibles of Boston at the beginning of the century. In *Fourscore* (1934) Grant wrote his autobiography, with some sidelights on the Sacco-Vanzetti Advisory Committee. See SACCO-VANZETTI CASE.

Grant, Ulysses S[impson] (1822–1885), soldier, 18th president. Born near Pt. Pleasant, Ohio, Grant graduated from West Point in 1843 and served in the Mexican War. He hated the routine of soldiering, took to solitary drinking, and resigned from the army in 1854. He worked as a farmer, real estate agent, and clerk. He entered the Union army in May 1861 and was given the rank of brigadier-general. His rise was rapid, as he continued to win first minor, then major, victories, culminating in Lee's surrender at Appomattox (April 9, 1865).

Grant's fame was great at the close of the war; with the debacle of Johnson's administration he became the inevitable Republican choice for president. He was elected in 1868 and again in 1872. His administration was marred by corruption and graft; he was overawed by men of wealth and social station and was a poor judge of human nature. During this time the Fifteenth Amendment was passed (providing equal voting rights for black citizens), the *Alabama* case was referred to arbitration, an amnesty act for Confederate veterans was passed, postal cards were first issued, and the Centennial Exposition at Philadelphia opened.

After his years in office, Grant lost his money in an investment scheme and almost went to jail. At the suggestion of Mark Twain, then conducting a successful publishing firm, Grant wrote his *Personal Memoirs* (2 v., 1885–86), completing the manuscript while dying of throat cancer. The *Memoirs* earned huge sums for Grant's widow. They have been praised for their straightforwardness and simplicity. Novels about the general and president include Max Byrd's *Grant* (2000), *Grant Speaks* (2000) by Ev Ehrlich, and *That Fateful Lightning* by Richard Parry.

Grapes of Wrath, The (1939), a novel by JOHN STEINBECK. In this moving book, Steinbeck wrote a classic novel of a family's battle with starvation and economic desperation. The story also tells in vivid terms the story of the westward movement and the frontier. The JOADS, Steinbeck's central figures,

are "OKIES," farmers moving west from a land of drought and bankruptcy to seek work as migrant fruit-pickers in California. They are beset by the police, participate in strike violence, and are harried by death. The book belongs to the PROLETARIAN LITERATURE that became more and more important in the first half of the 20th century and reflected growing economic and social unease. But Steinbeck was by no means committed merely to exploiting an ideology. His novel is one of absorbing interest, with powerful episodes and vivid descriptions. The book was based on a careful study Steinbeck made in 1936, when he followed groups of unemployed men and women to California; he embodied his observations in some newspaper articles, later published as a pamphlet called *Their Blood Is Strong*. It won the 1939 Pulitzer Prize, and was filmed by JOHN FORD in 1940.

Grass Harp, The (1951), a novel by TRUMAN CAPOTE. An eleven-year-old orphan, Collin Fenwick, goes to live with his two elderly aunts, Dolly and Verena Talbo; Dolly, shy, tender, and imaginative, is the complete antithesis of the grasping, shrewd Verena, who finally drives Dolly, in company with Collin and Catherine, the black cook, to take refuge in a treehouse in a chinaberry tree. They are joined by Riley Henderson and Judge Cool, two "outcasts" from the town, and the "five fools in a tree" find their "raft in a sea of leaves," suggestive of Huck's raft, a place where they feel they belong, where they can be honest, and where they are "free to find out who we truly are." Despite the pastoral and romantic interlude in the tree, reality dominates the end of the novel: Dolly and Verena are reunited, Dolly dies, Collin grows up to study law, and Riley Henderson becomes a public figure. But the private world of Dolly, although incompatible with the public world, is denied neither existence nor validity, and enriches the public world by its presence.

Grassroots Theatre: A Search for Regional Arts in America (1955), a personal account by Robert Gard. Gard tells of his experiences in fostering the growth of regional drama, in New York, Alberta Province, and Wisconsin.

Grattan, C[linton] Hartley (1902–1980), lecturer, teacher, author. Grattan, born in Massachusetts, contributed to many magazines and newspapers, lectured in this country and Australia, and won a reputation as a critic opposed to the NEW HUMANISM. (See IRVING BABBITT.) Among his books: *Bitter Bierce* (1929); *Why We Fought* (1929); *The Three Jameses: A Family of Minds* (1932); *The Deadly Parallel* (1939); *Introducing Australia* (1942, rev. ed., 1947); *In Quest of Knowledge: A Historical Perspective on Adult Education* (1955), also published in Persian, Urdu, Hindi, and Indonesian; *The United States and the Southwest Pacific* (1961); and *The Southwest Pacific: A History* (1961). He edited *The Critique of Humanism* (1930).

Grau, Shirley Ann (1929–), novelist, short-story writer. Born in New Orleans and educated at Tulane Grau has written fiction steeped in Louisiana local color and problems of race. Perhaps best among her novels, *The Keepers of the House* (1964) won praise for its treatment of a white family, interracial marriage, politics, and the Ku Klux Klan. Other novels are *The Hard Blue Sky* (1960), set on a Louisiana island;

The House on Coliseum Street (1961), a New Orleans novel of divorce and promiscuity; *The Condor Passes* (1971), covering three generations of a Louisiana family; *Evidence of Love* (1974), and *Roadwalkers* (1994). Short stories are collected in *The Black Prince* (1955), *The Wind Shifting West* (1973), and *Nine Women* (1986).

Graustark (1901), a novel by GEORGE BARR MCCUTCHEON. Subtitled "The Story of a Love Behind the Throne," this romance emulated Anthony Hope's popular *Prisoner of Zenda* (1894) in its account of how an American commoner named Grenfall fell in love with the Princess Yetive in a highly colored imaginary kingdom. It was followed by a series of other novels set in the same locale including *Beverly of Graustark* (1904) and *The Prince of Graustark* (1914).

Gravity's Rainbow (1973), a novel by THOMAS PYNCHON. Pynchon's monumental third novel might have been entitled *V-2*, for not only does it develop narrative voices, themes, and structural innovations introduced in Pynchon's first novel, *V* (1963), but it even adopts two major characters, Seaman Bodine and Lieutenant Weissmann, from the earlier work. Furthermore, *Gravity's Rainbow* deals with the development, during the Third Reich, of the V-2 rocket, the prototype of the guided missile, which would become the delivery system for the nuclear armaments being developed in America during the same period. The merging of the two technological advances culminates a "dream of annihilation" that in Pynchon's vision has obsessed Western civilization for centuries. "Gravity's rainbow" symbolizes both the arc of the rocket and the possible trajectory of civilization itself, as it proceeds toward its own seemingly inevitable destruction.

But the question of inevitability is a complicated one in this novel, not only in terms of theme but also in terms of narrative structure. The trajectory of the main plot, which deals with a G.I. named Tyrone Slothrop who appears to have erections when he is in parts of London that the V-2 eventually hits, is complicated by so many subplots that it is difficult to ascertain what happens to this boob-hero or what his denouement might mean. The divergences of the subplots paradoxically suggest that perhaps a trajectory is never fully determined; perhaps even the course of history allows for deviation and thus possibility. In an encyclopedic work that in the range of its reference and the brilliance of its execution invites comparison with *Moby-Dick* and *Ulysses*, Pynchon creates a form that echoes and augments its subject matter.
MOLLY HITE

Gray, Asa (1810–1888), scientist, teacher. Gray made Harvard a center of botanical study in the United States. He published a series of scientific studies of American flora, also several textbooks, including *Elements of Botany* (1836); *Flora of North America* (2 v., 1838–43, in collaboration with JOHN TORREY); *Manual of the Botany of the Northern U.S.* (1848); *How Plants Grow* (1858); *How Plants Behave* (1872); and *Darwinia* (1876).

Gray, Harold [Lincoln] (1894–1968), newspaper artist, creator of comic strips. Born in Kankakee, Illinois, Gray left newspaper work in Chicago to start his own studio. In

1924 he created the popular comic strip character *Little Orphan Annie*.

Gray, James (1899–1984), newspaperman, critic, essayist, novelist, dramatist. Gray's writings as drama critic and book reviewer for the St. Paul *Press & Dispatch* were well received. His literary column became widely syndicated, and he moved later to the staff of the Chicago *Daily News*. A collection of his reviews was published as *On Second Thought* (1946), and he published a number of other books, including the regional novels *Shoulder the Sky* (1935) and *Wake and Remember* (1936), a volume on *The Illinois* (1940) for "The Rivers of America Series," *The University of Minnesota 1851–1951* (1951), and several plays.

Graydon, Alexander (1752–1818), memoirist. Philadelphia-born, Graydon served as a captain of a Pennsylvania battalion during the Revolutionary War. His *Memoirs of a Life* (1811) depicts his brief military service in New York in 1776, his capture, and eight months imprisonment.

Grayson, David. Pen name of RAY STANNARD BAKER.

Grayson, William John (1788–1863), lawyer, public official, poet. Born in Beaufort, South Carolina, Grayson served in the South Carolina legislature, in Congress, and as port collector of Charleston. He was an ardent advocate of states' rights, but in 1850 published a pamphlet, *A Letter to Governor Seabrook*, opposing secession and pointing out the evils of disunion. His best-known poem is *The Hireling and The Slave* (1854). A work of frank and vigorous propaganda, it compares the advantages of the slave in the South with the harsh life of the pauper laborer in Europe, painting an idyllic picture of the slave's share in rural life and sports. Grayson continued with this theme in *The Country* (1858).

Graysons, The (1887), a historical novel by EDWARD EGGLESTON. Into this story of pioneer life in Illinois, Eggleston introduced the figure of Lincoln as a young lawyer. Lincoln wins freedom for the accused hero by proving from the almanac that, contrary to the evidence against him, there was no moonlight and hence no murder on the night in question. This episode is based on an actual event, Lincoln's successful defense of "Duff" Armstrong in a murder trial during the 1840s.

"Great American Novel, The." The frequent use of this phrase, especially toward the end of the 19th century, indicated the belief that it was possible to write a genuine epic of American life which would equal the best works of other literatures. It was an expression of profound nationalistic hope in the face of what seemed to be conclusive evidence that no individual American writer possessed the requisite genius or cultural background. JOHN WILLIAM DE FOREST precipitated the discussion in 1868 with an essay using the phrase as title, in which he suggested that UNCLE TOM'S CABIN might be the best candidate. The phrase was also used as the title of a novel (1938) by CLYDE BRION DAVIS. His hero, Homer Zigler, is a newspaperman who hopes someday to write "the great American novel"; in the meantime he works on newspapers in Cleveland, Kansas City, San Francisco, and Denver, an idealist who never achieves his great ambition.

Great Awakening. A religious revival movement that began with the preaching of JONATHAN EDWARDS and assumed formidable proportions in 1740–50, sweeping through New England, some of the Middle States, and the South. It was marked by an extreme emotionalism, which sometimes took erratic forms. Edwards's *Narrative of the Surprising Works of God* (1757) recorded conversions which often indicated states of mind at least temporarily not far removed from insanity. The movement was opposed by the "Old Lights," under the leadership of JONATHAN MAYHEW and CHARLES CHAUNCEY; their ideas in time led to the doctrine of Unitarianism.

Great Depression. From Black Thursday on October 24, 1929, until the Nazi-Soviet Non-Aggression Pact of August 24, 1939, an economic depression engulfed the United States. During the decade of the 1930s "the Great Depression" developed in three stages.

The first period (1929–1933) saw economic disaster and personal misery. In March of 1930 unemployed workers demonstrated in New York, Cleveland, Los Angeles, and 35 other cities; in 1931 New York had 82 breadlines serving 82,000 meals a day. Throughout the land hundreds starved, and untold thousands endured malnutrition. During the second stage of the depression (1933–36), President Franklin D. Roosevelt put into effect the New Deal, a complex series of government programs to restore the American economy and put people back to work. The labor union movement flourished; Marxism became socially influential; and with Hitler's rise to power in Germany, anti-fascist sentiment bloomed. The Depression's third phase (1936–1939) began with the outbreak of the Spanish Civil War. By that time Roosevelt's policies had strengthened the economy, and the number of jobs multiplied rapidly. The influence of Marxism declined among intellectuals and workers, and with increasing alarm Americans watched fascist powers hold practice wars in Spain, Ethiopia, and on the Czech border. The depression years came to a close with the Nazi-Soviet Non-Aggression Pact in August of 1939, and the United States braced for war.

During the Great Depression with all its human misery, serious American writers concerned themselves with social issues. The Roosevelt administration devalued the dollar and forced many expatriate writers to return home, but as part of the Works Progress Administration (WPA), it created the FEDERAL WRITERS' PROJECT and the FEDERAL THEATER PROJECT, both of which benefited many writers.

Leftist critics and theorists—among them Marxists such as Max Eastman, Granville Hicks, and John Howard Lawson—became influential. Lawson's *Theory and Technique of Playwriting* (1936), for example, not only became the leading manual for dramatists of the period but also established principles of dramatic writing for film that remain in effect. Other writers, such as Edmund Wilson, shunned the excesses of Marxism but examined social and cultural issues from a staunchly liberal stance. Often opposing the extremists of the left were such influential critics as Richard P. Blackmur, Kenneth Burke, Malcom Cowley, Joseph Wood Krutch, and Allen Tate. During the 1930s, three Writers' Congresses were held in which many writers—liberals, communists, and humanists alike—articulated their social concerns.

Attentive to the issues of the time, such established playwrights as Eugene O'Neill, Maxwell Anderson, and Thornton Wilder wrote meaningful and popular plays. Among established dramatists Elmer Rice and John Howard Lawson dealt with the social issues most directly. But new leftist theater companies such as the Group Theatre began producing the work of such new writers as Clifford Odets, Sidney Kingsley, Lillian Hellman, and Paul Green.

Among the leading American poets of the decade were Robert Frost, Archibald MacLeish, James Gould Fletcher, Mark Van Doren, Robert Hillyer, Conrad Aiken, and expatriates T. S. Eliot and Ezra Pound.

Margaret Mitchell's *Gone with the Wind* was one of the runaway best sellers and won a Pulitzer Prize in 1937, but three notable American writers won the Nobel Prize for Literature—Sinclair Lewis (1930), Eugene O'Neill (1936), and Pearl Buck (1938). Three other highly esteemed American novelists wrote significant books during the thirties—William Faulkner, Ernest Hemingway, and F. Scott Fitzgerald.

Waiting for Lefty, a play by Clifford Odets; *U.S.A.*, a trilogy of novels by John Dos Passos; and *The Grapes of Wrath* by John Steinbeck present perhaps the most detailed, original, and dramatic depictions of the state of American life during the Great Depression. Helpful books on the period include Daniel Aaron's *Writers on the Left* (1961), Walter Rideout's *The Radical Novel in the United States, 1900–1954* (1956), and Sam Smiley's *The Drama of Attack: Didactic Plays of the American Depression* (1972).

SAM SMILEY

Great Dictator, The (1940), a screenplay written, produced, and directed by CHARLIE CHAPLIN, with Chaplin in the two chief roles. For the first time in his career Chaplin played a speaking part. He was both the dictator of a mythical country (Hitler was the model) and a barber who was his double.

Great Dismal Swamp. See DISMAL SWAMP.

Great Divide, The (in 1906 produced as *The Sabine Woman*; present title, 1909), a play contrasting East and West by WILLIAM VAUGHN MOODY. Deserting verse for prose, Moody tried to present in this play a contrast between East and West. The heroine, representing the former, is attacked by three men while alone in her brother's cabin in Arizona; she saves herself by agreeing to marry one of them, who supposedly represents the free spirit of the West.

Great Gatsby, The (1925), a novel by F. SCOTT FITZGERALD. This is Fitzgerald's most nearly perfect work. The narrative thread is concerned mainly with marital infidelity and violent revenge, but the power of the novel derives from its sharp portrayal of wealthy society in New York City and Long Island as seen through the eyes of the midwestern narrator, Nick Carraway. Jay Gatsby is a man with a shady past who has achieved social rank; the world in which he moves is shown to be one of moral emptiness and desperate boredom.

The "Jazz Age," Fitzgerald's constant subject, is exposed here in terms of its false glamor and cultural barrenness. Yet in the end the novel transcends its own bitter view and is probably Fitzgerald's most humane work; certainly it is his most finished and is written in a fully developed and easy style. It has enjoyed a continuous popularity and is one of the chief texts of the American literary renaissance in the post–World War I period.

Great God Brown, The (1926), a play by EUGENE O'NEILL. In this experimental work O'Neill utilized expressionistic techniques to depict the complicated relationships existing between the self-divided artist, Dion Anthony, his wife, and their friend, a successful businessman, Brown. Masks similar to those of the classic Greek theater are worn by the actors to emphasize radical shifts in the apparent characters of the protagonists.

Great Meadow, The (1930), a novel by ELIZABETH MADOX ROBERTS. Roberts tells how Kentucky was settled by emigrants from Virginia, how they fought the Indians, and the hardships they endured as pioneers.

Great Stone Face, The (1851), a tale by NATHANIEL HAWTHORNE included in THE SNOW IMAGE AND OTHER TWICE-TOLD TALES. The story centers around a natural rock formation in New Hampshire, sometimes called "The Old Man of the Mountain," a subject of legends since Indian days. Ernest, a simple-minded but noble inhabitant of the region, awaits the day when someone will come to visit the mountains who will really look like the Great Profile. The poet who tells the story realizes at last that it is Ernest himself who resembles the image.

Great Train Robbery, The (1903), a movie written and produced by Edwin S. Porter (1870–1941). Porter had already produced for Thomas A. Edison *The Life of an American Fireman* (1899? or perhaps as late as 1903), which created great excitement. But he told his story with greater skill in *The Great Train Robbery*, which established the pistol-shooting desperado as a stock figure of American movies. It won a tremendous success and is credited with starting American movies on the path they were to follow for many years.

Great or Gay White Way. See BROADWAY.

Greek and Roman influence. The American colonists brought with them from Europe a regard for Greek and Latin as the basis of a true education. One of the earliest schools established was the Free Grammar School set up in Boston in 1635, better known as the Boston Latin School, which has trained generation after generation for college. The earlier schools were intended only for boys, who studied Latin from the time of their admission as young children and undertook Greek usually by their fourth year. They covered a wide range of Greek and Latin literature, and were fluent in reference and quotation. The same stress was laid on the classical languages in college, sometimes with Hebrew added.

The American Revolution was partly guided by classical ideals; its symbols and institutions, as Gilbert Highet pointed out, "were markedly Greco-Roman in inspiration." For example, the senior legislative body in the United States and most Latin-American countries is called the *Senate*; in the United States the Senate meets in the *Capitol*. The names of many American cities go back to Greece and Rome. Thomas Jefferson and John Adams were equally firm in their belief that the new American civilization must be based on that of ancient Greece and Rome. Monticello, Jefferson's private home, was a reminiscence of a Roman one; his plans for the University of Virginia recalled the spaciousness of a Roman villa, and its library was modeled on the Roman Pantheon.

Well into the 20th century, a knowledge of Greek and Latin was required of every cultured person. Innumerable textbooks were produced and often attained a wide circulation. But times changed and a variety of influences changed the practices of the educational system. Schools and colleges ceased to require the study of classical languages, and many began to drop them as elective studies.

Yet the influence of the classics remained strong. Those who studied them were often affected in new and vital ways. Many creative writers, going back to the ancient Hellenic world, found inspiration for compositions that reflected the present day under classic guise. Three American poets paricularly under this influence were T. S. ELIOT, EZRA POUND, and HILDA DOOLITTLE. In all of these writers Greek myths, techniques, and points of view may be found; often the verse shows an unexpected kinship with choruses in Greek plays. EUGENE O'NEILL and ROBINSON JEFFERS both employed Greek legends as a means of interpreting contemporary life. More recently, the influence is apparent in works otherwise as different as JOHN UPDIKE's *The Centaur* (1963) and John Barth's *Chimera* (1972).

Greeley, Horace (1811–1872), printer, editor, writer, political leader. Born in New Hampshire, Greeley worked as a printer in New York and started the first penny newspaper, *The New Yorker* (1834). Later he combined this and the weekly *Log Cabin* (begun in 1840), into the New York *Tribune* (April 10, 1841), made that paper famous, and remained its editor until 1872. He exerted wide influence in both literary and political spheres, although he held elected office for only three months (congressman, 1848–49). He was influential in Lincoln's nomination, and although many of Lincoln's ideas displeased him, he continued to support him. He was averse to the Republican policy of revenge on the South that followed the Civil War, and in 1872 ran for the presidency against Grant in a coalition of liberal Republican and Democrats, but was defeated.

He was a supporter of FOURIERISM and helped ALBERT BRISBANE fund his phalanxes. He favored the agrarian movement, with its emphasis on open land and a liberal policy for settlers. He sympathized with the laboring classes of the city and did what he could to improve their condition. He joined in the intellectual awakening of the 1840s; he employed MARGARET FULLER on the *Tribune* and even took her into his own household. He appears as a character in Irving Bacheller's EBEN HOLDEN (1900). Among Greeley's own books are *Hints Toward Reform* (1850), *Glances at Europe* (1851), *The American Conflict* (1866), *Recollections of a Busy Life* (1868), and *Essays on Political Economy* (1870).

Greely, Adolphus Washington (1844–1935), army officer, explorer, author. Greely made many important explorations of Arctic regions. When the San Francisco earthquake and fire took place (1906), he was placed in charge of relief work. He wrote *Explorers and Travelers* (1893), *True Tales of Arctic Heroism* (1912), *Reminiscences of Adventure and Service* (1927), and other books.

Green, Adam. Pen name of LEONARD WEISGARD.

Green, Anna Katharine (1846–1935), novelist, detective story writer, poet. Born in Brooklyn, Green began as a poet. Her father James Wilson Green was a noted trial lawyer, and her consequent interest in crime led her to write THE LEAVENWORTH CASE (1878), the first piece of detective fiction to be written by a woman. It became a best seller and was later dramatized. Other books of Green's include *The Hand and the Ring* (1883); *The Doctor, His Wife, and the Clock* (1895); *The Filigree Ball* (1903); *The House of the Whispering Pines* (1910); and a collection of verse, *The Defense of the Bride and Other Poems* (1882).

Green, Anne (1899–?), novelist, memoirist. Green was born in Savannah, Georgia, but her family early removed to Paris, where her father was in business. Green (her brother is JULIEN GREEN) described the household in a volume of reminiscences, *With Much Love* (1948). Her novels are set in France; they include *The Selbys* (1930); *A Marriage of Convenience* (1933); *Fools Rush In* (1934); *The Silent Duchess* (1939); *Just Before Dawn* (1943); and *The Old Lady* (1947), in which a French woman comes to the U.S. Her characters, many drawn from life, are treated satirically.

Green, Asa. See ASA GREENE.

Green, Joseph (1706–1780), distiller, merchant, satirist. A wealthy member of Boston society, Green was a loyalist in politics. He was regarded as the foremost wit of his day and exercised his talents in newspapers and pamphlets. His most widely circulated verse satire was *A Winter's Evening* (1750). He also wrote *The Poet's Lamentation for the Loss of His Cat, Which He Used to Call His Muse* (*London Magazine*, November, 1733). The poet in this case was Green's friend MATHER BYLES; the poem is sometimes called "Doctor Byles' Cat."

Green, Julien (1900–1998), French novelist of American parentage. Except for the years in which he attended the University of Virginia (1918–22) and the World War II years (1940–45), Green lived in France and wrote his books in French. He was as much influenced by his Puritan heritage as by the Catholicism to which he converted. His first novel, *Mont-Cinère* (1926; tr. *Avarice House*, 1927), set in Virginia, is the story of an American family caught between boredom and greed. *Adrienne Mesurat* (1927; tr. *The Closed Garden*, 1928) and *Léviathan* (1929; tr. *The Dark Journey*, 1929) reflect his obsessive sense of sin, his consciousness of the violence and sadism of which men are capable, and his fascination with and fear of madness and death.

With *Le Visionnaire* (1934; tr. *The Dreamer*, 1934) and *Minuit* (1936; tr. *Midnight*, 1936), Green entered into a more personal, dreamlike exploration of the constant battle between good and evil, passion and reason. Two of his best novels are *Moïra* (1950), with a setting drawn from the University of Virginia and *Chaque homme dans sa nuit* (1960, tr. *Each Man in His Darkness*). His last major fictional work was a planned trilogy, once again set in the American South before the Civil War. Drawing on the stories his mother had told him of life on plantations inhabited by gracious women and courtly men, Green wrote the massive novels *The Distant Lands* (1991), *The Stars of the South* (1993) and *Dixie*. A very prolific writer, his work included five plays, six collections of essays, and two works of history, in addition to his novels and journals. He began keeping a diary in his twenties and continued writing in it for the next seventy years. The published volumes of his journals ultimately comprised sixteen volumes, published first in French and sometimes translated into English. Nine volumes were translated as *Journal 1926–1972* (1972); other English volumes include *Personal Record 1928–1939* (1939); *Diary 1928–1957* (1962); *Memories of Happy Days* (1942); and *To Leave Before Dawn* (1967), the latter two translated by his sister, Anne Green. In his last decade two more volumes appeared in French: *On est si sérieux quand on a dix-neuf ans* (1993), covering the years 1919 to 1924, and *Pourquoi suis-je moi?* (1996), covering the years 1993 to 1996. In 1971, Green was elected to the Académie Française, the first American to be so honored.

Green, Paul E[liot] (1894–1981), teacher, dramatist, motion picture scriptwriter. Born in North Carolina, Green graduated from the University of North Carolina and did graduate work there and at Cornell. He taught philosophy and dramatic arts at the University of North Carolina and became known for plays set for the most part in North Carolina: *The Lord's Will and Other Plays* (1925); *Lonesome Road: Six Plays for Negro Theater* (1926); *The Field God* and IN ABRAHAM'S BOSOM, both of which appeared on Broadway in 1927, the latter winning the Pulitzer Prize; THE HOUSE OF CONNELLY AND OTHER PLAYS (1931); *Roll Sweet Chariot* (*Potter's Field*, 1934); NATIVE SON (with RICHARD WRIGHT, 1941); and *Peer Gynt* (an American version, 1951). During the thirties he lived and worked for a time in Hollywood, but his success there was far from unqualified, and he returned to teaching in North Carolina. He did, however, write several successful scripts for Will Rogers and George Arliss. In later years he became more interested in writing what he calls "plays derived from the people's history, their legends, folk-customs and beliefs, their hopes and ideals, and producing them in hillside amphitheaters built for that purpose." Among these pieces, which he calls "symphonic dramas," are: *The Lost Colony* (1937); THE COMMON GLORY (1947); *Faith of Our Fathers* (1950); *Wilderness Road* (1955); *The Founders* (1957); *The Confederacy* (1958); *Stephen Foster* (1959); *Texas* (1966); *Drumbeats in Georgia* (1973); *Louisiana Cavalier* (1976); and *We the People* (1976). Stories are collected in *Wide Fields* (1928); *Salvation on a String* (1946); *Dog on the Sun* (1949); and *Home to My Valley*. Essays on theater are collected in *The Hawthorn Tree* (1943); *Dramatic Heritage* (1953); *Drama and the Weather* (1958); and *Plough and Furrow* (1963).

Green, Samuel (1615–1702),   printer. Green came to Massachusetts about 1633 and managed in Cambridge the only printing establishment in the colonies until 1665. He printed Eliot's INDIAN BIBLE, THE BAY PSALM BOOK, and nearly 275 other books.

Green Bay Tree, The (1924),   a novel by LOUIS BROM- FIELD. Lily Shane, one of Bromfield's most successful women characters, begins life in a midwestern industrial town, goes to Paris to bear an illegitimate child. She is shown vividly against both French and American backgrounds and as a vital force in the life of her family, of her aristocratic friends, and of some workmen in her native town. The novel was dramatized (1927) as *The House of Women*. It forms the first novel in a tetralogy called *Escape*; the others are *Possession* (1925), EARLY AUTUMN (1926), and *A Good Woman* (1927).

Greenberg, Samuel (1893–1917),   poet. Brought from Austria to the United States at the age of seven, Green- berg lived in poverty on New York's Lower East Side. In his last years in a charity hospital for the tubercular he began reading good literature and writing poetry intensely and feverishly. Nothing he wrote was published in his lifetime. The manu- scripts fell into the hands of HART CRANE, who was influenced by Greenberg's sensuous and often striking metaphors. Green- berg's posthumous *Poems: A Selection from the Manuscripts* (1947) contains an appreciative preface by Allen Tate.

Greene [or Green], Asa (1789–c. 1837),   physician, editor, bookseller, humorist. Born in Massachusetts, Greene came to New York about 1830, abandoned medicine, and set up as a bookseller and author. Some of his own experiences apparently appear in *The Perils of Pearl Street* (1834), adven- tures of a poor boy in New York. He is best remembered, how- ever, for his satirical and burlesque novels: *The Life and Adventures of Dr. Dodimus Duckworth* (1833), which describes in mock-heroic style the experiences of a spoiled child who ultimately becomes a country doctor; *A Yankee Among the Nullifiers* (1833), a fictional account of a visit by Greene to South Carolina, also the story of tricks practiced by a crafty clock-peddler; and *Travels in America, by George Fibbleton, Esq., Ex-Barber to His Majesty, The King of Great Britain* (1833), a burlesque of Mrs. Trollope's famous book, *Domestic Manners of the Americans* (1832). Usually Greene wrote broad farce, but he had a quieter and more truly humorous side. *A Glance at New York* (1837) is more realistic than the other works.

Greene, Ward (1892–1956),   newspaperman, editor, novelist. Greene was born in North Carolina. His career as a newspaperman in the South and in New York was topped by his appointment as executive editor of King Features Syndicate (1921). In 1929 he began writing novels in the hard-boiled school. Among them: *Cora Potts* (1929); *Ride the Nightmare* (1930); *Weep No More* (1932); DEATH IN THE DEEP SOUTH (1936); *Route 28* (1940); and *The Lady and the Tramp* (1954).

Greenfield Hill (1794),   a descriptive poem by TIMO- THY DWIGHT. It was written in imitation of Sir John Denham's topographical poem *Cooper's Hill* (1642), and as a result of the author's residence as a minister in Greenfield, Connecticut

(1783–95). It praises village life, at least in America, and extols the leaders of the people. Historical events are described, such as the Pequot War and the burning of Fairfield, Connecticut, by the British (1779).

Greengroin, Artie.   A character created by HARRY BROWN for the World War II magazine YANK. He is a private 1st class who is constantly getting into trouble. Some of the Greengroin pieces are included in *The Best from Yank* (1945) and in a gathering made by Brown, *Artie Greengroin* (1945).

Green Grow the Lilacs (1931),   a folk play by LYNN RIGGS. This is in part a cowboy opus, in part a historical drama that describes Indian Territory (later Oklahoma) not long before its admission to the Union. A cowboy named Curly McLain is in love with a pretty and spoiled young woman who is attracted by him but makes use of her attraction for Jeeter Fry, a sinister character on the ranch where she lives, to spite Curly. The cowboy and Fry contend for her hand; she marries Curly. When Jeeter tries for revenge on their wedding night and accidentally kills himself in a fight, Curly is suspected of murder, then acquitted. The play was later transmuted into the outstandingly successful musical play *Oklahoma!* (1943) by Richard Rodgers and Oscar Hammerstein II.

Green Mountain Boys.   In the "war" (1775) between New York and Vermont a group of hastily organized militia under ETHAN ALLEN fought off the New York officers and declared the "New Hampshire Grants" an independent state under the name of Vermont. Later these same "boys" fought in the American Revolution and captured the fortress of Ticon- deroga. The play *The Green Mountain Boys* (1833), by Joseph Stevens Jones, and the novel *The Green Mountain Boys* (1839), by DANIEL PIERCE THOMPSON, were written about them. James Fenimore Cooper presents the "Yorker" point of view in THE CHAINBEARER (1845).

Greenough, Horatio (1805–1852),   sculptor, writer on art. Greenough made busts of some of the most famous men of his time, including Lafayette, Henry Clay, and James Fenimore Cooper. His gigantic statue of Washington as Zeus, half nude, is now in the Smithsonian Institution. He became a noteworthy lecturer and writer, and his functional theory of art was expressed in *Aesthetics in Washington* (1851). His *Essays on Art* were included in a *Memorial* biography of him by H. T. Tuckerman (1853); his *Letters to His Brother Henry* were collected (1887) by F. B. Greenough.

Green Pastures, The (1930),   a play by MARC CON- NELLY. This successful production ran for more than a year and a half and won a Pulitzer Prize. It was based on ROARK BRAD- FORD's retelling of Old Testament stories in *Ol' Man Adam an' His Chillun* (1928). Connelly stated that the play was "an attempt to present certain aspects of a living religion in the terms of its believers"; namely thousands of Southern blacks who accepted the Bible as a guide to conduct.

Greenslet, Ferris (1875–1959),   editor, publisher, lit- erary critic, biographer. Born in Glen Falls, New York, Greenslet became editor of the *Atlantic Monthly* (1902–07), then an editorial adviser and later editor-in-chief of Houghton Mifflin. He wrote *Joseph Glanville* (1900); *Walter Pater* (1903);

Life of J. R. Lowell (1905); *Life of T. B. Aldrich* (1908); and *The Lowells and Their Seven Worlds* (1946). His memoirs, *Under the Bridge* (1943), tell of the many New England literary figures he knew personally.

Greenwich Village. Often called "the Village," this is a region in New York City extending approximately from Spring Street on the south to 14th Street on the north and from the Hudson River east to Broadway. It was originally a village, in fact, reached by stage coach from other parts of Manhattan. Here or nearby lived Thomas Paine, Poe, Henry James, Mark Twain, Whitman, and Masefield. It attained fame during the early decades of the 20th century as an equivalent of the Latin Quarter of Paris. The population consisted of persons of Irish, Italian, and African-American descent; they were joined by writers, artists, actors, newspapermen, and other bohemians from all over the country. Magazines were founded; shows were produced, often of a quality that challenged Broadway and to some extent revolutionized the theater; art flourished on the sidewalks and in great studios; and political radicalism found a foothold. The Villagers made a point of flouting conventional dress and mores. MAXWELL BODENHEIM called it "the Coney Island of the soul."

After World War II, the Village began to flourish as a center of intellectual and literary activity for a new generation. Younger artists and writers moved in, new folk and jazz clubs opened, and theater thrived in an atmosphere in which serious plays began to depend less on Broadway and more and more on Off Broadway and Off Off Broadway for production and responsive audiences. Avant-garde movements, anti-establishment journals, and loosely connected groups such as the BEAT GENERATION and the NEW YORK SCHOOL POETS were generally located in or had strong affinities with the Village.

Gregg, Josiah (1806–1850), author of travel books, government agent, newspaper correspondent. Born in Tennessee, Gregg for reasons of health went to Santa Fe as a trader and for nine years traveled the plains regions nearby. He published a book on his adventures, *Commerce of the Prairies, or, The Journal of a Santa Fé Trader* (2 v., 1844). It was often reprinted in its own time and was included in Reuben G. Thwaites's *Early Western Travels* (v. 19 and 20, 1905). Maurice G. Fulton edited his *Diary and Letters* (2 v., 1941, 1944).

Gregory, Horace [Victor] (1898–1982), poet, critic, translator, teacher. Born in Milwaukee, Gregory was an important contributor to the many little magazines of the 1920s and later a faculty member at Sarah Lawrence College (1934–60). Among his books are *Chelsea Rooming House* (1930), *No Retreat* (1933), *Chorus for Survival* (1935), *Poems, 1930–1940* (1941), *Selected Poems of Horace Gregory* (1951), and *Medusa in Gramercy Park and Other Poems* (1961). In 1931 he brought out a memorable translation of *The Poems of Catullus*; this was followed by *Ovid, The Metamorphoses* (1958). *A History of American Poetry, 1900–1940,* in collaboration with his wife, MARYA ZATURENSKA, came out in 1946. He wrote critical biographies of Amy Lowell (1958), James McNeil Whistler (1959), and Dorothy Richardson (1967), and a study of D. H. Lawrence (*Pilgrim of the Apocalypse*, 1933). Essays are col-

lected in *The Dying Gladiator* (1961). A memoir is *The House on Jefferson Street* (1971).

Gregory, Jackson (1882–1943), teacher, writer of western and detective stories. A prolific writer, Gregory won acclaim for the readability and accuracy of his western tales. Among them are *The Outlaw* (1916), *Desert Valley* (1921), *Splendid Outlaw* (1932), *Across the Border* (1933), *Sudden Dorn* (1937), and *Hermit of Thunder King* (1945).

Grenfell, Sir Wilfred Thomason (1865–1940), physician, missionary, adventurer, memoirist. Born in England, Grenfell devoted his life to medical work in Newfoundland and Labrador and wrote numerous books about his experiences. Among them are *Harvest of the Sea* (1906), *A Man's Faith* (1908), *Adrift on an Ice-Pan* (1909), *Down North on the Labrador* (1911), *Tales of the Labrador* (1916), *A Labrador Doctor* (1923), *Labrador Looks at the Orient* (1928), *Forty Years for Labrador* (1932), and *A. Labrador Logbook* (1938). Norman Duncan had Grenfell in mind when he wrote his popular novel *Dr. Luke of the Labrador* (1904).

Grey, Zane (1875–1939), dentist, writer of western stories and articles on outdoor life. Grey was born in Zanesville, Ohio. In 1904 he made up his mind that writing rather than dentistry was to be his career, but not until the publication of *Riders of the Purple Sage* (1912) did he attain great popular success. He published many books after that, including *Desert Gold* (1913); *The Border Legion* (1916); *The U.P. Trail* (1918); *The Mysterious Rider* (1921); *The Thundering Herd* (1925); *Code of the West* (1934); and numerous posthumously published novels: *Rogue River Feud* (1948); *Lost Pueblo* (1954); etc. Possibly his best novel was *The Last of the Plainsmen* (1908). A great sports fisherman, he wrote many books on his experiences, including *Tales of Fishing* (1925). He was always a first-rate storyteller and dramatizer of a region. Jean Kerr wrote *Zane Grey: Man of the West* (1950).

Grey Champion, The (1837), a story by NATHANIEL HAWTHORNE. See WILLIAM GOFFE.

Grey Owl [Archibald Stansfeld Belany] (1888–1938), naturalist, writer. Born in England, Belany emigrated to Canada in 1906, joined an Ojibwa band and later became famous as the naturalist Grey Owl, assumed to be an Indian. In the 1930s he toured the United States and Great Britain as a lecturer, labeled by the London *Times* "A Canadian Thoreau." His books include *Men of the Last Frontier* (1929), on Ojibwa life; *Pilgrims of the Wild* (1935); *The Adventures of Sajo and Her Beaver People* (1935), a popular children's book; and, perhaps his best work, *Tales of an Empty Cabin* (1936), observations of human and animal life in the forest. Anahareo, an Iroquois woman with whom he lived, wrote *Devil in Deerskins* (1972), a memoir of their life. A biography is Lovat Dickson's *Wilderness Man* (1973).

Greyslaer (1840), a romance by CHARLES FENNO HOFFMAN. The scene is the Mohawk Valley at the time of the Revolution, but the plot is based on the famous Beauchamp Case or Kentucky Tragedy, a "triangle" murder that attracted several novelists by its sensational aspects. (See under BEAUCHAMP.) The hero, Max Greyslaer, is a patriot agitator who falls in love with Alida De Roos, but they cannot marry until the shame of a secret (but, as it turns out, invalid) marriage has been cleared from her name. See WILLIAM JOHNSON.

Grierson, Francis (1848–1927),   musician, essayist. Already well known as a singer and pianist under his real name BENJAMIN HENRY JESSE FRANCIS SHEPARD, Grierson took a pen name when he returned from a musical tour of Europe (1888) and began writing. His first book was published in France as *La Revolte Idealiste* (1889) and, in part, translated into English as *Modern Mysticism* (1899). Other titles are: *The Celtic Temperament and Other Essays* (1901); *The Valley of Shadows: Recollections, 1858–63* (1909); *Portraits* (1910); *La Vie et les Hommes* (1911); *The Invisible Alliance* (1913); *Abraham Lincoln, The Practical Mystic* (1921); *Illusions and Realities of the War* (1918); and *Psycho-Phone Messages* (1921), purported spirit communications of famous people written when Grierson was dying in poverty in Los Angeles.

Griffith, David W[ark] (1875–1948),   actor, playwright, movie scriptwriter, producer. Born in Kentucky, Griffith began as an actor, then became a dramatist; among his plays was *A Fool and a Girl* (1907). After the failure of this drama he decided to try the movies, first as an actor, then as a scriptwriter for Biograph Films. He soon turned to directing, doing work that was more convincing and exciting than any produced up to that time. He reached the peak of his reputation with the production of an epic film on the Civil War, *The Birth of a Nation* (1915), based on Thomas Dixon's novels THE CLANSMAN and THE LEOPARD'S SPOTS. Himself a Southerner whose father had fought in the Confederate Army, Griffith poured into the picture much that was personal. The picture attained the greatest success won by any movie up to that time, but also brought Griffith violent denunciation for having caused the revival of the Ku Klux Klan. He was both astonished and hurt, and to show his real feelings he sank his entire fortune in another play, INTOLERANCE (1916), which in its uncut form ran for twenty hours and tried to prove, in four parallel episodes, that intolerance never pays.

Griffith was the first movie director to extend films beyond one reel. His other innovations include the fade in and fade out, angle shots, back lighting, night photography, the moving camera, and many other techniques still in use. These techniques had a great influence in Germany, France, and Russia, where they were immediately appropriated.

Among his often revolutionary films were *Broken Blossoms* (1919), *Way Down East* (1920), *Orphans of the Storm* (1921), *One Exciting Night* (1922), and *Isn't Life Wonderful?* (1924). In *Abraham Lincoln* (1930) Griffith tried out the talkies and won an award as the best director of the year. He developed many stars, including Douglas Fairbanks, Sr.; Mary Pickford; Lillian Gish; and Mack Sennett.

Griffiths, Clyde.   The chief character in Theodore Dreiser's AN AMERICAN TRAGEDY (1925).

Grile, Dod.   A pen name of AMBROSE BIERCE.

Grimke, Sarah Moore (1792–1873) and **Angelina Emily** (1805–1879),   pamphleteers. Born in South Carolina, the sisters moved to Philadelphia, became Quakers, and were active participants in the American Anti-Slavery Society.

Among their works are Sarah's *Epistle to the Clergy of the Southern States* (1836) and *Letters on the Equality of the Sexes and the Condition of Women* (1838); and Angelina's *An Appeal to the Christian Women of the South* (1836) and *Appeal to the Women of the Nominally Free States* (1837). Together they compiled *American Slavery as It Is: Testimony of a Thousand Witnesses* (1839), a sourcebook for Harriet Beecher Stowe.

Grimke, Angelina Weld (1880–1958),   short-story writer, playwright. Raised in Boston, Grimke was the grandniece of Angelina Grimke Weld (1805–1879) and Sarah Moore Grimke (1792–1873), abolitionists and advocates for the rights of women. Their half-brother, Henry Grimke, had taken a slave, Nancy Weston, as his mistress; the son, Archibald, born to that union was Angelina Weld Grimke's father. Her mother was Sarah E. Stanley, of a prominent white family, who abandoned her husband and daughter.

Grimke was educated in Boston and Washington, D.C. where her father was a diplomat. She graduated from Wellesley College in 1902 and was a teacher in Washington. She wrote plays, stories, and poems, mostly before 1920. A few pieces were printed in such Harlem Renaissance journals as *Opportunity* and *The Crisis*, but the bulk of her work was not printed during her lifetime. "The Closing Door," a story of a mother killing her child out of fear of race hatred, was published in the *Birth Control Review* (1919). The majority of her writing is in the manuscript collection of Howard University.

Gringo, Harry.   See H. A. WISE.

Grinnell, George Bird (1849–1938),   explorer, Indian authority, editor. Born in Brooklyn, Grinnell spent his life exploring wild sections of the West, studying Indian tribes, and helping in the conservation movement. He wrote numerous books, among them *Pawnee Hero Stories and Folk-Tales* (1889), *Blackfoot Lodge Tales* (1892), *Travels of the Pathfinders* (1911), and *The Cheyenne Indians* (2 v. 1923), besides a series of books for boys. He edited (and partly owned) *Forest and Stream* (1876–1911).

Grisham, John (1955–   ),   novelist. Born in Jonesboro, Arkansas, Grisham went to Mississippi State and after law school at the University of Mississippi, settled in that state, practicing law in Southaven, serving in the state House of Representatives (1984–90), and living in Oxford, hometown of the state's most famous writer, William Faulkner. *A Time to Kill* (1989), Grisham's first novel, was based on observing the powerful testimony of a child against her rapist. With the vivid courtroom scene in his mind and musing about what would happen if the girl's father killed her attacker and had to be defended, Grisham developed the plot. With difficulty, he found a small publisher who printed 5000 copies. The author bought 1000 copies and gave them to family and friends; these first editions became quite valuable when, in its second publication, the book sold nearly nine million copies. *The Firm* (1991), concerning an idealistic young lawyer's investigation of a corrupt Memphis law firm, was also a best seller and was made into a movie. With the financial success he achieved, Grisham was able to quit his law practice, build his dream home, and concentrate on writing. Other titles turned into motion pictures include *The Pelican Brief* (1992) and *The Client* (1993). In both novels an innocent person knows more about murder than is healthy and must be protected. *The Chamber* (1994) deals with a Ku Klux Klansman, Sam Cayhall, on death row for killing the two young sons of a Jewish civil rights attorney. Adam Hall, his estranged grandson and an attorney, tries to get the sentence reversed, even though he believes his grandfather to be guilty as charged. Grisham's realistic depiction of life on death row raises questions about capital punishment. *The Rainmaker* (1995), also a movie, chronicles a recent law school graduate's difficulties in making a living and retaining his ethics. Current headlines are mirrored in *The Runaway Jury* (1996) on a lawsuit against the big tobacco companies, *The Partner* (1997) featuring a lawyer who defrauds his firm by faking his own death and absconding with millions, *The Street Lawyer* (1998), in which a rising star in a D.C. firm is challenged to think about his profession's ethics by a Vietnam vet, and *The Testament* (1999), where the greedy relatives of a fabulously wealthy man contest the will which leaves his money to a young woman missionary in Brazil. *The Brethren* (2000) describes an elaborate extortion-by-mail plot devised by three former judges from their prison in North Florida. When they target a congressman being groomed for the presidency by the CIA, they stumble into more intrigue than they planned for. Though, by some calculations, Grisham is the world's most successful author, he is caustic about reviewers' treatment of popular fiction, asserting that critics are incapable of being fair to the writers of best-selling books. With *A Painted House* (2001), Grisham tried something new. It is a fictionalized memoir of life on an Arkansas cotton farm in the 1950s. Luke, the ten-year-old protagonist, is able to escape the dreary reality of hardscrabble rural existence through family stories and the radio accounts of Stan "The Man" Musial's baseball prowess.

Griswold, Rufus W[ilmot] (1815–1857), newspaperman, critic, anthologist, editor. Born in Vermont, Griswold was employed on various newspapers and magazines, worked with EDGAR ALLAN POE on GRAHAM'S MAGAZINE and succeeded him as assistant editor, published numerous anthologies and personality sketches of contemporary writers, and in time attained prominence in the literary world. Griswold began as a printer; he was licensed to preach as a Baptist minister, but seems never to have occupied a pulpit. The degrees of D. D. and LL. D. that he assumed he apparently bestowed on himself.

Griswold was perhaps the worst liar in the history of American literature. Horace Greeley, one of almost twenty editors and publishers who employed him, called him "the most expert and judicious thief who ever handled scissors." His worst qualities were shown in connection with Poe, who thought him his friend and made him his literary executor. Griswold repaid him by perpetrating a long series of slanders that greatly influenced the estimate of Poe's character and writings. Arthur Hobson Quinn, in *Edgar Allan Poe: A Critical Biography* (1941), was one of the first to present the facts about Poe vs. Griswold. Griswold's anthology *The Poets and Poetry of America* came out in 1842 (and had many later edi-

tions); his *Prose Writers of America* appeared in 1847; and his *The Female Poets of America*—made up from appropriate sections of *The Poets and Poetry of America*—was published in 1848, and had several later printings.

Grogan, Tom.   See TOM GROGAN.

Gross, Milt (1895–1953),   cartoonist, writer, scenic artist. Gross began to work as a comic artist for newspapers in 1913, created a series of popular comic strips, including "Nize Baby," "Banana Oil," "Gross Exaggerations," "Dear Dollink," and others. Some of these appeared in book collections—*Hiawatta Witt No Odder Poems* (1926); *Dunt Esk* (1927); *Famous Females from Heestory* (1928); and *I Shoulda Ate the Eclair* (1946).

Grosvenor, Gilbert H[ovey] (1875–1966),   editor. Born in Turkey, Grosvenor was successively assistant editor, managing editor, and editor-in-chief of the *National Geographic Magazine* (1899–1954). He turned it from a stodgy periodical with a circulation of only nine hundred into a periodical for students of geography and lovers of nature and travel, with a circulation of over two million. He was the first United States editor to use natural color photographs. He made the NATIONAL GEOGRAPHIC SOCIETY wealthy, won contributions from many distinguished persons. He wrote *Young Russia* (1914), *The Hawaiian Islands* (1924), *Discovery and Exploration* (1924), *Maps for Victory* (1942), and other books.

Group, The (1775),   a satirical play by MERCY OTIS WARREN. It is a drama in name only; the lines consist of a discussion among supporters of the British cause. The play was published the day before the Battle of Lexington.

Group, The (1963),   a novel by MARY MCCARTHY.

Group Theater, The.   An association of actors, playwrights, and producers, many originally associated with the THEATRE GUILD, who in 1931 decided to form their own organization to produce plays of "social significance." After several trials they produced a Broadway hit, Paul Green's THE HOUSE OF CONNELLY (1931), went on to introduce new talents to the theater, and produced some important works; among them are Maxwell Anderson's *Night over Taos* (1932); Howard Lawson's *Success Story* (1932); Sidney Kingsley's MEN IN WHITE (1933); Irwin Shaw's THE GENTLE PEOPLE (1939); William Saroyan's *My Heart's in the Highlands* (1939); and several plays by CLIFFORD ODETS, beginning with WAITING FOR LEFTY (1935). The group in time suffered internal dissension and broke up. Its history is described in *The Fervent Years* (1945), by HAROLD CLURMAN, who with Cheryl Crawford and Lee Strasberg had furnished the original inspiration for The Group.

Grove, Frederick Philip (1879–1948),   novelist, essayist, poet. Born Felix Paul Greve in Prussia, he grew up in Hamburg. In 1909 he left a European literary career, debts and perhaps other troubles, faked a suicide, fled to Canada, and adopted a new identity. His books in English include *Over Prairie Trails* (1922), drawing on personal experience in Manitoba; and the novels *A Search for America* (1927), a semiautobiographical portrayal of immigrant hardship; *Settlers of the Marsh* (1925); *Our Daily Bread* (1928); *The Yoke of Life* (1930); *Fruits of the Earth* (1933); *Two Generations: A Story of*

Present-Day Ontario (1939); and *The Master of the Mill* (1944). His fictional autobiography *In Search of Myself* (1946) won a Governor General's Award.

Grove, Lena, a character in LIGHT IN AUGUST, by William Faulkner. Lena Grove offers an important contrast to the violence and death present in the plot. Her confinement symbolically reenacts the confinement of Joe Christmas's mother, and her placidity and animal unconcern make her a kind of Earth Mother, carrying out her natural function of reproduction in a context that seems, but for her, hostile to life and growth.

Gruelle, Johnny [John Barton] (1880–1938), author of books for children. Born in Illinois, Gruelle created the character RAGGEDY ANN, who appeared in various books bearing her name; also Raggedy Andy and other popular personages. He originated the comic strip "Brutus" (1910).

Grund, Francis Joseph (1798–1863), writer. A German who came to the United States, Grund wrote several books that portray America as seen through foreign eyes. The most important of these was *The Americans in Their Moral, Social and Political Relations* (1837). In Philadelphia he worked as a journalist, later became editor of *Age*; still later he served in Antwerp, Le Havre, and the South German states in the U.S. consular service.

Guardian Angel, The (1867), a novel by OLIVER WENDELL HOLMES. This novel shows how heredity may conflict with environment and how a kindly guardian may prevent the wreck of a life. All this is illustrated by an orphan, Myrtle Hazard, brought from the tropics to live in New England. The book was popular; by 1887 it had passed through twenty-three editions. It is an example of Holmes's opposition to Calvinism.

Guare, John (1938–   ), playwright. Born in New York City, Guare was educated at Georgetown University and the Yale University Drama School. Many of his plays have been produced in Off Broadway theater. *Muzeeka* (prod. 1967; pub. 1969) won an Obie Award. With *The House of Blue Leaves* (prod. 1971; pub. 1972), picked as best play of the year by the New York Drama Critics Circle and winner of a second Obie, and *Two Gentlemen of Verona* (music by Galt MacDermot), the Drama Critics Circle choice for best musical of 1971–72, he achieved national recognition. Urban life is his subject, and his method exploits theatrical conventions. He has also written for television and film. Other plays include *Marco Polo Sings a Solo* (1973); *Landscape of the Body* (1978); *A New Me* (1981); *Three Exposures* (1982); and *The Talking Dog* (1986). *Six Degrees of Separation* (1990) concerns a wealthy couple conned by a young man who claims to be the son of actor Sidney Poitier. It exposes the gap between blacks and whites as well as that between parents and children.

Guerard, Albert Joseph (1914–2000), novelist, critic. Born in Houston, Guerard did his undergraduate work at Stanford, went on to Harvard, and returned to Stanford to earn a Ph.D. He taught writing at his alma mater from 1961 to 1985, influencing the careers of Alice Hoffman and John Updike, among others. His nine novels include *Maquisard: A Christmas Tale* (1945), concerning the French underground resistance to the Nazis, and *Night Journey* (1950) dealing with experiences during World War II, when Guerard was a member of Army intelligence. *The Exiles* (1963) deals with political corruption in the Caribbean and *The Hotel in the Jungle* (1996) is set in a Mexican resort. Guerard wrote critical books on Conrad, Dickens, Dostoyevsky, Faulkner, Gide, and Hardy. His autobiography is called *The Touch of Time: Myth, Memory and the Self* (1980).

Guess, George. See SEQUOYA.

Guest, Barbara (1920–   ), poet. Born in Wilmington, North Carolina, she earned a degree at U.C.L.A. before marriage to Lord Stephen Haden-Guest. After the failure of that marriage and a second wedding, she moved to New York in the 1950s, where she worked in the editorial offices of *Art News* and became associated with the New York school of poets, including John Ashbery, Frank O'Hara, and James Schuyler and the painters who were their friends. Their painterly, experimental poetry was for a time an influence on her work. Her first poetry collection, *The Location of Things,* appeared in 1960, followed by more than a dozen others, including *Stripped Tales* (1995). The poems of *Fair Realism* (1988) demonstrate the influence of painting. Guest soon turned to an interest in language and the images evoked by the word on the page. Her *Selected Poems* appeared in 1995. *Seeking Air* (1978) is a novel; *The Ladies Choice* (1953), *The Office* (1961), and *Port* (1965) are plays. A study of the work of H. D. [Hilda Doolittle] and her circle netted a well-received biography of the poet entitled *Herself Defined: The Poet H. D. and Her World* (1984).

Guest, Edgar ["Eddie"] A[lbert] (1881–1959), newspaperman, columnist. poet. Born in England, Guest came to the United States in 1891, began working for the Detroit *Free Press,* and made his entire career on that paper. He became a verse columnist in 1899. He soon developed a facility for folksy verse, sentimental and moralistic. For several decades he wrote a poem a day, including Sundays. These verses were widely syndicated, gathered in numerous volumes, and personally recited on the air. He is said to have written more than 11,000 poems. His most famous line is: "It takes a heap o'livin' in a house t' make it home." Among his books are *A Heap o' Livin'* (1916), *Just Folks* (1917), *Collected Verse* (1934), and *Living the Years* (1949). Royce Homes wrote Guest's biography (1955).

Guggenheim Fellowships. These are awarded by the John Simon Guggenheim Memorial Foundation. Several hundred annual fellowships are given to Americans to support work in any scholarly or creative field.

Guild, Curtis (1827–1911), editor, poet, memoirist. Boston-born, Guild founded the Boston *Commercial Bulletin,* merged several other papers with it, and called the combination the *Morning Traveler* and *Evening Traveler.* He collected his poems in *From Sunrise to Sunset* (1894) and wrote *A Chat about Celebrities* (1897).

Guillén, Nicolás (1902–1989), Cuban poet. A leading figure of the *poesia negra* ("black poetry") movement, Guillen was born in Camaguey of mixed heritage, African and Spanish, and studied law in Havana. With *Motivos de son (Sound*

Themes, 1930), he began to build his poems on the myths and music of the Afro-Cuban world. *Sóngoro Cosongo* (1931) employs folklore motifs in a further experimental mélange of African words and rhythms and Cuban vernacular. In 1934, with the satirical *West Indies, Ltd.*, he turned abruptly to nationalistic, leftist political verse, which he continued in *España* (1937), his poetic defense of the Spanish Loyalists, with whom he fought in the Spanish Civil War. *El son entero* (1947), the title Guillén gave to his collected poems, refers to the unusual beat of Afro-Cuban music, which moves through all his poetry as its most subtle distinguishing quality. His subsequent books include *La paloma de vuelo popular* (1958), *Balada* (1962), *Tengo* (1964), and *Le gran zoo* (1967; tr. *The Great Zoo and Other Poems*, 1972).

Guimarães Rosa, João (1908–1967),   Brazilian novelist, short-story writer. Trained as a physician, Guimarães Rosa collected stories from his rural patients. His first book was a collection of short stories *Sagarana* (1946; tr. 1966). Ten years later he published his masterpiece novel *Grande sertão: veredas* (tr. *The Devil to Pay in the Backlands*, 1963) and a two-volume cycle of short novels, *Corpo de baile*, in the same year. *Grande sertão* is a first-person narration by Riobaldo of his search for his father; the chronology is disjointed and Riobaldo constantly deforms words, leaves thoughts incomplete, or retells the same incident with variations. The result is one of the most complex novels of Latin America. Other titles are *Primeiras estórias* (1962, tr. *The Third Bank of the River and Other Stories*, 1968), *Tutaméia* (1967), and *These Tales* (1969).

Guiney, Louise Imogen (1861–1920),   poet, essayist, journalist, librarian. Born in Massachusetts, a Catholic by birth and intense faith, Miss Guiney (pronounced *guynee*) spent many of her later years in England; she was buried near Oxford. Her delicate, musical verses won her early fame. They were modeled on old English ballads and the poems of the cavaliers; sometimes even the spelling is antique. Her poems were collected in *Songs at the Start* (1884); *The White Sail and Other Poems* (1887); *A Roadside Harp* (1893); *England and Yesterday* (1898); and *Happy Ending* (1909; rev., 1927). Her essays were gathered in several books, including *A Little English Gallery* (1894) and *Patrins* (1897), and her *Letters* were collected (1926) in two volumes.

Güiraldes, Ricardo (1886–1927),   Argentinian novelist and poet. His first four books (one poetry, three fiction) had been poorly received when he made his third trip to Paris and discovered the avant-garde of French writers. His prose poem *Xaimaca* (1923), clearly influenced by the SYMBOLISTS, fared better. But it was his masterpiece, DON SEGUNDO SOMBRA (1926, tr. 1935), a classic in GAUCHO LITERATURE, that ensured his reputation. Güiraldes had spent the summers of his childhood on the ranch where he was born and where he learned the lore of the *gaucho* from an older friend and storyteller, Segundo Ramírez. Güiraldes's attitude toward the *gaucho* is almost one of reverence, but his characters are convincingly of this world. His concern was always with the spiritual condition of the human creature, and he believed that the lifestyle and

mind of the *gaucho* offered a chance to consider that condition at both its best and its most transparent.

Guiterman, Arthur (1871–1943),   poet, newspaperman, editor. Born in Austria, Guiterman, a finished writer of light verse, first attracted attention with his *Rhymed Reviews in Life*. He rarely wrote serious verse, although his *Death and General Putnam* (in a collection of the same title, 1935) is an exception. He adapted Molière's *L'Ecole des Maris* for the Theatre Guild (1933), also wrote the libretto and lyrics for WALTER DAMROSCH's opera, *The Man Without a Country* (produced, 1937). Among his collections are *Betel Nuts* (1907), *The Laughing Muse* (1915), *Ballads of Old New York* (1920), *Lyric Laughter* (1939).

Gullah.   A name given to a group of African-Americans, also to the dialect of English they speak. They are descendants of slaves who now inhabit islands off the coast of South Carolina, Georgia, and northeastern Florida, also portions of the coast itself. The name may come from *Gola*, the name of a tribe and language of the Liberian hinterland, or from *Ngola*, the name of a tribe in Angola. The dialect is an anomaly among African-American dialects, being the only one not easily intelligible elsewhere. It is a mixture of 17th- and 18th-century English and a number of West African languages and dialects. Some of these words have now passed into the general American vocabulary: *buckra*, a white man; *gumbo*, *okra*; *hudu*, hoodoo. Among those who have discussed this dialect are John Bennett, *Gullah: A Negro Patois* (1908); Reed Smith, *Gullah* (1926); Lupton A. Wilkinson, *Gullah versus Grammar* (1933); and L. D. Turner, *Africanisms in the Gullah Dialect* (1949).

Gullah proverbs have been frequently collected (a selection is given in B. A. BOTKIN's *Southern Folklore*, 1949); a typical one is: "Yaas, bubbuh, uh haa'kee, but uh yent yeddy"—that is, "I hear what you are saying, but I am not paying any attention to it." About this group Charles C. Jones wrote *Negro Myths from the Georgia Coast* (1888); Ambrose E. Gonzales, *The Black Border* (1922); and Guy B. Johnson, *Folk-Culture on St. Helena Island, S.C.* (1930). Literature employing Gullah includes DuBose Heyward's PORGY (1925; made into a folk play, with Dorothy Heyward, 1927; made into an opera, with George Gershwin, *Porgy and Bess*, 1935) and MAMBA'S DAUGHTERS (1929); also Julia Peterkin's BLACK APRIL (1927).

Gullible's Travels (1917),   satirical tales about the newly rich by RING LARDNER.

Gunmaker of Moscow, The (1856),   a novel by SYLVANUS COBB, JR. This was a best seller in the year of its publication. A Russian armorer named Ruric Nevel loves and is loved by a young duchess. Peter the Great witnesses the skill of the young armorer in a duel and makes him one of his favorites. After many adventures Ruric is raised to the nobility, given a large estate, and permitted to wed the duchess.

Gunn, Thom (1929–   ),   poet and critic. Born Thomson William Gunn in Gravesend, England, during World War II he was sent to the countryside in Hampshire for protection from Nazi bombing. There he was exposed to the poetry of Marlowe, Milton, and Keats, which gave him an appreciation for metrical form. After service in the British Army, he studied at Trinity College, Cambridge (B.A. 1953; M.A. 1958). Since 1954, when he came to study poetry with Yvor Winters at Stanford University, Gunn has been a San Francisco resident. He began a long career teaching at the University of California, Berkeley in 1958. In his prize-winning poetry, Gunn typically puts contemporary subject matter, ranging from motorcycles to AIDS, in traditional poetic forms. Early poems were written in iambic pentameter; more recent work uses a wider variety of forms from syllabic to free verse. The diction also reflects long residence in California; as Donald Hall described the language in Gunn's *Selected Poems 1950–1975*, it "begins as English and progresses toward American." Gunn's first collection, *Fighting Terms* (1954), presenting love as combat, brought him attention in England, but Gunn had fallen in love with an American, Mike Kitay, and had decided to come to the United States. His second volume *The Sense of Movement* appeared in Britain in 1957 and the United States two years later. *My Sad Captains* (1961), in a looser style and showing a greater interest in nature, was followed by *Moly* (1971), containing several poems on drug experimentation. The two books were printed in a combined edition in 1973. *Jack Straw's Castle* (1976) explores drug use and the disenchantment of bad trips. *The Passage of Joy* (1982) deals explicitly with homosexual relations, as does *The Man with Night Sweats* (1992). *Collected Poems* appeared in 1994, and *Boss Cupid* in 2000. Gunn's criticism, often written for the London *Times Literary Supplement*, is gathered in *The Occasion of Poetry: Essays in Criticism and Autobiography* (1982) and *Shelf Life* (1993). Gunn never became an American citizen and defines himself as an Anglo-American poet.

Gunnar (1874), a "tale of Norse life" by HJALMAR HJORTH BOYESEN. Gunnar, of lowly birth, loves the niece of a landowner, and the romantic plot relates the dangers he encounters, the devotion of the lovers, the folk customs of the Norseland, and the wedding festivities.

Gunter, Archibald Clavering (1847–1907), civil engineer, chemist, broker, novelist. Born in England, Gunter turned from a career as an engineer to writing. His self-published MR. BARNES OF NEW YORK (1887) immediately became a best seller. Mr. Barnes was an engaging character, an excellent surgeon, a crack shot, a successful lover, and an adept at settling international complications. None of Gunter's thirty-eight later books duplicated his first success, although *Mr. Potter of Texas* (1888) and *Miss Nobody of Nowhere* (1890) did well. See FRESH THE AMERICAN.

Gunther, John (1901–1970), journalist, historian. Born in Chicago, Gunther became a reporter on the Chicago *Daily News* in 1922, and stuck to reporting throughout his career. In 1924 he became a foreign correspondent for the *News*, and thereafter the world was his beat. He wrote *Inside Europe* (1936, frequent revisions) and established a worldwide reputation; thereafter he wrote *Inside Asia* (1939); *The High Cost of Hitler* (1940); *Inside Latin America* (1941); INSIDE U.S.A. (1947); *Inside Africa* (1955); *Inside Russia Today* (1958); and *Inside Europe Today* (1961). Books on individuals include

Roosevelt in Retrospect (1950); *General Douglas MacArthur* (1951); and *President Eisenhower* (1952). *Death, Be Not Proud* (1949) is an affecting memoir on the death of his young son. *The Lost City* (1964), about Vienna, is one of several novels. *A Fragment of Autobiography* appeared in 1962.

Gurowski, Adam G. de (1805–1866), writer, scholar. Count Gurowski lived a stormy life in Europe as one of those who conspired for the freedom of Poland from Russia during the abortive revolution of 1830. In 1849 he came to the United States. During the Civil War he served as a translator in the State Department, and *My Diary: Notes on the Civil War* (1862–66) reports his observations. He also wrote *America and Europe* (1857).

Gustafson, Ralph [Baker] (1909–1995), poet. Born in Quebec, Gustafson attended Bishop's University, Quebec, and Oxford University and lived in England and New York as well as Canada. A prolific writer, he evolved from a traditional poet in his first book, *The Golden Chalice* (1935), to the modernist one evident in *Rivers Among Rocks* (1960), a personal travelogue, and later works. Some of his best travel poems are collected in *Sift in an Hourglass* (1966) and *Ixion's Wheel* (1969). Other titles include *Themes and Variations for Sounding Brass* (1972), a multimedia script lamenting the violence accompanying modern political upheavals; *Fire on Stone* (1974); *Soviet Poems* (1978); *Gradations of Grandeur* (1982); and *Selected Poems* (1983).

Gustavus Vasa (1690), a play by BENJAMIN COLMAN. Colman was the pastor of a church in Boston; he wrote verse as well as sermons and is said to have produced his play at Harvard. If this tradition is correct, his may have been the first performed play by an American writer.

Guterson, David (1956–), novelist. Born in Seattle and educated at the University of Washington, Guterson has taught high school English at Bainbridge Island in Puget Sound. Guterson's first publication is a story collection *The Country Ahead of Us, the Country Behind* (1989). His first novel, *Snow Falling on Cedars* (1994), won the 1996 American Booksellers Book of the Year Award and was made into a motion picture. It is set in remote San Piedro Island after World War II. When a local white fisherman is found drowned, Japanese-American Kabuo Miyamoto is charged with murder. The resulting trial exposes the dreams, prejudices, and suffering left over from the war. *East of the Mountains* (1999) traces the journey of a retired heart surgeon who has been diagnosed with terminal colon cancer. Ben Givens sets out for the Cascade Mountains, planning to kill himself and make it look like a hunting accident. In the natural setting, rendered with copious detail, doubts assail him. *Family Matters* (1992) is a nonfiction book advocating home schooling.

Guthrie, A[lfred] B[ertram], Jr. (1901–1991), newspaperman, novelist, lecturer. Guthrie got his first job as a printer's devil on the Choteau *Advocate* in Montana. In 1926 he went to Lexington, Kentucky, where he worked on the staff of the *Leader* for twenty years, finally becoming executive editor. His first novel, THE BIG SKY (1947), earned immediate critical and popular success. It treats the era of the 1840 mountain men with a mingling of realism and poetry, and gives a faithful and fascinating picture of Indian life in American literature. Although Guthrie was born in Indiana, his family moved to Montana when he was still an infant, and his love for the West is a rich part of his history and his writing. In 1949 he won a Pulitzer Prize for THE WAY WEST, which describes the passage of a small emigrant train over the Oregon Trail in 1847. Other novels include *These Thousand Hills* (1956), set in 19th-century Montana; *The Blue Hen's Chick* (1965), autobiographical; *Pertive* (1971), depicting a Montana town around 1900; *The Last Valley* (1975), set in Arfive a generation later; and *Fair Land, Fair Land* (1982), a sequel to *The Big Sky*. Short stories are collected in *The Big It* (1960). Other works include *Playing Catch-up* (novel, 1985); *Four Miles to Far Mountain* (poetry, 1987); and *Murder in the Cotswold* (1989).

Guthrie, Woody [Woodrow Wilson] (1912–1967), folk singer, song writer. Born in Oklahoma, Guthrie became from age thirteen an itinerant worker and singer, accompanying himself on guitar and harmonica. Continually involved in union activities and left-wing politics, he had some success as a radio personality in California in the 1930s and later wrote songs in support of the Columbia Basin Project; among these are "Roll On, Columbia" and "Grand Coulee Dam." From service in the Merchant Marine in World War II came "The Good Reuben James." Sympathy for the plight of migrant workers brought about "Plane Wreck at Los Gatos." Other titles include "Union Maid," "Philadelphia Lawyer," "So Long, It's Been Good to Know You," "Hard Travelin'" and "Pastures of Plenty." Best known of all is "This Land Is Your Land." For the most part, Guthrie failed to profit from his talent and his hundreds of songs passed into a legacy for others. Among singers and song writers he associated with were Huddie Ledbetter and Pete Seeger, and, as he lived out his last years in a hospital, dying of Huntington's chorea, younger singers began to pick up and extend his voice and manner, including Jack Elliott and BOB DYLAN. Guthrie's autobiography is *Bound for Glory* (1943, revised 1968). With Henrietta Yurchenco, his wife, Marjorie Guthrie, wrote *A Mighty Hard Road* (1970). His son, Arlo Guthrie (1947–   ), also a folk singer and song writer, is best known for "Alice's Restaurant."

Gutiérrez, Eduardo.   See GAUCHO LITERATURE.

Gutiérrez Nájera, Manuel (1859–1895),   Mexican poet, short-story writer, and critic. One of the pioneers of MODERNISMO in Spanish America, Gutiérrez was an aesthetic purist strongly influenced by the French romantics. Through his own poetry, but more through his critical writings and his role as founding editor of Mexico's first modernist journal, *Revista azul,* he did a great deal to encourage an expanded sensuality in the poetic vocabulary. His work is collected in *Poesias completas* (1953) and *Cuentos completas y otras narraciones* (1958).

Guy Rivers (1834),   a "tale of Georgia" by WILLIAM GILMORE SIMMS. The story is one of gold mining in the wilds of Georgia. See BORDER ROMANCES.

Guzmán, Martín Luis (1887–1976),   Mexican essayist, novelist. Guzmán studied law, but joined the Mexican Revolution as a reporter, covering the campaigns first of Venustiano Carranza, then of PANCHO VILLA. After 1914, he lived mostly in New York and Madrid until the 1930s. Meanwhile, he produced his best-known work, *El aguila y la serpiente* (2 vols. 1928; tr. *The Eagle and the Serpent*, 1930). The title, taken from the Mexican coat of arms, symbolizes for Guzmán the struggle characteristic of Mexico's history from Aztec times, especially apparent in the violence of the Revolution. He describes scenes from the times as an eyewitness, building an accurate and moving account indispensable to any study of the history of modern Mexico. Guzmán's novel *La sombra del caudillo (The Shadow of the Leader,* 1929) is based on a 1927 incident in the power struggle between two Mexican political leaders. *Memorias de Pancho Villa* (4 v. 1938–40; tr. *Memories of Pancho Villa,* 1965) is fictional autobiography. *Muertes historicas* (1959; tr. *Historical Deaths,* 1959) details the last moments of two revolutionary leaders.

H

Habberton, John (1842–1921), editor, novelist, playwright. Born in Brooklyn, New York, Habberton spent most of his life in editorial work. He won popular success with *Helen's Babies* (1876), based on the author's harrowing experiences with his two young sons (called Budge and Toddie in the book) during his wife's absence, and vainly tried to repeat his success with *Other People's Children* (1877), *The Worst Boy In Town* (1880), and *Some Boys' Doings* (1901). He also wrote a popular play, *Deacon Crankett* (1880).

habitant. A settler of French descent in French Canada or Louisiana. Habitants have been the subject of many amusing poems written in a mixture of French and English. Probably the best is WILLIAM HENRY DRUMMOND's *The Wreck of Julie Plante*.

Hackett, Albert (1900–1995), playwright, screenwriter, and **Frances Goodrich [Hackett]** (1891–1984), playwright, screenwriter. Their joint efforts resulted in a series of successful plays and movies, culminating in an adaptation of *The Diary of Anne Frank* (1956) based on *The Story of a Young Girl*. This play won a Pulitzer Prize, the New York Drama Critics' Circle Award, and the Antoinette Perry (Tony) Award. They also wrote the play *Western Union, Please* (1939); and screen plays for *The Thin Man; Easter Parade; Father of the Bride; Gaby*; and *Seven Brides for Seven Brothers*, among others.

Hagedorn, Hermann (1882–1964), poet, biographer. An admirer of Theodore Roosevelt, Hagedorn dealt frequently with him: *The Boy's Life of Theodore Roosevelt* (1918), *Roosevelt in the Bad Lands* (1921), *Roosevelt, Prophet of Unity* (1924), *The Rough Riders* (1927), and *The Bugle That Woke America—The Saga of Theodore Roosevelt's Last Battle for His Country* (1940). *The Roosevelt Family of Sagamore Hill* (1954) was a Book-of-the-Month Club selection. Hagedorn edited a selection from Roosevelt's writings (1923) and the *Memorial Edition* of his works (1923–24) and was active in the Roosevelt Memorial Association. In addition, Hagedorn wrote excellent biographies of General Leonard Wood (1920), William Boyce Thompson (1935), and Albert Schweitzer (1947). *The Hyphenated Family* (1960), "a kind of autobiography," relates the history of a family that tried to live both in Germany and the United States. Hagedorn issued several collections of verse, including *A Troop of the Guard* (1909), *Poems and Ballads* (1912), *Combat at Midnight* (1940), *The Bomb That Fell on America* (1946).

Hahn, Emily (1905?–1997), journalist, biographer, novelist, feminist, memoirist. Born in St. Louis, Hahn studied mining engineering at the University of Wisconsin. Against a background of adventure rivaled by few men, she contributed over 200 articles to *The New Yorker*, the first of these resulting from her 1924 cross-country trip in a Model T Ford. From the beginning, she set few limits on herself. After the first of her books, *Seductio ad Absurdum: The Principles and Practices of Seduction—A Beginner's Handbook* (1930), she went to Africa, where she worked in a hospital and lived with pygmies in the Belgian Congo; a diary, *Congo Solo*, and a novel, *With Naked Foot*, grew from these experiences. By 1935 she was China Correspondent for *The New Yorker*. "Though I'd always wanted to be an opium addict," she wrote, "I can't claim that as the reason I went to China." There she had an affair with Zau Sinmay, a Chinese artist and poet, and met the women (one of whom married Sun Yat-sen, another Chiang Kai-shek) featured in her biography *The Soong Sisters* (1941). She chronicled her public affair with Major Charles Boxer, a British spy in Hong Kong, with whom she had a daughter, in the bestseller *China To Me: A Partial Autobiography* (1944); the couple were married in 1945 and remained so until her death. After the war, she continued her flood of writing, with biographies of D.H. Lawrence, Aphra Behn, and Mabel Dodge Luhan, novels, and children's books, but she turned increasingly to monkeys, wildlife preservation, and primate intelligence, earning election to the American Academy of Arts and Letters. Her more than 50 books include: *Diamond: The Spectacular Story of Earth's Rarest Treasure and Man's Greatest Greed* (1956); *Once Upon a Pedestal: An Informal History of Women's Lib* (1974); *The Islands: America's Imperial Adventures in the Philippines* (1981); *Eve and the Apes* (1988), concerning women who own apes; and *Look Who's Talking* (1988), about animal and human communication. Ken Cuthbertson wrote a biography, *Nobody Said Not to Go: The Life, Loves, and Adventures of Emily Hahn* (1998).

Hail Columbia, Happy Land! (April 25, 1798, first performance; published three days later in *The Porcupine Gazette*), a lyric by JOSEPH HOPKINSON. It was adapted to the music of *The President's March*, said to have been composed by Philip Phile (or Pheil). Hopkinson's lyric was first sung by Gilbert Fox in a Philadelphia theater at a time when war with France threatened. It became very popular and remained so during the 19th century.

Hailey, Arthur (1920–   ),   English-born Canadian novelist. Hailey's best-selling novels are fast-paced fictional documentaries, loaded with carefully researched factual detail. The focus is on the airline industry in *Airport* (1968), the auto industry in *Wheels* (1971), banking in *The Moneychangers* (1975), the pharmaceutical industry in *Strong Medicine* (1984), television journalism in *The Evening News* (1990) and Miami police in *Detective* (1997). Hailey's popular success is due in part to his skillful construction of plots and his selection of subjects that affect the well-being, if not the survival, of every reader.

Hairy Ape, The (1922),   an expressionist play by EUGENE O'NEILL. It exhibits the brutalization of Yank, the leader of the stokers in the hold of a transatlantic liner. Later it shows Yank in New York, where his disillusioning adventures lead him finally to the zoo. There he realizes that an ape is his nearest kin in spirit. Yank frees him and is crushed to death by the beast. O'Neill said he drew Yank as a "symbol of man, who has lost his old harmony with nature."

Hakluyt, Richard (1552?–1616),   English clergyman, editor, geographer. Hakluyt gathered accounts of voyages made by his countrymen, and in 1582 published a collection of *Divers Voyages Touching the Discovery of America*. He continued to amass other material and to publish much that would otherwise have been lost. His chief collection appeared in 1589: *The Principal Navigations, Voyages, Traffics, and Discoveries of the English Nation* (greatly enlarged, 3 v. 1598–1600). In this work he included the voyages to the New World of the Cabots, Sir John Hawkins, Sir Francis Drake, Martin Frobisher, Sir Walter Raleigh, and others.

Halberstam, David (1934–   ),   writer on political and social issues, and sports. Deep research and detailed reporting are hallmarks of his work. *The Best and the Brightest* (1972) is a study of U.S. entry into the Vietnam War, and *The Powers That Be* (1979) examines CBS, *The Washington Post*, *Time*, and *The Los Angeles Times*. *The Fifties* (1993) is a study of popular culture, politics, and economics in that decade, and *The Children* (1998) a study of civil rights and race relations. Sports books include *The Summer of '49* (1989) and *October 1969* (1994), on baseball, and *Playing for Keeps: Michael Jordan and the World He Made* (1999). Novels include *The Noblest Roman* (1961), *One Very Hot Day* (1968), and *The Breaks of the Game* (1981).

Haldeman-Julius, E[manuel] (1889–1951),   publisher, editor, writer. Although Haldeman-Julius wrote books of his own—*Dust*, a novel written with his wife (1921); *The Art of Reading* (1922); *Literary Essays* (1923); *An Agnostic Looks at Life* (1926); *The First Hundred Million* (1928); and *My First 25 Years* (1949)—he was chiefly notable as a publisher and distributor of books written by others. His publications, which he sold primarily through the mails, were known as LIT-

TLE BLUE BOOKS. They were small, paperbound, inexpensive volumes, sometimes of trivial material but often of excellent writing from the past and present. They introduced millions of readers to the pleasures of reading. Haldeman-Julius also edited the controversial *American Freeman*.

Hale, Edward Everett (1822–1909),   clergyman, short-story writer, memoirist. Born in Boston, Hale was a man who did many things well and with ease. He preached to the pleasure of many audiences, and for six years was chaplain of the U.S. Senate. Someone asked him once, "Dr. Hale, do you pray for the Senate?" "No," he replied; "I look at the senators and pray for the people." He was a kindly and understanding critic, one of the first to print a warm approval of Walt Whitman's LEAVES OF GRASS. His originality and inventiveness are exhibited in his best-known piece of writing, THE MAN WITHOUT A COUNTRY (*Atlantic Monthly*, December 1863; published separately 1865; collected with other pieces in *If, Yes, and Perhaps*, 1868). The hero, Philip Nolan, soon became a national myth. Made into an opera by Walter Damrosch, it was produced at the Metropolitan Opera (1937). Hale wrote accounts of his career in *A New England Boyhood* (1893, enlarged in 1900) and *Memories of a Hundred Years* (2 v. 1902). His son, **Edward Everett Hale, Jr.** (1863–1932), wrote a biography, *The Life and Letters of Edward Everett Hale* (2 v. 1917).

Hale, Lucretia Peabody (1820–1900),   author of books for children, novelist. In 1880 appeared THE PETERKIN PAPERS, which made Hale's reputation as a significant writer of humor for young people. These sketches, originally printed in ST. NICHOLAS and OUR YOUNG FOLKS, were followed by *The Last of the Peterkins, With Others of Their Kind* (1886). The Peterkins are a Boston family always making ludicrous blunders (the earliest of the stories is called "The Lady Who Put Salt in Her Coffee"), and they are frequently saved by the benevolent "Lady from Philadelphia." Hale, sister of EDWARD EVERETT HALE and SUSAN HALE, was a social and educational crusader who also wrote novels with her brother and others. In 1874 she was the first woman elected to the Boston School Committee.

Hale, Nancy (1908–1988),   newspaperwoman, editor, novelist. This granddaughter of EDWARD EVERETT HALE wrote several lively novels, among them *The Young Die Good* (1932), *Never Any More* (1934), *The Prodigal Women* (1942), *The Sign of Jonah* (1950), *Black Summer* (1963), and *Secrets* (1971). Her short stories appeared in many magazines and are collected in *The Earliest Dreams* (1936), *Between the Dark and the Daylight* (1943), and *The Empress' Ring* (1955). *A New England Girlhood* (1958) is an autobiography. *The Pattern of Perfection* came out in 1960. Her other titles include *New England Discovery* (1963), *Life in the Studio* (1969), *Mary Cassatt* (1975), and *The Night of the Hurricane* (1978).

Hale, Nathan [1] (1755–1776),   teacher, soldier. At Yale the young soldier was an outstanding scholar and athlete, and during the Revolution he was hanged as a spy by the British. His regret at having only one life to give for his country was inspired by a line in Addison's play *Cato* (1713). An anonymous ballad, written soon after Hale's death, commemorated his patriotism. Clyde Fitch wrote a successful play (1898) about him, and he appears in J. R. Simms' *The American Spy* (1846), Howard Fast's *The Unvanquished* (1942), and other novels. Isaac W. Stuart (1856), Jane Tallman (1932), and George D. Seymour (1933) have written biographies of Hale. His family included the ancestors of EDWARD EVERETT HALE.

Hale, Nathan [2] (1784–1863),   publisher, editor, geographer. Hale, a nephew of NATHAN HALE [1], bought the Boston *Daily Advertiser* in 1814, edited it till 1854, and made it an influential paper. He was one of the founders of the *North American Review* and the *Christian Examiner*, and he published and edited the *Monthly Chronicle* (1840–46). He wrote *An Epitome of Universal Geography* (1830).

Hale, Sarah Josepha Buell (1788–1879),   editor, writer, feminist. Hale is an important figure in the annals of the emancipation of women. The death of her husband, David Hale, a brilliant lawyer, left her with five children to support. A poem of hers—MARY HAD A LITTLE LAMB (1830)—became a classic. In 1828 she assumed the editorship of *The Ladies' Magazine*, which in 1837 was bought by Louis A. Godey and was transformed into GODEY'S LADY'S BOOK. Together they made it a great success, especially because Hale encouraged new writers, including women. Her novel *Northwood, or, Life North and South* (1827), was among the first fictional denunciations of slavery. She wrote a valuable compilation, *Woman's Record, or Sketches of All Distinguished Women from the Beginning Till A.D. 1850* (1854). She compiled *The Ladies' Wreath* (1837), a gift-book; two annuals, *The Opal* (1845, 1848) and *The Crocus* (1849); and edited the letters of Madame de Sévigné and Lady Mary Wortley Montagu.

Hale, Susan (1833–1910),   illustrator, writer. Hale wrote, in collaboration with her brother EDWARD EVERETT HALE, a popular series of travel books. *A Family Flight Over Egypt* (1882) was followed by volumes on France, Germany, Spain, and other countries, and by *A Family Flight Around Home* (1885). She wrote a biography of Thomas Gold Appleton (1885) and an account of *Men and Manners in the 18th Century* (1898). A facile and humorous illustrator, she did the drawings for the limericks in Mrs. William G. Weld's *Nonsense Book*.

Haley, Alex [Palmer] (1921–1992),   historian, novelist. Haley was born to a professional family in Ithaca, New York. He served twenty years in the Coast Guard before becoming a writer. Although his early adventure stories were published in several magazines, including *Playboy*, and he collaborated with Malcolm X on *The Autobiography of Malcolm X* (1965), Haley was relatively unknown until the publication of *Roots* (1976, Pulitzer Prize 1977). In this combination of history and fiction, Haley traces his family back to an African ancestor, Kunte Kinte, who was enslaved. The book was made into a successful television miniseries (1977). A sequel for television, *Roots: The Gift*, based on a story outline by Haley, appeared in 1988. The book version is called *A Different Kind of Christmas* (1988). *Henning, Tennessee* (1989) is a memoir about the town his family moved to during his boyhood.

Half-Way Covenant, The (c. 1662),   a document drafted by RICHARD MATHER that indicated a decline in the rigid dogmatism of the Mather dynasty. It advocated the baptism of children of nonregenerate though baptized parents—such parents were regarded by Mather as "half-way" members of the church.

Haliburton, Thomas Chandler (1796–1865), humorist. A Nova Scotian who died two years before Canadian Confederation. Haliburton has been called the father of North American humor—a claim that has been both upheld and attacked, depending in part on North American critics' nationalities and the temper of their times. Although the origins of Sam Slick, Haliburton's best-known character, have been variously attributed—to DAVY CROCKETT and to SEBA SMITH's Jack Downing, for example—the qualities that have so engaged readers with Sam Slick are clear: Slick, the "Clockmaker," is a prototypical Yankee entrepreneur, a congenial, philosophizing, sharp-witted salesman who speaks in a vernacular liberally salted with homespun idioms as he sells his clocks to the gullible Bluenoses (Nova Scotians) while he derides their foibles and celebrates the virtues of Americans. But what has beguiled Canadian, American, and British readers since Slick's emergence in 1835 in *The Novascotian*, a Halifax newspaper, is the way in which Haliburton shaped Slick's pronouncements so that his apparent praise of American virtues and condemnation of Nova Scotian vices also function didactically and ironically, instructing Haliburton's countrymen as they looked both to Britain and to the United States for direction in forming the beginnings of a national identity.

Born in Windsor, Nova Scotia, into a prominent Tory family, Haliburton became a lawyer in 1820 and began his career as a politician when he was elected to the Nova Scotia House of Assembly in 1826. He became a judge in 1829 and a member of the Supreme Court in 1841, retiring in 1856 to move to England, where he died in 1865. Haliburton drew on his first book, *A General Description of Nova Scotia* (1823), to write his two-volume *An Historical and Statistical Account of Nova Scotia* (1829). *The Clockmaker; or, The Sayings and Doings of Samuel Slick, of Slickville* (1836) had its beginnings in a highly successful series of sketches that Haliburton published in *The Novascotian*; a pirated edition was soon published in England, and a second and third series followed in 1838 and 1840. Several more Sam Slick collections followed in 1843, 1844, and 1853. Of his other works, which include his three-volume *Traits of American Humor, by Native Authors* (1852), the best-known is *The Old Judge; or, Life in a Colony* (1849).

Sam Slick's views in *The Clockmaker* are reported to us through the Squire, a Bluenose who rides with Slick on his rounds, watching him sell his clocks and listening to his sermons on "human natur" and on Yankee energy, ingenuity, industry, and political acumen, as well as his laments on Nova Scotian inertia and complacency as Slick urges the Squire and his province to follow the American lead and "go ahead." Slick is the ideal vehicle for Haliburton's vision: although deeply conservative and loyal to Britain, Haliburton also admired American enterprise, so that Slick provided him with a sharp spur to goad Nova Scotians into reconsidering their status in relation to American and British aspirations. Immensely popular on both sides of the Atlantic in the mid-19th century, Sam

Slick's sharp-tongued musings on the Nova Scotian realities of his day remain popular both for their local humor and for the lasting insight they provide into the continuing ambiguities of New World visions on both sides of the forty-ninth parallel.

NEIL BESNER

Hall, Bayard Rush (1798–1863), clergyman, novelist. Hall's fictionalized depiction of life on the Indiana frontier, *The New Purchase: or, Seven and a Half Years in the Far West* (1843), was printed under the pseudonym Robert Carlton. *Frank Freeman's Barber Shop* (1852) is a story about an African-American barber.

Hall, Donald (1928–   ), poet, editor. Hall was poetry editor of the *Paris Review* and Professor of English at the University of Michigan before moving to rural New Hampshire. His first book of poems, *Exiles and Marriages* (1955), won several awards, including the Edna St. Vincent Millay Award of the Poetry Society of America. In editing *The New Poets of England and America* (1957, with Robert Pack and LOUIS SIMPSON) Hall answered the charge that academic poetry had become effete and specious, including mostly poets who employed traditional forms skillfully. For two decades his life revolved around his New Hampshire home, and his wife, poet Jane Keuyon, who died of leukemia in 1995. *Without: Poems* (1998) treats the illness and loss. *Winter Poems from Eagle Pond* (1999) and *Here at Eagle Pond* (2000), essays, focus on their home. *Life Work* (1993) is a memoir and meditation on poetry. Earlier collections of Hall's verse include *The Alligator Bride: Poems New and Selected* (1969); *Kicking the Leaves* (1978); *The Twelve Seasons* (1983); and *Old and New Poems* (1990).

Hall, James (1793–1868), banker, lawyer, judge, editor, historian, poet. Hall, one of the first to record the legends of the frontier, founded and edited the ILLINOIS MONTHLY MAGAZINE (1830–32), the first western literary periodical, and the *Western Monthly Magazine* (1832–36). Among his books are *Legends from the West* (1828), *Legends of the West* (1832), *The Harpe's Head: A Legend of Kentucky* (1833), *The Soldier's Bride and Other Tales* (1833), *Tales of the Border* (1835), *Sketches of History, Life, and Manners in the West* (2 v. 1834–35), and *The Romance of Western History* (1857). John T. Flanagan described him in *James Hall, Literary Pioneer of the Ohio Valley* (1950).

Hall, James Norman (1887–1951), novelist, short-story writer, historian, memoirist. First a social worker, Hall served in the British and American armies during World War I, was a prisoner in Germany for six months, then a resident of Tahiti. These adventures contributed background for his writings. In his fiction he had as an almost constant collaborator CHARLES NORDHOFF, with whom he wrote the trilogy MUTINY ON THE BOUNTY (1932), *Men Against the Sea* (1933), and *Pitcairn's Island* (1934), based on old records. The first volume of the trilogy was made into a movie (1935) that became a classic. The collaborators also wrote *The Lafayette Flying Corps* (1920), *Falcons of France* (1929), *The Hurricane* (1936), and *Botany Bay* (1941). Hall himself wrote *Kitchener's Mob* (1916); *High Adventure* (1918); *Mid-Pacific* (1928); *Flying with Chaucer* (1930); *Dr. Dogbody's Leg* (1940), short stories; *Lost Island* (1944); *A Word for the Sponsor* (1949), a poem; *The Far Lands* (1950); and *Tahiti: Voyage Through Paradise* (1953).

Hall, Oakley [Maxwell] (1920–   ), novelist. Born in San Diego, California, and educated at Berkeley and the University of Iowa, Hall taught for a number of years at the University of California, Irvine. He has won acclaim for his contributions to the serious western in novels that include *Warlock* (1958, filmed in 1959), *The Bad Lands* (1978), and *Apaches* (1986). *Separations* (1997) is set in Colorado in the 1880s. *Ambrose Bierce and the Queen of Spades* (1998) is a murder mystery set in San Francisco in the 1870s. Others are *The Adelita* (1975) and *The Coming of the Kid* (1985). He has published also as O. M. Hall and Jason Manor.

Hall, Samuel (1740–1809), printer, editor. Hall assisted Ann Franklin, Benjamin's sister-in-law, in publishing the Newport *Mercury* (1762). Later he founded the *Essex Gazette* in Salem (1768), the *New England Chronicle* in Cambridge (1775), and the *Massachusetts Gazette* in Boston (1785).

Hall, Sam[uel] S[tone] (1838–1886), dime novelist. One of the few dime novelists who had a firsthand knowledge of the West, Hall wrote under the names Major Sam S. Hall and Buckskin Sam. Among his novels are *Diamond Dick, The Dandy from Denver* (1882); *Bow and Bowie; or, Ranging for Reds* (1882); *Arizona Jack; or, Giant George's Tenderfoot Pard* (1882); *Desperate Duke, the Guadaloupe "Galoot"* (1883); and *Rocky Mountain Al; or, Nugget Nell, the Waif of the Range* (1883).

Halleck, Fitz-Greene (1790–1867), banker, secretary to John Jacob Astor, poet. Literature was an avocation with Halleck, and the mark of that fact, as Lowell pointed out in *Fable for Critics* (1848), is on almost everything Halleck wrote. He had a sense of fun that appeared in his association with a group of young writers in New York who called themselves the Ugly Club and advocated "ugliness in all its forms," and in his more fruitful association with JOSEPH RODMAN DRAKE, with whom he wrote the CROAKER PAPERS. These appeared first in the New York *Evening Post* and the *National Advocate* and were collected as *Poems by Croaker; Croaker & Co.*; and *Croaker, Jun.* (1819) and again as *Poems, by Croaker* (1860). Later Halleck wrote "Fanny" (1819), a burlesque in imitation of Byron. When Drake died in 1820 Halleck wrote an elegy, beginning "Green be the turf above thee, friend of my better days." Another popular poem was MARCO BOZZARIS (1825), again an imitation of Byron. *Alnwick Castle* (1827) was an imitation of Scott. Halleck made a gathering of his *Poetical Works* in 1847.

Hallet, Richard Matthews (1887–1967), novelist. Educated at Harvard, Hallet signed on the bark *Juteopolis* to sail from Boston to Sydney in 1912, intending to find material for a book. Later he worked on a steamship, returned to get a navigation degree at Harvard, and served as a junior officer on a World War I transport ship. *The Rolling World* (1938) is autobiographical. *The Lady Aft* (1915) treats the struggle between humans and the sea. *Trial by Fire* (1916), a story of life on a Great Lakes oar boat, has many similarities to O'Neill's later play "The Hairy Ape." Hallet's short fiction was much admired.

Halliburton, Richard (1900–1939), literary adventurer, writer of travel books. Halliburton spent most of his life wandering over the world and then writing about his experiences. Some of his books became best sellers, among them *The Royal Road to Romance* (1925), *The Glorious Adventure* (1927), *New Worlds to Conquer* (1929), *The Flying Carpet* (1932), and *A Book of Marvels* (1937). Halliburton swam the Hellespont and the length of the Panama Canal, and he followed the routes of Ulysses, Cortez, and Alexander the Great. In 1939, while attempting to sail in a Chinese junk from China to San Francisco, he disappeared. A selection of his travel writings, *The Romantic World of Richard Halliburton*, appeared in 1961.

Halper, Albert (1904–1984), novelist, short-story writer. Halper wrote naturalistic proletarian novels translated into many languages. Among his works are *Union Square* (1933), *Sons of the Fathers* (1940), *The Little People* (1942), *The Golden Watch* (1953), and *Atlantic Avenue* (1956). Much of his work stemmed from his personal experience of his native Chicago, and he edited an anthology of stories about the city, *This Is Chicago* (1952).

Halpern, Daniel (1945–), poet, editor. Halpern's verse has been collected in *Traveling on Credit* (1972), *Street Fire* (1975), *Life Among Others* (1978), *Seasonal Rights* (1982), *Foreign Neon* (1991), *Selected Poems* (1994) and *Something Shining* (1999). He has served as an editor of Ecco Press and *Antaeus* and is a prolific editor of anthologies.

Halpine, Charles Graham (1829–1868), soldier, newspaperman, poet. Irish born, Halpine fought in the Civil War, attaining the rank of brigadier-general. Already well known before the war as a newspaper wit, he reached his greatest success when under the pen name Miles O'Reilly. He found humor in his Civil War experiences, collected in *The Life and Adventures, Songs, Services, and Speeches of Private Miles O'Reilly* (1864) and *Baked Meats of the Funeral* (1866).

Halsell, Grace (1923?–2000), journalist, memoirist. Raised on a West Texas cattle ranch, she began newspaper work in Lubbock and later represented the Fort Worth *Star-Telegram* in Washington, D.C. After the 1968 assassination of Martin Luther King, and inspired by John Howard Griffin's *Black Like Me* (1968), she disguised herself as black to work as a cleaning woman in the Deep South. The resulting chronicle of degradation and attempted rape, *Soul Sister* (1969), was followed by *Bessie Yellowhair* (1973), an account of her life on a Navajo reservation and as an American Indian nanny in Los Angeles, and *The Illegals* (1978), telling of crossing the border with Mexican immigrants. *In Their Shoes* (1996) is an autobiography.

Halyard Harry. Pen name of an author whose real name is unknown. He wrote historical tales, among them *The Heroine of Tampico* (1847) and *The Mexican Spy* (1848), as well as *The Ocean Monarch* (1848) and *Wharton the Whale-Killer* (1848).

Hamilton, Alexander (1755–1804), statesman, essayist. Born in the West Indies to James Hamilton and Rachel Faucett Lavien, he was sent to North America for education in 1772. He studied at King's College (now Columbia University) and wrote pamphlets and articles espousing the colonial cause, including the anonymous *A Full Vindication of the Measures of Congress from the Calumnies of Their Enemies* (1774) and *The Farmer Refuted: or a More Comprehensive and Impartial View of the Disputes Between Great Britain and the Colonies* (1775).

Early in 1776 Hamilton was given a commission as commander of an artillery company, and during the remainder of that year he fought with Washington in the battles of Long Island, White Plains, Trenton, and Princeton. In 1777 he was made an aide-de-camp to Washington and promoted to lieutenant colonel. He was a valued advisor to his commander, but desiring a more active role, he resigned in 1781.

He was elected a member of the Continental Congress in 1782, but found the Congress disorganized and inefficient; he retired after a year to practice law, but did not give up his interest in government. In 1786 he was a delegate from New York to the Annapolis convention, at which he proposed that a convention meet the following May in Philadelphia to draft a constitution. Although his contributions to the Constitutional Convention were slight, he helped secure ratification of the Constitution in New York, even though two-thirds of the delegates had initially opposed it. Even more important was his work with John Jay and James Madison on THE FEDERALIST (1787–88), the most important and influential work of the post-Revolutionary era; Hamilton contributed more than two-thirds of the essays. *The Federalist* expressed the fundamental principles behind the Constitution and argued for a government based on centralization, conservatism, and unity.

The Department of the Treasury was established by Congress in 1789, and Hamilton was immediately asked to be Secretary. With his characteristic ability to quickly find the root of a problem he began to organize the Treasury, made plans for establishment of a mint and bank, arranged for the government to take over state debts, and set up a system of taxation. His *Report on Industry and Commerce* (1791) showed his grasp of the economic and financial problems of the time. Although Hamilton presented his plan for a national bank in 1790, the bank was not established until 1792; the constitutionality of the bill had been challenged by Thomas Jefferson and James Madison. In answer to their arguments, Hamilton presented his doctrine of the implied powers and of the loose construction of the Constitution, an interpretation since proven to be one of the cornerstones of American government.

Hamilton resigned as Secretary of the Treasury in 1795 and returned to his law practice, but continued his interest in government and used his influence to throw the disputed election of 1800 to Jefferson rather than AARON BURR. Although Burr, like Hamilton, was a Federalist, Hamilton distrusted the man, believing him to be dangerous. When Hamilton again opposed Burr's candidacy for governor of New York in 1804, Burr challenged him to a duel in which Hamilton was mortally wounded.

Although Hamilton's financial policies have often been criticized as overly stringent or favoring commerce and industry at the expense of agriculture, his contribution to American government remains on a par with that of the other great statesmen of the Republic. His distrust of the common people and their ability to rule themselves, his desire for a strong central government, and his general political philosophy, which was based on aristocracy, power, and wealth, needed the counterbalance offered by the philosophies of Jefferson and Madison—in the same way Jefferson's agrarianism and democratic idealism needed the political realism of Hamilton.

A dramatic study of Hamilton was made in Gertrude Atherton's novel *The Conquerer* (1902), based on a careful study of sources. He appears frequently in other historical fiction, including Jeremiah R. Clemens' *The Rivals* (1860), Charles F. Pidgin's *Blennerhassett* (1901), Joseph Hergesheimer's *Balisand* (1924), and Howard Fast's *The Unvanquished* (1942).

As a political economist, Hamilton was strongly influenced by Thomas Hobbes's *Leviathan* (1651) and Adam Smith's *Wealth of Nations* (1776). He was a clear, concise, logical, and convincing writer on economic subjects, in the form of reports and letters. He wrote most masterfully in *The Federalist* papers and undoubtedly provided ideas and phrases for Washington, as in the FAREWELL ADDRESS. Important collections of Hamilton material have been gathered for the Library of Congress and for the Stevens Institute of Technology.

Hamilton's papers have been published under the editorship of Harold C. Syrett (22 v., 1961 and after). Studies include Broadus Mitchell's *Alexander Hamilton, The Revolutionary Years* (1970) and Gerald Stourgh's *Alexander Hamilton and the Idea of Republican Government* (1969).

Hamlet, The (1931), **The Town** (1957), and **The Mansion** (1960),   a trilogy by WILLIAM FAULKNER. Spanning almost fifty years in time, the trilogy is centered on the innumerable and vicious SNOPES family, whose first member invades Yoknapatawpha County in the early years of the 20th century. In the hamlet of Frenchman's Bend, Flem Snopes begins as a clerk in Will Varner's store, and, through usury, conniving, and thrift, becomes part owner of the store and husband of Varner's daughter Eula. In the town of Jefferson Flem works his way into Colonel Sartoris's bank, finally becoming vice president. To enrich himself still further, he drives the bank president, Manfred De Spain, from town. In *The Mansion* Flem moves into the now-vacant De Spain mansion, one of the largest and oldest houses in Jefferson. Flem is mercenary, lacking human feelings of any kind and caring only for money and for the outward appearance of respectability. He imports a number of cousins—Mink, I. O., Lump, Ike, Eck—whom he installs in various positions in the community, until the local citizens feel they are overrun with Snopeses.

The novels are loosely episodic, humorous, and ironic. *The Hamlet* offers stories dealing alternately with horse trading and love—economic life vis-à-vis emotional life. *The Town* continues this contrast on a more sophisticated level, centering on the hopeless and almost comic love of Gavin Stevens, first for Eula Varner Snopes and then for her daughter Linda, and on the machinations used by Flem to acquire more

money. *The Mansion* departs from this scheme, dealing primarily with the attempts of Mink Snopes to return to Jefferson and murder Flem, and with the relationship between Gavin and Linda. Each of the novels is made up of sections narrated for the most part by characters whose main purpose is to observe the action rather than take part in it: V. K. Ratliff, the ubiquitous sewing-machine salesman; and Chick Mallison, the young nephew of Gavin Stevens.

Hamlet of A. MacLeish, The (1928),   poem by ARCHIBALD MACLEISH. In this dramatic monologue of fourteen sections in accentual meter, the story of Hamlet is used as a symbol for the way "the knowledge of ill is among us" and the ways in which man tries to deal with it. But MacLeish contrasts Hamlet's situation with his own (using himself as symbol for modern man), in that "in the old time" there at least was a name for the evil—murder, incest, revolution—whereas now the sensitive man is distressed by something he cannot fight because he cannot determine what it is.

Hamlin, Jack.   A professional gambler who appears in BRET HARTE'S GABRIEL CONROY (1876) and about twenty of Harte's short stories. He is courteous, melancholy underneath his gaiety, dissatisfied with the life he leads. He resembles JOHN OAKHURST, of *The Luck of Roaring Camp* and *The Outcasts of Poker Flat*. Both characters were apparently modeled on a real person about whom Harte wrote in *Bohemian Days in San Francisco*. Hamlin is a handsome man, pale and scrupulously elegant, always genial, who nonchalantly sets forth for the duel that ends in his death.

Hammerstein, Oscar [Greeley Glendenning] II (1895–1960),   librettist. Nephew of the impresario Oscar Hammerstein (1847?–1919), young Hammerstein was born in New York City and began working backstage on Broadway at an early age, learning by a process of trial and error the elements that make up a successful book and singable lyrics for a musical play. His best guide and tutor was the librettist OTTO HARBACH, with whom he collaborated on several plays. He also collaborated with Frank Mandel and Laurence Schwab. His lyrics—well over a thousand in all—were set to music by some of the most celebrated composers of the day: Jerome Kern, Sigmund Romberg, Rudolf Friml, Herbert Stothart, and above all RICHARD RODGERS. Among the plays featuring his songs are *Rose Marie* (1924), *Sunny* (1925), *The Desert Song* (1926), *Show Boat* (1927), *New Moon* (1928), OKLAHOMA! (1943), *Carmen Jones* (1943), *Carousel* (1945), *South Pacific* (1949), *The King and I* (1951), *Flower Drum Song* (1958), and *The Sound of Music* (1959). Some of these became movie hits as well, and Hammerstein also wrote lyrics for a number of movies with no previous ancestors on the stage. Among the songs that have made Hammerstein famous are "Old Man River"; "When I Grow Too Old to Dream"; "All the Things You Are"; "The Last Time I Saw Paris"; "Oh, What a Beautiful Morning"; "The Surrey with the Fringe on Top"; "Only Make Believe;" "Some Enchanted Evening"; and "Younger than Springtime." Hammerstein won a Pulitzer Prize (1944) for *Oklahoma!* His collection of *Lyrics* (1949) shows him as an adroit metrist, an unsophisticated sentimentalist, and a clever satirist. Deems Taylor has told the story of Rodgers and Hammerstein in *Some Enchanted Evenings* (1953).

Hammett, [Samuel] Dashiell (1894–1961),   writer of detective stories and movie scripts. Born in Maryland, Hammett worked as a newsboy, freight clerk, railroad laborer, messenger boy, stevedore, advertising manager, and Pinkerton detective. By 1922 he had published nothing but some verse, but then his career turned mostly to Hollywood. One of his notable scripts was for Lillian Hellman's WATCH ON THE RHINE (1943). Hammett is known best as the creator of the so-called hard-boiled detective story. His books include *Red Harvest* (1929); *The Dain Curse* (1929); *The Maltese Falcon* (1930), in which he created his sleuth Sam Spade; THE GLASS KEY (1931); THE THIN MAN (1932); *Adventures of Sam Spade* (1944); *Hammett Homicides* (1946); and *The Creeping Siamese and Other Stories* (1950). On radio the Thin Man and Sam Spade proved very popular. See HARD-BOILED FICTION.

Hammett, Samuel Adams ["Philip Paxton," "Sam Slick"] (1816–1865),   frontier humorist, memoirist. Hammett, born in Connecticut, was one of the earliest to set down in print his observations of the southwestern frontier. *A Stray Yankee in Texas* (1853) was followed by *The Wonderful Adventures of Captain Priest* (1855) and *Piney Woods Tavern, or Sam Slick in Texas* (1858). His hero, Sam Slick, is derived from T. C. Haliburton's character of the same name.

Hammon, Briton (fl. 1747–1760),   author of an early slave narrative, *A Narrative of the Uncommon Sufferings and Surprizing Deliverance of Briton Hammon, a Negro Man . . . How He Was Cast Away in the Capes of Florida; the Horrid Cruelty and Inhuman Barbarity of The Indians in Murdering the Whole Ship's Crew, and the Manner of His Being Confined Four Years and Seven Months in a Close Dungeon, and the Remarkable Manner in Which He Met with His Good Old Master in London, and Returned to New-England, a Passenger, in the Same Ship.* As the title indicates, Hammon did not actually escape slavery, but was reunited with his original master and confined in more pleasant circumstances.

Hammon, Jupiter (1720?–1800?),   a slave who wrote verses that won publication in his own lifetime and gained the praise of white critics. He lived in Long Island and Connecticut. He antedated PHILLIS WHEATLEY by several years, and one of his poems was *A Poetical Address* (1778) inscribed to her. Much of his poetry was of religious content, such as his *Address* (1787) urging patience on his fellow slaves. Oscar Wegelin wrote the study *Jupiter Hammon* (1915).

Hammond, John (mid-17th century),   English colonist. Hammond lived in Virginia and Maryland for twenty-one years, 1635–1656. He wrote glowingly of the new land in LEAH AND RACHEL, OR, THE TWO FRUITFUL SISTERS, VIRGINIA AND MARYLAND: THEIR PRESENT CONDITION, IMPARTIALLY STATED AND RELATED (1656).

Handy, W[illiam] C[hristopher] (1873–1958), composer, orchestra leader, publisher. The son of an Alabama clergyman, Handy did a great deal to popularize the blues, although he also incorporated elements of other folk tunes into his compositions. His more notable pieces include *Memphis Blues* (1909), *St. Louis Blues* (1914), *Joe Turner Blues* (1915), *Beale Street Blues* (1917), *Loveless Love* (1921), and *Got No Mo' Home Dan a Dog* (1926). Handy became his own publisher and an active worker in theatrical circles. His songs were popular all over the globe and he made a collection of pirated versions of the *St. Louis Blues*, including phonograph records in Japanese and Russian. Among his books are *Negro Authors and Composers of the U.S.* (1935), *Negro Spirituals* (1938), and *Father of the Blues*, an autobiography (1941). He edited an anthology, *Blues* (1926), which was reissued as *A Treasury of the Blues* (1949) with a critical text by Abbe Niles and pictures by Miguel Covarrubias.

Hanley, William (1931–   ),   playwright and novelist. He is best known for *Slow Dance on the Killing Ground* (1964), a play about "facing the darkness." Several of his plays are collected in *Mrs. Dally Has a Lover and Other Plays* (1965). His novels are *Blue Dreams* (1971), *Mixed Feelings* (1972), and *Leaving Mount Venus* (1977).

Hannah, Barry (1942–   ),   novelist. Hannah grew up in Clinton, Mississippi, an area that figures heavily in his fiction. After undergraduate premedical studies, he switched to literature and did graduate work at the University of Alabama. His lifelong interest in the past of the South, especially the Civil War and the career of cavalry officer Jeb Stuart, provides a substructure for the playing out of contemporary violence, including the Vietnam War and the racial unrest connected with the civil rights movement. He has worked as a screenwriter and taught at several colleges, most recently the University of Mississippi. In his first novel, *Geronimo Rex* (1972), the protagonist is an aspiring writer who emphasizes his physical resemblance to the Apache chief whose independence he admires. Hannah describes *Night-watchman* (1973) as his "most deliberately Gothic book." *The Tennis Handsome* (1983) portrays several generations of Vicksburg residents from the Twenties through the Vietnam War. *Boomerang* (1989) is a first-person narrative of a Mississippi boyhood and middle age. Some of his best work is in his story collections: *Airships* (1978), *Captain Maximus* (1985), *Never Die* (1991), *Bats Out of Hell* (1993), and *High Lonesome* (1996). In *Yonder Stands Your Orphan* (2001) he extends the Southern Gothic tradition in a novel of criminality, sex, and violence set in a small Mississippi town.

Hannibal, Missouri.   A town on the Mississippi River, where MARK TWAIN spent his boyhood and where his experiences provided the background for *Tom Sawyer* and *Huckleberry Finn*, as well as for chapters in *Life on the Mississippi*. Twain wrote for the Hannibal *Journal*, bought by his brother Orion Clemens in 1851. Many places in the town and nearby are Mark Twain memorials: his boyhood home, the Mark Twain Museum, the Mark Twain Cave, a statue of Twain in Riverview Park, and a Tom and Huck Monument at the foot of Cardiff Hill.

Hansberry, Lorraine [Vivian] (1930–1965),   playwright. Born to a middle-class African-American family on the south side of Chicago, Hansberry studied painting in Chicago and abroad before moving to New York City in 1950. Her *A Raisin in the Sun* was the first play by an African-American woman to be produced on Broadway (1959) and won the Drama Critics' Circle Award. It tells the story of a family's attempt to escape from the ghetto to the white suburbs, a struggle her own father had fought through to the Supreme Court. Hansberry won a special award at the Cannes Film Festival (1961) for her screenplay. Hansberry died of cancer on the day her second play, *The Sign in Sidney Brustein's Window* (1964), closed on Broadway. Robert Nemiroff, her ex-husband, has edited two collections of her work in *To Be Young, Gifted and Black* (1969) and *Les Blancs: The Collected Last Plays of Lorraine Hansberry* (1972).

Hans Pfaal. See THE UNPARALLELED ADVENTURES OF ONE HANS PFAAL.

Hapgood, Hutchins (1869–1944), newspaperman, student of social conditions, novelist. Born in Chicago, and educated at Harvard, Hapgood wrote for several New York newspapers and for magazines, and in his books did much to interpret the spirit of his day. Among his writings are *The Spirit of the Ghetto* (1902), *The Autobiography of a Thief* (1903), *The Spirit of Labor* (1907), *Types from City Streets* (1910), and *A Victorian in the Modern World* (1939), his autobiography. *The Story of a Lover* (1919) is a semi-autobiographical novel.

Hapgood, Norman (1868–1937), lawyer, newspaperman, editor, political and social crusader, diplomat, biographer, drama critic. Born in Chicago, this brother of Hutchins Hapgood exerted considerable influence not merely on the general thought of his time but also on some of its leading personages, among them ALFRED E. SMITH, about whom (in collaboration with Henry Moscowitz) he wrote a campaign biography, *Up from the City Streets* (1927), and Woodrow Wilson, whom he strongly supported as President. After a brief practice of the law, he turned to newspaper work. Later he became editor of *Collier's* and carried on effective campaigns against harmful drugs and foods. He served for a while as minister to Denmark. Among his books are *Literary Statesmen and Others* (1897), *Daniel Webster* (1899), *Abraham Lincoln: The Man of the People* (1899), *George Washington* (1901), *The Stage in America* (1901), *Industry and Progress* (1911), *Why Janet Should Read Shakespeare* (1929), and *The Changing Years* (1930), his autobiography.

Hapless Orphan, The (1793), an anonymous novel by "an American Lady." Caroline Francis, the heroine, a sort of Becky Sharp, follows her own path pretty selfishly, but when she tries to take away another girl's young man and the young man commits suicide, Caroline becomes the victim of a vendetta.

Happy Hooligan. A hobo who appeared in a comic strip by FREDERICK B. OPPER. Maud the Mule frequently abetted Hooligan.

Harbach, Otto [Abels] (1873–1963), newspaperman, playwright, librettist. Born in Salt Lake City, Harbach taught English and worked for newspapers and advertising agencies before turning to the stage. He became a noted librettist, working alone and with collaborators. His plays include *The Three Twins* (1907), *Bright Eyes* (1909), *The Fascinating Widow* (1910), *The Firefly* (1912), *High Jinks* (1913), *Katinka* (1915), *You're in Love* (1917), *No! No! Nannette* (1925), *Rose Marie* (1924), *The Desert Song* (1927), *Cat and the Fiddle* (1931), and *Roberta* (1933).

Harbaugh, Henry (1817–1867), clergyman, hymn writer, editor, poet. Born in Pennsylvania, Harbaugh published a collection of *Poems* (1860), *Hymns and Chants* (1861), and *The Religious Life of Washington* (1863). But he is chiefly remembered for his poems in German dialect, posthumously collected as *Harbaugh's Harfe* (1870). Among these the best known were *Das Alt Schulhaus an der Krik* and *Die Schlofschtub*.

Harbaugh, Thomas Chalmers ["Capt. Howard Holmes"] (1849–1924), poet, dime novelist. Born in Maryland, Harbaugh published at least two collections of verse, *Maple Leaves* (1884) and *Ballads of the Blue* (1892). But such fame as he won depended on his DIME NOVELS, issued mainly by Beadle & Adams, whose dates and exact authorships are far from fixed. Harbaugh undoubtedly had a hand in the NICK CARTER series. From the 1880s into the first two decades of the 20th century he wrote many other thrillers, including *Judge Lynch, Jr.; Navajo Nick; The Pampas Hunters; The Silken Lasso; Dodger Dick; The White Squadron; The Withered Hand*; and *Kit Carson's Chum*.

Harben, Will[iam] N[athaniel] (1858–1919), novelist, short-story writer. One of the early regional novelists. Harben made his native state of Georgia the background for some of his widely read stories, notably *White Marie: A Story of Georgian Plantation Life* (1889), *Northern Georgian Sketches* (1900), *The Woman Who Trusted* (1901), *Abner Daniel* (1902), *The Georgians* (1904), *Ann Boyd* (1906), and *Mam' Linda* (1907).

Harbinger, The (1845–1849), a weekly newspaper, edited by George Ripley. From 1845 to 1847 it was the official publication of Brook Farm. It treated social science, politics, and the arts. Lowell, Whittier, and Greeley were among its contributors.

Harbor, The (1915), a novel by ERNEST POOLE.

Hard, Walter (1882–1966), poet, historian, folklorist. Born in Vermont, Hard was regarded as a representative voice of the state, especially in his free verse vignettes and narratives. Hard wrote for local papers, dabbled in politics, and published four volumes of verse: *Salt of Vermont* (1931), *A Mountain Township* (1933), *Vermont Vintage* (1937), and *Vermont Valley* (1939). Hard's other books include *Some Vermonters* (1928); *This is Vermont* (1936), an informal guidebook written with his wife, Margaret Hard; *Walter Hard's Vermont* (1941); *The Connecticut [River]* (1947); and *A Matter of Fifty Houses* (1952).

hard-boiled fiction. A type of detective or crime story in which an air of realism is generated through laconic and often vulgar dialogue, depiction of cruelty and bloodshed at close range, and use of generally seamy environments. The genre was perhaps a product of the prohibition era, but it was also an attempt to apply the literary lessons taught by such serious American novelists as ERNEST HEMINGWAY and JOHN DOS PASSOS. Hard-boiled fiction appeared early in the magazine BLACK MASK (founded 1919), and its development was closely associated with the editor, Joseph T. Shaw. An example was DASHIELL HAMMETT's story "Fly Paper," which appeared in August 1929 in *Black Mask*. In 1946 Shaw compiled *The Hard-Boiled Omnibus: Early Stories from Black Mask*, including stories by Hammett, RAYMOND CHANDLER, Raoul Whitfield, and GEORGE HARMON COXE. To these names should be added W. R. BURNETT, Jonathan Latimer, and Peter Cheyney. Later, hard-boiled fiction in a particularly violent phase became hugely popular in the Mike Hammer novels of Mickey Spillane. Among more recent writers who owe something to the tradition are SUE GRAFTON, GEORGE V. HIGGINS, EVAN HUNTER, SARA PARETSKY, and ROBERT B. PARKER.

Harder They Fall, The (1947), a novel by BUDD SCHULBERG. In this story boxing is presented as a brutal sport transformed into a corrupt industry. The protagonist is an Argentinian named Toro Molina, a fighter of gigantic size, who is suggestive of Primo Carnera, the Italian fighter who became heavyweight champion of the world, earned more than $3,000,000 for his promoters, but returned partly paralyzed to his native land. The novel was made into a movie.

Hardwick, Elizabeth (1916–), novelist, essayist. Long identified as "the wife of Robert Lowell," to whom she was married from 1949 to 1972, Hardwick possesses formidable talent and has accomplished work of note, including the founding of *The New York Review of Books*. Her best novel is *Sleepless Nights* (1979), partly autobiographical. Earlier was *The Simple Truth* (1955), about a college student on trial for the murder of his sweetheart. Her essay collections include *A View of My Own* (1962), *Seduction and Betrayal: Women and Literature* (1974), and *Bartleby in Manhattan* (1983). Fifty years of essays on literature from Henry James to Richard Ford are collected in *Sight Readings: American Fictions* (1998).

Hardy, Arthur Sherburne (1847–1930), civil engineer, diplomat, editor, novelist, poet. Born in Andover, Massachusetts, Hardy was educated at West Point, spent a year in the army, taught and practiced civil engineering, served in diplomatic posts for several years in Europe and in Persia, edited the COSMOPOLITAN for two years, and wrote poetry and novels. Of his poems, *Francesca of Rimini* (1878) is best known. His most widely read novel is *Passe Rose* (1889), the story of a dancing girl at the court of Charlemagne. He also wrote *But Yet a Woman* (1878); *The Wind of Destiny* (1886); *Aurélie* (1912); *Diane and Her Friends* (1914); his autobiography, *Things Remembered* (1923); and some mathematics texts.

Hare, Robert (1781–1858), chemist, teacher, writer. Hare invented various laboratory devices. He wrote a *Brief View of the Policies and Resources of the U.S.* (1810) and *Spiritualism Scientifically Demonstrated* (1855); and two romances,

Standish the Puritan (1850) and *Overing, or, The Heir of Wycherly* (1852).

Hare, Walter Ben (1870–1950), actor, meteorologist, playwright. Hare first wrote plays for amateur groups. He attained an extraordinary success with some of his two hundred or so dramas, particularly a rural melodrama called *Aaron Slick from Punkin Crick* (1919), which made Hare wealthy. He said he wrote under three names: "I used the pen name Lt. Beal Carmack for the plays I'm ashamed of, the name Mary Modena Burns for religious plays, and the other stuff I wrote under my own name." Carmack received the credit for *Aaron Slick*.

Hargrove, [Edward Thomas] Marion [Lawton] (1919–), newspaperman, novelist. Born in North Carolina, Hargrove wrote the best-seller *See Here, Private Hargrove* (1942), compiled from his newspaper column "In the Army Now." After the war he wrote *Something's Got to Give* (1948), a satire on the radio industry, and *The Girl He Left Behind* (1956), a humorous account of draftees.

Hariot [sometimes **Harriot**], **Thomas** (1560–1621), English naturalist, historian, astronomer, explorer. Hariot, an able Oxford scientist, accompanied Sir Richard Grenville on a trip to the New World in 1585. He collected specimens of animals and plants on Roanoke Island, studied the Indians there, and later published his *Brief and True Report of the New-Found Land of Virginia* (1588), the first English book on the first British colony in America. Accurately and clearly written, the book was often reprinted and occasionally plagiarized. Stefan Lorant, in *The New World* (1946), reprinted Hariot's texts and the original water colors of John White.

Harjo, Joy (1951–), poet, musician, screenwriter. Born in Tulsa, Oklahoma, Harjo was descended on both sides from people who survived the Trail of Tears caused by the Indian Removal Act of 1830. Her father, a full-blooded Creek, was born into the wealth that resulted, ironically, from the discovery of oil on Indian lands in Oklahoma, but the land and wealth were lost in his youth. Her mother was Cherokee, Irish, and French. After boarding school at the Institute for American Indian Arts in Santa Fe, New Mexico, she began a premed program at the University of New Mexico, but turned to creative writing, graduating in 1976 and moving to the University of Iowa for an M.F.A. (1978). She has taught at Arizona State University, the University of Colorado, the University of New Mexico, and other schools. One of her earliest literary influences was the Bible, as she played "preacher" as a child, in imitation of her paternal grandfather, a Baptist minister. The influences of Keats, Dickinson, and Shelley also run through her poetry, but her subjects are herself, the margins between people and races, and the inner and outer landscapes of the American Southwest. Increasingly, her rhythms have displayed the influence of Creek and Cherokee music and the mixed jazz forms of her band, Poetic Justice, for which she plays tenor sax. In the title poem of *What Moon Drove Me to This* (1980), she portrays a "dangerous woman" pulled toward the music of her Creek identity but held back by a man who wants the white, the "other half." In the title poem of *She Had Some Horses* (1983), she treats symbolically a similar inner tension, as both the "horses she loved" and those "she hated" prove for all their differences to be identical. *Secrets from the Center of the World* (1989) combines prose poems with southwestern landscape photographs. *In Mad Love and War* (1990), highly praised, mixes gender and racial politics with messages of change. *The Woman Who Fell from the Sky* (1996) brings together present and past, myths and transformations. *A Map to the Next World* (2000) extends Harjo's poetic boundaries to Hawaii, the Middle East and elsewhere.

Harland, Henry ["Sidney Luska"] (1861–1905), novelist, short-story writer, editor. Harland, who was born in Russia of American parents, began writing under a pen name as an immigrant of Jewish background. These writings include *As It Was Written: A Jewish Musician's Story* (1885); *Mrs. Peixeida* (1886); *The Yoke of the Thorah* (1887); *My Uncle Florimond* (1888); *A Latin Quarter Courtship and Other Stories* (1889); and *Grandison Mather* (1889).

Harland went to England, where he came under the influence of Henry James and also became associated with a group of writers ostensibly in revolt against Victorian respectability. He was the first editor of the magazine *The Yellow Book* (1894–1897), which had as early contributors James, George Saintsbury, Richard Garnett, Max Beerbohm, William Watson, and Aubrey Beardsley. In his English period Harland wrote gay and witty romances. Best known was *The Cardinal's Snuff Box* (1900). Among the others are *Mademoiselle Miss and Other Stories* (1893), *Grey Roses* (1895), *Comedies and Errors* (1898), *The Lady Paramount* (1902), and *My Friend Prospero* (1904).

Harland, Marion. Pen name of MARY VIRGINIA TERHUNE.

Harlem. A section of upper Manhattan, founded in 1658 by Peter Stuyvesant and called Nieuw Haarlem. About the time of World War I, it became a predominantly African-American residential and cultural area.

Harlem Renaissance. A period of high productivity in African-American art and culture particularly identified with the 1920s. Important writers of the period include Countee Cullen, Claude McKay, Jean Toomer, Zora Neale Hurston, James Weldon Johnson and Langston Hughes. See AFRO-AMERICAN LITERATURE.

Harmonium (1923), the first volume of poems by WALLACE STEVENS. It consists of works printed in little magazines beginning with the "War Number" of *Poetry* in 1914. The first edition sold less than one hundred copies, although some of its poems—PETER QUINCE AT THE CLAVIER and LE MONOCLE DE MON ONCLE—have since become anthology pieces. *Harmonium* was reissued in 1931 with three poems omitted and fourteen new poems added.

Harmony, New Harmony. Communal experiments established in Pennsylvania and Indiana by followers of George Rapp (1757–1847), a German religious leader. He led a migration of six hundred adherents to the United States in 1803, settling in a town in Butler County, Pennsylvania, that he

called Harmony. In 1815 the Rappites moved to Harmony, or New Harmony, in Indiana. In 1825 they sold the colony to the Owen Community founded by Robert Owen (1771–1858), Welsh humanitarian and author of *A New View of Society* (1813). His colony failed (1828), but New Harmony became a cultural center, and a weekly magazine published there, *The New-Harmony Gazette* (in 1829 called *The Free Enquirer*), continued from 1825 to 1835 to preach Owen's brand of socialism. Meanwhile the Rappites returned to Pennsylvania and settled at Economy Town (now Ambridge), near Pittsburgh. In 1831 an adventurer who called himself Count Maximilian De Leon set up a secessionist movement and made off with most of the funds of the colony. In 1832 Bernard Mueller, who opposed Rapp's doctrine of celibacy, withdrew with 250 members to Monaca, a nearby town. After Rapp's death the colony declined, and in 1906 its property was taken over by the state.

Harper, Frances Ellen Watkins (1825–1911), poet, Abolitionist, prose writer. Born of free parents in the slave state of Maryland, Harper was educated at her uncle's school for free blacks. She moved several times to get to a free state, finally settling in Pennsylvania. She worked on the Underground Railway and gave antislavery speeches throughout the North. Her verse, largely narrative and written in ballad stanzas, also served the antislavery cause and focused on social ills and equal rights for women. She wrote essays, short stories, and one novel, *Iola Leroy; or, Shadows Uplifted* (1892). Her work was published under several variations of her initials and name. *Eventide* (1854), a collection of poems and tales, appeared with the pseudonym Effie Alton. Collections include *Forest Leaves* (c. 1845); *Poems on Miscellaneous Subjects* (1854, preface by William Lloyd Garrison); *Moses: A Story of the Nile* (2nd edition, 1869); *Sketches of Southern Life* (1891); and *Atlanta Offering: Poems* (1895). A modern edition, *The Poems of Frances E. W. Harper*, appeared in 1970.

Harper, Michael S[teven] (1938–   ), poet. Born in Brooklyn, New York, Harper was educated at Los Angeles State College and the University of Iowa. From 1970 on he taught at Brown University. Harper draws on family stories, African-American history, folklore, and literature to illuminate the American experience. His collections include *Dear John, Dear Coltrane* (1970); *Nightmare Begins Responsibility* (1974); *Images of Kin: New and Selected Poems* (1977); *Healing Song for the Inner Ear* (1985); and *Honorable Amendments: Poems* (1995).

Harper's Bazaar. A weekly magazine for women, first called *Harper's Bazar*, founded November 1867 by Harper and Brothers, it became a monthly in 1901. In 1913 it became a Hearst publication. The spelling of the name was changed in 1920. Early numbers had contributions by some of the foremost of American writers, but in recent years it has specialized in women's fashions and beauty enhancement. Articles for the professional designer and retailer, travel writing, profiles, and interviews are also included. In 1990 it had a circulation of about 750,000 and by 2000 it was available in ten foreign editions in addition to the New York one.

Harpers Ferry, West Virginia. See JOHN BROWN.

Harper's Magazine.   *Harper's New Monthly Magazine* was founded by Fletcher Harper, of Harper & Brothers, in 1850. It featured serials by popular English novelists of the time—Dickens, Bulwer, Trollope, Thackeray, and George Eliot—and copious woodcut illustrations. It was a sensational success, reaching 200,000 circulation by 1860, an unprecedented figure for a magazine selling for $3 a year.

For the first year or two, the English serials that furnished the body of the magazine were pirated; thereafter, advance sheets were purchased from the London publishers. *Harper's* long continued to draw heavily on English writers. In the 1850's, *Harper's* carried some non-English material, but mostly in the departments. The "Easy Chair"—devoted to comment on literature, art, music, and politics—was first filled by Donald G. Mitchell, and then in 1859, by the urbane and erudite George William Curtis. See EDITOR'S DRAWER and EASY CHAIR.

Henry Mills Alden began a half-century editorship in 1869. The new editorship and the competition of the new SCRIBNER'S MONTHLY caused some changes in *Harper's*. Illustrations by Edwin A. Abbey, John W. Alexander, Howard Pyle, and Winslow Homer; and serials by Howells, Henry James, C. D. Warner, and Constance Fenimore Woolson brought distinction to the magazine. In the "Editor's Study" department, begun by Howells in 1885, an important campaign for the new realistic fiction was waged. Warner succeeded Howells in that department in 1894, though Howells returned to the magazine to occupy the "Easy Chair" from 1901 to 1921.

At the end of the century, color had come into the illustrations, and more attention was being given to contemporary problems. Mark Twain, whose *Joan of Arc* had been an anonymous contribution in 1895–1896, continued to be an occasional contributor, as did Mary Johnston, Booth Tarkington, Frank R. Stockton, and other leading writers. Woodrow Wilson's *History of the American People* was serialized in 1901. The Harper bankruptcy and change in ownership of 1900 had little effect on the magazine. Alden retired in 1919, turning the editorship over to Thomas B. Wells, long an assistant editor and by then vice president of the publishing company.

After World War I, it became apparent that the old quality magazine was losing ground. Wells virtually abandoned illustration and concentrated on thoughtful articles about current social and moral problems, though he did not eliminate fiction. Lee F. Hartman was editor from 1931 to 1941; Frederick Lee Allen, editor from 1941 to 1953, stressed economic, political, and social problems. This emphasis continued under his successor, John Fischer.

In the early 1960s, Harper's became the property of *The Minneapolis Tribune* and nearly became defunct in the early 1980s, when it was rescued by a grant from the MacArthur Foundation and Atlantic Richfield. Under the leadership of Lewis H. Lapham, editor almost continually from 1976, *Harper's* has maintained its place as one of America's most thoughtful magazines, supported in the year 2000 by a Harper's Magazine Foundation endowment of $50 million and a circulation of 220,000.

Harper's Weekly.   Fletcher Harper of the publishing house of Harper & Brothers was responsible for founding the *Weekly* in 1857, as he had been for founding the *Monthly* seven years before. (See HARPER'S MAGAZINE.) Its editors were Theodore Sedgwick (1857–1858), John Bonner (1858–1863), George William Curtis (1863–1892), Carl Schurz (1892–1894), Henry Loomis Nelson (1894–1898), John Kendrick Bangs (1898–1901), George Harvey (1901–1913), and Norman Hapgood (1913–1916). *Harper's Weekly* was a small folio, originally of 16 pages, printed on good paper and fully illustrated. In the early 1870s it had a circulation of over 400,000; though it ran below that figure through most of its life, it was always a weekly of prestige and influence. It was especially distinguished in four fields:

1. In reports, editorials, and pictures, it gave much attention to current events.
2. It was a journal of opinion; most of its editors were mainly concerned with politics, leaving the general content to their managing editors. Henry Mills Alden, managing editor (1863–1869), called it "the fighting arm" of the House of Harper. At first a Buchanan paper, it came strongly to Lincoln's support by the middle of the war; later it battled for Grant, Cleveland, and Wilson. Its most spectacular campaign was the one against the Tweed Ring in New York in 1871; later it gave sturdy support to civil service reform, tariff reduction, and maintenance of the gold standard.
3. It was notable for its illustrations—woodcuts, later halftones. It carried full- and double-page pictures of news events and slashing cartoons. Its Civil War illustrations by Thomas Nast, A. R. and William Waud, and others made it a great pictorial history of that conflict. The Nast drawings pillorying the Tweed Ring mark a high point in the history of American political cartooning. Later artists, such as Edwin A. Abbey, William T. Smedley, and Howard Pyle, gave the paper distinction. R. F. Zogbaum's pictures of the War with Spain were memorable, and there was a fine pictorial record of the 1893 Columbian Exposition in Chicago. Pictures of the American girl by Charles Dana Gibson and James Montgomery Flagg were features after the turn of the century.
4. Throughout most of its career, the *Weekly* carried serial fiction and short stories—at first, like its sister monthly, the work of Dickens, Read, and Collins, and later that of Kipling, Barrie, Conan Doyle, Hamlin Garland, Howells, and James. In 1913 the old "Journal of Civilization," as it had loved to call itself, having made no profits for some two decades, was sold to the McClure organization (see MCCLURE'S MAGAZINE), but it survived the change; it was sold again two years later, and in 1916 was merged with the INDEPENDENT.

Harrigan, Edward (1845–1911),   comedian, playwright, producer, lyricist. Born in New York City, Harrigan made a happy theatrical connection with Anthony Cannon

(1855–1891), who called himself Tony Hart. Harrigan and Hart developed a special form of drama, usually a group of related sketches written by Harrigan and featuring kindly burlesques of various ethnic types. The main lead was usually Irish. Their first great success was *The Mulligan Guard Picnic* (1878), and a series of Mulligan plays followed, equally successful. The partnership broke up in 1885, but Harrigan continued to produce plays until 1896. E. J. Kahn wrote a lively account of the team in *The Merry Partners* (1955). See DAN MULLIGAN.

Harriot, Thomas.   See THOMAS HARIOT.

Harris, Benjamin (?–1716?),   publisher, book-seller, editor, writer for children. Harris began publishing pamphlets and newspapers in England in the late 1670s. In 1686 he sailed for New England, where he appears to have stayed until about 1695. He opened a bookshop in Boston and began printing writings of his own. He issued an almanac for 1687 and then, sometime before 1690, printed the NEW ENGLAND PRIMER, of which more than 5,000,000 copies were ultimately sold. For it he wrote the rhymed alphabet, intended to give young children some idea of the Calvinist universe. It had pictures and seems to have delighted children, who up to that time had to content themselves with the lengthy and dreary sermons of the time for listening and reading matter. The book was a revision and improved version of Harris's *Protestant Tutor*, published in London (1679). On Sept. 25, 1690, Harris put out the first newspaper in America, *Publick Occurrences Both Forreign and Domestick*. It had only three small pages and was immediately suppressed for "reflections of a very high nature." Back in England, Harris issued a *Bible in Verse* (1701?).

Harris, Charles K[assel] (1865–1930),   song writer, memoirist. Born in Poughkeepsie, New York, Harris wrote his first published song, "Kiss and Let's Make Up," in 1891. In the next year he hit it big with "After the Ball," and his next success was "Break the News to Mother" (1897). His last hit capitalized on a new invention: "Hello, Central, Give Me Heaven" (1901). Harris wrote an autobiography, *After the Ball: 40 Years of Melody* (1926). He also established a successful music-publishing firm in New York City.

Harris, Frank (1856–1931),   Irish-born American journalist, biographer, and novelist. Harris studied law, but turned to journalism. Through the years he served as editor of some of the leading journals of England and America, including the *Fortnightly Review*, the *Saturday Review*, and *Vanity Fair*. He is remembered primarily for his scandalous quasi-autobiography entitled *My Life and Loves* (3 v. 1923–27). The book presents much information about the Victorian literary figures Harris knew, but because of explicit sexual scenes, it was banned in America and England for many years. His other publications include a malicious and inaccurate biography of Oscar Wilde (1916).

Harris, George Washington ["Sut Lovingood"] (1814–1869),   jeweler, river pilot, railroad superintendent, humorist. Born in Pennsylvania, Harris became a skilled river pilot while still in his teens. He was a natural storyteller who liked to spin earthy yarns in a racy dialect. His first full-length sketch, *The Knob Dance*, was published in *The Spirit of the Times* in 1845. Later his newspaper and magazine pieces were collected in *Sut Lovingood: Yarns Spun by a "Nat'ral Born Durn'd Fool"* (1867), which immediately became popular and was frequently reprinted.

Harris, Joel Chandler (1848–1908),   journalist, humorist, short-story writer, novelist. Born in Georgia, Harris went to work at age thirteen as a printer's devil on *The Countryman*, a weekly newspaper published at the Georgia plantation Turnwold, and received much of his education through the help of the paper's owner, Joseph Addison Turner. Harris soon began printing some of his own writing anonymously in the paper, and, through his work on the estate, became acquainted with the plantation workers and their folklore. After two years at Turnwold, Harris worked on newspapers in Macon, New Orleans, and Savannah. In 1876 he joined the staff of the Atlanta *Constitution*, where he remained for twenty-four years. For his first assignments on the *Constitution*—humorous sketches of African-Americans—Harris drew on his boyhood knowledge of life at Turnwold, reproducing black speech and creating Uncle Remus as his main character. In the following year, an article by William Owens on African-American folklore in *Lippincott's Magazine* awakened Harris to the literary possibilities of the tales to which he had listened as a boy, and on July 20, 1879, the first Uncle Remus animal story appeared in the *Constitution*. Entitled "Negro Folklore. The Story of Mr. Rabbit and Mr. Fox, as Told by Uncle Remus," the sketch later became the introduction to UNCLE REMUS, HIS SONGS AND HIS SAYINGS (1880).

Although Harris claimed to have chosen one version of each tale for presentation "without embellishment and without exaggeration," his literary ability, his ear for spoken language, and his masterful characterization of Uncle Remus, who tells the tales to a small boy, turned the unvarnished folktale into a work of art. The difference between the characters of "Buh Rabbit" as recorded by Owens and Brer Rabbit in Harris's tales is significant. Instead of a vain, sharp, yet foolish character, he becomes shrewd, mischievous, and one of the most lovable of Harris's animal folk. The first sketch was immediately popular, and Harris continued the tales with "Brer Rabbit, Brer Fox, and the Tar Baby" (see THE TAR BABY) in the *Constitution* on November 16, 1879, dividing the tale into three installments—a technique he often used—to arouse the curiosity of the reader as to Brer Rabbit's ultimate escape.

Nights with Uncle Remus, a second series of tales, appeared in 1883; in it Harris introduced Daddy Jack as a storyteller, but his Gullah dialect is difficult to understand and the stories were less successful than those of Uncle Remus. Unlike the tales in the first collection, which are set after the Civil War, these take place during the days of slavery. There is little evidence of anything but affection between the slaves and their masters, although the life of the plantation is not idealized or treated as a part of the grand and gracious past. Uncle Remus is not a sentimental stereotype of the devoted slave, but an individual character of warmth, humor, superstition, and shrewdness.

Harris published several more collections of Uncle Remus stories, including *Uncle Remus and his Friends* (1892); *Told by Uncle Remus* (1905); and *Uncle Remus and the Little Boy* (1910), which appeared posthumously. He also wrote a series of stories specifically for children: *Little Mr. Thimblefinger* (1894), *Mr. Rabbit at Home* (1895), *The Story of Aaron* (1895), *Aaron in the Wildwoods* (1897), and *Plantation Pageants* (1899).

Harris also wrote many stories, two novels, and three novelettes on Southern life. *Mingo and Other Sketches in Black and White* (1884) deals with whites' and African-Americans and with the contrast between the aristocracy and the middle class. Perhaps the best story of the collection, "At Teague Poteet's," deals with the mountaineers of north Georgia. "Free Joe and the Rest of the World," in *Free Joe and Other Sketches* (1887), is an argument neither for nor against slavery, but a study of the tragic situation of the individual—in this case a freed slave— for whom society has no place. Harris's other collections of stories include *Balaam and His Master* (1891), *Tales of the Home Folks in Peace and War* (1898), *The Chronicles of Aunt Minervy Ann* (1899), *On the Wing of Occasions* (1900), and *The Making of a Statesman* (1902).

Harris published two novels, *Sister Jane, Her Friends and Acquaintances* (1896), a story of Georgia life before the Civil War, and *Gabriel Tolliver* (1902), which deals primarily with the Reconstruction period. *On the Plantation* (1892), a novelette, is largely autobiographical and contains vivid descriptions of Harris's boyhood and his experiences at Turnwold. Less interesting are two later novelettes, *A Little Union Scout* (1904) and *Shadow Between His Shoulder Blades* (1909, published posthumously), both of which deal with the Civil War.

In 1907 Harris and his son Julian established *Uncle Remus' Magazine*, with DON MARQUIS as an associate editor. The magazine was later merged with the *Home Magazine*, in which Harris continued to publish new Uncle Remus stories. His daughter-in-law, Julia Collier Harris, wrote *The Life and Letters of Joel Chandler Harris* (1918). R.L. Wiggin's *The Life of Joel Chandler Harris from Obscurity in Boyhood to Fame in Early Manhood* (1918) includes all his important early writings.

Harris, Mark (1922–),   novelist. Born in Mount Vernon, New York, Harris was educated at the University of Denver and the University of Minnesota. His novels, many featuring the protagonist Henry W. Wiggen, treat contemporary social ills with humor. The Wiggen novels include *The Southpaw* (1953), *Bang the Drum Slowly* (1956), and *A Ticket for a Seamstitch* (1957). Other titles are *Something about a Soldier* (1957), *Wake Up, Stupid* (1959), and *The Goy* (1970). *Mark the Glove Boy; or The Last Days of Richard Nixon* (1964), *Twenty-one Twice: A Journal* (1966) and *The Best Father Ever Invented* (1976) are autobiographical. *Friedman & Son* (1962) is a play. Later titles include *Saul Bellow, Drumlin Woodchuck* (1980), a wry biography with a title taken from a poem by ROBERT FROST, and the novels *Lying in Bed* (1985), *Killing Everybody* (1987),

Speed (1990), about growing up in Mount Vernon, and *The Tale Maker* (1994).

Harris, Thomas Lake (1823–1906),   poet, Christian socialist, mystic. Harris came to the United States from England when still a young child. Always deeply religious, he contributed to religious magazines and became a Universalist minister at age twenty. In 1850 he became a member of a religious community in West Virginia and there began dictating poems that had come to him, he said, from "divine wisdom." He organized a succession of agricultural, socialist, and spiritual societies at Amenia, New York, and Fountain Grove, California. He explained his ideas in a prose work, *The Brotherhood of the New Life* (1891). Among his verse collections are *The Epic of the Starry Heaven* (1854), *A Lyric of the Golden Age* (1856), *The Wisdom of the Adepts* (1884), and *The Song of Theos* (1903).

Harrison, Benjamin (1833–1901),   lawyer, public official, 23rd President. Harrison's grandfather, WILLIAM HENRY HARRISON, had been ninth President of the United States. Harrison was born in Ohio, served with distinction in the Civil War, and thereafter became one of Indiana's leading lawyers. In 1880 he was elected to the United States Senate, and was chosen to run against Cleveland (1888), whom he defeated. During his Presidency Idaho and Wyoming were admitted as states, and the Oklahoma Territory was opened to settlement. He lost the 1892 election to Cleveland and retired to his law practice. His biography was written by General Lew Wallace (1888). He published one book that had a wide sale, *This Country of Ours* (1897). *Views of an Ex-President* (1901) was compiled by his wife.

Harrison, Constance [Cary] (1843–1920),   novelist, memoirist. Born in Virginia, Harrison first won a reputation with her story *A Little Centennial Lady* (1876), derived from the diary of an aunt. She went on to other popular works, the best known of which was a satire on American social climbers abroad, *The Anglomaniacs* (1890). Others are *Bellhaven Tales* (1892), *Sweet Bells Out of Tune* (1893), and *A Bachelor Maid* (1894). She wrote her memoirs in *Recollections Grave and Gay* (1911).

Harrison, Henry Sydnor (1880–1930),   newspaperman, novelist, short-story writer. Dissatisfied with journalism, Harrison, a native of Tennessee, wrote a novel in six months and discovered he had created a best seller. It was *Queed* (1911), the story of a radical who is sobered by a spell of newspaper work. Among his later stories are *V.V.'s Eyes* (1913), *Angela's Business* (1915), and *Andrew Bride of Paris* (1925).

Harrison, Jim (1937–),   poet, novelist. Harrison grew up in northern Michigan and lived there on a farm for many years. After graduating from Michigan State, Harrison taught English at the State University of New York and wrote screenplays. It was *Legends of the Fall* (1979) that brought him acclaim and commercial success. *Legends* comprises three violent novellas, with vengeance as a primary theme. His other fiction includes *Wolf: A False Memoir* (1971); *A Good Day to Die* (1973); *Warlock* (1981); *Sundog* (1984); *The Woman Lit by*

Fireflies (1990), three novellas; *Julip* (1994), three more novellas; and *The Road Home* (1998), historical fiction set in Nebraska. His poetry is collected in *Plain Song* (1965), *Locations* (1968), *Outlyer* (1969), *Letters to Yesenin* (1973), *Returning to Earth* (1977), *Selected and New Poems* (1982), and *Shape of the Journey: New and Collected Poems* (1998). *Just Before Dark* (1991) collects nonfiction.

Harrisse, Henry (1830–1910),   international lawyer, historian, bibliographer. Born in France, for many years Harrisse lived in the United States, but some of his books are written in French. He became a specialist in the age of discovery and exploration of America. He compiled a bibliography of three hundred books relating to America between 1493 and 1551 (1866); studied Columbus in several volumes (1866, 1871, 1884); investigated the voyages of the Cabots (1892, 1996); and wrote on Amerigo Vespucci (1895).

Hart, Frances Noyes (1890–1943),   novelist. Born in Maryland, Hart introduced novelties such as legal proceedings and scientific detection to the detective story. The most widely circulated of her books was *The Bellamy Trial* (1927); others were *Hide in the Dark* (1929) and *The Crooked Lane* (1934).

Hart, Fred H. (*fl.* 1873–78),   frontier humorist. No information is available on Hart's life. He wrote a book called *The Sazerac Lying Club: A Nevada Book*, which Walter Blair judged the best book of tall tales published from 1855 to 1900. The only extant edition seems to be the fifth, published in San Francisco (1878).

Hart, John S[eely] (1810–1877),   teacher, editor, historian. Hart, a native of Stockbridge, Massachusetts, was among the pioneers in teaching American literature and in realizing the importance of American authors, such as Melville and Whitman. He edited *The Female Prose Writers of America* (1852; rev. ed., 1856) and *A Manual of American Literature* (1873). It is believed that in 1872 Hart taught at Princeton the first college course in American literature.

Hart, Joseph C. (1798–1855),   lawyer, novelist, public official. Hart lived at Nantucket for a while and in 1834 published MIRIAM COFFIN, OR, THE WHALE-FISHERMAN. This is said to be the first novel on whaling; its chief aim was to propagandize for the whaling industry. Later he issued a collection of essays on travel and literature, *The Romance of Yachting* (1848). At the time of his death he was American consul in the Canary Islands.

Hart, Lorenz (1895–1943),   lyricist, translator. For a time Hart, a New Yorker, made his living as a translator. For example, in 1921 he wrote the standard English version of Ferenc Molnár's *Liliom*. He and RICHARD RODGERS formed a partnership and began a brief, fertile collaboration writing shows successfully produced by amateurs. In 1925 their songs for the *Garrick Gaieties* helped the show run for a year and a half, instead of the one-night performance that had been planned. Further successful Rodgers and Hart collaborations were *Dearest Enemy* (1925); *Garrick Gaieties* (1926); *The Girl Friend* (1926); *Connecticut Yankee* (their greatest hit, 1927); *Jumbo*

(1935); *I Married an Angel* (1938); *The Boys from Syracuse* (1939); PAL JOEY (1940), and several musical plays for the movies.

Hart, Moss (1904–1961),   playwright, librettist. Hart was born in New York City and began his theatrical career with *The Hold-Up Man* (1925). His first success was *Once in a Lifetime* (1930, in collaboration with GEORGE S. KAUFMAN). He wrote the libretto for Irving Berlin's *Face the Music* (1933) and for Kurt Weill's *Lady in the Dark* (1941). Collaborating again with Kaufman, he wrote *Merrily We Roll Along* (1934); YOU CAN'T TAKE IT WITH YOU (1936), which won a Pulitzer Prize in 1937; *I'd Rather Be Right* (1937); *The American Way* (1939); and THE MAN WHO CAME TO DINNER (1939). He also wrote *Winged Victory* (1943), *Light Up the Sky* (1948), and *The Climate of Eden* (1952). He won the Antoinette Perry Award for his direction of the musical *My Fair Lady*. His autobiography, *Act One*, became a best seller in 1959. Hart said of himself that he had "the soul of a beachcomber" and left to himself would not write another line. But what he wrote, especially in combination with Kaufman, is one of the wittiest series of plays ever to appear on the American stage. His inclination to introduce some of his contemporaries into his plays, began, it was said, with *Once in a Lifetime*. Brooks Atkinson called *The Man Who Came to Dinner* "a merciless cartoon of ALEXANDER WOOLLCOT's bad manners, shameless egoism, boundless mischief, and widely assorted friendships." When *Light Up the Sky* was produced, the air was rife with rumors that the comedy caricatured actual Broadway personages. See GEORGE WASHINGTON SLEPT HERE.

Hart, Tony.   See EDWARD HARRIGAN.

Harte, [Francis] Bret (1836–1902),   editor, poet, short-story writer, novelist, dramatist, consul. Harte was born in Albany, New York, left school early, read widely, and published his first poem in *The Sunday Morning Atlas* (1847). In 1854 he and his sister sailed for San Francisco to join their mother. Harte worked an unsuccessful claim on the Stanislaus River, taught, and may have served as a guard on a Wells Fargo pony express. He finally entered the field of journalism, and his earliest extant piece, *The Valentine*, was contributed to San Francisco's *The Golden Era* (March 1, 1857). It was at this time that he began using the signature "Bret Harte." Jessie Benton Frémont, herself an able writer, assisted him in developing his style of writing, meeting influential people, and finding a position at the San Francisco mint.

Harte began his literary career with humorous sketches, went on to attract attention with his verses, some humorous and some serious, and finally won worldwide fame through his short stories. He helped C. H. WEBB start *The Californian* (1864) and he edited THE OVERLAND MONTHLY until 1870. He also edited a controversial anthology of California verse, *Outcroppings* (1865), and published a collection of his own, *The Lost Galleon and Other Tales* (1867). His CONDENSED NOVELS (1867) revealed his satirical and critical powers in parodies of various contemporaries. *The Overland Monthly* published many literary nuggets from Harte's California experiences: THE

LUCK OF ROARING CAMP (1868); the comic verse narrative PLAIN LANGUAGE FROM TRUTHFUL JAMES (1870, often called *The Heathen Chinee*); and enough others to round out the collection *The Luck of Roaring Camp and Other Stories* (1870).

In 1871 Harte accepted an offer of $10,000 a year from the *Atlantic Monthly* for any stories and verses he chose to write, and left California for Boston. The Boston experience in the end ruined him. He produced little worthwhile writing, and the *Atlantic* became weary of the sentimentality of his stories, perhaps even more so of his "unmoral treatment of immoral subjects." The contract not renewed, Harte soon found himself in desperate financial straits, from which a lecture tour and publication of a novel, GABRIEL CONROY (1875–76), did not rescue him; nor did the writing and production of a play, AH SIN (1877), in collaboration with MARK TWAIN, even though the drama was based on the popular *Heathen Chinee*. He served for a while as consul at Krefeld, Germany, and at Glasgow. Thereafter he lived in and around London, a favorite in literary and social circles, and added to his income by lecturing. He produced numerous short-story collections, several plays, and a second series of *Condensed Novels* (1902).

Much that Harte wrote was a Dickensian version of the Far West. Like Dickens, he found melodrama, sentimentality, sordidness, picturesqueness, and eccentricity in the scenes he was familiar with. He had a talent for mimicry, most obvious in his *Condensed Novels* and some of his verse. American local humor—stories told in barrooms, country stores, and elsewhere—had an immense influence on Harte's style and subject matter. In prose and meter he created a picturesque and idiosyncratic Bret Harte country. He could be astonishingly realistic and unconventional, though Mark Twain once remarked that the dialect employed by his characters was one that "no one on heaven or earth had ever used till Harte invented it." He was undoubtedly repetitive, made too much use of coincidence, and was often overly romantic.

Nevertheless, he helped make San Francisco the literary capital of the West and was the mentor of a group of early writers there that included Mark Twain. His influence on Western stories and movies has been potent, as R. R. Waterhouse points out in *Bret Harte, Joaquin Miller, and the Western Local Color Story* (1939).

Like Twain, Harte wanted to be a playwright, and sometimes dramatized his stories. *Two Men of Sandy Bar* was produced in 1876; *Sue* (written with T. Edgar Pemberton), in 1902; and *Salomy Jane* (dramatized by Paul Armstrong), in 1907. Many of his stories have been filmed. His other works include *Poems* (1871), *East and West Poems* (1871), *Stories of the Sierras* (1872), *Tales of the Argonauts* (1875), *Thankful Blossom* (1877), *The Twins of Table Mountains* (1879), *Poetical Works* (1880), *Cressy* (1889), *Colonel Starbottle's Client* (1892), *A Protégée of Jack Hamlin's* (1894), *Poetical Works of Bret Harte* (1896), *Some Later Verses* (1898), *Tales of Trail and Town* (1898), *From Sand Hill to Pine* (1900), *Trent's Trust* (1903), and *The Story of Enriquez* (1924). Material from *The Californian* by Harte and Mark Twain was collected in *Sketches of the Sixties*

(1926). His son Geoffrey Bret Harte edited his *Letters* (1926) and other letters were edited by B. A. Booth (1944).

Hartford Wits, The.   Known also as the Connecticut Wits, this loosely confederated group of writers collaborated, in various combinations, to produce a roughly homogeneous body of political satire during the last two decades of the 18th and the first decade of the 19th centuries. Chief among them were JOHN TRUMBULL (1750–1831), RICHARD ALSOP (1751–1816), TIMOTHY DWIGHT (1752–1817), DAVID HUMPHREYS (1753–1818), and JOEL BARLOW (1754–1812), all of Yale College, together with Dr. LEMUEL HOPKINS (1750–1801), an eccentric and talented physician of Hartford. They later were joined by THEODORE DWIGHT (1764–1846) and two other literary physicians, Mason F. Cogswell (17?–18?) and ELIHU HUBBARD SMITH (1771–1798). Barlow, Hopkins, Humphreys and Trumbull were probably mainly responsible for THE ANARCHIAD: A POEM ON THE RESTORATION OF CHAOS AND SUBSTANTIAL NIGHT, which appeared in twelve installments (1786–87) in the *New-Haven Gazette* and the *Connecticut Magazine*. Alsop and Theodore Dwight, with some assistance from Hopkins, Cogswell, and Smith, contributed twenty numbers of THE ECHO to the *Hartford American Mercury* (1791–1805). Alsop, Theodore Dwight, and Hopkins were the principal authors of THE POLITICAL GREENHOUSE FOR THE YEAR 1798 (1799). These satires were written in a strong, sometimes coarse burlesque style, modeled on the acrimonious tone of Pope's *Dunciad* or the broad ridicule of Butler's *Hudibras*, seasoned with the sharp political consciousness of such contemporary English satires as *The Rolliad*. The Wits were staunch Federalists, opposed to every threat of change. They drove sharp-pointed barbs of ridicule and recrimination deep into all opponents of established New England ways. To them French infidelism and Jeffersonian republicanism seemed equally disastrous, and against these tendencies the Wits fought a strenuous, though in the end a losing, battle. (See THE FEDERALIST PARTY.)

Each of these talented New Englanders was in his own right an author of some pretensions, and several are better remembered today for individual writings than for collaborations. Trumbull, for example, had gathered about him, when he was a tutor at Yale in the early 1770s, a group of somewhat younger men, including Dwight, Humphreys, and Barlow. He himself was soon known as the author of Addisonian essays called *The Medler* and *The Correspondent,* which reproved his contemporaries from the pages of the *Boston Chronicle* and the *Connecticut Journal.* He was more widely known as a satirist in rhyme when his THE PROGRESS OF DULNESS appeared in three parts from 1771 to 1773. His principal fame, however, came in 1775 with M'FINGAL, a favorite satire of early Revolutionary times. After expanding the poem in 1783, Trumbull virtually dropped from the literary scene and devoted himself to a career in the law.

Timothy Dwight, though he seems seldom to have collaborated in satire, is remembered as the second principal figure among the Wits. A man of supreme confidence, Dwight was for several years a clergyman and schoolmaster in Greenfield,

Connecticut. In 1795, he became president of Yale College, a post he held with honor until his death. His most important belletristic writings were THE CONQUEST OF CANAAN (1785), a biblical allegory in which his contemporaries read the triumphs of their own revolutionary armies, and GREENFIELD HILL (1794), a pastoral poem descriptive of New England. His *Triumph of Infidelity* (1788) was a satirical outburst against irreligion in America, so outspoken that in later years Dwight would not acknowledge it as his own. Many volumes of sermons and a posthumous account of *Travels in New-England and New-York, 1796–1815* complete his works.

David Humphreys, less talented as a writer, made up for his lack of imaginative skill by his industriousness in everything he did. An aide-de-camp to Washington, he later undertook a number of diplomatic missions abroad and from 1791 to 1802 was minister to Lisbon and Madrid. Returning to Connecticut, he devoted himself to agriculture, especially to raising Merino sheep. During his younger years he had written voluminously and with patriotic fervor—*A Poem Addressed to the Armies of the United States* (1780), *A Poem on the Happiness of America* (1780), *The Glory of America* (1783), and *A Poem on Industry* (1783), all of which sound didactic and imitative to modern ears. Richard Alsop of Middletown, Connecticut, said to have been one of America's first millionaires, was in many respects the most scholarly and bookish of the Wits. His published poems are chiefly graceful translations from the French, Italian, or Spanish, a *Versification of Ossian* (1793), and *The Twilight of the Gods* (1793), adapted from the Norse *Eddas*.

Joel Barlow, the youngest of the original group, was the most active and ultimately perhaps the most successful. Educated at Dartmouth and Yale under the influence of Trumbull and Dwight, he worked for years on an epic that would display the wonders of the New World. As published in 1787 it was called *The Vision of Columbus*, but for twenty years longer he worked at revising it and published it again in 1807 as THE COLUMBIAD, full of fine intention but without much fine poetry. After a varied career as chaplain, teacher, storekeeper, and editor, Barlow left New England in 1788 for France as agent for the ill-fated Scioto Land Company. Soon he was caught up by enthusiasm for the liberal ideas he saw in the French Revolution and joined forces with Thomas Paine and such Englishmen as Horne Tooke. He produced in verse *The Conspiracy of Kings* (1791) and in prose *Advice to the Privileged Orders* (1791), both inflammatory, even radical, which made him seem apostate to his former friends in Connecticut. Perhaps the best-known of Barlow's works is the *jeu d'esprit* called HASTY PUDDING (1796), which he composed in France in nostalgic memory of New England cornmeal. As time went on, he grew far beyond his former friends, became a confidant of Jefferson and Madison, a sponsor of young Robert Fulton, an American consul at Algiers, and in 1811 minister to France.

Other members of the group, each gifted within his limits, are perhaps of less individual importance. A good study of the entire group is Leon Howard's *The Connecticut Wits* (1943).

LEWIS LEARY

Hartley, Marsden (1877–1943),   poet, painter. Hartley spent his boyhood in Maine, moving at the age of fifteen to Cleveland. He studied painting in Cleveland, Paris, and Berlin, gaining his first successes as a painter in European exhibitions. In later life he lived in New Mexico, Nova Scotia, Bermuda, New York City, and Maine, winning recognition as one of America's most talented painters, one who particularly excelled in depicting the land and seascapes of his native state. For Hartley poetry was mainly an avocation, and the three small collections published during his lifetime—*Twenty-Five Poems* (1925), *Androscoggin* (1940), and *Sea Burial* (1941)—received no publicity. After his death a selection was made of these volumes and some five hundred poems left in manuscript: *Selected Poems of Marsden Hartley* (1945). Hartley wrote about many of the things he painted: Maine landscapes, the sea, animals, and persons contemporary and historical.

Hartmann, [Carl] Sadakichi (1867–1944),   playwright, poet, art critic. Born in Japan of a German father and Japanese mother, Hartmann came to the United States at an early age and was naturalized in 1894. He wrote four plays on the lives of famous men: *Christ* (1893), *Buddha* (1897), *Confucius* (1923), and *Moses* (1934) and one novel, *The Last Thirty Days of Christ* (1920). His poetry collections include *Drifting Flowers of the Sea* (1906) and *My Rubaiyat* (1913). He wrote several volumes of art criticism. *White Chrysanthemums: Literary Fragments and Pronouncements* appeared in 1971.

Haruf, Kent (1943–   ),   novelist. Born in Pueblo, Colorado, Haruf attended Nebraska Wesleyan University (B.A., 1965) and the University of Iowa (M.F.A., 1973). He has served in the Peace Corps in Turkey and taught English in high schools in Wisconsin and Colorado and at Nebraska Wesleyan University and Southern Illinois University. His three critically acclaimed novels—*The Tie That Binds* (1984), *Where You Once Belonged* (1991) and *Plainsong* (1999)—treat with spare, elegant prose the cruelty and compassion of small town and rural life on the high plains of Colorado.

Harvard Advocate, The.   A literary magazine edited, written, and published by Harvard students. It was founded in 1866. Donald Hall, who edited *The Harvard Advocate Anthology* (1950), called the magazine a "nursemaid of genius." Its distinguished contributors have included T. S. Eliot, Conrad Aiken, E. A. Robinson, James Agee, and Wallace Stevens.

Harvard Classics.   See CHARLES W. ELIOT.

Harvard Lampoon, The.   A humorous magazine published by Harvard students. Originally modeled after *Punch*, it was founded in 1876 by Ralph W. Curtis, John T. Wheelwright, Samuel Sherwood, and others. Its contents consist primarily of cartoons, anecdotes, and satirical pieces. *Lampoon*'s staff is traditionally fond of playing pranks on the Harvard community and has done numerous spoofs of popular magazines. Bernice O'Hara wrote *The Adventures of Bob Lampoon* (1939).

Harvey (1944),   a play by MARY C. CHASE. Harvey is a rabbit with two distinctions: it is six feet tall and visible only to the amiable drunkard who is the play's human protagonist. The point of the comedy turns on the futile attempts of eminent psychiatrists to exorcise Harvey. Psychiatrists and others are generously debunked, and there is a hint of the wisdom possible to the apparently loony. The play enjoyed a long success on Broadway, won a Pulitzer prize, and was made into a movie.

Hass, Robert (1941–   ),   poet, critic, translator. Born in San Francisco, Hass attended St. Mary's College of California (B.A., 1963) and Stanford University (M.A., 1965; Ph.D., 1971). A career marked by honors that include Woodrow Wilson, Danforth, and Guggenheim Fellowships, and a MacArthur Foundation grant, arrived at a pinnacle with Hass's two years as U.S. Poet Laureate and Poetry Consultant to the Library of Congress (1995–1997), where he worked diligently to give poetry a more prominent place in American daily life. "Poetry is a way of living," he has said, "a human activity like baking bread or playing basketball." His first collection, *Field Guide* (1973), a Yale Younger Poets Award book, displayed an engagement with birds, flowers, and animal life of the Bay area of California. *Praise* (1979), which won the William Carlos Williams Award, was widely acclaimed as heralding the emergence of a major American poet. More recent collections are *Human Wishes* (1989), including the long "Berkeley Eclogue," with its fundamental questioning of the place of poetry in his time ("*You want to sing?* / Tra-la. Empty and he wants to sing") and *Sun Under Wood: New Poems* (1996), winner of the National Book Critics Circle Award. The essays and reviews collected in *Twentieth-Century Pleasures: Prose on Poetry* (1984) provide insight into Hass's poetic interests and antecedents among American, European, and Asian poets. Professor of English at Berkeley since 1989, Hass has translated verse by CZESLAW MILOSZ in Milosz's *The Separate Notebooks* (1983), *Unattainable Earth* (1986), *Collected Poems* (1988), *Provinces* (1991), and *Facing the River* (1995). He has also edited *Rock and Hawk* (1987), a selection of poems by Robinson Jeffers; and *The Essential Haiku: Versions of Basho, Buson, and Issa* (1994).

Hastings, Lansford Warren (1818?–1868),   lawyer, explorer. The Ohio-born Hastings helped lead the first overland wagon migration to Oregon in 1842. His *The Emigrants' Guide to Oregon and California* (1845) was used by the ill-fated Donner Party expedition.

Hastings, Thomas (1784–1872),   musician, editor, composer. Born in Connecticut, Hastings was active in New York City churches, conducting choirs, editing collections of hymns, and composing hymns of his own. He wrote *A Dissertation on Musical Taste* (1822); gathered his own compositions in *Devotional Hymns and Religious Power* (with Lowell Mason, 1850); and edited *Spiritual Songs for Social Worship* (1831–32); *Musical Miscellany* (2 v. 1836); *The Sacred Lyre* (1840); and other similar compilations.

Hasty Pudding, The (1793),   a mock-heroic poem by JOEL BARLOW. This was written in a French inn, where Barlow happened to be served a dish of Indian corn mush, a favorite dish in his native Connecticut. He wrote three nostalgic cantos of four hundred lines in heroic couplets, describing how he came to write the poem, how the dish was made, how to eat it, and why it was worthy of praise. Although the verse often has all the false clangor of the heroic couplet at its worst, this very clangor greatly heightens the burlesque of the poem. The scenery in many passages is typically American—the sly raccoon, the bolder squirrel, the corn-husking ceremonies, the molasses, and the pumpkins.

Hatton, Anne Kemble (*fl.* 1790s),   playwright. Hatton was the author of *Tammany* (1794), the first in a series of plays by various authors popular in the early 19th century. They presented stereotypical romantic portraits of the woodland Indian as a noble creature in tune with nature. Other well-known plays in the genre were written by JOHN AUGUSTUS STONE and GEORGE WASHINGTON PARKE CUSTIS.

Haunted Palace, The (1839),   a poem by EDGAR ALLAN POE. It appeared first in the *Baltimore Museum* (April, 1839). Later it became one of the "rhymed verbal improvisations" that Poe attributes to Roderick Usher in THE FALL OF THE HOUSE OF USHER (*Burton's Gentleman's Magazine*, September 1839). Poe admits an "under or mystic current" in its meaning, and suggests that in it may be perceived "a full consciousness, on the part of Usher, of the tottering of his lofty reason upon her throne." Later, in one of his letters, Poe wrote, "By *The Haunted Palace* I mean to imply a mind haunted by phantoms—a disordered brain." Poe charged, unjustly, that Longfellow had plagiarized this poem in his "Beleaguered City" (1839); the latter was based on a footnote in Scott's *Border Minstrelsy*.

Havighurst, Walter [Edwin] (1901–1994),   teacher, historian, novelist. Havighurst was born in Wisconsin, taught mainly at Miami University in Ohio, and wrote numerous regional books, both fiction and nonfiction. Among his historical works are *Upper Mississippi* (THE RIVERS OF AMERICA SERIES, 1937); *The Long Ships Passing* (1942); *The Land of Promise: The Story of the Northwest Territory* (1946); *Annie Oakley of the Wild West* (1954), a biography particularly well received by the critics; *Wilderness for Sale* (1956); *The Miami Years* (1959), a history of Miami University; *Land of the Long Horizons* (1960); and *River to the West* (1970). His novels include *Pier 17* (1935), *The Quiet Shore* (1937), *The Winds of Spring* (1940), and *Signature of Time* (1949).

Having Wonderful Time (1937),   a play by ARTHUR KOBER. This comedy about the attempts of a group of vacationers in the Catskill Mountains to improve themselves culturally and socially ran for a year on Broadway and was later made into a successful musical called *Wish You Were Here* (1952).

Hawes, Charles Boardman (1889–1923),   teacher, writer. After teaching for a while, Hawes joined the staff of *Youth's Companion* and later became associate editor of *The Open Road*. All his life he was interested in and wrote about the sea. He published three long stories for boys: *The Mutineers* (1920), *The Great Quest* (1921), and *The Dark Frigate*

(1923). The last won a Newbery Award. He also wrote *Glouces-ter: By Land and Sea* (1923). *Whaling* (1924) was completed by his wife.

Hawkes, John (1925–1998), novelist, short fiction writer. Born in Stamford, Connecticut, Hawkes spent his childhood in New England, New York, and Alaska. During World War II, he served as an ambulance driver for the American Field Service in Italy and Germany. He began his career as a writer in Albert Guerard's creative writing seminar at Harvard University in the same year (1947) that he married Sophie Goode Tazewell. After working for several years at the Harvard University Press, Hawkes taught at Harvard and then at Brown University, where he remained for 30 years until his retirement in 1988. An inveterate traveler, Hawkes has written and placed many of his novels in foreign locales: France, Germany, Italy, Greece, and the Caribbean. He has taught at MIT, Stanford, the City College of CUNY, the Aspen Institute, and Bread Loaf; he is the recipient of Guggenheim, Ford, and Rockefeller Foundation Fellowships, and of many writing awards in the United States and abroad. He continues to write in and travel between Providence, Rhode Island, and France.

From the beginning, with the publication of the surrealistic novella *Charivari* in 1949, Hawkes has explored the lunar landscapes of the human psyche. In Hawkes's early novels, the landscapes are ruined and desolate: *The Cannibal* (1950) is set amidst the destruction of postwar Germany; *The Beetle Leg* (1951) depicts the desert wastelands of the Wild West; *The Owl* and *The Goose on the Grave* (novellas originally published in 1954 and republished as part of *Lunar Landscapes* in 1969) take place in nightmarish Italian settings destroyed by war and fascism; *The Lime Twig* (1961) portrays the criminal underworld of modern England. With the publication of *Second Skin* (1964), Hawkes's landscapes take on a more ambiguously exotic element. *Second Skin* alternates between a cold, bleak island off the coast of Maine and the imagined space of a warm, sunny island in the Caribbean; *The Blood Oranges* (1971) is set on an island in the Mediterranean; and *Death, Sleep & the Traveler* (1974) alternates between a house in the cold regions of Scandinavia and a suffocatingly hot Greek island. In *Travesty* (1976) and *The Passion Artist* (1979) the landscapes are increasingly internalized as the structure and mythology of a particular narrator's imagination is exposed. *Virginie: Her Two Lives* (1982) traverses history as it moves between a secluded chateau in 18th-century France and post–World War II Paris in portraying the dual lives of an eleven-year-old child. *Adventures in the Alaskan Skin Trade* (1985) returns to the frontier Alaska of Hawkes's childhood, and *Whistlejacket* (1988) to the scenes of horse racing Hawkes recounted in *The Lime Twig* and experienced as a child growing up in Connecticut. *Sweet William: A Memoir of an Old Horse* (1993) is told in the voice of the horse. *The Frog* (1996) tells of a French boy with a real or imaginary frog in his stomach. In *An Irish Eye* (1997) a foundling tells her tale.

As the alternating contrasts of his landscapes suggest, Hawkes's richly varied work explores the polarities and limits of the imagination. His fiction is authorial in that the ability to

ordain and control time and reality are set against the erotic urge to merge with the alien, the other, death. Hawkes explores eroticism in all its variety, as both the generative and destructive force of attraction and repulsion between bodies and psyches. For Hawkes, the means of exploration is style: though some works convey more recognizably traditional plots and structures than others, the stylistic experiments of all his fictions have enabled Hawkes to forge, over his forty-year career, a mythology of the contemporary imagination caught between the forces of life and death, both imagined and real. As with other contemporaries, such as Pynchon, Barth, and Nabokov, and predecessors such as Faulkner, Lautreamont, and Blake, Hawkes has succeeded in creating a stylized, imagined world that doubles for the one in which we live and read his novels.

Studies include Donald J. Greiner, *Comic Terror: The Novels of John Hawkes* (1973, 1978), Patrick O'Donnell, *John Hawkes* (1982), and Rita Ferrari, *Innocence, Power and the Novels of John Hawkes* (1996).

Patrick O'Donnell/GP

Hawks, Howard (1896–1977), screenwriter, director. Hawks was brought up in California, studied at Cornell and was a pilot during World War I. In 1922 he wrote and directed two comedy shorts he financed himself. His first commercially successful screenplay, *The Road to Glory* (1925), he sold to Fox on the condition that he direct it. His films, ranging from musicals (*Gentlemen Prefer Blondes*, 1953) and comedies (*Bringing Up Baby*, 1938) to gangster films (*Scarface*, 1932; *The Big Sleep*, 1946) and westerns (*Red River*, 1948; *Rio Bravo*, 1959), made him a highly regarded movie maker both in the United States and in Europe.

Hawks of Hawk-Hollow, The: A Tradition of Pennsylvania (1835), a novel by R. M. Bird about a Tory family in Pennsylvania the year after the battle of Yorktown. A case of false identities is cleared up in complex explanations, and the Tories turn out to be patriotic.

Hawthorne, Julian (1846–1934), novelist, historian, biographer. The son of Nathaniel Hawthorne was born in Boston and was a fluent writer of stories, none of which attained much success. Among them are *Idolatry* (1874), *Garth* (1877), *Fortune's Fool* (1883), and *John Parmelee's Curse* (1886). He also wrote *Nathaniel Hawthorne and His Wife* (2 v. 1884). His daughter, **Hildegarde Hawthorne** (1871–1952), wrote stories and biographies for young readers, as well as verse, essays, and histories for adults. Among them are biographies of Emerson, O. W. Holmes, John C. Frémont, and Matthew Fontaine Maury.

Hawthorne, Nathaniel (1804–1864), novelist, short-story writer. Born in Salem, Massachusetts, on July 4, Hawthorne sprang from five generations of New England Hathornes (as his name was spelled before he changed it as a young man). Among them were a judge in the Salem witchcraft trials and a grandfather who had commanded a privateer in the American revolution and had been commemorated in a ballad as "Bold Hathorne." Hawthorne's father, a merchant seaman who had risen to captain, had visited China, India,

Russia, and France before he died of yellow fever and was buried in Dutch Guiana (now Surinam) in 1808, when his son was four. After the loss of her husband. Hawthorne's mother, Elizabeth Clarke Manning Hathorne, took her children from the Hathorne house to live next door with the Manning family. There Hawthorne lived for the next several years with his mother, his two sisters (one younger, one older), his grandparents, and eight Manning uncles and aunts, all a dozen or more years older than he. Left behind in his old home were his grandmother Hathorne and two unmarried aunts.

Within this large extended family, Hawthorne's lifelong habits of solitude, reading, and introspection began early. Within three days of each other in April 1813, his grandmother Hathorne and grandfather Manning died. In the fall of that same year, he was hit on the foot by a ball. The injury kept him on crutches for a long while and mostly away from school for over two years. Encouraged in reading from childhood—he had read *Pilgrims' Progress* in his grandmother Hathorne's room on Sundays—he now had more time for that interest. Both the free time and the reading were extended after his convalescence ended, when his family spent the summer and early fall of 1816 in Raymond, Maine, where the Mannings owned several thousand acres they were hoping to develop in a wilderness not yet a state. In the next four years, Hawthorne was sometimes in Salem, for schooling and for work as a bookkeeper for his uncle's stagecoach line, and sometimes in Raymond, where, he wrote later, he first got his "cursed habits of solitude." He wandered in the woods, shot partridge, fished for trout, and skated on Sebago Lake. There and in Salem he continued his reading. By the time he was sixteen he had read Spenser's *Faerie Queene*, Thomson's *Castle of Indolence*, Shakespeare's plays, some of the *Arabian Nights*, Radcliffe's *The Mysteries of Udolpho*, Smollett's *Roderick Random*, Godwin's *Caleb Williams*, and all of Scott's novels prior to *The Abbott*, which in 1820 had just been published and which he intended to read as soon as he could get it. He was thinking, he wrote to his mother, of becoming an author, "But authors are always poor devils, and therefore may Satan take them."

In September 1821 he entered Bowdoin College, a small school not far from Raymond. There, he met Horatio Bridge, who became a lifetime friend; LONGFELLOW, a younger man destined for early fame; and FRANKLIN PIERCE, later a U.S. president. In 1825 he was graduated, having impressed a few people with his abilities, and returned to the Manning house in Salem with no clear goals in sight. He believed, he wrote to his older sister, "that he would never make a distinguished figure in the world" but must be content "to plod along with the multitude."

The next dozen years are part of the Hawthorne legend. Supported by Manning generosity and his own small share in the family estate, he lived mostly at home, earned very little, kept largely apart from society, and devoted himself to reading and writing. As the period drew to a close, in 1837 he wrote in a remarkable letter to Longfellow that "By some witchcraft or other—for I really cannot assign any reasonable why and wherefore—I have been carried apart from the main current

of life, and find it impossible to get back again. Since we last met . . . I have secluded myself from society; and yet I never meant any such thing. . . . I have made a captive of myself and put me into a dungeon; and now I cannot find the key to let myself out—and if the door were open, I should be almost afraid to come out." Responding to a comment of Longfellow's about his own "troubles and changes," he went on to write, "I can assure you that trouble is the next best thing to enjoyment, and that there is no fate in the world so horrible as to have no share in either its joys or sorrows. For the last ten years, I have not lived, but only dreamed about living." He then confessed that he had done some reading and writing, deprecating its value, and added "I see little prospect but that I must scribble for a living."

In fact, with single-minded purpose he had been scribbling for a living, as far as that was possible in his time and country, ever since leaving college. Approaching his thirty-third birthday, he was beginning to meet with some success, but it was not easy. At twenty-four—anonymously and at his own expense—he had published FANSHAWE (1828), a gothic romance set in a college like Bowdoin, but later retrieved and burned every copy he could find. Perhaps in college, certainly not long after, he had begun a collection called "Seven Tales of My Native Land"; these he burned when he failed to find a publisher. In 1830 he published five tales and sketches in *The Salem Gazette*. Almost simultaneously in the fall of 1830, he began his long association with THE TOKEN, when that annual (dated 1831) appeared with "Sights from a Steeple" and "The Haunted Quack." Contributions to NEW-ENGLAND MAGAZINE, *American Monthly Magazine*, THE KNICKERBOCKER MAGAZINE, and others followed. When he wrote his 1837 letter to Longfellow he had published in this way over forty fictional pieces as well as some biographical sketches of early New Englanders. Although all had appeared anonymously or pseudonymously, he was known as an author to a few influential friends and had emerged from his Salem seclusion long enough to edit in Boston *The American Magazine of Useful and Entertaining Knowledge* for a few months in 1836. He had also just had two books published. The first, *Peter Parley's Universal History on the Basis of Geography* (2 v. 1837), he had compiled for children with the assistance of his sister Elizabeth. The second was *Twice-Told Tales*.

With TWICE-TOLD TALES (1837) Hawthorne emerged in public as an author, with his name affixed to the volume. It was his fourth attempt to publish a collection of tales, the others failing because publishers could see no profit in a market dominated by English authors unprotected by copyright laws against American exploitation. Unknown to Hawthorne, publication this time had been guaranteed against failure by a college classmate, Horatio Bridge. Among the tales included were THE GENTLE BOY, THE MAYPOLE OF MERRY MOUNT, and THE MINISTER'S BLACK VEIL.

Within the next few years, Hawthorne became much more active in the world outside Salem, though he retained to the end of his life his preference for quiet and solitude. In 1837, Franklin Pierce proposed him as historiographer for a South Seas Expedition, but though the idea appealed to Hawthorne, nothing came of it. Drawn into society by ELIZABETH PALMER PEABODY, he soon met her sister Sophia, whom he courted for most of the next few years. Meanwhile, he sought an income in 1839–40 in the Boston Custom House, and tried communal living for several months in 1841 at BROOK FARM. Elizabeth Peabody published his *Grandfather's Chair* (1841), a history of early New England for young people, but his prospects for making a living were still not good when he and Sophia married in 1842 and moved into the Old Manse in Concord, which they rented from EMERSON and where they remained until 1845.

In MOSSES FROM AN OLD MANSE (1846) Hawthorne included some fine stories written in this period in which he turned away from his earlier obsession with 17th-century Puritanism: THE CELESTIAL RAILROAD, a satire on his transcendental neighbors; THE BIRTHMARK; "The Artist of the Beautiful"; and RAP-PACCINI'S DAUGHTER. But he also had to reach back to an earlier period for stories passed over for the two editions of *Twice-Told Tales*, including YOUNG GOODMAN BROWN. Although the Concord years had been good in some ways, writing was not providing him a living and now with two children he began his period as surveyor of customs in Salem, where he remained from 1846 to 1849.

As he reports in "The Custom-House," introductory to THE SCARLET LETTER (1850), Hawthorne produced little of literary interest during these years, but when he lost the position he turned immediately to writing, with the idea for another book of tales, one of which would be *The Scarlet Letter*. Convinced by his publisher, JAMES T. FIELDS, that the story, when accompanied by an autobiographical introduction, would be strong enough to stand on its own, he completed his best work in a fever of activity. Not long after its publication, he left Salem for Lenox, in the Berkshires of western Massachusetts.

By this time counted a major American author, Hawthorne was in a position to capitalize on his talents. Although he worked diligently, however, neither *The Scarlet Letter* nor any of his other writings ever presented him with more than a temporary stay against the fear of poverty that dogged him to the end of his days. Conditions were not yet ripe in the United States for an author to live from his pen alone. The Berkshire period was brief; Hawthorne soon moved from there to West Newton, and from there back to Concord, where he purchased the house known as Wayside. When his friend Franklin Pierce ran for president, he wrote a campaign biography. When Pierce won, Hawthorne became United States consul at Liverpool. During his years there (1853–57) he was rewarded at a level that far exceeded anything he had earned as a writer and enabled him to save enough to ease his life in his remaining years after he left.

The years between *The Scarlet Letter* and the Liverpool consulship were important for Hawthorne and for American literature. The meeting between Hawthorne and MELVILLE in the Berkshires was a high point in the lives of both authors. Melville's essay "Hawthorne and His Mosses" appeared during the month of their first acquaintance and remains a landmark

assessment. The two soon became fast friends. Melville, who was fifteen years younger, looked especially toward the older man for advice and approval, and Hawthorne was drawn to the adventurous spirit of the man who had lived among the cannibals. Melville's work particularly was affected, as MOBY-DICK (1851), which he was then writing, became less and less a story of the whale fisheries and more and more an allegory tinged with Hawthornian blackness. Conversely, Hawthorne was at the same time trying to lighten THE HOUSE OF THE SEVEN GABLES (1851) with touches of an unaccustomed sun. Leaving the lethargy of the custom house behind, spurred by the success of *The Scarlet Letter* and then of *The House of the Seven Gables*, and buoyed by his friendships with Melville and other writers and publishers, Hawthorne was producing at rapid pace and on a variety of subjects. In THE SNOW IMAGE (1852) he gathered pieces, some of them written much earlier, that included MY KINSMAN, MAJOR MOLINEUX and ETHAN BRAND. In a WONDER-BOOK FOR GIRLS AND BOYS (1852) and TANGLEWOOD TALES (1853) he retold classical myths for children. In a major new novel, THE BLITHEDALE ROMANCE (1852), he turned to his Brook Farm experience for material. Still the household bills remained worrisome, and the move to England was in large part a retreat from literature. He hoped to bank at least $20,000 before leaving office, and by the end of the second year was near that figure, though he stayed still longer.

After Liverpool, Hawthorne and his family lived in Italy long enough for him to absorb the materials of THE MARBLE FAUN (1860), which he wrote in England before returning to the United States a few months after its publication. Eight years had passed since *The Blithedale Romance*, and this new book proved to be his last major work, though OUR OLD HOME (1863), English sketches, appeared three years later. He died, probably of a brain tumor, in Plymouth, New Hampshire, while traveling with Franklin Pierce, and was buried in the Sleepy Hollow Cemetery in Concord, Massachusetts.

His work was dominated by a need to tell of what he knew best. Conscious from the beginning of his condition as American, he made Americanness a subject at a time when that had been not much tried in fiction. (CHARLES BROCKEN BROWN, WASHINGTON IRVING, and JAMES FENIMORE COOPER provide the significant earlier examples.) Much more than any earlier writer in the United States, he derived his fiction from his observation, keeping voluminous notebooks throughout his life and abstracting from them passages that gave solidity to even his most fanciful tales. More, too, than any writer earlier, his tales recorded not simply the external lives of his characters, but their internal confusions and anguished questionings, mirroring in this way the probing mind of the author who created them. In these respects, he was a forerunner of such realists as WILLIAM DEAN HOWELLS and HENRY JAMES, and both paid him the tribute of counting him among the greatest of their forebears. In Hilda of *The Marble Faun* he created the archetype of the innocent American girl abroad, a figure prominent later in both James and Howells. In taking from his notebooks the literal observations from life that became fiction in, for example, "Ethan Brand" and *The Blithedale Romance*, he employed a method much used later by Howells and still later a standard practice for many realistic writers. In shifting his focus from the externals of the action to the effects on the minds of the participants, he prefigured a concern of James that afterward became central to much modern fiction.

Specifically, his brand of American was the Puritan in New England, but it is well to remember that there were two hundred years between Hester Prynne and Ethan Brand, the first with her scarlet letter a product of the 17th century, the second with his lime kiln a man of Hawthorne's own time, the 19th century. By a strict count of years, we are now closer to Ethan—and to Hawthorne—than Hawthorne was to Hester when he created her. A great part of Hawthorne's achievement was to erase the difference, to make the past live again as though it were still with us. In this, he had before him the model of Scott.

From Scott, he learned the value of history and of immersion in the material close at hand. Like Scott, he developed an uncanny sense for the interest to be wrung from the clash of cultures in a changing time, reverence for the past mingled with thankfulness for its passing. And Scott was, of course, the great model in English of how local particularities—standing apart from the ongoing sweep of the strictly British novel—could be made to serve universal purposes. When Hawthorne began to write, Cooper had earned success in adapting Scott's materials and methods to novels set mostly in America's near past, the Revolution and surrounding decades. Irving excelled in tales of the Dutch in New York. Beginning his career with intensive reading in the history of his Salem ancestors and of the early New England world they lived in, Hawthorne gradually developed a dual focus: 17th-century Puritanism and its heritage in his own time.

To these materials he wedded an introspective and pessimistic temperament that he struggled at times, with only partial success, to subdue. In "Hawthorne and His Mosses," Melville wrote of "that great power of blackness in him" that "derives its force from its appeals to that Calvinistic sense of Innate Depravity and Original Sin, from whose visitations, in some shape or other, no deeply thinking mind is always and wholly free." Later readers have reacted in much the same way, suggesting that from a dark and brooding center arose an obsession with a few themes easily summarized. It is necessary for humans to develop warm human relationships, equally necessary to respect the sanctity of the individual. Sins are real, their effects long-lasting. The mind is less trustworthy than the heart. There is a fundamental ambiguity in the world and its appearances.

Matter and idea Hawthorne embodied in a lucid prose that like poetry is almost inseparable from its effects. His love of symbol and allegory, derived from early reading in Spenser and Bunyan, influenced Melville immediately, and many another writer since. His insistence on the ambiguous nature of experience undercut the authority of the narrator in ways that pointed toward the later restricted narrative strategies of

James and others. Refusing to call his longer fictions novels, designating them instead as romances, he at the same time treated them with complete moral and aesthetic seriousness—a practice that for the first time among major novelists had the effect of emphasizing the primacy of art over merely mimetic reproductions of reality. Melville compared him to Shakespeare; certainly he ranks with the great writers of fiction in English.

Ohio State's *Centenary Edition of The Works of Nathaniel Hawthorne* (23 v. 1992–1996), edited by William Charvat and others, has replaced the long standard *Complete Works* (12 v. 1883), edited by George P. Lathrop. Newton Arvin edited *The Heart of Hawthorne's Journals* (1929), Randall Stewart edited *The American Notebooks* (1932) and *The English Notebooks* (1941). Most complete among biographies are Arlin Turner's *Nathaniel Hawthorne* (1980) and Edwin H. Miller's *Salem Is My Dwelling Place: A Life of Nathaniel Hawthorne* (1992). Still useful are biographies by G. E. Woodberry (1902) and Randall Stewart (1948).

Hay, John [Milton] (1838–1905),   lawyer, secretary to Lincoln, diplomat, secretary of state, writer. Hay was born in Indiana, took his degree at Brown University and studied law with his uncle in Springfield, Illinois, next door to the law firm of Lincoln and Herndon. When Lincoln was elected President, JOHN G. NICOLAY, his secretary, persuaded Lincoln to "let Hay come along" as his assistant.

After the war Hay was made Secretary of Legation at Paris (1865–67), at Vienna (1867–68), and at Madrid (1869–70). Out of his Spanish experiences he drew *Castilian Days* (1871).

On Hay's return to the United States he wrote for five years for the New York *Tribune*; among his contributions were the *Pike County Ballads*, six poems in western dialect that were later included in PIKE COUNTY BALLADS AND OTHER POEMS (1871). In 1874 he married and later moved to Cleveland. The strike and riots of 1877 profoundly disturbed him, and he later wrote and published anonymously a novel, THE BREADWINNERS (1884), that sought to defend property against the "dangerous classes." Meanwhile he had been appointed First Assistant Secretary of State, and moved to Washington. He and Nicolay wrote *Abraham Lincoln: A History* (1890), making use of much valuable new material. Fifteen years later the two men edited the *Complete Works of Abraham Lincoln*. McKinley appointed Hay ambassador to Great Britain (1897–98), then secretary of state, an office he continued to hold under Theodore Roosevelt, helping to implement the Open Door policy in China and the negotiations for the Panama Canal.

After Hay's death his wife edited *The Letters of John Hay and Extracts from His Diary* (3 v. privately pub., 1908). In 1939 Tyler Dennett, author of *John Hay: From Poetry to Politics* (1933), issued the first public printing of this material, *Lincoln and the Civil War in the Diaries and Letters of John Hay*. Clarence L. Hay edited his father's *Complete Poetical Works* (1916), and *Addresses of John Hay* (1907) gave some of his speeches. Nonpolitical letters appear in Caroline Ticknor's *A Poet in Exile: Early Letters of John Hay* (1910) and in *A College*

Friendship: A Series of Letters from John Hay to Hannah Angell (1938).

Haycox, Ernest (1899–1950),   writer of western stories. A native of Portland, Oregon, Haycox wrote a swift-moving story with some regard for verisimilitude, and he had a strong sense of the historical development of the West. Among his books are *Free Grass* (1929), *Starlight Rider* (1933), *Sundown Jim* (1938), *Saddle and Ride* (1939), *Rim of the Desert* (1940), *Action by Night* (1943), *The Wild Bunch* (1943), *Bugles in the Afternoon* (1944) about George Custer; *Long Storm* (1946), and *The Earthbreakers* (1952), an ambitious, realistic treatment of the frontier experience. Several of his stories have been filmed.

Hayden, Robert E[arl] (1913–1980),   poet. Born Asa Bundy Sheffey in Detroit, he was given the name Robert Hayden by foster parents. A researcher for the Federal Writers' Project (1936–1940), Hayden used many of the facts of African-American history he unearthed in the formal poetry of his first collection, *Heart-Shape in the Dust* (1940). He was educated at Wayne State University and at the University of Michigan, where he worked with W. H. Auden. He taught at Fisk University (1946–1969) and the University of Michigan (1969–1980). In his poetry, he combined details of the lives of such historical figures as Nat Turner, Frederick Douglass, Harriet Tubman, and Malcolm X with personal experience. He was the first African-American poet to be chosen Consultant in Poetry to the Library of Congress (1976). His other titles include *Figure of Time: Poems* (1955); *Selected Poems* (1966); *Angle of Ascent: New and Selected Poems* (1975); and *Robert Hayden: Collected Poems* (1985).

Haydn, Hiram (1907–1973),   teacher, editor, novelist. Haydn was born in Cleveland, and after a career in teaching, became an executive officer for Phi Beta Kappa, editor of the *American Scholar* and editor for Crown Publishers, Bobbs-Merrill, and Random House. He edited anthologies and wrote three novels: *By Nature Free* (1943), *Manhattan Furlough* (1945), and *The Time Is Noon* (1948). The last was especially commended for its sharp and subtle college scenes. In 1959 he joined with Alfred Knopf, Jr., and Simon Michael Bessie to found Atheneum Publishers.

Hayes, Alfred (1911–1985),   poet, novelist, playwright. Hayes was born in England and grew up in New York City, where he worked as a newspaper, magazine, and radio writer. His first book of poems, *The Big Time* (1944), made extensive use of the city background. In 1943 Hayes went into the Army, serving in Italy. During this period he worked with Roberto Rossellini on the movie *Paisan* (1946) and gathered material for his two most successful novels, *All Thy Conquests* (1946) and *The Girl on the Via Flaminia* (1949). The latter, originally a play, was rewritten as a novel, and later readapted into a play (1954) and a movie (*Act of Love*, 1954). Two of Hayes's later novels are *Shadow of Heaven* (1947) and *In Love* (1953). These books are notable for their complex Jamesian prose style, differing from Hayes's earlier work, which was distinguished by its economy of detail and taut, poetic style. *The*

Stockbroker, The Bitter Young Man, and *The Beautiful Girl*, a novella, appeared in 1973. His verse includes *Welcome to the Castle* (1950), a book commended for its force and honesty, and *Just Before the Divorce* (1968).

Hayes, Isaac I[srael] (1832–1881),   physician, explorer, writer. Hayes was born in Pennsylvania. Among his books were three that described his own experiences and observations in the Arctic: *An Arctic Boat-Journey* (1860), *The Open Polar Sea* (1867), and *The Land of Desolation* (1872). One of his best books is *Cast Away in the Cold: An Old Man's Story of a Young Man's Adventures, As Related by Captain John Hardy, Mariner* (1868).

Haymarket Square Riot.   A clash between Chicago police and labor unionists on May 4, 1886, in which a bomb, thought to be thrown by anarchists, caused the death of seven policemen and wounded sixty-eight others. The arrest of eight anarchist leaders followed; although nothing could be proved, they were convicted of "constructive conspiracy to commit murder" and four of them were hanged. The others were imprisoned, and one committed suicide. The case caused widespread controversy, led to a temporary setback of the labor union movement, and resulted in much adverse criticism of the judicial proceedings. A petition bearing the names of prominent persons all over the country led Governor JOHN PETER ALTGELD to pardon the three men still in jail. Among the petitioners was WILLIAM DEAN HOWELLS, who from that time took a strong interest in American social and political reforms. In 1907 Frank Harris visited Chicago to study the case, then wrote his novel *The Bomb* (1908), which is sympathetic to the convicted men.

Hayne, Paul Hamilton (1830–1886),   poet, biographer, editor. Born in Charleston, South Carolina, Hayne began contributing to the *Southern Literary Messenger*, joined the staff of the *Southern Literary Gazette*, and by 1855 had written enough verse for a collection, *Poems*. This was followed by *Sonnets and Other Poems* (1857) and *Avolio: A Legend of the Island of Cos* (1860). In 1857 Hayne founded *Russell's Magazine*, named for Russell's Bookstore in Charleston, a gathering place for young men of literary ambition, including HENRY TIMROD. The magazine was terminated with the coming of the Civil War, in which Hayne saw only limited service, but his ardent patriotism expressed itself in a group of fervent poems, such as *The Battle of Charleston Harbor*. During Sherman's march to the sea, Hayne's mansion was destroyed, and all he had left was a small piece of ground on the Savannah River in the pines of Georgia. There, after the war, Hayne lived with his family, making his livelihood entirely from his writings. He published *Legends and Lyrics* (1872), *The Mountain of the Lovers* (1875), *Lives of Robert Young Hayne and Hugh Swinton Legaré* (1878), and *The Broken Battalions* (1885). He edited the *Poems* of his friend Timrod (1873), with a sketch of his life. All through his later years he maintained an active correspondence with literary men and women in both the North and the South. Some of his letters have been collected by Daniel M. McKeithan and others. Hayne's poetry is notable chiefly for its landscapes of the South, as in *Aspects of the Pines* and *The Cottage on the Hill.*

Haywood, William Dudley (1869–1928), labor leader. Identified most closely with the Industrial Workers of the World (IWW), the Utah-born Haywood is one of the figures described in the novel *The 42nd Parallel* (1930), by John Dos Passos. A miner at 15 and union member at 18, Haywood was several times accused of inciting to violence, and Clarence Darrow successfully defended him from such a charge in 1905. During World War I, he was tried and convicted of sedition and sentenced to twenty years in prison. While awaiting a new trial in 1921, he escaped to the Soviet Union, where he died. *Bill Haywood's Book*, his autobiography, was published posthumously in 1929.

Hazard, Ebenezer (1744–1817), public official, historian. Closely associated with JEREMY BELKNAP, an early American historian, Hazard, a Philadelphian, made it his business to collect material likely to be of use to future chronicles. As surveyor of post roads and later postmaster-general, Hazard became acquainted with places and conditions all through the colonies. He copied many documents and intended to publish a documentary history of the Revolution. Congress gave him permission to make copies of its own papers and voted him £1,000 for expenses; apparently, he never drew on the money and never published the history. He finally issued two volumes of *Historical Collections, State Papers, and Other Authentic Documents* (1792, 1794), which have been useful as source materials.

Hazard, Shepherd Tom [Thomas Robinson] (1797–1886), sheep farmer, manufacturer, spiritualist, reformer, folklorist, humorist. Born in Rhode Island, Shepherd Tom, having made a fortune from sheep-raising and textile manufacturing, retired to do his best to communicate with the next world, lend his help to worthy causes (such as better asylums for the insane, anti-slavery, abolition of capital punishment, feminism, and pacifism), and collect all the tall tales he heard throughout his native state. Among his books are *Recollections of Olden Times* (1879), *The Jonny-Cake Letters* (1882), and *Miscellaneous Essays and Letters* (1883). In 1915 appeared *The Jonny-Cake Letters of "Shepherd Tom."*

Hazard of New Fortunes, A (1890), a novel by WILLIAM DEAN HOWELLS. This is the longest of Howells's works. The plot involves the relationship of a rich man, Dryfoos, to the magazine he has casually bought and also the difficulties he and his family encounter, after suddenly becoming wealthy, in scaling the social barriers of New York. Basil March, who had already appeared in THEIR WEDDING JOURNEY (1871), is made the editor of the magazine; he resigns rather than discharge a freespoken radical from his staff. Dryfoos's son Conrad turns radical, and both he and the outspoken staff member die from injuries received in a labor riot. The book is one of Howells's most thoughtful commentaries on modern social and economic problems.

Hazel Kirke (1880), a play by STEELE MACKAYE (1842–1894). Hazel, against the wishes of her father, an English miller, refuses to marry Squire Rodney and runs off instead with Carringford, who is really a lord. The latter's mother, bitterly opposed, tells Hazel her marriage to Carringford isn't legal, and Hazel tries to drown herself. She is rescued by her husband, and all ends happily. The play was a revision of an earlier one by MacKaye, *An Iron Will* (1879). *Hazel Kirke* had a consecutive run of about two years in New York, was constantly revived for more than thirty years, and was produced frequently abroad.

Hazzard, Shirley, (1931–), novelist, short-story writer. Born in Australia, Hazzard worked in governmental positions in Hong Kong and New Zealand before being assigned to the United Nations and settling in New York. *The Evening of the Holiday* (1966) is a novella; *People in Glass Houses: Portraits from Organization Life* (1967) is a witty novel about bureaucrats; *The Bay of Noon* (1970) is set in Italy; and *The Transit of Venus* (1980) centers on two Australian sisters. *Cliffs of Fall* (1963) is a collection of stories. *Greene on Capri: A Memoir* (2000) traces her longtime friendship with the writer Graham Greene.

H. D.   Pen name of HILDA DOOLITTLE.

Headless Horseman, The.   See THE LEGEND OF SLEEPY HOLLOW.

Headsman, The (1933), a novel by JAMES FENIMORE COOPER. This is the third novel in the series that began with THE BRAVO (1831) and THE HEIDENMAUER (1832), the whole being an expression of some of Cooper's political views. The scene is Switzerland, and Cooper, following his long-continued attack on feudal society and aristocratic traditions, shows the folly of a custom that the son of a headsman (executioner) must follow his father's vocation. The horror felt toward an executioner and his family is skillfully described, but Cooper spoils his social idea by letting the plot develop along absurdly conventional lines— the executioner's son turns out to be really the son of the Doge of Genoa.

Heald, Henry (1979–?), surveyor, letter writer. Heald made a trip with two others into the unbroken West, ending his journey in Illinois. The letters he wrote home were printed as *A Western Tour in a Series of Letters* (1819).

Hearn, [Patricio] Lafcadio [Tessima Carlos] (1850–1904), journalist, novelist, travel writer, teacher. Hearn was born on the Greek Island of Santa Maura, also called Leucadio, the source of his name Lafcadio. His father was a British army surgeon, his mother Greek. Raised by relatives in Dublin, and educated there and in England and France, Hearn by 1869 had settled in the U.S. His multiethnic and multicultural background and experience included ancestry that has been said to be English, Irish, Gypsy, Greek, and Arabic; a wife of African-American ancestry, and another of Japanese; and years in residence in Europe, the United States, and Japan.

Living in the United States from 1869 to 1887, he became a reporter on the *Cincinnati Commercial* (1875–78) but lost his job after living with (and probably marrying) a woman of African-American and white parents. He went to New

Orleans, worked on the *New Orleans Item* (1878–81) and the *New Orleans Times-Democrat* (1881–87), then lived in Martinique and wrote for *Harper's New Monthly Magazine* before moving to Japan, where in 1895 he became a citizen, known by two names, Lafcadio Hearn and Koizumi Yakumo.

His reputation was largely as an interpreter of the exotic, mostly in nonfiction prose. His novels are *Chita: A Memory of Last Island* (1889), set in Louisiana, and YOUMA: THE STORY OF A WEST-INDIAN SLAVE (1890). Earlier works include *Strange Leaves from Strange Literature* (1884), a gathering of articles on legends and stories from many sources; and *Some Chinese Ghosts* (1887), a collection of Chinese legends. *Two Years in the French West Indies* (1890) is a travel book. GLIMPSES OF UNFAMILIAR JAPAN (2 v. 1894) was followed by many more books on Japan. These include *Out of the East* (1895), *Kokoro* (1896), *Gleanings in Buddha-Fields* (1897), *In Ghostly Japan* (1899), *A Japanese Miscellany* (1901), *Kotto* (1902), *Kwaidan* (1904), which helped popularize haiku in the West, and *Japan: An Attempt at Interpretation* (1904). Among his translations are *Gombo Zhebes: Little Dictionary of Creole Proverbs* (1885) and *Japanese Fairy Tales* (5 v. 1898–1922). *Writings* appeared in 16 volumes in 1922. Henry Goodman edited *Selected Writings* (1949). Memoirs are by his wife, Setsuko Koizumi, *Reminiscences* (1918); and a son, Kazuo Koizumi, *My Father and I* (1935). Studies are by Elizabeth Stevenson (1961), Arthur E. Kunst (1969), and Jonathan Cott (1991).

Hearne, Samuel (1745–1792).   An explorer in the employ of the Hudson's Bay Company. Hearne traveled on foot from Hudson's Bay to the Arctic Ocean with the help of a group of Cree guides. His *Journey from Prince of Wales's Fort in Hudson's Bay to the Northern Ocean . . .* (1795) is a classic text of Canadian history.

Hearst, William Randolph (1863–1951),   newspaper and magazine publisher. Hearst began his career on the San Francisco *Daily Examiner* (1887) and made it a financial success. He bought the New York *Morning Journal* (1895) and in active competition with JOSEPH PULITZER developed a sensational type of newspaper, characterized by what its opponents called yellow journalism, that proved very popular. In 1900 he bought the Chicago *American*, in 1904 the Boston *American*. Thereafter he became owner of the largest newspaper combine in the United States. He served in Congress (1903–07), unsuccessfully sought the governorship of New York, acquired a group of magazines (including COSMOPOLITAN and GOOD HOUSEKEEPING), and bought large properties in Mexico. In World War I he opposed U.S. participation; in later years he attacked communism. John K. Winkler has written two books on Hearst, *Hearst: An American Phenomenon* (1928) and *W. R. Hearst: A New Appraisal* (1955). Other books about him include *Hearst, Lord of San Simeon* (1936), by Oliver Carlson and E. S. Bates, and John Tebbel's rather journalistic *The Life and Good Times of William Randolph Hearst* (1952). W. A. Swanberg's *Citizen Hearst* (1961) is considered definitive. Hearst's life suggested Orson Welles's film *Citizen Kane* (1940).

Hearth and Home.   A magazine founded in 1868.

Among its editors were Donald G. Mitchell, HARRIET BEECHER STOWE, FRANK R. STOCKTON, and MARY MAPES DODGE. Aimed at first at a rural audience, the magazine went into financial decline and was rescued by EDWARD EGGLESTON, its literary editor, who contributed to it his novel THE HOOSIER SCHOOLMASTER (1870–71), after which the magazine enjoyed an immediate increase in circulation. It ceased publication in 1875.

Heart Is a Lonely Hunter, The (1940),   a novel by CARSON MCCULLERS. The story of a deaf and mute boy growing up in a small Southern town.

Heart of Maryland, The (1895),   a Civil War play by DAVID BELASCO. The play was inspired by Rose Hartwick Thorpe's poem CURFEW MUST NOT RING TONIGHT! (1870). Belasco visited Maryland and made good use of realistic details in his background. The heroine, Maryland Calvert, falls in love with a Union officer, and when he is condemned to die and his execution is scheduled for the time of the curfew bell, she seizes the bell's clapper and swings out from the tower in a successful stratagem to stop his execution. The play was Belasco's first great success.

Heart's Needle (1959),   an influential collection of CONFESSIONAL POETRY BY W. D. SNODGRASS, containing the title sequence and other poems.

Hearts of Oak (1879),   an adaptation of an English melodrama, H. L. Leslie's *The Mariner's Compass* (1865), by DAVID BELASCO and J. A. HERNE. The adaptation was made without Leslie's consent, but he did not succeed in stopping the production of the play or in being allowed to call his own play *Hearts of Oak*. Herne later bought all rights to the play, and he and his wife appeared in it many times.

Heath, James Ewell (1792–1862),   public official, novelist, playwright. Heath, a native of Virginia, held various state and national posts. He had a great interest in literary matters, was an adviser for the SOUTHERN LITERARY MESSENGER, and interceded in Poe's behalf with the publisher of that magazine. Both he and the publisher concurred, however, in rejecting *The Fall of the House of Usher*. Heath himself, so far as we know, wrote only two books: *Edge-Hill, or, The Family of the Fitzroyals* (1828), a story of plantation life; and *Whigs and Democrats, or, Love of No Politics* (1839), a satire on rural elections in Virginia. The play was produced and published anonymously.

Heathen Chinee, The.   The name popularly given to Bret Harte's humorous poem PLAIN LANGUAGE FROM TRUTHFUL JAMES (1870).

Heat-Moon, William Least [Trogdon, William] (1939–   ),   memoirist. Educated at the University of Missouri and a teacher at Stephens College in the same town, William Trogdon in 1978 took leave from his teaching, separated from his wife, and in a recreational vehicle began an odyssey around the U.S., recording accidental meetings and conversations in small towns along the secondary roadways marked in blue on maps. Out of this he crafted a big popular and modest critical success, *Blue Highways* (1983). In *PrairyErth (A Deep Map)* (1991) he describes in great detail the present and past of one small place, Chase County, Kansas. *River-Horse: A Voyage Across America* (1999) chronicles a trip by small boat from New York to Oregon.

Heavysege, Charles (1816–1876),   poet. Born in England, Heavysege came to Canada in 1853, settled in Montreal, and wrote epic closet dramas in verse, the best of which are *Saul: A Drama in Three Parts* (1857) and *Jephthah's Daughter* (1865). His work is available in the reprinted *Saul and Selected Poems* (1967). *The Advocate* (1865) is a novel.

Hébert, Anne (1916–   ),   novelist, poet. Born and brought up in Quebec, Hébert was much influenced by her father, a provincial civil servant, and her cousin, the poet Hector de Saint-Denys Garneau. Her first publication, *Les songes en equilibre* (1942), a collection of traditional poems, won the Prix David. The title poem of *Le tombeau des rois* (1953) is a major expression of Québecois culture. *Le torrent* (1950), a story collection, was reissued in 1963 (tr. 1967) with four new stories added. In the mid-1950s, Hébert moved to Paris, but she makes frequent visits to Canada.

Her best-known work is the fiction contained in a four-novel cycle. *Kamouraska* (1970, tr. 1974) is based on an actual 19th-century murder. *Les enfants du sabbat* (1975, tr. *Children of the Black Sabbath*, 1978), dealing with witchcraft, is set in the 1930s and 1940s. *Heloise* (1980, tr. 1982) concerns a Paris vampire. *Les fous de Bassan* (1982) includes multiple narrative perspectives on a double rape and murder. Other novels are *Le premier jardin* (1988) and *L'enfant chargé de songes* (1992). *Oeuvre poétique* (1993) contains the bulk of her verse.

Hecht, Anthony [Evan] (1923–   ),   poet. Hecht's verse of his early and middle years reflects the literary taste of the 1950s and 1960s: it is both erudite and ornate, as seen in *A Summoning of Stones* (1954) and *Struwwelpeter* (1958). With *The Hard Hours* (1967), *Millions of Strange Shadows* (1977), and *The Venetian Vespers* (1979), Hecht adopted a plainer style that yet remains oblique and displays tight command of technique. *The Transparent Man* (1990), *Collected Earlier Poems* (1990), and *Flight Among the Tombs* (1996) are more recent volumes of verse. Much honored, with awards that include the Bollingen Prize and fellowships from the American Academy of Poets and the Ford, Guggenheim, and Rockefeller Foundations, he has also written criticism that includes *The Hidden Law: The Poetry of W. H. Auden* (1993) and *On the Laws of the Poetic Art* (1995).

Hecht, Ben (1893–1964),   dramatist, journalist, novelist. Born in New York City, Hecht began writing for the Chicago *News* and lived in Chicago during its literary renaissance (1911–30) in which he took part, publishing stories in the *Little Review* and *Smart Set*. His first novel, *Erik Dorn* (1921), makes use of his experiences as Berlin reporter for the *News* (1918–19). It tells the story of a jaded intellectual who throws over his wife and his mistress for the excitement of European revolution. He returns, shoots the new lover of his mistress in self-defense and finds that his wife no longer wants him. The novel, which caused a great deal of furor, shows influences of Huysmans, whom Hecht admired. He left the

News in 1923 to begin his own paper, the *Literary Times*. He published more novels: *Gargoyles* (1922), *Fantazius Mallare* (1923), *Count Bruga* (1926), and *A Jew in Love* (1930). The last two are lampoons of MAXWELL BODENHEIM, who had drawn an unflattering portrait of Hecht in *Ninth Avenue* (1926). Thirty-two years later Hecht wrote a play about Bodenheim, *Winkelberg* (1958). His short stories are considered much better. *A Thousand and One Afternoons in Chicago* (1922) and *Tales of Chicago Streets* (1924) were early collections, and many are gathered in *The Collected Stories of Ben Hecht* (1945).

He collaborated with Charles MacArthur on two plays, *The Front Page* (1928) and *Twentieth Century* (1933), both made into successful films. They also wrote the scenario for *Wuthering Heights* (1939). *Spectre of the Rose* (1946), Hecht's most original scenario, is about a ballet dancer who commits suicide. He was very active in Hollywood during this period. *Notorious* (1946) and *A Flag Is Born* (1946) are typical Hecht movies.

Heckewelder, John Gottlieb [Ernestus] (1743–1823), missionary, authority on Native Americans. Heckewelder came to America from England as a boy, became a Moravian missionary to the Indians of Ohio and interested himself in other settlements nearer the Atlantic seaboard. With other Moravian missionaries he succeeded in converting a considerable number of Delawares and Mohegans. He became fond of them and felt a strong antagonism to their traditional enemies, the Iroquois. This partiality appears strongly in his *Account of the History, Manners, and Customs of the Indian Nations of Pennsylvania and the Neighboring States* (1822). The book influenced Cooper in his attitude toward Indian tribes, as manifested in THE LAST OF THE MOHICANS (1826) and the later books in the LEATHER-STOCKING TALES. Cooper also borrowed many factual details and the name Chingachgook. When Longfellow was in college, he read the book and was greatly impressed by it; his *Song of Hiawatha* (1855) shows its influence. See HIAWATHA.

Hedge, [Frederic] Henry (1805–1890),   clergyman, poet, translator, editor, teacher. Born in Cambridge, Massachusetts, Hedge was an infant prodigy, memorizing Virgil at age seven. At thirteen, in the company of GEORGE BANCROFT, he went to Germany, where he became fluent in German and was initiated into German idealism, which he was the first to introduce authoritatively in America. He returned to take a degree at Harvard, went on to four years in the Divinity School, becoming a Unitarian clergyman.

In March 1833, he wrote an article on Coleridge for the *Christian Examiner*, which he later described as "the *first word*, so far as I know, which any American had uttered in respectful recognition of the claims of transcendentalism." He knew Kant, Hegel, and Schelling at first hand; he was a sober transcendentalist, with no romantic ecstasies; he remained a conservative and a churchman, espousing idealism as a creed which taught both love and duty. He saw transcendentalism as a social philosophy, giving a viewpoint on institutions, and anticipated Emerson's AMERICAN SCHOLAR (1837).

On September 16, 1836, there was founded the Transcendental Club, often called the Hedge Club—perhaps because it met only when Hedge was in town. Hedge wrote numerous books, including *Conservatism and Reform* (1843), *Prose Writers of Germany* (1848), *Ways of the Spirit and Other Essays* (1877), *Atheism in Philosophy* (1884), and *Martin Luther and Other Essays* (1888). Perry Miller called his *Reason in Religion* (1865) "perhaps the classic statement of transcendentalized religion." Hedge wrote one greatly admired poem, called *Questionings* when it first appeared in the *Dial* (January, 1841), later renamed *The Idealist*—a combination of Kant and Emerson. See TRANSCENDENTALISM.

Hegan, Alice.   See ALICE HEGAN RICE.

Heggen, Thomas [Orlo] (1919–1949),   novelist. Heggen was born in Iowa and left the staff of the *Reader's Digest* to serve five years in the Navy during World War II, mainly on sea duty in the Pacific. Then he returned to the *Digest*. Using his experiences as a basis, he wrote *Mister Roberts* (1946), which sold more than a million copies in its original form, many hundreds of thousands more as a paperback. It was adapted for the stage by Joshua Logan (1948), and was also filmed. It is an uninhibited, uncensored depiction of the boredom of the men on a Navy cargo carrier during the war.

Heidenmauer, The (1832),   a novel by JAMES FENIMORE COOPER. The second of three novels that express Cooper's ideas on government, it followed THE BRAVO (1831) and was followed by THE HEADSMAN (1833). The scene is the Palatinate in the 16th century; and the plot turns on the conflict between the dominant Benedictine order and the increasing strength of Lutheranism.

Heinlein, Robert A. ["Anson MacDonald"] (1907–1988),   novelist, author of science fiction and nonfiction, TV and screen writer. Born in Missouri, Heinlein has been called the dean of science fiction writers. He was educated at Annapolis and U.C.L.A. and wrote his first story in 1939. His fertile imagination was the source for many of the major themes in science fiction writing. A story about nuclear fission, written while the Manhattan Project was still a secret, had to be suppressed because of its advanced ideas. His novels were usually published simultaneously in French, German, and Italian, and often in other languages.

Heinlein's novels, even when stylistically flawed, are so original in conception that they rarely fail to hold the reader's attention. Some of his books are *The Green Hills of Earth* (1951), short stories; *The Puppet Masters* (1951); *Rocket Ship Galileo*, which was made into the movie *Destination Moon* under the author's technical supervision; *The Door into Summer* (1957); *The Menace from Earth* (1960); *Stranger in a Strange Land* (1961), by far his most famous work, about a human brought to earth after being raised by martians; *I Will Fear No Evil* (1971); *The Notebooks of Lazarus Long* (1978); *Job: A Comedy of Justice* (1984); and *The Cat Who Walks Through Walls* (1985).

Heiress, The (1947),   a play by Ruth and Augustus Goetz, based on Henry James's novel WASHINGTON SQUARE.

Held, John, Jr. (1889-1958),   cartoonist, artist. Held, born in Salt Lake City, began his career as a cartoonist, went on to more serious work, but was always noted for his effective satire, especially of the flapper era. His collections include *Grim Youth* (1930), *Saga of Frankie and Johnny* (1931), *Women Are Necessary* (1931), *The Flesh Is Weak* (1932), *The Work of John Held, Jr.* (1932), *A Bowl of Cherries* (1933), and *Crosstown* (1934). A study is Shelley Armitage's *John Held, Jr.: Illustrator of the Jazz Age* (1987).

Held by the Enemy (1886),   a Civil War play by WILLIAM GILLETTE. The action takes place in a Southern city captured by Union forces. Eunice McCreery is betrothed to a Confederate lieutenant, but two Union officers are also in love with her.

Helicon Hall (Helicon Home Colony).   An experiement in community living that UPTON SINCLAIR founded near Englewood, New Jersey, and in which he invested his royalties from *The Jungle* (1906). Among the literary rebels who joined him was SINCLAIR LEWIS.

Hell-Bent for Heaven (1924),   a play by HATCHER HUGHES. This Pulitzer Prize–winner is set in the North Carolina mountains; the central character is a religious fanatic, hellbent for heaven, who is adept at using a religious camouflage to cloak his selfish desires.

Heller, Joseph (1923–1999),   novelist. Born in Brooklyn and educated at New York University, Columbia University, and Oxford University (Fulbright Scholar, 1949–1950), Heller served in the Air Force in World War II, an experience he drew on in his best-known work, *Catch-22* (1962), a black comedy. The title has entered the language as a phrase defining a circular trap. Yossarian, the antihero, is convinced that the officers, from General Scheisskopf on down, are insane and trying to kill him. Every time he completes a mission as a bombardier, the squadron loses another man, and the number of missions required for home leave is raised. On a ludicrous mission to bomb the incomplete bridge at Avignon, Snowden bleeds to death on Yossarian's flying suit. Yossarian stops wearing clothes. Heller's technique is to alternate the ridiculous with the starkly realistic scenes of war. *Closing Time* (1994) is an unsatisfactory sequel to *Catch-22*. His other fiction includes *Something Happened* (1974), *Good as Gold* (1979), *God Knows* (1984), *Picture This* (1988) and *Portrait of the Artist as an Old Man* (2000). *Catch-22* was dramatized by the author in 1971, and another play is *We Bombed in New Haven* (prod. 1967). *No Laughing Matter* (1986), with Speed Vogel, is autobiographical. *Now and Then: From Coney Island to Here* (1998) is a memoir.

Hell-Fire Club, The.   This actually was a group called The Couranteers, informally assembled by JAMES FRANKLIN to contribute to his magazine, the NEW-ENGLAND COURANT (founded August 14, 1721). The members attacked the MATHER family savagely, and in return the Mathers gave the group this nickname, implying a resemblance to the Hell-Fire Clubs of London in the early 18th century—groups of reckless and dissolute young men who made the streets of London a peril and a nuisance. The contributors to the *Courant* imitated the *Spectator* papers.

Hellman, Lillian (1905–1984),   playwright. She came from a family that spent half of the year in New York City and the other half in New Orleans, with two spinster aunts. A rebellious only child, she left New York University after her junior year. Later she taught at various universities, including Yale and Harvard. Her marriage (1925–32) to Arthur Kober, a press agent and playwright, ended in divorce. Dashiell Hammett, author of *The Thin Man*, lived with Hellman for many years and advised her on writing.

Hellman's successful plays in the 1930s and 1940s depicted selfishness, exploitation, and greed. *The Children's Hour* (1934) deals with a malicious girl ruining the lives of two female teachers by spreading rumors that they are lesbians. In *The Little Foxes* (1939), members of an aristocratic Southern family fight over money and inheritance. Hellman's mother was the model for Birdie, and Alexandra has many of Lillian's traits. After traveling in Europe during the 1930s and learning about fascist atrocities in the Spanish Civil War, Hellman wrote *Watch on the Rhine* (1941). Her anti-Fascist sentiments vitalize Kurt, the protagonist who is forced to kill a Nazi sympathizer. *Another Part of the Forest* (1946) deals with the same family as *Little Foxes*, but in this play the people are twenty years younger. The father-daughter relationship reflects similarities of Hellman's relationship with her own father.

Again drawing on family experiences, Hellman wrote *The Autumn Garden* (1951). It takes place in a Gulf Coast resort, similar to one she visited as a child. Two sisters, based on her New Orleans aunts who ran a boarding house, show their devotion to their brother, a character modeled after Hellman's father. It is a probing play about the middle years of life; the characters confront their weaknesses and suffer from what they see. *Toys in the Attic* (1960) deals with destructive love and the same two women as *The Autumn Garden*. The work projects the idea that when dreams are fulfilled, they sometimes lose their magic.

Hellman's plays reflect her compassion for others and her vigorous personality. A dedicated humanist, she professed the politics of the oppressed and liberal causes. Her plays have tightly woven plots that probe psychological weaknesses and offer striking insights into social issues of her time.

Hellman contributed to fifteen screenplays either as initial author, collaborator, or original screenwriter. Some of her movies include *Dead End* (1937), *The Little Foxes* (1941), *Watch on the Rhine* (1943), *Another Part of the Forest* (1948), *The Children's Hour* (1962), and *Toys in the Attic* (1963). In 1966 she wrote the screenplay for *The Chase*. The movie *Julia* (1976) was based on Hellman's book *Pentimento*. Although not written by Hellman, *Julia* deals with her life, her ideas, and her relationship with Dashiell Hammett.

During the 1960s and 1970s, Hellman wrote her memoirs: *An Unfinished Woman* (1969), *Pentimento* (1973), and *Scoundrel Time* (1976). There are two excellent biographies about her: *Lillian Hellman: Playwright* by Richard Moody and *Lillian Hellman: Her Legend and Her Legacy* by Carol Rollyson.

Sam Smiley

Helper, Hinton Rowan (1828–1909),   memoirist, crusader. One of the most influential writers of the antebellum era, Helper was a native of North Carolina devoted to the South and brought up on a plantation run by slave labor. He worked at miscellaneous jobs in his early years; in 1849 he went to California and didn't like what he saw there, as he told in *Land of Gold: Reality vs. Fiction* (1855). This book discusses what was to become the first and greatest of his causes: free labor. But the publisher deleted the passages on this topic.

Helper began doing research work in the South for a book that was to create an immense sensation, *The Impending Crisis of the South: How to Meet It*, which he finally published at his own expense in 1857. The book had a simple thesis: the South was economically and culturally far behind the North because of its slave labor. Make slavery impossible by taxing it out of existence, said Helper, and send all African-American men back to Africa. The South, he added, is "fast sinking into a state of comparative imbecility and obscurity," filled with "illiterate chevaliers of bowie-knives and pistols." He denounced the authors, clergymen, and politicians of the South in unmeasured language. As a result it became illegal in most parts of the South to own the book. In the North, on the contrary, the book was an immediate success. It went through over 100 printings, in addition to a pamphlet summary produced and circulated by the Republicans.

In 1861 Helper was made a consul at Buenos Aires. On his return he published three books denouncing blacks and all colored races as inferior and urging their deportation; one was called *The Negroes in Negroland* (1868). He also urged a project for a great north and south intercontinental railroad: *The Three Americas Railway* (1881).

Helprin, Mark (1947–   ),   novelist, short-story writer, conservative commentator. Raised in Ossining, New York, and educated at Harvard, Helprin has served in the Israeli armed forces. A moral fantasist, Helprin attracted critical attention with *Ellis Island and Other Stories* (1981), which combine the realistic and the fantastic in a compassionate vision of humanity. His novel *Winter's Tale* (1983) also combines history, fable, and myth in a utopian epic of Manhattan struggling to liberate itself from crime and poverty. *A Dove of the East* (1975) is stories, *Refiner's Fire* (1977) a novel. *A Soldier of the Great War* (1991) is set in Italy during World War I. In *Memoir from Antproof Case* (1995) an elderly American in Brazil writes of his many-faceted life.

Hemingway, Ernest [Miller] (1899–1961),   novelist, short-story writer. The son of an Oak Park, Illinois, doctor,

Clarence Edmonds Hemingway, known for his devotion to hunting and fishing, and of Grace Hall Hemingway, whose interests were music and religion, Ernest Hemingway made an unusual combination of these outdoor and indoor interests in his life and career. Educated at the local public schools, he was particularly active at Oak Park High, where he played football and began writing news columns, chiefly in imitation of Ring Lardner. He also wrote some light verse and several short stories, a few of which contain hints of the style he was later to make his hallmark. He spent many summers on Walloon Lake in upper Michigan, where he was later to set several of his better-known short stories. He decided against college, and went to Kansas City after graduation from high school. There he found employment on the Kansas City *Star*, then one of the country's leading newspapers, and received valuable training for his eventual career. He was repeatedly rejected by the army, but finally was able to get into the war as an ambulance driver and was severely wounded at Fossalta di Piave, Italy, just before his nineteenth birthday. He was decorated by the Italians for heroism, and after hospitalization in Milan he served with the Italian infantry until the Armistice.

Following a period of recuperation in northern Michigan and employment as a foreign correspondent for the Toronto *Star*, Hemingway settled in Paris, determined, under the informal guidance of GERTRUDE STEIN, EZRA POUND, and others, to become a writer. Before long his stories, several of them reflecting his boyhood, were collected in a volume called *In Our Time* (1925) and began to attract attention for the attitudes and technique that were soon to become famous. His next published work was THE TORRENTS OF SPRING (1926), a parody of the style of Sherwood Anderson, who had exerted an early influence on him. Although highly amusing to those familiar with Anderson's manner, the book was written in haste and is not of primary significance. But *The Sun Also Rises*, published in the same year, made his reputation and set him, at the age of twenty-six, in the limelight he both enjoyed and resented for the rest of his life.

Public attention was often attached to Hemingway for extraliterary reasons. His first three marriages—to Hadley Richardson, mother of his first son; to Pauline Pfeiffer, mother of his second and third sons; and to MARTHA GELLHORN, the novelist—all ended in divorce. His fourth wife was the former Mary Welsh of Minnesota, whom he met in England in 1944, and who remained with him until his death. Widely traveled, Hemingway lived for extended periods in Spain and Africa, and for most of the 1930s on Key West, Florida. He frequently was as much identified with sporting and fighting activities as with literature. In his prime he was an amateur boxer and a record-holding deep-sea fisherman, as well as an expert big-game hunter and a bullfight *aficionado*. He also fought informally in two more wars, first on the Loyalist side in the Spanish Civil War and then in World War II, particularly with the Fourth Division of the First Army. Ostensibly a correspondent, he led a small, irregular, and colorful unit of his own in several battles in Europe. Following the war and further deco-

ration, he settled more quietly on an elaborate estate called Finca Vigia, at San Francisco de Paula, near Havana, until the Castro revolution displaced him. He traveled once more to Spain to follow the bullfights, and finally settled in Ketchum, Idaho, near Sun Valley. There, in poor health, and following two periods of hospitalization in the Mayo Clinic, he died of a self-inflicted gunshot wound, and there he is buried.

Despite a highly colorful, at times flamboyant, career, Hemingway will be remembered for his books, which must be separated from the forceful, occasionally overriding personality of their author. He always considered himself primarily a writer, and he was deeply serious, dedicated, and hardworking. For many years he was probably the most widely known American writer. His style, his attitudes, and some of his characters became widely recognized throughout the world, and he was possibly the most influential writer of English prose in the first half of the 20th century.

His first wholly mature and important work, IN OUR TIME, reveals at the start many of the qualities for which he was to become known. Almost a novel, the book particularly establishes, in a series of chapters, a fragmentary but careful early biography of Nick Adams. This biography became the prototype for the boyhoods of most of his later protagonists. Most important, it records Nick's various exposures to a series of violent or otherwise upsetting experiences, beginning in Michigan and culminating with the wound he receives in World War I—an event with far-reaching psychological and ideological implications. The Hemingway hero, far from being the simple, wooden primitive he is often mistaken for, is in reality an inordinately sensitive figure. The decision of the wounded Nick Adams that he had made a "separate peace" with the enemy and was not a "patriot" forecasts a long estrangement from organized society for both the author and his typical protagonist.

THE SUN ALSO RISES presents this protagonist, now Jake Barnes, as having been wounded in the war in such a way as to make sexual experience impossible. Partly as a result, he is a member of the lost generation, as Gertrude Stein termed it, which is represented in Paris by an international collection of entertaining but aimless expatriates, collected mainly about the novel's promiscuous heroine, Lady Brett Ashley. This miscellaneous group includes Jake, an American newspaper correspondent; Robert Cohn and Bill Gorton, who are writers; Mike Campbell, whom Brett intends to marry when her divorce is final; and an unusual Greek count. The action involves considerable drinking, fishing, and going to the bullfights at a Spanish fiesta in Pamplona. Brett passes from Cohn to Romero, a young and gifted bullfighter whom she soon renounces for fear she will harm him, and finally she returns, hopelessly, to Jake. The fact that nothing really leads anywhere in the novel points to its central theme. The action comes full circle to imitate the sun, which, as described in Ecclesiastes, also rises only to hasten to the place where it arose. An extraordinarily fresh and sparkling novel, it is scrupulously planned and executed, lively and entertaining. Its message is clear: For these people, at least, life is futile, unavailing, and essentially empty.

Similarly successful and equally pessimistic was Hemingway's next novel, A FAREWELL TO ARMS (1929). Based on the sketch and the story that make up Chapter 6 of *In Our Time*, the novel relates the unhappy adventures of Frederic Henry, an American lieutenant in the Italian ambulance service in World War I. After falling in love with an English nurse, Catherine Barkley, he is wounded and hospitalized in Milan, where he and Catherine are again together. Following his recuperation, he returns to his company, which is suffering badly in the war, in time for the disastrous retreat from Caporetto. In the course of the retreat Henry is forced to desert in order to avoid a useless sacrifice of his life. He flees to Switzerland with Catherine, now pregnant with his child, and is left with nothing when she dies in childbirth. "If people bring so much courage to this world the world has to kill them to break them, so of course it kills them," the author says in comment. "The world breaks everyone and afterward many are strong at the broken places. But those that will not break it kills." Catherine is one of "the very good and the very gentle and the very brave" who are killed "impartially"; Henry, on the other hand, is broken at the end of the novel, and becomes strong only in a later appearance as the Hemingway protagonist under a different name.

Once again a cleanly and sparely written and impeccably constructed novel, it manages as few have done to fuse a war story with a love story by taking them in turn through subtly parallel stages of development. Incorporating a disillusionment with war—if not indeed, by extension, with modern society itself—the book is founded firmly on such moral values as belief in order, discipline, competence and, most of all, love. But it is nonetheless a tragic, desperate novel that portrays humanity as biologically and socially trapped and doomed. It ranks with *The Sun Also Rises*, in general critical opinion, as his best novel.

These early triumphs were followed by a marked decline, for although Hemingway published regularly during the 1930s and continued to have a wide following, none of his book-length efforts measured up to the high standard his work of the 1920s had set. First came two books of nonfiction, DEATH IN THE AFTERNOON (1932) and *Green Hills of Africa* (1935), which represent the author in escape from the society he had by implication renounced in *A Farewell to Arms*. The African book is an account of a big-game expedition, interspersed with numerous passages having to do with literature, Africa, and America, and punctuated by the author's repeated insistence that he has a right to do what he pleases where he pleases. *Death in the Afternoon* is about bullfighting in Spain, an activity to which Hemingway was long attracted—but more, he argued, as a tragic ritual in which the fighter is the high priest of a ceremonial, administering the death men seek to avoid, than as a sport. A remarkably learned book for one to whose country the sport, or rite, is not native, it also contains some amusing conversations with an Old Lady and some

excellent discussions of the problems of writing good prose. But it remains a minor work.

In 1937 Hemingway returned to Spain, then in the throes of civil war, as a reporter. During his visit he became ardently pro-Loyalist, and soon found himself involved in yet another war for democracy. This fact had an important bearing, at first indirect, on his next three book-length works. A radical change in his attitudes began with the novel TO HAVE AND HAVE NOT (1937), which evidences entirely different notions about the society he had scrupulously been avoiding in his recent work. This is a depression novel in which the author is for the first time concerned with social problems. Harry Morgan, finding it impossible to earn an honest living for himself and his family, strikes out on his own as an outlaw, smuggling rum and Chinese nationals into Cuba. At the end he is killed, but not before learning that a man has no chance alone. This message, which has some appearance of having been tacked on to the novel's action, is consonant with the burden of Hemingway's next work, a play called THE FIFTH COLUMN (1938). The play was written in praise of the fighters with whom the author had associated in Madrid, and whose cause had become his own. It is the story of an American in Spain, a seemingly dissolute but attractive newspaperman who is in reality deeply involved in the war. Despite some good dialogue, the work has never been counted a success. The most remarkable thing about it is the distance that Philip, the protagonist, has come since the days when his Frederic Henry said he was "always embarrassed by the words sacred, glorious, and sacrifice and the expression in vain . . ." and that "abstract words such as glory, honor, courage, or hallow were obscene. . . ."

The best work that came out of Hemingway's reconversion to the world was his next novel, FOR WHOM THE BELL TOLLS (1940). The title, referring to a devotion by John Donne, establishes the general theme of all men's involvement in mankind, as well as the more specific thesis that the loss of liberty anywhere reduces liberty everywhere. The novel, longest of Hemingway's works, deals with three days in the life of Robert Jordan, an American fighting as a volunteer guerrilla in the Spanish civil war. It is his assignment to blow up a strategic bridge located near Segovia. As he awaits the event, he falls in love with the daughter of a Republican mayor, María. Their affair is promoted by a powerful woman named Pilar, who is in reality the leader of the little band of Spanish patriots that includes, as do all Hemingway's better novels, several colorful and memorable minor characters. Signs of imminent disaster slowly pile up. After failing, because of Communist stupidity, to get a message to Loyalist headquarters warning that the advance will not succeed, Jordan blows the bridge as he had been instructed. The attack is not successful, as the generals realize too late; Jordan is badly wounded in the retreat and is left to die. But he has learned the purpose of such a sacrifice, and he faces his destruction at the end without bitterness: "I have fought for what I believed in. . . . If we win here we will win everywhere." Marred, in the opinion of some critics, by the idealized and romantic love story, as well as by the protagonist's somewhat rhetorical expressions of faith, this was the most successful of Hemingway's books as far as sales are concerned, and it is counted among his better novels.

Following it, however, the author lapsed into a silence that lasted for an entire decade. His next novel, *Across the River and into the Trees* (1950), met with a very poor reception. A peacetime army colonel, closely resembling the author, comes to Venice on leave to go duck shooting, to see the young Italian countess he loves, and to make a significant pilgrimage to the place where he, Richard Cantwell (and Nick Adams, Frederic Henry, and the author himself), was wounded in World War I. Apparently written during a period of ill health, the novel is Hemingway's weakest. It points up sharply the importance of that war injury in the author's life and work, but in some of its postures and mannerisms it seems to read like a parody of his better fiction, and Cantwell seems at times a caricature of his creator.

Only two years later, however, Hemingway published THE OLD MAN AND THE SEA (1952), a short novel widely acclaimed as a triumph and helpful in Hemingway's winning of the Nobel Prize for literature in 1954. An old Cuban fisherman, after a protracted spell of bad luck, ventures far into the Gulf Stream and hooks a giant marlin. He fights it for two days and nights before bringing it alongside, and then the sharks, which he fights until he has nothing left to fight with, eat all but the skeleton of the marlin, which he tows home. The sense some critics had that the author was trading on, rather than any longer creating, the style for which he became-known was probably compensated for by the abundance of meaning to be found in the narrative. Primarily the tale seems to emphasize that, given the fact of death, a man must always lose his battle in life; nevertheless, by the manner and dignity of his losing, he can win his own special victory. On another level the story may be read as an allegory of the author's own literary vicissitudes, and on the broadest level the short novel seems a representation of life itself as a potentially epic struggle in which man has the opportunity, while undergoing a sort of crucifixion, to establish his stature.

Following this success the author continued to write, but no more significant work was published during his lifetime. The main reason appears to have had something to do with his upper-bracket tax situation; furthermore, he is said to have felt that the best inheritance he could bestow on his wife and children was manuscript. Indeed, the profits from a single short story, THE SNOWS OF KILIMANJARO, had run well into six figures by the time of his death. Profits from all of his works since then, going to Scribner and to Hemingway's estate, have been immense.

Despite the fact that Hemingway published no important work in the shorter form after the 1930s, it is as a writer of short stories that some critics have primarily esteemed him. By that time three collections, *In Our Time*, MEN WITHOUT WOMEN (1927), and WINNER TAKE NOTHING (1932)—which were compiled and published with his one play in 1938 as *The Fifth Col-*

umn and the First Forty-Nine Stories—had established him as one of the most widely admired and imitated short-story writers. Such pieces as THE KILLERS, THE SHORT HAPPY LIFE OF FRANCIS MACOMBER, and "The Snows of Kilimanjaro" are as well known as the novels, and have become American classics. His influence on the form in America has been incalculable and was given strong new emphasis once again in the 1980s through the work of RAYMOND CARVER.

Hemingway's stories are remarkable for their objectivity and economy, occasionally for their complexity, and frequently for their subtlety. Many of them, though admired for the cleanness and freshness of the prose and the vigor and swiftness of the action, were long poorly understood. Sometimes the difficulty arose from a failure to discern their focus: "The Killers" and "Indian Camp," for notable instances, are not primarily about gangsters or Indians, but about the effect of certain highly unpleasant experiences, involving gangsters and Indians, on the central figure of Nick Adams. Further, the failure to consider Nick a consistent, developed character has sometimes caused difficulty; without remembering that he was badly wounded in World War I, for example, the reader can scarcely understand what is going on beneath the curiously tense surface of "Big Two-Hearted River." Another problem has been the frequent failure to detect the author's purposes, which are never simply to shock, and are frequently subtle; neither the structure nor the essential meaning of a story like "The Sea Change" is entirely available to one who has not perceived that the author is skillfully manipulating passages from Shakespeare's *Tempest* and Pope's *Essay on Man*. "The Snows of Kilimanjaro" makes use of Dante, Flaubert, and Ambrose Bierce, and stands as another example of Hemingway's debts to literature.

Hemingway's stories are of a piece with his novels in that most of the truly distinctive features of his longer works of fiction appear in them. The several protagonists who have been grouped together and called the Hemingway hero—Jake Barnes, Frederic Henry, Robert Jordan, and Richard Cantwell—have their genesis in Nick Adams, who appears only in the stories. Much less important in the work as a whole, and making no appearance in the stories although well known outside them, is the Hemingway heroine, who is presented as mistress of the hero, as the British Catherine Barkley in *A Farewell to Arms*, the Spanish María of *For Whom the Bell Tolls*, and the Italian Renata of *Across the River and into the Trees*. An idealized woman, selfless and compliant, she changes nationality as the hero never does, and grows younger as he ages. With each successive appearance she also becomes less of a person and more of a dream.

A slightly less consistent but much more significant figure who appears in the stories as well as in the novels is a man who introduces and exemplifies what is often called the Hemingway code. This is a set of controlling principles having to do with honor, courage, and endurance which, in a life of tension and pain, define a man as a man and distinguish him from people who are undisciplined and without a knowledge of the rules of the game. In a highly compromising world these principles enable certain figures in the author's work to conduct themselves extremely well in losing battles, and to show, in the well-known phrase, grace under pressure. The character who exemplifies the code, sometimes called the code hero, is often confused with the Hemingway hero, but is in reality distinct from him. The distinction is important, because the man with the code often presents the solution to the problems that the hero, in his extreme though muted sensitivity, regularly encounters. (In a story called "The Gambler, the Nun and the Radio," both figures are presented in clear and contrasted form.) Jack, the compromised but heroic prize fighter of FIFTY GRAND, is a man who illustrates the code, as are Manuel, the bullfighter of "The Undefeated," and Harry Morgan, the smuggler and protagonist of *To Have and Have Not*. Better known representatives are Wilson, the professional hunting guide of "The Short Happy Life of Francis Macomber," and Romero, the bullfighter in *The Sun Also Rises*. Best known is old Santiago, of *The Old Man and the Sea*, who is also the most rounded and complete personification of the code. Behaving perfectly while catching and losing his great fish, he expresses most effectively Hemingway's belief that what counts most in human existence is the dignity and courage with which the individual conducts himself in the process of being destroyed by life and the world.

The violence with which Hemingway was preoccupied in his life and work has proven to be the core of the man. The first short story in his first significant book, *In Our Time*, has turned out to be an uncanny forecast of this preoccupation and most of its eventual implications. Called "Indian Camp," it relates the visit of Dr. Adams and his young son, Nick, to a camp of Indians in northern Michigan. The doctor delivers a baby by Caesarean section, with a jackknife and without anesthetic. When the operation, which Nick attends, is over, they look in the bunk above and discover that the husband of the patient, who has been listening to her screams for two days, has cut his head nearly off with a razor. This violence exists not for its own sake but, as it eventually transpires, so that its effect on the little boy who witnesses it can be studied. This exposure is one of the sources of the bad nerves the hero has to contend with later on. Of equal interest is the fact that, not unnaturally, the story ends with the boy and his father discussing suicide. Readers are now unable to avoid the hindsight that the prototypes for both these figures were themselves destined, like the Indian who "couldn't stand things," to take their own lives. Dr. Hemingway shot himself with a Civil War pistol in 1929; it was a shotgun that took his son's life in 1961.

There is something fictionally appropriate about Ernest Hemingway's swift, wordless, and explosive departure, for seldom, anywhere in his work or life, was the author far from the essential fact of violence, and especially the fact of violent death. In DEATH IN THE AFTERNOON, while discussing how he really began his career, Hemingway relates how he "was trying to learn to write, commencing with the simplest things," and how he had decided to begin with violent death, which, now that the war was over, was best observed in the bullring.

Throughout his work the central theme is man in the face of violence, whether in war, bullring, or hospital, whether the violent deaths are of men or fish in the sea or big game or bulls on land. A line runs straight and true from "Indian Camp" through the hero's—and the author's—own repeated injuries in warfare and elsewhere to Hemingway's own violent and final destruction.

Hemingway's technical achievement was great enough so that his better books would survive if only for the style in which they are written. The Nobel Prize committee seemed to reflect this view when they cited in 1954 "his powerful style-forming mastery of the art of modern narration. . . ."

This prose style had a long and essentially American evolution. In *Green Hills of Africa* the author makes the remark that "all modern American literature" comes from Mark Twain's *Adventures of Huckleberry Finn* (1884). This is a broad overstatement, but Twain's successful attempt to write as an American boy might speak was indeed the beginning of a widespread contemporary style, informal and colloquial, fresh and occasionally poetic, to which Hemingway, after Twain, made the most notable contribution. However, a striking list of parallels between the lives and careers of Hemingway and Stephen Crane may help account for the fact that in Crane, to whom Hemingway has also acknowledged his debt, are also to be found several of the characteristics that mark this general tradition in American prose. At its best Crane's work shows the same intensity as Hemingway's, as well as the same terse and unliterary tone, the same understatements, and several of the features of the dialogue. In the days of Hemingway's apprenticeship, the efforts of Gertrude Stein and Sherwood Anderson to write simply, sparely, concisely, and yet repetitively were also instructive. A pamphlet published by Hemingway in Dijon in 1923, THREE STORIES AND TEN POEMS, contains two stories, "Up in Michigan" and "My Old Man," later reprinted in *In Our Time*, that reflect the debts to Stein and Anderson. (The third, called "Out of Season," is in its subject matter a little reminiscent of Scott Fitzgerald; the poems suggest debts to Stephen Crane and Vachel Lindsay.) It is here that one must turn to study the earliest manner of his adult work, since all the rest of that work was stolen from Hadley Richardson, his first wife, and appears to be permanently lost. Taken together with a short pamphlet of sketches called *In Our Time* (1924), which were also reprinted in the book *In Our Time*, these fragments and stories show clearly the author's earliest purposes; in their rigorous objectivity and extreme economy, and in the sharpness, clarity, and simplicity of the prose, they illustrate the principle that the author was later to state in *Death in the Afternoon*. Writing of the early days in Paris he says: "I was trying to write then and I found the greatest difficulty, aside from knowing what you really felt, rather than what you were supposed to feel, and had been taught to feel, was to put down what really happened in action: what the actual things were which produced the emotion that you experienced . . . the real thing, the sequence of motion and fact which made the emotion. . . ." A striking equivalent of the better-known theory of the objective correlative, previously formulated by T. S. Eliot in his *Sacred Wood* (1920), this is a key to an understanding of Hemingway's method of writing fiction.

Once Hemingway had begun to command a wider following than any of those who had had an immediate influence on him, he became an extraordinary influence himself. First in English, and then gradually in other languages, the hard spare prose made itself felt. It functioned chiefly as a purifying agent, acting against embellishment, padding, all forms of superficial artfulness, and any surface or self-conscious sign of thinking on the part of the author. In addition Hemingway did more than any single writer in English to vitalize the writing of dialogue. All his life a good listener, he managed, by stripping speech to the essentials typical of the speaker and by building patterns of mannerisms and responses peculiar to him, to produce the illusion that the people conversing in his work are actually speaking and not, as for instance in the work of Henry James, that he is speaking for them. Although the influence of his style has extended to the realms of subliterary fiction, particularly the tough-detective school where his effects have been radically cheapened and most of his meanings lost, his total effect has been generally applauded. Though some modern writers appear to have got stuck in it, many have been quick to concede that Hemingway was the gate through which they passed.

Another feature of his considerable significance as a 20th-century American writer has been the extraordinary way in which his views of life and the world have represented the shifting, evolving attitudes of his contemporaries, so that he became the bellwether of his age. *In Our Time* was an obscure but accurate forecast of the role that violence was to play in this century, and of the breakdown of peace in our time. In *A Farewell to Arms* the protagonist stood for countless Americans as he proceeded from complicity in a world war to bitterness to escape; in the development of his attitudes America as a whole could read its own history in the crucial period of Wilson to Harding. *The Sun Also Rises* is a memorable expression of the responses of a whole generation thrown off balance by the war and disillusioned of faith in many of the values that theretofore had sustained Western civilization. *Green Hills of Africa* and *Death in the Afternoon* are telling expressions of a resultant widespread desire for escape from social and international problems. *To Have and Have Not* reveals what the nation had learned in the Great Depression about the ultimate impossibility of the completely individualistic, even antisocial, existence the author, like many of his countrymen, had pursued since the war. A reborn concern for society coincided, in Spain, with a new realization of international responsibilities and a recognition of the necessity of resuming a democratic society's perennial war against tyranny. Thus, in *The Fifth Column* and *For Whom the Bell Tolls* his protagonist takes up the battle again, just as his compatriots were soon to involve themselves in World War II. And finally, as the American people began, following that war, to show a tendency to turn once again from public to private preoccupations, the Hemingway protagonist was once again a man alone, fighting his own

timeless battle far from the view of his fellows in *The Old Man and the Sea*. It would be hard, if not impossible, to find a reflection, or rather refraction, of modern American experience at once as accurate and artful in any other writer.

At the same time, viewed from a different perspective, the world of Hemingway's fiction was not broad and comprehensive. Since he concentrated on the significance of violence in our age and penetrated to what he found essential and distinctive, his world was a narrow and limited one that excluded a great deal of experience which would seem normal and representative to his readers. There are no families in Hemingway, no lasting marriages, no everyday lives, few ordinary places; indeed, most of the routine facts of average existence are conspicuously absent. His world is ultimately a world at war, either literally, as involved in calculated armed combat, or figuratively, as impregnated with violence—present, expected, or just past. The perpetually uprooted inhabitants of this world are limited to the urgencies of war; their lives are dictated by emergency, their pleasures seized in a hurry. They are in combat or transit or on leave, never at home; things about them do not grow or develop for long, but break or die off, or are lost or eaten away. Misery is not universal, because there are visions of stamina, courage, and competence; the body when it is not in pain can give great pleasure; and love, though never more than a temporary condition, profoundly exists. It is a fragmentary and special world which, although most of them do not live in it, his readers have found to be valid in some essential, important way.

Accused of lacking ideas, or more often and worse, of having adolescent ideas, Hemingway kept his thoughts for the most part from showing in his fiction, as he believed proper. Unless a deep and abiding interest in hunting, fishing, and certain sports is to be considered a sign of immaturity, the attitudes that can be found in his work are less often adolescent than simply timeless or perennial. Despite the fact that he was technically a convert to Roman Catholicism, though not for many years a practicing one, and that scattered through his work there is a certain amount of Christian symbolism, such occasional thoughts about the human condition as he permitted himself tended toward the stoical and pragmatic or, as suggested during his later life, the existential. Fundamentally, Hemingway believed that fiction and ideas are antithetical to each other, and the notion, sometimes encountered, that he was antiintellectual stems from that belief. Read *War and Peace*, he once remarked, and see how you will skip the "Big Political Thought passages" that Tolstoi "undoubtedly thought were the best things in the book when he wrote it . . . and see how true and lasting and important the people and the action are. . . . That is the hardest thing of all to do." At his best he did manage to do what he is here calling attention to, and he may on occasion have managed to do it in the prose that he labored so intensely to attain—the kind that "would be as valid in a year or in ten years or, with luck and if you stated it purely enough, always." His techniques, his attitudes, his sensitivity to the spirit of his age and to violence, which has played such a role in it, conspired to establish him as one of the greatest modern writers, and the best of his work seems likely to secure for him a permanent and prominent place in the history of American letters.

Works posthumously published include *A Moveable Feast* (1964), a memoir of Paris; *Islands in the Stream* (1970), a World War II novel set in the Caribbean; and *The Dangerous Summer* (1985), about bullfighting. *The Nick Adams Stories* were collected in 1972. *The Complete Short Stories* (1987) supersedes earlier collections and includes some previously unpublished. Full biographies are Carlos Baker, *Ernest Hemingway: A Life Story* (1969); Jeffrey Meyers, *Hemingway: A Biography* (1985); and Kenneth S. Lynn, *Hemingway: His Life and Work* (1987). Peter Griffin's *Along with Youth: Hemingway, the Early Years* (1985) and Michael Reynolds's *The Young Hemingway* (1986) both begin multivolume biographies.

PHILIP YOUNG/GP

Hémon, Louis (1880–1913),   newspaperman, novelist, short-story writer. Hémon emigrated from France to England, where he wrote fiction, and then in 1911 came to Quebec. He became acquainted with Eva Bouchard and made her the heroine of his novel MARIA CHAPDELAINE: her parents were modeled after a man and wife who had employed Hémon on their farm. After sending the manuscript to the editor of the Paris newspaper *Le Temps*, Hémon set out in search of further literary material, but was killed by a train in Ontario. When his novel was published as a serial in *Le Temps* (1914), it attracted little attention. Then it appeared as a book in 1916 and was translated into English in 1921. It was a great success, and Hémon's papers were searched for additional novels and stories. These appeared as *My Lady Fair* (1923), *The Journal of Louis Hémon* (1924), *Blind Man's Buff* (1925), *Monsieur Ripois and Nemesis* (1925).

Henderson, Alice Corbin (1881–1949),   poet, editor, writer. Henderson, born in St. Louis, published three collections of verse: *The Spinning Woman of the Sky* (1912), *Red Earth* (1920), and *The Sun Turns West* (1933). But her chief service to poetry was as associate editor of the magazine POETRY (1912–16), of which she was a cofounder. She is credited with having discovered for the magazine Carl Sandburg and Edgar Lee Masters. In her later years she became interested in New Mexico and bought a ranch not far from Santa Fe, where she edited an anthology of New Mexico poetry, *The Turquoise Trail* (1926). She also wrote an account of the Penitentes there, *Brothers of Light* (1937). With HARRIET MONROE she edited an anthology, *The New Poetry* (1917).

Henderson, Daniel McIntyre [1] (1851–1906), bookseller, poet. Henderson came to America from Scotland in 1873 and established himself in Baltimore, where he wrote numerous lyrics that attained considerable popularity, and some were set to music. He published *Poems: Scottish and American* (1888) and *A Bit Bookie of Verse* (1906).

Henderson, Daniel [McIntyre] [2] (1880–1955), poet, editor, biographer, novelist. Henderson, born in Baltimore and son of the foregoing Henderson, continued the family tradition of poetry and published several volumes of graceful, sincere verse: *Life's Minstrel* (1919), *A Harp in the Winds* (1924), and *Frontiers* (1933). He served on the editorial staff of several magazines, in particular some in the Hearst group (1924–48). He wrote biographies of Theodore Roosevelt, Daniel Boone, Mary Tudor, and Admiral Charles Wilkes as well as numerous works dealing with American history, several juveniles, and a historical novel, *A Crown for Carlotta* (1929). In 1943 he edited *Reveille*, war poems by members of the U.S. armed forces. With his wife, Ernestine, he wrote a biography of Alice and Phoebe Cary (1950).

Henderson the Rain King (1959),   seriocomic novel by Saul Bellow. The hero, Eugene Henderson—it is not coincidental that his initials match those of Ernest Hemingway—is a large, clumsy, and powerful man of 55 who is undergoing a middle-age crisis. In a humorous mix of dense literary and other allusions and rich colloquialisms, Henderson's first-person narrative relates how, although he is a millionaire, his life is foundering for lack of purpose. A World War II veteran, he is twice-married, given to irrational outbursts, uneasy as a father, and uncertain about his vocation. He decides to go to Africa in hope of finding himself. Underlying his angst is his feeling of rejection by his father, intensified by the fact of his brother's death. He suffers from a need for acceptance and approval, which he in turn frustrates by acting out his guilt and rage. Bellow constructs a fantasy-Africa in which Henderson can encounter the primitive realities he has lost touch with and so become healed.

The quest proceeds along two stages. Accompanied by Romilayu, his faithful guide, Henderson first encounters a gentle and peace-loving people called the Arnewi (are new?), from whom he learns that man wants to live. In gratitude, he tries to free the land of drought by ridding their cistern of frogs, but in his blundering and too-cocky way, he blows it up instead and is constrained to move on.

The second stage is much longer and more complex. Here he meets the Wariri (wary, weary, warrior?) and their king, Dahfu (daffy?), who has been to medical school in Syria. This tribe is much less gentle, and the lesson this time is that man has to die, which Henderson learns as Dahfu—teacher, healer, Reichian therapist, quack, a figure who recurs in various guises throughout Bellow's fictions—has him overcome his fear of death by playing with a pet lion.

True to his own teaching, and dethroned by a rival court faction, Dahfu accepts death at the claws of a wild lion during a ritual hunt. Henderson, on the other hand, having saved the tribe from drought *this* time by lifting a heavy cloud-goddess statue, is being eyed for the throne. He refuses, of course, and returns home intending to enter medical school himself. He has learned that Reality—the Given—includes Death as well as Life, and that this does not negate Worthwhileness. So he can let go of his need for father's approval, and he can father himself—a resolution symbolized by his bringing a lion cub representing Dahfu's spirit back home with him and befriending an orphan child on the plane.

One difficulty is to gauge how seriously Bellow intended all this. He is clearly poking fun at the trendy quest for self-fulfillment and the literary fashion of deep heart-of-darkness and wasteland symbolism, yet he is also engaging the reader sympathetically in his hero's sufferings and realizations. In satirizing itself, perhaps this novel is both endorsing the quest for renewal and at the same time saying it can only really succeed if it is taken with a dash of humor and self-awareness. Another difficulty is that the resolution has been found by a number of critics to be somewhat arbitrary and willed rather than flowing naturally from the material, and it may well be that these two difficulties stem from the same underlying uncertainty of tone and intention that gives the novel its curiously volatile and improvisatory air.

NORMAN FRIEDMAN

Henley, Beth [Becker] (1952–), playwright. Henley was raised in Jackson, Mississippi, where her mother was active in amateur theater. Henley studied drama at Southern Methodist University and there wrote her first play, *Crimes of the Heart* (1978). This story of three eccentric sisters in a small Mississippi town was produced in four other cities before it reached Broadway and won the Pulitzer Prize. Henley wrote the screenplay for the 1986 film version. Her other plays are *The Miss Firecracker Contest* and *The Wake of Jamey Foster*.

Hennepin, [Johannes] Louis (1640–1701?), Flemish missionary, explorer, historian, geographer. A Franciscan friar, Hennepin preached successfully in the Low Countries, in 1665 joined LA SALLE's expedition to Canada and began working with the Iroquois at Fort Frontenac, now Kingston, Ontario. In 1678 he accompanied La Salle's expedition toward the Great Lakes and then, as leader of an independent party, explored the upper Mississippi. He was captured by Sioux tribesmen, but was rescued in 1681. He returned to France and there published accounts, believed exaggerated by historians, of his explorations: *Description de la Louisiane* (1683), *Nouveau voyage* (1696), and *Nouvelle découverte d'un très grand pays situé dans l'Amérique* (1697). An English version of his *Description de la Louisiane* was made in 1880, a more authoritative one in 1938 by Marion E. Cross.

Hennessy. A character who appears frequently in the MR. DOOLEY sketches of Finley Peter Dunne. Hennessy is believed to have been modeled on John J. McKenna (1853–1941), one of Dunne's friends in James McGarry's saloon in Chicago. But McKenna appears in person in at least one of the Dooley pieces, *The Idle Apprentice*.

Henry, Marguerite (1902–1997), children's fiction writer. Born Marguerite Breithaupt in Milwaukee, Wisconsin, where her father owned a printing shop, she published her first story in *Delineator Magazine* at age 11. She wrote avidly at Milwaukee State College, graduated, married Sidney Crocker Henry, and began her professional writing career soon after. Most celebrated among her more than sixty books is *Misty of Chincoteague* (1947), one of the best horse stories ever written for children, about an orphan brother and sister who befriend a wild colt on the island of Chincoteague, off the coast of Virginia, a descendent of ponies washed ashore after a shipwreck hundreds of years ago. Turned into a 1961 movie, *Misty* has been translated into many languages, read by millions around the world, and spawned numerous other related books,

including *Stormy: Misty's Foal* (1963) and *Misty's Twilight* (1992). Among Henry's best horse stories unrelated to *Misty* are *Justin Morgan Had a Horse* (1945), about the first of the Morgan breed of horses; *King of the Wind* (1948), about an 18th century Arabian stallion; *Brighty of the Grand Canyon* (1953,) about a burro in the Old West; *Gaudenzia: Pride of the Palio* (1960), about an annual competition in Siena, Italy; and *San Domingo: The Medicine Hat Stallion* (1972). Others of her books include her first, *Auno and Tauno: A Story of Finland* (1940); *Robert Fulton: Boy Craftsman* (1945); *Benjamin West and His Cat, Grimalkin* (1947); *Cinnabar: The One O'Clock Fox* (1956); and *Muley-Ears, Nobody's Dog* (1959).

Henry, O. Pen name of **William Sydney** [earlier spelled **Sidney**] **Porter** (1862–1910), short-story writer, poet, newspaperman, editor. Porter grew up in Greensboro, North Carolina, and worked first in his uncle's drugstore. Then he drifted off to Texas, where he spent ten years as a clerk, a draftsman in a state land office, finally a bank teller. After a romantic elopement, he began writing pieces for newspapers in Texas and Michigan and for a magazine of his own called THE ROLLING STONE. Then came Porter's great tragedy: he was charged with embezzlement. In a panic, Porter did not wait to stand trial, but left for Central America (the scene of CABBAGES AND KINGS, 1904). There he met other fugitives, including the outlaw Al Jennings. Al later told about their friendship in *Through the Shadows with O. Henry* (1921). When Porter had news that his wife was ill, he returned to the United States, stayed with her until she died, and gave himself up to the authorities. He was tried, convicted, and sentenced to serve five years in the Federal penitentiary at Columbus, Ohio. He was released, with time off for good conduct, after three years and three months.

There has been debate about Porter's trial and conviction. A certain amount of unclear evidence indicates that Porter may have been shielding someone. The most persuasive analysis of the accusation and conviction is found in E. Hudson Long's *O. Henry: The Man and His Work* (1949). The records of the trial have been reproduced from the originals of the U.S. circuit court of appeals at New Orleans in *W. S. Porter, Plaintiff in Error, vs. United States, Defendant in Error* (1940).

Porter was well treated by prison officials and worked as prison pharmacist. To support his daughter, Porter turned to writing again. The first of his new stories to be signed O. Henry appeared in *McClure's Magazine* in 1899 and was called *Whistling Dick's Christmas Stocking*. Apparently, he sold twelve stories while in jail, but there may have been more, since he used other pseudonyms, among them Oliver Henry and S. H. Peters. Where he got the name O. Henry has been much disputed, but he probably adopted it to avoid questions about his term in prison. The most plausible derivation is that Porter found his pen name in the *U.S. Dispensatory*, a reference work consulted daily by American pharmacists. It was the name of a celebrated French pharmacist, Etienne-Ossian Henry, abbreviated to O. Henry.

Porter's time in Texas and Central America contributed much to his storehouse of incidents and personalities, and in prison he heard many stories that were the germs of his later narratives—among them the tale of Jimmy Connors, the thief who became the hero of A RETRIEVED REFORMATION and of Paul Armstrong's successful play ALIAS JIMMY VALENTINE (1909). The stories Porter wrote in prison had made an impression on editors; when he was released he made his way to New York and soon won acclaim as America's top short-story writer. Although he wrote extensively of the Southwest and occasionally of other writers, Porter became the prose laureate of Manhattan. To him the city was an opportunity for writing a new series of Arabian Nights stories, and in several of his tales he calls it Bagdad-on-the-Subway.

Porter was a marvelous spinner of yarns who possessed endless inventiveness of plot and character. C. Alphonso Smith, who in his *O. Henry Biography* (1916) was the first scholar to deal with Porter's career and writings, traced four stages in the telling of an O. Henry story: the arrestive beginning; the reader's first guess as to how the story will come out; the stage in which the reader discovers that his first forecast is wrong; and the triumphant conclusion, with a sudden surprise. Porter's success and the seeming facility of his formula turned critics and some writers against him. The continued popularity of his works, however, indicates that readers agree with his notion of what makes a good story.

In his own lifetime, collections of Porter's stories were published: THE FOUR MILLION (1906), *The Trimmed Lamp* (1907), *Heart of the West* (1907), *The Voice of the City* (1908), *The Gentle Grafter* (1908), *Roads of Destiny* (1909), *Options* (1909), *Strictly Business* (1910), and *Whirligigs* (1910). After his death appeared *Let Me Feel Your Pulse* (1910), *Sixes and Sevens* (1911), *Rolling Stones* (1912), *Waifs and Strays* (1917), *Seven Odds and Ends, Poetry and Short Stories* (1920), *Letters to Lithopolis* (1922), *Postscripts* (1923), and *O. Henry Encore* (1939). *The Collected Works of O. Henry* (2 v. 1953) includes all his stories and some of his poems. Porter was interested in the theater, and in collaboration with FRANKLIN P. ADAMS wrote a fairly successful play called *Lo* (prod. 1909). In 1952 a group of Hollywood scriptwriters produced *O. Henry's Full House*, a movie based on five of his stories.

In 1918, the O. Henry Memorial Awards were established for authors of the best stories published each year. The winning stories are also included in annual short-story collections. See THE GIFT OF THE MAGI; THE LAST LEAF [2].

Henry, Patrick (1736–1799),   lawyer, orator, statesman, public official. In 1760 Henry, born in Virginia, began to practice law and soon won renown as a fiery patriotic orator. His speeches on the Stamp Act increased his renown, especially one delivered on May 29, 1765, in the Virginia House of Burgesses. He had introduced seven resolutions, and in his peroration he shouted, "Caesar had his Brutus; Charles the First, his Cromwell; and George III—may well profit by their example!" At this point the Speaker of the House remonstrated with an interruption of "Treason! Treason!" and others echoed his words. But Henry replied, "If that be treason, make the most of it!" Even better known was his address to the Virginia Assembly of Delegates, March 23, 1775. Henry advocated the

immediate arming of the colony, and at the close of his speech said solemnly, "I know not what course others may take, but as for me, give me liberty, or give me death!" In May 1775, the Royal Governor of Virginia proclaimed him an outlaw. In the years after the Revolution, Henry became more conservative. He served five useful terms as governor of Virginia and declined a sixth after he had been elected. He also declined to accept the positions of Secretary of State and of Chief Justice of the Supreme Court offered to him by Washington.

In Virginia he became a folklore hero whose shrewdness was sometimes represented as passing the boundaries of honesty. Even as an orator Henry's fame would have been obscured without his first biographer, William Wirt, whose *Sketches of the Life and Character of Patrick Henry* (3 v. 1817) immortalized him. Wirt gathered as well as he could memories of Henry's addresses and wove them into his narrative. Henry's grandson, William Wirt Henry, edited a useful work, *Patrick Henry: Life, Correspondence, and Speeches* (3 v. 1891). Robert D. Meade's *Patrick Henry, Patriot in the Making* (1958) is the first of two authoritative volumes. Henry has appeared often in historical novels, including John Esten Cooke's THE VIRGINIA COMEDIANS (1854), Robert W. Chambers's CARDIGAN (1901), Irving Bacheller's *In the Days of Poor Richard* (1922), Hildegarde Hawthorne's *Rising Thunder* (1937), Elizabeth Page's *The Tree of Liberty* (1939), John Erskine's *Give Me Liberty* (1940), and Kenneth Roberts's OLIVER WISWELL (1940).

Henry St. John, Gentleman (1859),   a novel by JOHN ESTEN COOKE. This is a sequel to THE VIRGINIA COMEDIANS (1854), involving some of the same characters as that novel of colonial life in Virginia. But the leading character is St. John, a descendant of Pocahontas who joins the opposition to Lord Dunmore, arrogant governor of the colony. A love story involves beautiful Bonnybel Vane, in whose behalf St. John fights a duel.

Henry, Will.   See HENRY W. ALLEN.

Henson, Josiah (1789–1881),   clergyman, lecturer. Born in Maryland, Henson escaped from slavery, went to Canada, and became a Methodist minister. He traveled widely and met many celebrities, lecturing frequently on his experiences, which included assisting in the escapes of over 100 slaves and helping establish a cooperative colony in Canada. His fame rests chiefly on the fact that HARRIET BEECHER STOWE, by her own acknowledgment in her *Key to Uncle Tom's Cabin* (1853) and in her introduction to Henson's *Truth Stranger Than Fiction* (1858, originally published as *Life of Josiah Henson* or as *Autobiography* in 1849), used the incidents of his life for "many of the finest conceptions and incidents of Uncle Tom's character." She altered and augmented them, however, so that Henson and Uncle Tom are by no means identical. Henson's cabin still stands in Rockville, Maryland.

Hentoff, Nat (1925–   ),   writer, critic. Hentoff was born in Boston and educated at Harvard and the Sorbonne. In 1960 he became a staff writer for *The New Yorker* magazine. He has contributed drama reviews and articles on race relations and politics to various magazines. At first best known as a jazz critic writing in a lively contemporary idiom, he turned later to polemics on politics and free speech. His books include *Hear Me Talkin' To Ya* (1955); *The Jazz Makers* (1957); *Jazz* (1959); *Jazz Street* (1960); *The Jazz Life* (1961); *Black Anti-Semitism and Jewish Racism* (1970); *Does Anybody Give a Damn?* (1977), an essay on education; *The First Freedom* (1980), a history of free speech in America; *Free Speech for Me—But Not for Thee* (1992); *Speak Freely: A Memoir* (1997); and *Living the Bill of Rights: How to Be an Authentic American* (1998).

Hentz, Caroline Lee [Whiting] (1800–1856), novelist, dramatist. Born in Massachusetts, Hentz lived for many years in the South, and one aim of her fiction was to alleviate Northern prejudice against the South, especially in respect to slavery. Her books include *De Lara: or, the Moorish Bride* (1831); *Werdenberg: or, the Forest League* (1832); *Linda, or, The Young Pilot of the "Belle Creole"* (1850); *The Planter's Northern Bride* (2 v. 1854); and *Ernest Linwood, or, The Inner Life of the Author* (1856).

Hentz, Nicholas Marcellus (1797–1856), novelist. The French-born husband of Caroline Lee Hentz wrote *Tadeuskund, the Last King of the Lenape* (1825), a melodramatic novel about the Delaware Indians.

Herald of Gospel Liberty. This is believed to have been the first weekly in this country devoted to religious topics. It was founded in 1808 by Elias Smith, an event commemorated in J. Prester Barrett's *The Centennial of Religious Journalism* (1908).

Herbert, Frank (1920–1986), science fiction writer. Herbert was a newspaperman turned writer. His first novel was *The Dragon in the Sea* (1956), a psychologically intricate story of a search for a saboteur in an undersea war. *The Santaroga Barrier* (1968), about a utopian community, reveals Herbert's continuing interest in the evolution of intelligence. He is known best for an ecology-minded series of heroic adventures that includes *Dune* (1965), the name of the desert planet that provides its setting; *Dune Messiah* (1970); *The Children of Dune* (1976); *The God Emperor of Dune* (1981); and *The Heretics of Dune* (1985). His other works include *Lazarus Effect* (1983) and, with his son Brian, *Man of Two Worlds* (1986).

Herbert, Henry William ["Frank Forester"] (1807–1858), teacher, translator, editor, poet, novelist, writer on sports and nature, artist. Herbert emigrated from England to America in 1831. For several years he taught school, then became a newspaperman. He also did some translating from the Greek and helped found the *American Monthly Magazine*. Then he began writing conventional historical romances: *The Brothers: A Tale of the Fronde* (1835), *Cromwell* (1838), *Ringwood the Rover* (1843), *The Roman Traitor* (1846), *The Cavaliers of England* (1852), and *The Cavaliers of France* (1852). Under the name Frank Forester, he composed and published sketches of hunting and sporting life, becoming the first sports writer in the United States. Under his pen name he also wrote *The Warwick Woodlands* (1845), *My Shooting Box* (1846), *The Deer-stalkers* (1849), *Field Sports of the United States and British Provinces of North America* (2 v. 1849), *The Quorndon Hounds* (1852), *The Complete Manual for Young Sportsmen* (1856), and *Horses and Horsemanship of the United States and British Provinces of North America* (1857). In 1858 Herbert committed suicide.

Herbert's books are still readable, the work of a genuine lover of nature and sports. Perhaps the best of his sporting novels is *The Warwick Woodlands* (reprinted 1934). His *Sporting Sketches* were collected in 1879, his *Poems* in 1888. The best biography of Herbert is William S. Hunt's *Frank Forester: A Tragedy in Exile* (1933).

Herbert, Victor (1859–1924), musician, composer. Herbert came to the United States from Ireland in 1886 to join the orchestra of the Metropolitan Opera Company. A few years later he began conducting bands and orchestras, organized an orchestra of his own, and helped found ASCAP. He was always deeply interested in composing, especially light operas. His first opera to be performed was *Prince Ananias* (1894), and for the remainder of his career he was the country's leading representative of light, tuneful, memorable music. Between 1894 and 1917 Herbert wrote thirty-five operas and operettas, besides incidental music for other theatrical pieces. Among the operettas are *The Wizard of the Nile* (1895), *The Fortune Teller* (1898), *Babes in Toyland* (1903), *Mlle. Modiste* (1905), *The Red Mill* (1906), *Naughty Marietta* (1910), and *Sweethearts* (1913). His two grand operas are *Natoma* (1911), an Indian play, and *Madeleine* (1914), a one-act drama.

Herbst, Josephine [Frey] (1897–1969), novelist. Born in Iowa, Herbst belongs with the so-called proletarian novelists. Although her depiction of life among the lowly is powerful, she often forgets her story in her accumulation of physical and psychological details. Among her books are *Nothing Is Sacred* (1928), *Money for Love* (1929), *Pity Is Not Enough* (1933), *The Executioner* (1934), *Rope of Gold* (1939), *Satan's Sergeants* (1941), *Somewhere the Tempest Fell* (1947), *New Green World* (1954), and *The Watcher with the Horn* (1955). See PROLETARIAN LITERATURE.

Heredia, José María de (1803–1839), Cuban poet. Exiled at twenty for revolutionary activity against the Spanish regime in Cuba, Heredia imbued his poetry with the disillusion and frustration that was the lot of many Cuban intellectuals of his generation. After spending two unhappy years in the U.S., he settled in Mexico and except for a brief trip to Cuba in 1836 remained in Mexico for the rest of his life. Although Heredia's poetry is classical in form, he has been called the first romantic poet of Hispanic America because of the subjectivity and intensity that characterize his verse. The two poems generally considered his best are "En el teocalli de Cholula" (1820), in which Heredia reflects on the impermanence of all earthly endeavor, and "Niagara" (1824), in which the poet describes the scene in a style as torrential as the falls itself, and then laments his solitude, so far from home.

Herford, Oliver (1863–1935), poet, illustrator, playwright. Born in England, Herford came to the U.S. as a child, studied in London and Paris and at Antioch College. He established himself in this country as a contributor of verse and drawings to magazines. He wrote many books, illustrating most of them himself. Among them are *Pen and Inklings* (1892); *The Bashful Earthquake and Other Fables and Verses* (1898); *An Alphabet of Celebrities* (1899); *A Child's Primer of Natural History* (1899); *The Cynic's Calendar* (with ETHEL WATTS MUMFORD and Addison Mizner, 1902–17); *Rubáiyát of a Persian Kitten* (1904); *A Little Book of Bores* (1906); *The Simple Jography* (1908); *Cupid's Encyclopedia* (1910); *The Kitten's Garden of Verses* (1911); *The Mythological Zoo* (1912); *Confessions of a Caricaturist* (1917); *This Giddy Globe* (1919); *The Herford Aesop* (1921); *Excuse It Please* (1929); and *The Deb's Dictionary* (1931). Poems written for *Life* were collected in 1923. He adapted *The Devil* (1908) from a play by Ferenc Molnár and wrote plays of his own, among them *The Florist's Shop* (1909) and *The Love Cure* (1909).

Hergesheimer, Joseph (1880–1954), novelist, short-story writer, historian, biographer, travel writer. Early in his career Hergesheimer, who was born in Philadelphia, won the esteem of critics in this country and abroad. He began an unimportant novel, *The Lay Anthony* (1914), and went on to *Mountain Blood* (1915); THE THREE BLACK PENNYS (1917); two books of short stories, *Gold and Iron* (1918) and *The Happy End* (1919), which includes "TOL'ABLE DAVID"; LINDA CONDON (1919); JAVA HEAD (1919); *Cytherea* (1922); *The Bright Shawl* (1922); and *Balisand* (1924). Hergesheimer expressed vividly his love of beauty, adherence to old ideals of chivalry, melancholy at the passing of a world he loved, and interest in people who dared to be individuals. Some of the novels—*The Three Black Pennys, Java Head, Balisand*—have become minor classics of American fiction.

Herlihy, James Leo (1927–1993), novelist, playwright. Artistic chronicler of the bizarre, grotesque, and alienated, Herlihy is best known as the author of books and plays made into movies: *Blue Denim* (1958), a play; *All Fall Down* (1960); *Midnight Cowboy* (1965); and *Stop, You're Killing Me* (1970), three one-act plays.

Hernández, José (1834–1886), poet. Hernández grew up a genuine gaucho on the Argentine pampas. He founded a newspaper, *Rio de la Plata* (1869), which he used to lobby on behalf of the gauchos. Three years later he published the narrative poem on which his reputation rests, MARTIN FIERRO. The realism and accessibility of the poem made it as popular among the rural people of Argentina as R. W. SERVICE's Yukon ballads were among the pioneers of the Pacific Northwest. For years, Hernández was disdained by the more educated reader, but this changed greatly after the turn of the century.

Herndon, William Henry (1818–1891), lawyer, politician, biographer of Lincoln. In 1842 Herndon, a Kentuckian, entered the office of Logan and Lincoln in Springfield, Illinois, as a student. When that partnership was dissolved in 1844, Lincoln invited him to become his junior partner, and the law firm of Lincoln and Herndon continued to exist until Lincoln's death.

Lincoln's assassination gave Herndon a mission in life—to preserve Lincoln for posterity. He wrote down his own reminiscences, went to Kentucky and talked to men who had known Lincoln as a boy, and gathered a great mass of material.

Because of financial setbacks he was forced to sell much of his data to WARD HILL LAMON in 1870. In the 1880s Jesse W. Weik, an ardent student of Lincoln's life, began a correspondence with Herndon, and in 1889 the two men published *Herndon's Lincoln: The True Story of a Great Life*. The work aroused a good deal of controversy because of the inclusion of information concerning Lincoln's mother, his religious unorthodoxy, his marriage to Mary Todd, and his romance with Ann Rutledge, but recent critics have felt that Herndon's work contributed a good deal to the demythologizing of Lincoln's life. Herndon himself was the subject of David Donald's biography, *Lincoln's Herndon* (1948).

Herne, James A. [originally **James Ahern**] (1839–1901), actor, playwright. A capable actor—his daughters Julie and Chrystal also attained prominence on the stage—Herne developed as a writer into an impressive realist. Among his plays are HEARTS OF OAK (with DAVID BELASCO, 1879); *Drifting Apart* (1888); MARGARET FLEMING (1890); SHORE ACRES (1892); and THE REVEREND GRIFFITH DAVENPORT (1899). A collection, *Shore Acres and Other Plays*, was made in 1928 by Mrs. Herne. Herne's dramas dealt often with unsophisticated characters in rural environments, and they exerted a considerable influence on later playwrights.

Herr, Michael (1940–   ), writer. After covering the Vietnam War for *Esquire*, Herr published *Dispatches* (1977), a personal narrative considered one of the best books about that conflict. Herr also wrote the narration for the film *Apocalypse Now* (1979); *Walter Winchell: A Novel* (1990), a biography of the famed journalist, in the form of a screenplay; and *Kubrick* (2000), a brief memoir and study of the movie director.

Herrera y Reissig, Julio (1875–1910), Uruguayan poet. A representative of the baroque, or extravagant, wing of MODERNISMO, Herrera Reissig was the leader of a Bohemian literary group that met in the attic of his father's home in Montevideo. His poems—all written in sonnet form—were intended to appeal to the few. They are characterized by experimentation in vocabulary and by unusual imagery, though his themes were often drawn from everyday life. A posthumous edition of his *Poesias completas* was published in 1945.

Herrick, Robert (1868–1938), teacher, novelist, short-story writer. Born in Massachusetts, he sought in his fiction to describe and analyze the problems of modern industrial society, especially the corruption of the middle-class soul by commercialism.

In his novel *Chimes* (1926), for instance, he attacked the big business methods prevalent at the University of Chicago, where he taught for thirty years (1893–1923). He drew a distinction between most of his novels as realistic and a limited group that were, as he said, idealistic, manifesting a kind of broadminded Puritanism. Among his more notable novels are *The Web of Life* (1900), THE COMMON LOT (1904), *The Memoirs of an American Citizen* (1905), *A Life for a Life* (1910), *The Healer* (1911), *One Woman's Life* (1913), *Clark's Field* (1914), and *The End of Desire* (1932). His most widely read book was *The Master of the Inn* (1908), in which a cure for modern ills is sought in contemplation, quietude, and physical labor.

Herriman, George (1880–1944), cartoonist. Born in New Orleans, listed as "colored" on his birth certificate, he was raised by his family in Los Angeles and lived as white or "creole." In 1897 he began drawing for the *Los Angeles Herald*, and soon moved to New York as a cartoonist for various papers and strips. *The Family Upstairs*, about the Dingbat family, was his first successful strip. Krazy Kat first appeared there in 1910 and in 1911 *Krazy Kat* became an independent feature. Legend has it that the idea for this cartoon strip came from an office boy named Willie, who looked over his shoulder one day at a cartoon of a cat and mouse playing marbles and said, "Why don't you make the mouse chase the cat?" Krazy Kat, Ignatz Mouse, and Offisa Pup came alive in the strip. Krazy Kat loved Ignatz, and Offisa Pup loved Krazy Kat. Ignatz's constant joy was to "crease Kat's bean with a brick," thereby showing his affection, but Offisa Pup always tried to protect the Kat.

Hersey, Harold Brainerd (1893–1956), editor, poet. Much of Hersey's verse is set in his native Montana. Among his collections are *Gestures in Ivory* (1919), *Cylinders* (1925), *Singing Rawhide* (1926), *Bubble and Squeak* (1927), and *Verse* (2 v. 1939). He was the first editor (1917) of *The Quill: A Magazine of Greenwich Village* and, with Elinor Hersey, of *Main Street* (1929); he told his own life story in *Pulpwood Editor* (1937).

Hersey, John [Richard] (1914–1993), magazine writer, war correspondent, editor, historian. Hersey was born of American parents in China and spoke Chinese before learning English. At one time secretary to SINCLAIR LEWIS and later a writer for *Time* and *The New Yorker*, Hersey published his first book, *Men on Bataan* (1942), as a war correspondent's report. *Into the Valley* (1943) showed his increasing mastery of language and ideas in its brief, well-written account of a skirmish on Guadalcanal. *A Bell for Adano* (1944), based on Hersey's observation of the American occupation of Italy, shows deep sympathy with and an understanding of the Italian people. It won a Pulitzer Prize.

HIROSHIMA (1946) made Hersey's reputation. In China as a correspondent for *Time* and *The New Yorker*, Hersey had made a visit to Japan to see what had happened to Hiroshima's inhabitants when the atomic bomb was dropped. The remarkable report he sent back appeared in *The New Yorker* on August 31, 1946. Man's inhumanity and courage are also the theme of Hersey's novel *The Wall* (1950), his most ambitious work—the story of the extinction of the Warsaw ghetto by the Germans. It was made into a play produced on Broadway (1960) and in Europe (1961). His later publications include *The Marmot Drive* (1953), *A Single Pebble* (1956), *The War Lover* (1959), *The Child Buyer* (1960), *The Algiers Motel Incident* (1968), *The Writer's Craft* (1974), *Blues* (1987), *Fling and Other Stories* (1990), and *Antonietta* (1991).

Herskovitz, Melville Jean (1895–1963), anthropologist, explorer. Herskovitz was born in Ohio, taught at Columbia, Howard, and Northwestern, and became professor of anthropology at Northwestern. He led scientific expeditions to Dutch Guiana, Haiti, West Africa, Trinidad, and Brazil, with his wife, Frances Shapiro Herskovitz, as his assistant. Together they wrote *The Outline of Dahomean Religious Belief* (1933), *Rebel Destiny: Among the Bush Negroes of Dutch Guiana* (1934), *Surinam Folklore* (1936), *Trinidad Village* (1947), and *Dahomean Narrative, A Cross-Cultural Analysis* (1958). In addition Herskovitz wrote *The American Negro: A Study in Racial Crossing* (1928), *Life in a Haitian Valley* (1937), *Dahomey* (1938), *Acculturation* (1938), *The Economic Life of Primitive Peoples* (1940), *The Myth of a Negro Past* (1941), *Man and His Works* (1948), *Economic Anthropology* (1952), and *Cultural Anthropology* (1955). The special province of Herskovitz was the indigenous African and the displaced African, and he established some astonishing facts about the relationship that still prevails between the people of West Africa and African Brazilians.

Hervey, Harry C[lay] (1900–1951), newspaperman, explorer, novelist, short-story writer. Hervey, a Texan, traveled extensively in Asia, Africa, and the islands of the Pacific and led an archaeological expedition (1925) in the country that now is Vietnam. He sold his first story at age sixteen to H. L. Mencken; his first novel, *Caravans by Night* (1922), appeared when he was twenty-one. Among his other novels are *The Black Parrot* (1923), *Ethan Quest* (1925), *Congai* (1927), *Red Hotel* (1932), *The Damned Don't Cry* (1939), *School for Eternity* (1941), and *Veiled Fountain* (1947).

Herzog (1964), novel by SAUL BELLOW. At the center of Bellow's fiction stands a series of high-minded, earnest, and voluble monologists, prolific thinkers, stylish polemicists. Moses Elkannah Herzog is the most agonizingly articulate, comically self-conscious of them all. Beleaguered by the intensity of his introspection, Herzog worries over his life: an intellectual stumped in the middle of his second book—tellingly, an inquiry into Romanticism—a husband brooding over his second failed marriage, and above all a man trying to think his way into clarity, all the while wryly aware that he is the creator of his own paralysis. The epitome of this condition is the spate of letters that Herzog writes—to the living and the dead, to the famous and to his own circle of friends and enemies—but never sends. The letters document Herzog's detailed, vivid, and anxious apprehensions of contemporary American life in Chicago, in New York, and in the more pastoral setting of his retreat in the Berkshires. They also serve as a wonderfully colloquial venue for his irreverent, chatty, but also profound reflections on the fate of the individual in modern society. Herzog's storm of consciousness whirls him in all directions across the landscape of his past and present, but at the novel's end he is brought to the moment of equilibrium and silent repose—at one with his soul, with God, and with the natural and temporal world—that so many Bellow characters seek and that so often eludes them.

NEIL BESNER

Hester Prynne. Major character of Hawthorne's THE SCARLET LETTER.

Hewat, Alexander (1745?–1829), clergyman, historian. Hewat lived in South Carolina from 1763 until the outbreak of the Revolution, whereupon his Tory views led him to return to his native Scotland. His *An Historical Account of the*

Rise and Progress of the Colonies of South Carolina and Georgia (2 v. 1779) is reliable except for his information on the Revolution.

Hewitt, James (1770–1827), musician. Born in England, Hewitt came to America in 1772 and became active as a performer, conductor, and composer. He wrote one of the earliest of American operas, *Tammany, or, The Indian Chief*, which was performed under the auspices of the Tammany Society of New York. The libretto was written by Anne Julia Hatton. Hewitt's son, **John Hill Hewitt** (1801–1890), sometimes called the Father of American Ballad Poetry, wrote many popular songs, including "Minstrel's Return from the War" (1827) and "All Quiet Along the Potomac Tonight" (1864). He published *Miscellaneous Poems* (1838) and an autobiography, *Shadows on the Wall, or, Glimpses of the Past* (1877), which gives vivid pictures of the musical personalities of the mid-19th century.

Heyen, William (1940–), poet. His early work includes *Depth of Field* (1970); *Noise in the Trees: Poems and a Memoir* (1974); and *Long Island Light* (1979), containing "The Snapper," a much anthologized poem. Heyen has contemplated the Holocaust and written many poems about it, including those in *Swastika Poems* (1977) and twenty more poems on the subject in *Erika: Poems of the Holocaust* (1984). *The Host: Selected Poems, 1965–1990* appeared in 1994. More recent, focussed collections are *Crazy Horse in Stillness* (1996), and *Diana, Charles, and The Queen* (1998). *Pig Notes and Dumb Music* (1998) collects prose.

Heyward, Dorothy (1890–1961), playwright, novelist. Born in Ohio, and a distinguished alumna of the Harvard drama workshop presided over by G. P. BAKER, she wrote *Nancy Ann* at Harvard and saw it produced on Broadway (1924). Her other plays are *Love in a Cupboard* (1926), *Jonica* (1929), *Little Girl Blue* (1931), and *Set My People Free* (1948), but she is best known for her collaboration with her husband, DUBOSE HEYWARD, on the dramatization of his novels PORGY and *Mamba's Daughters*. Her own fiction includes *Three-a-Day* (1930) and *The Pulitzer Prize Murders* (1932).

Heyward, DuBose (1885–1940), poet, novelist, playwright. A descendant of Thomas Heyward, Jr., a signer of the Declaration of Independence, Heyward was forced into manual labor as a teenager because of his father's death. Working on the docks of his native Charleston, South Carolina, Heyward met many African-American laborers and observed sympathetically their way of life. He admired their "humor and genuine kindness of heart," qualities he portrayed in his first novel, PORGY (1925). In collaboration with his wife, DOROTHY HEYWARD, he turned it into a play that was produced in 1927. The operatic form, *Porgy and Bess*, with music by GEORGE GERSHWIN (1935), has become an enduring classic of American theater and is sometimes performed as grand opera. *Mamba's Daughters* (1929), another novel set in Charleston, was also, in collaboration with Mrs. Heyward, turned into a successful play (1939). *Peter Ashley* (1932) is a story of Charleston during the Civil War. *Star-Spangled Virgin* (1930) is set in the Virgin Islands at the onset of Franklin Roosevelt's New Deal. With HERVEY ALLEN, Heyward published a collection of poems based on folklore and local history of his native region, *Carolina Chansons* (1922). His verse also appears in *Skylines and Horizons* (1924) and *Jasbo Brown and Selected Poems* (1931). A biography is *DuBose Heyward: The Man Who Wrote "Porgy"* (1954) by Frank Durham.

H. H. Pen name of HELEN HUNT JACKSON.

Hiawatha, The Song of (1855), a long narrative poem by HENRY WADSWORTH LONGFELLOW. This poem, along with EVANGELINE (1847) and *The Courtship of Miles Standish* (1858), was an attempt on Longfellow's part to supply America with a legendary past. The plot deals with the adventures of Hiawatha, an Ojibway raised by Nokomis, the daughter of the Moon. After detailing his hero's accumulation of natural wisdom, the poet recounts the deeds of Hiawatha in revenging his mother, Wenonah, against his father, the West Wind. Hiawatha eventually becomes the leader of his people and teaches peace even in the face of the encroaching white man. When his wife, MINNEHAHA, becomes ill, he leaves with her for the land of the Northwest Wind, and departs with a message to extend brotherhood to the white man.

Longfellow used several prose narratives and Indian histories as his sources, notably the *Account of the History, Manners, and Customs of the Indian Nations of Pennsylvania and the Neighboring States* (1819) by the Rev. JOHN HECKEWELDER, and ALGIC RESEARCHES (1839) and other writings of HENRY R. SCHOOLCRAFT. By 1854 Longfellow had decided on the plan of the poem and its meter, although in June he was still calling the chief character Manabozho, apparently under the impression that Manabozho and Hiawatha were identical. The former was the name of a tricky Ojibway and Algonquin demigod, whereas Hiawatha is the name generally given to the reformer (*c.* 1500) credited with founding the Iroquois Confederacy. Many of Manabozho's wiles were transferred in the poem to Pau-Pau-Kee-Wis. The language and the names of various tribes were similarly confused.

In response to criticism of his use of a meter adapted from the Finnish epic *Kalevala*, Longfellow pointed out the common employment of trochaic tetrameter lines in some earlier poems on Native Americans, and the use of repetition and parallelism in Native American poetry.

Hickok, Wild Bill [James Butler] (1837–1876), soldier, scout, and U.S. marshal. Hickok, born in Illinois, fought in many frontier and Indian battles under Custer and Sheridan. As Marshal at Hays City and later at Abilene, Kansas, he faced some of the toughest men on the frontier, killing only in self-defense or in the line of duty. In 1872 he toured the East with Buffalo Bill (WILLIAM F. CODY). Four years later he was murdered by the notorious Jack McCall, and was buried in Mount Moriah Cemetery in Deadwood, South Dakota. He became a legend in his lifetime and a folk hero after his death. Many books and articles have been written about him, including Frank J. Wilstach's *Wild Bill Hickok, the Prince of Pistoleers* (1926); William E. Connelley's *Wild Bill and His Era* (1933); Mari Sandoz's *The Buffalo Hunters* (1954), and Joseph Ross's *They Called Him Wild Bill* (1964).

Hicks, Elias (1748–1830),   religious leader, memorist. Born a Quaker in Hempstead, New York, Hicks advocated views that led him to leave the orthodox Quakers and form a sect of his own, the Hicksites. They stressed "the inward light." Hicks, an ardent worker, is said to have traveled ten thousand miles on foot, another fifteen hundred by carriage after he was eighty, and to have preached in the open air more than a thousand times. He was a poor man, but would accept no money for his services and made his living by working his farm on Long Island. He wrote and preached constantly against slavery and by his efforts brought about passage of a New York law that abolished slavery in that state (1827). WALT WHITMAN as a boy heard him preach—his Quaker family were friends and neighbors of the Hickses. The poet's religious views were deeply influenced by those of Hicks, and in NOVEMBER BOUGHS (1888) he paid a warm tribute to the preacher, *Notes on Elias Hicks*. Among Hicks's writings are *Observations on the Slavery of the Africans* (1811) and *The Quaker* (4 v. 1827–28). His *Journal* appeared after his death (1832). In 1910, Henry W. Wilbur wrote *The Life and Labors of Elias Hicks*, and in 1956 Bliss Forbush wrote *Elias Hicks, Quaker Liberal*.

Hicks, Granville (1901–1982),   teacher, editor, writer. Hicks was born in New Hampshire, taught in various colleges, and served on the editorial staff of *New Masses*. For years on the far left politically, he resigned from the Communist Party in 1939 and from that time on became a strong opponent of Communist doctrines and Soviet policies; he became an ardent advocate of "the American way." (See PROLETARIAN LITERATURE.) Among his books are *The Great Tradition* (1933), *John Reed—The Making of a Revolutionary* (1935), *I Like America* (1938), *The First to Awaken* (1940), and *Where We Came Out* (1954). He edited *Proletarian Literature in the U.S.* (1935) and (with Ella Winter) *The Letters of Lincoln Steffens* (1938). Also he wrote three novels: *Only One Storm* (1942), *Behold Trouble* (1944), and *There Was a Man in Our Town* (1952). *Small Town* (1946) is a candid study of the New York community where he lived for much of his life.

Hidatsa Indians.   A part of the SIOUX family of tribes, sometimes called the Gros Ventre, that lived along the upper Missouri River. In the late 18th century, following a dispute about buffalo hunting, one village group separated from the rest and became nomadic. This group was known to white settlers in the 19th century as the Crow.

Hidden Hand, The (1859),   the first successful novel by E.D.E.N. SOUTHWORTH. It was published serially in the New York *Ledger* (the second half under the title *Capitola's Peril*), translated into several European languages, and produced in play form in both England and the United States.

Hidden Persuaders, The.   See VANCE PACKARD.

Hiebert, Paul (1892–?),   chemist, humorist Hiebert's popular, gently satiric *Sarah Binks* (1939) won Canada's Stephen Leacock Award. His other works include *Tower in Siloam*, nonfiction; *Willows Revisited* and *For the Birds* (1980), humor; and *Doubting Castle* (1976) and *Not as the Scribes* (1984), religious books.

Higgins, George V. (1939–1999),   novelist. Born in Brockton, Massachusetts, and educated at Boston College, Higgins became a newspaperman, a lawyer, then a Massachusetts and Federal prosecutor. With an insider's view of the criminal justice and political systems, Higgins had a deep interest in motive and a fascination with hoodlums, as seen in his strongest novel, *The Friends of Eddie Coyle* (1971), redolent of the seamy side of Boston. It is a study as dateless as Hemingway's "The Killers." Written entirely in dialogue, this grim book displays Higgins's virtually flawless ear. Among his many novels are *Digger's Game* (1973), *Cogan's Trade* (1974), *Kennedy for the Defense* (1980), *The Patriot Game* (1982), *Impostors* (1986), and *Trust* (1990). *The Progress of the Seasons* (1989) is a nonfiction tribute to the Boston Red Sox.

Higginson, Francis (1586–1630),   clergyman, memoirist. Higginson came to Salem, Massachusetts, from England in 1629 and became its first Congregational minister, but died in the next year as a result of the rigorous New England winter. From his *Journal* was taken a section published as *New-England's Plantation* (1630); the entire *Journal* was included in a *Life* (1891) of Higginson written by a descendant, T. W. Higginson.

Higginson, Thomas Wentworth (1823–1911), clergyman, soldier, editor, writer. Higginson was born in Cambridge, Massachusetts, and held pastorates for a number of years in several Massachusetts towns, was a strong Abolitionist, and served as a colonel in the Civil War. He related his experience as a white officer commanding African-American soldiers in *Army Life in a Black Regiment* (1870). He left the army in 1864 and thereafter (aside from a term in the legislature, 1880–81) devoted himself to writing. He knew all the prominent writers of his day and told about many of them in *Cheerful Yesterdays* (1898). He advised Emily Dickinson and edited (with MABEL LOOMIS TODD) Dickinson's *Poems* (1890).

Higginson was greatly interested in furthering the general welfare and the higher education of women and wrote a book entitled *Common Sense About Women* (1881). He also wrote biographies of Margaret Fuller (1884), his ancestor Francis Higginson (1891), Longfellow (1902), and Whittier (1902); several collections of essays, including *Atlantic Essays* (1871) and *Carlyle's Laugh and Other Surprises* (1909); histories of the United States and of its literature; a novel, *Malbone* (1869); and some verse. His *Writings* were collected in seven volumes in 1900, and his *Letters and Journals* were published in 1921. *The Complete Civil War Journal and Selected Letters of Thomas Wentworth Higginson* (2000) was edited by Christopher Looby. Howard N. Meyer edited an anthology, *The Magnificent Activist: The Writings of Thomas Wentworth Higginson* (2000).

Highsmith, Patricia (1921–1995),   novelist, short-story writer. Born in Texas, brought up in Greenwich Village, and educated at Barnard College, she lived most of her adult life in England, France, and Switzerland. Often using American characters and settings, Highsmith wrote in and often transcended the mystery and suspense genres. Her theme is obsessive guilt, as displayed in her best-known book, *Strangers on a Train* (1950). Bruno and Guy meet, share confidences, and agree to kill each other's most hated person because, lacking a motive, the police will be baffled. Guy backs out, but Bruno, who proposed the plot, goes through with his murder of Guy's wife. The Jungian implications of "the shadow" are carried out well. Alfred Hitchcock made the first film version in 1951. Among other Highsmith titles are *The Blunderer* (1954); *The Talented Mr. Ripley* (1955), introducing Tom Ripley, the talented, self-inventive murderer who also inhabits a world of violence and homoerotic sexuality in four of her other novels; *The Glass Cell* (1964); *Ripley Under Ground* (1970); *Slowly, Slowly in the Wind* (1979), a short-story collection; *People Who Knock on the Door* (1983); *Tales of Natural and Unnatural Catastrophes* (1987); and *Found in the Street* (1987), set in New York City. Writing as Claire Morgan, she also published *The Price of Salt* (1952, rev. 1991), a lesbian novel still in print with over a million copies sold. *The Selected Stories* appeared in 2001.

High Tor (prod. 1936, pub. 1937),   a play in prose and verse by MAXWELL ANDERSON. It mingles realism and satire, ghosts and real persons, the past and the present. A modern young man removes to High Tor, a mountain overlooking the Hudson, as an escape from civilization. He can sell his property for a good price, and his fiancée urges him to do so, but he is stubborn. A gang of robbers, ghostly sailors from an old Dutch ship, an old Indian, two rascally lawyers, and other characters add to the amusing and ingenious plot. The hero finally sells his land, marries, and goes west.

Highwater, Jamake (1942–   ),   anthropologist, novelist. Part Blackfoot, part Cherokee, and educated at Berkeley and The University of Chicago, Highwater is a premier interpreter of Native American sensibility, myth, and art. Among his many books are *Anpao: An American Indian Odyssey* (1977); *Journey to the Sky* (1978), a novel about two men in search of the lost Maya Kingdom; *The Sun, He Dies* (1980), a novel about the end of the Aztec world; *The Primal Mind: Vision and Reality in Indian America* (1981); *Myth and Sexuality* (1989); and *The Mythology of Transgression: Homosexuality as Metaphor* (1997). Highwater writes poetry and books on Native American painting as well as film-scripts and travel guides.

Hijuelos, Oscar (1951–   ),   novelist. New York City born and educated at City College (B.A., 1975, M.A., 1976), Hijuelos worked in advertising before becoming a professor of English at Hofstra University. Among the most accomplished of contemporary Hispanic authors, Hijuelos has written especially of people negotiating the pathway between a strong Cuban past and a culturally diverse and ever-changing New York. *Our House in the Last World* (1983) traces the lives of such a family in the 1940s, commemorating, says Hijuelos, "at least a few aspects of the Cuban psyche (as I know it)." In *The Mambo Kings Play Song of Love* (1989), most celebrated of his works, Cuban brothers become singers in Spanish Harlem in the 1950s, follow their brief fame to an appearance on the *I Love Lucy* show, and then fade from view. In *The Fourteen Sisters of Emilio Montez O'Brien* (1993), female narrators tell of several generations of a Cuban-Irish family in Pennsylvania. *Mr. Ives' Christmas* (1995) is a Christmas story of identity, self-searching, and spirituality. *Empress of the Splendid Season* (1999), another story of generations, tells of a daughter of a wealthy Cuban businessman, banished to New York to survive as a cleaning woman.

Hildreth, Richard (1807–1865),   lawyer, historian, economist, editor, novelist. Born in Deerfield, Massachusetts, Hildreth worked as a lawyer, but soon turned to journalism as offering a wider field for his exploitation of various causes. He was a Federalist and a decided rationalist. In economics he was a Benthamite and worked out an elaborate philosophical system that applied Jeremy Bentham's ideas to society, politics, ethics, and religion. He planned to expound this philosophy in a series of books, but published only *Theory of Morals* (1844) and *Theory of Politics* (1853).

A fanatical Abolitionist, he edited two antislavery papers while in British Guiana for his health. But his views were more effectively expressed in a novel, *The Slave, or, Memoirs of Archy Moore* (1836), often reprinted as *Archy Moore*. Archy, a slave of mainly white descent, tells the harrowing story of his adventures in the South, of his marriage and the birth of his son, and of his escape to the North. It is a bitter, realistic indictment of slavery.

A magazine editor and contributor for many years, Hildreth joined HORACE GREELEY's *New York Tribune* in 1855 and stayed till 1861, when Lincoln appointed him consul at Trieste, where he remained until 1864. The most important work by Hildreth is a six-volume *History of the United States* (1849–52), which discussed events up to 1821 from a strongly Federalist viewpoint.

Hill, Frederic Stanhope (1805–1851),   editor, poet, playwright, actor. Born in Boston, Hill abandoned the study of law to become the editor of two Boston periodicals, published *The Harvest Festival and Other Poems* (1826), and then went on the stage, first as an actor, later as a stage manager. Ill health forced his retirement, but he wrote two popular plays: *The Six Degrees of Crime, or, Wine, Women, Gambling, Theft, Murder, and the Scaffold* (1826) and *The Shoemaker of Toulouse* (1834).

Hill, George Handel ["Yankee Hill"] (1809–1848), actor, humorist, memoirist. A Boston native, Hill saw Alexander Simpson play the role of Jonathan Ploughboy in Samuel Woodworth's THE FOREST ROSE (1825) and as a teenager made up his mind to become a comedian in Yankee roles. He appeared first in such a role in 1826, but not until he played Jonathan Ploughboy some years later was he recognized as the leading stage interpreter of the Yankee. In 1836 Hill went to England and later to Paris, winning a huge success as Hiram Dodge, a Yankee sharper in Morris Barnett's extravaganza, *The Yankee Peddler, or, Old Times in Virginia* (1834). As he grew more popular, Hill tended more and more toward monologues, with occasional interruptions by the other players. Then he adopted the monologue outright. He would stand alone on stage to present "A Learned Society," a satire on the

New England thirst for abstruse discussion. His biography was written by W. K. Northall (*Life and Recollections of Yankee Hill*, 1850). In his own lifetime Hill published *Little Hill's Yankee Story Book* (1836), a gathering of monologues. After his death appeared *Scenes from the Life of an Actor, Compiled from the Journals, Letters, and Memoranda of the Late Yankee Hill* (1853).

Hill, Grace Livingston (1865–1947), novelist. Born in Wellsville, New York, Hill by the time of her death had published seventy-nine books and was at work on her eightieth, that vast output having sold in excess of 4,000,000 copies. Her first book was *A Chautauqua Idyl* (1887). Others were *Katherine's Yesterday* (1896), *Phoebe Dean* (1909), *Exit Betty* (1920), *Rainbow Cottage* (1934), and *Head of the House* (1940). Jean Kerr wrote of her in *Grace Livingston Hill: Her Story and Her Writings* (1948).

Hill, Joe (1879–1915), balladeer, labor organizer. A Swedish-born immigrant, Hill was also known as Joel Haglund and Joe Hillstrom. He joined the IWW (Industrial Workers of the World, also called Wobblies) in 1910 and composed many of the songs used by the group. "The Preacher and the Slave," with its ironic reference to "pie in the sky," was particularly well known. Convicted of a grocery store robbery and murder, he was executed by a Utah firing squad in 1915. His guilt or innocence has been much debated, but his farewell message to BILL HAYWOOD—"Don't waste any time in mourning. Organize."—has earned him a place among heroes of American folklore.

Hill, Kirkpatrick (1938–), children's author. After her early years in an Alaskan mining camp, where her father was a mining engineer, Hill attended public school in Fairbanks and attended the University of Alaska, and, later, Syracuse University (B.S. 1969). Thirty years of teaching in the Alaskan bush provided material for three highly praised novels about the lives of young Athabascan Indians: *Toughboy and Sister* (1990), in which a boy and a girl, who have already lost their mother, are marooned by the death of their father at their family's summer fishing camp in the Yukon; *Winter Camp* (1993), a sequel, in which an elderly Athabascan woman arranges to fly with the orphans into the winter wilderness so she can teach them trapping and other survival skillls; and *The Year of Miss Agnes* (2000), set in a one-room school in Alaska in 1948, and telling of a schoolteacher from England, her Athabascan students, and the changes coming to the native way of life after the end of World War II.

Hillerman, Tony (1925–), mystery novelist. Trained as an anthropologist, Hillerman writes his novels partly in imitation of Arthur Upfield, whose half-Aborigine detective, Napolean Bonaparte, is unmatched in crime-solving in Australia. Hillerman sets his books in the Navajo areas of northern New Mexico, and they often turn on a knowledge of Navajo culture or history. Joe Leaphorn, the experienced detective, and Jim Chee, the apprentice medicine man and fellow member of the Navajo Tribal Police Force, use their knowledge of the people and the reservation to solve crimes, usually murder. Among his best are *Thief of Time* (1988),

which treats the issue of preserving Native American artifacts from grave robbers; *Coyote Waits* (1990), involving the murders of a policeman, a history professor, and a former South Vietnamese colonel; *Sacred Clowns* (1993), about pueblo sacred ceremonies and murder; *The Fallen Man* (1996); *The First Eagle* (1998), with an eagle and a human killed; and *Hunting Badger* (1999), involving the robbery of an Indian casino by right-wing militia.

Hillhouse, James A[braham] (1789–1841), poet, dramatist, Congressman, merchant. Born in Connecticut, Hillhouse was fifty years a member of Congress. His drama in verse, *Demetria* (composed, 1813; pub., 1839), is considered his best piece. *Percy's Masque* (1819) was based on Bishop Percy's ballad *The Hermit of Warksworth*. *Sachem's Wood* (1838) is a sentimental and humorous description of his estate in New Haven. His two-volume collection of his writings appeared in 1839 as *Dramas, Discourses, and Other Pieces.*

Hillyer, Robert [Silliman] (1895–1961), poet, essayist, translator. Hillyer was born in New Jersey and taught at Harvard, Trinity, and Kenyon. His first book was *Sonnets and Other Lyrics* (1917), followed by many others—among them *Hills Give Promise* (1923), *The Seventh Hill* (1928), *A Letter to Robert Frost and Others* (1937), *Pattern of a Day* (1940), *The Death of Captain Nemo* (1949), *The Relic and Other Poems* (1957), *In Pursuit of Poetry* (1960), and *Collected Poems* (1961). His *Collected Verse* (1933) won a Pulitzer Prize. In *Poems for Music* (1947) he gathered what he considered his seventy best lyrics. He wrote several novels and made a rendering of the Egyptian *Book of the Dead*—*The Coming Forth by Day* (1923).

Hilton, James ["Glen Trevor"] (1900–1954), newspaperman, textbook author, novelist. Hilton first came to the United States from England in 1936, took up residence in California and applied for naturalization in 1948. Chiefly known as a novelist, he wrote such great successes as *And Now Goodbye* (1931), *Rage in Heaven* (1932), *Lost Horizon* (1935), *We Are Not Alone* (1937), *Random Harvest* (1941), *So Well Remembered* (1945), *Nothing So Strange* (1947), and *Time and Time Again* (1953).

him (1927), a play by E. E. CUMMINGS.

Himes, Chester [Bomar] (1909–1984), novelist. Himes was born in Missouri and attended Ohio State University. He began writing during his imprisonment in the Ohio State Penitentiary on an armed robbery charge. Released from prison in 1935, he worked on the Federal Writers' Project and in World War II defense plants. His first novel, *If He Hollers, Let Him Go* (1945), depicts the bigotry he encountered as an African-American in California shipyards and plants; *Lonely Crusade* (1947) concerns labor unions, and *Cast the First Stone* (1952) deals with race relations in a prison.

Himes in 1953 left the United States to live in Europe. *Third Generation* (1954) follows a family from slavery on. *The Primitive* (1955) is a semiautobiographical story of an African-American writer and a white woman. Himes became known for murder stories set in Harlem, which he wrote for the French publisher Marcel Duhamel's *Série Noir*, and featuring detectives "Coffin" Ed Jones and "Grave Digger" Johnson. These include *For Love of Imabelle* (1957, retitled *A Rage in Harlem* in 1965); *The Crazy Kill* (1959); *Cotton Comes to Harlem* (1965); *The Heat's On* (1966); *Come Back, Charleston Blue* (1967); and *Hot Day Hot Night* (1970). His two-volume autobiography is *The Quality of Hurt* (1972) and *My Life of Absurdity* (1977). *Black on Black: Baby Sister and Selected Writings* (1973) is a story collection.

Hindus, Maurice [Gershon] (1891–1969), author of books on Russia, novelist. Born in Russia, Hindus came to the U.S. in 1905, was educated at Colgate and Harvard, and began writing magazine articles. He visited Russia on numerous occasions to secure materials for articles and books. Among his books are *Russian Peasant and Revolution* (1920), *Broken Earth* (1926), *Humanity Uprooted* (1929), *Red Bread* (1931), *The Great Offensive* (1933), *Mother Russia* (1943), *The Cossacks* (1945), and *Crisis in the Kremlin* (1953). He also wrote an account of his youth, *Green Worlds* (1938), and several novels, including *Moscow Skies* (1936), *To Sing with the Angels* (1941), and *Magda* (1951).

Hine, Daryl (1936–), poet, translator. Born in Vancouver and educated at McGill and the University of Chicago, Hine edited *Poetry* magazine (1968–1978) and was a recipient of Guggenheim and MacArthur Foundation fellowships. He is the author of a dozen books of formally structured poetry, including *Five Poems* (1954), *The Devil's Picture Book* (1961), *The Wooden Horse* (1965), *Selected Poems* (1980), *Academic Festival Overtures* (1985), and *Postscripts* (1991). He has also written a novel, *The Prince of Darkness and Co.* (1961); a travel book, *Polish Subtitles* (1962); and translations from the Greek, *The Homeric Hymns and the Battle of the Frogs and the Mice* (1972).

Hinkle, Thomas C[lark] (1876–1949), author of juveniles. Born in Illinois, Hinkle was one of the best writers for young people in the mid-20th century. Most of his stories deal with animals. He began with numerous books for very young readers, about Tiny Cottontail and Doctor Rabbit; went on to *Tawny, A Dog of the Old West* (1927); *Shag, the Story of a Dog* (1931); *Silver, The Story of a Wild Horse* (1934); *Old Nick and Bob, Two Dogs of the West* (1941), and many others.

Hinojosa [-Smith], Rolando (1929–), novelist, poet, mystery writer. Born in Mercedes, Texas, Mexican-American on his father's side, Anglo-American on his mother's, Hinojosa was raised speaking Spanish, learned English in school, and has preferred to write in Spanish, although he translates his books into English and sometimes writes in that language. He earned a B.S. from the University of Texas at Austin in 1953 and postgraduate degrees from New Mexico Highlands University (M.A., 1963), and the University of Illinois (Ph.D., 1969). After stints in high school and other universities, from 1981 on he has taught at the University of Texas at Austin. His major work is found in the Klail City Death Trip series, eight novels with a thousand characters published between 1972 and 1993 in pursuit of his ambition "to set down in fiction the history of the Lower Rio Grande Valley."

These are: *Estampas del valle y otras obras* (1972; rev. in English as *The Valley*, 1983); *Klail City y sus alrededores* (1977; in English as *Klail City*, 1987); *Korean Love Songs from Klail City Death Trip* (1978), a novel in verse; *Claros varones de Belken* (1981; *Fair Gentlemen of Belken County*, 1987); *Mi querido Rafa* (1981; *Dear Rafe*, 1985); *Rites and Witnesses* (1982); *Los amigos de Becky* (1990; *Becky and Her Friends*, 1990); and *The Useless Servants* (1993). The Klail City Death Trip series is generally experimental, intertwining sketches, poems, letters, diaries, and many narrative voices to form a rich collage around the central figures of orphaned cousins, Jehu Malacara and Rafe Buenrostro, as they pass from childhood through service in the Korean War, the University of Texas, and into adulthood. In *Partners in Crime* (1985) and *Ask a Policeman* (1998), conventional detective thrillers, the cousins also appear.

Hinton, S[usan] E[loise] (1948–), writer. Born in Tulsa, Hinton was educated at the University of Tulsa and has continued to live mostly in Oklahoma. She won acclaim as a writer for young people with *The Outsiders* (1967, filmed 1983), narrated by a boy of fourteen as a theme written for school and telling of street gang conflicts in a city in the Southwest. This was the first of a series about alienation among teenagers. Best sellers as novels, they were later made into popular movies, including *That Was Then, This Is Now* (1971, filmed 1985); *Rumble Fish* (1975, filmed 1983); and *Tex* (1979, filmed 1982). More recent is *Taming the Star Runner* (1988).

Hiroshima (1946), a report by JOHN HERSEY. Hersey went to the Japanese city in May 1946 to report the results of the explosion of the first A-bomb on August 6, 1945. *The New Yorker* devoted its entire editorial space to the report in its issue of August 31, 1946. The American Broadcasting Company canceled all its regular 8:30–9:00 broadcasts on four successive evenings to read the entire piece to listeners all over the country. In November the account was published in book form, and within a year had been serialized and translated in a dozen languages and in Braille. The account, objective and horrifying, concentrated on the lives of six people who lived in Hiroshima and still is read as a masterpiece of reportage in which truth is permitted to make its own moral impact.

Hirst, Henry Beck ["Anna Maria Hirst"] (1817–1874), lawyer, newspaperman, poet. Hirst, born in Philadelphia, contributed articles to several magazines under the pen name of Anna Maria Hirst. His first book, *The Book of Caged Birds* (1843), gave hints to bird lovers and contained a few poems. ENDYMION (1848) was an imitation of Keats, and a year later he published *The Penance of Roland*.

Hispanic-American Literature. The literature of Americans of Spanish descent, especially the literature of the United States by writers whose ancestors came from Spanish-speaking parts of the New World, including the areas first explored and settled by Spaniards within the territory that is now the United States—in Florida, the Southwest, and California. "Hispanic" is a broad term, embracing such subdivisions as "Chicano" (for the literature written by

Mexican-American men), "Chicana" (for that of Mexican-American women), and "Nuyorican," a recent coinage for the writings of Puerto Ricans living in New York. The literature of early exploration and settlement includes such texts as CABEZA DE VACA's *Narrative* (1542) of his eight years of wandering through the American South and Southwest; Pedro de Castenada's *Narrative of the Expedition of Coronado* (c. 1565), and GASPAR PEREZ DE VILLAGRA's *History of New Mexico* (1610). Like these, other writings of the time were utilitarian, and most retain interest now primarily for historians. The later domination of the English language within these areas left much of the most vital Hispanic literature unwritten, captured only within the oral tradition. As a result, Hispanic-Americans were for a long time most visible in writings in English by authors standing outside of the Hispanic tradition, though many wrote intelligently and with feeling in accounts ranging from RICHARD HENRY DANA, JR.'s *Two Years Before the Mast* (1840), describing California before it was a state, through JOHN STEINBECK's novels and stories of the Depression era nearly a hundred years later.

In the second half of the twentieth century, Hispanic-American literature emerged with renewed vitality in the work of writers of Hispanic descent who wrote sometimes in Spanish and sometimes in English. Among the subjects are the rich Hispanic oral heritage, the dilemmas of bilingualism and acculturalism, and the rapidly changing world of the 20th century from Hispanic perspectives. In recent years, this literature has received important infusions from outside the longtime centers of Mexican-American population and the community of Puerto Ricans living in New York.

Chicano and Chicana authors and titles include OSCAR ZETA ACOSTA, *The Revolt of the Cockroach People* (1973); RUDOLFO ANAYA, *Bless Me, Ultima* (1972); Raymond Barrio, *The Plum Plum Pickers* (1969); NASH CANDELARIA, *Memories of the Alhambra* (1977); LORNA DEE CERVANTES, *From the Cables of Genocide: Poems of Love and Hunger* (1991); DENISE CHAVEZ, *Face of an Angel* (1994); SANDRA CISNEROS, *Woman Hollering Creek* (1991); ROLANDO HINOJOSA, *Klail City* (1987); JOHN RECHY, *City of Night* (1983); TOMAS RIVERA, *. . . y no se lo trago la tierra / And the Earth Did Not Part* (1971); RICHARD RODRIGUEZ, *Hunger of Memory* (1982); GARY SOTO, *Living Up the Street* (1985); Richard Vasquez, *Chicano* (1970); and Jose Antonio Villareal, *Pocho* (1959).

Nuyorican authors and titles include Jesus Colon, *A Puerto Rican in New York* (1961); Nicholassa Mohr, *Rituals of Survival* (1985); Pedro Pieti, *Puerto Rican Obituary* (1973); Edward Rivera, *Family Installments* (1982); Pedro Juan Soto, *Spiks* (1956); and Piri Thomas, *Down These Mean Streets* (1967).

Hispanic authors from outside the Mexican-American and Puerto Rican communities trace their heritages variously to Puerto Rico (without the Nuyorican tie), to Cuba, and to other Caribbean, Central American, and South American nations. Representative authors and titles include JULIA ALVAREZ, *How the Garcia Girls Lost Their Accents* (1991); REINALDO ARENAS, *Before Night Falls* (1993); JUNOT DIAZ, *Drown* (1996); ROSARIO FERRE, *Eccentric Neighborhoods* (1997); OSCAR HIJUELOS, *The Mambo King Plays Songs of Love* (1989); JAIME MANRIQUE, *Latin Moon in Manhattan* (1992); and HEBERTO PADILLA, *Self-Portrait of the Other* (1990).

See LATIN AMERICAN LITERATURE; SPAIN AND SPANISH INFLUENCE IN THE NEW WORLD.

History and Present State of Virginia, The (pub. London 1705, rev. 1722),   descriptive account by ROBERT BEVERLEY.

History of.   For books where this is the first principal word in the title, see the proper name instead, for example, for *The History of Maria Kittle*, see MARIA KITTLE, HISTORY OF.

History of American Literature: The European Exploration.   In the summer of 1001, a crew of thirty-five Vikings led by LEIF ERICSON set up a campsite in what is now Newfoundland. Over the next few years, additional Viking crews returned to explore and temporarily colonize the region. Ericson called the place Vinland, and the daring voyages found their way into two Norse prose narratives, the *Saga of Eric the Red* and the *Tale of the Greenlanders*. Though prophecies of a western land had long preoccupied the European imagination, these Norse stories remain the earliest literary representations of encounters with the New World.

The brief Viking experience in North America made no lasting geographical or literary impression. Not until 2:00 a.m., Friday, October 12, 1492, did the momentous impact of America on European consciousness begin. The Genoese navigator CHRISTOPHER COLUMBUS undeniably made the first recorded discovery of western lands, though his discovery had been preceded by that of the ancestors of Native Americans, who are believed to have emigrated from Siberia across the Bering Strait some 15,000 years earlier. Columbus, however, never understood what it was he had actually discovered. Throughout his four voyages to the New World between 1492 and 1502—and throughout his journals and letters—Columbus interpreted everything he saw within the context of his belief that he had successfully reached Asia. For all his navigational skills, Columbus—in Washington Irving's words—continually wandered "in lands of his imagination."

Credit for the discovery of America as a new land is often—though not without controversy—given to the Florentine navigator AMERIGO VESPUCCI. In 1501, sailing to Brazil under the Portuguese flag, Vespucci noted that "we arrived at a new land which . . . we observed to be a continent." Vespucci's *The New World* (1503) received far wider circulation than anything Columbus had published. When a German geographer, Martin Waldseemuller, encountered Vespucci's work while preparing an edition of Ptolemy, he took the liberty of feminizing Vespucci's given name and writing "America" across the new territory on his 1507 world map. Despite numerous objections—the Spanish and Portuguese continued to refer to the New World as "The Indies" until the 18th century—the name stuck. Vespucci's writings and Waldseemuller's geography convinced Europeans that what Columbus had found was no string of Asian islands but an entirely new region of the earth.

Exploration of the New World proceeded rapidly, with fresh maps and printed reports appearing almost annually throughout the early 16th century. Three years after HERNANDO CORTÉS conquered Mexico in 1521, GIOVANNI DA VERRAZANO explored the coast of North America from North Carolina to Maine. His highly polished *Letter to the King* (1524) is a narrative of confounded expectations. Like Columbus, he set out with a theory: "My ambition on this voyage was to reach Cathay and the extreme eastern coast of Asia." But finding only "an obstacle of new land," Verrazano is forced to conclude that "land has been found by modern man which was unknown to the ancients." In its narrative movement, Verrazano's *Letter* prefigures one of the dominant themes of American culture—the superiority of fact over a cherished belief.

Yet the obvious advantage of fact in a contest with long-held belief was often sapped by literary models, a tendency repeated throughout the literature of European exploration. For example, borrowing from Jacopo Sannazaro's *Arcadia* (1504), a popular chivalric romance—and ultimately from Virgil's *Eclogues*—Verrazano called Virginia's Accomack peninsula Arcadia. For Renaissance writers, Arcadia represented an idyllic landscape comfortably inhabited by courtly shepherds who live in hardy simplicity. This pastoral ideal evolved into a cultural attitude that helped shape the American writer's response to the natural world, and it led to a persistent devaluation of civilized society in favor of a return to simpler ways of life.

Behind the pastoral ideal was the age-old belief in a terrestrial paradise. On his third voyage, Columbus thought he had approached the original Garden of Eden. Later explorers possessing a less biblical sense of geography would still see the primeval American landscape as offering the possibility of another earthly paradise. This view influenced most descriptions of the new land. In his essay "Of Cannibals" (1580), Montaigne wrote of the inhabitants of America: "I think that what we have seen of these people . . . surpasses not only the pictures with which poets have illustrated the golden age, and all their attempts to draw mankind in the state of happiness, but the ideas and the very aspirations of philosophers as well. . . ." In his "Ode to the Virginia Voyage" (*c.* 1605), the English poet Michael Drayton succinctly expressed the general enthusiasm for the new Golden Age, calling Virginia "Earth's only paradise."

With this vision of a Golden Age went the vision of actual gold. All other motives for exploration—the investigation of new regions, the conversion of native populations, the discovery of previously unknown natural phenomena—were secondary compared to the acquisition of gold and silver. "We came here to serve God, and also to get rich," said the conquistador BERNAL DIAZ, whose *The True History of the Conquest of New Spain* was not published until 1632. The search for gold, not geographical curiosity, stimulated the earliest penetrations into the North American wilderness. One of the chief expeditions was led by FRANCISCO CORONADO, who traveled to the Colorado River region and the Great Plains in 1540 in search of the fabled Seven Cities of Gold. Coronado's trip, too, was one of confounded expectations; according to Pedro Casteneda's *Narrative of the Expedition of Coronado* (*c.* 1565), all the party found was "a little, crowded village."

Survival in the wilderness—the central action of many exploration narratives—would become a recurring theme of both popular and classic American literature. Out of the confrontation with the wilderness would emerge a new type of hero—tough, self-reliant, experienced, in contact with life at its most elemental levels. The origins of this heroic personality can be traced to such early wilderness tales as *The Narrative of Alvar Nunez Cabeza de Vaca* (1543). This harrowing account of how four shipwrecked men kept themselves alive while wandering for eight years through the hard country of the Texas Gulf remains one of the great documents in the literature of human endurance. Like many American survival and captivity tales, CABEZA DE VACA's narrative culminates in spiritual rebirth—the survivors in this case saving themselves by becoming faith healers among the various indigenous communities that held them prisoner.

The connection between physical survival and spiritual rebirth is best expressed by the explorer who perhaps more than any other typified the new American hero—Captain JOHN SMITH. "It is a happy thing to be born to strength, wealth and honour," Smith wrote, "but that which is got by prowess and magnanimity is the truest virtue; and those can the best distinguish content that have escaped most honorable dangers; as if, out of every extremity, he found himself now born to a new life. . . ." Though Smith's numerous accounts of the New World contain a few Edenic overtones, his paradise is primarily utilitarian. Though the new land abounded in natural resources, it required, Smith continually emphasized, discipline and hard work to forge an independent subsistence.

Smith wrote primarily to attract colonists. Like such earlier promotional efforts as THOMAS HARIOT's *A Brief and True Report of the New Found Land of Virginia* (1588), Smith's writing stressed the "incredible abundance" of the New World. Smith, however, went a step further by promoting the land as a means to individual well-being, liberty, and improved social status. In his books we find the earliest formulations of what would become a prevailing image of America—an open society in which someone without benefit of family connections, inheritance, or formal education can through hard work alone enjoy a happy, independent, and prosperous life. The role Smith played in the invention of America may be far more important than the part he played in its discovery.

With the appearance of Smith's *The Generall Historie of Virginia, New England, and the Summer Isles* (1624), the English language and the American colonial experience became inseparably united. For that reason, anthologies of American literature often begin with his writings. Yet the English, despite RICHARD HAKLUYT's *The Principal Navigations* (1589), at first participated only minimally in the colonization of the New World. While Smith struggled with an unprepared band of colonists to erect a dingy fort in Jamestown in 1609, Spain had already accumulated nearly a century of experience throughout many regions of America. Further, long before Smith reached Virginia, a black Spanish slave named Estevan had journeyed far into the wilderness of New Mexico. And about the time Smith finally gave up on Jamestown, Santa Fe was a successfully settled community. By the early 17th century, the French, too, were contributing to the literature of exploration. In *The Voyages of Samuel de Champlain, 1604–1618* (1619) can be found the prototypes of an enduring American character, the frontiersman—a rugged individual familiar with Native American customs and wholly adapted to life in the woods.

"We Americans," Walt Whitman wrote, "have yet to really learn our own antecedents. . . . They will be found ampler as has been supposed, and in widely different sources. Thus far, impress'd by New England writers and schoolmasters, we tacitly abandon ourselves to the notion that our United States have been fashioned from the British Islands only—which is a very great mistake." To survey the large body of writing that grew out of the European explorations is to encounter one of the great traditions of American literature itself—its enormous cultural diversity. Studies include S. E. Morison, *The European Discovery of America: The Northern Voyages* (1971) and *The Southern Voyages* (1974).

ROBERT ATWAN

History of American Literature: The Colonies.
Even before the American people created a new nation, they began the process of creating a new literature. What we have is a body of literature that was at first a kind of subset of English literature but one that gradually created a new tradition. Although American literature was not to have new forms until Walt Whitman and Emily Dickinson came on the literary scene well into the 19th century, early settlers in Virginia, Massachusetts, and elsewhere began to create literary works of continuing interest. Americans have for a long time thought of themselves as a particular people, and colonial American literature provides answers to the question, What does it mean to be an American? The people responsible for survival of the two earliest English colonies in America, Virginia's Captain JOHN SMITH (1580–1631) and Plymouth's Governor WILLIAM BRADFORD (1590–1657), were both able men of letters, though neither had much formal education, and both offer insights into the nature of the American experience.

Captain John Smith could consider that he was responsible for his own destiny. The son of a yeoman, he established himself by fighting in European wars. He wrote only because he was denied the opportunity to act. His leadership made possible the survival of the Jamestown colony, but when he was badly hurt in an accident, he was obliged to return to England. His efforts to return to America had distinctly limited success—he was able to return only once, for an exploratory trip to the New England coast in 1614—and as a result he had to use his pen to encourage the exploitation of America. His most valuable work is probably his "Description of Virginia," which appears both in *A Map of Virginia* (1612) and in the big

book that is both his composition and his compilation, *The Generall Historie of Virginia, New England, and the Summer Isles.* (The islands are the Bermudas, which Smith never saw.) Smith provides a remarkably learned report on flora, fauna, and the indigenous population. But his other writings, such as *Advertisements For the unexperienced Planters of New England, or anywhere* (1631), are more appealing because they reveal much about Smith himself—an attractive man, though an egotist. He was perhaps the first American dreamer, as he urged men to imitate the "brave spirits that advanced themselves from poor soldiers to great captains, their posterity to great lords, and their king to be one of the greatest potentates on earth."

William Bradford was long governor of the little Plymouth colony, created by Puritans who had separated from the Church of England and came to the New World not to exploit it but to practice their religion in a community of like-minded people. He differed in outlook from Smith in that he valorized community and continuity. Bradford's description of the heroism of the founders of the colony was intended to give the young people of Plymouth a strong sense of what had been done for their community. In *Of Plymouth Plantation* Bradford looks back from 1630 to the events of ten years before. "Being thus passed the vast ocean, and a sea of troubles before in their preparation . . . they had now no friends to welcome them nor inns to entertain their weather-beaten bodies; no houses or much less towns to repair to to seek for succour." But, he argued, God's providence had guided them to their refuge, and there God had continued to sustain them. Told in masterly rhythmical prose, this account of a step in the founding of America is the greatest book of American literature of the 17th century. Though it was read in manuscript by many people of Plymouth and by later historians, it was not published until 1856.

Both Smith and Bradford recognized that those who were here when the Europeans arrived had something to teach the immigrants about survival tactics, but neither recognized that the "savages" had any rights. In New England many Native Americans had died from early contact with Europeans, who brought with them germs that brought on unfamiliar diseases; some of the newcomers saw the weakening of the natives as God's way of preparing for their coming.

Ten years after Bradford's group arrived, a much stronger group of PURITANS (who differed from the Plymouth Pilgrims in not being separatists) created the Massachusetts Bay Colony. One of the early colonists in the Colony, ANNE BRADSTREET, was a substantial poet, one of the first women poets writing in English whose work is still read with pleasure. Her most admired poems are those in which the housewife and mother struggles to see herself and especially the deaths of her children in the context of her religious faith, as in her little elegy "Farewell, dear Babe." Bradstreet was not isolated by her interest in poetry. Instead she was isolated only because it was not expected that a woman could or should write poetry with the kind of dedication Bradstreet gave to her art. It has even been suggested that no place has produced more practicing poets in modern times than early Massachusetts.

The American colonies were still thinly settled by Europeans till well into the 18th century. In the year 1700 there were some 500,000 European Americans in all the colonies, and the largest town, Boston, had only seven thousand people in that year. Despite small numbers, the colonies produced a remarkably valuable literature. In New England, because printing presses were available there early and because the people, especially those of Massachusetts Bay, were the best educated in those early years, a substantial amount of writing was published. These works have attracted a great deal of attention from literary and historical scholars, in part because of the influence of Harvard's PERRY MILLER. Though it used to be said that the Puritans' strongly religious orientation was a deterrent to literary creativity, the record shows the reverse. A great deal of what was written in America in the days before there was a local literary marketplace was utilitarian, though even some of these writings were the work of people of literary ambition, such as the huge output of COTTON MATHER (1663–1728). The clergyman's great work is the *Magnalia Christi Americana*, which might be translated as "The Great American Works of Christ," a long, complex epic celebrating New England's achievements and by implication an assertion of the central place of America in world history.

Much that was written in colonies other than those of New England was promotional, intended to attract new settlers to America. Some writers were as much interested in pleasing as in instructing. One such is the best early Southern writer, WILLIAM BYRD II (1674–1744). A witty and polished writer, Byrd lived nearly as much in England as in the New World. He wrote elegantly crafted letters at a time when the epistolary art constituted a significant literary genre, but his most important work is *History of the Dividing Line betwixt Virginia and North Carolina Run in the Year of Our Lord 1728*, not published till the 19th century. For Europeans, surveying was the most essential work to be performed in the virgin land, since proper ownership of land was the prerequisite for a legal structure. Byrd's account of his visit to the frontier is that of an uninhibited gentleman deeply curious about the world around him. He saw much that he believed would prove valuable, much to exploit. Though he paints an unattractive picture of the uncivilized frontiersmen of North Carolina whom he encounters, he is charitably disposed toward the Native Americans. To convert them from infidelity and reclaim them from barbarity, he advocates intermarriage.

Elsewhere in the South, poetry was cultivated. The best poet there was the Marylander RICHARD LEWIS (1700?–1734), whose models were Dryden, Pope, and their English contemporaries. Perhaps the best of his several substantial poems is "A Journey from *Patapsco* to *Annapolis*, April 4, 1730." The poem not only describes the journey—and allegorically man's journey through life—but also explores the relationship of the new science of Newton and the new philosophy of Locke to theology. Lewis grounds his poem in America by means of references to such distinctly American creatures as the hummingbird, which to him excels the nightingale. The hummingbird

> . . . sucks his Food, the Honey Dew,
> With nimble Tongue, and Beak of jetty Hue.
> He takes with rapid Whirl his noisy Flight,
> His gemmy Plumage strikes the Gazer's Sight;
> And as he moves his ever-flutt'ring Wings,
> Ten thousand Colours he around him flings.

Another Maryland poet, EBENEZER COOK (c. 1667–1733?), is best known because the central figure of his satiric antipromotional poem "The Sot-Weed Factor" was made by JOHN BARTH into the dubious hero of his novel of the same name. Cooke makes fun of promotional literature but also of English ignorance of America. America seems to Cooke's innocent a land full of wolves, rattlesnakes, and Indians.

Unlike Southern writers, who thought of themselves as Englishmen and followed currently fashionable English literary models, the poets of early New England followed older models, such as that of George Herbert. Puritanism, the dominant mode of thinking, provided a basis for poetry. For the Puritans, the sensible world, the Word of God as found in Scripture, and even Jesus Christ were to be understood as metaphors. The world of nature was to be seen as analogous to the Deity. In "Contemplations," Anne Bradstreet wrote, "If so much excellence abide below, / How excellent is he that dwells on high?" Or, as EDWARD TAYLOR (c. 1644–1729) explained, "Natural things are not unsuitable to illustrate supernaturals by." Not only was Christ conceived of as a metaphor, but He left with mankind another metaphor, the gift of the Lord's Supper. With such precedents, the metaphor-rich poetry of Edward Taylor can be seen as a natural development of New England Puritanism. Taylor delighted in writing meditations on biblical texts that are metaphorical or refer to correspondences, as in the following, each the subject of a poem: "I am the living Bread"; "We have an Advocate with the Father"; "Which are shadows of things to come"; and "Which things are an allegory." Taylor's correspondences draw on the remote and the close at hand, as when he compared the process of sanctification to "Housewifery," in a poem with that title. Discovery of Taylor's verse in the 1930s and 1940s greatly enriched early American literature, though his knotty, witty poems are too demanding for him to have many admirers now.

Taylor was a clergyman. Naturally, the genre to which most ministers devoted their talents was the sermon. Of the huge quantity of surviving New England Puritan sermons, perhaps the best are those of THOMAS HOOKER (1586–1647), one of the founders of Hartford, Connecticut. Like Taylor, he sought to show how religious experience resembles everyday life. Hooker used homely images, as when he encourages his listeners to sweep their hearts and "cleanse every sink, and brush down every cobweb, and make room for Christ." Of the dozens of New England clergymen whose writings survive, the most important was the philosophical theologian JONATHAN

EDWARDS (1753–1758), known best for his severely threatening sermon "Sinners in the Hands of an Angry God." Using arguments drawn from contemporary empirical philosophy, he argued that God is all-powerful and sinful man powerless to do anything to promote his own salvation. Perhaps his most literary work is his "Personal Narrative," which tries to suggest on the basis of Edwards's own experience how salvation is manifested in the converted person's changed perception of reality, his sense of divine things. Edwards tells how after God had converted him he found it entertaining to "see the lightnings play and hear the majestic and awful voice of God's thunder." Though he served for a time as a missionary to the Indians on the Massachusetts frontier, Edwards's writings provide little sense of what it was to be an American in his time and place.

The most outstanding writer of colonial America, BENJAMIN FRANKLIN (1706–1790), had emphatically different views of God and man. Profoundly influenced by Enlightenment ideals, he devoted much energy to the establishment of such institutions as the public library. Despite his many activities, he also wrote a great deal: satires, promotional tracts, scientific treatises, almanacs, and much else. He was a supremely gifted letter writer, but his greatest work is his AUTOBIOGRAPHY, which he began in 1771 and reaches only to the year 1757. Though he was a more complicated and attractive figure than his account of himself suggests, Franklin effectively presented himself as imperfect but nonetheless the kind of man that he felt was most needed, one who was the friend of mankind. His story has provided memorable pictures of life in early America, as in the description of Franklin's arrival in Philadelphia with only money enough to buy three great puffy rolls. More significantly, it has provided many Americans with a model for success.

Franklin presents America, as had Captain John Smith, as a place where a person might make his way from humble origins to accomplishment and fulfillment. Franklin's story of himself is set forth as a model for others. More ambitiously, the emigré HECTOR ST. JOHN DE CRÈVECOEUR (1735–1813) both explored America from Nantucket Island to Charleston, South Carolina, and sought to answer the large question, What is an American? His masterful *Letters from an American Farmer* (1782), mostly written before the Revolution, gives an appealing presentation of America as "our great Alma Mater" where "individuals of all nations are melted into a new one." The American is "a new man who acts on new principles and must therefore entertain new ideas and form new opinions." Drawing on his own experiences as a farmer in Orange County, New York, but also on his observations in many corners of the continent, Crèvecoeur describes the "great metamorphosis" that the immigrant experiences as he is given "fields to feed and clothe" him and "a comfortable fireside to sit by and tell" his children how he has prospered so that he now possesses "the immunities of a freeman."

Although colonial literature has been read as an adumbration of the literature of the American Renaissance, it ought to be noted that its direct influence was limited, since not much of it was readily available until more recent times. One does find Herman Melville preoccupied with the figure of Franklin, and Perry Miller located a tradition that extended from Jonathan Edwards to Emerson. Such continuities, though much discussed, have also been much challenged.

But it can safely be asserted that readers of colonial American literature find a great deal of value and interest, whether they seek to learn how European Americans responded to the New World or are looking for books that continue to provide aesthetic pleasure. They learn less than might be wished about the lives of African-Americans who were brought to this country in increasing numbers to suffer slavery and about the situation, aspiration, and achievements of women, and they find that Native Americans were seen not as rightful possessors of the land but more often as a scourge to be eradicated. On the other hand, it is not too much to hope that the process by which scholars have brought the writings of Edward Taylor and William Byrd to our attention will continue to uncover neglected and unknown writers and works that will enrich our understanding of the beginnings of the American nation.

Studies include Perry Miller, *Errand into the Wilderness* (1956); Everett Emerson, ed., *Major Writers of Early American Literature* (1972); Robert Daly, *God's Altar: The World and the Flesh in Puritan Poetry* (1978); and Michael T. Gilmore, ed., *Early American Literature: A Collection of Critical Essays* (1980).

EVERETT EMERSON

History of American Literature: The Revolution to 1830. The years 1775–1830 spanned the American Revolution, creation of a new nation under the Constitution and Bill of Rights, and the trying out of a new system of government in relationships at home and abroad. In literature, these years were a time of consolidation and innovation, building on the lessons of the past and extending them in response to the new conditions. For the literature of the revolution itself, see THE AMERICAN REVOLUTION. The following paragraphs are devoted mostly to the years afterward.

American freedom from British rule gave renewed urgency to questions of identity and purpose that had concerned Americans from the first settlements. What is an American? remained the overriding question, but it encompassed a number of other questions, each in its own way important for the nation and, increasingly, for the world. The goddess Liberty had been enthroned, but at what point might her rule disintegrate into anarchy, with its concomitant threat of freedoms denied not by the rule of kings but of mobs? What was the boundary to be between individual freedoms and the constraints of law in a justly ordered society? Under what terms were Americans to possess the land that had been given to them? What was the future for the original possessors, the Native Americans scrambling to arrange new relationships with the Great White Father, George Washington, and his successors, who had replaced the more distant Great White Father overseas? How were the ideals of life, liberty, and pursuit of happiness to be squared with the institution of slavery? How were American authors, inheritors of a language with a long and distinguished tradition of literature centered in a small island, to adapt that tradition to a radically different situation?

Answers to these questions were sought in literature primarily in two ways. First, there was the literature of active engagement. Writers played a major part in creating the political, economic, and social institutions that provided the first answers to most of these questions for the emerging nation. Secondly, there was the literature of examination and report, including for the first time in American literature a substantial turn toward belles-lettres. Writers looked to the land and people of the new country for material for essays, travel accounts, fiction, poems, and plays that would illuminate the new conditions in the language of a rising national literature.

The Founding Fathers combined major political accomplishment and genuine literary ability in a measure unparalleled by any subsequent generation in the United States. Among them, THOMAS JEFFERSON stands preeminent for writing in most of the fields of his considerable genius. In THE FEDERALIST, ALEXANDER HAMILTON, JAMES MADISON, and JOHN JAY wrote a series of still-compelling arguments on the merits of unification under the Constitution. GEORGE WASHINGTON had an enduring effect not only for the example of his life but for the eloquent plain sense of his expression as recorded in documents including his FAREWELL ADDRESS. JOHN ADAMS was a worthy Federalist opponent of Jefferson, and their correspondence forms one of the major records of the period. His wife, ABIGAIL ADAMS, in her letters gave lasting expression to a woman's perspective on the period. Important though these writings are, however, the bulk of the memorable writing of the time belongs to authors who observed their new country mostly from positions outside of politics, reporting from that removed perspective the life and manners of their countrymen.

Among poets, JOEL BARLOW continued a career begun as one of the HARTFORD WITS. To a people still wondering who they were, he gave an amusing celebration of the homespun qualities of American life in THE HASTY PUDDING (1793) and held out promise of future greatness in THE COLUMBIAD (1807), the most ambitious of a number of American prophetic poems of the period. More skilled as a poet, PHILIP FRENEAU turned from his wartime satires and invective to become a poet of nature, combining an eye for the romance of American scenery with a mind nicely attuned to the reigning Deism of the day. In the next generation, but still within the period, he was followed and surpassed in power by WILLIAM CULLEN BRYANT, the first of the famed New England poets of the 19th century.

Meanwhile, theater became an active part of American cultural life, catering frequently to a desire to see American types in flesh on the stage. Definition by contrast was sometimes the game, providing the title and subject to the best play of the period, THE CONTRAST (1787), by ROYALL TYLER: English pretension against American plain sense. Among other playwrights were WILLIAM DUNLAP, JOHN HOWARD PAYNE, and JAMES NELSON BARKER, whose THE INDIAN PRINCESS (1808) introduced Pocahontas in the first American play on an Indian subject to reach the stage.

Books of travel and description proved important. JONATHAN CARVER's *Three Years' Travels Through the Interior Parts of North America* (1778) found an interested audience abroad, as did ST. JOHN DE CREVECOEUR'S LETTERS FROM AN AMERICAN FARMER (1782), a major work of observation and analysis, published after the war, but describing a prewar America. WILLIAM BARTRAM's *Travels Through North and South Carolina, Georgia, East and West Florida* (1791) contains uniquely valuable accounts of the wilderness. The journals of MERIWETHER LEWIS and WILLIAM CLARK, unpublished in their entirety for a century, were wonderfully detailed in ways that ensured them a high place in the literature of exploration.

The end of the 18th century saw the beginnings of the American novel in works like Susanna Rowson's CHARLOTTE TEMPLE (1791); Hugh Henry Brackenridge's MODERN CHIVALRY (1792–1815); Gilbert Imlay's THE EMIGRANTS (1793); William Hill Brown's THE POWER OF SYMPATHY (1789); and, most impressive of all, in Charles Brockden Brown's WIELAND (1798) and subsequent works. James Kirke Paulding's KONINGSMARKE (1823) came considerably later, as did John Neal's *Rachel Dyer* (1828), and both writers were prolific in various areas.

The major authors of the period, however, are WASHINGTON IRVING and JAMES FENIMORE COOPER, writers with whom the major American literature of the 19th century got its real start. SYDNEY SMITH's gibe, "In the four quarters of the globe, who reads an American book?" was answered convincingly in the same year it was made by the publishing in book form of Irving's THE SKETCH BOOK OF GEOFFREY CRAYON (1820), hugely successful at home and abroad. Cooper soon followed with THE PIONEERS (1823). It not only inaugurated THE LEATHERSTOCKING TALES but gave solid expression to themes important to American literature and life ever since, raising questions about freedom and law, ownership of the land, relationships with Native Americans, and the conservation of natural resources. Irving and Cooper, preeminent in the 1820s, continued producing distinguished work in the midst of the explosion of talent that marked the years 1830–1860.

Studies include Van Wyck Brooks, *The World of Washington Irving* (1944); Alexander Cowie, *The Rise of the American Novel* (1948); Perry Miller, *The Life of the Mind in America: From the Revolution to the Civil War* (1965); and Cathy N. Davidson, *Revolution and the Word: The Rise of the Novel in America* (1986).

History of American Literature: 1830–1865. During these years arose the first generation of indisputably great American writers, and they defined themselves as renegades. "I have written a wicked book and feel spotless as the Lamb," HERMAN MELVILLE wrote on completion of *Moby-Dick* (1851). Ten years earlier, RALPH WALDO EMERSON had proclaimed in SELF-RELIANCE: "If I am the Devil's child, I will live then from the Devil." Melville's wickedness and Emerson's deviltry are not metaphysical but social, one aspect of an edgy love-hate relationship to their nation. It is, in part, a protest against a rapidly urbanizing America in which the forces of economic progress were coming to dominate its motives and misshape its national morality. As the roar of the locomotive obscured the song of the thrush, these writers confronted the growing contradictions between the idealized image of America and its everyday reality. The ideal America was a holy project, figured as the New Eden before the nightmare of history, or alternatively as the New Jerusalem at the end of time. Here humankind would have its second chance to reunite the human, the natural, and the divine and lead the world to salvation. Yet the social reality of the period begins with the coining of the term "technology" and ends with the nation well on its way to becoming an aggressive capitalist power. If the constituted America had come to monopolize God and create Him in its own image, then the American writer must become, if not Satanic, a prophet in the wilderness, attempting to overthrow the self-satisfied, blinding certainties of the empowered with probing doubts and refusing protests.

Emerson's "I unsettle all things" serves as a motto for the others as well, and they proclaimed their outcast status. Some of them, like FREDERICK DOUGLASS, were outcasts literally and legally. Numerous SLAVE NARRATIVES detailed the horrors of an exclusionary idea of freedom and of a Christianity that sang hymns while separating families and treating souls as merchandise. MARGARET FULLER, as well as more strictly political suffrage writers, reminded readers of the real and strong existence of an entire excluded gender. Most of the major American romantics—the writers of prose fiction, Cooper, Poe, Hawthorne, and Melville; the essayists, Emerson and Thoreau; the poets, Longfellow, Whittier, Oliver Wendell Holmes, Lowell, and Whitman—were male, white, and upper-class, but they too protested against the national failure to confront forms of otherness. The young men of NATHANIEL HAWTHORNE's tales often treat women with fearful loathing and lustful voyeurism when they are not sentimentalizing them out of all living shape. Frequent renderings of intense friendships between a white and an other-colored man—Cooper's NATTY BUMPPO and Chingachgook, Melville's Ishmael and Queequeg—served as an expiatory rite for a culture that was daily and violently enacting its bigotries. More largely, personal eccentricity was upheld in the lives as well as in the pages of a Thoreau and a Dickinson; its victimization was dramatized in tales such as Melville's BARTLEBY THE SCRIVENER and Hawthorne's THE GENTLE BOY and given historical explanation by Hawthorne's sagas of Puritan intolerance.

Yet these writers did not see themselves as counter-cultural. Instead, their purpose was to recall America to its ideals. Thus Thoreau removes himself to Walden "by accident . . . on Independence Day, or the Fourth of July 1845." No accident! His Walden endeavor is to make real and deep the merely political status of the new nation. Likewise, Whitman's lifelong task is to totalize institutional democracy into a way of thinking and living.

The literature has a nationalist emphasis, then, even if nationalist-in-protest. Self-reliance meant cultural as well as personal independence. These writers were painfully aware that a cultural imperialism may continue and even increase long after a strictly political independence is achieved. "The country is tired of being be-Britished," wrote NATHANIEL WILLIS and GEORGE P. MORRIS in the 1840s. Most American books, Margaret Fuller said simply, "were English books," and Emerson spoke of "this tapeworm of Europe." The new nation was tied to England by language, history, and educational methods. The distrust of social norms and the common sense that supported it, the proposing of new social arrangements and the experiments with literary forms that would express a beyond-rational imagination, were themselves informed by the British and German romantic writers of a generation just ended. Veneration of England had increased, fueled by the guilt and insecurities that come with a successful revolution. Yet these writers felt less tied to England than tied down by it. The international copyright law would not be adopted until 1891, and the contemporaneous existence of the great Victorian novel meant that Dickens and Thackeray dominated the bookstalls of New York. Further, the period defined literature narrowly, as belles-lettres, and the New World literary heritage appeared barren where it was not gawkily embarrassing. A fear spread that, without a literary culture, the United States would exist as nothing more than an economic arrangement.

The requirement was not merely for artistic achievement but for a distinctly American literature. In addition to the pressure to match a political independence with a cognitive one, several factors caused writers to identify themselves with the fate of the republic. Literary nationalism, itself an import from German romanticism, argued that universal truth must spring from the customs and tales of a specific soil and led Americans to look to their own, worriedly thin heritage. Democracy, a controversial and derided term even to British liberals, demanded defense and application to the roles of reader and writer. ("I round and finish little," Whitman remarked of his technique, emphasizing the responsibilities of a democratic audience: "The reader has his work to do as I have mine.") The myth of the West, a myth that easily predates the discovery of the New World in classical and early Christian writings, added an archetypal goad for a distinctly, even apocalyptic, American literature. The myth compares the movement of civilization to the daily round of the sun, dawning in the east and seeing its flashing culmination in the west. It informs Columbus's interpretation of his discovery: "God made me the messenger of the new heaven and the new earth . . ." and two centuries later, HARRIET BEECHER STOWE, reading Mather's *Magnalia* as a youth, became convinced that America was "commissioned to bear the light of liberty and religion through all the earth and to bring in the great millenial day. . . ." Such a revelatory mission requires something more than smooth poems in old forms. And finally there was the Puritan habit of the exemplary representative, the individual as the community in microcosm. Thus Thoreau, in his essay "Walking," makes his short hike from Walden an emblem of the westward movement throughout all time. For all these reasons, one could not be a writer who happened to live in America; one was, like it or not, the American writer, and so private a poet as EMILY DICKINSON would affirm, "I see—New Englandly—."

The Young America clubs that concocted endless prolegomenae and bloated claims for incapable poets presented a sad if predictable spectacle of national inferiority. Less predictably, an American literature was securely founded. Aided more by their detractors than their would-be boosters, new writers capitalized on the very lacks in American life that the British mocked, and this is seen most clearly in the issue of history.

The European insistence that the present could be defined rightly only in relation to the past was so marked in this period that John Stuart Mill defined historicism as the "Spirit of the Times." Hawthorne supplied such a past by focusing on his Puritan ancestry, burrowing into some details and allegorizing others so that a distance of merely two centuries came to seem universalizing eons. Other writers substituted space for time, using the continental expanse rather than a long-ago for their legend-making machinery. Cooper chronicled the frontier conflicts of two groups with radically different senses of history, the pre-Columbian Indians in proud and embattled decline with the advancing European Americans seeking renewal from European agedness in a world that was new only to them. In such ways, the American present and near-present could seem a simultaneous landscape reenacting all of world history. As Lowell would write, "Here, as in a theater, the great problems of anthropology . . . are compressed, as it were, into the entertainment of a few hours."

Other writers refused the demand for history entirely. The past, that "small village tale" as Emerson called it, was blinding at worst and unnecessary at best. "All the past we leave behind," Whitman says of his pioneers, insisting on the freshest of starts: "We debouch upon a newer, mightier world. . . ." An envisioned future could replace a corrupted past as the guide to present action, especially on a continent not yet fully settled. But in seeking a grounds of authority, not even a future prospect so much as the immediate present would serve in history's stead. Whitman searches for history in libraries and legends only to find, "It is in the present—it is this earth today." Similarly, Emerson proclaims, "We are always coming up with the emphatic facts of history in our private experience and verifying them here—there is properly no history, only biography." Time itself is a democracy. "There was never any more inception than there is now," Whitman insists in "Song of Myself," "Nor any more youth or age" or "perfection" or "heaven or hell." Every moment is radically alike in providing the basic attributes of existence. To look to history for anything less than the universal is petty, so why look to it at all when the universal exists in the immediate, all-available present? Indeed, that present in which commonplaces blaze into ultimates affords something better than sober historical wisdom affords the infinite. "Forever—is composed of Nows," Dickinson writes. Permanent nature, human and environmental, was abundantly available here, more so than in an England personified by Thoreau as "an old gentleman who is travelling with a great deal of baggage, trumpery which has accumulated from long housekeeping, which he has not the courage to burn"; and nature could get to where habit and history could not go.

Providing a history or refusing such provision, Americans became aware of how malleable their world was, of how much freedom they could exercise still in imagining America. The resultant literature, especially writings that denigrated history, has its own past, but a past changed by a recognition of the mind's symbol-making power. This past is signaled by Dickinson's "I see—New Englandly," for this means seeing through Puritan eyes. Emerson echoes the church fathers when he insists, "The world is emblematic"; and while only Hawthorne thematized the Puritan inheritance, all the others responded to the decline of religion by reviving the Puritan habit of discovering spiritual truths in material phenomena. To the New England PURITANS, the history of migration and settlement and even the events of individual lives were explained by Scripture. Their migration from an English Babylon or oppressing Egypt across the Red Sea of the Atlantic had led them to an American Canaan. The hardships of settlement were the reliving of the temptations of Christ in the wilderness—again, not "like" those temptations, as a mere figure of speech, but a reenactment of them. The American romantics were latter-day Puritans and heretics at once. They wished to regain the Puritan sense of experience as constant crisis, as never accidental or trivial, with no separate category for spiritual experience because all experience was that. Thus, in THE SCARLET LETTER (1850) Hawthorne creates a scarlet A for his Hester Prynne that burns beyond rational explanation, and Melville's Ahab chases a whale to commit deicide. Thoreau finds an inverted heaven in Walden pond and tends beans to cultivate truths while Emerson announces "All meaning in a potato." "All meaning" cannot be limited by authorized holy books, however, and this symbolizing technique differs from, as much as it imitates, Puritan typology, for the new writers liberate speculation from dogma. They too journey toward essential truths, but they discard the doctrinal roadmap. Instead, they speculate endlessly, knowing that full meaning will escape even the totality of all thought. They mock consistency and court self-contradiction, throwing a trope as far as it can fly on one page and doing the same with an opposing trope on the next. Melville's Ishmael produces a nearly endless series of counter-commentaries on the meanings of the whale, boasting that his book is one of those "enterprises in which a careful disorderliness is the only true method," and confessing that it is but "the draught of a draught" informed by "Doubts of all things earthly, and intuitions of some things heavenly. . . ." EDGAR ALLAN POE's protagonists find terror and the Godhead, suffer insanity and gain vision, not sequentially but simultaneously, as the same event viewed from incongruent perspectives. Whitman silences criticism with "Do I contradict myself?/ Very well then. . . . I contradict myself; / I am large. . . . I contain multitudes." And Emerson terms his collected works "A Farmer's Almanac of mental moods." We will never know what these writers believe, for, in Dickinson's aphorism, "How destitute is he / Whose gold is firm." We can ascertain only what matters to them by the topics to which their contradicting thoughts frequently return.

These strains, themselves contradictory—an insistence on finding final truths in temporal things and a knowledge that all such discovered absolutes are nonetheless temporary and relative in the unstopping dynamism of thought—not only coexist but contribute to each other. There is a huge desire in these writers to make the imagination real on the landscape of daily living. "We must realize our rhetoric and our rituals," insists Emerson, and both Thoreau and his Walden compose just such a realization. The American text is an action that discovers the self that represents the nation, for instance Whitman's "Walt," his self-recreation. This round of art and life places extraordinary demands on both. Making the word flesh means that essence must become appearance and literary persona must become daily personality. However unreasonable the demand that any being literalize on the public surface of a life her or his private delvings, this is precisely the puritan-derived requirement of American authorship.

The attempt, of course, is impossible, potentially tragic, and even evil, as Melville's Ahab exemplifies. The creation of an American superperson fails not only because it cannot suppress any number of wayward elements in the psyche but because the blankness of American culture invites attempts to create and construct a self and a nation also deprives the ego of that stability granted by a long cultural inheritance. Thus Thoreau calls himself "a spiritual football" and "a mere collection of atoms." "Who are we? Where are we?" he cries as he climbs Katahdin seeking footholds, a grounding. This failure of the self to collect itself alerts the quester to the truth that even the most factual of apparent actualities, individual identity, is a fiction, not a lie but not a given either. Or if there is underneath all social posings a "real ME," in Whitman's phrase, it "still stands untouched, untold, altogether unreached,/ Withdrawn far, mocking me with mock-congratulatory signs and bows. . . ." Thus, five years after the grandly egoistic creation of his Walt in "Song of Myself," Whitman must make a retreating confession. Yet the retreat is also an advance, for if this radical ontological insecurity is cherished, it may become epistemological play, Ishmael's "careful disorderliness." Dickinson's plaint "I'm Nobody!" becomes a boast of the protean ego: "How dreary—to be—Somebody," she exclaims, for to be "Somebody" is to stop, to refuse the law she states in another poem, that "The Soul should always stand ajar," open to the trauma of the unexpected.

The literary result is a period of unprecedented experiment. No one had ever written a novel like MOBY-DICK, in which a plot occasionally interrupts meditations rather than the other way round, or an epic poem like SONG OF MYSELF with the poet and the hero one, and an enlargement of a single moment the only narrative. No one had merged autobiography with philosophical treatise with nature writing as Thoreau did, and no one had ever invented a "vocation," as Emerson called it when he left the fading Unitarian church to become a secular essayist-minister. Traditional literary genres are undermined, examined as they are made to jostle each other in unprecedented combinations. All literary "things" get "unsettled" indeed.

Nonetheless, the literature of this period veers toward the tragic. The promise of an unspeakable bliss is made seriously, and TRANSCENDENTALISM, that most literal of visionary philoso-phies, could have arisen only here. When Thoreau argues that "The unconsciousness of man is the consciousness of God" or Dickinson announces that "Paradise is of the Option," they are not intending hyperbole. Yet something retrograde in the human composition defeats us, so that insensibly we squander ourselves into the ordinary, "warp our cubits," as Dickinson says, "To avoid a crown." Or it is a matter of Dickinson's "thief ingredient" in experience itself, whereby paradises are granted for a moment only to be revoked forever after.

So too the literary careers of this generation have been aptly characterized as a fast sequence of flood and drought. After the great essays of the 1830s, Emerson increasingly became a fine observer of society but far less a creator of it, one of those "secondary men" he earlier scorned. Whitman altered forever our sense of poetic possibility but soon retreated to respectability, no longer "one of the roughs" but "the good grey poet" busily bowdlerizing his earlier poems. Hawthorne's last four romances are botched, left unfinished, stranded. Melville's fiction reached such an impasse of skeptical doubt that his only escape was to exit into poetry, not much of it very good. Dickinson lived with her thought so intensely that the mind rebelled in a breakdown she described as "Revenge of the nerves," and Poe's early death was unsurprising only because his life was wretched from the start. Even at their best, these writers are in someways inadequate. In seeking the big truths, they can overlook the ordinary social scene of real politics and domestic lives, of remediable evils and attainable reforms. They defend otherness but can themselves adopt nasty cultural stereotypes. In important ways, they fail to teach us how to live.

Despite the brevity and limits of their achievements, they nonetheless offer us something rare. Whitman writes that the only true poet is one "who glows a moment on the extremest verge." To glow on that verge and accept the consequences constitutes the reckless sincerity that unites these writers. They sacrificed any number of comforts available to common lives to possess a vision that might illuminate and then annihilate. They allowed for this destruction, sure in Dickinson's knowledge that "A Wounded Deer—leaps highest—." If, as Whitman says, "the reader has his job to do," he and the others deserve the strenuous labor they demand of us.

Most of the major writers of the period are named above. Among others that remain of interest are the historians WILLIAM HICKLING PRESCOTT, GEORGE BANCROFT, JOHN LOTHROP MOTLEY, and FRANCIS PARKMAN; the novelists CATHERINE MARIA SEDGWICK, JOHN PENDLETON KENNEDY, WILLIAM GILMORE SIMMS, and E. D. E. N. SOUTHWORTH; the playwright and novelist ROBERT MONTGOMERY BIRD; the author of TWO YEARS BEFORE THE MAST, RICHARD HENRY DANA, JR.; the humorists of the Old Southwest, AUGUSTUS BALDWIN LONGSTREET, GEORGE WASHINGTON HARRIS, JOSEPH GLOVER BALDWIN, and T. B. THORPE; the memoirist HARRIET A. JACOBS; the poets JONES VERY and FREDERICK GODDARD TUCKERMAN; the writers of miscellaneous prose and verse NATHANIEL PARKER WILLIS and BAYARD TAYLOR.

Studies include Van Wyck Brooks, *The Flowering of New England, 1815–1865* (1936); F. O. Matthiessen, *American*

Renaissance: Art and Expression in the Age of Emerson and Whitman (1941); Jane Tompkins, *Sensational Designs: The Cultural Work of American Fiction, 1790–1860* (1985); Lawrence Buell, *New England Literary Culture: From Revolution Through Renaissance* (1986); Robert Weisbuch, *Atlantic Double-Cross: American Literature and British Influence in the Age of Emerson* (1987); and David S. Reynolds, *Beneath the American Renaissance: The Subversive Imagination in the Age of Emerson and Melville* (1988).

ROBERT WEISBUCH

History of American Literature: 1865–1920.   No single decade in the long period between the end of the Civil War and the end of World War I was as richly creative as the 1850s or the 1920s. Henry James, the outstanding writer of his generation, settled permanently in Europe in 1875. But if this makes the period seem merely dim, or transitional, that would be far from true. These were the years that confirmed the vitality and scope of American literature, as the country itself fulfilled its continental destiny. At last the United States, in ever more rapid communication, began directly to respond to, and challenge, contemporary European movements in philosophy, psychology, and the arts.

The collapse of the Confederacy and slavery was followed by a feeling of relief: The war was over, the old world had survived, and nothing fundamental—Americans were reassured—had changed. The old guard, who had made their names before the Civil War, still dominated the scene: Emerson, Longfellow, Oliver Wendell Holmes, Whittier, James Russell Lowell, Charles Eliot Norton were all New Englanders; and for several decades New England continued its cultural dominance over the rest of the country. From that prewar culture, too, a certain hidden leaven survived, unsuspected by most contemporaries. MELVILLE, who had privately published poetry, also left the manuscript of a last prose romance, BILLY BUDD, SAILOR, on his death and not to be published until 1924. Nor was EMILY DICKINSON's amazing output of over a thousand lyrics—her "letter to the world"—to be given its initial, partial, posthumous publication until 1890. Only WHITMAN, after a paralytic stroke in 1873, continued to attract disciples to him in his retirement at Camden, New Jersey, while continually revising and reediting LEAVES OF GRASS.

It was not until the 1880s that new voices began to be heard, or that American literature can be said to have decisively shifted into a new phase of development. The rallying cry was Realism, which became rapidly identified with the Midwest, or frontier America. Yet this was not so much a protest against the grandees of New England conservatism as a riposte to the mode of sentimental fiction by such enormously popular women writers as Mrs. E.D.E.N. SOUTHWORTH, ELIZABETH WARD, FRANCES HODGSON BURNETT and even—the most gifted of them all—HARRIET BEECHER STOWE. Its key crusader was WILLIAM DEAN HOWELLS, son of a small-town Ohio printer, who eventually settled in Boston. In 1867 he became assistant on the ATLANTIC MONTHLY, and by 1871 he had succeeded Lowell as editor-in-chief to become the dean of a revived Brahmin culture. He aimed, he said, to "seek the universal in the individual rather than the social interests"; American novelists, he declared, should concern themselves with "the more smiling aspects of life, which are the more American." Yet Howells's concept of realism—a democratic attentiveness to the everyday texture of American life—was no more able to confront the speculative, unstable, and unscrupulous boom times of late Victorian America—the Gilded Age, as Twain christened it—than any other literary mode. A younger generation of writers soon followed, often called Naturalists, whose aim was not merely to "seek the universal in the individual," but precisely those "social interests" Howells had so far avoided. They intended to do no less than protest against the acquisitive and troubled age in which they lived. By 1900 much serious American literature had redefined itself as a literature of reform.

Something must be said, then, about the nature of these new allegiances to REALISM and NATURALISM, as well as about the massive changes whose transformations of American society continued to accelerate throughout this period. Howells's move in 1889 from Boston to New York, to become a member of the editorial staff of HARPER'S, can serve as the decisive date for this shift of literary focus, as well as for a shift of literary power from New England to Manhattan. A New York streetcar strike, the conviction of the so-called anarchists of the HAYMARKET SQUARE RIOT (1886), the Pullman Strike of 1894, and the study of social reformers such as HENRY GEORGE all united to push Howells to confront the problems of untrammeled capitalism. His novel A HAZARD OF NEW FORTUNES (1890) marks the transition. Howells's reading was vast, his correspondence wide. He admired Emile Zola (in France), and Giovanni Verga (in Italy), and Pérez Galdós (in Spain), and above all Tolstoy (in Russia). He befriended and encouraged all the most promising youngsters of the next generation: Hamlin Garland, Stephen Crane, Frank Norris, the Yiddish writer Abraham Cahan, and the African-American poet Paul Laurence Dunbar.

Realism claimed to be responsive to the day-to-day detail of ordinary life—including the domestic, genealogical, and financial detail: facts of location in space; facts of time and place; facts of family tangles and even more tangled bank accounts. Facts, facts, facts. But this hardly suffices to distinguish one realist text from another. Consider the works sometimes named as the three leading American realist novels: HUCKLEBERRY FINN (1884–85), THE RISE OF SILAS LAPHAM (1885), and WHAT MAISIE KNEW (1897). Their authors are certainly the three leading American novelists of the 1870s and 1880s. But what an odd trio Twain, Howells, and Henry James make! It would puzzle most readers to name their common elements. Only one thing in the end seems sure: Huck and Silas and Maisie all achieve moral victories, and it is those moral victories that their respective fictions celebrate. For the myth of heroism was dependent on free will. "All right, then, I'll *go* to hell," Huck Finn declares, following the dictate of his (open) heart at the expense of his (social) conscience; just as the (moral) rise of Silas Lapham confirms his (financial) fall. But such heroic ideals were becoming harder and harder to sustain.

For what Mendel, Ricardo, Marx, Darwin, Freud and Malthus had seemingly taught was that man was trapped; that he was the unsuspecting victim of genetic, economic, political, evolutionary, and psychological forces, including an ever-spiraling population growth. The myth of heroism, moreover, depended on a vision of an integrated society with its own economic and sexual hierarchies, its own natural and super-natural controls. By the end of the century, however, it seemed that the whole universe had disintegrated into a chaos of com-peting and anarchic forces, receding ever faster to a state of entropic collapse. Herbert Spencer, following Darwin's lead, declared that the doctrine of "the survival of the fittest" must be applied to contemporary human society. No counterattack, however defiant, could be waged by a lone individual. It was as if a blizzard had struck the old American certainties. "One viewed the existence of man then as a marvel," wrote Crane in "The Blue Hotel" in 1899, "and conceded a glamor of wonder to these lice, which were caused to cling to a whirling, fire-smote, ice-locked, disease-stricken, space-lost bulb." The new forces of Hegelian idealism and Darwinian biology and eco-nomic determinism—of evolution, class warfare, and hered-ity—were peculiarly stacked against the old Jeffersonian belief in personal self-control. Romantic individualism soon soured, in the *fin de siècle*, to a documentary pessimism.

The three matching naturalist fictions, by contrast, are often said to be Crane's THE RED BADGE OF COURAGE (1895), Norris's MCTEAGUE (1899), and Dreiser's SISTER CARRIE (1900). This is certainly a far more consistent trio, but consider the key issue of voluntary or involuntary determinism, whether naturalist characters in fact are wholly controlled and conditioned by environment, heredity, instinct, or chance. Crane, for one, wrote the most morally ambiguous fictions. Crane's spurious red badge ironically reunites the hero with his regiment, whose trust is an absolute good. Male survival depends, as in THE OPEN BOAT, on mutual trust; disaster, as in THE BLUE HOTEL, results from division and distrust. A naturalist novel is not necessarily flawed when freedom seems to coexist with deter-minism, or optimism with pessimism. This was a far-ranging, philosophical movement that would claim such vital 20th-century heirs as Wharton's ETHAN FROME (1911), Dos Passos's MANHATTAN TRANSFER (1925), Faulkner's THE SOUND AND THE FURY (1929), and Steinbeck's THE GRAPES OF WRATH (1939).

Whatever the European models, there were peculiar local cir-cumstances that led to this crisis of the individual conscience in America. One was the population explosion partly caused by a vast, new wave of immigration. In 1860 the population of the United States was under 40 million; by 1900 that figure had doubled; by 1920 it had reached almost 106 million. By the turn of the century immigration was running at a level of almost a million a year—about 14½ million southern and central Euro-pean immigrants arrived at Ellis Island between 1900 and 1915. Another factor was the rapid shift of population from farm to city. In 1860, 60 per cent of the work force worked on farms, 26 per cent in industry and transport; in 1900 only 37 per cent worked on farms, while 46 per cent worked in industry and transport—by 1920 more than 50 per cent. Between 1860 and 1900, American towns and cities grew at twice the speed of the nation as a whole. By 1900 well over a third of Americans—all 30 million of them—were city-dwellers. New York, already a million strong in 1860, grew to nearly 3½ million by 1900; Chicago, even more astonishingly, shot from nothing to become in two generations the country's second largest city. By 1860 the old colonial centers, Charleston, Salem, Providence, and Albany, had yielded to Cincinnati, St. Louis, Chicago, and Buffalo; by 1900 New Orleans, Newark, and Louisville had given way to Cleveland, San Francisco, and Pittsburgh.

Personal wealth had also skyrocketed. At the humblest level, per capita income had more than doubled. Consider the rich: when JOHN JACOB ASTOR died in 1848 he left an exceptional per-sonal fortune of 20 million dollars. ANDREW CARNEGIE (1835–1919) enjoyed an annual income of 25 million dollars and when he retired sold out his business interests for 450 mil-lion dollars. These were dizzying sums. From about 1870 the United States experienced the fastest rate of industrialization the world had ever known. By 1900 the U.S. had become the world's most advanced industrial nation, leading not only in production of raw materials (oil, coal, timber, copper) and foodstuffs (wheat), but overtaking both Britain and Germany in manufactured goods as well. Improved communications enabled quicker exploitation. Soon after the transcontinental railroads were completed, the frontier too was closed. By 1900 the old Jeffersonian dream of a continent developed by self-reliant, independent farmers had disappeared forever. By a series of mergers that shattered earlier, individual forms of enterprise, new corporate organizations controlled larger and larger concentrations of wealth. By 1904 less than one per cent of the nation's businesses (roughly 2,000 firms) controlled 40 per cent of industrial production. When U.S. Steel was founded in 1901, its capitalization of 41.4 billion was three times the annual budget of the federal government. Not only did natural-ism grow as a response to these demonic technological and eco-nomic forces—Henry James called them "the new remorseless monopolies"—but popular culture thrived on a glut of science fiction offering apocalyptic nightmares and utopian visions.

By 1900 the growing cleft between high art and popular art—"Highbrow" and "Lowbrow" VAN WYCK BROOKS called them—was rapidly dividing serious fiction from daydreams, or uplift, or mere fun. The heroic ideal was still noisily encour-aged by the western DIME NOVEL from Ned Buntline (E. Z. C. JUDSON) to ZANE GREY. Grey's sixty titles sold over 15 million copies during his lifetime. But there had never been such a surefire bestseller as HORATIO ALGER. From the 1860s to the 1890s, some 110 books with such alliterative titles as *Brave and Bold, Sink or Swim, Strive and Succeed, Strong and Steady, Try and Trust, Fame and Fortune,* and *Luck and Pluck* tumbled from the press at the rate of three or four a year. Alger's esti-mated sales range from 20 to 400 million, beating Mark Twain and Louisa May Alcott hollow. At this level of pulp the moral certainties of capitalism—of rags to riches, of Log Cabin to White House—had never been subverted. Such reading con-tinued to fire the imagination of the new urban masses. Their most literate successors, appealing to a widespread taste for exotic locations, were to be OWEN WISTER and JACK LONDON. Wister set THE VIRGINIAN (1902) among Wyoming cowpunchers of the 1870s and 1880s, establishing many of the patterns of fiction about the West, and London took readers to the Klondike and the Oakland waterfront. These works were the last universal bestsellers before the age of Hollywood.

Such subjects alone suggest the increasing range of American literature. No longer confined to New England or New York, its settings—extending from Chicago to Nebraska, from Ohio to Wyoming and San Francisco—now became as varied across the continent as its authors were diverse in ethnic origin. Before the Civil War, American writers by and large had been white middle-class males from the northeast shores of the Atlantic. Now, women and African-Americans and immigrants of Jewish, say, or German, or Norwegian stock were beginning to publish. What Israel Zangwill was to call *The Melting Pot* (1908) was already a tentative feature of the American literary scene, though each city, far from melting, still tended to be a jumble of separate nations, classes, and creeds. Early examples were *Yekl, A Tale of the New York Ghetto* (1896) and *The Rise of David Levinsky* (1917), by ABRAHAM CAHAN. But the most sensational was the extinction of a Lithuanian immigrant family in UPTON SINCLAIR'S THE JUNGLE (1906).

The universal question was: How does one plot a meaningful life? or rather, How does one plot a meaningful life in an increasingly frantic and racially, industrially, and heroically meaningless universe? One response was, So what? Or as William James put it, "What, in short, is the truth's cash value in experimental terms?" PRAGMATISM is the peculiarly American philosophy born of this period. Another was Crane's attempt to reassemble a fragile dignity, a nervous integrity for man— within a generation this was reduced to a mere code, a moral shorthand for stoic self-definition and self-control, often called Hemingway's code. A third was to project utopian or dystopian (optimistic or pessimistic) solvents to the contemporary blizzard. EDWARD BELLAMY, in *Looking Backward* (1888) from the year 2000 A.D., saw that by a process of industrial evolution, the American National State (stripped of all competitive and acquisitive ethics) had become organized as one huge monopolistic business trust into which all other corporations had become peacefully absorbed. IGNATIUS DONNELLY, in *Caesar's Column* (1891), projected a more brutal vision. Jack London drew up the gloomiest, most fascist blueprint of all, in which by 1918 America had become a police state, perpetuating supercartels by force until the 23rd century. *The Iron Heel* (1908) projects a plutocratic caste society supported by secret police, a military oligarchy, and powerfully subsidized unions combining to suppress organized labor, which responds with terrorist strikes.

A fourth response was just to drift and to chart that drift in socially upward or downward mobile terms, while desperately groping for self-fulfillment. The site for such chance encounters was now invariably the aggressively commercial and glamorous city, especially one of the boom cities of the Gilded Age—New York and Chicago (as in Dreiser's *Sister Carrie*). It was in urban anonymity, above all, that the new American woman was to find her ambiguous liberation. A fifth response was simply nostalgia.

For the postbellum decades were also decades pining for the youth of the nation. It was then that America's first great children's books were written: LOUISA MAY ALCOTT's LITTLE WOMEN: OR MEG, JO, BETH AND AMY (1868–69) and Twain's THE ADVENTURES OF TOM SAWYER (1876). But the backward glance was also the idyllic glance into every nook of pastoral America (untouched by war) from KATE CHOPIN's Louisiana tales to BRET HARTE's California tales to MARY WILKINS FREEMAN's New England tales to JOEL CHANDLER HARRIS's *Uncle Remus* tales. It ranged across the land from the Maine of SARAH ORNE JEWETT to the Indiana of EDWARD EGGLESTON to the Virginia of ELLEN GLASGOW to the New Orleans of GEORGE WASHINGTON CABLE. But this diversity of focus (often called LOCAL COLOR fiction) also trained a sharp ear on the variety of American speech: Cajun voices, Creole voices, New England voices, Hoosier voices, Missouri (Pike County) voices, drawling Southern voices, Yiddish voices, African-American voices. The old gardener in CHARLES W. CHESNUTT's *The Conjure Woman* (1899) is only one of many such black voices. Twain's *Adventures of Huckleberry Finn* (1884–85) was published at the height of the greatest flood of dialect literature that America has ever known. It glanced both backward in time—to the decade before the Gold Rush—and westward into the heartland of America—from small-town Missouri to rural Arkansas. As Twain boasted in a foreword: "In this book a number of dialects are used, to wit: the Missouri negro dialect; the extremest form of the backwoods South-Western dialect; the ordinary 'Pike-County' dialect; and four modified varieties of this last." For he was a master of dialect, and *Huckleberry Finn* is his incontestable masterpiece.

Though settled in the East like Howells, Twain remained loyal to the tradition of frontier humor he had imbibed on the Mississippi and first practiced as an apprentice journalist in Nevada and California. It had much to do with shifts of tone between the genteel and the vulgar. In earlier Southwestern fiction a gentleman always framed the story. Twain revolutionized this tradition by eliminating—or, at least, seeming to eliminate—this double focus. In the opening paragraph of *Huckleberry Finn* the gentlemanly narrator, "Mr Mark Twain," bows out *in propria persona*. Huck is left alone at stage center. The achievement of *Huckleberry Finn*, then, can hardly be grasped outside this native tradition. That adolescent voice is both the culmination of one strand of American humor and the birth of a modern American prose style.

But a more pressing problem remained, that of politics and an overweening capitalism. From DEMOCRACY (1880), HENRY ADAMS's novel of Washington political patronage, to HENRY BLAKE FULLER's THE CLIFF-DWELLERS (1893), and Upton Sinclair's *The Metropolis* (1908) and *King Coal* (1917), it was America's rapidly evolving business community—its abundant production but skewed distribution of wealth—that was at issue. This applies equally to the contradictory spokesmen for the marginalized and impoverished community of recently emancipated slaves. Both W. E. B. DUBOIS and BOOKER T. WASHINGTON were debating how blacks could ever gain their rightful share of the new prosperity. As Henry George wrote in PROGRESS AND POVERTY (1879): "The association of poverty with progress is the great enigma of our times. It is the central fact from which springs industrial, social, and political difficulties that perplex the world, and with which statesmanship and philanthropy and education grapple in vain."

It was an era of violent political protest. The People's Party, or Populists, a mixture of farmers and labor reform groups, was formed in 1891. EUGENE V. DEBS, who organized the American Railway Union in 1893 and led the strike against the Pullman Company in 1894, founded the Socialist Democratic party in 1899. MUCKRAKING was the term Theodore Roosevelt used in 1906 to mock "the lunatic fringe," so intent on muck, he thought, that they could not see the celestial crown held over them. (The image derives from Bunyan's *Pilgrim's Progress*.) Roosevelt was attempting to counter such investigative classics as LINCOLN STEFFENS's *The Shame of Cities* (1904) and T. W. Lawson's *Frenzied Finance* (1904–5), yet he staunchly supported JACOB RITS in his fight against New York's appalling slum tenements.

Another metaphor was that of the jungle, internationally the most widespread trope—from Kipling's *The Jungle Book* (1894) to Conrad's *Heart of Darkness* (1899) to Henry James's "The Beast in the Jungle" (1903). EDGAR RICE BURROUGHS gave it popular and permanent circulation with his fantasy *Tarzan of the Apes* (1914). The theme of hunters and hunted, aggressors and victims, in a nakedly savage world underlies the forest landscape of Crane's *The Red Badge of Courage* as much as the monstrous predators of Sinclair's *The Jungle* and Frank Norris's THE OCTOPUS (1901). The Lithuanian immigrant group of *The Jungle* is socially dismembered and almost literally flayed, as are the hogs from the Chicago stockyards. The book prompted an investigation not into immigrant conditions, but into the meat-packing industry by President Roosevelt, which culminated in the Pure Food and Drug Act of 1906. It was a rare instance of fiction instigating federal initiative and a change of law. For Jack London this world of ruthless brutality, forever oscillating between savagery and civilization, transferred to the frozen north, becoming the very stuff of his finest fiction: *The Son of the Wolf* (1900), THE CALL OF THE WILD (1903), and WHITE FANG (1906).

Progressive reformers sought to end the laissez-faire brutality of the free market by encouraging a more active view of government that might prevent the violent clashes, industrial strikes, and boom-and-bust business cycles of the 1890s. Though far from a coherent group—it included such diverse thinkers as JANE ADDAMS. Walter Lippmann, Herbert Croly, JOHN DEWEY, RANDOLPH BOURNE and Van Wyck Brooks and was further divided over Woodrow Wilson's war policy in 1917— these Progressive intellectuals conceived of scientific reforms, planned and executed by experts, which were to lay the foundations for Franklin Delano Roosevelt's New Deal. Well before the Depression, it had become clear—to such reformers, at least—that social harmony, based on a more equitable distribution of abundance, must be the absolute American priority. Free land was exhausted. The data of the 1890 census and FREDERICK JACKSON TURNER's "The Significance of the Frontier in American History" showed clearly that the frontier was closed. There was to be no more escape, no more territory, in Huck's phrase, "to light out for . . . ahead of the rest."

The best place, in retrospect, to view these teeming problems is none other than Chicago, "proud to / be Hog Butcher, Tool Maker, / Stacker of Wheat, Player with Railroads / and Freight Handler to the Nation," as described by CARL SANDBURG in 1914. Chicago was the very heart of the jungle. "Thousands of acres of cellular tissue, the city's flesh outspreads," as FRANK LLOYD WRIGHT put it,

layer upon layer, enmeshed by an intricate
network of veins and arteries, radiating into
the gloom, and in them, with muffled, persistent
roar, circulating as the blood in your veins,
is the almost ceaseless beat of the activity to
whose necessities it all conforms. (1904)

As Dreiser's Carrie conformed, drawn irresistibly by rail from Columbia City; or as Louis H. Sullivan's skyscrapers soared, plastic expressions of vertical aspiration in space, "to dazzle, entertain and amaze." For Chicago was both a field of force and a cellular growth, a "festive scene" in Sullivan's words; and thus it was a symptomatic site for the new naturalists like Dreiser, and Sinclair, and Norris, and even SHERWOOD ANDERSON. These, too, were the years of the Chicago Renaissance (c. 1912–25), celebrated by some for its jazz on the South Side, by others for HARRIET MONROE's *Poetry: A Magazine of Verse* (1912) which encouraged Midwestern talent, like Sandburg, EDGAR LEE MASTERS and VACHEL LINDSAY, mixed with more cosmopolitan, eclectic talents such as T. S. Eliot, Ezra Pound, Wallace Stevens, and Edwin Arlington Robinson.

Dreiser understood that theatrical city of glamour and illusion, desire and success, which beckoned like a mirage. For the city, in all its moods, seemed more like a woman, more like the unconscious itself, and so a fluid place where women might effortlessly float to the top. The city in its fanciful fashion was charged with sex, whose circuits Dreiser traced, not to condemn nor to smirk, but to test as yet another incalculable field of force. That is why the new woman was drawn to the city, despite the casualties signaled in fictions by KATE CHOPIN or EDITH WHARTON. (WILLA CATHER's heroines and Chopin's heroines tend to find their strength and happiness on farms or ranches.)

From this glance at the urban scene one item is still missing: the newspaper. To be a writer in this period was also, most commonly, to be a journalist. Whitman, Twain, Dreiser, Sinclair, D. G. PHILLIPS, London, Steffens, and Howells all were, or had been, journalists. From newspapers the novelists drew much of their information, even inspiration; from meeting deadlines, they learned to write rapidly and without fuss. London was a thousand-word-a-day man, completing some 50 books in 19 years. The turn of the century saw an information explosion. By 1900 there were six times as many American newspapers as in the 1860s; the four quality weeklies of 1890, with about 600,000 readers, had expanded by 1910 to twenty weeklies, read by four to five million people. The years 1880–1900 also saw the rise of photojournalism, best evoked in the word "snapshot," itself a metaphor from hunting. That split-second capture of life is as apt a term for Crane's brilliant succession of images as for the halftone reproductions that from 1880 began to appear in the New York *Daily Graphic*. By the 1880s cheap hand-held cameras proliferated: tiny cameras hidden in watches, canes, books, and dummy revolvers. Crane hunts his victims through the killing fields of *The Red Badge of Courage* for snapshots as the journalist stalks his prey. Even Henry James had the great New York edition of his works illustrated by Alvin Langdon Coburn's marvelous photographs.

But this emphasis on reality gave rise to a very different counter-aesthetic. In 1913 the Armory Show, which first presented Cubism, Expressionism, Fauvism, Futurism, and Surrealism to the New York public, sent shock waves through the whole establishment. Art was supposed to be genteel, uplifting, presentable. It was supposed to reflect a sensible, predictable world. This new modernist, abstract stuff was nothing of the kind. It challenged expectation as it dissolved reality to puffs of color or simultaneous projections of planes. But it also provided fertile stimulus. Within three years a new magazine, THE SEVEN ARTS (1916–17), was launched to spur on "that latent America" trapped within the "commercial-industrial organization" by the presentation of new fiction, poetry, and criticism. Battle lines were quickly drawn. Because of its opposition to war, *The Seven Arts* was closed down by government order. But the breakthrough was absolute and permanent. Its dissident themes—of cultural and industrial alienation in an unjust and fragmented world—were to be tellingly developed in the postwar years. One of its contributors, JOHN REED, who reported the Bolshevik coup of 1917 in *Ten Days That Shook the World* (1919), was to be buried one year later under the walls of the Kremlin.

It was now, too, that Henry James's stock began to rise in his home country. He had always been esteemed, but the sale of the New York edition (named in honor of his birthplace) had disappointed the elderly author, who died in 1916. For he had always been an internationalist, and it now gradually began to be understood that James had long ago blurred his initial realism by a kind of psychological impressionism whose verbal gusts and puffs from their overlapping planes and points of view anticipated the complex, volatile, contradictory essence of modernism. Finally, something became clear about the nature of James's artistic ambition: to harness and transcend both French and British and American culture. For he had aimed to be the Sainte-Beuve of English-speaking letters; he had attempted to extend to the novel the principles Matthew Arnold had applied to poetry; and, as an American, he had hoped to fulfill the promise held out by Hawthorne. Fluent in French, Italian, and German, he had aspired to an international role, since Americans alone—as he observed at age twenty-four—could "pick and choose and assimilate and in short (aesthetically, etc.) claim" their property wherever they

found it. James found it mainly in Goethe, Shakespeare, Dickens, George Eliot, Balzac, Stendhal, and Flaubert.

"Refinement" and "awareness" and "conscious moral purpose" were chiefly what he valued. He defined a novel as "a personal, a direct impression of life." The interpenetration was absolute. James's view of art, as of life, was wholly organic. As he asked in a celebrated formula: "What is character but the determination of incident? What is incident but the illustration of character? What is either a picture or a novel that is *not* of character?" His conscience was permanently torn between this moral vision and formalist needs. The solution was never easy. Only when goaded by H. G. Wells did he finally, in a private letter, make the pronouncement: "It is art that *makes* life, makes interest, makes importance . . . and I know of no substitute whatever for the force and beauty of its process." Art alone makes experience meaningful—Whistler had said as much, and so had Wilde. It is the uneasy weight of James's judgment that makes this statement so impressive. It was born of long battles with his critical conscience. Form alone was not enough. Documentation was not enough (thus his quarrel with Zola). It is moral awareness—the Arnoldian appeal to the "amount of felt life"—to which James always returned.

But if James seemed to reduce all experience to art, his friend Henry Adams reeled in the intellectual blizzard. All nature dissolved, in his view, not to color, or impressions, or moral perspectives, but into a play of forces. "All I can see," he wrote in 1900, "is that it is one of . . . terrific energy, represented not by souls, but by coal and iron and steam." In THE EDUCATION OF HENRY ADAMS (1907) the scientific and moral progressivism of the Theodore Roosevelt era received its most pessimistic check. For the irony of his whole education, so Adams claimed, was its failure to discover a controlling principle behind the facts. He had become an old man before he grasped that the play of forces was ultimately autonomous and uncontrollable: Man must accept his failure in the role of sorcerer's apprentice; we need to be educated out of the assumption of order into a perception of chaos and informed silence. Adams belatedly taught in his "Dynamic Theory of History" the powerlessness of human beings.

This was a peculiar shock to an American—indeed, Bostonian—sensibility trained with a Franklin-like faith in technology, optimism, rationality, and progress. Mind was no longer, it seemed, the cause of form and sequence; the world no longer the product of God-given, manmade progress. Adams longed for law and synthesis, not chaos and multiplicity; but life, he began to see, was a construct of irreconcilable opposites. Anarchy was the controlling principle and mind merely "millions of chance images stored away without order in the memory." The force of love had been displaced by the force of gravity; the Virgin Mary (in a memorable image), by the dynamo. The dissipation of energy, as expressed in Maxwell's second law of thermodynamics, not only ruled the universe but also our aimless, secular, fragmented confusion. The meaninglessness of the cosmos was echoed by the meaninglessness of human history. As the 20th century began, Adams preached the inevitable law of social entropy, of irreversible disorder, and decreasing intellectual energy. "As the mind of man enlarged its range," he wrote, "it enlarged the field of complexity, and must continue to do so even into chaos."

Since the *Education* was privately distributed in 1907 and not published posthumously until 1918, it is difficult to exaggerate the influence Adams had on the young generation of postwar expatriates. The acceleration of 20th-century history, they learned, would lead either to an explosion or sluggish deceleration; whichever way, it was "meaningless motion." Education was a force that crushed; society and its economic monopolies, just another such force; and the United States, simply the largest magnetic force, inviting an ever-accelerating consumption, restlessly spending energy and money. Only art seemed to offer a plausible alternative, and in Paris the expatriates met an American who had been there since 1902. GERTRUDE STEIN's salon was hung with paintings by Cézanne and Picasso and Matisse—the very artists who were to shock New Yorkers in 1913—and her prose bore witness to a dissolution of verbal sequence similar to the dissolution of pictorial realism shown on her salon walls. The direction in which Henry James had pointed was relentlessly explored in Stein's work, from THREE LIVES (1909) on; and her mentor in such experiments was none other than Henry's own brother, WILLIAM JAMES.

Stein had studied with James when was a student at Radcliffe, and two aspects of his teaching irrevocably stuck: All knowledge was held within the potentiality of the present, and the potentiality was like a stream, what James called the "stream of consciousness." So when—after dropping out of the Johns Hopkins medical school and joining her brother in Paris—she turned to writing, she abandoned linear time, plot, structure, and chronology. Everything had to express arbitrary, miscellaneous, liberated consciousness. And she boldly persisted in this program, never allowing herself to become immobilized, like the narrator of CHARLOTTE PERKINS GILMAN's "The Yellow Wallpaper" (1892); neither male opposition nor exhaustion could suppress her native comic buoyancy. It was impetus and motion she was after, not judgments, labels, names, or definitions. Far from viewing a solid-seeming world from the outside, like the realists and naturalists, she wanted to achieve unimpeded access to the flux of her own consciousness. In this she was the indispensable connection (with Joyce) between Victorian writers like Henry James and younger modernists like Faulkner. Just as the cubists had fragmented conventional perspectives into Cézanne's notorious triangles, cubes, and cones, Stein was intent on dismantling traditional forms and abandoning structures both visual and syntactic that had been imposed on time and space and, above all, on language.

Restlessly she experimented with moment-to-moment sequences, what she called her "movies," by a montage of repetitions with minute variations as in movie frames. The young men who came to sit at her feet owed much to these experiments, though both Sherwood Anderson and later Hemingway applied them resolutely back to a more formal, linear, normative prose. Anderson's aim was to write a series of sto-

ries with the consistency of atmosphere and scene of Hamlin Garland's MAIN-TRAVELLED ROADS (1891), set in Wisconsin and Iowa. He developed Garland's theme of yearning and futility in WINESBURG, OHIO (1919), telling of stunted, impoverished lives, of fearful isolation, of suppressed impulses, of a "vague and intangible hunger." This is, as it were, what Hawthorne's villagers from *The Scarlet Letter* had come to, two hundred years on, in the limitless plains of the Midwest. Edgar Lee Masters had sketched a similar desolation in his free-verse cycle, SPOON RIVER ANTHOLOGY (1915). Only here at the center of a small-town cluster of Hucks and Toms and Beckys (far older, though, than anything Twain had ever allowed himself to imagine, with their lusts and flirtations) Anderson placed an adolescent reporter for the local paper. If George Willard is ever to grow up, he must get out; he must slough off this set of queer, obsessive, grotesques pent up in their religious bigotry and sexual frustration. He must, that is, take the train, like Carrie, for the nearest city.

The rural population, as we saw, was fast diminishing; and if some local color authors were nostalgic for the old ways, others saw them only as prisons that distorted and cramped the lives—especially the sexual lives—of smalltown Americans. Escape was in the air. If reporters like Crane, and later Hemingway, were escaping abroad, so more obviously were the poets. EZRA POUND had arrived in London by 1908. It was through Pound's influence that WILLIAM CARLOS WILLIAMS's second book, *The Tempers* (1913), was published, in London. T. S. ELIOT arrived in 1914, and it was in England that he first heard of ROBERT FROST. It was Pound who persuaded Harriet Monroe in Chicago to publish Eliot's "The Love Song of J. Alfred Prufrock" in 1915. Frost's *A Boy's Will* (London, 1913) had been published before he met Pound, though Pound reviewed it, and his second book, *North of Boston* (1914), was also published in London. In that same year *Des Imagistes*, an anthology Pound had edited, appeared, but the quick-change poet soon ditched Imagism and turned to Vorticism, a movement fathered by a British author and artist, Wyndham Lewis, to combine Cubism and Futurism in a single *Blast* (the name he gave his journal). Like Stein in Paris, Pound in London was searching for a technical basis of modern art in fluidity, metamorphosis, and flux. Not the movie but the vortex became his "radiant node." By 1915 he had begun working on *Three Cantos* (1917) and his masterly translations of Chinese poems, found among Ernest Fenollosa's papers and published in *Cathay* (1915), were further to influence the ideogrammatic method of THE CANTOS.

By contrast, the literary scene back home seemed bleak. Yet the fruition of all this work was to become apparent only in the 1920s, which, as remarked at the opening, was one of the two most richly creative of all American literary decades. To see just how so much frustration, alienation, and need for expatriation transformed itself triumphantly into golden years, we must turn the page to the postwar era.

Studies include Warner Berthoff, *The Ferment of Realism: American Literature, 1884–1919* (1965); Dale Kramer, *Chicago Renaissance: The Literary Life in the Midwest, 1900–1930*

(1966); Jay Martin, *Harvests of Change: American Literature 1865–1914* (1967); and Donald Pizer, *Realism and Naturalism in Nineteenth-Century American Literature* (rev. 1984).

HAROLD BEAVER

History of American Literature: 1920–1940. Some of the most important writing ever produced in America was written during the height of MODERNISM. Much of the best work of Hemingway, Fitzgerald, Frost, Faulkner, Gertrude Stein, Pound, Sherwood Anderson, Dos Passos, T. S. Eliot, O'Neill, William Carlos Williams, Langston Hughes, E. E. Cummings, Robinson Jeffers, Susan Glaspell, Sinclair Lewis, Anzia Yezierska, Marianne Moore, Wallace Stevens, H. D., Willa Cather, Jean Toomer, Zora Neale Hurston, and others was published during this period. What was written during these twenty years changed the direction of literature throughout the world for the rest of the century.

Modernism resulted from a number of causes. The devastation of belief that had occurred in the later 19th century, when Darwin's findings forced most people to question their religious convictions, was intensified during World War I. For these young writers, that war had cataclysmic philosophical and emotional effects. Shocked by the immense losses of that conflict, losses of spirit and power as well as life, writers were forced to question all beliefs; and the role of literature became for them not its traditional one of confirming social vision, but of questioning it. The shape and tone of literature changed to parallel its purpose; instead of predictable rhymes and forms, modern writing was chaotic, its structure unexpected and seemingly whimsical, as if to mirror the randomness of modern life.

In the absence of religious conviction, the artist and writer took on the role of philosophical authority. Early in this period, EZRA POUND, T. S. ELIOT, and FORD MADOX FORD, who were writing hundreds of essays and reviews, created the figure of artist-god, and in their maxims, made literature matter: "Literature is news that stays news." "The mastery of any art is the work of a lifetime." The high seriousness that such treatment invested in the writer is shown in the earnest and somber products of the writers' effort. Although there was a great deal of comedy in the graphic art of the time, modern literature was a serious business. And because so many new publishing houses had been created, it could also be a profitable business—its attraction for many writers was partly its possible financial reward.

The newness of literature was reflected in its forms. The aim of the modernist was to charge verbal expression with new energy as well as meaning. Finding the work of many late Victorian writers dull and moralistic, 20th-century writers turned to an organic form. Whether called free verse or *vers libre* in poetry, expressionism in drama, or lyricism, impressionism, or stream of consciousness in fiction, styles and techniques were to be engaging and, above all, innovative. New truths could be expressed only in new forms.

The philosophic basis for the modernists' belief in the identity between meaning and form lay in the work of WILLIAM JAMES, Henri Bergson, ALFRED NORTH WHITEHEAD, F. H. Bradley,

JOHN DEWEY and others. All believed that knowing grew from concrete experience, from dealing with the objects of a culture as well as its less tangible thought. IMAGISM, the poetic movement that was current nearly a decade before the 1920s, had encouraged poetry that presented an image without didactic comment, so readers were forced to complete the poem's meaning for themselves. Few lines existed between poetry, drama, and fiction, because modernist writers all agreed with the primacy of this technique, and many of them wrote with little regard for genre. JOHN DOS PASSOS, E. E. CUMMINGS, WILLIAM FAULKNER, LANGSTON HUGHES, SUSAN GLASPELL, JAMES JOYCE, ELIOT, FORD, POUND, and certainly ERNEST HEMINGWAY and GERTRUDE STEIN—Hemingway considered himself first a poet, and Stein created new forms of genre whenever she wrote—wrote in all forms and regularly borrowed techniques from one to use in another.

The fusion of many kinds of literature, evolving from many traditions—Chinese, Japanese, Russian, Provençal, and Classic were as familiar to modernists as was English of the previous four hundred years—brought a health and vitality to modernism that was without precedent. Because of the rush of new materials into the literature of this period, writers often cited somewhat contradictory principles. For instance, if the role of the modernist writer was to be that of a reporter, using an objective tone and attitude, then how could the selection of subject matter remain subjective? Hemingway might have pretended in the vignettes of *In Our Time* (1925) to be reporting what he had seen during World War I and at the bullfights, but he slants the reader's reactions to that action by the way he presents each story, and the way he arranges his stories and vignettes within the book. To say that modernist writing is objective is not quite accurate.

Modern writing tried to avoid the sentimental and the overly didactic. It concentrated on the image or the scene, presented without extensive authorial comment. Irony was often used as a distancing device. The narrative was often told through a mythic, archetypal, or traditional literary pattern, with liberties taken in the accepted tradition so that readers would realize that innovation was confronting them. The Grail quest, a journey motif, the struggle between father and son—if these elements seemed familiar to the modern reader, so much the better. The modernist writer was trying to appear contemporary, but was also trying to tap into the deepest human responses. Even though it was important to appear modern, it was also important to realize the validity of the endurance of literature.

Being part of this new artistic movement helped modify the alienation many of these writers felt from mainstream American culture. For various personal reasons, many writers and artists had difficulty living in the kind of country America had become after World War I, with its attempts to legislate people's lives and their morality, and its self-satisfying prejudices. Prohibition was only a symptom of the attitudes and economics that pervaded America in the 1920s. Many American modernist writers lived abroad, and formed groups there that fostered the evolution of new aesthetic principles. The salons of Gertrude Stein and Natalie Barney; the influence of SYLVIA BEACH's Paris bookshop; the power of such little magazines as POETRY, *The Double Dealer, Transatlantic Review,* THE DIAL, AMERICAN CARAVAN, *Opportunity,* and others; the importance of small publishing ventures that brought into print the most experimental of the modernist work—these elements of modernism have yet to be adequately studied. As John Dos Passos recalled in his memoirs, these years were a "creative tidal wave," with "currents of energy breaking out everywhere. . . . Americans were groggy with new things in theatre and painting and music." Among the new things Dos Passos mentions are futurism, cubism, vorticism, Picasso, Modigliani, Marinetti, Chagall, Apollinaire, Eisenstein, Meyerhold, and Stein. Clearly, artistic influence came from sources other than writing.

Literary history, however, tends toward the neat and orderly, and conventional literary history has never accepted the randomness, the chaos, that marked the development of modernism. Rather, it places at the heart of modernism T. S. Eliot's long poem, THE WASTE LAND, published in 1922. The poem might more accurately be seen as the result of a decade of poetic and fictional experimentation, replicating in some ways Ezra Pound's HUGH SELWYN MAUBERLEY, his sequence poem published two years earlier, in 1920. Even though Pound's poem dealt more precisely with the devastation and disillusion of the Great War, Eliot's emphasis in his poem on the waste land character of modern life struck critics forcibly.

The Waste Land in its touchstone role provided the experience of nonsequential structure, conveying meaning through a collage of scene, dialogue, and allusion to other Western history and literature. One of the main narrative lines was that of the Fisher King trying to save his land from drought, searching for water to transform the waste land back to fruitfulness. The distancing of grief and anger that Eliot conveyed illustrated his notion of the objective correlative the artist would choose—some object, some concrete image, that would convey feelings. The correlative, rather than the writer's voice, would convey meaning to the reader. Language had become code, and only readers who had themselves experienced the angst most modern texts spoke about could become accurate readers.

If work by Eliot, Pound, Faulkner, and Stein—and only such work—is considered representative of modernism, then the period was aiming for a very limited set of readers. Such readers would know how to follow the disjointed narratives, interpret the intention of the ironic voice, and bring to the text their own knowledge of human life so that they could detect irony in the first place. The texts considered the most important achievements of the modern period—Faulkner's THE SOUND AND THE FURY, Dos Passos's *U.S.A.* trilogy, Hemingway's THE SUN ALSO RISES and A FAREWELL TO ARMS, Eliot's *The Waste Land*, Stein's *Tender Buttons*, Pound's CANTOS, O'Neill's DESIRE UNDER THE ELMS and Cummings's THE ENORMOUS ROOM and HIM—demanded sophisticated readers, trained in close reading techniques that were best acquired in college classrooms.

Following the same modernist principles, subject matter, like technique, was inherently restrictive. Because so many writers tried to repress emotion, in keeping with the caveat that point of view should be objective, many kinds of experience were omitted from serious literature. War and its brutality were appropriate, and writers as diverse as Hemingway, Cummings, Dos Passos, Robinson Jeffers, Cather, and Wharton wrote well about its waste. But seldom in the canon of modernism is there literature about positive relationships between sisters, resolved conflicts between parent and child, same-sex friendships, or women finding satisfaction in their lives—in short, the fulfillment of family life. (In O'Neill, instead of fulfillment, family life is a heart-breaking debacle.) The mythic patterns that occur are usually adventure and male-hero myths, and the result of this kind of emphasis is that modernist literature—for all its experimentation in craft and form—presents male experience and beliefs almost to the exclusion of female interests. It also appeals in its stories and attitudes to wealthy people and educated people, and it consistently offers texts that are narratively difficult.

Such a view of modernism, which is the one reified by anthology selections and some critical summaries, is shown to be inaccurate when one reads the actual books published year by year from 1920 to 1940. Dos Passos was right in calling the period one of creative energy; key publications during 1920 alone show the variety and excellence of the beginning of literary modernism. Sinclair Lewis's MAIN STREET shows in expert detail and wry voice the problems of staying home in provincial America; ANZIA YEZIERSKA's *Hungry Hearts* renders poignantly the Russian Jew as immigrant in New York streets, showing particularly the hardships endured by the women and children so often prisoners of their own households; O'Neill's EMPEROR JONES draws on Freudian and subconscious motivation to explain a life that was less fantastic than its expressionistic setting suggested; Fitzgerald's THIS SIDE OF PARADISE and Wharton's THE AGE OF INNOCENCE, in seeming to mourn past traditions, give rise to a new and deeply ironic sense of the so-called promise of the 1920s. These important works were followed the next year by Dos Passos's bitter THREE SOLDIERS; Susan Glaspell's remarkable *The Verge*, a play more revealing of a woman's psychology than any other yet produced on the American stage; WILLIAM CARLOS WILLIAMS's *Sour Grapes*, a collection of his radically simple poems; and SHERWOOD ANDERSON's story collection, THE TRIUMPH OF THE EGG. Coming two years after WINESBURG, OHIO, which influenced short-fiction writers throughout the world, the ironic *Egg* narratives helped bring sentiment back into the literary aesthetic.

A year-by-year account would be necessary to show the amazing wealth of writing being done by all kinds of modernist writers, with all kinds of subjects and themes. Wallace Stevens's careful and controlled HARMONIUM was published in 1923, the same year as Cummings's exuberant *Tulips and Chimneys.* JEAN TOOMER's *Cane*—structurally and tonally one of the most modern of collages—came a year before JESSIE REDMON FAUSET's first novel, *There Is Confusion*, and established the HARLEM RENAISSANCE of black writers before ALAIN LOCKE's anthology *The New Negro* appeared, in 1925. H. D.'s novel *Palimpsest* followed such modernist miniature fiction as

Cather's *A Lost Lady* and, a little earlier, Wharton's *Summer*, one of our first novels about abortion; and in some ways paralleled Gertrude Stein's immense 1925 work, THE MAKING OF AMERICANS. Faulkner was writing stories of his South in SARTORIS, AS I LAY DYING, and LIGHT IN AUGUST, while NELLA LARSEN was creating her South in her novels *Quicksand* and *Passing*—and CLAUDE MCKAY was avoiding the South entirely in his *Home to Harlem*. THOMAS WOLFE's LOOK HOMEWARD, ANGEL appeared just one year before the Fugitives' manifesto, I'LL TAKE MY STAND, both countered and intensified by ERSKINE CALDWELL's horribly comic TOBACCO ROAD and Ellen Glasgow's ironically sobering *The Sheltered Life*. What Fitzgerald had succeeded in creating in his 1925 THE GREAT GATSBY, that provocative questioning of American vision and American ambition, was being met—and in some ways was being answered—throughout the 1920s, especially in the works of Lewis, Faulkner, Hemingway, Cather, O'Neill, and Dreiser.

It was as if the 1920s were, literarily as well as economically, given to sailing richly colored, gaily decorated trial balloons—what kinds of novels would sell? How experimental could the American stage become? How cryptic could poems be and still find readers? How vivid could sexual passages become? How realistic could literary language be? Where were the boundaries? If the major fiction of 1929 implicitly answered those queries (*The Sound and the Fury*; *A Farewell to Arms*; *Look Homeward, Angel*), then the 1930s already brought a dramatic change. Eliot's sorrowful ASH WEDNESDAY and HART CRANE's fragmented and unsettling THE BRIDGE both appeared in 1930, along with Dos Passos's questioning THE 42ND PARALLEL and KATHERINE ANNE PORTER's *Flowering Judas*. In 1931, O'Neill's MOURNING BECOMES ELECTRA continued the tone of foreboding. As the country moved further and further into the economics of Depression, literature modified its technical high jinks, and the aesthetic emphasis on craft—on what could possibly be achieved through innovation with words and meanings—began to disappear.

Because there was less technical innovation, readers began to concentrate once again on theme. All modernist literature included a number of treatments of the by-now traditional American theme, the search for self. Identity—defined, circumscribed, or changed by the process of living in America—was as important to modernist writers as it had been to those of the 19th century. In modernist fiction, too, male identity was of greater interest than female; accordingly, the search for self was often made in the wilderness or at sea, in environments isolated from family or friends. So long as male characters—separate from family—were the subjects of literature, setting could be nearly anywhere. But once women's lives, or the lives of men who were part of a family or social unit, became the chief interest, literature would have to become concerned with the concept of community.

Literature of the 1930s changed that focus, and community—and the ways characters interacted with one another—grew to be more significant than consideration of a single character. Dos Passos's *U.S.A.* trilogy helped establish the theme of interaction, reemphasizing the injustice done to Sacco and Vanzetti (see SACCO-VANZETTI CASE) and using America's blindness to the power of the wealthy as one of its recurring themes. EDWARD DAHLBERG's *Bottom Dogs* and MICHAEL GOLD's *Jews Without Money* explored the poverty experienced by most recent immigrants, and pointed toward political radicalism. When EDMUND WILSON, WALDO FRANK, Langston Hughes, MERIDEL LESUEUR, MALCOLM COWLEY, Dos Passos, Sherwood Anderson, and forty-five other writers signed the 1932 "Manifesto," they believed that any revolution to come would be more than economic. It also needed to provide a new philosophic and imaginative basis for living. Wilson, Dreiser, and Sherwood Anderson reported on the plight of the Kentucky mining towns, and others wrote about textile workers in Gastonia, North Carolina; Erskine Caldwell wrote about the misery of Southern sharecroppers, and Meridel LeSueur chronicled the lives of desperately poor women during the 1930s. Any full recounting of important American writers during the 1930s would need to include the names of William Carlos Williams, Josephine Herbst, Josephine Johnson, James T. Farrell, Muriel Rukeyser, Michael Gold, Jack Conroy, Leane Zugsmith, Clifford Odets, Lillian Hellman, Zora Neale Hurston, Albert Maltz, Albert Halper, Thomas Bell, Arna Bontemps, John Howard Lawson, Archibald MacLeish, Tess Slesinger, Ruth Suckow, John Steinbeck, and Nathanael West.

Close reading of the work of these writers shows a number of traits in common with the writing produced during the beginning decade of modernism, the 1920s. Yet, because of the peculiarities of literary history, most of the writers named above are considered proletarian rather than modernist. Supposedly, they are more interested in message than in art and write from a concern with didacticism instead of formalism. The work itself belies this charge, and remains as a treasure for readers familiar only with Fitzgerald or Hemingway. The modernist aesthetic was to waken readers to new insights, new understandings—to bring literature back to a central position in human life so that reading became a means of gaining wider understanding. Forcing the reader's attention through coined words, slanted type, or punctuation used as words was one means of reaching a response. By the 1930s, the human subject matter of loss and waste was almost enough by itself: type face would not change the sad message, nor would fragmented story lines break into the pathos inherently present. As with all good writers, these American artists of the 1930s used what was before them with skill and seriousness of purpose, and created important literature that is still in the process of being discovered.

Studies include Malcolm Cowley, *After the Genteel Tradition: American Writers, 1910–1930* (rev. 1964) and *A Second Flowering: Works and Days of the Lost Generation* (1973); Hugh Kenner, *The Pound Era* (1971) and *A Homemade World: The American Modernist Writers* (1975); David Perkins, *A History of Modern Poetry: Modernism and After* (1987); and Linda Wagner-Martin, *The Modern American Novel, 1914–1945* (1989).

LINDA WAGNER-MARTIN

History of American Literature: 1940–1960. World War II brought historical and social changes that greatly affected literature. MODERNISM had long been established, but for the time being did not seem very relevant. The conditions of the GREAT DEPRESSION that fostered a socially conscious and politically aware literature in the 1930s were replaced by a wartime prosperity and an impetus to other kinds of political literature, mostly supportive of the war effort. Older writers like Hemingway and Steinbeck wrote directly antifascist works or served as correspondents alongside journalists, such as MARGARET BOURKE-WHITE, MARTHA GELLHORN, ERNIE PYLE, and JOHN HERSEY. ERSKINE CALDWELL reported on the Russian front and wrote of the effects of the war in the rural South, while HARRIET ARNOW absorbed the material for her masterly novel of life among families displaced from Kentucky to manufacture bombers at Michigan's Willow Run. Among older poets, Eliot drew on his experiences as an air raid warden in London for his "Little Gidding," and ARCHIBALD MACLEISH wrote propagandistic radio plays. Antifascism informed plays by ROBERT SHERWOOD, MAXWELL ANDERSON, and others. Hollywood's support of the war ranged from patriotic adventure films to the remarkable documentaries of FRANK CAPRA.

Much of the most important literature resulting from World War II came after the war, when returning soldiers turned their experiences into books that helped announce a new generation of American writers. Novels and their settings included JOHN HORNE BURNS'S THE GALLERY (1947), set in North Africa and Italy; NORMAN MAILER'S THE NAKED AND THE DEAD (1948), on an island in the South Pacific; IRWIN SHAW'S THE YOUNG LIONS (1948), Germany; JAMES JONES'S FROM HERE TO ETERNITY (1951), Pearl Harbor just before the Japanese attack; and HERMAN WOUK'S THE CAINE MUTINY (1951), aboard a minesweeper. In the company of these works, mostly grounded in a straightforward realism, JOHN HAWKES'S *The Cannibal* (1948) stood apart as a surrealistic picture of the war seen from the German side. Other writers, notably JOSEPH HELLER and KURT VONNEGUT, took much longer to get their major World War II fictions into print. Distinguished poetry directly related to the war came from RANDALL JARRELL, KARL SHAPIRO, RICHARD EBERHART, LOUIS SIMPSON, JAMES DICKEY, and W. D. SNODGRASS. ARTHUR MILLER'S first major play, *All My Sons* (1947), was a drama of wartime profiteering.

Despite the evidence of these and other works coming from younger writers, from the end of the war into the 1960s American literature was dominated by older masters still publishing. These included Hemingway, Cummings, Faulkner, William Carlos Williams, Frost, Eliot, Steinbeck, Dos Passos, and Pound. All but Steinbeck were born in the 19th century and all lived at least fifteen to twenty years after the war (they died between 1961 and 1972). Although most had done their best work earlier, they continued as strong presences; younger authors wrote in their shadows, consolidating but for the most part not extending the lessons of their theory and practice.

In the novel and the short story realism was dominant, though modified from its 19th-century origins by the econ-omy of Hemingway, the social consciousness of Steinbeck, the interior monologues of Faulkner, and the fragmentation of Dos Passos. Innovation was present, but not generally successful. Poetry was mostly under the spell of the NEW CRITICISM, strongly rooted in the work of Pound and Eliot, though the alternative voice of William Carlos Williams was in the postwar years emerging as a major force. In drama, the long career of Eugene O'Neill was capped by the posthumous production of his masterpiece, *Long Day's Journey into Night* (1956); other playwrights from an earlier period continuing strong included Maxwell Anderson, Thornton Wilder, and Lillian Hellman.

In fiction, following fast on the work of Faulkner and Katherine Anne Porter, the South became a major source of writers who drew much of their strength from the distinctive heritage and ongoing culture of their native region. Prominent among them were several masters of the short story. In her brief career, FLANNERY O'CONNOR produced two premier collections, *A Good Man Is Hard to Find* (1955) and *Everything That Rises Must Converge* (1965). EUDORA WELTY's *A Curtain of Green* (1941) began a career that was summarized four decades later in *The Collected Stories* (1980). PETER TAYLOR's collection *A Long Fourth* (1948) was the first in a similarly extended literary life that continued to surprise as recently as *The Old Forest* (1985). A sense of place and of character is strong in each of these writers, as in each it is united with a distinctive personal voice and a firm control over the mechanics of narration. Outstanding among Southern novelists was ROBERT PENN WARREN, also a distinguished poet, whose widely celebrated ALL THE KING'S MEN (1946) formed one in a string of accomplished prose fictions. Other writers of fiction only slightly less eminent include CARSON MCCULLERS, author of *The Ballad of the Sad Cafe* (1951); TRUMAN CAPOTE, who achieved early fame with the brilliantly evocative *Other Voices, Other Rooms* (1948); and WILLIAM STYRON, author of *Lie Down in Darkness* (1951), *The Confessions of Nat Turner* (1967), and other novels.

Fiction of the rural South was balanced in the postwar years by fiction of the urban North, much of it written by a suddenly prominent population of Jewish writers. Among them, Norman Mailer was the first to win fame, with *The Naked and the Dead*. He was soon followed by SAUL BELLOW, whose ADVENTURES OF AUGIE MARCH (1953) gave Americans a modern, streetwise Huckleberry Finn; this and Bellow's later novels, including HENDERSON THE RAIN KING (1959) and HERZOG (1964), constituted in time a body of work that made him one of the few novelists of his generation who could seriously be ranked in total accomplishment beside Hemingway and Faulkner. Another major Jewish writer was BERNARD MALAMUD, whose stories in THE MAGIC BARREL (1958) remain touchstones of the sensibilities of the period. Meanwhile, an older writer, ISAAC BASHEVIS SINGER, born in Poland, wrote in Yiddish in New York City the fiction that, beginning with *The Family Moskat* (1950), made him in English translation a major American writer; he and Bellow have thus far been the the only American novelists to win the Nobel Prize for work done primarily since 1945.

Parallel with the rise of Southern literature and Jewish literature was a huge increase in literature by African-Americans. RICHARD WRIGHT proved the great catalyst with NATIVE SON (1940) and BLACK BOY (1945). RALPH ELLISON won acclaim with INVISIBLE MAN (1952), one of the great American novels. WITH GO TELL IT ON THE MOUNTAIN (1953), an autobiographical novel of growing up in Harlem, JAMES BALDWIN began a distinguished career that included excellent later fiction and some of the strongest essays of his time. CHESTER HIMES and ANN PETRY contributed fine realistic fiction, and FRANK YERBY wrote best-selling historical romances.

The urban and suburban North and East formed the background for fiction by many other writers. J. D. SALINGER, Jewish and Irish Catholic, captured with unmatched skill the tensions of sensitive adolescents in THE CATCHER IN THE RYE (1951), *Nine Stories* (1953), and two other books before falling into mysterious silence. JOHN O'HARA and JOHN CHEEVER depicted a world mostly Protestant, mostly privileged. MARY MCCARTHY came from the West to write of Eastern intellectuals. JACK KEROUAC brought East Coast and West Coast together in ON THE ROAD (1957), the most memorable of the BEAT GENERATION fictions. In the West, A. B. GUTHRIE, JR., and WALTER VAN TILBURG CLARK wrote memorably of the mountains and, later, KEN KESEY wrote of life on the West Coast. WRIGHT MORRIS began in the 1940s his many fictions set mostly in the West.

The major poets who appeared during or not long after the war were THEODORE ROETHKE, ELIZABETH BISHOP, RANDALL JAR-RELL, JOHN BERRYMAN, ROBERT LOWELL, and RICHARD WILBUR. Along with older poets still writing, they formed a literary establishment resented by others. Celebrated by the media as leaders of revolt were the members of the Beat Generation, but apart from ALLEN GINSBERG'S HOWL (1956), and a few other pieces, Beat fame has on the whole lasted longer than its poetry. In the West, LAWRENCE FERLINGHETTI gave great impetus to the SAN FRANCISCO RENAISSANCE, in part a Beat phenomenon. Allied to the Beats, at least in their revolt against received forms, were the BLACK MOUNTAIN POETS. Followers of Williams and Pound, and led by CHARLES OLSON, they campaigned for an open poetry, released from the tradition-bound aesthetics dominant in the most admired poetry of their time. Meanwhile, the NEW YORK SCHOOL POETS, loosely grouped around FRANK O'HARA, were developing an open style of another kind, heavily influenced by abstract expressionist painters. During the same period, African-American voices were beginning to be heard with renewed vigor as LANGSTON HUGHES published important verse and GWENDOLYN BROOKS achieved her first success.

By the 1960s the proponents of open form had largely won, as colleges and universities instituted courses in creative writing and hired poets, often from outside of academia, to teach them. In the 1960s and after, open forms tended to be the rule rather than the exception even in poems written by poets with long-standing reputations: Lowell is the paradigmatic example.

Most accomplished of the writers of innovative fiction active in the 1950s and 1960s was VLADIMIR NABOKOV, an immigrant with a distinguished European career behind him. Some of his best fiction, including *Lolita* (1955) and *Pnin* (1957),

was written in English during the two decades of his American residence. The work of WILLIAM S. BURROUGHS was highly publicized and much imitated, as was that of HENRY MILLER, whose writing had begun in the 1930s in France, but only now became generally available in the U.S. Experimental writers with major reputations yet to emerge included John Hawkes and WILLIAM GADDIS.

In drama, the new wave began with TENNESSEE WILLIAMS and ARTHUR MILLER. Williams's THE GLASS MENAGERIE (1945) and A STREETCAR NAMED DESIRE (1947) and Miller's DEATH OF A SALES-MAN (1949) proved enduring classics followed by numerous other successes. Among playwrights of their generation, they were rivaled only by WILLIAM INGE. Later, LORRAINE HANSBERRY'S *A Raisin in the Sun* (1959) ushered in a period of significant accomplishment for African-American playwrights.

Studies include James E. B. Breslin, *From Modern to Contemporary American Poetry, 1945–1965* (1984); Ihab Hassan, *Radical Innocence: The Contemporary American Novel* (1961); and Gerald Weales, *American Drama Since World War II* (1962).

History of American Literature: 1960 and After. The 1960s were the third straight decade dominated by war. Americans had lived through World War II, a conflict widely supported, the Korean War, an undeclared so-called police action enforcing the United States's role in protecting democracy around the globe, and finally Vietnam, fought in a country few could find on a world map and resulting from a failed European colonial venture. It was too much. Public revulsion at continued conflict came together with other forces having their roots in wartime disruptions to produce the civil rights movement, the women's movement, and President Lyndon Johnson's war on poverty. Individuals, removed from their home regions and usual work, had glimpsed better personal possibilities and rejected the slots allotted to them under the old conventions. As a BOB DYLAN lyric announced in 1963, "The Times They Are A-Changin'."

Returning soldiers, often educated at public expense, moved their families to the new, affluent suburbs. Cities became increasingly the homes of the poor and of African-American and Hispanic minorities. Immigration quotas—used in the past to stabilize the ethnic mixture of the population in a 19th-century mold—were first liberalized and, under Presidents Kennedy and Johnson, eliminated; more non-European immigrants were added to the mix. A series of shootings of leaders associated with the civil rights movement—JOHN F. KENNEDY (1963); MALCOLM X (1965); MAR-TIN LUTHER KING (1968) and Robert Kennedy (1968)—brought the images of war home and further stretched the social fabric.

In this period of change, the first five years of the decade brought the deaths of Hemingway, Faulkner, Cummings, Frost, William Carlos Williams and Eliot, all males of Anglo-Saxon lineage whose views and methods dominated literature. Younger fiction writers experimented with the antinovel and turned to expressions of the absurd to communicate their experience. THOMAS PYNCHON'S V appeared in the same year, 1963, in which J. D. Salinger, a World War II veteran writing quality realistic fiction, dropped out of the literary scene and published his last book. Universities developed programs to teach creative writing and welcomed poets of the antiacademic mold into the classroom; the two opposing schools of poetry merged. As commercial Broadway theater weakened in taste-making power, serious playwrights began writing for off-Broadway and regional theaters, where less formal stage techniques and fewer financial demands allowed for experimentation. On the other hand, television and film fostered a type of writing strongly defined by commercial and temporal constraints. A few writers, such as SAM SHEPARD and ARTHUR KOPIT, were able to succeed in theater, film, and television.

Realistic fiction, drawing on everyday experience, continued to flourish. In the pages of *The New Yorker* the suburbanites of JOHN CHEEVER and JOHN UPDIKE's fiction coexisted with the postmodernist figures of DONALD BARTHELME. Updike chronicled the confusions of Rabbit Angstrom, a middle-class Everyman, in four novels: *Rabbit, Run* (1960), *Rabbit Redux* (1970), *Rabbit Is Rich* (1981), and *Rabbit at Rest* (1990), each appearing at the opening of successive decades, and to top off the century, he added a novella, "Rabbit Remembered," in the short story collection *Licks of Love* (2000). JOYCE CAROL OATES based her novel *them* (1969) on a student's description of the Detroit race riot of 1967 and defined postwar race relations in urban regions in *Because It Is Bitter, and Because It Is My Heart* (1990). JOHN GARDNER painted the details of life in upstate New York in *The Sunlight Dialogues* (1972) and *October Light* (1976) and brought on a critical storm with his attack on other writers for lack of ennobling purpose in *On Moral Fiction* (1978).

In novels like *Ragtime* (1975) and *Billy Bathgate* (1989), E. L. DOCTOROW provided a setting in which historical figures and fictional constructs interact. TONI MORRISON, with the exception of Steinbeck (1962) the United States's only native-born winner of the Nobel Prize in Literature from the 1950s to 2000, drew on African-American history and defined the experience of women in such novels as *Song of Solomon* (1977) and *Beloved* (1987). With Dickens as a model, JOHN IRVING mixed observed reality with absurdity in *The World According to Garp* (1978), *The Hotel New Hampshire* (1981), *The Cider-House Rules* (1985), *A Prayer for Owen Meany* (1989) and other works.

Southern regional literature continued strong. Writers such as WALKER PERCY, with fiction set in Louisiana, and REYNOLDS PRICE, a chronicler of North Carolina, were joined by BARRY HANNAH and LEE SMITH and by African-American narrators of a Southern woman's life, such as ALICE WALKER. ANNE TYLER, BOB-BIE ANN MASON, and JAYNE ANNE PHILLIPS dealt with life in the border states.

Northwest experience formed the basis for the work of KEN KESEY and RAYMOND CARVER. LARRY WORWODE and WRIGHT MOR-RIS chronicled the Plains region. LARRY MCMURTRY and ELIZA-BETH TALLENT portrayed the Southwest, as did CORMAC MCCARTHY, after he shifted from an earlier focus on the mountains of Tennessee; JOAN DIDION and SAM SHEPARD described California life.

The more diverse population was represented by an upsurge of ethnic writing. Literature by American Jews continued important. PHILIP ROTH, whose story collection *Goodbye, Columbus* (1959) soared at the beginning of the decade, continued with a series of novels. *Portnoy's Complaint* (1969), a comic vision of sexual misadventure and family tension, was followed by the Zuckerman novels, self-reflexive studies of a writer-professor and his art. Bellow, Singer, and Malamud published major works, and Bellow and Singer won Nobel Prizes (1976, 1978). TILLIE OLSEN's *Tell Me a Riddle* (1962) and the short stories of GRACE PALEY delineated the urban Jewish woman's life. CYNTHIA OZICK published her first work in the 1980s. Meanwhile a host of new writers emerged from newer immigration patterns.

African-Americans depicted their history and contemporary life. JAMES BALDWIN, who first came to prominence with fiction and essays published in the 1950s, continued to challenge the American conscience with essays on race relations and fiction depicting the African-American experience. ALICE WALKER's *The Color Purple* (1982), narrated in Southern African-American vernacular, was successful both as a book and a film. MAYA ANGELOU, in an ongoing autobiography, movingly detailed her abusive childhood. JAMAICA KINCAID detailed life in the West Indies. GLORIA NAYLOR's highly acclaimed *The Women of Brewster Place* (1982) reported the urban experience. CHARLES JOHNSON's *Middle Passage*, a novel of the slave trade, won the National Book Award in 1990.

The oldest residents, Native Americans, combined their strong oral tradition with contemporary experience. N. SCOTT MOMADAY described a man straddling two cultures in *House Made of Dawn* (1969). In *Ceremony* (1977), LESLIE MARMON SILKO portrayed the healing effect of traditional ritual on a soul-scarred veteran. JAMES WELCH defined the contemporary reservation experience in *Winter in the Blood* (1974) and recreated the life of his Blackfoot ancestors in *Fool's Crow* (1986). LOUISE ERDRICH's novel *Love Medicine* (1984) won the National Book Critics' Circle Award and introduced Chippewa characters developed further in later books.

Asian-Americans, a fast-growing group, branched out from the idealized autobiographies published during and immediately after World War II. LOUIS CHU realistically depicted the nearly all-male life of Chinatown in *Eat a Bowl of Tea* (1961). RICHARD KIM focused on the Korean War experience in *The Martyred* (1964). MAXINE HONG KINGSTON incorporated the anecdotes of her female and male progenitors in *Woman Warrior* (1976) and *China Men* (1980). JOHN OKADA's *No-No Boy*, ignored when it was published in 1957, gained recognition with the increased emphasis on Asian Studies. Writers who won both critical praise and wide readership include VED MEHTA, AMY TAN, GAIL TSUKIYAMA, and HA JIN.

Alternative visions of human experience and nontraditional forms appealed to writers disillusioned in the aftermath of war and haunted by the specter of nuclear destruction and continuing inequity. The traditional mimetic function of fiction seemed inadequate, and influences from abroad reinforced the concept of antifiction or metafiction. Existential ideas, the French *nouveau roman*, the MAGICAL REALISM of South Americans such as JORGE LUIS BORGES, and the fictional illusions of Nabokov, whose *Lolita* was one of the major texts of the period, all influenced literary experimentation. JOSEPH HELLER in *Catch-22* (1961) and KURT VONNEGUT in *Slaughter-house-Five* (1966) approached their World War II experiences with black comedy or parody. THOMAS BERGER turned the idealized Western formula inside out in *Little Big Man* (1964). THOMAS MCGUANE and BARRY HANNAH satirized business, small-town boosterism, and sex. JAY MCINERNEY produced a comic inversion of the career struggle in *Bright Lights, Big City* (1984). Pynchon and DON DE LILLO brought impressive erudition and arcane information to plots based on elaborate international conspiracies. WILLIAM GADDIS, JOHN HAWKES, and JOHN BARTH stressed the idea of fiction as an artificial construct. Others attacking the boundaries of fiction include ROBERT COOVER, RONALD SUKENICK, WILLIAM GASS, ALEXANDER THEROUX, JOSEPH MCELROY, and WILLIAM T. VOLLMANN.

Several who had experienced the Vietnam War tried to express its special horror. MICHAEL HERR gave a personal slant to the perspective of a war correspondent in *Dispatches* (1977). TIM O'BRIEN treated the war in a memoir and three novels, including a winner of the National Book Award, *Going After Cacciato* (1978). Others who wrote memorable novels include LARRY HEINEMANN and PHILIP CAPUTO.

A major increase in university creative writing programs led to academic support for such established poets as A. R. AMMONS, GWENDOLYN BROOKS, and JAMES DICKEY and created positions for many younger poets. In a spirit of new romanticism celebrating the individual, faculties and curricula changed rapidly. Such antiestablishment groups as the BLACK MOUNTAIN POETS, including CHARLES OLSON, ROBERT CREELEY, and ROBERT DUNCAN, achieved their first publication by major presses. Poets whose work had been ignored achieved recognition: LOUIS ZUKOFSKY's work was printed in the 1960s; SABELLA GARDNER published two collections at that time. AMY CLAMPITT emerged as a significant poet in the late 1970s, and most of LORINE NIEDECKER's oeuvre was not published until the 1980s.

The 1959 publication of ROBERT LOWELL's *Life Studies* and *Heart's Needle* by Lowell's student W. D. SNODGRASS ushered in a decade dominated by CONFESSIONAL POETRY. ANN SEXTON and SYLVIA PLATH, also students of Lowell, had major publications: Sexton's *To Bedlam and Part Way Back* (1960) was followed by other collections and *The Complete Poems* (1981) after her death; Plath's posthumously published work began with *Ariel* (1965). JOHN BERRYMAN's *The Dream Songs* (1969) closed out the decade.

Other poets, while referring to personal experience, spurned the confessional label. These include the Deep Image poets ROBERT BLY and JAMES WRIGHT, who share an interest in poetry in other languages, especially work from South America, with W. S. MERWIN and MARK STRAND. GALWAY KINNELL combines the personal with the mythical. WILLIAM STAFFORD's brief poems evoke the plains of the Midwest. GARY SNYDER uses the Far West locale. Posthumous publication of FRANK O'HARA's *Collected Poems* (1971) brought attention to the urban expression of the loosely defined NEW YORK SCHOOL, including KENNETH KOCH, JAMES SCHUYLER, and JOHN ASHBERY, the last being one of the most celebrated poets of his generation.

The experiences of women, given painful voice by Sexton and Plath, were chronicled by others. ADRIENNE RICH and MARGE PIERCY express feminist consciousness. Alice Walker depicts the lives of Southern women in verse.

Most post-1960s verse is written in open forms, but JAMES MERRILL's formal skill is a sharp contrast. HOWARD NEMEROV, RICHARD WILBUR, and CAROLYN KIZER have also maintained formal interests.

African-American voices continued to be prominent in other areas besides fiction. The oratory of MARTIN LUTHER KING, JR., echoing the cadences of the King James Bible and African-American folk music, was a dominating presence in the 1960s. Jesse Jackson continued the oratorical tradition. Poets evoked African-American history and experience. ROBERT HAYDEN, whose first work appeared in the 1940s, did not attain recognition until publication of his *Selected Poems* (1966). IMAMU AMIRI BARAKA, who changed his name from LeRoi Jones in 1965, DON L. LEE, ISHMAEL REED, NIKKI GIOVANNI, LUCILLE CLIFTON, MICHAEL S. HARPER, SHERLEY WILLIAMS, and RITA DOVE write of family history and express racial pride and anger in their verse.

Among other poets, the work of CATHY SONG represents the Chinese-American heritage, while BEI DAO writes poems in exile. Immigrants from Eastern Europe include CHARLES SIMIC and JOSEPH BRODSKY. PHILIP LEVINE depicts Northern blue collar experience, and DAVE SMITH and CHARLES WRIGHT celebrate their Southern backgrounds. NORMAN DUBIE and LOUISE GLUCK mix personal experience with historical reference; ROBERT PINSKY uses formal techniques with success; and ALBERT GOLDBARTH's work reveals his academic bent. STANLEY PLUMLY and BRAD LEITHAUSER paint strong visual images.

EDWARD ALBEE was the major new playwright of the 1960s. The influence of European Theater of the Absurd is apparent in his work and that of ARTHUR KOPIT. Realistic theater continued to be successful, and both TENNESSEE WILLIAMS and ARTHUR MILLER continued active. NEIL SIMON became Broadway's most commercially successful writer with such plays as *Barefoot in the Park* (1963) and *The Odd Couple* (1965). Baraka expressed his anger in *The Toilet* (1962) and *Dutchman* (1964). James Baldwin contributed *Blues for Mr. Charlie* (1964). AUGUST WILSON contributed a series of successful interpretations of African-American family life, including *Fences* (1985) and *The Piano Lesson* (1990). Frank Chin's *Chickencoop Chinaman* was produced at the American Place Theater in 1972. David Henry Hwang's *FOB* (fresh off the boat) won the 1981 Obie Award.

With the commercial pressures of Broadway forcing many of the best playwrights to find production elsewhere, SAM SHEPARD was spectacularly successful in the Off Off Broadway setting; his first production, in 1964, was followed by over forty plays, including *True West* (1980) and *Fool for Love* (1983). The sponsorship of Joseph Papp's Shakespeare in the Park program was crucial for DAVID RABE's *Sticks and Bones* (1971), about the legacy of the Vietnam War. Other significant playwrights include DAVID MAMET, and MARSHA NORMAN and BETH HENLEY, two of the most successful women in contemporary theater.

Studies include Frederick R. Karl, *American Fictions: 1940–1980* (1984); Alan Williamson, *Introspection and Contemporary Poetry* (1984); and Marjorie Perloff, *The Dance of the Intellect: Studies in the Poetry of the Pound Tradition* (1986). A comprehensive anthology for the four decades after 1945 is George Perkins and Barbara Perkins, *Contemporary American Literature* (1988).

Histories of American literature from its beginnings include Arthur Hobson Quinn and others, *The Literature of the American People* (1951); Robert E. Spiller and others, *The Literary History of the United States* (4th ed., 1974); Emory Elliott and others, *Columbia Literary History of the United States* (1988); Sacvan Berkovite, gen. ed., *The Cambridge History of American Literature* (1994–   ). An enduring favorite among comprehensive anthologies is George and Barbara Perkins, *The American Tradition in Literature* (9th ed., 1998).

For supplementary surveys in this volume see AFRO-AMERICAN LITERATURE; ASIAN-AMERICAN LITERATURE; CANADIAN LITERATURE IN ENGLISH; CANADIAN LITERATURE IN FRENCH; CHILDREN'S LITERATURE; COMICS; DIALECT IN AMERICAN LITERATURE; DRAMA; FEMINISM; GLOBALIZATION OF AMERICAN LITERATURE; HISPANIC-AMERICAN LITERATURE; HUMOR; JEWISH AMERICAN LITERATURE; LATIN AMERICAN LITERATURE; LITERARY CRITICISM; LITTLE MAGAZINES; LITTLE THEATER; MAGAZINES; MOTION PICTURES; NATIVE AMERICAN LITERATURE; NEWSPAPERS; NOVEL; POETRY IN THE U.S.; SCIENCE FICTION AND FANTASY; SHORT STORY; and THE SOUTH.

History of the Dividing Line Between Virginia and North Carolina: Run in the Year 1728 (first pub., 1841), by WILLIAM BYRD II. A later edition of the book, prepared by William K. Boyd (1929), added *The Secret History of the Line*, taken from manuscript. Byrd related his experience with a party of surveyors from Virginia. The story is spiced with humor, as when he writes of some of the inhabitants of North Carolina.

History of New York.   See NEW YORK, A HISTORY OF.

Hitchcock, Alfred (1899–1980),   director. Born and educated in England, Hitchcock got his start in the British film industry. His best known British films are *The Man Who Knew Too Much* (1934) and *The Thirty-Nine Steps* (1935), an adaptation of a John Buchan novel. He came to Hollywood in 1939. His first American movie, *Rebecca* (1940), an adaptation of a Daphne du Maurier novel, won the Oscar for best picture. *Suspicion* (1941) won an Oscar for Joan Fontaine as the woman whose husband is scheming to kill her. Among his best films are *Strangers on a Train* (1951), from a book by PATRICIA HIGHSMITH; *Rear Window* (1954); *Vertigo* (1958); *North by Northwest* (1959); and *Psycho* (1960). A technically gifted director, his work was much admired in the United States and Europe.

Hitchcock, Enos (1744–1803),   clergyman, novelist, biographer. Hitchcock served as a chaplain in the Continental army and wrote a life of Washington (1800). He is chiefly remembered as the author of the second American novel published in book form, *Memoirs of the Bloomsgrove Family*

(1790, see BLOOMSGROVE). The book is full of moral discourses and is noteworthy as an early protest against imitation of the British. Hitchcock wrote a *Treatise on Education* (1790) and another story, *The Farmer's Friend, or, The History of Mr. Charles Worthy* (1793).

Hitchcock, Ethan Allen (1798–1870),   soldier, teacher, critic, philosopher. Hitchcock was educated at West Point, taught there for many years, and served in the Mexican and Civil Wars, reaching the rank of major general. His books include *The Doctrines of Spinoza and Swedenborg Identified* (1846), *Swedenborg: A Hermetic Philosopher* (1858), *Remarks on the Sonnets of Shakespeare* (1865), and *Notes on the "Vita Nuova" and Minor Poems of Dante* (1866). Two posthumously published volumes tell about his own experiences: *Fifty Years in Camp and Field* (1909) and *A Traveler in Indian Territory* (1930).

H. M. Pulham, Esq. (1941),   a novel by JOHN P. MARQUAND. Unlike THE LATE GEORGE APLEY (1937), Pulham partially escapes from his Boston environment and inhibitions by way of World War I, and falls in love with a girl in New York City, but like George Apley he weds the girl his family selects for him. The book goes on to explore the cost of conformity for both Pulham and his wife. The book satirizes the Boston Brahmin society and the change in its mores after the war.

Hoagland, Edward (1932–   ),   essayist, novelist. Hoagland was born in New Canaan, Connecticut, and educated at Harvard. As honest, independent, and in love with details of everyday natural life as Thoreau, and with a prose style strong and supple, Hoagland started out as a novelist. *Cat Man* (1956) deals with life in the circus; *The Circle Home* (1960), with boxing; and *The Peacock's Tail* (1965), with slum life. As an essayist he gained national attention with his best seller, *Walking the Dead Diamond River* (1972). His subjects range from the habits of bears and foxes to married life in urban New York. Other essay collections include *Notes from the Century Before* (1969); *The Courage of Turtles* (1971); *Red Wolves and Black Bears* (1976); *African Calliope* (1979) about a voyage up the Sudan; *The Tugman's Passage* (1982); and *Tigers & Ice: Reflections on Nature and Life* (1999), published after a bout with blindness. *Compass Points: How I Lived* (2001) is a memoir. A novel is *Seven Rivers West* (1986), set in the western frontier.

hoaxes.   Practical jokes and the like have played a large part in American folklore and humor. In frontier conditions, greenhorns and tenderfeet were the butts of incessant and sometimes cruel pranks. The country yokel was a favorite target of urban tricksters. The "bad boy," immortalized by GEORGE W. PECK, was given license in his endeavors to disrupt the dignity of his elders. In literature, one of the first important figures associated with hoaxes was Poe, who turned them into an art form. A literary hoax reports fantasy under the false appearance of fact, with the intention of exposing reality as a literary effect. Poe had a great fondness for gulling the public, as was evident especially in THE BALLOON HOAX (1844) and *The Facts in the Case of M. Valdemar* (*American Review*, December 1845). In turn, Poe was the subject of hoaxes, especially after his death, when poems written by others were passed off as his. One of the best, "Leonainie," came from the pen of James Whitcomb Riley. William Cullen Bryant was the similar victim of a poem, entitled "A Vision of Immortality."

The western humorists of the Mark Twain era indulged constantly in hoaxes and spoofs in order to exploit Easterners' excessive credulity about the West. In 1854, for example, Ferdinand Cartwright Ewer, who later became a minister, wrote a burlesque of spiritualism, then sent a reprint of the article to a New York magazine ardently devoted to spirit communication. The editor printed the article in good faith, and one spiritualistic publication after another did the same. Ewer confessed the hoax, but the more ardent members of the cause chose not to believe him. At about the same time, GEORGE HORATIO DERBY, better known as John Phoenix and Squibob, contributed to the San Francisco *Herald* a scientific report by one Dr. Hermann Ellenbogen on certain zoological discoveries in the mountains of Washington Territory, including living specimens of the Gyascutus and the Prock. The parody was reprinted in the East and proved to the West how gullible Easterners were.

Not long after Mark Twain joined the staff of the Virginia City *Enterprise*, he described the discovery in the Sierras of a petrified man, with one hand extended from the tip of his nose. The story was widely reprinted. One of Twain's most solemn and most successful hoaxes was the paragraph in "The Double-Barreled Detective Story" (1902) describing a spicy morning in early October in which, among other details, he tells how "far in the empty sky a solitary oesophagus slept upon motionless wing."

In the East, Witter Bynner and Arthur Davison Ficke fooled the literary public with their SPECTRA poems, written under the pseudonyms Emanuel Morgan and Anne Knish. The BATHTUB HOAX of H. L. Mencken was a solemn article in the New York *Evening Mail* (1917), relating how the bathtub had been invented in Cincinnati in the 1840s and first installed in the White House by Millard Fillmore, and alleging that its use by the president had been opposed by many doctors as an unhealthful practice. The tale was widely accepted, even appearing in an encyclopedia. In 1925 Mencken exposed the hoax, but it continued to circulate as indubitable fact. It was reprinted with other essays in *The Bathtub Hoax* (1958). An unintentional hoax was the ORSON WELLES 1938 broadcast of Howard Koch's adaptation of H. G. Wells's *The War of the Worlds*, which panicked millions of listeners into believing that Martians were invading our planet. Curtis D. MacDougall described other examples in *Hoaxes* (1940). Daniel Hoffman provides an excellent account of the literary uses to which Poe put the hoax in *Poe, Poe, Poe, Poe, Poe, Poe, Poe* (1972). James M. Cox provides a brilliant discussion of the structure of the device in *The Fate of Humor* (1966). See HUMOR IN THE UNITED STATES; CARDIFF; GIANT TALL TALES.

DP

Hoban, Russell [Conwell] (1925–   ),   fabulist, children's writer. Born in Landsdale, Pennsylvania, and long respected as a writer for children, with more than 50 books, Hoban wrote for both children and adults in *The Mouse and*

His Child (1967), and in *The Lion of Boaz-Jachin and Jachin-Boz* (1973). His best-known adult books are *Turtle Diary* (1975), made into a movie, about two lonely people who conspire to liberate a sea turtle from a zoo; and *Riddley Walker* (1981), about a twelve-year-old in the distant postnuclear future, when the English language has metamorphosed into a sinister simplicity. Hoban emigrated late in midlife from Connecticut to England. *Pilgermann* (1983) is about the First Crusade. *The Moment Under the Moment* (1992) is a collection of essays. *A Russell Hoban Omnibus* appeared in 1999. *Amaryllis Night and Day* (2001) is a novel of fantasy, ghosts, myths, and magic set in contemporary London.

Hobart, Alice Tisdale [Nourse] (1882–1967),   historian, writer of travel books, novelist. Born in Lockport, New York, Hobart went with her husband, an American businessman, to China and spent twenty years in the cities of that country and on the Manchurian and Mongolian frontiers. She embodied accounts of her experiences first in such books as *Pioneering Where the World Is Old* (1917) and *Within the Walls of Nanking* (1928), then in a series of novels about the experiences of westerners with the people of Mongolia. Chief among these was *Oil for the Lamps of China* (1933). In *Their Own Country* (1940) the characters in the former book return and face the economic problems of America. Later, Hobart produced *The Peacock Sheds His Tail* (1945) about Mexico, and *The Cleft Rock* (1948) about four generations in California; also *The Serpent-Wreathed Staff* (1951) and *Venture into Darkness* (1955). *Gusty's Child*, her autobiography, was published in 1959.

Hobomok: A Tale of Early Times (1824),   a historical romance by LYDIA MARIA CHILD. The author, then only twenty-two, read a review by J. G. Palfrey that had appeared three years before in the *North American Review* (April 1821) urging American writers to treat American themes. Her story supposedly follows an old Puritan manuscript, and relates how a young girl, betrothed to a neighbor who has been reported lost at sea, falls in love with a handsome, refined Indian chief, marries him, and has a son by him. Then her betrothed returns, and the Indian nobly gives her up. It is one of the earliest novels laid in Puritan times.

Hobson, Laura Z[ametkin] (1900–1986),   novelist. Born in New York City, where most of her fiction is set, Hobson worked as a reporter for newspapers and magazines before turning to short stories in 1935. Her first novel, *The Trespassers* (1943), is an attack on immigration quotas that excluded European refugees in the period before World War II. Her best-known novel, *Gentleman's Agreement* (1947), concerns a young reporter who pretends to be Jewish in order to gain material for a magazine article on anti-Semitism and discovers that well-meaning people can be bigoted. *The Tenth Month* (1971) deals with unwed mothers; *Consenting Adult* (1975), with homosexuality. Her other novels include *The Other Father* (1950), *The Celebrity* (1951), *First Papers* (1964), and *Over and Above* (1979). *Laura Z: A Life* (1983) is an autobiography.

Hodge, Frederick Webb (1864–1956),   ethnologist, government official, explorer. Hodge, born in England, became an authority on Native Americans. He worked mainly with the Bureau of American Ethnology at Washington and museums in New York and Los Angeles. He conducted several ethnological expeditions in the Southwest, wrote numerous articles and monographs, and edited *Handbook of the American Indians North of Mexico* (1907–10), *Narratives of Cabeza de Vaca and Coronado* (1907), *Curtis's North American Indian* (20 v. 1907–10), and similar volumes.

Hodgins, Eric (1899–1971),   editor, novelist. Hodgins, born in Detroit, first wrote in collaboration with F. A. Magoun *Sky High* (1929, rev. ed. 1935), *A History of Aircraft* (1931), and *Behemoth* (1932). His two popular novels were *Mr. Blandings Builds His Dream House* (1946) and *Blandings' Way* (1950).

Hodgins, Jack (1938–   ),   novelist, short-story writer. Hodgins's setting is generally his native Vancouver Island and its people. *The Invention of the World* (1977) contains larger than life characters, including an evangelist who has convinced an entire Irish village to come to Canada, and the seven daughters of the Barclay family who appear in many of his fictions. *The Resurrection of Joseph Bourne* (1980) deals with the effects of a tidal wave on an isolated port. *Spit Delaney's Island* (1976) and *The Barclay Family Theatre* (1981) are story collections. *The Macken Charm* (1995) presents the Barclays again.

Hoffman, Charles Fenno (1806–1884),   lawyer, editor, novelist, memoirist, poet. Hoffman, who was born in New York City and trained in the law, abandoned law for writing, first as a contributor to newspapers and magazines, especially the *Knickerbocker*, then as a poet and novelist. He achieved celebrity for a novel he based on a Kentucky murder case, GREYSLAER: A ROMANCE OF THE MOHAWK (1840); and the lively descriptive letters he wrote during a journey across the Alleghenies and over the prairies were collected in *A Winter in the West* (1835). Later he wrote *Wild Scenes in the Forest and Prairie* (1839). He published three books of verse, later collected in *Poems* (1873). An unfinished novel, *Vanderlyn*, appeared in the *American Monthly Magazine* when he was its editor (1835–37). His last years were clouded by mental illness, and in 1850 he was committed to a hospital. Homer F. Barnes wrote Hoffman's biography (1930). WASHINGTON IRVING was betrothed to Hoffman's sister Matilda, and her early death was the great tragedy of his life. See KNICKERBOCKER SCHOOL.

Hoffman, Daniel [Gerard] (1923–   ),   poet, critic. Born in New York and educated at Columbia, Hoffman is a professor at the University of Pennsylvania. His poetry collections include *An Armada of Thirty Whales* (1954), selected for the Yale Series of Younger Poets; *A Little Geste* (1960); *Striking the Stones* (1968); and *Brotherly Love* (1980), a long poem about the history of Philadelphia. *Hang-Gliding from Helicon: New and Selected Poems, 1948–1988* appeared in 1988 and *Middens of the Tribe: A Poem* in 1995. He has written critical books on Poe and Stephen Crane and is the editor of *The Harvard Guide to Contemporary American Writing* (1979). *Zone of the Interior* (2000) is a World War II memoir.

Hogan, Linda (1947–   ),   poet, novelist, essayist. Born in Denver, Colorado, Hogan grew up in Colorado and in Oklahoma, where most of her Chickasaw relatives have lived since the 1830s. Educated at a variety of community colleges, she worked as a waitress, secretary, nurse's aid, and library clerk, began writing in her thirties, and received an M.A. in 1978 from the University of Colorado, where she has later taught. Her poems, on her life, her Native American heritage, and the natural world, are collected in *Calling Myself Home* (1978), *Daughters, I Love You* (1981), *Eclipse* (1983), and *Red Clay: Poems and Stories* (1991). Novels are *Mean Spirit* (1990), set during the rush for oil on Indian lands in Oklahoma in the 1920s; *Solar Storms* (1995), covering five generations of Native American women; and *Power* (1998), about the coming of age of a young Indian woman. *Dwellings* (1995) is an essay collection.

Holbrook, Josiah (1788–1854),   educational and social reformer. Holbrook founded the first branch of The American Lyceum at Millbury, Massachusetts, in 1826 and established more than a hundred branches before 1829. Within the next seven years, he set up nearly three thousand more. He wrote *The American Lyceum, or, Society for the Improvement of Schools and Diffusion of Useful Knowledge* (1829); issued *Scientific Tracts Designed for Instruction and Entertainment* (beginning 1832); and established and edited the *Family Lyceum* (1832). He secured as speakers many of the most eminent men of the country, including Daniel Webster, Emerson, Lowell, and Oliver Wendell Holmes. Some of the LYCEUMS were still in existence at the end of the 19th century. They encouraged the foundation of libraries and museums, and were influential disseminators of knowledge.

Holbrook, Stewart H[all] (1893–1964),   editor, historian, college lecturer. Holbrook spent his early years in his native Vermont and in New Hampshire, and for a time worked in his father's logging camps. Later he went to the West Coast, where he worked as a newspaperman, editor, and writer. His first book to gain a large audience was *Lost Men of American History* (1946). Among his other publications are *Ethan Allen* (1940); *Burning an Empire: America's Great Forest Fires* (1943); *Little Annie Oakley and Other Rugged People* (1948); *Yankee Exodus: An Account of Migration from New England* (1950); *Far Corner: A Personal View of the Pacific Northwest* (1952); *Down on the Farm* (1954); *The Columbia* (1956); *The Rocky Mountain Revolution* (1956); *Dreamers of the American Dream* (1957); *Mr. Otis* (1958); and a satire, *The Golden Age of Quackery* (1959).

Holiday (prod. 1928, pub. 1929),   a play by PHILIP BARRY. This is a dissection of a rich man's family, one member of which, Julia, shares her father's drab and conventional ideas, while her brother and sister seek freedom in a wider experience. A young lawyer falls in love with Julia, learns that she is really not what he wants, and marries her sister.

Holland, Edwin Clifford (1794?–1824),   poet, dramatist, editor, essayist. Born in Charleston, Holland became an editor of the Charleston *Times* and contributed to the *Port Folio* of Philadelphia. He won distinction as a poet with *Odes, Naval Songs, and Other Occasional Poems* (1813), and his romantic drift was further displayed in a dramatization of Byron's *The Corsair* (1818). It was produced in Charleston in 1818. *Essays; and a Drama in Five Acts* was posthumously published (1852).

Holland, Josiah Gilbert ["Timothy Titcomb"] (1819–1881), editor, novelist, poet, historian. Born in Massachusetts, Holland was editor of the Springfield *Republican*, then with Roswell Smith helped found SCRIBNER'S MONTHLY (1870), which he edited until his death. He wrote with frank didacticism, and his stories, poems, essays, and sayings appealed to his generation. Among his novels are *The Bay-Path* (1857), *Miss Gilbert's Career* (1860), *Arthur Bonnicastle* (1873), and SEVENOAKS: A STORY OF TODAY (1875). He wrote effective verse, and his *Poems* were collected in 1873. His *Timothy Titcomb's Letters to Young People, Single and Married* (1858) gave practical advice. His *Life of Abraham Lincoln* (1866) was among the most important of the early biographies of Lincoln. See BITTER-SWEET.

Holland, Rupert Sargent (1878–1952), lawyer, historian, writer. Holland, born in Louisville, wrote many books of historical and other fiction for young people. Among them are *The Boy Scouts of Birch-Bark Island* (1911), *Knights of the Golden Spur* (1912), *Blackbeard's Island* (1916), *The Pirates of the Delaware* (1925), *The Rider in the Green Mask* (1926), *Drake's Lad* (1929), *The Pirate of the Gulf* (1929), *A Race for a Fortune* (1931), *The Sea-Scouts of Birch-Bark Island* (1936), and *Secret of Blennerhassett* (1941). Popular also were Holland's *Historic Boyhoods* (1909) and *Historic Girlhoods* (1910) and his *Plays of the American Colonies* (1937).

Hollander, John (1929–   ), poet, critic. Born in New York, Hollander was educated at Columbia and Indiana University, taught at Yale from 1959, and has been awarded the Bollingen Prize and a MacArthur Fellowship. *A Crackling of Thorns* (1958), his first collection, was selected for the Yale Younger Poets series by the editor, W. H. AUDEN. A student of English metaphysical poetry and prosody, and an accomplished musician, he writes metrical, witty verse. In *Types of Shape* (1968) his shaped poems are reminiscent of George Herbert. His other collections include *Movie-Going* (1962) and *Visions from the Ramble* (1965), both using the landscape of Manhattan; *The Night Mirror* (1971); *Town and Country Matters: Erotica and Satirica* (1972); *The Head of the Bed* (1973); *Tales Told of the Father* (1975), written in syllabic lines; *Reflections on Espionage* (1976; reprinted with a new introduction, 1999), a long poem making espionage a metaphor for poetry and introducing real poets under spy names; *Spectral Emanations: New and Selected Poems* (1978); *Blue Wine and Other Poems* (1979); *Powers of Thirteen* (1983); *In Time and Place* (1986); *Selected Poems* (1993); *The Gazer's Spirit: Poems Speaking to Silent Works of Art* (1995); and *Figurehead and Other Poems* (1999). His books of criticism include *The Untuning of the Sky: Ideas of Music in English Poetry, 1500–1700* (1961); *Rhyme's Reason* (1981); *Melodious Guile*

(1988); and *The Poetry of Everyday Life* (1998). Among his verses for children are *Various Owls* (1963) and *The Quest of the Gole* (1966). He has been a tireless editor of many verse collections, including *American Poetry: The Nineteenth Century* (1993).

Holley, Marietta ["Samantha Allen"] (1836–1926), humorist. Using the pen names Josiah Allen's Wife and Samantha, Holley, who was born in Jefferson County, New York, advocated temperance and women's suffrage in popular essays. Samantha was unsophisticated and poorly educated, but wise in her observations of everyday events. Among Holley's collections of sketches are *My Opinions and Betsy Bobbet's* (1873), *Samantha at the Centennial* (1877), *Samantha at Saratoga* (1887), *Samantha Amongst the Colored Folks* (1892), *Samantha at the World's Fair* (1893), *Samantha in Europe* (1895), and *Josiah Allen on Women's Rights* (1914).

Holley, Mary [Austin] (1784–1846), biographer. Holley, born in Connecticut, began to write after the death of her husband, the president of Transylvania University. She wrote *A Discourse on the Genius and Character of the Rev. Horace Holley* (1828). In 1831 she visited Texas. Her letters about it became *Texas: Observations Historical, Geographical, and Descriptive* (1833), the first book on the subject. Later it was expanded into a fuller account, *Texas* (1835).

Hollingsworth. A character in Hawthorne's *Blithedale Romance*.

Hollister, Gideon Hiram (1817–1881), lawyer, poet, novelist, historian. Hollister, born in Connecticut, wrote two novels: *Mount Hope, or, Philip, King of the Wamapanoags* (1851) and *Kinley Hollow* (1882). He also wrote a *History of Connecticut* (1855) and a considerable amount of verse. His poem on Thomas à Becket (1866) was dramatized by Edwin Booth.

Hollow Men, The (1925), a poem by T. S. ELIOT. Occupying a position between THE WASTE LAND and ASH-WEDNESDAY, both with respect to content and the order in which the poems were written, *The Hollow Men* begins with references to human paralysis and ends with a juxtaposition of the human world of illusory dreams and the divine Kingdom beyond death. The first four sections of the poem deal respectively with the general sterility of the "living dead," the particular fear of reality and of the eyes of judgment, the desolation of the world between birth and death, and the faint hope for the appearance of the "perpetual star" and "multifoliate rose"; the fifth section recapitulates the themes of the first four in an alternation of fragmentary phrases. The ending is ambiguous, both a cry of despair at the emptiness of human life and a simultaneous assertion, "For Thine is the Kingdom."

Holm, John Cecil (1904–1981), actor, playwright. Holm, born in Philadelphia, went on the stage in 1925. His first play, *Three Men on a Horse* (1935), was written in collaboration with GEORGE ABBOTT. Other plays of his include *Best Foot Foward* (1941), *Banjo Eyes* (1941), *Brighten the Corner* (1945), and *Gramercy Ghost* (1947). He also wrote movie scripts.

Holm, Saxe.   See HELEN HUNT JACKSON.

Holmes, Abiel (1763–1837),   clergyman, historiographer, biographer. Born in Connecticut, the father of OLIVER WENDELL HOLMES, SR., was pastor of a church in Cambridge for forty years. He wrote (1798) a life of Ezra Stiles, the father of his first wife, president of Yale, and his highly revered teacher. Holmes's most important production was *American Annals, or a Chronological History of America* (1805, rev. ed. 1829), a scholarly collection of information in two volumes.

Holmes, [John] Clellon (1926–1988),   novelist, critic. Several years before the term "Beat Generation" became known to the American public, Holmes's novel *Go* (1952) had depicted a new, lost, wandering BEAT GENERATION. In 1958 appeared *The Horn*, a novel about jazz. A collection of essays, *Nothing More to Declare* (1967), is autobiographical. *Gone in October* (1985) presents memoirs of Kerouac. *Displaced Person* (1987) is a travel memoir.

Holmes, John (1904–1962),   teacher, poet. Holmes, born in Massachusetts, began teaching English at Tufts in 1934. His publications include several volumes of excellent verse: *Address to the Living* (1937), *Fair Warning* (1939), *Map of My Country* (1943), *The Double Root* (1950), *The Symbols* (1955), and *The Fortune Teller* (1961). He speaks of the "tight rhythm, harsh metaphor, disturbed or deliberately ambiguous or very private reference" in his poems, but readers have not found them as hermetic as the poetry of some other 20th-century writers. *Writing Poetry* appeared in 1960.

Holmes, Mary Jane [Hawes] (1825–1907),   novelist. Holmes, born in Massachusetts, began writing when she was fifteen, and in her lifetime published thirty-nine novels, all of them sentimental in tone and moral in purpose. Her books sold in the millions. Her first novel was *Tempest and Sunshine* (1854), and LENA RIVERS (1856) is her best-known book. Among her other books are *Ethelyn's Mistake* (1869), *The Tracy Diamonds* (1899), and *Rena's Experiment* (1904).

Holmes, Oliver Wendell, Sr. (1809–1894),   physician, teacher, scientist, poet, essayist, novelist, biographer, critic, lecturer, epigrammatist. Holmes was a descendant of ANNE BRADSTREET. His grandfather was a surgeon, his father the clergyman ABIEL HOLMES. Born in Cambridge, Massachusetts, Holmes was educated at Harvard and became in some ways a professional Harvardian—of his 408 poems, at least 108 have some reference or relationship to Harvard.

At first Holmes studied law, but then turned to medicine. After study at home and in Paris, he was given his degree by Harvard (1836). Meanwhile in 1830 he won nationwide acclaim with his passionately expressed resentment against the destruction of *The Constitution*, the famous war vessel from the War of 1812. His poem OLD IRONSIDES appeared in the Boston *Daily Advertiser* (September 16, 1830), was reprinted all over the country, and influenced the government not to destroy the vessel.

As a physician Holmes had a memorable career. He was a teacher at Dartmouth, later at Harvard, where he became dean of the Medical School; a practitioner; and a researcher. He was an enthusiastic and informative lecturer. In the classrooms and hospitals of Paris he said he had learned three principles: "Not to take authority when I can have facts; not to guess when I can know; not to think a man must take physic because he is sick." He brought back from Paris emphasis on the use of the microscope in medicine. More important was a conclusion he set forth in a paper that he read before a medical society and published in 1843: *The Contagiousness of Puerperal Fever.* This study of childbed fever showed that physicians careless about personal cleanliness themselves were the vehicles by which the fever was transmitted. Many lives were saved by Holmes's methods, and he was proved right by the researches of Pasteur and Lister. He published many other medical papers and collected some of them in book form, including *Boylston Prize Dissertations* (1838), *Homeopathy and Its Kindred Delusions* (1842), and *Medical Essays, 1842–1882* (1883).

Holmes took keen delight in observing the intricate order and symmetry of nature, especially of the human body. Some of this delight was expressed in one of his best poems, *The Living Temple* (1858), and his medical experiences were reflected also in *The Stethoscope Song* (1849) and *La Grisette* (1863). A more important link between Holmes the physician and Holmes the writer may be found in his three "medicated" novels—ELSIE VENNER (1861), THE GUARDIAN ANGEL (1867), and A MORTAL ANTIPATHY (1885).

Holmes the scientist and Holmes the man of imagination are inextricably interwoven in his attitude toward religion and his general philosophy of life. By descent Holmes was a Calvinistic Puritan, but he attacked Calvinism again and again in prose and verse. In his poem THE DEACON'S MASTERPIECE (1858), a wonderful one-hoss shay went to pieces all at once, like the Calvinistic system. Similarly, in *Elsie Venner* he sought to test the doctrine of original sin and human responsibility. Yet he once wrote to Harriet Beecher Stowe: "I do not believe you or I can ever get the iron of Calvinism out of our souls."

A Brahmin of Brahmins and in the main a conservative, in his free-thinking rationalism he was an ardent rebel. But he was not a transcendentalist, nor in politics anything but a Federalist. He appreciated wealth, but sincerely and actively preached humanitarianism.

Holmes was always ready with his neat and entertaining verses at a reunion or celebration. At his best he is America's finest writer of *vers de société*. He usually chose such familiar media as the ballad, the octosyllabic couplet, and the heroic couplet, although he also wrote blank verse and sonnets with great skill. Among his best poems are THE LAST LEAF (1833) and THE CHAMBERED NAUTILUS (1858). The salt of wit still preserves many of his other poems, among them "The Height of the Ridiculous" (1830), "The Ballad of the Oysterman" (1830), "To an Insect" (1831), "My Aunt" (1831), "Contentment" (1858), and "Dorothy Q." (1871). As a scientist, Holmes interested himself in what he called *The Physiology of Versification* (1883), an exposition of his belief in a vital connection between the laws of versification and the laws of respiration and the pulse.

He was especially at home in the casual and discursive essay. In the "Autocrat" series (THE AUTOCRAT OF THE BREAKFAST TABLE, 1858; *The Professor at the Breakfast Table*, 1860; THE POET AT THE BREAKFAST TABLE, 1872; and *Over the Teacups*, 1891) he developed what was almost a genre of his own, one based largely on his fondness for dominating a conversation and his quick wit and gift of phrase. Holmes had the idea for the series early; the two "Autocrat" papers he contributed to the *New England Magazine* (November 1831, February 1832) are close in manner to the series more formally begun in the *Atlantic Monthly* in 1857. The papers mix verse and narrative, speculation and homily, and he was at his best in this peculiar amalgam of soliloquy, conversation, anecdote, epigram, and story. The topics are multifarious, just as they were in Holmes's conversation or in his popular lectures.

The Writings of Oliver Wendell Holmes, Riverside Edition (13 v. 1891–92) is standard. H. E. Scudder edited *The Complete Poetical Works* (1895), in one volume. Biographies include J. T. Morse, *Life and Letters of Oliver Wendell Holmes* (2 v. 1986); Eleanor M. Tilton, *Amiable Autocrat* (1947); and Edwin P. Hoyt, *The Improper Bostonian: Dr. Oliver Wendell Holmes* (1979).

Holmes, Oliver Wendell, Jr. (1841–1935), lawyer, jurist, Supreme Court Justice. Born in Boston, the younger Holmes had a deep pride in his New England background; nevertheless, he had to escape "the shadow of his father." Although Dr. Holmes accepted the new theories of physics and biology as presented in Darwinism, he argued eloquently against their extension into the realm of moral freedom and spirit. The younger Holmes welcomed that extension. The father called mechanical force "the Deity himself in action." The younger man regarded the conservation of energy as in no need of divine concurrence.

Before he completed his senior year at Harvard, Holmes enlisted in the Union army. He served for three years and was wounded three times, twice severely. He was lost to sight for a while, and the elder Holmes reported his adventures in search of him in "My Hunt After 'The Captain'" (*Atlantic Monthly*, November 1862). In *Touched with Fire* (1946) Mark DeWolfe Howe collected Holmes's war letters and his diary. These writings are marked by boyish enthusiasm mixed with the outburst of a man growing older.

Holmes began to practice law in Boston in 1867, on his return from the first of many trips to England, and began to teach at the Harvard Law School in 1870. His lectures on *The Common Law* (1881) became a classic. In the next year he was appointed to the Supreme Judicial Court and became chief justice in 1899. In 1902 he was appointed by President Theodore Roosevelt to the Supreme Court, and after a notable series of opinions and dissents was regarded as the leading exponent of law in Anglo-Saxon countries. He retired in 1932.

Holmes deeply impressed himself upon the law and greatly influenced political and economic conditions in the United States. He believed that the law was made for society, not society for the law; and that judges must not allow their own opin-

ions and prejudices to interfere with social changes, even if they know these changes are harmful. He held that the life of law was not logic but experience, that law was not an absolute but "what the courts will enforce," that the law "must found itself on actual forces," that "the first call of a theory of law is that it should fit the facts." It was an axiom of his that "certainty generally is an illusion, and repose is not the destiny of man." He said, "The best test of truth is the power of thought to get itself accepted in the market." "Our Constitution," he once explained, "is an experiment, as all life is an experiment," and he believed that courts must allow experimentation to continue.

It was customary after a while to call Holmes "the great dissenter," but some of his dissents shaped history. He was also regarded as a great liberal, although Holmes by no means abandoned his father's and his native region's orthodoxy in politics and economics. His dissents often had great influence, so that in time many of his views were accepted as good law, such as his pronouncements, always based on the Constitution, on the plenary power of Congress over commerce, on the taxing power of Congress, on the meaning of "police power," and on the provisions of the Bill of Rights.

In addition to *The Common Law* Holmes published in his own lifetime a small volume of *Speeches* (1891, rev. 1913) and *Collected Legal Papers* (1920). Mark DeWolfe Howe, in addition to his edition of the letters and diary mentioned above, edited the *Holmes-Pollock Letters: The Correspondence of Mr. Justice Holmes and Sir Frederick Pollock, 1874–1932* (2 v. 1941). In 1953 appeared *The Holmes-Laski Letters, 1916–1935*, a long-range debate between Holmes and Harold J. Laski in England. Some of Holmes's opinions as a judge appear in *The Dissenting Opinions of Mr. Justice Holmes* (1929), edited by Alfred Lief; *The Judicial Opinions of Oliver Wendell Holmes* (1940), edited by Harry C. Shriver; and Max Lerner's *The Mind and Faith of Justice Holmes* (1943). A Pulitzer Prize biography of him was Catherine Drinker Bowen's YANKEE FROM OLYMPUS (1944). Emmet Lavery's play, *The Magnificent Yankee* (1946), was also made into a movie (1951).

Holmes, William Henry (1846–1933), artist, geologist, anthropologist, government official. Holmes was a member of the staff of the U.S. Geological Survey, later was head curator of anthropology of the U.S. National Museum and chief of the Bureau of American Ethnology. In 1920 he became director of the National Gallery of Art. He was greatly interested in the aesthetic side of the ancient American cultures he studied. Among his publications are *Art in Shell of the Ancient Americans* (1883); *Ancient Art of the Province of Chiriqui, Colombia* (1888); *Archaeological Studies among the Ancient Cities of Mexico* (1895–97); and *Handbook of Aboriginal American Antiquities* (1919). *The Holmes Anniversary Volume* (1916) paid tribute to him on his 70th birthday.

Homage to Clio (1960), a volume of poetry by W. H. AUDEN. It consists of thirty poems, a prose interlude, and some humorous "academic graffiti," short verse pieces on such poets and philosophers as Blake, Kierkegaard, Marx, and Eliot.

Homage to Mistress Bradstreet (1956), a long poem by JOHN BERRYMAN. Its subject is the Puritan poetess ANNE BRADSTREET.

Home Burial. A dramatic poem by Robert Frost, originally published in *North of Boston* (1914), in which the alternating voices of a man and wife reveal how the death of their child has ruptured the marriage.

Home as Found (1838), a novel by JAMES FENIMORE COOPER. See HOMEWARD BOUND.

Home Journal, The. A weekly magazine founded in 1846 by N. P. WILLIS and G. P. MORRIS. It contained much miscellaneous material—verse, essays, gossip. Willis edited the magazine until his death in 1867. In 1901 the name of the magazine was changed to *Town and Country.*

Home on the Range. JOHN LOMAX first recorded this song in *Cowboy Songs* (1910), getting it from an African-American singer who had often made the trip up the Chisholm Trail. It seems likely that Dr. Brewster Higley and Daniel E. Kelley, both of Kansas, composed the words and music, possibly as early as 1873, under the title "My Western Home." It was published for the first time in the Kirwin (Kansas) *Chief*, March 21, 1874.

Homeward Bound, or, The Chase (1838), a novel by JAMES FENIMORE COOPER. In the same year he published a sequel, *Home as Found.* He made use in his narrative of a book by Capt. Judah Paddock, *A Narrative of the Shipwreck of the Ship "Oswego" on the Coast of South Barbary* (1818). For the most part *Homeward Bound* is an entertaining account of life on an ocean liner, with social distinctions among the passengers and with a captain competent as a mariner and social arbiter. In *Home as Found* the leading characters of the earlier book, themselves descendants of Judge Temple of THE PIONEERS, come to grips with Cooper's theme—American manners. Much of the plot is devoted, in fictional guise, to some of Cooper's personal controversies; Edward Effingham is obviously a self-portrait. The book is severely critical of American dress, social intercourse, men of letters, businessmen, lawyers, and America itself. A contemporary review by William Gilmore Simms regretted the querulous tone of the book. Another critic, Thurlow Weed, called it "a skinning alive"; Cooper sued him for libel.

Hone, Philip (1780–1851), merchant, public official, diarist. Hone, born in New York City and an ardent Whig and sturdy defender of American ideas and institutions, became mayor of New York (1825) and was a friend of most of the prominent persons of his day. From 1828 until his death he kept a diary in which he recorded details of the social and cultural life of the times. The manuscript (twenty-eight quarto volumes) is in the New York Historical Society Library. Parts of it have been pubished in books by Bayard Tuckerman (1889), Allan Nevins (1927), and Louis Auchincloss (1989).

Honest John Vane (1875), a novel by J. W. DE FOREST. The title is ironical for the work is a realistic attack on inefficiency and corruption in national politics. The chief character is a dishonest congressman who nevertheless manages to get himself reelected.

Honey in the Horn (1935), a novel by HAROLD L. DAVIS. A realistic narrative of life among the pioneers of early Oregon, it won a Pulitzer Prize and debunked many popular notions of frontier gallantry.

Hongo, Garrett Kaoru (1951–), poet, memorist, anthologist. Born in Hawaii of Japanese ancestry, Hongo grew up in California, graduated from Pomona College (B.A., 1973) and studied at the University of Michigan (1974–1975) and the University of California, Irvine (M.F.A., 1980). Founder and director of the Seattle theater group Asian Exclusion Act (1975-1977), he produced plays by Frank Chin and Wakako Yamauchi as well as one of his own, "Nisei Bar and Grill." He taught at various universities in California and Texas before returning to the Northwest in 1989 to teach creative writing at the University of Oregon. *Yellow Light* (1982) includes his best early poetry. *The River of Heaven* (1988) won the Lamont Poetry Prize, was nominated for a Pulitzer Prize, and led to Guggenheim and Rockerfeller Foundation fellowships. Sometimes compared to Whitman in his repetitions, catalogs, anecdotes, and first-person perspective, but writing of the Asian-American experience, he proclaims himself "committed to a task of enlightenment." *Volcano: A Memoir of Hawaii* (1995) is a prose evocation of his family's past in Hawaii and California. He has edited *The Open Boat: Poems from Asian America* (1993); *Songs My Mother Taught Me: Stories, Plays, and Memoir*, by Wakako Yamauchi (1994); and *Under Western Eyes: Personal Essays from Asian America* (1995), with contributions from AMY TAN and CHANG-RAE LEE.

Honorable Peter Stirling, The (1894), a novel by PAUL LEICESTER FORD. A portrait of an honest and fearless politician, it enjoyed a great vogue in its time, partly because readers believed that Stirling was modeled on Grover Cleveland. This was denied by Ford.

Hood, Hugh [John] (1928–), short-story writer, novelist. Born in Toronto and educated at the University of Toronto, Hood taught at the University of Montreal. His story collections include *Flying a Red Kite* (1962); *Around the Mountain: Scenes from Montreal Life* (1967); *The Fruit Man, the Meat Man and the Manager* (1971); *Dark Glasses* (1976); *Selected Stories* (1978); *Not Genuine Without This Signature* (1980); *August Nights* (1985); and *You'll Catch Your Death* (1992). Among his novels are a projected *New Age/Le Nouveau Siècle* series of twelve books. These include: *The Swing in the Garden* (1975); *A New Athens* (1977); *Reservoir Ravine* (1979); *Black and White Keys* (1982); *The Scenic Art* (1984); *The Motor Boys in Ottawa* (1986); *Tony's Book* (1988); *Property and Value* (1990); *Be Sure to Close Your Eyes* (1993) and *Dead Men's Watches* (1995). They are narrated by Matthew Goderich, whose family history back to the 1880s is drawn upon in stories of Toronto from the 1930s to the present. Novels outside the series illustrate Hood's ability to describe the technical aspects and inner workings of various occupations. *White Figure, White Ground* (1964) details the life of a painter; *The Camera Always Lies* (1967), an actress; *A Game of Touch* (1970), a cartoonist; and *You Can't Get There from Here* (1972), multinational business.

Hood, John Bell (1831–1879),   soldier. Born in Kentucky, Hood fought with the Army of Northern Virginia at Gettysburg and lost a leg at Chickamauga. His army was virtually obliterated at Nashville by General George H. Thomas, the "Rock of Chickamauga" (December 1864), and Hood surrendered at Natchez, Mississippi, in May 1865. His well-titled memoir, *Advance and Retreat* (1879), is one of the most memorable books to come out of the Civil War.

Hooker, [William] Brian (1880–1946),   song writer, opera librettist, translator, novelist. Hooker was born in New York City. His greatest success was a translation of Edmond Rostand's *Cyrano de Bergerac*, made in 1923, produced on Broadway and made into a movie. Hooker collaborated with Horatio Parker on *Mona* (1911) and *Fairyland* (1915). He published a collection of *Poems* (1915). *White Bird* (1924) was another opera. Hooker and W.H. Post wrote the book and lyrics for Rudolf Friml's musical version (1925) of Justin H. McCarthy's novel *If I Were King* (1901). It was called *The Vagabond King*. Among Hooker's lyrics were "Song of the Vagabonds" and "Only a Rose." *White Eagle* (1927) was a musical version of Edwin Milton Royle's THE SQUAW MAN (1905), for which Hooker supplied the book and lyrics, as he did for *Through the Years* (1932), based on A.L. Martin's *Smilin' Through* (1919).

Hooker, Thomas (1586–1647),   Congregational clergyman, author of treatises on religion and government. Hooker, born in England, asserted the freedom of individuals to make their own decisions in politics and religion. He sought the abolition of all property and religious tests for the vote, contending that "the foundation of authority is laid . . . in the free consent of the people," and brought about (1643) a defensive organization of "United Colonies of New England" that prefigured the United States.

Hooker was educated at Cambridge and held doctrines so strongly opposed to those of Archbishop Laud that Laud planned to silence him. Hooker fled to Holland, where he remained for three years until his former congregation could emigrate to Newtown (later Cambridge), Massachusetts, and settle there. Later he and his congregation moved to Connecticut and founded Hartford, not without opposition from an autocratic governor. He has been called perhaps "the most powerful pulpit orator among the ministers of New England." Under his guidance there were adopted by the General Assembly at Hartford on January 14, 1639, certain "Fundamental Orders," which have been called "the first written constitution of modern democracy." At the behest of fellow ministers he undertook, with JOHN COTTON, a *Survey of the Sum of Church Discipline* (1648), a strong defense of the New England Congregational way against the criticisms of English Presbyterians.

Other compositions have come down to us only from the shorthand notes of admiring listeners. Among them are *The Poor Doubting Christian* (1629), *The Equal Ways of God* (1632), *The Soul's Exaltation* (1638), *Four Godly and Learned Treatises* (1638), *The Saint's Guide* (1645), *The Saint's Dignity and Duty* (1651), and *The Application of Redemption* (1656).

Hooper, Ellen [Sturgis] (1812?–1848),   poet. Hooper's fame is based largely on a six-line untitled poem that appeared in the first issue of *The Dial* (July 1840) with the opening lines: "I slept, and dreamed that life was Beauty;/ I woke, and found that life was Duty." Hooper also wrote some hymns.

Hooper, Johnson Jones (1815–1862),   humorist, newspaperman, lawyer, public official. Hooper drifted from his native North Carolina to Alabama and became identified with that state. He established the Montgomery *Mail* in the 1850s and edited it until 1861. His reputation as a humorist was founded chiefly on his account of *Some Adventures of Captain Simon Suggs, Late of the Tallapoosa Volunteers* (1846). Simon was depicted as an unmitigated rascal with the guiding principle: "It is good to be shifty in a new country." The rowdy and uninhibited tales Johnson told about Simon ridiculed many institutions and folkways of the South. Of similar character was *The Widow Rugby's Husband and Other Tales of Alabama* (1851). When war broke out Hooper became secretary of the Provisional Congress of the Southern States.

Hoosier.   The word means "Indianan" and may be applied to a resident, to locutions or pronunciations, to customs, vocations, etc., and Indiana is the Hoosier state. On January 3, 1832, the word was used in a carrier's poem, that is, a poem addressed to readers of the paper by newsboys, in the *Indiana Democrat*.

The derivation of the term is unknown. Some think it means "husher" and is connected with "whoosher," others that it is a corruption of "hussar." Still others believe it comes from a greeting, "Who's yere?"

Hoosier School.   About 1900 so many writers born in Indiana were active in the literary world that the term Hoosier School was given to them. These writers included EDWARD EGGLESTON, GEORGE CARY EGGLESTON, JAMES WHITCOMB RILEY, GEORGE ADE, THEODORE DREISER, JOHN JAMES PIATT, JAMES MAURICE THOMPSON, and BOOTH TARKINGTON. MEREDITH NICHOLSON discussed the Hoosier School in *The Hoosiers* (1900).

Hoosier Schoolmaster, The (1871),   a novel by EDWARD EGGLESTON. This was probably based in part on the experiences of Eggleston's brother George. It tells of a young man who takes a job in a one-man school and soon discovers that his success will depend more on muscle than on book learning. He manages to win the friendship of the worst bully in the school and gets along well. Boarding around in the neighborhood, he meets people of many kinds, falls in love, finds himself suspected of being an ally of some night riders, and has other entertaining adventures. Well-known scenes in the book are the spelling bee and the trial scene. The book has a strong religious undercurrent and exhibits Eggleston's interest in Indianan dialect. The story was first published in serial form in *Hearth and Home*, of which Eggleston was editor, and boosted its circulation fourfold; it was widely pirated all over the world. Eggleston wrote the book partly as a protest against the preoccupation of contemporary writers with New England; and he found inspiration in the axiom of the French critic Hippolyte Taine (1828–1893) that "the artist of originality will work courageously with the materials he finds in his own environment."

Hopalong Cassidy.   See CASSIDY, HOPALONG.

Hopedale Community.   A Christian Socialist settlement founded by ADIN BALLOU in 1841 near Milford, Massachusetts. Based on individual freedom—including women's rights, social responsibility and religious tolerance—it prohibited unchastity, intoxicating beverages, slavery, war, capital punishment, and personal violence. At its peak of prosperity in the early 1850s, Hopedale had over two hundred members, but an attempt to found a second colony in Minnesota (1854) was unsuccessful. The entire experiment had failed by the end of the decade.

Hope, Laura Lee.   See THE BOBBSEY TWINS.

Hope Leslie (2 v. 1827),   a novel by CATHARINE MARIA SEDGWICK. It is a story of the Pequod War in Massachusetts, about 1636, and Governor Winthrop and Thomas Morton are among the historical characters. At the same time it portrays the character and grievances of the disappearing Indians, and the men and manners of the 17th century.

Hopi Indians.   A part of the Uto-Aztecan linguistic family and Pueblo group of Native Americans, resident from before the 15th century in northeastern Arizona. Their religion, based on deep devotion to nature, includes such rituals as the Snake Dance, in which rattlesnakes are clasped in the dancer's arms and in his mouth as he dances to evoke the precious rain. *Kachinas*, supernatural beings who live in the neighboring mountains, are represented by masked dancers and small wooden dolls. An intimate view of the Hopi way of thinking is found in *Sun Chief, the Autobiography of a Hopi Indian*, edited by Leo W. Simmons (1942). Other as-told-to autobiographies include Louise Udall, *Me and Mine: The Life Story of Helen Sekaquaptewa* (1969), and Harold Courlander, *Big Falling Snow: A Tewa-Hopi Indian's Life and Times* (1978). A sympathetic portrayal of the Hopis is Walter C. O'Kane's *Sun in the Sky* (1950). They appear imaginatively in Edna Dean Proctor's *Song of an Ancient People* (1892), Willa Cather's DEATH COMES FOR THE ARCHBISHOP (1927), Dame Margaret Smith's *Hopi Girl* (1931), and the novels of TONY HILLERMAN.

Hopkins, Lemuel (1750–1801),   physician, poet, satirist. Hopkins, born in Connecticut, was an eminent physician whose own tendency toward tuberculosis led him to the study of medicine. One of the founders of the Connecticut Medical Society, he practiced in Hartford, became intimate with the group of literary men called the HARTFORD WITS, and contributed satiric verses to some of their enterprises—THE ANARCHIAD (1786–87), THE ECHO (1791–1805), and THE POLITICAL GREENHOUSE (1798). Among his separate writings were *The Democratiad* (1795), *The Guillotina, or A Democratic Dirge* (1796), and numerous short poems; his works have not yet been collected.

Hopkins, Pauline (1859–1930),   novelist. In *Contending Forces* (1900), Hopkins links pre–Civil War violence in the Caribbean and the South to racial oppression at the turn of the century with a chronicle of several generations of an African-American family. Her romance *Winona: A Tale of Negro Life in the South and the Southwest* was serialized in the *Colored American Magazine* in 1901.

Hopkins, Samuel (1721–1803),   clergyman, author of books on theology. Born in Connecticut, Hopkins lived austerely, showed constant unselfishness, freed his slaves, and wrote on theology. He was a disciple of JONATHAN EDWARDS in whose home he lived for several years. Among the best of his writings were those directed against slavery, *A Dialogue Concerning the Slavery of the Africans* (1776) and *A Discourse upon the Slave Trade* (1793). Widely read was his book on *A System of Doctrines Contained in Divine Revelation Explained and Defended* (1793). His theology was expounded most definitively in the posthumous *Dialogue Between a Semi-Calvinist and a Calvinist* (1805), in which the true believer is willing "to be damned for the glory of God." His *Works*, edited by Sewall Harding in three volumes, appeared in 1854.

Hopkins, Sarah Winnemucca (1844?–1891),   lecturer, historian. A descendant of Paiute chiefs, Hopkins was born in Nevada. Fluent in English from childhood, she acted as a liaison between her people and the white settlers. She made a tour of the East in 1879, giving over three hundred lectures to protest federal policy toward Native Americans. *Life Among the Piutes: Their Wrongs and Claims* (1883) was a further attempt to influence white attitudes. She founded a school for Paiute children on her brother's farm, but financial failure and her own ill health brought it to an end in 1887.

Hopkins, Stephen (1707–1785),   governor, pamphleteer. Hopkins was governor of Rhode Island, his native state, from 1755 to 1768; a member of the Continental Congress (1774–1776); and a signer of the Declaration of Independence. He wrote a pamphlet, *The Rights of Colonies Examined* (1765), which investigated the origin and nature of law, rejected the claims of parliamentary authority over the colonies, and claimed for them as "much freedom as the mother state from which they went out." See MARTIN HOWARD.

Hopkinson, Francis (1737–1791),   lawyer, signer of the Declaration of Independence, musician, writer. Born In Philadelphia, Hopkinson is said to have been the first student of the Academy of Philadelphia, later the University of Pennsylvania. He was an eminent lawyer, later a Federal judge. He was also an excellent musician and claimed to have been the first native American to produce a musical composition. Among his later works was *The Temple of Minerva* (1781), a "dramatic allegorical cantata." He also published some pieces for the harpsichord.

Hopkinson was deeply involved in the Revolution and was a member of the first CONTINENTAL CONGRESS. He wrote prose and verse assiduously in the cause of the colonies. Perhaps his best-known piece was the BATTLE OF THE KEGS (1778). In the same cause he wrote A PRETTY STORY (1774), *A Political Catechism* (1777), and a *Letter to Joseph Galloway* (1778). In addition to his other accomplishments Hopkinson was an artist; he designed the state seal of New Jersey and helped design the American flag. He prepared a collection of his works, *The Miscellaneous Essays and Occasional Writings of Francis Hopkinson* (3 v. 1792), but many of his writings are available only in their original periodical or manuscript forms. (See also LIBERTY'S CALL.) His son, **Joseph Hopkinson** (1770–1842), also was a lawyer and judge, served in Congress, took an active part in community life, and wrote a celebrated patriotic song, HAIL COLUMBIA (1798).

Hopscotch.   Title of the English translation (1966) by Gregory Rabassa of *Rayuela* (1963), a novel by JULIO CORTAZAR. Oliveira, an Argentine intellectual, leads a bohemian existence in the boulevards and attics of Paris. Two accidents change his life: falling in love with la Maga, a childlike woman, and finding the manuscripts of the revered Morelli. Tired of Oliveira's pretended irresponsibility, la Maga leaves him. He returns to Buenos Aires, where eventually his games of alienation lead to madness, although the reader may choose to believe that, in his room in the insane asylum, he alone has found the window that opens onto the beyond. The story is narrated in jarring segments interspersed, in a sort of hopscotch, with Morelli's ironic reflections on the death of the contemporary novel.

Hopwood, Avery (1882–1928),   newspaperman, playwright. Born in Cleveland, Hopwood wrote *Clothes* (1906) in collaboration with CHANNING POLLOCK. Its success led him to a career on the stage in the course of which he wrote many farces and mystery plays. The best known of his farces are *The Gold-Diggers* (1919), *The Demi-Virgin* (1921), *Getting Gertie's Garter* (with Wilson Collison, 1921), and *Why Men Leave Home* (1922). His mystery melodrama THE BAT was written with MARY ROBERTS RINEHART (1920). After his death his mother established the Hopwood Literature Prizes at the University of Michigan, Hopwood's alma mater. These cash prizes have been awarded to promising students since 1931, and are among the most prestigious given by any university.

Horgan, Paul (1903–1995),   librarian, historian, novelist. Horgan was born in Buffalo, New York, but much of his literary work centers in New Mexico. He won the Harper Novel Prize in 1933 with *The Fault of Angels*. Among his other works are *Men of Arms* (1931); *From the Royal City* (1934); *No Quarter Given* (1935); *Main Line West* (1936); *New Mexico's Own Chronicle* (with M.G. Fulton, 1937); *Far from Cibola* (1938); *Habit of Empire* (1938); *A Tree on the Plains* (an opera, 1942, music by Ernst Bacon); and a biographical introduction to *Diary and Letters of Josiah Gregg* (2 v. 1941–44). One of his major books is *Great River: The Rio Grande in North American History* (2 v. 1954), for which he won a Pulitzer Prize. It was followed by *The Centuries of Santa Fe* (1956); *A Distant Trumpet* (1960), a novel about Apache wars in the 1880s; *Citizen of New Salem* (1961); *Whitewater* (1970), a novel; and *Mexico Bay* (1982), a novel about a writer attempting a history of the Mexican War.

Horgan's strong religious belief is seen in such novels as *The Saintmaker's Christmas* (1955) and *Give Me Possession* (1957)

and in the nonfiction *Lamy of Santa Fe* (1975; Pulitzer prize), a biography of Father Jean Baptiste Lamy. The related "Richard" novels, including *Things As They Are* (1964), *Everything to Live For* (1968), and *The Thin Mountain Air* (1977), trace a life from boyhood to manhood. *Of America East & West* (1984) is a collection of essays from earlier works.

Horizon (prod. 1871, pub. 1885),   a play by AUGUSTIN DALY. It deals with an American army post at the frontier, introducing a West Pointer as the hero and including among its characters a girl who is loved by a gambler, an Indian chief, and the officer.

Horse-Shoe Robinson (1835),   a novel by J.P. KENNEDY. Using James Fenimore Cooper as a model, Kennedy wrote this historical romance of the South in the period of the American Revolution. The hero and the heroine favor the Revolution, but the young woman's father is a Tory. The most engaging character is Robinson himself—a hearty, salty, uninhibited old campaigner. The novel became popular immediately, won the praise of Irving and Poe, and continued a favorite for several decades.

Horton, George Moses (1798?–1880?),   poet. A slave in the area of Chapel Hill, North Carolina, Horton was a ghost writer of love poetry for college students. He published three collections of verse, including *Naked Genius* (1865).

Hosmer, William Howe Cuyler (1814–1877), lawyer, poet, historian. Born in Avon, New York, Hosmer became acquainted with the Indians of western New York, Wisconsin, and Florida and wrote sympathetically about them in prose and verse. Among his books are *The Pioneers of Western New York* (1838); *The Themes of Song* (1842); *Yonnondido, or, Warriors of the Genesee* (1844); *Bird Notes* (1850); *Legends of the Senecas* (1850); *Poetical Works* (1854); and *Later Lays and Lyrics* (1873).

Hospital Sketches (1863),   memoirs of LOUISA MAY ALCOTT's experiences as a nurse in Washington during the Civil War. The book won her wide recognition as a writer of power and promise, and earned for her the money for a trip to Europe.

Hostos, Eugenio María de (1839–1903),   Puerto Rican educator and man of letters. Hostos was educated in Spain, where he wrote *La peregrinación de Bayoán* (1863), a political novel, and fought for the short-lived republic of 1868. His hopes that Puerto Rico might be granted autonomy with Santo Domingo and Cuba in a confederation of the Antilles were dashed by the imperialist attitude of the Spanish republicans. Hostos is remembered not only as a patriot, but also as an enlightened teacher, dedicated to progress and truth. His best-known work, *Moral social* (1888), is a guide to ethical social conduct, which was designed as a school text. He also wrote an excellent essay (1872) on *Hamlet*.

Hotel New Hampshire (1981),   a novel by JOHN IRVING. The chronicle of a large family who experience violence from rural New Hampshire to Vienna.

Hot Ploughshares (1883),   a novel by ALBION W. TOURGÉE. The story, laid in the Reconstruction period, was one of the earliest to employ the miscegenation theme. The heroine is believed to be part African-American and has considerable difficulty in disproving this, but finally marries the hero.

Hough, Emerson (1857–1923),   teacher, newspaperman, lawyer, novelist. Hough, born in Iowa, did not care for teaching or the law and he gave them up for what he called "outdoor journalism." His first successful book was *The Story of the Cowboy* (1897), but it was not until he published a novel, *The Mississippi Bubble* (1902), that he was able to rely on writing for his livelihood. *The Law of the Land* (1904) followed, then four volumes of The Young Alaskans series (1910–18), *The Magnificent Adventure* (1916), *The Man Next Door* (1917), and other novels. His greatest success came in 1922 with *The Covered Wagon*, an exciting story with carefully studied historical background. *North of Thirty-Six* (1923) was also popular. Hough wrote his recollections of the Old West in *The Passing of the Frontier* (1923). *The Covered Wagon* has often been reprinted and was made into a movie in the year of its publication.

Hough, Henry Beetle (1896–1985),   public relations counselor, editor, publisher. Born in Massachusetts, Hough with his wife, Elizabeth Wilson Hough, in 1920 took over publication of the *Vineyard Gazette* at Edgartown, Martha's Vineyard. His best books, particularly *Country Editor* (1940) and *Once More the Thunder* (1950), deal with his experiences as an editor. He also wrote *Martha's Vineyard, Summer Resort* (1936), *Thoreau of Walden* (1956); *The New England Story* (1956), *Lament for a City* (1960), and several novels—*That Lofty Sky* (1941), *All Things Are Yours* (1942), *Roosters Crow in Town* (1945), *Long Anchorage* (1947), and *Singing in the Morning* (1951).

Hound and Horn.   A little magazine, published from 1927 to 1934, cofounded and edited by Lincoln Kirstein. R. P. Blackmur and Yvor Winters were also involved editorially. It printed work by Katherine Anne Porter, Gertrude Stein, T. S. Eliot, and Ezra Pound, whose verse "The White Stag" provided its title. *The "Hound and Horn" Letters* (1982) provides material about editors and contributors.

House, Edward Mandell (1858–1938),   historian, novelist. Born in Texas, House helped elect Woodrow Wilson and served him as an advisor. His anonymous novel *Philip Dru, Administrator: A Story of Tomorrow, 1920–1935* (1912) proposed governmental reforms. *The Intimate Papers of Colonel House* (4 v., 1926–1928) are a valuable source of information about American policy during World War I.

House by the Side of the Road, The.   A poem by SAM WALTER FOSS, included in his collection *Dreams in Homespun* (1897). Two lines have become a permanent part of the American memory: "Let me live in my house by the side of the road/And be a friend of man."

House of Mirth, The (1905),   a novel by EDITH WHARTON. This classic story satirizes the high society of New York Wharton knew so well. LILY BART is a poor relation who endeavors to secure a wealthy husband, becomes involved with a man who tries to blackmail her, is falsely accused of an intrigue with another woman's husband, retires from the vain

contest and becomes a milliner, and commits suicide just as the man she loves arrives with an offer of marriage. The book is a vivid picture of social life in New York in the days of the hansom cab. Clyde Fitch turned the novel into a play (1906), considerably altering the plot.

House of Night, The (1779, 1786),   a poem by PHILIP FRENEAU. The poem, which runs to 136 quatrains, belongs to the so-called Graveyard School of poetry, and is an allegory on death.

House of the Seven Gables, The (1851),   a novel by NATHANIEL HAWTHORNE. The story focuses on the house itself and on actions that took place in the past and have consequences in the present. The house, two centuries old by the time the story begins, was built on land fraudulently obtained by the ancestral Pyncheon from an ancestral Maule, whom Pyncheon caused to be executed for witchcraft. Maule's dying curse on the Pyncheon family continues to be effective through several generations, and the last surviving Pyncheons are still under its influence as the story opens.

Hepzibah Pyncheon, an old maid, and her brother Clifford are chained to the house, their link with the family and the past, and view the outside world only through closed windows and curtains. Clifford, a sensitive but ineffective man, has just returned from jail, where he spent thirty years for the supposed murder of his uncle, and Hepzibah is forced to open a shop to support her brother and herself. Their cousin, Judge Jaffrey Pyncheon, the last affluent member of the family, dies as the last victim of the curse and is revealed to be the man who wrongfully sent Clifford to prison and cheated him of his inheritance. Phoebe Pyncheon, a young and pretty country cousin, is saved from the curse by having been raised away from the house and its taints. Holgrave, the boarder, is revealed to be a descendant of the executed Maule, and proves himself worthy of Phoebe when he refuses to exert mesmeric power over her, as one of his ancestors had done to enslave an earlier Pyncheon. Thus, one member of each family is raised above the curse and manages to find love.

House of Usher, The Fall of the.   See FALL OF THE HOUSE OF USHER.

Houston, James D. (1933–   ),   nonfiction writer, novelist, short-story writer. Born in San Francisco, Houston was educated at San Jose State College (B.A., 1956), served in the U.S. Air Force (1957–1960), won an Air Force short-story contest, and pursued graduate work at Stanford University (M.A., 1962). Among his most acclaimed books are *Farewell to Manzanar: A True Story of Japanese American Experience during and after the World War II Internment* (1973), written with his wife, **Jeanne Wakatsuki Houston;** and *Californians: Searching for the Golden State* (1982), a travel narrative with interviews. Novels include *Between Battles* (1968), *Gig* (1969), *A Native Son of the Golden West* (1971), *Continental Drift* (1978), and *Love Life* (1985). *Gasoline: The Automotive Adventures of Charlie Bates* (1980) collects short stories.

Houston, Jeanne Wakatsuki (1934–   ),   memoirist. Houston and her husband, **James Houston** (1933–   ), wrote a powerful memoir of her Japanese-American family's forced removal to an internment camp during World War II. *Farewell to Manzanar* (1973) tells, through the eyes of a child, about the hardships and effects.

Hovey, Richard (1864–1900),   poet, dramatist. Born in Illinois, Hovey was educated at Dartmouth. In 1891 he published *Launcelot and Guenevere: A Poem in Dramas*, and went to England and France. He met Mallarmé and became interested in symbolism, which he thought held the key to a proper synthesis of realism and idealism. He was attracted also to Maurice Maeterlinck and translated eight of his plays into English.

In 1892 Hovey went to Nova Scotia and New Brunswick with his friend BLISS CARMAN. There they wrote SONGS FROM VAGABONDIA (1894), *More Songs from Vagabondia* (1896), and *Last Songs from Vagabondia* (published after Hovey's death in 1901). In 1893 appeared *Seaward*, an elegy on the death of the poet and translator THOMAS WILLIAM PARSONS; in 1898 *Along the Trail* was published, and in 1900 *Takesin, A Masque to the End of the Trail* (1908) was a posthumous collection of verse. Best remembered of Hovey's poems are "Men of Dartmouth," "Eleazar Wheelock," and "Stein Song."

Howadji, The.   Pen name of G. W. CURTIS.

How Annandale Went Out (1910),   a sonnet by EDWIN ARLINGTON ROBINSON. In its fourteen lines Robinson presents a drama of the conscience. A physician is called upon to attend a dying friend, a wreck of a man with "hell between him and the end." He uses "a slight kind of engine" (a hypodermic?) and puts him out of his misery. This vivid anecdote was one of the earliest realistic poems of the new poetic era to which Robinson belonged.

Howard, Bronson [Crocker] (1842–1908),   newspaperman, playwright. Born in Detroit, Howard founded the American Dramatists' Club (later the Society of American Dramatists and Composers), and was an active worker in the cause of international copyright. He won his first success with the farce *Saratoga* (1870). In general his plays deal with American upper classes. Among his successes were THE BANKER'S DAUGHTER (1878), *Young Mrs. Winthrop* (1882), *One of Our Girls* (1885), *The Henrietta* (1887), SHENANDOAH (1888), and *Aristocracy* (1892). He produced an interesting analysis of his craft in *The Autobiography of a Play* (1914).

Howard, George [Fitzalan] Bronson (1884–1922), newspaperman, novelist, playwright. Howard was born in Maryland and his best book is the novel *God's Man* (1915), a scarcely veiled attack on a New York City magistrate named Joseph Corrigan. He also wrote *Birds of Prey* (1918) and *The Black Book* (1920). Among his plays were *The Snobs* (1911) and *The Alien* (with Eric Howard, 1927).

Howard, Martin (?–1781),   lawyer, Loyalist, writer. A Newport, Rhode Island, lawyer, he wrote the pamphlet *A Letter from a Gentleman of Halifax, to His Friend in Rhode Island* (1765), a reply to *The Rights of Colonies Examined* (1765), by Governor STEPHEN HOPKINS of Rhode Island. Howard argued that if Parliament had given the colonies certain rights, Parliament could take them away. His pamphlet was answered by Hopkins and by JAMES OTIS, Howard retorting with a *Defense*

(1765). A mob burned Howard in effigy at Newport and he fled to England.

Howard, Oliver Otis (1830–1909),   soldier, government official. General Howard served as director of the Freedman's Bureau and negotiator with Native Americans in the Southwest. In 1872 he concluded a treaty with the Chiricahua Apache chief Cochise, but the peace was brief. He wrote a two-volume *Autobiography* (1907) and *My Life and Experiences Among Our Hostile Indians* (1907).

Howard, Richard (1929–   ),   poet, critic, translator. Howard was born in Cleveland and educated at Columbia and the Sorbonne. Poetry editor of *The Paris Review* and a Chancellor of the Academy of American Poets, he is known for translations of Gide, Genet, Robbe-Grillet, and many others, and for elaborate controlled, learned, and witty verse, often in the form of dramatic monologues. *Untitled Subjects* (1966), a series of fifteen dramatic monologues, won the Pulitzer Prize. *Two Part Inventions* (1974), *Fellow Feelings: Poems* (1976), *Misgivings* (1979), *Lining Up* (1984), and *No Traveller* (1986) are other collections. *Trappings: New Poems* (1999) displays him at the height of his form. *Second Growth* (1967) and *Alone with America* (1969, rev. 1980) are critical works on contemporary poetry.

Howard, Sidney [Coe] (1891–1939),   playwright. Howard, born in California, was a member of G. P. BAKER's 47 Workshop at Harvard. He began with an effort in blank verse, *Swords* (1921), went on to adaptations from foreign plays, and then to collaboration with EDWARD SHELDON in *Bewitched* (1924). His first original play to attract wide attention was *They Knew What They Wanted* (1924), which won a Pulitzer Prize with its depiction of an aging Napa Valley vintner who marries a mail-order wife and later magnanimously condones her brief infidelity. *The Most Happy Fella* (1957) is a musical version of this play. Howard went from one success to another. Perhaps the best of his plays are THE SILVER CORD (1926), a study of maternal possessiveness; and *Yellow Jack* (with Paul de Kruif, 1934), a documentary that tells with dramatic effectiveness how the army conquered yellow fever. He also wrote *Lucky Sam McCarver* (1925); *Ned McCobb's Daughter* (1926); *Salvation* (with CHARLES MACARTHUR, (1928); *Lute Song* (with WILL IRWIN, 1930); *The Late Christopher Bean* (an adaptation from the French of René Fauchois, 1932); and DODSWORTH (with Sinclair Lewis, 1934).

Howe, E[dgar] W[atson] ["The Sage of Potato Hill"] (1853–1937),   newspaperman, editor, novelist, aphorist, memoirist. Howe was always primarily the newspaperman and small-town editor. He owned and edited the Atchison (Kansas) *Daily Globe* (1877–1911), later started *E. W. Howe's Monthly* (1911–37). In 1883, after numerous rejections, his best novel, THE STORY OF A COUNTRY TOWN, appeared. *Plain People* (1929) was Howe's autobiography, but he was best known for various collections of his editorials and aphorisms—*Lay Sermons* (1911), *Ventures in Common Sense* (1919), and *The Indignations of E. W. Howe* (1933).

Howe, Helen (1905–1975),   monologist, novelist. Born in Boston, Howe made solo appearances in army and navy hospitals, New York and London theaters, and night clubs. Her literary reputation is based on her satiric novels about the foibles of New York, New England, and Hollywood society. They include *The Whole Heart* (1943), *We Happy Few* (1946), *The Circle of the Day* (1950), *The Success* (1956), and *Fires of Autumn* (1959).

Howe, Irving (1920–1993),   literary critic, social historian, educator. In addition to his critical works, *Sherwood Anderson: A Critical Biography* (1951) and *William Faulkner: A Critical Study* (1953), he wrote *The UAW and Walter Reuther* (1949, with B. J. Widick) and *The American Communist Party: A Critical History* (1957, with Lewis Coser). Howe contributed articles and reviews on literary and political subjects to magazines like PARTISAN REVIEW. He demonstrated his ability to synthesize his social and literary interests in *Politics and the Novel* (1957), a book of essays on Stendhal, Dostoevsky, Conrad, Turgenev, Hawthorne, Henry James, Henry Adams, Malraux, Silone, and Orwell. The book is concerned not with defining the political novel, but with examining what happens to novels that deal with politics—how they may be ruined by ideology or made truly significant by dealing with it. With Eliezer Greenberg, Howe edited *A Treasury of Yiddish Stories* (1955) and *A Treasury of Yiddish Poetry* (1969). Howe's other works are *World of Our Fathers* (1976), a highly praised and widely read social and intellectual history of New York City Jewish life; *Socialism and America* (1985); and *A Margin of Hope: An Intellectual Autobiography* (1982).

Howe, Julia Ward (1819–1910),   poet, dramatist, writer of travel books, biographer, memoirist. Born in New York City, Julia Ward in 1843 married a noted humanitarian and teacher of the blind, SAMUEL GRIDLEY HOWE, and soon came to know many of New England's distinguished men and women and formed a cultural link between New York and Boston. After her husband's death she continued his work and lectured on woman suffrage, prison reform, and international peace. She was an excellent linguist and a passionate lover of music. Among her writings were several collections of verse: *Passion Flowers* (1854), *Words for the Hour* (1857), *Later Lyrics* (1866), and *From Sunset Ridge: Poems Old and New* (1898). She also wrote *A Trip to Cuba* (1860), *Sex and Education* (ed. 1874), *Memoir of Samuel Gridley Howe* (1876), *Modern Society* (1881), *Reminiscences* (1899), and *At Sunset* (1910). Many of her letters appear in the Pulitzer Prize–winning biography of her prepared (2 v. 1915) by her two daughters, LAURA E. RICHARDS and Maud Ward Howe. Howe is chiefly remembered for the BATTLE HYMN OF THE REPUBLIC, written December 1861 to a Civil War soldiers' tune, published in the *Atlantic Monthly* (February 1862), and included in her *Later Lyrics*. She appears in Louise Hall Tharp's book *Three Saints and a Sinner* (1956).

Howe, M[ark] A[ntony] DeWolfe (1864–1960), biographer, historian, editor, poet. Howe worked on the staffs of *Youth's Companion*, the *Atlantic Monthly*, the *Harvard Alumni Bulletin*, and the *Harvard Graduates' Magazine*, and served as vice president of the Atlantic Monthly. He was an active author well into his nineties.

Howe's books have a wide range, but he was preeminent in biography. He wrote lives of Phillips Brooks (1899); George Bancroft (1908); Bishop Hare, apostle to the Sioux (1911); Charles Eliot Norton (1913); Mrs. James T. Fields (1922); Barrett Wendell (1924, a Pulitzer Prize book); James Ford Rhodes (1929); John Jay Chapman (1937); and Oliver Wendell Holmes (1939). Howe also edited the letters of many of these figures. He wrote about Boston (1903, 1910) and about *The Atlantic Monthly and Its Makers* (1919), edited the "Beacon Biographies" (31 v. 1899–1910), wrote and published six volumes of verse, the last—*Sundown*—when he was ninety-two.

Howe, Samuel Gridley (1801–1876),   physician, teacher, crusader, welfare worker. Howe was the husband of JULIA WARD HOWE and a noted teacher of the blind. He trained the blind deaf-mute girl Laura Bridgman (1829–1889) by means of raised type he had devised and by other methods that later also proved successful with Helen Keller. He was interested in helping other handicapped persons as well and was active in antislavery movements, with his wife founding an abolitionist paper, *The Commonwealth*. He interested himself in the cause of various groups in revolt against the Turks. He prepared manuals for the blind and wrote a *Historical Sketch of the Greek Revolution* (1828). His wife wrote a memoir of him (1876), and his daughter Laura E. Richards edited his *Letters and Journals* (2 v. 1906–09).

Howe, Tina (1937–   )   playwright. Born in New York City to a well-to-do family, she was educated at private schools and Sarah Lawrence College. *The Nest* (1969), her first Off Broadway play, deals with an overweight woman's disappointments. Plays with the difficulties of motherhood as a theme, such as *Birth and Afterbirth* and *Approaching Zanzibar*, met with so much critical hostility that she had difficulty getting them produced; *Zanzibar* waited more than twenty years for staging. *Museum* (1976) is a satire on art criticism. *Art of Dining* (1979) centers on Ellen and Cal and the patrons of their New Jersey restaurant. The action of *Painting Churches* (1983) takes place in a single room of the Boston townhouse of an aging poet. *Coastal Disturbances* (1986) treats the confusing lives of various bathers on a private beach, and *Approaching Zanzibar* (1989) deals with the fear of death. Mabel, the central figure of *Pride's Crossing* (1997), journeys through time from 1917 to the present. Published plays include *Coastal Disturbances: Four Plays by Tina Howe* (1989) and *Approaching Zanzibar and Other Plays* (1995).

Howe, Sir William (1729–1814),   English general. Howe took part in the engagement at Bunker Hill, then in October 1755 succeeded Gage as commander of British troops in America. He won several battles against Washington, but failed to follow up his victories. Severe criticism led to his resignation in 1778, and the following year he appeared before Parliament and was cleared of the charges against him. He published a *Narrative of Sir William Howe Before a Committee of the House of Commons* (1778). In 1793 he was made a full general.

Howe appears several times in American writings. In reply to General Burgoyne's play, THE BLOCKADE (1775), which ridiculed the Continental soldiers, some anonymous person (possibly MERCY OTIS WARREN) wrote *The Blockheads* (1776), concerned with Howe's unsuccessful attempt to storm Dorchester Heights. Francis Hopkinson made an amusing but scurrilous reference to Howe's amorousness in THE BATTLE OF THE KEGS (1778). Hawthorne wrote *Howe's Masquerade* (in *Twice-Told Tales*, 1842), the story of a ball given by Howe in Boston at which suddenly appeared a procession of ghostly figures representing the early Puritan governors whose coming presaged the end of royal authority in New England. Howe also appears in Richard P. Smith's *The Forsaken* (1831); S. Weir Mitchell's HUGH WYNNE, FREE QUAKER (1897); Irving Bacheller's *In the Days of Poor Richard* (1922); and Kenneth Roberts's OLIVER WISWELL (1940).

Howells, William Dean (1837–1920),   novelist, poet, editor, critic. The son of a newspaperman and journeyman printer, Howells was born in Martins Ferry and grew up in various towns in Ohio, went to school irregularly, and by the time he was fifteen was a contributor of poems, tales, and essays to Ohio papers. He gave an account of his boyhood in *A Boy's Town* (1890) and *My Year in a Log Cabin* (1893), and in *Years of My Youth* (1916) related his experiences after he went to work for the *Ohio State Journal*, in Columbus. By the time he was twenty-three he had published *Poems of Two Friends* (1860) and a campaign life of Lincoln (1860). His poetry had also appeared in the *Atlantic Monthly*, and when he made a literary pilgrimage to Boston in 1860 he was received as a promising young writer. When he dined with Lowell, Holmes, and Fields, Holmes described the event as "the apostolic succession . . . the laying on of hands."

The life of Lincoln resulted in Howells's appointment as consul in Venice, where he spent the Civil War years and enjoyed an opportunity to observe European culture and manners. He wrote a series of travel letters to the Boston *Advertiser* that were revised and published after his return to America as *Venetian Life* (1866). The book was a popular success and won him the further respect of the Cambridge group, particularly Lowell. Howells went to work for the *Nation*, then for the ATLANTIC, of which he became editor in 1871. During this period his power as a literary figure grew steadily. He maintained an alliance with the older New England group and regularly published contributions from Lowell, Emerson, and Longfellow in his magazine, but at the same time he encouraged new writers, notably Henry James, Mark Twain, and many of the local colorists. In part out of friendship with James and Twain, Howells evolved his theory of realistic fiction, which he elaborated in his reviews and essays and put into practice in his own novels. As early as 1872, in his first novel, THEIR WEDDING JOURNEY, he had announced his program: "Ah! poor Real Life, which I love, can I make others share the delight I find in thy foolish and insipid face?" Later he further developed this realism of the commonplace in the tradition of the novel of manners in such works as A MODERN INSTANCE (1882) and THE RISE OF SILAS LAPHAM (1885). By this time he was recognized as one of the leading exponents of serious writing in America and as one of its most rewarding novelists.

Meanwhile Howells had left the *Atlantic* and had begun to contribute the "Editor's Study" (1886–92) to *Harper's Monthly*. Influenced by Tolstoy and by the American socialist Laurence Gronlund, he took up a sharply liberal view to supplement his realism. In his so-called economic novels, especially A HAZARD OF NEW FORTUNES (1890) and A TRAVELER FROM ALTRURIA (1894), he made close studies of American political and social conventions. After 1894 his militant phase subsided, though he continued to be interested in reform. Nearly sixty, he continued to write fiction, approaching in *The Landlord at Lion's Head* (1897), *The Kentons* (1902), *The Son of Royal Langbrith* (1904), and *The Leatherwood God* (1916) the best of his earlier work. But most of his books during his later years were collections of articles that had been turned out for the several Harper magazines. *Literary Friends and Acquaintances* (1900) and *My Mark Twain* (1910) have charm and insight, and even his slighter essays are relieved by a delightful prose style. In 1908 he was elected president of the American Academy of Arts and Letters. Until the last ten years of his life he remained alert to new men and influences; he reviewed enthusiastically the posthumous poems of Emily Dickinson, championed the work of Stephen Crane, and recognized the potentialities of Frank Norris. Yet, in spite of himself, he had become for such younger men as Dreiser, Mencken, and Sinclair Lewis the personification of the old gentility.

During his career Howells wrote thirty-five novels, thirty-five plays, four books of poetry, six books of criticism, and thirty-four miscellaneous volumes. Among important works not mentioned above are *Suburban Sketches* (essays, 1871); A CHANCE ACQUAINTANCE (1873); THE LADY OF THE AROOSTOOK (1879); *The Undiscovered Country* (1880); INDIAN SUMMER (1886); *The Minister's Charge* (1887); *The Shadow of a Dream* (1890); *Criticism and Fiction* (1891); *The Quality of Mercy* (1892); *Stops of Various Quills* (poems, 1895); *My Literary Passions* (1895); *Heroines of Fiction* (2 v. 1901); and *The Vacation of the Kelwyns* (1920). The critical recognition of his work when it was published, more than fifty years of editorial activity, close relationship with most of the important authors of the time, and championship of early realism in American fiction combine to give Howells unquestioned historical importance. Beyond that, his best novels remain eminently readable and are more and more widely recognized as American classics. (See also AN IMPERATIVE DUTY.)

A multivolume *Selected Edition of William Dean Howells* (1968–   ) is in process at Indiana University. W. J. Meserve edited *Complete Plays of W. D. Howells* (1960). Mildred Howells edited *The Life in Letters of William Dean Howells* (1928). Biographical and critical studies include Edwin H. Cady, *The Road to Realism* (1956) and *The Realist at War* (1958); Edward Wagenknecht, *William Dean Howells: The Friendly Eye* (1969); Kenneth Lynn, *William Dean Howells: An American Life* (1971); John W. Crowley, *The Black Heart's Truth: The Early Career of W. D. Howells* (1985), and Rodney D. Olsen, *Dancing in Chains: The Youth of William Dean Howells* (1991).

GEORGE ARMS/GP

Howes, Barbara (1914–1996), poet, short-story writer. Howes was born in New York, raised in Massachusetts, and educated at Bennington College. She traveled extensively in England and Italy with her husband, the poet William Jay Smith, and for several years was editor of the literary quarterly *Chimera*, contributing poems and stories to numerous magazines and anthologies. Collections include *The Undersea Farmer* (1949), *In the Cold Country* (1955), *Light and Dark* (1960), *The Blue Garden* (1972); and *Collected Poems 1945–1990* (1995).

Howl. A poem by ALLEN GINSBERG (1956), one of the best examples of the Beat poetry of the 1950s, revolutionary in form and content. Its long, Whitmanesque line stood in sharp contrast to the tightly wrought poetry in vogue at the time. The violence of its highly personal lament for American civilization was strikingly different from the quiet, measured voice of most modern poetry. In 1957, San Francisco customs authorities seized part of the British edition of *Howl and Other Poems* on the charge that it was obscene literature. The book was ultimately cleared in a court case brought by LAWRENCE FERLINGHETTI's City Lights publishing company.

How to Write Short Stories (1924), a collection of ten stories by RING LARDNER. Lardner had won a wide audience but little critical recognition until this volume, with its sardonic preface, woke up the critics.

Hoyt, Charles Hale (1860–1900), critic, playwright. Born in New Hampshire, Hoyt wrote popular farces satirizing topical subjects. For many years he wrote and produced at least a play a year. One of them, *A Trip to Chinatown* (1891), ran for 650 nights. Weak in plot, they were intended as vehicles for songs and specialities. Songs still familiar include: "The Bowery," "The Man Who Broke the Bank at Monte Carlo," and "East Side, West Side." Among other plays by Hoyt are *A Bunch of Keys* (1882), *A Parlor Match* (1884), *A Tin Soldier* (1886), *A Hole in the Ground* (1887), *A Texas Steer* (1890), *A Temperance Town* (1893), *A Milk-White Flag* (1893), *A Contented Woman* (1897), *A Stranger in New York* (1897), and *A Day and a Night in New York* (1898). His plays remain in manuscript, with the exception of *A Texas Steer*, published in a collection of *Representative American Dramas* (1925).

Hubbard, Elbert [Green] (1856–1915), businessman, printer, editor, writer. As a young man Hubbard, born in Illinois, sold soap and might easily have become a millionaire. But he wanted to sell ideas instead, and he prospered in that business too. He toured Europe to see what was salable and was deeply impressed by William Morris's Kelmscott Press and his interior decoration ideas. On Hubbard's return he founded the Roycroft Press at East Aurora, New York, and issued innumerable arty productions—books in imitation leather, booklets, and magazines. He also produced pottery, metal and leather work, and furniture, intended to carry out Morris's ideas. As stock in trade Hubbard used familiar sentiments from Thoreau and Emerson. He made a specialty of biography, in accordance with Emerson's doctrine of hero worship, and wrote 170 LITTLE JOURNEYS recounting visits to the homes of notable men and women. He also published THE PHILISTINE

(1895–1915), largely devoted to his own effusions and epigrams, and later issued *The Fra* (1908–17). A self-conscious aesthete in appearance, Hubbard was known as Fra Elbertus or the Fra. His most successful publication was A MESSAGE TO GARCIA (1899), a sermon on a Spanish-American War episode. He befriended both Stephen and Hart Crane. He died aboard the *Lusitania* when it was sunk by a German submarine.

Hubbard's publications include *One Day: A Tale of the Prairies* (a novel, 1893); *Time and Chance* (1899); *Life of Ali Baba* (1899); *Thousand and One Epigrams* (1911); *The Roycroft Dictionary* (1915); *Memorial Edition of Little Journeys* (14 v. 1915); and *Selected Writings* (14 v. 1923).

Hubbard, [Frank Mc]Kin[ney] ["Abe Martin"] (1868–1930), cartoonist, humorist. Born in Ohio, Hubbard worked for his father, a newspaper publisher, and later joined the Indianapolis *News* as staff artist, cartoonist, and columnist. In 1914 he created the character of ABE MARTIN, a HOOSIER rustic whose ungainly figure adorned the top of a column quoting some of his cracker-barrel epigrams. Occasionally there would be an essay of some length in the same style, occasionally references to and quotations from other rustics—Fawn Lippincutt, the village belle; Tell Binkley, the village failure; and Young Lafe Bud, who fancied himself a dandy.

Hubbard, L[afayette] Ron[ald] (1911–1986), science fiction and mystery writer, founder of the Church of Scientology. Hubbard, whose interests and accomplishments ranged from experimental music to exploration, was widely known for his science fiction—*Fear* (1951), *Typewriter in the Sky* (1951), and *Final Blackout* (1948)—until his treatise *Dianetics: The Modern Science of Mental Health* (1950) made him rich.

Hubbard, William (1621–1704), clergyman, historian. Hubbard left England with his father to go to New England, was graduated in Harvard's first class (in 1684 he substituted for a while as president), was ordained in 1658, and served as minister of the Congregational Church in Ipswich, Massachusetts, until 1703. He was orthodox to an extreme, but opposed the persecution of witches and protected some of its victims. His best-known book was his *General History of New England from the Discovery to 1680*, first printed in part in 1815, in fuller versions 1848 and 1878. The history was based on earlier documents by Thomas Morton, William Bradford, and John Winthrop, but also included material obtained by Hubbard's own research.

Huckleberry Finn, Adventures of, novel by Samuel Langhorne Clemens, published under his pseudonym MARK TWAIN. Though advertised on the title page as "Tom Sawyer's Comrade," the book is not so much a sequel as a second shot at summoning up Twain's boyhood. "By & by I shall take a boy of twelve," he had written to Howells in 1875, "& run him on through life (in the first person) but not Tom Sawyer. . . ." By 1876 he was calling it "Huck Finn's Autobiography." It was composed in starts and stops. The 1876 fragment broke off near the end of chapter 16, though most of chapters 12 to 14 was as yet unwritten, just where a steamboat cuts the raft in two. An insoluble problem must have overwhelmed him, now that Huck was helping a runaway slave plunge farther and farther into the South. He continued work—with the Granger-ford feud, the entry of the king and duke—even before his return trip to the Mississippi in 1882. Finally, in the summer of 1883, he resumed at about chapter 22 and galloped the text home. It was published in London in December 1884; in New York in February 1885, omitting a chapter incorporated into LIFE ON THE MISSISSIPPI.

When the story opens Huck is living with the Widow Douglas and her sister, Miss Watson. His father, an illiterate boozer, puts in an appearance to demand Huck's share of the treasure found in the cave at the end of THE ADVENTURES OF TOM SAWYER, kidnaping Huck and imprisoning him in his lonely cabin by the Mississippi. Huck stage-manages his own apparent murder and escapes to Jackson's Island, where he meets Jim, Miss Watson's runaway slave. Fearing that a posse is after Jim, they make off on a raft in the hope of turning in to the Ohio river and making for free territory on the Illinois shore. But they miss the turning at Cairo, and soon after a steamboat runs down the raft.

Huck swims ashore and finds shelter with the Grangerford family, whose feud with the neighboring Shepherdsons ends in a bloodbath. Jim is discovered hidden in a swamp, and after the raft is retrieved and mended they set off south once more until they are hijacked by a couple of crooks. One is a journeyman printer and actor in his thirties who calls himself the Duke of Bridgewater, the other a fake evangelist in his seventies who calls himself the Dauphin, or Louis XVII of France. At various riverside towns in what must be Tennessee, Arkansas, and Louisiana, the king and duke join a revivalist camp meeting, mount farcical Shakespearean or pornographic productions, and finally masquerade as English claimants to a legacy of one Peter Wilks. Huck, who has been tagging along with the adventurers, turns against them on behalf of the dead man's daughters. Shortly afterward, the king sells Jim behind Huck's back to Silas Phelps, whose wife turns out to be Tom Sawyer's Aunt Sally. Huck impersonates Tom in a bid to rescue Jim, until the real Tom arrives masquerading as his brother Sid. Tom takes over the plot, concocting a "mixed-up and splendid rescue" in which he is shot and Jim is recaptured. But Tom now reveals that Miss Watson, before dying, had set Jim free in her will. Huck learns his fortune is safe and his father is dead. The rescue, Tom-fashion, had only been for "the *adventure* of it," from which Huck concludes, in the last lines: "But I reckon I got to light out for the Territory ahead of the rest, because Aunt Sally she's going to adopt me and sivilize me and I can't stand it. I been there before."

That final episode at the Phelps farm has attracted more commentary than all the rest of the book combined. There are the moral aspects: Did the episode reveal a failure of nerve? Had Huck learned nothing on his journey downstream? How could he so easily truckle again to Tom's schemes? Then there is the formal aspect: Does Tom's takeover aesthetically fulfill the book? An answer is best made by comparing *Tom Sawyer* with *Huckleberry Finn*. In *Tom Sawyer* boys' games are a constant rehearsal for the affairs of the real world. Aesthetic play, in other words, is resolved in moral action. But in *Huckleberry*

Finn this sequence is radically reversed. Again and again moral action is dissolved in aesthetic play. The reversal of sequence could not be more absolute. Rehearsal inevitably *follows* action as a farcical coda or burlesque. The king's and duke's fraudulent takeover of the Wilks household is mirrored by Tom's equally fraudulent stratagems for befuddling the Phelpses. It is this limping progress, inescapable by the finale, that has dismayed so many critics and seems to frustrate Huck's so-called moral education or quest.

But Huck's voice, to the end, reigns supreme. *Huckleberry Finn* is the first book in English ever to be written entirely in a vernacular. It was not just a trick on Twain's part or a spurt of colloquial gusto. It was rather a performance so complex that Twain was never able to repeat it himself. For it involved a triple voice. In the opening paragraph the gentlemanly narrator "Mr. Mark Twain" bows out *in propria persona* to leave Huck on stage alone; yet Huck had internalized the joker Twain, who had cocooned within himself the gentlemanly Mr. Clemens of Hartford, Connecticut. This is the very essence of Twain's humor. Broadly it comes to this: Twain is *always* the humorist, never Huck. Huck may combine, in Kenneth Lynn's phrase, "the Gentleman and the Clown." But it does not follow that Mr. Mark Twain is the Gentleman and Huckleberry Finn the Clown. To the contrary, it is one of the amazing paradoxes of *Huckleberry Finn* that it is the other way round. Inevitably it is Huck who is the Gentleman and Twain who is the Clown. Instead of a punctilious, poker-faced, gentlemanly narrative mask (traditional to Southwestern humor) for heightening the irruptions of laughter, Twain chose a 14-year-old boy. Instead of puncturing the complacencies of middle age, Twain bounces his subtlest effects off Huck's anxious and preoccupied head.

HAROLD BEAVER

Hudson's Bay Company.   An enterprise organized in the 17th century by a group of English businessmen to obtain furs in North America for the British market. It obtained a charter from King Charles II on May 2, 1670, and made many explorations, overcame opposition by the French, earned large dividends, established a continent-wide monopoly and eventually gave up some of its powers and privileges to the Dominion of Canada (1868). The company appears in Edison Marshall's *Seward's Folly* (1924), Vardis Fisher's *Pemmican* (1956), and H.S.M. Kemp's *Northern Trader* (1956). George Bryce related the *Remarkable History of the Hudson's Bay Company* (1900), and it is the subject also of Douglas MacKay's *Honorable Company* (1936).

Hudson Review (1948–   ),   literary quarterly published in New York. Its influence, like that of the *Kenyon Review*, was especially powerful in the early years of the New Criticism. Blackmur, Pound, Tate, and Yvor Winters were all contributors.

Hudson River School.   A group of landscape painters working between 1825 and 1875. Their work parallels that of such writers as WASHINGTON IRVING and JAMES FENIMORE COOPER; both the writers and the painters were influenced by European romanticism. Combining idealism about nature with a growing pride in the beauty of their country, particularly scenes such as Niagara Falls, the Hudson River Valley, and the White Mountains, they developed a new vision of wilderness in which humans are an insignificant intrusion. Thomas Doughty (1793–1856) was the first to be identified with the Hudson River School, and THOMAS COLE (1801–1848) was a leader during the group's most active years. Albert Bierstadt (1830–1902) painted the Rocky Mountains and other western scenes. Other painters in the group include Asher B. Durand (1796–1886); J. F. Kensett (1818–1872); S. F. B. MORSE (1791–1872); Henry Inman (1801–1846); Jasper Cropsey (1823–1900); Frederick F. Church (1826–1900); and George Inness (1825–1894).

Hughes, Hatcher (1881–1945),   teacher, dramatist. Born in North Carolina, Hughes taught at Columbia University. He also wrote several successful plays, among them *A Marriage Made in Heaven* (1918); *Wake Up, Jonathan* (with ELMER RICE, 1921); HELL-BENT FOR HEAVEN (Pulitzer Prize, 1923); *Ruint* (1924); and *The Lord Blesses the Bishop* (1932). The best of his plays deal with North Carolina mountaineers. *Hell-Bent for Heaven* deals with their superstitions and feuds.

Hughes, Langston (1902–1967),   poet, dramatist, short-story writer, journalist. Born in Joplin, Missouri, into an African-American family once zealous for abolitionism (an ancestor had died at Harpers Ferry fighting alongside John Brown), Hughes grew up mainly in Lawrence, Kansas, and in Cleveland, where he published verse and fiction in his high school magazine. After a year in Mexico, where his father lived, he entered Columbia University in 1921, but withdrew in 1922. In the next few years, while his verse appeared in magazines, he worked at odd jobs, including one as messman on ships to Africa and Europe, another as dishwasher in a Paris night club. In 1926, he entered Lincoln University, in Pennsylvania. By 1929, when he was graduated, he had published two books of verse, *The Weary Blues* (1926) and *Fine Clothes to the Jew* (1927), that confirmed him as the best poet of the so-called Harlem Renaissance of that decade. A novel, *Not Without Laughter* (1930), added to his reputation.

With the onset of the Depression, Hughes turned sharply toward the left. Visits to Haiti and Cuba led him to condemn American imperialism there, and in 1932–1933 he spent a year in the Soviet Union, where he had gone to help make a film on American race relations. Hailed as a revolutionary writer, he wrote his most radical verse there. His next book, the short-story collection *The Ways of White Folks* (1934), also showed increased bitterness. In the rest of the decade he concentrated on drama, especially after his *Mulatto*, a tragedy about miscegenation, opened on Broadway in 1935. After serving as a war correspondent in Spain, he returned home in 1938 to found the leftist Harlem Suitcase Theatre, whose first production was his *Don't You Want to Be Free?*

With World War II, his radicalism began to decline—as shown in his benign first volume of autobiography, *The Big Sea* (1940). In songs and radio scripts, he supported the war effort. In 1942, he began a more than twenty-year stint as a columnist with the Afro-American weekly *Chicago Defender*. In 1943, he introduced the character Jesse B. Semple, or "Sim-

ple," a black urban Everyman whose humor, vitality, droll language, and racial defensiveness quickly became the heart of the column. Eventually, Hughes published five collections of stories based on the Simple columns.

The success on Broadway in 1947 of the musical play *Street Scene*, with Hughes as lyricist and Kurt Weill as composer, enabled him to buy a home and settle in Harlem. His output became prodigious. He published volumes of verse, such as *Fields of Wonder* (1947), *One-Way Ticket* (1949), *Montage of a Dream Deferred* (1951), and *Ask Your Mama* (1961). In addition to the Simple stories, he wrote two books of stories, *Laughing to Keep from Crying* (1952) and *Something in Common* (1963), as well as another novel, *Tambourines to Glory* (1958). His second volume of autobiography, *I Wonder as I Wander*, appeared in 1956. Hughes also published many songs and opera libretti; a history of the NAACP, *Fight for Freedom* (1962); about a dozen books of fiction and nonfiction for children; and a similar number of anthologies and editions. He translated books by García Lorca, Gabriela Mistral, Nicolás Guillén, and Jacques Roumain. His main professional interest after 1947 was probably the musical theater. Several of his efforts, such as the highly acclaimed *Black Nativity* (1961) and *Jericho-Jim Crow* (1964), involved gospel music.

With his long career and wide range, Hughes was perhaps the most representative black American writer. His poetry was also the most original. His work exuded a profound, uncompromised love of his race and from the start offered inspired depictions—largely unprecedented—of its beauty and humanity. Early, too, he saw music as the heart of Afro-American expression and linked his writing to its initiatives. Thus, in the 1920s he worked to fuse the lowly blues with formal poetry; in the 1940s he turned to the disjointed be-bop style that reflected the new urban pressures affecting black culture; still later came experiments with progressive jazz and gospel. His populism, encouraged early by the examples of Whitman and Sandburg, has affected his critical reputation. Middle-class Afro-American reviewers often condemned his work in blues and jazz as exposing the worst element of the race; these and other critics also sometimes found Hughes insufficiently intellectual. But he was committed to an art that both reflected the realities of Afro-American culture and was accessible to a large section of the community. In general he succeeded. Especially among black Americans, his body of work continues to appeal to a surprisingly wide audience. His other titles include *The Langston Hughes Reader* (1958) and *Selected Poems* (1959). Akiba Sullivan edited *Selected Stories* (1996). The first three of a projected eighteen-volume *Collected Works* appeared in 2001. A biography is Arnold Rampersad, *The Life of Langston Hughes* (2 v.; 1986, 1988).

ARNOLD RAMPERSAD

Hughes, Robert (1938–   ),   art and cultural critic. Born in Sydney, Australia, a graduate of St. Ignatius College and Sydney University, Hughes has lived in the United States since he began writing art criticism for *Time* in 1970. *The Shock of the New* (1980), on modern art, and *American Visions:*

The Epic History of Art in America (1997), derived from acclaimed PBS television series, are sweeping surveys distinguished by broad knowledge and firm opinions. *The Fatal Shore* (1987) is a masterful history of the convict presence in Australia. *Culture of Complaint: The Fraying of America* (1993) is a polemic against the "hollowness at the cultural core" of his adopted country and *A Jerk at One End* (1999) a brief book on fishing.

Hugh Selwyn Mauberley (1920),   a poem by EZRA POUND. Through Mauberley, Pound expresses his hatred of war and commercialism in the arts, and his views of such contemporaries as Arnold Bennett (Mr. Nixon) and Ford Madox Ford (the stylist). At the same time, *Mauberley* is Pound's farewell to London and to the period in which almost alone he championed Frost, Eliot, Lawrence, and Joyce. Eliot himself called the poem "a document of an epoch," and the influence of its virtuosity in sound and rhythm could be seen two years later in *The Waste Land*.

Hugo, Richard (1923–1982),   poet. Born in Seattle, Hugo was abandoned by his parents and raised by grandparents. He served as a bombardier in World War II, and many of his war experiences and other personal experiences found their way into his poetry. He was educated at the University of Washington and taught at the University of Montana, where he directed the creative writing program (1964–1982). His poetry collections include *A Run of Jacks* (1961), *The Lady in Kicking Horse Reservoir* (1973), *What Thou Lovest Well Remains American* (1975), *Selected Poems* (1979), and *Making Certain It Goes On: The Collected Poems* (1984). *The Triggering Town* (1979) is a collection of short prose pieces. *Death and the Good Life* (1981) is a detective story.

Huguenots.   A French Protestant 17th- and 18th-century sect whose theology was Calvinistic. Subject to persecution, many emigrated to America after the Edict of Nantes was revoked in 1685.

Huidobro, Vicente (1893–1948),   poet. Born to a wealthy Chilean family whose real name was García Fernández, he devised his own assumed surname. He published four volumes of poetry in Chile before leaving for Europe in 1916. In Paris he wrote slight poetry in French, publishing it in *Nord-Sud*, and became friends with leading intellectuals. He published three volumes of Spanish poetry in Madrid in 1918 (*Arctic Poems; Equatorials; The Water Mirror*). In the last three decades of his life, he traveled between Chile and Europe, involving himself in literary and political disputes. His long poem *Altazor* (1932) contains explorations of the structure of words as well as an amazing variety of images in its description of the soaring and fall of the poet-bird. *Satyr, or the Power of Words* (1939) is a novel.

humanism.   Originally, humanism signified a movement of people who studied fields concerned with the moral and imaginative aspects of man—history, poetry, rhetoric, and moral philosophy—as opposed to theology, on one hand, and mathematics and science, on the other. Humanists studied classical texts—Aristotle, Plato, and Cicero—as opposed to theological texts. Although Renaissance humanists were

Christians, humanists tended to base truth more upon empirical evidence than upon supernatural creeds or dogma. In the Victorian period, using the concept of culture, Matthew Arnold was a leading exponent of the role of the humanities—English, history, the arts—in a liberal education and of reading the major works of Western civilization, especially the classical writers, to learn "the best that is known and thought in the world."

In America, the *new humanism* combined an attack on modern literature and a plea for classical standards of taste with a call for conservative moral values. IRVING BABBITT and PAUL ELMER MORE, the leaders of the movement, saw in humanism a protection against the decadence of modern life. In *Literature and the American College* (1908) Babbitt upheld the "inner principle of restraint" as a curb to naturalism, the gospel of progress, and the romanticism of Rousseau. More shared with Babbitt a general contempt for modern literature, describing Dos Passos's *Manhattan Transfer* as "an explosion in a cesspool." Both writers looked back to Emerson's distinction between "law for man" and "law for thing" as an alternative to what he believed was the undue influence of utilitarianism, specialization, and science. More developed his position in *Shelburne Essays* (1904–21) and *New Shelburne Essays* (1928–36); Babbitt furthered his ideas in *The New Laokoön* (1910), *Democracy and Leadership* (1924), and most notably in *Rousseau and Romanticism* (1919).

In the 1920s NORMAN FOERSTER gathered a humanist symposium, including T. S. Eliot, "to consider the requirements of Humanism in the various activities of modern thought and life." The symposium, published as *Humanism and America, Essays on the Outlook of Modern Civilization* (1930), was attacked by exponents of the NEW CRITICISM, who advanced a more formal criticism and chided new humanism for its snobbery and conservation.

Later, deconstructionists influenced by JACQUES DERRIDA would criticize New Criticism as "old fashioned humanism" because of its emphasis on the themes, values, and teleology of works at the expense of linguistic phenomena. Deconstructionists also criticized New Criticism as well as historical criticism for neglecting the gaps, fissures, and enigmas that undo readings that stress how organic form enacts consistent values.

Recently, Daniel R. Schwarz, among others, has used the term "humanistic formalism" to define a criticism that does not accept the tenets of deconstruction that "there is nothing outside the text" and that literary texts are "the free play of signifiers." These critics—often deriving some of their principles from Aristotle—stress the mimetic quality of literature and insist that literature is written by human authors, about human actions, and for human readers. Without neglecting formal considerations such as voice, genre, narrative structure, and linguistic patterns, these critics focus on the dialogue between the anterior or real world and the imaginative world of fictions as well as the author's creative process and how that is shaped by the historical period in which the author writes. These critics believe that (a) the form of a literary text—style, structure, narrative technique—expresses its value system;

(b) a literary text is a creative gesture of the author and the result of historical context; (c) a literary text imitates a world that precedes it; and (d) literary texts usually address how and why people behave—what they do, desire, fear, doubt, and need. Humanism does not mean "life-affirming," but concern with how and why people live, think, act, feel, read, write, and speak. While acknowledging variations in the diverse responses of readers, humanistic criticism believes there is the possibility of approaching a determinate meaning by studying authors, their periods, and their canons. It believes that readers and text meet at the seam of reading.

DANIEL R. SCHWARZ

Humble-Bee, The (composed, 1837; pub., 1839),   a poem by RALPH WALDO EMERSON. Emerson recorded in his journal (May 9, 1837), "Yesterday in the woods I followed the fine humble-bee with rhymes and fancie fine."

Humble Romance, A, and Other Stories (1887), by MARY E. WILKINS FREEMAN. These grim stories of New England are peopled by characters who are closemouthed and frequently joyless, but doggedly determined in their struggles against a bleak environment and stern, moralistic heritage.

Humboldt's Gift (1975).   In this novel, the Death Question in all its variations both highbrow and lowbrow presses on the protagonist, Charlie Citrine, a successful dramatist and yet another of Bellow's distracted intellectuals fighting against a life in great disorder. The immediate cause of Charlie's extended meditations—in Rudolph Steinerian anthroposophy, into Romantic flights and transcendental fits, into the very sources of the religious experience itself—is the death of his friend-turned-enemy, the extravagantly lyric poet and madman, von Humboldt Fleisher.

The character of Humboldt is based largely on the public facts associated with Delmore Schwartz (1913–1966). Bellow, however, also means to clear his own name and conscience from the ghostly presence of Schwartz's accusations. The result is a version of the confrontation Bellow had explored in *The Victim* (1947), but this time with a character who has more intellectual resources and who can fight harder against victimization.

America, Citrine argues, is too big, too tough, for lyric poets. On the other hand, the novel itself is an argument that the fiction writer can take on the entire range of contemporary American life—including its sharpers, con men, characters sporting "low life expertise," inexplicable women, and barracuda-like divorce lawyers—and still survive.

The result is a novel that often turns long-winded and preachy, that tangles its complicated plot—about Humboldt's twin "gifts" of a manuscript (that magically answers Citrine's financial prayers) and a letter that reconciles old wounds with the balm of love—but one filled with essential passages that tell us much about Bellow and what he calls "the actualities of religious life."

SANFORD PINSKER

Humes, H[arold] L. (1926–1992),   novelist, founder with PETER MATTHIESSEN of PARIS REVIEW. Humes is also known for his first novel, *The Underground City* (1958), set in postwar

France, and for his short, dark novel *Men Die* (1959). It concerns five black prisoners being guarded by a white lieutenant on an island in the West Indies.

Humor in the United States.   The spirit of comedy is all-pervasive in American literature; from the colonial wits who satirized the political currents of the day to contemporary novelists, poets, and dramatists who employ irony and dark humor to reflect on the absurdities of postmodern life. Humor is found in the works of major authors, such as Poe, Hawthorne, Melville, Thoreau, Whitman, and Emily Dickinson and, in the case of Twain and Faulkner, comedy is central to their styles and artistic visions.

Critics have devoted little attention to humor, despite its abiding presence in American culture—in everything from newspapers, magazines, and the comics to radio, television, film, and the stage. There is a common misconception that comedy is less important than tragedy and serious philosophic questions, even though the human condition and the nature of existence are central concerns of the humorist. It is also difficult to define humor or to describe the way it functions in cultural and social contexts. This is understandable since there is little agreement on what makes things funny.

It was Faulkner who noted, "We have one priceless universal trait, we Americans. That trait is our humor." Americans are thought to have a special sense of humor that often features exaggeration, hyperbole, and the tall tale. Comedy is encouraged by our democratic system in which we often posit higher ideals than we can live up to. It is the incongruity between the ideal and the real, between the dream and the failure to achieve it, to which much American humor is addressed.

We hold nothing above ridicule in the exercise of free speech—law, government, religion, president, or pope. Few nations so willingly celebrate their failures and foolishness through hilarity and the horse laugh as do Americans. Thus, a gauge of the success of our system is our willingness to abide and absorb ridicule and comic criticism. Many writers have taken advantage of the opportunity this offers and have demonstrated their own ultimate faith in the system and its ideals against which they measure human conduct and find it laughable.

While most writing in North America during the Colonial and Federal periods addressed practical economic and political questions, or engaged in theological debate, humorists were there to puncture pretensions about the same subjects. Having been twice deported from New England for encouraging unseemly liberal activities, the most notorious of which was dancing around a Maypole, THOMAS MORTON took his revenge through the *New English Canaan* (1737), a sometimes comic critique of the stiff-necked Puritan's bigotry, while from the other end of the spectrum *The Simple Cobbler of Agawam in America* (1647) by NATHANIEL WARD was a disaffected clergyman's satirical attack on religious tolerance, British politics, and the conduct of women. Ward found women frivolous, even though the Colony was shortly to have as its first poet a woman from Massachusetts Bay, ANNE BRADSTREET. While most of her poetry was imitative of British models in *The*

Tenth Muse (1650), her originality shone through her witty personal poems about being a housewife and a writer, such as those prefacing her collections. It was another woman, SARAH KEMBLE KNIGHT, who took a frank look at the populace and their manners and recorded in her *Journal* (1704–5, pub. 1825) with ironic detachment and amusement the quaint people and curious events she encountered in her travels through New England and New York.

South of New England, the Colonists also found that a satiric slant on things helped alleviate the frustrations of a frontier society. In *The Sot-Weed Factor* (1708), Marylander EBENEZER COOK's fictional and unreliable narrator laid a Hudibrastic curse on the doorstep of the New World because of the harsh treatment he received. And WILLIAM BYRD II, from the security of his Virginia estate, ridiculed North Carolinians for their seeming sloth and amorality in *A History of the Dividing Line* (1728, pub. 1841), when he wasn't keeping his remarkable diaries or writing poems and sketches in the 18th-century fashion of Swift, Pope, and Addison.

The best humor of the period came from BENJAMIN FRANKLIN in Philadelphia, whose *Dogood Papers* (1722), *Poor Richard's Almanacks* (1732–1757), periodical essays, and bagatelles displayed a brilliant wit and use of irony that earned for him a reputation as our first major literary humorist. His major work, the *Autobiography* (1771–1790, pub. 1818), is noteworthy not only for its irreverent enlightenment but also for the pungent, genial humor of its style.

The HARTFORD WITS were a loosely affiliated group of dedicated Federalists who resisted the changes that came in the wake of the Revolution as a result of Jeffersonian republicanism, and they produced several collaborative satires directed against the opposition. The most talented of the group were JOHN TRUMBULL, author of *M'Fingal* (1775, 1782), a burlesque epic attacking those of a loyalist sentiment, and JOEL BARLOW, best remembered for his mock heroic tribute to cornmeal and the virtues of the rural life, "The Hasty Pudding" (1793).

Like the other leading intellects of his time, HUGH HENRY BRACKENRIDGE was deeply involved in politics as an advocate of the Revolution, a leader of the Republican party, and a jurist, but he found the time to construct a four-volume comic novel called *Modern Chivalry* (1792–1815), modeled after *Don Quixote* but directed with a satiric gaze at the unresolved problems of American democracy and defects in the American character. Some consider it the first true American novel, and in its extravagant detail and coarse language, an antecedent of frontier humor. TABITHA TENNEY, the wife of a Congressman, also found inspiration in Cervantes for her novel *Female Quixotism* (1801), a cautionary tale for women about the dangers of reading the popular romances of the time. WASHINGTON IRVING was one of the first writers to break away from the political or business career model of his peers to make a profession of authorship. His short stories remain among some of the best in the English language, and while they often demonstrate a witty turn of phrase and a gentle irony, he established his fame and reputation as a humorist with his burlesque work

of history by the fictional Diedrich Knickerbocker, *A History of New York* (1809).

In 19th-century America, literary humor had two distinct regional centers—the North and the South. In the letters collected in *The Life and Writings of Major Jack Downing* (1833), SEBA SMITH used the traditional joke device of having a provincial observer from Maine comment on urban social institutions of the day, but by making Downing a confidential adviser to President Andrew Jackson, Smith demonstrated the usefulness of the humorist as a moral conscience in the shady manipulations of national political life. In Downing, Smith gave American literature the quintessential Yankee and exploited the rich potential of regional language.

The stereotype of the acquisitive and wily Yankee trader found its fullest embodiment in the adventures of the itinerant Sam Slick, created by Nova Scotian T. C. HALIBURTON and collected in *The Clockmaker; or, The Sayings and Doings of Samuel Slick* (1836) and subsequent volumes. Other explorations of the Yankee character are found in the crackerbarrel philosopher Hosea Biglow and the intemperate scoundrel Birdofredum Sawin in the dialect poems of James Russell Lowell, *The Biglow Papers* (1848, 1867), and in the witty monologist who held forth with sophistication and brilliance around a boardinghouse table in OLIVER WENDELL HOLMES's *Autocrat of the Breakfast Table* (1858). From these writings emerges the figure of the New England Yankee, materialistic yet pragmatic, by turns honest or corrupt and naive or wordly wise, at times a country bumpkin and at others an urban sophisticate. He was, then, like most Americans, a paradoxical and contradictory figure given consistency through the skeptical irony of comedy.

The female counterpart of the Yankee was created by BENJAMIN SHILLABER in the *Life and Sayings of Mrs. Partington* (1854) and later collections. Mrs. Partington's commonsensical eccentricities were countered by women who would have their own say. FRANCES WHITCHER's *The Widow Bedott Papers* (1856) satirized stereotypical characteristics of the female—sentimentality and frivolousness—which kept women from fulfilling their potential in a male-dominated culture, while MARIETTA HOLLEY took a more direct route. Her two dozen books published between 1873 and 1914, about a character named Samantha Smith Allen, ironically known as "Josiah Allen's Wife," directly assaulted with common-sense humor the attitudes and assumptions of her time that kept women repressed. Holley's eye for social absurdity caused her to be called the female Mark Twain, whose popularity she rivaled, despite her feminist stands against the trends of the day. Nearly all these Northeastern humorists used regional dialect, malapropisms, linguistic incongruities, and comic misspellings as sources of humor, which has discouraged a continuing popularity among readers.

The American South was also a center of literary humor in the antebellum period, when the frontier expanded. Using the sporting journals and newspapers of the time, especially the New York *Spirit of the Times*, Southern humorists wrote about matters of masculine interest and portrayed a world of violence and exaggeration through tall tales and expanded metaphor. They were not writers by trade nor necessarily humorists by intention, but rather were professional men—lawyers, doctors, editors, and politicians mainly—who tried to record what they heard from the mouths of yarnspinners as they traveled through what were then the frontier states, such as Georgia, Alabama, Mississippi, Tennessee, and Louisiana (the Old Southwest). In their use of regional idiom and elements of everyday life at the lowest social levels, they anticipated the local color and realism movements in the last part of the century.

The titles of the works by the major writers in this group suggest something of the geographic range and variety of subject matter they encompassed: AUGUSTUS BALDWIN LONGSTREET's *Georgia Scenes, Characters, Incidents, &c., in the First Half Century of the Republic* (1835); THOMAS BANGS THORPE's story "The Big Bear of Arkansas" (1841); WILLIAM TAPPAN THOMPSON's *Major Jones Courtship* (1843); JOHNSON JONES HOOPER's *Some Adventures of Captain Simon Suggs, Late of the Tallapoosa Volunteers, Together with "Taking the Census" and Other Alabama Sketches* (1845); Henry Clay Lewis's *Odd Leaves from the Life of a Louisiana "Swamp Doctor"* (1950); and JOSEPH GLOVER BALDWIN's *The Flush Times of Alabama and Mississippi* (1853). Related to the frontier humorists was DAVID CROCKETT, whose *Narrative of the Life of David Crockett of the State of Tennessee* (1834) contains much humorous folklore and comic exaggeration, but the book seems largely to have been written by Thomas Chilton. The most accomplished of these humorists was GEORGE WASHINGTON HARRIS, whose *Sut Lovingood, Yarns Spun by a "Nat-ral Born Durn'd Fool"* (1867) brought Southern dialect to unmatched heights of metaphoric power and gave American literature its liveliest and most outrageous social rebel before Huckleberry Finn. TWAIN, FAULKNER, and other writers would read and profit by Harris's example, and the character of Huck Finn owes much to his influence.

If comic misspellings and incongruities between formal speech and illiterate dialect were simply devices among the humorists of the Northeast and the Old Southwest, they became the stock in trade for the writers who have become known as the Literary Comedians or "Phunny Phellows." It was perhaps a tribute to the literacy of the American populace in the last half of the 19th century that they found them humorous—assuming one must know the correct word to find the distortion funny—but these writers intentionally misspelled words with little intention of recording dialect or imitating regional speech. This was a visual rather than a verbal humor, since what it looked like on the printed page was the source of its effect. What several of them did that was different, was to create public personalities to accompany their writings by making appearances on the stage platform at a time when the lecture circuit was a major source of entertainment in the United States.

Charles Farrar Browne initiated the trend by publishing a series of letters from an illiterate but clever showman, named ARTEMUS WARD, who traveled with his wax museum. By 1862, when he published his first collection, *Artemus Ward, His Book*, Browne had mounted the lecture platform to create a stage character modeled after the fictional letter writer. The popularity of the character overshadowed the existence of the author to such an extent that Browne practically merged with his own creation. Following in his footsteps was HENRY WHEELER SHAW, who lectured as Josh Billings, whose main talent lay in comic aphorisms and wise sayings. Also beginning with letters contributed to the press, Shaw collected his works in several best-selling volumes, beginning with *Josh Billings, His Sayings* (1865). Following Browne and Shaw, a long series of writers began moving from the humor columns of the newspapers to the lecture circuit and collected volumes of their letters and talks. A list of them and their first books must include ROBERT H. NEWELL, *The Orpheus C. Kerr Papers* (1862); CHARLES H. SMITH, *Bill Arp, So Called* (1866); and EDGAR WILSON NYE, *Bill Nye and Boomerang* (1881). But there were more than fifty others. Perhaps the most intriguing of the lot was David Ross Locke, who contributed the most memorably irascible and engagingly nefarious of the lengthy series of comic creations, PETROLEUM V. NASBY, a cowardly and bigoted defender of white supremacy and states' rights who effectively debunked the South through ironic exaggeration. Beginning with *The Nasby Papers* (1864), Locke's collections proved extremely popular. He was a special favorite of Abraham Lincoln, who is said to have been reading *The Nasby Papers* just before he left for Ford's Theater on the fateful evening.

Samuel L. Clemens would emulate, draw together, and build on all the major strands of American humor up to his time and improve on them. He cut his journalistic teeth on the boisterous humor of the frontier, contributed his first literary efforts as comic letters and sketches to the newspapers of his day, and turned to the lecture platform and book publishing as lucrative sources of income. Like the Literary Comedians before him, he created a persona for himself as Mark Twain, which was so masterfully brought to public attention through expert manipulation of the media that he was the best-known personality of his time. The fictional Mark Twain remains so powerful that even today we are more comfortable referring to Clemens as Twain rather than by his real name. He set a high standard for literary humor and made it more respectable by incorporating its techniques into mainstream American fiction. *Adventures of Huckleberry Finn* (1885), for example, betrays its roots in the dialect school of frontier humor, but Clemens goes on to demonstrate how the American colloquial language can be put to effective literary use and that a comic structure can be as effective as a tragic one in addressing such serious philosophic issues as the responsibilities human beings bear for one another, and the conflict between individual conscience and the laws of the state and society. Along with *Huckleberry Finn*, such books as *The Innocents Abroad* (1865), *Roughing It* (1872), *The Adventures of Tom Sawyer* (1876), *A Connecticut Yankee in King Arthur's Court* (1889), and *Pudd'nhead Wilson* (1894) remain among the masterworks of American fiction and literary humor. Neither the nation's literature nor humor would ever be the same after Clemens, and the image of Mark Twain, dressed in a white suit, puffing on a cigar, and delivering commonsense wisecracks on the failures of mankind and civilization, has come to represent everything quintessentially American.

The 19th-century newspaper was also an outlet for other types of humor besides sketches, tales, and letters. Puns, understatement, burlesque, clever wordplay, and the poker-faced anecdote were the specialties of GEORGE HORATIO DERBY, whose collected pieces in *Phoenixiana* (1856) and *The Squibob Papers* (1865) were widely popular, and Charles G. Leland achieved fame through comic ballads written in a German American dialect and collected in *Hans Breitmann's Ballads* (1868). The writer generally regarded as the first newspaper humor columnist is JAMES M. BAILEY, whose columns as "The Danbury News Man" increased the circulation of the Danbury (Connecticut) *News* from less than 2,000 to 30,000 in nine months' time. Bailey's pieces about ordinary events in a small town also found their way into hardcovers, beginning with *Life in Danbury* (1870).

In the 20th century, newspaper and periodical humorists have tended to fall into regional or affiliated groups as they have in the past. In Chicago, for example, three stellar wits worked within close proximity around the turn of the century and afterward. EUGENE FIELD, at the Chicago *Daily News* after 1883, was ridiculing local folly in prose and verse in his column "Sharps and Flats." His frequently sentimental poems about children, such as "Little Boy Blue" (1889), were balanced by his acerbic satires of social trends and human nature. At the Chicago *Morning News* (later the *Record*), GEORGE ADE was producing "Stories of the Street and Town," about interesting urban characters, and "Fables in Slang," impertinent lessons couched in colloquial language and unusual typography. A popular selection of the latter appeared as *Fables in Slang* (1900). Over at the Chicago *Post*, FINLEY PETER DUNNE was providing keen political and social commentary in Irish-American dialect through his fictional mouthpiece, Mr. Dooley, a saloon keeper in the tradition of the cracker-barrel philosopher. Although Dunne moved to New York to pursue magazine publishing, Dooley remained in his Chicago setting and reached millions of readers through a series of books, beginning with *Mr. Dooley in Peace and War* (1898).

New York was another city with more than its share of humorists in residence. While DON MARQUIS produced an astonishing quantity of fiction, poetry, drama, and comic commentary, he will be remembered best for the two characters he created in columns for the New York *Evening Sun* in 1916—Archy, the free-verse cockroach, and Mehitabel, the free-spirited cat. In column and book form, beginning with *archy and mehitabel* (1927), lowercased because Archy cannot operate the typewriter shift key, Marquis wrote some of the most original and lasting humor in American literature. About 1919, a group of writers, journalists, and artists began regularly to assemble for lunch or dinner at the Algonquin Hotel in New York City. Soon the Algonquin Round Table became the site of sparkling repartee and sophisticated wit as numerous leading humorists joined the group: ROBERT BENCHLEY, who celebrated the inept modern urban male; S. J. PERELMAN, whose satiric assaults on the English language stretched its comic potential; RING LARDNER, who skillfully transcribed the language and character of ordinary Americans; DOROTHY PARKER, celebrated for her sardonic comments and caustic stories and poems about love, hate, betrayal, and disenchantment in the urban jungle; GEORGE S. KAUFMAN, who was writing with several collaborators some of the most engaging comedies of manners ever to grace the American stage; and Alexander Woollcott, who carried the art of insult and egocentricity to new heights of irritation.

Many of these figures also contributed to *The New Yorker*, launched in 1925 as *the* satiric magazine for the sophisticated reader, and it would remain so for the rest of the century. Its two shining lights were E. B. WHITE, an urbane prose stylist whose keen wit sparkled through his anonymous contributions to the "Talk of the Town" columns, and JAMES THURBER, who through clever essay and eccentric cartoon made confusion and "emotional chaos remembered in tranquility" into tools of the comic muse. Thurber's fictional autobiography, *My Life and Hard Times* (1933), his story "The Secret Life of Walter Mitty" (1939), and many of his cartoons are classics of American humor and helped define what has come to be known as the "little man" in popular culture—a figure lacking in size and courage but who confronts the threats of modern technology and society and somehow survives through antic persistence and adaptability. *The New Yorker* has been a major source of American humor down to the present, when WOODY ALLEN and GARRISON KEILLOR have found a home there for their prose pieces.

Other humorists also were an important part of the cultural scene in the first half of the century: cowboy philosopher WILL ROGERS, more effective on the stage and radio than in his newspaper columns and probably the best loved man of his age; the sage of Baltimore, H. L. MENCKEN, merciless satirist of American manners and mores whose humor was often obscured by excessive venom in his newspaper columns and books; the master of light verse, OGDEN NASH, who toyed with the conventions of poetry and took winsome liberties with the sounds and meanings of words; and movie scriptwriter ANITA LOOS, best remembered for the title of her novel *Gentlemen Prefer Blondes* (1925) and its sequel *But Gentlemen Marry Brunettes* (1928), and their corrupt-innocent heroine, Lorelei Lee. The columns of America's newspapers and magazines have continued to be hospitable to humorous essays, sketches, stories, poems, and features. Among those who have achieved popularity in the last few decades through periodical publication (and subsequent books) are Art Buchwald, Russell Baker, RICHARD ARMOUR, Jean Shepherd, Peg Bracken, JEAN KERR, ERMA BOMBECK, JUDITH VIORST, Nora Ephron, Ellen Goodman, Fran Liebowitz, and Judith Martin. All but the first four are women, most of whom have taken as their subject matter the trials and tribulations of being a woman in a male-dominated society, thus continuing the work begun earlier by Frances Whitcher and Marietta Holley. The fiction of Betty MacDonald, Shirley Jackson, and Erica Jong also provides humorous slants on feminine issues.

The major writers of the Southern Literary Renaissance during the first part of the century and their heirs have incorporated a high degree of humor in their work. This was especially true of Faulkner, whose delight in epic exaggeration and belief in the saving grace of comedy informed nearly all of his fiction, but it was also true of the ironic allegories of JAMES BRANCH CABELL and poet JOHN CROWE RANSOM, the enthusiastic romanticism of THOMAS WOLFE and JESSE STUART, the sensitive character studies of EUDORA WELTY and CARSON MCCULLERS, the theological disquisitions of FLANNERY O'CONNOR and WALKER PERCY, and the outrageous sensuality of ERSKINE CALDWELL. More recently, the South has witnessed a revival of many of the techniques and characteristics of the humor of the Old Southwest, as in the books of William Price Fox, Guy Owen, Mac Hyman, Fred Chappell, Mark Steadman, Robert Y. Drake, Florence King, BARRY HANNAH, Lewis Grizzard, and Roy Blount, Jr.

A strain of cynical humor and a sense of the darkly absurd have always been a part of American literature, but the writer who specialized in it was AMBROSE BIERCE, who disappeared into Mexico about 1914. His mordant epigrams in *The Devil's Dictionary* (1911) and collections of short stories showed the terrors of human nature at its worst and earned for him the epithet Bitter Bierce. In the 1930s, NATHANAEL WEST reflected cynically on the emptiness of modern life in such satirical works as *Miss Lonelyhearts* (1933) and *The Day of the Locust* (1939). It was World War II, the horrors of Nazism, and the threat of a nuclear holocaust, however, that deepened this strain and provided visions of despair for a number of writers who came to be known among critics as Black Humorists. Identified with this group are such novelists as JOHN HAWKES, VLADIMIR NABOKOV, KURT VONNEGUT, JR., JAMES PURDY, J. P. DONLEAVY, THOMAS PYNCHON, DONALD BARTHELME, THOMAS BERGER, JOSEPH HELLER, JOHN BARTH, KEN KESEY, and the writer who gave black humor its name, BRUCE JAY FRIEDMAN. Nightclub comedian and sometime writer Lenny Bruce carried this kind of humor into extreme and obscene territory.

Among the unabashed believers in the eternal value of laughter have been the Jewish American writers, who have combined their ethnic experience with the comic resilience that is a part of their heritage. Under the pen name LEONARD Q. ROSS, LEO ROSTEN applied the comic dialect tradition to the experience of East European immigrants learning English at night school in *The Education of H*Y*M*A*N K*A*P*L*A*N* (1937) and subsequent books about the earnest but not always apt Mr. Kaplan. Rosten also wrote highly popular comic lexicons beginning with *The Joys of Yiddish* (1969), as exercises in erudition and the eccentric ways of Jewish language and culture. Working the humor column tradition was HARRY GOLDEN, whose paper the *Carolina Israelite* was entirely devoted to his comments on the social and political scene in postwar America, later collected into a series of best-selling books beginning with *Only in America* (1958). The good humor and gentleness of his style and approach, no matter how serious the subject matter, caused many to label Golden a Jewish Will Rogers. Several major novelists have made ethnic humor central to their treatments of the Jewish American experience, especially PHILIP ROTH, SAUL BELLOW, and BERNARD MALAMUD.

African-Americans have always had a rich vein of indigenous humor in their folklore, oral traditions, tales, and games, and it has functioned as a comedy of resistance and survival in a long history of enslavement and oppression. CHARLES W. CHESNUTT incorporated much traditional folk humor in his stories collected in such books as *The Conjure Woman* (1899), as did PAUL LAURENCE DUNBAR in his dialect poetry, such as *Lyrics of Lowly Life* (1896), although Dunbar all too often reflected conventional stereotypes of African-American life. CLAUDE MCKAY's novels, for example, *Home to Harlem* (1928), celebrated the richness and humor of African-American life in Harlem. ZORA NEALE HURSTON set out to collect folklore and preserved it in gracefully written accounts and stories, as in *Mules and Men* (1925) and *Their Eyes Were Watching God* (1937). The most versatile African-American writer, LANGSTON HUGHES, wrote a series of satiric sketches for a newspaper about streetwise philosopher Jesse B. Simple, who punctured the pomposities of African-Americans and whites alike. These were collected in several volumes, beginning with *Simple Speaks His Mind* (1950). Hughes also edited the standard anthology, *The Book of Negro Humor* (1966). The capstone of African-American humor is RALPH ELLISON's novel, *Invisible Man* (1952), which gathers all the hate, hurt, and humiliation of growing up black in America into a masterful satire of the larger society and a picaresque comedy of the first order. Outrage is transformed into art through the touch of comic genius.

It has been obvious throughout the history of American humor as outlined here that periodicals have been central to its existence. Nearly every humorist has been affiliated with or written for the press at one time or another, and there seems to be some charismatic connection between the columns of newspapers and magazines and the desire to amuse people. Several periodicals have been essential, however, to the survival of humorous writing. In the 19th century, there were *Spirit of the Times* (1831–56), *Vanity Fair* (1859–63), *Puck* (1877–1918), *Judge* (1881–1949), and *Life* (1889–1936). In the 20th century, the major humor publications were *The New Yorker* (1925–   ), *Mad* (1952–   ), *National Lampoon* (1970–   ), and *The Onion* (1988–   ).

Because of the prevalence of a cynical, aggressive, and often blasphemous spirit in contemporary comedy, some critics have believed that American humor has been in a state of decline. They look back fondly at what they see as a golden age—the days of Chaplin, Thurber, and Will Rogers, who have no counterparts today. For all the bleak nay-sayers, however, there have been an equal number of comic optimists, and affirmation is at the heart of all types of humor, after all. Otherwise, why bother? The truth is that the American comic spirit is as strong and alive as ever.

Useful books on American humor include Constance Rourke, *American Humor: A Study of the National Character* (1931); Walter Blair, *Native American Humor* (1937); Norris W. Yates, *The American Humorist: Conscience of the Twentieth*

Century (1964); Walter Blair and Hamlin Hill, *America's Humor: From Poor Richard to Doonesbury* (1978); Neil Schmitz, *Of Huck and Alice: Humorous Writing in American Literature* (1983); Nancy Walker, *A Very Serious Thing: Women's Humor and American Culture* (1998) and *What's So Funny? Humor in American Culture* (1998); and Mel Watkins, *On the Real Side: A History of African-American Comedy* (1999).

M. THOMAS INGE

Humphrey, William (1924–1997), novelist. Humphrey was born in Texas. The distinction of his first novel, *Home from the Hill* (1958), lies in the effective contrast between its finely etched prose and its subject matter—the passions of men who are remembered in legends, the excitement of a wild-boar hunt, cars speeding across the Texas flats. Humphrey's writing includes *The Ordways* (1965) and *Proud Flesh* (1973), Southern family chronicles; *The Last Husband* (1953) and *A Time and a Place* (1968), story collections. Humphrey celebrates fishing in *The Spawning Run* (1971) and *My Moby Dick* (1978). *Farther Off from Heaven* (1977) is a memoir. *September Song*, short stories, appeared in 1992.

Humphreys, David (1752–1818), diplomat, manufacturer, writer. A man of varied abilities, Humphreys, born in Connecticut, served in the Continental army as an aide to Washington, who employed him on several important missions abroad. He foresaw America's industrial development and wrote a pedestrian *Poem on the Industry of the United States* (1783) and established a woollen mill after introducing Spanish merino sheep into Connecticut. *A Poem on the Happiness of the United States* (1780), a satire called THE ANARCHIAD (1786–87), a life of General Israel Putnam (1788), and two plays—*The Widow of Malabar* (1790) and *The Yankey in England* (1814)—were among his other productions. He was one of the HARTFORD WITS.

Humphries, [George] Rolfe (1894–1969), poet, teacher, critic, translator. Humphries's verses appeared in many magazines and a number of collections. His best work is in the graceful smaller forms, in which he shows a skillful use of verse sounds and cadence. Humphries did translations from Virgil (the *Aeneid*) and Ovid (the *Metamorphoses*), as well as from the works of modern European authors, including Lorca's *The Poet in New York* (1940). Among Humphries's published volumes are *Europa and Other Poems* (1929), *Out of the Jewel* (1942), *Forbid Thy Ravens* (1948), *The Wind of Time* (1949), *Poems Collected and New* (1954), and *Green Armor on Green Ground* (1956). His last poems were published in *Coat on a Stick* (1969).

Huncke, Herbert (1915–1996), Beat character and writer. Born in Greenfield, Massachusetts, Huncke grew up in Detroit and Chicago, and was involved in the street world of drugs, sex, and crime from his teenage years. He was most famous for his association with **Beat Generation** writers, appearing in a number of their works: in Kerouac's *The Town and the City* as Junkey, in *On the Road* as Elmo Hassel, and in *Visions of Cody* and *Books of Dreams* as Huck; in John Clellon Holmes's *Go* as Ancke; in William S. Burroughs's *Junkie* as the

title character, Herbert; and in a number of Ginsberg's poems, including *Howl*. His own writings include *Huncke's Journal* (1965), *Elsie John and Joey Martinez* (1979), *The Evening Sun Turned Crimson* (1980), and *Guilty of Everything* (1990).

Huneker, James Gibbons (1860–1921), biographer, short-story writer, novelist, memoirist. Born in Philadelphia, Huneker was the chief American exponent of critical IMPRESSIONISM and wrote always with subjective luxuriance, leaving textual analysis to others. He introduced new ideas and techniques to the United States and influenced the young writers who began to publish after World War I. He wrote at first for Philadelphia periodicals, then came to New York (after a fruitful stay in Paris studying music), where he served on various newspapers and magazines, including the *Musical Courier*, the *Sun*, the *Times*, and the *World*.

Among Huneker's collections of critical and biographical pieces are *Mezzotints in Modern Music* (1899), *Chopin* (1900), *Overtones* (1904), *Iconoclasts* (1905), *Egoists* (1909), *Promenades of an Impressionist* (1910), *Franz Liszt* (1911), *Old Fogy: His Musical Opinions and Grotesques* (1913), *The Pathos of Distance* (1913), *New Cosmopolis* (1915), *Ivory, Apes, and Peacocks* (1915), *Unicorns* (1917), *Bedouins* (1920), and *Variations* (1921). His only novel, *Painted Veils*, appeared in 1920, as did his autobiography, *Steeplejack*. Huneker published two collections of short stories: *Melomaniacs* (1902) and *Visionaries* (1905). His wife, Josephine Huneker, collected his *Letters* (1922) and his *Intimate Letters* (1924, repr. 1936).

Hunt, Helen. See HELEN HUNT JACKSON.

Hunt, Isaac (1742?–1809), lawyer, political writer, clergyman. Born in Barbados, Hunt became first a student, then a tutor at the University of Pennsylvania. He wrote a series of satires he called *A Humble Attempt at Scurrility* (1765), and the college as a result refused him his degree, finally granting it in 1771. When dissension arose between the colonies and the mother country, he took the Tory side, issuing *The Political Family* (1775) and engaging in other political activities. Threatened with violence, he escaped to Barbados and then to England. There he became a clergyman, and his son Leigh Hunt became a noted writer. But the elder man lost his position as a tutor in a ducal family because he tried to intervene in behalf of the American painter John Trumbull, who was charged with being a spy. He was arrested for debt and lived in great poverty for the rest of his life. One of his later writings was called *The Rights of Englishmen: An Antidote to the Poison Now Vending by Thomas Paine* (1791).

Hunt, William Gibbes (1791–1833), editor, publisher. Born in Boston and educated at Harvard, Hunt went to Lexington, Kentucky, where he founded two magazines, among the earliest to be established in the West: *The Western Monitor* (1815–19) and *The Western Review and Miscellaneous Magazine* (1819–21). Hunt included biography, fiction, verse, and history as well as digests of English novels. He also ran a series of scientific articles by CONSTANTINE RAFINESQUE, a traveler from Turkey in the United States.

Hunter, Dard (1883–1966), printer, papermaker, writer. Born in Ohio, Hunt established a press of at Chillicothe

(1919), after working for several years as art director with Elbert Hubbard's Roycroft Press. In Chillicothe he made his own paper, designed his own fonts, did his own printing, and wrote and published a number of highly praised books. Among them are *The Etching of Figures* (1915), *The Art of Bookmaking* (1915), *The Etching of Contemporary Life* (1917), *Primitive Papermaking* (1972), *The Literature of Papermaking, 1390–1800* (1925), *The Story of Paper* (1937), *Papermaking: The History and Technique of an Ancient Craft* (1943), *Papermaking by Hand in America* (1950), *Papermaking in Pioneer America* (1952), and *My Life with Paper, an Autobiography* (1958).

Hunter, Evan ["Ed McBain"] (1926–   ), novelist, playwright, screenwriter. Born in New York City as Salvatore Lambino (he changed his name legally to Evan Hunter in the 1950s) and educated at Cooper Union and Hunter College, Hunter wrote pulp fiction and mainstream novels before beginning the widely admired (and translated) Ed McBain series, set in the 87th Precinct of Isola, a city like New York created by the author. These mystery thrillers began to appear in 1956, with three in that year—*The Pusher, Cop Hater*, and *The Mugger*—and *The Last Dance* (2000) was the fiftieth in 44 years. Hunter's first novelistic success was *The Blackboard Jungle* (1954), a sensational exposé of the brutal underworld of a big-city high school that established him as a master of narrative. He has thus far written more than ninety works of fiction and sold more than one hundred million books.

Hunter, Kristin (1931–   ), novelist, short-story writer. From her first novel, *God Bless the Child* (1964), on through a varied body of work, Hunter depicts realistically but optimistically the African-American ghetto existence, especially in Harlem. She has been an advertising copywriter and an information officer for the City of Philadelphia, and an English instructor at the University of Pennsylvania. Her works include *The Landlord* (1966), *The Survivors* (1975), *The Lakestown Rebellion* (1978), *Kinfolks* (1996), and *Do Unto Others* (2000). She has also written a series of young adult books, the best-known being *The Soul Brothers and Sister Lou* (1968).

Hunter, Robert. See ANDROBOROS.

Hunters of Kentucky. A song celebrating the Kentucky Rifle Company's part in Andrew Jackson's victory over the British at New Orleans in the War of 1812. First published in 1822, it was probably composed by Samuel Woodworth and passed into the folk tradition.

Huron Indians [more exactly, **Wyandot**]. They were of the same speech and culture family as the Iroquois, but did not reach as high a degree of political development. They lived in Ontario and nearby sections of what was later the United States and often fought the Iroquois but were vanquished by them. They also fought the United States during the Revolution and the War of 1812. Surviving Hurons live in Canada, Michigan, Ohio, and Oklahoma.

Hurst, Fannie (1889–1968), writer of fiction, plays, and movie scenarios. She won her first celebrity with collections of short stories, particularly *Every Soul Hath Its Song* (1916), *Gaslight Sonatas* (1918), and *Humoresque* (1919), eight

stories of Jewish life in New York City that were turned into a play (1923). Among her books are *Star-Dust* (1921), *Lummox* (1923), *A President Is Born* (1928), *Back Street* (1931), *Hallelujah* (1944), *Man with One Head* (1954), *Family!* (1959), and *God Must Be Sad* (1961). Her autobiography is *Anatomy of Me* (1958).

Hurston, Zora Neale (1891–1960), anthropologist, novelist, short-story writer, essayist. Hurston was born in Eatonville, Florida, the first black incorporated town in America. She was educated at Howard, Barnard, and Columbia University, where she studied under anthropologist Franz Boaz. Her writings focus primarily on rural black folk who represent the culture in which she grew up. He novels are *Jonah's Gourd Vine* (1934), the story of a black preacher who owes his reputation largely to the wife he treats badly: *Their Eyes Were Watching God* (1937), often cited as the first black feminist novel of the 20th century for its female protagonist's conscious development from girlhood through liberated womanhood; *Moses Man of the Mountain* (1941), a critique of philosophical and political meanings of freedom and black leadership, patterned on the biblical exodus from Egypt, and *Seraph on the Suwanee* (1948), a story of poor rural whites. Her folklore collections are *Mules and Men* (1935) and *Tell My Horse* (1938). *Dust Tracks on a Road* (1942), Hurston's autobiography, won an award for its treatment of race relations. There are two collections of her stories, published in 1979 and 1985. Hurston, a significant writer of the Harlem Renaissance, was often criticized by her peers for celebrating black folk culture in art and folklore instead of engaging in overt protest against racial oppression of blacks. Neglected as a writer for years before her death, Hurston is now widely read and celebrated by writers and critics. See Robert Hemenway, *Zora Neale Hurston: A Literary Biography* (1977) and Karla F. C. Holloway, *The Character of the Word, The Texts of Zora Neale Hurston* (1987).

NELLIE MCKAY

Huston, John (1906–1987), director, actor, screenwriter. Born in Missouri, Huston acted from the time he was three. After a vagabond existence that included service in the Mexican army and singing on street corners in London, he settled in Hollywood, directing his first hit, *The Maltese Falcon* (1941). After service in World War II, he brought Sartre's *No Exit* to Broadway. *Treasure of Sierra Madre* (1946) won two Oscars for him and one for his father, actor Walter Huston. His other notable films include *Asphalt Jungle* (1950), *The African Queen* (1951), *The Night of the Iguana* (1964), and *The Man Who Would Be King* (1975). His final film, a version of James Joyce's short story *The Dead* (1987), displayed his sure touch with a delicate and tender theme. *An Open Book*, his autobiography, appeared in 1981.

Hutchins, Robert Maynard (1899–1977), president of the University of Chicago, later chancellor. Born in Brooklyn, New York, Hutchins abolished intercollegiate football at the University and set up a program permitting gifted students to start college after two years of high school, and to further shorten their stay in college by passing examinations. Among his books are *No Friendly Voice* (1936), *The Higher Learning in*

America (1936), *Education for Freedom* (1943), *St. Thomas and the World State* (1949), *The Conflict in Education* (1953), and *What's a College For?* (1960).

Hutchinson, Anne (1591–1643),   religious teacher. Born in England, the daughter of a clergyman, Hutchinson emigrated in 1634 with her husband and children to Boston. There her kindliness and forceful character won a following for the antinomian doctrines she advocated (see ANTINOMIAN-ISM). She asserted the possibility that "the person of the Holy Ghost dwells in a justified person" and that there was salvation by personal intuition of divine grace. She was tried for her beliefs and banished (1637). She moved first to Rhode Island, then to Pelham Manor, at that time a settlement near New York City. There, in the following year, she died in an Indian massacre near the site of her home on the present Hutchinson Parkway, named in her honor. She was probably the first woman in America who dared take the lead in discussing questions of religion. She is the subject of a number of biographies, including Edith Curtis's *Anne Hutchinson* (1930), Winnifred Rugg's *Unafraid: A Life of Anne Hutchinson* (1930), and R. P. Bolton's *A Woman Misunderstood: Anne, Wife of William Hutchinson* (1931).

Hutchinson, Thomas (1711–1780),   public official, historian. Born in Boston, Hutchinson entered Harvard at twelve. By age twenty-one he had accumulated a modest fortune in business and thereupon entered public life. He developed strong Tory tendencies and was made by George III first chief justice, then royal governor of Massachusetts. One of his decisions caused James Otis to utter his famous statement that "taxation without representation is tyranny." He did not like the Stamp Act but accepted it as legal, and a mob destroyed his home. As governor his authority was so generally ignored that martial law had to be proclaimed (1774). When General Gage and his troops arrived in the following year, Gage assumed the governorship, and Hutchinson went to England to render an account of his administration. He never returned to America.

Hutchinson's *Diary and Letters* were published (2 v. 1884–86). His most important writing was *A Collection of Original Papers Relative to the History of the Colony of Massachusetts Bay* (2 v. 1764, 1767); a third volume appeared after his death (1828). The so-called *Hutchinson Letters* were written allegedly to the British Foreign Office in 1768–69 and advocated strong measures against the colonies. Somehow, they came into the possession of Benjamin Franklin and, apparently against Hutchinson's wishes, were published in 1772, causing much bad feeling against him. The publication brought about Franklin's removal from the office of deputy postmaster-general. Hutchinson was attacked in Mercy Otis Warren's play THE ADULATEUR (published 1773), and he was a prominent character in Lydia M. Child's novel *The Rebels* (1825).

Hutton, Joseph (1787–1828),   actor, playwright. Born in Philadelphia and one of the first American dramatists to see his work performed publicly, Hutton was imitative and rarely used American settings. Among his plays are *The School for Prodigals* (1808), *The Wounded Hussar* (1809), *Fashionable Follies* (1809), and *The Orphan of Prague* (1810).

Hutton, Laurence (1843–1904),   critic, writer, bibliophile, editor. Born in New York City, Hutton served as drama critic of the New York *Mail* and later became literary editor of *Harper's Magazine*. He was widely acquainted with the authors of England and the United States, and traveled a great deal in Europe. He wrote nearly fifty books. Among them are *Plays and Players* (1875), *Literary Landmarks of London* (1885), *Curiosities of the American Stage* (1891), *Literary Landmarks of Edinburgh* (1891), *Edwin Booth* (1893), *Literary Landmarks of Rome* (1897), and *Talks in a Library* (1905).

Hwang, David Henry (1957–   ),   playwright. Son of immigrant Chinese-Americans, Hwang was educated at Stanford and Yale Drama School. He won the Obie Award for *FOB* (1981), a play about the survival strategies of new immigrants—"fresh off the boat"; *Family Devotions* (1983) treats the same theme. His plays have been produced in Singapore and Hong Kong as well as across the United States. *The Dance and the Railroad* (1982), concerning a strike in 1867 among Chinese railroad workers, has been produced for television. *M. Butterfly* (1988) won the Tony Award as best play of the year and is his most celebrated work to date. He wrote the screenplay for *Golden Gate* (1994). *Trying to Find Chinatown* (1999) contains selected plays.

Hymn to the Night (1839),   a poem by HENRY WADSWORTH LONGFELLOW. One of Longfellow's best-known poems, *Hymn* was praised by Poe (no indiscriminate eulogist of Longfellow): "No Poem ever opened with a beauty more august."

Hyperion (1839),   a romance by HENRY WADSWORTH LONGFELLOW. Stemming from Longfellow's studies of German romanticism, *Hyperion* has been called his *Wilhelm Meister*. It narrates in thin disguise his love for Frances Appleton, later his wife. Paul Flemming, a typical romantic hero, is traveling in Europe when he falls in love with Mary Ashburton. She spurns him, and he continues his quest for the mythical blue rose, in German legend a symbol of the unattainable. During his picaresque travels he is accompanied by Berkley, an older and more experienced man who attempts to cure Paul of his romantic love. Berkley's counsel combines with unfavorable circumstances to keep Paul from attaining his dreams. The book is studded with many of the old legends Flemming hears in his travels, which foreshadows Longfellow's use of legend in such later works as *The New England Legends* and TALES OF A WAYSIDE INN.

I

Iberville, Sieur d' [Pierre Le Moyne] (1661–1706), explorer. Born in Quebec, Iberville has been called the first great Canadian. His achievements as an explorer and soldier were great, but he is chiefly remembered as one of the founders of Louisiana. He fought against the English as a member of the French navy later in expeditions to Hudson's Bay (1690). He was commissioned (1698) to found a colony in Louisiana, and made the first permanent settlement at what is now Biloxi, Mississippi. While preparing a naval expedition against England he died of yellow fever at Havana. He had planned to capture New York and Boston.

Icarians. See ETIENNE CABET.

Icaza Coronel, Jorge (1906–1979), Ecuadoran novelist, short-story writer, playwright. Icaza began by writing plays when he was an actor with the National Theatre in the late 1920s. His literary reputation, however, is based on his story collections and novels. His novels belong to the *Indigenista* movement, which protested the abject conditions to which the Indian population of the Andes had been reduced by colonial and neocolonial rule. By far his best-known work is *Huasipungo* (1934, tr. 1962, also tr. as *The Villagers*, 1973), a novel depicting with horrifying realism the appropriation of Indian lands, a brutal massacre to abort their protest, and the squalid conditions in which they are forced to exist.

Icebound (1923), a play by OWEN DAVIS. This Pulitzer Prize–winner depicts the Jordan family, a clan of assorted scoundrels who await the death of Mother Jordan. The mother disappoints them by leaving her money to Jane Crosby, a poor relative. Jane ultimately marries a reformed member of the family, for whom she has secretly been holding the money in trust.

Iceman Cometh, The (1939, produced 1947). A play by EUGENE O'NEILL. Through the conversations of a group of derelicts in the backroom of the End of the Line Cafe, O'Neill pursues a recurring theme in his work: existence derives its meaning from the fantasies and illusions we use to conceal reality. Among the last of his plays, it seems to conclude that hope is an important human resource to be salvaged only if illusion can be kept alive.

Ichabod (1850), a poem by JOHN GREENLEAF WHITTIER. The title of the poem is a Hebrew word meaning "inglorious"; it is sometimes translated as "the glory hath departed." The title may have been suggested to Whittier by a remark of James Russell Lowell's in the NATIONAL ANTI-SLAVERY STANDARD (July 2, 1846) concerning DANIEL WEBSTER: "Shall not the Recording Angel write *Ichabod* after the name of this man in the great Book of Doom?"

The poem was provoked by Whittier's hot anger at Webster when he read Webster's "Seventh of March" (1850) speech, delivered in support of the COMPROMISE OF 1850 and of the Fugitive Slave Law. Webster preached moderation, although he knew the speech would lose him many supporters. He was denounced by many New Englanders, including Emerson, Holmes, W. L. Garrison, and Wendell Phillips. *Ichabod* is surely one of the most powerful poems of denunciation ever written. Thirty years later Whittier repented of his violence, and in THE LOST OCCASION paid a tender tribute to Webster.

Ichabod Crane. The gawky schoolmaster whom the burly Brom Van Brunt outwits in Washington Irving's LEGEND OF SLEEPY HOLLOW (in *The Sketch Book*, 1819). Both are suitors for the hand of Katerina Van Tassel; Brom scares the schoolmaster out of the running by pretending to be a headless horseman. Irving says that on a windy day Ichabod looked like "some scarecrow eloped from a cornfield."

Ide, Simeon (1794–1889), printer. Ide, born in Vermont, was one of the earliest of American printers. At Claremont, New Hampshire, he printed *The New England Farmer's Diary and Almanac*. Among other books was *Scraps of California History Never Before Published: A Biographical Sketch of William B. Ide* (1880). His son Lemuel formed a publishing firm with E. P. Dutton: Ide & Dutton (1852).

idealism. A system of philosophy that emphasizes mind or ideas as the central reality of the universe. In various forms it is identified with Plato, Plotinus, Kant, Fichte, Hegel, Schelling, Berkeley, and other Old World metaphysicians, all of whom have exerted great influence on American philosophers. It was not until American writers and teachers became familiar with the names and works of the great German idealists of the 18th and 19th centuries that the movement made much headway in the United States. An early systematic expositor of German idealism was Laurens Perseus Hickock (1798–1888) of Union College, whose principal writings were *Rational Psychology, or, The Subjective Idea and the Objective Law of All Intelligence* (1848),

Moral Science (1853), and *Empirical Psychology* (1854). His influence was continued at Amherst, principally by Charles Edward Garman (1850–1907), whose *Letters, Lectures, and Addresses* were collected in 1909. Other notable teachers who spread the idealist gospel were George Herbert Palmer at Harvard, George Holmes Howison at MIT, John Bascom at Williams, A. C. Armstrong at Wesleyan, Noah Porter and George Trumbull Ladd at Yale, George Sylvester Morris at Johns Hopkins and Michigan, John Grier Hibben at Princeton, Jacob Gould Schurmann at Cornell, Nicholas Murray Butler at Columbia, Bowden P. Bowne at Boston University, and James E. Creighton at Cornell. Greatest of them all was Josiah Royce of Harvard, who advanced from what may be called a pure idealism to one that was influenced by the pragmatist Charles Peirce.

Numerous schools of idealism flourished. First and most important was the St. Louis School, joined with the names of Henry Brokmeyer, William Torrey Harris, and Denton J. Snider; for a time it formed an alliance with the Concord School of Bronson Alcott. Later came Thomas Davidson's Summer School of the Cultural Sciences at Glenmore in the Adirondacks and the Breadwinner's College in New York City. Widely influential was the Society for Ethical Culture, founded in 1876 by Felix Adler in New York City; branches were established in other cities and it is still active. Idealism was important in the intellectual development of Henry James, Sr., G. Stanley Hall, John Dewey, William James, Alfred H. Lloyd, and others generally not reckoned as professed idealists. Its influence was potent in the transcendentalist movement and in the development of what Schneider calls "idealistic democracy," particularly in the writings of the St. Louis School and in those of the Rev. Elisha Mulford. Walt Whitman, though probably not directly acquainted with the works of Hegel, professed a strong adherence to his doctrines. In general, American idealists have been greatly interested in the applications of idealist doctrines to government, law, the workings of society, the uses of logic, education, and behavior. See TRANSCENDENTALISM.

Idell, Albert E[dward] (1901–1958), novelist. Born in Philadelphia, Idell was widely experienced in many professions, including prize fighting. He used autobiographical materials in many of his novels, which include *Pug* (1941), *Centennial Summer* (1943), *Bridge to Brooklyn* (1944), *The Great Blizzard* (1948), and *The Corner Store* (1953).

Ides of March, The (1948), a novel by THORNTON WILDER. A fictionalization of the life of Julius Caesar, this novel deals with the dictator's last months and his assassination. The story is told through documents—letters, extracts from diaries, snatches of verse, proclamations, circulars—and reveals Wilder's knowledge of Roman antiquity. The book falls into four sections, each covering the same period of time. Thus, the novel presents four views of the same events.

Idiot's Delight (1936), a play by ROBERT E. SHERWOOD, in which he argues the issues of the oncoming World War II. Among the characters, all isolated in an Alpine hotel, are a young English couple, a German scientist, a French munitions manufacturer, and some American actors. After seeing the futility of the efforts of "the little people" to stop a war, one of the actors and a mysterious Irene resume an old love affair. The play, which won a Pulitzer Prize, reveals Sherwood's gloomy belief in the decay of Western civilization.

If I Should Die Tonight (published in the *Christian Union*, June 18, 1873), a meditative poem usually attributed to Arabella Eugenie Smith (1844–1916). It became very popular, but the parody that BEN KING (1857–1894) wrote under the same title did much to destroy the vogue of the verses.

Ignatow, David (1914–1997), poet and editor. Ignatow was among the poets who frequented Greenwich Village in the late 1930s and early 1940s and, under the tutelage of William Carlos Williams, espoused the tenets of IMAGISM. Daring in its use of meter and fantastic imagery, Ignatow's work is also marked by a keenly individual expression of humanism. His poems are primarily short, perceptive portraits or parables, centering on urban man's anxious existence. In 1967 he became coeditor of the distinguished literary journal *Chelsea*. Three years later he published a collected edition of his work, *Poems: 1934–1969* (1970). He was awarded the Bollingen Prize for Poetry in 1977. *Tread the Dark* (1978), his seventh book of poems, contains some of his most purely expressed meditations on the human condition. *Open Between Us* was published in 1979; it was followed by *Whisper to the Earth* in 1982 and *Leaving the Door Open* in 1984. *New and Collected Poems: 1970–1985* appeared in 1987. Other titles include *Shadowing the Ground* (1991), *I Have a Name* (1996) and the posthumous *Living Is What I Wanted: Last Poems* (2000).

I Have a Rendezvous with Death (*North American Review*, October, 1916), a poem by ALAN SEEGER. The young poet, who enlisted in the French Foreign Legion, wrote this poem shortly before he was killed in the Battle of the Somme. It immediately became popular and was perhaps better known than any other World War I poem by an American. It was included in Seeger's *Poems* (1916).

I Hear It Was Charged Against Me (1860), a poem by WALT WHITMAN. Whitman here replies to the charge that he was preaching destructive, anarchistic doctrines. He denies the charge, says that he has no interest in being either for or against institutions, but believes only in "the institution of the dear love of comrades."

Ikkemotubbe. Chickasaw chief in Faulkner's fiction, also known as Doom or The Man. He is mentioned in a number of works and appears as a character in "A Justice," "Red Leaves," and "A Courtship."

Ile (1919), a one-act play by EUGENE O'NEILL. This is the story of a sea captain who insists on continuing his hunt for whale oil (ile) at the cost of his wife's sanity and the risk of a mutiny. It is a powerful melodrama and has been a favorite of little theater and amateur groups. It was first produced (1917) by the PROVINCETOWN PLAYERS.

Iliad, The American (1947), the story of the Civil War narrated by eyewitnesses and contemporaries, as edited by Otto Eisenschiml and Ralph Newman. With the help of several hundred contributors, chosen from both sides of the

Mason-Dixon Line, the editors present a vivid and complete picture of the great struggle.

Illinois Monthly Magazine. Founded October 1830 in Vandalia, Illinois, by JAMES HALL, the magazine moved first to Cincinnati, then to Louisville, where it became widely known as the *Western Monthly Magazine.* It ceased publication in 1837. Hall wrote most of the contents: stories, poems, history, criticism, gossip.

I'll Take My Stand: The South and the Agrarian Tradition, by Twelve Southerners (1930), a symposium in which the participants were eminent Southerners, including ALLEN TATE, JOHN GOULD FLETCHER, ROBERT PENN WARREN, STARK YOUNG, and DONALD DAVIDSON. Most had been members of The Fugitives, a group at Vanderbilt University who published a little magazine of poetry, *The Fugitive* (1922–25). In this *Agrarian Manifesto*, as they called the book, they outlined an anticapitalist movement, drawing their inspiration from the past—from Plato, Jefferson, and Carlyle. They favored an intellectual aristocracy.

I'll Take You Home Again, Kathleen (1876), a favorite song, with words and music by Thomas Paine Westendorf. Westendorf's wife was visiting her home in New York, while he had to stick to his schoolteaching job in Plainfield, Indiana—hence this plaintive song.

I Love You Truly (in *Seven Songs*, 1901; separately published, 1906), a song by CARRIE JACOBS BOND, who also wrote the music. It became one of her greatest hits and still endures.

Images or Shadows of Divine Things (1948), by JONATHAN EDWARDS. These itemized manuscript notes by Edwards were gathered and published by PERRY MILLER, who saw in them an attempt "to work out a new sense of the divinity of nature and the naturalness of divinity." Miller argued that they established Edwards as "the first American empiricist," a theologian who was willing to subordinate biblical revelation to the authority of natural reason.

Imagism. A short-lived and sporadic movement whose origins, poetic theory, and significance for the development of modern poetry are matters of some debate. Initially, in 1908–09 in London, a group of poets including EZRA POUND gathered around the English critic T. E. Hulme, who championed the use of clear, concise images and free verse to revive a classicist spirit and combat the decadence of humanism and romanticism responsible for the excesses of late 19th-century English poetry. In 1912, Pound referred to Hulme's movement as the School of Images and thus acknowledged its continuity with the group he was then leading, *Les Imagistes* of 1912–14. Between 1915 and 1917 the movement was led by AMY LOWELL, whose three imagist anthologies did much to popularize its tenets and practitioners, while Pound's theory of the image evolved into Vorticism. After 1917, imagism as a movement dissolved, but by then its values were widely established.

In Pound's formulation, the three principles of imagism are: "direct treatment of 'the thing,' whether subjective or objective"; "to use absolutely no word that does not contribute

to the presentation"; and "to compose in the sequence of the musical phrase, not in the sequence of a metronome." For models of spare, nondiscursive presentation and meters other than the accentual-syllabic pentameter, imagists turned to a wide variety of literatures, including classical Greek and Latin poetry, Chinese and Japanese forms, and biblical, Old English, Provençal, and Symbolist verse. The technical innovations and originality inspired by these models, as well as the adoption of such an eclectic, ahistorical, and international tradition for modern poetry in English, have been important for 20th-century poetry in general. H. D., Richard Aldington, F. S. Flint, J. G. Fletcher, and Lowell were counted among the original *Imagistes*, but the work of such poets as T. S. Eliot, William Carlos Williams, Wallace Stevens, Marianne Moore, and D. H. Lawrence also registers the impact of imagism.

The rhetorical core of this poetic is the image, which Pound defined in 1913 as "that which presents an intellectual and emotional complex in an instant of time." He added that "the presentation of such a 'complex' instantaneously" gives a "sense of sudden liberation," and a "sense of freedom from time limits and space limits." The transcendent note sounded here suggests a longer genealogy for the image in symbolist and romantic poetics. Pound's description in 1914 of a one-image poem as a "superposition" or "one idea set on top of another" further elaborates this poetic, which ultimately yields one compositional principle of the CANTOS. Pound's two-line "In a Station of the Metro" (1914), in which he juxtaposes the "apparition" of faces in a subway crowd to "petals" on a "black bough," has become the paradigmatic imagist poem. This understanding of metaphor not as ornament but as structure is another legacy of imagism for 20th-century poetry.

Discussions of the sources, history, theory, and poetry of the imagist movement include René Taupin, *The Influence of French Symbolism on Modern American Poetry* (1929, 1985); Stanley K. Coffman, Jr., *Imagism* (1951); Frank Kermode, *Romantic Image* (1957); Herbert N. Schneidau, *Ezra Pound: The Image and the Real* (1969); J. B. Harmer, *Victory in Limbo: Imagism 1908–1917* (1975); and John T. Gage, *In the Arresting Eye* (1981).

MUTLU KONUK BLASING

Imlay, Gilbert (1754–1828?), novelist, writer of travel books, soldier, surveyor, adventurer. Had Imlay written a full and frank account of his own extraordinary career, it might well have been superior to his novel THE EMIGRANTS, OR, THE HISTORY OF AN EXPATRIATED FAMILY (1793). He fought in the Revolution and assumed the title of captain. In 1783 he went to Kentucky, where he bought land and became a surveyor. But he became entangled in financial and legal difficulties, fled to England (1792), and later to France, where he sought to persuade the government to seize Louisiana from the Spaniards. In France also he formed an attachment to Mary Wollstonecraft and was the father of her illegitimate daughter, Fanny. He deserted her and his daughter, though he seems to have continued to see them; his last meeting with Mary was recorded in 1796, shortly before Mary's marriage to William Godwin. From this time on, there is no definite information about Imlay. In 1828 a Gilbert Imlay was buried on the island of Jersey.

Imlay wrote two books, *A Topographical Description of the Western Territory of North America* (1792) and *The Emigrants*. Both are enthusiastic eulogies of the United States. The Irish poet Thomas Moore called the former a romantic work "which would seduce us into a belief that innocence, peace, and freedom had deserted the rest of the world for Martha's Vineyard and the banks of the Ohio." *The Emigrants* describes the adventures of an English family in America, drawing invidious comparisons between the evils of the Old World and the wonders of the New. In the spirit of English radicalism, Imlay argued in his novel for women's rights and advocated easier divorce.

Impending Crisis of the South, The (1857).   See HINTON ROWAN HELPER.

Imperative Duty, An (1891),   a novel by WILLIAM DEAN HOWELLS. This was probably the first novel that centered on a characteristically American social problem, the sudden discovery of African ancestry by a person apparently white. Rhoda Aldgate, the beautiful heroine, discovers that she is one-sixteenth African-American. She has pangs of conscience and finally decides to tell the man who wants to marry her. Already aware of the fact, he regards it as unimportant.

Imp of the Perverse, The (*Graham's Magazine*, July 1845),   a story by EDGAR ALLAN POE. This is the last of the group called Tales of Conscience. The story, which includes a discourse on phrenology, seeks to explain by morbid example the principle of "perversity."

impressionism.   This is a term for an artistic method emphasizing sense impressions of experience on the observer rather than objectivity. In painting it is applied to the French Impressionists of the 1870s, who experimented with light effects. In literature it is applied to a branch of realism. Gustave Flaubert used impressionist techniques to produce the illusion of reality: he described carefully selected details of a character or scene and left it to readers to organize the impressions for themselves. Impressionism later became a part of the technique of any writer who employed SYMBOLISM, NATURALISM, or EXPRESSIONISM and was never really thought of as a separate school of writing. Joseph Conrad was an impressionist in the tradition of Flaubert and Maupassant; among American authors, HENRY JAMES and STEPHEN CRANE have been called impressionists. A related technique in poetry was IMAGISM. In criticism, impressionism—often associated with fine writing like that of Walter Pater—emphasizes the individual response to a work of art; it has been described as "the adventures of a soul among masterpieces."

In Abraham's Bosom (1926),   a play by PAUL GREEN. It is a play of mingled pity and terror, in which a mulatto, Abraham McCranie, tries to help African-Americans by establishing a school for them in a North Carolina town. His white father helps him, but after the father's death his white half-brother, Lonnie, declines to give any further assistance and Abraham kills him. The play, praised for its tragic intensity, won a Pulitzer Prize.

In Cold Blood (1966).   TRUMAN CAPOTE called his account of the 1959 murder of a Kansas farm family a nonfiction novel. Using information he collected through interviews with townspeople and the killers, Capote created a vivid portrait of the criminals and graphically described the crime, the criminals' escape to Mexico, capture, trial, appeals, and hanging (1965).

Independence Hall.   This famous building on Independence Square, Philadelphia, was first erected as a capitol for the colony of Pennsylvania. In 1775 the Continental Congress met here and chose Washington as commander-in-chief; in 1776 the same body adopted the DECLARATION OF INDEPENDENCE in this building. THE ARTICLES OF CONFEDERATION and the CONSTITUTION were drawn up in sessions held in Independence Hall. Here is housed the Liberty Bell, which was cast in England in 1752.

Independent, The.   A weekly periodical published in New York City from 1848 to 1923, then in Boston until 1928. Originally a Congregationalist journal, it became interdenominational in later years, and in the 20th century engaged in much political discussion. It had some notable editors, including HENRY WARD BEECHER (1861–64), WILLIAM HAYES WARD (1896–1914), and Hamilton Holt (1914–20). Fine writers of the day contributed to its pages. In 1916 it absorbed HARPER'S WEEKLY and in 1928 was merged into THE OUTLOOK.

Indian and Oklahoma Territory.   A region long possessed by the FIVE CIVILIZED TRIBES, lying north of Texas. By presidential proclamation the land in this territory was thrown open to white settlement, as of noon on April 22, 1889. At the sound of a bugle, 50,000 men and women made a wild rush to stake out claims. Approximately a year later the Territory of Oklahoma was organized, but a small section continued to be called Indian Territory. In 1907 the two were combined to make the State of Oklahoma. Many portions of this region have appeared in romantic fiction, as in COURTNEY RYLEY COOPER's *Oklahoma* (1926), Edna Ferber's CIMARRON (1930), and Dora Aydelotte's *Trumpets Calling* (1938).

Indian Bible (New Testament, 1661; entire Bible, 1663), a translation of the Scriptures into the dialect of the Naticks, a Massachusetts tribe of the Algonquins, by JOHN ELIOT.

Indian Burying Ground, The (1788),   a poem by PHILIP FRENEAU. Always sympathetic to the Indians, Freneau in this poem portrays a huntsman who at his death is buried in a sitting posture, with venison, images of birds, bow and arrows, and other reminders of his life at his side. The penultimate stanza closes with two striking lines: "The hunter still the deer pursues,/The hunter and the deer, a shade!" The English poet Thomas Campbell liked the last line so well that he concluded the fourth stanza of his *O'Connor's Child* (1809) with the same words.

Indian captivity narratives.   Stories of white people abducted by Indians. These narratives constituted an early American literary genre and continued to appear from the colonial period to the last quarter of the 19th century. The subject matter was similar—sudden attacks on cabins and the burning of settlements, the scalping of men and women and the killing of children, horrible tortures of the captives carried away alive, and frightful sufferings as they went with the Indians from one camp to another, sometimes starving, often beaten, occasionally—it was alleged—even eaten.

The earliest narratives, simple, direct, and religious, begin with Mrs. Mary Rowlandson's book CAPTIVITY AND RESTAURATION OF MRS. MARY ROWLANDSON. Other examples are found in Increase Mather's ESSAY FOR THE RECORDING OF ILLUSTRIOUS PROVIDENCES (1684), Cotton Mather's MAGNALIA CHRISTI AMERICANA (1702), and John Williams's REDEEMED CAPTIVE RETURNING TO ZION (1707). The narratives became more literary, as in Samuel Bownas's version (1760) of Elizabeth Hanson's *God's Mercy Surmounting Man's Cruelty* (1728). Then hacks began to provide these narratives, supplanting pious individuals who were thankful to God for their rescue. Hatred is expressed for white men, especially Frenchmen and priests, as much as for the Indians, as in William Fleming's *Narrative of the Sufferings and Surprising Deliverances of William and Elizabeth Fleming* (1750) and Robert Eastburn's *The Dangers and Sufferings of Robert Eastburn* (1758). Even more popular was the gory and sensational volume *French and Indian Cruelty Exemplified in the Life and Various Vicissitudes of Peter Williamson* (1757). The material becomes a mélange of fact and fiction with salability rather than truth the main goal. Charles Brockden Brown modified the captive narrative in EDGAR HUNTLY (1799) by transferring it into the realm of avowed fiction.

In the 19th century the problem of authenticity became genuine and often insoluble, especially as historians began to turn to these narratives as a basis for their chronicles. Some of the earlier collections were still frankly sensational. More objective were the editions prepared by Samuel Gardner Drake (1832, 1839), J. Pritts (1839), and HENRY R. SCHOOLCRAFT (1844). Collections of narratives of captivity are to be found at the Newbery Library, the Huntington Library, and the Library of Congress. H. H. Peckham's *Captured by Indians* (1954) contains fourteen true tales of pioneer survivors.

Indian [Amerindian] languages.

Philologists have been attracted to the Indian languages ever since foreigners first came in contact with Native Americans. An early theory developed to the effect that Native Americans were the lost tribes of Israel and their languages variants of Hebrew; much ingenuity was expended in the pursuit of this conjecture. Later philologists attempted to reduce the confusing number of Indian languages to an acceptable order. One classification, made by J. W. POWELL for the Bureau of Ethnology (1891), listed fifty-six different linguistic families among tribes living north of Mexico. EDWARD SAPIR later reduced these to six: Eskimo-Aleut, Algonquian-Wakashan, NaDene, Uto-Aztecan, Penutian, and Hokan-Siouan. In all, more than two hundred separate languages have been defined. In spite of much speculation, the derivation of most Indian languages remains in doubt, although it is now thought that the Eskimo-Aleut family belongs to the Uralic group along with Finno-Ugric. Central and South American Indian languages are almost equally numerous and complex.

Words borrowed from the Indians were the earliest Americanisms and fell largely into two groups, those borrowed indirectly through Spanish and Portuguese, and those directly borrowed after the establishment of English colonies in North America. Among the former are *cacao* (cocoa), *canoe, hammock, hurricane, potato, tobacco, tomato, buccaneer, avocado, cashew, tapioca, cougar*, and *coyote*. Direct borrowings include *opossum, moccasin, terrapin, moose, powwow, wigwam, hominy, wampum, squaw, hickory, tomahawk, toboggan, chipmunk*, and *tepee*. In addition many American place names are of Indian origin.

Indian poetry.

Although various 18th- and 19th-century American poets had professed an interest in Indian poetry and had pretended to imitate Indian forms in their own works, it was not until almost 1900 that scholars and critics began a large-scale study of traditional Indian poetry in native languages. By far the greatest of those who first entered the field was FRANCES DENSMORE, whose many books and monographs, beginning in 1893, made Indian poetry and music accessible to everyone. Her translations have been highly praised for their accuracy and literary quality. Others who have worked in the field are WASHINGTON MATTHEWS (*The Mountain Chant: A Navaho Ceremony*, 1887; *The Night Chant*, 1902; *Navaho Myths, Prayers and Songs*, 1907); Franz Boas (*The Central Eskimo*, 1888; *Chinook Songs*, 1888; *Eskimo Tales and Songs*, 1894); NATALIE CURTIS BURLIN (*The Indians' Book*, 1908, rev. 1923); Eda Lou Walton (*Navajo Traditional Poetry*, 2 v. 1920); Nellie Barnes (*American Indian Love Lyrics*, 1925); William Thalbitzer (*The Ammassalik Eskimo*, 1923); Constance Lindsay Skinner (*Aztec Poets*, 1925; *Songs of the Coast Dwellers*, 1930); Ruth Underhill (*Singing for Power, The Song Magic of the Papago Indians*, 1938); and Paul Radin (*The Road of Life and Death: A Ritual Drama of the American Indian*, 1945). See NATIVE AMERICAN PROSE AND POETRY.

Indian Princess, The, or, La Belle Sauvage (1803),

a play by J. N. BARKER. This was the first play dealing with Indians to be produced and the first to introduce POCAHONTAS as the leading character. It was also the first original American play to be produced in England after initial performance in America. Barker saw that the historical rescue of JOHN SMITH by the Indian princess came too early to serve as a climax and made the love affair between her and JOHN ROLFE an important part of the plot. Her saving of the colonists became the climax. For a time Pocahontas and her fellow Indians talk rhythmically in an imitation of Indian speech but later in the rhythms of blank verse.

Indian Prophecy, The (1827),

a play by George Washington Parke Custis (1781–1857). Custis, George Washington's stepson, treated in this play an early incident in Washington's life. The Indian chiefs who brought about Braddock's defeat and death (1755) killed two horses under the young Virginian officer and pierced his clothing with bullets, but at last abandoned their attempt to kill him. They believed him invulnerable. This play started a vogue for Indian drama.

Indians, Tales of the North American (1929),

selected and annotated by Stith Thompson (1885–1976). The

tales are organized in nine groups: mythological stories, mythical incidents, trickster tales, hero tales, journeys to the other world, animal wives and husbands, miscellaneous tales, tales borrowed from Europeans, and Bible stories. These are further analyzed in his valuable notes into a series of motifs. A map indicates cultural areas.

Indian Student, The, or, Force of Nature (1788), a poem by PHILIP FRENEAU. Shalum, an Indian boy living on the banks of the Susquehanna, is persuaded by a priest to leave "Satan's waste" and attend Harvard. There he submits for a while to the boredom of studies, but determines at last to leave those "gloomy walls" and return to the delights of nature.

Indian Summer (1886), a novel by WILLIAM DEAN HOWELLS. Theodore Colville, a journalist of forty, meets in Florence a boyhood acquaintance, the widow Mrs. Lina Bowen. He becomes engaged to her young ward, Imogene Graham. When Imogene realizes she is in love with a younger man, Colville at last recognizes the maturer love that has developed between him and Mrs. Bowen, who had been helpless to interfere in what she knew to be a mismatch. Howells considered the book one of his best.

In Dubious Battle (1936), a novel by JOHN STEINBECK and one of the more important books to come out of the proletarian movement. This was Steinbeck's first successful novel. *In Dubious Battle* deals with a fruit strike in a California valley and the attempts of radical leaders to organize, lead, and provide for the striking pickers. Perhaps the most important, although not the central, character is Doc Burton, who helps the strikers and is concerned with seeing things as they exist, without labels of good and bad attached. The strike fails, and Jim, one of the two leaders, is senselessly killed. The title of the novel is from Milton's *Paradise Lost* and refers to the "dubious battle" of Satan and his angels with the hosts of heaven.

Industrial Valley (1939), a factual narrative by RUTH MCKENNEY. In it she employs the techniques of fiction, especially those introduced by JOHN DOS PASSOS. McKenney tells the story of the strike of the Akron, Ohio, rubber workers, which ran from January 1932 until March 1936. She introduces actual persons, scenes, incidents, newspaper headlines, and other contemporary data.

Industrial Workers of the World. See I.W.W.

Infidel, The (1835), a historical novel by ROBERT M. BIRD. A sequel to his CALAVAR (1834), it continues the story of Cortez's conquest of Mexico. Bird describes the scenery of Mexico and relates the events that marked Cortez's advance.

Ingalls, [Mildred Dodge] Jeremy (1911–2000), poet, teacher. Ingalls, born in Massachusetts, saw her first collection, *The Metaphysical Sword*, win the 1941 prize of the YALE SERIES OF YOUNGER POETS. Her major work, *Tahl* (1945), is a long poem in blank verse, contemporary in subject matter. In 1953 she published *The Galilean Way*, a synthesis of her philosophic and religious views. Among other titles are: *The Woman from the Island* (1958); *These Islands Also* (1959); and *The Stubborn Quantum* (1983). *The Epic Tradition and Other Essays* appeared in 1989.

Ingalls, Rachel (1941–), novella writer. Born in the United States, Ingalls moved to England soon after graduation from Radcliffe. She has had several books published there and became known to American audiences with the U.S. publication (1983) of her novella *Mrs. Caliban* (1982), the story of a lonely woman who escapes dismal reality through a love affair with Larry, a tall humanlike amphibian. Writing in the serious fantasy genre, Ingalls has produced *Theft* (1970); *The Man Who Was Left Behind* (1971); *Binstead's Safari* (1983), in which a folklorist's wife has an affair with a man who can transform into a lion; *I See a Long Journey* (1985), three supernatural tales; *The Pearl Killers* (1986), four gothic stories; and *The End of Tragedy* (1987), horror stories.

Inge, William (1913–1973), playwright. Inge was born and grew up in Independence, Kansas, the son of an overprotective mother. Intellectually precocious but socially shy, Inge possessed homosexual tendencies that apparently troubled him. He worked as a radio announcer, critic for a newspaper, and university teacher. Originally he wanted to be an actor, but he taught until age 37, when his first play was professionally produced. Inge started drinking early in life and went through years of psychoanalysis and membership in Alcoholics Anonymous, but eventually succumbed to depression and committed suicide.

During the 1950s, Inge was one of America's most successful playwrights, with four plays that did well in New York and became movies. Most of his dramas take place in small Midwestern towns and contain similar themes. His first Broadway show, *Come Back, Little Sheba* (1950), tells about an alcoholic, Doc Delaney, and his fantasizing wife, Lola. Childless, they battle with their loss of youth and ambition, but in the end they come to accept their situation. Some of Inge's other works also deal with a childless couple, based on his aunt and uncle, and Inge himself knew the problems of alcoholism.

Picnic (1953) concerns a group of lonely, frustrated women in a small Kansas town. A handsome, masculine stranger arrives to woo a beautiful young woman and persuade her to run away with him. The play deals with family life and love and associated failures, frustrations, and loneliness. *Bus Stop* (1955) is a romantic comedy set also in a Midwestern town. Bo, a naive cowboy, tries to force Cherie, a "sexually experienced" dancer, to marry him. The characters express Inge's favorite themes of loneliness and acceptance of life for what it is. He based his last successful play, *Dark at the Top of the Stairs* (1957), on his own boyhood. Sonny is Inge, and the other major characters resemble his own parents and sister. The characters of the drama express the complexity of family love, lonesomeness, and disappointment.

Inge also achieved success as a screenwriter. His screenplay for *Splendor in the Grass* (1961) won an Academy Award. The story takes place in a small Kansas town. Deanie Loomis and Bud Stamper grow up with overprotective parents. They suffer repressions that radically change their lives and force them to accept and cope with life's changes.

Inge was an important mid-century, Midwestern playwright who dealt chiefly with family conflict. His stories involve small-town people with complex problems of love, loneliness, and failure. His characters strive to accept life's traumas, something Inge never fully accomplished.

New York critics were often cruel to Inge, and he disliked Hollywood's control over his scripts. So he turned to novels. *Good Luck, Miss Wyckoff* came first. *My Son is a Splendid Driver* (1971) is autobiographical and deals with the same themes as his plays. *A Life of William Inge: The Strains of Triumph* (1989) by Ralph F. Voss sets forth the details of his life.

SAM SMILEY

Ingersoll, Charles Jared (1782–1862), lawyer, public official, writer. Born in Philadelphia, Ingersoll showed a deep interest in the philosophy of law and politics. He began by writing *Edwy and Elgiva*, a tragedy in blank verse produced in Philadelphia in 1801. Though his family held conservative political views, Ingersoll became a Jacksonian Democrat and served in Congress and in other public capacities. In 1808 he wrote *A View of the Rights and Wrongs, Power and Policy of the United States of America*, which attacked the British and urged a tariff war to achieve true independence. *Inchiquin, The Jesuit's Letters* (1810) denied the views of British travelers in America and provoked a bitter notice in the English *Quarterly Review* as well as important defenses of Ingersoll in this country. In 1823 Ingersoll, speaking before the American Philosophical Society in Philadelphia, delivered *A Discourse Concerning the Influence of America on the Mind*, in which he advocated a literature true to the utilitarian American character. He wrote a tragedy, *Julian* (1831), various historical works, and his *Recollections* (1861).

Ingersoll, Ernest (1852–1946), naturalist, museum curator, writer. Born in Michigan and a profound student of birds and animals, Ingersoll frequently attacked persons "who would not deal honestly with nature." He was gently admired by Theodore Roosevelt and by other naturalists, particularly JOHN BURROUGHS and WILLIAM BEEBE. He obtained his first important position as curator of the Oberlin College Museum; later he was on the staff of the Smithsonian Institution, the U.S. Geological Survey, the U.S. Fish Commission, and other official organizations. He contributed information to encyclopedias and dictionaries, wrote for newspapers and magazines, and published a series of books, among them *Knocking 'Round the Rockies* (1882), *Country Cousins* (1884), *Wild Neighbors* (1897), *Nature's Calendar* (1900), *The Wit of the Wild* (1906), *Primer of Bird Study* (1916), and *Dragons and Dragon Lore* (1928).

Ingersoll, Robert G[reen] (1833–1899), lawyer, orator, lecturer, soldier, public official, agnostic. His rationalistic views prevented his progress in politics, but he became a frequent orator at Republican meetings, particularly after his eloquent speech (1876) nominating James G. Blaine for president. No great philosopher, Ingersoll wrote under the influence of Voltaire and even more of THOMAS PAINE. Among his books are *The Gods* (1872), *Some Mistakes of Moses* (1879), and *Why I Am an Agnostic* (1896). *The Works of Robert G. Ingersoll* (12 v.) appeared in 1900.

Ingraham, Joseph Holt (1809–1860), sailor, newspaperman, teacher, minister, novelist. Ingraham's early career is obscure. Born in Maine, he became a clergyman and also ran a boys' school at Holly Springs, Mississippi. He wrote numerous historical romances, including the popular *Lafitte, the Pirate of the Gulf* (1836). Another book of his, *The Prince of the House of David* (1855), likewise became a best seller, and other books with a biblical setting are *The Pillar of Fire, or, Israel in Bondage* (1859) and *The Throne of David* (1860). His works also include *Jemmy Daly, or, The Little News Vendor: A Tale of Youthful Struggles and the Triumph of Truth and Virtue over Vice and Falsehood* (1843) and *The Beautiful Cigar Girl, or, the Mysteries of Broadway* (1850). See BRUISING BILL; JEAN LAFITTE.

Ingraham, Prentiss (1843–1904), soldier, adventurer, author of dime novels. Born near Natchez, Mississippi, the son of JOSEPH HOLT INGRAHAM, he was an even more prolific writer than his father. After service in the Confederate Army, he went west, became acquainted with Buffalo Bill Cody (see WILLIAM F. CODY) and turned to writing stories about the frontier. He is said to have composed about six hundred—a third of them devoted to Cody. Books attributed to Ingraham are *The Beautiful Rivals* (1884), *Cadet Carey of West Point* (1890), and *The Girl Rough Riders* (1903).

In His Steps (1896), a novel by CHARLES M. SHELDON. The subtitle of this immensely popular novel is "What Would Jesus Do?" and the story attempts to answer the question. A Protestant minister is shocked by conditions in his community. He asks his congregation to pledge to do always what they think Jesus would do in their place, and the book goes on to give various examples of how they carry out their pledge. After publication in a Congregational weekly called *The Advance*, the novel appeared (1897) in book form. Its popularity brought forth a swarm of pirated editions, since the book, in its serial form, had not been copyrighted.

Injun Joe. The villain in Mark Twain's *Tom Sawyer.*

Inman, Henry (1837–1899), soldier, newspaperman, historian. Born in New York City the son of the painter Henry Inman (1801–1846), the younger Inman joined the army and rose to the rank of lieutenant colonel by the time he was thirty-one, when he was dismissed from the service. He began writing about the frontier, with which he had become familiar in the Indian campaigns. Among his books are *Stories of the Old Santa Fe Trail* (1881), *The Old Santa Fe Trail* (1897), *Tales of the Trail* (1898), *The Great Salt Lake Trail* (1898), and *Buffalo Jones' Forty Years of Adventure* (1899).

Innocents Abroad, The. MARK TWAIN's first successful book (1869) is a revision of the letters he had written for the San Francisco *Alta California* concerning his 1867 trip on the *Quaker City*, with travelers motivated mostly by a desire to see the Holy Land. Twain's dominant purpose was to reveal what his own eyes had actually seen: reality uncolored by what had become his familiar enemies—pretense, conventionality, and gentility. Intended to be both informative and entertaining, the account is a somewhat loosely organized blend of irreverence and chauvinism, with the narrator's misleading expectations a central theme. The author achieves revenge for the victimization of his naive former self by debunking superstitions and legends through parody and burlesque, such as his tearful response to his visit to Adam's tomb. In addition, he makes fun of pious guidebooks and the hypocritical pilgrims with whom he traveled; at the same time he sought to gratify conventional people who purchased his book—sold to Middle Americans by subscription—by providing them with both reportage and passages of purple prose concerning such experiences as standing beside the Sea of Galilee at night.

In addition to the Holy Land, *The Innocents Abroad* describes Twain's adventures in Paris, his iconoclastic response to the Old Masters in Italy, and his irreverent reactions to Roman Catholicism in its many forms. The writer's artistic repertoire is varied, and Twain is alternately a good-humored skeptic and an ignorant philistine. The result is a work that has some delightful passages but seems painfully uneven and too long. Nearly 80,000 copies were sold, however, during its first sixteen months of publication, and the book was widely reviewed. With it Mark Twain became identified as a major American humorist.

EVERETT EMERSON

In Old Kentucky (1893),   a play by Charles Turner Dazey. One of the most popular plays of its era was this melodrama of a horse race, with plenty of local color. The details were based on personal observation and presented an effective contrast between the mountaineers of Kentucky and the bluegrass people. The heroine almost loses a young patrician's love by appearing in public in riding breeches.

In Ole Virginia (1887),   a collection of short stories by THOMAS NELSON PAGE. Several of them, particularly MARSE CHAN and "Meh Lady," became favorites of anthologists. These, like some of the other tales, deal with African-Americans.

In Our Time (1924 in France, 1925 in the United States), a collection of fifteen tales by ERNEST HEMINGWAY and his second book. Containing stories mostly about Nick Adams, as well as interchapters describing contemporary violence, *In Our Time* foreshadows in theme and style all of Hemingway's later work. The Paris edition, with the title uncapitalized, contained only the interchapters.

In Praise of Johnny Appleseed (*Century Magazine*, August 1921),   a poem by VACHEL LINDSAY later printed in *Collected Poems* (1923). Lindsay follows JOHN CHAPMAN's career over the Appalachian barricade, his wanderings among the Indians and in the wilderness, and his vigorous old age. The lines are rhymed, but the meter is irregular, with the customary exultant, leaping rhythm of Lindsay's other verses.

Inquiry into the Principles and Policy of the Government of the United States (1814),   a treatise by JOHN TAYLOR. The author, a radical agrarian, put into this work many concepts that later became commonplaces of American liberalism.

Inquiry on the Freedom of the Will, The (1753). See FREEDOM OF THE WILL.

Inscription for the Entrance to a Wood (composed 1815, published in *North American Review* September 1817, in *Poems* 1821),   a poem by WILLIAM CULLEN BRYANT. Bryant wrote this poem under two strong and not completely reconciled influences—Calvinism (one notes the reference to "the primal curse") and Wordsworth. As he revised the poem, the former influence receded somewhat. Retiring from the guilt and misery of the world, the poet finds solace in the tranquility and gladness of nature.

In the American Grain (1925),   a volume of essays by WILLIAM CARLOS WILLIAMS. Under the influence of D.H. Lawrence's *Studies in Classic American Literature*, Williams portrayed the developing American conscience in sketches of such major figures as Columbus, Cotton Mather, Washington, Franklin, and Poe, and such minor ones as Champlain, Thomas Morton, Père Sebastian Rasles, and Jacataqua. He sought the grain of American character especially in homely, rather than heroic, incidents of national history.

In the Baggage Car Ahead (1896),   a song by Gussie L. Davis (1863–1899). Davis had once been a Pullman porter, at another time had swept the halls of the New York Conservatory of Music, incidentally acquiring knowledge of musical composition. The lyric tells the story of a father accompanied in a train by several troublesome children; he explains to the protesting fellow passengers that "Their mother is in a casket in the baggage car ahead." The song became the most popular tear jerker of the Gay Nineties, and later was often employed as a burlesque.

In the Good Old Summer Time (1902),   a song with words by Ren Shields (1868–1913) and music by George ("Honey Boy") Evans, a blackface comedian.

In the Heart of the Heart of the Country, the title story of a 1968 collection by William Gass. The first-person narrator observes and meditates from a rural Indian town.

In the Midst of Life (published as *Tales of Soldiers and Civilians* 1891, retitled 1898),   a collection of twenty-six stories by AMBROSE BIERCE. These are not merely tales of grim horror in the manner of Poe; they are Bierce's commentaries on life as he saw it. The ten tales of soldiers in the first edition all end, for example, with the death of "the young, the beautiful, the brave." All the stories imply that life is dreadful, subject to frightening accidents and horrible coincidences. They show astounding powers of imagination and ingenuity, and they have twist endings rarely surpassed in literature. Among the best are "A Horseman in the Sky," "An Occurrence at Owl Creek Bridge," "The Man and the Snake," and "The Eyes of the Panther."

In the Shade of the Old Apple Tree (1905),   a song with words by Henry Williams (1879–1922), music by Egbert Van Alstyne. They were a popular team, and this song was their greatest hit.

In the Tennessee Mountains (1884),   eight short stories by Charles Egbert Craddock (MARY NOAILLES MURFREE.) These were the first writings to bring Murfree national recognition: they appeared originally in the *Atlantic Monthly*. Many of the stories have a tragic cast. All are realistic, if sometimes overly long depictions of life in the Great Smoky Mountains, and the dialect is reproduced with scrupulous exactness. The stories created a sensation. When it was revealed that Charles Egbert Craddock was a well-educated Tennessee spinster, she was promptly compared to George Eliot.

In the Valley (1890),   a historical novel by HAROLD FREDERIC. This is a realistic description of the bloody campaign around Oriskany. Frederic construes the battle there (1777) as the turning point of the war.

Intolerance (1916),   a film written, directed, and produced by DAVID W. GRIFFITH. A successor to Griffith's *The Birth of a Nation* (1915), this film was conceived and executed on an even grander scale, in part as an answer to criticisms of the earlier film. The plot ran in what Griffith called "four currents looked at from a hilltop," which in the last act mingled in one mighty river of drama and emotion. One stream of scenes deals with the fall of Babylon, another with Christ, a third with the massacre of the Huguenots on St. Bartholomew's Eve, and the last with a modern story involving the ruthless killing of strikers in an industrial dispute. The sections are joined by a repeated sequence suggested by Walt Whitman's line about "the cradle endlessly rocking." The film is sentimental and overdramatized, and the overemphasis on spectacle blurs the message.

Intruder in the Dust (1948),   a novel by WILLIAM FAULKNER. LUCAS BEAUCHAMP, an aging African-American who has long nettled the townsfolk of Jefferson because of his refusal to adopt the servile attitude white people expect, is wrongfully accused of murdering a white man and is threatened with violent death at the hands of a mob. Through the efforts of sixteen-year-old CHICK MALLISON, Aleck Sander, Chick's black friend, and seventy-year-old Miss Eunice Habersham, Lucas's innocence is proved and the real murderer captured. Having once failed to establish the barrier between white and black when Lucas refused to accept money for a meal, Chick is tormented by his obligation to Lucas. In defying the conventions of white society, both by attempting to defend a "stiff-necked nigger" and by violating a grave in his search for evidence, Chick rises above the restrictions of society and comes into manhood able to recognize other human beings as individuals, regardless of their color.

Invisible Man (1952),   a novel by RALPH ELLISON. The nameless protagonist at first has a rather unrealistic trust in the motives of others. He is dismissed from a Southern black college for disillusioning one of the founders by showing him the world in which blacks really live. In New York City he distinguishes himself by rousing a crowd at an eviction and is picked by Communist leaders for a political role. Ultimately, he realizes that the Communists are merely using him as a symbol of the African-American; as a person, he is as invisible to them as to anyone else. During a surrealistic Harlem riot, the hero realizes that he must contend with people of both races.

Opening his novel with a prologue inscribed in the language of his protagonist, Ellison provides his readers a fiction deriving from the classic description of double-consciousness by W. E. B. DuBois. "It is a peculiar sensation," DuBois wrote in *The Souls of Black Folk*, "this sense of always looking at one's self through the eyes of others. . . . One ever feels his twoness,—an American, a Negro; two souls, two thoughts, two unreconciled strivings; two warring ideals in one dark body. . . ." Similarly, the antihero of *Invisible Man* experiences the painful contradictions of African-American life as he seeks the fulfillment promised by the American Creed only to find its universality a pretense founded on willed blindness to the invisible other.

Entering the narrative through the prologue, the reader finds that all is already cached in the past, and the present is given over to a monologue conceding that history has driven the speaker into underground hibernation yet granting him power over events through the figurative idiom of his discourse. That discourse is intensely subjective, for as the narrator puts it, "In going underground, I whipped it all except the mind, the *mind*"; yet that is precisely the point. Reality is the objective occurrences of African-American experience that appear in the novel's main text as the events of a representative black life, but reality is also the themes and maps one conceives to make sense of events. The subjectivity of the prologue tells us that this novel is about cartography.

The dominance of a mental discourse signals too that a leading supposition of novelistic realism—the illusion of a text conforming to external reality beyond the margins of its pages—has been supplanted by narrative consciousness retaining the past in the patterns of a present subjectivity, thereby gaining validity for the narrator's outlook alone. The distinction between exterior reality and interior sensibility has been erased. Not surprisingly, then, the text of *Invisible Man* becomes progressively more surreal as it recollects discovery of existential identity.

Invisible Man was published in 1952—two years before the Supreme Court struck down school segregation, eight years before the Civil Rights Movement began with sit-ins by African-American college students—but the novel's fictive premise was prophetic. In politics, as in literature, African-Americans found liberation in singular consciousness.
JOHN M. REILLY

Invitation to a Beheading,   a novel by VLADIMIR NABOKOV. The Russian version (*Priglashenie na Kazn*) appeared in Paris and Berlin in 1938; the English translation was published in the U.S. in 1959.

Ioor, William (1780?–1830),   playwright. Ioor was one of a group of dramatists who made Charleston, South Carolina, something of a theatrical center in the early 19th century. The names of two of his plays have survived. One, a comedy based on an English novel, was called *Independence: Or, Which Do You Like Best, the Peer or the Farmer?* (produced 1805). The other, a historical play of patriotic character, was called *The Battle of Eutaw Springs and Evacuation of Charleston* (1813).

Iron Heel, The (1907),   a novel by JACK LONDON. Following the lead of Edward Bellamy, London peered into the future, but only as far as the years 1912–18 when, as he saw it, a right-wing revolution would occur, followed by an upsurgence of the socialists; much later would come a golden age.

Ironquill. The pen name of EUGENE FITCH WARE.

Iron Woman, The (1911), a novel by MARGARET DELAND; a sequel to *The Awakening of Helena Ritchie* (1906).

Iroquois. A group of Indian tribes who came close to developing a stable form of government, and whose customs, legends, and rituals greatly influenced American writers. About 1570 the Mohawk, Onondaga, Oneida, Cayuga, and Seneca Indians formed a confederacy to abolish war among themselves—but not to prevent them from making war on others. They became known as the Five Nations. In 1720 or thereabouts the related tribe of the Tuscaroras of North Carolina joined them, and their league was then called the SIX NATIONS. The lands they occupied or raided extended from the Valley of the St. Lawrence southward to the Carolinas and westward to the Great Lakes, but they mainly lived in New York State. They spoke languages of the Hokan-Siouxan stock and had similar social and religious customs. Their alliances played an important role in determining the destiny of the continent. They became bitter enemies of the French and strong allies of the British, and helped the British dominate North America. When the American Revolution broke out, they continued their alliance with the British until their power was broken by General Sullivan in August 1779.

The formation of the ancient Iroquois Confederacy was always attributed to a great chieftain and reformer, Hayenwatha, or Hiawatha, who lived about 1550. When Longfellow took Hiawatha's name and deeds as the subject for his poem, he did Hiawatha and his people a grave injustice by making Hiawatha an Ojibway.

Before Longfellow the Iroquois had already appeared in American writing and oratory. GADWALLADER COLDEN wrote *History of the Five Indian Nations* (1727). De Witt Clinton gave an elaborate *Discourse on the Iroquois* in an address (1811) before the New York Historical Society. James Fenimore Cooper introduced the Iroquois into the LEATHER-STOCKING TALES as the worst enemies of Chingachgook and his tribe. HENRY ROWE SCHOOLCRAFT wrote *Notes on the Iroquois* (1845, rev. 1847), but L. H. Morgan's *League of the Ho-dé-no-sau-nee, or Iroquois* (1851) was superior. Before Longfellow, a seven-thousand-line poem called *Frontenac, or, The Atotarho of the Iroquois* (1849), by Alfred B. Street, had appeared. An important volume was Horatio Hale's *Iroquois Book of Rites* (1883), based on written documents in the possession of chieftains who were in charge of these ancient ceremonies. Other studies include Alex T. Cringan's *Pagan Dance Songs of the Iroquois* (1900); Harriet M. Converse's *Myths and Legends of the New York State Iroquois* (1908); J. M. B. Hewitt's *The Requickening Address of the League of the Iroquois* (1916, 1944); George T. Hunt's *The Wars of the Iroquois* (1940); and Paul A. W. Wallace's *The White Roots of Peace* (1946, an account of the Confederacy). Over the years, the six tribes were widely dispersed. The Cayugas moved to Canada, Wisconsin, and Ohio; the Mohawks to Canada; the Oneidas now live on a small reserva-

tion in New York, although some fled to Canada, some to the West; some of the Onondagas removed to Canada and others to the West, but most of them remained in New York; and the Senecas now reside on three small reservations in New York. The Confederacy's continuing conflict with New York State officialdom is recounted in Edmund Wilson's *Apologies to the Iroquois* (1960).

Irving, John Treat (1812–1906), lawyer, broker, author of travel books, novelist. Born in New York City, Irving, a nephew of WASHINGTON IRVING, was a member of an expedition to the West in 1833 led by Henry L. Ellsworth. His experiences formed the basis for his *Indian Sketches* (1835, rev. 1888) and *Hunters of the Prairie, or The Hawk Chief* (1837). He contributed to the KNICKER-BOCKER MAGAZINE under the pen name John Quod, a name he also employed for several of his novels, including *The Quod Correspondence, or, The Attorney* (1842).

Irving, John [Winslow] (1942–   ), novelist. After writing three novels that attracted good reviews but little attention—*Setting Free the Bears* (1968), *The Water-Method Man* (1972), and *The 158-Pound Marriage* (1974)—Irving captured the American reading public's imagination in 1978 with THE WORLD ACCORDING TO GARP, which sold well over three million copies. In Irving's fictional universe, death is a capricious, omnipresent protagonist; family relations are always strained by tragicomic sexual conflicts and often complicated by physical and psychological deformities; individuals must contend with the violence and intolerance of social and political movements that are misguided more often than not; and the contemporary American writer must suffer the consequences of living in an age that, in its distrust of the imagination, reads fiction as autobiography, appropriating the writer's life instead of his work.

John Irving was born in Exeter, New Hampshire, an area he has often turned to for his fictional settings. He was graduated from Phillips Exeter Academy, the model for Steering School in *The World According to Garp*, and attended the University of Pittsburgh for a year before traveling to Europe, where he studied at the University of Vienna. Irving married Shyla Leary in 1964 before returning to complete his education at the University of New Hampshire and the University of Iowa. Irving has taught at the University of Iowa and Mount Holyoke College, but since the success of *The World According to Garp* has devoted himself more fully to his writing.

In *The World According to Garp*, Irving traces the career of a writer whose imaginative gift is consumed by the conflicts that embroil him in contemporary sexual politics and eventually lead to his assassination. We follow the decline of Garp's imagination from the rich, if morbid comedy of his first story, "The Pension Grillparzer," to his last novel—the luridly violent, melodramatically pornographic *The World According to Bensenhaver*. Many of Irving's fictional trademarks are in strong evidence here, among them a fascination with bears. In his next novel, *The Hotel New Hampshire* (1981), an old and decrepit bear named State O'Maine starts the Berry family along its melancholy decline as the father fails at successive attempts to establish a hotel business in America and in

Europe, and the family is riven both by its in-turning incestuous travails and by the madcap political forces that bomb their hotel in Vienna. With characteristically dark comedy and typical array of the improbably erotic and fantastic events that animate so many of Irving's plots, *The Hotel New Hampshire* exemplifies his distinctive fictional signature.

Teeming with the idiosyncratic characters that populate all of Irving's fiction, his sixth novel, *The Cider-House Rules* (1985), is a scathing exploration of the social history and the emotional and psychological realities of abortion; no other of his novels is as consistently forceful in its indictment of social mores. And in *A Prayer for Owen Meany* (1989), Irving's most sustained exploration of the nature of faith, he creates one of his most improbable and moving characters—the dwarflike figure of Owen Meany, with his uncannily high-pitched voice, eerie gift for prophecy, and unshakable belief that he is an instrument of God. Meany's tale is narrated in retrospect by Johnny Wheelwright, his best friend, who moved to Canada in the late 1960s. His recollections unfold against the background of the American experience in Vietnam and his obsession with understanding the nature of Owen Meany's faith.

At century's end, Irving had added three books. The novel *A Son of the Circus* (1994) features Dr. Farrokh Daruwalla, who returns from his home in Toronto to his native Bombay, where he uses his skills as an orthopedic surgeon to help crippled children. Before he left India, the doctor was the examining physician for two murder victims; twenty years later he is brought into contact with the murderer. *Trying to Save Piggy Sneed* (1996) is a collection of six short stories, tributes to the admired writers Gunter Grass and Charles Dickens, and memoirs about an influential grandmother, and the town garbage collector of the title, among others. *A Widow for a Year* (1998) is a novel centering on three periods in the life of writer Ruth Cole; the summer of 1958 when she was four, the fall of 1990 when her career is happier than her personal life, and the autumn of 1995 when, as a widow and mother, she falls in love for the first time. *My Movie Business* (1999) is Irving's memoir of the making of the film *The Cider House Rules.* He won an Oscar for the screenplay, and played a cameo part as station master in it. *The Fourth Hand* (2001), a novel, finds absurdity and honor in television journalism and stars a reporter whose left hand is eaten by a lion. Irving's novels offer a fictional world richly varied, by turn exuberantly imaginative and darkly brooding, sparked by bright comic flashes, but also imbued with elegaic reflections on mortality. Among his contemporaries, Irving is the American novelist who ranges most widely and confidently over the improbable profundities of the idiosyncratic, the quirky erotics of domesticity, and the exotic banality of the mundane.

NEIL BESNER

Irving, Peter (1771–1838),   physician, editor, merchant, writer. Born in New York City, this older brother of WASHINGTON IRVING was deeply devoted to him. He edited a daily paper, *The Morning Chronicle* (1802–05), to which Washington Irving contributed. He also assisted his brother in writing a HISTORY OF NEW YORK (1809). He himself published only

one book, *Giovanni Sbogarro* (2 v. 1820), a romance laid in Venice, issued under the pen name of Percival G—.

Irving, Pierre [Munro] (1803–1876),   lawyer, editor, biographer. Born in New York City, Pierre Irving was the son of WASHINGTON IRVING's oldest brother, WILLIAM. He became Irving's secretary and agent, collaborated with him on *Astoria* (1836), recorded their conversations, and became his literary executor. After his uncle's death he published an official biography, *The Life and Letters of Washington Irving* (4 v. 1862–64; 1869), which has remained the basis for all later biographies. He also edited some unpublished materials of Irving's and reprinted others in *Spanish Papers and Other Miscellanies* (2 v. 1866).

Irving, Washington (1783–1859),   essayist, historian, biographer, humorist. Born in New York City, Irving had a brief formal education, but was an avid reader in his father's library, which had a good assortment of English classics. Beginning at sixteen, he read law and then he practiced until 1803. When his health was threatened, he went to Europe in 1804 and remained for two years—the first of many visits.

Irving's first published writings were newspaper pieces, LETTERS OF JONATHAN OLDSTYLE GENT. (1802–1803). In 1807 appeared SALMAGUNDI, a series of satirical essays written in collaboration with his brother William and their friend JAMES PAULDING; the essays were slight, but their reception encouraged Irving to continue. In 1809 he published A HISTORY OF NEW YORK, using the pseudonym Diedrich Knickerbocker, and the book brought him immediate recognition. He was greatly depressed, however, by the death of his fiancée, and entered a period of aimlessness, eventually sailing again to England; he remained abroad, much of the time in England, for the next seventeen years. His best-known book was published there in 1820, THE SKETCH BOOK OF GEOFFREY CRAYON, GENT., a collection of stories and sketches mostly concerned with scenes he had known in childhood rambles in the New York countryside; RIP VAN WINKLE and THE LEGEND OF SLEEPY HOLLOW, two famous selections from the book, are an inseparable part of our national heritage.

Irving now signed his books Geoffrey Crayon, and his popularity was at its height. His reputation spread at home, in England, and on the Continent, where French and German translations brought him to a wide public, and he became the first American writer to achieve international fame, the first professional American writer in the full sense of the word. In 1822 he published BRACEBRIDGE HALL, which enjoyed a good sale, and this was followed by his least successful work, TALES OF A TRAVELER (1824). Financial worries began to plague Irving, and he gladly accepted ALEXANDER HILL EVERETT's invitation to join him in his embassy in Madrid. In 1826 Irving settled in Madrid and began his Spanish studies, which resulted in four original books: HISTORY OF THE LIFE AND VOYAGES OF COLUMBUS (1828), A CHRONICLE OF THE CONQUEST OF GRANADA (1829), *The Companions of Columbus* (1831), and THE LEGENDS OF THE ALHAMBRA (1832). Irving wrote enthusiastically about Spanish life and history. His narrative technique was lively, and readers took well to his new work. In 1842 Irving became minister to Spain, a post he occupied for four years.

In the meantime, during a brief stay in the United States, Irving had written ASTORIA (1836, rev. 1849), a history of the Astor family done on commission from them. It earned him $4,000 but little respect. *The Adventures of Captain Bonneville, U.S.A.* (1837) gives a fairly accurate picture of the times. (See CAPTAIN BONNEVILLE.) After completing his Spanish mission, Irving settled at his home, called SUNNY-SIDE, in Tarrytown, New York, and there spent his old age. He published his *Life of Oliver Goldsmith* in 1849 and a year later his two-volume biography *Mahomet and His Successors*. In 1855 appeared WOLFERT'S ROOST, a collection of essays, some of them revised from previous publications. His final years were spent in hard work on his life of George Washington—for whom he had been named—the fifth and final volume of which was published a few weeks before Irving died.

Irving's style was modeled on the work of such British authors as Scott, Addison, and Goldsmith; his subjects were often appropriated from English and German collections of legends and folktales; and his later books were less successful than the early ones. One looks in vain in his work for the moral concern, the intellectual vitality and acuteness, found in abundance in the works of Hawthorne, Melville, and Emerson among the succeeding generation of American writers. However, the grace and humor of Irving's prose, its delicate pictorial quality united with a strain of antiquarian romance and a strong sense of the melancholy of change, have given his best work lasting value. He greatly stimulated American cultural life by showing that American writers could become genuine men of letters in the European tradition. Our first great prose stylist, he established models for others to build on. He was our first familiar essayist, and his humor was an important step toward Twain. His wit preceded that of Holmes and Lowell, and his tales proved major sources for the short story as a genre.

The Works of Washington Irving (21 v. 1860–61) has long been standard. *A Complete Works of Washington Irving* has recently been begun by Twayne. W. P. Trent and G. S. Hellman edited *The Journals of Washington Irving* (3 v. 1919). Stanley T. Williams wrote *The Life of Washington Irving* (2 v. 1935).

Irving, William (1766–1821),   Indian trader, merchant, poet, public official. Born in New York City, the oldest brother of WASHINGTON IRVING was described by him as "the man I loved most on earth." He was primarily a businessman, but served several terms in Congress and was deeply interested in writing and in the welfare of his younger brother. He contributed verses and two letters to SALMAGUNDI (1807).

Irwin, Inez Haynes [Gilmore, Mrs. Will Irwin] (1873–1970),   novelist, short-story writer, writer of books for girls. Born in Brazil, and an adroit and ingenious story teller, Irwin early won a reputation. The best of her books is *Angel Island* (1914), an allegory in which angels, once married, turn into women. Among her other books are *June Jeopardy* (1908), *The Californiacs* (1916), *Gertrude Haviland's Divorce* (1925), *Family Circle* (1931), *Murder Masquerade* (1935), as well as the Maida series (1910–54) for girls and the Phoebe and Ernest stories (1910–12) for adolescents. Irwin was an active campaigner in the cause of woman suffrage, and she wrote *The Story of the Woman's Party* in 1921 and *Angels and Amazons* in 1933.

Irwin, Wallace [Admah] (1875–1959),   newspaperman, verse writer, humorist, novelist. Irwin, who was born in Oneida, New York, worked for the San Francisco *Examiner*, for a time edited the *Overland Monthly*, and won his first national recognition with *The Love Sonnets of a Hoodlum* (1902), Petrarchan verses in slang. He went back to New York in 1904 and later joined *Collier's* staff. There, under the pen name Hashimura Togo, he began writing the *Letters of a Japanese Schoolboy*, which reached book form in 1909 and continued to be popular for at least twenty years in magazines and syndicated reprints. Later he wrote *Mr. Togo, Maid of All Work* (1913); a number of detective stories; *The Rubaiyat of Omar Khayyam Jr.* (1902); various other collections of light verse; and *Seed of the Sun* (1921), a serious novel about the conflict of Japanese and Caucasians in California. He collaborated with Dr. Sylvester Lambert on *Yankee Doctor in Paradise* (1941).

Irwin, Will[iam Henry] (1873–1948),   newspaperman, war correspondent, writer. Born in Oneida, New York, the brother of WALLACE IRWIN was equally quick and skilled at all kinds of writing, a reporter above all else; his autobiography was fittingly called *The Making of a Reporter* (1942). He began by writing *Stanford Stories* (1900), in collaboration with C. K. Field, and with GELETT BURGESS he wrote two books of adventure in Californian settings. For a while he edited the San Francisco *Wave*, then served on the staff of the *Chronicle* (1901–04). In 1904 he joined the New York *Sun*. Two years later, when news of the great San Francisco earthquake and fire reached New York, he wrote an account under the headline "THE CITY THAT WAS" and won national renown. The articles were published in a book by that title in 1907.

S. S. MCCLURE called Irwin to *McClure's Magazine*, where he did muckraking stories. He went on to *Collier's*, and later he became a war correspondent. His war reports were collected as *Men, Women, and War* (1915) and *Reporter at Armageddon* (1918). He worked with HERBERT HOOVER on the Commission for Relief in Belgium and years later wrote the first biography of Hoover (1929). He wrote much fiction, an analysis of *Propaganda and the News* (1936), and two successful plays called *The 13th Chair* (with BAYARD VEILLER, 1916) and *Lute Song* (with SIDNEY HOWARD, 1930).

Isaacs, Edith J[uliet] R[ich] (1878–1956),   newspaperwoman, editor, public relations specialist, authority on the theater. Born in Milwaukee, Isaacs did newspaper work on the Milwaukee *Sentinel* and various publicity jobs during World War I. She came to her chief interest when she began editing the quarterly *Theatre Arts Magazine* (1918–23), then *Theatre Arts Monthly* (1924–46). Among her books are *Threatre* (1927), *Plays of American Life and Fantasy* (1929), and *The Negro in the American Theatre* (1947).

Isaacs, Jorge (1837–1895),   poet, novelist. Born in Colombia, Isaacs terminated his medical studies when his family lost its money in a civil war. In 1864 he joined the Bogota literary group, *El Mosaico*, which helped him publish his work. He served as editor of the newspaper *La Republica*, was Colombian consul in Chile, and fought on the liberal side in an 1876 civil war. In later life he explored the rural areas and studied Indian tribes. He is best known for his widely read novel MARIA (1867), about an orphaned beauty who dies while her beloved is studying abroad. The novel contains vivid descriptions of the Colombian countryside.

Isherwood, Christopher (1904–1986), novelist, playwright, biographer. Isherwood was born in England and educated at Cambridge, after which he worked as a tutor and studied medicine until he joined his friend W. H. AUDEN in Germany. His stories based on this period were collected in *Goodbye to Berlin* and later dramatized by John Van Druten for a Broadway play, *I Am a Camera*, which won the New York Drama Critics Award and also became a successful movie and musical, *Cabaret*. He wrote an autobiography, *Lions and Shadows* (1938), collaborated with Auden on several plays, and after extensive travel settled down finally in Santa Monica, California. There he became profoundly interested in the Vedanta Society, editing several anthologies on Vedanta, and for a time lectured at the Los Angeles State College. He was elected in 1949 to the National Institute of Arts and Letters. His novel *The World in the Evening* (1954) disappointed reviewers. In 1960 he collaborated with Charles Laughton in a dramatic project based on the dialogues of Plato. Some of his other books are *All the Conspirators* (1928), *The Memorial* (1932), *The Last of Mr. Norris* (1935), *Prater Violet* (1945), *The Condor and the Cows* (1949), and *Vedanta for Modern Man* (ed., 1951). In collaboration with Auden he wrote *Journey to a War* (1939) and several verse plays, the best known of which are *The Dog Beneath the Skin* (1935) and *The Ascent of F6* (1936). *Down There on a Visit*, a novel, appeared in 1962.

Ishmael, or, In the Depths (1863), a novel by Mrs. E.D.E.N. SOUTHWORTH; it was the first part of a novel called *Self-Made*, the second part published as *Self-Raised, or, Out of the Depths* (1864), a rags-to-riches romance that occasionally displays a sense of humor.

I Sing the Body Electric (1855), a poem by Walt Whitman that was given its present title in the 1867 edition of LEAVES OF GRASS. Whitman had included the poem in the first edition of his book, without a title, and then worked it over repeatedly, making the final changes in 1881. A candid poem of sexuality, it shocked many readers.

Israel Potter: His Fifty Years of Exile. HERMAN MELVILLE's eighth book (1855), based loosely on Henry Trumbull's *Life and Remarkable Adventures of Israel R. Potter*. Melville's narrative follows the life of a Revolutionary War soldier, Israel Potter, from his youth to his heroic efforts at Bunker Hill to his capture at sea, complex wanderings, and years of forlorn poverty during his fifty years abroad. Potter's exile includes such highlights as meeting King George III in his garden, acting as a courier between English pro-Americans and Benjamin Franklin in France, and serving with John Paul Jones during his campaign against the British navy, including

the battle between the *Serapis* and the *Bon Homme Richard*. In this attempt to regain the readership lost following publication of *Moby-Dick* and *Pierre*, Melville capitalizes on the adventurous elements in Potter's wanderings as well as on the pathos inherent in his poverty and exile. Melville also, however, mounts a sharp and often humorous criticism of various American philosophical tendencies as well as of several historical personages, including Franklin, Jones, and Ethan Allen. More important, Melville discovers within the career of Israel Potter themes fully coherent with his work from *Typee* through *Moby-Dick* and *Pierre*, demetaphorized and, seemingly, embedded within the fabric of American history. The ambiguities and paradoxes of Potter's life, a life of unrecognized and unrewarded heroism and patriotism, express Melville's deepening skepticism regarding the nature and outcome of the American Revolution, of the popular deification of the founding fathers, and of American culture itself.

RUSSELL J. REISING

Israfel (1831), a poem by EDGAR ALLAN POE. Poe prefaced this poem with a motto ascribed to the Koran: "And the angel Israfel who has the sweetest voice of all God's creatures." In 1845 the note was changed to read: "And the angel Israfel whose heartstrings are a lute, and who has the sweetest voice of all God's creatures." The original line was taken from George Sale's *Preliminary Discourse* to his translation of the Koran (1734); a lute, of course, is shaped like a heart. The poem expresses Poe's belief that poetry must be impassioned, and that a poet like himself might under other conditions sing as well as Israfel. It is a bold assertion of the power of a human poet.

Italian Father, The (produced 1799, published 1810), a play by WILLIAM DUNLAP based on Thomas Dekker's *The Honest Whore, Part II* (1630). Dunlap considered this the best of his sixty-odd plays. It tells how a father in disguise watches over his errant daughter.

Italian Journeys (1867), travel sketches by WILLIAM DEAN HOWELLS. Howells was appointed consul in Venice at the outbreak of the Civil War. With his young wife, he spent four years of almost undisturbed leisure in Italy, visiting places of interest, studying Italian literature, writing poetry, and forming the habit of close and sympathetic observation. Out of this long stay in a country he liked came two of his best books, *Venetian Life* (1866) and *Italian Journeys*. Among the places he describes in the latter are Padua, Genoa, Pompeii, Naples, Capri, Trieste, and Rome. His keen humor is as much in evidence as his sense of the picturesque.

It Can't Happen Here (1935), a novel by SINCLAIR LEWIS. The novel deals with the rise and establishment of a fascist dictatorship in the United States. Doremus Jessup, a liberal Vermont newspaper editor, sees with sorrow and horror the partisanship—not only of many of his friends and neighbors, but even of members of his own family—to the cause of Berzelius Windrip, seen as a veiled portrait of Huey Long. On election to the presidency in (presumably) 1936, Windrip resections the United States into eight provinces, gains control of both Congress and the Supreme Court by sheer force, and effectively overcomes all resistance by means of the Minute Men, his personal storm troopers. With members of an underground organization established by Walt Trowbridge, Windrip's opponent in the election, Jessup sets out to overcome the dictator's power. He is discovered and sent to a concentration camp, but eventually escapes to join Trowbridge in Canada. By the end of the novel, however, his own family has completely disintegrated. The novel was dramatized by Sinclair Lewis and John C. Moffitt in 1936, for production by the Federal Theater Project.

Ives, Charles Edward (1874–1954), composer, essayist. Born in Connecticut and educated at Yale, Ives went into the insurance business to make a living and worked passionately in his leisure time at composing music. His pieces, more than two hundred songs and other compositions, reveal him as a first-rate pioneer American composer. His most celebrated work is his second piano sonata, called *Concord, Mass., 1840–1860* (1920), a long, complex work "of satanic difficulty," according to Paul Moor. Ives called the sonata "one person's impressions of the spirit of transcendentalism that is associated with Concord of over half a century ago." The four movements bear the names of Emerson, Hawthorne, the Alcotts, and Thoreau. Ives wrote a slim accompanying volume called *Essays Before a Sonata.* The work was not performed *in toto* until 1939.

Ives, James Merritt (1824–1895).   See CURRIER & IVES.

I.W.W.   Familiar abbreviation for the organization named Industrial Workers of the World. The Wobblies, as they were often called, appear in several novels, including Winston Churchill's *The Dwelling Place of Light* (1917) and Josephine Herbst's *The Executioner* (1934).

J

Jack Downing. See DOWNING, JACK.

Jackson, Andrew (1767–1845), lawyer, soldier, public official, seventh president. Jackson was born and spent his boyhood in a frontier region near the border between North and South Carolina. The settlement was invaded by the British during the Revolution, and at thirteen Jackson fought in the battle of Hanging Rock, was captured and imprisoned by the British, and left an orphan at the end of the war. Although his early schooling had been sporadic, he began to read law at seventeen and was admitted to the bar before he was twenty.

Jackson was a delegate to the convention that drew up the Constitution of Tennessee in 1796 and was elected to the House of Representatives. He resigned his seat in the following year to fill a vacancy in the Senate, and again resigned to become a Supreme Court Judge in Tennessee from 1798 to 1804. From then until 1811 he was engaged in business ventures and in the management of his plantation, "The Hermitage," near Nashville. When war with England broke out in 1812 Jackson, who had been a major general in the Tennessee militia since 1802, was ordered to subdue the Creek Indians, who had recently gone on the warpath as a result of their friendship with the British and the incitement of Tecumseh. His victory over the Creeks at Horseshoe Bend (March 27, 1814) won him a commission as major general in the U.S. Army. In December 1814, he entered New Orleans and prepared the almost defenseless city for attack by the British. The attack was successfully repulsed with almost no losses to the Americans. Although a peace treaty with Britain had been signed before the battle was fought, Jackson had become a national hero.

In 1818 Jackson was sent to put down Seminole uprisings in Florida, and again acting without direct orders he pursued the Indians into Pensacola, seized the Spanish town, hanged two British citizens who he believed had incited the Indians, and nearly brought on war with England and Spain. Hostilities were avoided by diplomacy on both sides, and Jackson was made governor of Florida in 1821, after the territory was purchased from Spain.

Jackson was elected senator from Tennessee in 1823 and ran unsuccessfully for president in 1824; although he received more electoral votes than any other candidate, his votes were short of the majority necessary for election, and the House of Representatives elected John Quincy Adams. Jackson won the election of 1828 by a large majority, becoming the first president from a region west of the Appalachians. The common people felt that as a frontiersman and soldier, he was one of them. Jackson reciprocated by initiating the spoils system, whereby about one in ten government officials were removed and replaced by Jackson's friends. Many of the abuses of the spoils system have been exaggerated. Nevertheless, the advantages of the frequent rotation of officers introduced by the spoils system, which prevented a particular faction from becoming too long entrenched, were probably offset by a general lowering of the standard of officialdom as a result of Jackson's belief that a "man of intelligence" needed no special training or experience to fill a government post.

Jackson's kitchen cabinet gave him unofficial advice and strengthened his power as president, leaving the regular Cabinet with less influence. He surprised those who assumed him, as a Southerner, to be a partisan of states' rights, with his "Our Union, it must be preserved!" and Vice President Calhoun's "The Union, next to our liberty, most dear." He threatened South Carolina with a charge of treason if she persisted in defying the "tariff of abominations," a high tariff of 1828 thought by some to be unconstitutional and particularly unfair to the South. Although a man of property himself, Jackson opposed the Second Bank of the United States, chartered in 1816, which he believed tended to be monopolistic and against the interests of the agricultural South and West. The election of 1832 centered around the Bank issue, and Jackson interpreted his popular victory to mean the people empowered him to dissolve the Bank of the United States. He ordered government money to be deposited in various state banks, which encouraged speculation. As a result of high tariffs the national debt was liquidated, and Jackson ordered surplus funds divided among the states as loans, thus withdrawing government money from the banks and resulting in a sudden tightening of credit that created a financial panic. At the end of his second term he retired to The Hermitage, still the idol of his followers and still reviled by his opponents.

Studies on the Jacksonian period include Arthur Schlesinger, Jr.'s THE AGE OF JACKSON (1945). Novels in which Jackson appears as a character include Joseph B. Cobb's *The*

Creole, or, Siege of New Orleans (1850); Winston Churchill's THE CROSSING (1904); Ellery H. Clark's *The Strength of the Hills* (1926); Samuel Hopkins Adams's *The Gorgeous Hussy* (1934); Alfred Leland Crabb's *Breakfast at the Hermitage* (1945); Odell and Willard Shepard's *Holdfast Gaines* (1946); and Irving Stone's *The President's Lady* (1951). A play written by Laurence Stallings and Maxwell Anderson, *First Flight* (1925), deals with an episode in Jackson's youth.

Jackson, Charles [Reginald] (1903–1968),   newspaperman, bookseller, writer. Jackson's first novel was *The Lost Weekend* (1944), an immediate best seller and later a movie (1945). The novel describes the adventures, tragic and ridiculous, of an alcoholic. Jackson, who was born in New Jersey, once said the events were one-third autobiographical, one-third experiences of a friend, one-third "creative imagination." *The Fall of Valor* (1946) pictures the disintegration of a marriage because of the husband's homosexual tendencies. *The Outer Edges* (1948) tells of a sex maniac's murder of two children and how it affects various people. *The Sunnier Side* (1950) contains twelve stories reminiscent of Jackson's early days in an upstate New York village; *Earthly Creatures* (1953) is another collection of short stories.

Jackson, George Pullen (1874–1953),   folklorist, writer, teacher. Born in Maine, Jackson was educated in Dresden and at the University of Chicago and for twenty-five years taught at Vanderbilt University. Through his curiosity about the Sacred Harp hymnals, with their square, triangular, and diamond-shaped notes to indicate pitch, and his subsequent research on it, Jackson became a leading authority on American religious folk songs. He was the founder of the Tennessee State Sacred Harp Singing Association and became president of the Tennessee Folklore Society in 1942. Among his books are *Spiritual Folk-songs of Early America* (1937); *White and Negro Spirituals—116 Country Folk Songs as Sung by Both Races* (1943); *Down-East Spirituals* (1943), a supplement to his 1937 book; *The Story of the Sacred Harp, 1844–1944, Religious Folk Songs as an American Institution* (1944); and *Another Sheaf of White Spirituals* (1952), which he collected, edited, and illustrated.

Jackson, Helen [Maria Fiske] Hunt ["Saxe Holm"] (1830–1885),   poet, novelist, essayist. Some of Jackson's early work appeared anonymously or under the pseudonym Saxe Holm. Widowed in 1863, she turned to writing poetry: *Verses by H. H.* (1870) and *Sonnets and Lyrics* (1886). She first won a wide public with *Bits of Travel* (1872). After her second marriage in 1875, Jackson made her home in Colorado Springs, where she could not remain indifferent to the plight of the local Native Americans. She wrote a tract, A CENTURY OF DISHONOR (1881), dealing with the U.S. government's injustices toward the Indians, and circulated it at her own expense to every member of Congress. As a result, she was appointed to a special commission studying the status of the Mission Indians. RAMONA (1884) was her fictional plea for the Indian, although the personal romance of Ramona and Alessandro overshadows the fate of the Indian as depicted in the book.

Writings drawing on Jackson's friendship with EMILY DICKINSON, a fellow native of Amherst, Massachusetts, afford clues to the life of the poet, even though most of their correspondence has been lost. It has been suggested that *Esther Wynn's Love Letters*, the last one of the Saxe Holm stories (1874), and MERCY PHILBRICK'S CHOICE (1876), a novel, both made use of her knowledge of her friend's life.

Jackson, Joseph Henry (1894–1955),   editor, radio broadcaster, novelist, author of travel and historical volumes. Born in New Jersey, Jackson became prominent early in the 1920s in San Francisco literary circles, particularly as literary editor of the San Francisco *Chronicle* and as one of the first to broadcast literary commentaries. He was described in Gertrude Atherton's *My San Francisco* (1946). Among his books are *Mexican Interlude* (1936), *Tintypes in Gold* (1939), *Anybody's Gold* (1941), *The California Story* (1949), and *Bad Company* (1949). He edited *The Gold Rush Album* (1949).

Jackson, Laura Riding.   See LAURA RIDING.

Jackson, Shirley (1919–1965),   fiction writer. Jackson was born in San Francisco. Her work, embracing such varied forms as the novel, short story, and semiautobiographical sketch, is notable for its strong contrasts both in subject matter and in mood. She and her husband, the critic Stanley Edgar Hyman, lived in Vermont. Her two autobiographical books, *Life Among the Savages* (1953) and *Raising Demons* (1957), offer a humorous chronicle of the life of a middle-class intellectual family in a New England town.

Much of her short fiction and her novels contains a strong element of the fantastic and terrifying. Supernatural happenings, or the eerie phenomena of morbid mental states, occur disturbingly against the most ordinary backgrounds, among the most ordinary people. *The Road Through the Wall* (1948), *Hangsaman* (1951), and *The Bird's Nest* (1954) are novels about young people with abnormal mental conditions. THE LOTTERY (1949), a collection of short stories, *The Sundial* (1958), and *The Haunting of Hill House* (1959) feature fantastic and sometimes elusive allegories. *We Have Always Lived in the Castle* (1962) tells of a woman writer who poisons her family. *Come Along with Me* is a fragment that was published posthumously (1968). *The Witchcraft of Salem Village* (1956); *The Bad Children* (1959), a play; and *Nine Magic Wishes* (1963) are juveniles.

Jackson, Thomas Jonathan ["Stonewall"] (1824–1863), soldier. Jackson was born in Clarksburg, Virginia (now West Virginia). A graduate of West Point and a veteran of the Mexican War, Jackson gained fame as a general in the Civil War. He figured largely in Southern victories at the first Battle of Bull Run and especially in the Shenandoah Valley Campaign of 1862. While following up a victory at Chancellorsville he was accidentally wounded by his own men, and died several days later.

A poet of the North, John Greenleaf Whittier, paid tribute to Jackson after his death, in BARBARA FRIETCHIE (1863). Jackson's last words as he lay dying, "Let us cross the river and rest in the shade of the trees," have inspired poems: "Under the

Shade of the Trees," by his sister-in-law, Margaret Junkin Preston; "The Dying Words of Stonewall Jackson," by Sidney Lanier; and "In Which General Jackson Accompanied by His Foot Cavalry Crosses Jordan," by Martha Keller. The same words suggested the title of Ernest Hemingway's novel *Across the River and into the Trees* (1950).

He appears as a leading character in several novels: John Esten Cooke's *Surry of Eagle's Nest* (1866), B. K. Benson's *Bayard's Courier* (1902), Mary Johnston's THE LONG ROLL (1911), Randall Parrish's *The Red Mist* (1914), and Henry Kyd Douglas's *I Rode with Stonewall* (1940).

Jacobs, Harriet A. (1813–1897),   memoirist. Born as a slave in Edenton, North Carolina, Harriet Ann Jacobs wrote, under the pseudonym Linda Brent, the story of her life. *Incidents in the Life of a Slave Girl: Written by Herself* was first published in 1861, but not until a new edition, edited by Jean Fagan Yellin, appeared in 1987 was it taken seriously by students of African-American literature and feminist scholars. In her story Jacobs delineates the sexual exploitation that haunted slave women. To escape her lecherous white master, she becomes the lover of another white man who fathers her two children and, even after his election to Congress, refuses to fulfill his pledge to emancipate them. Threatened by her master, she hides for seven years in a confined space in her grandmother's home, observing her children although she cannot speak to them. Even after she and the children escape to the North in 1842, they are continually harassed by their former owners and fear they will be enslaved again.

Jakes, John (1932–   ),   novelist. After graduating from De Pauw in 1953, Jakes wrote advertising copy and tried science fiction, mysteries, and juvenile adventures before perfecting the combination of American historical detail, intricate plotting, and romance that produced his best sellers. His eight-volume Kent Family Chronicles, including *The Bastard* (1974), *The Rebels* (1975), *The Seekers* (1975), *The Furies* (1976), *The Titans* (1976), *The Warriors* (1977), *The Lawless* (1978), and *The Americans* (1980), covers the Revolution, the Civil War, and the westward expansion. *North and South* (1982) began a trilogy about antebellum life in both regions, the Civil War, and its aftermath, continued in *Love and War* (1984) and *Heaven and Hell* (1987). *California Gold* (1989) deals with the post–gold rush era, 1886 to 1921, when riches were won with oil, oranges, and land. In *Homeland* (1993) and *American Dreams* (1998) he wrote of a family of beer barons in Chicago at the end of the nineteenth century. *On Secret Service* (2000) brings together people of differing backgrounds and ideologies in Washington, D.C., during the Civil War.

James, Alice (1848–1892),   diarist. The youngest child and only daughter of Mary and HENRY JAMES, SR., was born in New York City. She was denied the education given her siblings, including the philosopher WILLIAM JAMES and the novelist HENRY JAMES, JR., and discouraged from the exercise of any profession. In her teens she suffered the first of a series of mental breakdowns and in her last years was a severely depressed invalid. During this period she began writing a diary, which she seems to have intended for publication. Her writing

reveals her as an astute critic of the careers of her famous brothers as well as a shrewd observer of her times. She writes of her awareness of approaching death, from breast cancer, and her philosophical acceptance of her death. Because brother Henry convinced her companion, Katherine Loring Peabody, that publication of the diary would embarrass the family, it did not appear in print until 1934. As *The Diary of Alice James*, edited by Leon Edel, it was reprinted in 1964. *The Death and Letters of Alice James* (1983) includes a selection of her correspondence.

James, Edwin (1797–1861),   explorer, physician, geologist, compiler of travel accounts. As a young man James, a Vermonter, accompanied Major Stephen H. Long in exploring the upper Arkansas. Using his own notes and manuscript journals kept by others, he compiled a narrative, *An Account of an Expedition from Pittsburgh to the Rocky Mountains* (2 v. 1822–23); it was reprinted in R. G. Thwaites's *Early Western Travels* (1905). James also issued *A Narrative of the Captivity and Adventures of John Tanner* (1830).

James, Henry, Sr. (1811–1882),   theologian, philosopher, lecturer. Born in Albany, New York, and the father of HENRY JAMES, JR., and WILLIAM JAMES, the senior James intended to become a lawyer, for a while attended Princeton Theological Seminary, but left because of an irreconcilable dissent from Calvinism. He adopted the religious ideas of Robert Sandeman, but later became to some extent a Swedenborgian (see SWEDENBORGIANISM). He was wealthy enough to do as he pleased and to write as he pleased. He traveled abroad, knew many eminent men personally, and enjoyed a rich family life, including the company of a daughter, Alice, as remarkable as his two sons. This family life is described in F. O. Matthiessen's *The James Family* (1947).

Among James's books are *Christianity, the Logic of Creation* (1857); *Substance and Shadow* (1863); *The Secret of Swedenborg* (1869); and *Society, the Redeemed Form of Man* (1879). His *Literary Remains* was edited (1884) by William James.

James, Henry, Jr. (1843–1916),   novelist, writer of short stories and *nouvelles*, literary criticism, accounts of his travels, autobiography, and a wealth of extraordinary letters. James is celebrated as the novelist whose concern with form gave to novelists writing in English a compelling example of the fruits of structural consistency. Joseph Warren Beach's emphasis (in *The Method of Henry James*, 1918, rev. 1954) on point of view has been most influential in this respect. Beach made plain James's principle: never allow anything to enter the novel or story that is not represented as a perception or experience of one of the characters.

Important though it is, this aspect of James does not of course account for the powers that made him a major novelist of the late 19th and early 20th centuries and one of the greatest who have written in English. Born in New York City, he was the grandson of one of the first American millionaires, William James of Albany, and the son of HENRY JAMES, SR., whose share of the family fortune was large enough to enable him to live comfortably in New York, Newport, and Cambridge, with extended intervals abroad. The novelist's father lost a leg as a consequence of fighting a fire while a child. After he had fallen into a severe depression, which began with a bout of panic, a friend recommended the works of Swedenborg, whom James Sr. later called "insipid with veracity." He accepted the doctrine and tried in his own extensive writings to combat the insipidity. His books harp so insistently on a few strings, however, that they are almost as boring as those of Swedenborg. In conversation and in his letters he was both gayer and wittier, though he was forever illustrating his all-inclusive system. (See *The Thought and Character of William James* by R. B. Perry and *The James Family* by F. O. Matthiessen, in which many of his letters appear.) "Father's ideas" were made game of by his lively family, although both WILLIAM JAMES (1842–1910), the future psychologist and philosopher, and Henry testified to their force and appeal when presented by their father, whose aberrant brilliance was recognized by Emerson and other well-known contemporaries.

Henry Jr. recorded memories of his childhood and youth in two autobiographical volumes, *A Small Boy and Others* and *Notes of a Son and Brother*. The latter title is suggestive. As his biographer Leon Edel insists, William, a vigorous and quick-witted elder brother, must have posed a formidable challenge. The father stood ready to interpret the whole world, and William was busy testing and exploring it. In these circumstances, what the novelist calls his "visiting mind" took command. Henry Jr. became consciously a spectator. Though New York had much to offer his infant sensibility (in particular its theaters, in which he acquired a lifelong passion for the stage), the chief spectacle, which absorbed the whole family, was Europe. Abroad, there was a world of high complexity and distinction, while America offered only three kinds of people: "the busy, the tipsy and Daniel Webster." The father of the family was somewhat anxious to secure the best possible education for his brood—there eventually were four boys and a girl. The boys went to a bewildering succession of schools and, in pursuit of what their father described as a better "sensuous education," were taken to Europe a number of times. There, under tutors and in Swiss and German schools, they acquired a cosmopolitan culture without a trace of cosmopolitan weariness. The passage in James's work most sharply suggestive of what Europe meant to him is an account of a visit to the Galerie d'Apollon at the Louvre in *A Small Boy and Others*.

William had thrown himself into painting—he soon gave it up for biology—and Henry briefly tried to emulate him. But Henry had always scribbled and in 1860 found needed encouragement from the artist John La Farge, who urged him to write more seriously. He undertook some translations from the French, and got his first editorial rejections. James was eighteen in that year. The two younger brothers fought with distinction in the Civil War, but William and Henry did not enter the army. Henry's memoir of the period suggests that an "obscure hurt" received while helping to put out a fire in Newport had incapacitated him. Edel's conclusion is that James had suffered a strained back, by no means incapacitating, but emotionally linked with his father's loss of a leg. The injury filled an emotional need—it was an excuse to be passive. He

need not fight; more important, he need not assert himself sexually. In 1862 James entered Harvard Law School, but left at the end of the school year. In 1864 appeared his first story, "A Tragedy of Error," and the *North American Review* published his first book review. The columns of the *Nation* and the *Atlantic Monthly* were soon open to him, and he profited much from the friendship and encouragement of WILLIAM DEAN HOWELLS, who became editor of the *Atlantic* in 1871. James's early fiction was gloomier and subtler than the popular taste would allow, but Howells stood by him staunchly. The reviews James wrote in these early years were biting and full of discrimination, which reflected not simply an early immersion in English fiction but a close acquaintance with contemporary French practice as well.

In the early stories Hawthorne counts for much, but the emotional state of the young author counts for more. James could not escape the theme of young love, but he handled it with elaborate detours suggestive of his own feeling of incapacity for the male role. This is particularly apparent in his first novel, *Watch and Ward*, which was serialized in the *Atlantic* in 1871. (Most of James's novels first ran in magazines. However, the dates of book publication are given below.) James's work improved greatly after his first independent journey to Europe, in his twenty-sixth year (1869). The effect of this visit was overwhelming. Florence, Venice, and Rome swept him off his feet. Yet he saw all these wonders as an American. "Travelling Companions" (1870) makes this very clear. A mere immersion in Europe was to be deplored. What is the right use of European experience for an American? This is a question that is handled in many ways by the stories of the seventies. "A Passionate Pilgrim" (1871), the most ambitious of James's works up to that time, is unhappily affected by his use of the rather clumsy device (it had haunted Hawthorne) of the American who returns to find his English heritage. After James returned home in 1870, stories and travel sketches poured forth in profusion. During a second trip to Europe (1872–74) James wrote his best story to date, A MADONNA OF THE FUTURE, and began his first novel of consequence, *Roderick Hudson*.

During these years James was much concerned with taking up a permanent residence abroad. Edel suggests that to his sense that the European scene offered the cultural complication necessary to a writer we ought to add James's embarrassed response to the demand of the elder Henry James that his boys marry and settle down. Marriage was never in question for the novelist, whose only serious interest in a woman had taken the form of a rather distant worship. His passionately admired cousin, Minny Temple, had died in 1870 while he was abroad. Minny had posed an awkward challenge, but her death enshrined her for him. She became in retrospect a kind of priestess of possibility, of "moral spontaneity," whose gift for life seemed to him as great as any he had ever known. The passages in *Notes of a Son and Brother* that describe Minny as he had known her in the summer of 1865 name her "the heroine of our common scene." She was to remain *his* heroine and appear in *The Portrait of a Lady* and *The Wings of the Dove*.

For whatever complex reasons, the son and brother left home in 1875, settling first in Paris, where Henry knew Edmond de Goncourt, Maupassant, Flaubert, and—most important to him—Turgenev. In 1876 he moved to England, where he was to spend the rest of his life. *Roderick Hudson* was published as a book in that year. A list of his notable works of the 1870s would include, in addition to those named above, "Madame de Mauves," THE AMERICAN (1877), "Four Meetings," *The Europeans* (1878), *An International Episode, Daisy Miller,* "A Bundle of Letters," and "The Pension Beaurepas." (A weak novel, *Confidence,* was published in 1879.) James's first book, A PASSIONATE PILGRIM AND OTHER TALES, had come out in 1875.

The international theme dominates the period. It represents not simply a rewarding device for making use of James's talents and personal history, but an adjustment to the question of expatriation. In juxtaposing his Americans with Europeans, James was, sometimes a bit anxiously, preserving his native note. He had a delightful gift of hitting off the consequences of an encounter between characters of differing national origins (as in "A Bundle of Letters," and more ambitiously in *International Episode*). "Madame de Mauves" had earlier demonstrated his insight into the dramatic possibilities of such collisions. The American girl in this story is a frightening figure who cares for nothing but status and external propriety. Her profligate husband, a member of the French aristocracy, is finally driven to suicide, and the young American who had admired her gives a thankful shiver at his escape.

James's first full-scale effort, RODERICK HUDSON, though it has fine passages of social observation of Northampton, Massachusetts, and presents us with a striking little group of Romans, including, of course, American expatriates, does not quite hold together. Rowland Mallet, who launches a talented American youth on his career as a sculptor, is too closely akin to the psychically disabled figures who had represented James himself in earlier work, and were fortunately to vanish after publication of *Confidence*. Roderick himself is too giddy and savage a figure for his creator to handle.

To find the right scale and the right situation for the sort of thing he was prepared to do at this stage was James's problem. He solved it brilliantly in THE EUROPEANS, which, though less ambitious than *Roderick Hudson,* is almost perfectly done. The encounter of Felix Young and the Baroness Münster, the Europeans of the title, with their New England relatives, the Wentworths, is sparely rendered, but it is not, as William James called it, "thin." Every stroke tells; it is a comedy of manners, but the manners are, as they are everywhere in James, the index of moral commitment or the lack of it.

DAISY MILLER, a long story that was serialized in England while *The Europeans* was being published month by month in the *Atlantic* (1878), was an immediate popular success and was quickly pirated in America. The American girl, armored and blinded by her innocence, who does what she likes—to the horror of the American colony in Rome, which is full of European suspicions of her conduct—became a figure all too representative of James's work for his own comfort. The pathos of Daisy, who dies of fever partly because the fatally expatriated Winterbourne has not found it possible to believe in her or discover her love for him, made her attractive to a wide public, and editors who kept asking for more international tales with attractive American girls were to plague James for years.

WASHINGTON SQUARE (1880), laid in the neighborhood in which James had grown up in New York City, is concerned with a struggle between father and daughter over the unattractive daughter's unworthy suitor. It is as close to Balzac as James was to come, depending as it does on characters whose beliefs and capacities are initially posited by the author and allowed to work themselves out to an inevitable consequence. It is much more characteristic of the later James to make character emerge as the felt consequence of actions described in the story itself.

James's life in London during this period is sketchily chronicled in *The Middle Years,* a posthumously published fragment of what was to have been a third autobiographical volume. But here as elsewhere his letters furnish much evidence. James floated on a rising tide of social success in these years. In one letter he reports that he dined out 107 times during the current season. Summer tours to France and Italy and visits to the great country houses whose amenities he celebrated in his fiction filled the time he could spare from writing in the succeeding years.

James's THE PORTRAIT OF A LADY (1881) is one of the finest novels in English. In it James launches the charming Isabel Archer on a great flight from the Albany of his childhood years to Europe, the locus of infinite possibilities. Endowed with a fortune by her disabled cousin, Ralph Touchett, she is caught by a fortune-hunting aesthete and condemned to a horrible marriage. The novel functions in terms of inverted perspectives: Isabel seems to demand and deserve a creative moral freedom; yet her demand is logically answered by spiritual enslavement, and the reader is made to realize how self-engrossed the original desire was. James's fine prose comes fully into its own in this novel. It is graceful, flexible, powerful, and metaphorically denser than his preceding work. He seems almost magically to find under his hand the very word that will make for a figurative extension and deepening of his meaning. The great theme of James's preceding decade, the question of how one is to take possession of the great world, is handled here by a finished novelist who succeeds in giving his central character a fullness of existence that defies abstract definition. Some critics, notably F. R. Leavis, in *The Great Tradition* (1949), find no greater achievement in the whole of James's work. If, as many have supposed, James has here imagined how it would have been had *he* died (in the person of Ralph Touchett), and Minny Temple had been endowed with the fullness of opportunity, he has not in the least compromised with his sense of actuality in imagining a career for his cousin.

Two other major works of the eighties, THE BOSTONIANS and THE PRINCESS CASAMASSIMA, are likewise novelistic in the sense that they offer more news of life than can be tidily summed up. The first, James's only big work with a wholly American setting, embraces a remarkable range of American experience without compelling it to the ends of form in the rigorous fashion of *The Portrait* or its other successors. Speaking generally, once James had finished his apprenticeship, he never dealt with society panoramically or as background, and this unaccustomed relaxation in *The Bostonians* must qualify our conclusions about the meaning of his uses of American and European experience. *The Princess Casamassima*, though it embraces much material that has to do with anarchist activity, the expression of widespread social unrest in the eighties, does so in stricter subservience to James's structural ends. While *The Bostonians* is a success of its kind, the success of *The Princess* is more questionable. James imposes on one character the task of discovering whether the glories of Europe's cultural accomplishments had been worth their cost in suffering and blood. Hyacinth Robinson has indeed had "more news of life than he knew what to do with," and the reader finds himself all too conscious of James's wide intention.

James made two journeys to America during the early eighties. His mother died during the first, and the second was occasioned by the fatal illness of his father. He was not thereafter to see his own country until his visit of 1904 and 1905. London was steadily his residence until, in 1898, he bought Lamb House in Sussex. Publication of THE TRAGIC MUSE (1890) is felt by some to mark the beginning of that elaboration of his style which, though both attacked and defended by his critics, is admitted by all to have changed the character of his work, if only in the sense that it demanded a fuller measure of attention from his readers. The fact that during the nineties James adopted the habit of dictating his extraordinarily long and complicated periods is a wonder, but not in itself an explanation of the increasing complexity of his prose. (This question will be discussed below in connection with *The Wings of the Dove* and *The Golden Bowl*.)

It is not an accident that at the end of the eighties James wrote *The Tragic Muse*, a novel that explores the meaning of pursuing the arts against the philistine background of contemporary English life. Both *The Bostonians* and *The Princess* had been commercial failures. He had done some other fine things during the eighties—THE ASPERN PAPERS, for example—but the novels after *The Portrait*, in which he sought to come to terms with a mass of social observations, had been meat too strong for both England and America. The question posed by Hyacinth Robinson is apocalyptic, truly radical, and the Boston of *The Bostonians* is shown to be spiritually bankrupt and threatened by mere money worship. This judgment on the Athens of America found no favor there.

The public had more of an excuse to ignore *The Tragic Muse*, which is somewhat awkwardly managed as narrative. James's interesting study of his muse, an actress, is a prelude to his serious theatrical ventures of the first half of the nineties. These were not uniformly unsuccessful, but they did not bring the returns James hoped for, nor was the stage much enriched by his plays. When, in 1895, he was hooted from the stage at the opening night of *Guy Domville*, he was moved to rededicate himself to fiction, although he never quite abandoned his hope of theatrical success.

James's work in the later nineties can be grouped in various ways. He produced an extraordinary group of stories having to do with artists, among them "The Real Thing," "The Lesson of the Master," "The Middle Years," and "The Death of the Lion." Between 1896 and 1901 larger works emerged steadily: *The Other House*, *The Spoils of Poynton*, *What Maisie Knew*, *The Awkward Age*, and *The Sacred Fount*. In addition James wrote two *nouvelles*, "The Turn of the Screw" and "In the Cage."

THE TURN OF THE SCREW is the most celebrated of the lot. James meant to mystify and alarm us, and he did, employing his principle that the imagined horror was worse than any that could be clearly specified. More critical articles have been written about this *nouvelle* than anything else James wrote.

James's choice of theme and method in the group of longer works listed above is more radically experimental than before. He had entered upon what for most writers would have been a fourth career. After his apprenticeship of the sixties, and his fine and enduring work of the seventies, the achieved greatness of the eighties had been followed by five years of dogged effort to learn the craft of the stage, interspersed with writing some distinguished stories. His rededication to fiction was accompanied by a resolution to make use of what he had learned in the theater. In *The Other House*, literally adapted from one of his plays, he achieves a hair-raising theatrical directness of effect, but formally the work is halfway between theater and book. To the anti-Jamesians, the most infuriating of this series of experiments is the last in the order of production, THE SACRED FOUNT (1901). In this parable on the wrong uses of the imagination the reader seldom knows where to pin his sentiments. But there is little doubt as to James's general moral intention, common to this work and many others, among which we may mention *The Spoils of Poynton* and *The Birthplace* (1903).

In James the great sin is, to use St. Augustine's term, *cupiditas*, which takes many forms, most simply the greed for things as, in the spoils of Poynton, a collection of precious bric-a-brac. James's work is full of collectors who entertain the delusion that they may grow spiritually fatter by grasping the creations of truly imaginative men. Another form is mere lust, which denies the creative uses of the other partner. Still another is the tourist's vice, as we may call it, the attempt to make a possession of one's exquisitely cultivated sensibility. A completely frozen and dead form of this vice is to think of one's social status as aristocrat or person of wealth as a guarantee of one's value. The opposed value we may call *caritas*, though in this use we somewhat extend Augustine's term. It is not simply a wide spiritual generosity, but the acts of the generous *imagination*, particularly the power of the artist to celebrate life rather than to try to possess things, or the power of the young American girl, a Milly Theale or a Maggie Verver, to sacrifice herself in the interests of life and growth. Either the artist or the girl carries the burden of asserting this value for James—never both in the same work, for their functions are analogous. This broad opposition is the root of the theological system of the elder James, which the novelist appears to have absorbed without being fully aware of the measure of his debt. James's own way of putting the nature of the highest possible value involves the term *consciousness*, the furthest possible extension of which would attest to the fullest realization of our common humanity.

The narrator of *The Sacred Fount* does not so much celebrate life as attempt to appropriate the events in the lives of those around him as material for his fantasy. He is an outsider, like the central characters of WHAT MAISIE KNEW and THE AWKWARD AGE. Maisie, the telegraphist of "In the Cage," Nanda Brookenham of *The Awkward Age*, and the narrator of *The Sacred Fount* are excluded from the scene on which they seek, with or without success, to interpose. Moreover, the scene from which they are excluded is predominantly the grown-up world in which sex plays a large part. *What Maisie Knew* is an extraordinary technical tour de force in which a child seeks to make sense of a world of sexual intrigue among her elders, and emerges not only unscathed, but equipped with a burgeoning moral sense. This took a supreme deftness on James's part, but the question is whether the choice of a central consciousness so bereft leads to more than a display of virtuosity. *The Awkward Age* is clearly the greater work. The title refers to the moment at which the adolescent girl must be allowed to leave the nursery and enter the drawing room, where she will inevitably stifle good, that is, sexually tinged, conversation. Mrs. Brook is wonderfully done. She is the center of a circle that prides itself on its conversational tone, and her efforts to maintain it against poverty and the shifting needs and desires of those who surround her may be thought of as a touching and poetic exploration of the fate of any established scene of communication—if only there were anything to talk about. Unfortunately, there is not. The substance of the talk may be described as the higher sniggering, and has in it so little of the meat of the converse of adult men and women that it is reminiscent of the dog's view of the family dinner as it lies under the table. A point of undeniable interest about this novel is its fictional method. It is not, like *The Other House*, a play turned into a novel; rather, it is a novel scenically conceived with very little interstitial tissue. As James puts it in his preface, each scene is to be a separate light on the total situation.

The three novels James composed just after the turn of the century, THE AMBASSADORS (1903), THE WINGS OF THE DOVE (1902), and THE GOLDEN BOWL (1904), named here in the order of composition, are thought by many to be James's greatest works. James himself believed *The Ambassadors* to be the most perfectly constructed of his novels. The elaboration of the prose reaches its full measure in these three books; to an extraordinary degree, it isolates his characters from the felt pressures of the commonplace in order to clear the ground for James's exquisite notation of their centers of consciousness.

Of course the awareness of these characters is not given to all alike. Strether, the center of consciousness of *The Ambassadors*, who has a measure of imagination, is dispatched by a New England matriarch to rescue her son Chad from a (presumably) designing woman in Paris. From Mrs. Newsome's point of view, that of fine cold thought, or New England righteousness, Strether's mission fails. Strether discovers Chad vastly improved in *appearance*; he discovers in fact the whole vast and enticing realm of appearance, most significantly in Madame de Vionnet, Chad's mistress, and seeks finally to persuade him *not* to desert her. This inversion of perspective is reminiscent of that of *The Portrait of a Lady*, the work which, after *The Ambassadors*, James thought most rounded. Strether, not being an artist or an American girl, has no means with which to reconcile appearance and morality; he retires ruefully with his capital of experience and the sense that his moral rightness depends on his not, out of the whole affair, having got anything for himself. The origin of the novel may be seen in a passage in James's notebooks. A friend had reported that William Dean Howells had, on the Parisian scene, urged a young man to live before it was too late, and these are the very words which Strether employs in Gloriani's garden. But James clearly saw limits to this injunction. All his great invokers and encouragers of life are artists or young girls whose actions are in some way morally creative. Indeed, it may be said that the strength of this novel *as* a novel derives from the fact that James had chosen a restricted consciousness, a comparatively imaginative man, as he calls him in his notebooks, for his hero. It is on this lonely particularity of Strether's, lost as he is between the realms of appearance and morality, that the novel finds its appeal to us. Isabel Archer and Strether may for this reason be called James's finest central characters. They are not used up when the book ends.

For many critics, the three last novels are the summit of James's achievement. Part of the problem for the critic here is a semantic one. If these are novels, they are certainly novels with a difference. For one thing there is the element one commentator has called "structural imagery" and which may also be called the emblematic element in these novels. An abstract statement of a complicated kind of artistic process must suffice here. What James has done is to make the novel, not a dramatic poem, but functionally akin to a dramatic poem, a new literary kind in which figurative definition has the same force and is to be apprehended on the same plane as his most explicit dialogue. When, in *The Golden Bowl*, Adam Verver likens the Prince to a smooth and golden surface, a bowl in fact, his metaphor is not tributary to his actions; it *is* one of his actions. When Densher sees the plaza at Venice as the "drawing-room" of Europe "profaned and desecrated" by the storm, he is putting forward something that is to be as immediately apprehended as part of the meaning of the book as the report of a pistol shot. A more general way of stating the matter is to say that just as in a medieval bestiary the meaning of the pictured beasts is their exhibition of a particular divine purpose, so in the James of these final novels appearance is completely at the service of consciousness. What this ultimately means is that every least thing that appears is figurative, because only in this guise does appearance have meaning. All is foreground; there is no background.

The Wings of the Dove concerns a pair of lovers who conspire to secure the wealth of a dying American heiress. The scheme to have the young man marry Milly Theale is thwarted by a disappointed suitor who gives away the plot. Milly nonetheless leaves a fortune to the young man, who finds himself unable to accept it or to marry his fellow conspirator if she does leave it. He is left with his memory of Milly and his mistress who had wanted everything, got nothing. The emblematic elements are more to the fore in this novel than in *The Ambassadors*. The temptation is to sort them out and call them allegorical. But in allegory things stand for abstract qualities or values. James's intention is to achieve an identity between what is represented and its value. Milly Theale is quite commonly called a redeemer by James's readers. But those who understand his work best are using "redeemer" as a sign, a pointer, not making an analogy with Christ. Milly is a redeemer insofar as she is seen to function as one. When she sees those who copy paintings in the National Gallery as living under water, submerged in appearance, far from the (creative) sacred fount, we recognize her authority as quasi-divine, just as we recognize it in her descent upon London from the high places of the Alps, and her inescapable spiritual power when her wings cover the lovers at the end.

The Golden Bowl, James's most difficult work, has the simplest possible germ. James set down in his notebook an anecdote about a father and daughter who married, only to discover that their spouses were lovers. This germ exfoliated into a very big novel, in which an apocalyptic pair of marriages, consummating a union between America and Europe, are saved by James's final redeemer. Adam Verver and his daughter, Maggie, are inexhaustibly wealthy Americans, engaged in one of those colossal raiding expeditions which, at the turn of the century, were common among American millionaires. Adam proposes to make the museum at American City unsurpassed. Fanny Assingham, herself a partner in an international marriage of an earlier day, brings together Maggie and Prince Amerigo, in whom Adam recognizes a collector's piece of the highest order. Maggie marries, and Adam finds himself by this stroke detached and vulnerable to prowling females. At this juncture Charlotte Stant returns from America. She and the Prince—like the conspiratorial pair in *The Wings of the Dove*—earlier had found themselves too poor to marry. The matter is arranged. Adam marries Charlotte. Yet, the old intimacy of father and daughter persists, despite Maggie's love for her husband. The Prince and Charlotte are thrown together—in this book it is the sexually alive who are excluded—and exclaiming, "What in the world else can we do?" they become lovers.

The work is largely composed of conversations among these four and Fanny Assingham, who recapitulates the situation for her husband, the Colonel, at the end of the first volume. Her summary is masterly and conclusive from the viewpoint of appearance. But in the second volume it is Maggie's consciousness that presides; the reality of a saving love must arrange appearances afresh. The process is initiated when, by an ironic inversion, Fanny destroys the golden bowl to preserve the appearances she had created in bringing about the marriages—but the bowl, evidence of the liaison between Charlotte and the Prince, is an index of reality, as its destruction shows. Maggie's blank American good faith becomes knowledge of the sinful world; she is in a position to help the Prince,

though she must protect Adam at all costs. Her function as redeemer is to deny herself; knowing the reality, she must affirm the appearances to save them all; she goes into society, and undergoes her Calvary at Fawns when, charged by Charlotte, she repudiates all her knowledge. In the end she wins. Charlotte, isolated, is led off to America as cicerone of the collection at American City. Adam's taste is vindicated.

After completing these three novels, James returned to America for a visit of ten months, during which he lectured widely and collected material for the book published in 1907 as THE AMERICAN SCENE. On his return to Lamb House in 1905 he began the extensive task of revising and prefacing his works for the New York Edition. He excluded certain novels and stories, yet the whole finally ran to twenty-six volumes, including two posthumously published novels left incomplete, *The Sense of the Past* and *The Ivory Tower*, added in 1917. The important prefaces to this edition, which detail the circumstances of composition and supply data as to the origin of many of his works, provide an extended commentary on the craft of fiction. They were edited separately by R. P. Blackmur in *The Art of the Novel* (1934). The general effect of the revision, the "reseeing" as James called it, was simply to tease more out of the work as originally conceived by adding qualifications and metaphors—never by changing his original intention.

In 1908, while still engaged on the New York Edition, James undertook a further theatrical venture. In 1909 a serious illness left him unable to work. He journeyed to Germany with his brother William, who was gravely ill; they returned to America together and William died there in 1910. In the following year James published a minor novel, *The Outcry*, and Harvard awarded him an honorary degree, as did Oxford in 1912. This was another year of grave illness for James. *A Small Boy and Others* appeared in 1913, *Notes of a Son and Brother* in the following year. When the war broke out, James found himself unable to continue *The Ivory Tower*, an ambitious novel with an American setting. He threw himself into the work of propaganda, hospital visiting, and the like, eager to serve his adopted country as best he could. To signalize his sense of the importance of the cause, he became a British subject in 1915. He died in London in the following year.

James was a great novelist, almost unparalleled as a critic among writers of fiction, and a major influence on the fiction of the 20th century. From his experiments in narrative perspective sprang, in greater or lesser extent, the narrative strategies of writers as different as Conrad, Fitzgerald, and Hemingway, and of many writers since. His concern for consciousness foreshadowed much of the 20th-century novel's emphasis on psychology, just as his direct interior narrations helped show the way to stream-of-consciousness as a technique. His overarching vision of humans bound to make sad and restricted choices within a world that appears on the surface to offer them limitless freedoms remains enlightening a century later in a world that seems in some ways to have expanded our human opportunities, in other ways to have increased our restrictions.

Among works unnamed above, the short story "The Beast in the Jungle," should be mentioned for its collapsing in small scale important themes and techniques from the period of the late novels. *The Novels and Tales of Henry James* (26 v. 1907–1917), The New York Edition, remains standard, but readers have sometimes preferred earlier, unrevised versions of a few of the novels. Leon Edel edited *Complete Plays* (1949), *Complete Tales* (8 v. 1964), *Letters* (4 v. 1974–84), and, with Lyall Powers, *Complete Notebooks* (1986). Edel's comprehensive biography *Henry James* (5 v. 1953–72) has been condensed and revised in one volume (1985). Among many studies are F.O. Matthiessen, *Henry James: The Major Phase* (1944); Dorothea Krook, *The Ordeal of Consciousness in Henry James* (1962); Ora Segal, *The Lucid Reflector: The Observer in Henry James' Fiction* (1969); Milicent Bell, *Meaning in Henry James* (1991); and Roslyn Jolly, *Henry James: History, Narrative, Fiction* (1993).

QUENTIN ANDERSON/GP

James, Jesse [Woodson] (1847–1882),   bandit. Sympathizers with the South, Jesse, a native of Kearney, Missouri, and his brother Frank (1843–1915) joined the Quantrill guerrilla band and served with it until the end of the Civil War. In 1866 Jesse was declared an outlaw, and for the next sixteen years stole from banks and railroads, caused the deaths of a number of people, and managed nevertheless to become a popular hero, an American Robin Hood. A price of $10,000 was placed on his head, and Robert Ford, a member of his band, earned it by shooting him. His murder was narrated in an anonymous ballad called "Jesse James," and he became the hero of innumerable dime novels, for example, *Life and Death of Jesse James* (1901) in *The James Boys Weekly*. William Rose Benét wrote a poem called "Jesse James" describing the bandit's career. Jesse James, Jr., wrote *Jesse James, My Father* (1899).

James, Marquis (1891–1955),   journalist, biographer. James spent his childhood in and near Enid, Oklahoma, and early worked on the local newspaper. From 1915 on, he lived in New York City. He was twice awarded the Pulitzer Prize, in 1930 for his biography of Sam Houston and in 1938 for his two-volume biography of Andrew Jackson. His published work also includes *The Cherokee Strip* (1945), which describes his Oklahoma boyhood.

James, William (1842–1910),   physiologist, psychologist, philosopher, teacher. After an education that offered him every cultural opportunity, this son of HENRY JAMES, SR., began in 1872 to teach at Harvard, his alma mater. He first taught physiology, then psychology, finally philosophy; and the three were correlated in his thinking. He continued to teach until 1907, meanwhile producing works on psychology, theology, ethics, and metaphysics that deeply influenced his contemporaries. James had considerable stylistic gifts and tried to shock his listeners and readers into awareness. Many of his phrases were memorable, as when he spoke of "the bitch goddess success," or when he wrote, "A great many people think they are thinking when they are merely rearranging their prejudices."

James was distinctly American in the concepts he advanced. His approach to metaphysics was frankly common-sensical. He objected to the pure and highly logical but unreal systems of so many metaphysicians. He emphasized strongly the part that the nature of the knower plays in the character and validity of the knowledge he gathers. Any concept of the world around us, James felt, is a compromise between the objectively given and the personally desired. He was led in the end to the concept of PRAGMATISM, the subject of his series of lectures at the Lowell Institute and later at Columbia that were published as *Pragmatism* in 1907; a sequel was *The Meaning of Truth* (1909). He urged that one turn away from abstractions, verbal solutions, fixed principles, and pretended absolutes and look for concreteness and facts, action and power. He argued that "the ultimate test for us of what a truth means is the conduct it dictates or inspires."

Something of the same revolt against absolutes is seen in James's deeply interesting THE VARIETIES OF RELIGIOUS EXPERIENCE (1902), which contends that any article of religious faith is true when it provides emotional satisfaction. *The Principles of Psychology* (2 v. 1890; abridged as a school text, 1892) shows James as a keen observer of the world of sense—one remembers that his first ambition had been to become a painter. One chapter, devoted to "The Stream of Thought," advances the concept of the stream of consciousness, which helped lead the way to an important and revolutionary fictional technique. In other books he discusses THE WILL TO BELIEVE (1897), *Human Immortality* (1898), *The Sentiment of Rationality* (1905), and *A Pluralistic Universe* (1909). A shorter piece, *Energies of Men* (1907), is a magnificent exhortation to courage.

James, Will[iam Roderick] (1892–1942),   rancher, cowboy, western writer and illustrator. Born in Great Falls, Montana, James wrote simple, adventurous stories of the cow country that enjoyed great popularity. From his first book, *Cowboys, North and South* (1924), to his last, *The American Cowboy* (1942), he wrote about what he knew and loved; he also illustrated his own works. Among his other books, several of which were made into movies are *The Drifting Cowboy* (1925); *Smoky* (1926), a classic of children's literature; *Cow Country* (1927); *Sand* (1929); *Lone Cowboy: My Life Story* (1930); *Sun-Up* (1931); and *Horses I've Known* (1940).

Jamestown.   The first permanent English settlement in the United States, located on the James River in Virginia. It was founded in May of 1607 by Sir Christopher Newport and about 100 followers. Threatened by hunger, disease, and hostile Indians, the colonists barely hung on in the next two years. More colonists arrived after 1610; growing tobacco gave the group financial resources, and they made peace with their Native American neighbors. As the capital of Virginia (1607–1698), Jamestown was host to the first legislative assembly to meet in America (1610).

Janeway, Elizabeth [Hall] (1913–   ),   short-story writer, novelist. While a student at Barnard, Janeway, born in Brooklyn, New York, won the *Story* magazine intercollegiate short-story contest. She made her early career as a novelist of psychological perception. Among her works are *The Walsh Girls* (1943), *Daisy Kenyon* (1945), *The Question of Gregory* (1949), *The Vikings* (1951), *Leaving Home* (1953), and *The Third Choice* (1958). She became a strong feminist voice with *Man's World-Woman's Place* (1971), a study of social mythology; *Between Myth and Morning: Women Awakening* (1974); *Powers of the Weak* (1980); *Cross Sections from a Decade of Change* (1982) and *Improper Behavior* (1987).

Janice Meredith (1899), historical novel by PAUL LEICESTER FORD. Ford was both a first-rate story teller and an accurate historian. The heroine is the beautiful, vivacious, and fickle daughter of a Tory in the Province of New Jersey in 1774. A mysterious and handsome bond-servant turns out to be Col. John Brereton of the Continental army; Janice ultimately marries him. In the Philadelphia and Virginia scenes General and Mrs. Washington are portrayed.

Janvier, Thomas A[llibone] (1849–1913), short-story writer, journalist. Born in Philadelphia, Janvier traveled widely and in his fiction used the four backgrounds he knew best: Philadelphia, New York, Mexico, and the south of France. His first book, *Color Studies* (1885), gave sketches of life in Mexico, where he had gone on a journalistic assignment. There followed *The Mexican Guide* (1886), *The Aztec Treasure-House* (1890), *Stories of Old New Spain* (1891), *The Uncle of an Angel, and Other Stories* (1891), *Embassy to Provence* (1893), *In Old New York* (1894), *In the Sargasso Sea* (1898), *In Great Waters* (1901), *The Passing of Thomas* (1900), *The Christmas Kalends of Provence* (1902), *The Dutch Founding of New York* (1903), *Henry Hudson* (1909), *Legends of the City of Mexico* (1910), *From the South of France* (1912), and *At the Casa Napoleon* (1914).

Jarrell, Randall (1914–1965), poet, critic. Born in Nashville, Tennessee, Jarrell spent his early years in Long Beach and Hollywood, California, before returning to Nashville. As a student at Vanderbilt, he was influenced by JOHN CROWE RANSOM and followed Ransom to Kenyon College, where Jarrell taught for two years, for a while sharing a room with ROBERT LOWELL. Later he taught at the University of Texas, Sarah Lawrence, and the University of North Carolina. He died when struck by a car.

Air Force service in World War II provided material for the striking war poems of *Little Friend, Little Friend* (1945) and *Losses* (1948). One of these poems is "The Death of the Ball Turret Gunner," with the grim concluding line "When I died they washed me out of the turret with a hose." Like Robert Frost, whom he much admired, Jarrell was skilled at imposing a careful metrical structure, frequently iambic pentameter, on the sounds of American speech. Many of his best poems, for example, the title poem of *The Woman at the Washington Zoo* (1960), are monologues in which the character of the poet is hidden behind the persona of the speaker. Only occasionally did Jarrell drop the mask, as in his late autobiographical poems "The Lost World" and "Thinking of the Lost World," collected in *The Lost World* (1965). *The Complete Poems* was

published in 1969. His other titles include *Blood for a Stranger* (1942) and *The Seven-League Crutches* (1951). *Selected Poems* appeared in 1990.

Jarrell's literary criticism, ranking with the best of its time, was collected in *Poetry and the Age* (1953), *A Sad Heart at the Supermarket* (1962), and in posthumous volumes. *Pictures from an Institution* (1954) is a satiric academic novel. Studies include Suzanne Ferguson, *The Poetry of Randall Jarrell* (1971), and William H. Pritchard, *Randall Jarrell: A Literary Life* (1990).

Jarves, James Jackson (1818–1888), newspaperman, editor, author of travel books, art critic, diplomat. Jarves's father, Deming Jarves, called Founder of American Glass, established glassworks at Sandwich, Massachusetts, to utilize the fine Cape Cod sand. The younger Jarves, who was born in Boston, traveled extensively and settled for a while in Hawaii. He founded the first newspaper there, *The Polynesian* (1840), and was made director of the government press. While on a diplomatic mission for Kamehameha III, he passed through Italy, resigned his post, and settled down in that country. From 1879 to 1882 he was United States vice consul at Florence.

Among his books are *Scenes and Scenery in the Sandwich Islands* (1843), *History of the Hawaiian or Sandwich Islands* (1843–47), *Parisian Sights* (1852), *Art Hints* (1855), *Italian Sights* (1856), *Art Thoughts* (1869), and *A Glimpse of the Art of Japan* (1876). Four of Jarves's six children predeceased him, and he wrote in memory of one of them, a talented artist who died at the age of fifteen, *Pepero: A Brief Memoir of James Jackson Jarves, Jr.* (1891).

Jasper, John J. (1812–1901), preacher. Jasper, an African-American born in Virginia, for many years attracted large audiences, African-American and white, to the Sixth Mount Zion Church in Richmond, Virginia. His best known sermon, called "De Sun Do Move," was printed (1850), along with introductory matter, by the Dietz Press of Richmond in its *Southern Masterpiece Series*.

Java Head (1919), a novel by JOSEPH HERGESHEIMER. In his examination of the American past, Hergesheimer turned to the China trade that helped make New England rich, and wrote *Java Head*, about a young sea captain and his Chinese wife.

Jay, John (1745–1829), lawyer, public official, judge. Jay was admitted to the bar in 1768 and five years later was a royal commissioner to settle the boundary line between New York and New Jersey. He was delegate to the First and Second Continental Congresses, chief justice of New York, minister to Spain, joint commissioner with Benjamin Franklin in making peace with England, secretary of foreign affairs under the Confederation, Chief Justice of the U.S. Supreme Court, and governor of New York.

As a member of the Continental Congress Jay wrote an *Address to the People of Great Britain* and composed appeals to Canada, Jamaica, and Ireland to rebel. He dealt with foreign affairs in five papers he contributed to THE FEDERALIST. His *Correspondence and Public Papers* (4 v. 1890–93) were edited by Henry P. Johnston.

Jayhawkers.   Members of a band of guerrillas who engaged in a border war involving Kansas and Missouri in the antebellum period on the question of free soil and slavery. The jayhawkers were antislavery. The name in time came to be applied to the inhabitants of Kansas. Thompson B. Ferguson wrote *Jayhawkers: A Tale of the Border War* (1892). In collaboration with Lloyd Lewis, Sinclair Lewis wrote the play *Jayhawker* (1934).

J. B. (1958),   a verse drama by ARCHIBALD MACLEISH. Suggested by the biblical story of Job, this play shows modern man in a universe whose laws he cannot understand, and comments on the various attitudes of faith and despair man may choose. A successful businessman, J. B. gives thanks for his happiness without claiming to have deserved it, while his wife, Sarah, believes that God directly rewards or punishes man's actions as they merit reward or punishment. As pointless catastrophes strike them, their positions change. Sarah will not believe her children guilty; she almost commits suicide in her despair at the absence of justice. In his agony, J. B. now demands to know a reason, a justification. A priest, a psychologist, and a cynical social historian offer unsatisfactory explanations. Even the Voice from the Whirlwind, while impressive, is not an answer relevant to the human problem of how to live. The ending affirms man's capacity to "endure and love."

Noted for its circus tent setting and play-within-a-play structure, the play received a Pulitzer Prize, MacLeish's third. Elia Kazan directed the Broadway production, the success of which, along with that of T. S. Eliot's *The Cocktail Party*, proved that poetry on the American stage could be popular.

Jeffers, Robinson (1887–1962),   poet. John Robinson Jeffers—the John, Jeffers noted, "never took"—was born in Sewickley, a suburb of Pittsburgh, Pennsylvania, the son of Dr. William Hamilton Jeffers, a Presbyterian minister and Old Testament scholar, and the former Annie Robinson Tuttle. Jeffers attended grammar schools in Switzerland and Germany, acquiring both French and German, and his father began to "slap" Latin and Greek into him from the age of nine, as he recalled, "literally, with his hands." The family moved to California in 1903 upon Dr. Jeffers's retirement, and Robinson entered Occidental College, from which he was graduated two years later. He then studied, successively, comparative literature, medicine, and forestry at the University of Southern California, the University of Zurich, and the University of Washington, but took no degree.

Returning to southern California, Jeffers took up the bohemian existence described in his first, self-published, book of poems, *Flagons and Apples* (1912). This period ended with his marriage to Una Call Kuster in 1913. The Jefferses settled in Carmel after plans to live in England were aborted by the outbreak of World War I, and twin sons, Donnan and Garth, were born to them in 1916. Supported by a modest bequest, Jeffers bought property near Point Lobos in 1919, and built the stone house he lived in for the rest of his life.

From the first, the majestic coast south of Carmel was the setting and the subject of most of Jeffers's verse, as is evident in the title and contents of his first commercially published volume, *Californians* (1916). It was not until after the war, however, that he shed earlier influences—Wordsworth, Tennyson, and Hardy among them—and, rejecting symbolism and imagism as well, found his own voice. TAMAR AND OTHER POEMS (including THE TOWER BEYOND TRAGEDY, an adaptation of the *Oresteia*) was printed privately in 1924 after his publisher, Macmillan, had rejected a second manuscript. A few critics were induced to read it, chiefly through the efforts of James Rorty. The response was immediate. Jeffers was hailed as a genuine talent, and compared immoderately to Aeschylus and Shakespeare. Boni and Liveright, which had rejected *Tamar*, put out an expanded edition that included a new poem, ROAN STALLION.

Over the next decade, Jeffers produced most of his major work, including *The Women at Point Sur* (1927), CAWDOR (1928), DEAR JUDAS (1929), *Descent to the Dead* (1931), THURSO'S LANDING (1932), *Give Your Heart to the Hawks* (1933), and *Solstice* (1935). The title poems of all these volumes, except for *Descent to the Dead*, a sequence inspired by a trip to Britain and Ireland, and *Dear Judas*, like "The Tower Beyond Tragedy" a verse drama, were lengthy narratives set on the California coast and dealing with themes of incest, Oedipal violence, and religious obsession that Jeffers took to be symptomatic of the cultural decline of the West. This view was more explicitly taken up in such poems as "Meditation on Saviors" and "The Broken Balance," while in the verse dramas "Dear Judas," "At the Fall of an Age," and "At the Birth of an Age," he explored the mythic sources—Greek, Judeo-Christian, and Nordic—of Western culture.

Solstice was an uneven book, and the title narrative of Jeffers's next volume, *Such Counsels You Gave to Me* (1937), seemed to emulate earlier and better work. By the time his *Selected Poetry* appeared in 1938, his reputation, never fully secure, was in decline, and his later books, *Be Angry at the Sun* (1941), *The Double Axe* (1948), *Hungerfield* (1954), and *The Beginning and the End* (1963), received mixed notice. His major success in those years was an adaptation of Euripides' *Medea*, which ran on Broadway with Judith Anderson in the title role, and represented the culmination of his long interest in Greek tragedy. But an attempt to stage "Dear Judas" encountered censorship and charges of blasphemy, while Jeffers's publisher, Random House, after prevailing on him to remove several poems bitterly critical of America's involvement in World War II from *The Double Axe*, still felt impelled to print a statement dissociating itself from his views at the head of the book. Jeffers's last decade brought some belated official recognition, including the Shelley Memorial Award and the award of the Academy of American Poets. For the most part, however, he was ignored in the court paid to Frost, Eliot, and Pound. By the time of his death, he had been largely relegated to the status of a regional poet whose chief interest was in the evocative landscape-painting of some of his shorter poems.

The generation since Jeffers's death has seen some revival of interest in his work, although no critical consensus has emerged. There is evidence, too, of his importance as a cultural icon among contemporary American poets, although, unlike the work of Pound or Stevens, his work has stubbornly resisted imitation or assimilation. Jeffers's early reception was in part a response to the territory he opened up to the Freudian revolution; for this, along with Faulkner and O'Neill, who rapidly followed him, he occupies a permanent place in the history of American literature. By the same token, his sudden eclipse was conditioned by the circumstances of the 1930s and 1940s; liberals who demanded social commitment decried his cultural pessimism and political isolationism, while the New Critics eschewed narrative and direct statement in favor of ellipsis and irony. The postwar attempt to fit 20th-century literature into the Procrustean bed of Modernism similarly excluded Jeffers, who had forthrightly distanced himself from Pound, Eliot, and their successors. Present perspective, however, enables us to see how Jeffers shared in the problematic of Modernism, however his poetic solutions differed, and suggests the need for a far more inclusive account of modern American letters. In such an account, Jeffers should occupy a place of honor and importance, both as part of the great generation that established the preeminence of American poetry in the English-speaking world, and as a poet of extraordinary range, philosophical complexity, and authoritative utterance.

Jeffers's strengths and weaknesses as a poet are inextricable, but he wrote nothing trivial. His narratives owe much to the example of Edwin Arlington Robinson, but they surpass the model and have not been equaled since. Their plots and characterizations are repetitive and even obsessive, but the narrative pulse of the ten and five stressed lines is both supple and controlled, while the interspersed authorial commentary varies the cadence and lends shrewd perspective. No reevaluation can ignore them. The shorter poems share the same rhythm of lyric thrust checked by terse observation and dicta. The influence of Schopenhauer, Nietzsche, and Spengler has been noted in his work, as well as that of Freud, Jung, and Frazer; but a great deal of critical work remains to be done on a poet whose culture and range of reference are as rich as any in modern American literature. Studies include Radcliffe Squires, *The Loyalties of Robinson Jeffers* (1956); Robert Brophy, *Robinson Jeffers: Myth, Ritual and Symbol in His Narrative Poems* (1973); Robert Zaller, *The Cliffs of Solitude: A Reading of Robinson Jeffers* (1983); and the work of William Everson, *Fragments of an Older Fury* (1969) and *The Excesses of God: Robinson Jeffers as a Religious Figure* (1988). Melba Berry Bennett's *The Stone Mason of Tor House* (1966) is importantly corrected by James Karman's *Robinson Jeffers: Poet of California* (1987), but a full-scale biography still awaits. The five-volume *Collected Poetry of Robinson Jeffers* (1988–2001), edited by Tim Hunt, supersedes earlier editions. Hunt also edited *The Selected Poetry of Robinson Jeffers* (2001).

ROBERT ZALLER

Jefferson, Joseph (1829–1905), actor, playwright, memoirist. Born in Philadelphia to the fourth generation of a theatrical family, Jefferson first appeared on the stage at age four and continued to play almost to the day of his death. His first great hit was Tom Taylor's *Our American Cousin* (1858).

In the following year he turned to Washington Irving's RIP VAN WINKLE, which had already been dramatized and altered by several writers. After some experimentation he asked DION BOUCICAULT to doctor it further. He appeared in 1865 in London for 170 nights in Boucicault's version, then brought it to New York in 1866 and scored a huge success. Rip was a standard role for him for forty years.

Jefferson became one of the most popular actors of his day, especially as a comedian. His *Autobiography* (1890) was reprinted in 1950 as *Rip Van Winkle.*

Jefferson, Thomas (1743–1826), statesman, diplomat, lawyer, scientist, architect, third president. Born in Albemarle County, Virginia, Jefferson was educated at the College of William and Mary. He was well read in classical literature, science, and philosophy, and after his graduation studied law. He was admitted to the bar in 1767 and continued to practice until just before the Revolution. He was elected a member of the Virginia House of Burgesses in 1769 and remained in the House until 1775; his greatest contributions were made in committees and in the drafting of documents. Unable to attend the Virginia convention of 1774 because of illness, he sent a paper entitled *A Summary View of the Rights of British America*, in which he argued for the natural rights of emigration and settlement, for an end of British taxation and a commercial agreement between England and America based on trade. The paper was rejected, but was probably instrumental in gaining Jefferson's election to draft the DECLARATION OF INDEPENDENCE two years later. Jefferson's clear, concise, and subtle prose made the *Declaration* the foremost literary work of the Revolution, as well as the most important single political document in American history. Based to a large extent on the philosophy of Locke, the *Declaration* emphasized the natural and unalienable rights of man, rather than those derived from the existing body politic.

Although Jefferson did not believe in absolute human equality, neither did he believe in the artificial aristocracy of birth and wealth then ruling in Virginia; accordingly, while in the Virginia House of Delegates from 1776 to 1779, he successfully worked for abolition of the right of primogeniture and land held in entail; he also introduced a bill for the establishment of religious freedom, separating religious opinions from civil authority. Although his *Bill for the More General Diffusion of Knowledge*, a summary of his views on education, was not adopted, he succeeded in establishing professorships of anatomy, medicine, modern languages, and law at the College of William and Mary.

Jefferson was governor of Virginia from 1779 to 1781, but had little power, due to the wartime limitations placed on his office, and in effect resigned when the British invaded Virginia. His conduct was investigated by the Assembly and, although his actions were fully vindicated, he suffered a loss of political prestige for some time after. His dislike of publicity, which had been apparent earlier in his career, was intensified after his governorship, and he retired to his home at Monticello, where he organized and enlarged memoranda about Virginia on which he had been at work for a number of years.

These NOTES ON THE STATE OF VIRGINIA, published in France in 1784–85 and later pirated in the United States, established his reputation as scientist and scholar and are still considered a valuable source of information about the natural history of Virginia, as well as about 18th-century political and social life.

Jefferson was elected a delegate to Congress in June 1783, and his voluntary retirement thus came to an end. During his six months' service he drafted thirty-one state papers, among them *Notes on the Establishment of a Money Unit*, in which he advocated adoption of a decimal system, and his reports on the western territory. Had these reports, anticipating the *Northwest Ordinance of 1787*, been adopted, they would have forbidden slavery in the western territory after 1800.

In 1784 Jefferson was appointed to assist Benjamin Franklin in negotiating commercial treaties with France, and the following year became Franklin's successor as minister to France. He was an excellent diplomat, succeeded in gaining several commercial concessions from the French, and contributed to the awakening French interest in America. He observed the beginning of the French Revolution with interest and was particularly sympathetic to the moderate reformers, although he disliked the later violence of the Revolution and the open imperialism of Napoleon. During his stay in Europe, Jefferson traveled to northern Italy, where he studied agriculture and classical architecture, and with his plans for the new capitol of Virginia helped initiate the growth of classical architecture in America.

Jefferson's work in France prevented his attendance at the framing of the American Constitution, and on his return he was concerned that the Constitution did not include provisions regarding the rights of individuals, and did not limit the number of times a president might be reelected. He was satisfied when a Bill of Rights was added to the Constitution, and accepted Washington's offer of the Secretaryship of State.

While Jefferson was Secretary of State he came into repeated conflict with ALEXANDER HAMILTON, Secretary of the Treasury, first over a movement for commercial discrimination against the British, which Hamilton opposed, and later because of Jefferson's fears that the Treasury was favoring commerce and finance at the expense of agriculture. Many of the basic differences between the two secretaries came to a head in 1791, when the Bank of the United States was established. Jefferson questioned the constitutionality of the Bank bill, arguing that it assumed powers not granted to the Federal government by the Constitution, but Hamilton's broad construction of the Constitution and the implied powers of the Federal government was finally accepted. By 1792 Hamilton's financial program had brought about a split in the cabinet that formed the foundation of an opposing political party, the Republicans (later Democrats), whose recognized leader was Jefferson. In the summer of 1792 Jefferson complained of Hamilton's financial policy to Washington, and the president presented Hamilton with a formal list of the objections cited against him, to which Hamilton made formal reply. Probably because of the campaign being waged against him by PHILIP FRENEAU, editor of the *National Gazette*, Hamilton attacked Jefferson in a series of vituperative articles in the *Gazette of the United States*, with the deliberate intent of driving Jefferson from office. However, the crisis following the outbreak of the war in Europe of 1793 brought a measure of unity into the cabinet and put at least a temporary end to the Jefferson-Hamilton hostilities.

Jefferson retired from his position as Secretary of State in December 1793 and returned to Monticello, where he devoted himself to agriculture and improvements on his estate. Although he wrote to Madison in 1795 that he had no desire to run for president, he did not refuse when the Republican party proved determined to support him. He lost the election to JOHN ADAMS [2], and under the election system at that time became vice president. Jefferson took little active part in the administration, but presiding over the Senate gave him the experience to write his *Manual of Parliamentary Practice* (1801), a basic work on parliamentary procedure. Probably his most important contribution to American democracy during the Adams administration was his work with James Madison on the Kentucky and Virginia Resolutions, which presented the "compact" theory of the Union, in which the states were authorized to attack unconstitutional laws in protest against the abuse of civil liberties.

Jefferson and AARON BURR were tied in the presidential election of 1800, and the choice between them was given to the House of Representatives. Due to dissension in the Federalist party and the fact that many abstained from the voting, Jefferson was elected despite the Federalist majority in the House. Finding almost all minor governmental offices filled with Federalist appointees, Jefferson proceeded to remove all officers whose appointment seemed to him to be of doubtful legality. He revoked the commissions of the midnight judges appointed by Adams at the very end of his term; the case of *Marbury v. Madison*, which arose as a result of Jefferson's action, was the first instance in which the Supreme Court asserted its right to declare an act of Congress unconstitutional. Jefferson also opposed renewal of the Alien and Sedition Acts, liberalized the Naturalization Act, and eased the national debt by cutting Federal expenses. Probably his most important contribution to the growth of America was made with the purchase of the Louisiana Territory from France in 1803, not only giving the United States complete control of the Mississippi River and its 800,000 acres of surrounding land but making possible the expansion of America from coast to coast.

Jefferson was easily reelected in 1804. War between Britain and France broke out shortly after and, in an attempt to prevent the United States from being forced to enter the war, Jefferson passed the Embargo Act (1807), closing American markets and depriving the combatants of American supplies. The Act was particularly unpopular in New England, where shipbuilding and trade had been growing rapidly, and Jefferson was forced to repeal the Act in 1809.

After forty years of public service, Jefferson was at last able to retire permanently to Monticello and enjoy the peace of a private life. He improved his lands by crop rotation, experimented with new farming methods and implements, studied, and pursued his varied interests. In 1814 he sold his personal library of ten thousand volumes to Congress to replace the books burned by the British during the Revolution. His advice was sought by his successors, Monroe and Madison; he was reconciled with his old friend John Adams; and the two men, from 1811 until their deaths in 1826, carried on a voluminous correspondence, perhaps the most interesting in American letters. Jefferson continued his interest in public education, and from the end of his presidency until his death he advocated a university "based on the illimitable freedom of the human mind to explore and to expose every subject susceptible of its contemplation." The University of Virginia—for which he had drawn plans, supervised construction, and designed the curriculum—was opened in 1825, a year before his death. Along with the *Virginia Statute for Religious Freedom* and the *Declaration of Independence*, Jefferson regarded it as one of his three greatest achievements.

Jefferson's writings fall into four classes: (1) state papers and political pamphlets, (2) the *Notes on Virginia*, (3) letters, and (4) miscellaneous pieces. In the first group, aside from the *Declaration*, formal publication was given to his *Address to the Senate on the 4th of March, 1801*, his First Inaugural; both this and his Second Inaugural Address are notable and eloquent documents.

Notes on Virginia has been constantly reprinted. Jefferson's letters still in existence run to more than 18,000; letters written to him number more than 25,000. P. Wilstach edited *The Correspondence Between John Adams and Thomas Jefferson* (1925). The miscellaneous writings cover a vast range: *Notes on the Establishment of a Money Unit* (1784); *Report on French Protests Against the Tonnage Laws* (1791); *Life of Captain [Meriwether] Lewis* (1817); and *Autobiography* (1821, pub. 1829).

The definitive edition is *Papers of Thomas Jefferson*, edited by Julian P. Boyd (1950–   ); *Thomas Jefferson, Writings* (1984) is a one-volume selection. Dumas Malone wrote a six-volume biography, *Jefferson and His Time* (1948–1981).

Jemison, Mary (1743–1833),   called the White Woman of the Genesee. At age fifteen Mary Jemison, living in western Pennsylvania, was captured by Indians. She adopted the name Deh-hewo-mis, married twice into the Delaware tribe, and regarded herself as a Delaware for the rest of her life. In 1797 the Indians granted her a large tract of land in the Genesee Valley in New York State. Her story was told in James E. Seaver's *A Narrative of the Life of Mrs. Mary Jemison* (1824).

Jen, Gish (1956–   ),   novelist, short-story writer. Born and raised in Scarsdale, New York, Lillian Jen was the child of immigrant parents who decided not to return to China after the Communist takeover of 1949. She changed her first name to Gish (after Lillian Gish, star of silent movies) when she was a teenager. An English major at Harvard (B.A., 1977), she studied business briefly at Stanford and taught English in China before completing an M.F.A at the Writer's Workshop of the University of Iowa. In her first novel, *Typical American* (1991), she tells of an exchange student's experi-

ences as he cuts himself off from home and tries to become an American after the 1949 revolution. In this and later books, her tone is often comic as she examines the question "What is an American?" from an Asian perspective. In *Mona in the Promised Land* (1996), a Chinese-American teenager decides to convert to Judaism. In the stories of *Who's Irish?* (1999), Jen continues her cross-cultural examination of lives both in the United States and in China.

Jenks, George Charles ["W. B. Lawson"] (1850–1929), newspaperman, editor, novelist. Jenks, born in London, emigrated to the U.S. and settled in Pittsburgh, where he worked on various newspapers and wrote a great number of dime novels. He created the popular character of DIAMOND DICK and many of the NICK CARTER stories, some written under his pseudonym. Typical titles are *Diamond Dick's Decoy Duck* (1891), *The Dalton Boys in California* (1893), and *Out with the Apache Kid* (1894).

Jenks, Tudor [Storrs] (1857–1922),   lawyer, writer of children's books. Jenks, born in Brooklyn, New York, practiced law and was on the staff of ST. NICHOLAS. A generation of young people were brought up on his stories and books, which combined entertainment with instruction in his popular treatments of historical, literary, and scientific subjects. Some of his titles are *The Century World's Fair Book for Boys and Girls* (1893), *The Boys' Book of Explorations* (1900), *In the Days of Chaucer* (1904), *In the Days of Shakespeare* (1905), *Our Army for Our Boys* (1906), *The Dolls that Talked* (1906), *Electricity for Young People* (1907), and *In the Days of Goldsmith* (1907). Jenks also wrote a comedy, *Dinner at Seven Sharp* (1917), in collaboration with his wife.

Jennie Gerhardt (1911),   a novel by THEODORE DREISER. Jennie's harsh German father forces her to leave home when he discovers she is pregnant. The baby's father, an Ohio senator, had promised to marry her but died before he could carry out his intention. She becomes the mistress of the scion of a wealthy family, who marries in his own class, becomes ill, and is nursed by Jennie. When he dies she steals in to his funeral, afraid to speak to his family.

Jennifer Lorn (1923),   a novel by ELINOR WYLIE. This was Wylie's first novel and one of her most amusing works, a "sedate extravaganza" laid mainly in England and India in the 18th century. The chief character is a pompous, aristocratic Englishman, seen through the eyes of his satiric wife as they go on a picaresque journey.

Jennings, John Edward, Jr. (1906–1973),   deckhand, salesman, historian, novelist. Born in Brooklyn, New York, Jennings won his first success with *Next to Valour* (1939), a story of New Hampshire in the days of the Rogers Rangers. Most of his later novels have a historical basis. They include *Call the New World* (1941), *Gentleman Ranker* (1942), *The Shadow and the Glory* (1943), *The Salem Frigate* (1946), *River to the West* (1948), *The Pepper Tree* (1950), *The Sea Eagles* (1950), *Banners Against the Wind* (1954), *Shadows in the Dusk* (1955), and *The Wind in His Fists* (1956). He also wrote *Our American Tropics* (1938); *Boston, Cradle of Liberty* (1947); *Clipper Ship Days* (1953); and *The Golden Eagle* (1959).

Jessel, Miss. The former governess in Henry James's THE TURN OF THE SCREW.

Jesuits in North America. A Catholic missionary order, the Jesuits were founded by St. Ignatius of Loyola in 1540 to combat Muslim influence. In later days its chief aim has been the propagation of the faith in many parts of the world. The Jesuits accompanied or closely followed conquest of the New World by the Spanish, French, and Portuguese. The Jesuit missionaries often suffered torture and martyrdom. The phrase "Jesuit Martyrs of North America" is applied to eight priests, including Isaac Jogues and John De Brébeuf, killed by Native Americans in the 17th century in New York and Canada, and later canonized by Pope Pius XI (1930). Around them an epic poem, *Brébeuf and His Brethren* (1940), was written by the Canadian poet E. PRATT.

The chief early literary account of the Jesuits in their North American missionary endeavors is *Jesuit Relations* (see FRENCH INFLUENCE IN AMERICA). Francis Parkman wrote *The Jesuits in North America in the 17th Century* (1867).

In the middle of the 18th century came severe attacks on the Jesuits in Portugal, France, Italy, and elsewhere; in 1773 the order was suppressed by Pope Clement XIV and went out of existence in all countries except Russia. It was universally restored by Pope Pius VII in 1814, but continued to suffer from exile and confiscation in several nations. In the United States it is an important teaching order. Among universities it sponsors are Fordham and Georgetown.

Jewett, [Theodora] Sarah Orne (1849–1909), writer of regional sketches and stories, novelist. Sarah Orne Jewett was born and chiefly lived in South Berwick, Maine, the locale, together with the Boothbay Harbor environs, she represents in her fiction. She was of patrician, seafaring, and professional New England stock, and as a child counted elderly relatives among her playmates. All these influences are perceptible in her fiction. As a young girl she enjoyed a close relationship with her father, Dr. Theodore Jewett. He encouraged his daughter's close observation of nature and of persons, interested her in medicine, and introduced her to English literature, thus fostering the keen perception and the cultivated perspective she would develop as a writer. Her first novel, *A Country Doctor* (1884), provides a fictional version of their relationship. Jewett's formal schooling was completed on her graduation from the Berwick Academy in 1865. The most important relationship of Jewett's mature years was her intimate friendship (1880–1909) with Annie A. Fields, widow of the Boston publisher and herself a distinguished hostess and philanthropist (see JAMES T. FIELDS). Jewett wintered with Fields in Boston and summered with her in Manchester, Massachusetts. Together they maintained a literary salon. They traveled in Europe (1882, 1892, 1898, 1900), where they were received by the literary elite, including Tennyson, Twain, Kipling, and James.

Jewett in 1868 began writing stories and poems for children, at first under the name A. C. Eliot. She entered the Boston publishing world effortlessly, discovering mentors in William Dean Howells and other editors of the *Atlantic Monthly*, where she published her first regional sketches. Augmented and collected, these became DEEPHAVEN (1877), an apprentice work for her best book, THE COUNTRY OF THE POINTED FIRS (1896), both these works being sequences of connected tales strung on the slender plot line of summer visitors' incursions into a rural community. Jewett's reputation rests most firmly on her fictions of 1885–96, which include the short-story collections *A White Heron* (1886), *The King of Folly Island* (1888), *Strangers and Wayfarers* (1890), *A Nature of Winby* (1893), and *The Life of Nancy* (1895), and culminate in *Pointed Firs*. A remarkable late story is "The Queen's Twin" in the collection by that name (1890). Her writing career ended abruptly in 1902, after an incapacitating accident. Jewett enjoyed popular and critical esteem throughout her career.

In her most characteristic attitude and voice Jewett resembles the familiar essayist; she referred to her tales as sketches. Her implied narrators and central consciousness characters have an observer's stance. They frequently locate their perspectives spatially—at a window, by the seashore, on a tree limb looking out over woodland. They are keen observers, noting the detail of natural and domestic settings with precision. When they turn their gaze on domestic interiors, the reader is made to see how the rooms of a house interconnect, where the furniture is placed and its state of elegance or decrepitude, and just what lies down the front walk, a tangled or a trim garden. Other senses are called into play, the odor of pine trees in the sunshine, the feel of the wind, the sound of an old house leaking after a rain shower. The implied narrators are meditative, compassionate, genial, sometimes ironic in their amused contemplation of the human subjects under scrutiny; frequently, a lambent humor informs their vision. Occasionally, they are judgmental. In the early fictions especially, there is a didactic or moralizing or interpretive attitude, frequently oriented toward Christian resignation, at other times toward a pragmatic criterion of usefulness. In this delicate balance of laughter and compassion, freighted with Christian moralizing, Jewett resembles Elizabeth Gaskell. She resembles Gaskell, too, in her documentary treatment of domestic interiors as the expression of character and in her fluent and authentic rendering of dialect. Hence, Jewett transforms local-color materials through a governing voice and attitude, a characteristic personal vision, expressed in a style celebrated for its economy, precision, nuance, and limpidity. Her luminous and vital description of landscape governed by a prevalent mood may be seen, for example, in the early sketch "River Driftwood," in the coastal vistas of *A Marsh Island* (1885), or in "A White Heron," commonly regarded as her finest single tale.

Jewett's narrative tone of gentle, reflective musing merges into her most characteristic theme of nostalgic reminiscence. Her fiction celebrates the past, both the ancestral New England forebears and the thriving shipbuilders and merchants. Perceived against these heroic older generations are the contemporary impoverished, desolate farmers; the survivors of 18th-century aristocratic families, living in solitude in antiquated great houses; and superannuated sea captains who subsist on anecdotal reminiscence. This leads to Jewett's concurrent theme—the contrast between past and present, expressed yet again in that of country vs. town. The rural and the elderly live at the tempo of the natural world, in harmony with the seasons and responsive to weather, expressing themselves in their relationship to nature, as fishermen, farmers, gardeners, and would-be conservators of natural creatures and resources. Modernity signifies disruption, destruction of the woodlands, obsolescence of aristocratic life styles, incursion of summer visitors into rural neighborhoods, and migration of the young and the male westward and into industrialized New England towns, leaving behind the figures in the foreground of her canvas, a plethora of spinsters and widows. Thus, another characteristic theme emerges, that of female friendships and bondings—those of sisters, of schoolgirls, of older women bound together in friendship, those of grandmothers and maiden aunts with younger relatives with whom they share a home. The older women may be perceived as earth mothers, sibylline figures, repositories of folk wisdom, for example, Almira Todd in *Pointed Firs*.

Historically, Jewett represents a continuum with the pioneering New England regionalist writings of HARRIET BEECHER STOWE and the romanticized realism of WILLA CATHER. For Jewett, Stowe's *Pearl of Orr's Island* was a seminal book, causing her to scrutinize anew the familiar Maine landscape and people. Jewett bequeathed to Cather the concept of the necessity of a detached and culturally enriched perspective for the writer who would utilize local materials without being submerged in regionalism. Henry James praised Jewett's art of fiction. His admiration for the finish, penetration, verisimilitude, and nuanced tone of her New England stories is still current. While Jewett is preeminent among the fashionable New England local-color writers of the post–Civil War era, including ROSE TERRY COOKE and MARY WILKINS FREEMAN, she is also commonly regarded as the most distinguished American regionalist writer of the 19th century. Charles G. Waugh and others edited *The Best Stories of Sarah Orne Jewett* (1988). Biographical and critical studies include Richard Cary, *Sarah Orne Jewett* (1962); Richard Cary, ed., *Appreciation of Sarah Orne Jewett* (1973); and Gwen L. Nagel, ed., *Critical Essays on Sarah Orne Jewett* (1984).

JEAN FRANTZ BLACKALL

Jewish American Literature.   The Jewish presence in American life dates back to 1654, when twenty-three Jews arrived in New Amsterdam (soon to be New York), refugees from seized Dutch colonies in Brazil. There are now between five and six million Jews in the United States. The Jewish literary presence can be said to begin in the 1880s, when the influx of East European Jews began, a migration that was to number about two million from these oppressive regions between 1880 and 1920, when immigrant restriction legislation began in earnest.

At the time of the American Revolution there were perhaps 2,000 Jews in this country, almost all Sephardim—that is, like the first refugees, descendants of Jews expelled from Spain in 1492. A hundred years later the numbers swelled to more than

half a million, most of them German Jews, or Ashkenazim. This group prospered by and large and produced some notable thinkers and theologians as well as merchants and bankers, but they made no lasting literary impact on the American scene. The East European Jews and their descendants did place their mark decisively on the character of American Jewish life and on American culture. Today the number of writers who were or are Jews is legion and still growing. One can only name and discuss briefly those whose Jewish lives and literary achievements have intersected with and had measurable impact on American literature.

One begins with a Sephardic Jew, EMMA LAZARUS (1849–1889), who is best known for her compassionate and stirring poem "The New Colossus," which is inscribed at the base of the Statue of Liberty. In welcoming "the tempest tossed" and "huddled masses . . . yearning to breathe free," the poem expresses the best side of America, as a redemptive land. An all but assimilated Emersonian for most of her life, Lazarus in her last years, moved by the oppression of Jews abroad, became a spiritual Zionist, publishing *Songs of a Semite, The Dance of Death, and Other Poems* in 1882.

The true originator, however, of the impressive line of achievement by Jewish American writers in our time must be said to be ABRAHAM CAHAN (1860–1951). Known best as the editor of the great Yiddish newspaper *The Jewish Daily Forward*, which he helped found in 1897 and then led continuously from 1903 until his death, he produced a considerable body of fiction in English—he also wrote some in Yiddish—between 1892 and 1917. His stories and novels deal largely with the effects of immigration and the themes of accommodation and acculturation. *Yekl: A Tale of the New York Ghetto* (1896)—the basis for the film *Hester Street* (1975)—tells the story of a callow youth who sheds his Old World values and adopts superficial and unfulfilling values of the New World. Cahan's work includes *The Imported Bridegroom and Other Stories* (1898), *The White Terror and the Red: A Novel of Revolutionary Russia* (1905), and his last and best novel, probably the best immigrant novel in American letters, *The Rise of David Levinsky* (1917)—the story of a wealthy garment manufacturer who starts as a penniless immigrant, but looks back on his life and material success with an ambiguous sense of unfulfilled psychic and spiritual yearning. This theme is echoed as well in Sidney Nyburg's *The Chosen People* (1917), an advance in sophistication over several earlier novels by other lesser writers—Ezra Brudno, Edward Steiner, Elias Tobenkin—who extolled the advantages of unambiguous assimilation to the new life.

Among serious early contributors to the line of American Jewish writers, there were none who wrote with greater skill and impact than MARY ANTIN (1881–1949) and ANZIA YEZIERSKA (1880–1970). These two may be fruitfully compared and contrasted, revealing in their differences the great range of responses to the complex stimulus of American life. Antin's *The Promised Land* (1912) has been denigrated recently as an example of "the cult of gratitude" to be found in some immigrant literature, but it is a vivid and beautifully written account of the heroine's journey from a benighted village in the Russian Pale to the intellectual riches of Boston and the higher learning she eventually received. It also is an indispensable American document, along with *The Rise of David Levinsky*, and Yezierska's powerful novel *Bread Givers* (1925) and collection of essays *Children of Loneliness* (1923). Unlike Antin, Yezierska evokes her sense of betrayal by America's promise even though in the spirit of prophecy she urges the country to assume its best self. *Bread Givers* is subtitled "A Struggle Between a Father of the Old World and a Daughter of the New," thus drawing attention to the ethnic and feminist themes that made it a popular college text in the 1970s and 1980s after decades in which Yezierska's reputation and work had largely been forgotten.

The period between World War I and World War II ushered in a new era of writers, largely American born, for whom the pace of Americanization was still problematic. The 1920s encouraged a freewheeling intellectual and economic climate, though it also witnessed a growth in anti-Semitism as evidenced in the policies of the emergent Ku Klux Klan, Henry Ford's circulation of "The Protocols of the Elders of Zion," and the racist immigrant exclusion act of 1924. Still, an optative or at least Bohemian mood often prevailed, as in MAXWELL BODENHEIM's *Naked on Roller-skates* (1930) or BEN HECHT's *A Jew in Love* (1931), or the expatriate experience of HAROLD STEARNS—the model for Robert Cohn in Hemingway's *The Sun Also Rises*. Cross currents were evident in the work of LUDWIG LEWISOHN, whose autobiographical *Up Stream* (1922) describes his anger at being refused an academic appointment because he was a Jew, despite his parent's early conversion to Christianity, and his embrace of fierce Jewish nationalism. Lewisohn also wrote novels, such as his highly praised (by Freud and Thomas Mann) *The Case of Mr. Crump* (1925), attacking puritanical attitudes toward sexuality. As Samuel Ornitz (1890–1957) asserts in *Haunch, Paunch, and Jowl* (1923), however, "There was not yet an American identity." This caustic tale of an unscrupulous drive for success by the ethnic arriviste is a forerunner of JEROME WEIDMAN's *I Can Get It for You Wholesale* (1937) and BUDD SCHULBERG's definitive Hollywood novel *What Makes Sammy Run* (1941). While refreshingly unsentimental, a more complex and ultimately enriching way of dealing with the many-sidedness of Jewish experience would only appear in significant and widespread ways after the World War II and the total breakthrough of Jewish writers into the mainstream of American culture.

This process was set in motion earlier, after the crash of 1929, when the center of American life seemed no longer to hold, all of its values were in question, and ethnic and regional working-class and lower middle-class writers of all sorts emerged in great numbers as the freshest voices of the depression period. Jews as well as Italians, Irishmen, and African-Americans began to be taken seriously and centrally, even as, paradoxically, in the general calamity, ethnic exclusivity seemed passé. Thus, MICHAEL GOLD's *Jews Without Money* (1930) set the tone for the vogue of proletarian literature in the turn leftward of many writers of the period. It chronicled in detail—often sentimentally and through

the tinted glass of the class struggle—the life of poor Jews in the tenements and streets of the Lower East Side in the early years of the 20th century.

CLIFFORD ODETS was the most talented leftist playwright of the period. His *Awake and Sing* (1933), the story of a middle-class Bronx Jewish family caught in the moil of the depression, and his *Waiting for Lefty* (1934), inspired agit-prop, are enduring achievements, although his departure for Hollywood inspired one of DOROTHY PARKER's—another splendid Jewish American writer—best lines, "Odets, where is thy sting?" His easy familiarity with the vernacular in these works, along with ELMER RICE's *Street Scene* (1929) and *Counsellor-at-Law* (1931) and SIDNEY KINGSLEY's *Dead End* (1935), among numerous contributions by Jewish dramatists and screen writers of the period, can be seen as mopping up the last vestiges of American literary gentility and as forerunners of the linguistic achievements of Saul Bellow and Philip Roth. Poets flourished as well—LOUIS ZUKOFSKY, CHARLES REZNIKOFF, GEORGE OPPEN, and MURIEL RUKEYSER, who attempted to apply the modernism of Eliot and Pound to a socially conscious verse. A vigorous literary criticism began to emerge from what Daniel Aaron (*Writers on the Left*, 1961) has called the literary political wars of the 1930s. Consider LIONEL TRILLING, Professor of English at Columbia University, and the first Jew to gain that appointment, writing in *The Menorah Journal*. (This journal was the precursor of *Commentary* in the 1960s, under the editorship of a former student of Trilling's, NORMAN PODHORETZ.) PHILIP RAHV and William Phillips assumed editorship of *Partisan Review* in 1935 and turned it toward an anti-Stalinist left but modernist position. Robert Warshaw wrote groundbreaking movie criticism. There was the pioneering and brilliant literary and cultural essays of Isaac Rosenfeld (whose one novel, *Passage From Home*, 1946, is a moving evocation of Jewish tensions and emotions in a Chicago family). Meyer Schapiro wrote outstanding art criticism, and out of long years of reading in the New York Public Library, ALFRED KAZIN produced *On Native Grounds*, 1942, a love affair with American literary culture, which is one half of his full identity—the other half, to Jewish American life and culture, was acknowledged in his influential autobiographical *A Walker in the City* (1951).

Among the most solid fictional achievements of the 1930s, as we see now, are those by literary sports—EDWARD DAHLBERG, *Bottom Dogs* (1930); DANIEL FUCHS, the Williamsburg Trilogy, not successful in its time but reissued in 1961; MEYER LEVIN, *The Old Bunch* (1937), a marvelous document of generational interaction among Chicago families (Levin went on to become in his last years one of the few genuinely Zionist novelists among Jewish American writers); and satiric gems by NATHANAEL WEST, *Miss Lonely-hearts* (1932) and *The Day of the Locust* (1939), unforgettable in their depiction of American grotesquerie and a spiritual shallowness that seems to await apocalyptic violence. The greatest Jewish American novel of the 1930s, perhaps, is *Call It Sleep* (1934) by HENRY ROTH.

This was Roth's only novel, although he later began to publish again. *Call It Sleep* is a beautifully rendered account of an acutely sensitive boy's growing up in an immigrant family dominated by a somewhat psychotic father in a coarse and bewildering social milieu. The book, like others of the period, was rescued from oblivion during the Jewish renaissance of the 1950s and 1960s. *Call It Sleep* was saved by the critics Leslie Fiedler and Alfred Kazin, and an influential review in the *New York Times* of a 1961 reprint by IRVING HOWE, a critic and scholar. Howe is also the author, with Kenneth Libo, of a Pulitzer Prize work, *World of Our Fathers: The World East European Jews Found and Made* (1976).

The emergence of the work of Saul Bellow, Bernard Malamud, and Philip Roth in the 1950s was the spark for a recognition of the major role of Jewish writers in American culture. And with the publication of *The Family Moskat* (1950), translated from Yiddish to English, I. B. Singer initiated a long career as a major American writer. The social and historical moment was propitious. Jews, who had been largely working class, benefited from the general economic expansion after World War II, becoming by then solidly middle-class and professional. The nation's conscience had been scarred by the revelations of the Nuremberg trials, and the attitude toward Jews changed, as Jewish writers themselves changed under the shadow of the Holocaust. Until 1947 anti-Semitism had been quite visible in the U.S.—LAURA HOBSON's *Gentleman's Agreement* (1947) and ARTHUR MILLER's *Focus* (1945) were efforts to convince the middle class of its evils, while Saul Bellow's *The Victim* (1947) dealt with the issue in a more complicated and ironic fashion—suitable to a writer who had begun his career associated with the left intellectuals of *Partisan Review*. By 1948 and the warm reception afforded the new state of Israel, the tide had turned.

SAUL BELLOW's first two novels, *Dangling Man* (1944) and *The Victim* (1947), were rather existentialist, brooding works. THE ADVENTURES OF AUGIE MARCH (1953) represented a significant shift and was to influence other Jewish writers. Exuberantly picaresque, its eponymous hero a Jewish American (born in Chicago) Huck Finn and Ishmael, it celebrated the promise and potential embodied in American life. Its language and attitudes were liberating to the new generation—a self-confident blend of the vernacular and the high style, of classic wisdom and ethnic street-smarts, by a writer whose first language had been Yiddish—it heralded a new maturity and self-assurance in the Jewish American writer. By 1964 Bellow's *Herzog* won a National Book Award and a large middle-class audience. This tale of a tragic-comic intellectual nebbish domesticated Abraham Cahan's early efforts to synthesize European thought with Jewish subjects and American concerns. Bellow won a Nobel Prize in literature in 1976 for his impressive total output—among the best, his short stories and novellas, such as *Seize the Day* (1956). It became apparent that a Jewish writer could be honored as a stellar world figure—in Bellow ethnic particularity and general or universal concerns were joined and transcended.

BERNARD MALAMUD burst on the literary scene in 1953 with *The Natural*, a mythic tale about baseball, but it was *The Assistant* (1957), a novel about a poor Jewish grocer and his Italian

assistant that equated being Jewish with being human, and his collection of extraordinary stories THE MAGIC BARREL (1958), with its linguistic and thematic echoes of the great Yiddish masters, that secured his reputation and role. He went through a bad phase in the 1970s marked by *The Tenants* (1970) and its pessimistic view of the future of American culture, especially in racial relations, as did Bellow in *Mr. Sammler's Planet* (1970). The 1970s and 1980s also gave birth to newer voices, reflecting the tensions and hopes of the Civil Rights Movement, the Vietnam War and its protests, and the rise of the women's movement.

The figure who spans all these decades with vitality and continuing relevance is PHILIP ROTH. His first book, *Goodbye, Columbus and Five Short Stories* (1959) won both the Jewish Book Council and the National Book Award—though several of the stories offended many Jews with their satiric thrust at unexamined contemporary Jewish pieties and complacencies. His *Portnoy's Complaint* ten years later, a novel rich in raw sexual language and a wild send-up of the Yiddish momma and good Jewish boy stereotype, outraged many, while it delighted more, propelling Roth into the best-seller category. His impeccable ear, perceptive eye, and literary sophistication are apparent in an astonishing variety of works that chronicle our times as few other works have. *My Life as a Man* (1974) projects a sense of male grievance, and his Zuckerman trilogy and *The Counter-Life* (1987) play with the process of fictionalization and reality while exploring deeper themes of Jewishness, life and death, and human suffering. *The Ghost Writer* (1979) shows Roth at the top of his form—audaciously imagining Anne Frank alive and the mistress of the literary apprentice's master (modeled on Malamud)—a bold and moving affirmation of the literary imagination. Major books, among them *American Pastoral* (1997), have continued to display Roth's strengths.

An entire essay needs to be written on American Jewish women writers. We began with the Mothers—Lazarus, Antin, Yezierska—and since the empowerment of the women's movement the number of important Jewish American women writers has increased exponentially and continues to grow. The long silence imposed on Jewish women by traditional Judaism and by the exigencies of immigrant poverty is over. The brilliant memoirs of growing up as Jewish American women by Kate Simon (*Bronx Primitive*, 1982) and the talented novelist Lynne Sharon Schwartz (*Leaving Brooklyn*, 1989) fill in vital and previously scanted territory. The stories by GRACE PALEY *The Little Disturbances of Man* (1959) and *Enormous Changes at the Last Minute* (1974) show how a secular and socially conscious feminine sensibility can intersect with Jewishness, as does the powerful and highly influential *Tell Me a Riddle* (1961) by TILLIE OLSEN. CYNTHIA OZICK is a major novelist and short-story writer who has combined a deep and conscious Jewishness with technical virtuosity and cosmopolitan literary antecedents. Her story "Envy: or Yiddish in America" is masterly; "The Pagan Rabbi" (1969) is a brilliant talmudic exegesis on the struggle between animism and orthodoxy; *The Shawl* (1989), a moving woman's view of the

Holocaust and a subject not often treated directly by Jewish American writers (E. L. WALLANT's *The Pawnbroker* (1961) and Art Spiegelman's comic book masterpiece *Maus: A Survivor's Tale* (1986) are exceptions, though the fact of the tragic moment in human history is never far from any Jew's mind.)

Consider in addition to all these writers (and more) such literary voices as ALLEN GINSBERG, whose "Howl" (1956) ushered in the 1960s, and NORMAN MAILER, the Peck's Bad Boy of American literature, author of the definitive account of the antiwar movement in *The Armies of the Night* (1968). Then there is ADRIENNE RICH, the doyenne of women's consciousness and poetry in the late 20th century, as well as hundreds of other poets, fiction writers, novelists, dramatists, and critics whose connections with something called "Jewish American literature" may seem tenuous or attenuated, but are nevertheless part of the stream, in some part enfranchised, too, by the general history here outlined. It is easy to see what a vast repertoire of cultural value has been created and has touched American life at its most essential points.

Helpful books include Allen Guttmann, *The Jewish Writer in America* (1971); Ira Bruce Nadel, *Jewish Writers of North America: A Guide to Information Sources* (1981); Daniel Walden, ed., *Twentieth Century American-Jewish Fiction Writers* (*Dictionary of Literary Biography*, v. 28, 1984); Louis Harap, *Creative Awakening, In the Mainstream*, and *Dramatic Encounters* (3 v. 1987); and Lewis Fried, ed., *Handbook of American Jewish Literature* (1988); Lynn Davidman and Shelley Tenenbaum, *Feminist Perspectives on Jewish Studies* (1994); and Alan L. Berger, *Children of Job: American Second-Generation Witnesses to the Holocaust* (1997).

JULES CHAMETSKY

Jhabvala, Ruth Prawer (1923–   ), novelist, screenwriter. Born in Germany to parents of Polish-Jewish heritage, she was forced to flee with her family to Britain in 1939. She earned a degree in English literature from London University, married an Indian architect, and moved to India. There, she and her husband raised three daughters. Since 1975, she has lived in New York City. Her first novels, *To Whom She Will* (1955; *Amrita* in the U.S.) and *Nature of Passion* (1956), comic in tone, depict life in Indian society. *Heat and Dust* (1975), winner of the Booker Prize, relates parallel stories of life in modern and colonial India; she wrote the prize-winning screenplay. Switching from Indian settings and subjects is *In Search of Love and Beauty* (1983); set in New York, it deals with German and Austrian immigrants. Also set in Manhattan is *Poet and Dancer* (1993), centering on a relationship between two women. As a screenwriter, she has been connected to the team of James Ivory, director, and Ismail Merchant, producer, in film adaptations of novels such as her own *Heat and Dust* (1984); Henry James's *The Europeans* (1979) and *The Bostonians* (1984); E. M. Forster's *A Room with a View* (1986) and *Howard's End* (1992); Evan S. Connell's *Mr. & Mrs. Bridge* (1990); and Kazuo Ishiguro's *The Remains of the Day* (1993).

Jim Bludso of the Prairie Belle (in PIKE COUNTY BALLADS, 1871), a poem by JOHN HAY. This tale of a Mississippi steamboat engineer who sacrifices himself to save his passengers when his boat catches fire was based on a real incident. The poem is in western dialect, which Hay and Bret Harte began using in verse at about the same time; Mark Twain had already made it popular in prose.

Jim Crow.   T. D. Rice, an American vaudeville performer and impersonator, was widely known for his song "Jump, Jim Crow," which he based on a song and shuffling dance done by an old African-American while grooming a horse. Rice's version was first given in Louisville in 1828, and the song was published and sung all over the country. The term "Jim Crow" soon became an insulting epithet and was applied to the segregation practiced in the South—"Jim Crow" cars, schools, sections, etc.

Jin, Ha [Xuefei Jin] (1956–   ),   novelist, poet. Born in the northern city of Jinzhou, China, Ha Jin served as a teenager with the People's Liberation Army during the Cultural Revolution. Afterward, with a B.A. in English literature from Heilongjiang University (1981) and an M.A. from Shandong University (1984) he came to the United States in 1985 to study at Brandeis University. In 1989, following the Tiananmen Square massacre, he decided not to return. After study at Boston University, and with a Ph.D. from Brandeis (1992), he began teaching at Emory University in 1993. He had already published a book of poems, *Between Silences* (1990). "Writing in English," he has said, "became my means of survival, of spending or wasting my life, of retrieving losses, mine and those of others." Praised for his early books, he achieved his first popular success with *Waiting* (1999), a story of eighteen years of frustrated love between a Red Army doctor and nurse who cannot marry until the doctor's first wife grants him the divorce she promises him annually. The book is a marvel of close observation rendered in the clean, precise prose of a writer whose second-language English proves exactly right for the subject matter. *Facing Shadows* (1996) is a second book of verse. Stories are collected in *Ocean of Words: Army Stories* (1996) and *Under the Red Flag* (1997). *In the Pond* (1998) is a comic novella of the bureaucratic frustrations of daily Chinese life. *The Bridegroom* (2000) collects twelve stories of life in a changing Chinese society. Though the authority figures may be different people, the tyranny of a rigid bureaucracy remains the same.

Joad.   The name of the family of Okies—former residents of Oklahoma—who in John Steinbeck's THE GRAPES OF WRATH (1939) make their way to California as migrant workers. Tom Joad is the principal character, and the others include his grandparents, parents, and Uncle John.

Joan of Arc, Personal Recollection of.   See PERSONAL RECOLLECTIONS OF JOAN OF ARC.

John Brent (1862),   a novel by THEODORE WINTHROP, set in California and Utah.

John Brown's Body [1].   A famous Civil War song of obscure origin. The tune dates back as far as 1856 and is generally credited to William Steffe, a South Carolinian who composed many camp-meeting tunes. The "John Brown" verses have been attributed to Charles Sprague Hall, Frank E. Jerome, T. B. bishop, and others. They were first popularized by Col.

Fletcher Webster's 12th Massachusetts Regiment, which used them as a marching song, and soon the song was adopted by all Union soldiers. The tune was also used for THE BATTLE HYMN OF THE REPUBLIC.

John Brown's Body [2] (1928),   an epic poem by STEPHEN VINCENT BENÉT. The poem follows the course of events leading to the Civil War, beginning in a Prelude with the introduction of slavery and going on to John Brown's raid on Harper's Ferry and his execution. Looking at both sides of the conflict with deep sympathy, Benét sketches the great figures of the war, its momentous battles, the hardships endured by those on the home front, events on the frontier, occasional romantic moments, the men of various types and origin who served in both armies, and the coming of peace. The poem has many notable portraits—Lincoln, Grant, Stonewall Jackson, Lee, "Beauty" Stuart, Jefferson, Davis, Judah P. Benjamin, and others. The narrative is based on extensive research. It was awarded a Pulitzer Prize.

John Bull and Brother Jonathan, The Diverting History of (1812),   a satire by JAMES KIRKE PAULDING. It was inspired by Francis Hopkinson's A PRETTY STORY (1774), and by the feelings that led to the War of 1812. Bullock Island represents England, Jonathan has thirteen farms, and there are references to the Manor of Frogmore of Lewis Baboon (Louis XVI). There is a British traveler in the United States who is called Corporal Smell-fungus. The satire of England is, however, so good-humored that the work was reprinted in a British journal. It ran through several editions in the United States and in revision was doubled in length. It was followed many years later by an inferior sequel, *The History of Uncle Sam and His Boys* (1835), in which Jonathan becomes Uncle Sam, with twenty-four sons.

John Bull in America (1825),   a satire by JAMES KIRKE PAULDING. In this work Paulding continued his defense of the United States against the attacks of British writers, especially travelers who returned home with sneering descriptions of this country. The subtitle of his book is "The New Munchausen," and the book purports to be a narrative of a tour in America made by a Cockney. Paulding satirizes broadly the ignorant blunders and silly prejudices of British travelers.

John Henry.   Legendary African-American hero of numerous folktales and ballads. He was employed in building railroads or as a roustabout on river steamboats. Always depicted as a man of gigantic strength, he even competed with a steam drill in driving steel on the railroad. The tales are apparently based on the exploits of a real person who worked on the Chesapeake & Ohio Big Bend Tunnel in the early 1870s. One of his earliest appearances in print came when Louise Rand Bascomb published a railroad song in the *Journal of American Folklore* (1909) beginning, "Johnnie Henry was a hardworkin' man,; she died with his hammer in his hand." Other collectors followed with additional material. Guy B. Johnson, in *John Henry: Tracking Down a Negro Legend* (1931), made a collection of ballads and variants.

John Marr and Other Sailors (1888),   a collection of twenty-five poems by HERMAN MELVILLE. *John Marr* is roughly divided in four parts: Sea-Pieces, Minor Sea-Pieces, Pebbles, and a prefatory section introduced by an essay on John Marr, who has lived most of his years on the prairies in stoic frustration, away from the seas of his young manhood. Marr and the other sailors invoke the spirits of their long-ago shipmates—Bridegroom Dick, Tom Deadlight, Jack Roy, and others. Although Marr's resemblance to his creator is fictitious rather than autobiographical, Melville, too, was somewhat sentimental, and here expresses his own heartfelt nostalgia.

"Sea-Pieces"—"The Haglets" and "The Aeolian Harp"—posits the ironic indeterminacy of the universe and the vanity of human wishes. Minor Sea-Pieces, the major poetic achievement of John Marr, reaffirms that wisdom. In "To Ned" he musingly recalls events of forty years before, when he and Richard Greene, "the Typee-truants," roved the Marquesas, and he wonders "if mortals twice/Here and hereafter, touch a Paradise." Another of the Minor Sea-Pieces, "The Tuft of Kelp," is, like the poetry of Emily Dickinson, gnomically expressive, a nugget of pure intelligence. Pebbles, the last section, proposes not merely the acceptance of wisdom but the wisdom of acceptance.

Johnny Appleseed.   See APPLESEED, JOHNNY.

Johnny Got His Gun (1939),   an antiwar novel by DALTON TRUMBO. It is a first-person narration by an armless, legless, faceless, deaf war veteran. It was made into a film in 1971.

Johnson, Burges   (1877–1963),   newspaperman, teacher, editor, writer. Born in Vermont, Johnson became a professor of English and as a writer was known for his humor. Among his books are *Beastly Rhymes* (1906); *The Well of English and the Bucket* (1917); *As I Was Saying* (1923); *New Rhyming Dictionary and Poets Handbook* (1931, rev. 1957); *Sonnets from the Pekinese* (1935); *Professor at Bay* (1937); *As Much As I Dare* (1944); *Campus Versus Classroom* (1946); and *The Lost Art of Profanity* (1948).

Johnson, Charles [Richard] (1948–   ),   novelist, short story writer. Born in Evanston, Illinois, Johnson graduated from Southern Illinois University (B.A., 1971; M.A., 1973) and spent the next few years in graduate study at the State University of New York at Stony Brook before entering teaching in 1976 as an assistant professor at the University of Washington. He had already published two collections of cartoons, *Black Humor* (1970) and *Half-Past Nation Time* (1972), and had won praise for a first novel, *Faith and the Good Thing* (1974). Written under the tutelage of John Gardner and informed by that author's vision of a moral fiction, which Johnson has continued to make a part of his practice, *Faith* mixes folk humor and philosophy in a tale of a Southern black girl's search for the "Good Thing" in Chicago. Johnson describes his second novel, *Oxherding Tale* (1982), as "a modern, comic, philosophical slave narative—a kind of dramatization of the famous 'Ten Oxherding Pictures' of Zen artist Kakuan-Shien." In it the hero, born in deception to a white mother and a black slave, learns something of Eastern mysticism, socialism, and philosophy as he passes through various levels of society and identity toward freedom. In *Middle Passage* (1990), a National Book Award winner, Johnson broke through to wide readership and acclaim, mixing fantasy and realism in a story of a free black man who escapes bill collectors in New Orleans by stowing away on a ship headed for Africa to pick up a cargo of slaves. In *Dreamer: A Novel* (1998) he fictionalizes events leading to the assassination of Martin Luther King, Jr., focusing on a double who, but for twists of fate, might have been King himself. *The Sorcerer's Apprentice* (1986) collects short stories. *Africans in America: America's Journey through Slavery* (1998), written with others, is a companion to the PBS series with the same title.

Johnson, Charles Spurgeon (1893–1956),   teacher, editor, author. Born in Virginia, Johnson became a teacher and later became president of Fisk University in 1946. He won many honors for his work on African-American culture and history. Among his books are *The Negro in American Civilization* (1930), *Shadow of the Plantation* (1934), *Preface of Racial Understanding* (1936), *Growing Up in the Black Belt* (1941), *Into the Main Stream* (1946), and *Education and the Cultural Crisis* (1951).

Johnson, Edward (1598–1672),   historian. A joiner by trade, Johnson came to Boston from England in 1630. In 1650 he began writing a history of the Massachusetts colony. He called it *The Wonder-Working Providence of Sion's Savior in New England*, although it was first published anonymously in England in 1654 as *A History of New England*. It was the first published large-scale history of the Puritan colonies.

Johnson, James Weldon (1871–1938),   lawyer, poet, teacher. Born in Jacksonville, Johnson became the first African-American admitted to the Florida bar since Reconstruction days. Thereafter he enjoyed a varied career, including successful songwriting in New York, a term as consul in Venezuela and Nicaragua, and teaching at Fisk. Among his books are *The Autobiography of an ExColored Man* (a novel, 1912); *Fifty Years and Other Poems* (1917); GOD'S TROMBONES (1927); *Black Manhattan* (1930); and *Along This Way* (autobiography, 1933). He edited *The Book of Negro Poetry* (1922) and two collections of spirituals (1925, 1926). *Saint Peter Relates an Incident; Selected Poems* appeared in 1935.

Johnson,   Josephine   W[inslow]   (1910–   ), painter, teacher, writer. After writing short stories successfully for several years, Johnson, born in Missouri, won a Pulitzer Prize with her first novel, *Now in November* (1934), a realistic but poetic story of life on a Midwestern farm. The award led to the collection of her short stories in *Winter Orchard and Other Stories* (1935). *Jordanstown* (1937) shifted the scene to an industrial region during the depression, and *Wildwood* (1946) sympathetically describes a girl's loneliness. *The Dark Traveler* (1963) is a novel about schizophrenia. *The Inland Island* (1969) portrays the America of its time. *Sorcerer's Son* (1965) collects short stories. *Seven Houses* (1973) is a memoir. She also published a book of verse, *Year's End* (1937), and a book for children, *Paulina* (1939).

Johnson, Martin (1884–1937),   explorer, author of travel books. Accompanied on many expeditions by his wife, OSA JOHNSON, Martin Johnson, who was born in Illinois and

was an explorer of little-known regions, invariably brought back entertaining and exciting accounts of his experiences. His books, usually prepared in collaboration, include *Through the South Seas with Jack London* (1913), *Cannibal-Land* (1917), *Camera-Trails in Africa* (1924), *Safari* (1928), *Lion: African Adventures with the King of Beasts* (1929), *Congorilla* (1931), and *Over African Jungles* (1935).

Johnson, Osa [Helen] (1894–1953),   explorer, author of travel books, movie producer, memoirist. Osa Johnson, born in Kansas, accompanied her husband, MARTIN JOHNSON, on photographic expeditions to the South Seas (1912), the Solomon Islands and the New Hebrides (1914), Borneo (1917–19), the African jungles (1921), and Borneo again (1935–36). In collaboration with Martin she wrote books about these expeditions and produced motion pictures based on their travels. After his death she continued to write. Among her books are *Osa Johnson's Jungle Friends* (1939), *Four Years in Paradise* (1941), and *Tarnish, The True Story of a Lion Cub* (1945). Her two volumes of autobiography had a wide sale: *I Married Adventure* (1940) and *Bride in the Solomons* (1944).

Johnson, Owen [McMahon] (1878–1952),   novelist, writer for boys. Born in New York City the son of the poet ROBERT UNDERWOOD JOHNSON, Owen Johnson is probably best remembered for *Stover at Yale* (1911), a campus story that mingles criticism with entertainment and which created something of a sensation. Lawrenceville School in New Jersey is the setting for *The Varmint* (1910), *The Tennessee Shad* (1911), and *Skippy Bedelle* (1923), all concerning ingenious young rascals. Johnson also wrote novels for adult readers, including *Children of Divorce* (1927) and *The Coming of the Amazons* (1931).

Johnson, Pauline (1861–1913),   poet. The daughter of a Mohawk father and an English mother related to William Dean Howells, she was born on the Six Nations Reservation near Brantford, Ontario. Her verse first appeared in the New York magazine *Gems of Poetry* in 1884. From 1892 until her retirement to Vancouver in 1909, she was a popular platform performer, reading her own work in Canada and parts of the United States. For her readings she often wore Indian dress and used her tribal name, Tekahionwake. Her collections include *The White Wampum* (1895), *Canadian Born* (1903), and *Flint and Feather* (1912). *Legends of Vancouver* (1911), *The Shagganappi* (1913), and *The Moccasin Maker* (1913) are collections of short prose pieces. Betty Keller's *Pauline* (1981) is a biography.

Johnson, Robert Underwood (1853–1937),   poet, editor, public official. Born in Washington, D.C., Johnson performed outstanding services in improving copyright protection for authors, in helping (with JOHN MUIR) to create Yosemite Park, in establishing the Hall of Fame at New York University (he was its director from 1919 to 1937), and in the American Academy of Arts and Letters. During World War I he originated the movement to provide American Poets Ambulances in Italy, and he was ambassador to Italy, 1920–21. *St. Gaudens, an Ode* (1910) won particular notice among his earlier poems. *Poems of Fifty Years* appeared in 1931. His memoirs are contained in *Remembered Yesterdays* (1923).

Johnson, Samuel (1696–1772),   theologian, philosopher, teacher, college administrator. Johnson, born in Connecticut and a graduate of Yale, became a Congregational minister, then went to England and was ordained in the Protestant Episcopal Church. On his return to America he won a wide reputation as a clergyman and a scholar. He became the first president of King's (later Columbia) College (1753), served for ten years, and then returned to his old church at Stratford, Connecticut. As a thinker Johnson moved away from harsh Calvinism toward the rationalism of some of his English instructors. Later he turned toward Bishop George Berkeley, becoming his friend and disciple during the years when the English prelate lived at Newport, Rhode Island. Johnson wrote *An Introduction to the Study of Philosophy* (1731), *A System of Morality* (1746), *Elementa Philosophica* (1752), and *English and Hebrew Grammar* (1767). H. W. and C. Schneider edited *Samuel Johnson: His Career and Writings* (4 v. 1929), the first volume of which contains Johnson's readable *Memoirs*, together with selections from his personal correspondence.

Johnson, Thomas.   See THE KENTUCKY MISCELLANY.

Johnson, Sir William (1715–1774),   colonist. Born in Ireland, Johnson was a land and fur trader in the colony of New York. During the French and Indian War (1754–63) he headed a force of Indians and colonial militia that defeated the French at Lake George. He was made a baronet, and in 1756–74 was Superintendent of Indian Affairs for all colonies north of the Ohio River. His estate was near the city of Johnstown, which he founded. He knew the Iroquois and their language well, married a Mohawk woman, and was made a sachem of the Mohawk tribe. He was greatly impressed by what he called the Attic elegance of diction and compelling rhythm of the Indian orators. Johnson appears in several historical novels, among them James Kirke Paulding's THE DUTCHMAN'S FIRESIDE (1831), C. F. Hoffman's GREYSLAER (1840), Robert W. Chambers's *Cardigan* (1901), Kenneth Roberts's NORTHWEST PASSAGE (1937), John Tebbel's *The Conqueror* (1951), and Margaret Widdemer's *The Golden Wildcat* (1954).

Johnston, Annie Fellows (1863–1931),   children's writer. Celebrated for *The Little Colonel* (1895) and subsequent volumes in the same series for children, Johnston was born in Indiana but spent the latter part of her life in Pewee Valley, Kentucky, the prototype of the Lloydsboro Valley in her books. She was a woman of deep religious interests and independent spirit; at the age of seventeen she had already begun to teach school. She wrote a number of books for children besides her Little Colonel Series, and a volume of reminiscence, *The Land of the Little Colonel* (1929).

Johnston, George (1913–   ),   poet, translator. Born in Ontario and educated at the University of Toronto, Johnston served in the Royal Canadian Air Force in World War II. His poetry is collected in *The Cruising Auk* (1959), *Home Free* (1966), *Happy Enough: Poems 1935–1972* (1972), *Taking a Grip* (1979), *Auk Redivivus: Selected Poems* (1981), *Endeared by*

Dark: The Collected Poems (1990), and *What Is to Come: Selected and New Poems* (1996). A college teacher expert in Old Norse and Icelandic sagas, Johnston has translated *The Saga of Gisli* (1963), *The Faroe Islanders' Saga* (1975), and *The Greenlanders' Saga* (1976), the last two revised as *Thrand of Gotu* (1994). *Rocky Shores* (1981) is a translation of modern Faroese poetry.

Johnston, Mary (1870–1936),   novelist. Johnston wrote some of the best of the historical romances that were so popular at the beginning of the 20th century. Her second novel, TO HAVE AND TO HOLD (1900), was her most popular. Of her twenty-three romances, fifteen have their backgrounds in her native Virginia, and most of the others are set on the ocean and in Great Britain. Toward the middle of her career Johnston became interested in mysticism, feminism, and socialism, and these found their way into books such as *Silver Cross* (1922). Among her other books are *Prisoners of Hope* (1898), *Audrey* (1902), *Sir Mortimer* (1904), *Lewis Rand* (1908), THE LONG ROLL (1911), *Cease Firing* (1912), *Foes* (1918), *Croatan* (1923), *The Slave Ship* (1924), *Miss Delicia Allen* (1933), and *Drury Randall* (1934).

Johnston, Richard Malcolm (1822–1898),   teacher, lawyer, writer, lecturer, humorist. Born in Georgia and a disciple of AUGUSTUS BALDWIN LONGSTREET, Johnston began in imitation of Longstreet's *Georgia Scenes* (1835)—Johnston called his book *Georgia Sketches* (1864). Like Longstreet he learned the art of storytelling as a lawyer on circuit. In an enlarged form, his book was renamed DUKESBOROUGH TALES (1871). They were reprinted in 1883, in the heyday of Southern dialect humor, and became widely popular. As a result Johnston enjoyed a new spurt of creative activity and produced *Old Mark Langston* (1884), *Two Gray Tourists* (1885), and *Mr. Absoalom Billingslea and Other Georgia Folk* (1888), among several others. His writing may be seen as establishing a clear relationship between the older humor and the newer local color writing. His *Autobiography* appeared in 1900.

Johnston Smith.   See SMITH, JOHNSTON.

John Street Theater.   The first permanent playhouse in New York City. It opened December 7, 1767. The first play given there was George Farquhar's *The Beaux Stratagem*; it also saw the first production in New York of plays by Shakespeare, Ben Jonson, and Congreve, as well as many contemporary plays and afterpieces. When the British occupied New York the playhouse was renamed the Theater Royal, and officers of the English garrison, especially the talented Major John André, used it for amateur productions; a professional company also occupied the theater. In 1785 an American company again occupied the theater for regular seasons. They produced British plays, but their stage also saw the first performances of two important American works: Royall Tyler's THE CONTRAST (1787), in the course of which Jonathan, the Yankee bumpkin, describes his first visit to a playhouse (the John Street Theater); and William Dunlap's THE FATHER (1789). The theater was used for the last time on January 13, 1798, and then was sold and demolished.

Jonathan. A character in Royall Tyler's play THE CON-TRAST (1787), the earliest stage Yankee.

Jonathan, Brother. See BROTHER JONATHAN.

Jonathan Corncob, Loyal American Refugee, Adventures of. Written by Himself (London, 1787). One of the earliest novels based on the American Revolution, this story describes—in the manner of Fielding and sometimes of Rabelais—the nautical and amatory adventures of the hero. This Massachusetts youth, whom chance throws into the British camp, participates in the occupation of New York City by Lord Howe and takes part in other episodes in Providence, in the Barbados during a hurricane, on a prison ship in Boston Harbor, and in a naval court-martial.

Jonathan to John (1861), a poem by JAMES RUSSELL LOWELL that formed part of the *Second Series* of the BIGLOW PAPERS. Published in February 1862, it was a vigorous protest against England's action when a Northern warship seized two Confederate envoys en route to Europe on the British mail steamer *Trent*. The British government demanded return of the envoys and began to mobilize armies. Lincoln yielded rather than risk war with Great Britain, but there was great anger throughout the North, voiced by Lowell in his vigorous but lengthy poem.

Jones, Casey. See CASEY JONES.

Jones, D[ouglas] G[ordon] (1929–), poet, editor. Born in Ontario, he has taught in Quebec and founded *Ellipse* (1969), which published both English and French poetry. His collections include *Frost on the Sun* (1957); *Sun Is Axeman* (1961); *Phrases from Orpheus* (1967); *Under the Thunder the Flowers Light Up the Earth* (1977; Governor-General's Award); *A Throw of Particles: The New and Selected Poetry* (1983); *Balthazar and Other Poems* (1988); and *The Floating Garden* (1995). *Butterfly on Rock* (1970) is a study of myths and symbols in modern Canadian writing.

Jones, Gayl (1949–), novelist, poet. Born in Kentucky, she was educated at Connecticut College and Brown University. Her early novels, *Corregidora* (1975) and *Eva's Man* (1976), feature African-American Southern female protagonists whose sexual experiences are explicitly described. *White Rat* (1977) is a collection of stories. Her poetry is collected in *Song for Anninho* (1981), *The Hermit-Woman* (1983), and *Xarque and Other Poems* (1985). After a twenty-one-year break from fiction, Jones published two more novels in the late 1990s. She lived in Paris and Kentucky with her husband, a fugitive from justice, until publicity from her novel *The Healing* (1998) brought police and tragedy to her door and she entered a mental hospital. *The Healing* tells of faith healing, of both mind and body. *Mosquito* (1999) is a long, sprawling tale, told orally, "the way true stories is," by a black woman who drives a truck between Mexico and the United States, gets involved in the transport of illegal aliens, and meditates on the art of transforming reality into fiction.

Jones, Howard Mumford (1892–1980), teacher, poet, critic, historian, translator, editor. Jones, born in Michigan, taught successively at the University of Texas, North Car-

olina, Michigan, and Harvard. He is known best for *The Theory of American Literature* (1948). His other books include *Guide to American Literature and Its Background Since 1890* (1953) and *O Strange New World* (1964, Pulitzer Prize), a study of American culture.

Jones, Hugh (c. 1670–1760), grammarian, historian, preacher. Jones came to Virginia from England to teach at the College of William and Mary. He is remembered for two books: *A Short English Grammar and Accidence to the English Tongue* (1724), the first English grammar written in America; and *The Present State of Virginia* (1724), which is both a secular and ecclesiastical history as well as a sunny promotional tract.

Jones, James (1921–1977), novelist. Born in Illinois, Jones could not afford college and enlisted in the Army in 1939. His service in Hawaii and on Guadalcanal gave him material for *From Here to Eternity* (1951) and *The Thin Red Line* (1962), and the reading he did convinced him that he needed to write. In 1945, he submitted a manuscript to Maxwell Perkins. The influential editor returned it but, sensing talent, offered him an advance on an unwritten second book; the result was FROM HERE TO ETERNITY, an immediate best seller and film. Set in Schofeld Barracks, Hawaii, it is a realistic—sometimes brutal—depiction of army life, ending with the Japanese attack on Pearl Harbor. *The Thin Red Line* is a sequel, following four infantrymen through the Pacific War. The final passages of the third book in the series, *Whistle* (1978), which takes place in a veterans' hospital, were dictated from Jones's own hospital bed; it was published posthumously. His other works include *Some Came Running* (1957), set in the Midwest in the aftermath of World War II; *The Pistol* (1959), a novella; and *Viet Journal* (1974), recording a 1973 visit to Vietnam. *To Reach Eternity: The Letters of James Jones* (1989) was edited by George Hendrick.

Jones, James Athearn (1791–1854), novelist, folklorist. Born in Tisbury, Massachusetts, Jones wrote some novels, but his main contribution to American literature was a collection of legends, *Tales of an Indian Camp* (3 v. 1829), revised as *Traditions of the North American Indians* (1830).

Jones, John Beauchamp (1810–1866), editor, novelist, diarist. Jones, born in Maryland, saw enough of frontier life in Kentucky and Missouri to write about it familiarly in his novels. He went back East, married, and edited the Baltimore *Sunday Visiter* and the *Madisonian*, President Tyler's personal magazine. He also began writing fiction, but had to publish his *Wild Western Scenes*, in which Daniel Boone appears as a character, at his own expense (1841). It sold 100,000 copies in his lifetime. He followed with a second volume in 1856 and with *Wild Southern Scenes* in 1859, but his later books failed to equal the success of his first. He also wrote *The Life and Adventures of a Country Merchant* (1854) and *The Monarchist* (1853). As the Civil War neared, he began the *Southern Monitor* (1858) in Philadelphia; with the outbreak of the war he retreated to Montgomery, Alabama, and became a clerk in the Confederate War Department. He lived in Burlington, New

Jersey, after the war, where he prepared for publication his most valuable book, *A Rebel War Clerk's Diary* (1866).

Jones, John Paul (1747–1792),   naval officer, memoirist. Born John Paul in Kirkcudbright, Scotland, and a seaman from age twelve, Jones emigrated to Virginia (1773) and was commissioned a lieutenant in the new American navy in 1775. He destroyed many British ships and successfully harassed their supply operations. His most famous engagement was as captain of the *Bonhomme Richard* (or Poor Richard, so-named to honor Benjamin Franklin), a refurbished old French vessel; with two other ships he attacked the British convoy escorts *Serapis* and *Countess of Scarborough*. His riposte to a surrender request, "Sir, I have not yet begun to fight," and his capture of the *Serapis* (1779) made Jones a hero; his ship was so badly damaged it sank not long after he abandoned it for the *Serapis*.

He served briefly in the Russian navy, winning victories against the Turks, went to Paris in 1790, and died there during the French Revolution. His grave was forgotten until 1905, but since 1913 his remains have been enshrined at the United States Naval Academy. His *Memoirs* (2 v. 1830) were reprinted in 1972. Biographies include Anna De Koven, *Life and Letters of John Paul Jones* (1913) and Samuel Eliot Morison, *John Paul Jones* (1959, repr. 1964). Jones has been celebrated in poems by Freneau and Whitman and appears as a character in Cooper's THE PILOT (1823), Melville's ISRAEL POTTER (1955), Winston Churchill's RICHARD CARVEL (1899), and Sarah Orne Jewett's *The Tory Lover* (1901).

Jones, Joseph Stevens (1809–1877),   actor, physician, playwright. Jones's career began as an actor, then he studied medicine, receiving his degree in 1843 from Harvard. He practiced medicine for a time, became city physician of his native Boston, and lectured on physiology. But his love of the stage led him to become manager of the Tremont Theater and begin writing plays. The total credited to him varies from 150 to 200, and they were of all kinds—melodramas, farces, local color plays (here he was something of a pioneer), and historical plays. Jones created a memorable Yankee character in Solon Shingle, a teamster in *The People's Lawyer* (1839), a long-running play sometimes produced as *Solon Shingle*. Possibly the best of his plays was *The Silver Spoon* (1852), which was revised and produced as late as 1911; it may have influenced Augustin Daly in *Horizon* (1871) and James A. Herne in *Shore Acres* (1892). Jones turned the play into a novel, *The Life of Jefferson S. Batkins* (1871).

Among his other plays are *The Liberty Tree* (1832), *Paul Revere* (1875), and *Captain Kyd, or, The Wizard of the Sea* (1830).

Jones, Le Roi.   See BARAKA, IMAMU AMIRI.

Jones, Major Joseph.   Pen name of WILLIAM TAPPIN THOMPSON.

Jones, Nard [Maynard Benedict] (1904–1972), newspaperman, editor, novelist. Born in Seattle, and a specialist in the Pacific Northwest, Jones won particular praise for two novels, *Oregon Detour* (1930) and *Swift Flows the River*

(1940). The former is set in a small wheat-farming community, and the latter portrays pioneering days on the Columbia River. Among his other novels are *The Petlands* (1931), *Wheat Women* (1933), *Scarlet Petticoat* (1942), *Still to the West* (1946), *The Island* (1948), *I'll Take What's Mine* (1954), *Ride the Dark Storm* (1955), and *Great Command* (1959).

Jones, Robert Edmond (1887–1954),   stage designer, author of books on the theater. Jones designed sets for some of the most notable theatrical productions of the first half of the 20th century, especially in connection with experimental troupes—the Washington Square Players, the Provincetown Players, the Greenwich Village Theater, and the Theatre Guild. Jones expressed his design doctrines in *The Dramatic Imagination* (1941).

Jong, Erica [Mann] (1942–   ),   novelist, poet. Jong was born in New York City and educated at Barnard. The treatment of female sexuality in her first novel, *Fear of Flying* (1973), initiated a vogue for frankness soon followed by other female novelists. Isadora Wing, the protagonist, has a huge sexual appetite and suffers no guilt over her infidelity and promiscuity. In the sequel, *How to Save Your Own Life* (1977), bisexuality is introduced. Seventeen years later, Wing serves as the narrator of *Any Woman's Blues* (1990), in which Leila Sand, a self-pitying and sexually driven artist, copes with her obsessions. Among other Jong novels are *Fanny* (1980) and *Parachutes and Kisses* (1984), *Half-Lives* (1973), and *Loveroot* (1975). *At the Edge of the Body* (1979), *Serenissima: Ordinary Miracles* (1983), *Becoming Light: Poems New and Selected* (1992) and *Fruits and Vegetables: Poems* (1971) collect poetry. *Fear of Fifty: A Midlife Memoir* (1994), *What Do Women Want?: Bread, Roses, Sex, Power* (1998) and *Witches* (1999) are nonfiction prose.

Jordan, Elizabeth (1867–1947),   newspaperwoman, editor, playwright, memoirist, novelist, shortstory writer. Born in Milwaukee, Jordan was on the staff of the old New York *World* for ten years, editor of the *Sunday World* for three years more. Her stories on the LIZZIE BORDEN murder trial were avidly read—she became convinced that the defendant was innocent. She became editor of HARPER'S BAZAAR, later literary adviser to Harper & Brothers. She was a close friend of Henry James, Mark Twain, William Dean Howells, and SINCLAIR LEWIS, whose first book she accepted for publication. She also wrote books and plays of her own: *Tales of the City Room* (1898); *Tales of the Cloister* (1901); *The Lady from Oklahoma* (a comedy, 1911); *The Story of a Pioneer* (with ANNA HOWARD SHAW, 1915); *Black Butterflies* (1926); *Page Mr. Pomeroy* (1933); *The Life of the Party* (1935); and *The Real Ruth Arnold* (1945). She told her own story in *Three Rousing Cheers* (1938), depicting a life of literary and editorial activity but also of devotion to many causes, especially woman suffrage and the welfare of authors.

Jordan, June (1936–   ),   poet, novelist, essayist. Born in Harlem, Jordan was educated at Barnard and the University of Chicago. She is known mostly for her free verse dealing with the everyday struggles of African-Americans and their political oppression. Her collections include *New Days:*

Poems of Exile and Return (1973), *Things That I Do in the Dark* (1977), *Passion: New Poems, 1977–1980* (1980), *Living Room: New Poems, 1980–84* (1985), *Haruko/Love Poetry: New and Selected Love Poems* (1993), *June Jordan's Poetry for the People: A Revolutionary Blueprint* (1995) and *Kissing God Goodbye: Poems, 1991–1997* (1997). She has written several books for young readers, a biography of Fannie Lou Hamer (1972), and collections of essays including *Civil Wars* (1981) and *Affirmative Acts: Political Essays* (1998). *Soldier: A Poet's Childhood* (2000) covers the 30s and 40s.

Joseph, Chief [Highn'moot Tooyalakekt] (1840?–1904), tribal leader and orator. A chief of the Nez Perce tribe, his name means "Thunder Going to the High Mountains." In 1877, after the federal government had failed to honor its treaty obligations, and warfare had failed to secure peace, he led his tribe out of Oregon in an attempted 1500-mile retreat into Canada. His surrender speech, printed under the title "I Will Fight No More Forever" in the *North American Review* (April 1879), is a classic statement of Native American pride and resolve in the midst of terrible suffering. *From Where the Sun Now Stands* (1960) by Will Henry (see HENRY W. ALLEN) is a fictional account of Chief Joseph and his struggle.

Josephson, Matthew (1899–1978), editor, biographer. Born in Brooklyn, New York, Josephson helped found the expatriate magazine *Secession* (Spring 1922–April 1924), worked on the staff of *Broom*, and was the American editor of *transition*, then assistant editor of the *New Republic*. In 1948 he was elected to the National Institute of Arts and Letters. Meanwhile he had turned to well-written biographies and muckraking books on business and politics. Among them are *Zola and His Time* (1928); *Portrait of the Artist as an American* (1930), biographical sketches joined by a thesis that industrial society defeats art; *Jean-Jacques Rousseau* (1932); *The Robber Barons* (1934); *The Politicos* (1938); *The President Makers* (1940); *Victor Hugo* (1942); *Stendhal* (1946); *Sidney Hillman* (1952); and *Edison* (1959). *Life Among the Surrealists* (1962) and *Infidel in the Temple* (1967) are memoirs.

Josiah Allen's Wife. A pseudonym of MARIETTA HOLLEY.

Josselyn, John (1638–75), naturalist. The Englishman made two visits to New England (1638–1639 and 1663–1671). His accounts, containing some fanciful anecdotes along with advice for settlers and local history, are called *New England's Rarities Discovered* (1672) and *An Account of Two Voyages to New England* (1674).

Journal of a Visit to London and the Continent, 1849–50 (1948), a journal kept by HERMAN MELVILLE during a trip abroad, edited by Eleanor Melville Metcalf and published a century after it was written.

Journal of Julius Rodman (*Burton's Gentleman's Magazine*, January to June 1840), a fictional travel narrative by EDGAR ALLAN POE, published anonymously and purporting to record a trip across the Rocky Mountains in 1792, predating Lewis and Clark.

Journey to the Land of Eden, A (1841), a journal by WILLIAM BYRD. Byrd kept this record of his trip to North Carolina in 1733, setting down his frank, often satirical observations on many subjects, including the country folk in the regions he visited.

Joutel, Henri (*c.* 1645–*c.* 1723), adventurer. He sailed with LaSalle in 1684, intending to help found a colony at the mouth of the Mississippi; the ships with colonists landed by mistake at Matagorda Bay in Texas. During an attempt to retrace their way to the Mississippi, LaSalle was murdered. Joutel went on to Quebec, and his account of the journey, *A Journal of the Last Voyage Perform'd by Monsr. de la Sale to the Gulph of Mexico to Find out the Mouth of the Missisipi River* (1713), describes the memorable exploit.

JR. A 1975 novel by WILLIAM GADDIS. The JR of the title is a sixth grader who becomes mastermind of a vast corporate empire.

J. S. of Dale. Pen name of FREDERIC JESUP STIMSON.

Juárez, Benito (1806–1872), Mexican statesman. A Zapotec Indian, Juárez led *La Reforma*, a liberal, anticlerical movement for political, economic, and social reform. Named president in 1857, he fought the French-supported regime of Maximilian, whom he defeated in 1867, and ruled Mexico until his death. Though *La Reforma* was not wholly successful Juárez occupies a place in Mexican popular imagination similar to that of Lincoln in the U.S.

Judah, Samuel B[enjamin] H[erbert] (1799?–1876), dramatist, novelist, poet, lawyer. Born in New York City, Judah tried to win recognition in the theater, but the ridicule he received offended his vanity and in a satire, *Gotham and the Gothamites* (1823), he sought revenge on his critics. The result was a suit for libel, which he lost; he was fined and imprisoned. Plays of his produced up to that time included *The Mountain Torrent* (1820), *The Rose of Arragon* (1822), *A Tale of Lexington* (1822), and *Odofriede the Outcast* (1822). In 1827 he published *The Buccaneers, A Romance of Our Own Country in Its Ancient Day*, one of the earliest novels to make use of the legend of Captain Kidd.

Judd, Sylvester, III (1813–1853), teacher, clergyman, novelist, poet. Born in Westhampton, Massachusetts, Judd broke with the Calvinism of his ancestors by becoming a Unitarian clergyman in Augusta, Maine (1840–1853). He seems to have exercised keen powers of observation during his pastoral calls, for some of his novels contain passages of considerable realism. But the books are more notable for their utopian ideas, especially those of Fourier, then popular with the Transcendentalists. Judd published anonymously MARGARET, A TALE OF THE REAL AND IDEAL, INCLUDING SKETCHES OF A PLACE NOT BEFORE DESCRIBED, CALLED MONS CHRISTI (1845, rev. 2 v. 1851), a novel designed "to promote the idea of a liberal Christianity." The heroine is the daughter of a German musician who completely transforms a New England village; the book strongly suggests the influence of Goethe's *Wilhelm Meister*. Judd espoused all the causes of his day—antislavery, pacifism, temperance, opposition to capital punishment—but always in a mild, non-aggressive spirit. He also wrote *A Young Man's Account of His Conversion from Calvinism* (1843); and in his biography, *The Life and Character of the Rev. Sylvester Judd*

(1854), by Arethusa Hall, is preserved a document for private family use that he called *Cardiography*, an exposition of his theological difficulties and conclusions.

Judge. This comic weekly was founded in 1881 by a group of writers and artists who had resigned from the staff of PUCK not long after H.C. BUNNER became its editor. James Albert Wales (1852–1886), a cartoonist, was the leader of the group. It had financial difficulties until it was recognized two or three years later as an organ for the Republicans, in opposition to *Puck* and the Democrats, but it did not reach the height of its influence till the first decade of the next century. During the depression period of the 1930s it became a monthly, but ceased publication in 1939.

Judgment Day. See YOUNG LONIGAN.

Judson, E[ward] Z[ane] C[arroll] ["Ned Buntline"] (1823–1886), midshipman, soldier, fur trader, magazine editor, organizer of the Know Nothing party, playwright, dime novelist. Judson's career reads like episodes in the four hundred dime novels he is said to have written. Born in Stamford, New York, he served in the navy and won a reputation as an inveterate duelist. Later, in Nashville, he fought a duel with the husband of his mistress, killed him, was taken out by a mob and lynched—but he was rescued at the point of death. He led the Astor Place Riots in New York against the English actor Macready, and was sent to jail for a year. He was a bitter anti-Catholic, and invented the name Know Nothing (a signal for secrecy) as the name of a faction opposed to the Catholics. Although dismissed from the Union army for drunkenness during the Civil War, he later claimed the title of colonel and stated that he had been Chief of Scouts for the Army of the Potomac.

In the meantime he had become a prolific writer of dime novels, a genre he is sometimes credited with originating. Some he published in a magazine he founded, *Ned Buntline's Own*, which preceded Beadle & Adams by at least a decade; in later years Judson worked for the latter firm. (See ERASTUS F. BEADLE.) On a trip to the West he met Col. WILLIAM F. CODY and wrote a play for him, *The Scouts of the Plains* (1872). It was Judson who named the scout Buffalo Bill. Judson also wrote hymns and lectured on temperance. His original Buffalo Bill story, written in 1869 after a hasty interview with the then unknown Cody, was called *Buffalo Bill, the King of the Border Men*; it was later brought out in book form and was repeatedly reprinted.

Judson's dime novels have become collectors' items. A few characteristic titles are *Magdalena, the Beautiful Mexican Maid* (1847); *The Black Avenger* (1847); *The Gals of New York* (1848); *Norwood, or, Life on the Prairie* (1849); and *Stella Delorme, or, The Comanche's Dream* (1860). Jay Monaghan wrote a biography of Judson called *The Great Rascal* (1952). See THE DIME NOVEL.

Julius Rodman. See JOURNAL OF JULIUS RODMAN.

Jumping Frog of Calaveras County, The Celebrated. See CELEBRATED JUMPING FROG.

Jungle, The (1906), a novel by UPTON SINCLAIR. Rarely has a book had as much direct influence on people's lives as did Sinclair's account of the appalling conditions in the Chicago stockyards. Sinclair takes Jurgis Rudkus, a poor Slav immigrant, as his central character, depicting with revolting realism his experiences as a worker in the stockyards. Jurgis becomes debased and then, in accordance with Sinclair's own creed, turns to Socialism as a way out.

The book's two theses—that the so-called Beef Trust was knowingly selling diseased meat to the public, and it paid its employees a bare subsistence wage—attracted tremendous attention. President Theodore Roosevelt read the book and was profoundly shocked. He sent for Sinclair, who was able to give him exact information based on long research in Packingtown. Sinclair, it is said, wanted to give other ideas to Roosevelt, but the president said, "Tell Sinclair to go home and let me run the government."

The book became the *Uncle Tom's Cabin* of its generation. The stockyards were literally cleaned up, a Pure Food and Drug Act was passed, and labor conditions were improved. Sinclair used the money he made to start a Socialistic colony called HELICON HALL in New Jersey, where Sinclair Lewis served briefly as a janitor. The book was translated into seventeen languages. In 1946 a new edition was issued, with an introduction by Sinclair.

Junípero, Serra. See MIGUEL JOSÉ SERRA.

Junkie (1953), a fictionalized account of the author's heroin addiction, published under the pseudonym William Lee by WILLIAM S. BURROUGHS.

Junto Club. A social and intellectual group founded by Benjamin Franklin in 1727. Its limited membership of artisans, first known as the Leather Aprons, formed a subscription library, the first public Library in America.

Jurgen (1919), a novel by JAMES BRANCH CABELL, which became a *cause célèbre* and established the author's fame. This book forms part of an elaborate series of novels laid in the imaginary medieval realm called Poictesme. Jurgen is a middle-aged pawnbroker married to a nagging wife who suddenly disappears. Jurgen goes in search of her but really is in quest of his lost youth. By magic he finds himself twenty-one again, and sets out on strange adventures, including visits to Heaven and Hell, in which he meets a lost sweetheart and encounters a host of mythical persons. At the end he goes home, finds his wife there, and is glad to be a middle-aged, henpecked husband again.

The New York Society for the Suppression of Vice, of which John S. Summer was the executive, banned *Jurgen* from the bookshops, an act that aroused the literati. For two years the novel was supposedly out of circulation—to the great profit of booksellers. An emergency committee was organized to battle for the book. When the case came to court, the judge advised acquittal.

Jusserand, Jean Jules (1855–1932), historian, diplomat. Jusserand, who had won a reputation with his books on English literature and history, was appointed French ambassador to the United States in 1902. Not long afterward appeared the last part of his best work, *Literary History of the English People* (3 v. 1895–1909). One of his books, *With Americans of*

Past and Present Days (1916), received the first Pulitzer Prize awarded for history.

Just Before the Battle, Mother (1863), a favorite Civil War song by GEORGE ROOT (1820–1895). A sequel, "Just After the Battle," was less successful.

Justice, Donald (1925–), poet. Born in Florida and educated at Miami University, North Carolina, and Iowa, Justice has been a college teacher of writing. His *Selected Poems* (1979) won the Pulitzer Prize. Other collections of his gentle, controlled verse include *The Summer Anniversaries* (1960), *Night Light* (1967), *Departures* (1973), and *The Sunset Maker* (1987), which also has stories and memoirs. *Platonic Scripts* (1984) is a book of essays. *A Donald Justice Reader* (1991) selects poetry and prose. *New and Selected Poems* appeared in 1995. *Oblivion: On Writers and Writing* (1998) is nonfiction prose.

Just, Ward [Swift] (1935–), journalist, novelist. Born in Indiana, Just was educated at Trinity College in Hartford. A long-time reporter for *Newsweek*, the *Washington Post*, and other magazines, he writes novels focused on the political, military, intellectual, and social life of contemporary Washington, D.C. These include *A Soldier of the Revolution* (1970), *Stringer* (1974), *Nicholson at Large* (1975), *The American Ambassador* (1987), *Jack Gance* (1989), *The Translator* (1991), *Ambition and Love* (1994) and *Echo House* (1997). His nonfiction includes *Report from Vietnam* (1968) and *Military Men* (1970). *Twenty-one: Selected Stories* appeared in 1990.

K

Kael, Pauline (1919–2001), film critic. Kael was a philosophy major at the University of California, Berkeley, and was working in the Bay Area when she published the book that established her professionally, *I Lost It at the Movies* (1965). Three years later she was regular film critic for *The New Yorker* and published the equally successful *Kiss Kiss, Bang Bang* (1968). Many books followed. Typically, she gave her second book its title "because that's what movies are about." In the 1960s Kael championed French filmakers, elevating Jean Luc Godard to godly status. Kael, more than any other important public movie critic, looked at film from all conceivable angles—technical, financial, psychic, artistic, historical. She was most concerned with impact, not with whether a film was commercially successful. Kael retired from *The New Yorker* in 1991. *5001 Nights at the Movies* (1991) and *For Keeps* (1996) collect reviews and essays.

Kah-ge-ga-gah-bowh.　See GEORGE COPWAY.

Kahler, Hugh M[acNair] (1883–1969), editor, novelist, short-story writer. Kahler, born in Philadelphia, was for some years a contributing editor of the *Ladies' Home Journal*. He wrote many novels, including *Babel* (1921), *The East Wind* (1922), *Father Means Well* (1930), *The Big Pink* (1932), and *Bright Danger* (1941).

Kalashnikoff, Nicholas S. (1888–1961), writer. The first of Kalashnikoff's five books, *They That Take the Sword* (1939), won him a MacDowell Fellowship. This passionate fictionalized history of the Russian Revolution and the early years of the Communist regime was based on the author's own experiences. At Moscow University, he had been arrested for revolutionary activities, and after a year of solitary confinement, he was sent to northern Siberia. Later he fought in the Czar's army in World War I with the rank of captain and during the Russian Civil War he was for a time a general. *Jumper*, his debt of gratitude to war horses, published in 1944, was acclaimed a classic to stand beside *Black Beauty*.

Kaler, James Otis (1848–1912), juvenile author. Born in Maine, Kaler used the name James Otis on his more than one hundred books. His great success was *Toby Tyler: or Ten Weeks with a Circus* (1881). His other titles include *Jenny Wren's Boardinghouse: A Story of Newsboy Life in New York* (1893) and historical tales such as *At the Siege of Quebec* (1897) and *With Perry on Lake Erie* (1899).

Kalloolah (1849), a novel by WILLIAM STARBUCK MAYO. Mayo, a physician affected by wanderlust, went off to the Barbary States, determined to explore the interior of Africa. He never got far, and soon returned home to practice his profession and write. His first book was *Kalloolah*, the narrative of Jonathan Romer, a young American who makes up his mind to explore Africa. After varied adventures he reaches the fictive city of Killoam, a sort of utopia invented by Mayo to poke fun at some aspects of civilization.

Kalm, Peter (1716–1779), botanist. Kalm was sent to America in 1748–51 by the Swedish Academy of Sciences. His observant, if somewhat naive, account of his experiences appeared in Sweden (3 v. 1753–61), in English translation as *Travels into North America* (2 v. 1770–71). He prepared a fourth volume, but it was destroyed in a fire. Notes on which this volume was based have been incorporated in Adolph B. Benson's *The America of 1750: Peter Kalm's Travels in North America* (2 v. 1937).

Kane, Elisha Kent (1820–1857), surgeon, explorer, writer. Born in Philadelphia, Kane in 1850 served as senior medical officer of a rescue expedition that searched in vain for Sir John Franklin (1786–1847), an Arctic explorer. Franklin was not given up for dead until 1857. Kane's account of the futile search was published as *The U.S. Grinnell Expedition in Search of Sir John Franklin* (1853). Kane made a second expedition in search of Franklin, this time as commander of the *Advance*. His party made some important explorations, and went overland to a Danish settlement in Greenland. Kane's *Arctic Explorations: The Second Grinnell Expedition* (2 v. 1856) is rich in scientific data and is written in a forcible style that is often unexpectedly poetic. It became an immediate best seller.

Kane, Harnett Thomas (1910–1984), newspaperman, novelist. Born in New Orleans, Kane was educated at Tulane University, was a reporter on the New Orleans *Item-Tribune*, and taught journalism at Loyola University in New Orleans. He was best known for *Louisiana Hayride: American Rehearsal for Dictatorship* (1941), an account of the career of Huey Long from his rise to power until his death and the victory of his political opponents in 1940. His other nonfiction works are *Bayous of Louisiana* (1943), *Gentlemen, Swords and Pistols* (1951), and *Spies for the Blue and Gray* (1954). His novels, which are based on fact, include *Bride of Fortune* (1948), the story of Varina Howell, wife of Jefferson Davis; *The Lady of Arlington* (1953), a story based on the life of Mrs. Robert E. Lee; and *The Gallant Mrs. Stonewall* (1957).

Kang, Younghill (1903–1972), teacher, translator, novelist. In the United States after 1921, Kang, born in Korea, interpreted the Far East for Americans. His first book was *Translations of Oriental Poetry* (1929). He spent two years in Europe as a Guggenheim Fellow and wrote an account of his experiences in his best-known book, *The Grass Roof* (1931). *East Goes West* (1937) is a novel dealing in a more general way with the lives of Asian-Americans.

Kanin, Garson (1912–1999), actor, playwright, director, writer. Born in Rochester, Kanin was actively connected with the theater, on Broadway and in Hollywood, and acted in many Broadway successes. He was an assistant to GEORGE ABBOTT and in 1937 joined the production staff of SAMUEL GOLDWYN. During World War II he and Carol Reed of England were appointed to direct General Eisenhower's *The True Glory*, a documentary of the war that won an Academy Award in 1945. One of Kanin's most notable plays was *Born Yesterday* (1946), which ran on Broadway for nearly four years and was made into a successful movie. Others are *A Double Life* (1948), in collaboration with his wife, Ruth Gordon (1896–1985); *Smile of the World* (1949); *The Rat Race* (1949); and the screenplays for *Adam's Rib* (1949) and *Pat and Mike* (1952), films starring Katharine Hepburn and Spencer Tracy. He wrote an English libretto for *Die Fledermaus*, by Johann Strauss, and directed it for the Metropolitan Opera. In 1955 he directed *The Diary of Anne Frank*. He also wrote short stories and published novels, including *Blow Up a Storm* (1959), *A Thousand Summers* (1973), *A Hell of an Actor* (1977), and *Moviola* (1979). *Hollywood* (1974) is a memoir.

Kantor, Mackinlay (1904–1977), newspaperman, columnist, writer. Born in Iowa, Kantor began as a reporter, won success with his early novels, and occasionally worked in *Hollywood*. He told the story of his childhood in *But Look, the Morn* (1947). His first novel, *Diversey* (1928), is a story of Chicago gangsters. *Long Remember* (1934, rev. 1956) is a realistic novel about the Battle of Gettysburg. *The Voice of Bugle Ann* (1935), the engaging story of a hound, was very popular. Later came *Arouse and Beware* (1936) and *The Romance of Rosy Ridge* (1937), the former laid in the Civil War period, the latter immediately after it. In *Valedictory* (1939), a high-school janitor watches graduates receive their diplomas and recalls incidents in their school lives. Among his other novels are *The Jaybird* (1932), *Gentle Annie* (1942), *Happy Land* (1943), *Midnight Lace* (1948), and *Signal 32* (1950). Kantor also wrote a novel in spirited verse, *Glory for Me* (1945), a story of three discharged service men that formed the basis for the Academy Award–winning film *The Best Years of Our Lives* (1946); and *Turkey in the Straw* (1935), ballads and other verse. His ANDERSONVILLE (1955), the story of the infamous Confederate prison, became a best seller. It was followed by *Spirit Lake* (1961); *Beauty Beast* (1968), set on the Gulf Coast; and a historical novel, *Valley Forge* (1975). *Storyteller* (1967) is a collection, and *The Day I Met a Lion* (1968) is a memoir.

Kaplan, Justin (1925–   ), biographer. Kaplan was born in New York City and worked for publishing houses before becoming a writer. He is the author of *Mr. Clemens and Mark Twain* (1966: Pulitzer Prize, National Book Award); *Lincoln Steffens* (1974); and *Walt Whitman* (1980: American Book Award). In 1992, he revised the standard reference work, *Bartlett's Familiar Quotations*, and with his wife, Anne Bernays, he wrote *The Language of Names* (1997), a study of how names affect lives.

Karig, Walter ["Keats Patrick"] (1898?–1956), newspaperman, artist, novelist, writer of juvenile stories, naval officer. Born in New York City, Karig worked for the Newark (New Jersey) *News*, part of the time as Washington correspondent. Under his own name, the pen name of Keats Patrick and other pseudonyms, he began writing books in the late 1920s and won critical approval with *Lower Than Angels* (1945), probably his best novel. Among his other novels are *Caroline Hicks* (1951), *Neely* (1953), and *Don't Tread on Me* (1954). Attached to the Navy Department during World War II as a public relations man, he attained the rank of captain (1946) and became co-author of an excellent series of *Battle Reports* (1944 and later).

Karr, Mary (1954–   ), poet, essayist, memoirist. Karr has made her youth in her native East Texas the subject of two striking memoirs: *The Liars' Club* (1995) and *Cherry* (2000). The first book finds humor in life with a mentally ill mother and an alcoholic father. Using the salty vernacular of the region, Karr relates her father's ability to keep the men gathered in a bait shop backroom enthralled with his stories, while the young daughter must cope with her mother's instability. *Cherry* begins with the seventeen-year-old leaving home to travel west where she hopes to realize her dream of becoming a writer, and looks backwards to reconstruct her adolescent juggling of sexual and substance abuse tensions while longing for intellectual companionship. Poetry collections include *Abacus* (1987) and *The Devil's Tour* (1993). *Viper Rum* (1998) combines poetry on death and suicide with the afterword "Against Decoration," an essay on the importance of intellectual content in poetry.

Kate Beaumont (1872), a novel by JOHN W. DE FOREST. Based on De Forest's experience as an official of the Freedmen's Bureau in the Reconstruction period, the novel deals with plantation society in Charleston and with poor whites in South Carolina. De Forest's depiction of poor whites anticipated the work of William Faulkner and Erskine Caldwell. William Dean Howells regarded *Kate Beaumont* as De Forest's best novel, but it sold poorly.

Katherine Walton (1851), a novel by W. G. SIMMS. See THE PARTISAN.

Kauffman, Janet (1945–   ), novelist, short-story writer. Kauffman was born in a predominantly Mennonite community in southeast Pennsylvania and educated at the University of Chicago. She teaches at Eastern Michigan University. *Places in the World a Woman Could Walk* (1984), a short-story collection, is especially evocative of the rural Michigan setting in which she lives. *Collaborators*, a novel, was published in 1986, and *Obscene Gestures for Women* in 1989. She often writes about rural women and depicts them with a poet's exactitude. *The Body in Four Parts* (1994) is a novel in four sections, one for each of the elements—earth, air, fire and water. *Characters on the Loose* (1997) is a collection of stories in an experimental mode. *Rot* (2001) is a novella about dying.

Kauffman, Reginald Wright (1877–1959),   editor, drama critic, novelist, poet. Born in Pennsylvania, Kauffman wrote numerous books popular in languages other than English. Among them are *Jarvis of Harvard* (1901, rev. 1923); *What Is Socialism?* (1910); *The House of Bondage* (1910); *Jim* (1915, reissued 1929 as *Jim Trent*); *The Mark of the Beast* (1916); *Our Navy at Work* (1918); *The Blood of Kings* (1926); *The Alabama Case* (1927); THE OVERLAND TRAIL (1927); and *Impossible Peace* (1943).

Kaufman, George S[imon] (1889–1961),   playwright, columnist, raconteur. Kaufman was born in Pittsburgh, Pennsylvania, and moved to New Jersey in 1910, where he worked as a ribbon salesman. Soon his fascination for the theater led him to New York City. Though Kaufman lived for a time in England and often worked in Hollywood, much of his life was spent in the sophisticated inner circle of literary wits who met daily at the Algonquin Hotel's celebrated round table. There he met other bright intellectuals from the theater who entertained each other in a viciously clever fashion that delighted readers in the city. Included in this group were Robert Sherwood, Alexander Woollcott, Heywood Broun, Robert Benchley, Marc Connelly, Deems Taylor, Howard Dietz, Edna Ferber, Peggy Wood, and Dorothy Parker.

Kaufman began contributing to "The Conning Tower," a column conducted by Franklin P. Adams, and through Adams's influence became a columnist on the *Washington Mail*. He then succeeded Adams as columnist on the *New York World*, joined the staff of the *New York Tribune* as a drama reporter, and later was drama reporter on the *New York Times*. Kaufman's first produced play was *Someone in the House* (1918). It had been written originally by Larry Evans and Walter C. Percival as a dramatization of two of Evans's short stories. The producer, George C. Tyler, was unsatisfied with their work and asked Kaufman to rewrite it. From then on, Kaufman was frequently called on to rework the plays of others, thus earning a reputation as a play doctor. Kaufman drew on some of his experiences in this capacity when he wrote *The Butter and Egg Man* (1925), which is about an accusation of plagiarism.

Kaufman wrote most of his plays with collaborators, and such works were to become the hallmark of his efforts in the theater. His long series of collaborations with MARC CONNELLY includes DULCY (1921), a satirical portrait of a cliché-ridden woman who had appeared first in Kaufman's contributions to "The Conning Tower"; *To the Ladies* (1922), a comedy of home life; MERTON OF THE MOVIES (1922), a merciless satire of Hollywood in which Kaufman himself took a role as an actor; *Helen of Troy* (1923), a musical; and BEGGAR ON HORSEBACK (1924), based on a German comedy by Paul Apel that satirizes big business and its relation to art. With EDNA FERBER, Kauf-

man wrote *Minick* (1924), based on one of Ferber's finest short stories. Kaufman then wrote another musical, *The Cocoanuts* (1925), as a showcase for the Marx Brothers. Working again with Edna Ferber, Kaufman produced *The Royal Family* (1927), an amusing revelation of the vagaries and eccentricities of a theatrical family resembling the Barrymores. *June Moon* (1929), a farce about Tin Pan Alley, was written with RING LARDNER, and *Once in a Lifetime* (1930), another satire of Hollywood, was written with MOSS HART. In 1931 Kaufman wrote the book for a musical called *The Band Wagon* in collaboration with Howard Dietz, called by Cecil Smith "one of the most perfect revues in the history of Broadway." The adroit exposé of high society called DINNER AT EIGHT (1932) was written next, again with Edna Ferber. With Morrie Ryskind he wrote OF THEE I SING (1932), a musical that satirizes American politics. GEORGE GERSHWIN wrote the music for the show, and his brother Ira wrote the lyrics. This successful collaboration won a Pulitzer Prize. Another show with Ryskind, *Let 'Em Eat Cake* (1933), was a sequel to *Of Thee I Sing*, but was less successful. *The Dark Tower* (1933) concerns an unsolvable murder and was written with ALEXANDER WOOLLCOTT; *Merrily We Roll Along* (1934) is a criticism of materialism written with MOSS HART; and *First Lady* (1935) is about Washington society, written with Katherine Dayton. The difficulties of young actresses are given sympathetic treatment in *Stage Door* (1936), written with Edna Ferber. Kaufman won another Pulitzer Prize for the farce YOU CAN'T TAKE IT WITH YOU (1936), which he wrote with Moss Hart. Together, he and Hart then wrote a series of plays: *I'd Rather Be Right* (1937), a satire on the New Deal; *The American Way* (1939), a paean to democracy; THE MAN WHO CAME TO DINNER (1939), an unflattering portrait suggestive of Alexander Woolcott; and GEORGE WASHINGTON SLEPT HERE (1940), a saga of a country house.

During the 1940s, Kaufman wrote the play *The Late George Apley* (1944) with JOHN P. MARQUAND; the musical play *Park Avenue* (1946) with NUNNALLY JOHNSON; and *Bravo!* (1948), his last collaborative effort with Edna Ferber. He and his second wife, Leueen MacGrath, wrote *The Small Hours* in 1951. *The Solid Gold Cadillac* was written in 1952 with Howard Teichmann, and *Silk Stockings* was completed in 1953 with Abe Burrows.

The list of Kaufman's plays is a long one, yet most were Broadway hits and were cordially received by the critics. Brooks Atkinson, writing an introduction for *Six Plays* (1942) by Kaufman and Moss Hart, described Kaufman as "master of the destructive jest," going on to say that "the fury of the gags, the bitterness and speed of the humor, the precision of the phrasing are remarkable in the field of popular comedy." If the essence of satiric comedy is verbal repartee that relentlessly attacks pomposity, self delusion, and moral hypocrisy, Kaufman's skill in this genre set the standard by which other American comedic writers for theater, film, and television have since been judged.

FRANKLIN D. CASE

Kavanagh (1849),   a romance by HENRY WADSWORTH LONGFELLOW. The central value of *Kavanagh* is the idyllic atmosphere it creates. It is a story of unfulfilled dreams and of literary as well as amatory aspirations. The most believable character is the local schoolmaster, Mr. Churchill. The book opens on his literary reflections, but his incapacity to become the poet of his dreams is made obvious by his failure to see the drama going on around him. Kavanagh is the new minister in the town of Fairmeadow, and two girls, initially great friends, fall in love with him. Alice Archer is poor and tied to a blind mother; Cecilia Vaughn is both beautiful and rich. Kavanagh, ignorant of Alice's love, marries Cecilia and leaves Fairmeadow, and Alice wastes away and dies. When Kavanagh and his wife return, Kavanagh has a long discussion with Mr. Churchill on the nature of affairs in town, and the latter has to report that his romance has not yet been written. The book delighted many discerning readers, among them Emerson and Hawthorne. Hawthorne recognized the quietness of the book to be its chief quality. It creates an amusing and romantic vision of a small New England town in which passions are either satirized or sentimentalized.

Kazan, Elia (1909–   ),   director. Kazan was born in Turkey of Greek parents. One of the most gifted of modern directors, Kazan turned to directing in 1940 after seven years of acting with the turbulent and vital GROUP THEATER. He has worked with some of the most distinguished plays of the American theater: *The Skin of Our Teeth, A Streetcar Named Desire, Deep Are the Roots, All My Sons, Death of a Salesman, Cat on a Hot Tin Roof,* and *J. B.* In 1944 he also began to direct movies, including *A Tree Grows in Brooklyn, Gentlemen's Agreement, A Streetcar Named Desire, On the Waterfront* (for which he received an Academy Award for 1954), and *East of Eden.* Kazan also co-founded the celebrated Actors Studio, to teach so-called method acting.

Kazan has published novels, for example, the semiautobiographical *America, America* (1962; made into a movie directed by Kazan, 1963); *The Arrangement* (1967); *The Assassins* (1972); *The Understudy* (1974); and *Acts of Love* (1978). His autobiography, *A Life,* appeared in 1988.

Kazin, Alfred (1915–1998),   American literary critic. Kazin's first book of criticism, *On Native Grounds* (1942), traced the development of American prose from the time of W. D. HOWELLS. Its sequel, *Bright Book of Life* (1973), continues his history and criticism from HEMINGWAY TO NORMAN MAILER. Aside from such other books of criticism as *The Inmost Leaf* (1955) and *Contemporaries* (1962), Kazin has written three autobiographical works: *A Walker in the City* (1951), an appealing memoir of his boyhood in Brooklyn; *Starting Out in the Thirties* (1965), about his young manhood; and *New York Jew* (1978), a personalized literary and political history from the Hitler-Stalin pact (1939) to the 1970s. *An American Procession* (1984) is a critical appraisal of all the literary greats in American literature from THOREAU through POUND, FAULKNER, and HEMINGWAY. In *Our New York* (1990), text by Kazin accompanies photographs by David Finn.

Keaton, Buster [Joseph Francis Keaton] (1895–1966), actor, director, screenwriter. Born to performers on the road,

Keaton got his nickname from Harry Houdini. A star of his parents' act from age three, Buster was an accomplished acrobat. He entered the movies in a series of comedy shorts directed by Fatty Arbuckle, and served briefly in World War I before settling into his own Buster Keaton Studio in 1919. *Our Hospitality* (1923), filled with amazing physical feats and visual gags, was his first feature-length film. Keaton typically portrayed a man facing adversity with a totally deadpan face. *The Navigator* (1924) was his greatest commercial success. *The General* (1927), a comic Civil War story involving a runaway locomotive, is one of his best movies. When he gave up his own studio and control over his films in 1928, Keaton's career faltered. Live appearances at the Cirque Medrano in Paris and a scene with Charlie Chaplin in *Limelight* (1952) helped restore his reputation.

Keenan, Henry Francis (1850–1928),   novelist. Born in Rochester, New York, Keenan is remembered for THE MONEY-MAKERS (1885), which was published anonymously. He also wrote *Trajan* (1885), *The Aliens* (1886), and other novels. *The Money-Makers,* subtitled *A Social Parable,* showed the corrupting influence of big business and was intended as a reply to John Hay's attack on labor unions in THE BREADWINNERS (1884).

Kees, Weldon (1914–1955),   poet. Born in Nebraska, Kees went to live first in New York City, then in San Francisco. His reputation stems from his posthumously published *Collected Poems* (1960, rev. 1975), edited by Donald Justice. Also posthumous is *Fall Quarter* (1990), an academic novel, edited by James Reidel Kees. He was a bibliographer, writer for *Time* magazine, painter, jazz pianist, and composer. His earlier collections of verse include *The Last Man* (1943), *The Fall of the Magicians* (1947), and *Poems 1947–1954* (1954). He was assumed a suicide when his car was found near the Golden Gate Bridge.

Keillor, Garrison (1942–   ),   humorist. Keillor achieved acclaim for his National Public Radio program "A Prairie Home Companion," which first ran in the late 1970s. In books such as *Happy to Be Here* (1982), *Lake Wobegon Days* (1985), and *Leaving Home* (1987), Keillor puts a weird comic twist on life in his imaginary rural community of Lake Wobegon, Minnesota. Other pieces are collected in *We Are Still Married* (1989). *Me, By Jimmy (Big Boy) Valente As Told to Garrison Keillor* (1999) is a tall tale satire inspired by the election of a professional wrestler, Jesse Ventura, as governor of Minnesota.

Keimer, Samuel (1688–1739?),   printer, publisher, editor, poet, writer of religious tracts. Keimer was an eccentric, the author of *A Brand Pluck'd from the Burning* and *A Search After Religion* (both 1718). In 1722 he came to Philadelphia from his native England and set up a printing shop. When BENJAMIN FRANKLIN was looking for work, Keimer gave him a job. They soon quarreled, and when word came to Keimer that Franklin was about to start a newspaper, Keimer hurriedly produced one of his own, *The Universal Instructor in All Arts and Sciences: and Pennsylvania Gazette* (December 1728). When Franklin realized he had been betrayed, he joined forces with Andrew Bradford in the *American Weekly Mercury* and in February 1729 began contributing to it his BUSY-BODY PAPERS, with an occasional attack on Keimer. Keimer soon sold out to Franklin, gave up his printing business, and left for Barbados. Franklin called the newspaper THE PENNSYLVANIA GAZETTE and ran it successfully until 1766. Keimer appeared in 1734 as the editor of the *Barbados Gazette*. A collection of papers from this periodical was published in London in 1741 in two quarto volumes under the title *Caribbeana*—supposedly as an imitation of *The Tatler*. Keimer is chiefly remembered today through Franklin's vivid, mocking portrait of him in his *Autobiography*.

Keith, Agnes Newton (1901–   ),   travel writer, memoirist. Keith, born in Illinois, was author of a best seller on life in Borneo, *Land Below the Wind* (1939). In January 1942, the Japanese came ashore in Borneo, and Keith, her husband, and their young son lived in horrible captivity. She told the story of her experiences in *Three Came Home* (1947), which was later made into a movie. In 1950, after a visit to the Keith family in British Columbia, the Keiths returned to Borneo. Mrs. Keith described what she saw in *White Man Returns* (1951). *Bare Feet in the Palace* was published in 1955. Other titles include *Children of Allah* (1966), *Beloved Exiles* (1972) and *Before the Blossoms Fall: Life and Death in Japan* (1975).

Keith, George (1638?–1716),   clergyman, teacher, controversialist. Keith, born in Scotland, put out more than a hundred publications, in the course of which he attacked many personages, especially in the colonies, where he came to avoid English persecution of Quakers. There he organized a separate sect called Keithians, or Christian Quakers, and then took Anglican orders, bitterly attacking Quakers who refused to become converted with him. He was denounced by WILLIAM PENN (1692) and replied in *The Deism of William Penn and His Brethren* (1699). He also wrote *A Journal of Travels from New Hampshire to Caratuck* (1706).

Kelland, Clarence Budington (1881–1964),   newspaperman, public relations expert, writer of boys' stories, novelist. Born in Michigan, Kelland worked as a reporter in Detroit and later became editor of the AMERICAN BOY there (1907–15). To this period belongs the popular series of books for boys about his character Mark Tidd as well as other juvenile books. Then Kelland turned to writing fiction for adults and in 1921 won fame with his stories about Scattergood Baines, his most vivid creation. Baines, a fat Yankee promoter, apparently guileless but in reality hard and shrewd, gets in and out of all kinds of scrapes. More of his adventures are related in *Scattergood Pulls the Strings* (1941). Among Kelland's numerous later books are *Dynasty* (1929), *Hard Money* (1930), *Jealous House* (1934), *Great Crooner* (1933), *Skin Deep* (1938), *Archibald the Great* (1934), *Stolen Goods* (1950), *The Key Man* (1952), *Murder Makes an Entrance* (1955), and *West of the Law* (1958).

Keller, Helen [Adams] (1880–1968),   counselor on international relations for the American Foundation of the Blind, memoirist, essayist. Born in Tuscumbia, Alabama, a normal child, but deprived of sight and hearing at nineteen months by a disease, Keller grew half-wild in her isolated state. When she was seven, Anne Sullivan Macy (1866–1936) undertook to educate her through a system of spelling a touch

alphabet into her hand. But the basic concept of communication, that of a relationship between words and things, was hard to teach. Understanding of this concept came suddenly. She and her teacher were standing by an outdoor pump when someone was pumping water; Miss Sullivan placed the child's hand under the spout and spelled out the word "water" in the palm of Helen's other hand. At last joining the thought of the fresh flowing liquid and the word, Helen stooped down and touched the earth, showing her desire to know its name. By nightfall she had learned thirty words. When she was ten years old she asked to be taught to speak.

Keller received an A.B. degree *cum laude* at Radcliffe in 1904. Sullivan was her constant companion throughout her school years and after, until "Teacher" died in 1936. Keller received honorary degrees and other honors from universities all over the world. She also wrote numerous books, among them the inspiring *Story of My Life* (1902, reissued 1947). Among her other writings are *Optimism* (1903), *The World I Live In* (1908), *The Song of the Stone Wall* (1910), *Out of the Dark* (1913), *My Religion* (1927), *Midstream—My Later Life* (1930), *Helen Keller's Journal* (1938), *Let Us Have Faith* (1940), and *The Open Door* (1957). She paid a warm tribute to her instructor in *Helen Keller's Teacher: Anne Sullivan Macy* (1955). Van Wyck Brooks wrote *Helen Keller: Sketch for a Portrait* (1955), an intimate and revealing work done in honor of Keller's seventy-fifth birthday.

The Miracle Worker, a successful play by William Gibson (1959), and later a movie, dramatized Anne Sullivan Macy's initial success in communicating with Helen as a child.

Kelley, Edith Summers (1894–1956),   novelist. The Canadian-born author worked with Upton Sinclair at the Helicon Home Colony before taking up tobacco farming in Kentucky, the setting for her novel *Weeds* (1923). *The Devil's Hand*, set in Southern California, did not see print during her lifetime, but was brought out by the Southern Illinois University Lost Fiction series in 1974.

Kelley, William Melvin (1937–   )   novelist and photographer. Kelley was born in New York City and educated at Harvard, where he studied creative writing with Archibald MacLeish and John Hawkes. His first novel, *A Different Drummer* (1962), a story about an African-American sharecropper, is supportive of nonviolence as a means of reducing racial bias. In his preface to the story collection *Dancers on the Shore* (1964), Kelley criticized the tendency to put all African-American writers into one category and defended his right to depict people and not symbols or ideas. *A Drop of Patience* (1965) is about a blind jazz musician; *dem* (1967) is a satire of the ways of white people. *Dunfords Travels Every Wheres* (1970) is an experimental novel.

Kellogg, Elijah (1813–1901),   clergyman, novelist, poet. Born in Maine, Kellogg wrote much juvenile literature, but is remembered only for SPARTACUS TO THE GLADIATORS (1846), a declamatory poem favored for recitations by schoolchildren of the last century.

Kelly, Eric P[hilbrook] (1884–1960),   teacher, author. Kelly, born in Massachusetts, taught at Dartmouth and later in Poland, where he spent some time during World War I. His writing falls into two categories—authoritative books on Poland, and books for young people. His works include *The Trumpeter of Krakow* (1928), *The Blacksmith of Vilno* (1930), *The Golden Star of Halich* (1931), *From Star to Star* (1944), and *The Amazing Journey of David Ingraham* (1949).

Kelly, George [Edward] (1887–1974), actor, playwright. Beginning in vaudeville, Kelly first wrote sketches, then full-length plays. The first was THE TORCH BEARERS (1922). Two years later Kelly sprang into sudden celebrity with THE SHOW-OFF, an amusing and timeless study of a braggart. Then came CRAIG'S WIFE (1925), an unpitying study of a cold, nagging woman that won a Pulitzer Prize. His later plays were *Behold the Bridegroom* (1927), *Maggie the Magnificent* (1929), *Reflected Glory* (1936), and *The Fatal Weakness* (1946).

Kelly, Jonathan Falconbridge (1817–1855?), humorist. Kelly, born in Philadelphia, often wrote under pseudonyms—"Falconbridge." "Jack Humphries," "O.K.," and "Cerro Gordo." After his death some of his stories and skits were collected as *The Humors of Falconbridge* (1856).

Kelly, Myra (1887–1910), teacher, children's writer. Educated at Teachers College, Columbia University (1899), Kelly taught at a school on the Bowery, where her students were immigrants. Her book of stories about them, *Little Citizens: the Humors of School Life* (1904), was a great success. Her other works include *The Isle of Dreams* (1907), *Wards of Liberty* (1907), *Rosnah* (1908), *The Golden Season* (1909), *Little Aliens* (1910), *New Faces* (1910), and *Her Little Young Ladyship* (1911).

Kelly, Robert (1935–), poet, playwright, fiction writer. Born in Brooklyn and educated at City College and Columbia University, Kelly has taught at Bard College in New York. A prolific writer, he emerged as an advocate of "Deep Image" poetics in the early 1960s. With Paris Leary, he edited *A Controversy of Poets: An Anthology of Contemporary American Poetry* (1965), and with his wife, Joan Kelly, and George Economou, he edited *Trobar*, a little magazine devoted to the deep image concept of using contemporary spoken language to portray vivid images from the author's subconscious. *Red Actions: Selected Poems, 1960–1993* (1995) selects from some twenty-five volumes of published poetry. *The Well wherein a Deer's Head Bleeds* is a play, produced in 1964 and published in 1968. Fiction titles include a novel, *The Scorpions* (1967), and stories collected in *A Transparent Tree* (1985); *Doctor of Silence* (1988); *Cat Scratch Fever* (1990); and *Queen of Terrors* (1994).

Kelly, Walt (1913–1973), cartoonist. Kelly was born in Philadelphia. His possum hero, Pogo, ran for president in 1952 on an independent ticket (*I Go Pogo*). Pogo failed to win election, but lost none of his tremendous popularity with readers of comic strips. From the first *Pogo* (1951) to the *Pogo Extra* (1960), there were twenty-two Pogo books. *Ten Ever Lovin' Blue-Eyed Years with Pogo*, an anthology, came out in 1959. His animal characters from the Okefenokee Swamp earned their celebrity by being of a generally pleasant disposition but not averse to an occasional barbed comment on contemporary life and politics.

Kemble, Edward Windsor (1861–1933), cartoonist, illustrator. This highly esteemed artist, born in California, worked for *Life* and for newspapers. Kemble also illustrated many books, including *Huckleberry Finn, Pudd'nhead Wilson, Uncle Tom's Cabin,* and other classics.

Kemble, Fanny [Frances Anne Kemble Butler] (1809–1893), actress, diarist, dramatist. Born into a celebrated English theatrical family, Kemble married an American, Pierce Butler (1834), and came to the United States to live on his plantation in Georgia, unaware that her husband was a slaveowner. At first she thought his slaves were content, but she gradually became convinced that this was not so. She recorded her enlightenment in *A Journal of a Residence on a Georgian Plantation in 1838–39* (1863, reprinted 1961), written as letters to a friend, Elizabeth Dwight Sedgwick. She was particularly incensed by the practice of driving women back to work with whips only three weeks after childbirth, and she recorded a dreary list of the ailments, miscarriages, and mortalities that were the consequence.

She divorced Butler in 1848, but continued to live in the United States from 1849 to 1868 and again from 1873 to 1878, giving readings from Shakespeare to earn a living. She was a vivacious woman, always active, often tactless, always popular with audiences. Her play *The Star of Seville* was published in 1837. Henrietta Buckmaster has written a well-documented novel, *Fire in the Heart* (1948), telling the story of Fanny Kemble's life. Margaret Armstrong's *Fanny Kemble: Passionate Victorian* (1938) is an excellent biography. Hawthorne is said to have drawn on Fanny Kemble for his portrait of Zenobia in THE BLITHEDALE ROMANCE.

Kemp, Harry [Hibbard] (1883–1960), poet, novelist, editor, dramatist, biographer. Born in Ohio, Kemp at first wrote quiet, competent poetry, but he broke out in the exhibitionist 1920s with verse of quite different quality and content, particularly his *Chanteys and Ballads* (1920), and with prose accounts of his life in fictional form—*Tramping on Life* (1922) and *More Miles* (1927). The basis of these novels was a trip around the world; he made special studies of night life in London and New York City and traveled over North America as a tramp. Kemp wrote a four-act play called *Judas* (1910) and also wrote *Boccaccio's Untold Tale and Other One-Act Plays* (1924). Among his other works are *The Thresher's Wife* (1914), a narrative poem; *The Sea and the Dunes* (1926); *The Golden Word: An Outline of a Non-Asectic Religion* (1930); *Harry Answers Omar: A Counterblast to the Rubaiyat* (poem, 1945); *The Poet's Life of Christ: Songs of the Living Lord* (1946); and *Rhyme of Provincetown Nicknames* (1954).

Kendall, G[eorge] W[ilkins] (1809–1867), newspaperman, war correspondent, historian. Born in New Hampshire and a printer by trade, Kendall along with a fellow printer in New Orleans, Francis A. Lumsden, founded *The Picayune* (1837). It was a four-page sheet, written well, and at once established itself. Kendall and Lumsden went on to what some authorities regard as the beginning of war correspondence and the gathering of news data under war conditions. In 1841, restless and desirous of establishing the fact that the people of New Mexico yearned for independence from Mexico, he set out on a trip in which he suffered harrowing hardships, was imprisoned in Mexico, and barely escaped with his life. On his return, he wrote an excellent account of his experiences in *A Narrative of the Texan Santa Fé Expedition, Comprising a Description of a Tour Through Texas and Across the Great Southwestern Prairies* (2 v. 1844, repr. in facsimile in the *Original Narratives of Texas History and Adventure*, 2 v. 1935). When war broke out, Kendall accompanied the Texas Rangers to the border, volunteered to serve as an aide, and saw most of the major actions of the war. His dispatches occasionally anticipated official bulletins and certainly were far in advance of any other newspaper correspondence. Kendall wrote an account of *The War Between the U.S. and Mexico* (1851). His own achievement is described in Fayette Copeland's *Kendall of the Picayune* (1943).

Kendrick, Baynard [Hardwick] (1894–1977), publisher, hotel manager, lawyer, writer. Kendrick, born in Philadelphia, saw service in World War I and did welfare work with hospitalized veterans. All this led to the creation of Duncan Maclain, a blind detective who appears in *The Last Express* (1937), *Blind Man's Bluff* (1943), and others of Kendrick's mystery novels. He was the first president of the Mystery Writers of America, Inc. Out of his work for blinded veterans also came his first general novel, *Lights Out* (1945). Long fascinated by Florida, Kendrick wrote a historical novel about that state, *The Flames of Time* (1948), laid in an era when it was a battleground for the Spanish, English, Americans and Native Americans. His other books include *You Die Today* (1952) and *Reservations for Death* (1957). His movies include *The Last Express* (1938), *Eyes in the Night* (1942), *Bright Victory* (1952), and *Clear and Present Danger* (1958).

Keneally, Thomas [Michael] (1935–   ), novelist, memoirist, playwright. Born in Sydney, Australia, Keneally first made his reputation there. Since his appointment as a visiting professor of writing at the University of California-Irvine in 1985, he has regularly taught and lived in the United States for part of the year and is a fellow of the American Academy of Arts and Sciences as well as similar organizations in Australia and England. A prolific writer, Keneally began his career with *The Place at Whitton* (London, 1964; New York, 1965). Five more novels followed before *The Chant of Jimmie Blacksmith* (1972), a novel loosely based on a real incident of an aborigine tragically unable to fit into white culture, appeared. It is a book often listed as required reading for university courses in Australian literature. In the next decade, Keneally wrote ten more novels.

With *Schindler's List* (1982, publ. in London the same year as *Schindler's Ark*), Keneally became one of Australia's best known writers. He had first heard the story of Oskar Schindler, owner of a German armament plant who saved Jewish concentration camp inmates by putting them on his list of essential war workers, from a Holocaust survivor in a Beverly Hills luggage shop. With extensive research, Keneally fleshed out the details of Schindler's building houses for Jewish workers on his plant site, reuniting them with their fami-

lies, providing them with adequate food and medical care, and saving them from the Nazis. By the end of the war, Schindler had about 1300 Jews under his protection. At the same time he socialized regularly with Nazi officers, left his wife, kept mistresses, and earned a personal fortune providing war materials to the German Army. When the book was nominated for Britain's Booker McConnell Prize for fiction, there was some controversy about whether it fit the criteria, but Keneally defended his use of fictional form for narrating historical events, asserting "the novel's techniques seem suited for a character of such ambiguity and magnitude as Oskar." The novel won the prize, and Steven Spielberg's Oscar-winning film version of 1993 further heightened Keneally's fame.

A Family Madness (1985) studies the repercussions of World War II on a Byelorussian immigrant family in Sydney. *To Asmara* (1989) treats African guerilla warfare of the 1980s. *Flying Hero Class* (1991) centers on the tour manager for a traveling troupe of aboriginal dancers. *Woman of the Inner Sea* (1992) treats a woman's attempt to escape the tragedy of her childrens' deaths by going into the interior of Australia. *A River Town* (1995) fictionalizes the immigration of some of Keneally's Irish ancestors at the beginning of the twentieth century. Among other novels are *The Fear* (1965); *Three Cheers for the Paraclete* (1968); *The Playmaker* (1987); and *Jacko the Great Intruder* (1994). Nonfiction titles include the memoir *Homebush Boy* (1995); and *The Great Shame: And the Triumph of the Irish in the English-Speaking World* (1999), concentrating on the 40,000 Irish men and women who were transported by law to Australia in the nineteenth century, and the effect their lives had on the wider world. *Childermass* (1968); *An Awful Rose* (1972); and *Halloran's Little Boat* (1975) are plays.

Keneally is one of a group of late twentieth century writers whose subject matter and readership transcend national boundaries.

Kennan, George (1845–1924),   newspaperman. Kennan, born in Ohio, wrote widely on foreign subjects. The Century Company commissioned him to visit Russia and Siberia, a trip that involved a 5,000-mile trek by dogsled. THE OUTLOOK sent him to the front in the Spanish-American and Russo-Japanese Wars. He visited Mt. Pelée after its eruption in 1902. He wrote *Siberia and the Exile System* (2 v. 1891), *Campaigning in Cuba* (1899), *The Tragedy of Pelée* (1902), and *E. H. Harriman* (2 v. 1922).

Kennan, George F[rost] (1904–   ),   diplomat, historian. Experience as a diplomat at strategic posts made Kennan, born in Milwaukee, a noted political authority, especially on the Soviet Union. In 1926, a year after graduating from Princeton, he entered foreign service, holding posts of increasing importance, climaxing in 1952 with the ambassadorship to the USSR. In 1956 he was appointed permanent professor in the School of Historical Studies at the Institute for Advanced Study. His books are astute analyses of foreign policy. *Russia Leaves the War* (1956), an investigation into the aims of Soviet policy, won the National Book Award and a Pulitzer Prize. *Russia, the Atom, and the West* (1958) was at first a series of lectures given over the BBC, with the aim of changing the climate of opinion from one favoring military containment of Russia to one favoring coexistence. Among his books are *Realities of American Foreign Policy* (1954), *The Decision to Intervene* (1958), *Soviet Foreign Policy* (1960), and *Russia and the West Under Lenin and Stalin* (1961). His *Memoirs* (1967) won both the Pulitzer Prize and the National Book Award. Other titles include *Sketches from a Life* (1989), *Around the Cragged Hill: A Personal and Political Philosophy* (1994) and *At a Century's End: Reflections 1982–1995* (1997). *An American Family: The Kennans: The First Three Generations* (2000) details rural life in the colonial period.

Kennedy, Adrienne (1931–   ),   playwright. Highly experimental and innovative, Kennedy's plays are most often performed and taught in universities. All kinds of characters—from history and from the movies—inhabit her dramas. In her best-known work, *Funnyhouse of a Negro* (1964), appear Jesus Christ, Queen Victoria, and Patrice Lumumba. She has written many one-acters, perhaps the best of which is *A Movie Star Has to Star in Black and White* (1976). *Deadly Triplets* (1990) is a combination mystery novel and autobiography set in 1960s London. *The Alexander Plays* (1992) is a collection of one-act plays. *People Who Led to My Plays* appeared in 1996.

Kennedy, Charles Rann (1871–1950),   actor, theatrical manager, writer, teacher. The English-born Kennedy made his first appearance in New York in 1903 in the medieval play *Everyman*. In 1917 he became a naturalized citizen. In 1908 he wrote a play that attained worldwide fame, *The Servant in the House*. A figure symbolizing or actually representing Jesus helps a modern family solve its problems through love and goodness. He wrote other plays of a religious or moralistic character—*The Winterfeast* (1908), *The Terrible Meek* (1911), *The Army with Banners* (1917), *The Chastening* (1922), *Flaming Ministers* (1932), *Face of God* (1935), and *The Seventh Trumpet* (1941).

Kennedy, Jonn Fitzgerald (1917–1963),   35th president, congressman, senator, author. Born in Brookline, Massachusetts, JFK was the second of nine children born to the wealthy Roman Catholic family of Joseph and Rose Fitzgerald Kennedy. He was educated at Harvard University, and his senior thesis on Britain's failure to prepare for conflict against the Nazis, *Why England Slept*, was published the year of his graduation. He served as secretary to his father, then the U.S. Ambassador to Great Britain, for six months before joining the Navy in the fall of 1941. He was cited for bravery under fire as commander of a torpedo boat (PT-109) sunk by the Japanese off the Solomon Islands. He injured his back in rescuing other survivors and, despite a series of operations, the injury never completely healed.

His father had intended that the oldest son, Joseph Jr., would go into politics, but Joe was killed in a plane crash during the war, so JFK ran as the Democratic nominee for the 11th district of Massachusetts and was elected to the House of Representatives in 1946 at the age of 29. He served three terms. In 1952, he ran for the Senate against the incumbent, Senator Henry Cabot Lodge, Jr. Despite a landslide victory for the

Republican presidential candidate, Dwight D. Eisenhower, Kennedy defeated Lodge by 70,000 votes.

As a Senator, Kennedy developed a reputation for responsiveness to constituents and an evolving liberal voting record. In 1956, he was narrowly defeated as the party's vice-presidential nominee, but became widely known because of his televised concession speech. Recuperating from one of a series of operations on his injured back, he wrote *Profiles in Courage* (1956), an account of eight political leaders who defied popular opinion in matters of conscience; it won a Pulitzer Prize. In 1958 he was reelected to the Senate by the largest margin in his state's history. A steady stream of national speaking engagements and magazine articles followed. His brothers Robert Francis (1925–1968) and Edward Moore (1932–   ), both later elected to the Senate, joined his staff.

In January 1960 Kennedy formally announced his candidacy for the presidency. Knowing that no Catholic had ever been elected president, he tackled head-on the issue of his religion in a televised address to a convention of Protestant ministers in Houston and in the West Virginia primary campaign. Nominated on the first ballot, he selected LYNDON B. JOHNSON of Texas, one of his chief rivals, as running mate. His acceptance speech introduced the phrase New Frontier, which was repeated in his Inaugural Address and became associated with his agenda.

Kennedy narrowly defeated the Republican nominee, Vice President RICHARD M. NIXON, by emphasizing the problems of unemployment, a sluggish economy, the Castro government in Cuba, and what he termed a missile gap with the Soviet Union. A series of four televised debates with Nixon proved crucial. Kennedy, the lesser known candidate, demonstrated his poise and grasp of the issues. He was the youngest man and the first Catholic to be elected to the presidency. His administration was to last little more than 1000 days.

Liberalizing immigration quotas was a major emphasis, and Kennedy detailed his argument in *A Nation of Immigrants* (posthumous publication, 1964).

The nation was shocked when the Kennedy potential was stopped by an assassin's bullet; he was riding with his wife and two others in an open convertible through the streets of Dallas, Texas, on November 22, 1963, when he was struck by two rifle bullets in the throat and head. Lee Havery Oswald, the accused slayer, was himself shot two days later. Lyndon Johnson, with a blood-spattered Jacqueline Kennedy standing at his side, took the oath of office on the plane that bore Kennedy's body back to the capitol. A presidential commission headed by Earl Warren, the chief justice of the Supreme Court, ruled that Oswald had acted alone, but suspicions of conspiracy persist.

Among the many studies of Kennedy are James MacGregor Burns's *John Kennedy: A Political Profile* (1960), covering his career up to the campaign for president; Theodore H. White's *The Making of the President* (1960), detailing the campaign; Theodore Sorenson's *Kennedy* (1965), a detailed history of his 11 years as senator and president by a chief aide; and Arthur M. Schlesinger, Jr.'s *A Thousand Days: John F. Kennedy in the*

White House (1965), the work of the historian JFK had designated to keep the record. The JFK Memorial Library in Boston houses many of his papers and memorabilia.

Kennedy, John Pendleton ["Mark Littleton"] (1795–1870), lawyer, public official, writer. Born in Baltimore, Kennedy practiced law for several years, served in Congress, was Speaker of the House and, under Millard Fillmore, secretary of the navy. In the latter capacity he organized the Perry expedition to Japan and Elisha Kent Kane's second Arctic expedition. He was greatly interested in education and was active in the affairs of the University of Maryland and the Peabody Institute.

Writing, always an avocation, was perhaps his deepest interest. He wrote on politics, often satirically, and his writing frequently took the form of fiction, as in *Quodlibet* (1840), a light satire on Jacksonian democracy. He published his fiction under the pen name Mark Littleton. SWALLOW BARN (1832), held together by a thin thread of story, was Kennedy's first novel and has been described as the first important fictional treatment of Virginian life. HORSE-SHOE ROBINSON (1835) was based on the personal recollections of its hero, a veteran of the Revolution whom Kennedy met while visiting South Carolina. *Rob of the Bowl* (1838), which many critics consider his best work, is laid in St. Mary's City, Maryland's first capital, in 1681; among the incidents is an attempt of Protestants to overthrow Catholic rule. Kennedy also wrote *Memoirs of the Life of William Wirt* (1849).

Kennedy, in his friendly way, helped Poe after reading the *Ms. Found in a Bottle* (1833) as a contest judge. He furnished Thackeray with information for *The Virginians* (1857–59)—a legend long current credited him with having written a chapter of that book. J. B. Hubbell edited *Swallow Barn* (1929), and E. E. Leisy edited *Horse-Shoe Robinson* (1937).

Kennedy, William (1928–), novelist. Born in Albany, New York, Kennedy has used his home town as the setting for a trio of novels. *Legs* (1975) is a fictionalized life of the gangster Jack "Legs" Diamond and his showgirl mistress, Kiki Roberts, seen through the eyes of attorney Marcus Gorman. *Billy Phelan's Greatest Game* (1978) is set in the Depression era and centers on the kidnapping of a political boss's son. *Ironweed* (1983, National Book Award) deals with Francis Phelan, an alcoholic ex-baseball player, returning to Albany's skid row, where he and his friend, Helen, fight to stay alive and come to terms with the past. Kennedy has also written *The Ink Truck* (1969); *O Albany!* (1983), an essay collection; the screenplay for *The Cotton Club* (1984); *Quinn's Book* (1988), a novel set in Civil War–era Albany; and *Riding The Yellow Trolley Car: Selected Nonfiction* (1993). *The Flaming Corsage* (1996) chronicles the marriage of an Irish-American and a member of a patrician family in turn-of-the-twentieth-century Albany.

Kennicott, Carol. Leading character in Sinclair Lewis's MAIN STREET (1921). It is she who tries to bring culture to Gopher Prairie.

Kent, James (1763–1847), lawyer, public official, jurist, writer on law. Kent, born in Putnam County, New York, practiced law after his graduation from Yale and admission to the bar, and served as professor of law at Columbia; Kent Hall at that university is named for him. He also served as a judge in New York courts. It is said that Kent was the first to deliver his judicial opinions in writing, and his views as a result became influential in later cases. He became known as the American Blackstone because of his *Commentaries on American Law* (4 v. 1826–30), which has gone through many editions. He was a lover of literature and a friend of Charles Brockden Brown. See BREAD AND CHEESE CLUB; FRIENDLY CLUB.

Kent, Louise Andrews (1886–1969), novelist. Born in Massachusetts, Kent wrote over twenty books, including a number of novels for children, a series of humorous books about life in New England, and two cookbooks. In 1935 *He Went With Marco Polo* became the first of six historical novels, including *He Went With Champlain* (1959). Her three Mrs. Appleyard books—*Mrs. Appleyard's Year* (1941), *County Mouse* (1945), and *With Kitchen Privileges* (1953)—were praised for their witty and knowledgeable depiction of life in Boston and rural Vermont. Kent's interest in New England is also evident in her cookbooks—*Mrs. Appleyard's Kitchen* (1942) and *The Summer Kitchen* (1942, with Elizabeth Kent Gay)—which combined favorite New England recipes with a running commentary by Mrs. Appleyard. Among her other books are *Douglas of Porcupine* (1931), *Two Children of Tyre* (1932), *The Red Rajah* (1933), *The Terrace* (1934), *He Went With Vasco Da Gama* (1938), *Paul Revere Square* (1939), *He Went With Christopher Columbus* (1940), *He Went With Magellan* (1943), *Village Greens of New England* (1948), and *He Went With John Paul Jones* (1958).

Kent, Rockwell (1882–1971), painter, illustrator, author of travel books. Born in Tarrytown Heights, New York, and a rebel in politics as well as in painting, Kent often stirred up controversies. He began to show in public in 1910, and thereafter wrote and illustrated numerous books based on his experiences in various sea voyages. Among the books are *Wilderness* (1920), *Voyaging Southward from the Strait of Magellan* (1924), *N. by E.* (1930), and *Salamina* (1935). He also wrote *Rockwellkentiana* (1933), *This Is My Own* (1940), and *It's Me, O Lord* (1955). Among editions of the classics he illustrated are *Candide* (1928), *The Bridge of San Luis Rey* (1929), *The Canterbury Tales* (1930), *Moby-Dick* (1930), and *Beowulf* (1931).

Kenton, Simon (1755–1836), Indian fighter, scout, soldier. Kenton, because of his many daring adventures and exploits, became a frontier legend. Born in Virginia, he was one of Boone's chosen company and served with George Rogers Clark and Anthony Wayne. A biography was written by Edna Kenton (1930), and he appears in Robert Montgomery Bird's *Nick of the Woods* (1837), Maurice Thompson's ALICE OF OLD VINCENNES (1900), Winston Churchill's THE CROSSING (1903), and Thomas Boyd's *The Shadow of the Long Knives* (1928).

Kentuckians, The (1898), a novel, by JOHN FOX, JR. One of Fox's better novels, this story contrasts the two main groups in the population of Kentucky—the richer, better educated group, mainly centered in the bluegrass region, and the illiterate, improverished group of the mountains.

Kentucky Cardinal, A (1894),   a novelette by JAMES LANE ALLEN. Adam Moss, more interested in birds than in human beings, falls in love with a neighbor's daughter of somewhat capricious character. Jealous of his interest in birds, she demands that he make captive one of the Kentucky cardinals who frequent the bird refuge he has set up and present it to her in a cage. He does so reluctantly, and the bird dies. The lovers are greatly distressed, quarrel for a time, and are reconciled. In a sequel, *Aftermath* (1896), the lovers are married, and the wife helps the husband take some interest in social life. But she dies in giving birth to a son, and he returns to his deep absorption in nature.

Kentucky Miscellany, The (1789),   a collection of verses by Thomas Johnson, Jr. It is said to be the first book of poems written and printed in Kentucky.

Kentucky Tragedy.   See BEAUCHAMPE.

Kenyon Review, The.   A quarterly founded in 1939 at Gambier, Ohio, by members of the faculty of Kenyon College, with JOHN CROWE RANSOM as editor. The magazine stressed close structural criticism and reviews of important new trends in music, literature, painting, and aesthetics, as well as studies of classic forms, stories, and poetry. Its initial advisory board included ALLEN TATE, MARK VAN DOREN, ROBERT PENN WARREN, and other writers of reputation. Its early circulation was aided by purchase of the subscription list of the *Southern Review* on that magazine's expiration in 1942. From its beginning the *Kenyon Review* presented some of the most thoughtful and capable writers of our time: R. P. Blackmur, Marianne Moore, and Eliseo Vivas.

Keokuk.   See SAUK AND FOX INDIANS.

Keppler, Joseph (1838–1894),   cartoonist, publisher. Born in Austria, Keppler came to the U.S. in 1867, founded *Die Vehme*, a German-language comic weekly, in St. Louis. In 1871 he also founded, in the same city, *Puck, Illustrierte Wochenschrift*. In 1876 he helped found in New York a weekly called *Puck, Humoristisches Wochenblatt*. In the following year it became an English-language weekly, the famous PUCK that would continue for some decades to purvey humor and commentary to the American audience. Cartoons prepared from lithographs rather than woodblocks were an early feature of the magazine.

Kern, Jerome [David] (1885–1945),   composer. Kern, born in New York City, showed musical talent even in childhood, which led to professional training. His first musical comedy, *Mr. Wix of Wickham*, was done in 1910. Thereafter, he wrote a long series of songs for musical shows and movies, including *Very Good, Eddie* (1915); *Leave It to Jane* (1917, revived 1959, for a long Off Broadway run); *Sally* (1920, revived 1948, with borrowings from *Leave It to Jane*); *Sunny* (1925); SHOW BOAT (1927); *The Cat and the Fiddle* (1931); *Music in the Air* (1932); *Roberta* (1933); and *Very Warm for May* (1939). Among his most successful songs are "They Didn't Believe Me," "I've Told Every Little Star," "The Last Time I Saw Paris," "Look for the Silver Lining," "My Bill," "Old Man River," and "Smoke Gets in Your Eyes." His songs set new standards for Broadway and greatly influenced later songwrit-

ers, for example, George Gershwin, Cole Porter, Vincent Youmans, and Richard Rodgers. *The Jerome Kern Song Book* (1955) collected fifty of his best-loved songs, with an introduction by Oscar Hammerstein II.

Kerouac, Jack (1922–1969),   novelist. Born Jean Louis Kerouac in Lowell, Massachusetts, of French Canadian heritage, Kerouac was educated in Lowell and then went on to the Horace Mann School and Columbia University on football scholarships. In New York City he met WILLIAM BURROUGHS and ALLEN GINSBERG and the three became the seminal figures of the BEAT GENERATION. During this early Beat period, he was involved in a scandal over the murder of Dave Kammerer by his friend Lucien Carr, which led to the first of Kerouac's two marriages, but the key woman in Kerouac's life was his mother.

Kerouac is best known as the writer of one book, ON THE ROAD (1957). Indeed, Kerouac thought of himself as the writer of "one book," "one vast book" (he even called it "a Divine Comedy of the Buddha") made up of the nineteen books he wrote, taken together, and to be called the Legend of Duluoz. Kerouac's true legend is the progression of his language through book after book in search of a linguistic equivalent of the breakdown of traditions, the new consciousness he saw all around him. His first novel, *The Town and the City* (1950), was well received but it was considered derivative of the work of Thomas Wolfe. It was not until the best-selling *On the Road* that he began to use a form that would reflect the fast-paced life of hitchhiking, sex, and drugs. The language of *On the Road* is speedy, and its composition on a roll of teletype was well publicized. His so-called spontaneous writing follows a jazz analogy. Kerouac explained his process as that of a hornplayer sounding one long unrevised note—although the manuscript underwent extensive revision, according to Viking editor Malcolm Cowley, before publication seven years after it was written. Kerouac accomplishes his artistic intentions in *Visions of Cody* (1972), published in an earlier form in 1959. Actually unrevised, the text is made up of sections of poetic prose much akin to jazz riffs, including verbatim taped conversations between the narrator and his hero. In *Desolation Angels* (1965), Kerouac completes the linguistic progression in prose sections that follow the contours of riffs with haikus serving as bridges to subsequent sections. While the musical comparison works to explain the experimentation in style and form of each separate book, it also explains the unity of Kerouac's grand design. This core grouping from *The Town and the City* to *On the Road* to *Visions of Cody* to *Desolation Angels* shows the progression of Kerouac's stylistic innovation. The development of his spontaneous bop prosody in these principal novels explains how his one vast book, his Legend of Duluoz, follows a poetic unity, not the linear unity we most identify with legends. That his writing even had unity was not understood during his lifetime.

Ironically, Kerouac reacted adversely to celebrity. He was either canonized as The King of the Beats (a sociological, not literary phenomenon) or, put down as the last decade's passing fad, his writing dismissed as rebellious, ragged, and ungrammatical. Worse, he was regarded as merely an autobiographical chronicler, so much of his writing depending on his childhood and early Beat history. Moreover, Kerouac suffered from the misbegotten celebrity of being confused with the Dean Moriarty figure in his book, an amoral rogue whose prototype was NEAL CASSADY, with whom he was traveling during his life on the road and who inspired the nonstop writing and fast lifestyle. The true poetic nature of his achievement is just now being recognized. An imaginative sensibility prevails over a historical one. His art is the re-creation of American myth: Kerouac's Sal Paradise, the narrator of *On the Road*, shambles after the "sparkling incandescent Roman candle" Dean Moriarty in a romantic Huck Finn/Jim relationship, the Mississippi River supplanted by the automobile.

His other books—*The Subterraneans* (1958), *The Dharma Bums* (1958), *Dr. Sax* (1959), *Mexico City Blues* (1959), *Tristessa* (1960), *Lonesome Traveler* (1960), *Visions of Gerard* (1963), and *Vanity of Duluoz* (1968), to name a few—repeat and revise early Beat history, transfiguring it in each retelling and providing variations on Kerouac's central preoccupations: America as paradise lost; the transience of human life and values; Christian dogma vs. Buddhism; and, above all, language.

The conclusion of Kerouac's legend is the end of his spiritual quest: he achieves the only solace he has ever had—as a writer writing. In writing lies his redemption. Several of Kerouac's novels are now regarded by many as classics of American literature. Indeed, Kerouac's total achievement, the books taken as a whole as he intended, records the process of a writer's art. Unfortunately, in his later years, no one could prevent his despair and journey downward. While living with his ailing mother and his third wife, and becoming increasingly more isolated from his friends, Kerouac died at age 47 in St. Petersburg, Florida, of an internal hemorrhage related to his alcoholism. Letters between Kerouac and Joyce Johnson were published as *Door Wide Open: A Beat Love Affair in Letters, 1957–1958* (2000).

REGINA WEINREICH

Kerr, Jean [Collins] (1923–   ),   novelist, playwright. Born in Pennsylvania, Kerr is best known for her autobiographical comic fictions about family life: *Please Don't Eat the Daisies* (1957), *The Snake Has All the Lines* (1960), and *How I Got to Be Perfect* (1978). She collaborated with her husband, WALTER KERR, in adapting Franz Werfel's *The Song of Bernadette* (1946) and on the musical comedy *Goldilocks* (1948). Her own plays include *Mary, Mary* (1961) and *Poor Richard* (1964).

Kerr, Orpheus C.   Pen name of ROBERT HENRY NEWELL.

Kerr, Walter (1913–1996),   drama critic. Kerr, born in Illinois, was educated at Northwestern University and taught at the Catholic University of America in Washington, D.C., until 1950, when he became drama critic for the New York *Herald Tribune*. His fresh, vigorous, and penetrating reviews established him as one of the foremost critics of the Broadway theater. In 1955, disheartened by what he considered the sad state of playwriting, he wrote *How Not to Write a Play*, which

called on playwrights to restore the theater to its original vitality. In 1966 he became theater critic for the *New York Times*. His plays include *Murder in Reverse* (1935) and adaptations of *Rip Van Winkle* (1937), *The Vicar of Wakefield* (1938), and Molière's *The Miser* (1942). *Sing Out Sweet Land* (1944) is an opera libretto. His other books include *Criticism and Censorship* (1956), *Pieces at Eight* (1957), *The Decline of Pleasure* (1962), *The Theatre In Spite of Itself* (1963), *Tragedy and Comedy* (1967), *Thirty Plays Hath November* (1969), *God on the Gymnasium Floor* (1971), and *The Silent Clowns* (1975).

Kesey, Ken [Elton] (1935–2001),   novelist, shortstory writer. Born in Colorado, Kesey was educated at the University of Oregon and in creative writing classes at Stanford University on a Woodrow Wilson scholarship. In 1961 Kesey volunteered for a series of government-sponsored experiments with what were called psychomimetic drugs at the Menlo Park Veteran's Hospital. Kesey's experiences and work as night attendant on the psychiatric ward provided inspiration for *One Flew over the Cuckoo's Nest* (1962), a highly acclaimed novel pitting a lusty and defiant individual against the life-denying order represented by Nurse Ratched's ward. In June 1961 Kesey moved with wife, Faye, to a small logging town in Oregon to collect material for *Sometimes a Great Notion* (1964). This ambitious epic of the Northwest revolves around the conflict between a fiercely individualistic clan of loggers and their local union, but the sociological analysis is sharper and the characterization more complex, less melodramatic. After a period of literary inactivity spent in the hip subculture of Menlo Park and, since 1967, on a farm in Pleasant Hills, Oregon, Kesey published *Kesey's Garage Sale* (1973), a collage of letters, comic strips, and an autobiographical screenplay chronicling Devlin Deboree's (an alias for Kesey) underground exploits. This was followed by *Seven Prayers by Grandma Whittier*, a series of narrative monologues and character studies serialized in Kesey's magazine *Spit in the Ocean*, and by *Demon Box* (1986), a collection of autobiographical stories and articles that examine the challenges and inadequacies of countercultural idealism. A recent publication is *Caverns* (1989), a collaborative novel composed with his creative writing class at the University of Oregon and signed O. U. Levon ("Oregon University Novel"). *The Further Inquiry* (1990) is Kesey's account of his Merry Prankster period, famously chronicled by TOM WOLFE in *The Electric Kool-Aid Acid Test*. *Sailor Song* appeared in 1993.

Critical studies include M. Gilbert Porter's *The Art of Grit* (1982) and Stephen L. Tanner's *Ken Kesey* (1983).

MARCEL CORNIS-POPE

Kesselring, Joseph.   See ARSENIC AND OLD LACE.

Kester, Paul (1870–1933),   playwright. Kester, born in Ohio, adapted foreign plays for the American and English stages. In the 1890s the vogue for historical novels led him to dramatize many of them. He often wrote or adapted plays for particular players, among them Julia Marlowe, Marie Tempest, E. H. Sothern, and Margaret Anglin. Of his original plays his first great success was *Sweet Nell of Old Drury* (1901), produced in England, the United States, Australia, and the Far

East, and frequently revived. His other plays were *Zamar* (1893); *Mademoiselle Mars* (1902); and a dramatic version of Charles Major's *When Knighthood Was in Flower*. His brother, **Vaughan Kester** (1869–1911), with whom he occasionally collaborated, was a novelist; his best-known work was *The Prodigal Judge* (1911), a tale of a boy's adventures in Ohio and western Tennessee.

Kettell, Samuel (1800–1855),   editor, essayist, public official. Born in Massachusetts, Kettell is chiefly remembered for the three-volume reply he made to Sydney Smith's query "Who reads an American book?" His reply took the form of an anthology, *Specimens of American Poetry, with Critical and Biographical Notices* (1829), which began with Cotton Mather and continued to Kettell's own day. He also assisted SAMUEL G. GOODRICH in the preparation of his *Peter Parley* series and translated one volume into modern Greek. As an original writer, he used at least two pen names—Timo Titterwell for *Yankee Notions: A Medley* (1838) and Sampson Short-and-Fat for *Daw's Doings, or, The History of the Late War in the Plantations* (1842).

Key, Francis Scott (1779–1843),   lawyer, poet, author of "The Star Spangled Banner." Key was educated at St. John's College, near Annapolis. In 1801, after a period of reading law under the tutelage of Judge J. T. Case, he began practicing in Frederick, Maryland, in partnership with R. B. Taney. Taney was later to become Key's brother-in-law, as well as one of the best-known chief justices of the Supreme Court.

The War of 1812 found Key living in Georgetown in the District of Columbia, where he practiced law with an uncle, Philip Barton Key. When the British evacuated Washington in 1814, they took with them as a hostage a prominent physician, Dr. William Beanes, and Key was asked to undertake Beanes's release. Traveling through the British lines, Key was successful in his negotiations, but was detained by the British commander, Admiral Cockburn, until after a planned attack on the city of Baltimore. It was after watching the attack on Fort McHenry, one of the defenses of Baltimore, on the night of September 13–14, 1814, that Key wrote his famous poem.

"The Star-Spangled Banner" was first published in the Baltimore *American* for September 21, 1814, and was soon thereafter set to the music of "Anacreon in Heaven," a song composed by John Stafford Smith, an Englishman, as the anthem of the Anacreontic Societies, groups of amateur musicians. The tune was well known in America, having been current during the Revolution as "Adams and Liberty."

Key went on to become a prominent lawyer in the nation's capital. Rejecting a notion of entering the ministry, he served as U.S. Attorney for the District of Columbia from 1833 until 1841. His collected works were published posthumously (1857); they comprise religious and love poems and some light humorous verses. His song was finally adopted as the United States national anthem in 1931, after years of being sung as such, unofficially, by the public.

Keyes, Daniel (1927–   ),   writer. Born in New York City and educated at Brooklyn College, Keyes won wide admiration for his story "Flowers for Algernon," told from the per-

spective of a retarded man and considered a classic of science-fiction. It was expanded to a novel (1966). Among his other novels are *The Touch* (1971), *The Fifth Sally* (1981), and *Charly* (1990).

Keyes, Frances Parkinson (1885–1970).   novelist, nonfiction writer. Born Frances Wheeler in Charlottesville, Virginia, Keyes was educated in private schools in Boston and Europe. At nineteen, she married Henry Wilder Keyes (surname rhymes with *wise*) who would be elected Governor of New Hampshire (1917) and a United States Senator (1919). Shortly after his death in 1938, she converted to Roman Catholicism, a change that would have an effect on her choice of nonfiction subjects. She wrote lives of several female saints including Anne, the grandmother of Christ; Therese, called the Little Flower; Mother Cabrini; and Catherine of Siena. Her novels, rich in romance and well-researched local color, concern themselves with characters of wealth in beautiful surroundings. Her first novel, *The Old Gray Homestead* (1919), was followed by dozens more over a period of fifty years. *Honor Bright* (1936) was first to make the best seller list; other popular titles include *The River Road* (1945); *Came a Cavalier* (1947); *Joy Street* (1950); *Steamboat Gothic* (1952); and *The Royal Box* (1954). Many were set in New Orleans, where Keyes lived in the Old French Quarter in a house that had belonged to the Confederate General Pierre Beauregard. The general and other prior occupants appear as characters in *The Chess Players* (1960) and *Madame Castel's Lodger* (1962). The house was acquired by the Keyes Foundation, a charitable trust to help writers and preserve historic buildings in 1948. *Dinner at Antoine's* (1948) is one of the most popular of her New Orleans titles; it deals with a murder during Mardi Gras. Keyes wrote a monthly column in *Good Housekeeping* for several years and contributed to other periodicals. Other novels include *The Explorer* (1964); *I, the King* (1966); and *The Heritage* (1968). *The Restless Lady* (1963) is a story collection; *All Flags Flying* (1972) is a memoir.

Key Into the Language of America, A.   A book by Roger Williams (1643), primarily a phrase book of the language of Indians native to Massachusetts and Rhode Island, especially the Narragansetts. Organized by topics such as "salutations" or "entertainment," each section contains a word list, some comments and descriptions of customs, and verses expressing sentiments of compassion and admiration.

Keystone Comedies.   See MACK SENNETT.

Kid, The (1947),   a poem by CONRAD AIKEN. There is a legend that a bookish recluse named William Blackstone greeted Boston's first settlers on what is now the Boston Common. Aiken, in a series of nine quietly written but eloquent poems, takes Blackstone as an emblem of the free spirit in American life, describes his later wanderings, and tells of other heroes, legendary and real, who appear as America moves west. Aiken discussed in his USHANT (1952) his discovery of Blackstone's "magical figure" in Justin Winsor's *Memorial History of Boston* (4 v. 1880–81).

Kidd, William ["Captain Kidd"] (1645?–1701), privateer and pirate. As a shipowner in New York, Kidd saw an excellent chance for personal profit in joining British ships engaged against French privateers in the West Indies, and later he was sent out against the pirates who infested the Indian Ocean. In all these expeditions the Scottish-born Kidd had royal warrants and was paid for his services. A man of means, he helped pay for the building of Trinity Church in New York City. In 1696 he set out from New York on an expedition against pirates off Madagascar. The story goes that a mutinous crew caused him to turn pirate himself. He joined forces with two other sea marauders, and orders were issued for his arrest. He captured a number of vessels, and in 1699, on his way back from the West Indies, he was induced to land at Boston. He expected to receive a pardon, but was sent back to England, put on trial, convicted not of piracy but of murder, and hanged. The trial was widely reported, and *A Full Account of Proceedings in Relation to Captain Kidd* (1701) went into several editions.

Justly or unjustly, Captain Kidd became the leading pirate of legend in both England and the United States. Many ballads were written and printed about him, for example, a *Dialogue Between the Ghost of Capt. Kidd and a Kidnapper* (1704). There was also *Captain Kidd's Farewell to the Seas* (1701), called in its American version *The Dying Words of Captain Robert Kyd*. It appeared in several broadsides, from the pre-Revolutionary period to 1820. For some reason Kidd was also supposed to have been more skillful than most pirates in concealing his wealth, and as far back as 1699 a New Jersey wag created great excitement by declaring that Kidd, during a visit to Cape May, had buried money there. That was the first of a number of similar hoaxes, among them the letter found in 1849 in a field near Palmer, Massachusetts, signed "Robert Kidd." In 1894 another hoax mentioned Deer Island, Maine, as a treasure site. Kidd's ghost has also occasionally appeared, as at Clark's Island, Massachusetts. His spirit broods over other parts of the country; in 1950 a mining engineer bought Oak Island, Nova Scotia, and began hunting a treasure cache supposedly left there by Captain Kidd.

Willard Hallam Bonner, in *Pirate Laureate: The Life and Legends of Captain Kidd* (1947), usefully reexamines the Kidd saga, with some attempt at the rehabilitation of Kidd's character. One section of Bonner's book analyzes the literary uses that have been made of the Kidd legends. These legends found their way into American writing, particularly fiction, between 1824 and 1849. Washington Irving was perhaps the first to make literary use of Kidd, in TALES OF A TRAVELLER (1824) and WOLFERT'S ROOST (1855); Kidd was a part of the Knickerbocker tradition. Samuel B. F. Judah wrote *The Buccaneers* (1827), a pretentious novel in which "Richard" Kidd becomes mixed up in all sorts of affairs. Then came Fenimore Cooper, who refers to Kidd favorably in his *History of the Navy* (1839) and THE DEERSLAYER (1841), again in the 1850 Preface to THE RED ROVER. In *The Sea Lions* his conception of the plot and characters was obviously influenced by incidents in Kidd's career. But his most important use of the Kidd saga was in THE WATER WITCH (1830), where the pirate is frequently mentioned. Joseph Holt Ingraham wrote *Capt. Kidd, or, The Wizard of the Sea* (1839).

Harriet Beecher Stowe's "Captain Kidd's Money" appeared in the *Atlantic Monthly* for November 1870 and was reprinted two years later in *Sam Lawson's Oldtown Fireside Stories*. A long-lasting tribute to the fascination Kidd exerted was a play by J. S. Jones, *Captain Kyd, or, The Wizard of the Sea*, first shown in 1830 and published in 1857. Possibly the most widely read reference to the Kidd legend in American literature is in Poe's THE GOLD BUG (1843).

Kieft, Willem (1597–1647),   governor of New Netherlands from 1638 to 1647. He appears as William the Testy in Washington Irving's first important work, (Diedrich Knickerbocker's) A HISTORY OF NEW YORK (1809), and was irascible, unpopular, and unsuccessful. His administration and character were defended by J. W. Gerard, who stressed the great difficulties Kieft faced, but when he was lost at sea on his homeward voyage, JOHN WINTHROP, in his *Journal* (which later became a *History of New England*, published in 1790), proclaimed his death a judgment of God.

Killens, John Oliver (1916–1987),   novelist, playwright. Born in Georgia, he was educated at Howard University and the Columbia University Law School, which he left to enter the Army. World War II service provided the material for his best-known novel, *And Then We Heard The Thunder* (1962), dealing with segregation and racism in the military. The protagonist, an African-American officer, soon discovers he is not on equal footing with white officers and he must make common cause with his fellow blacks. *Youngblood* (1954) treats the struggle for rights in rural Georgia. His other works include *'Sippi* (1967); *Slaves* (1969); *The Cotillion* (1971); *The Great Black Russian: A Novel on the Life and Times of Alexander Pushkin* (1988); and two books for juveniles: *Great Gittin' Up Morning* (1972), a biography of Denmark Vesey, and *A Man Ain't Nothin' but a Man: The Adventures of John Henry* (1975), a book for young readers. His plays include *Ballad of the Winter Soldier*, with Lofton Mitchell, (prod. 1964); *Lower than the Angels* (1964); and *Cotillion*, with music by Smokey Robinson and Willie Hutch (1975). As founder of the Harlem Writers Guild (1952), Killens played a key role in encouraging other African-American artists.

Killers, The   (first published in *Scribner's Magazine*, March 1927; repr. in MEN WITHOUT WOMEN, 1927), a short story by ERNEST HEMINGWAY. The first of Hemingway's works to win wide popularity, this story is a study in violence, revealing the effect of urban toughness on the mind of a small-town youth. It had an enormous influence on the development of HARD-BOILED FICTION and writing about gangsters.

Kilmer, [Alfred] Joyce (1886–1918),   poet, teacher, editor, essayist. After teaching for a while in the Morristown (New Jersey) High School, Kilmer worked as an editor, book reviewer, and lecturer on poetry. A collection of his verse, *Summer of Love*, appeared in 1911 without attracting much attention. Then his poem "Trees" was published in the August 1913 issue of *Poetry* and won him national celebrity. It became the title piece of his second collection, *Trees and Other Poems* (1914). His last collection appeared in 1917, *Main Street and Other Poems*. Kilmer, an enthusiastic advocate of the cause of the Allies in World War I, enlisted in the army and was killed in France. He was awarded a posthumous Croix de Guerre. His wife, **Aline Kilmer** (1888–1941), wrote good verse. Among her collections are *Candles That Burn* (1919), *The Poor King's Daughter and Other Poems* (1925), and *Selected Poems* (1929).

Kilpatrick, Major General Judson. See ALLATOONA.

Kim, Richard (1932–   ),   novelist. Kim was born and educated through secondary school in Korea and served in the Korean armed services. In the United States he attended Middlebury College, Johns Hopkins, the University of Iowa, and Harvard. He married an American and became a naturalized citizen in 1964. His novels, set in Korea, deal with the struggle to preserve private morality against the force of war. *The Martyred* (1964), a tightly plotted first-person narration written in an elegant spare style, begins in 1950 with the North Korean occupation of Seoul. *The Innocent* (1969) focuses on the leader of a coup d'état, Colonel Min. *Lost Names: Scenes from a Korean Boyhood* (1971) is a collection of stories dealing with a Korean family living under the Japanese occupation. *Lost Souls*, another novel, was published in 1974.

Kimbrough, Emily (1899–1989),   editor, humorist, travel writer. Kimbrough, born in Indiana, was editor of *Fashions of the Hour*, fashion editor of *Ladies' Home Journal*, and its managing editor before she turned to writing. The first of her many humorous books, *Our Hearts Were Young and Gay* (1942), was written in collaboration with CORNELIA OTIS SKINNER. *We Followed Our Hearts to Hollywood* (1943) is an amusing memoir of her adventures in Hollywood with Miss Skinner after they had been asked to adapt their novel for the screen. Kimbrough attracted a large and faithful readership and became well known as a writer of travel books such as *A Right Good Crew* (1958) and *Water Water Everywhere* (1956). Among her other books are *The Innocents from Indiana* (1950) and *Forty Plus and Fancy Free* (1954). *Pleasure by the Busload* (1961) is another travel book.

Kincaid, Jamaica (1949–   ),   novelist, short-story writer. Born Elaine Potter Richardson on the Caribbean island of Antigua, she came to New York as a seventeen-year-old, earned her high school diploma in night school, and attended the New School for Social Research and Franconia College. In 1974, after seeing her first article in print, she changed her name to Jamaica Kincaid. The following year she was introduced to William Shawn, the editor of *The New Yorker,* and began writing for the magazine. Five years later she married the editor's son, Allen Shawn; they live with their children in Vermont. Most of her fiction is set in her native West Indies. *At the Bottom of the River* (1983) is a collection of short stories. *Annie John* (1985), her first novel, tells the story of a young woman's nervous breakdown and her treatment with traditional potions and rituals by her mother and grandmother. *Annie, Gwen, Lily, Pam, and Tulip* (1986) is a second story collection. *A Small Place*, a long essay on colonialism, was refused for publication by *The New Yorker* because of its angry tone. It appeared in book form in 1988, both in England and the U.S., followed by an essay deploring the dominance of English culture in Caribbean education, "On Seeing England for the First Time" (*Harper's*, 1991). *Lucy* (1990) is a novel made up of five stories about a young black woman coming to New York to work as a nanny in a white family. Kincaid has also published a series of articles about gardening and the colonization of plants in *The New Yorker. Autobiography of My Mother*, a controversial work defined by the author as fiction, appeared in 1996. *My Brother* (1997) is a memoir about a death from AIDS and its effect on a family.

King, Alexander (1900–1965),   painter, writer, editor. Born in Austria, King came to America in 1913 and worked as an editor of *Life* and *Vanity Fair* and illustrator of special editions of plays of Eugene O'Neill. He recounted many of his activities in his extravagant, anecdotal autobiography, *Mine Enemy Grows Older* (1958), a witty and occasionally tender account of his unconventional life. *May This House Be Safe from Tigers* (1960) is also autobiographical and written in much the same ironic and strangely sensitive vein as the earlier book. In *I Should Have Kissed Her More* (1961), King continued his autobiographical journey, stopping to remember the women he had known and loved. He translated and edited poems of the German poet Peter Altenberg in *Peter Altenberg's Evocations of Love* (1960).

King, [William Benjamin] Basil (1859–1928),   a novelist. King, born on Prince Edward Island, served as an Episcopal minister in Halifax before accepting a call to Cambridge. His first novels attracted no special attention, but *The Inner Shrine*, serialized in *Harper's* and published anonymously in 1909, became a best seller. King's sight began to fail, but he was able to continue writing. His great interest in his later writings was in spiritualism and life after death. Among his books are *The Street Called Straight* (1912), *The Way Home* (1913), *The Lifted Veil* (1919), *The Discovery of God* (1923), and *Adventures in Religion* (1929).

King, Benjamin [Franklin] (1857–1894),   writer of light verse. King, born in Michigan, is remembered chiefly for his poem IF I SHOULD DIE TONIGHT. His eight-line lament "The Pessimist" has also been widely quoted.

King, Clarence (1842–1901),   geologist, mining engineer, author. King, who was born in Rhode Island, was educated at Yale. He crossed the continent on horseback and began working as a mining engineer at the Comstock Lode and in California, then worked on a government survey and wrote a report, with collaborators, in seven volumes. It was he who first explored and defined the boundaries of the Yosemite Valley. For several years he was in charge of the U.S. Geological Survey as its first head and wrote technical works on geology. A lover of nature, King expressed himself most fully in *Mountaineering in the Sierra Nevada* (1872, rev. ed. 1902), which appeared first in the *Atlantic Monthly*. The scientific description is accompanied by narratives of exciting experiences and by impressions of frontier characters.

In 1871 King met HENRY ADAMS in Colorado, and he has been credited with determining the noticeable turn toward scientific thinking that occurred thereafter in Adams's work. King's biography was written (1958) by Thurman Wilkins.

King, Edward Smith (1848–1896),   journalist, novelist, poet. After an early career on the *Springfield* (Massachusetts) *Republican*, King came to public notice with *The Great South* (1875), a gathering of reports on a trip in the post–Civil War South. On this trip he met and became friends with George W. Cable, whom he championed. His novel *The Gentle Savage* (1883) places an Oklahoma Native American among sophisticates. *A Venetian Lover* (1887) is a blank verse narrative. His best book, *Joseph Zalmonah* (1893), explores slum conditions in New York City.

King, Grace Elizabeth (1851–1931),   short-story writer, novelist. King wrote local color treatments of Louisiana, especially New Orleans. Her books include *Monsieur Motte* (1888); *Tales of a Time and Place* (1892); *Balcony Stories* (1893); and *The Pleasant Ways of St. Medard* (1916), a novel set during the Reconstruction. Her autobiography, *Memories of a Southern Woman of Letters* (1932), was published a few months after her death.

King, Martin Luther, Jr. (1929–1968),   minister, civil rights leader, orator, memoirist. The son and grandson of Atlanta, Georgia ministers, King was educated at Morehouse College and Boston University. Influenced by the teachings of THOREAU and Mahatma Gandhi, King advocated nonviolent civil disobedience to counter racial segregation and bigotry. The boycott of the bus system in Montgomery, Alabama (1955), led to a Supreme Court ruling that segregated transportation was unconstitutional; King's account is called *Stride Toward Freedom* (1958). As founder and leader of the Southern Christian Leadership Conference, King led protests throughout the South, was frequently arrested and jailed, stabbed, and had his home bombed three times. His "Letter from Birmingham Jail" (1963) is a reply to those who criticized his tactics. At the March on Washington, August 28, 1963, in support of civil rights legislation, he delivered the memorable "I have a dream" speech. In the following year he was awarded the Nobel Peace Prize.

King took a position against the Vietnam War while continuing to fight for racial justice with such activities as the 1965 voter registration drive in Selma, Alabama. In April of 1968, King went to Memphis, Tennessee, to show support for striking sanitation workers; he was shot and killed there by James Earl Ray. January 15th, his birthday, is celebrated in most states as a national holiday. Stephen B. Oates's *Let The Trumpet Sound* (1982) is a biography.

King, Stephen (1947–   ),   novelist, short-story writer. King was born in Maine and continues to make his home there. In his fiction, he creates terrifying situations using apparently ordinary people and places. His first novel, *Carrie* (1974), deals with an outcast schoolgirl who uses telekinesis to exact revenge on her classmates. *The Shining* (1977) concerns a family stranded in a haunted hotel, and *Christine* (1983) centers on a car possessed by an evil spirit. Among others in King's long list of titles are *The Dead Zone* (1979), *Firestarter* (1980), *Cujo* (1981), *Pet Sematary* (1983), and *The Dark Half* (1989). *The Stand*, published originally in 1978, tells of death from a virus that has escaped from a biological laboratory; in 1990 it was reissued at twice its original length. Many of his novels have been made into films. He also writes under the pseudonym Richard Bachman (*Thinner*, 1985). His short fiction is collected in *Night Shift* (1978), *Different Seasons* (1982), and *Skeleton Crew* (1985). *Hearts in Atlantis* (1999) contains two novellas, two short stories and an epilogue. In 2000, while he was recovering from being hit by a van, King put the novella *Riding the Bullet* on the Internet. The resulting "hits" tied up the Net for several days. *On Writing: A Memoir of the Craft* (2000) describes his near-fatal accident and advises writers.

King, Stoddard (1889–1933),   newspaperman, columnist, writer of humorous verse. King was born in Wisconsin. His newspaper column, "Facetious Fragments," often interspersed with verses, appeared in the Spokane *Review* (1916–33). It was widely read and quoted. He collected some of his pieces in *What the Queen Said* (1926), *Listen to the Mocking Bird* (1928), and *The Raspberry Tree* (1930). While he was an undergraduate at Yale he won a prize with a poem entitled "There's a Long, Long Trail A-Winding," later set to music.

King, Thomas Starr (1824–1864),   clergyman, poet, editor. King, born in New York City, is chiefly remembered for his descriptive account *The White Hills: Their Legends, Landscape, and Poetry* (1860), one of the earliest regional analyses. His lectures were collected by Edwin P. Whipple under the title *Substance and Show* (1877).

King Cotton.   A term current in the controversies preceding the Civil War. It was meant to indicate not merely the dominance of cotton in the Southern economy, but also its potent sway over the rest of the nation and Europe as well. David Christy (1802–?) is believed to have originated the phrase in the title of his book *Cotton Is King* (1855). James Henry Hammond (1807–1864), senator from South Carolina, popularized it in a taunting speech before the Senate: "You dare not make war on cotton. . . . Cotton is king."

King David (1923),   a narrative poem by STEPHEN VINCENT BENÉT. In ballad style Benét tells again the startling story of sin and repentance related in 2 *Samuel* 11–12. The poem won the *Nation's* Poetry Prize for 1923 and was separately printed in the same year.

King Philip and **King Philip's War**.   The date of birth of King Philip, whose Indian name was Metacom or Metacomet, is unknown; he died in battle on August 12, 1676, after serving as sachem of the WAMPANOAG INDIANS. His father, Massasoit, had been friendly to the settlers, and Philip realized that their encroachments would in the end drive out his people. He therefore called for an alliance of all the tribes in New England. When the war (1675–76) broke out, the issue for a time looked doubtful, but there was dissension within the ranks and Philip was killed by a Native American.

Contemporary Puritan historians who wrote about King Philip include INCREASE MATHER in his *Brief History of the War with the Indians* (1676) and William Hubbard in his NARRATIVE OF THE TROUBLES WITH THE INDIANS (1677). The account of a survivor appears in *A Narrative of the Captivity and Restoration of*

Mrs. Mary Rowlandson (1677). Daniel Gookin, a missionary, wrote *Historical Account of the Doings and Sufferings of the Christian Indians in New England*, dated by him December 18, 1677. Benjamin Tompson, first American poet born on this continent, in his NEW ENGLAND'S CRISIS (1676), described in skillful heroic couplets some of the episodes and actors in King Philip's War and flayed the degeneracy and backsliding of the colonists as responsible for the sufferings God had inflicted on them.

When writers in the early 19th century began to exhibit the wrongs Native Americans had suffered at the hands of the settlers, King Philip became a popular theme. For a time a poem in six cantos called *Yamoyden: A Tale of the Wars of King Philip* (1820) was the most popular literary production of its day. It was the work of two friends, both under twenty, JAMES W. EASTBURN and ROBERT C. SANDS; the poem shows Philip as a wise, bold hero who "fought because he would not yield his birthright." Although his piece was not generally known until the appearance of his *Sketch-Book* (1819), WASHINGTON IRVING earlier had written *Philip of Pokanoket* (1814), in which Philip appears in heroic proportions. James Fenimore Cooper made use of the story in THE WEPT OF WISH-TON-WISH (1829). In a plot that involves the kidnapping of a young white girl, the emphasis is laid on Philip's ally Conanchet, chief of the Narragansetts.

King Philip was effectively exalted in a prize play by John Augustus Stone called METAMORA, OR, THE LAST OF THE WAMPANOAGS (produced 1829). Edwin Forrest played the role for many years. The grandiloquence of this and other plays about Indians irritated James Rees into writing a rather weak burlesque, *Metamora, or the Last of the Pollywoags* (1847). King Philip found a natural defender in WILLIAM APES, a Pequod Indian who became a Methodist minister in 1829. In 1836 Apes delivered a stirring address, printed the same year, on the Indian monarch. He included in his address an oration such as Philip might have delivered in council to his chiefs and warriors.

Two early novels that dealt principally with King Philip's War were G. H. Hollister's *Mount Hope* (1851) and Daniel P. Thompson's *The Doomed Chief* (1860). William G. Schofield's *Ashes in the Wilderness* (1942), concerned with the same war, is based on a colonial diary. Esther Forbes's *Paradise* (1937) tells the story of a family nearly destroyed in the war with the Indians. See ALGONQUIN INDIANS.

Kingsblood Royal (1947), a novel by SINCLAIR LEWIS. Lewis sought in this controversial novel to show the absurdity of the taboo against mixed Caucasian and African-American parentage by depicting a man who suddenly discovers that a supposed Indian ancestor was really a black man. Lewis is savagely satiric in his depiction of types in an average American community, viewing the advocates of race prejudice as not only wicked but appallingly dull.

King's Henchman, The (1927), an opera by Deems Taylor with libretto by EDNA ST. VINCENT MILLAY. The action takes place in the 10th century, with an Anglo-Saxon king and his foster brother as the leading characters. They woo the same woman, unworthy of both, and the play ends in the tragic death of the foster brother. The opera was effective as drama, and the music won warm praise.

Kingsley, Sidney (1906–1995), actor, playwright. Kingsley, born in New York City, played small parts in stock companies and on Broadway and then saw his play *Crisis* produced on Broadway. With its title changed to MEN IN WHITE (1933), the play won a Pulitzer Prize and has been frequently revived both here and abroad. Even more successful was DEAD END (1935), which was an equal hit as a movie (1937). The play, like most of Kingsley's productions, had a social purpose, and to it was ascribed some of the credit for important laws aimed at slum clearance. Later Kingsley wrote *Ten Million Ghosts* (1936); *The World We Make* (1939); *The Outward Room* (1939); *The Patriots* (with his wife, Madge Evans Kingsley, 1942); *Detective Story* (1949; movie version, 1951); *Darkness at Noon* (1951, an adaptation of a novel by ARTHUR KOESTLER); *Lunatics and Lovers* (1954), a farce; and *Night Life* (1962).

Kingsolver, Barbara (1955–), novelist, short-story writer, poet, essayist. Born in Annapolis, Maryland, Kingsolver was educated at DePauw and the University of Arizona. Her first novel, *The Bean Trees* (1988), centers on Taylor Greer, a young woman from Kentucky who finds herself the caretaker of a Cherokee child in Tucson. The women she meets there, though abandoned or widowed, take her and her foster daughter, Turtle, into their compassionate circle. *Homeland* (1989) is a collection of twelve stories about women struggling for homes and security. *Holding the Line: Women in the Great Arizona Mine Strike of 1983* (1989) is a nonfiction book on the Phelps Dodge Copper Company strike. *Animal Dreams* (1990) traces Codi Noline's return to her rural Arizona roots, only to find that grief, bigotry and pollution have reached there, too. *Pigs in Heaven* (1993) is a sequel to Kingsolver's first novel and follows Taylor and Turtle as their pairing is threatened by a Cherokee lawyer's custody suit. *Another America/Otra America* (1992) pairs poems in English with Spanish translations. *High Tide in Tucson* (1995) is an essay collection. *The Poisonwood Bible* (1998), set in the Belgian Congo in 1959, follows the Price family—missionary Nathan, his wife and four daughters—as they cope with hostility, political turmoil, climate, and their own flaws. The title is a reference to the father's mispronunciation of a word in the local dialect, turning an adjective meaning precious into the name of a tree that causes skin irritation. The confusion is emblematic of how his personality defeats his religious goals. The lives of the five women are revealed in alternating chapters, covering the thirty years after they leave Africa. *Prodigal Summer* (2000) combines ecological concerns with a series of conflicts between humans, enforcing the notion that humankind constitutes a small part of the natural scene.

Kingston, Maxine Hong (1940–), memoirist, novelist. Born in California to parents from the Pearl River area of China who spoke little English, Kingston was educated at the University of California, Berkeley. Torn between the traditional attitudes of her family and the values of the outside world, Kingston explored the tension in two autobiographical fictions. *The Woman Warrior: Memoirs of a Girlhood Among Ghosts* (1976) weaves a tapestry from the "talk story" utilized by women in her family and her own experience. She notes an ironic disjuncture between the stated traditional message and the underlying meaning of the stories of militant women or disgraced girls. *China Men* (1980) is a similar treatment of the experience of male immigrants, including the hardships encountered in building the western railroad. In the picaresque *Tripmaster Monkey* (1989), Kingston moves to pure fiction. The protagonist is a male Berkeley graduate of Chinese heritage with the punning name Wittman Ah Sing who considers himself a reincarnation of the mythical Monkey King, said to have brought the Buddhist scriptures from India. His ambition is to write a play that will encompass the history of the world and unite all the divergent strains of culture he observes around him. *Hawai'i One Summer* (1987) is an essay collection. Paul Skenazy and Tera Martin edited *Conversations with Maxine Hong Kingston* (1998).

Kinnell, Galway (1927–   ),   poet. Born in Providence, Rhode Island, and raised in Pawtucket, Galway Kinnell may be the most peripatetic of American poets. He was educated at Princeton, where he became a friend of the poet W. S. MERWIN, and at the University of Rochester. He began his teaching career at the University of Chicago. Since then he has worked with the Congress of Racial Equality in Louisiana in the civil rights movement, given many readings of his work, and taught at numerous schools, including the University of Grenoble, the University of Teheran, the University of California at Irvine, and, most recently, New York University. He has been the recipient of many awards and fellowships, including a National Institute of Arts and Letters award, two Guggenheim fellowships, a Rockefeller grant, and a National Endowment for the Arts grant.

Kinnell's is a poetry of quest as well as a poetry of flight. Early work is contained in *First Poems: 1946–1954*, a limited edition published in 1970, and *The Avenue Bearing the Initial of Christ into the New World* (1974), in each of which are found the themes of selfhood, mortality, and the wilderness within and without that are the central concerns of his mature work. His first published book, *What a Kingdom It Was* (1960), announces Kinnell's principal strategies, in particular a proclivity for investing the material world with the willed shape and sense of human consciousness. Yet the self tends to remain lonely among its creations, and in *Flower Herding on Mount Monadnock* (1964) one finds solitary speakers among the objects of the wilderness. Aware of his separateness, the speaker engages in a poetry of naming through which the self discovers its essence in contrast to the emptiness about him.

Often grotesque and bleak, Kinnell's poetry is honest and large in conception, confronting the necessity of death which, in Keatsian fashion, the poet understands as the making of identity. In *Body Rags* (1968) the Eskimo hunter in "The Bear" crawls into the eviscerated but still warm carcass of a bear he has tracked and there dreams of becoming the bear. In *The Book of Nightmares* (1971), a poem of ten linked sections that crosses the psychic terrain from the birth of his daughter Maud to the birth of his son Fergus, Kinnell is partially successful but wholly courageous in his effort to sustain the

dream that can transcend death. The effort continues in *Mortal Acts, Mortal Words* (1980). Though perhaps his least coherent collection, it contains some of Kinnell's most personal and exuberant poems, such as "After Making Love We Hear Footsteps," "Saint Francis and the Sow," and "Blackberry Eating." In *The Past* (1985), the personal tone persists while the reader senses a reassertion of Kinnell's original interests in versification and stanza form. Other collections include *When One Has Lived a Long Time Alone* (1990) and *Imperfect Thirst* (1994).

Kinnell has been active as a translator, bringing to English readers René Hardy's novel *Bitter Victory* (1956), a new translation of the poetry of François Villon (1965), Yves Bonnefoy's *On the Motion and Immobility of Douve* (1968), and Yvan Goll's *Lackawanna Elegy* (1970). His stay in Iran inspired his one work of fiction, the short novel *Black Light* (1966). Selections from his many interviews are collected in *Walking Down the Stairs* (1978).

MARK A. R. FACKNITZ

Kino, Eusebio Francisco (1644–1711),   Jesuit missionary, explorer, mapmaker. Kino, born in Italy, came to Mexico in 1681, did missionary work in Lower California, northern Mexico, and southern Arizona, and was instrumental in the return of the Jesuits to the California peninsula in 1697. For nearly twenty-five years he worked as missionary, cattle raiser, and map maker, opened a road around the head of the Gulf to save the difficult passage by water, determined that California was not an island but a peninsula, and made a map that was widely circulated in Europe. He established a score of towns in California, in the river valleys of San Miguel, Magdalena, Sonóita, and Santa Cruz. One of them was Loreto, named after a shrine in central Italy. Kino discovered and described the Casa Grande ruins in Arizona and died at Magdalena. His autobiography, *Favores Celestiales*, was found, edited and published by Herbert E. Bolton as *Kino's Historical Memoir of Pimería Alta* (2 v. 1919).

Kinsella, W[illiam] P[atrick] (1932–   ),   novelist, short-story writer. Born in Edmonton, Alberta, Kinsella was educated at the University of Victoria and the University of Iowa (1978). His stories, focused on the eighteen-year-old Cree Indian Silas Ermineskin, are included in the collections *Dance Me Outside* (1977), *Scars* (1978), *Born Indian* (1981), *The Mocassin Telegraph* (1983), *The Alligator Report* (1985) and *Red Wolf, Red Wolf* (1987). A baseball fan, Kinsella turned the story "Shoeless Jackson Comes to Iowa" into the novel *Shoeless Joe* (1982) and collaborated on the screenplay for the movie version, *Field of Dreams* (1989). The protagonist, Ray Kinsella, obeys a voice that tells him to build a baseball diamond in his corn field. As the field is built, Shoeless Joe Jackson and the other members of the disgraced 1919 Chicago White Sox team appear and play ball, observed by the Kinsella family and J. D. SALINGER, who has been coerced into coming out of isolation. His other fiction about the sport includes *The Iowa Baseball Confederacy* (1986), *The Further Adventures of Slugger McBatt* (1988), *Box Socials* (1991) and *If Wishes Were Horses* (1996). *The Winter Helen Dropped By* (1995) is a non-sport novel.

Kinsey, Alfred Charles (1894–1956),   taxonomist, biological researcher. A graduate of Bowdoin College and Harvard University, Kinsey taught biology at Harvard, then at Indiana University, becoming a professor there in 1929. In 1938 he took charge of the study on human sexual behavior sponsored by the Institute for Sex Research at Indiana University and the National Research Council. He published the results of the study in *Sexual Behavior in the Human Male* (with W. B. Pomeroy and C. E. Martin, 1948) and *Sexual Behavior in the Human Female* (with Pomeroy, Martin and P. H. Gebhard, 1953).

Kirby, William (1817–1906),   poet, newspaper editor, novelist. Kirby came to Canada from England in 1832 and settled in Niagara seven years later, where he edited the Niagara *Mail* for the next twenty-five years. In 1871 he was appointed customs collector. His first major publication was *The U.E., a Tale of Upper Canada* (1859), an epic poem. *Canadian Idylls* (1894) and *Annals of Niagara* (1894) are nature poems. Kirby is best known for his novel THE GOLDEN DOG (1877, rev. ed. 1896).

Kirkland, Caroline [Matilda Stansbury] ["Mrs. Mary Clavers"] (1801–1864),   a novelist, author of travel books, essayist, editor. Born in New York City, Kirkland and her professor husband briefly settled in a frontier village in Michigan. She described life on the frontier in *A New Home— Who'll Follow? or, Glimpses of Western Life* (1839; new ed. edited by John Nerber, 1953); *Forest Life* (1842); and *Western Clearings* (1845).

Kirkland, Joseph (1830–1894),   editor, novelist. Kirkland, born in Geneva, New York, and a son of CAROLINE KIRKLAND, is remembered for one novel, ZURY: THE MEANEST MAN IN SPRING COUNTY (1887). In it and in a sequel, *The McVeys* (1888), he continued his mother's attempt to portray the West realistically, particularly the life of farmers there. *The Captain of Company K* (1891) is a Civil War story. Kirkland influenced others, especially HAMLIN GARLAND. He has been praised for the accuracy of his representations of western speech.

Kiss Me Kate (1948, publ. 1953),   a play within a play by BELLA and SAMUEL SPEWACK, with music by COLE PORTER, based on Shakespeare's *Taming of the Shrew*.

Kiss the Boys Good-Bye (1938),   a play by CLAIRE BOOTHE LUCE. It is a satirical account of a movie producer's search for someone to play Scarlett O'Hara in his version of *Gone with the Wind*. The play was made into a movie.

Kit Carson's Ride (publ. in *Poems of the Sierras*, 1871), a stirring poem by JOAQUIN MILLER. In this poem, probably the best that Miller wrote, the scout rescues his Native American bride from pursuing tribesmen and from a prairie fire—with the help of his good steed, 'Pache. The poem is obviously in the meter and manner of Robert Browning's *How They Brought the Good News from Ghent to Aix* (1846).

Kittredge, George Lyman (1860–1941),   teacher, scholar. Kittredge was graduated from Harvard in 1882 and taught there from 1888 until 1936. A popular, dramatic lecturer, Kittredge was known for his fiery readings of Shakespeare and his stinging rebukes of delinquent students.

In his scholarly techniques and the fields he chose, Kittredge largely followed FRANCIS J. CHILD, his predecessor at Harvard. Among his important writings are *The Language of Chaucer's "Troilus"* (1894); *Words and Their Ways in English Speech* (with J. B. Greenough, 1901); *English and Scottish Popular Ballads* (with H. C. Sargent, 1904); *The Old Farmer and His Almanack* (1904); *English Witchcraft and James I* (1912); *Chaucer and His Poetry* (1915); *A Study of Gawain and the Green Knight* (1916); *Shakespeare* (1916); *Sir Thomas Malory* (1925); *Witchcraft in Old and New England* (1929); and an edition of *The Complete Works of Shakespeare* (1936).

Kitty Foyle (1939),   a novel by CHRISTOPHER MORLEY. It chronicles a love affair between a young man of one of Philadelphia's Main Line families and an Irish office girl.

Kizer, Carolyn (1925–   ),   poet, critic. Kizer was born in Spokane and educated at Sarah Lawrence. She has studied in China, worked for the State Department in Pakistan, and was the first director for literature of the National Endowment for the Arts. A poet who explores the possibilities of form and utilizes humor, she was among the first to articulate feminist attitudes. *The Ungrateful Garden* (1961) was her first collection. Other titles include *Knock Upon Silence* (1965); *Midnight Was My Cry* (1971); *Mermaids in the Basement: Poems for Women* (1984); later gatherings include *Yin: New Poems* (1984), *The Nearness of You: Poems for Men* (1986), *Harping On: Poems 1985–1995* (1996); and *Cool, Calm & Collected: Poems 1960–2000* (2000). Critical essays are gathered in *Proses: Essays on Poems and Poets* (1993). She was a founder and editor of *Poetry Northwest* (1959–1965).

Klein, A[braham] M[oses] (1909–1972),   poet. Klein was brought to Montreal from the Ukraine as a baby. He was given a solid orthodox Hebrew education, but eschewed rabbinical studies and entered McGill University, where he began to write poetry expressing his Zionist sympathies. Though he got a law degree at the University of Montreal, he preferred other work as an editor, in public relations, or teaching. His first collection, *Hath Not a Jew* (1940), explored his relationship to his heritage. *Poems* and *Hitleriad*, a satire, followed in 1944. In his finest collection, *The Rocking Chair* (1948), he expressed sympathy for persecuted minorities, including Native Americans and French Canadians. "Portrait of the Poet as Landscape," an optimistic vision of the self-transformation of a writer, is the final poem of this book. The Canadian Jewish Congress sent him on a fact-finding trip to the refugee camps of Europe and North Africa and to Israel after World War II; the novel *The Second Scroll* (1951) was inspired by what he observed and is influenced in organization by the methods of James Joyce, whom Klein admired and studied. At this time he suffered severe mental illness and was suicidal; he ceased to write completely. Posthumous publications include *The Collected Poems of A. M. Klein* (1974); *Beyond Sambation: Selected Essays and Editorials 1928–1955* (1982) and *A. M. Klein: Short Stories* (1983).

Klein, Charles (1867–1915),   actor, playwright. Klein came to the United States from England when he was fifteen, played juvenile roles on the stage, and won his first popular success with *Heartsease* (1897). His best plays were written for production by DAVID BELASCO and performance by the noted actor David Warfield, among them *The Auctioneer* (1901) and *The Music Master* (1904). Other plays of popular appeal written by Klein were *The Lion and the Mouse* (1905), *The Third Degree* (1908), and *The Gamblers* (1910).

Klein, Joe (1946–   ),   journalist, novelist. Born in New York and educated at the University of Pennsylvania, Klein was a little-known Washington reporter and news-magazine editor until it was revealed that the political muck-raking novel *Primary Colors* (1996), which was published anonymously and which he had repeatedly denied writing, was indeed his work. The tale of southern governor Jack Stanton's quest for the presidency was a thinly disguised attack on President Bill Clinton, published as the president was seeking a second term in office. Numerous people inside the president's political circle were suggested as the author, along with reporters, such as Klein, who had covered the 1992 campaign. After both the *New York* magazine's computer analysis of the style and the *Washington Post*'s analysis of handwritten corrections to the novel manuscript named Klein as the likely writer, he admitted authorship. *The Running Mate*, in which Senator Charlie Martin attempts to become Stanton's vice presidential candidate, appeared in 2000.

Klondike gold rush.   In 1896 George Washington Carmack made a bonanza strike of gold in the Klondike territory in northwest Canada. The resulting gold rush reached its climax in 1898 and continued during the following years. By 1900 about $22,000,000 worth of gold had been taken out of the frozen ground. Dawson became a boom city, full of queer and sometimes sinful characters, but not as sinful as ROBERT W. SERVICE made them out; he did not get to the Klondike until 1906. Even more fantastic were the newspaper reports sent home by JOAQUIN MILLER.

Numerous authors found the gold rush a literary bonanza. Probably the most famous Klondike story is Jack London's THE CALL OF THE WILD (1903); WHITE FANG (1906) and *Smoke Bellew* (1912) used the same background. Service's *Songs of a Sourdough* (1907, later called *The Spell of the Yukon*, 1908), his *Ballads of a Cheechako* (1907), and his novel *Trail of '98* (1912) recall the Klondike scene. The most frequently recited of his Yukon poems are THE SHOOTING OF DAN MCGREW and "The Law of the Yukon."

Kluckhohn, Clyde K[ay] M[aben] (1905–1960), anthropologist, archaeologist, teacher, writer. Kluckhohn, born in Iowa, was educated at Harvard and began teaching there in 1935. Through the years he was active in various government agencies, especially during World War II. His interest centered to a large extent on Native Americans. Six years spent among the Navahos resulted in numerous papers and books. Among his books are *To the Foot of the Rainbow* (1927); *Beyond the Rainbow* (1933); *The Navaho* (1946); *The Children of the People* (1946, with Dorothea Leighton); *Personality in Nature, Society and Culture* (1948, rev. ed. 1953, with H.A. Murray); *Mirror for Man* (1949); and *Navaho Means People* (1951, with Leonard McCombe and E.Z. Vogt).

Knapp, Samuel Lorenzo (1783–1838),   lawyer, editor, miscellaneous writer. Knapp, born in Massachusetts, wrote biographies, naval histories, and a two-volume work on the Hudson River (1835–1836). He also wrote *Extracts from a Journal of Travels in North America* (1818) under the pen name Ali Bey, and *The Bachelor and Other Tales, Founded on American Incident and Character* (1836). Such of his reputation as survives is based on the fact that he was a pioneer historian of American literature in his *Lectures on American Literature, With Remarks on Some Passages of American History* (1829).

Knickerbocker, Diedrich.   See HISTORY OF NEW YORK, by DIEDRICH KNICKERBOCKER.

Knickerbocker, Holiday (1938),   a musical comedy with text by MAXWELL ANDERSON and music by Kurt Weill. The play was suggested to Anderson by Washington Irving's *Knickerbocker's History of New York* (1809). The lines and lyrics show Anderson at his best, and Weill's "September Song" is still widely sung.

Knickerbocker Magazine.   The Old Knick, founded in 1832, was New York's first monthly of wide national prestige. It almost perished in its first 16 months because of inept management despite editorial excellence under CHARLES FENNON HOFFMAN and TIMOTHY FLINT. Not until May 1834, when LEWIS GAYLORD CLARK took over as editor and part owner, did it begin to show the brilliance that later characterized it. Clark's own chatty and humorous "Editor's Table" was for many years an important part of the magazine, and he attracted a distinguished list of contributors. Among them were such New Yorkers as WASHINGTON IRVING (a contributing editor 1839–1841), Cooper, Bryant, James K. Paulding, N.P. Willis, R.H. Stoddard, and G.W. Curtis, as well as Philadelphians Robert Montgomery Bird, Charles Godfrey Leland, Mathew Carey, and Bayard Taylor. New England was represented most prominently by Longfellow, Hawthorne, Whittier, and Holmes. Clark came to pay much attention to the West, enlisting such writers as James Hall, Caroline Kirkland, H.R. Schoolcraft, and Francis Parkman. Most important of the western *matériel*, as Clark loved to call it, was Parkman's *Oregon Trail* (1847), and most prominent among the magazine's associate editors was Clark's brother, Willis Gaylord Clark. The *Knickerbocker*, suffering from too many changes of ownership, deteriorated toward 1850, and after that date competition from *Harper's* proved too much for it. It barely survived the Civil War, perishing in 1865.

Knickerbocker School.   A name given to a loosely associated group of writers living and working in New York City or nearby during the first half of the 19th century. Their chief point of relationship was not unity in doctrine or practice but rather the fact that they were all helping to make New York an important literary center. Among the members of the group were Washington Irving, J.K. Paulding, James Fenimore Cooper, William Cullen Bryant, J.R. Drake, Fitz-Greene Halleck, John Howard Payne, Samuel Woodworth, Epes Sargent, Lydia M. Child, George P. Morris, G.C. Verplanck, Robert C. Sands, William Cox, N.P. Willis, Lewis G. and Willis G. Clark,

C. F. Hoffman, Clement Moore, and Bayard Taylor. Kendall B. Taft's exhaustive study, *Minor Knickerbockers* (1947), shows that the group indulged in self-criticism as well as in creative activity and sought to foster a national literature.

Knight, Eric ["Richard Hallas"] (1897–1943), a writer, newspaperman, and cartoonist. Knight came to the United States from England in 1912 and remained in this country during the rest of his life, except for service in the Canadian Army during World War I and the American Army during World War II and an occasional visit to Yorkshire. His best-known tales are laid in Yorkshire, particularly *The Flying Yorkshireman* (collected with other novellas, 1936). Others of his books include *Invitation to Life* (1934); *The Happy Land* (1940); *Lassie Come Home* (a juvenile, 1940); *This Above All* (1941); and *Sam Small Flies Again* (short stories, 1942).

Knight, Henry Cogswell ["Arthur Singleton, Esq."] (1789–1835), clergyman, writer, lecturer. Born in Massachusetts, Knight was a clever versifier. He published his first collection, *The Cypriad* (1809), in his sophomore year at Harvard; this was later reworked as *The Trophies of Love*. He also issued *The Broken Harp* (1815) and *Poems* (2 v. 1821). After a tour of the country he wrote a series of amusing *Letters from the South and West* (1824) under the pen name Arthur Singleton, Esq. In 1831 appeared some of his *Lectures and Sermons*.

Knight, Sarah Kemble (1666–1727), diarist, businesswoman, conductor of a dame's or writing school, humorist. Born in Boston, Knight was the daughter of a merchant who was one of Oliver Cromwell's agents in America. Her husband died in London in 1706(?), but she took over many of his and her father's responsibilities, was a shrewd business adviser, and signed many public documents. One tradition is that Benjamin Franklin attended her school. In 1704 Knight made a trip to New York to expedite settlement of a wealthy relative's estate. She kept a diary of her journey on horseback—in those days a difficult if not dangerous undertaking—which was published in 1825, with Theodore Dwight as editor. The *Journal of Madame Knight* has always been regarded as one of the most vivid and authoritative pictures of the colonial period.

Knight's Gambit (1939), a book of related stories by WILLIAM FAULKNER. Dealing with the inhabitants of YOKNAPATAWPHA COUNTY, *Knight's Gambit* is a collection of detective stories in which GAVIN STEVENS, the county attorney, ferrets out culprits and saves the innocent. The book is ingenious and skillfully narrated; perhaps the best story is "Monk," which deals with an idiot who is imprisoned for a murder he did not commit and who finally is incited to kill the warden who has befriended him.

Knister, Raymond (1899–1932), novelist, poet. Knister was born and lived most of his brief life in Ontario. *White Narcissus* (1929), his only novel to be published during his lifetime, portrays the effects of obsession. *My Star Predominates* is a fictional version of the last years of John Keats. It was published in 1934, after Knister's death by drowning. Other posthumous publications include *Collected Poems* (1949), *Selected Stories of Raymond Knister* (1972), *Raymond*

Knister: Poems, Stories and Essays (1975), and *The First Day of Spring: Stories and Other Prose* (1976).

Knopf, Alfred A. (1892–1984), publisher. Knopf, born in New York City, was educated at Columbia University and founded a publishing firm in 1915 with Blanche Wolf, whom he married a year later. He became president of Alfred A. Knopf, Inc., in 1918, and chairman of the board in 1957, when his wife became president. In 1960 Random House, Inc., acquired the stock of the company, but the firm continued as an independent imprint. His son, Alfred, Jr., founded Atheneum Publishers in 1959 with Simon Michael Bessie and Hiram Haydn.

Knowles, John (1926–), novelist. Born in West Virginia and educated at Yale, Knowles is best known for *A Separate Peace* (1960), the story of friendship and treachery at a New England boys' school during World War II. *Peace Breaks Out* (1981) is a sequel. His other titles are *Morning in Antibes* (1962), *Indian Summer* (1966), *The Paragon* (1971), *Spreading Fires* (1974), *A Vein of Riches* (1979), the story of a West Virginia family whose fortune is based on coal, *A Stolen Past* (1983) and *The Private Life of Axie Reed* (1986). *Phineas* (1968) is a story collection, and *Double Vision* (1964) is a travel book. *Backcasts: Memories and Recollections of Seventy Years as a Sportsman* appeared in 1993.

Know-Nothing party. In U.S. history, a popular name for the American Party, which reached its greatest influence in 1854–55. Its program called for the exclusion of Catholics and foreigners from public office and for other nativist measures. It was originally a secret society, whose members answered questions with "I don't know." The party split over the slavery issue and faded after the election of 1856.

Knox, Samuel (1756–1832), minister and educator. After graduation from the University of Glasgow, Knox came to America in 1795. His ideas on education, expressed in *Essay on the Best System of Liberal Education, Adapted to the Genius of the Government of the United States* (1799), influenced Jefferson's ideas in founding the University of Virginia. Knox advocated a college for every state and a national university. He also argued for promotion on merit and the establishment of a university press.

Knox, Thomas W[allace] (1835–1896), newspaperman, traveler, author of books for boys. Born in New Hampshire and believed to have been a descendant of John Knox, Thomas Knox followed various occupations before turning to newspaper work. Then he made travel his chief occupation. The first of his journeys was across Siberia, and later he visited many other parts of the earth. He ordinarily turned out two books a year, including a popular series, "The Boy Travelers" and "The Young Nimrod" series. As a Civil War correspondent he collected his dispatches in *Camp-Fire and Cotton-Field* (1865). He wrote biographies of Robert Fulton (1886), Henry Ward Beecher (1887), and other noted men; and a manual entitled *How to Travel* (1881).

Kober, Arthur (1900–1975), press agent, producer, columnist, writer, playwright. Kober, born in Poland, wrote dialect stories set in the Bronx or Hollywood, and from these emerged several books: *Thunder Over the Bronx* (1935), HAV-ING WONDERFUL TIME (1937), *Pardon Me for Pointing* (1939), *My Dear Bella* (1941), *That Man Is Here Again* (1946), and *Oooh, What You Said!* (1956). A comedy based on *Having Wonderful Time* was produced in 1937. In addition, Kober wrote a successful musical, *Wish You Were Here* (1952), with Joshua Logan and Harold Rome. *Mighty Man Is He*, another play, written in collaboration with George Oppenheimer, was produced in 1960.

Koch, Kenneth (1925–   ),   poet, playwright, novel-ist. Born in Cincinnaati, Koch was educated at Harvard and Columbia. He has taught for many years at Columbia, but has never embraced intellectualism in poetry and has been associ-ated with the anti-academic NEW YORK SCHOOL POETS, including JOHN ASHBERY and FRANK O'HARA. Drawing on surrealism, these poets attempt to translate the unconscious into poetry by using dreamlike juxtapositions and emphasizing the present, ordinary, but often bizarre, moment. Koch's poems unify per-sonal free association around a central image or word pattern and often depend on parody as a way of expressing social con-sciousness. In addition to shorter poems, he has written two Byronic epics in ottava rima—*Ko, or A Season on Earth* (1959) and *The Duplications* (1977)—and a prose-poem exploration of life in New York City in the 1950s, *The Burning Mystery of Anna in 1951* (1979). In addition to poetry, Koch has written numerous plays and a novel, *The Red Robins* (1980), which he has also dramatized. Koch demonstrates his commitment to enlarging the audience for poetry in America by becoming involved with writing projects in elementary schools and in nursing homes. He has written about his experiences with these groups in *Wishes, Lies and Dreams: Teaching Children to Write Poetry* (1970) and *I Never Told Anybody: Teaching Poetry Writing in a Nursing Home* (1977). His *Selected Poems, 1950–1988* appeared in 1994 and his collection *Straits* appeared in 1998. Koch won the Bollingen Prize in 1995, the Rebecca Johnson Bobbitt National Prize for Poetry in 1996; the same year, he was inducted into the American Academy of Arts and Letters. *New Addresses*, a collection of fifty poems, was published in 2000.

SHARON L. DEAN

Kogawa, Joy (1935–   ),   novelist, poet. Born in Vancouver, Kogawa and her family were, like others of Japan-ese ancestry, forcibly moved into the interior of British Columbia during World War II, an experience Kogawa described in *Obasan* (1981). *Itsuka* (1992) follows one of the characters in her first novel into postwar life. *The Rain Ascends* (1995) treats a young woman's struggle in dealing with secrets in her father's life. Her first volume of poems, *The Splintered Moon* (1968), offers brief poems with short lines and spare direct phrases. Her other verse collections are *A Choice of Dreams* (1974), *Jericho Road* (1978), and *Woman in the Woods* (1985). *Naomi's Road* (1986) is a children's book.

Kolodny, Annette (1941–   ),   radical feminist writer. Among Kolodny's concerns are the pollution of land, mind, and body, by a generation which in her view has forgot-ten its own spirit of the 1960s. Her books include *The Lay of the Land: Metaphor as Experience and History in American Life and Letters* (1975); *Westering Women: Fantasies of the American Frontiers, 1630–1860* (1983); *Dancing Through the Minefield: Theory, Method, and Politics in Feminist Literary Criticism* (1983); and *The Hand Before Her: Fantasy and Experience of the American Frontier 1630–1860* (1984).

Komroff, Manuel (1890–1974),   writer, editor, war correspondent. Born in New York City and notable chiefly as a historical novelist, Komroff wrote novels of various kinds, many short stories, the manual *How to Write a Novel* (1950), and at least one play, *Don Quixote and Sancho* (1942). His nov-els are *Juggler's Kiss* (1927), *Coronet* (1930), *Two Thieves* (1931), *Waterloo* (1936), *The March of the Hundred* (1939), *The Magic Bow* (1940), *Feast of the Jesters* (1947), *Echo of Evil* (1948), *Jade Star* (1951), *The Story of Jesus* (1955), and *Mozart* (1956, a juvenile). Two story collections are *The Grace of Lambs* (1925) and *All in One Day* (1932). His autobiography is *Big City, Little Boy* (1953).

Köningsmarke, the Long Finne: A Story of the New World (1823),   by JAMES KIRKE PAULDING. This story relates the adventures of a Finnish immigrant to the colony of New Sweden on the Delaware. He is a noble fellow in appearance, and the daughter of the governor falls in love with him. Both are kidnapped by the Indians, and other obstacles arise, but all is well in the end.

Koontz, R[ay] Dean (1945–   ),   novelist, short-story writer. Born in Everett, Pennsylvania, Koontz began writ-ing as a child to escape his troubled and impoverished family life. A prolific writer, he has published over a hundred titles under his own name and pseudonyms including Brian Coffey, Deanna Dwyer, K. R. Dwyer, Leigh Nichols and Owen West. Though he published his first books while in college at Ship-pensburg State, Koontz dates the beginning of his career as a serious writer from the publication of *Chase* (1973), a sus-pense novel dealing with the effects of the Vietnam War on a veteran. In *Whispers* (1980), a screenwriter is brutally attacked by an obsessive stalker. In the best selling *Watchers* (1986), genetically altered life forms are being created in a secret gov-ernment lab. *Strangers* (1986) follows a group of people who have spent a weekend in the same Nevada motel and afterward experience nightmares and fears that drive them to uncover the mystery. *Dark Rivers of the Heart* (1994) pits an ex-policeman against a fascistic governmental agency. *Strange Highways* (1995) is a collection of stories and novellas. *Inten-sity*, another gruesome story of obsession, appeared in 1995. Chris Snow, whose light-sensitive genetic affliction forces him to work in the dark, is the hero of *Seize the Night* and *Fear Nothing*, both published in 1998. In *False Memory* (2000), four characters develop mysterious forms of mental illness. Despite his emphasis on violence, Koontz insists he is optimistic about the human condition and believes that the role of fiction is to "reinforce our noble traits."

Kopit, Arthur L[ee] (1937–   ),   playwright. Kopit was born in New York and brought up on Long Island. His plays are often characterized by dark humor, the juxtaposition of realistic and antirealistic elements, and some of the longest titles in theatrical history. His relationship to the so-called theater of the absurd is based more on these stylistic similarities than on a shared vision. While still an undergraduate at Harvard, he wrote nine plays, including *On the Runway of Your Life You Never Know What's Coming Off Next* (1957). He created a minor sensation with the production of *Oh Dad, Poor Dad, Mamma's Hung You in the Closet and I'm Feelin' So Sad* (1960), about an overprotective mother, Madame Rosepettle, who travels with her henpecked retarded son, a pet piranha, man-eating Venus-flytraps, and her dead husband who is carried in a coffin. After several unsuccessful plays and a time of relative obscurity, Kopit wrote *Indians* (1968), which established his reputation as a serious and inventive playwright. In *Wings* (1978) he suspended traditional narrative dramatic techniques to depict the fragmented perceptions of a stroke victim. Other plays include *End of the World* (1984), *Road to Nirvana* (1991), and *Three Plays* (1997).

Korean Conflict.   The treaties that followed World War II set up the organization of the United Nations as an instrument to prevent future aggression by nations. This instrument was tested and found only partially effective when North Korean troops invaded South Korea on June 25, 1950, in an attempt to overthrow the government there. The United Nations took action under U.S. leadership, and forces—for the most part American—were sent to Korea to stop the invasion from the north. In October of that year Chinese troops from Manchuria crossed the Yalu River to aid the North Koreans, and on November 26–27 four Red Chinese armies attacked and repulsed UN troops along their farthest line of advance in North Korea.

Major offensives did much to drive the North Koreans back toward the 38th parallel, and on March 15, 1951, the UN forces recaptured Seoul. In the following month a controversy arose between President Truman and General Douglas MacArthur, the commanding general in Korea, as a result of which MacArthur was recalled. On July 27 (Far Eastern Time), 1953, a truce was finally signed, after much negotiating, with provisions for exchange of prisoners and a cease-fire.

Books on the Korean Conflict include Walter Karig's *War in Korea* (1952); Samuel L. Marshall's *Pork Chop Hill: The American Fighting Man in Action* (1956); Carl Berger's *Korea Knot* (1957); Malcolm Cagle and Frank Manson's *Sea War in Korea* (1957); and John Spanier's *Truman-MacArthur Controversy and the Korean War* (1959).

The war produced several personal narratives: *Beyond Courage* (1955), by Clay Blair, Jr.; *Valley of the Shadow* (1955), by Ward Millar; and *Last Parallel: A Marine's War Journal* (1957), by Martin Russ. Novels dealing with the war include *The Bridges at Toko-ri* (1953), by James Michener; *Ride to Panmunjom* (1956), by Duane Thorin; *Tall Man* (1958), by A. M. Harris; *Band of Brothers* (1959), by Ernest Frankel; *Known But to God* (1960), by Quentin Reynolds; and the fiction of RICHARD KIM. *M*A*S*H* (1970), a film about a mobile Army surgical hospital where horror and comedy are juxtaposed, led to a long-running television series of the same name.

Kosinski, Jerzy [Nikodem] (1933–1991),   novelist. Born in Poland, Kosinski emigrated to the United States in 1957. *The Painted Bird* (1965) uses strong and shocking visual descriptions to record the nightmare experiences of a young boy wandering around Europe during World War II. *Steps* (1968, National Book Award) is a series of camera-eye observations in which the protagonist plays roles ranging from sniper to photographer. Kosinski's other works, also exploring themes of sex, violence, power and destruction, include *Being There* (1971), *The Devil Tree* (1973), *Cockpit* (1975), *Blind Date* (1977), *Passion Play* (1979), *Pinball* (1982), and *The Hermit of 69th Street* (1988). Under the pseudonym Joseph Novak, he wrote about the Soviets in *The Future Is Ours, Comrade* (1960) and *No Third Path* (1962).

Kostelanetz, Richard (1940–   ),   editor, poet, novelist. Born in New York and educated at Brown, King's College (London) and Columbia, Kostelanetz is an advocate of experimental techniques and editor for otherwise unpublished writers. He attracted attention with *The End of Intelligent Writing: Literary Politics in America* (1977), alleging a conspiracy by the New York literary establishment to silence innovative writing. Assembling Press, Future Press and RK Editions, his publishing labels, have been open to writers excluded by mainstream publishers. For the most part these have been the entities in which he published his own long list of titles, though *Wordworks: Poems Selected and New* (1993) and the critical essays in *The Old Poetries and the New* (1981) were published by well-known presses.

Kowalski, Stanley,   the brutal, sensual husband of Stella and ravisher of her sister, Blanche Dubois, in Tennessee Williams's STREETCAR NAMED DESIRE.

Kramer, Larry (1935–   ),   screenwriter, playwright, novelist. Born in Bridgeport, Conn., and educated at Yale, Kramer was nominated for an Oscar for his screenplay of D. H. Lawrence's *Women in Love* (1969). *Faggots* (1978) is a novel depicting the lifestyle of male homosexuals on New York's Fire Island. *The Normal Heart* (1985), a two act play dealing with gays and AIDS, was one of the first dramas to deal with the AIDS epidemic. Ned Weeks, the protagonist of that play, reappears in *The Destiny of Me* (1993); in the later play he is in the hospital seeking experimental treatment to stay alive. Kramer's essays are collected in *Reports from the Holocaust: The Making of an AIDS Activist* (1989). *Just Say No* (1988) is a satiric play. *Reforming the Civil Justice System* (1996) is nonfiction, and *Brilliant Windows: Poems* appeared in 1998.

Krantz, Judith (1927–   ),   novelist. Krantz was educated at Wellesley and worked as fashion editor of *Good Housekeeping* and contributor to *McCall's, The Ladies Home Journal,* and *Cosmopolitan* before becoming a bestselling novelist. She depicts her heroines' triumphs and perils in the world of glamour. Krantz's first novel, *Scruples* (1978), was published when she was 51. It was so successful that her next, *Princess Daisy* (1980), commanded a huge advance. *Mistral's Daughter* (1982), *I'll Take Manhattan* (1986), and *Till We Meet Again* (1988) have all been best-sellers. *Dazzle* appeared in

1990; other titles include *Scruples Two* (1992), *Lovers* (1994), and *Spring Collection* (1996). *Sex and Shopping: The Confessions of a Nice Jewish Girl* (2000) is a memoir.

Krause, Herbert (1905–1976), farmer, newspaperman, teacher, writer. Well acquainted with the farms and farmers of his native Minnesota and neighboring states, Krause in his novels depicts farm life with tragic realism and pity. His first novel, *Wind Without Rain* (1939), won the award of the Friends of American Writers. *The Thresher* (1946) is another regional novel, with strong emphasis on local folkways, morals, and landscapes. Other books by Krause are *The Oxcart Trail* (1954), *The Builder and the Stone* (1958), and *The Big Four* (1960). Also regional in texture is Krause's one-act play, *Bondsmen in the Hills* (1936). *Neighbor Boy* (1939) is a book of verse.

Kreymborg, Alfred (1883–1966), poet, editor, critic, literary historian. Born in New York City, Kreymborg has been called a patron saint of the modern little magazine movement. (See LITTLE MAGAZINES.) He founded *The Glebe* in September 1913 as an organ of the Imagist movement, and published contributions by Ezra Pound, James Joyce, Richard Aldington, and William Carlos Williams. In the following year he began publishing *Others*, a magazine that lasted until July 1919. It aimed to publish poems by "others," those who were bolder and more experimental than poets publishing in *Poetry*. Kreymborg gathered the best of its verse in *Others, An Anthology* (1916). In 1921 he was persuaded by the book-seller Harold Loeb to start still another little magazine, BROOM, an elaborate affair, edited first at Rome, then in Berlin, and finally in New York. While he and Loeb were in charge, it was conservative, but thereafter it became erratic and exciting. It ceased publication in January 1924. In 1927 Kreymborg established an annual publication, THE AMERICAN CARAVAN, an experiment carried on, along with Paul Rosenfeld, Van Wyck Brooks, and Lewis Mumford, until 1936. He made collections of his verses in *Mushrooms* (1916), *Funnybone Alley* (1927), and *Selected Poems, 1912–1944* (1945). Kreymborg was also interested in experimental theater. A charter member of the Provincetown Players and managing director of the Manhattan-Bronx Federal Theater Project, he wrote *Plays for Merry Andrews* (1920); *Rocking Chairs and Other Comedies* (1925); *Puppet Plays* (1926); *Manhattan Men* (1929); *Ballad of Youth* (1938); *The Ballad of Valley Forge* (1944), with music by Alex North; *Man and Shadow: An Allegory* (1946); and *No More War and Other Poems* (1950), a ballad-play. Kreymborg told his own story in *Troubadour* (1925) in prose, and in *Man and Shadow* in blank verse.

Kroetsch, Robert (1927–   ), novelist. Born and educated in Alberta, Kroetsch studied at the University of Iowa Writers' Workshop. *But We Are Exiles* (1965) is a realistic novel based on his experience with riverboats. Three related novels—*The Words of My Roaring* (1966), *The Studhorse Man* (1969, Governor General's Award), and *Gone Indian* (1973)—use metafictional techniques, comedy, and fable. *Badlands* (1975) deals with a paleontologist looking for dinosaur bones

in Alberta. *What the Crow Said* (1978), *Alibi* (1983), and *The Puppeteer* (1992) are novels. *The Stone Hammer Poems* (1975) contains mostly short pieces, and other verse collections include *The Ledger* (1975), *Seed Catalogue* (1977), *The Sad Phoenician* (1979), *Field Notes* (1981), and *Advice to My Friends* (1985). *Completed Field Notes* is a long poem. *A Likely Story: The Writing Life* (1995) is a memoir.

Kroll, Harry Harrison (1888–1967), teacher, novelist, memoirist. Born In Indiana, and a lifelong teacher, Kroll's earliest work was *A Comparative Study of Southern Folk Speech* (1925). His first novel, *The Mountain Singer* (1928), depicts the people of the Tennessee mountains. *Cabin in the Cotton* (1931) is set in West Tennessee; *The Keepers of the House* (1940) and *The Rider on the Bronze Horse* (1942) are set in Mississippi. Alabama is the setting for *Waters Over the Dam* (1944). *Their Ancient Grudge* (1946) is a retelling of the Hatfield-McCoy feud, and *Darker Grows the Valley* (1947) is an account of life in the Tennessee Valley from 1778 to the Great Depression. *Last Homecoming* (1950) tells of a novelist who returns to his home community. His later novels include *The Long Quest* (1953), *Summer Gold* (1955), *My Heart's in the Hills* (1956), *Cloi* (1957), and *For Cloi, With Love* (1958). Kroll tells the story of his life in *I Was a Sharecropper* (1937).

Kronenberger, Louis (1904–1980), drama critic, historian, essayist, novelist, editor. Kronenberger, born in Cincinnati, worked at two publishing houses, then at *Fortune*, before becoming drama critic for *Time*. He began lecturing on drama at Columbia University in 1950 and at Brandeis University in 1953, and editing an annual volume of *The Best Plays* in 1953. His other publications include an anthology of light verse (1934); a delicately satirical novel, *Grand Right and Left* (1952); *The Thread of Laughter* (1952), an account of English stage comedy; *Company Manners* (1954), "a cultural inquiry into American life" both honest and witty; *The Republic of Letters* (1955), appreciative essays on various writers; and *Marlborough's Duchess* (1958), a biography. *The Cart and the Horse* (1964) and *The Polished Surface* (1969) are essay collections. *No Whippings, No Gold Watches* (1970) are reminiscences.

Krutch, Joseph Wood (1893–1970), critic, essayist. Born in Tennessee, Krutch was drama critic for the *Nation* for many years, as well as a professor of English at Columbia and elsewhere. Krutch achieved renown for his critical work on the modern drama, his literary criticism, and his philosophic essays on the condition of modern man. He discussed the makers of modern drama in *The American Drama Since 1918* (1939, rev. 1957) and *Modernism in Modern Drama* (1954). His literary criticism includes *Edgar Allan Poe: A Study of Genius* (1926), one of the first psychoanalytical interpretations of literature; *Five Masters, a Study in the Mutations of the Novel* (1930); *Samuel Johnson* (1944); and *Henry David Thoreau* (1948). In *The Modern Temper* (1929), a series of essays centered on the antithesis between man and nature, he analyzed the scientific orientation of the age and its effect on man's need for extrascientific values. *The Measure of Man* (1954), a mellower and less pessimistic work, is partially an extension of

The Modern Temper and shows the abandonment of Krutch's earlier belief that modern philosophy must be based on the deterministic and materialistic findings of science.

Human Nature and the Human Condition (1959) is a critical analysis of modern society and its standards, and a clear and well-argued exposition on the necessity for humanistic values in a mechanized world. Krutch also wrote a number of meditative essays on nature and reflections on man's relationship to the universe, such as *The Twelve Seasons* (1949), *The Desert Year* (1952), *The Best of Two Worlds* (1953), *The Great Chain of Life* (1956), *The Grand Canyon: Today and All Its Yesterdays* (1958), and *The Forgotton Peninsula* (1961). He edited *The Gardener's World* (1959), a collection of essays on gardens and related subjects from the writings of authors ranging from Homer to John Burroughs. *More Lives than One* (1962) is a memoir.

Kubler-Ross, Elisabeth (1926–   ), physician, writer. Kubler-Ross is known for one book, her first. In a large-scale project, interviewing hundreds of dying people in hospitals, Kubler-Ross found that contrary to popular belief, the dying are mostly eager to talk about death, for a variety of reasons. *On Death and Dying* (1969) is her report of this study. *Remember the Secret* (1988) is a book for young people on dealing with death.

Ku Klux Klan, a name from the Greek word *kuklos* (band or circle) given to two secret societies. The original Ku Klux Klan was formed about 1866 in Pulaski, Tennessee, as a social organization for former Confederates, but it quickly developed into a secret organization and spread rapidly through the South. In April 1867, Nathan Bedford Forrest, the Grand Wizard, or Cyclops, of the Pulaski group, called a convention of delegates from all groups to meet at Nashville for reorganization. One important result of the Nashville convention was a declaration of principles of the Klan, which included recognition of the supremacy of the Constitution, its laws, and the Union; the Klan further stated that its purposes were to protect the weak from the depredations of the lawless, to protect the Constitution, and to aid in the execution of its laws. The Klan was formally disbanded by Forrest in 1869, when it became clear it was being used as an instrument of violence rather than as a check on it. Despite the disbandment, the Klan continued its activities, and Congress passed the Ku Klux Klan acts of 1870 and 1871 in order to deal with the offenders. The power of the Klan was broken, and as Reconstruction came to an end and the white Southerners regained a measure of political control, the need for such an organization ceased to exist.

In 1915 a new group, modeled on the structure of the original Klan, was organized in Georgia. The new Klan did not restrict its antipathies to African-Americans but attacked Catholics and Jews, as well as such ideas as birth control, Darwinism, pacifism, and the repeal of Prohibition. In the early 1920s the Klan was said to have a membership of five million throughout the United States, and had considerable political power in Indiana, Oklahoma, and Texas. After newspaper exposés of its terroristic activities, beginning in 1923, the Klan began to decline, though it continues to exist.

The Klan has furnished ample material to novelists. In Thomas Nelson Page's RED ROCK (1898) the protagonist, Steve Allen, leads the Klan when he returns after the war. The Klan was sensationally employed by a clergyman, THOMAS DIXON, JR., in a series of novels—THE LEOPARD'S SPOTS (1902), *The Clansman* (1905), and *The Traitor* (1907), all laid in the Reconstruction era. *The Clansman* became the basis of David W. Griffith's film *The Birth of a Nation* (1915).

Kumin, Maxine (1925–   ), poet, novelist. Born in Philadelphia and educated at Radcliffe, Kumin found in her life on a New Hampshire farm the material for some of her best work, including *Up Country: Poems of New England* (1973, Pulitzer Prize). Her first novel, *Through Dooms of Love* (1965), a semiautobiographical tale of conflict between a Radcliffe girl and her pawnbroker father, was followed by *Passions of Uxport* (1968) about married life in the suburbs. Her later novels include *The Abduction* (1971) and *The Designated Heir* (1974). Her first mystery novel, *Quit Monks or Die!* (1999), stars police chief Digger Martinez. Kumin's verse, usually in traditional forms, pays particular attention to natural events. Her poetry collections include *Halfway* (1961), *The Privilege* (1965), *Nightmare Factory* (1970), *The Retrieval System* (1978), *Our Ground Time Here Will Be Brief* (1982), *Closing the Ring* (1984), *The Long Approach* (1985), and *Nurture* (1989). *Looking for Luck* (1993) and *Connecting the Dots* (1996) were followed by *Selected Poems 1960–1990* (1997). Her essays are collected in *To Make a Prairie* (1979), *In Deep* (1987), *Women, Animals & Vegetables* (1996) and *Always Beginning* (2000). *Why Can't We Live Together Like Civilized Human Beings?* (1982) is a story collection. At the age of 73, Kumin's neck was broken in a horse carriage accident. *Inside the Halo and Beyond* (2000) describes her recovery from life-threatening injuries. *Always Beginning: Essays on a Life in Poetry* appeared in 2000.

Kunitz, Stanley (1905–   ), poet, translator. Born in Worcester, Massachusetts, and educated at Harvard, Kunitz edited reference books for the H. W. Wilson Company for many years. He served in the army during World War II and afterward went into college teaching and was on the Columbia faculty for many years.

His first collections, *Intellectual Things* (1930) and *Passport to the War* (1944), attracted little notice. He had difficulty getting his *Selected Poems 1928–1958* (1958) published, but it won the Pulitzer Prize. His other collections include *The Testing Tree* (1971), including some translations from Russian poets; *The Terrible Threshold: Selected Poems 1940–1970* (1974); *The Coat Without a Seam* (1974); *The Lincoln Relics* (1978); *The Poems of SK 1928–1978* (1979); *The Wellfleet Whale and Companion Poems* (1983); and *Next-to-Last Things* (1985). *Passing Through: Later Poems New and Selected* appeared in 1995 and *Collected Poems* in 2000. At the age of 95, Kunitz was named Poet Laureate of the United States.

Kushner, Tony (1957?–   ), playwright. Born in New York and educated at Columbia University, Kushner gained notice for his *Angels in America* series. The first part, *Angels in America: A Gay Fantasia on National Themes, Part One: Millennium Approaches* was produced first in San Francisco (1991) and then in New York. With its counterpart *Angels in America: A Gay Fantasia on National Themes, Part Two: Perestroika* (New York, 1992), Angels explores the experience of being gay during the 1980s and 1990s in the United States. Seven hours long, it has garnered both the Pulitzer Prize and the Tony Award (1993) for best play. Other plays include *A Bright Room Called Day* (1991), set in the pre-Nazi Weimar Republic, and *Slavs! Thinking About the Longstanding Problems of Virtue and Happiness* (1995). Kushner has also adapted works by Goethe, Corneille, the Yiddish playwright S. Ansky, and Bertolt Brecht for the stage.

Kyne, Peter B[ernard] (1880–1957), short-story writer, novelist. Born in San Francisco, Kyne served in the army in World War I. He published many popular books, but is best known for several collections of stories about a wealthy ship owner and sea captain whose name is the title of one of them, *Cappy Ricks* (1916). *The Go-Getter* (1922), the story of a shrewd businessman, was also a success.

L

Labat, Jean Baptiste (1663–1738), French missionary, explorer, memoirist. Labat in 1693 joined a mission leaving for Martinique, and in the West Indies from 1695 to 1705, he kept a voluminous diary. Like the diarist Pepys he had a devouring curiosity, a sense of humor, and a gift for the practical. He published his *Nouveau voyage aux îles de l'Amérique* (8 v. 1724–1742).

Ladyrinth of Solitude, The (*El laberinto de la soledad*, 1950, tr. 1961), a book by OCTAVIO PAZ. This penetrating essay on Mexican history has probably been read more widely and is thus more influential than any of the other essays or poetry of this talented writer. In search of the meaning of the Mexican and, by extension, the Latin American experience, Paz singles out the conquest of the Indians by Spanish invaders as the moment when the true Mexico became isolated and obscured by masks. Silence, dissimulation, *machismo*, hermeticism, violence, and the cult of death are the masks adopted by Mexicans to disguise their fundamental historical solitude. Paz argues, however, that solitude has become a universal part of the human condition and that all men, like the poet himself, must become conscious of this condition in order to find, in the plenitude of love and creative work, a glimpse of the way out of the labyrinth of solitude.

Lacy, Ernest (1863–1916), lawyer, teacher, dramatist, poet. Lacy, born in Pennsylvania, taught high school English in Philadelphia. He wrote a one-act play in verse, *Chatterton* (prod. 1894, publ. 1900 in Lacy's *Plays and Sonnets*). Lacy expanded the play into a five-act tragedy, *The Bard of Mary Redcliffe*, never produced but published in 1916. Another poetic tragedy, *Rinaldo, the Doctor of Florence*, was produced in 1895; *The Ragged Earl* was produced in 1899.

Ladd, Joseph Brown (1764–1786), physician, poet. See DELLA CRUSCANISM.

Ladd, William (1778–1841), pacifist writer. There is a direct line from Ladd's work to the founding of the League of Nations. Son of a New Hampshire shipbuilder, he was educated at Harvard and went to sea as a master. In 1819 he began devoting all his energies to promoting the cause of international peace. *On the Duty of Females to Promote the Cause of Peace* (1836) pioneers the relationship between pacifism and feminism. *An Essay on a Congress of Nations* (1840) presents a concrete plan for the organization not only of an international congress, but for a court of nations to settle differences. He lobbied incessantly and effectively.

Laddie (1913), a novel by GENE STRATTON-PORTER. This is an autobiographical account of Porter's childhood; the title character is based on her brother Leander, who was drowned at eighteen. Like some of her earlier books, it has as its setting the Limberlost Swamp of Indiana. In the course of the next thirty years or so, the book sold more than a million and a half copies.

Ladies' Companion, The. A monthly magazine founded in New York City in May 1834 by William W. Snowden in imitation of GODEY'S LADY'S BOOK. Among its contributors were J. K. Paulding, Longfellow, W. G. Simms, and Poe. *The Mystery of Marie Rogêt* by Poe appeared in its pages in 1842–43. It ceased publication in October 1844.

Ladies' Home Journal, The. In December 1883, the women's section of Cyrus H. K. Curtis's Philadelphia *Tribune and Farmer* began separate publication as a cheap small-folio monthly "conducted by Mrs. Louisa Knapp," who was in fact Mrs. Louisa Knapp Curtis. The paper looked like a success from the start, and Curtis was soon able to employ well-known contributors such as Elizabeth Stuart Phelps, Harriet Prescott Spofford, Rose Terry Cooke, Mary Jane Holmes, Will Carleton, and Robert J. Burdette. By 1893 the *Journal* was excluding patent-medicine advertising entirely, and a decade later it was leader in the campaign that resulted in enactment of a federal Food and Drug Act. The magazine prospered, and by 1903 it became the first upmarket monthly to reach a million circulation.

In 1889 EDWARD W. BOK began his thirty-year editorship of the *Journal*. The magazine became celebrated for its chatty, intimate advice on personal and household matters, revealing personality sketches of famous men (sometimes autobiographical), and the fiction and poetry of such writers as Howells, Twain, Kipling, Conan Doyle, Bret Harte, Mary E. Wilkins, Sarah Orne Jewett, Anthony Hope, and Hamlin Garland. The *Journal* was one of the first magazines to adopt four-color illustrations, and it was distinguished by the art work of Edwin A. Abbey, W. L. Taylor, Howard Pyle, Charles Dana Gibson, and W. T. Smedley. Beginning in 1912, the magazine published the best series of art works in color that had yet appeared in any magazine. During World War I the *Journal* published the writings of such leaders as F. D. Roosevelt, Taft, Hoover, McAdoo, and Queen Elizabeth of Belgium.

Bok retired in 1919. Though something of the old intimacy of the *Journal* went with him, the magazine continued its circulation advances and its use of big-name authors, including Calvin Coolidge, H. G. Wells, Galsworthy, Tarkington, and Cather. To the editorship in 1935 came a husband-and-wife team, Bruce and Beatrice Blackmar Gould. They increased the *Journal*'s attention to public affairs, national and international. Among popular serials in the 1940s were Franz Werfel's *The Song of Bernadette*, Margery Sharp's *Clung Brown*, and J. P. Marquand's *Melville Goodwin, USA*. But nonfiction serials by John Gunther, Margaret Mead, and Pearl Buck were even more important; and the contributions of Mrs. Eleanor Roosevelt (which began while her husband was still president) and of Dorothy Thompson underlined the increasing emphasis on public affairs. In 1960 circulation passed six million, and advertisers paid $38,500 for the back cover of a single issue.

In 1990, circulation was cut back to five million with one four-color page of advertising selling for $67,200. The magazine's emphasis is "contemporary women's service," including personal finance, lifestyles, and entertainment.

Ladies' Repository.   A magazine founded in 1841 by Samuel Williams and published in Cincinnati by the western agents of the Methodist Book Concern. It has listed many noted literary personages, including Alice and Phoebe Cary, among its contributors. Women's fashions and advocacy of temperance were frequent topics, and Frances E. Willard, founder of the Women's Christian Temperance Union, wrote articles for its pages. It ceased publication in December 1876.

Lady Eleanore's Mantle   (originally publ. in the *Democratic Review*, December 1838, repr. in the second series of *Twice-Told Tales*, 1842), a short story by NATHANIEL HAWTHORNE. In this study in pride and its fearful punishment, Lady Eleanore Rochcliffe comes to live in Boston, at the home of her guardian. She is a haughty beauty, perpetually draped in a strange mantle, and spurns all her suitors. Then an epidemic of smallpox sweeps through the community, and she is somehow associated with it, but is herself stricken and dies, repentant. Her mantle is burned; the epidemic ends. The picture of pride is clear, though the medical lesson seems obscure.

Lady Lazarus.   A poem by SYLVIA PLATH on her history of suicide survival. She described the speaker of the lines written in 1962 as "a woman with the great and terrible gift of being reborn." The poem was published in *Ariel* (1965).

Lady of the Aroostook, The (1879),   a novel by WILLIAM DEAN HOWELLS. The *Aroostook* is a vessel on its way to Europe; the lady is a young, beautiful, and delicate teacher, on a trip abroad for her health. The only female on board, she suffers the attentions of a drunken patrician passenger. She is rescued by another Boston blue blood, who gradually perceives the nobility beneath her native rusticity. When they get to Europe and Lydia meets the relatives she has come to visit,

their sole question is whether the young man is good enough for her.

Lady or the Tiger?, The   (*Century Magazine*, November 1882, in book form 1884), a story by FRANK R. STOCKTON. Stockton called the story originally *The King's Arena* and read it at a party given by a friend. Its reception there was so good that he elaborated it and sent it to the *Century Magazine*. It was the most enduring story the magazine ever published. In a barbaric land a handsome youth is audacious enough to fall in love with the king's daughter and she with him. His offense is discovered, and he is condemned: in a great arena he must walk up to two great doors and open one of them. Behind one door is a beautiful maiden who would be given to him in marriage; behind the other is a ravenous tiger. The princess learns the secret of the doors and signals the young man to open the door on the right. Who comes out, asked Stockton, the lady or the tiger? Stockton wrote another story that was supposed to solve the puzzle, *The Discourager of Hesitancy* (*The Century*, July 1887), but it also left the query still hanging.

lady's books.   The most famous lady's book was GODEY'S LADY'S BOOK, established in 1830; it captured a wide market through the use of many devices that had made ANNUALS popular, for example, elaborate title pages, steel engravings of romantic scenes, and expensive fashion plates. Among Godey's predecessors were *The Weekly Visitor and Ladies' Museum* (founded 1817), *The Ladies' Literary Cabinet* (1819), *The Ladies' Magazine* (1819), *The New York Mirror and Ladies' Literary Gazette* (1823), *The Album and Ladies' Weekly Gazette* (1826), *The Philadelphia Album and Ladies' Literary Portfolio* (1827), and *The Ladies' Magazine and Literary Gazette* (1828). The last-named magazine was Godey's chief competitor; he took it over in 1837, acquiring its capable editor, SARAH JOSEPHA HALE (1788–1879), who wrote MARY HAD A LITTLE LAMB (1830).

Laet, Johann De (dates unknown),   a director of the Dutch West India Company and a director of the publishing house of the Elzevirs. A learned man with a gift for style, De Laet wrote and had Abraham Elzevir publish his account of the *Nieuwe Wereldt* (1625), the first report on the Dutch colonies in North America.

La Farge, Christopher (1897–1956),   poet, novelist, architect, water colorist, war correspondent. Born in New York City, Christopher, like his brother OLIVER, was a grandson of JOHN LA FARGE (1835–1910), the artist and writer. At Harvard Christopher's interests were literary, although he specialized in architecture. His studies were interrupted by service in World War I—in World War II he served as a correspondent in the Pacific.

The Great Depression of the 1930s put an end to his architectural career, and he took his family to England, where he wrote a narrative poem, *Hoxsie Sells His Acres* (1934), a "restrained tour de force" of his recollections of childhood in Rhode Island. He returned to the United States shortly thereafter. He published *Each to the Other* (1939), a highly praised novel in verse about a happy marriage; *Poems and Portraits*

(1940); *The Wilsons* (1941), short stories about a snobbish family; and *East by Southwest* (1944), stories about the South Pacific. Like Oliver, Christopher was interested in Native Americans. *Mesa Verde* (1945), a play in verse, expresses this interest. *The Sudden Guest* (1946) is a novel in which a selfish and domineering woman recalls, during the hurricane of 1944, the ravages of the "sudden guest," the hurricane of 1938. *All Sorts and Kinds* (1949) is a collection of eighteen of his best short stories.

La Farge, John (1835–1910),   artist, memoirist. Born in New York City of French parents, La Farge studied painting in Europe and traveled in the Pacific with Henry Adams. His books include *Considerations on Painting* (1895), *An Artist's Letter from Japan* (1897), *Great Masters* (1903), *The Higher Life in Art* (1908), and *Reminiscences of the South Seas* (1912).

La Farge, Oliver [Hazard Perry] (1901–1963), novelist, short-story writer, anthropologist. La Farge, born in New York City, was always fascinated with Indian lore and specialized at Harvard in anthropology and archaeological research. After graduation he made a number of archaeological and ethnological expeditions to Arizona, Mexico, and Guatemala for Harvard, Tulane, and Columbia Universities.

His particular interest was the Navajos. LAUGHING BOY (1929), a novel about a Navajo, won a Pulitzer Prize. *Laughing Boy* was followed by *Sparks Fly Upward* (short stories, 1931); *The Year Bearer's People* (1931); *Long Pennant* (1933); *All the Young Men* (short stories, 1935); *The Enemy Gods* (1937); and *The Copper Pot* (1942), one of his few novels not concerned with Indians. He also wrote *The Eagle in the Egg* (1949), based on his experiences as an officer in the army's air transport command; *The Mother Ditch* (1954), a juvenile; and *Behind the Mountains* (1956), a nonfiction account of simple village folk in New Mexico. He also wrote *A Pictorial History of the American Indian* (1956) and *Santa Fe, The Autobiography of a Southwestern Town* (1959). *Raw Material* (1945) is autobiographical. D'ARCY MCNICKLE wrote *Indian Man: A Life of Oliver La Farge* (1971).

Lafayette, [Marie Joseph Paul Yves Roch Gilbert du Motier], Marquis de (1757–1834),   general, friend of America. A man of great wealth, Lafayette entered the French army and was active in French court life. When the American Revolution broke out, he offered his services and was made a major general. He saw much action and proved valuable as an intermediary with France; he also served as an aide to Franklin in the peace negotiations.

In France, in the years that followed, Lafayette showed strongly the influence of the ideas he had absorbed in the United States. During the French Revolution he sought to be a moderating force, strove to retain the monarchy with constitutional restraints and helped bring about adoption of laws that resembled those of the new American nation. He served in the French army but left when it was obvious that his moderate ideas were not in favor. Captured by the Austrian army, he remained in prison until his release was obtained by Napoleon. During the latter's control of the French regime, Lafayette, who disapproved of his ideas and methods, remained in retirement. After 1815 he again became politically active, invariably taking sides against reactionary rules and regimes. He visited the United States in 1824–25, and his visit became a great triumphal tour.

Lafayette's tour inspired a number of song writers. Samuel Woodworth wrote "Lafayette's Welcome," and the same title was used for "Grand March and Quick," by A. Clifton. Col. W. H. Hamilton composed "The Chivalrous Knight of France," W. Strickland wrote "Come Honor the Brave" to the tune of "My Heart's in the Highlands," and Major J. H. Barker presented "Hail Lafayette" as a tribute of respect. Several novels have introduced Lafayette as a character in stories of the Revolution: J. E. Heath's *Edge-Hill* (1828), Catherine Sedgwick's *The Linwoods* (1835), John Esten Cooke's *Canolles* (1877), and Howard Fast's *Conceived in Liberty* (1939).

Lafitte [also Laffite], Jean (1780?–1826?),   pirate, soldier. Lafitte seems to have reached the neighborhood of New Orleans around 1809 as the head of a band of smugglers and privateers. When the War of 1812 broke out, the British sought his cooperation, but he declined their offers and was accepted by General Jackson as an aide in resisting the invaders; Jackson gave him amnesty for his crimes. He took part in the Battle of New Orleans (January 8, 1815), and Jackson stated that Lafitte "was one of the ablest men on that morning." But after the war was over, Lafitte returned to his freebooting in Texas. He disappears from view historically around 1826.

During his lifetime and thereafter Lafitte was regarded as a hero by the people of Louisiana, and as a legend he seems to have entered literature when Lord Byron, in a note to *The Corsair* (1815), suggested some likenesses between his hero and Lafitte. In 1826 the anonymous *Lafitte, or The Baratarian Chief* gave a sentimental account of his life. Somewhat similar was a serial published (1831) in *The Casket* called *The Baratarian Chief*. The most noteworthy of all the stories was Joseph Holt Ingraham's *Lafitte: or, The Pirate of the Gulf* (1836). Ingraham showed him at the beginning of his career as a ruthless buccaneer, and at the end as a spiritualized hero converted by a woman's beauty to realization of his crimes. The book was immensely popular. Ingraham's son, the dime novelist Prentiss Ingraham, wrote *Lafitte, The Pirate of the Gulf* (1931) and *La Fitte's Lieutenant* (1931). Lafitte appears also in Joseph B. Cobb's *The Creole* (1850), Mary Devereaux's *Lafitte of Louisiana* (1902), Meredith Nicholson's *The Cavalier of Tennessee* (1928), Lyle Saxon's *Lafitte. The Pirate* (1930), HERVEY ALLEN's *Anthony Adverse* (1933), Mitchell V. Charnley's *Jean Lafitte* (1934), Sallie Bell's *Marcel Armand* (1935), Laura Krey's *On the Long Tide* (1940), Odell and Willard Shepard's *Holdfast Gaines* (1946), Paul T. Williams's *The Iron Mistress* (1951), and Madeleine Kent's *The Corsair* (1955). Harold W. Thompson found in circulation in New York a ballad called *The Brave Lafitte*, which recounts the story of the pirate's strange bride.

La Flesche, Francis (1860–1932),   ethnologist, lecturer, autobiographer. Francis La Flesche, the son of an

Omaha chief, was educated on a reservation in Nebraska. He became later an ethnologist of the Bureau of American Ethnology and with Alice Cunningham Fletcher, who adopted him as her son, was joint author of *The Omaha Tribe* (1911). He made other studies of the Osage tribe, which resulted in *A Dictionary of the Osage Language* (1932) and *War Ceremony and Peace Ceremony of the Osage Indian*, printed six years after his death. He also translated many Indian poems. His *The Middle Five—Indian Boys at School* (1900) is an account of his boyhood on the reservation. See SUZETTE LA FLESCHE.

La Flesche, Suzette (1854–1923), lecturer, essayist, biographer, sister of FRANCIS LA FLESCHE. La Flesche was educated on the reservation and at a private school in Elizabeth, New Jersey, and returned to her Nebraska birthplace to teach in the government school. In 1877, when the Poncas, a tribe related to the Omahas, were exiled from South Dakota and sent to Indian Territory, Suzette and her father visited them and began a campaign to acquaint the public with the injustice done to the Poncas. They were largely responsible for the abandoning of the cruel policy of driving tribes from one place to another. (See STANDING BEAR.)

In 1881 Suzette married Thomas H. Tibbles, an Omaha newspaperman, and assisted him with editorials and essays. She also edited and wrote an introduction to an anonymous narrative, *Ploughed Under, the Story of an Indian Chief* (1881).

La Follette, Robert M[arion] (1855–1925), U.S. Senator, leader of the Progressive Party movement, orator. La Follette, born in Wisconsin, rose steadily from District Attorney to Congressman to Governor of Wisconsin to Senator. He helped bring about striking reforms in railroad regulation, taxation, tariffs, and primary elections. He sought the presidency as the leader of the newly formed Progressive Party, but lost the nomination to Theodore Roosevelt, who was defeated (1912) by Woodrow Wilson. La Follette was an unceasing insurgent, and in 1924 again sought the presidency on a third-party ticket. He received about 5 million votes but was defeated by Calvin Coolidge. He was a remarkable orator; his addresses, particularly in the Senate, received wide attention. His *Autobiography* appeared in 1912; a collection of his writings, entitled *Political Philosophy*, in 1920. Bella Case La Follette, his widow, and his daughter Fola wrote a biography of him (2 v. 1953).

Lahiri, Jhumpa (1967–), short-story writer. Born in London of parents born and raised in India, Jhumpa Lahiri was raised in Rhode Island with frequent visits to Calcutta. A graduate of Barnard College, she earned a Ph.D. in Renaissance Studies from Boston University. A fellowship at Provincetown Fine Arts Work Center led to an agent, stories in *The New Yorker* and her first book, *Interpreter of Maladies* (1999), a widely praised collection of nine stories set in India and the United States. The title story, from Boston University's *Agni Review*, was selected for the O. Henry Award and *The Best American Short Stories* (1999).

Lahontan, Louis-Armand De Lom D'Arce, Baron de (1666–1713?), soldier, official, traveler, memoirist.

Born in France, Lahontan was in Canada for ten years (1683–93) and held some important official posts. His *Nouveaux Voyages de M. le Baron de Lahontan dans l'Amérique Septentrionale* (1703) gave Chateaubriand some of his notions about the noble savage. His book was immediately translated into English, with the addition of some supposed *Dialogues* with a Huron chieftain, Adario. There have been at least fifty editions of the book; a reprint of the 1703 English version was edited by R. G. Thwaites (2 v. 1905).

Laing, Alexander [Kinnan] (1903–1976), poet, seaman, teacher, librarian, editor. Laing, born in Great Neck, New York, wandered around and filled many posts before he settled down at Dartmouth as an English teacher and later as an assistant librarian. He wrote several volumes of verse—including *Fool's Errand* (1928) and *The Flowering Thorn* (1933)—as well as a discourse on poetry and language, *Wine and Physic* (1934). An epic poem of the clipper-ship era, *The Sea Witch* (1933, new eds. 1944, 1958), was supplemented by a prose work, *Clipper-Ship Men* (1945). He edited an anthology of horror stories, *The Haunted Omnibus* (1937), and wrote a macabre novel, *The Cadaver of Gideon Wyck* (with T. Painter, 1934).

Lamar, Mirabeau Buonaparte (1798–1859), editor, soldier, statesman, diplomat, planter, poet. Born in Georgia, Lamar was private secretary to the governor of Georgia, then became editor of the *Columbus Enquirer*, a states' rights newspaper; later he moved to Texas and joined SAM HOUSTON's army. He was promoted to major general, became secretary of war in the provisional cabinet of Burnet, served as vice president of Texas under Sam Houston (1836–1837), and became president of Texas in 1838. Though hotheaded and ruthless in many respects, he was not without statesmanlike qualities. He established a public school system, founded the city of Austin, and obtained formal recognition of the Lone Star Republic from the leading countries of Europe. His highly romantic *Verse Memorials* was published in 1857.

Lamb, Harold [Albert] (1892–1962), novelist. Born in New Jersey and educated at Columbia (1916), Lamb was fascinated by Asian history. His stories for *Adventure Magazine* led to books that were highly colored, romantic, historically accurate, and popular. Two of them, *The Plainsman* (1936) and *The March of the Barbarians* (1940), were made into successful movies. *Genghis Khan* (1927), his earliest full-length biographical narrative, was followed by many others, among them: *Tamerlane* (1928); *Alexander of Macedon: Journey to World's End* (1946); *Charlemagne: The Legend and the Man* (1954); *Cyrus the Great* (1960); and *Babur—The Tiger: First of the Great Moguls* (1961). Among his historical narratives are *The Crusades: Iron Men and Saints* (1930); *The Crusades: The Flame of Islam* (1931); *The March of Muscovy: Ivan the Terrible* (1948); *New Found World: How North America Was Discovered and Explored* (1955); and *Constantinople: Birth of an Empire* (1957). Lamb spent a number of years traveling in the Near East and China and at one time followed Marco Polo's route.

Lambert, Janet Snyder (1894–1973), author of books for children. Lambert wrote a large number of books for teenagers, beginning with the Parrish Series in 1941 which included *Star-Spangled Summer*, her first book; *Don't Cry Little Girl* (1952); and *A Song in their Hearts* (1956). Among her other books are *A Dream for Susan* (1954), *The Precious Days* (1957), *Spring Fever* (1960), and *Forever and Ever* (1961).

Lamming, George (1927–   ),   novelist. Born in Barbados, Lamming has for many years lived in England. Taken together, Lamming's early novels—*In the Castle of My Skin* (1953), *The Emigrants* (1954), *Of Age and Innocence* (1958), and *Season of Adventure* (1960)—form a continuum from childhood to adulthood and from the island home (the imaginary San Cristobal) overseas. While these are political novels about Caribbean society, they also become a chronicle of emotional dislocation and personal development. His books deal with the responsibility of the artist to himself, his society, and the community of man, "his third world." Among Lamming's other works are *Water with Berries* (1971), *Natives of My Person* (1972), and a long essay, *The Pleasures of Exile* (1960), about the problems of the emigrant West Indian writer.

L'Amour, Louis [Dearborn] (1908–1988),   novelist. Born in Jamestown, North Dakota, L'Amour left school at fifteen to work at various manual labor jobs. He was an avid reader and educated himself through books. After returning from service as a tank corps officer in World War II, he began writing stories and novels on the American West based on historical research. He published 105 books in his lifetime, many of them best sellers and over thirty of them made into movies. Among his books are *Guns of the Timberland* (1955); *Burning Hills* and *Silver Canyon*, both published in 1956; and *Shalako* (1962). *Education of a Wandering Man* (1989) is an autobiography completed just before his death.

Lampell, Millard (1919–1997),   songwriter, radio producer and script writer, novelist. Lampell has written many songs, including ballads for the Almanac Singers, a troupe noted for its performances at union meetings. In 1943 he wrote "The Lonesome Train," a poem that became a cantata with music by Earl Robinson; the train was Lincoln's funeral train journeying to Springfield. Later, another cantata, *Morning Star* (1946), was read at a New York *Herald Tribune* forum by the actor Robert Montgomery. Lampell's experiences with wounded veterans went into a series of broadcasts that were published in book form as *The Long Way Home* (1946). He did a series of ballads for *A Walk in the Sun* (1946), a movie depicting infantry warfare in Italy during World War II, based on Harry Brown's novel (1944) of the same title. His first book, *The Hero* (1948), a novel, portrays the difficulties that face the son of an immigrant seeking to rise above his environment. In 1961 he made a successful dramatization of John Hersey's *The Wall* for Broadway.

Lamplighter, The (1854),   a novel, anonymously published, by MARIA SUSANNA CUMMINS. This was the author's first book and an immediate success. Gerty, the heroine, spends her childhood in miserable and squalid surroundings, is rescued by a kindly old lamplighter named Trueman Flint, acquires a playmate named Willie, and is taken into the family

of Emily Graham, a rich blind girl, when Flint dies. She learns that her father is really Emily's brother, who had run away from home when by accident he blinded her, and she marries Willie, who has become very successful and wealthy. A sequel, *The Watchman* (1855), was written by Philip A. Maitland.

Hawthorne, who was receiving very small royalties from his books at the time, wrote resentfully: "America is now wholly given over to a d—d mob of scribbling women, and I should have no chance of success while the public taste is occupied with their trash—and should be ashamed of myself if I did succeed. What is the mystery of these innumerable editions of *The Lamplighter*, and other books neither better nor worse?—worse they could not be, and better they need not be, when they sell by the 100,000."

Lampman, Archibald (1861–1899),   poet, post office official. Born in Marpeth, Ontario, Lampman was influenced by English poets—Pope, Coleridge, Keats, Tennyson, and Swinburne, particularly Keats. His poems on nature are his best, and he was called in his own day Canada's greatest nature poet. His influence on the later Canadian poet BLISS CARMAN was marked. His poetry was collected in *Among the Millet* (1888), *Lyrics of Earth* (1895), *Alcyone* (1899), *Poems* (1900), *At the Long Sault and Other New Poems* (1943), and *Selected Poems* (1947).

Lampoon, The Harvard.   See HARVARD LAMPOON.

Lamprey, Louise (1869–1951),   author of children's books. Born in New Hampshire, Lamprey devoted much time to magazine and newspaper work, conducted a library story hour, and worked at a girls' camp. Her experiences with young people led her to believe that children prefer truth to make-believe, and in 1918 she published her first children's book, *In the Days of the Guild*. This was followed, at the rate of one or two a year for twenty-odd years, by *Children of Ancient Rome* (1922), *Days of the Colonists* (1922), *Children of Ancient Greece* (1924), *Days of the Pioneers* (1924), *Children of Ancient Egypt* (1926), and many others.

An authority on architecture, she contributed articles to the *Junior Encyclopaedia Britannica* (1935) on architecture and primitive dwellings, and wrote a number of juvenile books on the subject, such as *All Ways of Building* (1926), *Days of the Builders* (1926), and *Wonder Tales of Architecture* (1927). Her last years were spent in Limerick, Maine, where she wrote a *History of Limerick, Maine* (1933), *Limerick Pageant* (1937), *The Story of Cookery* (1940), and *Building a Republic* (1942).

Lancaster, Bruce (1896–1963),   State Department official, novelist. Lancaster began writing his popular historical novels while he was a consular official in Japan. The earliest, *The Wide Sleeve of Kwannon* (1938), is set in the Far East. Several deal with American history, among them *Guns of Burgoyne* (1939), *Bright to the Wanderer* (1942), *Trumpet to Arms* (1944), *The Scarlet Patch* (1947), *No Bugles Tonight* (1948), and *Blind Journey* (1953).

Lancelot (1920),   a narrative poem by EDWIN ARLINGTON ROBINSON. It forms part of a trilogy that retells the Arthurian legend in modern terms—the other two are MERLIN (1917) and TRISTRAM (1927). It describes the havoc and destruction that follows Lancelot's love affair with Guinevere and the king's discovery of the double infidelity. When Arthur orders that his queen be burned at the stake, Lancelot and his followers save her, and the pair spend several months at Joyous Gard. Then Lancelot returns Guinevere to Arthur, takes part in a war that destroys Arthur, visits Guinevere in the convent where she has taken refuge, but departs alone—to seek the light that may come even in darkness.

Land of Little Rain, The (1903),   fourteen sketches by MARY AUSTIN. Austin here depicts familiar characters of the Southwest, its winged scavengers and plants and strange places.

Landon, Melville De Lancy ["Eli Perkins"] (1839–1910),   journalist, humorist, lecturer. Born in Eaton, New York, Landon served in the U.S. Treasury and the Confederate Army and was a cotton planter in Arkansas and Louisiana before he settled down to a successful career as journalist and lecturer. In 1871 he published *A History of the Franco-Prussian War in a Nutshell*. A humorous correspondence from Saratoga for the New York *Commercial Advertiser*, originally signed "Lan," later "Eli Perkins," established him as a wit. These letters, collected as *Saratoga in 1901* (1872), were followed by *Eli Perkins at Large, His Sayings and Doings* (1875) and *Eli Perkins' Wit, Humor, and Pathos* (1883), which went through many editions and was followed by the equally successful *Thirty Years of Wit* (1890), partly autobiographical. After conducting Josh Billings's lecture tour, Landon ascended the platform himself and delivered thousands of humorous lectures. In 1875 he edited the complete works of ARTEMUS WARD and in 1891 compiled *Kings of Pulpit and Platform* (reissued under slightly different titles), a treasury of information about American humorists.

Landor's Cottage (1849),   by EDGAR ALLAN POE. This sketch was published as a pendant to POE'S DOMAIN OF ARNHEIM. It was apparently a dramatization or idealization of the cottage he and his wife occupied at Fordham, New York. There is very little story element in the sketch, but there appears in it for a short period a woman called Annie. We know that in drawing his exquisite portrait of her Poe had in mind Mrs. Annie Richmond, with whom he was deeply in love at the time. He made Annie's identification plain in letters to her and elsewhere.

Lane, Patrick (1939–   ),   poet. Born and educated in British Columbia, Lane worked as a logger, fisherman, and miner before becoming a university teacher of writing. His poetry, often dealing with the lives of working people, includes *Mountain Oysters* (1972); *Passing into Stone* (1973); *Unborn Things* (1975), with drawings by the poet; *Poems New and Selected* (1979, Governor General's Award); *The Measure* (1980); and *Old Mother* (1982). *Selected Poems* (1987) was followed by *Winter* (1990); *Mortal Remains* (1991); and *Too Spare, Too Fierce* (1995). Stories are collected in *How Do You Spell Beautiful?* (1992). He edited the verse of his brother Richard Stanley Lane, who died in 1964, as *The Collected Poems of Red Lane* (1968).

Langer, Susanne K. (1895–1985),   philosopher, teacher, author. Langer was born in New York City and edu-

cated at Radcliffe. A teacher at several colleges and universities, she joined Columbia University in 1945. Her first books were purely philosophical, and her later works concerned themselves with the rational aspects of art. She expressed in them the belief that "art is a basic human need." Langer's books are *The Practice of Philosophy* (1930), *An Introduction to Symbolic Logic* (1937), *Philosophy in a New Key* (1942), *Feeling and Form* (1953), *Problems of Art* (1957), and *Reflections on Art* (1958).

Langner, Lawrence (1890–1962),   patent agent, founder and director of the THEATRE GUILD. Born in Wales, Langner came to this country in 1911, started his own firm of patent agents, and then organized the Washington Square Players. In 1914 the Players produced Langner's play *License*, which dealt with marriage. This was followed by a number of one-act plays, the most popular of which was *Another Way Out* (1916). *The Family Exit* (1917), a farce comedy, was Langner's first full-length drama. Out of the Washington Square Players grew the Theatre Guild, of which Langner was the founder and after 1919 the director. He also founded the American Shakespeare Festival Theatre and Academy of Stratford, Connecticut. He was responsible for the first American productions of Shaw's *St. Joan* and *Back to Methuselah*. He also produced several of O'Neill's plays for the Guild. He adapted European plays for the American stage, such as *Don Juan* (1921) and Molière's *School for Husbands* (1933, in collaboration with ARTHUR GUITERMAN), and with Robert Simon rewrote *Die Fledermaus*, calling it *Champagne Sec* (1933).

His wife, Armina, collaborated with Langner in his most successful plays. *Pursuit of Happiness* (1934), in which a Hessian soldier becomes involved with the old American custom of bundling, was followed by *Suzanna and the Elders* (1940), a comedy on life in the Oneida colony. *The Magic Curtain: The Story of a Life in Two Fields* (1951) is not only an autobiography but a picture of many great playwrights and actors, a history of the Theatre Guild, and a fascinating record of the upsurge of creative activity which in the 1910s and 1920s gave rise to the little theater movement. He also wrote *The Importance of Wearing Clothes* (1959) and *The Play's the Thing* (1960).

Langstaff, Launcelot.   Pen name of J. K. PAULDING.

language poets.   A loosely allied group of experimental writers who came to prominence in the late 1970s and 1980s. Such figures as Charles Bernstein, Clark Coolidge, Lyn Heijinian, Jackson Mac Low, Michael Palmer, Bob Perelman, Leslie Scalapino, and Ron Silliman, while perceptibly distinct in their styles and techniques, share a desire to radically unsettle the ordinary workings of language by systematically disrupting features like syntax, referentiality, and structural principles like argument and narrative. What most clearly distinguishes this group from earlier experimental movements like DADAISM, Surrealism, OBJECTIVISM, the BLACK MOUNTAIN POETS, and the NEW YORK SCHOOL POETS is its programmatic linkage of linguistic and sociopolitical phenomena. This linkage is forged explicitly and repeatedly in the unusually large body of theoretical writings that the language poets have produced, partly under the influence of such recent intellectual movements as poststructuralism and cultural materialism. If a central tenet can be derived from the various and, in some cases, clashing positions these writers take, it is that an attack on the structures of discourse and meaning constitutes an attack on the hegemonic and oppressive structures of late-capitalist society. Whether or not this belief is wishful, as it seems to some, it has led to creation of some impressive, formidably difficult, sporadically interesting texts. These can be sampled in two anthologies: *In the American Tree* (1986), edited by Ron Silliman, which also includes a selection of theoretical writings; and *"Language" Poetries* (1987), edited by Douglas Messerli.

Roger Gilbert

Lanier, Clifford Anderson (1844–1908), poet. Born in Georgia, the brother of Sidney Lanier composed verse, some of which is included in Sidney's *Poems* (1884). He wrote *Thorn-Fruit* (1867) and *Sonnets to Sidney Lanier and Other Lyrics* (1915).

Lanier, Henry W[ysham] (1873–1958), engineer, editor, publisher, author. Born in Georgia, this son of Sidney Lanier served in various New York publishing offices after giving up work as a civil engineer in the West Indies, and then in 1925 founded, published, and edited the *Golden Book*, an attractive monthly reprint of the world's classics, old and new. He sold the magazine in 1930 and resumed writing. Among his books are *The Romance of Piscator* (1904), *The Runaway Pearls* (1922), *O Rare Content* (1930), *A. B. Frost* (1933), *Secret Life of a Secret Agent* (1938), and *The Village in the City's Heart* (1949).

Lanier, Sidney (1842–1881), poet, critic, musician. Born in Macon, Georgia, Lanier was educated at Oglethorpe University. The Civil War interfered with his plans for graduate study in Germany, and he served as a volunteer in the Confederate army, in 1864 captured and imprisoned for four months at Point Lookout, Maryland. He emerged from his war experiences afflicted with the tuberculosis that remained with him for the rest of his short life.

Lanier had early decided to devote his life to writing, but economic necessity prevented him from ever completely realizing his ambition. For a time after the war he worked at odd jobs. His marriage in 1867 to Mary Day and the birth of several children increased his responsibilities. In 1873 he finally settled in Baltimore, where he became first flutist with the Peabody Symphony Orchestra. An accomplished musician, his work attracted the attention of distinguished conductors. At the same time he undertook various literary pursuits, both scholarly and creative. He had already published a novel, Tiger-Lilies (1867), a Civil War story containing some of the first realistic descriptions of Southern life, but the book had not been a success. It was as a poet that Lanier first achieved a reputation, especially with the publication of Corn in *Lippincott's Magazine* (1875). For the remaining eight years of his life he produced a succession of important poems, including The Symphony (1875), The Song of the Chattahoochee (1877), The Marshes of Glynn (1878), *The Revenge of Hamish* (1878),

and such short lyrics as "Sunrise, the Ballad of Trees and the Master," and "Opposition."

Lanier also produced three important works of criticism. *The Science of English Verse* (1880) is an attempt to establish, through a systematic analysis of verse forms and techniques, the scientific basis of versification, and to demonstrate the close identity between music and poetry. In the analogy of literary and musical theory, Lanier sought precise rules of form governing rhythm, color, tone, and melodic tension. *The English Novel* (1883) bears as a subtitle "From Aeschylus to George Eliot: The Development of Personality," which more nearly describes its content. Lanier traces the growth of human personality in relation to the parallel development of music, science, and the novel as a literary form. There are critical appraisals of a wide variety of authors, including Aeschylus, Plato, Chaucer, Malory, Zola, Walt Whitman, and many others. Each author is interpreted in the light of his contribution to the emergence of human personality throughout Western civilization. In the course of the book Lanier touches on many social, ethical, and aesthetic problems, and reiterates his earlier thesis that science and poetry have developed simultaneously. *Shakespeare and His Forerunners*, which was not published until 1902, is a less important work. Much of Lanier's scholarly work at this time was done in conjunction with his lectureship in English literature at Johns Hopkins University, a post to which he was appointed in 1879. From his reading in medieval and Elizabethan literature, he produced four books for children, adaptations of Malory, *Gil Blas*, Percy's *Reliques*, and the *Mabinogion*.

Lanier's importance as a poet, aside from the enduring readability of his best work, lies in his skill as a technician. In this respect he was a follower of Poe; he believed poetic effects could best be produced by deliberate manipulation of prosodic devices. In *The Symphony*, for example, he strove for a succession of precise textures to suit the poem's content. The parts of the poem reflect the components of a symphony orchestra, the various instruments—violin, flute, clarinet, horn, bassoon—representing moods and sentiments consonant with the qualities of sound they characteristically produce. Thus the violins raise the plaintive cry of the poor and oppressed against the exploitations of industrialism and commercialism. The horn, on the other hand, sounds the challenge of the spirit of chivalry. The poem is a remarkable structure of shifting meters and tonal qualities, rich in rhyme, assonance, and alliteration. It is also a ringing protest against modern materialism. Lanier believed stoutly in the virtues of nature and love of the land, themes he developed in *Corn*; in *The Symphony*, despite his emphasis on verbal effects, he introduced clearly realistic illustrations of the brutality of business.

Two of the most striking examples of Lanier's lyrical genius are *Sunrise* and *The Marshes of Glynn*, both from the group called "Hymns of the Marshes." Rich in sensory imagery, these poems combine lights and shadows, "emerald twilights,—virginal shy lights," into a vibrant chiaroscuro of contrasting and blending scenic objects. Iambs and dactyls are interspersed in lines of varying length to produce a sustained harmony of rhythm, tone, and mood. In the same category of distinguished descriptive lyrics belong *The Mocking Bird, Evening Song,* and *The Song of the Chattahoochee.* The last-named ingeniously captures the spirit of the rushing mountain stream in the sprightly and rippling measures of "Out of the hills of Habersham, down the valleys of Hall."

The shortcomings of Lanier's poetry are the result partly of natural limitations of genius and partly of the difficult circumstances of his life. His essential mysticism remains always vague and amorphous. His major poems are a criticism of life, but the criticism lacks definiteness and solidity. His fervent moral indignation too often spends itself in sentimentality. Thus there is a lack of depth and clarity in the philosophic content of the poetry. Sound frequently takes precedence over sense, and the music overshadows the meaning. The completely right word is not always found. Yet despite these faults Lanier has a permanent place in the American literary tradition. His technical originality and skill, his sure lyrical instinct, his sweep of poetic imagination, his ingenious creation of pure music through the medium of verse, and his sensitiveness to human need and yearning—these qualities secure for Lanier a place among our poets of lasting value.

A centennial collection of Lanier's works (10 v. 1946) was edited by C. R. Anderson. Biographies and studies are by Aubrey H. Starke (1932), Lincoln Lorenz (1935), Jack De Bellis (1972), and Jane S. Gabin (1985).

HOWARD W. HINTZ/GP

Lanigan, George Thomas ["G. Washington Aesop"] (1845–1886),   newspaperman, humorous poet. Born in Québec, Lanigan worked from 1874 to 1883 on the New York *World.* He published *Canadian Ballads* (1864) and *Fables* (1878), the later under his pseudonym. He is chiefly remembered for his poem "Threnody for the Ahkoond of Swat," which was written when Lanigan read in the London *Times* (January 22, 1878) an item headed "The Ahkoond of Swat Is Dead."

Lanman, Charles (1819–1895),   newspaperman, public official, artist, explorer. Lanman, born in Michigan of partial Indian descent, was at first in business, then worked on a newspaper, but from 1849 on was for the most part in government service, usually as librarian or secretary. His books include *Letters from a Landscape Painter* (1845), *A Summer in the Wilderness* (1847), *A Tour to the River Saguenay* (1848), *Letters from the Allegheny Mountains* (1849), and *Adventures in the Wilds of America* (1854). He also wrote a life of Daniel Webster (1852) and prepared a *Dictionary of the U.S. Congress* (1859). He wrote thirty-two books and painted more than a thousand landscapes.

Lanny Budd.   See BUDD, LANNY.

Lantern in Her Hand, A (1928),   a novel by BESS STREETER ALDRICH. Perhaps the best of her stories, *Lantern* tells of a pioneer woman who comes to the Nebraska prairies in the 1860s and against great difficulties raises a large family. Many of its incidents come from the experiences of Mrs. Aldrich's grandparents.

Lapointe, Paul-Marie (1929–   ),   poet. Born in Québec and educated at the Ecole des Beaux Arts in Montreal, Lapointe has been a journalist, freelance writer, and program director for Radio-Canada. His first collection, published in 1948, attracted little attention, and Lapointe was silent for a dozen years until *Choix de Poèmes-Arbres* appeared in 1960, followed by *Pour les Ames* (1964). All the earlier work was gathered in *Le Réel Absolu: Poèmes 1948–1965* (1971), winner of a Governor General's Award and the Prix David. Two books illustrated by Gisele Verreault followed: *Tableaux de L'amoureuse* (1974) and *Bouche Rouge* (1976). *Écritures* (1979) is a lengthy work treating writing as gratuitous, devoid of meaning. *Tombeau de René Crevel* (1979) honors the French surrealist who influenced Lapointe.

Larcom, Lucy (1824–1893),   poet, teacher, abolitionist, autobiographer. Lucy Larcom, born in Beverly, Massachusetts, began writing poetry at seven. After her father's death, her mother moved the family to Lowell and was forced by poverty to put the children to work at the Lowell Mills. Lucy began working at a mill when she was eleven. Later she taught school in pioneer settlements in Illinois and in 1854 at Wheaton Seminary (later College) at Norton, Massachusetts. Larcom was one of the editors of OUR YOUNG FOLKS (later merged with *St. Nicholas Magazine*) from 1865 to 1873. A collected edition of her *Poems* was published in 1869 and reissued in a *Household Edition* in 1884. She collaborated with her friend JOHN GREENLEAF WHITTIER in his two anthologies, *Child Life* (1871) and *Songs of Three Centuries* (1883). *A New England Girlhood* (1889), her autobiography, repays reading today, not only for its idyllic picture of country life, but also for the light it throws on child labor practices in early American factories.

Lardner, John (1912–1960),   newspaperman, columnist. RING LARDNER's son, born in Chicago, won an early reputation as a sports writer and continued to be among the best in that field. During World War II he served as a correspondent in the Pacific, North Africa, and Italy for *Newsweek.* After the war he returned to *Newsweek* as a columnist, writing mainly about sports. Lardner also wrote for the North American Newspaper Alliance and was a frequent contributor to *The New Yorker.* He wrote *The Crowning of Technocracy* (1933) and *Southwest Passage: The Yanks in the Pacific* (1943) and made a selection of his occasional pieces in *It Beats Working* (1947). Among his other books are *White Hopes and Other Tigers* (1951) and *Strong Cigars and Lovely Women* (1951).

Lardner, Ring[old Wilmer] (1885–1933),   American humorist, short-story writer, newspaperman. Lardner was born in Niles, Michigan. Although widely known in his own day as a sports columnist and funny man, he was regarded by some critics as an important American fiction writer. Virginia Woolf in England and Edmund Wilson in the United States singled out for praise Lardner's ability to get beneath the surface of ordinary American life and reveal unpleasant truths. His remarkable ear for what has been called illiterate Midwestern American speech enabled him to create searing portraits of familiar American types—baseball players, boxers, a talkative nurse, a song writer, a Hollywood producer, etc. His favorite form was the dramatic monologue, in which a character who tells his own story unwittingly reveals the usually awful truth about himself. Lardner's first important book was YOU KNOW ME AL (1916), fictional letters from a baseball player, which came out originally in the *Saturday Evening Post*. His best short stories appeared in two collections: HOW TO WRITE SHORT STORIES (1924), which included "Some Like Them Cold" and "The Golden Honeymoon," and THE LOVE NEST AND OTHER STORIES (1926), which included "Haircut," probably his best story. In recent years, Lardner's reputation has declined, partly because of alleged misanthropy, but also because his stories now strike some readers as dated.

W. J. STUCKEY

Larpenteur, Charles (1807–1872), fur trader, memoirist. Born in France, Larpenteur came to Maryland as a child, then went west to St. Louis and worked as a clerk, later as a trader. After his death his reminiscences were published under the title *Forty Years a Fur Trader on the Upper Missouri* (2 v. 1898); the book has become a rich mine of material for historians.

Larreta, Enrique Rodriguez (1875–1961), Argentine novelist. Larreta was a romantic who wrote with great technical precision. He recreated the Spain of Philip II in *La gloria de don Ramiro* (1908; tr. *The Glory of Don Ramiro*, 1924). His dark and lyrical stories are remarkable for images that assault the reader's senses with colors, sounds, and smells. Other well-known works are two novels set in Argentina's cattle country, *Zogoibi* (1926) and *En la pampas* (1955). In addition there is *El Gerardo* (1956), a two-part novel set in the Alhambra and in Argentina shortly after the Spanish Civil War.

Larsen, Nella (1893–1964), novelist. Daughter of a Danish mother and a West Indian father, she studied at Fisk University and the University of Copenhagen. She was the first black woman to receive a Guggenheim Fellowship for creative writing (1930), but she wrote only two novels. *Quicksand* (1928), which W. E. B. DuBois praised, centers on Helga Crane, a woman of mixed parentage who feels alienated in the rural South, Harlem, and Denmark. Tormented by intense sexual desires she marries an African-American evangelist and goes to live in Alabama, a form of enslavement she cannot escape. *Passing* (1929), concerning African-Americans who live as whites, was reprinted as a Modern Library book in 2000.

La Salle, Réné Robert Cavelier, Sieur de (1643–1687), teacher, explorer. After spending some time as a Jesuit novitiate in his native France, La Salle set out in 1666 for New France and joined his brother in Montreal. He went in search of a great river—the Ohio—that Indians had told him about. He went as far as what is now Lake Ontario and built a fort at the outlet of the Niagara River. In 1679 he began new explorations along the Great Lakes as far as Green Bay. In 1681–82 he continued his explorations southward and was the first European to descend the Mississippi River to its mouth. He took possession of the entire region in the name of Louis XIV and named it Louisiana in his honor. Back in France, he was

named viceroy of the Mississippi territory. In 1684 he sailed on an expedition to establish a colony at the mouth of the Mississippi, lost his way, and came to what is now Matagorda Bay in Texas. His ships were wrecked or returned to France. La Salle tried to reach the Mississippi by land, but on the way his men mutinied and murdered him. Francis Parkman wrote memorably about this great explorer in *La Salle and the Discovery of the Great West* (1879).

Las Casas, Bartolomé de (1474–1566), Dominican missionary and historian. Born in Spain, Las Casas came to Santo Domingo in 1502 and was the first priest ordained in the New World (1510). In 1514, Las Casas suddenly became aware of how unjustly the Indians were being treated in America, and from then on devoted himself to promoting their welfare, usually with the support of the crown, but against the bitter opposition of the Spanish settlers. *Brevísima relación de la destrucción de las Indias* (1522), his vivid, but probably exaggerated, account of Indian sufferings, was instrumental in fostering the long-lived "black legend," which denigrated the colonial policies of Spain in America. His major work, *Historia general de las Indias* (1875), is an important source of the early period of colonization in Latin America.

Last Hurrah, The (1956), a novel by Edwin O'Connor, 1918–1968). Frank Skeffington, perennial mayor of his city, announces on his 72nd birthday that he will stand for reelection. The novel is veracious, though sentimental. Many critics have pointed out a similarity between O'Connor's protagonist and Mayor James Michael Curley of Boston.

Last Leaf, The [1] (1831), a poem by OLIVER WENDELL HOLMES. Holmes, strolling the streets of Boston, used to see an old gentleman, Major Thomas Melville, grandfather of Herman Melville, who was said to have been one of the members of the Boston Tea Party. Holmes said of him, "His aspect . . . reminded me of a withered leaf which . . . finds itself still clinging to its bough while the new growths of spring are bursting their buds and spreading their foliage all around it."

Last Leaf, The [2] (in *The Trimmed Lamp and Other Stories*, 1907), a short story by O. HENRY. None of O. Henry's other tales is more characteristic of his technique and sentiment than this account of a girl who lies dying of pneumonia in a Greenwich Village apartment and makes up her mind to go as soon as the last leaf of five remaining has dropped off a vine outside her window. One leaf hangs on, and she recovers—but there is an O. Henry twist to the ending.

Last of the Mohicans, The (1826), a novel by JAMES FENIMORE COOPER. Second of the LEATHER-STOCKING TALES, this historical romance concerns the attempt of Alice and Cora Munro to join their father at Fort William Henry near Lake Champlain, where he commands British forces fighting the French. The treacherous Magua and his Huron Indians are in league with the French, but Uncas, and his father, Chingachgook, with their friend NATTY BUMPPO try to assist the girls and their official escorts, the young British soldier, Heyward, and the comic psalm-singer, David Gamut. A series of attacks, captures, fights, and rescues constitutes the smoothest-knit action in the Bumppo series.

The two sisters represent the two types of women and love stories typical of Cooper and imitated thereafter in popular fiction, particularly in westerns, with their code of manly purity, honor, and heroics. The suit of the honest Heyward for the fair Alice, both generous-hearted but rather stiff and ineffectual in practical matters, at last receives paternal blessing. The love of UNCAS for Cora, who has black ancestors, is quietly passionate and efficiently courageous. The love is ended when both are killed in the last fight before victory and are buried in a double funeral in which Chingachgook and Bumppo express the identity of the noblest qualities in the Native American and the white. Cooper was attacked for giving too idealized a picture of the Indian as the noble savage, but the conflict of the different tribes of Indians and their different kinds of pride, with Uncas and Magua as antithetical extremes, provides some of the book's most powerful scenes. It is the skilled woodsman Bumppo who is an idealized image of the noble virtues of naturalness in contrast with those whom civilization has corrupted, like some of the French and their Indian allies, or rendered awkward, like Heyward and his fellow British. See MAHICANS; JOHN GOTTLIEB HECKEWELDER.

Late George Apley, The (1937),   a novel by JOHN P. MARQUAND. The story is told as "A Novel in the Form of a Memoir," and the memoirist is a staid and polished annotator who manages to satirize himself as he conveys the events of George Apley's life. Apley was born into an old and wealthy family—the first Apley had been graduated from Harvard in 1662. He falls in love with an impossible girl named Mary Monahan and is sent on a sea voyage. Returning home, he studies law and becomes a coupon-clipper. He marries, devotes his time to charitable enterprises and collecting Chinese bronzes, is disquieted about the younger generation, even more by the taking over of Boston by the Irish.

Lathrop, George Parsons (1851–1898),   poet, biographer, editor. Born in Honolulu, Lathrop founded the American Copyright League in 1883, was editor of the Boston *Sunday Courier* and associate editor of the *Atlantic Monthly*. He wrote a *Study of Nathaniel Hawthorne* (1876) and published several collections of verse, including *Rose and Roof-Tree* (1875) and *Dreams and Days* (1892).

Latin American Literature.   Latin American writing now reaches an international readership in translation and constitutes a major topic of academic research. Worldwide attention has gone to recent (post-1960s) fiction in such imaginative modes as magical or mythical realism (discussed below), and to modern Latin American poets who communicate social statements without sacrificing lyrical complexity. While these contemporary developments have excited widespread interest, Latin American writing is no new phenomenon. It began, at the latest, with the exploration of the New World and is thousands of years older if one includes pre-Columbian literature.

Ideally, Latin American literature would be considered and studied as encompassing the lyrical and narrative expression of the great native empires that flourished before the Conquest. Unfortunately, few examples of these literary traditions

have survived. The Incas did not use graphic writing, but rather a system of knots (quipu) together with mnemonic training. New research is discovering the complexity of this writing. Much Incan poetry and drama, orally transmitted, became lost, though some examples were transmitted after the Conquest. From Mexico and Central America, surviving codices and hieroglyphic inscriptions are nonliterary. Some pre-Columbian literature was reconstructed after the Conquest by missionaries and Indians, and one such work has influenced modern writers: the Mayan *Popol Vuh* (1554–58?), cosmology and divine and human history. The *Chilam Balam* (1500s) are multivolume Mayan prophetic scriptures. Classical literature vanished, but native tales and drama were transmitted as folklore, fusing with Catholic elements.

The writings of Spanish and Portuguese explorers, conquerors, missionaries, and settlers form the next phase of Latin American literature. *Crónicas de Indias* (chronicles of the Indies) is the categorical term for these works, composed in a variety of genres and styles by skilled and naive authors. The *crónicas* range from reports to the Spanish Crown to sometimes fantastic eyewitness accounts of exploration, conquest, and disaster, official and unofficial histories of regional conquests, polemical demands for justice, and administrative and legal writings. The earliest of these, which begin with the logbook of CHRISTOPHER COLUMBUS (1451–1506) and the letters of HERNÁN CORTÉS (1485–1547) to the Emperor Charles V, which relate the conquest of Mexico, are primarily historical documents. BARTOLOMÉ DE LAS CASAS (1474–1566) illustrates the clergy's defense of enslaved Indians. But works of clear literary value appear. The artfully unpretentious BERNAL DIAZ DEL CASTILLO (1492–1584) gives the common soldier's version of the conquest of Mexico and a warts-and-all portrait of Cortés. ALVAR NUÑEZ CABEZA DE VACA (1480?–1559), a castaway, lived closely with tribes in what is now the United States Southwest and Northern Mexico. Scholars have found much significant information in the historical works of "El Inca" GARCILASO DE LA VEGA (1539–1616), son of an indigenous princess and a Spanish conqueror. This author sets himself a paradoxical task: to present Incan culture and religion in the best light without questioning the Spanish Conquest and destruction of this empire and the imposition of Christianity. While few of the *crónicas* approach the elegant style and complex argumentation that "El Inca" achieved, these writings continue to excite scholars by revealing how New World colonies were perceived, understood, and represented by, chiefly, their colonizers. However, some documents show colonization through the eyes of the conquered: the Peruvian Indian Felipe Guamán Poma de Ayala (1530s–1610s), petitioning the Crown to restore the Incan empire, is the most studied example.

Early in the Colonial era, Latin American poets discovered the possibilities of renewing epic verse with fresh subject matter: the New World's natural splendors, peoples, and conquests. The Chilean national epic, LA ARAUCANA (1569–89), was composed by Alonso de Ercilla (1533–1594), a participant in the struggle to subdue the Araucanian Indians. The poem celebrates the bravery of Spaniards and the fierce defense of tribal lands. The poetic glorification of the New World motivated such notable works as *La grandeza mexicana* (1604) by Bernardo de Balbuena of Mexico (1562–1627).

As a European-style urban culture arose, there was abundant cultivation of poetry and drama, in part to prove the colonies equal in refinement to Spain and Portugal. A Mexican nun, SOR JUANA INÉS DE LA CRUZ (1648?–1695), became Latin America's first outstanding poet. Admired in the viceroy's court as a clever beauty, Sor Juana withdrew to a convent to concentrate on her studies and on poetry and drama. Sor Juana has fascinated subsequent generations with the scholarly life she led at a time when learning was for men, as well as her ingeniously crafted works. She is the most accomplished representative of the Baroque in Latin America, where many poets strove for the utmost intricacy of style and construction; the Mexican Carlos Sigüenza y Góngora (1645–1700) typifies this strenuously erudite and elevated manner.

As Latin Americans grew restless under colonial rule, their literature often stressed unique features of the region so as to suggest that it possessed a destiny apart from that of Europe. *El lazarillo de ciegos caminantes* (1775 or 1776), clandestinely published in Lima by Concolorcorvo (1715–1778?, real name Alonso Carrió de la Vandera), serves this function. Purporting to be a travel guide, it shows raucous disrespect toward colonial rule and attitudes, encouraging Latin Americans to conceive of their land and themselves as distinct from, and equal in importance to, Europe and the Europeans. Two Brazilian epics, *O Uruguay* (1769) by José Basílio de Gama (1740–1795) and *Caramurú* (1781) by José de Santa Rita Durão (1720?–1784), highlighting Brazilian nature and native peoples, display the patriotism that was one factor in the independence movement.

The literary figure who best exemplifies the spirit of Independence is JOSÉ JOAQUÍN FERNÁNDEZ DE LIZARDI (1776–1827), known as The Mexican Thinker, after his progressive journal of that name. After his polemical, Enlightenment-style social criticism and manifestoes brought him trouble with the authorities, Lizardi expressed his views in fiction, producing the picaresque *El Periquillo Sarniento* (1816), the first Latin American novel.

Independence for most of Latin America was achieved between approximately 1810 and 1823. Neoclassical verse on this theme has two purposes. One is to celebrate Latin America's accomplishment and establish that the new nations are no longer under colonial rule. The other is to counsel newly decolonized regions on the best conduct of their post-Independence affairs, urging unity, industry, and the building of an egalitarian society uncontaminated by the decadence believed to be undermining Europe. The foremost poet of the armed struggle is the Ecuadorian José Joaquín de Olmedo (1780–1847) with his ode *La batalla de Junín: Canto a Bolívar* (1825), emphasizing heroic accomplishments—not only recent victories, but the glories of the pre-Columbian past—and the distinctive mission incumbent on inhabitants of the unsullied New World. The Venezuelan-born ANDRÉS BELLO (1781–1865), later a leading figure in Chilean education and

intellectual life, complemented Olmedo's poem with his own 1826 *Silva a la agricultura de la zona tórrida*. This work enjoins Latin Americans to trade the sword for the plow, prescribing farm life to preserve Latin America's purity.

Romanticism in Latin America differed from the European movement. It appeared later and was often commingled with other tendencies, such as realism and a pro-development ideology unlike the anti-industrial bias of many European romantics. The long-exiled Cuban JOSÉ MARÍA HEREDIA DE HEREDIA (1803–1839) helped popularize the movement; his emotive poems "*En el teocalli de Cholula*" (1820) and "*Niágara*" (1824) had broad appeal. In Argentina, romanticism coincided with the dictatorship of Juan Manuel Rosas (1793–1877). Exile was the common fate of the nation's intellectuals, including ESTEBAN ECHEVERRÍA (1805–1851), author of verse and manifestoes, the essayist and educator DOMINGO FAUSTINO SARMIENTO (1811–1888), and the novelist José Mármol (1817–1871). These authors produced the three foremost examples of the passionate literature directed against Rosas and toward a new era of rationally planned progress for Argentina. Echeverría's "*El matadero*" (1939?), a short story that is also an exhortation to enlightened democracy, exemplifies the fusion of romanticism, realism, and social criticism frequent in contemporary Latin American writing. Sarmiento's *Vida de Juan Facundo Quiroga: Civilización i barbarie* (1845) is a hybrid work of biography, history, geography, and ethnography, but above all it is an urging to Argentinians to depose Rosas and construct a modern society. Mármol's novel *Amalia* (1851–1855), conveying the same social ideas, is notable for its hyperemphatic imagery and symbolism.

In Brazil, romanticism produced memorable lyric poetry. Its poets sang of the purity of the Indian and abundance of the land, appealing to the senses and sentiments of Brazilian readers. Domingos José Gonçalves de Magalhaes (1811–1882) inaugurated early romanticism, while ANTONIO GONÇALVES DIAS (1823–1864) produced its most popular verse. Mid- and late-century romanticism are represented by the satanic Manuel Antônio Alvares de Azevedo (1831–1852) and Antônio de Castro Alves (1847–1871), an abolitionist who turned poetry to social ends.

By far the most-read work of the century is the novel MARÍA (1867) by the Colombian JORGE ISAACS (1837–1894). A fictional memoir of a man haunted by a youthful, doomed love, *María* attracted sentimentalists as well as readers who admired its evocation of moods, often via description of landscape.

Details of local customs make *María* representative not only of romanticism but also of the contemporary search for literary images of Latin America's rural areas. This regionalism had many variants, ranging from critical social realism to rapturous bucolic idylls. Realistic regionalism was established in Chile by such novelists as Alberto Blest Gana (1830–1920), author of *Martín Rivas* (1862). In Brazil, *Indianismo* idealized the Indian and the native landscape. The novelist JOSÉ MARTINIANO DE ALENCAR (1829–1877) drew readers to his *O Guarani* (1857) and *Iracema* (1865) with ethereally lyrical Indian-white love stories allegorizing the national past. *Indianismo* had its equivalent in Spanish America: Two examples are the novel *Cumandá* (1871) by Juan León Mera (1832–1894), of Ecuador, and the long poem *Tabaré* (1886) by Juan Zorilla de San Martín (1855–1931), of Uruguay.

A tougher regionalism flourished simultaneously. The same Alencar who idealized Indians wrote relatively earth-bound novels of the Brazilian backlands. Rawer yet is the naturalism of *Memórias de um sargento de milícias* (1854–55) by Manuel Antônio de Almeida (Brazil, 1831–1861). Social protest appeared in various forms, such as antislavery narratives in Cuba and Brazil, and novelistic exposés of the exploitation of the Indians in Peru, and the fiction of ALUÍZIO DE AZEVEDO (Brazil, 1857–1913), which forced awareness of class and racial stratification. JOSÉ HERNÁNDEZ (1834–1886), an Argentinian, won sympathy for the endangered gaucho with his long poem MARTÍN FIERRO (1871–79).

Realism, romanticism, and regionalism were becoming exhausted when a great original, RICARDO PALMA (1833–1919), transcended them with his *tradiciones* (1872–1911). These are brief narratives, most of them set in Palma's home city of Lima in its colonial era. They resemble nostalgic compilations of history, legend, and rumor. Closer reading reveals a mockery of colonial society for its ostentation and snobbery. Palma developed a language distinctive in its rhythms and thoughtful, fresh lexical choices.

The renovation of literary language in Spanish became the principal business of modernism. If Palma was its forerunner, JOSÉ MARTÍ (1853–1895), the Cuban Independence hero, became its first major practitioner. Martí harbored competing desires to promote social justice through his writing—particularly on Cuban freedom—and to renew the store of Spanish prose and poetry. His essays are admirable for rhythmic, even musical effects, which strengthen their social message, and his poetry fuses populist simplicity with formal experimentation.

The drive to vivify literary Spanish with eloquent new rhythms and a replenished vocabulary motivated the first generation of modernists. Manuel Gutiérrez Nájera (Mexico, 1859–1895) stood out in journalism, fiction, and poetry for his balanced, harmonious expression. The poet JOSÉ ASUNCIÓN SILVA (1865–1896) of Colombia treated romantic themes with the flexible, variegated rhythmic patterns achieved by modernism. These writers' brief lifespans help account for their limited progress beyond romanticism. But RUBÉN DARÍO (1867–1916) lived to renew Spanish writing. His 1888 *Azul* (rev. 1890) summarized the movement for the public. Its poetry is less indicative of modernism than its prose sketches, which evoke sensory impressions. Darío was criticized as Frenchified and luridly sensual. Yet in retrospect his work is distinctively Latin American, for all its influences, and shows craftsmanly discipline. The poems of *Prosas profanas* (1896) prove Darío's genius for metrical innovation and creation of a realm of refined splendor. Appearing aloof from social issues, Darío rebels against his era's ideology of material progress. He was able to reconstitute the modernist movement with new colleagues: LEOPOLDO LUGONES (1874–1938), who gave modernism a home in his Buenos Aires; the Uruguayan JULIO HER-

RERA Y REISSIG (1875–1910); and a Bolivian in Argentina, Ricardo Jaimes Freyre (1868–1933), celebrated for adding Nordic mythology to modernist verse in his 1899 *Castalia bárbara*. To keep the movement fresh, members explored divergent routes that soon led beyond modernism, as in Darío's *Cantos de vida y esperanza* (1905) and Lugones's work in the second decade of the 20th century. Late modernist poets include the Mexicans AMADO NERVO (1870–1919), Enrique González Martínez (1871–1952), and Ramón López Verlarde (1888–1921) and the Peruvian José Santos Chocano (1875–1934). José Enrique Rodó (1872–1917) was foremost in the modernist essay.

In Brazil, Spanish-American modernism was paralleled by the Parnassian poetry of Raimundo Corréia (1860–1911), Alberto de Oliveira (1857–1937), and Olavo Bilac (1865–1918). More vital was the emergence of JOAQUIM MARIA MACHADO DE ASSIS (1839–1908), whose elegantly constructed fiction abounds in astute insight and mischievous ambiguity, irony, and reticence. Contemporaneous is the hybrid *Os sertôes* (1902) by Euclides da Cunha (1866–1902), an account of a backlands uprising that eloquently defends what was perceived as uncivilized Brazil. José Pereira da Graça Aranha (1868–1931) used fiction to analyze changes in Brazilian society.

After modernism, the expression of personal emotion regained favor. Delmira Agustini (Uruguay, 1886–1914), ALFONSINA STORNI (1892–1938), and Juana de Ibarbourou (Uruguay, 1895–1975) fascinated the public with poetry that artfully resembled confessions. The Nobelist GABRIELA MISTRAL (real name Lucila Godoy Alcayaga, Chile, 1889–1957) was foremost in this personalism.

In the 1920s so-called novel of the earth, rural Latin America is so described as to suggest forces—malign or benevolent—inherent in the land; authors may urge ways of coexisting with these irrational, but undeniable, powers. *La vorágine* (1924) by the Colombian JOSÉ EUSTASIO RIVERA (1889–1928) is a city man's nightmare of jungle swarming with evil. The 1926 DON SEGUNDO SOMBRA by the Argentine RICARDO GÜIRALDES (1886–1927) evokes the lessons to be had from Latin America's earth. DOÑA BÁRBARA (1929) by RÓMULO GALLEGOS (Venezuela, 1886–1969) allegorizes the savagery of the nation's plains and the accommodation civilization must make.

Many young writers of the 1920s joined avant-garde groups. JORGE LUIS BORGES (1899–1986) and others formed the Martín Fierro movement in Buenos Aires, and these experimentalists and their social-art rivals established the need to go beyond modernism. Brazil was gripped by avant-gardism, called modernism, following the 1922 Week of Modern Art. MÁRIO DE ANDRADE (1893–1945) emerged as its high priest, with OSWALD DE ANDRADE (1890–1954) providing anarchistic guidance. MANUEL BANDEIRA (1886–1968) was its outstanding poet, and Ronald de Carvalho (1893–1935) was its literary critic. For all their clowning, the modernists were thoughtful students of Brazil's identity, speech, folklore, and cultural future. Modernism was a broad, branching movement whose variants include the poetry of Cecília de Meireles (1901–1964), Jorge de Lima (1893–1953), and many others.

Avant-gardism is represented by individual talents as well as movements. CÉSAR VALLEJO (Peru, 1895–1938) continues to influence new poets with his fragmented expression, equally powerful in communicating personal rage and fear and a communal struggle to remake society. Nobelist PABLO NERUDA of Chile (1904–1973), after growing skilled at reflecting individual experience via surreal imagery, simplified his verse to reach a wider public and opened new possibilities in social-protest poetry. VICENTE HUIDOBRO (Chile, 1893–1948) self-styled creationist, experimented with extreme reliance on novel metaphors. Avant-garde poetry lived on in such resurgences as the Argentine Generation of 1940 and the Brazilian concretism of the 1950s.

Regional realism flourished in the 1930s in the novels of Brazil's northeast by RAQUEL DE QUEIROS (1910–   ), JOSÉ LINS DO REGO (1901–1957), and GRACILIANO RAMOS (1892–1953); the best-selling writer JORGE AMADO (1912–   ) emerged from this realist wave. Indians were seen sympathetically in the novels of CIRO ALEGRÍA (Peru, 1909–1967) and JORGE ICAZA (Ecuador, 1906–1978). Mexico's 1910 revolution gave novelists scenes of social change. Yet some authors gained renown while avoiding local specifics, as EDUARDO MALLEA (Argentina, 1903–1982) and ERICO VERISSIMO (Brazil, 1905–1975).

From the 1920s, much writing from Latin America mingled realism with fantasy. The dreamlike novels of MARIA LUISA BOMBAL (Chile, 1910–1980) criticized upper-class life. Uruguayans HORACIO QUIROGA (1879–1937) and JUAN CARLOS ONETTI (1909–1994) and Argentinian Roberto Arlt (1900–1942) gave verisimilitude and imagination equal weight in their fiction. JOÃO GUIMARÃES ROSA (Brazil, 1888–1967) narrated backlands conflict in an artistically transformed version of regional speech.

The same mixture was vital to the magical or mythical realism that flourished from the 1950s on, as in the innovatively constructed fiction of ALEJO CARPENTIER (Cuba, 1904–1980), GABRIEL GARCIA MÁRQUEZ (Colombia, 1928–   ), JUAN RULFO (Mexico, 1918–1986), MIGUEL ANGEL ASTURIAS (Guatemala, 1899–1974), and perhaps JOSÉ MARIA ARGUEDAS (Peru, 1911–1969), an insider to Indian life. All drew on the inherent magic of rural Latin America, marked by tribal, mythic thought. Authors more urban in emphasis also revealed the mythic or hallucinatory vein in everyday life, as the Argentinians Borges and JULIO CORTÁZAR (1914–1984); CARLOS FUENTES of Mexico (1928–   ); MARIO VARGAS LLOSA (Peru, 1936–   ); and JOSÉ DONOSO (Chile, 1924–1996). Leading poets examine culture and society: the understated CARLOS DRUMMOND DE ANDRADE (Brazil, 1902–1987); Nobelist OCTAVIO PAZ (Mexico, 1914–1998), critical and universalistic; NICANOR PARRA (Chile, 1914–1998), colloquial; Ernesto Cardenal (Nicaragua, 1925–   ), involved in revolution; NICOLÁS GUILLÉN (Cuba, 1902–1989), representative of African Caribbean culture; and JOÃO CABRAL DE MELO NETO (Brazil, 1920–1999), student of society.

Latin American fiction since the boom exibits greater diversity. All prominent boom novelists were Caucasian men who demonstrated a mastery of the norms of elegant writing, even if they broke the rules for effect. The postboom era saw writers from a broader range of backgrounds, including some whose writing seemed raw, inexpert, lurid, or trashy.

Among women, the Chilean ISABEL ALLENDE (1942–   ) has won most popularity; ROSARIO FERRE (Puerto Rico, 1942–   ) subtly mocks patriarchy; ELENA PONIATOWSKA (France-Mexico, 1933–   ) combines literature and journalism. Women such as the Mexican Angeles Mastretta (1949–   ), who, in a postmodern vein, bring popular elements into literary writing, have been derided as producers of "literature lite." Gay and lesbian writing from Latin America interests queer-theory researchers as well as a nonacademic readership. MANUEL PUIG (Argentina, 1932–1990), the writer who best exemplifies the postboom, is known both for his reliance on popular culture and his portrayals of gay characters. Lesbian and gay writing includes the work of the Cuban REINALDO ARENAS (1943–1990), Mexicans Luis Zapata (1951–   ) and Sabina Berman (1955–   ), and the Brazilian Silviano Santiago (1936–   ). Writers of African ancestry, such as the Colombian novelist-anthropologist Manuel Zapata Olivella (1920–   ), allow readers a glimpse of lesser-known ethnic cultures. The era of conquest and colonization exercises a renewed fascination. Readers seek special insights from writers of hybrid background, especially from those who, like the Inca Garcilaso and Guaman Poma, bridge written and oral cultures. The "new historical novel" of such authors as Abel Posse (Argentina, 1936–   ) often re-narrates the conquest and colonization of Latin America. Latin American testimonial writing, whose best-known practitioner is Rigoberta Menchu (Guatemala, 1958–   ; Nobel Peace Prize, 1992), continues to generate controversy by commingling literary and factual approaches to social phenomena.

General studies include Enrique Anderson Imbert, *Spanish-American Literature: A History* (2 v. 1969); David William Foster, ed., *Handbook of Latin American Literature* (1987); Carlos A. Sole and Maria Isabael Abreu, eds., *Latin American Writers* (1989); and Roberto González Echevarria and Enrique Pupo-Walker, eds., *The Cambridge History of Latin American Literature* (1996).

NAOMI LINDSTROM

Lattany, Kristin Hunter.   See HUNTER, KRISTIN.

Lattimore, Owen (1900–1989),   teacher, explorer, authority on Asia. Lattimore, born in Washington, D.C., and the brother of RICHMOND LATTIMORE, explored and wrote about many sections of Asia: *The Desert Road to Turkestan* (1929); *High Tartary* (1930); *Manchuria, Cradle of Conflict* (1932); *Mongol Journeys* (1941); *China, A Short History* (with Eleanor Lattimore, 1947); *The Situation in Asia* (1949); *The Pivot of Asia* (1950); and *Nationalism and Revolution in Mongolia* (1955). Some of his books aroused controversy because of his liberal political views. *Ordeal by Slander* (1950) describes his troubles with McCarthyism.

Lattimore, Richmond (1906–1984),   poet, translator, critic. Lattimore, a distinguished scholar born in China, was educated at Dartmouth and, with Rhodes and Fulbright scholarships, at Oxford, Rome, and Greece. Though chiefly regarded as a scholar and translator, Lattimore considered himself primarily a poet. His early poetry reveals the influence of such American moderns as Cummings, MacLeish, Stevens, and Hart Crane. His poetic gift contributed to the richness of his translations. Lattimore's books include *Themes in Greek and Latin Epitaphs* (1942); *The Odes of Pindar* (tr. 1944); *The Iliad of Homer* (tr. 1951); *The Complete Greek Tragedies* (1953–58, coeditor); *Greek Lyrics* (tr. 1955); *Poems* (1957); *The Poetry of Greek Tragedy* (1958); *Hesiod* (tr. 1959); and *The Odyssey of Homer* (tr. 1965).

Laudonnière, René Goulaine de (16th century), explorer, memoirist. A Frenchman, Laudonnière tried to found a colony in Florida, but failed. He wrote an account of his experiences, *L'Histoire Notable de la Floride* (1586). One of the expedition members, an artist named Jacques Le Moyne, brought his paintings of the American scene back to France; in 1592 Theodore de Bry, a publisher in Frankfurt-am-Main, published an edition of *La Floride* with Le Moyne's illustrations. In 1587 Laudonnière's account was translated into English and later included in Hakluyt's *Principall Navigations*. The book is especially valuable for its depiction of the Timucuan Indians, a tribe now vanished. A fellow colonist, Jean Ribaut, also wrote an account of the enterprise in his *Whole and True Discovery of Terra Florida* (1563).

Laughing Boy (1929),   a novel by OLIVER LA FARGE. Using his knowledge of Navajo customs, La Farge wrote this Pulitzer Prize winner, a novel of love and jealousy, deception and death. Laughing Boy elopes with Slim Girl, but later discovers she has a lover. He tries unsuccessfully to kill them both, but later is reconciled with Slim Girl. On their way back to their people she is killed from ambush, and Laughing Boy is purged of both love and grief.

Laughlin, James IV (1914–1997),   editor, publisher, poet. Born in Pittsburgh, Laughlin acknowledged the influence of DUDLEY FITTS, his teacher in preparatory school, in turning him to an interest in contemporary literature. At Harvard, Laughlin pursued his studies of avant-garde writing, became aware of the difficulties faced by experimental authors seeking an American publisher, and issued the first volume of *New Directions* (1936) to help overcome the deficiencies of the commercial literary marketplace. Soon Laughlin was publishing not only his annual but many books and pamphlets as well from his home in Norfolk, Connecticut, and *New Directions* became the most important avant-garde publishing house in the United States. It specialized in new writing by American and English authors, translations of important modern classics from abroad, and literary criticism in various contemporary modes. Laughlin's own poems have been issued from time to time in private editions. Among his works are *Wild Anemone, and Other Poems* (1957), *Selected Poems* (1960), and *The Bird of Endless Time* (1989). Hayden Carruth's *Beside the Shadblow Tree* (2000) is a memoir of Laughlin.

Laurence, [Jean] Margaret [Wemyss] (1926–1987), Canadian novelist. Born in Manitoba, Laurence married in 1947 and spent eight years in Africa, the setting of her early books: a novel, *This Side Jordan* (1960); a volume of short stories, *The Tomorrow-Tamer* (1963); and a travel book, *The Prophet's Camel Bell* (1963, publ. in the U.S. as *New Wave in a Dry Land*, 1964). Settling in England in 1962, she began her series of Manawaka novels, set in her birthplace, which dramatize the lives of prairie women: *The Stone Angel* (1964), *A Jest of God* (1966), *The Fire Dwellers* (1969), and *The Diviners* (1974), a complex novel about a writer striving to understand herself as she faces middle age. *A Bird in the House* (1970) is a set of linked stories set in Manawaka. Her other books include a juvenile story, *Jason's Quest* (1970), and a collection of essays, *Heart of a Stranger* (1976). *Dance on the Earth* (1989), a memoir, was completed by her daughter.

Laurens, Henry (1724–1792),   merchant, statesman, diplomat. Laurens, a leading merchant of his native Charleston, was greatly attached to Great Britian, but broke with its government over some of its maritime policies, against which he directed *Some General Observations on American Custom House Officers and Courts of Vice-Admiralty* (1769). He served in many official capacities in South Carolina, and when the new national government was formed he was president of the Continental Congress for a year. He sailed for Europe in 1780 to arrange for a loan to the American forces, was captured by the British and imprisoned in the Tower of London, and later was exchanged for Lord Cornwallis. He described his experiences in a *Narrative*, published in 1857 by the South Carolina Historical Society.

Laurents, Arthur (1918–   ),   playwright, screenwriter, director. Born in New York City and educated at Cornell, Laurents gained prominence with his *Home of the Brave* (1946), which won the Sidney Howard Playwright Award and a special grant from the National Academy of Arts and Sciences. He also wrote *The Time of the Cuckoo* (1953), later filmed as *Summertime*, and the book for *West Side Story* (1957), in which he transplanted the tragedy of Romeo and Juliet from Verona to New York's West Side, with music by Leonard Bernstein. *Gypsy* (1959), based on the life of stripper Gypsy Rose Lee; *Do I Hear a Waltz?* (1965); and *Hallelujah, Baby!* (1967) are other musicals for which he wrote the books. His *Invitation to a March* (1960) is a modern comedy based on the Sleeping Beauty legend. Laurents also wrote the screenplays for *Rope, Anastasia, The Snake Pit*, and *The Turning Point*. His novel *The Way We Were* (1972) was also filmed. *Original Story By* (2000) is "A Memoir of Broadway and Hollywood."

Laus Deo! (1865),   a poem by JOHN GREENLEAF WHITTIER. This poem celebrating the passage of the Thirteenth Amendment and the freeing of the slaves was composed (December 18, 1865) as Whittier sat in the Friends' Meeting House in Amesbury, Massachusetts, and listened to the clang of bells and the roaring of cannon that proclaimed passage of the amendment. When he returned home he recited passages of the poem—not yet written down—to his family. "It wrote itself," he told Lucy Larcom.

Laut, Agnes C. (1871–1936),   novelist, writer of historical nonfiction. As a child, Laut lived in Winnipeg, where she could observe frontier conditions and mingle with descendants of the great fur traders. Her novel *Lords of the North*

(1900) portrays the rivalry between the North West and Hudson's Bay companies. Laut later came to live in the United States. She was always deeply interested in the past of both countries. Among her books are *The Story of the Trappers* (1902), *Pathfinders of the West* (1904), *Freebooters of the Wilderness* (1910), *The Fur Trade of America* (1921), *The Conquest of Our Western Empire* (1927), and *The Overland Trail* (1929).

La Vérendrye, Pierre Gaultier de Varennes, Sieur de (1685–1749),   Canadian-born explorer. Persisting, despite official red tape and the murder by Sioux of his son and nephew, La Vérendrye explored Manitoba, the Dakotas, western Minnesota, and the northwest territories of Canada. He and his sons opened the West to the French fur trade. An account of his life appears in an edition of his *Journals and Letters*, edited by L. J. Burpee (1927).

Lavery, Emmet [Godfrey] (1902–1986),   lawyer, newspaperman, editor, actor, scriptwriter. After long service on his hometown Poughkeepsie *Sunday Courier*, Lavery was attracted to the theater in the 1930s, especially in connection with the FEDERAL THEATER PROJECT of Hallie Flanagan. His first stage play was *The First Legion* (1934), which dealt with the Jesuits. Later he wrote *Monsignor's Hour* (1935); *Second Spring* (on the life of Cardinal Newman, 1938); and *Hitler's Children* (a dramatization of Gregor Ziemer's *Education for Death*, 1942). His most successful play was *The Magnificent Yankee* (1946), about Justice Oliver Wendell Holmes. He wrote also *The Gentleman from Athens* (1948); *Fenelon* (1956); *American Portrait* (1958); and a television script, "Continental Congress" (1976).

Lawrence, D[avid] H[erbert] (1885–1930),   novelist, essayist, poet. Lawrence and his wife, Frieda, traveled widely, and in September 1922 came to America from England to live, staying until October 1925, mostly on MABEL DODGE LUHAN's ranch in New Mexico. (See MORNINGS IN MEXICO.) Lawrence's STUDIES IN CLASSIC AMERICAN LITERATURE (1923) is itself a classic. He was deeply impressed by Mexico and wrote some poems about primitive life or survival there, which he portrayed in *The Plumed Serpent* (1926), a powerful novel in which Lawrence tried to work out his own perplexed beliefs concerning human civilization. Two books dealing mainly with the Lawrences in America are Witter Bynner's *Journey with Genius: Recollections and Reflections Concerning the D. H. Lawrences* (1951) and Eliot Fay's *Lorenzo in Search of the Sun: D. H. Lawrence in Italy, Mexico, and the American Southwest* (1953).

Lawrence, Josephine (1890–1978),   newspaperwoman, novelist. Lawrence worked for her hometown Newark *Sunday Call* and Newark *Evening and Sunday News*. She began her career in fiction with a series for children, but after 1932 wrote for adults. In that year appeared *Head of the Family*, the first of many novels considering the everyday problems of commonplace people. Representative of her books are *Years Are So Long* (1934), *If I Have Four Apples* (1935), *But You Are Young* (1940), *Let Us Consider One Another* (1945), *Double*

Wedding Ring (1946), *The Pleasant Morning Light* (1948), *The Web of Time* (1953), *The Empty Nest* (1956), *All Our Tomorrows* (1959), *Not a Cloud in the Sky* (1964), *Retreat with Honor* (1973), and *Under One Roof* (1975).

Lawson, James (1798–1880),   businessman, critic, editor, writer. Lawson came to the United States from Scotland at age sixteen, worked in New York City as an accountant and a newspaper editor, and then became successful in marine insurance. A friend of William Gilmore Simms and other writers, he wrote an unsuccessful play, *Giordano* (1828), and published verse and essays anonymously. His *Ontwa: The Son of the Forest* (1822) was set among the Erie Indians.

Lawson, John (?–1711),   explorer, colonial official, author of travel books. Born in Great Britain, Lawson came to the Carolinas toward the beginning of the 18th century and traveled widely in that region. An account of his experiences was published in London (1709) as *A New Voyage to Carolina: Containing the Exact Description and Natural History of That Country*, later reprinted somewhat misleadingly as *The History of Carolina*. It was also reprinted (1711) in John Stevens's *A New Collection of Voyages and Travels* and was published in a German translation (1712, 1722). A reprint was edited by Francis L. Harriss (1937).

Lawson was one of the best of the early travel writers. He made every effort to be accurate and just—his account is constantly friendly to the Indians and is a plea for better treatment of them. For a while he was back in England, but then returned to the Carolinas as surveyor-general. In company with a Swiss baron he set out to make plans for a new colony, but was captured and killed by Tuscarora Indians.

Lawson, John Howard (1895–1977),   newspaperman, playwright. Born in New York City, Lawson was associated with radical movements in both literature and social concerns. His early plays were examples of expressionism, particularly *Roger Bloomer* (1923) and PROCESSIONAL (1925); his later plays were proletarian in outlook: *Loud Speaker* (1927), *The International* (1928), *Success Story* (1932), *The Pure in Heart* (1934), *Gentlewoman* (1934), and *Marching Song* (1937). Lawson also wrote several movie scripts, including *Action in the North Atlantic* (1943), *Sahara* (1943), and *Smashup* (1947). In addition, he was the author of *The Theory and Technique of Playwriting and Screenwriting* (1949); *The Hidden Heritage* (1950), a book about the cultural history of the United States; *Film in the Battle of Ideas* (1953); and *Film: The Creative Process* (1964).

Lawson, Sam.   A shiftless Yankee in Harriet Beecher Stowe's novel OLDTOWN FOLKS (1869). His droll remarks and action furnish the comic relief. He appeared again in *Sam Lawson's Oldtown Fireside Stories* (1872).

Lawson, W. B.   The pen name of GEORGE CHARLES JENKS.

Lay of the Scottish Fiddle, The (1813),   a burlesque of Sir Walter Scott's *Lay of the Last Minstrel* (1805), by JAMES KIRKE PAULDING. It appeared anonymously and was devoted mainly to criticism of the British invasion of Chesapeake Bay.

Oddly enough, it was published in a handsome edition in London, with a preface highly complimentary to Paulding. But a review in the London *Quarterly* was savage in its denunciation of Paulding. This and Paulding's other writings attracted the attention of President Madison, who appointed him (1815) secretary to the Commissioners of the Navy.

Layton, Irving (1912–   ),   poet, teacher. Born Israel Lazarovitch, in Romania, Layton grew up in Montreal in a community adjacent to the French working-class area. He was educated at Macdonald College and McGill. As a young man he tutored immigrants for a living and later became a lecturer at Sir George Williams University, Montreal, and York University, Toronto. Exuberant, quarrelsome, determinedly out of step with prevailing opinion, Layton established himself as the dominant figure in his generation of poets. He has also been its most prolific, with forty-seven volumes published to date. From his first collection of poems, *Here and Now* (1945), Layton has railed at what he sees as the philistine and puritanical character of Canadian society. In such volumes as *In the Midst of My Fever* (1954), *The Swinging Flesh* (1961), *Balls for a One-Armed Juggler* (1963), and *Lovers and Lesser Men* (1973), Layton repeatedly strikes out at bourgeois conformity and dullness. Layton wrote several erotically explicit love poems in order to shock and outrage his fellow citizens in what he called "a cold Presbyterian country." But his collections of verse include poems of great power and beauty that reflect on such universal questions as social injustice, life's transience, and immortality. Layton won a Governor General's Award for *A Red Carpet for the Sun* (1959). *Fortunate Exile* (1987) contains Layton's poems about Jews. A volume of memoirs, *Waiting for the Messiah*, was published in 1985, the same year in which appeared a controversial biography by Elspeth Cameron, *Irving Layton: A Portrait*. *The Collected Poems of Irving Layton* appeared in 1971. Other gatherings include *The Darkening Fire: Selected Poems 1945–68* (1975), *The Unwavering Eye: Selected Poems 1969–1975* (1975), *A Wild Peculiar Joy: Selected Poems 1945–1982* (1982), *Final Reckoning: Selected Poems 1982–1986* (1987), and *Fornaluxt: Selected Poems 1928–1990* (1992). *Irving Layton and Robert Creeley: The Complete Correspondence, 1953–1978* appeared in 1990.

DAVID STOUCK/BP

Lazarus, Emma (1849–1887),   poet, translator. Born in New York City a precocious child of wealthy and cultivated parents, Emma Lazarus published *Poems and Translations* (1867), written in her teens. A novel, *Alide: An Episode in Goethe's Life* (1874), followed, and in 1881 she published a translation of Heine's poems and ballads. Nevertheless, her early work, flowery and romantic, would not have won her a permanent reputation if her indignation had not been kindled by the Russian pogroms of 1882. She became a Jewish poet with a cause—to defend and glorify her people. *Songs of a Semite* (1882) contains a number of notable poems, including *The Crowing of the Red Cock, The Banner of the Jew*, and *Dance to Death*—considered her best work. Her sonnet "The New Colossus" (1883) is inscribed on the pedestal of the Statue of Liberty. Her *By the Waters of Babylon*, a series of poems printed in the *Century* in March 1887, attracted attention as an early example of the influence of Whitman. Her collected *Poems* appeared in 1889.

Lazarus Laughed (1927),   a play by EUGENE O'NEILL. This play apparently was performed in Pasadena, California, in 1927, but never made it to Broadway. It is an experimental, poetic play employing masks for all the characters except Lazarus. When Jesus brings Lazarus back from the dead, Lazarus immediately begins to laugh, symbolizing his profound joy in living, "the Eternal Life in Yes." His laughter infects others, and he goes about preaching a creed of love and eternal life, symbolized in laughter. He goes to Rome, where he converts some of the Roman legionnaires, but not Caligula or Tiberius. His wife, Miriam, is poisoned, and Lazarus is tortured and burned in the amphitheater, still averring that there is no death. There are seven choruses, wearing masks.

Lea, Henry Charles (1825–1909),   publisher, historian. Born in Philadelphia, a descendant of a partner in an old American publishing firm, Carey & Lea, which in Henry's time became Blanchard & Lea, Lea began to work for his father in 1843 and succeeded him as partner in 1851. He was greatly interested in medieval history, particularly the history of the Roman Catholic Church. He wrote *Superstition and Force* (1866), *Studies in Church History* (1869), and then his four most important works: *A History of the Inquisition of the Middle Ages* (3 v. 1888); *A History of the Inquisition of Spain* (4 v. 1906–07); *The Inquisition in the Spanish Dependencies* (1908); and *The Moriscos of Spain* (1901). From his papers was gathered another book, *Materials Toward a History of Witchcraft* (1939), arranged and edited by A. C. Howland. His books on the Inquisition have been described as among "the great triumphs of American scholarship."

Lea, Homer (1876–1912),   soldier, novelist. Born in Denver, Lea was in China during the Boxer Rebellion and served later as a general in the revolution of Sun Yatsen. In several novels—*The Vermilion Pencil* (1908), *The Valor of Ignorance* (1909), and *The Day of the Saxon* (1912)—Lea predicted the coming of world wars and the danger of world domination by Oriental invaders.

Lea, Tom (1907–2001),   artist, novelist, poet, historian. Born in Texas, Lea was educated at the Art Institute of Chicago and devoted himself to painting and illustrating. His work appeared frequently in the *Saturday Evening Post* and *Life*, and his murals decorated several public buildings in Texas. In 1941 he became artist-correspondent for *Life*. His experiences during World War II led to his first book, *Peleliu Landing* (1945). His first novel, *The Brave Bulls* (1949), about bullfighting, won acclaim. His other novels include *The Wonderful Country* (1952); *The Primal Yoke* (1960); *The Hands of Cantú* (1964), set in Mexico in the 16th century; *A Picture Gallery*; and *In The Crucible of the Sun* (1974). He also wrote *The King Ranch* (1957), a two-volume work on Texas history. *Art of Tom Lea*, compiled by Kathleen J. Hjerter, appeared in 1989, and

Rebecca Craver and Adair Margo edited *Tom Lea: An Oral History* in 1995.

Leacock, Stephen [Butler] (1869–1944), economist, essayist, humorist. Leacock emigrated to Canada from England with his parents in 1876 and was raised on a farm in Ontario. He was educated at Canadian and American universities and taught economics and political science at McGill. His *Elements of Political Science* (1906) became a standard textbook. He was known best, however, as the prolific author of sketches and essays in which he holds up for laughter all forms of sham and pretension. The first of Leacock's little humor books, *Literary Lapses* (1910), contains his most anthologized piece, "My Financial Career," an account of a naive young man's attempt to open a bank account. Leacock's most popular volume is *Sunshine Sketches of a Little Town* (1912), a classical portrayal of human foibles and pretensions in a country town. This collection of stories about life in Mariposa is generally viewed as genial satire, somewhat nostalgic, even idyllic, but Robertson Davies sees the Mariposa folk as a self-important, only moderately honest lot, and writes that Leacock's sunshine is really "the glare of a clinician's lamp" exposing human weakness. *Arcadian Adventures with the Idle Rich* (1914) is a companion volume poking fun at the money-eyed class in a large city. Leacock published a collection of humorous sketches almost every year for the Christmas trade. His other titles include *Nonsense Novels* (1911), *Further Foolishness* (1916), *My Discovery of England* (1922), and *My Remarkable Uncle* (1942). Leacock's life story is told in *Leacock: A Biography* (1985) by Albert and Theresa Moritz, and recent critical assessments can be found in *Leacock: A Reappraisal* (1986), edited by David Staines.

DAVID STOUCK

Leaf, Munro (1905–1976), teacher, writer of books for children, artist. Born in Baltimore, Leaf became an English teacher. An overheard conversation on the subject of *ain't* led him to write a short book called *Grammar Can Be Fun* (1934). He did a few rough sketches to help the artist with the proposed pictures, but his own sketches were used instead, and he illustrated nearly all his books from then on. A series followed his first book—*Manners Can Be Fun* (1936), *Safety Can Be Fun* (1938), and others. His Watchbird series begun in 1939. But his biggest hit was *Ferdinand the Bull* (1936). For this book Robert Lawson (1892–1957) did the illustrations, and it immediately became a sensational favorite not only with children but also with many adults. It is the story of a peaceable bull who loves flowers and refuses to fight in the bullring. Leaf also wrote *Wee Gillis* (1938), with drawings by Lawson. In 1957 he wrote *Three Promises to You* for the United Nations, and in 1958 *Science Can Be Fun*. Other titles include *Being an American Can Be Fun* (1964); *Who Cares? I Do* (1971); and *Metric Can Be Fun* (1976). Leaf did a monthly column, "Watchwords," 1931–1967, for the *Ladies' Home Journal*.

Leah and Rachel, or, The Two Fruitful Sisters, Virginia and Maryland (1656), a tract by JOHN HAMMOND. Hammond seems to have been a military man who spent nineteen years in Virginia and two in Maryland. He left Maryland when he was sentenced to death by the Puritans who had taken it over. His book extols life in America, even though he criticizes some aspects of it. The work was reprinted in Peter Force's *Tracts*, III (1844).

Leather Stocking and Silk, or, Hunter John Myers and His Times (1854), a novel by JOHN ESTEN COOKE. This story of the Virginia Valley at the beginning of the 19th century is laid in Martinsburg, really Williamsburg. The plot comprises a labyrinth of love affairs, but one of the characters, Hunter John, shows the influence of Cooper's Natty Bumppo, as does the title.

Leather-Stocking Tales. Five novels by JAMES FENIMORE COOPER, in which the chief character, NATTY BUMPPO, is sometimes called Leather-Stocking because of his leather leggings. DANIEL BOONE was an obvious prototype, but since Bumppo was definitely a "York Stater," efforts have been made to identify him with some of the Indian fighters of New York in the late 18th century. A special candidate for the honor is Nat Foster (1766–1840), a trapper who is said to have called himself Leather-Stocking long before Cooper wrote. A. L. Byron-Curtiss, who wrote *The Life and Adventures of Nat Foster* (1897), was confident that Cooper knew Foster, and that he adopted for Leather-Stocking an exploit of Nat's in rescuing two girls from a panther. Another candidate is Nick (sometimes called Major) Stoner (1762 or 1763–1853), who looked like an Indian, wore gold rings in his ears from boyhood, and engaged in adventures not unlike Bumppo's.

The novels appeared in print in the following sequence: THE PIONEERS (1823); THE LAST OF THE MOHICANS (1826); THE PRAIRIE (1827); THE PATHFINDER (1840); and THE DEERSLAYER (1841). The narrative sequence, following Leather-Stocking from youth to old age, is: *Deerslayer, Mohicans, Pathfinder, Pioneers, Prairie*. The changes in Bumppo's character are abrupt and obviously intended to meet the needs of each story. In the order of publication D. H. Lawrence saw the series as exhibiting "a *decrescendo* of reality, a *crescendo* of beauty." Despite all Bumppo's faults—his inconsistency of language in the various novels, the loose synthesis of his traits, and his long-winded ethical essays—he ranks with the great characters of literature. Sainte-Beuve and Thackeray praised him warmly. Mark Twain, on the other hand, satirized him and Cooper mercilessly in FENIMORE COOPER'S LITERARY OFFENSES.

Leaves from Margaret Smith's Journal in the Province of Massachusetts Bay, 1678–79 (1849), a novel by JOHN GREENLEAF WHITTIER. This is an imaginary diary supposedly kept by a young English woman who visits her relatives in New England in the colonial period. She visits not only Massachusetts but also what are now Maine and Rhode Island, and meets several historical characters. The novel appeared serially in the *National Era* (1848) and then as an anonymous novel.

Leaves of Grass. A collection of poems WALT WHITMAN first published in 1855 and revised and augmented until 1892. The 1855 edition was a quarto volume of ninety-five pages, bound in green cloth and stamped with designs of roots, leaves, and small flowers. The name of the author was omitted from the title page, but the frontispiece was an engraved portrait of the poet in shirt sleeves and nonchalant posture. Fewer than eight hundred copies were bound, and most of these remained unsold. Today they bring high prices. This first edition contained twelve poems without titles, the first and longest of which was later called SONG OF MYSELF. The poems were preceded by a long, oddly punctuated essay, also without title, though it is usually referred to as the "1855 Preface." It was Whitman's manifesto, often compared to Wordsworth's Preface to *Lyrical Ballads*, stating what the American poet should be and do. He is to be "commensurate" with the American people. "His spirit responds to his country's spirit," and he "incarnates" the geography and natural life of his nation. The program was thus nationalistic, but also religious, for the role of the poet was to be that of guide and example, taking over the work of the priests of the past. The inspiration of this poet would be "real objects," and his form would be "transcendent and new," taking shape organically like growing melons and pears, shedding "the perfume impalpable to form." The ideas were not entirely new, for Coleridge had expressed some in his lecture on "Shakespeare, a Poet Generally," and a number may be seen in Emerson's "The Poet."

In the following year, 1856, Whitman published a second edition of *Leaves of Grass*, revised and expanded. He omitted the 1855 Preface but printed a long public letter to RALPH WALDO EMERSON, whom he addressed as "Master." Emerson's influence on Whitman's poems is clear in Whitman's application and adaptation of many of Emerson's transcendental ideas. The most important new poem in the second edition was "Sun-Down Poem" (title changed in 1860 to CROSSING BROOKLYN FERRY).

An edition that scholars have come to regard as crucial in Whitman's development was the third, published by Thayer and Eldridge of Boston in 1860. It not only contained many new poems, the best being OUT OF THE CRADLE ENDLESSLY ROCKING, but also three new groups—the groups being composed of new poems and 1855–56 poems—"Chants Democratic," "Enfans d'Adam" (later changed to CHILDREN OF ADAM), and CALAMUS [1]. The first of these groups merely exemplified the nationalistic program announced in the 1855 Preface, but the other two groups launched a new program of the importance and sacredness of sex and the power of love. Several of the sex poems, such as "A Woman Waits for Me," profoundly shocked many of Whitman's readers and stirred up controversy that lasted well into the 20th century. In the third edition Whitman also attempted to arrange his poems in a symbolic order, beginning with the semiautobiographical STARTING FROM PAUMANOK (Indian name for Long Island) and ending with "So Long!" in which the poet envisioned himself as "disembodied, triumphant, dead," surviving in his poems.

During the remainder of his life Whitman continued to revise, rearrange, expand, and republish *Leaves of Grass*. In 1865 he published a small volume called DRUM-TAPS, and a sec-ond edition with "Sequel to Drum-Taps," containing the Lincoln elegies: O CAPTAIN! MY CAPTAIN! and WHEN LILACS LAST IN THE DOORYARD BLOOM'D. But this collection of war poems was annexed to *Leaves of Grass* in 1867 and incorporated in 1872.

In 1881 Whitman completely rearranged and extensively revised *Leaves of Grass*. This edition, published by James R. Osgood in Boston, established the final order and text of the poems included in the 1881 *Leaves of Grass*. Later poems were simply annexed without disturbing the established order. However, Whitman did make a few textual changes for a limited edition in 1888 that were not taken over into the 1892, or "Death-bed Edition." This final edition was printed while the poet was mortally ill, and friends had to do much of the proof-reading. A text intended to be definitive, and incorporating the poet's revisions for the rare 1888 edition, was edited by Sculley Bradley and others and appeared as *"Leaves of Grass": A Textual Variorum of the Printed Poems* (3 v. 1980). See I SING THE BODY ELECTRIC; A BACKWARD GLANCE.

Leaves of Grass, Preface to (1855),   by WALT WHITMAN. Whitman did not reprint this *Preface* when his second (1856) edition appeared and in later years sometimes spoke of it in deprecatory terms. Yet in 1890, when Horace Traubel questioned him about it, he remarked, "I may have underrated the *Preface*. . . . At the moment it seemed vital and necessary: it seemed to give the book some feet to stand on." The *Preface* is written in a vein that Whitman's poetry and prose tracts were to make familiar: "The United States themselves are essentially the greatest poem. . . . Of all nations the United States with veins full of poetical stuff most needs poets and will doubtless have the greatest and use them the greatest. . . . The greatest poet does not moralize or make applications of morale: he knows the soul. . . . The English language befriends the grand American expression. . . . It is the powerful language of resistance . . . it is the language of common sense."

Beginning in 1856 and continuing thereafter, Whitman used the *Preface* as a quarry for entire units of poems. It contributed largely to at least four poems: BY BLUE ONTARIO'S SHORE, "Song of Prudence," "To a Foil'd European Revolutionaire," and "Poem of the Singers and the Words of Poems," all in the 1856 edition. The last became the second part of *Song of the Answerer* (1881).

Leavitt, David (1961–   ),   novelist, short-story writer. Born in Pittsburgh, Leavitt was educated at Yale (B.A., Phi Beta Kappa, 1983). His first book, *Family Dancing* (1984), won immediate acclaim for its stories of troubled family relations involving cancer, sibling rivalry, alien hallucinations, and homosexuality. *The Lost Language of Cranes* (1986), a novel, depicts the tensions in a family confronting a son's homosexuality and a father's addiction to pornography. *Equal Affections* (1989) presents a woman dying of cancer, a husband having an affair, a gay son with lover problems, and a daughter who is folksinger, lesbian, and feminist. *A Place I've Never Been* (1990) collects stories of homosexuality, unfaithfulness, and AIDS. *While England Sleeps* (1993), a novel set during the Spanish Civil War, brought charges of plagiarism from

Stephen Spender, who claimed unauthorized use of his auto-biography, *World Within World*. After Viking withdrew the first edition, the novel was published with changes and a new preface by Houghton Mifflin (1995), who also published *Arkansas: Three Novellas* (1997), including "The Term Paper Artist," about a writer named David Leavitt reduced by scandal to writing term papers for sex. Other works include the novels *The Page Turner* (1998), about an aging pianist in Rome, *Martin Bauman* (2000), a *roman à clef* about a gay writer and the literary world, and *The Marble Quilt* (2001), stories.

Leavitt, Dudley (1772–1851), maker of almanacs, editor. He compiled *Leavitt's Farmer's Almanack* (1797–1851), occasionally varying the title, and edited the *New Hampshire Register* (1811–17).

LeConte, Joseph (1823–1901), geologist, zoologist, botanist. LeConte was educated at Harvard and taught at the University of California, Berkeley. A proponent of ideas of evolution drawn from Lamarck and Darwin, he was also influenced by Lombroso (1835–1909), known for his suggestion that criminal traits are inborn. For LeConte, humans were mixtures of high and low instincts: "True virtue consists, not in the extirpation of the lower, but in its subjection to the higher." What was true for individuals was also true for society, with lower classes balanced and controlled by upper classes. Among his works are *Religion and Science* (1874), *Elements of Geology* (1878), *Evolution and Its Relation to Religious Thought* (1818), and *Outlines of Comparative Physiology and Morphology of Animals* (1900). He also wrote an *Autobiography* (1903). His journal of service in the Confederate army was published as *'Ware Sherman* (1937). LeConte's influence on American literature is seen most directly in the works of FRANK NORRIS, who was one of his students.

Lederer, John (fl. 1669–1670), scholar, explorer. Little is known of Lederer except that he was of German origin. He wrote in Latin an account of the geography, geology, and inhabitants of Virginia that Sir William Talbot, a member of the Virginia Council, translated into English; it was published in London as *The Discoveries of John Lederer in three several marches from Virginia to the West of Carolina, March 1669–Sept. 1670* (1672).

Led-Horse Claim (1883), a novel by Mary Hallock Foote (1847–1938). Foote made a western variation of the old Romeo-and-Juliet theme. Two rival mines stand on the opposite banks of Led Horse Gulch in Colorado. When the sister of the manager of one of the mines comes to visit him, she meets by chance the manager of the other mine, and they fall in love. The ensuing complications are straightened out sentimentally but not implausibly. In the novel Foote gave one of the earliest descriptions of a western mining camp.

Ledoux, Louis V[ernon] (1880–1948), chemist, poet, critic, collector. Born in New York City, Ledoux made his living as head of the firm of Ledoux & Co., chemists and assayers. But his pleasure was in writing poetry, meeting poets, writing criticism, and collecting manuscripts and Japanese prints. He gathered his verse in several collections: *Songs from the Silent Land* (1905), *The Soul's Progress and Other Poems* (1906), and *The Shadow of Aetna* (1914). He wrote a book on George Edward Woodberry (1917) and several books on Japanese art, including *The Art of Japan* (1927) and *Japanese Prints of the Primitive Period* (1942). Toward the beginning of the century Ledoux met EDWIN ARLINGTON ROBINSON and until the death of the poet remained his close friend and benefactor.

Ledyard, John (1751–1789), traveler, memoirist. Born in Connecticut, Ledyard attended Dartmouth, then went to sea and subsequently served in Captain Cook's journey of exploration. He prepared a *Journal of Captain Cook's Last Voyage to the Pacific Ocean* (1783), a lively and apparently reliable account that gives the only eyewitness account of Cook's murder in Hawaii. Ledyard became convinced that the Pacific offered great opportunities for traders. After presenting his ideas to Robert Morris, Jefferson, and John Paul Jones, he went to Russia to see the Empress Catherine about his project, but he was arrested as a spy and expelled. Undaunted, he planned an expedition to Africa, but died at Cairo. Ledyard's career inspired JARED SPARKS to begin writing biography, and his first sketch was a *Life of John Ledyard, the American Traveler* (1828), which went through several editions and was later included in Sparks's *Library of American Biography* (1834–38, 1844–47).

Lee, Arthur (1740–1792), physician, lawyer, public official, writer. Born in Westmoreland County, Virginia, Lee earned a degree in medicine at Edinburgh (1764) and was admitted to the bar in London in 1775. In the meantime he had practiced medicine at Williamsburg. In London he found himself in the midst of a controversy over the authorship of the *Letters of Junius* (1768–72) and over the recalcitrant American colonies. In London, using the signature Junius Americanus, he published his satiric *Appeal to the Justice and Interests of the People of Great Britain* (1774) and *A Second Appeal* (1775). He was made an agent of the Continental Congress in London (1775) and in the next year joined Benjamin Franklin and Silas Deane in Paris to negotiate a treaty with France. There he made violent accusations of treachery against Deane and Franklin; as a result, Lee and Deane were recalled (1779). Lee served in the Continental Congress and opposed adoption of the Constitution, but he continued to take part in acrimonious controversies and he helped John Dickinson write THE LIBERTY SONG. C.H. Lee wrote *A Vindication of Arthur Lee* (1894).

Lee, Chang-rae (1965–), novelist. Born in Seoul, Korea, Lee was educated at Yale (B.A., 1987) and the University of Oregon (M.F.A., 1993). His prize-winning first novel *Native Speaker* (1995) treats a Korean-American private spy confronting his anomalous identity on the bridge where two cultures diverge and meet. His second, *A Gesture Life* (1999), examines a sixty-year-old Japanese immigrant living in a wealthy suburb of New York City. A retired storekeeper, respected in the community as "good Doc Hata," he is revealed as having a dark past involving a monstrous life in the Japanese army supervising Korean "comfort women" in Burma during World War II.

Lee, Charles (1731–1782),   general in the Continental Army. Born in England, Lee fought under Braddock and in various parts of Europe. He was an ardent enemy of the Tory government, and the *Letters of Junius* have sometimes been attributed to him. During the American Revolution he was captured by the British, and documents were later discovered showing that he had made traitorous proposals to Lord Howe. At the Battle of Monmouth, and contrary to Washington's orders, he retreated and was later court-martialed. He died a bitter and half-insane man. Lee has appeared in novels about the Revolution, generally in an unfavorable light, as in J. E. Heath's *Edge-Hill* (1828), H. Manford's *The Spur of Monmouth* (1876), Howard Fast's *The Unvanquished* (1924), and Willard Wiener's *Morning in America* (1942).

Lee, Dennis (1939–   ),   poet, editor, literary critic. Born in Toronto, Lee was educated at the University of Toronto and has taught and worked in publishing. His poems lament the loss of values and diminishing spirit he sees in contemporary Canada. His titles include *Kingdom of Absence* (1967), sonnets about "a cosmos gone askew"; *Civil Elegies* (1968, expanded 1972); *The Gods* (1979), combining earlier works, including the title poem and "The Death of Harold Ladoo" (1976), an elegy for a fellow writer; *Riffs* (1993), a verse mini-novel; and *Nightwatch: New and Selected Poems 1968–1996* (1996). He has also written children's nonsense verse, including *Alligator Pie* (1974), *Jelly Belly* (1983), and *Lizzy's Lion* (1984).

Lee, Eliza Buckminster (c. 1788–1864),   novelist, memoirist. A New Hampshire author and sister of JOSEPH STEVENS BUCKMINSTER, Lee wrote *Sketches of a New England Village* (1838), *Delusion, or, The Witch of New England* (1840), and *Naomi, or, Boston Two-Hundred Years Ago* (1848). She also published translations of German authors and *Memoirs* (1849), about her brother and their father.

Lee, Hannah Farnham [Sawyer] (1780–1865), novelist, biographer, historian. Lee was born in Newburyport, Massachusetts. Her writings were about domestic life and education. These include *Three Experiments of Living* (1837), *Elinor Fulton* (1837), and *Sketches and Stories from Life, For the Young* (1850). She also wrote about Thomas Cranmer and the Huguenots, sculpture, and old painters; and in 1853 she published a sketch of a slave (originally from San Domingo) who had been devoted to her sister, *A Memoir of Pierre Toussaint.*

Lee, [Nelle] Harper (1926–   ),   novelist. Harper Lee, born in Alabama, wrote her first novel, *To Kill a Mockingbird* (1960), and won a Pulitzer Prize. It is a compassionate, gripping tale of a little girl in a small Alabama town in the 1930s whose father, a lawyer, defends an African-American accused of raping a white woman.

Lee, Henry ["Light-Horse Harry"] (1756–1818), soldier, statesman. Lee was born in Prince William County, Virginia. By the time he was twenty-six, he had had one of the most brilliant military careers in the annals of the American Revolution. Thereafter, he tried his hand at local politics, espoused the Constitution, became governor of his state, and

later represented it in Congress. He tried in Baltimore to lead armed opposition to the War of 1812 and was severely mauled by a band of Federalists. He spent the rest of his life in the West Indies, returning to die in the home of his close friend, General Nathanael Greene.

In December 1799 Lee wrote and introduced into the House of Representatives resolutions on the death of Washington; a week later (December 26) he delivered a eulogy on Washington. Both contained his memorable characterization of Washington: "First in war, first in peace, first in the hearts of his countrymen." (Possibly he said "fellow citizens" instead of "countrymen.") Reflected fame came from the renown of his son, ROBERT E. LEE. Another son, Henry (1787–1837), became a soldier and author; as an author Henry was attracted mainly to military subjects and figures, for example, *The Campaign of 1781 in the Carolinas* (1824) and *Life of the Emperor Napoleon* (1835).

Light-Horse Harry himself wrote *Memoirs of the War in the Southern Department of the U.S.* (2 v. 1812). For the third edition of this work Robert E. Lee wrote a short biography, dealing almost entirely with his father's military achievements. *The Life and Letter of Col. Henry Lee*, compiled by John Torrey Morse, appeared in 1905. James Boyd wrote *Light-Horse Harry Lee* (1931).

Lee, Henry II.   See LEE, HENRY.

Lee, Li-Young (1957–   ),   poet. Born of Chinese parents in Jakarta, Indonesia, Lee spent his early childhood wandering through Southeast Asia with his parents, fugitives from political repression whose travels ended in 1964 when they settled in western Pennsylvania. He graduated from the University of Pittsburgh in 1979 and attended the University of Arizona and the State University of New York College at Brockport. In his poems he refers frequently to his family's past and to his father, once a physician to China's Mao Tse-tung, later a medical advisor to President Sukarno of Indonesia, still later a Presbyterian minister in Pennsylvania. Poems are collected in *Rose* (1986) and *The City in Which I Love You* (1990). *The Winged Seed: A Remembrance* (1995) is a memoir.

Lee, Manfred B.   See ELLERY QUEEN.

Lee, Richard Henry (1732–1794),   statesman, pamphleteer. This quiet, determined man—brother of ARTHUR LEE—was one of the most distinguished of the Virginia Lees. He was a radical, in the school of Jefferson. As early as 1759 he delivered a bold oration against slavery in the House of Burgesses; he took a leading part in the resistance to British measures; on June 7, 1776, he introduced into the Continental Congress resolutions that the colonies should be independent, form alliances, and organize a confederation; and he signed the DECLARATION OF INDEPENDENCE. After the war Lee opposed the Constitution because it did not contain a Bill of Rights. He was the ablest of those who replied to the *Federalist* papers—in his *Letters of the Federal Farmer* (1787–88). When he became a senator from Virginia he helped secure the adoption of the first ten Amendments, himself writing the tenth. His *Letters* (2 v. 1911–14) were edited by J. C. Ballagh.

Lee, Robert E[dward] (1807–1870), soldier. Born in Westmoreland County, Lee was the son of HENRY "LIGHT-HORSE HARRY" LEE, a member of a distinguished Virginia family and a hero of the Revolutionary War. Young Lee early showed a talent for mathematics and was graduated from West Point second highest in his class. He served seventeen years as an engineer, was promoted for gallantry during the Mexican war, and was superintendent at West Point from 1852 to 1855. He successfully put down John Brown's insurrection at Harper's Ferry in 1859.

As a Union soldier, a Whig, and a man deeply devoted to the Union, Lee had little sympathy with secessionist feelings in the South, but his family's long residence in Virginia and the tradition in which he had been brought up made it impossible for him, as a man of honor, to fight against his native state. Accordingly, he declined the offer of field command of the United States army in April 1861, and a few days later, when he learned that Virginia had seceded and felt that war was imminent, resigned from the army completely.

Virginia lost no time in choosing Lee as a commander of her army and, although he had hoped to avoid taking part in the war, he felt obliged to accept. He was made a field commander of the Army of Northern Virginia in May 1862 after a month of service primarily as military adviser to JEFFERSON DAVIS, and hurriedly fortified Richmond against attack. Lee's strategy was highly successful during the first year of his command, but he was handicapped by the loss of Stonewall Jackson (see THOMAS JONATHAN JACKSON) after the battle of Chancellorsville. After his defeat at the battle of Gettysburg, Lee sought to resign as commander. He was persuaded to carry on, but heavy casualties, lack of supplies, and the superior strength of the Union army made victories after Gettysburg small and sporadic. He surrendered to ULYSSES S. GRANT at Appomattox Court House on April 9, 1865.

Lee became president of Washington College in September 1865 and helped considerably to raise its standards. The school's name was later changed to Washington and Lee University in his honor.

An excellent soldier and strategist, Lee also had the ability to inspire confidence in his men and was often considered the ideal of Southern manhood. He was the subject of many poems by Southerners, among them Father Abram Joseph Ryan's *The Sword of Robert Lee*, John Reuben Thompson's *Lee to the Rear*, and Donald Davidson's *Lee in the Mountains* (1938), which is set in the period of Lee's college presidency. Lee also appears in poems by Northern writers, notably Edgar Lee Masters's *Lee: A Dramatic Poem* (1926). Among novels dealing with Lee are Mary Johnston's *Cease Firing* (1912) and MacKinlay Kantor's *Long Remember* (1934). A basic biography of Lee was written (1904) by his son, Capt. Robert E. Lee. Many other biographies have been written, most notably one by Douglas Freeman, which won a Pulitzer Prize (4 v. 1934), and a later one by the same author, *Lee of Virginia* (1958). *The Wartime Papers of R. E. Lee* were edited by Clifford Dowdey, 1961. Lee left no memoirs.

Lee, Robert E[dwin] (1918–1994), playwright. Born in Elyria, Ohio, Lee achieved his greatest successes in collaboration with Jerome Lawrence. *Inherit the Wind* was a thinly veiled story of the Monkey Trial of 1925 in Dayton, Tennessee, in which a young biology teacher, John T. Scopes, was called into court for violating state law by teaching evolution (see SCOPES TRIAL). The resulting debate between Clarence Darrow for the defense, and William Jennings Bryan for the prosecution, rocked the country during the 1920s. *Inherit the Wind*, which ran from 1955 to 1957 on Broadway, was later made into a successful movie. *The Gang's All Here* (1959) was suggested by the life of President Harding; in it a mediocre man is pushed to the forefront of public life by cynical politicians. Both *Auntie Mame* (1956), a play, and *Mame* (1966), a musical comedy, enjoyed long runs. On his own, Lee wrote the books for two Broadway musicals, *Look Ma, I'm Dancing* (1948), and *Shangri-La* (1956).

Lee, William. A pen name used by WILLIAM S. BURROUGHS.

Leech, Margaret (1893–1974), novelist, biographer, historian. Leech, who was born in Newburgh, New York, collaborated with Heywood Broun on *Anthony Comstock, Roundsman of the Lord* (1927), which was based largely on Anthony Comstock's reports written when he was secretary of the Society for the Suppression of Vice. In 1941 appeared her most widely read book, *Reveille in Washington*, a historical record of doings in the capital during the Civil War and winner of a Pulitzer Prize. In 1959 she published *In the Days of McKinley*, which also won a Pulitzer Prize.

Leeds, Daniel (1652–1720), almanac maker, author. The first job of the Philadelphia printer William Bradford was to do an almanac for Leeds, who was born in England. Leeds also wrote *The Temple of Wisdom for the Little World* (1688) and *News of a Trumpet Sounding in the Wilderness* (1697). He was a Quaker who quarreled with the Quakers of the colony. His sons, Titan and Felix Leeds, were also almanac makers. Titan (1699–1738) was the subject of a continuing hoax by Benjamin Franklin, who solemnly prophesied in the first issue of *Poor Richard's Almanack* (December 19, 1732) that Leeds would die on October 17, 1733. His joke was a repetition of one that Jonathan Swift in 1708 played on an English astrologer, John Partridge.

Lefevre, Edwin (1871–1943), stockbroker, newspaperman, novelist, short-story writer. Born in Columbia, Lefevre became a newspaperman and an authority on Wall Street. He wrote *Reminiscences of a Stock Operator* (1923) and *The Making of a Stockbroker* (1925). Among his other books are *Wall Street Stories* (1901), *The Golden Flood* (1905), *Sampson, Rock of Wall Street* (1907), and *The Plunderers* (1916). As a story teller, Lefevre possessed the O. Henry gift for the unexpected ending.

Le Gallienne, Eva (1899–1991), actress. Born in England and daughter of Richard Le Gallienne (1866–1947), English essayist, poet, and novelist who emigrated to the United States in 1903, she made her stage debut in London in 1915, but thereafter played in American theaters. She was founder and director of the Civic Repertory Theater (1926) in New York. She edited Henrik Ibsen's *Hedda Gabler* and *The Master Builder* (1955) and translated 12 other plays. *At 33* (1934) is her autobiography, continued in *With a Quiet Heart* (1953).

Legaré, Hugh Swinton (1797–1843), lawyer, public official, diplomat, scholar. Born in Charleston, Legaré was crippled at the age of five and devoted himself strenuously to literature and later to the law. He held various state and national offices, including serving as attorney-general in President Tyler's cabinet; when Daniel Webster resigned, he was appointed Secretary of State. He wrote learnedly on Demosthenes and Byron, assessed the significance of William Cullen Bryant, helped start the SOUTHERN REVIEW (1828), and contributed essays to many periodicals. His writings were collected in two volumes (1845–46) by his sister. His cousin, JAMES MATTHEWES LEGARÉ, dedicated an affecting poem to his memory, "On the Death of a Kinsman."

Legaré, James Matthewes (1823–1859), poet. Born in Charleston and distant cousin of HUGH SWINTON LAGARÉ, James Legaré published only one book, *Orta-Undis and Other Poems* (1848).

Legend of Sleepy Hollow, The (published in *The Sketch Book*, 1820), a story by WASHINGTON IRVING. At Sleepy Hollow, now Tarrytown, New York, Irving placed his rollicking tale of a headless horseman, which probably came from German folklore or from a story by J. K. A. Musäus (1735–1787). The really memorable character in the story is ICHABOD CRANE. According to tradition, Irving modeled Ichabod on Jesse Merwin, a local schoolmaster who was Irving's lifelong friend; he similarly used Katrina Van Alen, a buxom girl of Kinderhook, as the model for Katrina Van Tassel. Brom Van Brunt is a well-drawn study of the extrovert. See BROM BONES; SLEEPY HOLLOW; SKETCH BOOK.

Legends of the Alhambra, The (1832; rev. and enlarged, 1852), a "Spanish Sketch Book" by WASHINGTON IRVING. In 1826 Irving was appointed diplomatic attaché to the American Legation in Madrid, and his work left much time for travel, research, and writing. He was deeply attracted by the romantic ruins of the Alhambra at Granada, and *Legends* was the result. In dealing with the historic clashes of Spaniard and Moor, Irving inclines to the side of the Mohammedans who erected such a splendid civilization on Spanish soil. Some of his tales are based on legends, others his own invention. There are mysterious caverns, concealed treasures, phantom cavalcades, and deeds of magic and love.

Leggett, William (1801–1839), editor, political controversialist, teacher, poet, short-story writer. Although Legett was born in New York City, for a time his family lived in a pioneer settlement on the Illinois prairies. Leggett served in the navy for more than three years, and his sea experiences went into three books: two collections of poems, *Leisure Hours at Sea* (1825) and *Journals of the Ocean* (1826); and *Naval Sketches* (1834). His recollections of life in the Wild West went into *Tales and Sketches, by a Country Schoolmaster* (1829). In

1828 Leggett established a weekly newspaper, the *Critic*, largely written and printed by him. It ceased publication after six months. In 1829 he became an editor of the New York *Evening Post*. He sided with Jackson and wrote chiefly on such matters as free trade and the U.S. Bank. A drop in the *Post's* circulation, owing somewhat to his articles, caused him to withdraw, and he started a paper of his own, the *Plaindealer*. It suspended publication after six months. Leggett died just before setting out to fill an appointment as diplomatic agent to Guatemala. His articles appear in *A Collection of the Political Writings of William Leggett* (1840).

Legree, Simon. The chief villain in Harriet Beecher Stowe's UNCLE TOM'S CABIN. Brutal and mean, he flogs Uncle Tom to death when Tom refuses to reveal the hiding place of two runaway women slaves. He dies an appropriate death in the novel, but he underwent a strange resurrection in Thomas Dixon's THE LEOPARD'S SPOTS (1902).

Le Guin, Ursula K[roeber] (1929–   ), writer of science fiction and fantasy. Le Guin's mother, Theodora, was a psychologist and her father, Alfred Kroeber, an anthropologist in Berkeley, California. Le Guin was educated at Radcliffe College and Columbia University before going to France, marrying, and returning to live in Oregon, where she began her prolific writing career. She created a series of imaginative worlds in her fiction, incorporating elements of mythology, anthropology, and psychology and offering a vision of Taoist wholeness and balance. Her major achievement in fantasy is the *Earthsea* trilogy (1968–72), concerning the wizard Ged in his career as arch-mage in the pretechnological world of islands called Earthsea. *Tehanu: The Last Book of Earthsea* (1990) is a sequel. Her several science-fiction novels introduce an original cosmos, beginning with the Hainish trilogy (1965–67) and including two outstanding works: *The Left Hand of Darkness* (1969) explores gender relations on a distant, frigid planet where the inhabitants are androgynous. *The Dispossessed* (1974), subtitled "an ambiguous Utopia," probes the values of an idealistic anarchist colony in another world through a narrative structure demonstrating the opposing theories of sequential and simultaneous time. Le Guin's fantasy and science fiction, which she regards as thought experiments, transcend her genre through the complex level of ideas and the rich prose style. Her experimental novel *Always Coming Home* (1985) combines myth, anthropology, poetry, music, and documentary, and actively engages the reader in the authorial process of plot construction. Her novel *The Lathe of Heaven* (1971) was adapted for television. Among other novels are *The Word for World Is Forest* (1972), *The Beginning Place* (1980), and *The Telling* (2000). Collections of her short stories include *The Wind's Twelve Quarters* (1975), *Orsinian Tales* (1976), *The Compass Rose* (1982), *Searoad* (1992), and *Unlocking the Air* (1996). Her essays are collected in *Language of the Night* (1979) and *Dancing at the Edge of the World* (1989). She has also written poetry, plays, and several children's books. A study is Charlotte Spivack, *Ursula K. Le Guin* (1984).

CHARLOTTE SPIVACK

Leisler, Jacob (1640–1691),   colonial agitator. Born in Germany, Leisler led a successful rebellion (1689) to seize the government of New York City. He acted as governor for two years, but was not recognized by the British crown. He was deposed, tried for treason, and hanged. While in office Leisler called for a meeting in New York of delegates from all the colonies to make preparation for a war with Canada that he saw coming. Seven delegates, chiefly representing New England, actually met (1690), and thus constituted the first Colonial Congress in America. Many persons were greatly offended at Leisler's execution, and for many years there were two bitterly opposed factions in New York, the Leislerians and the anti-Leislerians. Leisler figured in two plays: Cornelius Mathews's *Jacob Leisler* (1848) and Elizabeth Smith's *Old New York, or, Democracy in 1689* (1853); and three novels: Joseph H. Ingraham's *Leisler* (1846), Edwin L. Bynner's *The Begum's Daughter* (1890), and Dorothy Grant's *Night of Decision* (1946).

Leithauser, Brad (1953–   ),   poet, novelist. Born in Detroit, Leithauser was educated at Harvard and lived for several years in Japan. He held a Fulbright Fellowship in Iceland (1989). Distinguished by verbal skill and technical mastery, his verse has reminded readers of the work of JAMES MERRILL, whom he admires. His first two books were *Hundreds of Fireflies* (1982) and *Cats of the Temple* (1986); most of their contents were reprinted in England as *Between Leaps: Poems 1972–1985* (1987). Later collections include *Mail from Anywhere* (1990) and *The Odd Last Thing She Did* (1998). Also impressive for their display of the author's narrative skills and creative intelligence are the novels *Equal Distance* (1985), drawn from his Japanese experience, and *Hence* (1989), set in Boston and Cambridge in 1993 and involving humans, computers, and chess. *Seaward* (1993) and *The Friends of Freeland* (1997) are later novels. *Penchants and Places* (1995) collects essays and criticism.

Leland, Charles Godfrey.   See HANS BREITMAN.

Lemelin, Roger (1919–1992),   novelist. Lemelin was born in Québec and self-educated after age fourteen. He earned praise for three novels set in Québec. *Au pied de la pente douce* (1944, tr. *The Town Below*, 1948) describes the life of the urban working class toward the end of the Depression. *Les Plouff* (1948, tr. *The Plouffe Family*, 1950) focuses on a single family striving to move upward during the war years; it inspired a popular Canadian TV series. In *Pierre le magnifique* (1952, tr. *In Quest of Splendour*, 1955) the movement upward is largely achieved. Another novel, *Le crime d'Ovide Plouffe* (1982), has been less admired. *Fantaisies sur les péchés capitaux* (1940) comprises seven stories on the deadly sins.

Lena Rivers (1856),   a novel by MARY JANE HOLMES. Lena's father has disappeared and is accused of a crime, and she goes from Massachusetts to Kentucky to live among her aristocratic relatives. When an eligible young man appears, it is of course Lena whom he chooses; moreover, Lena's father turns up—not guilty after all.

L'Engle, Madeleine (1918–   ),   novelist. Born Madeleine L'Engle Camp in New York City, she was educated at Smith. Although she has published over forty works in several genres and novels for all ages, she is best known for her tales for young people—*A Wrinkle in Time* (1962), *A Wind in the Door* (1973), *A Swiftly Tilting Planet* (1978), *An Acceptable Time* (1989), and *Troubling a Star* (1994)—combining science fiction with the themes of family love and moral responsibility. Many of her plots center on young women, convincingly portrayed. *The Small Rain* (1968) deals with a musician learning self-discipline. *Camilla Dickinson* (1951) is a first-person narrative by a maturing adolescent. The Austin family deals with love, death, and hope in *Meet the Austins* (1960), *The Moon by Night* (1963), *The Young Unicorns* (1968), and *A Ring of Endless Light* (1980). Her other titles include *The Summer of Great-Grandmother* (1974), autobiography; *The Sphinx at Dawn* (1982), stories; *Many Waters* (1986); *A Cry Like a Bell* (1987); *Two-Part Invention* (1988); *Certain Women* (1992); and *A Live Coal in the Sea* (1996).

Leni-Lenape Indians.   See DELAWARE INDIANS.

Lennox, Charlotte Ramsay (1720–1804),   poet, novelist, dramatist. Ramsay, daughter of a lieutenant governor of the colony of New York, was sent at the age of fifteen to be educated in England, where she remained for the rest of her life. She attained celebrity by burlesquing sentimental novels and by writing the same sorts of novels she had lampooned. *The Female Quixote; or, The Adventures of Arabella* (1752), which she dramatized in 1758 as *Angelica; or Quixote in Petticoats*, describes a young girl who tries to live like the heroines of fashionable French novels. *The Life of Harriot Stuart* (1750) is perhaps the first novel that had American scenes—the Hudson River, Albany, the Mohawk Valley. *The History of Henrietta* (1758, dramatized in 1769 as *The Sister*) *Sophia* (1762); and *Euphemia* (1790) were widely read sentimental novels.

Lenore (1831, 1843, 1845),   a poem by EDGAR ALLAN POE. This lament on the death of a beautiful young woman passed through three quite different drafts. Poe's theme was one he often employed. He said in THE PHILOSOPHY OF COMPOSITION (1846) that the death of a woman both young and beautiful "is, unquestionably, the most poetical topic in the world." He treated this topic in verse and in his stories, among them MORELLA, BERENICE, and LIGEIA.

Lenox, James (1800–1880),   philanthropist, collector, editor, publisher. After graduating from Columbia Law School in 1820, James Lenox worked in his father's business until the death of his father left him heir to a fortune. From that time he devoted himself to study, travel, and collecting paintings, rare books, and manuscripts. He collected Americana as well as incunabula and Shakespeareana. To house his treasures, he built the Lenox Library in 1870 on Fifth Avenue between 70th and 71st Streets.

He edited and privately printed a number of the books and manuscripts in his collection, among them *Washington's Farewell Address to the People of the U.S.* (1850); *Nicolaus Syllacius De Insulis Meridiani atque Indici Maris Nuper Inventus*

(1859), a 15th-century account of Columbus's second voyage by Niccolò Scillacio, with a translation by John Mulligan; Shakespeare's *Plays in Folio* (1861); and *The Early Editions of King James' Bible in Folio* (1861). He also published the *Letter of Columbus to Luis de Santagel* (1864), an account of the unique copy of the Spanish quarto edition in the Biblioteca Ambrosiano, Milan. His *Bibliographical Account of the Voyages of Columbus* (1861) appeared in the *Historical Magazine*.

One of the New York's greatest philanthropists, Lenox founded and supported the Presbyterian Hospital, endowed the New York Public Library, and left his priceless collection of books, paintings, and manuscripts to New York City. See BENJAMIN FRANKLIN STEVENS.

Lenski, Lois (1893–1974),   artist, illustrator, writer of books for children. After doing illustrations for other authors, Lenski, who was born in Ohio, began writing books of her own for children. The first was *Skipping Village* (1927), and many others followed, including *Bayou Suzette* (1944), *Boom Town Boy* (1948), *I Like Winter* (1950), *Prairie School* (1951), *Houseboat Girl* (1957), and *Little Sioux Girl* (1958). Several of Lenski's books won awards, among them *Strawberry Girl* (1946), the story of a child who lives an uncertain life as a member of a central Florida "strawberry family," which won a Newbery Medal. Among her later titles are *Lois Lenski's Christmas Stories* (1968) and *Lois Lenski's Big Book of Mr. Small* (1979). Her autobiography, *Journey into Childhood*, appeared in 1972.

Leonard, Daniel (1740–1829),   political controversialist, lawyer. Born in Norton, Massachusetts, and at first an adherent of the colonists, Leonard switched his views and went over to the crown. An able writer, under the pen name Massachusettensis, he contributed a series of letters (December 12, 1774–April 3, 1775) to the *Massachusetts Gazette*, presenting the Tory side with much logic and occasional threats. JOHN ADAMS [2] replied to the letters under the pen name Novanglus. Leonard's letters were reprinted as *The Origin of the American Contest with Great Britain* (1775). Leonard was later exiled and was made chief justice of Bermuda.

Leonard, Elmore [John] (1925–   ),   novelist, short-story writer. Born in New Orleans, the son of an automobile executive, Leonard became interested in writing while growing up in Michigan. After service with the Seabees in the South Pacific, he majored in English and Philosophy at the University of Detroit (Ph.B., 1950) and began a career as an advertising writer. After *Argosy* magazine published his first story, "Trail of the Apache," in 1951, he moonlighted for ten years as a writer of pulp westerns—thirty stories and four novels, *The Bounty Hunters* (1953), *The Law at Redondo* (1955), *Escape from Five Shadows* (1956), and *Last Stand at Saber River* (1957)—before the success of *Hombre* (1961), chosen by the Western Writers of America as one of the best westerns of all time, set him free from advertising. Other westerns followed, but when the market dried up in the early 1960s, he briefly abandoned fiction, then turned to crime novels, the genre for which he has been most celebrated, with nearly thirty published by 2000. Critics praise his spare style and wiseguy dialogue, frankly modeled more on Hemingway, Steinbeck, and John O'Hara than on other western or crime writers, his compelling plot lines, and his flair for dead-on, often satiric, evocations of times and places. These later works include: *Stick* (1983), his first bestseller; *LaBrava* (1983), awarded an Edgar as best mystery novel of the year; *Glitz* (1985), a Book-of-the-Month Club selection; *Get Shorty* (1990), a jokey view of Hollywood from an author thoroughly familiar with the subject; *Maximum Bob* (1991), about a Florida judge's fondness for the electric chair and desire to get rid of his wife, who believes herself possessed by the spirit of a girl eaten by an alligator; *Riding the Rap* (1995), the work, according to reviewer Martin Amis, of "a literary genius"; and *Cuba Libre* (1998), a political satire set in Cuba at the time of the Spanish-American War. *The Tonto Woman and Other Western Stories* (1998) collects nineteen early stories. *Pagan Babies* (2000) centers on Detroit priest Terry Dunn's efforts to set up a foundation benefitting the orphan survivors of Rwandan genocide, in spite of the inept gangsters and ex-cons who surround him.

Leonard, William Ellery (1876–1944),   teacher, poet, translator, critic. Leonard, born in New Jersey, taught at the University of Wisconsin. He wrote books and monographs on literary subjects, meanwhile leading a busy private life, the best record of which is found in his autobiography, *The Locomotive God* (1927), and the sonnet sequence *Two Lives* (1925) about his marriage and his wife's suicide. There also seems to be autobiography in the sonnets of *A Man Against Time* (1945). Leonard developed agoraphobia, which from 1922 on made him practically a prisoner in his home, and the disturbances furnished ample material for Leonard's sonorous poetry. He published many collections of verse, including *The Vaunt of Man and Other Poems* (1912); *The Lynching Bee and Other Poems* (1920); *A Son of Earth* (his collected verse, 1928); and *Man Against Time, an Heroic Dream* (posthumous, 1945). In addition he was an ardent student of Lucretius, translated his poems (1916, repr. 1921), wrote a study of his life and poetry (1942), and helped edit the Latin text.

Leonard, Zenas (1809–1857),   fur trapper and trader, explorer, memoirist. Born in Clearfield, Pennsylvania, Leonard went west to St. Louis, joined an expedition that was making its way to California, and became a fur trapper. In 1833 he joined an expedition to Utah, Nevada, and California organized by John Reddeford Walker for Capt. Benjamin Louis Eulalie de Bonneville. Leonard, as official clerk of the expedition, kept a journal. Part of his account was published in the Clearfield *Republican*, later published as *Narrative of the Adventures of Zenas Leonard, Written by Himself* (1839, ed. by W. F. Wagner, 1904, by Milo M. Quaife, 1934). It is regarded as one of the best depictions of a mountain man's life. Leonard became an Indian trader on the Santa Fe trail, at Fort Sibley, Missouri.

Leopard's Spots, The (1902),   a novel by THOMAS DIXON, JR. Following his usual line of thought, Dixon endeavored to show what frightful results would follow if the

African-American were "lifted above his station." His title was derived from Jeremiah xiii, 23, and was intended to suggest to the reader the words preceding the title phrase. Included in the narrative is an account of an African-American legislature. See SIMON LEGREE.

Leopold, Aldo (1887–1948),   conservationist. A graduate of Yale Forestry School, Leopold became supervisor of Carson National Forest in New Mexico in 1913. A pioneer in wildlife management, Leopold published a landmark textbook in 1933 and in the same year began teaching at University of Wisconsin, which created a chain of game management for him. In 1935 he helped found the Wilderness Society. His posthumously published *A Sand County Almanac* (1949) has sold over a million copies, inspiring those who find his concept of a land ethic especially persuasive. Studies are Susan Flader's *Thinking Like a Mountain* (1974) and Curt Meine's *Aldo Leopold: His Life and Work* (1988).

Le Page du Pratz, Antoine Simon (1690?–1775), historian. Probably a Fleming, Le Page du Pratz seems to have emigrated to Louisiana. He wrote *Histoire de la Louisiane* (3 v. 1758), which was translated as *The History of Louisiana* (2 v. 1763).

Le Pan, Douglas (1914–   ),   poet, novelist. Born in Toronto and educated at the University of Toronto and Oxford, Le Pan has twice won the Governor General's Award: for *The Net and the Sword: Poems* (1953), based on his experience as an artillery officer in Italy during World War II; and for his novel *The Deserter* (1964), about a soldier who has gone AWOL. He was a member of the Canadian Department of External Affairs (1945–59), a period recalled in the memoir *Bright Glass of Memory* (1979), and later a professor at Queen's University and the University of Toronto. His other verse collections are *The Wounded Prince* (1948); *Something Still to Find* (1982); *Far Voyage* (1985), poems to a cancer victim; *Weathering It: Complete Poems, 1948–1987* (1987); and *Macalister, or Dying in the Dark* (1995), a verse drama about a Canadian soldier in World War II.

Lerner, Alan Jay (1918–1986),   author, lyricist, producer. After graduating from Harvard in 1940 Lerner, born in New York City, went into radio writing. He began collaborating with FREDERICK LOEWE for the musical comedy stage in 1942, and their first successful production was BRIGADOON (1947). He worked with Kurt Weill on the musical *Love Life* (1948), and again with Loewe on *Paint Your Wagon* (1951), then went to Hollywood to write screenplays, first for *A Royal Wedding* and then for *An American in Paris*. Again in collaboration with Loewe he wrote *Gigi* (1953, film 1958); *My Fair Lady* (1956), which had a long and successful run on Broadway and became a film in 1964; and the Broadway musical *Camelot* (1960), based on T. H. White's book on King Arthur, *The Once and Future King* (1958). A memoir is *The Street Where I Live* (1978).

Lerner, Max (1902–1992),   teacher, lecturer, editor, radio commentator, columnist, essayist. Lerner, who was born in Russia, taught at Sarah Lawrence, Harvard, Brandeis, and Williams; he helped edit the *Encyclopedia of the Social Sciences*

and for two years edited the NATION; he contributed regularly to several New York newspapers and was a popular lecturer. Described as "a neo-Marxian liberal," he advocated social change but opposed Communism. Among his books are *It Is Later Than You Think* (1938), *Ideas Are Weapons* (1939), *The Consequences of the Atom* (1945), *Actions and Passions; Notes on the Multiple Revolution of Our Time* (1949), *America as a Civilization: Life and Thought in the United States Today* (1957), *The Unfinished Country* (1959), *The Age of Overkill: A Preface to World Politics* (1963), *Ted and the Kennedy Legend* (1980), and *Wrestling with the Angel: A Memoir of My Triumph over Illness* (1990).

Leslie, Eliza (1787–1858),   short-story writer, writer on domestic science. Born in Philadelphia, Eliza Leslie was one of the first women in this country to realize the financial returns possible in domestic science. In 1827 she published *Seventy-Five Receipts for Pastry, Cakes, and Sweetmeats* and then turned to writing children's stories. She was also successful as a short-story writer. Her "Mrs. Washington Potts" was awarded the *Godey's Lady's Book* prize in 1845. She wrote one novel, *Amelia, or a Young Lady's Vicissitudes* (1848), but was best known for her books on domestic life, such as *An American Girl's Book* (1831), *Domestic Cookery Book* (1837), *The Lady's Receipt Book* (1846), and *The Behavior Book* (1853).

Leslie, Frank [Henry Carter] (1821–1880).   *Frank Leslie's Ladies Gazette of Fashion and Fancy Needle Work*, which was first issued in January 1854, was started by a young engraver who had come to the United States from England in 1848, changing his name to avoid parental censure. Toward the end of that year, Leslie purchased the *New York Journal*, a "story paper," and combined the two publications. In 1855, he brought out *Frank Leslie's Illustrated Newspaper*, a sixteen-page weekly modeled after the *London Illustrated News*. One of its innovations was the speed with which illustrations followed the events they portrayed—appearing two weeks after publication of the news. This achievement went unmatched until after the Civil War. The weekly claimed a circulation of 100,000. Although *Harper's Weekly*, first published in 1857, offered strong competition, Leslie began to issue *Frank Leslie's New Family Magazine* in 1857 and *Frank Leslie's Budget of Fun* in the following year.

The *Illustrated Newspaper* was Leslie's outstanding venture. Its managing editor was Henry C. Watson, who had been an associate of Edgar Allan Poe on the *Broadway Journal*. Although writers such as Wilkie Collins and Walter Besant were contributors, the *Illustrated News* could not match the literary standards of *Harper's Weekly*. But it never lacked variety. Its features ranged from a series on America's "Great West" to the "House-wife's Friend Department" to prizefight news. Although given to sensationalism, the magazine also campaigned against political corruption. Unfortunate real estate investments nearly ruined Leslie and his enterprises. After his death, his widow continued the publications with considerable success, legally taking the name of Frank Leslie. In 1889, she sold the *Illustrated Newspaper* to W. J. Arkell and Russell B. Harrison, publishers of JUDGE. The magazine, later called

Leslie's Weekly, never succeeded in regaining its earlier popularity. Later yet, it became THE AMERICAN MAGAZINE and survived until 1956, thus covering a span of more than 100 years.

Leslie, Miriam Florence Folline Squier (1836–1914), editor, travel writer, feminist. *Frank Leslie's Lady's Journal* was edited in 1871 by Miriam F. Squier, the beautiful, much-married future wife of FRANK LESLIE. In 1871 she published a translation of *Travels in Central America* by Arthur Morelet. She wrote *California: A Pleasure Trip from Gotham to the Golden Gate* in 1877, an account of a luxurious trip made with Frank Leslie after they married.

Leslie's death in 1880 left his widow deeply in debt, but by a number of astute moves, one of them being the legal adoption of the name "Frank Leslie," she managed his magazines so shrewdly that by her death she had built a fortune of two million dollars. She wrote and published a number of feminist books: *Rents in Our Robes* (1888), *Beautiful Women of Twelve Epochs* (1890), *Are Men Gay Deceivers?* (1893), and *A Social Mirage* (1899). Joaquin Miller, meeting her on her California trip, was captivated by her charms and modeled Annette, the heroine of his novel *One Fair Woman*, upon her. Madeleine B. Stern told her extraordinary story in *Purple Passage: The Life of Mrs. Frank Leslie* (1953).

Lesson of the Master, The.   A story by HENRY JAMES. First published in *The Universal Review* in 1888, the story was collected in *The Lesson of the Master* (1892) and in volume XV of James's New York Edition. A young writer, Paul Overt, learns from an older one, Henry St. George, an ambiguous lesson about self-denial in pursuit of art, especially the sacrifice of marriage and family.

Lester, Charles Edwards (1815–1890),   lawyer, clergyman, consular official, translator, writer. A great-grandson of JONATHAN EDWARDS, Lester wrote of revolting living conditions in English industrial areas, observed during a trip abroad: *The Glory and Shame of England* (2 v. 184) and *The Condition and Fate of England* (1842). While serving as consul at Genoa, he translated Italian writings, and on his return he wrote *My Consulship* (1853). Although his books on England had aroused resentment in that country, he became New York correspondent of the London *Times*. He wrote many books thereafter—biographies of American heroes; a history, *Our First Hundred Years* (1874); and a book on hospital conditions during the Civil War.

Le Sueur, Meridel (1900–1996),   journalist, novelist, poet. Born in Iowa and raised in Texas, Oklahoma, and Kansas, Le Sueur was the child of a leftist lawyer. After quitting high school, she went to New York, where she lived in a commune with EMMA GOLDMAN and studied at the American Academy of Dramatic Art. During the Depression she worked in a factory, acted in Hollywood, and earned a reputation as a proletarian writer with contributions to *The Daily Worker* and *The New Masses*. In a novel, *The Girl* (1939), and in *Salute to Spring and Other Stories* (1940), she portrayed the hardships of women's lives during the 1930s. In *North Star Country* (1945) she described the Midwest of her childhood, and in *Crusaders* (1955) she told the story of her parents' lives. Pilloried during

the McCarthy era (see MCCARTHYISM), she published radical journalism in the next two decades, but few books. She reports some of this agony in *Song for My Time: Stories of the Period of Repression* (1977). Her other works include *Conquistadors* (1973); *The Mound Builders* (1974); *Rites of Ancient Ripening* (1975), a book of verse; *Women on the Breadlines* (1977); *I Hear Men Talking and Other Stories* (1984); and *The Dread Road* (1991), a novel about a Colorado mining strike. *Ripening: Selected Work, 1927–1980* appeared in 1982.

Letter to His Countrymen, A (1834),   by JAMES FENIMORE COOPER. Disgruntled with press attacks that had cost him much of his American audience, Cooper attacked the press, charging it with subservience to foreign opinions. He attacked President Jackson for certain diplomatic appointments, attacked Congress for seeking to destroy the executive branch of the government, and attacked Americans for being supine during these attempts to destroy their liberties. Cooper emphasized the difference between the English governmental system, in which an oligarchy had taken all powers away from the King, and the American system, with its carefully planned system of checks. At the end he said farewell to writing and offered a dignified reproof to his public. But he did not stop writing; in the next year appeared THE MONIKINS, an allegory and satire that continued the themes of his *Letter*.

Letters from a Farmer in Pennsylvania, to the Inhabitants of the British Colonies   (1767–68 in the *Pennsylvania Chronicle*; in pamphlet form, 1768), twelve letters by JOHN DICKINSON published anonymously. Dickinson, a Maryland lawyer who practiced and held public office in Delaware and Pennsylvania, assumed in these *Letters* the character of a small farmer with a few servants, a good library, and some well-read friends. He was impelled to share with his countrymen, he said, his "thoughts on some late transactions." His chief point was that in the heated controversy between the colonies and the mother country, it was England, not America, that was legally in the wrong. He supported his thesis with arguments taken from Locke to the effect that the purpose of government was to protect the inalienable rights of property, in accordance with the social compact involved. He urged the people to use the right of legal petition, then to employ measures against the purchase of British goods, and finally—when all else failed—to resort to arms.

The *Letters* made a sensation and were reprinted in most colonial newspapers. There were one Irish, one French, six American, and two English editions in book form. Burke probably was influenced by Dickinson, and Voltaire praised him. Dickinson was known from then on as the Pennsylvania farmer.

Letters from an American Farmer (1782),   by Michel-Guillaume Jean de Crèvecœur writing under the pen name of J. Hector St. John (see CRÈVECŒUR). Crèvecœur (1735–1813) was a French soldier who came to Canada to fight under Montcalm and later made explorations around the Great Lakes. He came to New York in 1759 after the fall of Quebec, took out naturalization papers six years later, and became a surveyor and trader, traveling far west in the course of his work. In 1769 he married and settled down as a farmer in Orange County, New York. During the Revolution he refused to support either side and remained a pacifist; the rebels forced him to leave his farm, and the royalists imprisoned him for two months. He finally managed to get to England, then to France. There he wrote his *Letters*, which were published in England (1782). Later he translated them into French, *Letters d'un Cultivateur Américain* (1783). Franklin became his friend, he was elected to the *Académie des Sciences*, and he was taken to visit the great naturalist Turgot. Under this new influence he veered to the side of the rebels and was appointed in 1783 French consul in New York. In America he found his wife dead, his farm ruined. His children had vanished, but he found them later in Boston. He wrote an additional book dealing with his second fatherland, VOYAGE DANS LA HAUTE PENNSYLVANIE ET DANS L'ETAT DE NEW-YORK (1801). More than a century later some suppressed letters, a number of essays, and a short play were collected in *Sketches of the 18th-Century America* (1925).

Crèvecœur was an ardent disciple of Rousseau; this strain somewhat weakens the vigor of his *Letters*, although he is realistic enough when considering the life of a frontier farmer. At times he writes merely rhetorically and elegantly, at other times he is eloquent, especially in the passage in which he answers his own question, "What is an American?" Many of the English Romantic poets and critics read the *Letters* with delight, and William Hazlitt found in them "not only the objects but the feelings of a new country."

Letters of Jonathan Oldstyle, Gent. (1802–1803), by WASHINGTON IRVING. Irving was nineteen when these nine essays appeared in the New York *Morning Chronicle*, edited by his brother Peter. They were pirated by a New York publisher in 1824, and five editions appeared in England. All traded on Irving's sudden burst of fame; the New York edition omitted his name and attributed the Letters to "the Author of the *Sketch Book*."

The *Letters* deal mostly with the theater, which Irving loved and wanted to improve. He satirizes the ranting plays, vulgar audiences, inaudible music, and critics. Some well-known personages of the day are held up for ridicule, under fictitious names. The style is obviously modeled on *The Spectator* and its American imitators and foreshadows Irving's later writing.

Letters of the British Spy, The (published anonymously in the *Virginia Argus*, 1803; in book form, 1803), by WILLIAM WIRT. These ten *Letters* described Southern society, sometimes satirically. Especially celebrated was Wirt's depiction of a blind preacher. The *Letters* were supposedly written to a member of Parliament by an English traveler in the United States.

Let Us Now Praise Famous Men (1936), a record of the lives of three tenant families during the Depression, in prose by JAMES AGEE, photographs by Walker Evans.

Levertov, Denise (1923–1997), poet. Born in Ilford, Essex, her mother Welsh and her father an Anglican clergyman converted from Judaism, Levertov received no formal educa-tion, but learned at home in an actively literary family with a houseful of books. Her first book, *The Double Image* (1946), published while she was still in England, showed her as a young poet of considerable promise. In 1947 she married Mitchell Goodman (1923–), an American author; in 1948 they moved to the United States and she began to develop an American voice, especially influenced by the verse of Wallace Stevens and William Carlos Williams. Among poets more nearly her contemporaries, she was associated especially with BLACK MOUNTAIN POETS Charles Olson, Robert Duncan, and Robert Creeley. The verse from this period is collected in *Here and Now* (1957), *With Eyes at the Back of Our Heads* (1959), *The Jacob's Ladder* (1961), and *O Taste and See* (1964). In 1961 she became poetry editor of *The Nation* and during the 1960s she and her husband actively opposed the Vietnam War. Since then much of her verse has been informed by politics, especially concern for women and the third world, though much remains personal. Her poetry titles include *The Sorrow Dance* (1967), *Embroideries* (1969), *Relearning the Alphabet* (1970), *To Stay Alive* (1971), *Footprints* (1972), *The Freeing of the Dust* (1975), *Life in the Forest* (1978), *Oblique Prayers* (1984), *Breathing the Water* (1987), *A Door in the Hive* (1989), *Evening Train* (1992), *Sands of the Well* (1996), and *This Great Unknowing: Last Poems* (1999). Her essays are collected in *The Poet in the World* (1973), *Light Up the Cave* (1981), and *Tessarae: Memories and Suppositions* (1995). Christopher Mac-Gowan edited *The Letters of Denise Levertov and William Carlos Williams* (1998).

Levin, Ira (1929–), novelist, playwright. Born in New York City, Levin was educated at New York University. A master of suspense, he has been best known for the novel *Rosemary's Baby* (1967)—also a film (1968)—in which the heroine bears Satan's child. It inspired many subsequent novels and films of occult and gothic horror. *Son of Rosemary* (1997) is a sequel. His play *Deathtrap* (1978)—also a movie (1982)—builds enormous tension as a writer of murder mysteries and a young admirer plot murder in their own lives. His other novels include *A Kiss Before Dying* (1953); *This Perfect Day* (1970); *The Stepford Wives* (1972); *The Boys from Brazil* (1976, film 1978), about Nazis in South America; and *Sliver* (1991), about voyeurism. His other plays include *No Time for Sergeants* (1955), a comedy; and *Critic's Choice* (1960).

Levin, Meyer (1905–1981), novelist. Born in Chicago and educated at the University of Chicago, Levin used his experiences with *Chicago Daily News* (1922–28) in his first novel, *Reporter* (1929). His other early novels include *Frankie and Johnny: A Love Story* (1930); *Yehuda* (1931), about life in a kibbutz; and *The New Bridge* (1933). These paved the way for the three novels generally perceived as his best, all set in Chicago: *The Old Bunch* (1937), mixing fact and fiction in a story of American Jews that followed the lives of nineteen high school graduates of 1921; *Citizens* (1940), about the 1937 strike at Republic Steel; and *Compulsion* (1956), based on the 1924 Leopold-Loeb murder case. His novels with settings in Palestine or Israel include *My Father's House* (1947),

Gore and Igor (1968), *The Spell of Time* (1974), and *The Harvest* (1978). Among others are *Eva* (1959); *The Stronghold* (1965), set in Germany; and *The Architect* (1982), based on the life of Frank Lloyd Wright. *The Fanatic* (1964) is a novel based on Levin's attempt to get his version of Anne Frank's diary produced on Broadway; *The Obsession* (1973) reports that battle again after it had stretched to two decades. *In Search* (1950) is an autobiography.

Levine, Norman (1923–), memoirist, novelist, poet. Born in Ottawa, Levine lived mostly in Cornwall, England, from the late 1940s until he returned to Canada in 1980. His most celebrated book, *Canada Made Me* (1958), is a memoir of the Canadian underside in the 1950s; reminiscent of works by George Orwell and Henry Miller, it reports the hand-to-mouth living of a working-and-bumming writer. It was not published in a Canadian edition until 1979, when it finally made his reputation at home. Similar materials appear in the novel *From a Seaside Town* (1970) and stories collected in *Selected Stories* (1975) and *Thin Ice* (1979). The novel *The Angled Road* (1952) tells of a young man's RCAF experience in World War II. Poetry is collected in *The Tight-Rope Walker* (1950) and *I Walk by the Harbour* (1976). *Champagne Barn* (1984) and *Something Happened Here* (1991) are story collections.

Levine, Philip (1928–), poet. Born in Detroit, Levine was educated at Wayne University and the University of Iowa. A spokesman for "the voiceless," he uses ordinary speech rhythms and colloquial language to celebrate the strength of the working people who taught him, he says, that his "formal education was a lie." *Selected Poems* (1984) draws from ten earlier books. These include *On the Edge* (1963), *Not This Pig* (1968), *They Feed the Lion* (1972), *The Names of the Lost* (1976), *Ashes* (1979), *Seven Years from Somewhere* (1979), and *One for the Rose* (1981). Later volumes, almost all saturated in memories of Detroit, include *What Work Is* (1991); *The Simple Truth* (1994), a Pulitzer Prize winner; and *The Mercy* (2000). *The Bread of Time: Toward an Autobiography* appeared in 1994.

Lewis, Alfred Henry ["Dan Quin"] (1858–1914), journalist, short-story writer. Born in Cleveland, Lewis was admitted to the bar at an early age. In 1881 he went west and became a hobo cowboy, writing for the Las Vegas *Optic* and wandering about southeastern Arizona. In 1885 he tried to practice law in Kansas City, Missouri, filling his spare time with politics and journalism. In 1890 he sent a story to the Kansas City *Times*, representing it as an interview with an old cattleman. It was copied by newspapers all over the country, and a character was born.

Lewis wrote many of these stories, all told by the Old Cattleman, whose dry philosophy and homely humor follow traditions established by the American humorists of the 19th century. His WOLFVILLE (1897), *Sandburrs* (1900), *Wolfville Days* (1902), *Wolfville Nights* (1902), *Wolfville Folks* (1908), and *Faro Nell and Her Friends* (1913) were very popular in their day. In 1894 Lewis became one of the ablest editors of the growing chain of Hearst newspapers. He also wrote a number of fictionized biographies and two books of underworld life, *Confessions of a Detective* (1906) and *The Apaches of New York* (1912).

Lewis, Charles Bertrand ["M. Quad"] (1842–1924), newspaperman, columnist, dime novelist, playwright. Born in Ohio and originally a printer, Lewis went to college for a while, served in the Union Army, worked on various newspapers in Michigan, particularly the Detroit *Free Press* (1869–91), and then on the New York *World*. Early in his newspaper career he was involved in a steamship fire on the Ohio, and his humorous account of *How It Feels to Be Blown Up* gave him a national reputation. As a columnist he wrote about the Lime-Kiln Club, a forerunner of humorous accounts of African-American social life. Among his books are *Quad's Odds* (1875), *Goaks and Tears* (1875), *Bessie Bane, or, The Mormon's Victim* (1880), *The Comic Biography* (1881?), *Brother Gardner's Lime-Kiln Club* (1882, 1887), *Sawed-Off Sketches* (1884), *Spark's of Wit and Humor* (1887), and *Trials and Troubles of the Bowser Family* (1889, 1902). His play *Yakie* was produced in 1884.

Lewis, Estelle [or Stella]. Pen name of SARAH ANNA BLANCHE ROBINSON LEWIS.

Lewis, Janet (1899–1998), novelist, short story writer, poet. Born in Chicago, Lewis was educated at the University of Chicago and in 1926 married YVOR WINTERS. Although she wrote much lyric poetry, she is remembered chiefly for her historical novels, three of them based on court cases involving circumstantial evidence. Of these, *The Wife of Martin Guerre* (1941) is her best. It concerns the actual court case of a man accused of deceiving the wife of another man. The accused was an exact double of the husband, thought dead. It is a close and evocative study of human nature under pressure. *The Invasion: A Narrative of Events Concerning the Johnston Family of St. Mary's* (1932) dramatizes from within an Indian culture, the Ojibway, and its gradual disappearance. *The Trial of Soren Qvist* (1947) depicts a 17th-century Danish pastor wrongly accused. *The Ghost of Monsieur Scarron* (1959) presents a Paris bookbinder of 1694 accused of libeling Louis XIV and Madame de Maintenon. Another novel, *Against a Darkening Sky* (1943), presents a woman in the center of "the incoherent civilization, the moral wilderness" of the 1930s. Her stories are collected in *Good-bye Son* (1946), and much of her verse is collected in *Poems Old and New, 1918–1978* (1981), and *The Dear Past* (1994).

Lewis, Meriwether (1774–1809), explorer, soldier, governor. Manager of his family plantation in Virginia at eighteen, Lewis served in the suppression of the Whiskey Rebellion of 1794, joined the regular army shortly afterward, and was stationed at several frontier posts, where he learned Indian languages and customs. When Jefferson became president he asked Lewis to serve as his private secretary. Lewis's project, to search for a land route to the Pacific, was encouraged by Jefferson, and Congress appropriated $2,500 for the purpose. With Capt. WILLIAM CLARK as joint commander, Lewis set out from St. Louis in the spring of 1804 on the now-famous Lewis and Clark Expedition. Undeterred by attacks from hostile Indians and great hardships, the expedition moved on to the Pacific coast. Lewis kept a detailed diary of the expedition, remarkable for its scientific accuracy and its stately 18th-century style. He was appointed governor of the Louisiana Territory, an office he held until his death.

Lewis appears in many novels, including Eva E. Dye's *The Conquest* (1902), Emerson Hough's *The Magnificent Adventure* (1916), Ethel Hueston's *Star of the West* (1935), Donald C. Peattie's *Forward the Nation* (1942), Odell and Willard Shephard's *Holdfast Gaines* (1946), Vardis Fisher's *Tale of Valor* (1958), and James Alexander Thorn's *From Sea to Shining Sea* (1985). Lewis appears also in Robert Penn Warren's *Brother to Dragons: A Tale in Verse and Voices* (1953). John Bakeless described *Lewis and Clark; Partners in Discovery* (1947). Vardis Fisher wrote of Lewis's death in *Suicide or Murder* (1961). Lewis and Clark's *History of the Expedition* was edited by Nicholas Biddle (1814). R. G. Thwaites collected all the *Original Journals of the Lewis and Clark Expedition* (8 v. 1904–05), a great work of which Bernard De Voto made a one-volume abridgment (1953). Stephen E. Ambrose's *Undaunted Courage* (1996), a history of the expedition, makes copious use of the journals. See SACAJAWEA.

Lewis, Oscar (1914–1970),   anthropologist. Lewis studied impoverished rural people, earning particular recognition for his work with Mexicans and Mexican-Americans in *Five Families* (1959) and *Children of Sanchez* (1961) and with Puerto Ricans in *La Vida* (1966), which won a National Book Award. His books, distilled from hundreds of hours of tape-recorded conversations, attained a beauty and power that elevated them above mere documentary. In studying poverty as a culture unto itself, transcending national distinctions, Lewis created what has been called the anthropology of poverty and has had a major impact on social analysis. His final work was a massive oral history of the Cuban revolution, *Living the Revolution* (3 v. 1977–78), based on interviews taken in 1969–70.

Lewis, Richard (1700?–1734),   poet. Lewis emigrated to Maryland as a young man and became a clerk in the Assembly and perhaps a schoolteacher. Long forgotten, he is now remembered for descriptions of nature in poems published, at times anonymously, in newspapers and magazines. Best known is "A Journey from Patapsco to Annapolis, April 4, 1730," which appeared in *The Gentleman's Magazine*, March 1732. Others are "Earth's Felicities, Heaven's Allowance," "Sea-Storm nigh the Coast," and "Food for Criticks." He also published a translation of Edward Holdsworth's *Muscipula* (1728), a satire on the Welsh.

Lewis, Sarah Anna Blanche Robinson [pen name **Estelle Lewis, sometimes Stella**] (1824–1880),   poet, dramatist. Lewis's fame rests on mentions of her by EDGAR ALLAN POE. He praised her poem "Forsaken" and later wrote a eulogistic article about the Maryland poet in the *Democratic Review* (August 1848). She was a sentimental poet whose verses were collected in *Records of the Heart* (1844) and *Child of the Sea and Other Poems* (1848). *Sappho* (a play, 1868) was translated into Greek and played in Athens. In *The Union* (March 1848) Poe addressed an anagrammatic poem, *An*

Enigma, to Lewis and in a letter to her in 1849 calls her "my dear sister Anna" and "my sweet sister." There is evidence that Lewis subsidized Poe, and that his attitude was hypocritically flattering toward what he elsewhere called her "rubbish."

Lewis, [Harry] Sinclair (1885–1951),   novelist. Born in Sauk Center, Minnesota, Lewis was the son of a country doctor. He was something of a dreamer, a gangling boy with few friends, self-conscious and unsure of himself. He spent his freshman year at Oberlin College in Ohio and then transferred to Yale. His first stories and poems, in imitative 19th-century verse, were published in Yale's literary magazine. In his last year he interrupted his studies at Yale and for a month worked as a janitor in Upton Sinclair's socialistic colony at HELICON HALL in Englewood, New Jersey. He contributed more short stories and poems to a number of magazines and after graduation in 1908 spent several years in newspaper and editorial work in various parts of the country. When living in New York City, he published his first novel, *Hike and the Aeroplane* (1912), a story for boys. *Our Mr. Wrenn: The Romantic Adventures of a Gentle Man* (1914) deals with an American in Europe, and was praised for its realism, humor, and mild satire. *The Trail of the Hawk* (1915), which Lewis thought prefigured Lindbergh's career, is based to some extent on Lewis's own boyhood and young manhood. The novel has passages of satire that foreshadow his later work, but it is primarily sentimental. It was also praised by reviewers, some of whom wrote that Lewis was one of the most promising young American writers. In *The Job: An American Novel* (1917) Lewis first presented controversial subjects, in particular the theme of the young woman entering the world of business and the resultant conflicts between marriage and career. Although better than the two preceding novels, *The Job* was viewed less favorably by the critics, many of whom objected to the realism of the book and its unidealized treatment of the American business world. *The Innocents* (1917), a sentimental picture of an elderly couple and of village life, and *Free Air* (1919) were neither as good or as well received as the earlier books.

Quite different are the novels of Lewis's next period. MAIN STREET (1920) is a devastatingly satiric novel of the dullness and cultural deadness of the small town. Lewis drew on his boyhood knowledge of the small midwestern town to create Gopher Prairie, which was to become a symbol of the provincialism and rigidity of small American towns. The novel was immensely successful and established Lewis as a significant American novelist, the first to thoroughly demolish the sentimental myth of the happy village that had dominated, with few exceptions, stories of American rural life since the 19th century. BABBITT (1922) is in many ways an extension of *Main Street*, with the emphasis shifted from the town to George F. Babbitt, citizen, booster, and epitome of small-town attitudes and interests. Yet Babbitt is also something more than an embodiment of an attitude. In his struggle for success, gregariousness, unimaginative and unperceptive acceptance of his surroundings, and averageness, he may be seen as a negative folk hero who, though the object of scorn and ridicule, is often pathetic and never quite despicable.

Lewis spent several months traveling in the Caribbean with the bacteriologist PAUL DE KRUIF in preparation for his next book, ARROWSMITH (1925), Lewis's favorite among his novels. A story of a young doctor and his struggle between personal desires and idealistic dedication to science, *Arrowsmith* is without much of the biting satire of *Main Street* and *Babbitt*. In its main character it presents a theme lacking in the earlier novels, that of a man in search of truth. *Arrowsmith* was awarded a Pulitzer Prize, which Lewis refused to accept on the grounds that the prize was awarded not for literary merit but for the best presentation of "the wholesome atmosphere of American life."

Mantrap (1926), based on an expedition Lewis made into the Canadian wilderness, was dismissed by most reviewers as "Lewis in a light vein." It was followed by ELMER GANTRY (1927), a mercilessly satiric story of a Midwestern minister and evangelist. It was received with even more outrage than *Main Street*, but those who liked it praised it highly for Lewis's ability to capture precisely the atmosphere and quality of a type of Midwestern revivalism. The characters of Frank Shallard and Andrew Pengilly, Lewis's ideal religious men, went unnoticed by those who denounced Lewis as an instrument of the devil. Also unnoticed was the import of the book, which was not so much an attack on religion itself as on the dehumanized society that made it possible for Elmer to get "everything from the church and Sunday School, except, perhaps, any longing whatever for decency and kindness and reason."

The Man Who Knew Coolidge (1928) was another attack on the small businessman but less successful than *Babbitt*. DODSWORTH (1929) returned somewhat to the tenor of Lewis's first books, in which the Midwesterner is compared favorably with the outsider. Sam Dodsworth, a prosperous businessman with some appreciation of literature and art, takes his shallow and well-groomed wife, Fran, to Europe, where most of the novel takes place. Fran has an affair with an Austrian count, and Sam finally leaves her to marry a more congenial woman. Sidney Howard collaborated with Lewis on a dramatic version of *Dodsworth* in 1934.

Lewis was awarded the Nobel Prize for literature in 1930, the first American novelist so honored. After *Dodsworth*, however, his work began to decline, although he continued to write prolifically. His works of this last period include *Ann Vickers* (1933), the story of a social worker. *Work of Art* (1934) deals with hotel-keeping. IT CAN'T HAPPEN HERE, perhaps the most arousing of Lewis's later work, gives a strong warning of the possibility of a fascist dictatorship in the United States. *The Prodigal Parents* (1938) shows the relations between generations. *Bethel Merriday* (1940) concerns a girl ambitious for success in the theater. *Gideon Planish* (1943) satirizes a materialistic college president. *Cass Timberlane* (1945) is the story of an older man's love for his young and unsuitable wife. KINGSBLOOD ROYAL (1947) deals with racial prejudice. *The God-Seeker* (1949) tells of a missionary in Minnesota in the 1840s. The posthumously published *World So Wide* (1951) returns to the theme of the American in Europe, which Lewis had treated in *Our Mr. Wrenn* and *Dodsworth*.

Lewis, always an excellent mimic and an irrepressible speaker, became interested in the theater and wrote a dramatic version of *It Can't Happen Here* (1936), in which he played the leading role of Doremus Jessup, a middle-aged newspaper editor. *Jayhawker* (1934), a play Lewis wrote in collaboration with Lloyd Lewis, amused audiences but was not notably successful.

Almost all of Lewis's books were based either on painstaking research into a subject—he worked with de Kruif for *Arrowsmith*, studied real estate for *Babbitt*, and visited ministers and churches for *Elmer Gantry*—or on situations or places Lewis knew well. Thus, his boyhood in Sauk Center provided the background for *Main Street*; his travels in Europe contributed to *Dodsworth* and *World So Wide*; and his experience as an actor and playwright contributed to *Bethel Merriday*. There is also much disguised biography in Lewis's work, and many suggestions of Lewis himself in some of his characters. Searching for the reality of America, he found the oppression of freedom and value by rigid provincialism; and searching for the innocence of the American ideal, he found the corruption of a money-oriented civilization. A romancer as well as realist and satirist, he loved the Babbitts and Main Streets of America even as he deplored them. Gifted with an amazing ability for mimicry, he could impersonate his characters or deliver a Babbitt-like Rotarian speech at will, as the accuracy of tone and verisimilitude of his novels demonstrate; yet his writing is rough and his style can best be described as reportorial.

Studies include Mark Schorer, *Sinclair Lewis: An American Life* (1961) and Martin Light, *The Quixotic Vision of Sinclair Lewis* (1975).

Lewis and Clark Expedition.   See WILLIAM CLARK; MERIWETHER LEWIS.

Lewisohn, Ludwig (1883–1955),   editor, teacher, critic, writer. Born in Germany, Lewisohn came to the United States in 1890, studied at the College of Charleston, South Carolina, and later taught at Wisconsin, Ohio State, and Brandeis. An authority on German literature, he translated books by Hauptmann, Wassermann, Rilke, and others. But he was also well acquainted with the literatures of other lands. Among his critical volumes are *The Modern Drama* (1915), *The Spirit of Modern German Literature* (1916), *The Poets of Modern France* (1918), *The Drama and the Stage* (1922), *The Story of American Literature* (1937), and *Goethe* (2 v. 1949). In his later years Lewisohn turned to Jewish problems and wrote *Israel* (1925), *Rebirth* (ed. 1935), *The American Jew* (1950), and other works. The Jewish theme also entered some of his fiction. Among his novels are *The Broken Snare* (1908); *Don Juan* (1923); *The Case of Mr. Crump* (1926), considered his masterpiece, about the implacability of a scorned wife; *Roman Summer* (1927); *The Island Within* (1928); *The Golden Vase* (1931); *The Last Days of Shylock* (1931); *Trumpet of Jubilee* (1937); *Renegade* (1942); *Anniversary* (1948); and *In a Summer Season* (1955). Lewisohn also wrote two volumes of reminiscence: *Up Stream* (1922) and *Mid-Channel: An American Chronicle* (1929).

Ley, Willy ["Robert Willey"] (1906–1969),   scientist, editor, author. Born in Germany, Ley forsook science fiction—and with it his pen name, Robert Willey—to concern himself with factual science. He served as a research engineer for the Washington Institute of Technology and was information specialist at the Commerce Department. Among Ley's books are *Rockets, Missiles and Space Travel* (1951), *Exotic Zoology* (1959), *Engineers' Dreams* (1954), and *The Exploration of Mars* (1956), which he wrote in collaboration with Wernher von Braun. Ley also wrote *Kant's Cosmogony* (1968) and *Another Look at Atlantis and Fifteen Other Essays* (1969).

Lezama Lima, José (1912–1976), Cuban poet, novelist, essayist. A moving force behind a resurgence of Cuban poetry, he published several literary reviews, notably *Orígenes* (1944–57). His books of verse—including *Muerte de Narciso* (1937), *Enemigo rumor* (1941), *La fijeza* (1949), *Dador* (1960), and *Las eras imaginarias* (1971)—reveal his surrealist tendencies and use of evocative metaphors, abrupt syntax, and literary allusions. His best work is his only novel, *Paradiso* (1966), a complex exposition of a view of man fallen from grace and forever cut off from his full creative potential.

Libbey, Laura Jean (1862–1924), novelist. Born in New York City, Libbey wrote sentimental stories that attained wide popularity. Among her books are *A Fatal Wooing* (1883), *Junie's Love Test* (1886), *Miss Middleton's Lover* (1888), *That Pretty Young Girl* (1889), *A Mad Betrothal* (1890), *Parted by Fate* (1890), and *We Parted at the Altar* (1892). It is said that Theodore Dreiser was influenced by Libbey.

Liberator, The. A name given to two magazines: [1] an abolitionist journal founded in Boston by WILLIAM LLOYD GARRISON (1831–65); and [2] a left-wing magazine founded by MAX EASTMAN that superseded the MASSES in 1918 and was absorbed in 1924 by the *Labor Herald*. Garrison's magazine aroused enthusiasm and violent opposition, and in the South laws were passed suppressing it. The second *Liberator* was a pale imitation of the *Masses*.

Liberty's Call (*Pennsylvania Packet*, 1775), a poem by John Mason. After publication in the *Packet*, it appeared as a broadside. It is also attributed to FRANCIS HOPKINSON.

Liberty Song, The (Boston *Gazette*, July 18, 1768), a poem by JOHN DICKSON. It was originally called *A Song for American Freedom*. Some of the lines were written by Dickinson's friend ARTHUR LEE. It was sung to the tune of William Boyce's *Hearts of Oak* and became the theme song of the Sons of Liberty, a group opposed to unjust taxation.

Library of America, The. A project originally proposed by Edmund Wilson in 1968, this is a series of works of American literature republished in good bindings on acid-free paper. Edited by a consortium of scholars, the series establishes reliable reading texts and brings back into print some works that long had been generally unavailable.

Library of Congress. Also called the Congressional Library. It is located in Washington, D.C., and faces the Capitol. As early as 1782–83 the Continental Congress debated the need for a library. On April 24, 1800, President John Adams signed "An Act to Make Provision for the Removal and Accommodation of the Government of the U.S.," in which the fifth clause provided an appropriation of $5,000 "for the purchase of such books as may be necessary for the use of Congress at the city of Washington and for fitting up a suitable apartment for containing them and placing them therein." About half the sum was promptly used to buy a collection of books in London. The books became ashes when the British burned the Capitol on the night of Aug. 24–25, 1814. The Library of Congress later managed, however, to obtain another or a similar copy of all but three of the books destroyed.

In 1815 Jefferson was in financial straits, and the Library purchased his excellent 6,457-volume library. It became the nucleus of the present collection, today the largest in the world in number of items. Its accretions come from many sources. Administration of the copyright law is one of the charges of the librarian of the Library of Congress, through a subordinate called the Register of Copyrights. By law the librarian received after 1846 one copy and after 1870 two copies of every book copyrighted. In addition the law provides for copyrighting unpublished plays; movie, radio, and television scripts; film strips; and published and unpublished music, so that the library possesses the world's largest collection of such material. Furthermore, the library has been made custodian of numerous special collections, for example, the papers of George Washington and Thomas Jefferson, the J. Pierpont Morgan collection of autographs of the signers of the Declaration of Independence, and a vast gathering of Americana. The oldest manuscript in the Library is a Babylonian clay tablet dating from several thousand years B.C. The oldest book printed from type is the Gutenberg Bible, printed between 1450 and 1455. The oldest newspaper of which the library has a complete file is the London *Gazette*, going back to 1665. Its collection of sources for the study of American history numbers more than twelve million items. In addition it owns the world's largest collection of maps and other cartographic material. Finally, there are the library's collections of several hundred thousand recordings and of several million photographic prints, slides, and motion-picture films. Reflecting its deep interest in contemporary American poetry, the Library has made recordings of readings by eminent poets, which it makes available to the public, and at one time it supervised awards to poets under the Bollingen Foundation, but ceased doing so in 1949 as a result of a dispute over an award to Ezra Pound. Yale University now supervises the awards.

The Library of Congress assists Congressmen with research for speeches, bills, and replies to constituents. The Library of Congress also renders important services to other libraries, printing catalogue cards they can purchase and use. In addition it long has been a practice for U.S. publishers to print the Library of Congress catalogue card number on the copyright page of all books. The Library also publishes a large number of special lists and guides. Increasingly, its material is available in electronic form, online.

Lieber, Francis (1800–1872), soldier, teacher, author of books on political economy. Lieber, born in Germany, served under Marshal Blücher at Waterloo (1815) and as a volunteer in the Greek War of Independence (1822). Then, since he was an active liberal, he came to the United States (1827), where he edited the *Encyclopedia Americana* in Boston for five years, then taught at South Carolina College in Columbia (now the state university). He was an impressive figure to the students and to the world at large. Longfellow said of him, "He is a strong man; and one whose conversation, like some tumultuous mountain brook, sets your wheels all in motion."

All the important leaders in political science felt Lieber's influence. The ideas expressed in his books show the influence of Edmund Burke, Henry Hallam, and others—as his biographer, Frank Freidel, points out in *Francis Lieber: 19th-Century Liberal* (1948). But what he taught, especially his idea of encouraging many independent institutions as a means of preventing absolutism, fitted in well with American ideas. Among his books are *The Manual of Political Ethics* (1838–39), *Essays on Property and Labor* (1841), *On Civil Liberty and Self-Government* (1853), *On Nationalism and Internationalism* (1868), and *On the Rise of the Constitution of the U.S.* (1872). Thomas S. Perry compiled his *Life and Letters* (1882), and his ideas are discussed in L. R. Harley's *Francis Lieber* (1899) and Bernard Edward Brown's *American Conservatives* (1951).

Liebling, A[bbott] J[oseph] (1904–1963),   reporter, columnist, war correspondent, satirist. In *The Wayward Pressman* (1947) Liebling described some of his own experiences as a newspaperman before he became a staff member of *The New Yorker* in 1935. Expelled from Dartmouth College, he worked on various papers, accumulating experiences that fitted him for the role he would fill on *The New Yorker*—gadfly to American journalism. He wrote for a column called "The Wayward Press," in which he discussed at length the shortcomings of newspapers and he conducted a longstanding feud with Col. McCormick and the Chicago *Tribune*. Liebling was also a gifted reporter, as he showed in his war sketches, *The Road Back to Paris* (1944). Among his other books are *Back Where I Came From* (1938); *The Telephone Booth Indian* (1942); *Mink and Red Herring* (1949); *Chicago: Second City* (1952); *The Sweet Science* (1956), a series of sketches on boxers and boxing, subjects he followed avidly and wrote on perceptively; *Normandy Revisited* (1958); *The Earl of Louisiana* (1961), a series on Governor Earl Long originally done for *The New Yorker; The Press* (1961), a collection of articles; *Between Meals: An Appetite for Paris* (1962); and posthumous collections, *Molly and Other War Experiences* (1964) and *Liebling at Home* (1982).

Lie Down in Darkness (1951),   a novel by WILLIAM STYRON. Set in the South, the novel deals with the Loftis family and is narrated by Milton Loftis as he accompanies the coffin of his daughter Peyton to the grave. The narrative technique is a Joycean stream of consciousness through which the other characters in the story and the events leading to Peyton's death are revealed. The story relates the moral and psychological breakdown of the Loftis family, showing as well the differences between African-Americans and whites, the reaction to fundamentalist religion, and the accompanying pervasive sense of guilt. The guilt of the Loftis family itself—Milton's incest desires, Helen's jealousy and Puritanism, Peyton's father complex—reflects the traditional Southern fears of inbreeding, overgentility in ladies, and fear of African-Americans.

Life [1].   *Life* was the third of a trio of humorous magazines founded in close succession: *Puck* in 1877, *Judge* in 1881, *Life* in 1883. All three are now dead as humorous magazines. JOHN AMES MITCHELL, an artist, founded *Life*. He had received a $10,000 legacy and wanted to try out a new zinc process for reproducing his black-and-white drawings, so he decided to start a magazine in competition with *Puck* and *Judge*. He had an excellent business manager, Andrew Miller, and a very good editor, Edward Sanford Martin. Even more important, however, were the drawings of CHARLES DANA GIBSON, who began contributing in 1886. Books of Gibson's drawings were popular all over the world, and the circulation of the magazine increased, reaching a quarter of a million at its peak in 1920. It also attracted many notable contributors: authors John Kendrick Bangs, James Whitcomb Riley, Agnes Repplier, and Brander Matthews; artists E. W. Kemble, Palmer Cox, A. B. Frost, and Oliver Herford. In 1892 Thomas L. Masson became editor. The magazine advocated causes and conducted crusades, some of them worthwhile and some eccentric. It fulminated against doctors; vivisection; hobble skirts ("Don't cry, Tommy; it's only a woman"); marriage of American girls to foreign fortune-hunters; and ticket speculators. It also advocated a Fresh Air Fund to assist city children by providing them the chance to summer in the country. John Mitchell hated John D. Rockefeller, Sr., J. P. Morgan, Sr., and William Randolph Hearst and never missed an opportunity to savage them in words and pictures. Mitchell once was warned that his home would be bombed, and libel suits were instituted against him, not one of which he lost.

When *Life* began to fail, Charles Dana Gibson bought it and made ROBERT E. SHERWOOD editor (1924–28). For a time brilliant contributors gave it a blood transfusion: Frank Sullivan, Robert Benchley, Dorothy Parker, Franklin P. Adams, Corey Ford, Don Herold, Art Young, John Held, Jr., Ellison Hoover, Ralph Barton, and Percy Crosby. In 1931 it was changed to a monthly and sold to a new group. In October 1936, it passed into the hands of Time, Inc., which wanted only the name.

Life [2].   On November 23, 1936, appeared the first issue of *Life* as a pictorial magazine. The aim was "to see life, to see the world, to eyewitness [the *Time* influence making itself felt] great events." At the beginning its text consisted of captions for pictures and short expository blocks. After a while the text was expanded by having at least one sustained, signed article each week, and later there were profiles of noted persons and lengthy historical and scientific articles that became regular features. For example, in 1952 *Life* paid an astonishing sum for the right to publish, in a single issue, Hemingway's *The Old Man and the Sea*. In 1972, the magazine failed, although "Special Report" issues appeared occasionally afterward. In 1978, *Life* was revived as a monthly, which ceased publication in 2000.

Life Amongst the Modocs: Unwritten History (1873),   an autobiographical narrative by JOAQUIN MILLER, in later editions called *Unwritten History: Life Among the Modocs* (1874), *Paquita: The Indian Heroine* (1881), *My Own Story* (1890), and *Joaquin Miller's Romantic Life Amongst the Indians*

(1898). There is much about Paquita, a modest, intelligent, industrious, and beautiful girl whom Miller finally married. In the course of their adventures she was fatally wounded by his enemies and died, says Miller, "in my arms." See MODOC INDIANS.

Life at the South, or, "Uncle Tom's Cabin" as It Is (1852),   a novel by W. L. G. Smith (1814–1878) in reply to Harriet Beecher Stowe's UNCLE TOM'S CABIN.

Life in the Far West (1848),   an account by GEORGE FREDERICK RUXTON. This is a description of the Rocky Mountain men of the 1840s, their battles with Indians, their women, their mode of speech, their amusements. Ruxton had come from England via Vera Cruz, making his way to Santa Fe and wintering with the mountain men in what is now South Park, Colorado. He wrote his account (somewhat fictionized) for *Blackwood's Edinburgh Magazine* (1847–48); his story was often reprinted during the 19th century.

Life of Reason, The (5 v. 1905–06),   a philosophical examination by GEORGE SANTAYANA. Under the influence of WILLIAM JAMES, JOSIAH ROYCE, and Hegel, Santayana attempted an analysis of common sense. His fundamental thesis was that "everything ideal has a natural basis and everything natural an ideal development." He employed James's psychology as an analysis of experience, substituting for "stream of consciousness" the term *flux*. Knowledge has two poles: physics, which explains the concretions of existence; and dialectics, which clarifies ideas, values, and objects. The life of reason takes shape in institutions: society, religion, art, and science.

Life on the Mississippi.   An autobiography and travel book (1883). Here MARK TWAIN combined "Old Times on the Mississippi," the amusing, fictionalized account of his experiences as a cub pilot written in the winter of 1874–75, with a description of the river as he had found it during a month-long trip undertaken to make notes for the book. The chapters written early are masterful; the others are uneven, for the author found the writing difficult and resorted to padding and the use of borrowed sources.

Twain portrays his former self as an innocent boy who suffers painfully at the hands of the master pilot Horace Bixby. The emphasis is on humor, but the account ends on a serious note—a strong sense of loss—when ignorance and innocence yield to knowledge and experience. In the account of his return to the river, the author's attempt to travel incognito fails early, and thereafter, without a fictional narrator, the report is on the whole sober. Readers looking for Twain's familiar humor are usually disappointed with the reportage. The original manuscript included much that was entertaining, but was deleted because Twain thought of himself as creating "a standard work." The deleted passages appear in the 1944 Limited Editions Club text.

EVERETT EMERSON

Life Studies (1959),   a collection by ROBERT LOWELL. This is the book that along with *Heart's Needle*, by W. D. SNODGRASS—published in the same year—heralded the turn to CONFESSIONAL POETRY that would be seen in the next decade, especially in the work of SYLVIA PLATH, ANNE SEXTON, and JOHN

BERRYMAN. Influenced especially by WILLIAM CARLOS WILLIAMS, Lowell here began to print open poems on personal subjects, though the book contains also some poems in his earlier, more structured mode. Modified in different printings, it appeared first in England without the autobiographical prose piece "91 Revere Street" that in the first American issue appeared as the book's second section; this and the fourth part, the title sequence "Life Studies," showed Lowell dealing frankly with his childhood, deaths in the family, his marriage, and his mental problems.

Life with Father (1935),   CLARENCE DAY, JR.'s memoir of his father. This book is a collection of humorous sketches reporting experiences of the author with his highly eccentric father. They began appearing in *The New Yorker*, *Harper's Magazine*, and the *New Republic* as early as 1920. A sequel is *God and My Father* (1932). The play *Life with Father*, based on Day's book and written by RUSSEL CROUSE and HOWARD LINDSAY, opened on November 8, 1939, and reached its 3,224th performance on July 12, 1947, when it finally closed on Broadway. A movie opened later that year.

Life Without Principle.   An essay by HENRY DAVID THOREAU. Originally a lecture frequently delivered by Thoreau, it was first given as "Getting a Living" in 1854. The present title was given to it by Thoreau for the *Atlantic*, where it was first printed in October 1863, and collected in *A Yankee in Canada* (1866). Other titles considered or used by Thoreau, including "The Higher Law," "Life Misspent," and "What Shall It Profit?" suggest the themes. It is an essay on "the way in which we spend our lives." Thoreau says, "The ways by which you may get your money almost without exception lead downward." The laborer should seek not merely to make a living, but to do a job well. We must think beyond today. "Read not the Times. Read the Eternities." All of the material wants of our days will pass, including concerns about slavery, trade, and industry. "In short, as a snow-drift is formed where there is a lull in the wind, so, one would say, where there is a lull of truth, an institution springs up. But the truth blows right on over it, nevertheless, and at length blows it down."

Ligeia   (pub. in the *American Museum*, September 1838; included in *Tales of the Grotesque and Arabesque*, 1840), a tale by EDGAR ALLAN POE. Poe reverts to a theme he treated in MORELLA (1835)—metempsychosis and the return of a dead wife from the grave. But his treatment of the theme in *Ligeia* is much more convincing. This was Poe's favorite of his stories, and it has always been highly regarded by critics. Ligeia, married to the man who tells her story and is deeply devoted to her, dies after a wasting illness despite her strong desire to live. The man goes to England and remarries, but with no love for his new wife, and she too dies. But as she lies in the coffin, she suddenly comes back to life—and her husband recognizes her as Ligeia. The poem THE CONQUEROR WORM was written in 1843 and added to *Ligeia* in 1845. Poe may have taken the name Ligeia from Ligea, in classic mythology one of the three Sirens.

Lighthall, William Douw (1857–1954),   lawyer, public official, poet, editor. Born in Hamilton, Ontario, Lightfall was active as a lawyer, founded the Union of Canadian

Municipalities, wrote the books *Canada a Modern Nation* (1904) and *The Governance of Empire* (1910), served in military units, and founded the Great War Veterans' Association. But his great interest was poetry. He published his first slim collection, *Thoughts, Moods, and Ideals*, in 1887, with the apologetic subtitle *Crimes of Leisure*. His "first real book" was *The Young Seigneur, or, Nation-Making* (1888), published under the pseudonym Wilfred Chateauclair. The characters were French Canadians. In the following year he edited *Songs of the Great Dominion*. He organized the Society of Canadian Literature (1889), which paved the way for the Canadian Authors' Association, and edited several other anthologies. He collected his verse in *Old Measures* (1922). He wrote in meter and in free verse, and Canadian patriotism animates many of his best poems.

Light in August (1932),   a novel by WILLIAM FAULKNER. *Light in August* has some of the familiar ingredients of popular fiction about the South: madness, racial hatred, miscegenation, and glorification of the Civil War. Faulkner's treatment and themes, however, are anything but typical. His main character, Joe Christmas, who is white in appearance but thought to be part African-American, is placed in an orphanage by his white grandfather, Doc Hines, who enjoys seeing him taunted by the other children. A pious farmer who adopts Joe beats him to make him learn his catechism, and a philanthropic spinster, Joanna Burden, with whom he has a violent sexual affair, attempts to exploit him for her charitable causes. When she tries to force Joe to assume a black identity, he kills her. Hounded by his grandfather, pursued and finally trapped by Percy Grimm, a local fascist, Joe is castrated and killed. In a moving conclusion, Faulkner elevates Joe Christmas to the status of crucified victim.

Two other major characters bear significantly on the story of Joe Christmas: Gail Hightower, an ex-clergyman who neglected his congregation to preach to them about the glorious deeds of his grandfather during the Civil War, and Lena Grove, who gives birth at the close of the novel after a futile search for the baby's father. As Doc Hines may be said to represent that mixture of religion and racial hatred that causes Joe's suffering and death, so Hightower represents the church's failure to preach sin and forgiveness. Lena Grove, in contrast, appears to be Faulkner's means of dramatizing the eternal verities—love, nature, acceptance of life—against which the tragedy of Joe Christmas and the pathetic story of Hightower are to be seen.
W. J. STUCKEY

Lightnin' (1918),   a play by WINCHELL SMITH and FRANK BACON. This play had a Broadway run of 1,291 performances. Bacon played the leading role, Lightnin' Bill Jones, who owns the Calivada Hotel, half of which lies in Nevada, half in California. The Nevada sheriff has trouble when he tries to arrest a man for whom he has a warrant; the threatened man merely jumps across the state line. Lightnin' has numerous troubles, especially when his wife sues him for divorce, but manages to solve them all. He denies indignantly that he is a liar when he boasts that he once drove a swarm of bees over the plains in the dead of winter without losing a bee.

Lihn, Enrique (1929–1988),   Chilean poet and short-story writer. Lihn writes with a sense of irony that leavens even his most political work and makes the author part of the world whose folly he describes. His images—in his stories as well as in his fully fleshed, richly lyrical poems—are among the most striking in the language. His books of poems include *La pieza oscura* (1963), *Poesta de paso* (1966), *Escrito en Cuba* (1969), *La musiquilla de las pobres esferas* (1969), and *Algunos poemas* (1972). A highly praised volume of short stories, *Aqua de arroz*, appeared in 1969. A selection of his poems in English translation, *The Dark Room and Other Poems* (1978), reveals his range of styles, from neorealist to antipoetry. *Mester de juglaria* (1987) collects poems from two decades. *La republica independiente de Miranda* (1989) is a story collection.

Lilacs (in *What's O'Clock*, 1925),   a poem by AMY LOWELL. One of Lowell's better-known and better free-verse poems, identifying the lilacs and herself with New England.

Lily Bart.   See BART, LILY.

Lincoln, Abraham (1809–1865),   lawyer, 16th president of the United States. Lincoln was born in Hardin County, Kentucky. Lincoln was largely self-taught, a lover of the Bible, Shakespeare, Robert Burns, Tom Paine, *The Pilgrim's Progress*, *Aesop's Fables*, and *Robinson Crusoe*. Lincoln learned the art of storytelling at the crossroads store and became a master of western humor. In 1828 he helped sail a flatboat down the Mississippi, saw a slave market in New Orleans, and acquired a strong dislike for slavery. He worked as a storekeeper in Salem, Illinois, later as a surveyor, postmaster, and again as a storekeeper (unsuccessful). It was at this time that he took up with Ann Rutledge, who died shortly after the couple became engaged.

In 1832 the Black Hawk War broke out and Lincoln served briefly as a captain. In 1834 he was elected to the State Legislature and served four terms as one of Henry Clay's Whig followers. In 1836 he was admitted to the bar, and in 1837 he moved to Springfield, Illinois. He married Mary Todd, a woman of good family and social standing, after a troubled courtship.

Meanwhile Lincoln was earning a reputation as a lawyer and went into partnership, in succession, with some of the best lawyers of Illinois, finally in 1843 with WILLIAM H. HERNDON. He had a knack for winning over juries. In 1846 he was elected to Congress, where he voted against abolitionist measures but refused to favor slavery. It was founded, he said, "on both injustice and bad policy." He also voted for a resolution censuring President Polk for engaging with Mexico in "an unnecessary and unconstitutional war." He did not run for reelection and his political career seemed finished.

Then came the movement that ended with the founding of the Republican party, and gradually Lincoln was drawn back into public life and away from Whiggism. When JOHN C. FRÉMONT ran for the presidency in 1856, Lincoln was the recognized leader of Illinois Republicans. The DRED SCOTT decision of the Supreme Court (1857) drove him further toward the antislavery cause. In 1858 he accepted nomination for the Senate, and then came the debates with STEPHEN A. DOUGLAS, in the course of which Lincoln became nationally known, even though he lost to Douglas. The House Divided speech, in which he accepted the nomination, and his speeches during the seven debates with Douglas were read everywhere and became part of the literature of argumentation. Lincoln showed a masterly command of logic and language. His reputation was heightened by the *Cooper Union Address* (1860), before an Eastern audience. At the convention held in the same year to nominate a candidate for the presidency, Lincoln won by a landslide on the third ballot. In the election campaign that followed, Lincoln remained silent, yet he carried every Northern state except New Jersey and lost every Southern state. He won a majority of the electoral votes, a plurality of the popular vote. As soon as the results were known, Southern states began to secede, but Lincoln continued his silence.

On February 11, 1861, Lincoln left Springfield and made a brief *Farewell Address* as he stood on the railroad platform. His remarks reveal a dark, foreboding mood, expressed in language that has the quality of poetry. It is believed that the official version was written down by Lincoln in the train after his departure, but it differs in several respects from newspaper versions published at the time. Lincoln's version tends to enhance the alliterative sequence and to strengthen the rhythmic pattern, in accordance with Lincoln's usual practice.

Lincoln delivered a conciliatory *Inaugural Address* (March 4, 1861) making it plain that his first concern was to save the Union, even if slavery had to continue. The coming of war forced Lincoln to assume dictatorial powers. He was deeply dissatisfied with the way in which McClellan and other Union generals conducted their campaigns, particularly in view of the great superiority of the North in men, supplies, and strategic advantages. Not until U.S. GRANT and W.T. SHERMAN appeared on the scene did he feel he had found field leaders of sufficient audacity. Some modern commentators believe that Lincoln was his own best general, that without his bold and intelligent guidance the war would have been lost.

Lincoln's conduct during the war was exemplary. He avoided acting like a dictator although he was one by the force of circumstances; the press remained free, as was shown by the violence of the personal attacks made on Lincoln. He fought the South, but refused to hate it. He wielded immense power, but was not corrupted by it. His cabinet was mostly unsympathetic, but he managed to keep the members working for him; and he kept Congress at bay. On January 1, 1863, he issued his EMANCIPATION PROCLAMATION, strictly as a military measure, although in time it became more than that. On November 19, 1863, he delivered his GETTYSBURG ADDRESS, the most majestic of all his speches. When he ran for reelection against General GEORGE B. MCCLELLAN, the Democratic candidate, many thought he would lose. But the military victories of Grant, Sherman, and PHILIP SHERIDAN turned the tide. Lincoln had a majority in the Electoral College (212 to 21), but the popular vote was closer. Lincoln began planning for a lasting peace, one in which the South would again take an honorable place in the nation's activities. His *Second Inaugural Address* (March 4, 1865) was a masterpiece of noble feeling and phrasing. But he was assassinated,

supposedly as an act of revenge for the South; JEFFERSON DAVIS himself acknowledged that no one suffered more than the South as a result of John Wilkes Booth's fateful act.

Lincoln's personality was deceptively simple; on examination he proves to have been a paradoxical combination of opposites. This is partially explained by his considerable histrionic ability. He was often sincerely humble, but as JOHN HAY, long his private secretary, insisted, "It is absurd to call him a modest man. No great man was ever modest. It was his intellectual arrogance and unconsidered assumption of superiority that men like Salmon P. Chase and Charles Summer never could forgive." He took a humorous and open pride in his own homeliness and had a natural friendliness that defeated the efforts of his secretaries, Hay and J.G. NICOLAY, to protect him against intrusions.

Lincoln's humor was the most paradoxical of his qualities but it helps explain much in his career, personality, and fame. The saddest-looking of men, Lincoln was an inveterate joker. His favorite contemporary humorists included ARTEMUS WARD, R.H. NEWELL ("Orpheus C. Kerr"), and PETROLEUM V. NASBY. A frontiersman in many ways, Lincoln keenly relished the humor of the frontier and himself contributed to its storehouse of stories. Aside from his genius in telling a story, he had the gift of epigram, often more wit than humor.

Lincoln the writer cannot be separated from Lincoln the politician or Lincoln the lawyer. His success in practical matters was in large part due to his command of words. He was marvelously articulate, making himself understood by the multitude despite his frequently poetic and elevated language, his soaring images, and his complex emotional and intellectual content. Repetition of sound, as well as of words and phrases, marks Lincoln's skillful blending of grammatical and logical parallelism. The result is often a distinctly poetic cadence. Without doubt, he was the greatest writer by far among American presidents.

The LIBRARY OF AMERICA has issued a complete Lincoln in two volumes: *Abraham Lincoln: Speeches and Writings* (1989), edited by Don E. Fehrenbacher. It is based on *The Collected Works of Abraham Lincoln* (8 v. 1953–55), edited by Roy P. Basler and others. Standard for many years, though less comprehensive, is *The Complete Works of Abraham Lincoln* (2 v. 1894), edited by John G. Nicolay and John Hay; this was enlarged (12 v. 1905), mostly by the addition of letters. A fine one-volume edition with an excellent critical introduction is *Abraham Lincoln: His Speeches and Writings* (1946), edited by Roy P. Basler.

The first life of Lincoln was one he wrote for campaign purposes, *Lincoln's Autobiography* (1859). This was followed by a campaign biography of Lincoln and his vice presidential candidate written by WILLIAM DEAN HOWELLS, *Life and Speeches of Abraham Lincoln and Hannibal Hamlin* (1860). Noteworthy biographies by Lincoln's associates are one by his law partner, WILLIAM HENRY HERNDON, *Lincoln: The True Story of a Great Life* (1889), another by his chief secretaries, John G. Nicolay and John Hay, *Abraham Lincoln: A History* (10 v. 1890). Among more recent biographies, CARL SANDBURG's *Abraham Lincoln:*

The Prairie Years (2 v. 1926), and *Abraham Lincoln: The War Years* (4 v. 1939) are classics. Satisfactory one-volume lives include those by Lord Charnwood (1917), Benjamin P. Thomas (1952), and Steven B. Oates (1984). Of special interest for its pictorial record is Stefan Lorant's *Lincoln: His Life in Photographs* (1941).

Lincoln appears in literature so frequently that a listing must necessarily be abbreviated. Walt Whitman wrote two poems about him, O CAPTAIN! MY CAPTAIN! and WHEN LILACS LAST IN THE DOORYARD BLOOM'D; the former has been the most frequently recited poem about Lincoln, and the latter the greatest and most affecting of all the tributes paid to him. James Russell Lowell in COMMEMORATION ODE wrote a magnificent passage with the line: "New birth of our new soil, the first American"; and elsewhere he spoke of him as "the incarnate common sense of the people." In his poem, "Lincoln, the Man of the People," Edwin Markham wrote: "He was a man to hold against the world,/A man to match the mountains and the sea." Other poets who wrote memorably about Lincoln include Edwin Arlington Robinson, Vachel Lindsay, Melville, Julia Ward Howe, Bayard Taylor, Whittier, Paul Laurence Dunbar, and Sandburg.

In fiction Lincoln has been a favorite character. Some of the novels and short stories in which he appears are Henry Ward Beecher, NORWOOD (1867); Edward Eggleston, THE GRAYSONS (1888); Bret Harte, *Clarence* (1895); Winston Churchill, THE CRISIS (1901); Upton Sinclair, *Manassas* (1904); S. Weir Mitchell, *Westways* (1913); Elsie Singmaster, *Gettysburg* (1913); John Buchan, *The End of the Road* (in *The Path of the King*, 1921); Ben Ames Williams, HOUSE DIVIDED (1947); Irving Stone, *Love Is Eternal* (1954); and Gore Vidal, *Lincoln* (1984).

Among plays that deal with Lincoln these may be noted: John Drinkwater, *Abraham Lincoln* (1919); Robert E. Sherwood, ABE LINCOLN IN ILLINOIS (1938); and Mark Van Doren, *The Last Days of Lincoln* (1959).

Lincoln, Joseph C[rosby] (1870–1944).   Born in Brewster, Massachusetts, and a descendant of Cape Cod sailors and captains, Lincoln knew the region well and loved it. At first he tried to make a living in business, then turned to writing and published a collection of *Cape Cod Ballads* (1902). When his first novel, *Cap'n Eri* (1904), appeared and made an immediate success, Lincoln's future was determined. In it, three retired sea captains, weary of housekeeping together, advertise for a wife. Thereafter, Lincoln's novels were surefire successes. They reflect the continuing changes in Cape Cod life from the turn of the century to World War II, as sand and seashell roads turn to macadam, cars replace horses, summer visitors come and go, attic relics turn into antiques, real estate speculators eye the seashore, young women and men pursue shaky paths to love, and retired sea captains try to maintain their heritage and their dignity. Lincoln's sense of eccentric character and humorous speech never deserted him. All his books are readable. Among the best are: *Mr. Pratt* (1906), *Cy Whitaker's Place* (1908), *Keziah Coffin* (1909), *The Postmaster* (1912), *Cap'n Dan's Daughter* (1914), *Shavings* (1918), *Galusha the Magnificent* (1921), *Queer Judson* (1924), *Rugged*

Water (1924), *All Alongshore* (1931), and *Storm Signals* (1935). In the year before his death appeared *The Bradshaws of Harniss*, with World War I as a background. *The Old Home House* (1907) is an early collection, reprinted as *Cape Cod Stories*.

Lincoln, Victoria (1904–1981),   novelist, short-story writer. Lincoln's first book, *February Hill* (1934), told a kindly, sometimes ribald story of her native Fall River, Massachusetts, that established her reputation as a writer of power and wit. It was adapted for the stage by GEORGE ABBOTT as *Primrose Path* (1939). For some years she wrote short stories exclusively, collected in *Grandmother and the Comet* (1944). *The Wind at My Back* (1946) contains three novelettes, one of which—*Before the Swallow Dares*—is autobiographical. *Celia Amberley* (1949) follows a woman's life from early childhood to maturity; *Out from Eden* (1951) returns to the manner and humor of *February Hill* in its amusing study of an artist's family. More recent works are *The Wild Honey* (1953) and *Dangerous Innocence* (1958). She returned to Fall River in *A Private Disgrace* (1967), about LIZZIE BORDEN.

Linda Condon (1919),   a novel by JOSEPH HERGESHEIMER. In this psychological study of a man and a woman, Hergesheimer analyzes the meaning of beauty to a woman and the meaning of his ideals to a sculptor. Linda, a frigid woman, is intent on preserving her beauty. All her life she has been the inspiration of Dodge Pleydon, who creates a statue inspired by her. A mob destroys it, and Linda is roused to emotion at last, but Pleydon refuses her, intent on keeping his own ideals alive.

Lindbergh, Anne Morrow (1906–2001),   author. Born in Englewood, New Jersey, Anne Morrow married CHARLES A. LINDBERGH. She was an able and often highly poetic writer, some of whose books dealt with experiences shared with her husband and were believed to reflect his opinions. *North to the Orient* (1935) and *Listen! the Wind* (1938) are vivid descriptions of her flying experiences. *The Wave of the Future* (1940) proposed not resisting the advance of fascism. She also wrote a charming novelette, *The Steep Ascent* (1944); the autobiographical and philosophical *Gift from the Sea* (1955), which spoke to women all over the country; *The Unicorn and Other Poems* (1956); and *Dearly Beloved* (1962). Her essays, diaries, and letters are contained in *Earth Shine* (1969), *Hour of Gold, Hour of Lead* (1973), *Locked Rooms and Open Doors* (1974), and *War Within and Without* (1980).

Lindbergh, Charles A[ugustus] (1902–1974),   aviator. Lindbergh was born in Detroit. His solo flight across the Atlantic on May 20–21, 1927, the first such flight in history, created a world sensation. With Fitzhugh Green he wrote an account of the flight called *We* (1927); the title refers to Lindbergh and his plane, *The Spirit of St. Louis*. He became internationally known, made good-will tours of several countries, and married Anne Morrow, the daughter of the U.S. Ambassador to Mexico, Dwight W. Morrow. The tragic kidnapping and death of their infant son, Charles, Jr., in March 1932, resulted in the passing of so-called Lindbergh laws, which make interstate kidnapping a Federal offense. The Lindberghs moved to Europe, where he worked with Alexis Carrel on the mechanical heart. In the years immediately preceding World War II, Lindbergh was an advocate of American neutrality. He wrote *Of Flight and Life* (1948) and an autobiography, *The Spirit of St. Louis* (1953), which won a Pulitzer Prize. His *Autobiography of Values* (1978) was posthumously edited.

Linderman, Frank B[ird] (1868–1938), trapper, miner, chemist, writer. Born in Cleveland, Linderman went to Montana as a young man and spent most of his life there. He knew Native Americans well and often wrote about them, especially for children. Among his books are *Indian Why Stories* (1915); *On a Passing Frontier* (1920); *Bunch-Grass and Blue-Joint* (verse, 1921); *How It Came About Stories* (1921); *Lige Mounts* (1922); *Indian Old-Man Stories* (1920); *American: The Life Story of a Great Indian, plenty-Coups* (1930); *Old Man Coyote* (1931); *Red Mother* (1932); *Beyond Law* (1933); and *Blackfeet Indians* (1935).

Lindeström, Peter Mårtensson (?–?), engineer. Lindeström visited New Sweden on the Delaware in 1653–54, then returned home to Sweden. During his last years he prepared an account of the new land, calling it *Geographia Americae*. It was translated from the original manuscript and published in 1925.

Lindsay, Howard (1889–1968), actor, director, producer, playwright. Born in Watertown, New York, Lindsay left Harvard to go on the stage, showed a talent for directing, and staged DULCY and *To the Ladies*, both by George S. Kaufman and Marc Connelly, as well as other plays. He and his frequent collaborator, RUSSELL CROUSE, produced and directed numerous plays, some of their own composition. The first play they wrote together was *Anything Goes* (1934), and their first partnership in production was ARSENIC AND OLD LACE (1941). Their greatest success came with their dramatization (1939) of LIFE WITH FATHER, in which Lindsay and his wife played the leads for five years. Lindsay also worked with DAMON RUNYON on *A Slight Case of Murder* (1935), with Crouse on STATE OF THE UNION (1945), with IRVING BERLIN on *Call Me Madam* (1950), and with RICHARD RODGERS and OSCAR HAMMERSTEIN II on *The Sound of Music* (1959).

Lindsay, [Nicholas] Vachel (1879–1931), poet. Born in Springfield, Illinois, Lindsay at first intended to be a missionary; although he gave up this idea in any literal sense, the crusading spirit was very strong in him, and he tried to convert America to a love of poetry and to a revival of agrarian society. For a time he wanted to be an artist. He lectured for the Anti-Saloon League through central Illinois, and spent the summer of 1912 walking from Illinois to New Mexico, preaching the Gospel of Beauty and exchanging his poems for meals and shelter.

Lindsay's verse, published in Harriet Monroe's magazine *Poetry*, became highly popular. Lindsay also become widely known through his public recitals, in which he would have his audience join him in his chanted refrains. Lindsay was welcomed in England, appeared at Oxford, and sometimes served as resident poet at small colleges. But he always came back to Springfield, which he celebrated in *The Golden Book of Springfield* (1920), a prose work. His native city was also the setting

for one of his best poems, "Abraham Lincoln Walks at Midnight" (1914). Gradually his poetry faded in quality, and he became weary and disillusioned. Robert Morss Lovett, who knew him well, says this disillusion and a morbid conscience brought about his suicide by drinking poison.

The study of influences on Lindsay sends one on strange paths. He read everything EDGAR ALLAN POE wrote, but tried, largely in vain, to escape Poe's and Swinburne's influences. SIDNEY LANIER was a model, also WALT WHITMAN, but Lindsay's verse was an imitation of Whitman's attitude rather than of his technique. Along with these one must consider hymns, revivalist sermons, the addresses of Lincoln, Salvation Army music, and jazz. His reputation rests on such poems as "A Gospel of Beauty" (1908), GENERAL WILLIAM BOOTH ENTERS INTO HEAVEN (1913), "A Net to Snare the Moonlight" (1913), THE EAGLE THAT IS FORGOTTEN (1913), THE CONGO (1914), THE SANTA FE TRAIL: A HUMORESQUE (1914), "The Chinese Nightingale" (1917), "The Ghost of the Buffaloes" (1917), and IN PRAISE OF JOHNNY APPLESEED (1921).

Among Lindsay's books are *Rhymes To Be Traded for Bread* (1912); *General William Booth Enters into Heaven and Other Poems* (1913); *Adventures While Preaching the Gospel of Beauty* (1914); *The Congo and Other Poems* (1914); *The Art of the Moving Picture* (1915); *A Handy Guide for Beggars* (1916); *The Chinese Nightingale and Other Poems* (1917); *The Golden Whales of California and Other Rhymes in the American Language* (1920); *Collected Poems* (1923, rev. ed. 1925); *Going-to-the-Stars* (1926); *The Candle in the Cabin* (1926); *Johnny Appleseed* (1928); *The Litany of Washington Street* (1929); and *Every Soul Is a Circus* (1929). *Selected Poems* (1931) was edited by Hazelton Spencer.

Stephen Graham wrote about Lindsay in *Tramping with a Poet in the Rockies* (1922). Biographical and critical works are A. E. Trombly, *Vachel Lindsay, Adventurer* (1929), and EDGAR LEE MASTERS, *Vachel Lindsay: A Poet in America* (1935). Both are based on personal knowledge. Biography and interpretation are found in Mark Harris, *City of Discontent* (1952), and Eleanor Ruggles, *The West-Going Heart: A Life of Vachel Lindsay* (1959).

Lin McLean (1897), a group of six sketches and a poem about a "charming cowboy" by OWEN WISTER. The scene is Wyoming "in the happy days when it was a Territory with a future, instead of a State with a past." Wister had begun publishing the sketches as early as 1891 when he wrote "How Lin McLean Went West" for *Harper's*.

Linn, John Blair (1777–1804), poet, clergyman. A graduate of Columbia College, he published verse in *The Poetical Wanderer* (1796), *The Death of George Washington* (1800), *The Powers of Genius* (1801), and, posthumously, *Valerian, a Narrative Poem* (1805). A play, *Bourville Castle, or the Gallic Orphan* was produced in 1797.

Lins do Rêgo, José (1901–1957), Brazilian novelist. Born into an aristocratic planter family in Parahyba, Lins do Rêgo achieved celebrity as part of a regionalist movement in Brazil, treating the sugar plantations of the northeast in a cycle of six novels. The first three of these— *Menino de Engenho* (1932), *Doidinho* (1933), and *Bagué* (1934)—were translated in one volume as *Plantation Boy* (1966). The story is of a powerful estate owner seen mostly through the eyes of his grandson. Two later novels of the cycle, *O Moleque Ricardo* (1934) and *Usina* (1936), feature a black companion of the white boy of the earlier books. The author's best work, FOGO MORTO (1943), is the last of the cycle.

Lin Yutang [also Yu-t'ang] (1895–1976),   teacher, editor, translator, writer. Born and educated in China, Lin attended Harvard graduate school and later studied in Germany. He went back to China to teach, wrote for various English and Chinese periodicals, some of which he founded, and edited texts for students. Lin joined revolutionary movements, of which he said, "I have always liked revolutions, but never revolutionaries." Among his novels are *Moment in Peking* (1939); *Chinatown Family* (1948), a popular treatment of life in an American Chinese community; *The Red Peony* (1961); and *The Flight of the Innocents* (1965). Other books written or edited by Lin include *My Country and My People* (1935), an analysis of China that did not entirely please the Chinese; *Confucius Saw Nancy* (1936); *A Nun of Taishan* (1936); *A History of the Press and Public Opinion in China* (1936); *The Importance of Living* (1937); *The Wisdom of Confucius* (1938); *A Leaf in the Storm* (1941); *Wisdom of China and India* (1942); *Between Tears and Laughter* (1943); *The Gay Genius* (1947); *Wisdom of Laotse* (1948); *Wisdom of America* (1950); *Widow, Nun, and Courtesan* (three stories, one original, two translated, 1951); *Famous Chinese Short Stories* (1952); *Vermilion Gate* (1953); *Looking Beyond* (1955); *The Chinese Way of Life* (1959); *The Importance of Understanding* (1960); and *The Chinese Theory of Art* (1968).

Lionel Lincoln, or, The Leaguer of Boston (1825), a novel by JAMES FENIMORE COOPER. The hero is a British officer whose family history involves a mystery. Lionel arrives at Boston in time to take part in the opening events of the Revolution and then goes back to England with a bride. The book has good descriptions of Lexington and Concord.

Lion of the West, The (1831),   a farce by JAMES KIRKE PAULDING. The play was written as a vehicle for James H. Hackett in the leading role, Col. Nimrod Wildfire, supposedly a takeoff on DAVY CROCKETT and other hunters and pioneers. It was rewritten several times and even renamed, finally being performed (1833) as *A Kentuckian's Trip to New York*; it may have inspired W. A. Caruthers's novel *The Kentuckian in New York* (1834).

Lippard, George (1822–1854),   journalist, novelist, playwright. Born in Chester County, Pennsylvania, Lippard at nineteen became a journalist for the *Spirit of the Times*, a Philadelphia daily. His column *Our Talisman* is somewhat in the style of Dickens's *Sketches by Boz*. Failing in health, he turned to writing novels. *The Monks of Monk Hall* (1844), retitled a year later *The Quaker City*, was a lurid story about the midnight orgies of a group of the best people. Influenced by gothic romances, it created a furor; a dramatization by the author was withdrawn by the mayor, who feared an outraged mob might destroy the theater. A watered-down version was performed in New York City in 1845.

Lippard became a popular lecturer on legends of the Revolution and wrote a number of books on the subject, as well as many romantic historical novels. Among them are *Blanche of Brandywine* (1846), *Paul Ardenheim* (1848), *Bel of Prairie Eden* (1848), and *The Man with the Mask* (1852). *New York: Its Upper Ten and Lower Million* (1853) and *Eleanor: or, Slave Catching in Philadelphia* (1854) deal with vice and debauchery in the two cities. In 1850 Lippard founded the Brotherhood of the Union, a benevolent society that aimed to eliminate poverty and crime by removing the social evils causing them.

Lippincott, Sara Jane [Clarke] (1823–1904),   newspaper correspondent, essayist. Writing as Grace Greenwood, Lippincott gained popularity with works that included sketches and letters collected as *Greenwood Leaves* (1850) and a travel book, *Haps and Mishaps of a Tour in Europe* (1854).

Lippincott's Magazine (1868–1914).   J. B. Lippincott & Co. began issuing this monthly magazine in Philadelphia in January 1868; it won recognition in competition with the *Atlantic*, particularly for its contributions from Southern writers, among them Sidney Lanier and William Gilmore Simms. It also printed works from England, including Wilde's *The Picture of Dorian Gray* and Kipling's *The Light that Failed*: Among other American contributors were Gertrude Atherton, Stephen Crane, Rebecca Harding Davis, Lafcadio Hearn, Henry James, Frank Stockton, and Constance Fenimore Woolson. In 1914, it was sold to McBride, Nast & Co., becoming briefly *McBride's Magazine*. In 1916 it merged with *Scribner's Magazine*.

Lispector, Clarice (1917–1977),   Brazilian novelist, short-story writer. Born in the Ukraine, Lispector grew up in Brazil, studied law in Rio, married a diplomat, and lived most of her life abroad. She became Brazil's best-known woman novelist, especially valued for explorations of the feminine consciousness in works of introspective anguish. Her best-known novels include *A maçã no escuro* (1961, tr. *The Apple in the Dark*, 1967), about a man who perhaps did or perhaps did not commit murder; *A paixão segundo G. H.* (1964, tr. *The Passion According to G. H.*, 1998), shorter and more concentrated; and *A hora da estrêla* (1977, tr. *The Hour of the Star*, 1986), her last novel, which attracted particular attention with its sad tale of a country girl who comes to the big city and dreams of movie-style success. Among her other works are three earlier novels: *Perto do coracao salvagem* (1944); *O lustre* (1946); and *A cidada sitiada* (1949). Her short fiction is collected in *Laços de familia* (1960, tr. *Family Ties*, 1972) and *A legião estrangeira* (1964, tr. *The Foreign Legion*, 1986).

Literary Criticism: Before 1960.   Meyer Abrams in *The Mirror and the Lamp* (1953) says there are four general approaches to literary criticism; (1) theories of mimesis, (2) pragmatic theories, (3) expressive theories, and (4) objective theories. At various times in Western and American literary history, one or another approach has tended to be dominant, but at no time has any one of these approaches been totally out of favor or in eclipse.

Plato and Aristotle appear to have initiated the *mimetic* theories. They assumed that a play was an imitation of an action.

Down through the ages critics have argued about the precise meanings of *imitation*—how close or how far criticism can or should get from actuality and from history. Probably no serious critic has ever denied it some validity.

Pragmatic theories emphasize the audience. Aristotle's doctrine of catharsis, purging the audience of pity and fear, is pragmatic. Literary criticism throughout the Christian era emphasized the audience's response—for good or evil—to the literary work. Horace stressed the utility (*utile*) as well as the beauty (*dulce*) of art. The moralistic theories of the 19th century or of the New Humanists are pragmatic.

Expressive theories held the largest appeal for the Romantic period and the 19th century generally. These theories stress the poet's imagination and moral nature, giving rise to the dictum, "*Le style, c'est l'homme.*" Coleridge was perhaps the greatest expressive critic, and his American disciple was Emerson.

Objective theories emphasize the work itself. Thus discussed, literature is seen impersonally, objectively, apart from the author. Formalist theories about the techniques of art are objective. Mark Schorer's "style is the subject" implies an acceptance of an objective theory of art. The major emphasis in 20th century criticism, especially in the so-called New Criticism, is objective.

Abrams says the four theories collectively endeavor to explain "the total situation of a work of art." They also, at times, tend to run together.

The mimetic theory has not been greatly emphasized in American criticism. Aristotle's *Poetics*, however, has long been taught respectfully in American universities, and modern novelists and critics have come to see the justness of the stress *Poetics* lays on plot. The so-called neo-Aristotelians at the University of Chicago (see CHICAGO CRITICS) have tried to build a theory of modern criticism based on the *Poetics*, centering attention on mimesis. Their work can be seen in *Critics and Criticism* (1952), edited by Ronald Crane. Imitation theories have also entered literary theory in other ways, through the historical study of literature—a climate of opinion, a world picture, a work's mirroring of its age—and through the study of myth. The historical method of VERNON PARRINGTON (*Main Currents in American Thought*, 3 v. 1927–30) relates the literary work to its milieu. Like all students of the historical method in literary study, Parrington was indebted to Hippolyte Taine (1828–93), the French critic, who said that a knowledge of "race, moment and milieu" could be equated with what was to be found in a given work of literature.

In the 19th century, critics were more given to pragmatic tests than were critics in the 20th century. Readers knew a line was true poetry if it caused them to catch their breath, raised gooseflesh, or caused hair to stiffen. William Wimsatt and M. C. Beardsley, in "The Affective Fallacy" (*Sewanee Review*, 1949), vigorously oppose such tests, declaring them vague and imprecise. They disapproved of Aristotle's catharsis doctrine, and of Longinus's discussion of the "transport" of an audience, holding that the poem itself should be the center of critical attention. As a matter of emphasis, Wimsatt and Beardsley are probably right. Yet even after reading a sophisticated critical analysis of a poem or story, it remains for the small private voice inside each reader to give or deny assent to the judgment. This finally is a pragmatic test.

William Cullen Bryant, in *On the Nature of Poetry* (1826), said the term *imitation* is of doubtful usefulness. He stressed the poet's imagination and the ability to create and evoke powerful feelings from symbols, thus aligning himself with expressionist theories. But he also emphasized the role of poetry in improving the morality of the audience, a pragmatic theory. Emerson once or twice mentions imitation, but generally the doctrines in "The Poet" (1844) are quite similar to those of Bryant. James Russell Lowell, in *The Function of the Poet* (1855), and Walt Whitman, in the Preface to *Leaves of Grass* (1855), also saw the poet as seer, projecting great moral truths. American criticism in the 19th century tended to follow Coleridge's expressionist theories, which are stated most explicitly in *Biographia Literaria* (1817).

Admiration of Coleridge's doctrine of the imagination has been expressed by such modern American critics as Kenneth Burke and Cleanth Brooks. Modern criticism does not to any considerable extent stress the poet or novelist's moral nature, but psychoanalytical criticism is in the romantic-expressionist tradition. Edmund Wilson, in *The Wound and the Bow* (1941), for example, discusses a writer's hurt, or "wound," relating it to the writer's imaginative gifts (his "bow") and literary work.

The objective theories are sometimes related to expressionist theories. For example, Coleridge emphasized the poet's imagination, but he also discussed patterns of imagery, metrics, characterization, and tone. Edgar Allan Poe was an objective, or formalist, critic. He stressed the beauty of the poem, not its power to teach. In THE POETIC PRINCIPLE he said, "A long poem is simply a contradiction in terms," and he insisted that the short story ("Hawthorne's Tales," 1847) be constructed after the writer has conceived what his *single* effect would be. Henry James also emphasized objective theories. In *The Art of Fiction* (1888), he is aware that fiction is an imitative art and that the quality of the writer's mind and the writer's moral nature profoundly influence the work created. But the major emphasis is on structure, and on the techniques through which a writer may create a work of art.

Almost all the terms current in American criticism prior to 1960 were employed in the service of one or another objective theory. John Crowe Ransom used the term *texture*, by which he meant images, metaphors, and meters. Robert Penn Warren, Allen Tate, and the writer of the present essay used the term *tension*, usually to mean the unity, sometimes paradoxical, resulting from a struggle of conflicting ideas. A proposition using appropriate language, characters, or episodes justifies itself by resisting convincingly a series of ironic questions. Cleanth Brooks's belief that the language of poetry is essentially paradoxical and ironic is also an objective theory.

During the early days of America, of course, neoclassical ideals were dominant. Most criticism appeared in periodicals. (See Lyon Richardson, *History of Early American Magazines*, 1741–1789.) Alexander Pope and Jonathan Swift were commonly praised. College textbooks of rhetoric were those used in England: Lord Kames's *Elements of Criticism* (1762), Hugh Blair's *Lectures on Rhetoric* (1783), and Archibald Alison's *Nature and Principles of Taste* (1790).

The glories of Newtonian science were in the air and gave rise to the belief that prose should be natural, precise, and without false ornaments—Franklin, Jefferson, and Paine held such notions. An early critic of this type was JOSEPH DENNIE (1768–1812), a conservative Federalist who wrote for *Farmer's Weekly Museum* (1796–98) and the *Port Folio* (1801–09). Forty of his essays were published as a book in 1796, and he was acclaimed as the American Addison—his reputation was soon eclipsed by Washington Irving's.

There were many discussions of American as opposed to English writing and literature. Walter Channing, a Harvard professor, saw no way for American literature to emerge because Americans used English, not a language of their own. Meanwhile, Noah Webster was busy standardizing American spelling, and through writers like Philip Freneau (1752–1832) and Charles Brockden Brown (1771–1801), America began to have its own literature. John Trumbull (1750–1831), a Connecticut poet, expressed the common sentiment of the day:

This land her Swift and Addison shall view
The former honors equall'd by the new;
Here shall some Shakespear charm the rising age,
And hold in magic chains the listening stage.

Literary criticism, as it has been more usually understood, began in America in the early 19th century. Bryant in his *Lectures on Poetry* (1825) derided sickly imitations of neoclassical writers. He praised the judicious combination of imagination and emotion, originality and metrical flexibility. Bryant was a transitional figure between neoclassicism and romanticism. Coleridge's influence swung the balance. James Marsh (1794–1842) wrote an elaborate introduction to Coleridge's *Aids to Reflection* (1829) and *The Friend* (1831); F. H. Hedge (1805–1890) wrote extensively about the German philosophers to whom Coleridge was indebted, and he wrote an influential essay on Coleridge in the *Christian Examiner* in 1833. These men introduced Coleridge's work to Emerson and his transcendental friends. GEORGE RIPLEY (1802–1880), one of the founders of the *Dial* and the organizer of Brook Farm, also wrote transcendentalist criticism, especially during his years as book reviewer (1849–80) for the New York *Tribune*.

Transcendental criticism, with Emerson as its chief spokesman, minimized external forms and stressed the transforming power of the writer's imagination. Having read Coleridge, Emerson borrowed Kant's distinction between Understanding (rationality) and the higher Reason (intuition, etc.). Also from Coleridge he took the distinction on the one hand between fancy, which works by association, and imagination, which creates; and on the other hand, the organic theory of composition, in which each detail is intimately involved with and modified by every other detail and by the whole.

The most active critic in Emerson's group was MARGARET FULLER (1810–1850), an editor of the *Dial*, ardent feminist, essayist, and reviewer. Her *Papers on Literature and Art* was published in 1846. In it, she divided critics into three types: the *subjective* simply responds or reacts to a work; the *apprehensive* enters imaginatively into the work, trying to identify himself with the author's intentions; the *comprehensive* acts as the *apprehensive* critic does, but also makes a judgment about the relative merits of the work. Critics, she said, can either apply the highest standards—those of Coleridge, for example—or enjoy lesser works of the fancy, recognizing that they are of a humbler order.

In EDGAR ALLAN POE America had its first truly original critic. Through his antididacticism and emphasis on the poem as a work of art, he influenced the symbolist writers in France, and thereby, indirectly, the art-for-art's-sake movement in England in the 1890s. Poe believed the artist needed knowledge, an idealizing imagination, and conscious artistry of a high order. He defined poetry "as the rhythmical creation of beauty." Poe argued, in a rather confused way, with Coleridge's doctrines, but was nonetheless indebted to *Biographia Literaria*. It was in his attack on "the heresy of the didactic" that Poe went most strongly against the drift of his time. Poetry is concerned with beauty, and if the beautiful should happen to give moral instruction, the gift is accidental. Taste alone—informed taste—is the basis for judgment.

The critic, Poe held, should be "frank, candid, and independent . . . giving honor only where honor is due." He should not be afraid of giving offense to an author, because his loyalty is to "the general cause of letters." He should respect tradition, but not at the expense of originality. General theory, he also said, is useful, but the practicing critic should get down to particulars, discussing a work in terms of its unique effects, its merits and defects. Poe had the courage to try to live up to these rules and thereby alienated many literary figures, including Emerson and Margaret Fuller. Quite possibly, too, his standards and frequently caustic tone discouraged the critical movement that might have been expected to develop in his wake.

Scholars have singled out a handful of mid-19th-century critics as representative of the criticism of the time. Two are EVERT DUYCKINCK (1816–1878) and his brother GEORGE DUYCKINCK (1823–1863), coeditors of the New York *Literary World* (1847–53), the leading literary review of its day. They were acquainted with Irving, Cooper, Bryant, and Melville and were sometimes instrumental in getting new writers into print. The brothers edited *Cyclopaedia of American Literature* (1855). Rufus Griswold (1815–1857) was a prominent New York and Philadelphia journalist. He compiled several anthologies of poems, writing introductions for them. E. P. Whipple, a prolific and generous-minded critic, is now almost forgotten. Poe believed he was a critic of great merit.

The New England Brahmins, especially OLIVER WENDELL HOLMES, SR. (1809–1894), and JAMES RUSSELL LOWELL (1819–1891), carried great weight in the literary world. Holmes prepared himself for giving a series of lectures on the English poets by reading in the files of the *Edinburgh Review* and by studying the critical works of Coleridge, the Schlegels,

William Hazlitt, and Leigh Hunt. He also knew Horace's *Ars Poetica* intimately. By 1857–58, when he wrote *The Autocrat of the Breakfast Table*, he had become familiar with a wide range of poetry and criticism and thought his own way through critical problems. For example, he did not subscribe to Wordsworth's "emotion recollected in tranquility"—he said composition was "a cold-blooded, haggard, anxious, worrying hunt" after rhymes and good effects. Holmes was a witty, sane, and undogmatic critic.

Lowell was an admirer of Emerson as a speaker, but he disapproved of the transcendentalist's desire to live "off the internal revenues of the spirit." Lowell, a born conservative, was stirred by his first wife to investigate liberal doctrines and programs. As a young man his mind and writings were vital and often original. He was also learned. *The Biglow Papers*, a series of satiric verses in a rustic idiom, implied an attack on bookish writing and urged a native American literature. As editor of the *Atlantic Monthly* he wrote many essays, later collected in book form as *Fireside Travels* (1864), *Among My Books* (1870), *My Study Windows* (1871), and others. Lowell has been called America's most distinguished 19th-century critic, but surely this is too great praise. Lowell may have been more judicious than Poe, but he lacked Poe's brilliance and originality.

Edmund C. Stedman (1833–1908), a poet and successful Wall Street broker, is rather difficult to categorize. As a poet he is clearly tepid and in the genteel tradition. As a critic he is antididactic and a follower of Poe. In *Nature and Elements of Poetry* (1892) he developed the theory that beauty is independent of moral considerations. He did not, however, possess the analytical powers necessary for serious criticism.

Walt Whitman (1819–1892) proposed a revolutionary theory in *Democratic Vistas* (1871). He treated the ideals of democracy and individualism, and condemned the degradation of democracy and the vulgar wealth of the post–Civil War era. He prophesied future greatness and asked for a cultural declaration of independence from Europe.

As a critic WILLIAM DEAN HOWELLS (1837–1920) is a curious amalgam of his age and country. He was at once a realist and a victim of the genteel tradition, a believer in Tolstoy's evolutionary ethics and in Taine's literary determinism. Art, he said, must tell the truth, and in doing so, it should serve morality and reveal the "smiling aspects" of American life and the virtues of democracy. His critical volumes include *Criticism and Fiction* (1891), *My Literary Passions* (1895), and *Literature and Life* (1902). Howells was good at sketching the lives of his literary acquaintances, and he helped secure public favor for Emily Dickinson, Stephen Crane, Hamlin Garland, and Frank Norris as well as many European writers.

HENRY JAMES, JR. (1843–1916), is without question America's most outstanding 19th-century critic, and possibly future generations will see that he surpassed the work of later American critics. He had a clear understanding of the value and limitations of any rules, and he had what Keats and Shakespeare had, "negative capability": that is, there is no need to force a theory or to arrive at a neat, logical conclusion when confronted by two seemingly contradictory ideas. James's *The Art of Fiction* is at once simple and sophisticated, useful and unpretentious. James on occasion worried points in a sophistical manner, but generally he could be depended on to see what is essential, what is peripheral, and what is beside the point. Some of his critical volumes are *French Poets and Novelists* (1878), *Notes on Novelists* (1914), and *Notes on Reviews* (1921). The prefaces he wrote for the New York edition of his novels have been a kind of *poetics* for the modern novelist. They were first collected in *The Art of the Novel* (1934) by R. P. Blackmur.

In general, 19th-century critics suffered from America's cultural involvement with the genteel tradition, which minimized the life of the body, separated spirit from flesh, ignored the actualities of American life, especially urban life, and fought off scientific knowledge. An especially effective criticism of the genteel tradition was George Santayana's THE GENTEEL TRADITION AT BAY (1911). Santayana held that James escaped the genteel tradition by comprehending it and turning it into subject matter. Poe, Hawthorne, and Emerson, he said, were highly endowed writers who "could not retail the genteel tradition; they were too keen and independent for that. . . . In their own persons they escaped the mediocrity of the genteel tradition, but they supplied nothing to supplant it in other minds." It is no exaggeration to say that the quarrel 20th-century writers and critics have had with the 19th century was over the failure of most writers in the earlier era to come to grips with the limitations of that tradition.

Modern American criticism is indebted to 19th-century criticism, especially to that of Coleridge, Poe, and James. But it also breaks with the genteel tradition and looks abroad for other sources of inspiration. Beginning with critics like James Gibbons Huneker (1857–1921), Lewis Gates (1860–1924), and Joel Spingarn (1875–1939), American criticism turned to Europe—to Walter Pater, Anatole France, Benedetto Croce, and others. The impressionist movement, extremely important in Europe, made some headway in America, but more with poets and fiction writers than with critics.

In *The New Criticism* (1910) Spingarn said literature is expression, and the critic should ask and answer only two questions: What did the writer intend to do? and How well did he do it? Ethical questions, the study of sources, and all the rest are beside the point. Spingarn made a little stir, but the big movement, culminating in the NEW CRITICISM, was getting under way in England. Ezra Pound and T. S. Eliot, through their contributions to little magazines here and abroad—*The Egoist, Criterion, Blast, Poetry, The Little Review, The Dial*, and so on—were undertaking to establish the modern movement. Both Pound and Eliot have declared their indebtedness to the French Remy de Gourmont.

Eliot published *The Sacred Wood* (1920), which he said was concerned with "the integrity of poetry," and Pound published *Instigations* (1920), with essays on a dozen French poets, on Henry James, Remy de Gourmont, Vorticism, Provençal poetry, and the "Chinese Written Character." In these two volumes one finds many of the preoccupations of modern criticism: the emphasis on the image, symbolism, art for art's sake, and the availability of certain earlier works from

Western and English literary tradition. T. E. Hulme, a British critic with whom Pound was friendly, influenced Eliot and Pound in their antiromantic stand—opposition to vague expressions and grandiloquence—and in their concern with literary conventions.

Eliot, Hulme, and also Ford Madox Ford, a friend of James and a proponent of impressionist fiction, exerted considerable influence on Allen Tate, John Crowe Ransom, Robert Penn Warren, and Cleanth Brooks, all of whom had a great deal to do with carrying modern criticism to the campus. Their criticism tended to be concerned with the language of poetry and literary structure, but also with questions of regionalism, nationalism, and traditionalism. More or less associated with them, especially through their contributions to the *Southern Review, Sewanee Review,* and *Kenyon Review,* are R. P. Blackmur, Kenneth Burke, Yvor Winters, William Troy, and Morton Zabel.

Concurrent with the careers of Eliot and Pound have been other critical movements. Randolph Bourne (1886–1916), Van Wyck Brooks (1886–1963), Ludwig Lewisohn (1882–1955), H. L. Mencken (1880–1956), Stark Young (1881–1963), Lewis Mumford (1895–1990), Carl Van Doren (1885–1950), Mark Van Doren (1894–1972), and Joseph Wood Krutch (1893–1970) may be said to have been deeply involved with what Brooks, in 1915, called "America's Coming of Age." They welcomed new talent, watched and commented as literature was influenced by Freud, Jung, Marx, and the depression, and as it fought a rearguard action against the genteel tradition. Thanks to them, O'Neill, Lewis, Dreiser, Fitzgerald, Cather, Faulkner, and other new talents got a hearing.

The New Humanists, Irving Babbitt (1865–1933) and P. E. More (1864–1937), insisted that man is a supernatural being, and that the center of concern in literature is with ethics. More published fourteen volumes of SHELBURNE ESSAYS, and Babbitt, the more astute of the two, a number of books that still are read, notably *Rousseau and Romanticism* (1919).

Society in the 20th century apparently could not afford men of letters like Lowell and Howells, but Malcolm Cowley, author of *Exile's Return* (1934) and *The Literary Situation* (1954), and Edmund Wilson, critic for *The New Yorker* and author of *Axel's Castle* (1931) and innumerable other books, managed to survive as professional critics.

An academic critic who merged a number of critical traditions was LIONEL TRILLING (1905–1975), especially in *The Liberal Imagination* (1943). Associated with the *Partisan Review* (founded in 1934, at first a strongly leftist journal but later independent), Trilling examined liberal assumptions, testing them against conservative and reactionary opinions. He also scrutinized Freudian theory, showing where it was and was not relevant to the understanding of literature. A student of Matthew Arnold, Trilling wrote with a sense of high seriousness, trying to relate the study of literature to an understanding of culture.

By the 1950s there were many good critics publishing articles and books: Leon Edel, Philip Rahv, John Gassner, Eric Bentley, Richard Chase, Philip Young, and perhaps twenty-five or thirty others. In the immediate post–World War II era, America had more good critics than at any earlier time in its history. They paved the way for the expansion of criticism that has followed.

The 20th century has been called an Age of Criticism and an Alexandrian Age. The latter term implies that criticism is sometimes seen as existing prior to poetry or drama or fiction, and also that critical preoccupations inhibit and stultify creative impulses. It does appear to be true that some of the major figures in modern literature—Yeats, Joyce, Eliot, and Wallace Stevens—wrote their poetry or fiction only after deliberately working out complicated rationales and symbolic systems. American criticism, of course, is a part of the modern literary milieu, a victim of whatever may be excessive in it, but it also participates in and enjoys its strengths and virtues.

For further reading about pre-20th-century American literary criticism, see Clarence A. Brown, ed., *The Achievement of American Criticism* (1954); William Charvat, *The Origins of American Critical Thought* (1936); Harry H. Clark, "The Influence of Science on American Literary Criticism, 1860–1910," *Transactions of the Wisconsin Academy of Sciences, Arts, and Letters,* 44; George De Mille, *Literary Criticism in America* (1931); Norman Foerster, *American Criticism* (1928); John P. Pritchard, *Criticism in America* (1956); John Stafford, *The Literary Criticism of Young America, 1837–1850* (1952); and Floyd Stovall, ed., *The Development of American Literary Criticism* (1955). *The Idea of an American Novel* (1961), edited by L. Rubin and J. R. Moore, is a useful anthology of criticism of the novel. Anthologies and histories for the period prior to 1960 include: Charles Glicksberg, ed., *American Literary Criticism, 1900–1950* (1953); Stanley Edgar Hyman, *The Armed Vision* (1948); Murray Kreiger, *The New Apologists for Poetry* (1956); William Van O'Connor, *An Age of Criticism, 1900–1950* (1952); William Van O'Connor, ed., *Forms of Modern Fiction* (1948); Robert W. Stallman, *The Critic's Notebook* (1950); and Morton D. Zabel, ed., *Literary Opinion in America* (1951). *The Shock of Recognition* (1943), edited by Edmund Wilson, contains the opinions American writers have had about the work of their contemporaries.

WILLIAM VAN O'CONNOR

Literary Criticism: Since 1960. *Poststructuralist, feminist, historicist, ideological, canonical, political*—these adjectives, now so much the common coin of critical discourse, were not in wide circulation—indeed, some had not yet been minted—in 1960. The NEW CRITICISM was still the dominant paradigm, and critics favored *organic, ironic, balanced, universal,* and *timeless.* Today there is no central paradigm: current American criticism is notable for the multiplicity of its discourses, the variety of its projects, and the diversity of its assumptions about authors, texts, readers, language, and history. Although many critics have carried on the work of formal criticism and historical scholarship over the past forty years, the greatest changes in critical practice have been the result of the rise of Theory.

For the New Critics, texts were autonomous, well-wrought verbal icons. Authors were the creators of these icons, but critics had to avoid the Intentional Fallacy of turning to authors for judgments of texts. Readers had to avoid the Affective Fallacy of equating their response to the text with its meaning and to seek instead the complexities emerging from the text's balanced structure of assertions and images. In the 1960s critics began to question these assumptions about authors and readers. The virtual erasure of the real reader's activity from the interpretive process became a problem for many critics. Early attempts to empower the reader included Stanley Fish's affective stylistics and Norman Holland's analysis of literary response. Although this work actually gave the text a different kind of control over the reader's activity, it effectively challenged the concept of the autonomous text and prepared the way for stronger claims about the reader's share in interpretation—by Fish and Holland themselves as well as by David Bleith, Wolfgang Iser, and many others.

In 1967, E. D. Hirsch, Jr., sought to bring down the second pillar of the New Critical house of faith, the intentional fallacy. In *Validity in Interpretation*, Hirsch argued that meaning resided not in the words on the page but in the consciousness of their author; consequently, the only valid interpretation is one that recovers the author's intention. Hirsch's position was initially both controversial and influential, but its influence waned as new movements have undermined many critics' faith in stable meanings.

As the New Criticism lost its power, critics turned in the late 1960s and early 1970s to developments in continental criticism, especially French structuralism. Following the model of Ferdinand de Saussure's *Course in General Linguistics*, which described language as a sign system, critics such as Roland Barthes, Tzvetan Todorov, and Gerard Genette sought to identify the underlying structures of the literary system: the grammar of narrative, the use of figures of speech such as metaphor and metonymy as devices to create thematic meanings, and the conventions governing the production of such effects as the realistic or the fantastic. Structuralism's insistence that literature was a structure of conventions paved the way for American critics to reflect on the conventions of criticism. In *Structuralist Poetics* (1975), Jonathan Culler welded Noam Chomsky's idea of linguistic competence onto structuralism's emphasis on rules and conventions. He proposed that learning how to interpret literature was a matter of acquiring literary competence, that is, learning the rules for producing acceptable interpretations. Also in the mid-1970s, Stanley Fish was responding to criticism of his affective stylistics by proposing a more radical version of Culler's linguistic competence—the theory of interpretive communities. In Fish's view, the rules of interpretation adopted by different communities of readers dictate the meanings of texts. Once the servants of texts, readers became their creators—though readers themselves could be seen as written by the rules and assumptions that constituted their interpretive communities.

The ferment in the mid-1970s and early 1980s was further enriched by the rise of new critical movements—deconstruction, feminist criticism—and by the new impetus behind older movements such as psychoanalytic and Marxist criticism. American critics were no sooner feeling familiar with structuralism than post-structuralism hit the coasts. (Students wore T-shirts reading "structuralism" on the front and "post-structuralism" on the back.) Post-structuralism, especially the deconstruction practiced by JACQUES DERRIDA, put into question structuralism's founding assumption that there were identifiable, stable structures underlying myth, literature, and other objects of the human sciences. Derrida's deconstruction questioned the whole of Western metaphysics and its belief that truth could be grounded in some firm foundation. As initially adopted by American critics, especially the so-called Yale School of Geoffrey Hartman, J. Hillis Miller, and Paul de Man (see YALE CRITICS), deconstruction in criticism became an operation of uncovering the indeterminacy of textual meaning through the dismantling of binary oppositions on which texts seemed to be built or through detailed analysis of some figure of speech or some apparently marginal element in the text. Although these critics were in effect pushing the envelope of New Critical formalism, their techniques of deconstruction proved useful to critics of an antiformalist bent.

Another consequence of the breakdown of the New Critical paradigm was that critics became more open to the insights of other disciplines. Work in psychoanalytic criticism in particular became more widespread and more sophisticated. In the 1970s HAROLD BLOOM set forth a theory of poetic influence based on Freud's notion of the Oedipus complex: In order to carve out his own poetic identity, each poet must overcome the power of a father-like predecessor through a creative misreading of the father's work. Norman Holland analyzed real readers' responses to texts and argued that these responses were determined by the readers' identity themes. Shoshana Felman suggested that literature and psychoanalysis ought not to be put into a master-slave relation but that each should be able to learn from the other. Peter Brooks, following Freud's analysis of desire in *Beyond the Pleasure Principle*, proposed a psychodynamics of narrative plots. Recently, American critics have been adopting the work of Jacques Lacan, whose rereading of Freud emphasizes the role of language in the development of identity, the experience of loss, and the creation of desire.

Among the critics who made fruitful use of work in other disciplines throughout the 1970s, 1980s, and 1990s were many feminists. Feminist critics have never all shared the same assumptions and goals but they are united in their agreement that the writing and reading of literature are actions bound up with the relations between gender and power. Some feminist work, for example, that by Kate Millet and Mary Ellman, has focused on critiquing the patriarchy and its stereotypical ways of representing women or of responding to women writers. Some projects, for example, those by Patricia Spacks, Elaine Showalter, Margaret Homans, and SANDRA GILBERT and Susan Gubar, have sought to uncover a distinct female literary tradition. Other work, especially by French feminists such as Helene Cixous and Luce Irigaray, has attempted to define an *écriture féminine*. Feminist critics have frequently adapted feminist analyses in the social sciences to inform their discussions of the nature and consequences of the woman writer's and the woman reader's social and psychological positions at different points in history. In addition, feminist critics' awareness of the political nature of reading and writing put them in the forefront of attacks in the 1980s on the traditional canon (see FEMINISM).

Some of the political impetus behind feminist criticism has been shared by Marxist critics, whose cause in America was advanced powerfully in the early 1980s by Frederic Jameson, Terry Eagleton, and Mikhail Bakhtin, who wrote in Russia in the 1920s and 1930s but only became widely known in the West in the 1980s. Jameson, who has been influenced by Louis Althusser's rereading of Marx, argued in *The Political Unconscious* (1981) that every text has a political dimension, often one that it does not acknowledge but that can be recovered by critics who follow his dictum to "always historicize!" In his widely read *Literary Theory* (1983), Eagleton offered a tour de force survey and critique of Theory (including everything mentioned here) and then concluded with a call for a Marxist rhetorical criticism that would focus on the social place and power of literature. Bakhtin argued that any use of language is implicated in ideology. Any utterance communicated not just a content and a form but also a set of social values associated with that way of speaking; consequently, to speak or write is to occupy some stance toward the world.

The most recent significant movements have been the burgeoning of African-American criticism and the rise of the New Historicism. Together with feminist and Marxist critics, African-American critics have been insisting on the necessity of including gender, class, and race as categories of literary analysis. African-Americanists such as Henry Louis Gates, Jr., Houston Baker, Hortense Spillers, and Deborah McDowell have been tracing an African-American literary tradition, exploring its relation to the oral tradition, and seeking to define a distinctive African-American criticism that would not necessarily be rooted in the models of white critics.

The NEW HISTORICISM, exemplified in the work of such critics as Stephen Greenblatt and Louis Montrose, alters the traditional relation between history and literature. History is not the stable background against which to read a foregrounded literature, but literature and history are unstable entities that mutually influence each other. In their analyses of these influences, New Historicists frequently draw on Michel Foucault's analyses of the dissemination of power as well as on techniques of deconstruction. The New Historicism at first had its greatest influence in Renaissance studies, but it is becoming increasingly influential in other areas, including the study of American literature.

Although this theoretical activity has not led to the emergence of new orthodoxy, the recurring emphasis on politics and ideology has had a widespread influence. Sometimes this emphasis has led contemporary critics to reevaluate their forebears: KENNETH BURKE's work, with its emphasis on literature as symbolic *action*, has been read with renewed interest. Sometimes the emphasis has led established critics to revise their thinking. WAYNE C. BOOTH's *The Company We Keep* (1988) shows how his ideas about the ethical dimensions of fictional form and technique have changed since *The Rhetoric of Fiction* (1961) under the pressure of recent feminist and African-American criticism. Another consequence of the emphasis on politics and ideology is that critics have begun to reflect on the institution of criticism. Gerald Graff's *Professing Literature* (1987) offers a valuable history of the concerns and conflicts of the profession since its beginning in the late 1800s.

The future of criticism will surely continue to be deeply affected by the ongoing dialogues of theory and the interactions of criticism and other disciplines, but it would be foolish to make any predictions. The developments of the past forty years do suggest, however, that it will be more than another generation before American criticism is again dominated by a single paradigm.

Three fine anthologies are *Contemporary Literary Criticism: Literary and Cultural Studies*, edited by Robert Con Davis and Ronald Schleifer (4th ed., 1998), *Contexts for Criticism*, edited by Donald Keesey (3rd ed., 1998), and *The Critical Tradition*, edited by David H. Richter (2nd ed., 1998). All three include excellent bibliographies. Useful studies of recent critical history are Frank Lentricchia's *After the New Criticism* (1980); William Cain's *The Crisis in Criticism* (1984); Vincent Leitch's *American Literary Criticism from the Thirties to the Eighties* (1988); and Bernard Bergonzi's *Exploding English: Criticism, Theory, Culture* (1990). David Richter edited *Falling into Theory: Conflicting Views on Reading Literature* (2nd ed., 1999). Two volumes edited by Gregory S. Jay in the *Dictionary of Literary Biography* series offer extended views of important individual critics of this century: *Modern American Critics, 1920–1955* (1988) and *Modern American Critics Since 1955* (1988).

JAMES PHELAN

Literary Digest.   I. K. Funk founded this magazine in New York City on March 1, 1890, and edited it until 1905. William Seaver Woods, editor from 1905 to 1933, led the magazine to a high degree of success. Emphasis was laid on current events and living persons, largely by means of quotations from newspapers and magazines; cartoons were freely reproduced, and humor was a frequent feature. The magazine reached more than 2 million in circulation and was a favorite in schools for study of current events. In 1937 it was merged with the REVIEW OF REVIEWS as *The Digest*; later that year publication was resumed under the original name. On February 19, 1938, it suspended publication and several months later was absorbed by *Time*.

literary histories of the U.S.   The first detailed attempt to describe American literature was a series of papers that JOHN NEAL contributed to *Blackwood's Magazine* in 1824–25. Four years later came a series of lectures by SAMUEL L. KNAPP, and the first anthology, SAMUEL KETTELL's *Specimens of American Poetry, with Critical and Biographical Notices* (3 v.). The undependable and biased RUFUS W. GRISWOLD wrote about American poets and prose writers in the 1840s, and the DUYCKINCKS produced an excellent *Cyclopaedia of American Literature* (2 v. 1855, *Supplement* 1866), with well-chosen selections. A milestone event was the publication of MOSES COIT TYLER's

History of American Literature, 1607–1765 (2 v. 1878), followed by his equally important *Literary History of the American Revolution, 1763–83* (2 v. 1897). Works of miscellaneous character and varied importance intervened, among them EDMUND C. STEDMAN's weighty anthology *Poets of America* (1885); CHARLES F. RICHARDSON's pioneer *American Literature* (2 v. 1887–88); Henry A. Beers's *An Outline Sketch of American Literature* (1887), a brief popular study published by the Chautauqua Press; E.C. Stedman and E.M. Hutchinson's *A Library of American Literature* (11 v. 1888–90); Greenough White's *The Philosophy of American Literature* (1891); and FRED LEWIS PATTEE's *History of American Literature Since 1870* (1915).

Such histories began to multiply. They were mostly of a conventional character, although few were as conservative as BARRETT WENDELL's *Literary History of America* (1900), which treated New England almost exclusively. Particularly sound were Walter C. Bronson's (1900) and William P. Trent's (1903). GEORGE E. WOODBERRY sounded a challenge in *America in Literature* (1903), as did John Macy in his *Spirit of American Literature* (1908), which sought to overturn many of our literary idols. VAN WYCK BROOKS began his remarkable career with *The Wine of the Puritans* (1909) and *America's Coming of Age* (1915), later continued in *The Flowering of New England* (1936), *New England: Indian Summer* (1940), and many other similar books. The first elaborate and cooperative work in this field was the *Cambridge History of American Literature* (4 v. 1917–21), edited by W.P. Trent, JOHN ERSKINE, STUART P. SHERMAN, and CARL VAN DOREN. A generation later appeared the *Literary History of the United States* (3 v. including one of bibliography, 1948; rev. 1953), edited by ROBERT E. SPILLER, Willard Thorp, Thomas H. Johnson, and HENRY SEIDEL CANBY, with HOWARD MUMFORD JONES, DIXON WECTER, and Stanley T. Williams as associates. A one-volume work of the same period, *The Literature of the American People* (1951), by Arthur Hobson Quinn, Kenneth B. Murdock, Clarence Gohdes, and George F. Whicher, remains useful for the sweeping perspectives over broad periods achieved by limiting the contributors to four distinguished scholars.

The most recent comprehensive one-volume history is revisionist: *The Columbia History of American Literature* (1988) general editor, Emory Elliot. A multivolume work, *The Cambridge History of American Literature* (1994–   ) is under the general editorship of Sacvan Bercovitch.

Literary Review.   A magazine founded in 1920 by HENRY SEIDEL CANBY. It was later called the *Saturday Review of Literature*, then the SATURDAY REVIEW.

Literary World   [1]. A weekly founded in February 1847 in New York City by the DUYCKINCKS and CHARLES FENNO HOFFMAN. Members of the New York literati reported on society and literature until it ceased publication in December 1853.

Literary World   [2]. A monthly founded in Boston in June, 1870, by S.R. Crocker, who edited it until 1877; BLISS CARMAN was editor in 1903–04. William J. Rolfe, the Shakespearean scholar, conducted a department dealing with his specialty, and entire issues were devoted to Whittier, Emerson, and others. The magazine became a fortnightly in 1879, was

absorbed by the *Critic* in 1904, and the latter was absorbed by PUTNAM'S MAGAZINE in 1906. *Putnam's* in turn was absorbed by the ATLANTIC MONTHLY in 1910.

Literati, The (1850),   EDGAR ALLAN POE's sketches of thirty-eight authors of the KNICKERBOCKER SCHOOL or resident in New York City. The sketches had appeared in six installments in *Godey's Lady's Book* (May to October 1846); a seventh appeared in 1848. Some were warmly eulogistic, others epigrammatically disparaging.

Littell, Eliakim (1797–1870),   editor, publisher. Littell, born in New Jersey, founded the Philadelphia *Register and National Recorder* in 1819, but is best known by the magazine called *Littell's Living Age*. It began publication on May 11, 1844, and he continued as its editor until his death. In 1897 it became the *Living Age*, and it lasted until 1941. It aimed to reprint the best fiction, essays, and verse published in magazines abroad.

Littell, William (1768–1824),   lawyer, poet, essayist. Littell, born in New Jersey and known best as a compiler of law books, scandalized his associates by publishing *Epistles of William, Sur-named Littell, to the People of the Realm of Kentucky* (1806), a collection of satirical essays on prominent men of his day. He also wrote serious works, including *Political Transactions in and Concerning Kentucky* (1806), *Narrative of the Settlement of Kentucky* (1806), and *The Statute Law of Kentucky* (5 v. 1809–19). Another light work was *Festoons of Fancy, Consisting of Compositions Amatory, Sentimental and Humorous in Verse and Prose* (1814).

Little Blue Books.   Paperbound, five-cent booklets sold by E. HALDEMAN-JULIUS by mail-order from Girard, Kansas. Thousands of titles were included, millions of copies sold, as Haldeman-Julius related in *The First Hundred Million* (1928). Books like Boccaccio's *Decameron* (sold in four sections) were popular, as were *Omar Khayydm* and *A Shropshire Lad*. It was Haldeman-Julius who first published WILL DURANT's *Story of Philosophy* in a group of booklets (collected, 1926) to make Simon & Schuster's first great success. Many of the booklets were didactic: *How to Improve Your Conversation, How to Play Golf, How to Write Advertising*. Some were joke books, and some were published to further the publisher's agnostic views.

Little Eva.   A character in Harriet Beecher Stowe's UNCLE TOM'S CABIN (1852). Eva is the small daughter of Uncle Tom's kindly owner, Augustine St. Clare. Her death scene is a high point in the story.

Little Foxes, The (1939),   a play by LILLIAN HELLMAN. It depicts unfavorably the rise of industrialism in the South, and shows the new breed of Southerners as rapacious and ruthless—like "the little foxes who spoil the vines" in the Song of Solomon, ii:15.

Little Journeys (1894–1908),   a series of biographical sketches by ELBERT HABBARD. First published separately, then together in fourteen volumes, these 170 sketches told of Hubbard's visits to the homes of famous men and women. They were immensely popular, were reprinted in a memorial edition in 1914, and appeared again in partial reprints during the 1940s.

Little Leather Library.   Harry Scherman, Robert Haas, and Maxwell Sackheim, newspapermen and advertising men, decided it might be a good idea for the Whitman Candy Co. to boost trade by giving away a tiny copy of *Romeo and Juliet* with each package of confectionery. The idea succeeded. Five-and-ten-cent stores and chain drugstores began giving away capsuled literature, and the list of titles grew to a hundred. The little books were found all over the country, and the three men founded the Little Leather Library (1916), which sold 40,000,000 copies of the classics at ten cents a copy. The enterprise was eventually given up, but led shortly thereafter to the founding of the BOOK-OF THE-MONTH CLUB, as described by Charles Lee in *The Hidden Public* (1958).

Little Lord Fauntleroy (1886),   a novel by FRANCES HODGSON BURNETT. Young Cedric Errol, an American boy, falls heir to an earldom and goes to England to claim it. He is a manly, considerate youngster with beautiful manners, long curls, and a lace-collared velvet suit, and he makes a deep impression on his selfish British relatives. Burnett took the idea for the costume from one worn by Oscar Wilde when he visited her, and the curls and manners from her son. Mothers all over America found in the book the complete answer to the problem of raising boys, thereby producing a generation to whom the young lord was anathema. Burnett made a dramatization of her book, and movie versions followed.

little magazines.   A name usually applied specifically to small, often short-lived avant-garde publications that serve as focal points for literary heterodoxy, are intended for a small audience, and are not commercially oriented. These periodicals have often been the only means of expression available to new and experimental writers swimming against the current of established literary tradition.

The DIAL may be regarded as the main trunk of the family tree. It appeared first as a New England transcendentalist organ published (1840–44) by MARGARET FULLER and RALPH WALDO EMERSON, then as a fortnightly in Chicago (1880–1916), then in New York as a liberal magazine drawing contributions from many distinguished writers, and finally as a literary monthly (1920–29) that championed modern movements. A few other little magazines began to make their appearance shortly before the turn of the century. Elbert Hubbard's THE PHILISTINE (1895–1915) published the work of STEPHEN CRANE and disregarded conventional notions of printing format. William Marion Reedy's MIRROR (1893–1920) first published the SPOON RIVER ANTHOLOGY (1914–15), and the works of other writers who were later to become well known. Other early little magazines include the Chicago CHAPBOOK (1894–98), *The Lark* (1895–97), M'LLE NEW YORK (1895–96, 1898–99), and *The Papyrus* (1903–12).

The literary revolution of 1910–20 was assisted by little magazines that began to appear in profusion about that time: *The Masses* (founded 1911); POETRY (1912); *Glebe* (1913); *Blast* (in London 1914, with some American contributors); THE LITTLE REVIEW (1914); *Bruno's Weekly* (1915); *Others* (1915); *Contemporary Verse* (1916); *The Seven Arts* (1916); *The Lyric* (1917); *The Quill* (1917); *The Country Bard* (1918); and *The*

Liberator (1918). They published the work of many writers then unknown who were to become the major voices in 20th-century literature: Sherwood Anderson, Van Wyck Brooks, Hart Crane, E. E. Cummings, John Dos Passos, Theodore Dreiser, Robert Frost, T.S. Eliot, William Faulkner, Ernest Hemingway, Vachel Lindsay, Marianne Moore, Eugene O'Neill, Katherine Anne Porter, Ezra Pound, John Crowe Ransom, Wallace Stevens, Allen Tate, William Carlos Williams, Edmund Wilson, Thomas Wolfe, and others. Between 1914 and 1929 *The Little Review*, one of the most important of the little magazines, had in its pages the early work of Carl Sandburg, Vachel Lindsay, T.S. Eliot, Wallace Stevens, Marianne Moore, and Robert Frost. Harriet Monroe's *Poetry*, founded in 1912 and now published in Chicago by the Modern Poetry Association, has had an exceptionally long life.

Some magazines succeeded in making their influence widely felt. *The Seven Arts* publicized the nationalism of Van Wyck Brooks and Waldo Frank. *Secession*, along with *Exile*, *Glebe*, and *Others*, represented the rebellious younger generation of the 1920s, and contributed to the reevaluation of American culture demanded by the new writers. Some magazines had more limited aims: to introduce a certain kind of new poetry or to assert the literary claims of a particular region.

During the 1920s, American expatriates in London and Paris published numerous little magazines, often aimed primarily at an American audience. Among these were *The Criterion* (London 1922), which T.S. Eliot edited for a time; *transition* (Paris, 1927), in which Gertrude Stein, Hemingway, and William Carlos Williams appeared; *Exile* (ed. in Paris, publ. in Chicago, 1927), Ezra Pound's vehicle; BROOM (Rome, then London, then New York, 1921–1924); *Secession* (Vienna, Berlin, and New York, 1922–1924). Published in the United States were *Contact* (1920); the new form of *The Dial* (1920); *The Frontier* (1920); *The Double-Dealer* (1921), which first published Hemingway and early work of Edmund Wilson and Robert Penn Warren; a new *The Lyric* (1921); *The Measure* (1921); *Voices* (1921); *The Fugitive* (1922) (see THE FUGITIVES); *Laughing Horse* (1922); *The Chicago Literary Times* (1923); *Palms* (1923); *S.N* (1919); *Bozart* (1927); *The Blues* (1929); *The Gyroscope* (1929); and *The Kaleidoscope* (1929, called *The Kaleidograph* after 1932).

By the mid-1920s the new movements were well under way. The period also saw a new form of the little magazine, which would eventually supersede the more purely literary titles of the earlier decade. Many of the magazines that began publication between 1925 and 1930 can be classified in two groups: the doctrinaire political-literary journal typified by the *New Masses* (1926, see THE MASSES), which became the predominant form of the little magazines published in the 1930s, and the quarterly or magazine review, such as *Prairie Schooner* (1927), which came into its own during the 1930s and 1940s.

Only a small percentage of the magazines of the early 1920s continued publication in the following decades. New titles in the 1930s and 1940s included *The Harkness Hoot* (1930), STORY (1931), *The American Spectator* (1932), *Wings* (1933), THE PAR-

TISAN REVIEW (1934), *The Spinners* (1934), *American Prefaces* (1935), *The Critic* (1934), *New Directions in Prose and Poetry* (1936), THE KENYON REVIEW (1939), *Furioso* (1939), *Accent* (1940), *Florida Magazine of Verse* (1940), *The Poet of the Month* (1941), *Chimera* (1942), *Quarterly Review of Literature* (1943), *Hudson Review* (1948), *Tiger's Eye* (1947), and *Cronos* (1947).

By the late 1940s the dominant form of the little magazine was the quarterly review. Some of these had ceased to be little magazines at all; usually supported by or affiliated with universities, they were financially secure, primarily critical rather than creative, and drew their contributors, not from among young experimental writers, but from established professors and critics.

After World War II a new group of literary magazines surfaced in reaction against established conventions. Opening their pages to younger writers and alternative subjects and styles, some became associated with BEAT WRITING, the BLACK MOUNTAIN POETS, and the San Francisco Renaissance. Important among these were CID CORMAN's *Origin* and ROBERT CREELEY's *Black Mountain Review*, as well as EVERGREEN REVIEW, which far outdistanced the others in readership and helped bring new fashions in writing, many imported from Europe, much closer to the American mainstream. *The Fifties* (later *The Sixties, The Seventies*, and so on), edited by ROBERT BLY, was prominent among journals opening up the tradition in English with its frequent translations from contemporary Latin American and European poets. CLAYTON ESHLEMAN's *Caterpillar* followed in the 1960s and was later metamorphosed into *Sulfur*.

Most of these alternative journals were exclusively or primarily devoted to poetry. *Evergreen Review* was not, and this and other journals of broader interest tried to reach the mass market created by the great surge in paperback publishing: *New World Writing, Anchor Review*, DISCOVERY, THE NOBLE SAVAGE and others appeared in paperback formats aimed at distribution through drugstores and other mass outlets. By the 1970s, little magazines had proliferated so as to defy easy summation; hundreds could boast some claim to attention, although for many the audience was local or cliquish. Among the best of those prominent then and after, and not yet named, are *Anteus, Carolina Quarterly, Chelsea, Malahat Review, Massachusetts Review, Ontario Review, Paris Review, Sewanee Review, Shenandoah, Tamarack Review, TriQuarterly, Virginia Quarterly Review*, and *Yale Review*. Some had established reputations much earlier, and in terms of longevity, prestige, and the level of their continuing support could hardly be called little except, for most, in circulation. Many older magazines and new ones created for the electronic age are now exploring possibilities of online publication and can be accessed through various search engines.

Little Men (1871), a novel by LOUISA MAY ALCOTT. A sequel to LITTLE WOMEN.

Little Orphant Annie (1885), a poem in Hoosier dialect by JAMES WHITCOMB RILEY. It was originally called *The Elf Child*. It presented the orphan girl who told the children in whose home she lived "witch tales" and stories of "the gobble-uns 'at gits you ef you Don't Watch Out!" Harold Gray called his comic strip "Little Orphan Annie."

Littlepage Manuscript Series. See SATANSTOE, THE CHAINBEARER, and THE REDSKINS.

Little Red Song Book (1909), a publication of the I.W.W. Revised and expanded in later printings, the *Little Red Song Book* contained songs important to the labor movement, including some by JOE HILL. Hundreds of thousands of copies were in print by the time of World War II.

Little Regiment, The: and Other Episodes of the American Civil War (1896), six short stories by STEPHEN CRANE. Like the earlier RED BADGE OF COURAGE, the stories in this collection treat the feelings and emotions of fighting men under trying battle conditions. All the stories concern events of the Civil War except for "The Veteran." Here the reader meets Henry Fleming, hero of *The Red Badge*, as an old man. Fleming dies a heroic death in a flaming barn while attempting to rescue some colts, thus vindicating his title to the badge of courage lost and won at Chancellorsville.

Little Review, The (March 1914–May 1929), a little magazine published by Margaret Anderson, first at Chicago, later in New York City and Paris. It was an exciting, individualistic magazine, which proclaimed its belief in "Life for Art's sake" and announced that it was written for "intelligent people whose philosophy is Applied Anarchism." Its contributions explored many varying ideas and personalities: Nietzsche, Bergson, anarchism, feminism, psychoanalysis, cubism, and dadaism. Among the contributors were Sherwood Anderson, Vachel Lindsay, Ezra Pound, Yeats, Hart Crane, Richard Aldington, T. S. Eliot, Wyndham Lewis, Ford Madox Ford, Ben Hecht, William Carlos Williams, Jean Cocteau, Guillaume Apollinaire, and Kenneth Burke. Most celebrated was James Joyce. When Anderson began to print *Ulysses* in her magazine in installments (1918–21), four issues were confiscated by the Post Office and burned. In December 1920, the Society for the Suppression of Vice brought the *Review* before a special sessions court. The judge fined Anderson $100. She told the story of her adventurous life in *My Thirty Years' War* (1930) and *The Fiery Fountains* (1951). *The Little Review Anthology* appeared in 1953.

Little Shepherd of Kingdom Come, The (1903), a novel by JOHN FOX. This popular story relates the experiences of Chad Buford, a shepherd, with whom two women fall in love. Of doubtful parentage, he lives for a while with the Turners in the Cumberland Mountains, at a settlement that gives its name to the book. The Turners' adopted daughter, Melissa, falls in love with Chad, but he wants to marry Margaret Dean, a Lexington girl who isn't sure about him because of a supposed "blot on his birth." In time he becomes established socially, but they are again estranged when he enlists in the Union Army. Melissa makes a dangerous trip to warn him his life is in danger, but dies of exposure; he marries Margaret after the war. The book was dramatized by EUGENE WALTER in 1916.

Little theater movement, the. The free theaters of Europe—such as the *Théâtre Libre* in France, the *Freie Buhne* in Berlin, and the Abbey Theatre in Ireland—inspired the little theater movement in the United States before World War I. Adopting the goals of European forerunners, the American visionaries who created the little theaters of the early 20th century were opposed to the shallowness of the commercial theater in New York and its derivative road companies. These new, idealistic producers dedicated themselves to experimentation, relevance, and higher quality in theatrical art. They wanted to present fresh plays by new American playwrights, and most of them also wished to stage the new plays from Europe—written by such playwrights as Henrik Ibsen, Anton Chekhov, and George Bernard Shaw—works that Broadway producers for the most part shunned. The leaders of little theaters were bound to create theater for the sake of art rather than dollars.

Some of the people who helped initiate the movement were Mrs. Lyman Gayle of the Toy Theatre, Boston, 1912; Maurice Browne of the Chicago Little Theatre, 1912; Irene and Alice Lewisohn of the Neighborhood Playhouse, New York, 1915; and Sam Hume of the Detroit Arts and Crafts Theatre, 1915. Two of the most significant early theater groups in this movement were the Washington Square Players of New York City, 1915, and the Provincetown Players of Massachusetts the same year.

In late 1911 and early 1912 with a flurry of theatrical activity, the little theater movement became a reality. During that season the Abbey Theatre of Dublin toured many American cities, and its leading personalities—Yeats, Lady Gregory, and Lennox Robinson—not only demonstrated their creative accomplishments on stage but also spread a gospel of new drama. Inspired by the example and the ideals of the Irish players, Mrs. Gayle transformed a stable on Lyme Street in the Back Bay area of Boston to establish the Toy Theatre. KENNETH MACGOWAN, who later helped with other experimental companies, witnessed the debut of the Toy Theatre as an apprentice critic, and he later wrote about it in his early study of the spread of American theater, *Footlights Across America* (1929). Although the Toy Theatre seated only 113 people and featured such amateur actors as AMY LOWELL, it was a striking success, until Mrs. Gayle moved the operation to a larger, less hospitable space and attempted too quickly to professionalize the company.

Also in 1912, Maurice Browne and his wife, Ellen Van Volkenburg, established the Chicago Little Theatre on the fourth floor of the Fine Arts Building. His theater was even smaller, seating only 91 spectators at a time. The building itself provided a fertile milieu, housing music and dance studios, editorial offices of two literary magazines, and the Baldwin Piano Company. Once a pupil of the British theater visionary Gordon Craig, Browne set out to develop a new type of American drama and to present plays by such writers as Yeats, Schnitzler, Strindberg, and Wilde. He even began to pay his actors a little, $10 a week, and himself $300 a year. The group lasted five years. Oliver M. Sayler in *Our American Theatre* (1923) claims that Maurice Browne when discussing his own operation coined the term "little theater."

The Neighborhood Playhouse, a longer-lived theater, was founded in 1915 in New York City under the direction of two young women, Alice and Irene Lewisohn. Their organization stands as the one thoroughly feminist theater in the movement. Others who helped the Lewisohns in the early years were Agnes Morgan, playwright and director; Helen Arthur, lawyer and play reader; Aline Bernstein and Alice Beer, costumers; and Sara Cowell Le Moyne, voice coach. For its first four years the Neighborhood Players succeeded well enough that the group raised the money to build the Neighborhood Playhouse. It opened on February 12, 1915. This theater group—staunchly a woman's theater with no man having any function except by invitation—slowly and wisely professionalized its personnel and eventually put together a permanent company that lasted until 1927. The name persists today as the Neighborhood Playhouse School of the Theatre.

The little theater spread as well to cities away from the East Coast. In 1915 Sam Hume, a multitalented man of the theater, convinced playwright Sidney Howard and actor Irving Pichel to help him put together an outdoor production in Detroit, and because of its success, he subsequently founded the Arts and Crafts Theatre. Later, on the West Coast, Hume helped initiate THEATRE ARTS, a magazine under the editorship of Sheldon Cheney that became the most important voice of new theater in America. Like Maurice Browne, Hume had been influenced by Gordon Craig, and he attempted to put into practice many of the ideas of the great innovator. Hume also gave many new theater artists a start. For example, he took newly graduated Frederic McConnell from Carnegie Tech and put him to work. McConnell would later create the Cleveland Playhouse, itself a little theater that became a leading community theater and eventually a significant professional repertory company.

A week after the opening of the Neighborhood Playhouse, the Washington Square Players gave their first public performance on February 19, 1915. Here was another, nearly ideal example of little theater. Some of the originators were young people who later became theater luminaries: ROBERT EDMOND JONES, PHILIP MOELLER, Samuel A. Eliot, Jr., Helen Westley, and LAWRENCE LANGNER. Attracting numerous other diligent and talented workers, the group encouraged such actors as Katherine Cornell, Frank Conroy, and Roland Young; designers Jones and Lee Simonson; and playwrights Zoe Akins, Susan Glaspell, Ben Hecht, and Eugene O'Neill. The Washington Square Players lasted for four years, and then its leaders launched a new professional production company called the Theatre Guild. By the end of the 1920s, the Guild was the leading company of the New York theater.

Of all the little theater groups that came into being during the teens, perhaps the most significant was the PROVINCETOWN PLAYERS. In the summer of 1915 the group came together on Cape Cod, and under the direction of GEORGE CRAM COOK produced two plays, *Suppressed Desires* by Cook and SUSAN GLASPELL, and *Constancy* by Neith Boyce. From the beginning and throughout its life, this theater group focused on playwriting and on producing new American plays. Because of their initial success, the Provincetown Players acquired a rickety fish house at the end of a wharf and rebuilt it into a theater space 25 feet square by 10 feet high. There they produced a second pair of plays. In the next summer, with 30 active members and 87 subscribers, the group produced four bills of three one-act plays each—giving a one-act play by Eugene O'Neill its first production.

In the fall of 1916, the Provincetown Players moved their operation to Greenwich Village in New York and established a theater at 133 MacDougal Street, and in the following year they moved down the street to number 139. There, and later in the larger Greenwich Village Playhouse on Sheridan Square, the Provincetown Players produced a remarkable group of new American plays, including *Bound East for Cardiff, The Emperor Jones, The Hairy Ape*, and *Desire Under the Elms* by Eugene O'Neill; *Trifles, Inheritors*, and *The Outside* by Susan Glaspell; and *The Princess Marries the Page* and *Aria da Capo* by Edna St. Vincent Millay.

Over the years many talented people worked with the Provincetown Players, for example, writers Djuna Barnes, Maxwell Bodenheim, Louise Bryant, Floyd Dell, Edna Ferber, Theodore Dreiser, Alfred Kreymborg, John Reed, Evelyn Scott, Wilbur Daniel Steele, and Wallace Stephens; performers E. J. Ballantine, Charles Ellis, Charles S. Gilpin, and Louis Wolheim; designers Millia Davenport and Cleon Throckmorton. The most noteworthy people, however, were directors George Cram Cook and Kenneth Macgowan, designer Robert Edmond Jones, and writers Susan Glaspell and Eugene O'Neill. From 1915 to 1929, the Provincetown Players surely operated a playwright's theater, and the company presented to the world some of the leading American dramatic writers of its time.

The little theater movement spread far beyond Boston, Detroit, Chicago, and New York. Beginning in 1911, Thomas H. Dickinson created the Wisconsin Players of Madison and Milwaukee. In 1913 Beulah E. Jay and F. H. Shelton brought the Philadelphia Little Theatre into being. In 1915 Samuel A. Eliot, Jr., started a little theater in Indianapolis, and Allen Crafton transformed an Illinois saloon into the Prairie Playhouse in Galesburg. In the 1920s, the Goodman Theatre came into being under the guidance of Thomas Wood Stevens, and Jasper Deeter established the long-lived Hedgerow Theatre in Pennsylvania. Other little theaters came into being during the teens in St. Louis; Duluth; Baltimore; Philadelphia; Berkeley; and Erie, Pennsylvania, as well as other cities and towns. STUART WALKER even established a little theater that toured, naming it the Portmanteau Theatre. Walker gave a start to such actors as Tom Powers, Gregory Kelly, Morgan Farley, and Ruth Gordon.

Despite the relatively short life of the little theater movement in its first incarnation, 1912–1920, its ideals never faltered, and the theater artists whom the movement introduced were as important as any who ever occupied the American stage, especially Eugene O'Neill. Perhaps even more important, the movement helped spawn numerous community and

college theaters, and it initiated a tradition of small, idealistic theater groups, a tradition that still endures.

During the first two decades of the 20th century, a more general type of little theater activity spread through the United States—the community theater. In 1900, Jane Addams, Ellen Starr, and Laura Pelham—at Hull House, in Chicago—initiated one of the first of the century's community theaters. With a strong sense of social mission, they created a settlement house to bring the stimulus of arts and crafts to the poor, and to these visionary women theater represented a worthy pursuit. PERCY MACKAYE also helped the cause of community theater early in the century by starting a tradition of outdoor productions. MacKaye also published a book entitled *The Civic Theatre* (1912) and in it argued that community theater productions offered an excellent means for local citizens to join together in creative enterprises and use their leisure time to good effect.

Perhaps the chief distinction between community theaters and little theater (or alternative theater) groups can be summarized thus: most community theaters produce plays with proven records in commercial theater, whereas little or alternative theaters tend to produce new American plays or little-known European or classic dramas. Most community theater personnel participate in theater as leisure activity, whereas most people involved with little or alternative theater see theater as their primary profession, even though they may have to work at other jobs to supplement their incomes. In any case, distinctions between the two sorts of theaters are difficult to draw, and many theater groups are a mixture of types.

The community theater movement developed so rapidly that by 1925 nearly 2,000 such groups had joined the Drama League of America. In the final years of the 1920s, the number of such theaters continued to increase. In the depression years of the 1930s, however, community theater along with most other enterprises suffered financial deprivation. With the creation of the FEDERAL THEATER PROJECT, funded by the United States government and lasting from 1935 to 1939, community theater found a new stimulus. Then throughout World War II community theater took another leap in popularity as people joined together in many communal causes, including entertainment and amateur theatricals. The movement remained strong until the 1960s when the new generation of young people turned their attention to political activities, and there was a lull in community theater activity from then until the early 1980s, when community theater began to flourish again, especially in cities of small and medium size. Currently, a system of regional and national drama festivals appears to be acting as a stimulant to local theater effort.

Examples of strong community theater operations abound, for example, in Midland, Texas; Indianapolis; Shreveport, Louisiana; and Columbus, Ohio. The Cleveland Play House and the Pasadena Playhouse are examples of organizations that were community theaters and then came to serve other functions. The Cleveland Play House began with living-room readings in 1915, and soon thereafter its leaders began to produce full-fledged theater as a part of the little theater movement. In 1921 when Frederic McConnell took charge, the Cleveland Play House became a community theater. Finally, McConnell—and later directors K. Elmo Lowe and Richard Oberlin—transformed the organization into a professional company. Gilmor Brown started the Pasadena Playhouse in 1916, and it succeeded well, for many years fulfilling the dual functions of community theater and theater school. After Brown's death in 1960, the organization weakened, and in 1969 it ended in a state of bankruptcy. Community theater, however, has continued to thrive elsewhere, with new theaters such as Jeff Daniels's *Purple Rose Theatre* in Chelsea, Michigan, arriving in the 1990s to strengthen the long tradition.

Outdoor theater, another offshoot of the little theater movement, also continues to grow. Many years after the productions of Percy MacKaye, playwright PAUL GREEN devoted the late portion of his artistic life, during the 1940s and 1950s, to writing and helping to produce such outdoor classics as *The Lost Colony*. The Institute of Outdoor Drama on the campus of the University of North Carolina continues to coordinate the many folk-oriented outdoor productions throughout the country.

No discussion of the little theater movement would be complete without mention of its influence on the beginning and continuing life of college and university theater. Some of the most significant teacher-directors who introduced ideals of little theater to campuses were GEORGE PIERCE BAKER, Harvard 1908, and Yale 1924; A. M. Drummond, Cornell 1912; Alfred G. Arvold, North Dakota Agricultural College 1914; Thomas Wood Stevens, Carnegie Institute of Technology 1914; and Frederick Koch, University of Grand Forks 1914, and University of North Carolina 1918. Others among the early leaders on campus were Allen Crafton, Alexander Dean, John Dolman, Jr., Sawyer Falk, Hallie Flanagan, Hubert Heffner, Glenn Hughes, Lee Norvelle, and ARTHUR HOBSON QUINN.

Later manifestations of little theater occurred in the Off Broadway movement of the 1950s and 1960s, the repertory theater movement of the 1960s, the Off Off Broadway movement of the 1970s, and the alternative theater movement of the 1980s and 1990s. Throughout the 20th century, little theater in the United States enjoyed a significant life, and it remains one of the nation's most persistent forms of theater. The innovative nature of many of these groups often outstrips the creativity of their fully professional but necessarily commercial counterparts. The spirit of the little theater movement, which initiated some of the best productions early in the 20th century, flourishes at the beginning of the 21st, and as long as visionaries with high ideals establish energetic companies, the spirit of little theater at its best will continue to stimulate theater of quality and excitement. See DRAMA IN THE U.S.
SAM SMILEY/GP

Littleton, Mark.   See JOHN PENDLETON KENNEDY.

Little Women, or, Meg, Jo, Beth, and Amy (in two parts, 1868, 1869),   a novel for young readers by Louisa

May Alcott. A suggestion by Thomas Niles, an editor with a Boston publishing firm, induced Alcott to write this book, a fictionalized account of life in her own family; it made her famous and wealthy. The story concerns four sisters of varying dispositions. Jo March, the heroine, is a tomboy and wants to become an author. Her older sister Meg, very pretty, aspires to be a young lady. Beth is shy and loves music. Amy hopes to be a great artist and also to overcome her selfishness. The rich boy next door, Theodore Lawrence (Laurie), would like to marry Jo, but marries Amy instead; Jo marries an elderly professor, Mr. Bhaer (see WILLIAM RIMMER); Meg marries John Brooke, Laurie's tutor. The story had a number of sequels.

Livesay, Dorothy (1909–1996),   poet. Born in Winnipeg, Livesay was educated at the University of Toronto and the Sorbonne. Her early poems, collected in *Green Pitcher* (1928) and *Signposts* (1932), were influenced by IMAGISM. During the Depression she was active with the Communist party in Canada and was employed as a social worker in Montreal, New Jersey, and Vancouver; her poetry in this period and afterward displayed the social consciousness apparent in *Selected Poems* (1956). Her wartime verse in *Day and Night* (1944) won the Governor General's Award, as did *Poems for People* (1947). Some of her best poetry dealt with women, love, and aging, themes apparent in *The Unquiet Bed* (1967), *Plainsongs* (1969), *Ice Age* (1975), and *The Woman I Am* (1977). Other poems are found in *The Raw Edges: Voices for Our Time* (1981) and *The Self-Completing Tree* (1986). Her essays, poems, and letters are collected in *Right Hand Left Hand* (1977). *A Winnipeg Childhood* (1973) is a fictional memoir, expanded in *Beginnings* (1988) and *The Husband: A Novella* (1990).

Living Age.   See ELIAKIM LITTELL.

Lloyd, Henry Demarest (1847–1903),   journalist, reformer, economist. Born in New York City, Lloyd was admitted to the bar in 1869 and became an active reformer, contributing to the defeat of Tammany in 1871. One year later he moved to Chicago to write for the *Tribune*. His articles pointed out the dangers of monopoly, the abuse of grain speculations, and the machinations of the railroads and of the Standard Oil Co. He investigated industrial oppression in the Spring Valley coal strike and championed the anarchists convicted in the Haymarket massacre of 1886. *A Strike of Millionaires against Miners* (1890) was a plea for the rights of labor; *Wealth against Commonwealth* (1894), his best known book, pointed out that the natural wealth was in the hands of a few people, rather than under control of the nation.

Lobel, Arnold [Stark] (1933–1987),   writer and illustrator of children's books. Born in Los Angeles, Lobel grew up in Schenectady, New York, and was educated at Pratt Institute. He married Anita Kempler (1934–   ) and collaborated with her on several books. Among his titles are *A Zoo for Mr. Muster* (1962), about the Prospect Park Zoo in Brooklyn; *Frog and Toad Together* (1973), one of a popular series; and *Fables* (1981), animal tales.

local color.   Associated with REALISM in American literature, the local color movement spanned the years from the end of the Civil War to the 1890s. A new sense of the size of the country and its regional differences followed from the war itself, the newly accessible West after completion of the transcontinental railroad in 1869, the abandonment of New England farmlands for those in the Midwest, the rise of the cities, and the waves of immigration. American readers began to look to their own country for writers and subjects. After the war, the realistic movement, particularly as embodied in WILLIAM DEAN HOWELLS and the ATLANTIC MONTHLY, provided impetus to writers to look close to home, to choose for their material the life they knew best. The result was local color, a derivative of realism that emphasized the folkways, speech patterns, manners, and traditions of a region.

Among the writers were, for the West, BRET HARTE; for Louisiana, GEORGE WASHINGTON CABLE, GRACE KING, and KATE CHOPIN; for the old South, JOEL CHANDLER HARRIS; for Connecticut, ROSE TERRY COOKE; for Tennessee, MARY NOAILLES MURFREE; for the Midwest, HAMLIN GARLAND; for Maine, SARAH ORNE JEWETT; for Massachusetts and Vermont, MARY E. WILKINS FREEMAN; and for North Carolina and Ohio, CHARLES W. CHESNUTT. Important forerunners included A. B. LONGSTREET, HARRIET BEECHER STOWE, and GEORGE WASHINGTON HARRIS. Although the term "local color" has ceased to be much used for them, efforts to derive fictional interest from the ways of distinctive communities have continued into our own time. See REGIONALISM.

Lochhead, Douglas (1922–   ),   poet, scholar. Born in Guelph, Ontario, and educated at McGill and the University of Toronto, Lochhead has taught at various universities. His poems, at first conventional and then more open, range in content from the Canadian landscape to more personal themes. *The Full Furnace: Collected Poems* appeared in 1975, and *Tiger in the Skull: New and Selected Poems* in 1986. *High Marsh Road: Lines for a Diary* (1980) is a sequence centered in New Brunswick. Other verse appears in *Upper Cape Poems* (1989), *Dykelands* (1989), and *Homage to Henry Alline and Other Poems* (1992). An authority on Canadian studies, Lochhead has written and edited works especially on Canadian poetry.

Locke, Alain [LeRoy] (1886–1954),   sociologist, teacher, art critic, philosopher, editor. Born in Philadelphia, Locke was educated at Harvard and Oxford and became professor of philosophy at Howard. In 1910 he toured the South to study the problems of his race. He became prominent as an authority on African-American culture with the publication of *The New Negro* (1925), an anthology of poetry and prose that demonstrated the vitality of the HARLEM RENAISSANCE. *The Negro in America* (1933) was soon followed by *Frederick Douglas, a Biography of Anti-Slavery* (1935); *The Negro and His Music* (1936); *Negro Art—Past and Present* (1936); and *The Negro in Art* (1940). With Bernard Stern he edited *When People Meet: A Study in Race and Culture Contact* (1942). He also edited a number of anthologies of African-American stories and plays.

Locke, David Ross.   See P. V. NASBY.

Locke, John (1632–1704),   English philosopher. Locke was one of the most influential thinkers and writers who ever lived, furnishing ideas for three revolutions—that of 1688 against James II of England, that of 1776 of the American colonies against George III, and that of 1789 of the French against Louis XVI. He was a highly respected adviser to many English statesmen and published numerous writings on philosophy, the human mind, education, religion, and economics, among them *Letters Concerning Toleration* (1689, 1690, 1692); *Two Treatises of Civil Government* (1690); *An Essay Concerning the Human Understanding* (1690); *Some Thoughts Concerning Education* (1693); and *The Reasonableness of Christianity* (1695). Locke rejected the notion of innate ideas and held that "there is nothing in the mind except what was first in the senses"; the mind at birth is a *tabula rasa* waiting to be written on, so everything in the mind is the result of experience. In his two *Treatises* on government he argued for natural rights and natural law, with government resting on a social contract and on inalienable rights of life, liberty, and property. Locke expounded the ideas of the dissenters: constitutional rights, toleration, security, and the sovereign will of the majority.

Jonathan Edwards read the *Essay Concerning Human Understanding* when he was only fourteen and was so impressed by Locke's doctrine of sense as the ultimate source of reflection that he worked out an empirical argument for supernatural or holy love. Benjamin Franklin also read Locke's *Essay*, and later was influenced by Locke's ideas on education. Tom Paine naturally followed Locke. Samuel Adams held he was "one of the greatest men who ever lived." Richard Henry Lee said the DECLARATION OF INDEPENDENCE was copied from Locke's treatise on government. In this Locke wrote: "The state of nature has a law to govern it, which obliges every one; and reason, which is that law, teaches all mankind, who will but consult it, that being all equal and independent, no one ought to harm another in his life, health, liberty, or possessions." Jefferson gave the words a new "felicity of expression," as John Adams phrased it, but the ideas are Locke's.

Lockridge, Richard [Orson] (1898–1982),   newspaperman, drama critic, novelist. Lockridge, who was born in Missouri, worked on Kansas City papers and the New York *Sun*. In 1936 he began writing, in collaboration with his wife, **Frances Lockridge** (?–1963), a series of detective stories featuring a married couple, the Norths. The stories began as a series in *The New Yorker*, and the Norths became popular on radio. Their books include *Mr. and Mrs. North* (1936), *The Norths Meet Murder* (1940), *Murder Out of Turn* (1941), *A Pinch of Poison* (1941), *Death on the Aisle* (1942), and *Killing the Goose* (1944). In collaboration with G. H. Estabrook, Lockridge wrote *Death in the Mind* (1945). The Lockridges' later works include *Cats and People* (1950) and *The Faceless Adversary* (1956).

Lockridge, Ross [Franklin, Jr.] (1914–1948), teacher, novelist. Born in Indiana, Lockridge was the son of a teacher at Indiana University. He was educated at the Sorbonne and Harvard and spent years writing a lengthy novel,

Raintree County (1948). The book was hailed as a major triumph, and Lockridge's future seemed secure, but he committed suicide. July 4, 1892, the day on which the entire action of the book takes place, is a great day in Raintree County, an imaginary county in Indiana. John Wickliff Shawnessy, principal of the local high school, is the chief actor, and flashbacks to earlier episodes of his life vividly illuminate the history.

Lockwood, Francis Cummins (1864–1948), teacher, historian. Born in Illinois, Lockwood taught at various universities, including Arizona, and for a time was acting president there. He became interested in Arizona history and wrote mainly on the Southwestern region. Among his books are *Arizona Characters* (1928), *Pioneer Days in Arizona* (1932), *With Padre Kino on the Trail and A Guide to His Mission Chain* (1934), *The Apache Indians* (1938), and *More Arizona Characters* (1943).

Lodge, George Cabot (1873–1909), poet, dramatist. This son of Henry Cabot Lodge was a Bostonian of Bostonians, but also a rebel who wrote several collections of poems and two dramas, *Cain* (1904) and *Herakles* (1908). He was deeply under the influence of Schopenhauer and of Buddhist thought. Among his books are *The Song of the Wave* (1898), *Poems* (1902), *The Great Adventure* (1905), and *The Soul's Inheritance* (1909).

Lodge, Henry Cabot (1850–1924), lawyer, editor, historian, public official. Born in Boston and educated at Harvard, Lodge was editor of *The North American Review* (1873–76). Following service in the Massachusetts legislature, he was elected to the House of Representatives in 1886, to the U.S. Senate in 1893, and served till his death. He is remembered by many for his opposition to the League of Nations. He wrote biographies of Alexander Hamilton (1882), Daniel Webster (1883), and George Washington (2 v. 1888–89), as well as several histories and a memoir, *Early Memories* (1913).

Loewe, Frederick (1904–1988), composer. Born in Vienna, Loewe came to the United States in 1924 intent on a musical career, but drifted about America working at goldmining, cattle-branding, even boxing as a bantam-weight. A chance encounter with ALAN JAY LERNER ignited his career, resulting in one of the great teams of contemporary theater. Their BRIGADOON (1947) ran for 581 performances. This was followed by *Paint Your Wagon* (1951). In 1956 Lerner and Loewe, taking George Bernard Shaw's *Pygmalion* as a basis, wrote *My Fair Lady*, and it became an American classic. *Gigi*, written for the screen in 1959, proved another box-office bonanza. *Camelot* (1961), a durable hit, was based on T. H. White's *Once and Future King*.

Lofting, Hugh [John] (1886–1947), author and illustrator of children's books. Born in England, Lofting studied civil engineering at MIT and London Polytechnic and worked on railways in Africa and South America, but soon turned to writing. He lived in the U.S. from 1912 to 1916, then created Doctor Dolittle in letters home to his children from his service with the Irish Guards in Europe. Wounded, he settled in Connecticut in 1919 and lived in the U.S. for the rest of his life. *The Story of Doctor Dolittle* (1920) was followed by *The Voyages of Doctor Dolittle* (1922) and others in the same series. His other books for children include *The Story of Mrs. Tubbs* (1923) and *Tommy, Tilly, and Mrs. Tubbs* (1936), both picture books; *Porridge Poetry* (1924), verse; *The Twilight of Magic* (1930), a fantasy about a magic seashell; and *Gub Gub's Book* (1932), a food book by Doctor Dolittle's pig friend. *Victory for the Slain* (1942) is adult verse, anti-war.

Logan, Cornelius Ambrosius (1806–1853), sailor, newspaperman, actor, playwright. Born in Baltimore, he became an actor and toured the country. In 1834 he wrote a play that proved a hit, *Yankee Land, or, The Foundling of the Apple Orchard*. Similar plays in the tradition of the Yankee rural wag were *The Wag of Maine* (1834) and *The Vermont Wool Dealer* (1840). Logan himself appeared as Aminadab Slocum in his *Chloroform, or, New York a Hundred Years Hence* (1849).

Logan, James [1] (1674–1751), public official, scholar. In 1699 Logan, an Irish-born Quaker, accompanied WILLIAM PENN to the New World as secretary and adviser. In Pennsylvania, Penn made him Secretary of the Province and Commissioner of Property and Receiver-General. As land agent for the proprietors, Logan negotiated with the Indians and obtained huge tracts of land for settlement. He published several books in Latin abroad. Benjamin Franklin printed Logan's verse translation of the *Moral Distiches* (1735) of Dionysius Cato and of Cicero's *De Senectute* (*M. T. Cicero's Cato Major, or, His Discourse of Old Age*, 1744). Franklin described the former as "the first translation of a classic which was both made and printed in the British colonies"; he spoke of the latter as "a happy omen that Philadelphia shall become the seat of the American Muses." By 1751 Logan had made a collection of nearly three thousand volumes, which he bequeathed to the city for public use.

Logan, James [2] (1725?–1780), Mingo chief. He took the name of James Logan in admiration for the Pennsylvania official (see above). He was long a friend of the English, but the murder of his family in the Yellow Creek massacre of April 1774 led to his participation in Lord Dunmore's War against the settlers. Later he sided with the British against the Americans in the Revolution. He was finally killed in a family quarrel. Brantz Mayer in 1851 published a *Discourse called Tah-gah-jute, or, Logan and Captain Michael Cresap* vindicating the captain of the charge of the murder.

In 1774 Logan sent a remarkable document to Lord Dunmore, then governor of Virginia. It gained wide currency and was long a standard recitation piece in American classrooms. In his *Notes on the State of Virginia* (1784) Jefferson printed it as proof that American Indians, contrary to European belief, were not degenerate savages. Dr. Joseph Doddridge's play *Logan, The Last of the Race of Shikellemus, Chief of the Cayuga Nation* (1823) and John Neal's novel *Logan, A Family History* (1822) were designed to do justice to the Indian chief.

Logan, John (1923–1987), poet. Born in Iowa, Logan was educated at Coe College and the University of Iowa and taught at several schools, including the University of Buffalo.

His work received major critical acclaim. Often personal, his poems focus also on landscapes and human relationships. His collections include *Ghosts of the Heart* (1960), *Spring of the Thief* (1963), *The Zig-Zag Walk* (1969), *The Bridge of Change* (1980), and *Only the Dreamer Can Change the Dream: Selected Poems* (1981). His prose is collected in *The House that Jack Built* (1974, rev. 1984), autobiographical; and *A Ballet for the Ear: Interviews, Essays and Reviews* (1983), edited by A. Poulin, Jr. His *Collected Poems* was published in 1988.

Logan, Joshua [Lockwood] (1908–1988),   producer, writer, director. Born in Texarkana, Texas, Logan was educated at Princeton and, under Konstantin Stanislavsky, at the Moscow Art Theater. His greatest hit was *South Pacific* (1949), which he directed and for which he was also coauthor and coproducer. Among other Broadway hits he directed, some of which he cowrote, are *I Married an Angel* (1938), *Knickerbocker Holiday* (1938), *Annie Get Your Gun* (1946), *Mister Roberts* (1948), *Wish You Were Here* (1952), *Picnic* (1953), *Fanny* (1954), and *The World of Suzie Wong* (1958). His films include *Picnic* (1971), *Bus Stop* (1956), *South Pacific* (1958), *Fanny* (1961), *Camelot* (1967), and *Paint Your Wagon* (1969). Long a sufferer from manic depression, he contributed to public awareness by open discussion of the disease and its effects. *Josh* (1976) is an autobiography, and *Movie Stars, Real People, and Me* (1978) is a memoir.

Logan, Olive (1839–1909),   actress, playwright, newspaper correspondent, lecturer. Born in Elmira, New York, Olive Logan was the daughter of CORNELIUS LOGAN and tried for a time to be an actress. Under the influence of ARTEMUS WARD she became a lecturer, and her talks on social and political topics proved successful. She made frequent trips abroad and contributed to newspapers in this country, England, and France, writing under the pen name Chroniqueuse. Logan also wrote two plays that Augustin Daly produced, *Surf* (1870) and *Newport* (1879), both social satires, as well as novels and other books, including *Apropos of Women and Theaters* (1869) and *The Mimic World* (1871).

Log of a Cowboy, The (1903),   a narrative by ANDY ADAMS, based on his experiences in a five-month cattle drive from Texas to Montana in 1882.

Lolita (France 1955; U.S. 1958),   a novel by VLADIMIR NABOKOV.

Loman, Willy.   The salesman in DEATH OF A SALESMAN, by ARTHUR MILLER.

Lomax, Alan (1915–   ),   ballad collector, author. Working with his father, JOHN LOMAX, and independently, Alan Lomax—he was born in Texas—recorded folk songs all over the United States and in the Bahamas, Haiti, England, Scotland, Ireland, Spain, and Italy. From 1937 to 1942 he was in charge of the American Folk Music Library of the Library of Congress. During the 1940s he produced radio programs, lectured, and continued to gather folk songs. He has written *Mister Jelly Roll* (1950), *Folk Songs of North America* (1960), *The Penguin Book of American Folk Songs* (1961), and *The Land Where the Blues Began* (1993).

Lomax, John A[very] (1867–1948),   teacher, businessman, ballad collector, memoirist. Lomax, born in Mississippi, began collecting ballads early. When he was a graduate student at Harvard, BARRETT WENDELL arranged for a three-year fellowship so he could go on collecting. His *Cowboy Songs and Other Frontier Ballads* (1910) was a landmark work. Lomax related his experiences as a collector in *Adventures of a Ballad Hunter* (1947). *Songs of the Cattle Trail and Cow Camp* (1918) followed *Cowboy Songs*. With the assistance of his son ALAN LOMAX, he collected *American Ballads and Folk Songs* (1934), *Negro Folk Songs as Sung by Lead Belly* (1936), and *Our Singing Country* (1941). Lomax also helped establish the Archive of American Folk Song at the Library of Congress.

London, Jack (1876–1916),   novelist, short-story writer, political essayist, adventurer, hobo, seaman, socialist, rancher, war correspondent. London was born in San Francisco, the son of Flora Wellman Chaney and (probably) William H. Chaney, a well-known philosopher/lecturer and self-proclaimed Professor of Astrology, who denied his paternity and deserted his common-law wife on learning of her pregnancy. When the child was nine months old, Flora married John London, a widower who had placed his two youngest daughters, Eliza and Ida, in an orphanage while he worked as a carpenter.

The circumstances of London's impoverished childhood strongly influenced the essential attitudes of his adulthood. "My body and soul were starved when I was a child," he later wrote, and he never outgrew his resentment of poverty and of his mother's spiritualistic fervor and emotional coldness. The only maternal affection he received was from the African-American woman "Aunt Jennie" Prentiss, who had been his wet nurse, and from his stepsister Eliza.

At age fourteen, London was forced to discontinue his education to work in a factory. At fifteen he quit work to become "Prince of the Oyster Pirates" on San Francisco Bay. At seventeen he shipped as an able-bodied seaman aboard a sealing schooner bound for the Northwest Pacific, subsequently winning $25 first prize in a contest sponsored by the San Francisco *Morning Call* for his "Story of a Typhoon off the Coast of Japan." At eighteen he joined Kelly's Army—the western contingent of General Jacob Coxey's Army of the Unemployed—in its March on Washington to protest the economic depression of 1893–94 but left the Army at Hannibal, Missouri, to hobo his way to the Midwest and the East Coast, was arrested as a vagrant in Niagara and served thirty days in the Erie County Penitentiary. At nineteen he resumed his education at Oakland High School. At twenty he joined the Socialist Party and, after intensive cramming, enrolled for a semester at the University of California. At twenty-one he joined the Klondike Gold Rush. At twenty-two, suffering from scurvy, he returned to Oakland and launched his career as a professional writer, selling his story "To the Man on Trail" to the *Overland Monthly* for $5. At twenty-three he made his major breakthrough into the literary marketplace by publishing "An Odyssey of the North" in the *Atlantic Monthly* for $120 and a year's free subscription to the magazine. At twenty-four he was hailed as the American Kipling with the publication of *The Son of the Wolf* by Houghton, Mifflin, and married Bessie Mae Maddern, who became the mother of his two daughters, Joan (1901) and Becky (1902). At twenty-six, after collaborating with Anna Strunsky in writing *The Kempton-Wace Letters*, an epistolary dialogue on love, he spent six weeks in the East End of London and wrote *The People of the Abyss* (1903). At twenty-seven he won worldwide acclaim as the author of *The Call of the Wild* and separated from Bessie after falling in love with Charmian Kittredge. At twenty-eight he reported the Russo-Japanese War for the Hearst Syndicate. At twenty-nine he bought the 130-acre Hill Ranch in Glen Ellen, California, married Kittredge, and was elected first president of the Intercollegiate Socialist Party, lecturing at Harvard, Yale, and several other major universities. At thirty he reported the San Francisco earthquake for *Collier's* and began construction of a sailboat, *The Snark*. At thirty-one he sailed to Hawaii on the first leg of an around-the-world cruise, which he was forced to abandon in Australia two years later because of multiple tropic ailments contracted in the Solomon Islands. At thirty-four he won recognition in California as a scientific farmer through his development of Beauty Ranch, in the Valley of the Moon, began construction of Wolf House, and mourned the loss of his and Charmian's infant daughter, Joy. At thirty-seven he was discovered to have diseased kidneys during surgery for appendicitis. At thirty-eight he reported the Mexican Revolution for *Collier's*, but was forced to return home following a severe case of bacillary dysentery. At thirty-nine, suffering from failing kidneys, he returned to Hawaii, hoping to regain his health. At forty he resigned from the Socialist Party "because of its lack of fire and fight," came home to devote his energies to the development of his ranch, and died on November 22, 1916, apparently of uremia (as diagnosed by attending physicians) but, more likely (as recent evidence attests) of stroke and heart failure.

In less than two decades London produced two hundred short stories, more than four hundred nonfiction pieces, twenty novels, and three full-length plays on an extraordinary variety of subjects: agronomy, alcoholism, animal and human psychology, animal training, architecture, assassination, astral projection, big business, ecology, economics, folklore, gold-hunting, greed, hoboing, love, mental retardation, mythology, penal reform, political corruption, prizefighting, racial exploitation, revolution, science, science fiction, seafaring, slum housing, socialism, stock-breeding, war, wildlife, and the writing game. His reputation was established initially on the basis of his Northland Saga, the largest single facet of his complex literary achievement, comprising twenty-eight stories, four novels, one play, and a half-dozen nonfiction pieces, informed by such naturalistic themes as primitivism, atavism, environmental determinism, and survival of the fittest in such stories as "The Law of Life" (1901), "Love of Life" (1905), and "To Build a Fire" (1908). His most famous Northland novels are THE CALL OF THE WILD (1903), the fabulous tale of a kid-

napped ranch dog that achieves mastery as a Klondike sled dog and ultimately becomes the great Ghost-Dog of Northland legend; and WHITE FANG (1906), written as a companion-piece to the earlier novel and reversing the process of devolution by presenting the story of a savage Northland wolf-dog that is transformed into a gentle ranch pet through human love.

Other well-known works are THE SEA-WOLF (1904), an initiation story reminiscent of Kipling's *Captains Courageous*; THE IRON HEEL (1908), an apocalyptic version of the war between capitalism and the working classes; MARTIN EDEN (1909), a *Bildungsroman* drawn largely from London's own struggle to achieve success; *John Barleycorn* (1913), a fictional memoir written in support of the prohibitionist movement; and THE VALLEY OF THE MOON (1913), a dramatization of London's agrarian vision. Not known as well, but important to understanding London, are *The People of the Abyss* (1903), his sympathetic first-person account of living conditions in one of the world's most notorious slums; *The Road* (1907), the account of London's hoboing experiences; *Burning Daylight* (1910), a novel incorporating in its central character the three major archetypes of the American hero as frontiersman, businessman, and yeoman farmer; THE STAR ROVER (1915), an exposé of brutal prison conditions comprising a series of vivid narrative sketches unified by the theme of astral projection; and *The Red One* (1918) and *On the Makaloa Mat* (1919), two short-story collections published posthumously and revealing London's philosophical shift from materialistic monism toward the theories of C. G. Jung, whose work he discovered six months before his death.

Strongly influenced by Herbert Spencer's "Philosophy of Style" and Rudyard Kipling's "plain style," London's literary techniques were predicated on functionalism, sincerity, and what he called "impassioned realism." He was instrumental in ushering into American literature a new prose for the modern fictionist: clear, straightforward, unpretentious, imagistic. He had mastered the principle of the objective correlative a generation before T. S. Eliot popularized the concept. A major force in establishing for fiction a respectable middle ground between the saloon and the salon, London had a pervasive and profound influence on modern writers, including such figures as Orwell, Hemingway, Ring Lardner, James Jones, Mailer, and Kerouac. Moreover, London has America's best claim to the title of Great World Author: his works have been translated into more than eighty languages, and he is regarded by many foreign critics as our most powerful writer.

Although there is no complete edition of the works, Stanford Press University has published *The Complete Short Stories* (1993). Eight of London's most important book-length works, along with twenty-five stories and four essays, capably edited by Donald Pizer, are included in the two volumes published by the Library of America (1982). Daniel Dyer's annotated edition of *The Call of the Wild—With an Illustrated Reader's Companion* (1995) is definitive. Complementing these publications are Richard Etulain's *Jack London on the Road: The Tramp*

Diary and Other Hobo Writings (1979) and Dale L. Walker and Jeanne Campbell Reesman's *No Mentor But Myself: Jack London on Writers and Writing* (1999). The most reliable biographies are Franklin Walker's *Jack London and the Klondike* (1966, 1994) and Russ Kingman's *A Pictorial Life of Jack London* (1979). Clarice Stasz's *American Dreamers: Charmian and Jack London* (1988) provides insights into the complex relationship between London and his second wife. Other rich sources include the three-volume Stanford Edition of *The Letters of Jack London* (1988), edited by Earle Labor, Robert C. Leitz III, and I. Milo Shepard, and Russ Kingman's *Jack London: A Definitive Chronology* (1992). Hensley C. Woodbridge's *Jack London: A Bibliography* (1966, 1973), listing both primary and secondary materials, is indispensable. Earle Labor's *Jack London* (1973, rev. ed. with Jeanne C. Reesman, 1994) is a concise critical introduction. The best studies of the fiction are Charles N. Watson's *The Novels of Jack London* (1983), Jacqueline Tavernier-Courbin's *The Call of the Wild: A Naturalistic Romance* (1994), and Jeanne Campbell Reesman's *Jack London: A Study of the Short Fiction* (1999).

EARLE LABOR

Long, Huey [Pierce] (1893–1935),   lawyer, politician, public official. Born in Winnfield, Louisiana, Long became governor in 1928 and created a political patronage system that controlled Louisiana for many years. He provided the state with excellent highways and good schools during his term as governor, built a new state capitol, and helped the Louisiana State University. But his financing methods were bizarre or worse. In 1929 he was impeached but not convicted. He was elected to the U.S. Senate in 1930. He called himself the Kingfish, announced a Share-the-Wealth Plan, and tried to run for president. Long was assassinated by Dr. Carl A. Weiss, Jr., who was in turn killed by Long's armed bodyguards.

Long wrote two books, *Every Man a King* (1933) and *My First Days in the White House* (posthumously published, 1935). Long inspired much fiction. Hamilton Basso's *Sun in Capricorn* (1942) is a savage attack on a scoundrel and dangerous demagogue not unlike Long. In John Dos Passos's *Number One* (1943) Long appears as a charlatan with a lust for power matched only by his lust for women. Adria Locke Langley sentimentalized Long in *A Lion in the Streets* (1945). Robert Penn Warren's Willie Stark in ALL THE KING'S MEN (1946) also resembles Long, as does Sinclair Lewis's Berzelius Windrip, the would-be dictator in *It Can't Happen Here* (1935). Irving Berlin's *Louisiana Purchase* (1940) is a satire of the Long regime.

Long, John Luther (1861–1927),   lawyer, short-story writer, playwright. Born in Pennsylvania, Long wrote a story entitled MADAME BUTTERFLY that was published in the *Century* magazine for January 1898. It caught the eye of DAVID BELASCO, who collaborated with Long on a play that had a successful run, and Giacomo Puccini used it as a basis for his opera. A second collaboration, THE DARLING OF THE GODS (1902), a Japanese melodrama, was followed by ADREA (1904), a Roman tragedy with a blind princess as heroine. Long began to write alone, but his own plays were less successful. *Dolce* (1906),

founded on his short story, and *Kassa* (1909) were followed by *Crowns* (1922), a drama of ideas.

Long Day's Journey into Night (1956),   a play by EUGENE O'NEILL. This extraordinary autobiographical drama, which was not produced until 1956, was written some time before July 22, 1941, when O'Neill presented the manuscript to Carlotta, his third wife, with a letter paying tribute to her for the way in which she had helped him "to face my dead at last and write this play—write it with deep pity and understanding for all the four haunted Tyrones." The *Tyrones* were the O'Neills—Eugene, his father, mother, and older brother. The father is the celebrated actor, the mother a drug addict, the older son a drunkard and ne'er-do-well. A harrowing domestic tragedy, the play offers a clear insight into O'Neill's character and stands as a masterpiece of American dramatic literature.

Longfellow, Henry Wadsworth (1807–1882),   poet, translator, dramatist, writer of prose fiction and non-fiction. Longfellow is among the rarest of American literary phenomena. A nation that has seldom been aware of its own poets, and even less of its good poets, made him an honored institution in his own time. That perception was validated by accolades from British and continental literary figures, as well as from such national literary lions as Emerson and William Cullen Bryant, whose considerable fame as poets became less than Longfellow's. The public not only knew and praised Longfellow but actually bought his poetry in sufficient quantities to enable him to quit his academic career in 1854 and live very comfortably for the remainder of his long life primarily on the proceeds of his writing. Since Longfellow, only Robert Frost among American poets has approached comparable status in the national culture.

Longfellow was born in Portland, Maine, then still part of Massachusetts. From his school days, he sensed a literary calling, but as scion of an old New England Puritan family who heeded the dicta of his formidable father, Longfellow by and large held his literary aspirations in abeyance while contemplating careers in the law, in medicine, and in the clergy. Finally, he and his father agreed upon a professorship in foreign languages, a new field at American universities, which was offered to young Longfellow when he was graduated from Bowdoin College in 1825—a decision that was to empower Longfellow to become a first-rate translator of Dante, among others, and to become an important conduit through which European culture would be transmitted to the United States. The arrangement with Bowdoin entailed his spending 1826 to 1829 in Europe to gain proficiency in Spanish, French, Italian, and German.

He would return to Europe three more times. In Scandinavia and Germany in 1835 and 1836 he tightened his grasp of German and added Scandinavian languages to his linguistic repertoire for his Harvard professorship, which commenced in 1836. He went back to Germany in 1842, and to Britain and the Continent in 1868 and 1869 to receive a number of honors, including an audience with Queen Victoria and honorary degrees at Oxford and Cambridge. The Queen, noting the familiarity that common people, including palace servants, had with Longfellow's poems, remarked, "Such poets wear a crown that is imperishable."

The first non-British citizen to be commemorated in the Poet's Corner of Westminster Abbey, his international following was legion. Among his publishers were seventy-odd British publishers—many of them literary pirates—who published almost three hundred editions of Longfellow's work in the second half of the century. He was more popular in Britain than even Tennyson and Browning. By 1900 there had been at least one hundred book translations in eighteen languages. Americans were lavish in their support of their favorite poet: figures for the sales of his work are astonishing, including 30,000 copies of THE SONG OF HIAWATHA (1855) in six months and 15,000 copies of THE COURTSHIP OF MILES STANDISH (1858) on the first day alone.

Yet, the seeds of the decline of Longfellow's reputation were planted in the very reasons for his enormous popularity. There is no more paradigmatic 19th-century American poet, no one possessed of a genuine lyrical talent and an extraordinary gift for using the great variety of traditional English prosody and poetic genres who reflected more sympathetically the Puritan, Romantic, and Victorian values of his people. Small wonder that Longfellow was their literary hero. But to new generations of Americans who came up in the ruins of those values at the end of the 19th century and thereafter he often seemed fossilized, though he continued to be widely read in school up until World War II.

EDGAR ALLAN POE—except when he needed Longfellow and wrote to him soliciting contributions to *Graham's* magazine, which Poe was editing—was among the few to attack the living icon. Poe may not have been entirely comfortable with the values that Longfellow promulgated, but it is also true that Poe was jealous of the literary, and perhaps the social, position of Longfellow and the other New England Brahmins. On more than one occasion, with all the resentment of an outsider barred from an exclusive club, Poe leveled charges of plagiarism against Longfellow and snidely applied the name Frogpondia to New England, and Boston its intellectual center.

Ironically, Longfellow's strong romantic proclivity created a gloominess of vision in much of his poetry that is reminiscent of Poe, though without Poe's tortured otherworldliness and necrophilia. At its best, the gentle darkness in Longfellow's outlook implies a sad isolation of humanity from God; it hints at the colder sense of cosmic alienation that was to characterize the world view of the literary naturalists at the end of the century. In his early work, HYMN TO THE NIGHT, for example, there were strong measures of both popular Byronic *Weltschmerz* and gothic chill: in the "haunted chambers of the Night," or death, is surcease from the tribulations of life. "Holy Night," he says wistfully, lays its "finger on the lips of Care,/And they complain no more." Fortunately, Longfellow could sing more than one note. The harder-headed Puritan in him was capable of fighting such depressing impulses in poems such as A PSALM OF LIFE, published in the same volume as "Hymn to the Night," the 1839 VOICES OF THE NIGHT. "Life is

real! Life is earnest/And the grave is not its goal," he could remind himself, "Let us be up and doing, . . . /Learn to labor and to wait." But the dominant mood of Longfellow's early work, heightened by the death of his first wife, Mary, in childbirth in 1835 on one of his trips to Europe, was melancholic. And that undertone persisted in his verse. In the 1850 poem "The Fire of Drift-Wood," for instance, against the bright fire and reminiscence of old friends, there is the deep regret "of what had been, and might have been,/And who was changed, and who was dead"; in the flames of the driftwood fire burn "The lost ventures of the heart,/That send no answers back again."

After the death of his second wife, Fanny, in 1861, from a fire in which Longfellow was burned in a futile effort to rescue her, he felt more ambivalent than ever about the relationship between humanity and Nature or God, although he could sense a cosmic beneficence beyond the human capacity to understand. The core simile of one of his loveliest and most contemplative sonnets, "Nature" (1878), postulates Nature's affection for us "As a fond mother, when the day is o'er,/Leads by the hand her little child to bed." She "takes away/Our playthings one by one," and then "Leads us to rest so gently, that we go/Scarce knowing if we wish to go or stay." She has, sadly, denied us our playthings—the people and things in which we invest our love—but Longfellow seeks to believe that gentle Nature means well after all; we are simply "too full to sleep to understand/How far the unknown transcends the what we know." Ultimately, Longfellow's God stands in relation to humankind essentially as the Puritan God did—as a parent to a child whose comprehension is all too small.

There is more than one poet Henry Wadsworth Longfellow, and there is the writer of unmemorable prose Longfellow. His prose includes nationalistic criticism, for example, "Defense of Poetry" (1832); sketches, for example, OUTRE-MER: A PILGRIMAGE BEYOND THE SEA (1835), modeled on Washington Irving's *Sketch Book*; and lightweight fiction, for example, HYPERION (1839) and KAVANAGH (1849).

The poet Longfellow that commanded most public attention in his time—and the one who tends to live in public memory in ours—is not the most resonant, not the Longfellow of "Nature" or of the broodingly beautiful "The Jewish Cemetery at Newport" (1858), say, or of the unromanticized, dignified Civil War poem "Killed at the Ford" (1867). Rather, it is the verse orator of topical matters as in THE ARSENAL AT SPRINGFIELD (1846) and the ballad THE WRECK OF THE HESPERUS (1841); the homey, preachy fireside poet of THE VILLAGE BLACKSMITH (1842); the author of long verse narrations of American historical and mythological figures, as in PAUL REVERE'S RIDE (1863), *The Song of Hiawatha*, *The Courtship of Miles Standish*, and EVANGELINE: A TALE OF ACADIE (1847); and the writer of heavy verse drama, such as CHRISTUS, A MYSTERY (1872). Widely forgotten is the fact that Longfellow was a first-rate translator, not only of Dante (his blank-verse translation of the *Divine Comedy* came out in 1865–1867), but of other writers in some eighteen languages. And largely ignored, too, is his superb achievement as composer of sonnets, including the "Divina

Commedia" cycle (1867) that he wrote in association with his translation of Dante; his incisive and melodic tributes to fellow writers (Chaucer, Shakespeare, Milton, Keats, and Hawthorne); and his pensive sonnets such as "Nature" and "The Harvest Moon" (1875), the latter with its elegant expression of the *ubi sunt* theme. It is difficult to think of anyone since Petrarch who has used the form of the Petrarchan sonnet more effectively.

There are ample grounds on which to maintain Longfellow's place in the pantheon of American poets. His own age had its own reasons; as his friend Oliver Wendell Holmes rightly said, Longfellow was America's "Chief Singer," the most beloved of her "Schoolroom Poets." Strangely, though, it was the generous and often critically perceptive WALT WHITMAN— in terms of poetic technique and of personality vastly different from Longfellow—who most precisely explained the contribution Longfellow made to American culture and the outpouring of love he received in return. On the poet's death in 1882, Whitman observed in "The Critic" that Longfellow:

> . . . is certainly the sort of bard and counteractant most needed for our materialistic, self-assertive, money worshipping, Anglo-Saxon races, and especially for the present age in America,—an age tyrannically regulated with reference to the manufacturer, the merchant, the financier, the politician, and the day workman; for whom and among whom he comes as the poet of melody, courtesy, deference,—poet of the mellow twilight of the past in Italy, Germany, Spain, and in Northern Europe, poet of all sympathetic gentleness, and universal poet of women and young people. I should have to think long if I were asked to name the man who had done more, and in more valuable directions, for America.

But the current age has reasons enough of its own, if it chooses to heed them, to recognize the worth—beyond the historical and cultural stature—of this accomplished lyricist, prosodist, sonneteer, and translator. We really should do better by him than regard his poems the way he viewed his books as he looked back on his life in 1881 and called them (in the sonnet "My Books") "my ornaments and arms of other days;/Not wholly useless, though no longer used, . . ."

The best editions of the works of Longfellow are the 1886 Riverside Edition (11 v.) and the 1891 Standard Library Edition (14 v. including Samuel Longfellow's respectful biography of his brother). An excellent early single-volume edition is H. E. Scudder's Riverside Edition (which relies on information provided by Samuel Longfellow), published by Houghton Mifflin, copyright from 1863 to 1920. An excellent recent single-volume edition is J. D. McClatchy, *Poems and Other Writings* (2001) in the Library of America series. The most useful modern study of Longfellow's life and work is Edward Wagenknecht's *Henry Wadsworth Longfellow, His Poetry and Prose* (1983).

See THE ARROW AND THE SONG; BALLADS AND OTHER POEMS; THE BIRDS OF KILLINGWORTH; THE BUILDING OF THE SHIP; THE CHILDREN'S HOUR; THE DAY IS DONE; EMMA AND EGINHARD; EXCEL-

SIOR; THE GOLDEN LEGEND; MEZZO CAMMIN; MORITURI SALUTAMUS; MY LOST YOUTH; NEW ENGLAND'S TRAGEDIES; SEAWEED; THE SKELETON IN ARMOR; THE SPANISH STUDENT; TALES OF A WAYSIDE INN.
ALAN SHUCARD

Longfellow, Samuel (1819–1892), clergyman. Author of a biography of his brother, HENRY WADSWORTH LONGFELLOW (2 v. 1886), Samuel Longfellow also published several volumes of hymns, including *Vespers* (1859) and, in collaboration with THOMAS WENTWORTH HIGGINSON, a book of poems, *Thallata: A Book for the Seaside* (1853).

Long Roll, The (1911), a novel by MARY JOHNSTON. This story of the Civil War, laid in the South, involves both battle action and a love affair. Stonewall Jackson is a leading character, and the Battle of Chancellorsville furnishes the climax of the book. In *Cease Firing* (1912), a sequel to *The Long Roll*, Johnston went on to the period from Vicksburg to the close of the war. The books were based on careful research and on personal information; Johnston's father, Major Albert Johnston, fought in the war.

Longstreet, Augustus Baldwin (1790–1870), lawyer, clergyman, college administrator, editor, writer. Born in Augusta, Georgia, Longstreet was educated at Yale and the Litchfield Law School. He was a judge and a clergyman; a president of Emory College, Centenary College, the University of Mississippi, and South Carolina College. He wrote first for the Milledgeville *Southern Recorder*, then founded the *States Rights Sentinel* at Atlanta in 1834 and continued as editor until 1836. His GEORGIA SCENES, CHARACTERS, INCIDENTS, ETC., IN THE FIRST HALF CENTURY OF THE REPUBLIC (1835, frequently reprinted) is a classic of down-to-earth humor and regionalism. Longstreet knew his Georgians, especially the poor whites; he could put over an anecdote and reproduced dialogue well. Fighting, baby talk, drunkenness, dancing, dueling, horse racing, and undomestic wives are severely reprimanded. One of the best pieces deals with "Georgia Theatrics." Longstreet later wrote *Stories with a Moral* (posthumously publ., 1912) and a novel, *Master William Mitten* (1864), semiautobiographical.

Longstreet, Stephen (1907–), novelist, playwright, editor, historian, artist, film critic. Born in New York City, Longstreet wrote the book for Broadway's *High Button Shoes* (1947) and the screenplay for Hollywood's *The Jolson Story* (1947). He wrote such histories as *The Real Jazz, Old and New* (1956), *Encyclopédie Du Jazz* (1958), and *Never Look Back* (1958). Out of his travel experience Longstreet wrote the bestselling *The World Revisited* (1953) and *The Boy in the Model-T* (1956), which is an account of his transcontinental tour of the United States at age twelve. In such novels as *The Pedlocks* (1951), *The Lion at Morning* (1954), and *The Promoters* (1957), he embarked on a long series of novels he called "a kind of native Human Comedy" covering all our history. Longstreet's novels include *Decade* (1940), *Sound of an American* (1941), *The Beach House* (1952), *Man of Montmartre* (1958), and *Geisha* (1960). Among his travelogues are *Last Man Around the World* (1941), *Chico Goes to the Wars* (1943), and *Last Man Comes Home* (1942). He also wrote *Nine Lives*

With Grandfather (1944), *The Sisters Liked Them Handsome* (1946), and *A Century on Wheels* (1952).

Long Tom Coffin.   See COFFIN, LONG TOM.

Long Valley, The (1938),   a collection of thirteen stories by JOHN STEINBECK. They deal with people in the Salinas Valley in California, especially in relation to the migrants who have come into the valley. Best known of the tales is *The Red Pony*, separately printed in 1945 and often reprinted.

Lonigan, Studs.   The central figure of three novels by JAMES T. FARRELL. The background is the Irish district of Chicago. Lonigan—first name, William—is a young tough whose career reveals the conflict between ancient ideals and modern corruption. YOUNG LONIGAN (1932) follows Lonigan in his middle teens, and *The Young Manhood of Studs Lonigan* (1934) takes him from high-school days to ten years later. *Judgment Day* (1935) shows him more and more corrupt until he dies at the age of 29, destroyed by alcohol and venereal disease. He starts with good impulses, but becomes a tough and ruthless hoodlum. The stories were collected (1935) in a single volume.

Look Homeward, Angel: A Story of the Buried Life (1929),   a novel by THOMAS WOLFE. This first novel by Wolfe remains his best. It is autobiography in a thin disguise. Eugene Gant, in appearance, early environment, parentage, domestic surroundings, and education is Thomas Wolfe. Always a voluble writer, Wolfe produced a deluge in this first effort, and at least a little credit for the book's success must be assigned to MAXWELL PERKINS of Charles Scribner's Sons, who edited the manuscript. The chief credit belongs to Wolfe, however, who made his book a powerful comedy—sometimes affectionate, sometimes satirical—of the life of a sensitive youth coming of age in North Carolina and later in the North. In 1957 a play was made from portions of the book by Ketti Frings.

Looking Backward 2000–1887 (1888),   a novel by EDWARD BELLAMY that offers a utopia into which Bellamy projected all his ideas for the realization of a good society. It has sold widely throughout the world and continues to be read. In 1897 Bellamy wrote a sequel, *Equality*, in which he replied to attacks on the earlier book and offered detailed suggestions for carrying out his plans.

Loos, Anita (1893–1981),   novelist, motion picture script writer. Born in Sisson, California, Anita Loos at age fifteen began writing film scripts for D. W. Griffith, and with her husband, John Emerson, wrote for Douglas Fairbanks and Constance Talmadge. In later years she prepared scenarios for such films as *Red Headed Woman, San Francisco, Saratoga, Alaska, The Women, Blossoms in the Dust*, and *I Married an Angel*. But her greatest celebrity came from the novel GENTLEMEN PREFER BLONDES (1925), an amusing story about the travels of a predatory blonde flapper. The novel inspired a play (1925); a sequel, *But Gentlemen Marry Brunettes* (1928); a musical comedy (1949); and a movie (1953). She was also the author of two successful plays, *Happy Birthday* (1946) and *Gigi* (1951, from the novel by Colette). Her memoirs are *Twice Over Lightly* (1972) and *The Talmadge Girls* (1978), on two silent-movie stars, Constance and Norma Talmadge. Her auto-

biographical works are *This Brunette Prefers Work* (1956), *A Girl Like I* (1966), *Kiss Hollywood Good-by* (1974), and *Cast of Thousands* (1976).

López Velarde, Ramón (1888–1921),   Mexican poet. Influenced by Laforgue and LEOPOLDO LUGONES López Velarde wrote about love, religion, and his homeland in a style characterized by use of colloquial speech involving eccentric, unexpected words and images. The poems in *La sangre devota* (1916) and *Zozobra* (1919) deal with the spiritual and carnal aspects of love, showing the poet's final disenchantment and dismay at his failure to satisfy either his physical appetites or the demands of his soul. *La suave patria*, his best-known poem, which appears in the posthumous *El son del corazón* (1932), is an ironic but tender tribute to his native province.

López y Fuentes, Gregorio (1895–1966),   Mexican novelist. His best-known novel is *El indio* (1935, tr. *They That Reap* 1937), in which he reveals the injustices inflicted on Mexico's indigenous Indians early in the 20th century and realistically describes tribal customs and institutions. *Campamento* (1931) and *Tierra* (1933) are novels of the Revolution, the second dealing with followers of Zapata. *Mi General* (1934) presents the problems of generals mixing in peacetime politics.

Lord, William Wilberforce (1819–1907),   clergyman, poet. Upon publication of *Poems* (1845) Lord, born in Madison County, New York, was hailed as the American Milton despite a castigating review by Poe, who had been infuriated by Lord's burlesque of his *Raven*. *Christ in Hades* (1851), a religious epic, and *André* (1856), a historical narrative in blank verse, were Lord's only other important publications. He served as chaplain in the Confederate army during the Civil War. His *Complete Poetical Works* was published in 1938.

Lorde, Audre [Geraldine] (1934–1992),   poet. Of West Indian parentage, but born and raised in New York City, Lorde was educated at the National University of Mexico, Hunter College, and Columbia University. Her poetry is often passionate about love, sometimes angry about race, sometimes feminist. Among her volumes of poetry are *The New York Head Shop and Museum* (1974); *Coal* (1976); *The Black Unicorn* (1978), poems about Africa; *Chosen Poems Old and New* (1982); and *Our Dead Behind Us* (1986). Her prose works include *The Cancer Journals* (1980), about her struggle with the disease; *Zami: A New Spelling of My Name* (1982), a novel or "biomythography"; *Sister Outsider* (1984); and *Burst of Light* (1988).

Lorimer, George Horace (1867–1937),   businessman, reporter, editor, author of inspirational books. Lorimer, born in Louisville, after working for Philip Armour in the canning industry and then for himself in the wholesale grocery business, became a reporter in Boston, went to work for the SATURDAY EVENING POST in 1898, and edited it from 1899 to 1936. The *Post* had been on the point of expiring, but Lorimer made it into a tremendous success, with a circulation of 3,000,000. He was convinced that big business and its ways spelled true romance and was able to translate this conviction into the weekly fiction and nonfiction of his magazine. Severe in his censorship of advertising, he encouraged bright young authors and paid them well. Among authors he published were Frank Norris, Theodore Dreiser, Stephen Crane, Jack London, Sinclair Lewis, and F. Scott Fitzgerald. He wrote two inspirational books, *Letters from a Self-Made Merchant to His Son* (1902) and *Old Gorgon Graham* (1904), as well as one or two others.

Loring, Emilie [Baker] (?–1951),   novelist, writer on domestic science, playwright. Loring began to write articles for women's magazines under the pseudonym Josephine Story. *For the Comfort of the Family* (1914) and *The Mother in the Home* (1917) are collections of essays on home-making. Her first novel, *The Trail of Conflict* (1922), was followed by twenty-eight more books of fiction, among them *It's a Great World!* (1935), *When Hearts Are Light Again* (1943), *Bright Skies* (1946), *Love Came Laughing By* (1949), and *To Love and To Honor* (1950). The author said her formula for success was "a wholesome love story." *Where's Peter?* (1928), a comedy, was popular with amateur groups.

Los de abajo (1915, tr. *The Underdogs* 1929),   a novel by Mariano Azuela. Ignored for years after its first appearance in a Spanish-language El Paso newspaper, *Los de abajo* is now generally regarded as the best of the many novels inspired by the Mexican Revolution. Written in a spare, colloquial style, the novel consists of a series of sharply etched vignettes that recount the career of Demetrio Macías, the leader of a band of ignorant, often bestial, peasants. Through Macías, Azuela recreates the blind, apparently futile struggle of the nameless masses who took up arms for a cause they did not understand and, swept along by the turbulence of the revolution, continued fighting because they did not know how to stop.

Lost Generation, The.   "You are all a lost generation," said GERTRUDE STEIN to ERNEST HEMINGWAY in Paris, as he recorded in the preface to THE SUN ALSO RISES (1926), still a central representation of the group of lost young people to whom she referred. Among later accounts by people who lived in Paris in the 1920s are several by MALCOLM COWLEY—*The Lost Generation* (1931); EXILE'S RETURN (1934, rev. 1951); and *A Second Flowering: Works and Days of the Lost Generation* (1973)—and ROBERT MCALMON's *Being Geniuses Together* (1938); SAMUEL PUTNAM's *Paris Was Our Mistress: Memoirs of a Lost and Found Generation* (1947); MORLEY CALLAGHAN's *That Summer in Paris* (1963); and Hemingway's *A Moveable Feast* (1964).

Lost in the Funhouse (1968),   a collection of short fiction, including the title story, by JOHN BARTH.

Lost Lady, A (1923),   a novel by WILLA CATHER. This story is sometimes called Cather's masterpiece. It shows her powers of style, subtle characterization, and moral import at their highest. The lost lady is Mrs. Marian Forrester, the young wife of a great western pioneer and builder of railroads. She is seen, with a naiveté that becomes the most delicate irony and revelation, through the eyes of Niel Herbert, an adoring young boy. Beautiful, charming, seemingly the perfect lady, she has a passionate nature and weakness for drink and cheap men that lead her astray. When her husband dies, her chief protection

against the world around her is taken away. She slowly coarsens, the placid existence to which she has been accustomed crumbles around her, and she disappears. She is heard of thereafter only in rumor as the cherished wife of a wealthy Englishman in South America. To Neil she represents the great age of the pioneers, but Cather saw in her life the way in which a generation of "shrewd young men," who had never dared anything, drove out "the dreamers, the great-hearted adventurers" who had won the Old West.

Lost Weekend, The (1944).   See CHARLES JACKSON.

Lothrop, Amy.   Pen name of ANNA BARTLETT WARNER.

Lothrop, Harriett Mulford Stone ["Margaret Sidney"] (1844–1924),   children's story writer. Born in Connecticut, Harriett Lothrop began to write stories at an early age, although her first contributions to WIDE AWAKE magazine did not appear until 1878. Her FIVE LITTLE PEPPERS AND HOW THEY GREW (1881) sold over 2 million copies; it is the story of a lively, courageous family of children whose widowed mother works as a seamstress to keep her family together. In spite of the author's tendency to sentimentalize and instruct, the book is written with a simple, cheerful gusto and reality that appealed to young readers. *So As by Fire* (1881), *The Pettibone Name, a New England Story* (1882), *A New Departure for Girls* (1886), *Dilly and the Captain* (1887), *How Tom and Dorothy Made and Kept a Christian Home* (1888), *Rob, a Story for Boys* (1891), and several further adventures of little Peppers did not approach the spectacular success of the original *Five Little Peppers*.

Lottery, The (1949),   a story by SHIRLEY JACKSON, originally in *The New Yorker* magazine. This, Jackson's best-known story, has become a small classic. A lottery is part of a spring ritual observed by everyone in a small American town. Most of the procedures of the ritual have been forgotten, and no one knows any longer the reason for the lottery, but it continues unquestioned. Until the last lines of the story, the reader does not discover why everyone must pick a slip of paper, nor why the family that gets the slip with a spot on it is disturbed. Then the horror is revealed, heightened by the adherence to ceremony that has surrounded the proceedings throughout the story: The woman chosen by the lottery is stoned to death by the other townspeople.

Loudon, Samuel (1727?–1813),   bookseller, printer, pamphleteer. After arriving in America, perhaps from Ireland, Loudon became an ardent patriot, although his *The Deceiver Unmasked* (1776), an anonymous reply to Thomas Paine's COMMON SENSE, offended some radicals. He published *The New York Packet*, which later printed some of the FEDERALIST papers, and printed THE AMERICAN MAGAZINE, edited by Noah Webster.

Louie, David Wong (1954–   ),   short-story writer, novelist. Born in Rockville Centre, New York, Louie was educated at Vasser College and in the creative writing program of the University of Iowa. His first story collection, *Pangs of Love and Other Stories* (1991), gathered several pieces that had already been selected for prize anthologies and Asian-American collections. Often the theme of his fiction is the conflict between the immigrant generation and their offspring.

The Barbarians Are Coming (2000) is a novelistic treatment of the same theme. Sterling Lung, son of a Chinese immigrant couple who live above their laundry business, has trained as a chef at the prestigious Culinary Institute of America, but his parents are disappointed that he did not choose to be a doctor. His father resents his lack of familiarity with Chinese culture, and his mother deprecates his cooking style. Lung is caught between his parents' world, in which arranged marriages are the rule, and the demands of his pregnant girlfriend.

Love and Friendship, or, Yankee Notions (prod. 1807, publ. 1809),   a comedy by A. B. Lindsley. This play revealed several Yankee characters against the background of Charleston, South Carolina. The Yankee is presented in vigorous style, displaying more greenness and more honesty than were customary in the stage Yankees of later vintage.

Lovecraft, H[oward] P[hillips] (1890–1937),   short-story writer, novelist. Born in Providence, Rhode Island, when Lovecraft died only two small books of his had been published, but he was recognized in a small circle of admirers as a master of fantastic tales of terror. Since Lovecraft's death, his celebrity has grown. A recluse, ill most of his life, he was learned in the lore of the 18th century, master of several languages, and versed in the sciences. He drew on "the problematic possibilities of science" for what Donald A. Wollheim called "his Poesque tales of cosmic dread." He had marked gifts of language, often poetic in phrasing.

In his lifetime he published *The Shunned House* (1928) and *The Shadow Over Innsmouth* (1936). Many of his other tales had appeared in the magazine *Weird Tales*. His writings were further collected in *The Outsider and Others* (1939), *Beyond the Wall of Sleep* (1943), *Marginalia* (1944), *The Lurker at the Threshold* (1945), *The Best Supernatural Stories of H. P. Lovecraft* (1945), *Something About Cats and Other Pieces* (1949), *Selected Letters* (1948), *Dreams and Fancies* (1962), *Dagon and Other Macabre Tales* (1965), and *The Dark Brotherhood* (1966). L. Sprague de Camp wrote *Lovecraft: A Biography* (1975).

Lovejoy, Elijah P[arish] (1802–1837),   teacher, clergyman, newspaper editor. Born in Albion, Maine, Lovejoy went to St. Louis and founded *The Observer*, which fought both slavery and intemperance. His strong views on lynching aroused so much feeling that Lovejoy left St. Louis and continued his newspaper at Alton, Illinois, as the Alton *Observer*. Mobs in Alton on four occasions destroyed his presses. During the fourth attack, Lovejoy and the mob exchanged shots, and Lovejoy was killed. His death strengthened abolitionist feeling throughout the North. His brother, **Owen Lovejoy** (1811–1864), also a clergyman, continued to fight slavery, became a strong supporter of Lincoln, and served in the House of Representatives (1856–64).

Love Nest, The, and Other Stories (1926),   a collection of nine tales by RING LARDNER. In it appear two of Lardner's best stories, the title story (dramatized by Robert E. Sherwood, 1927), and "Haircut."

Love Song of J. Alfred Prufrock, The   (*Poetry* magazine, June 1915; collected in *Prufrock and Other Observations*, London 1917; and *Poems*, 1920), a poem by T. S. ELIOT. Written in 1910–11, while Eliot was a graduate student, this poem was not published until he had gone off to England. A dramatic monologue, it presents the musings of a man whose youth is beginning to slip away from him and who is unable to bring himself to the point of speaking frankly to the lady of his choice. The poem can be read as a study in neurotic impotence and at the same time as a contrived specimen of the cultural decay Eliot perceived in his time. Except for scraps of juvenilia, this was Eliot's first published work, and it is doubtful that any other poet in modern times has won such admiration with his first poem. In it Eliot used many of the devices—associative progressions, precisely controlled free verse, literary allusions, etc.—he developed more fully in his later work.

Lovett, Robert Morss (1870–1956),   teacher, literary historian, educational administrator, public official, writer. Born in Boston, Lovett might have had a career teaching at Harvard, but chose to go to an exciting new institution, the University of Chicago, and taught there from 1892 to 1936. He held liberal views on political topics, although he avoided discussing them in class; he favored freedom for Ireland and India, battled for peace and civil liberty, and was a warm friend of JANE ADDAMS and her Hull House. During this period he collaborated with WILLIAM VAUGHN MOODY on *A History of English Literature* (1902), edited anthologies, and wrote *Richard Gresham* (1904) and *A Winged Victory* (1907), two novels that attracted little attention. He also published an analysis of *Edith Wharton* (1925) and, with Helen Sard Hughes, a *History of the Novel in England* (1932). In 1948 Lovett published his memoirs, *All Our Years*, a frank and amusing account of his career.

Lovewell, John (1691–1725),   Indian fighter. Lovewell, born in Massachusetts, fought Indians skillfully until he was finally ambushed and killed in Maine at what is now called Lovell's or Lovewell's Pond. His exploits were celebrated in several ballads. For example, Longfellow's first published poem was THE BATTLE OF LOVELL'S POND (1820). Frederic Kidder wrote *The Expeditions of Captain John Lovewell and His Encounters with the Indians, Including a Particular Account of the Pequauket Battle, and a Reprint of Rev. Thomas Symmes's Sermon* (1865). There is also an account of him in Francis Parkman's *Half-Century of Conflict* (1892). Hawthorne devoted a somewhat melodramatic story, ROGER MALVIN'S BURIAL (*The Token*, 1832; *Mosses from an Old Manse*, 1846), to two survivors of the battle.

Lovingood, Sut.   See SUT LOVINGOOD YARNS.

Lowell, Abbott Lawrence (1856–1943),   lawyer, teacher, political economist, university administrator. Lowell was a descendant of Lowells who settled in Newbury, Massachusetts, in 1639, and whose progeny have played major roles in Massachusetts life. His older brother, Percival Lowell (1855–1916), was an astronomer, and his sister was the poet AMY LOWELL. He practiced law from 1880 to 1897 and meanwhile wrote *Essays on Government* (1889), *Government and Parties in Continental Europe* (2 v. 1896), *The Influence of Party upon Legislation in England and America* (1902), and his most important work, *The Government of England* (2 v. 1908). As president of Harvard (1909–33), he modified the elective system, encouraged the advancement of scholarship by setting up and endorsing the Society of Fellows, and stressed the importance of a liberal education in preparation for any profession, especially public service.

Lowell continued to write and publish. Among his many books were *Public Opinion and Popular Government* (1913); *Public Opinion in War and Peace* (1923); *At War with Academic Traditions* (1934); and an outspoken autobiography, *What a College President Has Learned* (1938). After his retirement he completed a biography of his brother Percival (1935). Henry Aaron Yeomans, a friend of Lowell's, wrote a biography (1948).

Lowell, Amy (1874–1925),   poet, critic, biographer, translator. Born in Brookline, Massachusetts, the sister of ABBOTT LAWRENCE LOWELL, Amy Lowell was a member of the tenth generation of a wealthy and prominent New England family. Nevertheless, she was allowed only minimal education and reared for marriage and motherhood. Being suited to neither, Lowell in 1898 suffered a depression from which she did not recover for many years. In the meantime, in 1902, she found her vocation as poet while watching a stage performance by the Italian tragedienne Eleonora Duse. For the remainder of her life Lowell found inspiration in the company of gifted women, the actress Ada Russell serving as her muse and companion in the last decade of her life.

In 1913 the work of free verse imagist poets was published in America, and Lowell immediately identified herself with these literary insurgents. In 1914, after two trips to London to meet with these poets, she assumed direction of the movement by breaking with EZRA POUND and sponsoring the three imagist anthologies of 1915–17. Adherents of traditional verse were scandalized by poetry that demanded free choice of subject and form, and a literary war erupted in America. Because of her zest for controversy, intellectual keenness, and theatrical personality, Lowell became chief advocate for this new poetry, electrifying audiences on her lecture and reading tours and succeeding in bringing American poetry into the 20th century.

Unfortunately, Lowell's fame as a colorful public figure far overshadowed her work as poet, and since her untimely death her poetry has been largely neglected and undervalued. Her prolixity, her unevenness, and the amazing range of styles and subjects she adopted have confused readers and discouraged scholars from studying her seriously. Although she was seen mainly as a poetic innovator, her experiments with new forms often produced poetry of great intensity and a fresh and startling beauty. This is true of her lyrics, her descriptive pieces, and even occasionally of her narratives. In subject matter Lowell is strongest in treating the themes of love, human emotional deprivation, and the divinity of natural beauty. In treating the latter, Lowell produced a multitude of evocative and incandescent images unique in poetry and associating her with the impressionist painters and composers she admired. In commenting about this aspect of her work, John Livingston Lowes described her as the foremost master of the sensuous image in the English language.

Lowell's most notable collections are SWORD BLADES AND POPPY SEED (1914), *Pictures of the Floating World* (1919), and *What's O'Clock* (1925). In addition to six other books of poetry, Lowell produced the first American treatment of contemporary French poets in *Six French Poets* (1915), the first critical study of the new poetry movement in her *Tendencies in Modern American Poetry* (1917), and the first 20th-century collection of translations from Chinese poets in *Fir Flower Tablets* (1921). In 1922, she published A CRITICAL FABLE, a witty, versified treatment of the American poetry scene tossed off as a *jeu d'esprit* while she was recovering from one of many bouts of serious illness. Another achievement was her detailed treatment of the life and work of John Keats in a massive scholarly biography, but her need to complete this labor of love drained her last physical reserves and ended her life at age fifty-one.

A combination of worldly literary merchandiser, gifted poetic innovator, futurist, and transcendent nature mystic, Amy Lowell brought a unique viewpoint and gifts to American poetry, but neither her personality nor her work was understood in her lifetime, and today there is need for new studies and reinterpretation. S. Foster Damon, a friend of the poet, wrote the official biography, *Amy Lowell: A Chronicle* (1935). Her poetry was collected in *The Complete Poetical Works of Amy Lowell* (1955). Critical studies are Glenn Richard Ruihley, *The Thorn of a Rose: Amy Lowell Reconsidered* (1975) and Richard Benvenuto, *Amy Lowell* (1985).

GLENN RICHARD RUIHLEY

Lowell, James Russell (1819–1891),   poet, editor, teacher, critic, diplomat. Born in Cambridge, Massachusetts, Lowell had a patrician reserve, yet thought his way through to democratic ideas, took a firm stand on slavery, and was one of the first writers to pay significant tribute to the greatness of Lincoln, "the first American," in his *Ode Recited at the Harvard Commemoration* (1865). As a student at Harvard, Lowell preferred following his personal tastes in reading to plowing through the prescribed lists in his courses, and as a consequence he was rusticated for six months to Concord, but he was graduated in 1838. He took a degree in the law school, but did not find the practice of law congenial. He turned to journalism, contributed to the DIAL and to *Graham's* and became editor of a high-minded but short-lived magazine, THE PIONEER.

In 1844, after a long engagement, Lowell married Maria White (1821–53), herself a poet of strongly abolitionist tendencies. She encouraged her husband in his writing and is credited with deepening his humanitarian impulses, which found expression in antislavery and antiwar articles. The first work to bring Lowell national attention was THE BIGLOW PAPERS, FIRST SERIES (1848). The poems in this collection were interlarded with many prose passages, the whole forming a sort of dialogue between Hosea Biglow, a Yankee farmer, and his friends. Lowell's use of Yankee dialect, which had been anticipated by previous satirists, was the first in verse of genuine literary merit. In these papers, which had begun appearing in the Boston *Courier* on June 17, 1846, Lowell skewered the supporters of the Mexican War, viewed by many Northerners as a Southern scheme to extend slave territory. Later, in 1862, when the Civil War was not going well for the North, Hosea Biglow appeared again to attack the South and defend Northern policy with sharp and homely wit.

The year 1848 saw also publication of two more poems that rank among Lowell's best. THE VISION OF SIR LAUNFAL marked a high point in Lowell's and in American romanticism. Inspired by Arthurian legends of the pursuit of the Holy Grail, it held its popularity for a century, with its "Prelude" retaining its place during that period as one of the best-remembered poetic celebrations of nature in American literature. In A FABLE FOR CRITICS, he viewed the leading contemporary authors with a wit and verve that remain contagious in the best passages on those authors still read.

Between 1847 and 1853, when he was at the height of his fame and his powers, Lowell suffered the deaths of three of his four children and of his wife, Maria White. In 1855, when LONGFELLOW gave up his chair as Smith Professor of Modern Languages at Harvard, Lowell was appointed to succeed him, and he continued in that position until 1872.

In 1857, Lowell became the first editor of the ATLANTIC MONTHLY, a position he filled until 1861 while he continued to teach. In 1864, he joined Charles Eliot Norton as coeditor of the NORTH AMERICAN REVIEW, and he maintained his connection with the magazine until the end of his teaching career at Harvard. During the war, he wrote more *Biglow Papers* for the *Atlantic* (1862–1866) and collected them as a *Second Series* in 1867. He also began to appear as a poet of public occasions, delivering poems like the "Commemoration Ode" (1865) and the "Concord Centennial Ode" (1875). New volumes of poems included *Under the Willows* (1869) and THE CATHEDRAL (1870). His critical and familiar essays were gathered in *Among My Books* (1870, *Second Series* 1876) and *My Study Window* (1871).

He left Harvard in 1872 for a two-year trip abroad, where he was given honorary degrees by Oxford and Cambridge. Later, he served as American Ambassador to Spain (1876–80) and Great Britain (1880–80) and received an honorary degree from Edinburgh. Home in Cambridge in the last years of his life, he published the poems in *Heartsease and Rue* (1888), and several books of essays and addresses. The standard edition is *The Writings of James Russell Lowell* (10 v. 1890). Definitive for its time as a one-volume collection was *The Complete Poetical Works of James Russell Lowell*, Cambridge Edition (1897), edited by H. E. Scudder. Good biographies are H. E. Scudder, *James Russell Lowell* (2 v. 1901) and Martin Duberman, *James Russell Lowell* (1966). Also useful is C. David Heymann, *American Aristocracy: The Lives and Times of James Russell, Amy and Robert Lowell* (1980).

Lowell, Robert (1917–1977),   poet, playwright, autobiographer, essayist. Robert Traill Spence Lowell IV was born in Boston, the only child of Robert Traill Spence Lowell III, USN, and Charlotte Winslow Lowell. Belonging to a collateral branch of the Lowell family, he was a grandson of ROBERT TRAILL SPENCE LOWELL and was related to JAMES RUSSELL LOWELL

and AMY LOWELL, astronomer Percival Lowell (1855–1916), and Harvard president ABBOTT LAWRENCE LOWELL. On his mother's side, he counted among his ancestors Pilgrim patriarch Edward Winslow (1629–80), Plymouth colony governor Josiah Winslow (1629–1680), and Revolutionary War general John Stark (1728–1822). Unfortunately, Lowell's parents were financially marginal, and Lowell grew up amid painful contradictions between his mother's social aspirations and his father's downward mobility.

Furthermore, the family tree itself posed a problem as the young Lowell sought to construct his identity. James Russell Lowell and Amy Lowell were celebrated poets in their day but artistic embarrassments later on; Lowell viewed the former as a poet "pedestaled for oblivion" and said of the latter that it was "as if Mae West were a cousin." The politicians and educators in the family were even less a source of pride. Josiah Winslow and John Stark were warriors who committed brutal acts, and A. Lawrence Lowell helped send the quite possibly innocent Sacco and Vanzetti to their deaths (see SACCO-VANZETTI CASE). Robert Lowell became the most powerful historical poet and playwright of this age not because he was in love with the past but because he was haunted by it. As poems like "At the Indian Killer's Grave" make clear, he was shaken and possessed by the sins of the fathers.

After unsettled periods in Washington, D.C., and Philadelphia, Lowell and his parents moved to Massachusetts, where his father was for several years second in command at the Boston Naval Shipyard, living apart from his wife and son on weekdays. Eventually, he resigned this post and went into business; his earnings, as Lowell was later sardonically to write, "more or less decreased from year to year." Lowell's father was dull and withdrawn, his mother bright but imperious, and the two engaged in a marriage-long war over their son and over everything else. Young Lowell was graduated from prep school well educated but with retrograde social attitudes and marked behavior problems. His uncontainable anger earned him the nickname of "Cal" when he was at St. Mark's School. This was short both for "Caligula," the insane Roman tyrant, and for "Caliban," the man-animal of Shakespeare's *The Tempest*. Yet Lowell had also discovered poetry at St. Mark's and wrote sensitive lyrics with Christian themes.

Lowell studied for two years at Harvard (1935–37), where his poetic gifts went unrecognized. Finally, he knocked his father down in a dispute and soon after left home. He drove to Clarksville, Tennessee, with his mother's psychiatrist, MERRILL MOORE, and presented himself to Moore's friend, the poet and critic ALLEN TATE. The meeting changed Lowell's life. Tate acknowledged Lowell as a poet and assumed a mentoring relationship to him. Camping out on the Tates' lawn for the summer, his tent occasionally sidled by cows, Lowell took his meals with Tate and his wife, the novelist CAROLINE GORDON. He and Tate talked and wrote poetry. In the fall, he enrolled at Kenyon College to study with Tate's friend and colleague in the Fugitive group, JOHN CROWE RANSOM. He did well in his classes, graduating summa cum laude in Classics. And he wrote poetry that was clotted, awkward, often repellent in its unfocused anger, promising but generally unpublishable.

After graduating in 1940, Lowell married his first wife, the brilliant novelist and short-story writer JEAN STAFFORD, and he converted to Roman Catholicism. After an apparently aimless period—which included, however, a year of graduate study at LSU with CLEANTH BROOKS and ROBERT PENN WARREN—he returned with his wife for a year's stay with the Tates in Monteagle, Tennessee. There he wrote the poems that would appear in his first published book, the privately printed *Land of Unlikeness* (1944). Inducted into the army in 1943, he again rebelled by refusing service, partly on pacifistic grounds and partly because he disagreed with President Roosevelt's demand for Germany's unconditional surrender. He served five months in West Street Jail in New York City and federal prison at Danbury, Connecticut, a period he later represented in the poems "Memories of West Street and Lepke" and "In the Cage."

In 1946, Lowell published his first major volume of poetry, *Lord Weary's Castle*. It won him a Pulitzer prize and the kinds of notices poets dream about. In the most prominent review, his friend RANDALL JARRELL proclaimed him the leading poet of his generation, a position he more or less retained until the troubled last decade of his life. *Lord Weary's Castle*, which included revised versions of ten poems first published in *Land of Unlikeness* along with thirty-two new ones, brought MODERNISM and the kind of poetry prized by the NEW CRITICISM to one kind of culmination. The volume is allusive, ambiguous, intense, syntactically opaque, metrically complex, and filled with vivid, even violent imagery. Roman Catholic in outlook yet at times bordering on blasphemy, it is a sustained jeremiad against the American past and present, against war, materialism, misused authority, and cruelty in all its forms and occasions.

"Children of Light," for example, avers that the pilgrims planted "Serpent's seeds of light" when they "fenced their gardens with the Redman's bones." "Concord" mocks the mammonism and ignorance of modern Americans: "Ten thousand Fords are idle here in search/Of a tradition." The most powerful text may be a long, phantasmagorical elegy called "The Quaker Graveyard in Nantucket." Built of puns, figures, symbols, allusions, colloquialisms, and unforgettable images, this poem yearns for Christian transcendence even as it remains transfixed by war and greed. The penultimate section, a suddenly harmonious though perhaps chilling religious vision, yields to bitter lament in the poem's conclusion: "The Lord survives the rainbow of His will."

Lord Weary's Castle was new, yet familiar at the same time, since its values and forms had been prepared by avant-garde poets and critics since the 1920s. One can hear in it the influence of Eliot and Pound, Crane and Ransom, Brooks and Warren, and above all the arch Modernist and social reactionary Allen Tate. Lowell later observed that the book's style was Tate's. The poems expressed a longing for traditional values in charged, convoluted language that was ostentatiously untraditional. Yet if the volume was in a sense a culmination of a dominant ideology of form, it was also a conclusion. There was no place left to go in that mode, nothing left to write that would not seem anticlimactic. Lowell and to some extent poetry in English were left stranded by his very success.

Lowell's next volume, *The Mills of the Kavanaughs* (1951), contained several interesting poems with a strong narrative thread. Nevertheless, the volume did indeed feel anticlimactic to its author. As he was later to describe his dilemma: "What you really feel hasn't got the form, it's not what you can put down in a poem. And the poem you're equipped to write concerns nothing that you care very much about." Divorced in 1948 and remarried in the following year to novelist and essayist ELIZABETH HARDWICK, Lowell taught for short periods at the University of Iowa, Indiana University, and Kenyon College, and he lived for three years in Europe. This was a period in which he lost most of the stable anchors of his existence. His father died in 1950 and his mother in 1954; he lost or abandoned his Catholic faith and his Tate-like politics; and he was not writing with purpose. Following his mother's death, he suffered a psychotic break, thus commencing the recurrent cycles of manic-depressive illness that would afflict him for the rest of his life.

By 1957, Lowell was back in Boston, living with his wife and new-born daughter Harriet and teaching writing at Boston University. Spending the summer at Castine, Maine, he was "struck by the sadness of writing nothing" and began to write "Skunk Hour," a poem in a new, conversational style about the comedy and pain of his personal experience. Searching for new poetic models, Lowell turned his attention from Tate to WILLIAM CARLOS WILLIAMS and ELIZABETH BISHOP, both personal friends and both masters of the apparently casual yet resonant image. For his new sense of self-exposure, Lowell may have looked to W. D. Snodgrass, whose HEART'S NEEDLE (1959) he had read in manuscript—Snodgrass had been his student at Iowa—and to Allen Ginsberg's HOWL (1956), which he had heard recited while visiting San Francisco. But Lowell was on to something new—a blend of distance and revelation, wit and feeling, and his probing of the complex fabric of a human life while at the same time constructing a thick verbal fabric of reverberating images, puns, quotations, and ironies.

The title sequence of LIFE STUDIES (1959) sequence brings the plot and psychological depth of autobiography into poetry. It begins by representing Lowell as a young boy who silently observes a death in the family and who is unwillingly involved in his parents' lacerating conflicts. It concludes by portraying Lowell as an adult, experiencing the deaths of his parents, the tensions of his own unhappy marriage, and ultimately the breakdown of his mind. In "Skunk Hour," the poet describes the tragicomic circumstances of his mental and spiritual collapse: "I myself am hell" in an emptiness relieved only by skunks.

Beyond its social and psychological themes, *Life Studies* reflects on its own status as a literary text. Voyeurism and overhearing appear as a recurrent motif. In "91 Revere Street" the young Lowell overhears his parents' bedroom quarrels as a sort of primal scene, verbal rather than sexual; in "My Last Afternoon with Uncle Devereux Winslow" he looks out on the world "unseen and all-seeing"; and, finally, in "Skunk Hour" he spies on lovers as his own madness envelops him. Despite its pathological aspect, this activity of watching and representing lies at the heart of *Life Studies*, perhaps of all literary works. It is not simply Lowell as character who observes what he should not, but Lowell as author and we as readers. *Life Studies* is not simply a confession, as it was instantly labeled, but a meditation on the complicated roles that seeing, imagining, and writing play in human life.

Life Studies revolutionized poetry in English. Lowell's invention of the personal for our time had an evident impact on many subsequent texts: Ginsberg's *Kaddish* (1960), ANNE SEXTON's *To Bedlam and Part Way Back* (1960), Randall Jarrell's *The Lost World* (1965), SYLVIA PLATH's *Ariel* (1966), JOHN BERRYMAN's *The Dream Songs* (1969), and FRANK BIDART's *Golden State* (1973) and "The Confessional" (1983), among others. An even more important revolution, one that affected poems not personal at all, was that *Life Studies* freed poetry from the shadow of Modernism and the grip of a New Criticism grown old and narrow. After this volume, poetry could be anything, could go anywhere, since a normative style or subject matter no longer existed. Jarrell had observed that *Lord Weary's Castle* ached to enter a "realm of freedom" but could not; *Life Studies* entered the realm and demolished its opposite, the kingdom of necessity. Poetry thereafter exploded in a hundred different directions—though it increasingly went unread in a postliterate culture.

After *Life Studies* appeared, Lowell and his family moved to New York. *Life Studies*, together with the poem FOR THE UNION DEAD, represented his farewell to the city where he was born. New York City was to be a new start. Living on Manhattan's upper west side, Lowell wrote a sequence of innovative translations of European poems entitled *Imitations*, published in 1961. He began to write plays as well: a translation of Racine's *Phaedra* (1961), a trilogy based on stories by Hawthorne and Melville called *The Old Glory* (1964), a free adaptation of Aeschylus's *Prometheus Bound* (1969), and a version of Aeschylus's *The Oresteia* (1978). He also composed the poems of *For the Union Dead* (1964), which he later called "lemony, soured and dry" but which most critics regard as another landmark volume. Many regard the title poem—an elegy for the Massachusetts 54th regiment of black Union Army soldiers—as Lowell's finest single text. It revises and transforms his earlier prophetic mode. The poem depicts St. Gaudens's monument to the heroic regiment as being "out of bounds" in modern Boston, a city where "a savage servility/slides by on grease."

In 1965, Lowell protested the Vietnam War by publicly declining President Lyndon Johnson's invitation to the White House Festival of the Arts. This act, and the controversy it caused, sped him into a new phase of his life and art. He spent the next years participating in antiwar demonstrations and in Senator Eugene McCarthy's campaign for the 1968 Democratic presidential nomination. His writing reflected this activity. *Prometheus Bound*, performed in 1967 and published in 1969, and especially the poems of *Near the Ocean*, published in 1967,

question patriarchal power, political inequity, and the ideology of war. Echoing both Juvenal and William Carlos Williams, "Central Park" laments the plight of the urban poor. "Waking Early Sunday Morning" resumes Lowell's prophetic stance: in a world of "chance/assassinations, no advance."

Lowell's political and moral concerns also inform *Notebook 1967–68* (1969), an experimental volume of unrhymed sonnets that "mixes the day-to-day with the history." The sequence includes social reflection, commentary on literary works and artists through the ages, and memories of events in the poet's life. Unable to stop writing, Lowell produced a revised and expanded version of the work in 1970, now called simply *Notebook*. Still unable to free himself from the project, and increasingly unhappy with the "jumbled" form it had assumed, he expanded and reordered it once more, splitting it into two volumes: *History* (1973), arranged chronologically and stripped of some of the personal material, and the briefer *For Lizzie and Harriet* (1973), focusing on the poet's increasingly dissonant private life. Although *Notebook/History* is imperfect in structure, it contains some of Lowell's richest writing. Comparable to Pound's CANTOS, this long poem is one of the most erudite and challenging texts in American literature.

In 1970, Lowell moved to England, where he taught for several years at Essex University. In 1971, he and Caroline Blackwood, a writer of essays and fiction, had a son named Robert Sheridan. In the following year, Lowell divorced Elizabeth Hardwick and married Blackwood. These events, along with ruminations on aging, eros, and art, appear in *The Dolphin* (1973), Lowell's last sonnet sequence. The volume, an aesthetic summation of sorts, won a Pulitzer prize.

Lowell's last years were spent in pain. As his marriage to Caroline Blackwood threatened to dissolve, Lowell felt himself separated from each of his two families and each of his two countries. Furthermore, he suffered from an increasingly debilitating heart ailment. In 1977, he returned to the United States without Blackwood. On September 12 of that year, he died of heart failure in a New York City taxicab, returning from a visit with Blackwood and his son in Ireland to the home of Hardwick and his daughter in Manhattan. Just days earlier, his last book of poems had appeared, *Day by Day*, a collection of moving and lucid autobiographical poems.

Lowell learned from some of the greatest poets of the Modernist movement—Eliot, Pound, Tate, Ransom, Williams—and he in turn befriended and taught many of the strongest poets of his own generation: Elizabeth Bishop, John Berryman, Randall Jarrell, Delmore Schwartz, Sylvia Plath, Frank Bidart, and others. More than any other poet of his time, he changed the agenda of English-language poetry. Endlessly original and inquisitive, willing to risk failure and condemnation, using his verbal creativity the way other people use food and air, he made himself, in the estimation of some critics, a Milton or a Whitman for his time.

Lowell's *Collected Prose* appeared in 1987. Jeffrey Meyers edited *Robert Lowell: Interviews and Memoirs* (1988). A biography is Ian Hamilton, *Robert Lowell* (1982). Studies are Marjorie Perloff, *The Poetic Art of Robert Lowell* (1973); Stephen

Yenser, *Circle to Circle: The Poetry of Robert Lowell* (1975); Steven Gould Axelrod, *Robert Lowell: Life and Art* (1978); and Katherine Wallingford, *Robert Lowell's Language of the Self* (1987).

STEVEN GOULD AXELROD

Lowell, Robert Traill Spence (1816–1891), clergyman, teacher, novelist. Brother of JAMES RUSSELL LOWELL, this Robert Traill Spence Lowell (his son and grandson bore the same name) was the grandfather of ROBERT LOWELL. His novel *Anthony Blade: A Story of a School* (1874) was based on his experiences as headmaster at St. Marks, a school later attended by his grandson. He derived an earlier novel, *The New Priest at Conception Bay* (1858), from his time as an Episcopal clergyman in New Brunswick. For a period he taught at Union College and set *A Story or Two from an Old Dutch Town* (1878) in Schenectady, New York. He also published *Poems* (1864).

Lower East Side. A section of New York City below 14th Street and east of Broadway. This area of approximately two square miles was for many decades the haven of poor immigrants, a slum with picturesque aspects, and a community that produced many notable men and women. Its sweatshops, tenements, schools and welfare centers, theaters and cafés, and political clubs produced a myriad of industrialists, teachers, artists, musicians, gangsters, politicians, civic leaders, labor leaders, prizefighters, actors, theatrical producers, and writers of many different national origins. These nationalities came to the East Side in successive waves; it was perhaps the greatest melting pot in our annals. Identified with the East Side by birth or residence were Alfred E. Smith; sculptors Jo Davidson and Jacob Epstein; painter George Luks; actors Eddie Cantor, Fannie Brice, Milton Berle, and the Marx Brothers; Yiddish actors Bertha Kalich, Jacob Adler, Molly Picon; composers Edward MacDowell, Irving Berlin, and George Gershwin; and writers Jacob A. Riis, Ernest Poole, Konrad Bercovici, James Oppenheim, Alfred Kreymborg, Myra Kelly, Michael Gold, Abraham Cahan, and Henry Roth.

Typical books dealing with the region are JACOB RIIS's *How the Other Half Lives* (1890) and *Out of Mulberry Street* (1898); Oppenheim's *Dr. Rast* (1909); Cahan's THE RISE OF DAVID LEVINSKY (1917); Fannie Hurst's HUMORESQUE (1919); Bercovici's *Dust of New York* (1919); Alexander Woollcott's *Story of Irving Berlin* (1925); ALFRED E. SMITH's *Up to Now* (1929); MICHAEL GOLD's *Jews Without Money* (1930); Henry Roth's *Call It Sleep* (1934); and Harry Golden's *Only in America* (1958) and *For Two Cents Plain* (1959). Popular songs associated with the East Side are "Maggie Murphy's Home" (1890), "The Sidewalks of New York" (1894), and "The Sunshine of Paradise Alley" (1895).

Lowes, John Livingston (1867–1945), teacher, scholar, editor, essayist. Born in Decatur, Indiana, Lowes took his first degree at Washington and Jefferson College (1888) and taught mathematics there for three years, then taught English at several institutions, finally at Harvard (1918–39). He published several noteworthy books: *Convention and Revolt in Poetry* (1919), a persuasive account of action and reaction in the history of poetry; THE ROAD TO XANADU (1927), a widely influential examination of the sources of Coleridge's *Kubla Khan* and *The Ancient Mariner* and of the nature of inspiration; two books on Chaucer (1931, 1934); and two collections of essays, *Of Reading Books and Other Essays* (1930) and *Essays in Appreciation* (1936).

Lowie, Robert H[arry] (1883–1957), teacher, ethnologist, curator. Lowie, who came to the United States from Austria at the age of ten, became an assistant in the American Museum of Natural History in 1908, thereafter went on to positions in other museums and at various universities, eventually becoming professor of anthropology at the University of California. He took part in various expeditions among the Indians and wrote many learned papers. Among his books are *The Assiniboine* (1909), *Social Life of the Crow Indians* (1912), *The Sun Dance of the Crow Indians* (1915), *Culture and Ethnology* (1917), *Primitive Society* (1920), *Primitive Religion* (1924), *The Origin of the State* (1927), *Are We Civilized?* (1929), *The Crow Indians* (1935), *History of Ethnological Theory* (1937), *The German People* (1945), *Social Organization* (1948), and *Indians of the Plains* (1954).

Lowry, [Clarence] Malcolm [Boden] (1909–1957), novelist. Born in England and educated at Cambridge, Lowry traveled widely, living in the United States in 1935, in Mexico in 1936, and from 1937 to 1954 mostly in Dollarton, British Columbia, leaving occasionally for trips that included Mexico and Haiti. He died a suicide in Sussex, England. During his lifetime, he completed only two novels. *Ultramarine* (1933), an impressionistic account of a sea voyage, owed something to his friend CONRAD AIKEN's *Blue Voyage* (1927). *Under the Volcano* (1947), set in Mexico, is a masterful study, partly autobiographical, of the disintegration of an alcoholic British consul. Works published posthumously include *Lunar Caustic* (1958), fictionalizing Lowry's experience as an alcoholic in New York's Bellevue Hospital, and *Hear Us O Lord from Heaven Thy Dwelling Place* (1961), stories heavily influenced by his Canadian experiences.

Loy, Mina [Lowry, Mina Gertrude] (1882–1966), poet. A contributor to LITTLE MAGAZINES like *Other, Contact*, and *Broom*, Loy early established a minor reputation for avant-garde verse, disjointed in syntax and with irregular spacing and punctuation. Some of these were collected in *Lunar Baedecker* (1923) and *Lunar Baedeker and Time-Tables* (1958). *The Last Lunar Baedecker* (1982), with still more poems, was edited by Roger Conover.

Lucas, George (1945–   ), film director. Born in Modesto, California, he was educated at the local junior college and the University of Southern California Cinema School. His success in the 1965 National Student Film Festival won him a production scholarship at Warner Brothers, where he became a protegé of Francis Ford Coppola. With *American Graffiti* (1973), an autobiographical film about adolescents, he emerged as a leading director. The highly popular *Star Wars* (1977), a science fiction film based on a classic quest plot and using innovative special effects, spawned a series of sequels, made Lucas's reputation, and enabled him to open his own film studio. His other films include *THX-1138* (1971), *The Empire Strikes Back* (1980), and *Return of the Jedi* (1983).

Luce, Clare Boothe (1903–1987),   playwright, diplomat. Born in New York City, Boothe served on the staff of *Vogue* and *Vanity Fair* before turning to writing satirical plays: *Abide with Me* (1937), *The Women* (1937), KISS THE BOYS GOODBYE (1938), *Margin for Error* (1939), *Child of the Morning* (1951), and *Slam the Door Softly* (1970). Her observations of travel abroad in a dangerous time are keenly conveyed in *Europe in the Spring* (1940). She also wrote a novel, *Stuffed Shirts* (1931, as Clare Boothe Brokaw). Increasing interest in public affairs led her to stand for Congress, and she was elected for two terms from a Connecticut district (1943–47). She served as ambassador to Italy from 1953 to 1956. In 1935 she married HENRY R. LUCE.

Luce, Henry R[obinson] (1898–1967),   editor and publisher. Born in China and educated at Yale, Luce joined with college friend Briton Hadden (1898–1929) in 1923 to found the newsmagazine *Time*, which became the cornerstone of a publishing empire scarcely rivaled in history. *Fortune*, a magazine for businessmen, followed in 1930, and LIFE in 1936. Luce also published *Sports Illustrated, Architectural Forum*, and *House and Home*. His second wife was CLARE BOOTHE LUCE.

Luck of Roaring Camp, The   (*Overland Monthly*, August 1868, included in *The Luck of Roaring Camp and Other Sketches* 1870), a story by BRET HARTE. Cherokee Sal is a prostitute who frequents a miners' camp. A child is born to her, but she dies in giving birth. The miners adopt the child and call him Thomas Luck, but in the following year the camp is destroyed in a flood, and Kentuck, one of the miners, dies holding the infant in his arms. The story made Harte widely known.

Ludlow, Fitz Hugh (1836–1870),   editor, teacher, lawyer, writer. Born in New York City, Ludlow early became a narcotics addict and wrote *The Apocalypse of Hasheesh* for *Putnam's Magazine* while he was a senior at Union College; the article was expanded into a book, *The Hasheesh Eater*, in 1857. He taught for a while, was admitted to the bar but never practiced, worked as a critic on several New York magazines, and as a free-lance contributed to others. For the *Atlantic Monthly* he did in 1863 a series of travel sketches about the West, including a laudatory account of a then unknown author, Mark Twain. The sketches were collected as *The Heart of the Continent* (1870). Some of his short stories appeared in *Little Brother and Other Genre-Pictures* (1867).

Ludlow, Noah Miller (1795–1886),   actor, memoirist. Born in New York City, Ludlow formed one of the earliest theatrical chains on record, along with Sol Smith managing theaters in St. Louis, New Orleans, Mobile, and other towns simultaneously. He gave the first English plays in New Orleans and was the first actor to reach some of the remote regions in the West and South. He told of his experiences in *Dramatic Life as I Found It* (1880).

Ludlum, Robert (1927–2001),   suspense novelist. Born in New York City, Ludlum served in the Marine Corps from 1944 to 1946, graduated from Wesleyan University (B.A.,

1951), and was an actor and theatrical producer in New York and New Jersey before publishing his first novel in his forties. The *Scarlatti Inheritance* (1971) tells of corruption and espionage after World War I, as American financiers, by enriching a group of Germans, assist in the rise of Hitler. Twenty bestsellers have followed on similar subjects: corruption, terror, spying, and assassination in the tense contemporary world, some of them written as "Jonathan Ryder" or "Michael Shepherd." More than 200 million books have been sold, in thirty-two languages and forty countries. They include: *The City of the Halidan* (1974), about a geologist in Jamaica; *The Gemini Contenders* (1976), twin brothers and a secret document; *The Chancellor Manuscript* (1977), J. Edgar Hoover's death discovered to be a murder involving theft of his files; *The Bourne Identity* (1980); *The Bourne Supremacy* (1986); and *The Bourne Ultimatum* (1990), a trilogy set in motion when a spy awakens with amnesia; *The Aquitaine Progression* (1984), with generals from five countries plotting to take over the world; and *The Icarus Agenda* (1988), an American presidential election manipulated by five wealthy men. *The Hades Factor* (2000) was written with Gayle Lynds, who has also written thrillers under her own name.

Lugones, Leopoldo (1874–1938),   Argentine poet. Born in Cordoba, Leopoldo moved to Buenos Aires in the 1890s and there fell under the influence of RUBÉN DARIO, becoming an exponent of MODERNISMO and a militant socialist. His first volume of verse, *Las montañas de oro* (1897), was reminiscent of the grandiose romanticism of Victor Hugo and WALT WHITMAN, with only traces of the modernism that became more apparent in *Los crepúsculos del jardín* (1905) and still more so in *Lunario sentimental* (1909). This last, influenced also by Laforgue, contains some of his most celebrated poems. With *Odas seculares* (1910), he turned his verse toward patriotism and a greater poetic orthodoxy as he celebrated the centenary of Argentine independence. Among later volumes, more orthodox than the early ones and in some ways more personal, are *El libro fiel* (1912), *El libro de los paisajes* (1917), *Las horas doradas* (1922), and *Poemas solariegos* (1927). His ballads appear in *Romancero* (1924) and *Romances del Río Seco* (1938). Lugones's prose works include *La guerra gaucha* (1905), a historical novel; and *El payador* (1916), about gaucho troubadors. A collection of fantastic short stories, *Las fuerzas extrañas* (1906), was known to and perhaps influenced JORGE LUIS BORGES.

Luhan, Mabel Dodge (1879–1962),   art patron, memoirist. Born in Buffalo, New York, of the wealthy Ganson family, Mabel Dodge might have continued to lead a leisurely life of high society but for the early death of her first husband, Carl Evans. Soon afterward she married the architect Edwin Dodge, later divorced him and married the artist Maurice Sterne, and finally settled in Taos, New Mexico, in 1918, with her fourth husband, Tony Luhan, a Pueblo Indian. She is remembered for her salons in Italy (1902–12) and New York City (1912–18) where many artists and intellectuals gathered, among them Gertrude Stein, Lincoln Steffens, Bernhard Berenson, John Reed, Max Eastman, and Carl Van Vechten.

Her best-known protégé was D. H. Lawrence, about whom she wrote *Lorenzo in Taos* (1932). Lawrence and John Collier, among others, were influenced by her love of the Pueblo Indians—their ancient creed, their strange and brilliant speech rhythms, and their simple values. Her *Intimate Memories* are valuable records of her experiences among many great artists and writers. They are composed of *Background* (1933), *European Experiences* (1935), *Movers and Shakers* (1936), and *Edge of the Taos Desert* (1937). Other prose works are *Winter in Taos* (1935) and *Taos and Its Artists* (1947). She is said to be the model for characters in Eastman's *Venture*, Lawrence's *The Woman Who Rode Away*, and Van Vechten's *Peter Whiffle*. Gertrude Stein wrote *A Portrait of Mabel Dodge*.

Lukas, J[ay] Anthony (1933–1997),   journalist, non-fiction writer. Born in New York City, educated at Harvard (B.A., *magna cum laude*, 1955) and the Free University of Berlin (1955–1966), Lukas was a correspondent for the *New York Times* in Washington, D.C., at the United Nations, in the Congo, and in India. He taught at Yale, Boston University, and the Kennedy School of Government, and was awarded honorary degrees by Northeastern University and Colby College. In his most celebrated book, *Common Ground: A Turbulent Decade in the Lives of Three American Families* (1985), he examined the results of court-ordered busing to achieve racial integration in Boston. Following three families—affluent "WASP," welfare black, and disadvantaged Irish Catholic, whose roots he traced to pre-Revolutionary War America, slavery in Georgia, and Ireland—he composed a picture of contemporary American racial, class, and economic tensions. Of his impetus to write the book, Lukas said: "I believe that what happened in Boston was not a random series of events but the acting out of the burden of American history." Others of his books also treat social and political issues: *The Barnyard Epithet and Other Obscenities: Notes on the Chicago Conspiracy Trial* (1970); *Don't Shoot—We Are Your Children!* (1971), on the countercultural revolution of the 1960s; *Nightmare: The Underside of the Nixon Years* (1975); and *Big Trouble: A Murder in a Small Western Town Sets Off a Struggle for the Soul of America* (1997), on the class struggle as it featured labor and capitalism in early twentieth-century Idaho.

lumberjack songs.   The lumber industry of the late 19th century gave rise to some of the best American ballads. Some of the major collections are Roland P. Gray's *Songs and Ballads of the Maine Lumberjacks* (1925), F. L. Rickaby's *Ballads and Songs of the Shanty Boy* (1926), F. H. Eckstorm and M. W. Smyth's *The Minstrelsy of Maine* (1927), Harold W. Thompson's *Body, Boots, and Britches* (1940), Earl C. Beck's *Songs of the Michigan Lumberjacks* (1941), and William M. Doerflinger's *Shantymen and Shantyboys* (1951).

Lundy, Benjamin (1789–1839),   editor, abolitionist. Born in Sussex County, New Jersey, Lundy was ardent in his opposition to slavery, although he would not countenance the violent verbal attacks of WILLIAM LLOYD GARRISON when he appointed the latter associate editor of a magazine he founded in 1821, *The Genius of Universal Emancipation*, which appeared irregularly until 1839. Lundy traveled all over the country and also visited Canada and Haiti, the latter when he was in search of places in which colonies of freed slaves might be established. Wherever he went he agitated against slavery. He was assaulted in Baltimore by slave dealers, and in Philadelphia a mob destroyed his property. He organized in St. Clairsville, Ohio, the Union Humane Society (1815), one of the first antislavery societies. In his book *The War in Texas* (1836) he gave details of a plot on the part of slaveholders to have that region secede from Mexico. In 1836 he founded the *National Enquirer and Constitutional Advocate of Universal Liberty*, which JOHN GREENLEAF WHITTIER edited for a while. Thomas Earle edited Lundy's *Life, Travels, and Opinions* (1847).

Lurie, Alison (1926–   ),   novelist. Born in Chicago, Lurie was educated at Radcliffe. A teacher of English at Cornell University after 1968, she has written often on academic subjects. Most popular of these is *The War Between the Tates* (1974), a novel in which the breakdown of the marriage between a teacher and his wife parallels the ongoing progress of the Vietnam War. Her earlier novels are *Love and Friendship* (1962), of adultery in academia; *The Nowhere City* (1965), of Eastern academics in Los Angeles; *Imaginary Friends* (1967), in which sociologists observe a small-town religious cult; and *Real People* (1970), about a woman novelist. More recent are *Only Children* (1979); *Foreign Affairs* (1984, Pulitzer Prize), about teachers of English on sabbatical leave in London; *The Truth About Lorin Jones* (1988); and *The Last Resort* (1998), a literary satire set in Key West. *Don't Tell the Grown-Ups: Subversive Children's Literature* (1990) is a collection of essays. *The Language of Clothes* (1981) is also nonfiction. She has also written books for children.

Luska, Sidney.   Pen name of HENRY HARLAND.

Luther, Seth (fl. 1817–1846),   carpenter, pamphleteer, labor reformer. Luther was an early crusader in behalf of better conditions for industrial workers. Born in Providence, Rhode Island, he saw the mill system of New England as a cruel exaction "on the bodies and minds of the producing classes." His *Address to the Workingmen of New England* (1832) apparently helped bring about passage of a child labor law in Massachusetts (1842). He also wrote *An Address on the Right of Free Suffrage* (1833) and *An Address on the Origin and Progress of Avarice* (1834). He believed in extending the privileges of free public education and in abolishing monopolies, capital punishment, and imprisonment for debt. In 1834 he was made secretary to the General Trades Convention in Boston and in 1835 helped draw up the *Boston Circular*, which advocated a ten-hour day.

lyceums.   A lyceum was a system of adult education through lectures by noted persons. Often a library or a collection of minerals or other objects was part of the lyceum, and often local groups studied some subject, scientific at first, historical or literary later on, in connection with the lyceum.

JOSIAH HOLBROOK, of Derby, Connecticut, started the movement when in 1826 he published an article in the *Journal of Education* outlining his plan for informal popular education. He hoped to see a lyceum in every American town, and he envisioned lyceums as a national influence. The American Lyceum, a national group, was organized in 1831. In two years a hundred lyceums had been started under Holbrook's inspiration, in nearly every state of the Union; there were nearly 3,000 before the movement petered out. The Civil War had an unfavorable effect on the lyceums, and by 1870 they had mainly degenerated into what Bayard Taylor, once a highly popular lecturer, resentfully called "nonintellectual diversion." But in their time they had a great educational influence, encouraged reading, and helped to unify the nation. Holbrook published a book, *The American Lyceum* (1829), describing his plan, and in 1830 began issuing a number of *Scientific Tracts Designed for Instruction and Entertainment*. He also edited the *Family Lyceum* as a weekly newspaper.

Emerson and Thoreau lectured on the lyceum circuit, as did many others, treating a variety of topics. John Godfrey Saxe read his new humorous verses, Bayard Taylor took listeners with him on his lively travels, John B. Gough warned against the terrors of intemperance, mesmerists and phrenologists inducted listeners solemnly into these sciences, Anna Dickinson championed reforms, Henry Ward Beecher delivered his eloquent sermons, J. R. Lowell lectured amiably and wittily as far west as Wisconsin, Margaret Fuller produced learned "conversations" for Boston audiences, Theodore Parker talked eagerly to what he called "glorious phalanxes of old maids," Horace Greeley was a popular figure, W. G. Simms came up from the South, and many British lecturers were welcomed by large audiences—Dickens, Thackeray, Matthew Arnold.

In time commercial lecture bureaus began to take over the field. The comic lecturers—Mark Twain, Artemus Ward, David Ross Locke, Bill Nye, Will Rogers—formed a tribe of their own and were highly successful. The lyceum was also in large part replaced by CHAUTAUQUA, founded in 1874.

Lyell, Sir Charles (1797–1875),   geologist. Born in England, Lyell twice visited America on scientific expeditions and wrote two books that contain his general and scientific observations, *Travels in North America, Canada, and Nova Scotia, With Geological Observations* (1845) and *A Second Visit to the United States of North America* (1849). In contrast to the accounts written by most British travelers in America, his books praised the United States.

Lynd, Helen Merrell (1896–1982),   and **Lynd, Robert S[taughton]** (1892–1970),   teachers, sociologists. Together this husband and wife team studied Muncie, Indiana, as a typical American community, which they wrote about in MIDDLETOWN (1929). Later *Middletown in Transition* (1937) indicated changes that had occurred since their first visits.

She continued the story alone in *Update: Middletown Families: Fifty Years of Change and Continuity* (1982).

Lynes, [Joseph] Russell [Jr.] (1910–1991),   editor, critic, writer. Born in Massachusetts and educated at Yale, Lynes served as Director of Publications at Vassar College and principal at the Shipley School, Bryn Mawr, Pennsylvania, before becoming managing editor of *Harper's Magazine* (1947–67). His books include *Snobs* (1950); *Guests* (1951); *The Tastemakers* (1954); *A Surfeit of Honey* (1957); the fictional *Cadwallader* (1959); *The Domesticated Americans* (1963), on the American home; *The Art-Makers of Nineteenth-Century America* (1970); and *The Lively Audience: A Social History of the Visual and Performing Arts in America, 1890–1950* (1985).

Lyon, Harris Merton (1883–1916),   drama critic, short-story writer. Lyon was a brilliant writer who died young. Two collections of his stories and sketches were published: *Sardonics* (1909) and *Graphics* (1913). It is believed that Theodore Dreiser, who knew him well, was thinking of Lyon when he wrote "De Maupassant, Jr." in his *Twelve Men* (1919).

Lyon, James (1735–1794),   hymnologist. Born in New Jersey, Lyon was a graduate of Princeton and a clergyman in Nova Scotia and Maine. In 1761 he published an anthology, *Urania, or, A Choice Collection of Psalm-Tunes, Anthems, and Hymns*, a book described as having inaugurated a new epoch in church music. It was in use for a century. Lyon himself wrote hymn music that later anthologists reprinted.

Lytle, Andrew [Nelson] (1902–1995),   writer, teacher. Born in Murfreesboro, Tennessee, Lytle attended Vanderbilt University and was a member of GEORGE PIERCE BAKER's 47 workshop at Harvard. He worked as an actor in New York, then returned to Tennessee and contributed to the Agrarian symposium I'LL TAKE MY STAND (1930). He taught at several universities, was managing editor of the SEWANEE REVIEW (1942–43), and became its editor in 1961. Most of his writing is set in the South and is largely concerned with the impact of the prevailing Northern way of life on Southern traditions of strong family ties, matriarchy, and agrarianism. *The Long Night* (1936) and *The Velvet Horn* (1957) are historical novels, the former taking place during the Civil War and the latter shortly after. "A Name for Evil" (1947, repr. in *A Novel, a Novella and Four Stories*, 1958) is a modern ghost story dealing with the spirit of a dead man and its eerie effect on his living heirs. *Bedford Forrest* (1931, rev. 1960) is a biography of the Confederate general. *A Wake for the Living* (1975) traces his family history for nearly two centuries in Tennessee.

M

Mabie, Hamilton Wright (1845–1916), editor, critic, essayist. Born in Cold Spring, New York, Mabie practiced law for eight years, but in 1879, when EDWARD EGGLESTON asked him to help edit the *Christian Union*, later called the OUTLOOK, he found an occupation much better suited to his taste and ability. Editor of church news at first, he progressed to literary editor, editorial writer, and associate editor. He published a children's book, *Norse Stories Retold from the Eddas* (1882); *My Study Fire* (1890); *Books and Culture* (1896); *The Life of the Spirit* (1899), a popular uplift book; *William Shakespeare, Poet, Dramatist and Man* (1900); and *Heroines That Every Child Should Know* (1908). He also edited the *After-School Library* (1909), a twelve-volume set sold by subscription.

McAlmon, Robert [Menzies] (1896–1956), lawyer, cowboy, lumberjack, artist's model, writer. Born in Clifton, Kansas, McAlmon was one of the earliest expatriates of the LOST GENERATION. His career developed mostly in Paris, and most of his books were published in France. He helped edit some of the LITTLE MAGAZINES of the 1920s, including *Contact*, and contributed to others. He published several volumes of verse: *Explorations* (1921), *The Portrait of a Generation* (1926), *North America, Continent of Conjecture* (1929), and *Not Alone Lost* (1937). His best work is probably the semifictional sketches in *Village: As It Happened Through a Fifteen-Year Period* (1924), an account of a place called Westworth that recalls Sinclair Lewis's GOPHER PRAIRIE and Sherwood Anderson's WINESBURG, OHIO. He also wrote an autobiography, *Being Geniuses Together* (1938), extended in 1968 by KAY BOYLE. Robert E. Knoll wrote *Robert McAlmon: Expatriate Publisher and Writer* (1957) and *McAlmon and the Lost Generation* (1962).

McArone Papers. Satires of war correspondence contributed by GEORGE ARNOLD (1834–1865), a promising young poet of the time, to *Vanity Fair*, the *Leader*, and the *Weekly Review* from 1860 to 1865.

MacArthur, Charles (1895–1956), newspaperman, editor, dramatist, writer, movie producer. Born in Scranton, Pennsylvania, MacArthur became a reporter on the Chicago *Herald and Examiner*, the Chicago *Tribune*, and the New York *American* from 1914 to 1923. This period of his life is reflected in THE FRONT PAGE (1928), the frequently revived play about newspaper life that he wrote in collaboration with BEN HECHT. In New York City he became a member of the ROUND TABLE at the Hotel Algonquin and married the actress Helen Hayes. In 1924 he began doing free-lance magazine work and writing plays; among the latter were *Lulu Belle* (with EDWARD SHELDON, 1926), about an African-American Carmen; *Salvation* (with SIDNEY HOWARD, 1927), about a lady evangelist; *Twentieth Century* (with Hecht, 1932), a satire on Hollywood; *Ladies and Gentlemen* (with Hecht, 1939); *Johnny on the Spot* (1941); and *Swan Song* (with Hecht, 1946). In 1929 he began writing and producing movies in Hollywood. Beginning in 1948 he edited *Theatre Arts Magazine*.

Macauley, Robie [Mayhew] (1919–), novelist, editor, short-story writer. Born in Michigan and educated at Kenyon College and the University of Iowa, Macauley taught at Kenyon, edited the *Kenyon Review* (1959–66), became fiction editor of *Playboy* magazine, and after 1978 a senior editor at Houghton Mifflin. His fiction includes the novels *The Disguises of Love* (1952) and *A Secret History of Time to Come* (1979), and stories collected in *The End of Pity* (1957).

McBain, Ed. See EVAN HUNTER.

McCarthy, Cormac (1933–), novelist. Born in Rhode Island, McCarthy grew up in rural Tennessee, where his family moved when he was four, and was educated at the University of Tennessee. The world of his early fiction is the mountains of Tennessee. Against a backdrop of natural beauty he creates lives distorted by poverty, incest, murder, theft, and insanity in works that have earned him comparison to Faulkner, Carson McCullers, and Flannery O'Connor as a master of Southern lives twisted by circumstance. Early novels include *The Orchard Keeper* (1965), *Outer Dark* (1968), *Child of God* (1973), and *Suttree* (1979). *Blood Meridian: Or The Evening Redness to the West* (1985) starts out in Nagodoches, Texas in 1849, and follows a boy to Mexico. The three novels that follow make up his acclaimed *Border Trilogy*, with the settings moving back and forth to each side of the border between the United States and Mexico, the themes harsh, the landscapes and people unforgiving, and the prose reminiscent of Hemingway in its stark precision. In *All the Pretty Horses* (1992), first of the three, John Grady Cole and his friend Lacey Rawlins cross over into Mexico in the aftermath of World War II. In the second, time shifts backward to the time before the war, when teenage Billy Parham, protagonist of *The Crossing* (1994), transports a trapped wolf from New Mexico to the mountains of Chihuahua, and in the concluding volume, *Cities of the Plain* (1998), it moves forward again, as John Grady Cole and Billy Parham are cowboys on a New Mexico ranch encroached upon by the military in 1952. The novels were published together in 1999, and *All the Pretty Horses* was filmed in 2000. McCarthy has also written *The Stonemason* (1995), a five act play about a black family in 1970s Louisville. Narrated by young Ben, who has dropped out of graduate school to follow his grandfather's trade of stonemasonry, it tells a multigenerational story of family life.

McCarthy, Mary [Therese] (1912–1989), novelist, short-story writer, critic. Born in Seattle, Washington, and orphaned at age six, Mary McCarthy was raised by an aunt and uncle and two sets of grandparents of Catholic, Jewish, and Protestant backgrounds. Her childhood is minutely and memorably recalled in *Memories of a Catholic Girlhood* (1957). She was educated at Vassar, began writing book reviews for *The Nation* and the *New Republic*, and became drama critic for the *Partisan Review Sights and Spectacles, 1937–1956* (1956) is a collection of her theater pieces, revealing her as an informed, witty, and generally accurate, if severe, critic. After her divorce from EDMUND WILSON, she taught for a few years at Bard College and Sarah Lawrence, drawing on this experience in her satirical novel *The Groves of Academe* (1952). In this book, as in such novels as *The Company She Keeps* (1942), *The Oasis* (1949), *A Charmed Life* (1955), and *The Group* (1963), her special subject is the follies of the contemporary intellectual. To the treatment of this theme she brings keen powers of observation, a polished and brilliant style, and merciless, somewhat malicious wit. Her later novels include *Birds of America* (1971); and *Cannibals and Missionaries* (1979), about the hijacking of a plane on the way to Iran. She is the author of a collection of short stories, *Cast a Cold Eye* (1950); *Venice Observed* (1956) and *The Stones of Florence* (1959), pictorial studies of the two cities; *On the Contrary* (1961), a collection of articles on contemporary subjects; *Vietnam* (1967); *Hanoi* (1968); *The Writing on the Wall* (1978), essays; and *The Mask of State: Watergate Portraits* (1974); *Ideas and the Novel* (1980); *Occasional Prose* (1985); and *How I Grew* (1987).

McCarthyism.   In a narrow sense McCarthyism is the name given to the attitudes and practices of Senator Joseph McCarthy (1908–57) and his followers engrossed in investigating and purging purported security risks, especially those supposedly with ties present or former, actual or imagined, to Communist groups and governments during the late 1940s and early 1950s. More generally, McCarthyism has come to be associated with harassment and surveillance of suspected radicals beginning with the House Un-American Activities Committee in 1938 to the present, especially investigations intent on proving guilt by association, misstatement, and other procedures considered inimical to the guarantees of human rights inherent in the Bill of Rights. As David Caute documents in *The Great Fear* (1978), hundreds of high school and college teachers, writers, film makers, actors, actresses, and political figures were forced to sign loyalty oaths and had their lives disrupted, their marriages broken, their works censored, and their careers

destroyed by being investigated or even threatened with investigation by McCarthy and his followers. The exact number of suicides attributable to McCarthyite harassment is not known, though the numbers appear to be significant and tragic.

Books sympathetic to McCarthy and his followers include McCarthy's own *McCarthyism: The Fight for America* (1952) and in collaboration with his staff, *America's Retreat from Victory: The Story of George Catlett Marshall* (1951); and William F. Buckley and L. B. Bozell's *McCarthy and His Enemies* (1954).

Most other writing about McCarthy has been severely critical of the witch hunting conducted by the Wisconsin senator. Notable early statements include Jack Anderson and R. W. May's *McCarthy: The Man, the Senator, the Ism* (1952); L. Gore's *Joe Must Go* (1954); and James Rorty's *McCarthy and the Communists* (1954). More recently, David Caute's *The Great Fear: The Anti-Communist Purges Under Truman and Eisenhower* (1978) is a thorough and documented analysis of the social, cultural, intellectual, and political ramifications of McCarthyite purges. Other important contributions to an understanding of the era include Michael Paul Rogin's *The Intellectuals and McCarthy: The Radical Specter* (1967); Athan G. Theoharis's *Seeds of Repression: Harry S. Truman and the Origins of McCarthyism* (1971); David M. Oshinsky's *A Conspiracy So Immense: The World of Joe McCarthy* (1983); and Robert Griffith's *The Politics of Fear: Joseph R. McCarthy and the Senate* (1987).

During the 1980s and the reemergence of historical and political criticism and cultural studies, historians and literary critics began reassessing the impact and implications of McCarthyism and of the Cold War era in general on academic literary and historical practices. Among useful studies are Ellen W. Schrecker's *No Ivory Tower: McCarthyism and the Universities* (1986), Russell J. Reising's *The Unusable Past: Theory and the Study of American Literature* (1986), and Donald Pease's *Visionary Compacts: American Renaissance Writings in Cultural Context* (1987). Important literary works dramatizing aspects of McCarthyism include OWEN LATTIMORE, *Ordeal by Slander* (1950); ARCHIBALD MACLEISH, *The Trojan Horse* (1952); ARTHUR MILLER, *The Crucible* (1953); HOWARD FAST, *Silas Timberman* (1954); and Molly Kazan's *The Egghead* (1957).

RUSSELL J. REISING

McCaslin family,   characters in works by WILLIAM FAULKNER, primarily in the linked short stories of *Go Down, Moses* (1942). Among the first families to settle in Yoknapatawpha County (ostensibly modeled after Faulkner's own Jefferson County, Mississippi), the McCaslins evidence the guilt of miscegenation, incest, and slavery that continues to haunt their lives long after the Civil War is over. The members of this family include:

Lucius Quintus Carothers McCaslin. Founder of the family and its plantation, Old Carothers is the father of a daughter and twin sons by his white wife. He seduced a slave, Eunice, who bore him a daughter, Tomasina ("Tomey"), whom he later seduced in turn, thus compounding miscegenation with incest.

Theophilus ("Uncle Buck") McCaslin. A bachelor until his sixties, he and his twin brother, Amodeus ("Uncle Buddy"), legitimate sons of Old Carothers, do not believe in slavery and invent a system whereby their father's slaves can earn their freedom; most of them, however, refuse to leave. Buck and Buddy increase the thousand-dollar legacy of their father to his black son/grandson, Tomey's Turl (Terrel), to a thousand dollars each for Turl's three surviving children. Uncle Buck also appears in Faulkner's *The Unvanquished* (1938).

Sophonsiba Beauchamp. Sister of Hubert Beauchamp, married to Theophilus "Uncle Buck" McCaslin, and mother of Isaac McCaslin of "The Bear."

Isaac McCaslin. Hero of "The Bear" and several other related stories, Isaac was the last male McCaslin to carry the name. Ike later marries but has no children. He refuses his inheritance after he learns of the tangled guilt of Old Carothers.

Tennie Beauchamp. Wife of Tomey's Turl and mother of Lucas. She was won at poker by Uncle Buck from Hubert in 1859.

Lucas Quintus Carothers McCaslin Beauchamp. Part black grandson of Old Carothers, he is a principal character in Faulkner's novel, *Intruder in the Dust* (1948), as well as in "The Fire and the Hearth" in *Go Down.*

Carothers McCaslin ("Cass") Edmonds. Great-grandson of Old Carothers, he inherits the plantation after Ike, his younger cousin, refuses his inheritance.

Isaac ("Zack") Edmonds. Friend and rival of his part black cousin Lucas, Isaac commandeers Lucas's wife Molly to care for his infant son after the death of the child's mother. After six months, Lucas demands she be returned to him.

Carothers ("Roth") Edmonds. Isaac Edmonds's son. As a young man he has an affair with a very light-colored black woman, who is in fact a distant relative of his on the McCaslin side, and who bears him a child, but whom he refuses to marry. She reveals to old Ike that she is the great-great-granddaughter of the original McCaslin.

NORMAN FRIEDMAN

McCay, Winsor (1869?–1934), cartoonist. McCay was born in Spring Lake, Michigan, worked as an artist for a Cincinnati dime museum, went from there to the Cincinnati *Commercial Tribune* and then to the New York *Herald* in 1903. At the *Herald*, he created the comic strip "Little Nemo in Slumberland," which appeared first on October 15, 1905. Extremely popular, it inspired a Broadway production with music by VICTOR HERBERT. McCay's other comic strips were "Little Sammy Sneeze" and "Dream of the Rarebit Fiend." McCay also inspired later moviemakers with his animated films, including *Little Nemo* (1911); *The Story of a Mosquito* (1912); *Gertie the Dinosaur* (1914); and *The Sinking of the Lusitania* (1918). *The Dream of a Rarebit Fiend* (1906) was a live action film based on his strip. His later life was given over mostly to political car-

McCASLIN GENEALOGY

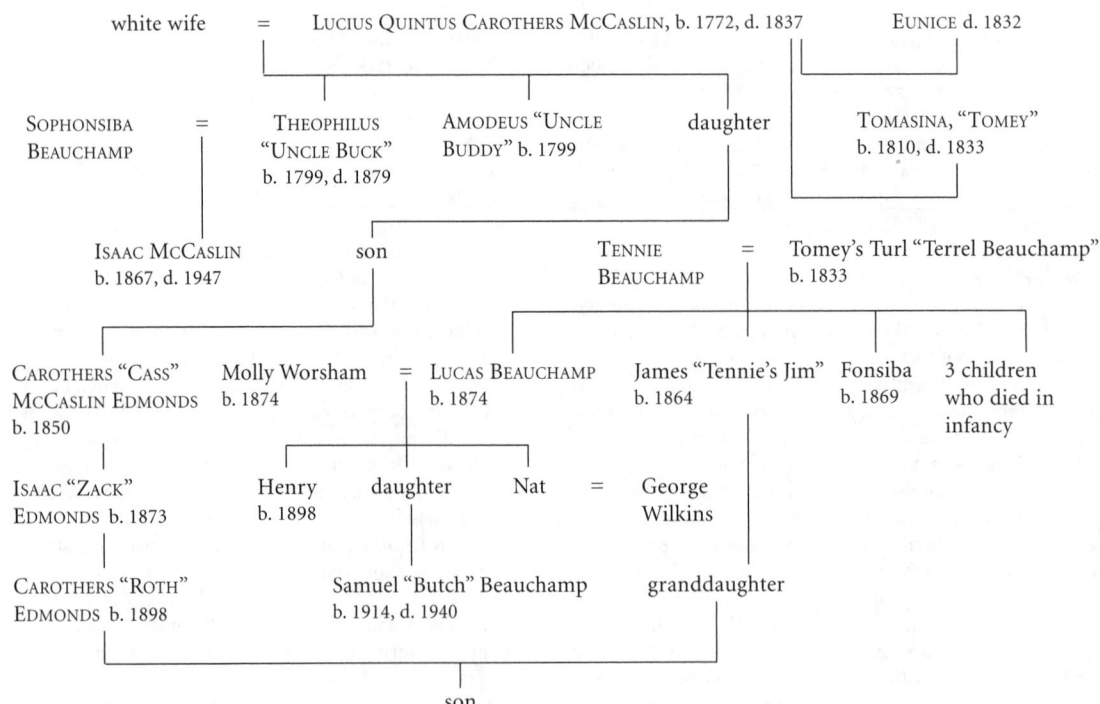

toons. His story is told in *Winsor McCay: His Life and Art* (1987), by John Canemaker.

McClellan, George B[rinton] (1826–1885), soldier, engineer, public official, memoirist. Born in Philadelphia, McClellan was educated at the University of Pennsylvania and at West Point, graduating second in his class. He saw his first combat in the Mexican War.

When the Civil War broke out in 1861, McClellan was commissioned a major-general. He became general-in-chief of the union forces when General Scott retired, but did not keep this rank for long. His reluctance to take offensive action, even after a retreating enemy, and his general indecision tried the patience of his superiors. He was relieved of one command after another, and finally retired. He attempted to vindicate himself by running against Lincoln in the presidential campaign of 1864.

He was elected governor of New Jersey in 1878 and served for three years. After this he retired to write *McClellan's Own Story* (1887), in which he defended his military career. His *Mexican War Diary* (1917) was edited by William Starr Myers.

McClellan appears in occasional poems of his own day, admiringly so in poems such as Thomas Dunn English's *The Charge by the Ford*. But George Henry Boker wrote of him as *Tardy George* (1865). Charles King introduced him in his lurid tale, *The General's Double* (1897).

McCloskey, [John] Robert (1914–), author of children's books, illustrator. Born in Ohio, McCloskey attended Vesper George School of Art in Boston and the National Academy of Design in New York. His books have been extremely popular with children, and two of them, *Make Way for Ducklings* (1941) and *Time of Wonder* (1957), won the Caldecott Award of the American Library Association. McCloskey has also written and illustrated *Lentil* (1940), *Homer Price* (1943), *Blueberries for Sal* (1948), *Centerburg Tales* (1951), *One Morning in Maine* (1952), and *Deep-Water Man* (1963).

McClung, John A[lexander] (1804–1859), novelist. Born in Kentucky, McClung, patterning himself on Scott and Cooper, wrote *Camden: A Tale of the South* (1830), about events during the Revolution after the fall of Charleston. He also wrote *Sketches of Western Adventure* (1832).

McClure, Alexander K[elly] (1828–1909), newspaper editor, author of travel books, historian. McClure was born in Pennsylvania. His most original work was *3000 Miles Through the Rocky Mountains* (1869). In 1875 he and Frank McLaughlin founded the *Philadelphia Times*, which he edited forcefully until 1902, when it was merged with the *Public Ledger*. McClure in the meantime continued to write and edit books. Among them were *Abraham Lincoln and Men of War Times* (1892) and *Old-Times Notes of Pennsylvania* (2 v. 1905). He edited a series called *Famous American Statesmen and Orators* (6 v. 1902). In 1902 he published *Recollections of Half a Century*.

McClure, Michael [Thomas] (1932–), poet, playwright. Born in Marysville, Kansas, McClure dropped out of college to become a BEAT GENERATION poet in San Francisco.

His work is frequently obscure, its images hallucinatory. Some of it takes the form of plays, for example, *The Beard* (1965), a poem-play in which Billy the Kid confronts Jean Harlow; *Gargoyle Cartoons* (1971); *Gorf* (1976); and *Josephine: The Mouse Singer* (1980). His collections of verse include *Star* (1970), *September Blackberries* (1974), *Jaguar Skies* (1975), and *Antechamber* (1978). His novels are *The Mad Cub* (1970); and *The Adept* (1971). *Selected Poems* appeared in 1986. *Huge Dreams* (1999) republishes *The New Book/A Book of Torture* and *Star*, both out of print for thirty years. *Rain Mirror: New Poems* also appeared in 1999.

McClure, S[amuel] S[idney] (1857–1949), editor, publisher. The most influential editor of his era, McClure, who was born in Ireland, came to the United States in 1866 with his mother and three brothers to join relatives near Valparaiso, Indiana. He worked his way through high school and Knox College in Galesburg, Illinois, where he edited the campus newspaper; became engaged to Harriet Hurd, a fellow student whom he later married; and was graduated with the class of 1882. Two years later, after editing *The Wheelman*, the house organ of a bicycle manufacturer in Boston, and working for the Century Company in New York, he founded the Literary Associated Press, a syndicate that bought articles and fiction to sell to newspapers throughout the country.

The success of the syndicate enabled McClure in 1893 to found *McClure's Magazine*, a monthly featuring articles on current affairs and poetry and fiction by new and established writers, including Robert Louis Stevenson. A. Conan Doyle, Rudyard Kipling, BOOTH TARKINGTON, and WILLA CATHER. Indefatigable in seeking new subjects and writers, McClure attracted to his magazine the most gifted journalists of the day, such as IDA TARBELL, RAY STANNARD BAKER LINCOLN STEFFENS, and WILLIAM ALLEN WHITE. According to Ellery Sedgwick, McClure's was "the most brilliant staff ever gathered by a New York periodical." Beginning with its January 1903 issue, the magazine exerted its greatest influence on American journalism and national policy during the next seven years, with the publication of its MUCK-RAKING articles exposing corporate and municipal corruption, for example, Tarbell's nineteen-part series on the history of the Standard Oil Company; Steffens's articles, "The Shame of the Cities"; and Baker's articles on railways, miners' strikes, and lynching. White credited *McClure's* with nationalizing local news, inspiring Theodore Roosevelt's reform policies, and bringing the nation close to "government by magazine."

In 1906, McClure's partner, JOHN PHILLIPS, joined by Tarbell, Baker, and others who opposed McClure's visionary schemes to enlarge his publishing empire, left his staff and started their own magazine, *The American*. *McClure's Magazine*, with Willa Cather as managing editor, maintained its standards of good writing and accurate reporting of controversial subjects, but in 1911 debt compelled McClure to cede control to a group of financiers who soon forced him out of the editorship. He was editor again from 1920 until 1925, when the declining magazine was sold to Hearst's International Publications.

McClure is portrayed in autobiographies and reminiscences

by Baker, Steffens, Tarbell, Frank N. Doubleday, and Ellery Sedgwick, among others. McClure narrated the substance of *My Autobiography* to Willa Cather, who wrote the chapters of the book first published in *McClure's* in 1914. Robert Louis Stevenson acknowledged that he had caricatured McClure in his novel *The Wrecker* (1901), but William Dean Howells denied the widespread assumption that Fulkerson in *A Hazard of New Fortunes* (1890) was based on McClure.

ELSA NETTELS

McClure's Magazine.   See S. S. MCCLURE.

McConkey, James [Rodney] (1921–   ),   novelist, memoirist. Born in Ohio, McConkey taught English at Cornell. Much of his most memorable work, sometimes presented as fiction, has the quality of spare, evocative autobiography—moments of a lifetime caught in lucid prose. *Crossroads* (1968) sketches experiences beginning in boyhood. *A Journey to Sahalin* (1971) presents racial violence on a college campus. In *The Tree House Confessions* (1979), a man visits a tree house built for a dead son. *Court of Memory* (1983) contains memoirs, including those of *Crossroads*. *Rowan's Progress* (1991) ponders the history of Rowan County, Kentucky. *Stories of My Life with the Other Animals* (1993) is comprised of seven essays covering the period from 1984 to 1991 in the author's life. *To a Distant Island* (2000) is a study of Anton Chekhov's 1890 trip to Sakhalin Island, off the coast of Siberia.

McConnel, John Ludlum (1826–1862),   lawyer, soldier, novelist. McConnel's brief life was devoted mainly to the Army—in the war with Mexico—and the practice of law. His most important novel was *Talbot and Vernon* (1850), which describes the Battle of Buena Vista as McConnel himself saw it and tells the story of a romance jeopardized by an accusation of forgery.

McCord, David [Thompson Watson] (1897–1997), poet, editor, critic, painter. Born in New York City, McCord was on the staff of the *Harvard Alumni Bulletin* and served as executive secretary of the Harvard Fund Council. He was drama and music critic for the old Boston *Evening Transcript* (1923–28). He published numerous collections of light verse and books of familiar essays, including *Oddly Enough* (1926), *Floodgate* (1927), *Stir-about* (1928), *The Crows* (1934), *Bay Window Ballads* (1935), *Twelve Verses from XII Night* (1938), *On Occasion* (1943), *A Star by Day* (1950), *The Old Bateau and Other Poems* (1953), and *Odds Without Ends* (1954). As an editor he produced a fine collection of humorous verse, *What Cheer* (1945), part of which was reprinted as the *Pocket Book of Humorous Verse* (1946) and again, revised, in the Modern Library (1955). *Selected Poems* came out in 1957. *One at a Time*, verse for children, appeared in 1977.

McCourt, Frank (1931–   ),   memoirist. Born in Brooklyn and brought up in Limerick, Ireland from age four, McCourt returned to New York at age nineteen and attended New York University. For thirty years he taught writing in the New York public schools. His first publication *Angela's Ashes* (1996), written after his retirement from teaching, turned McCourt into an immediate success and gained him both the National Book Critics Circle Award and the Pulitzer Prize. A reminiscence of his poverty-stricken boyhood, *Angela's Ashes* is a gripping read, detailing his mother, Angela's, struggles with an alcoholic husband, poor sanitation, inadequate medical care, and a miserly welfare system. Despite the misery of three dead siblings, and his own illnesses, McCourt's autobiography, written from the perspective of a young child, is often humorous and always entertaining. McCourt has said he had to rid himself of judgmental attitudes before he was able to write in the child's voice. The book ends with the teenager and one of his brothers arriving in New York in 1949. *'Tis* (1999) takes its title from the last words of the first book and describes McCourt's teaching experiences, stint in the Army, relations with his parents and surviving brothers, friendships, loves and marriages. The deaths of his mother—in New York—and his father in Ireland bring the book to a close.

McCosh, James (1811–1894),   clergyman, educator, philosopher. McCosh was a minister of the Established Church in Scotland until he left to join in the Free Church movement. The exclusion of the supernatural in J.S. Mill's *System of Logic* led him to write a refutation, *The Method of the Divine Government: Physical and Moral* (1850). He taught logic and metaphysics at Queen's College, Belfast, for sixteen years and in 1868 was appointed president of the College of New Jersey (now Princeton).

McCosh was one of the first theologians to accept Darwin. He saw no clash between science and religion, but contended that the doctrine of evolution proved God's method of creation. Among his works are *Typical Forms and Special Ends in Creation* (1855), *The Intuitions of the Mind Inductively Investigated* (1860), *The Supernatural in Relation to the Natural* (1862), *An Examination of Mr. J. S. Mill's Philosophy: Being a Defense of Fundamental Truth* (1866), *The Laws of Discursive Thought* (1870), *Christianity and Positivism* (1871), *The Scottish Philosophy* (1875), and *Realistic Philosophy Defended in a Philosophical Series* (2 v. 1887).

McCoy, Horace (1897–1955),   newspaperman, short-story writer, novelist. Born in Tennessee, McCoy began as a sports writer on the Dallas (Texas) *Journal*, but was interested in the theater, often made pilgrimages to Paris, knew F. Scott Fitzgerald and other expatriates, and began writing stories somewhat in their manner. Some of them were printed in small magazines and attracted the attention of EDWARD J. O'BRIEN and other anthologists. He also became a screenwriter in Hollywood. His first novel, *They Shoot Horses, Don't They?* (1935), is the story told on the eve of his execution by a man who had, at her request, killed his marathon-dance partner. Others are *No Pockets in a Shroud* (1937), a study of corruption in a small town; followed by *I Should Have Stayed Home* (1938), *Kiss Tomorrow Good-Bye* (1948), and *Scalpel* (1952).

McCracken, Elizabeth (1966–   ),   novelist, short-story writer. Born in Boston, she was educated at Boston University, the University of Iowa writing program, and Drexel University. *Here's Your Hat, What's Your Hurry* (1993), her first publication is a collection of nine short stories involving characters in often bizarre situations. *The Giant's House* (1996) is a novel about Peggy Cort, the librarian in a small Cape Cod town who befriends James Sweatt, already six-foot two-inches tall at age eleven. *Niagara Falls All Over Again* (2001) is a novel about a comedy team.

McCrae, John (1872–1918),   physician, poet. Born in Guelph, Ontario, McCrae received a medical degree from the University of Toronto and was made a fellow at McGill University. During World War I he served in the medical corps until his death from pneumonia. His rondeau *In Flanders Fields*, which appeared in *Punch* in 1915, soon became one of the best-known poems of the war. A posthumous volume, *In Flanders Fields and Other Poems*, was published in 1919.

McCullers, [Lula] Carson [Smith] (1917–1967), novelist, short-story writer, playwright. Born in Columbus, Georgia, McCullers attended Columbia University and New York University. Her success began with first novel, THE HEART IS A LONELY HUNTER (1940), a story of a deaf-mute's associations with various people in a small Southern town, among them an African-American and an adolescent girl. Her second novel, *Reflections in a Golden Eye* (1941), deals with violence at a peacetime army post in the South. Her third novel, THE MEMBER OF THE WEDDING (1946), again attracted a wide audience with its exploration of the loneliness and isolation of a twelve-year-old girl, Frankie, who wants to go along on her brother's honeymoon. McCullers wrote a dramatization of the novel (1950) that was later made into a movie (1952). She explores her theme of the lonely individual's search for love among children and misfits in society and is able to give it universal significance. *The Ballad of the Sad Café* (1951) contains the novelette and a selection of short stories; the title piece was made into a play by EDWARD ALBEE. *Seven* (1954) is a collection of stories. *The Square Root of Wonderful*, a play, appeared in 1958; the novel *Clock Without Hands* in 1961. Uncollected writings were gathered in *The Mortgaged Heart* (1971).

McCulley, Johnston (1883–1958),   novelist, playwright, screenwriter. McCulley, born in Ottawa, Illinois, began as a newspaperman, turned to fiction with *The Land of Lost Hope* (1908), the first of a series of more than sixty romantic novels that appeared under his own name and several pen names, including *The Jungle Trail* (1917), *The Masked Woman* (1920), *The Mask of Zorro* (1924), *The Crimson Clown* (1927), *Who Killed the Caretaker?* (1930), *Zorro Rides Again* (1931), *Reckless Range* (1937), *Range Lawyer* (1942), and *The Caballero* (1947). McCulley produced more than thirty Zorro novels, wrote television scripts for the Zorro series and also wrote plays, radio dramas, and screenplays.

McCulloch, Thomas (1776–1843),   clergyman, educator, humorist. Born in Scotland, McCulloch was a Presbyterian minister who settled in 1803 in Pictou, Nova Scotia, and in 1838 became first president of Dalhousie University. His chief contribution to literature was "Letters of Mephibosheth Stepsure," serialized in the *Acadian Recorder* (1821–23). Among the first humorous products of Canadian literature, they anticipated the writings of THOMAS HALIBURTON and have been

reprinted as *The Stepsure Letters* (1960). His other writings include *Popery Condemned by Scriptures and the Fathers* (1808), *Popery Condemned Again* (1810), and *The Nature and Uses of a Liberal Education* (1819).

McCutcheon, George Barr (1866–1928),   newspaperman, novelist. Born in Indiana, McCutcheon resigned his position with the Lafayette *Courier* in 1893 after the success of his second novel. His first, GRAUSTARK (1901), which he sold for $500, made a fortune for the publisher. BREWSTER'S MILLIONS (1902), which sold more than 5,000,000 copies, was made into a successful play by WINCHELL SMITH (1906) and was filmed a number of times. McCutcheon sandwiched realistic novels among his many swashbuckling moneymakers and claimed an affection for *Mary Midthorne* (1911), a quiet tale of Indiana life, but he is best known for *Graustark* and its sequels, *Beverly of Graustark* (1904) and *The Prince of Graustark* (1914).

McCutcheon, John T[inney] (1870–1949),   cartoonist, writer. The brother of GEORGE BARR MCCUTCHEON was one of the best-known American cartoonists. He began working for the Chicago *Record* in 1889. GEORGE ADE joined him, and together they wrote and illustrated a series called *Stories of the Street and of the Town*. In 1903 McCutcheon switched to the *Tribune* and remained there until his retirement in 1946. For many years McCutcheon's cartoons were a front-page feature of the *Tribune*. He drew some powerful political cartoons, but preferred the gentler aspects of life, as in his "Bird Center" extravaganzas and his "Boy in Springtime" drawings. Among his books are *Stories of Filipino Warfare* (1900), *Cartoons by McCutcheon* (1903), *Bird Center Cartoons* (1904), *The Mysterious Stranger and Other Cartoons* (1905), *Congressman Pumphrey, the People's Friend* (1907), *In Africa* (1910), *T. R. in Cartoons* (1910), *John McCutcheon's Book* (1948), and *Drawn from Memory* (autobiography, 1950).

McDermott, Alice (1953–   ),   novelist. Born in Brooklyn, McDermott was educated at the State University of New York and the University of New Hampshire. Her novels deal with aspects of love and family life, particularly among Irish-Americans. *A Bigamist's Daughter* (1982) centers on Elizabeth Connelly, an editor for a vanity press who becomes involved with a client who is writing a book about a bigamist. The problems raised by her client's unfinished novel cause her to question her own father's many absences from home. *That Night* (1987) involves teenage romance and pregnancy; it was a finalist for the National Book Award. *At Weddings and Wakes* (1991) tells the stories of individual family members against the background of ritual gatherings. *Charming Billy* (1998) won the National Book Award. It begins at a bar lunch after the funeral of Billy Lynch, a man of legendary humor and charm who has died an alcoholic. As relatives and friends remember his life, it becomes clear that not all they think they know about him is true.

MacDonald, Betty [Anne Elizabeth Campbell Bard] (1908–1958),   government official, memoirist. MacDonald served as a labor adjuster with the government and later worked in other official capacities. She took to writing and turned out a number of extremely popular books of comic reminiscence: *The Egg and I* (1945), filmed in 1947; *Mrs. Piggle-Wiggle* (1947); *The Plague and I* (1948); *Anybody Can Do Anything* (1950); and *Onions in the Stew* (1955). *The Egg and I* sold more than a million copies.

Macdonald, Dwight (1906–1982), essayist, critic. Macdonald's focus of interest moved gradually from Yale and his first job on *Fortune* magazine, to radical politics and a job on *Partisan Review*, to the founding of a journal of his own, *Politics* (1944–49), devoted at first to anarchist and pacifist views, with Leon Trotsky as a major influence, and finally to disillusioned criticism of any doctrinaire political stance. In 1952 he became a staff writer for *The New Yorker. Memoirs of a Revolutionist* (1957, reissued as *Politics Past* 1970) documents this progression. Macdonald's other works include *Henry Wallace: The Man and the Myth* (1948); *Against the American Grain* (1962), a collection of essays that includes "Masscult and Midcult," Macdonald's controversial analysis of popular culture; *The Ghost of Conspiracy* (1965), on the Warren Commission's report on the assassination of President Kennedy; and *Discriminations* (1974), essays.

MacDonald, John D[ann] (1916–1986), mystery writer. MacDonald was the creator of Travis McGee, a Florida-based private investigator. McGee is a mixture of the rough detective of HARD-BOILED FICTION and the compassionate investigator, like ROSS MACDONALD's Lew Archer. John MacDonald's plots are typically complex, the backgrounds investigated in depth. Among his many Travis McGee mysteries, all of which include a color in the title, are *The Deep Blue Good-By* (1964), *Nightmare in Pink* (1964), *The Dreadful Lemon Sky* (1975), *The Green Ripper* (1979), *Free Fall in Crimson* (1981), and *The Lonely Silver Rain* (1985). He also wrote numerous other works of suspense and a novel of ecological concern, *Condominium* (1977).

MacDonald, [John] Ross [pen name of **Kenneth Millar,** 1915–1983], novelist. Born in San Francisco and reared in Canada, Macdonald was one of the few mystery writers whose books were consistently taken seriously by literary critics. His series of detective stories featuring private investigator Lew Archer began with *The Moving Target* (1949). Archer has a deep compassion for people in trouble and a reluctance to employ violent methods. MacDonald shows deep psychological insight, frequently involving the pathological and the morbid, as in *The Underground Man* (1971), *Sleeping Beauty* (1973), and *The Blue Hammer* (1976), and a penchant for vivid metaphors and similes. His approach to the mystery novel was influenced by RAYMOND CHANDLER, with whom MacDonald shared the conviction that a well-written mystery is as artistically sound as any other type of fiction. His wife is MARGARET MILLAR. *Self-Portrait* (1982) collects essays.

MacDonald, Wilson (1880–1967), poet, etcher. Born in Cheapside, Ontario, MacDonald is essentially a lyric poet; his melody is constantly maintained, his metaphors apt and effective. He regards civilization as a failure and calls for a return to the soil. Among his books are *Song of the Prairie*

Land (1918), *The Miracle Songs of Jesus* (1921), *Out of the Wilderness* (1926), *A Flagon of Beauty* (1931), *The Song of the Undertow* (1935), *Comber Cove* (1937), and *The Lyric Year* (1952).

MacDowell Colony. A creative retreat established to honor Edward A. MacDowell (1861–1908), a composer, pianist, and teacher. After his death some of his admirers established the MacDowell Memorial Association. His widow deeded to the Association their home at Peterborough, New Hampshire, which thereafter became the MacDowell Colony, to which many composers and writers have come for quiet and inspiration.

MacDowell, Katherine Sherwood ["Sherwood Bonner"] (1849–1883), short-story writer, novelist. Born in Holly Springs, Mississippi, MacDowell was secretary to Henry Wadsworth Longfellow for a time, meanwhile contributing verse, articles, and stories to various magazines. Some of these were collected in *Dialect Tales* (1883) and *Suwanee River Tales* (1884), and for the most part they have Southern backgrounds. MacDowell used her memories of the Civil War and the Reconstruction in an autobiographical novel, *Like Unto Like* (1878).

McElheney, Jane ["Ada Clare"] (1836–1874), novelist, poet, actress. McElheney, a cousin of the poet Paul Hamilton Hayne, was born in Charleston, South Carolina. At age twenty-one she returned from France, unmarried, but with a small son she explained as a result of a love affair with the pianist and composer Louis Gottschalk. With Harry Clapp, editor, poet, and so-called King of Bohemia, whom she had known in Paris, she met regularly with friends in PFAFF'S CELLAR on lower Broadway, until her friends were scattered by the Civil War. As her fragile literary career waned, she became an actress. Her novel *Only a Woman's Heart* (1866), like her shorter works, was a thinly disguised account of her great love affair. The hero, Victor Doria, was a combination of Gottschalk and EDWIN BOOTH. The book was not a success. Even the critics who admired Ada Clare as a woman attacked her as a novelist.

McElroy, Joseph (1930–), novelist. Born in Brooklyn and educated at Williams and Columbia, McElroy first gained attention with *A Smuggler's Bible* (1966), a novel in which a Bible hollowed for smuggling becomes a metaphor for spiritual emptiness in our time of smugglers. This set the pattern for his later novels, postmodern in their confusions and disjunctions, their undercutting of structure and expectation. These include *Hind's Kidnap* (1969), about a man obsessed with solving a mysterious kidnapping where everyone is a suspect; *Lookout Cartridge* (1974), fracturing reality through the metaphor of a film that may not exist about things that may not have happened; *Plus* (1977), merging with science fiction as brain and machine interact; *Women and Men* (1987); and *The Letter Left to Me* (1988), in which a young man internalizes the effects of a letter from his father, received after the father's death.

McEvoy, J[oseph] P[atrick] (1895–1958), novelist, playwright. Born in New York City, McEvoy in 1919 published his first book, a volume of light verse called *Slams of Life*. In 1924, with the production of *The Potters*, he began a successful dramatic career. *The Comic Supplement* (a revue, 1925) was followed by *Americana* (1926) and *Allez Oop* (1927). *God Loves Us* (1926), a satirical comedy attacking the Babbitts and "those who put the jazz in Jesus," was extremely popular. *Show Girl* (1928) and *Hollywood Girl* (1929), novels, were followed by *Father Meets Son* (1937), a play, and *Stars in Your Eyes* (1939), a musical comedy. McEvoy wrote many magazine articles and created the comic strip "Dixie Dugan." *Charlie Would Have Loved This* (1956) is a collection of humorous sketches.

MacEwan, Gwendolyn (1941–1987), poet, novelist. Born in Toronto, MacEwan left school at eighteen and four years later published her first novel, *Julian the Magician* (1963). A historical fantasy, it was followed by another in a similar vein, *King of Egypt, King of Dreams* (1971). *Noman* (1972) collects quasi-mythological stories. Her poems are likewise informed by myth and mysticism. Her collections include *The Rising Fire* (1963); *A Breakfast for Barbarians* (1966); *The Shadow-Maker* (1969); *Magic Animals* (1975); *The T. E. Lawrence Poems* (1982), mimicking the voice of Lawrence; *Earthlight* (1982); and *After Worlds* (1985). *The Poetry of Gwendolyn MacEwen: The Early Years* (1993) and *The Poetry of Gwendolyn MacEwen: The Later Years* (1994) were edited by Margaret Atwood and Barry Callaghan.

Macfadden, Bernarr [or **Bernard**] (1868–1955), physical culturist, editor. Born in Missouri, Macfadden, an astonishing personality, furnished reading matter, advice, and stimulation to millions. He advocated a number of physical and dietary cults, which others called fads, but his own personal practice of them—including standing on his head and turning somersaults—continued to an extraordinary age. Among the evils against which he crusaded were alcohol, medicine, tobacco, corsets, prudishness, white bread, overeating, and muscular inactivity.

Macfadden had an exuberant gift for personal publicity. He began writing with a four-page pamphlet in the 1890s, but at the height of his success he was advocating the Macfadden road to physical and mental health and happiness to nearly fifteen million readers through ten newspapers, twenty magazines, and fifty books, including a multivolume *Macfadden Encyclopedia of Physical Culture*. He founded *Physical Culture* in 1898 and followed with a string of other magazines. Most influential was *True Story* (1919). Macfadden's first Physical Culture Show in Madison Square Garden (1904) was the forerunner of later bathing beauty contests. Macfadden went to jail and was heavily fined for nudity, another health fad he pioneered.

True Story started a flood of imitators among confession magazines, and this was also true of another innovation of Macfadden's. In 1924 he founded the first New York City tabloid, the *Graphic*. The paper died in 1932. He owned several other newspapers for a time. He published fiction in which heroines could always take care of themselves and any annoyers. His heroes often progressed from extreme emaciation and weakness to robust, handsome health—by following the Macfadden way and presumably by eating in the Macfadden Vegetarian Restaurants, of which he founded a large number. In the early 1940s Macfadden got into progressive financial difficulties, and minority stockholders bought out his string of publications, with a proviso that he would give them no direct competition for five years. In 1943 he bought back *Physical Culture*, which had lost circulation heavily when the new management tried to make it a beauty magazine. In 1946 he started a new magazine, *Bernarr Macfadden's Detective Magazine*. His divorced first wife, Mary Macfadden, in collaboration with EMILE GAUVREAU, wrote the story of their marriage in *Dumbbells and Carrot Strips: The Story of Bernarr Macfadden* (1952).

McFee, William [**Morley Punshon**] (1881–1966), novelist, short-story writer, essayist. Born in England, apprenticed at age seventeen to a firm of mechanical engineers, McFee ran away to sea in 1906 and served on ships until 1911, when he settled in the United States. His first book, *Letters from an Ocean Tramp* (1908), was followed by *Aliens* (1914, revised 1918) and *Casuals of the Sea* (1916), about an impoverished London suburban family, which he composed during his years at sea. In World War I he served in the British navy, and his experiences in the Mediterranean provided background for some of his later novels. *Command* (1922), one of his best novels, laid in Salonika, is the story of a mediocre man's rise to heroism. His other works include *Race* (1924); *Pilgrims of Adversity* (1928), set in Central and South America; *Sailors of Fortune* (1929), short stories; *North of Suez* (1930); *The Harbourmaster* (1932), the tragedy of a sea-loving man who stays on land; *The Beachcomber* (1935); *Derelicts* (1938); *Watch Below* (1940), about tramp steamers; *Spenlove in Arcady* (1941); *Family Trouble* (1949); and *The Adopted* (1952). Many of the stories are told by Chief Engineer Spenlove, whom McFee acknowledged as his "garrulous, ironic, goateed *alter ego*." His essays and autobiography are combined in *Harbours of Memory* (1921), *Swallowing the Anchor* (1925), *More Harbours of Memory* (1934), and *In the First Watch* (1946).

M'Fingal (1775, 1782), a burlesque epic by JOHN TRUMBULL. Trumbull was urged to write a satire on the loyalists, and this poem was the result. The first part appeared anonymously in 1775; later Trumbull divided this section into two cantos and added two more cantos. It was immensely popular, had numerous editions, and was widely pirated. Trumbull closely followed Samuel Butler's *Hudibras* (1663, 1664, 1678), using the same terse tetrameter couplets. The name M'Fingal recalls James Macpherson's alleged translation of the Gaelic bard Ossian; Fingal was an old Scots hero. In the poem M'Fingal is an inveterate loyalist who is such a blunderer in his arguments that they prove the opposite case; he is ultimately tarred and feathered. Toward the end of the poem M'Fingal gloomily foresees the triumph of the rebels. See HARTFORD WITS.

McGee, Travis.   See MACDONALD, JOHN D.

McGinley, Phyllis (1905–1978),   writer of light verse. Born in Oregon, McGinley was a frequent contributor to *The New Yorker* and other magazines, known for her clever and humorous poems about various aspects of modern life. Among her best-known collections of verse are *A Pocketful of Wry* (1940), *Love Letters* (1954), *Times Three: Selected Verse from Three Decades* (1960, Pulitzer Prize), and *Christmas Con and Pro* (1971). She also wrote essays and numerous books for children.

Macgowan, Kenneth (1888–1963),   drama critic, publicity director, play director, historian, teacher. Macgowan was a drama and movie critic, worked as a publicity man in Hollywood, directed plays, produced movies, and taught theater at the University of California. Among his books are *The Theater of Tomorrow* (1921), *Continental Stagecraft* (1922), *Masks and Demons* (1923), *Footlights Across America* (1929), *The Early Stone Age in the New World* (1948), *Early Man in the New World* (1950), and *A Primer of Playwriting* (1951). Macgowan became deeply interested in anthropology, an interest awakened by his book on the masks used by primitive peoples.

MacGrath, Harold (1871–1932),   newspaperman, novelist. Born in Syracuse, New York, MacGrath worked for various newspapers in his native state before turning to writing novels. His third book, *The Man on the Box* (1904), became a best seller. It was promptly dramatized and later made into a film. It tells the story of a young man of good family who works as a groom in the family of the young lady he loves, prevents her father from selling important documents to a foreign country, and marries the girl. Other novels followed: *The Princess Elopes* (1905), *The Carpet from Bagdad* (1920), *Drums of Jeopardy* (1911), and others. MacGrath called them "fairytales for grown-ups." He also wrote PERILS OF PAULINE, a silent-movie serial.

McGuane, Thomas [Francis] (1939–   ),   novelist, short-story writer. Born in Michigan and educated at Michigan State University, the Yale School of Drama, and Stanford, McGuane has lived for a number of years in Montana. He is a comic novelist of singular talent, with his best work rich in human understanding and effectively grounded in the locales he knows best. In his first novel, *The Sporting Club* (1969), he takes great delight in the destruction of a wealthy private club in northern Michigan. *The Bushwhacked Piano* (1971) finds humor on the road in a scheme to make money from bats. *Nobody's Angel* (1979) and *Something to Be Desired* (1984) display older Montana verities in conflict with lives defined in part by new money from elsewhere. His other novels are *Ninety-two in the Shade* (1973), about fishing off Florida; *Panama* (1978), set in Key West; and *Keep the Change* (1989), set in New York and Montana. His stories are collected in *To Skin a Cat* (1986). *An Outside Chance* (1980) contains essays on sports. *Some Horses* (1999) is a collection of essays about the cutting horses on his ranch. *The Longest Silence: A Life in Fishing* (1999) collects thirty-three essays on fishing in various parts of the world.

McGuffey, William Holmes (1800–1873),   educator, textbook complier. Born in Pennsylvania, McGuffey was edu-cated at Washington and Jefferson College. He taught at Miami University, was president of Cincinnati College and Ohio University, and later taught at Woodward College and the University of Virginia. McGuffey was known to thousands of Americans as the author of their first schoolbook; in fact, it is said of the author of the "Eclectic Readers" that he taught America to read. The series began in 1836 with the *First* and *Second Readers*. The *Primer*, *Third*, and *Fourth Readers* appeared in 1837, the *Speller* in 1838, the *Rhetorical Guide* in 1841, the *Fifth Reader* in 1844, the *Sixth* in 1857. His younger brother, Alexander Hamilton McGuffey, collaborated in the "Eclectic Series" and probably compiled the *Speller* and the *Fifth Reader* without his brother's assistance. In all, the books sold 122 million copies, with new editions appearing well into the 20th century. They combined moral lessons with extracts from literature and helped shape the tastes of generations of Americans.

Machado de Assis, Joachim María (1839–1908), Brazilian novelist and poet. Widely regarded as Brazil's greatest novelist, Machado de Assis was born in Rio de Janeiro, the son of a house painter and a Portuguese woman from the Azores. Orphaned early, he had only a primary school education, but read widely while he supported himself as a typesetter and journalist, and in his mid-twenties he began to gain recognition as a writer. In 1869 he married a Portuguese woman of distinguished family and, although afflicted with epilepsy, led a conventional private life. In 1897 he became the first president of the Brazilian Academy of Letters and served until his death.

His novels have been compared with the novels of HENRY JAMES in their concern for psychology and for problems of narrative perspective. In Machado's work the first-person narrator generally chosen proves also to be the major character. Questions of interpretation arise, with the reader forced to consider that the version presented may not be the only one. The most celebrated are *Memórias póstumas de Brás Cubas* (1881, tr. *Epitaph of a Small Winner*, 1952), a comic, Sterne-like narrative by a man who is dead; *Quincas Borba* (1891, tr. *Philosopher or Dog?* 1954); *Dom Casmurro* (1900), generally considered his masterpiece; *Esaú e Jacó* (1904, tr. *Esau and Jacob*, 1966); and *Memorial de Aires* (1908). All develop ironic visions of life, bleak and sometimes despairing, with more than a little attention paid, especially in *Dom Casmurro*, to the telling of the story rather than to the story itself. Two early works are *Helena* (1876, tr. 1984) and *Iaiá Garcia* (1878, tr. *Yayd Garcia*, 1976). Machado also wrote poetry and more than 200 short stories. His *Obras completas* appeared in 1952.

McHenry, James (1785–1845),   novelist, dramatist, poet, critic. McHenry, born in Ireland, admired Sir Walter Scott, Anne Radcliffe, and James Fenimore Cooper. His first publications were a collection of verse, *The Pleasures of Friendship* (1822), and a poem on the Revolution called *Waltham* (1823). Then appeared several historical romances, all published anonymously. In his periodical writings he sometimes used the pen name Solomon Secondsight. His two best-known novels appeared in 1823; *The Wilderness, or Braddock's Times* and *The Spectre of the Forest*. The former concerns an Irish family living in the wilderness near Fort Duquesne. The latter is set in 17th-century New England. McHenry also wrote *O'Halloran, or, the Insurgent Chief* (1824) and *Meredith* (1831), and he published a blank-verse tragedy, *The Usurper* (1827).

McHugh, Vincent (1904–1983), newspaperman, poet, novelist, critic folklorist, teacher, screenwriter. Born in Providence, Rhode Island, McHugh wrote the eccentric *Caleb Catlum's America* (1936), about a folk hero who roams through American history, meeting everyone from Ben Franklin to the latest radio comedian. Among McHugh's other novels are *Touch Me Not* (1930), *Sing Before Breakfast* 1933), *I Am Thinking of My Darling* (1943), and *The Victory* (1947). A volume of poems is *The Blue Hen's Chickens* (1947).

McInerney, Jay (1955–   ), novelist. Born in Hartford, Connecticut, McInerney was educated at Williams. For a time a fact checker for *The New Yorker*, he won praise with *Bright Lights, Big City* (1984), a novel narrated in the second person about the frenzied life of a young man with a similar position in Manhattan. His fine comic voice also animates *Ransom* (1985), a novel set in Japan. Another novel is *The Story of My Life* (1988). In *Brightness Falls* (1992), a successful couple fail in the New York stock market and publishing worlds. *Last of the Savages* (1996) covers three decades in the lives of prep school roommates. *Model Behavior: A Novel and 7 Stories* (1998) is a satire on celebrity in the 90s; *How It Ended* (2000) is a story gathering.

MacInnes, Helen [Clark] (1907–1985), novelist. Born in Scotland, MacInnes, wife of the distinguished scholar Gilbert Highet, was best known as the author of novels of adventure and espionage distinguished by their literate style. These include *Above Suspicion* (1941), *Assignment in Brittany* (1942), *Horizon* (1946), *Neither Five Nor Three* (1951), *Pray for a Brave Heart* (1955), *North from Rome* (1958), *Decision at Delphi* (1960), *The Salzburg Connection* (1968), *Message from Málaga* (1971), *Prelude to Terror* (1978), *The Hidden Target* (1980), and *Cloak of Darkness* (1982). Set in a wide variety of European and American backgrounds, these novels combine suspenseful action with an unusually accurate depiction of the local people and their surroundings.

MacInnes, Tom [Thomas Robert Edward] (1867–1951), lawyer, public official, poet. Born in Dresden, Ontario, MacInnes went to China and studied Chinese poetry and philosophy, later writing a book about Lao-tzu, *The Teaching of the Old Boy*. Vancouver became his home in later years. MacInnes's poetry shows the influence of such diverse poets as Villon, Poe, and Whitman, as well as the influence of Chinese philosophy. Among his collections are *Lonesome Bar and Other Poems* (1909), *In Amber Lands* (1910), *Rhymes of a Rounder* (1913), *The Fool of Joy* (1918), *Complete Poems* (1923), and *In the Old of My Age* (1947).

McIntyre, John T[homas] (1871–1951), newspaperman, writer. Born in Philadelphia, McIntyre wrote detective stories under the pen name Kerry O'Neil, juveniles—the Buckskin Series, and historical romances—*Blowing Weather*

(1923), *Stained Sails* (1928), and *Drums in the Dawn* (1932). The romances were about pirates, John Paul Jones, and the American Revolution, respectively. He also wrote realistic stories, such as *The Ragged Edge* (1902); *Slag* (1927); *Steps Going Down* (1936), a story of the Philadelphia underworld that he regarded as his greatest achievement; *Ferment* (1937); and *Signing Off* (1938). With Arnold Daly, the actor who appeared in it, he wrote the melodrama *Wedding Journey*, too strongly realistic for audiences of his time. Later he wrote a fantasy, *Young Man's Fancy*, produced in 1919 and turned into a novel in 1925.

McKay, Claude (1889–1948), poet, novelist. Born in Jamaica, McKay wrote one of the first novels by an African-American to reach a wide readership, *Home to Harlem* (1928), which tells the story of a black soldier returned from France after World War I. As a young man in Jamaica, McKay, a member of the native constabulary, had written dialect verses that were widely circulated in the colony. Two collections were published, *Songs of Jamaica* (1911) and *Constab Ballads* (1912). He came to the United States in 1912, attended school for a while, worked as a Pullman porter, and began to write again. He became an important figure in the Harlem Renaissance of the 1920s, drifted into Communism, visited Russia, and lived for a while in France. He published two more volumes of verse: *Spring in New Hampshire and Other Poems* (1920) and *Harlem Shadows* (1922); also several stories and novels, including *Banjo* (1929), a story of Marseilles; *Gingertown* (1931), short stories; and *Banana Bottom* (1933), set in Jamaica. His novels are often vividly realistic, *Banana Bottom* perhaps the best. McKay told the story of his life in *A Long Way from Home* (1937) and wrote *Harlem: Negro Metropolis* (1940).

MacKaye, Percy [Wallace] (1875–1956), teacher, poet, playwright. Born in New York City and educated at Harvard and Leipzig, Percy MacKaye taught in a private school in New York City and then became a member of the Cornish, New Hampshire, colony of artists and writers. *The Canterbury Pilgrims* (1903), a fanciful blankverse play concerning the Wife of Bath's pursuit of Chaucer, was followed by two more poetic dramas, produced by E. H. SOTHERN and Julia Marlowe, *Jeanne d'Arc* (1906) and *Sappho and Phaon* (1907). THE SCARECROW (1908), a prose play based on Hawthorne's FEATHERTOP, was successful here and abroad and was made into a film. MacKaye was much interested in pageantry, community theater, and folk drama. *The Playhouse and the Play* (1909), *The Civic Theatre* (1912), and *Community Drama* (1917) deal with production problems. *St. Louis* was a community masque for 7,500 actors (1914). His other works include *Sanctuary, A Bird Masque* (1913); *A Thousand Years Ago* (1914), a poetic drama laid in China; *Caliban, by the Yellow Sands* (1916), a community masque to commemorate the Shakespeare tercentenary; *Rip Van Winkle* (1920), a libretto for Reginald DeKoven's opera; *This Fine-Pretty World* (1923), a comedy of folk ways; *Kentucky Mountain Fantasies* (1926), one-act plays about mountaineers; *Tall Tales of the Kentucky Mountains* (1928); *Songs of a Day* (1929); *Poog's Pasture* (1938); and *What We*

Will (1943). He edited *The Modern Reader's Chaucer* (1912) with J. S. P. Tatlock and wrote a biography of his father STEELE MACKAYE. His early poetic works were collected in *Poems and Plays* (2 v. 1916). MacKaye's most ambitious work was a tetralogy of verse plays, *The Mystery of Hamlet, King of Denmark—or What We Will* (1949), tracing the histories of the major characters in Shakespeare's tragedy up to the time the play begins.

MacKaye, [James Morrison] Steele (1842–1894), dramatist, painter, actor, inventor. Born in Buffalo, New York, MacKaye studied painting with George Inness and other American painters and studied later in Paris. He served in the army during the Civil War and later acted at the Bowery Theater, painted, and ran an art store. After studying in Paris with François Delsarte (1811–1871), he established a school of acting in New York City. In 1872 he produced *Monaldi*, a play he adapted from the French. In 1873 he gave *Hamlet* in French in Paris, then went on to London to give it in English.

Back in the United States, he wrote and produced plays, established theaters, and initiated many innovations, including overhead lighting, the moving or "double" stage, the disappearing orchestra pit, and folding chairs. Meanwhile, his plays frequently were successful, particularly HAZEL KIRKE (1880), and *Paul Kauvar: or Anarchy* (1887), about the French Revolution. One of MacKaye's last achievements was the planning of a huge amphitheater, the Spectatorium, for the Chicago World's Fair (1892–93), where he gave a play about Columbus called *The World Finder*, for which Anton Dvořák wrote his *New World Symphony*. MacKaye's son PERCY MACKAYE wrote *Epoch, the Life of Steele MacKaye, Genius of the Theater* (1927).

McKenney, Ruth (1911–1972), newspaper-woman, memoirist, novelist, sociological writer. McKenney was born in Mishawaka, Indiana. Although known best as a humorist, she also wrote a careful investigation of economic and social conditions in Akron, Ohio, in the years 1932 to 1936: INDUSTRIAL VALLEY (1939). For a time McKenney was a member of the Communist Party, but was expelled for "left deviationism." Most of her writing has been devoted to humorous accounts of her family affairs. *My Sister Eileen* (1938) was a best seller and later was made into a successful play (1941) and a musical, *Wonderful Town* (1953). The play and the musical were filmed in 1942 and 1954, respectively. McKenney's sister Eileen and the novelist NATHANAEL WEST, Eileen's husband, were killed in an automobile accident three days before *My Sister Eileen* opened on Broadway. McKenney wrote about her grandfather in *The Loud Red Patrick* (1947). *Love Story* (1950) is about her own marriage. The books about her sister were gathered into an omnibus volume, *All About Eileen* (1952). *Far, Far from Home* (1954) is another volume of reminiscences, and *Mirage* (1956) is a novel.

MacKenzie, Sir Alexander (1764–1820), fur trader, explorer, memoirist. A Scottish immigrant, Mackenzie entered the fur trade in Canada and made many trips of exploration in western Canada. Later he wrote *Voyages from Montreal on the River St. Lawrence, Through the Continent of North America to the Frozen and Pacific Oceans, in the Years 1789 and 1793* (1801).

McKuen, Rod (1933–   ), poet, songwriter. Born in California, McKuen became a popular author of sentimental poems and songs gathered in books that include *Stanyan Street and Other Sorrows* (1966), *Listen to the Warm* (1967), *Come to Me in Silence* (1973), and *Looking for a Friend* (1980). A prose work is *Finding My Father* (1976), about his search for the father he never knew.

McLachlan, Alexander (1818–1896), poet. Born in Scotland, McLachan emigrated to Upper Canada in 1840, and later lived in Ontario. A farmer and tailor, he became known as the Burns of Canada for his poems of honest work and simple pleasures. His books include *The Emigrant and Other Poems* (1861) and *Poems and Songs* (1874). *Poetical Works* was published in 1900 (reprinted with additions, 1974).

McLean, Sarah Pratt (1856–1935), novelist. McLean, born in Connecticut, wrote some of her novels under her married name, Sarah P. McLean Greene. Her first book dealt with *Cape Cod Folks* (1881), and in all her books she emphasized New England local color. Among them are *Some Other Folks* (1882), *Towhead* (1883), *Vesty of the Basins* (1892), *The Moral Imbeciles* (1898), *Last Chance Junction* (1899), *Flood-Tide* (1901), *Winslow Plain* (1902), *Deacon Lysander* (1904), and *Everbreeze* (1913).

MacLeish, Archibald (1892–1982), poet, playwright, public servant, teacher. Born in Illinois, MacLeish was educated at Yale and Harvard Law School. With the entry of the United States into World War I in 1917, he shipped to France, where he saw action in the second Battle of the Marne. After graduation in 1919, MacLeish taught constitutional law at Harvard and practiced law in Boston. In 1923 he and his wife, Ada, moved to Paris with their two young children—he to devote himself to poetry and she to establish herself as a concert soprano.

"American Letter" in *New Found Land* (1930) announced his rediscovery of America—while expressing the poet's nostalgia for France—after his return to the States in 1928. From 1929 to 1938 MacLeish worked as an editor of Fortune. His articles in support of the New Deal—together with his controversial public poetry, such as the satirical FRESCOES FOR MR. ROCKEFELLER'S CITY (1933), and his topical, pioneering radio plays, THE FALL OF THE CITY (1937) and *Air Raid* (1938)—led to his official involvement in public affairs. Within a year after his appointment as the first curator of Harvard's Nieman Foundation of Journalism, MacLeish became Librarian of Congress. His reorganization of the institution transformed it into a modern library during his tenure (1939–44). He tried in *The Irresponsibles* (1940) to alarm his own disillusioned generation, betrayed into war by Wilsonian idealism, to the reality of a new German threat. Publication of this controversial pamphlet led to his appointment first as director of the short-lived Office of Facts and Figures and then as associate director of its successor, the Office of War Information, which disseminated propaganda. As an assistant secretary of state (1944–45), MacLeish was instrumental in the formation of UNESCO.

In 1949 he became Boylston Professor of Rhetoric and Oratory at Harvard. During the 1950s he spearheaded the successful campaign by T. S. ELIOT, ROBERT FROST, and ERNEST HEMINGWAY to obtain the release of EZRA POUND from St. Elizabeth's Hospital. *Poetry and Experience* (1961), MacLeish's only volume of literary criticism, derived from his lectures at Harvard. He retired to Conway, Massachusetts, in 1962.

A verse dramatist whose first play for the stage, PANIC (1935), featured Martha Graham and Orson Welles, and whose Broadway hit *J. B.* (1958) captured both a Pulitzer Prize and a Tony Award, MacLeish owes his literary reputation nonetheless to his poetry. From the early *Cantos* of Pound, Arthur Waley's translations of Chinese poems, the work of French poet St.-John Perse (Alexis Léger), and the descriptive prose of Hemingway, MacLeish forged his own distinctive idiom. "You, Andrew Marvell" and the lesser "Ars Poetica"— with its imagistic thesis, "A poem should not mean /But be"— remain his most often anthologized poems, but "Memorial Rain," " 'Not Marble Nor the Gilded Monuments," "Epistle To Be Left in the Earth," "Cook Country," and "Calypso's Island" are no less memorable. The best of his topical poems, "Invocation to the Social Muse," probes the literary and political tensions of the 1930s. The first of MacLeish's two Pulitzer Prizes for poetry went to CONQUISTADOR (1932), a lyric epic in experimental *terza rima* about the Spanish conquest of Mexico. *Collected Poems, 1917–1952*, since superseded by the posthumous *Collected Poems 1917–1982* (1985), won both the Pulitzer Prize and the Bollingen Prize in 1953. *Six Plays* (1980) collects much of the verse drama.

Volumes of occasional prose include *A Continuing Journey* (1967) and *Riders on the Earth* (1978). Warren V. Bush of CBS News assembled *The Dialogues of Archibald MacLeish and Mark Van Doren* (1964) from film. R. H. Winnick edited *Letters of Archibald MacLeish, 1907–1982* (1983). MacLeish saw as "the autobiography of my professional life" *Archibald MacLeish: Reflections* (eds., Bernard A. Drabeck and Helen E. Ellis, 1986). See THE HAMLET OF A. MACLEISH.

DAVID HAVIRD

McLellan, Isaac (1806–1899), poet, sportsman, lawyer. Born in Maine, McLellan wrote verses about hunting and nature. Many of his poems appeared first in magazines such as *Forest and Stream* and the *American Angler*. Collections of his poems include *The Fall of the Indian, with Other Poems* (1830), *Mount Auburn and Other Poems* (1843), *Poems of the Rod and Gun, or Sports by Flood and Field* (1886), and *Haunts of Wild Game* (1896).

MacLennan, Hugh (1907–1990), novelist, essayist. Born in Nova Scotia, MacLennan grew up in Halifax and was educated at Dalhousie, Oxford, and at Princeton, where he studied classics. He began writing while teaching at a boy's school near Montreal. His first novel, *Barometer Rising* (1941), tells of the devastating explosion in Halifax harbor in 1917 that MacLennan had experienced as a boy. A great success in Canada, it seemed to many to mark a new national consciousness for Canadian fiction, a strong initial thrust in a direction long awaited. Edmund Wilson called it "a landmark in Canadian writing" and an "authentic classic." With a Guggenheim Fellowship that enabled him to spend a year writing in New York City, MacLennan next completed *Two Solitudes* (1945), a novel bringing together French Canadians and English Canadians in a clarification of what seemed now his major theme: the unification of separate elements into a Canadian whole. A best seller, it enabled him to give up teaching for full-time writing. His later novels are *The Precipice* (1948), set in a fictional town in Ontario and in New York and Princeton; *Each Man's Son* (1951), set in his native town, Glace Bay; *The Watch That Ends the Night* (1959), hugely successful and praised for its psychological depth; *Return of the Sphinx* (1967), set amidst the disorders of the 1960s; and *Voices in Time* (1980), a postnuclear holocaust novel. His essays are collected in *Cross-Country* (1949), *Thirty and Three* (1955), *Scotchman's Return* (1960), *The Other Side of Hugh MacLennan* (1978), and *On Being a Maritime Writer* (1984).

Mac Low, Jackson (1922–   ), poet, playwright. Born in Chicago and educated there and at Brooklyn College, Mac Low began composing verbal texts by "nonintentional" methods in the 1950s. His series on the presidents of the United States (1963), for instance, is based on a structure of images taken from the Phoenician meanings of the letters of the presidents' names. His poetry, often performed with dancers and musicians, may utilize randomizing computer programs or acrostics to minimize authorial intrusion and emphasize language. Among his collections are *22 Light Poems* (1968), *Representative Works, 1938–1985* (1986) and *Barnesbook: Four Poems Derived from Sentences by Djuna Barnes* (1996). Plays include *Verdurous Sanguinaria* (1967), *The Twin Plays: Port-au-Prince and Adams County Illinois* (1966) and *The Pronouns: A Collection of 40 Dances—For the Dancers* (1971).

McLuhan, [Herbert] Marshall (1911–1980), cultural critic, communications theorist. Born in Edmonton, Alberta, McLuhan was educated at the University of Manitoba and Cambridge University. He taught in the U.S. before returning to Canada in 1944, where he taught mostly at the University of Toronto, founding the Center of Culture and Technology there in 1963. In *The Mechanical Bride: Folklore of Industrial Man* (1951), he examined the effects of popular culture and advertising. In *The Gutenberg Galaxy: The Making of Typographic Man* (1962), he examined the effects on humans of the invention of print and the spread of electronic technology; the world, he said, had become a global village. In *Understanding Media: The Extension of Man* (1964), he proposed that "the medium is the message," as "print man" is turned into "electronic man"; this idea was extended in *The Medium Is the Massage* (1967) to a view of humans passively accepting manipulation be by electronic signals. His witty, aphoristic style did not endear him to some readers, but many others found in his work a wellspring of sharp insights and stimulating ideas. His other books include *Peace and War in the Global Village* (1968) and *The Interior Landscape: The Literary Criticism of Marshall McLuhan 1943–62* (1969), edited by Eugene McNamara.

McManus, George (1884–1954),   cartoonist. Born in St. Louis, McManus created numerous enduring characters in his comic strips "Bringing Up Father," "The Newly Weds," "Let George Do It," and others. He began as a cartoonist with the St. Louis *Republic* in 1899 and went on to papers in New York and to syndication. "Bringing Up Father" began about 1913 and ran on for many years, appearing in more than 750 papers all over the world and in twenty-seven languages; seven shows featuring "Father" toured the country for more than a decade, and radio programs, television shows, and movies were based on it, and on its central characters, Maggie and Jiggs. McManus wrote *Fun for All* (1948).

MacMillan, Donald B[axter]   (1874–1970), explorer, teacher, ethnologist, writer. Born in Massachusetts, MacMillan began his career as a teacher of classical languages, first went to the northern polar regions in 1910, and conducted ethnological investigations among the Eskimos in 1911–1912. Thereafter, he headed numerous expeditions in the Arctic region, and added greatly to geographical and ethnological knowledge. He wrote *Four Years in the White North* (1918), *Etah and Beyond* (1927), *Kahda* (1929), *How Peary Reached the Pole* (1932), and *Eskimo Place Names* (1943). His wife, Miriam, recounted her voyages with him in *Green Seas and White Ice* (1948).

McMillan, Terry (1951–   ), short-story writer, novelist. Bom in Port Huron, Michigan, McMillan was educated at the University of Califonia-Berkeley and Columbia University. At age twenty-fve she sold her first short story. *Mama* (1987) started out as a short story and was expanded to a novel during a stay at the MACDOWELL artists' colony. It tells of Mildred Peacock's struggles to raise her five children alone. *Disappearing Acts* (1989) alternates the narrative between two main characters of different background who are in love, but struggling to stay together. *Waiting to Exhale* (1992), the story of four professional women with everything but love, and *How Stella Got Her Groove Back* (1996), about a successful business woman's trip to Jamaica, were both made into motion pictures. *A Day Late and a Dollar Short* (2001) is a survey of the multigenerational Price family's difficulties. McMillan is the editor of *Breaking Free: An Anthology of Contemporary African-American Fiction* (1990).

McMurtry, Larry [Jeff] (1936–   ), novelist. McMurtry grew up in North Texas on a family ranch near Archer City, surrounded by the scenes of much of his best fiction. He was educated at Rice and Stanford and from the start had a way with Texas and Texans and the narrative pull of a good Western story. His first novel, *Horseman, Pass By* (1961), formed the basis for the movie *Hud* (1963). This and *Leaving Cheyenne* (1963) dealt with conflicts between old ways of life and the new ways mandated by government and big business; nostalgia is not the main point, however, as the myth of the

Old West impacts in some ways negatively on the present. *The Last Picture Show* (1966) presents the town of Thalia (modeled on Archer City) as an emblem of a vanishing culture. McMurtry was coauthor of the script for the movie (1971). *Texasville* (1989) is set in the same town at a later time; the Pulitzer Prize–winning *Duane's Depressed* (1999) completes the trilogy. McMurtry's best work is *Lonesome Dove* (1985), a novel of epic scope that chronicles an 1870s cattle drive from Texas to Montana; it was made into a hugely successful television miniseries. *Streets of Laredo* (1993) continues the *Lonesome Dove* saga. Having brought back the body of his partner, Augustus McCrae, Woodrow Call now pursues two killers across the Pecos into northern Mexico. His other novels include *Terms of Endearment* (1975), turned into a major film (1983); *Somebody's Darling* (1978), set in Hollywood; *Cadillac Jack* (1982), set in Washington, D.C.; *The Desert Rose* (1983), set in Las Vegas; *Anything for Billy* (1988), the story of Billy the Kid narrated by a writer of bad dime novels; *Some Can Whistle* (1989), about a rich novelist and *Boone's Lick* (2000). In *Buffalo Girls* (1990), McMurtry again portrays the Wild West. His nonfiction is collected in *In a Narrow Grave: Essays on Texas* (1971), *Flim Flam: Essays on Hollywood* (1987), *Walter Benjamin at the Dairy Queen: Reflections at Sixty and Beyond* (1999) and *Roads: Driving America's Great Highways* (2000).

McNally, Terrence (1939–   ), playwright. Born in Florida, McNally grew up in Texas and was educated at Columbia University. *And Things That Go Bump in the Night* (1964) failed on Broadway, but impressed some audiences with its comic portrayal of a family protected from the outside world by an electric fence. Later plays have established McNally's continuing comic power. Among the best are *Where Has Tommy Flowers Gone?* (1971), about an innocent adrift in New York; *Bad Habits* (1971), pairing two short plays called *Ravenswood* and *Dunelawn* set in sanitoriums, one permissive, the other restrictive; and *The Ritz* (1974, filmed 1976), his most popular play, about a man trying to escape his homicidal brother-in-law by hiding in a Turkish bath patronized by gay men. *Lisbon Traviata* (1985) is a tragicomedy about two gay men who are fixated on a pirated version of a performance by the opera singer Maria Callas. *Frankie and Johnnie in the Clair de Lune* (1987) is a romantic comedy. Frankie is a waitress in the coffee shop where Johnny mans the grill; Frankie is reluctant to continue the romantic relationship that Johnnie badly wants. McNally wrote the screenplay for the film version. *Lips Together, Teeth Apart* (1991) is set in a Fire Island beach house willed to a woman by her brother who died of AIDS and deals with marital failure, homophobia, and fear of death. McNally won four Tony Awards in the 90s: for his book for the musical version of MANUEL PUIG's *Kiss of the Spider Woman* (1992), and for his book for the musical version of E. L. DOCTOROW's *Ragtime* (1993), *Love! Valour! Compassion*, a play about the lives and relationships of eight gay men who vacation in an upstate New York country house (1995), and *Master Class*, a biographical play about Maria Callas (1996). *The Full Monty*, a play based on the English film about male strippers, appeared on Broadway in 2000.

McNickle, D'Arcy (1904–1977),   novelist, historian. Born in St. Agnatius, Montana, McNickle grew up as a Flathead (or Salish) Indian on a reservation in Montana and was educated at the University of Montana, Oxford, and the University of Grenoble. He directed the Newberry Library Center for the History of American Indians and was a cofounder of the National Congress of American Indians. His first novel treated a man who, like McNickle, was of mixed descent; his protagonist in *The Surrounded* (1936) is torn between the world of his Flathead mother and the world of his Spanish father. *Wind from an Enemy Sky* (1978), another novel, also treats cultural conflicts. *Runner in the Sun* (1954) is a novel for young people about ancient cliff dwellers in New Mexico. McNickle's studies and histories include *They Came Here First* (1949), *The Indian Tribes of the United States* (1962), and *Native American Tribalism* (1973). *Indian Man* (1971) is a life of OLIVER LA FARGE. With Harold E. Fey, McNickle wrote *Indians and Other Americans* (1959).

McNulty, John (1896?–1956),   newspaperman, essayist, humorist. Born in Massachusetts and educated at Princeton, McNulty was an effortlessly funny journalist who contributed sketches about New York City's Third Avenue to *The New Yorker*. Chiefly reports of McNulty's observations in his favorite saloon, they were collected in *Third Avenue* (1946). Other adventures, recorded in *A Man Gets Around* (1951), concern Bellevue Hospital, the horse-breeding regions of Kentucky, and Ireland. McNulty also wrote *My Son Johnnie* (1955), a touching examination of the relationship between a father and a small boy. *The World of John McNulty* (1957) is a posthumous selection.

McPhee, John A[ngus] (1931–   ),   writer. Born in Princeton, New Jersey, and educated at Princeton, McPhee worked as an editor for *Time* magazine before becoming a staff writer for THE NEW YORKER. Since that time he has developed into one of America's finest writers of precise, lucid expository prose, a master at involving readers in his fascination with a wide range of earthly phenomena. Most of his work appears first in the pages of *The New Yorker*, shortly after in book form. His titles include *Oranges* (1967); *The Pine Barrens* (1968), about an unspoiled area of New Jersey; *Encounters with the Archdruid* (1972); *The Deltoid Pumpkin Seed* (1973), about experimental aircraft; *The Curve of Binding Energy* (1974), about the atomic bomb; *The Survival of the Bark Canoe* (1975), about a contemporary craftsman; *Coming into the Country* (1977), a masterful study of Alaska; *A Roomful of Hovings* (1979); *Giving Good Weight* (1980); and *La Place de la Concorde Suisse* (1984).

The *Annals of a Former World* series is comprised of four books on the geology of the United States: *Basin and Range* (1981) chronicles a cross-country trip with an advocate of plate tectonics theory; *In Suspect Territory* (1983) profiles Anita G. Harris, a geologist who feels that plate tectonics theory does not adequately explain the geology of the eastern

U.S.; *Rising from the Plains* (1986) and *Assembling California* (1993) complete the set. *Looking for a Ship* (1990) is the story of McPhee's voyage with the U.S. Merchant Marine. *Irons in the Fire* (1997) is a collection of essays on the men who enforce cattle-branding practices.

McPherson, James Alan (1943–   ),   short-story writer, essayist. McPherson, born in Georgia, was educated at Harvard and the University of Iowa (1969). An African-American, he has said that race as a factor should be kept in the background, and his cast of working class characters includes both African-Americans and whites. His stories are collected in *Hue and Cry* (1969) and *Elbow Room* (1977), for which he won a Pulitzer Prize. In 1981 he was made a MacArthur Fellow. *A Region Not Home: Reflections from Exile* (2000), an essay collection, follows the success of *Crabcakes* (1998) memoirs and essays.

McPherson, James M[unro] (1956–   ),   historian. Born in Valley City, North Dakota, McPherson is best known for his writing on the Civil War. He received his B.A. from Gustavus Adolphus College (1958) and his Ph.D. from Johns Hopkins University. His early writing focused on race relations and the Civil War. *The Struggle for Equality: Abolitionists and the Negro in the Civil War* (1962) won the Anisfield Wolff Award in Race Relations. McPherson won the Pulitzer Prize for *Battle Cry of Freedom: The Civil War Era* (1988), his bestselling and most highly acclaimed book. He has taught at Princeton University since 1962. His other works include *The Abolitionist Legacy: from Reconstruction to the NAACP* (1976); *Ordeal by Fire: The Civil War, and Reconstruction* (1981); *What They Fought For, 1861–1865* (1994) and *Is Blood Thicker than Water?: Crises of Nationalism in the Modern World* (1998).
SUZANNE PERKINS-HART

McPherson, Sandra (1943–   ),   poet. Born in California, McPherson was educated at San Jose State College and the University of Washington. Her poems of simple diction and precise observation are collected in *Elegies for the Hot Season* (1970), *Radiation* (1973), *The Year of Our Birth* (1978), *Patron Happiness* (1983), and *Streamers* (1988). *Edge Effect: Trails and Portrayals* and *The Spaces Between Birds: Mother/Daughter Poems 1967–1995* both appeared in 1996.

Macrae, David (1837–1907),   minister, missionary. Macrae, a Scotsman, visited America twice and wrote two books about his trips, *The Americans at Home* (1870, reprinted in the U.S. in 1952) and *America Revisited and Men I Have Met* (1908). He records his interviews with public men and authors, his observations on the post–Civil War South, and other topics.

MacSparran, James (1693–1757),   clergyman. An Anglican minister, MacSparran came from England to Rhode Island in 1721 and became embroiled in theological arguments when Calvinists attacked his book *The Sacred Dignity of the Christian Priesthood Vindicated* (1751). His *America Dissected* (1753) is a description of the colonies in letter form.

McTeague (1899),   a novel by FRANK NORRIS. A prime example of the American naturalistic novel, *McTeague* treats the gradual degeneration of a stupid, but initially harmless, giant of a man whose instincts are nearer brute than human. McTeague practices dentistry without a license in a poor section of San Francisco and marries Trina, who has just won $5,000 in a lottery. He soon loses his job and takes to drink. Trina becomes a miser, and McTeague murders her in a fit of rage and steals her money. Tracked down by her cousin, McTeague becomes the victim of his own violence.

McWilliams, Carey (1905–1980),   lawyer, sociologist, public official, biographer, editor. McWilliams wrote books on racial minorities: *Brothers Under the Skin* (1943); *Prejudice* (on Japanese in the United States, 1944); and *A Mask for Privilege: Anti-Semitism in America* (1948). Each book maintains the thesis that while prejudice cannot be outlawed by legislation, discrimination can be. McWilliams wrote on farm workers in *Factories in the Field* (1939) and *Ill Fares the Land* (1942). His other books are *Southern California Country* (1946); *California: The Great Exception* (1949); *Witch Hunt: The Revival of Heresy* (1950) about civil rights; and *The Education of Carey McWilliams* (1979), a memoir. From 1955 to 1979 he edited *The Nation.*

Macy, John [Albert] (1877–1932),   critic, literary historian, editor. Macy was literary editor of the Boston *Herald* (1913–14), of *The Nation* (1922–23). His book on *The Spirit of American Literature* (1913) encourages us to no longer put up with literary names that "persist by the inertia of reputation." He reviewed sixteen major authors from Irving to James and made a plea for regionalism and the use of native materials. He also wrote *Socialism in America* (1916), *The Story of the World's Literature* (1925), and *About Women* (1930). His wife, Anne Sullivan Macy, was the teacher of HELEN KELLER.

Madame Butterfly (*Century Magazine*, January 1898), a short story by JOHN LUTHER LONG, the basis for a drama by Long and David Belasco (1900) and the opera (1906) by Puccini (1858–1924). It is the story of a young Japanese woman who is tricked into believing she is the wife of an American naval officer; when he deserts her, she commits suicide.

Madame Delphine (1881),   a novelette by GEORGE WASHINGTON CABLE. A quadroon, devoted to her almost-white daughter, attempts to assure her a happy marriage by telling her she is really the child of white parents. It did not please Southern readers opposed to miscegenation. Together with other stories on similar themes, it was responsible for the harsh treatment that drove Cable to leave the South.

Madeleva, Sister Mary.   See MARY EVALINE WOLFF.

Madgett, Naomi Long (1923–   ),   poet. Born in Virginia and educated at Virginia State College, Wayne State University, and the University of Detroit, Madgett has taught in the Detroit public schools and at Eastern Michigan University and, through her Lotus Press, encourages other African-American writers. Among her collections are *Pink Ladies in the Afternoon* (1972) and *Exits and Entrances* (1978). *Phantom Nightingale: Juvenilia 1934–1943* appeared in 1981, and *Remembrances of Spring: Collected Early Poems* in 1993.

Madison, Dolly [Payne Todd] (1768–1849),   memoirist, wife of JAMES MADISON. Dolly Madison was born in Guil-

ford County, North Carolina. Her personal recollections were published as *Memoirs and Letters* (1886). After marrying Madison in 1794, she became an increasingly important social figure in Washington and was the unofficial first lady of the widower Jefferson's administration and official White House hostess after her husband's inauguration in 1809. She survived her husband for more than thirteen years. She came back to Washington in 1837 as a social leader. Her means were scanty, and Congress bought some of her husband's papers for $30,000 and others, in 1848, for $25,000. She sent the first personal message over S. F. B. Morse's telegraph wires. Her domination of Washington society and political influence have made her a popular figure in biographies and historical romances.

Madison, James (1751–1836),   public official, pamphleteer, 4th president. Born in Port Conway, Virginia, Madison attended Princeton (then called the College of New Jersey) and was there converted to the doctrines of the Enlightenment and to 18th-century political radicalism. He helped organize the American Whig Society and became intimate with a circle that included PHILIP FRENEAU and HUGH HENRY BRACKENRIDGE. When the war broke out, Madison was made chairman of the Virginia Committee of Safety and wrote its resolutions against the British. He wrote pamphlets and was elected to the Virginia Constitutional Convention in 1776. As a member of GEORGE MASON's Committee to Prepare a Bill of Rights, he revised Mason's clause on religious freedom. He was a member of the first Virginia Assembly held under the new constitution, a member of the Governor's Council, and a member of the Continental Congress. Madison's energy, ability, and integrity were recognized by his fellow members, and he was given various important tasks. In 1784 he was back in the Virginia Assembly, where he helped to secure passage of Jefferson's bill for religious freedom.

Madison's association with THOMAS JEFFERSON was constantly close. Both were outstanding exemplars of the Enlightenment, both of a philosophic turn of mind, both practical enough to know when to leave theory and consistency behind. Between them they were instrumental in framing the CONSTITUTION and Bill of Rights. Madison's work at the Constitutional Convention (1787) was monumental, and his journals are the best source of information on the proceedings. He won an unexpected triumph against PATRICK HENRY in the Virginia ratifying convention (1788) when the latter opposed adoption of the Constitution. He contributed at least fourteen papers to THE FEDERALIST in a further attempt to get the Constitution adopted.

Madison became a member of Congress and, fearful of ALEXANDER HAMILTON's attempts to build a financial oligarchy, founded with Jefferson the Republican (later called the Democratic) Party. In 1794 Madison married the efficient and gracious widow Mrs. Dolly Payne Todd (see DOLLY MADISON), and in 1797 he retired from Congress. After Jefferson's election he served as Secretary of State.

Madison was elected president in 1808 and reelected in 1812. The major event of his second term was the War of 1812, brought about in part by his attempts to resist British aggression on the sea by enforcing an embargo. This second war with England was called by many angry citizens "Mr. Madison's War." In the later years of his administration he advocated tariff protection and a strong army.

Madison spent his last years on his estate at Montpelier, Virginia, where he prepared for publication his notes on the Constitutional Convention. He was a constant supporter of the African Colonization Society, which founded Liberia, and was aware that the "dreadful calamity" of slavery was incompatible with the principles of equality and freedom. Madison's papers and writings were collected by Gaillard Hunt in *The Writings of James Madison, His Public Papers and His Private Correspondence* (9 v. 1900–1910). His *Autobiography* was published in the *William and Mary Quarterly* in 1945. The fullest biography of Madison is that prepared in six volumes by Irving Brant (1941–61, abridged 1970). M. D. Peterson compiled a biography in Madison's own words (1974).

Madoc [Madog ab Owain Gwynedd] (1150?–1180?), a Welsh prince who according to Welsh legends sailed with ten ships westward and discovered America, supposedly about 1170. Zella Armstrong, in *Who Discovered America? The Amazing Story of Madoc* (1950), describes her collation of many references and passages in old texts and her resulting conviction that Madoc actually did cross the Atlantic and that his party left descendants here—certain blue-eyed Indians who have long puzzled anthropologists. One explorer, George Catlin, believed that the Mandans, a Siouan people of North Dakota, are descendants of Welsh immigrants. Robert Southey wrote an epic poem called *Madoc* (1805), which told how the Welsh chieftain sailed to America and founded a settlement after defeating a local tribe called Aztecas.

Madonna of the Future, The (*Atlantic Monthly*, March 1873; in *Madonna of the Future and Other Tales*, 1879), a story by HENRY JAMES. It concerns an artist who never manages to paint his perfect madonna, although he has dreamed of doing so for twenty years.

magazines. The magazines of colonial America not only were periodicals published by English settlers on a British frontier, but were frank imitations of the new and increasingly popular monthly miscellanies of the mother country. Nine years after England's first successful general monthly, the *Gentleman's Magazine*, appeared in 1731, Benjamin Franklin was making plans to demonstrate to his countrymen on both sides of the Atlantic that such a publication could originate in the New World. This wish to exhibit American culture to the world, especially to Britain, was transformed during and after the Revolution into a passion for developing and displaying a national American culture. Motives were not wholly altruistic, for publishers then and thereafter always had the hope, often ill-founded, of making money from their ventures.

How ill-founded these hopes were is shown by the fact that the nine monthlies and seven weeklies issued before the Revolution had an average life of ten months. Though the first project for an American magazine was Franklin's, his plans were betrayed to his rival printer in Philadelphia, Andrew Bradford, who managed to get his AMERICAN MAGAZINE [1] out three days before Franklin's GENERAL MAGAZINE; both were dated January 1741 though they were issued in mid-February. Published on the eve of the Revolution was Isaiah Thomas's *Royal American Magazine* (1774–75), with notable patriotic cartoons engraved on copper by Paul Revere. Only two monthlies were issued—for limited periods—during the Revolution, both in Philadelphia and both under distinguished literary editorship. Thomas Paine was editor for seven months of the *Pennsylvania Magazine* (1775–76) and Hugh Henry Brackenridge edited the *United States Magazine* throughout 1779.

In the last fifteen years of the 18th century, 71 magazines were begun, including 27 weekly miscellanies. They ranged from Maine to South Carolina, though Philadelphia was the leading publication center. Of the 71, only 15 survived for more than two years and only seven for more than five. Indeed, the average life of the magazines founded in the 18th century was twenty months. "The expectation of failure is connected with the very name of a Magazine," observed Noah Webster as he started his AMERICAN MAGAZINE [2] (1787–88).

The early monthlies were commonly modeled on English prototypes, small octavo in size, with some 64 pages printed on the durable rag paper of the times, often with advertising on the flimsy covers and occasionally with sparse illustration by woodcuts or copper plates. Probably three-fourths of the content was borrowed from books, pamphlets, newspapers, and other magazines. The Addisonian essay was a chief stock in trade. Though these were borrowed right and left, some were notable original contributions, as CHARLES BROCKDEN BROWN's first identified work, "The Rhapsodist," in the *Columbian Magazine* and JOSEPH DENNIE's early essays in the *Farmer's Museum*, of Walpole, Vermont. Poetry, reprinted and original, was found in virtually all 18th-century magazines. Mathew Carey's *American Museum* (1787–92), perhaps the best of the magazines of its century, furnished a good anthology of early American poetry. Forerunners of the American short story are found in tales and fragments of the English "sensibility" and Gothic schools. Religion, news and discussions of public affairs, and science (medicine, agriculture, meteorology) held important places in the offerings of these magazines.

At the turn of the century Brown, often called America's first man of letters, attempted four periodicals—two in New York and two in Philadelphia. He failed to win public favor for any of them, but the most successful was the *Literary Magazine and American Register* (1803–07). The shining light of those years was Joseph Dennie's weekly PORT FOLIO (1801–27), of Philadelphia, in which that brilliant essayist discussed manners and politics with gusto—the latter from an extreme Federalist point of view.

Greatest among representatives of the review type of periodical in all the history of American journalism was the NORTH AMERICAN REVIEW (1815–1940), edited for the first half of its life by a succession of Harvard scholars. The *North American* was for some years a participant in the third war with England—the paper war. A considerable part of this wordy conflict was devoted to defense of the young American literature against sneers by the English Tory reviews. The famous query of Sydney Smith in the *Edinburgh Review* in 1820, "In the four quarters of the globe, who reads an American book?" continued to annoy American critics for nearly a hundred years. Articles by Edward Everett in the *North American* were that review's main contributions in defense of the new nationalism, but Robert Walsh, editor of a heavy Philadelphia journal called *American Quarterly Review* (1827–37), was a general in the war. Philadelphia's *Analectic Magazine* (1813–21) was chiefly notable for the brief editorship (1813–14) of Washington Irving.

With improvements in printing and papermaking, together with what has been called the rise of the common man, the 1830s saw the beginnings of the first great monthlies of general circulation. GRAHAM'S MAGAZINE (1826–58) of Philadelphia was distinguished in literary content and in illustration, and it set a new standard of liberal payment for contributions. The KNICKERBOCKER MAGAZINE (1833–65) was New York's best-known magazine of this period, with a list of contributors rivaling that of *Graham's*. Chief Southern magazine of these years was the SOUTHERN LITERARY MESSENGER (1834–64), of Richmond, Virginia, edited by EDGAR ALLAN POE from 1835 to 1837. These magazines were well printed and usually ran to ninety-six pages or more.

The *Democratic Review* (1837–59) and the *American Whig Review* (1845–52), though largely political, offered much literary material. The former published some twenty-five pieces by HAWTHORNE, early tales by Walter (*sic*) Whitman, and work by BRYANT, WHITTIER, LONGFELLOW, and LOWELL during its uneven history. Its Whig contemporary offered Poe, Bryant, Lowell, and Greeley, as well as such political leaders as JOHN QUINCY ADAMS, DANIEL WEBSTER, and John C. Calhoun.

Important quarterlies of these years were the DIAL (1840–44), Boston exponent of New England transcendentalism, edited successively by Margaret Fuller and Ralph Waldo Emerson; and the *Southern Quarterly Review* (1842–57). The latter was founded in New Orleans, but soon moved to Charleston, South Carolina, and its last few numbers were issued from Columbia, South Carolina. William Gilmore Simms was editor of the *Southern* from 1849 to 1855. The commercial organ to the South, and to some extent that section's political spokesman and literary voice, was *De Bow's Review* (1846–80), of New Orleans. The *Massachusetts Quarterly Review* (1847–50) was edited by Emerson, Theodore Parker, and J. Elliot Cabot, and was devoted mainly to politics and literary criticism; it was once dubbed "the *Dial* with a beard."

Though several 18th-century magazines catered to women readers, the first to be specifically designed for them was the *Ladies' Magazine* (1792–93) of Philadelphia. But the first successful women's magazine, and the most successful of all antebellum magazines (reaching 150,000 circulation by 1860), was GODEY'S LADY'S BOOK (1830–98), notable for its fashion plates but also for its literary fare. Though its fiction and verse often seemed sentimental in what later critics thought a ridiculous degree, its liberal pay schedule attracted

most of the leading American authors. The chief competitor of *Godey's* for many years was *Peterson's Ladies' National Magazine* (1842–98), long edited by Ann S. Stephens, prolific author of serial fiction.

The urban miscellany designed for weekend reading became popular early in the 19th century. Nearly every city in the land had one or more of them in the first two-thirds of that century. They carried some news, usually emphasizing local society, sports, and amusements, but in the hands of able, idiosyncratic editors they might turn to emphasis on politics, literature of special type, or some specialized interest. Their popularity increased toward mid-century, and in 1852 Philadelphia had no less than sixteen of them. Longest-lived was the SATURDAY EVENING POST, founded in 1821 by Charles Alexander and S. C. Atkinson, two Philadelphia printers. This periodical enjoyed great success in the 1840s and 1850s, when it published the most popular English and American writers of serial fiction and shorter pieces by several distinguished authors, thereby achieving a national circulation. After the Civil War, Sunday editions of daily newspapers put many of the urban weekenders out of business, and the *Post* declined slowly toward bankruptcy until Cyrus H. K. Curtis bought it in 1897 and brought it to what seemed like a national institution under George Horace Lorimer's editorship (1899–1936).

Another urban miscellany of the original *Post* type was the distinguished *New York Mirror* (1823–57), edited mainly by GEORGE POPE MORRIS, now remembered, if at all, by his lines beginning, "O woodman, spare that tree!" and NATHANIEL PARKER WILLIS, poet and essayist. The NEW YORK LEDGER (1847–1903) was a storypaper not originally designed for weekend reading, but after the war it changed its publication day from Monday to Saturday. It claimed 400,000 circulation in 1860 and featured the serials of MRS. E. D. E. N. SOUTHWORTH and SYLVANUS COBB under the leadership of Robert Bonner, its publisher. High prices lured into *Ledger* pages such contributors as Bryant, Longfellow, Mrs. Stowe, Greeley, and Everett. The SATURDAY PRESS (1838–66) was the organ of the PFAFF'S CELLAR group in New York, among whom its editor, Henry Clapp, reigned as "prince of the Bohemians." It printed early Walt Whitman poems and Mark Twain's "Jumping Frog" story.

Later examples of the weekly of parochial design were the San Francisco papers *Argonaut* (1877–1958) and WASP (1876–1935); AMBROSE BIERCE enlivened the former with his column for its first two years, and then transferred to the latter, where he could sting with less constraint. *Reedy's Mirror* (1891–1920) of St. Louis was best remembered for its introduction of a rising group of Midwestern writers, and particularly for its publication of EDGAR LEE MASTERS's *Spoon River Anthology* pieces (see THE MIRROR). THE NEW YORKER (1925–   ) was a latecomer among urban weeklies. Harold Ross, editor until his death in 1951, declared at the beginning that his magazine was "avowedly published for a metropolitan audience," though he expected "a considerable national circulation" for it. A great national circulation was achieved, partly because New York is regarded by many as the cultural capital of the nation, and partly because of the editors' ability to attract and choose good writing on a great variety of subjects that appeal to the cultivated reader.

Returning to the field of the general monthly, we may note a new era in magazine publishing with the founding of HARPER'S NEW MONTHLY MAGAZINE in 1850. It soon reached 200,000 circulation, based largely on its copious illustration by woodcuts and its serial use of the work of the English novelists so popular in America at mid-century. Though several cheaper magazines undertook competition with *Harper's* in the new pattern, not for twenty years did another great book publisher challenge *Harper's* on even terms. *Scribner's Monthly* (1870–1930), using the same lavish illustration but more American materials, became a powerful rival. In 1881 it broke away from Charles Scribner's Sons and was published as the CENTURY ILLUSTRATED MONTHLY MAGAZINE. Scribners kept out of the magazine field for five years, as bound by its contract when it sold its *Monthly*, and then established SCRIBNER'S MAGAZINE (1886–1939), an illustrated monthly of high quality. Another illustrated periodical issued by a New York book publisher was *Appleton's Journal* (1869–81). Though founded as a weekly, it turned to monthly publication in 1876. With a great variety of comments on manners and on the arts, it also published serials by English, French, and German writers, many engravings of American scenery on steel, and woodcut fold-ins of metropolitan subjects.

Meanwhile, three other book publishers undertook monthly magazines of a high level, but without emphasis on illustration. PUTNAM'S MONTHLY MAGAZINE (1853–57) was, for its first three years at least, the best all-round quality magazine ever published in America. GEORGE WILLIAM CURTIS, PARKE GODWIN, Longfellow, Thoreau, Melville, and Cooper were frequent contributors. But the competition of the times briefly drove Putnam's out of this field; after the war it issued a second series, *Putnam's Magazine* (1868–70), a brief and less brilliant attempt, followed many years later by a third series (1906–10), which was an illustrated literary-review magazine.

Second of the quality monthlies without illustration to appear in the mid-century era was the ATLANTIC MONTHLY (1857–   ), issued for its first half century by a succession of Boston book publishers. It enjoyed distinguished editorship, beginning with that of JAMES RUSSELL LOWELL. Its roll of contributors included most of the leading American authors, and its literary standards were high. By the 1960s *Atlantic* and *Harper's* were the only survivors of the quality magazines of the 19th century.

The *Galaxy* (1866–78) was a kind of New York *Atlantic*, notable for publication of the work of HENRY JAMES, Mark Twain, RICHARD GRANT WHITE, Anthony Trollope, and Justin McCarthy. LIPPINCOTT'S MAGAZINE (1868–1916) of Philadelphia was a good monthly with a varied history. It printed many leading writers, with some emphasis on the south and midwest; it used some illustration until 1885, when it adopted the policy of printing an entire novel or novelette in each number. The OVERLAND MONTHLY (1868–1935) of San Francisco was first edited briefly by Bret Harte. Though a good literary magazine during most of its long life, it was later much given to regional promotion. The *Chautauquan* (1880–1914) was the organ of the Chautauqua Literary and Scientific Circle, and in its early years gave much space to readings for that great organization for adult education; eventually, it introduced greater variety, with strong emphasis on public affairs.

Henry Carter was born in Ipswich, England, the son of a glovemaker who was unsympathetic with the boy's inclinations toward art. But Henry smuggled out some drawings to the London *Illustrated News* that were published under the name "Frank Leslie." Some years later he left for London to learn the engraver's art, and when he was twenty-seven, he came to America, soon becoming chief engraver for *Gleason's Pictorial Drawing-Room Companion* (1851–59), America's first successful picture paper. Still working as "Frank Leslie," which became his legal name in 1857, he began publishing periodicals of his own in 1855. These all bore his name in the title, and all were copiously illustrated by woodcuts. They were in various fields—women's journals, juveniles, comics, etc. Best-known and most successful were *Frank Leslie's Illustrated Newspaper* (1855–1922) and *Frank Leslie's Popular Magazine* (1876–1956). (See FRANK LESLIE.) *Illustrated Newspaper* was the first important illustrated news weekly in the United States. Its pictorial coverage of the Civil War was notable. After the mid-1890s it flourished as *Leslie's Weekly*, using large pictures, short articles on general news events, personalities, sports, the theater, and humor. The monthly *Popular* became the AMERICAN MAGAZINE [5] in 1906, surviving for half a century thereafter as a good popular magazine. As for Frank Leslie, he speculated in real estate and went bankrupt in the depression of the mid-1870s. Several of the dozen periodicals he was then publishing were discontinued, and he died in 1880. His wife, a remarkable person of business acumen and energy herself, thereupon took the name "Frank Leslie" and carried on for some years with six of the original Leslie periodicals.

Begun shortly after Leslie's *Illustrated Newspaper* was HARPER'S WEEKLY (1857–1916), also distinguished for copious illustration of current events, but conducted on a higher literary level; moreover, its succession of great editors made it an important journal of opinion for many years. Later entries in this field, combining news, comment, and illustration to make popular weekly miscellanies, were COLLIER'S (1887–1957) and *Liberty* (1924–51). *Collier's*, founded by the McCormick-Patterson newspaper organization, was very popular for several years. *Collier's* was begun as *Once A Week* by Peter F. Collier and wielded much influence under the editorship of such men as Norman Hapgood (1902–12) and William L. Chenery (1925–43).

The leading weekly journal of opinion, unsupported by either pictures or fiction, in the later 19th century was the NATION (1865–   ), founded by Edwin Lawrence Godkin, who gave it high standing, though never a large circulation. When he became editor of the New York *Evening Post*, he made it that paper's weekly edition. It was separated from the *Post* in

1918, under Oswald Garrison Villard's ownership, and it became increasingly liberal in social and political views. It was in the climate of fresh and radical inquiry represented by this development that the NEW REPUBLIC (1914–   ) was established by Willard D. Straight, with Herbert Croly as editor. Though it has enlisted many brilliant writers, its circulation has always been limited, and it has required subsidies from wealthy liberals to keep it going.

An early monthly of reform views, the *Arena* (1889–1909), conducted by Benjamin O. Flower, was a good index of the increasingly sensitive social conscience of the times. Another important monthly of inquiring disposition was the *Forum* (1886–1940). Its long career was uneven, but it was always notable for its symposia on controversial questions. The MASSES (1911–17) was far to the left. It was founded by a group of Greenwich Village socialists and recruited a remarkable company of brilliant writers of essays, fiction, and verse. Barred from the mails during World War I, it reappeared as the Marxist LIBERATOR (1918–24) and later as the *New Masses* (1926–48).

The subject of religion was prominent in most of the early American magazines. Slightly over an eighth of those published in the 18th century were devoted primarily to religious matters, and eventually every sect was represented not only by a monthly or quarterly review but by weeklies that were either national or regional in scope. Some denominations had a score of periodicals in publication at the same time by the mid-19th century, and by the 1890s the Methodists and Baptists, most prolific in periodical literature, each had over a hundred going at one time. The earlier religious weeklies contained much secular news, but with the growth of newspaper circulations, they began devoting themselves mainly to church news and family reading. In the 20th century there were many consolidations and suspensions; Methodist periodicals, for example, were reduced again to about a score. However, in 1989, some 744 publications classified as religious were in course of publication in the U.S.

One of the most important of reviews in the religious field was the Unitarian bimonthly, the CHRISTIAN EXAMINER (1824–69); it was distinguished not only for its exposition of a point of view in theology, but for its literary criticism and its comment on social, philosophical, and educational problems. The *Catholic World* (1865–   ), founded and conducted for nearly a quarter-century by Isaac T. Hecker, has always been a popular type of review, but one of high standards and a notable list of contributors. Best known of 20th-century Catholic weeklies is the COMMONWEAL (1924–   ), subtitled *A Weekly Review of Literature, the Arts and Public Affairs*, and written largely by laymen.

Two well-known Congregational weeklies were the INDEPENDENT (1848–1928) and the OUTLOOK (1870–1935). Among the editors of the former were Henry Ward Beecher, Theodore Tilton, and William Hayes Ward; and of the latter, Beecher and Lyman Abbott. In the early 1870s the *Independent*, influenced by its contemporary (founded as *Christian Union*), became more and more a secular miscellany for fam-

ily reading; and the two weeklies for many years followed that course, together with important commentary on public affairs.

Two interdenominational weeklies have long been outstanding. The CHRISTIAN HERALD began in 1878 as the American edition of a London journal that exploited the sermons of C. H. Spurgeon, and later featured T. DEWITT TALMAGE's sermons. Its good fiction and lively miscellany long maintained its leadership in its special field. The *Christian Century* was begun by the Disciples of Christ in 1884 as the *Christian Oracle*; in 1900 it changed its name and soon thereafter declared itself undenominational. Under able editorship it has long provided a limited readership with thoughtful commentary on social, political, international, and literary matters.

The transition between the old *Godey* type of women's magazine and the modern women's magazines was affected by (1) the dress-pattern business and (2) mail-order advertising. The path well worn by the great quartette comprising *Godey's*, *Peterson's*, *Arthur's Home Magazine* (1852–98, long conducted by the author of *Ten Nights in a Bar Room*), and *Frank Leslie's Lady's Magazine* (1857–82), with their colored fashion plates, household hints, and serial fiction, was followed by *Demorest's Monthly Magazine* (1865–99), but with one notable innovation—Demorest stapled tissue-paper dress patterns into each issue. Incidentally, *Demorest's* published many first-rate authors in its literary miscellany, and editor Jane C. ("Jenny June") Croly made the magazine the organ of Sorosis, the mother of the women's club movement in the United States. MCCALL's (1873–2001), founded by a New York garment maker under the title *The Queen*, followed the pattern idea, and through a series of inspired changes in magazine design and illustration became by mid-20th century a leading mass-circulation monthly.

The WOMAN'S HOME COMPANION (1874–1957) began in Cleveland, Ohio, supported by mail-order advertising and called simply *The Home*. Purchased after its first decade by the Crowell Publishing Company, it became known for excellent fiction, lively articles, and good illustration. It perished because of the perils of mass circulation, which will be discussed later. Paragon of cheap mail-order journals for the home was *Comfort* (1884–1942) of Augusta, Maine, which gained much of its circulation on its offer of "four years for a dollar," and was America's first million-circulation magazine, reaching that pinnacle in 1895. The LADIES' HOME JOURNAL (1883–   ), offshoot of a farm journal published by Cyrus H. K. Curtis in Philadelphia, also gained its start as a mail-order paper at fifty cents a year, but it improved its standing by paying good authors and offering much advice for home and family. When it reached its first million circulation in 1903, its annual subscription rate was one dollar.

Three *haut-ton* fashion magazines were notable also for their literary content: HARPER'S BAZAAR (1867–   ) became a Hearst publication in 1936; VOGUE (1892–   ) began as one of the numerous class of urban weeklies of society already referred to, but under Condé Nast as publisher (1909–42) and

Edna Woolman Chase as editor (1914–48) it became a magazine of excellent feature articles and a purveyor of the announcements of top stylists and garment makers. It was sold to S. I. Newhouse, the newspaper group owner, in 1959. VANITY FAIR (1913–36), edited by Frank Crowninshield, was a distinguished interpreter of the literature, theater, and arts of its period. Conde Nast Publications brought the title back to life in 1983.

Though magazines for the home often carried juvenile departments, there were some outstanding periodicals designed primarily for children. The YOUTH'S COMPANION (1827–1929) was the most widely known. Founded by the elder Nathaniel Willis as a rather preachy weekly, under Daniel S. Ford, who was associated in its management for over forty years, it printed not only some of the best fiction for children of its time but many interesting anecdotal articles by well-known men and women. ST. NICHOLAS (1873–1943), edited by Mary Mapes Dodge for over thirty years, was a monthly of high quality. The *American Boy* (1899–1941), which absorbed the *Youth's Companion* in 1929, was a somewhat livelier weekly, giving more attention to adventure and sports.

Political satire was connected, throughout the 19th century, more or less closely with the humor periodicals. They came in with the partisan journalism of the new century and on the whole were a rough lot. Four of them stand out for their high quality. VANITY FAIR [1] (1859–63) was edited for a time by Artemus Ward. PUCK (1877–1918) was distinguished by JOSEPH KEPPLER's aggressive political and social cartoons, presented in bold chromolithograph. In general it was Democratic in its sympathies, and so the Republicans took over JUDGE (1881–1947), which also used colored cartoons. Eventually, this once-respectable weekly was lost in the ruck of low-life peep-show periodicals. LIFE [1] (1883–1936) was the greatest of American satirical weeklies; eschewing both color and political affiliation, it was superior in art, verse, and fiction.

The infinite diversity of our periodical literature is demonstrated by our best-known professional journals. The *Medical Repository* (1797–1824) was edited by Samuel Latham Mitchill and associates in New York. The weekly *Journal of the American Medical Association* (1883–   ) has long exerted a powerful influence, and in the 20th century it has enjoyed the largest circulation of any medical journal in the world. The A.M.A. also publishes more than a dozen other journals in specialized fields, while all the state and large city medical societies have their own journals, supported mainly by pharmaceutical advertising. Most notable of early law reviews was the *American Law Journal* (1808–17) of Philadelphia, edited by John E. Hall, who was also a *Port Folio* editor. First of the great university law-school journals was the *Harvard Law Review* (1887–   ); it was followed by important law reviews from Columbia, Yale, Pennsylvania, and Michigan. Case reporters attained large circulations. *Green Bag* (1889–1914) was a unique journal devoted to the lighter side of the profession.

A large and important group of periodicals developed in the latter half of the 19th century to represent the various industries and fields of business in the country. Earliest of these were the farm papers, represented by John S. Skinner's *American Farmer* (1819–73) of Baltimore and Thomas Green Fessenden's *New England Farmer* (1822–46) of Boston. Later came the *American Agriculturist* (1842–   ), the *Country Gentleman* (1853–1955), and the *Farm Journal* (1877–   ), each with its definite quality and complicated history. But by the 1870s it was evident that the varied topographical and weather conditions throughout the country gave an advantage to the many state and regional farm papers that had sprung up. Not a few of these hundreds of agricultural journals had some importance as purveyors of popular essays, poetry, fiction, and humor and were leaders in more scientific farming operations as well.

Engineering periodicals began with a group of mechanics' magazines in the 1820s. The *Scientific American* (1845–   ), long edited by O. D. Munn and A. E. Beach and their sons and grandsons, was a weekly for seventy-six years, then a monthly; its file contains a marvelous history of American invention and scientific ideas. POPULAR SCIENCE MONTHLY (1872–   ), founded by E. L. Youmans to introduce Herbert Spencer to America, was long continued on philosophical lines, but in 1915 turned to the more popular theme of current invention. *Science* (1883–   ) had a brief predecessor founded by Thomas A. Edison, but the new magazine was financed by Alexander Graham Bell and eventually became the official organ of the American Association for the Advancement of Science. NATIONAL GEOGRAPHIC MAGAZINE (1888–   ) was a scientific journal at the outset.

Meanwhile, journals representing leading industries and trades had multiplied. Transportation, mining and oil, communications, construction—all had prosperous and increasingly specialized organs. Trade journals underwent tremendous proliferation.

Returning again to the succession of general literary monthlies, a group most readers intend to denote by the term "magazine," we find them revolutionized by the advent of the 10-cent magazine in the 1890s. Cheap but excellent half-tone reproduction of photographs took the place of expensive fine-line engravings on wood, hard times worked against the 35- and 25-cent magazines, and lively editorial leadership emphasized current events and public affairs—all combining to turn public favor away from the older stand-bys and toward MCCLURE'S MAGAZINE (1829–1929), John Brisben Walker's COSMOPOLITAN (1886–   ), *Munsey's Magazine* (1889–1929), and *Everybody's*—and all selling for 10 or 15 cents. These monthlies quickly built up circulations of some half-million each, with tremendous advertising patronage.

Cosmopolitan under Walker was an exciting and distinguished magazine. In 1905 it was sold to William Randolph Hearst, becoming that newspaper publisher's first venture into the magazine field and exploiting many well-known names. Hearst later acquired *The World Today*, which had begun as a news magazine in 1901, later called it *Hearst's International*, but in 1925 merged it into *Cosmopolitan*. FRANK

A. MUNSEY made his debut as editor-publisher-contributor of the *Golden Argosy* (1882–   ), originally a weekly for boys and girls, later an all-fiction monthly (dropping *Golden* from its title), and still later one of the growing list of men's magazines. Munsey's most successful venture was *Munsey's Magazine*, a failure initially as a weekly but an overwhelming success soon after it became a fully illustrated general magazine of great variety at ten cents in 1893. *Everybody's* (1899–1930) came on later, to distinguish itself in the muckraking movement.

A considerable literature of exposure had developed in such magazines as the *Arena*, *Forum* and *North American Review* through the 1890s, but the magazine cult of exposure of corruptions in government, finance, and society began definitely with the unexampled success of the January 1903 issue of *McClure's*, which contained an installment of IDA M. TARBELL's history of the Standard Oil Company, an article in LINCOLN STEFFENS's series on "The Shame of the Cities," and one of RAY STANNARD BAKER's exposés of labor-union "rackets." Here, more or less fortuitously, had developed an immensely popular pattern of articles on public affairs, in which *Everybody's*, *Cosmopolitan*, *Hearst's International*, *Collier's*, *Hampton's Magazine* (1898–1912), and other periodicals joined. In 1906 President Theodore Roosevelt, angered by *Cosmopolitan's* series on "The Treason of the Senate," dubbed the movement "muckraking," after the fable of the man with the muckrake in *Pilgrim's Progress* (see MUCKRAKING LITERATURE). The muckraking movement and its magazines waned around 1912.

Pulp magazines, so called because they were printed on cheap paper made of wood pulp, began with *Argosy's* experiment in 1896. They were without illustration, except for occasional line cuts, and were devoted to Westerns, mysteries, love stories, sports, wonder and horror stories, and such escape literature. They sold for ten cents a number, chiefly at the newsstands, and multiplied exceedingly until rising costs during World War II and the competition of paperback books put an end to the genre (see PULPS). The true-story magazine, its pattern set by Bernarr Macfadden's *True Story* in 1919, purported to give true narratives of sensational incidents, particularly those involving sex. *Motion Picture* (1911–   ), eventually a member of the Fawcett group, was the first successful moving picture fan magazine, and the forerunner of a large, varied, and generally profitable class of illustrated periodicals, also distributed mainly by newsstands. Some of these degenerated into the mass of peep-show and gag magazines. Daddy of all such was probably the *National Police Gazette* which began in 1845 as a crime reporter and later achieved national circulation, especially in barber shops, based on its pictures of prize fighters and burlesque queens. Comic books, based originally on newspaper comic strips, began their boom in the latter 1930s. Though mainly designed for children, they had a large readership among adults. Their exploitation of crime, sex, and terror brought a considerable degree of regulation by local and state authorities and by the industry itself. This caused some decline in circulation, but at their height in the mid-1950s they distributed an estimated 35,000,000 copies a month.

The mid-century group of men's magazines began with the success of *Esquire* (1933–   ), which originated as a medium for men's clothing advertising but made a spectacular record by including color pictures or color paintings of women wearing little clothing, for example, the Petty girl. In the later 1940s it dropped this feature and came to rely on sophisticated articles and fiction by name authors. Most of *Esquire's* herd of imitators were cheaper in content and format. *Argosy* and *True* (1937–   ) turned to the men's magazine class successfully, with sound editorial policies.

Another group, of greater importance from the literary point of view, was made up of the LITTLE MAGAZINES. These were often published outside the metropolitan areas and always disowned a commercial motive. They wanted to survive, but they wanted even more to publish good fiction, poetry, and essays, and to break new literary ground. Among the several hundred little magazines, not a few have been strikingly eccentric, many have striven for charm in typography and printing, and most have had small circulations and short lives. Herbert S. Stone's CHAP-BOOK (1894–98) is often regarded as first of the tribe. Others were Elbert Hubbard's PHILISTINE (1895–1915), Margaret C. Anderson's LITTLE REVIEW (1914–21), John T. Frederick's MIDLAND (1915–33), Alfred Kreymborg's *Others* (1915–19), the Vanderbilt University *Fugitive* (1922–25), and another Southerner, The *Double Dealer* (1921–26), of New Orleans. Harriet Monroe's POETRY (1912–   ) of Chicago holds the record for longevity in this class. The DIAL (1880–1929) became a little magazine in 1918. By mid-20th century most magazines of this class were sponsored by colleges and universities, as THE SEWANEE REVIEW (1892–   ) and the KENYON REVIEW (1939–   ). By 2000, many of these had online web versions and others, generally newer, were available only online.

Eclectics had been common among American magazines from the beginning of the 19th century. Most widely known was *Littell's Living Age* (1844–1941), which for many years was composed chiefly by excerpts from British periodicals. But it remained for the READER'S DIGEST (1922–   ), applying the abridgment process, spicing its pages with amusing anecdotes and sayings, and using pocket-size format, to reach a circulation unrivaled among American magazines until it was surpassed late in the twentieth century by *Modern Maturity*, the magazine of the American Association of Retired Persons (AARP).

The LITERARY DIGEST (1890–1938) was also an eclectic, but it was primarily a news magazine, taking the larger part of its content from newspapers. It was a weekly, but Albert Shaw's REVIEW OF REVIEWS (1890–1937) was a monthly and contained many valuable original articles on public affairs. Walter Hines Page's *World's Work* (1900–32) was also a monthly dealing with current events and problems, but not eclectic. All these periodicals, by a series of consolidations, came to rest in the bosom of *Time*.

Time (1923–   ) was founded by Briton Hadden and Henry R. Luce with the object of presenting each week an orderly, condensed review of the news for intelligent readers. It was a tremendous success. After Hadden's death in 1929, Luce carried on with *Fortune* (1930–   ), a dollar-a-copy magazine of business; the great smash-hit picture weekly LIFE (1936–2000); and the weekly *Sports Illustrated* (1954–   ). *Time* had many imitators, chief of which were two launched in 1933—*Newsweek* and *United States News*; the latter, conducted by David Lawrence from Washington, became the *U.S. News and World Report* in 1948. Lawrence's weekly was filled chiefly with articles on national and international affairs, as was Max Ascoli's fortnightly *Reporter*, begun in 1949. The SATURDAY REVIEW (first called the *Saturday Review of Literature*, 1924–   ) was an outgrowth of the book-review supplement of the New York *Evening Post*; but after Norman Cousins became editor in 1942, it challenged attention in a variety of currently interesting fields.

At mid-century, troubling signs emerged in mass circulation magazines. Publications with names that seemed indispensable and indestructible proved to be neither. *Collier's* magazine had a circulation of 3,500,000 when it died in 1956, along with another Crowell Publishing magazine, *Woman's Home Companion*. *Look, The Saturday Evening Post*, and *Life* all fought a losing struggle for survival. The cause of the decline seemed to be the rise of television as a competitor for the advertising dollar and the reader's time. The *Post*, which engaged in aggressive, investigative journalism near the end (with an inordinate amount of resulting libel cases), folded in 1969, though it was later reborn as a nine-issues-a-year publication. *Life* died in 1972. It, too, was resurrected, first as an occasional publication, eventually as a monthly whose circulation rose to 1,700,000 by 1990. It combined the written word and its old forte, the photo essay, in its climb to economic and market stability, but in 2000 it went out of business again. *Look* stayed dead.

The passing of these magazines in the 1960s and later was, after all, a consequence of the changing market, a selective and temporary weakness in mass magazines, and not in the magazine industry as a whole. At the same time that *Life, Look*, and the *Post* were facing difficulties, the magazine industry began to reflect its adaptability to market forces and a changing American culture.

New York magazine (1968–   ), for instance, established itself as a city magazine with a national reputation, having been spun off from the failed *New York Herald-Tribune* and put on its feet independently by Clay Felker. It and a number of other magazines served as platforms for a new genre of writers who practiced something called THE NEW JOURNALISM, for want of a better name. Whether it was new or not was hotly debated. Was it a resurrection of muckraking journalism? Was it just more and livelier writing at length and in depth? At its heart, it was nothing more or less than the use of fiction techniques to tell a nonfiction story, resulting in absorbing reading when it came from the typewriter of a reporter-writer who could handle the form in search of a view of reality. The writers typically linked with the New Journalism form included TOM WOLFE, GAY TALESE, JIMMY BRESLIN, Shana Alexander, GLORIA STEINEM, and Peter Maas along with novelists NORMAN MAILER and TRUMAN CAPOTE. Arnold Gingrich's *Esquire* turned more to serious prose in the 1960s, deemphasizing the female form along the way. Faced by multiple public issues—the Vietnam War, civil rights, the environmental movement, the women's movement, and consumerism—many other magazines did the same.

And, an *Esquire* staffer who thought it was time to appeal to the new American openness launched what some called sex journalism. Hugh Hefner's *Playboy* (1953–   ), hanging on to an entrepreneurial shoestring at the outset, soared to a circulation of more than seven million in 1973 before falling back to a still impressive 3,657,000 by 1990. Although repetitive displays of undraped young females seemed to be the main appeal, some substantial fiction and nonfiction prose was sandwiched between the expanses of exposed flesh. Robert Guccione's *Penthouse* (1969–   ) and other imitators followed suit. At the outer limits of sex journalism was Larry Flynt's *Hustler* (1974–   ), much scorned but also recognized for the court battles it fought—most of them successfully—for free expression.

Some new magazines succeeded by speaking to a common denominator. *People* (1974–   ), a Time, Inc. startup, reached a circulation of 3,347,000 by leaning heavily on telling about the lives of the rich and famous, while not ignoring the unusual in the life of the average American. Others, for example, *New Woman* (1970–   ) and *Ms.* (1972–   ), spoke of and for the emerging women's movement and all that it meant to the nation.

Older titles stayed on top by adjusting and changing. *National Geographic's* colorful views of the world became more serious, analytical, and pointed as it looked more closely at the world's problems and not just its travel attractions. Its staffers went repeatedly to cover the war in Vietnam. For Geographic reporter Dickie Chappelle and other journalists, the search for news and truth led to death in the rice paddies. *Reader's Digest's* middle-America approach was modified as its staff of reporters tackled troubles besetting the nation, while including traditional homey and personal features. *Rolling Stone* (1967–   ), launched by Jann S. Wenner, began as a rebellious platform for the counter-culture before turning its focus to the contemporary music scene, selling more than a million copies an issue by 1990. *Philadelphia* (1908–   ) and *Texas Monthly* (1973–   ) exemplified an increase in the number and quality of city and regional magazines. Not all were as aggressive in their investigative reporting on close-to-home issues as these two, but growing affluence in metropolitan areas fostered expansion of this class of magazine. Magazines traditionally linked with quality journalism changed in some ways and survived, if not they did not always prosper. *Atlantic* and *Harper's* dipped and recovered, and *New Republic* survived a near-death experience before stabilizing once more. *New Yorker* devotees gasped when the Newhouse organization purchased the magazine, and began to worry when editor William Shawn, a lineal descendant of the Ross line of editing philosophy, was replaced as editor by Robert Gottlieb, but the quality of its fiction and nonfiction seemed intact and survived the still-later controversial editorship of Tina Brown.

The leading newsweeklies—*Time, Newsweek,* and *U.S. News and World Report*—fared well by thorough reporting and analysis of national and world events, turning to more by-lined pieces, and unabashed point-of-view articles, based on the substantial editorial resources of their bureaus around the world. Magazines concerned with business and economics in general and personal finance in particular fared well, including *Forbes* (1917–   ), *Business Week* (1929–   ), and *Time*'s entry into the field, *Money* (1972–   ). Their editorial tone turned more critical and analytical than it might have been in an earlier era.

A precise figure on the number of periodicals that qualify as magazines became harder to obtain as the numbers increased in response to both mass and class needs. The typical classification of magazines into one of five categories—general consumer, business, literary and academic, newsletters, and public relations—covers the range from specialized academic or hobby interests to the mass market *Reader's Digest* type of publication. A phenomenon of the end of the century was the huge success of magazines tied to TV celebrities. *Martha Stewart Living* came first, followed, as the century turned, by *O, The Oprah Magazine* (2000) and *Rosie: The Magazine* (2001), designed as a successor to *McCall's.* One expert estimated 16,000 periodicals as America entered the 1990s. Another counted at least 500 new magazine start-ups in a typical year. In the final decade of the 20th century, there were dozens of magazines with circulations exceeding a million, led by *Modern Maturity* (1957–   ), with 20,500,000, and *TV Guide* (1953–   ) and *Reader's Digest*, both with more than 10,000,000. Magazines—in all their diversity—seemed alive, well, and able to adapt to the reading needs of a changing nation.

FRANK LUTHER MOTT/WALLACE B. EBERHARD/GP

Maggie: A Girl of the Streets (1893),   a novel by STEPHEN CRANE. Aged twenty-two, Crane, a journalist living in poverty in New York, published at his own expense his first novel, *Maggie*, destined to become the most celebrated picture of tenement life in the Bowery. In nineteen short chapters, this grim naturalistic tale chronicles the tragic life of Maggie Johnson, born in the slums and victimized by everyone in her squalid and violent world: her drunken and abusive mother reviles her and casts her out, a Bowery sharper seduces and deserts her, her brother condemns her, the neighbors shun her, and a minister whom she approaches in desperation shrinks from her. Destined to lose in the struggle for survival, she is last portrayed walking the streets soliciting men, an anonymous girl of "the painted cohorts of the city" who disappears in the darkness of the "final block" leading to the East River, where presumably she drowns. The novel exposes not only the degradations of slum life but the failure and corruption prevailing throughout American society—in religious institu-

tions, the factory system, popular culture, and false moral codes and double standards. The novel, rejected by Richard Watson Gilder, editor of *The Century Magazine*, was acclaimed by William Dean Howells, who promoted its publication by D. Appleton and Company in 1896. *Maggie* exemplifies the distinctive features that made Crane's work a landmark in American fiction: a terse ironic style, symbolic use of color, mock-heroic treatment of lowly subjects, and division into short chapters unified by recurrent motifs and parallel and contrasting scenes.

ELSA NETTELS

Magical Realism (*lo real maravilloso*),   A term introduced by ALEJO CARPENTIER in his prologue to *El reino de este mundo* (1949, tr. *The Kingdom of This World*, 1957). The Cuban novelist was searching for a concept broad enough to accommodate both the events of everyday life and the fabulous nature of Latin American geography and history. Carpentier, who was greatly influenced by French surrealism, saw in magical realism the capacity to enrich our idea of what is real by incorporating all dimensions of the imagination, particularly as expressed in magic, myth, and religion. Together with examples of magical realism by Latin American authors, the term has passed into international currency, influencing the theory, practice, and criticism of fiction around the world.

Magic Barrel, The (1958),   a collection of short stories by BERNARD MALAMUD. With a few exceptions, the volume offers short, powerful episodes concerning New York Jews. In the short-story form, Malamud reveals his sensitive gift of characterization even more clearly than in his novels. His sense of the bizarre is shown in the wild African-American angel named Levine, and his feel for almost demonic characters is shown in Susskind of "The Last Mohican" and Salzman of "The Magic Barrel." Malamud skillfully moves from the grimly natural to the fantastic and supernatural; the world of dreams and that of the real mix in a strange amalgam. In his unusual style—a mixture of plain speech with Yiddish expressions and haunting lyrical outpourings—he is able, despite his insistence on the hard facts of reality, to imply a significant spiritual world just beyond.

Magnalia Christi Americana (1702),   a history of the church in New England by COTTON MATHER. The book is in praise of "the great achievements of Christ in America." In this folio of nearly eight hundred pages, Mather intended to revive the spirit of religion in America. He gives a good picture of the settlement, governors, leading divines, Congregational church, remarkable providences in which God showed what a deep interest He took in the New England churches, and various disturbances—theological and military—such as the wars with the Indians. Mather had three themes: the virtues of New England's religious way, the danger of backsliding, and the need for reform. He deals with them in highly rhetorical fashion, embellishing at every point.

Magnificent Ambersons, The (1918),   a novel by BOOTH TARKINGTON that won a Pulitzer Prize. It forms part of a trilogy called *Growth* (1927), which appeared as *The Turmoil*

(1915), *The Magnificent Ambersons*, and *The Midlander* (1923). The middle volume tells the story of a snob, his numerous mean actions, and his final overthrow. He does a good deal to ruin the lives of his mother and other people, but is at last forgiven—by the author and by some of those he has injured. The book also traces the decay of one aristocracy and the rise of another in an American city.

Mahan, Alfred T[hayer].   See INFLUENCE OF SEA POWER UPON HISTORY, 1660–1783.

Mahicans.   The Mahicans were both a tribe and a confederacy of ALGONQUIN Native Americans. The MOHICANS constituted one tribe of the confederacy, distinct from the Mahicans. Uncas, who figures in Cooper's THE LAST OF THE MOHICANS, was a Mahican in the sense that he was of that confederacy, but his tribe was the Mohegans. The Mahican tribe occupied both banks of the upper Hudson River. At war with the MOHAWKS by the time of the Dutch settlements, the Mahican tribe was driven eastward, and by the middle of the 17th century had moved their council fire from Schodac, near Albany, to Stockbridge, Massachusetts. The tribe dispersed in time, some of them joining other members of the Mahican confederacy to form a group known as the Stockbridge Indians, which suffered badly in the FRENCH AND INDIAN WAR. By mid-19th century most of the remnant were living in Wisconsin.

Mailer, Norman (1923–   ),   novelist, journalist, playwright. Born in Long Branch, New Jersey, Mailer was educated at Harvard. He intended to become an aeronautical engineer, but after he published his first short story, "The Greatest Thing in the World," in the *Harvard Advocate*, he dedicated himself to becoming a "great American novelist." In pursuit of experiences equal to his immediate literary ambition of writing the best American novel about World War II, Mailer joined the U.S. Army in 1944. His experiences in the invasion of Luzon became the basis for *The Naked and the Dead*, which won critical acclaim as the most sophisticated novel about World War II. The contours of the rest of Mailer's literary craeer are describable in terms of his changed relationship to this novel.

In *The Naked and the Dead*, Mailer shaped his narrative materials out of the different ideologies with which his characters shaped their experiences: General Cummings' totalitarianism, Lieutenant Hearn's liberalism, and Sergeant Croft's primitivism. The enormously popular novel was self-consciously literary in its intertextural affiliations with the narrative experiments of FARRELL, DOS PASSOS, and HEMINGWAY.

As Mailer's narrative interests shifted to the experiences of returning veterans, he found it increasingly difficult to associate his personal experiences with theirs. In the two novels he published after *The Naked and the Dead*—*Barbary Shore* (1951) and *The Deer Park* (1954)—Mailer did not eradicate the combat soldier from his narrative consciousness, but adapted his readiness for military action to the psychology of invented social types—the hipster, the sociopath, the "white Negro"—who proposed new styles of postwar survival out of the residual energies of the battlefield. Mailer's early postwar novels presupposed the continued existence of a combat soldier within, for whom World War II served as an imaginary alternative to everyday life in the Cold War. Experiencing demands urged on by their perceptions, thoughts, and instincts—as if they had emerged out of a pervasive but invisible battlefield—Mailer's existential heroes were designed to meet the enemy within on familiar ground.

After some critics judged these novels self-indulgent and underdeveloped, Mailer turned to the prose essay as his medium, and the reactions of his own psyche to contemporary events for his subject matter. In 1955 he cofounded *The Village Voice*, a weekly newspaper dealing with politics and culture, and began writing columns of commentary that would become *Advertisements for Myself* (1959) and *The Presidential Papers* (1963). The persona he constructed out of his reaction to his sociopolitical environment inverted the psychology of the acculturated war veteran.

Every event Mailer's persona engaged threatened to turn back into an incident of war. "Literary form in general," explained Mailer, "is the record of war. It is the record as seen in a moment of rest, yet it is the record of a war which has been taking place. Don't you see, whatever is alive, or intent, or obsessed, must wage an actual war: it creates the possibility for form in its environment, by its every attempt to shape the environment. Whenever the environment resists, the result is form."

In *The White Negro* (1957), Mailer proposed that Americans continue the war in the form of a collective psychological reaction formation against the totalitarian encroachments of the media. As the record of this ongoing war with American culture, Mailer's literary form did not recall what had occurred in battle, but reinvested life-threatening sensations and impulses, which when experienced in battle exceeded his representational capacity, with a credo of hipster existentialism able to dispel their destructive influences. When Mailer described his writing as the record of a war, he claimed for his work of this period the power to separate the fragmented self from the shattering intensities of Cold War America and resituate that self within a medium in which it could recover its psychic integrity.

On the battlefield the self was required for purposes of survival to respond with the entire sensibility pitched to a level of complete psychological alertness. In *Advertisements for Myself*, Mailer superimposed this battlefield self onto the postwar environment to accrue related capacities of response for his persona. Because he generalized the imaginary battlefield onto the entirety of American culture, each of the social types Mailer invented for himself after the war elevated the incomplete socialization of the veteran's war mentality into a different social power: The white Negro gave him entry into the most dangerous urban and psychic zones, the existential hipster drew upon powers of visionary response able to discern the deep order in chaotic political events, and the cultural figure that was the collective result of Mailer's heterogeneous personae identified himself as an imaginary adviser to the president.

When Mailer returned to the novel in 1965 with the publication of *An American Dream*, Stephen Rojack, the protagonist, was an alias for the persona Mailer had developed in his nonfiction prose, and his actions—the murder of his estranged wife, the fight to the death with the master magician who was her father, and the love affair with Cherry, the most erotic woman in America—were reenactments of events that had already occurred in *Advertisements for Myself*.

Because Mailer had built his literary identity out of his reaction to great national issues—World War II, the Kennedy assassination, the Cold War—he empowered himself as official interpreter of the complex events that build the national history. In *Armies of the Night* (1968), Mailer recounted his reactions to the October 1967 march on the Pentagon; in *Miami and the Siege of Chicago* (1968) and *St. George and the Godfather* (1972), he covered the Democratic and Republican conventions; in *Of a Fire on the Moon* (1970), he reported the astronauts' space flight; in *The Prisoner of Sex* (1971), he reported on the ideology of Women's Liberation; and in *The Executioner's Song* (1979), he reported the execution of Gary Gilmore. In turning to events in his personal, as well as the national, life—the 1960 stabbing of his second wife, his *Voice* columns on the high magic of the CIA and the Mafia, the Liston-Patterson fights, his Reichian meditations on the "good orgasm"—into the bases for his fiction, Mailer eradicated the distinction between the fictional and the nonfictional. As a persona that had learned how to resist the cultural forces—media jargon, FBI surveillance, consumerism—that dominated the lives of others, Mailer claimed the power transcendentally to inhabit the culture, to be in American culture but not of it.

When Mailer returned to the topic of war in *Why Are We in Vietnam?* (1967), he constructed D. J., a protagonist who understood that war to be a form of collective violence directed not against North Vietnamese communists but the media's interference with the psychic lives of Americans. Mailer successfully transformed the disillusionment of Americans with the ideology that justified the Vietnam War into an excuse for constructing a character who replaced the collective violence of war with the redemptive violence of Mailer's hipster existentialist. The identification Mailer exploited between D. J.'s obsessional reactions against media encroachments and the antiwar movement returned him to the dream of becoming the great American novelist he had aspired to become from the beginning of his career. *Ancient Evenings* (1983), the novel Mailer published sixteen years later, and which is about reincarnation in ancient Egypt, bears witness to the difference between Mailer's aspiration to write The Great American Novel and his perennial failure to realize it—thus far.

Tough Guys Don't Dance (1984) is a novel. Mailer's additional works of nonfiction include *Cannibals and Christians* (1967), *Marilyn* (1973), about Marilyn Monroe, and *Portrait of Picasso as a Young Man* (1995). *Harlot's Ghost* (1992) is a massive novel about The Central Intelligence Agency (CIA). *The Time of Our Time* (1998) is a second anthology of his own writing, as selected by Mailer. Studies include Richard Poirier,

Norman Mailer (1972), and Robert Solotaroff, *Down Mailer's Way* (1974).

DONALD PEASE/BP

Maillet, Antonine (1929–), novelist, short-story writer. Born in New Brunswick, Canada, Maillet was educated at the Université de Montréal and Laval University, where she has taught literature and folklore. Celebrated as the foremost writer of Acadia, she won the Prix Goncourt—the first non-native of France to do so—for her novel *Pélagie—la Charrette* (1979, tr. *Pélagie: the Return to a Homeland*, 1982). It tells of the trials of a group of Acadians who make their way back to their homeland after the removal to Louisiana in the 1750s. She drew on Acadian folklore for her novel *Pointe-aux-Coques* (1958), set in a village; *La Sagouine* (1971, tr. *The Slattern*), sixteen monologues by the wife of an Acadian fisherman, frequently performed on stage; and *Par derrière chez mon père* (1972), humorous sketches. Later novels with Acadian materials include *Don l'Orignal* (1972, tr. *The Tale of Don l'Orignal*, 1978), a Governor General's Award winner; *Gapi et Sullivan* (1973); *Mariaagélas* (1973); and *Cent ans dans les bois* (1981), set in the late 19th century in New Brunswick. Plays include *La Contrebaudiere* (1981), *Garrochés Paradis* (1986) and *Margot la Folle* (1987). *Les Confessions de Jeanne de Valois* (1992) is a combination biography and autobiography.

Main Currents in American Thought, an Interpretation of American Literature from the Beginnings to 1920 (3 v. 1927–30), by VERNON LOUIS PARRINGTON. This remarkable work won a Pulitzer Prize when the first two volumes were issued in 1927. The third volume, incomplete at Parrington's death, was edited by E. H. Eby with a memoir of the author. A one-volume edition was issued in 1939.

Maine Woods, The (posthumously published, 1864), an account of three visits to Maine by HENRY D. THOREAU. Thoreau visited Maine in 1846, 1853, and 1857. He published accounts of the first two trips in *Union Magazine* (1848) and *Atlantic Monthly* (1858); these, together with an account of the third trip, were edited by his friend WILLIAM ELLERY CHANNING (1818–1901) to make the book. Thoreau describes the guides and other men of the Maine wilderness, giving a good account especially of Joe Polis, a Penobscot Indian.

Main Street (1920), a novel by SINCLAIR LEWIS. Lewis first achieved international renown with *Main Street*, an exposure of the ugliness, monotony, and intolerance of the Midwestern small town, here called Gopher Prairie, whose main street, according to its author, "is the continuation of main streets everywhere." The protagonist, Carol Kennicott, married to a kindly but unimaginative doctor, works to transform the drab town into a place of beauty and culture but is defeated by the complacency and hostility of the leading townspeople and by her own impracticality and sentimental illusions. Divided between her longing to rebel and desire to be accepted, she is most admirable in the resolute courage with which she fights bigotry and hypocrisy in the town and befriends those ostracized for their poverty or their unconventional views. Defeated in her efforts to conquer what Lewis called the "village virus," she leaves Gopher Prairie to work for two years in a government office in Washington during World War I and then returns to resume her life as Kennicott's wife and mother of their two children. According to Lewis's biographer, Mark Schorer, the publication of *Main Street*, the first popular best seller to attack cherished ideas about marriage, gender roles, and small town life, was "the most sensational event in twentieth-century American publishing history" and made Lewis "the spokesman for a literary generation."

ELSA NETTELS

Main-Travelled Roads (1891),   a collection of eleven short stories by HAMLIN GARLAND. The stories brought a harsh realism to the local color movement and drew angry criticism that Garland was "a bird willing to foul his own nest." The stories, laid in the Dakotas and Iowa, are often grim in tone. They show the farmer as the victim of storms and devastating crop pestilences, cut off from ordinary social intercourse, and in many instances crushed beneath a mortgage. Occasionally the stories portray good, as in "God's Ravens," an account of the kindliness of village folks to a newspaperman and his wife, and "A Good Fellow's Wife," an engaging tale of the wife who wins back the confidence of a community where her husband, a banker, has lost all their money by his unwise speculations. Garland collected similar tales in his *Prairie Folks* (1893).

Mair, Charles (1838–1927),   government official, poet. Born in Lanark, Ontario, Mair had published *Dreamland and Other Poems* (1868) before his role in suppressing the North West Rebellion of 1885 won him the title "the warrior bard." In *Tecumseh* (1886), a verse drama centered on the War of 1812, he attempted an epic sweep, with paeans to prairies and buffalo. His prose *Through the Mackenzie Basin: A Narrative of the Athabaska and Peace River Treaty Expedition of 1899* (1908) was based on personal experience.

Major, Charles (1856–1913),   lawyer, legislator, novelist. Born in Indianapolis, Major read history as a relief from his law practice and his work as a public official. He produced a novel of the early Tudor period in England, *When Knighthood Was in Flower* (1898), which tapped a public desire for historical romance and became an immense success. It was immediately and widely imitated. Major continued writing and produced one more best seller, *Dorothy Vernon of Haddon Hall* (1902), but his other works were less successful.

Major, Clarence (1936–   ),   poet, novelist. Born in Atlanta, Major has been praised for his surreal poetry and innovative fiction, both fracturing into shards of language his experience as an African-American, or the experiences of the African-Americans who constitute his major subject matter. His novels include *All-Night Visitors* (1969); *No* (1973), about the violent world of a black boy growing up in the South; *Reflex and Bone Structure* (1975); *Emergency Exit* (1979); *My Amputations* (1986), about a parolee who takes an author hostage and impersonates him on a lecture tour; *Such Was the Season* (1987), an Atlanta matriarch's story; and *Painted Turtle: Woman with Guitar* (1988), about a man's love for a Zuñi

singer. *Dirty Bird Blues* (1996) is a more conventional fiction about Manfred Banks, a blues musician struggling against his love for Old Crow whiskey, trying to reunite with his wife, and make a living with his music. Among his volumes of verse are *Love Poems of a Black Man* (1965), *Swallow the Lake* (1970), and *Some Observations of a Stranger at Zuni in the Latter Part of the Century* (1988). He also compiled a *Dictionary of Afro-American Slang* (1970), and collected African-American poetry in *The Garden Thrives* (1996) and short stories in *Calling the Wind* (1993).

Makemie, Francis (1658?–1708),   clergyman, missionary, pamphleteer. Makemie, sometimes called the father of American Presbyterianism, was born in Ireland, came to America in 1683, and subsequently organized the first American presbytery. He engaged in many controversies. Attacked by GEORGE KEITH, founder of the so-called Christian Quakers, or Keithians, he wrote *An Answer to George Keith's Libel* (1694). When he was attacked by the Anglican clergy, his reply was given in *Truths in a New Light* (1699). In England on a money-collecting mission, he issued *A Plain and Friendly Persuasive to the Inhabitants of Virginia and Maryland for Promoting Towns and Cohabitation* (1705). Later he was fined for preaching without a license and thereupon wrote *A Narrative of a New and Unusual American Imprisonment* (1707), as a result of which he was exonerated.

Making of Americans, The (1925),   by GERTRUDE STEIN. Spoken of sometimes as a novel, sometimes as "the alleged history of a family's progress," this lengthy production seems to some to be one of Stein's most important books. She composed it about 1906–08, but no publisher wanted it, and it accumulated dust for twenty years. Supposedly it deals with the wanderings and experiences, mainly mental, of three generations of Stein's family, but it is also supposedly the progress of everybody else. The style has many of Stein's characteristic devices, particularly repetition. There is no dialogue, no action. When ERNEST HEMINGWAY first came under Stein's influence, she set him to copying *The Making of Americans* for publication in Ford Madox Ford's *Transatlantic Review* and later to correcting the proofs. Hemingway is said to have stated that he learned much from this task.

Making of an American, The (1901),   an autobiography by JACOB A. RIIS. Riis came to the United States from Denmark in 1870, worked as a police reporter and was shocked by conditions he found in New York City slums. He wrote vigorously on the subject, attracted the attention of Theodore Roosevelt and won his support. Riis gives a vivid account of his life in this volume, first published serially in the *Outlook*.

Malaeska, The Indian Wife of the White Hunter (1860),   a novel by ANN S. STEPHENS. Well known in New York literary circles, Stephens has gone down in literary history as the first to write a Beadle Dime Novel. It sold 300,000 copies in its first year and encouraged her and others to continue producing stories for this library. See ERASTUS BEADLE.

Malamud, Bernard (1914–1986),   novelist, short-story writer. Malamaud was born in Brooklyn, the son of

Russian Jewish immigrants, and he grew up in the world of small grocery stores and grinding poverty he describes so poignantly in THE ASSISTANT (1957). He was educated at City College, in New York.

Malamud thought of himself as a writer who specialized in chronicles of "simple people struggling to make their lives better in a world of bad luck." Suffering ennobled his protagonists, giving them moral wisdom and an attitude about humanity that Malamud regarded as quintessentially Jewish. In his most representative work, fantasy and reality comingle to create a world simultaneously familiar and strangely exotic. The technique works its maximum power in the short story, where brevity and compactness heighten the contours of his moral fables. This is especially true in his best work, "The Magic Barrel," "The Angel Levine," and "The Last Mohican," from THE MAGIC BARREL (1958), and in the title story of *Idiots First* (1963).

Malamud began his career with *The Natural* (1952), a novel thick with allegorical implications and American archetypes. The novel has no Jewish characters, and Malamud retained a special fondness for it as he was increasingly grouped with SAUL BELLOW, PHILIP ROTH, and other Jewish-American writers. Nonetheless, the novel is every bit as much the morality play and every bit as much concerned with the equation of suffering-and-wisdom, as his subsequent, identifiably Jewish works.

The Assistant, which many critics consider his signature work, is set in the prison of a failing grocery store, where Morris Bober, its elderly, long-suffering Jewish owner, teaches his assistant, Frankie Alpine, what it means to be a Jew, and what it means to be a man. After decades in which Jewish protagonists struggled to assimilate to the non-Jewish world around them, *The Assistant* is a tale about reverse assimilation, one in which Frankie takes over the store on Morris's death and undergoes a painful conversion to Judaism. As Morris instructs Frankie, "A Jew suffers for the law." However, when Frankie points out that Morris doesn't attend synagogue services, that he doesn't wear a skullcap, and that he has seen Morris eating ham, Morris counters by saying: "I suffer for you." When Morris dies, Frankie returns the favor, suffering for Morris's sake as Morris had suffered for his.

However, such movements toward goodness and personal salvation are fraught with ironic undercuttings and comic complications. More often than not, Malamud's protagonists end up as moral bunglers, as schlemiels of good intention. This is precisely the case in "The Magic Barrel," as Leo Finkel moves toward his date with Stella, the prostitute whose love will redeem him as his goodness will save her, and the situation in *A New Life* (1961), Malamud's academic novel about the comic incongruities that greet S. Levin, a sad-eyed, transplanted New Yorker, as he fights for the Good, the True, and the Beautiful among the pragmatic philistines of Oregon's Cascadia College. Like Finkel, S. Levin takes on the heavy responsibilities of another man's wife and family and, jobless, drives off into the sunset in a car that threatens to break down within 100 miles.

With novels such as *The Fixer*, a historical novel based on the accusations of blood libel that swirled around Mendele Beiliss, and *The Tenants* (1971), an allegorical saga of relations between blacks and Jews that centers on two writers who share quarters in a condemned apartment building—one "established," Jewish, and failing in his imaginative powers; the other, black, undisciplined, angry, and filled with potential—Malamud made his mark as a writer of social conscience. Despite its setting in early 20th-century Russia, *The Fixer* is as much directed toward the Civil Rights Movement as it is toward its historical circumstances; and its message—that no man can be a nonpolitical animal—reverberates against Malamud's deep conviction that "the purpose of freedom is to create it for others." *The Tenants* is both a darker look at the same subject and a cautionary tale. For if Harry Lesser and Willie Spearmint are secret sharers, they are also each other's potential murderer. *Mercy*—repeated more than eighty times—is the note on which their respective dreams of vengeance and destruction end, and the litany says as much about Malamud's thinning hopes as it does about how he desperately clung to them.

Malamud never abandoned his public posture that "with me, it's story, story, story," but his later fiction raises serious questions about whether or not art helps make people free. *The Tenants* is a watershed novel in this regard, with *Dubin's Lives* (1979), a novel centered on a biographer whose own life begins to reduplicate the patterns of his prize-winning biographies, suggesting one answer while *God's Grace* (1982), a beast fable with a distinctly apocalyptic flavor, suggests another. Unlike Lesser, William Dubin gives every appearance of being the consummate professional. He wards off potential cases of writer's block by moving easily from one biographical project, for example, from Emerson to Thoreau, to another. When he takes up the case of D. H. Lawrence, however, he becomes entangled in the sort of sexual distractions one normally associates with novels by Saul Bellow. Indeed, even Dubin's musings have that weighty texture of ideas that look more akin to *Herzog* than to, say, the Morris Bober of *The Assistant*. *God's Grace* was even more troublesome because the gloominess of its tone—despite moments of parodic cheer—was too easy and not entirely convincing.

Malamud richly deserves being called one of our major writers, even though his best, most representative, work was done prior to the 1970s. Readers were reminded of this truth when *The Stories of Bernard Malamud* was published in 1983. It brought the best of Malamud's short stories between two covers, and if it made his so-called decline clear, it also served to highlight his impressive achievements. He was and will likely remain one of our best practitioners of the short story.

Critical studies include Sidney Richman, *Bernard Malamud* (1967); Sandy Cohen, *Bernard Malamud and the Trial by Love* (1974); and Jeffrey Helterman, *Understanding Bernard Malamud* (1985).

SANFORD PINSKER

Malcolm X (1925–1965),   black activist. Born Malcolm Little in Omaha, Nebraska, he was best known as Malcolm X. *The Autobiography of Malcolm X* (written with ALEX

HALEY) tells of his life as a target for racism, criminal, Black Muslim preacher, and founder of the Organization of Afro-American Unity (1964). Assassinated by three men (two of them Black Muslims) in the same year the book appeared, he has been increasingly recognized since his death as a charismatic leader in the struggle for Afro-American identity and power.

Mallea, Eduardo (1903–1982), Argentinian novelist, essayist, short-story writer. Born in Bahia Blanca, Mallea abandoned law studies in Buenos Aires to begin a career as a writer concerned with his own and his country's identity. His first two books, *Cuentos para una inglesa desesperada* (1925) and *La ciudad junto al rio inmovil* (1936), are collections of stories. Among his most important works of fiction is *Todo verdor perecera* (1941), with its desolate, lonely protagonist. It was published in English, along with *Fiesta en noviembre* (1938), *Los enmigos del alma* (1950), and *Chaves* (1953), as *All Green Shall Perish* (1966). His other novels are *La Aguilas* (1943), on the decline of a family of landowners; *El alejamiento* (1945); *El retorno* (1945); *Los enemigos del alma* (1950); *Simbad* (1957); and *La barca de hiel* (19670. Among his nonfiction works are *Historia de una pasion argentina* (1937, tr. *History of an Argentine Passion*, 1983), autobiographical; and *La vida blanca* (1960), a study of the Argentine mind. *Obras completas* was published in two volumes in 1965.

Mallison, Charles ["Chick"], a character created by WILLIAM FAULKNER. The nephew of Gavin Stevens, Chick grows from childhood to young manhood in four of Faulkner's novels; as a child he narrates part of *The Town*; as a sixteen-year-old boy he is instrumental in proving Lucas Beauchamp innocent of murder in INTRUDER IN THE DUST; and as a young man he narrates part of *The Mansion* and is an interested observer in KNIGHT'S GAMBIT.

Malone, Dumas (1892–1986), teacher, historian, biographer. After teaching at various universities, Malone became professor of history at Columbia. Among his important services was work as editor of the DICTIONARY OF AMERICAN BIOGRAPHY. For many years he devoted himself to the study and interpretation of Jefferson and published a magisterial biography, *Jefferson and His Times* (6 v. 1948–81). Malone also wrote *Saints in Action* (1939); *The Interpretation of History* (1943), with four collaborators; *Story of the Declaration of Independence* (1954); and with Basil Rauch a two-volume history of the United States, *Empire for Liberty* (1960).

Malone, Michael (1942–), novelist, playwright. Born in North Carolina and educated at the University of North Carolina and Harvard, Malone has written mysteries and several picaresque novels. *Dingley Falls* (1980), his third novel is set in the New England town of the title. The secrets of the police chief, newspaper editor, banker's wife and other residents are revealed against the backdrop of hate letters appearing in area mailboxes. *Uncivil Seasons* (1983) is a mystery novel set in a small southern town. In *Handling Sin* (1986), a southern minister leaves his church to travel with a young black woman, and his son—the protagonist—searches for him. *Time's Witness* (1989) is a mystery novel is set in the Piedmont area. The hero of *Foolscap* (1991) is a conservative young college professor selected to write the biography of Ford Rexford, an aging playwright whose vital life experience changes his young biographer. Other novels include *Painting the Roses Red* (1975) and *The Delectable Mountains* (1977). *Defender of the Faith* (1981) is a play; Malone has also written several screenplays and some nonfiction.

Maltz, Albert (1908–1985), playwright, short-story writer, novelist, movie scriptwriter. Maltz was born in Brooklyn, New York. While studying at Yale with G.P. BAKER, Maltz and a fellow student, GEORGE SKLAR wrote *Merry-Go-Round* (1932), a play on political corruption in New York City. With Sklar, Maltz also wrote *Peace on Earth* (1933), a pacifist play. *Black Pit* (1935) is Maltz's play that deals with a strike in a mining region and the psychology of a strikebreaker. Maltz's proletarian and propaganda writing is also evident in his short stories, *The Way Things Are* (1938), and in two novels: *The Underground Stream* (1940), about attempts to bring unions to the auto industry, and *The Cross and the Arrow* (1944), about a German's assistance to British bombers. As a screenwriter, he worked on *This Gun for Hire* (1942) and the patriotic films *Destination Tokyo* (1944) and *Pride of the Marines* (1945). Blacklisted after the war as one of the so-called Hollywood Ten (see MCCARTHYISM), he received no more significant film credits, except for *The Naked City* (1948), directed by Jules Dassin, himself a Hollywood exile. Maltz's other novels are *The Journey of Simon McKeever* (1949), about a search for a satisfying life; *A Long Day and a Short Life* (1957); and *A Tale of One January* (1966). A second collection of stories is *Afternoon in the Jungle* (1970). His essays are collected in *The Citizen Writer* (1950).

Mamet, David (1947–), playwright. Mamet's parents divorced when he was ten, and he spent time exploring the streets of Chicago. Before graduating from Goddard College he studied acting at the Neighborhood Playhouse. Mamet taught for a while and did various other jobs. Back in Chicago in the 1970s he organized an ensemble acting group called the Saint Nicholas Company, which performed many of his plays.

In 1976 a double bill of *Sexual Perversity in Chicago* and *Duck Variations* appeared Off Broadway. The turning point in Mamet's career came in 1977 with the production of *American Buffalo* on Broadway. The play concerns three men who meet briefly in a junk shop and plan a burglary that never comes off. Mamet says he writes about the missing communication in our society. *A Life in the Theater* (1977) contains 26 scenes with two egotistical actors. *Glengarry Glen Ross* won the Pulitzer Prize in 1984. The play deals with the unscrupulous manipulations of real-estate salesmen. Mamet also wrote the movies *The Untouchables* (1986) and *Things Change* (1988). Some of his other plays are *The Water Engine* (1978), *The Woods* (1979), *Speed-the-Plow* (1988), *Oleanna* (1992) and *Cryptogram* (1995). Nonfiction prose is collected in *Writing in Restaurants* (1986), *The Cabin* (1992), *A Whore's Profession* (1994), and *Jafsie and John Henry* (1999). Essays on the theater are gathered in *True and False* (1997) and *Three Uses of the Knife: On the Nature and Purpose of Drama* (1998). Mamet wrote and directed the film *State and Main* (2000), a satire on Hollywood.

David Mamet has a growing reputation as one of the important modern playwrights in America. His plays lack plot, but they excel in psychological interplay between characters. He writes realistic plays in acid gutter language that tell about the pervasiveness and destruction of the American dream.
SAM SMILEY/BP

Man Against the Sky, The (1916),   a poem by EDWIN ARLINGTON ROBINSON. The title poem in a collection of Robinson's, "Man Against the Sky" helped consolidate his fame. Brooding on man's destiny, the poet examines several creeds that attempt to explain this lonely figure against the sky. He is any man—mankind symbolized. The "world on fire" that appears in the second line of the poem is World War I; it is also the sunset that stands for death, and the universe described by modern science.

Manchester, William (1922–   ),   journalist, novelist, biographer, historian. Born in Attleboro, Massachusetts, he was educated at the University of Massachusetts and the University of Missouri. Although Manchester has published four novels, his reputation rests primarily on the biographies and histories that have established him as one of the premier chroniclers of the major figures and events of our times. These include *Disturber of the Peace: The Life of H. L. Mencken* (1951); *The Death of a President* (1967), about the assassination of JOHN F. KENNEDY; *The Glory and the Dream: A Narrative History of America, 1932–1972* (1968); *American Caesar: Douglas MacArthur* (1978); and two volumes of an ongoing life of Winston Churchill, *The Last Lion: Visions of Glory, 1874–1932* (1984) and *The Last Lion: Alone, 1932–1940* (1988). His other works include *Controversy and Other Essays in Journalism* (1976) *Goodbye, Darkness* (1980), a memoir of his service in the Pacific Theater of World War II, and *A World Lit Only by Fire: The Medieval Mind* (1992).

Manchild in the Promised Land (1965),   an autobiography by CLAUDE BROWN.

Mandan Indians.   The Mandans were a tribe belonging to the Sioux linguistic family. They had an agricultural economy and inhabited permanent villages on the Missouri, near the present Bismarck, North Dakota. The explorer Vérendrye visited them in 1738, and Lewis and Clark spent the winter of 1804–05 with them. They were friendly to the mountain men and fur traders. GEORGE CATLIN also visited, writing about them and studying them in a number of paintings. Unfortunately, contact with whites brought also the smallpox that wiped them out as a tribe in 1837. In 1870 their survivors settled with the Sioux on the Fort Berthold Reservation in North Dakota. Their songs are studied in FRANCES DENSMORE's *Mandan and Hidatsa Music* (1923).

Mandel, Eli [Elias Wolf] (1922–1992),   poet, editor, teacher. Born in Estevan, Saskatchewan, Mandel was educated at the University of Saskatchewan and the University of Toronto. He taught for many years at York University. From the beginning his poems were marked by violence and pessimism, guilt and fear, as seen in *Fuseli Poems* (1960), *Black*

and Secret Man (1964), and *An Idiot Joy* (1967). In *Stony Plain* (1973) his subjects included World War II and the death camps. His later books are *Out of Place* (1977), a long poem rooted in personal observation of failed Jewish settlements in Saskatchewan; *Life Sentence* (1981), including poems and journals from visits to India, Peru, and Ecuador; and *Dreaming Backwards: Selected Poems* (1981). His essays are collected in *Criticism* (1966) *Another Time* (1977), and *The Family Romance*. (1986) He is the editor of several anthologies of contemporary Canadian verse.

Manfred, Frederick Feikema ["Feike Feikema"] (1912–1994),   novelist. Born near Doon, Iowa, Feikema was educated at Calvin College and worked at various mostly menial jobs in the 1930s before becoming a journalist and then a prolific author of fiction. Like VARDIS FISHER, he has accumulated a record of his home area, which he calls Siouxland, in which the personal shades into the historical. His style is energetic, sometimes rough, at its best an effective conveyor of his vision. His novels written under the name Feike Feikema include *The Golden Bowl* (1944), about Midwest farmers; *Boy Almighty* (1945), based on his sanitorium bout with tuberculosis; *This Is the Year* (1947), another farm novel; *The Chokecherry Tree* (1948, revised 1961), about a boy at odds with his surroundings; and the trilogy *World's Wanderer*, comprising *The Primitive* (1949), *The Brother* (1950), and *The Giant* (1951), about a young man's search for identity from his farm home to a college like Calvin to New York and return. His novels written under his real name came later and include a number evoking the history of Siouxland. Among them are *Lord Grizzly* (1954), about the mountain man HUGH GLASS; *Riders of Judgment* (1957), of Wyoming cattle wars in the 1890s; *Conquering Horse* (1959), about an Indian boy; *Scarlet Plume* (1964), about a white woman carried off by Sioux in 1862; *The Man Who Looked Like the Prince of Wales* (1965); and *King of Spades* (1966), about the 1870s gold rush into the Black Hills. His short stories are collected in *Arrow of Love* (1961) and *Apples of Paradise* (1968). *The Wind Blows Free* (1980) is a memoir of hitchhiking during the Depression.

Man from Home, The (1907),   a play by BOOTH TARKINGTON and HARRY LEON WILSON that became a hit. It contrasts the simple American with the sophisticated European. Daniel Voorhees Pike, of Indiana, goes abroad to reclaim his ward, who is in danger of becoming an expatriate and marrying a fortune-hunting nobleman.

Mangione, Jerre [Gerlando] (1909–1998),   writer, editor. Born in Rochester, New York, Mangione was raised by Sicilian relatives in the area he describes in *Mount Allegro* (1943). It is a first-rate rendering of the American immigrant experience. He was educated at Syracuse University and worked for the government and in advertising and public relations before teaching at the University of Pennsylvania from 1961 on. Published as a novel, *Mount Allegro* nevertheless forms a trilogy with two works of nonfiction in which the author continues his ethnic observations abroad: *Reunion in Sicily* (1950) and *A Passion for Sicilians* (1968). His other books include two novels, *The Ship and the Flame* (1948) and *Night Search* (1965); a brief record of immigration, *America is Also Italian* (1969); and a history of the FEDERAL WRITERS' PROJECT, *The Dream and the Deal* (1971).

Manhattan Transfer (1925), a novel by JOHN DOS PASSOS. For several years during the 1920s, the Pennsylvania Railroad maintained a station in the New Jersey meadows between Newark and Jersey City which it called Manhattan Transfer, where passengers between New York City and points south and west changed trains. Thus, in the title of the Dos Passos novel, "Manhattan Transfer" stands for the shifting and variegated life of New York City. The novel is composed with the newsreel and cinema technique Dos Passos often used and includes a staccato succession of descriptive and narrative scenes. The novel is an imaginative sociological study, intended to give a panoramic impression of a swarming metropolis. The story revolves around an actress who marries, loves, and divorces. Many other characters appear only fleetingly. The final effect is one of frustration and defeat. It was the novelist's first mature work and set the technical pattern and philosophy for the novels that followed.

Mankiewicz, Joseph L[eo] (1909–1993), scriptwriter, director, producer. Born in Pennsylvania, Joseph Mankiewicz joined his brother Herman (1897–1953) in Hollywood in 1929. Among his many screenplays are a number he also directed, including *A Letter to Three Wives* (1949), *All About Eve* (1950), *People Will Talk* (1951), *Julius Caesar* (1953), *Guys and Dolls* (1955), *The Quiet American* (1958), and *Cleopatra* (1962). Films he directed include *The Late George Apley* (1947) and *The Ghost and Mrs. Muir* (1947).

Mann, Emily (1952–), playwright. Born in Chicago, Mann grew up in a time and place of social change, and has used the ferment in her work. The interest awakened when her father showed her documents he had assembled for an oral history of concentration camp survivors led to Mann's interviewing a survivor in London and writing the plays *Annulla Allen: Autobiography of a Survivor* (1977) and *Annulla, An Autobiography* (revised and staged in 1985). *Still Life* (1980), about violence in America, is based on interviews with a Vietnam veteran, his wife and his mistress. *Execution of Justice* (1982) is rooted in trial transcripts and interviews dealing with the shooting murders of San Francisco's Mayor, George Moscone, and openly homosexual city supervisor Harvey Milk, by Dan White, a Vietnam veteran. *Having Our Say: The Delaney Sisters' First 100 Years* (1995) tells the story of the two daughters of a slave who, during their long lives, witnessed and recorded a century of change in race relations and the lives of women. *Greensboro* (1996) recalls the 1979 murder of five members of the Communist Workers Party during a demonstration against the Ku Klux Klan. Though the deaths were captured on videotape, they went unpunished, in part because of collusion by members of the police department.

Mann, Horace (1796–1859), legislator, educator. Born in Franklin, Massachusetts, Mann was educated at Brown University. He passed the bar, practiced law in Boston

and Dedham, served as state representative (1827–33) and state senator (1833–37), and then as secretary of the newly created state board of education. During his twelve-year tenure schools were improved, teacher salaries increased, and teacher training institutions established. In 1848 he was elected to the House of Representatives as an antislavery Whig. In 1853 he became first president of Antioch College. His second wife, Mary Peabody Mann, sister of ELIZABETH PEABODY, edited with others *The Life and Works of Horace Mann* (5 v. 1891).

Mann, Thomas (1875–1955), novelist. Born in Germany, Mann emigrated to the United States in 1938, lived for a while at Princeton, New Jersey, then settled in Santa Monica, California. He became a citizen in 1944, but in 1953 went to Switzerland and remained there the rest of his life. His daughter **Erika Mann** (1905–1969) wrote several books in English, including *School for Barbarians* (1938) and *The Lights Go Down* (1940). Her younger brother **Klaus Mann** (1906–1949), novelist and essayist, also published a number of books in English, among them an autobiography called *The Turning Point* (1942).

Thomas Mann wrote no works for publication in English, but he continued his writing in America and wrote among other books the final volume of his *Joseph* tetralogy, *Joseph the Provider* (1944), which he characterized as reflecting the spirit of America and being essentially a success story—Joseph's administration of the national economy, he said, "unmistakably reflects the New Deal." *Dr. Faustus* (1948) was also written in the United States. In 1951 Mann was elected to membership in the American Academy of Arts and Letters.

Manners, J[ohn] Hartley (1870–1928), actor, playwright. Manners came to the United States in 1902, playing in Lily Langtry's company. In 1912 he married the actress Laurette Taylor, and wrote for her his greatest success, PEG O' MY HEART (1912), a comedy about a wealthy Irish girl who goes to live with her aunt in London, saves her cousin from scandal, and marries the right man. The play had a long run and was produced in several languages in Europe. Manners also wrote *The House Next Door* (1909), *The Woman Intervenes* (1912), *Happiness* (1917), and *The National Anthem* (1920).

Manning, Marie. Pen name of BEATRICE FAIRFAX.

Manningoe, Nancy, a character in Faulkner's "That Evening Sun" and REQUIEM FOR A NUN. Left alone and awaiting murder by her husband after the end of "That Evening Sun," Nancy nevertheless plays an important part in *Requiem for a Nun*, in which she is Temple Drake's confidante and nursemaid to Temple's children. Because Nancy's past was as sordid as Temple's, Nancy is the one person whom Temple can trust. Nancy, however, is able to face the questions of guilt and responsibility honestly, whereas Temple is not.

Manrique, Jaime (1949–), novelist and poet. Born in Colombia, Manrique came to the United States as a teenager and graduated from the University of South Florida. In the U.S. he felt free to write "from the perspective of a gay Latino living in New York City." His 1978 novella *El Cadavar de Papa*, in which a gay protagonist murders his father, and, in drag, attempts to seduce his macho father-in-law, became a best seller in Colombia. *Colombian Gold* (1983) combines some of the material of the earlier novella with themes of political corruption. *Latin Moon in Manhattan* (1992) reflects the author's years as a Spanish interpreter in the courts. *Twilight at the Equator* (1997) tells of a young traveler's romanticized homesickness for Colombia. *Eminent Maricones: Arenas, Lorca, Puig, and Me* (1999) is a collection of short nonfiction pieces describing his own youth and the lives of REINALDO ARENAS, FEDERICO GARCIA LORCA, and MANUEL PUIG, three gay Latin writers who influenced him. Poetry collections include *Scarecrow* (1990) and *My Night with Federico Garcia Lorca* (1997).

Mansfield, Richard (1854–1907),   actor, playwright. Mansfield was a monologist on the English stage and later took roles in Gilbert and Sullivan operas. He came to the United States in 1882 and made a great hit in *A Parisian Romance* (1883). Thereafter, he was one of the great stars of the American stage, a romantic actor and autocrat who regarded a play primarily as a vehicle for Richard Mansfield. Mansfield won celebrity in the leading roles of *Dr. Jekyll and Mr. Hyde* (1887) and *Beau Brummell* (1890). He acted in plays by Shakespeare and helped introduce Shaw and Ibsen to the American stage.

One of his later successes was Booth Tarkington's *Monsieur Beaucaire.* For *The First Violin,* a play he wrote in collaboration with J. I. C. Clarke (1898), he assumed the pseudonym Meridan Phelps. He is also credited with a play entitled *Don Juan* (1891). PERCIVAL POLLARD, who adapted various plays for Mansfield, wrote a satirical novel about him, *The Imitator* (1901).

Mansion, The (1959),   a novel by WILLIAM FAULKNER. See THE HAMLET.

Man That Corrupted Hadleyburg, The (1900),   a story by MARK TWAIN and title piece of a collection of stories and essays. It is the story of a sack of money—the gold turns out to be lead—that a stranger leaves with a bank cashier in Hadleyburg. A note authorizes delivery of the sack to the person who years before made a certain remark after befriending the clerk. A secret letter comes to nineteen of the town's prominent men, telling them the supposed remark. All of them prepare to claim the treasure. In time comes exposure. The hypocrisy of American small-town culture is ruthlessly laid bare, but the town achieves the wisdom to change its official motto—"Lead Us Not Into Temptation"—by deleting "Not."

Manuductio ad Ministerium (1726),   a manual for divinity students by COTTON MATHER. In it he discusses science, experimental philosophy, the classics, modern languages, and belles-lettres. One section is a treatise on style, in the course of which Mather gives his ideas on "loading the rifts with ore" by constant enlargement of the text with "touches of erudition" and "profitable references," without which the text would be "jejune and empty pages." He advises divinity students: "All your days make a little recreation of poetry in the midst of your painful studies." The book was highly esteemed and was reprinted in London (1781, 1789) as *Dr. Cotton Mather's Student and Preacher.*

Manuscript Found in a Bottle.   See MS. FOUND IN A BOTTLE.

Man Who Came to Dinner, The (1939),   a play by MOSS HART and GEORGE S. KAUFMAN. The leading character embodies what was supposed to be a friendly burlesque on ALEXANDER WOOLLCOTT, then at the height of his celebrity. Woollcott himself was so pleased with his portrait that he played the role on the road (Monty Woolley played it on Broadway). The main character, Sheridan Whiteside, is the guest of a Midwestern family; when he suffers an accident he is immobilized in their home for some weeks. He invites various well-known and eccentric friends to visit him, meddles in family affairs, insults virtually everyone in town, and when he has earned his hosts' gratitude by at last recovering his health and is preparing to depart, he breaks his leg again. A motion-picture version was made in 1941.

Man Who Died Twice, The (1924),   a blank verse narrative by EDWIN ARLINGTON ROBINSON. A musician ruins his life by debauchery and, in bitter self-reproach, destroys the manuscripts of two symphonies he has written. He then prepares to die of starvation in his garret. Suddenly he feels the impulse of genius again, resolves to live, is inspired with the music of his "Third Symphony," and becomes resigned to life. He joins some street evangelists and attains salvation.

Man Without a Country, The (*Atlantic Monthly,* December 1863),   a story by EDWARD EVERETT HALE. This story made a profound impression when it first appeared, was reprinted as a brochure in 1865, and was gathered into Hale's collection *If, Yes, and Perhaps* (1868). Written with the intention of inspiring patriotism for the Union during the Civil War, it may have been occasioned by the remark of the Northern Copperhead Clement L. Vallandigham (1820–1871) that he didn't want to live in a country ruled by Lincoln. Lincoln banished him to the Confederacy in 1863, but he returned to campaign against Lincoln's reelection. Hale's powerful story of the naval officer who makes a hasty wish never to see America again is laid in the era of the 1805 conspiracy of AARON BURR in the Louisiana Territory. Philip Nolan was Hale's own invention and in no way connected with a real Philip Nolan who had fought in the war between Texas and Mexico. Hale wrote a supplementary story, *Philip Nolan's Friends* (1876), dealing with the real Nolan. An opera, with ARTHUR GUITERMAN supplying book and lyrics, and WALTER DAMROSCH the music, was produced in 1937.

Man with the Blue Guitar, The (1937),   a volume of verse by WALLACE STEVENS. Taking its name from a painting by Picasso, the title poem, in thirty-three parts, is a meditation on the relationship of art to nature and of the artistic medium to the artist. Accused of distorting reality, the man with the guitar replies, "Things as they are / Are changed upon the blue guitar." So, Stevens suggests, with poetry: the words insist on a reality of their own, not that of the external objects they seem to represent.

Man with the Golden Arm, The (1949),   a novel by NELSON ALGREN. Frankie Machine (Francis Majcinek), a gambling-house dealer, is said to have a golden arm so sure is his touch with cards. It seems that he might extricate himself from the Chicago Polish slum environment he has always known, but in the end his drug addiction drives him to suicide. As Frankie makes his way along the back streets of Chicago, the places he sees take on a phantasmagoric cast: the bars, the pool hall, the jail, inhabited by the bums and small-time criminals of Skid Row. Here society clumsily tries to deal with those it has made no room for, and fails. The book received a National Book Award in 1950 and was later made into a motion picture.

Man with the Hoe, The (1899),   a poem by EDWIN MARKHAM. Inspired by the powerful Millet painting of the same name, this poem appeared first in the San Francisco *Examiner* on January 15, 1899. It was immediately reprinted and translated into many languages as a spirited protest against the wrongs inflicted on labor.

Map of Virginia with a Description of the Country, A (1612),   an account by JOHN SMITH and others. The book provides a map of the shores of Chesapeake Bay, gives facts concerning the natural history of Virginia and adds a chronicle of occurrences in the colony from June 1608 to the end of 1609.

Mapple, Father.   The preacher of the sermon in chapter 9 of MOBY-DICK.

Marble, Dan[forth] (1810–1849),   actor. A Connecticut Yankee, Marble won early celebrity as a portrayer of Yankee roles. He toured the country for some years, then appeared (1836) in a play especially written for him by E. H. Thompson called *Sam Patch*. In 1844 he went on to London, where he followed J. H. Hackett in winning enthusiastic audiences for plays with Yankee parts.

Marble Faun, The (1860),   a novel by NATHANIEL HAWTHORNE. This is the last impressive book written by Hawthorne, and in it are found the themes central to his writing: the effects of guilt and the sense of gain and loss when one attains maturity. These themes occur as early as FANSHAWE and are set forth most brilliantly in THE SCARLET LETTER.

DONATELLO, an Italian count, is the central character, and the story deals with his transition from innocence to experience. His resemblance to the Faun of Praxiteles, a symbol for Hawthorne of natural innocence, is noted by the three other important characters: the sculptor Kenyon, and the two young art students, MIRIAM and Hilda. The female characters are the blonde and dark types so familiar in Hawthorne's fiction. Miriam is an exotic, dark woman resembling Zenobia in THE BLITHEDALE ROMANCE and Hester in *The Scarlet Letter*. Hilda is a fair New England girl whose innocence is symbolized by the white pigeons in her care. Miriam's background is somehow tainted by her relation to a mysterious stranger. Hawthorne, as usual, does not attempt to clear up the ambiguity of the stranger's hold on Miriam, and her guilt becomes the guilt of experience common to all people.

Donatello's love for Miriam and his interpretation of her desires leads him to kill the stranger; the murder is witnessed by Hilda so that, by implication, no one is free from the taint of the act. In the new maturity that comes to Donatello after the crime, and in his decision to turn himself over to the authorities, Hawthorne develops the theme of the fortunate fall.

The location, Rome, is an integral part of the action. In addition to its geographic and artistic landmarks, Rome figures in the story as the home of the Catholic Church. Hilda is driven to a priest by her need to confess, and the moral problems of the *felix culpa* form a focal point for the growth of experience in Donatello.

March, Jo.   An important character in LOUISA MAY ALCOTT's novel LITTLE WOMEN (1868). She is in part an autobiographical portrait.

March, Joseph Moncure (1899–1977),   newspaperman, music critic, poet. Born in New York City, March, while a student at Amherst, took part in ROBERT FROST's poetry group there and was highly praised by Frost. He flourished briefly in the 1920s, published two remarkable narrative poems, *The Wild Party* (1928) and *The Set-Up* (1928). Both are written in staccato rhythms and highly colloquial, tough diction.

March, William [pen name of **William Edward March Campbell**] (1893–1954),   novelist, short-story writer. Born in Mobile, Alabama, March grew up in Southern sawmill towns. From his Marine Corps experience in World War I came *Company K* (1933), a fiction in which each soldier tells his own history to create a composite account. His other novels include *Come In at the Door* (1934); *The Tallons* (1936); *The Looking Glass* (1943); *October Island*, about a missionary's wife who becomes a goddess on a South Sea island; and *The Bad Seed* (1954), about a child murderess who is a genetic criminal. The novel was successfully dramatized by MAXWELL ANDERSON (1954). His stories are collected in *Some Like Them Short* (1939) and *Trial Balance* (1945). *A William March Omnibus* (1956) contains *Company K, October Island*, and a number of short stories.

Marching On (1927),   a historical novel by JAMES BOYD. Set in the time of the Civil War, it is in part a love story, the narrative of a young man's attempts to win a bride above his own social station, but the book is memorable chiefly for its descriptions of the battles of Antietam and Chancellorsville and a Federal prisoner-of-war compound.

Marching Through Georgia (1865),   a song by HENRY C. WORK, who wrote both the words and the music. It is a rollicking tune that celebrates General Sherman's march to the sea.

March to the Sea.   Gen. WILLIAM T. SHERMAN, in command of the Union Army of Tennessee, believed that only the total destruction of Southern resources and morale could bring an end to the Civil War. After his conquest of Atlanta he led his 62,000 troops on a march to Savannah, leaving a swath of destruction fifty miles wide behind him. The march lasted from November 12 until December 21, 1864. Later he turned north to meet the Union forces in Virginia. (See MARCHING THROUGH GEORGIA.)

Many books describe the march and its effects: *Lincoln Finds a General*, by K. P. Williams (1949); *Story of the Great*

March (1865), a contemporary account by Major George Ward Nichols; *Sherman's March Through the Carolinas* (1956), by John Barrett; Burke Davis, *Sherman's March* (1980); and *The Memoirs of William Tecumseh Sherman* (2 v., 2nd ed. 1886). *Gone with the Wind* (1936) by Margaret Mitchell is a memorable portrait of the terror and anguish of those who stood in Sherman's path.

Marcin, Max (1879–1948), newspaperman, dramatist, film and radio writer, short-story writer. Born in Germany, Marcin was a prosperous newspaperman and made large sums writing fiction for popular magazines. He dealt mainly with crime, both as journalist and fictionist. His first play, *The House of Glass* (1915), was a crime story written in collaboration with GEORGE M. COHAN. He wrote many hits, either alone or in collaboration with Cohan, DONALD OGDEN STEWART, SAMUEL SHIPMAN, and others. Among them were *Eyes of Youth* (1916), *Here Comes the Bride* (1916), *The Woman in Room 13* (1917), *The Night Cap* (1921), and *Los Angeles* (1927). He spent ten years in Hollywood, returned to Broadway to work as a play doctor, and then on the staff of CBS as director of various shows dealing with crime. He also wrote a four-act comic melodrama, *Cheating Cheaters* (1932).

Marco Bozzaris (*New York Review*, June 1825), a poem by FITZ-GREENE HALLECK. Marco Bozzaris was a Greek hero of the War of Independence against the Turks (1822–23). The battle in which Bozzaris died is the subject of Halleck's spirited poem, expressing the general admiration felt for the Greeks in the United States.

Marco Millions (1928), a play by EUGENE O'NEILL. The Marco of O'Neill's play is Marco Polo, who is used as a whipping boy to express the dramatist's scorn for mercenary people. Marco, interested only in making his millions, does not see that Kubla Khan's daughter is in love with him. He serves her only for the bonus he hopes to receive and at last marries a fat, commonplace Venetian. Contrasted with Marco's commercialism is the wiser insight of the Orient.

Marcuse, Herbert (1898–1979), political philosopher, sociologist. Marcuse, already a noted sociologist, fled Germany in 1933 and immigrated to the U.S. in 1934. He taught at Columbia, Harvard, Brandeis, and the University of California at San Diego. His dense and complex work attempted to apply the theories of Marx, Freud, and Hegel to modern technological society. In *Eros and Civilization* (1955), he relates sexual repression to political and social repression. In *One-Dimensional Man* (1964) he argues that the mass materialism of American culture stifles all diversity. Marcuse believed that revolutionary ideals of freedom can exist in a nonrevolutionary, industrial society. He saw American society as one that systematically impeded freedom, and believed that students and minority groups were the most effective agents of social change. Many of his radical libertarian ideals, sometimes imperfectly understood, were espoused by student radicals in the 1960s. Among Marcuse's other books are *Soviet Marxism* (1958), *Counterrevolution and Revolt* (1972), and *The Aesthetic Dimension* (1978).

Marcy, Randolph Barnes (1812–1887), army officer, explorer, memoirist. Born in Massachusetts, Marcy had a distinguished military career. He served as a major general during the Civil War and later became Inspector General. Before the war he had explored portions of the Southwest, as related in W. B. Parker's *Notes Taken During the Expedition Commanded by Capt. R. B. Marcy, U.S.A.: Through Unexplored Texas, in the Summer of 1854* (1856). Marcy himself wrote *The Prairie Traveler* (1859), *Thirty Years of Army Life on the Border* (1866), and *Border Reminiscences* (1872). W. E. Holden has written *Beyond the Cross Timbers: Travels of R. B. Marcy, 1812–1887* (1955).

Mardi: And a Voyage Thither (1849), a novel by HERMAN MELVILLE. In this, his third novel, Melville entertained questions of ethics and metaphysics, politics and culture, sin and guilt, innocence and experience. The complexity of the novel's content, in fact, destroys all pretensions to literary form. Originally a narrative of adventure, *Mardi* became an allegory of mind.

The most important sections of *Mardi* recount a symbolic quest for Absolute Truth, as undertaken by five men: Taji, the young monomaniacal hero; Babbalanja, a philosopher; Yoomy, a poet; Mohi, a historian; and King Media, a man of common sense. On King Media's boat, they sail through the island archipelagoes of Mardi (the World), stopping at various countries, including Vivenza (the United States), where Melville criticizes the institution of slavery and the tendency to mobocracy. In their travels Taji, who most nearly represents Melville, kills a South Sea Islander priest, Aleema, in order to rescue Yillah, a beautiful young white woman of seemingly prelapsarian innocence. But Yillah disappears, and in seeking her, Taji undertakes a double quest: for Final Truth and for Lost Innocence. At the same time that Taji seeks Yillah or Innocent Love, he is sought by Hautia, the incarnation of sophisticated sexuality, who speaks in the language of flowers. Hautia also represents retribution for sin, and haunts Taji for murdering the priest. Thus Taji becomes both pursuer and pursued. He is last seen alone, sailing his craft on desperate seas.

For Melville *Mardi* was a preparation for future work, which, after *Mardi*, took on new dimensions. For the first time he presented a questing hero, an analysis of metaphysical problems, and a book more important on the symbolic than on the realistic level, in these respects anticipating *Moby-Dick* and *Pierre*.

Margaret (1849, rev. 1851), a novel by SYLVESTER JUDD. Judd depicts a Maine community that is remodeled on Fourierist lines. The novel helped acquaint the public with the Transcendentalism and Unitarianism of Emerson and Alcott. As an early regional study, it gave an affectionate and accurate picture of the Maine landscape, human and natural.

Margaret Fleming (1890; revived 1907, 1915), a play by JAMES A. HERNE. Herne's play shocked his generation by its frank treatment of an act of adultery and its forgiveness; to a later generation it seems surprisingly sentimental. W. D. Howells, Hamlin Garland, Mary E. Wilkins, and other leaders of the realistic movement in fiction praised the play, which had a short run.

Margaret Howth (1862),   a novel by REBECCA HARDING DAVIS. The background is an Indiana milltown.

Margaret Smith's Journal (1849),   a story by JOHN GREENLEAF WHITTIER. Margaret is an English girl who comes to America in 1678 to visit relatives. She meets several persons of historical note, and Whittier makes use of the narrative to tell much about New England history. Margaret keeps a diary in which she reveals her liberal and generous character as she speaks of slavery, witchcraft, Indian warfare, bigotry, and other matters that were Whittier's own great concerns.

Marginalia.   Short essays by EDGAR ALLAN POE, some of them excerpted from earlier reviews or articles that had appeared in the *Democratic Review, Godey's, Graham's*, and the *Southern Literary Messenger* from 1844 to 1849. They are of varying character and merit, sometimes merely factual in a way that reveals Poe's deep interest in science, sometimes critical, sometimes imaginative, and frequently suggestive concerning Poe's literary methods. Among other things, he defended the idea that character could be read from handwriting, held that modern oratory was greater than that of the Greeks, exalted the importance of punctuation, and analyzed songwriting and dreams.

María (1867).   A novel by JORGE ISAACS (1837–95), Colombian poet and novelist. Perhaps the most widely read South American novel, *María* is a romantic idyll that describes the ill-starred love affair between the title character and her cousin Efraín. Although the plot is cloyingly sentimental by contemporary standards, the author's picture of life in Colombia's Cauca Valley, where the action takes place, retains its freshness and charm.

Maria Chapdelaine (1921),   a novel by LOUIS HÉMON, posthumously published. It is a story of French-Canadian pioneers who go out into the unbroken wilderness in the Lake St. John country beyond the Saguenay River in Quebec. Samuel Chapdelaine, his wife, and their six children work arduously at their task of making farmland.

Maria Kittle, The History of (1793),   a tale by ANN ELIZA BLEECKER. Probably the first piece of American fiction dealing chiefly with Native Americans—in general represented as cruel and bloodthirsty—this short novel relates the harrowing experiences of its heroine, who was carried off by Indians during the period of the French and Indian War.

Mariátegui, José Carlos (1895–1930),   Peruvian essayist, one of the major thinkers of the Latin American left. Mariátegui's *Siete ensayos de interpretación de la realidad peruana (Seven Essays Interpreting Peruvian Reality*, 1928) constitutes an original and probing Marxist analysis of Peruvian life and literature and of the neocolonial social and economic factors that shaped both. He founded the literary journal *Amauta* (1926–30), in which many of his own impeccably written essays were first published and which served as the intellectual nerve center of an entire genera-

tion. *Amauta* provided a forum for all manner of revolutionary aesthetic, religious, and political thought.

Marie Rogêt, The Mystery of. See MYSTERY OF MARIE ROGÊT, THE.

Marion, Francis ["The Swamp Fox"] (1732?–1795), Revolutionary soldier. Marion commanded militia troops that practiced guerrilla action against British forces in South Carolina, living in swamps and forests. He has been a favorite figure for novelists. W. G. Simms wrote a biography of Marion (1844) and then described him in a series of seven historical romances. Of the seven, five are related stories: *The Partisan* (1835), *Mellichampe* (1836), *Katherine Walton* (1851), *The Forayers* (1855), and *Eutaw* (1856). The remaining two novels are: THE SCOUT (1841) and *Woodcraft* (1853). Marion also appears as a minor character in John P. Kennedy's HORSE-SHOE ROBINSON (1835); in an anonymous novel, *The Swamp Steed* (1852); and in Jefferson Carter's *Madam Constantia* (1919). William Cullen Bryant celebrated Marion in a spirited poem, "Song of Marion's Men" (1831).

Marjorie Daw (1873),   a short story by T. B. ALDRICH, John Fleming, confined to his home during a spell of illness, receives from his friend Edward Delaney a series of letters describing in glowing terms Edward's neighbor, Marjorie Daw. His letters in reply are so ardent that Edward tells him Marjorie is ready to return his love. Then John recovers, telegraphs that he is coming to claim her hand, and is informed by Edward, who flees hurriedly, that there is no Marjorie Daw. When the story appeared in the *Atlantic Monthly*, it was regarded as a prime example of the new short-story techniques.

Marjorie Morningstar (1955),   a novel by HERMAN WOUK. This is the story of a Jewish girl in New York City and her progress via love affairs to suburbia and a family.

Markfield, Wallace [Arthur] (1926–   ),   novelist. Born in Brooklyn, New York, Markfield was educated at Brooklyn College and New York University. His novels humorously portray the Jewish experience in New York City and environs. They include *To an Early Grave* (1964); *Teitlebaum's Window* (1970), about growing up in Brighton Beach during the Depression; *You Could Live It If They Let You* (1974); and *Radical Surgery* (1991). His stories are collected in *Multiple Orgasms* (1977).

Markham, Edwin (1852–1940),   farmer, teacher, poet, lecturer. In his boyhood Markham herded sheep and worked as a farm hand, going to school for three months during the year. After attending the State Normal School at San Jose, he taught in various parts of California. In 1899 he completed his poem THE MAN WITH THE HOE, inspired by Millet's painting. Both the subject matter—a protest against exploitation of the poor—and the style, sonorous and rhetorical, were then at the height of fashion. Markham soon was able to abandon teaching and devote himself to writing and lecturing on poetry and on social and industrial problems. He won another great success with his poem "Lincoln, the Man of the People." Frank Norris is believed to have used, him as the model for his sensitive, mystical Presley in THE OCTOPUS. Markham's works include *The Ballad of the Gallows Bird* (1896), *The Man with* *the Hoe and Other Poems* (1899), *Lincoln and Other Poems* (1901), *Gates of Paradise and Other Poems* (1920), *New Poems: Eighty Songs at 80* (1932), and *Collected Poems* (1940).

Markoe, Peter (1752?–1792),   poet, satirist, dramatist. Markoe's father was a wealthy American with plantation holdings in the West Indies. Born in St. Croix, Markoe was educated at Oxford and possibly at Trinity College, Dublin. In 1775 he was listed as a captain in the Philadelphia City Militia. He began writing verse at an early age, but all his best-known writings come after the war. His tragedy *The Patriot Chief* (1784) was apparently never produced but was praised by John Parke (1754–1789) in a poem, *To Mr. Peter Markoe on His Excellent Tragedy Called "The Patriot Chief,"* although Parke urged Markoe to employ native themes. Markoe's *Miscellaneous Poems* appeared in 1787. *The Times* (1788) was a topical satire praised by contemporary critics. Markoe's comic opera *Reconciliation, or, The Triumph of Nature* (1790) never reached the boards. To Markoe are attributed *The Algerine Spy in Pennsylvania* (1787), described as "Letters Written by a Native of Algiers on the Affairs of the U.S. in America," and *The Storm, A Poem Descriptive of the Late Tempest* (1788). Sister Mary C. Diebels has written an account of *Peter Markoe, A Philadelphia Writer* (1944).

Marks, Jeannette [Augustus] (1875–1964),   writer of juveniles, poet, playwright. Born in Chattanooga and educated abroad and at Wellesley College, Marks taught English at Mt. Holyoke from 1901 until her retirement. In 1911 she won the Welsh National Theater prize for *The Merry Merry Cuckoo* and *Welsh Honeymoon*, plays that enjoyed great popularity in the U.S. and in Great Britain. She organized the Play and Poetry Shop (1916) at South Hadley, Massachusetts, where poets and dramatists were invited to lecture and read from their works. In addition to writing, directing plays, and teaching, she wrote children's books, poetry, and numerous scholarly articles. *The Family of the Barretts, a Colonial Romance* (1938) was the result of a study of Elizabeth Barrett Browning. As a liberal Quaker, she worked in various causes, including seven years spent in aiding Sacco and Vanzetti (see SACCO-VANZETTI CASE); she reported the trial in *Thirteen Days* (1929). Among her other works are *The Cheerful Cricket* (1907), *Through Welsh Doorways* (1909), *Early English Hero Tales* (1915), *Three Welsh Plays* (1917), *Willow Pollen* (1921), *The Sun Chaser* (1922), *Genius and Disaster: Studies in Drugs and Genius* (1925), *The Merry Merry Cuckoo and Other Welsh Plays*, (1927), and *Life and Letters of Mary Emma Woolley* (1955).

Marks, Percy (1891–1956),   teacher, novelist. Born in California and educated at the University of California and Harvard, Marks taught at Dartmouth, Brown, and elsewhere before he tossed a bombshell in the form of *The Plastic Age* (1924), a novel of undergraduate life considered shocking in its day. After the success of *The Plastic Age*, which he never again approached, Marks turned to writing to earn his livelihood. *Martha* (1925) is about a half-Indian woman. *Lord of Himself* (1927), a sequel to *The Plastic Age*, was followed by more than a dozen novels, among them *The Unwilling God*

(1929), *A Tree Grown Straight* (1936), *What's a Heaven For?* (1938), *No Steeper Wall* (1940), *Full Flood* (1942), *Shades of Sycamore* (1944), and *Blair Marriman* (1949). *Which Way Parnassus* (1926) was a nonfiction attack on higher education in America.

Mark Twain.   See TWAIN, MARK.

Marlatt, Daphne [Buckle] (1942–   ),   poet. Born in Melbourne, Australia, Daphne Buckle came with her parents to British Columbia in 1951 and was educated at the University of British Columbia and Indiana University before settling down as a writer in Vancouver in 1970. Her favorite mode of expression is long, prosaic lines presented as narrative verse. Her volumes include *Frames* (1968), retelling Andersen's "The Snow Queen" for its reflection on her own life; *Rings* (1971), musings of a woman whose marriage is disintegrating; *Vancouver Poems* (1972), the city seen through a single consciousness; and *Steveston* (1974), about a Japanese Canadian fishing village. *Zocalo* (1977), uses a long line to record a woman's experiences as a visitor to Yucatan. At the opposite extreme is *Leaf/leafs* (1969), images presented in lines of one word or syllable. *Net Work* (1980) is a volume of selected writings. Her poetry collections include *Here and There* (1981), *How Hug a Stone* (1983), and *Touch to My Tongue* (1984). *Ana Historic* (1988) is a novel. Her second novel, *Taken* (1996), focuses on an Australian couple whose experiences resemble those of her parents during World War II.

Marmion, or The Battle of Flodden Field (prod. 1812, pub. 1816),   a play by JAMES NELSON BARKER. This historical drama in blank verse, apparently a decorous production dealing with a conflict between James IV of Scotland and Henry VIII of England, was first attributed to Thomas Morton, an English dramatist, for fear the audience would spurn a play by an American. The play was intended to symbolize the conflict between the United States and England that led to the War of 1812. It held the stage for years and was played as late as 1848.

Marquand, John P[hillips] (1893–1960),   newspaperman, short-story writer, novelist, critic. Marquand was born in Wilmington, Delaware. In his boyhood Marquand's family moved to Newburyport, Massachusetts, a place that became a frequent background for his fiction. He went to Harvard, worked on the Boston *Transcript* and New York *Tribune*, wrote copy for an advertising agency, and saw action in World War I. After 1921, he lived in Newburyport, Boston, and New York City—with time off for visits to the Orient.

Marquand was a first-rate storyteller who dealt amusingly and sometimes profoundly with the characteristic dilemmas of his era. He began his writing career with *Prince and Boatswain* (1915), a collection of sketches. *The Unspeakable Gentleman* (1922) contains some Newburyport passages descriptive of an earlier day. *Four of a Kind* (1923) is a gathering of four tales. (Marquand's shorter writings were collected in *Thirty Years*, 1954.) *The Black Cargo* (1925) is concerned with the opium trade. *Lord Timothy Dexter* (1925) is the biography of an eccentric New Englander. *Warning Hill* (1930), with its emphasis on social status, is often regarded as a precursor of Marquand's later manner. There followed *Haven's End* (1933) and three tales set in the Orient: *Ming Yellow* (1934), *No Hero* (1935), and *Thank You, Mr. Moto* (1936). Marquand also contributed stories about Mr. Moto, a polite Japanese, to *Collier's* and *Saturday Evening Post*.

Marquand began the second stage in his career with THE LATE GEORGE APLEY (1937), which won a Pulitzer Prize for its ironic picture of a Boston family. *Wickford Point* (1939) carries the study a little further. In H. M. PULHAM, ESQ. (1941) a man writes his memoirs as he prepares to attend the twenty-fifth reunion of his Harvard class. *So Little Time* (1943) is the story of a play doctor in New York. *Repent in Haste* (1945) tells of a wartime marriage made too quickly. *B. F.'s Daughter* (1946) describes a domineering tycoon and his domineering offspring. *Point of No Return* (1949) is the story of a banker waiting for a promotion. In MELVILLE GOODWIN, U.S.A. (1951) a general is studied at all the stages of his development. *Sincerely, Willis Wayde* (1955) expresses satirically Marquand's disillusionment with business and its effect on human nature. *Women and Thomas Harrow* (1958) is chiefly about the New York theater of the 1920s. *Timothy Dexter Revisited* (1960), published posthumously, returns to the Newburyport setting of the first Timothy Dexter book.

Marquette, Jacques (1637–1675),   Jesuit priest, missionary, explorer. Père Marquette came to New France as a missionary in 1666. He spent two years studying Indian languages and customs and then began work among the Ottawa Indians at Sault Ste. Marie, Michigan. In 1671 he established a mission at Mackinac Island. In 1673, in company with Louis Joliet, he began explorations that resulted in increased knowledge of many regions now part of the United States, particularly those along the Mississippi. Marquette's journal of his discoveries and observations was first published in 1681 and was reprinted in Reuben G. Thwaites' *Jesuit Relations* (1896–1901, v. 59). It reveals him as a keen observer, a practical man, an able writer. Francis Parkman included an account of Marquette in his *Jesuits in North America* (1867).

Marquis, Don[ald Robert Perry] (1878–1937), newspaperman, writer. Born in Illinois, Marquis worked in Atlanta on JOEL CHANDLER HARRIS's *Uncle Remus's Magazine*, then became a columnist in New York for the *Sun* and the *Tribune*. His stories and verse about ARCHY AND MEHITABEL, the cockroach and the cat that lived in the *Sun* office, are still read. The roach writes the stories without capitalizations because he cannot hit the shift key on the typewriter: "coarse/jocosity/ catches the crowd/ shakespeare/ and i/ are often/ low browed." The cat, "toujours gai," roamed widely in search of ribald adventures. To these two figures, Marquis devoted *archy and mehitabel* (1927) and several sequels, all gathered from his column and collected after his death in an omnibus, *The Lives and Times of archy and mehitabel* (1940), illustrated by GEORGE HERRIMAN. Some of the stories were made into a musical (1954) by George Kleinsinger and Joe Darion. Among other characters created by Marquis were Clem Hawley, the Old

Soak, an uninhibited enemy of prohibition; Hermione and her Little Group of Serious Thinkers, all apostles of the platitudinous; and the Cave Man and his battered lady love. They appeared in several books: *Hermione* (1916); *The Old Soak* (1916, made into a play, 1926); *The Old Soak's History of the World* (1924, 1934); and *Love Sonnets of a Cave Man and Other Verses* (1928).

Marquis was chiefly a poet, a master of the folk style and the satiric vein, as in *Dreams and Dust* (1915), *Noah an' Jonah an' Cap'n Smith* (1921), *Poems and Portraits* (1922), *Sonnets to a Red-Haired Lady* (1922), and *The Awakening* (1924). Marquis deeply pondered and often rewrote a play on the last days of Jesus, *The Dark Hours* (1924), which he produced himself in 1932. He wrote fiction about the South in *Carter and Other People* (1921), and some of his striking short stories may be found in *The Revolt of the Oyster* (1922). Deep protest is heard in *The Almost Perfect State* (1927) and *Chapters for the Orthodox* (1934). He left an incomplete novel, *Sons of the Puritans*, largely autobiographical, which was published posthumously (1939). In 1946 *The Best of Don Marquis* was issued with an introduction by his friend CHRISTOPHER MORLEY. A biography by Edward Anthony, *O Rare Don Marquis*, appeared in 1962.

Marryat, Frederick (1792–1848),   naval officer, writer. Marryat served in the British navy for twenty-four years, retiring with the rank of captain. Thereafter he wrote first-rate adventure tales such as *Mr. Midshipman Easy* (1836) and *Masterman Ready* (1841). Marryat lived for two years (1837–39) in the United States and Canada and published *The Diary in America, with Remarks on Its Institutions* (6 v. 1839). The book, like others by British authors, aroused much resentment in this country. Marryat was hanged in effigy and his books burned. Among Marryat's later books were the novels *The Settlers in Canada: Written for Young People* (1844); *The Children of the New Forest* (1847); and a travel book *Travels and Adventures of Monsieur Violet in California, Sonora, and Western Texas* (1853), made up largely of extracts from JOSIAH GREGG's *Commerce of the Prairies* (1844). There also were passages from George W. Kendall's *Narrative of the Texan Santa Fe Expedition* (1844). Marryat's son **Frank Marryat** wrote observations of the California gold rush, *Mountains and Molehills* (1855).

Marse Chan (*Century Magazine*, April 1844; part of the collection *In Ole Virginia*, 1887),   a story in dialect by THOMAS NELSON PAGE. The tale is told by the servant of a likable Southerner called Marse Chan by his faithful retainer. The hero loves a girl who returns his affection but, because of family pressure, pretends to disdain him. They are reconciled just before he is killed on the battlefield, and she mourns him for the rest of her life. It became one of the best-known of Page's nostalgic stories of the antebellum South.

Marse Henry.   A name given to HENRY WATTERSON (1840–1921), editor of the Louisville *Courier-Journal* (1868–1918).

Marsh, George Perkins (1801–1882),   lawyer, public official, linguist, diplomat, conservationist. Born in Woodstock, Vermont, Marsh practiced law, was elected to various public offices, and served in the House of Representatives and as minister to Turkey. In 1861 he was appointed by Lincoln as our first minister to Italy, where he served till his death. Marsh discussed the English language and its Scandinavian and Anglo-Saxon elements in *Lectures on the English Language* (1860) and *The Origin and History of the English Language* (1862). In these volumes he anticipated linguistic views of later scholars. He was also a pioneer in the field of conservation. He wrote *Man and Nature* (1864, rev. 1874), which anticipated contemporary attempts to correct man's wasteful use of natural resources. David Lowenthal wrote *George Perkins Marsh: Versatile Vermonter* (1958).

Marsh, James (1794–1842), clergyman, teacher, educational administrator, translator, editor. Born in Hartford, Vermont, Marsh studied at Dartmouth and entered the ministry. He published a two-volume translation of Herder's *Spirit of Hebrew Poetry* (1833). He prepared young JOHN ADAMS [2] for Harvard, taught for three years at Hampden-Sydney, was appointed president of the University of Vermont in 1826, and later taught there as professor of moral and intellectual philosophy. Marsh edited Coleridge's *Aids to Reflection* (1829) with a "Preliminary Essay," also the same writer's *The Friend* (1831). His writings served to bolster the new movements of Unitarianism and Transcendentalism; they were collected by Joseph Torrey in *The Remains of the Rev. James Marsh, with a Memoir* (1842).

Marshall, Christopher (1709–1797), pharmacist, public official, diarist. Born in Ireland, Marshall came to Philadelphia about 1727 and became a leading pharmacist. When the Revolution began, he participated (1775) in a conference that laid the groundwork for a new state. Throughout the war Marshall kept a journal, first published in part in 1839 as *Passages from the Remembrance of Christopher Marshall* and supplemented ten years later. In 1877 came a still fuller version, covering the years from 1774 to 1781. He was interested in many matters besides the war, and his diary reveals him as a man of great kindliness and faithful to Quaker principles except in his support of the war, for which he was expelled from the Society of Friends.

Marshall, Edison (1894–1967), novelist, short-story writer, explorer. Born in Indiana, Marshall became a traveler in Alaska, Siberia, Central Africa, and other lands who wrote of adventure with carefully constructed backgrounds. Among his books are *The Voice of the Pack* (1920), *The Snowshoe Trail* (1921), *The Land of Forgotten Men* (1923), *The Deadfall* (1927), *Forlorn Island* (1932), *The White Brigand* (1937), *Benjamin Blake* (1941); *The Infinite Woman* (1951), *American Captain* (1954), *Inevitable Hour* (1957), *Pagan King* (1959), *Earth Grant* (1960), *West with The Vikings* (1961), *Cortez and Marina* (1963), and *The Lost Colony* (1964).

Marshall, Humphry (1722–1801), botanist. Marshall, like his cousin John Bartram, was deeply interested in botany. In 1785 he published the first book on American forest shrubs and trees, arranging them in Linnaean classifications: *Arbustrum Americanum: The American Grove.*

Marshall, Paule [Burke] (1929–   ), novelist, short-story writer. Born in Brooklyn, New York, Marshall was educated at Brooklyn College. In her first novel, *Brown Girl, Brownstones* (1959), she tells of a young woman growing up, as she herself did, as the child of immigrants from Barbados living in the Barbadian section of Brooklyn. Later work is similarly enriched by ties to black Caribbean sensibilities and the folkways and rhythms of New York immigrant speech. Her other novels are *The Chosen Place, the Timeless People* (1969), about an American research group on a Caribbean island, *Praisesong for the Widow* (1983), about a wealthy American confronted on a Caribbean vacation with reminders of her West Indian and African heritage, *Daughters* (1991), and *The Fisher King* (2000). Her stories are collected in *Soul Clap Hands and Sing* (1961) and *Reena and Other Stories* (1983).

Marshes of Glynn, The (pub. anonymously, 1878, in *The Masque of Poets*), a poem by SIDNEY LANIER. In this poem Lanier reaches the height of his lifelong attempt to reconcile the techniques of music and poetry. Its lush imagery sensuously depicts the sea marshes of Glynn County, Georgia, which Lanier visited in 1875.

Martí, José [Julian] (1853–1895), poet, essayist. Born in Havana of poor parents, he was sent by a patron to the Institute of Havana for his education. He became known not only as the apostle of Cuban independence but also as one of the most original and influential writers of Latin America. As a youth he was imprisoned and later deported from Cuba because of his opposition to Spanish rule and remained an exile for most of his life. From 1881 to 1895, he lived in New York City, working as a newspaper correspondent, Uruguayan consul, teacher, and translator. At the same time, he tirelessly collected funds, made speech after speech, and founded the Cuban Revolutionary Party in order to prepare a military expedition that would drive the Spaniards from the island. In 1895 Martí decided to return to Cuba to take advantage of renewed revolutionary sentiment there. His journal, *Diario de Cabo Haitiano a Dos Rios* (1941), and letters to family and friends record his emotions as he and General Máximo Gómez reached Cuba with four companions and joined other insurgents. During a skirmish at Dos Ríos, Martí disobeyed Gómez's order to retreat and was killed by Spanish soldiers.

Martí the poet is often regarded as a forerunner of MODERNISMO, though his work belongs to no school. His verses, written in a fresh, uniquely personal style, deal ardently, sometimes mystically, with familial and romantic love, freedom, and death. His best-known poems are in three collections: *Ismaelillo* (1882), addressed to his young son; *Versos libres*, written mainly in 1882 but not published until the 20th century; and *Versos sencillos* (1891). Many of his prose works, such as the essays *Nuestra América* (1891) and *Simón Bolívar* (1893), express his faith in the future greatness of Hispanic America. A perceptive critic of the U.S., Martí also wrote articles such as "Coney Island" (1881), "Emerson" (1882), "Jesse James" (1882), and "Walt Whitman" (1887). An *Obras completas* was published in 27 volumes in 1954.

Martin, Abe. An old farmer, of scarecrow figure and shrewd homespun wisdom, who appears in the writings of FRANK MCKINNEY ("KIN") HUBBARD. His pungent, often cynical sayings in Hoosier dialect were gathered from a column in the Indianapolis *News* in twenty-six volumes and two books of selections: *Abe Martin's Furrows* (1911) and *Abe Martin's Wise-Cracks* (1930).

Martin, Helen Reimensnyder (1868–1939), short-story writer, novelist. Martin's special field was the region of the Pennsylvania Dutch—she was born in Lancaster, Pennsylvania. Her first and best-known novel, *Tillie: A Mennonite Maid* (1904), is set in that background. Martin knew well the customs of the Mennonites. Among her other books are *Sabina: A Story of the Amish* (1905), *The Revolt of Anne Royle* (1908), *Barnabetta* (1914), *Martha of the Mennonite Country* (1915), *Ye That Judge* (1926), *Yoked with a Lamb and Other Tales* (1930), and *The Ordeal of Minnie Schultz* (1939). *Barnabetta* was turned into a play called *Erstwhile Susan* (1916) that was long a vehicle for Minnie Maddern Fiske.

Martin, William (1950–), novelist. Born in Cambridge, Massachusetts, Martin was educated at Harvard and the University of Southern California. His first novel *Back Bay* (1980) set the pattern for his use of historical subject matter served up with fictional techniques. A silver tea set, said to have been made by Paul Revere for George Washington, is traced through its theft from the White House during the War of 1812 and its loss overboard during a shipboard fight in Boston Harbor. *Nnerve Endings* (1984) has a kidney recipient investigating the boating explosion in which his donor, a film producer planning to expose corruption in the cable television business, was killed. *The Rising of the Moon* (1987) deals with the Easter Uprising of 1916 in Ireland. *Cape Cod* (1991) traces a rivalry between two families from the Mayflower voyage to the twentieth century. *Annapolis* (1996), a novel about American naval history, and *Citizen Washington* (1999) fill in the details of well-known places and people. Martin also wrote the script for the television drama *George Washington: The Man Who Wouldn't be King* (1992), part of the Public Broadcasting series *The American Experience*.

Martin Chuzzlewit (1843), a novel by Charles Dickens. Its hero visits America, is fleeced in a real-estate deal, and sees American manners and morals at their worst. He returns to England completely disillusioned, as Dickens himself had been after his own visit, recorded in AMERICAN NOTES FOR GENERAL CIRCULATION (1842).

Martin Eden (1909), a novel by JACK LONDON. This autobiographical novel tells of London's struggle to achieve success, his experiences with women, and his disgust with society.

Martín Fierro (1872), a narrative poem by JOSÉ HERNÁNDEZ. What is now considered the Argentine national classic was not recognized as such until the subject of its tale, the gaucho, had historically disappeared. This masterpiece of GAUCHO LITERATURE follows the transformation of a brutally conscripted cowboy into an army deserter and outlaw. Martín Fierro, in the tradition of the minstrel, tells his own life story: he suffers injustice under the abusive power of law officers, he fights duels, and he finally flees with his friend Cruz into the Indian-held territories. The second part, *La vuelta de Martín Fierro* (1879), portrays him ready to strike a pact with society. The political content of the poem was promptly acknowledged in Argentina, but its literary quality was first recognized by the Spanish poet de Unamuno some twenty years after its publication. Drawing from the gaucho oral tradition and expressing the gaucho sense of worth and rivalry with the educated folk from Buenos Aires, *Martin Fierro* became a favorite among the illiterate gauchos, who paid to hear it read in the camps and general stores of the *pampa*.

Martineau, Harriet (1802–1876), writer. A prolific English author, Martineau came to America in 1834, supported the abolitionist cause, visited New England, New York, the Midwest, and New Orleans. Her *Society in America* (1837) and *Retrospect of Western Travel* (1838) were critical of what she found, especially in the South.

Martone, Michael (1955–), poet, short-story writer. Born in Fort Wayne, Martone has degrees from Indiana University and Johns Hopkins. His interest in his native state is shown in *Alive and Dead in Indiana* (1984) in which each story is a fictional monologue by or about a public figure with some connection to Indiana. *Fort Wayne Is Seventh on Hitler's List* (1990) and *Pensees: The Thoughts of Dan Quayle* (1995) show similar interest. Poetry and prose poems are collected in *At a Loss* (1977) and *Return to Powers* (1985). *Safety Patrol* (1988) and *Seeing Eye* (1995) are story collections. *Townships* (1992) and *The Flatness and Other Landscapes* (2000) are essay collections.

Martyr, Peter [Pietro Martire d'Anghiera] (1457–1526), teacher, historian, diplomat. D'Anghiera, Italian ambassador in Egypt and teacher in Spain, was one of the first to write about the early explorers, many of whom he knew personally. *De Rebus Oceanicis et Novo Orbe*, or *Decades* (1516) gives the first account of the discovery of America. Richard Willes made an English version of *Decades* (1577).

Marvel, lk. See DONALD GRANT MITCHELL.

Mary Had a Little Lamb (*Juvenile Miscellany*, September, 1830), a poem by SARAH JOSEPHA HALE. Hale was editor of the *Miscellany*, and published the verses over her initials; she reprinted them in the same year in *Poems for Our Children, Designed for Families, Sabbath Schools, and Infant Schools*. In 1832 Lowell Mason set the words to music. They were reprinted in *McGuffey's Second Reader* (1857), probably responsible for establishing their reputation.

Maryland! My Maryland! (1861), a poem by JAMES RYDER RANDALL, which is sung to the tune of the German Christmas song *O Tannenbaum*. The anti-Union riots in Baltimore (1861) inspired Randall to write the poem. It was published in the New Orleans *Delta*, April 26, 1861, was widely reprinted, and was adopted as a battle song by the Confederate soldiers.

Mason, Arthur (1876–?),   novelist, short-story writer. Born in Ireland, Mason went to sea at seventeen, became an American citizen in 1899, and remained a sailor until the beginning of World War I. His novel *The Flying Bo'sun: A Mystery of the Sea* (1920) draws on his experience in the lumber trade from Puget Sound. *The Cook and the Captain Bold* (1924) is a collection of stories, and *Ocean Echoes* (1922) is a book of memoirs.

Mason, Bobbie Ann (1940–   ),   short-story writer, novelist. Mason was born and raised in western Kentucky. She was educated at the University of Kentucky, the State University of New York at Binghamton, and the University of Connecticut. For a while she pursued her teenage interest in popular music and the movies by writing for magazines like *Movie Life* and *T.V. Star Parade*. Then she taught at Mansfield State College in Pennsylvania (1972–79) and wrote her first two books: *Nabokov's Garden: A Guide to Ada* (1974) and *The Girl Sleuth: A Feminist Guide to the Bobbsey Twins, Nancy Drew, and Their Sisters* (1975). She discovered her true voice in the short stories collected in *Shiloh and Other Stories* (1982). In these, she returns to the country of her childhood, seeing it changed. Rural people crowd shopping malls, eat at Burger Kings, and interpret their lives by the light of TV talk shows. In the words of the narrator of "Shiloh": "Subdivisions are spreading across western Kentucky like an oil slick." In the stories of *Love Life* (1989) and *Zigzagging down a Wild Trail* (2001), she explores the same territory, as people with minimal expectations seek to discover meaningful lives in a world they understand primarily through the icons of mass culture. In a novel, *In Country* (1985), she tells of a visit to the Vietnam War Memorial in Washington by a young woman whose father died in Vietnam; by her uncle, a Vietnam veteran; and by her grandmother. Her short novel, *Spence + Lila* (1988), tells of love strung taut by a woman's bout with breast cancer. The novel *Feather Crowns* (1993) tells the story of Kentucky tobacco farmers Christie and James Wheeler, parents of quintuplets at the turn of the twentieth century. After the babies all die, Christie and James are exploited by promoters who have them touring the country with the five small embalmed corpses in glass cases. *Clear Springs* (2000) is a memoir of three generations of the Mason family and an autobiography of the author's early years in the Kentucky farming community where she was born and raised.

Mason, F[rancis] Van Wyck (1901–1978),   novelist, children's story writer. Born in Boston, Mason, upon graduation from Harvard in 1924, established an importing firm but soon became a prolific writer of popular fiction. His first book, *Seeds of Murder* (1930), was followed by more than a dozen other mysteries, all with exotic settings. Three juveniles—*Q-Boat* (1943), *Pilots, Man Your Planes* (1944), and *Flight into Danger* (1945)—grew out of his experiences in World War II. *Captain Nemesis* (1931), *Three Harbors* (1938), *Stars on the Sea* (1940), *Rivers of Glory* (1942), and *Eagle in the Sky* (1948) are popular historical novels dealing with the Revolutionary period. *Hang My Wreath* (1941), published under the pen name Ward Weaver, is a Civil War love story. *Cutlass Empire* (1949) is a fictionalized account of the 17th-century pirate Henry Morgan. In *Proud New Flags* (1951) Mason embarked on a tetralogy devoted to naval aspects of the Civil War. Among his later novels are *Winter at Valley Forge* (1954), *Silver Leopard* (1955), *Blue Hurricane* (1958), *Secret Mission to Bangkok* (1960), *Trouble in Burma* (1962), *Maracaibo Mission* (1965), and *The Deadly Orbit Mission* (1968).

Mason, John (1600–1672),   soldier, public official. Mason came to America about 1633, was active as a militiaman, and helped found Windsor and Norwich, Connecticut. He wrote an account of his victory over the Pequot Indians in 1637 that was included in Increase Mather's *A Relation of the Troubles That Have Happened in New England* (1677). Mather attributed the narrative to John Allyn, then secretary of the Connecticut colony, but Thomas Prince edited it as *Brief History of the Pequot War* (1736) and gave the correct authorship.

Mason, Perry.   The leading character in 82 novels by ERLE STANLEY GARDNER.

Mason and Slidell: A Yankee Idyll (1862),   a poem in the *Second Series* (1867) of Lowell's BIGLOW PAPERS. James Murray Mason and John Slidell were sent by the Confederacy as envoys to Great Britain and France. They set sail on the British mail steamer *Trent*. On November 8, 1861, the steamer was stopped by the American war vessel *Jacinto*, and the envoys were arrested. The incident brought the Union to the verge of war with England. They were released on January 2, 1862, and proceeded to London, but were unable to secure recognition of the Confederacy by England or France.

Masque of Judgment, The (1900),   a play in verse by WILLIAM VAUGHN MOODY. This play was the first of a trilogy and was followed by *The Fire-Bringer* (1904) and *The Death of Eve* (1912), the last never completed. In *Masque*, the archangel Raphael expresses his belief that God erred in allowing sin and then punishing the sinner; the Serpent is shown as the victor. The play is written in language that recalls John Milton's.

Masque of Mercy, A (1947),   a verse play by ROBERT FROST. The poet wrestles in this often amusing and always keen-witted discussion with some ancient problems of the relation between God's mercy and God's justice.

Masque of Reason, A (1945),   a verse play by ROBERT FROST concerned with Job's problem of the relationship of God and man.

Masque of the Red Death, The (*Graham's Magazine*, May 1842),   a story by EDGAR ALLAN POE. Poe's preoccupation with the idea of death led him here to one of his best tales of terror. The story of Prince Prospero's attempt to isolate himself from the plague is almost pure description, with only rare and short passages of dialogue. The allegorical imagery leads finally to the figure of the Red Death.

Massachuset Indians.   Native Americans belonging to the ALGONQUIAN linguistic family. They inhabited the area around and somewhat north of what is now Boston. In the early 17th century they numbered perhaps 3,000, but war and disease had reduced their number to only about 500 by 1631, when the great waves of immigration to the Massachusetts Bay Colony had just begun. Converted to Christianity by JOHN ELIOT, they soon lost their tribal identity and were numbered among the PRAYING INDIANS.

Massachusettensis.   The pen name of DANIEL LEONARD, also the title of a collection of his essays (1775), in which he argued for home rule for the colonies, but also for continued allegiance to Britain. John Adams thought these essays dangerous because of their wit and subtlety.

Massachusetts Bay Company.   This was the English chartered company that established the Massachusetts Bay Colony. In 1628 a small English association had received a land grant from the Council of New England and promptly established a settlement at Salem. The grant, covering territory between the Charles and Merrimack rivers and extending westward to the Pacific Ocean, was soon taken over by leading Puritans, including Sir Richard Saltonstall, Thomas Dudley, and JOHN WINTHROP, and in 1629 they received from Charles I a royal charter as the Massachusetts Bay Company. In the summer and fall of 1630, seventeen ships, carrying about a thousand passengers, sailed from England and founded Boston and several nearby towns. They carried their charter with them, thereby establishing a tradition of independence of signal importance to the future history of the colony and the country to follow. Government was by the corporation, with all freemen, or stockholders, voting. They set up a representative system with annual elections of all officers, and with no role reserved for either king or parliament. Conceived as a religious refuge for Puritans, the colony was in effect a theocracy, with voting restricted to church members. Fed by persecution in England, the colony established a judicial system, a press, and a college, and within a dozen years it numbered about 16,000 people. Company and colony remained identical until 1684, when the royal charter was withdrawn. In 1691, Massachusetts became a royal colony, and its jurisdiction was then extended to include Plymouth and Maine.

Massachusetts Centinel and the Republican Journal.   A magazine founded in 1784, which in 1790 became the *Massachusetts Centinel and the Federalist Journal* and in 1840 was merged with the Boston *Daily Advertiser*. Its most noted contributor was JOHN QUINCY ADAMS, who wrote attacks on the American sympathizers, especially TOM PAINE, with French revolutionary ideas.

Massachusetts to Virginia   (delivered in Ipswich, January 2, 1842; printed in *The Liberator* the same month; collected in *Voices of Freedom*, 1846), a poem by JOHN GREENLEAF WHITTIER. This poem was perhaps Whittier's greatest in the cause of abolition. Its fervor gives it the quality of a magnificent oration. The subject is the fugitive slave law, in particular the insults and threats some Virginians directed against Massachusetts for refusing to enforce the law. The poem replies with defiance, adds a strong appeal to Virginia to remember the ideals of Jefferson, and vividly depicts the scandals of the slave traffic. Most powerful of all is the sweeping and imaginative panorama of Massachusetts towns responding to the appeal to save a fugitive slave: "No fetters in the Bay State! no slave upon her land!"

Massa's in de Cold, Cold Ground (1852),   a song by STEPHEN FOSTER. It describes slaves weeping at the grave of their master.

Massasoit (c. 1580–1661),   Indian chief, sachem of the WAMPANOAGS. Massasoit, whose home was in what is now Warren, Rhode Island, was friendly to the Pilgrims and made a treaty of peace with them that was kept till the accession of his son, known as KING PHILIP. Massasoit also made a treaty with Roger Williams.

Masses, The.   A left-wing magazine (1911–18) originally sponsored by Piet Vlag, a restaurant manager. The first editor (January–April 1911) was Thomas Seltzer, but the magazine did not do well. MAX EASTMAN took hold in December 1912 and ran the magazine until its suppression by the Federal authorities in December 1917. He had as contributing editors some writers and artists who then or later were veryfprominent, including FLOYD DELL, JOHN REED, LOUIS UNTERMEYER, MARY HEATON VORSE, Art Young, George Bellows, and Boardman Robinson. It was a sparkling magazine, including essays on literature and art, but as war with Germany approached, the magazine became angry and less balanced. In August 1917, the Post Office Department barred it from the mails.

In March 1918, *The Masses* was succeeded by THE LIBERATOR, which assumed a doctrinaire tone; Eastman was its editor for a while. In 1924 it was merged with two Communist periodicals and became *The Workers' Monthly*. In May 1926 appeared the weekly *New Masses*, and it became a monthly in 1948 as *Masses & Mainstream*. The editor was Samuel Sillen, and among the contributing editors were John Howard Lawson, Howard Fast, W.E.B. DU BOIS, PAUL ROBESON, and William Gropper.

Masters, Edgar Lee (1868–1950),   poet, writer. Masters was born in Garnett, Kansas, but grew up in Petersburg and Lewistown, Illinois, not far from the Spoon River he later made famous. Typesetting as a teenager, a year at Knox college, and an apprenticeship in his father's law office preceded a law practice in Chicago that was to last for thirty years. He had been writing at least since college and finally found himself in SPOON RIVER ANTHOLOGY (1915), a book that quickly went through many editions. Talks with his aging mother apparently had given him the idea for a book of personal stories from the grave told by people like those they had known in Petersburg and Lewiston. He had read J. W. Mackail's *Selected Epigrams from the Greek Anthology* and found there an appropriate model for a compressed style that he chose to express in colloquial free verse. The poems began appearing first in 1914 in *Reedy's Mirror*, where Masters used the pseudonym Webster Ford. After the initial success of the book, Masters enlarged it; in 1916 an expanded version contained 243 lives that may be read to reveal nineteen intertwined stories, though some also stand apart from the texture of the whole. *The New Spoon River* (1924) contains another three hundred portraits. Quitting the law in 1921, Masters moved to New York City and devoted himself full time to writing, but he never duplicated the success of *Spoon River Anthology*. Among his later collections of verse are *Songs and Satires* (1916), *Starved Rock* (1919), *Domesday Book* (1920), *The Serpent in the Wilderness* (1933), *Poems of People* (1936), and *Illinois Poems* (1941). He also wrote plays, several books of fiction, books on Lincoln (1931), Vachel Lindsay (1935), Whitman (1937), and Twain (1938), and *Across Spoon River: An Autobiography* (1936).

Mather, Cotton (1663–1728), clergyman, historian. Born in Boston, Mather was one of the most remarkable men in America, a prodigy who entered Harvard at twelve, expert theologian, learned controversialist, determined Puritan, precursor of American deists, indefatigable author, able critic, researcher in superstition, man of scientific temperament who nevertheless was inclined to believe in witchcraft, and educational theorist. Perry Miller in *The New England Mind* (1953) called him "the greatest intellectual in the land" and "the most nauseous human being."

Mather was born to the clerical gown. His grandfathers were RICHARD MATHER and JOHN COTTON, and his father was INCREASE MATHER. His father taught him so well that when Cotton Mather entered Harvard he was anathema to his fellow students, but the darling of the tutors. He was eighteen when he took his M.A., became his father's assistant at North Church in 1685, and married the first of his three wives a year later. He became involved in one quarrel after another, some personal, some trivial, many theological, and at least one, his ardent and then dangerous advocacy of inoculation for smallpox, very much to his credit. Throughout his life he wrote unceasingly; the number of his titles has never been exactly determined, although a huge list is contained in Thomas J. Holmes's *Cotton Mather: A Bibliography of His Works* (3 v. 1940).

Some of his writings were *Memorable Providences Relating to Witchcrafts and Possessions* (1689), *The Present State of New England* (1690), *The Wonderful Works of God Commemorated* (1690), THE WONDERS OF THE INVISIBLE WORLD (1693), *The Short History of New England* (1694), *The Life of His Excellency, Sir William Phips* (1697), *Reasonable Religion* (1700), MAGNALIA CHRISTI AMERICANA (1702), *The Negro Christianized* (1706), *The Deplorable State of New England* (1707, 1708), BONIFACIUS (1710), *Psalterium Americanum* (1718), THE CHRISTIAN PHILOSOPHER (1721), *An Account of Inoculating the Small Pox* (in collaboration with Dr. Zabdiel Boylston, 1722), and *Manunductio ad Ministerium* (1726). His *Diary* was published in two volumes in 1911–12.

Of his interest in popular lore Richard Dorson noted that his *Magnalia* "accurately records folklore concepts which permeated the mind of 17th-century New England when the intellectuals shared with the folk an acceptance of the supernatural." He was greatly interested in education and drew up *Some Special Points Relating to the Education of My Children* (1708). He was elected to the Royal Society of London in 1713 and contributed to its *Philosophical Transactions*. There is no

collected edition of Mather's writings. A good selection is Kenneth B. Murdock's *Selections from Cotton Mather* (1926). Kenneth Silverman's *The Life and Times of Cotton Mather* (1984) is the first full biography.

Mather, Increase (1639–1723), clergyman, educational administrator, historian. Born in Dorchester, Massachusetts, and educated at Harvard and at Trinity in Dublin, Mather first preached in England, then came home to the pulpit of North Church (1664) and officiated there until his death. He went abroad to win a new charter for the colony, and brought about the appointment of SIR WILLIAM PHIPS as governor. But with the coming of the Salem witchcraft trials and Phips's participation in them, Mather became increasingly subject to attack, although his own attitude was not fanatical, as is evident in his *Cases of Conscience Concerning Evil Spirits Personating Men* (1693). He was president of Harvard from 1685 to 1701, retiring amidst heated quarrels. He was a man of immense influence whose hot temper and indomitable views provoked controversy—at the beginning of his career he even opposed his father RICHARD MATHER in a theological quarrel, although he finally changed sides. Like his son COTTON MATHER he took the unpopular scientific side in the smallpox inoculation controversy. He was deeply interested in science, but as an adjunct to theology, and sought to find the hand of Providence in many strange events, which he chronicled in *Doctrine of Divine Providence, Opened and Applied* (1684) and ESSAY FOR THE RECORDING OF ILLUSTRIOUS PROVIDENCES (1684).

Like his son he wrote endlessly—he wrote more than a hundred works. He wrote a biography of his father, *The Life and Death of Richard Mather* (1670); his son Cotton in turn wrote a biography of Increase Mather, *Parentator* (1724). Among other works by Increase Mather are *Some Important Truths About Conversion* (1674), *A Brief History of the War with the Indians in New England* (1676), *A Relation of the Troubles Which Have Happened in New England* (1677), *Kometographia, or, A Discourse Concerning Comets* (1683), *An Arrow Against Profane and Promiscuous Dancing* (1684), *A Narrative of the Miseries of New England* (1688), *The Order of the Gospel* (1700), *A Discourse Concerning Earthquakes* (1706), and *Several Reasons Proving That Inoculating the Small Pox Is a Lawful Practice* (1721). The last was reissued, with an introduction by George L. Kittredge, in 1921. Kenneth B. Murdock wrote *Increase Mather, the Foremost American Puritan* (1925). Thomas J. Holmes compiled *Increase Mather: A Bibliography of His Works* (2 v. 1931).

Mather, Richard (1596–1669), clergyman. Mather was an Oxford graduate, ordained about 1619, a Puritan who came to New England in 1635 as a pastor in Dorchester, Massachusetts. He is perhaps best known for the part he played in preparing the BAY PSALM BOOK (1640). He exerted great influence on church policies and church rules, particularly the *Platform of Church Discipline* (1649). His son INCREASE MATHER said of his preaching that it "was plain, aiming to shoot his arrows not over his people's heads, but into their hearts and consciences." Thomas J. Holmes includes a list of his writings, as well as those of twelve of his descendants, in his bibliography *The Minor Mathers* (1940). See THE HALF-WAY COVENANT.

Mather, Samuel (1706–1785),   clergyman, biographer, poet. The last of the Mathers wrote of his father in a *Life of the Very Reverend and Learned Cotton Mather* (1729). Born in Boston, Samuel Mather, was pastor for a while in the North Church but was dismissed and formed a new congregation. He wrote *Attempt to show that America Must be Known to the Ancients* (1773) and a poem called *The Sacred Minister* (1773). (See BONIFACIUS.)

Mathews, Cornelius (1817–1889),   writer, editor, lawyer. Born in Port Chester, New York, and admitted to the bar in 1837, Mathews never practiced law, but turned to writing stories and poems for magazines. *Behemoth: A Legend of the Mound Builders* (1839), a romance, was followed by *The Career of Puffer Hopkins*, published serially in *Arcturus* (1841–42). This novel, like some of Mathews's later works, deals with New York politics. *Poems on Man in His Various Aspects Under the American Republic* (1843) drew favorable comment from James Russell Lowell. His plays include a comedy on the New York electioneering rackets, *The Politicians* (1840); a drama in blank verse, *The Martyrs of Salem* (1846), which was a hit here and abroad; a historical drama, *Jacob Leisler* (1848); and a light comedy, *False Pretenses; or, Both Sides of Good Society* (1855). His *Indian Fairy Book* (1856) was republished in 1877 as *The Enchanted Moccasins*. He published a small humorous weekly, *Yankee Doodle* (1846–47), and was a contributing editor of the *New York Dramatic Mirror* from 1883 until his death.

Mathews, John Joseph (c. 1894–1979),   writer. Born in Pawhuska, Oklahoma, Mathews was an OSAGE educated at the University of Oklahoma and Oxford University. His works include *Wah'Kon-Tah: The Osage and the White Man's Road* (1932), covering the period from late 19th-century to the time of writing; *Sundown* (1934), a work of fiction; *Talking to the Moon* (1945), an autobiography; *Life and Death of an Oilman: The Career of E. W. Marland* (1951), a biography; and *The Osages: Children of the Middle Waters* (1961).

Matthews, [James] Brander (1852–1929),   teacher, critic, editor, essayist, novelist. Born in New Orleans, Matthews was educated at Columbia College and Columbia Law School, but never practiced law. He contributed to many magazines, wrote plays and fiction, became professor of English at Columbia (1892–1900), and then at the same University became the United States's first professor of dramatic literature (1900–1924). His books on drama include *The Theaters of Paris* (1880), *French Dramatists of the 19th Century* (1881), *Studies of the Stage* (1894), *The Development of the Drama* (1903), *Molière* (1910), and *The Principles of Playmaking* (1919). Especially noteworthy is his *Shakespeare as a Playwright* (1913), which stressed Shakespeare's competency in the theater rather than as a literary man. His essays ranged from the antiquity of jests to the serious subject of poker. He also stimulated the study of American literature in a history of its development (1896); wittily fought for usage against gram-

matical rules, and for simplified spelling; and in a study clarified the technique of the short story. His best novel was about New York City: *A Confident Tomorrow* (1899). He wrote short stories for *In Partnership* (in collaboration with H. C. Bunner, 1884), and *Vignettes of Manhattan* (1894). He also wrote plays: *Margery's Lovers* (1884); in collaboration, *A Gold Mine* (1887); and *On Probation* (1889).

Matthews, Washington (1843–1905),   surgeon, ethnologist. Born in Ireland, Matthews became a U.S. army surgeon and served mainly in the Southwest. He became deeply interested in the Navahos and wrote several books and many papers about them, including *The Mountain Chant: A Navaho Ceremony* (1887), *Navaho Legends* (1897), and *Navaho Myths, Prayers, and Songs* (1907).

Matthiessen, F[rancis] O[tto] (1902–1950), teacher, critic. Born in Pasadena, California, Matthiessen spent four years at Yale, two years in Europe as a Rhodes Scholar, and two more years at Harvard for his Ph.D. He was an instructor at Yale for two years, then returned to Harvard, where he spent the rest of his life. In 1947, Matthiessen taught on leave at Salzburg. He published his diary of the months in Salzburg and Czechoslovakia as *From the Heart of Europe* (1948). In 1949–50, again on leave from Harvard, he worked on a life of Dreiser and edited *The Oxford Book of American Verse* (1950). On April 1, 1950, overcome by severe depression and "terribly oppressed by the present tensions," he committed suicide.

The first of Matthiessen's major works was *The Achievement of T. S. Eliot: An Essay on the Nature of Poetry* (1935, enlarged ed. 1947). This was a landmark work, as was *American Renaissance: Art and Expression in the Age of Emerson and Whitman* (1941). Then Matthiessen turned to *Henry James* and produced *Henry James: The Major Phase* (1944) and *The James Family: Including Selections from the Writings of Henry James, Senior, William, Henry, and Alice James* (1947). He also contributed to anthologies and collaborative works, wrote numerous essays and reviews, and edited several books. He served as an editor for the *New England Quarterly* (1938–40).

Posthumously published were *Theodore Dreiser* (1951) and *The Responsibilities of the Critic: Essays and Reviews* (1952). Other books are *Sarah Orne Jewett* (1929) and *Translation: An Elizabethan Art* (1931). He also edited volumes of writings by HENRY JAMES and HERMAN MELVILLE. A novel said to have been suggested by Matthiessen's life and death is MAY SARTON's *Faithful Are the Wounds* (1955).

Matthiessen, Peter (1927–   ),   novelist, travel and nature writer. Born in New York City, Matthiessen was educated at Yale and the Sorbonne. After founding the PARIS REVIEW, he worked for three years as a commercial fisherman. He has traveled widely as a naturalist, observing and commenting on the potentially disastrous consequences of humankind's careless use of the environment. Similar concerns animate his fiction. Three novels have received particular acclaim: *At Play in the Fields of the Lord* (1965), bringing into cultural conflict the Indians of an Amazon jungle, North

American whites, and a North American Indian; *Far Tortuga* (1975), a sea novel set in the Caribbean; and *Killing Mister Watson* (1990), telling through twelve fictional voices the story of an actual killing in 1910 in the Florida Everglades. Two later novels, *Lost Man's River* (1998) and *Bone by Bone* (1999), complete the Everglades trilogy. His other novels are *Race Rock* (1954), *Partisans* (1955), and *Raditzer* (1961), a sea novel set at the end of World War II. *On the River Styx* (1989) collects his short stories. Among his many works of nonfiction are *Wildlife in America* (1959); *The Cloud Forest: A Chronicle of the South American Wilderness* (1961); *Under the Mountain Wall* (1962), on New Guinea; *The Shorebirds of North America* (1967); *Oomingmak: The Expedition to the Musk Ox Island in the Bering Sea* (1967); *Sal Si Puedes: Cesar Chavez and the New American Revolution* (1970), about the struggle for better conditions for agricultural workers; *Blue Meridian* (1971), about a search for a great white shark; *The Tree Where Man Was Born* (1972), on East Africa; *The Snow Leopard* (1978), about a trek through the mountains of Nepal in search of spiritual enlightenment; *Sand Rivers* (1981), on a safari in Tanzania; *In the Spirit of Crazy Horse* (1983), about the 1975 shootout between Native Americans and FBI agents in South Dakota; and *Men's Lives* (1986), about Long Island fishermen.

Maud Muller (1854), a narrative poem by JOHN GREENLEAF WHITTIER, part of his collection called *The Panorama and Other Poems* (1856). A wealthy judge stops to talk to Maud Muller, who is raking hay. Each is deeply impressed by the other, but the judge finally rides away; each dreams of marriage to the other, but each instead marries a social equal—with regrets later on. Whittier concludes with the lines: "For of all sad words of tongue or pen,/ The saddest are these, 'It might have been!'" BRET HARTE, in a clever parody, "Mrs. Judge Jenkins," imagined that the pair had really married, unhappily. His conclusion was: "More sad than these we daily see:/ It is, but hadn't ought to be." According to Whittier, "Maud Muller" itself was based on an actual incident near York, Maine, when he stopped to talk with a girl working in a hayfield. He may also have had in mind his unhappy attachment to Mary Emerson Smith, who rejected him because of his poverty and social inferiority.

Mauldin, Bill [William H.] (1921–), cartoonist. Mauldin worked his way through the Chicago Art Institute just in time to be drafted by the army in 1940. He fought as an infantryman in the Sicilian and Italian campaigns, was awarded a Purple Heart, but won most recognition for his cartoons of army life overseas. They appeared first in a division weekly, then in the Mediterranean edition of *Stars and Stripes*, becoming by far the most popular cartoons of the war. The two chief characters in the cartoons, Willie and Joe, are bearded, dirty GIs whose attitudes toward officers, army food—the war in general—are distinctly sardonic. Mauldin shunned sentimentality and false patriotism to portray army life realistically. In 1945 and again in 1959 he won a Pulitzer Prize. Two collections of Mauldin's war cartoons were published, *Up Front* (1945) and *Back Home* (1946). In 1949 Mauldin published an entertaining book about his boyhood,

A Sort of a Saga. He reported the Korean War for *Collier's*, and *Bill Mauldin in Korea* appeared in 1952. *What's Got Your Back Up?* (1961) is another collection, as is *I've Decided I Want My Seat Back* (1965). His autobiography, *The Brass Ring*, appeared in 1971.

Maum Guinea and Her Plantation Children, or, Christmas Among the Slaves (1861), a dime novel by METTA VICTORIA VICTOR (1831–1886). The book, abolitionist in sentiment, was widely read for a time.

Mauve Decade, The: American Life at the Close of the 19th Century (1926), a literary and historical survey by THOMAS BEER.

Maverick, Samuel (1602?–1676?), public official, trader, writer on colonial America. Maverick, a dim historical figure, seems to have been an associate of Sir FERDINANDO GORGES, the soldier and colonial proprietor. Some time in the late 1650s he returned to England and there issued a *Brief Description of New England and the Several Towns Therein* (1660); he was back in Massachusetts in 1664 as an appointee of Charles II.

Maximus Poems, The, a poetic sequence by CHARLES OLSON.

Maxwell, William Keepers (1908–2000), novelist, short-story writer. Born in Illinois and educated at the University of Illinois and Harvard, Maxwell is noted for his evocation of the American past, in particular, the Midwest of the decades before and after World War I. Primarily concerned with the subtle and often tragic relationships existing among families and close friends, he has also written insightfully about children and adolescents. Among his novels are *Bright Center of Heaven* (1934), *They Came Like Swallows* (1937), *The Folded Leaf* (1945), *Time Will Darken It* (1948), *The Chateau* (1961), and *So Long, See You Tomorrow* (1979). He has also written a number of short stories, some of which appear in *The Old Man and the Crossing* (1966), *Over by the River* (1977), and *Billy Dyer and Other Stories* (1992). In addition, he is the author of a children's book, *The Heavenly Tenants* (1946). *The Writer as Illusionist* (1955) is about the craft of writing. *Ancestors* (1971) is a family history. *The Outermost Dream*, an essay collection, appeared in 1989. His last book, *All the Days and Nights*, came out in 1995.

May, Samuel Joseph (1797–1871), Unitarian clergyman, reformer. Born in Boston, May engaged in so many good causes and crusades that Bronson Alcott called him "the Lord's chore boy." He was active as an abolitionist, fighter for the rights of women, and as a champion of temperance. Among his books are *The Rights and Conditions of Women* (originally a sermon, 1846); *The Revival of Education* (1855); and *Some Recollections of the Anti-Slavery Conflict* (1869). He also wrote *A Brief Account of His Ministry* (1867).

Mayer, Brantz (1809–1879), lawyer, historian, editor. In 1855 Mayer, born in Baltimore, left his law practice and began writing on historical topics. He wrote *Mexico as It Was and Is* (1844), edited the *Journal of Charles Carroll of Carrollton* (1845), also the journal of a notorious sea character, *Captain Canot, or, 20 Years of an African Slaver* (1854). The latter volume was used as a source by HERVEY ALLEN for *Anthony Adverse* (1933). The book was reprinted in 1928 with an introduction by Malcolm Cowley. Another book on Mexico (1851) and a memoir of Jared Sparks (1867) were among Mayer's other writings.

Mayflower.   A ship of about 180 tons, the *Mayflower* left Plymouth, England, on September 6, 1620 (old style calendar; September 16 by the modern calendar). Land was sighted at Cape Cod on November 9/19, and on November 11/21, after sixty-five days at sea, the ship entered Provincetown Harbor, and the PILGRIMS signed the MAYFLOWER COMPACT. For the next three weeks they explored the area, landing finally at Plymouth on December 11/21, 1620.

Mayflower Compact.   An agreement signed November 11, 1620 (old style calendar; November 21 by the modern calendar) on board the MAYFLOWER. The PILGRIMS agreed to "Covenant and Combine ourselves together into a Civil Body Politic" and "to enact, constitute and frame such just and equal Laws, Ordinances, Acts, Constitutions and Offices, from time to time, as shall be thought most meet and convenient for the general good of the Colony, unto which we promise all due submission and obedience." As a precedent they had the church covenants familiar to Puritans; the compact served in turn as an important precedent in America for the concept of civil government by mutual consent organized to promote the common good.

Mayhew, Experience (1673–1758),   missionary, translator, author. Born in Chilmark, Massachusetts, Mayhew worked for the Society for the Propagation of the Gospel in New England. He learned the local Indian language when he was a boy, preached to the Martha's Vineyard Indians in their own tongue, and converted many of them. In 1707 he translated Cotton Mather's *The Day Which the Lord Hath Made* into the Indian language; in 1709 his translation of the Psalms and the Gospel of St. John was published, entitled the *Massachusee Psalter*. Some authorities attribute to him the *Indiane Primer* (1720), a reading book for children. *Indian Converts: or, Some Account of the Lives and Dying Speeches of a Considerable Number of Christianized Indians of Martha's Vineyard* (1727) gave an account of his missionary activities. A man of boundless energy, Mayhew was unable to swallow all the pessimism of the Calvinist doctrine. His *Grace Defended* (1744) acknowledged a deviation from the orthodox belief in total depravity and expressed belief in a degree of free will.

Mayhew, Jonathan (1720–1766),   clergyman, pamphleteer. Born in Chilmark, Massachusetts, Mayhew was the son of EXPERIENCE MAYHEW. A graduate of Harvard, he became pastor of West Church in Boston in 1647, and held the post till his death. In theology Mayhew was a forerunner of Unitarianism. One of his most trenchant writings came out of the controversies that ensued when he maintained these views in *A Letter of Reproof to Mr. John Cleaveland* (1764). In politics he espoused liberal doctrines and was a fervent defender of the rights of man and the dignity of the individual. His *Discourse Concerning Unlimited Submission* (1850) was a polemic against tyranny. Mayhew became the chief clerical leader of

the opposition to British repression of the colonies, for example, in his sermon *The Snare Broken* (1766). Joseph Green wrote an *Eclogue, Sacred to the Memory of the Rev. Jonathan Mayhew* (1766).

Mayhew, Thomas, Jr. (1621?–1657),   Indian missionary. The grandfather of EXPERIENCE MAYHEW and the great-grandfather of JONATHAN MAYHEW, he was the owner of Martha's Vineyard and acted as governor and magistrate there. He maintained excellent relations with the Indians and sought to convert them to Christianity. He collaborated with JOHN ELIOT in writing *Tears of Repentance* (1652).

Maylem, John (1739–1762?),   soldier, poet. The dates and facts of Maylem's life are uncertain. He fought in the French and Indian Wars and described in bombastic heroic couplets *The Conquest of Louisburg* (1758), and his own capture by troops under Montcalm in *Gallic Perfidy* (1758). He called himself on the title page of these poems "Philo-Bellum." Some of his verses are preserved in manuscript; they are largely celebrations of wine and Venus.

Maynard, Theodore (1890–1956),   teacher, writer. Born in India, Maynard began living in the United States permanently in 1920 and became a citizen in 1941. He studied for the ministry and preached in Unitarian churches until he became a Catholic in 1913. He taught at various Catholic universities, but thought of himself as primarily a poet. Among his books of verse are *Poems* (1919), *Exile and Other Poems* (1928), and *Collected Poems* (1946). His prose works include *De Soto and the Conquistadores* (1930), *The Odyssey of Francis Xavier* (1936), *The Crown and the Cross: A Biography of Thomas Cromwell* (1950), and *The Long Road of Father Serra* (1954). He edited anthologies of Catholic verse (1926) and Catholic prose (1928). *The World I Saw* (1938) is an autobiography.

Mayo, Frank (1839–1896),   actor, dramatist. Born in Boston, Frank Mayo was for years one of the most popular actors of his day, both in the U.S. and in England. He made a specialty of rough-and-ready character parts, for example, appearing in *Davy Crockett* (1872), written by Frank Hitchcock. Mayo wrote as a vehicle for himself a dramatization (1895) of Mark Twain's PUDD'NHEAD WILSON.

Mayo, Katherine (1867–1940),   newspaperwoman, historian, writer. Mayo, born in Pennsylvania, wrote militantly against social injustice. The failure of an upstate New York sheriff to apprehend three known murderers led her to write *Justice to All* (1917), an account of the Pennsylvania State Police that led to establishment of a similar body in New York. She investigated the workings of the YMCA abroad during World War I and reported her favorable findings in *That Damn Y* (1920), but was not as kind to the United States administration of the Philippines in *Isles of Fear* (1925). *Mother India* (1927) was a controversial study of child marriage in India. In *Volume Two* (1931) she provided documentation for her book. She was one of the best and most useful muckrakers of her generation.

Mayo, William Starbuck (1811–1895),   physician, traveler, novelist. Mayo, born in Ogdensburg, New York, went abroad in search of health and adventure and spent several years in Spain and North Africa. His observations led to the writing of some striking novels, the best of which was KALLOOLAH (1849), which has been compared both with SWIFT's *Gulliver's Travels* and MELVILLE's *Typee*. *Berber* (1850) describes life among the Moors, but *Never Again* (1873) is about New York City and its social and commercial circles.

Maypole of Merry Mount, The (1836, reprinted in *Twice-Told Tales*, 1837), a story by NATHANIEL HAWTHORNE. See THOMAS MORTON.

Mc. Names beginning with MC- are alphabetized as if they began with MAC-.

Mead, Margaret (1901–1978), psychologist, anthropologist. Mead was born in Philadelphia. Before obtaining her Ph.D. degree from Columbia University, Margaret Mead went to Samoa as a Fellow of the National Research Council to study adolescent girls. The book she published as a result of her investigations, COMING OF AGE IN SAMOA (1928), became a classic work of anthropology and a popular success. She made a number of other expeditions to distant parts of the world to study the customs of primitive peoples. In *Growing Up in New Guinea* (1930), and *Sex and Temperament in Three Primitive Societies* (1935) she continued her investigation of marriage and sex in primitive societies. She applied her independent intelligence to a broad range of subjects, always examining the extent to which character is shaped by culture and vice versa. Her other important works include *Male and Female* (1949), *An Anthropologist at Work* (1959), and *Culture and Commitment* (1970). She lectured extensively, airing her progressive views on contemporary issues, and wrote frequently for scholarly journals and popular magazines. *Aspects of the Present* (1980) is a selection from her articles that had appeared in *Redbook* magazine between 1969 and 1979. She also wrote a biography of her teacher and collaborator, *Ruth Benedict* (1974), and an autobiography, *Blackberry Winter* (1972). *Letters from the Field: 1925–1975* (1977) contains her reflections on the methods of anthropological field work that she developed. She also wrote *A Rap on Race* (1971), with JAMES BALDWIN.

Meat Out of the Eater (1670), a poem by MICHAEL WIGGLESWORTH. The poet described his work in a subtitle: "Meditations Concerning the Necessity, End, and Usefulness of Affliction unto God's Children."

Mecom, Jane [Franklin] (1712–1794), BENJAMIN FRANKLIN's sister. Six years his junior, Jane was, Franklin said, "ever my peculiar favorite." He kept in constant touch with her by letter for more than sixty years, and a good deal of their correspondence has survived—more of his than hers—and was capably edited by Carl Van Doren in *The Letters of Benjamin Franklin and Jane Mecom* (1951). Van Doren had already written *Jane Mecom: Franklin's Favorite Sister* (1950).

Meek, Alexander Beaufort (1814–1865), poet, lawyer, public official, editor, historian. Born in Columbia, South Carolina, Meek was a successful lawyer, judge, federal official, and Speaker of the House in the Alabama legislature. He was influential in establishing a public school system for Alabama, and he was a secessionist, but reluctantly. For a time

he was on the editorial staff of the Mobile *Daily Register* and other papers. He wrote a history of *The Southwest* (1840) and *Romantic Passages in Southwestern History* (1857). His verses are preserved in *Songs and Poems of the South* (1857).

Meeker, Ezra (1830–1928), pioneer, memoirist, historian, novelist. Meeker was born in Huntsville, Ohio. Six years later than FRANCIS PARKMAN he traveled the Oregon Trail, and he related his experiences in several autobiographical volumes. Among them are *The Ox-Team, or, The Old Oregon Trail, 1852–1906* (1906), revised as *Ox-Team Days on the Oregon Trail* (1922); *Ventures and Adventures of Ezra Meeker, or, Sixty Years of Frontier Life* (1909), revised as *The Busy Life of 85 Years of Ezra Meeker* (1916); and *Seventy Years of Progress in Washington* (1921). He also wrote *Kate Mulhall, A Romance of the Oregon Trail* (1926).

Meeker, Nathan Cook (1817–1879), newspaperman, Indian agent, memoirist. Born in Euclid, Ohio, Meeker wrote a book of his experiences, *Life in the West* (1868). He was among those who became interested through Horace Greeley in Fourierist colonies, was for a time connected with a phalanx in Ohio, and later helped found the Union Colony in Colorado. (See CHARLES FOURIER.)

Megapolensis, Johannes (1603?–1670), clergyman. Megapolensis lived for six years on the shores of the upper Hudson, where he came into contact with Native Americans. He wrote letters about them that were made into a pamphlet (1644) entitled *Een Kort Ontwerp vande Mahakvase Indiaenen*. This was reprinted in 1651; its English versions are described in J. Franklin Jameson's *Narratives of New Netherland* (1909). Megapolensis found the local people friendly to white men, though he observed they were given to lying, thieving, lewdness, murder, and drunkenness.

Mehta, Ved [Parkash] (1934–), memoirist, autobiographer, journalist, novelist. Born in India, Mehta was stricken with meningitis and left blinded at age three. At fifteen he came to the United States to continue his education at the Arkansas School for the Blind in Little Rock. He completed it at Pomona College, Oxford, and Harvard. Settling in New York, in 1961 he became a staff writer for THE NEW YORKER, and much of his best work has first appeared in its pages. A luminous writer, he has composed a series of memoirs and autobiographies unique in our time, perhaps in history. They relate the history of his own life and the lives of his family and friends to create a panorama of Indian society and of the life of one Indian from the 1930s onward. Titles of this work are *Face to Face* (1957), an early work; *Daddyji* (1972), on his father; *Mamaji* (1979), on his mother; *Vedi* (1982), on his years at school in Bombay; *The Ledge Between the Streams* (1984), about his family life in the tumultuous years from 1940 to 1949; and *The Stolen Light* (1989), about his schooling in America. His other works include *Mahatma Gandhi and His Apostles* (1977) and *The New India* (1978). *A Family Affair: India under Three Prime Ministers* (1982) and *Rajiv Gandhi and Rama's Kingdom* (1994) are sequels to *The New India*. Mehta is a MacArthur Fellow.

Melanctha (1909), a story by GERTRUDE STEIN included

in THREE LIVES, her first published book. It is a study of the mind of an African-American girl as revealed in her natural speech rhythms.

Melish, John (1771–1822), textile manufacturer, cartographer. This Scotsman visited the United States several times and wrote *Travels in the U.S. of America in the Years, 1806 and 1807 and 1809, 1810, and 1811* (2 v. 1812). He finally settled in Philadelphia (1811). His description of this country is on the whole impartial and friendly. He sought to promote immigration from Great Britain and in 1819 issued *Information and Advice to Emigrants to the U.S.* For his travel volumes he drew numerous maps, and he published *A Military and Topograhical Atlas of the U.S.* in 1813.

Mellen, Grenville (1799–1841), lawyer, poet, storyteller, editor, historian. Born in Biddeford, Maine (then part of Massachusetts), Mellen wrote conventional verse, largely influenced by English models and collected in *The Martyr's Triumph and Other Poems* (1833). His short stories were collected and published under the pen name Reginald Reverie as *Sad Tales and Glad Tales* (1828).

Mellichampe, A Legend of the Santee (1836), a novel by WILLIAM GILMORE SIMMS. See THE PARTISAN.

Melville, Herman (1819–1891), novelist, poet. Emerging out of a background of faded gentility and financial insecurity, Herman Melville was plunged into the adventurous sailor's life that became grist for his fictional mill. In a remarkably productive twelve years (1845–57) he produced nine novels, fourteen tales and sketches, and a number of articles and reviews. Initially popular as a writer of escapist adventure novels, he alienated many contemporary readers as his fiction became increasingly complex. His capacious, energetic fiction explored uncharted philosophical territory and powerfully dramatized the condition of marginal figures such as impoverished sailors, exploited workers, and members of ethnic minority groups. He reached a point of mental and physical exhaustion in the late 1850s and entered a long period of literary silence interrupted only sporadically by bursts of creativity. Although he regained a coterie of followers shortly before his death, he probably could not have anticipated the 20th century's revival of him as one of the giants of American literary history.

Melville was born into comfortable circumstances in New York City. His father, Allan Melvill (the *e* was added in the 1830s), was a prosperous dry goods merchant who could trace his lineage back to a queen of Hungary and the kings of Norway. His mother, Maria, was descended from the illustrious Gansevoorts, one of the Dutch patroon families of New York. Both sides of the family could boast of ancestors who had distinguished themselves in the American Revolution: Allan's father, Major Thomas Melvill, had been one of the men disguised as Indians who fooled the British at the Boston Tea Party; Maria's father, the revered and wealthy General Peter Gansevoort, had been a hero in the defense of Fort Stanwix.

Herman was the third of eight children born to Allan and Maria between 1818 and 1830. His brilliant, charming older brother Gansevoort was the cynosure of the group; the more plodding Herman was marked for commerce rather than a profession. He attended the New York Male School during the late 1820s but had little formal education after that. His family life was loving and peaceful until his father suffered financial reverses. The economic panic of 1830 hit Melvill's business at a time when he had overextended himself to creditors. After a futile attempt to save his business, he accepted a job as manager of a New York fur company's branch in Albany. Through hard work he regained his financial footing but then suffered another setback. Thousands of dollars in debt, Allan Melvill collapsed physically and mentally. He died in delirium on January 28, 1832. His brother Thomas gave the opinion that he had become permanently insane and was better off dead.

In the years immediately following Allan's death, the family regained a measure of prosperity through borrowing and resourceful work. Maria Melville, establishing a pattern of indebtedness that Herman would later repeat, often called on her wealthy relatives, the Gansevoorts, for financial help. Her oldest sons took a variety of jobs to bring in additional funds. Gansevoort started a fur cap factory and store, which flourished for five years until it was wiped out by the panic of 1837. Allan apprenticed himself to a lawyer. Herman had attended Albany Academy from 1830 to 1832 but dropped out of school shortly after his father's death. He took on successive jobs as bank clerk, helper on his uncle Thomas's farm, and assistant in Gansevoort's fur company. The great depression of 1837 sent the Melvilles into an economic tailspin from which they would not emerge for several years. To save money, they left Albany for the modest nearby village of Lansingburgh. Herman, after teaching for a term at a country school in 1837, studied surveying and engineering at Lansingburgh Academy in the hope of getting an engineering job on the Erie Canal, but on completing the course found that no job was available. He had kept intellectually active by joining a local debating society, and in 1839 his "Fragments from a Writing Desk" were published in the *Democratic Press and Lansingburgh Advertiser*. They were imitative exercises in satire and romantic fantasy.

After years of struggling against poverty and job insecurity, Herman at twenty was ready for a change. Gansevoort, who had gone with Allan to New York City to study the law, learned in May 1839 that a packet ship, the *St. Lawrence*, had a berth for Herman, who went immediately to New York and signed on as a crew member. His four-month journey on the *St. Lawrence*, which ran between New York and Liverpool, was an experience he would later fictionalize in *Redburn: His First Voyage* (1849). The young man of aristocratic lineage was subjected to merciless hazing at the hands of rough sailors, and in Liverpool he witnessed the vice and squalor prevalent around the docks. On his return, Melville briefly resumed school teaching and then in 1840 took a trip west to visit his uncle Thomas Melville, who had moved to Galena, Illinois. Melville's search for a job there proved fruitless, but the trip was to have a literary dividend for him—he took a trip on a

Mississippi steamer that provided the background for *The Confidence-Man* (1857).

With no prospects for steady employment, Melville returned East and signed on as a common sailor on a whaling ship, the *Acushnet*, out of Fairhaven, Massachusetts. On January 3, 1841, the *Acushnet* set sail from New Bedford for the South Seas. The first year or so of the voyage was pleasant for Melville. Crew morale was high, and he wrote his family from Peru that he was satisfied with his work. But a poor whale catch and rising tensions between the captain and two of his officers dampened the crew's mood, and Melville decided to jump ship. On June 23, 1842, while the *Acushnet* was anchored in Nuka Hiva harbor in the Marquesas Islands, Melville and a shipmate, Richard Tobias Greene, slipped overboard. For a day or two they forged torturously through the hilly jungles of the island and then were taken in by a tribe of Taipi natives. They found the Taipis, who were reputed to be fierce cannibals, outwardly friendly, but within a month Melville and Greene began to feel like prisoners. After Greene failed to return from a trip for medical aid, Melville on August 9 was taken on by an Australian whaling ship, the *Lucy Ann*.

Conditions aboard the *Lucy Ann* were even less bearable than those on the *Acushnet*, and within two months the ship returned to Tahiti under the threat of mutiny. As one of the accused mutineers, Melville was put into light confinement to await trial. By October he was out of jail and, along with a physician-friend John B. Troy (Dr. Long Ghost of OMOO), he spent the next two months knocking about Tahiti and the neighboring island of Eimeo, where he worked briefly as a potato farmer. After many adventures, described in *Omoo*, Melville shipped with another whale ship, the *Charles and Henry*, which cruised in the South Pacific for six months before stopping over in the Hawaiian Islands, where Melville was discharged. After three months in Honolulu, Melville enlisted as an ordinary seaman aboard the warship *United States*. On October 14, 1843, the *United States* dropped anchor in Boston harbor, and Melville's stint in the U.S. Navy was over.

Melville was later to tell his friend NATHANIEL HAWTHORNE that he dated his life from his twenty-fifth year, and indeed it was then that his creative self came into being. When he returned to the family home in Lansingburgh, he regaled his sisters with exciting stories of his South Sea experiences. Doubtless at the urging of his relatives, he began to write them down. The result was his first novel, TYPEE (1846), a fictionalized rendering of his captivity among the cannibals on the Marquesas Islands. In the summer of 1845 Melville sent his manuscript for consideration by British publishers through Gansevoort, who had been appointed secretary of the United States legation in London. Gansevoort succeeded in placing the novel with a reputable publisher, John Murray, who published the novel as part of his Colonial and Home Library. Tragically, in the middle of publicity over *Typee* in May 1846, Gansevoort suddenly took ill and died. With Gansevoort gone, Herman was left as the head and chief breadwinner of the Melville family.

For a time it seemed as though he would fulfill this role admirably as a writer of popular fiction. When *Typee* was published in England, it was greeted with generally glowing reviews and strong sales. Signs of Melville's future difficulties with conventional readers, however, were not long in coming. When a New York publishing firm, Wiley and Putnam, agreed to publish the novel, Melville was forced to delete some thirty pages of material that seemed daring or sacrilegious, particularly passages that denigrated Christian missionaries.

Most of his contemporaries, however, saw *Typee* simply as a dramatic, charmingly readable account of a man's life among cannibals. Among the appreciative readers who praised the book were Margaret Fuller, Washington Irving, Walt Whitman, and Nathaniel Hawthorne. A temporary controversy over the authenticity of the narrative was happily resolved when Melville's companion among the Taipis, Richard Tobias Greene (the Toby of the novel)—who had become a housepainter near Buffalo—wrote a letter to a newspaper corroborating Melville's story. *Typee* was to sell some 20,000 copies in Melville's lifetime and was the book with which he was most commonly identified.

Buoyed up by the happy reception of *Typee*, Melville immediately produced a sequel, *Omoo* (1847), which was also well received by reviewers and the public. Based on Melville's participation in the mutiny aboard the *Lucy Ann* and his subsequent escapades on Tahiti, *Omoo* blended adventure, humor, and exoticism in a way that pleased readers in 1847 and would delight later South Sea travelers such as ROBERT LOUIS STEVENSON and HENRY ADAMS. Although some reviewers condemned the novel as erotic and profane, the popular audience appreciated its vivid characters and racy humor, which made up for its lack of unifying central narrative.

It was under these propitious circumstances that Melville married Elizabeth Knapp Shaw, the daughter of a longtime family friend and patron, Lemuel Shaw, Chief Justice of Massachusetts. The Melvilles moved into a spacious house at 103 Fourth Avenue, New York City, along with his brother Allan and Allan's new bride, as well as his mother and his four unmarried sisters. Eventually the crowded conditions in the home would become a nuisance to Melville, but for the time being he adapted well to the situation and became a literary man about town. Joining the circle of the noted editor and writer EVERT A. DUYCKINCK, he participated in such Duyckinck ventures as the short-lived comic weekly *Yankee Doodle*, for which Melville wrote the satirical "Authentic Anecdotes of 'Old Zack'" in 1847. He also was a reliable book reviewer and travel writer for another Duyckinck publication, *The Literary World*.

Melville set himself to work on another South Sea novel that seems to have been initially conceived as a sequel to *Omoo*. Indeed, the first third of MARDI AND A VOYAGE THITHER (1849), describing the rescue of an imperiled woman by a brave sailor, is in the romantic adventure vein of the previous novels, though Melville's language was far more richly textured than before. It is after the fair Yillah disappears that the novel veers toward philosophical and social allegory. The hero, Taji, embarks on a relentless search for his lost Yillah, making many stops in the mythic island chain of Mardi. His stopping places include Vivenza (the United States), where he is appalled by brawling politicians and oppressed chattel slaves; Dominora (England), where he witnesses the signs of heartless imperialism and class divisions; Maramma (the Roman Catholic church), with its retrograde creeds and harsh authoritarianism; and Franko (France), a nation aflame with revolutions. The people accompanying Taji on his journey are also representative: Babbalanja (the philosopher), Mohi (the story-teller), Yoomy (the bard), and King Media (the figure of authority). Taji's journey, while full of surprises and delights, proves fruitless, as he never finds Yillah. While some of his fellow travelers are finally content to remain on the island of Serenia (symbolizing creedless Christianity), Taji continues his relentless pursuit, at last heading chartless toward the open ocean.

Top-heavy with literary allusions, *Mardi* reflected Melville's deepening reflections on such authors as Rabelais, Sir Thomas Browne, Robert Burton, Spenser, and Coleridge. Taji's frustrated search for Yillah reflected Melville's own tormented quest for the truth of things. Most readers were not prepared to follow Melville on this quest. Though some perceptive reviewers saw *Mardi* as an ambitious philosophical romance, others blasted Melville for going off track and leaving behind the straightforward narration of his earlier novels. Melville's experiment in what he would later call the Art of Telling the Truth had jeopardized his standing with his readers.

Melville could not forget these readers, in part because he needed their financial support. *Mardi*, which was to sell only about 3,000 copies during his lifetime, was hardly the kind of work that would help provide for his growing family. A son, Malcolm, was born in early 1849, and within six years three more children—Stanwix, Elizabeth, and Frances—would arrive. He called his next two novels, REDBURN (1849) and WHITE-JACKET; OR; THE WORLD IN A MAN-OF-WAR (1850), "two jobs, which I have done for the money—being forced to it, as other men are to sawing wood." He abandoned the allegorical, philosophical mode of *Mardi* and returned to adventurous narration. In *Redburn* he embellished his experiences aboard the *St. Lawrence* and in Liverpool with many popularly oriented images, including sensational descriptions of drunkenness and spontaneous combustion, pictures of poverty and vice in the great city, and a portrait of a hypocritical captain and a horribly depraved sailor, Jackson. Although Melville was dismissive of what he called the "beggarly" *Redburn*, modern readers have found the novel a compelling story of a young man's initiation into the evils of society and human nature. *White-Jacket*, based on Melville's journey on the *United States*, puts to use the kind of lurid imagery popular in reform literature of the 1840s. Aimed largely at exposing the injustices aboard a U.S. warship, the novel contains moving accounts of the exploitation of common sailors, particularly punishment by flogging. On completion of *White-Jacket* in October 1849, Melville went to London to negotiate terms for British publication, and then went for a hurried pleasure and educational tour of part of the Continent. He sailed for home on Christmas Day 1849 and reached New York on February 1, 1850.

As living conditions in the Fourth Avenue house had become difficult, Melville moved with his wife and children to the Berkshire area in western Massachusetts, where a number-hof authors, including NATHANIEL HAWTHORNE and CATHARINE SEDGWICK, had homes. The Melvilles settled on a 160-acre property in Pittsfield, where Melville divided his time between farming and writing. His first work there was his masterpiece, MOBY-DICK; OR, THE WHALE (1851). Evidently, Melville at first planned to write another pot-boiler, for he wrote his British publisher Richard Bentley that the novel was to be "a romance of adventure founded upon certain wild legends of the Southern Sperm Whale Fisheries." But his questing, contemplative spirit could not be suppressed; he was drawn irresistibly to truth seeking. He was at the height of his creative powers, and the combined stimuli of his refreshing new environment, his intensified reading in such authors as Shakespeare and Carlyle, and his exhilarating friendship with his neighbor Hawthorne kindled his already active imagination. He expected to have the manuscript done by December 1850, but he undertook so many revisions that it did not reach the publisher until the next autumn.

Moby-Dick is centered around a symbolic quest, but Ahab's single-minded vindictive pursuit of the White Whale gives the novel a powerful, unifying plot line. With this plot line holding the novel together, Melville is free to experiment with a dazzling array of tones, styles, and levels of diction. The novel gathers together unique images from contemporary American culture and fuses them with archetypes from classic literature. From American culture, Melville derives grotesque native humor—visible in the characterization of Captain Peleg, the mate Stubb, the cook Fleece; a folksy religious idiom—manifested in Father Mapple's colorful sermon and in the secular use of religion throughout the novel; dark reform devices—especially in the portrait of the ex-drunkard Perth and in the raucous drinking scene in the Spouter Inn; and radical-democratic paradoxical characters—for example, the humane cannibal Queequeg, the oxymoronic oppressor Ahab, the querulous Quaker Bildad, and the entire wicked yet likable crew. He enriches these indigenous images and character types by coupling them with allusions to the Bible, Shakespeare, transcendental philosophy, and many other literary sources. Ishmael, the narrator, is both the brash "b'hoy" of the American streets and, figuratively, the wandering son of the Biblical Hagar, while Captain Ahab is at once the oppressor of popular culture and, by association, the evil Ahab of I Kings, the doomed overreacher of Renaissance drama, as well as Faust, Lear, and Prometheus. Ahab's destructive quest reflects Melville's search for the ungraspable truth of the universe. The object of the quest, the White Whale, is the most capacious symbol in American literature, embodying a whole range of archetypal and contemporary images, from the divine to the devilish.

After finishing *Moby-Dick* Melville wrote to Hawthorne, "I have written a wicked book, and feel spotless as the lamb. Ineffable sociabilities are in me." He bitterly recognized, however, that not many readers of his day would appreciate the novel. Although the reviews of *Moby-Dick* were predominantly favorable, few exhibited any understanding of its power and depth, and some showed nothing but outrage and bafflement—one reviewer stated that Melville should be served with "a writ *de lunatico*." Moreover, his first six books had earned him an average in royalties of $1200 apiece—not good money even in those days.

Melville quickly changed tack, aiming to attain popularity by producing what he called "a rural bowl of milk." But PIERRE; OR, THE AMBIGUITIES (1852) is hardly a bowl of milk, nor was it popular. What began as a village idyll became a searching study of the ineffectiveness of virtue in a flawed world. The novel begins happily enough, with descriptions of the young Pierre Glendinning of bucolic Saddle Meadows on the verge of marriage with the angelic Lucy Tartan, a match that receives the full blessing of his beloved mother. But Pierre soon discovers that he has a half sister, Isabel, who is living in obscurity in Saddle Meadows and who arouses his pity and concern. Pierre tries to exercise what he considers virtue by helping out the wretched Isabel, but his goodness bears evil fruit. His mother virtually disowns him and in the end dies of grief. Relatives of Lucy Tartan become enraged when the hapless Lucy moves in with Pierre and Isabel, who have gone to the city and are carrying on a semi-incestuous relationship in a strange tenement known as the Church of the Apostles. Pierre, who is an author, expresses his mounting disillusionment in his writings, as he leaves behind the sentimental magazine verse that had made him popular and writes a demonic book that is rejected by his startled publishers. *Pierre* culminates in disturbing pictures of murders, imprisonment, and suicides.

Melville believed *Pierre* would be popular, perhaps because he had brought together elements of the domestic novel and the sensational novel, both of which enjoyed great popularity in his day. But his odd coupling of these disparate genres, as well as his inevitably gloomy philosophizing, won few admirers. More than one reviewer declared that Melville had gone insane, and sales were abysmal.

Bitterly disappointed by the reception of *Moby-Dick* and *Pierre*, Melville resolved to avoid the kind of overt metaphysics that had alienated many readers. Late in 1853 he began a low-keyed career as a writer of short stories and sketches, mainly for *Harper's New Monthly Magazine* and *Putnam's Monthly Magazine*. The best of the tales, BARTLEBY, THE SCRIVENER and "Benito Cereno," were subtle studies of human perversity and social evils as perceived through the lens of the conventional consciousness. In "Bartleby" a decorous, highly conventional small-time lawyer is shocked out of his smug complacency by the bizarre behavior of one of his copyists, Bartleby, who decides he "prefers not to" work. Bartleby becomes a multilayered symbol of passivity, soul-deadening work, the dehumanization of Wall Street, and in the end death itself. The lawyer, who does an emotional St. Vitus's dance in response to his enigmatic employee, is the average man confronted with the ineffable.

"Benito Cereno" dramatizes a similar confrontation in a different context, this time with apocalyptic social overtones.

Captain Amasa Delano, while anchored off Chile, spots a strange ship drifting in the distance. Delano, a benign religious man, visits the ship—a slaver—only to be baffled by the strange situation he witnesses there. He spends the better part of the day trying to understand the disarray aboard the ship, whose captain, Benito Cereno, seems insidiously threatening and, paradoxically, under control of the blacks who are presumably under his charge. The truth is revealed at the climatic moment when Delano begins to leave in his skiff. Benito Cereno jumps into the boat after him, madly pursued by the blacks who, we learn, are slaves who had mutinied and were in control of the ship. Although in the end the leaders of the mutiny are punished by death, the formerly cheerful Delano is darkly haunted by the problem of "the Negro." By centering on Delano's ambiguous vision of the mutinous blacks, Melville exposes the incipient racism and misapprehension of the slavery issue on the part of middle-class whites.

Among the other stories Melville wrote at this time were "The Paradise of Bachelors and the Tartarus of Maids," a trenchant exposé of upper-class frivolity as contrasted with the dreary toils of women factory workers; "I and My Chimney," a humorous story, laced with sexual symbolism, about a chimney that remains standing—much to the narrator's delight—despite repeated attempts by others to tear it down; "Cock-A-Doodle-Doo!," about a poor family that dies of starvation but remains happy to the end because it owns a remarkable rooster, symbolizing proud religious faith; "Poor Man's Pudding and Rich Man's Crumbs," which portrays a stoical poor family and, in another scene, a desperate crowd of London poor people thronging to eat the scraps left over from an upper-class feast; "The Bell-Tower," about a clock-maker killed by his own invention; "Jimmy Rose," a sketch of a once successful man resigned to cheerful failure; and "The Two Temples," a satirical sketch rejected by *Putnam's* because of its bold contrast between a snobbish, aristocratic church and a humble yet friendlier public theater; and THE ENCANTADAS, ten sketches about the Galapagos Islands that depict a gray and barren world. A number of the *Putnam's* stories were gathered together and published as THE PIAZZA TALES (1856).

ISRAEL POTTER; OR, FIFTY YEARS OF EXILE, which appeared serially in *Putnam's* and then was published separately in 1855, is a tightly written adventure novel, with few metaphysical overtones, about a hero of the American Revolution who struggles for decades against poverty in London and returns home only to be rejected by the country he had served. The novel is notable for its ambivalent portraits of the shrewd Benjamin Franklin, the unprincipled John Paul Jones, and the bluff Ethan Allen, as well as for its vivid scenes of London squalor, and its lightly ironic undertones. Despite this flurry of literary activity in the mid-1850s, Melville's career was clearly running down. His best work had either been rejected outright or praised with vague politeness, and many of his magazine sketches were tossed off like hackwork. Melville was under a variety of other pressures as well. The combined work of magazine writing and farming was getting to be a burden for a man who was breaking down physically and, family members believed, mentally as well. In early spring 1855, while he was at work on "Benito Cereno," Melville suffered an attack of rheumatism that left him helpless for days. He had a history of eye trouble and was developing sciatica as well. It was under these difficult conditions that he wrote his bitterly comic novel, THE CONFIDENCE-MAN, HIS MASQUERADE (1857).

Based in part on accounts of American confidence men in popular fiction and newspapers, this novel follows the gambits of a costume-changing trickster who assumes seven—some say eight—different avatars. He variously appears as Black Guinea, an African-American cripple begging for coins; John Ringman, a man with a weed who weasels a loan from a merchant; a man in gray, who raises money for the bogus Black Rapids Coal Company; an herb doctor who purveys quack medicines; a philosophical intelligence officer, who tries to rent out boys to a Missouri bachelor; and a cosmopolitan who defends conviviality and trust even as he is cheerfully fleecing his dupes. The abstract names of the different personae point up the extraordinary complexity of the book; indeed, some critics claim that there is not *one* confidence man but *seven* (or eight). Whatever the true identity of the main character, Melville is cleverly playing here with the creation of fictions and the artful manipulation of surface appearances. Left behind is the earnest philosophical quest of *Mardi* and *Moby-Dick*. Instead, Melville delineates with sardonic humor the dodges and postures of an eternal charlatan. Set on a New Orleans–bound steamer and beginning on April Fools' Day, the novel, with its baffling circuities, is in some senses an April Fools' joke on the reader. In its fecundity and complexity, it is also a testament to Melville's creative spirit.

On completion of *The Confidence-Man*, Melville's family decided he needed a trip abroad for his health. With funds provided by Judge Shaw, Melville took a trip to Europe and the Levant from October 1856 to May 1857. He first stopped over in New York to talk with Dix and Edwards about publication plans for *The Confidence-Man*, and then on October 11, 1856, set sail for Glasgow. In November he was in Liverpool visiting Hawthorne, who since 1853 had been serving there as American consul. The old friends, who had been estranged for years, walked together on the dunes outside the city and talked metaphysics as of old. Hawthorne later recalled that Melville had "pretty much made up his mind to be annihilated" and that he "could neither believe nor be comfortable in his disbelief." Giving Hawthorne the authority to arrange for British publication of *The Confidence-Man*, Melville sailed on to Malta, Greece, Egypt, and at last the Holy Land, which he found a surprisingly barren, uninspiring place. After touring Greece and Italy, he returned to Liverpool, where he sailed for New York on May 5, 1857, arriving on May 20.

He wanted to resume writing, but his family was against it, and the reception of *The Confidence-Man* had been frigid; by June 1857 only 343 copies of the 1000-copy British edition had

sold. Although Melville would live for more than three more decades, *The Confidence-Man* proved to be the last novel he published in his lifetime.

Melville decided to go on the popular lecture circuit. Over three seasons (1857–60) he toured various states, lecturing successively on "Statues in Rome," "The South Seas," and "Travelling: Its Pleasures, Pains, and Profits." As he cleared only a little over $1,000 from his lectures, it is a wonder that he devoted three years to this vocation. It was only with the help of his father-in-law that his family remained financially solvent.

Since the mid-1850s his wife, tired of the Berkshire winters, had wanted to return to New York. Melville had sold half of his farm in 1856. In 1861 Judge Shaw died, and with part of Melville's wife's inheritance they were able to relocate. In 1863 Melville sold the remaining eighty acres of his farm and moved to 104 East 26th Street, New York City, where he was to spend the rest of his life.

Melville wrote a series of poems about central battles and figures of the Civil War, collecting seventy-two of them as BATTLE-PIECES AND ASPECTS OF THE WAR (1866). Although *Battle-Pieces* received only cursory notice in its day, it is now considered, along with Walt Whitman's DRUM-TAPS, the best of hundreds of volumes of poetry that emerged out of the Civil War. While forthright in support of the Union cause, Melville's poems display sympathy and admiration for the Southern experience as well.

The nation's tragic conflict and its difficult aftermath coincided with severe problems in Melville's personal life. Although the family was now relatively secure financially as a result of Elizabeth's inheritances, there was strain on the marriage in the mid-1860s. Melville, whose back had been severely injured in a carriage accident in 1863, had become moody and occasionally was very depressed. His wife, whose half brothers were convinced he was insane, at one point almost left him. The worst blow came in September 1867, when their son Malcolm died by his own pistol. The Melvilles took the calamity stoically, but they never fully recovered from the shock. In the coming years, they would confront pain or disappointment from their other children: the restless Stanwix became a jobless drifter in Central America and died in San Francisco in 1886; Elizabeth struggled against rheumatoid arthritis; Frances remained so bitter about her father that she refused to speak about him even after the Melville revival in the 1920s.

In some respects, though, Melville's fortunes improved. For years his family had tried to get him a government job and at last, in December 1866, he was appointed deputy customs inspector of the port of New York at a salary of $4.00 a day, a post he held for nineteen years. By the early 1870s Melville was writing again, this time a narrative poem based loosely on his 1856 tour of the Holy Land. Some 18,000 lines of rhyming octosyllabic couplets, CLAREL: A POEM AND PILGRIMAGE IN THE HOLY LAND was published with little fanfare in 1876. *Clarel* traces the travels of a variety of modern pilgrims—the world-weary sailor Nehemiah, the American wanderer Rolfe, the liberal Anglican clergyman Derwent, the misanthropic Swede Mortmain, the reclusive Vine—who, along with the central seeker Clarel, discourse endlessly on thorny religious and social issues. While tedious and sometimes exasperating, *Clarel* is the most detailed and powerful poetic representation of the collision between skepticism and faith produced in 19th-century America.

During the 1880s Melville continued writing poetry. His privately printed volume JOHN MARR AND OTHER SAILORS (1888) contained twenty-five poems, some about old sailors recalling their shipmate-spirits of long ago and other affirming the ironic indeterminacy of the universe and the vanity of human wishes. TIMOLEON (1891), another collection of miscellaneous verse, included "The Enthusiast," on the maintenance of high ideals), "Art" (on the agonies of artistic creation); "The Age of the Antonines," on the sterility of Western civilization; and "After the Pleasure Party," (on the frustration of unfulfilled sexuality). *Weeds and Wildings, With a Rose or Two* (1924) includes rather unsuccessful nature poems and nostalgic pieces recalling the early and blissful days of his marriage to Elizabeth Shaw.

The most exciting product of his pen from this period was a novelette left unfinished at his death and published as BILLY BUDD in 1924. In the story of the young Handsome Sailor victimized by a malicious master-at-arms, Melville created a classic tale of innocence versus evil. In the novel Melville deploys the kind of Biblical imagery—Adam vs. the serpent, Christ vs. his persecutors, the yardarm as the cross, the Lamb of God, and so forth—that had been treated only ironically in *The Confidence-Man*. In *Billy Budd* is Melville making a satirical portrait of ineffectual virtue, or is he proclaiming a final testament of acceptance? The question has long been debated on campuses and perhaps has no final answer. The least that can be said is that he has created a moving tale of ethical and psychological conflict.

At his death in 1891 Melville had a small but devoted group of followers, most of them in England. The centennial of his birth in 1919 prompted a revival of interest in him that has not abated since then. See also JOURNAL OF A VISIT TO LONDON AND THE CONTINENT.

The Works of Herman Melville (16 v. 1922–24) is being superseded by *The Complete Writing of Herman Melville*, edited by Harrison Hayford and others (1968–   ). Biographical and critical studies include Lewis Mumford, *Herman Melville* (1929); W. E. Sedgwick, *Herman Melville: The Tragedy of Mind* (1944); Richard Chase, *Herman Melville* (1949); Newton Arvin, *Herman Melville* (1950); Leon Howard, *Herman Melville: A Biography* (1951); James E. Miller, Jr., *A Reader's Guide to Herman Melville* (1962); Carolyn L. Karcher, *Shadow Over the Promised Land: Slavery, Race, and Violence in Melville's America* (1980); Michael Paul Rogin, *Subversive Genealogy: The Politics and Art of Herman Melville* (1983); James Duban, *Melville's Major Fiction: Politics, Theology, and Imagination* (1983); David S. Reynolds, *Beneath the American Renaissance: The Subversive Imagination in the Age of Emerson*

and Melville (1988); Hershel Parker's *Herman Melville: A Biography, Vol. 1, 1819–1851* (1996) is the first installment of a projected three-volume study.

DAVID S. REYNOLDS

Melville Goodwin, U.S.A. (1951),   a novel by J. P. MARQUAND. In a succession of episodes, a typical American military officer is depicted. The high point is a journalistic interview lasting several days, to which Goodwin is subjected, a fictional description of the ordeal Marquand had endured when he was made the subject of a cover story for *Time* (March 7, 1949).

Member of the Wedding, The (1946),   a novel by CARSON MCCULLERS. In this remarkable study in child psychology, Frankie is a lonely, motherless girl whose brother is being married. Somehow she gets the notion that she will accompany him and his wife into the world. The wedding is seen through her eyes; as a chorus to her remarks and thoughts one hears her six-year-old cousin and the African-American family cook. In 1950 a dramatic version of the novel by McCullers was produced in New York. It was later filmed (1952).

Mencken, H[enry] L[ouis] (1880–1956),   newspaperman, editor, writer. Born in Baltimore, Mencken was a reporter on the Baltimore *Herald*, became city editor and then editor. He joined the *Sunpapers* in 1906 and continued with them thereafter. He became literary editor of the SMART SET in 1908, a coeditor in 1914, continuing until 1923. In 1924 he and GEORGE JEAN NATHAN founded the AMERICAN MERCURY; he withdrew in 1933.

During the early decades of the 20th century, Mencken was at the direct center of a literary cyclone. He excited increasing vituperation from what he called the *booboisie*, especially in the *Bible belt*, another of his neologisms. His own insults were unmeasured. He denounced Hoover, Wilson, and Franklin D. Roosevelt. He flouted religion, excoriated newspapers, denounced traditional authors, eulogized radical new writers like Dreiser and Sinclair Lewis, and flayed politicians. He reported the SCOPES TRIAL in a series of masterly articles and directed raucous jeers at prohibition.

Mencken's first book was *Ventures into Verse* (1903), a collection of pieces in conventional style. His first prose books, on Shaw (1905) and on Nietzsche (1908), exhibited him as the most belligerent literary warrior of his generation in the United States. He then wrote a play, *The Artist* (1912), followed by *Heliogabalus* (1920), which he wrote with Nathan. Meanwhile he had been writing essays on numerous topics, many of them satiric. These he collected in *A Book of Burlesques* (1916), *A Little Book in C Major* (1916), *A Book of Prefaces* (1917), *Damn: A Book of Calumny* (1918), and *In Defense of Women* (1918). In a series of six books he vented his PREJUDICES (1919, 1920, 1922, 1924, 1926, 1927). He also wrote *Notes on Democracy* (1926); A TREATISE ON THE GODS (1930, rev. 1946); *Making a President* (1932); and *A Treatise on Right and Wrong* (1934). With THE AMERICAN LANGUAGE, he made a reputation in lexicography, for him an entirely new field. The book went into revised editions in 1921, 1923, and 1936. He later published two additional volumes, *Supplement One* (1945) and *Supplement Two* (1948).

Mencken wrote his autobiography in three volumes: *Happy Days* (1940), *Newspaper Days* (1941), and *Heathen Days* (1943). Out of his vast store of reading and clipping, he gathered a *New Dictionary of Quotations* (1942) that includes fresh and unconventional material. The *Mencken Chrestomathy* (1949) offers a wide and representative selection from his writings. On September 12, 1955, his seventy-fifth birthday, his publisher presented a paperbound selection from his writings, *The Vintage Mencken*, edited by Alistair Cooke. *Minority Report: H. L. Mencken's Notebooks* (1956); *A Carnival of Buncombe* (1956), sixty-nine political pieces from the Baltimore *Evening Sun*; and *The Bathtub Hoax, and Other Blasts and Bravos from the Chicago Tribune* (1958) were published posthumously (see BATHTUB HOAX). *The Letters of H. L. Mencken*, edited by Guy J. Forgue, appeared in 1961. Charles A. Fecher edited *The Diary of H. L. Mencken* (1989).

Mending Wall (in North of Boston, 1914), a poem by ROBERT FROST. Two farmers meet in spring to mend their stone wall. Both contend against that natural and mysterious something "which doesn't love a wall." But the neighbor holds doggedly to a saying of his father's, "Good fences makes good neighbors," while the speaker of the poem remarks, "There where it is we do not need the wall: / He is all pine and I am apple orchard; / My apple trees will never get across / And eat the cones under his pines, I tell him."

Men in White (1933), a play by SIDNEY KINGLEY. It presents a crisis in the life of a surgeon who finds himself faced with a conflict of love and professional duty. It won a Pulitzer Prize in 1934.

Menken, Adah Isaacs (1835–1868), actress, poet. Adah Menken's stage career started in her home city, New Orleans, in 1857; at about the same time her poems began to appear in the *Cincinnati Israelite* and the New York *Sunday Mercury*. Tongues wagged in tavern and pulpit when in the title role of Byron's *Mazeppa* she appeared half naked and strapped to the back of a horse. She radiated such charm, vitality, and generosity that she attracted writers of all sorts. In San Francisco and Virginia City she captivated Joaquin Miller. BRET HARTE wrote of her as Belle Montgomery in his poetry. MARK TWAIN admired her. In London Dickens, Charles Reade, Swinburne, Rossetti, and Burne-Jones sat at her feet. In Paris she became the last love of Dumas *père* and was worshipped by Gautier. Her marriages and divorces were a constant subject for scandal. Her autobiographical poems, entitled *Infelicia* (1868), were full of wild romanticism. Allen Lesser's *Enchanting Rebel* (1947) is a novel based on her life. Wolf Mankowitz's *Mazeppa: The Lives, Loves and Legend of Adah Isaacs Menken* appeared in 1982.

Men Without Women (1927), fourteen short stories by ERNEST HEMINGWAY. Some of the finest examples of Hemingway's mastery of description, dialogue, and atmosphere appear in this volume. THE KILLERS is a narrative remarkable for its atmosphere of impending doom and for Hemingway's

dramatic method of narration. "The Undefeated" and FIFTY GRAND deal with one of Hemingway's favorite subjects—the courage of an aging man. "Hills Like White Elephants" is another restrained masterpiece.

Mercedes of Castile (1840), a novel by JAMES FENIMORE COOPER It is an account of the first voyage of Columbus interwoven with a love story.

Mercy Philbrick's Choice (1876), a novel by HELEN HUNT JACKSON. Jackson had known EMILY DICKINSON well when both were children, but then for a long time did not see her, although they exchanged many letters. Using her knowledge of Emily's life and character, Jackson wrote a short story about her, "Esther Wynne's Love Letters," one of the anonymously published and never acknowledged *Saxe Holm's Stories* (1874); and a novel, *Mercy Philbrick's Choice*. Mercy is morbidly diffident, has an unhappy love affair, and writes poems that she refuses to publish.

Meredith, Janice. See JANICE MEREDITH.

Meredith, William (1919–), poet. Born in New York and educated at Princeton, Meredith served in the military in World War II and the Korean War. His *Love Letter from an Impossible Land* was given the Yale Series of Younger Poets Award in 1943. Other collections include *Ships and Other Figures* (1948), *The Open Sea and Other Poems* (1958), *The Wreck of the Thresher and Other Poems* (1964), *Earth Walk: New and Selected Poems* (1970), *Hazard, the Painter* (1975), and *The Cheer* (1980). A stroke brought an end to his teaching career at Connecticut College (1955–1983), but *Partial Accounts: New and Selected Poems*, published four years later, earned the Pulitzer Prize. Meredith writes personal poetry, largely in traditional forms. He has been compared to Robert Frost, and praised by James Dickey as "at his best . . . cultivated, calm, quietly original." *Effort at Speech: New and Selected Poems* (1997) is a National Book Award winner.

Merlin [1] (1874), a poem by RALPH WALDO EMERSON. Emerson, who always chafed at the rules of meter and rhyme, made a first draft of this poem for his *Journal* in 1845 and wrote it in practically free verse; later, he reworked it into a somewhat more conventional form. The poem is an analysis of the methods of poetry, and in it Emerson says of the poet, "He shall not his brain encumber/ With the coil of rhythm and number/ But, leaving rule and pale forethought,/ He shall aye climb/For his rhyme." Elsewhere he extols the poet's great powers, bids him avoid triviality and await genuine inspiration.

Merlin [2] (1917), a long blank-verse narrative poem by EDWIN ARLINGTON ROBINSON. It was followed by LANCELOT (1920) and TRISTRAM (1927). It expounds the fatalistic creed of the sage Merlin, who is called by Arthur to consult with him regarding the schemes of Arthur's illegitimate son Modred, and the illicit love affair of Guinevere and Lancelot, which together suggest that for Robinson, Arthur's world and the fate it suffered can be seen as a mirror for later times.

Merrill, James [Ingram] (1926–1995), poet. Born in New York City into a wealthy family, Merrill grew up there and in Southhampton. His parents' divorce in 1939 provides him with a dominant theme and a range of metaphors as he works and reworks the event throughout his poetry. He was educated at Amherst, with intervening service in the U.S. Army (1944–45).

Merrill's early work, *First Poems* (1951) and *The Country of a Thousand Years of Peace* (1959), introduces a romantic sensibility in formally accomplished, figurally complex, impersonal, often precious, and somewhat obscure poems—"early versions of desire" that "blaze tinily," from Merrill's perspective in 1972, "like fire deep / In windowglass far from the fire." His work has developed from these premises to become increasingly personal and autobiographical in subject matter, more intimate in voice, prosier, and more broadly witty, colloquial, and conversational in manner, while remaining highly formal. Among the influences on his work, Merrill cites ELINOR WYLIE's spiritualism; Proust's conception of memory; HENRY JAMES's luxuriant prose; AUDEN's combination of traditional forms and conversational language; WALLACE STEVENS's "odd glamorizing of philosophical terms"; and the human "scale" of ELIZABETH BISHOP, who foregoes "systems" in favor of the "elements," with no need for "oracular amplification" or elevation "on stilts to make her vision wider."

In *Water Street* (1962) Merrill defines his poetic interests with a sure sense of his historical position. "An Urban Convalescence," the important opening poem of the volume, reaffirms his rejection of modernist experiments and his commitment to traditional forms and personal memory. Here, while he chooses to rely on conventional devices and orders, he does not appeal to them for metaphysical authority. From this point on, his work exhibits a distinctly postmodern use of canonical forms, enlarging the resources and possibilities of verse after modernism while resisting nostalgia both for an authoritative tradition and for a "singular" or "individual" authorial voice. For Merrill, "voice in its fullest tonal range—not just bel canto or passionate speech," and not the "purely literary" speech of an immediacy and simplicity that is "never heard in life unless from foreigners or four-year-olds"—would be "utterly unattainable without meter and rhyme" and other "obsolete" forms. Admittedly, conventions "breed echoes" and lend "a lurking air of pastiche" to the diction, but then "no voice is as individual as the poet would like to think."

With *Water Street* Merrill dedicates himself to "making" some kind of formal "house" "Out of the life lived, out of the love spent." The house is a recurrent metaphor for poetic form in his work, but this house is no home. Rather, it figures a liminal structure, poised between the natural and historical entropy "outside" and a textual dissolution of the subject "inside" it. Another poem in the volume, "Prism," represents this "windless, compact and sunny" textual space as "a pea-sized funhouse," where subject and object alike are warped and consumed by the medium and its generic obsessions. Forms, like "houses" and the "fire screen" of a later poem, offer not so much protection as exposure to visions of the "really inhuman depths" and the "elements" of "terror, anger, love" inside as well as outside. While Merrill's voice has grown more personal

and intimate, it has also grown more clearly intertextual, resolving itself into a convention of other poets, poems, and voices. His "acoustical chambers so designed to endow the weariest platitude with resonance and depth" are at once "thrilling" and "maddening" for the scribe-poet, who suspects that "it's all by someone else!"

Merrill's other books of poems include *Nights and Days* (1966), *The Fire Screen* (1969), *Braving the Elements* (1972), *The Yellow Pages* (1974), *Divine Comedies* (1976), *The Changing Light at Sandover* (1982), *From the First Nine: Poems 1946–1976* (1982), *Late Settings* (1985), *The Inner Room* (1988) and *A Scattering of Salts* (1995). A comprehensive *Selected Poems* was published in 1992. His poetry won two National Book Awards, the National Book Critics Circle Award, the Bollingen Prize, and the Pulitzer Prize. By relying on exaggeratedly artificial forms, mixing different stanzaic patterns with blank verse and even prose, cultivating a composite tone, and referring to the writing process within his work, Merrill continued to resist and interrupt any illusions of unmediated speech. Whatever his ostensible subject, the poet is always placed at the scene of writing, choosing his words, revising, and commenting on what he is doing. "Manners for me are the touch of nature, an artifice in the very bloodsteam," Merrill remarks, bypassing the modern opposition of forms vs. nature. Yet this selfconsciousness about the built-in distance of his "cool"—mannerly and mannered—verse enables a remarkable frankness in dealing with "hot" emotional, psychological, and sexual material.

Rhetorically as well, Merrill does not oppose primal sources, natural origins, or unities to metaphoric distancing. For him, a primal experience, like a proper meaning, is often an effect of metaphor's deviation. The "transmissions" of translation, metaphor, interpretation, and tradition open access to origins, originals, truths, and even the past itself in the very process of divagating from them. "The unities of home and world, and world and page, will be observed through the very act of transition from one to the other," Merrill tells us in a statement that defines his "center" as, in fact, metaphoric passage.

The historical tradition of forms and the diachronic transport of metaphor have their synchronic double in the pun, Merrill's favorite device. Puns not only make for surface play, which helps domesticate his stylized forms as well as his visionary strain, but often serve as the structural pivot of the poems. His sense of "the relativity, even the reversibility of truths" finds its rhetorical expression in the synchronic doubleness of puns, which enables the poet "to see both ways at once" without privileging one way over another. Puns touch on a "secret, fecund place in language herself" and offer, in a parodic amplification, an uncanny double of supernatural truths. "If World War I snapped, as we hear tell, the thread of civilization," and if "a culture without Greek or Latin or Anglo-Saxon goes off the gold standard," Merrill writes, the "ill-gotten gains" of wordplay, "at once representing and parodying our vital wealth," offer a way of creating works "whose resonance" may last "more than a season." A triumphant illustration of this vision is THE CHANGING LIGHT AT SANDOVER, in which the historical treasure of an array of allegorical systems resolves into one cosmic pun. This epic trilogy, in part a transcription of voices from the so-called other world received through a Ouija board, is an homage as awesome as the generative power it celebrates—the wholly "human resource" of language, which reveals the source light itself by clothing it in the right discourse.

J. D. McClatchy edited *Collected Poems* (2001). Merrill's other works include two novels, *The Seraglio* (1957, 1987) and *The (Diblos) Notebook* (1965), and a book of essays, *Recitative* (1986). *A Different Person: A Memoir* appeared in 1993. *Memoirs of a Minotaur* (2000), by Merrill's nephew Robin Magowan, is in part a tribute to the poet, as is Alison Lurie's *Familiar Spirits: A Memoir of James Merrill and Alison Lurie* (2001). A major study of his work is Stephen Yenser's *The Consuming Myth* (1987).

MUTLU KONUK BLASTING/BP

Merrill, Stuart [Fitzrandolph] (1863–1915),   poet, translator. Born in Hempstead, New York, Merrill was one of the early American expatriates. He lived mostly in France and did all his writing in French. (He also published a collection of translations from Huysmans, Baudelaire, Mallarmé, and other French writers, *Pastels in Prose*, 1890.) His volume of poems *Les Gammes* (1887) confirmed his position in the French symbolist movement. For a while, he managed the New Art Theatre in Paris, and in 1892 published a second volume of poems, *Les Fastes*. His most important work, *Une Voix dans la Foule* (1909), expresses his deep sympathy for the sufferings of mankind.

Merritt, A[braham] (1884–1943),   reporter, archaeologist, short-story writer. Born in New Jersey, Merritt worked first on the Philadelphia *Inquirer*, later for the *American Weekly*, of which he became editor in 1937. In the meantime, he engaged in archaeological and historical studies relating mainly to the modern survival of ancient cults. He published several imaginative fantasy novels, including *The Moon Pool* (1919), *The Ship of Ishtar* (1926), *The People of the Abyss* (1931), and *Dwellers in the Mirage* (1934).

Merriwell, Frank.   A character created by WILLIAM GILBERT PATTEN, who wrote under the name Burt L. Standish. Patten, already a popular dime novelist, conceived this character in 1896 and wrote weekly stories about him for eighteen years. The stories were later collected in the Frank Merriwell Series, which ran into 208 volumes from 1900 to 1933, then was revived with *Mr. Frank Merriwell* in 1941. Patten presented Merriwell as an athletic hero at Yale; he had so many virtues that he seemed a caricature and indeed became a comic strip character in 1931. The series, the most extended in all juvenile literature, has sold more than 125,000,000 copies.

Merton, Thomas (1915–1969),   poet, writer, priest. Merton was born in the Pyrenees and grew up in France, mostly among artists. He received his early schooling in France. His father, a landscape painter, was British, his mother an American and a Quaker. He attended Cambridge University and Columbia University. He became a convert to Catholicism in 1938, and his first book, *Thirty Poems* (1944), shows the flame of his enthusiasm for the faith he chose. In 1941 Merton entered the strict Cistercian monastery at Gethsemani, in Kentucky, as a Trappist novice. His autobiographical *The Seven Storey Mountain* (1948) became an immediate best seller. Ordained a Catholic priest in 1949, Merton continued his monastic life, publishing nearly fifty books in his lifetime. Volumes of verse after his first include *Figures for an Apocalypse* (1948), *The Strange Island* (1957), and *Collected Poems of Thomas Merton* (1977). *Mystics and Zen Masters* (1967) is one of many prose works after *The Seven Storey Mountain*.

Merton of the Movies (1922),   a novel by HARRY LEON WILSON, dramatized in 1922 by MARC CONNELLY and G. S. KAUFMAN, filmed in 1924. In this portrayal of Merton Gill, the small-town dry-goods clerk who finally reaches Hollywood, Wilson satirized the dreams of the average American youth as well as Hollywood itself.

Merwin, Samuel (1874–1936),   editor, novelist, director, dramatist. Born in Evanston, Illinois, Merwin began his literary career by writing lively novels in collaboration with H. K. Webster on American railroad-building—*The Short Line War* (1899) and *Calumet K* (1901). The latter was a best seller. Later he wrote other novels, among them two about adolescents—*Temperamental Henry* (1917), and *Henry Is Twenty* (1918). He was associate editor of *Success* from 1905 to 1909, editor till 1911; in the course of his work on this magazine he investigated the opium trade in China and wrote *Drugging a Nation* (1908).

Merwin, W[illiam] S[tanley] (1927–   ),   poet, translator, prose writer. Born in New York City, Merwin was educated at Princeton and McGill before going to Majorca as tutor to the son of the poet Robert Graves. His earlier poems, mostly traditional subjects rendered in sharp images, were collected in *A Mask for Janus* (1952); *The Dancing Bears* (1954), *Green with Beasts* (1965), *The Drunk in the Furnace* (1960), and *The Moving Target*. With *The Lice* (1967), his poems began to take on a note of surrealism and to appear more meditative. His following volumes include *The Carrier of Ladders* (1963), *Writings to an Unfinished Accompaniment* (1973), *The Compass Flower* (1977), *Opening the Hand* (1983), and *The Rain in the Trees* (1988). His translations include *The Poem of the Cid* (1959), *The Song of Roland* (1963) and Dante's *Purgatorio* (2000). *The Miner's Pale Children* (1970) and *Houses and Travelers* (1977) are collections of prose parables, mostly brief, poetically intense, mysteriously minimal in their communications. *Unframed Originals: Recollections* (1982) consists of memoirs of his family in Pennsylvania.

Message to Garcia, A (1899),   an essay by ELBERT HUBBARD. First published in THE PHILISTINE, March 1899, the essay described an event of the Spanish-American War. An American officer, Andrew Summers Rowan (1857–1943), had carried a message to the Cuban revolutionary leader General Garcia y Inigues and reported his reply to Washington, encountering many difficulties on the way. Hubbard's essay was inspirational, drawing from the exploit a message for others. When you are given a job to do you ought to do it no matter what the odds are against you; be sure you deliver your message to Garcia.

Immensely popular, the essay was reprinted many times and translated into at least twenty languages. It has been estimated that during World War I a million copies were distributed. Businesses printed copies for their employees during the boom years of the 1920s and the Depression years that followed. Perhaps all told the essay had been printed in forty million copies by 1940. Rowan told his own story in *How I Carried the Message to Garcia* (1923). The exploit also inspired a movie, *A Message to Garcia* (1936).

Messer Marco Polo (1921),   a novel by BRIAN DONN-BYRNE. The story is narrated by Malachi Campbell, an Ulsterman who had fought all over the world and picked up many strange tales. He tells what he asserts to be "the real story of Marco Polo," an account of how Marco fell in love with the daughter of Kubla Khan. At her command her magicians save him from death in the desert. He stays and marries her, and then she dies and, when Marco is old, he goes back to Venice. The book became a best seller.

Metacomet.   See KING PHILIP.

Metamora, or, The Last of the Wampanoags (1829), a play by JOHN AUGUSTUS STONE. The play was written in response to an offer by the actor Edwin Forrest of a handsome prize for "the best tragedy in five acts, of which the hero, or principal character, shall be an original of this country." Stone won the prize, and Forrest continued to play in it for the rest of his career. In 1836 he commissioned R. M. Bird to revise it. The play exists in two incomplete manuscripts, printed in *America's Lost Plays* (1941). Metamora is the Indian monarch KING PHILIP.

Metaphysical Club.   This group of scientists, philosophers, and laymen was founded at Cambridge, Massachusetts, during the 1870s. Its members included WILLIAM JAMES, OLIVER WENDELL HOLMES, JR., CHARLES SANDERS PEIRCE, JOHN FISKE, CHAUNCEY WRIGHT, Francis E. Abbot, Nicholas St. John Green, and Joseph Warner. Green, a lawyer and a disciple of Jeremy Bentham, was credited by Peirce with having directed attention to a definition of "belief" by the British metaphysician Alexander Bain as "that upon which a man is prepared to act." From this definition, says Peirce, "pragmatism is scarce more than a corollary." He and James developed this idea when they spread the doctrine on PRAGMATISM. Peirce himself was apparently the first to put the idea down on paper, and then into print, when he wrote an article on the subject for *The Popular Science Monthly* (1878).

Methodism.   The doctrines, practices, and worship of Protestants whose central core of belief stems from the movement begun in England by John Wesley (1703–91). He, his brother Charles, and GEORGE WHITEFIELD were the important early figures. All were ordained as ministers of the Church of England, but as early as 1729 at Oxford they had begun meetings and discussions that led to the resolve to conduct their lives by "rule and method," the origin of the term "Methodism." Soon taking to evangelical preaching wherever they could assemble an audience, they were barred from most pulpits by a church hierarchy that disapproved of their methods of conversion. As their movement grew, they ordained lay preachers and sent them from congregation to congregation in a form of itinerant preaching that eventually became a major part of Methodism. In 1744 the Methodists held their first annual conference and drew up their Articles of Religion. On most points of doctrine they did not stray far from the teachings of the established church, but they placed greater stress on repentance, faith, and salvation open to all. Three years earlier, Whitefield had already broken away to become leader of a Calvinistic group of Methodists less certain of the Arminian idea of salvation extended beyond the bounds of the elect (see ARMINIANISM).

Methodism took root in America early and found especially fertile soil. The Wesleys visited Georgia in 1735 and Whitefield's visits from 1738 on contributed to the GREAT AWAKENING that helped create a climate for conversion. In 1769 Wesley sent several itinerant preachers over and in 1773 the first annual conference was held. In 1784 Thomas Coke arrived with authority from Wesley to organize the societies in America. In later years, Methodism split into a number of organizations, including the African Methodist Episcopal Church (1816), for African Americans; the Methodist Protestant Church (1830), with no bishops; the Primitive Methodist Church (c. 1830); the Wesleyan Methodist Connection (1843), antislavery; the Methodist Episcopal Church, South (1845), pro-slavery; and the Congregational Methodist Church (1852). In 1939 a number of groups united as the Methodist Church and in 1968 that church joined with the Evangelical United Brethren Church to become the United Methodist Church, the largest group of Methodists. By the 1980s Methodists numbered close to thirteen million in the United States.

Mexican War.   The successful revolt of Texans against Mexican control in 1836 planted seeds of future trouble between the United States and Mexico. Some Texans sought independence from Mexico and annexation by the United States simultaneously, but the policies of Jacksonian America could not accommodate such an acquisition of foreign territory, and Texas established itself as an independent republic. By the early 1840s, however, expansion was a national political issue, and notions of America's "Manifest Destiny" abounded. Indeed, they were the focus of the election of 1844, in which James K. Polk, a Democrat and an expansionist, carried the day against the incumbent Whigs. After the election, but before Polk's inauguration, Whig President John Tyler engineered the annexation of Texas by joint resolution of Congress, a move that had the effect of stealing considerable Democratic thunder over the expansion issue.

Annexation brought to a head the longstanding border conflict between Mexico and Texas. Mexico claimed the Nueces River as its northern boundary, but the United States embraced the Texan contention that the Rio Grande marked the border farther south. Polk, launching his expansionist program on several fronts, sent John Slidell to Mexico City with an offer to purchase New Mexico (then consisting of present-day Arizona, Nevada, Utah, and parts of New Mexico, Colorado, and Wyoming) and California. When the Mexican government, knowing beforehand the intent of the mission, refused to receive Slidell, Polk ordered General Zachary Taylor to occupy a position just north of the Rio Grande. On April 25, 1846, a Mexican force, having crossed into the disputed area between the Rio Grande and Nueces rivers, attacked a party of American troops, an event that Polk called an invasion of American soil. Within three weeks of the attack, Congress passed a declaration of war on Mexico.

The war proceeded on three fronts: Taylor and Winfield Scott invaded Mexico; Stephen Watts Kearny marched on Santa Fe and thence into California; and Commodore John D. Sloat blockaded major Mexican ports on the Pacific, from Mazatlan to Monterey. Militarily, the war was little more than a succession of American victories over poorly equipped Mexican forces. Peace negotiations begun in early January 1848 resulted in the Treaty of Guadalupe Hidalgo, which went into effect on July 4. The United States received California and New Mexico for the sum of $15,000,000—about half of what Polk had originally offered to pay Mexico for those lands before the war. Any savings were offset by the loss of nearly 13,000 American lives (most as a result of disease) and a military cost to the U.S. government of nearly $98,000,000.

The best brief history is Otis A. Singletary, *The Mexican War* (1960). A more detailed account is K. Jack Bauer, *The Mexican War, 1846–1848* (1974). The essential older work is Justin H. Smith, *The War with Mexico* (2 v. 1919), still useful because of Smith's virtually unlimited access to Mexican archives, something denied to subsequent researchers. Fiction based on the Mexican War has been undistinguished at best, and the principal literary contribution may be JOHN GREENLEAF WHITTIER's "The Angels of Buena Vista."

WILLIAM W. SAVAGE, JR.

Meyer, Annie Nathan (1867–1951), educator, dramatist, novelist. Born in New York City, Annie Nathan passed the Columbia University examinations, but was unable to receive credit because women were excluded from Columbia at the time. In order that other young women should not be similarly treated, she set about founding a women's branch of Columbia, after first obtaining permission from the university's trustees. The account of the founding of Barnard College in 1889 is told in her *Barnard Beginnings* (1935). *Helen Brent, M.D., A Social Study* (1892), a novel dealing with a woman's choice between love and a career, was followed by *Robert Annys, a Tale* (1901). Turning her attention to Broadway, Meyer wrote six plays: *The Dominant Sex* (1911), *The Dreamer* (1912), *The District Attorney* (1920), *The Advertising of Kate* (1921), *The New Way* (1925), and *Black Souls* (1932).

Mezzo Cammin (1842), a sonnet by HENRY WADSWORTH LONGFELLOW. Longfellow laments that his ambi-

tion to build "a tower of song with lofty parapet" has been defeated by "sorrow and a care that almost killed." It was written while he was on a trip to Europe for his health and was not published until 1886. The title, from Dante, refers to the fact that Longfellow, too, was in the "middle way" of his life—thirty-five years old. The sorrow was undoubtedly the death of his first wife; "the tower of song" not completed was probably his *Christus*, outlined in his notebooks of the period.

Michaels, Anne (1958–   ), poet, novelist, essayist. Born in Toronto, she was educated at the University of Toronto. Two early poetry collections, *The Weight of Oranges* (1985) and *Miner's Pond* (1991), were printed together in a Canadian publication (*The Weight of Oranges*, 1997) and, with a third title, as *Poems:The Weight of Oranges, Miner's Pond and Skin Divers* (2000) in the United States. Though her verse is often written in the first person, it is not directly autobiographical; some of the dramatic monologues are written in the voices of such historical figures Isak Dinesen or Marie Curie. Her novel *Fugitive Pieces* (1996) treats two perspectives of the Holocaust. *Sudden Miracles: Eight Woman Poets* (1991), edited by Rhea Tregevov, and *Poetry and Knowing* (1994), edited by Tim Lilburn, include some of her essays on poetry.

Micheaux, Oscar (Devereaux) (1884–1951), novelist, screenwriter. Born in Illinois, Micheaux went to high school there before establishing a homestead in South Dakota in 1904. His first novel, *The Conquest* (1913), subtitled *The Story of a Negro Pioneer, by the Pioneer* was published with borrowed money and sold to neighboring farmers and blacks in the South by the author. In 1915, he founded Western Book Supply Company to print and distribute his second and third novels *The Forged Note: A Romance of the Darker Races* (1915) and *The Homesteader* (1917). Four more novels followed. After writing the screenplay for his novel *The Homesteader*, Micheaux became an independent filmmaker and produced over forty movies primarily intended for black audiences. His film career was acknowledged after his death with a lifetime achievement award from the Directors Guild of America and a star on the Hollywood Walk of Fame. An annual award named for him recognizes black contributions to American film.

Michener, James A[lbert] (1907–1997), novelist. Born in New York City, Michener was educated at Swarthmore and the University of Northern Colorado. His experiences in the navy in World War II provided background for the stories collected in TALES OF THE SOUTH PACIFIC (1948), which won a Pulitzer Prize and was made into the Broadway musical *South Pacific* (1949). Michener followed this success with a series of semidocumentary novels, generally panoramic and crowded with facts, each novel illuminating the history of a particular place: *Hawaii* (1959); *The Source* (1965), about Israel; *Centennial* (1974), about Colorado; *Chesapeake* (1980), about Maryland's Eastern Shore; *The Covenant* (1980), about South Africa: *Poland* (1983); *Texas* (1985); *Alaska* (1988); and *Caribbean* (1989). His other novels include *The Fires of Spring* (1949), about a boy growing up in Pennsylvania; *The Bridges at Toko-Ri* (1953), about the Korean conflict; *Sayonara* (1954), about Japanese-American relations in Japan; *The Bridge at Andau* (1957), about the 1956 Hungarian revolt; *Caravans* (1963), set in Afghanistan; *The Drifters* (1971), about young people wandering around the world; and *Space* (1982), about astronauts. *Return to Paradise* (1951) is a second collection of short stories of the South Pacific. His nonfiction titles include *Kent State* (1971), an examination of the campus demonstrations and the shooting of four students by the National Guard.

Middle Border. See HAMLIN GARLAND.

Middleton, George (1880–1967), editor, playwright. Middleton was born in Paterson, New Jersey. After graduation from Columbia University, Middleton spent two years in Paris studying the theater and writing plays. His first play, *Cavalier* (1902), was written with PAUL KESTER. *Polly with a Past* (1917), a comedy written with Guy Bolton, was one of his successes. He was literary editor of *La Follette's Weekly* from 1912 until 1930. From 1929 until 1931 he was an associate producer in the Fox Film Corporation. His one-act divorce play, *Collusion*, was refused a license by the London censor in 1921, by the Los Angeles censor two years later. Among his published plays are *Embers* (1911), *Tradition* (1913), *Nowadays* (1914), *Masks* (1920), *The Light of the World* (1920), *Hiss! Boom!! Blah!!!* (1933), *That Was Balzac* (1936), and *The Dramatists Guild* (1939). *These Things Are Mine* (1947) is his autobiography.

Middletown (1929), a survey of a typical mid-American city in the 1920s by ROBERT S. and HELEN M. LYND, based on Muncie, Indiana. Later the Lynds published *Middletown in Transition* (1937), and Helen Lynd added *Update* (1982), extending the story to half a century.

Middle West. In general the terms *Middle West* and *Midwest* designate the region bounded on the east by the Appalachians, on the north by Canada, on the south by an extension of the Mason and Dixon Line, and on the west by the Rockies. This region would consequently include Ohio, Michigan, Illinois, Indiana, Wisconsin, Minnesota, Missouri, Iowa, Kansas, Nebraska, and the Dakotas. The literature of this region has a certain degree of unity, especially in its farm and small-town novels, in which American realism first flowered. See Ralph L. Rusk, *The Literature of the Middle Western Frontier* (2 v. 1925), and Dale Kramer, *Chicago Renaissance: The Literary Life of The Midwest, 1900–1930* (1966).

Midland, The: A Magazine of the Middle West. This was an influential little magazine, founded by John T. Frederick in Iowa City in 1915, and edited by him until 1933, when it was absorbed by *The Frontier* (see LITTLE MAGAZINES. FRANK LUTHER MOTT was associated with Frederick in the editorship from 1925 to 1933. The magazine was esteemed for the fine poems and short stories it published.

Midnight Ride of Paul Revere, The. See PAUL REVERE'S RIDE.

Miers, Earl Schenck (1910–1972), editor, historian, novelist, writer of juveniles. Miers was born in Brooklyn, New York. *The Ivy Years* (1945) tells of his college days at Rutgers and the battle he fought against cerebral palsy, the result of a brain injury at birth. This is also the subject, frankly treated, of *Why Did This Have to Happen?* (1958). Two other autobiographical books are *Where the Raritan Flows* (1964) and *Down in Jersey* (1973). Miers served on the staff of several publishing firms. His best-known books are historical, among them *Gettysburg* (with Richard A. Brown, 1948); an account of General Sherman, *The General Who Marched to Hell* (1951); *Web of Victory* (1955), a study of Grant at Vicksburg; and *The Last Campaign: Grant Saves the Union* (1971). *Valley in Arms* (1943) is a historical novel. Among his other books are *Backfield Feud* (1936); *Composing Sticks and Mortar Boards* (1941); *Career Coach* (1941); *Bookmaking and Kindred Amenities* (1942); *Ball of Fire* (1956); *Rebel's Roost* (1956); *America and Its Presidents* (1959); *Storybook of Science* (1959); and with Paul M. Angle the two-volume *Tragic Years, 1861–1865* (1960).

Mifflin, Lloyd (1846–1921), poet, printer. Born in Columbia, Pennsylvania, Mifflin wrote many sonnets and imitations of Greek poets. Among his collections are *At the Gates of Song* (1897), *The Slopes of Helicon* (1898), *Fields of Dawn and Later Sonnets* (1900), *Collected Sonnets* (1905), and *As Twilight Falls* (1916).

Miles, George H[enry] (1824–1871), lawyer, teacher, playwright, poet, novelist. Born in Baltimore, Miles turned from law to teach at Mount St. Mary's College for many years. His first play of any consequence, *Mohammed, the Arabian Prophet*, won in 1849 a prize offered by the actor Edwin Forrest, who never produced it. It was finally brought to the stage in 1851. Another play by Miles dealt with a favorite theme of his day, *Hernando de Soto* (1852). It was never published, but part of the manuscript survives. One of Miles's comedies, *Señor Valiente* (1859), was successfully produced in Baltimore and New York City.

Miles, Josephine [Louise] (1911–1985), poet, scholar. Born in Chicago, Miles was raised in California, where she has spent most of her life. She was educated at the University of California at Los Angeles and at Berkeley, where she remained throughout her teaching career. Her poetry is typically based on common speech, and reflecting the passing moment. *Collected Poems* appeared in 1983. Her earlier titles include *Line of Intersection* (1939), *Poems 1930–1960* (1960), and *To All Appearances: Poems New and Selected* (1984). Her critical works include *The Vocabulary of Poetry* (1946); *The Continuity of Poetic Language* (1951); *Eras and Modes in English Poetry* (1957, revised 1964); *Renaissance, Eighteenth-Century and Modern Language in English Poetry* (1960); *Style and Proportion: and The Language of Prose and Poetry* (1967).

Miles Wallingford (1844), a novel by JAMES FENIMORE COOPER. This story was a sequel to AFLOAT AND ASHORE, OR, THE ADVENTURES OF MILES WALLINGFORD, which was published several months earlier under the first part of the title.

Millar, Kenneth. See ROSS MACDONALD.

Millar, Margaret (1915–1994), novelist. Born in Kitchener, Ontario, Millar made a specialty of psychological mystery novels set in Toronto or Georgian Bay, Ontario. These include *The Devil Loves Me* (1941), *The Wall of Eyes* (1943), *The Iron Gate* (1945), *Vanish in an Instant* (1952), *Beast in View* (1955), *An Air That Kills* (1957), *Listening Walls* (1959), *Stranger in My Grave* (1960), *The Fiend* (1964), *Ask for Me Tomorrow* (1976), *The Murder of Miranda* (1979), *Mermaid* (1982), and *Banshee* (1983). Her husband, Kenneth Millar, wrote under the pen name ROSS MACDONALD.

Millay, Edna St. Vincent (1892–1950),   poet, dramatist. Born in Rockland, Maine, Millay was fortunate to grow up in a family that encouraged her literary talents. The three Millay sisters were avid readers of ST. NICHOLAS magazine, and it was in its pages that Edna Millay first found her welcome as a poet. Such early verses as *Forest Trees* and *Vacation Song* were published in it. RENASCENCE won publication in a poetry selection called *The Lyric Year* (1912). There seemed little chance that she might go to college until a family friend, Caroline B. Dow, undertook to help with Millay's education. After preliminary courses at Barnard, Edna Millay entered Vassar and was graduated in 1917, the year in which her first book, *Renascence and Other Poems*, was published. Upon graduation, Millay went to live in Greenwich Village, New York. For a while she acted with the PROVINCETOWN PLAYERS, who produced some of her plays. Like most of her Village contemporaries, the copper-haired, green-eyed poetess was "very, very poor and very, very merry," as she described it. Although she was known in literary circles where the sparks of genius find early recognition, the reading public in general became familiar with her work only through her second book, A FEW FIGS FROM THISTLES (1920). She was influenced particularly by Shakespeare, Keats, and to a lesser degree Gerard Manley Hopkins, and developed a special genius for the sonnet. In 1923 she won the Pulitzer Prize for THE HARP-WEAVER AND OTHER POEMS. Her books were selling well and she made dramatic personal appearances that further heightened her vogue. The ardent youth of her time found in Millay's verses a creed and a way of life. Undoubtedly, her most quoted quatrain remains: "My candle burns at both ends; / It will not last the night; / But ah, my foes, and oh, my friends— / It gives a lovely light."

In 1923 she married Eugen Boissevain, a New York importer. Soon after, they purchased a farm in Austerlitz, New York, which she called Steepletop after the wildflower named Steeplebush, which abounded in the region. They continued to live there for the rest of their lives. Some of Millay's finest work was written in a shack some little way from the main house.

As Millay approached the middle years, her writing showed less impudence and more seriousness, especially when political catastrophe overtook Europe. She wrote powerful verses against the barbaric developments there. Among her books are *Aria da Capo* (1920, a play, which she considered one of her best); *Three Plays* (1926); THE KING'S HENCHMAN (1927, a play that Deems Taylor turned into an opera); *The Buck in the Snow and Other Poems* (1928); *Fatal Interview* (1931), a sonnet sequence on a doomed love affair; *Wine from These Grapes* (1934); *Conversation at Midnight* (1937); *Huntsman, What

Quarry? (1939); and *Make Bright the Arrows* (1940). Her *Collected Sonnets* appeared in 1941, her *Collected Lyrics* in 1943. Published after her death were *Mine the Harvest* (1954) and *Collected Poems* (1956). She also wrote fictional and satirical sketches, such as *Distressing Dialogues* (1924), under the pen name Nancy Boyd. Nancy Milford, *Savage Beauty* (2001), is the authorized biography. Others are by Jean Gould (1969) and Daniel Mark Epstein (2001).

Miller, Alice Duer (1874–1942),   poet, playwright, novelist, short-story writer. She was born in New York City and wrote light, witty novels, some of which were dramatized, in particular *Come Out of the Kitchen* (1916) and *The Charm School* (1919). Another, *Gowns by Roberta* (1933), became the basis of the popular musical comedy *Roberta*, with music by Jerome Kern and book by Otto Harbach. She conducted a column for the New York *Tribune* called "Are Women People?" and wrote scripts for Hollywood and appeared in a Hecht-MacArthur movie called *Soak the Rich*. Several collections of her short stories were published. Her great popular success came with her fervid and sentimental verse eulogy of England's resistance to the Nazis in 1940, *The White Cliffs of Dover*. In 1941 she published *I Have Loved England*. After her death, Denning Duer Miller, her son, compiled a slim *Selected Poems* (1949).

Miller, Arthur (1915–   ),   playwright, essayist. Miller was born in New York City and grew up in Harlem and Brooklyn. His coming of age corresponded almost exactly with the stock market crash of 1929, and that event and the subsequent Depression were the most formative influences on his developing imagination. From the calamities came his conviction that behind the uncertainties of life there were certain hidden laws that the artist must probe and explain. He attended the University of Michigan planning to become a journalist, but his receipt of the Avery Hopwood Prize for his first dramatic script redirected his ambitions and changed his life.

Determined on a career as a writer, he worked briefly for the FEDERAL THEATER PROJECT after graduation and, after dissolution of the Project, wrote a number of radio plays. During the war he published an account of American military training, *Situation Normal*, which appeared in 1944, and his only novel, *Focus* (1945). But it was in the theater that he wanted to succeed, and after an initial disappointment with his first Broadway production, *The Man Who Had All the Luck* (1944), he skyrocketed to national prominence with *All My Sons* (1947), which won the Drama Critics' Circle Award and ran for more than a year. With the proceeds from *Sons* he bought a farm in Connecticut where he moved with his wife and two young children. There he wrote DEATH OF A SALESMAN, his second Broadway success and the work that established his international reputation.

Celebrity brought Miller financial security, but it also made him a more visible target for critics opposed to his humanitarian and left-wing views. His adaptation of Ibsen's *An Enemy of the People* (1950) and his own THE CRUCIBLE (1953) were resented by some as criticisms of the activities of the House Committee on Un-American Activities (see MCCARTHYISM). This led to attacks on Miller by the American Legion and several editorial writers, when it was learned that he was working on a film script for the Youth Board of New York City in 1955. Under pressure from these sources, the Youth Board dropped what had become an embarrassing project.

The following year Miller was subpoenaed to appear as a witness before the House Committee. His refusal to give the names of writers, already known to the Committee, whom he had seen at a communist writer's meeting in 1947 resulted in citation for contempt of Congress and a fine of $500. He appealed his case to the Supreme Court and was acquitted in 1958.

During these years, the turmoil in his public career was paralleled by developments in his private life. In 1956 he divorced his first wife, Mary Slattery, to marry Marilyn Monroe. Besieged by an insatiable press, the couple found temporary haven in England, where Miller worked on a revision of *A View from the Bridge*, which had originally appeared on Broadway in 1955. On their return to America, however, Miller found it increasingly difficult to write for the stage, partly because of his sense of alienation from a country moving increasingly to the right, and partly because of his involvement in his wife's career. During this period he wrote a number of short stories, turning one of them into his first film script. *The Misfits* (1960), produced by Frank Taylor, directed by JOHN HUSTON, and starring Marilyn Monroe, proved to be something less than an artistic success. For Miller and his wife, it was a disaster, and shortly after the completion of the film, they were divorced.

In 1964, after an absence of nine years, Miller returned to Broadway with what is probably his most deeply personal statement, *After the Fall*. The writing of the play had coincided with three important milestones in Miller's life—the death of his mother in 1961, his marriage to photographer Inge Morath in February 1962, and the suicide of Marilyn Monroe in August of that year. Reaction to the play was mixed. Few critics seemed able to separate their response to the work from their attitude to Miller's relations with Marilyn Monroe, which they took to be the subject of the drama.

In the years following Miller's return to the stage he found his relationship with the New York commercial theater increasingly strained. *Incident at Vichy* (1964), *The Price* (1968), and *The Creation of the World and Other Business* (1972) were produced on Broadway, but more and more Miller looked to other outlets for his work. Two one-act plays, *Fame* and *The Reason Why* (1970), were first presented at the New Theater Workshop; *The Archbishop's Ceiling* (1977) was performed at the Kennedy Center in Washington, and *The American Clock* (1980) first opened at the Spoleto Festival in Charleston, South Carolina, before moving to Broadway. *Elegy for a Lady* and *Some Kind of Love Story* (1982) were produced by the Long Wharf Theater in New Haven. The stage version of *Playing for Time* (1985) first appeared at the Studio Theater in Washington, and the one-act plays *I Can't Remember Anything* and *Clara* (1987) were presented at Lincoln Center.

Convinced that artists should be engaged in the world around them, Miller has spent much of his life actively promoting causes in which he believed. Through his long association with PEN International, including a year as president, he has worked tirelessly for the release of politically imprisoned writers. He has also been active in party politics, having served as a delegate to the 1968 Democratic Convention in Chicago. This relationship of art and active politics is vividly illustrated in his most recent work, the movie script *Everybody Wins* (1990), which is based on his campaign against the miscarriage of justice in Connecticut.

If one characteristic typifies Miller's work, it is his exploration of the relationship between public and private morality, what he describes as a man's attempt to "evaluate himself justly." For almost four decades, in plays, essays, stories, reportage, and personal interviews, he has struggled to understand the chaos of 20th-century American experience. That experience, encompassing as it has a Depression, the Cold War, racial strife, and Vietnam, has seemed to many a subject for despondency. Miller, almost alone among his contemporaries, has continued to cling to a stubborn optimism. Against all the evidence—the Holocaust, the hysteria of Cold War paranoia, even the painful discovery of his own capacity for evil—Miller has continued to believe in the forces of life and to invoke them against the advocates of nihilism and despair.

Miller's first real success on Broadway, *All My Sons* (1947), deals with the question of self-evaluation in the context of World War II. Joe Keller, a Midwestern aircraft manufacturer whose delivery of faulty piston heads during the war caused the death of several American airmen, has avoided punishment for his action by blaming his partner, and has assuaged his conscience by convincing himself that all was done in support of his family. Although melodramatic in form, the play gains its considerable power not from the moralizing, but from the conflict between the self-justifying father and his disillusioned son.

This strain in Miller's writing came to mature fruition in his masterpiece, *Death of a Salesman*, produced just two years later. Described as possibly the best play ever written by an American, *Salesman* marks the brilliant fusion of the ideas and formal problems that Miller had been wrestling with since he began writing. Originally to be called "The Inside of His Head" the play combines traditional naturalism with expressionistic techniques that enable Miller to explore areas of the subjective life inaccessible to conventional dramatic form. Its focus on the interior life of a single character produces a distorted perspective, but it permits intense concentration on the processes of self-delusion and rationalization. Willy Loman's flaw has been variously interpreted as a pitiable blindness to the realities of the American Dream, as the unrealistic hope of a doting father, and the bad luck of a salesman working a tough territory. The disagreement arises from the rich complexity of the play as well as from the fact that the social and psychological levels of the work are imperfectly related. The view of Willy as an exploited victim of an indifferent capitalistic system seems unconnected to the Freudian strains dealing with sexual repression and guilt, and the conflict between father and son. Self-accused of failure as father, provider, and husband, Willy can produce nothing in his own defense but crumbling dreams and a faltering sense of dignity. Tom between his refusal to accept the assessments of his son Biff and his inability to believe in the reassurances of his wife, he alternates between outrage and contrition. When, in his final confrontation with Biff, Willy comes to the realization that his son's knowledge of his affairs on the road has not destroyed his love, Willy is able at last to still his hidden accusers. Although Willy's attempt to rescue Biff with Willy's life insurance money is usually interpreted as an act of self-deception, Willy is not entirely deluded in his death. His fears that his son despised him had proven false, and the dignity he laid claim to was in some measure acquired.

The question of personal conscience becomes even more central in his next play, *The Crucible* (1953). The work is a product of Miller's increasing awareness of the corrosive influence of the ongoing investigations of the House Un-American Activities Committee. By its campaign of innuendo and intimidation, HUAC had been creating an atmosphere of suspicion and terror that reminded Miller and others of the witchhunting hysteria of the 17th century.

The figure of John Proctor, the New England farmer condemned and hanged for witchcraft, provided Miller with yet another opportunity to explore the problems of private and public conscience. As Miller portrays him, Proctor is a man whose opposition to the hysteria prevailing in Salem is undermined by his own sense of unworthiness stemming from a liaison with a former servant girl. This familiar combination of indignation and guilt is presented in an atmosphere of religious superstition that makes the issues seem starker and less complicated than in most of Miller's other works. The continuing popularity of the play may be due in part to this seeming lack of complexity. In fact, Proctor's ringing defiance of the corrupt court and his martyr's death at the end of the play obscure more subtle treatment of Proctor's ambivalent attitude to Abigail, and his self-justifying relations with his wife.

After the Fall, staged by Elia Kazan in 1964, illustrated the developing gap between the perceptions of Broadway audiences and the playwright's rather convoluted ruminations on history and guilt. The most free-form and innovative of Miller's plays, *Fall* like *Death of a Salesman* is a psychodrama, in that it externalises the protagonist's stream of consciousness—the interminable quarrel between ego and superego—the regretting, justifying, remembering Self and the implacable Conscience. In the course of a two-hour conversation with an invisible Listener, who may be a psychiatrist or God or simply his own conscience, Quentin attempts to find meaning in events that have brought him to the brink of despair. His recollections take him back to incidents in his youth during the 1920s and political involvements in the 1950s. But they focus on his relationship with his second wife, Maggie, a beautiful and self-destructive singer who seemed to the New York audiences to bear a disturbing resemblance to Marilyn Monroe. Haunted by the failure of two marriages,

Quentin is reluctant to enter a third relationship until he can assess his own responsibility for the death of love.

In the context of this situation, Miller explores his two reigning preoccupations—the relationship of selfishness and altruism, and the need to define an achievable code of morality for oneself. The first half of the play deals with the idealism of the 1930s and the hope that socialism represented a new pattern of social relationships. By the midpoint of the play Quentin has faced betrayals that challenge the optimistic interpretation of human nature implied by socialism, but he persists in his belief in the idea. The remainder of the work focuses on Quentin's discovery that he cannot live up to his own high conception of himself, and the disorientation and despair that discovery leads to. Realizing that the attempt to assert total innocence leads to the projection of blame onto others and ultimately to self-destruction, Quentin learns to accept his own evil. This recognition that we live in a fallen world and that, like Cain, all of us are capable of murdering our brother, seems to strengthen him to face the future.

There is little doubt that *After the Fall* is Miller's most personal statement. It not only confronts the failure of socialism, but at the same time foresees the collapse of the new paganism that seemed for a brief period in the 1960s to offer an alternative hope. As had happened so often in the past, however, audiences and critics failed to respond to the issues Miller was raising in the play. Blinded by what appeared to many to be embarrassingly frank autobiographical material, many spectators could not make the jump from the personal story to the universal issues Miller was illustrating. To such viewers the work seemed sanctimonious and self-serving.

Incident at Vichy (1964) explores themes of guilt and conscience in the context of the Nazi persecution of the Jews. This was a subject touched on in *After the Fall*, in which the concentration camp tower symbolized people's inherent capacity for evil. But *Incident* was Miller's first direct treatment of the Jewish holocaust, an event that haunted and challenged Miller's creative imagination. The work, based on a story Miller heard in 1955, is powerful theater, but it lacks the complexity of his other work. A German aristocrat is brought to an awareness of his complicity in the Nazi evil and tries to atone for his guilt by helping a Jew escape by changing places with him. Like some of the author's earlier works, the play seems more an illustrated thesis than a wholly convincing representation of human behavior. It may have been that the European characters were too remote from Miller's personal experience.

No such criticism can be leveled at his next Broadway play, *The Price* (1968), in which Miller returned once again to the familiar streets and accents of New York City. As in *Death of a Salesman*, Miller here deals with illusions and betrayals in a family that has lived through the Depression. The action takes place in the attic of a New York brownstone where two brothers meet to arrange the sale of the family furniture to a Jewish antique dealer. In the course of discussing the price they should ask for the furniture, the brothers review their relationship, for years poisoned by resentment and misunderstanding. Walter, the older brother, is a wealthy doctor whose material success is a reflection of a certain pragmatic selfishness. Victor is a New York policeman who feels that his own chances had been hampered by his brother's refusal to lend him $500 so he could attend medical school, and by the financial obligations he assumed to take care of their father during the Depression. As the brothers confront one another amid the relics of a vanished life, they dispute their interpretations of past events. Walter maintains that Victor's sacrifices had been unnecessary, since their father had money in the bank and could have looked after himself. Victor claims to have been ignorant of his father's duplicity but admits, in any case, that he would not have humiliated the old man by challenging him. Attacked on one side by his brother, who hopes to expiate his sense of guilt by buying him off, and on the other by his wife who feels he has deliberately deluded himself, Victor must try to come to an honest assessment of his actions. Did he pay too high a price to keep his father from the degradation he saw other men sinking into, or did he get fair value for his life? In the end Miller seems to leave the question unanswered. At least here there is none of the ethical clarity and moral self-righteousness that characterized *All My Sons*. At the play's end Victor seems satisfied with the bargain he has made and convinced that his evaluation of his life is just. And Walter leaves as sure as ever that he is in the right. The laughter of Solomon, the antique dealer, as the curtain comes down is disturbingly ambiguous. But by his example and his gnomic statements, Solomon seems to suggest that the highest wisdom consists of going forward and refusing to become entangled in retrospective recriminations. Harry Peters, the retired airplane pilot of *Mr Peters' Connection* (2000), reviews his life and finds it unsatisfying.

Miller's preoccupation with questions of personal worth and his courageous insistence on honesty are due in part, no doubt, to his nature. But they are also a consequence of the perspective from which he has been forced to view his world. For although Miller is the chronicler of middle America—of the small merchants, workers, and salesmen who constitute the silent majority—in fact he writes from the sidelines, almost indeed from the outside. As a Jew and left-wing liberal, Miller has experienced at first hand the alienation of the excluded, and felt the need to resist culturally imposed stereotypes whether they are the product of prejudice or the shibboleths of business and success. He understands the outsider's need to assert his worth in the face of society's condemnation or contempt. It is his genius to have found in this experience a metaphor for the existential human condition.

Two volumes of *Collected Plays* have appeared (1957, 1981). *I Don't Need You Any More* (1967) is a collection of stories. *Timebends: A Life* (1987) is autobiography. Robert A. Martin edited *The Theater Essays of Arthur Miller* (1978). *Echoes Down the Corridor: Collected Essays, 1944–2000*, edited by Steven R. Centola, appeared in 2000. A study is Dennis Welland's *Miller: The Playwright* (3rd ed., 1985).

NEIL CARSON/BP

Miller, Cincinnatus Hiner [or **Heine**].   See JOAQUIN MILLER.

Miller, Daisy.   See DAISY MILLER.

Miller, Henry (1891–1980),   writer. Born in the Yorkville section of Manhattan, Miller was brought up by his German-American parents in Brooklyn. He spent two months at City College in 1909, and took a job with a cement company. Then he traveled in the Southwest and Alaska. He returned home in the next year and went to work in his father's tailor shop. In 1920 he became employment manager for the Western Union, in 1927 he was operating a Greenwich Village speakeasy, and in 1930 he left for France, where he would live for nine years. During this period he published TROPIC OF CANCER (1934) and *Tropic of Capricorn* (1939), as well as *Black Spring* (1936). After his return to New York in 1940, he traveled in the United States, wrote voluminously, and finally settled in Big Sur, California.

Most of Miller's books are autobiographical. The first part of *Tropic of Capricorn* chronicles his frantic, hilarious years with Western Union. *Tropic of Cancer* covers his years of bumming around Paris. *Black Spring* consists of autobiographical sketches ranging from Brooklyn to Paris. *Big Sur and the Oranges of Hieronymus Bosch* (1956) tells about his life on a secluded mountain top overlooking the Pacific Ocean. But the period he kept returning to in most of his books is his childhood in Brooklyn's 14th Ward: "From five to ten were the most important years of my life; I lived in the street and acquired the typical American gangster spirit." Though an expatriate for many years, Miller always insisted that he was "just a Brooklyn boy." "At sixty-six," he wrote, "I am more rebellious than I was at sixteen . . . now I am positive that youth is right,—or the child in its innocence."

Miller was an American romantic, convinced that the secret of a man's life lies partly in his ability to recover his childhood innocence and purity of feeling. He turned to the events of his own life in search of this innocence as have other notable American writers: FITZGERALD, HEMINGWAY, WOLFE. With Whitman, whom he named as a major influence, he shared a compulsion to recognize the body.

The Colossus of Maroussi (1941), a travel book about Greece, is one of his most interesting works. Where thousands of tourists and scholars had sought the secrets of ancient Greece in its ruins, Miller found the spirit of Hellenism in living people, with whom he drank much wine, ate great meals, and talked long into the night. His short studies of outcasts, derelicts, and prostitutes display a warm compassion and tender humor, especially *The Alcoholic Veteran With the Washboard Cranium* and *Mademoiselle Claude*. Miller can be hilariously funny, not only about sex, but about odd characters, as in *Astrological Fricassee*, and about people he has known, as in *Max and the White Phagocytes* (1938), the story of a deracinated European Jew he befriended. His love for America comes out even in such a pointedly critical work as *The Air-Conditioned Nightmare* (1945), a collection of essays based on a nationwide tour he made in 1941, and its sequel, *Remember to Remember* (1947).

Miller's early works were long unavailable in English-speaking countries. Judged obscene, they were published in

France by the Obelisk Press. Only in the freer 1960s did it become possible for Americans to gain easy access to Miller's books. *Tropic of Cancer* was first printed in the U.S. in 1961, 27 years after its Paris printing. *Tropic of Capricorn* followed in 1962, *Black Spring* in 1963. Other works unavailable in the U.S. until the 1960s, even though they were written here, include an autobiographical trilogy, *The Rosy Crucifixion*, comprising *Sexus* (1949), *Plexus* (1953), and *Nexus* (1960). Release of all of these books in rapid succession did much to extend Miller's reputation considerably beyond the influence the Paris editions had already had on the BEAT GENERATION.

Among Miller's many other books are *Aller Retour New York* (1935), about a trip to New York during his Paris period; *The Cosmological Eye* (1939), his first American publication, stories and sketches; *The Wisdom of the Heart* (1941), sketches and essays; *Sunday after the War* (1944), sketches; *The Plight of the Creative Artist in the United States of America* (1944); *Obscenity and the Law of Reflection* (1945); *The Smile at the Foot of the Ladder* (1948), a tale of a clown; *The Books in My Life* (1952); *Nights of Love and Laughter* (1955), stories; *The Time of the Assassins* (1956), a study of Rimbaud; *To Paint Is to Love Again* (1960), with reproductions of some of his paintings; and *Selected Prose* (2 v. 1965). *My Life and Times* (1971) contains recorded interviews. Several volumes of his extensive correspondence have been published, including *Hamlet* (2 v. 1939, 1941), with Michael Fraenkel; *Lawrence Durrell and Henry Miller* (1963), edited by George Wickes; *Letters to Anaïs Nin* (1965); and *Letters of Henry Miller and Wallace Fowlie* (1975). Lawrence Durrell edited *The Henry Miller Reader* (1959). NORMAN MAILER wrote about Miller and printed selections from his work in *Genius and Lust: A Journey Through the Major Writings of Henry Miller* (1976).

Miller, Joaquin [pen name of **Cincinnatus Hiner** (or **Heine) Miller**] (1837–1913),   poet, journalist. Born in Liberty, Indiana, he moved with his family in 1852 to a farm in the Willamette Valley, Oregon. For several years he wandered on the Pacific Coast, living in gold mining camps and with the Digger (western SHOSHONE) and MODOC Indians, helping to establish a pony express route between Washington and Idaho, and editing the *Democratic Register* in Eugene, Oregon. He became a lawyer and judge in Oregon before gaining celebrity as the frontier poet during his visit to London in 1870–71. He took the name Joaquin Miller as a tribute to the Mexican bandit JOAQUIN MURRIETTA, whom he helped popularize. *Songs of the Sierras* (1871), published in London first as *Pacific Poems* (1870), made his reputation, and included KIT CARSON'S RIDE. Many other volumes of verse followed. *Complete Poetical Works* (1897, revised 1902) omits three subsequent books. LIFE AMONGST THE MODOCS (1873) is a prose work of embellished autobiography. *The Building of the City Beautiful* (1893) is utopian. THE DANITES IN THE SIERRAS (1882) is one of several plays. *Collected Works*, in six volumes, appeared in 1909–10.

Miller, Merle (1919–1986),   newspaperman, editor, novelist. Born in Iowa, Miller fought in World War II and

edited YANK, came back to work for *Time*, and was an editor of *Harper's Magazine* from 1947 to 1949. Two of his books—a novel, *Island 49* (1945), and *We Dropped the A-Bomb* (with Abe Spitzer, 1946)—appeared before his novel *That Winter* (1948), which first won critical and popular approval for him. It is a realistic tale of three war veterans in the first winter of peace. Miller was an antagonist of those who seek to abridge freedom of expression in the United States: his novel *The Sure Thing* (1949) and his nonfiction *The Judges and the Judged* (1952) both deal with this topic. Among his later works are *Reunion* (1954); *A Secret Understanding* (1956); *A Gay and Melancholy Sound* (1961); *On Being Different* (1971), on homosexuality; *Plain Speaking: An Oral Biography of Harry S. Truman* (1974); *Lyndon* [Johnson]: *An Oral Biography* (1980); and *Ike the Soldier: As They Knew Him* (1987).

Miller, Perry [Gilbert Eddy] (1905–1963),   teacher, historian. Born in Chicago, Miller taught at Harvard beginning in 1931. His principal theme was American history as rooted in the ideas of the Puritans. His doctoral thesis, *Orthodoxy in Massachusetts*, was published in 1933. Miller saw his study as part of a larger work that would show the intellectual history of New England through the 18th and 19th centuries. With T. H. Johnson he edited a comprehensive anthology, *The Puritans* (1938), and published *The New England Mind: The 17th Century* (1939) and *The New England Mind: From Colony to Province* (1953). In 1948 appeared his edition of Jonathan Edwards's IMAGES, OR, SHADOWS OF DIVINE THINGS, part of Miller's study of New England in the 18th century. *The Raven and the Whale* (1956) is a literary study of POE and MELVILLE. *Errand into the Wilderness* (1956) and *Nature's Nation* (1967) collect essays.

Miller, Sue (1943–   ),   novelist. Educated at Radcliffe, Harvard, Boston University and Wesleyan, Sue Miller lives in Cambridge, Massachusetts. She achieved recognition with her first novel, *The Good Mother* (1986). The able parent of the title is a divorcee who decides, because of a nasty custody battle instigated by her ex-husband, to relinquish her parental rights in the best interests of her daughter. *Inventing the Abbots* (1987) is a short story collection in which different aspects of family tension are treated. *Family Pictures* (1993) is the history of a Chicago family whose middle child, Randall, is autistic. The psychiatrist father, David, blames the mother, Lainey, for his son's condition and for giving birth to three younger children. When the family is forced to institutionalize Randall, it can no longer hold together and shatters. *For Love* (1993) concerns a middle-aged woman's quest for self-identity. *The Distinguished Guest* (1995) centers on an elderly author forced by failing health to move in with her youngest son's family. Her presence, and that of a journalist who comes to interview her, exacerbates the already tense family situation. In *While I Was Gone* (1999) the 1960s past of a New England veterinarian catches up with her. *The World Below* (2001) tells of a woman's discovery of her grandmother's past.

Miller, Walter M[ichael], Jr. (1923–   ),   writer of science fiction. Miller is the author of the highly respected novel *A Canticle for Leibowitz* (1959). In this after-the-bomb novel, a group of monks attempt to preserve the often indecipherable remnants of civilization. He has also published collections of short stories: *Conditionally Human* (1962), *The View from the Stars* (1964), and *The Darfstellar* (1982). Other collections are *The Best of Walter M. Miller, Jr.* (1980) and *The Science Fiction Stories of Walter M. Miller, Jr.* (1984).

Miller, William (1782–1849), millennialist. Born in Pittsfield, Massachusetts, and first a farmer then a Baptist preacher, Miller was an eloquent and convincing speaker. He came to believe that about 1843 Christ would return to earth and rule for the next thousand years and published *Evidence from Scripture and History of the Second Coming of Christ, about the Year 1843* (1836), originally given as sixteen lectures. It was widely read, and a new sect was formed, called Millerites. Various periodicals echoing his prediction appeared, particularly *The Midnight Cry* and *Signs of the Times*. A definite date was finally set, October 22, 1844, but it passed without disaster. Out of the Millerites came the Seventh-Day Adventists, led by Hiram Edson. Edward Eggleston's *The End of The World* (1872) deals with the sect. Jane Marsh Parker's novels *Barley Wood* (1860) and *The Midnight Cry* (1886) were rooted in the personal knowledge of a daughter.

Millerites.   See WILLIAM MILLER.

Millett, Kate [Katherine Murray] (1934–   ), writer, feminist. Millett earned a Ph.D. at Columbia University for the work that was published as *Sexual Politics* (1970), a seminal text for the women's movement. In it she analyzes works of NORMAN MAILER, HENRY MILLER, D. H. Lawrence, Jean Genet, and others, finding in them a persistent contempt for women. In two autobiographical works she attempted to extend the boundaries of women's speech: *Flying* (1974), about her marriage and her affairs with women; and *Sita* (1977), about a mental breakdown and a lesbian relationship. *The Basement* (1979) relates an actual case of torture and murder of a teenage girl. *The Loony-Bin Trip* (1990) is an account of Millett's struggle with mental illness. *The Politics of Cruelty: An Essay on the Literature of Political Imprisonment* appeared in 1994.

Millhauser, Steven (1943–   ), novelist. Born in New York City, Millhauser was educated at Columbia and Brown. His *Edwin Mulhouse: The Life and Death of an American Writer, 1943–1954, by Jeffrey Cartwright* (1972) is a postmodern comedy about a precocious novelist, written by his twelve-year-old friend; *Portrait of a Romantic* (1977), another self-conscious fiction, is a splintered account of high school years. A brief later work is *In the Penny Arcade* (1985). *Martin Dressler: The Tale of an American Dreamer* (1996) tells of a son of immigrants at the turn of the twentieth century who "dreams the wrong dream." Other titles include story collections *The Barnum Museum* (1997) and *The Knife Thrower* (1998). *Enchanted Night*, a novella, appeared in 1999.

Mills, C[harles] Wright (1916–1962), sociologist. Born in Waco, Texas, Mills was a professor of sociology at Columbia University. He wrote two widely known books:

White Collar (1951) and *The Power Elite* (1956). *White Collar*, subtitled "America's Middle Classes," calls attention to this segment of American society: managers, teachers, secretaries, nurses, salesgirls, insurance agents, receptionists, lawyers, even trade unionists. It was here that Mills introduced his relentless social criticism. In *The Power Elite* he shifts his focus to the three elites that he believed were in control of the United States: the men of corporate wealth, the militarists, and the politicians. Both books were influential indictments of our society. *Sociological Imagination* (1959) addresses itself to the shortcomings of contemporary sociology. In addition to studies of mass communications, Mills collaborated on *New Men of Power: America's Labor Leaders* (1948) and *Puerto Rican Journey* (1950). *The Causes of World War Three* appeared in 1958, *Images of Man* in 1960. Also in 1960 appeared *Listen Yankee: The Revolution in Cuba*, his most politically oriented work, intended to correct American misconceptions about the nature of the 1958 Cuban revolution.

Miln, Louise [Jordan] (1864–1933), novelist, short-story writer, memoirist. Born in Illinois, Louise Jordan married an actor and with him toured much of the world as an actress. She wrote about her experiences in *When We Were Strolling Players in the East* (1894) and *An Actor's Wooing* (1896). She also wrote *The Feast of Lanterns* (1920), *Mr. and Mrs. Sen* (1923), *In a Shantung Garden* (1924), *It Happened in Peking* (1926), *Peng Wee's Harvest* (1933), and other stories with a Chinese background. Her view of the Orient was sentimental, her depiction less realistic than that of Pearl Buck.

Milosz, Czeslaw (1911–   ), poet, essayist, novelist. Born in Lithuania, Milosz was educated at the University of Wilno (Vilnius). He survived the German occupation of Poland and spent 1945 to 1950 working in the Polish diplomatic service in Washington and Paris, before disenchantment with communism led to his permanent flight from his country in 1951. In 1961 he settled in California and taught Slavic languages at Berkeley. Already a leading avant-garde poet in Poland in the 1930s, he was led by his exposure to totalitarianism to focus on ideology, consciousness, choice, and necessity. The concern for humanity evident in underground poems of protest published during the war persists in his poems written much later in the security of exile.

Milosz first received serious attention in the U.S. with *Zniewolony umysl* (1953, tr. *The Captive Mind*, 1953), an examination of the power of communist ideology over Polish intellectuals. *Rodzinna Europa* (1959, tr. *Native Realm*, 1981) is a moral and intellectual autobiography from childhood to the 1950s. In his poetry, which is classical, often almost biblical in style, Milosz created a mythic world defined by memory and imagination through which to view the realities and cruelties of people. *Selected Poems* (1973, rev. 1981); *Bells in Winter* (1978); *Provinces* (1991); and *Facing The River* (1995) contain representative selections of his verse in translation. His fiction, also informed by acute moral awareness, includes *The Usurpers* (tr. 1955) and *The Issa Valley* (1955, tr. 1981), an autobiographical novel evoking the beauty of a Lithuanian countryside still insulated from the evils of the world. He also wrote *History of Polish Literature* (1969) and worked for years on a Polish translation of the Bible. Milosz won the Nobel Prize in Literature in 1980. *The Witness of Poetry*, a further volume of verse, was published in 1983. *The Land of Ulro* (1984) combines passages of intellectual autobiography with writings on literature and metaphysics. *The Collected Poems 1931–1987* appeared in 1988. In the preface, Milosz speaks of the "existence of this body of poetry in a language different from that in which it was written" as "for me the occasion of constant wonder." Writing in Polish, but achieving most of his reputation in the English that he collaborates on with others, he poses a challenge for those who hold that poetry must be appreciated in its original language. *Beginning with My Streets* (1991) contains essays and reminiscences. *Milosz's ABC's* (2001) is a memoir, alphabetically arranged. *New and Collected Poems* appeared in 2001.

Milquetoast, Caspar.   A character created by the cartoonist H. T. WEBSTER for the New York *Herald Tribune* and other newspapers. He is afraid of his own shadow, obeys all directions implicitly, and doesn't dare call his soul his own. Hence the epithet "a milquetoast."

Miners, Ballads of.   See COAL DUST ON THE FIDDLE.

Mingo.   A name employed by the DELAWARE INDIANS to refer generally to the Six Nations of the IROQUOIS. James Fenimore Cooper uses it frequently in his LEATHER-STOCKING TALES as a derogatory term suggesting cruelty and treachery, as in the case of Magua, the Huron in *The Last of the Mohicans*. The name was also applied specifically to a band of Iroquois Indians inhabiting western Pennsylvania and West Virginia. Among these was JAMES LOGAN [2], the Chief Logan celebrated in Jefferson's *Notes on the State of Virginia*.

Mingo and Other Sketches in Black and White (1884),   four stories by JOEL CHANDLER HARRIS about life in Georgia. The title story is about Mingo, a faithful African-American servant.

Minimalism.   Minimalism as an aesthetic term derives from the plastic arts, in which it denotes a simplicity of line or form, and from music and dance, in which it characterizes the suppression of harmony in favor of pure and isolated tones, or the reduction of motion to a few precise and often stark gestures. In fiction the minimalist tradition reaches back at least to the short works of Guy de Maupassant, though the work that emphatically proclaims the presence of minimalist principles in American letters is Ernest Hemingway's *In Our Time* (1925). His stories "Cat in the Rain" and "Hills Like White Elephants" are models of the type. Hemingway explained his method as a deliberate excision of significant scenes. In *A Moveable Feast* (1964) he argues that such deletions achieved a kind of verisimilitude, the sensation of encountering characters incompletely, just as in real life.

In the 1970s and 1980s, minimalism was the dominant manner of a minor renaissance of the short story. Growing out of the experimental fictions of DONALD BARTHELME, whose most influential works include *Come Back, Dr. Caligari* and

Unnatural Practices, Unnatural Acts (both 1968), as well as works like ROBERT COOVER's *Pricksongs and Descants* (1969), minimalism tended to drop the self-conscious surrealism of its antecedents in favor of a zero-degree realism of daily life. RAYMOND CARVER, the principal author of the movement, acknowledged his debt to Hemingway in the title of his first collection, *Will You Please Be Quiet, Please?* (1976). In later works, particularly *Furious Seasons* (1977) and *What We Talk About When We Talk About Love* (1981), Carver continued in the minimalist mode, but with the publication of *Cathedral* (1983) and *Where I'm Calling From* (1988), several of his stories made clear that he was headed in new directions.

Two major types of minimalist writers can be identified—the formal and the social minimalist. The formal minimalist is a technician with a taste for clear, colloquial language and uncluttered plots. The social minimalist has origins in narrative naturalism. The formal minimalists tend to employ narrow temporal frames, present tense, and first-person narrators while eliminating editorial or authorial intrusions. Of these writers, TOBIAS WOLFF (*In the Garden of North American Martyrs*, 1981), Jonathan Penner (*Private Parties*, 1983), and James Salter (*Dusk and Other Stories*, 1988) were notably successful in exploiting the formal limitations of minimalism.

Among many unflattering labels, social minimalism was also called dirty realism and K-Mart realism. *Family Dancing* (1984), a collection of stories by David Leavitt, and Mary Robinson's *An Amateur's Guide to the Night* (1984), show a large debt to Carver, not only in manner but in subject. The characters of dirty realism are the marginal members of American society. In the short fiction of BOBBIE ANN MASON (*Shiloh and Other Stories*, 1982), the characters are drawn from the lower-middle class of western Kentucky. In Richard Ford's *Rock Springs* (1987) and William Kittredge's *We Are Not In This Together* (1984), the characters are apt to be drifters, criminals, or disadvantaged children from the openly hostile and bleakly beautiful country of Montana and Wyoming. In general, however, the rootlessness of contemporary Americans is a common theme in social minimalism. Characters are apt to live nowhere in particular, though in the works of JAYNE ANNE PHILLIPS (*Black Tickets*, 1979; *Fast Lanes*, 1987) they tend to come from West Virginia and move on to nameless states. In the stories of Bobbie Ann Mason and Mary Hood (*How Far She Went*, 1984) the moribund traditions of small-town America are the background for the glitzy vitality of a new national culture of television advertising and enforced consumption.

MARK A. R. FACKNITZ

Minister's Black Veil, The (*The Token*, 1836; TWICE-TOLD TALES, 1837),   a short story by NATHANIEL HAWTHORNE. In this tale, The Reverend Hooper, on the eve of his marriage, assumes a veil and never thereafter discards it. His fiancée abandons him, his parishioners look at him with a sort of terror, and his life is one of apparent despair and gloom. As he dies, he sees on every face around him a black veil. Still veiled, Hooper is carried to his grave. The plot seems to have been suggested to Hawthorne by an incident he mentions in a note, telling how a clergyman in Maine had worn a veil as symbol of repentance for having accidentally killed a beloved friend.

Minister's Wooing, The (1859),   a novel by HARRIET BEECHER STOWE. This was the most ambitious of Stowe's New England stories, judged by some as the best of the group, although others are inclined to place OLDTOWN FOLKS (1869) higher. The setting is Newport in the latter part of the 18th century, and into the story Stowe wove many details of New England life as she had seen it as a girl, as well as some of her own religious trials. SAMUEL HOPKINS is the minister, somewhat straitly orthodox. Mary Scudder is the much younger girl he woos. She really loves her cousin James Marvyn, but refuses to marry him because he has not been saved. He goes to sea and is reported lost in a shipwreck. She accepts the minister and is prepared to wed him, when James returns. She declines to break her word to Hopkins, but he learns of her dilemma and frees her. James, in the meantime, has found his salvation in religion and, in addition, has made his fortune.

Miniver Cheevy (1907, included in *The Town Down the River*, 1910),   a poem by EDWIN ARLINGTON ROBINSON. One of Robinson's most famous poems, this character sketch depicts Miniver with sarcastic humor. Feeling himself born out of his time, Miniver looks back romantically to the Middle Ages: "He missed the mediaeval grace / Of iron clothing" and scorns money but "is sore annoyed without it" and keeps on drinking. The phrasing and technical skill show Robinson at his best.

Minnehaha.   A Sioux word meaning "waterfall" or "laughing water." In Longfellow's HIAWATHA (1855), Minnehaha is a Sioux maiden whom Hiawatha marries.

Minot, George Richards (1758–1802),   lawyer, historian. A Massachusetts jurist, Minot is remembered for his contemporary account of SHAY'S REBELLION: *The History of the Insurrection in Massachusetts in the Year 1786 and the Rebellion Consequent Thereon* (1788).

Minot, Susan (1956–   ),   novelist and short-story writer. Born and brought up in a Boston suburb, Minot was educated at Boston University, Brown, and Columbia. *Monkeys* (1986), her first novel, includes details of a large suburban upper-class family similar to her own, though the author insists on its basic fictionality. Composed of nine short narratives of events in the Vincent family over a thirteen year period, the novel centers on the mother's death in an auto accident, and is told from the perspective of the second oldest daughter, Sophie. Minot has been described as a minimalist writer for her economical style. After the success of her first publication, Minot moved to a small village in Tuscany to write the stories in *Lust and Other Stories* (1989) about young professionals in New York City. Back in the United States she has published *Folly* (1992), a novel set in 1917 New England, and written the screenplay for *Stealing Beauty* (1996) from a story by Bernardo Bertolucci. In *Evening* (1998) a dying woman, slipping in and out of consciousness, remembers the events of her earlier life.

minstrel shows.   The term *minstrels* was revived early in the 19th century to designate troupes of players in America who presented a miscellaneous series of acts in the guise of African-Americans. Before this period, slaves had been represented on the American stage, often as comic servants. Similar stereotyping was applied to Yankee and Irish servants. All were stage descendants of comic Irish servants and other servants in British comedy and farce. Frequently, the African-American characters danced and sang, and most of these roles were played by white men in blackface, sometimes by well-known actors like EDWIN FORREST. But some African-American performers became well known on the minstrel stage, particularly William Henry Lane, billed as Juba, who was a spectacular dancer.

In the 1820s it became more customary to interpolate African-American songs and dances in theatrical performances. Thomas D. Rice (1806–1860), in one of his shows, played the part of a shuffling and grotesque hostler called JIM CROW. In the early 1840s appeared DANIEL EMMETT, who wrote the tune of "Dixie" for one of his shows, and EDWIN P. CHRISTY, who used many of STEPHEN FOSTER's tunes for his Christy Minstrels. The technique became stereotyped: In the first part of the show, the *olio*, a row of minstrels, sat on chairs, a pompous interlocutor (or "straight man") sat in the center, and on the corners there were "Tambo" and "Brother (or Brudder) Bones," the "end men." In general, the interlocutor was the butt of the end men's jokes. In the second part of the show, individual minstrels performed as singers, players, dancers, monologists, and actors. The show usually concluded with a burlesque.

Innumerable minstrel troupes toured the country. Their popularity reached its height in the years from 1850 to 1870, but the companies continued to perform well into the 1920s, and amateur minstrel shows continued into the 1950s. The influence of these shows on the American stage was profound. Amos 'n' Andy, of radio and television fame, were their direct descendants, as was the entertainer Al Jolson. Accounts written while the shows were still in vogue include Leroy Rice, *The Monarchs of Minstrelsy* (1911); Dailey Paskman and Sigmund Spaeth, *Gentlemen, Be Seated! A Parade of Old-Time Minstrels* (1928); and Carl F. Wittke, *Tambo and Bones: A History of the American Minstrel Stage* (1930, reissued 1968).

Minuit, Peter (1580–1638),   colonial administrator. Minuit was director general of the colony of New Amsterdam from 1626 to 1631. He made peace with the Indians by buying from them the land occupied by the settlement (now the island of Manhattan) with cloth, beads, hatchets, and trinkets. Later Minuit fell out of favor with the Dutch and was dismissed. He led an expedition for the Swedish South Company to what is now Wilmington, Delaware, built Fort Christina there, and named the territory New Sweden. In the following year he bought from the Indians land near the present site of Trenton, *New Jersey*. He was lost in a hurricane in the West Indies while on a trading expedition.

Miranda, Francisco (1750–1816),   soldier, traveler. Born in Venezuela, Miranda traveled widely in Europe and America, knew many notables, and kept copious journals. In

1780 Miranda took part in a French and Spanish expedition intended to help the rebellious American colonists. When peace came, he traveled in the United States. Later he served as a general in the French revolutionary army, renounced allegiance to Spain, and plotted freedom for his own country. He led a patriot army in Venezuela (1810), became dictator (1812), was defeated by loyalist forces (1812), and then was imprisoned in Spain until his death.

His papers, carefully bound by him in sixty-three folio volumes, were left in trust in England, and lay forgotten until W. S. Robertson published a portion of them as a *Tour of the United States* (1928) and used them as a basis for a *Life of Miranda* (1929). In the meantime the papers were sold to the government of Venezuela, which began their publication in thirty-two massive volumes. Joseph F. Thorning wrote an account of *Miranda: World Citizen* (1952).

Miranda, in discussing democracy in his journals, suggested that America could hardly go further. At Sag Harbor, New York, he found a community of fishermen who operated off the coast of Brazil. Most of them were Native Americans, and Miranda perceived from the esteem in which they were held that they were, as a race, no whit inferior to any other. In Boston he met PHILLIS WHEATLEY, an African-American who had had a volume of poems published in England, and again he noted that "the rational being is the same whatever his form or aspect." When later he turned to making a constitution for his own New World, he always stipulated equality of rights among free men whatever their color.

Miriam.   A leading character in Hawthorne's THE MARBLE FAUN (1860). Miriam is an art student whose origin and nationality are veiled in mystery. She lives in obvious terror of Brother Antonio, a model who constantly follows her and who is killed by her friend Count Donatello.

Miriam Coffin, or, The Whale Fisherman (3 v. 1834), a novel by JOSEPH G. HART. This is believed to be the first work of fiction to deal with whaling. Melville was acquainted with it when he wrote MOBY-DICK (1851). Colonel Hart wrote the novel principally to obtain Congressional support for the whaling industry.

Miron, Gaston (1928–1996),   poet, editor, politician. Born in Quebec, he was educated in parochial schools. In Montreal he helped found Les Editions de l'Hexagone (1953), a publisher associated with a group of poets including PAUL-MARIE LAPOINTE. Miron's own poetry appeared mostly in periodicals until *L'homme rapaillé* (1970, partially tr. *The Agonized Life*, 1980). *Contrepointes*, a collection of poems written between 1954 and 1968, was published in 1975. Active in the Canadian separatist movement, Miron was briefly imprisoned for his political beliefs in 1970, the same year in which he won the Prix France-Canada for his first poetry collection.

Mirror, The [1].   A weekly magazine founded by GEORGE P. MORRIS in New York City in 1823. It became a widely circulated and influential magazine of high literary standards and continued until 1842. N. P. WILLIS in 1831 merged his *The American Monthly* with the *Mirror*, and joined its staff as European correspondent. Selections from his articles during the next four years appeared in book form as *Pencilings by the Way* (1835). Morris and Willis tried several times to revive the magazine.

Mirror, The [2].   A weekly magazine founded at St. Louis on March 1, 1891, by M. A. Fanning and James M. Calvin. For a time it seems to have been called the *Sunday Mirror*. From May 30, 1913, until September 2, 1920, it was called *Reedy's Mirror*. (See WILLIAM MARION REEDY.) In 1920 CHARLES J. FINGER took it over and called it *All's Well, or, The Mirror Repolished*. It ceased publication in December 1935. Under Reedy's editorship the magazine played an important role in the development of American, especially Midwestern, literature.

Mission Indians.   The name applies specifically to Native Americans converted to Christianity by Spanish missionaries and placed under the jurisdiction of 21 missions established between 1769 and 1823. More generally, it has been applied to Native Americans converted to Catholicism in various parts of the Southwest. Among books telling the story are John G. Shea's *History of the Catholic Missions Among the Indian Tribes of the U.S.* (1854), George Wharton James's *In and Out of the Old Missions* (1905), Z. Englehardt's *The Missions and Missionaries of California* (4 v. 1908–1916), Cleve Hallenbeck's *Missions of the Old Southwest* (1929), Agnes Repplier's *Junípero Serra* (1933), and John A. Berger's *Franciscan Missions of California* (1941).

Novels about the Mission Indians include Helen Hunt Jackson's RAMONA (1884) and Mary Austin's *Isidro* (1905). Jackson had earlier called attention to the plight of western Indians in A CENTURY OF DISHONOR (1881).

Mississippi River.   HERNANDO DE SOTO reached the Mississippi in May 1541. The French in Canada learned about the river from the Native Americans and began explorations toward the middle of the 17th century. Among them were LA SALLE (about 1669) and HENNEPIN (1680). Settlements began to spring up along the river. The source of the river was not definitely determined until 1832, when an expedition led by HENRY R. SCHOOLCRAFT reached Itasca Lake in Minnesota.

The Mississippi has as its principal tributary the Missouri, and together they form one of the world's largest river systems. In 1811 the first steamboats were launched on the river and became a picturesque part of the scenery. The height of the traffic was reached in the years immediately preceding the Civil War, a period immortalized in Twain's LIFE ON THE MISSISSIPPI (1883); the river and its people also appear memorably in HUCKLEBERRY FINN (1884).

The river has inspired much description and nonfictional analysis. Books of this type range back to Zadock Cramer's *The Navigator* (1808) and Zebulon Pike's *Account of an Expedition to the Sources of the Mississippi* (1810) and include such later volumes as Willard Glazier's *Down the Great River* (1888); S. W. McMaster's *60 Years on the Upper Mississippi* (1893); George Cary Eggleston's *The Last of the Flatboats* (1900); Julius Chambers' *The Mississippi River* (1910); Lyle Saxon's *Father Mississippi* (1927); Walter A. Blair's *A Raft Pilot's Log* (1930); Walter

Havighurst's *Upper Mississippi: A Wilderness Saga* (1937); and Edwin and Louise Rosskam's *Towboat River* (1948).

A poem about a common river tragedy, the blowing up of a steamboat during a race, was John Hay's JIM BLUDSO OF THE PRAIRIE BELLE (1871). John Gould Fletcher wrote a group of poems called *Down the Mississippi (Selected Poems*, 1938). "The River" is central to HART CRANE's *The Bridge* (1930). Works of fiction and folklore include Edna Ferber's SHOW BOAT (1926); Homer Croy's *River Girl* (1931); F. J. Meine and Walter Blair's *Mike Fink, King of Mississippi Keelboatmen* (1933); August Derleth's *Bright Journey* (1940); Cid Ricketts Sumner's *Tammy Out of Time* (1948); Katherine Bellamann's *The Hayvens of Demarest* (1951); and Frances Parkinson Keyes' *Steamboat Gothic* (1952). Ben Lucien Burman has written fiction and nonfiction about the river in the 20th century, in *Mississippi* (1929), *Steamboat Round the Bend* (1933), *Blow for a Landing* (1945), and *Children of Noah* (1951).

Miss Lonelyhearts (1933),   a novel by NATHANAEL WEST. This brief, brilliant novel is the story of a man who writes advice to the lovelorn in a New York newspaper. Haunted by the pathetic letters he receives, he tries to live his role of omniscient counselor. He is harried on the one hand by the cynicism of his editor, Shrike, who regards religion, art, and love as attempts to escape reality; on the other hand, by the demands of his girl, Betty, that he lead a normal bourgeois existence. The agonized hero's fumbling attempts to reach out to suffering humanity as a kind of modern Christ are somehow always twisted by circumstances, finally with fatal consequences. He tries to convey a message of love to the Doyles, an embittered, sordid couple. The result is that Mrs. Doyle tries to seduce him, and her husband murders him by mistake.

Though the novel comments strongly on the decay of religion, its theme is the helpless loneliness of the individual in modern society. However, it is the style and imagery that give the book its peculiar merit. West's language is tight and compressed. To an almost monotonous extent, he uses violent images to describe commonplace events, but his treatment of actual violence is almost starkly bare. At times his brilliant precision in handling symbol and image succeed in destroying the borderline between reality and nightmare, and devastating forces are presented with great power.

Missouri River.   The Missouri is a magnificent river whose headwaters rise in southwestern Montana, and it gathers the waters of many tributaries along its course. It was an early trade route, explored by the French. In 1804–05, Lewis and Clark came to the upper Missouri (see under MERIWETHER LEWIS), and their observations appear in Lewis's *History of the Expedition Under Captains Lewis and Clark* (1814, ed. by Elliott Coues 1893). The first steamboat appeared on the river in 1819, but the fluctuations in the depth of the river made navigation difficult. JOHN G. NEIHARDT descended the Missouri from its headwaters in a light boat as preparation for writing *Cycle of the West* (1949). Audubon knew it, as he reports in his *Journals* (ed. by Elliott Coues, 2 v. 1897); J. F. McDermott edited *Up the Missouri River with Audubon: The Journal of*

Edward Harris (1952). Henry Marie Breckenridge wrote his *Journal of a Voyage Up the River Missouri in 1811* (1814). Among other books on the river are J. V. Brower's *The Missouri River and Its Utmost Source* (1896); Charles Larpenteur's *40 Years a Fur Trader on the Upper Missouri* (ed. by Elliott Coues, 1898); Hiram M. Chittenden's *History of Early Steamboat Navigation on the Missouri River* (2 v. 1903); Joseph Mills Hanson's *Conquest of the Missouri* (1909, reprinted 1946), an account of the exploits and explorations of Captain Grant Marsh (1832–1916); Philip Edward Chappell's *History of the Missouri River* (1911); C. P. Deatherage's *Steamboating on the Missouri River in the 60's* (1924); Pierre A. Tabeau's *Narrative of Loisel's Expedition to the Upper Missouri* (tr. from the French by Rose Abel Wright, 1939); Stanley Vestal's *The Missouri* (1945); and Bernard De Voto's ACROSS THE WIDE MISSOURI (Pulitzer Prize, 1947) and his *Course of Empire* (1952).

Miss Ravenel's Conversion from Secession to Loyalty (1867),   a novel by JOHN W. DE FOREST. This is the best work of a significant early realist. De Forest tells the story of a New Orleans doctor who, at the beginning of the Civil War, exiles himself and his daughter Lillie to New Boston (obviously New Haven, where De Forest lived) because he is loyal to the Union. In New Boston two men woo Lillie, a Virginian lieutenant colonel who is likewise loyal to the Union and a Yale scholar as well. The book satirizes the puritanism of society in New Boston, and it has some powerful battle scenes that anticipate Crane's *Red Badge of Courage.*

Mr. Flood's Party (1920),   a narrative poem by EDWIN ARLINGTON ROBINSON. Eben Flood apparently goes on a spree once a year. He engages in a dialogue with himself, sings "Secure, with only two moons listening," and soon becomes pathetically alone again.

Mr. Higginbotham's Catastrophe   (*The Token*, 1834; *Twice-Told Tales*, 1837), a story by NATHANIEL HAWTHORNE. A young tobacco peddler hears that wealthy old Mr. Higginbotham has been hanged and spreads the story. But people tell him they have just seen the man—he isn't dead at all. Again he is told the same story, so he goes to Mr. Higginbotham's home—in time to save him from being murdered. As a reward the peddler gets Mr. Higginbotham's fortune and his niece in marriage. The story, one of Hawthorne's most lightheartedly humorous, was based on an actual murder case.

Mister Roberts (1946),   a novel by THOMAS HEGGEN concerning the men on board a cargo ship in World War II.

Mrs. Wiggs of the Cabbage Patch (1901),   a novel by ALICE HEGAN RICE. In the course of her active welfare work, Rice met the woman who suggested the character of Mrs. Wiggs. In the book she is a widow with five children to support, but she refuses to be downed by circumstances and keeps a cheerful outlook on life. She lives in a broken-down section of Louisville along the railroad tracks known as The Cabbage Patch. Her three daughters are called Asia, Australia, and Europena. A wealthy young man and his former fiancée befriend the Wiggs family and become reconciled in the process. A leading character in one of the episodes is Cuba, a half-dead horse that Mrs. Wiggs nurses and makes a valuable member of the family. The book sold 200,000 copies in three years.

Mistral, Gabriela [pen name of **Lucila Godoy Alcayaga**] (1889–1957),   Chilean poet. The daughter of a rural schoolmaster who often composed songs and poems for village fiestas, Mistral also became a teacher. Her first verses were inspired by an unhappy romance, with a man who commits suicide. In 1914 Mistral won a poetry contest in Santiago with her *Sonetos de la muerte*, which were later included in her first collection, *Desolación* (1922). All her work is a variation on the single theme of love. Initially she expressed her own tragic and frustrated passion, but as she grew older, her vision became broader. She was concerned especially with children and with the humble and persecuted everywhere. *Ternura* (1924) is a collection of children's songs and rounds. She donated the proceeds of *Tala* (1938) to the relief of Basque children orphaned in the Spanish Civil War. Acclaimed as an educator as well as a poet, she received the Nobel Prize in Literature in 1945, the first woman poet and the first Latin American so honored. Her works for children are translated in English in *Crickets and Frogs: A Fable* (1972). Translations into English of her selected poems have been published by Langston Hughes (1957) and by Doris Dana (1972).

Misty of Chincoteaque (1947).   Horse story for children by MARGUERITE HENRY.

Mitchell, Donald Grant ["Ik Marvel"] (1822–1908), farmer, essayist, author. Born in Connecticut, Mitchell was educated at Yale and then managed his family farm. He left for Europe in 1844 and spent the next ten years writing stories and reports, mostly for the New York *Morning Courier and Enquirer*, and traveling in Europe and the United States. His first two books, *Fresh Gleanings* (1847) and *The Battle Summer* (1850), concern his European travels and the French Revolution of 1848, respectively. His first popular book was REVERIES OF A BACHELOR (1850), which was followed by *Dream Life* (1851). He also became the first editor of "The Easy Chair" department of HARPER'S MAGAZINE. In 1852 he married and, nostalgic for the American countryside after a year in Venice as United States Consul, he settled with his family on a Connecticut farm. His love of agriculture and the pleasures of rural life dominate most of his subsequent writing, which is also infused with the warmth and candor that characterized his earlier writing. His mature work includes *Fudge Doings* (1855); *My Farm at Edgewood* (1863); *Seven Stories* (1864); *Doctor Johns* (1866), a novel; *Rural Studies* (1867); *About Old Story Tellers* (1877); *Bound Together* (1884); *English Lands, Letters, and Kings* (4 v. 1889–1897); and *American Lands and Letters* (2 v. 1897–1899).

Mitchell, Isaac.   See ALONZO AND MELISSA.

Mitchell, John (1680?–1750?),   physician, naturalist. Mitchell seems to have settled in Virginia as a physician sometime between 1700 to 1725. He returned to England in 1746. His interest in cartography led him to produce a valuable *Map of the British and French Dominions in North America* (1755).

He also prepared a paper on yellow fever that Benjamin Franklin turned over to Dr. Benjamin Rush, who made one of its suggestions on the use of purgatives the basis for his medical practice in that disease. He wrote an *Essay on the Causes of the Different Colors of People in Different Climates* that was published in the *Philosophical Transactions* of the Royal Society in London. To the same society he sent a paper describing thirty new genera of plants he had found around his home. *Mitchella repens*, the name of a little trailing vine, is a memorial to his deep interest in American botany.

Mitchell, John Ames (1845–1918),   editor, artist, novelist. Born in New York City, Mitchell studied architecture in Boston and Paris and practiced his profession for several years in Boston. Then he returned to Paris to study art and became expert at black-and-white etching. When he came back to New York in 1880, new methods of picture reproduction enabled him to use his skill to good effect. He founded the humorous weekly *Life*, contributing editorials, caricatures, and cartoons. He retained a controlling interest in the magazine even when later he began to write novels (see LIFE [1]). Best known of these are AMOS JUDD (1895) and *The Pines of Lory* (1901). Like all his books, which sold well in their day, but were far less important than his work on *Life*, they emphasize sensational action and juxtapose a wide variety of often exotic characters. His other novels include *A Romance of the Moon* (1886), *The Last American* (1889), *That First Affair* (1896), *Gloria Victis* (1897), *The Villa Claudia* (1904), *The Silent War* (1906), and *Pandora's Box* (1911).

Mitchell, Joseph [Quincy] (1908–1996),   reporter, essayist. Born near Iona, North Carolina, Mitchell attended the University of North Carolina, but left school to write in New York City in 1929 and never left Manhattan. He wrote for several newspapers and became a staff writer for *The New Yorker* in 1938. His interest was in little-known people and places. His essay called "The Mohawks in High Steel" describing the work of Indian bridge and skyscraper builders who walked unafraid hundreds of feet in the air, was used as the introduction for Edmund Wilson's *Apologies to the Iroquois* (1960). Other collections of Mitchell's magazine writings include *My Ears Are Bent* (1938); *McSorley's Wonderful Saloon* (1943), depicting life in a bar dating from 1854 where gas lights still functioned and old men spent their days; *Old Mr. Flood* (1948); and *The Bottom of the Harbor* (1960). *Joe Gould's Secret* (1965) collects a series of profiles of Joseph Ferdinand Gould, a 1911 Harvard graduate who hung around Greenwich Village coffee houses claiming to have mastered sea gull language and to be working on an oral history of our times. After Gould's death in a psychiatric hospital, Mitchell revealed the truth that the oral history was imaginary. The Gould features were praised for their fine writing, including an eleven-hundred-word paragraph written in stream-of-consciousness mode. *Up in the Old Hotel* (1992), a collection published after Mitchell had given up his writing career, was a commercial and critical success.

Mitchell, Langdon [Elwyn] (1862–1935),   playwright. Born in Philadelphia, the son of S. WEIR MITCHELL taught writing at the University of Pennsylvania. *Sylvian* (1885), his first play, is a romantic tragedy. *The New York Idea* (1906) is a comic treatment of marriage and divorce. Mitchell did stage adaptations of works by his father and of Thackeray novels. *Understanding America* (1927) is a book of essays.

Mitchell, Margaret (1900–1949),   novelist. Born in Atlanta, where she lived her entire life, Mitchell was educated at Washington Seminary there and at Smith College. Her one novel, GONE WITH THE WIND (1936, Pulitzer Prize) was a spectacular success. It depicts her native Georgia before, during, and after the Civil War. Millions of copies of it were sold, in English and 18 foreign languages. The movie made from it (1939) became a classic, shown repeatedly ever since it first appeared.

Mitchell, S[ilas] Weir (1829–1914),   physician, novelist, poet. Mitchell was born in Philadelphia. After obtaining a degree in medicine from Jefferson College, he continued his studies in Paris, specializing in neurology. His writings on toxicology, neurology, and clinical medicine became known throughout the medical world.

His experiences as surgeon in the Union Army during the Civil War formed the basis for "The Case of George Dedlow" (*Atlantic*, July 1866), a story of a quadruple amputee. *Hephzibah Guinness* (short stories, 1880) was the first volume to appear under Mitchell's own name; three anonymous books for juveniles were earlier. His first long novel, *In War Time* (1885), combined Mitchell's gift for historical narrative with his insight into human psychology in a study of an able, charming man lacking stamina and courage. *Roland Blake* (1886), another novel of the Civil War, contains a good example of a possessive woman. *Characteristics* (1891) is a novel written almost entirely as dialogue. *Hugh Wynne: Free Quaker* (1897), the story of a man's struggle to live up to his Quaker ideals in war-torn Philadelphia during the American Revolution is thought by many to be Mitchell's finest work. *Dr. North and His Friends* (1900) is a sequel to *Characteristics* and was followed by *Circumstance* (1901), a psychological study of the Civil War, and *Constance Trescott* (1905), the study of a woman obsessed with revenge. *The Red City* (1907), a novel laid in the red-brick dwellings of revolutionary Philadelphia, was the result of years of careful research. *Westways* (1913) tells of a Pennsylvania family divided by the Civil War. Dr. Mitchell depicted with remarkable skill the suffering of women in wartime. He also wrote volumes of verse, among them *The Hill of Stones* (1882), *The Masque and Other Poems* (1889), and *The Wager* (1900).

Mitchell, W[illiam] O[rmond]   (1914–1998), short-story writer, novelist, humorist. Born in Saskatchewan, Mitchell drew on his native provincial experience for the stories of his most popular book, *Jake and the Kid* (1962), based on characters he had created in a radio series for CBC, 1950–58. Jake is a kind of holdover frontiersman. Mitchell's *Who Has Seen the Wind* (1947), a *bildungsroman* of Saskatchewan life, holds a solid niche in Canadian literature. Other titles include *The Kite* (1962), *The Vanishing Point* (1973) *Daisy Creek* (1984) and *For Art's Sake* (1992).

Mittelholzer, Edgar Austin (1909–1965),   Guyanan novelist. Of Swiss and Creole heritage, Mittelholzer in his many novels treats themes of racial tension, psychological alienation, miscegenation, and violence. Determined from an early age to become a writer, Mittelholzer settled in London and eventually won critical attention with *Morning in Trinidad* (1950), a subtle exploration of the divisions created by race, color, and class, and with *Shadows Move Among Them* (1951), an interesting satire and probably his best book. His greatest popular success was the Kaywana trilogy—*Children of Kaywana* (1952), *Hubertus* (1955), and *The Old Blood* (1958)—a fictionalized history of the Caribbean from 1612 to 1953. Near the end of his life, his books were increasingly concerned with isolation, disintegration, and suicide. Shortly before his final novel was published, he immolated himself.

Mizner, Wilson (1876–1933),   miner, confidence man, entertainer, corporation promoter, gambler, hotelkeeper, prize fighter, writer, wit. Born in California, Mizner was a man of many adventures—in the Yukon and Alaska, in many parts of the Lower Forty-eight, on shipboard and abroad, in New York City and Hollywood. He knew the underworld, Broadway, and Hollywood. He helped Paul Armstrong with his ALIAS JIMMY VALENTINE (1909) by drawing on his knowledge of the underworld to provide characteristic incidents and language. BRONSON HOWARD persuaded Mizner to collaborate with him on an original play, *The Only Law* (1909), about a broker who kept a chorus girl, who in turn kept a gigolo. Mizner and Howard quarreled bitterly, and Howard wrote a novelette, *The Parasite* (1912), for *Smart Set*, in which Mizner appears in a venomous portrayal as Milton Lizard. Mizner and Paul Armstrong managed to compose two more plays, *The Deep Purple* (1910) and *The Greyhound* (1912), the former about city criminals, the latter about confidence men on an ocean liner. Alva Johnston wrote lengthy studies of Mizner for *The New Yorker* (1942, 1950), and Edward Dean Sullivan wrote *The Fabulous Wilson Mizner* (1935).

M'liss (1863–1864),   a novelette by BRET HARTE. This story of a neglected child who is revealed as fiery, jealous, and pathetic is set among the Dickensian characters Harte discovered in California mining camps. It was an expansion of an earlier story, "The Work on Red Mountain," which appeared in the December 1860 issue of *Golden Era*. None of his earlier work had attracted much attention, but Californians asked for more about M'liss, and Harte wrote this expansion as a serial in *Golden Era* from September 1863 on. It was not included in Harte's 1867 collection, but appeared in *The Luck of Roaring Camp and Other Sketches* (1870) and separately as *M'liss: An Idyl of Red Mountain* (1873).

M'lle New York.   A fortnightly magazine founded in New York City in August 1895 by VANCE THOMPSON. It appeared until April of 1896, then suspended until November 1898, when it resumed for a year. Thompson and JAMES HUNEKER made it one of the two or three most notable of the early experimental little magazines. Thompson reported literary gossip and inveighed against philistinism; Huneker dealt with the theater, the fine arts, and American prejudices. *M'lle New*

York introduced to American readers such writers as Ibsen, Maeterlinck, Strindberg, Verlaine, and Hamsun; and it expounded the ideas of Wagner, the Symbolists, and Nietzsche.

Moberg, Vilhelm.   See THE EMIGRANTS [2].

Moby-Dick.   Epic novel by HERMAN MELVILLE, first published in England in October 1851 as *The Whale*; complete American edition in November 1851 as *Moby-Dick; or, The Whale*. Received with mixed responses in its own time, *Moby-Dick* was rediscovered after 1920 and gradually acknowledged as a masterpiece of storytelling and symbolic realism. The plot is relatively simple, involving Captain Ahab's pursuit of an elusive and "evil" White Whale, as witnessed and retold by a young sailor-scholar, Ishmael. Almost every aspect of life on a whaler and the ensuing chase are assigned broader cultural significance. In Ishmael's retelling, *Moby-Dick* becomes the story of a double quest: man's quest for meaning and his pursuit of "the ungraspable phantom of life"; and America's quest for success and efficiency as embodied in whaling, its most flourishing 19th-century industry. At the center of both quests is strong-willed Captain Ahab, an individualist in search of absolute mastery over himself and the world. A transcendentalist at heart, Ahab projects personal meanings on a formless and incomprehensible reality, reducing it to an allegorical confrontation between himself as human Avenger and the White Whale as an assailable "incarnation . . . of all the subtle demonisms of life and thought." Ishmael, and occasionally other members of the crew, question Ahab's single-minded pursuit of the great whale, but they surrender their wills to Ahab's strong, idiosyncratic vision. By contrast to the "lucky livers" and cautious materialists who form much of the Pequod crew, Ahab emerges as a powerful, if somewhat ambiguous, cultural hero who maneuvers his crew toward a heroic clash with the White Whale.

Ishmael's role as sole survivor of the final chase is to provide a sympathetic, albeit critical, account of Ahab's confrontation with the White Whale. Against Ahab's allegorical-reductionist vision, Ishmael develops a more flexible, phenomenological view that recognizes the "intricate, overlapped, interweaved, and endless" nature of reality as embodied in the White Whale. By contrast to Ahab, who can only respond to the White Whale by trying to destroy it and being in turn destroyed by it, Ishmael approaches creatively a whale-like world, "weaving" and "spreading" a narrative text that becomes as spacious as the realities it describes. Combining a subjective, recreative response—as explained in chapter 42 on "The Whiteness of the Whale"—with a reading from the "whale's perspective," Ishmael achieves a balanced, participative vision that regards contradictions "with an equal eye." As Ishmael's interracial "marriage" with the "savage" harpooner Queequeg further hints, this vision can be extended to the world of social relations, replacing the patriarchal, autocratic order represented by Ahab, with an egalitarian emphasis on interracial collaboration.

The catastrophic ending of *Moby-Dick* suggests that Ishmael's world was not yet ready for a collaborative, phenomenological vision. Ahab's confrontational view seems to prevail in *Moby-Dick* and in the two novels that followed it, PIERRE (1852) and THE CONFIDENCE-MAN (1857). But Ishmael's approach still manages to humanize the story, refocusing attention away from the failed aspects of the quest plot to the ways in which human perception works, encircling "the everlasting elusiveness of Truth" with bold mythic constructions. This latter aspect has been particularly appealing to contemporary readers. Recent criticism has spoken of the "postmodern turn" of *Moby-Dick*, of the relevance of Melville's narrative and epistemological questions for the new fiction of NORMAN MAILER, KEN KESEY, JOSEPH HELLER, KURT VONNEGUT, RICHARD BRAUTIGAN, and THOMAS PYNCHON.

MARCEL CORNIS-POPE

Mocha Dick.   J. N. Reynolds published an account of this white whale in *The Knickerbocker Magazine* in 1839, twelve years before Melville's *Moby-Dick*. It was the earliest account of a white whale legendary among seamen for its fierceness and the difficulty of killing it.

Modern Chivalry (1792, 1793, 1797; rev. 1805; reprinted with an addition 1815),   a novel by HUGH HENRY BRACKENRIDGE. This four-volume novel is a sort of American *Don Quixote*, and its two main characters were obviously modeled on the principal characters of that work. The book, a satire on American politics, was based in large part on Brackenridge's own embittering political experiences. The scene is western Pennsylvania, and the adventures that are described, often with high humor, give a deep insight into conditions on the American frontier. Brackenridge, despite his thrusts at the defects of American life, was a staunch believer in democracy. Henry Adams called the novel "a more thoroughly American book than any written before 1833."

Modern Instance, A (1882),   a novel by WILLIAM DEAN HOWELLS. One of the earliest novels of social realism in America, it deals with the marital difficulties of Bartley and Marcia Hubbard, whose "love marriage falls into ruin through the undisciplined character of both." Howells originally entitled the novel *The New Medea*; there is a strong resemblance between the irrational, passionate nature of Marcia and that of her Greek counterpart.

modernism.   Broadly defined, *modernism* designates not a school or trend, but a synthesis of artistic and cultural developments spanning the first half of the 20th century that set out to reform literature and society, seeking new artistic idioms and modes of representing reality. The earliest positive use of this term can be found in Rubén Dario's coinage of *movimento modernista* in the early 1890s. Fully accepted by the 1920s, the term helped account for a diversity of innovative tendencies, integrating them in a dynamic system of common tenets and features. Chief among these are a desire to escape or reformulate the past, a radical critique of traditional metaphysics, philosophic and cultural relativism, an antiromantic concept of subject, artistic awareness and self-determination, reliance on symbolistic techniques, structural and thematic irony, and linguistic innovation.

The conflicting nature of modernism, divided between a poignant sense of relativism and historical instability—the very notion of what is modern becomes rapidly obsolete, pushing continually toward a more modern modern—and a militant form of cultural revisionism, interested in rearticulating the foundations of culture. "As much imbued with a feeling for [its] historical role . . . as with a feeling of historical discontinuity," said Richard Elman and Charles Feidelson, modernism straddled progress and decadence, continuity and rupture, an apocalyptic sense of crisis and a belief in a new beginning. The tension between these two sides of modernism was often so profound that in many cultures they have been regarded as separate, the militant and disruptive aspects of the literary experiment being relegated to the avant-garde, while modernism came to denote the synthetic, recuperative, and often conservative side of modernity.

In English, *modernism* has been used to designate a post-romantic, modern temper, or more narrowly the period of intense artistic experimentation between 1909, when FORD MADOX FORD founded *The English Review* to promote new literary approaches, and 1930 when the implications of the modernist revolution became fully realized and accepted. In retrospect, this period—reaching its peak about 1922, when *Ulysses*, THE WASTE LAND, *Aaron's Rod*, *Jacob's Room*, and ANNA CHRISTIE were published—appears as relatively unitary, with marked social and cultural characteristics reflected not only in literature, massive urbanization, rapid technological development, and intellectual mobility, but also in a postwar syndrome of "open breach with the past," said Frank Kermode, that encouraged a feverish search for new contexts and forms of expression. But this 20th-century renaissance could not be properly understood without reference to the late 19th-century work of Ibsen, Chekhov, Dostoevsky, Baudelaire, Mallarmé, James, or Conrad that constituted what might be called an early modernistic phase. Likewise, 1930 marks a waning of high modernism in England, but not in the U.S. Such novels as OF TIME AND THE RIVER (1935), ABSALOM, ABSALOM! (1936) and U.S.A. (1930–36) still represent highwater marks of modernism, though in a homemade vein. Playwrights such as EUGENE O'NEILL and MAXWELL ANDERSON continued to challenge the outworn conventions of the well-made European drama, creating a new American theater. Pound's injunction to "make it new" found fresh resonance in the later work of WILLIAM CARLOS WILLIAMS, E. E. CUMMINGS, and WALLACE STEVENS. The mid-century new criticism of JOHN CROWE RANSOM, CLEANTH BROOKS, ROBERT PENN WARREN, and W. K. Wimsatt canonized modernism as the dominant literary mode, building around it a comprehensive theory of aesthetic autonomy centered on the poetic text "as an organic system of relationships." A form of revamped, stylized modernism survived well into the 1950s in the innovative work of Beckett, NABOKOV, Durrell, BARTH, PYNCHON, and GADDIS, regarded variously as belatedly modernistic, neomodernist, or postmodernist.

The difficult, demanding art of the modernists has been criticized for its obscurity, highbrow aestheticism, or its intellectual and ethical dryness. While still admiring masters, such as Eliot, Proust. Yeats, and Joyce, EDMUND WILSON'S influential AXEL'S

CASTLE (1931) no longer found them helpful as guides because of their alleged separation of literature from social action. This line of criticism has often taken crude, dogmatic forms, as in Georg Lukács's blanket rejection of modernism as socially estranged and decadent, the expression of an elite class. Recent cultural criticism has taken a more balanced view, distinguishing—as did Jürgen Habermas—between an emancipatory side of modernism associated with rationality and the ideals of the Enlightenment, and a deconstructive, theoretical side that reenacts the Cartesian split between reality and the thinking subject.

Upon closer perusal, the innovative aesthetics of modernism is neither gratuitous, nor completely free and pure, displaying complex relations with the larger sociocultural *Zeitgeist*, or with prominent intellectual and literary traditions (Kantian aesthetics, political liberalism, romantic and symbolistic art, Victorian systemic realism). Aesthetic innovation had direct epistemological and political implications for the modernists. Their search for open-ended, polyphonous forms of expression made possible a more vivid, recreative response to life, not just an aesthetically satisfying account of it. The modernists openly confronted the bourgeois notion of modernity with its exclusive emphasis on material progress and commercialism, looking for more complex, spiritual-aesthetic patterns of order. Their opposition took two different forms:

(1) a *homeopathic* tactic that combatted middle-class philistinism and dehumanization through deliberate adoption of alienated and artificial artistic forms. The typical modernist vision is apocalyptic, provocative, highlighting the fragmentation of modern experience (Yeats: "Things fall apart; the center cannot hold") through its own textual discontinuity;

(2) a *utopian*, recuperative strategy, seeking spiritual enlightenment and wholeness against the fragmentation and divisiveness of modern life. As an antidote to the modern "dissociation of sensibility" (Eliot), the modernists resorted to complex organizational procedures designed to bring together "blood, imagination and intellect" (Yeats). Their main emphasis was on art as a dynamic, self-regulating order, capable of achieving an explosive fusion between the disparate areas of experience.

Particularly this utopian, globalizing ambition of modernism, manifested in elegant mythic structures and overarching metaphors, has been increasingly questioned after 1960 by critics and philosophers of culture affiliated with POSTMODERNISM. Though innovative in form, modernism perpetuates, according to J.-F. Lyotard, the grand narratives (comprehensive modes of assemblage and self-legitimation) that society has traditionally used to minimize risk and unpredictability. Feminists, more recently, have pointed out modernism's alignment with maleness and the power of tough rationality at the expense of other forms of expression (sentimental, subjective, romantic, etc.). But these critiques overlook the fact that modernist aesthetics and epistemology are far less homogeneous and integrative than alleged, relying simultaneously on formal control and performative (improvisational) looseness, global order, and local randomness. Instead of opposing modernism

and postmodernism, one could see them as two related faces of the same multivisaged, conflicting phenomenon of modernity.
MARCEL CORNIS-POPE

modernismo.   A literary movement that arose in Spanish America in the late 19th century and was subsequently transmitted to Spain. In searching for pure poetry, the modernists displayed a dazzling verbal virtuosity and technical perfection that revolutionized Spanish literature. According to some critics, the publication of MARTÍ's *Ismaelillo* (1882) marked the beginning of the movement. Others assert that, while Martí exerted enormous influence on Spanish-American writing and thought, his poetry is so individual that he cannot be considered to have been even a precursor of *modermismo*. There is no disagreement, however, as to the dominant role of DARÍO, whose work defined and stimulated modernism in America and in Spain. Publication of his *Azul* (1888) is said by these other scholars to signify the birth of modernismo, and *Prosas profanas* (1896) is considered *modernismo* at its zenith. Other early modernist poets (often considered precursors of the movement) were GUTIÉRREZ NÁJERA, SILVA, and Julián del Casal, the Cuban. Modernists of the later, post-1896, phase include LUGONES, RODÓ, HERRERA Y REISSIG, José Santos Chocano, NERVO, and BLANCO FOMBONA.

In rebellion against romanticism, from which they were not always able to free themselves, the modernists drew their initial inspiration and technique from European, particularly French, sources. From French PARNASSIANS and SYMBOLISTS such as Gautier, Coppée, and Verlaine, came their pessimism and melancholy, their belief in art for art's sake, their zeal for technical excellence and musicality, their love of exotic imagery, and a vocabulary in which abound swans (one of Darío's favorite symbols), peacocks, gems, and palaces. Another distinctive characteristic of the modernists was their unceasing experimentation with old and new verse forms. In their desire to escape from the sordidness of reality, the early modernists usually shunned political and native themes. Their successors, however, inspired no doubt by the impassioned verses that Darío hurled at THEODORE ROOSEVELT and by Darío's ode to Argentina, turned increasingly to American subjects, as exemplified by Chocano's *Alma América* (1906). In prose writing, particularly the essay, *morderniso* fostered a new simplicity and elegance, the finest examples of which are to be found in the works of RODÓ.

Modoc Indians.   The original home of these Native Americans was in the border region between Oregon and California. By treaties with the federal government they lost much of their land and retired to a reservation in southern Oregon. They attempted to return to their original home, but were defeated by government troops in the Modoc War (1872–73). Some went permanently to Oklahoma, and others returned to Oregon. The Modocs are renowned for their industry and are ordinarily peaceable, but they were superior fighters in tribal days. Many later became members of the Society of Friends. JOAQUIN MILLER wrote LIFE AMONGST THE MODOCS (1873). Other books on this tribe are A. B. Meacham's

Wi-ne-ma and Her People (1876), Jeremiah Curtin's *Myths of the Modoc* (1912), Jeff C. Riddle's *The Indian History of the Modoc War* (1914), and Leslie Spier's *Klamath Ethnography* (1930).

Moeller, Philip (1880–1958),   playwright, director. Born in New York City, Moeller was educated at Columbia University and traveled extensively in Europe. He helped found the Washington Square Players and wrote dramas displaying the comedy or irony behind historical events and personages. In 1918 a collection of his one-act plays was published as *Five Somewhat Historical Plays*. A three-act comedy, *A Roadhouse in Arden* (1916), was followed by *Madame Sand* (1917); *Molière* (1919); *Sophia* (1919); and *Camel Through the Needle's Eye* (1929). He adapted *Fata Morgana* (1931) from the Hungarian in collaboration with J. L. A. Burrell. He was active in the Theater Guild from its founding.

Mohawk Indians.   Of the Hokan-Siouan linguistic stock, the Mohawks were part of the Iroquois Confederacy. They lived in the most easterly portion of the Six Tribes region, in the area between present-day Albany and Utica, New York. Like the other tribes in the group, their family organization was maternal, with inheritance through the female line. They were allied with the British against the French and retained allegiance to the British during and after the Revolution. JOSEPH BRANT, one of their most famous chiefs, visited England twice, was a colonel in the British army and a member of the Episcopal Church. His sister married SIR WILLIAM JOHNSON, who made his home with the Six Nations. The white men's wars finally destroyed the Mohawks. They sold their lands to the State of New York in 1797, and some of them settled among the Senecas of Ohio, then moved with them to Indian Territory (now Oklahoma) in 1832. Others migrated to Ontario.

Mohawks appear frequently in history and legend. Their greatest leader was Hiawatha, who lived about 1570. H. R. SCHOOLCRAFT, writing down the myths of the Iroquois, confused him with Manabozho, the Algonquin or Chippewa deity, and Longfellow echoed Schoolcraft's confusion in his poem THE SONG OF HIAWATHA. PONTEACH, OR, THE SAVAGES OF AMERICA (1766), by Major Robert Rogers, which was the first American play to deal sympathetically with the Native Americans, introduces as a character Monelia, the daughter of the Mohawk chief Hendrik. Mohawks appear occasionally in Cooper, as in *Wyandotté* (1843) and THE REDSKINS (1846).

Mohawk River and Valley.   About 150 miles long, the Mohawk joins the Hudson at Cohoes, above Troy. It is the largest of the Hudson's tributaries. The Mohawk Valley was first seen by Europeans when Jesuit priests made their explorations. The Iroquois were driven out after the American Revolution, and a great migration of settlers poured through the valley. The Mohawk Trail leads from New England in this direction.

The Battle of Oriskany (August 6, 1777), near the present city of Utica, has particularly attracted historians and historical novelists, many of whom regard it as the turning point of the

Revolution. British General Barry St. Leger and his Indian allies were on their way to join General Burgoyne, but were defeated by the frontiersmen of the Mohawk Valley, led by General Nicholas Herkimer. Novels about historical events in the Mohawk Valley include Charles Fenno Hoffman's GREYSLAER (1840), Harold Frederic's IN THE VALLEY (1890), Robert Neil Stephens's *Philip Winwood* (1900), Elsie Singmaster's *The Long Journey* (1917), and Walter D. Edmonds's DRUMS ALONG THE MOHAWK (1936). Historical accounts and descriptions are found in William Maxwell Reid's *The Mohawk Valley* (1901), Nelson Greene's *History of the Mohawk Valley* (4 v. 1925), T. Wood Clarke's *The Bloody Mohawk* (1940), and other books.

Mohegan Indians.   Native North Americans whose language belongs to the Algonquian linguistic stock. Also called Mohican, they are the eastern branch of the MAHICAN. In the early 17th century they occupied most of southwestern Connecticut, especially along the Thames River. When European settlers first arrived, the Pequots and the Mohegans were united under the rule of Sassacus. Later, a group under Uncas assumed separate identity as Mohegan. At that period, the combined tribes numbered about 2,300, but they were practically extinct as a group by the 19th century. In the 20th century the tribes were revitalized by casino ownership. Mohegan writers include Hendrick Aupaumut, who wrote an autobiography *A Narrative of an Embassy to the Western Indians*, (1827) and Samson Occom (1723–1792) who wrote *A Choice Collection of Hymns and Spiritual Songs Intended for the Edification of Sincere Christians of All Denominations* (1774) and *A Sermon Preached at the Execution of Moses Paul, an Indian Who Was Executed at New Haven, on the 2d of September 1772* (1772). JAMES FENIMORE COOPER's *The Last of the Mohicans* (1826) reintroduced the tribe to American readers with the noble characters CHINGACHGOOK and his son UNCAS, companions of NATTY BUMPPO.

Mohicans, The Last of the.   See LAST OF THE MOHICANS.

Moïse, Penina (1797–1880),   teacher, poet, hymnologist. Born in Charleston, South Carolina, Moïse was obliged to leave school to help support her family, but continued her education and later conducted a school for girls. She published several volumes, among them *Fancy's Sketch Book* (1833) and *Hymns Written for the Use of Hebrew Congregations* (1856). Her *Secular and Religious Works* was published in 1911.

Möllhausen, Heinrich Balduin (1825–1905), travel writer. This German author made three trips across the U.S.: to Fort Laramine (1849–1853), from Fort Smith to Los Angeles (1853–1854), and down the Colorado River (1857–1858). He used his observations of the frontier in many romantic novels, including the trilogy *Der Halb Indianer* (1861), *Der Flüchtling* (1861), and *Der Majordomo* (1863). His *Diary of a Journey from the Mississippi to . . . the Pacific* (1858) is his only work that has been translated into English.

Molloy, Robert (1906–1977),   newspaperman, literary editor, novelist, translator. Born in Charleston, South Carolina, Molloy at first was a businessman, later did freelance

writing, then joined the New York *Sun* (1936) and edited its book page from 1943 to 1945. *Pride's Way* (1945), his first novel, was set in Charleston and became a best seller. Among his later stories are *Uneasy Spring* (1946), *The Best of Intentions* (1949), *Pound Foolish* (1950), *A Multitude of Sins* (1953), and *An Afternoon in March* (1958). He also wrote *Charleston: A Gracious Heritage* (1947) and translated various works from Spanish and French.

Molly Maguires.   This was originally an Irish secret society that used terrorism against landlords and their agents in Ireland. When conditions seemed equally oppressive in the anthracite coal regions near Scranton, Pennsylvania, a similar group was organized there, and from 1865 to 1877 it terrorized the entire region. In addition to ballads written on the subject, Francis P. Dewees wrote *The Molly Maguires* (1877); ALLAN PINKERTON described the methods employed in bringing them to justice in *The Molly Maguires and the Detectives* (1905); and J. Walter Coleman analyzed them in *The Molly Maguire Riots* (1936).

Molly Pitcher.   See PITCHER, MOLLY.

Momaday, N. Scott [Tsoai-talee] (1934–   ·), novelist, poet, memoirist. Momaday, a member of the Kiowa tribe, was born in Oklahoma and grew up on reservations in the Southwest. He was educated at the University of New Mexico and Stanford University. He has taught at Berkeley, Stanford, and the University of Arizona. His first novel, *House Made of Dawn* (1968), the story of a young Native American caught between his heritage and white culture, won a Pulitzer Prize. *The Way to Rainy Mountain* (1969) is a reworking of Kiowa folktales interspersed with reminiscences of his own childhood. *The Names* (1976) combines personal memories with anecdotes about his ancestors. His poetry collections include *Angle of Geese* (1973) and *The Gourd Dancer* (1976). *The Ancient Child* (1989) is a novel concerning Set, a successful San Francisco artist who was raised as an Anglo, but is actually part Kiowa. When his adoptive father dies and dissonant elements creeping into his paintings threaten his career, he is saved by the intervention of Grey, a Kiowa woman who brings him back to his Native American roots. *The Man Made of Words* (1997) is a collection of essays on such diverse topics as travel, the differences between oral and written cultures, and government policy towards Native Americans. *In The Bear's House* (1999) is a mixed media collection including forty paintings, poems, prose pieces and a dialogue between the Great Mystery, Yahweh, and the primal Bear, Urset. *Circle of Wonder: A Native American Christmas Story* (1999) recalls Momaday's childhood on the Jemez reservation.

Monahan, Michael (1865–1933),   poet, critic, editor. Born in Ireland, Monahan began as a journalist in Albany, New York, at age twenty-two. His early verses were collected in *Youth and Other Poems* (1895). He founded one of the earliest of the LITTLE MAGAZINES, *The Papyrus: A Magazine of Individuality*. This monthly appeared from July 1903 until May 1912, with a suspension from September 1906 to June 1907. In June 1914, Monahan founded *The Phoenix*, a similar magazine, which appeared monthly until November 1915. Among his books are *Benigna Vena* (1904); *Palms of Papyrus* (1908, 1909), a study of men of letters; *Nova Hibernia* (1914); and *At The Sign of the Van* (1914).

Monette, John Wesley (1803–1851), physician, explorer, historian. Born in Virginia, Monette is remembered chiefly for his *History of the Discovery and Settlement of the Valley of the Mississippi by Three Great European Powers* (2 v. 1846). Although he won an excellent reputation as a physician, too, a fortunate investment made him financially independent and he devoted much of his time to research and writing. During the yellow-fever epidemic of 1841, his advice to Natchez that it quarantine itself saved that city from the scourge. He was deeply interested in the effects of climate on health and civilization and anticipated some of Darwin's theories. What has survived from his pen is mainly papers contributed to medical journals and observations on yellow-fever epidemics (1838 and 1842).

Money-Makers, The (1885), a novel by H. F. KEENAN. See THE BREAD-WINNERS.

Monikins, The (1835), a novel by JAMES FENIMORE COOPER. Cooper's monikins are four monkeys, two male and two female, whose homeland is in the polar regions. They persuade Noah Poke, a Connecticut sea captain, and Sir John Goldencalf to accompany them to their homeland. The pair visit three countries, which stand for England, France, and the United States. Cooper deals with all three, especially the United States, in a bitterly sarcastic vein.

Monk, Maria (1817?–1849), fraudulent nun. At the height of the anti-Catholic demonstrations of the 1830s, Monk, who was born in Canada, made her appearance in New York City, claiming she had escaped from a convent in Montreal. Not long afterward appeared her *Awful Disclosures of the Hotel Dieu Nunnery of Montreal* (1836), which sold 200,000 copies. Its success led her to write *Further Disclosures* (1837). Meanwhile, her dissolute behavior led many to doubt her revelations, and two Protestant clergymen went to Montreal, inspected the Hotel Dieu Nunnery, and concluded that she was an impostor. Monk died in prison in New York, after an arrest for thievery. Laughton Osborn (c. 1809–1878), a poet and playwright, attacked the *Disclosures* in a satirical poem, *The Vision of Rubeta* (1838).

Monocle de Mon Oncle, Le (in HARMONIUM, 1923), twelve poems by WALLACE STEVENS. In these poems, each eleven lines long, Stevens examines faith and disillusionment, the inspiration of youth and the sadness of age, the passing of beauty and the freshness of experience, innocence and sophistication.

Monroe, Harriet (1860–1936), editor, poet, dramatist. Born in Chicago, Monroe had already attained some fame as a versifier when she was asked to write the *Columbian Ode* for the Chicago Exposition of 1893. In 1896 she published a biography of her brother-in-law, John Wellborn Root, the celebrated architect, and in 1903 five verse plays, *The Passing Show*. In 1912 she conceived the idea that brought her lasting recog-

nition. POETRY: A MAGAZINE OF VERSE appeared in October 1912 and soon became a strong force in the literary world. Monroe fought untiringly for many years to keep her magazine alive, to "open its pages to all sorts of experimental and unconventional work without neglecting the traditional forms," and to encourage and stimulate new poets. *Poetry* was the inspiration for dozens of ephemeral LITTLE MAGAZINES. As a critic Monroe was not unusually gifted and was hampered by prejudices. She published the work of a number of important poets, including Eliot, Sandburg, Vachel Lindsay, and Pound, who was for a time an assistant editor, but she repeatedly rejected the poetry of Robert Frost until his fame had been assured elsewhere.

Her anthology *The New Poetry* (1917), edited in collaboration with ALICE CORBIN HENDERSON, was one of the early collections of FREE VERSE, as well as other verse, and was received with a great deal of interest. Both the original and the revised edition (1932) contained a large section of Monroe's own verse, which she also collected in *Valeria and Other Poems* (1892), *You and I* (1914), and *Chosen Poems* (1935). Her autobiography, *A Poet's Life* (1937), gives an interesting account of her life and travels and her effort to make Chicago the literary center of the United States.

Monroe, James (1758–1831), soldier, lawyer, 5th president. Monroe fought in the Continental Army, rising to the rank of major. After the war he studied law with THOMAS JEFFERSON and became one of his most devoted followers. He served in various legislative bodies, advocated states' rights, opposed the adoption of the Constitution, but accepted it loyally after its ratification. He was minister to France in 1794, governor of Virginia in 1799. He was sent once more as minister to France and was instrumental in bringing about the LOUISIANA PURCHASE, but other missions to England and Spain proved failures. He became governor again, Secretary of State under Madison, then Secretary of War.

In 1816 and again in 1820 he was elected president. During his two administrations, Monroe obtained the cession of Florida from Spain, settled Canadian border disputes, and abandoned all fortifications on the Canadian border. In addition, the MONROE DOCTRINE was established, and the Missouri Compromise on slavery was accepted. When Monroe retired in 1825 he went back to Virginia and tried unsuccessfully to mend his shattered finances. In 1830 he moved to New York City, where he died in poverty.

Two early biographies, Daniel C. Gilman's *James Monroe* (1883) and George Morgan's *Life of James Monroe* (1921), have been superseded by Arthur Styron's lively *Last of the Cocked Hats* (1945) and W. P. Cresson's *James Monroe* (1946, repr. 1971). Monroe's writings were edited by S. M. Hamilton (7 v. 1898–1903, repr. 1973).

Monroe Doctrine. After the fall of Napoleon, European nations united in the Quadruple Alliance, directed against popular or democratic movements in Old World lands. But their eyes were also directed to the Western Hemisphere, and it was feared both by England and the United States that attempts would be made to seize portions of the

Spanish Empire as it fell to pieces, also some of the far western and still unsettled lands. George Canning (1770–1827), the British Foreign Secretary, suggested that a joint declaration be issued warning against European intervention on the American continents. But Monroe's Secretary of State, JOHN QUINCY ADAMS, advocated a unilateral statement by the United States. In a message to Congress on December 2, 1823, JAMES MONROE formulated his doctrine, which thereafter became a cornerstone of American foreign policy. The new republics of Latin America had just been recognized by the United States and England, and Monroe warned that "we could not view any interposition for the purpose of oppressing them, or controlling in any other manner their destiny, by any European power in any other light than as the manifestation of an unfriendly disposition toward the United States." A considerable portion of the Monroe Doctrine had been implicit or actually formulated in utterances of earlier Presidents—the doctrine of isolation from European entanglements, of the paramount interest of the United States in the fate of neighboring territory, of self-determination for American communities.

Monsieur Beaucaire (1900),   a novelette by BOOTH TARKINGTON. A French duke in the days of Louis XV, seeking adventure, goes to England disguised as a barber in order to find just the right bride. He falls in love with the beautiful Lady Mary Carlisle, but after many ups and downs his true identity is revealed and he returns to France to marry his cousin.

Monster and Other Stories, The (1899),   a collection by STEPHEN CRANE. It contains "The Monster," THE BLUE HOTEL, and "His New Mittens." It was reissued in 1901 with four additional stories. The *Century* rejected the title story on the grounds that it was "too horrible." "The Monster" tells the story of an African-American who, in saving a child from a burning laboratory, has his face disfigured by flaming acid. He becomes an object of horror and repugnance to the townspeople, who want to lock him up because of his transformation. Dr. Trescott, the father of the child, defends the "monster" and is ostracized by his fellow citizens.

Montalvo, Juan (1832–1889),   Ecuadoran essayist. A bitter foe of tyranny, Montalvo attacked Ecuadoran dictator Gabriel García Moreno in the pages of his journal *El cosmopolita*. When he heard of García Moreno's assassination, Montalvo declared, "My pen has killed him!" His savage polemical essays, *Catilinarias* (1880), were directed against a new dictatorship and contributed to his banishment from Ecuador. His best-known work, *Siete tratados* (1882), consists of seven treatises on moral and literary subjects, including a comparison of Washington and Bolívar. He also wrote *Capítulos que se le olvidaron a Cervantes* (1895), a successful imitation of Cervantes. Not considered a profound or original thinker, Montalvo is esteemed today largely because of the vigor of his style.

Montanus, Arnoldus (1625?–1683),   writer. Born in the Netherlands, Montanus produced a sumptuous volume on America, *De Nieuwe en Onbekende Weereld* (The New and Unknown World, Amsterdam, 1671). In 1671, there appeared in London a book called *America*, a large and handsomely illustrated folio ascribed to John Ogilby; it is mostly a translation of the book by Montanus. The latter was in small part also translated by E. B. O'Callaghan, who wrote the "Description of New Netherland" for the *Documentary History of the State of New York* (1851).

Montcalm de Saint-Véan, Marquis Louis Joseph de (1712–1759),   soldier. Born in France, Montcalm in 1756 became field marshal of the French troops fighting to save Canada from the British. In the crucial battle of Quebec (September 13, 1759), the French were defeated, and Montcalm was mortally wounded. Francis Parkman made a detailed study of the conflict in *Montcalm and Wolfe* (2 v. 1884).

Montezuma [sometimes **Moctezuma** or **Montezuma II**] (1480?–1520).   His reign as Aztec emperor (c. 1502–1520) was notable for incessant warfare and unrest. When CORTÉZ and his Spanish troops arrived in Mexico, he was able to exploit the tensions and make alliances with enemies of Montezuma. WILLIAM H. PRESCOTT, in *History of the Conquest of Mexico* (1843), describes how Montezuma, thinking the Spaniards were descendants of the feathered serpent god Quetzalcoatl, tried to induce them to leave by offering rich gifts, which further enflamed their greed. Montezuma's splendid court at Tenochtitlán which the Spanish visited in 1519 convinced them there was fabulous wealth to be had. Cortez seized Montezuma as a hostage and tried to govern through him, but the Aztecs rose up against them. Montezuma was killed, though it is not clear whether he was killed by a Spaniard or an Aztec. William Carlos Williams wrote "The Destruction of Tenochtitlan," in *In the American Grain* (1925). See CONQUEST OF MEXICO.

Montgomery, L[ucy] M[aude] (1874–1942),   novelist. A school teacher and wife of a Presbyterian minister, Montgomery became by accident a popular writer of juveniles. Asked to prepare a short serial for a Sunday School paper, she drew on memories of her girlhood on Prince Edward Island, where she was born, to produce ANNE OF GREEN GABLES (1908). It became an international success and was followed by *Anne of Avonlea* (1909), *Chronicles of Avonlea* (1912), *Anne of the Island* (1915), and many other books for girls.

Monthly Magazine and American Review, The (1799–1802),   a periodical edited by CHARLES BROCKDEN BROWN, based in New York. It switched to quarterly publication in 1801, and its name was changed to *The American Review and Literary Journal*. Brown published portions of his own *Edgar Huntly* (1799) in it.

Monti, Luigi (1830–1903),   teacher, writer. Monti fled from Italian tyranny to the United States in 1850, taught at Harvard, and was made American consul at Palermo. He published *The Adventures of a Consul Abroad* (1878). Monti knew all the members of the Cambridge group of his time and was introduced by Longfellow into the storytelling group of TALES OF A WAYSIDE INN (1863, 1872, 1874) to relate "King Robert of Sicily" and other tales.

Mont-Saint-Michel and Chartres (privately printed 1904, published 1913),   an historical essay by HENRY ADAMS. This classic study of medieval civilization is written as the commentary of Henry Adams to an imaginary niece as they tour the Abbey Church at Mont-Saint-Michel and the Chartres Cathedral. To Adams the great cathedrals express the unity of 12th-and 13th-century European culture. They reflect the deep, resonant faith and the clear purposes that enable people to work together efficiently and to the height of their powers. In his next book, THE EDUCATION OF HENRY ADAMS, Adams contrasted the coherence of this medieval universe and its high achievement with the confusion and wasted energy of the modern "multiverse." *Mont-Saint-Michel and Chartres* identifies three phases of the medieval synthesis. In the first, that of Mont-Saint-Michel and the *Chanson de Roland*, the feudal principle unifies church and state; in the second and highest phase, represented by Chartres Cathedral, love supersedes the will and is symbolized in the Virgin of Chartres; in the last phase, best exemplified in the *Summa Theologiae of Aquinas*, intellect prevails. For the first half of his book, Adams concentrates on church architecture—the physical evidence of spirit—until he can feel its emotion and grasp its ideal. Then he turns to the history, literature, and philosophy of the era to confirm and extend his insights. The work is a subtle evocation and, like the cathedrals Adams admired, a graceful but solid construction.

FRANK MCHUGH

Moodie, Susanna [Strickland] (1803–1885),   novelist, poet. After marrying J. W. D. Moodie, an army officer, Susanna sailed with him and her sister, CATHERINE PARR TRAILL, from England to Canada in 1832. She described the hardships experienced by pioneers like herself in the Canadian wilderness in *Roughing It in the Bush, or Life in Canada* (1852). Notable for its realism, sincerity, and dry humor, the work revealed the sentiments of a well-bred Englishwoman whose initial dislike for her new home eventually turned to affection and belief in Canada's potential greatness. She also wrote several poems and novels, including *Mark Hurdlestone* (1853) and *Geoffrey Moncton* (1856), most of which were conventionally sentimental.

Moody, Anne (1940–   ),   memoirist. Moody's candid description of life as a Southern black woman in *Coming of Age in Mississippi* (1968) is an important source of first-hand history for the period from the end of World War II through the civil rights struggles of the mid-Sixties. She has also published a collection of four stories called *Mr. Death* (1975).

Moody, Dwight Lyman (1837–1899),   evangelist. Born in Massachusetts, Moody left school at age thirteen to become a shoe clerk in Boston, later a traveling salesman for a wholesale shoe firm. In 1856 he moved to Chicago, where he built up a lucrative business. In 1860 he resigned from business to become an independent city missionary without salary or supervision. In 1867, 1870, and 1873 he visited Great Britain, where he preached to large numbers. On his third trip he was accompanied by Ira D. Sankey (1840–1908), his organist and singer, who collected the *Gospel Hymns* popularly referred to as "Moody and Sankey hymns." Sankey later wrote *My Life and the Story of the Gospel Hymns* (1906).

The profits from Moody's tours and the hymnal were used for philanthropic purposes. In 1879 Moody founded the Northfield Seminary for Girls, in 1881 the Mount Hermon School for Boys, and in 1889 the Chicago Bible Institute. Eighteen volumes of his sermons appeared during Moody's lifetime, with such titles as *"To the Work! To the Work!" Exhortations to Christians* (1884); *Secret Power, or, The Secret of Success in Christian Life and Christian Work* (1881); *Prevailing Prayer: What Hinders It* (1885); *Heaven: Where It Is, Its Inhabitants, and How To Get There* (1885); and *Sowing and Reaping* (1896). His sermons were translated into many languages.

Moody, Rick [Hiram F. III] (1961–   ),   novelist, short-story writer. Born in New York City, Moody was educated at Brown and Columbia. His first novel *Garden State* (1991) received little notice, but his second *The Ice Storm* (1994) gained immediate attention and was made into a movie. Set in an upper-class Connecticut town in November of 1973, it depicts the advent of an early winter storm as the inciting incident in the destruction of a family already riven by sex and drugs. *The Ring of Brightest Angels Around Heaven* (1996) is a story collection. *Purple America* (1997) is a postmodern treatment of upper-middle-class life and its accouterments, golf courses, station wagons and drinking.

Moody, William Vaughn (1869–1910),   poet, dramatist, teacher. Moody was born in Indiana, the son of a steamboat pilot who died when Moody was a child. Moody struggled for an education, became a high school teacher in Indiana and New York, and attended Harvard on a partial scholarship. He taught there briefly before going on to the University of Chicago, where he taught until he turned to writing for the last few years of his life. Born in the same year as Edwin Arlington Robinson and five years before Robert Frost, Moody achieved recognition and died before the two poets were widely known.

Moody's best poems touch on issues of the day. "Gloucester Moors" protests the unequal distribution of the world's goods. "The Menagerie" mocks man's sense of his place in the evolutionary scheme. ODE IN TIME OF HESITATION and "On a Soldier Fallen in the Philippines" satirize turn-of-the-century manifest destiny. He also wrote successful poetic dramas: THE MASQUE OF JUDGMENT (1900), a Miltonic play on God's relation to man, and *The Fire-Bringer* (1904). *The Sabine Woman* (1906), later titled THE GREAT DIVIDE (1909), contrasting the puritanical East and the Wild West, and *The Faith Healer* (1909) are prose plays. *Poems* appeared in 1901. John M. Manly edited *The Poems and Plays of William Vaughn Moody* (1912). Robert Morss Lovett edited *Selected Poems* (1931). A biography is Maurice F. Brown, *Estranging Dawn: The Life and Works of William Vaughn Moody* (1973).

Moon-Calf (1920),   a novel by FLOYD DELL. Felix Fay leaves a little Illinois community for the big city, Chicago, thinking he will find there a world closer to his heart's desire. He leaves behind him his childhood sweetheart whom he thinks he has outgrown, but in a sequel, *The Briary-Bush* (1921), Felix returns home and marries her—he has experienced to the fullest Chicago's literary maelstrom.

Moon Hoax. See BALLOON HOAX.

Moon of the Caribbees and Six Other Plays of the Sea (1919),   by EUGENE O'NEILL. This collection followed *Thirst and Other One Act Plays* (1914), a publication O'Neill financed. Both are based on the year O'Neill spent at sea in 1910, when he shipped aboard a vessel bound for Argentina.

Five of the plays are dramas of the sea, both realistic and poetic, dramaturgically effective yet rarely melodramatic. ILE portrays a mad sea captain more intent on oil than on people. The title play describes with pathos the scene on the *Glencairn*, a British steamer, when women come aboard as she lies at a West Indian port. In BOUND EAST FOR CARDIFF a sailor of the same vessel lies dying, and a shipmate tries to cheer him with talk of the fun they had been expecting on shore. In *The Long Voyage Home* the sailors are shown drinking in a London bar, and the *Glencairn* puts to sea in wartime for the drama of suspicion that *In the Zone* reports. *Where the Cross Is Made* shifts to America to present the tragic figure of Captain Bartlett, gone mad in his dreams of a treasure that his son Nat believes never existed—but the son too is finally infected with the dream. *The Rope* is likewise concerned with buried treasure, supposedly buried by a father to conceal it from his sons.

Moore, Brian (1921–1999),   novelist. Moore was born and educated in Northern Ireland and immigrated to Canada in 1948. After moving to the United States in 1959, he retained his Canadian citizenship. His first three novels and some of his later ones have an Irish flavor. *The Lonely Passion of Judith Hearne* (1955) deals with a middle-aged spinster in a Belfast boarding house who assuages her loneliness with an imaginary romance. *The Feast of Lupercal* (1957) centers on Diarmud Devine, who has been emotionally crippled by the same repressive educational system he now perpetuates. *The Luck of Ginger Coffey* (1960, Governor General's Award) concerns a middle-aged immigrant to Canada. *The Great Victorian Collection* (1975), a fantasy, also won a Governor General's Award. Moore's later novels include *Catholics* (1972) and *The Doctor's Wife* (1976). His more recent novels, such as *The Mangan Inheritance* (1979), *Cold Heaven* (1983), *Black Robe* (1985), *The Colour of Blood* (1987), *Lies of Silence* (1990), *No Other Life* (1993), and *The Statement* (1995) present a darker view of politics and humanity.

Moore, Clement Clarke (1779–1863),   scholar, poet. Moore, born in New York City, taught Oriental and Greek literature at the General Theological Seminary in New York City. His *Compendious Lexicon of the Hebrew Language* (1809) was for years the standard authority. He published *Poems* (1844), sentimental and conventional in nature. Moore is known today for a single poem, *'Twas the Night Before Christmas*, which appeared in 1823 in the *Troy Sentinel* under the title A VISIT FROM ST. NICHOLAS. See KNICKERBOCKER SCHOOL.

Moore, Douglas [Stuart] (1893–1969),   teacher, composer, writer. Moore, born in Cutchogue, New York, was

director of music at the Cleveland Museum of Art and taught music at Columbia University. His compositions include works for orchestra, chorus, chamber music, and opera. Moore set many of Stephen Vincent Benét's poems to music and collaborated with Benét on an opera based on THE DEVIL AND DANIEL WEBSTER (1938). Of literary interest, too, are a tone poem for orchestra, *Moby Dick* (1928); an opera, *White Wings* (1935), based on Philip Barry's play; an operetta, *The Headless Horseman* (1936); and *Giants in the Earth* (1951), an opera based on O. E. Rölvaag's novel, with the libretto by Arnold Sungaard. His opera *The Ballad of Baby Doe* (1955) achieved critical and popular acclaim. His later operas include *Gallantry: A Soap Opera* (1957) and *The Wings of the Dove* (1960). Moore also wrote two books, *Listening to Music* (1932) and *From Madrigal to Modern Music* (1942).

Moore, [Horatio] Frank[lin] (1828–1904),   editor, anthologist. Born in Concord, New Hampshire, Moore was greatly interested in history. He worked at the New York Historical Society and edited many compilations and anthologies. Among them are *Songs and Ballads of the American Revolution* (1856), *American Eloquence* (1857), *Materials for History* (1861), *Women of the War* (1866), and *Songs and Ballads of the Southern People* (1886).

Moore, George Henry (1823–1892),   historian, librarian. Born in Concord, New Hampshire, the elder brother of FRANK MOORE was librarian of the New York Historical Society, then of the Lenox Library (now part of the New York Public Library). He wrote on many historical topics, such as *The Treason of Charles Lee* (1860), *Negroes in the Army of the Revolution* (1862), *Notes on the History of Slavery in Massachusetts* (1866), *Notes on the History of Witchcraft in Massachusetts* (1883), *Washington as an Angler* (1887), *Libels on Washington* (1889), and *John Dickinson* (1890).

Moore, John (1858–1929),   novelist, short-story writer, poet, editor. Moore, born in Alabama, took the name of Trotwood from Dickens' *David Copperfield* and used it for a pen name, John Trotwood. He later took Trotwood as his middle name. His reputation as a novelist was sufficiently great in his own time for him to found a magazine, *Trotwood's Monthly*, in 1905. In the following year it was renamed the *Taylor-Trotwood Monthly*, and he continued to edit it until 1911. His verses and stories are laid in the South, particularly Tennessee. Among them are *Songs and Stories from Tennessee* (1897), *The Bishop of Cottontown* (1906), *Uncle Wash, His Stories* (1910), and *Hearts of Hickory* (1926).

Moore, J. Owen. See ALLATOONA.

Moore, Julia A. (1847–1920),   poet, novelist. Moore, who was born in Michigan, was known as the Sweet Singer of Michigan. Her first book, *The Sweet Singer of Michigan Salutes the Public* (1876), was later called *The Sentimental Song Book*. Later she issued *A Few Words to the Public with New and Original Poems by Julia A. Moore* (1878). Many years afterward came her *Sunshine and Shadow* (1915), a historical novel. Mark Twain parodied sentimental verse like hers in *Huckleberry Finn*.

Moore, [Marie] Lorrie [Lorena] (1957–   ),   novelist, short-story writer. Born in Glens Falls, NY, Moore was educated at St. Lawrence University and Cornell. She is a professor of writing at the University of Wisconsin-Madison. Her short stories are distinguished by a sense of humor about the young professional people who inhabit them. Six of the nine stories in her first collection *Self-Help* (1985) are narrated in the unusual second person voice of a how-to-do-it book used, according to the author, ironically because they demonstrate "how-not-to" in contemporary emotional relationships. *Like Life* (1990) is a second story collection. Critics were enthusiastic about the combination of tenderness and humor demonstrated in *Birds of America* (1998), her third story collection. *Anagrams* (1986), about a chain-smoking art history professor, and *Who Will Run the Frog Hospital?* (1994), the first person recollections of an American woman in Paris about her adolescent friendship in upstate New York, are novels. *The Forgotten Helper* (1987) is a juvenile, and Moore edited an anthology of stories about childhood by contemporary writers called *I Know Some Things* (1992).

Moore, Marianne [Craig] (1887–1972),   poet, essayist. Born in Kirkwood, Missouri, Moore moved with her mother, Mary Warner Moore, and her brother Warner to Carlisle, Pennsylvania, where she lived for over two decades. While she was a student at Bryn Mawr, her poetic style first showed its distinctive flair in the pages of the campus literary magazine.

In 1918, at the age of 30, Moore moved with her mother to New York City, where she lived for the rest of her life. The move to New York brought her into the center of a group of writers and artists associated with *Others* magazine, including WILLIAM CARLOS WILLIAMS, WALLACE STEVENS, Mina Loy, LOLA RIDGE, Marsden Hartley, and Alfred Kreymborg. In his memoir *Troubadour*, Kreymborg captured the remarkable impression Moore made on him and others as "an astonishing person with Titian hair, a brilliant complexion, and a mellifluous flow of polysyllables which held every man in awe." Her travels to England, France, Italy, and Ireland, as well as her visits to Washington State and Virginia provided rich material for her poetry. Moore was widely loved and honored, especially during the later years of her life.

Moore's first volume, *Poems* (1921), was published without her prior knowledge by friends, including Hilda Doolittle, at The Egoist Press in London. Her second volume, *Observations* (1924), won The Dial Award for that year. Between 1925 and 1929 Moore edited *The Dial*, then one of America's foremost journals of literary and artistic modernism. Her *Selected Poems* appeared in 1935 with an introduction by T. S. Eliot, in which he wrote, "Miss Moore's poems form part of the small body of durable poetry written in our time."

Many of Moore's earliest poems are epigrammatic portraits of people, but the move to New York brought with it an expansion in both the length and scope of her work. Her piece entitled "Poetry," beginning "I, too, dislike it," shows her characteristic use of the catalogue of particulars to define a general term and of quotations from a variety of literary and nonliterary sources woven through the lines. Moore was a writer of unusually wide-ranging interests and knowledge; she

had an arresting eye for detail and a virtuoso mastery of form. While some of her major longer poems of the early 1920s, such as "Marriage" and "An Octopus," were composed in relatively free verse, Moore's formal signature is her virtually unique development of a syllabic verse that both highlights the natural rhythms of the English language and maintains an intricate repeated pattern of rhymes, audible and inaudible. Her typical procedure can be seen in "The Steeple-Jack," one of the mature poems of the 1930s that open *The Complete Poems*. A rather freely composed model stanza, in this case the opening (or perhaps the closing) stanza, lends its pattern of syllables and rhymes to the body of the poem, which flows over and through the pattern in contrast and subtle complicity with it. Moore's skill creates a highly graceful and unusual interplay between the poem as written or seen and the poem as spoken or heard, between form and flow.

Moore brought to her work a prodigious reading and passionate interest in many fields, especially natural history, the arts, and contemporary affairs. Her poetic appropriation of the images and language of science and technology, news and conversation, enables it to offset traditional poetic tones with the rhythms of prose rhetoric and ordinary speech. The emblem and its verbal counterpart, the aphorism, are forms that appear repeatedly in her work. Two of Moore's finest volumes, *What Are Years* (1941) and *Nevertheless* (1944), weave a keen sense of the unfolding tragedies of World War II through studies of plants and animals, artifacts, American history, and the character of other countries. In her study of the ostrich, for instance, "He 'Digesteth Harde Yron,' " she notes that this bird "was and is / a symbol of justice"—endangered, vigilant, courageous, all-too-often slaughtered. Moore's observations of the natural world—like the ostrich "whose comic duckling head on its / great neck revolves with compass-needle nervousness"—are grounded in awareness of moral and spiritual realities: "the power of the visible," the poem continues, "is the invisible."

The poet's major long undertaking during the postwar years was a translation, *The Fables of La Fontaine*, published in 1954. In the following year, a selection of her essays, *Predilections*, brought her critical eye and dense, energetic prose to the attention of a wide readership. During her career Moore won virtually every literary honor America had to bestow—*Collected Poems* (1951) brought her the Pulitzer Prize and National Book Award in 1951, the Bollingen Prize and the Gold Medal of the American Academy of Arts and Letters in 1953. For *The Complete Poems* (1967) she won the Poetry Society of America's Gold Medal for Distinguished Achievement and also America's highest literary honor, the National Medal for Literature. More important, she won the respect and admiration of her fellow poets and the affectionate appreciation of the American public.

Moore's later verse, from the mid-1950s through the 1960s, is somewhat looser in form and more playful in tone than the work preceding it. In 1953 "Tom Fool at Jamaica," a poem in praise of champions (the race horse and jazz musicians), was the first of her many later poems to appear in the pages of *The*

New Yorker. One of her last great pieces, "Granite and Steel," explores through interlaced quotations and symbols the themes of technology, America, and international unity embodied in the Brooklyn Bridge.

In the wake of her many awards, Moore became a public figure of some renown, recognizable in Brooklyn and later in Washington Square Park in her tricorn hat and cape, and a favorite of news photographers, who snapped her throwing out the first ball in Yankee Stadium in 1968. Media attention to her love of sports and animals as subjects for her verse sometimes tended to obscure the liberating and vitalizing effect her work had on the early development of modernism. Behind her somewhat eccentric and always individual style was a mind of uncommon breadth and acuity, a spirit of uncompromising rectitude, and a hopeful belief in human beings. Moore's celebrations of the natural world and of man's productions wove an affirmative and formally elegant strand through the fabric of literary modernism during the first half of the 20th century.

The Complete Poems of Marianne Moore (1981 edition) is the best available collection and contains about two-thirds of her published poems; *The Complete Prose of Marianne Moore* (1986) contains her essays, reviews, and other prose of 1907–68. Critical studies include Laurence Stapleton's *Marianne Moore, The Poet's Advance* (1978), Bonnie Costello's *Marianne Moore, Imaginary Possessions* (1982), Margaret Holley's *The Poetry of Marianne Moore, A Study in Voice and Value* (1987), Charles Molesworth's *Marianne Moore, A Literary Life* (1990), and *The Web of Friendship: Marianne Moore and Wallace Stevens* (1995) by Robin G. Schulze.

MARGARET HOLLEY

Moore, Merrill (1903–1957),   psychiatrist, poet. Born in Columbia, Tennessee, Moore took his medical degree at Vanderbilt Medical School (1928), taught at Harvard, became a Harvard research fellow in psychiatry, and served in various hospitals and clinics in Boston. He came by his avocation, poetry, in his college days, when he was a member of the FUGITIVES, the group of Southern agrarians led by JOHN CROWE RANSOM. Unlike some other members of the group, who later became leaders among serious American writers, Moore in his later years took a rather lighthearted view of literature. He specialized in sonnets and claimed he had written at least one a day throughout his adult life. His themes were often, not always, comic. He broke all traditions for sonnet-writing, used many meters and rhyme schemes, and though most of his sonnets have fourteen lines, some do not. Among his collections are *The Noise That Time Makes* (1929); *Six Sides to a Man* (1935); *Poems from The Fugitive* (1936); *M: One Thousand Autobiographical Sonnets* (1938); *Clinical Sonnets* (1949); *Illegitimate Sonnets* (1950); and *More Clinical Sonnets* (1952). Henry W. Wells wrote *Poet and Psychiatrist: Merrill Moore, M.D.* (1955).

Moran of the Lady Letty (1898),   a novel by FRANK NORRIS. This short adventure novel, influenced by Robert Louis Stevenson, tells how a vigorous young Viking daughter of the captain of the *Lady Letty* takes over when he is drowned. She gets into rough company, from which she is protected by a shanghaied sailor who has fallen in love with her.

More, Paul Elmer (1864–1937),   critic, philosopher. More was born in St. Louis and educated at Washington University and Harvard. Influenced by IRVING BABBIT, his fellow student at Harvard, he articulated an antiromantic stance. He taught at Harvard and Bryn Mawr and spent thirteen years as a journalist in New York before seeking seclusion in Princeton, New Jersey. His reviews and essays were collected in SHELBURNE ESSAYS (11 v. 1904–21).

A leading figure in the New Humanism movement (see HUMANISM), More was critical of modern writers, particularly the Naturalists. His ideas on psychology and sociology as expressed in such works as *Aristocracy and Justice* (1915), drew scathing attacks from H.L. MENCKEN and VAN WYCK BROOKS. More replied in his preface to THE DEMON OF THE ABSOLUTE (1928). That work and NORMAN FOERSTER's *Toward Standards* (1930) engendered a major critical controversy in the early 1930s. In the pages of the *Bookman, The Nation, and New Republic,* writers such as EDMUND WILSON, KENNETH BURKE, and LEWIS MUMFORD attacked the New Humanists on historical and philosophical grounds. More stayed aloof from this controversy, working chiefly on his *The Greek Tradition* (5 v. 1921–31) and the *New Shelburne Essays* (3 v. 1928–36). *Pages from an Oxford Diary* (1937), an autobiographical work, was the last of his books.

Moreau de Saint-Méry, Médéric-Louis-Élie (1750–1819),   lawyer, bookseller, ambassador, writer. Moreau studied law in Paris and returned to his native Martinique to write on the laws of the French colonies in America (1784–90). In Paris at the time of the Revolution, he fled to the U.S. with his family in 1792. After various travels he settled in Philadelphia as a bookseller, returned to France in 1799. His *American Journey (Voyage aux Etats-Unis de l'Amérique)* was edited by Stewart Sims. An English version was made by Kenneth and Anna M. Roberts (1947) in preparation for Kenneth Roberts's writing of *Lydia Bailey* (1947).

Morella (*Southern Literary Messenger*, April 1835; included in *Tales of the Grotesque and Arabesque*, 1840),   a story by EDGAR ALLAN POE. Poe tells of a strange beloved dying of a disease that recalls Virginia Clemm's ailment and displaying an indomitable will to "return again." The tale is obviously a preliminary study for LIGEIA; at the time he wrote "Morella," Poe regarded it as his best work.

More Wonders of the Invisible World (1700),   by ROBERT CALEF. This attack on COTTON MATHER and his conduct of the witchcraft investigation included some spicy details of the way in which Mather investigated Margaret Rule. The title is a derisive one, in imitation of Mather's WONDERS OF THE INVISIBLE WORLD (1693).

Morford, Henry (1823–1881),   journalist, novelist. Morford, a New Yorker, served in the Civil War and used it as background for the novels *Shoulder-Straps* (1863) and *The Days of Shoddy* (1864), describing military incompetence and war profiteering, and for his memoir *Red-Tape and Pigeon-Hole Generals As Seen from the Ranks* (1964). His other works include *The Rest of Don Juan* (1846), a Byronic poem; *The Bells of Shandon* (1867), a play in collaboration with John

Brougham; and *The Spur of Monmouth* (1876), a novel of the Revolution.

Morgan, Henry (1635?–1688),   buccaneer. Born in Wales, Morgan went in his youth to the West Indies. Commissioned by the governor of Jamaica, he engaged in a series of daring exploits, finally capturing Panama City after an almost incredible march across the Isthmus of Panama (1671). His conduct was so ruthless that he was recalled to England to answer for it. But he won the favor of Charles II, was knighted (1674), and appointed lieutenant governor of Jamaica. He has been a favorite subject for biographers and novelists. One of the best biographies is Rosita Forbes's *Sir Henry Morgan: Pirate and Pioneer* (1946). Among the novels may be mentioned John Steinbeck's *Cup of Gold: A Life of Henry Morgan, Buccaneer, with Occasional References to History* (1929); F. Van Wyck Mason's *Cutlass Empire* (1949); and Gordon Daviot's *The Privateer* (1952). Laurence Stallings and Maxwell Anderson's play *The Buccaneer* (1925) portrays Morgan in Panama.

Morgan, Henry Lewis (1818–1881),   ethnologist. Morgan made the first scientific investigation of a Native American tribe in his *League of the Ho-dé-no-sau-nee, or Iroquois* (1851). In *Systems of Consanguinity and Affinity of the Human Family* (1871), he set forth the view that the kinship system of the Iroquois was similar to that of other tribes. His *Indian Journals, 1859–1862* was not published until 1958. His other books include *The American Beaver and His Works* (1868) and *Ancient Society; or Researches in the Lines of Human Progress* (1877).

Morgan, John (1735–1789),   physician, writer. Born in Philadelphia, Morgan took his medical degree at Edinburgh and returned to found the Medical School of the University of Pennsylvania. There he continued teaching while practicing medicine. He wrote *A Discourse upon the Institution of Medical Schools in America* (1765), issued four pamphlets pointing out the advantages of a continued union with Great Britain, and published *A Recommendation of Inoculation* (1776).

Morgan, Joseph (1671–1745),   clergyman, writer. Morgan, born in Connecticut, wrote many religious books, but the only one still remembered is the fictional *History of the Kingdom of Basaruah* (1715), an allegory that sets forth the Congregational view of the fall and redemption of man.

Morgan Library,   originally the private collection of J. Pierpont Morgan (1837–1913), the financier, it was established as a public institution by J. Pierpont Morgan, Jr. (1861–1943) in 1924. The paintings, rare books, manuscripts, and incunabula are housed in a building adjacent to the Old Morgan residence in Manhattan. The library is open to scholarly research and sponsors exhibitions.

Morgan, Sarah (1842–1909),   diarist. Born in New Orleans, Morgan was educated at home as was the custom for women in her time. Her parents were both Northerners by birth, but Judge Thomas Gibbes Morgan had lived in Louisiana for twenty years when his seventh child, youngest of four daughters, was born to his second wife, Susan Hunt Fowler Morgan. At the beginning of 1861, Louisiana had

seceded from the Union and become part of the Confederacy; in April, Sarah's favorite brother, Henry, was killed in a duel; and in November her father died. She began her diary in January of 1862, not yet twenty, father and one brother dead, three other brothers in the Army of the Confederacy (two would not survive the war), and she, with her mother and sister, trying to keep up the family home in Baton Rouge. Unlike the Civil War memoirs of MARY CHESNUT, an older, married woman who lived in South Carolina and knew key political and military figures, Morgan's account of life on the fringes of the Confederacy reveals what living during wartime was like for unprotected women who had to use their ingenuity to survive. She tells of the capture of the city, the burning of wharves and cotton bales, the family's flight, and return to a vandalized house. She describes the emotional response to hearing about her brothers' deaths, Lee's surrender and Lincoln's murder, and prays that God will "Have mercy on us as a people." After the war she never again lived in Louisiana; in South Carolina in the 1870s she had a minor literary career, publishing essays on the role of women in newspapers and magazines. She married the editor of the Charleston *News and Courier*, Frank Dawson, but after he was murdered in 1889, she lived alone. At the end of the century she joined her son, Warrington Dawson, in Paris, where she died. Portions of her memoir were first published in 1915 as *A Confederate Girl's Diary. The Civil War Diary of Sarah Morgan*, edited by Charles East (1991), is a complete version of the text.

Mori, Toshio (1910–1980),   short-story writer. Mori, an American of Japanese ancestry, depicts life in his California hometown and in the Topaz Center, a World War II detention camp. His view of segregated Asian-American community life seldom includes white characters or deals with questions of race relations. His story collections include *Yokohama, California* (1949); *Woman from Hiroshima* (1979); and *The Chauvinist and Other Stories* (1979).

Morin, Paul (1889–1963),   poet. Morin, born in Montreal, wrote in French about a world far removed from Canada. Educated in Montreal and Paris, he spent two years in a Jesuit school in France. He returned to Montreal to take a degree in law (1910) from the city university, and went back to France, where he earned a doctorate of letters from the Sorbonne. The subject of his studies at the Sorbonne was the sources of the work of HENRY WADSWORTH LONGFELLOW. After his early training Morin gave up law for teaching literature at McGill, the University of Minnesota, and Smith. Morin's most important early work was *Le Paon d'émail* (1911), a collection of short impressionistic poems.

His *Poèmes de Cendre et d'Or* (1922) won the Prix David. During the Depression, he published little and in the 1940s he suffered from angina, his wife died, and a fire destroyed all his possessions, including several manuscripts. He never recovered from the ensuing mental depression. His final collection, *Geronte et Son Miroir* (1960), brought together work published in periodicals and newspapers, some autobiographical verse, and an exotic bestiary. His *Oevres Poétiques*, edited by Jean-Paul Plante, appeared in 1961.

Morison, Samuel Eliot (1887–1976), historian. Born in Boston, Morison was a prolific writer whose work is outstanding both for its scholarship and its felicity of style. He taught at Harvard from 1915 to 1955 and, as official historian of the university, produced a three-volume history under the general title *Tercentennial History of Harvard College and University* (1936). Among his many works on early New England are *Harrison Gray Otis: Urbane Federalist* (1913, 1969), *Builders of the Bay Colony* (1930, rev. 1958), and *The Intellectual Life of Colonial New England* (1956, first pub. as *The Puritan Pronaos*, 1936). Morison did considerable work as a maritime historian, and, as official Navy historian during World War II, wrote his fifteen-volume *History of the United States Naval Operations in World War II* (1947–62). He won Pulitzer Prizes for his biography *Christopher Columbus, Admiral of the Ocean Sea* (2 v. 1942) and *John Paul Jones: A Sailor's Biography* (1959). His many other works include *The Oxford History of the American People* (1965) and a two-volume study, *The European Discovery of America* (1971, 1974).

Morituri Salutamus: Poem for the 50th Anniversary of the Class of 1825 in Bowdoin College (comp. 1874, read 1875), a poem by HENRY WADSWORTH LONGFELLOW. The poet pays tribute to Bowdoin and its teachers, greets his classmates and remembers those who have died, retells an appropriate tale from the *Gesta Romanorum*, introduces many apt literary allusions, and shows his craft in using a verse from he rarely used, the iambic pentameter couplet. He put into the poem his philosophy of life—the injunction that it is better to be too bold than not bold at all, a reminder that many old men have continued to produce important work.

Morley, Christopher [Darlington] (1890–1957), newspaperman, editor, poet, writer. After graduation from Haverford College, in the Pennsylvania town in which he was born and where his father was professor of mathematics, Morley went to New College, Oxford, as a Rhodes scholar and while there published his first book of poems, *The Eighth Sin* (1912). His short novel *Parnassus on Wheels* (1917), a story about what a later generation would have called a bookmobile, was an immediate success, as was its sequel, *The Haunted Bookshop* (1919). A second collection of poems was *Songs for a Little House* (1917), and a book of essays was called *Shandygaff* (1918). In 1920 Morley wrote a play, *Three's a Crowd*, with EARL DERR BIGGERS, and in the next year published *One-Act Plays*. From 1924 to 1941 he was contributing editor of the *Saturday Review of Literature*.

During the 1920s Morley, along with DON MARQUIS and FRANKLIN P. ADAMS, worked in the literary spotlight of New York. All three were literary columnists of a kind that has since vanished from the journalistic scene. In addition, Morley and Cleon Throckmorton founded the Hoboken Theatrical Company (1928) and produced a number of revivals. Morley continued to write novels, including *Thunder on the Left* (1925), *Human Being* (1932), and KITTY FOYLE (1939)—the last-named a best seller. His collections of verse appeared regularly, and he edited two revisions of Bartlett's *Familiar Quotations*.

Among Morley's other works are four books of essays: *Plum Pudding* (1921), *Streamlines* (1936), *Letters of Askance* (1939), and *The Ironing-Board* (1949); five books of verse: *The Rocking Horse* (1919), *Middle Kingdom* (1944), THE OLD MANDARIN (1947), *The Ballad of New York and Other Poems* (1950), and *Gentlemen's Relish* (1955); two collections of short stories: *Tales from a Rolltop Desk* (1921) and *I Know a Secret* (1927); five novels: WHERE THE BLUE BEGINS (1922), *The Swiss Family Manhattan* (1932), *The Trojan Horse* (1937), *Thorofare* (1942), and *The Man That Made Friends with Himself* (1949). *John Mistletoe* (1931) is an autobiography.

Mornings in Mexico (1927), essays by D. H. LAWRENCE. In this volume Lawrence gathered two different kinds of sketches he wrote in 1924. One group describes the dancing Indians of Arizona and New Mexico; the other group gives accounts of aspects of life in Mexico. The dancing Indians appear again in *The Plumed Serpent* (1926).

Moro, César [pen name of **Alfredo Quispez Asín**] (1903–1956), Peruvian poet. During his early years as a writer, Moro lived in Paris and became thoroughly immersed in SURREALISM; he wrote in French some of the most daring and fiery surrealist poetry of his time. He returned to Peru in 1934, then moved in 1938 to Mexico City, where he remained for ten years and where he published *Le Château de Grisou* (1943) and *Lettre d'amour* (1944). *Trafalgar Square* (1954) is his last book of verse published during his lifetime. His Spanish poems, *La tortuga ecuestre*, appeared posthumously in 1957. The despairing and hallucinatory eroticism of Moro's poetry introduced into an otherwise dry Spanish tradition a vocabulary of desire and forbidden love. After his death, his bilingual poetry consistently gained the recognition, he failed to earn in his lifetime.

Morrell, Benjamin (1797–1839), sea captain, memoirist. Born in Rye, New York, Captain Morrell made some adventurous voyages, which he chronicled in *A Narrative of Four Voyages to the South Seas* (1832). Some of his experiences were also described in Thomas J. Jacobs's *Scenes, Incidents, and Adventures in the Pacific Ocean under Captain Benjamin Morrell* (1844).

Morris, Charles (1833–1922), dime novelist, editor. In addition to editing anthologies and popularizations such as *Half-Hours with the Best American Authors* (4 v. 1887), *Tales from the Dramatists* (4 v. 1893), and *Famous Orators of the World* (1903), Morris wrote many dime novels, among them *Dick, the Stowaway; Cop Colt, the Quaker City Detective;* and *Mike Merry, the Harbor Police Boy*, all published in the 1880s.

Morris, George Pope (1802–1864), editor, poet, playwright. Born in Philadelphia, Morris worked in his youth in a printing office in New York and wrote verses for metropolitan newspapers. At twenty-one he founded the *New York Mirror*, a weekly paper now remembered for such notable contributors as Bryant, Cooper, Whitman, James K. Paulding, Nathaniel Willis, and Fitz-Greene Halleck. In 1842 the *New York Mirror* became the *New Mirror* and in 1844 was superseded by the *Evening Mirror*, a daily edited by Morris and

Nathaniel Willis with EDGAR ALLAN POE as literary critic. Poe's *The Raven* appeared in the *Evening Mirror* in February 1845.

Morris had some success as a playwright. His *Brier Cliff* (1826), a drama of the American Revolution, had a long run. *The Maid of Saxony* (1842), an operetta, was a less lucrative venture. His best-known prose work was *The Little Frenchman and His Water Lots* (short stories, 1839). *The Deserted Bride and Other Poems* (1838)—which contains the well-known "Woodman, Spare That Tree!"—and *Poems* (1840) enjoyed great popularity. See KNICKERBOCKER SCHOOL.

Morris, Gouverneur (1752–1816), lawyer, public official, diplomat, writer. Born in Morrisania, New York, Morris at age twenty-three represented Westchester County in the first sessions of the New York Provincial Congress, and helped draft the State constitution. He favored the Revolutionary cause from the beginning. He served a term in Congress, helped Washington reorganize the army, and published his *Observations on the American Revolution* (1779). Defeated for reelection, he went to live in Pennsylvania, in 1787 representing that State at the Constitutional Convention. He is believed to have written the Preamble to the CONSTITUTION.

He went to France on business in 1789, became United States Commissioner to England, then United States Minister to France, serving as Washington's confidential emissary. He was thus able to observe the French Revolution in its turbulent beginnings. *The Diary of the French Revolution* that he kept was not published until 1939 (edited by his great-granddaughter, Beatrix Cary Davenport). Parts of it had appeared in Jared Sparks' *The Life of Gouverneur Morris* (3 v. 1832), and in the *Diary and Letters of Gouverneur Morris* (2 v. 1888), edited by his granddaughter, Anna Cary Morris. From the beginning the *Diary* was recognized as having prime historical value as well as literary and human interest. It was in part politics, in part scandal. Hippolyte Taine was one of the many historians who used it to great advantage in writing on the French Revolution.

Morris later served as assistant to ROBERT MORRIS (no relation), then Superintendent of Finance, and drew up a plan for a decimal system of coinage, later perfected by Jefferson and Hamilton. He served in the United States Senate from 1800 to 1803. His last years were devoted to the promotion of the ERIE CANAL, and for several years he was chairman of the Erie Canal Commission. Morris, known as a man of fashion and aristocratic tastes, wanted to keep power in the hands of the wealthier classes. Theodore Roosevelt wrote a biography of Morris (1888).

Morris, Willie (1934–1999), novelist, essayist. Born in Jackson, Mississippi, Morris went to the University of Texas and studied as a Rhodes scholar at Oxford University. At the age of thirty-two, he was made editor-in-chief of *Harper's Magazine*, but after nearly two decades in New York, he returned to his native state. The South was his perennial subject. In his autobiography, *North Toward Home* (1967), Morris uses his own life history to cast light on the history of his native region as it was impacted by the social and political changes of the post–World War II period. In such books as *Yazoo: Integration in a Deep-Southern Town* (1971), *Good Old Boy: A Delta Boyhood* (1971) and *Terrains of the Heart and Other Essays on Home* (1981), Morris explores the end of segregation and other profound social changes. Other writings include *The Last of the Southern Girls* (1973), a novel; a collection of short stories entitled *Always Stand In Against the Curve* (1983); *The Courting of Marcus Dupree* (1983), about the recruitment of black athletes by southern schools; *My Dog Skip* (1995), a memoir of growing up in the South, made into a movie; and *The Ghosts of Medgar Evers: A Tale of Race, Murder, Mississippi and Hollywood* (1998). *My Mississippi*, a collection of photographs by his son David Rae Morris, with a text by Willie Morris, was published in 2000, after Morris's death.

Morris, Wright (1910–1998), novelist, photographer. Morris often uses Nebraska, his home state, as a background for his work. After graduation from Pomona College, he lived briefly in Paris. With multiple perspectives and subtle irony, in his novels he focuses on the American character. His early novels include *My Uncle Dudley* (1942), *The Man Who Was There* (1945), *The World in the Attic* (1949), and *The Works of Love* (1952). *Field of Vision* (1956), based on a stay in Mexico, won the National Book Award. He has published several books combining pictures and text, such as *The Inhabitants* (1946), *The Home Place* (1948), *God's Country and My People* (1968), and *Picture America* (1982).

His best novels combine tragedy and humor; these include *Love Among the Cannibals* (1957); *Ceremony in Lone Tree* (1960); *A Life* (1973); and *Plains Song* (1980), winner of the American Book Award. He has written several memoirs, including *Will's Boy* (1981), *Solo* (1983), and *A Cloak of Light* (1985). His *Collected Stories: 1948–1986* appeared in 1986.

Morrison, Toni (1932–), editor, novelist, educator, playwright. Morrison was born Chloe Anthony Wofford in Lorain, Ohio. Growing up in the depression with resourceful parents—her father often worked three jobs—she excelled in her studies and also earned money doing housework. She was educated at Howard University and Cornell and taught English at Texas Southern University and then at Howard, where she met and married Harold Morrison, a Jamaican architect. After their marriage ended, Morrison established a pattern of juggling two or more demanding jobs. While raising her sons, she worked for Random House in New York, editing, among others, books by Muhammad Ali, TONI CADE BAMBARA, ANGELA DAVIS, GAYL JONES, and Andrew Young, and taught at State University of New York at Purchase, Bard College, Yale, and Rutgers. In 1984 she was appointed to the Albert Schweitzer Chair at State University of New York at Albany and in 1989 to the Robert F. Goheen Chair at Princeton University.

Her first novel, *The Bluest Eye* (1970), was received with respect and some awe by the critics, and each of her subsequent novels—*Sula* (1974); SONG OF SOLOMON (1977, winner of the National Book Critics' Circle Award and the National Book Award); *Tar Baby* (1981); *Beloved* (1987, winner of the Pulitzer Prize and the Robert F. Kennedy Book Award); *Jazz* (1992) and

Paradise (1998)—has been received with growing interest and enthusiasm. She has also written plays: a musical, *New Orleans*, produced in a workshop in New York in 1983, and *Dreaming Emmett*, produced in Albany to mark the first national holiday commemorating the birthday of Martin Luther King.

As a black woman writer, a designation she embraces, Morrison has created many memorable female characters whose stories are informed by the difficulty of growing up in a predominantly white racist society. The complex narrative of *The Bluest Eye*, alternating between the voice of an omniscient narrator and that of young Claudia MacTeer, relates the tragic story of Pecola Breedlove, whose young life is irreparably damaged by poverty, racism, ignorance, and domestic violence. *Sula* explores the powerful bond between the rebellious Sula Peace and the conventional Nel Wright, whose friendship began when they were girls together in 1921 and was still alive for Nel in 1965, twenty-five years after Sula's untimely death.

In all her novels, Morrison places her characters in specific historical contexts, carefully relating their personal lives to public events. *Song of Solomon* opens with an account of the birth in 1931 of Macon Dead III, the protagonist, whose quest for his roots results in the unfolding of several generations of personal and public history, extending from before the Civil War to the fall of 1963. *Tar Baby*, Morrison's first novel with major white characters, is set mainly on a Caribbean island, where Jadine, a young light skinned African-American woman with a degree from the Sorbonne and a successful career as a high-fashion model, meets and falls in love with Son, a black American fugitive. They travel to New York and to Son's impoverished home in the rural South, their passion playing out in the larger context of clashing cultures and values.

Morrison's well-received *Beloved*—the first volume in a planned trilogy—set in the third quarter of the 19th century, focuses on the life of the runaway slave woman Sethe and her struggle with the unspeakable pain of her past. Like Morrison's earlier novels, *Beloved* is marked by rich and lyrical language, narratives shot through with exotic and magical elements, and a fragmented structure that requires readers to participate in the telling.

Jazz (1992) deals with a love triangle composed of Joe, a cosmetics salesman, his wife Violet, and his mistress Dorcas, whom he kills. Morrison was awarded the Nobel Prize for Literature in 1993. In her first novel after the award, *Paradise* (1998) she explores race and gender issues in an all-black town in Oklahoma. The book begins when four women who have sought refuge in a house on the outskirts of a town established by freed slaves are murdered by nine male residents of the town. The author indicated she was exploring the question of "where paradise is, and who belongs in it."

Nonfiction titles include *Playing in the Dark: Whiteness and the Literary Imagination* (1992), a collection of essays she first presented as lectures at Harvard University, and *Rac-ing Justice, En-Gendering Power: Essays on Anita Hill, Clarence Thomas, and the Constitution of Social Reality* (1992), on the controversial Supreme Court nomination, edited and introduced by Morrison. Along with Claudia Brodsky Lacour, Morrison edited a collection of essays on a famous murder case, *Birth of a Nation'hood: Gaze, Script, and Spectacle in the O. J. Simpson Case* (1997), for which she wrote an introduction. A recent study is Linden Peach's *Toni Morrison* (1995).

MELISSA WALKER/BP

Morrow, Elizabeth [Reeve Cutter] (1873–1955). The wife of Dwight W. Morrow (1873–1931), lawyer, banker, and diplomat, Elizabeth Morrow, born in Cleveland, was at one time acting president of her alma mater, Smith College, and was always active in community affairs. She wrote numerous appealing books for children, among them *The Painted Pig* (1930); *Beast, Bird, and Fish* (1993); and *The Rabbit's Nest* (1940). She wrote a book of poems, *Quatrains for My Daughter* (1931), for ANNE MORROW LINDBERGH.

Morrow, Honoré Willsie (1880–1940), editor, novelist. Born in Iowa, Willsie from 1914 to 1919 edited the DELINEATOR. In 1923, after divorcing her husband, she married the publisher William Morrow, and her books thereafter bore her new name. Her Western stories, like *The Heart of the Desert* (1913) and *Still Jim* (1915), were highly regarded as true studies of the West. Later she turned to history and to romances that offered realistic and accurate depictions of former times. Best-received was her trilogy devoted to Lincoln, collected as *Great Captain* (1935)—including *Forever Free* (1927), *With Malice Toward None* (1928), and *The Last Full Measure* (1930). She defended the President's wife in *Mary Todd Lincoln* (1928). The pioneer Marcus Whitman and his wife appear authentically in *We Must March* (1925); Amos Bronson Alcott, in *The Father of Little Women* (1927); John B. Gough, temperance advocate, in *Tiger! Tiger!* (1930); and Daniel Webster, in *Black Daniel* (1931). She wrote candidly and amusingly of her daughter in *Demon Daughter* (1939).

Morse, Jedidiah (1761–1826), clergyman, teacher, geographer, editor. Morse, born in Connecticut, was an important influence on his times and had two brilliant and influential sons, SAMUEL F. B. MORSE and SIDNEY EDWARDS MORSE. He taught in Connecticut schools and in 1789 became pastor of a Charlestown, Massachusetts, church. He was active in the New England Tract Society, the American Bible Society, the Society for Propagating the Gospel among the Indians, and the Andover Theological Seminary. Early in life Morse became deeply interested in geography, and his books, including textbooks, were so popular that he was called the father of American geography. His *American Geography* (1789) was, he said, "calculated early to impress the minds of American youth with the idea of the superior importance of their own country." His other books in this field included the first book on the subject in this country, *Geography Made Easy* (1784), which was later enlarged and called *The American Universal Geography: Elements of Geography* (1795); and *The American Gazetteer* (1797). He also compiled *Annals of the American Revolution* (1824).

Morse, Samuel F[inley] B[reese] (1791–1872), inventer, artist, memoirist. Born in Massachusetts, Morse was educated at Yale and studied painting in England under Washington Allston. He was a successful portrait painter and founder (1825) of the National Academy of Design. He spent 12 years perfecting the telegraph and his version of code and, in 1844, demonstrated to Congress its practicability. His letters and journals, edited by E. L. Morse, were published in 1914 (repr. 1973).

Morse, Sidney Edwards (1794–1871),   inventor, editor, geographer. Born in Massachusetts, as was his older brother, SAMUEL F. B. MORSE, Sidney Morse was an ingenious Yankee who made several important inventions. He devised a flexible piston pump, a bathometer for exploring ocean depths, and a special process for printing maps. Although Morse edited religious journals for the greater part of his life, his deep interest was in geography. His first important book was *The New States, or, A Comparison of the Wealth, Strength and Opulence of the Northern and Southern States* (1813). He assisted his father, JEDIDIAH MORSE, in revising his popular textbooks and continued to publish similar books of his own. Among them are *An Atlas of the United States* (1823), *A Geographical View of Greece* (1824), *North American Atlas* (1842), and *A System of Geography for the Use of Schools* (1844). With his younger brother, Cary Morse (1795–1868), he founded the New York *Observer* and edited it from 1823 to 1858.

Mortal Antipathy, A (1885),   a novel by OLIVER WENDELL HOLMES. This was an attempt to handle in fiction the scars left by childhood experience. A child is dropped accidentally into a thorn bush by his cousin Laura—and thereafter has a mortal antipathy to attractive young women. He is cured many years later, when an athletic young woman rescues him from a fire, and they marry.

Morton, Charles (1627–1698),   clergyman, teacher, educational administrator, author. Morton, an English nonconformist minister, came to Boston in 1686. Failing to become president of Harvard, he started a rival school. Harvard compromised by making him first a fellow (1692) and then vice-president (1697). He was among those who urged prosecution for witchcraft in Salem. He published a volume called *The Spirit of Man* (1693), and his textbooks on science and logic were used, in manuscript, at Harvard. His *Compendium Physicae* was partly inaccurate and clung too closely to the Aristotelian classification of physics, but it called the attention of American students to the great changes in physical science that were stirring the Old World. This document in the history of education was edited for the *Publications of the Colonial Society of Massachusetts* (1940) by Theodore Hornberger.

Morton, George (1585–1628?),   colonist, publisher. Morton accompanied the Pilgrims to Holland; when the others emigrated to America in 1620, he returned to London and acted as their agent. It is conjectured that WILLIAM BRADFORD [1] and EDWARD WINSLOW prepared an account of the happenings in Plymouth, *A Relation or Journal of the Beginning and Proceedings of the English Plantation Settled at Plymouth in New England*, and sent it to Morton. He published it anonymously in 1622 and signed the preface G. Mourt. Generally known as *Mourt's Relation*, it is the first story of the new colony. Morton himself emigrated to Plymouth in 1623. His

publication or compilation was published in abridged form in *Purchas His Pilgrims* (1625). It was reissued (1865) in an edition prepared by Henry M. Dexter.

Morton, Nathaniel (1613–1685),   colonist, public official, historian. Born in Holland, Morton accompanied his father GEORGE MORTON to Plymouth in 1623, and after his father's death came under the guardianship of WILLIAM BRADFORD [1]. He became secretary of the colony, drafted its laws, and was collector of taxes, member of land-survey committees, and town clerk. He drew freely on the papers of Bradford and EDWARD WINSLOW in writing *New England's Memorial* (1669), the first long historical narrative published in Massachusetts. Morton wrote another, fuller account, the manuscript of which was burned in 1674, rewritten by 1680, and not printed until 1855. The original *Memorial* has been reprinted several times.

Morton, Sarah Wentworth (1759–1846),   poet. Born in Boston, Morton wrote under the name Philenia and was called the American Sappho. As a member of the Della Cruscan group of poets in American she wrote with sensibility, and her contemporaries admired the "warbling eloquence" of her verses. She collected them in *Ouabi, or, The Virtues of Nature: An Indian Tale in Four Cantos* (1790); *Beacon Hill* (1797); and *The Virtues of Society* (1799). The only book she published under her own name was *My Mind and Its Thoughts* (1823), a miscellany of prose and verse.

Morton, Thomas (1575?–1646 or 1647),   colonist, trader, writer. Morton, representing the Anglican and antiPuritan faction in England, came to New England in 1622. With a group of immigrants he established a colony at what he called Merry Mount or Merrymount (now Quincy, Massachusetts). He alienated the neighboring Puritans because he competed successfully with them in trade with the Indians, sold guns to the Indians, was an Anglican, and set up a maypole for his people—and the Indians—to dance around. The Puritans finally cut down the maypole and shipped Morton back to England in 1628. A year and a half later he returned, obstreperous as ever, but was again deported. In England he joined the foes of the Massachusetts Bay Colony and wrote *New English Canaan, or New Canaan: Containing an Abstract of New England, Composed in Three Books: Written by Thomas Morton of Clifford Inn, Gent., Upon Ten Years' Knowledge and Experiment of the Country* (Amsterdam, 1637). Morton returned to New England ten years later, was again arrested, heavily fined, and released. He made his way to York, Maine, where he died.

The NEW ENGLISH CANAAN is first of all intended as a history and a memoir, of course with a bias. But it is also an exuberant geographical and ethnological description. CHARLES FRANCIS ADAMS edited it (1883) and set forth a careful analysis of Morton in his introduction. The colony at Merry Mount has been treated in Catherine Sedgwick's *Hope Leslie* (1827), Nathaniel Hawthorne's *The Maypole of Merrymount* (1836), John Lothrop Motley's *Merrymount: a Romance of the Massachusetts Colony* (1849), and Helen Grace Carlisle's *We Begin* (1932). Howard Hanson and Richard L. Stokes wrote an opera called *Merry Mount* (1934).

Mosby, John Singleton (1833–1916),   scout and ranger in the Confederate Army during the Civil War. After serving in the cavalry under General J. E. B. Stuart, Mosby left the regular forces early in 1863 and commanded a group of bold partisan adventurers, whose efficient operations foiled the Federal Army on numerous occasions. He wrote *Mosby's War Reminiscenes, and Stuart's Cavalry Campaigns* (1887) and *Stuart's Cavalry in the Gettysburg Campaign* (1908).

Mosel, Tad (1922–   ),   playwright, poet. Mosel, born in Ohio, was educated at Amherst and the Yale School of Drama. Five unproduced plays and a year of acting finally were followed by recognition as the writer of a superior television dramas. His major success; however, came with his adaptation of JAMES AGEE's novel *A Death in the Family*, retitled *All the Way Home* (1960). His dramatic version of the novel also won a Pulitzer Prize for drama in 1961. Among his original plays are *Star in the Summer Night* (1954), *The Lawn Party* (1954), *My Lost Saints* (1956), and *The Out-of-Towners* (1957). *Impromptu* and *That's Where the Town's Going* were printed in 1998.

Mosley, Walter (1952–   ),   novelist, short-story writer. Born in Los Angeles to a white mother and black father, Mosley was educated at Goddard College, Johnson State College and the City College of New York. He left computer programming to become a writer and published his first novel *Devil in a Blue Dress* in 1990, introducing the black private detective, Ezekiel "Easy" Rawlins. Easy is an accidental crime fighter; when he loses his job in the post–World War II L.A. aircraft industry, he is hired by a wealthy white man to find a beautiful blonde named Daphne Monet, who hangs around black jazz clubs. The sequel *A Red Death* (1991), finds Easy, who has used stolen money to buy real estate, cooperating with the FBI to investigate a union organizer. In *White Butterfly* (1992), Easy works to solve the serial murders of three black women and the daughter of a city official who has appeared as a stripper named White Butterfly. Before the publication of his next novel Mosley was identified by President Bill Clinton as a favorite writer. *Black Betty* (1994) was a financial success and earned a multi-book contract for its author. *R. L.'s Dream* (1995) is a non-detective book in which Atwater "Soupspoon" Wise, dying and poor, is taken in by a young white neighbor, Kiki Waters. The two share love of the blues music of Robert "R. L." Johnson, which enables them to form a human bond despite their obvious differences. Two collections of stories, *Always Outnumbered, Always Outgunned* (1997) and *Walkin' the Dog* (1999) deal with the character Socrates Fortlow, a sixtyish former convict on parole from an Indiana prison where he was incarcerated for 27 years for a double murder and rape. Having settled in L.A., Fortlow is not free of his past or police surveillance. *Blue Light* (1998) is a science fiction novel. The biracial narrator, Chance, chronicles a struggle between the Blues, who have been irradiated by a blue light from outer space that gives them superhuman powers, and their enemies, the Gray Men. *Workin' on the Chain Gang. Shaking Off the Dead Hand of History* (2000) is a nonfiction study of the effects of capitalism on black Americans. *Fearless Jones* (2001) is a detective novel set in Los Angeles.

Moss, Howard (1922–   ),   poet, editor, playwright. Moss won the National Book Award in 1971 for *Selected Poems*. As poetry editor of *The New Yorker* after 1948, he had a wide influence. His later books of poetry are *Buried City* (1975) and *Notes from the Castle* (1979). His prose includes *The Magic Lantern of Marcel Proust* (1962) and *Whatever Is Moving* (1981). *Instant Lives* (1974) provides capsule biographies of writers written in parodies of their own styles. He has also written plays, including *The Oedipus Mah-Jongg Scandal* (1968) and *The Palace at 4 A.M.* (1972).

Mosses from an Old Manse (1846),   a collection of twenty-five tales and sketches by NATHANIEL HAWTHORNE. The Manse in the title and the initial sketch was owned by Ralph Waldo Emerson and was occupied by Hawthorne from 1842 to 1845, the first years of his marriage. The initial sketch is important in revealing something of Hawthorne's attitude toward nature as a symbol of spiritual truth. Some of Hawthorne's best stories, such as YOUNG GOODMAN BROWN, THE BIRTHMARK, RAPPACCINI'S DAUGHTER, "The Artist of the Beautiful," and THE CELESTIAL RAILROAD are included in this collection. Melville hailed it as an American masterpiece and found much of it "deep as Dante." Poe recognized Hawthorne's contribution to the art of the short story, but felt that the stories were too allegorical.

motion pictures.   American motion pictures begin in 1893 with the brief films made at Thomas Alva Edison's Black Maria Studio in East Orange, New Jersey, by W. K. L. Dickenson, the man largely responsible for the Kinetograph camera with which these films were photographed and the Kinetoscope peephole machine in which they first were viewed. These half minute to one minute films, featuring dancers, trained animals, fighters, skits, and small bits of reality, were viewed in Kinetoscope parlors throughout the country beginning in 1894. Motion pictures moved out of the peephole machine and onto a large screen before an audience during a vaudeville show on April 23, 1896, in Koster and Bial's Music Hall in New York City, when some of these Kinetoscope films were projected with the Vitascope, a machine first developed by Thomas Armat and C. Francis Jenkins. Within a few years a number of companies were producing short films that were first shown as a part of vaudeville shows, but were soon featured by themselves in converted stores, arcades, halls, and restaurants called nickelodeons, where urban audiences could find about twenty minutes of entertainment for a nickel. Films became longer, more varied in subject. Stories were developed more fully. But the next chapter in the making of American movies is highlighted by the contribution of Edwin S. Porter, who worked for Edison's company, especially in his *Life of an American Fireman* and *The Great Train Robbery* (both 1903). The crosscutting between parallel actions in these films and the concluding closeup in *Great Train Robbery* may not have been new to film, but the skillful dramatic editing of *Great Train Robbery*, focusing on thirteen separate shots to develop an exciting narrative, was innovating and influential.

In January 1909 the Motion Picture Patents Company (MPPC) was formed, a monopoly trust comprising the important film companies: Edison, Biograph, Vitagraph, Essanay, Kalem, Selig, and Lubin; the French companies Pathé and Star-Film; and the distributing company of George Kleine. The goals of the trust were to end fighting over patents among members and to monopolize film production, exhibition, and distribution. But the MPCC members proved unable to supply the number and quality of films necessary for winning their war with independent film companies, which were able to lure many technicians and performers away from the trust companies, popularize their own films by developing the star system, and make longer and more innovative films. Long before the MPPC was legally dissolved in 1918 because of its monopolistic tactics, such independents as Fox, Universal, Bison, Mutual, and Keystone were making the major films, while the film industry itself had moved its center of operation to Hollywood because of the location's excellent weather, geographic variety, and cheap real estate. By 1920, Hollywood and its environs could boast some fifty studios that produced ninety percent of the films made in America.

Probably no filmmaker had a greater impact on the development of the motion picture as both a popular entertainment and an art form than D. W. GRIFFITH. A former actor and writer, Griffith joined the American Mutoscope and Biograph Company in 1908, for which he would make more than 400 one- and two-reel films by 1913. Griffith established the basic techniques of film narrative—he was not the first to use a number of these techniques, but no one before had used them with such skill and in such combinations to enthrall audiences. With the help of his cinematographer, Billy Bitzer, Griffith employed shots from a variety of distances to create an individual scene; followed action by panning or moving the camera; employed a number of dramatic perspectives by his sophisticated placement of the camera; gave great attention to the *mise en scène*, composing scenes in depth and with dramatic lighting; developed his narrative with parallel actions; and elicited from his performers a natural level of acting new to the cinema. The artistic culmination of Griffith's career was undoubtedly *The Birth of a Nation* (1915), based on Thomas Dixon's novel *The Clansman*. It was a three-hour epic work of tremendous cinematic achievement, but one unfortunately qualified by its condescending portrayal of African-Americans and glorification of the Klu Klux Klan.

CECIL B. DE MILLE and Eric von Stroheim seem to represent opposite facets of Griffith's achievement—De Mille encapsulated Griffith's capacity for creating popular entertainment, and Stroheim had his dedication to artistic integrity. De Mille began his career by codirecting *The Squaw Man* in 1914, a six-reel Western of immense popularity, and later made a series of titillating romantic comedies until the newly formed Motion Picture Producers and Distributors of America (MPPDA), commonly called the Hays Office after its president Will H. Hays and organized to clean up the film industry, deflected him into making less overtly sexual films. De Mille went on to make spectacles such as *The Ten Commandments* (1924), which allowed him a good deal of violence and sex under a moral veneer. De Mille's showmanship and hypocrisy were

distinctly opposite to Stroheim's meticulous realism and psychological cynicism. Driven to make his films the way he saw them, Stroheim's greatest works, *Greed* (1924), based on Frank Norris's novel *McTeague*, and *The Wedding March* (1928) were both finally taken out of his hands by the studios and reduced considerably in size.

The films of the silent period that seem to have the most appeal for modern viewers are the comedies. The so-called Golden Age of Comedy began with the Keystone films of MACK SENNETT in which the cinema's world of motion gave new meaning to *slapstick* and *farce*. CHARLIE CHAPLIN first developed the character of the little tramp for Sennett, taking the character with him to Essanay in 1915 and then to Mutual in 1916, where he made a number of remarkable shorts during the next two years, including *The Rink* and *Easy Street*. Chaplin's feature film, *The Gold Rush*, made in 1925 for United Artists, remains one of the great film comedies of all time. Equally esteemed by film historians is BUSTER KEATON, the remarkable acrobat with the deadpan face. After a series of short comic gems, Buster Keaton Studio turned to making feature films, the most notable of which are *Sherlock, Jr.* (1924), *The General* (1924), and *Steamboat Bill, Jr.* (1928).

The American documentary also began during the silent period with ROBERT FLAHERTY's *Nanook of the North* in 1922. The documentary in this country was never to have the popularity of the feature fictional film and was rarely to be shown in commercial theaters, but the tradition was to be a strong one, leading to the films of PARE LORENTZ during Depression years, the war documentaries of such Hollywood directors as FRANK CAPRA and JOHN HUSTON, and to the "direct cinema" of Frederick Wiseman beginning in the 1960s.

On October 5, 1927, *The Jazz Singer* opened in New York City, and the voice of Al Jolson thrilled audiences while also marking the death toll of silent cinema. By 1930 nearly two-thirds of the theaters in America were equipped for sound and ninety-five percent of the motion pictures coming from Hollywood were sound films. The result of sound was a cinema that seemed closer to the world as we know it and that could involve our social awareness while also making credible and immediate a world of exaggeration and fantasy that appealed to our dreams, our aspirations, and our fears.

By this time the film audience itself had greatly expanded and included people of all backgrounds, but motion pictures catered significantly to the expanding middle class, frequently presenting the desirable world of the rich and the world of struggling humanity with a decidedly middle-class perspective and morality. In the throes of the Depression years of the 1930s, motion pictures were a significant force in giving both escape and hope to a significant part of the American public.

As the film audience grew and the feature film replaced an anthology of short films, larger and more comfortable theaters were built for showing motion pictures, an expansion peaking with the opening of the Roxy Theater in New York City in 1927—an extravagant colossus that could seat sixty-two hundred patrons. There were some twenty thousand movie theaters of all sizes spread throughout the United States by the early 1920s. By the end of the 1930s eighty million tickets were sold for the motion pictures in an average week.

From the 1920s through the early 1950s most commercial films in America were the product of the studio system, a method of mass producing films in a rapid and efficient manner through division of labor, supervision of a group of films by a production head, and creation of formula films. Motion pictures were sold through the star system, which appealed to the fantasies of the public by glamorizing the screen appearances and private lives of the most attractive performers. By the middle of the 1930s the major film studios were MGM, Paramount, Twentieth Century-Fox, Warner Brothers, Columbia, Universal, RKO, and United Artists, the last basically a distributor for independently made motion pictures. Except for United Artists, each of these companies had its own stable of stars and directors as well as individual departments for various technicians. Although Hollywood was turning out more than six hundred films a year by the end of the 1930s to satisfy its vast public, it still managed to produce a significant number of classic films that are a positive contribution to American culture.

The studio system was ready to repeat the same formulas as long as people continued filling the theaters, but there was more to the development of American film genres than box-office success. On an artistic level, such motion pictures offered filmmakers the opportunity to present variation and innovation within the well-established conventions of story and technique. On a psychological and emotional level, such films repeated themselves without boring audiences because they embodied the mythic and universal. A case in point is the extreme popularity of the gangster film during the early 1930s, a genre undoubtedly given reality and power by the new sound systems that filled the theater with the noise of gunfire, shattering glass, and screeching cars. But films such as Mervyn LeRoy's *Little Caesar* (1930), William Wellman's *The Public Enemy* (1931), and HOWARD HAWKS's *Scarface* (1932) also dealt with the perennial American conflicts between isolation and the collective, between individualism and law and order, while also offering audiences a vicarious means of dealing with the pressures of the Depression.

The musical was a product of film's conversion to sound, beginning both with a breathtaking vulgarity in the motion pictures choreographed by Busby Berkeley, such as *42nd Street* in 1933, and an elegance and grace in the films of Fred Astaire and Ginger Rogers, such as *The Gay Divorcee* in 1934. The 1930s also gave the horror film a decade of respectability, starting with Tod Browning's *Dracula* and James Whale's *Frankenstein*, both in 1931. But while the horror film may have dealt with the fears and anxieties produced by reality in a covert way, the screwball comedy—especially such films as Frank Capra's *It Happened One Night* (1934) and Howard Hawks's *Bringing Up Baby* (1938)—met them head on by overtly confronting social conflict and the war between the sexes in a zany, unpredictable, and totally unthreatening way. Although the Western had a period of relative quiet, it seemed jump-started again in 1939, perhaps to assert American values

against the threatening political situation in Europe, with Cecil B. De Mille's *Union Pacific*, JOHN FORD's *Stagecoach*, and George Marshall's *Destry Rides Again*.

Another type of film that benefited from sound was the animated cartoon, especially in its development by the WALT DISNEY studio. The wonderfully matched music, voices, and images of Disney's *Silly Symphony* series in 1929 pointed the way to the high achievement of the studio's first feature-length cartoon, *Snow White and the Seven Dwarfs* in 1937. During the 1940s cartoon series from other studios with characters such as Tom and Jerry as well as Bugs Bunny brought mayhem and madness to the screen; and in 1945 United Productions of America (UPA) was organized by former Disney animators, reaching its greatest success with the Mr. Magoo and the Gerald McBoing-Boing series in the early 1950s.

In 1941, at the very time that Europe was in the midst of chaos, ORSON WELLES's *Citizen Kane* was released, a film now universally acclaimed for its innovative camera work, editing, and sound. Based on the life of William Randolph Hearst, the motion picture tells the story of Charles Foster Kane largely through a number of flashbacks as recalled by various characters in the film. Welles, along with his cinematographer, Gregg Toland, created a series of striking visual images, often with deep focus, chiaroscuro lighting, and low-angle shots. Welles was to achieve many of the same effects in his next work, *The Magnificent Ambersons* (1942), adapted from BOOTH TARKINGTON's novel, but the film was taken out of his hands by RKO, cut in size, and given a totally inappropriate ending.

World War II brought to the screen a number of patriotic war films and dramas, but the ending of the conflict and return to Hollywood of many significant directors and performers did not necessarily lead to films of celebration. Hollywood became serious and moralistic, examining American values in such social-conscience films as Edward Dmytrk's attack against anti-semitism, *Crossfire* (1948); Clarence Brown's moving treatment of racism in his adaptation of William Faulkner's *Intruder in the Dust* (1949); and Robert Rossen's classic adaptation of Robert Penn Warren's novel about political corruption, *All the King's Men* (1949). Hollywood also responded to the darker side of human nature and American society with the *film noir*, a type of motion picture that presented a brutal and corrupt urban world of unsavory, neurotic figures with an emphasis on bleak settings, high contrasts, and dark shadows. Robert Siodmak's *The Killers* (1946), adapted from the Hemingway short story, Edmund Goulding's *Nightmare Alley* (1947), and Raoul Walsh's *White Heat* (1949) are notable examples of these films.

In significant ways both groups of films are indicative of the introspection and reaction that were appearing in our culture in response to the Cold War and the sudden possibility of atomic annihilation; such external forces also led to one of the bleakest pages in the history of American motion pictures, the witchhunt for subversives and communists in the movie industry, in 1947 and 1951, by the House Un-American Activities Committee (HUAC), a hunt that impelled the industry to blacklist any person even suspected of associating with communists. See MCCARTHYISM. But American exuberance could not be repressed: at the same time, Hollywood was also turning out its brightest, happiest, and most energetic musicals, especially such films as Stanley Donen and Gene Kelly's *On the Town* (1949) and *Singing in the Rain* (1952).

This period also saw the rise of the New American Cinema, the high point of this nation's avant-garde, experimental motion pictures. The movement technically begins with the films of Maya Deren made during the 1940s, especially her *Meshes of the Afternoon* (1943); and later includes the subjective films of Stan Brackhage, the graphic works of Stan Vanderbeek, and the structural films of Michael Snow. Such motion pictures were a reaction against commercial movies and played to a small clientele. Lacking the finances and equipment of the Hollywood studios, the makers of these films carried on their investigations into the nature of film and the possibilities of the medium in creating various states of consciousness and evoking various perceptual experiences in the audience.

The ending of the studio system began with the Supreme Court's Paramount Decision in 1948, which allowed studios to continue making and distributing films, but prohibited them from owning the theaters that showed these motion pictures. In the 1950s, television seriously cut into motion-picture audiences, while independent and European filmmakers were pushing their products into American theaters. American filmmakers were also finding it cheaper to make their films abroad. A positive aspect of this general situation was the advanced technology with which the studios sought to win patrons back to the theaters, especially color and wide-screen cinematography; the negative aspects were the reduction of the studios to mere agencies for financing and distributing films made by independent groups, sometimes with the studio's facilities, and the ultimate takeover of most of the studios, starting in the 1960s, by large conglomerates for which filmmaking was only one of many business activities.

In the midst of all these changes, however, a number of directors did some of their best work. John Huston continued to turn out such quality films as *The Treasure of the Sierra Madre* (1948) and *The African Queen* (1952); ALFRED HITCHCOCK was reaching the peak of his American career with films such as *Rear Window* (1954) and *Psycho* (1960); John Ford brought the Western to a high level of maturity with *The Searchers* (1956); and Elia Kazan achieved a new realism in the cinema with, for example, *On the Waterfront* (1954).

Two films appeared in the mid-1960s that heralded the beginning of a new period in American motion pictures: Arthur Penn's *Bonnie and Clyde* (1967), which featured a pair of gangsters and murderers as anti-establishment heroes, a high intensity of violence, and a stylistic virtuosity in image and sound; and Stanley Kubrick's *2001: A Space Odyssey* (1968), a work that made science fiction not only respectable but high poetry and that brought special-effects cinematography to a new degree of sophistication and visual beauty.

The 1970s introduced to the film industry a group of directors called the movie brats, so named because their education in film was basically derived from movie theaters and film schools, not from years of experience in the industry. The first of these, FRANCIS FORD COPPOLA, made two very successful and certainly artful gangster films, *The Godfather, Part 1 and Part II* (1972–1974); another, MARTIN SCORSESE, achieved remarkable psychological portrayals and an impressive gritty realism in *Taxi Driver* (1976) and *Raging Bull* (1979); while two of them, GEORGE LUCAS and STEVEN SPIELBERG, became the new mythmakers of the motion picture, creating works based on the movies of their childhood and the fantasies of children and adolescents. Lucas's *Star Wars* (1977) initiated in movie houses a long series of science-fiction and special-effects films that raised the motion picture to a new height of unreality and technological splendor; and Spielberg's *E. T.—The Extraterrestrial* (1982) diffused the terrors of space and brought a new charm and whimsy to fantasy films. The films of Lucas and Spielberg announced the new dominance of young people in motion-picture audiences, though films by idiosyncratic talents such as WOODY ALLEN still found mature audiences.

The last two decades are more notable for technological changes in cinema rather than any significant artistic development. Sound has finally caught up with image in quality, while the computer has brought incredible sights to the screen and advanced the way films are made. Digital technology now promises to take both filmmaking and exhibition a giant step into the future. At the same time, the movie industry has become part of vast busniess conglomerates, producing the software for a multitude of hardware—theatrical distribution is only the prelude to the film's exhibition on VCR, DVD, cable and network television, not to mention the sales of its novelization, musical track, and various tie-ins with restaurants and toy stores.

This ubiquity of film and its very extensive foreign market have led to a dumbing down of Hollywood's film products. The saving grace to this decline in story and character has been the development of an exciting and intelligent independent cinema which is finding an appreciative, albeit smaller, market.

American films have always drawn heavily from the novels and plays of our own culture, relying on stories and characters already developed but also capitalizing on the popularity of such works. Best-selling fiction such as MARGARET MITCHELL's *Gone with the Wind* has been made into extravagant films by Hollywood (in this case in 1939), but a number of classic novels have also been the source of motion pictures for example, Hawthorne's SCARLET LETTER, Melville's MOBY-DICK, Twain's HUCKLEBERRY FINN, Fitzgerald's THE GREAT GATSBY, and Hemingway's A FAREWELL TO ARMS have been made into films more than once. Some of the most successful adaptations of significant American novels into film are Stroheim's *Greed* (mentioned above), John Ford's version of Steinbeck's THE GRAPES OF WRATH, released in 1940; George Stevens's 1951 film version of Dreiser's AN AMERICAN TRAGEDY, retitled *A Place in the Sun*; Fred Zinnemann's adaptation of James Jones's FROM HERE TO ETERNITY, released in 1953; and Milos Forman's 1975 film version of KEN KESEY's *One Flew Over the Cuckoo's Nest*. The film industry has also absorbed a steady stream of plays from the world of the theater, including a number by such distinguished playwrights as EUGENE O'NEILL, TENNESSEE WILLIAMS, and ARTHUR MILLER—certainly Elia Kazan's 1951 adaptation of A STREETCAR NAMED DESIRE deserves special mention in this context. American literature in general has been a steady source of material and, on occasion, inspiration for the American film industry—and sometimes the two have combined to create a rare amalgamation, a rare fusion of two art forms.

IRA KONIGSBERG

Motley, John Lothrop (1814–1877), diplomat, historian. Born in Massachusetts, Motley entered Harvard at thirteen, obtained a doctorate from Göttingen, and returned to this country, where he published *Morton's Hope: or, The Memoirs of a Young Provincial* (1839), a semiautobiographical novel, and *Merry-Mount: A Romance of the Massachusetts Colony* (1849). After a few months with the United States legation in St. Petersburg, he returned home and published a historical essay on Peter the Great in the *North American Review* in 1845. After five years of concentrated work, he completed *The Rise of the Dutch Republic* (3 v. 1856), the history on which his reputation rests. It was an immediate success, and new editions and translations followed rapidly. *History of the United Netherlands* (1861–68); *Democracy the Climax of Political Progress* (1869); and *The Life and Death of Joen of Barneveld, Advocate of Holland* (1874) were the first three parts of a vast history of the Netherlands that Motley did not live to finish.

Motley, Willard [Francis] (1912–1965), novelist. Motley was born and educated in Chicago; he traveled around the country and worked at many jobs before deciding to concentrate on writing. His first novel, *Knock on Any Door* (1947), the story of a young man who grows up in a Chicago ghetto and becomes a killer was hailed as a major work. *Let No Man Write My Epitaph* (1958), a sequel dealing with the son of the protagonist of the first book, was less successful. The main characters are ethnic whites; Motley replied to critics who complained that an African-American writer should write about his own people, "My race is the human race." His other publications are *We Fished All Night* (1951), *Let Noon Be Fair* (1966), and *The Diaries of Willard Motley*, (1979).

Mott, Frank Luther (1886–1964), literary historian, editor. Born in Keokuk County, Iowa, Mott became an authority on American newspapers, magazines, and best-selling books. In 1927 he was appointed professor of journalism and director of the School of Journalism at the State University of Iowa, and in 1942 joined the staff of the journalism school at the University of Missouri. For his *History of American Magazines* (3 v. 1930, 1938) he received a Pulitzer prize; volume 4 appeared in 1957. Among his other books are *Six Prophets out of the Middle West* (1917), *Literature of Pioneer Life in Iowa* (1923), *Rewards of Reading* (1926), *American Journalism: A*

History (1941), *Jefferson and the Press* (1943), GOLDEN MULTITUDES: THE STORY OF BEST-SELLERS IN THE U.S. (1947), *The News in America* (1952), and *Five Stories* (1957).

Mott, Lucretia Coffin (1793–1880), abolitionist, feminist, reformer. Mott, a Quaker, was born on Nantucket Island and lived in Boston and Philadelphia. She taught at a Friends school and was active in the American Anti-Slavery Society and in the Underground Railway. When women were denied delegate status to the World Anti-Slavery Convention in London (1840), she and ELIZABETH CADY STANTON organized the first Women's Rights Convention (1848) at Stanton's home in Seneca Falls, New York. Her husband, James Mott (1788–1868), abolitionist and women's rights advocate, presided. A. D. Hollowell edited *James and Lucretia Mott: Life and Letters* (1884).

Mountaineering in the Sierra Nevada (1872), sketches by CLARENCE KING.

Mountain Interval (1916), a collection of lyric and narrative poems by ROBERT FROST. This collection contains some of Frost's most enduring poems—THE ROAD NOT TAKEN, "Christmas Trees," "In the Home Stretch," "The Oven Bird," BIRCHES, "A Time to Talk," "The Cow in Apple Time," and "Brown's Descent."

Mountains of California, The (1894, rev. and enlarged 1911), a description by JOHN MUIR. Muir was particularly enthusiastic about the wilder aspects of Californian scenery. In this volume he is at his best in his description of the geology, flora, fauna, and landscapes of the Sierra Nevada, the Coast Range, and the intervening Central Valley.

Mount Rushmore. See GUTZON BORGLUM.

Mourning Becomes Electra (1931), a trilogy of plays by EUGENE O'NEILL: *Homecoming, The Hunted*, and *The Haunted*. The playwright took his story from the *Oresteia* of Aeschylus, setting it in 19th-century New England and giving it a generous interlarding of Freudian theory. Agamemnon is represented by Ezra Mannon, a general returning from the Civil War. His wife Christine corresponds to Clytemnestra, his daughter (Electra) is Lavinia, and his son (Orestes) is Orin. The play takes its force from the conflict between Puritanism and romantic passion.

Mourning Dove (1888–1936), novelist. Mourning Dove, whose tribal name was Hum-Ishu-Ma, was one of the first Native-American women to publish a novel, *Cogewea the Half-Blood: A Depiction of the Great Montana Cattle Range* (1927). She also collected and recorded several Okanagari tales and songs.

Mourt's Relation. See GEORGE MORTON.

Moveable Feast, A (1964). Memoir by ERNEST HEMINGWAY. The posthumously published work summarizes his experiences in Paris and is especially valuable for observations of GERTRUDE STEIN and F. SCOTT FITZGERALD.

Moviegoer, The (1961), a novel by WALKER PERCY.

movies. See MOTION PICTURES.

Mowat, Farley [McGill] (1921–), Born in Ontario and educated at the University of Toronto, Mowat served in World War II and spent two years in the Arctic. In his first book, *People of The Deer* (1952), he blamed government officials and missionaries for the plight of the Ihalmiut, an inland Eskimo people whose living depends on the caribou. *The Desperate People* (1959) is an eloquent defense of their way of life. *The Snow Walker* (1975) is a collection of short stories and sketches about the human struggle to survive a hostle environment and modern technology. Mowat edited the journals of both celebrated and unknown explorers in *Coppermine Journey* (1958), from a narrative of Samuel Hearne; *Ordeal by Ice* (1960); *The Polar Passion* (1967); and *Tundra* (1973). He described his own trip to Arctic Russia in *Sibir: My Discovery of Siberia* (1970). His books on ecology include *Canada North* (1967), a pictorial study; *Canada North Now: The Great Betrayal* (1976); *This Rock Within the Sea: A Heritage Lost* (1968), about Newfoundland. Mowat has written with humor about dogs in *The Dog Who Wouldn't Be* (1957) and about wolves in *Never Cry Wolf* (1963); but seriously about the killing of seals and whales, *A Whale for the Killing* (1972). He told the story of Dian Fossey, the American naturalist who studied the mountain gorilla before she was murdered by poachers, in *Virunga* (1987), republished as *Woman in the Mist*. Books for young readers include *Lost in The Barrens* (1956) and *The Boat Who Wouldn't Float* (1969). Autobiographical titles include *My Father's Son* (1992) and *Aftermath* (1995).

Mowatt, Anna.   See FASHION, OR, LIFE IN NEW YORK.

Mowrer, Paul Scott (1887–1971),   newspaperman, foreign and war correspondent, writer on foreign affairs, poet. Born in Illinois, Mowrer long reported for the Chicago *News* at home and abroad. In 1928 he won a Pulitzer award for foreign correspondence. Among his books are *Belkanized Europe* (1921); *Our Foreign Affairs* (1924); and an autobiography, *The House of Europe* (1945). He also published several collections of poems, among them *Hours of France* (1918), *Poems Between Wars* (1941), *Twenty-One and Sixty-Five* (1958), and *The Mothering Land* (1960).

M. Quad.   The pen name of C. B. LEWIS.

Mr.   See MISTER.

MS. Found in a Bottle   (*Baltimore Saturday Visiter*, October 19, 1833; *Southern Literary Messenger*, December 1835; *The Gift*, 1836; collected in *Tales of the Grotesque and Arabesque*, 1840), a tale by EDGAR ALLAN POE. *The Visiter* had announced a prize competition with an award of $50 for the best story, $25 for the best poem. Poe submitted a poem, THE COLISEUM, and several stories. The tales deeply impressed the judges, and they gave the award to "MS. Found in a Bottle." This story tells how a vessel is swallowed up in a monstrous current; the narrator has been keeping a journal, which survives. Poe combined the legend of the Flying Dutchman with John C. Symmes's idea that the world is hollow, with water pouring into the interior from the ocean at the poles. The descent of the wave on the vessel is magnificently and horrifyingly described.

muckraking literature.   The term derives from Bunyan's *Pilgrim's Progress* (1678), in which one character is so busy raking muck that he cannot perceive the celestial crown held above him. Theodore Roosevelt applied the term to journalists who exposed corruption in business and government. Though used denigratingly at first, the term soon became one of praise, at least in the minds of some.

Spearhead of the movement was *McClure's Magazine* (see S. S. MCCLURE), with other militant periodicals following its lead. For *McClure's* IDA TARBELL contributed articles on Standard Oil, ROY STANNARD BAKER wrote about the anthracite coal industry, and LINCOLN STEFFENS did a piece on corruption in Minneapolis city government. Such writing attracted wide attention and increased circulation and advertising revenues. Particularly noteworthy in this era were volumes made up of material gathered from some of these magazines: Stefens' *The Shame of the Cities* (1904), *Struggle for Self-Government* (1906), and *The Upbuilders* (1909); Tarbell's *History of the Standard Oil Company* (1904); and SAMUEL HOPKINS ADAMS's *The Great American Fraud* (1906).

Fiction writers were, of course, influenced by the success of muckraking journalists. The fiction of the period was profuse and made a deep impression on the public. Most sensational was UPTON SINCLAIR's THE JUNGLE (1906); in practically all his later fiction Sinclair remained the militant reformer. An inveterate muckraker was DAVID GRAHAM PHILLIPS, whose novels in this field included *The Master Rogue: The Confession of a Croesus* (1903), *The Cost* (1904), *The Deluge* (1905), *The Plum Tree* (1905), *Light-Fingered Gentry* (1907), and *The Fashionable Adventures of Joshua Craig* (1909).

Phillips was at his best in *Susan Lenox: Her Fall and Rise* (1917), a study of a modern prostitute's acquisition of money and social triumph. Frank Norris's THE OCTOPUS (1901) and THE PIT (1903) were widely read, as was ROBERT HERRICK's *Memoirs of an American Citizen* (1905). THEODORE DREISER told the story of one rich man in a trilogy: THE FINANCIER (1912), THE TITAN (1914), and *The Stoic* (1947). WINSTON CHURCHILL wrote two exposure novels: *The Inside of the Cup* (1912) and *A Far Country* (1915). JACK LONDON treated the theme in two striking novels, THE IRON HEEL (1908) and *Burning Daylight* (1910).

Mudjekeewis.   The father of HIAWATHA in Longfellow's poem. He is given dominion over the winds for killing a great bear.

Mudville.   Usually thought to be a section of Somerville, Massachusetts. It is the scene of various ballads by George Whitefield D'Vys (1860–1941) as well as the site of the baseball game described in Ernest Lawrence Thayer's CASEY AT THE BAT (1888).

Muir, John (1838–1914),   naturalist, essayist. As a small boy in Scotland, John Muir read Audubon and dreamed of exploring in the New World, a dream that was realized after his father migrated to a farm in Wisconsin. In *The Story of My Boyhood and Youth* (1913) Muir described the hardships of his life on the farm, his boyhood delight in nature and books. Between 1863, when he left the University of Wisconsin, and 1868, when he settled for six years in the Yosemite Valley, Muir traveled thousands of miles on foot through Wisconsin, Illinois, Indiana, and Canada, and made a journey from Indiana to Mexico, the journal of which he published as *A Thousand Mile Walk to the Gulf* (1916). He had the naturalist's keen eye, a poetic appreciation of nature, and a gift for style. A lover of animals, he disliked the notion of a world made for man alone, with animals to serve him. He repeatedly expressed his wonder and admiration for the intelligence of beasts. *Stickeen* (1909) is a loving tribute to the loyalty and resourcefulness of his little half-wild dog.

Much of Muir's life was devoted to saving the natural beauties of the West from destruction by commercial exploitation. He roused the public to the need for a conservation program, and under his friend President Theodore Roosevelt the system of national parks was established. His letters report his constant, heartbreaking struggle to prevent humanity from ruining the beauties of nature (*Life and Letters of John Muir*, edited by W. F. Badé, 1923–24). Among his other works are THE MOUNTAINS OF CALIFORNIA (1894), *Our National Parks* (1901), *The Yosemite* (1912), *Travels in Alaska* (1915), and *The Cruise of the Corwin* (1917). His *Writings* were collected by Badé (10 v. 1916–24). Linnie M. Wolfe made an excellent anthology of selections, *The Wilderness World of John Muir* (1954).

Mukherjee, Bharati (1940–   ),   novelist, short-story writer. Born in Calcutta, India, Mukherjee was educated at the University of Calcutta and the University of Baroda before coming to the United States to study at the Iowa Writer's Workshop in 1963. In 1966 she began teaching at McGill University in Montreal, in 1969 received a Ph.D. from Iowa. In 1980 she and her family moved to the U.S., where she has taught at Iowa, Skidmore, Queens College, and Berkeley.

In three novels she portrays the lives of Indian women confronting two cultures: in *The Tiger's Daughter* (1972), the woman, educated in the United States, faces the shock of a return home; in *Wife* (1975), the woman goes to New York to meet her husband in an arranged marriage and later drifts into madness and murder; in *Jasmine* (1989), a woman goes from an Indian marriage to an American one, exchanging a life in the Punjab with its random violence for another in Iowa, where farmers are violently protesting foreclosures. *The Holder of The World* (1993) echoes HAWTHORNE's *Scarlet Letter* with its 17th-century heroine who returns to Salem, Massachusetts with her daughter, Pearl. *Leave It to Me* (1997) features a girl abandoned in India by her hippie mother. In two collections of stories, she portrays the immigrant experience in North America: *Darkness* (1985), mostly about Indians; and *The Middleman and Other Stories* (1988), winner of a National Book Critics Circle Award, about people from various, mostly Third World, countries who are adapting to new lives. Her nonfiction includes, with her husband, CLARK BLAISE, *Days and Nights in Calcutta* (1977), a chronicle of a visit, and *The Sorrow and the Terror: The Haunting Legacy of the Air India Tragedy* (1987).

Mulford, Clarence E[dward] (1883–1956),   writer of westerns. Born in Streator, Illinois, Mulford worked as a

municipal clerk in New York City when he began writing stories. His first book was *Bar-20* (1907), in which he introduced the character called HOPALONG CASSIDY, who later appeared in twenty-seven other books by Mulford. He had never been to the West, although in 1924 he finally visited the scene of his novels. Millions of copies of his books have been sold. Among them are *Hopalong Cassidy* (1910), *The Coming of Cassidy* (1913), *Rustlers' Valley* (1924), *Hopalong Cassidy Returns* (1924), *Me an' Shorty* (1929), *The Round Up* (1933), *Hopalong Cassidy Takes Cards* (1937), and *Hopalong Cassidy Serves a Writ* (1941). In 1935 appeared the first of many Hopalong Cassidy movies.

Mulford, [Amos] Prentice (1834–1891),   clerk, sailor, teacher, miner, newspaperman, writer, public relations counselor. Mulford, born in Sag Harbor, New York, worked on a New York newspaper for several years before building a cabin in the woods near Passaic, New Jersey, and living there as a hermit. He wrote an account of his experiences in *The Swamp Angel* (1888). He was an early columnist, writing for six years a piece called "The History of a Day" for the New York *Daily Graphic*. A popular work was his *Your Forces and How to Use Them* (6 v. 1888), which expounded what came to be called the New Thought. He described his western adventures humorously in *Prentice Mulford's Story* (1889).

Mulligan, Dan.   Mulligan and his wife Cornelia were leading characters in a series of vaudeville sketches, later a series of plays, written by EDWARD HARRIGAN. They were performed with great success on the stage with Harrigan in the male role, his partner Tony Hart in the female. The characters were Irish immigrants sympathetically observed from life. They appeared for the first time in *The Mulligan Guard* (1873). Harrigan's later plays include *The Mulligan Guard Ball* (1879), *The Mulligan Guard Chowder* (1879), *The Mulligan Guards' Christmas* (1879), *The Mulligan Guard Surprise* (1880), *The Mulligans' Silver Wedding* (1881), and *Cornelia's Aspirations* (1883).

Mumford, Ethel Watts (1878–1940),   novelist, playwright, humorist. Mumford, believed to have been born in New York City, is best remembered as coauthor with OLIVER HERFORD and Addison Mizner of *The Complete Cynics' Calendar*, which made its first appearance in 1902 and continued until 1917. She wrote a novel, *Dupes* (1901), and a play, *Sick-A-Bed* (1918).

Mumford, Lewis (1895–1990),   writer, philosopher, historian, and teacher. Mumford, born in New York City, brought his varied interests and learning to writings that explore the relation of man, especially modern man, to his natural and self-created surroundings. Mumford's work in city and regional planning was stimulated by reading the works of Patrick Geddes, a Scottish biologist and sociologist, and in 1924 Mumford helped found the Regional Planning Association of America. In his books, *The Brown Decades* (1931), *The Culture of Cities* (1938), *City Development* (1945), and *The City in History* (1961), he showed how the city is an expression of the growth of civilization and in turn influences that growth.

The Culture of Cities is also a part of a four-volume study called *The Renewal of Life* that includes *Technics and Civilization* (1934), *The Condition of Man* (1944), and *The Conduct of Life* (1951). In this, his major work, he examined the emergence of the modern scientific and technological world, and he pleaded for a realization of humanity's obligation to create a better life from the infinite resources still at its command.

Some of Mumford's articles written for *The New Yorker* are collected in *From the Ground Up* (1956). His other books include *The Story of Utopias* (1922); *Sticks and Stones* (1924), one of the first histories of American architecture; THE GOLDEN DAY (1926); *Herman Melville* (1929); *Green Memories* (1947), an affectionate biography of his son, Geddes, who was killed in World War II at age nineteen; *Art and Technics* (1952); *In the Name of Sanity* (1954); and *The Transformations of Man* (1956). In the two volumes of *Myth and Machine* (1967, 1970), as in many other works, Mumford tackles the dehumanizing effects of modern technology, urging a return to humanitarian values and moral regeneration. *My Works and Days: A Personal Chronicle* (1979) contains selected writings from 1914 to 1977 with autobiographical notes. It was followed by *Sketches from Life: The Early Years* (1982).

Mundy, Talbot (1879–1940),   traveler, writer. Mundy traveled extensively in Asia and Africa. He came to the United States from England in 1911, became a citizen in 1917 and frequently made additional trips to Europe and Mexico. *Rung Ho* (1914), his first book, exhibits his realism, his ability to tell a story well, and his emphasis on adventure. Among his works are *King of the Khyber Rifles* (1916), *The Ivory Trail* (1919), *The Eye of Zeitoon* (1920), *Om* (1923), *Jungle Jest* (1932), *The Lion of Petra* (1933), *Full Moon* (1935), and *Old Ugly Face* (1940).

Munford, Robert (1730?–1784),   legislator, dramatist, poet. Munford, a Revolutionary patriot, showed the faults and virtues of both sides in the war in what may be the earliest of all American plays, THE CANDIDATES (probably 1770), and in THE PATRIOTS (1776). Munford later served as a county official in Virginia, his home state, as well as in the House of Burgesses and the General Assembly. During his lifetime none of his productions appeared in print, but after his death his son William (1775–1825), himself a public official, poet, and dramatist, made a *Collection of Plays and Poems* (1798) by his father. This included the two plays mentioned, in addition to a partial translation of Ovid's *Metamorphoses* and ten poems. *The Candidates* was reprinted (1948), with an introduction by Jay B. Hubbell and Douglass Adair, and *The Patriots* was reprinted in the *William and Mary Quarterly* in July 1949, with an introduction by Courtlandt Canby.

Municipal Report, A   (*Hampton's Magazine*, November, 1909; later collected in *Strictly Business*, 1910), a short story by O. HENRY.

Munro, Alice [Laidlaw] (1931–   ),   short-story writer. Born in Wingham, Canada, Munro grew up on an impoverished farm in western Ontario where her father raised silver foxes and her mother fought a losing battle with Parkinson's disease. She was educated at the University of Western Ontario, then moved with her first husband, James Munro, to British Columbia. There she raised three daughters and helped her husband establish Munro's Books in Victoria. In 1972 she returned to Ontario where she married Gerald Fremlin in 1976. She began writing stories at university but her work progressed slowly and even when her first volume, *Dance of the Happy Shades* (1968), won the Governor General's Award, she drew very little public attention. However, her second book, *Lives of Girls and Women* (1971), concerning an adolescent girl coming to terms with family and small town, drew praise for its feminist interest and its carefully crafted, almost photographic style. It is often remarked that Munro draws heavily on her personal experiences for her stories, but she asserts that her work is "autobiographical in form but not in fact." In her best stories, nonetheless, there is a vivid sense of the region where she grew up and a recurring preoccupation with her eccentric and disabled mother. Further, several of the stories in *Something I've Been Meaning to Tell You* (1974) and *Who Do You Think You Are?* (1978) are set in British Columbia, tracing Munro's move to the West Coast and back. *Who Do You Think You Are?* earned Munro a second Governor General's Award and was short listed for the Booker Prize. Munro won a third Governor General's Award for *The Progress of Love* (1986). Munro's form is exclusively that of the short story—although *Lives of Girls and Women* was published as a novel, it was first written and submitted as a series of stories. Munro has honed her craft to perfection and her work is sought by magazines such as *The New Yorker* and *Redbook*. Her most recent collections are *Friend of My Youth* (1990), *Open Secrets* (1994), and *The Love of a Good Woman* (1998). Her work is discussed in numerous collections of critical essays including, *Probable Fictions: Alice Munro's Narratives Acts*, edited by Louis K. MacKendrick (1983), *The Rest of the Story: Critical Essays on Alice Munro*, edited by Robert Thacker (1999), and in W. R. Martin's *Alice Munro: Paradox and Parallel* (1987) and Magdalen Redekop's *Mothers and Other Clowns* (1992).
DAVID STOUCK

Munsey, Frank A[ndrew] (1854–1925),   novelist, editor, publisher. In 1882 Munsey, who was born in Maine, founded a magazine for young people called *The Golden Argosy*, which in 1888 became *The Argosy*, a successful magazine for adults, and in 1920 *The Argosy All-Story Weekly*. In 1889 he founded *Munsey's Weekly*, later called *Munsey's Magazine*. In 1929 this was merged with *Argosy All-Story*. *The All-Story Magazine* had been founded in 1904. In 1906 Munsey founded the *Railroad Man's Magazine*. In 1891 he purchased the New York *Star*, renamed it the *Daily Continent*, and published it, unsuccessfully, as a pioneer tabloid. Later he bought the Baltimore *News* (1908), the New York *Press* (1912), the New York *Sun* in both editions (1916), the New York *Herald*, the New York *Telegram* (1920), and newspapers in Washington and Boston. Although Munsey's habit of buying and then selling or killing distinguished newspapers earned him strong disapproval among journalists, these tactics soon became standard as newspapers came to be regarded as big business.

While he kept them, Munsey's papers lacked distinction and were devoted to an uninspired support of conservatism.

Munsey wrote novels, some of them stories for boys. Among them are *Afloat in a Great City* (1887), *The Boy Broker* (1888), *Derringforth* (1894), and *A Tragedy of Errors* (1899). He also wrote *The Founding of the Munsey Publishing House* (1907).

Munsey's Magazine.   See FRANK A. MUNSEY.

Munson, Gorham   (1896–1969),   critic, editor, teacher, writer. Munson was on the staff of various publishing firms and engaged extensively in economic journalism. He founded *Secession* in 1922, an avant-garde magazine that printed poems by HART CRANE, E. E. CUMMINGS, MARIANNE MOORE, and many other experimental writers of the 1920s. He founded and edited a fortnightly, *New Democracy* (1933–1936), devoted to the advancement of Social Credit, an economic theory holding that the world's ills can be cured by public control of credit. Munson also wrote many critical articles and published numerous volumes of criticism. For over two decades he gave a popular course in creative writing at the New School for Social Research in New York City. Among his books are *Waldo Frank: A Study* (1923), *Robert Frost: A Study in Sensibility and Good Sense* (1927), *Destination: A Canvass of American Literature Since 1900* (1928), *Style and Form in American Prose* (1929), *Dilemma of the Liberated* (1930), *Twelve Decisive Battles of the Mind* (1942), *Aladdin's Lamp: The Wealth of the American Nation* (1945), *The Written Word* (1949), *The Writer's Workshop Companion* (1951), and *Penobscot: Down East Paradise* (1959).

Murat, [Napoleon] Achille, Prince   (1801–1847), elder son of Joachim Murat (1767–1815). Joachim, a French soldier who married Napoleon's sister Marie Annunciata, was made King of Naples, and was executed by the Allies after Waterloo. Achille Murat emigrated to America in 1821. He settled in Florida, became a citizen, was appointed postmaster at Lipona, practiced law, and served in the militia in the Seminole War. He published three books about the United States: *Lettres sur les États-Unis* (1830); *Esquisse Morale et Politique des États-Unis* (1832, in English, *America and the Americans*, 1849); and *Exposition des Principes du Gouvernement Républicain, Tel Qu'il A Eté Perfectionné en Amérique* (1833). He was a keen observer and especially useful in presenting a picture of the South. He has figured in American literature principally because of his friendly correspondence with Emerson after the latter visited the South during the winter of 1826–27. A. J. Hanna wrote *A Prince in Their Midst: The Adventurous Life of Achille Murat on the American Frontier* (1946).

Murder in the Cathedral (1935),   a play in verse by T. S. ELIOT. This was Eliot's first completed drama and remains his most popular, although he expressed dissatisfaction with it. It is a work in the full tradition of the modern lyric theater, employing a herald, a lyric chorus, a cast of symbolical personages, and passages in poetry alternating with others in prose. It was written for performance in a church and is a favorite work for church theatrical groups. An operatic ver-

sion, *Assassinio nella Cathedrale*, composed by Ildebrando Pizzetti in 1958, was well received; an earlier film version (1952) was not.

The action of the drama depicts the last weeks in the life of Thomas à Becket; the quarrel between church and state is the main theme. Four Tempters, representing youthful love of pleasure, yearning for power, desire for the company of wealthy men, and pride as a longing for martyrdom, importune Becket, but he rejects all four and emphasizes his wish to serve the Law of God rather than the Law of Man. Four knights, perhaps reincarnations of the Four Temptations, carry out the assassination ordered by Henry II, justifying themselves in speeches.

Both Greek and medieval antecedents are observable in the play, but it remains thoroughly modern in tone and techniques and exhibits many of the rhythms and characteristic turns of speech of Eliot's lyric verse. Whereas in his later works for the stage Eliot moved closer to the techniques of the naturalistic theater, *Murder in the Cathedral* is drawn with an ideal visual and poetic simplicity that lends it great force and a classical somberness of movement.

Murders in the Rue Morgue, The   (*Graham's Magazine*, April 1841, reprinted in *Prose Romances*, 1843, and in *Tales*, 1845), a story by EDGAR ALLAN POE. Poe emphasizes the detector, or detective, as well as the crime, and makes the interest depend on analysis rather than guesswork. In the original draft it was called *Murders in the Rue Trianon*. The plot deals with the brutal murders of a mother and a daughter. The police are baffled, but C. AUGUSTE DUPIN, like innumerable amateur detectives to follow, is able to put the police on the track of an extraordinary solution of the crime. To stories of this type Poe gave the designation, "tales of ratiocination." He regarded *The Murders* as one of his best stories.

Murdoch, Frank Hitchcock (1843–1872),   actor, playwright. Born in Massachusetts, Murdoch played in juvenile and light-comedy productions. He wrote several striking plays, none ever published. The best, produced shortly before his death, was *Davy Crockett* (1872), highly successful. The leading role was taken by FRANK MAYO, who helped write the play. Murdoch also wrote *Light House Cliffs* (probably produced in 1870); *Bohemia, or The Lottery of Art* (1872); and *Only a Jew* (1873).

Murfree, Mary Noailles ["Charles Egbert Craddock"] (1850–1922),   short-story writer, novelist. Born in Murfreesboro, Tennessee, Murfree lived most of her life in Tennessee. She published her first stories as R. Emmet Denbry, a pseudonym she later changed to Charles Egbert Craddock, the name of one of her characters. A collection of stories, IN THE TENNESSEE MOUNTAINS (1884), one of the first realistic treatments of the southern mountaineer, presented a detailed picture of the people and region. *The Prophet of the Great Smoky Mountains* (1885), considered her best novel, deals with the enormous Cayce family; their daughter Dorinda, a beautiful girl; and the prophet, a local preacher who sacrifices his life to save a *revenooer*. Like Murfree's other works, *The Prophet* is full of poetic description, picturesque language, and difficult orthography. It was followed by *Down the Ravine* (1885), a juvenile; In the *"Stranger People's" Country* (1891); *The Mystery of Witchface Mountain and Other Stories* (1895); and half a dozen other local-color books. She also wrote a series of Southern historical novels, among them *Where the Battle was Fought* (1884), *The Story of Old Fort Loudon* (1889), and *The Frontiersman* (1904).

Murray, Albert (1916–   ),   novelist, essayist, intellectual historian. Born in Nokomis, Alabama, Murray attended Tuskegee Institute as well as New York University, the University of Michigan, Northwestern and the University of Paris. He served nearly two decades in the United States Air Force, retiring in 1962 as a major. An essay collection *The Omni-Americans: New Perspectives on Black Experience and American Culture* (1970) gained him recognition for his argument that African-American culture is unique and not a substandard version of white culture. He angered some people by insisting that the use of identifying nouns that emphasize unrealistic skin color—like black and white—exacerbates prejudice; he prefers "colored" or "Negro" as racial designations. His interest in music is shown in such essay collections as *The Hero and the Blues* (1973), *Stomping the Blues* (1976) and *The Blue Devils of Nada* (1996) as well as in his work with Count Basie on the musician's autobiography *Good Morning Blues* (1985). Other nonfiction includes *South to a Very Old Place* (1972). His novel trilogy about a boy growing up in the deep South shows influence of his own experience. The first, *Train Whistle Guitar* (1974) covers the childhood of a character called Scooter, and the influence of teachers and barbershop philosophers. *The Spyglass Tree* (1991) follows Scooter to a school similar to Tuskegee, and the concluding volume *The Seven League Boots* (1996) finds the protagonist a successful jazz musician and lover of beautiful women. Race is not a major theme in these novels; the characters surmount segregation coolly, demonstrating the author's unwillingness to relinquish "the human proposition underlying the American promise" by accepting any racial limits.

Murray, Judith Sargent (1751–1820),   essayist, playwright, poet. Born in Gloucester, Massachusetts, Judith Sargent was educated at home along with her brother Winthrop, until he went to Harvard College, where she could not follow. At eighteen, she married Captain John Stevens, a merchant seaman, who built her a mansion in Gloucester. Stevens went bankrupt during the Revolution, and in 1786 he escaped his creditors, fled to the West Indies without his wife, and died there. Under the pseudonym "Constantia," she published (1784) her first essay "Desultory Thoughts upon the Utility of Encouraging a Degree of Self-Complacency, Especially in Female Bosoms." The widow married Reverend John Murray in 1788. Her best known essay "On the Equality of the Sexes" was written in 1789, the same year her first child was born and died. Her poem, "Lines, Occasioned by the Death of an Infant" appeared in the January 1790 issue of the new *Massachusetts Magazine*. Subsequent issues printed poems written fifteen years earlier, at the start of the Revolutionary War. Poems and

essays, sometimes under the pseudonym Mr. Virgilius the Gleaner, continued to appear in the same magazine, along with prologues or epilogues to plays which could not be commercially performed because of the Commonwealth's law against playacting. The law was repealed in 1793, the same year the Murrays moved to Boston, where the new Federal Street Theater was calling for original dramas by American writers. Mrs. Murray's first play, *The Medium or, The Happy Tea-Party* was presented in March of 1795. *The Traveler Returned*, her second and final play appeared the next year. Her writings were collected in *The Gleaner* (3 v. 1798). She edited her husband's letters and sermons in three volumes, and wrote the last three chapters and supervised the publication of his autobiography, *Records of the Life of John Murray* (1816) after his death. Aside from a few verses published in the *Boston Weekly Magazine* from 1802 to 1805, Murray's literary life was over. She died at the home of her married daughter in Natchez, Mississippi.

Murrieta [or Murieta], Joaquin (1829?–1853), miner, bandit. Born in Mexico, he mined in the California gold fields from 1849 to 1851. When he and his family were mistreated and driven from their claim, he became the leader of a gang of outlaws. After two years of robberies and murders, the legislature authorized a deputy sheriff to hunt him down, and he was shot in his camp at Tulare Lake. The publication of JOHN R. RIDGE's *The Life and Adventures of Joaquin Murieta* (1854) was the first step in a process of turning him into a legendary romantic figure. Cincinnatus Hiner Miller, the poet, changed his name to JOAQUIN MILLER in Murrieta's honor.

Musser, Benjamin [Francis] (1889–1951),   poet, essayist, critic. Born in Lancaster, Pennsylvania, Musser was converted to Catholicism in 1908. He wrote on *Franciscan Poets* (1933), was cofounder (1931) of *The Trend*, and contributed to many of the little magazines. *Chiaroscuro*, his first book of verse, appeared in 1923. Thereafter, he published more than forty volumes, many of them collections of his own verse. *Selected Poems* was published in 1930, *Poems* in 1930–33. His writings were always marked by gentleness and love of mankind.

Mutiny on the Bounty (1932),   a novel by JAMES NORMAN HALL and CHARLES NORDHOFF. This vivid narrative is based on the mutiny by the crew of a British war vessel carried out in 1787 against a cruel commander, Captain William Bligh. The authors kept the historical characters and background, using as narrator an elderly man, Captain Roger Byam, who had served as a midshipman on the *Bounty*. The book was followed by two others, forming a trilogy: *Men Against the Sea* (1934), telling how Bligh and seventeen others were set adrift in an open boat, and *Pitcairn's Island* (1934), telling of the mutineers' life on a tiny Pacific island for twenty years.

The idea for a book on the famous mutiny had occurred to Hall as far back as 1916 when he was browsing in a Paris bookstore. He and Nordhoff read contemporary accounts of Captain Bligh and his voyage over 3,600 miles of sea in an open boat, also of the arrest, trial, and execution of the mutineers.

Hall wrote the English, Nordhoff the Polynesian chapters, but each contributed heavily to the work of the other. In 1935 a movie version of the book was made.

Muybridge, Eadweard [originally Edward James Muggeridge] (1830–1904), photographer. Muybridge came to the United States from England as a boy and made photography his lifework. He helped the U.S. Coast and Geodetic Survey, specialized in photographs of animals in motion, and published *The Horse in Motion* (1878) and *Animal Locomotion* (1887). Sections of the latter were reprinted in 1955 as *The Human Figure in Motion*. He invented the zoopraxiscope, an early movie projector.

My Ántonia (1918), a novel by WILLA CATHER. One of the most successful realistic portrayals of the Midwest, this novel tells the story of an immigrant Bohemian farm family in Nebraska, especially the fortunes of Ántonia Shimerda, a daughter of the family. She longs for a life of greater sensitivity than she finds on the farm. She escapes to a town, is betrayed by a philanderer, bears an illegitimate child, and finally returns to the farm and marries a fellow immigrant, Anton Cuzak. *My Ántonia* is notable particularly for its lucid and moving depictions of the prairie and the people who live close to it—the farmers whose lives are controlled by storm and drought and the spring rains.

My Aunt (*New England Magazine*, October 1831), a humorous poem by OLIVER WENDELL HOLMES. Holmes mingles mild ridicule with kindly sentiment in this account of an unmarried member of his family. It affords an amusing sidelight on oldtime education for girls of good family.

Myers, Gustavus (1872–1942), historian, reformer. Born in New Jersey, Myers is best known for his attack on political bossism, *The History of Tammany Hall* (1901, rev. 1917). He wrote a similar muckraking expose of financiers in *History of the Great American Fortunes* (1910). Other subjects he treated include the Supreme Court and bigotry.

Myers, Peter Hamilton (1812–1878), lawyer, writer. Born in Herkimer, New York, Myers practiced law in Brooklyn and was active as a writer in his earlier years. He began with a poem, *Ensenore* (1840), reprinted many years later in *Ensenore and Other Poems* (1875). In 1848 he published anonymously *The First of the Knickerbockers: A Tale of 1673*, followed by *The Young Patroon, or, Christmas in 1690* (1849) and *The King of the Hurons* (1850), both also anonymous. *The King* was reprinted in England as *Blanche Montaigne: The Prisoner of the Border* (1857).

My Friend Flicka. See MARY O'HARA.

My Heart and My Flesh (1927), a novel by ELIZABETH MADOX ROBERTS. This novel of the New South anticipated Faulkner in some of its episodes and attitudes but found a gentler and more conventional solution for its problems. The story concerns the three love affairs of Theodosia, whose father has given her two mulatto half sisters. Her first lover is burned to death, and her second deserts her. Only with the third, a simpleminded, honest cattle rancher, does she find peace. Some of the dialogue appears in the form of speeches, as in a play.

My Kinsman, Major Molineaux (*The Token*, 1832, collected in THE SNOW IMAGE AND OTHER TWICE-TOLD TALES, 1851), a story by NATHANIEL HAWTHORNE. Young Robin comes to Boston in the hope that his uncle, an influential man, will help him get started on his career. The very evening he arrives in town the citizens are preparing to tar and feather Major Molineaux, but until the end Robin remains ignorant of this fact and merely persists in trying to find out where his uncle lives. Hawthorne stresses the irony of the situation, and nothing but disappointment and disillusionment befall Robin.

My Lady Pocahontas: A True Relation of Virginia (1885), a novel by JOHN ESTEN COOKE. Elaborating on the Pocahontas story, Cooke describes the rescue of John Smith by Pocahontas, the supposed death of Smith, Pocahontas's marriage to John Rolfe and their trip to England—where POCAHONTAS finds that Smith is still alive—and the death of the Indian princess. An effective series of scenes involves Shakespeare and a performance of *The Tempest*, a play that may have been suggested to Shakespeare by incidents in the settlement of the New World.

My Life Is Like the Summer Rose (1819), a poem by RICHARD HENRY WILDE. Wilde wrote this song as part of an epic on the Seminole War, *The Lament of the Captive*. The song was published without his consent or knowledge and was reprinted all over the country. Then an Irish poet named Daniel O'Kelly and other poets claimed its composition, and it was even attributed to the ancient Greek poet Alcaeus. In 1834, in the first issue of the *Southern Literary Messenger*, the poem was definitely assigned to Wilde. It was set to music by Charles Thibault in 1822 and was popular as a song. Other musical settings included one, never published, by Sidney Lanier.

My Lost Youth (1855), a poem by HENRY WADSWORTH LONGFELLOW. Written in stanzas of nine lines, this lyric tells of the author's boyhood in Portland, Maine. It describes Portland's history and countryside, more particularly its ships and harbor. The poem contains the well-known nostalgic refrain, "A boy's will is the wind's will, / And the thoughts of youth are long, long thoughts." Robert Frost's *A Boy's Will* derived its title from the Longfellow poem.

My Old Kentucky Home (1853), a song by STEPHEN FOSTER, for which he wrote both lyrics and melody. It is considered second in popularity to Foster's OLD FOLKS AT HOME.

My Playmate (1860), a poem by JOHN GREENLEAF WHITTIER. *My Playmate* was called by Tennyson "a perfect poem; in some of his descriptions of nature and wild flowers, Whittier would rank with Wordsworth." The poet recalls childhood days spent with a playmate who has been identified as Mary Emerson Smith, whom Whittier later wanted to marry.

Myrer, Anton (1922–1996), novelist. Born in Worcester, Massachusetts, Myrer was enrolled at Harvard University when World War II erupted; he enlisted in the Marine Corps, imbued with the "concept of this country's destiny as the leader of a free world and the necessity of the use of armed force." His service in the Pacific (1942–1946) left him with the "angry awareness of war as the most vicious and fraudulent self-deception man had ever devised." Returning to finish school and graduate *magna cum laude* (1947), Myrer was soon at work on his first war novel *Evil Under the Sun* (1951). Other anti-war fictions followed, but it was his fifth publication, *Once an Eagle* (1968) that made his reputation. Sam Damon, the protagonist of the book, and his nemesis Courtney Massengale, are well known to military readers and the book has often been reprinted on the basis of demand for it as required reading in military school ethics and leadership classes. Sam Damon is a hard-fighting commander whose prime concern is the welfare of his troops. He dies trying to convince his superiors to keep out of the Vietnam War, and his dying advice, ". . . If it comes to a choice between being a good soldier and a good human being—try to be a good human being . . ." is prized by top brass. Other titles include *The Big War* (1957), *The Violent Shore* (1962), *The Intruder* (1965), *The Tiger Waits* (1973), and *The Last Convertible* (1978), about forty years of friendship among Harvard classmates.

Mysterious Stranger, The (written 1898, pub. 1916), a story by MARK TWAIN. Toward the end of his life Mark Twain reached a pessimism and fatalism that found voice in this story, published posthumously. The scene is Eseldorf (Jackass Village), Austria, in 1590. The narrator is a teen-age boy who is sitting on a hillside with two friends when a well-dressed young man of pleasing face and easy manners makes friends with them. It turns out that the young man is Satan, and he tells the three friends that his name on earth is Philip Traum (dream). The boy is a willing listener to the strange ideas of Satan, since he himself has been revolted by the cruelties of life and the burning of witches. Satan denounces morals as the cause of wars and inequalities, tells the boys there is no heaven or hell, shows his kindness by killing a boy who is a hopeless cripple, insists that everything one sees or knows is an illusion, completely upsets the ideals the boys have cherished—and then disappears.

The story is an expression, the bitterest in all his writings, of Twain's feeling about "the damned human race" and about religion. It also expresses Twain's delight in antique speech and in the pomp and ornament of chivalry, and his indignation against churches and monarchies. An unpublished version of the story was laid in Hannibal, Missouri.

Mystery of Marie Rogêt, The (published in *Snowden's Ladies' Companion*, November and December 1842–February 1843; later in Poe's *Tales*, 1845),   a story by EDGAR ALLAN POE. Poe's THE MURDERS IN THE RUE MORGUE, the first detective story, had attracted so much attention when it was published in 1841 that Poe looked around for a successor to the tale. He found one in the murder of Mary Rogêt, a beautiful girl of indifferent morals who had worked in a cigar store on lower Broadway in New York City and whose body had been found floating in the Hudson River on July 28, 1841. Poe read all the details he could find, transferred the scene to Paris, again enabled his detective C. AUGUSTE DUPIN to show his contempt for the police, and gave his own theory of the murder.

mystery stories.   See DETECTIVE FICTION.

N

Nabokov, Vladimir (1899–1977), novelist, short-story writer, poet, scholar. Son of a distinguished Russian jurist who would become cabinet secretary for the Provisional Government formed after the February Revolution of 1917, Nabokov spent most of his early summers on the family's country estate fifty miles south of his native St. Petersburg. There began his long preoccupation with lepidoptery, which, like his interest in chess, would find reflection in his literary work. From 1913 to 1916 he attended the liberal Tenishev school in St. Petersburg. At seventeen he published his first collection of verse. He was hurt by its cold reception in literary circles, yet he continued to write poetry, in Russian and later also in English, throughout his life. His prose showed the translucent euphoric quality of poetry, its subtle cadences and complex suggestiveness of connotation.

After the Bolshevik coup of October 1917, the Nabokovs stayed in the Crimea until they left by sea in 1919, just before the Red Army overran the peninsula. The family settled in Berlin, but Nabokov was sent to study at Cambridge. In 1922, while presiding over a meeting, his father was killed as he shielded a speaker with his own body from a militant monarchist's bullet. Some of the most poignant pages of Nabokov's autobiographical work *Speak, Memory* (revised edition 1966), are devoted to the extraordinary personality of his father. After completing his degree, Nabokov returned to Berlin, which then competed with Paris in importance as a major enclave of Russian emigrants. In 1925 he married Vera Evseevna Slonim, and their son Dmitri was born in 1934. To help "keep body and pen together," Nabokov gave English and tennis lessons, wrote a weekly review column, and composed crossword puzzles for an émigré newspaper. He published his Russian-language works—plays, poems, short stories, and novels—under the name V. Sirin. Many years afterward, having settled in the U.S., he supervised the translation of most of his novels and short stories into English, often making substantial revisions in the process.

A few years before the outbreak of World War II Nabokov underwent a radical artistic transformation. In 1936 he translated his novel *Despair* into English—owing to a British governess, English had been his first literary language. In 1938, he translated his *Kamera Obscura* for publication in America,

turning it into the heavily revised *Laughter in the Dark*. These trial runs encouraged him to write his first novel in English, *The Real Life of Sebastian Knight*. By 1940, with his wife and child, Nabokov had sailed to America from France—on the eve of the Nazi invasion. In the U.S. he became a college teacher of literature, the most important of his academic positions being his appointment at Cornell. He left it in 1959, when the success of *Lolita* enabled him to devote himself entirely to his literary work, and moved to Switzerland in order to be closer to his sister and his son, who was making a career as an opera singer in Italy. From then on Nabokov and his wife lived in Montreux, in the vicinity of Alpine butterfly haunts.

Early critics of Nabokov's work tended to regard him as a brilliant yet cold virtuoso aesthetician; later criticism recognized the profoundly humanist concerns of his work. One of the most frequently recurrent themes of Nabokov's fiction is that of the tension between artistic or metaphysical pursuits and moral commitments. His first novel, *Mary* (1926, tr. 1970) embodies this conflict in a clash between the moral and the aesthetic levels of significance attached to the protagonist's choices. *King, Queen, Knave* (1928, tr. 1968), an intricate web of cross references, recurrent images, and vibrant lyrical passages alternating with merciless satire, is based on a witty variation on the classical adultery triangle. It examines the banal uncreative modes of living which, under the influence of lust and greed, lead to a murder conspiracy. This novel also initiates the Nabokovian theme of the artist as an authentic individual, whether he is a businessman, a scholar, or, as in *The Defense* (1930, tr. 1964), a chess player. The artist, however, is not exempt from error: Grandmaster Luzhin of *The Defense* turns away from a painful chaotic reality to the involute harmonies of chess, only to have reality avenge itself on him. The structure of this novel bears affinities to that of chess puzzles, but despite its intricacy, *The Defense* is among the most touching of Nabokov's works.

Tension between a person's inner and outer life is explored in Nabokov's short novel *The Eye* (1930, tr. 1965), and again, from a different angle, in *Glory* (1932, tr. 1971). In *Glory* the protagonist, is a keenly sensitive, poetic, well-meaning young man who asserts his victory over fear in practically futile yet poetically meaningful acts, nevertheless emerging as an egotist whose misdirected private metaphysical pursuits encroach on his commitments to others.

Kamera Obscura (1932, tr. *Laughter in the Dark*, 1938) is another intricate variation on the adultery plot. Here, however, the pursuit of a sexual phantom replaces the transcendental quest, suppressing the protagonist's better impulses and feelings and placing him at the mercy of the greedy and sadistic young woman whose face seems to bear marks of his spurious ideal of beauty. The texture of this novel is closely related to cinematographic images and techniques of the early 1930s, but the darkness of the title refers, among other things, to the dampening of human sympathies that occurs both on the level of the plot and on that of reader response.

In *Despair* (1934, revised translation 1965) the theme of a metaphysical mistake is transformed into that of the error of an evil mind. This is a story of a deranged murderer who thinks of himself as an artist and despairs on discovering that the execution of his crime has fallen short of desired perfection. In Nabokov's code, murder is the polar opposite of an act of artistic creation and is the worst possible crime. The novel has a pronounced anti-Dostoevskian drive: the grimness of the crime at the center of the plot conflicts with the relative lightness of the protagonist-narrator's tone. This suggests that the distinctive feature of the modern type of murder is the callousness rather than the cruelty of the perpetrator. The novel shows how pseudoaesthetic considerations can be used to blot out the possibility of moral constraints.

In 1935, responding to the political climate of Germany and, perhaps, to whatever information about Stalin's regime making its way from Russia, Nabokov, in a powerful burst of inspiration, created a surrealistic dystopia entitled *Invitation to a Beheading* (tr. 1959). The world of this novel is dominated by a prison fortress in which the protagonist, Cincinnatus—Nabokov's Everyman—spends the days between his death sentence and execution. His crime, variously explained in the novel, consists in his having preserved his individuality in a grotesque version of a totalitarian state where everyone is supposed to be transparent. Written in highly evocative and at times hilariously witty prose that unfolds different layers of meaning—political, metaphysical, aesthetic—this polyphonic narrative satirizes the banal languages of private and public communication—totalitarianism disseminates banality—shows their connection with atrocities, and paints the portrait of an artist as a young man who strives to preserve his values and his inner freedom.

Invitation provides a clue to most of Nabokov's works by showing how, in a world made up of the words of others, the style of one's discourse may be a measure and an assertion of freedom of perception and thought. The novel is characterized by a limpid flexibility of prose that matches Shelleyan feats of arresting the elusive by translexical devices that almost break out from the prison of language to capture mystical moments. Extended anacoluthon structure combines with occasional ornateness. Labyrinthine literary reminiscences reinterpret

their sources. Parodies of other texts intertwine with original discourse—balancing on the edge of self-parody in its gusto. Tongue-in-cheek pedantry alternates with alphabetic iconism and chameleonic gliding. And all this occurs within the same sentence or paragraph, between echoes of different stylistic registers or literary genres. The cumulative effect of these techniques is the sense of carefully treasured spiritual freedom.

Such an inner freedom, not necessarily related to outward moral autonomy, is celebrated with particularly frank vigor in Nabokov's last novel written in Russian, *The Gift* (censored serialized version 1937–38, full version 1952). The major significance of this book in Nabokov's work lies in its telling the story of a young émigré writer's apprenticeship in such a way as to demonstrate the possibility of achieving a balance between moral commitments and lofty aesthetic pursuits. Among other things, *The Gift* contains beautiful verse passages that graphically merge with the surrounding prose because they are printed without lineation. The rendering of these passages in the 1963 English version (on which Nabokov collaborated with Michael Scammell) is one of the greatest feats of translation.

The composition of Nabokov's first English-language novel, *The Real Life of Sebastian Knight* (1941), was completed in 1940 on European soil. The epistemological concerns of this book enter into a complex interplay with the problem of moral insight. The plot is based on a young Russian gentleman's attempt to understand the life of a recently dead English novelist who is his half brother. *Sebastian Knight* is now one of the most widely read of Nabokov's novels, but the author seems to have been vaguely dissatisfied with it and to have reverted, for a while, to writing in Russian. Yet no new Russian novel was ever produced—two chapters were eventually published as fragments, and the remaining material was incorporated into Nabokov's subsequent American fiction.

The American literary scene proved congenial to Nabokov. From the 1940s his fiction gave fuller development to the cautious symbolism, subtle self-referentiality, and Romantic assertion of spiritual autonomy that his work had always displayed and that now brought him within the framework of the tradition shaped by Hawthorne and Melville. Apart from the intensification of these tendencies, no pronounced turning point occurred to match the language switch. The first book Nabokov wrote on American soil was the critical biography *Nikolai Gogol* (1944), an answer to the brilliantly iconoclastic biography of the 19th-century literary and social critic N. G. Chernyshevski written, as it were, by the protagonist of *The Gift*. Likewise, *Bend Sinister* (1947), for all its brilliance, is a tortured reply to *Invitation to a Beheading* and bears traces of the author's increasingly painful awareness of Stalin's and, in particular, Hitler's atrocities. Nabokov was deeply troubled by the death of his younger brother at the hands of the Nazis in occupied France, as well as by newly received information about the Holocaust. Symbolically, the protagonist of his *Lolita* spends the wartime years shuttling in and out of psychiatric wards.

Nabokov's *Lolita* places in an American setting the theme of pedophilia he had explored in his 1939 novella *The Enchanter* (published in the English translation in 1986) and develops it into a story of a perverse obsession that turns into a true though belated love. When the novel was completed in 1954, several American publishers turned it down. It first came out in 1955 between the rather disreputable green covers of the French Olympia Press. The literary value of the book was immediately recognized by great numbers of readers, and its shock value by even greater numbers. In fact, Nabokov has called attention to that stage in a little girl's life when inexperience joined with the keen sensitivity and intensity of the transition period make her particularly vulnerable. Yet, he is also held responsible for giving shape to one of the myths of modern culture, the myth of the nymphet, a mystically attractive preadolescent girl. While the smooth physique of childhood, on the verge of yielding its place to adult looks, seems to be a precious and fleeting visitation of transcendent beauty—the pedophiliac protagonist of *Lolita* endows this effect with a demoniacally sexual significance. The book shows how a mystical image projected on a flesh-and-blood child diverts Humbert Humbert from the moral attention he owes Dolly Haze to an unappeasable sexual desire for her. Faced with the effect of this desire on Dolly's fate, Humbert eventually gives up his attempts to explain away its criminality.

Like most of Nabokov's novels, *Lolita* is a vertiginous aesthetic maze constructed out of lyrical and satiric descriptions, lively double-talk, literary allusions, philosophical issues, tortured wit, and sad wisdom. Its ornate sophistication is enhanced in order to demonstrate Humbert's deliberate distancing of moral consciousness. Humbert believes that the demoniac qualities of nymphets as well as the metaphysical dimension of his lust absolve him from restraints. Between the lines of his first-person narrative, however, the novelist presents young Dolly Haze as a tough yet sensitive teenager caught up in circumstances that foster misplaced dreams, a misguided sense of honor, and a misconceived sense of security—a predicament that turns her into the pervert's victim. The satire on artificial cultural stereotypes from which Dolly eventually breaks away is lined with tragedy. One of the most touching episodes of the novel is the account in a kind of epilogue of the way Dolly rejects middle-class glamour and tries to cope with the genuine realities of existence.

In the intervals of his work on *Lolita* Nabokov wrote chapters of what in 1957 would come out as his novel PNIN. This story of a Russian émigré professor's life in America is, in many ways, Nabokov's meta-novel, though autodescriptive remarks are scattered throughout his fiction. Despite the dandyish narrator's implicit disdain for human interest, the book paints a loving paradox-laden portrait of an eccentric individual whose emotional plight—in an alien culture he respects and a beautiful world in which terrible things have but recently happened—stands for general human experience in postcataclysmic years.

PALE FIRE (1962), written in Switzerland, is set in an American university town—and in the imaginary country of Zembla. It consists of a 999-line poem by an academic poet John Shade; an introduction written by the editor, Shade's neighbor and colleague, Charles Kinbote; and lengthy annotations that have far less to do with the poem than with the editor's fantasy life. It is never made completely clear how much of the material is invented by Kinbote, or by Shade, and how much is supposed to have actually happened. The novel does not sanction any unambiguous interpretation of its structure, let alone of its themes: Nabokov reality makes sense only within inverted commas and a literary work is part of this reality and therefore cannot be objectively and univocally described. The structure of a literary artifact is as much a matter of personal perspective as any social, political, or aesthetic issue in the modern world. And yet the ambiguities do not extend to the ethical distinctions that run through the text of Nabokov's novels.

The basic pattern of *Pale Fire* involves an element of self-parody: while working on it Nabokov was also completing his literal translation of Pushkin's *Eugene Onegin*, preceded by an extended introduction, and followed by three volumes of comments and two appendices—"Notes on Prosody" and an essay on Pushkin's black great grandfather, "Abram Gannibal." In addition to being a major contribution to scholarship, this monumental work, published in 1964 (revised 1975), contains portions that—like parts of Nabokov's posthumously published lectures and letters—are valuable as literary works in their own right.

Nabokov's last three novels use different versions of the international situation to explore new facets of the relationship between moral commitments and aesthetic or metaphysical pursuits. *Ada, or Ardor* (1969) is set, as it were, on an imaginary planet, Antiterra, where the counterpart of the U.S. is an Anglo-Russian society with some francophone citizens, while the counterpart of the USSR is given the Swiftean name of Tartary. Luscious imagery dominated by the vision of an Edenic garden of childhood and an aesthetic sophistication that surpasses Humbert Humbert's serve the protagonist-narrator as means of distancing the pain which his love for his sister has inflicted on most other people around them. In *Transparent Things* (1972), a young American goes to Switzerland to face his own tragedy as a man who allows his talent to be wasted on humdrum tasks, storing up a tinderbox of unexpended psychic energy. *Look at the Harlequins!* (1974) is a story of a Russian émigré writer who becomes an American novelist and whose books seem to be inferior versions of Nabokov's own novels—inferior because, it seems, he neglects one of the hardest problems faced by a creative artist, the problem of moral commitment, of moral attention that might disrupt his absorption in his work yet perhaps ultimately makes his work all the more genuine.

Just before his death Nabokov was working on a manuscript provisionally entitled "The Original of Laura." The manuscript is preserved in the shape of index cards in a box: Nabokov liked to write his first drafts on many separate cards, using eraser-capped pencils—the graphite, he would say, tended to outlast the erasers.

Each of Nabokov's novels is built on a specific structural principle through which the thematic content and the structure are adjusted to each other, so that the story of the relationship between the reader and the text becomes a modifying commentary on the story of what happens to the characters. The relationship between the moral and the aesthetic thus becomes a matter not only of theme but also of the experience of reading. Though Nabokov rejected much in Plato, in the worlds of his creation, aesthetics correctly understood is inseparable from morality or truth.

While it is helpful to place Nabokov's work on the borderline between MODERNISM and POSTMODERNISM, his refusal to be labeled in terms of literary influences or movements, religious beliefs, and political ideologies must be taken seriously. A master of language games, he was acutely aware of alienating simplifications to which one condemns phenomena of the spiritual life by defining them. His insistence on individual inner freedom and consistency is held in check by constant attempts to transcend the limits of the self, by an eschatological alertness that partakes of gnostic mysticism but cannot be identified with it. His explicit sociopolitical views do not extend beyond an uncompromising condemnation of totalitarian regimes and of the practice of torture. Yet despite this demonstratively apolitical attitude, and despite his preference for personal truth over claims to objectivity, Nabokov's fiction captured some of the crucial processes taking place on, and beneath, the cultural agenda of his times.

There is so far no standard edition of Nabokov's collected works in English. Apart from the books mentioned above, his major works include four collections of short stories: *Nabokov's Dozen: A Collection of Thirteen Stories* (1958), *A Russian Beauty and Other Stories* (1973), *Tyrants Destroyed and Other Stories* (1975), and *Details of a Sunset and Other Stories* (1976); and a collection of poems and chess problems entitled *Poems and Problems* (1970); an important collection of interviews and articles *Strong Opinions* (1973); an innovative translation of Lewis Carroll's *Alice in Wonderland* into Russian (1923); and a precise annotated translation of *The Song of Igor's Campaign* into English (1960). Among posthumous publications are four collections of his college lectures on literature and *Selected Letters* (1989). *Vladimir Nabokov: The Russian Years* (1990) and *Vladimir Nabokov: The Russian Years* (1991), by Brian Boyd, comprise a comprehensive biography. Major critical studies include Michael Wood, *The Magician's Doubts: Nabokov and the Risks of Fiction* (1994); Leona Toker, *Nabokov: The Mystery of Literary Structures* (1989); D. B. Johnson, *Worlds in Regression: Some Novels of Vladimir Nabokov* (1985); Ellen Pifer, *Nabokov and the Novel* (1980); and G. M. Hyde, *Vladimir Nabokov: America's Russian Novelist* (1977).

LEONA TOKER

Nabuco, Joaquim (1849–1910),   Brazilian statesman and writer. The son of a wealthy landowner, Nabuco was a leader in the struggle against slavery, which he combatted by political activity and in writings such as *O abolicionismo* (1883, tr. *Abolitionism: The Brazilian Anti-slavery Struggle*, 1977). After the overthrow of the Brazilian monarchy, Nabuco retired from public life temporarily but later served as ambassador to the U.S. (1905–10). Cosmopolitan in outlook, he spent many years in France and England and was an enthusiastic supporter of the Pan-American movement. His finest literary work is probably his autobiography, *Minha formaçao* (1900), in which he gives a vivid portrait of slaveholding society in 19th-century Brazil.

Naipaul, V[idiadhar] S[urajprasad] (1932–   ), novelist, nonfiction writer. Born in Chaguanas, Trinidad, Naipaul was educated at Oxford. While there, he worked at the BBC as an editor, presented "Caribbean Voices," a weekly literary program, and reviewed books for the *New Statesman*. Knighted by Queen Elizabeth in 1990, Naipaul has made his home in England and devoted his entire life to writing. The winner of many prestigious awards, Naipaul has seen his writings translated into sixteen languages. Thus far Naipaul has produced over twenty books and innumerable articles. His first published novel, *The Mystic Masseur*, appeared in 1957 even though *Miguel Street* (1959) was the first novel he wrote. *A House for Mr. Biswas* (1961), his most acclaimed work, captures the tragedy of the East Indian in the Caribbean. *The Mimic Men* (1967) examines the problems of ex-colonials in the age of independence. *Guerrillas* (1975) and *A Bend in the River* (1979) represent an alienated vision of Third World societies and can be classified as apocalyptic works. *The Enigma of Arrival* (1987), a transparently autobiographical novel, captures the delight Naipaul felt when he accepted England as his second home. *A Way in the World: A Novel* (1994), partly autobiographical links stories examining the colonial and postcolonial history of Trinidad.

Naipaul's nonfiction frees him from his novelistic persona to speak more directly about his world. *The Middle Passage* (1962) records his response to Trinidad after being away for twelve years, and *An Area of Darkness* (1964) records his response after his first visit to India, the home of his grandparents. *The Loss of El Dorado* (1969) penetrates more deeply into Trinidad's history. *India: A Wounded Civilization* (1977) provides an account of his second visit to India. *Among the Believers* (1981) records his repulsion against the rise of Islamic fundamentalism. *Beyond Belief: Islamic Excursions Among the Converted People* (1998) chronicles a trip through non-Arab Islamic countries. *Finding the Center* (1984) and *A Turn in the South* (1989) catalogue Naipaul's final attempt to come to terms with his racial and ethnic past. *India: A Million Mutinies Now* (1990) chronicles a visit.

Naipaul's fiction and nonfiction are a part of the same strand and, as he acknowledged in *The Return of Eva Peron*(1980), the nonfiction sometimes bridges "a creative gap" between the two modes of writing. Perhaps, the best-known writer from the English-speaking Caribbean, Naipaul has been characterized as "one of the finest living novelists writing in English." His other works include *The Suffrage of Elvira* (1958), *Mr. Stone and the Knight's Companion* (1963), *A Flag on the Island* (1967), *In a Free State* (1971), and *The Overcrowded Barracoon and Other Articles* (1972). *Reading & Writing: A Personal Account* (2000) is a brief memoir. G. R. Aitken edited *Between Father and Son: Family Letters* (2000).

SELWYN R. CUDJOE/GP

Naked and the Dead, The (1948),   a novel by NOR-
MAN MAILER about World War II. Set on an island in the South
Pacific, it tells the stories of the American general directing the
invasion; of Lieutenant Hearn, his assistant; and of the men in
the platoon that Hearn takes over after a falling-out with the
general. Through flashbacks into the lives of the dozen or so
major characters, Mailer gives a picture of the America that
went into the war; through the detailed descriptions of fighting and the men under strain he examines the immediate
effects of the war; and finally, in the relationship between
Lieutenant Hearn and the general, he suggests the more subtle
and far-reaching effects of the war on men's minds and personalities. The book is encyclopedic yet particular, both realistic and symbolic. It is one of the best novels by an American
about World War II.

Naked Lunch (Paris 1959, New York 1966),   a book by
WILLIAM S. BURROUGHS that is a montage of fact and fiction
including, in the final version, excerpts from the obscenity trial
conducted to prevent publication of the book in the U.S.

Narragansett Indians,   part of the Algonquin-
Wakashan linguistic stock resident in Rhode Island. Roger
Williams made a study of their language, *Key into the Language
of America* (1634). They were nearly annihilated in a battle
called the Swamp Fight (1675) in King Philip's War.

Narrative of Arthur Gordon Pym, The (1838),   a
novelette by EDGAR ALLAN POE. A Nantucket youth with a passion for the sea stows away on a New Bedford whaler. He helps
suppress a mutiny and survives a storm that leaves only four
men alive. At one point a vessel floats by that is manned only
by dead men—which some may suppose to be a suggestion of
Coleridge's *Ancient Mariner*. In the end two survivors are left
drifting in a canoe toward the South Pole, where a great
human figure, its skin white as snow, stands guard.

The narrative is full of realistic details, and even some of the
names are real. Poe relied on a number of factual accounts of
travel and sea adventures, chiefly on information supplied him
by J. N. Reynolds, whose pamphlet *South Sea Expedition* Poe
had reviewed in the *Southern Literary Messenger* (January
1837). When Poe lay dying in Baltimore, scenes from this story
apparently haunted his last dreams, and he called repeatedly,
"Reynolds! Oh, Reynolds!" in a voice that echoed through the
hospital corridors.

Narrative of Colonel Ethan Allen's Captivity, A
(1779),   by ETHAN ALLEN. Allen told how he and other prisoners of war were mistreated by the British during the Revolution. The book was frequently reprinted and was reproduced
from the original Philadelphia edition, with an introductory
note by John Pell, in 1930.

Narrative of Surprising Conversions (1737),   by
JONATHAN EDWARDS. The actual title of this book was *A Faithful Narrative of the Surprising Work of God in the Conversion of
Many Hundred Souls*. The book was Edwards's account of
some of the manifestations of the GREAT AWAKENING that
began in 1734. The narrative takes the form of a letter to a fellow clergyman of Boston, BENJAMIN COLMAN, and describes

the growth and decline of a spiritual revival in Edwards's own
parish at Northampton and in neighboring towns between
1733 and the spring of 1735. There was, says Edwards, a stirring in the consciences of the young, including a child of four,
who was overheard by her mother in her closet wrestling with
God in prayer, from which she came out crying aloud and
"wreathing her body to and fro like one in anguish of spirit."
He gives other instances of the combination of spiritual exaltation and physical convulsions. But as the fervor of conversion soon began to subside, Edwards laments, "Satan seemed
to be let loose and raged in a dreadful manner." An epidemic
of attempted suicides swept through the community, and
many suffered from strange delusions. Common sense in
time got the upper hand, although Edwards continued to
defend the Awakening in *Some Thoughts Concerning the Present Revival of Religion in New England* (1742). One of ROBERT
LOWELL's most striking poems, *After the Surprising Conversions* (in Lord Weary's Castle, 1946), is based on Edwards's
document.

**Narrative of the Troubles with the Indians in New
England** (1677),   by WILLIAM HUBBARD. Hubbard's book
appeared after KING PHILIP'S WAR had ended, when the people
of New England were still aroused against the Native Americans. But Hubbard, a clergyman, was fair in his treatment and
sought to give a natural rather than a providential explanation
of events. He displayed a similar attitude in his *General History
of New England* (completed 1680, pub. 1815), in which he
ascribes the success of the colonists to their "industry and diligent pains" and to "the salubriousness of the air in this country" as much as to "God's benevolence." His *Narrative* was
reprinted in S. G. Drake's *History of the Indian Wars* (Volume I,
1865).

narratives of captivity.   See INDIAN CAPTIVITY NARRA-
TIVES.

Nasby, Petroleum Vesuvius [pen name of **David Ross
Locke**] (1833–1888),   journalist, editor, political satirist,
humorist. Born in Vestal, New York, Locke at age ten worked as
a printer's devil for the *Cortland Dermocrat* (New York),
became an itinerant printer in his early teens, and at age nineteen founded, with James G. Robinson, the *Plymouth Advertiser* (Plymouth, Ohio). As soon as it was well established he
left to take a position as coeditor of the *Jeffersonian* in Findlay,
Ohio. One evening in 1861 he met the town loafer and drunkard attempting to obtain signatures to a petition advocating
the exile of all African-Americans from the town. The few
families of African-Americans in Findlay were respectable,
industrious citizens, and the irony of the occurrence amused
and angered Locke. A few days later a letter appeared in the *Jeffersonian* signed Petroleum V. Nasby, an alleged Copperhead, a
name destined to become famous. See COPPERHEADS. The letter
was an bitter attack on those whose views paralleled the views
of the town drunkard.

In 1865 Locke became editor, later owner, of the Toledo
Blade, which took over the letters of this unregenerate Copperhead and printed them for the next 16 years. He followed

the type of humor associated with America at this time—bad spelling, worse grammar, braggadocio, hyperbole, and anticlimax. Funny as he seemed to the readers of his day, Nasby was a serious satirical creation. This drunken, bigoted, cowardly advocate of white supremacy and state's rights by espousing the Southern cause made it look ridiculous. Secretary of the Treasury George S. Boutwell publicly attributed the overthrow of the rebels to "the Army and Navy, the Republican Party, and the *Letters of Petroleum V. Nasby*," and Lincoln once opened a Cabinet meeting by reading from Nasby. A large number of collections of Nasby letters appeared between 1864 and 1893, among them *The Nasby Papers* (1864), *Swingin' Round the Cirkle* (1867), *Inflation at the Cross Roads* (1875), *The Diary of an Office Seeker* (1881), and *Nasby in Exile, or, Six Months of Travel* (1882). Cyril Clemens wrote an account of *Petroleum V. Nasby* (1936), as did James C. Austin (1965).

Nash, Ogden (1902–1971),   poet. Nash, born in Rye, New York, worked as a young man as a schoolteacher, editor, bond salesman, and advertising copywriter, but his chief interest was in light verse. He wrote with such winsome outrageousness that he soon became the most popular writer of light verse of his time and by 1935 was able to devote himself entirely to writing. Any subject suited Nash, but he was especially fond of the inanities of modern urban society—his sardonic mood stops just short of helpless exasperation. As a regular contributor to *The New Yorker* in the 1920s and 1930s, he helped establish the tone of sophisticated disaffection identified with it in those days.

Nash's books include *Free Wheeling* (1931), *Hard Lines* (1931), *Happy Days* (1935), *The Bad Parent's Garden of Verse* (1936), *I'm a Stranger Here Myself* (1938), *The Face is Familiar* (1940), *Good Intentions* (1943), *Many Long Years Ago* (1945), *Versus* (1949), *Parents Keep Out: Elderly Poems for Youngerly Readers* (1951), *The Private Dining Room and Other New Verses* (1953), *The Christmas That Almost Wasn't* (1957), *Verses From 1929 On* (1959), and *Boy Is A Boy* (1960). He wrote lyrics for the musical comedies *One Touch of Venus* (1943, with S. J. PERELMAN), and *Two's Company* (1952).

Nashoba Community.   This community of slaves was established at Nashoba, Tennessee, in 1825 by FRANCES [FANNY] WRIGHT. Her intention was to give the slaves a chance to earn their freedom and then colonize them in the West Indies, but when she became ill and had to leave, a free-love scandal brought about a public outcry that doomed the experiment.

Nast, Thomas (1840–1902),   cartoonist, illustrator. Brought to New York City from Germany at age six, Nast began regular work with HARPER's in 1862. At first he turned out sentimental and patriotic pictures, and his first caricature appeared in January 1863. He developed this medium until Thomas Nast and *Harper's* became the greatest power in print of the period. He chastised Andrew Johnson, and supported Grant in two presidential campaigns. The greatest fight of his career was that with the Tweed Ring, which had the finances of New York City completely in its control. Numerous devastat-

ing anti-Tweed cartoons flowed from Nast's pen. The circulation of *Harper's* greatly increased, and ultimately public opinion became informed enough to demand prosecution of Tweed and his associates.

Nast, always conservative and usually Republican, came out strongly against racial prejudice and attacked the income tax, inflation, and reduction of the armed forces. He is credited with having first used the donkey to symbolize the Democratic Party, the elephant for the Republicans, and the tiger (emblem of Tweed's old Americus Fire Company) for Tammany Hall, the Democratic Party club in New York City. He also illustrated books for children and the humorous writings of PETROLEUM V. NASBY.

Nast left *Harper's* in 1886 and tried one paper after another unsuccessfully. With his son he had his own paper—a lifelong ambition—but *Nast's Weekly* was the most dismal failure of all. At last John Hay, Theodore Roosevelt's Secretary of State, offered him a consulship in Guayaquil, Ecuador, in 1902. Nast accepted, but died there of yellow fever within the year. Albert B. Paine wrote his biography (1904).

Natchez, Les (1826),   a romance by FRANÇOIS RENÉ DE CHATEAUBRIAND. This story was originally part of the manuscript that contained the stories of ATALA and "René" and was written between 1797 and 1800. Like the others it was a recollection of his own experiences in America in 1791 and a restatement of his ideas of life under so-called natural conditions. René, the hero, marries Celuta, a Natchez Indian girl. Celuta thinks René has betrayed her tribe and is torn between a conflict of duties, although the real traitor turns out to be someone else. The Natchez massacre of the French settlers in 1729 forms a setting for the story. Some of Chateaubriand's descriptions were based on passages in WILLIAM BARTRAM's *Travels* (1791).

Nathan, George Jean (1882–1958),   drama and social critic, editor, memoirist. Born in Indiana, he was a wise, witty, sardonic drama critic for several magazines and newspapers, notably *The New Yorker*, and collected his more important reviews in yearbooks: *The Theater Books of the Year* (1943–51). He was a colleague of H. L. MENCKEN and WILLARD HUNTINGTON WRIGHT in editing SMART SET during its greatest years, for a time joined Mencken in editing AMERICAN MERCURY, and later founded his own periodical, the *American Spectator*. With Mencken he wrote *Europe After 8:15* (1914) and *The American Credo* (1920). Among his other books are *Mr. George Jean Nathan Presents* (1917), *The Autobiography of an Attitude* (1925), *The World of George Jean Nathan* (1952), and *The Theater in the Fifties* (1953).

Nathan, Robert (1894–1985),   poet, novelist. Born in New York City, Nathan was educated at Harvard and abroad. *Peter Kindred* (1919), a semiautobiographical novel, was followed by *Autumn* (1921), in which he revealed an individual style, poetic, tender, mocking, and occasionally vapid. *The Puppet Master* (1923), *Jonah* (1925), *The Fiddler in Barly* (1926), and *The Woodcutter's House* (1927) are all short novels, but close to poetry. His many other books include *The Bishop's*

Wife (1928); *There Is Another Heaven* (1929); *The Orchid* (1931); *One More Spring* (1933); *The Road of Ages* (1935); *The Enchanted Voyage* (1936); *The Barly Field* (1938), a collection of five early novels; *Tapiola's Brave Regiment* (1941); *But Gently Day* (1943); *Mr. Whittle and the Morning Star* (1947); *Long After Summer* (1948); *River Journey* (1949); *The Innocent Eye* (1951); *Sir Henry* (1955); *So Love Returns* (1958); *The Color of Evening* (1960); *The Wilderness Stone* (1961); and *A Star in the Wind* (1962). Among Nathan's volumes of poetry are *Youth Grows Old* (1922); *The Cedar Box* (1929); *The Winter Tide* (1940); *Dunkirk, A Ballad* (1942); *The Darkening Meadows* (1945); *The Green Leaf* (1950); and *Winter in April* (1958). He also wrote several plays, including *Jezebel's Husband & the Sleeping Beauty* (1953) and *Juliet in Mantua* (1966).

Nation, Carry [Amelia] (1846–1911), temperance agitator. Carry Nation was born in Pope's Landing, Kentucky. As a result of an unfortunate experience with her intemperate first husband, Nation became a violent crusader against liquor. She was often arrested and imprisoned, and became a national figure, storming into saloons with a hatchet and destroying liquor and furnishings. She lectured extensively and gave an account of her life in *The Use and the Need of the Life of Carry A. Nation* (1904). Herbert Asbury (1929), Carleton Beals (1962), and Robert L. Taylor (1966) wrote biographies.

Nation, The. A weekly journal of politics, literature, and the arts, founded by E. L. GODKIN in 1865 and still going. Although it has passed through a number of changes in ownership, *The Nation* has been a consistently liberal and sometimes radical publication; it has numbered among its editors and contributors many of the most distinguished literary figures of the United States. During the 1920s it was one of the few established periodicals open to the new literature, and much important criticism appeared in its pages. During the 1940s and 1950s it lost some of its support among intellectuals when it advocated a policy regarded as too favorable toward the Soviet Union. By 1990 its editorial policy swung noticeably toward a centrist position.

National Anti-Slavery Standard. Founded in 1840, the *Standard* was insistent on immediate abolition of slavery. It won some distinguished contributors. JAMES RUSSELL LOWELL was its editor in 1848 and 1849 and continued to contribute to it until 1852. Some of his BIGLOW PAPERS appeared in its pages. Some of his otherwise uncollected articles have been gathered in W. E. Channing's edition of *The Anti-Slavery Papers of James Russell Lowell* (2 v. 1902). The magazine ceased publication in 1872.

National Book Awards. Awards given annually by American publishers for the best books of the previous year. Two cash awards are presented, one in fiction, one in nonfiction. Established in 1950, they were called the American Book Awards from 1980 to 1986.

National Book Critics' Circle Awards. Established in 1974, these awards are given annually to the best books of the previous year as established by panels of critics and authors. There is one winner in each of five categories: fiction, nonfiction, biography or autobiography, poetry, and criticism.

National Era, The. An important abolitionist periodical, the *National Era* was founded in 1847, flourished vigorously before the war, and expired in 1860. It was edited by Gamaliel Bailey and had as contributors some of the most prominent abolitionists of the time. The most famous of its projects was UNCLE TOM'S CABIN, serialized from June 1851 to April 1852.

National Gazette, The. This pro-Jefferson periodical, edited by PHILIP FRENEAU, engaged in heated controversy during its brief life (1791–93). The *Gazette* expressed opinions in violent opposition to those in the GAZETTE OF THE UNITED STATES, a pro-Hamilton organ edited by John Fenno. The two papers engaged in virulent party abuse, which infected their news reports, editorials, even poems and skits they published. In later years Jefferson asserted that the *Gazette* had "saved our Constitution, which was galloping fast into monarchy." It died when public opinion turned against revolutionary excesses in France.

National Geographic Society, The, and **The National Geographic Magazine**. The Society was founded in 1888 by a group of scientists in Washington, and its membership has grown to almost two million. It has financed expeditions to unexplored and obscure regions of the world, and has made oceanic and cosmic-ray investigations. In its elaborately illustrated monthly *National Geographic Magazine* the beauties and wonders of many lands are described. The Society also prepares superbly drafted maps. A fine history is C. D. B. Bryan, *The National Geographic Society: 100 years of Adventure and Discovery* (1987).

National Institute of Arts and Letters. See AMERICAN ACADEMY OF ARTS AND LETTERS.

National Intelligencer and Washington Advertiser (1800–1870), published as a triweekly at first, it became a daily after 1813. S. H. Smith founded it as a continuation of his *Philadelphia Independent Gazatteer*, a masthead retained as the title of the weekly edition. Its editorial stance favored the administrations of Jefferson, Madison, and Monroe, and it served as the only printed record of Congressional debates until 1825. It suspended publication after the Civil War, and when transplanted to New York in 1870 became a completely different publication.

Native American Humor, 1800–1900 (1937), a history, with many examples, by WALTER BLAIR. Blair's work considers the changing attitudes of humorists toward native comic characters, the changing techniques of humor, and the changing attitudes of readers toward native humor. The range is from the *Farmer's Almanac* to Mr. Dooley, with a full section on Mark Twain.

Native American Prose and Poetry. This nation's first literature originated in the verbal arts of the native peoples who migrated to this continent over 28,000 years ago. When Western Europeans arrived, 18 million people inhabited native North America and 5 million lived in what is now the United States. At the time of contact, the native peoples were divided into more than 300 cultural groups and spoke 200 different languages, plus many dialects, derived from seven basic language families. By 1940, one hundred forty-nine of these languages were still in use.

Native Americans continue to create and perform their oral literatures, which strongly influence their written works. The power of oral tradition is expressed in this song by Big Tree (Kiowa):

They carried dreams in their voices;
They were the elders, the old ones.
They told us the old stories,
And they sang the spirit songs.

Oral literatures reflect the diversity of Native American religious beliefs, social structures, customs, languages, and manners of living. Themes commonly expressed in these literatures include the importance of living in harmony with the physical and spiritual universe, respect for the power of thought and word, reverence for the land, and the need for community and cooperativeness within the tribe.

Although most Native American literatures were transmitted orally, some tribes in North America, such as the Ojibwas and tribes on the Plains and Northwest Coast, made pictographic records. Although traditional ceremonies, myths, and songs follow general patterns established within the group over time, ceremonialists, storytellers, and singers create their own performances within these patterns. The personal style of the performer is important, and significant aspects of style and performance include choice of ritual or ordinary language, use of repetition, structure of the work, revisions of the text to incorporate relevant allusions to the present, appeals to the audience, and use of the performer's voice and body to dramatize content. Audience response is another important dimension.

Oral literatures include such genres as ritual drama— chants, ceremonies, and rituals—as well as narrative, song, and oration. Ritual drama is a sacred form of oral literature that contains both narrative and song and sometimes includes oratory as well. Religious ceremonies express a tribe's attempts to communicate with and to control its spiritual and physical world through the power of the word, whether chanted, sung, or spoken. Ceremonies—and the songs, narratives, and orations included in them—may be expressed in special forms of language. While some are performed seasonally as parts of rituals intended to ensure renewal of the earth or fertile crops, others mark communal events, such as entrance into a tribal society. Many pertain to special occasions in people's life— receiving a name, puberty, marriage, death, and honoring the dead. Ritual dramas are performed by priests or singers, shamans, and social organizations.

Songs constitute the largest part of American Indian oral literatures. Although the performance of songs is generally accompanied by some form of percussion, usually the drum or rattle, musical bows and wind instruments are also used. Some tribes ascribe the origin of songs to such sources as visions of the supernatural, individual creation, or borrowing from other tribes. Composed both communally and individu-

ally, songs may sometimes be the possessions of individuals or families. Sacred songs express the religious rites and supplication of the group. Like other genres of oral literature, they utilize repetition, enumeration, and incremental development, as illustrated in this excerpt from the "Flower Wilderness Song" in *Yaqui Deer Songs*, by Larry Evers and Felipe Molina:

Over there, in the center
of the flower-covered wilderness,
in the enchanted wilderness world,
beautiful with the dawn wind,
beautifully you lie with see-through freshness,
wilderness world

Songs also express the personal experiences of the individual, such as vision or dream, love, personal sorrow or loss, and the singer's own death. Among the special occasions celebrated in song are victory and defeat of individual warriors. Other personal songs include lullabies, women's work songs, hunting songs, and elegies. Others are social songs that are performed for pleasure and have no connection with personal power.

Storytelling has been a major way of entertaining and educating Native Americans in tribal culture. Stories are sometimes divided into those that are true and those that are fictional, the sacred and nonsacred, or some combination of these. Further, stories originally categorized as sacred may sometimes be reclassified as nonsacred. Myths generally describe a world peopled by animals in human form and monstrosities of nature. During the succeeding transformation age, a culture hero or transformer orders the world, turning animal people into animals, and other beings into natural landmarks. This period is followed by the historical age of human memory.

Plots of stories generally are episodic and include considerable humor. Stories often have one-dimensional characters who rarely express thought or emotion and emphasize only the external aspects of behavior necessary to advance the action. Tribes sometimes use archaic language for myths. These narratives usually include stories about the creation of the world, origins and migrations of the tribe, culture heroes, and trickster-transformers. Emergence myths, common in the Southwest, describe the ascent of beings from under the earth to its surface and their subsequent settlement or migration. Movement from an earlier sky world to a water world, accomplished by means of a fall, characterizes the origin stories of the Iroquoian tribes of the Northeastern Woodlands. This myth incorporates the earth-diver motif, which includes a flood that occurred after the creation of the universe and resulted in the re-creation of the present world out of mud brought up from under the water by the earth-diver, often a muskrat or waterfowl.

Also widespread are stories about the culture hero, whose father is divine and mother is a lesser being. The culture hero can be a sly trickster who relies on cunning and tricks to reach his goals, such as getting food or possessing a woman. The trickster is an overreacher who is frequently brought low after a temporary victory. Other motifs often present in Native American myths include star-husband, about an earth woman who yearns to marry a star; Orpheus, concerning the attempts of a spouse or loved one to bring a beloved person back from the world of the dead; animal husband or wife; abduction; and witches and monsters. While myths are true stories of the age before recorded history, tales may be either true or fictional and usually are set in the historical period. They may describe events significant to the history of the tribe, family, or individual.

Oratory has long been a highly regarded skill in many tribes, such as the Iroquois, Sioux, and Pima. Though most Native American orators were men, women sometimes play important roles as speakers. Ceremonies often contain addresses by shamans or priests to the supernatural powers or to the community. Nonceremonial speeches can include those made at council meetings, descriptions of victories over enemies, formal petitions, addresses of welcome, battle speeches to warriors, and statements of personal feeling or experience. Speeches made at meetings of Native Americans and settlers have been a major form of oratory since the arrival of the settlers.

Personal narratives, which achieved considerable popularity during the 19th and early 20th centuries, span both oral and written literatures, incorporating elements of oral storytelling and personal statement as well as narrated life history and written autobiography. Most of the life histories were narrated to translators or collaborators. As Native Americans became educated in the English language and literature, they began to write autobiographies that frequently combined oral history, myths and tales, and personal experience. The first published autobiography was *A Son of the Forest* (1829) by WILLIAM APES (Pequot), which reflects the tradition of the spiritual confessions of the period. Other significant autobiographies written in the 19th century include *The Life, History, and Travels of Kah-ge-ga-gah-bowh* (1847) by GEORGE COPWAY (Ojibwa), which reveals the influence of spiritual confessions and missionary reminiscences, and *Life Among the Piutes* (1883) by SARAH WINNEMUCCA [HOPKINS] (Paiute). Both of these volumes include ethnohistory and personal experience. One of the most widely read autobiographers during the early 20th century was CHARLES EASTMAN (Sioux). His *Indian Boyhood* (1902) chronicles his life to age fifteen, and *From the Deep Woods to Civilization* (1916) describes his experiences in the white world. Both were written with his wife Elaine. Others who wrote autobiographies in the first half of this century include Luther Standing Bear (Sioux), Zitkala-Sa (Sioux), and FRANCIS LA FLESCHE (Omaha). Among those who have recorded their autobiographies more recently are Anna Moore Shaw (Pima), Ted Williams (Tuscarrora), and James McCarthy (Papago). An example of literary autobiography is *Talking to the Moon* (1945) by JOHN JOSEPH MATTHEWS (Osage), whose work is influenced by Osage culture as well as by Thoreau and John Muir. Equally sophisticated are the autobiographies of N.

SCOTT MOMADAY (Kiowa). His *Way to Rainy Mountain* (1969) chronicles the Kiowas' origin and migration to Oklahoma, their life both before and after the reservation period, and his own quest for tribal roots. His *The Names* (1976) is a more conventional autobiography that also traces his maternal ancestry and describes his childhood. *Interior Landscapes* (1990) by GERALD VIZENOR (Ojibwa) recreates his early life, army experiences, and emergence as a writer.

The genre of narrated autobiographies was introduced in *Black Hawk, an Autobiography* (1833), told by BLACK HAWK (Sauk), collected and translated by Antoine Le Claire, and edited in final form by John B. Patterson. A memoir contemporary to Black Hawk's is that of Governor Blacksnake (Seneca), recorded in Seneca-style English by Benjamin Williams and recently edited by Thomas Abler under the title *Chainbreaker* (1989). Twentieth-century Native American narrators who have collaborated with scholars in preparing excellent ethnographic autobiographies include Sam Blowsnake [Big Winnebago and Crashing Thunder] (Winnebago); Mountain Wolf Woman (Winnebago); Maria Chona (Papago); John Stands in Timber (Cheyenne); James Sewid (Kwakiutl); and Left Handed (Navajo). *Me and Mine* (1969), narrated by Helen Sekaquaptewa (Hopi) and written by Louise Udall, typifies the autobiography narrated by the subject to a friend. The most widely read oral life history is *Black Elk Speaks* (1932), narrated by BLACK ELK (Sioux) to author JOHN G. NEIHARDT. Far more literary than other such works, *Black Elk Speaks* records the life and visions of a Sioux holy man in his progress toward becoming a medicine man.

Falling somewhere between narrated and written personal narratives are those recorded in writing by subjects and later edited by scholars. Among these are *The Warrior Who Killed Custer*, recorded in Dakota by Chief White Bull (Sioux) but not published until 1968, and *Sun Chief* (1942), by Don Talayesva (Hopi) and revised and restructured by Leo W. Simmons. Important for the study of Indian women is MOURNING DOVE's autobiography and ethnohistory, edited by Jay Miller and published under the title *Mourning Dove: A Salishan Autobiography*.

The first Native American author to publish in English was SAMSON OCCOM (Mohegan, 1723–1792), who became a missionary to the Indians. His *A Sermon Preached at the Execution of Moses Paul, an Indian* (1772), the first Indian bestseller, reflects the tradition of the execution sermon then so popular in America and exemplified in the work of Increase and Cotton Mather. During the 19th century, many Indians wrote nonfiction prose. William Apes was a forceful writer of Indian protest literature whose works include "The Indian's Looking-Glass for the White Man," appended to the 1833 edition of his *The Experience of Five Christian Indians of the Pequod Tribe*, which charges whites with prejudice against Indians; *Indian Nullification of the Unconstitutional Laws of Massachusetts Relative to the Marshpee Tribe* (1835), which chronicles the attempts of this mixed-blood group of Wampanoags to regain self-government; and *Eulogy on King Philip* (1836), which attacks the inhuman treatment of Native Americans by the Pilgrims.

Many Native Americans in the 19th century wrote tribal histories that often contain myths and legends. Among these authors are GEORGE COPWAY (Ojibwa), William Whipple Warren (Ojibwa), Peter Dooyentate Clarke (Wyandot), Chief Elias Johnson (Tuscarora), David Cusick (Tuscarora), and Chief Andrew J. Blackbird (Ottawa). JOHN ROLLIN RIDGE (Cherokee, 1827–1867) wrote a series of essays on Native Americans recently collected in *A Trumpet of Our Own*. Ridge was one of the few Native Americans to write fiction and poetry in the 19th century. His *The Life and Adventures of Joaquin Murieta* (1854) is the first novel by a Native American author. In this romance, Ridge portrays the mixed-blood Murieta as a Byronic "noble outlaw" who turns to crime after he is victimized by white miners. It is also an early example of local color. Ridge's posthumous *Poems* (1868), most of which were written in his youth, is the only volume of poetry published by a Native American in the 19th century.

Perhaps the first novel to be written by an American Indian woman is *Wynema, a Child of the Forest* (1891) by Sophia Alice Callahan (Creek, 1868–1893). In this romance, Wynema, a Creek child who yearns for an education, introduces her teacher at a Methodist mission school to life in the Creek nation.

The first Native American woman to achieve acclaim as a poet and performer of her own works was EMILY PAULINE JOHNSON (Canadian Mohawk, 1861–1913), author of *The White Wampum* (1895), which includes many poems on Indian themes, and *Canadian Born* (1903). Her collected poems appear in *Flint and Feather* (1912). Johnson was also the first Native American woman to publish short fiction. Her *Moccasin Maker* (1913) contains short stories about Canadian Indian and non-Indian women.

During the 20th century, Native American authors increasingly wrote novels. Many of these deal with the quest by mixed-blood protagonists to find their place in society and with the importance of oral tradition to the survival of tribalism. In the first half of the century, Mourning Dove [Christal Quintasket] (1888–1936). John Joseph Matthews (Osage, c. 1894–1979) and D'ARCY MCNICKLE (Cree-Salish, 1904–1977) incorporate these themes in their novels. *Cogewea, the Half Blood* (1927), written by Mourning Dove in collaboration with Lucullus V. McWhorter, is one of the earliest novels written by a Native American woman. In the novel, Mourning Dove combines the portrayal of a strong-willed heroine who temporarily rejects her tribal heritage with plot elements from Westerns.

Mathews's *Sundown* (1934) focuses on the problems of a mixed-blood Osage whose abandonment of his ancestral past and inability to adjust to the white-dominated present result in alcoholism. Mathews' earlier *Wah-Kon-Tah* (1932) is a fictional account of the Osages' struggles to retain their traditions after they were forced onto reservations. The most polished novel by a Native American writer in the 1930s is McNickle's *The Surrounded* (1936), which chronicles the

dilemma of a mixed-blood hero inadvertently caught up in unpremeditated murders that his mother and girl friend commit. His strongly traditional mother and a tribal elder lead the protagonist back to the Salish culture he had rejected. McNickle later wrote *Runner in the Sun* (1954), a novel for young people that evokes the life, customs, and beliefs of the ancient cliff dwellers of Chaco Canyon in what is now northwestern New Mexico.

Closer in theme to mainstream American fiction of the 1930s is *Brothers Three* (1935) by John Oskison (Cherokee, 1874–1947), which is a fine example of the regional novel and a vivid portrait of a part-Cherokee family trying to regain their Oklahoma land and their values. An example of an ethnographic novel is *Water Lily* by Ella Deloria (Sioux, 1888–1971), an anthropologist. Completed by 1944 but not published until 1988, it is a valuable portrayal of 19th-century Sioux life that chronicles Water Lily's life from birth through adulthood. The only Native American author of mystery and detective fiction during the first half of the 20th century is [George] Todd Downing (Choctaw, 1902–1974), whose many novels, usually set in Mexico include *Murder on Tour* (1933), *The Cat Screams* (1934), and *Night Over Mexico* (1937).

Good examples of Native American satire are the prose writings of ALEXANDER POSEY (Creek, 1873–1901) and WILL ROGERS (Cherokee, 1879–1935). Using real Creek elders as characters, and writing in Creek-style English, Posey satirized in his "Fus Fixico Letters" the politics of Indian Territory and the nation as a whole. Posey's use of dialect and regionalism was influenced by Robert Burns, whom he greatly admired, and by FINLEY PETER DUNNE, whose satires featuring Mr. Dooley and Mr. Hennessey first appeared in the 1890s. National and international politics was the main theme of Rogers' satire. His books and miscellaneous writings are now being published as *Complete Works*, ed. Joseph A. Stout.

Little poetry was published by Native American writers during the first half of the 20th century. Mrs. Posey, after her husband's death, published *The Poems of Alexander Posey* (1910), most of which are romantic evocations of nature written in his youth. An interesting example of Indian dialect poetry is *Yon-doo-sha-we-ah* (1924) by Bertrand N. O. Walker [Hen-toh] (Wyandot), which contains some interesting character sketches and narratives. Far more sophisticated is [Rolla] LYNN RIGGS'S *Iron Dish* (1930), which contains delicate lyrics and perceptive descriptions of nature.

During the first half of the 20th century, Riggs (Cherokee, 1899–1954) was the only major Native American dramatist. He is best known for *Green Grow the Lilacs* (1931), a folk drama that became the hit musical *Oklahoma!* (1954). Also widely praised was his *Borned in Texas*, produced as *Roadside* (1930). *Cherokee Night* (1936) describes the sense of loss faced by Oklahoma mixed bloods.

In the late 1960s a new generation of highly sophisticated Native American writers emerged. The first of these to achieve national attention was N. SCOTT MOMADAY, whose *The House*

Made of Dawn (1968) won the Pulitzer Prize. The novel describes the ritual quest of a mixed-blood Pueblo World War II veteran for healing and suggests, at the end of the novel, the possibility that he may regain his sense of place, tribe, and self. *The Ancient Child* (1989) focuses the search for ritual healing by a mixed-blood artist, who becomes transformed into a bear through the aid of his lover, a Kiowa-Navajo visionary. Through the visions of the shaman and the experience of the protagonist, Momaday blends Native American myths of transformation and Western tales about Billy the Kid.

Ceremony (1977) by LESLIE MARMON SILKO (1948–   ) demonstrates the healing power of tribal ritual and storytelling by reuniting her mixed-blood hero, a World War II veteran, with his tribe at the end of the novel. PAULA GUNN ALLEN (Laguna-Sioux, 1939–   ) brings a feminist perspective to her treatment of the ritual quest in *The Woman Who Owned the Shadows* (1983). The heroine gradually accepts herself as a mixed-blood woman only after she relives—through memory, Keres oral traditions, and psychotherapy—her relationships with her family and the destructive men in her life. *Darkness in Saint Louis Bear-heart* (1978) by Gerald Vizenor (Ojibwa, 1934–   ) also uses the theme of the quest. His surrealistic and satiric novel chronicles the journey of a bizarre group in search of ritual knowledge, which takes them from Minnesota to the Southwest.

In *Winter in the Blood* (1975), JAMES WELCH (Blackfeet-Gros Ventre, 1940–   ) focuses on the nameless hero's search for the truth about his family background and about his fierce Blackfeet grandmother's early life. In Welch's *The Death of Jim Loney* (1979), a mixed-blood protagonist also seeks information about his Indian family and the white father who psychologically abandons him. The protagonist finds his release from his psychic dilemma in an act that brings about his death. Welch's *Fools Crow* (1986) is a historical novel that describes the impact of white settlement on a Montana band of Blackfeet in 1870.

Native Americans have incorporated themes other than the ritual quest in their novels. LOUISE ERDRICH (Ojibwa, 1954–   ) focuses on family and community relationships in *Love Medicine* (1984), *Beet Queen* (1986), and *Tracks* (1988). Set in Erdrich's native North Dakota and part of a projected series of four novels, they have gained Erdrich national recognition. *Tracks* and *Love Medicine* chronicle the relationships between members of a North Dakota Chippewa tribe from 1912 to 1983. *Beet Queen* deals primarily with the relationships between non-Indian characters in the off-reservation town of Argus. *A Yellow Raft on Blue Water* (1987) by MICHAEL DORRIS (Modoc, 1954–1997) also takes the family as its theme. Set on a Montana reservation, the novel portrays three generations of women torn apart by secrets but bound by kinship. Erdrich and Dorris, who are married, collaborate on each other's works.

Contemporary Native American novelists have used a variety of approaches and themes in treating Indian life. McNickle's *Wind from an Enemy Sky* (1978) demonstrates again the narrative power of his earlier *The Surrounded* in this story of the clash between Indian and non-Indian values that ends in tragedy for both groups. Vizenor's latest novel, *Griever: An American Monkey King in China* (1987), is a satire that deals with the adventures of a mixed-blood Indian who teaches English in a Chinese university and triumphs *over* Chinese bureaucracy as he becomes transformed into a Monkey King, the Chinese trickster. His *Trickster of Liberty: Tribal Heirs to a Wild Baronage at Petronia* (1988) describes a whole family of Indian tricksters who rebel against conventional systems and establish ingenious enterprises. *Medicine River* (1990) by Thomas King (Cherokee, 1943–   ) combines humor and realism in this novel describing his mixed-blood protagonist's attempts to understand his family background; to readjust to his home town of Medicine River, an Indian community outside the Blackfoot reserve in Alberta; and to cope with the schemes of his friend Harlen Bigbear. In *Jailing of Cecilia Capture* (1985), Janet Campbell Hale (Coeur d'Alene-Kootenai, 1947–   ) portrays the attempts of an urban Native American woman to restructure her life. This novel and her earlier *Owl Song* (1974), about a young boy, are among the few works dealing with urban Native Americans. Anna Walters (Otoe-Pawnee, 1946–   ) blends mystery and Navaho-white relations in her *Ghost Singer* (1988), which attacks whites' inhumane practice of storing Indian skeletons and possessions in museums. Other Native American novelists include Hyemeyohsts Storm (Cheyenne, 1935–   ), whose *Seven Arrows* (1972) aroused controversy because of its treatment of Cheyenne religion. His *The Song of the Heyoehkah* (1981) deals with a heroine's quest for ritual knowledge to become a shaman. The only novel by an Eskimo writer is. Markoosie's *Harpoon of the Hunter* (1970).

One of the few American Indian mystery writers, MARTIN CRUZ SMITH (Senecu del Sur-Yaqui, 1942–   ), has achieved national acclaim for four mystery novels, two of which have Indian themes. Both *Nightwing* (1977) and *Stallion Gate* (1986) have Indian protagonists who have left their pueblos, served in overseas wars, and returned to their homelands, where they feel separated from their people and their traditions. Far different are Smith's *Gorky Park* (1981) and *Polar Star* (1989), which deal with characters from both the Soviet Union and the United States.

Native American authors have also written much short fiction. Leslie Silko's short stories, which strongly reflect Laguna traditions, are collected with her poetry in *Storyteller* (1981). Simon Ortiz (Acoma, 1941–   ) has also published a collection of short fiction, *The Howbah Indians* (1978) and *Fightin'* (1983).

Gerald Vizenor's *Wordarrows* (1978), *Earthdivers* (1981), and *The People Named the Chippewa* (1984) combine satiric short fiction and nonfiction. The most widely published Indian writer of nonfiction prose is VINE DELORIA, JR. (Sioux, 1933–   ). His works combining political insight, wit, and satire are *Custer Died for Your Sins* (1969), which contains an interesting essay on Indian humor, and *We Talk, You Listen*

(1970). He has also written numerous books on Native American religion, philosophy, Indian-white relations, and politics. Michael Dorris's *The Broken Cord: A Family's On-Going Struggle with Fetal Alcohol Syndrome* (1989) portrays the author's efforts to raise his adopted son, Adam, a victim of the syndrome.

Since 1968, Native Americans have become prolific writers of poetry that reflects considerable variety in theme and form. Among the most widely published are Paula Gunn Allen (Laguna-Sioux), Jim Barnes (Choctaw), Barney Bush (Shawnee), Joy Harjo (Creek), Linda Hogan (Chickasaw), Maurice Kenny (Mohawk), Duane Niatum (Klallam), Simon Ortiz (Acoma), Wendy Rose (Hopi-Miwok), and Ray Young Bear (Mesquakie). Though primarily fiction writers, Louise Erdrich, N. Scott Momaday, Leslie Silko, James Welch, and Gerald Vizenor have also published poetry. Other talented poets include Peter Blue Cloud (Mohawk), Joe Bruchac (Abnakie), Elizabeth Cook-Lynn (Sioux), Diane Burns (Ojibwa-Chemehuevi), Gladys Cardiff (Cherokee), Anita Endrezze-Danielson (Yaqui), Nia Francisco (Navajo), Diane Glancy (Cherokee), Lance Henson (Cheyenne), Adrian Louis (Paiute), William Oandasan (Yuki), Carter Revard (Osage), Mary Tall Mountain (Athabascan), and Luci Tapahonso (Navajo).

The forms of contemporary Native American poetry vary from traditional chants and songs to highly individualistic verse. Many poets incorporate into their poems such tribal myths as creation and emergence, earthdiver, and the trickster. Common themes include a sense of loss of tribal roots, often associated with a specific space that is part of the history of the author's tribe, and closeness to nature and animals. Native American poets also deal with the problems of identity that mixed-bloods face, the sense of displacement that urban Indians experience, and the injustice inflicted on their people by the dominant society. They describe how family and tribal values provide Native Americans with the sources of strength to withstand attempts to alter their culture. Native American women poets frequently focus on the family and the role of women. Many emphasize and pay tribute to the grandmothers who traditionally helped raise the children and educated them in tribal culture. Although much of this poetry deals with Indian themes, writers are increasingly turning to other subjects as well. Several women writers have focused some of their recent poems on their reactions to maturation and aging.

From the time Native Americans migrated to this continent, they have created a rich heritage of oral and written literatures. Only by acknowledging the contributions of Native Americans to the rich mosaic of American literature can we understand the real history of our nation. To experience the imaginative world of Native American, we need only accept Paula Gunn Allen's challenge to "follow the winding corridors of winter tales/enter into the moving paths of shape and time." Studies include *Handbook of North American Indians* (in progress, edited by William C. Sturtevant, 20 v.); Paula Gunn Allen, *The*

Sacred Hoop: Recovering the Feminine in American Indian Tradition (1986); H. David Brumble III, *American Indian Autobiography* (1988); Arnold Krupat, *For Those Who Come After: A Study of Native American Autobiography* (1985) and *The Voice in the Margin: Native American Literature and the Canon* (1989); Charles R. Larson, *American Indian Fiction* (1978); A. LaVonne Brown Ruoff, *American Indian Literatures: An Introduction, Bibliographic Review and Selected Bibliography* (1990); and Andrew O. Wiget, *Native American Literature* (1985).

A. LAVONNE BROWN RUOFF

Native Son (1940).   Conceived on the template of a criminal thriller, RICHARD WRIGHT's cautionary tale of Bigger Thomas transformed readers' expectations about racial fiction through bold management of the techniques of recognition and identification. Taking the outline of plot from an actual Chicago murder case, and investing his fictional character with verisimilitude derived from felt experience and the research of social science on lower class urban African-American life, Wright gave his fiction the power of naturalism. Yet, sensitive to the limitations of documentation and aware that an account of victimization could confirm bias, he applied his craft to rendering the theme of his protagonist's brief life in terms of growing self-awareness. Writing against the prevailing American racial discourse, which portrays a young man of Bigger's circumstances either as a near brute or as a pitiable case, Wright drew on the character of the bad man in African-American popular literature to skirt the edge of stereotype. Like the unknown author of the ballad of Stagolee, and the inventors of the distinctive toasts that tell of "Shine" or "the signifying monkey," Wright encoded the straight story with an alternative message.

The message is carried by the third-person narrative voice that articulates events through much of the novel in an idiom suggestive of Bigger's mental processes, if not of his language. This voice of inner life privileges the reader to participate in Bigger's psychology, comprehend its social origins, and recognize its authentic expression in the motive for murder. As the novel reaches closure, Bigger achieves the capacity to speak without the mediation of authorial voice. His novel becomes incipient autobiography. Recognition that Bigger had a story worth hearing made *Native Son* shocking to readers in 1940. It also made the book a best seller that brought African-American prose fiction to the attention of a till-then oblivious literary establishment.

JOHN M. REILLY

Natty Bumppo.   See BUMPPO, NATTY.

naturalism.   The rise of naturalistic fiction in the latter half of the 19th century was influenced by Darwin's theory of evolution, Marx's historical determinism, and the mechanistic school of philosophy. Although the term is often used synonymously with REALISM, naturalism refers particularly to works in which the author emphasizes the control exerted by the forces of heredity and environment over human life, and the animalistic and instinctual elements in man. It is similar to realism primarily in its objectivity and careful attention to detail, but goes beyond realism in its tendency to take as its subject matter lower-class situations and characters, and particularly in its deterministic philosophy that frequently emphasizes the operations of blind chance. Human life is viewed as being at the mercy of uncontrollable exterior forces—the environment—or of interior drives—fear, hunger, sex. The slum girl crushed by her surroundings, such as Maggie, or the brutal and moronic man, such as McTeague, are typical characters. Crane's MAGGIE: A GIRL OF THE STREETS (1893), Norris's MCTEAGUE (1899), LONDON's *The Son of the Wolf* (1900), and Dreiser's SISTER CARRIE (1900) are the earliest examples of American naturalism.

The proletarian literature of the 1930s is in some ways an outgrowth of naturalism and similar to it primarily in its emphasis on the lower class; however, the major naturalistic novel to appear during the 1930s was FARRELL's *Studs Lonigan* trilogy (1932, 1934, 1935). Studies of naturalism include Richard Hofstadter's *Social Darwinism in American Thought* (1944); Lars Ahnebrink's *The Beginnings of Naturalism in American Fiction* (1950); and Charles C. Walcutt's *American Literary Naturalism, A Divided Stream* (1956).

Nature. [1] An essay by RALPH WALDO EMERSON on which he began working in 1833. Published anonymously in 1836, it was Emerson's first major work. Emerson sees nature as "Commodity" in its practical functions, as "Beauty" in the delight it arouses, as "Language" in its symbolical significance, and as "Discipline" in the education it gives the Understanding and the Reason. When man is in communion with nature he says to himself, "I become a transparent eyeball; I am nothing; I see all; the currents of the Universal Being circulate through me; I am part or parcel of God."

[2] A poem by Emerson that he used to preface his book *Nature, Addresses and Lectures* (1849); it was written in 1836.

nature writing in the U.S. Both the fact of wilderness and the mythic notion of a Virgin Land have long fascinated Americans; it is not surprising, then, that natural history—or nature writing—has long found its place in American literature. The tradition sinks its roots deeply into early American experience. Thomas Jefferson's *Notes on Virginia* (1781) "breathes with the excitement of some fabulous first encounter," in Alfred Kazin's phrase. William Bartram, a Quaker and the first American botanist, devoted his *Travels* (1791) to rich descriptions of the Southeast. Coleridge praised its "high merit," partly because it advanced the idea of "the natural man." In the 19th century, with the exploration of vast new territories, nature writing became more important. Meriwether Lewis and William Clark published their *History of the Expedition* (1814), and Francis Parkman wrote of his frontier adventures on *The Oregon Trail* (1849).

Unquestionably the finest nature writers of this period were Henry David Thoreau and John Muir. With Thoreau's classic *Walden* (1854), nature writing took a more subjective, often political, philosophical, and religious direction, while Thoreau's *Journals* contain some of the keenest observations by this "inspector of snowstorms." John Muir's equally subjec-

tive but more rhapsodic celebrations include *The Mountains of California* (1894), *My First Summer in the Sierras* (1911), and *Travels in Alaska* (1918). Muir's friend John Burroughs wrote more popular essays for periodicals and published *Ways of Nature* (1905).

Four outstanding desert writers assumed prominence in this century. Art historian John C. Van Dyke's *The Desert* (1901) paints colorful landscapes. About this same time, the young Mary Austin wrote her best book, *Land of Little Rain* (1903), lyrical sketches rooted in the Mojave drylands. She followed with *The Land of Journeys Endings* (1924), a loving depiction of the Southwest. Still later Joseph Wood Krutch moved to Arizona, where he wrote *The Desert Year* (1952) and *The Voice of the Desert* (1955).

The twentieth century's most influential nature writers have included Aldo Leopold, whose *Sand County Almanac* (1949) proposed a new "land ethic," Rachel Carson, whose *Silent Spring* (1963) sounded the alarm about the effects of pesticides on wildlife, Edward Abbey, whose comic tales and passionate ecopolemics energized several books, most notably *Desert Solitaire* (1968), and John McPhee, whose books include *Coming into the Country* (1977), on Alaska.

Other naturalists have celebrated regions of the country. Sigurd Olson captured the North Woods in *The Singing Wilderness* (1956), and Edwin Way Teale rendered his native New England in *Wandering Through the Winter* (1965), for which he received a Pulitzer Prize. Anne Dillard also won a Pulitzer for her remarkably heartfelt *Pilgrim at Tinker Creek* (1974), depicting Appalachia, and a more scientific Ann Zwinger focused on areas of Utah in *Run, River, Run* (1975, Burroughs Medal) and *Wind in the Rock* (1978). Barry Lopez's *Arctic Dreams* (1985) treated Alaska.

Nature writing is both traditionally American and increasingly popular, partly because of increasing reader fondness for nonfiction, partly because of heightened public concern about the natural environment. Among recent books, Wendell Berry's *What Are People For?* (1990) presents the essays of a quiet observer; Marc Reisner's *Cadillac Desert: The American West and Its Disappearing Water* (1996) and Jared Farmer's *Glen Canyon Damned: Inventing Lake Powell and the Canyon Country* (1999) treat the arid West, and Bill Bryson's *A Walk in the Woods: Rediscovering America on the Appalachian Trail* (1998) finds new truths on an old walk.

PAUL W. REA/GP

Nauset Indians, a part of the Algonkin-Wakashan linguistic stock. In *Of Plymouth Plantation*, William Bradford describes how a party from the *Mayflower* observed Nausets cutting up a grampus—probably a beached pilot whale—on the bay shore of Cape Cod near present-day Eastham, Massachusetts. Members of the tribe still live on the Cape, near Mashpee. Nausets were largely friendly to the Puritans and helped them through the first winter's hardships.

Navajos. An Indian tribe of the Southwest, one of the greatest of the Indian groups. They came into early conflict with white men and resisted boldly. They were finally subdued by Colonel KIT CARSON in 1863. The Navajos express their intense religious feeling in long chants, usually parallel in structure. Their everyday life is inseparable from their religion; they have no formal priesthood, and everybody takes part in the ceremonies. Fictional works dealing with the Navajos include Adolph Bandelier's *The Delight Makers* (1890), Willa Cather's DEATH COMES FOR THE ARCHBISHOP (1927), and Oliver La Farge's LAUGHING BOY (1929). Among nonfictional books are E. Sapir and H. Hoijer's *Navaho Texts* (1942); Clyde Kluckhohn and D. Leighton's *The Navaho* (1947); John Collier's *Patterns and Ceremonies of the Indians of the Southwest* (1949); A. Grove Day's *The Sky Clears* (1951); Kluckhohn and Evon Z. Vogt's *Navaho Means People* (1951, with photographs by Leonard McCombe); Ruth Underhill's *The Navajos* (1956); and Margaret Link's *The Pollen Path* (Navaho myths, 1956). A Navajo autobiography is *Navajo Blessingway Singer: The Autobiography of Frank Mitchell, 1881–1967* (1978). Luci Tapahonso, Navajo poet, has published *A Breeze Swept Through* (1987) and other books.

Naylor, Gloria (1950–   ),   novelist. Born in New York City, Naylor was educated at Brooklyn College and Yale. Naylor is best known for *The Women of Brewster Place* (1982), which deals with seven women whose diverse experiences illuminate the lives that African-American women live. *Men of Brewster Place* (1998) is a sequel. Her other fiction includes *Linden Hills* (1985), *Mama Day* (1988), and *Bailey's Café* (1992).

Neal, John ["Jehu O'Cataract"] (1793–1876), lawyer, poet, novelist, critic. Born in Maine, John Neal, after a scanty education, became a clerk, itinerant drawing teacher, and drygoods merchant. When his business failed he began to read law and edited *The Portico*, a monthly literary magazine published by the DELPHIAN CLUB. He wrote prose and poetry for the magazine and in 1817 published *Keep Cool: A Novel*. This story of a man who suffers feelings of guilt because he killed someone in a duel added to Neal's growing reputation as a writer, though it was not a financial success. *The Battle of Niagara: A Poem Without Notes* (1818); *Goldau: or, The Maniac Harper* (published under the pen name of Jehu O'Cataract, 1818); *Otho* (a verse tragedy, 1819); and *Logan, A Family History* (1822) increased his reputation. *Logan*, a novel, combines an attack on the United States Indian policy, debtors' prisons, and capital punishment with a fantastic story, partly fact, about a Herculean Englishman who marries an Indian queen. In 1823 Neal turned out three novels; the first, *Seventy-Six*, is a Revolutionary tale somewhat resembling Cooper's *The Spy*. Neal believed it to be his best work. In *Randolph* there were some uncomplimentary references to the recently deceased father of the poet Edward Pinkney, who challenged Neal to a duel. Neal ignored the challenge, was branded a coward, and immediately turned the experience into material for his next novel, *Errata, or The Works of Will Adams* (1823).

Sailing for England in 1823, Neal served as Jeremy Bentham's secretary for some time (and acted as his spokesman years later after he returned to America.) He stormed *Blackwood's Magazine*, overcame its well-known dislike for Ameri-

can authors, and wrote a series of sketches of American literary men, the first attempt at a literary history of the United States.

Brother Jonathan, or, The New Englanders (1824) was published in Edinburgh. On his return in 1827 to Portsmouth, Neal established *The Yankee*, a weekly newspaper. He continued to pour forth novels: *Rachel Dyer* (1828), the story of a Salem witch, considered by many his best work; *Authorship* (1830); THE DOWN-EASTERS (1833); *True Womanhood* (1859); *The White Pacer* (1863); *The Moose Hunter* (1864); and *Little Moccasin; or Along the Madawaska* (1865). The last three were written for the Beadle series of DIME NOVELS. *Wandering Recollections of a Somewhat Busy Life* (1869) is an autobiography.

Neal, Joseph Clay (1807–1847),   essayist, humorist, editor. Neal, born in New Hampshire, often placed among the practitioners of CRACKER-BARREL HUMOR, was decidedly under the influence of Charles Dickens. His first book, much of which appeared in a Philadelphia magazine he founded in 1836, *Neal's Saturday Gazette and Ladies' Literary Museum*, was *Charcoal Sketches, or, Scenes in a Metropolis* (1st series, 1838; 2nd series, 1848), a satire on Philadelphia ways and peoples. Dickens thought so highly of it that he reprinted the series in England as *The Pic Nic Papers* (1841). Several editions appeared in the United States, the last as late as 1865 (3 v.). Other writings of Neal were *In Town and About* (1843), *Peter Ploddy and Other Oddities* (1844), and *The Misfortunes of Peter Faber and Other Sketches* (1856).

Nearing, Scott (1883–1983),   radical pacifist, environmentalist. With a Ph.D. in economics, an impressive publishing record, and a promising career at the Wharton School of the University of Pennsylvania, Nearing, who was born in Pennsylvania, changed the course of his life by being fired as a radical in 1915 for denouncing capitalism in general and child labor in particular. After the U.S. entered World War I, the University of Toledo fired Nearing after a trial on charges of sedition even though he was acquitted. He was also expelled from the Communist Party for disavowing some of Lenin's views. In 1932 he and his wife Helen (1904–1995) decided to live outside the organized economic and political system entirely, if possible. They built a stone house in Vermont, raised their own food, and lived without electricity. They ate vegetables, grains, and fruits in season, and summed up their lives in a book that became a classic of its genre, *Living the Good Life* (1954), which in the 1960s and 1970s made them inspiring examples to youth, many of whom made pilgrimages to the seacoast Maine tree farm where the couple lived during Scott's last decade. Among the other books Nearing wrote are *The Making of a Radical: A Political Autobiography* (1972) and, with his wife their other classic, *The Maple Sugar Book: Together with Remarks on Pioneering as a Way of Living in the Twentieth Century* (1950).

Necessary Angel, The (1951),   a collection of essays on poetry by WALLACE STEVENS. Delivered mostly as talks at various universities, the essays are difficult, serious, and contradictory: "The accuracy of accurate letters," Stevens says at one point, "is an accuracy with respect to the structure of reality." The major theme of the essays is the relation of the imagination to reality and the way in which the imagination, in transforming reality, enriches it. Some critics accused Stevens of using poetry as an escape from reality. He answers this charge in a discussion of the poet's "supreme fictions." These fictions of the imagination, far from an escape, invest stark reality with meaning. Thus does Stevens make poetry equal, even superior, to philosophy.

Ned Myers (1843), a narrative by JAMES FENIMORE COOPER. Although this story of a sailor's experiences is written as fiction, the book is a factual record taken down from the lips of an old salt who in his youth had sailed with Cooper on the *Sterling*. It is a much more realistic picture of life at sea than one finds elsewhere in Cooper. Cooper himself spoke of the book as "edited by J. Fenimore Cooper." He gave as a subtitle, "A Life Before the Mast"—Dana's TWO YEARS BEFORE THE MAST had appeared in 1840, and the author had timidly sent a copy to Cooper.

Negro spirituals. Spirituals had a mixed heritage: African traditions, the slave experience, and white music, especially as transmitted through Methodist hymns and camp meeting songs. The first collection with music was *Slave Songs in the United States* (1867), compiled by William Francis Allen, Charles P. Ware, and Lucy McKim Garrison. The earliest critical study, which appeared in the *Atlantic Monthly* (June 1867), was written by THOMAS W. HIGGINSON, who as colonel of a regiment of African-American soldiers became familiar with their songs. In 1871 the Fisk University Jubilee Singers began touring the country and aroused great interest in their songs. Theodore Seward's *Jubilee Songs, as Sung by the Jubilee Singers of Fisk University* appeared in 1872, and G. D. Pike's *The Jubilee Singers* in 1873. Since then dozens of collections have been made.

Neighbor Jackwood (1856, rev. 1895), novel by J. T. TROWBRIDGE. The beautiful Camille Delisard, daughter of a Frenchman and his light-skinned slave, is sold after her father's death by his wife. She is rescued by Robert Greenwich, who helps her travel the UNDERGROUND RAILWAY to the Green Mountains of Vermont where she is befriended by Abimelech Jackwood of the title. Under an assumed name she becomes a servant to the Dunbury family; when Hector Dunbury proposes marriage, she describes her origins. Greenwich, who loves her passionately, seeks to claim her as a fugitive slave, but deviled by his conscience, he commits suicide and the lovers are finally married.

Neihardt, John G[neisenau] (1881–1973), short-story writer, dramatist, novelist, poet, professor. Born in Sharpsburg, Illinois, John Neihardt was educated at the Nebraska Normal College. From 1897 to 1907 he lived among the Native Americans, working at odd jobs. *The Lonesome Trail* (1907), a collection of short stories of pioneering heroes and Indians, utilized his experiences during this period. In 1907 he also published *A Bundle of Myrrh*, lyric poetry, and in 1921 a play entitled *Two Mothers*. The first of his epic poems of the West, *The Song of Hugh Glass* (1915), was followed by *The Song*

of Three Friends (1919), *The Song of the Indian Wars* (1925), *The Song of the Messiah* (1935), and *The Song of Jed Smith* (1941). In 1949 all five appeared in a single volume entitled *A Cycle of the West*. He also wrote four novels: *Life's Lure* (1914), *The Splendid Wayfaring* (1920), *When the Tree Flowered* (1951), and *Eagle Voice* (1953). Neihardt was the recorder of *Black Elk Speaks* (1932, repr. 1972), the story of a Sioux medicine man. See BLACK ELK and NATIVE AMERICAN PROSE AND POETRY.

Nelligan, Émile (1879–1941), poet. Educated in Montreal, Nelligan early revealed his poetic gift in a volume of poems entitled *Le Samedi* (1896), which was published under the pen name Émile Kovar. He continued to write poetry for various Montreal periodicals and was one of the first Canadians to be influenced by the French symbolist school. In 1899 he went insane and spent the remainder of his life in mental institutions. His collected poems, *Émile Nelligan et son œuvre* (1903), published by Louis Dantin, went into several editions.

Nelson, Antonya (1961–), short-story writer, novelist. Born in Wichita, Kansas, Nelson was educated at the University of Kansas and the University of Arizona. After winning the Flannery O'Connor award for her first collection of stories, *The Expendables* (1990), Nelson went on to write two more highly-praised story gatherings: *In the Land of Men* (1992) and *Family Terrorists* (1994). The third book combined a novella with seven stories. Her first novel, *Talking in Bed* (1996), centers on how the friendship forged between two men who meet while visiting their dying fathers in a hospital influences their marriage partners and their own lives. Birdy Stone, a high school teacher in New Mexico, is the protagonist of *Nobody's Girl* (1998). In the sequel *Living to Tell* (2000) another educator struggles with tragedy. The Mabie family of Wichita, Kansas is composed of a retired college professor and his wife and their three adult children, all returned to live in the family home. The son's return from prison, where he served time for a drunk-driving accident in which his grandmother was killed, causes the entire family to reassess relationships.

Nelson, Richard (1950–), playwright. Born near Manhattan, Nelson moved to Detroit as a child. In both places he was an early attendee at live theatrical productions, particularly musicals. Returning from study in England in 1973, he joined a theater group doing plays for Philadelphia's public radio station. Experimentation with theatrical convention is evident in *Jungle Coup* (1978) in which the central character speaks directly to the audience from a jungle setting. *Rip Van Winkle or "The Works"* (1981) deals, as Washington Irving's story does, with transition in American society during the Revolutionary War. In Nelson's treatment, Rip intends to sell his valley to a factory owner. He wanders into the hills and falls into an enchanted sleep, but returns to reclaim the land for agriculture. Both he and the factory owner are killed, but the conflict between them highlights tensions inherent in postrevolutionary America. Charlie, of the satiric *An American Comedy* (1983, and in *An American Comedy and Other Plays*, 1984), is a borderline schizophrenic who aims to be an investigative reporter. In *The Return of Pinocchio* (1983) a rich American immigrant returns to Italy after World War II to find poverty and moral confusion; comic book-like titles are projected on a backdrop during scenes. Such projected titles are also used in *Between East and West* (1985) dealing with a Czech director and his actress wife, who have escaped the Iron Curtain and are struggling in New York. *Principia Scriptoriae* (1986) concerns two writers who find themselves imprisoned in an unnamed Latin American country. With two plays (*Some Americans Abroad* and *Two Shakespearean Actors*) written for London's Royal Shakespeare Company, Nelson's career shifted to Britain at the end of the 80s. The latter and more substantial play treats the conflict between William Macready, the English actor, and the American Edwin Forrest. When the two performed Macbeth in rival productions in May of 1849, thirty-four people died in the ensuing riot. Other plays produced in London include *Columbus and the Discovery of Japan* (1994); *New England* (1994) dealing with a group of expatriate Brits in Connecticut; and *The General from America* (1996) returning to the period of the American Revolution for characters and subject matter.

Nemerov, Howard (1920–1991),   poet, novelist, essayist. Nemerov first left his native New York City to go to Harvard; upon graduation in 1941 he went into service as a pilot in World War II. After the war he worked as an editor of *Furioso*, a literary periodical, and completed his first book of poems, *The Image and the Law* (1947). Later he taught at Washington University. The *Melodramatists* (1949), his first novel, was well received. Nemerov was trained to admire the poetry of Eliot and Yeats, and his early work shows the same kind of wit and ambiguity, but his verse evolved and he came to regard "simplicity and the appearance of ease in the measure as primary values, and the detachment of a single thought from its ambiguous surroundings as a worthier object. . . ." Often the conjunction Nemerov saw between seemingly unrelated objects is unexpected, witty, sometimes jarring. His collections include *Guide to the Ruins* (1950), *The Salt Garden* (1955), *Mirrors and Windows* (1958), *New and Selected Poems* (1960), *The Next Room of the Dream: Poems and Two Plays* (1962), *Departure of the Ships* (1966), *Dangers of Reasoning by Analogy* (1966), *The Blue Swallows* (1967), *A Sequence of Seven* (1967), *The Winter Lightning: Selected Poems* (1968), *The Painter Dreaming in the Scholar's House* (1968), *Gnomes and Occasions* (1972), *The Western Approaches: Poems 1973–1975* (1975); *By Al Lebowitz's Pool* (1979), *Sentences* (1980), *Inside the Onion* (1984), and *War Stories* (1987). *The Collected Poems of Howard Nemerov* (1977) won a Pulitzer Prize. Other novels are *Federigo; or, The Power of Love* (1954) and *The Homecoming Game* (1957). *A Commodity of Dreams and Other Stories* (1959) is one of several story collections. *Reflections on Poetry and Poetics* (1972) is among his essay collections. *Journal of the Fictive Life* (1965) is a memoir.

Neruda, Pablo (1904–1973),   poet, politician. Born Ricardo Eliecer Neftalí Reyes in a small town in Chile, Neruda was an infant when his mother died. He was raised by his father, a railroad worker who did not want his son to be a poet. Neruda's invention of a poetic pseudonym is probably related to his father's objection. In 1921 he went to Santiago to complete his degree in French literature, but he dropped out and joined a group of experimental poets instead. His first volume of verse, *Crepusculario* (1923), showed the influence of French poetry. His most successful book, *Veinte Poemas de Amor y Una Canción Desesperada* (1924, tr. *Twenty Love Poems and a Song of Despair* 1969) combined avant-garde techniques and a gift for erotic expression. After its publication had established Neruda as one of Chile's most promising poets, the Chilean government appointed him to various consular posts in Europe and Asia. In 1934 he was assigned to Madrid, where he mingled with Spanish writers, such as *Manuel Altolaguirre*, with whom he founded (1935) a literary review called *Caballo verde para la poesía*. In the same year, Neruda published a translation of William Blake's "The Visions of the Daughters of Albion" and "The Mental Traveller." His outspoken sympathy for the Loyalist cause during the Spanish Civil War led to his recall in 1937, but he soon returned to Europe to help settle Republican refugees in America. From 1939 to 1943, he was Chilean consul in Mexico. Upon returning to Chile, Neruda became active in politics, was elected to the senate, and joined the Communist Party. When the party was declared illegal in Chile, Neruda was expelled from the senate. After several years in exile, he returned to Chile in 1953.

Neruda's earliest poetry—*La canción de la fiesta* (1921), *Crepusculario* (1923), and *Veinte poemas* (1924)—is reminiscent of MODERNISMO in form and tone. In the poems of his next period, particularly in *Residencia en la tierra* (tr. *Residence on Earth*, 1973), which appeared in two parts in 1932 and 1935, he gives full play to his intuition and experience. Written in an often surrealistic style, these poems depict an anguished world of chaos, desolation, and decay. The poet's experience in the Spanish Civil War and the impact of World War II turned him in new directions. In *Tercera residencia* (1947) and in such works as *Canto general de Chile* (1943), *Odas elementales* (1954), and *Extravagario* (1959, tr. *Extravagaria*, 1972), Neruda—by then a militant communist—became the people's poet and a polemicist. Though there is considerable debate over the merits of Neruda's later work, he is widely regarded as the greatest Spanish-American poet since DARÍO. Much of his poetry appears in translation in *The Selected Poems of Pablo Neruda* (1970). He was awarded the Nobel Prize in Literature in 1971. Stricken with cancer, which forced him to withdraw from the diplomatic position he had received under President Allende, he was living in Chile and suffered a fatal heart attack just twelve days after the successful right-wing coup in 1973. In his last days, between Allende's death and his own, Neruda completed his *Confieso que he vivido* (*Memoirs*, 1974), which appeared in translation in 1977.

Nervo, Amado Ruiz de (1870–1919),   Mexican poet. As a young man, Nervo studied for the priesthood, an experience reflected in the mysticism that characterizes much of his work. When forced to leave the seminary for financial reasons, he turned to journalism and became cofounder of the *Revista moderna*, an influential modernist review. From 1905 to 1918, he held a diplomatic post in Madrid and, at his death, was Mexican minister to Argentina and Uruguay. Nervo's early works, such as *Perlas negras* (1898), *Poemas* (1901), and *Jardines interiores* (1905), place him in the mainstream of MODERNISMO. Subsequently, however, his poetry became more subjective and revealing, and such works as *Serenidad* (1914) and *Elevación* (1917) express the asceticism and tranquility of his later years.

Neugeboren, Jay (1938–), novelist, short-story writer. Born in Brooklyn and educated at Columbia and Indiana University, Neugeboren has taught in high schools and colleges. The subjects of his early fiction are often marginal figures in urban settings. The main character in *Big Man* (1966) is an African-American star basketball player caught in the betting scandals of the early 1950s; *Listen Ruben Fontanez* (1968) centers on an elderly Jewish teacher and his Hispanic students. Several Brooklyn boys are treated in the short fiction of *Corky's Brother and Other Stories* (1969). Other novels are *Sam's Legacy* (1974), *An Orphan's Tale* (1976), *The Stolen Jew* (1981), and *Before My Life Began* (1985). *Imagining Robert* (1997) is a memoir of his brother's thirty-year history of mental illness and of other family instabilities. *Transforming Madness: New Lives for People Living with Mental Illness* (1999) examines the mental health system. *Don't Worry about the Kids* (1997) collects stories, mostly of affluent northeasterners.

Nevins, Allan (1890–1971), teacher, journalist, writer, historian. Nevins did editorial work for the New York *Evening News, The Nation,* the New York *Sun,* and the New York *World.* In 1927 he began to teach history at Cornell University, and in 1931 joined the faculty of Columbia University. He retired in 1958. Nevins wrote histories of outstanding merit and interest. His writings include *The Life of Robert Rogers* (1914); *The Evening Post—A Century Of Journalism* (1922); *Frémont: the West's Greatest Adventurer* (2 v. 1928); *Henry White—Thirty Years of American Diplomacy* (1930); *Grover Cleveland—A Study in Courage* (1932, Pulitzer Prize, 1933); *Hamilton Fish—The Inner History of the Grant Administration* (1936, Pulitzer Prize 1937); *Frémont, Pathmarker of the West* (1939, an enlargement and revision of *Frémont: the West's Greatest Adventurer*); *The Heritage of America,* with HENRY STEELE COMMAGER (1939); *John D. Rockefeller: the Heroic Age of American Business* (2 v. 1940); *The Ordeal of the Union* (1946, Scribner Centenary Prize); *The Emergence of Lincoln* (2 v. 1952); *Study in Power* (1953); *Ford: the Times, the Man, the Company,* in collaboration with Frank E. Hill (v. 1 1954, v. 2 1957); and *The War for the Union* (2 v. 1959). For a time, Nevins was editor of the *Chronicles of America.*

Newbery, John, and **the Newbery Award**. Newbery (1713–1767), born in England, was a printer and bookseller who in 1744 began the publication of volumes of quaint rhymes and stories for children. The American Library Association has offered a Newbery award each year since 1922 to the best book written for children.

New Criticism. A philosophy of criticism and an approach to literature that largely dominated the academy—not without various challenges—from 1940 to 1960. While never entirely homogeneous, the movement can be characterized as a reaction against traditional historical-philological scholarship on the one hand and impressionistic adventures of the soul on the other, matters held to be extrinsic to literature as an art. These are replaced by close and objective reading of the work itself—an approach in some ways not unlike the French method of detailed analysis known as *explication de texte.* The aim is thus to analyze the internal and reflexive part-whole relationships constituting the form of the work, which involves interpreting multiple layers of meaning and interactions of meanings on the assumption that this process will reveal the nonparaphrasable content of the work. This content is then seen as a special type of knowledge, a meaning not separable from its embodiment, hence organic—a higher kind of truth than that conveyed by abstractions of scientific and expository prose.

Aesthetically, such a concept reaches back through W. B. Yeats and the Aesthetes and Decadents of *fin de siècle* England and France—Walter Pater, Oscar Wilde, Arthur Symons, for example—who led the art-for-art's-sake revolt against the supposedly excessive moralizing of the Victorians. And this movement reaches back in turn to Kant through Coleridge and Keats, and to Aristotle through Sidney. Historically, it represented a reaction against the divided and specialized nature of modern secular and technological civilization, placing the emphasis back on the unity, concreteness, complexity, inclusiveness, and wholeness of art. The concept is thus a difficult one—how can a work be self-referring and meaningful at one and the same time?—and it perpetually threatened to crack at the seams.

The actual 20th-century beginnings of this new formalism emerged about 1909 in England, when the American EZRA POUND met the British T.E. Hulme and they launched an assault on Victorian verbosity and sentimentality. The outcome was the formation of a group during 1912–1914 calling itself *Les Imagistes,* and including H. D. (Hilda Doolittle), F. S. Flint, and Richard Aldington that promoted free verse, short and tightly organized lyrics, and concrete images.

Later in this second decade the influence of another American expatriate, T.S. ELIOT, was making itself felt. In a series of groundbreaking essays, his ideas of impersonality—"Tradition and the Individual Talent" (1917); the objective correlative, "Hamlet and His Problems" (1919); and the dissociation of sensibility, "The Metaphysical Poets" (1921)—pervaded critical thought for years to come. And, although he came later to repudiate the "lemon-squeezer approach" to criticism, his own dense and allusive poetry became a favorite subject of interpretation by the New Critics.

In the 1920s and 1930s the British semanticist I. A. Richards rose to practically equal prominence, publishing *Science and Poetry* in 1926, in which he argued that the language of poetry, in opposition to that of science and practical prose, had its own justification as the expression of emotive experience. In

Practical Criticism (1929) Richards initiated a method of close reading, and in The *Philosophy of Rhetoric* (1936) he coined the terms *tenor* and *vehicle* to analyze subject, analogue, and their interaction, *poetic metaphor*. William Empson, a former student of Richards, published the influential *Seven Types of Ambiguity* in 1930, an extension of the close-reading approach.

Meanwhile, at Vanderbilt University in Nashville, Tennessee, during the 1920s a group of young poets and critics—including JOHN CROWE RANSOM, ALLEN TATE, ROBERT PENN WARREN, and CLEANTH BROOKS—was forming a literary club. They published a periodical called *The Fugitive* from 1922 to 1925 and soon moved into social criticism in I'LL TAKE MY STAND (1930), a collection of essays attacking Northern industrialism in the name of Southern agrarianism. They soon returned to literature, however, but without abandoning their conservativism—their social and aesthetic concepts were, after all, parallel.

Drawing on the pioneering work of Pound, Hulme, Eliot, Richards, and Empson, they began issuing a series of influential books: Tate's *Reactionary Essays* (1936); the widely-used textbook by Brooks and Warren, *Understanding Poetry* (1938); Brooks's *Modern Poetry and the Tradition* (1939); and Ransom's *The New Criticism* (1941). By these means, an additional cluster of critical terms for discussing the inner organization of a work came into currency: texture and structure, denotation and connotation, irony, paradox, tension, and the heresy of paraphrase. W. K. Wimsatt and Monroe Beardsley added two additional sets of terms in 1946—*intentional fallacy* and *affective fallacy*— to further emphasize the concept of the work's autonomy.

By the 1960s, however, with the explosive emergence of various liberation movements shaking the academy and the world at large, the New Critics were attacked for their conservativism and their apparent separation of literature from practical concerns. It is doubtful, nevertheless, whether some sort of close reading, no matter what other approaches may come to the fore, will ever outlive its usefulness—for that is, after all, the basis upon which other approaches should be constructed in the first place.

Although KENNETH BURKE, R. P. BLACKMUR, and YVOR WINTERS are other prominent American critics who have been named in connection with the New Critics, their work is really too individual and diverse to fit comfortably into this category— Winters especially has in fact attacked the New Criticism.

NORMAN FRIEDMAN

New Directions,   a press founded in 1936 by JAMES LAUGHLIN IV specializing in avant-garde poetry and prose. It has published, among others, W. C. WILLIAMS and HENRY MILLER.

New Eclectic (1868–1875),   a monthly magazine published in Baltimore; it printed work by WILLIAM GILMORE SIMMS and SIDNEY LANIER. When it became the publication of the Southern Historical Society in 1871, it was renamed the *Southern Magazine*.

Newell, Robert Henry ["Orpheus C. Kerr"] (1836–1901),   journalist, humorist, novelist, poet. Born in New York City, Newell contributed to hometown newspapers, in 1858 becoming assistant editor of the New York *Sunday Mercury*, for which he wrote sentimental verses and comments on current topics. During the Civil War he was a war correspondent for the New York *Herald*. He invented his pen name as a pun on the swarm of wartime office-seekers in Washington and signed that name to the Orpheus C. Kerr letters—supposedly coming from Washington and originally printed in the *Mercury*, later in other journals, and finally as *The Orpheus C. Kerr Papers* (5 v. 1862–71). This correspondence was compounded of the same devices used by the creators of Sut Lovingood and Petroleum V. Nasby—bad spelling, overstatement, and anticlimax. Oddly mingled with this fashionable humor were imaginary episodes, war incidents, and sentimental verses. Although most of the *Papers* are unreadable today, one genuinely funny letter gives the results of an imaginary contest for a new national anthem. Entries supposedly submitted by Emerson, Holmes, Aldrich, Whittier, Longfellow, and others display Newell's wit and skill as a parodist.

Newell also published *The Palace Beautiful and Other Poems* (1865) and *Versatilities* (1871), poems; *The Cloven Foot* (1870), an attempted completion of Dickens's *The Mystery of Edwin Drood*. He also wrote *The Walking Doll*, or the *Asters and Disasters of Society* (1872), a novel of New York life, and *There Was a Man* (1884), a novel attacking the Darwinian theory. Newell was married for a short time to the actress ADAH MENKEN; from 1869 to 1874 he was an editor of the New York *World*. A neurological disease forced him to retire from active life two years later.

New England.   New England's often agonizing conflict between a Puritanical tradition and a rebellious nature; its commercial, intellectual, and social dominance; its granite landscapes; its flinty humor—all these have made the home of the Yankee a favorite theme for American writers of all generations. The grass-roots culture of the region has been collected in such volumes as Richard M. Dorson's *Jonathan Draws the Long Bow* (1946) and B. A. Botkin's *Treasury of New England Folklore* (1947); native Yankee wit appears in Richardson Wright's *Grandfather Was Queer: Early American Wags and Eccentrics from Colonial Times to the Civil War* (1939). The New England dialect was a stock prop of 19th-century humorists, as in SEBA SMITH's *Letters of Jack Downing* (1830) or in the Sam Slick sketches of THOMAS C. HALIBURTON (1835). James Russell Lowell used Yankee talk skillfully in his BIGLOW PAPERS (1846, 1867). A study of New England speech is to be found in *The Linguistic Atlas of New England* (1939–43).

Until near the end of the 19th century New England was the literary center of the United States, and writing produced there established standards for writers elsewhere. Major studies of New England literature include Van Wyck Brooks's THE FLOWERING OF NEW ENGLAND (1936) and NEW ENGLAND: INDIAN SUMMER (1940); Perry Miller's *The New England Mind: The Seventeenth Century* (1939) and *The New England Mind: From Colony to Province* (1953); Kenneth B. Murdock's *Literature and Theology in Colonial New England* (1949); and Lawrence Buell's *New England Literary Culture: From Revolution Through Renaissance* (1986).

So much fiction has been written about New England that only a few outstanding titles can be mentioned in this space:

Hawthorne, THE HOUSE OF THE SEVEN GABLES (1851); Harriet Beecher Stowe, THE MINISTER'S WOOING (1859); Oliver Wendell Holmes, ELSIE VENNER (1861); Louisa May Alcott, LITTLE WOMEN (1868–69); Thomas Bailey Aldrich, THE STORY OF A BAD BOY (1869); Mary E. Wilkins Freeman, A NEW ENGLAND NUN AND OTHER STORIES (1891); Sarah Orne Jewett, THE COUNTRY OF THE POINTED FIRS (1896); Wharton, ETHAN FROME (1911); Henry James, THE EUROPEANS (1878) and THE BOSTONIANS (1886); GEORGE SANTAYANA, *The Last Puritan* (1936); J. P. Marquand, THE LATE GEORGE APLEY (1937); Edwin O'Connor, THE LAST HURRAH (1956); JOHN UPDIKE, *Couples* (1968); John Irving, THE HOTEL NEW HAMPSHIRE (1981); and CAROLYN CHUTE, *The Beans of Egypt, Maine* (1986).

New England Poets have been central to the American tradition, from ANNE BRADSTREET, MICHAEL WIGGLESWORTH, and EDWARD TAYLOR, through the nineteenth-century writers WILLIAM CULLEN BRYANT, RALPH WALDO EMERSON, HENRY WADSWORTH LONGFELLOW, JOHN GREENLEAF WHITTIER, OLIVER WENDELL HOLMES, JAMES RUSSELL LOWELL, and EMILY DICKINSON to the twentieth century's EDWIN ARLINGTON ROBINSON, ROBERT FROST, WALLACE STEVENS, E. E. CUMMINGS, ROBERT LOWELL, ANNE SEXTON, SYLVIA PLATH, and MARY OLIVER.

New England: Indian Summer, 1865–1915 (1940), fourth volume of VAN WYCK BROOKS's *Makers and Finders* series. It surveys the years between the Civil War Boston of Oliver Wendell Holmes and the New England of Robert Frost and Eugene O'Neill. Writing of New England as it merged in these years with the spirit of the nation at large, Brooks also treats Henry James, Henry Adams, and William Dean Howells.

New England Courant.   This newspaper, founded by JAMES FRANKLIN on August 7, 1721, became noteworthy for its attacks on the authorities and its satiric sketches in imitation of *The Spectator*. It denounced COTTON MATHER for advocating vaccination against smallpox—Mather called the contributors to the *Courant* the HELL-FIRE CLUB. Among the contributors was Franklin's younger stepbrother, BENJAMIN FRANKLIN, who assumed the pen name of Silence Dogood and saw his first essay appear on April 2, 1722. James was a bit jealous, but when his attacks in the paper put James Franklin in jail he made Benjamin temporary publisher. Later the brothers quarreled, and Benjamin left for New York and Philadelphia in search of a job. The paper ceased publication on June 4, 1726.

New Englander, The.   This magazine was founded at Yale (1843) by Edward Royall Tyler, son of the playwright ROYALL TYLER. Its purpose was to support evangelical Christianity. In time its interest shifted to history and economics. It became one of the best-known reviews of the mid-19th century. In 1885 its name was changed to *The New Englander and Yale Review*. In 1892 it became the *Yale Review*. In 1911 Professor WILBUR L. CROSS of Yale took the publication over and made it a distinguished magazine of wide literary and general interests.

New England Magazine.   A monthly magazine founded by Joseph T. Buckingham and published in Boston. Its first issue appeared in July 1831, and it ceased publication in December 1836. During its short existence it had a reputa-

tion for quality unrivaled until the appearance of *Atlantic Monthly* in 1857. It had numerous noted contributors, including Hawthorne, Longfellow, Whittier, Noah Webster, Edward Everett, and Oliver Wendell Holmes, Sr. It was taken over by the *American Monthly Magazine*.

New England Nun, A, and Other Stories (1891), twenty stories by MARY E. WILKINS FREEMAN. They are written with that combination of realism and irony for which the author became known—as in the opening story, in which a young woman's fiancé goes to Australia to make a fortune, comes back after fourteen years, and marries another woman to the relief of the heroine, who does not want her accustomed domestic ways disturbed.

New England Primer, The.   The earliest extant edition of this widely circulated "little Bible" of the colonies is dated 1727 and is a collector's item. Who prepared the Primer is not known; it was an obvious imitation of many similar English volumes, which had long been imported and circulated in the colonies. It was a tiny textbook that fitted snugly in a child's pocket. The Primer immediately won an immense popularity, circulating not only in New England but also in other English settlements. Millions of copies were sold as late as the 19th century. Most young colonists learned to read from its pages. Deeply religious in tone, the 1749 edition contained, among other material, an alphabet with verses and illustrations, rules for behavior, several hymns, the prayer "Now I lay me down to sleep," the shorter catechism, and pious stories of several martyrs.

By 1800 the *Primer* began to look beyond the church walls for its contents, as when the alphabet read, "A was an Angler, and fished with a hook. B was a Blockhead, and ne'er learned his book." The book was imitated in *The New York Primer, The American Primer*, and similar texts; only the title page was different. *A Columbian Primer* is attributed to Benjamin Franklin. See BENJAMIN HARRIS.

New England's Annoyances (1630?).   This anonymous poem, sometimes called "the first verses by an American colonist," is said to have been taken down in 1685 from the lips of a woman of ninety-six. The lines describe the hardships, hazards, and privations of the New World, but bid the reader to have "a quiet and contented mind, / And all needful blessings you will find."

New England's Crisis (1676),   a narrative poem by BENJAMIN TOMPSON. Probably the first epic written on American soil, Tompson's poem describes KING PHILIP's War in 650 lines of heroic couplets. The Prologue pictures New England society as being in a state of decadence sufficient to bring on the war. The narrative has many classical allusions, but the Prologue, with its lament at the passing of early American ways when "the dainty Indian maize" was eaten out of clam shells in thatched huts, remains the most striking part of the poem.

New England's First Fruits (London 1643),   a pamphlet published anonymously but probably written by Henry Dunster, Hugh Peter, and Thomas Weld. It was in part a reply to Thomas Lechford's charges in his PLAIN DEALING (1642) that nothing was being done for the Indians in New England. The authors give a list of Indian conversions, go on to tell about the founding of Harvard College, and give other information about New England.

New England's Memorial.   See NATHANIEL MORTON.

New England's Prospect (1634),   a guide by William Wood (1580?–1639). Wood came to New England in 1629 and remained there for four years, then returned to England and published his book in London. He makes no attempt to minimize the difficulties of living in the colonies, provides a guidebook to the country, offers suggestions on equipment needed, and gives an account of the Indians. The book was reprinted in 1865.

New England Quarterly (1928–   ),   a scholarly periodical emphasizing literary and historical studies of life in the region, founded by SAMUEL ELIOT MORISON, ARTHUR M. SCHLESINGER, SR., and others.

New England's Rarities Discovered (1672),   a description by John Josselyn. Josselyn, who made two visits to this country, was not a Puritan and was often candidly critical of the colonies. His was the first systematic attempt to record New England flora and fauna. It also gives a general description of the region, provides some medical hints, and mentions new dishes—stewed pumpkins, for example. Josselyn's book was reprinted in the *Transactions* (1860) of the American Antiquarian Society. A later book of his was *An Account of Two Voyages to New England* (1674), reprinted in the *Collections* (1833) of the Massachusetts Historical Society.

New England Renaissance,   a term sometimes applied to the mid-19th century when writers of the region, inspirited by theological and philosophical ideas associated with UNITARIANISM and TRANSCENDENTALISM, dominated the cultural scene in the United States. The concept of a renaissance in American literature received widespread exposure through F. O. MATTHIESSEN's *American Renaissance: Art and Expression in the Age of Emerson and Whitman.*

New England's Trials (1620, 2nd ed. 1622),   a narrative of experiences and observations written by Captain JOHN SMITH. This was in part a tract on the fisheries, in part Smith's plea for employment to help develop them. In the 1622 edition it was enlarged to include an account of Plymouth. His story of Plymouth is strictly factual and says nothing of the religious motives that had led to the settlement. Smith's book was reprinted, in an edition edited by Charles Deane, in the *Proceedings* of the Massachusetts Historical Society (1873).

New England Tragedies, The (1868),   a drama by HENRY WADSWORTH LONGFELLOW. This drama—Longfellow called it a dramatic poem—was later made part of a work called CHRISTUS (1872), a trilogy comprising *The Divine Tragedy*, THE GOLDEN LEGEND, and *The New England Tragedies*. The plays imitated the form of medieval mystery plays and were intended to illustrate Hope in the age of Christ, Faith in the Middle Ages, and Charity in modern times. Longfellow divided *The New England Tragedies* into two parts: *John Endicott*, illustrating the cruel persecution of the Quakers by the Puritans; and *Giles Corey of the Salem Farms*, portraying the witchcraft madness. See GILES COREY.

New England Weekly Journal (1727–1741),   a Boston newspaper, the fourth to be established, founded by Samuel Kneeland and later merged with the *Boston Gazette* to become the *Boston Gazette, or Weekly Journal*. Increase Mather was one of its contributors; it printed essays and poetry as well as news.

New English Canaan (1637),   an account by THOMAS MORTON. The Puritans, themselves Dissenters, did not care much for Morton, a dissenter from Puritan views, and drove him out of his settlement at Merry Mount. In his *New English Canaan*, published in Amsterdam, Morton gives his side of the story. The first two sections are seriously intended, with a description of the Indians and the characteristics of the land. In the third section Morton accuses the Puritans of ousting him because they envied his success as a trader. Charles Francis Adams edited a reprint (1883) of *New English Canaan* for the *Publications* of the Prince Society of Boston. John L. Motley used the book as a basis for two novels, *Morton's Hope* (1839) and *Merry Mount* (1849); Hawthorne used it as a basis for his story THE MAYPOLE OF MERRYMOUNT (1836).

New Hampshire: A Poem with Notes and Grace Notes (1923),   a collection by ROBERT FROST that won the Pulitzer Prize for poetry in 1924. It contains some of his best-known poems, including the long title poem, THE AXE-HELVE, "The Grindstone," STOPPING BY WOODS ON A SNOWY EVENING, and "Fire and Ice."

New Harmony.   See HARMONY.

New Historicism.   A method of literary criticism, new historicism, also called cultural materialism, developed in the 1970s in reaction to the new critics' and deconstructionists' conception of literature as autonomous or self-referential, detached from historical contexts. Interdisciplinary in its approach, new historicism conceives the literary work to be inseparable from the cultures in which the work is produced and read, therefore embedded in social history, which itself is a construct reflective of the critic's culture. Interpretation of literature, which to the new historicist includes all forms of discourse, requires analysis of the interplay of political and social institutions and forms on which the meaning of literature is believed to depend. New historicists claim that their work differs from the old historicism of such critics as E. M. W. Tillyard and Dover Wilson in that it replaces a monolithic vision of a dominant ideology with a vision of diversity and struggle among competing centers of power, in which struggle literature itself engages. New historicism, which is grounded in the theories of Michel Foucault and Marxist critics such as Raymond Williams and Louis Althusser, first gained prominence in the work of Stephen Greenblatt, Jonathan Goldberg, and other critics of English Renaissance literature. Studies of American literature that exemplify ideas and methods of new historicism include Mark Seltzer, *Henry James and the Art of Power* (1984); Walter Benn Michaels, *The Gold Standard and the Logic of Naturalism* (1987); Amy Kaplan, *The Social Construction of*

American Realism (1988); Walter T. Herbert, *Dearest Beloved: The Hawthornes and the Making of the Middle-Class Family* (1993); and Walter Benn Michaels, *Our America: Nativism, Modernism, and Pluralism* (1995). A general study is Catherine Gallagher's *Practicing The New Historicism* (2000).

ELSA NETTELS/GP

Newhouse, Edward (1911–), novelist, short story writer. Newhouse came to the United States from Hungary at age twelve and learned English in New York City public schools and libraries. When he was eighteen and consumed by curiosity about the United States and Mexico, he set out to explore them by hopping freight trains. His first stories were published in *New Masses*, and his first two novels, *You Can't Sleep Here* (1934) and *This Is Your Day* (1937), are examples of proletarian literature. He subsequently lost faith in the movement and disowned his early efforts as childish. Many of his later stories appeared in *The New Yorker*. They have been collected in several books: *Anything Can Happen* (1941), *The Iron Chain* (1946), *Many Are Called* (1951), and *The Temptation of Roger Heriott* (1954), a novel.

New Humanism, The.   See HUMANISM.

New Journalism.   A style of reporting arising in the 1960s and associated particularly with the work of TOM WOLFE and NORMAN MAILER. Abandoning traditional journalistic objectivity, these authors and others created a literature characterized by strong evidence of the author's personality and opinions. Often, as in Mailer's *Armies of the Night* (1968), the author appears as a character. (See NON-FICTION NOVEL.)

Newlove, John (1938–), poet. Born in Regina, he has traveled extensively throughout Canada and now lives in British Columbia. The poetry in Newlove's earlier volumes— *Grave Sirs* (1962), *Moving in Alone* (1965, repr. 1977), *Notebook Pages* (1965), and *What They Say* (1967)—depicts an alienated sensibility traumatized by a predatory environment. In *Lies* (1972) and *The Fat Man* (1977), the poet's focus shifts from intense self-scrutiny to a search for the truth about Canada's history and present dilemmas. Convinced that traditional poetic devices hinder authentic expression, Newlove uses direct statement, visual precision, and irony. His other works include *Dreams Surround Us* (1977) and *The Green Plain* (1981).

Newman, Christopher.   A representative American, he is the major character in THE AMERICAN (1877), by Henry James.

New Masses.   See THE MASSES.

New Negro, The (1925).   An anthology edited by ALAIN LOCKE and associated with the HARLEM RENAISSANCE. The preface to the collection of essays, stories, a play, and bibliographies of African-American writers argued that self-expression, increasingly liberated from racial bigotry, would enrich American culture as a whole.

New Republic, The.   A weekly, founded in New York City in 1914 by Willard D. Straight, with Herbert D. Croly as editor; he was succeeded by Bruce Bliven. It aimed to be a liberal magazine and strongly supported Woodrow Wilson when he declared war on Germany, but later broke with him. It has always had a small but influential circulation, has been especially noted for its excellent book, drama, and moving picture reviews. Among its contributors have been Walter Lippmann, Randolph Bourne, Clarence Day, Henry Blake Fuller, Robert Morss Lovett, Stark Young, Malcolm Cowley, and James Agee.

News from Virginia: The Lost Flock Triumphant (1610),   a ballad by Richard Rich. This is one of the earliest poems to come out of America. Its purpose was less aesthetic than utilitarian. The author was one of the Virginia pioneers and described himself as "a soldier, blunt and plain," who to feed "his own humor" printed his impression of Jamestown in 1610. Scenes from the poem may have influenced Shakespeare's *The Tempest*.

newspapers.   The first news sheets and newspapers in the English colonies in America were a part of English journalism. Published by English pioneers in a new land, they imitated the home papers in from and content. Thus, the earliest American papers resembled the London *Gazette*, printed on both sides of a single leaf about six by ten inches, without display heads. News was derived chiefly from four sources: (1) extracts from the latest papers received from overseas, (2) extracts from papers published in other colonial towns, (3) private letters from a distance brought in by obliging readers and oral reports of travelers and sea captains, and (4) local news of general public importance, for example, great storms, celebrations, the governor's activities, and hangings.

Local news usually appeared under a local date line, forerunner of the editorial flag. Purely local matters were generally disregarded as being already well known to the community, though there were brief notices of deaths and marriages. These were noted in accordance with the concept of news as historical record rather than as sensation, entertainment, human interest, or timely report.

Disregarding earlier news sheet broadsides, the first papers designed for regular publication in America was *Publick Occurrences*, issued by Benjamin Harris in Boston, September 25, 1690. It was a three-page paper, the fourth left blank for written communications when sent to friends at a distance, thus pointing up the connection between written newsletters and early newspapers. Its printed pages were packed with well-reported news, but some gave offense to the colonial government, and no further issues were permitted. The first continuously published paper in the colonies was the Boston *News-Letter* (1704–76), founded by John Campbell, postmaster and writer of newsletters. It labeled itself conspicuously as "published by authority." Not so the NEW-ENGLAND COURANT (1721–27), also of Boston, founded by JAMES FRANKLIN, elder brother of BENJAMIN FRANKLIN. James was thrown into jail in 1722 because of a sarcastic reference to the governor, and he then named his sixteen-year-old apprentice Ben as editor, by that trick continuing publication. In the next year James got out of jail and Ben broke his indentures and ran away to Philadelphia to find fame and fortune.

In that city Andrew Bradford had founded the *American Weekly Mercury* (1719–49), for some years the town's only paper. In 1728 SAMUEL KEIMER, an eccentric printer and philosopher, began his *Universal Instructor in All Arts and Sciences and Pennsylvania Gazette.* It was not a success, and in the next year Franklin, by this time conducting a prosperous printing business, bought the paper, decapitated the high-sounding title, and continued the PENNSYLVANIA GAZETTE until his retirement from the printing business in 1748. Franklin retained an interest in the paper until 1766, by which time his partner, David Hall, was able to buy him out. Hall, along with his son, grandson, and their partners continued the paper until 1815.

Meanwhile, William Bradford, Andrew's father, who had been Philadelphia's first printer, moved to New York City and founded that city's first newspaper, the *Gazette* (1725–44). Having had his troubles with the authorities in Philadelphia, he made his newspaper definitely a government organ. But when the popular party in New York was engaged in a struggle with avaricious Governor William Cosby, leaders of that party helped JOHN PETER ZENGER, a German immigrant, to establish his *Weekly Journal* (1733–51) and fire repeated volleys of liberal political philosophy and satire at Cosby and his supporters. Late in 1734 Zenger was jailed, though his paper continued to be issued. His trial for seditious libel in August 1735 was a landmark in the American struggle for freedom of the press. Swayed by the oratory of Andrew Hamilton, a Philadelphia lawyer brought in to replace the attorneys who had been disbarred for supporting him, the jury acquitted Zenger, though the principle on which this popular action was based did not become law until many years later.

By 1750 fourteen newspapers were being published in the colonies, from Massachusetts south along the coast to South Carolina. A newspaper was commonly a by-product of a printing office, and the profit margin was represented by advertising patronage. Papers often increased to four or to six pages eleven by seventeen inches in size, and by mid-century the more successful publishers were often able to fill three or more pages with advertising, all single-column in width, with modest headings and a few stock cuts. All papers were printed by hand on rag paper.

Essays, in the form of letters to the editor on public affairs or moral questions, or arranged in series, in *Spectator* fashion, became important in colonial journalism. The *New England Courant* was the first paper to feature imitations of the Addisonian essay; of these, Franklin's Dogood Papers are the most notable. Later Franklin wrote "The Busy-Body" (1729) for Bradford's *American Weekly Mercury.* Other outstanding essays were those of Mather Byles in the *New England Weekly Journal* (1727–41); some "little pieces" by Franklin in his own *Gazette*; the excellent original essay series in William Parks's papers; "The Plain Dealer" in the *Maryland Gazette* (1727–34); and "The Monitor" in the *Virginia Gazette* (1736–50). All appeared anonymously.

Proceedings of the colonial assemblies and political matters were a major concern of the colonial papers. They unanimously rebelled against the regulations requiring the use of stamped paper in 1765, and many of them encouraged the growing movement toward independence. JOHN DICKINSON's

"Letters from a Farmer in Pennsylvania," published 1767–68 in William Goddard's *Pennsylvania Chronicle* (1767–74) and later reprinted in nearly all the colonial papers, were moderate, though they complained of taxation without representation and did not advocate independence. Not so Thomas Paine's COMMON SENSE, first published as a pamphlet early in 1776, and later reprinted piecemeal in most American papers. It produced a greater sensation than anything ever before published in the country and forced American public opinion to face the idea of separation from the mother country.

Newspapers gained in influence during the Revolution, though the war represented a great ordeal for all of them. At the time of the battle of Lexington thirty-seven colonial newspapers were being published, of which only twenty survived—some with suspensions—through the six and a half years to the surrender at Yorktown; but thirty-three new papers made courageous beginnings during the war, of which thirteen survived. Thus, by the end of the war there were almost as many papers as at the beginning. Leading patriot spokesmen were the *Massachusetts Spy* (1770–1904), founded in Boston by Isaiah Thomas, but moved to Worcester when the British occupied that city; the Boston *Gazette*, published by the "trumpeters of sedition," Benjamin Edes and John Gill, and written largely by such members of the Caucus Club as Samuel and John Adams, Josiah Quincy, and Joseph Warren; the *Pennsylvania Journal* (1742–93), conducted by William Bradford III, outstanding soldier-editor of the war; and John Holt's New York *Journal* (1766–1800), which was chased about over the country and its plant repeatedly destroyed by the British. Leading Tory papers were [James] *Rivington's New York Gazetteer* (1773–83), which, before the war, was one of the best and most widely circulated (3,600) papers in the colonies, but whose brilliant editor became the most hated royalist of them all; and the New York *Mercury* (1752–83), published by Hugh Gaine, the turncoat.

THE FEDERALIST, a series of papers discussing the proposed constitution, written by Alexander Hamilton, James Madison, and John Jay, appeared first in the New York *Independent Journal* (1783–1840). It was widely reprinted throughout the country, and in book form it has long exerted a worldwide influence. Following Washington's inauguration, John Fenno's GAZETTE OF THE UNITED STATES (1789–1818) became a government spokesman, while the NATIONAL GAZETTE (1791–93), conducted by the poet Philip Freneau, was the organ of the dissident party. In fact, the former represented the policies of Hamilton, and the latter, those of Jefferson. After the end of the brief but stormy career of Freneau's paper, the Philadelphia *Aurora* (1793–1843), conducted by Benjamin Franklin Bache—sometimes called Lightning-Rod Junior because of the achievement of his famous grandfather—took up the cudgels for the anti-Federalists. Bache's printing plant was wrecked by partisans who resented his criticism of Washington, and he was later attacked on the street by Fenno. Both belligerent editors died of yellow fever in the Philadelphia epidemic of 1798. Bache was followed in the editorship of the *Aurora* and its war against the Federalists by his able son-in-law, William Duane.

Washington was so highly regarded throughout the country that criticism of him personally was limited to comparatively few papers, though such was the President's sensitiveness to press attacks that these may have affected his decision to retire at the end of his second term. On the other side, William Cobbett, later a celebrated English writer but at this time living in America, issued his *Porcupine's Gazette* (1797–99), leading the Federalist journals in stinging satire until libel suits drove the editor home. All this marked the beginnings of what may be called the dark ages of American journalism, in which arrant partisanship distorted the reporting of public affairs. A phase of this situation was the passage of the Alien and Sedition Acts in 1798, ostensibly designed to curb seditious utterances on what seemed the brink of a war with France, and to deport dangerous aliens. The Acts were not reenacted in 1801, but resentment against them had helped Jefferson into the Presidency, and the spread of newspapers into the country west of the Appalachians had a tendency to redress the balance between the Federalists and what was now called the Republican Party in the control of the press. But it was not until the appearance of the penny press in the 1830s that bigoted partisanship showed signs of relaxing its hold.

The first daily paper in America was a shabby sheet issued by Benjamin Towne, who had changed sides twice in the Revolution. His daily of 1783–84 was one phase of his *Pennsylvania Evening Post* (1775–84). A far better daily appeared when John Dunlap and David C. Claypoole transformed their *Pennsylvania Packet*, begun in 1771, by adding to its name *"and Daily Advertiser"* in 1784; under various publishers the *Daily Advertiser* continued until 1839. The first New York daily was the transformed *Morning Post* (1782–92), but it was surpassed by the *Daily Advertiser (1785–1809)*, which was founded about a week after the *Post* became a daily under Francis Childs. The chief purpose of these early dailies was to furnish current information of the arrival of ships and the offerings of imported goods. Once started, however, the mercantile journals usually took strong partisan positions in politics and, of course, they carried general news. By 1820, of the 512 newspapers being published, forty-two were dailies, many of them carrying the word *Advertiser* in their titles or subtitles.

In the next decade the number of dailies increased by a third or more, some of them mainly political organs. Andrew Jackson developed a press that would "wheel and fire at word of command," and there was much outrageous scurrility in political comment on both sides. Less combative was the Washington *National Intelligencer* (1800–69), long conducted by Joseph Gales, Jr., and W. W. Seaton, and depended on by other papers for Washington news. Jefferson had encouraged Samuel Harrison Smith to establish it when the government was first transferred to the new capital, but it was later superseded as an administration organ by Jacksonian papers.

These papers, sold at $8 or $10 a year, were too expensive for common laborers, whose wages were less than $1 a day, but with the advent of power presses and machine-made paper, and with the rise of the common people, papers of smaller size

selling on the street at a penny a copy gradually gained ascendancy over the mercantile "blanket sheets." Benjamin Day's New York *Sun* was the first of these small four-page penny papers to make a resounding success. Its emphasis on local news, including its police-court reports in a witty vein, set the pattern for the penny press. Begun in 1833, it kept its price, while increasing its page size, until Civil War times. After the war CHARLES A. DANA became its editor (1868–97), emphasizing human-interest stories and an entertaining editorial page. In 1916 Frank A. Munsey bought it, and in 1950, twenty-five years after Munsey's death, it was merged with the *World-Telegram*. Some of the 19th-century's greatest papers began at one cent, though the *Sun* was the only one to keep that price after becoming successful. Five more that started at a penny will be mentioned here.

After several false starts in pursuit of fame and fortune in America, JAMES GORDON BENNETT, born in Scotland, founded the New York *Herald* in 1835, achieving by 1860 a circulation of 77,000—the largest in the world—and profits which, by his death in 1872, had made him one of the country's wealthiest men. The *Herald* was inclined to sensationalism. Bennett was a great innovator, having more firsts in newspaper techniques than any other publisher in the history of American journalism. On his death, James Gordon Bennett, Jr. edited the paper from 1872 to 1918, operating for many years by cable from his Paris residence. The *Herald* was merged with the *Tribune* in 1924.

Three New York printers, William M. Swain, Aruna S. Abell, and Azariah H. Simmons, together founded the Philadelphia *Public Ledger* (1836–1942), and in 1837, the Baltimore *Sun*. After Simmons's death Swain ran the *Public Ledger* and Abell, the *Sun*. Both were outstanding successes, encouraging the new magnetic telegraph and other improvements. Swain retired with a fortune in 1864, and George W. Childs was editor of the *Public Ledger* for thirty years. The *Sun* had its troubles during the Civil War but managed to retain outstanding editorship even after the administrations of Abell's son and grandson had ended, and it is still highly regarded by many.

HORACE GREELEY had tried a cheap-for-cash newspaper in New York several months before the *Sun* appeared, but he and his printer partner failed dismally in the attempt. In 1841, when he founded the *Tribune*, he tried again and was losing money when he brought in the astute Thomas McElrath as business partner. From then on things went better, and the *Tribune* and *Herald*, each now sold at two cents, became great competitors for many years. The *Herald* was always ahead in circulation, but the *Weekly Tribune* was remarkably popular and influential, especially in transplanted New England groups settled now from New York State westward to Kansas. Greeley himself, with all his eccentricities, stands out as probably the greatest editor in the history of American journalism. Distinguished as an enterprising newsman, even more distinguished as an effective editorial writer with a style that makes his *Tribune* articles as fresh, lucid, and persuasive today as when they were penned, Greeley was most notable for a lifelong devotion to the principle of giving a hearing to minorities and majorities alike. Following Greeley's death in 1872, after his defeat for the Presidency in that year, another great editor, WHITELAW REID, came to the *Tribune*; and the Reid family controlled it until the sale to John Hay Whitney in 1958 of what had become the *Herald Tribune*.

The *New York Times* was founded by HENRY J. RAYMOND and two financiers, George Jones and Edward B. Wesley, in 1851. During its first year it was a penny paper, then raised to two cents. Raymond, an experienced journalist, made the paper a news success and in its editorials tried to avoid the "low moral tone" of the *Herald* on the one hand and the "isms" of the *Tribune* on the other. His brilliant career was cut short at the age of forty-nine (1869), and Jones took over, making his most spectacular contribution by a crusade against the Tweed Ring. But in competition with the new Pulitzer-Hearst journalism of the 1880s and 1890s the *Times* had sunk to a friendly receivership, losing $1,000 a day, when ADOLPH S. OCHS took it over in 1896. Only two years later, when he challenged the "yellow papers" on their own price level of one-cent a copy, did Ochs start the upsurge that was to make the *Times* America's foremost newspaper. His policy was to forego sensationalism as such, print a large quantity and great variety of important news, and include in full many public documents. On the death of Ochs in 1935, Arthur Hays Sulzberger, a son-in-law, came into control.

One other great New York journal, a survivor from the early partisan era and never a penny paper, was the *Evening Post*, founded by Alexander Hamilton and friends in 1801 and edited from 1829 to 1878 by WILLIAM CULLEN BRYANT. As editor, Bryant was a great liberal, ever defending free commerce, free speech, and free soil. Henry Villard bought the paper in 1881 and soon made Edwin Lawrence Godkin editor. Godkin, English born and educated, had a critical mind, was a moderate liberal, and doubtless exerted no little influence. In its later phase the New York *Post*, under the ownership of Dorothy Schiff and her successors, became a tabloid of strongly liberal tendencies.

Meanwhile some great papers had grown up in the West and South. The earliest western papers were precarious weeklies designed to promote settlement in their regions, or to uphold party doctrines, or both. Pioneer adventurers were the Pittsburgh *Gazette* (1786–   ), sponsored in its early years by Hugh Henry Brackenridge, author of *Modern Chivalry*, a classic picaresque novel of early American politics; and the Lexington *Kentucky Gazette* (1787–1848).

By the 1890s Chicago had grown to be a great newspaper center second only to New York City. John Calhoun founded its first paper, the *Weekly Democrat*, in 1833; three years later "Long John" Wentworth bought it, edited it aggressively, made it a daily, and sold it in 1861 to the burgeoning *Tribune*. The latter paper was begun in 1847 and had a hard time until Joseph Medill, Charles H. Ray, and three other partners gained control in 1855. Ray and Medill did much to promote the political fortunes of Abraham Lincoln. The able Horace White was the *Tribune's* editor from 1866 to 1874, but it was not until

Medill, who had been serving as the city's mayor, bought complete control and took over as editor in 1874 that it began to win the dominance in Chicago journalism that it still retains. Fifteen years after Medill's death in 1899, two of his grandsons, Robert R. McCormick and Joseph Medill Patterson, came into management of the paper and ran it successfully as a strong local and Republican newspaper. Patterson's interests were eventually drawn away mainly to New York journalism, but Colonel McCormick's control did not falter until his death in 1955. Chief competitor of the *Tribune* in the pre-Medill years was the *Times* (1854–95), which, under Wilbur F. Storey's editorship (1861–78), was a sensational and eccentric paper; for a few days during June 1864, it was suspended by the military because of its Copperhead sympathies. Outstanding among other Chicago papers was the *Daily News*, founded by Melville E. Stone in 1876.

Among the South's great papers was the New Orleans *Picayune*, begun in 1836 by GEORGE W. KENDALL and Francis Lumsden, who named it for the coin at which it was sold. In the war with Mexico (1846–47) Kendall became the first outstanding regularly employed war correspondent in history, and much of the news of that war came to eastern papers through New Orleans. Through a series of mergers, New Orleans, which for half a century had several competing newspapers at a time, became in the 20th century a city with a single newspaper ownership—the *Times-Picayune* in the morning and the *States* in the evening. In Atlanta the *Constitution* (1868–   ) gained much prestige through the editorship of HENRY W. GRADY in the 1880s, and later of Evan P. Howell and his son Clark. In Louisville, GEORGE D. PRENTICE, a poet, wit, and journalist, founded the *Journal* in 1831; after the war it gained wide recognition as the *Courier-Journal* under the editorship of the brilliant HENRY WATTERSON.

No previous war in history had been covered so thoroughly by eyewitness correspondents as was the American Civil War. More than 150 correspondents served northern papers during the conflict, and at least that many more wrote occasional reports of military operations for newspapers or magazines. The New York *Herald* was said to have had thirty or forty correspondents on various fronts during the last year of the war, and several other papers sent out more than a dozen each. Telegraph facilities were not always available, and correspondents often had to make long journeys on horseback or on foot to get their reports through. Although the great papers were limited in size to eight six-column pages, they often gave more than a dozen columns to war reports, and some were able to provide occasional maps of the war areas.

In the decade following the Civil War the number of daily papers in the United States increased by about three-fourths; but it was not until the mid-1880s, under the stimulation of JOSEPH PULITZER's New York *World*, that what came to be called the New Journalism was developed. Pulitzer had come to St. Louis from Hungary in 1865, a penniless immigrant boy, and soon distinguished himself as a reporter on the *Westliche Post*

(1857–1938), then conducted by CARL SCHURZ and Emil Preetorius. By 1878 he was able to combine the expiring *Dispatch* and the recently established *Post* to form the *Post-Dispatch*, which soon became the leading morning paper of St. Louis and a strong competitor of the morning *Globe-Democrat* (1872–   ), then under the editorship of Joseph B. McCullagh. But Pulitzer was not satisfied with success in a midwestern city; his eyes were upon the country's greatest journalistic forum—New York City. He was thirty-seven when he came to that city in 1883 and bought the *World*. It had begun as a religious daily in 1860 and was ably edited with a political emphasis by Manton Marble in the 1870s. Now it was rescued from the doldrums and the grasp of Jay Gould and made into the most sensational, newsy, stuntloving, and crusading paper the country had yet seen. It was soon issuing the largest paper, sixteen pages for two cents, to the largest circulation and had the largest advertising patronage of any American newspaper. Its editorial page was strong and advocated many reforms, and the record-breaking Sunday supplements promoted newspaper illustration.

WILLIAM RANDOLPH HEARST, son of a California mining magnate, George Hearst, studied the Pulitzer methods with care and first experimented with them on a paper his father had bought for political purposes, the San Francisco *Examiner* (1865–   ). Journalism in that city had begun in 1847, and the chief papers in the early period had been the *Alta California* (1849–91), notable for contributions of such literary figures as Mark Twain and Bret Harte; and the *Chronicle* (1865–   ), founded by Michel H. and Charles de Young. Young Hearst's *Examiner* soon outdistanced competition, and when, after his father's death, his mother made available to him $7,500,000, Hearst invaded New York to challenge Pulitzer's supremacy. In 1895 he bought the *Journal*, which had been founded in 1882 by Joseph Pulitzer's estranged brother Albert, hired away from the *World* some of its best talent, and outdid that paper in its sensational news and Sunday features and also in its large-type scare heads. By 1897 the *World* and the *Journal* were running rival series of comic pages in their Sunday supplements, featuring the "Yellow Kid," and plastering the town with advertisements of this curious figure. This practice gave rise to the expression "yellow journalism," denoting a formula that included scare-head makeup, lavish use of pictures, frauds of various kinds (faked interviews, pseudo-science, "composite" photography), Sunday supplements with colored comics, and ostentatious crusades in behalf of the common people. Shortly after the turn of the century, with the *World's* gradual withdrawal from this kind of rowdy competition and Ochs's success with the *Times*, which confined itself to "all the news that's fit to print," yellow journalism as a movement tended to subside.

The Spanish-American War received much of the yellow treatment. Indeed, it is probable that the sensational coverage of Spanish atrocities in Cuba by a number of papers contributed to provoking that conflict. For several months during and after the war the circulations of the *Journal* and *World* ran well above the million mark.

A western paper that long followed the yellow formula was the Denver *Post* (1892–   ), conducted for many years by Fred G. Bonfils and Harry H. Tammen. The first Denver paper was the *Rocky Mountain News*, established during the Colorado gold rush in 1859; but when Bonfils and Tammen bought the little *Post* in 1895, they proceeded to make it blatant with red headlines and sensational content and treatment. It was, however, decidedly paternalistic in its attitude toward the people of the "Rocky Mountain Empire." Tammen died in 1924, but Bonfils continued his belligerent career until his death in 1933. Under E. P. Hoyt the *Post* maintained a position of less obstreperous but no less real influence in its region.

A distinguished paper that attained success, as did the *New York Times*, on the basis of opposition to yellow journalism was the CHRISTIAN SCIENCE MONITOR, founded by Mary Baker Eddy in Boston in 1908. Though sectarian in only a page or two, the *Monitor* gave minimal attention to crime and disaster, and emphasized the arts and mutual understanding of peoples.

A postscript to the yellow journalism period was the one marked by what was dubbed the "gutter journalism" of some of the early tabloid newspapers. Small page-size was not new in the long history of American papers, but when Joseph M. Patterson and Robert R. McCormick (of the Chicago *Tribune*) started the New York *Daily News* in 1919 with sixteen four-column pages containing copious illustration and emphasis on crime-and-sex sensation, it was a new departure. Easy to read on the subway, lively and entertaining, by the early 1940s it reached 2,000,000 circulation, the largest ever attained by an American daily. By that time Patterson, the paper's manager, had toned down its sensationalism considerably. Not so the competitive tabloids that had sprung up—BERNARR MACFADDEN's *Daily Graphic* (1924–32), nicknamed the "Pornographic"; Hearst's *Daily Mirror* (1924–1963), which immediately became a strong competitor in the war of the tabloids; and eleven papers appearing in nine other cities in the five years following the appearance of the *Daily News*. After the reform of Patterson's paper, however, the tabloids began to lose their more sensational character and to be distinguished by (1) smaller page size, (2) copious illustration, and (3) condensed and lively news presentation. Among the later tabloids established on this formula was the Chicago *Times* (1929), combined in 1948 with Marshall Field's *Sun* (1941) as the *Sun-Times*.

Coverage of two world wars and an undeclared war in Korea was an ordeal by fire for the United States press. Old-style war correspondence was impossible, it was soon learned, in a new-style war. In the early stages of World War I only one correspondent was accredited to accompany British forces in France, Frederick Palmer of the Associated Press. Nevertheless, many American correspondents were working out of Paris, Brussels, and "somewhere in France," and more came with the American Expeditionary Force. By 1915 it was estimated that as many as five hundred reporters were at work on the various fronts for American newspapers and periodicals. During

World War II the U.S. War Department accredited 1,186 American correspondents and news officials, and the Navy Department 460 more. (These figures are for the whole of the war, and there were probably not much over five hundred on duty at any one time.) Press coverage of the Korean conflict was expensive in lives, in suffering, and in money. Semiofficial estimates place the number of those who visited the war area during the hostilities at six hundred, of whom seventeen were killed.

Critics of the press had much to say in the 20th century about the disappearance of "personal journalism." It is true that the increased complexity of newspaper organization—with publishers, editors, managing editors, executive editors, news editors, and assorted managers—has tended to reduce the prestige of any star reporter, but many newspaper personalities nevertheless became well known nationally in this century. The syndicated columnists writing on public affairs represented one phalanx of this new personal journalism—such men as David Lawrence, Mark Sullivan, Walter Lippmann, Arthur Brisbane, Heywood Broun, Westbrook Pegler, Drew Pearson, Marquis Childs, and James Reston. Another phalanx—this one of publisher-editors—was equally well known through individual personalities. W.R. Hearst and Colonel McCormick were celebrities even though they did comparatively little writing; on the other hand, John S. Knight, of the Knight Newspapers, Erwin D. Canham, of the *Christian Science Monitor*, and Roy Roberts, of the Kansas City *Star* were highly articulate. Roberts carried forward the tradition of the *Star*, which had been founded in 1880 by William Rockhill Nelson, a man of strong personality. Its policy through the years had been low circulation rates, heavy regional coverage, and strong advocacy of local progress and reforms.

The small-city daily field also developed some interesting personalities. This had been true in earlier years, when SAMUEL BOWLES made the Springfield, Massachusetts, *Republican* (1844–1947 as a daily) a paper of high prestige and influence, and Joseph R. Hawley made the Hartford, Connecticut, *Courant* (1837–   as a daily) respected and powerful. In the latter decades of the 19th century two Kansas editors achieved fine reputations for their writing—WILLIAM ALLEN WHITE of the Emporia *Gazette* (1890–   ), and EDGAR WATSON HOWE, of the Atchison *Globe* (1877–   ). Both distinguished themselves as well in fiction and the essay.

Editors of community newspapers, better known earlier as the country weeklies of the smaller towns, tended to become prominent in their communities. Community newspapers hit a peak of nearly 14,000 in 1928; by 1989 they had declined to 7,600. Although numbers had declined, circulation had increased to an estimated 53,000,000 copies weekly, an average of 7,000 per newspaper. The term *country weekly* no longer seemed accurate and gave way to *community journalism*. It applied to the once-a-week, small newspaper still serving rural communities as well as those published more frequently—but still less than daily—in large towns, growing suburbs, and identifiable communities within bigger cities. As business enterprises, they ranged from small, single proprietorships to multimillion dollar corporations, such as the Princeton, New

Jersey-based Ingersoll Publications or the Neighbor newspapers headquartered in Marietta, Georgia. The latter published a string of community newspapers around the city of Atlanta. The editorial quality of community newspapers reflected the degree of commitment and journalistic standards of the publisher and editors. The excellence often found in community newspapers has merited honors from the Pulitzer committee. In 1973, for instance, a Pulitzer for reporting went to the Omaha (Nebraska) *Sun* newspapers for a series on Boys' Town. The Point Reyes (California) *Light* earned one for Meritorious Public Service in 1979, and Albert Scardino of the *Georgia Gazette* in Savannah won for editorial writing in 1984. The printing of community newspapers became easier and cheaper with the development of various photo and electronic typeseting devices, as well as cost-efficient, central offset printing plants that produced high-quality printing. Introduction of desktop publishing equipment promised further publishing economies, improved appearance, and low-cost start-up opportunities where markets appeared ready for new community publications.

The great wire news agencies were, of course, more impersonal, though the increasing use of bylines helped overcome that shortcoming. The New York Associated Press was organized by six papers of that city in 1848 to cooperate in newsgathering, and it was soon selling its service to groups in other cities and regions. In the 1880s the growth of one of these groups, the Western Associated Press, and the competition of an independent service called the United Press forced a realignment and the organization in 1893 of the modern Associated Press. The old UP collapsed in 1897, and immediately the Scripps-McRae papers set up their own Press Association, to become ten years later the modern United Press. Hearst set up his International News Service in 1909, to be merged with the U.P. in 1958 to become United Press International.

By 1990, UPI had gone through a number of owners and reorganizations, becoming controversial along the way. It generally was regarded as a less complete and competitive alternative to the AP, and the number of subscribers to its services dropped. But if UPI was less of a challenge to the reliable, worldwide news net of the AP, other choices emerged. The first general syndicates handling news and feature materials started business about the time of the Civil War. Typical were those offered by Irving Bacheller and S.S. McClure when they launched their syndicates in 1883 and 1884, respectively. Their services emphasized fiction, humor, news not found on the wire services, and gossip. By 1990, the number of syndicate services was in the hundreds, with thousands of offerings ranging from humor to how-to information to political analysis. As the number of newspapers owned by groups increased, the groups expanded their own individual feature and column offerings to include a repackaging of their deadline and background reporting, ready for use by daily newspapers. The AP's first-day story on a breaking news event was often challenged by one from the New York Times service, Knight-Ridder newspapers, or the Gannett Co., to name a few.

The growth of alternatives to the AP did little to answer the criticism that easy availability of wire services and syndicated features lead to sameness in the American daily newspaper, no matter where it published. Coupled with that problem was the increase in common ownership of growing numbers of newspapers, with a resulting decline in locally owned daily newspapers.

Newspaper chains, later to be called ownership groups, doubtless began with the interests that Benjamin Franklin, James Parker, and Isaiah Thomas held for a time in papers they had helped their apprentices set up in various colonial towns. But the first spectacular group was the one organized by E. W. Scripps in the last two decades of the 19th century. Scripps's first paper was the Cleveland *Press* (1878–1980), originally called the *Penny Press*. He bought the Cincinnati *Post* (1881–   ) in 1883 and put Milton A. McRae in as business manager, but it was not until 1895 that the Scripps-McRae League began to expand rapidly. By 1914 it was publishing twenty-three dailies. The Scripps formula was to choose a city of 50,000 to 100,000, start a new paper at one cent, put in a promising young man as manager on a stock-ownership basis, and champion the causes of labor and the common people. If the paper appeared to be a failure after a year or two, it was dropped. In 1920 Roy W. Howard was brought in as a partner; when Scripps retired in 1922 in favor of his son Robert P. Scripps, the firm became Scripps-Howard. Altogether, E. W. Scripps, Scripps-McRae, and Scripps-Howard founded or purchased fifty-seven daily papers—many resulting from mergers—twenty of which remained to the group in 1960. Scripps-Howard entered the New York field in 1927 by the purchase of the *Telegram*, the evening associate of the *Herald*, and four years later they created the sensation of those times by buying the *World* from the Pulitzer heirs. The morning *World* was killed at once, and the evening edition was merged in the *World-Telegram*. In 1950 they bought the *Sun* and merged it into the title.

The *Telegram* and the old *Sun* had been the only papers left of the ambitious attempt of Frank A. Munsey to build a great newspaper group of his own. Munsey made, in fact, two such attempts. The first, pursued during the first fifteen years of the 20th century, consisted of buying, founding, merging, and killing papers in Boston, New York, Philadelphia, and Baltimore. Though this first round was unsuccessful, Munsey soon returned to the game, this time not so much with the intention of putting together a chain of papers as of cleaning up the New York newspaper field by buying, killing off, and merging properties in order to create a more profitable situation for the industry. His manipulations, in which he destroyed four papers, ended with his death in 1925. He left a fortune of $20,000,000, mostly to the Metropolitan Museum of Art.

The basis of the great Hearst group comprised the San Francisco *Examiner*, the New York *Journal* (with the *American* as morning edition 1901–37), the Boston *American* (founded in 1904 and merged with the Hearst-owned *Record* in 1961), and the Chicago *American* (founded as *Journal* 1900, then called *American* and since 1937, *Herald-American*); but in the years

1913–29 Hearst bought or founded twenty-seven more papers, as well as six magazines, two wire services, a leading feature syndicate and a syndicated Sunday supplement, a newsreel service, and a motion-picture production company. He was in financial trouble, however, when the money panic of 1929 came along, and in 1937 he was forced to turn over his newspaper and magazine properties to a voting trust, which succeeded in bringing order out of the confusion of holding companies, and sold a number of the less profitable operations. But the Hearst group has owned, at one time or another, as many as thirty-seven dailies, chiefly in large cities. The founder died in 1951, and the group was thereafter conducted by his sons.

Newspapers and the newspaper industry changed in several fundamental ways by the end of the twentieth century. Fewer communities had competing dailies. More newspapers became part of media corporations that usually owned radio and television stations, billboard companies, book publishing houses, magazines, and syndicated services. Total daily newspaper circulation figures leveled, although Sunday newspapers increased dramatically in numbers and circulation. By 1988 only 43 communities had competing daily newspapers, as opposed to more than 500 in 1923. Half were kept alive by special legislation passed by the Congress in 1970 permitting Joint Operating Agreements (JOAs). The JOAs permitted two newspapers owned by different companies to pool printing and other facilities, along with general management, circulation, and advertising sales functions. Editorial independence was to be maintained, usually with separate newsrooms and editorial departments. The arrangement was criticized as monopolistic by some but was said to keep two editorial voices alive in a community, where otherwise one might fail. Daily newspaper managers—independent or corporately owned—reminded critics that they had no monopoly on the news or advertising in a community, even though they might be the only daily newspaper published in a community.

More dailies were controlled by media corporations, usually with interests in other media fields. The Gannett Co., under the aggressive leadership of Allen Neuharth, led in circulation by 1988, with 89 dailies, including the controversial *USA Today*, and 6,104,578 daily circulation. Thomson Newspapers, based in Toronto, Canada, owned the most newspapers, 109 that sold 1,907,184 copies daily, primarily in small and middle-sized communities.

Total daily circulation of the nation's 1520 newspapers totaled 56,990,000 in 1996, not significantly changed from the immediately preceding years and the 1960 total of 58,900,000. But Sunday newspapers increased in number from 586 in 1970 to 890 in 1996, with a circulation of 60,798,000. The decline in the number of daily newspapers led some to predict the death of the industry. But newspapers, 72 percent of which were published in communities under 50,000 population in 1988, were fiscally healthy for the most part. The problem area in competition, circulation, and profitability was urban America. The nation's capital was down to one dominant newspaper, the Washington *Post* (1877–   ), by 1990, with only a lightly regarded competitor in the Washington *Times* (1982–   ).

New York was down to two major dailies, the *Times* and *Daily News*, plus the third-place New York *Post*. A suburban newspaper, *Newsday* (1940–   ) led in circulation on Long Island and made inroads into Manhattan. The balance sheets on most surviving newspapers continued to show comfortable profits. A rumor that a daily newspaper was for sale usually brought bidders into the open. The newspaper industry still earned more advertising dollars than any other segment of the media industry, 26 percent of those dollars in 1988, for an estimated total of $30,680,000,000. Although they competed with other media forms for the citizen's time, no other communication medium reported the news in such a comprehensive, convenient, and economical package as the American newspaper.

The birth of *USA Today* in 1982 seemed to be a case in point in the willingness of a media giant to experiment and gamble. Under Neuharth's direction, the Gannett Co. evolved a plan to use satellite transmission of content from a central location to its printing plants nationwide to produce a newspaper that would be colorful and comprehensive but tightly written. Its influence, most critics agreed, was obvious in terms of changing the appearance and content of many other newspapers. Whether the bright splotches of color of *USA Today* and its short, closely edited stories, would help or hurt the industry was uncertain. Metropolitan newspapers in particularly seemed to experiment with techniques borrowed from *USA Today* as they tried to increase circulation.

But other large daily newspapers expanded by continuing the traditions of commitment to complete coverage and explanation of the world's events. The *New York Times* national edition circulated more than a million copies daily, giving readers the best of the *Times'* worldwide reporting resources. The Los Angeles *Times* became a respected package of regional, national, and international reporting. The *Wall Street Journal*—largest daily in the nation with nearly 2,000,000 circulation—emphasized readable, complete and thorough business reporting, while winning Pulitzers for national and international stories. By the end of the century, newspapers, like magazines and book publishers, had established Websites, but the long-term effect on print media remained uncertain.
FRANK LUTHER MOTT/WALLACE. B. EBERHARD/GP

Newton, A[lfred] Edward (1863–1940), businessman, bibliophile, publisher. Born in Philadelphia, Newton made a fortune in the electrical equipment business and thereafter devoted himself to collecting, studying, and writing about books. Among his writings are *The Amenities of Book-Collecting and Kindred Affections* (1918), *A Magnificent Farce and Other Diversions of a Book-Collector* (1921), *This Book-Collecting Game* (1928), *A Tourist in Spite of Himself* (1930), and *End Papers* (1933). Two plays he wrote, *Doctor Johnson* (1923) and *Mr. Strahan's Dinner Party* (1930), testify to his dominant interest, which brought about his election in 1930 as the first American president of the Johnson Club in London.

New York, A History of, from the Beginning of the World to the End of the Dutch Dynasty, by Diedrich Knickerbocker (1809),   a satirical account by WASHINGTON IRVING. Irving began the book as a burlesque, became

more serious as he advanced, and in the course of his narrative gave a good many historical facts. The book began as a satire on the Dutch, but Book IV goes beyond the Dutch to satire of Jefferson, pictured as Governor WILLEM KIEFT. In later editions Irving made some expurgations. Knickerbocker is a character Irving also used later in *The Sketch Book* (1819), to tell the story of RIP VAN WINKLE. The book begins ironically with the creation of the world, the discovery of America, and the settlement of the New Netherlands. There are descriptions of the Battery, the Bowerie, Bowling Green, Dutch manners and morals, and leading Dutch personages—some treated not too gently. Legends of an older day are recorded. Irving, defending himself against attacks, asserted justly, "Before the appearance of my work the popular traditions of our city were unrecorded; the peculiar and racy customs and usages derived from our Dutch progenitors were unnoticed or regarded with indifference, or adverted to with a sneer."

New Yorker, The.   HAROLD ROSS founded the weekly magazine in 1925. Begun on the pattern of other city magazines giving special attention to amusements, society, and local interests, it soon attracted a staff of distinguished talents and grew into a successful literary periodical. Full schedules of the theater, concerts, supper clubs, and museum exhibits are still included, and columns such as "Talk of the Town" often emphasize New York activities and people, but the fiction, verse, reviewing, and special articles are far wider in scope. Its PROFILES are well received as informal biographical treatments of interesting people.

After the death of Ross in 1951, William Shawn became the editor. Under his leadership the magazine retained its tone and format, but branched out into editorial involvement in public affairs and began to serialize complete books of exceptional interest. In 1987 Robert Gottlieb replaced Shawn as editor. Tina Brown took over from 1992 to 1998, and then David Remnick. The magazine has published work by ROBERT BENCHLEY, WOLCOTT GIBBS, OGDEN NASH, JOHN O'HARA, DOROTHY PARKER, S. J. PERELMAN, J. D. SALINGER, Rebecca West, EDMUND WILSON, JOHN CHEEVER, E. B. WHITE, JAMES THURBER, and JOHN HERSEY. Among more recent contributors are JOHN ASHBERY, ANN BEATTIE, RAYMOND CARVER, RITA DOVE, PAULINE KAEL, GALWAY KINNELL, JAMAICA KINCAID, JOHN MCPHEE, BOBBIE ANN MASON, JOHN UPDIKE, and William T. Vollmann.

New York Idea, The (first prod. November 19, 1906), a comedy by Langdon Mitchell. This is the story of the tangled marital affairs of two prominent social figures.

New York Ledger, The.   *The Merchants' Ledger*, an illustrated weekly magazine founded in 1847, was purchased in 1851 by Robert Bonner, who changed the name in 1855 to *The New York Ledger*. He edited it until 1887 and made it the most successful magazine of its day, partly by startling innovations in advertising technique, partly by recruiting well-known writers. Bryant, Tennyson, Longfellow, and the Cary sisters contributed poems; Harriet Beecher Stowe, E.D.E.N. Southworth, Dickens, and Sylvanus Cobb wrote fiction.

Readers could submit their problems to Bonner, and advice would be given by men like Henry Ward Beecher and Edward

Everett. In 1898 the *Ledger* became a monthly, and in 1903 it ceased publication.

New-York Mirror (1823–1860),   a weekly newspaper on the arts, literature, and society founded by Samuel Woodworth. In 1831 the Mirror bought out the *American Monthly Magazine*. Among its contributers were Cooper, Whittier, and Irving. It went through several changes of name: the *New Mirror* (1842), the *Evening Mirror* (1844), a daily with Poe as literary critic (1844–1845).

New York Public Library, The.   Consolidated by the union of the Astor, Lenox, and other libraries in 1895, this great New York City institution has two main divisions: the reference department, concentrated in a massive building at Fifth Avenue and 42nd Street, and a circulation division of many branches.

New York Review and Athenaeum Magazine, The, a short-lived (1825–1826) monthly literary journal. Bryant was among its editors. It merged with the *United States Literary Gazette*.

New York Review of Books, The (1963–   ),   a biweekly with single issues in July and August. It came into being because of a lengthy newspaper strike. A companion *London Review of Books* was founded in 1979.

New York School Poets.   A group of experimental poets, including JOHN ASHBERY, FRANK O'HARA, JAMES SCHUYLER, KENNETH KOCH, and BARBARA GUEST, who are linked by friendship, shared place and time—New York City in the early 1950s—and close connections to the New York School of abstract expressionist painters, whose work was transforming New York City into the capital of the art world. The poets were influenced by experiments in the plastic arts, wrote art criticism, were friends with the artists, and engaged in many collaborative projects. From this cosmopolitan and avant-garde perspective, they challenged repressive provincial values as well as the prevailing academic formalist verse.

O'Hara seems to have been the magnetizing presence in this informal community. "We were a bunch of poets who happened to know each other," Ashbery has said, pointing to the "vast differences" among the poets' work. John Bernard Myers—who, Ashbery says, "foisted" this "label" on the poets in a 1961 article—suggests that the term "coterie" might be more appropriate than "school" for this group, which he expands to include Joseph Ceravolo, Kenward Elmslie, Frank Lima, and Tony Towle in *The Poets of the New York School* (1969). In *An Anthology of New York Poets* (1970), Ron Padgett and David Shapiro include nineteen more poets and affirm that O'Hara's essay "Personism" speaks "for us all," thus acknowledging a common commitment to vanguardism and experimentation, a resistance to symbolism and moralizing, and an emphasis on surfaces, play, process, improvisation, and chance.

MUTLU KONUK BLASING

New York Times.   See ADOLPH S. OCHS; HENRY JARVIS RAYMOND; NEWSPAPERS.

Nez Percé Indians.   The name, meaning "pierced noses" was given by French trappers and others to a branch of the Sahaptin or Shapahtin tribe living on the middle Columbia and lower Snake Rivers in what is now Oregon, Idaho, and Washington. They were a wandering tribe, living mainly on salmon and roots. They are described in Washington Irving's *Adventures of Captain Bonneville, U.S.A.* (1837). Discovery of gold in 1860 brought a swarm of prospectors and land-hungry squatters to Oregon. Some of the less farsighted Indians signed away their lands, but a group led by CHIEF JOSEPH refused to give up the beautiful Wallowa Valley in eastern Oregon. In 1877 American troops attempted to force them to leave and enter a reservation. Rather than do this, Chief Joseph and his people struck their tepees and headed for the Canadian border. With less than three hundred warriors, Chief Joseph outmaneuvered and outfought American troops in fifteen engagements, but was finally obliged to surrender. He told his story in *An Indian's View of Indian Affairs (North American Review*, April 1879). Robert Payne wrote a novel about him, *The Chieftain* (1953).

The Nez Percés were settled on a reservation in Indian Territory in 1879; they were then described as a most intelligent, religious, and industrious people. But the climate was unsuitable, and their numbers shrank to 1,400 by 1885, when they moved to a reservation in Washington. They are now on an Idaho reservation. Herbert J. Spinden wrote a full account of their religion, poetry, and oratory in *The Nez Percé Indians* (1908); Lucullus V. McWhorter told the story of the Nez Percé War of 1877 in *Hear Me, My Chiefs* (1952); and Francis Haines wrote on *The Nez Percés: Tribesmen of the Columbian Plateau* (1955). Franz Boas edited *Folk-Tales of Salishan and Sahaptin Tribes* (1917), and other stories were told by Archie Phinney in *Nez Percé Texts* (1934).

Nichol, Barry P[hillip] (1944–1988),   poet. Born in Vancouver, British Columbia, and educated at the University of British Columbia, Nichol moved to Toronto. He first attracted international notice with hand-drawn "concrete" poems in the mid-1960s; his anthology *The Cosmic Chef* (1970) won a Governor General's Award. *Journeying and the Returns* (1967) is in more conventional free verse, as are his best-known works *The Martyrology: Books 1 and 2* (1972); *Books 3 and 4* (1976); *Book 5* (1982); *Book 6: Continental Trance* (1983); and *Books 7 and 8: Gifts* (1990).

Nichols, Anne.   See ABIE'S IRISH ROSE.

Nichols, John (1940–   ),   novelist. Born in California and educated at Hamilton College, Nichols has lived much of his life in New Mexico, the setting for his best-known work. His New Mexico trilogy comprises *The Milagro Beanfield War* (1974), *The Magic Journey* (1978), and *The Nirvana Blues* (1981). The three novels follow the changing of a New Mexico town from a traditional Hispanic farming community to a modern commercial society and the concomitant destruction of values. *If Mountains Die: A Memoir* (1979), *The Last Beautiful Days of Autumn: A Memoir* (1982), and *On the Mesa* (1986) chronicle fifteen years in Taos, New Mexico. *American Blood* (1987), *An Elegy for September* (1992), and *Conjugal Bliss* (1994) are novels. *Dancing on the Stones* (2000) is a selection of essays.

Nichols, Mike [Michael Igor Peschkowsky] (1931–), director, satirist. Born in Berlin to a family of Russians who fled Nazism, he came to America at age seven. Nichols was educated at the University of Chicago and studied acting under Lee Strasberg. He and Elaine May formed an improvised satirical duet that, in 1960, scored a hit on Broadway. His satiric wit and improvisational skill are apparent in his work on the stage, including many productions of plays by NEIL SIMON for which he often received writing credit, and such films as *Who's Afraid of Virginia Woolf* (1966), from the play by EDWARD ALBEE; *The Graduate* (1967, Academy Award for direction); and *Catch-22* (1970), from the book by JOSEPH HELLER; *Silkwood* (1983); and *The Birdcage* (1995).

Nichols, Thomas Low (1815–1901), novelist, reformer, memoirist. Nichols, born in New Hampshire, was a rebel and a radical who took refuge in England when he disagreed with the government about the Civil War. He wrote several novels, one named *Marriage* (1854, with his wife Mary Sargent Nichols [1810–1884]); *Ellen Ramsay* (1843); *The Lady in Black* (1844); and *Raffle for a Wife* (1845). Among his nonfictional works are *Journal in Jail* (1840); *Women, in All Ages and Nations* (1849); and his astute *Forty Years of American Life, 1821–61* (2 v. 1864). His wife also wrote an autobiographical novel, *Mary Lyndon, or, Recollections of a Lifetime* (1855).

Nicholson, Meredith (1866–1947), novelist, diplomat. Nicholson is best remembered for three mystery novels: *The House of a Thousand Candles* (1905), *Rosalind at Red Gate* (1907), and *The Siege of the Seven Suitors* (1910). He was U.S. minister to Paraguay (1933–34) and Nicaragua (1938–44).

Nick Adams, the focal character in Ernest Hemingway's *In Our Time* (1925).

Nick Carter, the hero of perhaps a thousand DIME NOVELS by various writers. John Russell Coryell may have been the first author to use the name, in the 1880s, but others appropriated it.

Nick of the Woods, or the Jibbenainosay (1837), a novel by ROBERT MONTGOMERY BIRD. Bird's best novel, it was extremely popular in its day. Bloody Nathan, scorned by pioneers as a timid Quaker who abhors all violence—his nickname is mere mockery—is later identified as the feared killer of Indians, Nick of the Woods. Yet he is seldom aware of the conflict between his two personalities. Bird describes the causes and symptoms of Nathan's split personality with remarkable psychological insight.

Most of the other characters are stereotypes. The virtuous hero and heroine utter platitudes; the Indians are brutish savages; and Roaring Ralph Stackpole, the picaresque horse thief, is mildly amusing. But Bird's background as a dramatist shows up in his handling of plot. He keeps the reader's interest by maintaining unrelieved suspense for many pages.

Nicolay, J[ohn] G[eorge] (1832–1901), journalist, historian, biographer. Nicolay was brought to this country from Bavaria at the age of six. His father, a flour mill operator, moved frequently, so the boy had little formal schooling. Nicolay clerked in a store and then became a printer's devil for the

Pittsfield (Illinois) *Free Press.* He worked his way up until by 1854 he was editor and proprietor of the paper. In 1851 Nicolay met his future collaborator, JOHN HAY. He sold the paper to become clerk to the Secretary of State of Illinois and in 1860 was appointed private secretary to ABRAHAM LINCOLN. Through Nicolay's efforts Hay was added to Lincoln's secretarial staff. They were intimate witnesses of most of the important acts of Lincoln's administration. Nicolay took many notes and Hay kept a diary. The two young men, with Lincoln's approval, embarked on a projected biography of Lincoln which was also to be a history of his era. After Lincoln's death the work had to be postponed for some years while Nicolay served, from 1865 to 1869, as United States Consul in Paris, and from 1872 until 1887 as marshal of the U.S. Supreme Court. While still holding this position, Nicolay began to collaborate with Hay on *Abraham Lincoln: A History*, which appeared in ten volumes in 1890. He produced two other works, *The Outbreak of the Rebellion* (1881) and *A Short Life of Abraham Lincoln* (1902), and also edited Lincoln's *Complete Works* (12 v. 1905) with Hay, although the actual editorial work was done by Francis D. Tandy.

Nicollet, Joseph Nicholas.   See BALLOON HOAX.

Niebuhr, Reinhold (1892–1971) theologian. Neibuhr was born in Missouri. After thirteen years as pastor of the Bethel Evangelical Church in Detroit, during which he took an active interest in labor problems, Niebuhr joined the faculty at the Union Theological Seminary in New York City, where he taught from 1928 to 1960. Allied with the socialist movement in the 1930s, Niebuhr dealt with questions of political morality and with the failure of Christianity to confront social problems in *Moral Man and Immoral Society* (1932). *The Children of Light and the Children of Darkness* (1944) contains his attack on the moral irresponsibility of those who fail to come to grips with the problem of power.

In *Christian Realism and Political Problems* (1953), he maintained that the church was actively sanctioning social ills by refusing to confront them. Among his many books are *Beyond Tragedy: Essays on the Christian Interpretation of History* (1937), *Essays in Applied Christianity* (1959), and *A Nation So Conceived* (1963), an analysis of the American character. *Justice and Mercy* (1974, ed. Ursula Niebuhr) is a posthumous collection of his sermons and addresses.

Niedecker, Lorine (1903–1970), poet. Niedecker used the natural surrounding of her native Wisconsin in many of her spare and musical verses. She wrote in almost complete social and artistic isolation. Toward the end of her life Niedecker supervised publication of *My Life By Water* (1970), her collected works, but at the time of her death her work was largely unknown. CID CORMAN helped make her work available by printing several pieces in *Origin* magazine and editing *The Granite Pail: The Selected Poems of Lorine Niedecker* (1985). *Between Your House and Mine* (1986) is a record of the correspondence between them in the last decade of her life. Niedecker also corresponded for many years with LOUIS ZUKOFSKY and sent him carbon copies of her typewritten work; those typescripts, often with his marginal suggestions for revision, are included in the collection of his papers at the University of Texas Humanities Research Center. The edited texts in *From This Condensery: The Complete Writings of Lorine Niedecker* (1985) are not wholly reliable.

Nigger, The (pub. and prod. 1910),   a play by EDWARD SHELDON. This is one of the earliest of the plays based on the familiar plot theme: a man, in this instance the governor of a state, is told he is partly African-American. The governor is about to sign a bill that will harm the financial interests of a cousin. The latter threatens to reveal the secret, but the governor signs the bill anyway. His fiancée at first rejects him, then rejoins him.

Nigger Heaven (1926),   a novel by CARL VAN VECHTEN. Set in Harlem in the jazz era, this novel has its melodramatic episodes and closes with a murder of which the hero is falsely accused. The book takes its title from an old term for the topmost gallery of the theater—"That's what Harlem is," says the writer. "We sit in our places in the gallery of this New York theater and watch the white world sitting down below us in the good seats."

Niggli, Josephina (1910–1983),   short-story writer, folklorist. Niggli wrote *Mexican Village* (1945), a collection of ten closely related stories and the first work of fiction by a Mexican-American to reach a large audience. It concerns Bob Webster, the illegitimate son of a Mexican woman and an Anglo father. Rejected by his father because of his Hispanic appearance, Webster settles comfortably in Hidalgo, the home of his maternal grandmother.

Night Before Christmas, The   (Troy *Sentinel*, December 23, 1823), a poem by Clement C. Moore. See A VISIT FROM ST. NICHOLAS.

Niles, Blair [Rice] (1888?–1959),   travel writer, novelist. Rice, born in Virginia, traveled extensively with her first husband, WILLIAM BEEBE. Their trip to Mexico resulted in *Two Bird Lovers in Mexico* (1905), and she collaborated on *Our Search for a Wilderness* (1910). She continued her nomadic life after her marriage to Robert Niles, an architect and expert photographer. *Casual Wanderings in Ecuador* (1923), *Colombia, Land of Miracles* (1924), and *Black Haiti* (1926) were illustrated by her husband's photographs. In 1944 she received a gold medal from the Society of Women Geographers. *Condemned to Devil's Island* (1928), a sensational account of prison life, was followed by *Free* (1930), a sequel; *Strange Brother* (1931), a fictional study of a homosexual, was praised by Havelock Ellis. Her other works include *Light Again* (1933), *Day of Immense Sun* (1936), *East by Day* (1941), *The James* (1939), and *Martha's Husband: An Informal Portrait of George Washington* (1951).

Niles, Samuel (1674–1762),   clergyman, historian, poet, writer on theology. Born on Block Island, Rhode Island, Niles took a post in Braintree, Massachusetts, and there won considerable renown as a preacher and writer. His *Tristitiae Ecclesiarum* (1745) is an account of the New England churches, and *God's Wonder-Working Providence for New England in the Reduction of Louisburg* (1747) is a tract in verse. He

also wrote *Divers Important Gospel-Doctrines* (1752) and *Summary Historic Narrative of the Wars in New England with the French and Indians*, published long after his death in the *Collections* (1837, 1861) of the Massachusetts Historical Society.

Nin, Anaís (1903–1977),   novelist, memoirist. Nin was born in Paris and came to the United States as a teenager. She was not widely known until the publication of *The Diary of Anaís Nin 1931–1966* (7 v. 1966–1980), a record of avant-garde life in Paris and New York. A major focus of the memoirs is establishment and psychological acceptance of a feminine identity. Portraits of friends such as HENRY MILLER add to the interest. Her first novel, *House of Incest* (1936), is a prose poem dealing with psychological torments. The second, *Winter of Artifice* (1939), examines a daughter's relationship to her father. The series *Cities of the Interior* includes *Ladders to Fire* (1946), *Children of the Albatross* (1947), *The Four-Chambered Heart* (1950), *A Spy in the House of Love* (1954), and *Solar Barque* (1958). In her fiction and her diaries, a dreamlike, sensuous prose expands personal concerns to a universal level. Nin's essays on literary theory include *Realism and Reality* (1946) and *The Novel of the Future* (1968). *The Delta of Venus* (1977) and *Little Birds* (1979) are books of erotica she wrote in the 1940s.

1919 (1932),   a novel by JOHN DOS PASSOS. This, the second novel in the trilogy *U.S.A.*, carries into World War I the careers of the characters in THE FORTY-SECOND PARALLEL, beginning with Joe Williams, the wandering, battered, and hapless sailor. Four new characters are introduced: Dick Savage, an esthetic, idealistic young Harvard man; Eveline Hutchins, bored and seeking new sensations; "Daughter" (Anne Elizabeth Trent), a relief worker; and Ben Compton, a young Jewish anarchist. The grim stories of their lives are interspersed with passages of "the Newsreel," "the Camera Eye," and short, sardonic biographical sketches, all lending historical background and social dimension to the narrative episodes, as they did in *The Forty-Second Parallel*.

Nissenson, Hugh (1933–   ),   short-story writer, novelist. Contemporary Jewish life and its connections to the past are thematic in his two volumes of short stories, *A Pile of Stones* (1965) and *In the Reign of Peace* (1972), and in his novel *My Own Ground* (1976). Nissenson departed radically from earlier themes in his 1985 novel, *The Tree of Life*, in which a young Harvard divinity graduate keeps a diary of events on the Ohio frontier during the troubles between settlers and Indians at the beginning of the 19th century. *The Elephant and My Jewish Problem: Selected Stories and Journals 1957–1987* was published in 1988.

Niven, Frederick (1878–1944),   novelist. Born in Chile to Scottish parents, he was educated in Scotland before being sent, in his late teens, to British Columbia for his health. *The Lost Cabin* (1908) is the first of several adventure novels set in the Canadian West. Others are *Hands Up!* (1913), *Cinderella of Skookum Creek* (1916), and *Penny Scot's Treasure* (1919). *Above Your Heads* (1911) and *Sage-brush Stories* (1917) are story collections. His books of verse include *Maple-leaf*

Songs (1917) and *A Lover of the Land* (1925). A trilogy of romance novels dealing with the fur trade on the Red River comprises *The Flying Years* (1935), *Mine Inheritance* (1940), and *The Transplanted* (1944). Nivens also published several novels set in Europe and a great deal of nonfiction.

Nixon, Richard M[ilhous] (1913–1994), politician, lawyer, and 37th president of the United States (1969–74). Nixon was educated at Whittier College and Duke Law School, practiced law in his home state of California, served in the navy during World War II, and after the war was elected to the U.S. House of Representatives and then the Senate. His reputation as an anti-Communist made him a desirable running mate for EISENHOWER in the 1952 presidential campaign, at the height of the Cold War. Defeated by JOHN F. KENNEDY in the 1960 presidential election and later by Pat Brown in the California gubernatorial race, Nixon announced his retirement from politics and began to practice law in New York City. During this period, he published *Six Crises* (1962), an account of pivotal experiences during his political career. In 1968 he ran for president again, defeating Hubert Humphrey, and announced what came to be known as the Nixon Doctrine, which reduced U.S. military forces abroad and used the funds saved to help smaller countries defend themselves; he also began withdrawing U.S. troops from Vietnam (see VIETNAM WAR). In 1972 relations with China were reopened, and détente with the Soviet Union was encouraged. In the same year, Nixon defeated the Democratic challenger, George McGovern, in a landslide reelection victory and effectively ended U.S. participation in the war in Vietnam. The remainder of Nixon's second term was dominated by the so-called Watergate scandal; when his participation in the efforts to cover up the scandal became public, Nixon lost political support in his own party. The House of Representatives voted three articles of impeachment against him (July 1974), but before a trial for impeachment could begin, he became the first president to resign from office (August 1974). He was granted a pardon by President GERALD FORD, and he published his memoirs, *R. N.*, in 1978. *In the Arena: A Memoir of Victory, Defeat and Renewal* (1990) is an informal treatment of several crises in which Nixon tries to influence the judgment of history on his life and career.

Nixon has been an object of fascination for many writers. Apart from Woodward and Bernstein's books on Watergate, *All the President's Men* (1974) and *The Final Days* (1976), views of Nixon have been expressed by disparate writers in such works as Garry Wills's *Nixon Agonistes* (1970), Philip Roth's *Our Gang* (1971), Theodore H. White's *The Making of the President* (1960, 1968, 1972), Robert Coover's *The Public Burning* (1977), and J. Anthony Lukas's *Nightmare* (1977). Bob Woodward's *Shadow: Five Presidents and the Legacy of Watergate, 1974–1999* (2000) traces the effects of the scandal on the presidency.

Noah, Mordecai M[anuel] (1785–1851), playwright, lawyer, editor, public official. Born in Philadelphia, Noah founded two or three papers, including *Noah's Times*

and Weekly Messenger, studied law and was admitted to the bar, served as sheriff, surveyor of Port of New York, and a judge of the court of sessions. In his theatrical ventures Noah was fervently patriotic. Perhaps his best-known play was a comedy, SHE WOULD BE A SOLDIER (1819). He also wrote *Paul and Alexis* (1812), later revived as *The Wandering Boys* (1821); *The Siege of Tripoli* (1820); *Marion, or, The Hero of Lake George* (1821); and *The Grecian Captive* (1822). His plays were popular and were often revived. In addition Noah wrote *Travels in England, France, Spain, and the Barbary States* (1819).

noble savage (1960–1962), a semiannual paperback *literary miscellany* described as "a magazine for writers, edited by writers." SAUL BELLOW was one of the founding editors; contributors included Ralph Ellison, Herbert Gold, Arthur Miller, Wright Morris, and Harvey Swados. An "Ancestors" feature reprinted works from the past.

Nock, Albert Jay (1873–1945), clergyman, editor, writer. From his childhood Nock was a maverick. He opposed American participation in the two World Wars and attributed it to the malign domination of our diplomacy by England. He wrote on Rabelais and Artemus Ward and edited their writings. With Francis Neilson he wrote *How Diplomats Make War* (1915, 2nd ed. 1916). Under the pen name Historicus he analyzed *The Myth of a Guilty Nation* (1922). He wrote a witty book on *Jefferson* (1926) and another on *Henry George* (1939), and under the pen name Journeyman he published *The Book of Journeyman* (1930) and *A Theory of Education in the U.S.* (1932). Collections of his essays were made in *Doing the Right Thing and Other Essays* (1928) and *Free Speech and Plain Language* (1937). His autobiographical works were *Journal of These Days: June 1932–December 1933* (1934); *Memoirs of a Superfluous Man* (1943), largely an attack on democracy; and the posthumous *Journal of Forgotten Days: 1934–35* (1949).

Nokomis. The grandmother who reared HIAWATHA and taught him the legends of the Ojibways. Her name means "Daughter of the Moon."

Nolan, Philip. See MAN WITHOUT A COUNTRY.

nonfiction novel. An account of actual events dramatized by the use of fictional techniques such as dialogue (see NEW JOURNALISM). TRUMAN CAPOTE's *In Cold Blood* (1965) is an example.

Nook Farm. A real estate development on the western limits of Hartford, Connecticut, that attracted some notable residents. Between 1871 and 1891 they included Harriet Beecher Stowe and her husband Calvin Stowe, Isabella Beecher Hooker, the Rev. Joseph Hopkins Twichell, Frederick Beecher Perkins, Charles Dudley Warner, and others. Mark Twain brought his bride Olivia to Hartford in 1871 and built a house on the land he bought at Nook Farm. A great scandal that rocked the community was the Tilton divorce suit that involved Henry Ward Beecher as an alleged adulterer. Kenneth R. Andrews wrote a description of the group in *Nook Farm: Mark Twain's Hartford Circle* (1950).

Noon Wine (1937), a novella by KATHERINE ANNE PORTER. The scene is a dairy farm in Texas run reluctantly by

Mr. Thompson, who regards chores as woman's work, but who is married to an invalid, Ellie. The silent hard work of Mr. Helton, a taciturn and strange new hired man, puts the farm on a paying basis. After nearly nine years, their peace is disturbed by the arrival of Homer T. Hatch, a sly and devious man who inspires distrust in Thompson at once. When he accuses Helton of being an escaped lunatic and tries to capture him for profit, Thompson kills him, believing that Hatch has knifed Helton. Although no marks or wounds are found on Helton, Thompson is acquitted of Hatch's murder. Nevertheless, he is overwhelmed by guilt and finally kills himself. The story is told in a simple, clear manner with the touches of irony usual in Porter's work.

Nordhoff, Charles (1830–1901), newspaperman, author. Nordhoff came from Prussia to the United States as a child, served in the U.S. Navy and later in the merchant marine and on sailing vessels, and wrote about his experiences in *Man-of-War Life* (1856), *The Merchant Vessel* (1856), and *Whaling and Fishing* (1856). This trilogy was published in a single volume, *Nine Years a Sailor* (1857), as *Life on the Ocean* (1874), and as *In Yankee Windjammers* (1940), the last edited by his grandson CHARLES BERNARD NORDHOFF. Nordhoff also wrote for the New York *Evening Post* (1861–71) and the New York *Herald* (1874–90). Among his other books are *Stories of the Island World* (1857), *Secession Is Rebellion* (1860), *Cape Cod and All Along the Shore* (1868), *Communistic Societies of America* (1875), and *The Cotton States* (1876).

Nordhoff, Charles Bernard (1887–1947), novelist. Nordhoff, born of American parents in England, was educated at Stanford and Harvard. He drove an ambulance in France in 1916 and later joined the Lafayette Flying Corps, where he met JAMES NORMAN HALL. In 1920 the two future collaborators went to Tahiti, where they remained for many years. *The Fledgling* (1919) is an account in diary form of Nordhoff's flying experiences during World War I. Both *The Pearl Lagoon*, adventures in the South Seas, and *Picaro*, a novel about two brothers in Guadaloupe whose destinies were bound up with airplanes, appeared in 1924. The *Derelict* (1925), another novel of adventure in the South Seas, was the last book Nordhoff wrote alone. From then until his death he worked with Hall. Their best-known collaboration was a trilogy: MUTINY ON THE BOUNTY (1932), *Men Against the Sea* (1934), and *Pitcairn's Island* (1934).

Norman, Marsha (1947–), playwright. Born in Kentucky and educated at Agnes Scott College in Georgia, Norman was slow to settle on writing as a profession, but met with success from the start. *Getting Out* (1977) depicts the struggle of Arlene to free herself from prostitution, even if it means doing menial work for low pay, *'night Mother* (1983), Norman's best-known play, also deals with a lonely woman's options, in this case whether to keep on living. Her other plays include *Third and Oak* (1978), *Circus Valentine* (1979), *The Holdup* (1983), *The Shakers* (1983), and *Traveler in the Dark* (1984). *Collected Plays* (1996) includes introductions and essays on playwriting.

Norris, [Benjamin] Frank[lin] (1870–1902), novelist. Norris was born in Chicago and grew up there and San Francisco. At age seventeen he acquired a serious interest in painting, and his father took him to Europe to study. The experiment did not last long, however, and Norris entered the University of California in 1890. There he read Zola, Kipling, and Richard Harding Davis, and in 1894 when he went on to Harvard he took with him the beginnings of his novel *McTeague*. Under Professor LEWIS E. GATES, who recognized his talent, he worked on this and on a second novel, *Vandover and the Brute*, though neither was published until several years later. After his year at Harvard, Norris traveled, reporting the Boer War for the San Francisco *Chronicle* and *Collier's*. Back in California he joined the staff of the *San Francisco Wave*, and in 1898 published his first novel, MORAN OF THE LADY LETTY. He worked briefly for a publisher in New York and then went to Cuba to report the Santiago campaign for *McClure's Magazine*, an assignment that left him in poor health.

MCTEAGUE appeared in 1899, followed by a sentimental romance, BLIX (1899), and a sensational story, *A Man's Woman* (1900). His most ambitious work, THE OCTOPUS (1901), heralded a great naturalistic trilogy on the production and distribution of wheat; but Norris died in 1902 after an operation for appendicitis. THE PIT, the second volume of the trilogy, appeared posthumously in 1903.

Norris's reputation as a major naturalist rests on *McTeague*, *Vandover and the Brute* (the manuscript of which was lost in the San Francisco earthquake and not recovered and published until 1914), and *The Octopus*. These books embody Norris's debt to Zola, his attempt to transfer Zola's literary technique to American materials, and his great contribution to the liberation of the American novel from the vapid sentimentalism of the 1890s. *McTeague* tells of a brutal, stupid dentist who is pushed from his profession, becomes a drunkard, murders his wife, and is trapped fleeing across the California desert toward the hills where he had spent his youth. The plot is sensational, but the story is told with a care for detail and with a fairly successful use of scientific concepts of heredity and environment. It is also true that *McTeague* produces outsized, grotesque effects, sensational rather than scientific, and in this respect is perhaps more romantic than naturalistic. But this is the kind of romance that Norris found in Zola. *Vandover and the Brute* is a study of a degenerative disease, lycanthropy, which reduces a charming and talented young man to abject poverty, misery, and attacks of mania during which he crawls about naked, barking and snarling like a wolf. Zola believed that such a novel could give so minute and circumstantial an account of disease that it would be a valuable scientific document, treating psychological phenomena as if they were chemical reactions. Norris did not adhere strictly to the formula, however, so *Vandover* is really a moral tale, somewhat confused, in which the responsibility for the protagonist's degeneracy is sometimes placed on himself, sometimes on a remorseless and purposeless universe, and sometimes on society.

In *The Octopus* Norris attempted an epic portrayal of the operation of economic determinism, such as Zola had carried out so triumphantly in *Germinal*. Norris's story fails to embody a consistent determinism, and the reason for the failure is that his epic is laid on the frontier and his ranchers, who begin the story as free agents possessed of more than the usual amount of force and self-sufficiency and engage in a heroic conflict with the forces of evil represented by the railroad. The evil of the railroad is personified by the figure of S. Behrman, whose villainous deeds are prompted by an evil within him that is not explained as the product of determining economic pressure. The uncertainty of Norris's philosophical position is brought out by the inconsistency of his economic viewpoint. At one moment the railroad is evil, at another the apathy of the voting public is to blame, at another the evils of competition are justified by the ultimate fact that the wheat is somehow grown and distributed, and at still another the wheat is presented as a force in itself that mystically *wills* to be grown and eaten. The story is continued in *The Pit*, Norris's weakest serious novel. Here his renunciation of a naturalistic technique in favor of popular sentimental romance is nearly complete. The novel was written for money, in all probability, and was the author's greatest popular success. Norris's essay, THE RESPONSIBILITIES OF THE NOVELIST, was published posthumously (1903).

The accomplishments of Norris should not be underrated. He was a groundbreaker for the great flowering of American fiction that followed him in the 20th century. Beyond that, his best novels remain readable and intelligent. But Norris was probably more interested in the purely novelistic aspects of Zola's technique than he was in the philosophical implications of NATURALISM. Because his novels express a confused view of reality, they fail to achieve the degree of consistency and integration usual in permanently viable works of art.

Norris has been studied in Franklin Walker's *Frank Norris: A Biography* (1932, 1963); Ernest Marchand's *Frank Norris: A Study* (1942); Donald Pizer's *The Novels of Frank Norris* (1966); and Don Graham's *The Fiction of Frank Norris* (1978).
CHARLES CHILD WALCUTT/GP

Norris, Kathleen [Thompson] (1880–1966), short-story writer, novelist, memoirist. Born in San Francisco and educated at home, Kathleen Thompson went to work at nineteen. She worked as a bookkeeper, clerk, and teacher, entertaining her small brothers and sisters by telling them stories she later would sell to magazines. In 1909 she married the novelist Charles Norris and moved to New York City, where she sold stories and serials to the women's magazines. Her first novel, *Mother* (1911), a sentimental tale of family life in California, was a best seller. Among Norris's later writings are *Noon* (1925); *My San Francisco* (1932); *My California* (1933); *Victoria* (1933); a play; *Bakers' Dozen* (1938), short stories, and more than seventy novels. *Certain People of Importance* (1922) is considered her best. Other novels by Norris include *The Heart of Rachel* (1916), *The Barberry Bush* (1928), *The Venables* (1941), *Mink Coat* (1946), *High Holiday* (1949), *Shadow Marriage* (1952), *Dear Miss Harriet* (1955), and *Family Gath-*

ering (1959). An omnibus volume collected *The Best of Kathleen Norris* (1955).

North, Sterling (1906–1974), critic, poet, novelist. Born in Wisconsin, North began his career as a poet. His work appeared during the 1920s in *The Dial, Poetry,* and *Harper's*. In 1929 he became a reporter on the Chicago *Daily News* and from 1933 to 1943 was book reviewer. Later he became literary editor of the New York *Post* and then of the New York *World-Telegram and Sun* (1949–1956). As a critic he was influential and widely syndicated. He wrote a number of novels, including *Plowing on Sunday* (1934); *Night Outlasts the Whippoorwill* (1936); *Seven Against the Years* (1939); *So Dear to My Heart* (1947, a best seller later made into a movie); and *Reunion on the Wabash* (1952). Among his juveniles are *The Birthday of Little Jesus* (1952); *Abe Lincoln, Log Cabin to White House* (1956); *George Washington* (1956); *Young Thomas Edison* (1958); *Thoreau of Walden Pond* (1959); and *Mark Twain and the River* (1960).

North American Phalanx. A Fourierist colony founded near Red Bank, New Jersey, by ALBERT BRISBANE in 1843. It lasted twelve years and was the most enduring of such colonies established in the United States. ALEXANDER WOOLLCOTT was born in the town of Phalanx in 1887.

North American Review. The most important of all American periodicals of the review type, the *North American Review* was founded in 1815. A large proportion of the country's most widely known men of letters and of public affairs contributed to its pages, and its file is an unmatched repository of American thought covering a century and a quarter. It never had a large circulation (76,000 in 1891 was its peak). It changed ownership many times and was really profitable only in the 1880s and early 1890s. It varied from time to time between quarterly, bimonthly, monthly, and fortnightly publication.

Editors and their terms were WILLIAM TUDOR, 1815–1817; JARED SPARKS, 1817–1818, 1824–1830; EDWARD T. CHANNING, 1818–1819; EDWARD EVERETT, 1820–1823; ALEXANDER H. EVERETT, 1830–1835; JOHN G. PALFREY, 1836–1842; Francis Bowen, 1843–1853; A. P. Peabody, 1853–1863; JAMES RUSSELL LOWELL, 1863–1872; HENRY ADAMS, 1872–1876; Allen Thorndike Rice, 1877–1889; Lloyd S. Bryce, 1889–1896; David A. Munro, 1896–1899; George B. M. Harvey, 1899–1926; Walter Butler Mahony, 1926–1935; and John H. G. Pell, 1935–1940. Among associate editors were Charles Eliot Norton and HENRY CABOT LODGE.

The *North American Review* was an outgrowth of the *Monthly Anthology* (1803–1811), conducted by a group of Harvard men organized loosely as the ANTHOLOGY CLUB. One member of the club, William Tudor, founded the *North American Review and Miscellaneous Journal* as a bimonthly in 1815. It immediately entered the third, or paper, war with England in defense of a national American literature, although it was itself more New England than national in its scope. Bryant began his contributions to the review with *Thanatopsis* in 1817. Like everything else for many years, *Thanatopsis* appeared anonymously. In its first five years the journal carried contributions from Edward and A. H. Everett, John Adams, Daniel Webster, H. W. Longfellow, and Francis Parkman; under later editors the old review became notoriously dull. As late as 1861, it was renewing its traditional opposition to immediate emancipation of the slaves, and it had little influence in the war years.

After the war, James Russell Lowell enlisted a group of contributors who regained much of the *Review's* former prestige: Edwin L. Godkin, Charles Francis Adams. Jr., George William Curtis, James Parton, and Goldwin Smith. Emerson appeared again. Henry Adams' editorship in the 1870s gave more force to the journal; Lowell observed that Adams was making the old tea kettle think it was a steam engine. Politics, science, and philology were emphasized; literary criticism came from Howells, Henry James, H. E. Boyesen, and many others.

In 1877 Allen Thorndike Rice, wealthy, energetic, Boston-born and Oxford-educated, bought the *North American*. The next year he moved the Boston-and-Harvard journal to New York and into the arena of controversial political, industrial, social, and religious questions. Symposia by leading thinkers, such as a debate by Robert G. Ingersoll and Jeremiah S. Black on the Christian religion, were frequent. Literature was not neglected: Emerson's later essays were printed, as were several by Whitman, a debate on the Shakespeare-Bacon controversy, and work by Bryce, Anthony Trollope, and others. After Rice's untimely death in 1889, Lloyd Bryce carried forward much the same policy, with outstanding work by Gladstone, Bryce, Howells, Andrew Carnegie, and Mark Twain.

In 1899 George Harvey purchased the *North American*, making it as lively in politics and social questions as it had been under Rice. Twain's *To a Person Sitting in Darkness* (February 1901) created a sensation. Tolstoy, Maeterlinck, and d'Annunzio became contributors. Serial fiction appeared for the first time, by Henry James, Howells, and Joseph Conrad. Harvey was absentee editor in 1921–1924 while Ambassador to Great Britain, and circulation declined. W. B. Mahony, lawyer and financier, bought the *Review* in 1926 and though he enlisted many well-known commentators on political and literary affairs, he was unable to make headway against the newer illustrated reviews, and the Winter, 1939–1940 issue of the *North American* was the last. A quarterly with the same name made its appearance in 1963 under sponsorship at the University of Northern Iowa.

North of Boston (London 1914), Robert Frost's second collection, it contains some of his best-known poems, including "Mending Wall," "The Death of the Hired Man," and "Home Burial."

Northwest Passage (1937), a novel by KENNETH ROBERTS. This sprawling novel describes Major ROBERT ROGERS'S expedition in 1759 to destroy the Indian town of St. Francis and then his idea of finding an overland route to the Northwest. Rogers's experiences in the Northwest are described in his own *Concise Account of North America* (1765). In preparing this novel, Roberts made extensive research and unearthed documents that historians had believed were lost. The book is one of Roberts's best works. See SIR WILLIAM JOHNSON.

Northwest Passage. When Pope Alexander VI in 1493 gave Spain a monopoly of the Western world, French and English expeditions tried to find a way to Cathay by sea through a Northwest Passage. JOHN CABOT was one of the first to believe that such an all-sea route existed. Among early navigators who sought to break a way across the Arctic seas north of Canada were Martin Frobisher, George Weymouth, John Davys, Luke Fox, John Knight, and HENRY HUDSON in the 16th and 17th centuries, JAMES COOK in the 18th and Sir John Franklin in the 19th. Actually no one made the passage until Roald Amundsen went through in 1906. The term was also applied to overland expeditions to the Pacific coasts. A complete history of the various expeditions is given by L. H. Neatby in his *In Quest of the Northwest Passage* (1958). WILLIAM T. VOLLMANN's novel *The Rifles* (1994) fictionalizes the search, with emphasis on the doomed Franklin expedition.

Norton, Andrews (1786–1853), biblical scholar. Norton, associated from 1811 until 1830 with Harvard, founded and edited the *General Repository and Review* (1812–1813), a Unitarian publication. *The Evidences of the Genuineness of the Gospels* (3 v. 1837, 1844), a study of the New Testament, is his most important work. *On the Latest Form of Infidelity* (1939) is an attack on Emerson's *Divinity School Address*.

Norton, Charles Eliot (1827–1908), teacher and man of letters. Professor of the history of fine art at Harvard, Norton was a frequent contributor to periodicals. In 1865 he helped found and edit *The Nation* and, with James Russell Lowell, edited the *North American Review*. Norton was active as translator, editor, biographer, and bibliographer. He edited the correspondence and reminiscences of Carlyle and the poetry of Donne and ANNE BRADSTREET. His friendships with well-known men and women of his time make his *Letters* (1913) valuable documents.

Norton, John (1606–1663), clergyman, controversialist, biographer. Norton fled to New England in 1635 when Archbishop Laud launched his offensive against Puritan preachers in England. He immediately became one of the leaders of the colony. He wrote *The Orthodox Evangelist* (1654); *Abel Being Dead yet Speaketh, or, The Life and Death of John Cotton* (1658), reprinted with notes by Enoch Pond (1834) (see JOHN COTTON); and *Heart of New England Rent, or, The Blasphemies of the Present Generation* (1659), directed against the Quakers, whom he persecuted with zeal.

Notes of a Native Son (1955), the collection of essays written between 1948 and 1955 that established JAMES BALDWIN (1924–87) as a major American essayist. These early essays form a Baldwin manifesto. They establish the themes that will mark all of the author's work during the next thirty-two years: the African-American's lonely search for identity in a world blinded by its own myths, and the power of love as a force to transcend those myths. Baldwin's method is at once prophetic, objective, and autobiographical. With passion derived in part from Old Testament rhetoric, he accuses his nation, the American nation and the larger nation of western civilization, of having betrayed its law and its ideals. His passion is made more effective by a cool objectivity, a biting irony, and an ability to make use of events in his own life for metaphorical purposes.

Notes of a Native Son is in three parts. The first is concerned with African-American identity, especially as it relates to the artist, and contains two controversial essays, "Everybody's Protest Novel" and "Many Thousands Gone," which criticize RICHARD WRIGHT. The general subject of Part II is life in black America. The central work here is the title essay, "Notes of a Native Son," a study of Baldwin's relationship with his father. The autobiographical approach prevails as well in Part III, in which "Equal in Paris" and "Stranger in the Village" use incidents from Baldwin's expatriate life in Europe as metaphors for the overall dilemma facing African-Americans and other oppressed people.

DAVID LEEMING

Notes of a Son and Brother (1914), the second volume of autobiographical narration by HENRY JAMES, covering the period from the late 1850s to 1870. The earlier years are treated in *A Small Boy and Others* (1913).

Notes on the State of Virginia (1784), a book by THOMAS JEFFERSON about his native state. It was first published in France and widely pirated there and in England. No American edition appeared until 1787. The book, rich in facts, shows Jefferson's classical learning. He denounces the lack of taste and the unseemly appearance of colonial architecture in Virginia and expounds his agrarian philosophy.

Notes Toward a Supreme Fiction (1942), a long poem by WALLACE STEVENS. It reflects Stevens's tendency to shift away from the rich metaphor and imagery of his earlier poetry toward a more abstract poetic statement about the nature of poetry. It begins with a flat, almost conversational statement and becomes progressively more metaphoric. The poem is divided into three sections labeled "It Must Be Abstract," "It Must Change," and "It Must Give Pleasure." The poem, the supreme fiction, says Stevens, "refreshes life so that we share/For a moment, the first idea." The "first idea" must be abstract, the semi-Platonic idea of the thing; it must change, since life and perspective are constantly changing, and it must give pleasure when the abstraction is blooded by human thought.

Notions of the Americans, Picked up by a Traveling Bachelor (1828), by JAMES FENIMORE COOPER. Lafayette asked his good friend Cooper to write an account of his triumphal American tour of 1824–25. Cooper feared that an undiluted account of official proceedings and welcomes would be dull, so he wrote a book about the United States through the letters of a supposed English traveler. This person was described as coming to the United States when Lafayette did, meeting him often, and witnessing his triumphs. Cooper excuses slavery by blaming Europeans for its introduction, and he defends the treatment of the Indian. Everywhere he mini-

mizes the wild and eccentric elements of American life in the 1820s. The book, which made many disparaging remarks about England, had a bad reception there and to it Cooper later traced the decline of his literary fortunes: he alienated Englishmen and even repelled Americans by the chauvinistic tone of the book. Cooper was later more severe in commenting on the United States.

Nott, Henry Junius (1797–1837), lawyer, teacher, humorist. Born in South Carolina, Nott practiced law before turning to literature. He served as professor of belles-lettres at the College of South Carolina. In 1834 he published, in two volumes, *Novelettes of a Traveller, or, Odds and Ends from the Knapsack of Thomas Singularity, Journeyman Printer*. In these picaresque sketches he made good use of local characters and incidents.

Novanglus. The pen name used by JOHN ADAMS [2] in his controversy with DANIEL LEONARD.

Novel: Before 1960. Americans read and enjoyed novels before they themselves wrote them or publicly approved of them. The slow rise of native fiction was partly due to the Puritans' condemnation as immoral of anything that did not remind man of his duty to God and, therefore, of secular tales that might seduce him into idleness. But there were other factors: Americans were colonials for more than a century and a half; it took time to develop a national point of view; and the business of clearing a wilderness and settling into it meant emphasis on practical matters and little attention to nonutilitarian, imaginative literature. The land was vast, uncultivated, and lacking in sophisticated urban centers. There were printers but no publishers, and it was easier to import or pirate fashionable works from abroad than to create, advertise, and distribute American fiction. Moreover, the novel as a genre was comparatively young, and only slowly did the new form make its way into all areas of a distant country. The novel in English was a product of the 18th century. One of its earliest exponents, Daniel Defoe, produced his first novel, *Robinson Crusoe*, in 1719; it was some years before he was followed by Samuel Richardson (*Pamela*, 1740); Tobias Smollett (*Roderick Random*, 1748); Henry Fielding (*Tom Jones*, 1749); and Laurence Sterne (*Tristram Shandy*, 1760). In the latter half of the 18th century England produced a spate of popular stories: sentimental and domestic, adventure and historical, and the type of tale of terror we call Gothic. Americans were able to sample these and other new works, but only after a time lag; Benjamin Franklin, for example, offered *Robinson Crusoe* in 1734 and his own reprinting of *Pamela* in 1744.

American fiction was at first derivative. Since all our early tales were comparatively short and of inferior quality, the question of priority is not highly important. There had been elements of fiction in travel accounts, narratives of Indian captivities, anecdotes, and folk tales, but no one writer's name stands out until late in the 18th century. Historians have put forth several candidates for first American novel. Among those often named have been JOSEPH MORGAN's *The History of the Kingdom of Basaruah* (1715), a religious allegory; CHARLOTTE

LENNOX's *The Female Quixote* (1752); Edward Bancroft's *The History of Charles Wentworth Esq.* (London 1770); FRANCIS HOPKINSON's A PRETTY STORY (1774); and THOMAS ATWOOD DIGGES's *The Adventures of Alonso* (London 1775). All these fail on one or more counts: They are too short. Their authors lived in America only briefly. Their scenes are not recognizably American. They do not exhibit an attitude or cast of mind that is significantly American. Most critics now agree that the rise of the American novel may be dated from WILLIAM HILL BROWN's THE POWER OF SYMPATHY (published anonymously 1789, and sometimes attributed to Sarah Wentworth Morton). This tale, told in the form of letters and showing the marked influence of Richardson, was set in Boston, where it was published, and was written by an American who drew his materials from a local scandal. Though dull, digressive, and piously moralistic, the tale had sensational elements, which included seduction, near incest, abduction, and suicide. Brown recognized that his story was open to attack; his preface contains a plea to the effect that if he had exposed vice, he had still recommended virtue.

This double quality was to remain for some years characteristic of the fiction most popular in the early days of our republic—the sentimental, domestic tale of a chaste heroine in regular danger of losing her virtue to a devilish seducer. Writers of such tales wanted it both ways—lure readers by an appeal to pruriency but haul them back to morality by sermonizing conclusions. Notable examples of the seduction story are SUSANNA ROWSON's *Charlotte Temple* (London 1791), which was one of the most popular American novels, and Hannah Foster's THE COQUETTE (1797). None of these seduction stories has much more than historical interest today. Their styles were overly ornate, their characters insufficiently motivated, their settings poorly rendered, and the motivation of their authors somewhat suspect. But they attracted readers, and their influence on popular fiction was to extend far into the next century.

A second type of novel that had been popular in England, the Gothic tale of terror (see GOTHIC FICTION), was generally beyond the power of native writers; America had no ruined castles, ancestral portraits, aristocracy, or corrupted church to portray. One sample of such a tale (with a foreign setting) is SARAH WOOD's *Julia and the Illuminated Baron* (1800)—the baron is enlightened, not lighted up. More successful was the use of Gothic elements in works like Charles Brockden Brown's WIELAND (1798).

The historical novel had a better fate in this early period, but it did not become prominent until the first quarter of the 19th century. Though America had a past of no great depth, there was to be some attempt to mine it in the purportedly autobiographical THE FEMALE AMERICAN; OR, THE ADVENTURES OF UNCA ELIZA WINKFIELD (London 1767), an Indian tale; JEREMY BELKNAP's *The Foresters* (1792); ANN ELIZA BLEECKER's THE HISTORY OF MARIA KITTLE (1793), set in the French and Indian wars; and JOHN DAVIS's THE FIRST SETTLERS OF VIRGINIA (1802). Satire, a fourth type of fiction, was not extensively practiced by novelists; it was too sophisticated, too topical, and too ironical for the average taste. The few notable satirical novels include GILBERT IMLAY's THE EMIGRANTS (London 1793), which depicted the contrast between the New World and the Old World; and ROYALL TYLER's THE ALGERINE CAPTIVE (1797), which attacked piracy and slavery. By far the best of the lot—and one of the finest American books before 1800—was HUGH HENRY BRACKENRIDGE's MODERN CHIVALRY published in installments between 1792 and 1815. Brackenridge (1748–1816) wrote an extremely long, picaresque novel with little continuous plot; although not distrustful of democracy itself, he was concerned with the failures of the American democratic experiment, and his pictures of corruption and demagoguery still have force.

Only one other American writer before 1800 ranks with Brackenridge. He is the CHARLES BROCKDEN BROWN (1771–1810), who produced six novels in four years. *Wieland* (1798) is a tale of religious mania; ORMOND (1799) involves the conflict of a high-minded woman and a hero-villain; ARTHUR MERVYN (1799–1800) is set partly in Philadelphia during a yellow fever epidemic; EDGAR HUNTLY (1799) treats of murder and Indian adventure; and *Clara Howard* (1801) and *Jane Talbot* (1801) are minor works. Brown has been called a Gothic novelist, and his use of ventriloquism, spontaneous combustion, sleepwalking, disguises, and other sensational elements gives some support to the claim. But Brown was primarily a rationalist, an enthusiast for science and the rights of women, and he was concerned with portraying the fate of reason in a not yet perfect world. His style was elaborately Latinate and balanced, and his intricate plots sometimes resemble a nested set of boxes, but his analyses of bizarre mental states and his ability to create and maintain suspense lift him far above his contemporaries. If anyone deserves the title of father of the American novel, it is Brown—one of the first to attempt to be a professional writer.

Before 1820 America had produced about ninety novels, but few of them ranked with the best work of Brackenridge and Brown. WASHINGTON IRVING won a reputation at home and abroad with THE SKETCH BOOK (1819–20) and with later collections of tales; he wrote no long fiction, but his style and subjects had some influence on Hawthorne and Poe. The next writer of importance to appear was JAMES FENIMORE COOPER (1789–1851), who is best remembered for the five Leather-Stocking tales: THE PIONEERS (1823), THE LAST OF THE MOHICANS (1826), THE PRAIRIE (1827), THE PATHFINDER (1840), and THE DEERSLAYER (1841); these added to a growing American mythology the figures of the frontiersman NATTY BUMPPO, the Indian CHINGACHGOOK, and a host of others. Cooper was remarkable for the range of subjects in his more than thirty novels; he wrote of the American Revolution (THE SPY, 1821), the sea (THE PILOT, 1823), Europe (THE BRAVO, 1831), the Dutch background of New York (SATANSTOE, 1845); he also wrote political satire (THE MONIKINS, 1835; HOME AS FOUND, 1838) and a Utopian novel (THE CRATER, 1847). Cooper, like others in the first half of the 19th century, called his books romances; his tales shied away form the commonplace domestic novel and concentrated on wild and exciting actions set in remote or otherwise unusual surroundings. Cooper's romances were weak in style and depended too much on coincidence for plot resolution, but they did much to awaken Americans to the significance of their own past, and they created a vogue for historical fiction similar to that initiated by Sir Walter Scott on the other side of the Atlantic.

The followers of Scott and Cooper were numerous, and the subjects of their novels varied. Among the more memorable were JOHN NEAL, whose Rachel Dyer (1828) dealt with witchcraft in Salem; LYDIA MARIA CHILD, who wrote of the pre-Revolutionary period in *The Rebels* (1825); JAMES KIRKE PAULDING, who examined Dutch colonialism in THE DUTCHMAN'S FIRESIDE (1831); CATHARINE MARIA SEDGWICK, whose *Hope Leslie* (1827) was concerned with Indians in 17th-century New England; TIMOTHY FLINT, who opened up interest in the West with *Francis Berrian* (1826); ROBERT MONTGOMERY BIRD, who left a fascinating portrait of an Indian-hater in NICK OF THE WOODS (1837); and JOSEPH HOLT INGRAHAM, whose LAFITTE (1936) deals with the famous pirate. Southerners, too, were arousing interest in the backgrounds of their region. The best known was WILLIAM GILMORE SIMMS (1806–70), whose thirty-four works of fiction include tales of the colonial period in South Carolina (*The Yemassee*, 1835), the Revolution (THE PARTISAN, 1835), and the border areas (RICHARD HURDIS, 1838). Less notable were GEORGE TUCKER (*The Valley of Shenandoah*, 1824), NATHANIEL BEVERLEY TUCKER (GEORGE BALCOMBE, 1836), WILLIAM ALEXANDER CARUTHERS (*The Cavaliers of Virginia*, 1835), and JOHN PENDLETON KENNEDY (HORSE-SHOE ROBINSON, 1835). The Civil War added a new subject for the historical romancer, but for many years fictional treatment of the conflict was subliterary. Still worthy of note, however, are JOHN WILLIAM DE FOREST's *Miss Ravenel's Conversion from Secession to Loyalty* (1866) and JOHN ESTEN COOKE's more romantic view of war in *Surry of Eagle's-Nest* (1866) and other books. Antislavery sentiment accounted for RICHARD HILDRETH'S THE SLAVE (1836) and HARRIET BEECHER STOWE's popular UNCLE TOM'S CABIN (1852).

A few authors better known as poets or short-story writers also attempted the novel in the period before 1870. EDGAR ALLAN POE wrote one extended piece of fiction, THE NARRATIVE OF ARTHUR GORDON PYM (1838), a sea adventure tale with a mysterious ending in the south polar region; HENRY WADSWORTH LONGFELLOW contributed two mild, dreamy romances, HYPERION (1839) and KAVANAGH (1849); WALT WHITMAN produced a ludicrous temperance tract in FRANKLIN EVANS (1842); and OLIVER WENDELL HOLMES, SR., wrote three books that foreshadow modern psychiatric findings: ELSIE VENNER (1861), THE GUARDIAN ANGEL (1867), and A MORTAL ANTIPATHY (1885). To this group may be added a few other minor works: THEODORE FAY's *Norman Leslie* (1835), CHARLES FENNO HOFFMAN's GREY-SLAER (1839), GEORGE LIPPARD's Gothic *The Quaker City* (1844), and CORNELIUS MATHEWS's *Big Abel and the Little Manhattan* (1845).

Women had been responsible for some of our earliest sentimental domestic fiction, and they continued in force in the first seventy years of the 19th century—so much so that

Hawthorne called them that "damned mob of scribbling women." They won a following in their day that was not achieved by the period's more serious writers. Most prominent were SUSAN WARNER (THE WIDE, WIDE WORLD, 1850); E.D.E.N. SOUTHWORTH, who wrote more than sixty novels in her eighty-year life span; MARIA CUMMINS (THE LAMPLIGHTER, 1854); and AUGUSTA JANE EVANS, widely renowned for her *St. Elmo* (1866). Two equally well-received and prolific sentimentalists were men: TIMOTHY SHAY ARTHUR and EDWARD PAYSON ROE.

With the exception of Cooper and Poe, none of the aforementioned writers contributed much to the development of fiction as a serious art between 1820 and 1870. The discovery that the romance could offer intellectual fare as well as entertainment was reserved for the two men whose names now loom above all others in this period. NATHANIEL HAWTHORNE and HERMAN MELVILLE. Hawthorne (1804–64) produced a number of distinguished short stories before 1850; in the next decade he wrote four important romances: THE SCARLET LETTER (1850), THE HOUSE OF THE SEVEN GABLES (1851), THE BLITHEDALE ROMANCE (1852), and THE MARBLE FAUN (1860). Hawthorne was deeply concerned with the essential nature of man, his proper role in life, and his ultimate fate. Unlike the transcendentalists, he could come to no optimistic conclusion. To him, man was by nature a being in whom good and evil were inextricably bound up. Again and again his major fiction treats one central theme: the individual who turns away from society, either literally or by experimentation on the souls of others, and thus becomes isolated and convinced that evil exists in the hearts of all. For some of his protagonists no return to society is possible; others find that they can live with their knowledge of evil, accept man's mixed nature, and continue to exist in their semifallen state. To portray the problem of mankind, Hawthorne developed a symbolic method that went beyond the allegory of his favorite authors, Edmund Spenser and John Bunyan, and that foreshadowed more modern fiction. He dramatized the fundamental conflicts of the heart versus the head, isolation versus society, innocence versus experience, pride versus humility, introspection versus prying into the minds of others, and triumph over sin versus destruction by it. In *The Scarlet Letter*, set in 17th-century New England, he examines the effect of the sin of adultery on HESTER PRYNNE the Reverend Arthur Dimmesdale, and Hester's wronged husband, the icily intellectual physician Roger Chillingworth. In *The House of the Seven Gables* the wrong of an ancestor is traced through seven generations of the Pyncheon family of Salem. *The Blithedale Romance*, based loosely on Hawthorne's connection with the utopian experiment of Brook Farm, muses on human motivations, interpersonal relations, and the enigma of appearance and reality. The last of the four romances, *The Marble Faun*, set in Italy, analyzes the regenerative, educative power of experience, through which the naively innocent individual, confronted by sin and guilt, is able to rise to a higher perception that includes knowledge of evil. Hawthorne's achievement was striking, but full appreciation of his subtleties did not come until the 20th century.

Celebrity was won early by HERMAN MELVILLE (1819–1891), but as his vision of man became increasingly deep and complex, he lost a wide readership; his rediscovery, beginning in the 1920s, was a major effort of scholarship. Melville first captivated the public with two romances drawn from his adventures in the South Seas, but also combined with material from his reading and with imaginative additions. These were TYPEE (1846) and OMOO (1847). He tried to repeat his success with a long allegorical voyage narrative, MARDI (1849), but the public was less interested in this first evidence of Melville's more serious concerns. His next book, REDBURN (1849), deals with the adventures of a young man on a voyage to Liverpool and back to New York. WHITE-JACKET, of the next year, has as its setting a United States Navy vessel on a cruise from Peru to Boston. In 1851 Melville poured the fruit of his speculations on fate, free will, evil, and reality into MOBY-DICK, a work so vast and intricate that a library of explication has grown up around it. The book puzzled and irritated readers who had enthusiastically bought his earlier tales. Melville completed the alienation of a popular audience with PIERRE (1852), a painful work with a contemporary domestic setting that has invited psychological interpretation because of its supposed evidence of the author's disturbed state of mind. ISRAEL POTTER (1855), a minor tale dealing with figures of the Revolution, was followed by the last work of fiction to appear in Melville's lifetime, THE CONFIDENCE-MAN (1857). A difficult, bitter story of the Devil and his wiles aboard a Mississippi River boat, this work has recently been acclaimed by some critics. One final short novel, BILLY BUDD, composed 1888–91, was not published until 1924. Melville was committed to probing the ambiguities of man's nature, but he reached no conclusions he could accept with finality. As Hawthorne remarked of him, he could "neither believe, nor be comfortable in his unbelief." Melville's central image in all his best books was the voyage of discovery; of all American novelists of the first half of the 19th century, he voyaged the farthest.

During the silent years before his death in 1891, Melville lived through several new directions in fiction. Between 1870 and 1900 many writers and critics cried out regularly for more realism in the novel. The term is not susceptible of precise definition, since it meant somewhat different things to various writers, but a few characteristics of the movement can be noted. There was castigation of sentimentality and of what was called literary lying in contrived popular stories; there was a strong influence of the scientific method, as the author tried to study man in the crucible of life; and there was increased emphasis on reporting the American scene as it was actually observed, with more precise rendering of setting, speech peculiarities, customs, and occupations. The realistic writer tried to become both more objective and more daring in subject matter; he shied away from intrusion of himself, and he strove to open fiction to franker consideration of sex, politics, business, and inequities in American society. The realistic writer wanted Americans to reject servile dependence on Europe for cultural innovations, but at the same time he was much impressed by the experiments in fiction made by foreign writers like Turgenev, Zola, Balzac, Flaubert, Stendhal, Tolstoy, and Dostoevsky. The realist was to be opposed both by the genteel author, who desired fiction to be idealistic and uplifting, and by the popular romancer, who continued to ply his trade with great success. But in the end the realist set his impress on serious fiction for many decades.

One phase of this new insistence on realism may be observed in the work of that group of writers loosely called local colorists. The Civil War had made many Americans more aware of the diversity and size of the nation they had created, and there was new pride in the recognition of cultural differences in New England, in the Old South, in the raw West—even in the rising melting-pot cities. And so there sprang up a group intent on reporting to the rest of the nation the peculiarities characteristic of their own sections. Most were short-story writers: SARAH ORNE JEWETT and MARY E. WILKINS FREEMAN in New England; THOMAS NELSON PAGE, JOEL CHANDLER HARRIS, and MARY NOAILLES MURFREE in the South; MARGARET DELAND in the Middle Atlantic States; and BRET HARTE in the West. At their most effective they created believable localized settings, regional dialects, curious characters; at their weakest they were apt to fall into nostalgia or into mere quaintness or picturesqueness. A few writers attempted to expand local materials into a long novel, and a few had a notable success: GEORGE WASHINGTON CABLE (THE GRANDISSIMES, 1880, dealing with the Creoles in Louisiana); KATE CHOPIN (THE AWAKENING, 1899, another study of Creoles); Sara Orne Jewett (THE COUNTRY OF THE POINTED FIRS, 1896, set in Maine); Edward Eggleston (THE HOOSIER SCHOOLMASTER, 1871); and LAFCADIO HEARN (CHITA, 1889, a tale of the Gulf Coast). As several critics have pointed out, insofar as the local colorist tended toward the local, he emphasized the factual; insofar as he gave prominence to the color in locale, he veered toward a more sweetly tinged view of life. Later the movement was to evolve into the more austere work of the regionalists (see REGIONALISM).

A few other writers were to describe certain aspects of region but contrived to give their novels more universal application. Henry Adams wrote of Washington politics in DEMOCRACY (1879); HAROLD FREDERIC depicted the narrowness of small-town New York life in THE DAMNATION OF THERON WARE (1896) and other books; EDGAR WATSON HOWE produced a biting STORY OF A COUNTRY TOWN (1883); and ALBION WINEGAR TOURGÉE revealed Reconstruction turmoil in North Carolina in A FOOL'S ERRAND (1879). SILAS WEIR MITCHELL tried a more realistic approach to historical fiction in HUGH WYNNE, FREE QUAKER (1897). There was looking forward as well as back in EDWARD BELLAMY's utopian, socially oriented fantasy, LOOKING BACKWARD: 2000–1887 (1888).

As the realists were to complain, there was no dearth of bestselling sentimental fiction in the period. HORATIO ALGER ("Luck and Pluck" series, 1869 ff.) and LOUISA MAY ALCOTT (LITTLE WOMEN, 1868) pacified and edified children while parents reveled in the gaudy or touching scenes invented by LEW WALLACE (BEN HUR, 1880); FRANCIS MARION CRAWFORD (*A Roman*

Singer, 1884); HELEN HUNT JACKSON (RAMONA, 1884); FRANCES HODGSON BURNETT (LITTLE LORD FAUNTLEROY 1886); JAMES LANE ALLEN (A KENTUCKY CARDINAL, 1894); and hosts of others. The detective story, initiated by Poe in the 1840s, got a boost in ANNA KATHARINE GREEN's *The Leavenworth Case* (1878); and the historical romance continued popular in the work of CHARLES MAJOR (*When Knighthood Was in Flower*, 1898) and PAUL LEICESTER FORD (ANICE MEREDITH, 1899).

It is no wonder that WILLIAM DEAN HOWELLS contemplating such productions, would ask plaintively: "Ah! poor Real Life, which I love, can I make others share the delight I find in thy foolish and insipid face?" Howells was to try to rechannel public taste through reviews, articles, editorial comments, and more than forty volumes of fiction. Realism was, he said, "nothing more and nothing less than the truthful treatment of material"; somewhat timid in his own approach to fiction, he gave willing and influential aid to the more daring realists at home and abroad. Howells's own best work can be studied in A MODERN INSTANCE (1882), which deals unsparingly with an unhappy marriage; THE RISE OF SILAS LAPHAM (1885), one of the earliest treatments of a materialistic businessman who comes to see the light; and A HAZARD OF NEW FORTUNES (1890), which reveals his concern for social justice. Howells's special interest in social theory is also shown in A TRAVELER FROM ALTRURIA (1894) and a sequel, *Through the Eye of the Needle* (1907). He spurned the historical romance, the Gothic tale, the surprise ending, the contrived love story, and the sensational employed for its own sake. From first to last he was remarkably consistent in his approach; he wanted to photograph the plain face of America, and he succeeded admirably in creating believable characters and situations. He occasionally seems tepid to readers steeped in the more hard-boiled realists, but he created a valuable panorama of social life in the latter half of the century.

Other directions in realism were to be taken by Howells's two close though utterly different friends, Twain and James. MARK TWAIN (1835–1910) was a Southerner-Westerner who was to prove one of the most popular of American authors. His career began with the freewheeling satire of the Old World in THE INNOCENTS ABROAD (1869), and he was never entirely to lose his fondness for exaggeration and brash humor. TOM SAWYER (1876) and HUCKLEBERRY FINN (1884) have been loved by generations, but behind the surface nostalgia for a vanished America lies trenchant criticism of the contrarieties and failures of our civilization. Twain attacked corrupt politics in THE GILDED AGE (written with Charles Dudley Warner, 1874) and feudalism and caste in THE PRINCE AND THE PAUPER (1882) and A CONNECTICUT YANKEE IN KING ARTHUR'S COURT (1889); but many readers, conditioned by the image of the popular humorist and lecturer, were to miss his deeper satire. In later years Twain's constitutional pessimism about man's basic nature deepened. It is reflected in THE TRAGEDY OF PUDD'NHEAD WILSON (1894), a flawed study of the slavery both of body and mind in a small Mississippi River town, and in THE MYSTERIOUS STRANGER (published 1916, written earlier), a fantasy on determinism that is set in Austria of the 1590s. Twain's interest in

twin characters and in violent contrasts reveals the basic duality in his own nature; remembered most often as a humorist, he was also responsible for some of the most despairing pages in our fiction. Howells called Twain "the Lincoln of our literature," emphasizing his essential American roots.

Whether one counts HENRY JAMES (1843–1916) among American authors depends somewhat on how seriously his long residence abroad and his becoming a British subject late in life are to be counted. But James's cast of mind and the themes of his fiction show an unmistakable impress of his homeland, and his shift of allegiance was no strong repudiation of it. Critics have traditionally divided the long, highly productive career of James into three chief periods. From the middle 1860s to the 1880s he used principally American characters, in both European and American settings (RODERICK HUDSON, 1876; WASHINGTON SQUARE, 1881). For the next decade or so he most often employed English characters and scenes (THE PRINCESS CASAMASSIMA, 1886; THE SPOILS OF POYNTON, 1897). After 1900 he renewed his interest in the international theme and concentrated on Americans caught up in European situations. His style and form also underwent noticeable change. James began writing in the general tradition of the English novel, moved toward greater verbal and structural complexity in his middle period, and closed his career with works of great density and difficulty (THE WINGS OF THE DOVE, 1902; THE AMBASSADORS, 1903; THE GOLDEN BOWL, 1904). James was passionately dedicated to the art of fiction, and he contributed a valuable body of critical theory as well as practice. No brief statement can do justice to James's aesthetics, but a few of his central principles may be summarized. He was a psychological rather than a photographic realist, and he held that it was the duty of the artist to represent life, not to reproduce it. He was much concerned with technical problems, such as narrative perspective, and he developed to a high degree the symbolic method initiated in America by Hawthorne and Melville. He was less interested in surface story than in the significance inherent in his plots, and he evolved an elaborate allusive style that demands the full attention of the reader. His themes were varied, but a few have been associated predominantly with his work: the conflict of societies (innocent American and cultured, decadent European), the failure of the general public to appreciate the meaning of true art, and the sensitive individual in quest of an ideal freedom. Because he refused to compromise with the demands of popular taste, James was never a best seller despite his general renown, but he exerted a strong influence on later writers and theoreticians of the craft of the novel.

In the decade of the 1890s a group of younger authors began to practice a branch of realism that has generally been identified as NATURALISM. Not all the writers of the group were to be equally affected, but most showed the influence of recent trends in science and economics, which led toward a deterministic view of mankind—the theory that man's nature and actions were controlled by his biological inheritance and by his social environment. The naturalistic novel emphasized brutality and sordidness; it introduced elements formerly considered taboo (like sex, alcoholism, depravity, drug addiction); and it became more panoramic, sprawling, and documentary. Generally, it preached pessimism about man's fate, but often expressed compassion for man's condition and therefore seemed to imply some lurking hope. Important in this period were HAMLIN GARLAND, who portrayed man against nature and a crushing social system in his stories of the Midwest MAIN-TRAVELLED ROADS, 1893); and in novels like ROSE OF DUTCHER'S COOLLY (1895); FRANK NORRIS, whose powerful California novels combined melodrama, determinism, and a vague mysticism (MCTEAGUE, 1899; THE OCTOPUS, 1901); STEPHEN CRANE, whose MAGGIE: A GIRL OF THE STREETS (1893) is often called the first naturalistic novel, but who is better known for his antiromantic Civil War novel THE RED BADGE OF COURAGE (1895) and is by far the most accomplished of the group in style and technique; and JACK LONDON, who concerned himself with class warfare, evolution, animals, and primitive men (THE CALL OF THE WILD, 1903; MARTIN EDEN, 1909). For all their obvious faults of careless writing and occasional tediousness, the naturalists performed a valuable service. Against genteelism, aestheticism, and pseudoculture they opposed a strong sense of fact, a drab reality that was for many Americans the true condition of life. They worked hard to break the confines of fiction: to widen the vocabulary, deal as honestly and directly with sexual matters as they could, and force greater public realization of the seamier sides of the American scene. If they themselves had few outstanding successes, they did suggest the direction that one important branch of fiction was to take in the 20th century.

THEODORE DREISER (1871–1945) was to continue naturalism both as philosophy and technique in a series of elephantine, but effective novels. Dreiser's career began with SISTER CARRIE (1900), which provoked wounded cries from genteel critics. He was to go on to write a searching trilogy about an American tycoon in THE FINANCIER (1912), THE TITAN (1914), and *The Stoic* (1947); in the moving AN AMERICAN TRAGEDY (1925) he analyzed social classes and the attempt of his protagonist to rise higher in the scale. Two other important books were JENNIE GERHARDT (1911) and THE "GENIUS" (1915). Upton Sinclair, a contemporary, came suddenly to notice in 1906 with his exposé of the Chicago meatpacking industry, THE JUNGLE; he wrote a few other socially conscious studies, but in later years was best known for his series of popular stories about contemporary events involving the central character of Lanny Budd.

In addition to Dreiser and Sinclair, several other significant novelists first published in the period between 1900 and 1920. SHERWOOD ANDERSON showed the influence of Freudian psychology in his sketches of the inhabitants of (WINESBURG, OHIO (1919) and in later books like *Poor White* (1920) and DARK LAUGHTER (1925). New regionalists arose, more objective and sociological in their approach than the local colorists. Among them were ELLEN GLASGOW, whose long cycle about Virginia began with *The Descendant* (1897) and continued through such later stories as BARREN GROUND (1925) and VEIN OF IRON

(1935); and WILLA CATHER, creator of the powerful Nebraska novels *O Pioneers!* (1913) and MY ANTONIA (1918), and of the later story of New Mexico history, DEATH COMES FOR THE ARCHBISHOP (1927). Cather's distinguished work also included THE SONG OF THE LARK (1915), A LOST LADY (1923), and THE PROFESSOR'S HOUSE (1925). EDITH WHARTON composed a brief, tragic tale of New England in ETHAN FROME (1911), but more characteristic were her novels of society, like THE HOUSE OF MIRTH (1905) and THE AGE OF INNOCENCE (1920).

Highly respected in their day, but treated less kindly by modern critics, were JAMES BRANCH CABELL, a mannered romanticist remembered for his once-scandalous JURGEN (1919), and BOOTH TARKINGTON, who captivated children with PENROD (1914) and their elders with such tales as THE MAGNIFICENT AMBERSONS (1918). Popular romancers and historical novelists charged ahead undeterred by naturalism, regionalism, or other new directions in serious fiction. Representative of them were MARY JOHNSTON (TO HAVE AND TO HOLD, 1900); JOHN FOX, JR. (THE LITTLE SHEPHERD OF KINGDOM COME, 1903); WINSTON CHURCHILL (THE CROSSING, 1904); EMERSON HOUGH (54-40 OR FIGHT! 1909); GENE STRATTON PORTER (A GIRL OF THE LIMBERLOST, 1909); KATHLEEN NORRIS (*Mother*, 1911); and HAROLD BELL WRIGHT (THE WINNING OF BARBARA WORTH, 1911); OWEN WISTER (THE VIRGINIAN, 1902) and ZANE GREY continued to supply the craving for Western fiction, as did MARY ROBERTS RINEHART (THE CIRCULAR STAIRCASE, 1908) and others, for the detective story. EDGAR RICE BURROUGHS merits mention for his *Tarzan of the Apes* (1914) and for his creation of a minor science-fiction shelf. Male readers were coming into their own with such appeals to escapist desires, and writers with an eye on the market were to pay increasing attention to them in later years.

By 1920 a number of influential forces were combining to give new shape and scope to our fiction. The findings of Freud and other psychologists about human drives and motivations were eagerly seized upon by writers, with particular emphasis placed on the dire effects of sexual inhibitions. World War I, the first foreign conflict in which a large number of our citizens had engaged, created disillusionment and bitterness, but it also brought attacks on complacency and opened up new worlds for men who had their first experience of Europe under wartime conditions. Some writers, disgusted with Prohibition and provincialism, remained in Paris to practice their art and to enjoy their membership in the LOST GENERATION; others remained at home to snipe at American folly, pretension, and the get-rich-quick spirit. In retrospect, the novels produced in the astonishingly fertile decade of the 1920s are most significantly characterized by their disquiet and questioning of America's future, despite their iconoclasm and frequent attention to wild parties and clandestine love affairs.

The roll call of writers who first published important fiction in the 1920s is a list of those who proved most influential for the next three decades: Sinclair Lewis, Fitzgerald, Dos Passos, Hemingway, Faulkner, Wolfe, and Wilder. Experimental in technique and often cynical in tone, their novels surveyed an American scene in which so-called normalcy was only a catchword. SINCLAIR LEWIS (1885–1951) opened the decade with a bang with his bestselling MAIN STREET (1920), the story of a citified heroine who tried to bring some semblance of culture and intellectualism to a small Midwestern town. Lewis followed up this triumph with a sardonic portrait of a booster businessman, BABBITT (1922); a dissection of the career of an idealistic doctor, ARROWSMITH (1925); and a depiction of the confrontation between a self-made tycoon and superficial European high society in DODSWORTH (1929). In 1930 he won the first Nobel Prize for literature ever bestowed on an American, but his talents thereafter failed him and he went into a long creative slump from which he never managed to pull out. Lewis's baiting of the boobs (as Mencken called them) now appears superficial, and his once praised slang-filled dialogue has dated painfully. There was a sentimentalist, too, behind the satirist's mask, and he could never determine for himself whether he really enjoyed or despised the objects of his derision.

If anyone epitomized the spirit of the Jazz Age for most readers it was F. SCOTT FITZGERALD (1896–1940), who began his blazing career with two exuberantly youthful novels, THIS SIDE OF PARADISE (1920) and THE BEAUTIFUL AND DAMNED (1922). His best book, THE GREAT GATSBY (1925), has been acclaimed as an American classic. Drink, easy success, and the collapse of the decade into the Great Depression effectively stultified Fitzgerald as an artist; he attempted a comeback with TENDER IS THE NIGHT (1934) and the unfinished Hollywood novel *The Last Tycoon* (published 1941), but he was not to return to critical favor until a decade after his early death.

JOHN DOS PASSOS (1896–1970) produced an effective war novel in THREE SOLDIERS (1921), but his panoramic view of New York City in MANHATTAN TRANSFER (1925) better foreshadowed his major trilogy of the 1930s, *U.S.A.*—THE 42ND PARALLEL (1930), *1919*, (1932), and THE BIG MONEY (1936). In this giant work he developed the technique of the collective novel, in which an entire city or country is the hero. The effect at first may be that of aimlessness, but gradually the reader realizes that all the varied characters are caught up in a common social situation—which is the book's real theme. A second trilogy Dos Passos called *District of Columbia*—*Adventures of a Young Man* (1939), *Number One* (1943), and *The Grand Design* (1949). *Mid-century* (1961) was an attempt to return to some of the experimental devices he had employed in *U.S.A.* Dos Passos's political convictions were radical in his earlier works; in later years he swung sharply to the right and was unable to recapture the fire and force of the 1920s and early 1930s.

ERNEST HEMINGWAY (1899–1961) became one of the best-known men of his era, both as a writer and as a public figure. His first long work of fiction, THE SUN ALSO RISES (1926), definitively captured the world of the expatriate in Europe; its terse dialogue and its action scenes were to impress a generation of younger authors. Hemingway's World War I novel, A FAREWELL TO ARMS (1929), skillfully constructed and highly symbolic, was one of his best works. His record of the Spanish Civil War, which attracted the attention and presence of a number of his contemporaries, appeared as FOR WHOM THE BELL TOLLS (1940).

Far less successful were TO HAVE AND HAVE NOT (1935), set in Florida and Cuba, and ACROSS THE RIVER AND INTO THE TREES (1950), a story of World War II that occasionally lapses into self-parody. The final novel published in his lifetime, THE OLD MAN AND THE SEA (1952), was highly praised, but some critics felt it did not rise to the level of his excellent short stories. Hemingway's style, fresh and individual when it first drew notice, became less effective with imitation and his own later efforts. His subjects were limited (war, sport, love), but he remains among the most significant writers of the first half of the century.

WILLIAM FAULKNER (1897–1962), who stands with a handful of our greatest authors, began publication with two minor novels, *Soldiers' Pay* (1926) and *Mosquitoes* (1927). In 1929 he initiated what was to become his saga of the mythical Mississippi county of Yoknapatawpha in SARTORIS and THE SOUND AND THE FURY, the latter one of the most successful experimental works in American fiction. Other installments were published at intervals; among the longer stories the most important were AS I LAY DYING (1930), LIGHT IN AUGUST (1932), and ABSALOM, ABSALOM! (1936). Widespread recognition came slowly to Faulkner. On the basis of horrific episodes, such as those in SANCTUARY (1931), he was first considered a naturalist or a Southern decadent, but by the late 1940s he was acclaimed as a major symbolist in the dark tradition of Hawthorne and Melville, and his myth of the South received elaborate analysis and explication. Faulkner became a master of varied styles, narrative techniques, and subjects; his influence at home and abroad was one of the most powerful in the 20th century. Like Hemingway, he won the Nobel Prize for his contributions to world literature.

Other important writers were contemporaries of these major figures. THOMAS WOLFE (1900–1938) revealed a genuine but unharnessed talent in his four massive autobiographical novels: LOOK HOMEWARD, ANGEL (1929), OF TIME AND THE RIVER (1935), THE WEB AND THE ROCK (1939), and YOU CAN'T GO HOME AGAIN (1940)—the last two issued posthumously. THORNTON WILDER (1897–1975) wrote two mannered but impressive novels in *The Cabala* (1926) and THE BRIDGE OF SAN LUIS REY (1927). There were others of lesser rank who drew appreciative readers: JOSEPH HERGESHEIMER (JAVA HEAD, 1919, and other works throughout the next decade); WALDO FRANK (*Rahab*, 1922); CARL VAN VECHTEN (NIGGER HEAVEN, 1926); and OLE EDVART RÖLVAAG (GIANTS IN THE EARTH, 1927). Representative fictionists on the popular level were EDNA FERBER (SO BIG, 1924); FLOYD DELL (MOON-CALF, 1920); LOUIS BROMFIELD (THE GREEN BAY TREE, 1924); GERTRUDE ATHERTON (*Black Oxen*, 1923); PERCY MARKS (THE PLASTIC AGE, 1924); and JOHN ERSKINE (*The Private Life of Helen of Troy*, 1925).

The depression years of the 1930s stimulated a powerful literature of social protest, though much of it has not worn well. Several writers combined a naturalistic literary technique with a political philosophy that was leftist in sympathy—often blatantly so. JAMES T. FARRELL (1904–1979) analyzed his generation in an outspoken trilogy: YOUNG LONIGAN (1932). *The Young*

Manhood of Studs Lonigan (1934), and *Judgment Day* (1935). They traced the gradual corruption of a Chicago youth by his environment. Farrell's many later works have repeated the form and themes of these books. ERSKINE CALDWELL (1903–1987) joined sexual sensationalism with a depiction of the plight of back-country Georgia farmers to produce TOBACCO ROAD (1932), GOD'S LITTLE ACRE (1933), and *Journeyman* (1935). A natural for paperback reprints, these and other stories made him one of the most widely read American authors. Californian JOHN STEINBECK (1902–1968) showed great promise in TORTILLA FLAT (1935), IN DUBIOUS BATTLE (1936), and the THE GRAPES OF WRATH (1939), all of which depicted lower classes in conflict with a capitalistic, materialistic society. In later years he lapsed into frequent sentimentality and displayed less immediate concern for social causes. Two African-American writers who came to prominence in the period were LANGSTON HUGHES (*Not Without Laughter*, 1930) and RICHARD WRIGHT (NATIVE SON, 1940). In the hands of such men as these the novel became more documentary and proletarian, tougher in vocabulary and action, and less concerned with individual character—since the future of mankind in the mass was the author's chief interest. The movement lost force with widespread disillusionment over the direction taken by communism and with the outbreak of World War II at the end of the decade.

Two authors of the 1930s who treated a different social level were JOHN P. MARQUAND and JOHN O'HARA. Marquand produced an excellent satiric treatment of Bostonian manners in THE LATE GEORGE APLEY (1937); his many later novels tended to be slick and conventional. O'Hara, who wrote a series of frank novels about the fictional community of Gibbsville, Pennsylvania, is well represented by his early *Appointment in Samarra* (1934); KATHERINE ANNE PORTER wrote a short, incisive novel in NOON WINE (1937), as did NATHANAEL WEST in *Miss Lonelyhearts* (1933). Of the bestselling authors of the time, HERVEY ALLEN (*Anthony Adverse*, 1933) and Margaret Mitchell (GONE WITH THE WIND, 1936) had sensational successes with racy historical romances; other practitioners of the genre were KENNETH ROBERTS (NORTHWEST PASSAGE, 1937); MACKINLAY KANTOR (*Long Remember*, 1934); and Stark Young (*So Red the Rose*, 1934). MARJORIE KINNAN RAWLINGS wrote moving stories of Florida crackers in *South Moon Under* (1933) and THE YEARLING (1938); other regionalists were CARL CARMER (*Stars Fell on Alabama*, 1934) and JULIA PETERKIN (SCARLET SISTER MARY, 1928). PEARL BUCK, another Nobelist, wrote of a Chinese family in THE GOOD EARTH (1931). The old-fashioned inspirational novel was kept alive by LLOYD C. DOUGLAS (*Magnificent Obsession*, 1929; *Green Light*, 1935). WILLIAM SAROYAN began his offbeat career with short stories and plays, but went on to write novels like *The Human Comedy* (1943). Detective stories and other escapist fiction generally overshadowed more serious work on the bestseller lists of the period, and book clubs and lending libraries contributed to the growth of a middlebrow art by arranging wider distribution than most American writers had ever enjoyed before. Largely ignored were a few other novels later acclaimed, including HENRY ROTH's *Call It Sleep* (1935) and ZORA NEALE HURSTON's *Their Eyes Were Watching God* (1937).

The 1940s were marked by America's participation in World War II and the aftermath in which the Cold War began. Novels about the armed conflict started to appear even while battles still raged: JOHN STEINBECK, *The Moon Is Down* (1942) and JOHN HERSEY, *A Bell for Adano* (1944). As the experience of the 1920s had indicated, many younger writers were to return from the front to pour out their experiences in ever franker and more profane novels: JAMES JONES, FROM HERE TO ETERNITY (1951); NORMAN MAILER, THE NAKED AND THE DEAD (1948); IRWIN SHAW, THE YOUNG LIONS (1948); and HERMAN WOUK, THE CAINE MUTINY (1951). Several of these men were to continue their writing careers into the next three decades, usually with less acclaim. Older authors also tried their hand at wartime fiction; JAMES GOULD COZZENS (*The Just and the Unjust*, 1942) published *Guard of Honor* in 1948, then returned to other fields in *By Love Possessed* (1957).

The Southern renascence in literature begun by Glasgow, Faulkner, Wolfe, and others continued with EUDORA WELTY (*Delta Wedding*, 1946); TRUMAN CAPOTE (*Other Voices, Other Rooms*, 1948); CARSON MCCULLERS (THE MEMBER OF THE WEDDING, 1946); and CAROLINE GORDON (*Green Centuries*, 1941). Probably the best of the younger Southern writers was ROBERT PENN WARREN (1905–1989), who began his career in fiction with *Night Rider* (1939) and *At Heaven's Gate* (1943), but won his first popular and critical success with ALL THE KING'S MEN (1946), one of the best novels of the decade; his later works included WORLD ENOUGH AND TIME (1950), *Band of Angels* (1955), and *The Cave* (1959).

NELSON ALGREN continued the big-city novel in THE MAN WITH THE GOLDEN ARM (1949) and *A Walk on the Wild Side* (1956). In the same period devotees of less intellectual fiction were reading KATHLEEN WINSOR (FOREVER AMBER, 1944); TAYLOR CALDWELL (*This Side of Innocence*, 1946); FRANK YERBY (*The Foxes of Harrow*, 1946); SAMUEL SHELLABARGER (*The Prince of Foxes*, 1947); and Frances Parkinson Keyes (*Crescent Carnival*, 1942). Science fiction, perhaps stimulated by general interest in atomic physics, attracted a growing band of enthusiasts.

One phenomenon of the 1950s was the appearance of the so-called BEAT GENERATION, one member of which was JACK KEROUAC, whose ON THE ROAD (1957) chronicled the beats' pursuit of sex, jazz, drugs, drink, and spiritual enlightenment. More formally structured were other novels of the decade: WRIGHT MORRIS (*The Field of Vision*, 1956); SAUL BELLOW (THE ADVENTURES OF AUGIE MARCH, 1953); RALPH ELLISON (INVISIBLE MAN, 1952); RANDALL JARRELL (*Pictures from an Institution*, 1954); and HERBERT GOLD (*The Man Who Was Not With It*, 1956). Another new talent was welcomed in WILLIAM STYRON, whose LIE DOWN IN DARKNESS (1951) suggested discipleship to the Faulknerian method. Perhaps the greatest critical and popular triumph was that of J. D. SALINGER, whose *The Catcher in the Rye* (1951) caught exactly the idiom and rhythm of speech of an outwardly hard but inwardly sensitive teenager.

Histories and studies include Alfred Kazin, *On Native Grounds* (1942); Alexander Cowie, *The Rise of the American Novel* (1948); Marius Bewley, *The Complex Fate* (1954); Richard Chase, *The American Novel and Its Tradition* (1957); W.M. Fronhock, *The Novel of Violence in America* (rev. 1957); Frederick J. Hoffman, *The Modern Novel in America* (1957); Leslie Fiedler, *Love and Death in the American Novel* (1960); Ihab Hassan, *Radical Innocence: The Contemporary American Novel* (1961); Robert A. Bone, *The Negro Novel in America* (rev. 1965); Frederick J. Hoffman, *The Art of Southern Fiction* (1967); Michael Millgate, *American Social Fiction: James to Cozzens* (1967); Joel Porte, *The Romance in America: Studies in Cooper, Poe, Hawthorne, Melville, and James* (1969); Philip Fisher, *Hard Facts: Setting and Form in the American Novel* (1985); Jane Tompkins, *Sensational Designs: The Cultural Work of American Fiction 1790–1860* (1985); Cathy N. Davidson, *Revolution and the Word: The Rise of the Novel in America* (1986); and George Dekker, *The American Historical Romance* (1988).

JOSEPH V. RIDGELY / GP

novel since 1960, the.   More than at any other time in our history, the American novel since 1960 has truly represented the kaleidoscope of American life. The novel became no longer exclusively white, mainly Protestant, and usually male (Hemingway, Faulkner, Fitzgerald, Wolfe, Dos Passos, Dreiser, Lewis of a previous generation), but all colors, races, and ethnic mixes. In the 1960s emerged the black novel, the female novel, the Jewish novel (accelerated from the 1950s), the gay novel, and the Chicano novel. Yet there was also a resurgence of writing by white male: JOHN BARTH, WILLIAM GADDIS, JOSEPH MCELROY, THOMAS PYNCHON, WILLIAM STYRON, DONALD BARTHELME, WILLIAM GASS, and others. The mix of so many types, including the entrance of large numbers of female writers, may be attributed to the legislated opening up of opportunity that occurred in the decade and to the growth of egalitarianism. While power structures remained basically intact, they became more flexible and lent themselves to alternate life styles. The novel both foreshadowed and reflected these new manners and mores, including a new freedom in the use of language.

In the process began a gradual separation of fiction into two major streams: those who have rejected innovation and experimentation, the realists and so-called neorealists (SAUL BELLOW, JOYCE CAROL OATES, JOAN DIDION, BERNARD MALAMUD, JOHN UPDIKE, NORMAN MAILER, PHILIP ROTH, JAMES BALDWIN, and, with some qualification, TONI MORRISON); and those who have tried to perpetuate an innovative, modernistic fiction (Gaddis in *JR* and *Carpenter's Gothic*, Barth in *Lost in the Funhouse* and *Letters*, McElroy in *Lookout Cartridge* and *Women and Men*, Barthelme in his short fictions and in *Snow White* and *The Dead Father*). The result on one hand is a broad mix and on the other a curious bifurcation in American fiction, further intensified by the reassertion of the short story after nearly two decades of relative dormancy.

American themes have changed in the decades after 1960, from that of certainty of America's place in the world to a far

more ambiguous positioning. Gaddis's *JR* (1975) is both unique and representative. It reaches back into 1960s egalitarianism and looks ahead to 1970s and 1980s bourgeois striving and belief in upward mobility through financial deals. As an acoustical novel—dependent almost entirely on dialogue—*JR* borrows from and parodies communications systems. That other representative mega-novel of the 1970s, Pynchon's GRAVITY'S RAINBOW, is also deeply concerned with information, misinformation, and disruptive communication. Both novels assimilated the enormous growth of television since the 1960s, a development that uses visual effects to convey incomplete information and influences nearly every aspect of American fiction. Made up of small bytes, *JR* has within it the compactness television demands as well as the shifting of attention television has accustomed us to. Some of this same sense of foreshortened, disrupted language and attention span also reveals itself in Mailer's *Why Are We in Vietnam?* and in HELLER's CATCH-22 (a large presence in 1960s and early 1970s fiction). It is also present in Barth's acoustical short pieces, in McElroy's saga-like *Women and Men*, and in somewhat more narrowly based work like BARRY HANNAH's *Ray*.

One key to what has occurred in American fiction since 1960 is found in the proliferation of languages. Experimentation here cuts across all gender, racial, ethnic groups, from effervescent ISHMAEL REED and KATHY ACKER to more studied Donald Bathelme and PAUL AUSTER, WILLIAM BURROUGHS was a large presence in this development—his *Naked Lunch* in particular; and then in writers seemingly as distinct as Barth (*Giles Goat-Boy, Lost in the Funhouse*), Pynchon (*V., The Crying of Lot 49, Gravity's Rainbow*), Barthelme (stories of the late 1960s and early 1970s), and McElroy (the metaphysical excursions in *Hind's Kidnap*). In Barth and Barthelme, we find the problematics of language, voice, tone; in Pynchon, language is subtext, infinite possibility, as if an act of vengeance on previous fiction, but always distinguished by attention to the linguistic innovations of MODERNISM. The group succeeding or paralleling these writers in the 1970s and 1980s offers fewer pure forms of innovative language and more of a bottoming-out, as in the work of the neorealists: RAYMOND CARVER in the short story, Paul Auster in his deliberately flattened-out novels, and in the lyrical-realistic narratives of RICHARD FORD.

Even so, not all is flatness, since in 1981, running against the realistic trend, the stories by GUY DAVENPORT in *Eclogues*, make fiction an assemblage, a verbal collage. We have also the continuation of the mega-novel trend, with Barth's *Letters* and McElroy's *Women and Men*, in which language swamps the subject, offers unlimited extension, and disallows closure. And in novels whose structures are traditional, such as Toni Morrison's *Beloved*, a lyricism pushes against realistic narrative to create unique zones of meaning.

The re-emergence of the short story as a force—a development in the 1970s and 1980s that may be related to the brief segments of television and to the growth of magazines such as *People*—indicates a concern with design. These story writers—Raymond Carver, ANN BEATTIE, FREDERICK BARTHELME,

BOBBIE ANN MASON, Barry Hannah, TOBIAS WOLFF, and MARK HELPRIN—are not homogeneous. Some reveal almost negative resonances, a throwback to planes of abstraction in nonrepresentational art. Donald Barthelme is a large presence here. But others have attempted ornamentation, an imposing rhetorical intrusion, for example, in Barry Hannah's *Airships* stories. Short-story writers have fallen into two basic categories: those who fill and those who empty. The fillers are mainly representational (Carver, Mason, Beattie); the emptiers are minimalists or abstractionists (Donald and Frederick Barthelme, Davenport, WALTER ABISH in his earlier pieces). The emptiers perceive objects, things, events, even history as the enemy; and its landscapes, when they can be discerned, are more saturated with language than with representation. Since these trends in the short story cannot be separated from ongoing work in the novel, we see the emptiers helping to continue an innovative strain in our fiction, while the fillers are traditionalists. The divisions here in the short story fit well into the larger split between those who have rejected innovation and those who favor experimentation.

Writers such as Bellow, Roth, Malamud, and Updike, who by the 1950s and 1960s had displaced Fitzgerald, Hemingway, and Faulkner (except in the universities), have themselves been displaced by those who insist on different voices. Their critical moment and apex of achievement came in the 1960s, with Bellow's HERZOG, Heller's *Catch-22*, Roth's PORTNOY'S COMPLAINT, Malamud's stories (in the late 1950s and after), John Hawkes's *Second Skin*, Joan Didion's *Play It As It Lays* (1970), Mailer's *Why Are We in Vietnam?*, Joyce Carol Oates's THEM, KURT VONNEGUT'S SLAUGHTERHOUSE FIVE, JERZY KOSINSKI'S *The Painted Bird* and *Steps*, JOHN WILLIAMS's *The Man Who Cried I Am*, ROBERT COOVER's *The Universal Baseball Association: J. Henry Waugh, Prop*, and Updike's RABBIT, RUN. The uproariousness of the decade, with its antiwar demonstrations, civil rights marches, and emergence of women's rights, brought that generation of novelists to their peak. By the 1970s and 1980s, when their failure to be innovative or adventurous hobbled them, a new generation emerged, with new structures and languages: Toni Marrison, Walter Abish (especially his *How German Is It*), CYNTHIA OZICK, Ishmael Reed, RUSSELL BANKS Richard Ford, ALICE WALKER, DON DELILLO, and Paul Auster (in his New York Trilogy). Joining up with Pynchon and Gaddis from the 1970s, Abish, Reed, and Auster, among this group, work within a somewhat experimental frame.

At the end of the 1990s, there was no clearly defined direction in American fiction, and the struggle continued between traditionalists (now called neorealists) and those who, for better or worse, were trying to stretch the limits of fiction. Since that battle began well back in the 1950s and 1960s, almost the entire second half of the century appears to be a fictional battleground: an old guard trying to hang on, a new guard not as yet certain of itself; and the old warriors such as Gaddis, Pynchon, and McElroy have not wavered.

A full survey for the indicated dates is Frederick R. Karl, *American Fictions: 1940–1980* (1984). Narrower studies include Jonathan Baumbach, *Landscape of Nightmare: Studies in the Contemporary American Novel* (1965); and Joanne S. Frye, *Living Stories, Telling Lives: Women and the Novel in Contemporary Experience* (1986). For a basic list of works on the American novel see NOVEL BEFORE 1960, above. See GLOBALIZATION OF AMERICAN LITERATURE.

FREDERICK R. KARL

November Boughs (1888), a collection of poems and prose pieces by WALT WHITMAN. Many of the poems had already appeared in the New York *Herald* and were later gathered into the 1889 edition of *Leaves of Grass*. The preface, A BACKWARD GLANCE O'ER TRAVEL'D ROADS, was also included in this edition.

Nowlan, Alden (1933–1983), poet, short-story writer. Born in Nova Scotia, Nowlan worked on newspapers in New Brunswick and taught writing at the University of New Brunswick. His first poetry collection, *The Rose and the Puritan* (1958), introduced his style of short anecdotal and conversational lyrics. *Bread, Wine and Salt* (1967) won the Governor General's Award. *Playing the Jesus Game* (1970) is a selection of poems. Other collections include *A Darkness in the Earth* (1959), *Under the Ice* (1960), *Wind in a Rocky Country* (1961), *Things Which Are* (1962), *The Mysterious Naked Man* (1969), *Between Tears and Laughter* (1971), *I'm a Stranger Here Myself* (1974), *Smoked Glass* (1977), and *I Might Not Tell Everybody This* (1982). *Various Persons Named Kevin O'Brien* (1973) is an autobiographical novel; *Miracle at Indian River* (1968), a collection of short stories. Nowlan has also written plays and a travel book and published a collection of his magazine articles.

Noyes, John Humphrey (1811–1886), Utopian, primitive communist. Born in Vermont, Noyes trained for the ministry at Andover and Yale. He urged the overthrow of the government of the United States so that Jesus Christ might take immediate control. He established a communistic colony at Putney, Vermont, in 1836, but had to make a hasty departure ten years later when charges of adultery, based on the colony's system of marriages, were brought against him. Later he founded the Oneida Community, where similar doctrines were preached, including polygyny and polyandry. Again Noyes fled, this time to Canada. For a time he edited a magazine called *The Perfectionist* (founded 1834). He was a facile and explosive writer. Among his books are *The Berean* (1847), *Male Continence* (1848), *Scientific Propagation* (about 1873), and *Home Talks* (1875). His *History of American Socialisms* (1870) gives an account of colonies like his own. George W. Noyes edited *The Religious Experience of John Humphrey Noyes* (1923) and *John Humphrey Noyes: The Putney Community* (1931); Robert Allerton Parker wrote *A Yankee Saint: John Humphrey Noyes and the Oneida Community* (1935).

Nuñez Cabeza de Vaca. See CABEZA DE VACA.

Nuttall, Thomas (1786–1859), printer, botanist, ornithologist, explorer. In 1808 Nuttall came from England to America as a journeyman printer. BENJAMIN SMITH BARTON of the College of Philadelphia aroused his interest in botany to such an extent that Nuttall joined an expedition to the Platte and Mandan regions and almost lost his life. In 1817 he became a member of the American Philosophical Society and in the next year published *Genera of North American Plants* (2 v.). About this time he began explorations in Arkansas, visiting territories never before visited by white men. He published his observations in *A Journal of Travels into the Arkansas Territory* (1821). In 1824 he began teaching botany at Harvard. He is said to have discovered more new genera and species of plants in North America than any other single scientist, with the possible exception of Asa Gray. He returned to England in the middle 1840s.

Nuyorican Literature.   See HISPANIC AMERICAN LITER-ATURE.

Nye, Bill [Edgar Wilson] (1850–1896),   humorist, farmer, lawyer, justice of the peace, postmaster, legislator, newspaperman, playwright. Born in Shirley, Maine, Nye went to live in Wyoming and in 1881 founded the Laramie BOOMERANG, continuing as its editor until 1885. For this newspaper he wrote humorous sketches which were widely copied. In 1886 he began writing regularly for the New York *World*. About that time, too, he began his successful lecture tours.

Nye put out a great many books. A few of them are *Bill Nye and Boomerang* (1881); *Forty Liars and Other Liars* (1882); *Baled Hay* (1884); *Bill Nye's Chestnuts, New and Old* (1887); *Bill Nye Thinks* (1888, republished as *Sparks from the Pen of Bill Nye*, 1891); *Nye and Riley's Railway Guide* (1888, later called *Nye and Riley's Wit and Humor*, 1896); and *Bill Nye's History of the U.S.* (1894).

Nye's drama *The Cadi* (1891) was successfully produced; *The Stag Party*, written with PAUL POTTER (1895) was a failure. Everybody knew Nye in the last quarter of the 19th century; he was one of the chief public figures of the American scene. Frank W. Nye edited *Bill Nye: His Own Life Story* (1926). *Letters of Edgar Wilson Nye* was edited by Nixon Orwin Rush (1952).

O

Oakes, Urian (1631–1681),   clergyman, teacher, poet. Oakes came to the Massachusetts colony about 1640, was graduated from Harvard in 1649, later served as fellow and tutor there, but returned to England. After serving as a clergyman and teacher in England for some years, he came back to this country and took over a church in Cambridge in 1671. He became a censor of the Massachusetts press and served briefly as president of Harvard. He expressed his emphatic views chiefly in *New England Pleaded With* (1673), denouncing freedom of worship as the "first-born of all abominations." His finest literary production was his *Elegy Upon the Death of the Rev. Mr. Thomas Shepard* (1677).

Oakes-Smith, Elizabeth [Mrs. Seba Smith].   See ELIZABETH OAKES SMITH.

Oakhurst, John.   A character in Bret Harte's THE OUT-CASTS OF POKER FLAT, THE LUCK OF ROARING CAMP, and other tales of early California. Oakhurst is a professional gambler who finds his marks in mining camps. He is presented as having "the melancholy air and intellectual abstraction of a Hamlet," and he is capable of noble acts, one of which brings him death in the story of Poker Flat.

Oates, Joyce Carol (1938–   ),   novelist, short-story writer, poet, playwright, nonfiction writer. Oates was born in Millerport, New York. This rural area of upstate New York is the setting of many of her novels and numerous short stories. Her early novels reflect her parents' experiences in the Depression, which is depicted as the source of subsequent anomalies in American culture.

Oates attended Syracuse University on a scholarship, majored in English, and as one of her professors relates, produced a manuscript of a novel nearly every semester. She continued her education at the University of Wisconsin, where she met Raymond J. Smith, whom she married in 1961. They moved to Texas, where Oates began her doctoral studies, which she dropped after discovering one of her stories on Martha Foley's *The Best American Short Stories* honor roll. When she began teaching English at the University of Detroit, she was already gaining a reputation, and in 1963 she published her first book, a volume of short stories, *By the North Gate*. With the exception of 1965, she has published at least one volume in every year since then. A prolific and brilliant writer, she has

been honored with numerous awards, including the National Book Award for *them*, a Guggenheim fellowship, membership in the National Institute of Arts and Letters, the Lotos Club Award of Merit, and the Continuing Achievement Award in the O. Henry Award Prize Stories series. After teaching at the University of Detroit and the University of Windsor, in Ontario, she became writer-in-residence at Princeton, where she became the Roger S. Berlind Distinguished Professor in the Humanities. Like Virginia and Leonard Woolf, Oates and her husband have their own press, The Ontario Review Press, which publishes the prestigious *Ontario Review: A North American Journal of the Arts*, as well as handsomely printed books of poetry, plays, novels, and collections of essays on contemporary writers.

Titles such as "Dreaming America," a chapter in *Wonderland* (1971), as well as the title of a book of poems (1973), and *American Appetites* (1989) reveal the main theme of Joyce Carol Oates's fiction—America itself. All her works probe the heart, imagination, and landscape of America. Her settings encompass the country, city, suburbs, and even the 19th century in America. She has portrayed farmers, lawyers, scientists, terrorists, a pentecostal preacher, academics, cultists, politicians, mobsters, car racers, old age, adolescence, and with equal fierceness the middle class and the middle-aged. She characterizes her fiction as psychological realism despite the wide diversity of forms she has adopted and transformed for her own purposes. These forms include the classical American romance, as in *Wonderland, With Shuddering Fall, A Garden of Earthly Delights* (1967) and *Do With Me What You Will* (1973); postmodernism, as in *The Assassins* (1975), *Childwold* (1976), *Son of the Morning* (1978), *Unholy Loves* (1979), *Angel of Light* (1981); the Gothic feminist trilogy *Bellefleur* (1980), *A Bloodsmoor Romance* (1982), and *Mysteries of Winterthurn* (1984); and realism, as in *Solstice* (1985), *Marya: A Life* (1986), *You Must Remember This* (1989) and *American Appetites* (1989). Indeed, she has published a volume of short stories, *The Poisoned Kiss and Other Stories from the Portuguese* (1975), "dictated" to her by a dead Portuguese writer, "Ferdinand." She has even published mystery-thrillers, such as *Lives of the Twins* (1987), *Nemesis* (1990), and *Starr Bright Will Be with You Soon* (1999), under the pseudonym Rosamond Smith, an act wryly iterating the theme of doubles that the novels explore. With each novel Oates offers new content and imposes a new artistic problem to solve.

Despite her restless experimentation, a constant in her fiction is attentiveness to the historical and the political. She repeatedly interprets the American collective experience. In her 1969 novel *them* she weaves the true story of one of her students during the Detroit race riots into a novel that not only depicts this particular riot, but explores the reasons for race riots in America and the reasons for violence in America. She leads her reader to the insight that violence in America is connected to the way Americans mythologize their lives. *Mysteries of Winterthurn* explores racism, sexism, and antisemitism in their ugliest manifestations in 19th-century America.

In *Solstice* (1985) she creates a unique portrait of a friendship between two women. Although there have been other works about such friendships, they have been, in the main, polemical vehicles in which the friendships are viewed in the context of a hostile society. *Solstice* may be the first novel in which women are defined—not in relation to men and not in relation to society—but purely and simply in relation to one another. It is an enormous achievement in terms of literary history. Virginia Woolf in 1929 complained that in fiction, as well as in life, women are always defined in relation to men. She pleaded for women to write novels in which they are defined in relation to themselves, that their freedom from a restrictive patriarchy depended on it. Oates, half a century after Woolf called for it, has done it.

In that she intuits what is in the national unconscious, Oates is a prophetic writer. The most striking example is her 1978 novel *Son of the Morning*. This extraordinary book is about a destructive and enormously popular evangelical minister, Nathanael Vickery. The novel's publication preceded by only a few weeks the news of the Reverend Jim Jones and the catastrophe at Jonestown in Guyana. Oates recognized a fierce spiritual hunger in the United States that she expressed in her novel and that also expressed itself in the actual phenomenon of Jonestown.

Her sense of membership in a literary community is deep. In an article written for *Psychology Today*, entitled "The Myth of the Isolated Artist," Oates states emphatically that the isolated artist is a myth: "In surrendering one's isolation, one does not surrender his own uniqueness; he only surrenders his isolation." Her novels are filled with the presence of other writers and with literary allusions. The Bible, The Upanishads, Joyce, Beckett, Nabokov, Thoreau, D. H. Lawrence, William James, Sylvia Plath, Lewis Carroll, William Wordsworth, Mark Twain, St. Augustine, and scores of others enrich her texts. The understructures of her novels contain conversations and quarrels with her contemporaries and her predecessors. Other novels include *Because It Is Bitter, and Because It Is My Heart* (1990), on race relations; *Zombie* (1995), about serial murders; *We Were the Mulvaneys* (1996), chronicling the disintegration of a happy family; *Man Crazy* (1997), detailing the drugged adolescence of a teenage girl; *My Heart Laid Bare* (1998), set in the first quarter of the twentieth century; *Broke Heart Blues* (1999), on celebrity in an affluent suburban high school; and

Blonde (2000), a thinly disguised recounting of the life and death of Marilyn Monroe. The short-story collection *Marriages and Infidelities* (1972) revises works by such authors as Henry James and Anton Chekov. In addition, *Childwold* reworks the material of Nabokov's *Lolita*, weaving in his imagery while damning what she sees as his insular vision.

John Gardner described Oates's novel *Bellefleur* as "the most ambitious book to come so far from that alarming phenomenon Joyce Carol Oates." In this Gothic novel, Oates weaves a shimmering tapestry made of odd and contradictory threads: a hermaphroditic birth, a vulture that devours an infant, a dwarf with "powers," a vampire, a cannibal, religious mystics and clairvoyants. Such are the Gothic trappings of this epic about the Bellefleurs, an old and powerful American family whose estate is located in the Adirondacks and whose history is an interpretation of American history from pioneer days to the present. Oates is a passionate, restless, obsessed writer, and—as Gardner asserted in his review of *Bellefleur*—"one of the great writers of her time."

Her other works include *Upon the Sweeping Flood and Other Stories* (1966), *A Garden of Earthly Delights* (1967), *Expensive People* (1968), *Women in Love and Other Poems* (1968), *Anonymous Sins and Other Poems* (1969), *Cupid and Psyche* (1970), *Love and Its Derangements* (1970), *The Wheel of Love* (1970), *The Edge of Impossibility: Tragic Forms in Literature* (1972), *Angel Fire* (1973), *The Hostile Son: The Poetry of D. H. Lawrence* (1973), *A Posthumous Sketch* (1973), *The Girl* (1974), *The Goddess and Other Women* (1974), *The Hungry Ghosts: Seven Allusive Comedies* (1974), *New Heaven, New Earth: The Visionary Experience in Literature* (1974), *Where Are You Going, Where Have You Been?* (1974), *The Fabulous Beasts* (1975), *The Seduction and Other Stories* (1975), *Crossing the Border* (1976), *The Triumph of the Spider Monkey* (1976), *Women Whose Lives Are Food, Men Whose Lives are Money* (1978), *All the Good People I've Left Behind* (1979), *Cybele* (1979), *The Lamb of Abyssalia* (1979), *Queen of the Night* (1979), *The Step-Father* (1979), *Celestial Timepiece* (1980), *Three Plays* (1980), *Contraries: Essays* (1981), *Nightless Nights; Nine Poems* (1981), *Invisible Women: New and Selected Poems, 1970–1982* (1982), *The Profane Art: Essays and Reviews* (1983), *Last Days* (1984), *Wild Saturdays and Other Stories* (1984), *On Boxing* (1987), *Raven's Wing* (1987), *(Woman) Writer: Occasions and Opportunities* (1988); *American Appetites* (1989); *The Time Traveler: Poems 1983–1989* (1990); *I Lock My Door Upon Myself* (1990); and *Middle Age: A Romance* (2001). *First Love: A Gothic Tale* (1996) is a novella; *Twelve Plays* (1991), *The Perfectionist and Other Plays* (1995) and *New Plays* (1998) collect dramas; *Where Are You Going, Where Have You Been?* (1993), *"Will You Always Love Me?"* (1996), *The Collector of Hearts* (1998) and *Faithless: Tales of Transgressions* (2001) are story gatherings. *Tenderness* (1996) is a poetry collection.

Critical studies include Eileen Bender, *Joyce Carol Oates: Artist in Residence* (1987) and Ellen G. Friedman, *Joyce Carol Oates* (1980).

ELLEN G. FRIEDMAN/BP

Oath of a Free Man (1639). This document, published as a broadside, was the first piece of printing done in the English settlements in America. It has come down to us in the form given it by Major John Child in his *New England's Jonas Cast up at London* (1647). Child attacked the oath as opposed to the laws of England, which permitted non-Puritan religious worship in the colonies. In reply the General Court of Massachusetts declared: "Our allegiance binds us not to the laws of England any longer than while we live in England."

Objectivism. A short-lived but influential movement in the early years of the Great Depression (1931–1934), led by WILLIAM CARLOS WILLIAMS and including the notable Jewish poets LOUIS ZUKOFSKY, GEORGE OPPEN, CARL RAKOSI, and CHARLES REZNIKOFF. Objectivism attempted in Williams's words, to shape the "formal necessity" of IMAGISM, an earlier poetic doctrine formulated by Ezra Pound in which the image is central, not merely ornamental, in verse language. Objectivism, in Zukofsky's view, was the desire to make a poem "an inclusive object" composed of "historic and contemporary particulars—a desire to place everything—everything aptly, perfectly, belonging within, one with, a context—A poem." Though sometimes mistaken as an antiromantic reaction in verse to the harsh years of the Depression, the objectivist poem—spare, intense, brief—implied a sensuous perception of the relations inhering among things. Taciturnity did not prevent such poetry from making claims for the spiritual coherence underlying seemingly inert, disjoint reality. Objectivism's main intent was to rid lyricism of commentary and embellishment, what GERTRUDE STEIN once described as "art by subtraction," and to present in an uncluttered foreground particulars whose relations, though unspecified, were accessible by inference.

The term *objectivist* was formally applied to the group in the Objectivist issue of *Poetry* (February 1931), edited by Zukofsky, whose notes in "Program 'Objectivists' 1931" set forth the terms and objectives of the new poetic. In 1934, members of the group and others raised money to publish Williams's *Collected Poems* by the Objectivist Press, its only publication, after which the movement faded. At its best, objectivist poetry is subtle, of fluid rhythms, and expressive of the intricate verbal complexities of what Milton Hindus, in discussing the work of Reznikoff, has called "the Talmudic imagination." Reznikoff may have summarized the poetic best when he remarked that he "believed in writing about the object itself . . . let[ting] the reader, or listener, draw his own conclusions." Objectivism's influence has been widespread among postmodern writers.

PAUL CHRISTENSEN

O'Brien, Edward J[oseph] (1890–1941), newspaperman, writer, editor. Although O'Brien, born in Boston, published a volume of poems and wrote several plays, he was best known for a long series of collections in which he passed judgment on contemporary short stories. His first collection, *The Best Short Stories of 1915* (see BEST AMERICAN SHORT STORIES), was followed by annual volumes until 1940, after which the series was continued by other hands. In 1921 he began a

similar series of *Best British Short Stories*. He also edited *The Great Modern English Stories* (1919), *Elizabethan Tales* (1937), and other compilations.

O'Brien, Fitz-James (*c.* 1828–1862), poet, playwright, short-story writer. Before he was twenty-four, O'Brien, born in Ireland, had published a large number of stories, poems, and articles in Irish and English periodicals. In 1852 he arrived in New York City and soon established himself as a member of the Bohemian circle that met in PFAFF'S CELLAR at 647 Broadway. He turned out a flood of stories, poems, plays, and sketches, the best of which appeared in *Putnam's Magazine*, *Harper's*, and *Atlantic*. His plays, mostly in one act, were written for James W. Wallack (1791–1864), a noted actormanager. The most successful, *A Gentleman from Ireland*, was revived as late as 1895. When the Civil War broke out, O'Brien volunteered, was decorated for bravery, and died of an infected wound. O'Brien had remarkable inventiveness and was a forerunner of the science fiction writer. His best-known tales—THE DIAMOND LENS, WHAT WAS IT?, and "The Wondersmith"—reveal a lively and unusual fancy and a fine style. His poetry has not stood the test of time so well. *Poems and Stories of Fitz-James O'Brien, Collected and Edited, With a Sketch of the Author*, by William Winter, appeared in 1881.

O'Brien, Frederick (1869–1932), newspaperman, author. Born in Baltimore, O'Brien as a youth shipped out in a cattle boat, tramped through several South American countries, and hoboed in the United States. Then he began working for newspapers, and ended as the publisher of two California papers. He spent a year in the Marquesa Islands and wrote a book on his adventures, *White Shadows in the South Seas* (1919). *Mystic Isles of the South Seas* (1921) described a visit to Tahiti and Moorea, and *Atolls of the Sun* (1922) dealt with life on Paumotu. His books are credited with bringing about a revival of interest in the South Seas.

O'Brien, Howard Vincent (1888–1947), editor, novelist, autobiographer. In 1911 O'Brien, born in Chicago, founded the magazine *Art*, serving as editor from 1911 to 1914. From 1928 to 1932 he was literary editor of the Chicago *Daily News* and wrote a column for it from 1932 until his death. Among his published works are *New Men for Old* (1912); *Trodden Gold* (1922); *The Terms of the Conquest* (1923, under the pseudonym Clyde Perrin); *The Thunder Bolt* (1923); *The Green Scarf* (1924), a novel; *What a Man Wants* (1925); *Wine, Women and War: A Diary of Disillusionment* (1929, pub. anonymously); *An Abandoned Woman* (1930), a novel; *Folding Bedouins* (1936), dealing with trailer travel; *Memoirs of a Guinea Pig* (1942); *So Long, Son* (1944), a personal narrative; and *All Things Considered: Memories, Experiences and Observations of a Chicagoan* (1948).

O'Brien, [William] Tim[othy] (1946–), novelist, short-story writer. Born in Minnesota, O'Brien was educated at Macalester College. Almost immediately after college, he was drafted to serve in the Vietnam War and was wounded near My Lai. This experience has provided his major subject: almost all of his books explore to some extent the meaning of the Vietnam conflict for Americans and the difficulty of understanding or interpreting it. In 1970 he began graduate study in government at Harvard, working summers for the *Washington Post*. During a two-year stint of national affairs reporting for the *Post*, he published his first book, *If I Die in a Combat Zone, Box Me Up and Ship Me Home* (1973), a series of sketches based on his experience as a foot soldier. *Northern Lights* (1974), a novel, followed. It examines the relationship between a returning veteran and his brother in the northern Minnesota home of their childhood. In 1976 he gave up his graduate study, remaining in the Boston area and writing. Portions of his second novel, GOING AFTER CACCIATO (1978) were prize-winning stories when published separately, and the book won the National Book Award in 1979. Again set in Vietnam, it merges Spec Four Paul Berlin's imaginary cross-country trip to the Peace Talks in Paris with his memories of his five months "at the war."

The Nuclear Age (1985) treats a middle-aged man's fear of nuclear disaster. *The Things They Carried* (1990) is a collection of linked stories about a platoon of foot soldiers. In it O'Brien patrols the border between fiction and fact. One of the characters is a twenty-three-year-old Tim O'Brien, but the incidents and authorial commentary emphasize the impossibility of establishing truth or seeing clearly in a war. *Going after Cacciato* and *The Things They Carried* rank among the best fiction about war in American literature. Lesser novels, still of interest, include *In the Lake of the Woods* (1994), with a politician haunted by accusations of his Vietnam past and by the disappearance and possible murder of his wife; and *Tomcat in Love* (1998), a comedy, with the unreliable narrator a deceived husband pursuing his wife's lover, and pursued in turn, perhaps, by Vietnam vets with a wartime grudge.

Obscure Destinies,   a 1932 collection of stories by WILLA CATHER.

O Captain! My Captain! (1865, rev. 1867),   a poem by WALT WHITMAN. This memorial on the death of ABRAHAM LINCOLN was first published in DRUM-TAPS, then included in the 1867 and 1871 editions of LEAVES OF GRASS. It is one of the few poems that Whitman wrote using conventional rhyme and meter.

Occom [also spelled **Occum** and **Ockum**], **Samson** (1723–1792),   missionary, hymnist, editor. A Mohegan Indian, Occom was converted in 1739 and thereafter educated by Eleazar Wheelock, who later became the first president of Dartmouth. Occom became a clergyman in 1759 and a missionary to various Indian tribes, and later visited England to raise money for the founding of Dartmouth, originally a college for Indian students. His first publication was *A Sermon Preached at the Execution of Moses Paul, an Indian Who Was Executed at New Haven* (1772). In 1774 he published *A Choice Collection of Hymns and Spiritual Songs*. He was credited with writing several of these, particularly *Awaked by Sinai's Awful Sound*. A brief autobiography remained unpublished until collected in Bernd Peyer's *The Elders Wrote: An Anthology of Early Prose by North American Indians* (1982).

Occomy, Marita B[onner] (1899–1971),   short-story writer, essayist, dramatist. Occomy was born in Boston, edu-

cated at Radcliffe, and became influential in African-American intellectual circles in Washington and Chicago. She was a regular contributor to *Crisis* and *Opportunity* in the 1920s and 1930s, writing innovative fiction and drama on race relations, conflict between generations, and thwarted ambitions of young people in urban ghettos in stories such as "Nothing New" (*Crisis*, 1926). Her play *The Purple Flower* (*Crisis*, 1928) is an allegory of the black quest for freedom and happiness in the North. A posthumous collection is *Frye Street and Environs: The Collected Works of Marita Bonner Occomy* (1987).

Occurrence at Owl Creek Bridge, An.   A story from *Tales of Soldiers and Civilians* (1891, later titled *In the Midst of Life*) by Ambrose Bierce, noted for its narrative technique.

Ochs, Adolph S[imon] (1858–1935),   publisher, editor. Born in Cincinnati, Ochs began work as a newspaper carrier at age eleven, worked as a printer and compositor, and bought his first newspaper, the *Chattanooga Times*, in 1878. He purchased the failing *New York Times* in 1896, and by stressing objective, nonpartisan reporting, and accuracy he built it into one of the most influential papers in the country. He also published the *Philadelphia Times* (1902–12) and the *Philadelphia Public Ledger* (1902–12). At his death he was succeeded as publisher of the *Times* by his son-in-law, Arthur Hays Sulzberger. In 1946 Gerald W. Johnson wrote *An Honorable Titan: A Biographical Study of Adolph S. Ochs*.

O'Connor, Edwin (1918–1968),   novelist. O'Connor, born in Rhode Island, became a radio announcer after graduation from college, and his first novel, *The Oracle* (1951), derived from his experiences in radio. THE LAST HURRAH (1956), a fictional portrait of a Boston political boss, was a bestseller and later a movie. *The Edge of Sadness* (1961), which won a Pulitzer Prize for fiction, was a perceptive study of the working of God's grace in the lives of a pastor and his charges—second- and third-generation Irish immigrants—in a decaying parish in a thinly disguised Boston. *I Was Dancing* (1964) concerns an aged entertainer's fight to stay out of a retirement home.

O'Connor, Flannery (1925–1964),   short-story writer and novelist. O'Connor was born in Savannah, Georgia, and spent most of her life on her mother's farm in Milledgeville, Georgia, where she raised peacocks and wrote fiction. She was educated at the Georgia State College for Women and the University of Iowa. Her master's thesis at Iowa contained many of the first stories she published, as well as an early version of a chapter of her first novel, *Wise Blood* (1952). In 1950, O'Connor contracted disseminated lupus, a disease that restricted her to life at home, though she would with great difficulty travel occasionally to universities and colleges to read her work or participate in symposia. She died of lupus at age thirty-nine.

O'Connor began by publishing short stories in literary magazines, but her first collection, *A Good Man Is Hard to Find*, was not published until 1955, three years after her novel *Wise Blood* had appeared. *Wise Blood* tells the story of Hazel Motes and an itinerant preacher who comes to the Southern town of Taulkinham in order to form "The Church Without Christ," and who ends up dead by the roadside, self-blinded, a human testament to the extremities of insight and zealotry. The stories of *A Good Man Is Hard to Find* are allegories of the intrusion of the sacred into the profanities of the modern world. O'Connor's second novel, *The Violent Bear it Away* (1960), is the tale of Tarwater, a fourteen-year-old prophet who alternatively rebels against and succumbs to the religious visions of his uncle. Posthumously published were *Everything That Rises Must Converge* (1965), O'Connor's second collection of short fiction; *Mystery and Manners: Occasional Prose* (1969), a collection of essays and reviews; and *The Complete Stories of Flannery O'Connor*, which contains all of O'Connor's collected and uncollected short fiction. *The Habit of Being* (1979), a collection of letters edited by O'Connor's friend and adviser, Sally Fitzgerald, is an invaluable assemblage of statements about her life and fiction from an author whose privacy was enforced, and whose works—in their depictions of the grotesqueness and extremity of contemporary existence—only appear to be quite separate from the modest, secluded presence who generated them.

O'Connor wrote as a Catholic and a Southerner—her fiction reflects the spiritually of the former and the regionalism of the latter. More largely, her works portray sacred invasions of the profane lives of her characters in the form of violence—a violation, O'Connor remarked at various times, that appears as extreme or grotesque only because the modern world is bereft of its sense of the sacred, so that the appearance of the sacred will be perceived as uncanny and defamiliarizing. Thus, "The Misfit" of "A Good Man Is Hard to Find" appears to be a vicious and insane criminal, but is also the means by which the petty and blind grandmother of the story, in the moments before her death, attains a kind of beatific vision. O'Connor is concerned with vision in the fullest sense, as a way of seeing, interpreting and transforming reality or, alternatively, the way in which the world is reduced to the narrowed constraints of the fanatic. For O'Connor, the dividing line between the prophetic and the demonic, the sacred and the profane, is often imperceptible, and her fictions both figure and transgress that line.

PATRICK O'DONNELL

O'Connor, William Douglas (1832–1889), newspaperman, government clerk, writer. Born in Syracuse, New York, O'Connor was the government employee who helped WALT WHITMAN get a job in the Department of the Interior. When James Harlan, head of the department, dismissed Whitman because he had written an "obscene" book (LEAVES OF GRASS), O'Connor wrote a vigorous pamphlet in Whitman's behalf, THE GOOD GRAY POET: A VINDICATION (1866), and found him another job in the Attorney General's office. O'Connor also wrote an antislavery novel, *Harrington* (1860). After O'Connor's death Whitman wrote a preface for the collection *Three Tales* (1892), by O'Connor.

Octopus, The (1901), a novel by FRANK NORRIS. Inspired by the naturalistic studies of Zola, Norris tried to write the great American Novel in *The Octopus*, which depicts the struggle for power between California wheat ranchers and

"the Railroad," the octopus that encircles and strangles the ranchers. The climax of the novel, a pitched battle between farmers and railroad men, was founded on a historic incident known as the Mussel Slough affair. In spite of many faults, *The Octopus*, with its epic sweep, its vivid descriptions, its thoughtful presentation of social and economic problems, was a landmark in the development of the American novel. THE PIT (1903) was a sequel, and the third volume of a proposed trilogy was never written.

Octoroon, The (1859), a play by DION BOUCICAULT. This popular play on a favorite theme of American fiction and drama was based by the Irish dramatist on a novel, *The Quadroon* (1856), by the English author Captain Mayne Reid. Zoe, a slave of mixed race, must be sold by a man who loves her to a man they both hate. *The Octoroon* was the ancestor of many other treatments of the social problem of racially mixed parentage.

Ode Inscribed to W.H. Channing (1847), by RALPH WALDO EMERSON. This is a key statement of Emerson's views regarding the practicality of humanitarian reform. He had apparently been asked by W. H. CHANNING, a nephew of WILLIAM ELLERY CHANNING and like him a Unitarian minister and ardent humanitarian, to make a pronouncement on slavery. Emerson refused—he later changed his mind. In this poem, however, Emerson lamented that "Things are in the saddle,/And ride mankind"; and he said he did not believe, as Channing seemingly did, that it would do any good to "rend the Northland from the South." Yet he was confident that "the over-god" would somehow bring good things to pass: "Wise and sure the issues are." In a paper on *New England Reformers* Emerson remarked that "society gains nothing whilst a man, not himself renovated, attempts to renovate things around him." On another occasion he said: "I have quite other slaves to free than those Negroes; to wit, imprisoned spirits, imprisoned thoughts." In his address on John Brown he nevertheless spoke out vigorously against slavery, as he did in the *Boston Hymn* (1863).

Ode in Time of Hesitation, An (*Atlantic Monthly*, May 1900), a poem by WILLIAM VAUGHN MOODY. The imperialistic spirit aroused by easy victory in the Spanish-American War threatened to result in the annexation of the Philippines. A vigorous voice raised against imperialism was that of Moody in this noble poem, which is also a tribute to Robert Gould Shaw.

Odell, Jonathan (1737–1818), clergyman, physician, satirist. Born in Newark, New Jersey, Odell became a physician and also was an Anglican clergyman. Thus, during the Revolution Odell served in the British forces as both chaplain and physician. He wrote songs for the British soldiers, directed violent satires against American leaders, and served as a spy for the British government. His most prolific year as a writer seems to have been 1779, when he wrote *The Word of Congress; The Congratulation; The Feu de Joie*; and *The American Times*. In 1783 Odell went to England as assistant secretary to Sir Guy Carleton. In the following year he settled in the loyalist province of New Brunswick in Canada.

Ode Recited at the Harvard Commemoration (July 21, 1865), by James Russell Lowell. Not long after Lee's surrender at Appomattox the President and Fellows of Harvard asked Lowell to prepare an ode for a day of commemoration for Harvard students who had died in the war. Although dubious of his ability to write lofty poetry, Lowell consented, deciding on a form featuring lines of irregular length but provided with a pattern of rhyme. He wrote the poem a night or two before its delivery. He was discouraged by its reception and his own public reading. When he preparing the poem for publication in a private printing in 1865, he added sixty-six lines—the magnificent sixth strophe that begins, "Such was he, our Martyr-Chief." In 1877 the poem was included in the collection called THE CATHEDRAL.

Ode Sung on the Occasion of Decorating the Graves of the Confederate Dead (1867), by HENRY TIMROD. This poem, printed in Timrod's *Poems* (1873), praises the "martyrs of a fallen cause." It was delivered at Magnolia Cemetery in Charleston.

Offutt, Chris (1958–), memoirist, short-story writer, novelist. Offutt draws on his Kentucky Appalachian background to write about escaping from poverty and deprivation for a life of wandering and loneliness accompanied by the inescapable urge to return. *The Same River Twice: A Memoir* (1993) tells of leaving home at nineteen for years on the underside of society, surviving as he could—wearing a walrus costume in a circus, painting houses—and then facing the challenges of marriage and fatherhood. *Kentucky Straight* (1992) and *Out of the Woods* (1999) collect stories of lost and alienated Kentuckians, at home and away. *The Good Brother* (1997) is a novel of murder in the Kentucky hills.

Ode to the Confederate Dead (*The American Caravan*, 1927; rev. in *Mr. Pope and Other Poems*, 1928; rev. again in *Selected Poems*, 1937), by ALLEN TATE. Probably the best known of Tate's poems, this is a meditation in a Confederate graveyard—less a tribute to dead soldiers than an ironic comment on death, change, and modern times. It is an obscure poem, as Tate himself admitted implicitly by writing a prose commentary, and reminiscent of T. S. Eliot in tone and cadence.

Odets, Clifford (1906–1963), playwright. Odets was born in Philadelphia and grew up in New York City. On leaving high school he turned to acting and writing. He worked for the Theater Guild until the Group Theater was formed to apply the methods developed by Stanislavski and the Moscow Art Theater. In 1931 he joined the Group Theater, and his early plays were well suited to its naturalistic methods. His first two plays, often considered his best, dealt with social conflicts: WAITING FOR LEFTY (1935) and AWAKE AND SING (1935). They brought him celebrity, and he continued to treat socialistic themes in his succeeding plays: *Till the Day I Die* (1935), *Paradise Lost* (1935), *I Can't Sleep* (1936), GOLDEN BOY (1937), *Night Music* (1940), and *Clash By Night* (1941). Odets turned to writing screen plays for Hollywood. His distaste for the commercialism and corruption in filmland is evident in *The Big Knife* (1948).

Odets's main problem was living up to the triumph of his early works. With *The Country Girl* (1950) he managed to renew his success. The play marks the end of his preoccupation with political themes and centers on the struggle of a young woman to remain faithful to her dissolute husband. *The Flowering Peach* appeared in 1954. *The Time Is Ripe: the 1940 Journal of Clifford Odets* (1988) reveals the conflicts he felt, as a Jew and a socialist, in the early years of the war.

Odiorne, Thomas (1769–1851), poet. A graduate of Dartmouth College, Odiorne was a nature writer whose work presaged the Romantic Movement. His long poem *The Progress of Refinement* (1792) mixes natural description and philosophy to describe the ideal state of humanity in harmony with environment.

Odum, Howard Washington (1884–1954), sociologist, teacher, writer, administrator. Born in Georgia, Odum was educated at Clark University and Columbia University. He taught at many universities, primarily in North Carolina and Georgia. In his writings he attempted to explain the racial and regional dilemmas of the South by analyzing its history. His proposed solutions to these problems have provided inspiration for Southern liberals. He also wrote fiction and collected folklore. His works include *Social and Mental Traits of the Negro* (1910); *Sociology and Social Problems* (1925); *The Negro and His Songs* (1925), with G. B. Johnson; *Rainbow Round My Shoulder* (1928), *Wings on My Feet* (1929), and *Cold Blue Moon* (1931), all novels; *Southern Regions of the United States* (1936); *American Social Problems* (1939); *Race and Rumors of Race* (1943); *The Way of the South* (1947); and *American Sociology* (1951), a history of the subject.

Of Mice and Men (1937), a novel by JOHN STEINBECK, dramatized by the author in the same year. As Steinbeck consciously wrote this short novel "like a play," the dramatic unities are apparent throughout. The plot concerns George and his powerful, simple-minded friend Lennie. Both are casual laborers who travel from one ranch to another, dreaming constantly of a place of their own. Written with great compassion and simplicity, *Of Mice and Men* was an outstanding success as a novel; as a drama it won the Drama Critics Circle Award for 1937. It was also made into a film (1939).

Of Thee I Sing (prod. 1931, pub. 1932), a musical comedy with music by GEORGE GERSHWIN and text by GEORGE S. KAUFMAN, IRA GERSHWIN, and Morris Ryskind. This funny political satire and collection of first-rate songs is built around a Presidential campaign with John P. Wintergreen as the leading candidate. His running mate is Alexander Throttlebottom, an insignificant little man who aptly satirizes the Vice-Presidency. The campaign managers decide that Wintergreen must marry, and his mate is to be the winner of an Atlantic City beauty contest. It was the first musical to win a Pulitzer Prize.

Of Time and the River: A Legend of Man's Hunger in His Youth (1935), a semiautobiographical novel by THOMAS WOLFE. A sequel to LOOK HOMEWARD, ANGEL, this novel appeared at the publisher's office as an enormous, diffused manuscript of several thousand pages entitled *The October Fair*. Working long hours with editor MAXWELL PERKINS of

Scribner's, Wolfe was persuaded to prune away a good part of the manuscript and divide the remainder into two works. The second half was included in THE WEB AND THE ROCK, published posthumously in 1939. *Of Time and the River* deals with Eugene Gant's studies in a playwriting course at Harvard, his work as an English instructor at New York University, and his European tour. Wolfe's powerful and exuberant style, his poignant descriptions, his "chants and soliloquies and prose poems," and the violence of his reactions make this novel an exciting and important work. Carl Van Doren, expressed the commonly held critical view that Thomas Wolfe's four novels are really only one, "a tumultuous series of scenes held together by the unity of a single giant hunger and desire . . . haunted by the perpetual image of time as an infinite river in which men lead their short and trifling lives, so soon to be forgotten in the universal flood."

Ogilvie, James (1775–1820), orator and writer. A Scottish immigrant to Virginia, he wrote for *The Port Folio* and published his *Philosophical Essays* in 1816.

Oglethorpe, James Edward (1696–1785), philanthropist, colonist, administrator, member of the House of Commons. In 1722 Oglethorpe was elected to Parliament. In 1729 he acted as chairman of a parliamentary committee to investigate debtors' prisons and three years later obtained a charter for the foundation of a colony in America—to be called Georgia after George II—that would be an asylum for persons newly released from debtors' prison. He obtained many private contributions in response to an appeal, *A New and Accurate Account of South Carolina and Georgia* (1732). In October he sailed for this country with 120 settlers and founded Savannah. He acted as governor of Georgia until 1743, when he returned to England. He was again elected to Parliament and spent thirty-two years there. He was also a member of the Johnson circle in London.

O'Hagan, Howard (1902–1982), Canadian novelist and short-story writer. His major novel, *Tay John*, (1939) received little notice on first publication, but following a 1974 reprinting, it was critically acclaimed and is now regarded as a Canadian classic. It deals with a mythic character, part Shuswap Indian and part Irish, caught between two cultures. O'Hagan also published two collections of stories, *Wilderness Men* (1958) and *The Woman Who Got on at Jasper Station* (1963), and a second novel, *The School Marm Tree* (1977).

O'Hara, Frank (1926–1966), poet, art critic, playwright. A prolific, unique voice in poetry from the mid-1950s to the mid-1960s, O'Hara, born in Baltimore, grew up in Massachusetts and, after a hitch in the navy during World War II, was educated at Harvard and at the University of Michigan, where he won the Hopwood Award. Unlike many poets of his generation, O'Hara never taught, except for giving a poetry writing workshop at the New School for Social Research in 1963. Instead, moving to New York City in 1951, he joined the staff of the Museum of Modern Art, where he remained until his death. From 1953 to 1955, he was also on the editorial staff of *Art News*, writing reviews and articles, and in 1961, he served as art editor for *Kulchur*. He and his friends John Ash-

bery and Kenneth Koch became the nucleus of the NEW YORK SCHOOL of poetry, with O'Hara its most prominent member. He also found support for his antiliterary poetry from the Abstract Expressionist painters Willem de Kooning, Jackson Pollock, and Larry Rivers, among others.

His ties to the New York art scene were further strengthened when his first two collections—*A City Winter, and Other Poems* (1952) and *Oranges* (1953)—were published by Tibor de Nagy Gallery. Influenced by the artists of his time, many of whom are mentioned in his work, he also found inspiration in surrealism and dadaism, in music and film, and in the poetry of William Carlos Williams, Whitman; Pasternak, Mayakovsky, and Rimbaud, among others. He summarized his poetics in the tongue-in-cheek essay "Personism: A Manifesto."

O'Hara's posthumous *Collected Poems* (1971) reveals the extraordinary range of his ability. An experimentalist, O'Hara nevertheless occasionally wrote formal poetry, such as his brilliant, effective odes ("Ode to Michael Goldberg['s Birth and Other Births]") and elegies ("For James Dean"), working within the genres' limitations to expand their possibilities, as he did with the loose sequence of forty-four love poems written for Vincent Warren between 1959 and 1961 and including "Joe's Jacket," "Having a Coke with You," and "Poem V (F) W."

His work was founded on voice—colloquial in diction, natural in cadence—more than metaphor, at once vivacious ("Poem" ["The eager note on the door said 'Call me'"]) and camp ("Poem" ["Lana Turner has collapsed!"]), filled with chatter ("Meditations in an Emergency") and mocking ("Ave Maria"), sarcastic ("Yesterday Down at the Canal") and serious ("The Day Lady Died"), surrealistic ("Chez Jane"), and flat ("Autobiographia Literaria").

Personal, not confessional, O'Hara's poetry documents daily experiences—traffic jams, meals, friends' names, partygoing, the theater and cinema, neon lights, buying cigarettes—of one more at home among skyscrapers than pastures. Appropriately labeled "I-do-this; I-do-that" poetry, his is a poetry of observation, not meditation; he never analyzed events nor judged. Such a poetry implies that O'Hara did not distinguish between art and life—for him the two were inexorably fused. Although known as a poet, O'Hara also wrote plays, a number of which were produced, first at Harvard, later in New York, and critical monographs on art. At age forty, he was struck by a beach buggy on Fire Island, New York, and died from injuries a few days later.

Collections published during O'Hara's lifetime are *A City Winter* (1952), *Oranges* (1953), *Meditations in an Emergency* (1957), *Second Avenue* (1960, *Odes* (1960), *Lunch Poems* (1964), and *Love Poems. (Tentative Title)* (1965). His posthumous works are *In Memory of My Feelings*, edited by Bill Berkson (1967); and gatherings edited by Donald Allen: *Collected Poems of Frank O'Hara* (1971); *Selected Poems of Frank O'Hara* (1974); *Early Poems: 1946–1951* (1976); and *Poems Retrieved*: 1951–1966 (1977). Art criticism and other prose are collected in *Art Chronicles 1954–1966* (1974) and *Standing Still and Walking in New York*, edited by Donald Allen (1975). *Selected Plays* was published in 1978. Studies are Marjorie Perloff,

Frank O'Hara: Poet Among Painters (1977) and Jim Elledge, ed. *Frank O'Hara: To Be True to a City* (1990).

JIM ELLEDGE

O'Hara, John [Henry] (1905–1970),   novelist, short-story writer. Born in Pottsville, Pennsylvania, O'Hara had a successful career in journalism, writing for newspapers in Pennsylvania and New York City and for *Newsweek, Time,* and *The New Yorker. Appointment in Samarra* (1934), his successful first novel, freed him to concentrate on writing fiction. Like much of his best work, it is an ironic picture of the members of a county club in a fictional Pennsylvania town. *Butterfield 8* (1935), based on a New York murder, was made into a film. *Ten North Frederick* (1955) deals with the contrast between the public and private lives of a leading citizen. *From the Terrace* (1958) detailed the life of a wealthy man, and *Elizabeth Appleton* (1963) the life of a privileged woman. O'Hara wrote screenplays, and many of his novels were made into films. Two of them, *Hope of Heaven* (1938) and *The Big Laugh* (1962), are set in Hollywood. His other novels include *A Rage to Live* (1949), *The Farmers Hotel* (1951), *Ourselves to Know* (1960), *The Lockwood Concern* (1965), *The Instrument* (1967), *Lovey Childs* (1970), and *The Ewings* (1972).

O'Hara collaborated with Richard Rodgers and Lorenz Hart in turning the title story of his collection PAL JOEY (1940) into a classic musical comedy (1949), later a movie. O'Hara was an acknowledged master of the short story and was especially admired for a dozen story collections, including *The Doctor's Son* (1935), *Sermons and Soda Water* (1960), *The Cape Cod Lighter* (1962), *The Hat on the Bed* (1963), and *Good Samaritan* (1974). *Sweet and Sour* (1954) is a selection of journalistic pieces on literature, and some of O'Hara's correspondence was published in *Letters* (1978).

O'Hara, Mary [Mary O'Hara Alsop] (1885–1980), novelist, composer. Born in New Jersey, Mary O'Hara Alsop moved after her first marriage to California, where she wrote scenarios. In 1930 she began living on a ranch in Wyoming that formed the background for her three novels about horses: *My Friend Flicka* (1941), *Thunderhead* (1943), and *The Green Grass of Wyoming* (1946). Flicka is a colt belonging to Ken McLaughlin, a boy who appears as a young man in the later novels. She discusses her novel *The Son of Adam Wingate* (1952) in *Novel-in-the-Making* (1954). She also composed a number of popular musical works, of which *Wyoming Suite for Piano* (1946) is the most ambitious.

O'Hara, Scarlett.   The heroine of Margaret Mitchell's GONE WITH THE WIND (1936).

O'Hara, Theodore (1820–1867),   poet, teacher, editor, lawyer, soldier. O'Hara, born in Kentucky, taught Greek, was admitted to the bar, and edited newspapers in Alabama and Kentucky. He fought in the Mexican War, was wounded during the Cuban rebellion against Spain (1849), and commanded a regiment in the Civil War. He was a popular orator and wrote verse fluently. "The Bivouac of the Dead" and "The Old Pioneer" are almost his only poems remembered today. George W. Ranck wrote about *O'Hara and His Elegies* (1875), and E. E. Hume wrote *Colonel Theodore O'Hara* (1936).

O. Henry.   See HENRY, O.

O. Henry Prize Stories.   In 1918 the Society of Arts and Sciences founded the O. Henry Memorial Awards for the best American short stories published each year. Since 1919 an annual volume of the prize-winning stories and others considered worthwhile has been issued. See BEST AMERICAN SHORT STORIES.

O'Higgins, Harvey Jerrold (1876–1929),   Canadian novelist and journalist who collaborated with experts to popularize political and social topics. *The Beast* (1910), written with Judge Ben B. Lindsey deals with the problems of urban youth. *Under the Prophet in Utah* (1911), with Frank J. Cannon, detailed the organization of the Mormon Church. *The American Mind in Action*, with Dr. Edward H. Reade (1924), is a study of psychoanalysis. O'Higgins's fiction includes *Some Distinguished American Minds* (1922); *Julie Crane* (1924) and *Clara Barron* (1926), sympathetic treatments of the American woman; and *Polygamy* (1914). He also dramatized Sinclair Lewis's *Main Street* (1921).

Oil! (1927),   a novel by UPTON SINCLAIR. The Teapot Dome oil scandal of the Harding administration, which broke in the middle 1920s, resulted in Sinclair's best novel, *Oil!* Its plot is familiar and not unrealistic: a son breaks away from his father's old-fashioned ideas. In this instance, in a California milieu, the son of a wealthy oil operator, an independent doing his best to resist the encroachments and deadly competition of the big corporations, discovers that politicians are insidious creatures, that oil magnates are unscrupulous, and that public officials are venal.

Ojibwa [Chippewa] Indians,   part of the Agonquian-Wakashan family of eastern woodland Native Americans. Eventually they settled in the Great Lakes and north-central region, where they had fewer enemies than tribes east of the Appalachians. In the upper Great Lakes region, the tribe is also called the Saulteaux. After the introduction of horses to the northern plains, a group of Plains Ojibwa lived the buffalo hunter life typical of PLAINS INDIANS. Allied with the French, the Ojibway fought with the armies of PONTIAC, an Ottawa leader, against the English forts at Pittsburgh and Detroit. The legends collected by SCHOOLCRAFT and utilized by LONGFELLOW in *Hiawatha* feature Ojibwa heroes, though Longfellow gave his character an Iroquois name. GEORGE COPWAY, an Ojibwa friend of Longfellow's, wrote several books on himself and his people. Ojibwa characters appear in Cooper's *Oak Openings* (1849), set in Michigan at the outbreak of the War of 1812. William Whipple Warren, an Ojibwa, wrote *History of the Ojibway, Based upon Traditions and Oral Statements* (1885, rep. 1957). JANET LEWIS's *The Invasion* (1932) is a fictional treatment of the tribe's decline. Contemporary writers of Ojibwa descent include LOUISE ERDRICH and GERALD VIZENOR. See ALGONQUIN INDIANS.

Okada, John (1923–1971),   novelist. Born in Seattle to immigrant Japanese parents, Okada was educated at the University of Washington and Columbia University. He served in the U.S. Air Force during World War II. His one novel, *No-No Boy* (1957), was not favorably received when published. It is a realistic treatment of the effects of racism and generational tension in the Japanese-American community of Seattle after World War II. Ichiro, the young American-born protagonist, returns to his parents' home after they have all been interned in relocation camps, and he has served a prison term for resisting the draft. His mother, still fiercely loyal to her native land, cannot understand how torn her son is between his ancestry and his citizenship. Okada was at work on a novel about Japanese immigrants when he died. His widow destroyed it and other writings after UCLA refused his papers for their manuscript collection.

Okie.   A term for an inhabitant of Oklahoma, used specifically in reference to the many who fled the state in the mid-1930s because of dust storms, the depression, and farm foreclosures. John Steinbeck's THE GRAPES OF WRATH (1939) deals with a group of Oklahomans who fled to California. The book describes the migration and brought *Okie* into common usage. Among the other factual accounts of these people are *Deserts on the March* (1935), by Paul Sears; *Rich Land, Poor Land* (1936), by Stuart Chase; *Factories in the Field* (1939), by Carey McWilliams; and *An American Exodus* (1940), by Dorothea Lange and Paul Schuster Taylor.

Oklahoma! (1943).   This musical comedy, with music by RICHARD RODGERS and book and lyrics by OSCAR HAMMERSTEIN II, is an adaptation of LYNN RIGGS's *Green Grow the Lilacs* (1931), a folk comedy set in the Indian Territory. The musical, with its memorable songs (especially "Oh, What a Beautiful Morning," "People Will Say We're in Love," "Pore Judd" and "The Surrey with the Fringe on Top"), opened on March 31, 1943, and closed on May 19, 1948. Its imaginative choreography, the work of Agnes De Mille, brought her to the first rank.

Olcott, Frances Jenkins (1872?–1963),   librarian, children's writer. Born in France, Olcott became assistant librarian of the Brooklyn Public Library and later was chief of the children's department of the Carnegie Library of Pittsburgh. After her retirement she compiled many valuable book lists and pamphlets for teachers, parents, and professional storytellers. Among her numerous books for children are *The Arabian Nights Entertainments* (1913), *Bible Stories to Read and Tell* (1916), *Wonder Tales from China Seas* (1925), *Wonder Tales from Baltic Wizards* (1928), *Island of Colored Shells* (1934), *The Book of Nature's Marvels* (1936), *The Bridge of Caravans* (1940), and *In the Bright Syrian Land* (1946).

Old Chester Tales (1898),   short stories by MARGARET DELAND. Old Chester is actually Manchester, now a part of Pittsburgh. At the time this book was written it was a small, independent town populated by families of Scotch, Irish, and English descent. The various stories make up a single picture, with all the action revolving around Dr. Lavender, the elderly rector who appears in a number of Deland's books.

Old Corner Bookstore.   A bookstore in Boston that was opened in 1828 by Timothy Carter. Many noted authors and publishers have made it a favorite rendezvous.

Old Creole Days (1879),   short stories by GEORGE W. CABLE. The setting for all seven of these stories, and for the novelette MADAME DELPHINE which was included in the later editions, is 19th-century New Orleans.

Old Farmer's Almanac, The (1793–   ).   Published first in Massachusetts by Robert Bailey Thomas and originally called *The Farmer's Almanac*, this annual compilation was the backbone of many an oldtime farmer's library. The *Almanac* consists of the "Farmer's Calendar," adorned with oldfashioned cuts and short poems; weather forecasts for the entire year; planting, gestation, and reproductive tables; digests of fish and game laws; anecdotes, recipes, charades, astrological lore (told with a skeptical note); and other odd bits of information. G. L. Kittredge's entertaining account of *The Old Farmer and His Almanack* (1904) points out the importance of this publication to the student of early American life.

Old Folks at Home (1851),   also called "Swanee River," by STEPHEN FOSTER. This, perhaps Foster's greatest song, was at first attributed, at the author's wish, to the minstrel E. P. Christy, who paid Foster ten or fifteen dollars for the immediate rights. Six months later Foster asked Christy to let him put his own name to the song. Apparently, Foster received royalties thereafter. Its enormous success convinced Foster that he should aim at becoming "the best Ethiopian song writer."

Old Ironsides   (Boston *Daily Advertiser*, September 16, 1830), a poem by OLIVER WENDELL HOLMES, SR. Old Ironsides was the popular name for the United States frigate *Constitution*, which played a notable part in the War of 1812, especially in a fight with the British frigate *Guerriere*, August 19, 1812. In 1830 the navy decided the ship was no longer seaworthy, and she was condemned to be broken up and sold. Holmes saw the announcement and in great indignation sat down and wrote "Old Ironsides," which made him widely known and saved the *Constitution* from destruction. The ship was rebuilt and remained in active service for many years. It is now on exhibition at Charleston, Massachusetts. Books about the famous vessel include C. W. Denison's *Old Ironsides and Old Adams* (1846); Justin Jones's *Mad Jack and Gentleman Jack, or, The Last Cruise of "Old Ironsides" Around the World* (1850); F. Alexander Magoun's *The Frigate Constitution and Other Historic Ships* (1928); and Edward Buell's *Fighting Frigate* (1947).

Old Maid, The (1924),   a novelette by EDITH WHARTON. Appearing originally as one in a series of four small volumes entitled OLD NEW YORK *The Old Maid* tells the story of Tina, Charlotte Lovell's illegitimate daughter, who is brought up by Charlotte's cousin Delia in ignorance of her parentage. As she grows up she regards Aunt Chatty as a typical old maid; her devotion is given to Delia. The situation is almost too much for Charlotte, but to save the girl's happiness she finally reconciles herself to it. The story was dramatized by ZOË AKINS in 1935, won a Pulitzer Prize, and was later filmed.

Old Man and the Sea, The (1952),   a novelette by ERNEST HEMINGWAY. Considered by many critics to be one of Hemingway's finest works, *The Old Man and the Sea* deals with an old Cuban fisherman who has had eighty-four days without a catch. Far from port on the eighty-fifth day he hooks a gigantic marlin. Outmatched in the two-day fight, the old man brings the fish alongside and harpoons it. Soon sharks appear, and the old man breaks his knife after he has killed only a few; during the last night of the voyage home the sharks devour all but the head of the great fish. The story is often interpreted as an allegory of man's inevitably losing struggle with existence; though the old man fights the great fish with courage and stoicism he is defeated in the end not by the fish—or by life itself—but by the sharks, or death.

Old Mandarin, The (1922, 1927, 1933, 1947), pretended translations from the Chinese by CHRISTOPHER MORLEY. Morley created the figure of a Chinese mandarin, to whom he credited short and usually witty pieces in free verse.

Old Manse, the Concord, Massachusetts, home of the Ralph Waldo Emerson family. Nathaniel Hawthorne wrote *Mosses from an Old Manse* during the period (1842–46) when he and his family lived in the house.

Oldmixon, John (1673–1742), poet, historian, dramatist. Born in England, Oldmixon published volumes of verse in 1696 and 1697, and had a play produced in 1703. Thereafter he seems to have devoted himself mainly to writing history, in which the Tories came off badly. His *British Empire in America* (2 v. 1708, rev. 1741) is the first work in which the British settlements on the Atlantic coast are examined as a unit, including the West Indies. Oldmixon examined critically all available authorities, checking one against the other; in his revision he made use of new information. In his trenchant comments on the Puritan persecution of Roger Williams and other dissenters, he called the Massachusetts officials "as real bigots in their way as Archbishop Laud was in his."

Old New York (4 v. 1924), four historical novelettes by EDITH WHARTON. In this series, as often, Wharton deals with people who come into conflict with conventional mores. It was written to present a chronological sequence from 1840 to 1880, each novelette dealing with a decade. In the first, *False Dawn*, the young New Yorker Lewis Raycie makes a grand tour of Europe, buying pictures so far in advance of the taste of his time that his father disinherits him. He leaves the pictures to his descendant, who sells them at auction for five million dollars. The second is THE OLD MAID, considered the most successful of this quartet. *The Spark* tells of a simple, chivalrous elderly man who comes under the strong spiritual influence of Walt Whitman. *New Year's Day* relates the heroic self-sacrifice of a wife who needs money for her ailing husband and is exposed to the scorn of New York's rigid society of the day.

Old Oaken Bucket, The (printed in the New York *Republican-Chronicle*, 1817; in *Poems, Odes, Songs* 1818; in *Melodies, Duets, Trios, Songs, and Ballads,* 1826), by SAMUEL WOODWORTH. The poem, originally called *The Bucket*, was inspired, it is said, by a well in Scituate, Massachusetts, where Woodworth was born. The lyric was first sung to the tune of *Jessie, the Flow'r o' Dumblane*, a lyric by Robert Tannahill with music by Robert Archibald Smith. In the 1830s E. Ives, Jr., wrote a parody on *The Old Oaken Bucket* that he called

Farewell to Home, but set to the tune associated with Thomas Moore's poem, *Araby's Daughter*. This tune was composed by George Kiallmark. Ives's joke was a boomerang; people forgot his parody but thereafter sang *The Old Oaken Bucket* to Kiallmark's tune. George S. Kaufman and Marc Connelly took from the poem the name of their short-lived satirical play, *The Deep-Tangled Wildwood* (1923).

Old Possum's Book of Practical Cats (1939) by T. S. ELIOT a collection of fifteen humorous poems beginning with "The Naming of Cats" and including portraits of such feline figures as "Old Deuteronomy" and "Macavity: the Mystery Cat," narratives of cat adventures, and a concluding poem on "The Addressing of Cats." Andrew Lloyd Webber wrote the music for a dramatic adaptation of the poems called *Cats*, produced in London (1981) and New York (1982) and hugely successful.

Old Southwest, the southern frontier of the early 19th century, including present-day Georgia, Alabama, Louisiana, Mississippi, Arkansas, Kansas, and Tennessee. A distinctive form of humor consisting of tall tales and sketches of rural characters emerged from this section. Well-known writers include A. B. LONGSTREET, DAVY CROCKETT, G. W. HARRIS, T. B. THORPE, and JOSEPH G. BALDWIN.

Olds, Sharon (1942–), poet. Born in San Francisco, raised in Berkeley, Olds was educated at Dana Hall School in Wellesley, Massachusetts, and at Stanford (B.A., 1964) and Columbia University (Ph.D., 1972). A longtime resident of Manhattan and a professor in the writing program at New York University, she has mined her personal life before, during, and after her thirty-two year marriage to a psychiatrist, for poems that speak frankly and with sexual explicitness of a woman's relationships to her father, her husband, and her children. Among her books, *The Dead and the Living* (1984) has been especially popular, selling perhaps 50,000 copies in fifteen years. *The Father* (1992) collects poems focused on her father's death from cancer. Other volumes include her first, *Satan Says* (1980); *The Gold Cell* (1987); *The Sign of Saturn* (1991); *The Wellspring* (1996); and *Blood, Tin, Straw* (1999).

Old Stormalong. Captain Alfred Bulltop Stormalong was a fictional folk hero of the Atlantic Coast in the days before the steamer. He sailed to England often, and once was in a boat so big that he barely scraped through the Cliffs of Dover, in fact rubbed off a bit of his topside paint and left the cliffs all white. His favorite vessel was a clipper ship so large that it was Wednesday in the fo'c's'le when it was still Monday aft. It is said that the initials A. B., which attached to a sailor's name allegedly mean able-bodied, are really derived from Stormalong's initials. Charles Edward Brown collected *Old Stormalong Yarns* (1933); Joanna C. Colcord included the ballad of *Stormalong* in her *Songs of American Sailormen* (1938); Frank Shay told his story at some length in *Here's Audacity! American Legendary Heroes* (1939); and Walter Blair joined him with other early folk heroes in *Tall Tale America* (1944).

Oldstyle, Jonathan. A pen name employed by WASHINGTON IRVING in nine letters he contributed to the New York

Morning Chronicle (1802–03). The letters satirized dueling, dress, marriage customs, ranting actors, vulgar audiences, inaudible music, and the critics of the day; they foreshadow the more mature Irving.

Old Swimmin' Hole and 'Leven More Poems (1883), a book of poems by JAMES WHITCOMB RILEY. The original edition was signed "Benj. F. Johnson, of Boone," with Riley's name after it. The first of Riley's books in Hoosier dialect, it contains "When the Frost Is On the Punkin," one of the author's best-known works. In the *Old Swimmin' Hole* was the first appearance of that sentimental nostalgia for boyhood scenes that was to make Riley's fortune, influence newspaper versifiers for years to come, and cause a violent reaction in writers like HAMLIN GARLAND.

Oldtown Folks (1869),   a novel by HARRIET BEECHER STOWE. "It is more to me than a story. It is my resumé of the whole spirit and body of New England," wrote the author of this saga of life in Oldtown (based on South Natick, Massachusetts, birthplace of her husband). The action, which takes place not long after the Revolutionary War, verges on melodrama, but the characters are depicted with skill. The story is related by Horace Holyoke, a young man with a mystical turn of mind whose spiritual visions are based on similar experiences of the author's husband, Calvin Stowe. See SAM LAWSON.

Oliver, Mary (1935–   ),   poet. Born in Maple Heights, Ohio, a Cleveland suburb, Mary Oliver attended Ohio State University (1955–56) and Vassar College (1956–57). Although she has taught elsewhere, she has been most identified with New England. She divides her time between Cape Cod, where she has lived for many years and has taught at the Fine Arts Work Center in Provincetown, and Bennington, Vermont, where she teaches at Bennington College. Her poems are most often spare, precise evocations of nature, frequently reminiscent in subject and method of earlier New England poets such as Emerson, Dickinson, and Frost. The observer learns, and is lifted in spirit. In "The Black Snake" a snake killed on the road brings thoughts of mortality. In "Picking Blueberries, Austerlitz, New York, 1957" a deer stumbles upon the sleeping "I" of the poem. Elsewhere, a hawk circles, a hummingbird dips "his dark tongue / in happiness." Cape Cod is rich in ponds, whales, mussels, turtles, and herons. She won the Pulitzer Prize for *American Primitive* (1983) and the American Book Award for *New and Selected Poems* (1992). Her other volumes of verse include her first collection, *No Voyage, and Other Poems* (1963); *The River Styx, Ohio* (1972); *Twelve Moons* (1978); *Dream Work* (1986); *White Pine: Poems and Prose Poems* (1994); and *West Wind: Poems and Prose Poems* (1997), with nineteen new poems and twenty-one previously published ones. Other books include *A Poetry Handbook* (1994); *Blue Pastures* (1995) essays; *Rules for the Dance: A Handbook for Writing and Reading Metrical Verse* (1998); and *Winter Hours: Prose, Prose Poems, and Poems* (1999).

Olmsted, Frederick Law (1822–1903),   landscape architect, author. Born in Connecticut, Olmsted designed such notable landscapes and parks as Central and Riverside Parks in New York City, the World's Fair in Chicago (1893), and the grounds of the Capitol in Washington. He was a highly observant writer who reported his conclusions about the South in three separately published volumes that were combined as *The Cotton Kingdom* (1856, 1857, 1860; 2 v. 1861–62; reprinted 1953). He also wrote *An American Farmer in England* (1852). Theodora Kimball wrote his biography (2 v. 1922, 1928). A more recent study is Charles E. Beveridge and Paul Rocheleau, *Frederick Law Olmsted: Designing the American Landscape* (1995).

Olney, Jesse (1798–1872),   teacher. Olney, born in Connecticut, developed new ways of teaching geography. He started with the familiar in his *Practical System of Modern Geography* (1828), then went on to the unfamiliar. He emphasized acquaintance with the student's own environment.

Olsen, Tillie (1913–   ),   author, political activist. Olsen's slender work emphasizes how gender, race and class can render people inarticulate. Olsen's own life illustrates the problem. She began working on her novel *Yonnondio* before she was twenty; a chapter from it was published in the *Partisan Review* in 1934, but she married in 1936, had four children, worked, and participated in union activities. She did not resume writing until the 1950s. In her prize-winning story "Tell Me a Riddle" (1961), an elderly couple must reevaluate their past in the face of the wife's impending death. The completed *Yonnondio*, a chronicle of a working family in the Depression, was published in 1974. Since that publication Olsen has been teaching writing and championing works by neglected woman writers such as Rebecca Harding Davis. Her *Silences* (1978) is a collection of lectures and essays.

Olson, Charles (1910–1970),   poet, essayist. Born in Worcester, Massachusetts, Olson spent his childhood summers in the seacoast resort of Gloucester, Massachusetts, whose history and character as a fishing center became the focus of his three-part *Maximus Poems*. After attending Wesleyan and Yale, Olson entered Harvard's new American Civilization program in 1936, an interdisciplinary curriculum emphasizing historical research, which he left in 1939 before completing doctoral work. Historical method influenced much of his thinking and poetry, but as he noted to his friend, poet ROBERT CREELEY: "The trouble is, it is very difficult, to be both a poet and an historian." Olson's brief political career began with the American Civil Liberties Union in 1941 and ended in 1945 after representing the Foreign Nationalities Division at the Democratic National Convention. His interest in minority cultures and races in America pervades his poetry and theoretical writings.

Olson's first important work, *Call Me Ishmael* (1947), interpreted Melville's *Moby-Dick* as an allegory in which the imperious individual of Western thought, Ahab, perishes and a new age of community relations begins with the lone survivor of the shipwreck, the compassionate Ishmael. "The shift was from man as a group to individual man," Olson wrote. "Now, in spite of the corruption of myth by fascism, the swing is out and back. Melville is one who began it." Olson's PROJECTIVE

VERSE essay, published in 1950, set forth the principles by which poetry could begin to express a new concept of self as post-individualistic, a poetry of keen attention to others without "the lyrical interference of the ego." This essay and others, "Human Universe" and "The Gate and the Center," declared the existence of a new tradition of literature at midcentury, one set against the academic and Anglo-American writing headed by Robert Lowell. In 1949, Olson's poem "The King-fishers" was published in which he declared his kinship with the tribal civilizations of pre-Columbian Central America, and not with the Western traditions of Greek and Roman thought. From 1951 to its close in 1956, Olson was rector of BLACK MOUNTAIN COLLEGE, where his influence on other poets led critics to refer to his movement as the Black Mountain school of poetry.

Olson's short poems in *In Cold Hell, In Thicket* (1953) and in *The Distances* (1960) trace aspects of mind linking individual and group awareness—the intuitive, mythological, archetypal patterns that enter an individual's thought as echoes of universal human thinking. His poems are cast in fluid and dissolving forms intended to reproduce the mental processes by which they were composed. These and other short poems gathered posthumously in *The Complete Shorter Poems* (1985) are Olson's effort to show in poetry how individual experience refreshes the mythical paradigms underlying all of human thought, the collective mental realm Olson called the "human universe."

His most important work, *The Maximus Poems*, is a poetic sequence of three hundred poems conceived in 1945 and worked on from 1950 to Olson's death by cancer in 1970. Its form of sequential narrative and lyric interlude derives in part from Ezra Pound's *Cantos* (1975) and WILLIAM CARLOS WILLIAMS's *Paterson* (1963), but is a unique account of the history and development of Gloucester, near where the Massachusetts Bay Colony was first established, and viewed as the microcosm of America's evolution. The poem traces parallel communities elsewhere in history as a pattern of social evolution. The second volume shifts from literary to mythological narratives of Gloucester's development. The third, unfinished volume returns to modern-day Gloucester as an emblem of contemporary society and its travails. Maximus, Olson's persona, is modeled on a 2nd-century A.D. philosopher from Tyre, Gloucester's "sister city" in ancient Phoenicia, who functions as a historical memory, drawing parallels and relations to the present. In the great second volume of the poem, Olson reconstructs the shape of ancient human consciousness by means of intersecting myths and cultural relics, much as an archaeologist pieces together fragments of ancient artifacts.

Olson's essays and poetry expanded the concept of self to include its psychological and spiritual bonds to the community. He wrote during the social upheavals of the post–World War II era and championed cultures long suppressed by Western imperialism. He wanted to separate American literature from Anglo-American tradition, to combine in new literature "red, white, and black" racial perspectives in the postimperial-

ist age. His influence on other writers has been pervasive and continues to arouse interest in myth and ancient literature as sources of communal vision. See Robert von Hallberg, *Olson: The Scholar's Art* (1978), and Paul Christensen, *Olson: Call Him Ishmael* (1979).

PAUL CHRISTENSEN

Olson, Elder (1909–1992),   poet, critic. Long associated with the University of Chicago, Olson was a notable critic of the Neo-Aristotelian school whose essays on poetry and literature were published in many magazines and anthologies. Among his collections of poetry are *The Cock of Heaven* (1940), *Things of Sorrow* (1943), and *The Scarecrow Christ* (1945). He was a thoughtful poet of a religious and humanist orientation.

Omoo: A Narrative of Adventures in the South Seas.   In *Omoo* (1847), his sequel to TYPEE (1846), Herman Melville fictionalizes his experiences in Tahiti in 1842, although it was presented to the public as a travel narrative. This is a comical novel, more picaresque and less cohesive than *Typee*, and written, as Walt Whitman noted in his review, in a "richly good-natured style." However, it also includes an even sharper attack than *Typee* on the missionaries and on the colonialist French in Polynesia. Reacting to the incompetent Captain Guy, the unnamed narrator proposes to his fellow sailors a Round Robin (a circular set of signatures) declaration of mutiny. After their incarceration in the "Hotel de Calabooza" (the jail), the narrator and his comrade, the waggish Doctor Long Ghost, roam around Tahiti. According to Melville, *omoo* is Marquesan for wanderer. Included in their adventures is a comic period of potato farming with the Yankee Zeke and the Cockney Shorty. After experiencing native hospitality, the adventures, in hopes of a royal sinecure, journey to the court of the Queen of Tahiti, Pomaree Vahinee I, a just ruler but an unfaithful wife to her henpecked husband, Tanee. When Pomaree denies them an interview and tosses them out of her court, the narrator signs aboard the whaler *Leviathan* for a year's voyage off the coast of Japan.

Melville's contemporary reviewers generally appreciated *Omoo*'s picturesque, comedic style. IN STUDIES IN CLASSIC AMERICAN LITERATURE (1923), D. H. Lawrence found Melville "at his best, his happiest, in *Omoo*." But later critics for the most part rank the novel as one of Melville's minor works.

NEAL L. TOLCHIN

O'Nan, Stewart (1961–   ),   short-story writer, novelist, nonfiction writer. Born in Pittsburgh, O'Nan was educated as a scientist at Boston College and worked as a test engineer for Grumman Aerospace. After winning prizes for his fiction, he turned to professional writing and completed a master of fine arts degree at Cornell University. *Snow Angels* (1994), set in western Pennsylvania, centers on two dysfunctional families. The Vietnam veteran at the center of *The Names of the Dead* (1996) has flashbacks to his war experiences. *The Speed Queen* (1997) records the thoughts of a female death row inmate on the day of her execution. *Everyday People* (2001) deals with the residents of an African-American community near Pittsburgh, especially an 18-year-old left paralyzed by an accident. Other novels include *A World Away* (1998), and *A Prayer for the Dying* (1999). *In the Walled City* (1993) is a short-story collection. O'Nan edited *The Vietnam Reader: The Definitive Collection of American Fiction and Non-fiction on the War* (1998). Utilizing police reports and eyewitness accounts, he recounts the true story of a July, 1944 blaze in Hartford, Connecticut. *The Circus Fire* (2000) tells how 167 spectators at the Ringling Brothers, Barnum and Bailey Circus were killed and hundreds more injured.

Once I Pass'd Through a Populous City   (1860, in *Leaves of Grass*, 3rd ed.; present title, 1867, 4th ed.), a poem by WALT WHITMAN. The city is New Orleans, which Whitman and his brother visited in 1848, and where he stayed long enough to edit the New Orleans *Crescent* for three months.

Ondaatje, Michael (1943–   ),   teacher, poet, novelist, editor, filmmaker. Born in Colombo, Ceylon [Sri Lanka], Ondaatje immigrated to Canada by way of England in 1962. He received a master's degree from Queen's University and has taught literature at York University in Toronto since 1971. Ondaatje's first books of poetry include *The Dainty Monsters* (1967), *The Man with Seven Toes* (1969), and *Rat Jelly* (1973). As their titles suggest, Ondaatje's work is characterized by a surreal blend of the ordinary and the fantastic: a woman fights off a rat with her umbrella, a horse falls from the top of a skyscraper. *The Collected Works of Billy the Kid*, both a factual and fictional life of William Bonney, won the Governor General's Award in 1970 and has been adapted for stage production in Stratford, Toronto, and New York. Ondaatje won a second Governor General's Award for poetry in 1979 with *There's a Trick with a Knife I'm Learning to Do*. Ondaatje's prose narratives also bear the special mark of the ordinary illuminated by the exotic. *Coming Through Slaughter* (1976) tells of the real and imagined events surrounding the madness and death of New Orleans jazz musician Buddy Bolden. *Running in the Family* (1982) describes the bizarre life of Ondaatje's parents and grandparents in colonial Ceylon. In both books documentary sources such as newspaper articles, photographs, and interviews are juxtaposed with imaginary voices and events creating surreal narratives with startling, often violent, images. *In The Skin of a Lion* (1987), set in the Toronto of the 1930s, is more conventionally a novel although impressionistic and poetic in style. *The English Patient* (1992), made famous by an award-winning film, weaves a complex tapestry out of the lives of four people with no fixed identity who come together during the last days of the Second World War. *Anil's Ghost* (2000) is a novel about a forensic anthropologist sent by the United Nations to investigate deaths that took place during the long civil war in her native Sri Lanka. Ondaatje has made several short films, including one about poet B. P. NICHOL entitled *Sons of Captain Poetry*. He has edited three collections of Canadian writing: *The Broken Ark: A Book of Beasts* (1971); *Personal Fictions: Stories by Munro, Wiebe, Thomas, and Blaise* (1977); and *The Long Poem Anthology* (1977). Ondaatje's work is discussed in

Sam Solecki's *Spider Blues: Essays on Michael Ondaatje* (1985), and Nell Waldman's *Michael Ondaatje* (1983).
DAVID STOUCK

One Flew Over the Cuckoo's Nest (1962),   a novel by KEN KESEY narrated by the Chief, a patient in a mental ward dominated by the Big Nurse. The docile patients are transformed when the eccentric McMurphy has himself transferred in from a prison and contends with the nurse for control. When McMurphy is lobotomized, the Chief suffocates him as an act of mercy and escapes.

One-Hoss Shay.   See THE DEACON'S MASTER-PIECE.

Oneida community,   a utopian socialist group established in 1848 by the Society of Perfectionists, led by JOHN HUMPHREY NOYES. The Perfectionists believed that the Second Coming had already occurred and that they were living in a state of sinlessness where monogamous marriage was no longer appropriate and jealousy had no place. Appalled by the suffering of women in childbirth, Noyes advocated Complex Marriage, in which sexual freedom and romantic friendships were encouraged, but reproduction was regulated by a group of elders, and women bore children only when they chose.

The group held property communally, encouraged manual labor and group study, and held weekly sessions of Mutual Criticism, a form of group therapy intended to foster individual spiritual development. The community manufactured steel traps, traveling bags, preserved fruit and silk, and developed a wide reputation for skilled craftsmanship and innovation. Its membership grew from 87 in 1849 to 306 in 1878, and branch communities were formed in Wallingford, Connecticut, and elsewhere in the northeastern states. They published several newspapers, including the weekly *Circular*, and encouraged free inquiry, education and the arts.

Members presided over 48 administrative departments and hired outside workers. The department heads met weekly as a Business Board in which women served equally with men in controlling community finances. Women wore loose trousers for convenience and cut their hair short. After being weaned, babies were cared for communally. Talented men were sent to universities; youths of both sexes were sent to factories to learn new manufacturing techniques. By 1870 a new generation, removed from the religious basis of Perfectionism, strained the solidarity of the community, and pressure from outside critics was building. John Noyes left Oneida in 1876 and established a new group on the Canadian side of Niagara Falls.

In deference to public sentiment, the group gave up its practice of Complex Marriage in 1879. Two years later a joint stock company called Oneida Community Limited was set up; members were given financial settlements and gradually left New York to settle in other parts of the country.

O'Neill, Eugene [Gladstone] (1888–1953),   playwright. In LONG DAY'S JOURNEY INTO NIGHT, by common critical consent the greatest play by America's most important dramatist, O'Neill confronts his own family by putting on stage "the four haunted Tyrones." "Written in tears and blood," filled with "deep pity and understanding and forgiveness" for the characters he portrays, O'Neill gives us a revealing portrait of himself as a young man in the crucial year of his life, 1912. Whatever happened to him up to that year, when he was twenty-four years old, helped form the dramatist to come. In the early part of that year, he attempted to commit suicide at "Jimmy-the-Priest's" saloon; at the end of that year, he entered a tuberculosis sanitarium, Gaylord Farm, in Connecticut, commencing a six-month stay that gave him a chance to pause and think about his life for the first time. "It was in this enforced period of reflection that the urge to write [plays] first came to me." During that period he began to read seriously every play he "could lay hands on: the Greeks, the Elizabethans—practically all the classics—and of course all the moderns. Ibsen and Strindberg, especially Strindberg, who first gave me the vision of what modern drama could be." He is determined "to be an artist or nothing," he writes to GEORGE PIERCE BAKER in whose playwriting course he enrolls at Harvard in 1914. The artist he becomes is America's most prolific and internationally renowned playwright.

O'Neill was born in a hotel room on Broadway, the appropriate place for this child of the theater. The son of James O'Neill, the Irish-born actor—who, as we learn in *Long Day's Journey*, could have become a great Shakespearean actor had he not sold out to financial success by playing repeatedly the title role in a moneymaker, *The Count of Monte Cristo*— O'Neill spent his earliest years being nursed in the wings of many different theaters by his mother, Ella Quinlan O'Neill, whose respectable background did not prepare her for becoming the wife of an actor. Eugene was their third son. James O'Neill, Jr. (Jamie) was born ten years before Eugene. Another son, Edmund, was born four years before Eugene, but caught measles from Jamie and died before reaching age two. Eugene's birth was extremely difficult for Ella, and it started her on her drug addiction, a fact that haunted Eugene throughout his life. When he was fifteen he learned that his mother was a drug addict. At that age he also turned away from Catholicism and began his hard drinking, which he continued, off and on, sometimes with frightening persistence and intensity, until 1926, when he made a choice between alcohol and his work.

Touring with his father and mother ended when O'Neill was seven years old. He went to a Catholic Sisters' boarding school in New York, then to a Catholic school in Manhattan operated by the Christian Brothers, then to a nonsectarian boarding school, Betts Academy in Stamford, Connecticut, from which he was graduated in 1906. O'Neill attended Princeton for one academic year, but didn't take his final examinations and was dropped for academic reasons and for misbehavior, having thrown a rock in the stationmaster's window during a drunken spree. Although this ended his formal education, it had no effect on his informal education. He was an avid reader reading the likes of Shaw, EMMA GOLDMAN, and Nietzsche, whose *Thus Spake Zarathustra* "has influenced me more than any book I've ever read."

In October of 1909 O'Neill hastily married Kathleen Jenkins, left for Honduras on a gold prospecting expedition a few days

later, and returned to New York in April 1910 with a touch of malaria but without any gold. In May of that year Eugene O'Neill Jr. was born, the son O'Neill would not see for almost twelve years. After a stint as assistant manager with his father's touring company, he went to sea as a deck-hand on a Norwegian sailing ship, the "Charles Racine." The sea always seemed to beckon to O'Neill; his closeness to it seems to have been both a physical and a spiritual necessity. He was an excellent swimmer and would swim farther from shore than seemed possible, returning spent and satisfied. His lifelong search for a home usually led him, like Ishmael, to the sea. He lived always near the ocean, in Cape Cod; Bermuda; Sea Island, Georgia; and Marblehead, Massachusetts. When he had no home in his early years of manhood he lived along the waterfront. He spent his boyhood summers in the New London, Connecticut, summer home of his parents—the setting of *Long Day's Journey*— located near the Thames River. His two-month trip as a sailor on the "Charles Racine," bound for Buenos Aires from Boston, helped inspire his early sea plays and gave him his most mystical experiences—"I felt synchronized with the rhythm of life." He jumped ship in Buenos Aires, worked at various jobs there, but usually lived the life of a bum on the waterfront, sleeping on benches, and scrounging for alcohol and food. He returned to New York in 1911 on a British tramp steamer, the "S. S. Ikala," which was the model for the "S. S. Glencairn" in his early sea plays. In New York he lived in a waterfront saloon on Fulton Street, called "Jimmy-the-Priest's." A drink of whiskey cost a nickel and a room cost three dollars a month. It was a "hell hole," in O'Neill's phrase. Then he shipped out again as an ordinary seaman on a passenger liner to England, and returned to New York as an ablebodied seaman. This trip gave him more material for his sea plays and enabled him to meet the stoker, Driscoll, who appears in the *Glencairn* plays and will eventually emerge as Yank Smith in *The Hairy Ape*. O'Neill's experiences at sea will feed his creative imagination throughout his career.

Incredibly ambitious and energetic, O'Neill began writing one-act plays in 1913, while he was reporter on the New London *Telegraph*, and stopped thirty years later, when he could no longer hold a pencil in hand. The rest of O'Neill's biography is ostensibly a record of his artistic development; what happened to him in the years before 1912—his family relationships, his personal experiences—will inform all the plays he writes in the years ahead. But some further biographical facts are of interest. In 1918 he married his second wife, Agnes Boulton, a short-story writer, with whom he had two children—Shane, born in 1919, and Oona, born in 1925. He divorced Agnes in 1929 and later disowned both children— Shane because of his alcoholism and derelict behavior, Oona because of her marriage at age eighteen to Charlie Chaplin, age fifty-four, O'Neill's own age at the time. Eugene O'Neill, Jr., became a professor of classics at Yale University, traveled the alcoholic path of self-ruin, and committed suicide in 1950, as did Shane years later.

O'Neill achieved celebrity in 1920 with *Beyond the Horizon* and *The Emperor Jones*. It was also the year of his father's death. Two years later, his mother died, after having cured herself of her drug addiction with the help of her belief in the Virgin Mary. Her death caused Jamie O'Neill—forever tied to his mother, he abandoned alcoholism when his mother abandoned morphine—to resume his alcoholic orgies. Jamie died a year later at age forty-five. O'Neill's third wife, actress Carlotta Monterey, whom he married immediately after his divorce from Agnes Boulton, survived O'Neill. She protectively provided the conditions for O'Neill's creativity. Some claim that O'Neill was her prisoner, which in some sense is true, but his bondage enabled him to write his last great plays. Perhaps his dedication of *Long Day's Journey* to Carlotta puts their relationship in the proper perspective—the play is "a tribute to your love and tenderness which gave me the faith in love that enabled me to face my dead at last."

From the 1930s O'Neill suffered a nervous disease that subjected his hands to a tremor, the tremor increasing with the passing years. Because he could compose only in longhand, the eventual loss of his ability to put pencil on paper was the end of his writing career. For the last ten years of his life, he would write nothing, although his mind, unaffected by the disease, was filled with a multitude of ideas and plans. Although O'Neill officially died on November 27, 1953, of bronchial pneumonia in a Boston hotel room—"Born in a goddam hotel room and dying in a hotel room!"—his life, which was his work, ended ten years earlier.

When the amateur PROVINCETOWN PLAYERS, headed by GEORGE CRAM COOK and SUSAN GLASPELL, put out its call for new plays in the summer of 1916 in Cape Cod, O'Neill dipped into his trunkful of plays and pulled out his manuscript of *Bound East for Cardiff*, thereby changing the course of American drama. Avoiding the basic ingredients of conventional drama and exploiting his knowledge of men at sea, O'Neill offered America a realistic, brooding, one-act play of high value about a dying sailor who talks to his friend about the past. *Bound East for Cardiff*, performed by the Provincetown Players on the rickety boards of the Wharf Theater on Cape Cod on the evening of July 28, 1916, marks the auspicious debut of the first modern dramatist of America.

From that date to 1920, when fame suddenly arrived for O'Neill, other one-act plays were performed by the Provincetown group in Cape Cod and in Greenwich Village, the most important being the three one-acters that constitute the *S.S. Glencairn* plays along with *Bound East: The Moon of the Caribbees, The Long Voyage Home,* and *In the Zone.* (The last was performed by the Washington Square Players, an amateur group that would eventually become the THEATRE GUILD, the most important producer of O'Neill's plays.) The realistic *Glencairn* plays display O'Neill's abiding interest in man's position in relation to large outside forces, here represented by the sea. They also reveal a theatrical virtuosity, a mastery of mood and melodramatic plotting, that will never leave him.

O'Neill's first important full-length play, written in 1918 and produced in 1920, became a Broadway success, thereby reaching O'Neill's widest audience up to then. The realistic

BEYOND THE HORIZON, which gave O'Neill his first Pulitzer Prize, deals with the dreams and frustrations of authentic farm people. It affected O'Neill's audience deeply, offering a vision of life that touched the tragic. Something new was happening to American drama: a serious playwright was presenting serious dramatic fare to a Broadway audience that usually went to the theater for escapist entertainment.

The year that ushered in the 1920s brought O'Neill fame with *Beyond the Horizon* and solidified that fame with THE EMPEROR JONES. The expressionism of *The Emperor Jones* so captivated American audiences that it is not inaccurate to claim that the play introduced expressionism to America. A short play in eight rapidly shifting scenes, it tells the story of the fall of Brutus Jones from "emperor" of a West Indian island to a crawling savage killed by his rebellious people. The expressionistic scenes, punctuated by the beating of tom-toms, powerfully suggest the panic of Jones as he makes his journey through the forest, a journey that is physical and psychological, racial and universal, a veritable *tour de force* for O'Neill. The play contains the first important part for a black actor in America. Charles Gilpin made theatrical history with the boldness of his performance as Brutus Jones, a part played later by PAUL ROBESON.

The combined success of the realistic *Beyond the Horizon* and the expressionistic *The Emperor Jones* made O'Neill America's most important dramatist, but a dramatist difficult to categorize. His artistry was bold; his aim was to stretch his medium to its utmost. With ANNA CHRISTIE, produced in 1921, O'Neill turned to realism tinged with symbolism. Its heroine-as-prostitute, colloquial dialogue, and saloon setting place it firmly in the realistic tradition, but the fog and the sea give the play a convincing behind life dimension. The play brought O'Neill his second Pulitzer Prize. With THE HAIRY APE, produced a year later, O'Neill returned to the expressionism of *Jones*, dramatizing the journey of the rough stoker Yank Smith toward self-realization and death. The play has a strong social and political dimension, condemning a capitalistic society, but it has an even stronger existential dimension, dramatizing the search for meaning in modern society, with death as the only answer to Yank's tortured thinking. In his next important play, ALL GOD'S CHILLUN GOT WINGS, produced in 1924, O'Neill again uses expressionistic devices in a primarily realistic treatment of the marriage of black Jim Harris (played by Paul Robeson) and white Ella Downey. Boldly confronting the issue of race relations, the playwright offers convincing insights into the psychological problems that can arise from mixed marriage. O'Neill wrote his best play of the 1920s near the middle of that decade by going back to the New England farm and stressing elemental passions in a story of conflict between father and son, a story of love between son and stepmother. Although it contains many elements of sensational melodrama—greed, onstage violence, sex, incest, adultery, infanticide—these elements are controlled by a larger frame of reference, a determinism based on the power of desire and the power of Mother, making DESIRE UNDER THE ELMS one of O'Neill's most powerful tragedies.

In the late 1920s O'Neill's artistic restlessness became a kind of frenzy; he aimed for a depth and a largeness that usually eluded him. In THE GREAT GOD BROWN, produced in 1926, O'Neill wanted to present directly "a drama of souls," and because he believed that the new psychology of Freud and Jung was essentially "a study in masks, an exercise in unmasking," he used the device of masks to bare the human soul on stage. This bold attempt to dramatize the agony of divided souls proved so puzzling to the audience that O'Neill was forced to make many public comments on his intention and on the play's meaning. In the 1928 MARCO MILLIONS, the first O'Neill play produced by the Theatre Guild, O'Neill offered his audience a romantic extravaganza about Marco Polo, filled with satire against American materialistic values. In LAZARUS LAUGHED, written in 1926, O'Neill pulled out all stops to present what he called "A Play for the Imaginative Theater," requiring hundreds of actors, about 400 costumes, about 300 masks. In his ambitious desire to return modern drama to its ritualistic and communal origins, O'Neill wrote a play so theatrically challenging that it has never been tested by professional performance. O'Neill's bold experimentation continued with STRANGE INTERLUDE, produced in 1928, which proved to be not only stageworthy but enormously popular. In this novelistic nine-act drama, O'Neill covers twenty-five years in the life of Nina Leeds, a middle-class woman looking for happiness. Here O'Neill uses the device of the interior monologue, allowing his characters to speak aloud their true inner thoughts, a variation of the Elizabethan soliloquy but also comparable to Joyce's stream of consciousness in the novel. The play's novelistic device, its popularization of current Freudian ideas, and its length—allowing for a dinner break—made it the most popular play the Theatre Guild ever produced and won for O'Neill his third Pulitzer Prize. But his next play, Dynamo, produced in 1929, the last O'Neill play of the 1920s, was a disaster both artistically and financially. Attempting to confront the big issues of science and religion, dramatizing a modern search for God that uses the dynamo as symbol, O'Neill offers a mechanical melodramatic plot informed by a fuzzy philosophical idea.

During the 1930s, when other dramatists were confronting the Depression, social problems, and the threat of fascism, O'Neill was becoming more interested in private worlds, even when found in universal myths. With the trilogy MOURNING BECOMES ELECTRA, produced in 1931, O'Neill ambitiously competed with the Greek dramatists for size in drama. He uses the Electra story to probe the minds of the Mannons, a New England family, during the Civil War. In an absorbing tragedy of death and determinism, presented without the help of experimental devices and remaining close to the realism that was his strength, O'Neill gave America perhaps the best play of the decade, certainly the play possessing the greatest tragic depth and scope. How surprised, therefore, was the American public when the Theatre Guild in 1933 presented O'Neill's next play, Ah, Wilderness!, the only pure comedy O'Neill wrote and one of the most popular plays in the American repertoire. He

called it a "comedy of recollection," but what it recollects is a time and place—1906 and small-town America—not his personal life, which is closer to the experience he presents in Long Day's Journey, although both plays are set in the New London summer home of the O'Neills. Both his Greek tragedy, Mourning Becomes Electra, and his nostalgic American comedy, Ah, Wilderness!, received lavish praise from an admiring public and press. Then came Days Without End, produced in 1934, probably O'Neill's worst play, which reflects O'Neill's own search for faith in the modern world. To present the conflict within his divided hero, John Loving, O'Neill has two actors play the split character, one John, the other Loving, but this striking device does not redeem a play whose affirmative ending, in which the hero returns to the Catholicism of his childhood, lacks conviction. The play's failure did not prevent O'Neill from receiving the Nobel Prize for Literature in 1936.

From 1934 until 1946, no O'Neill play was produced on Broadway. His silence after the failure of Days Without End led many to believe he had found his faith and lost his artistic powers. But O'Neill did not embrace Catholicism, and his silence reflected neither his artistry nor the intensity of his labors. Through the silent years he was working on an ambitious cycle of history plays and on his finest accomplishments: THE ICEMAN COMETH, Hughie, Long Day's Journey Into Night, and A Moon for the Misbegotten. Always thinking in large terms, O'Neill planned to write a cycle of plays dealing with almost 200 years of American history, from the Revolutionary War to the Depression. The cycle would offer his evaluation of his country's history; its overall title, "A Tale of Possessors Self-dispossessed," indicates the thrust of his criticism of American possessiveness and greed. Only one play of the cycle, A Touch of the Poet, not produced until 1957, was completed. The other plays, in various states of composition, were destroyed by O'Neill when he realized he would be unable to complete the enormous task. The manuscript of More Stately Mansions, another play of the cycle, survived by accident and has been performed in edited versions.

O'Neill's last four plays crown his formidable career and display him at the height of his creative power. The Iceman Cometh, produced in 1946, marked the return of O'Neill to Broadway. The crucial year in O'Neill's life, 1912, is the year of the play, set in a saloon in New York City modeled on the ones O'Neill frequented. The lodgers at the saloon are kept alive by alcohol and by their pipe dreams. The arrival of Hickey, the salesman, disrupts their sleepy existence. The interaction of Hickey with the other drinkers produces a powerful drama of crime and punishment, a complex realistic play that hearkens the symbolic, a play that evokes understanding compassion for the poor naked creatures whose souls are stripped bare. The play is important in any discussion of O'Neill's career because it broke O'Neill's silence in 1946 and triggered the revival of interest in O'Neill in 1956, three years after his death. The reaction to the 1956 Circle-in-the-Square Iceman, directed by Jose Quintero and starring Jason Robards as Hickey, was unequivocally enthusiastic. No other O'Neill play had a longer run than this production, before or since—a total of 565 performances. *Hughie*, the one-act play O'Neill wrote after *Iceman*, seems a natural extension of the long four-act play, because it stresses that illusions must be shared in order for man to endure. The only surviving part of a projected cycle of six one-act plays—collectively titled *By Way of Obit*—*Hughie* manages to present in forty-five minutes of playing time a picture of lonely men, two living and one dead, and it captures the atmosphere of a city by means of stage directions and sounds. It had its first American performance in 1964, with Quintero directing and Robards starring as Erie Smith.

O'Neill returned to the year 1912 for what has come to be regarded as his greatest play, *Long Day's Journey*, the highest achievement in American realistic theater. The play gives us a very long day in the life of the Tyrones, a day in which each member of the family makes an agonizing journey into night—the night of the play, the night of dreams, the night of death. It was psychologically necessary for O'Neill to confront his family by way of his art, and in *Long Day's Journey* he confronts them more directly than ever before. It was his way to better understand himself and his mother and father and brother and to forgive himself and his family for the hell they created for each other. Quintero's 1956 success with *Iceman* led Carlotta Monterey O'Neill to permit the young director to present *Long Day's Journey* on Broadway in that same year, thereby solidifying admiration for the reborn O'Neill. The production received high praise and gave O'Neill a posthumous Pulitzer Prize, his fourth, thirty-six years after his first, for *Beyond the Horizon*. This remarkable tragedy, so personal to O'Neill and so universal in its appeal, continues to invite interpretations and insights. Also intensely personal is O'Neill's last play, *A Moon for the Misbegotten*, written in 1943 and produced in 1947. It completes the story of Jamie, presenting a fuller picture of his deep love for his mother, and it gives Jamie a peaceful death, a closure that probably satisfied some deep need within O'Neill himself because in real life Jamie O'Neill died of apoplexy, nearly blind and somewhat mad from too much alcohol. The mother-substitute in the play, Josie Hogan, is one of O'Neill's most memorable characters. A tender giantess, she nurses into peace the fragile alcoholic in a play containing both lyricism and robust Irish comedy.

Throughout his career O'Neill offered theater audiences excitingly fine plays and disappointingly poor plays. The uneven quality of his work produced a mixed critical reaction, understandably so because O'Neill was a passionate playwright who boldly confronted big ideas and calculatingly stretched the possibilities of his artistic medium. His ambitions were immense and his accomplishment was greater than that of any other American playwright before or since. Whatever his deficiencies, his status as America's most important dramatist is beyond questioning. Before O'Neill, American theater was usually escapist entertainment; after O'Neill the phrase American drama took on significance. He offered emotional themes—love, death, frustration, illusion, fate—that touch the very nature of existence, always pursuing the truth

of man's experience as measured by feeling. He said about his writing: "I shall never be influenced by any consideration but one: Is it the truth as I know it—or, better still, feel it?" Many labels have been attached to O'Neill, ranging from realist to romanticist, from naturalist to mystic, but the one that seems most appropriate is dramatist of the emotions, and the single vision that informs most of his work is the tragic vision. In 1945, after O'Neill's work was over, he said that he was "always conscious of the Force behind—Fate, God, our biological past creating our present, whatever one calls it—Mystery certainly—and of the one eternal tragedy of Man in his glorious, self-destructive struggle to make the Force express him instead of being, as an animal is, an infinitesimal incident in its expression." The sincerity of his attempt to express the mystery of the force behind, the frustrations of our lives, and the nobility of our endurance often seems palpable. Always aware that the darkly inexpressible cannot be expressed, giving voice to his own inadequacy through the words of Edmund Tyrone in *Long Day's Journey*: "I couldn't touch what I tried to tell you just now. I just stammered. That's the best I'll ever do, I mean if I live. Well, it will be faithful realism, at least. Stammering is the native eloquence of us fog people." He nevertheless managed in his best work to write plays that place him with the giants of modern drama.

The best standard edition of O'Neill's work is *Eugene O'Neill: The Complete Plays*, ed. Travis Bogard (1988). The best biographies have been Arthur and Barbara Gelb, *O'Neill* (1962) and Louis Sheaffer, *O'Neill: Son and Playwright* (1968) and *O'Neill: Son and Artist* (1973) but the Gelbs' *O'Neill: Life with Monte Cristo* (2000) is the first of a projected three volumes, a major revision of their earlier works. Valuable critical studies are Travis Bogard, *Contour in Time: The Plays of Eugene O'Neill* (1988); Frederick I. Carpenter, *Eugene O'Neill* (1979); John Henry Raleigh, *The Plays of Eugene O'Neill* (1965); and Normand Berlin, *Eugene O'Neill* (1982).

NORMAND BERLIN

One's-Self I Sing, the first poem in Walt Whitman's LEAVES OF GRASS. A long version first appeared as "Inscription" in the 1867 edition. The nine-line version appeared first in the 1871 edition. The poem is a statement of Whitman's inclusive, democratic theme.

Ones Who Walk Away from Omelas, The, a story by URSULA K. LE GUIN from the collection *The Wind's Twelve Quarters*, published in 1975.

Onetti, Juan Carlos (1909–1994), Uruguayan novelist and short-story writer. Onetti never completed his secondary education, but became an erudite and profound novelist. He writes with a haunting mixture of sharply honed comedy and deep sadness about the loneliness of life, the futility of religions, and the crumbling of civilization. His books include a three-volume cycle of novels and stories often called the Santa Maria Sagas: *La vida breve* (1950, tr. *A Brief Life*, 1976); *Los adioses* (1954); and *Una tumba sin nombre* (1959). His most widely known book outside South America, *El astillero* (1961, tr. *The Shipyard*, 1968) is also set in Santa Maria. The main character, Larsen, seeks to climb socially by attaching himself to the shipyard owner's daughter, unable to see that the society he aspires to has disintegrated. *Juntacadaveres* (1965) takes Larsen back to a time before the beginning of *The Shipyard*. Onetti's *Cuentos completas* was published in 1968 (rev. 1974); his *Novelas cortas completas* appeared in 1968, and *Obras completas* in 1970. Onetti's experimental narration is often compared to Faulkner's, a writer he paid tribute to in *Requiem por Faulkner* (1975).

On Moral Fiction,   a 1978 essay by JOHN GARDNER in which he states that fiction has the high purpose to teach "what is necessary to humanness." He faults postwar novelists for lack of moral seriousness, love and hope for mankind, and consistency or clarity, and concludes that most contemporary fiction writers fail because they are too concerned with form over content. The essay brought a fire-storm of criticism from other writers; Gardner spent most of the rest of his life defending himself.

On Native Grounds (1942),   a brilliant study of American prose literature from 1890–1940 by ALFRED KAZIN.

Onondaga Indians.   This tribe was part of the Iroquois Confederacy, sided with the British in the French and Indian Wars, and now lives mostly in Ontario. It figures occasionally in JAMES FENIMORE COOPER's novels, especially those composing the *Littlepage Manuscripts* (1845–46). The Onondagas had some interesting myths, but their most important literary memorial is the so-called *Onondaga Book*, translated by Horatio Hale in the *Iroquois Book of Rites* (1883). This was first taken down in the Onondaga language in the late 18th century by Protestant missionaries. It gives the ritual employed by the tribe when a chief was mourned at his death. Hale noted that the book, sometimes called the *Book of the Condoling Council*, might be called an Iroquois Veda. It comprises speeches, songs, and other ceremonies, beginning with a long prose address.

On the Road (1957),   a novel by JACK KEROUAC. This novel was written in 1951 but did not find a publisher until 1957. It is now regarded as one of the best expressions of the BEAT GENERATION's way of life. It is also a major study of the promise and shortcomings of America. *On the Road* is a five-part first-person narrative. A young writer, Sal Paradise, describes four road trips across the American continent that he took between 1946 and 1950. The narration is firmly controlled but stays close to immediate experience, with its excitement and danger. And it is filled with the quick scene changes and picaresque episodes that suggest freedom and drift. At the center of the novel is Dean Moriarty, the exemplar of Beat life. Restless and primitive, Dean likes fast cars, alcohol, and jazz. He seeks "IT" or God as well and rejects the materialism and conformity of his time. Sal Paradise, Dean's friend and follower, is more sensitive and deliberate than Dean. He sees more, including Dean's limitations and his own disappointments, and he sets it all down in his narrative. Like Kerouac himself, he respects the facts and does not judge them. *On the Road*, in fact, is remarkable for its concreteness. Its anecdotes

and images from life off the beaten path of American experience are allowed to speak for themselves.

FRANK MCHUGH

On Trial (1914),   "a dramatic composition" by ELMER RICE. This story of a noble assassin who wants to be sentenced without a trial and of a harassed female was written by a young law clerk who abandoned the law after this play made a great hit on Broadway. He made good use of his legal knowledge in the play. He was also among the first to use the flashback as a dramatic device. The drama was originally called *According to the Evidence*, and dealt with a Kentucky mountain feud. Arthur Hopkins persuaded Rice to shift the locale to New York City with a banker as the victim.

Open Boat and Other Tales of Adventure, The (1898),   a collection of stories by STEPHEN CRANE. The title story is based on Crane's experience after the wreck of the steamer *Commodore*, on which he had sailed for Cuba as a war correspondent. Accounts of the wreck in dispatches to the New York *Press* and the Florida *Times-Union*, together with "Stephen Crane's Own Story," were collected for the first time in *Stephen Crane: An Omnibus*, edited by R. W. Stallman (1952). In the short story that Crane reconstructed from his experience, each detail is charged with significance and patterned into a scheme of relationships, so the difference between what happened and what he reconstructed is immense. Realistic details have been converted into symbols, and their sequence forms a designed whole possessing a life of its own.

The collection was published in England as *The Open Boat and Other Stories* (1898). Besides the title story, the best story in it is "The Bride Comes to Yellow Sky." "The Bride" is structurally a paradoxical reversal of situation and has close affinities, therefore, with Crane's "A Mystery of Heroism," "The Upturned Face," and "An Episode of War." In all four Crane stories, that which is predictable—a code, a theory, or an ideal—is discovered to be unpredictable when faced with unexpected realities.

Oppen, George (1908–1984),   political activist, poet. In France from 1929 to 1933 Oppen and his wife published a series of books including titles by Ezra Pound and William Carlos Williams and *An Objectivist's Anthology* (1932), edited by Louis Zukofsky. In New York he helped found The Objectivist Press, which published his first collection, *Discrete Series*, in 1934. An active Communist in the late 1930s, he set poetry aside while he organized the unemployed and supported his family as a tool and die maker in Detroit. After fighting in World War II, he was investigated by the House Un-American Activities Committee in 1950 and moved to Mexico City to avoid prison. He worked there as a furniture maker for eight years, returning after the death of Senator Joseph McCarthy. See MCCARTHYISM.

Oppen returned to poetry in the late 1950s. His second book, *The Materials*, appeared in 1962; *This in Which* was published in 1965, and *Of Being Numerous* won the Pulitzer Prize in 1968. His other books are *Seascape* (1973), *Collected Poems* (1975), and *Primitive* (1978). See OBJECTIVISM.

Oppenheim, James (1882–1932),   poet, essayist, novelist, editor, social worker. Born in Minnesota, Oppenheim studied at Columbia University before becoming a social worker on the New York City's lower east side. His observations of slum life were the background for his first book of short stories, *Dr. Rast* (1909). His first book of poetry, *Monday Morning*, appeared in the same year. *Songs for the New Age* (1914) combined social commentary and a loose poetic line in a style Louis Untermeyer described as "the Bible retranslated by Walt Whitman in collaboration with Dr. Freud." Oppenheim founded and edited *The Seven Arts* (1916–17). The failure of this venture, the entry of the U.S. into World War I, and personal problems weighed heavily on him and he turned to psychoanalysis. *The Book of Self* (1917), *Your Hidden Powers* (1923), and *Behind Your Front* (1928) all treat the topic. Poems from *Songs for the New Age, The Solitary* (1919), a free verse autobiography *The Mystic Warrior* (1921), and *The Golden Bird* (1923) were collected in *The Sea* (1923).

Opper, Frederick Burr (1857–1937),   cartoonist. Born in Ohio, for a quarter of a century Opper drew his cartoons for PUCK and then worked for the Hearst papers. His best-known cartoon was the bloated and repulsive picture of Big Business that he called "the Trusts." His most noted comic strips were a hobo, HAPPY HOOLIGAN, and his comic Frenchmen, Alphonse and Gaston. He published collections of some of his productions, among them *Our Antediluvian Ancestors* (1902), *Happy Hooligan* (1902), and *Alphonse and Gaston* (1902). In addition he did excellent illustrations for books by Twain, Finley Peter Dunne, and Bill Nye. His drawings for Nye's *History of the U.S.* (1894) were particularly funny.

Optic, Oliver.   The pen name of W. T. ADAMS.

Oralloossa, Son of the Incas (1832),   a tragedy by ROBERT MONTGOMERY BIRD. Bird was one of the first North American writers to interest himself in South America; his play deals with Peru immediately after the Spanish conquest. Bird created Oralloossa, the son and heir of the emperor Atahualpa, who leads a rebellion against Pizarro and kills the invader. (The incident is not historical.) But his own people finally betray him and bring about his death. EDWIN FORREST made the play one of his favorite acting vehicles. It was first printed in Clement E. Foust's *Life and Dramatic Works of Robert Montgomery Bird* (1919).

Oregon Trail, The (1849),   by FRANCIS PARKMAN. An autobiographical narrative of a tour of the West, originally called *The California and Oregon Trail*. It was first published serially in the *Knickerbocker Magazine* in 1847, and has since become a classic. It is an account of a trip made in 1846 by the author and his cousin Quincy Adams Shaw. They traveled together from St. Louis to Fort Laramie; there they separated, Parkman going to live for some weeks with a tribe of Sioux Indians. *The Oregon Trail* provides valuable descriptions of the prairies and a remarkable ethnological study of the Indians. On the basis of his own close observations, Parkman charged James Fenimore Cooper with lack of realism in his portrayals of Indian characters, especially UNCAS.

O'Reilly, John Boyle (1844–1890),   journalist, poet, novelist. The Irish-born O'Reilly was jailed for his activities in the Fenian movement. He was transported to Australia and in 1869 made a daring escape to the United States. He became a citizen, bought a part interest in the *Pilot*, the most influential Irish paper in America at the time, and was its manager and editor-in-chief until his death. His books include *Songs from Southern Seas* (1873), *Songs, Legends, and Ballads* (1878), *Poems and Speeches* (1891), and *Selected Poems* (1913). *Moondyne* (1879) is a powerful novel of convict life in Australia. He also wrote *Ethics of Boxing and Manly Sport* (1888). W. C. Schofield wrote a biography of O'Reilly entitled *Seek for a Hero* (1956).

Origin (1951–71),   a little magazine. Published by CID CORMAN, *Origin* welcomed avant-garde writers, including the BLACK MOUNTAIN POETS.

Ormond, or, The Secret Witness (1799),   a novel by CHARLES BROCKDEN BROWN. A melodramatic narrative in which the hero, Ormond, returning from travel abroad and contact with the French philosophers, feels himself freed from all ethical considerations. But when he tries to violate the heroine, Constantia, she kills him. Fortunately there is a secret witness to her crime, and she is acquitted.

Orphan Angel, The   (1926, in England 1927 as *Mortal Image*), a novel by ELINOR WYLIE. The novel reflects Wylie's passionate admiration of Shelley. In this romantic story she imagines that Shelley, instead of drowning, was picked up by a Yankee brig and carried to America. The year is 1822 and Shelley, a profound republican, is delighted by the land and the people. His romantic search for Silver Cross (Sylvie La Croix) carries him across America on a journey that Wylie depicts with a mixture of realism and poetry.

Orpheus C. Kerr.   See NEWELL, ROBERT.

Orphic Sayings   (*The Dial*, July 1840 and later issues), by BRONSON ALCOTT. Alcott dealt, as clearly as he could, with such topics as enthusiasm, hope, vocation ("Engage in nothing that cripples or degrades you"), temptation, conscience, speech, originality, nature.

Ortiz, Simon J[oseph] (1941–   ),   poet, short-story writer. An Acoma Pueblo Indian, Ortiz was born in Albuquerque and received his early education at the Bureau of Indian Affairs school on the Acoma reservation and Fort Lewis College (1961–1962). After service in the Army (1963–1966), he attended the University of New Mexico (1966–1968) and the University of Iowa (1968–1969), where he received an M.F.A. He has taught at various schools, including the University of New Mexico, and has been active in advancing Native American affairs, particularly in his home state. From the beginning, his goal in writing, he has said, was to express "the integrity and dignity of an Indian identity, and at the same time I wanted to look at what this was within the context of an America that had too often denied its Indian heritage." His collections of verse include: *Naked in the Wind* (1971), his first book; *Going for the Rain* (1976), his first from a major press, with poems ranging from the Acoma creation myth, through the trickster Coyote, to contemporary Albuquerque; *From Sand Creek: Rising in This Heart which Is Our America* (1981), poems set in a veterans' hospital, with parallels between an 1864 massacre of Indians and massacres in Vietnam; and *Woven Stone* (1984), a compilation from earlier volumes. *Fight Back: For the Sake of the People, for the Sake of the Land* (1980), verse and prose, highlights years of struggle from the Acoma defeat of the Spanish in the seventeenth century through twentieth-century conflicts over the development of New Mexico's uranium riches. *After and Before the Lightning* (1994) contains journal entries in prose and verse from a winter spent teaching on the Lakota Sioux reservation in South Dakota. Short stories are found in *Howbah Indians* (1978), *Fightin': New and Collected Short Stories* (1983), and *Men on the Moon: Collected Short Stories* (1999). He has also written juveniles and edited various books, including *Speaking for the Generations* (1998), essays on writing by nine Native American authors.

Osage Indians.   These Native Americans belong to the Sioux linguistic group and are among the original hunting tribes of the Great Plains. They were widely feared for their courage and aggressiveness. They liked horses; they were gentle with children and had developed a highly symbolic religion; and they were tall, dignified, and sometimes haughty. Their history is a long one, beginning with the earliest French and Spanish trade with Native Americans, and concluding in the present with their accumulation of enormous wealth from the gas and oil fields in Oklahoma—to which place they had reluctantly migrated under pressure from the white men. They numbered a probable 6,500 when Lewis and Clark first discovered them in 1804. Missionaries first appeared among them in 1820 and they eventually became strongly Roman Catholic. Full-blooded Osage form a relatively small percentage of the tribe. Many of the others bear names handed down from the days of the French traders. They have produced notable figures, among them JOHN JOSEPH MATTHEWS, a graduate of Oxford and an author of books dealing with Indian life; Maria Tallchief, a prominent ballerina; and WILLIAM LEAST HEAT-MOON, a writer.

The most extensive study of the Osages was made by a member of the Omaha tribe, the excellent ethnologist and writer FRANCIS LA FLESCHE. His volumes, issued by the Bureau of American Ethnology, are *Rite of the Chiefs; Sayings of the Ancient Men* (1921); *The Rite of Vigil* (1925); *Two Versions of the Child-Naming Rite* (1928); *Songs of the Wa-xó-be* (1930); and *War Ceremony and Peace Ceremony of the Osage Indians* (1939). Some of their chants show an extraordinary maturity of thought. Washington Irving refers often to the Osage in his *Tour of the Prairies* (1835). In CIMARRON (1930), Edna Ferber portrays the Osage Indians as wealthy parvenus who act like anyone who has suddenly struck it rich.

Osborn, Laughton (c. 1809–1878),   novelist. Osborn's *Sixty Years of the Life of Jeremy Levis* (2 v. 1831) is an episodic novel similar to *Tristram Shandy*. *The Vision of Rubeta* (1838) is a historical romance. Osborn also wrote poems and plays.

Osbourne, Lloyd (1868–1947),   novelist, short-story writer. At the time of his mother's marriage to ROBERT LOUIS STEVENSON, the San Francisco-born Osbourne, then a boy of twelve, received a toy printing press with which he and his stepfather spent long hours printing stories, poems, and woodcuts. After trying to live in California, Switzerland, England, and France, the Stevensons set out in 1887 on a cruise to the South Seas. In 1888 both Osbourne and Stevenson were adopted by one of the native tribes. Lloyd Osbourne's skill in the Samoan language fitted him admirably for his post as United States vice-consul in Samoa. He collaborated with Stevenson on *The Wrong Box* (1889), *The Wrecker* (1892), and *The Ebb Tide* (1894). After Stevenson's death in 1894, Osbourne returned to this country, where he continued to write light fiction, detective stories, and plays. Among his titles are *The Queen vs. Billy* (1900), *The Motor Maniacs* (1905), *Three Forward* (1906), *Wild Justice* (1906), and *The Grierson Mystery* (1928). Of more importance are his *Memoirs of Vailima* (1902), a valuable account of Stevenson in the South Seas that Osbourne wrote with his sister Isobel Strong, and *An Intimate Portrait of R.L.S.* (1924).

Osceola (1800?–1838),   Seminole Indian warrior. When the United States tried to force the Seminoles to leave Florida, they withdrew from their villages under Osceola's leadership and took refuge in the Everglades. They were never defeated and never signed a peace treaty. Osceola was treacherously seized while negotiating with army officers under a flag of truce, and he died a prisoner in Fort Moultrie, South Carolina. He is the chief figure in J. B. Benton's *Osceola, or, Fact and Fiction: A Tale of the Seminole War* (1838) and Theodore Pratt's *Seminole* (1954). See SEMINOLE INDIANS.

Osgood, Frances Sargent (1811–1850),   poet. Osgood, born in Boston, wrote simple, sentimental verses that were published in *Wreath of Wild Flowers from New England* (1838), *The Casket of Fate* (1840), and other collections. Her name lives chiefly because of her association with Edgar Allan Poe, who praised her verses in "The Literati." Mary E. Hewitt wrote her biography (1851).

O'Sheel [Shields], Shaemas (1886–1954),   poet. Born in New York City and an American follower of the Irish renaissance, O'Sheel wrote one poem that became widely known: "They Went Forth to Battle, but They Always Fell." Among his collections are *The Blossomy Bough* (1911), *The Light Feet of Goats* (1915), *Jealous of Dead Leaves* (1938), and *Antigone and Selected Poems* (1960).

Osmond, Gilbert, a character in *The Portrait of a Lady*, by Henry James.

Oskison, John Milton (1874–1947),   novelist, short-story writer, biographer. Born in Vinita in the Indian Territory (now Oklahoma) to a part-Cherokee mother and a white father, Oskison attended Willie Halsell College in Vinita before graduating from Stanford University (B.A., 1898) and undertaking postgraduate study in literature at Harvard. In 1899 his short story "Only the Master Shall Praise" won a *Century Magazine* prize and led to a career as a writer. He published fiction in major periodicals and worked for *The New York Evening Post, Collier's Weekly Magazine* and other journals as an editor, editorial writer and financial expert up to World War I, when he served in Europe as a lieutenant with the American Expeditionary Forces.

His first two novels, *Wild Harvest* (1925) and *Black Jack Davy* (1926), are set in the Indian Territory in the period before statehood. A third, *Brothers Three* (1935), examines the lives of mixed-blood siblings who try and fail to succeed in the white world. *A Texas Titan: The Story of Sam Houston* (1929) and *Tecumseh and His Times: The Story of a Great Indian* (1938) are biographical.

Ossoli, Margaret.   See FULLER, MARGARET.

Ostenso, Martha (1900–1963),   novelist. Brought to North America from Norway at an early age, Martha Ostenso lived in Minnesota, South Dakota, and Manitoba. Her first book, *A Far Land* (1924), was a collection of verse; it was followed by *Wild Geese* (1925), a prize-winning novel and her best-known work. Among her other novels are *The Dark Dawn* (1926), *The Mad Carews* (1927), *The Young May Moon* (1929), *The Waters Under the Earth* (1930), *The White Reef* (1934), *Milk Route* (1948), *Sunset Tree* (1949), and *A Man Had Tall Sons* (1958). They are for the most part set in scenes familiar to Ostenso and realistically described, even though the plots are romantic.

Others,   a poetry magazine founded in 1915, edited by ALFRED KREYMBORG during its four-year life. Ezra Pound described it as "a harum scarum vers libre American product." It was intended to counter Harriet Monroe's more conservative POETRY by encouraging experimentation. It sold about 500 copies of each issue, printing the works of Max Bodenheim, Eliot, John Gould Fletcher, Amy Lowell, Mina Loy, Marianne Moore, Pound, Lola Ridge, Sandburg, Wallace Stevens, and William Carlos Williams. Some of the group, notably Bodenheim, Williams, and Loy helped edit the magazine and exercised influence over its contents. They became known as part of the avant-garde "Others group."

Other Voices, Other Rooms (1948),   a novel by TRUMAN CAPOTE, written when Capote was in his early twenties. Thirteen-year-old Joel Knox arrives at the dilapidated mansion called Skully's Landing and enters a world imbued with dream and fantasy. The house is inhabited by the perfumed, effeminate Randolph, the African-American Jesus Fever and his daughter, Zoo, and Joel's invalid father. Beyond lies the Cloud Hotel, the mysterious retreat of the lunatic African-American Little Sunshine, the place "folks go . . . when they died but were not dead," and where Joel discovers self-awareness and a precocious wisdom that enables him to see the emptiness and paralysis of the inhabitants of Skully's Landing.

Otis, James (1725–1783),   politician, pamphleteer. Born in West Barnstable, Massachusetts, Otis was an ardent patriot during the Revolutionary period whose pamphlets attracted much attention. Beaten on the head in a quarrel with loyalist Tories in 1769, he never completely recovered. He is depicted as Brutus in his sister MERCY OTIS WARREN's play, THE ADULATEUR (1773). Among his writings are *A Vindication of the Conduct of the House of Representatives of the Province of Massachusetts Bay* (1762) and *The Rights of the British Colonies Asserted and Proved* (1764). The *University of Missouri Studies* for 1929 contains his pamphlets, edited by C. F. Mullett.

Ottawa Indians,   part of the Algonquian-Wakashan family of Native Americans. In 1615 Samuel de Champlain noted their settlements on Georgian Bay. They controlled trade with the French in the Ottawa River region, but the Iroquois forced the Ottawas to move west to Wisconsin. Later they settled in Michigan; modern settlements are on islands in Lake St. Clair and Lake Huron. Allied with the French to resist the western movement of English settlers, they took part in the unsuccessful siege of forts at Pittsburgh and Detroit led by a tribesman, PONTIAC. After the Revolution, when colonists secured title to all the lands east of the Mississippi, several expeditions were sent to subdue the Indians. None succeeded until Anthony Wayne defeated the allied tribes at Fallen Timbers, near Maumee, Ohio, in 1794, and they were forced to sue for peace, agreeing to give up all of Ohio and part of Indiana. Andrew J. Blackbird, an Ottawa, wrote *History of the Ottawa and Chippewa Indians of Michigan* (1887, repr. 1977)

Ottley, Roi (1906–1960),   newspaperman, broadcaster, author. Ottley, born in New York City, wrote for numerous magazines and New York City newspapers. He won celebrity with his first book *New World A-Coming* (1943), a brilliant description of African American life in Harlem and elsewhere. Ottley went abroad during the war as correspondent for *Liberty, PM*, and the Pittsburgh *Courier. Black Odyssey* (1948) is a history of African-Americans. *No Green Pastures* (1951) is a survey of race relations in Europe and Africa. *The Lonely Warrior* (1955) is the story of Robert S. Abbott, founder of a crusading newspaper that greatly influenced the African-American press.

Ouâbi, or, The Virtues of Nature (1790),   by SARAH WENTWORTH MORTON. See DEATH SONGS, INDIAN.

Our American Cousin,   a comic play first produced in 1858. Written by the British dramatist Tom Taylor, it pokes fun at Yankees. Lincoln was watching it at Ford's Theater in 1865 when he was shot by John Wilkes Booth.

Our Gang (1971),   a satire on the excesses of the Richard Nixon presidency by PHILIP ROTH.

Our Old Home   (1863, pub. in part in *Atlantic Monthly* in 1862), a series of sketches by NATHANIEL HAWTHORNE. The book was drawn from the period between 1853 and 1858 that Hawthorne spent in England, first as American Consul at Liverpool and later as a tourist. It gives artistic form to many of the details recorded in Hawthorne's *English Notebooks* and is among the best works written by an American about England. After a brief description of his consular duties and the people he met in fulfilling them, Hawthorne's narrative takes the reader through the country of his beloved Dr. Johnson and some of the haunts of Burns. The book concludes with sketches of English poverty and a satiric view of civic banquets.

It is a view of England through honest eyes and is worth attention for its revelations of 19th-century England and America.

Our Town (1938), a play by THORNTON WILDER. Presented without scenery of any kind, utilizing a narrator and a loose episodic form, adventurous and imaginative in style, this unique play won the Pulitzer Prize for Drama in 1938 and is one of the most distinguished in the modern repertoire. It deals with the simplest and most touching aspects of life in a small town. A stage manager casually introduces the characters, and his narration bridges the gap between the audience and the play's action. At times he also enters the scene and becomes part of the play. The play's action centers around the life of the Webb family and the Gibbs family, their neighbors. George Gibbs and Emily Webb fall in love and marry, and she dies while the life of the town continues to move about them.

Our Young Folks. A magazine for younger readers, founded in January 1865 by Ticknor and Fields; it merged with ST. NICHOLAS eight years later. Its chief editors were LUCY LARCOM, Mary Abigail Dodge, and J. T. TROWBRIDGE, who printed in it his serial *Jack Hazard and His Fortunes*, thereafter one of his most popular books. Other contributors included Harriet Beecher Stowe, Whittier, T. W. Higginson, T. B. Aldrich, Elizabeth Stuart Phelps, E. E. Hale, Rose Terry Cooke, Bayard Taylor, Mayne Reid, "Oliver Optic," and Horatio Alger.

Outcasts of Poker Flat, The (*Overland Monthly*, January 1869), a short story by BRET HARTE. This famous tale by Harte is a characteristic mixture of Dickensian sentimentality and Wild West sardonics. In it a group of ne'er-do-wells—the gambler JOHN OAKHURST, two prostitutes, and a drunkard—are expelled from Poker Flat, a western mining camp. They are joined by a naive young couple who are eloping. A blizzard traps them on a mountain pass, and the outcasts, one after another, sacrifice themselves for the young woman, who dies with them. Her lover in the meantime has left to bring help, but returns too late. Whatever the merits or demerits of the story, it helped found the local-color school of American fiction, and its influence is still observed in current writing.

Outcault, R[ichard] F[elton] (1863–1928), cartoonist. Outcault, born in Ohio, created some widely known comic strips, including "Hogan's Alley" (1895) for the New York *World*, the "Yellow Kid" (1896) for the New York *Journal* (the term "yellow journalism" was first applied to the *Journal* as a result of Outcault's drawings), and "Buster Brown" (1902) for the New York *Herald*. A little before any of these, Outcault had published in the Sunday supplement of the New York *World* a colored sequence that in six boxes unfolded the singular transformation of an anaconda that swallowed a succulent yellow dog. The sequence was entitled "The Origin of a New Species," which it was indeed—one of the first comic strips in color. Among his books are *Tige—His Story* (1905), a juvenile book with illustrations; and *My Resolutions: Buster Brown* (1906).

Outland, Tom, a character in *The Professor's House* (1925), by WILLA CATHER.

Outlook, The. A weekly magazine that appeared from 1870 until 1935. Originally it was called the *Christian Union* and was edited by HENRY WARD BEECHER, who had announced in THE INDEPENDENT (1861) that he "would assume the liberty of meddling with every question which agitated the civil or Christian community." In 1893 the name was changed to *The Outlook*, and by that time LYMAN ABBOTT was editor. A sensation was created when THEODORE ROOSEVELT joined its staff in 1909; he wrote articles agitating for many reforms. HAMILTON WRIGHT MABIE was another noted staff member. In 1928 the magazine absorbed *The Independent*. It became a monthly in 1932 as *The New Outlook*.

Out of the Cradle Endlessly Rocking (pub. 1859 in the New York *Saturday Press* as "A Child's Reminiscence"; in the 1860 ed. of LEAVES OF GRASS as "A Word Out of the Sea"; included under its present title in the *Sea-Drift* section of the 1881 ed.), a poem by WALT WHITMAN. Many critics find the poem to have at least three levels: a memory of childhood, a mature expression of love, and a philosophical discovery. The poem describes how a child walking the beach on Long Island hears the call of a bird, a "visitor from Alabama" mourning his lost mate, and ends with the poet being given the "word out of the sea," the word "death." The moment of the revelation from the sea becomes a turning- or maturation-point for the poet, who can never again be the child he once was, having come to an understanding of the real meaning and beauty of death.

Outre-Mer (1835), a series of travel sketches by HENRY WADSWORTH LONGFELLOW. The material for the sketches was gathered during Longfellow's years of study and travel through Europe, in particular, Germany.

Outsider, The, a novel by RICHARD WRIGHT, published in 1953. When Cross Damon, a post office employee is mistakenly reported as dead in a subway accident, he takes the opportunity to escape his debts and romantic entanglements and flee to New York. There he joins the Communist Party under an assumed name. He is manipulated into murder and is killed by a party member.

Overland Monthly (July 1868–July 1935), a magazine founded by a San Francisco bookseller, Anton Roman, and first edited by BRET HARTE. The magazine was intended to be regional, although Harte took care to go beyond the West Coast in his search for authors and material; in fact, he made the *Atlantic Monthly* his model. Harte was then comparatively unknown; in a short time the *Overland* made him celebrated, since in its second issue he printed his story THE LUCK OF ROARING CAMP. The story was a new departure for Harte, and he followed it up with three great stories: THE OUTCASTS OF POKER FLAT, *Miggles*, and TENNESSEE'S PARDNER. In the *Overland* also appeared his best-known poem, "The Heathen Chinee" (called in the magazine PLAIN LANGUAGE FROM TRUTHFUL JAMES). Harte conducted a column called "Etc.," in which he satirized local pecularities like the suppression of news of earthquakes and municipal corruption. He was adroit in winning noted contributors, including Mark Twain, and was particularly friendly to young writers.

When Harte left the *Overland* to go east on a tempting offer from the *Atlantic*, he became something of a lost soul. The *Overland*, too, began to decline. However, it continued to attract notable names: George Sterling, Joaquin Miller, Josiah Royce, Frank Norris, Robinson Jeffers, Edgar Lee Masters, and Jack London. London tells of his experiences as a contributor in his autobiographical novel MARTIN EDEN (1909), where the magazine is called the *Transcontinental Monthly*. See AMBROSE BIERCE.

Over-Soul (1841),   an essay by RALPH WALDO EMERSON. It was included in the *Essays, First Series*. The central thought of a primal mind, a cosmic unity in its Platonic sense, is one found everywhere in Emerson's writings. Here he defines it again: "It is the soul of the whole; the wise silence; the universal beauty to which every part and particle is equally related; the Eternal One."

Over the Hill to the Poor House (*Harper's Weekly*, June 17, 1871),   a poem by WILL CARLETON, included in his *Farm Ballads* (1873). "Over the hill to the poor-house I'm trudgin' my weary way," says the speaker in the poem; and includes details of his family life: "She had an edication, an' that was good for her; But when she twitted me on mine, 'twas carryin' things too fur."

Owen, Robert Dale (1801–1877),   social reformer, author, statesman. Born in Scotland, Robert Dale Owen was the eldest son of the English reformer Robert Owen. He represented his father's ideas in the United States in numerous articles and pamphlets beginning with his editorship of the New Harmony *Gazette* from 1825 to 1827. Soon after the failure of his father's utopian community at New Harmony, Indiana, Dale Owen came under the influence of Frances (Fanny) Wright and became editor of her paper, the *Free Enquirer*, patterned after the defunct *Gazette*. When this too failed, he turned to politics and served in Congress and in the Indiana Legislature. He managed to effectuate some of his educational and legal reforms and is responsible for the bill that established the Smithsonian Institution. While he was U.S. Minister at Naples (1855–58) he became interested in spiritualism and wrote two explanatory books: *Footfalls on the Boundary of Another World* (1860) and *The Debatable Land Between This World and the Next* (1872). His most influential work, however, is in the field of social or political reform: *The Policy of Emancipation* (1863), *The Wrong of Slavery* (1864), *The Future of the Northwest* (1863), and *Divorce: Being a Correspondence Between Horace Greeley and Robert Dale Owen* (1860). His miscellaneous works in other fields include *Hints on Public Architecture* (1849); *Pocahontas: An Historical Drama* (1838); and *Beyond the Breakers* (1870), a novel. His autobiography is called *Threading My Way* (1874).

Ox-Bow Incident, The (1940),   a novel by WALTER VAN TILBURG CLARK. Set in Nevada in 1885, this powerful story tells how three supposed cattle rustlers are lynched—just as word comes that they are innocent. The novel had implications of World War II and the struggle between democracy and totalitarianism, justice and ruthlessness. It was filmed in 1942.

Oz, The Land of.   This was an imaginary realm created by L. FRANK BAUM and made the scene of fourteen stories for children. The first, THE WONDERFUL WIZARD OF OZ (1900), was the most successful and was made into a popular musical comedy, *The Wizard of Oz* (1901), and an equally successful film (1939). The series was continued by Ruth Plumly Thompson and other writers.

Ozark Mountains, the.   These mountains constitute an eroded tableland that extends from southwestern Missouri across northwestern Arkansas into eastern Oklahoma. It is part of the speech region called Appalachia; for centuries it was a backwater of American culture, in which survived many folk beliefs, folktales, and locutions not found elsewhere in the United States.

Among books on the Ozarks are Vance Randolph's *The Ozarks* (1931), *Ozark Mountain Folks* (1932), *Ozark Superstitions* (1947), *Ozark Folksongs* (1950), *Tall Tales from the Ozarks* (1951), *Who Blowed Up the Church House? and Other Ozark Folk Tales* (1952), *Down in the Holler: A Gallery of Ozark Folk Speech* (with George P. Wilson, 1953), and *The Devil's Pretty Daughter* (1955). Fiction includes H. B. Wright's *That Printer of Udell's* (1903) and *The Shepherd of the Hills* (1907); and MacKinlay Kantor's *The Voice of Bugle Ann* (1935) and *Daughter of Bugle Ann* (1953).

Ozick, Cynthia (1928–   ),   novelist, short-story writer, essayist. Cynthia Ozick was born in The Bronx, New York. The author of four novels, three collections of short fiction, and two collections of essays, Ozick is a writer who blossomed late, but gradually emerged as the dominant voice for new directions in Jewish-American writing. Unlike many fiction writers identified with the American Jewish renaissance, Ozick brings considerable Jewish learning to her imaginative work. The result has been a series of fictions that pit Pan against Moses, unbridled passions against the fences of law. Moments in her first long, and largely unsuccessful novel, *Trust* (1966), intimate this theme, but the stories in *The Pagan Rabbi* (1971) make it breathtakingly clear. For many years Ozick worried so about the idol-making character of fiction—in the essays collected as *Art & Ardor* (1983)—as well as in fictions ranging from *Bloodshed* (1976) and *Levitation* (1982) to *The Cannibal Galaxy* (1983) and *The Messiah of Stockholm* (1987) that critics began to worry about her obsessive self-abnegation. However, her latest collections of essays—*Metaphor & Myth* (1989), *Fame & Folly* (1996), and *Quarrel and Quandary* (2000)—demonstrate that literature need make no apologies for its potential as an abiding, even necessary, moral force. That force is amply demonstrated in *The Shawl* (1989), Ozick's harrowing tale of a Holocaust survivor. Studies of Ozick's work include S. Pinsker's *The Uncompromising Fictions of Cynthia Ozick* (1987), J. Lowin's *Cynthia Ozick* (1988), E. Kauvar's *Cynthia Ozick's Fiction* (1993), S. Cohen's *Cynthia Ozick's Comic Art* (1994), and V. Strandberg's *Greek Mind/Jewish Soul* (1994).

SANFORD PINSKER

P

Pacing Mustang, the. A widespread legend of a magnificent stallion that was often seen but never captured. The first printed report of its presence is found in Washington Irving's TOUR ON THE PRAIRIES (1835). JOSIAH GREGG heard "marvelous tales," reported in his *Commerce of the Prairies* (1844), of a stallion of "perfect symmetry, milk-white, save a pair of black ears." These stories circulated, he said, in the northern Rockies, on the Arkansas, near the borders of Texas. In 1851 Melville introduced the Pacing Mustang into MOBY-DICK in his chapter "The Whiteness of the Whale."

Pack, Robert (1929–   ),   poet, editor. Born in New York City, Pack came to be associated with modern poetry when he was coeditor with Donald Hall and Louis Simpson of the anthology *The New Poets of England and America* (1957). His own work has been collected in *The Irony of Joy* (1955), *A Stranger's Privilege* (1959), *Guarded by Women* (1963), *Home from the Cemetery* (1969), *Nothing but Light* (1972), and *Keeping Watch* (1976). Selections from five books (1980–1992) appear in *Fathering the Map: New and Selected Poems* (1993). More recent volumes of poems include *Minding the Sun* (1996) and *Rounding It Out: A Cycle of Sonnetelles* (1999), verse in a sixteen-line form, derived from the sonnet and villanelle, invented by Pack. Prose is collected in *The Long View: Essays on the Discipline of Hope and the Poetic Craft* (1991). Pack has also been an active anthologist, especially of work connected with his years teaching writing at Breadloaf.

Packard, Vance (1914–1996),   social critic. His best-selling books criticize the American social scene. *The Hidden Persuaders* (1957) deals with the use of motivational research by advertising agencies. *The Status Seekers* (1959) is an analysis of attempts to achieve higher social standing. *The Waste Makers* (1960) is a criticism of the business practice of using built-in obsolescence to increase consumption. *The Ultra Rich: How Much Is Too Much* (1989) examines the new wealth in the U.S.

Padilla, Heberto (1932–2000),   poet, novelist, memoirist. Born in Pinar del Rio, Cuba, Padilla was employed in the United States as a translator and radio commentator when support for the revolution brought him home in 1959 to work for the Castro regime as an editor, journalist and foreign correspondent. His international renown came later, as a dissident. For *Fuera del juego* (1968, tr. *Out of the Game*), poems, he

was denounced as a counterrevolutionary. Briefly jailed in 1971 and forced into a "confession," he found his case taken up by the international literary community and in 1980 he was allowed to leave Cuba for the United States, where he taught and wrote until his death. In a novel *En mi jardin pastan los heroes* (1981, tr. *Heroes Are Grazing in My Garden,* 1984) and a memoir *Self-Portrait of the Other* (1990), he expressed his disillusionment with Castro's Cuba. Later volumes of poems are *Selected Poems* (1982) and *A Fountain, a House of Stone* (1991, bilingual).

Page, Elizabeth (1889–?),   teacher, welfare worker, novelist. The diary of her great-uncle Henry Page, who was a Forty-Niner, gave Vermont-born Elizabeth Page information for one of her best-known novels, *Wagons West* (1930). Her most admired work is *The Tree of Liberty* (1939), which portrays the conflict between the Jeffersonians and the Hamiltonians. Among her other books are *Wild Horses and Gold* (1932) and *Wilderness Adventure* (1946).

Page, P[atricia] K[athleen] (1916–   ),   poet, short-story writer. Born in Southern England, Page came to Canada as a child. She has been called the most brilliant member of the group of experimental writers associated with the magazine *Preview* during the 1940s. Her work appeared in their anthology, *Unit of Five* (1944). Though she shares with the other poets of this group a concern with social realities, "her flair," it has been pointed out, "is psychological rather than political." Her publications include *As Ten as Twenty* (1946); *The Metal and the Flower* (1954, Governor General's Award); *Cry Arafat!* a poetry collection published in 1967 after Page's many years abroad as the wife of W. A. Irwin, Canadian Ambassador to Australia, Brazil, and Mexico, *Poems Selected and New* (1974); *Evening Dance of the Grey Flies* (1981); *The Glass Air* (1985); *The Glass Air: Poems Selected and New* (1991); and *Hologram; A Book of Glosas* (1994). Page also edited *To Say the Least: Canadian Poets from A to Z* in 1979.

Page, Thomas Nelson (1853–1922),   lawyer, diplomat, novelist, historian, essayist. Page, born and brought up on a Virginia plantation, was related to many Southern first families. He practiced law in Richmond, but soon found his calling as a romantic writer. After his dialect story MARSE CHAN was printed in the *Century Magazine* (April 1884), he wrote other stories, collected in IN OLE VIRGINIA (1887). His *Red Rock* (1898), long a bestseller, thrilled readers with its picture of the Southern revolt against Reconstruction that gave rise to the Ku Klux Klan. The same sentimental and romantic spirit is seen in *The Old Gentleman of the Black Stock* (1897), a love story; *Two Little Confederates* (1888), a story for children; the novels *Gordon Keith* (1903) and *John Marvel, Assistant* (1909); and *The Red Riders* (1924), finished by Rosewell Page, his brother. Page's other books are *The Old South* (1892), *Social Life in Old Virginia* (1897), *The Old Dominion* (1908), and *Robert E. Lee, Man and Soldier* (1911). From 1913 to 1919 Page was ambassador to Italy. His writings were collected in 18 volumes issued from 1906 to 1918. A biography, *Thomas Nelson Page*, was published in 1923 by Rosewell Page. Theodore L. Gross, *Thomas Nelson Page* (1967), is a brief study.

Page, Walter Hines (1855–1918),   journalist, diplomat. Born in North Carolina, Page edited the St. Joseph (Missouri) *Gazette*, then worked on the New York *World* from 1881 to 1883. After he gained control of the Raleigh (North Carolina) *State Chronicle*, he advocated drastic reforms in the South. In 1891 he took over the *Forum* and in 1898 became editor of *Atlantic Monthly* and revitalized it. In the next year he launched the publishing firm of Doubleday, Page (later, Doubleday & Co.). In 1913 Woodrow Wilson appointed him ambassador to England. His enthusiasm for the Allied cause and his generally pro-British bias are evident in his *Letters* (1922–25). His other writings include *The Rebuilding of Old Commonwealths* (1902); *A Publisher's Confession* (1905); and, under the pen name Nicholas Worth, *The Southerner* (1909).

Pain, Philip,   a poet whose only known work is *Daily Meditations* (1668), printed in Massachusetts. Details of his life are unknown; the title page of his book states only that the author "lately suffering shipwreck, was drowned." The book is subtitled *Quotidian Preparations for, and Considerations of Death and Eternity.*

Paine, Albert Bigelow (1861–1937),   biographer, editor, dramatist, novelist, writer for children: Born in Massachusetts and raised in Illinois, Paine has been remembered chiefly for his association with MARK TWAIN. After Twain accepted Paine's 1906 proposal of collaboration, Paine used a stenographer to record Twain's memories and anecdotes. Paine published a volume of Twain's *Speeches* (1910), the three-volume *Mark Twain, A Biography* (1912), *Mark Twain's Letters* (2 v. 1917), and *Mark Twain's Autobiography* (2 v. 1924). Some critics have castigated his lack of objectivity, but he performed a valuable service in preserving materials that might otherwise have been lost.

Paine's long list of titles includes *The Bread Line* (1900); *The Van Dwellers* (1901); *The Great White Way* (1901), which gave its name to Broadway; *The Commuters* (1904); *Thomas Nast* (1904); *Joan of Arc—Maid of France* (1925), for which he received the Legion of Honor in 1928; and *Life* and *Lillian Gish* (1932). He also wrote more than twenty volumes of stories and rhymes for children, the best-known being *The Arkansaw Bear* (1898).

Paine, Ralph D[elahaye] (1871–1925),   newspaperman, novelist, short-story writer, historian. Paine was born in Illinois and served as a war correspondent during the Spanish-American War. He wrote more than thirty books, at least twenty of them dealing with the sea. He described many of his own experiences in *Roads of Adventure* (1922). He wrote both fiction and nonfiction for young people, wholesome books now neglected. Among them are *The Praying Skipper and Other Stories* (1906), *The Ships and Sailors of Old Salem* (1909), *The Book of Buried Treasure* (1911), *The Judgments of the Sea and Other Stories* (1912), *The Adventures of Captain O'Shea* (1913), *The Long Road Home* (1916), *Lost Ships and Lonely Seas* (1921), and *Joshua Barney* (1924).

Paine, Robert Treat   [the younger] (1773–1811), poet, drama critic, editor, lawyer. Born in Massachusetts, Paine was a younger son of Robert Treat Paine (1731–1814), the noted patriot, and was an ardent supporter of the Federalists. His most important poems were *The Invention of Letters* (1795), *The Ruling Passion* (1797), and "Adams and Liberty" (1798), a campaign song. His drama criticism is probably the best of his writing. Much of it is included in *The Works in Verse and Prose of the Late Robert Treat Paine, Jr.* (1812). See DELLA CRUSCANISM.

Paine, Thomas (1737–1809),   editor, writer. Paine, born in England, was the son of a Quaker father—Paine liked to think of himself as a Friend—and a mother who was a member of the Church of England. He left school at age thirteen and worked at various jobs without any great success. For a time he was a tax collector, a job that left him with a hatred of social inequality. During one of BENJAMIN FRANKLIN's visits to England the two met; Franklin was impressed with Paine and persuaded him to emigrate to America. Paine arrived in Philadelphia in 1774 and on Franklin's recommendation was made editor of the *Pennsylvania Magazine*, the first issue of which appeared in January 1775. In his essays for the magazine Paine advocated ideas far in advance of his time, among them women's rights, freedom for slaves, a system of international arbitration, national and international copyright, and kindness to animals.

When the Battle of Lexington was fought, Paine's course was set. He left his editorship and gave all his energy to the new cause. He joined Washington's army in its retreat across New Jersey in 1776 and seems to have won at once the esteem of the commander-in-chief. When the troops reached Newark, Paine sat on a log alongside a campfire and with a drumhead for a desk wrote the first of the series of pamphlets called THE AMERICAN CRISIS. The opening lines of the first number became the most famous that Paine ever wrote: "These are the times that try men's souls. The summer soldier and the sunshine patriot will, in this crisis, shrink from the service of his country, but he that stands it now deserves the love and thanks of man and woman. Tyranny, like hell, is not easily conquered; yet we have this consolation with us, that the harder the conflict, the more glorious the triumph. . . ." Washington ordered the words read to his shivering men, and the pamphlet helped inspire the surprising defeat of the British at Trenton a few days later. When the first number of *The Crisis* was published, it continued to exert a great effect, prepared for by Paine's earlier publication COMMON SENSE (1776), which had made him a leading propagandist of the patriot cause. Paine continued to write issues of *The Crisis* at Morristown and perhaps at Trenton. To commemorate his stay at Morristown, a statue by George J. Lober showing Paine writing on his drumhead was unveiled on July 4, 1950.

The last number of *The Crisis* was published in 1783. All the issues had had a considerable effect on public opinion, because they spoke for the man in the street or in the field; they were a passionate expression of all men's desire for freedom. Paine, though poor, refused all royalties and gave the copyright to the United States.

In 1787 Paine began a new career in Europe. A man of considerable inventive ability, he returned to the Old World with an entirely peaceful intention—to perfect an iron bridge. But he soon found himself in the midst of a new revolutionary turmoil. He was invited by the French to become a member from Pas-de-Calais in the National Assembly, an honor that made him the first modern international. To Franklin's remark, "Where Liberty is, there is my country," came Paine's amendment, "Where Liberty is not, there is mine. My country is the world; to do good, my religion."

The French Revolution divided opinion in America almost as deeply as in Europe. Among those affected were Paine and THOMAS JEFFERSON; and the difference in their outlook—Paine an internationalist, Jefferson still a nationalist—caused a break between them. Elsewhere Paine met violent opposition. JOHN ADAMS [2] had once said of him: "Washington's sword would have been wielded in vain had it not been supported by the pen of Paine. History is to ascribe the American Revolution to Paine." But now Adams called him "the filthy Tom Paine," starting a vicious epithet on its way down the centuries. In London clubs men wore TP nails in their boot heels to bear witness to their trampling on his principles. He was proscribed and his books burned by the hangman. Yet he kept on writing. When Edmund Burke published his *Reflections on the French Revolution* (1790), Paine wrote a reply that he called THE RIGHTS OF MAN (1791), which appeared with a dedication to George Washington. It was a vindication of the republican form of government of the United States, whose constitution he declared was "to liberty what a grammar is to language." Against Burke's theory of a single, static contract, Paine reaffirmed the doctrine of natural rights, arguing that each new generation has the right to decide how it shall be governed. The book was widely circulated, and a *Second Part* appeared in 1792.

Vituperation against Paine reached such heights that his life was in danger. He managed to escape from England and return to France, where he was enthusiastically received in the convention drafting a constitution for the Republic. He was one of the few persons active in the early years of the Revolution who escaped the guillotine. But it was not because he ceased to be outspoken. One of his most courageous acts was

to vote and write against the execution of the French monarch. He lined up with the moderates and incurred Robespierre's suspicions, was imprisoned, and escaped death only because the French tyrant himself was executed just as he was about to order Paine's death.

At the time, Paine was writing his last important book, THE AGE OF REASON (Parts I & II, 1794, 1796), part of it in prison. It was his most controversial work and his most misunderstood. Actually his views were held by many who shared in the 18th-century Enlightenment, and he was emphatically not an atheist. But he undertook a rational scrutiny of the Scriptures, much in the spirit of the later "higher criticism," and his analysis of Biblical revelation offended many readers deeply. Yet he was sincere, even impressive, in his affirmation of faith as a product of Nature and Reason. One English bishop held that many of Paine's ideas of God have a "philosophical sublimity."

Paine returned to America in 1802. He lived in New York City, in Bordentown, New Jersey, and in New Rochelle, New York. He was poverty-stricken and in poor health, and he was ostracized and attacked bitterly and unjustly. Even when he died he was not allowed to rest in peace. He had asked to be buried on his little farm at New Rochelle, but William Cobbett, the eccentric English pamphleteer, visited America in 1819 and dug up the coffin and took it to England. There he was not allowed to bury the body, so what became of Paine's bones is unknown.

One of Paine's earliest biographers was James Cheetham, a personal enemy whose *Life of Thomas Paine* (1809) first applied the phrase "filthy little atheist" to Paine. The epithet made Americans forget that Congress on August 26, 1785, had "*Resolved*, That the early and continued labors of Thomas Paine and his timely publications merit the approbation of this Congress." It was *The Age of Reason* that primarily caused the trouble, along with Paine's uncomplimentary letter of 1796 to Washington, written because Washington, like Burke, saw anarchy in the French Revolution. When Paine came to the United States in 1802, President Jefferson was embarrassed to receive him publicly, even though he, better than most, understood Paine's views and motives. Unfounded, ridiculous stories of Paine's drunkenness and personal slovenliness proliferated. A frightened stage driver refused to give him a seat, in 1806 he was denied the right to vote, and he was reported to have been overcome by horror and remorse on his deathbed. During his own lifetime two unfriendly biographies were published, the one by Cheetham and another by George Chalmers (London, 1791). These were somewhat corrected by Thomas C. Rickman's *Life* (London, 1819). Even friendlier was a biography by Calvin Blanchard (1860, 1877). But the ideas of the revilers persisted despite defenses by such men as Lincoln and Whitman. On the eve of the Civil War the City Council of Philadelphia refused a portrait of Paine intended for Independence Hall. For a long time the New York Historical Society kept a bust of Paine hidden in order to protect it. Theodore Roosevelt repeated the epithet "filthy little atheist." The first energetic attempt at rehabilitation was made by Rev. Moncure

D. Conway, a Congregationalist minister, in his biography of Paine (1892) and his four-volume *Writings of Thomas Paine* (1894–96). Since then, despite outcroppings of the old calumnies, Paine's reputation has continued to grow, and today there is a considerable Paine cult. His cottage in New Rochelle has been made a memorial under the care of the Huguenot and Historical Society, and his home in Bordentown is also a memorial.

Besides the publications mentioned above, these writings by Paine may be listed: *The Case of the Officers of Excise* (1772, 1793); *Epistle to the People Called Quakers* (1776); *Public Good* (1780); *Reasons for Wishing to Preserve the Life of Louis Capet* (1793); *Dissertation on First-Principles of Government* (1795); *The Decline and Fall of the English System of Finance* (1796); *Agrarian Justice* (1797); *Letter to the People of France and the French Armies* (1797); *Letters to the Citizens of the United States of America* (1802–03); and *Miscellaneous Poems* (1819). In addition to Conway, the following have edited collections of Paine's writings: Daniel E. Wheeler (10 v. 1908); William M. Van der Weyde (10 v. 1925); and Philip S. Foner (2 v. 1945).

Books on Paine include Hesketh Pearson's *Tom Paine, Friend of Mankind* (1937); John Dos Passos's *The Living Thoughts of Tom Paine* (1940); Alfred O. Aldridge, *Man of Reason: The Life of Thomas Paine* (1959); Owen Aldridge, *Thomas Paine's American Ideology* (1984); David Powell, *Tom Paine: The Greatest Exile* (1985); Jack Fruchtman, *Thomas Paine: Apostle of Freedom* (1994); and John Keane, *Tom Paine: A Political Life* (1995). Howard Fast's *Citizen Tom Paine* (1943) is a fictionalized biography.

HERBERT FAULKNER WEST/BP

Painted Veils (1920), a novel by JAMES HUNEKER. Huneker used as background the art world of New York City that he knew so well, introducing many people under their real names. In addition he digressed readily into discussion of the art movements of the day. The morals of the fictional characters are for the most part free-and-easy. The book was privately printed and was regarded as very daring in its day.

Pale Fire (1962), a novel by VLADIMIR NABOKOV containing a 999-line poem by the fictional John Shade and notes and commentaries on the poem by the dead poet's neighbor, Charles Kinbote. In his exegesis, Kinbote claims to be Charles Xavier, the last king of Zembla, hunted by the revolutionaries who deposed him. Shade is said to have been killed by accident by Gradus, one of the assassins. The many-layered novel parodies pedantic literary scholarship.

Pale Horse, Pale Rider (1934) is a collection of three short novels by KATHERINE ANNE PORTER including *Old Mortality, Noon Wine*, and the title story, one of the author's masterpieces.

Paley, Grace (1922–), short-story writer, poet. Born and educated in New York City, where many of her spare stories are set, Paley has been a politically active writer. She helped found the Greenwich Village Peace Center in 1961 and is an active feminist. Faith, who appears as a narrator or character in many of the fictions, is similarly political. Her story

collections are *The Little Disturbances of Man* (1959), *Enormous Changes at the Last Minute* (1974), *Later the Same Day* (1985), and *The Collected Stories* (1994). Other books include *Just as I Thought* (1998), prose pieces forming a record of her activist life, and *Begin Again: Collected Poems* (2000).

Palfrey, John Gorham (1796–1881), clergyman, historian, editor, teacher. Palfrey, born in Boston, owned and edited the NORTH AMERICAN REVIEW (1835–43), taught sacred literature at Harvard (1831–39), delivered and published the *Lowell Lectures on the Evidences of Christianity* (2 v. 1843), analyzed the *Relation Between Judaism and Christianity* (1854), and wrote an elaborate *History of New England* (5 v. 1858–90).

Pal Joey (1940), a collection of twelve stories by JOHN O'HARA. Celebrated stories about an infamous character, "a tap-dancing heel," these first appeared in *The New Yorker* (October 22, 1938–July 13, 1940), then in book form. They were transformed into a hit musical (1940), with music and lyrics by RICHARD RODGERS and LORENZ HART, the book by O'Hara.

Palma, Ricardo (1833–1919), Peruvian writer and politician. In his youth, Palma fought in civil wars. The high point of his political career came when he served as senator (1868–1872). In 1872 he published his first series of *Tradiciones Peruanas*, witty anecdotes based on Peruvian history and legend. Eight other collections appeared between 1974 and 1910. These skillfully written anecdotes, presenting a skeptical view of human behavior, made his reputation as a leading Peruvian writer. Palma was Director of the National Library from 1883–1912. He added thousands of volumes to replace books lost during the war between Peru and Chile (War of the Pacific, 1879–1883), and his forced retirement from the position saddened his later life.

Palmer, Alice Freeman (1855–1902), educator, poet. Born in Colesville, New York, Palmer in 1882 became president of the young Wellesley College. Under her administration the Academic Council was formed, entrance examinations were stiffened, courses of study standardized, and the faculty strengthened. She founded the Association of Collegiate Alumnae, forerunner of the American Association of University Women, in 1882. In 1887 she married Professor GEORGE HERBERT PALMER of Harvard. After her death her husband published a little volume of her poetry entitled *A Marriage Cycle* (1915), a touching tribute to the felicitous partnership of two extraordinary individuals. He also wrote *The Life of Alice Freeman Palmer* in 1908.

Palmer, George Herbert (1842–1933), philosopher, teacher. Palmer was born in Boston and educated at Harvard and the Andover Theological Seminary. After teaching Greek at Harvard, he transferred to the Philosophy Department. He was one of the first professors at Harvard to abandon textbooks and work out his ideas in lecture form. Among his numerous philosophical works are *The Field of Ethics* (1901), *The Nature of Goodness* (1903), *The Problem of Freedom* (1911), and *Altruism: Its Nature and Variety* (1919). His literary and critical works include *The English Works of George Herbert* (3 v. 1905), *The Life of Alice Freeman Palmer* (1908),

Intimations of Immortality in the Sonnets of Shakespere (1912), and *Formative Types in English Poetry* (1918). He also wrote a much-admired translation of Homer's *Odyssey* (1884). His *Autobiography of a Philosopher* appeared in 1930.

Palmer, Michael [Stephen] (1943–   ),   poet. Born in New York City, Palmer was educated at Harvard (B.A., French, 1965; M.A., Comparative Literature, 1967). With Clark Coolidge, an editor of a little magazine, *Joglars* (1964–1966) in Providence, Rhode Island, he has also, with Coolidge and others, been associated with CLAYTON ESHLEMAN's influential *Sulfur*. A long-time resident of San Francisco, where he has taught at the New College of California, he has been classed with the LANGUAGE POETS, but accepts more narrative and referential content in his verse than others of that movement. *The Lion Bridge: Selected Poems, 1972–1995* was published in 1998. Newer poems appear in *The Promise of Glass* (2000), as Palmer enriches his reputation among significant experimental poets of our time. Earlier volumes include his first, *Plan of the City of O* (1971); *Blake's Newton* (1972); *The Circular Gates* (1974); *Without Music* (1977); *Notes for Echo Lake* (1981); *First Figure* (1984); *Sun* (1988); and *At Passages* (1995). He edited *Code of Signals: Recent Writings in Poetics* (1983) and has written a number of dance scenarios for the Margaret Jenkins Dance Company.

Palmer, Ray (1808–1887),   teacher, clergyman, hymn writer. Palmer, born in Rhode Island, was at first a teacher in New York and Connecticut and then served in Congregational pulpits in Maine, New York, and New Jersey. His hymns and other verses were collected in *Hymns and Sacred Pieces* (1865), *Hymns of My Holy Hours* (1867), and *The Poetical Works by Ray Palmer* (1876).

Palóu, Francisco (1722?–1789?),   missionary. In 1749 Palóu, who was born in Majorca, accompanied JUNÍPERO SERRA to Mexico. He was one of the Spanish Franciscan group that replaced the Jesuits in Baja California (1768). Five years later he moved northward and founded the Mission Dolores (1776), still standing in San Francisco and its oldest building. He wrote a *Life of Junípero Serra* (1787, English tr. 1913); his numerous reports and letters have been gathered as *Historical Memoirs of New California* (4 v. 1926).

Papp, Joseph (1921–1991),   theater producer and director. Born Joseph Papirofsky in Brooklyn, New York, Papp founded the New York Shakespeare Festival and Public Theater. He studied acting and directing at the Actor's Laboratory Theatre in Hollywood (1946–48) before signing on as a stage manager for the *Death of a Salesman* national touring company. He also served as stage manager for Columbia Broadcasting System's television network in the 50s. In 1954 he founded the New York Shakespeare Festival, a unique project presenting free performances of Shakespearean plays in such outdoor locations as Central Park. He worked for little or no pay, produced and directed most of the productions himself, and remained artistic director of the group until his death. An offshoot of the first group, the New York Shakespeare Festival Public Theatre, founded in 1967, concentrated on contemporary and experi-

mental drama. Several of its productions ended up at the Public's Broadway theaters, including the musicals *Hair* (1967) and *A Chorus Line* (1975), and David Rabe's *Sticks and Bones* (1971). Papp was a major innovator who recognized the talent of such writers as DAVID RABE and JOHN GUARE, and encouraged actors including George C. Scott and Meryl Streep.

Paretsky, Sara (1947–   ),   writer of mystery thrillers. Born in Ames, Iowa, Paretsky was educated at the University of Kansas (B.A., 1967) and the University of Chicago (Ph.D., 1977; M.B.A., 1977). A career in business was transformed to one in writing when she conceived the character V.I. Warshawsky, private investigator, a woman "who was doing what I was doing, which was trying to make a success in a field traditionally dominated by men." Warshawsky, half Polish, half Italian, from the South Side of Chicago, is a first-person narrator, city-wise in the Raymond Chandler tradition, whose fans appreciate her blue-collar origins and the gritty toughness with which she pursues her quarry. She is featured in novels rich in the politics of time and place, written, Paretsky has said, "right up against the place where people's basest and basic needs intersect with law and justice." They include *Indemnity Only* (1982), in which Warshawsky tracks a woman missing from the University of Chicago; *Deadlock* (1984), a Chicago dockside murder mystery; *Killing Orders* (1985), with five million dollars in stocks missing from a Chicago monastery; *Bitter Medicine* (1987), corruption in the medical profession; *Blood Shot* (1988), pollution of natural resources; *Burn Marks* (1990), arson and politics; *Guardian Angel* (1992), exploitation of the elderly; *Tunnel Vision* (1994), flooding threatens the homeless; *Hard Time* (1999), contrasting the extremes of rich and poor in Chicago; and *Total Recall* (2001). *Windy City Blues* (1995) is a collection of Warshawsky short stories. *Ghost Country* (1998) follows debutante sisters through a series of bizarre events, with no V.I. Warshawsky in sight.

Paris Review, The (1953–   ),   a highly influential quarterly publication including literary and art criticism, poetry, fiction, and social comment. Founded by GEORGE PLIMPTON and other young Americans living abroad, the first issue inaugurated a series of detailed interviews with major contemporary writers. The first of these, with E. M. Forster, set the pattern of insightful discussion of the craft of fiction. A series of these collected profiles, *Writers at Work*, has appeared as separate publications beginning in 1958. *The Paris Review Anthology*, edited by George Plimpton, appeared in 1990.

Parish, Elijah (1762–1825),   a Congregational minister from Connecticut who wrote with Jedidiah Morse *A Compendious History of New England* (1804).

Parke, John (1754–1789),   soldier, poet, translator. Parke, born in Dover, Delaware, was educated at Newark College in Delaware and the College of Philadelphia and became an excellent classical scholar. He served in the Continental Army from 1775 to 1778 in the Quartermaster's Department and lived thereafter in retirement. He published only one volume, which also contains contributions by his friend David French. The collection was called *The Lyric Works of Horace, to*

Which Are Added a Number of Original Poems (1786). His renderings of Horace anticipate some of the later efforts of American verse writers like EUGENE FIELD and FRANKLIN P. ADAMS, who take their themes and viewpoints from Horace but give the renderings a contemporary setting. The collection included some original verses in the then current neoclassical style, and a play, *Virginia*.

Parker, Arthur Caswell (1881–1955), ethnologist, archaeologist, writer. Parker was born on the Cattaraugus Reservation of the Senecas. His great-uncle General Ely S. Parker was the "last grand sachem of the Iroquois and General Grant's military secretary," according to a biography of his kinsman that Parker published in 1919. Parker occupied important posts as an archaeologist and ethnologist, being especially interested in American Indians. Among his books are *Erie Indian Village* (1907), *Maize and Other Plant Foods* (1909), *Code of Handsome Lake* (1913), *Constitution of the Five Nations* (1916), *Archaeological History of N.Y.* (1922), *Seneca Myths and Folk Tales* (1923), *Indian How Book* (1927), *Gustango Gold* (1930), and *Manual for History Museums*.

Parker, Charlotte Blair (1868–1937), a playwright whose *Way Down East* (1898) enjoyed two decades of success.

Parker, Dorothy [Rothschild] (1893–1967), poet, short-story writer. Parker, born in New Jersey, began her career by writing occasional verse, playing the piano in a dancing school, and writing captions for a fashion magazine—she is credited with the advertising epigram "Brevity is the soul of lingerie." She became drama critic of *Vanity Fair* in 1917, but was discharged in 1920 because her reviews were too harsh. Thereafter, she frequently wrote drama and book reviews for *The New Yorker*, which turned a deaf ear to the cries of the wounded. Parker was noted for the sharpness of her critical sallies, as when she described Katherine Hepburn in *The Lake* as running "the whole gamut of emotion from A to B." A good many other trenchancies, dispensed in prose, verse, or random discourse, earned her a reputation for caustic wit probably unequaled by any other female American of her generation.

Parker's publications include ENOUGH ROPE (verse 1926, new ed. 1933); *Sunset Gun* (verse 1928); *Laments for the Living* (stories 1930); *Death and Taxes* (verse 1931); and *After Such Pleasures* (stories 1933). The verse has been collected in *Not So Deep as a Well* (1936), the stories in *Here Lies* (1939). She also wrote a play with ELMER RICE, *Close Harmony* (1924). *The Viking Portable Dorothy Parker*, which contains all her major works, appeared in 1944. In her verse Parker loved to write on departed or departing love, the fickle female, various types of suitors, memories of love, and occasionally more weighty themes. She was sardonic, rather limited in range, and drily elegant in meter and rhyme, although she could at times leave this realm and write a beautiful Christmas poem like "Prayer for a New Mother." Her stories are as profound in their knowledge of human nature as they are deep in disenchantment. Some, like "Big Blonde," have become classics; others, like "Lady with a Lamp," "Glory in the Daytime," and "A Telephone Call," are almost as good. They are often dramatized wisecracks at the expense of sentimentality.

Parker, Sir [Horatio] Gilbert (1862–1932), novelist. Parker, born in Ontario, wrote verse at sixteen, studied for the ministry at Trinity College, Toronto, and taught English there. In poor health, he went around the world, and for four years was associate editor of the Sydney (Australia) *Morning Herald*. Returning to Canada, he wrote short stories, collected in *Pierre and His People* (1892), and became the Dominion's best-known novelist. *The Seats of the Mighty* (1896), a novel of the fall of Quebec, was a best seller, and so was *The Right of Way* (1901). From 1898 on he lived in England and was knighted in 1902. He also wrote *A Ladder of Swords* (1904), *The Weavers* (1907), *The Judgment House* (1913), *The Power and the Glory* (1925), and many short stories as well as propaganda for the Allied cause during World War I.

Parker, Jane Marsh (1836–1913), author. The daughter of WILLIAM MILLER, she wrote two novels about the Millerites.

Parker, Robert B[rown] (1932–), novelist, writer of detective fiction. Born in Springfield, Massachusetts, Parker graduated from Colby College (B.A., 1954), served in the Army (1954–1956) during the Korean War, and began graduate work at Boston University (M.A., 1957). Working as a technical writer and film consultant in Boston and vicinity and writing advertising for a Boston agency, he taught in several Massachusetts colleges, and completed a Ph.D. at Boston University in 1970. For his doctoral thesis on the American hero, he wrote of the novels of the hard-boiled detective writers RAYMOND CHANDLER, DASHIELL HAMMETT, and ROSS MACDONALD. In *The Godwulf Manuscript* (1974), he introduced Spenser, a Boston policeman turned private investigator who has now appeared in about thirty novels. Among them, the early *God Save the Child* (1974), *Mortal Stakes* (1975), *Promised Land* (1976), and *The Judas Goat* (1978) gave Parker the confidence and income to retire from teaching. Other Spenser novels have appeared at the rate of one or two a year and Spenser has appeared in a popular television series, *Spenser for Hire*, and in television movies. Most of the time the setting is Boston, with Spenser's sidekick Hawk and his psychologist girl friend Susan Silverman playing prominent roles, but in *Hugger Mugger* (2000), Spenser investigates the shooting of race horses in Georgia, and in *Potshot* (2001) he confronts gangsters in a small town in Arizona. Parker's other books include the mainstream novels *Wilderness* (1979), *Love and Glory* (1983), and *All Our Yesterdays* (1994). *Night Passage* (1997) and *Trouble in Paradise* (1998) feature another sleuth, Jesse Stone, police chief in a small Massachusetts town. In *Poodle Springs* (1989), Parker completed an unfinished Raymond Chandler novel, and *Perchance to Dream* (1991) is a sequel to Chandler's *The Big Sleep*. Parker's female investigator Sunny Randall, in *Family Honor* (1999), was created at the request of Helen Hunt as a movie vehicle.

Parker, Samuel (1779–1866), Congregational clergyman, missionary. For several years Parker, who was born in Ashfield, Massachusetts, preached in western New York and engaged in missionary activities there. He represented the American Board of Commissioners for Foreign Missionaries in Oregon, and his activities there helped establish American claims to that region. He explored the countryside, established friendly relations with the Indians, and chose sites for missions. His literary fame rests on his *Journal of an Exploring Tour Beyond the Rocky Mountains* (1838).

Parker, Theodore (1810–1860), clergyman, abolitionist, writer. Born in Lexington, Massachusetts, Parker was graduated from Harvard Divinity School, became pastor of the Unitarian congregation of West Roxbury, Massachusetts, and married Lydia Cabot. A member of the Transcendental Club, he expounded its philosophy in *Discourse of Matters Pertaining to Religion* (1842). His sermon *On the Transient and Permanent in Christianity* (1841) was the first statement of his unorthodox beliefs. In it he rejects the Scriptures and the established church as the source of divinity and instead invokes personal intuition with God. These apparent heresies earned him the censure of his fellow clergymen, but he refused to resign and retained a loyal congregation. In 1845 he became preacher to the new Twenty-Eighth Congregational Society, with 7000 members. He actively supported abolitionism, hiding slaves in his home and aiding John Brown. His *Letter to the People of the United States Touching the Matter of Slavery* (1848) attempts to prove the evil of that system. Mr. Power, the inspired preacher in Louisa May Alcott's novel *Work* (1873), derives from Parker. His sermons were collected in three volumes (1853–5) and his collected works in fourteen volumes (1863–70). He is the subject of a biography (1936) by Henry Steele Commager and appears in the novel *The Sin of the Prophet* (1952) by Truman John Nelson.

Parker, Thomas (1595–1677), a Calvinist minister who arrived in Massachusetts from England in 1634. He taught preparatory school students, including Samuel Sewall. His works include *True Copy of a Letter Written by Mr. T. Parker* (1644) and *The Visions and Prophecies of Daniel Expounded* (1646).

Parkman, Francis (1823–1893), historian, horticulturist. Born in Boston, Parkman was graduated from Harvard in 1844 and directed by his family to study law thereafter. Parkman confessed an inability to concentrate on torts and contracts, owing to what he identified as a bad case of "Injuns on the brain." Indeed, if subsequent autobiographical remarks are to be believed, Parkman had already established his own agenda as early as 1842, laying plans for a life spent writing a history of the French and Indian War, which he later expanded to include "the whole course of the American conflict between France and England." He spent a great deal of time outdoors in the early 1840s, pacing battlesites, making notes, and generally absorbing atmosphere. He traveled west to Michigan in 1845 to collect information for what became HISTORY OF THE CONSPIRACY OF PONTIAC (1851), and in 1846 he journeyed to the northern Great Plains and lived among the Sioux. His journal of that experience was published as THE OREGON TRAIL (1849), his best-known book.

Parkman's health was never very good, and his predilection for wilderness did nothing to improve it, although few ever knew how fragile his physical condition really was. He began

writing *History of the Conspiracy of Pontiac* when illness had rendered him nearly blind. Composing in black crayon with a wire frame to guide his hand, he averaged six lines a day for the first six months of the project, which required an additional two years to complete. By 1856, he had produced VASSALL MORTON, an autobiographical novel. By 1858, his health was so bad that he went looking for cures in Europe. When he returned to the United States in 1860, he began a study of the rose, and working in his garden seemed to improve his health. In 1866 he published *The Book of Roses*, and in 1871 he became professor of horticulture at Harvard.

In 1865, with the publication of *Pioneers of France in the New World*, Parkman returned to the program of writing he had established some two decades earlier, and his histories appeared with some regularity thereafter: *The Jesuits in North America in the Seventeenth Century* (1867); *The Discovery of the Great West* (1869, reprinted as *La Salle and the Discovery of the Great West* in 1879); *The Old Regime in Canada* (1874); *Count Frontenac and New France under Louis XIV* (1877); *Montcalm and Wolfe* (1884); and *A Half Century of Conflict* (1892). Mason Wade, who published *Francis Parkman* (1942), edited Parkman's *Journals* (2 v. 1947), which, together with Wilbur R. Jacobs's *The Letters of Francis Parkman* (2 v. 1960) and Charles H. Gardiner's *The Literary Memoranda of Francis Parkman* (1961), provide insight into the man and his work. Other biographies include Howard Doughty, *Francis Parkman* (1962) and Robert L. Gale, *Francis Parkman* (1973). An assessment of his work is Otis A. Pease, *Parkman's History: The Historian as Literary Artist* (1953).

Parkman's legacy is one of paradox. His histories concentrate on the French, but his heroes are British. He was a strident critic of the Catholic Church in the New World, and especially of the Jesuits, but he had once considered joining a Catholic order. He accepted the inevitability of Anglo-Saxon expansion and favored the democracy of England over the military despotism of France, but his political convictions included belief in a conservative republic with restricted suffrage, "where intelligence and character and not numbers hold the reins of power," and he would have accepted a "good constitutional monarchy." He was fascinated by Indians, but his view of them was undeniably racist, as were his perceptions of, among others, blacks and Irishmen. And, despite that fascination, he knew, as William R. Taylor has shown, quite a bit less about Indians than his contemporaries supposed.

WILLIAM W. SAVAGE, JR.

Parley, Peter.   See S. G. GOODRICH.

Parley's Magazine.   See S. G. GOODRICH.

Parra, Nicanor (1914–   ), poet. Born to a poor family in a small town in southern Chile, Parra had a difficult time completing his education. He studied mathematics at Santiago University and later at Brown University and Oxford and became a teacher of mechanics. As a student in the United States and England, he read the modernist poets, especially Eliot and Auden. His first book, *Cancionero sin nombre* (1937), is relatively traditional. *Poemas y antipoemas* (1954, tr. *Poems and Antipoems*, 1967) signaled a sharp turn in the direction of his work, away from what he called the "formalism and rhetoric, grandiloquence, posturing, preciosity, limpness of character, softness" of much Spanish poetry. His antipoetry is carefully flat, nonsyllabic, antiromantic, and nonlogical, with the leap of association and surreal images as important elements.

Versos de salón (1962) is similar in tone and style to Poemas y antipoemas. In Obra gruesa (1969, tr. in part as Emergency Poems, 1972), Parra cut back further the use of metaphor, and the diction was even more matter-of-fact. Small, fragmentary poems, published intermittently as Artefactos, are distillations of the antipoetry principle so spare that the original antipoems seem almost lyrical in comparison. Poems of the 1970s focus on a figure he calls The Christ of Elqui (1977, tr. 1979).

Parra, Teresa de la (1895–1936),   novelist. De la Parra was born into a wealthy Venezuelan family and educated in Paris. Her partly autobiographical novels—Ifigenia: diario de una señorita que escribó porque se fastidiaba (1924) and Las memorias de Mamá Blanca (1929, tr. Mama Blanca's Souvenirs, 1959)—evoke memories of the declining plantation aristocracy and include meditations on time and time passing. She also comments on the second-class status of women of her position.

Parrington, Vernon L[ouis] (1871–1929),   teacher, historian, biographer, critic. Born in Aurora, Illinois, Parrington was brought up in the heart of Kansas Populism, a movement whose ideas molded his development. After attending the College of Emporia, Parrington went to Harvard University for two years and emerged with an intense desire to get "the last lingering Harvard prejudices out of my system." His long teaching career began at the College of Emporia, continued at the University of Oklahoma, and ended at the University of Washington. He was a superb teacher and theorist, reaching the climax of his career with The Colonial Mind (1927), which won a Pulitzer Prize and became the opening section of his MAIN CURRENTS IN AMERICAN THOUGHT (1927–1930), left unfinished at his death. Parrington's sense of architecture was everywhere evident in the harmony, balance, and proportion of his work. He refused, however, to write a belletristic account of American literature. He attempted instead a history of American in terms of the writings, of whatever kind, produced on its soil. He was deeply influenced by Taine's hypothesis that the literature of a people is the inevitable outgrowth of racial peculiarities, environment, and epoch. He made a frank avowal in the foreword to his first volume. "The point of view from which I have endeavored to evaluate the materials is liberal rather than conservative, Jeffersonian rather than Federalistic." He is at his best, therefore, when treating authors who are in some way exponents of liberalism: Roger Williams, Franklin, Paine, Emerson, Thoreau, Channing, Theodore Parker, Garland, above all Jefferson.

Parrish, Anne (1888–1957),   painter, novelist. Born in Colorado Springs, Colorado, into a family that included some noted artists (**Maxfield Parrish** was her cousin), Anne Parrish at first intended to become a painter. But in the early 1920s she began writing novels and proved an adept and entertaining storyteller. The Perennial Bachelor (1925), which won the Harper's Prize, is an ironic study of a man who never marries and at sixty goes as a beau to parties of young people, unaware of their laughter. In later novels she made similarly clever and convincing studies of odd personalities. The great crises in Europe and America that came with the rise of the dictators gave her books a more serious mood, as in Mr. Despondency's Daughter (1938) and Pray for Tomorrow (1941). A Clouded Star (1948) centers on some of the experiences of HARRIET TUBMAN, an ex-slave who assisted many slaves in their flight to freedom on the Underground Railroad. The Lucky One was published posthumously in 1958.

Parsons, Elsie Clews (1875?–1941),   anthropologist. Parsons became a leading authority on Amerindian lore. Among her books are Notes on Zuni (1917), Folk Tales of Andros Islands, Bahamas (1918), Folklore of the Sea Islands (1923), Ceremonial of Zuni (1924), Pueblo of Jemez (1925), Tewa Tales (1926), Taos Pueblo (1936), Pueblo Indian Religion (1939), and Taos Tales (1940). She began her writing career by publishing books of a more general nature, such as The Family (1906), The Old-Fashioned Woman (1913), Fear and Conventionality (1914), Social Freedom (1915), and Social Rule (1916).

Parsons, T[homas] W[illiam] (1819–1892),   dentist, poet, translator. Born in Boston, Parsons practiced dentistry, but his great interest was in perfecting his translation of the Divine Comedy. In 1867 his Inferno was published in Boston with illustrations by Gustave Doré; between 1870 and 1883, about two-thirds of the Purgatorio appeared in the Catholic World. Parsons's original verse was published in Poems (1854), The Magnolia (1866), The Old House at Sudbury (1870), The Shadow of the Obelisk (1872), and The Willey House, and Sonnets (1875). In 1893 a posthumous Complete Poems was published. After his death C. E. Norton gathered his translations in The Divine Comedy of Dante Alighieri (1893).

Particular, Pertinax.   Pen name of TOBIAS WATKINS.

Partington, Mrs.   This name became legendary through a humorous speech made by Sydney Smith in England in 1831 in which he ridiculed the rejection of the Reform Bill by the House of Lords by inventing a Dame Partington who, during a great storm, got out her mop and broom and vigorously pushed back the Atlantic Ocean. The speech helped to put the bill through. B. P. SHILLABER took over the name, called his character Mrs. Ruth Partington, and placed all kinds of malapropisms in her mouth as she discussed everything under the sun, from Calvinism to patent medicines. Yet she spoke often with Yankee wisdom.

Partisan Leader, The: A Novel, and an Apocalypse of the Origin and Struggles of the Southern Confederacy (1836, fictitiously dated 1856),   by NATHANIEL BEVERLY TUCKER. Tucker published the book under a pseudonym, Edward William Sidney. His chief aim was to influence the country against the election of MARTIN VAN BUREN. His book prophesied, in a fictional projection of the future, that Van Buren would set up a dictatorial rule and would so offend the Southern states that in 1849 South Carolina would secede and Virginia would be on the point of doing so. The book produced no effect on the election, but during the Civil War it was reprinted on both sides of the Mason-Dixon line for propaganda purposes.

Partisan Review.   A magazine founded in 1934. Though first closely connected with the radical left wing in politics, it soon began to diverge from Marxism. In 1936 it merged with the *Anvil*, edited by William Phillips, who joined the editorial board of the *Partisan Review*. In 1937, after suspending publication for fourteen months, a new board of editors was formed, which took a strongly independent political stand. In addition to PHILLIP RAHV, one of the founders, and Phillips, it included F. W. Dupee, Dwight MacDonald, and MARY MCCARTHY. The magazine has published creative work by most of the prominent writers of the contemporary Anglo-American literary world, without regard to private political convictions and with special emphasis on the most serious aspect of avant-garde literature. *Partisan Review* also has introduced much Continental writing to American readers through translations. Lionel Trilling did some of his most distinguished work for the *Partisan Review*, as have other critics such as Richard Chase and Robert Gorham Davis. Saul Bellow's work was first published in its pages; part of James T. Farrell's STUDS LONIGAN appeared there in installments. Throughout its existence the magazine has been a rallying point for American intellectuals. It is particularly well known for its symposia on contemporary questions affecting writers and other intellectuals. Past volumes containing collections of material from the magazine include William Phillips's edited *60 Years of Great Fiction from Partisan Review* (1997). *The Partisan Reader— 1934–44* (1946), edited by Phillips and Rahv, with an introduction by Trilling; *The New Partisan Reader* (1953); *Stories in the Modern Manner* (1953); *More Stories in the Modern Manner* (1954); and *The Partisan Review Anthology* (1962).

Parton, Ethel (1862–1944),   writer for young people. Born in New York City as Ethel Thompson, she was taken in by her grandmother, SARAH WILLIS, when her parents died. She took the surname of her grandmother's third husband. JAMES PARTON. She was a staff member of YOUTH'S COMPANION for more than forty years and also contributed to ST. NICHOLAS. She wrote *Melissa Ann, A Little Girl of the 1820s* (1931); *Tabitha Mary, A Little Girl of 1810* (1933); *Penelope Ellen and Her Friends: Three Little Girls of 1840* (1936); and similar historical narratives, based on research and on family recollections.

Parton, James (1822–1891),   teacher, biographer, essayist. Born in England, Parton came to America as a child. In 1848 his essay demonstrating that a woman had written *Jane Eyre* was noted by NATHANIEL PARKER WILLIS, editor of the New York *Home Journal*, who hired him to work on the paper. In 1854 he was commissioned to write a life of Horace Greeley. The success of the Greeley biography led him to write many others. Among them are *The Life and Times of Aaron Burr*

(1857, enlarged ed. 2 v. 1864); *Life of Andrew Jackson* (3 v. 1859–60); *Life and Times of Benjamin Franklin* (2 v. 1864); *Life of John Jacob Astor* (1865); *Life of Thomas Jefferson* (1874); and *Life of Voltaire* (2 v. 1881). His wife was Sara P. Willis. M. E. Flower has written *James Parton: The Father of Modern Biography* (1951).

Parton, Sara Payson Willis.   See SARA PAYSON WILLIS.

Partridge, Bellamy (1878–1960),   author, editor, critic. Although a prolific writer of fiction and nonfiction for many years, Partridge, born in Phelps, New York, did not gain popular favor until his sixties, with *Country Lawyer* (1939), a book based on the life of his father, which was later made into a film. *The Big Family* (1941) related the story of a lawyer's household of eight lively children. *As We Were* (1946) recollected family life between 1850 and 1900, with pictures collected by Otto Bettmann. *January Thaw* (1945), which told the adventures of a city couple determined to renovate a Connecticut farmhouse, became a Broadway play. *The Old Oaken Bucket* (1949) was about a rundown house with a spurious past. His other books are *The Roosevelt Family in America* (1936), *Excuse My Dust* (1943), *The Big Freeze* (1948), *Salad Days* (1951), *Fill 'er Up* (1952), and *Going, Going, Gone* (1958).

Passage to India (1868, pub. 1871 in "Annex" to *Leaves of Grass*),   a poem by WALT WHITMAN. Three great material triumphs prompted this poem: the laying of the Atlantic cable in 1866, the opening of the Suez Canal, and the completion of the Union Pacific Railroad in 1869. Whitman felt that these events heralded a great era of peace in which a superior civilization would be created by captains and engineers, noble inventors and scientists. To him the opening of the Suez Canal meant union with India, where civilization had perhaps been born. But the whole poem rests on Whitman's recognition that his faith in democracy had been premature and that much remained to be done before the New World could achieve the ideals he had celebrated in his earlier work. From the world as it was he turned aside in *Passage to India* to imagine a future utopia.

Passionate Pilgrim, The, and Other Stories (1875), a collection by HENRY JAMES. In 1873, in a letter to his mother, James mentioned his intention of making "a volume of tales on the theme of American adventures in Europe, leading off with *The Passionate Pilgrim*," which had appeared in 1871. The title story was one of a number of pieces stimulated by his trip abroad in 1869–70. It tells of Clement Searle, who goes to England, long the object of his dreams, to claim a rich estate. He is penniless, ill, and morbid. His misadventures lead to his death just at the moment when his desire is on the point of being gratified. The tale is ironic and tragic, but full of James's passionate love of England.

Pastorius, Francis Daniel (1651–1720),   theologian, lawyer, colonist, public official, teacher, geographer, historian, poet. Born in Germany, Pastorius was among the most learned of the American colonists, adept in seven languages, and well acquainted not only with legal and theological writings, but with science and medicine. Early in life he was greatly attracted by the teachings of a group of Quakers in Frankfurt; he has been described as a Friend who was also part Lutheran and Pietist. His ability attracted immediate attention, and he was sent (1683) as an agent of the Frankfurt Quakers to buy land in Pennsylvania for a settlement. He bought 15,000 acres of land on favorable terms from WILLIAM PENN, founded Germantown (he was its first mayor), was a member of the Assembly (1687, 1691), taught in Germantown and Philadelphia, and was a good friend of the local Indians. He wrote many important documents, particularly a noble protest against slavery, the first on record in America. He married Ennecke Klostermanns in 1688; they appear as characters in John Greenleaf Whittier's important but little known poem THE PENNSYLVANIA PILGRIM (1872).

Pastorius was a prolific writer. Much that he wrote, still unpublished (particularly numerous poems), is in five volumes of manuscripts in the library of the Historical Society of Pennsylvania. He called this collection his *Bienenstock* or *Melliotrophium* (beehive); it bears witness to his encyclopedic learning and his skill as a linguist. But he published a considerable body of work, including his doctoral thesis on a legal topic at Altdorf (1676); a report (1684) in German on the Pennsylvania colony (printed in an English version in A.C. Myer's *Narratives of Early Pennsylvania*, 1912, as *Pastorius' First Account of Pennsylvania*); *Vier Kleine Doch Ungemeine und Sehr Nuetzliche Tractaetlein* (1690); an epistle to the Pietists of Germany (1697); *Henry Bernard Koster, William Davis, Thomas Rutter, and Thomas Bowyer: Four Boasting Disputers of This World Briefly Rebuked* (a publication in the lively theological dispute with GEORGE KEITH, 1697); *A New Primmer or Methodical Directions to Attain the True Spelling, Reading, and Writing of English* (1678?); and *Umstaendige Geographische Beschreibung der zu Allerletzt Erfundenen Provintz Pensylvaniae* (1700; in an English version in Myer's *Narratives of Early Pennsylvania*). The last is regarded as Pastorius's most important production. A full account of him appears in S.W. Pennypacker's *The Settlement of Germantown* (1899). A list of his writings was given in Oswald Seidensticker's *First Century of German Printing in America, 1728–1830, Preceded by a Notice of the Literary Works of F.D. Pastorius* (1893).

Patchen, Kenneth (1911–1972), poet, painter. Born in Niles, Ohio, Patchen is noted especially for his poems, most of them short observations or narratives, written in free forms and strikingly original language. They merge humor and fantasy, sometimes veering toward satire, sometimes merely sentimental. He often illustrated his poems with his own abstract paintings, and some of his verse has appeared in portfolios and hand-printed illustrated sheets. He published many books, which found a wider audience than most of his fellow avant-garde poets. Among his books are *Before the Brave* (1936), *Dark Kingdom* (1942), *Sleepers Awake* (1946), *Panels for the Walls of Heaven* (1947), *Selected Poems* (1947), and *Red Wine and Yellow Hair* (1949). His many prose works include *The Journal of Albion Moonlight* (1941), *Memoirs of a Shy Pornographer* (1945), *See You in the Morning* (1948), and

Because It Is (1960). *The City Wears a Slouch Hat* (1942) is a radio play. The plays produced but unpublished in his lifetime appeared in *Patchen's Lost Plays* (1977).

Paterson, a poem by WILLIAM CARLOS WILLIAMS. Paterson was Williams's major work, conceived as four books. Book 1 appeared in 1946, the others in 1948, 1949, and 1951. Williams added a fifth book in 1958, and fragments of a sixth, found among his papers, were added in 1963 after his death. *Paterson* proved to be the poem that certified Williams's claims to major status as a poet after his many years with a secondary reputation. In scope, it was his challenge to other long poems of the 20th century, and in method it suggested alternatives that seemed peculiarly Williams's own. Specifically, it was a new model for poetry to replace, for Americans at least, the model provided by Eliot's THE WASTE LAND (1922). More generally, it invited comparison with such other long poems as Pound's CANTOS and Crane's THE BRIDGE.

Williams designed *Paterson* as a wholly American poem, deriving its materials from American history, folklore, and myth, and expressing them in an American vernacular voice. It was also a personal poem, deriving strength from the poet's struggle to live in the world as a human, to record that struggle honestly, and to evolve a strategy for expression appropriate to time, place, and person. As a result the poem is about the city of Paterson, New Jersey, its present and past. It is also about a man named Paterson, a doctor, who lives and loves in Paterson. And the doctor is a poet named Paterson who searches in the library for materials and wanders in the streets and parks reflecting on how to merge the personal and the observed in a work of creative vitality.

To help achieve his effect, Williams merged prose with his poetry, inserting historical accounts from books and newspapers as well as personal letters from aspiring poets Marcia Nardi (C. in the poem) and ALLEN GINSBERG (A.G.). The poem was frankly exploratory, as Williams made one of his subjects the difficulty of finding language to express those things that matter most and worked his way in his poetic line toward a clearer formulation of the "variable foot" he had long been seeking as fundamental meter.

Paterson had a tremendous influence on American poetry in the 1950s and after as its qualities were greatly admired by the BLACK MOUNTAIN POETS and by poets of the BEAT GENERATION and the SAN FRANCISCO RENAISSANCE. To younger poets Williams's poetry seemed more worthy of emulation than the work of T.S. ELIOT admired by their elders. Finally, the newer, more open poetry received a gigantic boost when ROBERT LOWELL, already celebrated as a poet in the Eliot mold, moved in the midst of *Life Studies* (1959) to a poetic practice inspired in large part by his reading of *Paterson*.

Pathfinder, The, or, The Inland Sea (1840), a novel by JAMES FENIMORE COOPER. It was next to the last in order of publication of the five books making up the LEATHER-STOCKING TALES, the third in order of narrative sequence. The Pathfinder is NATTY BUMPPO, otherwise Leatherstocking and the Deerslayer. The background is the Lake Ontario country, the time is

1760, and the plot is set against the background of the FRENCH AND INDIAN WARS. There is a love affair: beautiful Mabel Dunham's father would like her to marry Natty, but he gives her up to Jasper Western when he realizes Mabel is in love with Jasper. But Jasper also has his troubles; he is suspected of being a traitor, mainly because he can speak French. The true villain is, of course, revealed in time. D. H. Lawrence called Natty as portrayed here "a saint with a gun." Balzac was ecstatic in praise of the novel; "It is beautiful, it is grand. Its interest is tremendous."

Patrick, John (1905–1995),   playwright. Born John Patrick Goggan in Louisville, he was abandoned by his parents and shunted from foster home to boarding school until he struck out for the West Coast and began a writing career. Dropping his last name at 19, he wrote extensively for radio, Broadway theater, movies, and regional theater using the name John Patrick. Experience as an ambulance driver in World War II provided the background for his first successful Broadway production, *The Hasty Heart* (1945). *The Story of Mary Surratt* (1947), *The Curious Savage* (1950), and *Lo and Behold!* (1951) followed in quick succession. Patrick's Pulitzer Prize *Teahouse of the August Moon* (1953) is an adaptation of a novel by Vern Schneider about American soldiers who build a teahouse to please Okinawans during the occupation of their island.

Patriotic Gore: Studies in the Literature of the American Civil War (1962),   by Edmund Wilson, is a collection of sixteen essays on writing related to the war including the memoirs of Union generals Grant and Sherman and Confederates Mosby and Lee, diaries, political writing, and fiction by writers such as Ambrose Bierce and John De Forest. The title is taken from "Maryland, My Maryland" by JAMES RYDER RANDALL.

Patriots, The (1776),   a play by ROBERT MUNFORD. Munford depicted extremists on both sides unfavorably. Kenneth B. Murdock called it "one of the best American plays dealing with the Revolution." It was probably never produced and first appeared in print in Munford's *Collection of Plays and Poems* (1798). It was reprinted in the *William and Mary Quarterly* (July 1949), edited by Courtlandt Canby.

patroons.   On June 7, 1629, the States General of the Netherlands confirmed a Charter of Freedom and Exemptions under which the Dutch West India Company was empowered to grant certain privileges to colonists. To those who transported fifty settlers, they gave estates fronting sixteen miles along navigable rivers and extending inland as far as settlement would permit. The grantees, called *patroons*, were given feudal rights and granted exemption from taxation for eight years. By the end of January 1630, five patroonships had been granted along the Hudson, Connecticut, and Delaware Rivers. The privileges of the patroons remained undisturbed during English rule and after the Revolution. It was not until the 1840s that tenants made determined efforts to end all feudal privileges. Anti-Rent Associations brought on what was called the Anti-Rent War in the manor of Rensselaerswyck in the Albany region (1839–46). Finally, in 1846, a more liberal constitution

was adopted by New York State, by which perpetual leases were gradually replaced by fee-simple tenure. The unrest and violence were described in James Fenimore Cooper's trilogy *The Littlepage Manuscripts* (1845, 1846). See ANTI-RENT LAWS.

Pattee, Fred Lewis (1863–1950),   literary historian, teacher. Pattee was born in New Hampshire, studied at Dartmouth College and in Germany, and came back to teach, mainly at Pennsylvania State College. A pioneer in the study of American literature, he viewed literature as a popular expression rather than as the work of an elite. Among his histories are *A History of American Literature* (1896), *A History of American Literature Since 1870* (1915), *Sidelights on American Literature* (1922), *The Development of the American Short Story* (1923), *The New American Literature* (1930), *The First Century of American Literature* (1935), and *The Feminine Fifties* (1940). *Penn State Yankee: The Autobiography of Fred Lewis Pattee* appeared in 1953.

Patten, William Gilbert ["Burt L. Standish"] (1866–1945),   author of boys' books. Patten, a native of Maine, began to write in his late teens and won immediate success, writing Western stories under the name William West Wilder. His great celebrity, however, came when as Burt L. Standish he began to publish a series of novels about a character named FRANK MERRIWELL, a highly virtuous, manly Yale student. All together Patten's books have sold more than 100 million copies; the Merriwell series alone numbered more than two hundred titles.

Patterson, [Horace] Orlando (1940–   ),   sociologist and novelist. Jamaican in his origins, and a distinguished professor of sociology at Harvard, Patterson is the author of the *Children of Sisyphus* (1964), a much-admired novel set in the slums of Kingston in the 1950s. Other novels are *An Absence of Ruins* (1967), about an alienated West Indian intellectual, and *Die the Long Day* (1972), an examination of the effects of slavery. His sociological and historical works are major contributions to the study of minorities, and include *The Sociology of Slavery* (1967), a study of slavery in Jamaica; *Ethnic Chauvinism: The Reactionary Impulse* (1977); *Slavery and Social Death* (1982), a comparative study of slavery from ancient to modern times; *The Ordeal of Integration: Progress and Resentment in America's "Racial" Crisis* (1997); and *Rituals of Blood: Consequences of Slavery in Two American Centuries* (1999). With Julius P. Rodriguez he compiled *Chronology of World Slavery* (1999).

Pattie, James Ohio (1804–1850?),   explorer, memoirist. In the 1820s Pattie, born in Kentucky, undertook several expeditions to Baja California, New Mexico, and Mexico. He told of his adventures in a book that was edited and probably largely written by Timothy Flint: *The Personal Narrative of James O. Pattie, of Kentucky, During an Expedition from St. Louis, through the Vast Regions Between That Place and the Pacific Ocean* (1831). One B. Bilson, otherwise unknown, wrote an abridged account of adventures supposedly his own, but based on Pattie's work: *The Hunters of Kentucky, or, The Trials and Toils of Trappers and Traders* (1847). Pattie's *Personal*

Narrative was included in Reuben G. Thwaites's *Early Western Travels* (1905) and was edited by Milo M. Quaife (1930). Little is known of Pattie's later life, except that he was in California at the time of the 1849 gold rush.

Patton, Frances Gray (1906–2000), short-story writer, playwright, poet. Born in Raleigh, Patton has been called "a Jane Austen of North Carolina." Educated at Duke and the University of North Carolina, she was thoroughly acquainted with the Carolina scene and wrote about it with quiet irony and gracious wit. She wrote plays in her earlier days and published a few poems, but is known mainly for her short stories, some of which are collected in *The Finer Things of Life* (1951) and *A Piece of Luck* (1955). *Good Morning, Miss Dove* (1954) is a novel about a schoolmarm. *Twenty-Eight Stories* appeared in 1969.

Paul, Elliot [Harold] (1891–1958), journalist, editor, novelist. Paul was born in Massachusetts. After serving in World War I he remained in France to write for the Associated Press and the Paris editions of the Chicago *Tribune* and the New York *Herald Tribune*. His novels *Indelible* (1922), *Impromptu* (1923), and *Imperturbe* (1924) were hailed by a small circle of admirers. In 1927, with Eugene Jolas, he founded and edited the avant-garde periodical *transition*. *The Life and Death of a Spanish Town* (1937) tells the story of the beautiful village of Santa Eulalia, Ibiza, in the Balearic Islands, where Paul lived from 1931 until it was destroyed by Franco armies during the Spanish Civil War; it is undoubtedly his best book. His other works of this time were *Lava Rock* (1928), *Low Run Tide* (1928), *The Amazon* (1929), *Concert Pitch* (1938), *Stars and Stripes Forever* (1939), and *All the Brave* (1939), written with L. Quintanilla. His most popular book was the nostalgic memoir *The Last Time I Saw Paris* (1942). The great success of *The Mysterious Mickey Finn* (1939), a burlesque detective extravaganza, led him to concentrate on detective fiction. *Hugger-Mugger in the Louvre* (1940), *Mayhem in B-Flat* (1940), *Fracas in the Foothills* (1941), *The Black Gardenia* (1952), and other crime novels brought Paul thousands of readers who had never heard of *transition* or the expatriate colonies in the Balearics. Paul also wrote for the films; his best-known scenario was *A Woman's Face* (1941). Paul's autobiographical books of his life in the United States are *Linden on the Saugus Branch* (1947), *Ghost Town on the Yellowstone* (1948), *My Old Kentucky Home* (1949), and *Desperate Scenery* (1954).

Paul, John.   Pen name of CHARLES HENRY WEBB.

Paul, Louis (1901–1970), writer of fiction, poet. Born in Brooklyn, Paul enlisted in the army during World War I, thereafter wandering all over the United States for three years working as a laborer and hospital orderly, movie extra, motorman, elevator operator, typist, miner, ditchdigger, and sailor. His short story called *No More Trouble for Jedwick* brought him his first recognition when it was accepted by *Esquire* and awarded first prize in the O. Henry Memorial Awards for 1934. His novels include *The Pumpkin Coach* (1935), *A Horse in Arizona* (1936), *The Wrong World* (1938), *A*

Passion for Privacy (1940), *This Is My Brother* (1943), *Breakdown* (1946), *A Husband for Mama* (1950), *The Man Who Came Home* (1953), and *Dara the Cypriot* (1959). *Breakdown*, the story of an alcoholic, was dramatized (1948) as *A Cup of Trembling*.

Paulding, Hiram (1797–1878), naval officer, memoirist. A native of New York, Paulding had a distinguished naval career as acting lieutenant of the *Ticonderoga* in the Battle of Lake Champlain (1813), in service against the Barbary pirates (1815), in a campaign against Walker's filibusterers in Nicaragua (1857), and as commandant of the New York navy yard (1861–65). He described two of his exploits in books: *Journal of a Cruise of the U.S. Schooner Dolphin* (1831), an account of his pursuit of mutineers in the South Seas, and *Bolivar in His Camp* (1834), which tells how Paulding carried dispatches to Simón Bolívar in a 1,500-mile horseback trip across the Andes.

Paulding, James Kirke ["Launcelot Langstaff"] (1778–1860), novelist, dramatist, historian. Paulding's almost ideal boyhood was spent in fishing, hunting, and reading omnivorously. At eighteen he worked in a public office with his brother, and there he met fellow New Yorkers WASHINGTON IRVING and William Irving. A lively friendship sprang up among the young men, who formed the nucleus of a group they called The Nine Worthies of Cockloft Hall. In 1807 and 1808 Paulding and Irving published a humorous periodical, SALMAGUNDI; OR, THE WHIM-WHAMS AND OPINIONS OF LAUNCELOT LANGSTAFF, ESQ., AND OTHERS, which contained essays styled after the *Spectator*. Years later Paulding wrote a second series, *Tellers from the South, A Sketch of Old England, Salmagundi; Second Series* (1819–20). *The Diverting History of John Bull and Brother Jonathan* (1812) was a thinly disguised allegory attacking the pugnacious old despot John Bull. Paulding later wrote a sequel, called *The History of Uncle Sam and His Boys* (1835). *The Lay of the Scottish Fiddle* (1813), a burlesque poem, ridiculed the romanticism of Scott. THE BACKWOODSMAN (1818) celebrated, in rather dull verse, the adventures of a New York pioneer in Ohio. A number of histories, some serious, some more in the spirit of the *Diverting History*, appeared between 1815 and 1825; *The United States and England* (1815); *Letters from the South* (2 v. 1817); *A Sketch of Old England, by a New England Man* (2 v. 1822); and JOHN BULL IN AMERICA; OR, THE NEW MUNCHAUSEN (1825).

KONINGSMARKE, THE LONG FINNE: A STORY OF THE NEW WORLD (1823) was his first important work of fiction, a historical romance dealing with the Swedes in Delaware in the 17th century and satirizing the romances of Scott. THE LION OF THE WEST (1831), a drama of a rough American frontiersman, won a prize, was a great stage success, and laid the foundation for Paulding's popularity. THE DUTCHMAN'S FIRESIDE (1831), like Cooper's *Satanstoe* (1845), was based on Mrs. Grant's *Memoirs of an American Lady* (1808) and is believed by some critics to be Paulding's best novel. He also wrote WESTWARD HO! (1832); *A Life of Washington* (1835); *Slavery in the United States* (1836); *The Old Continental; or, The Price of Liberty* (1846);

and THE PURITAN AND HIS DAUGHTER (1849). *The Bucktails: or Americans in England* (1847), a satiric drama, portrays a shrewd Yankee type.

Paulding was a member of the Board of Navy Commissioners (1815–23) and Secretary of the Navy under Van Buren (1838–41). His novels, all but forgotten today, merit a better fate because of his impatience with false romanticism and his skillful use of the American scene. Paulding's son William Irving Paulding did a *Literary Life* of his father (1867). A.L. Herold wrote *James Kirke Paulding: Versatile American* (1926). A selection of his *Letters* was published in 1962.

Paul Revere's Ride   (in *Tales of a Wayside Inn*, 1863), a ballad by Longfellow. The story is told by the Landlord and opens the book. It narrates how Revere waited for the signal from the tower of the Old North Church, and then carried word from Boston to Lexington and Concord that British troops were approaching.

Paumanok.   This Indian name for Long Island became widely known through WALT WHITMAN's use of the name. He used it in the titles of two of his poems, "A Paumanok Picture" (1881) and "Paumanok" (1888). It also appears in "Out of the Cradle Endlessly Rocking" (1859–1881) and in *Specimen Days* (1882).

Pavilion of Women (1946),   a novel by PEARL BUCK set in China.

Pawnee Indians.   A tribe of Plains Indians who belonged to the group speaking the Caddoan language. Originally they lived in the Lower Mississippi Valley. The Pawnee entered history when a member of the tribe served as a guide for CORONADO (1541). Great lovers of horses, they made frequent raids on Spanish territory in New Mexico up to the beginning of the 19th century. French traders managed to become friendly with them; present-day Pawnee are likely to have an admixture of French as well as English ancestry. Their power declined as a result of cholera and other diseases. After cession of the Louisiana Territory to the United States (1803) the Pawnee became firm friends of the United States. They gave up all their lands except for a tract in Nebraska, then removed to a reservation in Oklahoma.

The Pawnee appear in Washington Irving's *Tour of the Prairies* (1835). Even earlier the Pawnee, along with the Sioux, had supplanted the Delaware and the Hurons in the third of James Fenimore Cooper's *Leather-Stocking Series* to appear, THE PRAIRIE (1827). Cooper carefully studied the region in which the story is laid and talked with representatives of the tribes he portrayed. He gained a favorable impression of the wisdom and moderation of these Indians. He spent more time writing *The Prairie* than any of his other novels because he was fascinated by the natural setting and the Indian information he accumulated.

The poetry and music of the Pawnee have been explored since the close of the 19th century. A thorough survey was made by Alice C. Fletcher in *The Hako: A Pawnee Ceremonial* (1904). FRANCES DENSMORE, the best known collector of Indian poetry and music, wrote a book on *Pawnee Music* (1929).

George E. Hyde in his *Pawnee Indians* (1951) emphasizes their highly developed political and religious organization. Other books include James R. Murie's *Pawnee Indian Societies* (1914); G.B. Grinnell's *Pawnee Hero Stories and Folk Tales* (1889); and W.R. Wedel's *Introduction to Pawnee Archaeology* (1936).

Paxton, Phillip.   See SAMUEL ADAMS HAMMETT.

Payne, John Howard (1791–1852),   actor, playwright, poet. Born either in New York City or East Hampton, New York, Payne at fourteen edited a weekly paper of dramatic news, the *Thespian Mirror* (1805–06); at fifteen he wrote a drama, *Julia, or, The Wanderer* (1806). On the basis of his success as Young Norval in John Home's popular tragedy, *Douglas*, he went to England in 1813, where he acted and wrote plays and was always on the verge of bankruptcy. An adaptation of a play called BRUTUS, OR THE FALL OF TARQUIN (1818) brought him some recognition but little money. In debtors' prison he wrote *Therese, Orphan of Geneva* (1821), making enough money to gain his freedom. Then came his triumph, *Clari, The Maid of Milan* (1823). It contained the song called "Home, Sweet Home," with music by Sir Henry Bishop. It became immensely popular, but Payne had sold the play outright and collected no royalties. He wrote and adapted other plays but remained poor. While in England he met Mary Shelley, widow of the poet Percy Bysshe Shelley, and courted her fervently and in vain. He returned to America penniless. Theatrical benefit performances were arranged for him and brought in almost $10,000. Daniel Webster and other friends got him the job of consul in Tunis, which he held on and off until his death.

Eleven of his plays were rescued from manuscripts and published in *America's Lost Plays* (v. 5 and 6, 1940), edited by Codman Hislop and W.R. Richardson. *Charles II* was included by A.H. Quinn in *Representative American Plays* (1917). This was a version of a French play and was done with Payne's friend WASHINGTON IRVING. Quinn calls it his best comedy, and regards Payne as a playwright of great skill. Biographies were written by Gabriel Harrison (1884), W.T. Hanson (1913), Rosa P. Chiles (1930), and Grace Overmyer (1957). Maude Barragan wrote a biographical novel, *John Howard Payne, Skywalker* (1953). See KNICKERBOCKER SCHOOL.

Paz, Octavio (1914–1998),   Mexican poet, essayist, social philosopher, and critic. Born in Mexico City, of Spanish and part Indian ancestry, Paz published his first book of poems, *Luna silvestre* (1933), when he was nineteen. Along with his lifelong absorption in literature, Paz has had a profound interest in the Mexican past, a keen social and political consciousness, and a somewhat mystical philosophical bent. After twenty-five years in the diplomatic service Paz resigned his post as ambassador to India in 1968 to protest his government's suppression of a demonstration by students and workers.

His poetry is lyrical and erotic and expresses his sense of the deep loneliness of man, which can be transcended only through attempts at communion, through sexual love, compassion, and faith. It is rich with images of Mexico's landscape and allusions to his Indian past. *The Collected Poems of Octavio Paz* appeared in 1987. Earlier books of poems include *Aguila o sol?* (1951, tr. *Eagle or Sun?* 1970); *Piedra de sol* (1957, tr. *Sun Stone*, 1963), perhaps his most important long poem, addressed to the planet Venus; *Salamandra* (1962); *Ladera este* (1969); and *Poemas 1935–75* (1979). Among the English translations are *Selected Poetry* (1963) and *Early Poems 1935–1955* (1973, both translated by MURIEL RUKEYSER) and *A Drift of Shadows* (1979). A further collection of poems, *Selected Poems* (ed., Eliot Weinberger), was published in 1984. His outstanding prose work is THE LABYRINTH OF SOLITUDE, a compelling, highly original, and influential study of the Mexican national character. Along with studies of Lévi-Strauss (1967, tr. 1970) and Marcel Duchamp (1968, tr. 1970), he has written the critical essays on poetry *El arco y la lira* (1956, tr. *The Bow and the Lyre*, 1973); *Conjunciones y disjunciones* (1969, tr. *Conjunctions and Disjunctions*, 1974), essays on sex and religion; *Posdata* (1970, tr. *The Other Mexico*, 1972), written after his resignation from the diplomatic corps; *El orgo filantrópico* (1979), essays on modern history; and *Essays on Mexican Art* (1993). Paz's major biographical and literary study of the 17th-century poet SOR JUANA INES DE LA CRUZ (1982, English tr. 1988) *Sor Juana: or, The Traps of Faith* reintroduced this remarkable figure to the world. In 1990 he was awarded the Nobel Prize in Literature.

Peabody, Andrew Preston (1811–1893),   a Unitarian minister who became a professor of Christian morals at Harvard in 1860. He produced nearly two hundred works and edited *The North American Review* from 1853 to 1863.

Peabody, Elizabeth Palmer (1804–1894),   educator. Elizabeth Peabody's remarkable teaching career began when, still in her teens, she taught at her mother's private school in Billerica, Massachusetts, where Peabody was born. Later she and her sister Mary opened a school in Boston. She also served as a devoted secretary for WILLIAM ELLERY CHANNING [1] during these years. In 1834 she became assistant to BRONSON ALCOTT in his Temple School. Difficult as Alcott was, she remained with him for two loyal years, carrying his burdens, fighting his battles, and working selflessly for the ideals of the school— and overlooking the fact that Alcott frequently forgot to pay her salary. *A Record of a School* (1835) gives an account of her work with Alcott.

Her early thirst for learning brought her into contact with some of the great thinkers of the day; at the age of eighteen she was tutored in Greek by RALPH WALDO EMERSON. It was through Elizabeth that NATHANIEL HAWTHORNE met her sister Sophia, his future wife. The bookstore Elizabeth opened in Boston in 1839 became a meeting place for writers, philosophers, Harvard professors, liberal clergymen, and Transcendentalists. Here plans for BROOK FARM were laid, and THE DIAL, the organ of the Brook Farm community, was published in the rear of the store (1842–43). Peabody contributed articles to the magazine that were reprinted, with some of her memoirs, as *A Last Evening with Allston* (1886). In 1844, after a fire destroyed her bookstore, she returned to teaching. At about this time

Peabody met HORACE MANN (1796–1859), with whom she entered into a platonic friendship. If she was surprised when Mann married her sister Mary, she was too generous to feel any resentment; throughout her life she remained on excellent terms with the Manns. She was a fervid Abolitionist; her antislavery feelings bound her closer to the Manns but strained her relations with the Hawthornes, who refused to enter into the controversy.

The first kindergarten in the United States was opened by Peabody in 1860. It was founded on the educational ideas of Friedrich Froebel. She studied Froebel's methods abroad and lectured and wrote books and articles on the new kindergarten methods. From 1873 until 1875 she published a magazine called *Kindergarten Messenger*, and from 1879 until 1884 she lectured at Alcott's School of Philosophy in Concord. By this time she had established herself as a wonderfully energetic, keen, headstrong old lady. Her works include *Chronological History of the United States* (1856), *Reminiscences of William Ellery Channing* (1880), and *Lectures in the Training Schools for Kindergartens* (1888).

Miss Birdseye in Henry James's *The Bostonians* (1886) may be a portrait of her, though James denied that any resemblance was intended. A delightfully humorous and sympathetic study is *The Peabody Sisters of Salem* (1950), by Louise Hall Tharp, who also wrote *Until Victory: Horace Mann and Mary Peabody* (1953).

Peabody, Josephine Preston (1874–1922),   poet, playwright. From the age of thirteen the Brooklyn-born Josephine Peabody wrote poems, many published in leading magazines. Her first book, *Old Greek Folk Stories* (1897), was followed by several volumes of verse: *The Wayfarers* (1898), *The Singing Leaves* (1903), *Pan: A Choric Idyll* (1904), *The Book of the Little Past* (1908), *The Singing Man* (1911), and *Harvest Moon* (1916). At Radcliffe College she came under the influence of WILLIAM VAUGHN MOODY and turned to writing poetic dramas: a one-act play, *Fortune and Men's Eyes* (1900); the much more ambitious and successful *Marlowe* (1901); *Wings* (1905), a one-act play laid in medieval Northumbria; *The Piper* (1910), the author's best-known work, based on the story of The Pied Piper of Hamelin; *The Wolf of Gubbio* (1913), about St. Francis; *The Chameleon* (1917), a comedy of modern life; and *Portrait of Mrs. W.* (1922), a prose play about the love affair of Mary Wollstonecraft and William Godwin. In 1925 her *Diary and Letters* appeared, followed in 1927 by *Collected Poems* and *Collected Plays*.

Peale, Norman Vincent (1898–1993),   clergyman, writer, editor. After holding several pulpits in various cities, the Ohio-born Peale became minister of the Marble Collegiate Reformed Church, New York City, in 1932. An effective preacher and writer, he called on the findings of psychiatry to help him inspire the troubled. He defined Christianity as "the science of successful living." Among his many widely read books, *A Guide to Confident Living* (1948) and *The Power of Positive Thinking* (1952) are the best known. Arthur Gordon has written *Norman Vincent Peale, Minister to Millions* (1958).

Peale, Rembrandt (1778–1860), son of Charles Willson Peale (1741–1827). Like his father he was a portrait painter but also painted allegorical subjects. His *Notes on Italy* (1813) describes his life abroad, some of his poetry is included in *Portfolio of an Artist* (1837).

Pearl. The child born of the adultery of Arthur Dimmesdale and Hester Prynne in Hawthorne's SCARLET LETTER (1850).

Pearl, The (1947), a novelette by JOHN STEINBECK. When a baby is stung by a scorpion, the child's father, pearl-fisher Kino, sets out to find a pearl to pay the doctor. He finds a huge one, but his neighbors plot to steal it and tragedy follows. The story is based on a folktale.

Pearl of Orr's Island, The (1862), a novel by HARRIET BEECHER STOWE. Whittier called it "the most charming New England idyll ever written." Mara Lincoln, the "pearl of great price," is brought up in the Maine fishing village of Orr's Island by her grandparents, who also adopt Moses, a Spanish boy. Mara comes to love Moses, but after many complications she dies and he marries her friend Sally.

Pearson's Magazine. A monthly equivalent of the London magazine of the same name; it was started in 1899 and ceased publication in 1925. For a time it reprinted some of the contents of the British magazine. Its chief celebrity comes from the fact that the brilliant and erratic Frank Harris bought it in 1916. He edited it until September 1922, but brought himself into disfavor because of his attacks on big business and the conduct of World War I. After he left the magazine it changed its policies, but survived for only three years.

Peary, Robert Edwin (1856–1920), explorer. Peary entered the United States Navy as a civil engineer. He began his Arctic explorations in 1886; on April 6, 1909, he reached the North Pole. Dr. Frederick Cook claimed he had reached the pole a year earlier; in 1911 Congress recognized Peary's claims and made him a rear admiral. Peary wrote *Northward over the "Great Ice"* (2 v. 1898), *Nearest the Pole* (1907), *The North Pole* (1910), and *Secrets of Polar Travel* (1917). His biography was written by Fitzhugh Green (1926) and by W. H. Hobbs (1936). Peary's wife, **Josephine Diebitsch Peary** (1863–1895), accompanied him on early expeditions and wrote *My Arctic Journal* (1893); *The Snow Baby* (1901), an account of her daughter who was born farther north than any other foreign child; and *Children of the Arctic* (1903).

Peattie, Donald Culross (1898–1964), naturalist. Born in Chicago, Peattie was a botanist for the Department of Agriculture after graduation from Harvard. From 1926 until 1936 he conducted a nature column in the Washington *Star*. Although he published four novels—*Up Country* (1928, with his wife Louise Redfield), *Port of Call* (1932), *Sons of the Martians* (1932), and *The Bright Lexicon* (1934)—as well as a number of children's books, he is known best for his nature writings, which combine science, poetic prose, and popular philosophy. *An Almanac for Moderns* (1935) was highly praised by the critics. In *Singing in the Wilderness: A Salute to John James Audubon* (1935), the lyric prose verges on senti-

mentality. *Immortal Village* (1945) is a history of the town of Vence in southern France. With his son Noel, Peattie wrote *A Cup of Sky* (1950). Among his other books are *Green Laurels: The Lives and Achievements of the Great Naturalists* (1936); *A Book of Hours* (1937); *Flowering Earth* (1939); *The Road of a Naturalist* (1941), an autobiography; *Forward the Nation* (1942); *American Heartwood* (1949); *Sportsman's Country* (1952); *A Natural History of Western Trees* (1953); *Lives of Destiny* (1954); and *Parade with Banners* (1957).

Peck, Annie Smith (1850–1935), explorer, archaeologist, memoirist. Peck was born in Providence, Rhode Island. A famed mountain climber, who made ascents of the Matterhorn (1895), Popocatepetl and Orizaba (1897), and Huascarán in Peru (the first ascent ever made, 1908), Annie Smith Peck gathered much scientific data in the course of her remarkable climbing feats. She recorded her experiences and observations in *A Search for the Apex of America* (1911), *The South American Tour* (1914), and *Flying over South America* (1932).

Peck, George Wilbur (1840–1916), newspaperman, public official, humorist. Peck, born in Henderson, New York, made his reputation in LaCrosse, Wisconsin, as a humorous writer; he collected some of his sketches in *Adventures of One Terence McGrant* (1871). He founded a newspaper called *The Sun* in 1874; four years later he moved the paper to Milwaukee. There his views as an editor proved so popular that he was elected mayor of the city and then governor of the state (1890–94). Meanwhile he had continued to publish in his paper and then in book form many humorous sketches. The most popular dealt with two characters he called *Peck's Bad Boy and His Pa* (1883). Peck continued to write his popular books, including *Peck's Bad Boy and His Pa, No. 2* (1883); *Peck's Boss Book* (1884); *Peck's Irish Friend, Phelan Geohagan* (1887); *Peck's Uncle Ike and the Red-Headed Boy* (1899); and *Peck's Bad Boy with the Cowboys* (1907). *How Private George W. Peck Put Down the Rebellion* (1887) gave humorous memories of the Civil War. *Mirth for the Million* (1883) was later reprinted as *Peck's Fun* (1887).

Peck, John Mason (1789–1858), Baptist minister and founder of missionary schools. He wrote books on the West including *A Guide for Emigrants* (1831), *Life of Daniel Boone* (1847), and *Father Clark; or The Pioneer Preacher* (1855).

Peck, Samuel Minturn (1854–1938), poet, writer of sketches. Peck wrote sugary verses, mainly about his native Alabama. Among his collections are *Cap and Bells* (1886), *Rings and Love Knots* (1892), *Rhymes and Roses* (1895), *Fair Women of Today* (1896), and *The Autumn Trail* (1925). He also gathered his prose sketches in *Alabama Sketches* (1902) and *Swamp Tales* (1912).

Peckham, Richard. A pseudonym of RAYMOND HOLDEN.

Peck's Bad Boy. See GEORGE WILBUR PECK.

Pecos Bill. This folk hero of the Southwest is the cowboy's equivalent of the logger's PAUL BUNYAN. He cleared Texas of badmen, taught the broncos to buck, invented tarantulas and scorpions as a joke on his friends, dug the Rio Grande, and invented roping. His horse, WidowMaker, was raised on a special diet of nitroglycerin and barbed wire and killed everyone who rode him except Bill. Pecos Bill's exploits are told in *Tall Tales from Texas* (1934), by Mody C. Boatright, and in shorter pieces by Edward O'Reilly and J. Frank Dobie. Carl Sandburg in *The People, Yes* (1936) calls him Pecos Pete.

Peder Victorious (1923, tr. from the Norwegian 1929), the second novel in a trilogy by OLE RÖLVAAG, the first being GIANTS IN THE EARTH and the third THEIR FATHER'S GOD. The scene is the Dakotas. The story involves the experiences of a family of Norwegian immigrants, their difficulties, church affairs, social diversions, etc. The hero is Peder Victorious Holm, who is urged by his mother and the local minister to enter the clergy; instead, as a result of a love affair, he chooses to become a farmer.

Peg o' My Heart (1912), a comedy by J. HARTLEY MANNERS.

Peirce, Charles Santiago Sanders (1839–1914), logician, scientist, philosopher. Peirce, born in Cambridge, Massachusetts, attributed his abilities and ideas to the influence of his father, Benjamin Peirce (1809–1880), a brilliant mathematician, who supervised much of his education. After his graduation from Harvard, where he developed an interest in philosophy, he joined the United States Coast Survey, which employed him for thirty years (1861–91). His scientific work on astronomy, gravity, and geodetics was original and competent but did not attract much notice. During the same period he studied under LOUIS AGASSIZ, lectured at Harvard on the philosophy of science (1864–65), was a member of the group that gave the Harvard lectures in philosophy (1869–70), and published a number of important papers on logic.

His connection with the Cambridge METAPHYSICAL CLUB in the 1870s and his friendship with Chauncey Wright and WILLIAM JAMES contributed to his formulation of the philosophy of PRAGMATISM. A paper in the *North American Review* (October 1871), in which he defended the philosophical realism of Duns Scotus and attacked Berkeley's nominalism, contains some elements of pragmatism, but his article *How to Make Our Ideas Clear*, which appeared in *Popular Science Monthly* in January 1878, is considered to be the progenitor of the philosophy of pragmatism in the United States. William James, to whom pragmatism owes its fame as a movement, first used the term in 1898, crediting Peirce as the originator; however, Peirce's pragmatism is of a different variety, more similar to the idealism of Josiah Royce, and including universals and an Absolute, which James and his followers rejected.

Peirce's teaching was sporadic, and by far the majority of his papers—on logic, metaphysics, mathematics, religion, psychology, science, and a wide range of other subjects—were not published in his lifetime. He devoted the last twenty-five years of his life to writing, hampered toward the end by financial difficulties and poor health. Never given much recognition outside of small professional circles before his death, he has come to be regarded as one of the most brilliant minds of his time and one of the most outstanding American philosophers.

The Charles Hartshorne and Paul Weiss six-volume edition of the *Collected Papers* (1931–35) is being replaced by a chronological edition edited by Christian Kloesel, Nathan Houser and others, *The Writings of Charles S. Peirce*. Six volumes are now in print. *The Essential Peirce: Selected Philosophical Writings* was issued by the same editors in two volumes (1992, 1998).

Peirce, William (1590?–1641), shipmaster, almanac compiler. In 1638 Peirce, born in England, issued his *Almanac for the Year of Our Lord 1639*, probably the first almanac put out in America. It was printed by the Stephen Daye Press.

PEN. A world association that preserves international ties among writers, PEN was founded in London on October 6, 1921, by Catherine Dawson Scott, an English writer, and John Galsworthy, who became its first president and who established a trust fund for the organization with the Nobel Prize money awarded to him in 1932. The first PEN center in the United States was opened in New York City (1922) under the presidency of BOOTH TARKINGTON.

Penhallow, Samuel (1665–1726), merchant, public official, historian. Born in England, Penhallow emigrated to New Hampshire in 1686. A wealthy tradesman, he also served the colony as chief justice. His interest in the wars with the Indians, wars he accounted for as a punishment from God for the sins of the Puritans, particularly for their not Christianizing the Indians, resulted in a popular book, *The History of the Wars of New England with the Eastern Indians* (1726, reprinted 1859).

Penn, William (1644–1718), statesman, religious and political writer. After his expulsion from Oxford University in 1662 because of his religious convictions, Penn traveled in France and Italy until recalled by his father. He gave up a brief naval career to study law. When he wearied of Lincoln's Inn, his father sent him in 1666 to manage his Irish estates. In Ireland Penn was imprisoned for his avowal of Quaker beliefs. When released, he returned to London and continued to express his beliefs. His first important work, *No Cross, No Crown* (1669), was a powerful plea for the Friends' religion and a scathing attack on the established clergy. During the next three years he was imprisoned a number of times but did not cease his activities. *The Great Case of Liberty of Conscience* (1670), written in prison, is a defense of religious toleration. On his release in 1671 he visited Holland and Germany, founding a Quaker society at Emden. He married in 1672 and settled down in Hertfordshire, where he wrote the *Treatise of Oaths, England's Present Interest Considered*, and a number of other tracts.

Penn acted as arbitrator in a dispute between Fenwick and Byllinge, two Friends who had bought land in America from the Crown. When a portion was put up for sale, Penn bought it, becoming one of the five proprietors. He visited the new colony and drew up its constitution. Soon many Quakers settled in what became West Jersey. In 1677 he returned to Holland and Germany to continue his missionary work, this time accompanied by George Fox. As a result of this expedition, a number of Germans from Kirchheim were drawn to the New World, where they settled in Germantown, the earlier name for Philadelphia. When in 1678 a new threat of "popish terror" appeared, Penn wrote his *Epistle to the Children of Light in This Generation*, followed a year later by *An Address to Protestants of All Persuasions*, and then by several lively and timely political tracts. But things looked grave for all dissenters, and he once more thought of America. He asked King Charles II for territory in America in payment of a debt owed to his father. On March 14, 1681, Penn received "a tract of land in America north of Maryland," which he named Sylvania—to which the king, over the new owner's protests, prefixed the name Penn in honor of Penn's father. Penn spent the next year drawing up a constitution. In September 1682, after writing his *Farewell to England*, Penn sailed without his family to the New World. On arrival he gathered together an assembly and passed "The Great Law of Pennsylvania," which stated that the territory was to be a Christian state on a Quaker model. His *Some Account of the Province of Pennsylvania* was published in 1681. Penn was notable for his just and friendly relations with the Indians. Voltaire said that his pact with the Indians was the only treaty made with them which was never sworn to and never broken.

Trouble with Lord Baltimore over the treatment of Quakers in Maryland brought Penn back to England in 1684; five months later King Charles died and Penn found himself in a powerful position. He managed to obtain the release of 1200 imprisoned Quakers, as well as a pardon for John Locke. *Information and Direction to Such Persons as Are Inclined to America* was published in 1684. He undertook a third mission to Holland and Germany in 1686; on his return he set out on a preaching tour in England. *Good Advice to the Church of England, Roman Catholics, and Protestant Dissenters* appeared at this time.

During the absence of its governor, troubles were brewing in Pennsylvania, and finally the Council in London removed Penn as governor. He lived for some time in retirement, during which he wrote *Some Fruits of Solitude* (1693), a book of maxims often regarded as the most literary of his writings, and a remarkable scheme for establishing *The Present and Future Peace of Europe* through a European parliament (1693).

On August 20, 1694, his governorship was restored. He did not, however, return to Pennsylvania until 1699, when he was forced to wrestle with the problem of slavery, which he was unable to abolish. In 1700 he made another successful treaty with the Indians and worked with Lord Bellomont in New York on a consolidation of the laws in America. He was forced to return to England in 1701, and once again affairs in America went from bad to worse. Penn decided to give his province back to the Crown if Queen Mary would take the Quakers under her protection. His mind was affected by a stroke before arrangements could be completed, and he died a few years later.

Among Penn's other works are *Fruits of a Father's Love* (1727), *An Account of W. Penn's Travails in Holland and Ger-*

many (1694), *A Brief Account of the Rise and Progress of the People Called Quakers* (1694), *The Harmony of Divine and Heavenly Doctrines* (1696), and *The Christian Quaker and His Divine Testimony* (1674). H. J. Cadbury and Isabel Grubb have edited Penn's *My Irish Journal* (1952). The most nearly complete edition of Penn's works is *A Collection of the Works of William Penn* (2 v. 1726), with a biography by Joseph Besse. Penn appears in Anna L. B. Thomas's novel *Nancy Lloyd, The Journal of a Quaker Pioneer* (1927). Pennsbury Manor, a recreation of Penn's home in Bucks County, Pennsylvania, has been established as a memorial.

Pennell, Elizabeth Robins (1855–1936),   biographer, travel writer. Elizabeth Robins was born in Philadelphia. After she wrote the text for a volume of illustrations by the painter JOSEPH STANLEY PENNELL, she and Pennell were married. They lived for over thirty years (1884–1918) in London, where they knew James, Shaw, and other celebrated authors and artists. They collaborated on many books, including *A Canterbury Pilgrimage* (1885), *The Life of James McNeill Whistler* (1908), and *Our Philadelphia* (1914). Elizabeth Pennell wrote *The Life of Mary Wollstonecraft* (1884), a biography of her writer-uncle *Charles Godfrey Leland* (1906); *Our House and London Out of Our Windows* (1912); and *The Life and Letters of Joseph Pennell* (2 v. 1929).

Pennell, Joseph Stanley (1857–1926),   painter, biographer. Pennell was born in Philadelphia. As a result of his success as the illustrator of George Washington Cable's *The Creoles of Louisiana* (1884), Pennell was sent to Italy to illustrate a series of articles on Tuscan cities written by William Dean Howells. Pennell and his wife, ELIZABETH ROBINS PENNELL, settled in England where they socialized with writers and artists and collaborated on several books; she wrote the texts and he provided illustrations. He became art editor of the *Star* in 1888, but turned the column over to his wife; she wrote that column and another under her own name in the *Daily Chronicle* for many years. Whistler gave his private papers to the Pennells and asked them to write his biography. Their *Life of James McNeill Whistler* (1908) was published five years after Whistler's death. Under Whistler's influence, Pennell first tried etching and then lithography of landscapes and factories. One series, "The Wonder of Work" (1909–1912), illustrated the industrial midlands of England and the construction of the Panama Canal. During World War I Pennell produced a series of drawings published as *Pictures of War Work in England* (1917). After the war, the Pennells returned to the United States where he was an art critic for the *Brooklyn Eagle*. He published *The Adventures of an Illustrator* (1925).

Pennsylvania Dutch,   an inaccurate term for the German-American people of eastern Pennsylvania and for their dialect, derived from German idiom. The region was settled by German immigration beginning in 1683 and continuing through the 18th and 19th centuries. Many of the people were members of religious sects that advocated separation from the general population, so their language and customs have persisted until recent times. The dialect is used in humorous writings such as the poetry of CHARLES FOLLEN ADAMS and CHARLES GODFREY LELAND. ELSIE SINGMASTER and THAMES WILLIAMSON both wrote novels set in the region.

Pennsylvania Farmer.   Pen name of JOHN DICKINSON.

Pennsylvania Gazette, The.   SAMUEL KEIMER, who was BENJAMIN FRANKLIN's first employer and later his constant rival, began to issue on December 24, 1728, a weekly periodical, *The Universal Instructor in All Arts and Sciences and Pennsylvania Gazette*. After nine ponderous and unsuccessful months, Keimer was glad to get rid of the paper and sold it to Franklin, who published the first issue under his editorship on October 2, 1729, and continued to own and edit the weekly until 1766. Franklin promptly dropped the adult education section of the paper's title and issued it simply as *The Pennsylvania Gazette*. In 1732 he began to issue a German edition called *Die Philadelphische Zeitung*, but this soon failed. The English version was very successful. It was as lively as Franklin could make it, and he contributed his *Dialogue Between Philocles and Horatio Concerning Virtue and Pleasure*; the letters of Anthony Afterwit and Alice Addertongue; *The Meditation on a Quart Mug; A Witch Trial at Mount Holly*; and *An Apology for Printers*, the last being a statement (June 10, 1731) on freedom of the press. He introduced weather reports and wrote for the man in the street. In 1754 he published in the *Gazette* what was probably the first cartoon in an American paper, a snake cut into pieces representing American colonies, with the motto "Join, or Die." David Hall and his descendants continued the paper. The last issue appeared on October 11, 1815.

Pennsylvania Magazine (January 1775–July 1776), a magazine nominally edited by THOMAS PAINE who contributed many articles to it. Robert Aitken published the monthly, which included reports on the progress of the Revolutionary War, letters from leaders such as George Washington, the text of the proposed *Declaration of Independence*, and scientific articles and literature.

Pennsylvania Packet or General Advertiser (1771–1839),   a triweekly newspaper founded in Philadelphia by John Dunlop. THOMAS PAINE used its columns to carry on a controversy with WILLIAM SMITH, writing in the *Pennsylvania Gazette*. It became a daily paper in 1784. When Dunlop's partners took over operation of the paper in 1795, the name was changed to *Claypoole's American Daily Advertiser*. Washington's "Farewell Address" (1796) was published in it. Zachariah Poulson (1761–1844) bought it in 1800. *The Philadelphia North American* took it over in 1839.

Penrod (1914),   a novel by BOOTH TARKINGTON. This humorous account of the adventures of a twelve-year-old boy in a Midwestern community (drawn from the author's nephews) won wide popularity and was followed by *Penrod and Sam* (1916) and *Penrod Jashber* (1929). All three were gathered in an omnibus volume, *Penrod: His Complete Story* (1931).

Pentecost, Hugh.   See PHILIPS, JUDSON PENTECOST.

Peony (1948),   a novel by PEARL BUCK. This is a narrative concerning racial conflict, exemplified in the story of a Jewish family living in China.

People, Yes, The (1936),   a poem by CARL SANDBURG. This is a conglomerate poem, composed in alternating passages of prose and free verse, narrative and homily, copybook English and slang. The whole is intended to present the poet's faith in the United States and democracy.

Pepperell, Sir William (1696–1759),   public official, soldier. Born in Maine, Pepperell in 1722 became a colonel in the state militia; in 1727 he was elected to his majesty's Council for the Commonwealth of Massachusetts, and held this office for 32 years. Pepperell was a successful merchant, a member of the governor's council, for a time chief justice of the colony. In 1745 he led an expedition against Fort Louisburg at Cape Breton and helped capture it. In the French and Indian War he raised a regiment and was appointed lieutenant general. He kept a *Journal* of the Louisburg expedition (pub. 1911).

Pequod.   The whaling ship in Melville's MOBY-DICK (1851).

Pequot Indians.   The Pequots were an Algonquian tribe who moved out of northern New England into Connecticut, Rhode Island, and Long Island under pressure from Puritan settlers. When a trader named John Oldham was murdered by the Pequots (July 20, 1636), JOHN MASON led a group of Puritans and Indians in an attack (1638) on the Pequots at Fort Mystic, which they burned to the ground. Mason wrote a *Brief History of the Pequot War*, which was included without his name in Increase Mather's *Brief History of the War with the Indians in New England* (1677) and separately published in an edition prepared by Thomas Prince (1736). One of his lieutenants, John Underhill, in *News from America* (1638), gave a less reliable account. Philip Vincent, a young English clergyman in New England at the time, wrote *A True Relation of the Late Battle Fought in New England* (1637), which was free from personal bias. Lion Gardiner, an observer rather than a participant, gave some important additional information in his *Relation of the Pequot Wars* (about 1660). The conflict forms the background for Catharine Maria Sedgwick's novel *Hope Leslie* (1827).

Perch, Philemon.   The pen name of R. M. JOHNSTON.

Percival, James Gates (1795–1856),   poet, physician, geologist. Born in Connecticut and trained in medicine at Yale and the University of Pennsylvania, Percival served as medical officer and taught chemistry at West Point. He translated poetry from Russian, Serbian, and Hungarian and wrote poetry in English and German. He was a journalist for the Connecticut *Herald* and Bond's *American Athenaeum*. As state geologist for Connecticut (1835–1842) and Wisconsin (1854–1856) he made several technical contributions to the field.

His long poem "Prometheus" (published in *Poems*, 1821) was compared favorably with Byron's *Childe Harold* by American critics of his time. Percival also published *Prometheus Part II with Other Poems* (1822), *Clio I and II* (1822), and *Clio III*

(1827). In *The Dream of a Day* (1843) Percival experimented with various metrical patterns. Throughout his life Percival suffered from mental illness and for ten years lived voluntarily on the grounds of the State Hospital at New Haven, Connecticut.

Percy, Florence.   The pen name of ELIZABETH AKERS.

Percy, George (1580–1632),   colonist. Percy, a son of the Earl of Northumberland, was deputy governor of Virginia Colony in 1609–10 and again in 1611. He prepared three manuscripts on his experiences (1608, 1612, *c.* 1622). His *Observations Gathered out of a Discourse of the Plantation of the Southern Colony in Virginia* seems to have combined the 1608 and 1622 manuscripts and was printed in *Purchas His Pilgrims* (1652). The second manuscript was printed in 1922.

Percy, Walker (1916–1990),   novelist, essayist. Percy, a resident of Covington, Louisiana, from 1950 until his death, was the son of a Birmingham, Alabama, lawyer who committed suicide in 1929, Walker was adopted by his father's first cousin, WILLIAM ALEXANDER PERCY, of Greenville, Mississippi. He received his M.D. from Columbia in 1941, but shortly thereafter contracted tuberculosis and abandoned a career in medicine.

The recipient of many awards, Percy published six novels: *The Moviegoer* (1961), *The Last Gentleman* (1966), *Love in the Ruins* (1971), *Lancelot* (1977), *The Second Coming* (1980), and *The Thanatos Syndrome* (1987). His other volumes include a collection of his essays on language and culture, *The Message in the Bottle* (1975), and the predominantly nonfictional potpourri *Lost in the Cosmos* (1983). His work has been discussed in hundreds of journalistic and scholarly articles and several books. The effects of his medical training, as well as his Catholic existentialism, his studies in language and semiotics, and his Southern class-consciousness as a member of the aristocratic Percy family, are readily apparent in his fiction. His novels of philosophical and spiritual quest—notable for their mingling of hilarity and high seriousness, their narrative ingenuity and strong sense of place and character—successfully combine romance with comedy of manners, melodrama, folklore, thriller and science fiction, millenialist fantasy, and various modes of satire. Despite his great respect for scientific thought, a major target of his satire is the popular, superficially optimistic faith of scientism, which he saw as in reality a doctrine of despair.

Studies include John Edward Hardy, *The Fiction of Walker Percy*; William Rodney Allen, *Walker Percy: A Southern Wayfarer*; Kieran Quinlan, *Walker Percy: The Last Catholic Novelist*; Patrick H. Samway, *Walker Percy: A Life*; and Michael Kobre, *Walker Percy's Voices*.

JOHN EDWARD HARDY

Perelman, Bob [Robert] (1937–   ),   poet. Born in Youngstown, Ohio, Perelman received his early education at the University of Michigan, where he received a B.A. in English and an M.A. in classics (1969), and the University of Iowa (M.F.A. in poetry, 1970). Active in the poetry scene in San Francisco in the late 1970s and 1980s, he published a number of books before receiving his Ph.D. in English from Berkeley

in 1990. In the 1990s he has been a teaching poet and scholar at the University of Pennsylvania. Long identified with the LANGUAGE POETS, he is more political than some, using the incoherences of language to demonstrate "the pain of repression that comes with the territory of world dominion," in a time when Americans seem uncertain both of their contemporary mission and of their place in history. In *The Marginalization of Poetry* (1996), he suggests that Language Poetry has reached its end as a movement, and analyzes the work of some of its practitioners. *Ten to One: Selected Poems* appeared in 1999. Earlier volumes of verse include *Braille* (1975), his first book; *Seven Works* (1978); *Primer* (1981); *The First World* (1986); *Face Value* (1988); *Captive Audience* (1988), a long poem; *Virtual Reality* (1993); and *The Future of Memory* (1998). Other books include *Writing/Talks* (1985), a collection of poets' presentations and audience responses; and *The Trouble with Genius: Reading Pound, Joyce, Stein, and Zukovsky* (1994).

Perelman, S[idney] J[oseph] (1904–1979),   humorist. Born in Brooklyn, New York, Perelman was educated at Brown, wrote first for *Judge* and then *The New Yorker*, as well as for the movies. His satire, with much word play he said was influenced by Joyce, dealt particularly with the entertainment industry, advertising and popular culture. His collected writings include *Dawn Ginsberg's Revenge* (1929); *Parlor, Bedlam and Bath* (1930); *Strictly from Hunger* (1937); *Keep it Crisp* (1946); *Crazy Like a Fox* (1944); *Acres and Pains* (1947); *The Best of S. J. Perelman* (1947); *Westward Ha! or, Around the World in 80 Cliches* (1948); *Listen to the Mocking Bird* (1949); *The Swiss Family Perelman* (1950); *The Ill-Tempered Clavichord* (1953); *Perelman's Home Companion* (1955); *The Road to Miltown, or, Under the Spreading Atrophy* (1957); and *The Rising Gorge* (1961). He also wrote three plays, the best known of which is *One Touch of Venus* (with OGDEN NASH, 1943). A collection, *The Most of S. J. Perelman*, was published in 1958.

Perfectionism,   a religious doctrine advanced by JOHN HUMPHREY NOYES (1811–1886) grounded in biblical passages (*Matthew* v. 48) suggesting that humans could regain sinlessness through Christ. Utopian communities based on the doctrine were founded in Putney, Vermont; Oneida, New York; and Wallingford, Connecticut. Neighbors reacted so strongly to the practice of complex marriage, a form of polygamy practice in the communities, that Noyes had to flee to Canada in 1879, and the communities dissolved. See ONEIDA COMMUNITY.

Perils of Pauline, The (1914? and thereafter),   a series of movies produced in weekly installments for many years. The script writer was CHARLES WILLIAM GODDARD (1880–1951), and the leading actress was Pearl White. Pauline was always in danger, but always managed to escape. She hung at the edge of cliffs, sank in quicksand, was swept down mill-races—and enjoyed it all. Goddard also wrote or helped to write *The Exploits of Elaine*, *The Mysteries of Myra*, and similar movie series. See HAROLD MACGRATH.

Perkins, Eli. Pen name of MELVILLE DE LANCEY LANDON.

Perkins, Frederick Beecher (1828–1899), librarian, editor, biographer. The Connecticut-born Perkins was the father of Charlotte Perkins Gilman and a nephew of Henry Ward Beecher and Harriet Beecher Stowe, and a brother-in-law of Edward Everett Hale. He worked on newspapers for a while, later became librarian of the Connecticut Historical Society (1857–61), and then of the San Francisco Public Library (1880–87). He was an associate editor of the *Library Journal* (1877–80). Among his books are *Charles Dickens* (1870); *The Best Reading* (1872); a novel, *The Lost Library* (1874); and DEVIL PUZZLERS AND OTHER STUDIES (1877).

Perkins, Lucy Fitch (1865–1937), artist, writer for children. Born Lucy Fitch in Indiana, Perkins was both a clever writer and a capable illustrator. In 1911 she wrote *The Dutch Twins*, and this was so successful that she followed it up with a series of similarly named stories: *The Japanese Twins* (1912), *The Irish Twins* (1913), *The Eskimo Twins* (1914), *The Belgian Twins* (1917), and many others. Among them were historical tales such as *The Puritan Twins* (1921) and *The Colonial Twins of Virginia* (1924). Perkins sought to promote friendliness with other nations by her portrayal of their young people. Her daughter Eleanor Ellis Perkins wrote her biography, *Eve Among the Puritans* (1956).

Perkins, Maxwell Evarts (1884–1947), editor, publisher. Perkins, born in New York City, became vice-president and editor-in-chief of Charles Scribner's Sons. Perkins had the insight to encourage new writers, such as Lardner, Fitzgerald, Hemingway, and Wolfe. Perkins worked with Wolfe to revise his cumbersome first manuscript of *Look Homeward, Angel* (1929) for publication; Wolfe's next novel, *Of Time and the River* (1935), was dedicated to Perkins, but Wolfe took his third novel to a different publisher, and in *You Can't Go Home Again* (1940), introduced a character named Foxhall Edwards apparently modeled on Perkins. Perkins's correspondence was collected and published after his death as *Editor to Author: The Letters of Maxwell E. Perkins* (1950).

Perley. Pen name of BENJAMIN PERLEY POORE.

Perrot, Nicholas (1644–1718?), French fur trader, explorer. He acquired great skill in Indian languages and was used by Frontenac as an envoy to encourage the Sioux and other tribes to make war on the Iroquois, who were unfriendly to the French. In the name of France he took possession of the Upper Mississippi region. He wrote a *Mémoire* on the Indians and their habits and religions (1864, tr. 1911).

Perry, Bliss (1880–1954), editor, scholar. Born in Massachusetts, Perry edited the *Atlantic Monthly* (1899–1909) and taught English at Williams, Princeton, and Harvard. He wrote and edited many books on English and American literature, for example, *Little Masterpieces* (18 v. 1895–1900) and the *Cambridge Edition of the Poets* (1905–1909). He wrote critical biographies of Whitman (1906), Whittier (1907), Carlyle (1915), and Emerson (1931); studies such as *The Amateur Spirit* (1904), *The American Mind* (1912), and *The American Spirit in Literature* (1918); and works of fiction including *The Broughton House* (1890), *Salem Kit-*

tredge and Other Stories (1894), *The Plated City* (1895), and *The Powers at Play* (1899). His autobiography is entitled *And Gladly Teach* (1935).

Perry, George Sessions (1910–1956), war correspondent, writer, editor. Perry was born in Texas and wrote chiefly of life in the United States. His best-known book is *Cities of America* (1947), an account of twenty-one cities that appeared chapter by chapter in the *Saturday Evening Post*. *My Granny Van* (1949) is a biography of his grandmother. *Families of America* (1949) describes nine American families of varying national origins. He also wrote two novels—*Walls Rise Up* (1939) and *Hold Autumn in Your Hand* (1941)—and *The Story of Texas A. & M.* (1951).

Perry, Matthew Calbraith (1794–1858), naval officer. Born in Rhode Island, the younger brother of Commodore OLIVER HAZARD PERRY opened communication with Japan by delivering a letter from President Fillmore to the Emperor in 1853; in the following year a treaty of amity between Japan and the United States was concluded. He described his accomplishments in *Narrative of the Expedition of the American Squadron to the China Seas and Japan* (3 v. 1856), reissued in an edition by Sidney Wallach in 1952.

Perry, Nora (1831–1896), poet, novelist. Born in Massachusetts, Perry wrote simple lyrics collected in *After the Ball and Other Poems* (1875) and books for young people such as *Hope Benham* (1894) and *Mary Bartlett's Step-Mother* (1900).

Perry, Oliver Hazard (1785–1819), naval officer. Perry, a native of Rhode Island, took part in the naval war against France and in the Tripolitan War. When the War of 1812 broke out he was given command of the naval forces on Lake Erie. On September 10, 1813, he defeated the British fleet with vessels he had himself constructed and sent a famous message to General W. H. Harrison: "We have met the enemy and they are ours." While on a diplomatic mission to Venezuela he died of yellow fever. Perry's shipbuilding exploit is well described in Carl D. Lane's novel *The Fleet in the Forest* (1943); the Battle of Lake Erie appears vividly in Irving Bacheller's D'RI AND I (1901) and Robert S. Harper's *Trumpet in the Wilderness* (1940). A. S. Mackenzie wrote *The Life of Commodore Oliver Hazard Perry* (2 v. 1840); more recent lives have been written by James C. Mills (1913) and Charles J. Dutton (1935).

Perry, Ralph Barton (1876–1957), teacher, philosopher, biographer. Born in Vermont, Perry, as a professor at Harvard became the chief authority on his friend WILLIAM JAMES, preparing *An Annotated Bibliograhpy of the Writing of William James* (1920); *The Thought and Character of William James* (2 v. 1935, Pulitzer Prize); *In the Spirit of William James* (1938); and numerous articles on the man whose ideas he chiefly followed. He called his own version of pragmatism "neorealism." He also wrote *The Approach to Philosophy* (1905); *The New Realism* (1912); *General Theory of Value* (1926); *A Defense of Philosophy* (1931); *On All Fronts* (1941); *Puritanism and Democracy* (1945); *Characteristically American* (1949); *Realms of Value* (1953); and other books—all showing James's influence in the vigor and vitality of their style.

Perry, Thomas Sergeant (1845–1928), critic, teacher, biographer, historian. Edwin Arlington Robinson, who edited his letters in 1929, called Perry "one of the great appreciators." Perry, who was born in Rhode Island, wrote *The Life and Letters of Francis Lieber* (1882), *English Literature of the 18th Century* (1883), *From Opitz to Lessing* (1885), *The Evolution of a Snob* (1887), *A History of Greek Literature* (1890), *John Fiske* (1906), and many articles and book reviews. He taught at Harvard University for two brief periods (1868–72, 1877–82) and in Japan (1898–1901). Perry was deeply interested in foreign literatures and was active in popularizing Turgenev and other Russian novelists, as well as some of the naturalistic French novelists. Biographies of Perry were written by John T. Morse, Jr. (1929), and by Virginia Harlow (1951).

Pershing, J[ohn] J[oseph] (1860–1948), soldier, teacher, lawyer. Born in Missouri and a graduate of West Point, Pershing spent his entire adult life in the army. During the Spanish-American War he served in Cuba. In 1913 he suppressed an insurrection in the Philippines and in 1916 took part in the pursuit of the Mexican bandit Francisco Villa. In 1917 he was put in command of the American Expeditionary Forces in France. When the great offensive of July 1918 began, the American Army under Pershing opened the way for the collapse of the German forces. He became Chief of Staff in 1921. In 1931 he published *My Experiences in the World War* (2 v.), a work for which he received a Pulitzer Prize in history.

Personae, title of Ezra Pound's second volume of poetry (1909); in 1926) poems from that book and another called *Exultations* (1909) were reissued under the title *Personae*.

Peter [or Peters], Hugh (1598–1660), clergyman. Born in England, he lived in Massachusetts from 1636 to 1641, where he followed Roger Williams as pastor of the Salem church, took part in colonial government, and helped found Harvard. Returning to England as an agent for the Massachusetts Bay Colony, he (along with Thomas Weld) edited *New England's First Fruits* (1643), a pamphlet probably intended to encourage potential settlers. An active member of the Cromwell faction, he was executed after the collapse of the Commonwealth.

Peterkin, Julia [Mood] (1880–1961), novelist, short-story writer. Peterkin became a specialist in the life and language of the Gullahs of her home state of South Carolina and regions farther south. Her treatment of the Gullahs is sympathetic, yet realistic in its depiction of their hard, humble, often tragic lives. Her novel SCARLET SISTER MARY (1928) won a Pulitzer Prize and was dramatized (1930) by Daniel Reed; the play was performed by a white cast, headed by Ethel Barrymore, in blackface. Peterkin's other books include *Green Thursday* (1924); BLACK APRIL (1927); *Bright Skin* (1932); *Roll, Jordan, Roll* (1933, a collection of photographs with text by Peterkin); and *Plantation Christmas* (1934).

Peter Quince at the Clavier (in HARMONIUM, 1923), a poem by WALLACE STEVENS.

Peter Rugg, the Missing Man (1824), a story by WILLIAM AUSTIN. It appeared first in the *New England Galaxy* (September 10, 1824) and has been reprinted in numerous anthologies. Peter Rugg, driving to Boston and overtaken by a severe squall, stubbornly refuses to take shelter, and is condemned to go on driving for fifty years. Rugg never finds the city, and the vision of his galloping horse signals for New Englanders an approaching storm. The tale is a variation of the folk motif of the man who never returns (in folksong, the ship that never returns, or, more recently, the man lost on the Boston subway). Louise Imogen Guiney and Amy Lowell both have poems on the subject, and the tale has some resemblance to RIP VAN WINKLE (1819) and the story of the Wandering Jew. Hawthorne makes Peter Rugg the doorkeeper to the museum that houses "A Virtuoso's Collection" in MOSSES FROM AN OLD MANSE.

Peters, Samuel Andrew (1735–1826), Anglican clergyman, loyalist. Born in Connecticut, Peters fled to England in 1774 in protest against the coming Revolutionary War and expressed his disapproval of the political situation in *General History of Connecticut* (1781). Later historians copied some of his exaggerated descriptions of Puritan attitudes. He also wrote *A History of the Reverend Hugh Peters* (1807), claiming to be related to the Puritan clergyman. In 1805 he returned to press some land claims, but Congress disallowed the claims. J. H. Trumbull wrote *The Rev. Samuel Peters: His Defenders and Apologists* (1877).

Peterson, Charles Jacobs (1819–1887), editor, historian, novelist, publisher. Peterson was a powerful figure in the literary life of his native city, Philadelphia, when it was at the height of its prosperity as a publishing center. He was an editor of *Atkinson's Casket*, which later became GRAHAM'S MAGAZINE (1842), and of the SATURDAY EVENING POST. He founded the *Ladies' National Magazine* (1842), later called *Peterson's Magazine*, and with ANN S. STEPHENS edited it until his death. Meanwhile he wrote several historical novels: *Grace Dudley; or, Arnold at Saratoga* (1849), *Kate Aylesford* (1855), and others. He also wrote popular histories, including *The Military Heroes of the Revolution* (1848) and *Naval Heroes of the United States* (1850).

Peterson, Henry (1818–1891), editor, publisher, poet, novelist. Like his cousin CHARLES JACOBS PETERSON, Henry Peterson, born in Philadelphia, was an important figure in the magazine world of that city. He was on the editorial staff of the *Saturday Gazette* and then became editor of the SATURDAY EVENING POST, which he and Edmund Deacon purchased in 1848. He also wrote a good deal of verse and several novels. In 1863 he collected his *Poems* and in 1869 published *The Modern Job* in free verse. Among his novels were *Pemberton* (1873), *Confessions of a Minister* (1874), and *Bessie's Lovers* (1877). In 1864 Deacon and Peterson bought the *Lady's Friend*, which Peterson's wife Sarah edited until 1874.

Peterson, Roger Tory (1908–1996), nature writer, artist, teacher. Peterson, born in Jamestown, New York, combined artistry with science in a series of authoritative books on birds, shells, wildflowers, reptiles and amphibians for which he received numerous awards. Beginning with his *Field Guide to Birds* (1934), he regularly published carefully illustrated volumes on wildlife and birds in several regions of the United States, Mexico, and Europe that are used extensively by serious students as well as by amateur naturalists.

Petry, Ann (1908–1997), novelist, short-story writer. Born in Connecticut, Petry wrote her first novel, *The Street* (1946), about people trapped in Harlem ghetto life. *The Street* was one of the first novels by an African-American woman to gain critical attention. *Country Place* (1947) depicts class conflict in a small New England town, and *The Narrows* (1953) is the love story of a racially mixed couple. *Miss Muriel* (1971) is a collection of short stories. Petry's books for children include *The Drugstore Cat* (1949), *Harriet Tubman: Conductor on the Underground Railway* (1955), and *Tituba of Salem Village* (1964).

Pfaff's Cellar. A tavern at 653 Broadway near Bleecker Steet, New York City, this was the meeting place for the bohemians of the 1850s. WHITMAN, Henry Clapp, Ada Clare, FITZ-JAMES O'BRIEN, BAYARD TAYLOR, GEORGE ARNOLD, ADAH MENKEN, and WILLIAM WINTER were among the regular members. The group was scattered by the Civil War, but the bohemians had written so much in praise of Pfaff's that it flourished as a tourist attraction for many years. A lively account of Pfaff's Cellar is found in Albert Parry's *Garrets and Pretenders* (1933).

Phaenomena Quaedam Apocalyptica ad Aspectum Novi Orbis Configurata (1697), an interpretation of *Revelations* by SAMUEL SEWALL. Some political events of the day, particularly the difficulties with Governor Andros, turned Judge Sewall to the prophecies of St. John. He published this pamphlet as tending "toward a description of the New Heaven," namely, New England. For the most part he wrote of defects and weaknesses, but despite its blemishes Sewall foresaw a great future for the country he loved. While contemporary New England writers were still talking about English landscapes, Sewall wrote in loving detail about Plum Island, where he had played as a boy. Whittier refers to the work in his poem "The Prophecy of Samuel Sewall."

Phalanx. See NORTH AMERICAN PHALANX.

Phelps, Elizabeth [Stuart] ["H. Trusta"] (1815–1852), novelist. She was born in Andover, Massachusetts. Using her own experiences as a basis, Phelps wrote many popular books, largely religious in content: *Sunny Side, or, The Country Minister's Wife* (1851); *A Peep at Number Five, or, A Chapter in the Life of a City Pastor* (1851); *The Angel Over the Right Shoulder* (1852); *The Tell-Tale* (1853); and others. She also wrote books for children, including the four-volume Kitty Brown series (1850 and later). Her daughter, Elizabeth, also became an author. See ELIZABETH STUART PHELPS WARD.

Phelps, William Lyon (1865–1943), professor, columnist. Professor of English literature at Yale from 1892 to 1933, Phelps, born in Connecticut, wrote *The Beginnings of the English Romantic Movement* (1893) and *Browning: How to Know Him* (1915). His *Essays on Russian Novelists* (1911) was influential in bringing Russian works to popular attention. He

also wrote studies on American literature: *Some Makers of American Literature* (1923) and *Essays on American Authors* (1924). From 1922 until his death he wrote a column entitled AS I LIKE IT for *Scribner's Magazine*. Several collections of his popular essays were published, including the *Scribner's* pieces. *Autobiography with Letters* appeared in 1939.

Phi Beta Kappa, an honorary scholarly fraternity founded at the College of William and Mary in 1776. Chapters were soon founded at other schools, and women were first admitted in 1875. Emerson delivered his "American Scholar" address before the Harvard chapter in 1837; the same title is used for the society's quarterly magazine.

Philadelphia Story, The (1939), a play by PHILIP BARRY. Tracy Lord, a young heiress, finds her old Philadelphia family traditions too restrictive, especially after an escapade with a reporter on the eve of her second marriage. The action is hilarious and often startling, and Barry aims some sharp barbs at Philadelphia society. Yet his most sympathetic and tolerant character is C. K. Dexter Haven, a man of Tracy's own social set. He was her first husband, and when everything becomes mixed up on the morning of the second wedding, he takes the place of the pompous, priggish new bridegroom and remarries Tracy. The play made a hit on Broadway and was also filmed.

Philenia. Pen name of SARAH WENTWORTH MORTON.

Philip, King. See KING PHILIP.

Philips, Judson Pentecost (1903–1989), mystery writer. Under his pseudonym Hugh Pentecost, as well as under his own name, Philips wrote over 100 mystery and detective novels; at his peak he turned out three books a year. He began writing for pulp magazines in the 1920s. His *Cancelled in Red* won the first prize in Dodd, Mead's mystery competition in 1939. Philips continued working until his death. *Pattern of Terror* (1990) was his last book. Some other titles are *The Obituary Club* (1958); *The Wings of Madness* (1966), one of the many Peter Styles novels; *The Beautiful Dead* 1973); and *Death After Breakfast* (1978).

Philistine, The. A monthly magazine founded in 1895 at East Aurora, New York, by ELBERT HUBBARD. A disciple of the British poet and storyteller William Morris (1834–1896), Hubbard sought to do for the American public what Morris seemed to be doing in England—stigmatize modern machine culture as unesthetic and revive an interest in the arts and crafts. The magazine, a vehicle especially for Hubbard's apothegms, was an instrument of adult education. The best-remembered piece to appear in it was A MESSAGE TO GARCIA (1899), an inspirational exhortation that was later reprinted many times. The magazine suspended publication in 1915, shortly after Hubbard went down with the *Lusitania*.

Phillips, David Graham ["John Graham"] (1867–1911), journalist, novelist. Born in Indiana, Phillips worked for the Cincinnati *Times-Star*, the New York *Tribune*, the New York *Sun*, and the New York *World*. From 1901 to 1911 he published many muckraking articles; the series entitled *The Treason of the Senate* was published in *Cosmopolitan* in 1906. He also wrote twenty-three problem novels, among them *The Great God Success* (1901), *The Cost* (1904), *The Deluge* (1905), *Light-Fingered Gentry* (1907), *The Fashionable Adventures of Joshua Craig* (1909), *The Conflict* (1911), and *George Helm* (1912). A number of his novels, as well as his only play, *The Worth of a Woman* (1908), deal with his era's changing attitudes toward women. His most important novel, SUSAN LENOX: HER FALL AND RISE (1917), a well-documented account of a country girl who becomes a prostitute, led his friends to call him an American Balzac. His career was cut short by a madman who shot him when he was walking near Gramercy Park in New York; the assailant believed Phillips had maligned his sister in *Joshua Craig*. I. F. Marcosson published *David Graham Phillips and His Times* in 1932.

Phillips, Henry Wallace (1869–1930), miner, teacher, writer. Although he was born in New York City, Phillips was one of the best writers of Western stories. He created a cowboy hero named Red Saunders, who contrived to get himself, his friends, and his foes into innumerable difficulties, mostly funny. The stories were illustrated by a master artist, A. B. FROST. Phillips was a good friend of another writer of Westerns, EUGENE MANLOVE RHODES, and occasionally collaborated with him. Among Phillips's books are *Red Saunders* (1902); *Plain Mary Smith: A Romance of Red Saunders* (1905); *Mr. Scraggs: Introduced by Red Saunders* (1906); *Red Saunders' Pets and Other Critters* (1906); *The Mascot of Sweetbriar Gulch* (1908); and *Trolley Folly* (1909).

Phillips, Jayne Anne (1952–   ), poet, short-story writer, novelist. Born and raised in West Virginia, Phillips was educated at the University of West Virginia and the University of Iowa. After two small press books, *Sweethearts* (1976) and *Counting* (1978), Phillips gained attention with *Black Tickets* (1979), a collection of short stories with interspersed vignettes. Her first novel, *Machine Dreams*, appeared in 1984. *Fast Lanes* (1987) is a story collection. Phillips draws on her experiences in West Virginia, the West Coast, and New England. *Shelter* (1994), a novel, is a gothic tale of a girls' summer camp in West Virginia. *Motherkind* (2000), a novel, drowns birth, marriage, and death in too many daily details.

Phillips, Wendell (1811–1884), lawyer, orator, reformer. Born in Boston, Phillips was graduated from Harvard Law School and was admitted to the bar in 1834. In 1835 he witnessed the mobbing of WILLIAM LLOYD GARRISON by proslavery sympathizers, an incident that changed the course of his life. Joining Garrison in the Anti-Slavery Society, he devoted all his time to lecturing in favor of abolition. A brilliant and gifted speaker, he introduced a direct and colloquial manner of public speaking as opposed to the elaborate and flowery style then in vogue. After the Civil War he labored for prohibition, women's suffrage, prison reform, and various administrative changes. The first volume of his *Speeches, Lectures, and Letters* appeared in 1863, the second in 1891.

Philological Society (1788–89), an organization whose members, including Noah Webster, were dedicated to the promotion of American language. The group was later called the Friendly Club of New York.

Philosophy of Composition, The (*Graham's Magazine*, April 1846), an essay by EDGAR ALLAN POE. It seeks to explain the nature of literary composition by taking the reader into the workshop of Poe's mind when he was composing THE RAVEN. Poe insists that careful planning must precede the writing of any poem, and that the plan must foresee the *dénouement* from the beginning. A pattern must be elaborated, and the exact nature of the effect to be produced must be analyzed. To show what he means, Poe explains how in planning *The Raven* he deliberately kept the poem brief, included a refrain in order to achieve the poetic effect he wanted, chose a single word ("nevermore") for this refrain, and selected the death of a beautiful woman as the most poetic of all topics.

Philo Vance. See VANCE, PHILO.

Phips [or Phipps], Sir William (1651–1695), soldier, governor. A skilled mariner, Phips was knighted for recovering treasure from a vessel sunk off Haiti. Born in Maine, He commanded Massachusetts troops in the capture of Port Royal (1690) and in an unsuccessful attack on Quebec, and was made royal governor of Massachusetts Bay Colony. He named a commission to try persons accused of witchcraft, but when he returned to the colony after an absence to discover that spectral evidence was being used to accuse people and that his own wife was among many prominent citizens who had been named, he ordered the trials to end. Involved in many disputes, he was called to London to answer charges against him in 1694 but died before the hearings began. Phips appears as an elephant in Cotton Mather's *Political Fables* (1692) and under his own name in Nathaniel Hawthorne's *Fanshawe and Other Pieces* (1876). Alice Lounsbury wrote *Sir William Phips* (1941).

Phoenix, John. The pen name of GEORGE HORATIO DERBY (1823–1861), California newspaperman. One of his books, a volume of sketches and burlesques, was called *Phoenixiana* (1856).

Piatt, John James (1835–1917), newspaperman, writer, editor, consul. Born in Indiana, Piatt first worked for the *Ohio State Journal* when WILLIAM DEAN HOWELLS was a member of the staff. They published together *Poems of Two Friends* (1860). From 1882 to 1893 he served as American consul at Cork, then at Dublin. Meanwhile, Piatt published many books of verse, including *Poems in Sunshine and Firelight* (1866), *Western Windows and Other Poems* (1869), *Idyls and Lyrics of the Ohio Valley* (1881), and *Odes in Ohio and Other Poems* (1897). He and his wife, **Sarah Morgan [Bryan] Piatt** (1836–1919), often published volumes together, such as *The Nests at Washington and Other Poems* (1864) and *The Children Out-of-Doors: A Book of Verses by Two in One House* (1885).

Piazza Tales, The (1856), a collection of six stories by HERMAN MELVILLE. All the tales except "The Piazza," which Melville wrote as an introductory sketch for the collection, appeared in *Putnam's Monthly Magazine* and are among his finest.

"The Bell Tower" is a story of the artist Bannadonna, who, in creating a mechanical man, strives to rival the power of God. Bannadonna is destroyed by his own creation, and Melville invokes the obvious moral: "And so pride went before the fall." Somewhat similar in theme to "The Bell Tower" is "The Lightning-Rod Man," which tells how a lightning-rod salesman tries to sell his wares one stormy afternoon. But the householder refuses to purchase a rod, believing that, though man cannot control the acts of Deity, he should not fear Him.

THE ENCANTADAS, OR, THE ENCHANTED ISLES is a collection of ten sketches set in the Galápagos Islands, which Melville visited as a seaman in 1841. The sketches are uneven in quality; probably the best are the powerfully sentimental tale of the Chola Widow and the magnificent descriptions of "The Isles at Large." In this latter sketch Melville describes the general appearance of the Encantadas—ashy, barren, inhabited by enormous tortoises—until he transforms them into symbols of hell on earth.

"The Piazza" and "Benito Cereno" bear some resemblance to one another in their investigation into the difference between appearance and reality, but "The Piazza" is by far the less important of the two. "Benito Cereno" is a triumph. Most of the action takes place aboard the *San Dominick*, a slave ship commanded by Benito Cereno. Although the captain appears to be in command, in reality he is the prisoner of the slaves, who are led by the Senegalese Babo, posing as Cereno's valet. The narrative gradually unfolds through the consciousness of Captain Amasa Delano of Massachusetts, who, in his innocence, never more than suspects the evil he cannot quite plumb. Eventually the conspirators are undone and Babo is put to death, but Cereno dies soon afterward. Melville based the story on information taken from *A Narrative of Voyages and Travels in the Northern and Southern Hemispheres* (1817), by AMASA DELANO.

BARTLEBY THE SCRIVENER, perhaps the best story of the collection, deals with an enigmatic young scrivener who refuses to work but will not leave his employer's office. Strongly disturbed by Bartleby, for whom he feels somehow responsible, the employer moves his office elsewhere, and Bartleby is taken to prison, where he dies.

Pickering, John (1777–1846),   lawyer, diplomat, linguist. Pickering, born in Salem, Massachusetts, was attached to the legations in Lisbon and London and then returned to the United States and was admitted to the bar. In 1829 he became City Solicitor in Boston. Adept in many languages, he was most interested in the languages spoken by Native Americans and the special locutions that English-speaking residents of the United States had adopted. On the former subject he wrote an article for the *Memoirs* (1820) of the American Academy entitled *On the Adoption of a Universal Orthography for the Indian Languages of North America*. On the other subject he wrote the first formal work on the American language: *A Vocabulary, or, Collection of Words and Phrases Which Have Supposed to Be Peculiar to the U.S. of America* (1816). In 1817 Noah Webster wrote *A Letter to the Honorable John Pickering on the Subject of His Vocabulary*. In this he took exception to some of Pickering's assertions. See TIMOTHY PICKERING.

Pickering, Timothy (1745–1829),   public official. Born in Salem, Massachusetts, Pickering was active in anti-British activities leading to the Revolution. He served as an adjutant to General Washington. After the war he moved to Pennsylvania, where he served in the Pennsylvania Constitutional Convention, became postmaster-general, secretary of war, secretary of state (1745–1800), United States Senator, and Congressman. The best known of his writings is the *Political Essays Series of Letters Addressed to the People of the U.S.* (1812), in connection with his ideas for a New England Confederacy. JOHN PICKERING was his son. Octavius Pickering and C. W. Upham wrote *The Life of Timothy Pickering* (4 v. 1867–73).

Pickthall, Marjorie L[owrey] C[hristie] (1883–1922), Canadian poet, novelist. Pickthall was brought by her parents from England to Toronto in 1890. She worked for a short time as a librarian and published short stories and some novels, including *Little Hearts* (1915), but it was her poetry that won a wide reputation. She issued several collections: *Drift of Pinions* (1912), *Lamp of Poor Souls* (1916), and *The Wood Carver's Wife and Other Poems* (1922). Her father, Arthur C. Pickthall, edited her *Collected Poems* (1927). Her verses are melodic, in traditional forms, with a constantly wistful note. She came under the influence of the Celtic Renaissance, but often employed Canadian themes and backgrounds.

Pierce, Lorne (1890–1961),   editor, biographer, literary historian. Pierce, born in Ontario, received degrees in theology and letters from various Canadian and American universities, was ordained in 1916, and became editor-in-chief of the Ryerson Press in 1920. In that capacity he encouraged numerous young Canadian writers and published their work. He also founded several awards for literature. He wrote numerous articles and textbooks as well as many volumes about the Canadian people and their arts, including *Marjorie Pickthall, a Book of Remembrance* (1925); *William Kirby: the Portrait of a Loyalist* (1929); *Master Builders* (1937); *A Canadian People* (1945); and *Grace Coombs: Artist* (1949). He also edited collections of Canadian prose and poetry, such as *The Makers of Canadian Literature* (13 v. 1922); *Alfred Lord Tennyson and William Kirby* (1929), correspondence between the two poets; and *Bliss Carman's Scrapbook* (1931).

Piercy, Marge (1936–   ),   poet, novelist. Born poor and white in a predominantly black neighborhood of Detroit, Piercy writes from a political stance. She rarely uses a persona in her poetry, speaking instead in her own voice about social issues and events of everyday life with humor and sensuality. Her poetry collections include *Breaking Camp* (1968), *Hard Loving* (1969), *To Be of Use* (1973), *Living in the Open* (1976), *The Twelve Spoke Wheel Flashing* (1978), *The Moon is Always Female* (1980), *Circles on the Water: Selected Poems* (1982), *Stone, Paper, Knife* (1983), *Available Light* (1988), *Mars and Her Children* (1992); *What Are Big Girls Made Of* (1997) and *The Art of Blessing the Day: Poems with a Jewish Theme* (1999). Active in the civil rights movement and a feminist, she intends her writing to be "of use" in raising the consciousness of other women. She attended the University of Michigan on a scholarship, an experience described in the novel *Braided Lives* (1982). Her other fiction titles include *Going Down Fast* (1969), *Dance the Eagle to Sleep* (1973), *Woman on the Edge of Time* (1976), *The High Cost of Living* (1978), *Vida* (1980), *Fly Away Home* (1984), *Gone to Soldiers* (1987), *He, She, and It* (1991), *City of Darkness, City of Light* (1996), and *Three Women* (1999).

Pierpont, John (1785–1866),   clergyman, poet. Pierpont, born in Connecticut, turned from the bar to literature, publishing *Airs of Palestine*, his first book of poems, in 1816. He attended Harvard Divinity School and became pastor of the Hollis Street Church in Boston in 1819. His antislavery views and advocacy of temperance and other unpopular causes led to his transfer to a Unitarian church in Troy, New York, and then to West Medford, Massachusetts. From 1861 until his death he served as clerk in the Treasury Department in Washington. He published two later books of poetry, *Airs of Palestine and Other Poems* (1840) and *The Anti-Slavery Poems of John Pierpont* (1843). He also edited two school readers, *The American First Class Book* (1823) and *The National Reader* (1827). J. P. Morgan was his grandson.

Pierre: or, The Ambiguities.   Herman Melville's seventh book, published in 1852, the first in which Melville abandoned first person narration. Like *Moby-Dick*, *Pierre* draws heavily on Shakespearean sources, especially the tragedies, and this, along with Melville's allusions to Dante, establishes an intertextual matrix of futility and disaster for Melville's narrative. *Pierre* traces the history of Pierre Glendinning of a landed and illustrious Revolutionary family, from his early teens and illusions of security, of family pride, and pastoral bliss through his receipt of a letter written by a young woman claiming to be his illegitimate half-sister to the murder, suicide, and death precipitated by Pierre's total rejection of his family and culture and by his total dedication to the cause of Isabel, his putative half-sister. Melville complicates the history of Pierre by punctuating it with the various ambiguities obscuring nearly every facet of Pierre's idealistic quest, from the familial and social implications of his decision to devote himself to Isabel to the theological and aesthetic implications of his course of action, to the credibility of Isabel's claim to be the daughter of Pierre's father, to the very nature of the human being and the meaning of human action.

While almost universally scorned by contemporary reviewers for its stylistic eccentricities, its strained and digressive narrative, and its violation of genteel sexual taboos, Melville's astute and prescient negotiations of the aesthetic and philosophical ambiguities inherent in Pierre's life has, according to the views of many 20th-century literary critics and theorists, elevated *Pierre* to the ranks of Melville's greatest works.

RUSSELL J. REISING

Pike,   a stereotypical character in mid-nineteenth century humor. A backwoodsman native of Pike County, variously located in any one of a half dozen states near the Mississippi River or on the frontier. In *At Home and Abroad*

(1960), BAYARD TAYLOR describes such a character as an "Anglo-Saxon relapsed into semi-barbarism." A Pike is characterized by rural dialect, alcoholism, crude manners, suspicion, greed, and ignorance, but general good nature. GEORGE DERBY was the first to describe the character, in 1854. BRET HARTE's *East and West Poems* (1871) and JOHN HAY's *Pike County Ballads* (1871) further popularized the figure.

Pike, Albert (1809–1891),   lawyer, soldier, editor, writer. Born in Boston, Pike went west as a young man. He had several careers, first as a hunter and trapper in the Southwest, then as an editor and lawyer in Arkansas and as the compiler of many volumes of reports of law cases, and thereafter as a soldier in the Mexican War and in the Confederate army. He was accused of atrocities in his use of Indian troops under his command in the Confederate army and for a time was forced to flee to Canada; his property was confiscated in 1865. He practiced law not only in Little Rock but also in New Orleans, Memphis, and Washington. He became a Mason in 1850 and after the Civil War devoted himself to making revisions of the Scottish Rite ceremonials.

Pike was a fluent and energetic writer who hoped to be remembered for his poetry. His *Prose Sketches and Poems Written in the Western Country* (1834) has been praised for its vivid depiction of the early Southwest. The attacks on him during the Civil War led to his *Letter to the President of the Confederate States* (1862). As a Mason he wrote *The Morals and Dogma of the Ancient and Accepted Scottish Rite* (1872). Two collections of Pike's verse appeared: *Nugae* (1854) and *Hymns to the Gods and Other Poems* (1872, pub. in enlarged form in 1873 and 1882). These and many uncollected poems were gathered by his daughter in three volumes (1900, 1916, 1916).

Pike, Mary Hayden [Green] (1824–1908),   novelist. Born in Maine, Pike is remembered for her abolitionist sentiments revealed in *Ida May* (1854), the story of an enslaved child, and *Caste* (1856) about a forbidden romance between a woman of mixed ancestry and a white man. *Agnes* (1858) is a historical romance set during the Revolutionary period.

Pike, Zebulon Montgomery (1779–1813),   explorer, soldier. The son of an army officer, Zebulon Pike entered his father's company at fifteen and at twenty-six was commissioned by James Wilkinson, governor of the Louisiana Territory, to explore the West. He made several important expeditions, on one of which he caught his first glimpse of the mountain that bears his name and declared it unclimbable. He died in battle during an invasion of Canada in the War of 1812. His *Account of an Expedition to the Sources of the Mississippi and through the Western Parts of Louisiana* was published in 1810. The standard edition (3 v. 1895) has a memoir and notes by Elliott Coues. *Zebulon Pike's Arkansaw Journal* was edited by S. H. Hart and A. B. Hulbert in 1932. Pike was a man of vivid imagination and considerable gift of style. W. Eugene Hollon wrote *The Lost Pathfinder: Zebulon Montgomery Pike* (1949).

Pike County Ballads (1871),   a collection of poems by JOHN HAY. These verses were written in western dialect and immediately became popular, starting a fashion in regional literature (see PIKE). Many Eastern aesthetes objected bitterly to the popularity that Hay and BRET HARTE gave to the Pike County personalities and their dialect. This attitude affected Hay himself, who wanted people to forget that he had ever written the half-dozen or so poems in dialect that gave him celebrity. Best-known of the *Ballads* are JIM BLUDSO OF THE PRAIRIE BELL and "Little Breeches." MARK TWAIN earned much from both Hay and Harte, and his Missouri characters are likely to talk the Pike dialect. See GEORGE HORATIO DERBY.

Pilgrims, the first settlers of New England, who came to Massachusetts on the Mayflower. They are to be distinguished from the later Puritan settlers of the Massachusetts Bay Colony. The Pilgrims originated in Scrooby, England, about 1606 as a group opposing the episcopal organization and rituals of the Church of England. They were Separatists who sought to restore the church to "its primitive order, liberty, and beauty." They emigrated to Holland in 1608. About half the group followed William Bradford to Plymouth in 1620. Other names among the Mayflower passengers are William Brewster, EDWARD WINSLOW, MYLES STANDISH, Priscilla Mullins, and JOHN ALDEN. Before they landed the travelers signed THE MAYFLOWER COMPACT, creating the first American settlement based on a social contract. They came ashore on Cape Cod on November 21, 1620, calling their first landfall Provincetown because the Lord had seen them safely across the Atlantic. At the present site of Eastham, they had their first encounter with the people of the region. Shots and arrows were fired, but there were no casualties; later experiences between this group and the tribes around Plymouth, where they landed, according to tradition on Plymouth Rock, on December 21, were largely friendly. SQUANTO, a Pawtuxet Indian, helped them in planting and fishing and in negotiating a treaty with Chief MASSASOIT.

Bradford described their experiences in "Of Plimouth Plantation," and later historians consulted Bradford's manuscript before it disappeared in the mid-18th century and was lost for nearly a hundred years. See *Of Plymouth Plantation, 1620–1647*, edited by Samuel Eliot Morison, New York, 1952.

Pillsbury, Parker (1809–1898), abolitionist and leader of woman suffrage movement. He wrote a history of the New England abolitionists called *Acts of the Anti-Slavery Apostles* (1883).

Pilot, The (1823), a novel by JAMES FENIMORE COOPER. With this book Cooper entered the third of the fictional realms in which he did his greatest work: first, history, in THE SPY (1821); then, the frontier, in THE PIONEERS (1823); finally, the sea, which Cooper himself knew best of all from his own experience. He was attempting to demonstrate that he could write a sea story better than Sir Walter Scott's *The Pirate* (1822)—at least in nautical details. The mysterious central figure, Mr. Gray, is obviously modeled on JOHN PAUL JONES. There is some of the customary lovemaking Cooper always thought necessary to bring into his stories, but the exciting action at sea makes the novel enduring. The notable character-drawing is found in lesser figures, especially LONG TOM COFFIN of Nantucket, usually regarded as a counterpart at sea of NATTY

BUMPPO on land. The book, with its patriotic appeal and its breezy sea episodes, was an immediate success in the United States and England.

Pinckney, Josephine [Lyons Scott] (1895–1957), poet, novelist. Pinckney began as a poet and later wrote humorous novels, using her home state of South Carolina as the subject of both. Her collection of verse, made in 1927, was called *Sea-Drinking Cities*. Among her novels are *Hilton Head* (1941), *Three O'Clock Dinner* (1945), *Great Mischief* (1948), and *Splendid in Ashes* (posthumous, 1958).

Piñera, Virgilio (1912–1979), playwright, novelist, short-story writer, poet. A Cuban famed for his bohemian lifestyle, his homosexuality, and the avant-garde qualities of his work, Piñera lived in the 1950s in Buenos Aires, where he came to know Borges and others of his circle. Back in Cuba, he was arrested in 1961 for "political and moral crimes" and lived and wrote thereafter largely on the fringes of Cuban cultural circles, emphasizing coldness, alienation, and cruelty in his writing. Among the most memorable of his thirty plays are the early *Electra Garrigó* (1943); *Jesús* (1948); and *Falsa Alarma* (1948); and the later *Aire Frío* (1958), family satire; *La boda* (1957), on marriage; *El no* (1965), on death; and *Dos viejos pánicos* (1968), which won the Casas de las Americas Award. Short stories, ironic and Kafkaesque, are collected in *Cuentos Fríos* (1956, tr. *Cold Tales*, 1988), and *Pequenas mañiobras* (1963). Novels include *La Carne de René* (1952, tr. *René's Flesh*, 1989), on sexual domination.

Pinkerton, Allan (1819–1884), detective, memoirist. Pinkerton came to the United States from Scotland in 1842 and established a detective agency, said to be the first in this country, in Chicago in 1850. He gained recognition by solving express company thefts and by guarding President-elect Lincoln against an attempted assassination. He organized the Secret Service of the North during the Civil War and did important espionage and counterespionage work. Later he won notoriety by his ruthless suppression of labor agitation, especially in the Homestead Strike (1892); his methods occasioned a Congressional investigation. He helped break up the notorious gang called the MOLLY MAGUIRES. He wrote many memoirs. Among them were *The Expressman and the Detective* (1874), *The Molly Maguires and the Detectives* (1878), *Criminal Reminiscences and Detective Sketches* (1879), *The Spy of the Rebellion* (1883), *Bank Robbers and Detectives* (1883), and *30 Years a Detective* (1884).

Pinkney, Edward Coote (1802–1828), midshipman, lawyer, teacher, poet. Born in England, the son of William Pinkney (1764–1822), a distinguished lawyer and diplomat who had been serving his country abroad as a minister dealing with controversial issues between the United States and England. The younger Pinkney entered the navy at age fourteen and served until he challenged his commander to a duel and was forced to resign. He studied law and was admitted to the bar, edited *The Marylander*, taught at the University of Maryland, and published some small collections of verse: *Look Out Upon the Stars, My Love* (1823); *Rodolph: A Fragment* (1823); and *Poems* (1825).

Pins and Needles,   a 1937 revue with music and lyrics by Harold Rome, first performed by members of the International Ladies Garment Workers Union. Originally intended as entertainment for union members, it became an immediate success and ran for over a thousand consecutive performances.

Pinsky, Robert (1940–   ),   poet, scholar. Born in New Jersey, he was educated at Rutgers (B.A., 1962) and Stanford (Ph.D., 1966), and has taught at Wellesley, the University of California-Berkeley and Boston University. His critical works include a study of Landor (1968), *The Situation of Poetry: Contemporary Poetry and Its Tradition* (1976) and *Poetry and the World* (1988). For several years after 1978 he served as poetry editor of the *New Republic. The Figured Wheel: New and Collected Poems 1966–1996* (1996) includes all of *Sadness and Happiness* (1975), *An Explanation of America* (1979), *History of My Heart* (1984), and *The Want Bone* (1990). *Jersey Rain* (2000) is more recent. He is the cotranslator of *The Separate Notebooks: Poems by Czeslaw Milosz* (1984), and in 1987 he published a reader interactive quest romance on computer disks called *Mindwheel*. His translation of Dante's *Inferno* (1994) has received high praise. Appointed poet laureate in 1997, he actively promoted poetry and edited *Americans' Favorite Poems* (1999)

Pioneer, The (January, February, March, 1843),   a magazine founded by JAMES RUSSELL LOWELL and Robert Carter. Some striking contributions appeared in the magazine, among them Hawthorne's *The Birthmark* and *The Hall of Fantasy*, Poe's *The Tell-Tale Heart* and *Notes Upon English Verse*, and much excellent poetry by Whittier, Elizabeth Barrett, and others. Some writings by Lowell appeared anonymously. In the February issue appeared, anonymously, the first published poems of Maria White, two sonnets addressed to Lowell. The three issues were reprinted in facsimile (1947) in an edition edited by Sculley Bradley.

Pioneers! O Pioneers!   (in *Drum-Taps* 1865, in "Annex" to *Leaves of Grass* 1867), a poem by WALT WHITMAN. In twenty-six stanzas, Whitman addresses a paean to the pioneers of America. The stanzas consist of four lines—the first short, the next two long, and the last a refrain, "Pioneers! O pioneers!" The poem is unusually regular in its metrics, compared with most of Whitman's work.

Pioneers, The, or, The Sources of the Susquehanna (1823),   a novel by JAMES FENIMORE COOPER. This was the first of the LEATHER-STOCKING TALES to be published, but in the order of events in NATTY BUMPPO's life, it is next to the last of the five. Cooper was especially fond of the book because of the many memories of COOPERSTOWN, New York, and his own youth that were found in the story. Judge Temple is drawn from his father. The main plot is concerned with the ownership of an estate in upper New York, in 1793. More important is the scrape Natty—now an elderly man—gets into when he shoots a buck out of season, and still more important are the incidental details of background and time, including the early calls for conservation of natural resources.

Pirsig, Robert M[aynard] (1928–   ),   novelist, teacher. Pirsig's *Zen and the Art of Motorcycle Maintenance* (1974), a philosophical account of a cross-country motorcycle trip with his young son, has attracted a devoted readership. *Lila: An Inquiry into Morals* (1991) continues some of the same concerns on a sailboat trip.

Pisan Cantos, The (1948),   ten sections of the longer *Cantos* of EZRA POUND. These sections were written while the poet was imprisoned in an army stockade in Italy for his Fascist radio broadcasts. Many of the obscurities of the poems are to be explained as allusions to personnel of the detention center. "The ripper," for example, represents a sergeant who tore unfastened buttons from the uniforms of trainees. The volume created a controversy when a group of poets chosen by the Library of Congress, and including Conrad Aiken, W. H. Auden, and T. S. Eliot, selected *The Pisan Cantos* for the library's Bollingen Prize of 1948.

Pit, The (1903),   a novel by FRANK NORRIS. The second part of the unfinished trilogy *Epic of the Wheat*, of which THE OCTOPUS was the first, this posthumously published novel has three distinct elements: the adventures of Curtis Jadwin, who attempts to corner the Chicago wheat market; the love story of Jadwin's wife Laura; and the story of the wheat itself, the life force that Norris intended as the central theme of the trilogy.

Pit and the Pendulum, The   (1842, pub. in *The Gift* 1843), a story by EDGAR ALLAN POE. Poe imagines a man who, after long suffering, is dragged before a court of the Spanish Inquisition in Toledo and given a death sentence—with tortures that were ingeniously and fiendishly contrived. Exploring his rat-infested cell, he almost plunges into a deep pit. Later, as he lies bound, he perceives above him a knife-edged pendulum that gradually swings lower and lower. He smears food on his ropes, and in the nick of time the rats gnaw them through. Even this is not enough torment. The walls of the cell become heated and force him in terror to the edge of the pit—but he is saved at the last moment when French soldiers capture the city. Poe gathered elements of his plot from several sources: Juan Antonio Llorente's *Critical History of the Spanish Inquisition*; Charles Brockden Brown's EDGAR HUNTLY (1799); William Mudford's story *The Iron Shroud*, from *Blackwood's Magazine*; and two other stories in the same periodical: *The Iron Bell* and *The Involuntary Experimentalist*.

Pitcairn's Island.   See MUTINY ON THE BOUNTY.

Plain Language from Truthful James (*Overland Monthly*, September 1870),   a humorous poem by BRET HARTE. It tells how the humorist BILL NYE and the mining camp character Truthful James try to get the better of a Chinese named Ah Sin in euchre. The Chinese player is too good for them, until they discover that he has a card or two up his sleeve—including twenty-four jacks. An agile parodist, Harte cast his poem in Swinburnian rhythms. It was included in the first edition of Harte's *Poems* (1871), but immediately was widely reprinted and pirated, usually under the title *The Heathen Chinee*, and dramatized as AH SIN by Harte and MARK TWAIN in 1877.

Plains [or Great Plains], The.   Roughly, the region extending from the Mississippi to the Rockies, but excluding the arid portions of the Southwest and the Dakota badlands.

Before the white man came, the plains were covered with tough grass that supported huge herds of bison, and there were few trees. The land was perfect for grazing cattle, and they replaced the depleted bison herds. The eastern section became a grain growing area. Erosion of the topsoil and drought led to the Dustbowl of the 1930s, especially in Oklahoma and Texas. PARKMAN's *Oregon Trail* (1849) describes the western migration of pioneers; WILLA CATHER describes farming life in Nebraska in books like *O Pioneers* (1913); STEINBECK's *Grapes of Wrath* (1913) tells of the Dustbowl refugees; and LARRY MCMURTRY's *Lonesome Dove* 1985) describes a cattle drive.

Plains Indians, a generic term for members of the several tribes who inhabited the Great Plains and prairies and centered their religious and ceremonial life on the buffalo and sun worship. They were first described by members of the Coronado expedition of 1541, who noted how completely the buffalo ruled their diet, housing, clothing, and tools. The tribe they observed, the Apaches, were described as gentle, faithful friends who were skilled in the use of signs and carried on an active trade with the Pueblos. They lived in movable housing (tipis) and traveled to follow the buffalo, using dogs as pack animals. The introduction of horses, acquired from the Spaniards, increased their mobility and they perfected the skill of hunting from horseback. As life on the plains became more attractive, the Sioux, Cheyenne, and Arapaho from the east, and the Cománche and Kiowa from the west joined the plains dwellers.

The buffalo hunt was the crucial event of the year for the Plains Indian; the men hunted and the women cured the hides and dried the meat. They lived on this meat through the winter camp where the men worked on their weapons and horse equipment while the women tanned and decorated the hides and made clothing. In the spring they began their wandering over the prairies in small groups, killing the amount of game needed for day-to-day living. Young men went on raiding parties, mostly to obtain more horses. At intervals they met as a tribe to conduct tribal business or hold religious ceremonies, especially the sun dance. Some tribes adopted only parts of this pattern: the Caddo, the Osage and the Mandan hunted buffalo but lived in permanent agricultural settlements; the Wichita had woven grass houses supported on pole frames; and the Pawnee, Arikara, and Mandan lived in timber houses covered with earth. LEWIS and CLARK observed Plains Indians; COOPER described them in *The Prairie*; and they appear in the work of PARKMAN and NEIHARDT. A modern novel detailing their way of life is *Fool's Crow* by JAMES WELCH, a Native American writer. See NATIVE AMERICAN LITERATURE.

Plath, Sylvia (1932–1963), poet, essayist, short fiction writer, and novelist. The older child of well-educated Boston parents, Otto and Aurelia Schober Plath, Sylvia was encouraged to do and be whatever she attempted. Her father was a brilliant German immigrant, an authority on bees, who taught zoology and German at Boston University. He married his student, Aurelia Schober, and lived another nine years, when the effects of untreated diabetes mellitus led to his death. Aurelia returned to teaching and managed with some difficulty to support her two children and her parents.

Sylvia conformed to the notion of the model child—excelling in school and whatever intellectual activities interested her, being docile and responsive to her family's wishes, and aiming steadily for honors and success in the American tradition of the 1950s. That conformity had heavy costs, however, and Sylvia experienced a severe breakdown following her junior year at Smith, where she was a scholarship student. Treated with electroconvulsive shock treatments during the summer of 1953, Plath achieved news headlines throughout the country as she mysteriously disappeared after one of these out-patient treatments. When she was found by her brother Warren under the crawl space of the breezeway, nearly dead from the overdose of sleeping pills she had taken in her suicide attempt, her depression only increased. It was six months before she returned to Smith, seemingly cured from an intensive period of psychotherapy and both electroconvulsive and insulin shock treatments.

As a college student, Plath published her poems and fiction in a number of literary and commercial magazines—always with an eye to earning money through her writing, given the tight finances of her family. She was graduated from Smith *summa cum laude* in 1955 and won a Fulbright fellowship to study English at Cambridge. When she left for England that fall, she promised herself that she would not return unmarried: social pressure on women in America was great. The average marriage age for women in the 1950s was 20.3, and when she sailed for England, Sylvia was nearly 23. Her career evinces the frustrating pressure that a woman should date and marry and have children even if she intends to be a professional person of some kind. In the 1950s ideology, only superwomen could meet the demands of this prescribed double identity.

Even though she knew she wanted to become a successful writer, Plath also wanted to marry. In June of 1956, she secretly became the wife of the young Yorkshire poet Ted Hughes (later Poet Laureate of England). Neither was wealthy, and both wanted only to write. After Sylvia finished her second year at Cambridge, the couple moved to America where she taught freshman English at Smith for a year. They then moved to Boston where each concentrated on writing (which Ted had been doing since his own graduation from Cambridge), with Sylvia taking the part-time secretarial jobs she describes in "Johnny Panic and the Bible of Dreams." Though she was never satisfied with what she wrote, Sylvia wrote a great deal of poetry and short fiction and was always on the edge of beginning her novel.

Ted's progress as a writer was easier to chart; his prize-winning book of poetry, *The Hawk in the Rain*, had created a market for his work, and he was writing poetry, children's stories, and plays with great regularity and success. Sylvia acted as Ted's agent, as well as his typist, along with doing her own writing. During these early married years, she also put together collection after collection of her poems, but never found a publisher for the book. After a stay at Yaddo, the writers' colony, during the fall of 1959, Sylvia made important changes in her voice as poet, and the collection she assembled after being at Yaddo was published in 1960 as *The Colossus and Other Poems*. In late 1959, she and Ted returned to England to live, and there, in April of 1960, Frieda Hughes was born. Sylvia was ecstatic about her child, but living in a crowded London flat with a baby was not conducive to two writing careers, so they used their savings from their American years and bought a Devon manor house. Despite the crowded conditions, Sylvia had written her first novel, *The Bell Jar*, which would be published in early 1963. Moving to Devon in the late summer of 1961 gave new impetus to Sylvia's writing. When Nicholas Farrar was born in January of 1962, Sylvia's life was—temporarily—joyous. She wrote the poignant *Three Women*, a radio play about women giving birth in a hospital, using effectively the subject matter, language, and insight that only a woman could convey, and a number of important poems, among them "The Moon and the Yew Tree" and "Elm." In both her novel and the radio play, Plath was leaving behind the consciously intellectual voice that she had practiced during her college and early professional years. In place of that, she had found a wry, comic, sometimes macabre tone and diction that seemed better to express contemporary woman's life as she saw it.

Once Ted had begun an affair with another woman and he and Sylvia had separated, Plath's more comic, more realistic, subject matter grew into the important "October poems." The anger of a woman who felt she had been betrayed—by her parents, in wanting too much of her; by society, in demanding conventional obeisance to meaningless forms and rules; by a husband who had not valued her contributions to what she saw as their joint venture—was brilliantly voiced in such unusual poems as "Lady Lazarus," "Daddy," "Fever 103," "Purdah," "The Detective," "Poppies in July," "Ariel," "The Rabbit-Catcher," and many others. Plath knew she had broken through into new territory, and that she was writing extremely well. Unfortunately, her depression returned, and her life—both alone in Devon and then alone in Yeats's flat in London, after she and the children moved there in December of 1962—seemed relentlessly bleak and fatiguing. Despite the best efforts of her doctor, she committed suicide by sleeping pills and gas inhalation on February 11, 1963.

Plath's poems show a steadily developing sense of her own voice, speaking of subjects that—before the 1960s—were considered inappropriate for poetry: anger, grotesque humor, sorrow, and defiance, contrasted at times with a rarer joy and a deep understanding of women's various roles. Her expansion of the conventional poetic patterns she had studied so carefully during her career set an example that shaped a great deal of poetry for the next thirty years—her reliance on unexpected metaphor, quick shifts from image to image, and a frantic yet always controlled pace that mirrored the tensions of her single-parent life during 1962 and 1963. In contrast to the late poems such as "Daddy" and "Lady Lazarus," Plath's final

poems—"Edge" and "Totem"—were icily mystic, solemn, and resigned. The full range of her poetry is evident in the 1981 *Collected Poems*, which won the Pulitzer Prize for Poetry in 1982. Much of her fiction remains unpublished, though Ted Hughes, the executor of her estate, edited *Johnny Panic and the Bible of Dreams and Other Prose Writings*, (1970), a small collection of short fiction and essays. *The Bell Jar* maintains wide sales throughout the world, speaking for a number of women's concerns in a manner still vital after nearly thirty years. An incomplete novel has disappeared, as have several volumes of her journals. Once all of Plath's work has been assembled, her reputation may rise even higher.

Her posthumous collection ARIEL (1965) won her belated recognition and what her teacher, ROBERT LOWELL, termed "appalling and triumphant fulfillment." Her other verse collections are *Crossing the Water* (1971) and *Winter Trees* (1971). Her prose includes *Letters Home: Correspondence* 1950–1963 (1975, edited by Aurelia Schober Plath), *The Journals of Sylvia Plath* (1982, edited by Ted Hughes and Frances McCullough) and *The Unabridged Journals of Sylvia Plath, 1950–1962*, edited by Karen V. Kukil (2000). Studies include Linda Wagner-Martin's *Sylvia Plath: A Biography* (1987); Anne Stevenson, *Bitter Fame: A Life of Sylvia Plath* (1989); Ronald Hayman, *The Death and Life of Sylvia Plath* (1991); and Janet Malcolm, *The Silent Woman: Sylvia Plath and Ted Hughes* (1994).

LINDA WAGNER-MARTIN

Pledge of Allegiance to the Flag, a statement written by James B. Upham (1845–1905), a contributor to YOUTH'S COMPANION, for use by school children celebrating the 400th anniversary of the discovery of America (1892).

Plimpton, George [Ames] (1927–), sports writer, editor, memoirist. Born in New York City, Plimpton served in the army from 1945 to 1948 and graduated from Harvard (A.B. 1950) and King's College, Cambridge (B.A., 1952; M.A., 1954). An editor of THE PARIS REVIEW from its inception in 1953, he edited the series *Writers at Work: The Paris Review Interviews* (1957–1992), and the selections *Poets at Work: The Paris Review Interviews* (1989), *Women Writers at Work* (1989), and *The Paris Review Anthology* (1990). As a sports writer he gained fame by immersing himself in the sports he covered, an amateur sporting with professionals in football, basketball, baseball, hockey, golf, boxing, and bullfighting; books include *Out of My League* (1961), baseball; *Paper Lion* (1966), football; *The Bogey Man* (1968), golf; *One for the Record: The Inside Story of Hank Aaron's Chase for the Home Run Record* (1974); *Shadow Box* (1977), boxing; and *Open Net* (1985), hockey. *The Curious Case of Sidd Finch* (1987) is a novel about a pitcher with a 150 mph fastball. Plimpton has also acted in films and written television scripts. *The Best of Plimpton* was published in 1990.

Plumly, Stanley (1939–), poet. Plumly uses imagery of Ohio and Virginia where he grew up. His first volume of poetry, *In the Outer Dark* (1970), was published when he taught at Louisiana State University. *Now that My Father Lies Down Beside Me: New and Selected Poems 1970–2000*

(2000) summarizes his career up to his distinguished professorship at the University of Maryland. He has continued a clear, lyric voice, rich in natural imagery, and won numerous awards, including a Guggenheim Fellowship. Other volumes are *Giraffe* (1973), *Out-of-the-Body Travel* (1977), *Summer Celestial* (1985), *Boy on the Step* (1989), and *The Marriage in the Trees* (1997).

Plummer, Jonathan (1761–1819),   preacher, pawnbroker, professional writer of love letters, balladist, peddler. Plummer, born in Newbury, Massachusetts, was appointed by the self-acclaimed TIMOTHY DEXTER as his poet laureate and responded by writing, among other pieces, *The Author's Congratulatory Address to Citizen Timothy Dexter on His Attaining an Independent Fortune* (1793). Another piece of his was called *Parson Pidgin, or, Holy Kissing, Occasioned by a Report That Parson Pidgin Had Kissed a Young Woman* (1807). He peddled in Newbury's Market Square an odd conglomeration of sermons, poems, and notions. His poems were the familiar broadsides of his time, providing both news and scandal. He wrote an autobiography in three successive pamphlets, *A Sketch of the History of the Life of Jonathan Plummer* (1797?). He is described in John P. Marquand's *Lord Timothy Dexter* (1925).

pluralism.   A general metaphysical term meaning a belief in the diversity of ultimate reality, which is often applied specifically to the philosophical system of WILLIAM JAMES. James set forth his beliefs in a series of lectures at Oxford University (1908) and published them in *A Pluralistic Universe* (1909).

Plymouth Colony,   a settlement founded on the Massachusetts coast in 1620 by the passengers of the Mayflower. (See PILGRIMS.) John Carver was the first governor. Plymouth was independent until its merger with the Massachusetts Bay colony in 1684. The early history of the group is recorded in Bradford's *History of Plymouth Plantation*, Winslow's *Good News from New England*, and Winthrop's *Journal*.

Plymouth Plantation, A History of (pub. 1856),   a chronicle by WILLIAM BRADFORD [1]. A description begun about 1630 of the events in the lives of the Pilgrim settlers from 1609 to 1649. A list of Mayflower passengers was added in 1651.

The first section covers the years in Holland and the sailing and settlement. It is clear and graceful in style, influenced by the Geneva Bible. The second part presents the early years in the colony in the form of annals from 1620 to 1646. Bradford's use of details and letters made the manuscript an important source of primary materials for early historians such as Nathaniel Morton, Thomas Prince, and Cotton Mather. Morton, Bradford's nephew, first owned the manuscript and based his *New Englands Memoriall* on it; Prince took information from it for his *Chronological History of New England*; and Thomas Hutchinson used it for his *History of the Colony of Massachusetts*. Prince bequeathed it to the Old South Church, but it disappeared during the Revolutionary War and was lost until it was discovered in 1855 in an English ecclesiastic's library. After being returned to America, it was published for the first time in 1856.

Pnin,   a seriocomic novel by VLADIMIR NABOKOV (1957), deals with the life of Timofey Pnin, a middle-aged Russian exile teaching in a college in upstate New York. Four of the seven chapters appeared first in *The New Yorker* and helped establish Nabokov's reputation as an American writer.

Pocahontas (1595?–1617),   a Native American woman who befriended white settlers in Virginia. The daughter of Powhatan, she was perhaps no more than twelve or thirteen when she rescued JOHN SMITH by interposing her head between his and the warriors' clubs that would smash it. This famous story, told by Smith in his *General History of Virginia* (1624), has been doubted, but it seems probable enough; in any case, the help of Pocahontas in subsequent years was crucial to the survival of the Jamestown settlement. In 1613, she was taken hostage by the English. Converted to Christianity and baptized Rebecca, she married JOHN ROLFE in 1614 and accompanied him to England in 1616. She was, in John Smith's words, as he recommended her to the attention of Queen Anne, "The first Christian ever of [her] nation, the first Virginian ever spake English, or had a child in marriage by an Englishman." She died and was buried at Gravesend, England, not long after her presentation to the queen.

Podhoretz, Norman (1930–   ),   editor, social commentator, memoirist. Born in Brooklyn and educated at Columbia University and Clare College, Cambridge, Podhoretz gained a following for his conservative thought after becoming editor of *Commentary* in 1960. Early essays were collected in *Doings and Undoings: The Fifties and After in American Writing* (1964). In *Making It* (1967), he writes of the struggle toward success in the New York literary world. *Breaking Ranks* (1979) is a memoir describing his turn to the right in political views. *Why We Were in Vietnam* (1982) defends American intervention. *The Bloody Crossroads: Where Literature and Politics Meet* (1986) brings his chief interests together. *Ex-Friends: Falling Out with Allen Ginsberg, Lionel and Diana Trilling, Lillian Hellman, Hannah Arendt, and Norman Mailer* (1999) is personal, gossipy, and one-sided, but occasionally tempered by humor as it revisits old friendships. *My Love Affair with America: The Cautionary Tale of a Cheerful Conservative* (2000) is an unabashedly patriotic celebration.

Poe, Edgar Allan (1809–1849),   poet, short-story writer, critic. Poe was the son of a talented actress, Elizabeth Arnold, and her second husband, David Poe, Jr., an actor and the son of a prominent officer in the Revolution. Orphaned in Richmond late in 1811, Poe was taken into the home of John Allan, a wealthy merchant. Allan, who regarded the boy as a genius, became his godfather but did not formally adopt him. The Allan family went to England in 1815, where Poe attended the classical academy of Dr. John Bransby at Stoke Newington. In the summer of 1820 the family returned to Richmond, where the boy entered the school of Joseph H. Clarke and composed a number of verses in honor of local schoolgirls. These are lost, but a satire, written when Poe was enrolled at the school of William Burke in 1823 and 1824, has survived.

Poe fell in love with Elmira Royster and was secretly engaged when he went to the University of Virginia in February 1826, but the engagement came to nothing, for her family intercepted the letters of the pair, and shortly thereafter arranged for her to be married to Alexander Barrett Shelton of Richmond. At the University Poe stood high in Greek, Latin, French, Italian, and Spanish, but remained only one term; apparently Allan had refused Poe spending money, and the young man gambled in hopes of raising funds. When Poe went into debt, Allan withdrew his godson from the university. Tales of Poe's heavy drinking at that time are probably exaggerated, since Poe was constitutionally unable to tolerate liquor, and even small amounts often had disastrous effects on him.

On his return to Richmond, Poe quarreled with his godfather and ran away to Boston, where he arranged for his first volume, TAMERLANE AND OTHER POEMS (1827), to be published anonymously. Some of the poems concerned his unhappy love affair with Elmira Royster; the best one, "The Lake," is about the legends told of the Lake of the Dismal Swamp, near Norfolk. Poe was unable to find employment, and, in desperate financial straits, enlisted in the army under the name Edgar A. Poe. He was sent to Fort Moultrie on Sullivan's Island, the scene of his later story, "The Gold Bug." He wrote to Allan, asking him to help secure his release from the army, but Allan refused until the death of his wife, who pleaded Poe's cause on her deathbed. Allan sent for Poe on the condition that Poe enter West Point, and the two were reconciled, at least temporarily.

Poe published another volume, *Al Aaraaf, Tamerlane, and Minor Poems* (see AL AARAAF), in Baltimore in 1829. Included is "Fairyland," an archly humorous poem owing something to *A Midsummer Night's Dream* and entirely unlike anything else Poe wrote. He returned to Richmond and quarreled again with John Allan before entering West Point in the summer of 1830. When Allan remarried in October of that year, it was apparent to Poe that he could expect little further aid from that quarter; shortly thereafter, Allan disowned him because of a disparaging remark made by Poe in a letter that Allan was given. With no immediate financial resources and no hope of any from the Allan family, Poe set about getting himself expelled from West Point.

Poe came to New York, where he published *Poems* (1831). The preface to this volume shows he took an interest in Coleridge's critical theories, by which some critics feel Poe was influenced. Others find in Poe a kinship to Byron, Moore, and Shelley alone among the great romantics. The influence of the Baltimore lyrist, Edward Coote Pinckney, also seems sure. But Poe was already much his own man, as is evidenced in the great brief lyric TO HELEN, in ISRAFEL, and in "The Sleeper," a macabre verse of which the poet was curiously fond. The two strange landscapes, THE CITY IN THE SEA, which describes the ruins of Gomorrah, and the "Valley of Unrest," about the Hebrites, show great originality.

Poe went to Baltimore and began to write short stories. Some of these, submitted in a prize contest, were published in the Philadelphia *Saturday Courier* in 1832. In 1833 MS. FOUND IN A BOTTLE won a $50 prize from the Baltimore *Saturday Visiter* and brought Poe some national recognition. He set to work on a play, POLITIAN, which he never finished. Through the novelist JOHN P. KENNEDY he established a connection with the SOUTHERN LITERARY MESSENGER of Richmond, became its assistant editor and then, in December 1835, its editor. He urged high literary standards, and during his editorship the *Messenger*'s subscription list increased from 500 to over 3,500. However, his castigations of unimportant books led to literary quarrels from which he was never to be free thereafter. Meanwhile Poe's aunt, Mrs. Maria Poe Clemm, with whom he had lived in Baltimore, arranged a marriage there in September between Poe and her daughter Virginia, who was then only thirteen years old (see VIRGINIA CLEMM). The couple lived for two years as brother and sister, but the marriage led to some social disapproval. Virginia was a devoted and sometimes a tolerant wife, but "never read half" of her husband's poetry. During her life Poe addressed no poems to her. He was apparently very much attached to Mrs. Clemm, who was the mainstay of the family during their long bouts of poverty and Virginia's illness. Poe wrote for her his charming sonnet "To My Mother" (1849).

For the *Messenger* Poe wrote BERENICE and MORELLA, as well as "Hans Pfaal," a comic tale of a voyage to the moon (see THE UNPARALLELED ADVENTURES OF ONE HANS PFAAL). Two poems, "Bridal Ballad" and "To Zante," may have related to a meeting with his first love, Elmira Royster, now Mrs. Shelton. Poe also began a serial, "Arthur Gordon Pym" (see THE NARRATIVE OF ARTHUR GORDON PYM), installments of which appeared in January and February of 1837; however, he then resigned from the *Messenger* and came to New York, where he published the complete serial as a book in 1838. An account of sea adventures based on fact, *The Narrative* is a grotesque and imaginative tale that ends in wildly incredible scenes near the South Pole. It was greatly admired by Baudelaire, though Poe himself called it a silly book.

In the summer of 1838 Poe was in Philadelphia, helping a Professor Thomas Wyatt bring out two books on natural history. Finally he became an editor of *Burton's Gentleman's Magazine* in May 1839. The magazine was owned by the comedian WILLIAM E. BURTON, with whom Poe remained until they quarreled in June 1840. Poe had plans for a magazine of his own to be called, punningly, the *Penn*, and later the *Stylus*. Beyond several prospectuses, the last in 1848, nothing came of the *Stylus*. He also solved ciphers in a paper called *Alexander's Weekly Messenger* and wrote miscellaneous papers, including a few news articles. In the *Saturday Evening Post* for May 1, 1841, Poe predicted the ending of Dickens's *Barnaby Rudge* from the first chapters.

George R. Graham bought Burton out and established GRAHAM'S MAGAZINE in December of 1840. Poe became an editor in charge of reviews with the April issue, and remained until May

1842. As had been the case with the *Southern Literary Messenger*, the circulation of the magazine increased dramatically while Poe was associated with it.

Although TALES OF THE GROTESQUE AND ARABESQUE (1840), containing twenty-five pieces, sold badly, Poe was busy with short stories and produced some of his masterpieces. THE MURDERS IN THE RUE MORGUE was in *Graham's* for April 1841; if not the first DETECTIVE STORY, that story set the form. Poe was also to invent almost all the species of the genus. He made an attempt, not wholly successful, to solve a real crime in THE MYSTERY OF MARIE ROGET in 1842; he dismissed the crime itself as of no interest in THE PURLOINED LETTER (1844); and in the same year he wrote the little-read "Thou Art the Man," the first story in which the criminal is at first undetected because he looks like a wholly respectable person. His other notable stories written between 1838 and 1843 include LIGEIA, THE FALL OF THE HOUSE OF USHER, WILLIAM WILSON, the enigmatic ELEONORA, THE MASQUE OF THE RED DEATH, THE TELL-TALE HEART, THE BLACK CAT, THE PREMATURE BURIAL, and the most popular of all, THE GOLD BUG, perhaps the greatest of all tales of buried treasure.

Misfortune struck the Poe household in January of 1842 when Virginia broke a blood vessel while singing. Her life was despaired of, and although she recovered somewhat, her health continued to be poor until her death from tuberculosis five years later.

Poe met Charles Dickens in Philadelphia in 1842 and hoped, vainly, to form some connection in England through him. Poe was also in correspondence with JAMES RUSSELL LOWELL; they met in 1845 and did not like each other. In April 1844 Poe, with Virginia, Mrs. Clemm, and the celebrated pet, Cat-erina, came to New York. He sold his BALLOON-HOAX to the New York *Sun* and went to work on the genial Major Mordecai M. Noah's paper, the *Sunday Times*. In October he joined N. P. Willis and General George P. Morris on the new "paper for the upper ten thousand," the *Evening Mirror*. He lived for a time "in the country" (near what is now Eighty-seventh Street and Broadway), and there wrote a final draft of THE RAVEN. After it was rejected by Graham, it was sold to George H. Colton for pseudonymous publication in the February issue of a new magazine, the *American Review*. Willis saw it in proof and published it in the *Mirror* on January 29, 1845, with an enthusiastic introduction and the author's name. Success was instantaneous. "Mr. Poe the poet" was to be permanently world famous.

He became an editor of a weekly paper, the *Broadway Journal*, and published a series of papers on Longfellow's "plagiarisms"—although Poe meant only that Longfellow was a derivative poet. He lectured on poetry at the Society Library. He met Mrs. FRANCES SARGENT OSGOOD (temporarily separated, though not publicly, from her husband), and fell in love with her—perhaps platonically, and in any case with Virginia's approval. He also frequented the salon of Anne Charlotte Lynch, later Mrs. Botta. And he was pursued by Mrs. Elizabeth F. Ellet, a woman of bad character—vain, ambitious only of reputation, and given to writing anonymous letters. This all led to complicated quarrels that may be left to the major biographers. He published *The Raven and Other Poems* and a selection of a dozen of his *Tales*. He went to Boston to lecture, became drunk, and read his poem "Al Aaraaf," which the audience found baffling, although T. W. Higginson testified to its beauty. He became the sole proprietor of the *Broadway Journal*, in which he published revised versions of most of his stories. But the paper collapsed, the last issue being that of January 3, 1846.

At the advice of the eccentric though melodious poet, Dr. THOMAS HOLLEY CHIVERS, he moved again from the city to the cottage at Fordham, his last home. He published THE PHILOSOPHY OF COMPOSITION in *Graham's Magazine* in April 1846. For *Godey's Lady's Book* he wrote a series of papers called THE LITERATI OF NEW YORK, most of which were innocuous; however, one on Dr. THOMAS DUNN ENGLISH, with whom Poe had had a fist fight (remotely connected with Mrs. Ellet and Mrs. Osgood), led to bitter controversy. Poe ultimately sued for libel and won his case, but at the expense of all reputation for sobriety or reliability. Godey gave up the *Literati* series, but printed THE CASK OF AMONTILLADO, a story of revenge now thought to be in part inspired by the author's own bitter quarrels. The story is ironic—a villain murders his enemy and is not found out, but at the end he realizes that the victim has rested in peace, while he has not.

Early in 1847 Virginia died. Poe was also very ill and was nursed by Mrs. Clemm and Mrs. Marie Louise Shew; the latter was the daughter of a physician and had been trained as one at home. To her Poe wrote several poems; one, "The Beloved Physician," of some length, is lost save for ten lines. She is supposed to have suggested THE BELLS to him. Mrs. Shew consulted Dr. Valentine Mott about her patient; she was told Poe had had a brain lesion in youth and would not live long. The lesion is thought to have produced manic and depressive periods, which might account for some of Poe's wild freaks and for occasional references to his being kept under sedation. All medical men who knew the poet or have studied his case agree that he did not use drugs habitually. The poet's one important work of 1847 was ULALUME.

Early in 1848 Poe gave a lecture on the universe, which was revised as a book, EUREKA. In September he went to Providence and became engaged to the local poet SARAH HELEN WHITMAN, to whom he had written a second "To Helen" (now sometimes called "To Helen Whitman") before their meeting. This affair produced a number of impassioned and literary letters, but soon ended. Poe had visited Lowell, Massachusetts, in July and lectured on the "Poetic Principle"; while in Lowell he first met Mrs. Annie Richmond, with whom he fell in love. In 1849 he addressed to her a long poem, "For Annie," ascribing his recovery from illness to the thought of the beloved lady's presence.

Poe began to write for the Boston *Flag of Our Union*, a cheap paper that paid well. To it he sent his last horror story, "Hop-Frog," his sonnet "To My Mother," and the short poem "Eldorado," which is about a search for beauty rather than gold. Poe also found a patron, Sarah (or Estelle) Anna Lewis, who employed him as her press agent. Poe and Mrs. Clemm spent a good deal of time visiting the Lewis home in Brooklyn.

Late in June of 1849, after having composed a final version of "The Bells" and ANNABEL LEE, Poe went south. He had a horrible spree in Philadelphia, but was rescued by C. Chauncey Burr, a minor writer, and John Sartain, the engraver who now ran the *Union Magazine*. They sent the poet to Richmond, where he had a happy summer, becoming engaged again to the sweetheart of his youth, the widowed Elmira Royster Shelton. He was also received in society and enjoyed the friendship of the young poet Susan Archer Talley, later Mrs. Weiss. Poe lectured both in Richmond and Norfolk. He went on two sprees, however, and on August 27 joined the Sons of Temperance.

Late in September he started for the North by boat and arrived in Baltimore probably on the twenty-eighth. There, according to Bishop O. P. Fitzgerald, he attended a birthday party, pledged his hostess in wine, and went on a spree. His whereabouts are unknown from then until October 3, an election day, when he was found in great distress by a compositor, Joseph W. Walker. The story that he had been taken, drunken or drugged, to polling places by "repeaters" is a hoax, though widely related. Friends brought him to the Washington Hospital where, under the care of Dr. John J. Moran (who later published overcolored reminiscences), he died without ever becoming completely conscious. The last words attributed to him, "Lord, help my poor soul," seem to be authentic. He was buried in what is now Westminster Churchyard on October 8, 1849, where a monument to him was erected in 1875. Mrs. Clemm and her daughter now rest beside him.

Poe was primarily and by choice a poet. He held three important ideas besides his insistence on brevity: poetry is close to music, beauty is the chief aim of poetry, and a poem may be composed logically (see THE PHILOSOPHY OF COMPOSITION. He was deeply interested in prosody and other technical aspects of verse, and published on the subject *The Rationale of Verse* (October and November 1848, in issues of the *Southern Literary Messenger*).

For reasons of economic necessity, Poe wrote little verse between 1831 and 1845, concentrating instead on the tales. Nevertheless, THE HAUNTED PALACE, an allegory of madness, and THE CONQUEROR WORM, the most pessimistic yet the most powerful of all his poems, belong to this period. With the sudden recognition brought by the publication of "The Raven" in 1845, he turned more to poetry. In the last years of his life he wrote the cheerful short lyric "Eulalie"; "The Bells," which had been begun by Mrs. Shew; "For Annie," the simplest of his ballads; and the courageous brief lyric "Eldorado."

Poe cared less for his tales than for his poems. Nevertheless, he had a firm and workable theory about the short story, which he expounded in his review (GRAHAM'S MAGAZINE, April–May 1842) of Hawthorne's *Twice-Told Tales*. A skillful literary artist, said Poe, does not fashion his thoughts to accommodate his incidents, "but having conceived, with deliberate care, a certain unique or single *effect* to be wrought out, he then invents such incidents—he then combines such

events as may best aid him in establishing this preconceived effect . . . In the whole composition there should be no word written, of which the tendency, direct or indirect, is not to the one pre-established design." He insisted on unity of mood as well as of time, space, and action. Poe is credited with the invention of the modern detective story with its amateur detective. He was similarly original in his version of the treasure hunt, "The Gold Bug," particularly in his introduction of a cryptogram.

Although Poe fancied his humorous work, the best of it is too much taken up with the faults and foibles of the world around him. "Some Words with a Mummy," for instance, deals with a brief American fad for Egyptology, and "The Literary Life of Thingum Bob," the best of the humorous tales, was a satire on the magazines of his day. Both are too dated to give pleasure to any but a few students of the period. He also wrote a gentle little love story, "Three Sundays in a Week," but his great stories, beyond any doubt, are the tales of horror, ratiocination, or pure beauty. The style of Poe's stories progressed from highly decorated and elaborate, as in THE ASSIGNATION, to straightforwardly simple, as in THE IMP OF THE PERVERSE and "Hop-Frog." He said that the stories of pure beauty, most notably THE DOMAIN OF ARNHEIM, had in them much of his soul. Toward the end of his life he remarked that he thought he had accomplished his purpose in poetry, but that he saw new possibilities in prose. These were almost certainly in the realm of pure beauty. Besides the books of criticism mentioned above, there is a great deal extant of Poe's work as a day-to-day critic. Much of it is about works that came unchosen to a reviewer's table. It often contains keen remarks of great significance, although too much of it is devoted to the examination of flies in amber.

Poe had a tremendous influence abroad. His special kind of poetry was echoed by Tennyson, Swinburne, and Rossetti; his stories influenced Stevenson, Conan Doyle, Jules Verne, Huysmans, and many others. It was in France that Poe's influence attained its widest range, largely owing to the deep respect of Baudelaire for Poe's poems, stories, and aesthetic theories. Between 1856 and 1864 Baudelaire wrote three articles on Poe and translated, with singular felicity, several of his works. Lois and Francis E. Hyslop, Jr., translated and edited *Baudelaire on Poe* (1952), which contains Baudelaire's three major essays and various prefaces and notes. Mallarmé, Valery, and Rimbaud, as well as the whole flock of Parnassians, symbolists, and surrealists, exhibit the influence of Poe (see SYMBOLISM). Covering the entire range of influences is a volume on *Poe in Foreign Lands and Tongues* (1941), edited by John C. French.

Poe was given to telling romantic stories of himself, and the construction of an accurate biography has been fraught with the greatest difficulties. The first formal biographer, R. W. GRISWOLD, published in the *Works* a memoir (1850) that was bitterly unfriendly to the poet but cannot be wholly neglected. In 1859 SARAH HELEN WHITMAN published *Edgar Poe and His Critics*, the first full-length defense of her fiancé. In 1885 appeared GEORGE EDWARD WOODBERRY's valuable *Edgar Allan Poe* (rev. ed. 2 v. 1909). In 1926 HERVEY ALLEN published ISRAFEL, widely read but nevertheless misleading; it was begun as a novel, and the author never completely eliminated all fictional passages. A recent and thorough biography is Kenneth Silverman's *Edgar Allan Poe: Mournful and Never-Ending Remembrance* (1991). The first accurate scholarly biography was ARTHUR HOBSON QUINN's *Edgar Allan Poe* (1941), though it is too much for the defense to be wholly satisfactory. He also prepared in collaboration with R. H. Hart an edition of *Edgar Allan Poe Letters and Documents* in the Enoch Pratt Free Library. Other biographies are Edward Wagenknecht's *Edgar Allan Poe: the Man Behind the Legend* (1963) and Julian Symons, *The Life and Works of Edgar Allan Poe* (1978).

Most of the many editions of Poe's works are founded on Griswold's (1849–56). Ingram's edition (1874–75) made a few additions to the canon, as did that of Stedman and Woodberry (1895). The only edition that even approached completeness was the seventeen-volume work (1902) of James A. Harrison. T. O. Mabbott edited the poems, tales, and sketches in a three-volume *Collected Works of Edgar Allan Poe* (1969–1978). A one-volume selection, edited by Patrick F. Quinn and G. R. Thompson, is *Edgar Allan Poe: Poetry, Tales, and Selected Essays* (1996).

See also: POETRY IN THE U.S.; LITERARY CRITICISM; SHORT STORY; BON BON; THE COLISEUM; A DESCENT INTO THE MAELSTROM; THE DEVIL IN THE BELFRY; DUC DE L'OMELETTE; A FABLE FOR CRITICS; GOTHIC MELANCHOLY; JOURNAL OF JULIUS; LANDOR'S COTTAGE; LENORE; MARGINALIA; THE PIT AND THE PENDULUM; THE POETIC PRINCIPLE.

THOMAS OLIVE MABBOTT/BP

Poet at the Breakfast Table, The (1872),   essays and dialogues by OLIVER WENDELL HOLMES, SR. This is the third in the series of rambling talks that began with THE AUTOCRAT OF THE BREAKFAST TABLE (1858), continued with *The Professor at the Breakfast Table* (1860), and closed with *Over the Teacups* (1891). The chief persons at the table are the Poet; the Old Master, given to philosophy; the Scarabee, an entomologist; the young astronomer, with his poetic outlook; Scheherazade, a young girl who writes stories; and the Lady. The papers, like the earlier ones, first appeared in *Atlantic Monthly*. See BREAKFAST TABLE SERIES.

Poetic Principle, The (1850),   by EDGAR ALLAN POE. Poe lectured on this subject in several cities during 1848–49. The essay was published posthumously in *Sartain's Union Magazine* (October 1850). The ideas expressed in it were favorites with Poe and may be found in some of his earlier writings, including AL AARAAF, one of his longest poems, written in 1827–29. In the essay Poe criticized the inartistic didactic elements in the literature of his day, but included as material suitable for true poetical effect "all noble thoughts—all unworldly motives—in all holy impulses—all chivalrous, generous, and self-sacrificing deeds." The essay contains eleven poems, English and American, offered as examples of fine poetry.

Poet Lore.   A monthly magazine founded in Philadelphia in 1889 by Charlotte Endymion Porter, poet and Shake-

spearean scholar, and Helen Archibald Clarke, an ardent student of Browning. The magazine discussed English and American poets and "the comparative study of literature." In 1892 it was transferred to Boston and became a quarterly. It expired in 1953 and was reestablished in 1962.

Poetry: A Magazine of Verse.   An important American magazine of verse founded in October 1912 by HARRIET MONROE, who edited it until her death in 1936. It is published in Chicago. When it was founded in 1912 the magazine quickly became the foremost platform for the new movement in American literature. It published much of the early work of such poets as Pound, Eliot, Wallace Stevens, William Carlos Williams, Lawrence, Millay, Elinor Wylie, Jeffers, Marianne Moore, and many others. Much distinguished as well as controversial criticism has appeared in its pages. See IMAGISM.

Poetry: Before 1960.   American poetry was at first not merely provincial, but colonial. In the cultural sense there was no America during the first years of occupation by Europeans: there were only Europeans living, for one reason or another, away from home, and at what point one chooses to say that a genuinely American cultural differentiation emerges depends more on subjective insight than upon calculable information. In the prose of the 17th century one may perhaps discern an American element before the century runs out: in Bradford's HISTORY OF PLYMOUTH PLANTATION (written before 1650, published 1856), for instance, or Samuel Sewall's *Diary* (written 1674–1729, published 1878–82) or Robert Beverley's *History* (mostly written before 1700, published 1705). In poetry, however, not even these slight indications of a rising native genius can be found. One may say two things about colonial poetry in America: all of it copied English models, and almost all of it was bad.

Neither point is unexpected when one considers the cultural milieu of the English colonies. The highly cultivated strata of British society did not emigrate to America—there were a few brilliant adventures, gentlemen like Raleigh, but very few. Most of the colonists, north and south, were literate but far from intellectual—sufficiently interested in reading to follow the literary fashions but rarely knowledgeable in the technical aspects of literary theory. Hence their taste was often second-rate. They imported books, including some good books, but the biggest trade, outside purely doctrinal materials, was in the works of inferior poets, and this continued until well after the Revolution. In 1732, for instance, the Bostonian bookseller Richard Fry imported twelve hundred copies of the works of Stephen Duck, the Wiltshire poet; and ANNE BRADSTREET, whose poetic talent and devotional fervor ought to have brought her close to John Donne or George Herbert or Richard Crashaw, or at least to Giles Fletcher or the honest Puritan George Wither, seems instead to have chosen as her models the labored conceits of Francis Quarles and Josuah Sylvester's uninspired translations from the uninspired French verse of Seigneur Du Bartas. Shakespeare was well known in America, though the Bay colonists were generally unfriendly to the theater, but *Paradise Lost* was apparently and surprisingly not known to more than a handful of colonists until well after 1700. The most popular work of versification by far among those written by colonists was Michael Wigglesworth's DAY OF DOOM (1662), an execrably written tract on damnation, the government of hell, and allied horrors. Terrified children were still required to memorize its choice bits in the 19th century.

Nevertheless, Mistress Bradstreet was a talented poet. Some of her poems were published in London in 1650 as THE TENTH MUSE LATELY SPRUNG UP IN AMERICA, a title she had no part in choosing. Occasionally, the sense of her religious conviction comes to us through her verses with genuine force, and if her metaphors were not notably original in conception, her imagination at least found turns of phrase that could give them the appearance of independent generation. Her works gain force when understood as the writings of a colonial housewife who lived with the wilderness scarcely a stone's throw from her back door, and she is remembered also a pioneer of the view point of women and a tutelary spirit of poets (see John Berryman's HOMAGE TO MISTRESS BRADSTREET, 1956).

EDWARD TAYLOR enjoyed the advantage of being discovered 250 years after his death in 1729. A preacher at Westfield, Massachusetts, he wrote verses for private ends alone and kept them in a manuscript that his heirs were enjoined to leave unpublished. He wrote in the metaphysical manner, notably after Donne, and got into his poems a sensuousness of feeling that Donne would have recognized. Perhaps this explains Taylor's reticence about publication—fear that the poems, though mostly religious in theme, were still too agreeable to accord with the reputation of a dissenting minister. What is more important, Taylor also got into his poems a certain amount of detail—for us the local habitation without which no poetry can endure. Taylor's manuscript turned up in the Yale Library in 1937 and was promptly published (*The Poetical Works of Edward Taylor*, Thomas H. Johnson, ed., 1939). Kenneth Murdock called Taylor the "greatest poet of New England before the nineteenth century." This still isn't saying much: against the crushing dullness of most of the rest, the slightest talent would stand out. But in fact Taylor deserves a place with his colleagues overseas, the minor English poets of the 17th century who wrote much that we now consider the best the language affords, and beyond this he was able to capture something of the local temper in America.

As the 18th century wore on, American poets became somewhat less preoccupied with doom and somewhat more aware of the new spirit in English poetry, represented by Dryden and Pope. Suppose, for the sake of the narrative, that the classical impetus in modern literature reached its height, its moment of splendid poise, in 1666, the year of *Le Misanthrope*. It is impossible to say precisely when the moment broke upon America, but certainly not before 1745, when *Poems on Several Occasions* by JOHN ADAMS [I] (not the future president) appeared; these contained a trace of classical delicacy and regularity. Hence there was a lag of at least seventy-five years; and it would be possible to write the whole cultural history of North America in terms of the progressive means by which

this lag was shortened. In 1747 William Livingston, later a prominent Revolutionary figure, published his *Philosophical Solitude*, a poem in tolerable heroic couplets. The young Philadelphian THOMAS GODFREY also showed talent in classical meters, though he died too young to develop them; his friend Nathaniel Evans, also a poet, edited a posthumous edition of Godfrey's *Juvenile Poems on Various Subjects* (1765). In Boston, PHILLIS WHEATLEY published at nineteen her *Poems on Various Subjects* (1773), mostly in heroic couplets. In all these poets, however, classicism was never more than a password to the *haut ton*, sincerely as it may have been imitated on occasion. In America the taste for classicism existed, but never the need; the land itself did not ask for it, so its meaning for the pre-Revolutionary American mind must have been—in the full sense—problematical.

As Revolutionary sentiment grew in strength, however, one element of the English classical movement was seized by American poets and put to an immediately practical use—the element of satire, turned inevitably against the country of its flowering. Even in this case American poets preferred, not the toughness of Dryden or the suavity of Pope, but the boisterousness of Charles Churchill and the bathos of Mark Akenside. The type can be seen in its full vigor among the HARTFORD WITS, a group of poets led by JOHN TRUMBULL, TIMOTHY DWIGHT, and JOEL BARLOW, the authors respectively of M'FINGAL (1775), THE CONQUEST OF CANAAN (1785), and THE COLUMBIAD (first version 1787, final version 1807). These were patriotic verses, as fiery in their way as any oration by John Adams or Patrick Henry, and as full of bad rhetoric. But they were popular and they served their purpose admirably; moreover, they constituted the first effective, large-scale adaptation of native materials to the ends of selfconscious literary composition in verse. The mark of provincialism is still abundantly on them, but it was now definitely provincialism, not colonialism. Nor should the Wits be downgraded on account of their rough technique; they were outstanding men—Barlow a diplomat, Dwight a president of Yale, and Trumbull a prodigy and one of the most brilliant men in America.

The Wits by no means exhaust the topic of Revolutionary poetry, for a finer talent than any of them was also producing patriotic verses. PHILIP FRENEAU was the first American poet who pointed the way toward a genuinely *poetic* solution to the dilemma of provincialism. He was a soldier, politician, and journalist; much of his verse was written for patriotic or political ends. But there remains a body of work poetic in the fullest sense, a personal amalgam of experience and feeling. After the Revolution, Freneau continued to write poetry—nature poems, love poems, and some important experiments with themes from Indian life. Beginning with a neoclassical metric, he loosened his verse, made it a personal vehicle, and introduced natural diction (independently of Wordsworth). Neither Romantic nor Gothic, Freneau drove his technique before him toward the goal of style. Here is the opening of his THE HOUSE OF NIGHT:

Trembling I write my dream, and recollect
A fearful vision at the midnight hour;
So late, death o'er me spreads his signal wings,
Painted with fancies of malignant power!

To the present day, much in American poetry stems from this plain line. Not another major poet in America before Emily Dickinson, not even Edgar Allan Poe, would have resisted the temptation to rhyme the first and third lines—a significant resistance. In America, Freneau occupies something like the stage that Chatterton, Smart, Gray, and Blake occupy in England: pre-Romantics freed of neoclassical academicism. Freneau did not go as far in most respects as his English contemporaries—this would have been impossible in the circumstances—but he did well. Americans should honor his work by reading it more than they do.

Freneau leads directly into the Romantic movement and the American 19th century in general with its two great figures, Poe and Walt Whitman, whose influence extends throughout world literature, and a third, Emily Dickinson, who in a less direct way has exerted an equal force. But a word or two must be said first about literary activity below this level. In the eastern cities the beginning of the 19th century was a time of relaxation and refinement; the wilderness was tamed, independence was won, the great urban fortunes had been founded. Women, emancipated from domestic chores by their husbands' wealth, became the poet's chief readers—a condition from which American poetry has yet to emerge. The romantic, subjective poetry of Wordsworth and Coleridge, and more especially of Shelley, Byron, Leigh Hunt, Joseph Blanco White, Thomas Moore, Thomas Hood, and others found an ardent audience among such readers, as did a number of American versifiers ready to embark on imitation. FITZ-GREENE HALLECK wrote mainly sentimental verses, though a Byronesque satire, FANNY (1817), was praised rather unaccountably by Ezra Pound. Halleck's friend JOSEPH RODMAN DRAKE wrote technically unobjectionable verses full of fays and sprites. Eaglesfield Smith wrote verse romances in the manner of Scott, fake dialect and all, and Samuel Woodworth wrote THE OLD OAKEN BUCKET (1826). Gothic melodrama flourished on the stage in New York, Philadelphia, and Charleston—Boston still took a dim view of theatrical entertainments—and the mood was sustained in architecture by Joseph Latrobe and his followers.

In 1820 the English critic and wit Sydney Smith asked: "In the four quarters of the globe, who reads an American book? or goes to an American play? or looks at an American picture or statue?" The taunt was widely circulated in America and widely approved by citizens who comprised the self-appointed elite. When JAMES N. BARKER dramatized in 1812 Scott's *Marmion* for production in a New York theater, the playbill read, "By Thomas Mortan, an Englishman." The public took well to the play, but when word leaked out that the adapter was really Barker, an American, the production folded in three weeks. In the face of this, no wonder American poets seldom were able to take their own work seriously.

Yet some of these poets possessed genius. WASHINGTON ALLSTON, for instance, rebelled against his family's decision that he become a doctor, and ran off to London to study. The British acclaimed him. Clearly he was one of the most brilliant young men of the age, both a painter and a poet, but in the long run he was paralyzed by his sense of being an American, and he failed to produce anything like the important work that was expected of him, though he left some charming fugitive pieces. WILLIAM CULLEN BRYANT is another case in point. His THANATOPSIS (1817), written when he was seventeen though not published until six years later, leaves no doubt of his high gift, and a few of his later poems are unequivocally good. But these few are scarcely vigorous enough to clamber above the dull, pedantic mishmash of the rest—imitative works written under a compulsion to bring European culture to America. As lifelong editor of the New York Post, Bryant made this his main concern; no doubt his learned, fluent editorials, articles, and reviews did a good deal to elevate the cultural tone of 19th-century America, but the same energy put into the shaping of American experience in verse might have resulted in something more important. Finally, there is the case of HENRY WADSWORTH LONGFELLOW. Longfellow's genius was enormous. Some of his love poems and other personal lyrics are good enough to deserve more readers than they have today. Moreover, he obviously did not shirk his responsibility toward the American scene: his verse narratives almost all sprang from native sources. Yet in nearly everything he wrote one detects a weakness, a failure of aesthetic daring or aesthetic faith at the heart of the poem; the poet retreats at the point where a bold word or exceptional meter might win victory, that is, in a full, unified poem. Longfellow was an assiduous scholar, particularly attracted to German and Scandinavian literatures. Too much of his work is imitative and lacks realism: the spirit of locality is not much in evidence in EVANGELINE (1847), for instance, or HIAWATHA (1855), though both purport to be American experiments in American mythology. His best effort in narrative was no doubt his slightest, *Paul Revere's Ride* (1861), tossed off quickly and with no thought of foreign models. In the end Longfellow became the most popular American poet of the century and the cultural arbiter of the American middle class, deeply committed to gentility. He presided in Cambridge, the leader of the New England school of poets—prosperous, gentle, kindly, and conventional; and he ended as a bearded countenance gazing benignly down from ten thousand classroom walls. Bryant and Longfellow achieved fame as poets, but judged by strict critical standards they lost their way. To what extent their provincialism can be blamed for the misadventure, no one will ever determine precisely, but aside from any other historical or biographical considerations, the texts of their poems alone give plenty of evidence that provincialism was an important factor. Nor was the loss to American poetry limited to these two.

"What does the poet make and what does his work create?" The question was asked by L. A. Richards, and he supplied his own answer: "Himself and his world first, and thereby other worlds and other men." Clearly no poet who has been considered here so far thought of his role in such terms as these. On the contrary, these poets took themselves and their worlds as given, inalterable, fixed, in a sense the reliable components of an existence fraught with the contingency of God's will, certainly not in need of self-creation; and for this reason, perhaps, they failed largely to affect the selves or worlds of their readers. Richards' statement of the poet's office is crucially modern, the base of modern literary theory; and it is significant that the first American poet who regarded himself as in any sense a "maker" or "creator" was also our first modern poet, EDGAR ALLAN POE. No one who has studied Poe's poems in relation to his life can doubt that the latter was as deeply influenced by the former as the other way round. Experience was meaningless for Poe until it had been poeticized; poetry was valueless until it had been lived. Beyond this, he buttressed his poetry with a critical theory that was both personal and prescriptive. No American writer before him had attempted anything so comprehensive. Poe hadn't the integrative sensibility that has become almost second nature for poets today. His verse and criticism were not always congruent, but both were illuminating and both—especially the criticism—produced effects that have been pervasive in all Western literature.

Coleridge defined the twofold force of poetry as "the power of exciting the sympathy of the reader by a faithful adherence to the truth of nature, and the power of giving the interest of novelty by the modifying colours of imagination." Conceivably, Poe read these words as a boy, for he attended school in England not long after publication of *Biographia Literaria*. In any case, he was an admirer of Coleridge, and in theory subscribed to the sound Romantic doctrine contained in the elder poet's critical precept. In practice, however, Poe was attracted more by the second half of Coleridge's definition than by the first. Poe's criticism says little about nature, but much about the use of language to sustain a mood, both through the meanings of words, considered primarily under their connotative aspects, and through the sounds of words. He came close to advocating automatic writing. If he fell short of that, he at least insisted on the primacy of the subconscious mind as the source of poetry's images and symbols, and he was an unquestioning believer in the efficacy of affective form. His trouble was that he failed to achieve in his poetry the spontaneity that his critical precepts required. His mood in verse was generally narrow, confined at one limit by melancholy and at the other by the macabre, and he attempted to sustain his mood in studied meters and assonances that too often strained his technique. Modern readers are likely to find his effect more a contrived euphoniousness than a genuine liberation of feeling, with the result that they prefer his short stories to his poetry. Even so, a dozen or more of Poe's lyrics succeed marvelously and are probably the best things of their kind in Anglo-American literature. Together with his stories, they have become so deeply ingrained in American culture that they are touchstones of the historical consciousness.

Poe's theories of language and symbolism were almost completely ignored by succeeding American poets for a hundred years, and the art of symbolism, so natural to American temperament and civilization, was left in the hands of the novelists, particularly Hawthorne and Melville. In part this was owing to the ascendancy of the Pre-Raphaelite movement in England and its consequent acceptance in America. The failure of the Rossettis and their friends to understand the real nature of the symbol in art allowed them to neglect Poe. But Baudelaire was more receptive—and more astute. He read and translated Poe's work and expanded Poe's concepts of the poetic act. Thus Poe's theories passed into French literature at a point where they could be most usefully absorbed, combining with the effects of Baudelaire's *Fleurs du mal* (1857) and Gautier's *Emaux et camées* (1852) to produce, in the ensuing works of Mallarmé, Rimbaud, the Parnassians, and the Symbolists, a literary development of great intrinsic vitality. In the course of time, the Pre-Raphaelites declined, the Rhymers ascended; and when Arthur Symons brought the French poets to the Anglo-American audience in his *The Symbolist Movement in Literature* (1899), which was widely read by young poets in the first years of the 20th century, Poe's influence reentered American literary life. At the same time it was spreading elsewhere by analogous means, until today the Poesque element in Western poetry taken as a whole is incalculably large.

Behind Poe, in a manner of speaking, the ordinary work of literary production went on, centered chiefly in New England. The transcendentalists and abolitionists used verse for their lucubrations when the mood to do so overtook them, and RALPH WALDO EMERSON turned out occasional poems of a certain intellectual vividness, though his verse-writing technique was slapdash; his friend HENRY DAVID THOREAU did little in poetry of any account. Probably the best of the transcendental poets was JONES VERY, whose brilliant, anxiety-ridden, intense mind was capable of only a small output of compressed and tightly formal poems, testimonials of ecstatic mysticism less akin to Emerson's religion than to the Mathers'. JOHN GREENLEAF WHITTIER, a low-born New Englander, wrote crudely but with an attention to homely detail, as in his minor masterpiece of descriptive verse, SNOW-BOUND (1866), but much of his ability was submerged in volatile antislavery diatribes. JAMES RUSSELL LOWELL was the epitome of Brahminism, urbane and learned. These men formed a close and usually closed circle, the Academy of their day, headed by Longfellow, deriving a locus from Longfellow's graciously appointed home in Cambridge. (See BRAHMINS.) Among them, they controlled the editorial policies of the NORTH AMERICAN REVIEW and ATLANTIC MONTHLY and hence the literary tastes of most of cultivated America. Their reviews could make or break young writers. Probably the most genial of them was OLIVER WENDELL HOLMES, SR. who wrote entertaining essays and several novels that remain interesting for their pre-Freudian excursions into psychotherapeutics, but he wrote primarily occasional poetry. When WILLIAM DEAN HOWELLS came East as a young man to seek his literary fortune, he went to Cambridge, for he knew his career hung in the balance until Lowell had condescended to pronounce judgment. A favorable judgment was given, as it turned out, and eventually Howells succeeded to Lowell's kingdom. But the American writer who most needed and most deserved the help of the Cambridge circle never got it. HERMAN MELVILLE worked all his life in a state of almost total critical neglect, and his poems, highly regarded today, were mainly published at his own expense and read by only a few people during his lifetime.

Meanwhile, Southern poets of the middle 19th century wandered into an attenuating dilettantism. As the crisis of Fort Sumter approached, the patriarchal planters and their more or less humanistic, later 18th-century culture gave way to the newly rich cotton kings, western farmers, and red-necked politicos. "The southern farmer of this period had neither the culture, the breadth of view, nor the tolerance of the Virginia planter of the eighteenth century," wrote Jay B. Hubbell, the eminent Southern literary historian. It can be argued that culture, breadth of view, and tolerance are no guarantors of good writing and may even be inimical to it, but in the South of 1830 to 1865, at any rate, the point seems well taken. By and large, Southern taste of the period, like Western taste, was subliterary—there was no one for poets to write for. Southern scholars usually claim Poe as their own, on the strength of his having been brought up in Richmond, but the claim is tenuous; and aside from Poe what was there? JAMES RYDER RANDALL, HENRY TIMROD (the most popular proslavery poet), FRANCIS ORRAY TICKNOR, ABRAM JOSEPH RYAN, Innes Randolf, WILLIAM J. GRAYSON—for the most part are forgotten figures. This is not to say that there was no vigorous writing in the South, but most of it was prose, the work of WILLIAM GILMORE SIMMS, JOHN PENDLETON KENNEDY, WILLIAM ALEXANDER CARUTHERS, JOHN ESTEN COOKE and Philip Pendleton Cooke, and others, strong writers who contributed to the progress of fictional realism in America. Nor should the Western Southerners and the humorists be forgotten—DAVY CROCKETT, AUGUSTUS B. LONGSTREET, and GEORGE W. HARRIS. But it is difficult to find still readable Southern poetry from this period.

WALT WHITMAN was thoroughly individual. He said his "God be with you" to the European poets and parted company with them irrevocably, at the same time and in consequence parting company with his American colleagues, too. He sang no sweet songs, but long, loosely metered chants. He put no history in his poems, but only the broad democratic present and the radiant future. He cared nothing for empire, unless it was the empire of free men—and women. Yes, sex was overt in Whitman's poems—not the coy naughtiness of most previous erotic poetry, but an open, even naïve acclamation of joy in sexual love, accompanied sometimes by an implicit recommendation of indiscriminateness. His aim was the perfection of the individual person through immersion in the commonalty of persons, and the anointing oil of the ritual was love. Whitman dealt more frankly with the physiological aspects of existence than any poet had before. With him, universal nature was a generative force, moving confidently forward toward the realization of Democratic Man. Even in death, nature retained its somewhat inscrutable *élan*. Of all the optimistic philosophies and literatures that derived from the general 19th-century ferment over evolutionary theory, Whitman's was by and large the happiest, and perhaps also the most successful. Spencer fell into confusion, Nietzsche into shameless posturing, Huxley into witticism, and Marx into wardheeling pettifoggery. Whitman, with only the flimsiest conceptualizing apparatus, outlives them all—read today not only with pleasure but with a sense of shared conviction by millions of like-minded people in every part of the world. This fact does not by any means place Whitman above the flaws of his own insight, the shortcomings of his historical consciousness. Whitman's zeal, enthusiasm, fervor, his grand cadences and liturgical phrasings, his irrepressible, highhanded love of word-making, cannot entirely conceal his shallowness. In spite of his tender, moving funeral song for President Lincoln, in spite of his invocations to nature's darker forces, Whitman lacked the tragic sense, and to the extent that knowledge of tragedy is prerequisite to composing genuinely and humanly affective poetry, Whitman failed. But in the context of 19th-century American optimism and expansionism, the failure seems slight.

Whitman published his poems first in 1855 as LEAVES OF GRASS, a small pamphlet he printed and sold himself. It did not attract much notice. Most people who did read it didn't like it. Nevertheless, Whitman persevered, and in the course of his life published a number of further editions, each an expansion and revision of its predecessor. Gradually his audience formed. Before his death he had acquired a gratifying enthusiastic following at home and abroad. Other poets began imitating him. To what extent his unmetered but highly rhythmical lines affected later experiments in vers libre it is difficult to say, for other poets during Whitman's lifetime were writing unmetered verse, especially in France. Perhaps in the long run Whitman's influence has been less than Poe's. But influence is not the only measure of a poet's success, nor even the chief one, and there is no doubt that Whitman's acceptance throughout the world has been wide and appreciative. Considering the nature of Whitman's poetic materials, this is nothing less than astonishing. For what personality was Whitman offering to view? Precisely that which had been the butt of the world's ridicule for decades—the naïve, optimistic, self-assured, democratic American, the Yankee Doodle. One measure of Whitman's genius is the degree to which he—Walt Whitman, the singer, the poet, the public personality, the collective "I"—converted this image of ridicule into one of the modern world's most compelling identities: Everyman as the principle of promise and faith.

The difference between Whitman's poetry and that of EMILY DICKINSON is so great that it scarcely seems possible the two were contemporaries. Perhaps the fact that they lived and worked at about the same time is as good an indication as any of the floundering quality of American literature before the 20th century. No conceivable movement or school or even period (in the usual literary sense) could unite two so dissimilar poets. Where Whitman was the democratic poet, the public poet, the celebrator of men's collective motives, Dickinson was personal, introspective, private. Where Whitman was optimistic, Dickinson was wryly pessimistic. Where Whitman was credulously pantheistic, Dickinson was apprehensively Calvinistic. Where Whitman rewrote and polished his poems continually, and did all that he could to secure their acceptance, Dickinson jotted down her poems on odd scraps of paper, scarcely ever went back to them, and left them concealed in a drawer, where they remained until after she died. Where Whitman was expansive, rhetorical, long-winded, Dickinson was lyrical, cryptic, compressed. Where Whitman acclaimed sex and freedom, implying at least that the two were necessary concomitants, Dickinson was so disturbed by her one mildly incorrect attachment to a married man that she buried herself in neurotic seclusion for the rest of her life. And so on and so on—the disparities are almost endless.

In an important sense, Emily Dickinson was a profoundly American poet, although she seldom incorporated any explicitly American materials in her poems. But, owing to her spiritual locus in the center, so to speak, of the conflict between New England's early and later theologies, she felt and expressed, often in dimly realized terms, a characteristically American anguish. She lived in Amherst, Massachusetts, and as a child learned the Calvinist creed and the Calvinist morality of her forebears, but she also picked up in her adolescent reading a smattering of the 19th-century revolt. Not enough of it, clearly, to fix her unequivocally with the transcendentalists or the Unitarians, but enough to turn her mind toward problems of doubt, guilt, purpose, and all the rest. Her neurotic anxieties gave her general quest a driving personal force. Without much formal education and with few intellectually disposed friends, she lacked the means of conceptualizing these cultural and moral conflicts as they were conceptualized by other troubled New Englanders—Hawthorne, Harriet Beecher Stowe, or Henry Adams. Hence, she never attempted anything on the grand scale, but instead captured her fears and resolutions in fugitive scraps of verse, shaped on the rhythms of the hymn tunes she remembered from childhood, cast up in images taken from her garden, her house, her reading. The result was a large body of mediocre verse surrounding twenty or thirty poems of shattering brilliance. The faults of the poems are easy to pick out: huge abstractions left unwedded to the context; allegories either flatly obvious or unanchored and cryptic; exoticisms (from her reading) tagged on without meaning or necessity; and, worst of all, what the critic Yvor Winters called her "quality of silly playfulness," and apparently deep need to meet questions of ultimacy with an attitude of childish irresponsibility and coquetry. Yet, in the twenty or thirty brilliant poems—some critics would say thirty or forty; the number is open to dispute, though the general proportion

of good to mediocre is not—she transcended these defects of poetic skill and temperament with an accession of genius probably greater than anything of its kind elsewhere in literature written in English. These poems offer much of value to readers and critics, but the manner of their composition offers even more to those who are willing to speculate about the psychology of the procedural imagination.

After Dickinson's death, a considerable tangle developed in respect to the publication rights to her literary remains, and in consequence the poems were published only gradually, a little at a time, in a number of succeeding volumes, and sometimes the texts were inaccurate. A scholarly, variorum edition didn't appear until early in the 1950s. But the main impact of her poems on readers and other poets was immediate. Her influence spread through American poetry like—for once the simile is not exaggerated—wildfire, especially among poets who came to prominence after World War I and more especially among female poets—LÉONIE ADAMS, LOUISE BOGAN, EDNA ST. VINCENT MILLAY, ELINOR WYLIE, and many others. Her style became so widely disseminated through American poetry—the figure is apt though bizarre—that it became virtually indistinguishable from *the* American style, and Whitman's chanting sentences for a while almost vanished from the poetic consciousness. Styles wear out, but we may be confident that twenty or thirty or forty of Emily Dickinson's poems will remain classics of American literature as long as American literature exists.

Southern intellectual life was seriously disrupted by the Civil War. The main intellectual and artistic currents in the United States during the first half of the 19th century—TRANSCENDENTALISM, Unitarianism, Owenism, the various other ramifications of Romantic theory—had been closely and doubtless inevitably tied to abolitionism, while at the same time abolitionism itself had been driven into such an uncompromising position by its radical wing, men like Whittier, Garrison, and the supporters of John Brown, that Southern intellectuals who might have desired to align themselves with a less bellicose but nevertheless progressive program of national development in the arts were prevented from doing so and were left instead to cultivate their own turnip patches. In some respects these turnip patches turned out to be remarkably fertile. But not for poetry. After 1865, prose was able to break from the 18th-century sentimentalism that dominated Southern taste, and the new prose writers who sought their inspiration in the language they heard around them, instead of in Addison or Walpole, gave to American literature a necessary infusion of local color and folk symbolism. This ranged from the subliterary, though culturally important, dialect tales of JOEL CHANDLER HARRIS and THOMAS NELSON PAGE to such formal masterpieces as HUCKLEBERRY FINN and THE GRANDISSIMES. Even in music Louis Gottschalk could make something like the same break, introducing Creole materials into his highly sophisticated compositions. But poetry, bound in a tight prosodic heritage, could not manage it. With one exception, the South produced not a single important poet between 1860 and 1900, and it is significant that a poet who did succeed in creating, in a few poems, a serious modern Southern style was a Northern African American, PAUL LAURENCE DUNBAR. These forty years of Southern literary history form a lucidly heightened illustration of the predicament of provincial culture—provincialism with a vengeance—for the South was, during this period, a provincial culture within a provincial culture.

Of course the exception was SIDNEY LANIER. In the 20th century his poetry, with its Pre-Raphaelite and Swinburnian affinities, became unpopular. Many readers would be inclined to deny that Lanier actually is an exception to the run of Southern mediocrity. The last popular edition of his poems was issued in 1915. Nevertheless, Lanier must be accorded respect for the quality of his mind and the seriousness of his intent, since both of these, aside from his poems themselves, have entered and augmented the main current of American poetry. It is tempting to say that Lanier was a kind of second-rate Poe, since like his predecessor he was deeply interested in the musical elements of verse and the techniques by which they are manipulated. But in reality he pursued a highly individual course. In the first place, he was both a professional musician and a creditable literary scholar and was able to give to his essays in criticism an authenticity that Poe's more fanciful cerebrations might never have achieved on their own. In the second place, Lanier was more deeply committed than Poe to the content of his work, at least in the sense that he was concerned not only for its emotional coherence but for its social and philosophical utility. Charles Anderson, editor of Lanier's *Works* (1945), observed that Lanier inclined toward the Emersonian conception of the poet as a religious seer "in charge of all learning to convert it into wisdom." This conversion, provided we use "learning" in the philosophical sense to mean all perceived experience, lies also at the heart of the modern or symbolist conception of the poet's role, and it seems fair to say that Lanier, however oldfashioned his poems may seem now, came close to our view of the poetic act. But, working apart from the center of literary activity, he gave much of his energy to poetically tangential enterprises. He was convinced that poetic technique could be reduced to a science if prosodists only would apply the analogy of music, and he wrote two books, *The Science of English Verse* (1883) and *Music and Poetry* (1889), to prove his point. They are tedious books, though here and there they contain interesting technical analyses. In his own poetry he applied his principles as well as he could, ending up too often with an exaggerated onomatopoeia that obscures his metrical experiments and novel imageries. In spite of this, however, there is enough substance in some of his poems to suggest that they may come into favor again as taste in literature continues on its spiral course.

In the North, meanwhile, affairs were not much better. The old Cambridge school declined and was replaced by a new one, more cosmopolitan, more refined, and occasionally more daring. William Dean Howells advocated a judicious realism in prose fiction. WILLIAM VAUGHN MOODY faced up intelligently to sexual taboos, as in THE GREAT DIVIDE (1906), a drama that won considerable success. But he didn't really go far in this direction; neither did TRUMBULL STICKNEY nor GEORGE SAN-

TAYANA, who were the two other most distinguished members of the group. These men were without question excellent poets and truly critical intellects—they were perhaps the first Americans who constructed literary careers exhibiting in some degree the qualities we attach to the great Europeans, men like Arnold, Leconte de Lisle, and Carducci; in other words, they were the first American men of letters. Moreover, they may have had more influence on their successors than most readers suspect. The intense originality of the poetry of WALLACE STEVENS, for instance, has led critics to seek its origins, no doubt with reason, in distant sources—Rimbaud and Laforgue—but the movement of his verse is often prefigured in passages from the works of Moody, whose poems were popular when Stevens was a young man. This is not to insinuate that the end of the century in America brought forth much memorable poetry: it didn't. Moody, Stickney, and Santayana were gifted poets, they gave American readers a touch of salutary professionalism at a high level, and they dealt often enough with themes from American life. Good writers in certain circumstances can make themselves useful by other means than the production of masterpieces. If these poets had not yet found the combination of matter and manner that could raise American poetry to the level of English poetry, this is to say that beneath their veneer they were still provincial poets.

There were poets residing in the rest of the country too, of course. But most of them contributed little to the main task at hand. Indiana had JAMES WHITCOMB RILEY, Chicago had EUGENE FIELD, Kentucky had MADISON CAWEIN; BLISS CARMAN and RICHARD HOVEY worked mainly in the East; in California a curious mixture of frontier roughhouse and yellow-book preciosity, stemming from AMBROSE BIERCE, issued in the poetry of GEORGE STERLING, JOAQUIN MILLER, C. W. STODDARD, EDWIN MARKHAM, and others; two women whose poems remain readable were LIZETTE WOODWORTH REESE and ANNA HEMPSTEAD BRANCH; other poets who were notable for one reason or another were EDWARD ROWLAND SILL, Philip Henry Savage, JOHN B. TABB, FRANK DEMPSTER SHERMAN, Louise Chandler Moulton, and Henry Jones; and PERCY MACKAYE wrote admirably for the verse theater and the opera. By the end of the 19th century, cultural life in the United States, in its aspects of organization and management, had become as extensive as cultural life anywhere. But although these poets and others produced works that have value as folklore, history, entertainment, social commentary, or occasionally as still valid poems in their own right, none made an enduring contribution to the development of a soundly based and balanced American poetry.

Success in removing the burden of provincialism from American poetry fell finally to the men and women who created the "revolution of the word," as it has been called, or more simply the "modern poetry," as we still refer to it. Conventionally, the date of the revolution is given as 1912, when HARRIET MONROE founded POETRY: A MAGAZINE OF VERSE in Chicago; the magazine quickly became the principal organ of the new poetry (another common designation). But without in the least diminishing the importance of *Poetry* or extenuating the genuinely revolutionary effects of much that the new poets did, one may believe that the movement did not occur overnight. The old turn-of-the-century poets in America, as noted already, were sophisticated writers, like their contemporaries in England, and they were aware of Baudelaire and the Symbolists. At the same time, the new poets did not acquire much following until after World War I. Thus, the period of emergence for the new poetry lasted at least fifteen years, probably longer. Moreover, one important transitional poet, like Yeats in England, spanned the whole era, and one protorevolutionary preceded it. EDWIN ARLINGTON ROBINSON's first book was published in 1896, his last in 1935. In toughness and psychological daring, his verse foreshadowed many elements of the revolutionary poetry, while his metric remained fixed in conventional usage. He wrote with power, often of themes from New England history and society. His work has been dimmed by Robert Frost's success with similar themes, which is an unfortunate outcome, for whereas Frost's attitudes have generally been ironic and metaphysical and touched with Emersonian softness, Robinson conceived his subjects in terms of tragic purity. No poet has brought lyrical narrative, that difficult form invented by Wordsworth, to a tenser development, and such poems of Robinson's as "Luke Havergal" and "Eros Turannos" should not be forgotten. STEPHEN CRANE, whose poems embodied a tough, realistic content in an ironic free verse that owed something to Whitman and something to journalese, would not have earned much of a reputation on the ground of his verse alone: he didn't write enough of it and his technique was primitive. But there is no doubt that he anticipated many innovations of the new poetry in the small number of poems he did write and publish, all before 1900. Moreover, because his novels attracted widespread attention and were praised by Howells, Huneker, and other influential critics, his verse undoubtedly was read and studied by the young writers who came along in the early years of the new century.

The new poets began their revolution as a rebellion against poetic practices and purposes that had gone stale. Their motives were for the most part negative rather than affirmative. They reacted against Victorianism, Georgianism, genteelism, the academy, the establishment, the rules and conventions, Wordsworth, Tennyson, Swinburne, Bridges—the whole suffocating past. Off they went, hellbent for leather, unfurling their banners as they rode—female emancipation, abolition of sexual taboos, down with American commercialism, abolition of deans and professors and, at the head, resplendent in gory hues, vers libre! As the ranks swelled, some banners were torn down and replaced by others, divisive (not to say derisive) slogans were hurled back and forth, squadrons wheeled away on new lines of march, platoons were lost and never heard from again, and the scene took on the appearance of a melee. Anything like a complete disentanglement of the conflicting elements is beyond the scope of an encyclopedia article. From here on, these observations will be abbreviated, exclusive, and general.

In geographical terms, the charge of the revolutionaries was more in the nature of an exodus—away from the former centers of culture in the East, particularly Cambridge and New York. The new poets were fed up with the conservative policies of the established publishing firms and the universities. The new centers of American poetry were two: Chicago and Europe. They represented two broadly divergent forces in American poetry; and for a quarter of a century a conflict between them invigorated the literary scene, though the two parties were so equally drawn that much of the time the conflict was subdued and antagonists from either side could mingle together on terms of mutual respect. Only when the Chicagoan school finally succumbed to the European were cries of triumph, anger, and misery plainly heard.

In Chicago, HARRIET MONROE ruled. Although she welcomed members of the European school to the pages of *Poetry*, it is clear in retrospect that her sympathies lay first with the Westerners, the Whitmanians, the ebullient democrats. Monroe was a good editor and a sensitive reader, she recognized the great verbal talents of Ezra Pound and his friends; but she lacked their erudition. Like many others in the same fix, she was unwilling to commit herself to an unreserved judgment—which was of course what the Poundians wanted. CARL SANDBURG was the leader of the Chicago group; others were EDGAR LEE MASTERS (whose candid SPOON RIVER ANTHOLOGY, 1915, used to be cited as a liberating force for American letters, though today its importance seems less decisive), VACHEL LINDSAY, LEW SARETT, STEPHEN VINCENT BENÉT, and FLOYD DELL. The historical importance of these poets, together with that of their colleagues who wrote in prose—HAMLIN GARLAND, FRANK NORRIS, THEODORE DREISER, SINCLAIR LEWIS, ERNEST HEMINGWAY—cannot be overemphasized. In a real sense they were the van of the avant-grade, without whom the less aggressive combatants could have made no headway. Besides, they represented an aspect of the American character, its expansive and progressive mood, that is never submerged for long.

But a significant omen of the future was the migration of THE LITTLE REVIEW, founded in 1914 by Margaret Anderson, from Chicago to New York and then to Europe. Anderson took a more esoteric line than Monroe, and soon she was attracting away from *Poetry* the American writers of the European branch whose sophisticated nostrils had begun to detect the aroma of prairie dust that clung to some of Monroe's protégés. The most important were EZRA POUND, who had been *Poetry's* foreign editor, and T.S. ELIOT. Pound had gone to Europe in 1908, had settled in London; there he and T. E. Hulme, a minor English philosopher, had established the imagist movement, advocating extreme precision of imagery and realism of outlook, together with free metric. They chose as models the verse of Greek antiquity, the ideographic poems of the Orient, the song forms of the troubadours and Villon, and the associative and evocative techniques of the symbolists. They attracted to their group such poets as H. D. (HILDA DOOLITTLE), JOHN GOULD FLETCHER, WILLIAM CARLOS WILLIAMS, and MARIANNE MOORE. Soon IMAGISM was taken over by AMY LOWELL and turned into a universal society for vers-librists, and Pound, a fast-moving young man, went on to other affairs. Eliot, also in London, found himself attracted to the older man's tough intellectuality, and the two became friends and collaborators.

Two main points should be emphasized about these American poets who lived in London and Paris during the years immediately before and after World War I. First, Pound had a knack of attracting to himself some of the finest writers who have ever appeared in the English-speaking world, and he had the further knack of bringing out their best and publicizing it to any part of the literate community that would listen. Besides the poets already mentioned, Pound worked with such writers as Hemingway, Joyce, and Cummings; even older writers—Frost, Yeats, Ford Madox Ford—have acknowledged his example. Pound insisted on clarity, precision, a reasoned technique; it wasn't so much that he enforced these notions on unwilling followers as that he gave other writers who already shared his ideas an aggressive sense of solidarity and support, which was just what they needed at that point. Secondly, many of these poets and novelists were fine critics too, and here they enjoyed a considerable advantage over the Chicagoans. Pound and Eliot especially were important. Between them they had produced by 1925 a core of critical theory, announced chiefly in short essays and reviews, which established not only the tone but the main areas of interest for the next three decades of literary activity. It has been called by its enemies the cult of form. This is unfair so far as it suggests a denial of feeling, but it is true that Pound and Eliot and the critics who followed their example were profoundly interested in the way the poem works on the page, and hence insisted on close textual analysis as the beginning of all literary appreciation, however it may be followed up by ancillary methods of interpretation.

By 1920 or thereabouts the main lines were drawn, and the rest may be quickly sketched in. Back in the United States various writers, mostly in the East, were following in the footsteps of the European school. ROBERT FROST, who had published his first book in England in 1913, soon returned to the United States, where he found an appreciative audience for his work, and took up a career that led ultimately to the popular leadership of American letters. WALLACE STEVENS entered on his determinedly individualistic course. William Carlos Williams also refused to be classified; admiring Pound but detesting Eliot, he used the symbolist and imagist techniques to develop an ideologically American aesthetic, which had a very wide influence on younger poets. The female poets who became popular in the 1920s mostly favored the formalists—EDNA ST. VINCENT MILLAY and ELINOR WYLIE, both of whom successfully feminized the decade's attitude of sentimental bitterness, and LOUISE BOGAN and LÉONIE ADAMS, who came later and were more reserved. The expatriate groups in London and Paris included CONRAD AIKEN, who had begun publishing his poems before the war and was now clearly a leader of the new movement; E. E. CUMMINGS, whose lyric intensity and formal eccentricity quickly attracted an audience; and ARCHIBALD MACLEISH,

whose early poems were gently metaphysical in tone. In the South a considerable renaissance was under way, particularly in Nashville, where the group variously known as the FUGITIVES, the Secessionists, and the Southern Agrarians was active in literature and political philosophy. The literary branch included JOHN CROWE RANSOM, ALLEN TATE, ROBERT PENN WARREN, and the novelist CAROLINE GORDON. These were writers of the first rank, who put not only learning but good tough thinking back into Southern poetry, and their reputations quickly ascended from the regional to the national plane. In criticism they exerted an enormous influence, especially Ransom, Tate, and Warren, who extended and refined the policies of Pound and Eliot, working closely with such British critics as I. A. Richards, William Empson, and F. R. Leavis. In politics, under the leadership of DONALD DAVIDSON, the group took a frank stand for the social values of the Old South, advocated reestablishment of an agrarian aristocracy, and then gradually relaxed its dogmatism. Two more strong personalities of the decade were HART CRANE, whose stormy, dense, splendidly eloquent poems attracted much attention, and YVOR WINTERS, a young Chicagoan living in California who turned from Chicagoesque experiments in imagist technique to a strict classical form, in which he composed poems of great perspicuity and force. At the same time Winters devoted himself to hottempered, trenchant criticism of his contemporaries, making Crane his special anathema, and he bore down heavily on what he called the fallacy of expressive form, which he found infecting the work of virtually every major 20th-century poet.

In the 1930s, the proletarian impulse turned many poets away from narrow concern with form and expression. Such expatriates as Archibald MacLeish and MALCOLM COWLEY returned home and put their poetic skill to the service of frankly political ends. New poets like MURIEL RUKEYSER and ALFRED HAYES took up proletarian themes, betraying in their style the great influence of W. H. AUDEN on American literature. Others, like KENNETH FEARING, leaned toward Whitman and Sandburg in their use of language. LOUIS ZUKOFSKY and the objectivists followed Pound and Williams in treating social themes in the larger context of cultural history. A group of young Californian poets, associated with Winters, included J. V. CUNNINGHAM and Howard Baker, whose formally quiet poems often conveyed acute social bitterness. The older poets, of course, continued their work. Eliot's ASH WEDNESDAY (1930) was received with mixed feelings by many admirers who found his acceptance of church dogma too easy, and the new installments of Pound's *Cantos* aroused considerable debate. MARIANNE MOORE found among younger poets many who praised her elegant, intricate poems.

The 1940s introduced two fine Jewish poets, DELMORE SCHWARTZ and KARL SHAPIRO, who dealt with urban themes in a clipped rhetoric that owed at lest something to the style of political writing adopted by the Anglo-American left. Other poets who chose somewhat the same tone were RANDALL JARRELL, JOHN FREDERICK NIMS, HARRY BROWN, RICHARD EBERHART, and JOHN MALCOLM BRINNIN, and bitter war poems predominated in the early part of the decade. THEODORE ROETHKE became one of the few poets who successfully cultivated two distinct styles, in his case a freely metered, highly metaphorical, Rimbaud-like abstractionism, used for the evocation of dream states and the psychology of children, and a more formal, metered and rhymed lyricism, recalling Waller or Sir John Davies and used for expressions of selfconscious feeling. After the war ROBERT LOWELL marked a return to the strict metaphysical style of Tate and Eliot. ELIZABETH BISHOP revealed the influence of Marianne Moore, and JEAN GARRIGUE of the Surrealists. RICHARD WILBUR pushed the classical motif in the direction of rococo minuteness, and at the other end of the scale KENNETH PATCHEN and KENNETH REXROTH worked in strictly ametrical forms, often very beautifully. But after World War II there could be no doubt that the European element in modern American writing had triumphed over the Chicagoan. The examples of Pound, Eliot, Joyce, Yeats, and Ford Madox Ford—to name only English-speaking contemporaries—were too powerful to be overcome or denied. The internationally oriented criticism of John Crowe Ransom and Allen Tate was supreme in the country, and the KENYON REVIEW, edited by Ransom, was regarded as the fount of authority, though its editor was actually a good deal more openminded than many of his admirers and detractors liked to believe.

This disposition of forces persisted in the 1950s, a decade of academicism. Ransom's prosy style in verse was imitated by ANTHONY HECHT and HOWARD NEMEROV, his lighter moods by DANIEL HOFFMAN and W. S. MERWIN, his moral vigor by DONALD JUSTICE and W. D. SNODGRASS. REED WHITTEMORE turned to openly mock-critical verse (on the analogy of Dryden's mock-heroics) with considerable success. DONALD HALL, who edited the *Paris Review*, an American magazine in spite of its name, became a leader of the young academicians. By the end of the decade a strong reaction set in against academicism, chiefly among the Beats, as they proclaimed themselves (see BEAT GENERATION). This was a vestigial outcropping of Chicagoism, but debilitated by bad writing and false sentimentality though some gained celebrity, a few produced good poems, and they had a widespread influence. Other poets who had already been working successfully in the broadly Williamsesque tradition were for a while attracted to the Beats by their claim to marshal the forces of anti-academicism, but it is significant that the best of these writers—KENNETH REXROTH, DENISE LEVERTOV, ROBERT CREELEY, ROBERT DUNCAN—had renounced the association, openly or privately, by the end of the decade.

At the end of so brief an account of the American poetry written since 1920, one thinks of names, a great many, that ought to have been included if simple justice were to be served—such individualists as ADELAIDE CRAPSEY, ROBINSON JEFFERS, José Garcia Villa, Samuel Greenberg, R. P. BLACKMUR, MINA LOY; such important poets as STANLEY KUNITZ, WITTER BYNNER, MARK VAN DOREN, THOMAS MERTON, MARYA ZATURENSKA; such minor but often marvelous poets as Norman Macleod, JOHN WHEELWRIGHT, THEODORE SPENCER, PAUL ENGLE, JESSE STU-

ART, JOSEPHINE MILES, JOHN PEALE BISHOP, Phelps Putnam, GENEVIEVE TAGGARD, WINFIELD TOWNLEY SCOTT, COUNTEE CULLEN, WILLIAM ELLERY LEONARD, ROBERT FITZGERALD, LANGSTON HUGHES, EUNICE TIETJENS, ALFRED KREYMBORG, SARA TEASDALE, EDMUND WILSON, Henry Rago, Marsden Hartley, Rosalie Moore, GEORGE DILLON, Barbara Howes, ROLFE HUMPHRIES, Ruth Stone, BABETTE DEUTSCH, ELDER OLSON, Reuel Denny. Even in the earlier periods, many poets who merit discussion have been omitted; RICHARD ALSOP, THOMAS FESSENDEN, EMMA LAZARUS, FREDERICK TUCKERMAN, STEPHEN FOSTER—these names must at least be set down.

May anything be added about the point raised at the beginning—had the poets of the modern era overcome American provincialism by the decade of the 1950s? The answer must be no and then yes. No, provincialism will never be overcome, if by this one means eradicated; it is as much a part of American culture as our accent. But yes, provincialism was overcome, if one means that the poets of the 20th century turned all American culture, and specifically its provincialism, into material for a mature, authentic literature. Some poets, for example, Wallace Stevens, virtually eradicated provincialism by being denationalized personalities, ignorant of cultural relativity. Such is the ingenuousness of total cosmopolitanism. Others, like William Carlos Williams, were determinedly provincial, aggressively aware of national cultural values. But most, like Tate and Jarrell and Bogan, simply assumed that the American is what he is, that he must write about himself, and that he may do so without hostility and in self-confidence and self-respect. They created a national, not a provincial, poetry—and this makes all the difference. A national poetry is one, equal, indwelling, receptive. The poets were not the first to secure such a cultural identity. Henry James in the novel, Edward A. MacDowell and Charles Ives in music, Louis Sullivan in architecture, and Charles Sanders Peirce in philosophy—all these came before the poets. But a good case could be made for the hypothesis that the poets did more than the rest to consolidate the position. In any event, the pleasure of reading American poetry need not be diminished by the fear that it betrays an inferior national genius. This was the fear that distorted much of the cultural life of our forefathers.

Histories and critical studies of American poetry include Horace Gregory and Marya Zaturenska, *A History of American Poetry, 1900–1940* (1946, 1969); Louis Bogan, *Achievement in American Poetry, 1900–1950* (1951); Roy Harvey Pearce, *The Continuity of American Poetry* (1961); Robert H. Walker, *The Poet and the Gilded Age: Social Themes in Late Nineteenth-Century Verse* (1963); L. S. Dembo, *Conceptions of Reality in Modern American Poetry* (1966); Hyatt H. Waggoner, *American Poets from the Puritans to the Present* (1968); Hugh Kenner, *The Pound Era* (1971); David Perkins, *A History of Modern Poetry* (2 v. 1976, 1987); James E. Miller, Jr., *The American Quest for a Supreme Fiction: Whitman's Legacy in the Personal Epic* (1979); William H. Pritchard, *Lives of the Modern Poets* (1980); R. Baxter Miller, ed. *Black American Poets Between*

Worlds, 1940–1960 (1984); Alicia Ostriker, *Stealing the Language: The Emergence of Women's Poetry in America* (1986); M. L. Rosenthal and Sally M. Gall, *Modern Poetic Sequence: The Genius of Modern Poetry* (1986); Mutlu Konuk Blasing, *American Poetry: The Rhetoric of Its Forms* (1987); William Drake, *The First Wave: Women Poets in America 1915–1945* (1987); and Albert Gelpi, *A Coherent Splendour: The American Poetic Renaissance, 1910–1950* (1988).

HAYDEN CARRUTH/GP

Poetry: Since 1960. The unprecedented variety of poetic theories and practice in this period attests to a widespread questioning of Modernist poetics. A pervasion reaction against the Modernists' impersonal, universal speaker makes for poetry more personal in tone and voice and more autobiographical and historical in subject, Poets like ROBERT LOWELL, SYLVIA PLATH, ADRIENNE RICH, JOHN BERRYMAN, RANDALL JARRELL, ROBERT PENN WARREN, and ELIZABETH BISHOP, who all started out as the formalist heirs of MODERNISM, modify or disown their early esthetics by turning to autobiographical material. Younger poets, who define themselves after 1960, begin with this focus on the personal and the historical.

Although the shift to personal verse may have been instigated by the perceived social and political threats to the individual in the 1950s, this change goes deeper than a defensive reaction. Implicitly or explicitly, postmodern poetry challenges the humanist and Romantic figuration of the poet as a central "man speaking to men" and the underlying universalist assumptions of this position, which survive in the modern poets for all their hostility to Romanticism. As the politics of universal speakers becomes suspect and universal truths become philosophically and scientifically untenable, truth comes to be seen as a matter of position and perspective—in a word, politics. Although the poets turn to individual and local truths, they need suffer no loss of scope. For the poet's self is now seen as an intertextual construct, in which such transpersonal forces as historical, sociopolitical, and familial contingencies; biological, psychological, and linguistic processes; and the broader cultural and institutional uses of language come into play. Thus, issues like the connection between private and public experience and the social position of poetry are engaged in the figuration of the poet's self.

Formally, poets after 1960 start with a wide range of options and proceed by defining the necessities for their choices and consciously engaging the rhetoric of their forms, whether free or traditional. While the norm is free verse, a few poets like Bishop, RICHARD WILBUR, ANTHONY HECHT, DONALD JUSTICE, MONA VAN DUYN, and JAMES MERRILL retain traditional forms. In the 1980s, Bishop's and Merrill's examples are especially influential in reviving an interest in formal poetry and enabling such younger poets as Katha Pollitt, Mary Jo Salter, and William Logan to use traditional forms without subscribing to formalist assumptions.

A broad spectrum of postmodern poetry redefines the figure of the poet in forms that continue the experiments of early Modernism. The BLACK MOUNTAIN POETS—led by CHARLES OLSON and including ROBERT CREELEY, DENISE LEVERTOV, ROBERT DUNCAN, AMIRI BARAKA, PAUL BLACKBURN, and EDWARD DORN—reject poetic and grammatical conventions, as well as abstract or deductive thinking, in favor of open forms, which follow from the body's kinetic knowledge of the world and are based on speech, breath, and physiological participation in the "harmony of the universe." An emphasis on particulars and an underlying organicism links this group to EZRA POUND, but with a difference: they view the poet's ego as another repressive structure, whose will to power over process must be resisted. In theory if not always in practice, Olson's Projectivism (see PROJECTIVE VERSE) construes the poet as a "postindividual," open self, a somatic organism that is continuous with natural and cosmic energies and has no authority to stand above other creatures. The implications of Black Mountain poetics have been developed in various directions. ETHNO-POETICS also emphasizes psychic and linguistic process in an attempt to integrate visionary and historical experience and to recuperate a native American tradition, while language poetry (see LANGUAGE POETS) focusing on linguistic processes within a social and historical matrix, analyzes the construction of the postindividual writing subject.

The antiformalism of BEAT GENERATION poets like ALLEN GINSBERG, LAWRENCE FERLINGHETTI, GARY SNYDER and GREGORY CORSO follows from Olson's theories, but their work is more accessible and polemical. Their protest poetry relies on a spiritual authority in its revolt against decorum on all fronts—in form, subject, diction, and tone. The Beats also regard reason and logical discourse as repressive structures implicated in the system and, "constantly risking absurdity," they deploy a broad humor to tackle "Moloch whose name is the Mind," whose mind is "pure machinery," whose "blood is running money."

The group of poets commonly called Deep Imagists or Surrealists—ROBERT BLY, JAMES WRIGHT, GALWAY KINNELL, W. S. MERWIN, MARK STRAND, CHARLES SIMIC—invoke Jung's archetypal unconscious and draw images from primitive myths, nature, and poets outside the Anglo-American tradition in order to shortcircuit conventional and rational modes of thinking. Transcending the bounds of the individual will and the rational ego, the speaker in this poetry is a hieratic, enigmatic voice sounding the depths of the true self, contemplating essences and working toward harmony with and respect for all creatures. Poets like CHARLES WRIGHT and David St. John allude to the conventions of Deep Image verse but address temporal experience and loss, both appealing to and distrusting the solace of nature. A number of less mystical poets—WILLIAM STAFFORD, John Haines, A. R. AMMONS, DONALD HALL, DAVID WAGONER, and MAXINE KUMIN—likewise turn against civilization and to nature for their themes and inspiration.

Distinct from these poetries, which appeal to a natural and/or cosmic authority for their formal, political, or spiritual programs, are poetries that opt for a historical ground. For example, the so-called NEW YORK SCHOOL POETS—FRANK O'HARA, JOHN ASHBERY, JAMES SCHUYLER, KENNETH KOCH, and BARBARA GUEST—attend to the historical texture of urban life.

They value spontaneity and improvisational forms that accommodate the random and the accidental. Their irreverence not only toward New Critical standards but toward all highfalutin poetic pronouncements and political agendas distinguishes them from the more programmatic antiformalists, and their free forms, which manage without the mystifications of nostalgic organicism and technetronic iconoclasm alike, have proven widely influential.

The Confessional poets—Lowell, Plath, Berryman, W. D. SNODGRASS, and ANNE SEXTON—also use historically, sociopolitically, and psychologically specific speakers (see CONFESSIONAL POETRY). Although the Confessionals deal with extreme experiences and emotions, they cast their suffering speakers as culturally representative. Their tone tends to the theatrical and sensational, as they rail against repressive political and psychological histories, and their self-imposed forms align with the social structures that repress the individual voice.

The Confessionals' emphasis on the personal and the historical prepares the way for other poets who use personal material representatively but are not limited to Freudian myths and psychosexual subjects. For the first time, a large number of poets marginalized by gender, race, ethnicity, class, or even geography project speakers who are not universal but are authenticated and empowered precisely by their marginal status. Poets like Rich, GWENDOLYN BROOKS, and Thomas McGrath write explicitly political verse, exploring hitherto marginalized experiences in the context of American poetry and history. But a great many poets feel free to speak from specific perspectives on the margins without being constrained to write polemical verse. LOUISE GLÜCK, CAROLYN KIZER, ROBERT HAYDEN, MICHAEL HARPER, RITA DOVE, GARY SOTO, GARRETT HONGO, PHILIP LEVINE, C. K. WILLIAMS, DAVE SMITH, and RICHARD HUGO are some examples.

While these groupings designate only loose associations, they are convenient for a synoptic history, for the period is marked by a poetry explosion. In part, this development reflects significant sociological changes affecting the production and dissemination of poetry: accompanying the reaction against the elitist formalism of Modernist poetry is a relaxation of standards, which has granted celebrity to a greater number of poets; a broader and more eclectically educated public has turned to poetry to answer needs not traditionally served by poetry; and, most important, the growth of creative writing programs has created an expanded market for teachers of poetry writing. All the same, the number of indispensable poets remains small. Except for O'Hara and Plath, the most distinguished poets—Bishop, Charles Wright, Ashbery, and Merrill—do not fit easily into these categories. They stand out for the complexity, range, and quality of their work. Often engaging traditions that Modernism evades—such as neoclassical and Romantic poetry—they explore the resources of language, the temporality of the poetic medium, and the history of forms and the ideologies inscribed therein to forge distinctive idioms at once thoroughly intertextual and unmistakably personal.

A comprehensive history of the first half of the period is David Perkins, *A History of Modern Poetry: Modernism and After* (1987). Volume 8 of *The Cambridge History of American Literature*, ed. Sacvan Bercouitch (1996), brings the record closer to the present. Critical studies of the period and of selected writers mentioned in this essay include David Kalstone, *Five Temperaments* (1977); Richard Howard, *Alone with America* (1980); Helen Vendler, *Part of Nature, Part of Us* (1980) and *The Music of What Happens* (1988); James E. B. Breslin, *From Modern to Contemporary* (1983); Alan Williamson, *Introspection and Contemporary Poetry* (1984); Charles Altieri, *Self and Sensibility in Contemporary American Poetry* (1984); Robert von Hallberg, *American Poetry and Culture, 1945–1980* (1985); Marjorie Perloff, *The Dance of the Intellect* (1985); Lynn Keller, *Re-making It New* (1987); Paul Breslin, *The Psycho-Political Muse* (1987); J.D. McClatchy, *White Paper* (1989); and Bob Perelman, *The Marginalization of Poetry* (1996).

MUTLU KONUK BLASING/GP

Poetry Society of America, The. This organization, established in 1910, boasts a membership that has included some of the most distinguished poets of the country—ROBERT FROST became its honorary president. It issued *The Poetry Society of America Anthology* (1947) and *In Fealty to Apollo* (1950). Current support includes a general Annual Award for poetry and the Frost Medal and Shelley Memorial Awards for distinguished achievement.

Poets and Poetry of the West, The (1860), an anthology edited by William Turner Coggeshall. This collection, with its biographical and critical commentaries, was one of the earliest to explore and arrange the poetic productions of the Midwest. Coggeshall made a plea for recognition of literary regions in the United States in his volume *The Protective Policy in Literature* (1859). His only predecessor in the field was WILLIAM D. GALLAGHER, who had issued *Selections from the Poetical Literature of the West* in 1841.

Pogo. A comic strip by WALT KELLY.

Pohl, Frederik (1919–), science-fiction writer. Pohl is very prolific, often writes with a collaborator, and views his writing as cautionary. Among his novels and story collections are the Undersea trilogy written with Jack Williamson—*Undersea Quest* (1954), *Undersea Fleet* (1956), and *Undersea City* (1958)—*Gladiator-at-Law* (1964) and *The Space Merchants* (1969) written with C. M. Kornbluth, and *The Reefs of Space* written with Jack Williamson (1965).

Poictesme. An imaginary region in the Middle Ages that is the setting for several novels by JAMES BRANCH CABELL.

Pokagon, Chief Simon (1830–1899), novelist. A Potawatomi who printed a pamphlet called *Red Man's Greeting* on birch bark for distribution at the World's Columbian Exposition in Chicago in 1893; the text reminded readers that the land on which the city and the fair stood still belonged to his tribe and had not been paid for. His novel *Queen of the Woods* (O-Gî-Mäw-Kwĕ-Mit-I-Gwä-Kî, 1899) uses many Algonquin words with English translation; it is partly autobiographical.

Politian: A Tragedy (1835–36), an unfinished drama in verse by EDGAR ALLAN POE. Three scenes were published by Poe in the December 1835 *Southern Literary Messenger* as "Scenes from an Unpublished Drama." Two more were added in January. Actually he wrote eleven scenes, one of them a poem called "The Coliseum," which had already appeared in the *Saturday Visiter* (October 26, 1833) and was later reprinted in magazines and in *The Raven and Other Poems* (1845). The other omitted scenes were of varied character, some of them low comedy. The text of all the scenes was first published in its entirety (1923) by Thomas O. Mabbott, who later made some corrections (*Notes & Queries*, July 14, 1945). Poe took the plot of his play from a murder case known as the "Kentucky Tragedy." His scene is Italy, the lover who takes revenge is not yet the husband of the injured heroine, and the medium is blank verse. Poe found neither drama nor blank verse congenial. See BEAUCHAMPE.

Political Greenhouse, The (*Connecticut Courant*, 1799), a satire in verse by RICHARD ALSOP, LEMUEL HOPKINS, and THEODORE DWIGHT. It represented the prevailing Federalist point of view among the Hartford writers active at that time. See HARTFORD WITS.

Politician Outwitted (prod. 1788, pub. 1789), a patriotic drama attributed to Samuel Low. It dramatized the great contest for and against the new Constitution.

Pollard, Edward A[lfred] (1831–1872), editor, historian, biographer. Virginia-born Pollard edited the *Daily Richmond Examiner* from 1861 to 1867. An ardent supporter of the South, he wrote *Southern Spy, or Curiosities of Slavery in the South* (1859); *Letters of the Southern Spy* (1861); *Southern History of the War* (1863, enlarged 1866); *The Lost Cause* (1866); and a life of Jefferson Davis (1869).

Pollard, [Joseph] Percival (1869–1911), critic, playwright, novelist. Pollard was born in Germany, was educated in England, came to the United States in 1885, began to write critical articles in the 1890s, and was a reviewer for *Town Topics* from 1897 until his death. He established a reputation as an authority on European, especially German, literature and wrote about American authors. The best of his critical writing was gathered in *Their Day in Court* (1909). *Masks and Minstrels of New Germany* (1911) introduced American readers to many little known German writers. He also wrote plays of his own, adapted others for RICHARD MANSFIELD, and satirized Mansfield in a novel, *The Imitator* (1901).

Pollock, Channing (1880–1946), critic, playwright. Pollock, born in Washington, began as a drama critic for the Washington *Post* and the Washington *Times*, and then wrote drama reviews for several New York magazines, including *Smart Set*. Among his more than thirty plays were *A Game of Hearts* (1900), *Napoleon the Great* (1901), a dramatization of Frank Norris's THE PIT (1904), *In the Bishop's Carriage* (1902), *The Little Gray Lady* (1906), *Clothes* (with AVERY HOPWOOD, 1906), *The Sign on the Door* (1919), *The Fool* (1922), *Mr. Moneypenny* (1928), and *The House Beautiful* (1931). Pollock also wrote many books and several popular songs, including "My

Man" for Fannie Brice, and wrote his memoirs in *The Adventures of a Happy Man* (1939, enlarged 1946) and *Harvest of My Years* (1943).

Pollyanna (1913), a children's novel by ELEANOR HODGMAN PORTER. This resolutely cheerful story of an appealing orphan who invents the "glad game" when she is sent to live with a stern aunt sold over a million copies. Apartment houses, a brand of milk, a game, and innumerable babies were named for "the Glad Girl." *Pollyanna* was dramatized in 1916 by Catherine Chisholm Cushing, later made into a movie for Mary Pickford. *Pollyanna Grows Up* (1915), the only sequel by Porter, was followed by a series of Pollyanna books by Harriet Lummis Smith, Elizabeth Borton, and Virginia May Moffitt. "Pollyanna" became a part of the language, defined in *Webster's New World Dictionary* as "an excessively or persistently optimistic person."

Pomerance, Bernard (1940–), playwright. Brooklyn-born Pomerance settled in England in the early 1970s and has made his career there. His work *The Elephant Man* (1979) was a success in London before its Broadway production. The play is based on the life of John Merrick, a Victorian figure whose disfigurement from disease made him an isolated freak show attraction before he was befriended by Frederick Treves, a surgeon. *We Need to Dream All This Again: An Account of Crazy Horse, Custer, and the Battle for the Black Hills* (1987) is a book-length narrative poem.

Ponceau, Pierre Étienne Du. See DU PONCEAU, PIERRE ÉTIENNE.

Ponce de Leon, Juan (1460?–1521). See FOUNTAIN OF YOUTH.

Pond, Frederick Eugene ["Will Wildwood"] (1856–1925), sportswriter, editor. An authority on field sports, Pond wrote a *Handbook for Young Sportsmen* (1876) and *Memoirs of Eminent Sportsmen* (1878), and edited HENRY WILLIAM HERBERT's *Sporting Scenes and Characters* (2 v. 1881). When Pond came east from his native Wisconsin to edit *Turf, Field, and Farm*, he immediately got in touch with E. Z. C. JUDSON (Ned Buntline) as a possible contributor, and after Judson's death Pond wrote *The Life and Adventures of Ned Buntline* (1888), containing much information obtained from conversations with that remarkable person. Pond edited other books about sports and several magazines, including *Wildwood's Magazine*.

Pond, James B[urton] (1838–1903), lecture manager, memoirist. Pond, born in Cuba, New York, was the most successful lecture manager of his day. Among his clients were Mark Twain, Henry Ward Beecher, George W. Cable, James Whitcomb Riley, Ralph Waldo Emerson, William Dean Howells, and Bill Nye. He wrote amusing reminiscences in *A Summer in England with Henry Ward Beecher* (1887) and *Eccentricities of Genius: Memories of Famous Men and Women of the Platform and Stage* (1900).

Poniatowska, Elena (1933–), nonfiction writer. Poniatowska's father, an emigré Polish aristocrat, and her mother, the daughter of wealthy landowners, fled Mexico during the Revolution. The family returned when Elena was nine. She was educated at an English school and learned Spanish from the family servants, but she has struggled to integrate herself into Mexican life and to communicate the tragic experiences of recent times. *Hasta no verte Jesus mio* (1969, tr. *Until We Meet Again*, 1987) details the life of Jesusa Palancares, a woman from the rural interior who has lived most of her life as a working class resident of Mexico, City. *La noce de Tlatelolco* (1971, tr. *Massacre in Mexico*, 1975) describes a 1968 incident in which the author's own brother was killed. *Nada, nadie* (Nothing. No One, 1988) treats the suffering of Mexico City residents in the 1986 earthquake. Her other works include *Querido Diego, te abraza Quiela* (1978, tr. *Dear Diego*, 1986); *Lilus Kilus* (1976); *La Flor de Lis* (1988); and *Tinísima* (1992, tr. 1996) a novel. *Here's to You, Jesusa*, translated by Deanna Heikkinen, appeared in 2001.

Ponteach, or, The Savages of America (1766), a play by Major ROBERT ROGERS. Rogers had fought Indians since his boyhood and as commander of Rogers's Rangers had played a leading role in the siege of Detroit by the Ottawa chieftain PONTIAC. *Ponteach* was not only the American play about Native Americans but also the first friendly treatment of them. The plot is complicated and includes a love affair; the medium is the somewhat pompous blank verse of the period. It was never produced, but Rogers's portrait of Pontiac helped establish his reputation as a so-called noble savage and a great leader. Another play on the same subject was Gen. Alexander Macomb's *Pontiac, or, The Siege of Detroit* (1835), produced in 1838 at the National Theater in Washington. Macomb also exhibited Pontiac in a noble light, introduced Major Rogers as a leading character, and gave the worst of it to the British officers.

Pontiac (1720?–1769), Ottawa Indian chieftain. Pontiac was probably born in northwestern Ohio. After he became leader of his tribe, he seems to have conceived the idea of forming a loose confederacy of several Algonquian tribes. When the French were defeated in the French and Indian Wars, Pontiac and his fellow chieftains distrusted the new British rulers. War broke out in 1763, and Detroit was besieged by Pontiac and his allies. Pontiac was a clever tactician, but was defeated by the British and signed a treaty of peace on July 25, 1766. He was murdered by another Native American in 1769. FRANCIS PARKMAN's classic *The History of the Conspiracy of Pontiac* (1851) has been updated by Howard H. Peckham's *Pontiac and the Indian Uprising* (1947). Pontiac appears as a character in Louis Zara's *This Land Is Mine* (1940) and Hervey Allen's *The Forest and the Fort* (1943). For plays about him see PONTEACH.

Poole, Ernest (1880–1950), journalist, novelist. Poole, born in Chicago, was educated at Princeton and went to live in the University Settlement House in New York, writing magazine articles advocating elimination of child labor, sweat shops, and slum conditions. After reporting on labor unrest in Chicago and an abortive revolution in Russia, he helped UPTON SINCLAIR gather information for *The Jungle* and published his own first novel, *The Voice of the Street* (1906). The

Harbor (1915) depicts the immigrant's experience and champions workers and unions. He served as a war correspondent in Europe during World War I and as a sympathetic observer of the Russian Revolution. *His Family* (1917), again treating the immigrant experience, won a Pulitzer Prize. Poole published over twenty fiction and nonfiction titles. *The Village* (1918), *The Dark People* (1918), and *The Little Dark Man* (1925) grew out of his Russian trips. His later novels are *His Second Wife* (1918), *Blind* (1920), *Beggar's Gold* (1921), *Millions* (1922), *Danger* (1923), *With Eastern Eyes* (1926), *The Destroyer* (1931), *Great Winds* (1933), and *The Nancy Flyer* (1949). *Nurses on Horseback* (1932) is an account of the remarkable work done in the Kentucky mountains by the Frontier Nursing Association. *The Bridge* (1940) is an autobiography. Other nonfiction titles are *Giants Gone: Men Who Made Chicago* (1943) and *The Great White Hills of New Hampshire* (1946).

Poole, William Frederick (1821–1894), librarian, historian. While still a student at Yale, Poole, who was born in Massachusetts, became interested in library work, was appointed to the staff of the university library, and in 1848 published his useful work *Poole's Index to Periodical Literature*, which he enlarged in later editions and which was continued after his death by other compilers. He became head librarian of the Boston Athenaeum (1856), of the Cincinnati Public Library (1871), of the Chicago Public Library (1874), and of the Newberry Library in Chicago (1887). Among his books are *The Battle of the Dictionaries* (1856), *Cotton Mather and Salem Witchcraft* (1869), *Anti-Slavery Before 1800* (1887), and *Columbus and the Founding of the New World* (1892).

Poore, Benjamin ["Perley"] (1820–1887), newspaperman, biographer. Poore, born in Massachusetts, was one of the most widely known Washington correspondents of his day. Under the pen name Perley, he wrote newspaper columns for the Boston *Journal* (1854–84), meanwhile writing numerous popular biographies. Among others, he wrote lives of Zachary Taylor, U. S. Grant, General A. E. Burnside, and Louis Philippe. He also edited the first issue of the *Congressional Record*.

Poor Richard's Almanack (1733–1757), an annual compilation prepared by BENJAMIN FRANKLIN. He ascribed the almanac to Richard Saunders, the publisher of an English compilation, *Apollo Anglicanus*, and also a Philadelphia customer of his. The *Almanack* became a vehicle for Franklin's common-sense philosophy, and many of his maxims have become familiar sayings, for example: "Nothing but money is sweeter than honey." "Approve not of him who commends all you say." He also drew on the proverbs of all ages. The *Almanack* was very popular. Franklin sold it in 1757, and it continued to be published until 1796.

Popeye, a character in SANCTUARY, a novel by William Faulkner. An embodiment of pure evil, Popeye is a perverted gangster and murderer who rapes Temple Drake and kills the halfwit Tommy. Popeye is finally hanged in Alabama for a murder he did not commit, having been busy at the time of the crime murdering a man in Memphis.

Porgy (1925), a novel by DUBOSE HEYWARD. It is a story of the Charleston, South Carolina, waterfront and the African-Americans who live on Catfish Row. Most notable among them is the crippled beggar Porgy, who becomes involved in a murder and is jailed as a witness by a white detective. Other important characters are Bess, Sportin' Life, Crown, and Serena. Heyward and his wife Dorothy adapted the novel into a successful play called *Porgy* (1927).

The effective use of spirituals in this play suggested to GEORGE GERSHWIN the possibility of turning it into a folk opera. The libretto was prepared by Heyward in collaboration with IRA GERSHWIN. Then George Gershwin began writing the music. In order to get the feel of the background, he lived for several weeks in a shack on the Charleston waterfront and sought in particular to absorb the music of the Gullahs. The opera *Porgy and Bess* opened in 1935 and has since been recognized as an American classic. Its songs have become universally known—"Summertime," "I Got Plenty of Nuttin'," "It Ain't Necessarily So," "Bess, You Is My Woman Now," and others.

Porgy, Captain. A comic character appearing in WILLIAM GILMORE SIMMS's trilogy of the Revolutionary War—THE PARTISAN (1835), *Mellichampe* (1836), and *Katharine Walton* (1851)—and in *The Forayers* (1855) and *Woodcraft* (1854). Captain Porgy combines a Falstaffian paunch and love for food and drink with bravery, gallantry, and generosity. He is bawdy, humorous, inventive, and a tireless practical joker.

Porter, Cole (1893–1964), composer, lyricist. Born in Indiana and musically inclined from childhood, Porter went to Yale, then to Harvard to study law. But he soon switched to music and obtained a thorough musical education in Cambridge and Paris. His musical comedy successes include *Anything Goes* (1934), *Red Hot and Blue* (1936), *Panama Hattie* (1940), *Something for the Boys* (1943), *Kiss Me, Kate* (1948), *Can-Can* (1953), and *Silk Stockings* (1955). Robert Kimball edited *The Complete Lyrics of Cole Porter* (1983).

Porter, David (1780–1843), naval officer, memoirist. Born in Boston, Porter saw sea duty during the War of 1812 and later in the Caribbean, but was court-martialed because of difficulties with the Spanish authorities in Puerto Rico. He served in the Mexican navy, 1826–29, then received from President Jackson consular and diplomatic appointments in Algiers and Constantinople. His memories of the Pacific were published as *A Journal of a Cruise Made to the Pacific Ocean, 1812–1814* (2 v. 1815), a book read with profit by Herman Melville. Porter also wrote *Constantinople and Its Environs* (2 v. 1835), in which he included letters he had written to James K. Paulding.

Porter, David Dixon (1813–1891), naval officer, historian. The son of DAVID PORTER was born in Pennsylvania and entered the navy at the age of sixteen. He served under his father in the West Indies and in the Mexican navy. During the Civil War he commanded the mortar fleet under Farragut and helped bring about the surrender of Vicksburg. After the war Porter was made superintendent of the Naval Academy, became an admiral in 1870, and held important positions in

the Navy Department. He edited *Memoir of Commodore David Porter* (1875) and wrote his own memoirs of the Civil War (1885), a *History of the Navy During the War of the Rebellion* (1887), and two novels.

Porter, Edwin S. Author and producer of THE GREAT TRAIN ROBBERY.

Porter, Eleanor H[odgman] (1868–1920), teacher, singer, novelist. Born in New Hampshire, Porter wrote sentimental novels, beginning with *Cross-Currents* (1907). She created two particularly popular characters, *Miss Billie* (1911), whose fortunes she continued to relate in *Miss Billie—Married* (1914), and POLLYANNA (1913), about whom she wrote one sequel, *Pollyanna Grows Up* (1915). Later she published *Just David* (1916), also a best seller.

Porter, Gene [va] Stratton (1863–1924), naturalist, novelist. Just south of Wabash, Indiana, where Porter's farmer-clergyman father moved when she was eleven, is the great Limberlost Swamp. There she studied birds, feathers, bees, moths, eggs, other forms of nature. HER LADDIE (1913) tells in fiction the story of her own childhood in the Limberlost country; *Freckles* (1904) portrays a lad whose days are spent in the Limberlost Swamp; and A GIRL OF THE LIMBERLOST (1909) has the same background. Other books of hers are *The Song of the Cardinal* (1902), *At the Foot of the Rainbow* (1908), *The Harvester* (1911), *Michael O'Halloran* (1915), and *The Keeper of the Bees* (1925). Her books sold in millions. Her daughter, Jeanette Porter Meehan, wrote her biography, *The Lady of the Limberlost* (1928).

Porter, Katherine Anne (1890–1980), short-story writer, novelist. Born in a log cabin in Indian Creek, Texas, and raised in grinding poverty with little formal schooling, Callie Russell—later changed to Katherine Anne—Porter gained a national and international reputation as a writer of brilliant short fiction. Her biographer, Joan Givner, documents Porter's passionate commitment to the art of literature amid the struggles of a hectic personal life. Porter's early reputation was limited to a small group of readers—many of them writers—who read her stories as they appeared in obscure little magazines. Later these were collected in *Flowering Judas* (1930) and in *Pale Horse, Pale Rider* (1939), containing besides the title story, NOON WINE and "Old Mortality." Her last single volume of new stories was *The Leaning Tower* (1944). *The Collected Stories* (1965) won a Pulitzer Prize. It was not until the appearance of her only novel, *Ship of Fools* (1962), and its conversion into a popular movie that Porter's reputation spread beyond academic and literary circles.

Porter's stories are generally admired for their perfection of form and style. Disagreements arise over assessments of her vision, whether she is negative or ironic, a realist or a truth teller. In an introduction to a second edition of *Flowering Judas* (1940) and later reprinted in *The Days Before* (1952), her collection of nonfiction pieces, Porter attempted to put her fiction in historical perspective, remarking that her life and that of her generation had been lived "under the heavy threat of world catastrophe" and that most of her energies of mind and spirit had been "spent in the effort to grasp the meaning of those threats, to trace them to their sources and to understand the logic of this majestic and terrible failure of the life of man in the Western world." This assertion would seem to place Katherine Anne Porter, by intention at least, in the company of writers such as T. S. Eliot and William Faulkner. Robert Penn Warren classed her achievement with that of Joyce, Hemingway, and Sherwood Anderson. *The Letters of Katherine Anne Porter*, edited by Isabel Bayley, appeared in 1990.

W. J. STUCKEY

Porter, Noah (1811–1892), clergyman, philosopher, educator. Born in Connecticut and associated with Yale as a student, professor of moral philosophy and metaphysics (1846–1871), and president (1871–1886), Porter was a Calvinist and an opponent of Darwin and Herbert Spencer. His book *The Human Intellect* (1868) was an early work on psychology. His educational philosophy, set forth in *The American College and the American Public* (1870, 1878), was widely read. He edited the 1864 edition of *Webster's American Dictionary of the English Language* as well as *Webster's International Dictionary* (1870). *The Sciences of Nature Versus the Science of Man* (1871), *Science and Sentiment* (1882), *The Elements of Moral Science, Theoretical and Practical* (1885), *Kant's Ethics* (1886), and *Fifteen Years in the Chapel of Yale College, 1871–1886* (1888) are his other principal works.

Porter, William Sydney. See O. HENRY.

Porter, William Trotter (1809–1858), humorist, newspaperman, editor. Born in Newbury, Vermont, Porter worked on newspapers in Vermont and New York City. In 1831 he founded a weekly sporting journal called SPIRIT OF THE TIMES and edited it until 1856, when the magazine was sold to George Wilkes and the name was changed to *Porter's Spirit of the Times*. It continued to be published until 1861. In his pages appeared the best of Southwestern and a good deal of national humor. Porter compiled three collections from his magazine: *The Big Bear of Arkansas and Other Tales* (1845), *A Quarter Race in Kentucky* (1847), and *Colonel Thorpe's Scenes in Arkansas* (1858). Francis Brinley wrote a *Life of William T. Porter* (1860).

Port Folio, The. JOSEPH DENNIE, Harvard graduate, lawyer, dandy, and essayist, founded the *Port Folio* in Philadelphia in 1801. It was a weekly miscellany devoted chiefly to literature and politics. John Quincy Adams, Charles Brockden Brown, Alexander Wilson, Thomas G. Fessenden, and William Dunlap were among the contributors to the early volumes of the magazine. But Dennie himself, often using the pen name Oliver Oldschool, was the chief writer throughout his editorship. He was an extreme Federalist; his eloquent denunciation of the democratic system in his series "The Progress of Democracy" (1803) caused him to be tried for seditious libel, but he was acquitted through a brilliant defense by Joseph Hopkinson. Dennie attacked Jefferson with poison-pen brilliance in 1802–1803, but in 1809 he abandoned political discussion. Commentary on English, classical, and Continental writers was important in the *Port Folio*, with travel, biography, American speech, and social customs lending great variety to the con-

tents of the journal. Dennie died in 1812 and was succeeded by Nicholas Biddle, who made the *Port Folio* a monthly review, but the magazine declined in popularity. Later editors were Charles Caldwell (1814–1816) and John E. Hall (1816–1827).

Portico, The, a monthly literary magazine published by the DELPHIAN CLUB.

Portnoy's Complaint (1969), a novel by PHILIP ROTH. In telling his life story to his psychiatrist, Alexander Portnoy complains of the effects of his mother's domination, especially on his sex life.

Portrait of a Lady, The (1881), a novel by HENRY JAMES. The *Portrait* is the greatest novel of James's early period. It is both an expansive Victorian work, treating James's characteristic theme of international contrast, and a harbinger of the subjective, inward fictions that he would write after 1900. Stream-of-consciousness technique is prefigured in the celebrated chapter 42. The lady of the title is Isabel Archer, a romantic, vital, but ignorant young woman, who is rescued from Albany, New York, by her Europeanized aunt. Mrs. Touchett proposes to give Isabel the advantages of European travel and manners, and the acquaintance of such persons as her sophisticated friend Mme. Merle. In England Isabel meets her aunt's husband, their charming but consumptive son Ralph, and their friend, Lord Warburton. In Italy she meets an expatriate, Italianate aesthete, Gilbert Osmond. Meanwhile, a resolute American suitor, Caspar Goodwood, pursues her to Europe. Isabel's sense of developing selfhood is played out in her responses to the suits of Warburton, Osmond, and Goodwood, who are both individuals and national types. Ralph Touchett has become a loving but detached spectator, having prevailed on his father to leave a fortune to Isabel so that she may be free to fulfill her sense of personal destiny. Isabel's disastrous choice of Osmond, subtly engineered by Mme. Merle, mother of his illegitimate daughter, results in knowledge, disillusion, and suffering. James anticipated criticism of the unresolved open ending: "The *whole* of everything is never told; you can only take what groups together," a remark indicative of his acute sense of form.

JEAN FRANTZ BLACKALL

Pory, John (1572–1635), geographer and colonist. In his native England, Pory studied with Richard Hakluyt. He came to Virginia in 1619 as secretary for the colony. His experiences were included in John Smith's *Generall Historie*.

Posey, Alexander Lawrence (1873–1908), Creek Indian poet, humorist, editor. Posey edited the *Indian Journal* from 1901 to 1903 and published in it some of his verses and his satirical *Fus Fixico Letters*. The latter were written in Indian-English dialect. Minnie H. Posey edited *The Poems of Alexander Lawrence Posey*, with a memoir by W. E. Connelly (1910).

Post, Emily [Price] (1873–1960), novelist, writer on etiquette. Post, born in Baltimore, wrote the novels *The Flight of the Moth* (1904), *Purple and Fine Linen* (1906), and others, dealing with Americans living elegantly in Europe. *Etiquette* (1922), written at the request of her publisher, sold half a million copies, establishing its author as social arbiter of America.

It was revised in 1927 and frequently thereafter. Her other titles are *How to Behave Though a Debutante* (1928), *The Personality of a House* (1930), and *Children Are People* (1940). She also conducted a radio program and wrote a syndicated newspaper column.

Post, Melville Davisson (1871–1930),   lawyer, storyteller, novelist. Post, born in West Virginia, wrote detective and mystery stories, the best known of which had a shrewd character named Uncle Abner as detective. Out of observations during his legal practice he wrote *The Strange Cases of Randolph Mason* (1896), adventures of an unscrupulous lawyer who knew how to find loopholes in the law. Among his other books are *The Man of Last Resort* (1897), *Dwellers in the Hills* (1901), *The Corrector of Destinies* (1908), *Uncle Abner, Master of Mysteries* (1918), *The Mystery at the Blue Villa* (1919), *The Man Hunters* (1926), and *The Silent Witness* (1930).

Postl, Karl Anton.   See CHARLES SEALSFIELD.

Postman Always Rings Twice, The (1934),   a novel by JAMES M. CAIN. This is a celebrated specimen of the hardboiled school of American fiction, the story of a young wife and her lover plotting to murder her aging husband and collect his insurance. The scene is primarily a roadside café in California.

postmodernism.   The first uses of the term "post modern" to designate a new sensibility in postwar literature can be found in RANDALL JARRELL's review of ROBERT LOWELL's *Lord Weary's Castle* (1946), and in CHARLES OLSON's poetic essays published in the early 1950s. Limited initially to discussions of poetry and architecture, the term was extended to other art forms that shared a common criticism of modernism. Reacting against the aesthetic foundation of high modernism with its emphasis on transcendent reason and its separation of art from history and mass culture, the early postmodernists encouraged an eclectic, anti-elitist poetics concerned with sensuous immediacy and performance (William Van O'Connor, LESLIE FIEDLER, SUSAN SONTAG). This poetics was subsequently developed along two theoretical lines: the first emphasized existential spontaneity, process art, ontological pluralization (Richard Wasson, William Spanos, Richard Palmer, Brian McHale); the second direction recommended narrative disruption and a radical epistemology based on indeterminacy, multiperspectivism, and a "new immanence of language" (Ihab Hassan). Hassan was the first to define postmodernism as a broad epistemic and structural "mutation in Western humanism."

Despite persistent disagreement regarding its definition, the term "postmodernism" was accepted by the mid-1970s as a comprehensive sociocultural paradigm. In the work of the French poststructuralist J.-F. Lyotard, postmodernism designates a recent phase in the development of Western societies characterized by mass consumption, electronic reproduction, eclecticism of taste, and informational and discursive proliferation. The two definitions of postmodernism, one artistic, the other sociocultural, are brought together in Lyotard's analysis of contemporary narration, which both constructs views of reality and makes them accord with the interests of a particular social order. Much of the postmodern debate has therefore centered on narrative as a mode of sociocultural construction and self-representation. Reacting against the traditional master narratives that projected an orderly and coherent universe, the postmodern writers have chosen narrative openness over closure, fiction over truth, and fragmentation over unity and coherence. But their emphasis on disruptive, self-reflexive procedures has often obscured an important ideological component in postmodern fiction: its critique of traditional narrative epistemologies. In the novels of Walter Abish, KATHY ACKER, ROBERT COOVER, RAYMOND FEDERMAN, MARILYN FRENCH, CLARENCE MAJOR, GRACE PALEY, THOMAS PYNCHON, ISHMAEL REED, RONALD SUKENICK—to name but a few—the disruptive techniques participate in a broad critique of narrative and cultural articulation. Innovative fiction uses its intense "metafictional" focus to challenge the traditional models on which narrative constructions have relied.

Using the example of recent fiction, it is helpful to distinguish two varieties of postmodernism: the first one—complacent, hedonistic, playfully antireferential—deserves the criticism that it has alienated fiction from "significant external reality." The second variety, more radically innovative and "resistant," has contributed significantly to a critique of the basic mechanisms of storytelling.

Studies include J.-F. Lyotard, *The Postmodern Conditions: A Report on Knowledge* (1979, tr. 1984); Matei Calinescu, *Five Faces of Modernity: Modernism, Avant-Garde, Decadence, Kitsch, Postmodernism* (1987); Ihab Hassan, *The Postmodern Turn: Essays in Postmodern Theory and Culture* (1987); Linda Hutcheon, *A Poetics of Postmodernism: History, Theory, Fiction* (1988); and Larry McCaffery, ed., *Postmodernist Fiction* (a critical bibliography, 1987).

MARCEL CORNIS-POPE

Potash and Perlmutter.   The chief characters in numerous stories by MONTAGUE GLASS. They are partners in the cloak-and-suit business, later in motion pictures; their joys and troubles, conveyed in dialect, amused a host of readers. For years there was a steady demand for the tales, which were collected in *Potash and Perlmutter* (1910), *Abe and Mawruss* (1911), *Potash and Perlmutter Settle Things* (1919), and other volumes. The characters were even more popular on the stage, beginning with *Potash and Perlmutter* (1913, in a dramatization by CHARLES KLEIN), *Abe and Mawruss* (1915, Glass in collaboration with Roi Cooper Megrue), and *Keeping Expenses Down* (1932, in collaboration with Dan Jarrett).

Potawatomi Indians,   a part of the Algonquian linguistic group settled in the Great Lakes region. During the War of 1812, they followed Tecumseh in siding with the British. Near the end of the 19th century many settled in their assigned allotments near the Canadian River in the Indian Territory, now known as Oklahoma. They are featured prominently in Cooper's *The Oak Openings* (1848), set in Michigan during the War of 1812.

Potiphar Papers (1853),   seven essays by GEORGE WILLIAM CURTIS dramatized as *Our Best People* (1854). Curtis, an ardent reformer, in these papers satirizes the so-called high society of this times; the newly rich, the old families, the young hangers-on who are good for such emergencies as a dance or a dinner. The chief character is Mrs. Potiphar, a climber, whose husband endures her as best he can.

Potok, Chaim (1929–   ),   Potok was born in New York City and educated at Yeshiva University and the University of Pennsylvania. Trained as a rabbi, he served as an Army chaplain. *The Chosen* (1967), his first novel, deals with two generations of Brooklyn Hasidic Jews. His other titles include *The Promise* (1969), *My Name Is Asher Lev* (1972), *In the Beginning* (1975), *Wanderings: Chaim Potok's History of the Jews* (1978), *Davita's Harp* (1985), *The Gift of Asher Lev* (1990), *The Tree of Here* (1993), and *The Sky of Now* (1994).

Potter, Paul [Meredith] (1853–1921),   dramatist. English-born, Potter was a skillful adapter of novels for stage production, as in his dramatizations of Du Maurier's *Trilby* (1895), Ouida's *Under Two Flags* (1901), and Balzac's *Honor of the Family* (1907). He also wrote some original plays, among them *The Ugly Duckling* (1890), *The American Minister* (1892), and *The Conquerors* (1898)

Pound, Ezra [Loomis] (1885–1972),   poet, translator, critic, editor. Pound was born in Hailey, Idaho, a mining town. When Ezra was three, his father, Homer, obtained an assayer's job at the U.S. Mint, and the Pound moved to a suburb of Philadelphia. On both sides, his family claimed colorful American roots. His father's father, Thaddeus Coleman Pound, had been a pioneer lumberman, railroad-builder and U.S. Congressman from Wisconsin, and his mother, Isabel, was related to the Wadsworths, Longfellows, and Westons of Massachusetts. These connections would incline Pound toward American history even as a grand tour at the age of twelve with his charismatic aunt, Frances Weston, directed him toward the glamor of Europe. Pound's travel inspired him to take up Romance languages and model himself on the poets of the Middle Ages. He once wrote that "I knew at fifteen pretty much what I wanted to do" and resolved that by thirty "I would know more about poetry than any man living." This resolve led to Pound's early achievement in Latin, his matriculation at the University of Pennsylvania at the age of sixteen, his work in the nascent field of Provençal studies at Hamilton College, and his graduate work on Lope de Vega back at Penn.

At college, Pound met other budding poets. WILLIAM CARLOS WILLIAMS was a medical student at Penn, and HILDA DOOLITTLE, who attended Bryn Mawr for a year, was the daughter of a Penn astronomer. In 1907–8 Pound taught Romance languages at Wabash College in Indiana, but his tenure was abruptly terminated when the college discovered he had sheltered a penniless actress in his boardinghouse room. (Pound maintained even years afterward that his actions had been innocent.) He returned to Philadelphia, proposed marriage to Hilda—her father forbade it—and gathered his resources to pursue a career as a poet abroad.

Pound headed for Venice, his beloved Browning's favorite city. There he privately printed his first book of poems, *A Lume Spento* (1908), bearing the postscript "Make strong old dreams lest this our old world lose heart." After a brief stay, he went to London, eager to talk with William Bulter Yeats, whom he thought the greatest living poet writing in English. Within a short time he made Yeats's acquaintance through the auspices of the Irishman's friend and former lover, Olivia Shakespear. (Pound married her daughter, Dorothy, in 1914.) On Yeats's part, though he had reservations about Pound's early poetry, he was flattered by the young poet's admiration and impressed with the shrewdness of Pound's practical criticism. "Ezra," he wrote Lady Gregory, "is full of the middle ages and helps me to get back to the definite and concrete . . . To talk over a poem with him is like getting you to put a sentence into dialect. All becomes clear and natural." During the winters of 1913, 1914, and 1915, Pound and Yeats married Georgie HydeLees, a friend of Dorothy Pound's, in 1917, Pound was best man at the wedding.

In London, Pound traveled in Yeats's circles—he visited Victor Plarr and other former members of the Rhymer's group, for example—but soon moved beyond them. Thanks to friendship with the novelist and feminist May Sinclair, Pound gained entry into a set of young radicals that included Rebecca West, and he began to write for *The New Freewoman*. Sinclair introduced Pound to Ford Madox Ford (then Hueffer) and through Ford Pound met HENRY JAMES. Ford also published Pound with James, Hardy, and Wells in the *English Review*, and interested Pound in the practice of contemporary fiction.

During the same period, Pound was making the acquaintance of musicians, artists, and the youn ger poets, many of whom shared a sympathy with the continental avant-garde. His troubadour studies brought him together with the pianist Walter Rummel, a devotee of medieval music who also happened to be part of the Debussy circle in Paris and a onetime lover of Isadora Duncan's. Meanwhile, friendships with the painter and novelist Wyndham Lewis and with the sculptors Jacob Epstein and Henri Gaudier-Brzeska brought Pound into the world of modern art, and discussions with T. E. Hulme and F. S. Flint made him aware of recent developments in French verse. In line with contemporary movements in Paris, most notably the Italian Marinetti's Futurism, Pound began to conceive his work as a part of the modern movements in the arts. Ford had encouraged him to bring his style up to date, and in 1913 he touted himself, Hilda Doolittle (now in London, where Pound rechristened her H.D.), William Carlos Williams, Richard Aldington, F. S. Flint, James Joyce, and others as "imagiste" poets. Pound's efforts included editing an anthology (*Des Imagistes*, 1914) and composing a manifesto that appeared after a few minor revisions under Flint's name. The manifesto announced what would later be considered the central principles of modernist poetry: "1. Direct treatment of the 'thing', whether subjective or objective. 2. To use absolutely no word that did not contribute to the presentation. 3. As regarding rhythm: to compose in sequence of the musical phrase, not in sequence of a metronome."

Even before *Des Imagistes*, however, Pound had understood that editing would bolster his own writing's chance to shape an audience for modern poetry. Invited to contribute to HARRIET MONROE's new journal POETRY in 1912, he talked her into appointing him foreign editor. Later, he obtained consulting editorships at *The New Freewoman* (beginning in 1913 and continuing when the journal became *The Egoist*), *The Little Review*, and *The Dial*—the most important avant-garde magazines of the day. He was also an important influence on the beginnings of Eliot's *Criterion* and for a brief time in 1927 and 1928 edited his own magazine, *The Exile*. Pound followed *Des Imagistes* with other anthologies, including the *Catholic Anthology* (1915), which introduced Eliot's Prufrock to English readers, the *Active Anthology* (1933), which published Basil Bunting and LOUIS ZUKOFSKY, and *Confucius to Cummings* (1964).

Translation was another part of Pound's program to modernize English poetry. Starting with medieval Italian and Provençal verse, Pound set about collecting and translating specimens of poetry in other languages to enrich the possibilities of English style. A great deal of his early criticism and poetry grew out of this project, including dramatic lyrics modeled on the Chinese in *Cathay* (1915), epigrammatic poetry based on Martial in *Lustra* (1916), verse drama based on the Japanese in *Certain Noble Plays of Japan* (1916), the long witty lines of "Homage to Sextus Propertius" (1919), and experiments with the French of Laforgue, Corbière, and Gautier.

From 1910 on, Pound went out of his way to promote the work of gifted contemporary stylists. In reviews and essays, he talked up D.H. Lawrence, ROBERT FROST, MARIANNE MOORE, James Joyce and T.S. ELIOT when their work was almost unknown. He was instrumental in getting Joyce published and noticed, and worked indefatigably to ensure recognition of *Ulysses*. With Eliot he became still more involved. The two Americans met in London in September 1914 and soon coordinated their struggle to modernize English literature. Between 1914 and 1922, Pound arranged for and financed Eliot's first book of poems, helped Eliot obtain an assistant editorship on *The Egoist*, and blue-penciled drafts of Eliot's poems, most famously THE WASTE LAND. (Eliot later said Pound's suggestions for revision provided "irrefutable evidence of his critical genius.") At the height of their collaboration Pound composed the satirical suite HUGH SELWYN MAUBERLEY (1920), like Eliot's quatrain poems modeled after Gautier and like *The Waste Land* received as a landmark of the modernist movement. (Pound, however, always regarded the poem as inferior to "Homage to Sextus Propertius," which he believed was both a better mask of the essential poet and a better piece of social criticism.)

THE CANTOS, an epic project that became Pound's lifework, also emerged out of his collaborative activities in London. Begun when he was with Yeats at Stone Cottage in 1915, the poem represents Pound's attempt to win back for poetry the scope and the sophistication that in the 19th century had been appropriated by the novel. Pursued over fifty-five years and

published in periodicals beginning in 1917 and in serial volumes beginning in 1925, the poem became the century's paradigmatic work-in-progress, embodying all the virtues and risks of open-endedness. Pound's aim was to represent the contours of civilization, Western and Eastern, and his ambitions at times included an ideological critique of Western values and a universal moral anatomy on the order of Dante's *Divine Comedy*. A "poem including history," *The Cantos* survey important moments in medieval and Renaissance Florence and Venice, the founding of the American republic, and vast stretches of dynastic China. Although readers disagree about the success of the whole, sections of *The Cantos* have become touchstones of 20th-century poetry and important models for subsequent writers. Yeats said he found in Pound's work "at moments more style, more deliberate nobility and the means to convey it than in any contemporary poet known to me." Eliot maintained, "I cannot think of any one writing verse, of our generation and the next, whose verse (if any good) has not been improved by the study of Pound's. His verse is an inexhaustible reference book of verse form." HEMINGWAY was stronger still. "Any poet born in this century or in the last ten years of the preceding century," he wrote, "who can honestly say that he has not been influenced by or learned greatly from the work of Ezra Pound deserves to be pitied rather than rebuked. . . . The best of Pound's writing—and it is in *The Cantos*—will last as long as there is any literature."

About 1918, Pound discovered C.H. Douglas, the English proponent of Social Credit, and swerved away from pure literature toward politics and economics. Recoiling from the human and cultural losses of the war, including the death of Gaudier-Brzeska, Pound also soured on Britain. At the end of 1920 he and his wife moved to Paris, where they became part of the American colony in Montpamasse. Pound remained in Paris for four years and associated himself with forward-looking artists, including the sculptor Constantin Brancusi and especially with the Dadaist group. He regularly saw Jean Cocteau and Francis Picabia, contributed to the Dadaist review, *391*, and patronized the avant-garde composer George Antheil. It was at this time that Pound and Hemingway became friends, and that he began a lifelong relationship with the exiled American violinist Olga Rudge. In Paris Pound also tried his hand at the other arts. He dabbled in painting and sculpture, wrote *Le Testament de Villon*, an opera that was performed at the Salle Playel, and collaborated with Antheil, Fernand Léger, and the American cameraman Dudley Murphy on an experimental film, *Ballet mécanique*.

In a few years, though, Paris seemed too frenetic and too frivolous. Having sampled life in Rapallo, Italy, in 1923 and 1924, Pound and his wife settled there in early 1925. Part of Italy's attraction was its peacefulness, but for Pound the chance to work in quiet was augmented by his enthusiasm for the political experiment of Mussolini, then viewed sympathetically by commentators as diverse as George Bernard Shaw and *The New Republic*. In Pound's view, Mussolini's economic and cultural programs held promise of a new Renaissance, and in

1935 Pound published an homage entitled *Jefferson And/Or Mussolini*. After Italy's invasion of Ethiopia in 1935, by which time most of Mussolini's American admirers had given him up, Pound continued to support the regime. This isolated him intellectually and hardened his political stance. In 1941 he began to broadcast his views on political and cultural matters on Italian radio. The broadcasts harped on economics and demonstrated a nasty streak of anti-Semitism. After Pearl Harbor Pound attempted to return to the States. When the attempt failed, he made a fateful decision to continue his broadcasts. In the summer of 1943 the U.S. government indicted him for treason. In May 1944 he was captured by Italian partisans and released. He made contact with the American authorities, was incarcerated, and was finally transferred to the Disciplinary Training Center at Pisa. There, after spending three weeks in an cage-like cell exposed to the Italian summer, he collapsed. It was between the time of his transfer to a medical tent and October 16th, when he was removed to Washington, that he wrote THE PISAN CANTOS, perhaps his finest work. Reflecting the confusion and intensity of his situation, and mixing self-questioning with defiance, these cantos were to cause a sensation in the postwar world of letters.

Back in Washington, legal mechanisms had been initiated to put Pound on trial. In the event, he was judged incompetent to stand trial on grounds of insanity and remanded to St Elizabeth's Hospital for the Criminally Insane, where he remained for almost thirteen years. In 1948, upon publication of *The Pisan Cantos*, a committee that included CONRAD AIKEN, AUDEN, Eliot, ROBERT LOWELL, KARL SHAPIRO, and ALLEN TATE awarded the volume the first annual Library of Congress Bollingen Award for American Poetry. The award, announced in 1949, raised a public controversy that echoed for many years. Meanwhile, Pound continued to write and translate in his hospital quarters, and continued to influence young poets as diverse as CHARLES OLSON and Robert Lowell (two of his many visitors at St. Elizabeth's). In April 1958 ROBERT FROST, ARCHIBALD MACLEISH, Eliot, and Hemingway helped obtain Pound's release. He returned to Italy, where he published the last two sections of *The Cantos*. Pound died in Venice and was buried on the cemetery island of San Michele.

Pound's most important volumes of poetry include *A Lume Spento* (1908), *Riposte* (1912), *Cathay* (1915), *Lustra* (1916), *Quia Pauper Amavi* (1919), and *Umbra* (1920). The best poems from these volumes, along with *Hugh Selwyn Mauberley*, were collected in 1926 in *Personae* and subsequently reprinted. A volume of *Collected Early Poems* was published in 1976. Many of Pound's translations were collected in *Translations* (1953). The first limited editions of *Cantos* Pound published were *A Draft of XVI Cantos* (1925) and *A Draft of the Cantos 17–27* (1928). These were incorporated into *A Draft of XXX Cantos* (limited edition 1930, commercial edition 1933). Subsequently published were *Eleven New Cantos XXXI–XLI* (1934), *The Fifth Decad of Cantos* (1937), *Cantos LII–LXXI* (1940), *The Pisan Cantos* (1948), *Section: Rock-Drill* (1955), *Thrones* (1959), and *Drafts & Fragments of Cantos CX–CXVII*

(1969). *The Cantos* appeared in a collected edition in 1948 and then in expanded collected editions in 1964 and 1970.

Pound wrote a great deal of influential critical prose scattered among his books, essays, and letters. Among his most important books of criticism are *The Spirit of Romance* (1910, rev. 1953), *Pavannes and Divisions* (1918), *Instigations* (1920), *How to Read* (1931), *ABC of Reading* (1934), *Make It New* (1934), *Polite Essays* (1937), and *Guide to Kulchur* (1938). Many of his essays are now reprinted in *Literary Essays* (1954), *Selected Prose 1909–1965* (1973), *Ezra Pound and Music* (1977), and *Ezra Pound and the Visual Arts* (1980). For a more complete list of Pound's poetry and criticism, readers should consult Donald Gallup's authoritative *Bibliography* (1963, rev. 1983). Collections of his letters include *Letters 1907–1941* (1950) and individual volumes of correspondence between Pound and Joyce (1967), Ford Madox Ford (1982), Dorothy Shakespear [Pound] (1984), Wyndham Lewis (1985), Louis Zukovsky (1987), and Margaret Cravens (1988).

The standard commentaries on Pound's work include K. K. Ruthven's *A Guide to Ezra Pound's Personae* (1969) and Carroll Terrell's two-volume *Companion to the Cantos* (1980, 1984). A record of his reception can be found in Eric Homberger's *Critical Heritage* volume (1972). The two best biographies are by Noel Stock (1970) and Humphrey Carpenter (1988). Criticism of his career as a whole can be found in Donald Davie, *Ezra Pound: Poet as Sculptor* (1964); Hugh Kenner, *The Pound Era* (1971) and Michael Alexander, *The Poetic Achievement of Era Pound* (1979). Discussions of *The Cantos* include Ronald Bush, *The Genesis of Ezra Pound's Cantos* (1976); Michael André Bernstein, *The Tale of the Tribe: Ezra Pound and the Modern Verse Epic* (1980); and Massimo Bacigalupo, *The Formed Trace: The Later Poetry of Ezra Pound* (1980).

RONALD BUSH

Powell, Dawn (1897–1965),   press agent, writer. An often ruthlessly realistic writer, the Ohio native's chief fame has come from her novels. Some are laid in small towns in the West, others are satires of the literary and entertainment world of Manhattan. Several have been reissued in paperback. *Angels on Toast* (1940, reissue 1990) is a comic treatment of New York City businessmen on the make; *The Wicked Pavilion* (1954, reissue 1990) deals with habitués of a Manhattan café; and *The Golden Spur* (1962, reissue 1990) is set in the Greenwich Village of the late 1950s and concerns a young man's search for his father among Abstract Expressionist artists. Among her other novels are *Whither* (1925); *She Walks in Beauty* (1928); *The Bride's House* (1929); *Dance Night* (1930); *The Tenth Moon* (1932); *Turn, Magic Wheel* (1936); *The Happy Island* (1938); *A Time to Be Born* (1942); *My Home Is Far Away* (1944); *The Locusts Have No King* (1948); *Sunday, Monday, and Always* (short stories, 1952); and *Cage for Lovers* (1957). Tim Page edited *The Selected Letters of Dawn Powell, 1913–1965* (1999).

Powell, John Wesley (1834–1902),   geologist, teacher, ethnologist. As director of the Bureau of Ethnology (1879–1902), he sought to reform the outmoded and corrupt administration of public lands in the post–Civil War period.

He advanced his ideas in *Exploration of the Colorado River of he West* (1875; edited in part by Horace Kephart as *First Through the Grand Canyon*, 1915) and in his revolutionary *Report on the Arid Region of the United States* (1878), William Culp Darrah wrote a life of *Powell of the Colorado* (1951), showing his great services to conservation and to knowledge of the Indians.

Powell, Thomas (1809–1887), playwright, editor, biographer, poet. Powell came to the United States in 1849 after he had assisted several English authors in the production of a modernized Chaucer. In this country he associated with the group that met in PFAFF'S CELLAR and edited or helped to edit several periodicals, among them *Frank Leslie's Illustrated Newspaper*. He collected a series of *Dramatic Poems* (1844) and wrote a play, *The Wife's Revenge* (1842). Other titles include *The Living Authors of England* (1849), *The Living Authors of America* (1850), and *Chit Chat by Pierce Pungent* (1857).

Power of Fancy, The (1770), a poem by PHILIP FRENEAU. Freneau combines a budding romanticism with an older deistic faith in the divinity of nature. Fancy, a "vagrant, restless" spirit, can roam freely through the world and discover there, rather than in the Bible, the word of God. Critics have suggested that the poem's form, a musical tetrameter, anticipates Keats and departs from the artificialities of American and English verse of the time.

Power of Sympathy, The (1789), by WILLIAM HILL BROWN, is often called the first American novel.

Powers J[ames] F[arl] (1917–1999), novelist, short story writer. Born in Illinois, Powers saw his first novel, *Morte D'Urban* (1962), win the National Book Award and soon go out of print. His second novel, *Wheat That Springeth Green* (1988), coming more than twenty-five years later, revived attention to the earlier title, which was reissued. The novels and three short-story collections—*Prince of Darkness*, (1947), *The Presence of Grace*, (1956), and *Look How the Fish Live* (1975), collected in one volume as *The Stories of J. F. Powers* (2000)—communicate the author's fascination with the lives of Roman Catholic priests in the Midwest.

Powhatan, father of POCAHONTAS and the most powerful of the chieftains of the POWHATAN CONFEDERACY when the English settled in Jamestown in 1607.

Powhatan Confederacy, tribes of the Algonquian linguistic stock that occupied tidewater Virginia and the Eastern shore of Chesapeake Bay when the English arrived in Virginia. Their chief, POWHATAN, at first opposed the English. After some early skirmishes an uneasy truce was achieved, in large part through the agency of POCAHONTAS, but the peace was broken when Powhatan died in 1618. His brother Opechancanough led attacks in 1622 that killed 347 settlers, and brought equally severe reprisals. When the Indians regrouped and attacked again in 1644, killing another 300, Opechancanough was captured and killed, destroying the power of the confederacy.

Pownall, Thomas (1722–1805), English colonial administrator. Pownall was secretary to the governor of New York, later lieutenant governor of New Jersey, then governor of Massachusetts. In 1760 he returned to England and was elected to Parliament. He was against all attempts at curtailing American liberties and proposed a centralized administration and union of the colonies in a book called *The Administration of the Colonies* (1764).

pragmatism. A form of philosophy of which WILLIAM JAMES, its most prominent representative, said that "it has no dogmas and no doctrine save its methods." James is largely responsible for its formulation and ideas; he gave much of the credit for it to CHARLES S. PEIRCE and F. C. S. Schiller. Pragmatism rejects absolutes, substitutes pluralism for monism, sees everything in the context in which it occurs, believes that truth is not something to be found but something to be forever sought, that ideas must be put to work in order to see the results—and if they work, they are good. James described it, not without irony, as "a method of settling metaphysical disputes that might otherwise be interminable." Philip Wiener, in *Evolution and the Founders of Pragmatism* (1949), discusses its background in science and natural theology, its birthplace in Peirce's METAPHYSICAL CLUB and Peirce's own ideas, the contributions of Chauncey Wright, Darwinism in James's psychology and pragmatism, its relationship to John Fiske's philosophy of history, the pragmatic legal philosophy of Nicholas St. John Green, evolutionary pragmatism in the legal theory of the younger OLIVER WENDELL HOLMES, and the philosophical legacy of the founders of pragmatism. Among the most prominent of James's followers was JOHN DEWEY.

Pragmatism has often been identified with Americanism. As H. S. Commager said, "Practical, democratic, individualistic, opportunistic, spontaneous, hopeful, pragmatism is wonderfully adapted to the temperament of the average American." The beginning of the school may be found in an article of Pierce's, "How to Make Our Ideas Clear" (*Popular Science Monthly*, January 1878). James wrote *Pragmatism: A New Name for an Old Way of Thinking* (1907).

Prairie, The (1827), a novel by JAMES FENIMORE COOPER. The third of the LEATHER-STOCKING TALES to be published, this is chronologically the last in NATTY BUMPPO's life. Set in 1805–1806 in western Nebraska and Wyoming, the novel was completed in Paris and depicts an area Cooper had never seen. His sources included reports of the Lewis and Clark expedition; the *Account of the Expedition from Pittsburgh to the Rocky Mountains* compiled by EDWIN JAMES (1823); and the impression made on him by a Pawnee chief he met who became the model for Hard-Heart in the novel. The novel has an elegiac quality suitable to an account of Leather-Stocking's old age and death, but has also some stirring episodes, including a buffalo stampede, a prairie fire, and a fight between Pawnee and Sioux warriors. In his good Pawnees and bad Sioux Indians, Cooper continues his opposition of types established in his Delawares and Mingoes. His evocation of the prairies rivals his depictions of sea and forest. The novel is remarkable also for the portrayal of the frontiersman Ishmael Bush and his family, Cooper's embodiment of characteristics formed on the fringes of society, necessary to the westward march of civilization.

Prairies, The (1833), a poem by WILLIAM CULLEN BRYANT. This eloquent description of the prairie lands was suggested to the poet by a visit to his brothers in Illinois. Bryant stresses the immensity of the plains, the character and history of the ancient Indians, the startling beauty of the reptiles, and the presence of the honeybee.

Prairie Schooner, The. Founded at the University of Nebraska in 1927, this magazine announced itself as the interpreter of the prairie country, but its contributors came from all sections. It has been one of the best of the little magazines and one of the longest-lived. In 1955 Paul R. Stewart told *The "Prairie Schooner" Story: A Little Magazine's First 25 Years.*

Pratt, E[dwin] J[ohn] (1882–1964), professor, poet. Son of Methodist minister, Pratt was born in New-foundland and grew up in a series of Newfoundland outports. After working as a teacher and student minister for five years, he left the island and was educated at Victoria College, University of Toronto, where he taught in the English department until 1953. During his lifetime he published thirteen collections of verse, establishing himself as Canada's preeminent poet. In his first book, *Newfoundland Verse* (1923), Pratt identifies his poetic vision as rooted in the hard realities of life in a bleak northern land. His major poems are long narratives whose subjects involve contests of epic proportion. "The Great Fued," from *Titans* (1926), dramatizes a critical struggle in the time of the dinosaurs. *The Titanic* (1935) recounts the clash between an iceberg and human technology, while *Towards the Last Spike* (1952) describes the vanquishing of a continent to construct the Canadian-Pacific Railway across its back. In these poems evolution is a central metaphor, wherein brute nature is gradually replaced by human intelligence and a moral order. Yet, according to Pratt, humanity has not entirely shed the brutal phase; he warns in poems written before World War II that "the snarl Neanderthal is worn/Close to the smiling Aryan lips," that humankind is poised between the instinct to kill and the ideal of self-sacrifice. This theme is dramatized in *Brebeuf and His Brethren* (1940), where Pratt recounts the martyrdom of the Jesuits in 17th-century Huronia. Pratt wrote with simplicity about the heroic phases of Canadian history but as a major poet he stands curiously apart from his contemporaries, a Victorian rather than a modernist, offering Christian certainties rather than existential doubts. His life is recounted by David G. Pitt in *E. J. Pratt: The Truant Years 1882–1927* (1984) and *E. J. Pratt: The Master Years 1927–1964* (1987). *E. J. Pratt: Complete Poems*, ed. by Sandra Djwa and R. G. Moyles (1988), is a scholarly edition of all his work.

DAVID STOUCK

Pratt, Theodore (1901–1969), novelist, playwright. Born in Minneapolis, Pratt wrote the play *Big Blow* (1938), dramatized from his book, and saw it produced on Broadway. He also wrote a trilogy about Florida: *The Barefoot Mailman* (1943), *The Flame Tree* (1950), and *The Big Bubble* (1951). His other books include *Spring From Downward* (1933), *Not Without the Wedding* (1935), *Mercy Island* (1941), *Mr. Limpet* (1942), *Mr. Winkle Goes to War* (1943), *Thunder Mountain* (1944), *Miss Dilly Says No* (1945), *The Tormented* (1950), *Cocotte* (1951), *Handsome* (1951), *The Golden Sorrow* (1952), *Escape to Eden* (1953), *Smash-Up* (1954), *Seminole* (1954), and *The Lovers of Pompeii* (1961). His short-story collections are *Perils in Provence* (1944) and *Florida Roundabout* (1959).

Praying Indians, a term used by the New England colonists to describe Native Americans who had befriended them and had converted to Christianity, especially members of the Nauset and Massachusetts tribes. See JOHN ELIOT.

Precaution, or Prevention Is Better Than Cure (2 v. 1820), JAMES FENIMORE COOPER's first novel. A novel of manners, it was published anonymously and was at first assumed to be the work of an English woman.

Prejudices (1919, 1920, 1922, 1924, 1926, 1927), essays by H. L. MENCKEN. A volume of selections appeared in 1927; some of the essays were reprinted in *The Mencken Chrestomathy* (1949). The essays appeared originally in the *Smart Set*, the *American Mercury*, the Baltimore *Sun*, and the New York *Mail*. They show Mencken as an iconoclast. Mencken lauded Germany, denounced the condition of American letters, but espoused such new writers as Theodore Dreiser, James Branch Cabell, and Sinclair Lewis.

Premature Burial, The (*Dollar Newspaper*, July 31, 1844), a "tale of terror" by EDGAR ALLAN POE. A man subject to cataleptic seizures, which to anyone unacquainted with them may seem like death itself, takes every possible precaution against being buried alive. He awakens from one such seizure in a berth in a small sloop; the coffin lid that he imagines above him is really the bottom of the berth above. The terror that has him in its grip disappears, and he is cured of his ailment. Poe cites in his story cases of premature burial, but W. T. Bandy suggests the most likely source of the story (*American Literature*, May 1947), a poem by Mrs. Seba Smith called "The Life-Preserving Coffin," which appeared in the *Columbian Lady's and Gentleman's Magazine* (January 1844). Another source often suggested is "Buried Alive" (*Blackwood's Magazine*, October 1821).

Prentice, George Dennison (1802–1870), newspaperman, editor. Prentice, born in Connecticut, was the first editor of the *New England Review*, published at Hartford; later he edited the Louisville *Daily Journal*, which became the Louisville *Courier-Journal*. Some of his contributions were collected as *Prenticeana, or, Wit and Humor in Paragraphs* (1860). Prentice also wrote a biography of Henry Clay (1831), and his *Poems* were collected in 1876.

Prentiss, Elizabeth Payson (1818–1878), novelist. Known chiefly as a writer of religious fiction and books for young people, her most popular work was *Stepping Heavenward* (1869), a novel of everyday life in the form of a woman's diary.

Presbyterianism, a form of ecclesiastical administration by a hierarchy of clerical and lay presbyters rather than by bishops (episcopal) or congregational assemblies. The first churches in America were organized through the agency of Francis Makemie in the early 18th century. During the GREAT AWAKENING the group was temporarily divided into the Old Side, who rejected evangelism and revivals, and the New Side, who favored them. Princeton University, first called the College of New Jersey, was founded by Presbyterians before the Revolutionary War. A Plan of Union brought the Presbyterians together with New England Congregationalists during the early 19th century; this alliance was especially strong on the frontier. The church later subdivided into the main body, called the United Presbyterian Church in the United States of America; the smaller Presbyterian Church in the United States, based largely in the South, which broke from the main body over the issue of slavery; and the Cumberland Presbyterian Church in the United States and Africa, composed largely of African American members.

Prescott, William Hickling (1796–1859), historian. Prescott, born in Salem, Massachusetts, lost the sight of his left eye in an accident as a Harvard undergraduate; he had to give up the law when his other eye began to fail. After travel in Europe, he returned to Boston, where he collected a large library and, with the help of readers and secretaries, prepared his manuscripts. *The History of the Reign of Ferdinand and Isabella the Catholic* (1838) sold its first printing in a few weeks and received praise from historians. His most enduring work, *The History of the Conquest of Mexico* (1843), went through numerous editions (see CONQUEST OF MEXICO). *History of the Conquest of Peru* (1847) followed; at the time of his death he had published three volumes of his unfinished *History of Philip II* (1855–1888). Prescott was more interested in action than in theory. He delighted in thrilling narrative and vivid descriptions; unlike other great historians, he expounded no philosophy of history. W. H. Munro edited Prescott's works with many additional footnotes (22 v. 1904, repr. 1968).

Present, The (September 1843–April 1844), a monthly periodical edited by W. H. CHANNING. Margaret Fuller, James Russell Lowell, and Charles Dana were among the contributors.

Present State of the New-English Affairs (1689), a broadside printed by Samuel Green of Boston after the overthrow of the unpopular governor, Sir EDMUND ANDROS. It described an interview between Increase Mather and King William III and printed a letter from Increase to his son, Cotton, and the order from the king recalling Andros.

Presidential Medal of Freedom Since 1963 it has been given to acknowledge contributions in the arts as well as for government service. Among writers so honored are RALPH ELLISON, EUDORA WELTY, and TENNESSEE WILLIAMS.

Preston, Margaret Junkin (1820–1897), memoirist, poet. Born in Pennsylvania, in the North, Preston nevertheless devoted herself to the Southern cause. She took the dying words of her sister's husband, Stonewall Jackson, for the refrain of her best-known poem, "Under the Shade of the Trees." *Silverwood: A Book of Memories* (1856), her first book,

is prose. Her poetry titles are *Beechenbrook: A Rhyme of the War* (1865), *Old Song and New* (1870), *Cartoons* (1875), and *For Love's Sake* (1886). Elizabeth P. Allen prepared *The Life and Letters of Margaret Junkin Preston* (1903).

Pretty Story, A: Written by Peter Grievous, Esq. (September 1774), a pamphlet by FRANCIS HOPKINSON. Published while the Continental Congress was assembling in Philadelphia, this satirical allegory was intended to portray the events leading to the establishment of the Congress. The pamphlet went into three editions before 1775.

Price, [Edward] Reynolds (1933–), novelist, short-story writer, essayist, poet. Born in North Carolina, he was educated at Duke and Merton College, Oxford, where he was a Rhodes Scholar. Since 1958 he has been a member of the Duke faculty. Price often centers his work on denizens of his home region such as the Mustian family of *A Long and Happy Life* (1962, dramatized in *Early Dark*, 1977); *A Generous Man* (1967); *Good Hearts* (1988), and some of the stories in *The Names and Faces of Heroes* (1963). In each case he tries to isolate what he has defined as "the central error of act, will, understanding which, once made, has been permanent, incurable, but whose diagnosis and palliation are the hopes of continuance." Rosacoke Mustian, the naive protagonist of *A Long and Happy Life*, erroneously assumes that marriage to Wesley Beavers will lead to the romantic state of the title. As a more experienced woman in *Good Hearts*, she survives, after 28 years of marriage, Wesley's desertion, a mysterious attack, and reunion with her husband. *Kate Vaiden* (1986), a prizewinning novel, is a first-person narrative of a memorable woman. Later works continue to explore life in North Carolina with a renewed commitment to faith brought about by Price's struggle with cancer and paralysis as chronicled in *A Whole New Life* (1994). *Letter to a Man in the Fire: Does God Exist and Does He Care?* (1999) was prompted by a letter from a fellow cancer sufferer. *Clear Pictures* (1989) is a memoir of growing up in North Carolina. Novels include *Love and Work* (1968); a trilogy formed by *The Surface of the Earth* (1975), *The Source of Light* (1981), and *The Promise of Rest* (1995); and *The Tongues of Angels* (1990); *Blue Calhoun* (1992); and *Roxanna Slade* (1998). *The Collected Stories* appeared in 1993, *The Collected Poems* in 1997. Essays are gathered in *Things Themselves* (1972), *A Common Room* (1987), and *Feasting the Heart* (2000). Price discusses his writing in *Learning a Trade: A Craftsman's Notebooks, 1955–1997* (1998).

Priest, Judge. See IRVIN S. COBB.

Priestley, Joseph (1733–1804), scientist, philosopher, theologian. He was trained for the Presbyterian ministry and served in several English churches, but soon gave up orthodox opinions and showed an interest in political philosophy; his *Essay on the First Principles of Government* (1768) influenced Jeremy Bentham. Experimenting with the property of gases, he discovered what he called "dephlogisticated air," later named oxygen by Lavoisier (1743–1794). He carried on an extensive scientific and philosophical correspondence with BENJAMIN FRANKLIN. When his political views, expressed in pamphlets sympathetic to the American colonies and the French Revolution, caused a mob to destroy his home and laboratories in 1791, he emigrated to the United States, settling in Philadelphia in 1794. His presence in America was attacked by WILLIAM COBBETT in *Observations on Dr. Priestley's Emigration* (1794). He lived and worked for the remainder of his life in Northumberland, Pennsylvania, where he wrote *Unitarianism Explained and Defended* (1796) and *A General History of the Christian Church* (1802).

Primary Colors.   See JOE KLEIN.

Prime, Benjamin Youngs (1733–1791),   physician, poet. Dr. Prime, born in Huntington, New York, practiced in New York City and published two collections of poems. *The Patriot Muse* (1764), dealing principally with the French and Indian Wars, was ardently pro-British. *Columbia's Glory, or, British Pride Humbled* (1791) upheld the American cause during the Revolution and one fine passage paid tribute to General Washington.

Prince, Thomas (1687–1758),   clergyman, historian. Born in Massachusetts, Prince studied law, theology, and medicine in England and was co-pastor of Old South Church in Boston until his death. He was a conservative in thought, but an ardent colonial patriot and a defender of civil liberties. He issued many publications, including twenty-nine sermons. His most important work was his *Chronological History of New England in the Form of Annals* (1736), a world history from the time of Adam to the Puritan colonies. It was continued in three pamphlets published in 1755.

Prince and the Pauper, The (1881),   a novel by MARK TWAIN. The idea for the book came to Twain when he was reading Charlotte M. Yonge's *The Prince and the Page* (1865), in which a medieval nobleman lives for years disguised as a blind beggar. As early as November 23, 1877, Twain set down this idea for a story in his notebook: "Edward VI and a little pauper exchange places by accident a day or so before Henry VIII's death. The Prince wanders in rags and hardships and the pauper suffers the (to him) horrible miseries of princedom, up to the moment of crowning in Westminster Abbey, when proof is brought and the mistake rectified." He read the book to his two little girls as it progressed and dedicated it "To Those Good-Mannered and Agreeable Children, Susy and Clara Clemens."

Prince of India, The, or, Why Constantinople Fell (1893),   a novel by LEW WALLACE. It took Wallace approximately twelve years to write this 300,000-word novel. President Garfield, who admired *Ben Hur* and who had appointed Wallace minister to Turkey, suggested a book with Constantinople as its setting.

Prince of Parthia, The (prod. 1767),   a blank verse tragedy by THOMAS GODFREY. See DRAMA.

Princess Casamassima, The (1886),   a novel by HENRY JAMES. The Princess Casamassima is the former Christina Light, the beloved of the sculptor in RODERICK HUDSON (1876). Now, separated from her husband, she decides to make a firsthand study of poverty and radicalism in London.

In London society she meets Hyacinth Robinson, the illegitimate son of an English nobleman and a Frenchwoman. Robinson, recruited by a group of social revolutionaries, is selected to commit an assassination and, torn between the opposing interests of socialism and society, ends his life in suicide.

Priscilla,   a character in Nathaniel Hawthorne's THE BLITHDALE ROMANCE (1852). Priscilla Mullins, one of the Plymouth settlers, appears as a character in Longfellow's THE COURTSHIP OF MILES STANDISH (1858).

Processional (1925),   an expressionistic play by JOHN HOWARD LAWSON, set in a West Virginia town during a coal mine strike. The characters are stereotypical, and the Ku Klux Klan is the object of much of the humor.

Proctor, Edna Dean (1829–1923),   poet, travel writer. Her youth was spent in the small New England town of Henniker, New Hampshire, her birthplace, where she wrote antislavery poems and articles during the Civil War. After the war she traveled in Russia, writing a series of letters to the New York *Independent* that were published as *Russian Journey* (1872). During the 1870s she lived in Brooklyn, writing articles for the *Tribune. Poems* (1866) was followed by *The Song of the Ancient People* (1892), *The Mountain Maid and Other Poems of New Hampshire* (1900), *Songs of America* (1906), and *The Glory of Toil* (1916). In a trip to the West she was aroused by the plight of Native Americans and wrote a flurry of newspaper articles urging more humane treatment of them. *The Complete Poetical Works of Edna Dean Proctor* appeared in 1925.

Professor at the Breakfast Table, The (1860),   the first of the three sequels to Oliver Wendell Holmes's *Autocrat of the Breakfast Table.* See BREAKFAST TABLE SERIES.

profile.   A variety of biographical sketch, variously called *character, description, interview, psychograph, closeup, cover story, personal sketch.* It is likely that the great popularization of the personal sketch came when JAMES GORDON BENNETT in the 19th century developed the newspaper interview in the New York *Herald.* Successive generations of reporters began to augment their reports with bits of intimate description. A specialized form of the personal sketch was GAMALIEL BRADFORD's *psychograph,* exemplified in his *Damaged Souls* (1923).

THE NEW YORKER adopted the term *profile* for the sketches that appeared in its pages. Other magazines followed: *Time* with its *cover stories, Life* with its *close-ups,* and many other magazines with feature stories intent on personalities. The form has been expanded to television documentaries and interviews.

Progress and Poverty (1879),   a treatise by HENRY GEORGE. George's fundamental idea was easily grasped. He stressed that progress and poverty seem to go hand in hand. He found the secret of this undesirable partnership in the systems of taxation practiced everywhere, which in his judgment shackled labor and punished capital and enabled landlords to profit through increased rents when the value of their property went up because of social advances. He advocated a simple remedy: impose only a *single tax* (the two words became the symbol of the movement he founded), a tax on land, and confiscate all unused land. "Appropriate all rent by taxation," he urged. The ideas expressed by George were not original, even if the combination of them was novel. He derived his ideas from Jefferson, Emerson, Comte, Condorcet, Fourier, John Stuart Mill, and other reformers. His book won instantaneous popularity and was translated into many languages. Organizations sprang up to carry his ideas into effect. His theories are considered to have influenced tax policy in the U.S., Canada, Australia, and Western Europe.

Progress of Dulness, The (1772–73),   a satirical poem by JOHN TRUMBULL. This poem in three parts deals with three typical characters—Tom Brainless, a shallow and conservative clergyman; Dick Brainless, a dissipated and stupid fop; and Miss Harriet Simper, a modish young woman who takes her code of life from romantic novels. Harriet, in love with Dick, loses him and marries Tom. The poem entertainingly satirizes college education, long sermons, the fiction of the day, religious bigotry, and oddities of dress and manners.

Progress to the Mines (1841, 1928),   a journal by WILLIAM BYRD. This portion of Byrd's account of his various journeys was written in 1732. He visited Fredericksburg and the iron mines around Germanna and gave careful descriptions of the methods of manufacturing iron in his time, also the fear among colonial manufacturers that England planned to restrict their industry, a fear realized in 1750.

Projective Verse,   essay by CHARLES OLSON. First published in *Poetry New York*, number 3, 1950, "Projective Verse" served as a rallying point for American poets in search of open forms. Olson urged that poetry not be controlled by preconceived patterns, that it must be written to the sound of the human voice, that the lines must be determined by breathing patterns, and that the typewriter could be used to score the work as "its space precisions" permit the poet to "indicate exactly the breath, the pauses, the suspensions even of syllables, the juxtapositions even of parts of phrases, which he intends." Most of the ideas were from other poets, including WHITMAN, WILLIAMS, CUMMINGS, and CREELEY, but the essay had an immediate and long-lasting influence. It gained wide distribution through its appearance in Donald M. Allen's *The New American Poetry: 1945–1960* (1960) and was collected in Olson's *Selected Writings* (1966), edited by Robert Creeley.

Prokosch, Frederic (1908–1989),   novelist and poet. Prokosch was born in Madison, Wisconsin, and educated at Haverford, Yale, and King's College, Cambridge, England. During World War II, he was cultural attaché at the American Legation in Sweden. He taught at Yale and the University of Rome. His extensive travels served as background for such novels as *The Asiatics* (1935, reissue 1983); *The Seven Who Fled* (1937); and *Night of the Poor* (1939).

World War II and its aftermath were the subject for *The Skies of Europe* (1941), *The Conspirators* (1943), *Age of Thunder* (1945), and *The Idols of the Cave* (1946). *Storm and Echo* (1946) details a trip across Africa. The lives of celebrated people are the subject for *A Tale for Midnight* (1955) about Beatrice Cenci, and *The Missolonghi Manuscript* (1968) about

Byron. *America, My Wilderness* (1972) deals with an African-American's attitude toward his country. Prokosch's poetry was collected in *The Assassins* (1936), *The Carnival* (1938), *Death at Sea* (1940), and *Chosen Poems* (1947). Other Prokosch novels are *A Ballad of Love* (1960), *The Seven Sisters* (1962), *The Dark Dancer* (1964), and *The Wreck of the Cassandra* (1966). *Voices* (1983) is a memoir describing his relationships with many of the major literary figures of the century.

proletarian literature.   The combined effect of the Great Depression and the socioeconomic emphasis of the New Deal fostered the only significant appearance of proletarian literature and criticism the United States has known. Although a handful of writers, notably WILLIAM DEAN HOWELLS and EDWARD BELLAMY, had expressed some socialistic and utopian ideals toward the end of the 19th century and Frank Norris argued against economic exploitation in THE OCTOPUS (1901), these writers were advocates of social reform rather than writers committed to radical political change. The earliest popular example of a proletarian novel is Upton Sinclair's THE JUNGLE (1906); like most of Sinclair's books it was socialist rather than Marxist in sympathy.

With the onset of the Depression some writers and intellectuals began to turn to theoretical Marxism as a possible solution to the evils of the American economy, and within a ten-year period at least seventy proletarian novels appeared. The proletarian novel portrayed the struggle between workers and employers, living conditions of poor workers, and often more specific themes that showed the benefits of Marxism and disparaged capitalism. However, few novels entirely propagandistic or adhering closely to party lines were successful as literature. The best writing of the period was often the work of authors whose books were more than vehicles for their political beliefs. A representative selection of proletarian literature may be found in GRANVILLE HICKS's *Proletarian Literature in the U.S.* (1935), which contains Clifford Odets's play, WAITING FOR LEFTY (1935), and selections from several novels, among them *Jews Without Money* (1930) by MICHAEL GOLD. Daniel Aaron wrote an extensive study: *Writers on the Left: Episodes in American Literary Communism* (1961).

Among the memorable novels of the Depression period are James T. Farrell's STUDS LONIGAN trilogy; John Dos Passos's U.S.A. (1938); JOSEPHINE HERBST's trilogy *Pity Is Not Enough* (1933), *The Executioner Waits* (1934), and *Rope of Gold* (1939); Henry Roth's *Call It Sleep* (1935); and John Steinbeck's IN DUBIOUS BATTLE (1936) and THE GRAPES OF WRATH (1939). Other writers of the era include NELSON ALGREN, SHERWOOD ANDERSON, MAXWELL BODENHEIM, ERSKINE CALDWELL, WALDO FRANK, MEYER LEVIN, Grace Lumpkin, IRWIN SHAW, DALTON TRUMBO, and RICHARD WRIGHT. After 1940 there were relatively few proletarian novels. Disillusion with communism as a result of the Soviet-Nazi pact of 1939, the end of the Depression, and the outbreak of World War II ended proletarian writing as a movement.

Promised Land, The (1912),   an autobiography by MARY ANTIN.

Prose, Francine (1947–   ),   novelist, short-story writer. Born in Brooklyn, New York, educated at Radcliffe (B.A., 1968) and Harvard (M.A., 1969), Prose first gained critical attention with a series of folktale-like fictions heavily laced with magic, myth, prophecy, and the supernatural. Among these are *Judah the Pious* (1973), set in Poland, about a rabbi, a king, and religious toleration; *The Glorious Ones* (1974), in which wandering players tell tales that intersect with their lives; *Marie Laveau* (1977), set in New Orleans, about a nineteenth-century mulatto woman gifted with second sight; *Household Saints* (1981), concerning God's grace in everyday life; and *Hungry Hearts* (1983), about a 1920s stage star possessed by a dybbuk. Later novels, still highly imaginative, but veering more toward contemporary realism dipped in the comedy of the absurd, include *Bigfoot Dreams* (1986), about a writer for a weekly tabloid; *Primitive People* (1992); and *Blue Angel* (2000), a satire on gender politics and sexual harassment codes, with its pivotal point a relationship between a college professor and a student. *Guided Tours of Hell* (1997) contains two novellas of Americans in Europe. *Women and Children First* (1988) and *A Peaceable Kingdom* (1993) are short story collections.

Protestant Episcopal Church,   the U.S. counterpart of the Church of England. The first regularly scheduled church services in this country were Church of England observances in Virginia (Jamestown, 1607). No Anglican worship was allowed by the Puritans until after revocation of the Massachusetts colonial charter (1686); three years later King's Chapel was established in Boston. The College of William and Mary (1693) was the first educational institution founded by Anglicans. There was serious internal dissension in the church during the Revolutionary War because so many clergymen were Loyalists, while the majority of the laity, including George Washington and many of the signers of the Declaration of Independence, favored a break with England. The Episcopal Church in America was established as a separate entity in 1789; Samuel Seabury was the first bishop. The standard doctrine of the denomination is included in the Thirty-Nine Articles and the *Book of Common Prayer*.

Prouty, Olive [Higgins] (1882–1974),   novelist. Prouty, born in Massachusetts, was known best for STELLA DALLAS (1922). Her first book was *Bobbie, General Manager* (1913). *Home Port* appeared in 1947, and *Fabia* in 1951.

Proulx, E[dna] Annie (1935–   ),   novelist, short-story writer. Born in Norwich, Connecticut, Proulx lived as a child also in North Carolina, Vermont, Rhode Island, and Maine, and attended Colby College briefly in the 1950s. Later, she returned to college, graduating from the University of Vermont (B.A., 1969) and receiving an M.A. in 1973 from Sir George Williams University in Montreal. Abandoning doctoral work in 1975 for freelance journalism, she wrote magazines articles and books such as *The Complete Dairy Foods Cookbook* (1982) and *Plan and Make Your Own Fences* (1983) before gaining attention in her forties for the stories of hard-scrabble northern New England lives collected in *Heart Songs* (1988). "All these stories were just bottled up inside me," she

said, "waiting to get out." Three novels followed: *Postcards* (1992), about the decline of a New England farm family; *The Shipping News* (1994), a National Book Award winner, set in Newfoundland; and *Accordion Crimes* (1996), following a Sicilian accordion to New Orleans and then from owner to owner, each a member of a different immigrant group, for a hundred years in different American settings. After many years in Vermont, Proulx moved to Wyoming, the setting for *Close Range: Wyoming Stories* (1999), a highly-praised collection that includes the novella "Brokeback Mountain," a story of two hard-up cowboys that Proulx counts at the top of her writing.

Providence Plantations.   The name given to a group of settlements made by ROGER WILLIAMS and others in what is now Rhode Island. Williams, an expatriate from Massachusetts because of his religious views, founded the first colony (1636) at what is now Providence. Later came ANNE HUTCHINSON, William Coddington, John Clark, and SAMUEL GORTON, the last-named a secessionist from Williams's colony. In 1644 all the settlements were united by a royal charter as Providence Plantations.

Provincetown Players.   An influential group of actors, producers, and playwrights who in various forms of organization from 1915 to 1929 produced about a hundred plays by almost fifty playwrights and laid the groundwork for modern American drama. The group started as an acting company in Provincetown, Massachusetts, under the direction of GEORGE CRAM COOK; their first theater, called the Wharf Theater (1916), was an abandoned fish house on a pier owned by Mary Heaton Vorse. Among the plays given were SUPPRESSED DESIRES, by Cook and his wife SUSAN GLASPELL; *Change Your Style*, by Cook; and *Contemporaries*, by Wilbur Daniel Steele. Even more important was the first production of EUGENE O'NEILL's BOUND EAST FOR CARDIFF. Later the group moved to New York City, where it established the Playwrights' Theater in a private home on Macdougal Street, and two years later the Provincetown Playhouse on the same street. In 1929 the group moved uptown to the Garrick Theater and, after an unsuccessful season, it disbanded.

In New York the Players continued to produce plays by O'Neill, as well as works by FLOYD DELL, THEODORE DREISER, EDNA ST. VINCENT MILLAY Susan Glaspell, SHERWOOD ANDERSON, PAUL GREEN, E. E. CUMMINGS, and EDNA FERBER. The great service of the group was the attention it focused on native writers. Helen Deutsch and Stella Hanau wrote *In Provincetown* (1931), and Susan Glaspell gave an account of her and her husband's experiences in *The Road to the Temple* (1926). Agnes Boulton, Eugene O'Neill's second wife, has also given a valuable account in her *Part of a Long Story* (1958).

Prue and I (1856),   seven sketches by G. W. CURTIS. A middle-aged bookkeeper living with his devoted wife on a meager salary imagines romantic travels.

Prufrock and Other Observations (1917),   poems by T. S. ELIOT. This was Eliot's first collection of verses, a paperbound pamphlet containing only twelve poems. The title is derived from the first poem in the collection, THE LOVE SONG OF J. ALFRED PRUFROCK.

Prynne, Hester.   The protagonist of Hawthorne's THE SCARLET LETTER (1850). She must wear a scarlet A on her dress to identify her as a convicted adulteress.

Psalm of Life, A.   Poem in *Voices of the Night* (1839), by HENRY WADSWORTH LONGFELLOW. The poet said the poem came to him in a flash and was quickly written on the morning of July 26, 1838. It was extremely popular and widely anthologized. It contains the well-known lines "Life is real! Life is earnest!" and "Footprints in the sands of time."

psychographs.   A term devised by Gamaliel Bradford. See AMERICAN PORTRAITS; GAMALIEL BRADFORD; PROFILE.

psychology and literature.   Although it may seem natural for the critics of literature to make use of psychology—critics are, after all, analysts—psychology is in reality equally the business of writers, committed as they must be to imagining the inner workings of character and motivation, a commitment that clearly overlaps that of psychology itself. There is something special, though, about how the interest in psychology has worked its way through the evolution of American literature, just as there is something characteristic about America and its literature. Historically, the U.S. is the product of the adventurer-explorers and religious dissenters of the Renaissance and Reformation, as well as of the iconoclastic philosophers of the Enlightenment. Thus, it was in America that humans sought to escape from the past and were confronted simultaneously by the openness of the frontier and of the future—at once a threat and a promise in space and time. Being alone in such a landscape, Americans are brought face to face with themselves—and the universe—with nothing in between.

We may see, therefore, that many of America's greatest writers were, among other things, constrained willy-nilly to become self-made explorers of the unconscious. One has only to think of POE's psychological romances and their intense focus on morbid mental and emotional states. Or of Hawthorne's THE SCARLET LETTER with its juxtaposition of the little town against the dark forest and its story of a man's mind breaking under the weight of its own freedom—assisted by the psychotherapy administered by his doctor-rival. Or of Melville's MOBY-DICK and its portrayal of another powerful mind cracking under the strain of its naked confrontation with the implacable enigma of the wild whale, the bottomless sea, and the endless universe. The essays of EMERSON and THOREAU seek in their own less demonic way a home for the naked self, as does WHITMAN's appropriately titled "SONG OF MYSELF." In EMILY DICKINSON's tightly organized lyrics, where the frontier has shrunk to the size of her little room, the mystery of the self's struggle with the Infinite is encountered even more frighteningly.

The fiction of HENRY JAMES forms a bridge between the 19th and 20th centuries in American literature. Although his great psychological mystery story, THE TURN OF THE SCREW (1898), has aroused storms of controversy over the question of the sanity of the governess, it is due more to his subtle portrayal of inner consciousness that he can be called a pioneer of the psychological novel—even as his older brother William can be called a pioneer of American psychology proper. This form became a major style of the novel during the first half of the 20th century. And when Freud visited this country along with his then disciple C. G. Jung in 1909—he was first translated here in 1913—he added an impetus for American writers to deepen their already natively endowed interest in psychology. Concern for hidden motivation, repressed sexuality, forgotten childhood traumas, stream of consciousness, dreams, alogical structures, etc. supplied an extra dimension to the existing obsession with the existential dilemma of self and universe.

It was especially during the 1920s and 1930s that these ideas fell on fertile soil. Some writers, such as CONRAD AIKEN, deliberately adopted psychoanalytic theory—his *Blue Voyage* (1927) and *Great Circle* (1933) reflect this influence in their intense subjectivity and subtle character realization. Others, such as Sherwood Anderson, seemed intuitively Freudian, as in WINESBURG, OHIO (1910), whose characters all suffer to a greater or lesser degree from sexual frustration. The Imagist poet H. D. (Hilda Doolittle) was actually in analysis with Freud himself in Vienna during 1933–34. HEMINGWAY's fiction, notable for its stoical facing of the darkness, is equally notable for the rigidity of its defenses against it.

Such Southern novelists as FAULKNER, CARSON MCCULLERS, and WILLIAM STYRON turned almost congenitally to the portrayal of the deeper and more conflicted layers of the mind. Faulkner's Benjy, for example, in THE SOUND AND THE FURY (1929), is a remarkable rendering of the inner consciousness of a mental retardate. Further, the plays of ARTHUR MILLER and TENNESSEE WILLIAMS reveal an intense preoccupation with family conflict and repressed sexuality. It has also been shown how NABOKOV (1899–1977) and Freud are similar as writers, despite—or because of—the former's explicit dislike of Freud. Others wrote works, such as Fitzgerald's TENDER IS THE NIGHT (1934), in which people have breakdowns and undergo psychological treatment—a subgenre carried on in more recent years in T. S. Eliot's THE COCKTAIL PARTY (1950), J. D. Salinger's THE CATCHER IN THE RYE (1951), SYLVIA PLATH's *The Bell Jar* (1963), PHILIP ROTH's *Portnoy's Complaint* (1969), JUDITH ROSSNER's *August* (1983), and many more works.

A related trend in poetry appeared in the 1960s and 1970s with the emergence of such confessional poets as ROBERT LOWELL, ANNE SEXTON, Plath, and JOHN BERRYMAN, all of whom suffered emotional breakdowns and subsequently underwent treatment, and all of whom—except Lowell—eventually committed suicide (as did Hemingway also).

Psychologies other than Freud's have had an impact as well, principally Jung's—differing from Freud's chiefly in postulating a collective unconscious beneath the individual unconscious, which contains the potential for generating universal primordial images that he called archetypes. Sir James G. Frazer's *The Golden Bough* (16 v. 1890–1915) anticipated and supported Jung's theory in tracing resemblances among myths and rituals of different times and places. Eliot acknowledged his debt to this tradition in the design of *The Waste Land* (1922). Others influenced by Jung are the projectivist poet CHARLES OLSON (1910–1970)—also influenced by PAUL GOODMAN (1911–1972) and gestalt therapy—and such deep-image poets as ROBERT BLY (1926–   ) and JAMES WRIGHT (1927–1980). And the theory and therapy of Wilhelm Reich (1897–1957), which emphasize how neurosis affects the body, had an interesting symbolic appearance in Saul Bellow's HENDERSON THE RAIN KING (1959), a seriocomic quest-romance.

Therapies come and go in the consumer-oriented culture of the U.S., and the American loneliness continues to motivate its citizens—and its writers—to undertake the endless search for the secret of the self in its confrontation with the frontier and the future. For it is here that people still persist in believing in the Fresh Start, and they still look, although somewhat apprehensively, to psychology for help in making the change, and to their writers for imaginative visions of that process.

Studies of the treatment of psychological material in literary works are numerous. *Psychoanalysis and American Fiction* (1965), ed. Irving Malin, contains essays by various hands on Cooper, Poe, Hawthorne, and others. David R. Saliba's *A Psychology of Fear* (1980) examines how Poe creates the terror of his tales. Martin L. Pop's *The Melville Archetype* (1970) sees the novels as psycho-religious voyages. Two studies of Whitman's psychological question are E. H. Miller, *Walt Whitman's Poetry: A Psychological Journey* (1968), and Stephen A. Black, *Whitman's Journeys into Chaos* (1975). Leon Edel's *The Modern Psychological Novel* (1955) is a pioneering study of that genre. Frederick J. Hoffman's *Freudianism and the Literary Mind* (1945, rev. 1957) contains studies of Sherwood Anderson, Fitzgerald, Henry Miller, and others. Gordon O. Taylor's *The Passages of Thought* (1969) examines the representation of mental states in James, Howells, Crane, Norris, and Dreiser. H. D.'s *Tribute to Freud*, written in 1944, was published in 1956; Norman N. Holland's *Poems in Persons* (1973) contains a psychological analysis of that work and its relation to her other writings. Lee Jenkins's *Faulkner and Black-White Relations* (1981) is a psychoanalytic study of how African-Americans come to represent the shadow-self of whites. Richard I. Evans's *Psychology and Arthur Miller* (1969) contains taped conversations with Miller about his artistic processes. Geoffrey Green's *Freud and Nabokov* (1988) attempts to define the similarities between the two. Jeffrey Berman's *The Talking Cure* (1985) is an excellent study of the processes of psychological treatment in *Tender Is the Night* and other works. Elizabeth Drew's *T. S. Eliot: The Design of His Poetry* (1949) traces Frazer's and Yung's effects on Eliot. Katherine Wallingford's *Robert Lowell's Language of the Self* (1988) examines the poet's use of psychoanalytic techniques; and Paul Breslin's *The Psycho-Political Muse* (1987) analyzes the psychological assumptions in the confessionals, the deep-image poets, and others, and relates these ideas to their political context in the 1960s.

NORMAN FRIEDMAN

Publicola.   The pen name used by JOHN QUINCY ADAMS for eleven articles that appeared in the *Columbian Centinel* of Boston from June 8 to July 27, 1791. Adams, then in his early twenties, was opposing such doctrinaires as Thomas Paine in their argument that the majority had an absolute right to rule. Adams, as a Federalist, appealed to an ethical absolute, as represented in the judiciary, in behalf of the minority.

Publishers' Weekly.   The first issue of this indispensable journal of the book publishing business appeared on January 18, 1872. The founder and first editor was Frederick Leypoldt, who had earlier conducted two short-lived periodicals, the *Literary Bulletin* (founded 1868) and the *Monthly Book Trade Circular* (founded 1869). He called his new magazine the *Publishers' and Stationers' Weekly Trade Circular*, in 1873 becoming known by its present name. Very early in the magazine's career Leypoldt secured the able assistance of Richard Rogers Bowker, who on Leypoldt's death in 1884 succeeded him as editor and continued in charge of the *Weekly* until his death in 1933. The *Weekly* is a record of the book trade from week to week and season to season.

Publius.   The pen name attached to essays by the three contributors to THE FEDERALIST papers (1787–88): Alexander Hamilton, James Madison, and John Jay.

Puck.   This humorous weekly was originally a German-language publication, founded in St. Louis by JOSEPH KEPPLER in 1869 as *Puck, Illustrierte Wochenschrift* and then issued in New York City in 1876, still in German, as *Puck, Humoristisches Wochenblatt*. In March 1877 an English edition began to appear, with Sydney Rosenfeld as editor for one year. He was succeeded by H. C. BUNNER (1878–96); he in turn by HARRY LEON WILSON (1896–1902), JOHN KENDRICK BANGS (1904–05), A. H. Folwell (1905–16), and Karl Schmidt (1916). The magazine was sold in 1917 to WILLIAM RANDOLPH HEARST and ceased publication in the next year, although the name was used for many years as the title of a Hearst Sunday magazine section.

Pudd'nhead Wilson, The Tragedy of (1894),   a novel by MARK TWAIN. Twain's last novel of the antebellum South exposes the evils of slavery, greed, and conformity in Dawson's Landing, a slaveholding town on the Mississippi River, below St. Louis. The protagonist, a white-skinned mulatto slave named Roxana seeks to protect her infant son, fathered by one of the town's Virginia aristocrats, from the horrors of slavery by exchanging in their cradles her child and her master's son, who was born on the same day. The deception is discovered some twenty years later by the title character, David Wilson, an outsider attempting to establish a law practice who is ostracized by the dullwitted townspeople for his mordant humor and quasi-scientific pursuits. In a climactic courtroom scene that concludes the novel, Wilson reveals the true identities of the children when he uses fingerprints he has collected to prove that the false heir, Tom Driscoll, was the murderer of his presumed uncle and guardian, the leading citizen of Dawson's Landing. Wilson's detection frees Italian twins falsely accused of the murder but leaves the rightful heir, raised in slavery, bereft of any place. Tom, sold down the river, suffers the fate his mother plotted to spare him. The novel exemplifies Twain's fascination with twinship and reversed identities, seen in THE PRINCE AND THE PAUPER (1882) and the fragment "Those Extraordinary Twins," in which Twain introduced the characters of *Pudd'nhead Wilson*. His portrayal of the child reared in slavery brilliantly demonstrates the thesis of the novel, that "training is everything," that the traits of the slave are learned, not inborn. Whether or not the viciousness of the mulatto child, Tom, can be entirely explained by training has been a recurrent subject of critical debate.

ELSA NETTELS

Pueblo Indians, a name given to members of four diverse linguistic groups who lived for centuries in their multistoried stone or adobe houses in the area where the borders of Arizona, New Mexico, Utah, and Colorado meet. Hopi, Zuni, Navajo, and others are included in the group. Spaniards from Cortez's expedition visited Zuni Pueblo in 1539; Coronado's army, in 1542 passing near what is now Sante Fe, initiated a period of Spanish domination. The villagers enjoyed independence from the Spaniards from 1680 to 1692. When Mexico gained its independence from Spain in 1800, the Pueblos were formally acknowledged as selfgoverning towns and their land holdings guaranteed. The U.S. government agreed to respect these rights when it took over the territory in 1848.

Religious observances in this dry region center on rain and corn. An advanced culture when first observed by Europeans, the Pueblos used irrigation, hunted for meat, and wove cotton for clothing. Their elaborate communal dwelling units are admired. Their skill in pottery, dating back to the 7th century A.D., is legendary. SIMON ORTIZ and LESLIE MARMON SILKO are distinguished Pueblo writers.

Puig, Manuel (1932–1990), novelist. Born in Argentina, Puig studied philosophy at the University of Buenos Aires and film in Italy. Puig fled the dictatorship of Juan Peron in 1973 and afterward lived in Mexico and New York City. His work details the influences of mass culture. *El beso de la mujer arana* (1976, tr. *The Kiss of the Spider Woman*, 1979), his best-known work, consists of conversations between men sharing a prison cell. Molina, a middle-class homosexual, retells the plots of films he has seen to the political prisoner Valentin. Initially hostile, their mutual dependence leads to an emotional and sexual bonding. It was made into a film and, like Puig's other books, is banned in his native country. A failed screenplay was the basis for *La traicion de Rita Hayworth* (1968, tr. *Betrayed by Rita Hayworth*, 1971). Among his other titles are *Boquitas pintadas* (1969, tr. *Heartbreak Tango*, 1973); *Publis Angelical* (1979, tr. 1986); *Maldicion eterna a quien lea estas paginas* (1980, tr. *Eternal Curse on the Reader of These Pages*, 1982); *Sangre de amor correspondido* (1984, tr. *Blood of Requited Love*, 1984); and *Cae la noche tropical* (1988, tr. *Tropical Night Falling*, 1991) on old age, loneliness, and exile. A study is *Manuel Puig and the Spider Woman* by Suzanne Jill Levine (2000).

Pulitzer, Joseph (1847–1911), newspaper editor and publisher. After coming to New York from Hungary, Pulitzer served in the Civil War and then became a reporter on the St. Louis daily German paper the *Westliche Post*. He became a part owner of the paper and was successful in local politics. After a trip abroad, he bought the St. Louis *Dispatch* in 1878 and turned it into one of the most profitable Western papers. When an editorial campaign against corruption led to a shooting in the newspaper offices, he went back to New York and bought the *World* from Jay Gould, in seven years building the circulation from 20,000 to over 200,000. A bitter circulation battle with WILLIAM RANDOLPH HEARST's *Journal* followed. Pulitzer, blind and in failing health, retired from active life. His bequest of two million dollars to Columbia University enabled the founding of a School of Journalism and the Pulitzer Prizes for journalism and literature.

Pulitzer Prizes. JOSEPH PULITZER set aside a fund of $500,000 to provide for these awards, which were to be given "for the encouragement of public service, public morals, American literature, and the advancement of education." The first prizes were awarded in 1917. Eight prizes are awarded in journalism: for the most meritorious service rendered by a newspaper, the best local reporting, the best local reporting with no edition-time pressure, the best reporting on national affairs, the most distinguished international reporting, the most distinguished editorial writing, the best cartoon, and the outstanding example of news photography. Six awards are given in letters: for the most distinguished fiction; the best American play; the finest book on American history; the best biography or autobiography; the most distinguished volume of verse; a nonfiction category was added in 1962. A prize is also awarded in music, usually to a work of some magnitude, such as an opera or long orchestral piece. All the awards are made annually under the control of the School of Journalism at Columbia University.

pulps, the. Three types of material are used in making paper: rag pulp, straw pulp, and wood pulp. The last, the least expensive, was used extensively in the so-called pulp magazines, as opposed to the slick magazines. The pulps published mainly escape fiction: dime novels, adventure stories, romances, westerns, detective stories, fantasy, and science fiction. Their heyday lasted from the early 1900s to the 1940s.

Pulsifer, Harold Trowbridge (1886–1948), poet, editor. Pulsifer was born in Connecticut. His maternal grandfather was cofounder of THE OUTLOOK with LYMAN ABBOTT, and when Pulsifer left Harvard he joined the staff of that magazine, acting as managing editor from 1923 to 1928. He introduced many new poets to the public through *The Outlook* and himself wrote verse. It was collected in *Mothers and Men* (1916), *Harvest of Time* (1932), *Elegy for a House* (1935), *Rowen* (1937), and other volumes. In 1931–32 he served as president of the Poetry Society of America.

Pumpelly, Raphael (1837–1923), geologist, explorer, memoirist. Born in Owego, New York, Pumpelly made important geological expeditions to Siberia, China, and Central Asia. He also explored the copper and iron resources of Michigan and the Lake Superior region and investigated the mineral resources of the United States for the 10th United States Census. He recounted these experiences in several books, including *Across America and Asia* (1869), *Explorations in Central Asia* (1905), and *My Reminiscences* (2 v. 1918).

Pupin, Michael I[dvorsky] (1858–1935), physicist, inventor. Born in Austria-Hungary, Pupin was educated at Columbia University and in Europe. His most important research involved magnetics; his so-called Pupin coil was essential to development of long-distance telephony. His autobiography, *From Immigrant to Inventor* (1923), won a Pulitzer Prize.

Purchas, Samuel (1575?–1626), travel writer. The English clergyman's first book, *Purchas His Pilgrimage* (1613), was a study of the regions and religions of the world. In *Hakluytus Posthumus, or Purchas his Pilgrimes* (4 v. 1625) he used Hakluyt's papers and the records of the East India Company to expand travel narratives, including descriptions of voyages to America.

Purdy, Al[fred Wellington] (1918–2000), poet. Born in Wooler, Ontario, Purdy left school at seventeen, rode the rails, worked in a mattress factory in Vancouver, served in the Royal Canadian Air Force, and emerged as a poet with *The Enchanted Echo* (1944). Scraping by, frequently impoverished into his forties, he accumulated over thirty more volumes of verse. He won the Governor General's Award for poetry in 1965 and 1986. When he died, he was hailed as Canada's "unofficial poet laureate." DENNIS LEE called him "without a doubt the greatest poet English Canada has ever produced," the one "that younger poets were measuring themselves against" for the last third of the century. Six foot three, two hundred pounds, a legendary drinker and restless traveler, he wrote of his youthful hobo years, the Canadian wilderness, and the Eskimos of Baffin Island all in a direct, lucid, and conversational style that brought him back insistently to the touchstone of Roblin Lake and its surroundings, near Ameliasburg and not far from his birthplace, in the Loyalist country on the northern shore of Lake Ontario. Collections include Russell Brown, ed., *The Collected Poems of Al Purdy* (1986), actually a selected edition, and *Beyond Remembering: The Collected Poems of Al Purdy* (2000). Other verse titles include *The Crafte So Long to Lerne* (1959); *Poems for All the Annettes* (1962); *The Cariboo Horses* (1965); *Wild Grape Wine* (1968), including the celebrated "Roblins Mills II," "Wilderness Gothic," and "Lament for the Dorsets;" *In Search of Owen Roblin* (1974), a cycle of local history; *A Handful of Earth* (1977); *The Stone Bird* (1981); and *Naked with Summer in Your Mouth* (1994). *A Splinter in the Heart* (1990) is a novel about the explosion of a chemical plant in Trenton, near Ameliasburg, in the year of his birth. *Reaching for the Beaufort Sea* (1993) is an autobiography. Sam Solecki edited *Starting from Ameliasburg: The Collected Prose of Al Purdy* (1995) and wrote *The Last Canadian Poet: An Essay on Al Purdy* (1999). Lewis K. MacKendrick's *Al Purdy* (1990) is an earlier study.

Purdy, James (1923–), novelist, short-story writer, poet. An Ohioan who moved to Brooklyn, Purdy is the author of over forty books. His mixed reception in the United States has been countered by the generally high praise accorded him in England. *Malcolm* (1959), his first novel, is the story of a 15-year-old boy's search for his lost father; it was dramatized in 1965 by Edward Albee. *The Nephew* (1960), set in Purdy's native Midwest, concerns the unwanted information Alma Mason unearths in filling in her memories of Cliff, her nephew, who has been reported missing in action in the Korean War. *Cabot Wright Begins* (1964) is a satirical novel about a rapist; *Eustace Chisholm and the Works* (1967) treats relationships between homosexuals. *I Am Elijah Thrust* (1972), about men of different ages and backgrounds, and *In a Shallow Grave* (1975), about a disfigured veteran and his childhood sweetheart, explore different kinds of alienation. *Jeremy's Version* (1970), *The House of the Solitary Maggot* (1974), and *Mourners Below* (1981) detail the strains in a Midwestern family. *On Glory's Course* (1984) is another Midwestern novel, set in the 1930s. *In the Hollow of His Hand* (1986) follows the adventures of a part-Indian illegitimate child. *Narrow Rooms* (1978) concerns homosexuality. *Garments the Living Wear* (1989) is a messianic novel of a plague in New York City. *Out with the Stars* (1994) depicts the gay community in New York just before the onset of AIDS. *Gertrude of Stony Island Avenue* (1996) treats a woman's mourning for her daughter. Stories are collected in *The Color of Darkness* (1957); stories and plays in *Stories Is All* (1962); plays and poems in *A Day After the Fair* (1977); and stories in *The Candles of Your Eyes* (1987). *63, Dream Palace: Selected Stories, 1956–87* (1991) takes its title from one of his most celebrated works, first published in 1956. Poetry volumes include *The Running Sun* (1971), *Sunshine Is an Only Child* (1973), and *Collected Poems* (1990).

Puritan and His Daughter, The (1849), a novel by JAMES KIRKE PAULDING. The story depicts Puritanism in the Old World and the New World as it shifts from England in the days of Cromwell to Virginia and then to New England.

Puritans and Puritanism. The Puritans sought to reform the Church of England by ridding it of its remaining Roman Catholic trappings, but their difficulties with the Crown and Anglican officials led a considerable number of them to advocate separatism (see SEPARATISTS). Attempts to suppress them led many Puritans to become refugees, first in the Netherlands and then in America. The Puritans who settled PLYMOUTH COLONY were separatists; those who settled Massachusetts (see MASSACHUSETTS BAY COMPANY) were not. Both groups, however, emphasized the independence of the parish church from the control of a central church government. The resulting CONGREGATIONALISM in the early days in Massachusetts provided a strong model for civil government based on the will of the people, even though in Massachusetts for many years that will was restricted to the vote of church members and was hence inimical to dissenting views.

Strongly Calvinistic, the New England Puritans insisted on a strict distinction between the elect and the damned, although by 1662 the adoption of the so-called half-way covenant made it somewhat easier to join the elect, and in 1692 a new charter of for Massachusetts extended the vote beyond the bounds of church membership. American Puritanism, then, was matter of place and time, early softening its harshest aspects outside of Massachusetts, and within that state changing considerably over the years. The GREAT AWAKENING begun in Massachusetts about 1734 was in some respects a last gasp of the old order, but Puritanism remained a major force in American life for at least another century, and some would argue for its persistence in some respects down to our own time.

Among American writers, NATHANIEL HAWTHORNE did more than any other to provide lasting embodiment in literature of the climate of Puritanism in Massachusetts at its early peak, the middle of the 17th century, but Hawthorne wrote two centuries after the fact. American literature is rich with records of the time. From the beginning the Puritans derived from their strong sense of the importance of their mission a great impetus to record. Histories and diaries poured from the pens of early officials like WILLIAM BRADFORD and JOHN WINTHROP, and MARY ROWLANDSON told of her capture by the Indians. In poetry ANNE BRADSTREET reflected on her experiences and MICHAEL WIGGLESWORTH framed the tenets of his religion in widely popular verse; religious controversies erupted and prompted ROGER WILLIAMS' rebukes of the Massachusetts theocracy. Somewhat later, EDWARD TAYLOR expressed his private musings in poetry to be discovered two centuries later; SAMUEL SEWALL recorded in diary form the private life of a prominent jurist; COTTON MATHER wrote voluminously on all aspects of the history of the colony and of his own time; and JONATHAN EDWARDS gave brilliant expression to an uncompromising Puritan theology already passing into history.

Puritanism as a historical phenomenon and as a living presence in American life has enriched American literature in ways far too numerous to detail here. The SALEM WITCHCRAFT TRIALS alone, for example, have engendered a large bibliography. Hawthorne's examination of male and female relationships under Puritanism in THE SCARLET LETTER has in turn fueled many other works, both scholarly and literary. The first century in New England continues to provide material for novelists and poets, and Puritanism as a heritage forms an important part of the background of many literary works set in much later times and in parts of the country far removed from New England.

Histories and critical studies include M. C. Tyler, *A History of American Literature During the Colonial Period, 1607–1765* (2 v. 1878); Perry Miller, *The New England Mind: The Seventeenth Century* (1939); K. B. Murdock, *Literature and Theology in Colonial New England* (1949); S. E. Morison, *Intellectual Life in Colonial New England* (1956); Austin Warren, *The New England Conscience* (1966); Sacvan Bercovitz, *The Puritan Origins of the American Self* (1975); Everett Emerson, *Puritanism in America: 1620–1750* (1977); William H. Shurr, *Rappaccini's Children: American Writers in a Calvinist World* (1980); Charles L. Cohen, *God's Caress: The Psychology of the Puritan Religious Experience* (1986); and Harry S. Stout, *The New England Soul: Preaching and Religious Culture in Colonial New England* (1986).

Purloined Letter, The (*The Gift*, 1845),   a story by EDGAR ALLAN POE. This is usually regarded as the greatest of Poe's three detective stories, with his French detective C. AUGUSTE DUPIN displaying even more than his customary acumen. A woman of royal rank has been blackmailed by a cabinet minister; she appeals to the police and they turn to Dupin. He visits the blackmailer and promptly finds the letter—hidden where anyone can see it.

Purple Cow, The.   See GELETT BURGESS.

Putnam, Israel (1718–1790),   Revolutionary soldier and hero. When the Revolutionary agitations began, Putnam became one of the Sons of Liberty, was commissioned a brigadier general, then a major general, and participated in many important actions in 1776–77. He wrote an account of an expedition against Havana (1762), and a trip to Florida published in 1931 in *The Two Putnams*. He is mentioned in James Fenimore Cooper's LIONEL LINCOLN (1825).

Putnam's Monthly Magazine.   Founded in January 1853, this magazine included among its contributors Melville, Longfellow, James Russell Lowell, Thoreau, James Fenimore Cooper, and William Cullen Bryant. After two years *Putnam's* was merged with another magazine, which itself soon ceased publication (1857). Then came *Putnam's Magazine*, founded in January 1868, with Frank R. Stockton, W. D. Howells, and John Burroughs among its contributors. In 1870 it was merged with the newly founded SCRIBNER'S In 1906 *Putnam's Monthly and The Critic* appeared, a new magazine that absorbed an older one. It attracted some good authors, mainly humorists; among them were Don Marquis and Gelett Burgess. In 1910 it was merged with ATLANTIC MONTHLY.

Puzo, Mario (1920–1999),   novelist. His first novel, *The Dark Arena* (1955), was set in Germany. A novel about an Italian immigrant family, *The Fortunate Pilgrim* (1964), followed but Puzo did not achieve wide recognition until he wrote *The Godfather* (1969), a best seller made into a successful movie. The main character, Don Vito Corleone, head of a New York crime family, is locked in a struggle for underworld power. *The Last Don* (1996) and *Omerta* (2000) complete a trilogy on the family. *Fools Die* (1978) details the life of a successful novelist; *The Sicilian* (1984) treats the Mafia in Sicily after World War II.; *The Fourth K* (1990) deals with a terrorist kidnapping of the daughter of a future President Kennedy.

Pyle, Ernie [Ernest Taylor Pyle] (1900–1945), columnist, war correspondent. Pyle had a successful career as a syndicated columnist, but it was his writing during World War II, depicting the lives of soldiers with sympathy and clarity, that made him widely known. These columns were collected in *Ernie Pyle in England* (1941), *Here is Your War* (1943), *Brave Men* (1944), and *Last Chapter* (1946). Pyle was awarded the Pulitzer Prize for distinguished reporting in 1944, and in the following year he was killed by machine gun fire in the South Pacific. His other collections are *An Ernie Pyle Album* (1946) and *Home Country* (1947).

Pyle, Howard (1853–1911),   illustrator, art teacher, children's writer. After a brief stay in New York City, Pyle returned to his native Delaware. He taught art in Philadelphia and in his own art school in Wilmington. Among his students were N. C. WYETH and MAXFIELD PARRISH. He wrote and illustrated many books for children, including *The Merry Adventures of Robin Hood* (1883), *Pepper and Salt* (1885), *The Wonder Clock* (1887), *Otto of the Silver Hand* (1888), *Men of Iron* (1892), *The Ghost of Captain Brand* (1896), *The Price of Blood* (1899), *The Story of King Arthur and His Knights* (1903), *The Story of the Champions of the Round Table* (1905), and *The Story of Sir Launcelot and His Companions* (1907). He revivified colonial life and medieval legends in his strongly individual paintings, many of which were reproduced in *Harper's Magazine*.

Pyncheon.   The Pyncheon family plays the chief role in Hawthorne's THE HOUSE OF THE SEVEN GABLES (1851).

Pynchon, Thomas [Ruggles] (1937–   ), novelist, short-story writer. Thomas Pynchon was born in Glen Cove, New York, and attended Cornell University, spending two years in the U.S. Navy between his sophomore and junior years. After graduation he lived in Greenwich Village for a year, then worked as a technical writer in Seattle, and lived in Mexico before dropping out of public view. His novel *Vineland* (1990) suggests that he had at that time lived part of the time in northern California. The most reclusive of all contemporary American writers, Pynchon has given no interviews and released no photographs of himself. His whereabouts have been a secret carefully protected by his publisher, agent, and close friends. The winner of the Faulkner Award (for *V.*), the Rosenthal Foundation Award (for *The Crying of Lot 49*), the National Book Award (for GRAVITY'S RAINBOW), the Howells Medal from the National Institute and American Academy of Arts and Letters (for the whole body of work, in 1975), and a MacArthur Foundation Award (in 1988), the man whom Edward Mendelson called "quite simply, the best living novelist in English," has virtually no public identity. He is intensely private, perhaps intensely shy, certainly uninterested in directly addressing the questions that critics have raised about his work.

Of course, these critics have also noted that Pynchon's attitude toward publicity is provocatively consonant with themes in his novels. Pynchon's fictional universes are permeated with intimations of a conspiracy so omnipresent and annihilating that it throws the future of civilization into doubt. In *V.* (1963), these intimations cluster around a mysterious woman whose appearances coincide with key moments of violent crisis in the history of the 20th century. In *The Crying of Lot 49* (1967), they are aligned with an organization called the Tristero, a cabal-like group of outcasts who may have been intervening in Western systems of communication since the Renaissance. In the encyclopedic *Gravity's Rainbow* (1974), the conspirators are known only as Them, and the possible extent of Their power is so vast that They may at last be inseparable from Us. In *Vineland*, the plotters are affiliated with the Federal Drug Enforcement Agency and the Justice Department. In each of these novels, individuals find themselves threatened by the machinations of malign forces to the point where having a public identity is an obvious source of danger.

But Pynchon's fiction cannot be reduced to the level of biographical statement; indeed, it is difficult to make any statement about the novels without doing damage to their complexity and innovation. One reason is that they are inherently about communication, structure, and plotting—the last as perhaps the most elaborate and self-reflexive pun running through Pynchon's writing. In one sense, a plot is a story line, the bare outline of what happens in a work of fiction. In another sense, however, a plot is a conspiracy, an underlying story of secret manipulation that reveals what really happened. Insofar as history is plotted, it may entail both these meanings: if it tells a story, it may do so precisely because somebody has created that story, arranged things to produce certain results.

Mason & Dixon (1997), in part a historical novel, takes the reader away from our complex present and back to the eighteenth century, when Charles Mason and Jeremiah Dixon arrived from England to run the boundary that became the Mason-Dixon Line. Plots in all senses abound in another polymath novel, with complexities enriched by the parodies of its times played off against the jokes, understandings, and fears of the present.

A conspirator and an author clearly have something in common, given this pun on "plot." By the same token, someone manipulated by a conspiracy is very much like a reader. Both the fascination and the difficulty of Pynchon's work derive from ways in which Pynchon intertwines acts of writing and reading, on the one hand, and acts of conspiring and perceiving possible conspiracy, on the other. Incorporating literary influences from writers as diverse as Melville, James, Conrad, Henry Adams, Vladimir Nabokov, and Jack Kerouac, and drawing on physics, chemistry, information theory, folklore, and popular culture for his allusions and structural metaphors, Pynchon is both the most eclectic and the most radically experimental of contemporary American fiction writers.

Slow Learner (1984) is a collection of short stories, including ENTROPY. Studies include Molly Hite, *Ideas of Order in the Novels of Thomas Pynchon* (1983), Steven Weisenburger, *A Gravity's Rainbow Companion* (1988), and J. Kerry Grant, *A Companion to V.* (2001).

MOLLY HITE/GP

Q

Quad, M. Pen name of CHARLES BERTRAND LEWIS.

Quadroon, The (1856), a novel by MAYNE REID, used by Dion Boucicault as a basis for his play THE OCTOROON (1859). The heroine is Aurore, a slave of mixed racial ancestry beloved by Edward Rutherford, an Englishman who has saved her and her mistress from drowning in a steamboat accident. Failing to buy her at a slave auction, Rutherford kidnaps her. The villain's dishonesty is exposed during the hero's trial, and the lovers are free to marry.

Quakers, a religious group founded in England in the middle of the 17th century by George Fox. The proper name of the group is the Religious Society of Friends; the name Quakers, originally a derisive term, is a common designation. The basis of the religion is intensely personal: Fox taught that no priest or formality is needed to establish communication with God and that each worshipper has an inner light of divine truth to guide his actions. Originally the Friends dressed in plain gray clothing and addressed each other with "thee" and "thou"; these outward forms have gradually disappeared. Quakers came to America in the 1650s to escape religious persecution, and though mistreated by the Puritans, flourished in Pennsylvania under the leadership of WILLIAM PENN. They were leaders in philanthropic movements, including peaceful relations with Native Americans, abolition of slavery, and prison reform. JOHN WOOLMAN, LUCRETIA MOTT, and JOHN GREENLEAF WHITTIER are among the best-known Quaker reform writers. Split in the 19th century over the doctrines of ELIAS HICKS, the group is now largely unified.

Quayle, Mary Jane Ward. See MARY JANE WARD.

Québécois literature. See CANADIAN LITERATURE IN FRENCH.

Queen, Ellery, the pseudonym used by Frederick Dannay (1905–1982) and Manfred B. Lee (1905–1971) in their series of nearly a hundred detective novels beginning with *The Roman Hat Mystery* (1929) and in *Ellery Queen's Mystery Magazine* (1941–).

Queequeg. Ishmael's tattooed companion in MELVILLE's *Moby-Dick*. He is a native of an island called Kokovoko, which Melville describes as "not down in any map; true places never are." At first frightened by Queequeg's shrunken head and his idol worship, Ishmael quickly decided, "I'll try a pagan friend . . . since Christian kindness has proved but hollow courtesy." Queequeg's death befits his stoicism and nobility.

Queiróz, Rachelde (1910–), Brazilian novelist and journalist. Her realistic novels deal with the position of women and with socioeconomic problems in northeast Brazil. *O quinze* (1930) treats the drought of 1915; *Jodo Miguel* (1932), *Caminho de Pedras* (1937), and *As três Marias* (1939, tr. *The Three Marias*, 1963) deal with female love and sacrifice. She wrote a collaborative novel with JORGE AMADO, JOSÉ LINS DE RÊGO, and GRACILIANO RAMOS, *Brandão entre o mar e o amor* (1942). Following a journalistic period, she returned to the novel with *Dôra, Doralina* (1975, tr. 1984).

Quin, Dan. Pen name of ALFRED HENRY LEWIS.

Quincy, Josiah (1772–1864), lawyer, public official, educator. Quincy, born in Braintree, Massachusetts, served in the House of Representatives, in the Massachusetts Senate, as mayor of Boston, and finally as president of Harvard (1829–45). He wrote a *History of Harvard University* (2 v. 1840) and *A Municipal History of Boston* (1852). His grandson, **Josiah Phillips Quincy** (1829–1910), wrote poetry, novels, short stories, and many essays.

Quint, Peter, a manservant in Henry James's THE TURN OF THE SCREW whose ghost apparently haunts the children, Miles and Flora.

Quinto Sol Publications, founded in Berkeley, California, in 1967 to publish Mexican American writing, it introduced the work of TOMÁS RIVERA, ROLANDO HINOJOSA-SMITH, RODOLFO ANAYA, and others in the decade of its operation.

Quiroga, Horacio (1878–1937), Uraguayan short-story writer, poet, novelist. His best-known stories are set in the jungles of Argentina, and in some the characters are animals. His collections include *Cuentos de la selva* (1919, tr. *South American Jungle Tales*, 1922, reprinted 1950); *Anaconda* (1921); *Cuentos de amor, de locura y de muerte* (1917); and *La gallina degollada y otros cuentos* (1925, tr. *The Decapitated Chicken and Other Stories*, 1976).

R

Raban, Jonathan (1942–   ), journalist, novelist, travel writer. Born in Norfolk, England, Raban was educated there at the University of Hull. His early interest in American themes is shown by his book on an American classic novel, *Mark Twain: Huckleberry Finn* (1968), as well as his account of a solo boat trip down the Mississippi River, *Old Glory: An American Voyage* (1981). In 1990, he moved to Seattle, Washington. In the United States, he has written several more books about the American experience: *Hunting Mister Heartbreak: A Discovery of America* (1990); *Bad Land: An American Romance* (1996), about early 20th-century pioneers to Montana; and *Passage to Juneau* (1999), recounting his experiences on a solo sail up the Inside Passage from Seattle to Alaska. Other titles include *Arabia: A Journey through the Labyrinth* (1978); *Coasting* (1986), about a boat trip around the coast of England; and a novel, *Foreign Land* (1985), about a middle-aged man who returns to England after a long absence to be shocked at how it has changed.

Rabbit, Run (1960),   a novel by JOHN UPDIKE. The main character is Harry Angstrom, whose nickname "Rabbit" came from high school basketball heroics. His decision to run from his pregnant wife, child, and stultifying job leads to tragedy. *Rabbit Redux* (1971) is set ten years after the first book. Rabbit and his wife, Janice, are still together, but the marriage is shaky. At loose ends when his wife leaves him, Rabbit gets involved with a pair of 1960s radicals. *Rabbit Is Rich* (1981) proceeds after another decade. Rabbit has now inherited a half interest in the auto dealership he works for and has found a place in middle-class society. He sets out to look for a daughter he thinks he fathered in his early flight. A fourth, perhaps final, *Rabbit* novel, *Rabbit at Rest*, appeared in 1990.

Rabble in Arms (1933),   a novel by KENNETH ROBERTS. This is a continuation of the history of the Revolution, which Roberts began in ARUNDEL (1930), his story of Benedict Arnold's expedition against Quebec. *Rabble in Arms* describes Arnold's halting of Burgoyne's invasion.

Rabe, David (1940–   ), playwright. Rabe was born, grew up, and attended college in Dubuque, Iowa. From his middle-class Catholic parents he acquired traditional American values and small-town upbringing. Rabe was drafted and served in the Army from 1965 to 1967. Working with a hospital support group in Vietnam, he acquired strong negative feelings toward the war. He returned to study and then teach at Villanova University. By 1974 his writing enabled him to make his livelihood.

Rabe's plays present contemporary America as a violent battleground with bursts of physical and verbal violence. Joseph Papp produced his plays in the New York Shakespeare Festival. *The Basic Training of Pavlo Hummel* (1971), *Sticks and Bones* (1972), and *Streamers* (1976) involve army life, the insecurity of Vietnam, and death. After the war, Rabe haunted go-go bars, where his play *In the Boom Boom Boom* (1974) takes place. It tells the sad story of Chrissie, who has been abused, wants to be a dancer, but ends up as a go-go girl. After working in Hollywood as a screenwriter, Rabe wrote *Hurlyburly* (1984), a play about unhappy Hollywood people struggling for power, taking drugs, and doing violence on children.

Rabe's plays depict rootlessness, a drug culture, racial problems, sexuality, and inevitable violence. Although he writes with elements of impressionism and surrealism, his newer plays are more realistic. He describes the male world in America, and he often ridicules American middle-class values. Rabe's language is obscene yet lyrical. His plays contain characters full of tension and scenes of intense confrontation. Rabe has also written screenplays and a novel, *Recital of the Dog* (1993).

Sam Smiley/GP

Rabinowitz, Solomon J.   See SHALOM ALEICHEM.

Raddall, Thomas (1903–1994),   novelist, short-story writer, historian. Born in England, Raddall came to Canada with his soldier father who later died in World War I. That death forced Thomas to leave school as a teenager. His novels deal with the history of his home province of Nova Scotia. When his stories, printed in the English *Blackwell's Magazine* in the 1930s, won the attention of Rudyard Kipling and John Buchan, he left his bookkeeping job to become a writer. His novels include *His Majesty's Yankees* (1942), *Roger Sudden* (1944), *Pride's Fancy* (1945), and *The Nymph and the Lamp* (1950). His story collections are *The Pied Piper of Dipper Creek and Other Tales* (1939), *Tambour and Other Stories* (1945), and *A Muster of Arms and Other Stories* (1954). *The Tide's Turn and Other Stories* (1959) is a selected collection. He also wrote histories and travel books.

Radical Club,   an informal group of New England Unitarian and Transcendalist thinkers who wanted to abolish supernaturalism from the Christian religion. The group flourished in the years immediately following the Civil War. The members contributed articles to *The Radical* (1865–72).

radio writing.   Because of commercial pressure, writing for the radio has not been generally creative. Notable exceptions are ARCHIBALD MACLEISH, who wrote verse dramas for the medium in the 1930s; STEPHEN VINCENT BENÉT, whose work was collected in *We Stand United and Other Radio Scripts* (1945); and ORSON WELLES, whose 1938 radio adaptation of *War of the Worlds*, by H. G. Wells; caused a panic. Others who wrote for the medium include PEARL BUCK, ARTHUR MILLER, LANGSTON HUGHES, and THOMAS WOLFE.

Radisson, Pierre Esprit (1636–1710?),   French fur trader, explorer. Radisson came to Canada about 1651 and was for a time a captive of the Iroquois. Later he formed an exploring partnership with his brother-in-law Médart Chouart, Sieur des Groseilliers. In a manuscript, various parts of which are in the Bodleian Library at Oxford, in the Hudson's Bay House, and in the British Museum, he described four voyages—some firsthand, some from the descriptions of others. Part of the account is in French, part in English. Radisson was a keen observer, not unsympathetic to the Indians, and his writings have a vivid interest surpassed by few other early narratives. His *Voyages* was printed in 1885, again in 1943.

Rafinesque, Constantine Samuel (1783–1840), naturalist, historian, economist. A European scholar, born in Turkey, Rafinesque settled in Kentucky in 1815. His widespread interests included Indian culture and language, and a modern bibliography of his works runs to nearly a thousand entries. Among his writings are *Annals of Nature* (1820); *Ichthyologia Ohiensis* (1820); *History of Kentucky* (1824); *Medical Flora, or, Manual of the Medical Botany of the U.S.* (1828–30); *American Manual of the Grape Vines* (1830); *American Florist* (1832); *A Life of Travels and Researches in North America and South Europe* (1836, reprinted 1944); *New Flora and Botany of North America* (1836); and *Safe Banking, Including the Principles of Wealth* (1837). Richard E. Call wrote *The Life and Writings of Rafinesque* (1895)

Ragged Dick (1867),   a novel by HORATIO ALGER. This was Alger's first successful book and started the immense vogue for his stories. *Ragged Dick* was first published serially in OLIVER ONTIO's *Student and Schoolmate* and became the title of two series. Dick starts out as a bootblack in New York City, makes the most of his chances, saves the little daughter of a rich man from drowning, and advances to inevitable success.

Raggedy Ann.   A character who first appeared in JOHNNY GRUELLE's book (1918) by that name and immediately became popular with children. The first book was followed by *Raggedy Andy* (1920) and other books about both characters. Dolls made up to look like the illustrations in the books have long been popular.

Raggedy Man, The (1890),   a poem by JAMES WHITCOMB RILEY. Written in the speech of a little boy, the poem tells of a hired man who performs odd jobs around a farm and wins the child's admiration through his storytelling.

Ragtime,   a 1975 novel by E.L. DOCTOROW depicting American life at the turn of the 20th century. Its fictional characters mix with historical personages, and actual events and fictional ones are depicted in the same realistic manner.

Rahv, Philip (1908–1973),   critic. He came to America from Russia as a child and was educated in Rhode Island. A leftist political theorist, he and others founded the PARTISAN REVIEW in 1933. He edited *The Great Short Novels of Henry James* (1944), *The Short Novels of Tolstoy* (1946), and *Discovery of Europe: The Story of American Experience in the Old World* (1947). His criticism, placing strong emphasis on the social forces underlying literature, included *Image and Idea* (1949), a collection of essays, and *Literature in America* (1957).

railroad folklore and literature.   An extensive body of railroad lore grew up around the thin bands of steel, officially joined at Promontory, Utah, in 1869 that spanned the country. It centered on heroes dedicated to fast trains (Casey Jones, the Wabash Cannonball), outlaws who robbed trains (the James brothers), and workers who built the railroad (John Henry). Railroading had a unique vocabulary, and terms such as "gandy dancer" found their way into the general speech. The ballad "I've Been Workin' on the Railroad" was first printed in *Carmina Princetonia* in 1894. B. A. Botkin and Alvin F. Harlow's *Treasury of Railroad Folklore* (1953) is a useful collection.

Fiction and nonfiction on railroads include S. R. Smith's *Romance and Humor of the Rail* (1873); Cy Waram's *Tales of an Engineer* (1895), *Snow on the Headlight* (1899), *Short Rails* (1900), and *The Last Spike and Other Railroad Stories* (1906); Frank Norris's THE OCTOPUS (1901); Francis Lynde's *Empire Builders* (1907), *Young Blood* (1929), and *The Fight on the Standing Stone* (1925); Robert Herrick's *Together* (1908); Upton Sinclair's *Money* (1908); Theodore Dreiser's THE TITAN (1914); Bruce V. Crandall's *After 40 Years* (1925), *Railroading on the Rails and Off* (1927), and *Reveries of an Editor* (1932); Lucius M. Beebe's *High Iron: A Book of Trains* (1938) and *Highliners: A Railroad Album* (1940); Frank P. Donovan, Jr.s' *The Railroad in Literature: A Brief Survey* (1940); and Taylor Caldwell's *Never Victorious, Never Defeated* (1954). The decline of the railroads has made them an object of nostalgia, as in the title poem of DAVE SMITH's *The Roundhouse Voices* (1985).

Raine, William MacLeod (1871–1954),   novelist. Raine, who came to the United States from England at the age of ten, turned to writing Westerns after some experience with the Arizona Rangers. Beginning with *Wyoming* (1908), he wrote eighty books, averaging two a year. Among them are *Ridgway of Montana* (1909), *A Texas Ranger* (1911), *The Yukon Trail* (1917), *Gunsight Pass* (1921), *Bonanza* (1926), *Colorado* (1928), *The Fighting Tenderfoot* (1929), *Roaring River* (1934), *Sons of the Saddle* (1938), *Justice Deferred* (1942), *The Bandit Trail* (1949), and *Dry Bones in the Valley* (1953).

Râle [or Rasles], Sebastien (1657?–1724),   Jesuit missionary, explorer, lexicographer. Assigned to New France in 1689, Father Râle established a mission among the Abnaki in Maine. He wrote a *Dictionary of the Abnaki Language*, not published until 1833. Nathaniel Deering, Maine editor and dramatist, wrote a tragedy entitled *Carabasset* (1830), in which a Jesuit named Rallé, apparently based on Father Râle, appears most favorably.

Raleigh, Sir Walter [also **Ralegh**] (1551?–1618), English soldier, poet, historian, explorer. Educated at Oxford, Raleigh fought in France and Ireland and commanded privateering ships against the Spaniards, gaining the approval of Queen Elizabeth. In 1583 he took part in his half-brother Sir HUMPHREY GILBERT's expedition to America. When Gilbert's ship was lost on the return voyage, his patent for exploration passed on to Raleigh. He organized several expeditions to the region he called "Virginia" in tribute to the Virgin Queen—it included all the land between Florida and Newfoundland. Colonist under Raleigh's patent settled on Roanoke Island off the coast of North Carolina; they disappeared, and the settlement is now commemorated in a yearly pageant by PAUL GREEN called *The Lost Colony* (1937).

Raleigh helped in the defeat of the Spanish Armada (1588); engaged in literary pursuits; and wrote in 1591 his *Report of the Truth of the Fight about the Islens of Azores*, the story of the defeat of *The Revenge*. He also wrote some very good verse, collected as *The Poems of Sir Walter Ralegh* (1591). In 1595 he led an expedition to Guiana, and on his return wrote *The Discoverie of the Large, Rich, and Bewtifyl Empyre of Guiana* (1596). When James I ascended the throne in 1603 Raleigh lost favor, was accused of conspiracy against James, and spent thirteen years in the Tower of London. There he made chemical experiments and wrote portions of a *History of the World* (1614), which got as far as 130 B.C. James released him for another expedition to Guiana, but when he returned home without any gold he was again arrested, given a biased hearing, and beheaded.

Many books have been written about Raleigh, among them Increase N. Tarbox's *Sir Walter Ralegh and His Colony in America* (1884); Irvin Anthony's *Ralegh and His World* (1934); and Ernest A. Strathmann's *Sir Walter Ralegh: A Study in Elizabethan Skepticism* (1951). Barrett Wendell wrote a play about him, *Ralegh in Guiana* (1902). Novels set in Raleigh's Roanoke and neighboring regions were written by Inglis Fletcher. Raleigh also appears in Charles Kingsley's *Westward Ho!* (1855); Maxwell Anderson's *Elizabeth the Queen* (1930); Van Wyck Mason's *The Golden Admiral* (1953); and Rosemary Sutcliff's *Lady in Waiting* (1957).

Ralph, James (1695?–1762), editor, teacher, writer, pamphleteer. Ralph was a friend of BENJAMIN FRANKLIN, with whom he sailed to London in 1724. His efforts at writing failed and he went off to teach in the provinces. He composed long poems, attacked Pope in *Sawney* (1728), and was the first American-born author to have plays produced on the London stage, *The Fashionable Lady* (1730) and others. He wrote a *History of England* in two huge folios (1744–76), a treatise on *The Use and Abuse of Parliaments* (1744), and another—his last book and based on his own experiences—on *The Case of Authors by Profession or Trade Stated, with Regard to Booksellers, the Stage, and the Public* (1758). He was in the employ of the politician George Bubb Dodington (1691–1762) and of Frederick, Prince of Wales, as a pamphleteer.

Ralph, Julian (1853–1903), newspaperman, short-story writer, autobiographer. Born in New York City, Ralph joined the New York *Sun* in 1875, after serving on the New York *World* and the New York *Daily Graphic*. In 1895 he went over to the New York *Journal*. He became a celebrated war correspondent, reporting, among others, the Greco-Turkish War and the Boer War. Among his books are *The Sun's German Barber* (1883); *On Canada's Frontier* (1892); *Our Great West* (1893); *Dixie, or, Southern Scenes and Sketches* (1895); *A Prince of Georgia and Other Tales* (1899); and *The Making of a Journalist* (1903).

Ramona (1884), a novel by HELEN HUNT JACKSON. It appeared serially in the *Outlook* and was published in book form in 1885. Ramona, an orphan of Scottish and Indian ancestry, is brought up as a foster sister to Felipe Moreno, who falls in love with her, as does Alessandro, a Mission Indian. When Ramona and Alessandro elope they experience prejudice. He is driven mad and dies, and Ramona marries Felipe. The story is believed to have been based on the life of a real person whose last descendant, Condino Hopkins, died on a reservation near Banning, California; Ramona herself is said to be buried in the Cahuilla Reservation near San Jacinto. Jackson treated the same theme earlier in a nonfiction work, A CENTURY OF DISHONOR (1881).

Ramos, Graciliano (1892–1953), Brazilian novelist. Ramos used the northeastern state of Alagoas, where he was a businessman and public official, as a setting. His first novel *Caetés* (1933) remained unpublished for nearly ten years after it was written. In 1936 he was imprisoned for his political views, a story told in *Memórias do Cárcere* (1953, tr. *Prison Memoirs*, 1974). He spent the last years of his life proofreading for a Rio de Janeiro newspaper. His novels express impatience with the social and economic tensions of his region, and he experimented with several narrative methods. *São Bernardo* (1935; tr. 1975) is a first-person narrative; *Angústia* (1936, tr. *Anguish* 1946) is a stream of consciousness narrative of a man driven mad by sexual passion; and *Vidas Sêcas* (1938, tr. *Barren Lives*, 1961), his best work, details the sufferings of an illiterate cowhand. *Infância* (1945, tr. *Childhood*, 1979) is a memoir.

Ramsay, David (1749–1815), teacher, physician, legislator, writer. Ramsay, born in Pennsylvania and an ardent supporter of colonial rights, is best known for his *History of the American Revolution* (1789). He also wrote pamphlets in defense of the American cause, several medical works, a *Biographical Chart, on a New Plan, to Facilitate the Study of History*, and several histories, among them *A History of the Revolution in South Carolina* (1785), *A History of the United States* (1816–17), and *Universal History Americanized* (1819). The last was his most ambitious work and appeared posthumously in twelve volumes.

Rand, Ayn (1905–1982), philosopher, novelist. Born and educated in Russia, Rand came to the United States as a young woman. She used her novels as a medium for her Objectivist philosophy, which glorified extreme individualism, emphasizing "rational self-interest" instead of altruism. Her four novels are *We, the Living* (1936); *Anthem* (1938); *The Fountainhead* (1943); and *Atlas Shrugged* (1957). *For the New Intellectual* (1961) and *The Romantic Manifesto* (1969) are nonfiction.

Randall, Dudley (1914–   ), poet, editor, publisher. Trained as a librarian at the University of Michigan, Randall founded the Broadside Press in Detroit, beginning with single sheets of his own work in 1963. He served as its general editor from 1965 to 1977; during that period Broadside published almost sixty books of poetry, providing a forum for African American poets. Collections of his work include *Poem Counterpoint* (1966, with Margaret Danner), *Cities Burning* (1968), *More to Remember: Poems of Four Decades* (1971), *After the Killing* (1973), and *A Litany of Friends: New and Selected Poems* (1981).

Randall, James Ryder (1839–1908), poet, teacher, newspaperman, editor. Randall's poem MARYLAND! MY MARYLAND was first printed in the New Orleans *Delta* (April 26, 1861) and reprinted all over the South. After 1865 Randall worked for the Augusta, Georgia, *Constitutionalist* and other newspapers. His *Poems* was published in 1910.

Randolph, Edmund [Jennings] (1753–1813), lawyer, public official. Randolph served his state and his country in many capacities—as a member of the Virginia Constitutional Convention (1776), in the Second Continental Congress (1779, 1780, 1782), and in the Federal Constitutional Convention (1787); as attorney-general of Virginia (1776–86), governor of Virginia (1787–88), Federal attorney-general (1789–94), and secretary of state under under Washington (1794–95). An eminent lawyer, he was senior counsel for AARON BURR in his trial for treason (1807) and won his acquittal. At the Constitutional Convention he advocated a plan known as the Virginia or Randolph plan, which would have greatly centralized the government and included a triumvirate of executives from three regions. He wrote *Vindication* (1795). His *Essay on the Revolutionary History of Virginia* appeared in the *Virginia Historical Magazine* (1935–37).

Randolph, Vance (1892–1980), folklorist, teacher. Born in Kansas, Randolph taught at the University of Kansas and collected materials for the Archive of American Folklore at the Library of Congress. In the 1920, he wrote, under his own name and various pseudonyms, books on subjects from bee keeping to Freud, but his speciality was the life and folklore of the Ozark region. Among his books are *The Ozarks* (1931); *Ozark Mountain Folks* (1932); *From an Ozark Holler* (1933); *Ozark Outdoors* (1934); *Ozark Anthology* (1940); *Ozark Folksongs* (4 v. 1946–50); *Ozark Superstitions* (1947); *We Always Lie to Strangers* (1951); *Who Blowed Up the Church House?* (1952); *Down in the Holler* (with George P. Wilson, 1953); *The Devil's Pretty Daughter and Other Ozark Folk Tales* (1955); *Talking Turtle and Other Ozark Folk Tales* (1957); and *Sticks in the Knapsack, and Other Ozark Folk Tales* (1958). See OZARK MOUNTAINS.

Rankin, Jeremiah Eames (1828–1924), clergyman, writer of hymns and other poems, teacher. Rankin is best remembered for his hymn *God be With You Till We Meet Again*, popularized by Dwight Lyman Moody and Ira D. Sankey. Rankin was born in New Hampshire, named pastor of the First Congregational Church in Washington, D.C., and later became president of Howard University (1889–1903). He

loved to write in Scottish dialect, which he knew well. He collected some of his verses in *The Auld Scotch Mither and Other Poems* (1873) and *Ingleside Rhaims* (1887).

Ransom, John Crowe (1888–1974), poet, critic, editor, teacher. Ransom, the son of a Methodist minister, was born in Pulaski, Tennessee. After graduation from Vanderbilt University in 1909, he read The Greats as a Rhodes scholar at Christ Church College, Oxford (1910–13). In 1914 he returned to Vanderbilt as a member of the English department. It was at this time that he and his colleague DONALD DAVIDSON, among others, formed the group that later—after Ransom's two-year stint in France during World War I (1917–19)—published *The Fugitive*, a journal of poetry whose run from 1922 to 1925 signaled the literary renascence of the South. With the publication of *God without Thunder: An Unorthodox Defense of Orthodoxy* in 1930, Ransom laid the aesthetic foundation for Southern Agrarianism, the subject of the symposium I'LL TAKE MY STAND (1930), to which he contributed the introduction and an essay. In 1937 Ransom moved to Kenyon College in Ohio, where he founded and edited the influential KENYON REVIEW (1939–59). He retired from teaching in 1958.

A perspicacious editor and the respected mentor at Vanderbilt of ALLEN TATE, ANDREW LYTLE, ROBERT PENN WARREN, CLEANTH BROOKS, and RANDALL JARRELL and at Kenyon of PETER TAYLOR, ROBERT LOWELL, and JAMES WRIGHT. Ransom owes his enduring popularity with students of Southern literature to a small body of poems, which he wrote as one of the FUGITIVES, and to a lesser extent to the criticism that occupied him during the succeeding four decades. Ransom's characteristic poems—he never reprinted his immature *Poems About God* (1919)—appeared in two slender volumes, *Chills and Fever* (1924) and *Two Gentlemen in Bonds* (1927). These poems boast an unmistakable idiom, that of a "displaced scholar," as Robert Penn Warren describes Ransom's typical persona. An ironical voice, whose timbre hints of the poet's training in classics and of his education at Oxford, it is nonetheless capable of relating with tenderness and pity such incidents as the death of children and their pets ("Bells for John Whiteside's Daughter," "Dead Boy," and "Janet Waking"). In "Antique Harvesters," which is unusually rich in local color, Ransom ridicules the Old South even as he expresses piety toward the mythic dimension of the region.

His typical theme, as dramatized in such poems of courtship as "Spectral Lovers" and "The Equilibrists" and most baldly announced in the meditative "Painted Head," a celebrated later poem, is the conflict between two forms of abstraction: the head, which Ransom depicts as a "rock garden" or an "iron acropolis," and the "body bush"—that is, between sense and sensibility. Ransom received the 1950 Bollingen Prize for Poetry; his *Selected Poems* (1963), containing controversial revisions, won the National Book Award.

The aim of much of Ransom's theoretical criticism is to differentiate between analytical prose and poetry. His criticism complements his poetry in its insistence on an ontological distinction between the world as known through prose, which Ransom scornfully identifies with science, and the world as known through poetry, whose combination of logical structure and local texture represents a fusion of science and myth. The New Criticism owes its designation to the title of his second volume of critical essays. Besides *The New Criticism* (1941), Ransom published *The World's Body* (1938) and *Beating the Bushes* (1972). Thomas Daniel Young, author of the biography *Gentleman in a Dust-coat* (1976), has edited with others *Selected Essays of John Crowe Ransom* (1984) and *Selected Letters of John Crowe Ransom* (1985). Young's anthology *John Crowe Ransom: Critical Essays and a Bibliography* (1968) remains useful. *John Crowe Ransom's Secular Faith* (1989) by Kiernan Quinlan is the most sophisticated book-length study of Ransom's work.

DAVID HAVIRD

Raphaelson, Samson (1896–1983), writer, movie director. He wrote his first successful play, *The Jazz Singer*, in 1925, began writing screenplays in 1929, and later became a movie director. His list of notable screenplay credits includes *Suspicion* (1941), *Heaven Can Wait* (1943), and *Green Dolphin Street* (1947). His plays include *Accent on Youth* (1934), *Jason* (1942), and *Hilda Crane* (1950).

Rappaccini's Daughter (*Democratic Review*, 1844; *Mosses from an Old Manse*, 1846), a story by NATHANIEL HAWTHORNE. This is one of the most effective of Hawthorne's short stories, in which a brooding symbolism pervades the incidents of an ingenious plot. A scientist whose absorption in his experiments is deeper than his love for his child feeds his daughter poison to study its effects. A young student falls in love with her and seeks to cure her with an antidote, but it kills her. As his *American Notes* testifies, Hawthorne had found the germ of his story in Sir Thomas Browne's *Vulgar Errors*. Browne had discovered the idea as far back as the medieval *Gesta romanorum*. *Rappaccini's Daughter* forms the basis for CHARLES WAKEFIELD CADMAN's opera, *The Garden of Mystery* (1925).

Rappists, a communal religious sect founded in Germany by George Rapp (1757–1847). The sect came to America and founded the communities of HARMONY (1804) in Pennsylvania and New Harmony (1814) in Indiana. Their doctrine included celibacy and the dissolution of marriages.

Rascoe, [Arthur] Burton (1892–1957), editor, columnist, critic. Rascoe was born in Kentucky. His books include *Theodore Dreiser* (1925), *A Bookman's Daybook* (1929), *Titans of Literature* (1932), *Belle Starr* (1941), and two autobiographical titles, *Before I Forget* (1937) and *We Were Interrupted* (1947).

Rationale of Verse, The, an essay by POE first published as "Notes on English Verse." It is the most complete account of his theory of metrics.

Raven, The (*American [Whig] Review*, February 1845; *The Raven and Other Poems*, 1845), a poem by EDGAR ALLAN POE in which the poet, steeped in melancholy memories of a lost love, is haunted by death in the guise of a raven. This poem made Poe famous and aroused much discussion because of Poe's account of how he wrote it (THE PHILOSOPHY OF COMPOSITION, 1846). It has sometimes been regarded as a mere tour de force and has been often parodied. In his essay on the poem Poe explained how he had selected his theme, how he had chosen the meter and refrain, and his theories about the most

suitable topics for poetry. Poe said he pondered the poem for years, but the final draft was written at a single sitting late in 1844. He said the metrical form was a modification of that used in *Lady Geraldine's Courtship* by Elizabeth Barrett Browning. The poem depends less on onomatopoeia than does THE BELLS, but it is rich in alliteration.

Rawlings, Marjorie Kinnan (1896–1953), reporter, poet, novelist. Born in Washington, D.C., Rawlings was a reporter and wrote syndicated verse before settling in Cross Creek, Florida, in 1928. Her novels and stories, including THE YEARLING (1938), use Florida scenery and folklore. Her other fiction titles are *South Moon Under* (1933), *Golden Apples* (1935), *When the Whippoorwill* (1940), and *The Sojourner* (1953). *Cross Creek* (1942) is a nonfiction account of her region; *Cross Creek Cookery* (1942) is a collection of regional recipes.

Raymond, Henry Jarvis (1820–1869), newspaper editor, historian. Jarvis was associated with HORACE GREELEY on several New York newspapers before he, with George Jones, founded the New York *Times* (1851). Raymond wrote *Disunion and Slavery* (1860) and a *History of the Administration of Lincoln* (1864). Much has been written about him, especially in histories of the *Times*. An excellent biography is E. Francis Brown's *Raymond of the Times* (1951).

Raynal, Guillaume Thomas François, Abbé (1713–1796), French historian, philosopher. The six-volume history of colonization in Asia and America that Raynal compiled with the help of Diderot and other *philosophes*—*L'Histoire philosophique et politique des établissements et du commerce des Européens dans les deux Indes* (1770) —was translated into English in 1776. Chateaubriand, Jefferson, and Crévecoeur were enthusiastic about it; Crévecoeur dedicated his *Letter from An American Farmer* (1782) to Raynal. In 1781, the *Parlement de Paris* branded Raynal's work impious and dangerous for its idea that people had the right to revolt against and withhold taxes from government. Raynal's *The Revolution of America* (1781) drew a response, *Letter to Abbé Raynal* (1782), from THOMAS PANIE.

Raynolds, Robert (1902–1964), novelist, poet, essayist. Raynolds was born in New Mexico. His novel *Brothers in the West* (1931) was a Harper Prize novel. It was followed by *Saunders Oak* (1933); *Fortune* (1935); *May Bretton* (1944); *The Obscure Enemy* (1945); *Paquita* (1947); *The Sinner of Saint Ambrose* (1952), a Book-of-the-Month-Club selection; *The Quality of Quiros* (1955); *Far Flight of Love* (1957); and two books of essays, *The Choice to Love* (1959) and *In Praise of Gratitude* (1961). In 1941 he wrote a verse drama, *Boadicea*.

Rayuela, a 1963 novel by JULIO CORTAZAR about the life of an Argentine intellectual in Paris, his return to Buenos Aires, and his confinement to an insane asylum. The protagonist's story is interspersed with portions of a manuscript he has discovered on the death of the contemporary novel. *Rayuela* was translated into English as *Hopscotch* (tr. by Gregory Rabassa, 1966).

Razaf, Andy [Andreamenentania Rasafkeriefo] (1895–1973), jazz lyricist. Razaf was the grandson of John Waller, a freed slave who became U.S. consul to Madagascar;

Waller's daughter married the queen's nephew and, when the French took over the island, the family had to flee to the U.S. to escape imprisonment because of their connection to the royal family. Andy Razaf was born a few weeks after their arrival in Washington. He sold his first song, "Baltimo," at age 17. During World War I he wrote verses protesting racial bigotry for *The Messenger, The Emancipator, The New Negro,* and *The Crusader.* After a brief time as a pitcher in semipro baseball, he returned to Harlem to write lyrics in 1921. He wrote the words for over 500 songs, including "Ain't Misbehavin'," "Black and Blue," "Memories of You," "Honeysuckle Rose," "Stompin' at the Savoy," and "In the Mood." He collaborated with Fats Waller, Eubie Blake, James P. Johnson, and W. C. HANDY.

Read, Opie [Percival] (1852–1939), newspaperman, humorist, novelist, editor, lecturer. Born in Nashville, Tennessee, Read claimed he had lectured in every county in the country. He edited *The Arkansas Traveler,* a magazine he founded in 1882. It became very popular and lasted till 1916. His novel *The Jucklins* (1895) sold about two million copies. He also wrote *The Kentucky Colonel* (1890), *Judge Elbridge* (1899), *My Young Master* (1896), *Son of the Sword-Maker* (1905), *By the Eternal* (1906), and *The Gold Gauze Veil* (1927). *I Remember* (1930) and *Mark Twain and I* (1940) are autobiographical. Maurice Elfer wrote *Opie Read* (1940).

Read, Thomas Buchanan (1822–1872), poet. Read was born in Pennsylvania. Beginning as an itinerant sign painter and portraitist, he soon had verse published in the Boston papers. His collected *Poems* appeared in 1847. During the Civil War he toured the North with the actor James Edward Murdoch, who recited Read's patriotic verses including *Sheridan's Ride. The Wagoner of the Alleghenies* was a popular narrative poem (1862). His *Summer Story, Sheridan's Ride, and Other Poems* appeared in 1865, his *Poetical Works* (3 v.) in 1866.

readers. Children once had no special provision made for their reading, but during the Victorian era more and more books were written especially for children, and carefully prepared readers—collections of material chosen for moral, literary, or patriotic value—were published. Such books seem to have been a characteristically American product, with W. H. MCGUFFEY's *Eclectic Readers* (6 v. 1836–57) the pioneer and most widely known example. These books were graded according to the age of the children for whom they were intended. They exerted wide influence, which is studied in revealing detail by Richard D. Mosier in *Making the American Mind: Social and Moral Ideas in the McGuffey Readers* (1947). The McGuffey readers had innumerable competitors.

Reader's Digest. Founded by DeWitt and Lila Acheson Wallace in 1922 as a pocket-size monthly offering what are represented as condensed articles from other American magazines.

Realf, Richard (1834–1878), newspaper writer, poet. His first collection of verses, *Guesses at the Beautiful* (1852), was published with the help of contributions by friends when he was eighteen. Leaving his native England, he came to Kansas (1854) where, as a newspaperman, he met JOHN BROWN, whose abolitionist principles he supported. He served in the Union Army in the Civil War and migrated to San Francisco, where he committed suicide when his bigamy was revealed. Twenty years after his death appeared *Poems by Richard Realf, Poet, Soldier, Workman.*

realism. Attempts to portray life accurately in America began with the accounts of the first settlements. These were not fictional, however, or not intentionally so, and the movement called "realism" did not begin for another two hundred years. Realism, a concerted effort to depict in fiction those elements counted real in life, was a movement of the latter half of the 19th century, most active from 1870 to 1900 and already losing force to NATURALISM in the last of its three decades. It had its roots in similar movements in Europe, but even these did not much predate the middle of the 19th century. Among important models for Americans were Balzac, Turgenev, Flaubert, Dostoevsky, and Tolstoy. The English novel, which they understood as being on the right track as early as Jane Austen, they perceived as losing its way in some respects in the work of Thackeray, Dickens, and many who came after. Among earlier Americans, Hawthorne, for all that he called his works romances, was highly respected for his selection of telling details and his care for inner reality, or what was only much later to be called psychological realism.

The three major realists were TWAIN, HOWELLS, and HENRY JAMES. Howells spearheaded the drive with the example of his works, the precepts of his critical essays and reviews, and his editorial positions on ATLANTIC MONTHLY (1866–81) and HARPER's (1886–92). Twain mocked romanticism and provided a model for plain style and for the use of dialect, regional materials, and American humor. James demonstrated the technical uses of restricted narrative perspectives, emphasized the role of artistic illusion in creating what is after all only the appearance of reality, and played a major role in shifting the focus of fiction from outer to inner reality.

Howells provided the best brief definition: "Realism is nothing more and nothing less than the truthful treatment of material." The concern for truth meant that the realist would write about things known to the writer. Never, in the best practice, however, did it mean a limitation to things directly experienced. As James observed, and demonstrated in his writing, a small insight into a moment of life can be turned into a great truth if the writer has the necessary imagination and the technical resources to embody it in convincing prose. The concern for truth meant also that the writer would prefer the representative to the extraordinary, since a work built on the extraordinary presents a face of life that is in general untrue. The concern for treatment meant that the writer would develop literary techniques to enforce the sense of reality—chiefly these involved selection of material, objectivity of reporting, and careful control of narrative perspective.

Realism thus described left no room for certain kinds of things that were in some sense real, and to a certain extent the move toward naturalism was an attempt to extend the boundaries to include the extraordinary and to capture from romance some measure of the power of authorial subjectivity. But the lessons of realism for American literature had been learned, and they have continued to reverberate. Associated with realism in its own time was the LOCAL COLOR movement. See also REGIONALISM.

Realms of Being, The, the general title of GEORGE SANTAYANA's major philosophical work. Individual volumes are *The Realm of Essence* (1927), *The Realm of Matter* (1930), *The Realm of Truth* (1937), and *The Realm of Spirit* (1940). *Skepticism and Animal Faith* (1923) is an introduction to *The Realms of Being*.

Reaney, James [Crerar] (1926–   ), poet, playwright, short-story writer. Reaney's first collection of lyric poems, *The Red Heart* (1949), drawing on rural life in southwestern Ontario near his Stratford birthplace, won the Governor General's Award, as did his second collection, *A Suit of Nettles* (1958), and his third, *Twelve Letters to a Small Town* (1962). He began to write for the theater with *The Killdeer* (1960). A trilogy of plays—*Sticks and Stones* (1973); *The St. Nicholas Hotel, Wm. Donnelly, Prop.* (1974); and *Handcuffs* (1975)—concern the Donnelly family who were massacred by a mob of their neighbors in 1880. His other plays dealing with Ontario history are *Baldoon* (1976), *The Dismissal* (1977), *Wacousta!* (1978), *King Whistle!* (1979), *Antler River* (1980), and *Gyroscope* (1983). His poetry was collected in *Selected Shorter Poems* (1975) and *Selected Longer Poems* (1976). *The Box Social and Other Stories* appeared in 1996.

Reason the Only Oracle of Man; or, A Compendious System of Natural Religion (1784), a work attributed to ETHAN ALLEN. The author attacks impostures of the church, revelation and miracles, appeals to authority, and Christianity in general. But he believed in God and immortality and seeks to justify his belief on rational, that is, deistic, principles. In his youth Allen had come under the influence of Dr. Thomas Young (1732–1777), a freethinker. It is believed that most of *Reason* was actually the work of Dr. Young, to whose manuscripts on these subjects Allen had access. See DEISM.

Rebecca of Sunnybrook Farm (1903), a novel by KATE DOUGLAS WIGGIN. Rebecca Rowena Randall, ten years old, leaves her impoverished and widowed mother and her sisters and brothers and goes to live with two maiden aunts, Miranda and Jane, in Riverboro. She makes friends, eventually wins an admirer, graduates from an academy, and in general radiates unquenchable charm and good humor in the face of considerable harshness from Aunt Miranda. The story was successfully dramatized in 1910 and was followed by *New Chronicles of Rebecca* (1907).

Rechy, John [Francisco] (1934–   ), novelist. Son of a Mexican mother and brought up in Texas, Rechy has lived in New York and Los Angeles. His *City of Night* (1963) is considered a classic novel of the urban homosexual experience. *The Sexual Outlaw* (1978) is a nonfiction study of gay promiscuity. *Coming of the Night* (1999) returns to the same subject, depicting a day and night in Los Angeles just before the advent of the AIDS epidemic. *The Fourth Angel* (1973) treats four abused Texas teenagers who band together. *Marilyn's Daughter* (1988), set in Hollywood, examines the power of myth. The Mexican single mother at the center of *The Miraculous Day of Amalia Gomez* (1992) lives in the violence of Los Angeles. *Our*

Lady of Babylon (1996) retells the stories of history's "fallen" women. Other titles include *Numbers* (1967), *This Day's Death* (1970), *The Vampires* (1971), *Rushes* (1979), and *Bodies and Souls* (1983).

Recognitions, The. WILLIAM GADDIS's first novel, published in 1955. Wyatt Gwyon, a member of an old New England family, finds his art through forgery of Flemish masters.

Reconstruction. At the end of the Civil War, Lincoln's policy toward the South, which was also followed by Johnson, was one of leniency. The radical Republicans, however, wanted to punish the South and forestall attempts of the Southern states to reduce former slaves to peonage by means of the Black Codes. They overcame the lenient faction and passed the Reconstruction Act (March 2, 1867), with other legislation and Constitutional amendments that protected the new rights of the former slaves and guaranteed them the ballot. To enforce these laws the Republicans sent officials to the South, whom the people there called carpetbaggers. Their misrule and corruption, together with the humiliation of having Northerners and former slaves in power, produced a reaction in the form of the KU KLUX KLAN and a new spirit of unity creating the Solid South. For more than a decade the Southern states were socially, politically, and economically ruined. Finally President Hayes ordered the troops removed from the South in April 1877. The carpetbag governments immediately fell, and the native whites came back into power. Except for providing a Constitutional basis for future emancipation, the radical Republicans had done little more than ensure that for more than two generations the South would vote solidly Democratic.

Historians and others have described the Reconstruction Era in detail. Among nonfiction works on the period are G. W. Cable, *The Silent South* (1885); W. A. Dunning, *Reconstruction, Political and Economic* (1907); Claude Bowers, *The Tragic Era* (1929); J. G. Randall, *The Civil War and Reconstruction* (1937); W. E. B. Du Bois, *Black Reconstruction* (1935); C. V. Woodward, *Reunion and Reaction* (1956); Hodding Carter, *Angry Scar* (1959); and Paul Buck, *Road to Reunion* (1937). Novels dealing with the period include A. W. Tourgee, *A Royal Gentleman* (1881), A FOOL'S ERRAND (1879), and BRICKS WITHOUT STRAW (1880); John W. De Forest, *The Bloody Chasm* (1881); Mary Noailles Murfree, *Where the Battle Was Fought* (1884); G. W. Cable, *John March, Southerner* (1894); T. N. Page, *Red Rock* (1898) and *The Red Riders* (1924); Ellen Glasgow, *The Voice of the People* (1900) and *The Deliverance* (1904); Thomas Dixon, Jr., THE LEOPARD'S SPOTS (1902), *The Clansman* (1905), and *The Traitor* (1907); Joseph Hergesheimer, *The Limestone Tree* (1931); Margaret Mitchell, GONE WITH THE WIND (1936); and Ben Ames Williams, *The Unconquered* (1953).

Red Badge of Courage, The (1895), a novel by STEPHEN CRANE. Subtitled *An Episode of the Civil War*, the novel that made Crane internationally celebrated was published when the author was twenty-four, before he served as a war correspondent or had even seen a battle. This extraordinary work of the imagination focuses on the mind of a young Union soldier, Henry Fleming, as he and his untried regiment undergo their first trials under fire. During the first day of battle, Henry runs in blind panic as others fall wounded and dying, but on the second day, conscious of "a little flower of confidence growing within him," he fights ferociously, leads the charge, and is praised by the commanding officers. Critics have debated whether Henry actually achieves the "quiet manhood" in which he rejoices at the end. Crane's comparisons of war to a blood-swollen god, the men in battle to frightened or maddened animals, imply that cowardice and heroism alike are matters of blind instinct. The novel is distinguished from purely naturalistic treatments of war by Crane's impressionistic techniques, which render Henry's experiences as an inward stream of images of sounds, shapes, colors, fragments of landscape, parts of bodies, and surreal forms generated by his fear-haunted mind. *The Red Badge of Courage* was acclaimed by the writers Crane later knew in England—Henry James, Ford Madox Ford, H. G. Wells, and Joseph Conrad, who wrote an introduction to the novel in 1924. The novel has influenced many writers, including DOS PASSOS, FAULKNER, HEMINGWAY, and JAMES JONES, and remains, in Eric Solomon's words, "a touchstone for modern war fiction." The first edition, published by D. Appleton & Co., is a shortened version of Crane's original text, edited by Fredson Bowers, *The Red Badge of Courage: A Facsimile of the Manuscript* (1972).

ELSA NETTELS

Redburn (1849), a semiautobiographical novel by HERMAN MELVILLE. The author, with gentle, ironic detachment, remembers and playfully distorts the memory of his own first trip across the Atlantic. The major theme of *Redburn* is expressed through the figure of the alert young man who wanders the path from innocence to experience. Other themes in the novel are found frequently in Melville's work: the inhumanity of man to man, which provoked Melville's antimissionary propaganda in TYPEE and OMOO and which would find expression again in WHITE JACKET, is shown here in the scenes of Liverpool squalor. Another significant theme is the distinction between appearance and reality, though it is less emphasized here than in MARDI and later in PIERRE. Redburn discovers to his chagrin and the reader's amusement that Captain Riga is not what he seems. Thus Redburn recounts a young boy's first confrontation with the larger world, an encounter that helps him mature but does not render him cynical. Redburn becomes the man satisfied—or not too dissatisfied—with life, a man who can become righteously—but not maniacally—indignant. The result in *Redburn* is a comic hero, and Melville's only comic novel.

Redding, J. Saunders (1907–1988), historian, editor. Believed to be the first African-American member of an Ivy League faculty, Redding joined the faculty of his alma mater, Brown University, in 1949 and retired from Cornell University in 1975. He also taught at Hampton Institute, Southern University, and Morehouse College. As a member of the staff of the Joint Center for Political Studies, he helped develop policies for dealing with racism in the 1970s. His autobiography is *No Day of Triumph* (1944), and his other works are *To Make a Poet Black* (1939), *Stranger and Alone* (1950), *They Came in*

Chains (1950), and *An American in India* (1954). He coedited *Cavalcade* (1970), an anthology of African American literature, with A. P. Davis.

Redeemed Captive Returned to Zion, The (1707), a narrative of captivity among the Indians written by JOHN WILLIAMS. Next to Mary Rowlandson's CAPTIVITY AND RESTAURATION (1682), this was the best seller among the widely read captivity narratives. Williams gives a vivid account of a massacre and of the sufferings undergone on long forced marches to the north. Williams made much of his resistance to attempts by Jesuits to convert him. See INDIAN CAPTIVITY NARRATIVES.

Redfield, James (1950–), philosopher, novelist. Born in Alabama and educated at Auburn University, Redfield worked as a counselor for abused children. He gave up that career to write and self-publish his first book, *The Celestine Prophecy* (1993). The book attracted considerable attention among followers of New Age philosophy and was bought by a major publishing house. The reissue sold millions of copies and stayed at the top of the *New York Times* best seller list for over two years. The novel recounts the narrator's travel to Peru in search of an ancient manuscript; enlightened people he meets during his quest provide him with nine insights about human potential. A similar search for meaning, this time in the Appalachian Mountains, is at the center of *The Tenth Insight* (1996). *The Secret of Shambhala: In Search of the Eleventh Insight* (1999) continues the search in Tibet.

Red Jacket, Seneca Chief. See SENECA INDIANS.

Redpath, James (1833–1891), newspaperman, lecture bureau manager, school official, writer. When Redpath was seventeen his parents emigrated from Scotland to Michigan. He worked for the New York *Tribune* for thirty years. He was especially interested in obtaining a refuge for African-Americans in Haiti, and he acted as a consular official for Haiti for several years. He was a correspondent during the Civil War, then superintendent of schools at Charleston, South Carolina. A good speaker, he decided in 1868 to organize a lecture bureau; his agency became well known in this country and abroad. For a time he edited the NORTH AMERICAN REVIEW. In the 1880s he became deeply interested in Ireland and agitated for its freedom. Among his books are *Tales and Traditions of the Border* (with his father, 1849); *The Roving Editor* (1859); *Echoes of Harper's Ferry* (1860); *The Public Life of Captain John Brown* (1860); *A Guide to Hayti* (1860); and *Talks About Ireland* (1881).

Red Rover, The (1827), a novel by JAMES FENIMORE COOPER. The plot of this romance is somewhat tortuous, with the hero taking three names during its course. At first he is Lt. Henry Ark, an officer in the British Navy about the middle of the 18th century, who takes the name Wilder and enlists as a common sailor on board the *Dolphin* in the hope of tracking down a mysterious pirate, the Red Rover. He finally encounters the pirate, who actually saves his life, at the same time rescuing Gertrude Grayson and her governess Mrs. Wyllys. Later it turns out that the lieutenant is really the son of Mrs. Wyllys and that his name is Paul de Lacey. The Red Rover turns out to be a punctilious gentleman who left the service of his Britannic Majesty because of indignation over the wrongs inflicted on the colonies. In an epilogue it is revealed, twenty years later, that he had joined the American patriots and fought with them against England. There are some good sea scenes and one fierce battle. Comic relief is furnished by an admiral's widow who constantly commits malapropisms with maritime terms. There is an affecting death scene, that of Black Scipio.

Redskins, The, or, Indian and Injin (1846),   a novel by JAMES FENIMORE COOPER, the third of the *Littlepage Manuscripts*. It deals with the dangerous situation created in New York State when bands of agitators rose up against the patroon system; the result was the Anti-Rent War (1839–46). The agitators disguised themselves as "Injins"; one of the important characters in Cooper's book is a real Indian, Susquesus. In 1846 a constitutional convention provided measures whereby the great manors were broken up. Cooper sympathized with the patroons and strongly favored them in his novels on the subject. *The Redskins* was the most polemical of these novels. See ANTI-RENT LAWS.

Reece, Byron (1917–1958),   poet, novelist, farmer. After leaving college, Reece taught for a while, then decided to be a farmer in his native Georgia. He also continued to write and publish ballads and lyrics that show the influence of A. E. Housman but strike an individual note. His collections include *Ballad of the Bones and Other Poems* (1945) and *Bow Down in Jericho* (1950). *Better a Dinner of Herbs* (1950) and *The Hawk and the Sun* (1955) are novels.

Reed, Ishmael (1938-),   poet, novelist. Born in Chattanooga, he grew up in Buffalo and attended the State University of New York. *Yellow Back Radio Broke-Down* (1969) introduced Hoodoo (or Voodoo) folklore precepts, especially the combination of beliefs and practices with divergent cultural origins, a nonlinear depiction of time, and the character Loop Garoo, an African-American cowboy. Reed's first major poetry collection, *Conjure: Selected Poems, 1963–1970* (1972), was followed by *Chattanooga: Poems* (1973); *A Secretary to the Spirits* (1977); and *New and Collected Poetry* (1988). His verse demonstrates an interest in Egyptian symbolism ("I am a cowboy in the boat of Ra") and in American and African-American history.

Mumbo-Jumbo (1972), a novel set in New Orleans in the 1920s, explores the origin and composition of an African-American aesthetic. *The Last Days of Louisiana Red* (1974) has three related plots concerned with racial violence. *Flight to Canada* (1976) traces the history of slavery through the story of Raven Quickskill's escape and explores the relationship between writers and editors. *The Terrible Twos* (1982) is a deconstruction of Thanksgiving and Christmas customs and an allegory on the Reagan presidency. *Reckless Eyeballing* (1986), its title taken from one of the charges leveled at lynching victim Emmett Till, contrasts the receptions given to African-American male and female writers. *The Terrible Threes* (1989) is a rambling text, continuing the assault on feminism and popular culture. *Japanese by Spring* appeared in 1993.

Reed's essay collections include *Shrovetide in Old New Orleans* (1978), *God Made Alaska for the Indians* (1982), *Selected Essays* (1982), *Writing Is Fighting: Thirty-Seven Years of Boxing on Paper* (1988), and *Airing Dirty Laundry* (1993).

Reed, John (1887–1920),   newspaperman, poet. Born to a wealthy Portland, Oregon, family and a graduate of Harvard (1910), Reed was sent to Mexico by the *Metropolitan Magazine* to report on the Mexican Revolution, he won national celebrity for his reporting, and out of this experience grew his first book, *Insurgent Mexico* (1914). His news reports on World War I, written for the same magazine, were republished as *The War in Eastern Europe* (1916). During 1916, also, a book of his poems was published, entitled *Tamburlaine and Other Poems*. He was an enthusiastic observer and supporter of the October Revolution in Russia, became a friend of Lenin, and wrote propaganda material for the Bolsheviks. After his return to the United States, he wrote *Ten Days That Shook the World* (1919), an eyewitness account of the Russian revolution and his most important book. After his expulsion from the Socialist Party in 1919, Reed founded the Communist Party in America, wrote its manifesto, and edited its newspaper, *The Voice of Labor*. Again he left America for Russia, was refused readmission to the United States, and remained in Russia until he died of typhus in 1920.

Reese, Lizette Woodworth (1856–1935),   teacher, poet, memoirist. Reese, born in Maryland, taught school for forty-five years. She published several small collections: *A Branch of May* (1887), *A Handful of Lavender* (1891), *A Quiet Road* (1896), *A Wayside Lute* (1909), *Spicewood* (1920), *Wild Cherry* (1923), *Selected Poems* (1926), *Little Henrietta* (1927), *White April and Other Poems* (1930), *Pastures and Other Poems* (1933), and *The Old House in the Country* (1936). She also wrote two autobiographical volumes, *A Victorian Village* (1929) and *The York Road* (1931).

regionalism.   Regionalism in literature is as old as the first colonies. The geographical, religious, and national differences of the original settlements in America inspired sentiments of separateness, and these were accentuated by the formation of separate states, by westward expansion, and by the Civil War. The size of the country made regionalism inevitable. The distance from Boston to New York is about the same as the distance from London to Paris; from New York to Los Angeles, about the same as from Paris to Teheran. Further, as immigrants from different cultural and ethnic backgrounds settled different portions of the land, the differences occasioned by geography were in many instances increased by differences in population.

The fact of regionalism is reflected in virtually all periods by the differences in literature produced in more or less separable and coherent areas: New England, the Middle Atlantic states, the South, the old Southwest, the Midwest, the Southwest, the West, the Far West, and the Northwest. Only briefly did a recognition of this diversity manifest itself as a literary movement, in the LOCAL COLOR writers of the later 19th century, and this was in part an extension of the drive toward a truly national literature that arose with the patriotic fervor of the Revolution and continued strong to at least the beginning of the 20th century. In the years since the local color period, many writers have continued to draw strength from regional differences and, increasingly, from pockets of ethnic and cultural differences within those regions.

Reid, [Thomas] Mayne (1818–1883),   novelist, journalist, actor. Born in Ireland, Reid lived in America from 1840 to 1850 and again from 1867 to 1870, but he wrote about the American frontier and his adventures as an officer of the U.S. Army in the Mexican War in books such as *The Rifle Rangers* (2 v. 1850). He wrote over ninety titles, including such popular books for boys as *The Scalp Hunters* (1851) and *The Boy Hunters* (1852), and romances like *The Quadroon* (1852). Especially popular was *Afloat in the Forest* (1866), the story of a family adrift on the Amazon. A friend of EDGAR ALLAN POE, he wrote "A Dead Man Defended" in *Onward* (April 1869) in answer to Poe's critics.

Reid, Whitelaw (1837–1912),   newspaperman, editor, diplomat, historian. Reid, born in Ohio, was a war correspondent who wrote notable dispatches on the fall of Richmond and the assassination of Lincoln. With the close of the fighting he toured the South, reporting his observations in *After the War* (1866). For a time he owned and supervised cotton plantations in two Southern states. He then returned to the North and completed a history of *Ohio in the War* (1868).

In 1868 Reid joined the staff of the New York *Tribune*, then edited by HORACE GREELEY. He was made managing editor in the following year. When Greeley ran for president against Grant (1872), Reid took charge of the paper and campaigned vigorously in its columns for him. In 1881 he placed JOHN HAY in charge of the paper and turned much of his attention to politics. He was appointed minister to France by Benjamin Harrison; McKinley and Theodore Roosevelt both sent him on special missions abroad; Roosevelt appointed him ambassador to England. Reid's other books include *Our New Duties* (1899), *Problems of Expansion* (1900), and *American and English Studies* (1913). Royal Cortissoz wrote *The Life of Whitelaw Reid* (2 v. 1921). Reid's son, Ogden Mills Reid (1882–1947), became editor of the *Tribune* after his father died.

Reiner, Max.   See TAYLOR CALDWELL.

Reitzel, Robert (1849–1898),   poet, polemicist, lecturer, editor, translator. Born in Germany, he wandered all over the U.S. as a lecturer and settled down in Detroit as the editor of the weekly *Der arme Teufel* (1884). This served as an appropriate medium for his writings, in prose and verse, on many subjects. He was a fiery and witty crusader who espoused social democracy, world citizenship, materialism, the workers' movement, and other causes. Long after his death a collection of his writings in this magazine was made, *Des armen Teufels gesammelte Schriften* (1913). A posthumous autobiography also appeared, *Abenteuer eines Gruenen* (Adventures of a Greenhorn, 1902).

The Reivers (1962),   a novel by WILLIAM FAULKNER. Set in 1905, this humorous tale involves an eleven-year-old,

Lucius Priest; Boon Hogganbeck, the Priest family's retainer; and Ned, their African-American coachman. These three "reivers," or plunderers, "steal" Lucius's grandfather's new motorcar and set off for Memphis, where they stay at a brothel. They swap the car for a race horse, and the intrigue that follows is the basis for the plot of this near-farcical addition to the saga of YOKNAPATAWPHA COUNTY.

religion in U.S. literature.   Many European settlers migrated to America to secure freedom of religious worship, but this quest was no guarantee of their toleration of other faiths. Of all the colonies Maryland, with its mixture of Protestants and Catholics; Rhode Island, with its chartered freedom of conscience; and Pennsylvania, with its Quaker creed, came closest to complete tolerance of other religions. In addition, the Dutch in New Amsterdam allowed freedom of worship.

The history of religion in the United States has been, for practically all sects, a movement away from formal theology toward what is most often a placid and nondogmatic faith. Theologically this has meant a revulsion against the doctrine of man's insignificance and innate depravity, a greater acceptance of the majesty and loving-kindness of God. In the days of the Enlightenment, of which THOMAS JEFFERSON is a major representative, reason was stressed in matters of belief and biblical interpretation. Later, Pragmatism and other practical forms of thinking had great appeal, and some clergymen gladly sought a union between theology and psychiatry. The Bible is still America's greatest best seller, although there is no longer the same extent of close reading of its verses that characterized the Puritan era. With the weakening of sectarianism and a deeper realization of the essential unity of mankind, members of the clergy have led Americans toward fellowship with other creeds and toward a deeper interest in social and economic problems.

Religious education is conducted outside the classrooms of public schools. In the churches themselves, aside from parochial schools, instruction is generally given in Sunday School classes. To assist in such instruction a vast literature has grown up. During the 19th century Sunday School books acquired an unfavorable reputation because of their frequent saccharinity and lack of realism. More recent books of this type are much more skillfully written.

Religious writing in America began with Puritan, Quaker, and other refugees. Native-born theologians began with men like the later Mathers and have been vigorously represented by a long line of writers. A brief selection of outstanding books in this field might include John Cotton, *A Model of Church and Civil Power* (1634) and *The Keys of the Kingdom of Heaven* (1644); Thomas Hooker, *A Survey of the Sum of Church Discipline* (1648); John Eliot, *The Christian Commonwealth* (1659); Increase Mather, *The Order of the Gospel* (1700); Cotton Mather, MAGNALIA CHRISTI AMERICANA (1702); Jonathan Edwards, SINNERS IN THE HANDS OF AN ANGRY GOD (1741) and FREEDOM OF THE WILL (1754); John Woolman, *Works* (including his *Journal*, 1774); Ethan Allen, REASON THE ONLY ORACLE OF MAN (1784); Joseph Priestley, *Discourses on the Evidences of Revealed Religion* (1794);

Timothy Dwight, *Theology* (5 v. 1818); Mary Baker Eddy, SCIENCE AND HEALTH (1875); Asa Gray, *Natural Science and Religion* (1880); H. W. Beecher, *Evolution and Religion* (2 v. 1885); Robert G. Ingersoll, *Why I Am an Agnostic* (1896); William James, VARIETIES OF RELIGIOUS EXPERIENCE (1902); George Santayana, LIFE OF REASON (5 v. 1905–06, 1 v. 1954); Josiah Royce, *Sources of Religious Insight* (1912); Felix Adler, *An Ethical View of Life* (1918); Harry Emerson Fosdick, *Christianity and Progress* (1922); Alfred North Whitehead, *Religion in the Making* (1926); Rufus M. Jones, *New Studies in Mystical Religion* (1927); Reinhold Niebuhr, *Moral Man and Immoral Society* (1932) and *Beyond Tragedy* (1938); John Dewey, *A Common Faith* (1934); Paul Blanshard, *American Freedom and Catholic Power* (1949); and H. W. Schneider, *Religion in 20th-Century America* (1952).

Inspirational volumes have enjoyed a tremendous sale; those with a psychiatric slant have found special popularity in recent years. Most of them are sincere endeavors to help people in mental or spiritual distress, but their language is closer to the brisk business world than to either the ministry or medicine. Religion has naturally always fascinated the storyteller. Some of their works more directly concerned with life in the Americas are Nathaniel Hawthorne, THE SCARLET LETTER (1850) and THE BLITHEDALE ROMANCE (1852); Harriet Beecher Stowe, THE MINISTER'S WOOING (1859); Edward Eggleston, THE CIRCUIT RIDER (1874) and ROXY (1878); Harold Frederic, THE DAMNATION OF THERON WARE (1896); Charles Sheldon, IN HIS STEPS (1897); Helen R. Martin, TILLIE A. MENNONITE MAID (1904); Winston Churchill, THE INSIDE OF THE CUP (1913); William Dean Howells, *The Leatherwood God* (1916); Sinclair Lewis, ELMER GANTRY (1927); Willa Cather, DEATH COMES FOR THE ARCHBISHOP (1927) and SHADOWS ON THE ROCK (1931); Thornton Wilder, THE BRIDGE OF SAN LUIS REY (1927) and *Heaven's My Destination* (1935); Oliver La Farge, LAUGHING BOY (1929) and *The Enemy Gods* (1937); O. E. Rölvaag, THEIR FATHER'S GOD (1931); Lloyd Douglas, *Green Light* (1935); Pearl Buck, *The Exile* (1936); LeGrand Cannon, *A Mighty Fortress* (1937); Gwethalyn Graham, *Earth and High Heaven* (1944); Jessamyn West, *The Friendly Persuasion* (1945); Theodore Dreiser, *The Bulwark* (1946); Henry Morton Robinson, *The Cardinal* (1950); John Updike, *A Month of Sundays* (1975); and J. F. Powers, *Wheat That Springeth Green* (1988).

The clergy has as a rule been handled tenderly on the stage and in the movies. An early and sympathetic treatment was James A. Herne's THE REVEREND GRIFFITH DAVENPORT (1899). During the 1920s, however, ministers—rarely priests or rabbis—were sometimes shown in all too human roles, like the minister in John Colton and Clemence Randolph's *Rain* (1922), based on Somerset Maugham's story. Other plays on religious themes are Percy MacKaye, *Jeanne d'Arc* (1905); Charles Rann Kennedy, *The Servant in the House* (1908) and *The Terrible Meek* (1912); William Hurlbut, *The Bride of the Lamb* (1926); Eugene O'Neill, LAZARUS LAUGHED (1927) and *Days Without End* (1933); Sidney Howard and Charles MacArthur, *Salvation* (1928); Marc Connelly, THE GREEN PASTURES (1930); T. S. Eliot, MURDER IN THE CATHEDRAL (1935) and THE COCKTAIL PARTY (1949); and Ten-

nessee Williams, *The Night of the Iguana* (1959). Radio and television have proven hospitable to a friendly presentation of religious themes, both in direct discourses by clergymen of all faiths and in occasional dramatizations.

In poetry one finds early examples such as Michael Wigglesworth's THE DAY OF DOOM (1662), but often its ecstatic Calvinism, as in Jonathan Edwards, reached poetic heights in prose more strikingly than in verse. But in the 19th century spiritual insight is manifest in Emerson, Whitman, and Whittier; and it continues in 20th-century poets like Stephen Vincent Benét, Sandburg, Hart Crane, and Mark Van Doren. Religion has provided important substance for major poets as recent as Robert Lowell and John Berryman. The first periodical devoted exclusively to news of religion was probably the *Christian Magazine*, founded in 1802 by the Rev. Elias Smith. It lasted for two years, then was replaced in 1806 by the HERALD OF GOSPEL LIBERTY, the precursor of innumerable similar magazines. Among important recent and contemporary religious magazines are the following: *America, American Judaism, American Lutheran, Catholic World, Chicago Jewish Forum, Christian Advocate, Christian Century,* CHRISTIAN HERALD, *Christian Register, The Churchman, Commentary,* COMMONWEAL, *Forward, Jubilee, The Living Church, The Lutheran, Messenger of the Sacred Heart, The Pastor, Presbyterian Life, Presbyterian Outlook, Pulpit Digest, The Pulpiteer, Religion in Life, The Sign,* and *Voice of St. Jude.* One great newspaper, the *Christian Science Monitor,* strikingly represents a religious viewpoint in the selection and description of news. See THE BIBLE IN THE U.S.

Remarkable Providences (1684), an essay by INCREASE MATHER. See AN ESSAY FOR THE RECORDING OF ILLUSTRIOUS PROVIDENCES RELATING TO WITCHCRAFTS AND POSSESSIONS.

Remarque, Erich Maria (1898–1970), novelist. Remarque was working as a sports writer in Germany when he wrote his first and most celebrated novel, *All Quiet on the Western Front* (1929), a realistic depiction of war based on the author's own experiences. He lived in Switzerland for a while and was permanently exiled by the Nazis. He came to the United States in 1939 and became a citizen in 1947. Among his later books were *The Road Back* (1931), *Three Comrades* (1937), *Flotsam* (1941), *Arch of Triumph* (1946), *A Time to Love and a Time to Die* (1954), *Black Obelisk* (1957), and *Heaven Has No Favorites* (1961). He usually wrote about the sufferings of soldiers and of veterans after the wars.

Remington, Frederic [Sackrider] (1861–1909), artist, writer. Remington attended the Yale School of Fine Arts, then worked on ranches in the West and brought back many striking sketches of cowboys and Indians in action. He soon began to write stories and sketches intended largely as vehicles for his illustrations. After he did the drawings for Theodore Roosevelt's *Ranch Life and the Hunting Trail* (1888), his reputation was established. Remington's books include *Pony Tracks* (1895), *Crooked Trails* (1898), *Sundown Leflare* (1899), *Stories of Peace and War* (1899), *Men with the Bark On* (1900), *John Ermine of the Yellowstone* (1902), and *The Way of an Indian* (1906). Collections of his pictures include *Drawings* (1897),

Remington's Frontier Sketches (1898), *A Bunch of Buckskins* (1900), *Western Types* (1902), and *Done in the Open* (1902).

Remus, Uncle.   See UNCLE REMUS.

Renascence (1912),   a poem by EDNA ST. VINCENT MILLAY, thought to have been written when Millay was seventeen.

Repplier, Agnes (1855–1950),   essayist, historian, biographer, poet, memoirist. She was an inveterate Philadelphian and wrote *Philadelphia—The Place and the People* (1898). In later years she wrote *In Our Convent Days* (1905) and several biographies that showed the deep influence of her convent training: *The Life of Père Marquette* (1929), *Mère Marie of the Ursulines* (1931), and *Junipero Serro* (1933, rev. 1947). Among her other works are *Books and Men* (1888), *Points of View* (1891), *Essays in Miniature* (1892), *Essays in Idleness* (1893), *The Fireside Sphinx* (1901), *Compromises* (1904), *A Happy Half-Century* (1908), *Americans and Others* (1912), *The Cat* (1912), *Counter Currents* (1915), *Points of Friction* (1920), *Under Dispute* (1924), *In Pursuit of Laughter* (1936), and *Eight Decades* (1937).

Representative Men (1850),   biographical sketches by RALPH WALDO EMERSON. These were lectures delivered in the United States and England from 1845 to 1848. The volume discusses Shakespeare the poet, Plato the philosopher, Goethe the writer, Swedenborg the mystic, Napoleon the man of the world, and Montaigne the skeptic. There is also an introductory piece, "On the Uses of Great Men." Unlike Thomas Carlyle, who in *On Heroes, Hero Worship and the Heroic in History* (1841) wrote admiringly of the dominance and ruthlessness of heroic figures, Emerson saw heroes as representative of their time and nation.

Requiem for a Nun (1951),   a novel by WILLIAM FAULKNER. Written in three prose sections, which provide the background, and three acts, which present the drama in the courthouse and jail, *Requiem for a Nun* centers on Temple Drake, one of the main characters of SANCTUARY. In the interval of eight years separating the events of the two novels, Temple has married Gowan Stevens and borne two children. She is being blackmailed by Pete, brother of her lover in *Sanctuary*, and is planning to run away with him when Nancy Manningoe, her black servant, kills Temple's youngest child. Her attempts to gain a gubernatorial pardon for Nancy finally bring out Temple's own involvement in and responsibility for the crime.

Resistance to Civil Government (1849),   an essay by HENRY DAVID THOREAU. The title is usually given as CIVIL DISOBEDIENCE.

Responsibilities of the Novelist, The (1903),   an essay by FRANK NORRIS. Like his contemporary, Hamlin Garland, Norris proclaimed that fiction has a purpose beyond mere narrative. He rejects the realism of William Dean Howells and Henry James as concerned with trivia, "the drama of a broken teacup." In its place Norris offers "romance," which portrays characters larger than life controlled by forces greater than they. Romance, he argues, will appeal not to the aesthete or the artist alone, but to the people—the responsibility of the novelist lies in appealing to the people.

Retrieved Reformation, A (in *Roads of Destiny*, 1909), a story by O. HENRY. It relates the ironic fate of Jimmy Valentine, a burglar who makes up his mind to reform but is foiled when he shows his skill in opening a safe during an emergency. Jimmy is said to have been modeled on Jimmy Connors, O. Henry's fellow prisoner in the Ohio State Penitentiary. Paul Armstrong based his successful play ALIAS JIMMY VALENTINE (1909) on the story.

Return of Peter Grimm, The (1911),   a play by DAVID BELASCO. Grimm, a botanist and old bachelor, completely mistakes the character of his worthless nephew Frederik and even extracts a promise from his foster daughter Kathrine that she will marry him. Peter dies suddenly at the end of Act I, then comes back to life determined to prevent or undo the mischievous marriage he has arranged. He is successful in the end.

Revere, Paul (1735–1818),   patriot, craftsman, cartoonist. Revere, a successful silversmith in his native Boston, experimented with engraving and portrait painting, carved frames, and manufactured false teeth. His greatest interest, however, was in politics, and when trouble arose between England and her colonies he turned out crude but effective cartoons for the Revolutionary cause. Of his many patriotic services the most famous was his midnight ride from Boston to Lexington on April 18–19, 1775, to warn the colonists there that the Redcoats were approaching from Boston. There are probably few poems as well known in America as Longfellow's account of the ride (see THE MIDNIGHT RIDE OF PAUL REVERE). As a military man Revere was less successful than as courier and craftsman. After the war he spent his time making beautiful gold and silverware, experimenting with engraving processes, casting church bells, making cannon, and discovering a process for rolling sheet copper. His silverware is some of the finest that America has produced, and many examples are displayed in the Boston Museum of Fine Arts.

Paul Revere's Own Account of His Midnight Ride, April 18–19, 1775, with a short account of his life by S.E. Morison, was printed in *Old South Leaflet No. 222* (1922). Other accounts are *The Life of Colonel Paul Revere* (2 v. 1891) by Elbridge H. Goss; *Paul Revere and His Engravings* (1901) by William L. Andrews; *The True Story of Paul Revere* (1905) by Charles F. Gettemy; *Paul Revere and the World He Lived In* (1942) and *America's Paul Revere* (1946) by Esther Forbes; and *Paul Revere and the Minute Men* (1950) by Dorothy Canfield Fisher. Revere figures vividly in Esther Forbes' novel *Johnny Tremaine* (1943).

Reverend Griffith Davenport, The (1899),   by JAMES A. HERNE. Herne based this play on the novel *An Unofficial Patriot* (1894), by Helen H. Gardener. Of the manuscript of the play nothing survives except Act 4, but the plot has been reconstructed from contemporary accounts and from data supplied by some of the surviving actors. The play, laid in the Civil War period, showed a Methodist circuit rider who owns a large plantation in the South but hates slavery. Davenport frees his slaves and incurs the ill will of his neighbors. He has numerous misadventures, including capture by a Confederate contingent of which his son is captain.

Reveries of a Bachelor, or, A Book of the Heart (1850), by Ik Marvel (DONALD G. MITCHELL). The book contains four reveries, the first of which appeared in the *Southern Literary Messenger* (1849). A sequel entitled *Dream Life* appeared in 1851. All the papers are mildly sentimental, gently humorous. They reveal a bachelor's thoughts of love and marriage; the last tells of a happy conclusion when he marries. The scenes are in city and country, in America and abroad. The book became widely popular.

Reviewer, The, a little magazine published in Richmond, Virginia, from 1921 to 1925. Its stated purpose was to showcase Southern literature. Its editors included EMILY CLARK, JAMES BRANCH CABELL, and PAUL GREEN.

Review of Reviews, The. Founded in 1890 as the American counterpart to a British magazine of the same name, this periodical took on an independent existence when ALBERT SHAW became editor (1894). Always deeply interested in European affairs, it was influential for many years but gradually faded away. In 1937 it merged with another dying magazine, *The Little Digest*. The combination, called *The Digest*, suspended publication in 1938.

Revolt of Mother, The (1890), a short story by MARY E. WILKINS FREEMAN. A Yankee farmer faces a revolt by his wife, who insists that some of the money he spends on agricultural equipment and big barns be spent instead on her and their young son and daughter. He yields after she and her children set up housekeeping in the new barn.

Revolutionary War. See AMERICAN REVOLUTION IN U.S. LITERATURE.

Rexford, Eben E[ugene] (1848–1916), poet, writer on gardening. Rexford published several collections of verse—*Brother and Lover* (1886), *Pansies and Rosemary* (1911), and others—as well as several books on gardening. He is chiefly remembered for his 1873 poem "Silver Threads Among the Gold," set to music by Hart Pease Danks.

Rexroth, Kenneth (1905–1982), poet, translator, critic. Rexroth was a largely self-educated man who absorbed and consolidated the ideas of others. Among his volumes of verse are *In What Hour?* (1940); *The Phoenix and the Tortoise* (1944); *The Dragon and the Unicorn* (1952); *In Defense of the Earth* (1956); *Natural Numbers: New and Selected Poems* (1963); *The Complete Collected Shorter Poems* (1967); *The Heart's Garden, The Garden's Heart* (1967); *The Collected Longer Poems* (1968); *The Spark in the Tinder of Knowing* (1968); *Sky Sea Birds Trees Earth House Beasts Flowers* (1970); and *New Poems* (1974). His essays and criticism include *The Alternative Society: Essays from the Other World* (1970), *American Poetry in the Twentieth Century* (1971), and *Communalism: From Its Origins to the 20th Century* (1975). He edited the poems of D. H. Lawrence (1948) and CZESLAW MILOSZ (1973) among others and translated from Japanese, Chinese, Spanish, and classical Greek and Latin. He wrote plays and a ballet, *Original Sin*, performed in 1961 by the San Francisco Ballet.

Reyes, Alfonso (1889–1959), essayist and poet. After receiving his law degree in his native Mexico in 1913, Reyes lived in Spain and served as a diplomat in France, Argentina, and Brazil. He returned to Mexico in 1939. Part of the Mexican intellectual group known as the *Ateneo de la Juventud*, Reyes was an authority on Spanish literature, author of *Capítulos de Literatura Española* (1939, 1945). His best-known book is *Visión de Anahuac, 1519* (1917), a depiction of Aztec civilization before the Spaniards came. His collections of essays include *Pasado Immediato y Otros Ensayos* (1941), *Ultima Tule* (1942), and *Tentativas y Orientaciones* (1944). His *El Deslinde* (1944) is an introduction to literary theory, and *Letras de la Nueva España* (1948) and *La X en la Frente* (1952) are studies of Mexico. *Ifigenia Cruel* (1924) is a dramatic poem. English translations of his collected essays are *Mexico in a Nutshell* (1964, tr. by C. Ramsdell) and *The Position of America* (1971, tr. by H. de Onis).

Reyles, Carlos (1868–1938), novelist. Reyles was born into a prominent family of Uruguay. With the advantage of inherited wealth, he was able to devote his life to writing. His early naturalistic novels such as *Por la Vida* (1888) and *Beba* (1894) were attempts to apply the theories of Zola. *La raza de Cain* (1900) is a study in abnormal psychology; *El Terruño* (1916) is a contrast between urban and rural life. His best-known novel, *El Embrujo de Sevilla* (1922, tr. by J. LeClercq as *Castanets*, 1929) is a lyrical novel in which the Andalusian city plays a role. *El Gaucho Florido* (1932) is a realistic treatment of rural life.

Reynolds, Jeremiah N. (1799?–1858), explorer, writer. Reynolds is chiefly remembered for the influence he exerted on research in the Antarctic and on Melville and Poe. Melville probably read Reynolds's account of a fierce white whale called Mocha Dick in the *Knickerbocker Magazine* (1839). Poe introduced Reynolds's polar theory into his UNPARALLELED ADVENTURES OF ONE HANS PFAAL (1835) and used a portion of an address that Reynolds made to Congress (published in 1836) in his NARRATIVE OF ARTHUR GORDON PYM (1838). Reynolds's fantastic notions apparently stirred Poe deeply; when he lay dying in a Baltimore hospital, he cried over and over, "Reynolds! Reynolds!" Reynolds wrote about the *Voyage of the U.S. Frigate Potomac, 1831–34* (1835). He also prepared the pamphlet *A South Sea Expedition* (1837) and undoubtedly stimulated interest in exploring the southern parts of the Atlantic and Pacific oceans.

Reynolds, John (1788–1865), novelist, historian. Born in Pennsylvania, he grew up on the frontier, serving in the Illinois state legislature, as governor, and as member of Congress. His *Pioneer History of Illinois* (1852) and *My Own Times* (1855) detail frontier life. *The Life and Adventures of John Kelly* (1853) is a semiautobiographical novel.

Reznikoff, Charles (1894–1976), poet. Reznikoff was an OBJECTIVIST. His lyrics are collected in *Inscriptions* (1959) and *By the Waters of Manhattan* (1962). Reznikoff completed work on only a few years of a projected four-volume history to be called *Testimony: The United States 1885–1915* (1965). *Holocaust* (1975) is a collection of poems based on the Nuremberg trials. *By the Well of Living and Seeing*

(1974, ed. Seamus Cooney) is a selected volume of poetry. *Family Chronicle* (1969) is a prose description of the lives of poor New York Jews.

Rhodes scholarships, founded by Cecil John Rhodes (1853–1902) to provide study at Oxford for men from British colonies, the United States, and Germany. The first recipients were selected in 1903. The German awards were suspended during World War I and eliminated after World War II. Scholarships for women were added in 1976.

Rhodes, Eugene Manlove (1869–1934), cowboy, government scout, writer. Rhodes, born in Nebraska, is regarded as one of the leading writers of Western stories. Many of his stories appeared in the *Saturday Evening Post* and led to creation of a Rhodes cult. His best-known story was "The Little Eohippus" (*Saturday Evening Post*, November–December, 1912), which later was expanded into a novel and published as *Bransford in Arcadia* (1914); in 1917 it was reprinted as *Bransford of Rainbow Range*. Rhodes was also a facile verse writer. Among his principal books are *Good Men and True* (1910), *West Is West* (1917), *Beyond the Desert* (1934), and *The Proud Sheriff* (1935).

Rhodes, James Ford (1848–1927), newspaperman, businessman, historian. Rhodes was born in Cleveland and all through his career as a businessman in the coal and iron industries was deeply interested in American history, which he viewed against the background of Henry Thomas Buckle's scientifically written *History of Civilization* (1857–61). His reputation rests chiefly on his most elaborate production, done after his retirement from business, a *History of the United States* (7 v. 1893–1906), which covered the years from 1850 up to the administration of Theodore Roosevelt. Two later volumes continued the narrative to 1908 (1919, 1922). His one-volume *History of the Civil War* (1917) won a Pulitzer Prize.

Rhodora, The: On Being Asked, Whence Is the Flower? (completed 1834, first published in the *Western Messenger*, July 1839), a poem by RALPH WALDO EMERSON. The poem has been variously interpreted. One critic explained that the poem represents Emerson's most effective expression of "the relations of the Primal Mind to the Individual Mind," and others have marked its transcendental flavor. On the surface the poem seems simple enough. Emerson says that the shrub called the rhodora is beautiful even if no one sees it, but he is thankful that God brought him there to see it.

Rhys, Jean (1894–1979), novelist, short-story writer. Rhys was born Jean Williams on the island of Dominica, West Indies, of a family settled for several generations there. After going to Europe for schooling at age sixteen, she lived most of the rest of her life there, but references to her native region pervade her work. Ford Madox Ford, who suggested her pen name, wrote the introduction to her first publication, *The Left Bank and Other Stories* (1927). Her novels *After Leaving Mr. Mackenzie* (1930), *Voyage in the Dark* (1934), and *Good Morning, Midnight* (1939) all treat the problems of women forced by economic necessity to be dependent on men, and many of the protagonists have West Indian backgrounds. In *Wide Sargasso Sea* (1966), Rhys imagines the life story of the Creole

bride from the West Indies hidden away by Mr. Rochester in Brontë's *Jane Eyre*. This most successful Rhys novel uses West Indies descriptions and symbolism. Two later story collections are *Tigers are Better-Looking* (1968) and *Sleep It Off Lady* (1976). Her unfinished autobiography, *Smile Please* (1979), was published after her death.

Ribaut [Ribault?], Jean (1520?–1565), French navigator, explorer. See RENÉ GOULAIN DE LAUDONNIÈRE.

Ribeiro, João Ubaldo (1940–), novelist. In his best-known novel, *Viva o povo brasileiro* (1984, tr. *An Invincible Memory* by the author, 1988), Ribeiro treats the quest for a national identity throughout the history of his native Brazil from 1647 to the late 1970s. He also translated his *Sergeant Getulio* (1971, tr. 1984) for publication in English.

Ribeyro, Julio Ramon (1929–1994), short-story writer, novelist. Born in Peru, Ribeyro lived in Paris after 1960. His short fiction follows classical European models of style to portray desolate urban life. His collected stories *Cuentos Completos*, containing 86 fictions written from 1952 to 1994, were published in 1994, the same year he was awarded the most important literary award in Latin America, the Juan Rulfo Prize. *Los Geniecillos Dominicales* (1969) is a novel about nightlife in Lima. *Confusión en la Prefectura* (1975) and *Cambio de Guardia* (1976) are political novels. *Prosas Apátridas* (1975) is a collection of 200 short, witty prose pieces, and his diaries were published in two volumes as *La Tentación del Fracaso* (1992 and 1993).

Rice, Alice Hegan [Caldwell] (1870–1942), Kentucky-born and known chiefly for her first book, MRS. WIGGS OF THE CABBAGE PATCH (1901), she produced more than a dozen novels, three volumes of short stories, and an autobiography, *The Inky Way* (1940). Her books include *Lovey Mary* (1903), *Sandy* (1905), *Captain June* (1907), *Mr. Opp* (1909), *A Romance of Billy Goat Hill* (1912), *Miss Mink's Soldier and Other Stories* (1918), *Quinn* (1921), *The Buffer* (1929), *Mr. Pete and Co.* (1933), and *The Lark Legacy* (1935).

Rice, Anne (1941–), novelist. Raised in New Orleans, Anne Rice at birth was named Howard Allen O'Brien. She had her first name changed to Anne in childhood and later became Anne Rice when she married Stan Rice. Anne Rice was educated at San Francisco State College and lived in San Francisco until 1988, when she and her husband moved to New Orleans. Each of the volumes of her vampire trilogy—*Interview with the Vampire* (1976), *The Vampire Lestat* (1985), and *The Queen of the Damned* (1985)—has been highly successful. Critics have praised her adept mixture of Gothic horror and eroticism, and her skill in manipulating her popular fictions in a context of believable people and places. *The Witching Hour* (1990), continues her critical and popular success.

Writing as Ann Rice, she has published two historical novels, *The Feast of All Saints* (1979), set in New Orleans in 1840, and *Cry to Heaven* (1982), set in Italy. Writing as Anne Rampling, she has published two contemporary novels, *Exit to Eden* (1985) and *Belinda* (1986). Writing as A. N. Roquelaure, she has also published pornographic novels, beginning with *The Claiming of Sleeping Beauty* (1983).

Rice, Cale Young (1872–1943),   poet, dramatist, novelist, critic. Upon marrying ALICE HEGAN, a fellow Kentuckian and popular novelist, Rice gave up teaching to devote himself to poetry. He published twenty-six volumes of verse and poetic drama, among them *From Dusk to Dusk* (1898), *Song Surf* (1900), *Many Gods* (1910), and *Far Quests* (1912). *Yolanda of Cypress* (1907), a poetic drama, was made into an opera in 1929. *Turn About Tales* (1920) and *Winners and Losers* (1925) are books of short stories written in collaboration with his wife. Rice also wrote novels and an autobiography, *Bridging the Years* (1939). After the death of his wife, Rice committed suicide.

Rice, Elmer (1892–1967),   playwright, director, novelist. Rice, born in New York City, gave up his law career early, although he continued to be interested in questions of censorship, arbitration, and legal rights. ON TRIAL (1914), Rice's first play—the first stage production to employ motion-picture techniques—was a hit. Other successful plays followed. THE ADDING MACHINE (1923) dextrously adapts German expressionist techniques in a satire on the growing robotization of man. Rice stressed sheer realism, however, in STREET SCENE (1929, Pulitzer Prize), which depicts slum conditions; *The Left Bank* (1931), a portrayal of ineffectual expatriates; and COUNSELOR-AT-LAW (1931), an unflattering picture of the legal profession. The Depression and the Nazi and Soviet menace are central to *We, the People* (1933), *Judgment Day* (1934), *Between Two Worlds* (1934), *Two on an Island* (1940), and *Flight to the West* (1940). These later plays were less successful, but *Dream Girl* (1945) and an operatic version of *Street Scene* (1947), for which KURT WEILL supplied the music, were very popular. Rice also wrote several novels, including *A Voyage to Purilia* (1930) and *The Show Must Go On* (1949). His autobiography, *Minority Report*, was published in 1963.

Rice, Grantland (1880–1954),   newspaperman, sportswriter, poet. Rice, born in Tennessee, wrote a newspaper column called "The Sportlight," which became a syndicated feature in 1930. He also wrote verse with facility and wit. Two collections (1917 and 1941) contain a number of pieces that have been very popular. He described his life entertainingly in *The Tumult and the Shouting: My Life in Sport* (1954). *The Final Answer and Other Poems* (1955) was edited by John Kieran.

Rice, T. D.   See JIM CROW.

Rich, Adrienne (1919–   ),   poet. Rich was born in Baltimore and educated at Radcliffe, where during her senior year she had her first volume of poetry, *A Change of World* (1951), accepted by the Yale Series of Younger Poets. In his preface to the volume, W. H. AUDEN described the work as "neatly and modestly dressed." Among the pieces in this apprentice work is "Aunt Jennifer's Tigers." She married Alfred Conrad two years later and bore three sons before she was thirty. A second collection, *The Diamond Cutters*, appeared in 1955. A year's residence in the Netherlands (1961–62) brought contact with contemporary Dutch poetry, and a number of her translations were published in *Necessities of Life* (1966).

The difficulties of combining the female role with poetic achievement, referred to in her journals of that time, began to surface in her poetry, beginning with *Snapshots of a Daughter-in-Law* (1963). With this collection she also began to date individual poems as though to emphasize their role as a record of her evolving ideas. Rich continued to wrestle with the tension in poems collected in *Leaflets* (1969) and *The Will to Change* (1971). The Vietnam War and her experience in teaching New York City minority youth further heightened her political awareness. Her poetic techniques evolved into a more jagged and urgent style. After her husband's suicide in 1970 she became increasingly involved in the women's movement and in the foreword to her second essay collection, *Blood, Bread and Poetry* (1986), she identified herself as a radical feminist and a lesbian. In an earlier essay "It Is the Lesbian in Us . . ." (1976), she had defined the term "lesbian" as not limited to sexual experience but as a "primary intensity between women" and the creative force that "drives us to feel imaginatively, render in language, grasp, the full connection between woman and woman." Some of her other prose is collected in *Of Woman Born: Motherhood as Experience and Institution* (1976) and *On Lies, Secrets, and Silence* (1979). Her poetry collections include *Selected Poems* (1967); *Diving into the Wreck* (1973); *Poems: Selected and New* (1975); *The Dream of a Common Language* (1978); *A Wild Patience Has Taken Me This Far* (1981); *Your Native Land, Your Life* (1986); and *Time's Power* (1989). *Adrienne Rich's Poetry and Prose*, edited by Barbara Charlesworth Gelpi and Albert Gelpi, appeared in 1995. *Midnight Salvage: Poems 1995–1998* appeared in 1999 and *Fox: Poems 1998–2000* in 2001.

Rich, Louise Dickinson (1903–1991),   teacher, writer. Born in Massachusetts, Rich and her husband, Ralph Eugene Rich, lived for six years in the deep woods of Maine. Her account of her experiences, *We Took to the Woods* (1942), became a nonfiction best seller. Among her later books are *Happy the Land* (1946), *The Start of the Trail* (1949), *My Neck of the Woods* (1950), *Trail to the North* (1952), *Only Parent* (1953), *Innocence Under the Elms* (1955), and *The Peninsula* (1958). She was also the author of many historical books for juveniles.

Rich, Richard.   See NEWS FROM VIRGINIA.

Richard Carvel (1899),   a historical novel by WINSTON CHURCHILL. One of the most popular novels about the Revolution, *Richard Carvel* is an account of adventures aboard a slaver from which he is rescued by JOHN PAUL JONES.

Richard Cory (1897),   a poem by EDWIN ARLINGTON ROBINSON. This sixteen-line Browningesque portrait is one of the poet's admired works. It is not only a portrait but also a narrative and an epigram, telling of the suicide of a supposedly successful man.

Richard Hurdis (1838),   a novel by WILLIAM GILMORE SIMMS. See BORDER ROMANCES.

Richards, Laura Elizabeth [Howe] (1850–1943), children's author, poet, biographer. Richards, born in Boston, produced more than eighty titles. *Captain January* (1890) and *Tirra Lirra* (1932) are two of her popular children's books. The biography of her mother, *Julia Ward Howe* (1916), written in collaboration with her sisters, MAUD HOWE ELLIOT and FLORENCE

HOWE HALL, won a Pulitzer Prize. She also edited her father's letters and journals and wrote a biography, *Samuel Gridley Howe* (1935). *E.A.R.* (1936) is a biography of Edwin Arlington Robinson, and *Stepping Westward* (1931) is an autobiography. Some of her other books are *Five Mice* (1881), *Rita* (1900), *Snow White* (1900), *Geoffrey Strong* (1901), *Grandmother* (1907), *Florence Nightingale* (1909), *Miss Jinny* (1913), *Abigail Adams and Her Times* (1917), *Joan of Arc* (1919), *Honor Bright* (1920), *Star Bright* (1928), and *Laura Bridgman* (1928).

Richardson, Charles Francis (1851–1913), teacher, poet, literary historian. Richardson, born in Maine, published several miscellaneous volumes, including a collection of poems, *The Cross* (1879), but he is remembered chiefly as a pioneer in the study of American literature. He published a primer on the subject in 1878 before writing his *American Literature*, 1607–1885 (2 v. 1887–88).

Richardson, Jack C[arter] (1935–   ), playwright, novelist, short-story writer. *The Prodigal* (1960) is a play on the Orestes theme, interpreted as a struggle between idealism and political opportunism, and treated with wry, sophisticated humor. *Gallows Humor*, a tragicomedy, was seen in 1961. In the same year Richardson, who was born in New York City, published a novel, *The Prison Life of Harris Filmore*. Another, *Memoir of a Gambler*, appeared in 1980.

Richardson, John (1796–1852), soldier, writer. Born in Ontario, Richardson fought for the British in 1812 and after the war went to England and joined the British army. He wrote a careful account of *The War of 1812* (1842). Richardson returned to Canada, where he became Canadian correspondent of the *London Times*. For a time he also edited a magazine and was superintendent of police on the Welland Canal. He died in New York City in extreme poverty. His best-known work was a novel, *Wacousta, or, The Prophecy* (1832), which deals somewhat romantically with the PONTIAC conspiracy and is regarded as the beginning of Canadian fiction. He also wrote *Personal Memoirs* (1838), *Eight Years in Canada* (1847), and the poem *Tecumseh* (1828).

Richie, Helena. Chief character in MARGARET DELAND's novels *The Awakening of Helena Richie* (1906) and *The Iron Woman* (1911), usually regarded as her best work.

Richler, Mordecai (1931–2001), novelist. Born in the Jewish area around St. Urbain Street, Richler used the geography of his native Montreal in many of his most successful novels as well as in the autobiographical sketches collected in *The Street* (1969). After dropping out of college, Richler lived briefly in Paris and worked for the Canadian Broadcasting Company before settling in England (1959–1972) and becoming a writer. Some of his best-known work was published while he was living in England. The main character of *The Apprenticeship of Duddy Kravitz* (1959) is obsessed with acquiring wealth to escape the ghetto. *The Incomparable Atuk* (1963) and *Cocksure* (1968) are satirical fables. Jake Hersch of *St. Urbain's Horseman* (1971), a Canadian Jew on trial in London for crimes he did not commit, fantasizes about an avenger who will set things right and punish the real evildoers. Joshua Shapiro of *Joshua Then and Now* (1980) is haunted by his failure to take a stronger stand against fascism. *Solomon Gursky Was Here* (1989) deals with a wealthy family in ways reminiscent of MAGICAL REALISM. *Barney's Version*, with a hero that critics have compared to Richter, appeared in 1997. Richler's journalistic writings are collected in *Life at the Top* (1965), *Hunting Tigers Under Glass* (1968), *Shoveling Trouble* (1972), *Notes on an Endangered Species* (1974), *Images of Spain* (1977), *Fun with Dick and Jane* (1977), and *The Great Comic Book Heroes* (1978). *Broadsides: Reviews and Opinions* appeared in 1990. *Jacob Two-Two Meets the Hooded Fang* (1975) is a children's book. His other novels include *The Acrobats* (1954), *Son of a Smaller Hero* (1955), and *A Choice of Enemies* (1957). Richler has emerged as a spokesman for Quebec's English speakers in the controversy about language laws. *Oh Canada, Oh Quebec! Requiem for a Divided Country* (1992) speaks of this. *This Year in Jerusalem* (1994) is a memoir.

Richman, Arthur (1886–1944), dramatist, screenwriter. Born in New York City, Richman wrote numerous plays, some of them adaptations. His most highly esteemed play is *Ambush* (1921), the poignant story of a family tragedy. His other dramas include *The Serpent's Tooth* (1922), *The Awful Truth* (1922), *A Proud Woman* (1927), and *The Season Changes* (1935).

Richter, Conrad [Michael] (1890–1968), short-story writer, novelist. Richter, born in Pennsylvania, published his first work, *Brothers of No Kin and Other Stories*, in 1924. His first novel, *Sea of Grass* (1937), the story of a cattle baron, demonstrated his interest in the Southwest, where he lived for many years. His most elaborate production was a trilogy depicting a pioneer group over the years: *The Trees* (1940), *The Fields* (1946), and *The Town* (Pulitzer Prize, 1950). *Always Young and Fair* (1947) is based on Richter's recollections of Spanish-American War days. *The Freeman* (1943) is laid in Ohio during the Revolution. *Tracey Cromwell* (1942) is about a woman in Arizona in the 1890s. Among his later books are *The Light in the Forest* (1953), *The Mountains and the Desert* (1955), and *The Water of Kronos* (1960).

Ricketson, Daniel (1813–1898), poet, historian. One of the minor transcendentalists, Ricketson, born in Massachusetts, is chiefly remembered for his association with Emerson, Alcott, and particularly Thoreau (see TRANSCENDENTALISM). He wrote a *History of New Bedford* (1858); his *New Bedford of the Past* (1903) appeared posthumously. He also published two collections of poems (1869, 1873).

Riddell, John. See COREY FORD.

Ridge, John R[ollin] (1827–1867), poet. Ridge was the son of John Ridge, a Cherokee chieftain who negotiated, with others, a treaty with the government giving away Georgia tribal lands. The father was murdered by resentful tribesmen on June 22, 1839, in the presence of his family. His son later described the scene. At the same time, in another part of the reservation, his grandfather, also a prominent leader of the tribe, was murdered. As a writer Ridge was known as "Yellow Bird," a translation of his Indian name, Chees-quat-a-law-ny. His *Poems* (1868) and *The Life and Adventures of Joaquin Murieta* (1854) were his chief publications. He also wrote for several California newspapers.

Ridge, Lola (1883–1941),   poet. Born in Dublin, Ridge went with her mother to Australia and then New Zealand. She fled to the United States to escape an unwise marriage in 1907, living first in San Francisco before settling in New York City. There she was associated with the anarchist-feminist Ferrer Association and school, dominated by EMMA GOLDMAN, and was the first editor of the association's magazine, *The Modern School*. Ridge's *The Ghetto and Other Poems* (1918) with its realistic portrayals of the poor challenged the anti-Semitism of her time. *Sun-Up* (1920), her second collection of poetry, describes Australia. Ridge worked on the literary magazine *Others* and traveled the country delivering a feminist lecture entitled "Woman and the Creative Will" in the 1920s. Her third book of poetry, *Red Flag*, appeared in 1927. She and Edna St. Vincent Millay were arrested in the same year for protesting the execution of Sacco and Vanzetti (see SACCO-VANZETTI CASE); her sonnet sequence *Firehead* (1929) recorded her emotional commitment to that case. Her final book, *Dance of Fire* (1935), warned of the appearance of Nazism.

Riding, Laura (1901–1991),   poet, novelist, critic. Born in New York City as Laura Reichenthal, she studied for three years at Cornell University and spent many years abroad before settling in Florida in 1938. Her critical work includes *A Survey of Modernist Poetry* (1927), with Robert Graves, and *Contemporaries and Snobs* (1928). Among her fiction titles are *A Trojan Ending* (1937), *Lives of Wives* (1939), and *Progress of Stories* (1935). Her *Collected Poems* (1938) includes work from nine earlier volumes and was reissued as *The Poems of Laura Riding: A New Edition of the 1938 Collection* (1980). *Selected Poems: In Five Sets* was published in the United States in 1973 and reprinted after her death (1993). *A Selection of the Poems of Laura Riding* appeared in 1997. *The Telling* (1975) is a philosophical essay. After her 1938 marriage to Schuyler B. Jackson, some of her work appeared under the name Laura Riding Jackson.

Ridpath, John Clark (1840–1900),   teacher, historian, editor. Ridpath, born in Indiana, taught English and history first at Asbury College, later at De Pauw University. In 1898 he edited *The Ridpath Library of Universal Literature*, which appeared in 25 volumes.

Riedesel, Friederike Charlotte Luise, Baroness von (1746–1808),   diarist. Married to a German officer attached to the British General Burgoyne's army, she and her daughters accompanied the troops on the march south from Canada. Following the army's defeat at Saratoga in October 1777, they were imprisoned and did not return to Europe until 1783. Her *Journal*, describing these events, was published first in a German edition (1800) and translated into English in 1827.

Riesenberg, Felix (1879–1939),   master mariner, engineer, novelist. Riesenberg, born in Milwaukee, wrote two technical books on the merchant marine, *The Men on Deck* (1918) and *Standard Seamanship* (1922)—authoritative works in a neglected field. He also wrote a number of novels. *P.A.L.* (1925), later issued as *Red Horses* (1928), is set between World War I and the boom of the 1920s. *East Side, West Side* (1927) is a novel of New York City. *Passing Strangers* (1932) is a story of the Depression. His other books tell of the sea: *Under Sail*

(1915), *Vignettes of the Sea* (1926), *Shipmates* (1928), *Log of the Sea* (1933), and *Mother Sea* (1933). *Living Again* (1937) is autobiographical. Riesenberg also wrote for the screen, stage, and radio and edited the *Nautical Gazette*.

Riggs, Lynn (1899–1954),   playwright. His first play, *Knives from Syria* (1921), was produced in 1925. In 1926 Riggs left his native Oklahoma for New York City and devoted himself to writing. *Big Lake* was produced in 1927 by the American Laboratory Theater. Riggs's first successful play, GREEN GROW THE LILACS, a remarkably fresh and appealing folk drama, formed the basis for the even more successful musical comedy OKLAHOMA! (1943), by Oscar Hammerstein and Richard Rodgers. *Russet Mantle* (1936), a comedy, and *The Cherokee Night* (1936), a tragedy, were followed by *The Cream of the Well*, which closed in 1941 after a few performances. Riggs enlisted as an army private in 1942 and settled in New Mexico after the war. He issued *Four Plays* (1947), and wrote *Hang on to Love* (1948) and *Toward the Western Sky* (1951).

Riggs, Stephen R[eturn] (1812–1883),   missionary, translator, memoirist. The Ohio-born Riggs recorded his experiences as a missionary in *Mary and I: 40 Years with the Sioux* (1880). He became well acquainted with the Sioux language and published grammars and dictionaries in that language. With John P. Williams he translated and compiled a book of hymns, *Dakota Odowan* (1853).

Rights of Man, The (1791–1792),   a tract by THOMAS PAINE, published in two parts in London. It was a reply to Edmund Burke's *Reflections on the Revolution in France* (1790), an attack on the doctrine of natural rights lamenting that "the age of chivalry is gone." Paine's rejoinder was dedicated to George Washington and sold so widely that the British government suppressed it and prosecuted Paine for treason. The suppression merely increased underground circulation of the tract, and to escape prosecution Paine fled to Paris and became a French citizen. In the United States the tract made a similar sensation and was immediately adopted by the Republicans (later called Democrats). Its ideas were commonplace with men like Jefferson; for example, no man or government had a right to bind succeeding generations. Jefferson wrote a letter that was used as an introduction for the Philadelphia edition of the tract without his authorization and embarrassed him greatly; it was regarded as a direct attack by the secretary of state (the office Jefferson then held) on Vice-President John Adams. The pamphlet set up numerous other repercussions in this country.

Riis, Jacob A[ugustus] (1849–1914),   journalist, reformer. Born in Denmark, Riis came to America at twenty-one and worked at odd jobs until 1877, when he got a job as a reporter. For more than ten years he crusaded for reform of slum conditions. His book *How the Other Half Lives* (1890) drew the attention of Theodore Roosevelt and probably influenced Stephen Crane's *Maggie, A Girl of the Streets* (1893). THE MAKING OF AN AMERICAN (1901) is Riis's account of his life and crusades and his most enduring book. His other books are *The Children of the Poor* (1892), *Out of Mulberry Street* (1898), *The Battle with the Slum* (1902), *Children of the Tenements* (1903), *Theodore Roosevelt the Citizen* (1904), *Is There a Santa Claus?*

(1904), *The Old Town* (1909), and *Hero Tales of the Far North* (1910).

Riley, James Whitcomb (1849–1916),   poet, lecturer, newspaperman. Riley, born in Indiana, lost his job as a reporter on the Anderson (Indiana) *Democrat* for the Leonainie hoax he published as a poem supposedly by EDGAR ALLEN POE, actually an imitation he had written himself. While working for the Indianapolis *Journal* in 1877, he began contributing a series of Hoosier dialect poems on rural subjects under the pen name "Benjamin F. Johnson, of Boone." A group of these poems was published in 1883 as *"The Old Swimmin' Hole" and 'Leven More Poems.* This book and his subsequent books launched him on a wave of popularity that brought him greater financial returns than any other American poet had known to that time. His most popular and enduring poems are WHEN THE FROST IS ON THE PUNKIN, "The Old Man and Jim," LITTLE ORPHANT ANNIE, "Knee-Deep in June," and THE RAGGEDY MAN.

Riley's collections include *Afterwhiles* (1887), *Pipes o' Pan at Zekesbury* (1888), *Old-Fashioned Roses* (1888), *Rhymes of Childhood* (1891), *Green Fields and Running Brooks* (1892), *Poems Here at Home* (1893), *Riley Child Rhymes* (1899), and *Book of Joyous Children* (1902). A Biographical Edition was issued in six volumes in 1913, in one volume in 1937. His *Letters* was edited (1930) by W. L. Phelps.

Riley, [Isaac] Woodbridge (1869–1933),   teacher, historian, philosopher. Riley, born in New York City, taught at Vassar from 1908 to 1933. His most important books are those he wrote on American philosophical thought and religious movements, among them *The Founder of Mormonism* (1902), *American Philosophy: The Early Schools* (1907), and *American Thought from Puritanism to Pragmatism* (1915). He also wrote *From Myth to Reason* (1926), *Men and Morals* (1929), and *The Meaning of Mysticism* (1930).

Rimmer, William (1816–1879),   physician, artist, teacher, author. Rimmer was brought to the United States from England in 1826 by his father, a French refugee who Rimmer claimed was the lost Dauphin. In 1876 he became professor of anatomy and sculpture at the Boston Museum of Fine Arts, publishing the lectures he delivered as *Art Anatomy* (1877). Earlier he had written *Elements of Design* (1864). One of his students was Louisa May Alcott, and some scholars believe Rimmer was the inspiration for the character of Professor Bhaer in LITTLE WOMEN.

Rinehart, Mary Roberts (1876–1958),   novelist, detective-story writer, playwright. Rinehart, born in Pittsburgh, started writing because of financial troubles brought on by the panic of 1903. At first she wrote verses, short articles, and children's stories, but THE CIRCULAR STAIRCASE (1908) and *The Man in Lower Ten* (1909) established her as the writer of a new type of detective story, one in which a well-knit plot was combined with lifelike, sometimes humorous characterizations of normal people. During World War I she served as war correspondent for the *Saturday Evening Post* on the Belgian and French fronts.

In addition to her detective stories, Rinehart was also the author of a series of amusing stories about a dauntless woman and her two friends: *The Amazing Adventures of Letitia Carberry* (1911), *Tish* (1916), *More Tish* (1921), *Tish Plays the Game* (1926), *Tish Marches On* (1937), and *The Best of Tish* (selected stories, 1955). Of her more serious novels, *K* (1915) and *The Breaking Point* (1922) are considered her best. AVERY HOPWOOD collaborated with her on four plays, one of which, THE BAT (1920), based on *The Circular Staircase*, had a phenomenal run.

My Story, which is autobiographical, was written in 1931 and revised in 1948. Among her other books are *When a Man Marries* (1909); *The Street of Seven Stars* (1914); *Kings, Queens, and Pawns* (1915); *Through Glacier Park* (1916); *The Amazing Interlude* (1918); *Love Stories* (1919); *The Out Trail* (1923); *Temperamental People* (1924); *The Red Lamp* (1925); *The Door* (1930); *The Wall* (1938); *A Light in the Window* (1948); and *The Frightened Wife* (1953).

Ringwood, Gwen Pharis (1910–1984),   playwright, novelist. Ringwood was born in the United States but has spent most of her adult life in Alberta. Her sole novel is *Younger Brother* (1959). She has written more than sixty plays, less than half of which appear in *The Collected Plays of Gwen Pharis Ringwood* (1982). Several plays, including *Lament for Harmonica* and *The Stranger*, concern the exploitation of Indians. Ringwood's musical plays include *Look Behind You, Neighbor* (music by Chet Lambertson) and *The Road Runs North* (music by Art Roseman), both written for public celebrations. Her best work, such as *Still Stands the House* (1938) and *Dark Harvest* (1945), deals with life on the Canadian prairies.

Rios, Alberto (Alvaro) (1952–   ),   poet and short-story writer. Born in the border town of Nogales, Arizona, Rios was educated at the University of Arizona and has taught there and at Arizona State University. Child of a Mexican father and English mother, Rios grew up in a language-rich family. He first gained recognition with the poems in *Whispering to Fool the Wind* (1982). Rios's verse has a narrative thrust and elements of the Latin American MAGICAL REALISM tradition. Other poetry titles include *Five Indiscretions* (1985), which deal with romantic and sexual relationships from both the male and the female perspectives; *The Lime Orchard Woman* (1988); and *Teodoro Luna's Two Kisses* (1990). Rios's short fiction is collected in *The Iguana Killer: Twelve Stories of the Heart* (1984), *Pig Cookies and Other Stories* (1995), and *The Curtain of Trees* (1999).

Ripley, George (1802–1880),   editor, reformer, literary critic. Ripley, born in Massachusetts, was educated at Harvard and taught mathematics there while attending the Divinity School. He became a Unitarian minister in Boston. For fifteen years he remained at the same church, studying German theology and editing the *Christian Register*. In 1838 Ripley began to edit *Specimens of Foreign Standard Literature* (14 v. 1838–52), translations of Victor Cousin, Théodore Simon Jouffroy, and Friedrich Ernst Schleiermacher, whose philosophies formed part of the basis for the American transcendental movement. Andrew Norton's *The Latest Form of Infidelity* (1839), a reply to Emerson's *Divinity School Address*, contained an attack on Ripley's *Discourses on the Philosophy of*

Religion (1836). Ripley answered in a series of letters that later was published as *Letters on the Latest Form of Infidelity* (1840). A year later he resigned from the ministry.

In 1841 Ripley, with twenty other members of the Transcendental Club, moved to West Roxbury, Massachusetts, where he became president of the experiment in communal living, BROOK FARM. There he taught mathematics and philosophy, edited THE DIAL, and worked on the farm. (See TRANSCENDENTALISM.) After the disastrous fire of 1846, Ripley, loaded with debts, moved to Brooklyn, New York, where he edited *The Harbinger*. In 1849 he abandoned *The Harbinger* and became literary critic of the New York *Tribune*. He soon became an outstanding influence in the world of letters. He recognized at once the value of such works as *The Scarlet Letter* and *The Origin of Species* and rarely allowed a single important publication to escape his notice. He became one of the founders of *Harper's New Monthly Magazine*, and with the income from this magazine, the *Tribune*, and his *History of Literature and the Fine Arts* (1852), prepared with BAYARD TAYLOR, he managed to work his way out of debt. In 1858 he brought out the first volume of the *New American Cyclopedia* (16 v. 1858–63), later revised as the *American Cyclopedia* (1873–76). O. B. Frothingham's *George Ripley* (1882) appeared in the American Men of Letters series. J. T. Codman's *Brook Farm, Historical and Personal Memoirs* (1894), Lindsay Swift's *Brook Farm, Its Members, Scholars, and Visitors* (1900), and Katherine Burton's *Paradise Planters* (1939) contain additional information.

Ripley, Robert L[eroy] (1893–1949),   cartoonist. In December 1918, Ripley, who was born in California, drew for the New York *Globe* the first of his *Believe It or Not* cartoons, showing seven unusual if not incredible achievements. The cartoon soon became a daily feature and several years later was syndicated by King Features, which at one time needed a staff of eighty to collect material and handle the letters Ripley received. His first book of *Believe It or Not* cartoons appeared in 1928.

Rip Van Winkle (1819),   a tale by WASHINGTON IRVING. This most famous piece in Irving's SKETCH BOOK immediately became a popular favorite. Irving tells how henpecked Rip Van Winkle in the days before the Revolution wanders into the Catskills with his faithful dog Wolf and there meets a dwarfish and strangely costumed man whom he helps carry a keg of liquor. They go into the mountains and come to a gathering of other strange persons who are playing ninepins, but no one says a word. Rip, after a nip or two at the keg, soon falls into a stupor and sleeps for twenty years. He awakens to find his beard full-grown and white, returns to his village to find his wife dead, his daughter married and a mother, and the whole country changed: now George Washington's image, and not George III's, adorns the village inn's signboard. Rip goes on to a happy old age.

The plot is an ancient folk theme. Although it appears in many times and places, Irving presumably based his story particularly on the German folk tale of Peter Klaus. Herman Melville, who had great respect for Irving, wrote *Rip Van Winkle's Lilac* (1890), relating a final episode in Rip's life. A lilac he had planted in his youth had furnished shoots for hundreds of bushes nearby, turning the neighborhood into a garden of lilacs. Like Rip's lilac bush, the story of his life has also sprouted freely in the theater. A pirated version of Irving's tale was played in Albany, New York, in 1828. Another version was produced in 1829, a copy of which has survived—it was the work of John Kerr, an English actor and play adaptor. It is held to be the basis of all later adaptations. Another version was made by WILLIAM BAYLE BERNARD in 1832 or 1834. Charles Burke made a new version in 1850. In 1855 appeared an opera by G. F. Bristow based on the tale. Then the actor JOSEPH JEFFERSON commissioned DION BOUCICAULT to do a revision. The resulting version, first produced in London in 1865, became the standard form of the play and was Jefferson's major vehicle until 1904. JAMES A. HERNE made a version about 1874. In 1920 PERCY MACKAYE composed a folk opera for which REGINALD DEKOVEN wrote the music. A French composer, Robert Jean Planquette, wrote yet another opera, produced in 1881 and given in the United States in a modernized version in 1933.

Rise of David Levinsky, The (1917),   a novel by ABRAHAM CAHAN. Cahan, who escaped from Czarist persecution in 1882 and fled to New York City, established himself as a successful editor of a Yiddish daily. The book presents a vivid picture of the needle trades in New York City and the unions in their early days, and is recognized as the first important immigrant novel. See LOWER EAST SIDE.

Rise of Silas Lapham, The (1885),   the best-known novel of WILLIAM DEAN HOWELLS. Lapham, a newcomer to Boston, has discovered the materials for a paint formula that makes him rich. He and his family attempt to break into the closed circles of society; the novel's best-remembered scene is one in which Silas attends an important dinner party and disgraces himself by drinking too much. At its deepest level, however, the novel is a work of morality, showing Lapham's moral rise from ruthlessness to a recognition of ethical standards. In the end Silas even contributes to his own financial defeat by refusing to engage in practices he now considers immoral. Throughout the story is woven a love affair between the son of a Brahmin family and Penelope Lapham, daughter of Silas; at the end the two find happiness by escaping to Mexico.

The novel is Howells's best and one of the triumphs of American fiction. The figure of Silas is skillfully drawn and presents an important American type: the self-reliant businessman, tough and shrewd and ambitious, although essentially honest and willing to accept what is right so far as he can understand it. The novel is a complex of social and moral feeling that probes the significance of American civilization in its growing aspect.

Rittenhouse, Jessie B[elle] (1869–1948),   poet, teacher, editor, critic. Rittenhouse, born in Mt. Morris, New York, published numerous collections of verse, including *The Younger American Poets* (1904), and wrote reviews, specializing in poetry. She was a founder of the Poetry Society of America. Among her books are *The Door of Dreams* (1918), *The Lifted Cup* (1921), *The Secret Bird* (1930), and *The Moving Tide: New and Selected Lyrics* (1939). *My House of Life* (1934) is an autobiography.

Rivera, José Eustacio (1889–1928),   Colombian novelist and poet. Rivera's work as a lawyer took him into the flatlands and jungles, where he encountered the exploitation of peasants in the cattle and rubber businesses. His only novel, LA VORÁGINE (1924, tr. *The Vortex*, 1935), tells of the poet Arturo Cova and his lover Alicia, who go mad in the face of the hardships of the jungle. His poetry appears in *Tierra de promisión* (1921).

Rivera, Tomás (1935–1984),   short-story writer. Rivera's major work, . . . *y no se lo tragó la tierra* (And the Earth Did Not Part, 1971), is a series of fourteen related stories and sketches written in Spanish. They tell of the lives of Mexican-American immigrant farm workers in Texas and the Southwest. Rivera himself came from that background, earned a Ph.D., and was Chancellor of the University of California, Riverside, at the time of his death.

Rivers of America Series.   This series began with ROBERT P. TRISTRAM COFFIN's *The Kennebec* (1937), was followed by STRUTHERS BURT's *Powder River* (1938) and CARL CARMER's *The Hudson* (1939). Since then the series has been extended into many volumes. Numerous noted authors have contributed. Each volume has included geographical and economic data, as well as accounts of historical happenings, descriptions of persons and places, and folklore. Constance Lindsay Skinner, until her death in 1939, was the series editor. Later editors have included STEPHEN VINCENT BENÉT, HERVEY ALLEN, and Carl Carmer.

Rives, Amelie.   See PRINCESS TROUBETZKOY.

Roa Bastos, Augusto (1917–   ),   novelist. Born to the family of a sugar plantation worker in Paraguay, Roa Bastos received a minimal education before joining the army at 17. He worked as a journalist and spent some time in Britain, but began to write seriously only after being exiled to Buenos Aires in 1948. His short-story collection *El trueno entre las hojas* (1953) was followed by the novel *Hijo de hombre* (1960, tr. *Son of Man*, 1965). Treating the histories of two rural towns during the Chaco war with Bolivia, in which the author fought, it emphasizes the sufferings of the poor, especially the indigenous Guarani Indians, and their capacity for heroism. The labyrinthine and important novel *Yo el Supremo* (1974, tr. *I the Supreme*, 1986) asserts that writing and politics are inseparable. Centering on the life of José Gaspar de Francia, the Supreme and Perpetual Dictator of Paraguay from 1814 to 1840, it explores the distance between the novelist and his readers. His other titles include *Madera quemada* (1967), a story collection; *Los pies sobre el agua* (1967); *Vigilias del Almirante* (1992); and *El Fiscal* (1993).

Road Not Taken, The (*Atlantic Monthly*, August 1915, the opening poem in *Mountain Interval*, 1916),   a poem by ROBERT FROST. This frequently anthologized poem is obviously symbolical. The speaker comes to a fork in a road and is undecided about which way to go. Both roads seem much alike, even if one "was grassy and wanted wear." He takes the one less traveled—and "that has made all the difference."

Road to Xanadu, The (1927, enlarged ed. 1930),   by JOHN LIVINGSTON LOWES. Lowes subtitled his critical and psychological masterpiece "A Study in the Ways of the Imagination." His title is a combination of a bit of dialogue from Goethe's *Faust* used as a motto, *Faust: "Wohin der Weg?"* [Whither the way?], *Mephistopheles: "Kein weg! Ins Unbetretene"* [No way, but into the unexplored], and the place name that Coleridge made famous in his poem "Kubla Khan" (1797). On the surface the book is a study of how Coleridge came to write some of his poems. In reality it is a unique study of the workings of the imagination, with Coleridge as an example.

Roan Stallion (*in Roan Stallion, Tamar and Other Poems*, 1925),   a narrative poem by ROBINSON JEFFERS. Set in the mountains near Monterey, California, "Roan Stallion" deals with the almost religious love of a woman named California for a magnificent red stallion, in which she sees a power and beauty equivalent to that of a divinity. When her brutal husband is trampled to death by the horse, she shoots the animal "out of some obscure human fidelity," but feels she "has killed God."

Roark, Garland (1904–1985),   cartoonist, advertising man, novelist. Roark, born in Texas, had his first literary success with *Wake of the Red Witch* (1946), which was made into a movie. His later books include *Rainbow in the Royals* (1950), *Star in the Rigging* (1954), *Tales of the Caribbean* (1959), and *Should the Wind Be Fair* (1960).

Robb, John S. ["Solitaire"].   Robb was a Missouri newspaperman and humorist. Little is known of his life aside from the fact that he wrote humorous stories of the West and Southwest around the middle of the 19th century. Some of his contributions appeared in the SPIRIT OF THE TIMES. He prepared one or two collections of his material. Best-known is *Streaks of Squatter Life and Far Western Scenes: A Series of Humorous Sketches Descriptive of Incident and Character in the Wild West* (1846, 1847), which was reprinted as *Western Scenes, or, Life on the Prairie* (1858). In this book were several tales of MIKE FINK, among the earliest to appear and apparently gathered from oral tradition.

Robbins, Harold (1916–1997),   novelist. Born Francis Kane, he took the name Harold Rubin when he was adopted in 1927 and later had it changed to Robbins. With little formal education, he worked at several jobs, including that of organizing a food distribution system that made him a millionaire at age twenty. He did his first writing for Universal Pictures. His first publication *Never Love a Stranger* (1948), with its candid treatment of sex, became a best seller. His output since then has been steady and no work has sold less than 600,000 copies. *The Carpetbaggers* (1961), his best-known book, is an adventure novel about chicanery in industry. *A Stone for Danny Fisher* (1952) draws on Robbins's experience as a poor boy in his native Manhattan. Other titles among his fast-paced narratives include *Where Love Has Gone* (1962), *The Betsy* (1971), *Spellbinder* (1982), *The Storyteller* (1985), *Piranha* (1986) *The Raiders* (1994), *The Stallion* (1996), and *Tycoon* (1997). Several have been made into films.

Robbins, Leonard H. (1877–1947),   newspaperman, humorist, columnist, poet. Robbins did newspaper work in his native Lincoln, Nebraska; Philadelphia; Newark; and New York City. In *The New York Times* magazine section he conducted a column called "About." He collected some of his verses in *Jersey Jingles* (1907).

Robbins, Tom (1936–   ),   novelist. Bizarre plot situations and eccentric characters are typical of Robbins's work. *Another Roadside Attraction* (1971) features the use of the mummified body of Christ as a sign for a hot dog stand. *Even Cowgirls Get the Blues* (1976) is a picaresque story of a girl hitchhiker with outside thumbs. *Still Life with Woodpecker* (1980) concerns the daughter of a king exiled in Seattle and her boyfriend, who deciphers popular icons, including a cigarette pack. *Jitterbug Perfume* (1984) sends a janitor who finds a mysterious blue bottle on a search for immortality. *Skinny Legs and All* (1990) follows Ellen Cherry Charles and her husband, Boomer Petway, on a cross-country trip in a vehicle made to look like a roast turkey. Other titles include *Half Asleep in Frog Pajamas* (1994) and *Fierce Invalids Home from Hot Climates* (2000), whose protagonist is an ex-CIA agent in search of answers in exotic locations.

Rob of the Bowl: A Legend of St. Inigoes (1838),   a historical novel by J. P. Kennedy concerned with a 1681 attempt by Protestants to overthrow the Catholic Lord Baltimore.

Robe, The (1942),   a novel by LLOYD C. DOUGLAS. Douglas, a clergyman-novelist, was once asked what became of the robe for which the Roman soldiers who had crucified Jesus cast lots. Douglas wrote this enormously popular novel by way of reply.

Roberts, Brigham Henry (1857–1933),   Mormon leader, historian, newspaperman, biographer. Roberts was brought to Utah from England in 1866 and became a leader of the Mormon Church. He worked on the Salt Lake City *Tribune* (1890–96) and served as an army chaplain in France (1918–19). He wrote *The Life of John Taylor* (1892), *New Witnesses for God* (3 v. 1895), *The Missouri Persecutions* (1900), *The Rise and Fall of Nauvoo* (1900), and *A Comprehensive History of the Church of Jesus Christ of Latter Day Saints, Century I* (6 v. 1930).

Roberts, Charles G[eorge] D[ouglas], Sir (1860–1943),   writer, teacher, editor. Born in New Brunswick, Canada, Roberts belonged to a distinguished literary family. His brother THEODORE GOODRIDGE ROBERTS was a noted poet and novelist, and BLISS CARMAN was a first cousin. In the opinion of Canadian critics, when Roberts published *Orion and Other Poems* (1880), the modern era of Canadian literature began. He was knighted in 1935. Roberts also wrote historical novels and stories about animals, usually against a background of Canadian nature. Among his novels, *The Heart of the Ancient Wood* (1900), "a deeply felt sylvan romance," may be reckoned a classic work. Among his books of poetry are *In Divers Tones* (1887), *Songs of the Common Day* (1893), *New York Nocturnes* (1898), *Collected Poems* (1900), *The Book of the Rose* (1903), and *Selected Poems* (1936). His prose works include *Earth's Enigmas* (1896), *A History of Canada* (1897), *The Forge in the Forest* (1897), *The Kindred of the Wild* (1902),

The Haunters of the Silences (1907), *the Feet of the Furtive* (1912), *Children of the Wild* (1913), and *Eyes of the Wilderness* (1933).

Roberts, Elizabeth Madox (1886–1941),   poet, novelist. Born in Kentucky, Roberts was educated at the University of Chicago. Her first publications were collections of poetry: *In the Great Steep's Garden* (1915) and *Under the Tree* (1922, enlarged 1930). Using her native Kentucky as setting, *The Time of Man* (1926), her first novel, dealt with poor whites becoming pioneers. *My Heart and My Flesh* (1927) details the decay of a Southern family. *The Great Meadow* (1930) is a historical novel of Kentucky pioneers. *A Buried Treasure* (1931), *The Haunted Mirror* (1932), a story collection, and *He Sent Forth a Raven* (1935) are also set in rural Kentucky. *Black Is My Truelove's Hair* (1938) and *Not by Strange Gods* (1941) focus on the lives of women. Her later poetry is collected in *Song in the Meadow* (1940).

Roberts, Kenneth [Lewis] (1885–1957),   newspaperman, editor, translator, author. Born in Maine, Roberts wrote voluminously and engaged lustily in controversy about his concept of American history and just as eagerly over whether it is possible to discover underground sources of water by dowsing. He wrote some of the best historical novels in American literature, among them ARUNDEL (1930), *The Lively Lady* (1931), RABBLE IN ARMS (1933), NORTHWEST PASSAGE (1937), OLIVER WISWELL (1940), and LYDIA BAILEY (1947). He made use of journals of some of the men who accompanied Benedict Arnold to Canada in writing *Arundel* and later compiled and edited these journals as *March to Quebec* (1939). Roberts and his wife wrote an excellent translation (1947) of Morceau de St. Méry's *Voyage aux États-Unis d'Amérique*. Roberts's later historical works are *Boon Island* (1956) and *The Battle of Cowpens* (posthumously pub. 1958). The *Kenneth Roberts Reader* was issued in 1945. His other volumes include *Trending Into Maine* (1938) and *Good Maine Food* (with Marjorie Mosser, 1939). *I Wanted to Write* (1949) is his autobiography.

Roberts, [George Edward] Theodore Goodrich (1877–1953),   poet, novelist. Roberts's career was long and distinguished, as befits a member of his well-known New Brunswick, Canada, family, which is described in Lloyd Roberts's *The Book of Roberts*. Theodore Goodrich Roberts was a journalist, writing for the *Newfoundland Magazine* and serving as special correspondent for the New York *Independent* in the Spanish-American War. During World War I, Roberts served as a captain in the Canadian army and later wrote several volumes of military history. In his poetry he employed traditional forms, including the ballad in English folk speech. The poems usually evoke the atmosphere of the seacoast in the Canadian Maritime Provinces, where he spent the greater part of his life. The same setting provided backgrounds for most of his thirty romantic novels, among them *The Red Feathers* (1907), *The Wasp* (1914), and *Stranger From Up Along* (1924). His poetry includes *Northland Lyrics* (1899), *The Lost Shipmate* (1926), and *The Leather Bottle* (1934).

Robert's Rules of Order (1876), a widely accepted compilation by Gen. Henry M. Robert (1837–1923) of rules of parliamentary procedure. With the rules of the U.S. House of Representatives as a base, Robert developed a pocket manual that proved so popular it was revised during its first year in print. A major revision was published in 1915, and it has remained in print ever since.

Robertson, Frank C[hester] (1890–1969), farmer, author of Western novels, stories, articles. In 1914 the Idaho-born Robertson settled a homestead and farmed it until 1922, when he wrote and sold his first story. His writings since then include more than a thousand short stories and more than 150 books. Among his better-known books are *Foreman of the Forty-Bar* (1925), *Fall of Buffalo Horn* (1928), *The Hidden Cabin* (1929), *Riders of the Sunset Trail* (1930), *The Mormon Trail* (1931), *Forbidden Trails* (1935), *The Pride of Pine Creek* (1938), *Longhorns of Hate* (1949), *Wrangler on the Prod* (1950), *Saddle on a Cloud* (1952), *Cruel Winds of Winter* (1954), and *Life and Times of Soapy Smith* (1961).

Robertson, Morgan [Andrew] (1861–1915), short-story writer. Morgan was born in Oswego, New York. After a few years of schooling he went to sea as a cabin boy and from 1877 until 1886 he was in the merchant marine. Later he tried to earn a living first as a jeweler, later as a writer of sea stories. Unable to support himself, Robertson died in poverty. Among his collections of sea stories are *Futility* (1898), telling of a disaster resembling the sinking of the Titanic; *Spun Yarn* (1898); *Shipmates* (1901); *Sinful Peck* (1903); *Down to the Sea* (1905); *Land Ho!* (1905); and *Masters of Men* (1914). One of his best tales is "The Derelict Neptune from Spun Yarn."

Robertson, William (1721–1793), Scottish historian and Church of Scotland clergyman. His major work was *The History of the Reign of the Emperor Charles the Fifth* (1769, repr. 1857) His two-volume *History of America* (1777) showed his interest in the New World.

Robeson, Paul [Leroy Bustill] (1898–1976), lawyer, singer, actor, writer. Son of an escaped slave, Robeson was a star athlete and a valedictorian at Rutgers, in his home state of New Jersey. He took a law degree at Columbia, but racial bigotry forced him out of the legal profession. He first performed as an actor with the Provincetown Players in EUGENE O'NEILL's *Emperor Jones* in 1924 and then in *All God's Chillun Got Wings*. He opened in Jerome Kern's *Show Boat* in Paris and played Othello in London in the late 1920s. He made numerous recordings, movies of *The Emperor Jones* and *Show Boat*, and concert tours. His 1943 production of *Othello*, the first with a black actor in that role, set a record for a Broadway run of Shakespeare.

He went to Russia in 1934 to work with the great movie director, Sergei Eisenstein. There he found an absence of racial bigotry that attracted his emotional allegiance. While other intellectuals became disillusioned by the Stalin purges, Robeson maintained his loyalty to Russia and paid dearly for it during the McCarthy era, when his passport was revoked, his career was shattered, and he was ostracized. During this period he wrote his autobiography, *Here I Stand* (1958). The Supreme Court ruled in 1957 that his passport should not have been revoked and that no American can be denied the right to travel because of his political views, but Robeson was ill and in seclusion. He did not attend the Carnegie Hall celebration of his seventy-fifth birthday and died of a stroke a few years later. A recent study is Martin Bauml Duberman, *Paul Robeson: A Biography* (1989).

Robins, Elizabeth [1]. See JOSEPH STANLEY PENNELL .

Robins, Elizabeth [2] [C. E. Raimond] (1865?–1952), actress, novelist, feminist. At sixteen Robins, born in Ohio, left school for the stage. On the death of her young actor-husband, she was taken to Norway by Mrs. Ole Bull, wife of the great Norwegian violinist, and there she made an intensive study of Ibsen. Not long afterward she settled in London, where she became acquainted with Wilde, Henry James, and Shaw. She was the first woman to play *Hedda Gabler* in London and also played other Ibsen roles.

Under the pen name C. E. Raimond, she published *Below the Salt* (1896), *The Open Question* (1898), and *The Magnetic North* (1904). She abandoned that name when she turned to feminist writing. Robins dramatized her novel *The Convert* (1906) as *Votes for Women* (1906). *My Little Sister* (1913), the story of a well-born girl who is abducted and forced into prostitution, proved so alarming that many readers wrote to newspapers demanding an investigation of the white slave traffic. *Theater and Friendship* (1932), a volume of letters written by Henry James to Robins and containing autobiographical notes written by her, was followed by *Both Sides of the Curtain* (1940), an autobiography.

Robinson, Charles (1818–1894), physician, welfare worker, political leader, public official. After practicing medicine in his native state of Massachusetts, Robinson went to California, where he tried to prevent the introduction of slavery. He returned to Massachusetts to resume his medical practice, but was sent to Kansas as an agent of the New England Emigrant Aid Committee and there became the leader of the Free-State group. In 1856 he was chosen governor, but was arrested and imprisoned on a charge of treason and usurpation. In 1861 he was again elected governor and later served in the state senate. He was a benefactor of the state university and while living in Sacramento he founded and edited the *Settlers' and Miners' Tribune*. He wrote *Kansas: Its Interior and Exterior Life* (1856) and *The Kansas Conflict* (1892).

Robinson, Edwin Arlington (1869–1935), poet. Gardiner, Maine, where Robinson's family moved shortly after his birth, in nearby Head Tide, is celebrated under the name Tilbury Town in his poetry. As a boy Edwin led a quiet life and in high school was already writing verse, and he continued after graduation, but without success. Enrolled as a special student at Harvard (1891–93), he was called home because of his father's failing health, and returned to Gardiner suffering from an old ear injury and obsessed by a sense of failure, which had dogged him from childhood. In 1896 he published his first book of poems at his own expense, *The Torrent and the Night Before*. Republished with changes the following year at the expense of a friend, the 1897 edition, called THE CHILDREN OF THE NIGHT, became Robinson's first public volume.

At that point he fell into a pattern that never was really broken—a pattern of restlessness, financial insecurity, loneliness relieved only by a few friends, and periods of depression in which he drank. He went to New York in 1896, returned to Harvard as a secretary, not as a student, in 1897, and went again to New York in the next year. *Captain Craig* (see THE BOOK OF ANNANDALE) appeared in 1902, backed by John Hays Gardiner and Laura Richards. Robinson worked in the building of the subways, making just enough to keep going. When Theodore Roosevelt, then in the White House, became interested in Robinson's work, he secured for the poet a sinecure in the New York Custom House at $2,000 a year. With the coming of the Taft administration (1909), however, Robinson lost his government position. In the following year he brought out his third book of verse, *The Town Down the River*.

In the summer of 1911 Robinson made his first visit to the MacDowell colony at Peterboro, New Hampshire, and found it such an inviting place to work that he returned each summer until his death. The first book of verse to come out of these summers was THE MAN AGAINST THE SKY (1916). MERLIN, the first of three long Arthurian poems, appeared in 1917. LANCELOT and *The Three Taverns* followed in 1920. AVON'S HARVEST was published in 1921, the same year in which his first *Collected Poems* received a Pulitzer Prize. Though now recognized as an important poet, Robinson was still largely dependent on friends for a livelihood.

Peterboro in summer, Boston in spring and fall, New York in winter—this became Robinson's routine. TRISTRAM, in 1927, brought him wide recognition at last and a measure of financial independence, thanks to Carl Van Doren and the Literary Guild. Robinson devoted the rest of his life to writing long narrative poems, struggling in this way to retain his hold on financial security, but his narratives are less admired now than his earlier short poems. He entered New York Hospital in January 1935, suffering from cancer, and died three months later, just after completing the proofreading of his final work, *King Jasper*. His ashes were buried in Gardiner.

Robinson's faults were many. Often his poetry is obscure, owing to its lack of concrete imagery or indirectness of statement; at times, however, his fondness for abstraction is part of his power. He inclined toward verbosity and circumlocution, perhaps a compensation for his inarticulateness in private life; nevertheless, his concern for inner reality foreshadowed the psychological interests of later writers, and his long poems explore character in ways that in the 20th century have been more generally left to prose fiction. At a time when American poetry was at a low ebb, Robinson introduced a new honesty, concentration, austerity, and dignity as well as a precision and plainness of diction, which his successors made into a poetic renaissance. In a career that began in a time of flowery sentimentality and ended in the midst of untrammeled experimentation, he stayed close to earlier conventions of form and technique. His short poems are mostly

traditional formal structures in meter in rhyme, and his long poems are mostly blank verse. Although he denied he was a pessimist, he anticipated many other poets of the 20th century with his emphasis on themes of alienation and failure. His best work continues to impress. See DEMOS AND DIONYSUS, FLAMMONDE, MINIVER CHEEVY, MR. FLOOD'S PARTY, RICHARD CORY.

In addition to the collections of verse already mentioned, Robinson published THE MAN WHO DIED TWICE (1924); DIONYSUS IN DOUBT (1925); CAVENDER'S HOUSE (1929), the first of his long studies of modern character; TALIFER (1933); and other titles. The final *Collected Poems* appeared in 1937. Letters have been edited by Ridgely Torrence in *Selected Letters* (1940), Denham Sutcliffe in *Untriangulated Stars* (1947), and Richard Cary in *Edwin Arlington Robinson's Letters to Edith Brower* (1968). Biographies are by Herman Hagedorn (1938) and Emily Neff (1948).

RICHARD CROWDER/GP

Robinson, Edwin Meade.   See TED ROBINSON.

Robinson, Harriet Jane Hanson (1825–1911), novelist, memoirist, woman suffragist. Robinson, born in Boston, in her youth was a mill worker in Lowell, Massachusetts. She became deeply interested in woman suffrage in her later years and wrote as propaganda *Captain Mary Miller* (1887) and *The New Pandora* (1889). She also wrote *Loom and Spindle; or Life Among the Early Mill Girls* (1898).

Robinson, Henry Morton (1898–1961),   teacher, editor, poet, novelist, critic. Robinson, born in Boston, was at first an English teacher at Columbia and later became a freelance writer. He published three verse collections: *Buck Fever* (1929), *Second Wisdom* (1936), and *The Enchanted Grindstone and Other Poems* (1952). Verse was perhaps Robinson's favorite and natural medium. In 1935 he became an associate editor of *Reader's Digest*, in 1942 a senior editor. *A Skeleton Key to Finnegans Wake* (with Joseph Campbell, 1944) established him as a Joyce authority. His novels *The Perfect Round* (1945) and *The Great Snow* (1947) were widely read. His next novel, *The Cardinal* (1950), was a best seller over a long period. Prominent Catholic prelates appear in the story, and some critics guessed that Robinson had based his main character on the late William Cardinal O'Connell of Boston. His last novel was *Water of Life* (1960).

Robinson, James Harvey (1863–1936),   teacher, historian. After traveling in Europe and spending a year in business in Bloomington, Indiana, his birthplace, Robinson decided to go to Harvard. He was graduated in 1887, studied in Germany, and received a doctorate from the University of Freiburg in 1890. In the following year he became professor of European history and assistant editor of the *Annals of the American Academy of Political and Social Science* at the University of Pennsylvania. From 1895 until 1919 he taught at Columbia University, resigning in protest against the unfair treatment of certain Columbia professors who were opposed to World War I. He helped found the New School for Social Research, where he taught until 1921. After the success of his remarkable book *The Mind in the Making* (1921), which some critics consider one of the most influential books of our time, he resigned to devote himself to writing. Robinson's other principal works are *Introduction to the History of Western Europe* (1903); *The Development of Modern Europe* (1907, with Charles Beard); *The New History* (1911, essays); *The Middle Period of European History* (1915); *Medieval and Modern Times* (1916); *The Relation of Intelligence to Social Reform* (1921); *The Humanizing of Knowledge* (1923); and *The Ordeal of Civilization* (1926).

Robinson, Marilynne (1944?–), novelist, essayist. Born in Idaho and educated at Brown University and the University of Washington where she earned a Ph.D. In English, Robinson is the author of a highly praised first novel. *Housekeeping* (1981) earned the Ernest Hemingway Foundation award for a first novel, received critical acclaim, and was made into a film. The tale is narrated by Ruth, who with her sister Lucille is cared for by a series of female guardians ranging from her grandmother, who tries to insulate the girls from their mother's and grandfather's deaths in a nearby lake by emphasizing routine and stability, to their aunt Sylvie, an eccentric whose view of life is that nothing is stable and everything changes. The novel ends with Lucille choosing normalcy and going to live with one of her teachers, and Ruth leaving her burning house and the town of Fingerbone by walking across a railroad trestle over the lake with Aunt Sylvie. Robinson's prose style has been especially praised for its economy and clarity. Robinson has also published nonfiction including *Mother Country: Britain, the Nuclear State, and Nuclear Pollution* (1989) and *The Death of Adam: Essays on Modern Thought* (1998).

Robinson, Rowland Evans (1833–1900), wood carver, cartoonist, writer. Robinson's work as an engraver and cartoonist impaired his eyesight and in 1893 brought on total blindness. He was, however, a prolific writer, at first on sports and country life in his native Vermont, later in other fields. For a time he served as an editor of *Forest and Stream*. He was at his best in portraying and interpreting the folkways and humor of a pioneer Vermont community. Uncle Lisha, a shoemaker and the autocrat of a convivial group, appears in several of his books, including *Uncle Lisha's Shop: Life in a Corner of Yankeeland* (1887), semicentennial ed. 1933); *Sam Lovel's Camps: Uncle Lisha's Friends Under Bark and Canvas* (1889); and *Uncle Lisha's Outing* (1897). He also wrote *Forest and Stream* (1886); *Vermont: A Study of Independence* (1892); *In New England's Fields and Woods* (1896); *A Hero of Ticonderoga* (1898, repr. 1934); *Hunting Without a Gun and Other Papers* (1905); and *Silver Fields and Sketches of a Farmer-Sportsman* (1921). The Centennial Edition of his writings (7 v. 1933–36) includes other titles.

Robinson, Solon (1803–1880), farmer, writer, public official. Born in Connecticut, Robinson ran a farm, wrote numerous reports and articles, published a magazine called *The Plow*, and was farm editor of the New York *Tribune*. He also wrote fiction and verse. Among his books are *Guano: A Treatise of Practical Information for Farmers* (1852); *Hot Corn-Life Scenes in N.Y.* (1854); *Facts for Farmers* (1864); and *How to Live:*

Saving and Wasting; or, Domestic Economy Illustrated by the Life of Two Families of Opposite Character (a novel, 1873). *Selected Writings* of Robinson were edited by H. A. Kellar (2 v. 1936).

Robinson, Ted [Edwin Meade] (1878–1946), poet, teacher, newspaperman. Robinson was born in Indiana and worked for Indianapolis papers, then for the Cleveland *Leader*, finally for the Cleveland *Plain Dealer*. He began conducting a column for the *Leader* in 1905 and became known nationally through his "Philosophy of Folly" column in the *Plain Dealer*. He published several collections of verse, including *Mere Melodies* (1918); *Piping and Panning* (1920); and *Life, Love, and the Weather* (1945).

Robotics, Three Laws of. See ISAAC ASIMOV.

Robison, Mary (1949–), novelist, short-story writer. Born in Washington, D.C., Robinson credits the Johns Hopkins writing program and her teacher, John Barth, with turning her into a serious writer of fiction. Her first collection of stories, *Days* (1979), was praised for spare prose and careful selection of the details of ordinary life. *Oh!* (1981) is a comic novel about an eccentric family of substance abusers. *An Amateur's Guide to the Night* (1983) and *Believe Them* (1988) are story collections. *Subtraction* (1991) is a quest novel centering on Paige Deveaux, a writer and college professor searching for her alcoholic husband with the help of his college friend. Robison has acknowledged that the university teaching she does detracts from her ability to focus on writing.

Rochambeau, Jean Baptiste Donatien de Vimeur, Comte de (1725–1807), soldier, memoirist. At seventeen Rochambeau entered the French army and soon became a colonel. In 1780 he was sent with 6,000 men to aid the Americans in the Revolution. He remained for a year at Newport, Rhode Island, and then joined Washington for the march on Yorktown. While the French fleet controlled the Chesapeake, Washington and Rochambeau took Yorktown and forced Cornwallis to surrender. After the war Rochambeau returned to France and served in the Revolution. Later Napoleon made him an officer in the Legion of Honor. Rochambeau's *Mémoires* (1890) were translated in part into English by W. E. Wright as *Memoirs of the Marshall Count de Rochambeau Relative to the War of Independence of the United States* (1838). Jean Jules Jusserand wrote *Rochambeau in America* (1916).

Roche, James Jeffrey (1847–1908), journalist, consul, writer. Roche's family migrated from Ireland to Prince Edward Island, where he was educated by his father and at St. Dunstan's College. In 1866 he moved to Boston and served as assistant editor of the Boston *Pilot*, a Catholic journal. Seven years later he succeeded John Boyle O'Reilly as editor. His first novel, *The Story of the Filibusters* (1891), was reprinted ten years later as *By-Ways of War*. With Lady Gregory, Douglas Hyde, and others he helped prepare *Irish Literature* (1904). In 1904 Roche was appointed consul to Genoa by Theodore Roosevelt and later was consul at Berne. In 1891 he published *A Life of John Boyle O'Reilly*. Among his books of humorous verse are *Songs and Satires* (1886), *Ballads of Blue Water and Other Poems* (1895), *Her Majesty the King: A Romance of the*

Harem (1898), *The V-a-s-e and Other Bric-a-Brac* (1900), and *The Sorrows of Sap'ed* (1904).

Rock Me to Sleep, Mother,   a poem by ELIZABETH AKERS.

Rockwell, Norman (1894–1978),   illustrator. Rockwell, born in York City, became celebrated particularly for his magazine covers and story illustrations, especially in the *Saturday Evening Post*, in which he showed special skill in depicting the common man and familiar scenes. His autobiography, *My Adventures as an Illustrator*, was published in 1960 and ran serially in the *Saturday Evening Post*.

Rocky Mountain region.   The Rocky Mountains extend for more than four thousand miles from the Mexican frontier to the Arctic in Canadian territory. In the United States Colorado, Utah, Nevada, Wyoming, Montana, and Idaho are included in this area. Highest peak in this range within the United States is Mt. Ebert in Colorado; the state contains 1,064 peaks exceeding 10,000 feet in elevation. The Rockies form the Continental Divide separating Pacific drainage from Atlantic (Gulf of Mexico) and Arctic drainage. They contain rich mineral deposits, fertile mountain pastures, and forest wealth, as well as providing a habitat for much wild life. They also are a great reservoir of water and power. In the American Rockies are Yellowstone, Glacier, Grand Teton, and Rocky Mountain National Parks.

In 1540 Coronado's scouts penetrated into the region, where the Pueblo Indians had a notable civilization. There were other Spanish explorers at the beginning of the 18th century, and French explorers came from Canada in 1742. But the mountain area was not very well known until the United States acquired part of it by the Louisiana Purchase, and the Lewis and Clark Expedition (see MERIWETHER LEWIS) explored it (1805–06). Their *Journal* has many references to the region, which soon became familiar to fur traders and trappers who, along with missionaries, entered it in large numbers during the early decades of the 19th century. In 1847 the Mormons found their Zion here and introduced irrigation. After the Mexican War the United States obtained title to the entire region. Settlements were set up in portions that later became states, especially when miners who had made no finds in California came back to Colorado, Nevada, Idaho, and Montana and made discoveries as rich as those in the Pacific state. Then began a new mythology, that of the mountain miners, with Mark Twain, Bret Harte, and others as their chroniclers. The wealth of the region increased and with it a deepening interest in the arts. The states and their people are individualists, with some distrust of the capitalist East.

Mark Twain's ROUGHING IT (1872) is the literary classic of the region; in the days of the great silver-mining boom, Twain got his literary start working on the Virginia City (Nevada) *Territorial Enterprise*.

Rocky Mountain Review,   a quarterly founded as the *Intermountain Review* in 1937. Retitled, it was printed in Utah until 1946. When Ray B. West took over as editor it was moved to Lawrence, Kansas, and then to the State University of Iowa in 1949. Originally a regional magazine, it became more generally literary. It ceased publication in 1959.

Roderick Hudson (1876),   a novel by HENRY JAMES. This was James's first major work and was written after he had emigrated to Europe. The titular hero is a precocious sculptor from Massachusetts whom Rowland Hallett, a rich patron of the arts, takes abroad. Rowland expects Roderick to develop his talent under the influence of classical sculpture. Roderick becomes engaged to Mary Garland before he leaves America but in Italy falls passionately in love with the beautiful but inconstant Christina Light. Roderick abandons his art, in spite of his early success, to pursue Christina, even after she marries Prince Casamassima and travels to Switzerland. His patron denounces him, his fiancée joins him in Switzerland, but Roderick is unable to recover his moral balance. He wanders off into the mountains during a storm and is found dead at the foot of a cliff. The ultimate tragedy is Rowland's. His hope that Mary would some day return his smoldering love for her is stifled under her silent accusation that he had abandoned Roderick. In this early novel James uses several techniques characteristic of his later works: the point-of-view shifts but usually resides in Rowland's mind, the intricate but precise structure unifies the story, and the style hints at the complexities of James's mature prose. James revised it extensively in later years. Christina reappears in THE PRINCESS CASAMASSIMA.

Rodgers, Richard (1902–1979),   composer. Rodgers, born in New York City, wrote the music for many popular musical comedies. His collaboration with LORENZ HART began in the autumn of 1919 when Rodgers entered Columbia College and wrote the music for the varsity show, the first freshman in Columbia's history to achieve this distinction. With Hart he created such hit shows as *A Connecticut Yankee* (1927), *I Married an Angel* (1937), *The Boys from Syracuse* (1938), *Pal Joey* (1940), and many others. His collaboration with OSCAR HAMMERSTEIN II began in 1942, when they turned LYNN RIGGS's play GREEN GROW THE LILACS into a spectacularly successful folk opera, OKLAHOMA! (1943, Pulitzer Prize). They went on to write *Carousel* (1945), based on Ferenc Molnár's *Liliom*; *South Pacific* (1949), with JOSHUA LOGAN, based on JAMES A. MICHENER's TALES OF THE SOUTH PACIFIC (1949, New York Drama Critics Circle Award; 1950, Pulitzer Prize); *The King and I* (1951); *Me and Juliet* (1953); *Flower Drum Song* (1958); and *The Sound of Music* (1959). Most of these were later filmed. After Hammerstein's death, Rodgers supplied music and lyrics for *No Strings* (1962).

Among Rodgers's best-known songs are "If I Loved You," "This Can't Be Love," "There's a Small Hotel," "My Heart Stood Still," "Oh, What a Beautiful Morning!" and "Some Enchanted Evening." *The Rodgers and Hart Song Book* was issued in 1951, *Six Plays* by Rodgers and Hammerstein in 1955. Deems Taylor's *Some Enchanted Evenings* (1953) is an account of the Rodgers and Hammerstein partnership.

Rodman, Selden (1909–   ),   art critic, writer, editor. Rodman, born in New York City, has been codirector of the remarkable *Centre d'Art* in Port-au-Prince; he was also a pioneer in encouraging Haitian primitive artists and has written two enthusiastic and stimulating books on Haiti: *Renaissance in Haiti* (1948) and *Haiti: the Black Republic* (1954). As a poet he pioneered in writing about air flight in *The Airmen* (1941). Among his other works are *Lawrence: The Last Crusade* (1937); *The Revolutionists* (a play, 1942); *The Amazing Year: A Diary in Verse* (1947); *Portrait of the Artist as an American* (1951); *The Eye of Man: Form and Content in Western Painting* (1955); and *Conversations with Artists* (1957). *The Insiders* (1960) is a study of modern painting, and *Where Art Is Joy* (1988) is about Haitian art. *Tongues of Fallen Angels* (1974) recounts Rodman's conversations with writers such as ALLEN GINSBERG and NORMAN MAILER.

Rodriguez, Richard (1944–   ), memoirist, essayist. Born to a Mexican-American family in San Francisco, Rodriguez was educated at Stanford; Columbia; the University of California, Berkeley; and the Warburg Institute, London. *Hunger of Memory: The Education of Richard Rodriguez* (1982) details the loss of ethnicity that is the by-product of education. In it and the subsequent *Days of Obligation: An Argument with My Mexican Father* (1992), Rodriguez attacks bilingual education and affirmative action as ineffectual remedies for social ills.

Roe, E[dward] P[ayson] (1838–1888), clergyman, novelist. Roe, born in New Windsor, New York, was ordained in 1862, served as a chaplain during the Civil War and then as minister to the Highland Falls, New York, Presbyterian Church for eight years. His curiosity and compassion were aroused by reports of the great Chicago fire of 1872. He visited the city, examined the ruins, and wrote his first novel, *Barriers Burned Away*, as a magazine serial. It was published in book form in 1872 and became an immediate best seller. His second novel, *Opening a Chestnut Burr* (1874), was so favorably received that Roe resigned his pastorate to devote himself to writing. He published seventeen more novels, most of them best sellers. Among his other titles are *From Jest to Earnest* (1875), *A Knight of the Nineteenth Century* (1877), *A Face Illumined* (1878), *Without a Home* (1881), *A Young Girl's Wooing* (1884), *Driven Back to Eden* (1885), *He Fell in Love with His Wife* (1886), and *Found Yet Lost* (1888). *Play and Profit in My Garden* (1873) and *A Manual on the Culture of Small Fruits* (1880) show his interest in horticulture. His sister Mary A. Roe wrote *EPR, Reminiscences of His Life* (1899).

Roethke, Theodore (1908–1963), poet. Roethke was born in Saginaw, Michigan, where his sternly Prussian father ran a successful floral business. Roethke grew up surrounded by the enterprise of bringing plants into life, and a preoccupation with literal and symbolic growth and transfiguration prevails in his poetry, as does a search for the acceptance and nurture he evidently missed as a child. He was educated at the University of Michigan, and beginning in 1931 taught at Lafayette College, Michigan State, Penn State, and Bennington, before settling finally at the University of Washington in Seattle in 1947. Friendships with ROLFE HUMPHRIES, STANLEY KUNITZ, and LOUISE BOGAN helped him decide on a career as a poet. Fiercely competitive, and sometimes clownish or vulgar in speech, he was a bear

of a man with an ego to match, but his aggressive manner masked a sometimes debilitating psychic vulnerability. He suffered the first of a series of breakdowns in 1936, and his struggles with alcohol sometimes led to personal and professional difficulties. His growing reputation never eased his need to be perceived as the best poet alive, but he was known as an fine teacher, and his commitment to the draining process of self-exploratory writing was genuine. He found comparative stability and happiness with his young wife, Beatrice, after their marriage in 1953 but died suddenly of a heart attack in 1963.

His first book, *Open House* (1941), was rather conventional, but his second, *The Lost Son and Other Poems* (1948), broke new ground, beginning with a collection of arrestingly vivid greenhouse poems and concluding with a cycle of related lyric sequences that are harrowing, dreamlike explorations of childhood, nature, and an exposed psyche. The surreal element in Roethke's work intensified in the meditative sequences of *Praise to the End!* (1951). *The Waking* (1953), which won a Pulitzer Prize, was marked by a return to a more traditional formal elegance. *Words for the Wind* (1958), generally considered his finest book, won the National Book Award and the Bollingen Prize. His last collection, *The Far Field*, posthumously published in 1964, is sometimes criticized for its echoes of Yeats, but it demonstrated Roethke's continued command of the meditative sequence. A prose collection, *On the Poet and His Craft*, appeared in 1965, followed by *Collected Poems* in 1966. Selections from his notebooks and letters have also been published.

JOHN BERRYMAN aptly characterized Roethke's work as "Teutonic, irregular, botanical, psychological, irreligious, personal . . . witty, savage, and willing to astonish." Roethke insisted that "we must permit poetry to extend consciousness as far, as deeply, as particularly as it can," and his longer poems often entail psychic journeys sharply objectified in the context of nature. His refreshingly original rhythms are keenly articulated and often hypnotic. Although his work is uneven and he sometimes gives way to self-indulgence or to surprising naiveté, many of his best poems re-create disconcertingly intense psychic or mystical experience. He also had a flair for the seductively lyrical and the brashly irreverent. He ranks as one of the best poets of the first postmodern generation. There are many critical studies, and Allan Seager's *The Glass House* is an engaging biography.

THOMAS J. TRAVISANO

Roger Malvin's Burial (*The Token*, 1832, collected in *Mosses from an Old Manse*, 1846),   a story by NATHANIEL HAWTHORNE. The background of this story is the battle described in the old ballad of *Lovewell's Flight*, which—together with a prose document—Hawthorne uses to start his narrative. He relates how Roger Malvin and Reuben Bourne, the young man betrothed to Malvin's daughter Dorcas, are returning wounded from the battle. The older man knows he must die soon and begs Reuben to go on without him. But he exacts a pledge that Reuben will return and give him proper burial. Reuben fails to fulfill his promise and all through the years is a moody, stricken man. Much later, through personal tragedy, the curse is removed. See also HUGH GLASS; JOHN LOVEWELL.

Rogers, John (1648–1721), Connecticut religious leader whose opposition to formal clergy and advocacy of total separation of church and state brought him into conflict with religious and political authority. He defended his ideas in *The Book of the Revelation of Jesus Christ* (1720).

Rogers, Robert (1731–1795), explorer, soldier, memoirist. Rogers, born in Methuen, Massachusetts, was one of the great adventurers of American history, but a man of unstable character and doubtful morals. He loved hunting, fishing, and fighting, and traded with the Indians and fought them. To escape prosecution for counterfeiting he enlisted as a scout and spy in the French and Indian War. He found favor with Sir William Johnson and became a ranger, a term denoting a soldier, usually mounted, whose business it was to range over an area for its protection, especially against Indians. Johnson placed Rogers in charge of a company of rangers, later of nine companies. He performed many daring and heroic deeds, helped capture Montreal, and in 1763 assisted in putting down PONTIAC's rebellion. He was a popular hero for his exploits against the Indians, but also engaged in illicit deals with them that left him heavily in debt.

In 1765 Rogers went to England, eager for political appointments and literary fame. He took three manuscripts, the first two published in 1765, the third in 1766. *A Concise Account of North America* gave, for the first time in English, a full account of the Old West, which Rogers had traversed on horse, on foot, and by canoe. His *Journals* (reprinted 1883) are about his early years as a ranger. His play PONTEACH, OR, THE SAVAGES OF AMERICA is a curious work, the first known play to deal primarily with Native Americans. The hero, about whose tragic life Rogers wrote in blank verse of little merit, is Pontiac, against whom Rogers had fought but whom apparently he admired.

Rogers succeeded in getting himself appointed to a post at Mackinac from which he could send out exploring expeditions into the Northwest, but he was accused of dealing illegally with the French and aiming to set up a realm of his own. He was arrested by General Thomas Gage, tried by court-martial, acquitted, and in 1769 was again in England, where he sued General Gage unsuccessfully. In 1774 he went into the service of the Bey of Algiers. In the following year he returned to America. He offered his services to both sides in the Revolution, but Washington had him arrested as a spy. He was paroled but nevertheless entered the service of the British as captain of a company of the Queen's American Rangers. He was defeated in a skirmish near White Plains, New York. In 1780 he returned to England, where he died in obscurity and poverty. Kenneth Roberts built NORTHWEST PASSAGE, one of his best novels, around Rogers (1937). The Queen's American Rangers appear in Frank Hough's *The Neutral Ground* (1941).

Rogers, Robert Cameron (1862–1912), poet. Rogers is remembered chiefly for his poem "The Rosary" (1894), which appeared in *The Rosary and Other Poems* (1906) and was set to music by Ethelbert Nevin (1898). Rogers issued other collections, including *The Wind in the Clearing and Other Poems* (1895) and *For the King and Other Poems* (1899).

Rogers, Will[iam Penn Adair] (1879–1935), rancher, actor, humorist. The Oklahoma-born Rogers was one of the most striking and original figures to appear in American literature and on the American stage. He became a rancher, then sold his holdings to make a trip around the world. Partly of Indian ancestry, he joined a Wild West show in the Argentine in 1902 under the name Cherokee Bill. He was a skilled horseman and an expert with the lasso, and later his expertness became part of a vaudeville act in which the circlings of the lasso were interspersed with seemingly naive, but in reality very shrewd, wisecracks. By 1905 he had reached New York City, where he performed in Hammerstein's Roof Garden. In 1914 he became a leading member of the cast of the Ziegfeld Follies. His wisecracks became popular sayings and led to his starting a newspaper column (1926), speaking as a radio commentator, and appearing in numerous movies. He played characteristically homely roles and made sage and witty remarks; among these movies were *State Fair*, *A Connecticut Yankee*, *David Harum*, *Judge Priest*, *Lightnin'*, and *Steamboat Round the Bend*. He wrote a series of books: *The Cowboy Philosopher on Prohibition* (1919), *The Cowboy Philosopher on the Peace Conference* (1919), *What We Laugh At* (1920), *The Illiterate Digest* (1924), *Letters of a Self-Made Diplomat to His President* (1927), *There's Not a Bathing-Suit in Russia* (1927), and *Will Rogers' Political Follies* (1929). An early aviation enthusiast, he was killed in an accident while flying in Alaska with the noted aviator Wiley Post. In 1949 Donald Day made a selection from his writings that was called *The Autobiography of Will Rogers*. Day also compiled selections from Rogers' newspaper columns in *Sanity Is Where You Find It* (1955). Several books about Rogers were written by people who knew him—P. J. O'Brien's *Will Rogers* (1935), Jack Lait's *Our Will Rogers* (1936), and Homer Croy's *Our Will Rogers* (1953).

Rohlfs, Mrs. Charles. Married name of ANNA KATHARINE GREEN.

Rojas [Sepúlveda], Manuel (1896–1973), Chilean novelist. Rojas wrote realistic fiction about urban life in Chile and Argentina. *Hombres del sur* (1927) is a story collection about the lives of working people. *Hijo de ladrón* (1951, tr. *Born Guilty*, 1955) is the first of a trilogy of autobiographical novels. His *Obras completas* appeared in 1961.

Rolfe, John (1585–1622), colonist. In 1609 Rolfe sailed from England for Virginia with his bride. After her death he began to cultivate Indian tobacco and succeeded in producing a variety that was "pleasant, sweet, and strong." The sale of tobacco brought prosperity to Virginia and insured the permanency of the settlement there. In 1613 Rolfe fell in love with POCAHONTAS, who was brought to Jamestown as a hostage. He married her a year later and in 1616 sailed with her to England. After she died in 1617 Rolfe wrote an *Account of Virginia*, which was first printed in the United States in the *Southern Literary Messenger* (June 1839). He returned to Virginia and is believed to have been killed by Indians. *A True*

Relation of the State of Virginia Left by Sir Thomas Dale in May Last 1616, by Rolfe, was printed in 1951. Ralph Hamor's *A True Discourse of the Present State of Virginia* (1615) and John Smith's *The Generall Historie of Virginia* (1624) show the importance of Rolfe in the development of the colony.

Rolling Stone, The,   the name William Sydney Porter (O. HENRY) gave to W. C. BRANN's *Iconoclast* when he purchased it in 1894 and began issuing it at Austin, Texas. The magazine was resold to Brann in 1895, and he changed the name back to *Iconoclast*. Porter's estate in 1913 published a collection of stories, poems, and sketches called *Rolling Stones*, which included some pieces from the magazine.

Rolling Stones Magazine,   a successful periodical on popular culture founded in 1967 by Jann Wenner. Among the first to note the influence of the Beatles and Bob Dylan, Wenner championed rock and roll as the message of rebellious youth. Robert Draper's *Rolling Stone Magazine: The Uncensored History* appeared in 1990.

Rollins, Philip Ashton (1869–1950),   lawyer, historian of the West. Rollins, born in New Hampshire, was deeply interested in the West and in 1920 began collecting early Western Americana. In 1945 he and his wife presented three thousand items from this collection to Princeton, his alma mater. Rollins wrote *The Cowboy: His Characteristics, His Equipment, and His Part in the Development of the West* (1922); *The Cowboy: An Unconventional History* (1936); and *Gone Haywire* (1939). He also edited Robert Stuart's *The Discovery of the Oregon Trail* (1935).

Rollo Books.   See JACOB ABBOTT.

Rölvaag, Ole Edvart (1876–1931),   novelist. Born into a fishing family in Norway, Rölvaag emigrated to South Dakota as a young man (1896). He worked for three years to earn the money he needed to attend Augustana College, a preparatory school. He was graduated from St. Olaf's College in Minnesota in 1905, and after a year at the University of Oslo, came back to teach Norwegian there. All of his novels were written in Norwegian. His first, *Amerika-Breve*, or *Letters from America* (1912), published under the pseudonym Paal Morck, was followed in 1914 by *On Forgotten Paths. Giants in the Earth* (1927, tr. by Lincoln Colcord), his masterwork, was first published as two separate titles, *In Those Days* (1924) and *The Kingdom Is Founded* (1925), in Norway. The sequel, *Peder Victorious* (1929), was followed by *Pure Gold* (1930), an English version of the Norwegian *Two Simpletons* (1920). His other titles are *Their Father's God* (1931) and *The Boat of Longing* (1933).

Roman Catholic Church in the United States. Catholic churches were established in Santo Domingo, Haiti, Puerto Rico, and Cuba in the first half of the 16th century. The first parish in the continental United States was that of St. Augustine, Florida (1565). The Jesuits were active missionaries to Indian tribes around the Great Lakes. Beginning in the 1770s, missions were built along the California coast under the leadership of JUNÍPERO SERRA, a Franciscan. Catholicism was not tolerated in most colonies. Maryland, which was founded by the Catholic Calvert family, was an exception, and the atmosphere of religious tolerance fostered by Roger Williams in Rhode Island and the Quakers in Pennsylvania offered some protection. JOHN CARROLL, a Jesuit who was the first Catholic bishop in the United States, consecrated in Baltimore in 1790, helped found Georgetown University. Nineteenth-century immigration by Irish, German, and Italian settlers increased the numbers of U.S. Catholics dramatically, and religious bigotry predictably found voice in movements such as the Know-Nothings in the 1840s and 1850s.

Romance (1913),   a play by EDWARD SHELDON. When a young man comes to tell his grandfather, a clergyman, of his intention to marry an actress, the older man tries to dissuade him by relating the great romance of his own youth, when he fell in love with an Italian opera singer. The grandson sticks to his resolution, and the grand accepts his decision. The play was one of the first to make use of the flashback as a stage device.

Romance of Dollard, The (1888),   a historical novel by MARY HARTWELL CATHERWOOD. This romantic story of New France in 1660 was Catherwood's first important success. A young woman of noble birth comes to Quebec with a shipload of other women who are ready to choose husbands among the eager frontiersmen. She marries the commandant of Montreal, who had known her in France. He returns to his post, is compelled to leave her to fight an Indian invasion, and she insists on joining him and is killed when the fort is taken by the Iroquois. Francis Parkman wrote a preface for the book and vouched for the truth of the main incidents.

Roman influence.   See GREEK AND ROMAN INFLUENCE.

Romans, Bernard (c. 1720–c. 1784),   natural historian. A native of the Netherlands, Romans was sent as a surveyor to Georgia and Florida in the mid-18th century by the British government. He served in the Continental Army in the Revolution. In addition to mapping and drawing nautical charts, he wrote *A Concise Natural History of East and West Florida* (1775).

Romantic Comedians, The (1926),   a novel by ELLEN GLASGOW. Like Glasgow's *They Stooped to Folly* (1929) and *The Sheltered Life* (1932), this novel is a satirical comedy of manners.

Roosevelt, [Anna] Eleanor (1884–1962),   diplomat, writer. Born into the prominent Roosevelt family, the niece of President THEODORE ROOSEVELT, she was involved in social causes before her marriage to her distant cousin FRANKLIN DELANO ROOSEVELT in 1905. When Franklin was crippled by poliomyelitis in 1921, she became his link with the world of politics. She was particularly active, as wife of the governor of New York and then the president, in issues relating to women and young people and in civil rights. In 1935 she began writing a syndicated daily column, "My Day." During World War II she was assistant director of the Office of Civilian Defense and traveled to Europe and Asia for the president. After FDR's death, from 1945 to 1953 and again in 1961, she was the U.S. delegate to the United Nations; in 1946 she was made Chairman of the U.N. Commission on Human Rights. Her writings include *This Is My Story* (1937), *The Moral Basis of Democracy* (1940), *I Remember* (1949), *On My Own* (1958), *You Can*

Learn by Living (1960), and *The Autobiography of Eleanor Roosevelt* (1961). Biographies are by T. K. Hareven (1968), J. R. Kearney (1968), and Joseph P. Lash (2 v. 1971–72, 1984).

Roosevelt, Franklin D[elano] (1882–1945), 32nd president. Roosevelt was a fifth cousin of THEODORE ROOSEVELT, who was also his wife's uncle. His family, of Dutch and English descent, was wealthy, and he was educated at Groton and Harvard. He then attended Columbia University Law School and there married ANNA ELEANOR ROOSEVELT. Admitted to the bar in 1907, he entered politics in 1910 as the leader of a group of insurgents against Tammany Hall in New York City; he won election to the state legislature. He supported WOODROW WILSON in 1912, and in 1913 was made an Assistant Secretary of the Navy under Josephus Daniels. In 1920 he was nominated as vice-presidential candidate on the Democratic ticket with James M. Cox and battled eloquently for the League of Nations. In August 1921, Roosevelt was stricken with poliomyelitis; he went to Warm Springs, Georgia, to take the cure but, although his condition was somewhat alleviated, he remained crippled for the rest of his life. He later established a foundation at Warm Springs.

Roosevelt never gave in to his affliction. He supported Governor Alfred E. Smith of New York for the Democratic presidential nomination, and Smith in turn urged Roosevelt to accept nomination for the governorship of New York. Smith lost to Hoover, but Roosevelt was elected governor and served for two terms, winning national recognition for his progressive policies. In 1932 he won the presidential nomination and was elected by a tremendous majority. He was reelected three times—a unique and, to some opponents, a dangerous achievement in American political history. In combatting the effects of the Depression, he introduced a series of drastic reforms, creating many new kinds of governmental agencies: the Civilian Conservation Corps, the Agricultural Adjustment Administration, the Tennessee Valley Authority, the National Recovery Administration, the Works Progress Administration, the Public Works Administration, and others. Many denounced the increasing invasion of private business by these agencies. Roosevelt suffered defeat only when he tried to enlarge the Supreme Court in order to facilitate the legislation needed to establish some of his remedial measures.

The national debt increased enormously during Roosevelt's terms, but so did national income. World War II brought a new phase of the Roosevelt era. With masterly command of propaganda techniques Roosevelt aroused the country against the Fascist threat. He and Winston Churchill from the beginning looked beyond the war to a world in which wars would cease. America built up history's greatest fighting machine up until Roosevelt's time, defeated its enemies on all the continents, and began preparing the atom bomb.

In failing health, Roosevelt took part in the Yalta Conference (February 1945) with Churchill and Stalin. Roosevelt has been criticized for making concessions to Stalin there that allowed for eventual Soviet domination of Eastern Europe. When Roosevelt died in April 1945 of a cerebral hemorrhage, the war in Europe was nearly over, and Allied forces were closing in on the Japanese in the Pacific.

Roosevelt had an extraordinary gift for communication. Even more effective than his personal appearances for political addresses were his radio Fireside Chats. Although earlier presidents had held press conferences somewhat casually, Roosevelt made them a potent instrument of communication with the public. A transcript of the proceedings was always made, and these were published in the *Public Papers and Addresses of Franklin D. Roosevelt*, edited by Samuel I. Rosenman (1928–45). Roosevelt had help with his speeches, as have many other presidents, but according to Robert E. Sherwood, no matter who contributed suggestions, phrases, or whole passages, the speech in its final version was Roosevelt's. His ghostwriting personnel changed from time to time, but the tone and rhythm of his speeches remained the same. Among the presidents he stands next to Lincoln as an orator and a phrase-maker. One may recall a few of his statements: "I pledge you, I pledge myself, to a new deal for the American people" (*Address at Chicago*, July 2, 1932); "Let me assert my firm belief that the only thing we have to fear is fear itself" (*First Inaugural Address*, March 4, 1933); "I see one-third of a nation ill-housed, ill-clad, ill-nourished" (*Second Inaugural Address*, January 20, 1937); "We have learned that we cannot live alone, at peace; that our own well-being is dependent upon the well-being of other nations far away. We have learned that we must live as men and not as ostriches, not as dogs in the manger" (*Fourth Inaugural Address*, January 20, 1945).

Roosevelt wrote *The Happy Warrior, Alfred E. Smith* (1928); *Government—Not Politics* (1932); *Looking Forward* (1933); and *On Our Way* (1934). Collections of his writings include J. B. S. Hardman, *Rendezvous with Destiny: Addresses and Opinions of Franklin D. Roosevelt* (1944); Dagobert Runes, *The American Way: Selections from the Public Addresses and Papers of Franklin D. Roosevelt* (1944); B. D. Zevin, *Nothing to Fear: The Selected Addresses of Franklin D. Roosevelt, 1932–46* (1946); *F.D.R.: His Personal Letters* (4 v. 1947, 1948, 1950); *F.D.R.: Columnist* (1947); *As FDR Said: A Treasury of His Speeches, Conversations, and Writings* (edited by Frank Kingdon, 1950); and *Franklin D. Roosevelt's Own Story, Told in His Own Words from His Private and Public Papers* (selected by Donald Day, 1951).

Roosevelt has been treated in many books, by friend and foe. Among them are Earle Looker, *This Man Roosevelt* (1932) and *The American Way: Franklin Roosevelt in Action* (1933); Charles A. Beard, *The Recovery Program, 1933–34* (with G. H. E. Smith, 1934); Rexford G. Tugwell, *The Battle for Democracy* (1935); Joseph Alsop and Turner Catledge, *The 168 Days* (1938); Emil Ludwig, *Roosevelt: A Study in Fortune and Power* (1938); Thomas E. Dewey, *The Case Against the New Deal* (1940); Robert H. Jackson, *The Struggle for Judicial Supremacy* (1941); Gerald W. Johnson, *Roosevelt: Dictator or Democrat?* (1941); Harold L. Ickes, *The Autobiography of a Curmudgeon* (1943) and *Secret Diary* (published in 1953 and following years); Frank Kingdon, *"That Man" in the White House* (1944); Edward R. Stettinius, *Lend-Lease: Weapon for Victory* (1944) and *Roosevelt and the Russians* (1949); Josephus Daniels, *The Wilson Era* (2 v. 1944, 1946) and *Shirt Sleeve Diplomat* (1947); Frances Perkins, *The Roosevelt I Knew*

(1946) and *The Roosevelt Myth* (1948); Cordell Hull's *Memoirs* (2 v. 1948); Henry L. Stimson and McGeorge Bundy, *On Active Service in Peace and War* (1948); Robert Sherwood, *Roosevelt and Hopkins* (1948); John Gunther, *Roosevelt in Retrospect* (1950); Allan Nevins, *The New Deal and World Affairs* (1950); James N. Rosenau, *Roosevelt Treasury* (a symposium, 1950); Harold F. Gosnell, *Champion Campaigner: Franklin D. Roosevelt* (1952); the correspondence of *Roosevelt and* [Josephus] *Daniels: A Friendship in Politics* (1952); Samuel I. Rosenman, *Working with Roosevelt* (1952); J.M. Burns, *Roosevelt: The Lion and the Fox* (1956); Arthur M. Schlesinger, Jr., *The Age of Roosevelt* (several volumes, 1957–1960); and Joseph P. Lash, *Eleanor and Franklin,* 1971. A one-volume biography is Frank Freidel's *Franklin D. Roosevelt: A Rendezvous with Destiny* (1990). Doris Kearns Goodwin won the Pulitzer Prize for *No Ordinary Time* (1994), a study of Franklin and Eleanor Roosevelt during World War II.

In a musical satire, *I'd Rather Be Right* (1937), by George S. Kaufman, Lorenz Hart, and Richard Rodgers, George M. Cohan gave a lifelike impersonation of Roosevelt. Dore Schary wrote a moving play about him, *Sunrise at Campobello* (1958), which ran on Broadway for over a year and was made into a film. It showed the effect on Roosevelt's character of the paralysis from which he suffered.

In *The Roosevelt Era* (1947) Milton Crane collected many contemporary pieces to reveal the kaleidoscopic background against which Roosevelt moved. He speaks with admiration of the effect of the New Deal in the field of letters and art, as shown by the admirable State Guides, the Federal Theater, and frescoes and murals all over the land. The WPA in cultural life was described in Wilson Whitman, *Bread and Circuses* (1937); *Federal Theater Plays* (2 v. 1938); Grace Overmyer, *Government and Arts* (1939); and Harold Clurman, *The Fervent Years: Group Theater* (1945).

Roosevelt, Kermit (1889–1943),   explorer, soldier, author of travel books. Kermit Roosevelt was THEODORE ROOSEVELT's son, born in the family's Oyster Bay, New York, home. Kermit accompanied his father on a hunting trip to Africa (1909–10) and in an exploration of Brazil (1914). He engaged in several business enterprises and became acquainted with various parts of the world, some of which he described in his writings. He served with the British army in World War II, later with the United States Army, and died while on active duty. Among his books are *War in the Garden of Eden* (1919); *The Happy Hunting Grounds* (1920); *Quentin Roosevelt—A Sketch with Letters* (1921), an account of his brother, killed in World War I, written in collaboration with another brother, Theodore, Jr.; *East of the Sun and West of the Moon* (1926); *Cleared for Strange Ports* (1927); *American Backlogs* (1928); and *Trailing the Giant Panda* (with Theodore, Jr., 1929).

Roosevelt, Theodore (1858–1919),   soldier, writer, 26th president. After graduation from Harvard, Roosevelt turned to writing history, in which he was intensely interested all his life. His first book was *The Naval War of 1812* (1882). He entered politics and served from 1882 to 1884 as a Republican member of the New York legislature. His health was fragile and

he restored it by engaging, sometimes recklessly, in strenuous physical activities; he published a book called THE STRENUOUS LIFE AND OTHER ESSAYS (1900). After the death of Alice Lee (1884), his first wife, Roosevelt went to the Dakota Territory, where he ranched and won the respect of the local inhabitants. At this time he completed several books: *Hunting Trips of a Ranchman* (1885), *Thomas Hart Benton* (1886), and *Ranch Life and the Hunting-Trial* (1888). Back home in New York, he reentered politics and married Edith Carow. He was appointed by President Harrison to the U.S. Civil Service Commission (1889–95). Then he was made police commissioner of New York City under a reform mayor, and his vigor and determination in that office won him national repute. At this time he published the last of the four volumes of THE WINNING OF THE WEST (1889–96).

In 1897 President McKinley made Roosevelt Assistant Secretary of the Navy; but when war with Spain broke out in 1898 Roosevelt resigned and organized the Rough Riders, a volunteer cavalry group he led into battle in Cuba. Roosevelt led a charge up San Juan Hill with great exuberance, although historians aver that the hill had already been captured. The commander returned to New York, was hailed as a hero, won nomination for governor, and was elected (1898). But Tom Platt, Republican boss of the state, feared Roosevelt's independence and induced the Republican convention in 1900 to get Roosevelt out of the way by nominating him as McKinley's running mate in the presidential campaign. Roosevelt accepted gloomily and was duly elected vice-president, but in 1901 McKinley was assassinated and Roosevelt became president.

Roosevelt had a reputation as a firebrand, alarming conservatives in his own party. He was the first president to recognize that a policy of isolation for the United States was dead. He realized further the primacy of economic issues and interfered actively in the business life of the nation. He was uncompromising in his view that all Americans were entitled to equal treatment, irrespective of race, creed, or color. An increasingly able politician who managed to get most of what he wanted from Congress, he was also a master of public relations, always the center of attraction. Anything—economic, social, ethical, literary, scientific, historical, journalistic—in which he happened to be interested was likely to be shoved into the headlines by one of his remarks.

Opinion has varied as to the profundity of Roosevelt's mind and the importance of his measures. In general historians feel he was not as radical as he seemed. The Square Deal he proclaimed anticipated the New Deal of his cousin Franklin Delano Roosevelt in many ways and equally alarmed many contemporaries. In his trust-busting activities Roosevelt brought about numerous reforms that made business competition at least somewhat more decorous and provided important ground rules for business practice. Aroused by Upton Sinclair's THE JUNGLE (1906), he brought about passage of the Pure Food and Drug Act. He sought somewhat unsuccessfully to conserve natural resources. He did effect the building of the Panama Canal. He settled the Alaska boundary dispute and helped negotiate an end to the Russo-Japanese War. He had a firm maxim for international affairs: "Speak softly and carry a big stick." As John Morton Blum shows in *The Republican Roosevelt* (1954), the president had three chief political ideas: he believed in power, in the strong executive; he believed in order, enforced by the executive; and he believed in morality for everybody.

In 1908 Roosevelt decided not to run again for president, fearing "the concentration of power in one hand." In March 1909, he turned the presidency over to his lieutenant, WILLIAM HOWARD TAFT, and departed on a hunting trip in Africa and a tour of Europe. He came home to find the Republican Party he had hoped to make one of "sane, constructive radicalism" returned to rank conservatism, and soon it was open war. Unable to win the Republican nomination in 1912, Roosevelt organized the progressive Bull Moose party, ran against both Taft and Woodrow Wilson, and took enough votes away from Taft to make Wilson the winner. In World War I Roosevelt spoke and wrote steadily in favor of intervention. His son Quentin was killed in action; in World War II his sons Kermit and Theodore died in active service. In his last years Roosevelt was embittered and frustrated, often violent in expressing his views.

Of all American presidents, with the possible exception of Woodrow Wilson, Roosevelt was probably the most deeply interested in books and the nearest to being a professional writer. The help he gave Edwin Arlington Robinson when that poet was in need is well known. (See CHILDREN OF THE NIGHT.) He often talked about books in public, and his endorsement could make a best seller. His own books sold well, especially *The Winning of the West*. He felt that historical writing must be vivid as well as accurate.

He also wrote, in addition to the books noted above, *American Ideals and Other Essays* (1897); *Oliver Cromwell* (1900); *Outdoor Pastimes of an American Hunter* (1905); *The New Nationalism* (1910); *History as Literature and Other Essays* (1913); *Theodore Roosevelt, An Autobiography* (1913); *Through the Brazilian Wilderness* (1914); *America and the World War* (1915); *A Book-Lover's Holidays in the Open* (1916); and *The Great Adventure* (1918). His *Diaries of Boyhood and Youth* were published in 1928, selections from his *Letters* (8 v.) in 1951–54.

His collected works have appeared in several editions. Samuel E. Morison wrote an introduction for *Three Great Letters by Theodore Roosevelt* (1954) and edited *The Hunting and Exploring Adventures of Theodore Roosevelt* (told in his own words, 1955). Hermann Hagedorn edited selections called *The Free Citizen* (1956) and wrote *Roosevelt in the Bad Lands* (1921), *The Rough Riders* (1927), and *The Roosevelt Family of Sagamore Hill* (1954).

Other books dealing with Roosevelt include Henry Cabot Lodge, *Theodore Roosevelt* (1919); Corinne Roosevelt Robinson, *My Brother, Theodore Roosevelt* (1921); Earle Looker, *The White House Gang* (1929); Owen Wister, *Roosevelt: The Story of a Friendship* (1930); H. U. Faulkner, *The Quest for Social Justice* (1931); Claude Bowers, *Beveridge and the Progressive Era* (1932); G. E. Mowry, *Theodore Roosevelt and the Progressive Movement*

(1946) and *The Era of Theodore Roosevelt, 1900–1912* (1958); and Edward Wagenknecht, *The Seven Worlds of Theodore Roosevelt* (1959). John Hall Wheelock prepared a *Bibliography of Theodore Roosevelt* (1920), and A. B. Hart and H. R. Ferleger prepared a *Theodore Roosevelt Cyclopedia* (1941).

Root, George Frederick (1820–1895),   composer, music publisher. Some of the most popular martial songs of the Civil War period were composed by Root, who was born in Sheffield, Massachusetts. Among them are "There's Music in the Air, Boys"; "Tramp! Tramp! Tramp!"; and "Just Before the Battle, Mother." In his later years Root joined the publishing firm of Root & Cady in Chicago—the Root in the firm name was his brother. He also wrote many hymns, including "The Shining Shore," and several cantatas, among them *The Pilgrim Fathers* (1854). "Rosalie, the Prairie Flower" (1855) was his most successful sentimental ballad. Root wrote his autobiography in *The Story of a Musical Life* (1891).

Rootabaga Stories (1922),   juvenile fiction by CARL SANDBURG. The author called these whimsical sketches moral tales. Written in a style nearer poetry than prose, and rich in the language and cadence of folk songs, *Rootabaga Stories* is directed toward very young children. It was followed by *Rootabaga Pigeons* (1923).

Roots (1976),   a book-length description by ALEX HALEY of his search for the genealogical history of his family. He describes his trip to Gambia, the African homeland of his ancestors, and recounts the lives of his forebears. The Pulitzer Prize book was made into a successful television documentary.

Rosary, The.   See ROBERT CAMERON ROGERS.

Rose, Aquila (1696?–1723),   sailor, printer, poet. When Benjamin Franklin applied for a job at SAMUEL KEIMER's shop, he found him setting type for an elegy on Rose, who had been Keimer's assistant. Some years later Rose's son Joseph became Franklin's assistant and collected all his father's available poems as *Poems on Several Occasions* (1740).

Rosenbach, A[braham] S[imon] W[olf] (1876–1952), bibliophile, teacher, editor, writer. Rosenbach was an eminent collector of rare books and manuscripts; at his death his Philadelphia home was turned into a museum under the care of the Rosenbach Foundation. He also established (1930) the Rosenbach Fellowship in Bibliography at the University of Pennsylvania, where he had taught English from 1898 to 1901. Among Rosenbach's own books are *The Unpublishable Memoirs* (1917), *An American Jewish Bibliography* (1926), *Books and Bidders* (1927), *The All-Embracing Doctor Franklin* (1932), *Early American Children's Books* (1933), *The Libraries of the Presidents of the United States* (1934), *A Book Hunter's Holiday* (1936), and *The First Theatrical Company in America* (1939). *To Dr. R.: Essays Collected and Published in Honor of His 70th Birthday* was published in 1946, and a biography, *Rosenbach*, by Edwin Wolf and John F. Fleming appeared in 1960.

Rosenfeld, Monroe H.   See CHARLES K. HARRIS.

Rosenfeld, Morris (1862–1923),   poet. Born in Poland, Rosenfeld emigrated to America in 1886 and was submerged in the crowded New York City ghetto, where he worked as a presser in the sweatshops. Barely able to make a living, he wrote poems about the misery he saw about him that were printed in the Yiddish press. He published a collection of folk and revolutionary songs, *Die Glocke* (1888), followed in 1890 by *Die Blumenkette*. Leo Weiner published in *Songs of the Ghetto* (1898) some of Rosenfeld's poems in prose translations. *The Works of Morris Rosenfeld* (3 v.) appeared in 1908.

Rose of Dutcher's Coolly (1895, rev. ed. 1899),   a novel by HAMLIN GARLAND, it is the story of a Midwestern farm girl who attends the University of Wisconsin and then goes on to Chicago to become a writer, in rebellion against the restrictions of farm life. She rejects marriage as a hindrance to her literary development, but later changes her mind.

Rose Tattoo, The (1951),   a play by TENNESSEE WILLIAMS. Set in a Sicilian community on the Gulf Coast, the play deals with a passionate and earthy dressmaker, Serafina Delle Rose, whose truckdriver husband, Rosario, has just been killed. Serafina abandons herself to grief, keeps Rosario's ashes in a marble urn in the house, storms and rages and refuses to believe rumors that Rosario had been unfaithful, and, finally, after three years of widowhood and frustration, meets a young truckdriver who, like the dead Rosario, wears a rose tattoo on his chest.

Rosier, James (1575–1635),   explorer. Rosier may have been a priest; he accompanied George Waymouth when the latter in 1605 undertook to find for Sir Thomas Arundel a refuge for Roman Catholics somewhere along the eastern shore of North America. The voyagers investigated Nantucket and various sites on the present Massachusetts coast. Rosier wrote *True Relation of the Most Properous Voyage Made This Present Year 1605 by Captain George Waymouth* (1605). His account was reprinted in 1887, with notes, and in H.S. Burrage's *Early English and French Voyages* (1906).

Ross, Alexander (1783–1856),   explorer. Born in Scotland, Ross settled in Canada in 1804 and taught school for a few years before becoming a clerk in the Pacific Fur Company. He helped establish Fort Astoria in what is now Oregon. Later he was in charge of Fort Nez Percé. After fifteen years he moved back to Canada, where he became the first sheriff of the Red River Colony. He was a man of considerable influence as well as a valuable recorder of Northwestern history. *Adventures of the First Settlers on the Oregon or Columbia River* (1849) was followed by *The Fur Hunters of the Far West* (2 v. 1855) and *The Red River Settlement* (1856).

Ross, Barnaby.   A pen name used by Frederic Dannay and Manfred B. Lee, whose better known pseudonym is ELLERY QUEEN.

Ross, Harold [Wallace].   See THE NEW YORKER.

Ross, Leonard Q.   Pen name of LEO CALVIN ROSTEN.

Ross, Lillian (1927–   ),   journalist. Ross was born in Syracuse, New York, but throughout most of her career as a staff writer for *The New Yorker*, she worked hard to separate herself from the subjects of her writing and to keep details of her personal life from being publically known. All of this vigilance was cast aside in her memoir *Here but Not Here: A Love Story* (1998) in which she detailed her secret decades-long affair with her editor, William Shawn, who maintained, with her, an apartment separate from his wife and children. Other books are gatherings from pieces first published in the magazine. The best known of these is *Portrait of Hemingway*, a *New Yorker* profile in 1950 and book in 1961. Other gatherings of magazine pieces include *Picture* (1952), on the making of a film version of STEPHEN CRANE's *The Red Badge of Courage; Reporting* (1964); *Talk Stories* (1966); *Reporting Two* (1969); and *Takes: Stories from "The Talk of the Town"* (1983). *The Player: A Profile of an Art* (1962) was done with her sister, Helen Ross. *Vertical and Horizontal* (1963) is a collection of short stories. *Adlai Stevenson* (1966) is a reminiscence of the unsuccessful Democratic candidate for president, and *Moments with Chaplin* (1980) relates interviews with film legend Charlie Chaplin.

Ross, [James] Sinclair (1908–1996),   Canadian novelist. Ross treated life in rural Saskatchewan, where he was born, in *The Lamp at Noon* (1968), a story collection. His novels with similar subject matter are *As for Me and My House* (1941) and *Sawbones Memorial* (1974), and his other novels are *The Well* (1958) and *Whir of Gold* (1970). *The Race* (1982) is a story collection.

Ross, W. W. E[ustace] (1894–1966),   Ross was born in Peterborough, Ontario, and trained in geophysics at the University of Toronto. He served in England during World War I and then returned to a long career in Ontario, working at his chosen scientific profession. His first poems were printed in *Poetry Magazine* and *The Dial* in 1923. He was pronounced Canada's "first Imagist poet" by the editor of a retrospective collection, *Experiment 1923–29*, edited by Raymond Souster (1956), published late in his life. Exploring the landscape of Canada and using Canadian vocabulary in his spare lyrics, Ross was a departure from traditional European-style verse. His other collections are *Laconics* (1930) and *Sonnets* (1932). *Shapes and Sounds* (1968) is a posthumous selection.

Rossner, Judith [Perelman] (1935–   ),   novelist. Rossner was born and educated in New York City, and most of her fiction is set there. She is known best for *Looking for Mr. Goodbar* (1975), a graphic portrayal of the sexual dilemma of contemporary women. *Emmeline* (1980) is the story of a teenager sent to work in an 1830s cotton mill to support her family. *His Little Women* (1990) concerns father-daughter ties in the complex stepfamily relations of Hollywood. *Olivia* (1994) and *Perfidia* (1997) detail mother-daughter relations. Her other titles include *To the Precipice* (1966), *Nine Months in the Life of an Old Maid* (1969), *Any Minute I Can Split* (1972), and *Attachments* (1977).

Rosten, Leo Calvin ["Leonard Q. Ross"] (1908–1997),   political scientist, teacher, research worker, consultant, humorist. As a scholar Rosten, born in Poland, produced a number of informative studies, the best known of which is probably *Hollywood: The Movie Colony, the Movie Makers* (1941). His other books are *The Washington Correspon-*

dents (1937), an analysis of news gathering in the capital, and *A Guide to the Religions of America* (1955). Undoubtedly Rosten's most widely read book, however, is a book of comic sketches written under his pen name and concerned with the activities of a night school for immigrant adults, THE EDUCATION OF H*Y*M*A*N K*A*P*L*A*N (1937). *The Joys of Yiddish* (1968) popularized many expressions in that vernacular language.

Rosten, Norman (1914–1995),   poet, radio writer, playwright. Rosten, born in New York City, wrote a verse drama, *This Proud Pilgrimage*, which was produced first at the University of Michigan Theater in 1938; *First Stop to Heaven* appeared on Broadway in 1941. He has also written plays for radio, including some on American historical figures for the *Cavalcade of America*. His poems were collected in *Return Again, Traveler* (1940) and *The Fourth Decade and Other Poems* (1943). *The Big Road* (1946) describes the building of the Alcan highway to Alaska. This was followed by *Songs for Patricia* (1951) and *The Plane and the Shadow* (1953). His play *Mister Johnson*, based on the novel by Joyce Cary, was produced on Broadway in 1956.

Roth, Henry (1906–1995),   novelist, short-story writer, essayist. When Roth was eighteen months of age, his mother, Leah, brought him to New York from Austria in circumstances not unlike those described in Roth's major work, *Call It Sleep* (1934). Despite its abject poverty and terrible squalor, the Lower East Side, where the family moved when Henry was age four, provided a sense of community that Roth was never again able to recover. Roth was a freshman at City College of New York when he published a sketch entitled "Impressions of a Plumber" in the school magazine. The piece brought him to the attention of Eda Lou Walton, a member of City College's English Department. Already estranged from his family, Roth began living with Walton in 1928, encountering somewhat uneasily the intellectual figures and ideas of Walton's friends Ruth Benedict and Hart Crane, the popularized Freud, and perhaps most influential of all, the writings of James Joyce. *Call It Sleep*, written during his relationship with Walton, is dedicated to her.

Call It Sleep received largely favorable reviews, but Roth found it difficult, if not impossible, to continue his career as a writer. A planned second novel was never completed, and Roth spent the years between 1940 and the early 1960s working as a substitute teacher, precision grinder, psychiatrist's aide, and, finally, a raiser of water fowl in Maine. At the urging of critics Leslie Fiedler and Alfred Kazin, and with the help of anthologist Harold Ribalow, *Call It Sleep* was republished in 1964. No study of Jewish-American literature can ignore the central place that *Call It Sleep* now has in the canon. Dozens of articles have been written about it, and B. Lyons has published a book-length study entitled *Henry Roth: The Man and His Work* (1977). In 1987, at the age of 81, Roth published his second book, *Shifting Landscape*, a collection of short writings.

SANFORD PINSKER

Roth, Philip (1933–   ),   novelist, short-story writer, essayist. Roth was born and raised in lower middle-class Newark, New Jersey. After a freshman year at Newark College of Rutgers University, Roth completed his education at Bucknell University and the University of Chicago. In 1955, his story "The Contest for Aaron Gold" was published in *Epoch* magazine and anthologized in Martha Foley's *Best American Short Stories*.

Roth came to national attention when GOODBYE, COLUMBUS AND FIVE SHORT STORIES won the 1959 National Book Award. If an older generation of Jewish-American writers had insisted, in Bernard Malamud's phrase, that "All men are Jews," Roth's vision was the converse. In Roth's fiction, all Jews are men. Defenders of the official Jewish community were upset by Roth's satirical, often scathing, portrait of the manners and mores of life in suburbia, but critics were quick to defend both the voice and the social criticism.

Roth's next novels—*Letting Go* (1962), a thick, Jamesian account of graduate student angst, and *When She Was Good* (1967), a tale of Midwestern gentiles—attracted serious attention without adding to the controversies that still swirled around Roth's earlier stories. However, *Portnoy's Complaint* (1969), a wildly comic novel about Alexander Portnoy's ill-fated struggle to free himself from the Jewish jokes and tribal fears that define his life, turned Roth into a *cause célèbre* and forever branded him an *enfant terrible*. As Roth put it in *Reading Myself and Others* (1975): "I was . . . strongly influenced by a sit-down comic named Franz Kafka and a very funny bit he does called 'The Metamorphoses'. . . . [and] not until I got hold of guilt, you see, as a comic idea, did I begin to feel myself lifting free and clear of my last book and my old concerns."

Indeed, Kafka remains one of Roth's abiding spirits, along with Henry James, Chekhov, Joyce, and other Modernist masters. Roth's protagonists, however, tend to be comic victims of the High Art they hope will be forever separated from the messy interferences of Life. In *The Breast* (1972), a slim, and ultimately unsuccessful book, Alan David Kepesh, a professor of comparative literature, awakes one morning to discover that he has been metamorphosed into a human breast, rather than into the beetle of Kafka's tale or the nose of Gogol's story. He is, in short, the victim of too much teaching, too intensely done. As Kepesh insists, in a burst of agony and recognition, what happened to him "might be my way of *being* a Kafka, being a Gogol, being a Swift. They would *envision* these marvelous transformations—they had the language and those obsessive fictional brains. I didn't. So I had to live the thing."

After a parodic romp through every possible joke and counterjoke about baseball (*The Great American Novel*, 1973), Roth returned to the painful autobiographical centers of *My Life as a Man* (1974). As Roth pointed out in *The Facts* (1988), the fictional account of Peter Tarnopol's disastrous marriage needed few, if any, embellishments. As Tarnopol/Roth puts it: "A reader of Conrad's *Lord Jim* and Mauriac's *Therese* and Kafka's 'Letter to His Father,' of Hawthorne and Strindberg and Sophocles—of Freud—and still I did not know that humiliation could do such a job on a man. . . . For I cannot fully believe in the hopelessness of my predicament, and yet the line that concludes *The Trial* is as familiar to me as my own face: 'it was as if the shame of it must outlive him!' Only I am not a character in a book, certainly not that book. I am real. And my humiliation is equally *real*."

To tell his story—and *tell* it, and *tell* it yet again—becomes Tarnopol's fate, as it has become Roth's. In this sense, *My Life as a Man* is a confessional novel. But that said, the contradictory impulses to defend and to attack, to seek revenge and to gain approval, generate a series of dazzling narrative structures. Tarnopol creates an fictional voice, an alter ego named Nathan Zuckerman, and in two stories that Tarnopol calls "Useful Fictions," he is able to begin the slow process of patterning his pains into the contours of Art. *My Life as a Man* is divided, then, into two unequal parts: the Zuckerman stories, and then how a wide variety of readers, including Tarnopol, respond to them. The result is a postmodernist hall of reflecting mirrors, each one casting a partial truth about what Tarnopol calls his "True Story."

Curiously enough, Peter Tarnopol does not appear in Roth's subsequent books; rather it is Nathan Zuckerman who takes over both center stage and Roth's fictive voice. *The Ghost Writer* (1979) launched a series that has now stretched to include *Zuckerman Unbound* (1981), *The Anatomy Lesson* (1983), *The Prague Orgy* (1985), *The Counterlife* (1987), and even a long section—by way of critical response—in Roth's memoir *The Facts*. The trilogy of *American Pastoral* (1997), *I Married a Communist* (1998), and *The Human Stain* (2000) all include Zuckerman.

Of the early Zuckerman novels, most critics agree that *The Ghost Writer*—an account of how the young Nathan sought the approval and the sponsorship of E. I. Lonoff, an older, more established Jewish writer—is the most absorbing and the most artistically successful. The young Nathan has just completed the manuscript of his most ambitious tale to date—a saga of a family's squabbling over money entitled "Higher Education." Nathan's father and, later, Judge Wapter, the Newark's Jewish community's unofficial spokesperson, worry that the story will confirm anti-Semitic stereotypes and end in renewed persecutions. Nathan, on the other hand, insists that his story is merely that—a story. Roth suffered similar attempts at censorship when he published *Goodbye, Columbus* and it is clear he is writing close to the bone.

As Lonoff puts it, Nathan is "not so nice and polite" in his fiction. Indeed, there are those who think of him as a dangerous person with a pen in his hand. That number increases dramatically when Zuckerman publishes *Carnovsky*, a novel that bears more than a few resemblances to *Portnoy's Complaint*. *Zuckerman Unbound* recounts the pains that befall a writer who becomes rich and famous because he has written a controversial best seller. *The Anatomy Lesson* continues the dissection, this time using the central metaphor of Rembrandt's painting of an autopsy and a particularly scathing critical attack mounted by Milton Appel that is modeled on an unflattering 1972 *Commentary* article by Irving Howe. Never has Roth's abiding need for approval been more evident, and never

before has he tongued his aching tooth with such a furious obsession.

What never faltered, however, was the brilliance of Roth's sentences and his ability to project Zuckerman's distinctive voice over the long haul that novels demand. This was especially true of *The Counterlife*, an exercise in postmodernist storytelling that pitted voice against countervoice, Nathan's life against various imaginatively rendered counterlives. *The Facts* is yet another example of countervoices in operation—this time, Roth speaking autobiographically about the untransformed facts, the way his life *really* was, and Zuckerman, in a long response, commenting on why *his* voice is vastly superior to, however much it is dependent on, Roth's. In *Deception* (1990) Roth uses a character called Philip to explore the boundary between fiction and autobiography. *Patrimony: A True Story* (1991) is an autobiographical account focused on the death of Roth's father.

Roth retired from teaching at the University of Pennsylvania and Hunter College in 1992. The following year he won the PEN/Faulkner award for *Operation Shylock* (1993); *Sabbath's Theater* (1995) won the National Book Award. Roth was awarded the National Medal of Arts by President Bill Clinton in 1998.

Philip Roth turned the corner to the twenty-first century with a trio of books detailing how the trials of postwar nation impacted the lives of individual men. In *American Pastoral* (1997; Pulitzer Prize), "Swede" Levov, a legendary high school athlete and successful glovemaker, is devastated by his daughter's involvement in 1960s violent radical politics. *I Married a Communist* (1998) concerns the blacklisting and ruin occasioned by McCarthy-era witch-hunts. Coleman Silk of *The Human Stain* (2000) is a college professor forced into retirement when his chance reference to missing students as "spooks" is taken as a racial slur. The action unfolds in 1998 against the backdrop of the Clinton impeachment frenzy.

If Roth has collected a wide array of detractors—including outraged rabbis and offended feminists—he has also been the subject of a considerable body of serious literary criticism. Book-length studies include J. McDaniels's *The Fiction of Philip Roth* (1974), S. Pinsker's *The Comedy That "Hoits"* (1975), G. R. Searles's *The Fiction of Philip Roth and John Updike* (1985), and Alan Cooper's *Philip Roth and The Jews* (1996).

SANFORD PINSKER/BP

Rothenberg, Jerome (1935–   ),   poet. Educated at the City College of New York and the University of Michigan, Rothenberg has taught at schools in New York, California, and Wisconsin. His interest in ethnicity is reflected in his anthologies, including *Technicians of the Sacred* (1968), tribal and oral poetry, and *Symposium of the Whole* (1983), writings on ETHNOPOETICS. His own verse collections are *The Seven Hells of Jigoku Zoshi* (1962), *Poland/1931* (1969, 1974), *Poems for the Game of Silence 1960–1970* (1971), *Horse Songs for 4 Voices* (1978), *Vienna Blood and Other Poems* (1980), *That Dada Strain* (1983), *New Selected Poems* (1989), *Khurbn and Other Poems* (1989), and *The Lorca Variations* (1993). *Pre-Faces*, a collection of his writings on poetics, appeared in 1982.

Roueché, Berton (1911–1994), novelist, medical reporter, travel essayist. Roueché, born in Missouri, was educated at the University of Missouri and after his first novel, *Black Weather* (1945), turned to factual narratives of medical detection, usually published first in *The New Yorker*. *The Incurable Wound* (1958) comprises six stories of medical detection. Roueché deals with Northeastern Americana in *The Delectable Mountains* (1959), a series of offbeat interviews with unusual personalities. He won a Special Award in 1954 from the Mystery Writers of America. Among his other books are *Eleven Blue Men* (1953); *The Last Enemy* (1956), a novel; *The Neutral Spirit: A Portrait of Alcohol* (1960); *The River World and Other Explorations* (1978); *The Medical Detectives* (1980, 1984); *Special Places: In Search of Small Town America* (1982); *Sea to Shining Sea* (1985); and *The Man Who Grew Two Breasts* (1995).

Roughing It (1872), a narrative by MARK TWAIN. In this book Twain relates how he and his brother Orion made their way to Nevada in the early 1860s and worked in the mining camps. He then tells about his trip to San Francisco and the Sandwich Islands. He met numerous entertaining characters, among them desperadoes and vigilantes, newspapermen, and Brigham Young. He gives a marvelously vivid and fundamentally veracious picture of the Far West in the early days. He fictionalized himself and some of his companions, anticipating the techniques he later used in his novels. The book was written after INNOCENTS ABROAD had scored its great success and apparently as a result of that success. Elisha Bliss, publisher of the first book, proposed one of this kind, and on July 15, 1870, Twain wrote to Orion Clemens that he had begun the book that day and asked his brother to send him some notes he could use. Orion did so, as did Joseph Goodman and others. The book was published in February and did very well, but not as well as *Innocents*.

Round Table. This name was given to at least two informal groups of literary men and women and their friends who met for dinner or luncheon. The earlier one, chronicled in Brander Matthews's *Roster of the Round Table Dining Club* (1926), was founded in 1867 and continued to meet well into the 20th century. The other, sometimes called the Algonquin Round Table because its meetings were held in the Algonquin Hotel dining room in New York City, seems to have started about 1919 and soon included the best-known writers, newspapermen, artists, and musicians about town. A full account of the group is found in *Tales of a Wayward Inn* (1938), by Frank Case, the hotel's able and genial proprietor, and in *The Vicious Circle* (1951), by his daughter, Margaret Case Harriman.

Rouquette, Adrien Emmanuel (1813–1887), poet, novelist, priest. As a young boy in New Orleans, in his native state of Louisiana, he was fascinated by the nearby Choctaw Indians, and after becoming a priest, ministered to them. At his death he was working on a dictionary of the Choctaw language. He was opposed to slavery and wrote poetry in the *gombo* dialect. His poetry is collected in *Les Savanes* (1841);

Wild Flowers: Sacred Poetry (1848); *Patriotic Poems* (1860); and *L'Antoniade, ou La Solitude avec Dieu* (1860). *La Nouvelle Atala* (1879) is a romance novel. Under the pseudonym E. Junius, he wrote *Critical Dialogue Between Aboo and Caboo* (1880), an attack on GEORGE WASHINGTON CABLE's depiction of Creoles.

Rouquette, François Dominique (1810–1890), poet. Like his younger brother, François was deeply interested in the Choctaw Indians in the St. Tammany forest near their home. After his return from France where, like his brother, he was educated, François took up the life of a hermit in the woods. Later he taught in New Orleans and ran a grocery store in Arkansas. He published two poetry collections, *Les Meschacébéennes* (1839) and *Fleurs d'Amérique* (1856). He shared his brother's hatred of slavery and wrote about the nobility of Indians and African-Americans.

Rourke, Constance M[ayfield] (1885–1941), teacher, biographer, critic, historian. Rourke, born in Cleveland, wrote an important study: AMERICAN HUMOR: A STUDY OF THE NATIONAL CHARACTER (1931), as well as a book on Davy Crockett (1934) and others, including *Trumpets of Jubilee* (1927), *Troupers of the Gold Coast* (1928), *Audubon* (1936), and *Charles Sheeler: Artist in the American Tradition* (1938). Her posthumously published *The Roots of American Culture and Other Essays* (1942) expounds the view that the native American genius was not literary.

Rousseau and Romanticism (1919), a study of the romantic character by IRVING BABBITT. This prolonged attack against Naturalism as represented by Rousseau treats Romanticism as the emotional aspect of Rousseau's philosophy. In the romantic emphasis on the ego and on whim, Babbitt saw the chief menace to civilization. Against the Romantic ideal he posed the Humanist ideals of ethical restraint and classical standards of taste.

Rover Boys Series. A popular series of books for boys. It included more than thirty titles, the first published in 1899. The books were written by EDWARD STRATEMEYER under the pen name Arthur M. Winfield.

Rovere, Richard [Halworth] (1915–1979), political and literary critic. Rovere was educated at Bard College, then part of Columbia University. At various times he was an editor for the *New Masses, The Nation, Common Sense, Harper's* magazine, the *Spectator* of London, the *American Scholar*, and *The New Yorker*. His books deal largely with political controversy. *The General and the President* (1951), written with ARTHUR M. SCHLESINGER, JR., went into the bitter controversy between Douglas MacArthur and Harry Truman. His other books include *Howe and Hummel: Their True and Scandalous History* (1947), *The Eisenhower Years* (1956), *The Orwell Reader* (ed. 1956), and *Senator Joe McCarthy* (1959).

Rowan, Andrew Summers. See A MESSAGE TO GARCIA.

Rowlandson, Mary. See CAPTIVITY AND RESTAURATION OF MRS. MARY ROWLANDSON.

Rowson, Susanna [Haswell] (1762–1824), writer, actress, educator. Susanna Haswell, born in England, spent

1767 to 1778 in America, where her father, a naval lieutenant, was stationed in Massachusetts. Her first novel, *Victoria* (1786), published the same year she married the actor William Rowson, was not particularly successful, nor were *The Inquisitor, or, Invisible Rambler* (1788); *Poems on Various Subjects* (1788); *A Trip to Parnassus* (1788); or *Mary, or, the Test of Honour* (1789). In 1791 CHARLOTTE, A TALE OF TRUTH caught the popular fancy, particularly in America, where much of the sentimental and instructive romance is laid. When a business failure wiped out their fortune, the Rowsons appeared in plays by Mrs. Rowson, including *Slaves of Algiers* (1794), *The Female Patriot* (1795), *Trials of the Human Heart* (1795), and *Americans in England* (1796). They performed in England and America from 1793 to 1796.

Mrs. Rowson left the stage in 1797 and opened a girls' school in Boston. She edited the *Boston Weekly Magazine* and wrote *Reuben and Rachel, or, Tales of Old Times* (1798), a historical novel; *Miscellaneous Poems* (1804); *Sarah, or, the Exemplary Wife* (1813), a semiautobiographical novel; and *Charlotte's Daughter, or, The Three Orphans*, usually called *Lucy Temple* (posthumously pub. 1828).

Roxy (1878),   a novel by EDWARD EGGLESTON. It presents the trials and renunciations of a young woman in Indiana in the early 19th century.

Roy, Gabrielle (1909–1983),   Canadian novelist. Roy's first novel, *Bonheur d'occasion* (2 v. 1945, tr. *The Tin Flute* 1947 and 1980) is her best-known work. Set in the St. Henri district of Quebec and written in the patois of the area, it tells the story of Rose-Anna Lacasse, mother of eleven children, and their struggles in a crowded and impoverished household. It is set against the background of World War II, ironically a means of escape for the men of the district; the women must accept the "bargain basement happiness" of the French title. Her second novel, *La Petite poule d'eau* (1950, tr. *Where Nests the Water Hen*, 1951), which is set in rural Manitoba, also centers on a woman with many children, but the tone is more positive. With this novel and later works, Roy worked closely with her translators. Her other novels are *Alexandre Chenevert* (1954, tr. *The Cashier*, 1955); *La Montagne secrète* (1961, tr. *The Hidden Mountain*, 1962); and *La Route D'Altamont* (1966, tr. *The Road Past Altamont*, 1966). *La Rivière sans repos* (1970) comprises three short stories and the title novella; the novella was translated in *Windflower* (1970). *Rue Deschambault* (1955, tr. *Street of Riches*, 1957), *Un Jardin au bout du monde* (1975, tr. *Garden in the Wind*, 1977), and *Ces Enfants de ma vie* (1977, tr. *Children of My Heart*, 1979) are story collections. *Cet Eté qui chantait* (1972, tr. *Enchanted Summer*, 1976) is a gathering of sketches.

Royall, Anne Newport (1769–1854),   novelist, editor, travel writer. Born in Maryland, Anne Newport's early childhood was spent on the frontier of Pennsylvania. Her father died when she was thirteen, and she returned to the South, where she worked with her mother as household help for Captain William Royall of Virginia. In 1797, after educating Anne, Captain Royall married her. When he died sixteen years later, his fortune was given to another heir. His widow

turned to a career of writing. From 1824 until 1831 she traveled continually, recording her impressions of the life and manners she saw around her. In 1831 she published in Washington, D.C., the newspaper *Paul Pry*, which was succeeded by *The Huntress*. In them she constantly attacked fraud and graft in government circles, and as a result she was frequently reviled and ridiculed.

Her principal works are *Sketches of History, Life, and Manners in the United States* (1826); *The Black Book, or, A Continuation of Travels in the United States* (1828–29); *Mrs. Royall's Pennsylvania* (1829); *Mrs. Royall's Southern Tour* (1830–31); *Letters from Alabama* (1830); and a novel, *The Tennessean* (1827). *The Life and Times of Anne Royall*, by Sarah Harvey Porter (1909), was supplemented by George Stuyvesant Jackson's *The Uncommon Scold, the Story of Anne Royall* (1937).

Royce, Josiah (1855–1916),   philosopher, teacher, essayist. Taught at home by his mother until he was eleven, Royce, born in California, entered high school in San Francisco in 1869 and excelled in mathematics. At the newly established University of California he studied under Joseph Le Conte, a geologist. He received a Ph.D. from Johns Hopkins University in 1878, returning to teach English at the University of California for the next four years. In 1882 Royce went to Harvard to replace William James, who was absent on leave, and remained there for the rest of his life. *The Religious Aspect of Philosophy* (1885) established Royce's theory of the Absolute. He held that if one admits the presence of evil in the world, it necessarily follows that there is also an absolute principle of truth, an all-knowing mind, or Universal Thought. William James assailed this theory vigorously.

Royce was the leader of the post-Kantian idealistic school in this country. (See IDEALISM.) *The Spirit of Modern Philosophy* (1892), which weighs positivism and evolution and finds them wanting, was followed by *The Concept of God* (1897), *Studies in Good Will and Evil* (1898), *The World and the Individual* (2 v. 1900–01), *The Philosophy of Loyalty* (1908), *The Problem of Christianity* (2 v. 1913), and *Lectures on Modern Idealism* (1919). *His Fugitive Essays* (1920) deal with Shelley, George Eliot, and Browning. *The Feud of Oakfield Creek* (1887) was the philosopher's one attempt at fiction. Studies of Royce are found in *Papers in Honor of Josiah Royce on His 60th Birthday* (1916) and in Santayana's CHARACTER AND OPINION IN THE UNITED STATES (1920).

Royle, Edwin Milton (1862–1942),   playwright, actor, producer. Royle, born in Missouri, was educated at Princeton. His first play, *Friends* (1892), was based on the struggles of men like himself—musicians, singers, and writers. *Captain Impudence* (1897), a one-act sketch, had a long run in vaudeville. *My Wife's Husbands* (1903), a farce, was made into a musical comedy entitled *Marrying Mary* (1906). THE SQUAW MAN (1906), one of the most successful plays of its day, showed Royle's interest in absolute realism. The Indian chief was drawn from life; both he and his daughter spoke an authentic Ute dialect that Royle had learned from the Indians. The play became Cecil B. De Mille's first movie (1914) and the first movie made in Hollywood. *The Struggle Everlasting* (1907), a modern morality play, was followed by *The Unwritten Law*, another melodrama, and *Lancelot and Elaine* (1921), a dramatization of Tennyson's poem. Royle costarred with his wife, Selena Fetter, and produced many of his own plays. He also dramatized a number of novels. He wrote *Edwin Booth as I Knew Him* (1933), as well as poems and songs.

Ruark, Robert [Chester] (1915–1965), newspaper columnist, parodist, novelist. Ruark, born in North Carolina, worked for the Washington (D.C.) *Daily News*, first as a sportswriter, later as assistant city editor. After serving in the navy, he became Washington correspondent for the Scripps-Howard papers and a columnist for United Features. There are forty essays lampooning the American scene in *I Didn't Know It Was Loaded* (1948), others in *One for the Road* (1949). A trip to Africa resulted in *Horn of the Hunter* (1953) and a novel, *Something of Value* (1955). *The Old Man and the Boy* (1957) is autobiographical. *Poor No More* (1959), a novel, tells of the rise and fall of a North Carolina boy.

Rudder Grange (1879), a novel by FRANK R. STOCKTON. Published serially, *Rudder Grange* established the author's reputation as a notable humorist.

Ruggles of Red Gap (1915), a comic novel by HARRY LEON WILSON. Ruggles, an English butler, is taken across the Atlantic to Red Gap, a western town. He becomes the social arbiter of the community and is appointed to read the Declaration of Independence at a Fourth of July celebration. Harrison Rhodes wrote a play from the novel (1915), with music by Sigmund Romberg. Successful movie versions were made in 1919, 1923, and 1935, the last with Charles Laughton as Ruggles.

Rukeyser, Muriel (1913–1980), poet, biographer, lecturer. Rukeyser, born in New York City, wrote poems that are acute refractions of an industrial and technological world. Her first collection, *Theory of Flight* (1935), in its title poem reflects her serious researches at the Roosevelt School of the Air. *U.S. 1* (1938) shows the poet's conviction that workmen were being exploited along Route 1. Her later collections indicate a trend toward the psychological and the pathological, including *A Turning Wind* (1939), *Beast in View* (1944), *The Green Wave* (1948), *Orpheus* (1949), *Selected Poems* (1951), *Chain Lightning* (1955), *Body of Waking* (1958), *Sun Stone* (1961), *I Go Out* (1961), *Selected Poems of Octavio Paz* (1961), *Poems 1935–1961* (1961), *The Speed of Darkness* (1968), *Breaking Open* (1973), *The Gates* (1976), and *The Collected Poems of Muriel Rukeyser* (1978). *Out of Silence: Selected Poems* (ed. Kate Daniels) appeared in 1992. Her interest in modern science and thought are apparent in her biography of *Willard Gibbs: American Genius* (1942) and *The Traces of Thomas Hariot* (1971). She paid tribute to Wendell Willkie in *One Life* (1957). *The Life of Poetry* (1949) is prose. *Selected Poems of Octavio Paz* (1963) is a translation.

Rule, Jane (1931–   ), novelist. Rule, born in New Jersey, was educated at Mills College in California and University College, London. In 1956 she moved to British Columbia, finally settling on Galiano Island, British Columbia. She is best known for the portrayal of lesbian themes. *Desert of the Heart* (1964) is set in Reno against the glitter of the casinos and the surrounding desert. *This is Not for You* (1970) is an epistolary novel. *Against the Season* (1971) is set in a small town. *The Young in One Another's Arms* (1977) concerns the residents of a Vancouver boarding house who work together to start a restaurant on Galiano Island. *Contact with the World* (1980) deals with the life and work of six Vancouver artists; multiple perspectives subtly alter the reader's view of the characters. *Memory Board* (1987) centers on a retired doctor seeking reconciliation with her twin brother. *After the Fire* (1989) reviews the lives of five women. Her story collections include *Themes for Diverse Instruments* (1975) and *Outlander* (1981). *Lesbian Images* (1975) is a critical study. Her other titles are *Inland Passage and Other Stories* (1985) and *A Hot-Eyed Moderate* (1985).

Rules by Which a Great Empire May Be Reduced to a Small One, a satirical essay published by Benjamin Franklin in the *London Public Advertiser* (September 1773). The solution he offers lists the actual complaints of the American colonists about harsh governors, high taxes, overregulation of business, and failure to respond to petitions as ways a government can lose colonies it wants to dispose of.

Rulfo, Juan (1918–1986), Mexican novelist and short-story writer. Both his father and his grandfather were murdered in the 1920s. After his mother died, he lived in an orphanage from age ten to fourteen. In colloquial language Rulfo tells stories of the rural poor in Jalisco, the region where he was born. His reputation rests primarily on his one novel, *Pedro Páramo* (1955, tr. 1959; reissued 2000, tr. Margaret Sayers). *El llano en llamas* (1953, tr. *The Burning Plain and Other Stories*, 1967) is a story collection.

Rumford, Count. See BENJAMIN THOMPSON.

Runyon, [Alfred] Damon (1884–1946), journalist, short-story writer. Born in Kansas, Runyon grew up in Colorado, where his first articles were printed in the Pueblo *Chieftain*. At fourteen he enlisted in the army and was sent to the Philippines during the Spanish-American War. After ten years of reporting for western papers he became a sportswriter for the New York *American* (1911). He was war correspondent for the Hearst papers in Mexico in 1912 and 1916, in Europe during World War I. From 1918 until his death he wrote a column for the Hearst Syndicate. Many of his stories about Broadway characters appeared in the *Saturday Evening Post* and other popular magazines, and he had a large following long before his first book, *Guys and Dolls* (1932), was published. It was followed by *Blue Plate Special* (1934), *Money from Home* (1935), *The Best of Runyon* (1938), *Take It Easy* (1938), *My Wife Ethel* (1939), *My Old Man* (1939), *Runyon à la Carte* (1944), and *Runyon First and Last* (1949). *A Slight Case of Murder* (1935), with HOWARD LINDSAY, was Runyon's only play, although many of his stories were made into successful movies. The musical comedy *Guys and Dolls* (1952), by Jo Swerling and Abe Burrows, with a score by Frank Loesser, was based on Runyon characters and incidents.

Rush, Benjamin (1745–1813),   physician, chemist, teacher, public official, author. Rush, born in Pennsylvania, was an admirer of Thomas Jefferson. He called agriculture "the true basis of national health, riches, and populousness." He made advances in dentistry and veterinary medicine. His *Medical Inquiries and Observations Upon the Diseases of the Mind* (1812) helped to found modern psychiatry. He argued for abolition of slavery and for women's education, opposed excessive study of Greek and Roman classics, and defined man as a religious as well as a social and domestic animal. He wrote constantly, and his pamphlets compare with Benjamin Franklin's in breadth of interest. It was Rush who suggested to Thomas Paine the writing of COMMON SENSE. He was also a signer of the Declaration of Independence. He wrote *A Syllabus of a Course of Lectures on Chemistry* (1770), *Sermons to Gentlemen Upon Temperance and Exercise* (1772), *An Address to the Inhabitants of the British Settlements in America Upon Slave-Keeping* (1773), and *An Inquiry into the Influence of Physical Causes Upon the Moral Faculty* (1786). He collected his *Essays: Literary, Moral, and Philosophical* in 1798, his *Medical Inquiries and Observations* in 1789. *The Autobiography of Benjamin Rush*, which included his *Travels Through Life* and his *Commonplace Book for 1789–1813* as he left it for his children, appeared in 1948 with George W. Corner as editor. L. H. Butterfield edited his *Letters* (2 v. 1951).

Rush, James (1786–1869),   physician, psychologist, satirist. Born in Philadelphia, the son of BENJAMIN RUSH was a distinguished man and an eccentric. He married a wealthy woman, withdrew from the practice of medicine, and devoted himself to study of the human mind. In this field he published two books of some note: *The Philosophy of the Human Voice* (1827) and *A Brief Outline of an Analysis of the Human Intellect* (1865).

Rusk, Ralph L[eslie] (1888–1962),   literary scholar. Rusk, born in Illinois, taught literature at several universities, among them Indiana and Columbia. Among his publications are *Literature of the Middle Western Frontier* (2 v. 1925), *Emerson's Letters for the Years 1813–1881* (6 v. 1939), and *The Life of Ralph Waldo Emerson* (1949).

Russ, Joanna (1937–   ),   novelist, short-story writer. Born in New York and educated at Cornell and Yale, Russ has taught at several universities. In the critical essay "What Can a Heroine Do? Or Why Women Can't Write" (1972), Russ sets forth her conviction that the traditional literary myths emphasize male potency and female dependency. *What Are We Fighting For? Sex, Race, Class and The Future of Feminism* (1998) restates Russ's commitment to the basic tenets of feminism. Her best-known work, *The Female Man* (1975), was described by the author as an attempt to combine propaganda and fiction. Her stories and novels often use the methods of science fiction and fantasy to present female characters with unique powers to escape or overcome contemporary reality. Her works include *Picnic on Paradise* (1968); *And Chaos Died* (1970); *Alyx* (1976), a collection of stories about the same character; *We Who Are About To . . .* (1977); *The Two*

of Them (1978); *Kittatinny: A Tale of Magic* (1978); *The Hidden Side of the Moon* (1988), a collection of 27 stories from various periods of her career; and *To Write Like a Woman: Essays in Feminism and Science Fiction* (1995).

Russell, Charles Edward (1860–1941),   poet, journalist, sociologist, biographer. Russell, born in Iowa, wrote for newspapers in Minneapolis, Detroit, Chicago, and New York before shifting to magazine writing and becoming celebrated for his muckraking articles. He dealt with a number of subjects—southern prison camps, northern prisons, the Michigan copper strike, women's suffrage, and slums owned by the Trinity Church Corporation—but his particular targets were the railroads and the meat packers. President Wilson appointed him to Elihu Root's mission to Russia in 1917, and out of his experiences came *Unchained Russia* (1918). His interest in drama and music led him to write *Julia Marlowe: Her Life and Art* (1926) and *The American Orchestra and Theodore Thomas* (Pulitzer Prize, 1927). Among his other works are *Such Stuff as Dreams* (1902) and *The Twin Immortalities* (1904), verse; *The Greatest Trust in the World* (1905), an exposé of the meat packers; *The Uprising of the Many* (1907); *Lawless Wealth* (1908); *Thomas Chatterton: The Marvelous Boy* (1908); *Songs of Democracy* (1909); *Why I Am a Socialist* (1910); *Business: The Heart of the Nation* (1911); *Stories of the Great Railroads* (1912); *Wendell Phillips* (1918); *A-Rafting on the Mississipp'* (1928); *Blaine of Maine* (1931); and his autobiography, *Bare Hands and Stone Walls* (1933).

Russell, Irwin (1853–1879),   poet. Russell became a lawyer at age nineteen, but found the law dull. He escaped frequently on trips to Texas and New Orleans and observed life on the Mississippi. His early poems, usually in black dialect, were printed in *Puck, St. Nicholas,* and *Scribner's.* In 1878 he exhausted himself helping his father, a physician, fight a yellow fever epidemic in his native Port Gibson, Mississippi, and died some months later. Little is remembered today of his once-popular verse except "Christmas Night in the Quarters." *Poems by Irwin Russell* (1888), edited by Joel Chandler Harris, was reprinted in 1917 as *Christmas Night in the Quarters and Other Poems.*

Russell, John (1885–1956),   explorer, newspaperman, short-story writer, novelist. Born in Iowa, the son of CHARLES EDWARD RUSSELL traveled widely, was a special correspondent of the New York *Herald* in Panama and Peru, and later did miscellaneous writing for that paper. His reputation is based chiefly on his well-constructed short stories, usually with exotic settings. Among his collections are *The Red Mark and Other Stories* (1919), *Where the Pavement Ends* (1921), and *The Lost God and Other Adventure Stories* (1947).

Russell, Osborne (1814–1865?),   frontiersman, memoirist. Russell, said to have been born in Maine, spent 1834 to 1843 in the Far West and kept a *Journal of a Trapper*, not published until 1921. This is an important commentary on the mountain men and the BLACKFEET INDIANS. Russell's factual accounts are detailed and significant.

Russell, Sir W[illiam] H[oward] (1820–1907),   British journalist. Russell came to the United States as a correspondent for the London *Times*. His experiences in America during the first years of the Civil War and later are recorded in *Pictures of Southern Life, Social, Political, and Military* (1863); *My Diary North and South* (1863); and *Hesperothen: Notes from the West* (2 v. 1882). *My Diary North and South* was reissued in abridged form in 1954.

Russell's Bookstore Group, a group of Southern literary figures meeting informally during the 1850s at John Russell's store in Charleston, South Carolina. *Russell's Magazine* (1857–1860), edited by PAUL HAMILTON HAYNE, was an outgrowth of their meetings. Other members of the group were HENRY TIMROD, WILLIAM GILMORE SIMMS, WILLIAM JOHN GRAYSON, and S. H. DICKSON.

Rutledge, Archibald [Hamilton] (1883–1973), teacher, poet, short-story writer. Rutledge, poet laureate of his native South Carolina, wrote much in prose and verse to celebrate the beauty and traditions of the region. His verse is pleasant and skillful, some of his most effective work being in quatrains. Among his poetry collections are *Under the Pines* (1907), *New Poems* (1917), *Collected Poems* (1925), *The Everlasting Light* (1949), and *The Heart's Chalice* (1953). Rutledge's prose contains many effective descriptions of nature, and *Home by the River* (1941, 1955) describes a fine old house. *Those Were the Days* (1956) is autobiographical.

Ruxton, George [Augustus] Frederick (1820–1848), English traveler, soldier, ethnologist. Into his short life Ruxton compressed a dozen lifetimes of adventure. At fifteen he was expelled from the Royal Military Academy. At seventeen he was fighting in the Carlist Wars in Spain and was knighted. At twenty he was hunting in Canada. By the time he was twenty-four he had made two trips to Africa and had contributed a paper on the Bushmen to the Ethnological Society of London. In 1846 he was in Mexico, traveled north to Colorado, and crossed the Great Plains. Back in England he published *Adventures in Mexico and the Rocky Mountains* (1847) and LIFE IN THE FAR WEST (1848). He died of dysentery before he could begin a second trip to the Rockies. Both his books are valuable accounts of life in the Rockies and are immensely readable. In 1924 the second half of Ruxton's *Adventures* was reprinted as *Wild Life in the Rocky Mountains. Life in the Far West* was reprinted in 1951.

Ryan, Abram Joseph (1838–1886), priest, poet. The son of an Irish immigrant, Abram Ryan, born in Maryland, studied at the Christian Brothers' School and at Niagara University, where he prepared for the priesthood. He was ordained in 1856, and after a few years of teaching returned to the South, where he served as chaplain in the Confederate Army. He was deeply moved by the loss of the Confederate cause, the death of his younger brother in battle, and the suffering he saw everywhere. His grief expressed itself poignantly in his poems. After the war "the poet of the Lost Cause" served as priest in Augusta, Mobile, New Orleans, Biloxi, Nashville, Knoxville, Macon, and Mobile. He also edited for brief periods *The Pacificator* and the *Banner of the South* in Augusta, and *The Star*, a Catholic weekly in New Orleans. His poems were very popular in the South, and many of them were set to music and sung in the schools. The best known are "The Conquered Banner," "The Lost Cause," and "The Sword of Robert E. Lee." *Father Ryan's Poems* (1879) was followed by *A Crown for Our Queen* (1882), a book of religious verse.

Ryga, George (1932–1987), playwright, novelist. Born of Ukrainian immigrant parents on a farm in northern Alberta, Ryga has written plays for radio and television and short and long fiction. His published novels are *The Hungry Hills* (1960), *Ballad of a Stone Picker* (1962), *Night Desk* (1978), and *In the Shadow of the Vulture* (1986). The Vancouver Playhouse produced *The Ecstasy of Rita Joe* in the late 1960s, and *The Ecstasy of Rita Joe and Other Plays* was published in 1971. Two posthumous volumes, *The Athabasca Ryga* (1990) and *Summerland* (1992), bring together unpublished writings.

Rynning, Ole (1809–1838), travel writer. Born in Norway, he came to Illinois in 1837. His book on America, published in Norway (1838, tr. *A True Account of America for the Information and Help of Peasant and Commoner*) was so useful in its description of American soil, climate, government, language, and opportunities that it is credited with encouraging the large Norwegian immigration of the 19th century.

S

Saadi (*The Dial* 1842, *Poems* 1847), a poem by RALPH WALDO EMERSON. Emerson uses the Persian poet Saadi [Sadi] (1184?–1291?) to present Emerson's own view of poetry. In the poem he praises the poet's aloofness and his search for beauty in the commonplace.

Sábato, Ernesto (1911–), Argentinian novelist and essayist. After his initial encounter with SURREALISM in Paris in the 1930s, Sábato abandoned his career as a physics professor and turned to writing. His first book, *Uno y el universo* (1945), along with subsequent essays and criticism like *Heterodoxia* (1953) and *El escritor y sus fantasmas* (1963), addresses existential and metaphysical concerns that are echoed in his fiction. His novel *El túnel* (1948, tr. *The Outsider*, 1950, also *The Tunnel*, 1988) presents the confessions of a convicted murderer. *Sobre héroes y tumbas* (1961, tr. *On Heroes and Tombs*, 1981) is an existential tragedy of incest, fire, and death. *Abaddón, el exterminador* (1974) portrays man as an alienated creature, obsessed with and plagued by guilt. In 1984, Sábato won the Spanish-speaking world's highest literary accolade, the Cervantes Prize in Literature. *The Writer in the Catastrophe of Our Time* (1990) is a selection of essays in translation.

Sabbath Scene, A (1850), a poem by JOHN GREENLEAF WHITTIER. Nowhere else in Whittier's poetry does he speak with such violence against slavery and its friends in the North. He directs his denunciation especially against Northern clergymen who smugly urged execution of the Fugitive Slave Law and defended the system of slavery as a Biblical institution. He imagines a scene in which a slave takes refuge in a church on a Sabbath morning, and the parson helps return her to her master. The poet denounces the clergyman and the church: "Down with pulpit, down with priest,/And give us nature's teaching!" He awakes to find it was all a dream. The poem was written in the hope of preventing passage of Henry Clay's Fugitive Slave Law, which was supported by Daniel Webster.

Sabin, Joseph (1821–1881), bookseller, bibliographer. Sabin came to the United States from England in 1848 and opened a bookstore. By 1865 he was a specialist in rare books and prints. In 1868 he started an enterprise that took sixty-eight years to complete. It was his *Bibliotheca Americana: A Dictionary of Books Relating to America, from Its Discovery to the Present Time.* Of its twenty-nine volumes, he edited the first fourteen; the rest were edited by WILBERFORCE EAMES and R. W. G. Vail.

Sabine, Lorenzo (1803–1877), historian. Lorenzo is known best for his work on colonial loyalists of the Revolutionary War era. His *The American Loyalists* (1847) was revised as *Biographical Sketches of the Loyalists of the American Revolution* (2 v. 1864).

Sacajawea (1788?–1884), a Shoshone guide for the Lewis and Clark expedition. The spelling of her name and the dates of her birth and death are subjects of dispute among historians. In 1800 she had been captured by an enemy tribe and sold to Toussaint Charbonneau, a French trader who married her. Lewis and Clark persuaded the couple, together with their infant child, to accompany them to the headwaters of the Missouri, Sacajawea's birthplace, and on to the Pacific and back again. In their *Journals* Lewis and Clark make frequent and friendly mention of her. She served as interpreter and was helpful in securing horses and guides and in pointing out native food plants. Later she left Charbonneau, married a Comanche (1856), and went with him to the Wind River Reservation in Wyoming, where she is said to have been seen by a missionary in 1875 and to have died in 1884. Novels and biographies about Sacajawea include Emerson Hough's *The Magnificent Adventure* (1916), James W. Schultz's *Bird Woman* (1918), Grace R. Hebard's *Sacajawea* (1933), Ethel Hueston's *Star of the West* (1935), and Donald C. Peattie's *Forward the Nation* (1942). A good biography is H. P. Howard's *Sacajawea: Indian Girl with Lewis and Clark* (1971). Her value to the Lewis and Clark expedition is detailed in Stephen Ambrose's *Undaunted Courage* (1996). See MERIWETHER LEWIS.

Sacco-Vanzetti case. A celebrated murder trial (May to July, 1921) in which two Italian immigrants were condemned to death in the murder of paymaster and a guard at South Braintree, Massachusetts, on April 15, 1920. The trial and conviction brought repercussions throughout the country, including a review of the case by a committee appointed by Governor Fuller of Massachusetts—President Lowell of Harvard, President Stratton of the Massachusetts Institute of Technology, and Judge Robert Grant—but the two men were finally executed seven years later, on August 22, 1927. The case probably created more public controversy than any other criminal trial in the previous history of the United States, and many literary men and women engaged actively in the debate, mostly in behalf of the two defendants. David Felix analyzed the reverberations in the intellectual community in *Protest: Sacco and Vanzetti and the Intellectuals* (1965).

Nicola Sacco and Bartolomeo Vanzetti were avowed anarchists. In addition to the murder charge against them they were accused of evading the draft during World War I. They denied any part in the murder, and a witness who claimed he had participated in the crime exonerated them. Notwithstanding, the two were condemned. As a result of the Bolshevik revolution in Russia and of the activities of the I.W.W. and other radical groups in this country, antiradical feeling ran high in the United States during the early 1920s, and this feeling obviously became involved in the public response to the trial. How much this extralegal sentiment had to do with the actual court proceedings is still a matter of debate. Ballistic tests on the pistol found on Sacco done in 1961 seemed to show that the gun had been used to kill the guard. Some authorities have concluded from these tests that Sacco was guilty, but Vanzetti was innocent.

The two men knew little English at the time of their arrest, but they—especially Vanzetti—took a keen interest in learning the language during their imprisonment. They wrote hundreds of letters in Italian and English to friends, relatives, and sympathizers. Though the letters often were ungrammatical, they possessed considerable literary power. Vanzetti's final appeal has become a classic. A collection of *Letters of Sacco and Vanzetti* appeared in 1928, and a transcript of the case appeared in five volumes in 1928–29, edited by Newton D. Baker. Felix Frankfurter wrote *The Case of Sacco and Vanzetti* (1927), and Judge Michael Angelo Musmanno analyzed the case in *After 12 Years* (1939). Francis Russell wrote *Tragedy in Dedham* (1962, repr. 1971), and H. B. Erdman analyzed *The Case That Will Not Die* (1969)

In 1948 appeared *The Legacy of Sacco and Vanzetti* by C. Louis Joughin and Edmund M. Morgan, analyzing 144 poems, six plays, and eight novels on the Sacco-Vanzetti theme. Upton Sinclair made the case the center of his novel BOSTON (1928). James Thurber and Elliott Nugent introduced *Vanzetti's* letter into their social comedy *The Male Animal* (1940). Edna St. Vincent Millay wrote the poem "Justice Denied in Massachusetts," (1927). H. L. Mencken, John Dos Passos, Lola Ridge, and many others spoke in warm protest against the way the trial had been conducted. Maxwell Anderson's plays *Gods of the Lightning* (1928) and *Winterset* (1935) were based on the case, and Ben Shahn created a series of paintings that were published under the title *The Passion of Sacco and Vanzetti* (1961).

Sackler, Howard (1929–1982),　　dramatist, director, film writer. Sackler's best-known play is *The Great White Hope* (1967, pub. 1968) based on the life of Jack Johnson, the first African-American to become world heavy-weight boxing champion. His other plays are *Uriel Acosta* (1954), *Mr. Welk and Jersey Jim* (1960), *The Nine O'Clock Mail* (1965), and *The Pastime of Monsieur Robert* (1966). His poetry is collected in *Want My Shepherd* (1954).

Sacred Fount, The (1901),　　a novelette by HENRY JAMES. The title refers to the theory of the narrator that in an unequal marriage or liaison the older or weaker partner is refreshed and invigorated at the sacred fount of the younger or

stronger personality, which in turn becomes depleted. The scene of the story is an English weekend house party. The narrator uses his theory to attempt to discover the relationships among the guests. In the end he confides his hypothesis to one of the principals, who dismisses it as a house of cards, leaving the narrator and the reader uncertain whether the denial is dictated by honesty or policy.

Sacred Wood, The (1920),　　a collection of essays by T. S. ELIOT. The role of tradition is emphasized, both in creative writing and in literary criticism. The book was of major importance in determining the modern evaluation of the Metaphysical poets and the Elizabethan and Jacobean playwrights.

Saffin, John (c. 1626–1710),　　poet, pamphleteer. In answer to Judge Samuel Sewall's *The Selling of Joseph* (1700), the first antislavery tract published in America, Saffin wrote his *Brief and Candid Answer to . . . The Selling of Joseph* (1701). His poetry, kept in a personal notebook, includes elegies on the deaths of his eight sons, satires, acrostics, and love poetry. One or two of the poems were published during his lifetime, but only after the notebook was given by a descendant to the Rhode Island Historical Society (1900) and printed as *John Saffin: His Book* (1928) did the poems come to light.

Said, Edward W. (1935–　　),　　literary critic, political commentator. Born in Jerusalem, Said immigrated first to Egypt then to the United States, where he was educated at Princeton and Harvard (Ph.D., 1964). During his tenure as professor of comparative literature at Columbia University, Said emerged as a leading commentator on the Palestinian-Israeli conflict, and in 1977 became a member of the Palestine National Council. *Orientalism* (1978), one of his best-known works, argues that traditional Western critics have created a stereotype of the culture of the Middle East that precludes objective evaluation, and serves to justify economic and political domination of the region. *Culture and Imperialism* (1993) expands on the themes of the earlier book, with emphasis on the influence of imperialism on Western art, particularly the novel. *Out of Place* (1999) is a memoir focused on Said's family and his education in the United States. Books dealing more directly with the Palestinian question include *The Question of Palestine* (1979); *The Politics of Dispossession: The Struggle for Palestinian Self-Determination, 1969–1994* (1994); *Peace and Its Discontents: Essays on Palestine in the Middle East Peace Process* (1995); and *The End of the Peace Process: Oslo and After* (2000). *Reflections on Exile and Other Essays* appeared in 2001. *The World, The Text and the Critic* (1983) is an award-winning book of literary criticism. Said is an amateur musician who, for several years, wrote a music column for *The Nation*, and *Musical Elaborations* (1991), a book of music criticism. With Jeffrey Kallberg, he edited *Chopin at the Boundaries: Sex, History and Musical Genre* (1996).

Sailors' songs [shanties, chanteys].　　The practice of singing such songs is very ancient, as some of them indicate by their obsolete technical details. During the 18th and early 19th centuries the American merchant marine experienced a great growth, and shantying became an art. Forecastle songs, not sung as work songs, are largely variants of old English,

Irish, and Scottish ballads. Other types with cadences adapted to the work at hand were referred to as short-drag shanties, halliard [halyard] shanties, and windlass or capstan shanties. Even on American ships Irish sailors were considered the best shantymen, though in time they were outstripped by African-Americans. There was little partsinging, except occasionally among African-American crews.

Lincoln Colcord made the first collection of American sailors' songs, *Roll and Go* (1924), later revised by his daughter Joanna as *Songs of American Sailormen* (1938). Other collections are Frank Shay, *Iron Men and Wooden Ships: Deep Sea Chanties* (1924); Fannie H. Eckstorm and Mary W. Smyth, *Minstrelsy of Maine* (1927); Robert W. Neeser, *American Naval Songs and Ballads* (1938); and Frank Shay, *American Sea Songs and Chanteys* (1948).

St. Clair, Arthur (1736–1818), soldier. St. Clair, born in Scotland, served in the American army during the Revolution, but was court-martialed (1778) when he abandoned Fort Ticonderoga before Burgoyne's advance. He was exonerated and later became a member of the Continental Congress and its president (1787). He was the first governor of the Northwest Territory (1787–1802), but when he was defeated by the Indians in a battle near Fort Wayne (November 4, 1791), he resigned his army command and was later removed from his post as governor. He wrote a vindication of his conduct, *A Narrative of the Manner in Which the Campaign Against the Indians Was Conducted* (pub. 1812). His *Papers* were edited by W. H. Smith (2 v. 1882).

Saint-Denys-Garneau, Hector (1912–1943), Quebec poet, the great-grandson of François-Xavier Garneau (1809–1866), Canadian historian. Saint-Denys-Garneau's *Regards et jeux dans l'espace* (1937) marks the beginning of modern poetry in Quebec and is the most extreme exploration of a traditional Jansenist Christianity. Flexible and spare, his poems vary from the delicately impressionistic to symbolist and metaphysical; extended mathematical conceits dramatize the barrenness of a world emptied of spiritual presence. His works are contained in *Poésies complètes* (1949, tr. *Complete Poems*, 1975) and *Journal* (1954, tr. 1954).

St. Elmo (1866), a novel by Augusta Evans Wilson (see AUGUSTA JANE EVANS). With the spectacular popularity of this novel, Wilson's third, a kind of St. Elmo's fire ran through the South. Plantations, schools, hotels, steamboats, merchandise, infants, and thirteen towns were named for the Byronic hero of the melodrama. When Edna Earle, an impossibly gifted and erudite young prude, finally succeeded in taming St. Elmo, the South's womanhood swooned with delight, and strong men wrote to the author to tell her they had been saved by her novel.

Saint-Gaudens, Augustus (1848–1907), sculptor, memoirist. Brought to the United States from Ireland in infancy, Saint-Gaudens studied art in America, France, and Italy and produced many fine works, including the statue of Admiral Farragut in Madison Square, New York City; the equestrian monument to General Sherman at the 59th Street entrance to New York City's Central Park; and portrait statues of Lincoln,

Robert Louis Stevenson, and many others. Two of his pieces are intimately linked with literature. One is his monument on Beacon Hill in Boston to Robert Gould Shaw (1837–1863), who was killed while storming Fort Wagner at the head of the 54th Massachusetts, the first enlisted black regiment; this monument evoked in 1900 William Vaughn Moody's AN ODE IN TIME OF HESITATION and is described in Robert Lowell's "For the Union Dead" (1960). The other is the impressive hooded and shrouded figure in Rock Creek Cemetery, Washington, D.C., dedicated to the memory of HENRY ADAMS's wife, Marian. Adams, an intimate friend of Saint-Gaudens, introduced him into his novel ESTHER (1884); the heroine is a portrait of Adams's wife, who had committed suicide. Saint-Gaudens's *Reminiscences* (2 v.) appeared after his death (1913).

St. John, Hector. Pen name of MICHEL-GUILLAUME ST. JEAN DE CRÈVECŒUR.

St. Nicholas. A magazine for young people founded in November 1873 by Roswell Smith and published in New York City. It ceased publication in February 1940. Its most noted editor was MARY MAPES DODGE, author of *Hans Brinker, or, The Silver Skates* (1865). Practically every author of juvenile literature contributed sooner or later to the magazine; some became celebrated because of their contributions. Among the contributors were Twain, Kipling, Robert Louis Stevenson, Edward Eggleston, Howard Pyle, Palmer Cox (author of the *Brownie Books*), Frank Stockton, Frances Hodgson Burnett, Dorothy Canfield Fisher, and Louisa May Alcott. Talented young contributors were awarded prizes and membership in the magazine's literary society, the St. Nicholas League. When times and tastes changed, the magazine lost its popularity. However, the *St. Nicholas Anthology* (1948), with selections made by Henry Steele Commager and an introduction by May Lamberton Becker, the magazine's last editor, proved very successful. This anthology was followed by a similar volume in 1950.

Sala, George Augustus (1828–1895), war correspondent. Sala, born in England, covered the Civil War for the London *Telegraph* and wrote *My Diary in America in the Midst of War* (1865). In 1879–80 he made an extensive tour of the United States and in his second report, *America Revisited* (1882), he tried to reach a better understanding of the country.

Sale, Chic [pen name of **Charles Partlow**] (1885–1936), actor, humorist. A native of South Dakota, Sale won wide popularity on the vaudeville stage as an impersonator of rural types, from small girls to old men. Later he played similar parts in movies and in Broadway revues. He had some facility as a writer and published his extraordinary *The Specialist* (1929), a small book on a subject never before treated in print—the construction of outhouses. Sale also wrote *A Corn-Husker Crashes the Movies* (1933) and other books.

Salem witchcraft trials. The Puritan clergy has suffered a bad press for three centuries because of the Salem witchcraft trials. However, after the Glorious Revolution, it was the power of the state, untrammeled by clerical restraints under a new charter, that led to the massacre. To be sure, Calvinism furnished the ideology that animated the proceedings, but the belief in witchcraft was not limited to New England. It was almost universal in the Western world, and its consequences in Europe were far more hideous than in Massachusetts. Nearly all of the Puritan divines counseled moderation and restraint. Cotton Mather even hinted that the court would be well-advised to include one or two ministers in its proceedings. But his diffident suggestions were not heeded. The magistrates, operating under a simplistic belief in witchcraft whose devious subtleties were not apparent to them, sent the condemned to the gallows. In effect, they were applying secular sanctions to spiritual sins. This fact was not lost on many of the accused, who confessed to being witches, thereby saving their lives at enormous cost to their souls. Those who died maintaining their innocence did not deny the reality of witchcraft; they simply insisted they were God-fearing Puritans who had had no traffic with the devil. Consequently, in order to account for the horrors of the Salem witchcraft trials, it is necessary to understand not only the religious, but also the historical, political, and even scientific context out of which they grew.

From 1689 to 1692 Massachusetts was without a legal government. Its original charter, abrogated by England in 1684, had been replaced with an administration headed by Sir Edmund Andros. But in England, the Glorious Revolution of 1688 replaced the Catholic James II with the Protestant William and Mary early in 1689, and in April the colonists overthrew Andros, wanting their pre-1684 charter restored. Instead, the Dominion of New England was abolished in 1691; and Massachusetts, whose population had reached 50,000 by 1690, was reconstituted as a separate royal colony with a governor and lieutenant governor appointed by the Crown but chosen by the Reverend Increase Mather, Massachusetts' agent in London from 1688 to 1692. His candidates were Sir William Phips, a wealthy Boston ship's carpenter who had been knighted in 1687, and the learned divine William Stoughton. Nevertheless, the new charter seriously weakened the theocracy because the franchise was no longer restricted to church members.

On March 29, 1692, Phips and Mather left England for Massachusetts. When they arrived on May 14, they found the colony in an uproar. Operating under the provisional government, magistrates—one was Nathaniel Hawthorne's great-great-grandfather, Colonel John Hathorne [sic]—had been hearing accusations against a number of persons charged with being witches by a group of girls and young women. The symptoms of the accusers indicate that they were probably suffering from convulsive egotism brought on by eating infected rye bread. However, lacking our scientific hindsight, they interpreted their afflictions according to the prevalent belief in witchcraft, and looked for people in league with the devil who were tormenting them.

The accusations had been made in Salem Village (now Danvers), but Salem Village, like Massachusetts, had no real government. It was a loose collection of farms adjacent to Salem Town, whose mercantile prosperity the Salem Village farmers regarded with envy. Moreover, Salem Village itself was split between fac-

tions led by two feuding families, the Porters and the Palmers. The Porters were much the more prosperous and had closer ties with Salem Town than did the Palmers. The charges of witchcraft came primarily from the socially and economically inferior group, and they were leveled at those with connections to its wealthier rivals. But in the absence of a duly constituted government, the *ad hoc* authorities could hold no legal trials. Meanwhile, more and more victims were being named as witches, and one prisoner had already died in the overflowing jails. A major crisis had developed in Massachusetts.

Governor Phips acted promptly and decisively by appointing a seven-person special court of *oyer* and *terminer*, composed of distinguished jurists and directed by the stern and implacable Stoughton—both a cleric and magistrate—to conduct the trials. The judges then made the fateful decision to admit so-called spectral evidence, or descriptions of apparitions of the witches that were invisible to everyone except the afflicted. Although the accusations had been made in Salem Village, the trials, which began in early June 1692, were held in Salem Town. The witch hunt was thus neither the aberration of a few hysterical individuals nor a lynching bee, but a program of Massachusetts' secular authorities. The state itself was condemning individuals for witchcraft. As Ambrose Bierce pointed out in *The Devil's Dictionary* under his definition of *inadmissible*, "The evidence (including confession) upon which certain women [and men] were convicted of witchcraft and executed was without a flaw; it is still unimpeachable. The judges' decisions based on it were sound in logic and in law. Nothing in any existing court was ever more thoroughly proved than the charges of witchcraft and sorcery for which so many suffered death."

Contrary to popular opinion, most of the Puritan clergy—including Increase and Cotton Mather—were far more cautious than the secular authorities, recommending restraint and pointing out that the devil was capable of presenting himself in the *personae* of innocent people. Spectral evidence, therefore, by itself should not be used as conclusive evidence of guilt. But their cautionary advice was unheeded by the representatives of the state. By the end of September, twenty of those charged had been executed. Nineteen were hanged. Giles Cory, husband of one of the victims, refusing to plead either guilty or not guilty to his indictment, was slowly crushed to death.

Initially the victims had been helpless old women, but as the accusers fingered more and more scapegoats, even a Puritan minister was executed. Eventually, according to rumor, Lady Phips, the wife of the governor, was accused. Late in October 1692, however, Sir William, on Increase Mather's advice, decided against the admissibility of spectral evidence, dissolved the old special court, and created a new Superior Court to hear the cases. But without spectral evidence, only a few more witches were indicted, and none were executed. By April 1693 Salem's reign of terror was over. After its collapse, Hawthorne's ancestor, unlike most of his colleagues, refused to repent of his role in it. And his descendant, in the Preface to *The Scarlet Letter*, wrote that his great-great-grandfather had "made himself so conspicuous in the martyrdom of the witches, that their blood may fairly be said to have left a stain upon him."

Both Hawthorne's romantic short story "Young Goodman Brown" (1835) and Arthur Miller's realistic play *The Crucible* (1953) are based on the Salem trials. Although *The Crucible* purports to be firmly grounded in history, it fails to communicate their intellectual plausibility and legal rigor. "Young Goodman Brown" conveys accurately the spirit of the period just before they began. It includes many of the leading citizens of Salem Village and refers to the accusation against Lady Phips. But the protagonist is a garden-variety good man, as is indicated by both his title—a term of respect for someone qualified to serve on a jury—and his common last name. Thus he represents those who would be called on to serve as jurors weighing the guilt of the accused. Three of the actual unfortunates who were later hanged are also introduced into the fable: Goody Cloyse, Goody Cory (who would be condemned by Magistrate Hathorne), and Martha Carrier, described in a phrase picked up from Cotton Mather as a "rampant hag."

The story is, in part, an allegory for Calvinism, emphasizing the doctrines of innate depravity and predestination. Calvinism leads men and women to evil, yet it had seized on a profound truth, for it is far more than a black mass that is being held in the forest: it is the communion of the human race. In the effort to extirpate sin—as in the persecution of the witches and the slaughter of twenty innocent people—men and women sink deeper into the morass of evil. Thus, by a twist of fate, the worst excess of Calvinism in America—carried out by good and respectable people with noble and exalted aims—was a conclusive illustration of the wickedness predestined as an ineradicable part of human mortality. Studies include Marion L. Starkey, *The Devil in Massachusetts: A Modern Inquiry into the Salem Witch Trials* (1950); Chadwick Hansen, *Witchcraft at Salem* (1969); and Paul Boyer and Stephen Nissenbaum, *Salem Possessed: The Social Origins of Witchcraft* (1976).

M. E. GRENANDER

Salinas, Luis Omar (1937–   ),   poet. Born in Texas, Salinas spent a few early years in Mexico before moving in with an aunt and uncle in California. He was educated at Fresno State University. His images and metaphors are often fantastic and surreal, tending to create "the fullness of the unreal" that is, in his view a better medium for illuminating the poverty and alienation experienced by Mexican-Americans. Widely anthologized in collections of Chicano and ethnic writing, including *Entrance: Four Chicano Poets; Leonard Adame, Luis Omar Salinas, Gary Soto, Ernesto Trejo* (1975), Salinas has published several collections including *Crazy Gypsy* (1970), *I Go Dreaming Serenades* (1979), *Afternoon of the Unreal* (1980), *Prelude to Darkness* (1981), *Darkness under the Trees: Walking behind the Spanish* (1982), and *The Sadness of Days: Selected and New Poems* (1987). With Lillian Federman, he edited *From the Barrio: A Chicano Anthology* (1973).

Salinger, J[erome] D[avid] (1919–   ),   novelist, short-story writer. Salinger was raised in and around his native New York City, attended Valley Forge Military Academy—on

which many of the incidents in *The Catcher in the Rye* are based—and briefly attended Ursinus College and Columbia University, failing to graduate from either. He served as a counterintelligence officer with the Infantry regiment 12th in France during World War II and published his first short story at age twenty-one. Although Salinger hoped to become a poet, he was apparently destined to be a writer of fiction. Soon other stories appeared in a number of magazines, including *Story* and *Colliers*, and eventually Salinger found a home for his work in the pages of *The New Yorker*, the ideal venue for his vision of religious angst and contemporary urban neurosis. *The Catcher in the Rye* (1951), a novel dealing with two days in the life of Holden Caulfield—a prep school version of Huck Finn who taxis through the streets of Manhattan much as Huck rafted down the Mississippi—has retained its popularity and its critical stature as a minor classic.

Nine Stories (1953), a collection of stories that appeared originally in *The New Yorker*, introduced various members of the Glass family who would dominate the remainder of Salinger's work. Critical response divided itself between high praise and cult worship. Most of the stories deal with precocious, troubled children, whose religious yearnings—often titling toward the East—are in vivid contrast to the materialistic and spiritually empty world of their parents. The result was a perfect literary formula for the 1950s. One story in particular was singled out by critics and young writers alike for special attention—"A Perfect Day for Bananafish," which briefly details the suicidal death of Seymour Glass, older brother, patron saint, and guru for his siblings. Meanwhile, Salinger continued to parcel out bits and pieces of the Glass family history: *Franny and Zooey* in 1961, and *Raise High the Roof Beam, Carpenters,* and *Seymour: An Introduction* in 1963.

"Hapworth 16, 1924" is the last installment of the Glass saga, and its date of publication in *The New Yorker* (June 19, 1965) also indicates the effective end of Salinger's public career. He prefers a reclusive life in Cornish, New Hampshire, where rumor has it that he continues to write, and where he occasionally engages in lawsuits against those who publish pirated editions of his early stories or otherwise invade his privacy. The most spectacular of these suits was brought against Ian Hamilton, author of *In Search of J. D. Salinger* (1988), for the unauthorized use of material from his private letters. Joyce Maynard, who as a nineteen-year-old lived for a year with the author, wrote about her experience in *At Home in the World* (1998). She also auctioned off their correspondence; the buyer, Peter Norton, returned the letters to Mr. Salinger. Margaret Salinger, his daughter, wrote *Dream Catcher: A Memoir* (2000), which filled in many of the biographical spaces, particularly of his military experiences in some of the bloodiest battles of World War II. Perhaps no other author of so few works has been the subject of so many analyses in the scholarly journals and in book-length collections. In addition, there are at least seven full-length volumes devoted to Salinger's work, ranging from early studies such as F. L. Gwynn and J. L. Blotner's *The Fiction of J. D. Salinger* (1958) and W. French's *J. D.*

Salinger (1963) to more specialized books such as G. Rosen's *Zen in the Art of J. D. Salinger* (1977) and E. Alsen's *Salinger's Glass Stories as Composite Novel* (1984).

SANFORD PINSKER/BP

Salisbury, Harrison E. (1908–1993), newspaper correspondent. Salisbury, born in Minneapolis, attended the University of Minnesota and worked for the United Press from 1930 to 1948. A year later he joined *The New York Times* and won a Pulitzer Prize for International Correspondence in 1955. His book *American in Russia* (1955) describes his experiences and observations from 1949 to 1958. Among his several other books on Russia are *Moscow Journal* (1961), *The Nine Hundred Days: The Siege of Leningrad* (1969), and *Russia in Revolution* (1978). He also covered events in China and wrote memorable accounts including *To Peking and Beyond* (1973), *China: 100 Years of Revolution* (1983), and *The Long March: The Untold Story* (1985). Among his other distinguished nonfiction books are *Without Fear or Favor: The New York Times and Its Times* (1980), *A Time of Change* (1988), *The Great Black Dragon Fire: A Chinese Inferno* (1989), and *Heroes of My Time* (1993).

Salmagundi; or, The Whim-Whams and Opinions of Launcelot Langstaff, Esq. and Others, a humorous periodical published by WILLIAM IRVING, JAMES KIRKE PAULDING, and WASHINGTON IRVING. It was issued in twenty numbers (January 24, 1807–January 25, 1808), and in 1808 was collected in book form. According to the preface the magazine, which stands as an American link between *The Spectator* and the *Pickwick Papers*, was designed to "instruct the young, reform the old, correct the town, and castigate the age." Under pseudonyms the writers aired their views on such topics as "the conduct of the world," politics, the theater, music, and the fashions of the day. In politics they were Federalist, in taste, aristocratic and conservative. This was the first writing of its kind to appear in the United States and was an immediate success. William Irving is known to be the author of the light verse and Paulding of the Oriental letters. In 1819 Paulding issued a second series by himself, but since it lacked the mixture of minds and variety of tastes needed to make it a true salmagundi, it was not a success. Much of the discussion that led to the papers took place at Mount Pleasant, the home of Gouverneur Kemble on the banks of the Passaic near Newark, N.J.; in the papers, it was called Cockloft Hall.

Salter, James (1925–), novelist. Born in New York City with the name James Horowitz, Salter was educated at West Point and had a career in the Air Force until 1957, when his first novel was published. James Salter, his pen name, eventually became his legal name. Highly praised among his novels are *A Sport and a Pastime* (1967), a love story set in France; *Light Years* (1975), memories of the decay of an affluent marriage; and *Solo Faces* (1981), about a rock climber. Two earlier novels, *The Hunters* (1957) and *The Arm of the Flesh* (1961), are highly acclaimed treatments of fighter pilots. *Dusk and Other Stories* (1988) won a PEN/Faulkner Award. Salter has also written for film and television. *Tasting Paris: An Intimate Guide* appeared in 1996. *Burning the Days: Recollection*

(1997) is a novel like memoir in elegant prose. *Cassada* (2000) is a revision of *The Arm of The Flesh*, "meant to be the book the other might have been."

Saltus, Edgar [Evertson] (1855–1921), essayist, novelist. Born in New York City, Saltus studied at Heidelberg, Munich, and Paris. He was graduated from the Columbia Law School in 1880 and plunged into the kind of social life he later described in his novels. His first book, a biography of Balzac, appeared in 1884. There followed two epigrammatic condensations of garbled Schopenhauer and Spinoza entitled *The Philosophy of Disenchantment* (1885) and *The Anatomy of Negation* (1886). They caught the popular fancy with their sophisticated pessimism. *Mr. Incoul's Misadventure*, the first of Saltus's so-called diabolical novels, came out in 1887, followed by *The Truth About Tristrem Varick* (1888), *The Pace That Kills* (1889), *Madam Sapphira* (1893), *Vanity Square* (1906), and others. Saltus early recognized the appeal of exotic and erotic history. His *The Imperial Purple* (1892), a history of the Roman emperors; *Historia Amoris* (1906), a history of love; and *The Imperial Orgy* (1920), a history of the Romanoffs, found avid readers. Saltus parallels Wilde, whom he met in London and about whom he later wrote *Oscar Wilde: An Idler's Impression* (1919).

H. L. Mencken and Carl Van Vechten both tried to reestablish his popularity. James Huneker portrayed him as a minor character in PAINTED VEILS (1920) and was influenced by his style, as was Van Vechten. *Edgar Saltus, the Man* (1925) is a biography by his third wife, Marie Saltus. See THE EROTIC SCHOOL.

Salut au Monde (called "Poem of Salutation" in *Leaves of Grass*, 1856 ed.; given its present title in 1867), a poem by WALT WHITMAN. This extraordinary composition proclaims in minute and specific detail Whitman's kinship with all mankind. Whitman reviews a multitude of scenes all over the world and sees people working and traveling, performing their religious rites and their daily tasks.

Salzman, Mark (1959–), novelist, memoirist. Born in Greenwich, Connecticut, and educated at Yale (B.A., 1982), Salzman has also studied cello and the martial arts. His first book, *Iron and Silk* (1986), dealt with a trip to Changsha, Hunan Province, China, where he taught English at a medical college and studied martial arts. *The Laughing Sutra* (1991) is a picaresque novel, tracing the adventures of a Chinese orphan and his traveling companion, a two-thousand-year-old warrior. *The Soloist* (1994) echoes Salzman's own musical experience. Prior to his matriculation at Yale, where he planned to major in cello performance, Salzman heard Yo-Yo Ma play Bach's fifth suite for unaccompanied cello. Mr. Ma's playing was so perfect that Salzman decided he could not achieve that level of excellence; he entered Yale as a Chinese major. The protagonist of the novel, no longer satisfied with his technical abilities, also gives up the cello. Instead he guides the concert career of a little Korean prodigy and finally learns to enjoy his own music making in private. *Lost in Place: Growing Up Absurd in Suburbia* (1995) is a memoir. A spiritual crisis in the life of a Carmelite nun is the basis of *Lying Awake* (2000). Sister John of the Cross has suddenly and mysteriously acquired the ability to write beautiful poetry. She attributes the gift to divine intervention, but when she seeks medical help for the physical ills that accompany her talent, the CAT scan reveals a small temporal lobe tumor may be the cause of both poems and headaches. The nun must decide whether to have the tumor removed and risk losing her vision of God.

Sam Slick. See T. C. HALIBURTON and S. A. HAMMETT.

Sam Spade. See DASHIELL HAMMETT.

Sanborn, Franklin Benjamin (1831–1917), teacher, biographer, editor, journalist, abolitionist. Sanborn, born in New Hampshire, was a friend of EMERSON, BRONSON ALCOTT, and THEODORE PARKER and claimed he was more indebted to them for his education than to Harvard. While still an undergraduate he started a little school at Concord, at Emerson's request, where he taught the children of Emerson, Hawthorne, Horace Mann, and John Brown, conducting his classes according to Alcott's so-called progressive methods. A staunch abolitionist, Sanborn assisted in the underground railroad and toured the West in 1856 to report on the progress of the Free Soil group. He was involved in the plans for John Brown's raid on Harper's Ferry, and for a while was in trouble with the law.

Sanborn edited the Boston *Commonwealth* and was a resident editor of the Springfield *Republican*. Much of his life was spent collecting material about the great New Englanders. He published *Henry D. Thoreau* (1882); *The Life and Letters of John Brown* (1885, 4th ed. 1910 called *John Brown, Liberator of Kansas and Martyr of Virginia*); *Dr. S. G. Howe, the Philanthropist* (1891); *Bronson Alcott: His Life and Philosophy* (with W. T. Harris, 2 v. 1893); *The Personality of Thoreau* (1901); *Ralph Waldo Emerson* (1901); *Hawthorne and His Friends* (1908); *Recollections of Seventy Years* (2 v. 1909); and *The Life of Henry David Thoreau* (1917).

Sánchez, Florencio (1875–1910), Uruguayan dramatist. Considered the outstanding dramatist of the Río de la Plata region, Sánchez turned to the theater after working as a journalist and participating in anarchist agitation. He wrote his first play, *M'hijo el dotor* (1903), to earn enough money to marry his sweetheart, whose parents viewed his bleak prospects with disfavor. Dealing with the conflict between an old gaucho and his urbane, self-centered son, the play met with notable success. The struggle between the old order and new is also the theme of other plays by Sánchez, notably *La Gringa* (1904), which is concerned with racial animosity between native Argentines and Italian immigrants, and *Barranca abajo* (1905), an elegy on the gaucho threatened by progress. Sánchez's work has been likened to IBSEN's because of its realism and emphasis on contemporary problems. His most important plays have been translated into English in *Representative Plays of Florencio Sánchez* (1961 tr. by W. K. Jones). See GAUCHO LITERATURE.

Sanchez, Sonia (1934–   ), poet, short-story writer, playwright. Born Wilsonia Benita Driver in Birmingham, Alabama, Sanchez was educated at Hunter College and New York University. Sanchez's poetry, based on her African-American heritage, emphasizes the spoken word and jazz rhythms. Some of her poetry titles are *Homecoming* (1969), *We a BaddDDD People*

(1970), *A Blues Book for Blue Black Magical Women* (1973), *I've Been a Woman: New and Selected Poems* (1978), *homegirls and handgrenades* (1984), *Under a Soprano Sky* (1987), *Wounded in the House of a Friend* (1995), *Does Your House Have Lions* (1995), and *Like the Singing Coming Off the Drums: Love Poems* (1998).

Sanctuary (1931), a novel by WILLIAM FAULKNER. The acts of violence—Temple Drake's rape and Tommy's murder—central to the story set the lawyer Horace Benbow on a quest for justice that ends in his realization that the law is often more closely related to public opinion than to the unbiased aims of justice. Believing the accused murderer, Lee Goodwin, to be innocent, Benbow unsuccessfully attempts to give shelter to Goodwin's common-law wife and their infant son, and to find out the truth from TEMPLE DRAKE, a witness to the murder. Temple falsely testifies against Goodwin to protect POPEYE, the rapist and real murderer, and Goodwin is killed by the townspeople. See REQUIEM FOR A NUN.

Sandbox, The (1960), an early play by EDWARD ALBEE.

Sandburg, Carl (1878–1967), poet, biographer. The son of Swedish immigrants, Sandburg attended public schools until he was thirteen and then went to work in his hometown, Galesburg, Illinois, and in the West: driver of a milk wagon, porter in a barber shop, scene shifter in a theater, worker in a brick kiln, carpenter's assistant, dishwasher, house painter, etc. In the Spanish-American War he served for eight months in Puerto Rico. After the war he entered Lombard College, where he became a student of Philip Green Wright. Sandburg's first book, a 39-page paperbound pamphlet called *In Reckless Ecstasy* (1904), was set and printed on a hand press in Wright's basement. Of the fifty copies printed, only two or three are known to exist.

Later Sandburg traveled for a while as a representative of Underwood & Underwood, selling stereopticon slides. In 1907–08 he worked as a district organizer for the Wisconsin Social-Democratic party, then wrote for several Milwaukee newspapers, notably the *Leader*. On June 15, 1908, he married Lillian Steichen, a schoolteacher and sister of the photographer Edward Steichen. From 1910 to 1912 he served as secretary to Emil Seidel, first socialist mayor of Milwaukee.

Sandburg moved to Chicago to continue his newspaper career on the *Daily News* and the *Daybook*. His first poems to gain a wide audience appeared in Harriet Monroe's POETRY: A MAGAZINE OF VERSE in 1914. Two years later appeared his *Chicago Poems*, and in 1918 he published *Cornhuskers*. Both volumes were well received by fellow poets and by a fairly wide general audience. Meanwhile, Sandburg set out to make himself an authority on Lincoln, whose personality and achievements greatly attracted the poet, who had made the virtues of American democracy his principal subject. His exhaustive biography of the Civil War president, requiring many years of preparation and writing, appeared as *Abraham Lincoln: The Prairie Years* (2 v. 1926) and *Abraham Lincoln: The War Years* (4 v. 1939), which won a Pulitzer Prize. The first twenty-six chapters from the biography were issued separately as *Abe Lincoln Grows Up* (1931), and an abridgment of all six volumes, *Abraham Lincoln*, appeared in 1954.

Sandburg's growing reputation during the 1920s and 1930s enabled him to give up newspaper work and live on his writing and his lecturing. He toured the country several times, reading from his poems and singing folk songs, which he accompanied on the guitar. His collections of local ballads, THE AMERICAN SONGBAG (1927) and *The New American Songbag* (1950), have been an important contribution to the literature of American folklore. For a time the poet conducted a syndicated newspaper column. He served as narrator for the radio series called Cavalcade of America, took part in foreign broadcasts of the Office of War Information, and contributed his services as writer to other wartime projects. For several years he lived with his wife and three daughters near Harbert, Michigan. He later retired to a farm at Flat Rock, North Carolina.

Sandburg's principal books of poetry, besides those already mentioned, are SMOKE AND STEEL (1920); *Slabs of the Sunburnt West* (1922); *Selected Poems* (1926); GOOD MORNING, AMERICA (1928); *Early Moon* (1930); and THE PEOPLE, YES (1936). In 1950 appeared his *Complete Poems*, for which he won a second Pulitzer Prize. In prose, besides the Lincoln biography, Sandburg wrote the biography *Steichen the Photographer* (1929); *The Chicago Race Riots* (1919); *Mary Lincoln, Wife and Widow* (1932); four books for children, ROOTABAGA STORIES (1922), *Rootabaga Pigeons* (1923), *The Rootabaga Country* (1929), and *Potato Face* (1930); *Remembrance Rock,* a novel (1948); *Always the Young Strangers* (1952), an autobiographical account of his youth; and *Prairie Town Boy* (1955), a reprint of one section of *Always the Young Strangers.*

In mood Sandburg's poetry ranges from his brutal attack on Billy Sunday, "To a Contemporary Bunkshooter," to the vigor of his paeans to American democracy and the tenderness of such wispy fantasies as "Fog." His style is made of equal parts of Whitman, the Imagists, and original Sandburg, with a passing debt to the Lincoln of the *Gettysburg Address.* Rhymeless and unmetered, his poems nevertheless employ strong cadences derived from Midwestern speech, and the diction ranges from a strong, sometimes hackneyed rhetoric to easygoing slang. He was not above invective, for among his poems are powerful denunciations of hypocrisy and political and commercial chicanery. He often wrote about the uncouth and the vulgar, the muscular and the primitive. Yet behind this vigor and animal force lies a large fund of pity and lovingkindness, the primary motive for his poetry. His work remains popular with a large and loyal audience. There is no doubt that his poems offer a representation of his time and place that is at once widely characteristic and poetically significant.

A complete biography is North Callahan, *Carl Sandburg: His Life and Works* (1987). Earlier studies include Richard Crowder, *Carl Sandburg* (1963), and Gay Wilson Allen, *Carl Sandburg* (1972).

RICHARD CROWDER/BP

Sandeman, Robert (1718–1771),   religious leader. Sandeman spent most of his life in Scotland, where he was a follower of John Glas (1695–1773). He and Glas protested against the Church of Scotland and advocated separation of church and state. His *Some Thoughts on Christianity* (1764) was published after his immigration to New England where, despite opposition from the Congregational clergy, he established his Sandemanian sect.

Sanderson, John (1783–1844),   teacher, author. Sanderson, born in Pennsylvania, was a contributor to several periodicals, particularly *The Port Folio* and *The Aurora.* He and his brother Joseph wrote two volumes of *Lives of the Signers of the Declaration of Independence* (1820, completed in seven additional volumes by Robert Waln, Jr.). His health failed in 1835 and he went to France and then to England. His impressions of France were given in *Sketches of Paris: Familiar Letters to His Friends, by an American Gentleman* (2 v. 1838). Those of England appeared in several papers in the *Knickerbocker Magazine.*

Sandoz, Mari [Susette] (1901–1966),   novelist, historical writer. Sandoz, the Nebraska-born daughter of Swiss emigrants, did not speak English until she started school at age nine, but her informal education was strictly western American, including much contact with the Sioux. She served as research worker and associate editor of the *State Journal of the Nebraska Historical Society.* Her biography of her father, *Old Jules* (1935), won the Atlantic Monthly prize. Her novels include *Slogum House* (1937), *Capital City* (1939), *The Tom-Walker* (1947), and *Miss Morissa* (1955). Her best work, however, is found in her nonfiction narratives: *Crazy Horse* (1942); *Cheyenne Autumn* (1953); *The Buffalo Hunters* (1954); *The Cattlemen* (1958); and two books in 1961, *Love Song to the Plains* and *These Were the Sioux.* Her other works on Sioux history include *The Battle of the Little Bighorn* (1966) and *A Pictographic History of the Oglala Sioux* (1967). *The Story Catcher* (1973) is a novella. *Sandhill Sundays and Other Recollections* (1970) is a collection of stories. Her other titles include *Beaver Men* (1964) and *The Battle of Little Big Horn* (1978). *The Christmas of Phonograph Records* (1966) is autobiographical.

Sands, Robert C[harles] (1799–1832),   poet, essayist, editor. Sands, born in Brooklyn, New York, a writer of the KNICKERBOCKER SCHOOL, wrote verse and edited several magazines and yearbooks in collaboration with WILLIAM CULLEN BRYANT and G.C. VERPLANCK. His best-known poem, written with JAMES W. EASTBURN, is called *Yamoyden* and is about King Philip. *The Writings of Robert C. Sands, in Prose and Verse* (2 v. 1834) was edited by Verplanck. Bryant wrote a memoir of Verplanck in the *Knickerbocker Magazine.*

Sandys, George (1578–1644),   colonist, translator. He lived in Virginia from 1621 to 1625, where he completed the verse translation of Ovid's work, *Ovid's Metamorphosis Englished by G. S.* (1626), that he had begun in England. This was the first translation of a classic done in America, and there are many references to America in Sandy's text.

San Francisco Renaissance.   The phrase refers to the literary ferment in the San Francisco Bay area between 1955 and 1965. The most public manifestation of this era was the Beat movement as it was played out in North Beach and made widely known through ALLEN GINSBERG's "Howl" (1956) and

JACK KEROUAC's *On the Road* (1957), but there were many other strands, all of which contributed to a romantic revival. Whether in Allen Ginsberg's long-lined poems of social protest or in ROBERT DUNCAN's open-ended so-called field poems or in MICHAEL MCCLURE's "beast" language experiments or in Helen Adam's ballads, the San Francisco Renaissance revived Emersonian ideals of individual vision and natural divinity and combined them with Whitmanian vitalism and communality. Reacting against the New Critical aesthetics of personal detachment and formal complexity then prevalent, poets of the San Francisco Renaissance treated the poem as an expressive vehicle, whose unmediated rhetoric and direct diction would reach the reader by more than semantic means. The evolution of public poetry readings contributed to this aesthetic, taking the poem off the page and putting it into the public sphere.

The origins of the San Francisco Renaissance can be found in California's long tradition of counterculture social and literary movements, extending back to the bohemian days of GEORGE STERLING, JACK LONDON, and ROBINSON JEFFERS. Later poets such as KENNETH REXROTH, WILLIAM EVERSON, GARY SYNDER, PHILIP WHALEN, and JACK SPICER who were in San Francisco during the early 1950s identified themselves with what Rexroth called the "alternative society," which mixed anarcho-pacifist political ideals and avant-garde literary experimentation. Lawrence Ferlinghetti's CITY LIGHTS BOOKSTORE and publishing firm provided the first literary venues, and bars and gallery spaces provided public spaces for readings. The media attention on the Beats brought a new, populist audience to literature. While the media projection of bohemian lifestyles often distorted history and overlooked the movement's literary contributions, the San Francisco Renaissance contributed to the vitality of literature and served as a major event in the evolution of a postmodern poetry. (See BEAT GENERATION.) Studies include David Meltzer, *The San Francisco Poets* (1971); Lawrence Ferlinghetti and Nancy Peters, *Literary San Francisco* (1980); Michael Davidson, *The San Francisco Renaissance* (1989); and Lewis Ellingham and Kevin Killian, *Poet Be Like God: Jack Spicer and The San Francisco Renaissance* (1998).

MICHAEL DAVIDSON

Sanger, Margaret [Higgins] (1883–1966), family planning pioneer. A leader in the birth control movement, Sanger wrote *Happiness in Marriage* (1927), *My Fight for Birth Control* (1931), and an autobiography, *Margaret Sanger* (1938).

Sangster, Charles (1822–1893), Canadian poet, post office official. Sangster has been called the first poet to make appreciative use of Canadian subjects. He contributed verse and prose to several periodicals; for a time edited *The Courier* in Amherstburg; and published *The St. Lawrence and the Saguenay and Other Poems* (1856), *Hesperus and Other Poems* (1860), and *Our Norland* (1893).

Sangster, Margaret E[lizabeth] (1838–1912), newspaperwoman, editor, poet, writer of juveniles. Sangster's name was associated as editor or subeditor with many important magazines of her time, including *Hearth and Home*, the *Christian Intelligencer*, *Harper's Young People*, *Harper's Bazaar*, the *Christian Herald*, the *Ladies' Home Journal*, and the *Woman's Home Companion*. She wrote *Little Janey* (1855), *Poems of the Household* (1882), *Easter Bells* (1897), *Winsome Womanhood* (1900), *Good Manners for All Occasions* (1904), *My Garden of Hearts* (1913), and many other books. *An Autobiography: From My Youth Up* (1909) described her career.

Sankey, Ira David.   See DWIGHT LYMAN MOODY.

San Martín, José de (1778–1850),   Argentine general and revolutionary leader. After taking part in Argentina's struggle for independence from Spain, San Martín became governor of Cuyo province (1814–17), where he organized an army to lead against Chile and Peru, the stronghold of Spanish power in South America. After a trek across the Andes, San Martín and the Chilean patriot Bernardo O'Higgins defeated the Spaniards at Chacabuco and Maipu and declared the independence of Chile. Rejecting the political honors grateful Chileans offered him, San Martín turned to the liberation of Peru. Although he was able to declare Peru's independence in 1821, most of the territory included in the viceroyalty of Peru still remained in royalist hands, and San Martín, who was named dictator of Peru, resolved to seek the aid of Bolívar. After a meeting between the two liberators at Guayaquil (1822), San Martín, perhaps believing that his continued presence in Peru would delay the final victory, resigned his post and left the country, leaving a clear field for Bolívar. He spent his last years in Europe and died in France. His achievements were belatedly recognized by his countrymen, who had ignored or vilified him during his lifetime, and in 1880 his remains were brought to Argentina for final burial in Buenos Aires.

Santa Anna [or **Ana**], **Antonio López de** (1795–1876), Mexican soldier, politician. Santa Anna was a soldier in the Spanish army for a while, returned to Mexico, and after several revolts became president in 1833. When Americans in Texas talked about separation from Mexico, he made himself dictator. He besieged the Alamo, a fort, and massacred all its defenders. He suffered a severe defeat by Sam Houston at the Battle of San Jacinto, was captured by the Texans, and was released only on condition that he would approve the independence of Texas. He defended Vera Cruz unsuccessfully against a French invasion and in 1841 again became president. During the Mexican-American War he led the Mexican Army, but was severely defeated. He resigned and left the country. In 1853 he was recalled to become president again, but another revolution soon drove him out. He died in poverty. His *Letters Relating to War* were edited by J. H. Smith for the American Historical Association *Report* (1917).

Santa Fe Trail.   The main overland route to the Southwest and southern California in the years before the railroad. Innumerable explorers, traders, military expeditions, and travelers traversed the Santa Fe Trail, and it is still the route of a transcontinental highway and of the Atchison, Topeka, and Santa Fe Railroad. The trail began at Independence (originally at Franklin), Missouri, proceeded along the prairie divide to the great bend of the Arkansas River, followed the river upward almost to the mountains, and then turned south to Santa Fe. It was originally traced by WILLIAM BECKNELL in 1821.

Josiah Gregg's *Commerce of the Prairies* (2 v. 1844) is the classic account of the trail; additional information is contained in Gregg's *Diary and Letters* (1941), edited by M. G. Fulton. Other nonfiction is George W. Kendall, *Narrative of the Texan Santa Fe Expedition* (2 v. 1844); G. F. RUXTON, LIFE IN THE FAR WEST (1859); Henry Inman, *The Old Santa Fe Trail* (1897); R. L. Duffus, *The Santa Fe Trail* (1930); STANLEY VESTAL, *The Old Santa Fe Trail* (1939); and *The Santa Fe Trail* (1946), complied by the editors of *Look* magazine. Novels about the trail include Stanley Vestal, *'Dobe Walls* (1917); R. L. Duffus, *Jornada* (1935); HARVEY FERGUSSON, the trilogy *Followers of the Sun* (1936); and Ottamar Hamele, *When Destiny Called* (1948). It is also the subject of Vachel Lindsay's poem "The Santa-Fé Trail: A Humoresque" (1914).

Santayana, George (1863–1952),   philosopher, critic, poet, novelist. Santayana's life and mind were shaped by two very different cultures: Avila, Spain, where he lived in his early childhood years and to which he often returned, and Cambridge, Massachusetts, where he studied and taught. "My real nucleus," he observed, "was this combination, not easily unified." At age eight Santayana left Avila with his father to join his mother in Boston, where she had settled in 1869 with her three children by a previous marriage. She had thus fulfilled the wish of her first husband, George Sturgis, a Boston merchant, that their children be schooled in Boston. Santayana remained in America with his mother, and his father returned to Spain.

His transplantation was, Santayana wrote, "a terrible moral disinheritance," adding, "The extreme contrast between the two centers and the two influences became itself a blessing: it rendered flagrant the limitations and the contingency of both." Consigned to kindergarten to learn English, the Spanish boy quickly proved his aptitude in language, and subsequently his precocity as a student, first at the Boston Latin School, then at Harvard. He was graduated in 1886 and won a fellowship for a year's study in Berlin. He returned to Cambridge to finish his doctoral dissertation on Lotze, and joined his former mentors, WILLIAM JAMES, JOSIAH ROYCE, and GEORGE HERBERT PALMER, as an instructor in Harvard's department of philosophy. After twenty-two years of teaching, Santayana abruptly resigned his chair—he had often felt there, he said, "a caged philosopher"—and in 1912 settled in Oxford, England. His travels in Europe after World War I led him to Rome, which became his principal residence from 1922 until his death.

Santayana began to write English verses during his Latin School days. A collection of his poems, *Sonnets and Other Verses* (1894), was his first book. Thirty additional sonnets were included in a second edition (1896). A later collection is *A Hermit of Carmel and Other Poems* (1901). Santayana thought his poetry authentic in inspiration but hackneyed in expression, and he soon turned to prose. A revival of his poetic impulse, as he termed it, occasioned two later prose works, *Soliloquies in England and Later Soliloquies* (1922) and *Dialogues in Limbo* (1926), the latter a *jeu d'esprit* that gives free play to radical intuitions and contending voices within him.

In *The Sense of Beauty* (1896), the first American treatise on aesthetics, Santayana examines formal properties common to what is found beautiful and the psychological ground of aes-

thetic response. His analysis yielded his controversial judgment that the beautiful is pleasure objectified. *Interpretation of Poetry and Religion* (1900) is informed by the recurring idea that religion and poetry are identical in essence: "Poetry is called religion when it intervenes in life [in practical affairs], and religion, when it merely supervenes upon life, is seen to be nothing but poetry." His most ambitious early work is *The Life of Reason: Or, The Phases of Human Progress* (1905–06), five volumes surveying episodes in the history of Western consciousness. Arguing that reason, the drive toward harmony and perfection, is rooted in prerational instinct, emotion, and desire, Santayana explores the ends of human activity and their partial fulfillments in the sciences, religions, the arts, and everyday life. Another work of his Harvard years is *Three Philosophical Poets: Lucretius, Dante, and Goethe* (1910), in which he envisions a supreme poet who should accommodate the perspectives of the naturalist, the Christian, and the humanist.

Following Santayana's self-exile from the academy, he wrote prolifically. His books include *Winds of Doctrine* (1913), *Egotism in German Philosophy* (1915), CHARACTER AND OPINION IN THE UNITED STATES (1920), *Platonism and the Spiritual Life* (1927), *The Genteel Tradition at Bay* (1931), *The Idea of Christ in the Gospels* (1946), and *Dominations and Powers* (1951). The major work of this period is Santayana's greatest work, *Realms of Being* (1927–40), a four-volume systematic statement of his mature philosophy. Distinguishing four minimum postulates of thinking and discourse, he calls them matter, essence, spirit, and truth. An introduction to these volumes is *Skepticism and Animal Faith* (1923), an advanced exercise in Cartesian skepticism that seeks to reconcile the claims of philosophic idealism and realism.

Santayana's first and only novel, THE LAST PURITAN (1935), is close to his personal history as a young man. In his late years he wrote his autobiography, *Persons and Places* (1944–53), in three volumes. *The Letters of George Santayana* (1955), containing a small portion of the letters now known to exist, were edited by Daniel Cory.

Santayana sustained a lifelong meditation on the vexed relations of the imagination and reality, philosophy's perennial problem. To his resolution of the question he brought incisive analytic powers and a sweeping historical imagination. He sought to assimilate and include in his reckonings a wide range of the intuitions and perspectives of Western poets, historians, and philosophers from classical times down to his own. He has been called, with Emerson, a dramatist of ideas and, like Emerson, his style is aphoristic and lapidary, suggesting a poet's view of clarity and precision as best served by metaphor, compression, and variations on a theme.

Santayana held that all human knowledge is imaginative construction—the hypotheses and theories of the sciences no less than theologies, philosophies, poems, or novels. Awareness proceeds through the employment of essences, the ideal terms, the immaterial aesthetic and logical identities, that mark difference, enabling discernment of a "this" as distinct from a "that." Such figments or fictions are the medium of perception and conception alike. Since the imagination (mind) may indefinitely outrun what happens to exist, essences are infinite in number.

Those essences that prove indicative of the external world in its structure and movement, ideas that prove applicable or prophetic in practice—Santayana was a pragmatist—comprise our always tentative, indirect, symbolic knowledge of reality.

An idealist and transcendentalist with respect to the contents of mind, Santayana was a materialist with respect to its origin and ground. Ideas and ideals are born of the body in the midst of circumstance—they are epiphenomenal—and the body is born of material elements and energies whose nature the physical sciences seek to discover. Santayana waged a sustained war on the principle of egotism, "the fond delusion that man and his moral nature are at the center of the universe." Questions of morality and the ends of living are paramount for humankind, but their wise resolution requires the humility of a full-blown naturalism.

In literary studies Santayana's influence has been many-sided. At a time when Symbolism had scarcely been heard of in America, he formulated, in 1900, a poetic theory incorporating many of the Symbolists' principles and methods. His early defense of classical form against romanticism, in the context of a naturalistic psychology, continues to be debated. Literary historians have found indispensable his term and conception, "the genteel tradition." But Santayna's influence in American literature can perhaps best be traced in the work of his students, chief among them T. S. ELIOT and WALLACE STEVENS. R. P. Blackmur has contended that Eliot said little about Santayana because "he incorporated so much of him," including Santayana's theory of the objective correlative. Santayana's central concern for accommodating and harmonizing the claims of both imagination and reality is pervasive in the poetry of Stevens, whose theory of the "supreme fiction" lies close to Santayana's reflection on poetry. Stevens paid his tribute to the "Master" in his poem "To an Old Philosopher in Rome." Late in his life Santayana was a friend and correspondent of EZRA POUND, who proposed that they write a book together and who observed that he had never known anyone who "faked less," and of ROBERT LOWELL, who wrote two poems about him.

The Works of George Santayana (1936–37) is now superseded by a critical edition of his writings, including his complete letters, edited by Herman Saatkamp and William Holzberger: *The Works of George Santayana* (1986–   ). Numerous critical studies of his work have been published. *The Philosophy of George Santayana* (1940), edited by Paul Arthur Schilpp, is a collection of critical essays to which Santayana responds in his "Apologia Pro Mente Sua," an essay he once called "perhaps the clearest exposition of my views." John McCormick's *George Santayana: A Biography* (1987) is comprehensive and informed.

RICHARD C. LYON

Santee, Ross (1888–1965),   artist, novelist. Santee, born in Iowa, attended the Chicago Art Institute, ambitious to become a cartoonist. Instead he went to Arizona to work on the range, and it was there that he embarked on a long career of illustrating and writing stories mostly concerned with the West. Some of his books are *Men and Horses* (1926), *Cowboy* (1928), *The Pooch* (1931), *The Bar X Golf Course* (1933), *The Bubbling Spring* (1949), *Rusty* (1950), and *Hardrock and the*

Silver Sage (1951). *Lost Pony Tracks* (1953) and *Dog Days* (1955) are autobiographical.

Santmyer, Helen Hooven (1895–1986),   novelist. Born in Cincinnati, educated at Wellesley College and as a Rhodes Scholar at Oxford, Santmyer published her first novel when she was thirty, but she is known best for a novel published when she was nearly ninety, . . . *And Ladies of the Club* (1982, Ohio State University Press; reissue Putnam's, 1984). This account of life in a small Ohio town from 1868 to 1932 centers on two members of the local women's club. Her other novels are *Herbs and Apples* (1925) and *The Fierce Dispute* (1929). *Ohio Town: A Portrait of Xenia* (1962; 1984) is a non-fiction memoir of the town in southwest Ohio where she lived for most of her adult life.

Santos, Bienvenido (1911–1996),   poet, novelist, short-story writer. Born in Manila, Philippines, he was educated there and at the University of Illinois. After teaching in his native country, he received a Fulbright professorship to teach at the University of Iowa (1966–1969) and became a naturalized citizen in 1976. His fiction concerns the experiences of Filipinos at home and abroad, especially the "pinoys," who have been in the U.S. for so long they are out of touch with their native culture. Stories are collected in *You Lovely People* (1955), *Brother My Brother* (1960), *Scent of Apples* (1979), and *Dwell in the Wilderness* (1985). *The Wounded Stag* (1956) and *Distances in Time* (1983) are poetry collections. Novels include *Villa Magdalena* (1965), *The Volcano* (1965), *The Man Who (Thought He) Looked Like Robert Taylor* (1983), and *What the Hell for You Left Your Heart in San Francisco* (1987). *The Praying Man* (1982), a controversial novel, was censored by the Philippine military when it was serialized in a magazine. *The Day the Dancers Came* (1967) contains essays, and reminiscenses are collected in *Memory's Fictions: A Personal History* (1993) and *Postscript to a Saintly Life* (1994).

Sapir, Edward (1884–1939),   anthropologist, linguist. Sapir came to the United States from Germany at an early age and was educated at Columbia, where he began his learned studies in Germanics and the Indo-European languages. Franz Boas gave him the opportunity to study Native American languages, one of which—Takelma, spoken in Oregon—became the subject of his doctoral thesis. The best-known book by Sapir is his semipopular *Language, An Introduction to the Study of Speech* (1921). He also wrote on the *Southern Paiute Language* (1931) and edited *Wishram Texts* (1909) and *Takelma Texts* (1909). His *Selected Writings* were edited by David Mandelbaum (1949).

Sapphira and the Slave Girl (1940),   a novel by WILLA CATHER. In New Testament history Sapphira and her husband Ananias were struck dead for lying. The scene of Cather's novel is Virginia, and the chief characters are several white families of distinction and a mulatto girl, Nancy Till, born of an affair between the housekeeper of the Henry Colbert household and a painter who had done portraits of Colbert and his wife, Sapphira. Sapphira, an invalid, becomes more and more jealous of Nancy. She conspires against her unsuccessfully, and the girl is assisted through the Underground Railroad to escape to Canada. Many years later she returns to visit her mother and the people who had helped her escape.

Sarduy, Severo (1937–1993),   novelist. Born in Cuba, Sarduy lived in voluntary exile in France after 1960. In Paris he became a member of the Tel Quel group, producing neo-baroque linguistic puzzles, including *Gestos* (1963); *De donde son los cantantas* (1967, tr. *From Cuba with a Song*, 1973); *Cobra* (1973, tr. 1975); *Maitreya* (1978), tr. 1987); and *Colibri* [hummingbird] (1982). *Cocuyo* (1990) describes the adolescence of a strange child, and *Pajaros de Playa* (1993) is about the AIDS epidemic that caused the author's own death. Plays are collected in *Para la Voz* (1977; tr. *For Voice: Four Plays*, 1985).

Sarett, Lew (1888–1954),   poet, lecturer, teacher. Sarett, born in Chicago, served as a woodsman, guide, and United States Ranger in the Rockies and Canada. His poetry is often concerned with Native Americans and wild animals. Among his collections are *Many Many Moons* (1920), *The Box of God* (1922), *Slow Smoke* (1925), *Wings Against the Moon* (1931), and *Collected Poems* (1941).

Sargent, Epes (1813–1880),   writer, editor. Sargent, born in Massachusetts, wrote his earliest work, a series of letters written from Russia during a trip with his father, for the Boston Latin School newspaper. He later worked for several Boston and New York papers before he started *Sargent's New Monthly Magazine*, which lasted from January to June 1843.

SPARTACUS TO THE GLADIATORS, Elijah Kellogg's once-famous elocution piece, was first published in Sargent's *School Reader* (1846). Among Sargent's chief works are *Fleetwood; or, The Stain of Birth* (1845), a novel; *Songs of the Sea and Other Poems* (1847); *Change Makes Change* (1854) and *The Priestess* (1854), dramas; and *Peculiar: A Tale of the Great Transition* (1864) and *The Woman Who Dared* (1870), poems. *Planchette; or, The Despair of Science* (1869); *The Proof Palpable of Immortality* (1875); and *The Scientific Basis of Spiritualism* (1880) reflect his interest in the supernatural. See KNICKERBOCKER SCHOOL.

Sargent, Lucius Manlius (1786–1867),   poet, antiquarian, translator. Sargent turned from the study of law to translating Virgil, wrote poetry of his own, and engaged in antiquarian research. He was especially interested in two crusades—temperance and the defense of slavery. Among his books are *Hubert and Ellen and Other Poems* (1812), *The Stage Coach* (1838), *Temperance Tales* (6 v. 1863–64), and *The Ballad of the Abolition Blunder-buss* (1861).

Sargent, Winthrop (1825–1870),   historian, editor. Sargent, a Philadelphian, was interested chiefly in historical research on the Revolutionary period. He wrote some notable works, among them *A History of an Expedition Against Fort Duquesne, Under Major General Braddock* (1855), and *The Loyalist Poetry of the Revolution* (1857). His *Life and Times of Major John André* (1861) eulogized the British spy. He also edited the loyalist poems of Joseph Stansbury and Jonathan Odell (1860).

Sarmiento, Domingo Faustino (1811–1888), Argentine statesman, educator, and writer. The self-educated Sarmiento once wrote that he had tried to pattern himself on Benjamin Franklin. His political career began when he opposed the dictatorship of Juan Manuel de Rosas, whom he

denounced in FACUNDO. He spent many years as an exile in Chile, where he became known as an innovative educator. He returned to Argentina after Rosas had been overthrown and held several important political posts, including minister of the U.S., a country he unabashedly admired. Elected president of the republic in 1868, he reformed the country's educational system, encouraged large-scale immigration, and furthered advances in transportation and communications. He was, however, unable to diminish the personalism in Argentine politics, and when his term ended the country was divided by civil war. A prolific writer whose complete works fill fifty-two volumes, Sarmiento was a romantic in style and literary outlook. His important works include *Viajes* (1849), an account of a trip to Europe, Africa, and the U.S., and *Recuerdos de provincia* (1850), an engaging memoir of his childhood.

Saroyan, William (1908–1981),   short-story writer, novelist, playwright, songwriter. Saroyan, born in Fresno, California, lived in an orphanage until his widowed mother was able to support her numerous children. He attended Fresno Junior High School, read avidly, and left school at twelve to become a telegraph messenger. His first short story to be published—in the Armenian magazine *Hairenik*—was reprinted in O'Brien's *Best Short Stories of 1934*. In the same year appeared THE DARING YOUNG MAN ON THE FLYING TRAPEZE. Its breezy, impertinent, tender style made it an immediate success. There followed *Inhale and Exhale* (1936); *Three Times Three* (1936); *Little Children* (1937); *Love, Here Is My Hat* (1938); *The Trouble with Tigers* (1938); and *Peace, It's Wonderful* (1939). The autobiographical *My Name Is Aram* (1940) contains some of his best stories. *The Human Comedy* (1942), an exuberant novel about a boy who delivered telegrams during World War II, was largely autobiographical. His play *My Heart's in the Highlands* (1939) was a Broadway success, and THE TIME OF YOUR LIFE (1939) won a Pulitzer Prize, which Saroyan refused to accept. *Love's Old Sweet Song* (1940) and *The Beautiful People* (1941) were less successful. In 1961, *Two by Saroyan* (including *The Cave Dwellers*, 1958) was revived off Broadway. His later writings include *The Adventures of Wesley Jackson* (1946); *The Assyrian and Other Stories* (1950); *Rock Wagram and Tracy's Tiger* (1951); *The Bicycle Rider of Beverly Hills* (1952); *The Laughing Matter* (1953); *The Bouncing Ball and Mama, I Love You* (1956); and *Papa, You're Crazy* (1957). The *William Saroyan Reader* was published in 1958. *Here Comes, There Goes You Know Who* (1961) is a volume of reminiscences. His other autobiographical volumes are *Not Dying* (1963) and *Short Drive, Sweet Chariot* (1966). *Boys and Girls Together* (1963) and *One Day in the Afternoon of the World* (1964) are novels.

Sarton, May (1912–1995),   poet, novelist, playwright. Sarton came to the United States from Belgium as a child. She taught literature and creative writing at Harvard, Wellesley, and elsewhere. Her books of poetry include *Encounter in April* (1937); *Inner Landscape* (1939); *The Lion and the Rose* (1948); *The Land of Silence and Other Poems* (1953); *In Time Like Air* (1957); *Cloud, Stone, Sun, Vine* (1961); *A Private Mythology* (1965); and *Collected Poems* (1974). Her novels, set in Belgium and New England, include *The Single Hound* (1938); *The*

Bridge of Years (1946); *Shadow of a Man* (1950); *A Shower of Summer Days* (1952); *Faithful Are the Wounds* (1955), about a Harvard professor's suicide under the pressures of MAC-CARTHYISM; *The Birth of a Grandfather* (1957); *The Small Room* (1961); *Mrs. Stevens Hears the Mermaids Singing* (1965); *Crucial Conversations* (1975); *A Reckoning* (1978); and *Anger* (1982). Her autobiographical works include *I Knew a Phoenix* (1959), *A Plant Dreaming Deep* (1968), *A World of Light* (1976), *Journal of a Solitude* (1973), and *Recovering* (1980). *The Underground River* (1947) is a play.

Sartoris (1929),   a novel by WILLIAM FAULKNER. A saga of the Sartoris family, the novel deals primarily with young Bayard Sartoris's urge for self-destruction. His beloved twin brother John having been killed in World War I, Bayard returns home haunted by the memories of his brother and becomes involved in a number of accidents. Because of his reckless driving, his grandfather, old Bayard Sartoris, rides with him in an attempt to force him to drive carefully, but young Bayard runs the car off a cliff, and his grandfather dies of a heart attack. Unable to face either himself or his family, Bayard goes to Ohio to become a test pilot and is killed. Faulkner's first novel to deal with YOKNAPATAWPHA COUNTY, *Sartoris* contains many of his later themes: the disappearing positive values of the Old South, the sterility and destructiveness of the industrial and machine age following World War I, and the inability of the heirs of the old world to adjust to the new. Faulkner picks up the beginnings of the Sartoris family in THE UNVANQUISHED.

Sartoris, Col. John.   A leading character in Faulkner's SARTORIS (1929), THE UNVANQUISHED (1938), and other novels and stories. He has numerous descendants and kinfolk. The Sartoris family is believed to be reminiscent of the Faulkner family, descendants of Col. William C. Faulkner (or Falkner).

Satanstoe (1845),   a novel by JAMES FENIMORE COOPER. This was the first novel of a trilogy called *The Littlepage Manuscripts*, which includes also THE CHAINBEARER (1845) and THE REDSKINS (1846). It is autobiographical in form. Cornelius Littlepage is the heir of an aristocratic family of Dutch descent living at Satanstoe, a strip of land in Westchester County, New York. Cornelius is educated at Princeton, makes fun of Yankees, is enthralled by the sights of New York City, comes out in society, saves a girl from a caged lion, rescues her again from the Hudson in flood, and fights the French at Lake George. In *The Chainbearer* Cornelius's son Mordaunt works on the patent of land the Littlepages hold in northern New York and comes in contact with squatters; in *The Redskins* Mordaunt's grandson takes part in the Anti-Rent War. Cooper made much use of material from Anne Grant's *Memoirs of an American Lady* (2 v. 1808). See ANTI-RENT LAWS.

Saturday Club.   A Boston dinner club that came into existence in 1855 and was later called the Magazine Club or

SARTORIS GENEALOGY

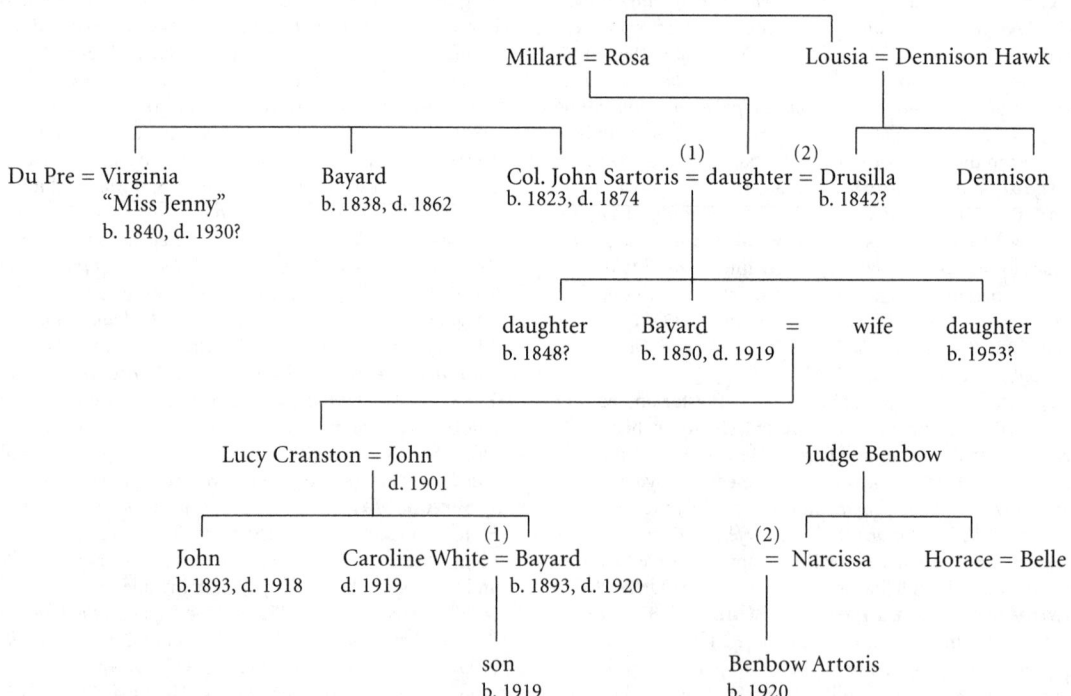

Atlantic Club. Among its members were EMERSON, LONGFEL-LOW, JAMES RUSSELL LOWELL, LOUIS AGASSIZ, HAWTHORNE, JOHN LOTHROP MOTLEY, CHARLES SUMNER, and WHITTIER. They dined together once a month at the Parker House. OLIVER WENDELL HOLMES, the leader and perhaps the wittiest conversationalist of the group, immortalized the club in his poem "At the Saturday Club" (1884). Edward W. Emerson wrote about *The Early Years of the Saturday Club, 1855–1879* (1918), and M.A. DeWolfe Howe continued the narrative to 1920 in *The Later Years of the Saturday Club* (1927).

Saturday Evening Post, The.   Volume I, Number 1, of the *Saturday Evening Post* was issued on August 4, 1821, joining scores of weekend miscellanies for Sunday reading then springing up all over the country. The founders were Charles Alexander and Samuel C. Atkinson, both ambitious young printers. Alexander brought to the partnership the subscription list of the *Bee*, a similar venture that had lasted only briefly, and Atkinson an interest in a printing plant that had once produced the defunct PENNSYLVANIA GAZETTE. During its first five years the *Post* was edited, chiefly by the use of scissors and pastepot, by Thomas Cottrell Clarke. The paper contained some tales and poems by amateur writers, a serial of the seduction novel pattern then popular, a "Dramatic Summary" reviewing plays, an essay series, some household hints, and a considerable amount of news in single-paragraph form.

The paper did well. The *Casket*, later GRAHAM'S MAGAZINE, which Atkinson and Alexander began as a monthly sister publication in 1826, passed on some of its own material to the *Post* for more than twenty years, including contributions by Poe, Nathaniel Parker Willis, James Kirke Paulding, and John Neal. RUFUS W. GRISWOLD was literary editor of both publications in 1842–1843.

When the *Post* absorbed the *Saturday Bulletin* in 1832, it became one of the leading weekend miscellanies in America and in the next decade absorbed three more such papers. In 1846 HENRY PETERSON, poet, novelist, and book publisher, became editor of the flourishing periodical. Two years later he and his publishing partner, Edmund Deacon, purchased the business, and the golden age of the early history of the *Saturday Evening Post* began. It still had only four pages, but they measured two feet wide by four feet long. The paper's leading contributors were E.D.E.N. Southworth, the immensely popular writer of serial fiction, and the scarcely less popular Emerson Bennett, Mary A. Denison, Grace Greenwood, and "Fanny Fern" Willis. In the 1850s it added, mostly through literary piracy, the work of such English novelists as Dickens—*A Tale of Two Cities* appeared in 1858—Reade, Mrs. Mulock, "Ouida," and G. P. R. James. Though virtually unillustrated in its earlier years, the *Post* made a feature of its large front-page woodcut beginning in 1863, and during the Civil War, pictures borrowed from *Frank Leslie's Illustrated Newspaper* accompanied some news of military operations.

The *Post* declined after the war. Peterson retired in 1873 and four years later the paper was sold at sheriff's sale to Andrew. E. Smythe. The weekend miscellanies were being supplanted by Sunday editions of daily papers, and the *Post* had a meager existence as a cheap story-paper until, following Smythe's death in 1897, the virtually bankrupt sheet was sold to Cyrus H. K. Curtis for $1,000.

Curtis had made a spectacular success with his monthly *Ladies' Home Journal* and at first made the *Post* a kind of weekly version of the *Journal*. By 1899 he had found a brilliant new editor, GEORGE HORACE LORIMER, and a successful new policy based on the interests of the young man in the dawning 20th century. Three types of subject matter dominated—business, public affairs, and romance—but all were more or less oriented in the direction of business and the young man's opportunities in an era of expansion and America's so-called manifest destiny. Business, outdoor adventure, sports, and humor were exploited. Typical series were Lorimer's *Letters of a Self-Made Merchant to His Son*, George Randolph Chester's *Get Rich Quick Wallingford* tales, Frank Norris's *The Pit* serial, and Arthur Train's stories of *Mr. Tutt*, the tricky lawyer. Writers of virile fiction included Kipling, London, Stephen Crane, and Rex Beach. Among humorists were Irvin Cobb, Ring Lardner, George Fitch, and Montague Glass.

By 1909 circulation had reached a million, and five years later that figure had doubled. Curtis's techniques of promotion included using Benjamin Franklin's name as founder. The *Post* had long been proud of its age, and for four months after he purchased the magazine Curtis had continued the big blackface line in the frontpage nameplate "Founded A.D. 1821"; then on January 29, 1898, this suddenly gave place to "Founded A.D. 1728," with the explanation that Benjamin Franklin had edited it in 1729–1765. (This was all later simplified to "Founded in 1728 by B. Franklin.") At the same time the volume number was jumped from 77 to 170. Thus, in one week the *Post* gained 93 years in age, as well as a new patron saint. The claim on Franklin was not fabricated by Curtis—others had prepared the myth for him, basing it on the fact that the *Post* was first issued from a shop that had formerly produced the PENNSYLVANIA GAZETTE, a newspaper Franklin conducted from 1729 to 1748. Franklin had not founded the *Gazette*, however, nor was the *Post* a continuation of it. The *Gazette* expired in 1815, six years before the *Post* was founded, on a very different plan, by men who had not been connected with the management of the *Gazette*. All of this is a mere footnote to the promotional history of a highly successful magazine.

After ten years under Lorimer, the editorial policy of the *Post* was somewhat altered, chiefly to appeal to women as well as to men. Robert W. Chambers, David Graham Phillips, William J. Locke, G. K. Chesterton, Corra Harris, and J. P. Marquand became familiar contributors, as did P. G. Wodehouse, whose numerous books first appeared there from 1914 until the end of the 1930s. Detective serials came to be constant fare. Illustration was copious and colorful. For years Samuel G. Blythe was the leading writer of political editorials, and the *Post* swung from what was originally a leftist position to one well to the right. Lorimer was strongly opposed to F. D. Roosevelt.

Curtis died in 1932 and Lorimer five years later. Wesley W.

Stout carried on the Lorimer editorial policies for five years, but when Ben Hibbs became editor in 1942, changes in typography, illustration, and design were accompanied by a marked change in the direction of nonfiction, though C. S. Forester's serial stories of sea adventure and Erle Stanley Gardner's and Clarence Budington Kelland's detective stories kept on. Norman Rockwell's cover designs were featured. Circulation rose to 6,000,000 in 1960. However, mass circulations, sought after as they may be, bring difficult problems of high solicitation and production costs, and the early 1960s were years of trial for the old *Post*. Executive Editor Robert Fuoss was responsible for the facelifting and policy changing that brought out a new *Post* in September 1961. Its political policy was more liberal, its articles often more striking, and its appearance more in accord with the spirit of the times among leading American magazines. Plagued by litigation as a result of strong investigative reporting, the *Post* ceased publication in 1969. It was revived as a glossier publication appearing nine times a year.

Saturday Press.   A weekly magazine founded in New York City (1858) by Henry Clapp and others; it continued to appear until 1866. The group that met at PFAFF'S CELLAR contributed to it freely. It was known as a bohemian and what was later called an experimental magazine. It won a high reputation, and to writers of a literary bent it was placed on a par with the *Atlantic Monthly*. Mark Twain's first literary appearance in the East came with the publication in the *Saturday Press* (November 18, 1865) of his "Jumping Frog" story. Walt Whitman liked the magazine and sent it some of his best work.

Saturday Review.   A weekly literary review founded in 1924 by HENRY SEIDEL CANBY, CHRISTOPHER MORLEY, Amy Loveman, and WILLIAM ROSE BENÉT. Originally named *The Saturday Review of Literature*, it changed in 1952 to the *Saturday Review*, since by then it covered world events, recordings, drama, radio, television, and travel, as well as books. Canby was editor-in-chief until 1936; he was succeeded by BERNARD DE VOTO (1936–38), George Stevens (1938–40), and NORMAN COUSINS, an important influence on the publication for forty years. Several columns were widely read, notably "Trade Winds," first written by Christopher Morley, later by Bennett Cerf and John G. Fuller; "Broadway Postscript," once written by John Mason Brown, later by Henry Hewes; "Booked for Travel," by Horace Sutton; and "Manner of Speaking," by John Ciardi.

Sauk and Fox Indians,   allied tribes that functioned as a single unit, members of the Algonquian linguistic stock located originally in Wisconsin and Michigan, and later drifted south and west toward the Mississippi. They were allied with the French and with PONTIAC (1772–1776) in opposition to the westward movement of English settlers. BLACK HAWK (1767–1838) and Keokuk (1780–1848) represented the two approaches of the tribe to relations with American authorities. Black Hawk was warlike. He supported Tecumseh's attempts at Indian confederation and allied with the British in the War of 1812. In 1832 his repudiation of the sale of tribal lands east of the Mississippi resulted in the Black Hawk war in which the young frontiersman Abraham Lincoln fought against the Indians. Black Hawk's cause was lost; he surrendered and was

taken as a prisoner to Washington, D.C., and on a tour of eastern cities where people flocked to see him. Keokuk favored negotiation and petition. His most celebrated advocacy for his people was an 1837 land control negotiation in Washington, D.C., under the auspices of the Bureau of Indian Affairs, with their traditional enemies, the Sioux. He spoke eloquently, won his case, and toured the east to great acclaim.

The present-day tribe, split into two sections, occupies land in Iowa and in Oklahoma. Sauk and Fox people are featured in JONATHAN CARVER's *Travels Through the Interior Part of North America* (1778); WILLIAM J. SNELLING's *Tales of the Northwest; or Sketches of Indian Life and Character* (1830); and fiction by AUGUST DERLETH.

Saunders, George (1958–   ),   short fiction writer. Born in Texas, Saunders was educated at the Colorado School of Mines and worked as an engineer and technical writer before entering the creative writing program at Syracuse University (M.A., 1988). His darkly satiric stories have been collected in *CivilWarLand in Bad Decline* (1996) and *Pastoralia* (2000). The protagonists of his fiction are often exploited by unscrupulous bosses in the service or entertainment industries. The narrator of "Daily Partner Performance Evaluation Form," for instance, portrays prehistoric man in a theme park; he is used by his faceless bosses to get Janet, who shares his cage, fired. Jeffrey of "The 400-Pound CEO" expresses the view that "God is unfair and preferentially punishes his weak, his dumb, his fat, his lazy." Other pieces demonstrate that the poor and good lose out, and that self-interest has become an ethical standard. However, the possibility of redemption is suggested by the narrator of "Isabelle," who moves in with the severely handicapped woman he mocked as a child and finds that "the sum total of sadness in the world is less than it would have been."

Saunders, Richard.   The pen name under which Benjamin Franklin wrote POOR RICHARD'S ALMANACK.

Savage, Philip Henry (1868–1899),   poet. His small body of lyric poetry is collected in *First Poems and Fragments* (1895) and *Poems* (1898).

Savage, Thomas (1915–   ),   novelist. Born in Salt Lake City, Savage was raised in Montana. His most characteristic work is set in the West. *The Power of the Dog* (1967), about two brothers and closet homosexuality, and *The Corner of Rife and Pacific* (1988), with its central character "The Sheep Queen," are set in Montana and illustrate well Savage's focus on family. Often cited along with WRIGHT MORRIS as a major but unread novelist, Savage has earned critical acclaim. His other novels include *The Pass* (1944); *Lona Hanson* (1948); *The Liar* (1969); *I Heard My Sister Speak My Name* (1977), semiautobiographical and considered by some his best work; and *For Mary With Love* (1983).

Sawyer, Tom.   See TOM SAWYER, THE ADVENTURES OF.

Saxe, John Godfrey (1816–1887),   journalist, poet, humorist. Saxe, born in Vermont, published many humorous poems and was much in demand as a lecturer. He wrote *Progress: A Satirical Poem* (1846); *Humorous and Satirical Poems* (1850); *The Money-King and Other Poems* (1860); *Complete Poems* (1861); *The Flying Dutchman, or, The Wrath of*

Herr Vonstoppetnoze (1862); *Clever Stories of Many Nations Rendered into Rhyme* (1865); and *Leisure Day Rhymes* (1875).

Say, Thomas (1787–1834), entomologist, explorer. Say, born in Philadelphia, in 1825 published *Narrative of an Expedition to the Source of St. Peter's River.* He began to specialize in entomology and in 1824 issued the first volume of his *American Entomology*, in 1828 two additional volumes. His papers were collected in 1869 (2 v.).

Scalapino, Leslie (1947–), poet, novelist. Born in California, she was educated at Reed College and the University of California, Berkeley. Scalapino's work blurs the distinction between poetry and prose, often retelling actual events but altering beginnings and endings. An experimental writer associated with the "Language" writing movement of the 1970s West Coast, she owns her own press and sometimes combines writing with visual art. Her prose poem *That They Were at the Beach—Aelotropic Series* (1985) is, according to the writer, meant to be read as a comic book, even though it does not contain actual pictures. *Way* (1988) mixes homeless people, middle-class teens in trendy clothes, and ships unloading imported goods to symbolize the impact of politics on American life. The essays and play of *How Phenomena Appear to Unfold* (1990) use a review of a book on Picasso as a starting point. *Crowd and Not Evening or Light* (1990) includes 75 photos of homeless people and beach-goers printed at angles on the page. *The Return of Painting, The Pearl, and Orion: A Trilogy* (1991) blurs the line between fictional narrative and verse. Other titles include *Goya's L.A., A Play* (1994) and *Green and Black: Selected Poems* (1996).

Scarecrow, The (1908), a play by PERCY MACKAYE. This drama was first produced by the Harvard Dramatic Club (1909); then at a theater in Middletown, Connecticut; on Broadway (1911); then in England and Germany (1914). Based on Nathaniel Hawthorne's FEATHERTOP, it tells of a scarecrow that is given life by a witch and assumes the title Lord Ravensbane.

Scarlet Letter, The (1850), a novel by NATHANIEL HAWTHORNE. In a preface to his novel, Hawthorne assumes the role of finder of the manuscript and a scarlet letter A, faded and worn, in the Salem Custom House attic. He claims merely to have transcribed the story, thus creating a dispassionate role for himself. Set in 17th-century Boston, the novel is built around three scaffold scenes, which occur at the beginning, the middle, and the end. The story opens with the public condemnation of Hester Prynne and the exhortation that she confess the name of the father of Pearl, her illegitimate child. Hester's husband, an old and scholarly physician, just arrived from England, assumes the name of Roger Chillingworth in order to seek out Hester's lover and revenge himself upon him. He attaches himself as physician to a respected and seemingly holy minister, Arthur Dimmesdale, suspecting that he is the father of the child.

The Scarlet Letter traces the effect of the actual and symbolic sin on all the characters. Hester, who wears the visible sign of the sin, finally learns to live with it. She embroiders with gold thread the scarlet letter she has been forced to wear and makes it the mark of her ties with the community that shunned her.

She ennobles herself by accepting her lot and devoting herself to the community, by which she is respected, although not forgiven. Although Dimmesdale's preaching helps the community, he is unable to expiate his sin by mortification of the flesh. He finally confesses publicly, but dies immediately thereafter. Chillingworth is revealed as the worst sinner of the three, because he sins out of hate, while the others sin out of love. He becomes the devil's tool when he commits what is to Hawthorne the cardinal sin, the invasion of the sanctity of the human heart, in attempting to assert his will over Dimmesdale. The novel is not about adultery, for the act occurred before the opening of the story, nor about sin *per se.* Rather, it is about the effect of sin on the mind and spirit of the characters. The scarlet letter comes to stand not for adultery, but for the guilt that is the common experience of all men.

Scarlet Sister Mary (1928), a novel by JULIA PETERKIN. The heroine of this local color story is a Gullah living on a South Carolina plantation. Her rich and joyous spirit survives despite her desperate poverty, her desertion by a worthless husband, and a number of casual affairs that leave her with nine children. She is expelled from the church but is readmitted after her confidence has been shaken by the death of her favorite son and by a vision of Christ's suffering. Starkly realistic throughout, the novel is written with a deep sympathy for the bitter lives of the fieldworkers. It won a Pulitzer Prize in 1929 and was dramatized in the following year by Daniel Reed.

Schaefer, Jack (1907–1991), novelist, short-story writer. Born in Cleveland, he studied at Oberlin College and Columbia University. He began his writing career as a reporter and editor for East Coast papers, but the publication of his first and best-known novel *Shane* in 1949 was followed by other fiction and nature writing about the American West. Shane, the title character, is a gunfighter trying to settle in to a more normal ranch hand's life, but forced to fight for his employer's family against the cattle ranchers who are trying to force them off their homestead. Other well-researched novels include *First Blood* (1953), *The Canyon* (1953), and *Company of Cowards* (1957). *The Kean Land and Other Stories* (1959) and *Heroes Without Glory* (1965) preceded his *Collected Stories* (1966). *The American Bestiary: Notes of an Amateur Naturalist*, his last book, appeared in 1975.

Schary, Dore (1905–1980), playwright, screenwriter, director. Born in New Jersey, Schary began as an actor, making his Broadway debut in a play with Spencer Tracy in 1930. His screenplay for *Boys Town* (1938) won an Oscar. *Sunrise at Campobello* (1956), a play about Franklin Roosevelt's struggle with polio, won five Tony awards. A staunch liberal, Schary resisted the blacklisting of Hollywood figures during the McCarthy era. (See MCCARTHYISM.) His book titles include *Case History of a Movie* (1950); *For Special Occasions* (1962); and, with Sinclair Lewis, *Storm in the West* (1963).

Schauffler, Robert Haven (1879–1964), poet, writer on music. Schauffler, a native of Austria, wrote several books intended to produce a better understanding of music, among them *Music as a Social Force in America* (1927), *Beethoven— The Man Who Freed Music* (1929), and *The Unknown Brahms*

(1933). He is perhaps known best for a poem, "Scum o' the Earth" (1912), a denunciation of race and religious prejudice, and the title poem in a collection. Two other gatherings of verses were *The White Comrade and Other Poems* (1920) and *The Magic Flame and Other Poems* (1923). His second wife was MARGARET WIDDEMER.

schlemiel figure, a type character from the Yiddish tradition. The word *schlemiel* passed into the American idiom in the 1890s, but only after World War II did the type play a large part in American fiction. A schlemiel is an innocent, but unlike innocents in the mold of Huck Finn who often triumph, the schlemiel is always unlucky: Things never turn out the way he had hoped. He is awkward, isolated from the mainstream. Often, like the character ISAAC BASHEVIS SINGER created in "Gimpel the Fool," he is an anti-hero whose foolishness is a form of wisdom.

Schlesinger, Arthur M[eier], Jr. (1917–), teacher, historian. Schlesinger followed his father as a teacher and writer of books on history, but wrote extensively on current problems. He has won the Pulitzer Prize for History (1946), the Francis Parkman Prize (1957), and the Bancroft Prize (1958). Among his writings are *Orestes A. Brownson: A Pilgrim's Progress* (1939); THE AGE OF JACKSON (Pulitzer Prize, 1945); *The Vital Center* (1949); *The General and the President* (with R. H. Rovere, 1951); and *The Age of Roosevelt*, now including *The Crisis of the Old Order* (1957), *The Coming of the New Deal* (1959), and *The Politics of Upheaval* (1960).

Schlesinger served as a special assistant in the administration of John F. Kennedy, about whom he wrote *A Thousand Days* (1965, Pulitzer Prize and National Book Award). The Vietnam War is treated in *The Bitter Heritage* (1967); *The Crisis of Confidence* (1969) is a collection of essays about the Sixties. *The Imperial Presidency* (1973) depicts the growing power of that office. *Robert F. Kennedy and His Times* (1978) won the National Book Award. *The Cycles of American History* appeared in 1986, and *A Life in the 20th Century: Innocent Beginnings, 1917–1950* in 2000.

Schlesinger, Arthur M[eier], Sr. (1888–1965), historian. Schlesinger taught at Ohio State and Iowa before going to Harvard as professor of history in 1924. His many important historical works include *The Colonial Merchants and the American Revolution* (1918); *New Viewpoints in American History* (1922); *Political and Social History of the U.S.* (1925, rev. in later editions); *The Rise of the City* (1933); *Learning How to Behave: A Historical Study of American Etiquette Books* (1940); *Paths to the Present* (1949); *The American as Reformer* (1950); *Harvard Guide to American History* (1954); and *Prelude to Independence: The Newspaper War on Britain, 1764–1776* (1958). *The Atlantic Migration*, written with M. L. Hansen, won a Pulitzer Prize (1941).

Schmitt, Gladys (1909–1972), novelist. Schmitt, born in Pittsburgh, wrote eleven novels and served on the faculty of Carnegie-Mellon University. Among them are *The Gates of Aulis* (1942), about a German immigrant family; his-

torical novels such as *David the King* (1946), *Rembrandt* (1961), *Electra* (1964), and *The Godforgotten* (1974). Other titles are *Confessors of the Name* (1952), *The Persistent Image* (1955), and *A Small Fire* (1957).

Schoolcraft, Henry Rowe (1793–1864), geologist, explorer, ethnologist, writer. Born in Watervliet, New York, Schoolcraft traveled in Missouri and Arkansas, accompanied the Lewis Cass expedition (1820) to Lake Superior as a geologist, was appointed an Indian agent there, and discovered the source of the Mississippi in 1832. He married the granddaughter of a Chippewa chieftain and from her gathered much Indian lore. He was Superintendent of Indian Affairs for Michigan (1836–41) and wrote about his explorations and researches in a number of influential books. He was the first Caucasian to translate Indian poetry and among the first to report Indian legends and religious beliefs seriously. He wrote *A View of the Lead Mines of Missouri* (1819); *Travels in the Central Portions of the Mississippi Valley* (1825); *Narrative of an Expedition Through the Upper Mississippi to Itasca Lake* (1834); *Algic Researches, Comprising Inquiries Respecting the Mental Characteristics of the North American Indians* (2 v. 1839, later reprinted as *The Myth of Hiawatha* (see ALGIC RESEARCHES); *Oneonta, or, The Red Race of America* (8 v. 1844–45, rev. and reissued, 1851, as *The American Indians: Their History, Condition, and Prospects*); *Notes on the Iroquois* (1846); *Personal Memoirs of a Residence of Thirty Years with the Indian Tribes* (1851); and *Scenes and Adventures in the Semi-Alpine Region of the Ozark Mountains of Missouri and Arkansas* (1863, in it was reprinted his *View of the Lead Mines*). *Indian Legends* (1955), based on his books, was compiled by M. L. Williams. Schoolcraft's writings, especially *Algic Researches*, had a profound influence on LONGFELLOW, who repeated Schoolcraft's great blunder—confusing the Iroquoian Hiawatha with the Chippewa Manabozho and placing on the southern shores of Lake Superior adventures that had taken place in central New York.

Schorer, Mark (1908–1977), novelist, critic, biographer. Mark Schorer was born in Wisconsin and educated at the University of Wisconsin. He wrote his first novel, *A House Too Old* (1935), a year before he acquired his Ph.D. He published short stories, mostly in *The New Yorker*, and literary articles in the quarterlies, later teaching and writing at Dartmouth, Harvard, and the University of California. His book *William Blake* (1946) took ten years to write. His other books are *The Hermit Place* (1941); *The State of Mind* (thirty-two stories, 1946); a biography, *Sinclair Lewis: An American Life* (1961); *The World We Imagine* (collected essays, 1968); and *Pieces of Life* (1977).

Schulberg, Budd (1914–), short-story writer, novelist. Born in New York City and the son of a film producer, Schulberg observed people associated with films in Hollywood. As a result, he wrote his first best seller, WHAT MAKES SAMMY RUN? (1941), the satirical story of a tough movie careerist. His next novel, THE HARDER THEY FALL (1947), was an equally sardonic account of the prize-fighting world. In THE DISENCHANTED (1950) Schulberg again obviously had a life model, in this case F. SCOTT FITZGERALD. The two had met when they worked together on a motion picture. It was dramatized and produced on Broadway in 1958. Schulberg also wrote a number of spirited but thoughtful short stories, collected in *Faces in the Crowd* (1953), and his screenplay *On the Waterfront* (1954) won wide critical acclaim. *Love, Action, Laughter and Other Sad Tales* (1990) is a collection of 16 tales, some centered on the film industry.

Schultze, Bunny [Carl Emil] (1866–1939), cartoonist. Schultze's most noteworthy character was Foxy Grandpa, who made his first appearance in the New York *Herald* on January 7, 1900.

Schulz, Charles M[onroe] (1922–2000), cartoonist. Born in Minneapolis, Schulz served in France and Germany with the 20th Armored Division during World War II. After the war, he studied cartooning and freelanced before launching his successful *Peanuts* strip in 1950. The strip, which he wanted to call "Li'l Folks," grew over a period of nearly fifty years from printing in seven newspapers and earnings of ninety dollars a week to syndication in more than 1,000 papers in 75 countries, television specials, merchandise and product endorsements, and gross earnings of over a billion dollars a year. Featuring Charlie Brown, a lovable and gentle boy who is, according to his creator, "sometimes put upon, and not always the brightest person"; his sister Sally; and their friends— aggressive Lucy, piano-playing Schroeder, Linus clutching his security blanket, and Snoopy the beagle who doesn't know he's a dog—the strip was read by 355 million at the time of Schulz's death. The National Cartoonists Society twice (1955, 1964) awarded Schulz the Reuben as outstanding cartoonist of the year; he also received the Yale Humor Award (1956) and the National Education Association's School Bell Award (1960). His first book, *Peanuts,* was published in 1952, and compilations came out continually thereafter in English and 15 other languages. "A Charlie Brown Christmas," a teleplay written with Lee Mendelson and animated by Bill Melendez and first broadcast in 1960, was awarded an Emmy and a Peabody award, and after 1965, aired annually. Fourteen more television shows, including "It's the Great Pumpkin, Charlie Brown" (1966), have appeared since. Five of them won Emmys. Schulz wrote the screenplays for feature-length animated films including *Snoopy, Come Home* (1972) and *Bon Voyage, Charlie Brown, and Don't Come Back!* (1980). The musical *You're a Good Man, Charlie Brown* was produced Off Broadway in 1967 and won two Tony awards in a 1999 Broadway revival. Schulz's work has been shown at the Louvre, and he has been awarded the *Ordre des Arts et des Lettres* from the French Ministry of Culture. Robert L. Short, a minister, wrote two books of theology based on the *Peanuts* strip, concertos inspired by the cartoon have been performed in Carnegie Hall, and the internationally known novelist Umberto Eco wrote an introduction for the first *Peanuts* book in Italian.

Unlike many cartoon strips, *Peanuts* was the work of one man's hands and mind. When he felt he was too ill to continue, Schulz announced the end of the strip. The last Sunday cartoon, with a signed farewell by the artist, appeared in papers the day after his death.

Schurz, Carl (1829–1906), soldier, statesman, journalist. Schurz joined the unsuccessful revolutionary movement of 1848 and was forced to flee Germany. In 1852 he came to the United States and in 1855 settled in Watertown, Wisconsin, where he studied law and was admitted to the bar. He soon became interested in the antislavery movement and the young Republican Party. He campaigned for Lincoln against Douglas and made a tour of New England, speaking against the Know-Nothing Party and in support of full rights for naturalized citizens. In the campaign of 1860 he made effective speeches in both English and German.

Lincoln appointed him minister to Spain, but he resigned to become an officer in the Union army. In the summer of 1865 he toured the South and wrote a report on conditions there. This report, although of extraordinary value, was suppressed by President Johnson because it recommended the extension of the franchise to blacks as a condition of readmission to the Union of the seceding states. It was made public only at the demand of Congress. Schurz then went into newspaper work, working for the New York *Tribune* and the Detroit *Post.* In 1867 he became a partner and joint editor of the St. Louis *Westliche Post.* In 1868 he was temporary chairman and keynote speaker for the Republican National Convention and was elected senator from Missouri. In 1876 he was appointed Secretary of the Interior by Hayes. After his cabinet term he was coeditor of the New York *Evening Post* and later wrote the leading editorials for *Harper's Weekly.* He was president of the National Civil Reform League in 1892–1901.

Schurz was at his best campaigning and in the Senate. Various editions of his speeches have been published, among them *Speeches of Carl Schurz* (1865) and *Speeches, Correspondence, and Political Papers of Carl Schurz* (1913), edited by Frederic Bancroft. Other works of his are *The New South* (1865), a pamphlet; *Life of Henry Clay* (1887); *Abraham Lincoln: An Essay* (1889); and *The Reminiscences of Carl Schurz* (1907–08).

Schuyler, James (1923–1991), poet, playwright, novelist, art critic. Born in Chicago and educated in West Virginia, Schuyler served in the Navy in World War II and lived in Italy briefly before moving to New York. A member of the NEW YORK SCHOOL OF POETS, Schuyler in his early work was encouraged by JOHN ASHBERY and FRANK O'HARA. Like them, he has been professionally involved with modern art, working as an editorial associate with *Art News* (1956–1962) and on the staff of the Museum of Modern Art. His poetry collections include *Salute* (1960), *Freely Espousing* (1969), *The Crystal Lithium* (1972), *Hymn to Life* (1974), and the Pulitzer Prize winning *The Morning of the Poem* (1980). Among his novels are *Alfred & Guinevere* (1958); *A Nest of Ninnies*, written with John Ashbery, (1969); and *What's for Dinner?* (1978). His plays include *Shopping and Waiting* (1953) and *A Picnic Cantata*, with music by PAUL BOWLES (1955). *Selected Poems* appeared in 1988. *The Diary of James Schuyler*, edited by Nathan Kernan, appeared posthumously (1997).

Schwartz, Delmore (1913–1966),   poet, short-story writer. Schwartz, born in Brooklyn, held several editorial positions, including an editorship at the *Partisan Review* (1943–1955). Among his works are *In Dreams Begin Responsibilities* (verse, 1938); *Shenandoah* (verse drama, 1941); *Genesis* (verse, 1943); and *Vaudeville for a Princess* (verse, 1950). He translated Rimbaud's *A Season in Hell* (1939). His short stories, many of them dealing with problems of Jewish life, have been collected in *The World Is a Wedding* (1948). A volume of new and selected earlier poems, *Summer Knowledge* (1959), won the Bollingen Prize in 1960. His *Last and Lost Poems* appeared in 1979. Schwartz was fictionalized by SAUL BELLOW as the character Von Humboldt Fleisher in *Humboldt's Gift*.

Science and Health, with Key to the Scriptures (1875),   a devotional textbook by MARY BAKER EDDY. In 1862 Eddy came under the influence of the mental healing system of Dr. Phineas Parkhurst Quimby and was cured of a long invalidism. Her reflections on her experience led her to write *Science and Health*, which underwent some revisions until 1910 and which has circulated in millions of copies and been translated into many foreign languages. Her doctrines attracted numerous converts; in 1879 the First Church of Christ Scientist was chartered. In 1895 Eddy abolished personal preaching in her church and ordained the Bible and *Science and Health* as pastor for her followers.

science fiction and fantasy.   Broadly speaking, science fiction and fantasy are branches of romantic literature, sharing with other romances an emphasis on adventurous plots and a lesser concern for mimetic representation of ordinary life. Such stories are escapist or wish-fulfilling on one level, speculative on another, mythmaking on a third. Stories of science fiction and fantasy differ from other forms of popular romance—detective stories, love stories, Westerns— primarily in extrapolating the lessons of science or the fancies of the imagination into settings significantly different from the world we recognize from experience and history. Frequently they emphasize ideas illustrated through examinations of future, alternative, or past civilizations.

Modern science fiction and fantasy may be seen as products of the conflicting values created at the end of the 18th century and the beginning of the 19th by the rise of science and the divergent pull of romanticism. From this perspective Mary Shelley's *Frankenstein* (1818) is the great progenitor. In the United States, the work of POE bulks large: in science fiction with THE UNPARALLELED ADVENTURES OF ONE HANS PFAAL (1835) and THE NARRATIVE OF ARTHUR GORDON PYM (1838), in fantasy with a number of his TALES OF THE GROTESQUE AND ARABESQUE (1840). After these beginnings, for a long while the great names appeared abroad and included especially Jules Verne and H. G. Wells. In the U.S. by the end of the 19th century, a number of works had appeared that were suggestive of things to come. Prominent among them are Fitz-James O'Brien's THE DIAMOND LENS (1850), in which a scientist finds love in a world viewed through a microscope; FRANK R. STOCKTON'S THE LADY OR THE TIGER? (1882), "A Tale of Negative Gravity" (1884), and *The*

Great War Syndicate (1889); Edward Bellamy's LOOKING BACKWARD (1888), a view of a Utopian future that inspired hundreds of other books; IGNATIUS DONNELLY's *Caesar's Column: A Story of the 20th Century* (1891); and ROBERT W. CHAMBERS's *The King in Yellow* (1895). Among DIME NOVELS were the anonymous *Frank Reade and His Steam Man of the Plains, or, The Terror of the West* (1883); Richard B. Montgomery's *Two Boys' Trip to an Unknown Planet* (1889); and LUIS PHILIP SENAREN's *Frank Reade and His Queen Clipper of the Clouds* (1900).

The turn of the twentieth century brought an increase in science fiction and fantasy, partly in response to the popularity of Verne and Wells. GARRETT P. SERVISS followed up on Wells's *The War of the Worlds* (1898) with *Edison's Conquest of Mars*, serialized in the New York *Evening Journal* in the same year, and then wrote *The Moon Metal* (1900), *A Columbus of Space* (1911), and *The Second Deluge* (1912). In 1911 HUGO GERNSBACK published in his magazine *Modern Electrics* his serial *Ralph 124C41+: A Romance of the Year 2660*. Beginning with *A Princess of Mars* (1917, serialized in 1912), EDGAR RICE BURROUGHS wrote at least ten Martian books as well as several that are set on Venus. In his Tarzan stories he created human-like apes and various lost cities, one inhabited by Atlanteans (this last picked up an interest given wide circulation earlier in Ignatius Donnelley's 1882 work of nonfiction, *Atlantis: The Antediluvian World*). With *The Moon Pool* (1919), A. MERRITT began a career combining science fiction, fantasy, and the occult in works of continuing popularity and wide influence that include *The Ship of Ishtar* (1926), *The Face in the Abyss* (1931), and *Burn, Witch, Burn!* (1933).

In 1926 Gernsback founded *Amazing Stories*, the first magazine devoted entirely to science fiction and giving great impetus to a field that had earlier found space in more general magazines such as *Argosy*. The hospitality given by *Weird Tales* in the late 1920s and 1930s to the stories of H. P. LOVECRAFT encouraged dimensions of cosmic terror not much visible in the field earlier. Other magazines, including *Astounding Stories* in the 1930s, *The Magazine of Science Fiction and Fantasy* in the 1940s, and *Galaxy* in the 1950s, helped turn the two decades after about 1935 into a golden age of science fiction. Writers who emerged in those years include ISAAC ASIMOV, RAY BRADBURY, L. SPRAGUE DE CAMP, LESTER DEL REY, ROBERT A. HEINLEIN, THEODORE STURGEON, and JACK WILLIAMSON.

Writers of the mid-1950s and since then have come to an established genre with a history of frequently repeated subjects and motifs. These include utopian and dystopian fictions, technological or biological experimentation, lost worlds, alien cultures, space and time travel, imperialistic wars, artificial life, postcatastrophe societies, abnormal mental states, parallel or alternate worlds, and sword and sorcery romances. In some of these areas entire cosmologies, histories, and mythologies have been constructed, with writers borrowing from and building on the works of one another.

Among social conditions affecting science fiction and fantasy in recent years have been the fears of the postnuclear world, growing distrust of the military-industrial complex, increasing ecological concerns, changing concepts of gender, and nostalgia for simpler times. Books, authors, and readers have multiplied rapidly. Increased attention to the genre and a greater sophistication in some of its writers has produced a more frequent crossover than in the past, as KURT VONNEGUT and URSULA K. LE GUIN, for example, have achieved general readership and extended critical reputations. MICHAEL CRICHTON, perhaps the most financially successful writer of his time, has largely erased the line between traditional science fiction and mainstream novels in *Jurassic Park, Timeline,* and others of his works. Others with fiction mostly since the 1950s include SAMUEL DELANEY, PHILIP K. DICK, HARLAN ELLISON, JACK FINNEY, FRANK HERBERT, DANIEL KEYES, FREDERICK POHL, JOANNA RUSS, CLIFFORD D. SIMAK, and ROBERT SILVERBERG.

Although most science fiction and fantasy has been written by writers identified with the genre, mainstream writers have sometimes employed key subjects or motifs in their works. In addition to Poe, a short list includes Hawthorne's RAPPACCINI'S DAUGHTER; Melville's MARDI; Cooper's THE CRATER; Twain's A CONNECTICUT YANKEE IN KING ARTHUR'S COURT; William Dean Howells's A TRAVELER FROM ALTRURIA; HENRY JAMES's "The Jolly Corner"; Jack London's BEFORE ADAM; UPTON SINCLAIR's *The Millennium: A Comedy of the Year 2000*; JOHN BARTH's *Giles Goat-Boy*; GORE VIDAL's *Myra Breckenridge*; VLADIMIR NABOKOY's *Ada: or Ardor*; JOHN GARDNER's *Grendel*; WALKER PERCY's *Love in the Ruins*; DON DE LILLO's *Ratner's Star*; MARGE PIERCY's *Woman on the Edge of Time*; MARGARET ATWOOD's *The Handmaid's Tale*; and NORMAN MAILER's *Ancient Evenings.*

Science of English Verse, The (1879),   a treatise on versification by SIDNEY LANIER.

Scientology.   See L. RON HUBBARD.

Scobie, Stephen (1943–   ),   poet, critic. Scobie was born in Scotland and earned degrees at St. Andrews before immigrating to Canada in 1965. Since completing the Ph.D. at the University of British Columbia, he has taught at the University of Alberta and the University of Victoria. His most significant poetry collections are *The Birken Tree* (1973), *McAlmon's Chinese Opera* (1980), *The Ballad of Isabel Gunn* (1987), *Remains* (1990), and *Gospel* (1994). *Leonard Cohen* (1978) is a critical study. Scobie also has edited *The Malahat Review. Alias Bob Dylan* (1991) is an examination of North American pop culture.

Scollard, Clinton (1860–1932),   poet, novelist. Scollard studied at Hamilton College and Harvard and Cambridge. From 1888 to 1896 he was professor of rhetoric and English literature at Hamilton, but retired to devote himself to creative work. In 1884 *Pictures in Song* was published, the first of a series of books that ended in 1932 with *Songs from a Southern Shore.* He wrote *A Boy's Book of Rhyme* (1896), *Songs of a Sylvan Lover* (1912), *The Epic of Golf* (1923), *The Crowning Years* (1929), and historical romances such as *A Man-at-Arms* (1898), *The Son of a Tory* (1901), *The Cloistering of Ursula* (1902), and *Count Falcon of the Eyrie* (1903).

In 1924 he married JESSIE B. RITTENHOUSE, poet and critic, with whom he produced two anthologies: *Bird-Lovers' Anthology* (1930) and *Patrician Rhymes* (1932). He also collaborated

with FRANK DEMPSTER SHERMAN on *A Southern Flight* (1905) and edited his poems in 1917. *The Singing Heart* (1934) is a selection of his poems edited by Scollard's wife with a memoir.

Scopes trial.   A famous court contest (July 1925) in which John T. Scopes, a Tennessee science teacher, was found guilty of teaching the doctrine of evolution. The antagonists were CLARENCE DARROW, who defended Scopes, and WILLIAM JENNINGS BRYAN, who led the prosecution forces to a temporary victory for religious conservatism and died five days after the end of the trial. The verdict was later reversed by the Tennessee Supreme Court. H. L. Mencken reported the so-called monkey trial in sardonic dispatches. In 1955 the trial was turned into a successful play, *Inherit the Wind,* by Jerome Lawrence and Robert E. Lee, and was later filmed.

Scorsese, Martin (1942–   ),   film director. He earned degrees in film studies from New York University and as a student produced a series of prize-winning short subjects. His first major film was *Mean Streets* (1973), followed by *Alice Doesn't Live Here Anymore* (1975). *Taxi Driver* (1976) won the International Grand Prize at the Cannes Film Festival. His other films include *New York New York* (1977), *The Last Waltz* (1978), and *The Raging Bull* (1979). His film of Nikos Kazantzakis's *The Last Temptation of Christ* (1987) prompted widespread protests.

Scot, George (17th century),   colonist. Scot had the task of encouraging emigration to New Jersey. In 1685 he embarked for America after composing a promotion tract called *The Model of the Government of East Jersey* (1685). Both he and his wife died on the voyage, but a daughter remained in the colony. His tract gave a history of colonization from biblical days, then pictured contemporary New Jersey with the help of testimonial letters. He presented many human as well as economic and legalistic details. His book was reprinted in W. A. Whitehead's *East Jersey Under the Proprietary Governments* (1846).

Scott, Dred (1795?–1858),   Virginia-born slave owned by Dr. John Emerson. He was taken (1834) by his master from St. Louis to Rock Island, Illinois, later to Fort Snelling in Wisconsin Territory. In Illinois, slavery had been forbidden by the Ordinance of 1787; in Wisconsin, slavery was forbidden by the Missouri Compromise (1820–21). In 1846 Scott sued for his freedom in the Missouri courts on the ground that he had been freed by his stay in a free territory. His case reached the Supreme Court in 1857. In the so-called Dred Scott decision, the Court ruled on several questions: (1) Scott as a black was not a citizen; (2) Congress could not prohibit a citizen from carrying any property, including slaves, into any territory; and (3) the Missouri Compromise was unconstitutional since under the Fifth Amendment Congress was prohibited from depriving persons of their property without due process of law. The decision created a furor, especially in the North. In the Lincoln-Douglas debates (see LINCOLN) Douglas tried to win Northern favor by enunciating a doctrine of local sovereignty to counterbalance the Dred Scott decision; as a consequence Douglas lost backing in the South. The Fourteenth Amendment (1868) annulled the decision.

Scott, Duncan Campbell (1862–1947), Canadian poet, short-story writer, public official. Well acquainted with the Canadian wilds and the Indians living there, Scott spent many years in the Canadian department of Indian affairs. He wrote much poetry and many short stories besides contributing articles to magazines. He also knew French Canada, and his first fiction, *In the Village of Viger* (1896), was a collection of French Canadian stories. Among his other books are *The Magic House and Other Poems* (1893), *Labor and the Angel* (1898), *New World Lyrics and Ballads* (1905), *Lundy's Lane* (1916), *Beauty and Life* (1921), *The Green Cloister* (1935), and *The Circle of Affection* (1947). He issued his *Collected Poems* in 1926. In 1951 Edward Killoran Brown edited a group of *Selected Poems*.

Scott, Evelyn (1893–1963), poet, novelist, memoirist. Scott, born in Tennessee, experimented with various narrative techniques, most notably in *The Wave* (1929), in which she made the Civil War a character and wove letters, stream-of-consciousness fragments, newspaper accounts, army reports, and plantation and war songs into the narrative. *Escapade* (1923), her first novel, is an autobiographical account of a stay in Brazil. *Background in Tennessee* (1937) is an account of her youth. Her other novels include *The Narrow House* (1921), *Narcissus* (1922), *The Golden Door* (1925), *A Calendar of Sin* (1931), *Eva Gay* (1933), *Breathe Upon Those Slain* (1934), *Bread and a Sword* (1937), and *The Shadow of the Hawk* (1941). Her poetry collections are *Precipitations* (1920) and *The Winter Along* (1930); *Love* (1920) is a play. *Migrations: An Arabesque in Histories* (1927) and *Ideals* (1927) are short-story collections. *Blue Rum* (1930), an adventure story, was published under the pseudonym E. Souza.

Scott, F[rancis] R[eginald] (1899–1985), Canadian poet. Son of the poet Frederick George Scott, F. R. Scott was a member of the so-called Montreal School influenced by T. S. Eliot in the 1920s and an editor of the magazine *Preview* in the 1940s. He taught law at McGill University, served as U.N. Representative to Burma (1952), and wrote on national and international affairs. His books of poetry include *Overture* (1945), *Events and Signals* (1954), and the collection *The Eye of the Needle: Satires, Sorties, Sundries* (1957). His other titles include *Evolving Canadian Federalism* (1958) and *Civil Liberties and Canadian Federalism* (1959).

Scott, Natalie Anderson (1906–), novelist, painter. Scott, a descendant of Russian Cossacks, came to the United States in 1922. She published her first novel, *So Brief the Years* (1935), under her original name, Natalie B. Sokoloff. It was an account of the conflict between White and Red Russians. *The Sisters Livingston* (1946) was followed by *The Story of Mrs. Murphy* (1947). Her later novels are *The Husband* (1948), *Romance* (1951), *The Little Stockade* (1954), *Salvation Johnny* (1958), and *The Golden Trollop* (1961).

Scott, Winfield (1786–1866), soldier, memoirist. Scott was a distinguished soldier who fought bravely in the War of 1812 and commanded the American Army during the Mexican War. In 1852 he ran unsuccessfully against FRANKLIN PIERCE for the presidency. Though a Virginian, he remained loyal to the Union, and when he published his *Memoirs* (2 v.

1864) he inscribed a set to General Grant. He wrote other books, among them *General Regulations for the Army* (1825) and *Infantry Tactics* (1835).

Scott, Winfield Townley (1910–1968), teacher, poet. Scott, born in Massachusetts, worked for a number of years as a newspaperman, especially on the Providence (Rhode Island) *Journal*, and taught at Bard College. Scott's poetry is noted for its supple colloquial strength. He dealt often with New England characters and ideas, as in *Elegy for Robinson* (1936) and *Mr. Whittier and Other Poems* (1948). His other collections are *Biography for Traman* (1937), *Wind the Clock* (1941), *The Sword on the Table* (1942), and *To Marry Strangers* (1945). *The Dark Sister* (1958) is an epic on the theme of Viking explorations in North America. *Poems: 1937–1962* (1962) is a comprehensive collection of Scott's verse.

Scottsboro case, a series of trials in which nine African-Americans, aged thirteen to nineteen, were charged with the rape of two white women on a freight train in Alabama. The first trial was held in 1931, but the case dragged on until 1937 even though one of the women withdrew her accusation. At some point in the long ordeal, all but the youngest defendant were sentenced to death; none was executed, but all served time in prison. The case was twice brought to the U.S. Supreme Court. In 1935 the Court ruled that the defendants' rights had been violated by the exclusion of African-Americans from jury service. In the retrial, four defendants were convicted and sentenced to life imprisonment; charges against the other five were dropped. Clarence Norris (1912–1989), who served fifteen years in prison before escaping to New York—he was the last surviving member of the group—wrote his memoir, *The Last of the Scottsboro Boys*, with Sybil D. Washington (1979). The case was a cause célèbre and many writers came to the young men's defense. LANGSTON HUGHES wrote "Christ in Alabama" (1931) and *Scottsboro Limited*, a play (1932); JOHN WEXLEY wrote *They Shall Not Die* (1934); and LINCOLN STEFFENS wrote *Essays on Scottsboro*.

Scout, The (1841), a novel by WILLIAM GILMORE SIMMS. Originally called *The Kinsmen*, this novel is set against the background of the Revolution and, as its original title suggests, is an episode in the life of a family—the struggle of two half-brothers in war and love.

Scribner's Magazine. When *Scribner's Monthly* was sold to the newly formed Century Company in 1881 and became the CENTURY ILLUSTRATED MONTHLY MAGAZINE, it was part of the bargain that Charles Scribner's Sons would not reenter the magazine field for at least five years. As soon as that time was up, in January 1887, the new *Scribner's Magazine* appeared, obviously competing with the *Century* and *Harper's*. Edward L. Burlingame was editor; leading contributors for fifteen years or more were Robert Louis Stevenson, Harold Frederic, James M. Barrie, H. C. Bunner, W. C. Brownell, Theodore Roosevelt, and Jacob A. Riis. The magazine was strong in fiction, travel, biography, and criticism of art and letters. Throughout its first four decades, the magazine was beautifully illustrated. In its early years it was distinguished by such wood engravers as George Kruell and Frederick Juengling; in the 1890s it was quick to adopt halftones based on the work of such artists as J. W. Alexander, C. D. Gibson, Will H. Low. W. T. Smedley, and Maxfield Parrish. After the turn of the century it became a leader in full-color illustration by Parrish, Howard Pyle, N. C. Wyeth, Frederic Remington, A. B. Frost, and H. C. Christy.

In 1914 Robert Bridges became editor; an excellent essayist and literary critic himself, he maintained the magazine's high quality. John Galsworthy, Edith Wharton, and Theodore Roosevelt were leading contributors. The magazine gave much attention to the World War. By 1925 it had begun to place a greater emphasis on public affairs. In the late 1920s the great fiction hits were Hemingway's A FAREWELL TO ARMS and the S. S. Van Dine mysteries. A downward trend in circulation was temporarily halted by such work, but continued after the retirement of Bridges in 1930 in spite of such newcomers to its pages as Thomas Wolfe, Sherwood Anderson, D. H. Lawrence, Erskine Caldwell, and a number of distinguished leftist nonfiction writers. In 1929 the subscription list was sold to *Esquire* and the name to the *Commentator*. In 1942 the publisher of *Scribner's Commentator* was found guilty of accepting subsidies from Japan for publishing propaganda for that government.

Scribner's Monthly.   See CENTURY ILLUSTRATED MONTHLY MAGAZINE.

Scudder, Antoinette [Quinby] (1898–1958),   poet, playwright, novelist, painter, critic, theater sponsor. Scudder, born in New Jersey, wrote several collections of verse, among them *Provincetown Sonnets and Other Poems* (1925); *The Soul of Ilaria* (1926); *Huckleberries* (1929); *Out of Peony and Blade* (1931); *The Henchman and the Moon* (1934); *East End, West End* (1935); and *Italics for Life: Collected Poems* (1947). Her dramatic works were published as *The Cherry Tart and Other Plays* (1938) and *The World in a Match Box* (1949). *The Grey Studio* (1934) was a novelette.

Scudder, Horace E[lisha] (1838–1902),   editor, writer for children. Scudder, born in Boston, wrote much of his work anonymously, including that done during his term as editor of the *Atlantic* (1890–1898) and the children's books while he was a teacher: *Seven Little People and Their Friends* (1862) and *Dream Children* (1864). He also worked behind the scenes with the *Riverside Magazine for Young People*, contributing his own stories and enlisting for its pages such prominent writers as Hans Christian Andersen, Frank R. Stockton, and Sara Orne Jewett. Under his own name he wrote *David Coit Scudder, a Missionary in Southern India* (1864), an account of his older brother; the *Bodley Books* (1875–1887), popular juvenile books of travel; and *Childhood in Literature and Art* (1894). He wrote biographies of Noah Webster (1882); George Washington (1890), one of the Riverside series; and James Russell Lowell (1901). He also wrote *Stories and Romances* (1880) and *A History of the United States* (1884).

Seabrook, William [Buehler] (1886–1945),   newspaperman, writer. Seabrook, born in Maryland, worked for papers in Georgia and New York, later did feature articles for news syndicates, and began traveling widely in 1924. He reported his experiences in *Adventures in Arabia* (1927), *The Magic Island* [Haiti] (1929), *Jungle Ways* (1931), *Air Adventure*

(1933), and *Witchcraft* (1940). *Asylum* (1935) tells of his stay in a hospital in an attempt to cure his alcoholism. *No Hiding Place* (1942) is also autobiographical.

Seabury, Samuel (1729–1796),   Episcopal clergyman, author. Born in Connecticut, Seabury studied at Yale and in Scotland, held pastorates in New Jersey, Long Island, and Westchester, and in 1783 was elected the first Episcopalian American-born bishop. He was a Loyalist during the Revolution and his pamphlets were widely read. His *Letters of a Westchester Farmer, 1774–1775* were edited (1930), with an introduction by Clarence H. Vance. He published *Discourses on Several Subjects* (2 v. 1793) and additional *Discourses on Several Important Subjects* (1798).

sea fiction in the United States.   Many American writers in various genres have considered the sea, as Melville put it—Freneau, Whitman, Dana, O'Neill, and Steinbeck, for example. But a major contribution to American literature exists in a tradition of sea fiction that has typically found in the voyage idea an affirmative means of exploring the meaning of life and the democratic possibility. The main figures in this tradition—often experienced as working seamen—are Cooper, Poe, Melville, Stephen Crane, London, Hemingway, and Peter Matthiessen.

When the novel first began to emerge as a promising medium for recording the American experience, it reflected the importance of maritime affairs in the early republic—as in Royall Tyler's *The Algerine Captive* (1797). But Cooper originated the sea novel proper. At least twelve of his novels—from *The Pilot* (1824) to *The Sea Lions* (1849)—deal predominantly with the traditional elements of sea fiction: sea, sailor, and ship. Cooper's lifelong interest in the sea is evident in his service both as a merchant sailor before the mast and as a midshipman in the U.S. Navy during a time when the United States became a world leader in maritime affairs. He also was part owner of the whaling vessel *Union* and wrote *History of the Navy of the United States of America* (1830).

His interest in maritime history is constant in his long work as a sea novelist, but there is a distinct development in his use of maritime materials. His initial romances of American naval heroics during the Revolution were followed by several novels in which the Byronic sea hero in the democratic cause was replaced by seamen of more believable proportions. The developing realism in his sea novels of the 1840s, particularly in *Ned Myers* (1843), reflects the influence of Dana's *Two Years Before the Mast*; and in his last and perhaps greatest sea novel, *The Sea Lions*, he drew on Charles Wilkes's *Narrative of the United States Exploring Expedition* and similar accounts to create sublime scenes of Antarctica, which contribute to the spiritual progress his main character experiences as a result of the voyage.

During Cooper's lifetime a number of others expressed the national interest in maritime affairs through their short stories of the sea, among them Nathaniel Ames, William Leggett, and John Codman. But Poe's *The Narrative of Arthur Gordon Pym* (1838), another work reflecting the public fascination with polar exploration, is the only other American sea novel from this period that successfully presented themes of larger human significance through the voyage idea.

This would of course be Melville's goal in *Moby-Dick*. Even his apprentice works *Typee* (1846) and *Omoo* (1847) indicated that he aspired to address the larger questions, but in his first attempt to do so with all his energy—in the allegorical *Mardi* (1849)—his voyaging mind would not attend to mere nautical realism. *Mardi* failed with his reading public, but as a prolonged meditation on life and death, faith and knowledge, it did more to prepare Melville for *Moby-Dick* than any of his other efforts, including the more realistic and successful, but still somewhat meditative, *Redburn* (1849) and *White-Jacket* (1850), semiautobiographical stories of his first voyage as a merchant seaman and his experience on the man of war *United States*.

In *Moby-Dick* he celebrated the whaling life—his Harvard and Yale—in a voyage narrated with a degree of realism; but he also exploited the voyage motif more fully than any writer in history. Here, in "landlessness," he sought "the ungraspable phantom of life." Envisioning the sea as life itself, he was the first to emphasize the sea's importance as the essential element of the genre. Thus, in his cetological meditations he introduced the idea that the sea life is ungraspable, indeed, without reference to biological thought (which was for him natural theology). As vehicles for his lyrical meditations on life, he created two of the greatest voices in our literature, expressing through Ahab and Ishmael both his sense of the blackness, sharkishness, and ambiguity of life, and his vision of a coherent universe in which a brotherhood of working seamen could embody his Christian-democratic values.

After 1851, Melville's long silence as a writer of sea fiction parallels, but was not caused by, the decline in American maritime activity, the passing of the sailing ships, the nation's increasing interest in the inland frontier, and a sharp decline in the publication of sea fiction. But by the late 1880s, partly in elegiac response to the expiration of the sailing life he had known, Melville renewed his interest in sea fiction and finally produced his second masterpiece, *Billy Budd, Sailor*. Also at this time several other sailor-writers, born between the 1860s and 1890s—MORGAN ROBERTSON, THORNTON JENKINS HAINS, ARTHUR MASON, FELIX RIESENBERG, BILL ADAMS, LINCOLN COLCORD, RICHARD MATTHEWS HALLET, and ARCHIE BINNS—began to commemorate the sailing life in its final years, and to reinterpret the sea life in light of the new biology that had developed after the *Origin of Species*. They created a small renaissance of American sea fiction that attracted a sizable and sympathetic reading public, like that to which the regionalists appealed. And some of them contributed to a body of Great Lakes maritime fiction that is still relatively unknown.

But the public's interest in sea fiction during these years— apparent also in the careers of Joseph Conrad, Joshua Slocum, and Eugene O'Neill—is best known today in the work of Stephen Crane and Jack London. Crane's "The Open Boat" is perhaps the all-time greatest short story of the sea, rivaled in American literature only by Melville's "Benito Cereno." London entered the literary world in the tradition of Dana and Melville by writing of his experience as a foremast hand on the sealer *Sophia Sutherland*. He wrote several sea stories and novels, but *The Sea-Wolf* (1904) is one of the major works of American sea fiction—memorable for the great captain, Wolf Larsen, and for its full development of the voyage idea. London projects a Darwinian reality that he believed had displaced the romantic or biblical visions projected in the voyages of Cooper, Poe, or Melville.

By the time Ernest Hemingway began writing about the sea in the late 1930s, aspiring young authors had ceased to imagine that stints as working seamen could lead to literary careers, as in Cooper, Dana, and Melville. Hallett and Binns had been the last to do that successfully, in *The Lady Aft* (1915) and *Lightship* (1934). But on the basis of his considerable experience with the sea and his interest in biological thought, Hemingway—and after him, Peter Matthiessen—contributed significantly to American fiction by dramatizing the struggles of modern men not only to survive, but to know and accept themselves as participants in the violent biological reality of all life as it has evolved from the sea. In *To Have and Have Not* (1937) Harry Morgan's brutal, almost reptilian vitality—like that of Wolf Larsen—makes him superior at least to the degenerate Wastelanders who surround him. In *Islands in the Stream* (1970), Thomas Hudson—a painter of marine life for the Museum of Natural History—explores his own biological reality in warfare and the violence of sex. And in *The Old Man and the Sea* (1952), Santiago's simple economy as a fisherman in the Gulf Stream offers an illuminating parable of what Hemingway called "the sea in being."

In the most recent achievement of American sea fiction, *Far Tortuga* (1975), PETER MATTHIESSEN projects a modern voyage in the New World waters that Columbus first explored. Living in discord aboard the *Lilias Eden*, Matthiessen's turtle men struggle to survive in a depleted sea, but even as their venture ends in shipwreck and dissension, Matthiessen—one of the most accomplished naturalists in American literature— affirms life and, tentatively, the possibility that humanity may yet discover ways to exist with dignity and a degree of harmony within the violent but fragile order of life on the watery world. More recently, popular books about the struggle between humans and the sea have been nonfiction. Sebastian Junger's best seller *The Perfect Storm* (1997) recounts the true story of the loss of the *Andrea Gail*, a fishing boat with a crew of six, 500 miles from its home port of Gloucester, Massachusetts. Caught in "the storm of the century," the men battled fiercely before succumbing to the ferocious waves. Linda Greenlaw, captain of the *Hanna Boden*, sister ship of the *Andrea Gail*, described her successful month-long 1,000-mile trip with a crew of five men in *The Hungry Ocean: A Swordboat Captain's Journey* (1999). Basic studies are T. Philbrick's *James Fenimore Cooper and the Development of American Sea Fiction* (1961) and B. Bender's *Sea-Brothers* (1988).

BERT BENDER

Seager, Allen (1906–1968),   scholar, novelist, short-story writer, memoirist. Seager taught at his alma mater, the University of Michigan, and at Oxford. *Equinox* (1943), *The Inheritance* (1948), *Amos Berry* (1953), *Hilda Manning* (1956), and *Death of Anger* (1960) are novels; *The Old Man of the Mountain* (1950) is a story collection; and *A Frieze of Girls: Memoirs as Fiction* (1964) is autobiography. *The Glass House* (1968) is a biography of THEODORE ROETHKE.

Sea Lions, The (1849), a novel by JAMES FENIMORE COOPER. Cooper had long been interested in CAPTAIN KIDD, and in his *History of the Navy* (1839) had given an account of Kidd's life and of the treasure the pirate had reputedly buried. In *The Sea Lions* novel Cooper interwove an account of whaling in the Antarctic and treasure hunting in the West Indies. The treasure hunt is based on a treasure island chart found among the belongings of a mysterious deceased sailor.

Sealsfield, Charles [also **C. Seatsfield** and **C. Sidons,** pen names of **Karl Anton Post**], (1793–1864), novelist, short-story writer, travel writer. All his life Sealsfield concealed his real name and the fact that he was originally a monk who escaped from a Bohemian monastery and in 1822 fled to the United States. He became an American citizen, but also lived in various parts of Europe. He traveled extensively in this country, especially in the Southwest and the Mississippi Valley, and visited Mexico. He wrote his books in German and translated them himself into English. Sealsfield wrote voluminously. The first fruit of his travels in the United States was *Die Vereinigten Staaten von Nordamerika, Nach Ihren Politischen, Religioesen, und Gesellschaftlichen Verhaeltnisse Betrachtet,* published in Germany (2 v.) in 1827. It appeared in London as *The United States of North America as They Are* (1827) and *The Americans as They Are* (1828).

He invented what he called the ethnographic novel, which deals with an entire people through the depiction of individuals. Typical was *Tokeah, or, The White Rose* (1829, rewritten in German, 1833). His other novels were grouped to produce the same effect: *Die Deutschamerikanischen Wahlverwandtschaft* (4 v. 1839–40) and *Sueden und Norden* (3 v. 1842–43). One of his best books was *Das Kajuetenbuch* (*The Cabin Book,* 1841), stories dealing mainly with the Texas War of Independence. His works were in part collected in a 15-volume edition published in Germany (1845–47).

Seaman, Augusta Huiell (1879–1950), writer of juvenile fiction. Seaman, born in New York City, began her career as a staff member of ST. NICHOLAS, in which her earlier work appeared. She wrote more than forty mystery stories, including *Jacqueline of the Carrier Pigeons* (1910), *The Pine Barrens Mystery* (1937), *The Case of the Calico Crab* (1942), and *The Vanishing Octant Mystery* (1949).

Seaman, Elizabeth Cochrane. See BLY, NELLIE.

Chief Seattle [Seathl] (1786–1866), Indian leader and spokesman. Seattle was chief of the Northwest Duwamish and Squamish tribes. He was converted to Christianity in the 1830s, and that conversion may have been a factor in his policy of peaceful coexistence with the advancing white settlers. Because he was known as a forceful orator, Seattle was called upon to express the views of his people on many occasions. His most famous address is that given in response to a proposal by Governor Isaac Stevens of the newly designated Washington Territory that the native

people be settled on reservations. The speech, called variously "Tears of Compassion" after a phrase in the first line, or "The White Man Will Never Be Alone" after a concluding phrase, is a plea for justice and compassion for his tribe. In the speech, Seattle acknowledges the declining numbers of his people and the power of the white settlers, but warns that even if the native people should die out, "these shores will swarm with the invisible dead of my tribe . . . the White Man will never be alone." An English version first appeared in the Seattle *Sunday Star* for October 29, 1887, more than twenty years after Seattle's death and thirty years after the speech was delivered in the Squamish language. There is no evidence that Dr. Henry A. Smith, the man who claimed to have reconstructed the words from his own notes, knew the Indian language. Whether the extant text accurately records Seattle's words, it is clear that he delivered a major speech on the subject of resettlement soon after the 1853 organization of the Washington Territory, and that he agreed to the Port Elliot Treaty (1855) assigning the native people to reservation lands. The city of Seattle was named for him.

Seaweed (1844), a poem by HENRY WADSWORTH LONGFELLOW. In this poem Longfellow sets forth a theory about the origin of poetry. He states that just as a storm causes seaweed to be torn from its base and tossed up on shore, so "storms of wild emotion/Strike the ocean/Of the poet's soul" and tear off "some fragment of a song" that is "at length in books recorded."

Sea-Wolf, The (1904), a novel by JACK LONDON. The ruthless power of Wolf Larsen, captain of the sealing schooner *Ghost,* is challenged when he rescues Humphrey Van Weyden, a literary critic, and Maude Brewster, a lady poet, after the ferry boat in which they were crossing San Francisco Bay collided with a steamer. Although Wolf cannot accurately be called a Nietzschean superman, he probably evolved from London's interest in Nietzsche. The story breaks into two parts: the first takes place on shipboard, the second on a desert island where Humphrey, Wolf, and Maude Brewster are wrecked.

Seccomb, John (1708–1792), Congregational clergyman, humorist. Seccomb, born in Medford, Massachusetts, was ordained minister of the town of Harvard in 1733. In 1757 he resigned and later became the minister of a dissenting congregation in Chester, Nova Scotia. He published an ordination sermon in Nova Scotia (1770) and a funeral sermon on the death of Governor Jonathan Belcher's wife (1771). His fame as a humorist is based on a cleverly rhymed poem, *Father Abbey's Will* (1730), written in honor of a bedmaker and sweeper at Harvard.

Secret Life of Walter Mitty, The, a JAMES THURBER short story (*The New Yorker,* 1939) collected in *My World—and Welcome to It* (1942). Walter Mitty, bullied by his wife and his associates, daydreams about himself as a hero in several situations, ending with his facing a firing squad with no blindfold, "undefeated, inscrutable to the last."

Sedgwick, Anne Douglas (1873–1935), novelist. Sedgwick was born in New Jersey, married Basil de Selincourt (1908), and thereafter resided in England. Her best-known novel was *The Little French Girl* (1924). She also wrote *The Dull Miss Archinard* (1898), *Franklin Winslow Kane* (1910), TANTE (1911), *Adrienne Toner* (1922), and other stories.

Sedgwick, Catherine Maria (1789–1867),   novelist, biographer. Sedgwick was born into a prominent family in western Massachusetts. Her fiction, admired in Europe as well as the United States, depicted domestic social life and values. Her first novel, *A New England Tale* (1822), was published anonymously. *Redwood* (1824), popular in England and France, elicited comparisons with the fiction of Maria Edgeworth, Scott, and JAMES FENIMORE COOPER. *Hope Leslie, or Early Times in the Massachusetts* (1827) is a romantic tale of colonial times, including depictions of frontier massacres and captivity. *Clarence: or, A Tale of Our Own Times* (1830) contrasts the social lives of two women—one conventional, the other more adventurous—in New York City. In *The Linwoods: or, "Sixty Years Since" in America* (1835), set in New York during the Revolution, she invited comparison with Scott's *Waverley, or 'tis Sixty Years Since*. Her other novels are *Live and Let Live* (1837) and *Married or Single?* (1857). She was a feminist and active in the Unitarian movement. She wrote biographies of Lucretia M. Davidson (1837) and John Curtis (1858). *The Life and Letters of Catherine M. Sedgwick* (1871), edited by Mary Dewey, included "Reminiscences of Miss Sedgwick" by William Cullen Bryant.

Sedgwick, Susan [Ridley] (1789?–1867),   children's writer. Like her sister-in-law, Catherine M. Sedgwick, she was interested in domestic virtues. *Young Emigrants* (1836) tells of a New York family's move to Ohio in the late 18th century. Her other works are *Allen Prescott: or, the Fortunes of a New England Boy* (1834) and *Alida: or, Town and Country* (1844).

Seeger, Alan (1888–1916),   poet. Seeger, born in New York City, when recently graduated from Harvard, went to Paris at the beginning of World War I. He enlisted in the French Foreign Legion and was killed at the Battle of the Somme. His poem "I Have a Rendezvous with Death" (*North American Review*, October 1916) was included in *Poems* (1916). His *Letters and Diary* appeared in the following year.

Seitz, Don Carlos (1862–1935),   biographer, poet. Seitz, born in Ohio, was the business manager for PULITZER's New York *World* and, near the end of his life, associate editor of the *Outlook*. He published two books of verse, *The Buccaneers* (1912) and *Farm Voices* (1918), but he is chiefly known for his biographies: *Artemus Ward* (1919); *Joseph Pulitzer* (1924); *Braxton Bragg, General of the Confederacy* (1924); *Horace Greeley* (1926); *Charles Curtis* (1928); *James Gordon Bennett* (1928); and *Lincoln the Politician* (1931). Among his other volumes are *The Dreadful Decade* (1869–1879) (1926); *The Great Island*, a book about Newfoundland (1926); *The Also Rans* (1927); and *Famous American Duels* (1929).

Seize the Day,   a novelette by SAUL BELLOW first published in the *Partisan Review* (1956) and later in the same year in book from with other stories. It depicts how material loss can lead to spiritual gain. See SAUL BELLOW.

Selby, Hubert, Jr. (1928–   ),   novelist. Born and raised in Brooklyn, Selby became a writer as a self-taught high-school dropout. His first novel, *Last Exit to Brooklyn* (1964), with its cast of homosexuals, prostitutes, and criminals in setting of urban violence, became the subject of an obscenity trial in England, was banned in Italy, and became a controversial best seller in the United States and made him widely known. His other novels are *The Room* (1971), *The Demon* (1976), *Requiem for a Dream* (1978), and *The Willow Tree* (1998). *Song of the Silent Snow* (1986) is a collection of short stories.

Seldes, George (1890–1995),   journalist. Seldes, born in New Jersey, was known for his outspoken attacks on censorship and demagoguery. During the 1940s he edited a liberal newsletter, *In Fact*. His autobiography is *Tell the Truth and Run* (1953). His works include *You Can't Print That! The Truth Behind the News, 1918–1928* (1929); *Can These Things Be!* (1931); *Sawdust Caesar* (1935), an attack on Mussolini and fascism; *Freedom of the Press* (1935); *Lords of the Press* (1938); *Witch Hunt* (1940); *Never Tire of Protesting* (1968); and *Even the Gods Cannot Change History* (1976). His memoirs *Witness to a Century* appeared in 1987.

Seldes, Gilbert [Vivian] (1893–1970),   journalist, critic, writer. Brother of GEORGE SELDES, and like him born in New Jersey, Gilbert Seldes edited *The Dial* (1920–23) and wrote books on popular culture, such as *The Seven Lively Arts* (1924), *The Movies and the Talkies* (1929), *The Movies Come from America* (1937), *The Great Audience* (1950), and *The Public Arts* (1956). His books of social analysis include *The United States and the War* (1917), *The Stammering Century* (1928), *The Future of Drinking* (1930), *Against Revolution, The Year of the Locust* (1932), and *Mainland* (1936). He wrote the novel *The Wings of the Eagle* (1929) and many radio and television scripts and reviewed those media for *Saturday Review*. Under the name Foster Johns he wrote detective stories: *The Victory Murders* (1927) and *The Square Emerald* (1928).

Self-Portrait in a Convex Mirror,   JOHN ASHBERY's long introspective, meditative poem used as the title piece of his 1975 book of poems. The central metaphor and title derive from a self-portrait by Francesco Mazzola (1503–1540) of Parma done on a convex piece of wood.

Self-Reliance (in *Essays, First Series*, 1841),   an essay by RALPH WALDO EMERSON. In this essay Emerson preached a doctrine of independence and individualism. Some of the essay's epigrammatic statements immediately became widely quoted: "Whoso would be a man must be a non-conformist." "Society everywhere is in conspiracy against the manhood of every one of its members." "Nothing is at last sacred but the integrity of your own mind." "A foolish consistency is the hobgoblin of little minds." "An institution is the lengthened shadow of a man."

Sellers, Colonel Beriah.   A character in THE GILDED AGE (1873), by Mark Twain and Charles Dudley Warner. One of Twain's most memorable comic creations, Sellers is a perpetual optimist whose impractical schemes and dreams of future glory contrast ironically with his unprepossessing station in life and talents. Later named Mulberry Sellers, he appeared in the plays *Colonel Sellers* (produced 1873; as *The Gilded Age*, 1880) and *Colonel Sellers as a Scientist* (1887), the latter written with

William Dean Howells, and in the novel THE AMERICAN CLAIMANT (1892). Sellers was a composite of traits drawn from many models, including perhaps Twain himself, his father, his brother Orion, and more distant relatives James Lampton and Jesse Madison Leathers.

Sellers, Isaiah (1802?–1864), steamboat pilot, newspaper correspondent. In LIFE ON THE MISSISSIPPI (1883), MARK TWAIN described Sellers as the patriarch of river pilots and claimed to have appropriated the pen name Mark Twain from Sellers, who used it to sign his river reports to the New Orleans *Picayune*. Twain said he took the name as a form of penance because by satirizing Sellers in the New Orleans *True Delta*, he had driven the old pilot out of newspaper work, an explanation doubted by literary historians.

Sellers, Mulberry. See COLONEL BERIAH SELLERS.

Selling of Joseph, The (1700), a tract by SAMUEL SEWALL. This tract was the first in America to denounce slavery and it also spoke of women's rights.

Selvon, Samuel [Dickson] (1923–1994), Trinidadian novelist. Selvon moved to London in 1950 and soon thereafter began to write and publish, while supporting himself by working as a clerk in the Indian embassy. Whether using Trinidad as a setting—as in *A Brighter Sun* (1952), *An Island Is a World* (1955), *Turn Again Tiger* (1958), and *I Hear Thunder* (1963)—or London—as in *Lonely Londoners* (1956) and *The Housing Lark* (1965)—Selvon explores the mistrust and prejudice between races with a compassionate humor and with a keen ear for dialect. Selvon moved to Canada in 1978. Among his other works are the stories in *Ways of Sunlight* (1958, repr. 1979) and the novels *Those Who Eat the Cascadura* (1972) and *Moses Ascending* (1975). *Foreday Morning: Selected Prose 1946–1986* appeared in 1989.

Seminole Indians. The name Seminole means "separatist" and was given to a Muskhogean tribe of Florida that left the Creek tribe and was later joined by Yamassee and Yuchi Indians and runaway black slaves. From the first sightings by Europeans, Seminoles have been known for their costumes made from brightly colored cloth strips sewn together. They were under Spanish rule during the War of 1812 and were hostile to the United States. After the first Seminole War (1817–1818) they were forced to sign the Treaty of Payne's Landing (1832), agreeing to cede their land holdings and move west. Many chiefs refused to abide by the arrangement, and the second Seminole War (1835–1842) resulted. It was the most costly Indian war in United States history. OSCEOLA was a leader in this war until he was captured, imprisoned, and died. M. M. Cohen described Osceola and other leaders in *Florida and the Campaigns* (1836). Most of the tribe moved west, suffering a loss of 40% from hardships along the way. A few hundred were allowed to remain in the Florida swamps; in 1962 a new treaty formally allotted 235,000 watery acres to their descendants. Those who moved to the Indian Territories formed a federation (1859) with the Cherokee, Choctaw, Chickasaw, and Creek—the five becoming known as the Five Civilized Tribes. Over a period of several years, the Dawes Commission forced the tribes to liquidate their holdings; in 1901 they were granted United States citizenship, and in theory, the Five Civilized Tribes were integrated into the general population. Only the tribally owned land in Florida remains.

Novels dealing with the Seminoles include Robert Wilder's *Bright Feathers* (1948), Theodore Pratt's *Seminole* (1954), and Frank G. Slaughter's *The Seminole* (1956). Frances Densmore made a penetrating study of their history and culture in *Seminole Music* (1956).

Semmes, Raphael (1809–1877), naval officer, lawyer, memoirist. Born in Maryland, Semmes was perhaps the best-known Confederate naval officer during the Civil War, commanding two raiders that inflicted great damage on Northern commerce, the *Sumter* and the *Alabama*. After the war he practiced law in Mobile, Alabama, and wrote several books about his experiences, including *Service Afloat and Ashore During the Mexican War* (1851), *Campaign of General Scott in the Valley of Mexico* (1852), *Cruise of the Alabama and the Sumter* (1864), and *Memoirs of Service Afloat During the War Between the States* (1869).

Senarens, Luis Philip (1863–1939), dime novelist. Senarens, believed to have been born in Brooklyn, New York, is said to have written more than 1,500 books—but the books were usually only sixteen pages long, three columns to the page. He employed many pen names. His most popular hero was Frank Reade, who appeared in a long series of stories, some of them published in the *Frank Reade Weekly* (1902 and thereafter).

Sendak, Maurice (1928–   ), writer and illustrator of children's books. Sendak is known for the playfully grotesque monsters in *Where the Wild Things Are* (1963) and the anatomically realistic child of *In the Night Kitchen* (1970). *The Sign on Rosie's Door* (1960) was produced on television as an animated television special, *Really Rosie* (1975), and as a musical play (1978), with the same name. Sendak was chosen to illustrate *Dear Mili* (1988), a Wilhelm Grimm fairy tale undiscovered for over 150 years. Some of his other titles are *Nutshell Library* (1962), *Higglety Pigglety Pop, or There Must Be More to Life* (1967), and *Outside Over There* (1981). A tireless illustrator of books by others, including Else Minarek, Randall Jarrell, Isaac Bashevis Singer, and Herman Melville, he collaborated with Iona and Peter Opie on *I Saw Esau: The Schoolchild's Pocket Book* (1992) and has been active designing scenes and costumes for the stage. He was the first American to be awarded the Hans Christian Andersen International Medal.

Seneca Indians, the westernmost of the Five Nations of the Iroquois, located in central and western New York. Seneca land lay between Seneca Lake and Lake Erie. The Iroquois Confederacy, traditionally said to have been sponsored by Hiawatha, was originally composed of the Mohawk, Seneca, Cayuga, Onondaga, and Oneida; later (about 1715) the Tuscaroras joined them, and the group was called the Six Nations. The Six Nations had an unwritten constitution and representative government. They joined with Pontiac against the English, but chose the English during the Revolutionary War. When troops sent by Washington defeated an army of

Tories and Indians near Elmira and marched through the Indian lands (1779), the power of the Iroquois Confederacy was broken. Many Iroquois moved across the border into Quebec and Ontario; a small group moved to northeast Oklahoma. Those who stayed in New York were confined to separate reservations. For 170 years the Senecas lived, according to a treaty signed during Washington's presidency, on a reservation on the Allegheny River. In the 1960s a dam built by the Army Corps of Engineers to protect Pittsburgh from flooding caused the Senacas' land to flood. They were awarded 15 million dollars in damages and relocated, but their sacred religious sites and cemeteries had been obliterated.

Two of the most celebrated Seneca chiefs are Cornplanter (1732?–1836) and Red Jacket (c. 1756–1830). In 1780, Cornplanter led an invasion of the settlements of the Schoharie valley; his white father, John O'Bail, was among the captives, but Cornplanter spared his father and his father's white family. As a guest of JEFFERSON, with whom he had carried on a correspondence, Cornplanter visited Washington, D.C., in the winter of 1801–1802. Both chiefs were called to Philadelphia by WASHINGTON in 1792. Red Jacket, a celebrated orator, spoke for his people. Though he complained that neither the English nor the Americans had provided for their Indian allies, he agreed that the Six Nations would advocate for peace between the U.S. and the western Indians.

Senecas are treated sympathetically in *Yonnondio, or Warriors of the Genesee* (1844) by William H.C. Hosmer, and Edmund Wilson discusses them in *Apologies to the Iroquois* (1960).

Sennett, Mack [stage name of **Michael Sinnott**] (1884–1960),   actor, film producer, director. Sennett, who was born in Canada, worked as an actor for DAVID W. GRIFFITH. In 1912 he joined the Keystone Co. and began producing the comic films with which his reputation is associated. In addition he developed a number of comedians who earned fame in their own right—Charlie Chaplin, Ben Turpin, Roscoe (Fatty) Arbuckle, Harold Lloyd, Harry Langdon, Buster Keaton, and others. Pretty girls—to whom no favoritism was shown in the usual roughhouse—and a corps of spectacularly ineffectual policemen, the Keystone Cops, were invariable features of Sennett's pictures. Sennett joined Paramount in 1917, and his comedy began to become more refined. With Cameron Forbes he wrote *Mack Sennett, King of Comedy* (1954).

Sense of Beauty, The.   George Santayana's treatise on aesthetics, based on lectures delivered at Harvard from 1892 to 1895 and published in 1896. See SANTAYANA.

Separatists,   groups of Christians who withdrew from the Church of England. The movement began with the Brownists, led by Robert Browne (c. 1550–1633), who advocated self-government by congregations. The term "Independents" was used in the 17th century. Separatist groups that emigrated to the colonies included the Pilgrims, Quakers, and Baptists. The aim of Puritans, including those who settled at Massachusetts Bay, was to purify the church, not to separate from it.

Septimius Felton, or A Romance of Immortality (1871),   a novel by NATHANIEL HAWTHORNE. Existence of this story was discovered after Hawthorne's death, and a large part of the manuscript was prepared and subsequently published by his wife. The manuscript was referred to in the preface to OUR OLD HOME, but it seems to have functioned merely as a preliminary to THE DOLLIVER ROMANCE. The plot of *Septimius Felton* is set in England and America and centers on a hero of mixed English and Indian ancestry.

Sequoya (1770?–1843),   CHEROKEE INDIAN artisan, inventor of an alphabet. Born in Tennessee, Sequoya was the son of a Caucasian and an Indian. In later life he called himself George Guess, George Gist, and George Guest. He is said to have been injured in a hunting accident and therefore prevented from engaging in the customary sports and war activities of his tribe. About 1809 he began to develop a Cherokee syllabary, or alphabet. After about ten years he produced a workable alphabet, which immediately went into general use and is still employed. It is so simple that all the Cherokees became literate in a matter of months. In 1825 a version of the New Testament was made in Cherokee with the help of Sequoya's symbols. In 1827 a Boston firm cast a font of type in Cherokee characters. It was used in the publication (1828–34) of a newspaper called the *Cherokee Phoenix*, later the *Cherokee Phoenix & Indian's Advocate*. The *Cherokee Messenger*, established in August 1844, was also printed in the Cherokee language.

Sequoya served on the delegation that signed a treaty (1828) resulting in moving the Cherokees to Indian Territory. G.E. Foster wrote *Sequoyah, the American Cadmus and Modern Moses: A Complete Biography of the Greatest of Redmen* (1885).

Serling, [Edward] Rod[man] (1924–1975),   television writer. He won the first of his five Emmy awards with *Patterns* (1957), but is best known for his long-running science fiction and fantasy series *The Twilight Zone* (1959). Among his other scripts are *Requiem for a Heavyweight* (1956), *The Comedian* (1957), and *The Velvet Alley* (1959).

Serra, Miguel José [Junípero] (1713–1784),   missionary. Born in Majorca, Serra took the name Junipero when he joined the Franciscan Order. In 1749 he and his friend and biographer Francisco Palou sailed for Mexico, where their first assignment was to the Pamé Indians in the Sierra Gorda Mountains. He wrote a catechism in the Pamé language. After seven years of preaching in Mexico City, where he gained a following and the legends about him began to grow, Serra joined an expedition commanded by Gaspar de Portolá up the California coast. He founded the first of his missions at San Diego in 1769. The missions San Carlos Barromeo (Monterey, 1770), San Antonio de Padua (1771), San Gabriel Arcángel (1771), San Luis Obispo (1772), San Juan Capistrano (1776), San Francisco de Asís (1776), Santa Clara de Asís (1777), and San Buenaventura (1782) were founded under his leadership. *Father Serra's Diary: an Account of his Journey from Loretto to San Diego, 1787* was published in 1935. Palou's books are *Life and Apostolic Labors of the Venerable Father Junipero Serra* (tr. 1958) and *The Founding of the California Missions Under the*

Spiritual Guidance of the Venerable Padre Fray Junipero Serra (tr. 1934).

Service, Robert W[illiam] (1874–1958),   Canadian poet, novelist. Service came from Scotland to Canada at age twenty. Leaving a banking job, he traveled for eight years in the area near the Arctic Circle. After service as an ambulance driver in France, he settled there but in 1940 he and his family escaped just ahead of the German army and returned to Canada for the duration of the war. He lived the remainder of his life in France. Service is best known for his frontier ballads, including THE SHOOTING OF DAN McGREW, collected in *Songs of a Sourdough* (1907, later retitled *The Spell of the Yukon*). His other titles are *Ballads of a Cheechako* (1909), *Rhymes of a Rolling Stone* (1912), *Rhymes of a Red Cross Man* (1916), *Ballads of a Bohemian* (1920), *Bar-Room Ballads* (1940), *Rhymes of a Roughneck* (1951), *Rhymes of a Rebel* (1952), and *Carols of a Codger* (1954). Among his novels are *The Master of the Microbe* (1926) and *The House of Fear* (1927). *Ploughman of the Moon* (1945) and *Harper of Heaven* (1948) are autobiographies. See KLONDIKE GOLD RUSH.

Serviss, Garrett P[utnam] (1851–1929),   newspaperman, science popularizer, science fiction writer. Born in Sharon Springs, New York, Serviss was educated at Cornell and Columbia, wrote for the New York *Sun* and POPULAR SCIENCE, and after 1892 became a popular lecturer, especially on astronomy. Among his widely read nonfiction are *Astronomy with an Opera Glass* (1888); *Other Worlds: Their Nature, Possibilities, and Habitability in the Light of the Latest Discoveries* (1901); *Astronomy with the Naked Eye* (1908); and *Curiosities of the Sky* (1909). As a pioneer in science fiction, he wrote the novels *Edison's Conquest of Mars* (1947, serialized 1898); *The Moon Metal* (1900); *A Columbus of Space* (1911), about a voyage to Venus in a spaceship powered by atomic energy; and *The Second Deluge* (1912), depicting humanity threatened with extinction after a cosmic collision.

Seth Jones, or, The Captives of the Frontier (pub. 1860 as No. 8 of *Beadle's Dime Novels*),   by EDWARD S. ELLIS. Orville J. Victor, for thirty years editor of Beadle & Adams, called this work "the perfect dime novel." The hero, of good station in life, assumes the disguise of an aged and eccentric hunter because he has heard that while he was away fighting in the Revolution his sweetheart had ceased to care for him. The story sold close to half a million copies in six months. This success determined Ellis's career, and he continued for three decades to write similar stories, mainly about hunters. See DIME NOVEL.

Seth's Brother's Wife (1887),   HAROLD FREDERIC's first novel, which appeared serially in *Scribner's Monthly*, then was published in book form. It was not a success. In this story of a triangular love affair and a murder involving two brothers and the wife of the older one, Frederic wrote realistically of soured lives and drabness, although in a later story, "The Editor and the Schoolma'am," (*The New York Times*, September 9, 1888), he satirized the way that Russian pessimism and gloom were penetrating American fiction.

Seton, Anya (1916–1990),   novelist. Seton, born in New York City and the daughter of ERNEST THOMPSON SETON, the Canadian naturalist, is known for historical novels focused on the lives of women. *My Theodosia* (1941) concerned the daughter of Aaron Burr; *Katherine* (1954) treated Katherine Swynford, wife of John of Gaunt. Her other titles are *Dragonwyck* (1944), *The Turquoise* (1946), *The Hearth and the Eagle* (1948), *Foxfire* (1951), *The Mistletoe and Sword* (1955), *The Winthrop Woman* (1958), *Devil Water* (1962), *Avalon* (1965), and *Green Darkness* (1973).

Seton, Ernest [Evan] Thompson (1860–1946), naturalist, illustrator, nature writer. Born in England, Seton grew up on a Canadian farm and was trained in art at London's Royal Academy. His first book, *Wild Animals I Have Known* (1898), was so successful that it launched him on a writing career. His titles include *The Biography of a Grizzly* (1900), *Lives of the Hunted* (1901), *Two Little Savages* (1903), *Scouting for Boys* (1910), *Woodcraft and Indian Lore* (1912), *Wild Animals at Home* (1913), *Bannertail* (1922), *Lives of Game Animals* (1925), *The Gospel of the Redmen* (1936), *The Biography of an Arctic Fox* (1937), *Mainly About Wolves* (1937), and *The Trail of an Artist-Naturalist* (1940), an autobiography. *America: Selections from the Writings of the Artist Naturalist* (1954) has an introduction by Farida A. Wiley.

Seuss, Dr. [pen name of **Theodor Seuss Geisel**] (1904–1991),   writer-illustrator of children's books. His pen name is a compound of his mother's maiden name and a Ph.D. degree he said he never took the trouble to earn. His books are written in verse and illustrated by the author. Among them are *And to Think I Saw It on Mulberry Street* (1937), *The 500 Hats of Bartholomew Cubbins* (1938), *The King's Stilts* (1939), *Horton Hatches the Egg* (1940), *Horton Hears a Who* (1954), *If I Ran the Circus* (1956), *How the Grinch Stole Christmas* (1957), *The Cat in the Hat* (1957), *Yertle the Turtle* (1958), *Happy Birthday to You* (1959), *Green Eggs and Ham* (1960), *Speeches and Other Stories* (1961), and *Oh, The Places You'll Go!* (1990). *The Seven Lady Godivas* (1939) is a book for older readers. Serious messages are often included. For example, *The Lorax* (1971) is an ecological warning; *The Butter Battle Book* (1984) counters the arms race; and *You're Only Old Once!* (1986) deals with aging.

Seven Arts, The,   a monthly magazine published during 1916–1917 to encourage American talent. Its editors included JAMES OPPENHEIM, VAN WYCK BROOKS, and WALDO FRANK. When financial backers withdrew support because of the magazine's pacifist editorial stance, the publication failed.

Seven Cities of Cibola.   See CIBOLA, THE SEVEN CITIES OF and FRANCISCO VÁSQUEZ DE CORONADO.

Sevenoaks (1875),   a novel by JOSIAH GILBERT HOLLAND. The New England village of Sevenoaks is the scene of the machinations of Robert Belcher, an unscrupulous millionaire who obtained his wealth by stealing a patent from an inventor, Paul Benedict.

Seventeen (1916),   a novel by BOOTH TARKINGTON. Written in much the same style as PENROD, *Seventeen* presents

William Sylvanus Baxter, "Silly Billy," an adolescent in the throes of his first love affair. The creature on whom he lavishes his attention is Lola Pratt, the "Baby-Talk Lady." The novel was dramatized in 1918 by Hugh S. Stange and Stannard Mears; it has been filmed a number of times and in 1951 was made into a musical by Sally Benson.

Seventh of March Speech by Daniel Webster (1850), a Senate speech replying to JOHN C. CALHOUN's attack on HENRY CLAY's Compromise Bill. Webster advised abolitionists to modify their principles in order to prevent dissolution of the Union. WHITTIER articulated the abolitionists' conviction that Webster had betrayed them in "Ichabod" (1850). Many years later, in "The Lost Occasion," Whittier admitted he had been too harsh on Webster.

Sewall, Jonathan (1729–1796),   lawyer, playwright. A grandnephew of Judge SAMUEL SEWALL, he later changed his name to Sewell. He was educated at Harvard, practiced law, and served as the Crown's last Attorney General of Massachusetts. His satirical play *The Americans Roused in a Cure for the Spleen* (1775), written under the pseudonym Roger de Coverley (printed version, *The American's Counsel, in a Cure for the Spleen*, 1775), displays his Loyalist sympathies. When war broke out, Sewell left for New Brunswick, Canada, where he died.

Sewall, Jonathan Mitchell (1748–1808),   poet. Sewall, born in Salem, Massachusetts, wrote the song "War and Washington," which was sung by American troops during the Revolution. An ardent Federalist, Sewall wrote *A Versification of President Washington's Excellent Farewell-Address* (1798) and *Eulogy on the Late General Washington* (1800). His *Miscellaneous Poems* appeared in 1801.

Sewall, Samuel (1652–1730),   jurist, diarist. Sewall's parents arrived in New England from England when Sewall was nine. In 1671 he was graduated from Harvard and two years later became a resident fellow at the college, and soon keeper of the library. He was manager of the colony's only licensed printing press from 1681 to 1684. He was deputy to the General Court for Westfield in 1683, and from 1684 to 1686 a member of the Council. In 1691 he was named councilor for the new charter forced on Massachusetts by the Crown. In the same year Governor Phips appointed him one of the special commissioners to try the Salem witchcraft cases. Later, convinced of the innocence of the nineteen persons condemned in court, Sewall stood up in the Old South Church in Boston while a bill was read in which he took "the blame and shame" for the miscarriage of justice. He was appointed justice of the Superior Court in 1692 and made a commissioner for the Society for the Propagation of the Gospel in New England in 1699.

Sewall, a strict Calvinist, believed that Indians and slaves should be kindly treated. His tract THE SELLING OF JOSEPH (1700) was the first antislavery work to be printed in America. He also wrote *Proposals Touching the Accomplishment of Prophecies Humbly Offered* (1713); *A Memorial Relating to the Kennebeck Indians* (1721); and, with Edward Rawson, anonymously, *The Revolution in New England Justified* (1691). He also produced numerous uncollected verse that he liked to read aloud, but he is chiefly known for his *Diary*, which extended from 1674 to 1729, with a break from 1677 to 1685. In it he gave a valuable and vivid account of day-to-day life in New England. *The Letters of Samuel Lee and Samuel Sewall Relating to New England and the Indians* was published in the *Massachusetts Historical Society Collections* in 1913. The *Diary* appeared in three volumes of the *Massachusetts Historical Society Collections* (1878–82), and an abridged edition, edited by Mark Van Doren, was published in 1927. A scholarly edition edited by M. Halsey Thomas was published in 1973. G. E. Ellis's *An Address on the Life and Character of Chief Justice Samuel Sewall* (1885), N. H. Chamberlain's *Samuel Sewall and the World He Lived In* (1897), and Whittier's "The Prophecy of Samuel Sewall" give accounts of Sewall. See PHAENOMENA.

Sewanee Review, The.   A quarterly magazine founded in 1892 at the University of the South, Sewanee, Tennessee. It is now reckoned the oldest quarterly of its kind in the United States and has been directed by a long succession of editors, including WILLIAM P. TRENT, Benjamin W. Wells, J. B. Henneman, GEORGE HERBERT CLARKE, William S. Knickerbocker, ALLEN TATE, John Palmer, and Monroe K. Spears. The editors have always been especially interested in Southern affairs, but under Tate and his successors, the magazine was chiefly noted as an organ of the NEW CRITICISM.

Seward, William Henry (1801–1872),   statesman, public official, orator. Seward, born in Florida, New York, began his career as a Democrat and served in the New York legislature. Later he switched to the Whig party and was elected (1838) governor of New York. In 1849 he became a United States Senator, and in 1852 he allied himself with the Know-Nothing Party to secure reelection and in 1855 joined the newly formed Republican Party.

Seward hoped to obtain the Republican nomination for president in 1860, but when Lincoln was chosen he campaigned for him. As Lincoln's Secretary of State, he negotiated the purchase of Alaska, often called "Seward's Folly." At the time of Lincoln's assassination an attempt was made on Seward's life as well, but he recovered. When Johnson became president, Seward supported him staunchly and wrote many of his addresses. He retired from office in 1869. Seward wrote an *Autobiography* (1877), and his *Works* were collected (5 v.) in 1884. Olive R. Seward edited *William H. Seward's Travels Around the World* (1873).

Sewell, Elizabeth (1919–2001),   scholar, poet, novelist. Born in India, educated at Cambridge University in England, Sewell emigrated to the United States in 1949. She taught at Vassar, Notre Dame, and the University of North Carolina at Greensboro. Scholarly and critical works include *The Structure of Poetry* (1952); *The Field of Nonsense* (1952), on wit and humor, with emphasis on Edward Lear and Lewis Carroll; and *The Orphic Voice* (1962), about poetry, literature, and science. Her novels include *Now Bless Thyself* (1962), about life in academia, and *The Dividing Time* (1951). Verse was collected in *Poems 1947–1961* (1963).

Sexton, Anne (1928–1974),   poet. Born in Newton, Massachusetts, into a family of New Englanders dating from the 17th century, Sexton lived an upper middle-class life in the family home in Weston and the family's summer compound on Squirrel Island. Mary Gray Staples, her mother, had literary aspirations, but being the competent wife of a successful woolen manufacturer, Ralph Harvey, took most of her time. Anne, their third daughter, was never quite at ease with the life prescribed for her and found solace in her relationship with her maiden aunt "Nana."

Academic success eluded her. From elementary school on, authorities urged her parents to get counseling for her. They did not, and her disobedience and inability to concentrate continued. In 1945, she was sent to a boarding school in Lowell, Massachusetts, where she wrote poetry, acted in plays, and played basketball. After graduation, she was briefly sent to what she termed a finishing school. Sexton's beauty and vivacity made her the ideal date for countless lovesick boys, and at nineteen she eloped with Alfred "Kayo" Sexton II. There followed five years of living with Kayo as a college student couple, sometimes with parents; then modeling while Kayo was fighting in Korea; and, finally, giving birth to their first child, Linda Gray, in 1953.

What had been instability and wide mood swings in Anne's behavior became deep depression. Over the next two years she was intermittently hospitalized, while her mother cared for Linda Gray. After the death of Anne's beloved "Nana" in 1954, her condition grew worse and, even though she had a second child in 1955, her psychiatric state continued to decline. It was at the advice of a therapist in 1957 that she began seriously to write poetry, enrolled in John Holmes's Boston Center for Adult Education writing course—where she met Maxine Kumin, who was to become her closest friend—and learned to transfer her personal anxieties and insights into meaningful art. Such poems as "You, Dr. Martin," "The Bells," and "The Double Image," written after Sexton read work by Robert Lowell and W. D. Snodgrass, marked her clear and unusual ability.

After studying with Snodgrass at the Antioch Writers' Conference in the summer of 1958, Sexton began working with Robert Lowell in his workshops at Boston University. There she met George Starbuck, Don Junkins, Stephen Sandy, Sylvia Plath, and others and came to understand that her work was distinctive. Sexton would understand that others could learn from her experimentation, and she grew in craft from a writer in tightly formal structures into the more voice-oriented rhythms of her later poems. Her first book, *To Bedlam and Part Way Back*, was published in 1960 and was followed in 1962 by *All My Pretty Ones*. So successful were these collections that a "selected poems" was issued in England, where Sexton's work was well received, and by the time *Live or Die*, her 1966 collection, appeared, it won a Pulitzer Prize.

The restlessness of Sexton's personal life during these years of high poetic visibility continued—she took trips to Europe and with Kayo went on an African safari—and sometimes her depression recurred. After her 1969 *Love Poems* and the unexpectedly comic 1971 *Transformations*, cynical and feminist poems based on the tales of the Brothers Grimm, Sexton's work grew more religious, more mythic, and—in the opinion of many critics—less effective. After *The Book of Folly* in 1972 came her divorce from Kayo, and then *The Death Notebooks* in 1974. At the

time of her suicide by inhaling carbon monoxide in 1974, Sexton had completed what would be her 1975 collection, *The Awful Rowing Toward God*. Since her death, several other posthumous collections have appeared, as well as *The Complete Poems* and *Anne Sexton, A Self-Portrait in Letters*. Linda Gray Sexton has become her mother's editor, as well as a writer herself.

Sexton also wrote some important essays about poetry and made insightful comments in her many interviews. She understood the fictive impulse and, like Wallace Stevens, saw her art as the supreme fiction. Much of what Sexton wrote was in no way autobiographical, and for her writing to be maligned because it is in some way confessional, drawing too intimately on personal experience, is unfair. She used her knowledge of the human condition—often painful, but sometimes joyful—to create poems readers can share. Her creation of incisive metaphor, her unexpected rhythmic patterns, and her ability to grasp a range of meaning in short works will keep Sexton's work available to readers. Though comparatively short, her writing career was important, as was her art. Studies include Diana Hume George's *Oedipus Anne: The Poetry of Anne Sexton* (1987) and Diane Wood Middlebrook's *Anne Sexton: A Biography* (1990).

LINDA WAGNER-MARTIN

Shaara, Michael (1929–1988), short-story writer, novelist. Born in New Jersey, Shaara got his B.A. from Rutgers, did graduate work at Columbia and the University of Vermont, served as a paratrooper and merchant seaman, and lived abroad for several years. His first book, *The Broken Place* (1968), is reminscent of Hemingway with its insistence on physical exertion as a mental healer. Shaara won the Pulitzer Prize with his second novel, *The Killer Angels* (1974). The story of the Civil War battle of Gettysburg, it is told from the multiple perspectives of officers and men of both armies. Shaara stated as his goal to reveal "what it was like to be there, what the weather was like, what men's faces looked like." It was turned into a 1993 television miniseries *Gettysburg*. Throughout his career Shaara wrote science fiction and fantasy. *The Herald* (1981) is an example; Nick Tesla lands his plane in a town where a mad scientist is killing off the residents in an attempt to create a master race. *Soldier Boy* (1982) is a collection of science fiction stories. *For the Love of the Game* (1991), the story of an aging pitcher who pitches a perfect game, was published posthumously.

Shadows on the Rock (1931), a novel by WILLA CATHER. A product of Cather's interest in Catholicism, this work is an episodic narrative of life in Quebec during the last days of Frontenac, centered on the life of Cécile Auclair, a child recently emigrated from Old France.

Shange, Ntozake (1948–), poet, playwright, novelist. Born Paulette Williams and educated at Barnard and the University of Southern California, she changed her name in 1971 and began to write poetry. The play she termed a choreopoem, *for colored girls who have considered suicide/when the rainbow is enuf*, was produced on Broadway in 1976. *Sassafrass, Cypress & Indigo* (1976, 1982) and *Betsey Brown* (1985) are novels. Her poetry titles include *Nappy Edges* (1978) and *A Daughter's Geography* (1983). Her plays include

A Photograph: A Study of Cruelty (1977), *Boogie Woogie Landscapes* (1978), *Spell #7: A Geechee Quick Magic Trance Manual* (1979), and *From Okra to Greens: A Different Kinda Love Story* (1984). *See No Evil: Prefaces, Essays and Accounts, 1976–1983* appeared in 1984.

shanties or chanteys.   See SAILORS' SONGS.

Shapiro, Karl [Jay] (1913–2000),   poet, critic, editor. Shapiro was born in Baltimore. His reputation was shaped by poems he wrote while serving in the Pacific in World War II, the best of which appeared in the rhymed stanzas of *V-Letter and Other Poems* (1944), for which he won a Pulitzer Prize. His poetry collections include *Poems* (1935), *Person, Place and Thing* (1942), *The Place of Love* (1942), *Essay on Rime* (1945), *Trial of a Poet and Other Poems* (1947), *Poems 1940–1953* (1953), *The House* (1957), and *Poems of a Jew* (1958). In *The Bourgeois Poet* (1964) Shapiro turned to the prose poem, free verse set in prose paragraphs. *His Selected Poems* appeared in 1968. He returned to traditional forms in *The White-Haired Lover* (1968) and *Adult Bookstore* (1976), and *Collected Poems 1940–1977* appeared in 1978. Stanley Kunitz and David Ignatow edited *The Wild Card: Selected Poems, Early and Late* in 1998. His critical works include *Beyond Criticism* (1953), *Start With the Sun* (1960), *Prose Keys to Modern Poetry* (1962), *Randall Jarrell* (1967), and *To Abolish Children and Other Essays* (1968). In *The Poetry Wreck: Selected Essays 1950–1970* (1975) Shapiro praised AUDEN, WILLIAM CARLOS WILLIAMS, WHITMAN, and JARRELL and criticized POUND and ELIOT. In addition to editing *Poetry* (1950–1956) and *The Schooner* (1956–1966, see THE PRAIRIE SCHOONER), he taught at the University of Nebraska and Northwestern. He wrote one play, *The Tenor* (1956), and one novel, *Edsel* (1970). *Poet: Volume One: The Younger Son* appeared in 1988.

Shaw, Anna Howard (1847–1919),   clergywoman, physician, reformer. Brought as a child from England to Massachusetts and then to the Michigan frontier, Shaw took a degree in theology and served as pastor of a Cape Cod church (1878), took an M.D. degree from Boston University (1886), and actively campaigned for temperance and women's rights. In 1904 she was elected president of the National American Woman Suffrage Association, and she earned a Distinguished Service Medal for her work on the Council of National Defense during World War I. Her memoir of life in the Michigan wilderness is called *The Story of a Pioneer* (1915).

Shaw, Henry W.   See JOSH BILLINGS.

Shaw, Irwin (1913–1984),   novelist, short-story writer, playwright. Shaw was born in New York City. His successful pacifist drama *Bury the Dead* (1936) was followed by other socially conscious plays, including *Siege* (1937), *The Gentle People* (1939), *Retreat to Pleasure* (1940), *Sons and Soldiers* (1944), and *The Assassin* (1944). *Children from Their Games* (1963) is a comedy. His novels include *The Young Lions* (1948), a World War II story of two American soldiers, one a Jew, the other a Gentile; *The Troubled Air* (1951), concerning actors harassed by charges of Communist sympathy; *Lucy Crown* (1956); *Two Weeks in Another Town* (1960); *Voices of a Summer Day* (1965); *Rich Man, Poor Man* (1970) and its sequel *Beggarman, Thief* (1977), recounting the lives of two brothers;

Evening in Byzantium (1973); *Nightwork* (1975); *The Top of the Hill* (1979); *Bread Upon the Water* (1981); and *Acceptable Losses* (1982). His story collections include *Sailor Off the Bremen* (1939), *Welcome to the City* (1941), *Act of Faith* (1946), *Mixed Faith* (1950), *Tip on a Dead Jockey* (1957), *Love on a Dark Street* (1965), *God Was Here But He Left Early* (1973), and *Five Decades* (1978). *In the Company of Dolphins* (1964) and *Paris! Paris!* (1977) are travel books. In *Report from Israel* (1950), Shaw wrote the text for photographs by Robert Capa.

Shawnee Indians.   A tribe of Algonquian stock. The name meant "southerner," although the tribe is believed to have originated in the north. One branch settled in Illinois and Ohio and along the Cumberland Valley; another went farther south to the Savannah River but about 1707 was forced back to Pennsylvania by the Cherokees and Catawbas. The Shawnees were a warlike people, fighting with other tribes, with the French, and later with the United States. Early in the 19th century Tenskwatawa, called the Prophet, and a brother of the great TECUMSEH, exhorted them to return to the old order of things and collected many followers at the mouth of the Tippecanoe River in Indiana, where they were defeated in the Battle of Tippecanoe in 1811 by General W. H. HARRISON. In 1825 they were sent to a reservation in Kansas, but large numbers went on to Texas, where they remained until they were driven out in 1850. Many of them now live in Oklahoma.

Cause of Alienation of the Delaware and Shawnee Indians from British Interests (1759), by C. Thomson, listed Shawnee grievances and proposed more justice for them. David Jones described the Shawnees in *A Journal of Two Visits Made to Some Nations of Indians on the West Side of the River Ohio in the Years 1772 and 1773* (1865). *A True Account of the Sufferings of Mary Kinnan* (1795) is a Virginia woman's account of her captivity from 1791 to 1794. The Shawnees appear in such fiction as R. M. Bird's *Nick of the Woods* (1837), Emerson Bennett's *The Pioneer's Daughter* (1866), and Edward Sylvester's *Footprints in the Forest* (1866).

Shay, Frank (1888–1954),   bookseller, publisher, editor, writer. Shay, born in New Jersey, owned bookshops in New York City and Provincetown, Massachusetts, and organized Frank Shay's Traveling Bookshop. Deeply interested in the stage, he organized the Caravan Theater and was a founder of the PROVINCETOWN PLAYERS. He also at times was a publisher, particularly of some of EDNA ST. VINCENT MILLAY's early poems. He edited several play anthologies and wrote or compiled many books about the sea and sea songs, among them *Iron Men and Wooden Ships* (1924), *American Sea Songs and Chanties* (1948), *The Bos'n's Locker* (1949), and *The Ships Flying* (1953). Among his other books are *My Pious Friends and Drunken Companions* (1927), *Here's Audacity* (1930), *Incredible Pizarro* (1932), *The Best Men Are Cooks* (1938), and an anthology of Cape Cod literature, *Sand in Their Shoes* (1951, ed. with his wife Edith Foley Shay). He was the originator of the outdoor art exhibits at Provincetown.

Shays's Rebellion,   an agrarian rebellion in Massachusetts in 1786–87, named for Daniel Shays, a Revolutionary War veteran. He and other debt-ridden farmers petitioned the Massachusetts legislature to issue paper money, reduce taxes and governmental salaries, and stop mortgage foreclosures. Shays led a force of 1,200 against the government arsenal at Springfield, where Federal troops broke up the insurrection. However, the legislature avoided imposing a direct tax in 1787 and exempted from debt collection people's clothing, household goods, and the tools of their trade. Ralph I. Lockwood wrote a novel, *The Insurgents* (1835), about Shays and his so-called broomstick army. In 1879 Edward Bellamy wrote his historical novel *The Duke of Stockbridge*, with the rebellion as a background.

Shea, John Dawson Gilmary (1824–1892), Catholic historian, editor, philologist. Shea, born in New York City, performed important service in gathering facts about Catholic missionaries in early days and in the field of Indian linguistics. One of his important works was his *History of the Catholic Church in the U.S.* (4 v. 1886–92). He also wrote *The Discovery and Exploration of the Mississippi Valley* (1853), *Early Voyages Up and Down the Mississippi* (1862), and a *Lincoln Memorial* (1865). An important linguistic work was *Library of American Linguistics* (15 v. 1860–74). He edited the original text of the *Jesuit Relations* (26 v. 1857–87) and founded the U.S. Catholic Historical Society.

Sheean, [James] Vincent (1899–1975), novelist, biographer, reporter, memoirist. Sheean, born in Illinois, was educated at the University of Chicago and became European correspondent for the Chicago *Tribune*. He reported, among other events, the Fascist march on Rome and the Spanish and French wars on the Riff tribesmen. *Personal History* (1935), his best-known work, relates Sheean's spiritual autobiography up to that point. His other nonfiction works include *An American Among the Riffi* (1926); *The New Persia* (1927); *Not Peace but a Sword* (1939), a denunciation of Fascism; *Between the Thunder and the Sun* (1943), which contains portraits of his father-in-law, Sir Johnston Forbes-Robertson, and his aunt, Maxine Elliot; *This House Against This House* (1946); *Lead Kindly Light* (1949), a tribute to Mahatma Gandhi; *The Indigo Bunting, A Memoir of Edna St. Vincent Millay* (1951); *Orpheus at Eighty* (1958), a tribute to Guiseppe Verdi; *Nehru, the Years of Power* (1959); *Dorothy and Red* (1963), a memoir of DOROTHY THOMPSON and SINCLAIR LEWIS; and *Faisal: The King and His Kingdom* (1975).

Sheean's novels reflect his varied cosmopolitan experiences and his concern with the individual's relationship to society. Among them are *The Anatomy of Virtue* (1927); *Gog and Magog* (1930); *The Tide* (1933); *Sanfelice* (1936); *The Pieces of a Fan* (short stories, 1937); *A Day of Battle* (1938); *An International Incident* (comedy, 1940); *Bird of the Wilderness* (1941); *A Certain Rich Man* (1947); *Rage of the Soul* (1952); *Lily* (1954); and *Beware of Caesar* (1965).

Sheed, Wilfred [John Joseph] (1930–), essayist, novelist, short-story writer. Born in London, Sheed came to the United States as a child, returned to Oxford for his education, and settled in New York City. He has written for *Commonweal* (1964–1967), the *New York Times Book Review*, and other periodicals. His fiction features realistic details of contemporary life and treats with humor the problems of individuals searching for their place in it. His novels include *Middle*

Class Education (1961); *The Hack* (1963); *Square's Progress* (1965); *Office Politics* (1966); *The Blacking Factory and Pennsylvania Gothic* (1968), a pair of novelettes; *Max Jamison* (1970); *Transatlantic Blues* (1978); and *The Boys of Winter* (1987). His nonfiction includes *The Morning After* (1971); *The Good Word and Other Words* (1979); *Three Mobs: Labor, Church and Mafia* (1974); *Essays in Disguise* (1990); *Baseball and Lesser Sports* (1991); and biographies of Muhammad Ali (1975) and Clare Boothe Luce (1982). Memoirs include *Frank and Maisie: A Memoir with Parents* (1985); and *In Love with Daylight: A Memoir of Recovery* (1995), about his battles with polio, alcoholism, and cancer.

Shelburne Essays (14 v. 1904–35),   literary, philosophical, and religious essays by PAUL ELMER MORE. More, along with IRVING BABBITT, was a founder of the New Humanist movement. See HUMANISM.

Sheldon, Charles M[onroe] (1857–1946),   clergyman, editor, novelist. Sheldon, born in Wellesville, New York, dramatized in his novel IN HIS STEPS (1896) his notion of the Christian Socialist trying to live his life as Christ would have done. It was serialized, pirated, and translated into sixteen languages. He edited the CHRISTIAN HERALD (1920–1925), and wrote an autobiography, *Charles M. Sheldon: His Life and Story* (1925).

Sheldon, Edward Brewster (1856–1946),   dramatist. In GEORGE PIERCE BAKER's Harvard playwriting course, Chicago-born Sheldon completed his first play, *Salvation Nell* (1907), which was produced in 1908. *The Nigger* (1909) dealt with the status of blacks and presented sympathetically a love story of people of mixed racial ancestry. Other plays followed quickly: *The Boss* and *Princess Zim-Zim* in 1911; *Egypt* and *The High Road* in 1912; *Romance* in 1913; and *The Song of Songs* and *The Garden of Paradise* in 1914. *The Jest* (1919), in blank verse, is an adaption of an Italian play. Though stricken with paralysis in 1923, Sheldon collaborated with SIDNEY HOWARD on *Bewitched* (1924), CHARLES MACARTHUR on *Lulu Belle* (1926), and MARGARET AYER BARNESS on *Dishonored Lady* (1930). Eric Barnes wrote a biography, *The Man Who Lived Twice* (1956), and Sheldon Rosen wrote a play about Sheldon and JOHN BARRYMORE, *Ned and Jack* (1981).

Shellabarger, Samuel (1888–1954),   historian, novelist. Born in Washington, D.C., and educated at Princeton, Harvard, and Munich universities, Shellabarger taught at Princeton from 1914 to 1923 and then retired to write. His work fell into three categories. He wrote scholarly biographies, *The Chevalier Bayard* (1928) and *Lord Chesterfield* (1935, rev. 1951). He wrote mysteries and light romances under the pseudonyms John Esteven and Peter Loring. He also wrote historical romances. Three deal with the Renaissance—Spain and Mexico in *Captain from Castile* (1945), Italy in *Prince of Foxes* (1947), and France in *The King's Cavalier* (1950). *Lord Vanity* (1953) recounts the fall of Quebec.

Shelton, Frederick William (1815–1881),   Protestant Episcopal clergyman, humorist. For a time Shelton, who was born in New York City, tried to make a living by writing humorous sketches for the KNICKERBOCKER MAGAZINE. In 1837, irritated by the descriptions of America that Mrs. Trollope and other visitors had published, he wrote *The Trolliopiad, or, Traveling Gentleman in America*, and dedicated the work, written in satirical couplets, to Mrs. Trollope. In 1847 he was ordained a minister of the Protestant Episcopal Church and occupied country parishes in New York and Vermont. He used some of his experiences as a preacher in his later writings. Among his books are *The Rector of St. Bardolph's, or, Superannuated* (1852); *Up the River* (1853); and *Peeps from a Belfry, or, The Parish Sketch Book* (1855).

Shenandoah (1888),   a play by BRONSON HOWARD. This Civil War play covers the entire period of the struggle. It involves two couples who go through many exciting experiences and present both the Northern and Southern points of view.

Shepard, Benjamin Henry Jesse Francis.   See FRANCIS GRIERSON.

Shepard, Odell (1884–1967),   scholar, essayist, novelist. Born in Illinois and educated at Northwestern, the University of Chicago, and Harvard, Shepard worked as a church organist, journalist, and English professor and served as lieutenant-governor of Connecticut (1940–1941). His published works include *Shakespeare Questions* (1916); *A Lonely Flue* (poems, 1917); *Bliss Carman* (1923); *The Harvest of a Quiet Eye* (1927); *The Joys of Forgetting* (1928); *The Lore of the Unicorn* (1929); *Thy Rod and Thy Creel* (1930); *Pedlar's Progress, The Life of Bronson Alcott* (Pulitzer Prize, 1937); and *Connecticut Past and Present* (1939). He also edited works of Thoreau, Alcott, and Longfellow, as well as several essay collections and college literature surveys. With his son Willard Odell Shepard, he wrote two historical novels—*Holdfast Gaines* (1946), whose hero is a Mohegan Indian, and *Jenkins' Ear* (1951), a narrative set in Horace Walpole's era.

Shepard, Sam (1943–   ),   playwright, actor, director. Born Samuel Shepard Roger, Jr., he began calling himself Sam Shepard when, after graduation from high school in Southern California, he began touring with a repertory company. His father was a bomber pilot in World War II, and Shepard was born on an Illinois army base. Until his father left the service in 1955, Sam lived on several bases, often alone with his mother.

He left his family's farm to write and tour as an actor, arriving in Greenwich Village in 1963. Soon he was writing for Off Off Broadway theater. His first two plays, *Cowboys* and *The Rock Garden*, premiered at the Theater Genesis in October 1964 and were favorably reviewed by the *Village Voice*. For the next few years, Shepard had two or three plays a year produced in small theaters, won several Obie Awards and Rockefeller and Guggeheim grants. He coauthored the screenplay for *Zabriskie Point* with Michelangelo Antonioni in 1970. Shepard and his wife and son moved to London, where he had several plays, including *The Tooth of Crime* (1972), successfully produced. They returned to California in 1974.

A trio of related plays on the theme of family discord—*Curse of the Starving Class* (1977); *Buried Child* (1978, Pulitzer Prize); and *True West* (1980)—confirmed Shepard's reputation as a gifted dramatist. His characters, fierce amalgams of lyricism and violence, struggle to define and assert their identities. The resulting tension, especially between fathers and sons and brothers, is a major theme. In twenty years, Shepard wrote more than forty plays and screenplays. *Fool for Love* (1983) won four Obie awards during its off Broadway run and was made into a movie (1985), with Shepard writing the screenplay and playing the male lead. Shepard has acted in several films, including the 1982 film biography of Frances Farmer. He was nominated for an Oscar in 1984 for his portrayal of test pilot Chuck Yeager in *The Right Stuff*.

His other important plays are *Angel City* (1976), *A Lie of the Mind* (1985), and *The Late Henry Moss* (2000). Collections include *Five Plays* (1967); *Action and the Unseen Hand: Two Plays* (1975); *Buried Child and Other Plays* (1979); *Four Two-Act Plays* (1980); *Seven Plays* (1981); and *Fool for Love and Other Plays* (1984). His stories are collected in *Hawk Moon* (1972) and *Cruising Paradise* (1996). *Rolling Thunder Logbook* (1977) is Shepard's account of the 1975 Bob Dylan tour. Critical studies include Bonnie Marranca, editor, *American Dreams: The Imagination of Sam Shepard* (1981); Ron Mottram, *Inner Landscapes: The Theater of Sam Shepard* (1984); and David DeRose, *Sam Shepard* (1992).

Shepard, Thomas (1605–1649),   clergyman, writer. Silenced in England because of his nonconformity, Shepard emigrated to New England and became pastor of a church in Newtown (later Cambridge), Massachusetts, succeeding THOMAS HOOKER, whose daughter he married. He was active in founding Harvard College. Among his books are *The Sincere Convert* (1641), which went through twenty editions up to 1812; *New England's Lamentation for Old England's Present Errors* (1645); and *Theses Sabbaticae* (1649). Other writings appeared posthumously, including a diary in 1747. N. Adams edited his *Autobiography* in 1832. *His Works* (3 v.) appeared in 1834.

Sheridan, Philip Henry (1831–1888),   soldier, memoirist, Sheridan, born in Albany, New York, was one of the chief Northern cavalry commanders in the Civil War. He took part in numerous battles, such as Chickamauga and the Battle of the Wilderness. During the Reconstruction period he was military governor of Texas and Louisiana. In 1867 he commanded the Department of Missouri and in 1883 succeeded Sherman as commander of the United States Army. Sheridan wrote *Personal Memoirs* (1888).

Sherman, Frank Dempster (1860–1916),   architect, teacher, poet. This noted architect, born in Peekskill, New York, taught graphics at Columbia University and was also a skilled writer of light verse. Among his volumes of verse are *Madrigals and Catches* (1887), *Lyrics for a Lute* (1890), *Little Folk Lyrics* (1892), and *Lyrics of Joy* (1904). Clinton Scollard edited a collection of his poems in 1917.

Sherman, Stuart P[ratt] (1881–1926),   teacher, critic, editor. Sherman, born in Iowa, was educated at Williams and Harvard and taught at Northwestern, then at Illinois (1907–1924). He engaged in many spirited contests with H. L. MENCKEN, who once refused to meet him. As editor of the book section of the New York *Tribune* (1924) he made it a lively place for criticism and discussion. Among his books are *Matthew Arnold: How to Know Him* (1917); *On Contemporary Literature* (1917); *Americans* (1922); *The Genius of America* (1923); *My Dear Cornelia* (1924); *Points of View* (1924); *Critical Woodcuts* (1926); *The Main Stream* (1927); and *The Emotional Discovery of America* (1932). Jacob Zeitlin and Homer Woodbridge prepared *The Life and Letters of Stuart P. Sherman* (2 v. 1929).

Sherman, William T[ecumseh] (1820–1891), soldier. Born in Ohio, Sherman served in the Mexican War and then was superintendent of a military academy in Alexandria, Louisiana. He was an outstanding Northern commander during the Civil War, became a major general in 1862, and succeeded Grant in the western command. On November 15, 1864, he ordered the burning of Atlanta and started his "march to the Sea," which cut the Confederacy in half. In a speech he made in Columbus, Ohio, on August 11, 1880, he remarked: "There is many a boy here today who looks on war as all glory, but, boys, it is all hell."

His *Memoirs* was published in 1875 (2 v.). Books about Sherman include J. D. Cox's *The March to the Sea* (1909); B. H. Liddell Hart's *Sherman—Soldier, Realist, American* (1929); Lloyd Lewis's *Sherman, Fighting Prophet* (1932); Earl Schenck Miers's *The General Who Marched to Hell* (1951); and R. G. Ahearn's *W. T. Sherman and the Settlement of the West* (1956). A potent war song was Henry Work's MARCHING THROUGH GEORGIA (1865). Sherman figures in Maurice Thompson's *His Second Campaign* (1883), Winston Churchill's THE CRISIS (1901), Mary Johnston's *Cease Firing* (1912), and John Brick's *Jubilee* (1956).

Sherwood, Robert E[mmet] (1896–1955), playwright, editor, biographer. Sherwood was preeminently a man of the theater, but his wide interests, particularly in politics, led him into many other fields and greatly affected the outlook in his plays. He was born in New Rochelle, New York, and attended Milton Academy. His education at Harvard was interrupted by World War I. He served in the Canadian Black Watch Regiment, was gassed at Vimy Ridge, and was wounded in both legs at Amiens. The war left him with a bitter resolution to do all he could to stop future wars. This attitude is apparent in *Acropolis* (1933), a play opposing militarism, and *Idiot's Delight* (1936), a pacifist drama that won a Pulitzer Prize. When Sherwood returned from the war, he became drama critic of *Vanity Fair* (1919), from which he and Robert Benchley resigned in 1920 because their coworker Dorothy Parker had been discharged for writing an unfavorable review. He then became associate editor and later editor of *Life* (1920–28). He also served as movie critic for *Life* and was one of the first to apply serious critical standards to motion pictures. Sherwood was also one of the wits and writers who gathered at the Algonquin Hotel's Round Table.

Sherwood's first play to be viewed seriously was *Barnum Was Right* (1917), written while he was still at Harvard; it was produced by the Hasty Pudding Club. At the time he was also editor of the Harvard *Lampoon*. His first Broadway production was *The Road to Rome* (1927), an attack on the concept of military glory. There followed *The Love Nest* (1927), an unsuccess-

ful work based on a Ring Lardner short story; *The Queen's Husband* (1928), an unflattering portrayal of Queen Marie Alexandra Victoria of Rumania; *Waterloo Bridge* (1930), a sentimental story of love between a prostitute and a young man; *This is New York* (1930), a play in which New York City's sophistication is contrasted with the Midwest's provincialism; *Reunion in Vienna* (1931), a superb comedy of 1930 Viennese society; *The Petrified Forest* (1935), in which gangsters who take over a desert filling station embody his theme of materialism versus idealism; ABE LINCOLN IN ILLINOIS (1938), a masterful portrait of Abraham Lincoln that won a Pulitzer Prize; *There Shall Be No Night* (1940), about a Finnish pacifist who decides to fight against the Nazis and thereby sacrifices his life; *The Rugged Path* (1945), an uneven work about a lonely journalist posthumously awarded the Congressional Medal of Honor; and *Small War on Murray Hill* (1957). He wrote one novel, *The Virtuous Knight* (1931). He wrote the screenplay for the movie based on Daphne du Maurier's *Rebecca* (1940). The movie of his screenplay *The Best Years of Our Lives* (1946), based on MACKINLAY KANTOR's *Glory for Me*, won seven Academy Awards. He also wrote for television and, at the time of his death in 1955, was under contract with NBC to write nine plays.

A number of Sherwood's plays contributed to a cause he espoused in the 1930s, the endeavor to hold the line against European totalitarian regimes and marshal American opinion against them. In opposition to fascism, he helped organize the Committee to Defend America by Aiding the Allies, and he gave generously of his royalties to the American Red Cross and Finnish Relief. In World War II, Franklin D. Roosevelt made Sherwood special assistant to the Secretary of War and the Secretary of the Navy, then director of overseas operations in the Office of War Information. Sherwood helped Roosevelt write some of his most memorable speeches. He recorded his war service in *Roosevelt and Hopkins* (1948), a book that won a Pulitzer Prize and other awards.

Sherwood's emotionally devastating experiences in World War I created his strong antiwar position. However, his equally strong opposition to the rise of European fascism led to a modification of this position and found expression in his tension-filled plays emphasizing idealism and opposing materialism. Using a variety of dramatic forms, such as melodrama, satire, and biography, Sherwood became one of the most notable American writers of pacifist and antiwar plays in the first half of the 20th century. John Mason Brown wrote *The Worlds of Robert E. Sherwood: Mirror to His Times* (1962) and *The Ordeal of a Playwright: Robert E. Sherwood and the Challenge of War* (1970).

FRANKLIN D. CASE

She Would Be a Soldier, or, The Plains of Chippewa (1819), a play by Mordecai M. Noah. Set during a battle of the War of 1812, it concerns Christine who, in the folk tradition, disguises herself as a man to visit her soldier-lover, Lenox. She is seized as a spy but is rescued by her lover.

Shields, Carol (1935–   ), novelist. Born Carol Warner in Oak Park, Illinois, she was educated at Hanover College (B.A., 1957) and the University of Ottawa (M.A.,

1975). After her marriage to Donald Shields, she moved to Canada and became a naturalized Canadian (1971) with dual citizenship. For years she lived the traditional life of a professor's wife, bearing five children and managing her household. At forty she began to write. Her first books were poetry collections, *Others* (1972) and *Intersect* (1974), and literary criticism, *Susanna Moodie: Voice and Vision* (1976). Alice Munro's letter of praise for Shields's first novel, *Small Ceremonies* (1976), began a friendship between two of Canada's best known writers of fiction. Other novels include *The Box Garden* (1977), *Happenstance* (1980), *A Fairly Conventional Woman* (1982), *Swann: A Mystery* (1987), and *The Republic of Love* (1992). Shields came to international attention when *The Stone Diaries* (1993) won the Governor General's Award and the Pulitzer Prize, and was short-listed for the Booker Prize. The novel is a biography of the fictional octogenarian Daisy Goodwill Flett, illustrated with carefully selected antique photos. Straddling geographical and genre borders, it traces the lives of ordinary people from a Manitoba mining town through Indiana, back to Canada, and finally to Florida. With Blanche Howard, Shields wrote an epistolary novel *A Celibate Season* (1991). *Various Miracles* (1989) and *The Orange Fish* (1990) are collections of short fiction. *Coming to Canada*, poetry, appeared in 1992, and the novel *Larry's Party* in 1997. With her daughter Catherine she wrote *Fashion, Power, Guilt, and the Charity of Families* (1995). *Departures and Arrivals* (1990) and *Thirteen Hands* (1994) are plays.

Shillaber, Benjamin Penhallow ["Mrs. Partington"] (1814–1890), printer, newspaperman, humorist. Shillaber, born in New Hampshire, after working as a printer and on the Boston *Post*, found that a character he had created for the *Post*, MRS. RUTH PARTINGTON, was so popular with the public that he could make a career out of reporting her misadventures and remarks. He founded a humorous weekly named THE CARPET-BAG, which won wide circulation in the West and Southwest. In it appeared the first recorded publication of MARK TWAIN, a sketch of life in Hannibal entitled *The Dandy Frightening the Squatter* (May 1, 1852). He followed up *The Life and Sayings of Mrs. Partington* (1854), a best seller, with *Partington Patchwork* (1872). Shillaber wrote an account of his life in the *New England Magazine* (June 1893–May 1894).

Shipman, Samuel (1883–1937), playwright. Shipman, born in New York City, was a skillful theatrical technician who wrote a number of successful plays, including *The Crooked Square* (1923); *Friendly Enemies*, with Aaron Hoffman (1918); *Children of Today* (1926); *Cheaper to Marry* (1924); and *Crime*, with John B. Hymer (1927).

Shirer, William (1904–1993), foreign correspondent, radio newscaster, novelist. Shirer, born in Illinois, was a reporter for the Paris edition of the Chicago *Tribune* and a CBS radio newscaster who observed the rise of Nazi power in Europe. His *Berlin Diary* (1941), *End of a Berlin Diary* (1947), *The Rise and Fall of the Third Reich* (1960), *The Rise and Fall of Adolph Hitler* (1961), and *The Collapse of the Third Republic* (1969) detail the history of German fascism and World War II.

His other nonfiction works are *Midcentury Journey* (1952) and *20th Century Journey* (1976). In 1990, Shirer updated his memoirs with *20th Century Journey: Volume Three 1945–1988*. *The Traitor* (1950), *Stranger Come Home* (1954), and *The Consul's Wife* (1956) are novels. *This Is Berlin* (1999) is a posthumous collection of Shirer's radio reports of the late 1930s.

Shirley, William (1694–1771), colonial administrator, military leader. Shirley came to America from England (1731) with strong imperialistic views and expressed them freely when he was made governor of Massachusetts in 1741. He planned the expedition against Louisburg (1745) and wrote *A Journal of the Siege of Louisburg* (1746). He continued as governor until 1749, when he went to England and France to serve on the commission that determined the boundary line between New England and French North America. On his return he was again appointed governor and became a major general at the outbreak of the French and Indian Wars. But his campaigns were unsuccessful. He became unpopular, was recalled to England in 1756, and from 1767 was governor of the Bahamas. He defended himself in a publication called *Conduct of General William Shirley* (1758). His *Correspondence, 1731–60* was edited by C. H. Lincoln (2 v. 1912).

Shock of Recognition, The (1943), an anthology edited by EDMUND WILSON. This is a gathering of literary documents chronicling the progress of literature in the U.S. It includes important essays, poems, parodies, biographical sketches, letters, and other materials. It begins with James Russell Lowell and Edgar Allan Poe and concludes with H. L. Mencken, John Dos Passos, and Sherwood Anderson.

Shooting of Dan McGrew, The (1907), a poem by ROBERT W. SERVICE. The poem, which has circulated in millions of copies, concerns the fate of "Dangerous Dan McGrew," a Yukon desperado. See KLONDIKE GOLD RUSH.

Shore Acres (1893), a play by JAMES A. HERNE. This was a radical revision of his earlier play *The Hawthornes* (1889) and was itself first performed as *Shore Acres Subdivision* and as *Uncle Nat*. It is the story of two brothers, one self-sacrificing, the other aggressive, and is on the whole a somewhat somber study of life in Maine.

Short Happy Life of Francis Macomber, The (1938), a short story by ERNEST HEMINGWAY. In this compact, suspenseful story, the Macombers, an American couple, are on a safari in Africa with the Englishman Wilson as their guide. Macomber's courage is tested when he wounds a lion and then runs away in fear; his wife is disgusted at his actions. Next day he is charged by a wounded buffalo; his wife, shooting from a car, misses the buffalo and kills her husband.

Short, Luke [Frederick D. Glidden] (1908–1975), novelist. Frederick Glidden, born in Illinois, took a degree in journalism at the University of Missouri (1930). He tried newspaper work, trapping, and mining before becoming a successful writer of Western novels, using the pseudonym Luke Short. His more than sixty titles range from early cowboy adventures to modern Western detective plots. The scenes often were set in New Mexico or Colorado. Several titles, including *Gunman's Chance* (1941), *Ambush* (1949), and *Rimrock* (1955), were serialized in the *Saturday Evening Post, Adventure,* or *Collier's.* The plots of *Dead Freight for Piute* (1940), *Ramrod* (1943), *High Vermilion* (1948), and many others were used in movies.

Short Story: Before 1945.   The short story, the most recent of recognized literary forms, is the only genre in which American authors could participate from the beginning. It was in the United States, early in the 19th century, that the short story emerged as a form capable of engaging the interest of all major writers of fiction. An American author was the first to use the term "short story" to describe his collection of prose tales, and it was an American writer who attempted the first significant definition.

This does not mean that the short prose narrative was unknown before the early 1800s. We have examples from ancient cultures that go as far back as the 8th century B.C. There are, however, significant differences between early narratives, generally known as tales, and what we have come to know as the short story. Early tales were either parts of a larger whole, as in Boccaccio's *Decameron,* or were other than literary, as in the Greek legends and the parables of the New Testament. By the 19th century, tales had turned into the beginnings of the modern short story, most notably in Washington Irving's THE SKETCH BOOK OF GEOFFREY CRAYON and Sir Walter Scott's *Chronicles of the Canongate.*

The concept of the short tale as a individual work of art, however, received its most memorable early expression in EDGAR ALLAN POE's review of NATHANIEL HAWTHORNE's *Twice-Told Tales in Graham's Magazine* (1842). Poe professed to have discovered genius of a high order in Hawthorne's book and proceeded to generalize on the critical principles that seemed to provide the order of the tales. The first use of the term "story," however, appears to have come somewhat later, when Henry James, also an admirer of Hawthorne, titled one of his collections *Daisy Miller: A Study; and Other Stories* (1883). Since that time "short story" has become the commonly accepted name for the form Poe first sought to define.

Perhaps the most significant fact about Poe's writing on the short story—aside from his serious and sympathetic reading of Hawthorne—was his emphatic statement that this form belongs "to the loftiest region of art." He said further that the writer of short fiction should not fashion his thoughts to accommodate his incidents, "but having conceived with deliberate care a certain unique or single *effect* to be wrought out, he then invents such incidents—he then combines such events as may best aid him in establishing his preconceived effects." Poe warned that "if his very initial sentence tend not to the out bringing of this effect, then he has failed in his first step. In the whole composition there should be no word written, of which the tendency, direct or indirect, is not to the one pre-established design."

Poe's emphasis on unity, economy, and self-containment is an attitude that has guided short-story writers to the present day; and it is one of Poe's concepts that so impressed the French poet Charles Baudelaire, and through him influenced a whole generation of 19th-century European writers. Less significant was Poe's method, which probably appears more mechanical than he intended and was possibly aimed at authors whose writing was too didactic to serve his higher purpose. Behind Poe's attempts at definition, however, resides the significant recognition that the importance of the short story lies in its capability to examine and portray the inner workings of the mind, either as it affects experience or is affected by it. Such well-known stories by Poe as THE GOLD BUG and THE PURLOINED LETTER exemplify the first type, which he called ratiocinative, in which the mind exercises a certain control over nature. Such stories as THE FALL OF THE HOUSE OF USHER and LIGEIA portray the second, which Poe called "tales of atmosphere or effect," in which the mind is affected by the unusual and the unknown.

Most of Hawthorne's tales contained the atmosphere and singleness of effect that Poe demanded. They appear, however, to have been motivated by Hawthorne's essential disagreement with the dominant New England attitude of his day, as exemplified by Ralph Waldo Emerson and the transcendentalists, the attitude that celebrated the virtue of innocence and saw in nature a fundamental benevolence. Hawthorne's short fiction examined past and present American life, revealed beneath its surface a world of evil, and warned against the dangers of failure to recognize and come to grips with that evil. More so than Poe's style, Hawthorne's style incorporated the voice of the native American as it had come to him through the oral tradition and from his New England Yankee neighbors, a style which was to be extended by the school of native humorists culminating in Mark Twain.

Although Hawthorne was later to refer to his stories as "blasted allegories"—they contained a didactic element that sometimes troubled Poe—he produced a notable body of work, particularly in such volumes as TWICE-TOLD TALES, MOSSES FROM AN OLD MANSE, and THE SNOW IMAGE AND OTHER TWICE-TOLD TALES. The best of them convey a sense of reality that make them moving human experiences, not merely thought-provoking exercises.

Hawthorne's most immediate influence among his contemporaries was made on HERMAN MELVILLE, who read Hawthorne when he was preparing to write his masterwork, MOBY-DICK, and in the same period in which he discovered Shakespeare. In his enthusiasm for Hawthorne, Melville did not hesitate to rank him almost as Shakespeare's equal, finding in him, as he expressed it, the soul of America as well as its voice. Most significantly, Melville accepted Hawthorne's antitranscendentalist attitude, particularly as it reflected the dangers of innocence and the reality of evil.

Melville arrived at the short-story form late in his career. PIAZZA TALES appeared in 1856, ten years after his first novel, *Typee,* and five years after publication of *Moby-Dick.* His stories appeared at a time when his reputation had ebbed, so that full appreciation of such works as BENITO CERENO and BARTLEBY THE SCRIVENER, two masterpieces of the American short story, had to await the revival of Melville's reputation in the 20th century.

HENRY JAMES, probably the most prolific of all American short-story writers, was also affected by Nathaniel Hawthorne. Early in his career he wrote an appreciative study of Hawthorne that appeared as the first volume in the distinguished English Men of Letters series. James published two volumes of stories before producing his first novel; eight more collections followed. He also wrote brilliantly on the craft of fiction, examining both the novel and the short-story forms. At one point he stated: "To write a series of good little tales I deem ample work for a lifetime." He was concerned with the matter of the form of fiction, as Poe had been, but his interest in problems of form and style came probably from the French writers whom Poe influenced, not directly from Poe himself. James discussed the obligations of the writer of fiction with a thoroughness, sensitivity, and erudition unusual in an American of his day. Among James's best-known short stories are "The Real Thing," "The Liar," "The Lesson of the Master," "The Beast in the Jungle," and "The Altar of the Dead," and these are just a few of his many excellent short works.

Contemporary with James, but offering an interesting contrast, is MARK TWAIN, who emerged as a writer of fiction directly from the school of native American humorists that flourished in the popular press and on the lecture platforms of the country in the 19th century. His first and probably best-known tale is THE CELEBRATED JUMPING FROG OF CALAVERAS COUNTY (1867). Much of Twain's early work was more suited to the lecture platform than to the pages of literature, told as it was in the voice of the humorous narrator, relating exaggerated anecdotes and tall tales from the folk tradition (see TALL TALES AND TALL TALK); but it was in the telling of such crude tales that he learned the particular craft that was to produce one of America's finest novels and a group of excellent short stories. This craft, which was the use of the American voice as a mask through which significant aspects of American life could be presented and commented upon, was to have a marked effect on most American short-story writing to follow. Twain's best stories were written late in his career, some of them colored by the pessimism that clouded that period of his life. Among them are "The £1,000,000 Bank-Note," THE MAN THAT CORRUPTED HADLEYBURG, and THE MYSTERIOUS STRANGER.

By the close of Twain's career the first important period in American fiction had come to an end. In the years that followed—roughly, the last decade of the 19th century and the first decade of the 20th—American fiction-writing languished, and the authors who represented it were divided into two contrasting factions. One of these was marked by self-conscious aestheticism and sentimentality; the other, by a kind of energetic and rugged honesty. Among the first group were the writers of the genteel tradition, writers for the popular press and pseudo-aesthetes. They included such writers as T. B. ALDRICH, LAFCADIO HEARN, AMBROSE BIERCE, O. HENRY, and BRET HARTE. Among the second were the realists and naturalists, such as WILLIAM DEAN HOWELLS, SARAH ORNE JEWETT, KATE CHOPIN, MARY E. WILKINS FREEMAN, HAMLIN GARLAND, EDITH WHARTON, FRANK NORRIS, and JACK LONDON. Some of the latter group, however, were more significant as novelists than as writers of short stories.

There is, however, an outstanding exception in the person of STEPHEN CRANE, whose writing career lasted only eight years, from publication of his novel *Maggie: A Girl of the Streets* (1892) to his death in 1900. In his early work in the short story, as in his first novel, Crane began by choosing to ally himself with the social realists, particularly Howells and Garland, because he believed them to be mostly concerned with "the truth." As his career continued, his subject matter broadened and his craft improved. From a preoccupation with the plight of the socially dispossessed, such as he displayed in his *Bowery Tales*, he moved to a concern with mankind confronted by a violent but impassive nature. This theme is explored most skillfully in such stories as THE OPEN BOAT, "The Bride Comes to Yellow Sky," and THE BLUE HOTEL. Crane's style contains elements of the school of native humorists, sobered and refined. This style, as well as his concern for man's action when confronted by an indifferent nature, was to have great effect on short-story writers to follow in the 20th century. Before the full effects of Crane's example could be felt, however, two writers intervened whose interests were more nearly allied to those of the social realists. They were THEODORE DREISER and SHERWOOD ANDERSON. Dreiser's early novels appeared at the turn of the 20th century, but his first collection of short stories was not published until 1918. Anderson, whose first novel appeared in 1916, published his first collection of short stories in 1917, and his collection WINESBURG, OHIO in 1919. Dreiser's short stories are, for the most part, less works of genuinely literary interest than they are case histories of characters suffering social injustice. Sherwood Anderson, much impressed by the new psychology and disheartened by a society moving from an agrarian culture to industrialism, likewise wrote many stories that appear to be more psychological or sociological studies than genuine short stories.

At their best, however, both authors wrote a few stories of lasting interest. In "The Lost Phoebe," Dreiser presented a self-contained and pathetic instance of the failure of American rural family life. Anderson, in THE TRIUMPH OF THE EGG, displayed a genuine flair for comedy of the gentler sort, while in such stories as "I'm a Fool" and "I Want to Know Why," he portrayed the gropings and yearnings of adolescence with an understanding and an objectivity that avoided the sentimentality so obvious in much of his work. Perhaps the greatest service Dreiser and Anderson performed in the American short story lay not so much in their own work as in the role they played in opposing the timid editorial standards that prevailed during most of their careers. By so doing, they prepared the way for the significant work that was to appear after World War I, a considerable body of short stories by such authors as HEMINGWAY, FAULKNER, FITZGERALD, KATHERINE ANNE PORTER, RING LARDNER, and STEINBECK.

Hemingway's acknowledged masters were Mark Twain and Stephen Crane. In Twain he believed he had found the true voice of America. In Crane he saw not only a further development of Twain's style, but also an attitude toward nature that seemed more vital for his time than Twain's relative benevolence, and an attitude toward society more appropriate than that of Henry James. Hemingway chose as subject for his stories those moments of physical crisis that demand courage. Like Crane, he adopted the concept of the code as a means of achieving "grace under pressure," Hemingway's definition of courage. He seems to have taken a hint from Crane's use of simple sentences and terse speech to develop his own stylistic method of ironic understatement. During his apprentice years in Europe Hemingway came under the tutelage of Ford Madox Ford and Gertrude Stein and was introduced to the works of Henry James, Conrad, and such French authors as de Maupassant, Dumas, Daudet, Stendhal, Flaubert, Baudelaire, and Rimbaud (from whom he said he learned his craft). From these authors, particularly the French poets and novelists, Hemingway received the influence of Edgar Allan Poe in perhaps its most significant form. From this time on few Americans would take the craft of the short story more lightly than had Poe or those Europeans whom Poe had affected.

Hemingway published three volumes of short stories—IN OUR TIME (1924), MEN WITHOUT WOMEN (1927), and WINNER TAKE NOTHING (1933)—in addition to his collected edition, THE FIFTH COLUMN AND THE FIRST FORTY-NINE STORIES (1938), in which appeared four previously uncollected stories. Among his best-known stories are "The Undefeated," THE KILLERS, "A Clean Well-Lighted Place," THE SHORT HAPPY LIFE OF FRANCIS MACOMBER, "The Capital of the World," and THE SNOWS OF KILIMANJARO.

Faulkner, growing up in the South, found his subject in the changes that had taken place in society as reflected primarily in pre–Civil War times and our own day. Of a generation that still felt the effects of the destruction of the Old South and yet was aware of the rise of a new society, Faulkner reflects in his short stories, as in his novels, a pervading sense of loss as well as a concern for what superseded the old manners and customs. He presents a postwar society that is made up almost equally of characters who cling futilely to the old ideals and characters who have accepted, or come to terms with, the present. In addition, he hints at an overriding judgment based on natural virtues that will "endure" and "prevail." Faulkner published two volumes of short stories, These Thirteen (1931) and Doctor Martino, and Other Stories (1934), in addition to his Collected Stories (1950). However, he wrote other collections of related short stories, such as The Unvanquished (1938), GO DOWN MOSES, AND OTHER STORIES (1942), and Knight's Gambit (1949), none of which are included in the Collected Stories. He is best known for such stories as "A Rose for Emily," "That Evening Sun," "Wash," "Spotted Horses," and "The Bear."

Fitzgerald, along with Hemingway, has long been considered a spokesman for the so-called lost generation, the writers who started their careers after World War I. The term "lost generation" appears today to have less significance than was once thought, but it does serve a purpose if it is seen as merely another manifestation of what has existed from the start in the writing of the American short story. Insofar as the writers of the 1920s reflected disillusion with the past, they made common cause with earlier writers who portrayed the decay of Western traditions in the art and society of Europe—such as Hawthorne, who surveyed a world of evil in human society, or Melville, who saw the years since the French Revolution as "a crisis of Christendom," or Henry James, who portrayed the decay of the old morals and the old manners.

Fitzgerald's "sad young men" sought meaning and beauty in a world that could provide them with only momentary sensation. Such an attitude was a reaction to the idealism and the optimism of the past, as well as a representation of the sterility of the present, but it offered little hope except the example of individual heroism at great cost and against great odds. The young men of Fitzgerald's stories generally came out of the West, as he himself had come from St. Paul, to astound and captivate but finally to succumb to the weight of social restrictions of which they appeared to be unaware. That their frantic search for happiness was more innocent and less evil than the glitter that attracted them we learn from the pictures of the rich and successful in such short stories as "A Diamond as Big as the Ritz," "May-Day," and "The Rich Boy." The full consequence of that innocence is explored in a late story, "Babylon Revisited," in which Fitzgerald has his principal character recognize and acknowledge his irresponsibility. These and other stories appeared in four volumes: Flappers and Philosophers (1920), Tales of the Jazz Age (1922), All the Sad Young Men (1926), and Taps at Reveille (1935). A posthumous collection, Selected Stories, appeared in 1951.

Katherine Anne Porter, a native of Texas, began publishing her short stories in the late 1920s. Her output was not large, but she maintained a consistently high quality in her writing. Her subjects were drawn from her own background: life in the South, in Mexico, and in Europe. Her attitude toward her material shows clearly the result of her Roman Catholic upbringing, her travels, and her interest in social causes. Her first published volume was a limited edition of a few stories published under the title Flowering Judas (1930). In 1935 this book was expanded and printed in a regular trade edition. A second volume, Pale Horse, Pale Rider, containing three long stories, appeared in 1939. The Leaning Tower and Other Stories, which contained eight short stories and the long title story, was published in 1944.

Ring Lardner, a Midwestern sports reporter at the time he began writing stories about baseball in 1918, developed a style similar to Mark Twain's in that it used the vernacular as a source of ironic comment on American society just prior to and following World War I. His best work is contained in two volumes, The Big Town (1921) and Round Up (1929). His most widely known stories are "Haircut" and "Golden Honeymoon."

John Steinbeck, a Californian, began publishing in the late 1920s, but he remained singularly unaffected by the influences on most of his contemporaries. Steinbeck produced a respectable body of short fiction, the best of which is contained in the volume The Long Valley (1938). His stories are concerned mostly with people in their relationship to nature, but less the indifferent nature of Crane and Hemingway than the more benevolent kind of Twain's *Huckleberry Finn*. Wary of sophistication and of urban social values, Steinbeck celebrates the virtues of a life lived close to the soil.

One of the most interesting features of the American short story in the period after World War I was the rise of a group of writers from the Southern states, many of whom seemed more at home in the short story than in the novel. Besides Faulkner and Porter, this group includes ERSKINE CALDWELL, CAROLINE GORDON, ROBERT PENN WARREN, and EUDORA WELTY. After World War II, new voices arose from other areas and from a variety of cultural backgrounds.

Useful studies include Arthur Hobson Quinn, *American Fiction: An Historical and Critical Survey* (1936); Ray B. West, Jr., *The Short Story in America: 1900–1950* (1952); and Arthur Voss, *The American Short Story: A Critical Survey* (1973).

RAY B. WEST, JR./GP

Short Story: Since 1945.   The writers in the period since 1945 cannot be discussed with the same assurance with which Hawthorne and Hemingway can be discussed. It is impossible to predict with certainty which of the established and rising authors of the 20th century will be read in the 21st century. Nevertheless, it is clear enough that in the years since the end of World War II the short story developed partly through trends that are indices of the social changes in the nation as a whole. With few exceptions, such as SARAH ORNE JEWETT, KATE CHOPIN, and KATHERINE ANNE PORTER, the short story had largely been the province of white Christian men. Since 1945 this has ceased to be the case, as the work of women, African-Americans, Jews, Orientals, Native Americans, and other marginalized groups has become increasingly important on the literary scene.

A roll call of important women short-story writers since 1945 would include ANN BEATTIE (1947–   ), GAIL GODWIN (1937–   ), SHIRLEY JACKSON (1919–65), URSULA K. LEGUIN (1929–   ), BOBBIE ANN MASON (1940–   ), CARSON MCCULLERS (1917–67), JOYCE CAROL OATES (1938–   ), FLANNERY O'CONNOR (1925–64), TILLIE OLSEN (1913–   ), GRACE PALEY (1922–   ), and JAYNE ANNE PHILLIPS (1952–   ). At present the firmest candidate for immortality among these is O'Connor, a Catholic writer whose Gothic narratives of pain, loss, crime, and violent death in the South are revealing of the paradoxes of Christianity: the last shall be first, out of hatred comes love, and he that would save his life shall lose it. Her most frequently reprinted story, "A Good Man Is Hard to Find," centers on a sociopath, The Misfit, whose crimes, like those of Dostoevsky's great sinners, are a perverse response to his faith. O'Connor's collections include *A Good Man Is Hard to Find* (1953) and *Everything That Rises Must Converge* (1965). Her *Complete Stories* appeared in 1971.

Some of the African-American short-story writers of this period are JAMES BALDWIN (1924–1987), TONI CADE BAMBARA (1939–1995), RALPH ELLISON (1914–1994), ERNEST J. GAINES (1933–   ), PAULE MARSHALL (1929–   ), JAMES ALAN MCPHERSON (1943–   ), ALICE WALKER (1944–   ), and RICHARD WRIGHT (1908–1960), whose *Uncle Tom's Children*

(1938) and *Eight Men* (1960) helped initiate this rich tradition. Perhaps the best-known tale by this group is Baldwin's "Sonny's Blues," from *Going to Meet the Man* (1965). It is an emotionally wringing story, structured musically with the theme-and-variations form of a jazz composition, about the varied response to suffering and prejudice in three generations of an African-American family. It centers on a jazz pianist, recently released from drug treatment in prison, and his efforts to reclaim his creativity while remaining "clean."

Jewish writers since 1945 have included SAUL BELLOW (1915–   ), HAROLD BRODKEY (1930–1996), STANLEY ELKIN (1930–1995), BERNARD MALAMUD (1914–86), NORMAN MAILER (1923–   ), Leonard Michaels (1933–   ), CYNTHIA OZICK (1928–   ), PHILIP ROTH (1933–   ), and ISAAC BASHEVIS SINGER (1904–1991), whose magical tales set in prewar Poland and refugee-strewn America—written in Yiddish and published in translation—have been influential on these and other American writers. The American-born Jewish writer whose work most resembles Singer's is Malamud, whose best stories—like "The Magic Barrel," from a volume of the same title (1958)—speak in a vivid nervous idiom and convey Talmudic wisdom, resignation in the face of suffering, and the irony inherent in the Jewish experience. Other minority writers of importance include the Chinese-Americans MAXINE HONG KINGSTON (1940–   ) and AMY TAN (1952–   ), the Indian-American BHARATI MUKHERJEE (1940–   ), and the Native Americans N. SCOTT MOMADAY (1934–   ) and LESLIE MARMON SILKO (1948–   ).

Fiction since 1945 also ceased to be primarily the product of the East and Midwest; in fact, the Southern and Appalachian regions, hard hit by the Depression of the 1930s and long bypassed by postwar prosperity, have played an unusually large part in the development of the short story. In addition to the Southern-born women and African-Americans already mentioned above, this group would include TRUMAN CAPOTE (1924–87), BARRY HANNAH (1942–   ), WALKER PERCY (1916–1990), and PETER TAYLOR (1917–1994).

These Southern writers have tended to operate within the framework of realism but with a strong lyrical streak in the tradition of Faulkner and Katherine Anne Porter.

A second form of influence on the development of the short story has been the collapse of the national weekly periodicals, like the *Saturday Evening Post*, that had previously been important markets for established writers and showcases for new talents. There remain periodicals publishing stories for relatively sophisticated tastes—*The New Yorker, Atlantic*, and some of the LITTLE MAGAZINES—and those publishing stories for popular tastes, such as *Cosmopolitan* and *Playboy*, but the middlebrow magazines that brought Fitzgerald and Faulkner to the masses are gone. The result is that periodical publication is less lucrative for all but a few authors. Proportionally fewer stories are published and read—aside from the weekly *New Yorker*, the main vehicles are monthlies and quarterlies—and a rift developed between highbrow and mass audiences that had once had important points of contact. *The New Yorker* has taken the place once held by the *Saturday Evening Post* as the center of the more artistically respectable market, and there has developed an easily recognizable genre known as the New Yorker short story—realistic in mode, cosmopolitan in values, ironic in tone, essentially Chekhovian in structure, and recounting a small incident that results in a major epiphany.

The central practitioners of this genre have been, successively, J. D. SALINGER (1919–   ), JOHN CHEEVER (1912–1982), JOHN UPDIKE (1932–   ), and ANN BEATTIE (1947–   ) Salinger's stories were immensely admired and imitated for their freshness of language and sensitivity to eccentric characters until the author's withdrawal into total silence since 1965 cast doubt on their aesthetic, which has since come to seem elitist and sentimental. "For Esme, With Love and Squalor," from *Nine Stories* (1953), perhaps his most reprinted piece, recounts the descent of an American intelligence officer into wartime despair and his rescue by the memory of a few moments in the company of a precocious orphan. Salinger's other collections include *Franny and Zooey* (1961) and *Raise High the Roofbeam, Carpenters* (1959).

Cheever's larger output was devoted almost exclusively to the mating customs and leisure pursuits of the martini-sipping upper-middle-class commuters of Westchester County, north of Manhattan, whom he treated with baleful affection and savage irony. Cheever's realism sometimes slips through the looking-glass into a more surrealistic mode, as in "The Swimmer," whose initially prosperous and uxorious protagonist, Neddy Merrill, starts swimming home through the pools of his neighbors, and ends what seems to be a single afternoon exhausted, aging, divorced, and unemployed. Cheever's stories are collected in *The Way Some People Live* (1943), *The Enormous Radio* (1953), *The Housebreaker of Shady Hill* (1958), *Some People, Places and Things That Will Not Appear in My Next Novel* (1961), *The Brigadier and the Golf Widow* (1964), and *The World of Apples* (1973). *The Stories of John Cheever*, a collection, was published in 1978.

John Updike's characters, like Cheever's, are sometimes from Manhattan or from its suburbs, more often from the New England or Mid-Atlantic hinterlands. Updike is a more dogged realist than Cheever, an explorer of the religious convictions remaining in today's secular society, the class barriers remaining in the open weave of suburbia, and the ambiguity of contemporary sexual mores. His stories are collected in *The Same Door* (1959), *Pigeon Feathers* (1962), *The Music School* (1966), *Museums and Women* (1972), *Problems*, (1979), *Too Far to Go* (1979), *Trust Me* (1987), and *The Afterlife: And Other Stories* (1994).

Anne Beattie is a realist closer to Updike than to Cheever, but as a woman from a later and hipper generation, she is more apt to chronicle the misprisions and disappointments of the bohemian lumpen-intelligentsia whose reading of Kafka and Proust has not prepared them for the emptiness of their own lives. Beattie's collections include *Distortions* (1976), *Secrets and Surprises* (1978), *The Burning House* (1982), and *Park City* (1998).

This is not to say that *The New Yorker* published only "New Yorker short stories." Simultaneously with Updike and Beattie, *The New Yorker* also published the surrealistic short stories of DONALD BARTHELME (1931–89), perhaps the most popular and accessible of the postmodern storytellers. Barthelme's stories operate without conventional plots and characters. Instead, we hear voices parodying the commonplace patter and rhythm of contemporary speech and writing, together with a sort of literary montage that comically or satirically juxtaposes fads with philosophy, fine art, and advertising jingles. His art was designed to situate itself on what he called "the leading edge of the trash phenomenon." Barthelme's pieces are collected in *Come Back, Dr. Caligari* (1964), *Unspeakable Pleasures, Unnatural Acts* (1968), *City Life* (1970), *Guilty Pleasures* (1974), *Great Days* (1979), *Paradise* (1986), and *Forty Stories* (1987).

Barthelme typifies a branch of postmodern literary art that tends to parody and stylize modes of current discourse. Other experimental practitioners of the short story, such as ROBERT COOVER (1932–   ) and JOHN BARTH (1930–   ), have taken as their principal theme the need of man to make fictions; the stories themselves become a vertiginous hall of mirrors in which reality is always revealed as another level of artifice. Coover's stories in *Pricksongs and Descants* (1969) and *A Night at the Movies* (1987), such as "The Babysitter" and "The Gingerbread House," recreate in a variety of literary styles the central myths of American culture: folk tales, dirty jokes, and other familiar fictional forms spiral apparently out of control into anti-versions revised beyond imagination. Barth's stories in *Lost in the Funhouse* (1968) present, sometimes in a vivid and poignant human context, but often quite abstractly, the paradoxes of the self-contained fictional world. Less programmatic in his postmodernism was VLADIMIR NABOKOV (1899–1977), born in Russia and perhaps the finest stylist ever to write English as an adopted language. Nabokov's acknowledged master was James Joyce—another expatriate—and, his stories, like those of Joyce, recreate with a complex multi-leveled technique the longings and disillusionments of nostalgic exiles within the vulgar and healthy-minded American society that Nabokov both hated and loved. Nabokov's American stories are primarily collected in *Nabokov's Dozen* (1971) and *Details of a Sunset* (1976).

In addition to Barthelme, Barth, Coover, and Nabokov, postmodernism is represented in the stories of WILLIAM GASS (1924–   ) with *In the Heart of the Heart of the Country* (1968), KURT VONNEGUT, JR. (1922–   ) with *Welcome to the Monkey-House* (1968), THOMAS PYNCHON (1937–   ) with *Slow Learner* (1984), Jonathan Baumbach (1933–   ) with *Return of Service* (1979), and WOODY ALLEN (1935–   ) with *Getting Even* (1971), *Without Feathers* (1975), and *Side Effects* (1980).

As a movement within American fiction, postmodernism peaked about 1970 and then began to decline. The backswing of the stylistic pendulum—a rejection of the idea of self-conscious illusion in fiction—inspired the neonaturalistic movement of a group of short-story writers centered on RAYMOND CARVER (1938–88). Carver's stories return to the tradition of Hemingway, with sharply drawn characters, vivid dialogue, and brief, clear, violent sentences. Carver's stories, however, have few noble wanderers. They center on, and are generally narrated in, the first person by working-or middle-class characters, laboring to talk about feelings and thoughts, trapped between dull jobs and the packaged pleasures of the mass market, recounting the desperation—and occasionally the flickering moments of transcendence—of their domestic lives. Carver's most admired stories include "What We Talk About When We Talk About Love," "Cathedral," and "Fever"—Carver's personal favorite—in which a teacher of art history, deserted by his wife, racked by influenza, and afflicted by incompetent and irresponsible babysitters for his two small children, manages to talk through and to come to terms with the passing of his marriage and his love. Realists associated with Carver include Jayne Anne Phillips (1952–), author of *Black Tickets* (1979), *Machine Dreams* (1984), and *Fast Lanes* (1987); and RICHARD FORD (1944–), author of *Rock Springs* (1987). A cross between the neonaturalism of Carver, whose work is typically is set in Western or Midwestern locales, in the strip-developments of suburbia, with the surrealistic patter of Barthelme can be found in writers like Amy Hempel (1951–), author of *Reasons to Love* (1985), and Tama Janowitz (1957–), whose *Slaves of New York* (1987) centers on the urban underclass of dogwalkers and artistic hangers-on.

The most recent of the stylistic movements is MAGICAL REALISM. Just as Carver's neonaturalists were in reaction against the insistent of postmodernism, so the magical realists might seem to be in favor of wonder and the marvelous in reaction against the tawdry and depressing subject matter and limited emotional range of the neonaturalists. Aside from dialectical reaction, the magical realists are stylistically affiliated with writers from the so-called third world—Latin Americans such as GABRIEL GARCIA MARQUEZ, Asians such as Salman Rushdie—whose matter-of-fact portrayals of fantasies, legends, primitive myths, the improbable and the impossible, have reshaped the world literary scene. In yet another sense, however, magical realism might be seen as a return from the short story to the older tradition of the tale, the short fictional genre of the SKETCH BOOK (1819) of Washington Irving or Hawthorne's MOSSES FROM AN OLD MANSE (1846). Among the important magical realists currently writing are T. CORAGHESSAN BOYLE (1948–), author of *If the River Was Whiskey* (1989), and Mark Helprin (1947–), whose *A Dove of the East* (1975), *Ellis Island* (1981), and *Winter's Tale* (1985) are central to the movement in the U.S. Helprin's most reprinted work, "The Schreuderspitze," portrays a German commercial photographer who conquers the Alps—and comes to terms with the sudden death of his wife and son—in a series of preternaturally vivid dreams; the story concludes with a vision of cosmic harmony "above time, above the world" that summons up the oldest legends of the human race.

Despite what might seem to be a set of dialectical oppositions, none of the fictional modes popular after World War II, from realism to postmodernism to neonaturalism to magical realism, has ever succeeded in displacing any of the others. Rather, these antinomies reflect the rich pluralistic diversity of fiction in the period, a diversity that seems likely to continue into the indefinite future. Useful annual collections are Katrina Kenison, *The Best American Short Stories*, and William Abrahams, *Prize Stories, The O. Henry Awards*. See GLOBALIZATION OF AMERICAN LITERATURE.

DAVID H. RICHTER

Shoshone [Shoshoni] Indians. Members of the Shoshonean tribe, one of the three groups of the Uto-Aztecan linguistic family; they are sometimes referred to as Snake Indians. They lived on the northern plains between the Black Hills and the eastern slopes of the Rocky Mountains. They fell into two groups: those toward the east were nomadic horsemen, skilled as warriors and buffalo hunters; farther west were those who sometimes were called Digger Indians, plant cultivators living in brush shelters.

The best-known Shoshone is SACAJAWEA, guide for the Lewis and Clark expedition. Chief Washakie (c. 1804–1900) was friendly to the white man and represented his people in many treaty negotiations and conferences. He was buried with full military honors, and his tombstone reads, "Always loyal to the Government and to his white brothers." JOAQUIN MILLER took a Shoshone wife and lived among her people in the mid-19th century. In January 1863 a large portion of the tribe, perhaps as many as 500, was massacred at Bear River, Idaho, by Federal soldiers. The tribe never recovered fully. In the 1870s the Shoshone allowed their traditional enemies, the Arapahoe, to live in the Wind River, Wyoming, reservation after their surrender. Though Washakie regarded this as a temporary courtesy, the government saw it as a solution to their problem. Only after repeated petitions were the Shoshone awarded a cash settlement (1927). Shoshone reservations are located in Idaho and Wyoming. A scholarly study is *The Shoshonis* (1964) by Virginia C. Trenholm and Maurine Carley.

Show Boat (1926), a novel by EDNA FERBER. In this popular book appear three theatrical generations. First there is Captain Andy Hawks, who runs a showboat on the Mississippi and marries Parthy Ann, a prim New England schoolmarm. They have one daughter, Magnolia, who becomes an actress and runs off with the leading man, Gaylord Ravenal. Their daughter Kim is born on the showboat. The captain dies and Parthy Ann takes over; Ravenal takes Magnolia to Chicago, but ultimately leaves her, and she returns to the showboat. Kim meanwhile grows up to be a Broadway star. The novel has been filmed twice and was made into an operetta (1927) by the librettist OSCAR HAMMERSTEIN and the composer JEROME KERN. It is one of Kern's best scores and includes his song *Old Man River*, which had become both a classic and a folksong. The operetta is often revived.

Shulman, Irving (1913–1995), novelist and screenwriter. Born in Brooklyn, he was educated at Ohio University and Columbia. During World War II, he served with the War Department. His first novel *The Amboy Dukes* appeared in 1947, followed by a dozen works of fiction in the next decade.

Shulman is best known for his screenplay *Rebel without a Cause* (1955) based on his novel of the same year, *Children of the Dark*. Turning to biography, he wrote *Harlow: An Intimate Biography* (1964), *Valentino* (1967), and *Jackie: The Exploitation of a First Lady* (1970). In 1972, the University of California at Los Angeles awarded him a Ph.D. *The Devil's Knee* (1973) and *Saturn's Child* (1976) rounded out his writing career.

Shute, Henry Augustus (1856–1943),   lawyer, judge, humorist. Shute, who served as a judge in his native New Hampshire from 1883 to 1936, loved to reminisce about his lively boyhood and did so in numerous books about a character named Plupy Shute: *The Real Diary of A Real Boy* (1902), *Real Boys* (1905), *Plupy* (1911), *Plupy, The Wirst Yet* (1929), and others. In addition he wrote *A Profane and Somewhat Unreliable History of Exeter* (1907) and *A Country Lawyer* (1911).

Siegel, Eli (1902–1978),   printer, poet. Born in Latvia, Siegel won early recognition with "Hot Afternoons Have Been in Montana," a poem published in the *Nation* in 1925. In later years he published *Is Beauty the Making One of Opposites?* (1955), *Art as Life* (1957), and *Hot Afternoons Have Been in Montana: Poems* (1957).

Sigourney, Lydia Howard Huntley (1791–1865), poet, novelist. Born and educated in Connecticut, Sigourney became known as a writer of popular verse based on happenings reported in the newspapers—especially the death notices. Her preoccupation with death and her habit of writing elegies for prominent people caused a contemporary wit to call her verse "death's second terror." She also wrote novels, among them *Lucy Howard's Journal* (1858) and a *History of Marcus Aurelius* (1836). *The Faded Hope* (1853) is a memoir of her son, who died in 1850; *Letters of Life* (1866) is an autobiography. Altogether she published sixty volumes, many of them verse. *Poetical Works of Mrs. L. H. Sigourney* (1850), edited by F. W. N. Bayley, was published in England. Gordon Haight's *Mrs. Sigourney, The Sweet Singer of Hartford* appeared in 1930.

Silas Lapham, The Rise of.   See RISE OF SILAS LAPHAM, THE.

Silko, Leslie Marmon (1948–   ),   poet, novelist short-story writer. Born in Albuquerque, Silko was brought up on the Laguna Pueblo Reservation, where members of her family have lived for many generations, and learned traditional stories from her great-aunt and great-grandmother. *Laguna Woman: Poems* (1974) was her first publication.

Ceremony (1977), her first novel, was widely praised. It tells the story of Tayo, a World War II veteran haunted by his experiences, especially the facial resemblance between his own people and the Japanese he was ordered to kill. Led by Old Betonie, like Tayo a man of mixed ancestry, Tayo finds peace through the power of ritual to conquer isolation and guilt. In this novel and in other works, Silko weaves in chants and legends; readers and characters must interpret the relevance and meaning of these traditional elements.

During the 1970s Silko lived for a time in Bethel, a remote Inuit village in Alaska, learning stories from that tradition. The title story of her collection *Storyteller* (1981) draws on Inuit myth. *Storyteller* combines poetry, family history, stories, and photographs. The photos, many taken by her father and grandfather, are of her family and the landscape she grew up in. The stories in the collection often mix modern experience and tribal lore as characters, steeped in tradition, confuse or equate the events of their own lives with the old stories. In "Yellow Woman," for example, a young Pueblo woman confuses her cattle-rustler abductor with one of the *ka'tsina* mountain spirits who in old stories lured women away.

A MacArthur Foundation Fellowship (1981) enabled Silko to take a leave from her teaching position at the University of Arizona. Silko's correspondence with the poet JAMES WRIGHT was edited by Anne Wright under the title *The Delicacy and Strength of Lace* (1986). *Almanac* (1991) is a wide-ranging novel about people caught between the current culture of the Southwest and the traditions of the native peoples of the region's past. *Gardens in the Dunes* (1999) begins and ends in a desert garden on the California-Arizona border, tended by Grandmother Fleet, one of the few remaining Sand Lizard Indians. Set at the turn of the 20th century, the novel graphs the conflict between native and European ways through the travels of Indigo, an orphaned girl taken in by a white woman, Hattie Palmer.

Sill, Edward Rowland (1841–1887),   poet, essayist. Born in Connecticut, Sill was orphaned young and brought up by an uncle in Ohio. He sailed around Cape Horn to California; studied law, music, and divinity; and worked at various jobs before becoming a professor at the University of California (1874–82). He spent his last years back in Ohio, writing essays and poetry for magazines under the pen name Andrew Hedbrooke. His poetry is collected in *The Hermitage and Other Poems* (1868), *The Venus of Milo and Other Poems* (1883), and *Poems* (1887). His collected *Prose* appeared in 1885.

Silliman, Benjamin (1779–1864),   educator, scientist, travel writer. Silliman, born in Connecticut, was educated at Yale and became professor of chemistry and natural history at age twenty-three. A few years later he journeyed to Europe and on his return in 1806 published a *Journal of Travels in England, Holland, and Scotland* (1810), which went through many editions.

Silliman, Ron (1946–   ),   poet. Born in Washington and raised in California, Silliman attended several schools, including the University of California at Berkeley. He has worked as an organizer in prison and tenant movements and edited the *Socialist Review*. One of the original members of the San Francisco LANGUAGE POETS movement, he has experimented with form and questioned the assumptions of "mainstream poetry." In *Nox* (1974), the pages are quartered by crossed lines; a word, several words, or letters are printed in the quarters. Each section can be read separately or in the reader's chosen order. *Ketjak* (1974) shows an interest in the boundaries between poetry and prose, especially in length of paragraphs. His book-length prose poem *Tjanting* (1981) continues this interest with each paragraph equaling the number of sentences in the previous two paragraphs. The pattern for his long ongoing poem, *The Alphabet,* may have been inspired by Louis Zukofsky's Objectivist poem *A*. Silliman's piece is planned for twenty-six volumes and has appeared in *ABC* (1983); *Paradise* (1985), *LIT* (1987), *What* (1989), *Manifest* (1990), *Demo to Ink* (1992), *Toner* (1992), *Jones* (1993) *N/O* (1994), and *Xing* (1996). His style mixes puns with intricate forms and descriptions of daily life.

Silva, José Asunción (1865–1896),   Colombian poet, considered a precursor of MODERNISMO. A tragic figure of acute sensibility, Silva felt oppressed by the smug provincialism of his native Bogotá, against which he rebelled in bitter, though highly lyrical, verse. The death of a beloved sister is said to have inspired his best-known poem, "Nocturno III," which displays the musicality and morbid melancholy, akin to POE's, that mark his poetry. Another characteristic note is a nostalgic yearning for the past, evident in the short poem "Vejeces." He died a suicide. An edition of his *Obra completa* appeared in two volumes in 1968.

Silverberg, Robert (1935–   ),   science fiction writer. Born in New York City and educated at Columbia, Silverberg is one of the most prolific American science fiction writers, with over seventy novels, more than four hundred short stories and novellas, over fifty nonfiction works, and more than forty edited collections, mostly on science fiction and fantasy. During the 1960s he is reported to have written nearly two million words a year. His novels include *Nightwings* (1969), a story of a society far in the future that is dominated by guilds, including Watchers and Rememberers; *A Time of Changes* (1971), about love in a repressive society that despises the self; *Dying Inside* (1972), about a man losing his telepathic powers; and *Shadrach in the Furnace* (1976), about mind and body transplants. *Lord Valentine's Castle* (1980) is a massive work mixing science fiction and fantasy. The several volumes of Majipoor novels, including *Majipoor Chronicles* (1982), *The Mountains of Majipoor* (1995), and *Sorcerers of Majipoor* (1996), have also been praised for their rich invention. *The Collected Stories, Volume 1* appeared in 1992. His pen names include Ivar Jorgensen and Calvin M. Knox.

Silver Cord, The (1926),   a play by SIDNEY HOWARD. This was one of the earliest and best psychological studies on the stage of a dominant mother.

Simak, Clifford D[onald] (1904–1988),   science fiction writer. Born in Wisconsin, Simak was for many years a journalist. He has written often of time travel, horror, and parallel universes in works that include *A City* (1952) and *Way Station* (1962), generally considered his best works; *All Flesh Is Grass* (1965); *Cemetery World* (1973); *A Heritage of Stars* (1977); *The Fellowship of the Talisman* (1978); and *The Visitors* (1980). Collections of short fiction include *Skirmish* (1977) and *The Civilisation Game* (1997).

Simic, Charles (1938–   ),   poet. Born in Belgrade, Yugoslavia, Simic was uprooted by World War II and finally settled in Chicago in 1954. His family's language was Serbian, but he began writing poetry in English in high school. He was educated at the University of Chicago and New York University, served in the Army (1961–1963), and published his first collection of poetry, *What the Grass Says* (1967). He has taught at the University of New Hampshire and has won a Guggenheim and a MacArthur Fellowship. *Selected Poems* (1963–1983) appeared in 1985. His poetry is at times surrealistic or mythic, sometimes rooted in his wartime experience. Among his other titles are *Somewhere Among Us a Stone Is Taking Notes* (1969), *Dismantling the Silence* (1971), *White* (1972), *Return to a Place Lit by a Glass of Milk* (1974), *Biography and a Lament* (1976), *Charon's Cosmology* (1977), *Classic Ballroom Dances* (1980), *Austerities* (1982), *Weather Forecast for Utopia and Vicinity* (1983), *Unending Blues* (1986), *The Book of Gods and Devils* (1990), *Hotel Insomnia* (1993), *A Wedding in Hell* (1994), *Walking the Black Cat* (1996), and *Jackstraws* (1999). *Uncertain Certainty* (1985) is nonfiction prose, and *The World Doesn't End* (1989) is a collection of prose poems that won a Pulitzer Prize. *The Unemployed Fortune-Teller: Essays and Memoirs* appeared in 1994 and *A Fly in the Soup, Memoirs* appeared in 2001. Simic has translated the work of Yugoslav poet Vasco Popa and, with MARK STRAND, edited a collection of European and South American poetry, *Another Republic* (1976).

Simms, William Gilmore (1806–1870),   novelist, poet. Raised in poverty and poorly educated, Simms was excluded from the aristocratic social and intellectual life of his native Charleston, South Carolina. His mother died when he was very young, and he was cared for by his maternal grandmother, who told him tales of local Indians, the Revolutionary War, and pirates along the coast. At eighteen, while staying with his father on a frontier farm near Georgeville, Mississippi, he visited the Creek, Choctaw, and Cherokee Nations. He wrote poetry about them and described their life in travel letters to the Charleston *City Gazette*. His observations convinced him that contact with whites was harmful to the Native American character. Back in Charleston, Simms practiced law, wrote for newspapers, and published verse, including *The Lost Pleiad* (1829, revised 1859). From 1849 to 1854 he edited *The Southern Quarterly Review*.

Simms's interest in historical fiction was influenced by Sir Walter Scott, whose work was popular in the South. Tragedy in the conflict of two cultures—one old and one new—was a crucial factor in the definition of the historical novel Scott set forth in the Preface to the Waverley Novels, and such conflict undergirds the plots of Simms's most successful romances.

The Yemassee (1835), his best-known novel, depicts the struggle between Carolina colonists and Indians in 1715. Sanutee, the chief of the Yemassee, is a tragic hero dying in defense of his culture and lands. Matiwan, his wife, kills their son Occonestoga, a betrayer of his people, to save him from the shame of tribal punishment so that his soul can gain eternal life. Sympathetic portrayals of Native Americans also appear in short stories collected in *The Wigwam and the Cabin* (1845–46) and in *The Cassique of Kiawah* (1859).

Like Cooper, Simms thought American writers should use American subjects and locales for fiction. Seven of his historical novels deal with the Revolutionary War as fought in his native region. *The Partisan* (1835), featuring the humorous Lt.

Porgy, depicts the 1780 guerilla campaigns of Marion and Sumter in the South Carolina swamps. *Melichampe* (1836) is a sequel. Major Singleton, the hero of *The Partisan*, reappears as the protector of the title character of *Katharine Walton* (1851). *The Sword and the Distaff* (1853), revised in 1856 as *Woodcraft*, features some of the same characters as the earlier books and realistically portrays Charleston at the end of the war straddling the thin line between poverty and wealth. *The Kinsman* (1841) was reissued as *The Scout* (1854). *Eutaw* (1856) describes the crucial battle at Eutaw Springs in 1781. *Joscelyn: A Tale of the Revolution in Georgia* appeared in 1867.

The Border Romances—including *Guy Rivers* (1834), set in Georgia; *Richard Hurdis* (1838) in Alabama; and *Border Beagles* (1840) in Mississippi—all have a similar plot. A young hero struggles with a gang of robbers, probably based on the real life Murrell Gang. *Beauchampe: or, The Kentucky Tragedy* (1842), also based on local history, deals with seduction, desertion, and revenge. Simms returned to the same case in *Charlemont* (1846). Among his more than thirty volumes of fiction are three on crime—*Martin Faber* (1833); *Confession: or, The Blind Heart* (1841); and *Castle Dismal* (1844)—and books about Spanish exploration of the New World such as *Vasconselos* (1853).

Simms showed enthusiasm for the theater and Edwin Forrest, the actor, and wrote several plays, including *Norman Maurice* (1851) and *Michael Bonham* (1852). *Poems: Descriptive, Dramatic, Legendary, and Contemplative* appeared in 1853. Simms wrote biographies of Francis Marion (1844) and Nathanael Greene (1849), who appeared as characters in his romances, and of Captain John Smith (1846). Among his historical studies are *Slavery in America* (1838), *The History of South Carolina* (1840), and *South Carolina in the Revolution* (1853). His *Works*, in twenty volumes, was published from 1853 to 1859; the revised Centennial edition was issued by the University of South Carolina Press in 1969. His granddaughter, Mary C. Simms Oliphant, helped edit his *Letters* (5 v. 1952–1956).

Simon Legree.   See LEGREE, SIMON.

Simon, [Marvin] Neil (1927–   ),   playwright. Simon began his career in a collaboration with his brother Daniel. They produced a review, *Catch a Star!* (1955), and a play, *Come Blow Your Horn* (1961). On his own Simon has written a series of long-running plays that have made him the most financially successful playwright in the history of American theater. They include *Barefoot in the Park* (1963), *The Star Spangled Girl* (1966), *Plaza Suite* (1968), *The Last of the Red Hot Lovers* (1969), *The Prisoner of Second Avenue* (1971), *The Sunshine Boys* (1972), and *California Suite* (1976). Known for plots emphasizing comic aspects of contemporary life, Simon's plays have often been turned into films with screenplays by Simon. *The Odd Couple* (1965)—two divorced men of completely opposite character trying to share an apartment—was made into a film (1968) and a long-running television series. *The Goodbye Girl* (1977) is a screenplay he wrote for his second wife, the actress Marsha Mason. Simon drew on his boyhood in New York City in *Chapter Two* (1977), *Brighton Beach Memoirs* (1983), and *Rumors* (1988). *Lost in Yonkers* won the Pulitzer Prize for Drama

in 1990. *Laughter on the Twenty-Third Floor*, featuring the interplay of writers for a television comedy series, appeared in 1994. *Dinner Party*, an untypically somber 2000 production, takes place in a Paris restaurant, where six antagonistic characters are locked together in a private room. *Rewrites* (1996) and *The Play Goes On* (1999) are memoirs. See MIKE NICHOLS.

Simple Cobbler of Agawam in America, The (pub. in London, 1647),   by NATHANIEL WARD under the pseudonym Theodore de la Guard. Ward was at the time a clergyman in Agawam (later called Ipswich), Massachusetts. The Cobbler of the title is metaphoric; Ward said he was willing to help mend the country "both in the upper leather and sole, with all the honest stitches he can take." The book is a satirical denunciation of England and New England for being tolerant of England in the quarrel between Parliament and the Crown, of the human race in general, and women in particular.

Simpson, Louis [Aston Marantz] (1923–   ), poet, critic, novelist, editor. Born in Kingston, Jamaica, Simpson has described growing up there in his autobiography, *North of Jamaica* (1972), but also discussed influences on his poetry, such as his mother's Eastern European Jewish background, his life in America beginning in 1940, and his service in World War II, the subject for a number of his important poems. Critics often divide Simpson's work into three periods: the first three books—*The Arrivistes* (1949), *Good News of Death* (1955), and *A Dream of Governors* (1959)—contain poems traditionally structured in meter and rhyme, with a frequent use of classical myth. The next two—*At the End of the Open Road* (Pulitzer Prize, 1963) and *Adventures of the Letter I* (1971)—mark a move to free verse, more surreal imagery, and an increasing emphasis on the poet's vision of American life. The later books—*Searching for the Ox* (1976), *Caviare at the Funeral* (1981), and *The Best Hour of the Night* (1983)—reveal Simpson's desire to adopt the subjects and methods of writers like Wordsworth and Chekhov, to narrate incidents of everyday life in language that gives the impression of an ordinary person speaking to others. These poems have been faulted for being prosaic, perhaps because the voice of narration, often very subtle in its movement and its condensations of expression, creates an understated lyricism more appropriate to the poems' characters and situations but less easily discernible than the traditional rhythms of his earlier poetry. More than any other major contemporary poet Simpson has used compressed narratives in which disjunctions and juxtapositions capture a sense of important emotion in apparently ordinary events of modern suburban life. His other works include *Riverside Drive* (1962); *Three on the Tower: The Lives and Works of Ezra Pound, T. S. Eliot, and William Carlos Williams* (1975); *A Revolution in Taste: Studies in Dylan Thomas, Allen Ginsberg, Sylvia Plath, and Robert Lowell* (1978); *A Company of Poets* (1981); *The Character of the Poet* (1986); *People Live Here: Selected Poems 1949–1983* (1983); *In the Room We Share* (1990); and *Ships Going Into The Blue* (1994).

JOHN BENSKO

Simpson, Mona (1957–   ),   novelist. Born in Green Bay, Wisconsin, Simpson was educated at the University of California at Berkeley and at Columbia (M.F.A., 1983). She received high praise for her first novel *Anywhere But Here* (1986), the story of a mother and daughter traveling west from Wisconsin to make a new life for themselves in California. Adele, the mother, hopes her daughter Ann will become a successful child film star, but has to work at mundane jobs while her daughter finds only limited success as a performer. *The Lost Father* (1991) is a semi-sequel to the first, although some details of the family's life are different. In this book, Ann is enrolled as a medical student in New York. She becomes obsessed with finding the father who abandoned her and her mother and tries everything to locate him, even changing her name to Mayan Atassi, the name he would have given her. After trips to the various schools where he has taught and to Egypt to locate his family, she finally finds him in California, only to discover that knowing where he is physically does not solve the mystery. *A Regular Guy* (1996) also deals with a father who has abandoned his wife and child, and a daughter who is determined to make him acknowledge her. Tom Owens, the father of this tale, is a successful biotech entrepreneur; critics have noted the similarity between his business success and that of Steve Jobs, co-founder of Apple Computer and Mona Simpson's real life brother. *Off Keck Road* (2000) is set in Simpson's hometown, and focuses on two single women of different economic backgrounds who find themselves involved with the same wealthy real estate tycoon. In her novels, Simpson concentrates on the tension between domesticity and independence, between stability and abandonment, and the effect of broken relationships on women.

Sims, Lieutenant A. K.   Pen name of JOHN HARVEY WHITSON.

Sinclair, Harold (1907–1966), musician, clerk, author. Sinclair, born in Chicago, wrote several novels that had a wide circulation. His first, *Journey Home* (1936), was a picaresque narrative. *American Years* (1938), *The Years of Growth* (1940), and *Years of Illusion* (1941) tell the history of an Illinois town from 1830 to 1914. He wrote about Benedict Arnold's march on Quebec in *Westward the Tide* (1940). He also wrote *Port of New Orleans* (1942), *Music Out of Dixie* (1952), *The Horse Soldiers* (1956), and *The Cavalryman* (1958).

Sinclair, Upton [Beall] (1878–1968), novelist, editor. Born in Baltimore, Sinclair began writing at 15 during his student days at the City College of New York and Columbia. His early novels include *Springtime and Harvest* (1901, retitled *King Midas*); *Prince Hagen* (1903); *The Journal of Arthur Stirling* (1903); *Manassas* (1904), about the Civil War; and *A Captain of Industry* (1906). Sinclair won an international reputation with his exposé of meat-packing houses, *The Jungle* (1906). This book was widely credited with forcing the Federal government to strengthen food adulteration laws. Sinclair invested the proceeds from this widely sold book in a cooperative socialist community, The Helicon Home Colony, in Englewood, New Jersey. He moved to California in 1915 where, in 1934, he forged an alliance of the unemployed and progressives (EPIC, End Poverty in California) that controlled the

state Democratic Party and nearly won him the governorship. He made several more unsuccessful tries at public office.

Between 1901 and 1940, Sinclair published more than 100 works. Titles from this period include *The Metropolis* (1908); *The Money-changers* (1908); *Love's Pilgrimage* (1911), in part autobiographical; *King Coal* (1917); *They Call Me Carpenter* (1922); OIL! (1927); BOSTON (1928), which deals with the SACCO-VANZETTI CASE; *The Wet Parade* (1931); *Plays of Protest* (1912) and other plays; many political and industrial studies, including THE BRASS CHECK, A STUDY OF AMERICAN JOURNALISM (1919); *American Outpost: A Book of Reminiscences* (1932); and *Upton Sinclair Presents William Fox* (1933). He also edited an anthology, *The Cry for Justice* (1915). His papers, collected at the Lilly Library of Indiana University, include more than a quarter of a million letters to the known and the unknown. Sinclair published a selection of this material in *My Lifetime in Letters* (1960). His *Autobiography* appeared in 1962.

World's End (1940) initiated a series of eleven novels centered on Lanny Budd, an international traveler who figures in intrigues and politics from World War I to the Cold War. The titles in this series are *Between Two Worlds* (1941); *Dragon's Teeth* (1942, Pulitzer Prize), on Anti-Nazi activities in the early 1930s; *Wide is the Gate* (1943), on the Spanish Civil War and the French Resistance; *The Presidential Agent* (1944), in which Budd serves President Franklin Roosevelt; *Dragon Harvest* (1945), set in France under Nazi seige; *A World to Win* (1946) and *A Presidential Mission* (1947), which take place in Europe, North Africa, and the Orient from 1940 to 1943; *One Clear Call* (1948) and *O Shepherd, Speak* (1949), which describe the war's end and its aftermath; and *The Return of Lanny Budd* (1953), which warns of the dangers of Soviet Russia.

Sinclair's later fiction includes *What Didymus Did* (1954, reissued as *It Happened to Didymus*, 1958); *The Cup of Fury* (1956); *Affectionately Eve* (1961); and *The Coal War: A Sequel to King Coal* (1977). Sinclair used pen names that include Clarke Fitch, Frederick Garrison, and Arthur Stirling.

Singer, Isaac Bashevis (1904–1991), novelist, short-story writer, Nobel prize in literature (1978), the first writer in Yiddish so honored. Singer was born in the village of Leoncin, Poland, but when he was young, his family moved to Warsaw which, except for time spent in the *shtetl* (small village) of Bilgoray during World War I, remained his home until he came to the United States in 1935. His father and paternal grandfather were rabbis, Chassidim—an ultra-orthodox and frequently enthusiastic, mystical branch of Judaism—while his maternal grandfather, also a rabbi, was in the Maskilic, or enlightened, tradition. Singer had a thoroughly traditional Jewish upbringing in which these two elements often collided. More significant influences on Singer's growing skepticism and his ultimate, personal resolution of the various contradictory claims to belief and doubt that he embraced were his elder brother, writer ISRAEL JOSHUA SINGER, the pantheistic philosophy of Spinoza, secular and modernist writers like Knut Hamsun, August Strindberg, and E. T. A. Hoffman, and his abiding interest in—though by no means uncritical acceptance—of psychic research and phenomena. He once described his credo as "a sort of kasha of mysticism, deism, and skepticism."

His brother I. J. Singer, eleven years Isaac Bashevis's senior, had become converted to science, rationalism, and socialism in pre–World War I Warsaw and was an important member in the 1920s of its lively and modernist world of Jewish intellectuals and artists. Isaac Bashevis was influenced by these ideas and currents but always stood outside and frequently opposed them. As a consequence of the success of his novel *Yoshe Kalb*, I. J. Singer had become Warsaw correspondent for the *Jewish Daily Forward*, in New York City. Some years after I. J. had come to the United States as a *Forward* writer, and as the situation of Polish Jews became increasingly ominous, he helped Isaac Bashevis to emigrate to New York in 1935. Isaac Bashevis had by then published only a few stories, sketches, and translations in generally obscure Yiddish journals in Vilna and Warsaw, along with an extraordinary but controversial and not very accessible short novel *Der Sotn in Goray* (Warsaw, 1935), but he was hired by the *Forward*. He continued to publish in the *Forward* for the rest of his life—in the early days, a stream of popular articles and features, usually under the name of Yitskhok Varshavski; later, his stories and serialized novellas and novels, usually under the name Yitskhok Bashevis. Singer did not break through to a wider non-Yiddish audience until the 1950s. In 1950 *The Family Moskat*, Isaac Bashevis Singer's second novel, became his first publication in English, but his appeal to the imagination of American readers and others did not really begin until Saul Bellow's fine translation of Singer's masterful short story "Gimpel the Fool" appeared in the *Partisan Review* in 1953. ("Gimpel the Fool" is the title story of the first English collection of Singer's stories in 1957.) There followed rapidly *Satan in Goray* in English (1955) and *The Magician of Lublin* (1957). With the appearance of *The Spinoza of Market Street and Other Stories* (1961) and *The Slave* (1962), which is considered by many to be Singer's finest novel, his reputation was ensured. This reputation was consolidated by at least eight more volumes of short stories and a half dozen additional novels—chief of which are his two epic novels of Polish Jewish life, *The Manor* (1967) and *The Estate* (1969), and his only novel set in the United States, *Enemies: a Love Story* (1972). His late work was seen by some critics as repetitious, perhaps diminishing in power—a charge made against Dostoyevsky, Faulkner, and many other major writers. Singer's work written in advanced age restates some of his chief themes with power and originality. The overwhelming impression remains that Isaac Bashevis Singer, writing in Yiddish—though always playing a close and vital, occasionally exclusive, role in the translation of his work into English—was a treasure of American and world literature.

Despite the size and variety of Singer's literary work—it includes as well two original plays in addition to stage and screen adaptations by others of several of his works, notably the story "Yentl the Yeshivah Boy" and about a dozen children's books, a form and an audience he took very seriously—his characteristic themes, concerns, and patterns recur, creating a distinctive Singerian universe. This universe is based largely on Singer's observation of the colorful and raffish, if impoverished, life on Krochmalna Street, the Jewish neighborhood in Warsaw where he grew up and where his father held Chassidic court (richly described in *In My Father's Court*, 1966). It also is based on his study of arcane episodes of Jewish history—he was fascinated by the so-called false messiahs, Sabbatai Zevi, in the 17th century, Joseph Frank in the 18th—and in his later years on the experience of Jewish survivors transplanted to America.

Paradoxically, Singer's work represents a flowering of Yiddish literature while standing apart from its mainstream. He often claimed that most Yiddish literature, which began seriously about the 1880s, was stamped by provinciality, sentimentality, and a tendentious social commitment. This claim is itself tendentious—it can be argued that there were forerunners of Singer in other works and that, for example, "Gimpel the Fool," in which simple faith and holy innocence in the face of every provocation become a reproach to the worldly and merely material, leans on the tradition of the exaltation of the humble and simple evident in much of classic Yiddish literature. Nevertheless, it is true that Singer's prevailing concern with the esoterica of cabala, demons, and *dybbuks* (spirits of the dead that invade the bodies of the living), and his frank, sometimes obsessive treatment of sexuality and carnality, his special mix of realism and fantasy, burst the bounds of that literature. It may also account for his imaginative appeal to a wider and modern audience.

As if to confound categorization, Singer wrote sprawling novels covering generations of Polish Jewish experience—*The Family Moskat, The Manor, The Estate*—as well as tightly controlled, highly structured novels such as *Satan in Goray, The Magician of Lublin*, and *The Slave*. Yet through them all we can discern common concerns—chiefly the unending struggle between the forces of order and the forces of chaos, manifested in the universe, the world, and individual men and women.

In *Satan in Goray*, in the wake of the Chmielnicki massacres of 1648, Rabbi Benish has left the disorder of the city of Lublin for a fresh start in the village of Goray. He restores a calm and orderly life for himself and the survivors of the massacres, based on strict observance of traditional religious practices. This harmony is shattered by followers of the false messiah, zealots, and sowers of discord, who temporarily and disastrously take over the town's life. In *The Slave*, which also takes place after 1648, the Jew Joseph is sold into slavery to a Polish farm family. He endures three years of bondage—living literally among the beasts—through faithful adherence to the rituals of orthodox religious observances and with the love and help of Wanda, a daughter of the farm family. After deliverance from bondage by the Jewish community, he returns for Wanda, whom he secretly marries, and who ultimately becomes Sarah, a converted Jew. She dies in childbirth, and he is expelled from Poland and wanders widely. After a spell as a Zevi follower, he returns in the end to Poland and to a life of traditional observances as a chief element of an orderly existence, though also believing that the inner spirit of the law is more important than the merely ritualistic. *The Magician of Lublin* displays a similar opposition and balancing of forces, but set in a more contemporary milieu. Yasha Mazur, the magician and confidence man of the title, is a modern existential hero, amoral, skeptical, sensual, seemingly boundless in his belief in his powers of self-fulfillment. His schemes and romantic dalliances end in failure and a kind of despair. He returns to his faithful and pious wife, renounces the world, and devotes his days to prayer and meditation. In the novel's epilogue he is widely regarded as a sage and a rabbi, Reb Jacob the Penitent, despite his own continuing skepticism.

Singer's novels of wide canvas display similar patterns, though they seem to move more in the stream of modern history. *The Family Moskat* weaves together scores of individual and family histories that touch on the Moskat family of Warsaw between 1900 and 1939. Until World War I the elderly patriarch Meshulam Moskat has presided over the family as its unifying center. After that, the disintegrating forces of history and unrestrained personality and desire dominate. In *The Manor* and *The Estate* we follow the fortunes of Calman Jacoby and his family and connections as they rise and fall from 1863—the date of a failed Polish insurrection against Russia—until the beginning of the 20th century. Jacoby has prospered, but he sees his life as a veritable hell. Images of the order and grace of the religious study hall and of the synagogue are juxtaposed against a family history rich in madness, sexual wantonness, and apostasy. Modern secular existence offers no salvation to the Jew, though it is equally obvious that the alternative religious life is hardly a viable one for intellectuals or the masses. At the end of *The Family Moskat*, as the Germans are nearing the gates of Warsaw, one doomed Jew says to another: "Death is the Messiah. That's the real truth." This chilling note writes finis to the messianic hope that threads its way, in various characters' commitments, throughout this and other Singer fictions. What we are left with is a subtle balancing in his work between the past and present claims of belief and doubt, myths and realities. His dybbuks and demons are images of disorder and the vagaries of human experience, the world and values of the faithful images of order. The bizarre, obsessive, driven quality of many of his characters are testimony to the extraordinary vitality of human desire and aspiration in the face of a baffling universe.

A person of immense sophistication, with the persona often of a naif, Singer in dedicating *The Family Moskat* to his brother said something that probably applies more to himself: "a modern man [with] all the great qualities of our pious ancestors." Above all, Isaac Bashevis Singer was a consummate storyteller, as demonstrated by *The King of the Fields* (1988), which is a mythic tale about the origins of the Polish nation and the introduction to it of Christianity. *Scum* (1991) and MESHUGAH (1994) are novels.

Singer's other fiction includes *Shasha* (1978) and *The Penitent* (1983); and story collections, *Short Friday* (1964); *The Seance* (1968); *A Friend of Kafka* (1970); *A Crown of Feathers* (1973); *Passions* (1975); *Old Love* (1979); *The Image* (1985);

and *The Death of Methuselah* (1985). Memoirs are *A Little Boy in Search of God* (1976), *A Young Man in Search of Love* (1978), *Lost in America* (1979), and *More Stories from My Father's Court* (2000). Edward Alexander's *Isaac Bashevis Singer* (1980) and Paul Kresh's *Isaac Bashevis Singer: The Magician of West 86th Street* (1979) are biographies.

JULES CHAMETZKY/BP

Singer, Israel Joshua (1893–1944),   novelist. Like his younger brother, ISAAC BASHEVIS SINGER, Israel wrote in Yiddish. He began his literary career in Poland, but with the support of publisher Abraham Cahan, came to the U.S. in 1934. His works written in America are *The Brothers Ashkenazi* (1936), set in Poland; *In die Berg* (1942), set in the United States; and *The Family Carnovsky* (1943), about the European wanderings of a Jewish family.

Single Hound, The (1914),   a group of 146 poems by EMILY DICKINSON. They were published by her niece, Martha Dickinson Bianchi, and were described as for the most part verses sent, along with flowers, to Dickinson's sister-in-law, Susan Gilbert Dickinson, her next-door neighbor. An analysis of the poems by Millicent Todd Bingham in *Ancestors' Brocade* (1945) shows that not all of them had previously gone unpublished.

single tax.   See PROGRESS AND POVERTY.

Singmaster, Elsie (1879–1958),   novelist. Singmaster was born in Pennsylvania Dutch environment she described in her novels. She began writing when she was eleven and in her maturity turned out over a score of novels, both juvenile and adult. Among them are *Katy Gaumer* (1914), *Keller's Anna Ruth* (1926), *The Young Ravenels* (1932), *The Loving Heart* (1937), and *A High Wind Rising* (1942). Singmaster's several nonfiction works include *A Short Life of Martin Luther* (1917).

Sinners in the Hands of an Angry God,   a sermon preached by Jonathan Edwards to his Enfield, Connecticut, parishioners on July 8, 1741, and published in the same year. Using the text "Their foot shall slide in due time" (Deut. XXXII, 35), Edwards warned that, being human, his parishioners were by nature depraved and could not assume salvation simply as a result of church membership. Particularly noted for its vivid descriptions of the torments of Hell, this sermon came at the height of the GREAT AWAKENING, a period of religious fervor in the first half of the 18th century.

Sioux Indians,   about thirty tribes speaking allied languages of the Hokan-Siouan language family, including the Dakota, Teton, Crow, and Mandan. As PLAINS INDIANS, their range was west of the Mississippi and they were bordered by Algonquin and Muskhogeon tribes to the east and north and Caddoes to the south and west. The stereotype of "the Indian" is strongly based on Sioux customs and appearance, and their costumes have become the standard ceremonial dress for Native Americans. They were the favorite antagonists of dime novels and Western movies. Isolated from white settlements during the 17th and 18th centuries, they took little part in wars between the French, English, and Americans. The westward expansion of the 19th century brought the Sioux into conflict with the white man as settlements and railroads encroached on buffalo hunting and horse raiding, and smallpox and cholera decimated the villages along the Mississippi River.

Red Cloud (1822–1909) lost the war against the western forts to troops armed with breech-loading rifles and retired to Pine Ridge Reservation in South Dakota after he was forced to sign a treaty in 1869. When CRAZY HORSE, Gall (c. 1840–1894), and SIT-TING BULL defeated GEORGE ARMSTRONG CUSTER at Little Big Horn (1876), they and their people were hunted down, killed, and imprisoned. Buffalo hunters hired by the railroads to clear the tracks wiped out the herds and with them the Sioux way of life. They had used every part of the animal for food, shelter, clothing, decoration, tools, and ritual objects. Without buffalo the Sioux were hungry, homeless, and unemployed. Sioux adherence to the Ghost Dance religion after 1888, with its promise of a return to the old ways and a messiah, frightened the army, and soldiers sought out Sitting Bull and his followers, killing the chief and imprisoning the others. At Wounded Knee Creek (December 1890) near the Pine Ridge Agency, the troops killed about a hundred and fifty men, women, and children, mostly unarmed. After surrender in 1891, the Sioux retired to reservations in the north-central region, including Minnesota, North and South Dakota, Iowa, Nebraska, and Montana.

Sioux songs recorded by ethnologists are particularly interesting in imagery and form. James Mooney rendered several for his *Ghost-Dance Religion* (1896). War and peace songs are prevalent among them, like the patriotic ode *You May Go on the Warpath*, translated by Frances Densmore. She prepared a valuable bulletin on *Music in Its Relation to the Religious Thought of the Teton Sioux* (1916). Much poetry is joined to the name of Sitting Bull, as recorded in Stanley Vestal's *Sitting Bull* (1932, rev. 1957).

Sioux appear frequently in early accounts of explorers and from time to time in imaginative literature. The Lewis and Clark *Journals* (1814) contain numerous references to them. Louis Deffebach placed the scene of his blank-verse drama *Oolaita, or, The Indian Heroine* (1821) among the Sioux. James Fenimore Cooper, journeying westward in search of new material, studied the Sioux. Washington Irving has much to say about them in ASTORIA (1836). FRANCIS PARKMAN reported his visit with the Sioux in *The Oregon Trail* (1849). In Stanley Vestal's biography and in W. Fletcher Johnson's *Sitting Bull* (1891) appear many details of life among the Sioux. Hamlin Garland's classic story "The Captain of the Gray Horse Troop" (1902) has as its locale old Fort Smith among the Tetongs, a Sioux tribe. Charles A. Eastman, whose Indian name was Ohiyesa, told of his life among the Sioux in *An Indian Boyhood* (1902). Chief Luther Standing Bear wrote several books about the Sioux, among them *My People the Sioux* (1928), *My Indian Boyhood* (1931), and *Land of the Spotted Eagle* (1933). Similar details are given in *Black Elk Speaks* (1932), a narrative taken down by John G. Neihardt. Joseph Epes Brown edited the same medicine man's *The Sacred Pipe: Black Elk's Account of the Seven Rites of the Oglala Sioux* (1953). G. E. Hyde wrote of the last stand of the Sioux in *A Sioux Chronicle* (1956). VINE

DELORIA, JR. is a Sioux writer whose works include *Custer Died for Your Sins* (1969).

Siringo, Charles A. (1855–1928),   cowboy, detective, memoirist, biographer. Siringo, a Texan, in his early years was a cowboy; in 1886 he joined the Pinkerton Agency. He looked back with constant pleasure to his cowboy days and wrote frequently about them. His book *A Texas Cowboy, or, 15 Years on the Hurricane Deck of a Spanish Cow Pony* (1885) became a classic. Among his books are *A Cowboy Detective* (1912), *A Lone Star Cowboy* (1919), *A History of "Billy the Kid"* (1920), and *Riata and Spurs* (1927).

Sister Carrie (1900),   Theodore Dreiser's first novel. "A picture of conditions," as Dreiser characterized it, *Sister Carrie* represents the contrasting fates of its two central characters. Carrie Meeber, a poor country girl, seeks her fortune in Chicago and New York and in a few years rises to stardom on the Broadway stage, only to discover that money does not buy happiness. George Hurstwood, the well-to-do manager of a fashionable bar in Chicago, falls in love with Carrie, and the infatuation leads to his decline and death. On her way to success, Carrie drudges in a Chicago shoe factory, lives for several months with a traveling salesman, and attracts the more polished and affluent lover, Hurstwood, who sacrifices his name, his marriage, and his position when he steals ten thousand dollars from his employer's safe and tricks Carrie into going with him to New York City. In the most powerful chapters of the novel, he loses his job during the Panic of 1893, sinks into paralyzing apathy, descends to beggary after Carrie leaves him, and commits suicide in a Bowery flophouse. The novel is naturalistic in its documentation of conditions in factories, bars, hotels, and theaters, and in its portrayal of the city as a powerful determinant of people's physical and mental states. Refusing to treat seduction and poverty in didactic or melodramatic terms, the novel is pathbreaking in its revelation of the humanity of characters who violate society's moral codes. Hostile critics condemned *Sister Carrie* as depressing and immoral, but to later novelists, such as Sherwood Anderson, John Dos Passos, James T. Farrell, and Sinclair Lewis, Dreiser's realism was liberating in its rejection of genteel convention. The original manuscript of *Sister Carrie*, some 30,000 words longer than the Doubleday, Page edition of 1900, was published by the University of Pennsylvania Press in 1983.
ELSA NETTELS

Sitting Bull (c. 1831–1890),   Sioux leader in warfare against the whites, especially at the Battle of Little Big Horn (June 25, 1876), where GEORGE A. CUSTER was killed. Sitting Bull escaped to Canada but returned in 1881 on promise of a pardon. He toured with Buffalo Bill's Wild West Show in 1885. He advised the Sioux to refuse to sell their land to settlers and advocated the Ghost Dance religion, which promised a return to the old ways of buffalo hunting. He was killed when Indian police tried to arrest him. Originally buried in North Dakota, Sitting Bull's remains were moved to South Dakota in 1954. A body of poetry has been ascribed to him. See *Sitting Bull, Champion of the Sioux* (1957) by Stanley Vestal. See also SIOUX INDIANS.

Siwash, Old. GEORGE FITCH wrote a series of stories about this college—supposedly Knox College in Illinois. The stories first appeared in the *Saturday Evening Post*, then in book form as *The Big Strike at Siwash* (1909) and *At Good Old Siwash* (1911).

Six Nations. The Indian confederacy known first as the League of the Five Nations—Mohawks, Senecas, Oneidas, Onondagas, Cayugas—later, after the admission of the Tuscaroras (about 1715) by its present name. See IROQUOIS.

1601 (c. 1876), a long unpublished sketch by MARK TWAIN. This piece had as a subtitle "Conversation as It Was by the Social Fireside in the Time of the Tudors." Twain apparently wrote the sketch for circulation in a small circle of friends. It was surreptitiously printed in his lifetime by John Hay and others but was not offered publicly until 1939.

Skeever, Jim. Pen name of JOHN ALEXANDER HILL.

Skeleton in Armor, The (1841), a ballad by HENRY WADSWORTH LONGFELLOW. In Touro Park, in Newport, Rhode Island, stands a mysterious structure, a round tower of rough-hewn stones, based on eight round columns. The first reference to the tower occurs in 1766, when it was called a stone-built windmill. In 1839 a Danish authority, C. C. Rafn, concluded that it was an ancient Norse building. Longfellow accepted Rafn's conclusion and made the skeleton of the builder the speaker of his poem.

Sketch Book of Geoffrey Crayon, Gent., The (1819, 1820), a collection of stories and essays by WASHINGTON IRVING. This volume became one of the most influential in American literary history and may be regarded as marking the beginning of the American short story. In his earlier writings Irving was close to the 18th-century mood. Here he moved into the romantic realm of Sir Walter Scott and his contemporaries. Like most of the American romantic writers, Irving was heavily influenced by German authors, particularly in RIP VAN WINKLE and THE LEGEND OF SLEEPY HOLLOW, and he also made pioneer and striking use of American folklore. American readers liked his travel sketches, especially *Westminster Abbey* and *Stratford on Avon*.

Skinner, B[urrhus] F[rederick] (1904–1990), behavioral psychologist, utopian writer. In *Walden II* (1948) Skinner envisioned a harmonious peaceful community where children are raised using positive reinforcement, and the principles of mass production are applied to domestic economy.

Skinner, Constance Lindsay (1879–1939), novelist. Born in Canada, Lindsay wrote several novels about life in the Far North, including *Builder of Men* (1913); *Good-Morning, Rosamund* (1917); *The Search Relentless* (1925); and *Red Willows* (1929). She wrote *Pioneers of the Old Southwest* (1919) and *Adventurer of Oregon* (1920) for the Yale Chronicles of America series and was the first editor of the Rivers of America series. Her other titles include *Songs of the Coast Dwellers* (1930) and *Beaver, Kings and Cabins* (1933).

Skinner, Cornelia Otis (1901–1979), actress, humorist, biographer. The daughter of two actors, Otis and Maud Skinner, it was almost inevitable that Cornelia Otis Skinner, born in Chicago, would go on the stage. She attended Bryn Mawr and made her first Broadway appearance with her father in *Blood and Sand* (1921). Four years later her play *Captain Fury* was produced, and in that same year she began to appear as a solo performer in character sketches that she wrote. In 1937 she performed the remarkable feat of turning Margaret Ayer Barnes's novel *Edna His Wife* into a full-length drama in which she played all the parts.

When the birth of her son brought a temporary halt to her acting, Miss Skinner tried her hand at humorous writing. Her titles include *Tiny Garments* (1932); *Excuse It, Please* (1937); *Dithers and Jitters* (1938); *Soap Behind the Ears* (1941); *Bottoms Up!* (1955); and *The Ape in Me* (1959). *Our Hearts Were Young and Gay* (1942), written with Emily Kimbrough, became a best seller, and was dramatized by Jean Kerr in the same year. *Family Circle* (1948) is a biography of her parents. *That's Me All Over* (1948) is an omnibus of earlier writings. With Samuel Taylor, she wrote *The Pleasure of His Company* (1948), a play in which she appeared on Broadway.

Skinner, Otis (1858–1942), actor, author. Born in Cambridge, Massachusetts, Skiner at age nineteen was hired by the Philadelphia Museum to play in the museum stock company. He made his New York City debut in 1879 and soon became one of the most popular of the younger actors. He married the actress Maud Durbin in 1895. One of his celebrated roles was that of the beggar in *Kismet*, a play that ran from 1911 to 1914. He was the author of *Footlights and Spotlights* (1924); *Mad Folk of the Theatre* (1928); *One Man in His Time* (1938), which he wrote in collaboration with his wife; and *The Last Tragedian: Booth Tells His Own Story* (1939). He was the father of CORNELIA OTIS SKINNER.

Skinners. See COWBOYS.

Skin of Our Teeth, The (1942), a play by THORNTON WILDER. This is an amusing combination of fantasy, morality, and satire, for which Wilder won his third Pulitzer Prize (1943). The play is unconventional in form; characters frequently address the audience, either explaining incidents or expressing bewilderment at their meaning. Its theme is universal—man's escape from disaster through the ages. The central character is George Antrobus, who invents the lever and the wheel and who is elected President of the Ancient and Honorable Order of Mammals (Subdivision: Humans). He is almost lured away from his wife by Sabina, the Eternal Temptress, but returns home in time to escape despair and disaster.

Skipper Ireson's Ride (1857), a ballad by JOHN GREENLEAF WHITTIER. This poem denounced a hardhearted Marblehead sea captain who "Sailed away from a sinking wreck, / With his own towns-people on her deck," and who was tarred and feathered by the women of Marblehead when he returned home. Whittier based the poem on a rhyme he had heard in childhood. Later he learned that he had done Skipper Ireson an injustice; it was established by Samuel Roads, Jr., in *History and Traditions of Marblehead* (1880), that Ireson's own crew had prevented him from going to the rescue.

Sklar, George (1908–1988), playwright, novelist. Sklar, born in Connecticut, was trained under GEORGE PIERCE BAKER at Yale, where he wrote with ALBERT MALTZ the play *Merry-Go-Round* (1933). After college he wrote several proletarian plays, including *The Stevedore* (with Paul Peters, 1934), an indictment of racial bias. Among his novels are *Two Worlds of Johnny Truro* (1947), *The Promising Young Man* (1951), *The Housewarming* (1953), and *The Identity of Dr. Fraser* (1962).

Slaughter, Frank G[ill] ["C. V. Terry"] (1908–   ), physician, novelist. There have been many literary physicians, but few have relied so heavily on the subject of medicine for fictional material as has Frank Slaughter. He was graduated from Duke University in 1926, obtained a medical degree in 1930, and entered the Army Medical Corps in 1942. He wrote three nonfiction books: *The New Science of Surgery* (1946); *Medicine for Moderns* (1947), a treatise on psychosomatic medicine; and *Immortal Magyar* (1950), a biography of Dr. Ignaz Philipp Semmelweis. His medical novels include *That None Should Die* (1941); *Spencer Brade, M.D.,* (1942); *Air Surgeon* (1943); *A Touch of Glory* (1945); *In a Dark Garden* (1946); *The Golden Isle* (1947); *Sangaree* (1948); *Divine Mistress* (1949); *The Stubborn Heart* (1950); *The Road to Bithynia* (1951); *The Healer* (1955); *Sword and Scalpel* (1957); and *Epidemic* (1961). *The Curse of Jezebel* (1961) is a retelling of an Old Testament story.

Slaughterhouse Five; or The Children's Crusade (1969),   a novel by KURT VONNEGUT, JR. Billy Pilgrim, a prisoner of war, has survived the bombing of Dresden in World War II and is on display in a zoo on Tralfamodore, a planet light years away. Living simultaneously in the past, present, and future, he sees repeated evidence of the absurdity of human actions and motives. Vonnegut uses disjointed chronology and impressionistic description.

Slave, The, or, Memoirs of Archy Moore (1836),   a novel by RICHARD HILDRETH. This work, the first of the antislavery novels, influenced HARRIER BEECHER STOWE. Archy, mostly of white descent, tells his own story, and his harrowing adventures show the cruelties of the slavery system at its worst. Hildreth, a Massachusetts lawyer, obtained his facts from personal observations in Florida, where he lived for two years, and from much reading. He emphasized the economic superiority of free enterprise in New England over the slave system of the South.

slave narratives.   American slave narratives are accounts that slaves wrote or dictated to record their experience of legal bondage in the Southern states. The term usually refers only to works published before 1865. Over one hundred book-length slave narratives were printed and reviewed during this period, usually by abolitionists in England and America. Those written after 1830, when abolition activity in America intensified, tend to make stronger demands for freedom and civil rights while the earlier narratives often stress religious themes.

The narratives exhibit typical traits, some common to slave experience, others imposed by the works' sponsors and audiences. The first requirement concerned the narratives' authenticity. Many believed that slaves were incapable of acquiring the skills necessary for writing a narrative, slavery proponents were eager to prove damaging eyewitness stories false, and in some instances, narratives were falsified or fictionalized. Readers had to be convinced that the narrators were indeed slaves telling the plain truth. When the subjects did not have the skills to write their own stories, their accounts were presented as "told to" a respectable amanuensis. The works actually composed and written down by literate slaves always appended the words "written by himself" or "written by herself" to the titles. Also attached were prefaces and authenticating letters from prominent white citizens. Often in the narrative proper one can distinguish more than a single authorial voice. In tone the language is highly formal, sometimes embellished with romantic flourishes or conventional pulpit oratory added by ghostwriters or editors.

Abolitionists directing the publication of the narratives called for certain obligatory scenes, including whippings, separations of families, seductions of beautiful slave girls, deprivation of food and shelter, and almost always a suspenseful, ultimately successful escape attempt. A key element was a discourse on the slave's struggle, either before or after escape, to become educated and mentally equipped to meet the challenges of freedom. The narratives contained, in addition to these standard features, sermons on the hypocrisy of Christian masters and on the evils of slavery in general.

Apart from supplying what audiences expected, some narratives risked employing a complex symbolism in order to lay claim to a broader range of powers beyond physical freedom. The most carefully designed of these narratives stress self-creation and self-knowledge by correlating three achievements: successful journey to the North, achievement of literacy, and conversion to a true Christianity. Potentially, in writing these narratives, slaves could assert their humanity, make themselves masters of their fate by mastering the word, and exercise self-actualizing powers of perception and interpretation.

The history of the slave narrative begins in 1760 with a fourteen-page dictated work, *A Narrative of the Uncommon Sufferings, and Surprizing Deliverance of Briton Hammon, A Negro man,—Servant to General Winslow of Marshfield, in New-England*. This account details the slave's capture by Indians and his eventual reunion with his master. Other early dictated narratives are those of James Gronniosaw (1770) and James Marrant (1780). The first slave to write his own story was George White, whose *Brief Account* appeared in 1810. By far the most sophisticated and the best-known of the early narratives is *The Interesting Narrative of the Life of Olaudah Equiano, or Gustavas Vassa, The African*, published first in London in 1789. Equiano's story records his transformation from ignorant enslaved African boy to free man and articulate international statesman.

In the 1830s the classic form of the slave narrative took shape. One unusual example is Charles Ball's *Slavery in the United States* (1836), a broad survey of slavery's horrors that was used by Mark Twain in *Connecticut Yankee in King Arthur's Court*. A unique narrative is *The Confessions of Nat Turner* (1831), dictated to Virginia attorney Thomas Gray while Turner awaited execution for leading the bloodiest uprising in the South during the period of slavery. The 1840s were the genre's most productive years. In 1845 Frederick Douglass published the first of three autobiographies, *Narrative of the Life of Frederick Douglass, an American Slave*, which he revised and updated ten years later in *My Bondage and My Freedom*

(1855). Both works represent the high point of the form both in style and in innovations in content. Three other accounts of the 1840s are noteworthy. *Narrative of William W. Brown, a fugitive slave* (1847) was a polished work by the author of the first African-American novel, *Clotel* (1853). *The life of Josiah Henson, formerly a slave, now an inhabitant of Canada, as narrated by himself* (1849) told the story of the man who claimed to be the model for Harriet Beecher Stowe's Uncle Tom, a boast she first corroborated and later dismissed. James W. C. Pennington's *The Fugitive Blacksmith* (1849) was written by an escaped slave who became a scholar, minister, and author of the first history of slavery. His narrative contains an ingenious escape borrowed by Twain for Huck Finn's smallpox lie. The only slave narrative known to have been written by a woman is Harriet Jacobs's *Incidents in the Life of a Slave Girl*, published under the pseudonym Linda Brent in 1861. Her work alters the staples of the male-oriented genre, scenes of journeying and isolation, in order to stress the power of women's communities in the North and South.

Although appreciated in their time, by the early 20th century the slave narratives were ignored by most historians and literary scholars. To cultural historians they now provide a valuable perspective on slavery. In literary studies, they represent a formative influence not only on 19th-century writers like Twain and Stowe but more significantly on central African-American texts of the 20th century, including Richard Wright's *Black Boy* (1945), Ralph Ellison's *Invisible Man* (1952), Ishmael Reed's *Flight to Canada* (1976), and Toni Morrison's *Beloved* (1989). See AFRICAN-AMERICAN LITERATURE.
LUCINDA MACKETHAN

Sleepy Hollow.   Tarrytown, North Tarrytown, and Irvington in New York State on the east bank of the Hudson together are sometimes called Sleepy Hollow Country. The region was made memorable by Washington Irving in his LEGEND OF SLEEPY HOLLOW (1819); he himself lived here in the house called Sunnyside, which is now restored.

Slesinger, Tess (1900–1945),   novelist. Slesinger's one novel, *The Unpossessed* (1934), drew on her relation to intellectuals associated with the *Menorah Journal* in New York City. Using modernist narrative structure, Slesinger describes how a marriage is destroyed by the husband's insistence that parenthood would compromise the couple's political ideals. A section describing abortion was published independently as "Missis Flinders." Slesinger worked in Hollywood as a screenwriter in the late 1930s and left a novel on the movies unfinished at her death.

Slick, Sam.   See T. C. HALIBURTON and SAMUEL ADAMS HAMMETT.

Slobodkin, Louis (1903–1975),   architectural sculptor, designer, writer for children. Slobodkin, born in Albany, New York, studied at the Beaux Arts Institute of Design and wrote and illustrated a long list of books for children. Among them are *Magic Michael* (1944), *The Seaweed Hat* (1947), *Mr. Mushroom* (1950), *Space Ship Under the Apple Tree* (1952), *The Little Owl Who Could Not Sleep* (1958), and *Gogo* (1960). He

also wrote articles on sculpture and a book for adults, *Sculpture Principles and Practice* (1949).

Slocum, Joshua (1844–1909?),   sailor. Born in Nova Scotia, his most noteworthy adventure came when he was fifty-one. He built a ship for himself, the thirty-six-foot *Spray*, and set out alone on a three-year voyage around both capes and across both great oceans. He was called "a Thoreau of the Sea" when he told the story in *Sailing Alone Around the World* (1900), which created a sensation. Earlier, he had written and published *Voyage of the Libertade* (1890), an account of a voyage with his family along the North and South American coasts for 5,500 miles. On November 14, 1909, he set forth on another voyage and was never heard from again.

Sloluck, J. Milton.   A pen name of AMBROSE BIERCE.

Small Boy and Others, A (1913),   an autobiographical narrative by HENRY JAMES in which he describes the learned household in which he, his sister Alice, and his older brother William were brought up. The period after 1859 is covered in *Notes of a Son and Brother* (1914).

Smalley, George W[ashburn] (1833--1916),   newspaperman, foreign correspondent, memoirist. Smalley, born in Massachusetts, covered the Civil War for the New York *Tribune* and after the war organized the *Tribune's* London bureau and covered European events until 1895, when he returned to the United States to serve as American correspondent for the London *Times*. He knew important people on both sides of the Atlantic and described them in several books, in which he did much to promote friendship between the two countries. Among his titles are *A Review of Mr. Bright's Speeches* (1868), *London Letters* (1890), *Studies of Men* (1895), and *Anglo-American Memories* (2 v. 1911–12).

Smart, Elizabeth (1913–1986),   novelist, poet. Born to a prominent Ottawa family, Smart lived in Canada, the United States, and England. Her first novel, the prose poem *By Grand Central Station I Sat Down and Wept* (1945), was written when she lived in British Columbia. During World War II she worked in Washington, D.C., and for the Ministry of Defence in London. For the next two decades, she supported herself by writing for fashion magazines. She had four children, fathered by the English poet George Barker, of whom her family vehemently disapproved. In 1977, more than thirty years after the appearance of her first book, she published a poetry collection called *A Bonus* and her second novel, *The Assumption of Rogues and Rascals*. Set in postwar England, it deals with a young woman's struggle with depression. Other writings include *In the Meantime* (1984), *Necessary Secrets* (1985), and the posthumous *Autobiographies* (1987), *The Collected Poems* (1992), and *On the Side of Angels* (1994).

Smart Set, The.   A magazine founded in 1890 by William D'Alton, who called himself Colonel Mann. Many young writers were attracted to the *Smart Set*, but it was not a financial success, and the colonel sold it (1900) to John Adams Thayer. Thayer found a capable editor in WILLARD HUNTINGTON WRIGHT, who took complete control in 1912 and hired some of the boldest young men of his day, in particular H. L. MENCKEN and GEORGE JEAN NATHAN. Thayer let Wright go and put Mencken and Nathan in charge in December 1914. They continued until December 1923, when William Randolph Hearst bought the magazine; it ceased publication in 1930.

During its heyday *Smart Set* made sprightly war on gentility and the *booboisie*, especially in its department called "Americana." But it also published much serious writing by contributors who included William Rose Benét, Frank Harris, Elinor Wylie, Lord Dunsany, William Butler Yeats, F. Scott Fitzgerald, Thorne Smith, Sinclair Lewis, James Branch Cabell, Dashiell Hammett, Aldous Huxley, Dorothy Parker, D. H. Lawrence, George Moore, Joseph Conrad, Oliver Gogarty, Maxwell Anderson, James Joyce, Eugene O'Neill, Arthur Schnitzler, Harriet Monroe, Lizette Woodworth Reese, Gelett Burgess, and others. Burton Rascoe edited *The Smart Set Anthology* (1934). See AMERICAN MERCURY.

Smet, Pierre-Jean de (1801–1873),   Jesuit missionary. Father de Smet came to the United States from Belgium in 1821, received training in Maryland and Missouri, and in 1827 was ordained. He began working with the Indians in 1838 and was known to them as "Blackrobe." He visited Sitting Bull in 1868 to attempt to conciliate him, and he founded missions throughout the Oregon country and on the Great Plains. He wrote of his experiences in *Letters and Sketches, with a Narrative of a Year's Residence among the Indian Tribes of the Rocky Mountains* (1843, repr. in R. G. Thwaites's *Early Western Travels, 1748–1846,* 1904–07, Vol. XXVII); *Oregon Missions and Travels Over the Rocky Mountains* (1847, repr. in Thwaites, Vol. XXIX); and *New Indian Sketches* (1863). H. M. Chittenden and A. T. Richardson edited the *Life, Letters, and Travels of Pierre-Jean de Smet* (1905).

Smiley, Jane [Graves] (1949–   ),   novelist, short-story writer. Born in Los Angeles, she was educated at Vasser and the University of Iowa (M.F.A., 1976; Ph.D., 1978). *Barn Blind* (1980) her first novel, centers on the troubled relations between Kate Karlson, a ranch wife, and her teenage children. *At Paradise Gate* (1981) explores family tensions in the face of the father's imminent death. *Duplicate Keys* (1984), set in Manhattan, is a mystery novel. *The Age of Grief* (1987) is a collection of the title novella and five stories, particularly praised for the gently humorous narration of the novella. *The Greenlanders* (1988), a novel of fourteenth-century Norse settlers based on the sagas, illustrates Smiley's range of subject and method. *Ordinary Love* and *Goodwill* (1989) are novellas, and *The Life of the Body* (1990) is a short story. It was *A Thousand Acres* (1991) that clarified Smiley's reputation as an accomplished writer of fiction. It won both the Pulitzer and National Book Critics Circle prizes and was made into a film. A feminist recasting of the King Lear plot, it focuses on Ginny, the oldest of the three daughters of a farmer who decides to divide his multimillion-dollar farm among his offspring. The women are the victims in this version, perhaps even victims of incest, and the effect is the same—total destruction of the marriages and relationships of everyone concerned. *Moo* (1995) and *Horse Heaven* (2000) are more sunny novels, the first a satire of academic life at an agricultural university and the second a well-researched look at the

world of horse racing in Southern California, with both equine and human characters. Nonfiction titles include *Catskill Crafts: Artisans of the Catskill Mountains* (1987) and, with others, *The True Subject: Writers on Life and Craft* (1993).

Smith, Alfred E[manuel] (1873–1944),   political leader, public official. Born on New York City's East Side, Al Smith joined Tammany Hall at an early age, served in the New York legislature (1903–15), as sheriff of New York County, and Governor of New York (1918–1920; 1922–1928). In 1928 he was nominated as the Democratic candidate for the presidency by Franklin D. Roosevelt (who wrote *The Happy Warrior: Alfred E. Smith,* 1928). Smith lost, largely because he was a Catholic. He published *Progressive Democracy* (1928); *Up to Now* (an autobiography, 1929); and *The Citizen and His Government* (1935).

Smith, Arthur James Mitchall (1902–1980),   poet. Smith, who was born in Montreal, was part of a literary group at McGill University, where he began publishing poems that attracted attention for their wit and freshness of language and imagery. Some of his poems appeared in the *Dial*. He earned a Ph.D. at Edinburgh and taught at various North American universities, including Michigan State. With F. R. Scott he edited an anthology, *New Provinces* (1936). Smith's poetry appeared in *News of the Phoenix* (1943), *A Sort of Ecstasy* (1954), and *Collected Poems* (1962). *Poems New and Collected* (1967) added twenty-two new poems. *The Classic Shade: Selected Poems* appeared in 1978. Smith edited several influential anthologies of Canadian poetry, including *The Oxford Book of Canadian Verse in English and French* (1960). His critical essays are collected in *Towards a View of Canadian Letters: Selected Critical Essays 1928–1971* (1973).

Smith, Betty [Wehner] (1904–1972),   playwright, novelist. Smith, born in Brooklyn, New York, had only primary schooling, and a broken early marriage left her with two children to raise. When the children were old enough, Smith studied at the University of Michigan, where she won the Avery Hopwood award in drama and gained the courage to make a career in playwriting. Her works include more than seventy one-act plays. She acted in stock and on the radio and for the Federal Theater Project. In 1943 her partly autobiographical novel of a Brooklyn childhood, A TREE GROWS IN BROOKLYN, was published, became a best seller, and was made into a movie. In collaboration with GEORGE ABBOTT, she turned the novel into a successful musical play (1951). She then joined the faculty of the University of North Carolina as a drama lecturer. Two further novels, *Tomorrow Will Be Better* (1948) and *Maggie-Now* (1958), did not equal her first success.

Smith, Chard Powers (1894–1977),   poet, novelist, historian, paleontologist. Smith, born in Watertown, New York, published much verse, including *Along the Wind* (1925); *Lost Address* (1928); *Hamilton* (a verse drama, 1930); *The Quest of Pan* (1930); and *Prelude to Man* (1936). The author of valuable critical works such as *Pattern and Variation in Poetry* (1932) and *Annals of the Poets* (1932), he also described *The Housatonic* (1946) in the Rivers of America series. Among his novels are *Artillery of Time* (1939); *Ladies' Day* (1941); *Turn of* the *Dial* (1943), a satire on advertising; and *He's in the Artillery Now* (1943).

Smith, Charles H[enry] ["Bill Arp"] (1826–1903), lawyer, humorist, newspaperman. Born in Georgia, Smith served in the Confederate Army and contributed numerous dialect letters under the pen name of Bill Arp to a newspaper in Rome, Georgia, called *Southern Confederacy*. After the war he continued these letters in the Atlanta *Constitution* for more than twenty-five years. Among the collections made of Smith's material are *Bill Arp So Called* (1866), *Bill Arp's Peace Papers* (1873), *Bill Arp's Scrap Book* (1884), and *Bill Arp: From the Uncivil War to Date* (1903).

Smith, Dave [David Jeddie] (1942–   ), poet, novelist, editor, essayist. Born in Portsmouth, Virginia, Dave Smith was educated at the University of Virginia, Southern Illinois, and Ohio University. After serving in the Air Force (1969–73), Smith began a distinguished literary career, writing, lecturing, teaching, and editing. In 1969 he founded *Back Door* (1969), a poetry magazine; he has also served as literature editor of the *Rocky Mountain Review* and as editor of *Southern Review*. He has received many awards including the prestigious Virginia Prize in poetry.

Smith's early collections, *Mean Rufus Throw Down* (1973), *The Fisherman's Whore* (1974), and *Drunks* (1975), reveal a penchant for evocative narrative, dramatic masks, and elemental human experiences. In *Cumberland Station* (1976) and *Goshawk, Antelope* (1979), the metaphoric-biographic exploration is more sharply anchored in specific cultural locales: tidewater Virginia or the "half-light" of "distant" places like Wyoming and Utah. *Goshawk, Antelope* established Smith's reputation. The books that followed displayed other facets of his talent: *Dream Flights* (1981) was praised for its realistic pathos and historical observation. These qualities were reconfirmed in *Onliness* (1981), a novel of character and allegorical situation set in Virginia. In *In the House of the Judge* (1983) blends narrative and metaphor, tracing subtle relations between personal and cultural history. *The Roundhouse Voices: Selected and New Poems* (1985) highlights Smith's capacity for thematic growth, evident also in *Cuba Night* (1989), and for stylistic renewal. New and selected poems have appeared in *Night Pleasures* (1992) and *Wick of Memory* (2000), both praised for their subtle blend of memory and reflection. He has also written about poetry in *Local Assays: On Contemporary American Poetry* (1985).

MARCEL CORNIS-POPE

Smith, Elihu Hubbard (1771–1798), physician, poet, playwright, editor. Smith, born in Connecticut, showed considerable promise as a writer before dying of yellow fever. Among his several interesting works were an anthology, *American Poems, Selected and Original* (1793), perhaps the earliest book of its kind in the United States, and an opera, *Edwin and Angelina* (1796). He was active in the HARTFORD WITS while he lived in Connecticut and in the FRIENDLY CLUB after he moved to New York City.

Smith, Elizabeth Oakes ["Ernest Helfenstein"] (1806–1893), poet, novelist. Smith, born in Maine, in her lifetime had a reputation considerably greater than that of SEBA SMITH, her husband. She was deeply interested in woman suffrage and other causes, and frequently worked them into the plots of her novels and plays. She began as a poet and in 1845 collected her *Poetical Writings*. Her novels include *The Western Captive* (1842), *The Sinless Child* (1843), *The Newsboy* (1854), and *The Bald Eagle* (1867). *The Newsboy* was one of the earliest sociological novels. *Selections from the Autobiography of Elizabeth Oakes Smith* was published in 1924.

Smith, F[rancis] Hopkinson (1838–1915), engineer, illustrator, painter, short-story writer, novelist. Smith, born in Baltimore, worked in his brother's iron foundry until the end of the Civil War, then moved to New York. He entered into partnership with James Symington and turned to engineering. He built the Block Island breakwater, the Race Rock Lighthouse, and the foundation for the Statue of Liberty. He also sketched and painted. Two books of travel sketches, *Well-Worn Roads of Spain, Holland, and Italy* (1887) and *A White Umbrella in Mexico* (1889), caught the public's attention. In 1891 he published a novelette based on his well-known after-dinner stories, COLONEL CARTER OF CARTERSVILLE. It was so successful that he abandoned engineering for writing. Among his principal works are *A Day at Laguerre's and Other Days* (short stories, 1892); *Tom Grogan* (1896); *The Fortunes of Oliver Horn* (1902); *The Tides of Barnegat* (1906); and *Kennedy Square* (1911). He also published books of charcoal sketches, among them *In Thackeray's London* (1913) and *In Dickens' London* (1914).

Smith, H[arry] Allen (1907–1976), newspaperman, humorist. Smith, born in Illinois, became a feature writer for the United Press in 1929, contributed many articles to the New York *World-Telegram*, and put together his first books from his newspaper pieces. Bergen Evans compiled an anthology, *The World, The Flesh, and H. Allen Smith* (1954). Books by Smith include *Low Man on a Totem Pole* (1941), *Life in a Putty Knife Factory* (1943), *Lost in the Horse Latitudes* (1945), *Rhubarb* (1946), *We Went Thataway* (1949), *People Named Smith* (1950), *London Journal* (1952), *The Compleat Practical Joker* (1953), *Rebel Yell* (1954), *Don't Get Perconel with a Chicken* (1959), and *How to Write Without Knowing Nothing* (1961).

Smith, Harry B[ache] (1860–1936), librettist. Smith, born in Buffalo, New York, knew the American stage so well and was such a rapid workman that he was called on again and again to supply book and lyrics for musical comedies and light operas—three hundred times or more according to the best accounts. Some first-rate musicians worked with him, among them REGINALD DEKOVEN on *Robin Hood* (1890) and other operas. Smith also did book or lyrics or both for *The Wizard of the Nile* (1895), *The Fortune Teller* (1898), *Babette* (1899), *The Girl from Utah* (1912), *The Red Canary* (1914), *Princess Flavia* (1925), *Countess Maritza* (1926), and *Cherry Blossoms* (1927).

Smith, Henry Nash (1906–1986), teacher, editor. Smith, born in Dallas, taught at several universities before becoming professor of English at the University of California at Berkeley (1953). He was also on the editorial staff of the *Southwest Review* (1927–41). He is best known for *Virgin*

Land: The American West as Symbol and Myth (1950) and for editing works of James Fenimore Cooper and Mark Twain.

Smith, James (1737?–1814?),   soldier, pioneer, public official, missionary. In 1755 Smith, born in Pennsylvania, was captured by Indians and lived for four years among them. In 1760 he returned to Pennsylvania, became a farmer, and engaged in exploring and Indian fighting. In 1778 he became a colonel in the militia, in 1788 moved to Kentucky and was a member of the constitutional convention there in 1792 and a member of the legislature. But he became interested in religion and served as a missionary to the Indians. Returning from one of his trips, he found that his son James had become a Shaker. He visited a settlement of Shakers near Lebanon, Ohio, and wrote two violent pamphlets denouncing them (1810). He also wrote *Treatise on the Mode and Manner of Indian War* (1812), but is chiefly remembered for his *Account of the Remarkable Occurrences in the Life and Travels of Col. James Smith, During His Captivity with the Indians* (1799), which has often been reprinted.

Smith, Jedediah Strong (1798–1831),   fur trader, explorer. Smith, born in New York, was among the first white men to cross the Sierra Nevada mountains. A member of the Ashley-Smith expedition, he explored the Missouri River (1823), traveled from the Great Salt Lake to southern California (1826–1827), and from California to Oregon (1828). He was killed by Indians on the Santa Fe Trail. His career is described in *The Ashley-Smith Explorations* (1918) by H.C. Dale, and he is a central character in JOHN G. NEIHARDT's novel *The Splendid Wayfaring* (1920).

Smith, John (1580–1631),   explorer, promoter, soldier of fortune. Born in England, Smith received a grammar school education but left home for a brief apprenticeship in business at fifteen, and then, after his father's death when John was sixteen, enlisted for military service in France and the Netherlands. Within the next ten years he traveled all over Europe, had been captured and sold into slavery in Turkey, escaped, traveled to Morocco, and returned to England.

Smith reached Virginia with the first colonists on April 26, 1607, and was designated as one of seven members of the governing council, but was stripped of his powers at first under suspicion that he might usurp the government. His contributions to the stability of the enterprise were so great, however, that by June he was readmitted to the council and eventually made president. During the extreme rigors of the early period—of the 100 people left in Jamestown in June 1607, only 38 remained when the first supply ship arrived in January 1608—Smith was largely responsible for keeping the enterprise viable. When he was captured by the Indians, he was apparently saved by Pocahontas, who later assisted the English by bringing them food and warning them of attack. Smith remained in Virginia until 1609, when, wounded in a gunpowder explosion, he returned to London.

In 1614 he resumed his explorations, mapping New England, which he named, from Maine to Cape Cod. On another expedition, in the following year, he was captured by French pirates. Unable to secure financing for later expeditions, he

worked on writings, books that proved to be major influences on the colonists of Plymouth and Massachusetts Bay. Dissatisfied with the Jamestown experience, he envisioned for New England a colony of farmers, craftsmen, and fishermen—small landowners free of the domination of landlords. The wealth he stressed was to be found in fishing and farm produce, not the gold that had lured so many earlier immigrants to the New World. Eager to return, he offered himself as a guide to the Pilgrims, who found it "better cheap" to use his maps and reports than hire him.

Smith's writings are sometimes confusing or contradictory in details and often promotional in tone. The story of the rescue by Pocahontas does not appear in his earliest accounts of Virginia, but only in the 1624 *General History*. On balance, however, he seems a creditable witness. His most important work, *The General History of Virginia, New England, and the Summer Isles* (1624), includes later, often expanded versions of *A Map of Virginia, with a Description of the Country, the Commodities, People, Government and Religion* (1612); *A Description of New England* (1616); and *New Englands Trials* (1620). Philip L. Barbour, ed., *The Complete Works of Captain John Smith* (1986), includes these and *A True Relation* (1608), *The True Travels, Adventures, and Observations of Captain John Smith* (1630), *Advertisements for the Unexperienced Planters of New England, or Any Where* (1631), and other pieces. Studies include Bradford Smith, *Captain John Smith* (1953); P.L. Barbour, *The Three Worlds of Captain John Smith* (1964); Everett H. Emerson, *Captain John Smith* (1971); and A.T. Vaughan, *American Genesis: Captain John Smith and the Founding of Virginia* (1975).

Smith, Johnston.   A pen name used by STEPHEN CRANE in privately printing his novelette MAGGIE: A GIRL OF THE STREETS in 1893. When a regular edition appeared (1896), it carried his real name.

Smith, Joseph (1805–1844),   Mormon prophet. In 1820 the Vermont-born Smith began to have supernatural visions appointing him prophet of a new religion; in 1827, according to his account, he got from the angel Moroni a book written in strange characters on golden plates. He translated the message as the *Book of Mormon* (1830), and on this book was founded the Church of the Latter-Day Saints in the same year. Smith decided to move westward and with his followers went first to Ohio (1831), then to Missouri (1838), and then to Nauvoo, Illinois (1840). There, on July 12, 1843, he proclaimed the doctrine of polygamy. Much opposition was aroused, especially in the columns of the Nauvoo *Expositor*. When Smith's followers destroyed the press of this paper, a warrant was issued for Smith's arrest. He resisted and was ultimately placed in a jail at Carthage. A mob invaded the jail and killed him. J.H. Evans wrote *Joseph Smith: An American Prophet* (1933); F.M. Brodie, *No Man Knows My History: The Life of Joseph Smith* (1945); and Ray B. West, Jr., *Kingdom of the Saints* (1957).

Smith, Lee (1944–   ),   novelist, short-story writer, journalist. Born in Grundy, Virginia, Smith earned her bachelor's degree at Hollins College and attended the Sorbonne. She worked as a journalist and public school teacher before joining the faculty at North Carolina State University. Her first novel,

The Day the Dogbushes Bloomed (1968), earned her a Book-of-the-Month Club fellowship. *Fancy Strut* (1973) is a comic novel of life in the New South, taking its name from a step used by drum majorettes. *Black Mountain Breakdown* (1960) follows the life of Crystal Renee Spangler from a rural childhood to paralysis and catalepsy. Critics particularly praised the use of Southern phrasing in its narrative voice. *Oral History* (1983) brought comparison with Faulkner, Welty, and O'Connor for its portrayal of family life in the South. It recounts one hundred years in the generations of the Cantrell family. *Family Linen*, also a multigenerational chronicle, appeared in 1985. *Fair and Tender Ladies* (1988) is an epistolary novel using the candid and ungrammatical letters of Ivy Rowe to relate her own and her female relations' stories. *Saving Grace* (1995) is narrated in the first person by Florida Grace Shepherd, the daughter of an itinerant snake-handling preacher. Other novels include *Something in the Wind* (1971) and *The Devil's Dream* (1992). Stories are collected in *Cakewalk* (1980), *Me and My Baby View the Eclipse* (1990), and *News of the Spirit* (1997). *The Christmas Letters* (1996) is a novella.

Smith, Lillian (1897–1966), author, editor, civil rights advocate. Growing up in a small Florida town, Smith saw racial bigotry: a three-year stint as a teacher in China showed her a different kind of racial tension. Returning to Georgia, she took up civic work, founded a girl's camp, and, with a friend, founded the quarterly *South Today*, publishing literary and social criticism. Her novel STRANGE FRUIT (1944) attracted much attention with its love story of a mulatto girl and a white man; it was later dramatized. *One Hour* (1960) is set in a small southern town. Her nonfiction titles include *Killers of the Dream* (1949, revised 1961); *The Journey* (1954); *Now Is the Time* (1955), recommending implementation of school integration; and *Our Faces, Our Words* (1964). *Memory of a Large Christmas* (1962) is autobiographical.

Smith, Logan Pearsall (1865–1946), epigrammatist, critic, essayist. Smith was born in New Jersey into a wealthy family. Walt Whitman came often to their later home in Philadelphia, and William James was a family friend. Declining to work in the family business, Smith lived abroad after 1888 and became a British subject in 1913. He won a reputation on both sides of the Atlantic as a polished and witty writer. His titles include *Trivia* (1902), *More Trivia* (1921), *Afterthoughts* (1931), *Last Words* (1934), the collection *All Trivia* (1935), and *Reperusals and Re-collections* (1936). *The Youth of Parnassus* (1895) is short stories, *Sonnets* (1908) and *Songs and Sonnets* (1909) are verse, and *On Reading Shakespeare* (1933) and *Milton and His Modern Critics* (1941) are literary criticism. His books on language are *The English Language* (1912) and *Words and Idioms* (1925). *Unforgotten Years* (1938) is autobiographical.

Smith, Margaret Bayard (1778–1844), Washington socialite, novelist. Her fiction includes *A Winter in Washington* (1824) and *What is Gentility?* (1828). Smith is known especially for *The First Forty Years of Washington Society* (1906), a collection of letters.

Smith, Martin [William] Cruz (1942–), novelist. Born in Reading, Pennsylvania, Smith grew up in Philadelphia and was educated at the University of Pennsylvania. *The Indians Won* (1970), written under the name Martin William Smith, begins with the Battle of Little Big Horn and imagines an Indian nation in the middle of the country. On the title page of his first commercially successful publication, *Nightwing* (1977), a horror story about bats, Smith substituted his Pueblo Indian maternal grandmother's name as his middle name. For *Gorky Park* (1981), a murder mystery set in Moscow with Arkady Renko, a Soviet policeman, as the protagonist, Smith demanded and got a million dollar advance. It was made into a successful film. *Stallion Gate* (1986) includes Native American characters and is set in New Mexico; it deals with the construction of the atom bomb. *Polar Star* (1989) takes place on a Soviet ship. Arkady Renko returns to Moscow in *Red Square* (1992) to discover he has become a target for the Russian Mafia. Fleeing to Cuba to stay alive in *Havana Bay* (1999), Renko finds, when a colleague is found dead floating in an inner tube in the Bay, that murder still stalks him. *Rose* (1996) is a historical novel set in 19th-century Lancashire, England.

Smith, Nora Archibald (1859?–1934), teacher, children's author. Smith, with her sister KATE DOUGLAS WIGGIN, wrote fifteen books, including *Kindergarten Principles and Practice* (1897). Born in Philadelphia, she spent most of her professional life in San Francisco. She also wrote *The Message of Froebel* (1900), *The Doll's Calendar* (1909), and *Action-Poems and Plays for Children* (1923). In 1925 she wrote *Kate Douglas Wiggin as Her Sister Knew Her*.

Smith, Red [Walter Wellesley] (1905–1982), sports writer. Smith, born in Green Bay, Wisconsin, worked for Milwaukee, St. Louis, and Philadelphia newspapers before joining the staff of the New York *Herald Tribune* in 1945 and becoming known as one of the best sportswriters of all time. Some of his pieces have been collected in book form. Among his books are *Out of the Red* (1950) and *Views of Sports* (1954).

Smith, Richard Penn (1799–1854), lawyer, editor, playwright, novelist. Smith practiced law, bought and edited his hometown Philadelphia newspaper *The Aurora* (1822–27), but was greatly attracted to the theater, and wrote about twenty plays. Unfortunately, not all the plays have been preserved, even in manuscript. Smith drew freely on French plays, and among his adaptations were *The Disowned* (1829) and *The Sentinels, or, The Two Sergeants* (1829). Another play, *The Actress of Padua* (1836), seems to have been a free adaptation of Victor Hugo's *Angelo, Tyran de Padoue* (1835). Smith's adaptation exists only in another version he made of Hugo's play in fictional form, *The Actress of Padua and Other Tales* (1836). He also dealt with American themes, as in *William Penn* (1829) and *The Triumph at Plattsburg* (1830). He also wrote THE EIGHTH OF JANUARY (1829), *The Deformed* (1830), and *Caius Marius* (1831) as well as a novel about the Revolution, *The Forsaken* (1831).

Smith is supposed to have ghostwritten DAVY CROCKETT's autobiography, *Col. Crockett's Exploits and Adventures in Texas* (1836); the title is sometimes given as *Davy Crockett and His*

Adventures in Texas, Told Mostly by Himself and the date as 1834. Smith's *Miscellaneous Writings* (1856) was edited by his son Horace W. Smith. *The Triumph at Plattsburg* was printed from manuscript by A. H. Quinn in his *Representative American Plays* (1917); several other plays were edited by R. W. Ware and H. W. Schoenberger for Volume 13 of *America's Lost Plays* (1941). Bruce W. McCullough wrote *The Life and Writings of Richard Penn Smith, with a Reprint of His Play, "The Deformed"* (1917).

Smith, Samuel (1720–1776), public official, historian. Smith was the author of a pioneer history of New Jersey, *History of the Colony of Nova-Caesaria, or New Jersey* (1765). He prefaced his narrative with speculations on pre-Columbian history and started the history itself with an account of what happened after the English took over the Jerseys from the Dutch in 1664. He discussed the confused Jersey land titles, Indian culture, local resources, and governors of the colony, concluding with an account of the condition of the region at the time.

Smith, Rev. Samuel Francis.   See AMERICA.

Smith, Samuel Stanhope (1750–1819), Presbyterian clergyman, college president, philosopher, historian. Smith, born in Pennsylvania, entered the ministry in 1773, became professor of moral philosophy at the College of New Jersey (later Princeton) in 1779, and president of the college in 1795. Among Smith's writings are *Lectures on Evidences of the Christian Religion* (1809); *Lectures on Moral and Political Philosophy* (2 v. 1812); a sequel to David Ramsay's *History of the United States* (1816–1817); and *Essay on the Causes of the Variety of Complexion and Figure in the Human Species* [and] *Strictures on Lord Kames's Discourse on the Original Diversity of Mankind* (1787).

Smith, Seba [Major Jack Downing] (1792–1868), editor, humorist. Born in Maine and educated at Bowdoin, Smith knew Maine's villages and people. After founding the Portland *Courier* in 1829, he began to contribute letters under the pen name Major Jack Downing, the first one appearing on January 18, 1830. He satirized the legislature and customs of Maine at first and then went on to the national scene, where "the Major" was supposedly a member of President Jackson's kitchen cabinet. The letters were reprinted and collected throughout the country, and several imitators appeared, including CHARLES AUGUSTUS DAVIS. The Downing letters continued until the Civil War. In 1839 Smith and his wife ELIZABETH OAKES SMITH moved to New York City, where they both contributed sketches, stories, and verse to magazines, and he served as editor of various magazines. Among his publications are *The Life and Writings of Major Jack Downing of Downingville, Away Down East in the State of Maine* (1833); *The Select Letters of Major Jack Downing* (1834); *May-Day in N.Y.* (1845); *'Way Down East* (1854); and *My 30 Years Out of the Senate* (1859).

Several skits about Jack Downing were performed in New York City theaters. In 1834 JAMES HACKETT produced *Major Jack Downing*. In June 1836, "Yankee" Hill appeared as Jack in *The Lion of the East*; in September Jack was a leading character in *Moonshine*. The major had numerous literary progeny: T. C.

Haliburton's Sam Slick, Charles Farrar Browne's ARTEMUS WARD, James Russell Lowell's Hosea Biglow, and other Yankee oracles and humorists who posed as semiliterate and wrote in dialect. Alice Wyman wrote *Two American Pioneers: Seba Smith and Elizabeth Oakes Smith* (1927).

Smith, Sol[omon Franklin].   See NOAH MILLER LUDLOW.

Smith, Sydney (1771–1845), clergyman, critic. Smith's dismissive comments on American culture in the *Edinburgh Review* (January 1820) made him notorious in the United States. In a review of Seybert's *Annals of the United States* he wrote: "In the four quarters of the globe, who reads an American book? or goes to an American play? or looks at an American picture or statue?" Smith could not have foreseen the almost immediate worldwide popularity of Irving and Cooper and the rapid following of the works of Poe, Emerson, Longfellow, Hawthorne, and Melville. Among American responses to Smith was one by Melville. "The day will come when you shall say, who reads a book by an Englishman that is a modern?" in "Hawthorne and His Mosses," 1850.

Smith, Thorne (1892–1934), humorist. Smith, born in Maryland, published an early novel, *Biltmore Oswald*, in 1918, but did not achieve success until 1926, when TOPPER appeared. In that novel a dead couple, seen only by Topper, complicate his life. Thereafter, he published *The Stray Lamb* (1929); *Did She Fall?* (1930); *The Night Life of the Gods* (1931); *Turnabout* (1931); *The Bishop's Jaegers* (1932); *Topper Takes a Trip* (1932); *Skin and Bones* (1933); *The Glorious Pool* (posthumous, 1934); and *The Passionate Witch* (completed by Norman Matson, 1935).

Smith, Walter Wellesley.   See RED SMITH.

Smith, William [1] (1727–1803), Episcopal clergyman, teacher, historian. Smith came to America from Scotland (1751) as a tutor. *His General Idea of the College of Mirania* (1753) led to his appointment as teacher at the Academy and Charitable School—forerunner of the University of Pennsylvania—and he became president of Washington College (1782–1789). His Loyalist writings aroused great opposition among the patriotic colonists. Particularly pro-British was his *Sermon on the Present Situation of American Affairs* (1775). Earlier he had denounced the pacifism of Quakers in his *Brief State of the Province of Pennsylvania* and his *Brief View of the Conduct of Pennsylvania for the Year 1755* (1756). He edited the *American Magazine and Monthly Chronicle* (1757–58), which encouraged poets to write verse as art rather than for didactic purposes. He wrote for the magazine a series of essays under the pen name "The Hermit" and published his *Discourses on Public Occasions in America* in London (1762). H. W. Smith issued *The Life and Correspondence of the Rev. William Smith, D.D.* (2 v. 1879, 1880).

Smith, William [2] (1728–1793), lawyer, judge, historian. Smith, born in New York City, attended Yale, studied law, and was admitted to the bar in 1750. He was made chief justice of the province of New York in 1767. In politics he was a moderate under suspicion from both sides; he finally went over to the British. In 1786 he was made chief justice of Canada, where he lived until his death. His literary fame rests on his *History of the Province of New York, from the First Discovery to the Year 1732* (1757).

Smith, William Jay (1918–   ),   poet. Born in Louisiana, he taught at Williams and Hollins colleges. His early poetry collections include *Poems* (1947), *Celebration at Dark* (1950), *The Tin Can* (1966), and *The Traveler's Tree* (1980). A recent collection is *The World Below the Window: Poems 1937–1997* (1998). He has done translations from Russian and Italian and has written light verse for children. *Army Brat* (1980) is an autobiography. *Laughing Time: Collected Nonsense* (1990) is verse for children. In *The Cherokee Lottery: A Sequence of Poems* (2000) he writes of the removal to Oklahoma.

Smith, Winchell (1871–1933),   actor, director, playwright. Smith, born in Connecticut, first appeared on the stage in 1892; by 1904 he had become a successful producer and director. In 1906 he collaborated with Byron Ongley on BREWSTER'S MILLIONS (based on George Barr McCutcheon's novel of 1902), which was a great success; *The Fortune Hunter* (1909) first gave prominence to John Barrymore. Greatest of all Smith's hits, however, was LIGHTNIN' (1918), written in collaboration with FRANK BACON, who took the leading role. His other plays include *The Boomerang* (with Victor Mapes, 1915); *Turn to the Right* (1916); and *Thank You* (with Tom Cushing, 1921).

Smoke and Steel (1920),   a collection of poems by CARL SANDBURG. The title poem is an attempt to find some kind of beauty—if only the beauty of terror and repulsion—in modern industrialism.

Snake Indians.   See SHOSHONE INDIANS.

Snelling, William Joseph (1804–1848),   trapper, newspaperman, satirist. Snelling, born in Boston, began as a western trapper, became well acquainted with Indian life, and wrote a widely read book, *Tales of the Northwest, or, Sketches of Indian Life and Character* (1830), reissued with an introduction by John T. Flanagan, 1936). In 1827 he helped subdue a revolt among the Winnebago Indians, returned to Boston, and became a poverty-stricken hack writer. He made fun of poets and poetasters of his day in *Truth: A New Year's Gift for Scribblers* (1831). His other titles are *Exposé of the Vice of Gaming as It Lately Existed in New England* (1833) and *The Rat-Trap, or Cogitations of a Convict in the House of Correction* (1837).

Snodgrass, W[illiam] D[ewitt] (1926–   ),   poet. Born and educated in Pennsylvania, Snodgrass served in the Navy before studying at the University of Iowa, for a time with ROBERT LOWELL. Snodgrass has taught at many universities, including Rochester and Delaware. His first volume of poems, *Heart's Needle* (1959), brought him a Pulitzer Prize. With Lowell's *Life Studies* of the same year, *Heart's Needle* inaugurated the vogue for confessional poetry in the 1960s. *The Remains* (1970), a sequence of family poems, was published under the pen name S. S. Gardons, an anagram of Snodgrass; it was published fifteen years later under his own name. *The Fuhrer Bunker: A Cycle* (1977) was the first printing of a continuing work, sometimes

produced as a play, that uses the imagined voices of prominent Nazis in dramatic juxtaposition. *Magda Goebbels* (1983) and *Heinrich Himmler* (1983) were additional segments published by small presses; other passages were added in productions at the American Place Theater (1981) and Eastern Michigan University (1987). The complete *Fuhrer Bunker* appeared in 1995. *After Experience: Poems and Translations* (1968) and *The Death of Cock Robin* (1989) are other collections. Most of his titles are represented in *Selected Poems: 1957–1987* (1987). A later collection is *Each in His Season* (1993). *After Images: Autobiographical Sketches* appeared in 1999.

Snopes family.   Inhabitants of William Faulkner's mythical YOKNAPATAWPHA COUNTY, the Snopeses appear in several of Faulkner's novels—notably THE HAMLET, *The Town*, and *The Mansion*—and are representative of the inhuman aspects of modern commercial civilization. The members of the Snopes family include *Ab Snopes*. The first of the Snopeses to be mentioned, Ab is involved with a gang of horse thieves and killers in THE UNVANQUISHED and reappears much later in "Barn Burning" (in *Collected Stories*). While a tenant on land belonging to Major De Spain, he ruins a valuable rug and is ordered to deduct the cost from his forthcoming crop. In revenge he burns De Spain's barn. Still later he is a minor character in *The Hamlet*.

Byron Snopes, a character in *The Town*. Byron, a clerk in COLONEL SARTORIS's bank, writes anonymous letters to Narcissa Benbow in *Sartoris*, and in *The Town* robs the bank and flees.

Clarence Snopes, son of I. O. Snopes, a character in SANCTUARY and *The Mansion*. Clarence is a Mississippi state senator; in *Sanctuary* he is willing to sell to the highest bidder information to be used in a murder trial.

Colonel Sartoris Snopes ["Sarty"], a character in "Barn Burning." The only true Snopes whom Faulkner treats sympathetically, the boy Sarty is torn between loyalty to his father and his knowledge of his father's meanness.

Eck Snopes, a character in *The Hamlet*. Supposedly not a true Snopes, Eck is a blacksmith and an honest man.

Eula Varner Snopes, a character in *The Hamlet* and *The Town*. The beautiful and voluptuous daughter of Will Varner, Eula marries Flem Snopes, who is "a crippled Vulcan to her Venus," when she is already pregnant with another man's child. She has an 18-year love affair with Manfred De Spain after her marriage to Flem, and kills herself to prevent her daughter, Linda, from being involved in a scandal.

Flem Snopes, son of Ab Snopes, a central character in *The Hamlet, The Town*, and *The Mansion*. The cleverest and most mercenary of the Snopeses, Flem works his way from clerkship in Varner's store to the vice-presidency of Colonel Sartoris's bank in Jefferson. He is largely responsible for the suicide of his wife and drives Manfred De Spain, her lover, from town in order to become president of the Bank of Jefferson and move into the De Spain mansion. He exploits the greed of others for his own gain and is concerned with obtaining and preserving a patina of respectability.

I. O. Snopes, a character in *The Hamlet*. For a time a schoolteacher, I. O. is characterized by his habit of lengthy and non-sensical stringing together of proverbs.

Ike Snopes, a character in *The Hamlet*. An idiot and the ward of Flem Snopes, Ike has a pathetic and tender love affair with Jack Houston's cow. The animal is finally bought and slaughtered by Ike's scandalized relatives.

Lump Snopes, a character in *The Hamlet*. Lump is Flem's successor as clerk in Varner's store.

Linda Snopes, a character in *The Town* and *The Mansion*. A Snopes in name only, Linda is the illegitimate child of Eula Varner and Hoake McCarron and is courted by Gavin Stevens, a lawyer twenty years her senior.

Mink Snopes, a character in *The Hamlet* and *The Mansion*. Mink allows his cow to stray into Jack Houston's pasture and is ordered to pay a pound fee to reclaim the animal. Feeling that he has been wronged, Mink ambushes and murders Houston and is sent to prison. He is released forty years later and returns to Jefferson to murder Flem Snopes, who refused to help Mink during his trial.

Montgomery Ward Snopes, son of I. O. Snopes, a character in *The Town* and *The Mansion*. Montgomery Ward runs a "French postcard peep-show" behind a supposed photography studio. He is discovered, but to prevent the name of Snopes from being soiled with a charge of pornography, Flem plants whiskey in Montgomery Ward's studio and has him jailed on a charge of moonshining.

Wallstreet Panic Snopes, son of Eck Snopes, a character in *The Hamlet* and *The Town*. Like his father, Wallstreet is honest, therefore not a true Snopes. He buys a grocery store and becomes a prosperous wholesaler.

Snow, Edgar Parks (1905–1972), editor, journalist. Snow was born in Kansas City, Missouri. *Red Star Over China* (1938), a firsthand report of rising Communist power in China, established Snow's reputation. *People on Our Side* (1944) grew out of his experience as a war correspondent in World War II. Among his many books are *The Pattern of Soviet Power* (1945), *Stalin Must Have Peace* (1946), *Random Notes on Red China* (1957), *China* (1957), and *Journey to the Beginning* (1958).

Snow, [Charles] Wilbert (1884–1977), teacher, poet, public official. Snow, born in Maine, taught English at several colleges and universities, joined the faculty at Wesleyan University in 1921, and served as Governor of Connecticut (1946–1947). His poetry appears in *Maine Coast* (1923), *The Inner Harbor* (1926), *Down East* (1932), *Selected Poems* (1936), *Before the Wind* (1938), *Maine Tides* (1940), *Sonnets to Steve* (1957), and *Collected Poems* (1963). *Codline's Child* (1974) is autobiography.

Snow-Bound, A Winter Idyll (1866), a poem by JOHN GREENLEAF WHITTIER. *Snow-Bound* is an idealized memory of being snowed in on his father's Massachusetts farm.

Snow Image, The, and Other Twice-Told Tales (1851), a collection of seventeen tales and sketches by NATHANIEL HAWTHORNE. The stories are an assemblage of early works and new material. The only unifying factor is perhaps the idea of the brevity of human life and fame. The title story, subheaded "A Childish Miracle," contrasts the practical world of the father with the imaginative world of the children, symbolized by the snow sprite they create. The concluding story, MY KINSMAN, MAJOR MOLINEAUX, shows the fleeting glory of one

SNOPES GENEALOGY

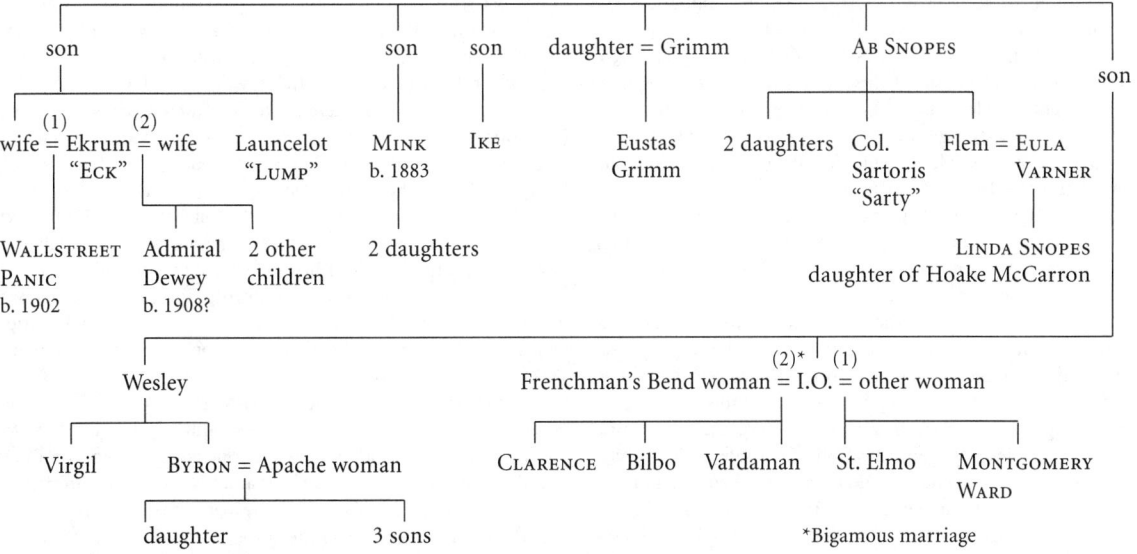

man, and another man's subsequent initiation into life. ETHAN BRAND, the best story of the collection, deals with a man in search of the unpardonable sin who finds, after wandering across the earth, that the search itself causes the sin to reside in his own heart.

Snows of Kilimanjaro, The (*Esquire*, August 1936, included in *The Fifth Column and the First 49 Stories*, 1938), short story by ERNEST HEMINGWAY. With a wealthy woman who has been keeping him, a writer named Harry goes on a safari in Africa. There he hopes to "work the fat off his mind" so he can set to work on all the things he has dreamed of writing. This dream is shattered when he develops gangrene in his leg. In the knowledge of death he reviews his life, a life that has sacrificed talent for pleasure. In a dream just before he dies he sees the legendary gigantic frozen leopard on the summit of Mt. Kilimanjaro, a symbol of death in the pursuit of vain, fleshly pleasures.

Snyder, Gary (1930–), poet and essayist. Snyder was born in San Francisco and educated at Reed College, Indiana University, and Berkeley. He shipped out as a seaman and later worked as a logger and forest lookout in the Pacific Northwest. These work experiences are vital parts of his aesthetic, and he has spoken of how the rhythm of the job enters the rhythm of the poem. Returning from Japan to America in the 1970s, Snyder helped form a commune with friends and built himself a house on the west slope of the Sierra Nevadas. He has taught at the University of California at Davis and been associated with the Naropa Institute of Disembodied Poetics in Colorado.

Interested in Native American culture from early in his life, Snyder added to this a growing interest in the life and culture of the Far East. He spent several years as a practicing monk in a Buddhist community in Japan and traveled widely in that part of the world. He has said he believes in the values of archaic culture: "the fertility of the soil, the magic of animals, the power-vision in solitude, the terrifying initiation and rebirth, the love and ecstasy of the dance, the common work of the tribe." His collection of essays *Earth House Hold* (1969) was widely read as one of the founding texts of the ecology movement. Snyder has continued to expound related ideas and has been a strong proponent of the Gaia theory, advanced by James Lovelock, which argues for the truly organic and self-regulating wholeness of the biosphere.

Snyder's literary roots go back to the San Francisco Renaissance and the so-called Beat movement, which included Allen Ginsberg and Jack Kerouac. Snyder is depicted as Japhy Ryder, a transcendent bohemian, in Kerouac's novel *The Dharma Bums* (1958). His poetic practice is indebted to the imagism of Ezra Pound, which prized the natural symbol and the pared-down description, as well as to objectivism, as practiced by Charles Olson and others. Objectivism continued and intensified imagism's emphasis on perceptual energies and an avoidance of misleading generalizations and safe philosophical nostrums. Against a background of existentialism and political radicalism, Snyder moved from early work such as *Myths & Texts* (1960) to travel and meditation poems in *The Back Country* (1968). Later books, such as *Regarding Wave* (1970)

and *Turtle Island* (1974) explored the need for community and cultural renewal. *Axe Handles* (1983) continued along these lines, with an even sparer sense of diction and a tighter, almost Zen-like intensity. *No Nature*, a volume of selected poems, appeared in 1992. *Mountains and Rivers without End*, a collection Snyder worked on for forty years, was published in 1996. *A Place in Space* (1995) contains new and selected prose. Often read as a spokesman of the counterculture, Snyder is really best seen as being in the tradition of such American visionaries as Thoreau. For him poetry is a spiritual discipline and a cultural resource, and it must be used wisely and reverentially, as should all forms of nature. A full study of the writings is found in *Gary Snyder's Vision: Poetry and the Real Work*, by Charles Molesworth.

CHARLES MOLESWORTH/BP

So Big (1924), a novel by EDNA FERBER. This story deals with the struggles of the widowed Selina DeJong to make a living for herself and her baby son Dirk.

Society and Solitude, essays by RALPH WALDO EMERSON, derived from lectures delivered after 1858 and published in 1870. Topics include art, civilization, courage, domestic life, farming, and old age. The title piece deals with the conflict in the mind of a person of intellect and integrity between the desire for solitude and the need for the company of other people.

Soglow, Otto (1900–1975), cartoonist. Soglow, born in New York City, began drawing cartoons for leading magazines in 1925, and in 1933 joined King Features Syndicate. A number of his drawings have been collected in books: *Pretty Pictures* (1931); *Everything's Rosy* (1932); *The Little King* (with David Plotkin, 1933); and *Wasn't the Depression Terrible?* (1934). Soglow's illustrations appear in books of verse by OGDEN NASH and others.

Solzhenitsyn, Alexander (1918–), novelist, short-story writer, historian, playwright, poet. Born in Kislovodsk, Russia, Solzhenitsyn was trained in physics and mathematics at the University of Rostov. He was a Red Army officer during World War II, but was arrested in 1945 for making a disrespectful reference to Josef Stalin. He served eight years in prison, and was exiled to Kazakhstan to teach in a rural school until 1957. His earliest book, the only one initially published in the USSR, *One Day in the Life of Ivan Denisovich* (1962, U.S. publication 1963), follows Ivan Denisovich Shukhov through an "almost . . . happy day" in a Siberian prison camp. Premier Khrushchev liked the full picture of the camp, the lack of any special horrors, and the nonverbal perspective of a peasant, and he personally approved publication in the literary journal *Novy Mir*. Its appearance brought world fame to the author.

As a result of this fame, ex-prisoners wrote to Solzhenitsyn of their prison-camp experiences, and he replied, asking for further details and documentation. Solzhenitsyn combined these with extensive interviews and his own unjust imprisonment to write *The Gulag Archipelago* in three volumes (1974, 1975, 1978), a history of the gulag prison system.

The First Circle compared the gulag to Dante's inferno, in the highest circle of which lived the pagan philosophers and poets who, although in hell, suffered no physical torments. It descibes Stalin's imprisonment of too many of the nation's scientists and his bizarre solution: to group privileged prisoners in *sharaska* research institutes. Gleb Nerzhin in 1949 debates with two fellow prisoners. He is drawn first to Lev Rubin's argument that the Leninist revolution had started idealistically before being corrupted by Stalin, but he is eventually convinced by Dmitri Sologdin's condemnation of the Communist rejection of personal morality and faith. Nerzhin faces a test of his new belief when he, as had Solzhenitsyn, refuses to work on a device for the secret police to use against innocent citizens; instead, the character accepts shipment to the lower circles of Stalin's hell.

Solzhenitsyn based *Cancer Ward* on his own experience in a clinic. Denying any symbolic intent, Solzhenitsyn described the characters so aptly that they emerge for most readers as representative types in Soviet society, especially Oleg Kostoglotov, the Solzhenitsyn-surrogate, and the Stalinist, Pavel Russanov.

Drawn partly from the experience of Solzhenitsyn's father, *August 1914* (1972) is the first in a projected cycle called *The Red Wheel*. Begun in praise of the October Revolution by the teenage Solzhenitsyn, it emerged as an anti-Communist work depicting the origin of a catastrophic revolution.

In 1973 the KGB confiscated a manuscript of *The Gulag Archipelago*; the following year, after the book had been published in the West, he fled Russia to avoid arrest. In *Pismo vozhdyam Sovetskogo Soyuza* (tr. *Letter to the Soviet Leaders* 1974), he advocated the end of Communist rule. In 1976, he settled in Vermont, where he continued to write about his native land.

Lenin in Zurich (1976) consists of a chapter on Lenin removed from *August 1914* to avoid antagonizing the censors and of Lenin chapters for future volumes. Solzhenitsyn restored the Lenin chapter in a republication of *August 1914* (1989), adding two hundred pages. *The Oak and the Calf* appeared in 1980. Solzhenitsyn returned to Russia in 1994.

In his acceptance speech for the 1970 Nobel Prize (published 1972), Solzhenitsyn lists two goals for literature: to enable people divided by barriers to empathize with one another, and to reveal "the lie" on which political terror thrives. Solzhenitsyn seeks a pure language. Aided by Vladimir Dahl's linguistic principles, historical dictionary, and collection of proverbs, Solzhenitsyn re-enriches the Russian literary vocabulary. However, his place in world literature is better ensured by the high degree to which he succeeds in his two goals. Studies include Michael Scammell, *Solzhenitsyn: A Biography* (1984), and Christopher Moody, *Solzhenitsyn* (1976).

RAYMOND J. WILSON III/BP

Sometimes a Great Notion, a 1964 novel by KEN KESEY about a strike in the Oregon lumber industry.

Sondheim, Stephen (1930–), composer and lyricist. Born in New York City, Sondheim established himself with the lyrics for Leonard Bernstein's *West Side Story* (1957). Musicals with both words and music by Sondheim include *A Funny Thing Happened on the Way to the Forum* (1962), *Company*

(1970), *Sweeney Todd* (1979), *Sunday in the Park with George* (Pulitzer Prize, 1984), *Into The Woods* (1987), and *Passion* (1994).

Sone, Monica (1919–), memoirist. Monica Sone's *Nisei Daughter* (1953) recounts the experiences of Japanese-Americans in detention camps during World War II.

Song, Cathy (1955–), poet. Born in Hawaii, Cathy Song was educated at the University of Hawaii, Wellesley, and Boston University. The title poem of *Picture Bride* (1982) tells of the author's Korean grandmother, a mail-order bride in Hawaii. *Frameless Windows, Squares of Light* appeared in 1988, and *School Figures* in 1994. Her book titles show an interest in forms and patterns to order her experiences.

Song of Hawatha. See HIAWATHA.

Song of Myself, a poem by WALT WHITMAN, originally published at the head of the first edition of LEAVES OF GRASS (1855) but not given its present title until the sixth edition (1881). By design and accomplishment a revolutionary manifesto, it announces new subject matter for poetry, the American democratic self, and a new style for embodying it—a combination chant and ordinary speech, with a few foreign phrases thrown in—in just over 1300 varying free verse lines.

In accordance with this program, and striving for openness and inclusiveness, the structure of the poem, rather than following a narrative, dramatic, logical, or lyrical order, unfolds in a mixture of all four incrementally around an associative sequence of widening spirals, circling through a number of topics a number of times, yet adding to their meaning in the process, somewhat in the manner of the theme-and-variations of musical form. Embodying a religious, political, and psychological journey, it is not only a poem about *self* but also a poem about *itself*—a poem in which the speaker is in the process of discovering and creating himself, his vocation, and the form of his poem—form embodying meaning in the organic fashion promulgated by romantic and modernist writers. At the same time, its 52 sections—matching the number of weeks in a year—fall into a traditional and natural 3-part division. The first 5 sections constitute an opening statement of the poem's vision of the underlying unity in all things, and the last 15 form a conclusion, with the middle 32 sections containing the body of the poem. Here, within the largest section, is found an alternating structure, which varies in focus from people to nature, from the positives in life to the negatives, and from self-assurance to doubts. Within *that* structure is an alternation from statement to exemplification, and it is in relation to the latter that Whitman created the so-called catalogue technique for giving the effect of inclusiveness at the heart of the poem's vision.

Resembling the mysticism of both East and West, yet differing in its insistence on the physical, as in William Blake— everything that lives is holy—and in the foremost New England Transcendentalist, RALPH WALDO EMERSON—the visible world bodies forth the invisible—the poem's vision seeks to annihilate the characteristic dualisms of Judeo-Christian culture, and to affirm that literature and life, the many and the one, self and other, matter and spirit, body and soul, good and evil, chastity and sexuality, city and country are parts of a single overall process rather than representing opposing forces in life. Thus, to sing of oneself is to sing of all, and to affirm an "optimistic" view of life, while taking inventories of pain and suffering, is to "contradict" oneself—which he of course affirms in turn.

"Song of Myself" has proven an inspiration and a challenge to many modernist and contemporary poets—from Pound, Hart Crane, and W. C. Williams to Charles Olson, Galway Kinnell, and James Merrill—in their efforts to create American epics, forms, or visions for the 20th century. Studies include James E. Miller, Jr., ed., *Whitman's "Song of Myself"—Origin, Growth, Meaning* (1964); and Edwin Haviland Miller, *Walt Whitman's "Song of Myself": A Mosaic of Interpretations* (1989). NORMAN FRIEDMAN

Song of Solomon. This, TONI MORRISON's third novel (1977), chronicles how a young African-American comes to terms with his family's painful and sometimes mysterious history. Adopting the magical realist technique of Gabriel Garcia Márquez, the novel is rich in eccentric characters and it successfully synthesizes stark and convincing naturalistic detail with a lyrical narrative style rooted in black speech that includes strong threads of the symbolic and the supernatural.

The main character, Milkman, so named because he was nursed by his mother until he was six, is reluctantly drawn into a quest to understand his troubled family's past. A central mystery is how names are acquired and what they mean. Milkman's wealthy father, Macon Dead, is obsessed with owning things and people. Milkman's mother, Ruth, is equally obsessed, perhaps to the point of incest, with the memory of her dead father. Milkman's aunt, Pilate, a woman uniquely in touch with her own feelings as well as with the supernatural, is unreasonably hated by her brother Macon. But she shows Milkman an unpossessive love that he cannot find from his parents. Milkman's intelligent friend Guitar grows absorbed in a conspiracy bent on violent revenge against whites, and gradually turns this violence against his own "brother" Milkman. At the same time, Milkman's return to his family's native ground, Virginia, and his serial ordeal in quest of knowledge of his family's past brings him to comprehend and even take pride in its present. The book's remarkable conclusion blends tragedy with the ambiguous hope of soaring above the limits of time and human failure. THOMAS J. TRAVISANO

Song of the Broad-Axe (1856), a poem by WALT WHITMAN. This poem appeared first in the 1856 edition of *Leaves of Grass* and was considerably revised in later editions. It describes the use of the axe in feudal lands abroad and in democratic lands at home.

Song of the Chattahoochee, The (probably written in 1877, pub. in 1883; in posthumous poems, 1884), a poem by SIDNEY LANIER. Throughout his career Lanier, a skilled musician, sought constantly to arrive at an artistic marriage of verse and music, perhaps never more successfully than in this poem. It is a triumph of alliteration, onomatopoeia, and melody.

Song of the Lark, The (1915), a novel by WILLA CATHER. The author said this was both her favorite novel and the one that satisfied her least. It deals with the transformation of Thea Kronborg, daughter of a Swedish preacher in Moonstone, Colorado, from a passionate, troubled, eager adolescent into an opera star.

Song of the Open Road (1856), a poem by WALT WHITMAN. In the 1856 and 1860 editions of *Leaves of Grass* this poem was called *Poem of the Road*. It was given its present title in 1871. Other revisions were made in subsequent editions.

Songs from Vagabondia (1890), poems by BLISS CARMAN and RICHARD HOVEY. These poems are melodious songs in the bohemian tradition and were widely popular, especially in college circles, toward the end of the 19th century. Carman wrote "A Vagabond Song," which set the key. Hovey contributed the celebrated "Stein Song," also "Comrades" and "At The Crossroad." The two poets later issued *More Songs from Vagabondia* (1898) and *Last Songs from Vagabondia* (1901).

Songs of Labor and Other Poems (1850), poems by JOHN GREENLEAF WHITTIER. Whittier called these verses "my simple lays of homely toil." The Dedication, in verse, is followed by "The Ship-Builders," "The Shoemakers," "The Drovers," "The Fishermen," "The Huskers," "The Corn-Song," and "The Lumbermen." The poems express much of the poet's philosophy of life, especially his belief in the nobility of manual labor. The songs appeared originally in the *Democratic Review* and the *National Era* in 1845–47.

Sonny's Blues, a short story by JAMES BALDWIN. Published first in the *Partisan Review* (1957), it was collected in *Going to Meet the Man* (1965). It is a first-person narrative of a man remembering his younger brother, who has been arrested as a drug dealer.

Son of the Middle Border, A (1917), an autobiographical narrative by HAMLIN GARLAND. The book was followed by A DAUGHTER OF THE MIDDLE BORDER (1921), *Trail-Makers of the Middle Border* (1926), *Memories of the Middle Border* (1926), and *Back-Trailers of the Middle Border* (1928).

Sontag, Susan (1933–), essayist, critic, novelist, short-story writer. Born Susan Rosenblatt to a couple engaged in the fur trade in China, she was brought up in New York City by a nanny. When she was five she learned that her father, whom she had rarely seen, had died overseas. The name Sontag came from her stepfather. Entering the University of Chicago at fifteen, she married a professor at seventeen, and gave birth to her son, David Rieff, before she was nineteen. She completed her education at Harvard.

In *Against Interpretation* (1966) Sontag made the case for sensory response to art; *Styles of Radical Will* (1969) and *On Photography* (1977) are also collections of aesthetic criticism. In *Illness as Metaphor* (1978) and *AIDS and Its Metaphors* (1989) Sontag treats the social and artistic perceptions of serious illness. THE VOLCANO LOVER (1992) recounts the famous love affair between Admiral Nelson and Lady Hamilton from the perspective of the cuckolded husband, Sir William Hamilton. *In America* (2000) is a historical novel loosely based on the life of the immigrant Polish actress, Helena Modjeska, at the turn of the twentieth century. It has been criticized for using other writers' words without attribution. Other novels include *The Benefactor* (1963) and *Death Kit* (1967). *I, etcetera* (1978) is a story collection, and *A Trip to Hanoi* (1968) deals with views of the Vietnam War.

Sophie's Choice, a 1979 novel by WILLIAM STYRON concerning the life of a survivor of Auschwitz whose father and husband were killed by the Nazis.

Sorensen, Virginia (1912–), novelist. Sorensen's novels reflect her childhood as a Mormon in Utah. They include *A Little Lower Than the Angels* (1942), *On This Star* (1946), *The Evening and the Morning* (1949), *Many Heavens* (1954), and *Kingdom Come* (1960). *Where Nothing Is Long Ago* (1963) is autobiography. Sorensen has also written books for children, including *The Miracles on Maple Hill*, a Newbery Medal winner.

Sorghum, Senator. A satirical character in the writings of PHILANDER CHASE JOHNSON, particularly his *Senator Sorghum's Primer of Politics* (1906).

Sorrentino, Gilbert (1929–), poet, novelist. Sorentino edited *Neon* (1956–60), a magazine featuring Beat writers. His fiction adopts various experimental narrative devices. *Sky Changes* (1966) parodies a quest; *Steelwork* (1971) and *Imaginary Qualities of Actual Things* (1971) are fictions without plot; *Mulligan Stew* (1979) is a literary potpourri with authors, characters, critics, and publishers thrown together; *Aberrations of Starlight* (1980) features multiple points of view; and *Crystal Vision* (1981) is almost exclusively dialogue. *Misterioso* (1990) is the final volume in a trilogy including *Odd Number* (1985) and *Rose Theatre* (1987). *Red the Fiend* (1995) is set in Depression-era New York. His poetry titles include *The Darkness Surrounds Us* (1960), *Black and White* (1964), *The Perfect Fiction* (1968), *Corrosive Sublimate* (1971), *The Orangery* (1978), and *Selected Poems* (1981). *Splendide Hotel* (1973) deals with the role of the poet. Reviews and essays are collected in *Something Said* (1984).

Soto, Gary (1952–), poet, memoirist. Born in Fresno, California, Soto was educated at the local branch of California State University and the University of California-Irvine. His first two books of poetry, *The Element of San Joaquin* (1977) and *The Tale of Sunlight* (1978), trace a journey from the grit of urban Fresno and the sweat of farm work in the San Joaquin valley to central Mexico where his family's odyssey began. *Black Hair* (1985) is a poetry collection. *Living Up the Street* (1984) and *Summer Life* (1990) are reminiscences. *Lesser Evils* (1988) and *Who Will Know Us?* (1990) collect essays. *Baseball in April* (1990) is a sports story collection for young readers.

Sot-Weed Factor, The, novel by JOHN BARTH (1960, rev. 1966). A picaresque fictional biography of EBENEZER COOK, writer of the earlier poem of the same name.

Sot-Weed Factor, The; or, A Voyage to Maryland (1708), a satire by EBENEZER COOK. The author may have been, as he says in this poem, an Englishman who came to Maryland in order to act as a factor, or agent, of a British merchant dealing in tobacco, but his true identity is problematical.

The poem is a Hudibrastic narrative of the author's dealings in America, his effort to recover property stolen from him, and his mistreatment in the courts. It ends with a trenchant curse on America and all its inhabitants. In 1730 appeared a sequel, *Sotweed Redivivus, or The Planter's Looking-Glass,* by "E. C. Gent." It is a much more serious and less readable production, directed against overproduction of tobacco. In a revised version this was also printed in THE MARYLAND MUSE (1731), which was edited by Lawrence C. Wroth for the *Proceedings* of the American Antiquarian Society (1934).

Soul on Ice (1968), a collection of essays by ELDRIDGE CLEAVER. The work, written after his release from Soledad Prison and based on his reading of PAINE, Marx, Lenin, BALDWIN, and MALCOLM X, described his state of mind at that time about the African-American experience in America.

Souls of Black Folk, The (1903), a collection of fifteen essays and sketches by W. E. B. DU BOIS. In it he describes the lives of African-American farmers, sketches the role of music in their churches, details the history of the Freedman's Bureau, discusses the career of Booker T. Washington, and advocates a commitment to higher education for the most talented African-American youth.

Sound and the Fury, The (1929), a novel by WILLIAM FAULKNER. Faulkner's fourth novel, his first radical experiment in form and technique, is one of his most successful works. Three of the book's four sections are interior monologues of the three Compson brothers who, with their hypochondriac mother and their vanished sister Caddy, are the sole surviving members of a decaying aristocratic family in Mississippi. The first section, seen through the eyes of the idiot Benjy, is literally "a tale told by an idiot, full of sound and fury." The second follows the thoughts of Quentin, a Harvard student whose world, built on a dying view of family honor and on his abnormally close ties to his sister Caddy, has been shattered by her seduction and hasty, loveless marriage. In their cryptic, often confusing changes of period, these two sections reflect respectively the disorder and the hypersensitivity of their protagonists' minds.

The third section is related in straightforward language by greedy, petty-minded Jason, who has kept for himself the money Caddy has been sending for support of her illegitimate daughter Quentin. Quentin manages to steal it back and runs off with a traveling carnival performer. The final section is a third-person narrative focused on Dilsey, the African-American cook, whose patience and compassion are implicitly contrasted with the self-absorption and self-destructiveness of the Compsons.

Sousa, John Philip (1854–1932), bandmaster, composer. Well educated in music, Sousa in 1880 became bandmaster of the U.S. Marine Corps band stationed at the White House; the band soon won national fame. In 1892 he was released from duty and formed his own band, with which he toured at home and abroad. He wrote music of much variety but won recognition particularly with his marches: "Semper Fidelis" (1888), "Washington Post March" (1889), "The Stars and Stripes Forever" (1897), and many others. He also wrote two comic operas, *El Capitan* (1896) and *The Bride Elect*

(1897); and two novels, *Pipetown Sandy* (1905) and *The Fifth String* (1907). His autobiography *Marching Along* was published in 1928.

Souster, Raymond (1921–   ),   poet, editor. Souster helped disseminate new Canadian poetry in the 1940s and 1950s, especially through the Contact Press of Toronto. He is himself the undisputed poet of that city, which he celebrates in short poems of strong rhythm and colloquial manner. His major collections are *The Color of the Times* (1964), *Ten Elephants on Yonge Street* (1965), *So Far So Good* (1969), and *Selected Poems* (1972). His later volumes include *Double-Header* (1975) and *Extra Innings* (1977). His work has been collected in seven volumes (1980–92). Other collections include *Riding the Long Black Horse* (1993) and *No Sad Songs Wanted Here* (1995).

South, The.   The American South was recognized early as a region set apart by the crops that flourished in its warm climate, the plantation system that developed to serve its agriculturally based economy, and the slaves who, beginning at Jamestown in 1619, were imported to work the fields of tobacco, cotton, indigo, sugar cane, and rice. By the time of the Revolution, coastal Virginia and South Carolina boasted a landed gentry that imitated the society of the English manor, and the Southern cavalier was in place as a contrasting type to the Northern yankee. Along with the so-called darky and poor white, the figures of the plantation master and his retinue were well established by the early 19th century as staple regional characters. When the Civil War swept away the plantation regime, it simply added one more factor, the element of lost glory, to Southern distinctiveness.

The uniqueness of Southern speech represents another basis for the idea of a South that is set apart, even though Southern language practices can hardly be considered uniform. Commonly held perceptions range from the notion of the Southern drawl to a belief in the special powers of Southern oratory. Explanations of why original and colorful language patterns persist in the South include the rural and small-town traditions of extended conversation and storytelling, the existence of close-knit communities that long remained isolated from mainstream culture, the Bible belt's emphasis on the poetic cadences of the King James version, and clear categories of caste and class that tended to encourage the use of speech patterns to verify a speaker's membership in a particular social group.

Geographically, the South is made up of the states that left the Union in 1860–61 to form the Confederacy: Alabama, Arkansas, Florida, Georgia, Louisiana, Mississippi, North Carolina, South Carolina, Tennessee, Texas, and Virginia. Most would add to the list at least the portions of Kentucky, Maryland, and Missouri where slavery was entrenched. Yet the South is both more and less than any geographic location. Few shared traditions link the people who settled regions as disparate as the Texas plains, Appalachian Mountains, Louisiana bayous, Florida everglades, Natchez river plantations, Charleston mansions, and the Outer Banks. In fact, there are many Souths but even so, as an emotional and intellectual construct, the South is a potent social and political force.

Specifically, writers who are Southern by cultural identification, no matter where they were born or grew up, have for three centuries made enduring contributions to American literature and since the 1920s have often dominated the American literary scene.

The earliest works to give some indication that the South would establish a separate literary tradition were written by an explorer, Captain John Smith; a gentleman landowner, William Byrd II; and a statesman, Thomas Jefferson. Smith's *A True Relation of Occurrences and Accidents in Virginia* (1608) was the first of several accounts the adventurer wrote to describe the southern section of the New World. In 1728, Byrd wrote a colorful record of his participation in an expedition to survey a line dividing Virginia and North Carolina. Entitled *The History of the Dividing Line*, this work establishes an ideal of the Virginia gentleman at the expense of North Carolina lubberlanders. Thomas Jefferson's letters are also an indispensable guide to the life of the Virginia gentleman. *Notes on the State of Virginia* (1785) provides comments on all aspects of the life of Jefferson's region during the early years of the Republic.

By the early 19th century Charleston, South Carolina, had replaced Virginia as the seat of Southern culture. Charleston was home to two influential antebellum magazines, the *Southern Review* (1828–32) and *Russell's* (1857–60), as well as to many writers, including HUGH SWINTON LEGARÉ, poet PAUL HAMILTON HAYNE, and novelist WILLIAM GILMORE SIMMS. Simms's border romances provide a starting point for Southern versions of the historical novel. An instructive contrast to Simms's is EDGAR ALLAN POE, born in Richmond, who left the South after attempting to edit the *Southern Literary Magazine* there and who rejected regional materials entirely in the poetry and fiction that gave him far more lasting fame than any other antebellum writer of Southern background achieved.

The plantation novel, the South's most specifically Southern literary tradition, received its definitive expression in Maryland author JOHN PENDLETON KENNEDY's *Swallow Barn* (1832), although many other authors, including NATHANIEL BEVERLY TUCKER, WILLIAM ALEXANDER CARUTHERS, and JOHN ESTEN COOKE, practiced the form. The pre–Civil War genre of the plantation romance, along with more overtly polemical writings—notably WILLIAM GRAYSON's "The Hireling and the Slave" (1851)—provided models of stock literary figures such as the master, mistress, mammy, and belle, and such familiar trappings as pillared mansions, magnolias and porticoes, darkies serenading, and dashing gentlemen fighting duels or riding to hounds. Plantation literature received a goad from HARRIET BEECHER STOWE's *Uncle Tom's Cabin* (1852), which itself drew on commonly held stereotypes of slaves, plantation owners, and overseers. Stowe relied as well on accounts of fugitive slaves who penned memoirs known as SLAVE NARRATIVES. The narratives of FREDERICK DOUGLASS, James Pennington, Solomon Northup, Henry Bibb, WILLIAM WELLS BROWN, and HARRIET JACOBS challenged the plantation romance's vision of the idyllic life on the plantation.

Particularly after the Civil War had destroyed the Old South as fact, many Southern writers responded to the call from

Northern literary magazines such as *Scribner's* and *Atlantic Monthly* for literature that could paint quaint pictures of the world memorialized as a lost cause. One successful response came from Middle Georgia humorist JOEL CHANDLER HARRIS. Beginning with *Uncle Remus: His Songs and His Sayings* (1880), Harris developed his black storyteller in several collections that dramatized the exploits of the folk hero Brer Rabbit within frame sketches emphasizing benign master-slave relations. THOMAS NELSON PAGE, especially in the stories of *In Ole Virginia* (1887), charmed readers with cavaliers and loyal black retainers, while GEORGE W. CABLE presented a somewhat grimmer picture of race relations among whites, Creoles, and blacks in his novel of New Orleans, *The Grandissimes* (1880). SIDNEY LANIER gave the New South the beginnings of a native tradition in poetry, particularly with his late marshland verses: "The Marshes of Glynn" (1878) and "A Ballad of Trees and the Master" (1881).

During this so-called reconstruction period the South's first great novelist, MARK TWAIN, created his most compelling works—*The Adventures of Tom Sawyer* (1876), *Life on the Mississippi* (1883), *Adventures of Huckleberry Finn* (1884), *A Connecticut Yankee in King Arthur's Court* (1889), and *The Tragedy of Pudd'nhead Wilson* (1894). For these books Twain drew on memories of boyhood adventures in Hannibal, Missouri, and on Mississippi riverboats, but also on his personal witness of how slavery, clannishness, and social pretension affected Southern society. He expressed in realistic, vernacular dialect the tensions that haunted life in the South both before and after the Civil War.

Twain was influenced by the antebellum South's popular tradition of Southwestern humor, produced by writers who scorned the sentimental plantation lore. They created instead rogues, con men, and assorted low characters for newspaper and magazine sketches collected in books such as AUGUSTUS BALDWIN LONGSTREET's *Georgia Scenes* (1835), JOHNSON JONES HOOPER's *Some Adventures of Simon Suggs* (1845), THOMAS BANGS THORPE's *The Big Bear of Arkansas* (1845), JOSEPH GLOVER BALDWIN's *Flush Times in Alabama and Mississippi* (1853), and GEORGE WASHINGTON HARRIS's *Sut Lovingood* (1867). After the Civil War, local color literature harped on themes designed to present the region in a favorable light. However, CHARLES CHESNUTT gave unsentimental portrayals of how Southern racism affected blacks in five books written between 1899 and 1905. Missouri-born KATE CHOPIN in *The Awakening* (1899) gave a sensitive and, for the time, shocking dramatization of the restricted roles assigned to women in the late 19th century South through her story of a young Louisiana Creole wife and mother who longs for freedom.

ELLEN GLASGOW, a native of Richmond who in the 1890s began her long career as a novelist, complained that what Southern literature at the end of the century lacked was "blood and irony." In her best novels, from *Virginia* (1913) to *Barren Ground* (1925) to *The Sheltered Life* (1932), she provided an example of the sensibility that would eventually create the phenomenon now known as the Southern renascence, a flowering of literature that contained elements of tension, complexity, and irony often missing in the works of earlier Southerners.

In 1917, the year when Baltimore-born satirist H. L. MENCKEN designated the South as a culturally sterile "Sahara of the Bozart," a group of young men were meeting at Vanderbilt University in Nashville, Tennessee, to discuss their passion for poetry and their ambivalent feelings about the "Brahmin" South. Four of them, JOHN CROWE RANSOM, ALLEN TATE, DONALD DAVIDSON, and ROBERT PENN WARREN, were the force behind two of Southern literature's most important ventures: *The Fugitive*, a poetry magazine published in Nashville from 1922 to 1925, and the agrarian treatise I'LL TAKE MY STAND, which they published with eight other Southern intellectuals in 1930. Modern Southern literature, from the renascence to the present, exhibits many of the tendencies that the fugitive-agrarian writers highlighted in praising the South of memory. In the works of the Southern renascence, one finds a rurally ordered society whose people have been shaped by their closeness to nature, shared tragic history, deeply felt religious sense, respect for family, reliance on memory and, as we have seen, a special ear for speech—what Faulkner called a heritage of oratory. Thus, modern Southern writers can be expected to treat the past as memory rather than fact. They emphasize the concrete in both language and setting. The conflicts propelling their characters involve communally derived moral imperatives—personal responsibilities imposed on a particular time and place and tinged with religious consequences. The South's history, its experience of defeat in the Civil War, guilt over the institution of slavery, and moral compromise in the segregating of its black citizens has continued to be the material of its fictions, along with equally compelling myths— the lost cause, the golden age before the war, the patriarch, the cavalier, and the lady.

The year 1929 saw publication of the earliest important works of two of the South's most noted and dissimilar novelists: the first two novels of WILLIAM FAULKNER's Yoknapatawpha saga, *Sartoris* and *The Sound and the Fury*, and THOMAS WOLFE's *Look Homeward, Angel*. While Faulkner went on to publish over a dozen more major works, *Look Homeward, Angel*, which received more acclaim than Faulkner's books on first appearance, was to be Wolfe's only completely self-directed novel. Wolfe, a native of Asheville, North Carolina, drew on the town, his family, and his beloved mountains to create his sprawling autobiographical novel, part bildungsroman, part satire, part prose poem. All of Wolfe's work is more intensely romantic and lyrical, more overtly autobiographical, and much less formally disciplined than the work of other modern Southern writers, yet with many others he shared an obsessive concern with family, with time, with loss, and with language.

Faulkner's genius and phenomenal output made him the South's greatest writer, one who left his mark on all the literature that followed. Beginning with *Sartoris*, he created one of the world's fullest fictional lands, Yoknapatawpha County, a mythical place reflecting the Mississippi that went back to his great-grandfather's times but stretched forward to display his own and America's concerns from the 1930s through the 1950s. *As I Lay Dying* (1930), *Light in August* (1932), *Absalom, Absalom!* (1936), *Go Down Moses* (1942), the Snopes trilogy—*The Hamlet* (1940), *The Town* (1957), *The Mansion* (1959)—and

The Reivers (1962) all developed different facets of his mythical county through changing narrative voices and designs. As different as are the characters and techniques in these works, the Yoknapatawpha novels constitute a continuous saga, all the stories exploring people bound together through confrontation with the manners, values, and vision of their community.

Faulkner's works mine the themes that have given Southern literature its enduring matter: the past as burden, alive in the present; the human need to assert identity and to claim greatness; man's responsibility to and for others; the inevitable clash between man's limitations and his vision; the bonds that the land, family, and place exert; and nature's mysterious, compelling hold over human endeavor. Beginning in the 1920s and continuing to the present, many Southern writers have developed these themes. Their efforts have been accepted to such a degree that Southerners dominated American literature for close to thirty years and up to 1990 continued to draw a large readership worldwide. From 1920 to 1960 the Fugitives, the Agrarians, and the New Critics were among America's most energetic and influential literary groups, and individual writers who lived in or wrote about the South were at the center of the American literary scene. Ransom, Tate, Davidson, and Warren continued after their Fugitive years to publish remarkably diverse poetry. Warren, Wolfe, and Faulkner were joined by JAMES AGEE, EUDORA WELTY, KATHERINE ANN PORTER, CAROLINE GORDON, ANDREW LYTLE, and ERSKINE CALDWELL in writing highly successful novels and short stories. In drama DUBOSE HEYWARD, PAUL GREEN, TENNESSEE WILLIAMS, and LILLIAN HELLMAN took Southern scenes and characters to Broadway and beyond.

In fiction alone, and apart from Faulkner, Southern writers in the 1930s and 1940s contributed works of remarkable range in style and subject. Erskine Caldwell's *Tobacco Road* (1932) voiced an angry, often comically grotesque protest against the dehumanization of the Southern tenant farmer, while Allen Tate produced in *The Fathers* (1939) one of the few modern Southern works to look imaginatively at the South's interior agony during the Civil War. The 1940s saw publication of CARSON MCCULLERS's *The Heart is a Lonely Hunter* (1940), which colors a modern Southern setting with grotesque overtones; the gothic mode is even more evident in her best and most Southern work, the novella *The Ballad of the Sad Cafe* (1941). The year 1946 saw publication of Robert Penn Warren's *All the King's Men*, inspired in part by the career of Louisiana governor Huey Long, and Eudora Welty's first novel, *Delta Wedding*. Like *The Golden Apples*, her story collection of 1949, *Delta Wedding* combines myth, an unerring eye for revelatory gestures, and a gifted ear for Southern speech. Two books of this period are in a class by themselves: MARGARET MITCHELL's *Gone with the Wind* (1936), which more than any other Southern work both capitalized on and perpetuated the Old South's most alluring myths, and James Agee's *Let Us Now Praise Famous Men* (1941), a documentary of sharecropper families that combines Walker Evan's photographs with Agee's lyrical, intensely introspective prose. In nonfiction, 1941 brought two very different meditations on the South, Wilbur J. Cash's often satirical study of the Southern psyche, *The Mind of the South*,

and WILLIAM ALEXANDER PERCY's nostalgic self-portrait of a Southern patrician stoic, *Lanterns on the Levee*.

The period of the Southern renascence was also a period of flowering in African-American writing, and many of the participants turned to the South in search of scenes to dramatize their quest for identity. As Americans trapped by the burden of the past and the prejudice of the present, they defined the doubleness of Southern experience. In their works are seen the commingling of past and present, pain and beauty, guilt and pride that were the heritage of all Southerners. Some of the writers who in this period began to define the imaginative possibilities that the South held were poets JAMES WELDON JOHNSON (*God's Trombones*, 1927) and JEAN TOOMER (*Cane*, 1922); RICHARD WRIGHT with his autobiography *Black Boy* (1945); ZORA NEALE HURSTON in her anthology of African-American folklore *Mules and Men* (1935) and in her haunting novel *Their Eyes Were Watching God* (1937); and RALPH ELLISON, whose *Invisible Man* (1952) has been rated one of the most important novels of the 20th century.

Beginning in the 1950s, Southern literature took some new directions while still treating identifiably Southern concerns. The ear for Southern speech, the eye for concrete details of place, the emphasis on a religious dimension and man's need for wholeness continued to enrich Southern works that contained more urban themes, often more twisted violence and more alienation. Eudora Welty enhanced her distinguished career with the novels *Losing Battles* (1970) and *The Optimist's Daughter* (1972) which, like her earlier works, celebrate memory as a way of seeing and ordering place and experience. Yet another Mississippian, WALKER PERCY, emerged as a writer for whom the South becomes, metaphorically, a way to explore the condition of modern man trapped in everydayness and looking for spiritual answers. In *The Moviegoer* (1961) and *The Last Gentleman* (1966) Percy takes Faulknerian characters and rechannels their quests to include central religious themes of 20th-century Christian philosophy. Another writer who exploited the South's "mystery and manners" in order to express a religious dimension to life was FLANNERY O'CONNOR, of Milledgeville, Georgia. Her short stories, in collections like *A Good Man Is Hard to Find* (1955) and *Everything That Rises Must Converge* (1965), combine Catholic doctrine, elements of the grotesque, a sharp ear for comic folk speech, and relentless exposures of the sin of pride.

Since the midpoint of the 20th century, Southern literature has exhibited more diversity in theme and point of view, but no lessening of intensity in the creation of imaginative worlds that draw on distinctively Southern language, values, and settings. The South continues to be central in the poetry and fiction of Fred Chappell, JAMES DICKEY, REYNOLDS PRICE, and Robert Morgan; the poems of A. R. AMMONS, James Seay, and GEORGE GARRETT; the fiction of Appalachian writers like LEE SMITH and CORMAC MCCARTHY; the themes and settings of novels by African-American writers, including MARGARET WALKER, ALICE WALKER, ERNEST GAINES, and TONI MORRISON; the novels of male experience by BARRY HANNAH, HARRY CREWS, PAT CONROY, and CHARLES FRAZIER; and the stories of women's voice by ANNE

TYLER, GAIL GODWIN, ELLEN GILCHRIST, and JAYNE ANNE PHILLIPS. As the cultural forces that stimulated the Southern renascence have changed, so have the modes of Southern writers. Still, the South—a place of distinctive traditions, beliefs, and accents—remains intact and so, therefore, does its substantial impact on American literature.

LUCINDA H. MACKETHAN/GP

Southern Literary Messenger, The.   A magazine founded in Richmond, Virginia, by Thomas W. White in 1834. POE's "Berenice" and "The Unparalleled Adventures of One Hans Pfaal" were printed in March and June of 1835. In December, Poe took over the editorship. Contributing book reviews and literary essays, poems and stories, Poe raised the circulation from 500 to 3500 during his two-year stint. A study of his editorship is David K. Jackson's *Poe and the Southern Literary Messenger* (1934). The magazine ceased publication in 1864. A revival (1939–44) reprinted earlier material.

Southern Review [1].   The first of the magazines of this title was founded in 1828 at Charleston, South Carolina, by Stephen Eliott and HUGH SWINTON LEGARÉ, and expired four years later. The two men sought to foster literature in the South.

[2] A quarterly with the same name was published in Baltimore from January 1867 to October 1879. It was founded by A. T. Bledsoe and Sophia Bledsoe Herrick and was an ardent advocate of Southern ideas and writers, with PAUL HAMILTON HAYNE as its chief critic.

[3] The third magazine called *Southern Review* was also a quarterly, published at Louisiana State University from July 1935 to April 1942 under a succession of editors—C. W. Pipkin, CLEANTH BROOKS, and ROBERT PENN WARREN. It became one of the more important little magazines. In its critical essays it aligned itself with the New Critics and their techniques of close textual examination of poems. It had many notable contributors, among them John Crowe Ransom, F. O. Matthiessen, Yvor Winters, Wallace Stevens, W. H. Auden, Randall Jarrell, Donald Davidson, Mark Van Doren, Caroline Gordon, Katherine Anne Porter, and Eudora Welty. *Stories from the Southern Review* (1953) was edited by Brooks and Warren.

Southern, Terry (1924–2000),   screenwriter, novelist, short-story writer. Born in Texas, Southern began his education at Southern Methodist University and the University of Chicago, served in World War II, earned a Northwestern University B.A., and studied at the Sorbonne after the war. He is best known for the screenplays that earned him Academy Award nominations: *Dr. Strangelove or: How I Learned to Stop Worrying and Love the Bomb* (1964, with Stanley Kubrick and Peter George), considered one of the most important films of the 1960s; and *Easy Rider* (1969, with Peter Fonda and Dennis Hopper), chronicling some of the myths of the drug and "road" cultures. Southern's best known novel is *Candy* (Paris, 1958; New York, 1964), with Mason Hoffenberg, a parody of Voltaire's *Candide* that was attacked as obscene. Other books include *Red Dirt Marijuana and Other Tastes* (1967); a collection of short pieces; and the novels *Flash and Filigree* (1958),

The Magic Christian (1959), *Blue Movie* (1970), and *Texas Summer* (1991), the story of a young white boy's relationship with a black hired hand. Mr. Southern was a staff writer for *Saturday Night Live* in the 1980s and taught screenwriting at New York University and Columbia University.

Southern Vanguard, A.   See JOHN PEALE BISHOP.

Southwest, The.   A region comprising Oklahoma, Texas, Colorado, New Mexico, Utah, Arizona, Nevada, and California. The Southwest is a land of dramatic contrasts in topography and climate. Its rare beauty is evidenced by its many national parks. The Grand Canyon, Yosemite, Mesa Verde, Carlsbad, Zion, and the rest are witness to the region's uniqueness—and to the tertiary nature of much of its economic base, since tourism has been the one constant in a regional economy of boom and bust in extractive industry centered on oil, gas, copper, uranium, and other resources. Historically a hinterland, first to the great Spanish colonial empires in Central America, and later to the eastern United States, the region received identification by early 19th-century explorers like Zebulon Montgomery Pike and Stephen F. Long as part of something Long called the Great American Desert. The negative connotation led the Federal government to use eastern portions as a dumping ground for Native Americans forcibly removed from the Southeastern states. The Southwest was as well a refuge for particularist groups like the Mormons, seeking freedom from harassment in more settled areas. After Reconstruction, large numbers of Southern African-Americans fled to the area to escape Jim Crow.

In the last quarter of the 19th century, the region sustained large-scale pastoral economies and, with technologies developed in the Industrial Revolution, large-scale mining, which brought new cycles of boom and bust reminiscent of the California gold rush of the 1850s. Expansive agriculture, made possible only by irrigation in that arid and semiarid environment, has, since the late 19th century, proved more reliable than extractive industry. Yet, it has always been subject to the vagaries of nature, of which the Dust Bowl of the 1930s remains the most persistent reminder.

Owing to its vast and frequently vacant stretches, the Southwest has been used increasingly by the Federal government as a weapons testing area. Development and testing of the atomic bomb and related activities at Los Alamos, Alamagordo, White Sands, Frenchman's Flats, Yucca Flats, and other sites contributed significantly to the Southwestern economy, as have a disproportionate number of military bases and training centers. (Ten of the nation's fifteen Air Training Command Bases, for example, were located in the Southwest in 1988.) The military presence, like tourism, indicates the extent of the region's reliance on tertiary industry. Reno, Las Vegas, Lake Tahoe, Aspen, and Vail, among others, are further evidence of it.

Almost despite the fragile economic circumstances in a hostile environment where water is often the most precious commodity, Southwesterners maintain an enviable sense of place, facilitated to a considerable degree by the intermingling—sometimes willingly, sometimes not—of diverse cultural traditions, notably Native American, Hispanic, Anglo,

African-American, and Asian. The popularity of the Southwestern Sunbelt, especially after the energy crisis of the mid-1970s, and the resulting immigration of Americans from colder climes hardly affected the character of the region, except in burgeoning urban areas that are no more or less homogeneous than any other such American centers.

The best historical introductions are W. Eugene Hollon's *The Southwest: Old and New* (1961) and *Great American Desert: Then and Now* (1966). California, so much of an exception to the Southwestern pattern that many scholars refuse to consider it a part of the region, regardless of geography, is best explained in Kevin Starr, *Americans and the California Dream, 1850–1915* (1973).

The Native American looms large in Southwestern iconography, as do the cowboy, the oilman, the paisano, the prospector, the outlaw, and the nuclear scientist. Less commonly perceived is the figure of the artist or the scholar, but these too have significance on the region's cultural landscape. All these types have inspired countless volumes of fiction and nonfiction. J. FRANK DOBIE, *Guide to Life and Literature of the Southwest* (1942; 1952), is a good, if dated, introduction to the writing, and may be supplemented by Walter S. Campbell (Stanley Vestal), *The Book Lover's Southwest* (1955), and John Q. Anderson, Edwin W. Gaston, Jr., and James W. Lee (eds.), *Southwestern American Literature* (1980).

Novels by OLIVER LAFARGE, *Laughing Boy* (1929); JOHN JOSEPH MATHEWS, *Sundown* (1934); Frank Waters, *The Man Who Killed the Deer* (1942); Thomas Fall, *The Ordeal of Running Standing* (1970); Thomas Sanchez, *Rabbit Boss* (1972); R. A. Lafferty, *Okla Hannali* (1972); and LESLIE MARMON SILKO, *Ceremony* (1977), deal with adjustments to life by Native Americans living in proximity to Anglo society. EDWARD ABBEY, *The Brave Cowboy* (1956); Jack Schaefer, *Monte Walsh* (1963); John Culp, *The Bright Feathers* (1965); and LARRY MCMURTRY in the *Lonesome Dove Series* (1985–   ) carry the cowboy to a level far above the norms established by ZANE GREY and LOUIS L'AMOUR for the archetypal Southwesterner. JOHN NICHOLS's trilogy—*The Milagro Beanfield War* (1974), *The Magic Journey* (1978), and *The Nirvana Blues* (1981)—treats the Hispanic experience in the context of economic development in New Mexico. All of these broaden the literary perspectives established by such fictions as MARY AUSTIN's *The Flock* (1906) and WILLA CATHER's *Death Comes for the Archbishop* (1927).

Mark Twain, in ROUGHING IT (1871), describes Nevada's COMSTOCK LODE. John Walton Caughey, *Gold Is the Cornerstone* (1948), is a good historical treatment of the California gold rush. J. Frank Dobie, *Coronado's Children* (1930), celebrates the folklore of buried treasure and lost mines of the Southwest. John Joseph Mathews, *Life and Death of an Oilman: The Career of E. W. Marland* (1951), remains the best biography of an entrepreneur in the petroleum industry. Perhaps the best fiction about the impact of boom-and-bust economy on individual lives is Robert Lewis Taylor, *The Travels of Jaimie McPheeters* (1958).

BILLY THE KID was the region's most notorious outlaw, at least from the standpoint of the enormous literature he inspired. The best surveys are Ramon Adams, *A Fitting Death for Billy the Kid* (1960), and Stephen Tatum, *Inventing Billy the Kid* (1982). The best novels are EDWIN CORLE, *Billy the Kid* (1953), and Charles Neider, *The Authentic Death of Hendry Jones* (1956). The outlaw tradition is debunked in William Cunningham, *Pretty Boy* (1936), a fictional treatment of Charles Arthur ("Pretty Boy") Floyd. The concept of the outlaw as an individual of highminded purpose is advanced in John Steinbeck, THE GRAPES OF WRATH (1939), the great novel of the Dust Bowl; and in Edward Abbey, *The Monkey Wrench Gang* (1975), the novel that established the eco-raider—one who wages war against real estate developers, dam-builders, et al.—as a cult figure. The detective fictions of DASHIELL HAMMETT, RAYMOND CHANDLER, ROSS MACDONALD, WALTER MOSLEY, and others present the darker side of criminal activity and thus of society, particularly in Southern California.

Thomas McMahon's *Principles of American Nuclear Chemistry: A Novel* (1970) and Peggy Pond Church's altogether remarkable memoir *The House at Otowi Bridge* (1960) offer perspectives on Los Alamos in the heyday of atomic bomb development. Arrell Morgan Gibson's *The Santa Fe and Taos Colonies: Age of the Muses, 1900–1942* (1983) is a historical study of the relationship between environment and art, a topic also explored in Lawrence Clark Powell's *The Creative Literature of the Arid Lands: Essays on the Books and Their Writers* (1977).

WILLIAM W. SAVAGE, JR.

Southwick, Solomon (1773–1839),   poet, editor. Born in Rhode Island, Southwick was editor of the Albany *Register* from 1808 to 1817. In 1819 he founded *The Ploughboy*, one of the earliest newspapers intended for farmers, and wrote articles for it under a pen name that became widely known—Henry Homespun, Jr. In 1823 he published a long didactic poem, *The Pleasures of Poverty*, and in 1837, *Five Lessons for Young Men*.

Southworth, E[mma] D[orothy] E[liza] N[evitte] (1819–1899),   novelist. Southworth, born in Washington, D.C., became one of the most prolific and most widely read novelist of her day. Deserted by her husband, and with two children to support, she turned to teaching and writing to earn her living. Southworth's first novel, *Retribution*, was published in 1847. THE HIDDEN HAND (1859), her best work, was serialized in *The New York Ledger* and was dramatized by Robert Jones (1867, pub. 1889). She went on to write more than sixty novels that altogether sold millions of copies. Among her books are *The Curse of Clifton* (1852); *The Missing Bride* (1855); ISHMAEL, OR, IN THE DEPTHS (1863); *Self-Raised, or From the Depths* (1864); *The Fatal Marriage* (1869); *The Maiden Widow* (1870); and *A Leap in the Dark* (1881). Her *Works* (42 v.) appeared in 1872.

Sovereignty and Goodness of God, The.   See CAPTIVITY AND RESTAURATION OF MRS. MARY ROWLANDSON.

Spain and Spanish influence in the New World. Spain's conquest of the greatest empire in all history presents two figures side by side, the conquistador and the Jesuit priest. Columbus's discoveries were consolidated by the conquistadors. Portugal had seized a great realm on the east coast of South America, and when word of the richness and extent of the new lands reached other nations of Europe, the French, English, and Dutch began to loot the Spanish Empire. The last Spanish outposts in the New World fell in the SPANISH-AMERICAN WAR. However, Spanish culture survives vigorously in the eighteen Latin American republics carved from the Empire. They occupy about 4,500,000 square miles of territory.

The history of Mexico over the centuries is somewhat typical. For three hundred years it was a Spanish colony, and during this period education was promoted and printing presses established. More than 10,000 churches were built, some of great beauty. Fierce conflict between the white man and the Indian marked Spanish advances on every frontier, as Philip Wayne Powell wrote in *Soldiers, Indians, and Silver: The Northward Advance of New Spain, 1550–1600* (1952). But it should also be pointed out that the Spaniards were more successful in assimilating native populations and cultures than were the colonialists to the north.

In the United States Florida was one Spanish outpost, the Southwest another, California still another. Spain sent its viceroys to organize governmental control. The Jesuits and Franciscans worked diligently in their missions among the Indian tribes, and their *Relations* are among the most important early documents about the New World.

The Southwest is still deeply imbued with Spanish influence. In New Mexico the legislature is officially bilingual. Through Mexico, as J. Frank Dobie points out in *Life and Literature of the Southwest* (rev. ed. 1952), "the Spaniards have had an abiding influence on the architecture and language of the Southwest. They gave us our most distinctive occupation, ranching on the open range. They influenced mining greatly, and our land and irrigation laws still go back to Spanish and Mexican sources."

Spanish-speaking groups have offered some problems of assimilation. Mexicans in search of work have sought entry across the Mexican border, sometimes by swimming the Rio Grande (giving rise to the objectionable term "wetbacks"), and legal and illegal entrants are found in considerable numbers in Texas, California, and elsewhere. Great numbers of Puerto Ricans, who are U.S. citizens, though most have clung to Spanish as a mother tongue, have entered the United States to congregate in New York and other cities, and they often live under wretched conditions in urban slums. John H. Burma wrote a documented account of *Spanish-Speaking Groups in the U.S.* (1954). Useful accounts of Spanish influence are Aurora Lea's *Literary Folklore of the Hispanic Southwest* (1953) and Stanley T. Williams's *Spanish Background of American Literature* (2 v. 1955).

Among the earliest fiction dealing with Hispanics in the Southwest are two novels by Eusebio Chacon (1869–1948) published in Sante Fe in 1892: *El hijo de la tempestad* (The Son of the Storm) and *Trans de la tormenta la calma* (The Calm after the Storm). From the 1850s a form of mostly anonymous

folk ballad, the *corrido*, has flourished—particularly in the border region of Texas.

Archibald MacLeish's poem CONQUISTADOR (1932) is based on Bernal Diaz Castillo's account (1632) of the Spanish conquest of Mexico. Eugene O'Neill used the Ponce de Leon story of the Fountain of Youth in his play THE FOUNTAIN (prod. 1925). Novels about the Spaniards in the New World include Charles Kingsley's *Westward Ho!* (1855); Lew Wallace's THE FAIR GOD (1873); Joseph Conrad's *Nostromo* (1904); Peter B. Kyne's *Tide of Empire* (1927); Thornton Wilder's THE BRIDGE OF SAN LUIS REY (1927); Vicente Blasco Ibáñez's *Unknown Lands* (1929) and *Knight of the Virgin* (1930); Gladys Malvern's *If Love Comes* (1932); Honoré Willsie Morrow's *Beyond the Blue Sierra* (1932); Blair Niles' *Maria Paluna* (1934) and *Day of Immense Sun* (1936); John Steinbeck's TORTILLA FLAT (1935) and THE PEARL (1948); Kyle Crichton's *The Proud People* (1940); James Branch Cabell's *First Gentleman of America* (1942); and Samuel Shellabarger's *Captain from Castile* (1945).

Mexican Village (1945) by JOSEPHINA NIGGLI is a collection of ten closely related stories. Mario Suárez has depicted life in the Tucson *barrio*. *Pocho* (1959), by José Antonio Villarreal, treats a family saga from the Mexican revolution to World War II.

The Teatro Campesino, established in 1965, was an outgrowth of César Chávez's farm workers' union. Plays, performed in fields, universities, or theaters, attacked the practices of greedy growers. Two years later, QUINTO SOL Publications was founded in Berkeley, California, to foster Mexican-American writing. The press published work by poet José Montoya (1932–   ) and fiction writers such as TOMÁS RIVERA (1935–1984), ROLANDO HINOJOSA-SMITH (1929–   ), and RODOLFO ANAYA (1937–   ). Rivera's major work, . . . *y no se lo tragó la tierra* (*And the Earth Did Not Part*, 1971) is a series of fourteen related stories and sketches depicting the lives of farm workers. Hinojosa-Smith is the author of *Estampas del valle y otras obras* (*Sketches of the Valley and Other Works*, 1972) and *Generaciones y semblanzas* (*Generations and Biographies*, 1977). Anaya's novel *Bless Me, Ultima* (1972), set in New Mexico at the end of World War II, uses the atomic testing at White Sands as a symbol of change. JOHN NICHOLS treats the experience of rural Hispanics in novels such as *The Milagro Beanfield War* (1974). Feminists include SANDRA CISNEROS, author of *The House on Mango Street* (1984), and the poet LORNA DEE CERVANTES (1954–   ). See HISPANIC LITERATURE.

Spanish-American War.   This conflict marked the emergence of the United States as a world power. The war was brought on by various causes, particularly the oppressive rule of Spain in Cuba. Soon after WILLIAM MCKINLEY became president in 1896, a new Cuban rebellion broke out. It was ferociously suppressed by the Spanish General Valeriano Weyler, and the American so-called yellow press fanned public opinion against Spain. After further provocative incidents came the sinking of the United States battleship *Maine* on February 15, 1898, in Havana Harbor. Despite sincere efforts to avoid war, the president was forced by popular clamor to send a message to Congress asking for forcible intervention of the United States to establish peace in Cuba. This was done in a joint resolution, which stated that Cuba would be left to its own people after peace had been declared. McKinley signed the resolution on April 20, a blockade of Cuba began on April 22, and Spain declared war on the United States April 24.

On May 1 Admiral George Dewey won the resounding victory of Manila Bay, as a result of which the Philippines—then ruled by Spain—fell into American hands. Cuba was invaded and Spanish forces were defeated at the Battles of El Caney and San Juan Hill, June 30, 1898. A naval victory was won in Santiago Harbor on July 3. Santiago surrendered on July 17. On July 26 Spain sued for peace. In the peace treaty the United States gave Spain twenty million dollars in payment for the Philippines, and Puerto Rico and Guam were ceded to the U.S. After the war came a strong anti-imperialist movement, fostered by such diverse personalities as Senator George F. Hoar of Massachusetts, Samuel Gompers, Andrew Carnegie, Jane Addams, and William Vaughn Moody. THEODORE ROOSEVELT's personal participation in the war brought him the vice-presidential nomination in 1900 and, after McKinley's death, the presidency.

The finest piece of literature that arose out of this conflict was published before the war began. Stephen Crane's THE OPEN BOAT (1897) relates Crane's experiences in a lifeboat after the vessel in which he was trying to get to Cuba was wrecked off the Florida coast. Later Crane served as war correspondent in Cuba, helped wounded men under fire, and wrote some memorable stories, which were collected in *Wounds in the Rain* (1900). Richard Harding Davis, a war correspondent on the same front, wrote about Crane in *Notes of a War Correspondent* (1910) and in several articles. He also wrote *Cuba in War Time* (1897) and *The Cuban and Puerto Rican Campaigns* (1898). Frank Norris was also on the scene, reporting the war for *McClure's Magazine*. Two contemporary poems, Richard Hovey's *Unmanifest Destiny* (1898) and John Jerome Rooney's *The Men Behind the Guns* (1898), have survived the war; Elbert Hubbard's A MESSAGE TO GARCIA (1899) had a circulation of more than forty million copies. The favorite marching song of the soldiers in the war was "A Hot Time in the Old Town Tonight" (1896), by Joe Hayden and Theodore A. Metz.

Unquestionably the best treatment of the Spanish-American War is Walter Millis's *The Martial Spirit* (1931). Other nonfiction books on the conflict include Stephen Bonsal's *The Fight for Santiago* (1899), George Kennan's *Campaigning in Cuba* (1899), Harry Thurston Peck's *Twenty Years of the Republic* (1906), George Dewey's *Autobiography* (1913), C. E. Chapman's *The Cuban Republic* (1927), M. M. Wilkerson's *Public Opinion in the Spanish-American War* (1932), and J. W. Pratt's *Expansionists of 1898* (1936). Among novels on the war are Joseph Hergesheimer's *The Bright Shawl* (1922), Herman Hagedorn's *The Rough Riders* (1927), Elswyth Thane's *Ever After* (1945), and Conrad Richter's *Always Young and Fair* (1947).

Spanish Bayonet (1926), a historical novel by STEPHEN VINCENT BENÉT.

Spanish Main, The. Originally this term was applied to the mainland of South America or to a portion bordering on the Caribbean Sea from the Isthmus of Panama to the Orinoco River. The term is also customarily applied to the entire Caribbean area, through which Spanish ships loaded with gold would sail on their way home. With the defeat of the Spanish Armada by England (1588), this region became the hunting ground of buccaneers who in the name of England looted the Spanish galleons. Their cry was "Westward Ho!"—a slogan which Charles Kingsley adopted as the title of a novel (1855) that depicts these Elizabethan adventures.

Spanish Student, The (pub. serially 1842, in book form 1843), a dramatic poem by HENRY WADSWORTH LONGFELLOW. It was one of several poems Longfellow wrote on Spanish themes. In the introduction he acknowledges his indebtedness to *La Gitanilla*, a story by Cervantes, and to three Spanish plays. Preciosa, the daughter of a nobleman, is stolen by gypsies, becomes a dancer, is wooed by a young man of high birth, and marries him when she is discovered to be of good family. Edgar Allan Poe in reviewing the play attacked Longfellow as a plagiarist, charging that it contained passages stolen from his own dramatic fragment, *Politian*. Longfellow's play was never produced in his lifetime in this country, but was staged in Dessau, Germany, (1855) in a German translation by Adolf Boettger.

Sparks, Jared (1789–1866), clergyman, professor, editor. Born in Connecticut, Sparks was a student, professor, and finally president (1849) of Harvard. Under his leadership as editor (1817–1819) and owner-editor (1823–1829), the NORTH AMERICAN REVIEW became one of the most important magazines in the United States. His scholarly interest was the American Revolution, and he edited the diplomatic correspondence of the war (12 v. 1829–1830), the writings of Washington (12 v. 1834–1838) and Benjamin Franklin (10 v. 1836–1840), and other papers. He wrote biographies of Benedict Arnold, Ethan Allen, Pere Marquette, La Salle, and others and edited two series of the *Library of American Biography* (10 v. 1834–1838; 15 v. 1844–1847). In addition he founded and edited the *American Almanac and Repository of Useful Knowledge* (1830–1861). See JOHN LEDYARD.

Sparrowgrass Papers, The (1856, repr. 1869), humorous sketches by FREDERICK SWARTHOUT COZZENS.

Spartacus to the Gladiators (1846), a declamation written by ELIJAH KELLOGG. Spartacus, a Thracian gladiator, organized a slave revolt in Rome in 72 B.C. that appeared for a time to have a chance of succeeding. He finally was defeated and killed.

Specimen Days and Collect (1882), a collection of WALT WHITMAN's diaries, notes, and essays first published by Rees Welsh in Philadelphia and republished in the same year by David McKay as *Specimen Days*. (A collect is a miscellaneous collection of essays on many subjects, but mostly literary.) Whitman's book begins with accounts of the poet's ancestry and boyhood on Long Island, but more extensive coverage is given to his experiences during the Civil War. Many of these paragraphs were transcribed from the notebooks he carried with him through hospitals on his visits to the soldiers. Others were jotted down during visits to recent battlefields or while staying in army camps. Later sections deal with his recovery from stroke in old age.

Speck, Frank G[ouldsmith] (1881–1950), teacher, anthropologist. Speck, born in Brooklyn, New York, concentrated on the ethnology and linguistics of the Native American. Among his books are *Ceremonial Songs of the Creek and Yuchi Indians* (1911), *Penobscot Shamanism* (1920), *The Rappahannock Indians of Virginia* (1925), *Native Tribes and Dialects of Connecticut* (1926), *A Study of the Delaware Indian Big House Ceremony* (1931), and *The Midwinter Rites of the Cayuga Long House* (1949).

Spectra and the Spectrist School, a literary hoax perpetrated by WITTER BYNNER and ARTHUR DAVISON FICKE. Irritated with the schools of poetry fashionable in 1915, Bynner (calling himself Emanuel Morgan) and Ficke (using the pen name Anne Knish) created so-called Spectric poems, wrote glowing reviews of the pseudonymous work under their real names, and published *Spectra: A Book of Poetic Experiments* (1916). Over thirty years later, Bynner revealed the hoax in *Word Study* (October 1948).

Spectre Bridegroom, The (1819), a story by WASHINGTON IRVING, included in *The Sketch Book.* Sir Hermann von Starkenfaust gains his dead friend's intended bride by playing the role of a specter.

Spencer, Cornelia Phillips (1825–1908), historian. Spencer was an outspoken advocate of the South. Born in New York City, she lived and wrote in Chapel Hill, North Carolina. Among her books are *The Last 90 Days of the War in North Carolina* (1866) and *First Steps in North Carolina History* (1889). Louis R. Wilson edited her *Selected Papers* (1953).

Spencer, Elizabeth (1921–), novelist, short-story writer. Born in Mississippi, Spencer has lived in Italy and Canada. Her early fiction, such as *Fire in the Morning* (1948), *This Crooked Way* (1952), and *The Voice at the Back Door* (1956), details changes in Southern custom and practice. *The Light in the Piazza* (1960) and *Knights and Dragons* (1965) focus on Americans traveling and living in Italy. *The Snare* (1972) is set in New Orleans. Her story collections are *Ship Island* (1968), *The Stories of Elizabeth Spencer* (1981), and *Marilee* (1981), the last a group of three stories on growing up in the South. *The Salt Line* (1984) is set on the Mississippi Gulf Coast; *The Night Travellers* (1991) deals with radicalism during the Vietnam War. *On the Gulf* (1991) is a story collection. *The Southern Woman* (2001) collects new and selected fiction.

Spencer, Theodore (1902–1949), teacher, editor, poet. Spencer, born in Pennsylvania, held the Boylston Chair of Rhetoric at Harvard. He was particularly interested in Elizabethan drama and metaphysical poetry and wrote critical books in both fields. His verse collections include *The Paradox in the Circle* (1941), *The World in Your Hand* (1943), *An Act of Life* (1944), *Poems: 1940–1947* (1948), and *An Acre in the Seed* (1950).

Spewack, Bella (1899–1990), and **Samuel Spewack** (1899–1971), playwrights. The Spewacks, both born in Eastern Europe, met when they worked as newspaper reporters. They are known for their plays, but Bella Spewack also wrote short stories, and Samuel Spewack wrote detective stories and served with the Office of War Information. Among the plays the Spewacks wrote or produced together are *Solitaire Man* (1926); *Poppa* (1928); *War Song* (1928); *Clear All Wires* (1932); *Spring Song* (1934); *Boy Meets Girl* (1935); *Leave It to Me* (1938); *Miss Swan Expects* (1939, pub. as *Trousers to Match*, 1941); KISS ME, KATE (1949); *My Three Angels* (1953), adapted from the French; and *Festival* (1955). COLE PORTER wrote the songs and lyrics for *Leave It to Me* and KISS ME, KATE.

Speyer, Leonora (1872–1955), violinist, poet. Speyer, born in Washington, D.C., wrote poetry that presents personal subject matter with formal virtuosity. Her titles include *Canopic Jar* (1921); *Fiddler's Farewell* (1926), a winner of the Pulitzer Prize; *Naked Heel* (1931); And *Slow Wall* (1939, enlarged 1946).

Spicer, Jack (1925–1965), poet. Spicer, a friend of ROBERT DUNCAN, lived most of his life in San Francisco. *After Lorca* (1957) is a collection of Spicer's translations and poetry dedicated to the poet, who died in the Spanish Civil War. *Billy the Kid* (1959) is a tribute to the legendary outlaw. His other books are *The Heads of the Town Up to the Aether* (1962), *Language* (1965), and *Book of Magazine Verse* (1966). *The Collected Books* appeared in 1975.

Spiegelman, Art (1948–), cartoonist. Born in Stockholm, Sweden, where his parents fled after their releases from Nazi concentration camps, Spiegelman immigrated with them to the United States and became an naturalized American. He was educated at Harpur College, now the State University of New York at Binghamton. Much of his work has been done in collaboration with his wife, Francoise Mouly; together, in the early in the 1980s, they produced the underground comic anthology *Raw*, which grew into an alternative press. His most famous production is the *Maus* series: *Maus: A Survivor's Tale, My Father Bleeds History* (1986) and *Maus II: A Survivor's Tale: And Here My Troubles Began* (1999). In these cartoons the mice are imprisoned by the cats in a place called "Mauschwitz." The events are narrated by a mouse named Vladek (Spiegelman's father's name) and concern the capture of Vladek and Anja (his mother's name) and their separation from their son Richieu, whom they never see again. The second book continues Vladek's narration with the couple's escape from Auschwitz, their flight to Sweden, where Art is born, and to America, where Anja commits suicide. The cartoonist has said the books were "motivated by an impulse to look dead-on at the root cause of my own deepest fears and nightmares." Spiegelman was awarded a special Pulitzer Prize for the series in 1992.

Spielberg, Steven (1947–), movie director, producer. Spielberg was born in Cincinnati and trained in film at California State College. He won a contract with Universal Studios after the showing of one of his student films at the 1969 Atlanta Film Festival. His first successful film was *Jaws*

(1975); its high earnings made him much sought after. His other films include *Close Encounters of the Third Kind* (1977), for which Spielberg wrote the story; *I Wanna Hold Your Hand* (1978); *1941* (1979); *Raiders of the Lost Ark* (1981); *E.T.* (1982); *Jurassic Park* (1993); *Schindler's List* (1993); and *Saving Private Ryan* (1998).

Spillane, Mickey [Frank Morrison] (1918–   ), writer of detective stories. Spillane created the character Mike Hammer, a hardboiled detective introduced in *I, the Jury* (1947), and went on to achieve great commercial success. Spillane combines sex and sadistic crime in books such as *My Gun Is Quick* (1950), *Kiss Me Deadly* (1952), *The Twisted Thing* (1966), and *Tomorrow I Die* (1984).

Spirit of the Times.   A magazine founded on December 10, 1831, by WILLIAM T. PORTER and devoted to sports and humor. It became highly influential and published contributions by many leading humorists and sportswriters of the era, including Thomas B. Thorpe, Henry William Herbert (Frank Forester), Albert Pike, W. T. Thompson, J. J. Hooper, J. M. Field, George W. Harris, and Richard Malcolm Johnston. Porter also encouraged contributions from amateur writers, especially tales and anecdotes from the frontier. Porter made two collections of material from his magazine: *The Big Bear of Arkansas and Other Sketches, Illustrative of Characters and Incidents in the South and Southwest* (1845, 1855) and *A Quarter Race in Kentucky* (1846, 1847; repr. as *Colonel Thorpe's Scenes in Arkansas*, 1858). In 1856 Porter sold the magazine to George Wilkes but continued to edit it until 1858. Wilkes, founder of the *National Police Gazette*, changed the name to *Porter's Spirit of the Times*, then in 1859 founded *The Spirit of the Times and Sportsman*; in 1861 he ceased publication of Porter's magazine. He started *Wilkes's Spirit of the Times* and continued until 1902, when it was merged with *The Horseman*.

Spofford, Harriet [Elizabeth] Prescott (1835–1921), novelist, poet, short-story writer, essayist, autobiographer. A native of Maine, Spofford was a popular writer of the late 19th century. Her novels include *Sir Rohan's Ghost* (1860) and *Marquis of Carabas* (1882); her verse is collected in *Poems* (1881) and *Ballads About Authors* (1887); and her short stories are collected in *The Amber Gods and Other Stories* (1863) and *Azarian* (1864).

Spoils of Poynton (1897),   a novel by HENRY JAMES. Mrs. Gereth, finding her taste in furnishing shared by young Fleda Vetch, invites her to visit her home, Poynton, and meet Owen, her unmarried son. Fleda admires the antiques and art at Poynton and falls in love with Owen, but he has agreed to marry Mona Brigstock. His mother dislikes Mona and, when asked to leave the house for the use of the engaged couple, Mrs. Gereth takes with her all her treasures. Mona threatens to break the engagement unless the possessions are returned. Fleda refuses to defend Mrs. Gereth's seizure of the treasures even though she knows that loss of the items would break up the match. Though Owen loves Fleda, he marries Mona. He writes to offer Fleda her choice of the beautiful things at Poynton, but she arrives to find that a fire has destroyed the house and all its contents.

Spoon River Anthology (1915),   a series of verse epitaphs by EDGAR LEE MASTERS. They were first serialized in WILLIAM MARION REED's *Mirror* (1914–1915) under the pseudonym Webster Ford; Master's real name was used in the book publication. The names in this still-read book are taken from tombstones in the Lewiston, Illinois, cemetery where Masters was himself buried in 1950. The *New Spoon River* (1924) did not rival the success of the first collection.

Spotswood, Alexander (1676–1740),   British soldier, administrator. Spotswood was appointed lieutenant governor of Virginia in 1710 and remained in America for the rest of his life. He served as deputy postmaster general of the American colonies from 1730 to 1739. R. A. Brock edited his *Official Letters, 1710–1722* (2 v. 1882–85).

Sprague, Charles (1791–1875),   poet. Sprague, born in Boston, became a banker and went on to write poetry, including the prize-winning "Ode to Shakespeare" (1823), that shows the influence of such English meditative poets as Collins and Gray. His poems include "Centennial Ode," in praise of the Pilgrims and "The Funeral," and he wrote a prose piece on "The American Indian." His collected *Writings* appeared in 1841 and was revised in 1876.

Spy, The (1821),   a novel by JAMES FENIMORE COOPER set in Westchester County, New York during the Revolution. It was Cooper's second novel and was influenced by Sir Walter Scott's successful historical fiction, especially *Waverley* (1814), The main character, Harvey Birch, is a Yankee pedlar who serves George Washington and is also friendly to the Loyalist Wharton family. The complex plot includes marriage and bigamy, disguise and flight, threatened execution and escape. All ends happily when the lovers are married, the Loyalist brother escapes hanging, the villain is killed in battle, and the pedlar resumes his itinerant life.

Squanto or **Tisquantum** (d. 1622),   guide and interpreter. A member of the Pawtuxet tribe who lived for some time in England. He may have been captured on the Maine coast by George Weymouth in 1605 and returned to New England by John Smith in 1615. He certainly was kidnapped by Captain Thomas Hunt in 1615 and lived in England until 1619, when he returned to North America with Captain Thomas Dermer. He befriended the Plymouth Colonists, gave them advice on planting and fishing that saved their lives in the harsh winter, and negotiated a treaty between them and Chief MASSASOIT in 1621. In the following year, while serving as guide and interpreter for WILLIAM BRADFORD's expedition around Cape Cod, he contracted smallpox and died.

Squaw Man, The (1905),   a play by EDWIN MILTON ROYLE. This romantic drama, one of the most successful of its day, concerns an English aristocrat and the Indian girl he marries after she has saved his life. The girl bears him a son, but commits suicide in order to avoid standing in his way when he becomes heir to an English title.

Squibob Papers, The (1865),   a series of humorous sketches by GEORGE DERBY, who often employed Squibob as a pseudonym. The sketches represent one of the earliest developments in American humor, employing puns, grotesqueries, exaggerated understatement, and rowdy burlesque. A number of them originally appeared in the San Francisco *Pioneer*.

Squier, E[phraim] G[eorge] ["Samuel A. Bard"] (1821–1888), newspaper editor, diplomat, archaeologist, writer. The New York–born Squier was one of the first to investigate the ancient mounds of Ohio and later became interested in similar mounds in New York. Appointed as special chargé d'affaires in Peru, he made investigations of that country's archaeological remains (1849–50), returning in 1853 and 1863–64 for further surveys. Among his books are *Ancient Monuments of the Mississippi Valley* (with E. H. Davis, 1848); *Antiquities of the State of New York* (1851); *Travels in Central America* (1852); *The States of Central America* (1858); and *Peru* (1877).

Stafford, Jean (1915–1979), novelist, short-story writer. Born in California and educated in Colorado, Stafford also spent time in Boston, New York City, and Europe. The poet ROBERT LOWELL was her first husband (1940–48). Her first novel, *Boston Adventure* (1944), concerns Sophie Marburg, the unwanted child of an immigrant family, whose dream of being adopted by her wealthy employer proves hollow. *The Mountain Lion* (1947) treats teen siblings Ralph and Molly, struggling to mature during summers in the natural environment of their uncle's ranch. *The Catherine Wheel* (1952) and *A Winter's Tale* (1954) are also novels. She wrote books for children and *A Mother in History* (1966), about the mother of the man who assassinated President John F. Kennedy. Her story collections are *Children Are Bored on Sunday* (1954) and *Bad Characters* (1965). Her Pulitzer Prize winning *Collected Stories* (1969), organized by the various places Stafford lived, is not a complete collection. Her best stories deal with the painful transitions of adolescence.

Stafford, William (1914–1993), poet. Born in Kansas and educated in Kansas and Iowa, Stafford taught at Lewis and Clark College in Oregon. The regions he lived in are central to his conversational poetry. Stafford did not publish his first book of poems, *West of Your City*, until 1960. His other titles are *Traveling Through the Dark* (1962), *The Rescued Year* (1966), *Eleven Untitled Poems* (1968), *Allegiances* (1970), *Someday, Maybe* (1973), *That Other Alone* (1973), *In the Clock of Reason* (1973), *Going Places* (1974), and *A Glass Face in the Rain* (1982). *Stories That Could Be True: New and Collected Poems* appeared in 1978. Stafford's correspondence with Marvin Bell is in *Segues: A Correspondence in Poetry* (1983). He edited *The Achievement of Brother Antoninus* (1967) and wrote *Writing the Australian Crawl: Views on the Writer's Vocation* (1978). *Down in My Heart* (1947) is a memoir of his experiences in World War II as a conscientious objector.

Stallings, Laurence (1894–1968), playwright, novelist, drama critic. Born in Georgia, Stallings treated his early life, education, and loss of a leg in World War I in the novel *Plumes* (1924). In collaboration with MAXWELL ANDERSON he wrote the antiwar play *What Price Glory?* as well as *First Flight* (1925) and *The Buccaneer* (1925). His graphic *The First World War* (1933) was a best seller. He wrote musicals such as *Deep River* (1926), which utilized jazz music, and *Rainbow*, with OSCAR HAMMERSTEIN (1928). He dramatized ERNEST HEMING-

WAY's *Farewell to Arms* (1930). *The Big Parade* (1925) is a novel.

Standing Bear, Luther (1868–1947?), Sioux chieftain, writer on Indian life. Standing Bear spent his boyhood in Nebraska and in South Dakota, where he was born, and at age eleven was sent to the Indian School at Carlisle, Pennsylvania. His Ponca Sioux tribe was assigned land in the Oklahoma Indian Territory, but many died in the forced relocation. A lecture tour by Standing Bear, Joseph La Flesche, and his daughter SUZETTE LA FLESCHE attracted the support of Eastern writers, including LONGFELLOW and HELEN HUNT JACKSON, and some restitution was made. Standing Bear was a successful lecturer, part of Buffalo Bill's Wild West Show (1898), and a movie actor. His books include *My People, The Sioux* (1928); *My Indian Boyhood* (1931); *Land of the Spotted Eagle* (1933); and *Twenty True Stories* (1934).

Standish, Burt L. Pen name of GILBERT PATTEN.

Standish, Miles [or Myles] (1584?–1656), soldier, colonist, public official. Born in England, Standish was a professional soldier who fought in the Netherlands. The Pilgrims hired him to accompany them to the New World in the *Mayflower*. He showed marked ability as a soldier, engineer, and administrator. On two occasions he ejected THOMAS MORTON from New England. Morton retaliated by making sneering references to Standish in THE NEW ENGLISH CANAAN (1632). Standish appears in Longfellow's poem THE COURTSHIP OF MILES STANDISH.

Stanley, Sir Henry M[orton] (1841–1904), newspaperman. Born in Wales, his name was originally John Rowlands; he adopted the name Stanley in tribute to a merchant in New Orleans who hired him when he worked his way as a cabin boy to that city. He served in the United States Navy and the Confederate Army and went on various expeditions as a newspaperman. In 1869 the New York *Herald*, which had previously employed him in Ethiopia, sent him in search of David Livingstone (1813–73), the Scottish missionary and explorer who was lost somewhere in the heart of Africa. Stanley started from Zanzibar in 1871 and found Livingstone in November at Ujiji. When the men met, Stanley uttered the words, "Dr. Livingstone, I presume?" In the following year Stanley published *How I Found Livingstone*. He remained in Africa as a *Herald* correspondent, made some important explorations, and gave up his American citizenship to become a British subject again (1892); he was knighted and became a member of Parliament. His *Autobiography*, edited by his widow, appeared in 1909. Among his books are *Through the Dark Continent* (2 v. 1878), *The Congo and the Founding of Its Free State* (2 v. 1885), and *In Darkest Africa* (2 v. 1890).

Stansbury, Joseph (1742?–1809), merchant, poet. Stansbury, who emigrated to Philadelphia from England in 1767, was a Loyalist who wrote songs to encourage British soldiers. *The Loyal Verses of Joseph Stansbury and Jonathan Odell*, collected by Winthrop Sargent, appeared in 1860.

Stanton, Elizabeth Cady (1815–1902), suffragist, editor, writer. As a girl, Stanton was allowed to attend school in her native Johnstown, New York, only because the death of her brother had created a vacancy. No college would accept her because of her sex, so she studied law in her father's office but was not allowed to take the bar examination or practice. After seeing LUCRETIA MOTT denied the right to speak at the World Anti-Slavery Convention in London, in 1840, she joined with Mott to agitate for women's suffrage. They organized the first Women's Rights Convention in 1848 at Seneca Falls, New York. Stanton ran for Congress in 1868 and became president of the National Woman's Suffrage Association in 1869. She and SUSAN B. ANTHONY edited *Revolution* during the same period.

Stanton wrote *A History of Woman Suffrage* with Susan B. Anthony and M. J. Gage (6 v. 1881–1922) and wrote her autobiography, *Eighty Years and More* (1898). Theodore Stanton and Harriet Stanton Blatch edited *Elizabeth Cady Stanton, As Revealed in Her Letters, Diary, and Reminiscences* (2 v. 1922).

Stanton, Frank L[ebby] (1857–1927),   newspaperman, poet. Stanton wrote for the Atlanta *Constitution*. One of his verses, "Mighty Lak' a Rose" (1901), became nationally known as set to music by Ethelbert Nevin. His lyrics were collected in 1892, 1898, 1900, 1902, and 1904.

Starr, Frederick (1858–1933),   anthropologist. Starr, born in Auburn, New York, was an authority on the Indian civilizations of Mexico and taught for many years at the University of Chicago. Among his books are *American Indians* (1898), *Truths About the Congo* (1907), *In Indian Mexico* (1908), *Philippine Studies* (1909), and *Liberia* (1913). He also compiled *Readings from Modern Mexican Authors* (1904).

Starrett, [Charles] Vincent [Emerson] (1886–1974), journalist, critic, writer. Starrett, born in Toronto, began as a reporter for the Chicago *Inter-Ocean* and went on to the Chicago *Daily News*. He lived in many cities, including New York, London, Paris, Rome, Reno, St. Louis, and Peking. His writings include well over a hundred books of every kind: poems, short stories, humorous sketches, biographies, novels. Among them are *Arthur Machen* (1918); *Ambrose Bierce* (1920); *Buried Caesars* (essays, 1923); *The Private Life of Sherlock Holmes* (1933); *The Great Hotel Murder* (1934); *Books Alive* (1940); *Bookman's Holiday* (1942); *Autolycus in Limbo* (poems, 1943); *Murder in Peking* (1946); and *Great All-Star Animal League Ball Game* (1957).

Star Rover, The (1915),   a series of related stories by JACK LONDON. A California convict, in prison for life, learns how to escape by leaving his body and incarnating himself as another person. Each time he does this, he undergoes strange adventures. The chief character was apparently based on a Californian named Ed Morrell, who professed to have taken part in many train holdups and made off with numerous sacks of gold. During the latter part of his life Morrell lectured and wrote on "The Folly of a Life of Crime," which was based on a short stretch in San Quentin; he also headed the Honor League of Reformed Criminals. Morrell wrote *The 25th Man: The Strange Story of EM, the Hero of Jack London's "Star Rover"* (1924, repr. 1956).

Star-Spangled Banner, The.   See FRANCIS SCOTT KEY.

Starting from Paumanok (1860),   a poem by WALT WHITMAN. This first appeared in the 1860 edition of *Leaves of Grass* under the title *Proto-Leaf*. The present title was substituted in the 1867 edition. The poem was frequently revised, mainly in 1867, but some further changes were made in 1881 when a section was transferred to SONG OF MYSELF. *Paumanok* was the Indian name for Long Island; it means fish-shaped.

State of the Union (1945),   a play by HOWARD LINDSAY and RUSSEL CROUSE. This amusing and effective political satire won a Pulitzer Prize (1946), ran on Broadway for 765 performances, and was filmed in 1948.

Stead, Robert J.C. (1880–1959),   novelist. Born in Alberta, Stead set most of his fiction in the Canadian West. He began his career during World War I with *The Bail Jumper* (1914), *The Homesteader* (1916), and *The Cow Puncher* (1918), but made his reputation with the realistic novels of pioneer life he wrote in the 1920s—*Neighbours* (1922), *The Smoking Flax* (1924), and *Grain* (1926).

Stead, William Thomas (1849–1912),   novelist. Stead's novel *If Christ Came to Chicago!* (1894) was one of several on the theme popular in the 1890s.

Stedman, Edmund Clarence (1833–1908),   poet, critic, anthologist. Born in Connecticut, Stedman studied at Yale for two years before going to New York City, where he worked as a journalist and stockbroker. His early poetry, including abolitionist verse, was collected in *Pan in Wall Street* (1867). Stedman, an influential critic in his day, was an admirer of EDGAR ALLEN POE and one of the first to recognize the abilities of WALT WHITMAN. In *The Nature and Elements of Poetry* (1892) he decried prosaic moralism. In collaboration with GEORGE EDWARD WOODBERRY he edited a 10-volume edition of *The Works of Edgar Allan Poe* (1894–95). Two volumes of Stedman's criticism, *Victorian Poets* (1875) and *Poets of America* (1885), were supplemented by two anthologies, *A Victorian Anthology* (1895) and AN AMERICAN ANTHOLOGY (1900), both of which became widely popular.

In addition to the books mentioned Stedman wrote *Poems, Lyrical and Idyllic* (1860); *Alice of Monmouth, An Idyll of the Great War, With Other Poems* (1864); *The Blameless Prince and Other Poems* (1869); and *The Poetical Works of Edmund Clarence Stedman* (1873). With Ellen M. Hutchinson he edited *A Library of American Literature from the Earliest Settlement to the Present Time* (11 v. 1888–90).

Steegmuller, Francis (1906–1994),   writer, biographer. Steegmuller, born in Connecticut, was educated at Columbia University, where he began contributing to *The New Yorker*. His biographies include *O Rare Ben Jonson* (1927), *Sir Francis Bacon* (1930), *Flaubert and Madame Bovary* (1939), *Maupassant, A Lion in the Path* (1949), and *The Two Lives of James Jackson Jarves* (1951). He also translated and edited *The Selected Letters of Gustave Flaubert* (1954) and translated *Madame Bovary* (1957). Steegmuller also wrote the novel *States of Grace* (1946) as well as murder mysteries, under the pseudonyms Byron Steel and David Keith.

Steele, Danielle (Fernande) (1947–   ),   novelist. Born in New York and educated at Parsons School of Design and New York University, Steele has been prolific and highly successful in the romance novel field, consistently landing on both the hardcover and softcover best-seller lists. Typically her books center on women in powerful or glamorous situations who have hard choices to make. In *Changes* (1983), a New York anchorwoman must decide between her career and her marriage to a Beverly Hills surgeon. The American-born Duchess of Whitfield struggles to raise her children in the years leading up to World War II in *Jewels* (1992). *Accident* (1994) details a family's struggle when a teenage daughter is seriously injured in a car crash. In *Malice* (1996) Grace Adams murders her abusive father in self-defense and must deal with the consequences. *The House on Hope Street* (2000), Steele's forty-ninth novel, has Liz Sutherland, a Marin County, California, divorce lawyer, picking up the pieces after her husband and law partner is murdered by a disgruntled client. Many Steele novels have been successfully made into television dramas; she has also written love poetry and books for children.

Steele, Wilbur Daniel (1886–1970),   short-story writer, novelist. Born in North Carolina, Steele was educated first at the University of Denver, studied art at home and abroad, and in 1910 began publishing stories that won popular and critical approval. Two collections of his stories are *The Best Short Stories of Wilbur Daniel Steele* (1946) and *Full Cargo* (1952), which selected from earlier gatherings: *Land's End* (1918); *The Shame Dance* (1923); *Urkey Island* (1926); *The Man Who Saw Through Heaven* (1927); *Tower of Sand* (1929); and others. Steele's stories are notable for their great variety of background, their constant ingenuity, and their grasp of psychopathology.

Steele's first novel was *Storm* (1914). Later came *Isles of the Blest* (1924), *Taboo* (1925), *Meat* (1928), *Undertow* (1930), *That Girl from Memphis* (1945), *Diamond Wedding* (1950), and *Their Town* (1952). He also wrote one-act plays, and with Norma Mitchell, his second wife, the full-length drama *Post Road* (1935). In collaboration with Anthony Brown he dramatized one of his most popular short stories, *How Beautiful with Shoes* (1935).

Steendam, Jacob (1616?–1672?),   poet. Usually regarded as New York's first poet, Steendam came to the New Netherlands from Holland about 1650, when he bought land on Long Island. His poetical works were issued in three volumes: *Den Distelvink* (The Goldfinch, 1649–50); *Klacht van Nieuw Nederlandt tot Haar Moeder* (Complaint of New Netherlands to Her Mother, 1659); and *'T Lof van Nieuw Nederlandt* (The Praise of New Netherlands, 1661). In the second volume he urged better treatment for the Dutch colony, and in the third he praised the colony in warm terms. Later he published a collection, *Zeede-Zanger voor de Batavische Jonkheyt* (Moral Songs for Batavian Youth, 1671).

Steere, Richard (1643?–1721),   colonist, poet. Nothing is known of Steere's early life except that he was a "Citizen of London" and that he published a narrative poem, *The His-*

tory of the Babylonish Cabal (1682), which took the Earl of Shaftesbury's part in the Whig dispute with the King's Party. He came to New England about this time, lived for a while in Providence, Rhode Island, and then moved to Long Island. In this country he published *A Monumental Memorial of Marine Mercy* (1684) and *The Daniel Catcher* (1713). The latter volume contains his two most striking poems, "Earth Felicities, Heavens Allowances" and "On a Sea-storm Nigh the Coast." "Earth Felicities" is written in blank verse, unusual in its time, and both poems reflect a protoromantic appreciation of nature.

Stefansson, Vilhjalmur (1879–1962),   explorer, anthropologist, writer. Born in Manitoba and raised in North Dakota, Stefansson spent most of his life in exploration, especially in the Arctic. He was convinced that people could live comfortably in northern climates and expressed his views forcibly in *The Northward Course of Empire* (1922) and *Not by Bread Alone* (1946). Among his other books are *My Life with the Eskimos* (1913); *The Friendly Arctic* (1921); *The Adventure of Wrangel Island* (1925); *The Standardization of Error* (1927); *The Three Voyages of Martin Frobisher* (1938); *Arctic Manual* (1941); *The Arctic in Fact and Fiction* (1945); *Great Adventures and Explorations* (an anthology, 1947); *New Compass of the World* (1949); and *Northwest to Fortune* (1958).

Steffens, [Joseph] Lincoln (1866–1936),   newspaperman, memoirist. Born in San Francisco, Steffens settled in New York City and, from 1892 to 1911, wrote for the *Evening Post*, the *Commercial Advertiser*, *McClure's*, the *American*, and *Everybody's*. This was the muckraking era, and Steffens became a leader in exposing the sins of politicians and business leaders (see MUCKRAKING LITERATURE). His 1902 *McClure's* article on corruption in St. Louis is regarded as having launched the muckraking movement. Steffens went on to many similar articles and books: *The Shame of the Cities* (1904), *The Struggle for Self-Government* (1906), *Upbuilders* (1909), *The Least of These* (1910), and *Out of the Muck* (1913). His autobiographical materials are *Lincoln Steffens Speaking* (1936), *Autobiography* (2 v. 1931), and *Letters* (2 v. 1938).

Stegner, Wallace [Earle] (1909–1993),   novelist, short-story writer, biographer, essayist. Born in Iowa and educated in Utah, Stegner taught at several universities, including Stanford. His realistic novels, many with rural settings, include *Remembering Laughter* (1937); *The Potter's House* (1938); *On a Darkling Plain* (1940); *Fire and Ice* (1941); *The Big Rock Candy Mountain* (1943); *Second Growth* (1947); *Country Dance* (1948); *The Preacher and the Slave* (1950), about the I.W.W. and JOE HILL; *A Shooting Star* (1961); *All the Little Live Things* (1967); *Angle of Repose* (1971), a fictionalization of MARY HALLOCK FOOTE's life made into an opera by Oakley Hall and Andrew Imbrie; *The Spectator Bird* (1976); and *Recapitulation* (1979). His story collections are *The Women on the Wall* (1950), *The City of the Living* (1956), *A Shooting Star* (1961), and *Collected Stories of Wallace Stegner* (1990). His nonfiction includes *Mormon Country* (1942); *One Nation* (1945); a biography of the explorer John Wesley Powell, *Beyond the Hundredth Meridian* (1954); *Wolf Willow* (1962); *The Gathering of*

Zion (1964); *The Sound of Mountain Water* (1969); *The Uneasy Chair* (1974); and *One Way to Spell Man* (1982). Stegner edited the letters of Bernard De Voto (1975).

Stegner's *Collected Stories* appeared in 1990. Although they were written over thirty years earlier—Stegner had stopped writing short fiction because he believed it to be a form more suitable for young writers—the pieces still appear fresh and solidly crafted. Characters from the novels *Recapitulation, The Big Rock Candy Mountain*, and *Wolf Willow* appear in this collection at earlier stages of their development.

Steichen, Edward (1879–1973), photographer, painter. Steichen, born in Luxembourg, was one of the first photographers to explore the aesthetic possibilities of the camera. A photographer in World Wars I and II, he became in 1947 director of the department of photography at the Museum of Modern Art. His historic exhibit there, *The Family of Man*, was later published as a collection (1955). His brother-in-law, CARL SANDBURG, wrote an account of him, *Steichen the Photographer* (1929).

Steig, William (1907–), artist, cartoonist. Steig has developed his special style of cartoon humor in the pages of *The New Yorker, Vanity Fair, Collier's*, and other magazines. At the same time he has won a reputation as a watercolorist and wood sculptor. His cartoons have been published in a number of collections—*About People* (1939), *The Lonely Ones* (1942), *All Embarrassed* (1944), *Small Fry* (1944), *Persistent Faces* (1945), *Till Death Do Us Part* (1947), *The Rejected Lovers* (1951), *Dreams of Glory* (1953), and *The Steig Album* (1959). *Drawings*, with an introduction by Lillian Ross, appeared in 1979, and *Strutters and Fretters; or the Inescapable Self* in 1994. *The World of William Steig* (1998), edited by Lee Lorenz, with an introduction by John Updike, contains 400 illustrations, including unpublished pieces selected by the artist. Late in his career Steig turned to writing, and often illustrating, books for children. Among the most popular are *Sylvester and the Magic Pebble* (1969), *Dominic* (1972), *The Amazing Bone* (1976) and *Wizzil* (2000).

Stein, Gertrude (1874–1946), novelist, essayist, playwright, poet, librettist, biographer. Throughout Stein's career she produced accessible texts that create characters and stories, but most of her major work aims to revolutionize not only our sense of literature but our sense of what meaning is. Obscure sentences inform her writing: "Why is a feel oyster an egg stir," from *Tender Buttons*, is characteristic. Even her directly communicative work is strongly marked by such experimentation. Stein's life as a writer is a paradoxical, dual-sided series of attempts to preserve her revolutionary, hermetic aims, and simultaneously to find the widest popular audience for them. Her attempts take the form of explaining her difficult art in terms of democratic American experience and history.

Stein was born in Allegheny, Pennsylvania, of a wealthy family of German-Jewish descent that moved on to Oakland, California. Stein's parents died during her adolescence. In 1893 she followed her brother Leo Stein to Harvard and studied psychology at the Harvard Annex (Radcliffe) under WILLIAM JAMES. In Baltimore she did graduate work in psychology and medicine at Johns Hopkins, but lost interest and failed her examinations. In 1903 and 1905 she wrote, but did not publish, her first short novels: *Q.E.D.*, about the relations—including lesbian relations—between three women; and *Fernhurst*, a study of gender conflicts and politics at a women's college.

During the next decade Stein wrote voluminously, developing and intensifying her modernist aims. In 1904 Gertrude and Leo set up house in Paris at 27 rue de Fleurus, where they collected works by Cezanne, Matisse, and Picasso. A Cezanne portrait, intimacy with Picasso, and memories of Baltimore life—including Gertrude's experience delivering babies in the city's African-American community—inspired Stein in 1906 to compose THREE LIVES, which she published at her own expense in 1909. These are stories about immigrant women servants and an American mulatto woman, MELANCTHA. As Picasso became a brother-in-art for Stein, tension developed with her brother, who was to attack Picasso for his venture into cubism, and to attack Gertrude for her next massive experiment, THE MAKING OF AMERICANS, written in 1906–08 (published in 1925). In 1907, in Paris, Stein met a Californian, Alice B. Toklas, who was to become Gertrude's lover and life-long companion. In 1909, Toklas moved into the Stein household, further freeing Gertrude from dependence on Leo. She continued to innovate, undertaking *Tender Buttons* (1914), which is considered a verbal equivalent of Picasso's cubism. The result was a lifelong break with Leo that began in 1913. This work, which abandons conventional syntax and semantics, can be read in part as a secret celebration of Stein's domestic and erotic relation with Toklas.

Stein's two publications by 1914 gained attention from such American writers, art patrons, and critics as SHERWOOD ANDERSON, MABEL DODGE LUHAN, HUTCHINS HAPGOOD, AVERY HOPWOOD, Henry McBride, and CARL VAN VECHTEN. Stein's art collection, writing, and developing connection with surrealism brought her into contact with the English modernists Clive Bell, Roger Fry, Wyndham Lewis, and Edith Sitwell. At the same time, World War I returned Stein to American demotic experience by bringing American soldiers to France. Stein had donated a Ford and her services as a driver to the American Fund for French Wounded. After American entry in the war, she felt as if she had gone back to the U.S. through contact with "military god-sons." Even while Stein, in another avant-garde effort, *Geography and Plays* (1922), was reinventing dramatic form as a new kind of landscape in writing and was practicing her cubist writing on American themes in *Useful Knowledge* (1928), she was touring the Army with Toklas in the Ford, and meditating on the specifically American motivation of her work.

In the postwar years Stein's celebrity continued to grow. FITZGERALD, HEMINGWAY, MARIANNE MOORE, KATHERINE ANN PORTER, THORNTON WILDER, and WILLIAM CARLOS WILLIAMS were influenced by, and championed, her. The HARLEM RENAISSANCE artists LANGSTON HUGHES, NELLA LARSEN, JAMES WELDON JOHNSON, and PAUL ROBESON paid tribute to "Melanctha," and composers GEORGE ANTHEIL and Virgil Thomson set various of her works to music. But most of Stein's work continued to be unpublished. *The Making of Americans* was 16 years old when Hemingway secured its partial appearance in *Transatlantic Review* in 1924. Yet publication did not, after all, mean increased audience. When printed in its entirety by ROBERT MCALMON's Contact Press in 1925, *The Making of Americans* did not sell. *Geography and Plays* and *Useful Knowledge* were also commercial failures. Undaunted, Stein entered a new phase of neoromantic experiment, producing such poems as "Patriarchal Poetry" (1927) and *Stanzas in Meditation* (1932). Meanwhile, four volumes of Stein appeared between 1930 and 1932 under the imprint of Toklas's privately financed Plain Edition. Yet Toklas's publishing strategy proved inadequate.

To help gain a wider reading of her work Stein had begun to write accessible explanations of her poetics. At Oxford and Cambridge, in 1926, Stein had delivered "Composition as Explanation," which explains her apparent nonsense as an attempt to use writing to embody "a prolonged present" and to forecast new awarenesses of time, of likeness, and of difference generated by postwar consciousness. This lecture was followed by a further explanation, in 1927, in Eugene Jolas's *Transition*; ironically, the explanation was garbled by the typesetter. Stein was now ready for one more radical departure: to write a book "As simply as Defoe did the autobiography of Crusoe." In the AUTOBIOGRAPHY OF ALICE B. TOKLAS (1933) Stein puts Toklas's personality in place of her own, thereby playfully dramatizing the problematic relations between her own identity and her perception by her audience.

Toklas became a best seller. The success was consolidated by publication of an abridged *The Making of Americans* in 1934; by an acclaimed production of *Four Saints in Three Acts*, which Virgil Thomson had composed to Stein's libretto in 1928; and by Stein's lecture tour of the United States in 1934–35. There, she found she had become a household name. She was taken up by Bennet Cerf of Random House, who reissued *Three Lives* in the Modern Library and brought out *Portraits and Prayers* (1935) and *The Geographical History of America* (1936). In Stein's *Lectures in America* (1935) and *Narration* (1935), she continued her explanations of the sense made by even her most obscure work; in "What Are Masterpieces," a lecture given in 1936 in a return visit to the English universities, she continued this explanatory project.

Yet, having at last secured the broad recognition she had sought, Stein nevertheless felt dissatisfied. Her puzzled fascination with problems of identity and audience, of how identities can or cannot be described, cognized, or read preceded her return to the States, and intensified thereafter, informing *The Geographical History of America, Everybody's Autobiography* (1936) and *Ida: A Novel* (1941). At the same time it became clear that her explanations did not further the close reading of her work she had hoped for. Stein's FOUR IN AMERICA (1932–33), a fantasy on the possible interidentity of Generals Washington and Grant, HENRY JAMES, and Wilbur Wright, was rejected by Cerf, as were the play *Doctor Faustus Lights the*

Lights (1938) and the children's story "The World Is Round" (1938), all on grounds of their audience-alienating obscurity.

The emergence of another world war, and Stein's life as an alien of Jewish descent in Vichy France, once again intensified Stein's reflections on her unpopular efforts in relation to American popular life. In 1942, Stein and Toklas left defeated Paris for their country house in southern France; soon after, the Nazi occupation cut the couple off from communication with the U.S. for two years. During this time Stein wrote *Wars I Have Seen* (1945), a meditation on the relation of American modernity and American wars to historical contingency and coincidence, and *Mrs. Reynolds* (1952), a hermetic translation of *Wars I Have Seen* into an allegorical novel about Hitler and Stalin.

With the liberation of France, Stein and Toklas returned to Paris in 1944. She surrounded herself again with military godsons, even touring the Army in Germany. Stein's last writings especially emphasize American themes. She wrote *Brewsie and Willy* (1946), an exploration of GI speech and of the problematic effects of postwar employment worries on American character. She collaborated with Virgil Thomson on an opera about SUSAN B. ANTHONY, *The Mother of Us All* (1947). One of Stein's last enthusiasms was RICHARD WRIGHT's *Black Boy*. Thus, Stein's interests at the end of her career came full circle, with a return to *Three Lives'* meditation on the experiences and hopes of the people. She died of cancer in Paris on July 27, 1946.

Notable artists influenced by Stein's styles or her ideas, in addition to those already named, include English novelist Henry Green; American novelists JANE BOWLES, PAUL BOWLES, and WILLIAM H. GASS; American poets FRANK O'HARA, JOHN ASHBERY and the so-called LANGUAGE POETS; and American composer JOHN CAGE.

Criticism remains divided over how much sense Stein's work makes or *should* make, even in spite of her explanations. And although Stein is central not just to avant-garde traditions but to Emersonian and Whitmanian traditions, criticism is also divided because Stein has been regarded more as eccentric than essential. Feminists claim that this marginalizing of Stein results from prejudice against thinking of women, especially of lesbians, as transformers of culture. But how much Stein can be enlisted for feminism also stays open to debate. Stein replaced father figures and brothers too with Toklas, but her directly accessible work represents a cultural nationalism that appears to transcend, or ignore, questions of gender and of gender antagonisms.

Stein's self-division is the root of the critical controversy. She was committed to the idea of literature as a use of writing and of language that makes them transcend immediate sense and social-historical relevance. Stein's use of words, cut away from their ordinary meanings and relations, intends to make words act as independent, abstract (yet vivid) entities. Words are not used by Stein for the sake of describing anything, because for her description is a relational mode. Stein prefers what is nonrelational, disconnected. Repetition, memory, and resemblance are also, according to Stein, relational modes. Her experiments seek to replace these modes with insistence—a presence and process of continuous mental and verbal movement, for which the ever-different still pictures that constitute a film strip are an analogy. Stein offers this movement in writing as an alternative to description, remembrance, resemblance, and the rest. Her problem with audiences is that audiences expect to have their desire for resemblance and for memory stirred by art. Stein asks that writers and audiences be stirred instead by mutually producing only whatever can "be a recognition by never before that writing having it be existing."

The Geographical History of America and "What are Masterpieces" illustrate the paradoxical nature of Stein's aims to transcend meaning and history, and at the same time to explain her aims as meaningful historical ones. Stein opposes human mind, an autonomous entity without identity—an abstract but vital Being—to human nature, which is characterized by identity and memory. "Mostly," Stein says, "a master-piece is about identity and in being so it must not have any"; and "we live in time and identity but as we are we do not know time and identity." Masterpieces do not express human universals—such universals would have to be identifiable. Moreover, masterpieces are not necessary, nor are they privileged expressions of forms of relationship. "The business of living . . . is relation and necessity"; masterpieces may picture this business but themselves stand clear of it. We can see that Stein is equating her writing with the human mind and its masterpieces. Yet just at such moments of maximal emphasis on mind's entity rather than identity, we find Stein relating her emphasis to human nature's domain. In *Lectures in America*, Stein's experimentation, she explains, issues from differences between English and American history. In contrast to English daily life—isolated, static, and intelligibly ordered—American life is an unsettled mobility, resistant to description, memory, and intelligibility. This is why, after all, Stein cannot use words fixedly and descriptively. Another English-American contrast matters: English island life creates a hierarchical split between what is inside daily life, and what is outside, an opposition intensified in English imperialism; by contrast, the movement of American life subverts such oppositions, implying a democratic resistance to invidious differences. (The subversion of opposition here also echoes Stein's hope to break down the difference between the inside of the writer and the outside of the writer's audience.) Stein's literary innovations, then, much as they belong to transcendent mind, *are* rooted in an American history that is not easy to extricate from human nature; and yet, at the same time, it paradoxically appears that for Stein American experience is a crossroad where human nature lets go of all traditional forms of relation, and brings history as we have known it to a close.

Does Stein's cultural nationalism comprehend a female component of human mind? Are we to think that feminist concerns belong only to human nature? *Toklas* says that "the cause of women does not happen to be [Stein's] business." Yet we know that Stein's heroines in her adolescence were the feminist CHARLOTTE PERKINS GILMAN, Saint Theresa (a feminist archetype), and George Eliot's rebel against father *and* brother, Maggie Tulliver; that *Q.E.D.*, *Fernhurst*, and *Three Lives* fit

feminist concerns; that Stein "liked to read about the suffragettes." *Tender Buttons* focuses on domestic objects, traditionally coded female, as it expresses antipatriarchal sexuality; "Patriarchal Poetry" parodies the dominance of male sense. In *Everybody's Autobiography*, surveying the world's dictators and presidents, Stein declares "there is too much fathering going on just now . . . fathers are depressing." *Ida* can be read as a real woman's witty response to James Joyce's imaginary heroines, and *The Mother of Us All* can be regarded as the American equivalent of Virginia Woolf's feminist tracts.

Carl Van Vechten edited *Selected Writings* (1946) and *The Yale Edition of the Unpublished Writings of Gertrude Stein* (8 v. 1951–58), from which Richard Kostelanetz derived *The Yale Gertrude Stein: Selections* (1980). A biography is John Malcolm Brinnin, *The Third Rose: Gertrude Stein and Her World* (1959).
ROBERT L. CASERIO

Steinbeck, John [Ernest] (1902–1968),   short-story writer, novelist. Some of Steinbeck's best work is set in Monterey County, California, where Steinbeck was born and spent most of his life. Self-supporting from youth, he attended Stanford University as a major in marine biology, but dropped out to work his way to New York City through the Panama Canal (1925). His first publication was a fictionalized life of Sir Henry Morgan (1929). After a period as a newspaper reporter, he went home again. For two winters he lived alone in the high Sierras, then worked in a trout hatchery, on fruit ranches, as a surveyor, an apprentice painter, and a chemist, but always kept on writing. Out of this period he emerged with a profound understanding of manual laborers that manifested itself in many of his books.

His next book, *Pastures of Heaven* (1932), was a collection of short stories dealing with the inhabitants of the secluded valley of that name, and the first evidence of Steinbeck's concern with people of simple needs, uncorrupted by materialism or sophistication, who have the potential to be closely related to the land and to their fellow men. Often, as in these stories, the characters have an incomplete knowledge of themselves and their potential or do not fully appreciate their role in a larger humanity.

To a God Unknown (1933), a mixture of pantheism and mysticism, is Steinbeck's strongest statement about man's relationship to the land, a theme present to a lesser degree in most of his writings. TORTILLA FLAT (1935) and IN DUBIOUS BATTLE (1936) established Steinbeck's reputation. The former deals with the Paisanos (Mexican-Americans) of Monterey. The latter tells of a violent strike among California fruit pickers. Partially a protest against the conditions under which the picker worked, it was another link in his developing philosophy of the relationship between man and man. OF MICE AND MEN (1937) is especially notable for its depiction of the mentally retarded giant Lennie, one of nature's unfinished children. It was first conceived as a play and was dramatized in the year of its publication, winning the Drama Critics' Circle Award. *The Long Valley* (1938) was a book of short stories.

In 1939 Steinbeck published THE GRAPES OF WRATH, sometimes described as "the 20th-century *Uncle Tom's Cabin*." In its depiction of the Joad family, fleeing the disastrous Dust Bowl of Oklahoma, this book sums up the despair of the early 1930s. It appears to have been as effective as Upton Sinclair's *The Jungle* (1906) was earlier in crystallizing public opinion against allowing such conditions to continue. Beyond its importance as a social document, however, it is also an affirmation of the solidity of mankind and the sanctity of life; "Everything that lives," says Tom Joad, "is holy." The novel won a Pulitzer Prize and was made into a classic motion picture in 1940.

Following the *Grapes of Wrath* Steinbeck's interest in marine biology led him to publish two books primarily about sea life, but interspersed with other observations on men and nature: *Sea of Cortez* (with Edward F. Ricketts, 1941) and *The Log from the Sea of Cortez* (1951), a reissue of the narrative part of the former volume with a short biographical sketch of Ricketts, who was killed in 1948. Doc, a leading character of *Cannery Row* (1945), strongly resembles Ricketts. Both CANNERY ROW and its sequel *Sweet Thursday* (1954) deal with Mac and the boys, a group of happy indigents whose lack of sophistication and acquisitiveness permits them to live in a state of nature. *The Red Pony* (1945) is a still popular account of four episodes in the life of a boy on a California ranch. *The Wayward Bus* (1947) describes the sexual misadventures of a group stranded overnight at a California wayside station. THE PEARL (1947), a novelette, shows how the finding of a magnificent pearl by a simple Mexican fisherman brings him only misfortune. *Burning Bright* (1950) tells of a wife who, when she finds her husband sterile, seeks to have a child by another man. Perhaps the best—and certainly the most ambitious—novel after *The Grapes of Wrath* is EAST OF EDEN (1952). His most ambitious treatment of the background of his home region, the story—centering on the conflict of two brothers—treats social history through three generations of the Trask family.

The novelette *The Short Reign of Pippin IV* (1957) is an amusing satirical "fabrication" of French politics today. His novel *Winter of Our Discontent* appeared in 1961. *The Acts of King Arthur and His Noble Knights*, an adaptation of Sir Thomas Malory's text left incomplete at his death, was edited by Chase Horton and published in 1976.

In general, Steinbeck's shorter fiction is humorous, warm sometimes to the point of being sentimental, and concerned with the small tragedies in the lives of simple people. It implicitly contrasts the good life of the natural man close to the soil with the depersonalization and dehumanization of the commercial world. Steinbeck's longer fiction is often subject to a philosophic tendentiousness, but is primarily concerned with the growth and development of men to whom it is necessary to be good group men in order to be good individuals.

Two collections of Steinbeck's writings have been made: *The Portable Steinbeck* (1943, rev. 1946) and *The Short Novels of John Steinbeck* (ed. by Joseph Henry Jackson, 1953). Steinbeck won the Nobel Prize for Literature in 1962. His nonfiction includes *Bombs Away: The Story of a Bomber Team* (1942); *Russian Journal* (1948, with Robert Capa as photographer); *Once There Was a War* (1958), excerpts from his work as a war correspondent;

Travels with Charley (1962), an account of cross-country travel with his dog; and *America and Americans* (1966).

Two books were privately printed: *Saint Katy the Virgin* (1936) and *How Edith McGillicudy Met R.L.S.* (1943). Besides dramatizing *Of Mice and Men* (1937), Steinbeck wrote a dramatization of his novel *The Moon Is Down* (1942), dealing with the Nazi threat. As a novel, *Burning Bright* was already so close to theatrical techniques that little was needed to make it ready for production in the year of its publication. Steinbeck also wrote the film scripts for *The Forgotten Village*, *The Pearl*, and *Viva Zapata!* In 1969, *Journal of a Novel: The East of Eden Letters* was published. Elaine Steinbeck and Robert Wallsten edited *Steinbeck: A Life in Letters* (1976). Jackson T. Benson's *The True Adventures of John Steinbeck* (1983) is a complete biography. John H. Timmerman's *John Steinbeck's Fiction: The Aesthetics of the Road Taken* (1986) is a critical study. *Working Days: The Journals of "The Grapes of Wrath,"* 1938–1941, edited by Robert DeMott, was published as part of the celebration of the fiftieth anniversary of the novel's appearance in 1939.

Steinberg, Saul (1914–1999),   cartoonist. Born in Romania and trained in architecture in Italy, Steinberg became a U.S. citizen in 1943. His satiric drawings, using precise line and buildings, reflect his education. His work frequently appeared in *The New Yorker* and has been collected in books, including *All in Line* (1945), *The Art of Living* (1949), *The Passport* (1954), *The Labyrinth* (1960), *The Catalogue* (1962), *Confessions* (1965), *The Inspector* (1973), and *Documents* (1979). *Discovery of America* appeared in 1992.

Steinem, Gloria (1934–   ),   publisher, editor, writer, feminist. Born in Ohio and educated at Smith, Steinem did graduate study at Delhi University and the University of Calcutta. Her writing appeared in *Esquire, Vogue, Life* and *Cosmopolitan.* In 1972 she cofounded MS. magazine and served as its editor until 1987. *Outrageous Acts and Everyday Rebellions* (1983) is a collection of twenty years of her writing on feminist issues. *Marilyn: Norma Jean* (1986) is a biography of Marilyn Monroe intended as a rebuttal to Norman Mailer's portrayal of the star. Steinem also wrote *Bedside Book of Self-Esteem* (1989). She has often been the spokesperson for a feminist perspective in public forums. *Revolution from Within: a Book of Self-esteem* (1991) describes the negative psychological and societal forces that influence personality development. Steinem draws on her own experience and that of other well-known people. *Moving Beyond Words/Age, Rage, Sex, Power, Money, Muscles: Breaking the Boundaries of Gender* (1994) contains new and revised essays on topics such as Freud and aging.

Stella Dallas (1923),   a novel by OLIVE HIGGINS PROUTY. A New England woman sacrifices her own life and interests to help her daughter achieve happiness. A best seller, it was made into a play, silent movie, talkie, and radio serial.

Stephansson, Stephan G[udmundsson] (1853–1927), farmer, poet, social agitator. Stephansson emigrated from Iceland to North America in 1873 and settled as a farmer in Alberta, Canada, in 1889; he remained there for the rest of his life. His poems are ranked among the best written in Icelandic in his day. His collected poems, *Andvokur* (Wakeful Nights, 1909) appeared in six volumes. He also wrote prose. All his work reveals him as a lover of nature and an opponent of social injustice.

Stephens, Alexander Hamilton (1812–1883), lawyer, public official, writer. Stephens studied law, served in the Georgia legislature, and U.S. Congress (1843–59); was Vice President of the Confederacy and a member of the U.S. Senate (not allowed to take his seat), again a member of Congress (1873–82), and finally governor of Georgia from 1882 until his death. Stephens discussed the war issues in *Constitutional View of the War Between the States* (2 v. 1868, 1870), and later replied to his critics in *The Reviewers Reviewed* (1872). He also wrote a *History of the United States* (1882) and his *Recollections* [and] *Diary Kept When a Prisoner, 1865* (1910).

Stephens, Ann S[ophia Winterbotham] (1813–1886), novelist, humorist, poet, short-story writer, editor. One of the most popular authors of the mid-19th century, Mrs. Stephens, a native of Connecticut, appears to have started her career when she was widowed. Stephens's best-known book was MALAESKA (1860), the first number issued in the Beadle Dime Novels. *Esther, A Story of the Oregon Trail* (1869) introduces one of nature's noblemen, an amalgam of DANIEL BOONE and James Fenimore Cooper's LEATHERSTOCKING. Like some other writers of the day, she imitated T. C. Haliburton's Sam Slick and wrote a book, supposedly by Jonathan Slick, called *High Life in New York* (1843) She also wrote *Mary Derwent* (1838), *Alice Copley* (1844), *Fashion and Famine* (1854), *The Rejected Wife* (1863), and *The Indian Queen* (1864). She founded the *Portland Magazine* (1834) and *Mrs. Stephens' Illustrated New Monthly* (1856) and served on the editorial staffs of other magazines.

Stephens, John Lloyd (1805–1852), lawyer, diplomatic agent, railroad builder, archaeologist. Stephens, born in New Jersey, traveled extensively in Europe and the Near East, and on his return published *Incidents of Travel in Egypt, Arabia Petraea, and the Holy Land* (2 v. 1837) and *Incidents of Travel in Greece, Turkey, Russia, and Poland* (2 v. 1838). With Frederick Catherwood he made extensive explorations in Central America, and their observations were vividly set down by Stephens in *Incidents of Travel in Central America* (2 v. 1841) and *Incidents of Travel in Yucatan* (2 v. 1843), with drawings by Catherwood.

Stephens, Robert Neilson (1867–1906), newspaperman, theatrical agent, playwright, novelist. Stephens, born in Pennsylvania, joined the staff of the Philadelphia *Press*, became its drama critic, and began writing melodramatic plays of his own. The most popular of them was *An Enemy to the King* (1896), later a novel (1897). He also wrote other novels, including *A Gentleman Player* (1899), *Captain Ravenshaw* (1901), and *The Bright Face of Danger* (1904).

Sterling, George (1869–1926), poet, dramatist, critic. Born in Sag Harbor, New York, and educated under JOHN B. TABB in Maryland, Sterling moved to California and became a writer. He was an active member of the Bohemian Club and wrote plays for its celebrated Bohemian Grove shows; he com-

mitted suicide in the club. Much admired by Western writers such as AMBROSE BIERCE, he was known in the East mainly as the author of the poem "A Wine of Wizardry" (*Cosmopolitan*, September 1907). Among Sterling's books are *The Testimony of the Suns and Other Poems* (1903); *The Triumph of Bohemia: A Forest Play* (1907); *A Wine of Wizardry and Other Poems* (1909); *Beyond the Breakers and Other Poems* (1914); *Yosemite: An Ode* (1916); *The Caged Eagle and Other Poems* (1916); *The Play of Everyman* (1917); *Thirty-five Sonnets* (1917); *Lilith: A Dramatic Poem* (1919); *Rosamund* (a play, 1920); *Sails and Mirage and Other Poems* (1921); *Truth* (a play, 1923); *Strange Waters* (1926); *Sonnets to Craig* (1928); and *After Sunset* (1939).

Sterling, James (1701?–1763), playwright, poet, clergyman. Born in Ireland, Sterling wrote several plays and pamphlets before being ordained an Anglican clergyman (1733). *The Poetical Works of the Rev. James Sterling* was published in 1734. In 1737 he came to Maryland, where he was a pastor in several parishes, wrote verses for periodicals, and served as customs collector at Chester. Among his later writings are *An Epistle to the Hon. Arthur Dobbs in Europe* (verse, 1752) and *Zeal against the Enemies of Our Country, Pathetically Recommended* (1755).

Stern, Philip Van Doren (1900–1984), historian, novelist, anthologist. Stern, born in Pennsylvania, wrote many books, including a historical novel, *The Drums of Morning* (1942); *The Man Who Killed Lincoln* (1939); *The Life and Writings of Lincoln* (1940); and *An End to Valor: the Last Days of the Civil War* (1958), an account of the period between March 4 and May 24, 1865. He also compiled numerous anthologies and a *Pictorial History of the Automobile* (1953) and wrote *The Confederate Navy* (1962), *Robert E. Lee: The Man and the Soldier* (1963), and *Henry David Thoreau: Writer and Rebel* (1972).

Stern, Richard G[ustave] (1928–), novelist, short-story writer, essayist. Stern's novels include *Golk* (1960); *Europe: or Up and Down with Baggish and Schreiber* (1961), the story of two American bureaucrats in postwar Germany; *In Any Case* (1963); *Stitch* (1965), depicting an expatriate artist said to be modeled on Ezra Pound; *Other Men's Daughters* (1973), on a professor-student love affair; *Natural Shocks* (1978); and *A Father's Words* (1986). His story collections are *Teeth, Dying and Other Matters* (1964); *1968: A Short Novel* (1970); *Packages* (1980); *Noble Rot: Stories 1989–1988* (1988); and *Shares* (1992). *The Books in Fred Hampton's Apartment* (1973) and *The Invention of the Real* (1982) are miscellaneous collections. *Sistermony* (1995) is a memoir of his sister's battle with cancer.

Sternberg, Josef von (1894–1969), film director. Born in Vienna, Sternberg served in the U.S. Army in World War I and settled in Hollywood in 1924. *Underworld* (1926) was Hollywood's first serious movie about gangsters. In 1930 he found Marlene Dietrich on the Berlin stage and cast her in the lead of *The Blue Angel*; together they did six more films in the United States: *Morocco* (1930), *Dishonored* (1931), *Shanghai Express* (1932), *Blonde Venus* (1932), *The Scarlet Empress*

(1934), and *The Devil Is a Woman* (1935). This work marks the height of his career. His autobiography is entitled *Fun in a Chinese Laundry* (1965).

Stevens, Abel (1815–1897),   Methodist clergyman, historian, biographer, editor. Stevens, born in Philadelphia, served as editor of *Zion's Herald* (1840–52) and the *National Magazine* (1852–56). He also wrote numerous works of historical character, among them *A History of the Religious Movement of the 18th Century Called Methodism* (3 v. 1858–61), *A History of the Methodist Episcopal Church in the U.S.* (4 v. 1864–67), and *Madame De Staël* (2 v. 1881). He also wrote *Sketches and Incidents* (2 v. 1844–45).

Stevens, Benjamin Franklin (1833–1902)   and his brother **Henry Stevens** (1819–1886), booksellers, bibliographers. These Vermont-born Americans became London booksellers specializing in Americana. They acted as agents for American bibliophiles and for the Library of Congress; some of their research material is now deposited in the latter institution. Henry Stevens prepared an *Introduction to the Catalogue Index of Manuscripts in the Archives of England, France, Holland, and Spain Relating to America, 1763 to 1783*, also a *Report on American Manuscripts in the Royal Institution of Great Britain*. Material relating to America was also collected for the British Museum. Benjamin Stevens wrote *Historical Nuggets* (1862), *Bibliotheca Historica* (1870), and *Recollections of Mr. James Lenox of New York and the Formation of His Library* (1886).

Stevens, Gavin,   a character created by WILLIAM FAULKNER. Stevens, a lawyer and later the county attorney in Jefferson, appears in several of Faulkner's novels. Educated at Harvard and Heidelberg, Stevens is a philosophic observer and commentator on events in YOKNAPATAWPHA COUNTY, although he rarely is directly involved in them. He develops a hopeless love for Eula Varner Snopes in *The Town* and later for her daughter, Linda, in *The Mansion*. He solves murders in KNIGHT'S GAMBIT and is a somewhat ineffectual but philosophic presence in INTRUDER IN THE DUST. Finally, to cure himself of his unrewarded love for Linda Snopes, he marries Melisandre Backus Harriss, a wealthy widow who appears in the title story of *Knight's Gambit*.

Stevens, James [Floyd] (1892–1971),   public relations counsel, storyteller. A native Iowan, Stevens won a notable success with his first book, *Paul Bunyan* (1925), and then dealt with Paul in three other works, *Saginaw Paul Bunyan* (1932), *Paul Bunyan's Bears* (1947), and *Paul Bunyan's Tree Farm* (1954). He also wrote novels, based largely on his experiences in the Northwest. Among them are *Brawny-man* (1926) and *Big Jim Turner* (1948). *Mattock* (1927) describes experiences in World War I, and *Homer in the Sagebrush* (1928) contains thirteen short stories about the West. *Green Power* appeared in 1958.

Stevens, Wallace (1879–1955),   poet, lawyer. Stevens, whose name is associated with the poetic experiments of the early 20th century, lived an outwardly conventional life. When an editor asked him for biographical information to be pub-

lished with several of his poems in 1922, he replied, "Do, please, excuse me from the biographical note. I am a lawyer and live in Hartford. But such facts are neither gay nor instructive." He was right, inasmuch as the external facts of his life fail to suggest the originality and exoticism of his work.

Stevens was born and grew up in the final decades of the 19th century in Reading, Pennsylvania, an industrial city of 43,278 population in 1880 and not far from Daniel Boone's birthplace. Stevens remained deeply attached to the rivers, valleys, and wooded hills of eastern Pennsylvania, which figure in many of his poems. While attending Harvard as a special student in 1897–1900, he served on the college literary magazine, the *Harvard Advocate*, and contributed poems and short stories to the *Advocate* and the *Harvard Monthly*. He also enjoyed the friendship of the philosopher-poet GEORGE SANTAYANA.

After briefly trying his hand at journalism in New York City, he attended New York Law School, worked as a law clerk for a year, and was admitted to the bar in 1904. His career in law, like his career in literature, got off to a slow start. His first partnership failed, and he held several other positions before joining the home office legal staff of the Hartford (Connecticut) Accident and Indemnity Company in 1916. He lived in Hartford for the rest of his life, handling surety and fidelity claims up to the time of his death of cancer at the age of 75. Except for brief trips to Canada and Cuba, and a cruise through the Panama Canal, he did not travel outside the United States. He lived within walking distance of his office and never owned an automobile. Like Thoreau, however, Stevens could claim to have "traveled a good deal" without leaving home. Particularly during the years when he lived in and around New York City (1900–16), he read voraciously and tried his hand at the poetic modes then fashionable among the avant-garde: French *symbolisme*, the aesthetic dandyism of the English *fin de siècle*, and imitations of oriental forms. Harvard classmates introduced him to postimpressionist painting and published his poems in the little magazines with which they were associated.

Nearly as important to his poetic development during these years was his marriage, in 1909, to a young woman from his hometown. The poems he wrote for Elsie Viola Kachel were the first he published after college. Though their relationship later became strained and distant, Elsie served as an incentive to his poetry, even as a kind of muse. The early poetry in particular betrays intense but unsatisfied desire, erotic feeling displaced onto the physical world. Their marriage produced a daughter, Holly, in 1924, the year after Stevens published his first book of poems. Appropriately, Stevens dedicated HARMONIUM to his wife. Collected in this volume are some of his best-known and most often anthologized poems: SUNDAY MORNING, "The Emperor of Ice-Cream," "The Snow Man," "Disillusionment of Ten O'Clock," PETER QUINCE AT THE CLAVIER, and THIRTEEN WAYS OF LOOKING AT A BLACKBIRD. Many of the poems are set in the South, especially Florida, to which Stevens traveled each year on trips that combined business and pleasure. In the later poetry, this tropical lushness would give way to the more austere, often autumnal landscapes of New England.

Stevens postponed publishing a book of poems because he feared the result would be too heterogeneous. Despite his careful attention to the arrangement of the poems, *Harmonium* remains a study in contrasts. For every poem celebrating color and light and the pleasures of this world, there is another devoted to ennui and the inevitability of death. *Harmonium* also embraces contrasting poetic styles. Some poems treat the grand themes of Romanticism in an appropriately grand rhetoric. Others deflate any form of high seriousness with irreverent wit and an elliptical idiom.

"Sunday Morning," for example, is virtually a 19th-century poem in its eloquence and concern for the loss of religious faith. The poet shares a meditating woman's nostalgia for belief and tries to ease her acceptance of a merely natural world by describing that world in the most attractive terms possible. It is a place of deer, quail, mountains, and sweet berries ripening in the wilderness. In "A High-Toned Old Christian Woman," by contrast, the poet attempts to shock a believer out of her complacency by literalizing her creed into a heavenly orgy, a "bawdiness/Unpurged by epitaph."

These two poems suggest why many readers find Stevens's work obscure. It is not that he alludes to an unfamiliar tradition, like Pound and Eliot, or a body of specialized knowledge, like Yeats, nor that he uses words that cannot be found in a dictionary. Rather, he frustrates the reader's desire for a consistent persona, a recognizable character whose life might serve as a narrative thread on which to string the poems like so many beads. Often faulted for being impersonal, Stevens's poetry might be more accurately described as multipersonal. Personal experience and emotion are not expressed directly, but are projected onto many different, often exotic personae who speak in a variety of voices. Thus "The Comedian as the Letter C," in which he uses allegory to tell the story of his own poetic pilgrimage, is more typical of his work than "Red Loves Kit," in which he quarrels—still obliquely, to be sure—with his wife.

This kind of indirection characterizes not only his poems about personal experience but also those about contemporary politics and social change. The books he published during the Depression—*Ideas of Order* (1935), *Owl's Clover* (1936), and *The Man with the Blue Guitar and Other Poems* (1937)—were criticized by many reviewers for their apparent indifference to the distress of millions of people. In fact, the grim realities of the 1930s cast a shadow over these volumes, though not in a way the journalist or social reformer would recognize. Stevens believed that the poet is not obliged to address social and political issues directly. Indirectly, however, he serves the community by constantly renewing its fund of spiritual resources. In this sense, Stevens affirmed again and again, the poet helps people live their lives.

THE MAN WITH THE BLUE GUITAR, his most ambitious poem of the 1930s, takes this dialogue between the poet and the community as its subject matter, though it affirms that poetry itself is ultimately the subject of any poem. Another well-known

piece, "The Idea of Order at Key West," pays tribute to the mind's capacity to give form and meaning to a chaotic world. Though very much a poem of its time, it has remained a timely poem because it represents all kinds of disorder, including the social and political turmoil of the 1930s, as the natural disorder of a Florida seascape. When Stevens tried to write more explicitly about contemporary affairs, as in *Owl's Clover*, he was usually disappointed with the result.

During World War II he undertook the most ambitious project of his career. The imagination, he maintained in *Owl's Clover*, is "source and patriarch of other spheres." That is, the mind begets political systems, philosophies, social rituals, science, mathematics, art, music, literature, and all other structures for ordering and interpreting the world. It also—here Stevens agreed with Santayana—creates both the gods and the religions that pay them homage. In time, any product of the imagination will lose its ability to compel admiration or belief. But the imagination itself remains vital. When one of its offspring fades, it creates another to take its place, one more in keeping with the spirit of the age.

Consequently, as Stevens saw it, the modern era is not necessarily a period of terminal skepticism. It might instead be a period of transition from one object of ultimate belief, or supreme fiction, to another. Having traced the supremacy of the gods to their source in the human mind, Stevens might logically have chosen to celebrate the creative source, the patriarch, rather than any of its creations. But he understood that human emotion cannot attach itself to such an abstraction. The ideal supreme fiction would mirror its source, yet be sufficiently concrete to elicit affection and awe.

Stevens never specified the form of his supreme fiction, since he knew that a specific fiction would be subject to the same fate as other superannuated products of the imagination. However, in NOTES TOWARD A SUPREME FICTION and other poems collected in *Parts of a World* (1942) and *Transport to Summer* (1947) he speculated that it might take the form of a quasi-Nietzschean hero, a major man. Such a hero would be credibly grounded in empirical experience, since in time of war soldiers were daily exemplifying nobility and self-sacrifice on the battlefields of Europe. But to qualify as *supreme* fiction the hero would also have to meet the criteria set forth in the three subheadings to "Notes": "It Must Be Abstract," "It Must Change," and "It Must Give Pleasure."

Stevens considered adding a fourth section to "Notes toward a Supreme Fiction," to be entitled "It Must Be Human." However, he understood that he could not proceed further in the direction of anthropomorphism without violating the other criteria for his supreme fiction. Major man would have to remain an ideal, what Stevens called "the impossible possible philosophers' man" in his poem "Asides on the Oboe." In his next book of poems, *The Auroras of Autumn* (1950), he abandoned the hero but not the supreme fiction, which appears in several guises. It is the central poem of "A Primitive Like an Orb," composed of all the poems ever written. Alternatively, it is the godlike figure of imagination represented in "The Auroras of Autumn" who controls cosmic change. In "Final Soliloquy of the Interior Paramour" Stevens went so far as to equate his supreme fiction with the divinity of traditional religion: "God and the imagination are one." Though it would be tempting to read this as Stevens' belated return to orthodoxy, he more likely was reaffirming the godlike powers of the human mind. Some, including a hospital chaplain who visited him during his final illness, have testified that he converted to Roman Catholicism shortly before his death. If so, this represents a later stage of his spiritual pilgrimage, one he did not live to record in his poetry.

"Final Soliloquy" is one of the new poems Stevens added to his previous books to make up the *Collected Poems* (1954). Like "To an Old Philosopher in Rome"—ostensibly about Santayana's last days—"The Poem That Took the Place of a Mountain," "The Planet on the Table," and "Of Mere Being"—the last of these published posthumously—it is a poem of valediction and summing-up. As he approached the end of his career, Stevens took pleasure and pride in his accomplishment. Yet he also understood its limits. Far from being contained in his poems, reality remained "The palm at the end of the mind, / Beyond the last thought" ("Of Mere Being").

During Stevens's lifetime, his achievement was recognized publicly with a Bollingen Prize (1949), two National Book Awards (1951, 1955), and a Pulitzer Prize (1955). He was inducted into the National Institute of Arts and Letters in 1946, and subsequently received honorary degrees from seven colleges and universities, including Harvard, Columbia, and Yale. He was frequently invited to read his poems and to lecture on the subject of poetry. Though uncomfortable in the role of public performer, he used these occasions to elaborate his ideas on the social and spiritual functions of poetry.

In the most satisfactory of these lectures, "The Noble Rider and the Sound of Words," Stevens argues that the style of poetry, irrespective of its subject matter or argument, supplies people with the spiritual resources they need to face the pressures and distractions of the 20th century. His other lectures and essays, collected in THE NECESSARY ANGEL (1951) and *Opus Posthumous* (1951, 1989), play variations on this theme, as do many of the aphorisms collected under the title "Adagia." Stevens was not a systematic thinker, and the aphorism was his natural mode of expression. Many of his poems and prose writings began as aphorisms, and some retain an aphoristic style and structure.

His *pensées* have proven highly suggestive to philosophers and religious thinkers, who have appropriated and sometimes attempted to systematize them. Few books have been so often plundered for book titles and epigraphs as Stevens's *Collected Poems*. Literary critics of each generation have found something to admire in his work and have often used it as a vehicle for their theories. Formalist critics of the 1950s and 1960s reveled in the irony, ambiguity, and formal integrity of his poems. Poststructuralist critics of the 1970s and early 1980s enlisted the later poems in a thoroughgoing critique of the metaphysical grounds of discourse. Since the early 1980s, biographical and historical critics have been recovering the

occasions that gave rise to Stevens's poems. In the process, they are humanizing a poet whose sophistication has long since been established.

Stevens's influence on other poets is harder to specify, since he never attracted a group of disciples in the manner of Pound or William Carlos Williams. Among the poets said to have learned much from him are John Ashbery, Robert Duncan, A. R. Ammons, and James Merrill. His indirect influence is more extensive and probably more profound. As Theodore Roethke put it in one of his poems, "Wallace Stevens—are we for him? / Brother, he's our father!" His legacy is manifest whenever a poetic son or daughter celebrates the power of the mind over brute reality; turns to human creations for the satisfactions once found in religious belief; or fuses wit, elegant phrasing, and musical cadence into a memorable poetry.

The Collected Poems of Wallace Stevens (1954) contains the bulk of his poetry. *The Necessary Angel: Essays on Reality and the Imagination* (1951) collects six lectures and an essay. *Opus Posthumous* (1989) reprints his three plays together with the "Adagia" and the poetry and prose not included in the other volumes. Holly Stevens's *The Palm at the End of the Mind* (1971) provides a useful selection of the poetry. While there is no definitive biography of Stevens, three studies provide extensive biographical information: Peter Brazeau's *Parts of a World: Wallace Stevens Remembered* (1983); Milton J. Bates's *Wallace Stevens: A Mythology of Self* (1985); and Joan Richardson's two-volume study, *Wallace Stevens: The Early Years, 1879–1923* (1986) and *Wallace Stevens: The Later Years, 1923–1955* (1988). Among works of criticism, Helen Vendler's *Wallace Stevens: Words Chosen Out of Desire* (1984) is a valuable short introduction to the poetry. Harold Bloom's more comprehensive *Wallace Stevens: The Poems of Our Climate* (1977) places the poet in the tradition of English and American Romanticism.

MILTON J. BATES

Stevenson, Adlai E[wing] (1900–1965), lawyer, statesman. Stevenson, born in Los Angeles, was graduated from Princeton, attended Harvard Law School and Northwestern University Law School, and was admitted to the bar in 1926. He worked in various government agencies in Washington, practiced law in Chicago, served as special assistant first to Secretary of the Navy Frank Knox, later to two Secretaries of State, Edward Stettinius and James Byrnes. He handled press relations at the San Francisco United Nations Conference, was senior adviser to the United States delegation to the United Nations General Assembly. In 1947 he was elected governor of Illinois and instituted many vigorous reforms. He was Democratic nominee for President in 1952 and again in 1956, but both times lost the election to Dwight D. Eisenhower. He was appointed Ambassador to the United Nations by President Kennedy in 1961.

His speeches have been published in *Speeches of Adlai Stevenson* (1952); *Adlai's Almanac: The Wit and Wisdom of Stevenson of Illinois* (1952); *Major Campaign Speeches of Adlai E. Stevenson* (1953); and *Call to Greatness* (1954). Among

Stevenson's books are *What I Think* (1956); *Friends and Enemies* (1959); and *Putting First Things First, A Democratic View* (1960).

Stevenson, Burton E[gbert] (1872–1962), newsman, librarian, compiler of reference works, novelist. A librarian in his native Chillicothe, Ohio, and founder of The American Library in Paris, Stevenson formed his chief reputation as the compiler and editor of a number of useful reference works. Among them are *Poems of American History* (1908); *The Home Book of Verse* (1912); *The Home Book of Verse for Young Folks* (1915); *The Home Book of Modern Verse* (1925); *The Home Book of Quotations* (1934); *The Home Book of Proverbs, Maxims, and Familiar Phrases* (1948); *The Home Book of Bible Quotations* (1949); and *Standard Book of Shakespeare Quotations* (1953). The eighth edition, revised and enlarged, of the *Home Book of Quotations* appeared in 1956. His works include about forty novels, mystery stories, books for children, and a play, *A King in Babylon*, (1955).

Stevenson, Robert Louis (1850–1894), novelist, short-story writer, essayist, poet. The Scottish writer had several connections with the United States. He came to California (1879) to be near Fanny Osbourrie and married her a year later, after her divorce. LLOYD OSBOURNE, her son, became Stevenson's collaborator. During his time in the United States, he wrote "The Pavilion on the Links," an essay on Thoreau; a draft of *Prince Otto* (1895); *The Silverado Squatters* (1883); and *The Master of Ballantrae* (1889). Always in search of favorable climates because he had been tubercular from childhood, Stevenson moved with his family to Samoa in 1889. His other writings about America are ACROSS THE PLAINS (1892); *The Wrecker* (1892), written with Osbourne; *The Ebb-Tide* (1894), with Osbourne; and *The American Emigrant* (1895).

Stewart, Donald Ogden (1894–1980), actor, humorist, film writer. After serving in World War I, Stewart began writing popular satirical novels. Among them are *A Parody Outline of History* (1921), *Aunt Polly's Story of Mankind* (1923), *Mr. and Mrs. Haddock Abroad* (1924), *Mr. and Mrs. Haddock in Paris* (1926), and *Father William* (1929). He won success as an actor in a play by his college friend, PHILIP BARRY, *Holiday* (1928–1929) and in his own play *Rebound* (1930). His Hollywood writing began in 1925. He won an Oscar for his screenplay of Barry's *Philadelphia Story* (1940) and worked on many other successful films. He left Hollywood and moved to London in 1951 because he was among the many screenwriters blacklisted during the McCarthy hysteria. *By a Stroke of Luck!* (1975) is his autobiography.

Stewart, George R[ippey] (1895–1980), professor, novelist, nonfiction writer. A native of Pennsylvania and a graduate of Princeton (1917), Stewart taught English at Columbia, Michigan, Berkeley, and elsewhere. Among his conventional novels are *East of the Giants* (1938); *Doctor's Oral* (1939), a harrowing account of a Ph.D. examination; *Storm* (1941); *Fire* (1948); *Sheep Rock* (1951), details of events at a Nevada site; and *The Years of the City* (1955), a history of a Greek city. *Earth Abides* (1949), recounting a return to the

Stone Age after civilization is destroyed by a virus, is counted a classic of science fiction. Both the fiction and nonfiction reveal his talent for communicating detailed information readably. His nonfiction titles include a biography, *Bret Harte* (1931); *Ordeal by Hunger* (1936) about the Donner party; *Names on the Land* (1945, rev. 1957); *Man, an Autobiography* (1946); *U.S. 40* (1953), a biography of the highway; *American Ways of Life* (1954); *Pickett's Charge* (1959); *The California Trail* (1962); *Not So Rich as You Think* (1968), on ecology; *American Place Names* (1970); and *American Given Names* (1979).

Stickney, [Joseph] Trumbull (1874–1904), poet. Educated at home by his classicist father, and at Harvard and the Sorbonne, the Swiss-born Stickney shared with his friend WILLIAM VAUGHN MOODY an interest in Greek literature. Stickney's dramatic work *Prometheus Pyrphoros* (1900) predates Moody's *The Firebringer* (1904) on the same theme. He saw his *Dramatic Verses* (1902) published, but *Poems* (1905) was edited by Moody, George Cabot Lodge, and J. E. Lodge after Stickney's death of a brain tumor.

Sticks and Bones, a play by David Rabe produced in 1971. Rabe, a veteran of the Vietnam War, uses expressionistic staging in his play about the inability of a stereotypical American family to understand the actions and attitudes of their maimed son and brother David, returned from the war.

Stiles, Ezra (1727–1795), scholar, clergyman. Stiles, born in Connecicut and a Yale graduate, taught there and became its president (1778–1795). He spent over twenty years as a Congregational clergyman in Rhode Island and New Hampshire. Only his *An Account of the Settlement of Bristol, Rhode Island* (1785), *History of Three of the Judges of King Charles I* (1794), and a few of his sermons—including "The United States Elevated to Glory and Honor" (1783)—were published in his lifetime. From the forty-five volumes of his writings preserved at Yale, F. B. Dexter edited *Literary Diary* (1901) and *Extracts and Miscellanies* (1916). I. M. Calder edited *Letters and Papers* (1933). *The Life of Ezra Stiles* (1798) was written by his son-in-law, Abiel Holmes.

Still, James (1906–   ), poet, novelist, short-story writer. Still, born in Alabama, worked as a librarian in rural Kentucky, an experience that provided him with the settings and imagery for his work. *Hounds on the Mountain* (1937) is a poetry collection; *River of Earth* (1940) and *Sporty Creek* (1977), about boyhood in Appalachia, are novels. Story collections include *On Troublesome Creek* (1941); *Pattern of a Man* (1976); and *The Run for the Elbertas* (1983). *The Man in the Bushes* (1988) reprints journal entries from 1935–1987, as does *The Wolfpen Notebooks* (1991). He has also written several books for juveniles.

Stimson, Frederic Jesup ["J.S. of Dale"] (1855–1943), lawyer, teacher, diplomat, author. A distinguished lawyer and professor of law at Harvard, Stimson also served as ambassador to Argentina and Brazil. Under his own name he wrote *Government by Injunction* (1894), *Labor in Its Relation to Laws* (1895), *The American Constitution* (1908), and *My United States* (1931). Under his pseudonym he wrote lighter works of various kinds: *Rollo's Journey to Cambridge* (1879), *The Crime of Henry Vane* (1884), *The Sentimental Calendar* (1886), *King Noanett* (1896), *Jethro Bacon of Sandwich* (1902), *In Cure of Her Soul* (1906), and *My Story: Being the Memoirs of Benedict Arnold* (1917).

Stith, William (1707–1755),   clergyman, teacher, historian, educational administrator. Stith was probably born in Virginia and was educated at Oxford and ordained in the Church of England. On his return to the colonies in 1731 he was elected master of the grammar school in William and Mary College, and five years later took charge of Henrico Parish, where he wrote his most celebrated book, *History of the First Discovery and Settlement of Virginia* (1747). In 1752 he was appointed president of William and Mary, and at the same time served as minister of York-Hampton Parish. Among his other publications were *A Sermon Preached Before the General Assembly* (1745) and *The Sinfulness and Pernicious Nature of Gaming* (1752).

Stobo, Robert (1727–1772?),   soldier, memoirist. Born in Glasgow, Stobo served under Washington at Fort Necessity (1754). Held as a hostage by the French, he was sentenced to death (1755) but escaped from Quebec, joined the British at Louisburg and assisted Wolfe in his attack on Quebec (1759). Later he served in the West Indies and England. His *Memoirs* appeared in 1800. Tobias Smollett used him as a model for the character of an eccentric Scottish soldier in *The Expedition of Humphry Clinker* (1771). In Sir Gilbert Parker's novel *Seats of the Mighty* (1896), Stobo was the model for Robert Moray.

Stockton, Francis [Frank] R[ichard] (1834–1902), novelist, short-story writer, editor. Stockton, born in Philadelphia, was widely admired in his time. At first a wood engraver and draftsman, Stockton wrote for newspapers in Philadelphia and New York, contributed humorous pieces to *Vanity Fair*, joined the staff of *Scribner's Magazine*, and later was assistant editor of *St. Nicholas*, a children's magazine. His first book, RUDDER GRANGE (1879), won him celebrity. This story of newlyweds who live in an abandoned canal boat was followed by two sequels: *The Rudder Grangers Abroad* (1891) and *Pomona's Travels* (1894). Stockton's story THE LADY OR THE TIGER? appeared first in the *Century* (November 1882), was collected in *The Lady or the Tiger? and Other Stories* (1884), and furnished material for an operetta (1888).

The success of this story made it possible for Stockton to devote all his time to writing for adults. Yet, there was a close connection between his stories for a juvenile audience and his more mature work. In the latter one finds the same love of the marvelous, the same fanciful humor that appear in *Ting-a-ling* (1870), *Roundabout Rambles in Lands of Fact and Fancy* (1872), *Tales Out of School* (1875), *A Jolly Fellowship* (1880), *The Floating Prince and Other Fairy Tales* (1881), *The Story of Viteau* (1884), and *The Bee Man of Orn and Other Fanciful Tales* (1887). Stockton wrote one of the earliest science-fiction stories, *A Tale of Negative Gravity* (*Century Magazine*, December 1884). Among his stories most likely to be remembered are

The Love Letters of Smith, Zenobia's Infidelity, The Remarkable Wreck of the Thomas Hyke, and *The Griffin and the Minor Canon*.

The funniest of Stockton's novels is probably THE CASTING AWAY OF MRS. LECKS AND MRS. ALESHINE (1886). His other books include *The Late Mrs. Null* (1886); *The Adventures of Captain Horn* (1895); *The Great Stone of Sardis* (1898); *Kate Bonnet* (1902); also the short-story collections, *A Christmas Wreck and Other Stories* (1886); *The Clocks of Rondaine* (1892); *Fanciful Tales* (1894); *The Magic Egg* (1907). His *Novels and Stories* (23 v.) appeared in 1899–1904. Martin J. Griffin, Jr., wrote *Frank R. Stockton: A Critical Biography* (1939).

Stoddard, Charles Warren (1843–1909),   poet, teacher, travel writer. Stoddard, born in Rochester, New York, attended college in Oakland, California, and contributed to magazines, especially Bret Harte's *Golden Era*. In 1867 Harte edited Stoddard's *Poems* for publication. Stoddard's poor health sent him abroad on travels, and he wrote many books about places he visited. The most influential was *South-Sea Idyls* (1873, English ed. 1874), which was read by Robert Louis Stevenson and many others and started the literary vogue for Polynesia. Among his other books are *Mashallah!* (1881), *The Lepers of Molokai* (1885), *Hawaiian Life: Lazy Letters from Low Latitudes* (1894), *A Cruise Under the Crescent from Suez to San Marco* (1898), *Over the Rocky Mountains to Alaska* (1899), *In the Footprints of the Padres* (1902), and *The Island of Tranquil Delights* (1904). Ina Coolbrith edited his *Poems* in 1917. His *A Troubled Heart* (1885) tells the story of his conversion to Roman Catholicism.

Stoddard, Elizabeth Barstow (1823–1902),   novelist, short story writer. Born on the Massachusetts coast and educated at Wheaton College, she married RICHARD STODDARD and moved to New York. She wrote a column for a San Francisco newspaper and stories for *Harper's New Monthly Magazine*. Her first novel, *The Morgesons* (1862), largely ignored in the excitement of the Civil War, was revived a hundred years later by editors Lawrence Buell and Sandra Zagarell in *The Morgesons and Other Writings, Published and Unpublished* (1984). Her other fiction is *Two Men* (1865), *Temple House* (1867), and a miscellany, *Lolly Dink's Doings* (1874).

Stoddard, Richard Henry (1825–1903),   poet, editor. Stoddard, born in Massachusetts, wrote verse influenced by the Romantic and Victorian poets and found that it never provided sufficient income for his family. HAWTHORNE helped him obtain a job as customs inspector, a favor Stoddard later repeated for MELVILLE. He wrote respected book reviews for the *New York Mail and Express* and the magazine *Aldine* and introduced contemporary authors in his *Bric-a-Brac Series* and *San-Souci Series*. Among his books are *Footprints* (1849), *Poems* (1852), *The King's Bell* (1863), *The Book of the East and Other Poems* (1871), *The Lion's Club with Other Verse* (1890), and *Recollections, Personal and Literary* (1903).

Stoddard, Solomon (1643–1729),   Congregational clergyman, librarian. Stoddard, born in Boston was educated at Harvard and served as librarian there before taking up his pastorate in Northampton (1672–1729). He carried on a continuing controversy with INCREASE MATHER over qualifications for church membership. Stoddard defended repentance and a profession of faith as adequate, while Mather demanded the relation of a personal experience of grace. Stoddard's views are set forth in *The Doctrine of Instituted Churches* (1700), *The Inexcusableness of Neglecting the Worship of God, Under a Pretense of Being in an Unconverted Condition* (1708), and *An Appeal to the Learned* (1709). He recommended hellfire as a sermon theme in *The Efficacy of the Fear of Hell to Restrain Men from Sin* (1713) and *A Guide to Christ* (1714). In *An Answer to Some Cases of Conscience Respecting the Country* (1722), he attacked immorality, drinking, and materialism. His grandson, JONATHAN EDWARDS, succeeded him in the Northampton pulpit.

Stoddard, William Osborn ["Col. Cris Forrest"] (1835–1925), editor, public official, inventor, author. Stoddard, born in Homer, New York, while working on an Illinois newspaper met Abraham Lincoln. When Lincoln was elected, Stoddard became an assistant private secretary. Later he wrote *Abraham Lincoln* (1884), *Inside the White House in War Times* (1890), *The Table Talk of Abraham Lincoln* (1894), *Lincoln at Work* (1900), and *The Lives of the Presidents* (10 v. 1886–89). He served as U.S. marshal in Arkansas, patented inventions in the fields of telegraphy, manufacturing, and railways, and still managed to write more than a hundred books, more than seventy of them for boys. Among these juveniles are *Dab Kinzer* (1881), *The Red Mustang* (1890), *Little Smoke: A Tale of the Sioux* (1891), *The Lost Gold of the Montezumas* (1897), and *The Spy of Yorktown* (1903).

Stolz, Mary Slattery (1920–   ), novelist, short-story writer. Stolz, born in Boston, has written many novels and short stories intended for children and young adults. Among her books are *To Tell Your Love* (1950), *The Seagulls Woke Me* (1951), *The Leftover Elf* (1952), *Ready or Not* (1953), *In A Mirror* (1953), *Pray Love Remember* (1954), *Truth and Consequence* (1953), *Two by Two* (1954), *Rosemary* (1955), *The Day and the Way We Met* (1956), *Hospital Zone* (1956), *Because of Madeline* (1957), *Goodbye My Shadow* (1957), *Second Nature* (1958), *And Love Replied* (1958), *Some Merry-Go-Round Music* (1959), *A Dog on Barkham Street* (1960), *Emmett's Pig* (1960), *The Beautiful Friend* (1960), *Belling the Tiger* (1961), *The Edge of Next Year* (1974), and *Go Fish* (1991).

Stone, Grace Zaring ["Ethel Vance"] (1891–1991), novelist. Stone, born in New York City, made two careers in fiction, writing her more serious books under her own name, her more sensational books under her pen name. Both kinds have been very popular. Among the former are *Letters to a Djinn* (1922), *The Heaven and Earth of Doña Elena* (1929), *The Bitter Tea of General Yen* (1930), *The Almond Tree* (1931), *The Cold Journey* (1934), *Althea* (1962), and *Dear Deadly Cara* (1968). Under her pen name she wrote *Escape* (1939), *Reprisal* (1942), *Winter Meeting* (1946), *The Secret Thread* (1948), and *The Grotto* (1951).

Stone, Irving (1903–1989), novelist. Stone, born in San Francisco, wrote a great number of successful fictionalized biographies beginning with *Lust for Life* (1934), on Vincent Van Gogh. He treated writers—Jack London is the subject of *Sailor on Horseback* (1938); artists—*The Agony and the Ecstasy* is on Michelangelo; and scientists such as Freud (*Passions of the Mind*, 1975) and Darwin (*The Origin*, 1980). Some of his most popular books concern wives of famous men: *Immortal Wife* (1944) deals with Jesse Benton Frémont; *The President's Lady* (1951) is on Rachel Jackson; Mary Todd Lincoln is the subject of *Love Is Eternal* (1954); and *Those Who Love* (1965) treats Abigail and John Adams. His more scholarly nonfiction includes *Dear Theo: The Autobiography of Vincent Van Gogh* (1937), edited from the correspondence between Vincent and his brother Theo; *Clarence Darrow for the Defense* (1941); *They Also Ran* (1943), biographies of failed presidential candidates (1943); *Earl Warren* (1948); *I, Michelangelo, Sculptor: An Autobiography Through Letters* (with Jean Stone, 1962); and *The Great Adventure of Michelangelo* (1965).

Stone, John Augustus (1800–1834), actor, playwright. Stone was born in Massachusetts. He wrote METAMORA, OR THE LAST OF THE WAMPANOAGS (1829) for the actor EDWIN FORREST. Following the success of that work, Stone wrote several similar plays: *Tancred, King of Sicily* (1831); *The Ancient Briton* (1833); *The Knight of the Golden Fleece, or, the Yankee in Spain* (1834); and revised James K. Paulding's LION OF THE WEST for JAMES H. HACKETT in 1831. Forrest and ROBERT MONTGOMERY BIRD profited from Stone's work but paid him no royalties; in desperation he drowned himself in the Schuylkill River. Forrest raised a handsome monument over Stone's grave.

Stone, Lucy (1818–1893), social reformer. Born in Massachusetts and educated at Oberlin College, Stone devoted her life to the causes of abolition of slavery and women's suffrage. She retained her maiden name as a matter of principle. The *Woman's Journal*, which she founded in 1870, was for nearly fifty years the official publication of the National American Woman Suffrage Association.

Stone, Robert [Anthony] (1937–   ), novelist. Stone, born in Brooklyn, New York, set his first novel, *Hall of Mirrors* (1967), in New Orleans. *Dog Soldiers* (1974), concerning drug dealing in Vietnam, won the National Book Award. *A Flag for Sunrise* (1982) deals with revolution in Latin America. *Children of Light* (1986) is about filmmakers in Mexico. *Outerbridge Reach* (1989) tells of a Vietnam Vet caught up in a solo around-the-world yacht race. *Damascus Gate* (1998) deals with terrorism in Jerusalem.

Stone, Samuel (1602–1663), clergyman. Stone was a nonconformist who emigrated from England with THOMAS HOOKER in 1633 and settled in Hartford, Connecticut, in 1636, where he was a leader of the New England synods and succeeded Hooker as minister of the Hartford church (1647). His views on church organization, set forth in *A Congregational Church Is a Catholike Visible Church* (1652), put him in conflict with Cotton Mather and others.

Stone, William Leete (1792–1844),   journalist, historian. Stone, born in New Paltz, New York, owned and edited the New York *Commercial Advertiser* (1821). JAMES FENIMORE COOPER successfully sued him for "slanderous criticism" over book reviews printed in the paper. Stone contributed tales and sketches to the popular annuals published in his time and in *The Lounger*, a literary journal he edited in Hudson, New York. His interest in local history, particularly the lives of Indians, led to *Life of Joseph Brant* (2 v. 1838), *The Life and Times of Red Jacket* (1841), *The Poetry and History of Wyoming* (1841), *Uncas and Miantonomoh* (1842), and *Border Wars of the American Revolution* (1843). His other works are *Matthias and His Impostures* (1833), *Tales and Sketches* (2 v. 1834), *The Mysterious Bridal and Other Tales* (3 v. 1835), and *Maria Monk and the Nunnery of Hotel Dieu* (1836).

Stong, Phil[ip Duffield] (1899–1957),   teacher, newspaperman, editor, writer. Strong, born in Iowa, had a great success with his novel *State Fair* (1932) and went off to Hollywood, where he worked with Will Rogers on the first of three successful movie versions of the novel. Thereafter, he wrote a long succession of stories, some of them for young people, for example, *Farm Boy* (1934) and *The Hired Man's Elephant* (1939); and some nonfiction, including *Horses and Americans* (1939); *Hawkeyes*, a history of Iowa (1940); and *Marta of Muscovy*, a biography of the wife of Peter the Great (1945). Among his other novels are *The Stranger's Return* (1933), *Career* (1936), *The Iron Mountain* (1942), *Jessamy John* (1947), *Return in August* (1953), *Blizzard* (1955), and *Gold in Them Hills* (1957). *If School Keeps* (1940) is an autobiography.

Stopping by Woods on a Snowy Evening   (*New Republic*, March 7, 1923; in *New Hampshire*, 1923), a poem by ROBERT FROST. Frost said on one occasion that the poem contains "all I ever knew"; at another time that it was the kind of poem he'd like to print on one page, to be followed with "forty pages of footnotes."

Stormalong, Old.   See OLD STORMALONG.

Storni, Alfonsina (1892–1938),   Argentine poet. Her poetry is guided by a thwarted eroticism and a deep resentment against a male world that left no role, other than submission, for women of talent. Although she desperately sought love, it became for her the simultaneous experience of hope, disillusion, and disgust. The tortured erotic poetry in *Dulce daño* (1918) and *Ocre* (1925) registered a uniquely feminine and feminist note. In a later volume, *El mundo de siete pozos* (1934), her erotic themes gave way to a more balanced, intellectual poetry. She drowned herself in 1938, the same year in which her final, haunting poems were published in *Mascarilla y trébol* (Death-Mask and Clover). Her *Obra poética completa* appeared in 1961.

Story.   A magazine founded in Vienna in April 1931 by WHIT BURNETT and his wife MARTHA FOLEY. It was published there and later in Majorca until 1933, when the editors and their magazine moved to New York City. There the magazine became known widely as the only periodical devoted exclusively to the short story as an art form. It was at various times a monthly, a bimonthly, a quarterly, and in 1951 a semiannual. The editors had by that time separated. In *Story: The Fiction of the Forties* (1949), Whit Burnett and Hallie Burnett, his second wife, chose fifty-one stories that had appeared in the pages of *Story* over a decade. *The Story of Story Magazine* (1980) is a memoir interrupted by Martha Foley's death.

Story, Isaac (1774–1803),   editor, poet, essayist. Story, born in Massachusetts, used many pseudonyms, including Peter Quince. A collection of his satirical verses was published, by Peter Quince, as *A Parnassian Shop Opened in the Pindaric Stile* (1801). He also wrote poems with patriotic and romantic themes. Among his writings are *Liberty* (1795) and *An Eulogy on the Glorious Virtues of the Illustrious George Washington* (1800).

Story, Joseph (1779–1845),   lawyer, public official, writer. Born in Massachusetts and appointed to the U.S. Supreme Court in 1811, Story shares with John Marshall the credit for establishing the strength of that court. In his twenties he published a collection of verse, *The Power of Solitude* (1804), which he tried later to suppress. Among his books are *Commentaries on the Constitution of the United States* (3 v. 1833), *On the Conflict of Laws* (1834), *On Equity Jurisprudence* (2 v. 1835–36), *Equity Pleadings* (1838), and *Law of Promissory Notes* (1845). His *Miscellaneous Writings* were gathered in 1852 by his son, the sculptor and poet WILLIAM WETMORE STORY, who had previously prepared his father's *Life and Letters* (2 v. 1851) and sculpted a statue of the noted jurist.

Story, William Wetmore (1819–1895),   lawyer, sculptor, poet, actor, biographer, author of travel books, novelist, dramatist, author of law books. William Story, JOSEPH STORY's son, was born in Massachusetts and grew up to become a man of many talents, known best as a sculptor. He disliked New England and lived in Italy for the greater part of his life, becoming friendly with the literary expatriates of his day. One of Henry James's least known books is *William Wetmore Story and His Friends* (1903), in which James seeks to explain the expatriates of the earlier years of the 19th century. Story's *Poems* were collected in 1845, again in *Graffiti d'Italia* (1868). One of his most popular books was a collection of essays, *Roba di Roma* (1862); he also wrote *Fiammetta* (1886), and a play, *Nero* (1875). He wrote several law books while practicing law in Boston.

Story of a Bad Boy, The (1870),   a semiautobiographical narrative by THOMAS BAILEY ALDRICH. Aldrich tries to explain in the opening sentences that he doesn't really mean a *bad* boy, but just "a real human boy." The adventures he relates as happening to Tom Bailey coincide more or less with his own experiences in Portsmouth, New Hampshire, but he adds to them episodes entirely fictional. The story ran originally for an entire year in *Our Young Folks* (1869).

Story of a Country Town, The (1883),   a novel by E. W. HOWE, offering a realistic depiction of life in the Midwest during the 19th century.

Story Teller's Story, A (1924),   an autobiographical narrative by SHERWOOD ANDERSON.

Stoughton, William (1631–1701), clergyman, public official. Stoughton, a Harvard graduate, attended Oxford but left England because of his nonconformist views. After his return to Massachusetts (1662), he held several religious and political posts, including acting governor (1694). He is remembered as the harsh judge of the Salem witch trials. His sermon *New England's True Interest, not to Lie* (1670) sets forth the view that because "God sifted a whole nation that he might send choice grain over into the wilderness," New Englanders had a strong obligation to strict morality.

Stout, Rex [Todhunter] (1886–1975), novelist, detective fiction writer. Stout, born in Indiana, introduced his orchidist and gourmet crime solver Nero Wolfe in *Fer-de-Lance* (1934). Novels featuring the detective who solves crimes without leaving his desk appeared at a brisk pace and include *The League of the Frightened Men* (1935), *The Hand in the Glove* (1937), *Too Many Cooks* (1938), *Some Buried Caesar* (1939), *Black Orchids* (1942), *Not Quite Dead Enough* (1944), *Murder by the Book* (1951), *Before Midnight* (1955), *If Death Ever Slept* (1957), *Death of a Doxy* (1966), and *A Family Affair* (1975). Other Stout novels, sans Wolfe, include *How Like a God* (1919), *Seed on the Wind* (1930), and *Forest Fire* (1933).

Stover, Dink. A character in several stories by OWEN JOHNSON. Stover is introduced first in *The Varmint* (1910) and *The Tennessee Shad* (1911), which relate his adventures in prep school, supposedly Lawrenceville School, in New Jersey. *Stover at Yale* (1911) sounds a more serious note and attacks the character of undergraduate life.

Stowe, Harriet Beecher (1811–1896), novelist, reformer, writer of short stories and domestic manuals. When Harriet Beecher, of Litchfield, Connecticut, was seven years old—three years after her mother, Roxana Foote, had died—her father wrote of her to a friend: "Hattie is a genius. I would give a hundred dollars if she was a boy." Her gender has colored posterity's perception of her genius as well: she is commonly identified first as "daughter of influential Calvinist minister LYMAN BEECHER, sister of famous pulpit orator HENRY WARD BEECHER, wife of professor Calvin Stowe," then as author of the most widely read and controversial novel written in the 19th century. Indeed, Harriet's childhood was indelibly marked by all the attitudes associated with her father's Calvinism, with its earnest anticipation of a life after death, strict standards of behavior, and distrust of art and entertainment. The future novelist read no profane literature until she was eleven, when Lyman's sudden enthusiasm for Sir Walter Scott meant that novels were no longer proscribed. At twelve, Harriet nearly memorized *Ivanhoe* and devoured clandestine copies of Byron's poetry. Like her older siblings, she had a conversion experience in her early teens, brought on by listening to her father preach. By the time she was eighteen, she was a committed, though troubled, Calvinist; in her early fifties she was to convert to her mother's more merciful Episcopalianism.

At thirteen, Harriet was both pupil and instructor at the Hartford Female Seminary, run by her sister Catharine—eventually one of the leading educators of women and propo-

nents of domestic science. Harriet taught Latin, rhetoric, and composition, unusual subjects for a girl of the period. The Beechers moved from Litchfield to Boston in 1826; from there they went in 1832 to Cincinnati, where Lyman became President of Lane Theological Seminary and Catharine opened the Western Female Institute. Still working under Catharine, Harriet wrote a children's geography; read and loved Mme. de Staël's *Corinne*; and joined the Semi-Colon Club, a literary society that encouraged its members to write. Among her closest friends were Calvin Stowe, a professor of Biblical literature at Lane, and his wife, Eliza; when Eliza died in 1836, Calvin's and Harriet's mutual grief became one of the bonds that led to their marriage. After their 1836 wedding, Harriet's immediate pregnancy—with twins—prevented her from accompanying Calvin to Europe. Pregnancy, viewed in 19th-century America as an illness rendering middle-class women perilously delicate, was an impediment to any woman who wished, as Stowe did, to see the world and to accomplish something in it. Pregnant six times in all, Stowe found the condition increasingly difficult. While carrying her fourth child, in 1840, she developed a chronic neuralgia that impaired her vision during her subsequent pregnancies. Her childbearing years were marked by lengthy separations from Calvin, ostensibly for their health—both separately underwent year-long water cures in Brattleboro, Vermont—but evidently also as a means of birth control. All six of her children survived infancy; a son died of cholera in 1849. Calvin, an eminent Hebrew scholar, taught at Bowdoin College and later at Andover Theological Seminary. The family moved to the East in 1850.

Since 1833 Stowe—despite the heavy household demands accepted as a matter of course by any faculty wife with a large family—had been publishing stories and sketches, by her own report "for the pay. I have determined not to be a mere domestic slave." Calvin encouraged her, writing in 1842: "My dear, you must be a literary woman. It is so written in the book of fate." Troubled by the Fugitive Slave Law of 1850 and by the biography written by Rev. Josiah Henson, an ex-slave, Stowe decided to "write something" to raise the nation's consciousness against slavery. The critical tradition of accusing *Uncle Tom's Cabin* (1851–52) of excessive sentimentality has probably been fed by Stowe's claim that the novel originated in a vision she experienced in church. She is said to have pictured a white-haired slave beaten to death by fellow slaves under a master's orders. The novel that grew up around this image was an immediate best seller, bringing fame in the North, notoriety in the South. Stowe first experienced the extent of her celebrity when she was lionized on a trip to England in 1853, where she made contact with such important women writers as Elizabeth Gaskell and Elizabeth Barrett Browning.

Stowe remained prominent in antislavery activity until Lincoln issued the Emancipation Proclamation in 1862. Disagreeing with the president's emphasis on preserving the Union, Stowe maintained that slavery must end immediately, because it was an oppression of human rights that undermined the nation's Christianity. She met Lincoln in 1862, when he is said to have joked, "So this is the little lady who made this big war."

When Stowe's oldest son drowned unregenerate in early adulthood, she became involved in spiritualism, an interest she shared with Elizabeth Barrett Browning and about which she corresponded with a skeptical George Eliot. In later years she and Calvin divided their time between Hartford, Connecticut, and an orange plantation in Mandarin, Florida. Stowe continued writing books, sketches, sermonettes, and columns; in the early 1870s she conducted public reading tours in the Northeast and Midwest. She survived Calvin by ten years and died senile at their Hartford home in 1896.

Traditionally considered a local color novelist, Stowe actually worked in many genres. Her first book, *The Mayflower* (1843), collected sketches of New England characters. THE MINISTER'S WOOING, set in the late 18th century and considered among Stowe's finest novels (1859), THE PEARL OF ORR'S ISLAND (1862), OLDTOWN FOLKS (1868), and *Poganuc People* (1878) return to her native scene and draw on family anecdotes. UNCLE TOM'S CABIN, by far her most influential book, was not her only antislavery work. To answer the work's detractors, she issued *The Key to Uncle Tom's Cabin* (1853) as a documentary defense of the novel's contents. She also published *Dred: A Tale of the Great Dismal Swamp* (1856), which highlights slavery's ill effects on its white perpetrators, and which George Eliot praised in an unsigned book review in the *Westminster Review* as the kind of novel women should write. Stowe's final reforming project was an elaborate defense of the reputation of Lord Byron's widow, whose cold personality was popularly supposed to have been responsible for her husband's troubles. *Lady Byron Vindicated* (1870) renewed the widow's charge that Byron lived incestuously with his half-sister, and once again made Stowe's name controversial. Stowe's interest in Lady Byron was a product of her European travels, as was *Agnes of Sorrento* (1862), a historical romance set in Savonarola's Italy. Her travel books include *Sunny Memories of Foreign Lands* (1854), recording her impressions of celebrities she met abroad, and *Palmetto Leaves* (1873), describing life in Florida.

Stowe's career had made her conscious of the difficulties of housekeeping, and she wrote domestic manuals, though seldom under her own name. As "Christopher Crowfield" she shielded her public identity to publish *Little Foxes* (1865) and *The Chimney Corner* (1868); she and her sister Catharine signed *The American Woman's Home* (1869). Crossing the genres of fiction and domestic manual, Stowe wrote what she called "society novels": *Pink and White Tyranny* (1871), *My Wife and I* (1871), and *We and Our Neighbors* (1873). Her interest in the woman's sphere surfaces again in *Women in Sacred History* (1873), which posits Christianity as a feminine faith.

Stowe's fictional techniques are those of the classic realist novelist, including close attention to dialects, detailed descriptions of domestic settings, careful inquiry into characters' motivations, and continual insistence on the plausibility of plots. Her works are didactic. She told George Eliot that "art as

an end, not instrument, has little to interest me." Her novels usually reiterate moral and theological messages through carefully constructed, repeated parallel scenes and through earnest exhortation of the audience, a technique Stowe adapted from the pulpit rhetoric of her day. Suffused in Christianity, her works idealize motherhood, sympathy, forgiveness, and woman's spiritual influence on the domestic sphere; they are also drily humorous. Until recently, Stowe—along with many of her female contemporaries—has been dismissed as one of what Hawthorne called the "scribbling women" of her era. New critical approaches to popular literature are redirecting serious attention to her work, however, and *Uncle Tom* now hovers at the margin of the literary canon. Conservative critics have questioned her novels' artistry, but no one questions their influence on the culture, which was—in *Uncle Tom*'s case—immense.

Forrest Wilson's *Crusader in Crinoline* (1941) is marred by condescension to its subject. Milton Rugoff's *The Beechers: An American Family in the Nineteenth Century* (1981) is more satisfactory. *Harriet Beecher Stowe: A Life* (1994) by Joan D. Hendrick is thorough and balanced. The classic commentaries on Stowe are by EDMUND WILSON, *Patriotic Gore*; LESLIE FIEDLER, *Love and Death in the American Novel*; Ann Douglas, *The Feminization of American Culture*; and, most recently, Jane Tompkins, *Sensational Designs*.

ROBYN R. WARHOL/BP

Strachey, William (early 17th century),   colonist, public official. Little is known of Strachey's life. After serving as secretary to the ambassador to Constantinople (1606), he joined the Gates-Somers expedition to Virginia. He survived the 1609 wreck of the *Sea Adventure*. His account of the wreck in a July 15, 1610, letter to "an Excellent Lady" in London may have influenced Shakespeare's *The Tempest* (1611), although it was not published until 1625 in SAMUEL PURCHAS's *Hakluytus Posthumus, or, Purchas His Pilgrims*. After the *Sea Adventure* separated from the rest of the fleet and ran aground in Bermuda, Strachey and his companions reached Virginia, May 1610, in two small boats they built. Strachey served as secretary of the Virginia Company until 1611. He wrote *History of Travaile into Virginia Britannia* (inscribed to Francis Bacon in 1618 but not printed until 1849) and helped edit and compile the legal code, *For the Colony in Virginia: Laws Divine, Moral and Martial* (1612). The laws were called Dale's Laws, after acting governor Sir Thomas Dale.

Strand, Mark (1934–   ),   poet, translator, writer of short stories and children's stories. Strand was born on Prince Edward Island, Canada, grew up in the United States, and was educated at Antioch, Yale, and the University of Iowa. He has been a teaching poet, mostly in the United States. In his first three books—*Sleeping with One Eye Open* (1964), *Reasons for Moving* (1968), and *Darker* (1970)—stark poems with lean diction and imagery frequently put a narrator in confrontation with irrational events and characters, somewhat surreal and somewhat in the manner of Borges and other Latin American or European writers. In its apparent certitude of simple declarations and narration, Strand's style, which he has described as a "new international style," acts with the dreamlike mystery and uncertainty of events to evoke emotions of isolation and a disquieting exploration of the boundaries between self and what may or may not be outside it. Strand's early poems eschew the naturalistic, vivid detail found in confessional poetry in favor of a more limited, dreamlike, symbolic imagery exciting the emotions rather than the senses. He often relies on blunt repetition of diction and syntax to create a lyricism of compelling movement, at times reminiscent of a litany. In later books—*The Story of Our Lives* (1973), *The Late Hour* (1978), and *Selected Poems* (1980)—longer poems, situations more directly related to the poet's life, and details drawn from his past, especially his childhood, add new range while further investigating reflexive relationships between art and the poet's inner and outer life. His other works include *Mr. and Mrs. Baby and Other Stories* (1985), a collection of brief, often surreal and whimsical prose pieces. *The Continuous Life* (1990) ended a ten-year hiatus from volumes of verse. In the same year, strand was selected as Poet Laureate of the United States. *Dark Harbor* (1993), a long poem, followed.

JOHN BENSKO/GP

Strange Fruit (1944),   a novel by LILLIAN SMITH. It is the story of an African-American woman and a white man caught in a coil of prejudice, misunderstanding, and violence. A murder and a brutal lynching are described vividly. The book sold widely, and was dramatized (1945) by the author and Esther Smith.

Strange Interlude (1928),   a play in nine acts by EUGENE O'NEILL. The plot concerns the emotional reactions of Nina Leeds, who subconsciously hates her father, a professor, holding him responsible for preventing her from sleeping with her fiancé before he went off to war and death in France. She becomes a nurse, marries good-natured Sam Evans, but when she learns she is about to have a child resorts to abortion to thwart the strain of insanity in his family. However, she has an affair with Dr. Darrell, and their child is very fond of his supposed father but hates his real father. When Evans dies, Nina marries a childhood admirer who reminds her of her father. O'Neill, to make clear the thoughts, reactions, and inner yearnings of his characters, effectively revived the asides and soliloquies of Elizabethan drama.

Stratemeyer, Edward (1863–1930),   juvenile author. Stratemeyer, born in New Jersey, wrote under several pen names a great number of popular series. The 20-book ROVER BOYS series, his most popular (1899–1916), was written under the name Arthur M. Winfield. Ten more titles (1917–1926) dealt with the second generation of prep school and college students. TOM SWIFT (beginning in 1910) ran to 40 volumes about the boy inventor, and the Motor Boys began in 1906. Under the name Laura Lee Hope, Stratemeyer wrote the Bobbsey Twins books. For three Nancy Drew Mysteries he used the name Carolyn Keene; his daughter, Harriet Stratemeyer Adams (1894–1982), continued to write Nancy Drew stories under that pseudonym. She also wrote the Hardy Boys

stories. Stratemeyer's work was so popular that in 1914 he hired a group of writers to produce new volumes from his outlines. The Stratemeyer Literary Syndicate continued to operate after his death. Among pseudonyms used by Stratemeyer and the Syndicate are Allen Winfield and Ralph Bonehill.

Stratton-Porter, Gene.   See GENE STRATTON PORTER.

Street, Alfred Billings (1811–1881),   poet. Street's nature poetry, including *The Burning of Schenectady* (1842) and *Frontenac* (1849), was much admired.

Street, James [Howell] (1903–1954),   novelist, journalist. Street spent his youth in his native Mississippi and began writing his first short stories while reporting for the New York *World-Telegram*. He also wrote several novels. *The Gauntlet* (1945), set in Missouri, is based on Street's experiences as a Baptist minister. In the sequel, *The High Calling* (1951), London Wingo, the hero, accepts a call to a North Carolina church. His other novels include *Look Away!* (1936); *Oh, Promised Land* (1940); *The Biscuit Eater* (1941); *In My Father's House* (1941); *By Valour and Arms* (1944); *Tomorrow We Reap* (1949); *Velvet Doublet* (1953); and *Good-bye, My Lady* (1954). His two books of nonfiction are *The Civil War* (1953) and *The Revolutionary War* (1954).

Street, Julian (1879–1947),   newspaperman, fiction writer, essayist. Street, born in Chicago, wrote short stories, one of which won an O. Henry Memorial Award and became the title story in *Mr. Bisbee's Princess* (1925). He collaborated with BOOTH TARKINGTON on a comedy, *The Country Cousin* (1916). Some of his other titles are *My Enemy the Motor* (1908), *Welcome to Our City* (1913), *American Adventures* (1917), *Mysterious Japan* (1921), *Where Paris Dines* (1929), and *Wines* (1933, rev. 1948).

Streetcar Named Desire, A (1947),   a play by TENNESSEE WILLIAMS. The play is set in the French Quarter of New Orleans, where two streetcars, one named Desire, the other named Cemetery, run on a single track. Blanche DuBois, the central character, is a fading Southern belle who tries to maintain illusions of gentility despite poverty and moral degeneration. Forced to sell what is left of the family plantation, she comes to live with Stella, a sister married to Stanley, an animalistic man who resents Blanche. His friend Mitch thinks of marrying her until Stanley tells him of Blanche's notorious and neurotic sexual escapades. Her hopes of marriage destroyed, Blanche confronts Stanley, and he rapes her. Finally, unable to impose her illusions on reality, she breaks down mentally and is led away to an asylum, still clinging to her fantasies and appealing to the "kindness of strangers." The play won a Pulitzer Prize, and a movie version (1951) was also widely successful.

Streeter, Ed[ward] (1891–1976),   banker, humorist. Streeter, born in New York City, became a vice-president of the Bank of New York in 1931. Several of his humorous books were extremely successful. The first, *Dere Mable* (1917), was based on World War I and was followed by *That's Me All Over Mable* (1918). Other books followed, all based on his own experiences, among them *Same Old Bill* (1918); *Daily Except*

Sunday (1938); *Father of the Bride* (1949, made into a successful movie, 1950); *Skoal Scandinavia* (1952); *Mr Hobbs' Vacation* (1954); and *Mr. Robbins Rides Again* (1958).

Street Scene (1929),   a play by ELMER RICE. The play presents life in a slum tenement and was one of the first stage productions to include realistic sound effects throughout the performance. Characters of various racial and temperamental components figure in the story, which reaches its climax in a double murder. The play won a Pulitzer Prize, and a musical version was made in 1947 with a score by KURT WEILL.

Strenuous Life, The (April 10, 1899),   an address delivered in Chicago by THEODORE ROOSEVELT. It was published in *The Strenuous Life: Essays and Addresses* (1900). Roosevelt here preached the doctrine "that the highest form of success comes, not to the man who desires mere easy peace, but to the man who does not shrink from danger, from hardship, or from bitter toil."

Stribling, T[homas] S[igismund]   (1881–1965), novelist. Born in Tennessee and educated at the University of Alabama, Stribling set several of his novels in the South, including his first, *Birthright* (1922), dealing with race relations. A stay in Venezuela provided material for *Fombombo* (1923), *Red Sand* (1924), *Strange Moon* (1929), and *Clues of the Caribees* (1929). His other novels with Southern settings are *Rope* (1928) and *Bright Metal* (1928), both set in Tennessee, and *Backwater*, with an Arkansas background. His Civil War trilogy—*The Forge* (1931), *The Store* (1932), and *Unfinished Cathedral* (1934)—treats several generations of the Vaiden family of Alabama, who rise from poverty to wealth, often by unscrupulous dealings. *The Sound Wagon* (1935) is political satire, and *These Bars of Flesh* (1938) pokes fun at education and politics in the North.

Stringer, Arthur [John Arbuthnott]   (1874–1950), writer. Born in Ontario, Stringer was at first a clerk in a railroad office, later a writer for newspapers and magazines and literary editor of the magazine *Success*. In 1917 he went to Hollywood to work on movie scenarios, and one of his earliest scripts was prepared (1918) for the serial PERILS OF PAULINE. He became a U.S. citizen in 1937. In his long literary career Stringer wrote more than fifty novels, among them *The Man Who Couldn't Sleep* (1919), *Prairie Child* (1922), and *Star in a Mist* (1943). His poetry collections include *Watchers of the Twilight and Other Poems* (1894), *Irish Poems* (1911), *Open Water* (1912), and *New York Nocturnes* (1948). *Red Wine of Youth* (1948) is a biography of the English poet Rupert Brooke.

Strong, Austin (1881–1952),   architect, playwright. Strong, born in San Francisco, worked as a landscape artist until 1905. His first plays were written in collaboration with Robert Louis Stevenson's stepson LLOYD OSBOURNE, who was Strong's uncle. They are *The Exile*, produced in London in 1903, and *The Father of the Wilderness*, produced in London and New York in 1905. One of his most celebrated plays is the one-act *The Drums of Oude* (1906). His later plays were *Rip Van Winkle* (1911), *Three Wise Fools* (1918), *Seventh Heaven*

(1920), and *A Play Without a Name* (1928). A collection, *The Drums of Oude and Other One-Act Plays*, appeared in 1926.

Strong, George Templeton.   See THE DIARY OF GEORGE TEMPLETON STRONG.

Strong, Josiah   (1847–1916),   clergyman, social reformer. Born in Illinois and educated at Western Reserve University, Strong deplored the moral vacuum left by transition from agrarian to industrial life and advocated renewed humanitarian values in *Our Country* (1885), *The Twentieth Century City* (1898), *Religious Movements for Social Betterment* (1900), and *The Next Great Awakening* (1902).

Stryk, Lucien (1924–   ),   poet. Born and educated in the Midwest, Stryk traveled and taught in Japan and Iran before teaching at Northern Illinois University. His interest in Oriental poetry is demonstrated in translations from both Chinese and Japanese, particularly poetry associated with Zen Buddhism. His collections include *Taproot* (1953), *The Trespasser* (1956), *Notes for a Guidebook* (1965), *The Pit and Other Poems* (1969), *Awakening* (1973), *The Duckpond* (1978), *Willows* (1983), and *Collected Poems* (1984). *Where We Are: Selected Poems and Zen Translations* appeared in 1996 and *And Still Birds Sing: New and Collected Poems* in 1997.

Stuart, Charles (1783–1865),   anti-slavery writer. Born in Jamaica, Stuart emigrated to the United States and joined the abolition movement. His *The West India Question: Immediate Emancipation Safe and Practical* (1823) became the guide for the antislavery movement in the U.S. and Great Britain.

Stuart, Jesse [Hilton] (1907–1984),   poet, novelist, teacher, editor. Stuart wrote more than a score of books that show his passionate love for the mountain country of Kentucky, where he was born. He is also known for his verse, in *The Man With a Bull-Tongue Plow* (1934), a sonnet collection, *Album of Destiny* (1944), and *Kentucky Is My Land* (1952). He won his earliest successes, however, with short stories, first collected in *Head o' W-Hollow* (1936). His later collections include *Men of the Mountain* (1941), *Tales from the Plum Grove* (1946), *Clearing in the Sky* (1950), and *Plowshare in Heaven* (1958). *The Best-Loved Stories of Jesse Stuart* (2000), a selection of thirty-four of the more than 400 Stuart published, is a testament to his continuing popularity. His first novel, *Trees of Heaven* (1940) is about a farm couple's struggle over their son's love for a poor white girl; *Daughter of the Legend* (1965) treats a similar conflict, this time the girl is of mixed race. Other novels include *Taps for Private Tussie* (1943), about a mountain family's attempt to spend the insurance money paid after their son in erroneously reported killed in action; *Mongrel Mettle* (1944), about a dog; *Foretaste of Glory* (1946); *Hie to the Hunter* (1950) and *The Good Spirit of Laurel Ridge* (1953). *Beyond Dark Hills* (1938) is an autobiographical essay written for a graduate class at Vanderbilt. Stuart's most influential book is the classic *The Thread that Runs So True* (1949), about the experience of teaching in a small mountain school. Stuart's love for his profession and his students is so convincingly portrayed that the book has often been required reading in education courses, and has been reprinted numerous times. *To Teach, To Love* (1970) is a further tribute to his own teaching and those who influenced it. Autobiographical works include *Year of My Rebirth* (1956) about his recovery from a heart attack; *God's Oddling: The Story of Mick Stuart, My Father* (1960); *The Seasons* (1976, a poetic reminiscence; and *If I Were Seventeen Again* (1980). *Lost Sandstones and Lonely Skies* (1979) is an essay collection.

Stuart, Robert (1785–1848),   fur trader, explorer, diarist. After Stuart, a Scotsman, and others had made their way by sea to found Astoria (1811), he made an eastward journey to St. Louis over a route at that time was practically unknown to white men. In the course of his explorations he discovered South Pass, later part of the route used by immigrants to California and Oregon. Washington Irving tells about him in ASTORIA (1836), and P. A. Rollins edited *The Discovery of the Oregon Trail: Robert Stuart's Narratives, 1811–13* (1935).

Stuart, Ruth McEnery (1849–1917),   short-story writer, novelist. Stuart is especially known for the authentic dialect of her stories of the South, many set in her native Louisiana. Among her books are *A Golden Wedding and Other Tales* (1893), *Carlotta's Intended and Other Tales* (1894), *Solomon Crow's Christmas Pockets and Other Tales* (1896), *Sonny* (1896), *In Simpkinsville: Character Tales* (1897), and *Aunt Amity's Silver Wedding and Other Stories* (1909).

Stuck, Hudson (1863–1920),   Protestant Episcopal clergyman, missionary. In 1885 Stuck came from England to the United States, served in Texas, and then, in 1904, was appointed archdeacon of the Yukon. He labored in that region until his death. He recorded his experiences in *Ten Thousand Miles with a Dog Sled* (1914), *Voyages on the Yukon and Its Tributaries* (1917), *The Alaskan Missions of the Episcopal Church* (1920), and *A Winter Circuit of Our Arctic Coast* (1920).

Studies in Classic American Literature (1922),   a series of essays by D. H. Lawrence. Following an introductory essay on "The Spirit of Place," Lawrence writes significant and provocative essays on Benjamin Franklin, Hector St. John Crevecoeur, Cooper, Poe, Hawthorne, Richard Henry Dana, Melville, and Whitman.

Studs Lonigan.   A character in novels by JAMES T. FARRELL.

Sturgeon, Theodore [Hamilton] (1918–1985), writer of fantasy and science fiction. Born Edward Hamilton Waldo in Staten Island, New York, he became Sturgeon on adoption in 1929 and grew up in Philadelphia. Widely published, he is remembered especially for fantastic stories exploring loneliness, alienation, extrasensory perception, shared consciousness, and other psychological states. His novels include *More Than Human* (1953), with children linked by complementary parapsychological powers; *The Cosmic Rape* (1958), with Earth's mental forces compelled to unite to repel invasion by an interplanetary mind; and *Venus Plus X* (1960), contrasting Earth and its sexual problems with a utopian society of bisexuals. Among his stories, "Bianca's Hands" and

"Baby Is Three" show particular force. His many collections include *E Pluribus Unicorn* (1953), *Caviar* (1955); *A Touch of Strange* (1958), *Aliens 4* (1959), *Sturgeon in Orbit* (1964), *Sturgeon Is Alive and Well* (1971), *Case and the Dreamer* (1973), *Visions and Venturers* (1978), *The Golden Helix* (1979), and *The Stars Are the Styx* (1979). Some of his best work is collected in *Selected Stories* (2000). He published also as Frederick R. Ewing, *I, Libertine* (1956) and as Ellery Queen, *The Player on the Other Side* (1963).

Sturges, Preston (1898–1959),   playwright, screenwriter, film director, producer. Sturges, born in Chicago, worked in his mother's cosmetics firm before beginning to write songs and work in the theater. He then began to write plays, the most successful being *Strictly Dishonorable* (1929). In Hollywood he wrote movie scripts and often directed and produced them. He won an Academy Award for *The Great McGinty* (1940). Among his other successful movies are *The Power and the Glory* (1932), *The Green Hat* (1933), *If I Were King* (1938), *Remember the Night* (1939), *Sullivan's Travels* (1941), *The Miracle of Morgan's Creek* (1944), *Hail the Conquering Hero* (1944), and *The Sin of Harald Diddlebock* (1946).

Stuyvesant, Peter (1592–1672),   soldier, colonial administrator. Stuyvesant was employed as a colonial administrator by the Dutch West India Co. In 1643 he was made governor of Curaçao and adjacent islands belonging to the Dutch. In 1644, while making an attack on the Portuguese island of St. Martin, he lost his right leg and was forced to return to Holland. There he was provided with a wooden leg, which he decorated with silver bands and called his "silver leg." In 1646 he was appointed director-general of New Netherland. From the start he announced and carried out a policy in which the interests of the colonists were bluntly subordinated to those of the company, and he was not popular. But he was successful for a while in settling disputes with other colonies, sometimes by force. He attacked and captured New Sweden in 1655. In 1664 he was obliged to surrender his colony to England because he lacked local support. In 1665 he returned to Holland, but came back in 1667 and until his death lived on his farm on the Bowery, in New Amsterdam (New York City). He was a man of violent temper, strong prejudices, and stubborn will. Washington Irving drew a satirical portrait of him as Peter the Headstrong in *A History of New York by Diedrich Knickerbocker* (1809).

Styron, William (1925–   ),   novelist. Born in Newport News, Virginia, William Styron has always been associated with the American South in his fiction, even despite the phenomenal success of his novel on the Holocaust, *Sophie's Choice* (1979). His mother died after his sophomore year in high school, and he has always revered his father, who died in 1978, as the gentlemanly, open-souled Virginian liberal. Several fathers in his fiction play a similar role, as they make a plea for the tolerance and understanding the contemporary world always disregards.

Polarities permeate Styron's life. He is the Southern Episcopalian who married the Jewish poet. He is the southerner who has lived most of his life in New England. He is a white man who has written as a black, an only child who craves connectedness and yet backs away from it, an antiwar marine, and a man who grew up in a sexually repressive era, yet who at times seems sexually obsessed. He is a man and writer in whom resistance breeds internal revolt and spiritual consciousness, as if authority and rebellion require one another to exist.

At the center of Styron's fictional realm there exists an encapsulated self or fictional character, who, often overwhelmed by a sense of anxiety, guilt, doom, self-scrutiny and dread, overwhelms the fictional universe he or she inhabits. This is a self so mired in its own problems and complications—whether of 1950s suburbia, slavery, Nazism, the southern past—that it nearly drowns in them. Styron exposes all the contradictions, paradoxes, and emotional ambiguities that drive these larger-than-life characters to their certain doom.

Styron reveals in his powerful fictions that shock of recognition and complicity in which sex, death, language, self-exploitation, slavery and Nazism are all inextricably bound up, not resulting in absolute paralysis but revealing the psychic and social depths of such forces. His bravely dark vision exposes the fact that we are all simultaneously victims and accomplices as we speak to, pursue, and use one another.

Styron's first novel, *Lie Down in Darkness* (1951), was praised for its Faulknerian rhythms and Joycean monologues. In it he castigated the mindless, liquor-ridden angst of modern suburban life. *Long March* (1953) was based on a forced march he underwent after being recalled to active duty in the Marine Corps during the Korean War. *Set This House on Fire* (1960), a brilliantly uneven book about murder and the existential agonies of Americans in Italy, was castigated by American critics but praised by the French.

Styron's most controversial book, which won the Pulitzer Prize, was *The Confessions of Nat Turner* (1967)—celebrated and vilified for its first-person narration of the slave rebellion in Virginia in 1831. *Sophie's Choice* fully illuminates Styron's lifelong concerns with human domination, the nature of evil, and the military. These themes, along with his sweeping rhetorical style, have made him one of the most critically and financially successful, serious, and popular American writers. A miscellany is *This Quiet Dust and Other Writings* (1982). *Darkness Visible: A Memoir of Madness* (1990) is an account of Styron's struggle with mental depression, and the public response was so overwhelming that he frequently gives public talks and leads discussions about it. *Tidewater Morning: Three Tales from Youth* appeared in 1993.

James L. West III has written a fine biography, *William Styron: A Life* (1998). Critical works include Samuel Coale's *William Styron Revisited* (1991), Elisabeth Herion-Sarafidis's *A Mode of Melancholy* (1995), and David Hadaller's *Gynicide: Women in the Novels of William Styron* (1996).

SAMUEL COALE

Suckow, Ruth (1892–1960), novelist, short-story writer. Although Suckow's works cover many themes and settings, her specialty was stories set in small Iowan towns like the

one in which she was born and grew up, and other parts of the Midwest, usually with German American characters. *Country People* (1924), her first novel, told the story of three generations of these people. Among other titles are *Iowa Interiors* (1926), *Cora* (1929), *Children and Older People* (1931), *The Folks* (1934), and *New Hope* (1942). Much that is autobiographical appears in *Some Others and Myself: Seven Stories and a Memoir* (1952). In 1959 she published *The John Wood Case*.

Suggs, Simon, featured in *Some Adventures of Captain Simon Suggs* (1845), by JOHNSON J. HOOPER. Suggs is a hard-drinking, witty backwoodsman whose philosophy is "It's good to be shifty in a new country." The sketches were first printed in O. Henry's SPIRIT OF THE TIMES and then were collected in book form.

Sui Sin Far. See EDITH MAUD EATON.

Sukenick, Ronald (1932–   ), novelist, short-story writer. Born in Brooklyn, New York, and educated at Cornell and Brandeis, Sukenick writes fiction, typologically experimental and chronologically disjointed, that deals with contemporary malaise. *Up* (1968) is a semiautobiographical novel of a young professor who is trying to finish his first novel. *Out* (1973) concerns a group of political radicals who wander the country blowing things up, and *98.6* (1975) deals with life on a commune. *The Death of the Novel* (1969) is a story collection. Sukenick has also written a study of WALLACE STEVENS (1967). His other titles include *Long Talking Bad Conditions Blues* (1979), *The Endless Short Story* (1986), *Blown Away* (1985), *Down and In: Life in the Underground* (1987), *Doggy Bag* (1994), *Mosaic Man* (1999), and *Narralogues: Truth in Fiction* (2000).

Sullivan, A[loysius] M[ichael] (1896–1980), advertising executive, poet. Sullivan, born in New Jersey, and an editor of business publications, was for several years president of the Poetry Society of America and published many collections of verse. Among them are *This Day and Age* (1944); *Tim Murphy Morgan, Rifleman, and Other Ballads* (1948); *Incident in Silver* (1950); *Choral Poems for Radio* (1951); *Psalms of the Prodigal and Other Poems* (1953); and *The Three-Dimensional Man* (1956).

Sullivan, Frank [Francis John] (1892–1976), columnist, writer. Sullivan, born in Saratoga Springs, New York, was long a columnist for the New York *World*. His satirical collection of clichés became widely appreciated often through his pieces for *The New Yorker*. Among his books are *Life and Times of Martha Hepplethwaite* (1926); *The Adventures of an Oaf*, with Herbert Roth (1927); *Innocent Bystanding* (1928); *Broccoli and Old Lace* (1931); *In One Ear* (1933); *A Pearl in Every Oyster* (1938); *Sullivan at Bay* (1939); *A Rock in Every Snowball* (1946); *The Night the Old Nostalgia Burned Down* (1953); *Sullivan Bites News*, with Sam Berman (1954); and *Moose in the Hoose* (1959).

Sullivan, John (1740–1795), public official. Sullivan, born in New Hampshire, was a member of the Continental Congress and took an active part in many important Revolutionary battles, attaining the rank of general. Along with James

Clinton he was sent to northern New York to punish the Six Nations for their part in the massacre of Wyoming. He defeated the Indians and their English allies, but failed to follow up his advantage, and engaged in a controversy with Washington. In 1779 he resigned from the army, became attorney general and then president of New Hampshire. His *Journals of the Expedition Against the Six Nations* appeared in 1887, and his *Letters and Papers* (2 v. ed. by O. G. Hammond) was published in 1930–31.

Sullivan, Mark (1874–1952),　　journalist, historian. Sullivan, born in Pennsylvania and trained in law at Harvard, never practiced and turned to journalism. In 1923 he joined the staff of the New York *Herald Tribune*, writing a column that was widely syndicated. In 1926 he began writing *Our Times: The United States 1900–1925*, annals of the 20th century, which reached six volumes. He also wrote the autobiographical *Education of an American* (1938).

Sullivan County Sketches (1949),　　ten pieces by STEPHEN CRANE collected and edited by Melvin Schoberlin. Only three of these stories or sketches appear in Crane's collected writings; the editor found the others in newspapers and magazines in which they had originally been published.

Sumner, Charles (1811–1874),　　public official. Born into a prominent Boston family and educated at Harvard, Sumner was first elected to the U.S. Senate in 1851 and served four terms. Known for his fiery speeches, he was assaulted on the Senate floor by Representative Preston S. Brooks after his antislavery address "The Crime Against Kansas" (May 20, 1856). He edited his *Orations and Speeches* (1850) and *Speeches and Addresses* (1856). A fifteen-volume collection, *Works*, was published (1870–1883), and E. L. Pierce wrote and edited *Memoir and Letters of Charles Sumner* (4 v. 1877–1893). Longfellow wrote a memorial poem at his death.

Sumner, William Graham (1840–1910),　　economist, professor. Sumner, born in New Jersey and educated at Yale, became a Yale professor of social science in 1872. An advocate of unrestricted capitalism, he championed free trade and opposed labor unions and governmental control of all kinds, including child labor laws. In *Folkways* (1907) he attempted to describe the evolution of social institutions. His writings on economics include *What Social Classes Owe to Each Other* (1883) and *Protectionism* (1885). He wrote biographical studies of Andrew Jackson (1882). Alexander Hamilton (1890), and Robert Morris (1892). A.G. Keller edited an unfinished manuscript as *Science in Society* (4 v. 1927). His other posthumous essay collections are *War and Other Essays* (1911), *Earth Hunger and Other Essays* (1913), and *The Forgotten Man and Other Essays* (1919).

Sun Also Rises, The (1926),　　a novel by Ernest Hemingway set in the period just after World War I. Jake Barnes, the narrator and principal character, is shown with his friends drifting through the cafés and dance halls of Paris, then fishing in the Spanish mountains, and afterward attending the bull fights in Pamplona. The fishing interlude seems to represent an idyllic existence, standing in contrast to the sexual

intrigue and violence that swirl about Lady Brett Ashley. Jake, impotent from a war wound, yearns for Brett and, therefore, suffers. Brett has an affair with Robert Cohn, an amateur boxer, and then seduces Pedro Romero, a young matador who embodies many of the qualities Hemingway admired. Romero, beaten by the jealous Cohn, goes off to a hotel with Brett. In the view of Romero's manager, Brett will be Romero's ruin. The novel ends happily when Brett sends Romero away. She tells Jake, ". . . it makes one feel rather good deciding not to be a bitch. . . . It's sort of what we have instead of God."

An epigraph quoting Gertrude Stein encouraged reviewers to regard the novel as a book about the lost generation, though a second epigraph, from Ecclesiastes, seemed to suggest otherwise. More recent critics have called the novel a prose version of Eliot's *The Waste Land*, a view first advanced by Malcolm Cowley. Hemingway himself said the point of the novel was that "promiscuity [is] no solution." It seems fair, however, to suggest that any judgment about *The Sun Also Rises* must take into account the fact that during much of the novel the characters are thoroughly enjoying themselves. The British title, *Fiesta*, emphasizes that aspect of the novel.

W. J. STUCKEY

Sunday Morning,　　a poem in blank verse by Wallace Stevens, written in 1915 and published in HARMONIUM (1923). On a tropical patio, a woman muses about life and death, religion, and the beauties of the world.

Sunnyside.　　WASHINGTON IRVING's home on the Hudson, not far from Tarrytown, New York, where Irving lived from 1836 to 1842 and again from 1846 until his death in 1859. It was originally built as a Dutch farmhouse in 1656, was burned by the British during the Revolution, and was rebuilt in 1785. When Irving bought it in 1835, he enlarged it from a four-room colonial saltbox to a fifteen-room mansion. John D. Rockefeller, Jr., donated half a million dollars to restore the house as a national shrine, which was opened to the public in October 4, 1947.

Sunthin' in the Pastoral Line (*Atlantic Monthly*, 1862; *Biglow Papers, Second Series*, 1867),　　a poem by JAMES RUSSELL LOWELL. Hosea Biglow falls asleep and dreams that an old Puritan Father appears and gives him some practical ideas on how to deal with the slavery issue. In good Yankee dialect he talks to him on how Charles I was beheaded because he was a tyrant and urges that Hosea, his descendant, must overthrow slavery in similar fashion.

Sun-Up (1923),　　a play by Lula Vollmer, one of the first American folk dramas, set in the mountains of North Carolina.

Superstition (prod. 1823, pub. 1825),　　a play by JAMES NELSON BARKER. The complicated plot deals with the Stuart house of England and at the same time the witchcraft trials in New England, where the action takes place.

Suppressed Desires (1915),　　a one-act play by SUSAN GLASPELL and her husband GEORGE CRAM COOK. This was one of the earliest plays produced by the PROVINCETOWN PLAYERS at their Wharf Theater. It deals satirically with the Freudian notion that suppressed desires, usually sexual, cause most neurotic conditions, but if brought to the surface and permitted to express themselves, lose their harmful effect.

Suri, Manil (1959–   ),   novelist. Born in Bombay, Suri received a Ph.D. from Carnegie-Mellon University and has taught mathematics at the University of Maryland, Baltimore County since 1983. His first novel, *The Death of Vishnu* (2001), part of which was published earlier in THE NEW YORKER, earned him comparison with other Indian writers in English, including, in the United States, BHARATI MUKHERJEE and JHUMPAR LAHIRI. Set in Bombay, the novel begins with the death of a drunken, near-beggar named Vishnu on the landing of an apartment and ranges into the Hindu and Muslim lives of others in the building, bringing in directly or through allusion the god Vishnu and his avatar Krishna, the *Bhagavad-Gita*, the Hindi movies and HAROLD ROBBINS novels of the author's youth, and the physicist Robert Oppenheimer's reaction to the first atomic blast. See THE GLOBALIZATION OF AMERICAN LITERATURE.

Survey Graphic, The.   Founded in 1897 as *Charities*, an official organ of the New York Charity Organization Society, this magazine took the name *The Survey* in 1897. In 1912 the society withdrew its support when the magazine published an article advocating election of Theodore Roosevelt. It continued as a liberal magazine, appealing especially to social workers. In 1902 Paul Kellogg joined its staff, in 1912 became its editor and continued in that position until 1952, when illness forced his withdrawal and the suspension of the magazine.

Susan Lenox: Her Fall and Rise (1917),   a posthumously published novel by DAVID GRAHAM PHILLIPS. The novel at first was suppressed because of its depiction of a girl of loose morals who frequently works as a prostitute. The book eventually was recognized as an attack on society rather than an indecent story. It received warm praise from Edith Wharton. Susan is an illegitimate child whose mother died at her birth. Revelation of this fact by a cruel cousin drives her away from the home of her aunt and uncle when she is seventeen. Thereafter, hers is a checkered and complicated life, involving many men of varied character.

Susann, Jacqueline (1921–1974),   novelist. Born in Philadelphia, Susann studied ballet and drama; she began as a model, appeared in Broadway and road company productions and, with Beatrice Cole, wrote a play called "Lovely Me" which was produced on Broadway in 1946. In a writing career spanning less than a dozen years, she produced three bestselling novels, including the spectacular success *Valley of the Dolls* (1966), about three glamorous substance-abusing women. Though critics called her fiction pornographic, Susann claimed that the descriptions of sex acts were necessary to the characterization, ". . . if I didn't sometimes show these characters at their more bestial, weaker moments, I'd have written a dishonest book." The other novels published while she was alive, *The Love Machine* (1969) and *Once Is Not Enough* (1973) also set sales records. Other titles are: *Every Night, Josephine!* (1963), a tribute to her pet poodle, *Dolores* (1976) and *Yargo*

(1978). Interest in Susann's flamboyant life style and her marriage to Irving Mansfield, a publicist who tirelessly promoted her career, has continued. *Lovely Me* (1987), by Barbara Seaman, is a biography; the film *Isn't She Great?* (2000) is loosely based on Michael Korda's 1995 *New Yorker* profile called "Wasn't She Great?"

Sut Lovingood Yarns (1867),   tales by GEORGE WASHINGTON HARRIS.

Sutpen family, The.   A family in ABSALOM, ABSALOM!, by William Faulkner. Its complex relationships include both African-Americans and whites. The following are members of the Sutpen family:

Charles Bon. The son of Thomas Sutpen and Eulalia Bon, who is of mixed racial ancestry, Charles marries a New Orleans octoroon by whom he has a son, Charles Etienne St.-Valery Bon. He is later engaged to his half-sister, Judith Sutpen, but is killed by her brother, Henry, before the marriage can take place.

Eulalia Bon. The daughter of a Haitian plantation owner, Eulalia is divorced by Thomas Sutpen when he discovers she is of mixed racial ancestry.

Jim Bond. The idiot son of Charles E. St.-Valery Bon and an African-American woman, Jim is the last remaining descendant of Thomas Sutpen. He disappears after Sutpen's house is burned in 1909.

Ellen Coldfield. The daughter of a respected merchant in Jefferson, Ellen is married to Thomas Sutpen, by whom she has two children, Henry and Judith. She is largely responsible for the engagement between Judith and her half-brother, Charles Bon.

Rosa Coldfield. The spinster sister-in-law of Thomas Sutpen, Rosa narrates part of *Absalom, Absalom!* She is engaged, but never married, to Sutpen who, in his desire to have male offspring to bear his name, insults her by suggesting that "they try it first and if it was a boy and lived, they would be married."

Wash Jones. The grandfather of the girl who bears an illegitimate daughter to Sutpen, Jones is a poor white squatter and handyman on the Sutpen estate. He murders his granddaughter, her newborn child, and Sutpen, and then kills himself.

Clytie [Clytemnestra] Sutpen. The daughter of Thomas Sutpen and a slave, Clytie burns the Sutpen house over her own and Henry Sutpen's head in 1909 to prevent Henry from being jailed for the murder of Charles Bon.

Henry Sutpen. The son of Thomas Sutpen by his second wife, Ellen Coldfield, Henry meets Charles Bon at the University of Mississippi and forms an intimate friendship with him, unaware that Bon is his half-brother. Learning of their relationship and of Bon's African-American ancestry, Henry murders him to prevent his marriage to Henry's sister, Judith. Henry disappears after the murder and is discovered in 1909, ill and hiding in Sutpen's almost-deserted house, cared for by his mulatto half-sister Clytie.

Judith Sutpen. The daughter of Thomas Sutpen and Ellen Coldfield, Judith is engaged to marry her half-brother Charles Bon. After his death she brings up his part-African-American son, Charles Etienne St.-Valery Bon.

Thomas Sutpen. Descended from a family of Southern poor whites, Sutpen came to Mississippi in 1833 and acquired a hundred square miles of fertile bottom land from the Chickasaw chief Ikkemotubbe on which he built a plantation called Sutpen's Hundred. He married Ellen Coldfield to connect himself with the local gentry and properly carry out his great design to found an aristocratic Southern family. He is murdered by his handyman in 1869 after a last, futile attempt to beget a white son to become master of Sutpen's Hundred.

Sutter, John Augustus (1803–1880),   colonist. Born in Switzerland, Sutter settled at the New Helvetia Colony, near Sacramento, California, in 1839. When his partner, James W. Marshall, discovered gold near their sawmill on the south fork of the American River on January 22, 1848, the resulting gold rush ruined their property. Sutter's *Diary* was first published in the San Francisco *Argonaut* (1878) and was reprinted in book form in 1932. His *New Helvetia Diary* (1845–1848) appeared in 1939.

Swados, Harvey (1920–1972),   novelist, short-story writer. Born in Buffalo, New York, Swados was educated at the University of Michigan and taught at Sarah Lawrence, the University of Iowa, and San Francisco State College. His first novel, *Out Went the Candle* (1955) portrays an American family during World War II; *On the Line* (1957) is a realistic view of workers in a large automobile plant. His other books are *False Coin* (1959), *Nights in the Gardens of Brooklyn* (1960), *A Radical's America* (essays, 1962), *The Will* (1963), *A Story for Teddy* (1965), *Standing Fast* (1970), and *Celebration* (1975).

Swallow Barn: A Sojourn in the Old Dominion (1832),   a novel by JOHN PENDLETON KENNEDY. It has been described by Kennedy himself as "a series of detached sketches linked together by the hooks and eyes of a traveler's notes. . . . There is a rivulet of story wandering through a broad meadow of episode." Influenced by Addison and Irving, the book is chiefly notable as one of the earliest to present the American stereotypes of the Southern gentleman and plantation life.

Swanson, Neil H[armon] (1896–1983),   newspaperman, historian, historical novelist. Swanson, born in Minneapolis, worked as a newspaperman almost throughout his life and early became interested in writing histories in fictional style. Two of his early books fall in this class: *The First Rebel* (1937) and *The Perilous Fight* (1945). In 1939 he began a series designed to show the development of the Middle Atlantic states during the 18th century. In the projected series he included some novels he had already published—*The Judas Tree* (1933) among them. Others are *Unconquered* (1947) and *The Calico Tree* (1955). With Anne Sherbourne Swanson he published *Star-Spangled Banner* (1958).

Swap, Solomon.   A Yankee character who appears in American comedies of the first half of the 19th century, though the name and some of the traits were taken from a farce by the English dramatist George Colman the Younger, Solomon was made popular by such actors as JAMES H. HACKETT and GEORGE HANDEL HILL.

Swarthout, Glendon [Fred] (1918–1992),   novelist. Born and educated in Michigan, Swarthout's first novel, *Willow Run* (1943), treats the lives of factory workers in this World War II defense plant. *They Came to Cordura* (1958) describes a campaign against Mexican bandits in 1916, and *The Eagle and the Iron Cross* (1966) concerns German prisoners of war who escaped from an Arizona detention center. In *Bless the Beasts and the Children* (1970) six boys try to free a buffalo heard after they see the killing of a buffalo. His other titles include *Where the Boys Are* (1960), *Welcome to Thebes* (1962), *The Cadillac Cowboys* (1964), *Loveland* (1968), and *The Tin Lizzie Troop* (1972). With his wife Kathryn, Swarthout has written several books for children.

Swedenborgianism.   This small but influential religious sect was founded on the doctrines of Emanuel Swedenborg (1688–1772). He was in the earlier part of his life an eminent scientist. Then, in April 1744, he had a vision of Christ and thereafter devoted himself largely to expounding a mystic doctrine of God and the world. He founded no church, in the belief that Protestant sects could incorporate his ideas into their own teaching. His writings appeared mainly in Latin, among the best-known being *Heaven and Hell* (1758) and *The Apocalypse Revealed* (1766). His doctrines include a special interpretation of the Trinity, emphasis on certain books of the Bible, three descending levels or "degrees of being in God," and the prediction of a new dispensation. Swedenborgians were first organized, in 1778, as a church in London. The sect was called the Society of the New Church Signified by the New Jerusalem, more often, the New Church.

James Glen preached Swedenborgianism in Philadelphia and Boston in 1784. A society was organized in Baltimore in 1792, and a national group in 1817. Swedenborg's deepest influence was exerted on the Concord School during the early 19th century. Emerson called him a "colossal soul," and the dwellers at BROOK FARM revered him. Henry James the elder was influenced by Swedenborgianism in his concept of "divine-natural humanity," and influenced his son, the novelist.

Sweeney.   A character, at one point called Apeneck Sweeney, who appears in a number of poems by T. S. ELIOT, notably *Sweeney Among the Nightingales* (1918), *Mr. Eliot's Sunday Morning Service* (1918), *Sweeney Erect* (1919), THE WASTE LAND (1922), and two fragments entitled *Sweeney Agonistes* (separately published [1926, 1927; then together, 1932). Sweeney is intended as a satirical portrait of sensual, materialistic man, particularly in the 20th century.

Sweet Singer of Michigan, The.   See JULIA A. MOORE.

Swenson, May (1919–1989),   poet. Born and educated in Utah the daughter of Swedish Mormons, Swenson moved to New York City after completing college. Her first published work, *Another Animal: Poems* (1954), printed in *Poets of Today 1*, attracted praise and won awards for its vivid imagery and experimental technique and typography. *A Cage of Spines* (1958) was her first solo collection, followed by *To Mix with Time* (1963). *Half Sun Half Sleep* (1967) includes descriptions of life in New York and Europe along with her translations of six contemporary Swedish poets. *Iconographs* (1970) includes shaped poems. *New and Selected Things Taking Place* (1978) is a sampler. *Poems to Solve* (1966) and *More Poems to Solve* (1971) contain verse for children. *Windows and Stones* (1972) is translated from Swedish.

Swift, Tom. A boy inventor, hero of a long series of novels for boys. Tom's exciting adventures with all kinds of contrivances, some of which anticipated actual inventions, became widely popular and brought considerable wealth to Tom's creator, EDWARD L. STRATEMEYER.

Swinton, William (1833–1892), newspaperman, teacher, historian, textbook author. Swinton's parents took him from Scotland to Canada in 1843. He taught as a young man in New York City and North Carolina, then joined the staff of *The New York Times* and helped cover the Civil War. Later he wrote several books about the war, one attacking General McClellan (1864), another describing *The Twelve Decisive Battles of the War* (1867). From 1869 to 1874 he taught at the University of California. A disagreement with the university president led to his resignation, and he thereafter wrote successful textbooks for use in elementary schools. His *Readers* were especially popular. He won a gold medal at the Paris Exposition of 1878 for his work in this field.

Sword Blades and Poppy Seed (1914), a collection of poems by AMY LOWELL. This second collection of Lowell's verse is important particularly for its inclusion of poems written in free verse and the first English examples of polyphonic prose, rhythmical prose characterized by the devices of verse except for strict meter.

symbolism. Primarily a European movement, symbolism originated in France midway through the 19th century and became of great importance and influence during the 1880s. It arose largely as a part of a romantic reaction that freed French verse from the rigidity and rhetoric of the classicism that had dominated French literature during the 18th century. Charles Baudelaire, who is considered one of the founders of symbolism, was deeply impressed by the poetry of Poe. He translated Poe's works into French and brought Poe more recognition in Europe than he was receiving in America. The musicality of Poe's verse and his use of synaesthesia were influential in the development of the poetry of Baudelaire, whose sonnet *Correspondances*, treating all objects as symbols, finds a correspondence between visual, auditory, and sensory perceptions.

Arthur Rimbaud provided the literary movement with its empowering myth when he remarked that the poet transformed himself into a visionary through "the derangement of all the senses." Throughout the history of symbolism, this description accompanied the movement as its tutelary spirit. Stéphane Mallarmé, perhaps the most important of the symbolist poets, focused this derangement on the relationship between poetic image and material referent. Mallarmé sought to divorce language from its particularity, creating poems whose obscurity became the more dense as he approached his abstract—and inaccessible—ideal. Influenced by Poe and Baudelaire, Mallarmé's salons and his aesthetic theories came closest to creating a school of symbolism and were highly influential both in France and in the spreading of symbolism to England.

Disdaining nature as chaotic and repugnant, the symbolists cultivated artifice in their personal lives to complement the artifice of the work of art, thus establishing the cult of the dandy, which was paralleled by Oscar Wilde and other English decadents of the 1880s and 1890s. Symbolism first made itself felt as an influence in England toward the end of the 19th century in the development of free verse and may have had some indirect effect on Pound and Amy Lowell's Imagism. American critical and little magazines began to pay attention to French symbolism at the beginning of the 20th century, and American expatriates in Europe furthered the introduction of French poetry and aesthetics into America.

In *The Twenties* (1955), Frederick J. Hoffman concludes that "French symbolism was not a negligible factor in the development of modern American poetry"; however, since no American poet has been a symbolist exactly after the fashion of the French, and the French developed their theory out of a misreading of Poe's American verse, it is difficult to differentiate between influence and individual development. Certainly, during the 1920s there was a marked vogue toward difficult, tightly constructed poetry in which words, singly and in combinations, were used in new or unusual ways—poetry that suggested rather than stated; that was highly evocative, often musical; or that depended, in Hart Crane's words, on "the illogical impingements of words on the consciousness," rather than on their logical connotations. Crane, particularly in his early poems, when he followed Rimbaud's imperatives quite literally, is possibly the only American poet who can truly be classified as a symbolist. Some critics consider that Eliot adapted some of the techniques of symbolism for his own uses, and some of the poems of William Carlos Williams and Archibald MacLeish are broadly symbolic in their use of subject matter but not, like Wallace Stevens in certain of his works, in their technique as well.

As a general term, and particularly with reference to prose writings, symbolism should not be confused with symbolist poetry, which refers to a particular literary movement characterized by the desire to express a state of mind by purely sensory images, and to suggest rather than describe. Symbolism in general may refer to any one thing being made to stand for another, a literary technique that is widespread. When distinguished from allegory, a literary symbol is said to partake wholly of the nature of the thing symbolized, while an allegorical figure calls attention to the difference between its signs and referents. The best examples of this distinction are the novels of Hawthorne and Melville, particularly *The Scarlet Letter* and *Moby-Dick*. *The Scarlet Letter* is an allegorical figure that has lost its power to refer, a fact that Hawthorne underlines in the chapter on the Custom House, where he finds a faded and worn letter A that still seems to exert some of its mysterious force. Hester's child, Pearl, is an allegorical figure for natural energy, and the wicked Chillingworth for revenge, and the scaffold and forest scenes take on multiple allegorical meanings. *Moby-Dick*, on the other hand, is almost inexhaustible in symbolic meaning. Ahab, the ship, the strange crew, Ishmael, and the whale itself are all susceptible to a variety of symbolic interpretations, each of which calls attention to the inherence of the symbol in the thing signified.

For further discussion of 19th-century American symbolism, see *Symbolism and American Literature* (1953), by Charles J. Feidelson, Jr. Works dealing with the symbolist poets in France include Arthur Symons, *The Symbolist Movement in Literature* (1899), and Ruth Z. Temple, *Critics' Alchemy: A Study of the Introduction of French Symbolism into England* (1953). For a general discussion of modern symbolism, see William York Tindall, *The Literary Symbol* (1958); Leo Bersani, *The Death of Stéphane Mallarmé*; and Tzvetan Todorov, *Theories of the Symbol* (1982).
DP

Symphony, The (1875), a poem by SIDNEY LANIER. In this extraordinary poem Lanier deliberately created some striking effects intended to demonstrate the close relationship between poetry and music that he constantly asserted. The poem closes with Lanier's most evocative phrase, "Music is Love in search of a word." The poem is a strong denunciation of industrialism and the commercial attitude of "glozing and lying." It is a plea for greater humanity and for attention to "the poor-folks' crying." The pattern of the poem consists of the successive use of various instruments in the orchestra: violins, flute, clarinet, horn, and oboe.

syndicate features. See NEWSPAPERS.

T

Tabb, John Banister (1845–1909), poet, clergyman. The Virginia-born Tabb was rejected for poor eyesight by the Confederate Army and became a blockade runner. After a number of runs to Europe, he was captured and imprisoned at Point Lookout, where he and fellow prisoner SIDNEY LANIER discussed poetry and became friends. Converted to Catholicism in 1872, Tabb was ordained a priest in 1884. His poetry deals with nature and religion; his first collection, *Poems* (1894), ran to seventeen printings. His other books are *An Octave to Mary* (1893), *Lyrics* (1897), *Child Verse* (1899), *Later Lyrics* (1902), *The Rosary in Rhyme* (1904), and *Quips and Quiddits* (1907). He also wrote an English grammar.

tabloids. See NEWSPAPERS.

Taft, William Howard (1857–1930), lawyer, judge, public official, teacher, author, twenty-sixth president of the United States. Born in Cincinnati, Ohio, Taft went to Yale University, was graduated from the Cincinnati Law School in 1880, and was admitted to the bar. He occupied a long series of public offices: assistant prosecuting attorney, assistant county solicitor, judge of the Superior Court, U.S. solicitor general, judge of the Federal Circuit Court, head of the Philippines Commission, governor of the Philippines, Secretary of War, and provisional governor of Cuba. Then, at Theodore Roosevelt's insistence, he was nominated for President and elected over William Jennings Bryan (1908). But Taft was fundamentally more conservative than Roosevelt, and offended not only his old friend, but numerous progressive voters; he ran unsuccessfully for a second term against Woodrow Wilson and against Roosevelt, who had founded the Bull Moose party in anger against Taft. In 1913 Taft became professor of constitutional law at Yale Law School and served until 1921, when he was appointed chief justice of the Supreme Court.

Taft wrote several books, among them *Popular Government* (1913) and *Our Chief Magistrate and His Powers* (1916). Mrs. William Howard Taft wrote *Recollections of Full Years* (1914).

Taggard, Genevieve (1894–1948), poet, professor, biographer. Born in the state of Washington, Taggard grew up in Hawaii, a location important to her poetry. Her collections include *For Eager Lovers* (1922), *Hawaiian Hilltop* (1923), *Words for the Chisel* (1926), *Not Mine to Finish* (1934), *Poems 1918–1938*, and *Slow Music* and *Origin Hawaii* (1947). In addition to founding and editing *The Measure, a Journal of Verse* (1920–1926), she compiled several anthologies of verse and wrote *The Life and Mind of Emily Dickinson* (1930). She taught at Mount Holyoke and Sarah Lawrence.

Tailfer, Patrick (fl. 1741), 18th-century physician, satirist, pamphleteer. Little is known of Tailfer save that in his sole published work he identified himself as an M.D. and that in a reply to this work he was accused of cruelty to his servants, even of having murdered one of them. He and several others quarreled bitterly with JAMES OGLETHORPE, founder of the Georgia colony, and fled to Charleston, South Carolina. There, in 1741, they issued a pamphlet of considerable length entitled *A True and Historical Narrative of the Colony at Georgia . . .*, by Patrick Tailfer, M.D., Hugh Anderson, M.A., David Douglas, "and Others, Landholders in Georgia." Tailfer, to whom the pamphlet is usually ascribed, indulged in scathing satire at the expense of Oglethorpe and other Georgia officials, but presented sufficient documentary evidence to make the attack effective. The pamphlet was reprinted in *Peter Force's Historical Tracts* (4 v. 1836–46), also in the Georgia Historical Society's *Collections* (Volume II, 1842), which also reprinted an official reply by Benjamin Martyn, secretary of the Georgia trustees. Another reply was made by the Rev. William Best in a sermon to these trustees, *The Merit and Reward of a Good Intention* (1742).

Tales of a Traveller (1824), thirty-two stories and sketches by WASHINGTON IRVING. The first of four groupings of stories, told by a number of convivial English gentlemen, contains a humorous ghost story, "The Bold Dragoon." The second deals with the adventures of Buckthorne, a young English literary hopeful. The third is concerned with Italian bandits. In the last and best section, "The Money Diggers," Irving is again creating his own special brand of American folklore. "The Devil and Tom Walker," which has been called "a comic New England Faust," deserves to rank beside the best legends from THE SKETCH BOOK (1820). Despite the romantic background and sentimental situations in many of the stories, they are all solidly based in realistic detail.

Tales of a Wayside Inn (1863), a collection of twenty-one long narrative poems by HENRY WADSWORTH LONGFELLOW. The tales are built around a framework similar to that used by Chaucer in the *Canterbury Tales* and Boccaccio in the *Decameron*. Each is narrated by a member of a group gathered at a fireside in a New England tavern. The tales reflect Longfellow's strong interest in history—early European in the case of "The Saga of King Olaf" and American in "Paul Revere's Ride." See LUIGI MONTI; BIRDS OF KILLINGSWORTH; EMMA AND EGINHARD.

Tales of Soldiers and Civilians (1891),   by AMBROSE BIERCE. See IN THE MIDST OF LIFE, the title given this collection in 1898.

Tales of the Grotesque and Arabesque (2 v. 1840), twenty-five stories by EDGAR ALLAN POE. This was Poe's first published collection and includes some of his most memorable stories, notably THE FALL OF THE HOUSE OF USHER. In his preface Poe replied to the charge made frequently, that his work was permeated with "Germanism and gloom." He said: "If in many of my productions terror has been the basis, I maintain that terror is not of Germany but of the soul." The volumes were rather favorably received but sold slowly, and Poe received no encouragement when he proposed a second enlarged edition. See THE ASSIGNATION; BERENICE.

Tales of the South Pacific (1947),   eighteen stories by JAMES A. MICHENER. Michener made rich use of his World War II naval experiences in this collection, which won the 1948 Pulitzer Prize for fiction. Although each tale can be read independently, various characters, American and native, reappear from time to time to form a connecting link. OSCAR HAMMERSTEIN II and RICHARD C. RODGERS drew together themes from several of the stories for the successful musical *South Pacific* (1949).

Taliaferro, Harden E. (1818–1875),   clergyman, writer. Taliaferro (whose name is pronounced TOLiv'r) was born in the mountainous western part of North Carolina and became a Baptist preacher at an early age. His book *The Grace of God Manifested* (1857) was published by the Southern Baptist Publication Society. He also collected folklore, especially tall tales, among the mountain folk of his region. He made a collection, *Fisher's River: Scenes and Characters* (1859), published under the pen name "Skitt."

Talifer (1933),   a novel in blank verse by EDWIN ARLINGTON ROBINSON. Two men—a businessman and a doctor—are deeply interested in two women—one somewhat mentally immature, the other an intellectual. The businessman, engaged to the former, gives her up and marries the latter, and the marriage proves to be unhappy. A divorce is arranged, and the businessman marries his first love and lives happily. The intellectual woman, under the doctor's care, stays abroad and studies at Oxford.

Talisman, The (1827–1830).   This periodical, issued annually by Edam Bliss, was originally undertaken by GULIAN C. VERPLANCK, WILLIAM CULLEN BRYANT, and ROBERT C. SANDS as a joint collection of miscellanies in the fashion of the 18th century. It was edited by the imaginary "Francis Herbert, Esq." and was continued until three volumes had been published. In 1833, the three volumes were republished as *Miscellanies first*

published under the name of The Talisman. Each author contributed some of his best work to the annual. Verplanck wrote a piece called "Reminiscences of New York," with help from Bryant, who contributed "The Indian Spring" and a poem in blank verse, "The Dream of the Princess Papantzin."

Tallant, Robert (1909–1957),   folklorist, novelist. New Orleans, his birthplace, served as the background for all of Tallant's work. In collaboration with LYLE SAXON and Edward Dryer he wrote and edited *Gumbo Ya-Ya, A Collection of Louisiana Folklore* (1945), *then wrote Voodoo in New Orleans* (1946), *Mardi Gras* (1948), and *The Romantic New Orleanians* (1950). His first novel, *Mrs. Candy and Saturday Night* (1947), is a story of his native city. *Angel in the Wardrobe* (1948) and *Mr. Preen's Salon* (1949) are also set in New Orleans.

Tallent, Elizabeth (1954–   ),   short-story writer, novelist. Born in Washington, D.C., and trained in anthropology at Illinois State University, Tallent published stories in major magazines in her twenties. Her first book was a collection of critical essays, *Married Men and Magic Tricks: John Updike's Erotic Heroes* (1982). *In Constant Flight* (1983) is a gathering of stories about young people whose lives fall short of their dreams. Her novel *Museum Pieces* (1985), set in New Mexico, parallels the struggle of a young couple and their daughter to reconstruct their family with restoration of Native American pottery shards in the museum. *Time with Children* (1987) and *Honey: Stories* (1993) continue to demonstrate her mastery, mostly with tales of domestic life.

tall tales and tall talk.   Constance Rourke was probably correct in setting down the Rev. Samuel A. Peters in her *American Humor* as a conscious rather than unconscious humorist, in which case his *General History of Connecticut* (1781) may be said to contain some of our earliest specimens of satirical lying. Had he not been conscious of their satiric effect, his entries would exemplify the form of tall talk that motivated Benjamin Franklin, originator of so much else in American civilization, to write the first spoof for a newspaper. On May 20, 1765, Franklin wrote a letter to a London newspaper as a satirical reply to statements being made about the American colonies. His letter called attention to the origins for these statements in a collective wish to believe in a fabulous, rather than actual, America. He mentioned particularly the story "in all the papers last week" that the people of Canada were preparing to set up "a cod and whale fishery this summer in the upper lakes"; he noted that "the grand leap of a whale in that chase up the fall of the Niagara is esteemed, by all who have seen it, as one of the finest spectacles in nature."

Peters's satiric lies and Franklin's satirical reply expose the source of the tall tale in a wish to trick a reader or listener into belief in a deception. When the gull for the tale is a stranger, his gullibility structures the difference between the members of the community who are in on the game and an outsider whose entry into the community coincides with his being taken in by the tale. The American tall tale made its formal bow in Washington Irving's *History of New York by Diedrich Knickerbocker* (1809), with its profile of Governor Wouter Van Twiller, for example, who was "exactly five feet six inches in height and six feet five inches in circumference." Generally, however, it is held that the tall tale first began to flourish on the Western frontier, a land without history about which travelers were eager to believe anything. The backwoodsman, represented by such historic figures as Daniel Boone and Davy Crockett, would supply endless wild tales of his exploits, some of them true and others exaggerated. To match the fooleries of Crockett, the West invented Mike Fink, king of the flatboatmen, whose vast hyperboles made other men's boasts seem like understatement. The Crockett *Almanacs*, about fifty of which appeared between 1835, and 1856, purported to be the work of Crockett himself or his heirs, and told many tall tales about Crockett, Fink, Boone, and others. This tall talk had a deep influence on many writers, including Twain and Whitman. Fine examples are given in Twain's *Life on the Mississippi* (1883), whose effect James Cox described in *The Fate of Humor* as the narrator's conversion of "his humiliation, failure, and anger into a tall tale which will both move and rouse the listener . . . move him to laughter and rouse him to skepticism."

The Yankee never went to the lengths the Westerner did. His humor was still spare and comparatively restrained. Richard Dorson found "the casual lie" characteristic of Yankee humor. His *Jonathan Draws the Long Bow* (1896) covers a wide and constantly entertaining range of supernatural stories; yarns of greenhorns, tricksters, and originals; tall tales of hunting and fishing, strong men, and the constantly reappearing sea serpent; and literary folk tales. Dorothy Canfield Fisher, in an article entitled "Old Salt and Old Oak," in the *Saturday Review of Literature*, May 22, 1943, mentions another class of New England tales, those that give a vivid glimpse into the tangled brain of somebody who isn't quite all there. A familiar one concerns a hired man who hears someone talking about a dead body found near a river. He asks anxiously, "Did it have on a brown coat?" "Yes," comes the answer. He shrinks back, then asks, "Did it have on black buttoned shoes?" "No." "Oh, then, 'twan't me." The chief folk hero of New England is Captain Stormalong, the sailor giant and hero of the sea. He appears in an old sailors' shanty and in Walter Blair's accounts in *Tall Tale America* (1944). Lewis Pendleton endeavored to rival the exploits of Stormalong in *Down East: The Remarkable Adventures on the Briny Deep and Ashore of Captain Isaac Drinkwater and Jedediah's Peabody* (1937).

Paul Bunyan is the greatest mythical hero America has provided. Tales about Bunyan have been gathered in several books, for example, H. W. Felton's *Legends of Paul Bunyan* (1937). Other folk heroes—some of them modeled on actual persons—are JAMES BRIDGER, FEBOLD FEBOLDSON, Gib Morgan of the oil fields, PECOS BILL, JOHN HENRY, TONY BEAVER, BILLY THE KID, and BIG-FOOT WALLACE. Other real people whose size has been magnified in American narratives include Captain JOHN SMITH, JOHNNY APPLESEED, WILLIAM F. CODY, ANNE OAKLEY, JESSE JAMES, the pirate LAFITTE, and KIT CARSON. Mody C. Boatwright, discussing "The Art of Tall Lying" (*Southwest Review*, Autumn 1949), suggested that the men who moved west with the fron-

tier had "in the tall tale developed one of America's few indigenous art forms." H. L. Mencken, in *The American Language*, 4th ed. (1936), found in the grotesque metaphors and farfetched exaggerations of American tall talk the source of a great many Americanisms.

There have been numerous collections of regional tall tales, or stories about individual heroes. Among these are J. H. Ingraham, *Lafitte, the Pirate of the Gulf* (1836); John C. Duval, *Adventures of Big-Foot Wallace* (1870); W. N. Burns, *The Saga of Billy the Kid* (1926); Percy MacKaye, *Tall Tales of the Kentucky Mountains* (1926); Frank Shay, *Here's Audacity! American Legendary Heroes* (1930); F. J. Meine, *Tall Tales of the Southwest* (1930); Roark Bradford, *John Henry* (1931); Walter Blair and F. J. Meine, *Mike Fink* (1933); Bernard De Voto, *Mark Twain's America* (1932); James H. Daugherty, *Their Weight in Wildcats* (1936); A. P. Hudson, *Humor of the Old Deep South* (1936); Vincent McHugh, *Caleb Catlum's America* (1936); C. Bowman, *Pecos Bill, the Greatest Cowboy of All Time* (1937); Richard Dorson, ed., *Davy Crockett: American Comic Legend* (1939); Harold W. Thompson, *Body, Boots, & Britches* (1940); B. A. Botkin, *Treasury of American Folklore* (1944), *Treasury of New England Folklore* (1947), and *Western Folklore* (1951); M. C. Boatwright, *Gib Morgan, Minstrel of the Oil Fields* (1945); Ben C. Clough, *The American Imagination at Work: Tall Tales and Folk Tales* (1947); Paul R. Beath, *Tall Tales from the Great Plains* (1948); Vance Randolph, *We Always Lie to Strangers: Tall Tales from the Ozarks* (1951); J. Frank Dobie, *Tales of Old-Time Texas* (1955); Bill Gulick, *White Men, Red Men, and Mountain Men* (1955); John J. Flanagan and Arthur Palmer Hudson, *American Folklore Reader: Folklore in American Literature* (1958); James M. Cox, *The Fate of Humor* (1966); and Neil Schmitz, *Of Huck and Alice: Humorous Writing in American Literature* (1983). See HUMOR IN THE UNITED STATES.

DP

Talmage, T[homas] De Witt (1832–1902), clergyman, editor. Talmage, born in New Jersey and ordained in 1862, became celebrated for eloquent sermons on temperance and morality. He drew large crowds to his Central Presbyterian Church in Brooklyn, New York, and his sermons were printed in more than 3,000 newspapers. Talmage edited *The Christian at Work* from 1874 to 1876 and *Frank Leslie's Sunday Magazine* from 1881 to 1889. He became editor of the CHRISTIAN HERALD in 1890 and nine years later resigned his pulpit to give all his time to this periodical. Among his many volumes of sermons are *Crumbs Swept Up* (1870), *Every Day Religion* (1875), *The Marriage Tie* (1890), and *Fifty Short Sermons* (1923). *T. De Witt Talmage as I Knew Him* (1912) is an autobiography.

Tamar (in *Tamar and Other Poems*, 1924), a narrative poem by ROBINSON JEFFERS. Jeffers's first attempt at a narrative poem, *Tamar* contains many themes he developed more successfully in his later work. The poem is loosely based on the Biblical story of Tamar, a daughter of King David who was seduced by her brother. A modern Tamar living on the Monterey coast seduces her brother, a neighbor, and her father. She communicates with the dead and finally brings down destruction on her entire family. Tamar is both the avenger, expiating the bloodguilt incurred by incestuous love, and a symbol of the destructiveness of narcissism and introversion.

Tamerlane and Other Poems (1827),   the first published collection of verses by EDGAR ALLAN POE. His name did not appear on the title page, which read simply, "By a Bostonian." The Byronic title poem is a narrative based on Poe's love affair with Sarah Elmira Royster, of Richmond. The speaker is the great Mongol conqueror, who here describes a love affair of his own time, though the poem does not aim at historical accuracy. In the poem Poe stressed the four themes that later dominated his work: pride, love, beauty, and death. The collection also includes "Visit of the Dead," "The Lake," "Evening Star," and "Imitation." The last poem, after much revision, was later called "A Dream Within a Dream."

Tan, Amy [Ruth] (1952–   ),   novelist, short-story writer. Born in Oakland, California, of Chinese immigrant parents, Tan was educated at San Jose State University (B.A., 1973, M.A., 1974). She began Ph.D. study at the University of California, Berkeley (1974–1976), before spending a dozen years as a language consultant, technical writer, and editor in the San Francisco area. She began to write fiction (and play jazz piano) as therapy for the tensions of her workaholic life. Stories drawn from her mixed cultural background surfaced in *The Joy Luck Club* (1989), an immediate best-seller and popular film (1993). The sixteen linked stories of the book come from four pairs of immigrant mothers and their American-born daughters, who have difficulty bridging the generational and cultural gap between growing up in China and growing up in the United States. When one mother dies, the daughter who takes her place at the club of the title helps pull the generations together as she makes a trip to the mothers' Chinese homeland and confronts the daughters' cultural heritage. In *The Kitchen God's Wife* (1991), a daughter again learns of her mother's Chinese past, a harrowing tale of women from different classes thrown together in desperate circumstances in China, separated and then reunited in the United States. *The Hundred Secret Senses* (1995) tells of half-sisters, one of whom speaks with spirits and believes the two shared another life in China in an earlier century. *The Bonesetter's Daughter* (2001) centers on Ruth Young's attempt to heal the rift with LuLing, her Chinese immigrant mother recently diagnosed with Alzheimer's disease and determined to record the events of her early life before her mind is destroyed. Ruth hires a translator to decipher the two packets of Chinese calligraphy her mother has sent. The documents describe a girlhood among a family of ink makers in a remote mountainous region from which LuLing and her sister escape with difficulty. *The Moon Lady* (1992) and *The Chinese Siamese Cat* (1994) are children's books.

Tanglewood Tales (1853),   six Greek myths retold by NATHANIEL HAWTHORNE. Issued as a sequel to Hawthorne's A WONDER-BOOK FOR GIRLS AND BOYS (1851), the *Tanglewood Tales* includes "The Minotaur," "The Pygmies," "The Dragon's Teeth," "Circe's Palace," "The Pomegranate Seeds," and "The Golden Fleece."

Tanner, Edward Everett, III.   See PATRICK DENNIS.

Tanner, John (1780?–1847),   Indian scout. Tanner, born in Kentucky, was captured by the Indians, and in 1830 published his *Narrative of the Captivity and Adventures of John Tanner During 30 Years' Residence Among the Indians*. The book became one of Longfellow's sources for HIAWATHA (1855).

Tar: A Midwest Childhood (1927),   a fictional autobiography by SHERWOOD ANDERSON. It is complementary to his *Story-Teller's Story* (1924).

Tar Baby, The.   A tar doll in JOEL CHANDLER HARRIS's Uncle Remus stories. The Tar Baby appears in *The Tar Baby Story and Other Rhymes by Uncle Remus* (1904), and elsewhere in Harris's prose tales, for example, "How Mr. Fox caught Mr. Rabbit" (in *Uncle Remus, His Songs and His Sayings*, 1880). Variants of the story have been found all over the world. The Tar Baby, a tar doll set up by the roadside, irritates Br'er Rabbit to such an extent that he strikes it until he himself is stuck tight.

Tarbell, Ida M[inerva] (1857–1944),   muckraking journalist, biographer, historian. Tarbell was born in Erie County, Pennsylvania, and was educated at Allegheny College. She worked on the *Chautauquan* magazine until 1891 and then spent three years in France. That stay led to a serialized biography of Napoleon in *McClure's Magazine* in 1895, which was followed by several popular works on Abraham Lincoln. Tarbell believed that her father, who had worked in the Pennsylvania oil fields, had been a victim of the Standard Oil Company. Her critical study *The History of the Standard Oil Company* (1902) embodied that point of view. She gained national celebrity as one of a number of journalists who were exposing corruption and waste in American society. As one of the so-called muckrakers, Tarbell helped launch the *American Magazine* in 1906 and wrote *The Tariff in Our Times* (1911) on behalf of the low-tariff reform position she held with the Democratic Party. Tarbell lectured widely and served on several presidential panels that addressed industrial and social issues through the early 1920s. A conservative feminist who opposed woman suffrage, she became less reformist later in life. She wrote favorable studies of such business leaders as Elbert H. Gary and Owen Young. Her autobiography, *All in the Day's Work* (1939), is a blend of anecdotes and comments on the events she had seen. Tarbell by the end was not as much of a reformer as she had seemed during the Progressive Era, but her later turn to the right did not diminish the contributions she had made to the muckraking tradition in American writing. A biographical study is Kathleen Brady, *Ida Tarbell: Portrait of a Muckraker* (1984).

LEWIS L. GOULD

Tarkington, [Newton] Booth (1869–1946),   novelist, playwright. Tarkington, born in Indianapolis, was educated at Purdue and at Princeton, where he founded the Triangle Club. In 1902–03 he was a member of the Indiana House of Representatives. The cynicism and dishonesty of the lawmakers affected him profoundly, and his first novel, THE GENTLEMAN FROM INDIANA (1899), deals with political corruption. His legislative experiences also figure in a later political novel, *In the Arena* (1905). There followed MONSIEUR BEAUCAIRE (1900), a romantic comedy, and *Cherry* (1903), an amusing satire on a college professor. The CONQUEST OF CANAAN (1905) depicts life in a small town.

Tarkington's greatest success was PENROD (1914), a story of a twelve-year-old boy who for a time rivaled Tom Sawyer and Peck's Bad Boy in the esteem of the American reading public. SEVENTEEN (1916) concerns Willie Baxter, a somewhat older Penrod, who is in the throes of his first love affair. Tarkington went on to other adult novels and achieved success as a local colorist, as in *Growth* (1927), a trilogy of urban life in the Middle West. He wrote more than forty novels altogether, won Pulitzer Prizes for THE MAGNIFICENT AMBERSONS (1918, filmed by Orson Welles in 1941) and for *Alice Adams* (1921). He also wrote twenty-five plays, eleven of them in collaboration with HARRY LEON WILSON.

The World Does Move (1928) is his autobiography. He left an uncompleted novel, *The Show-Piece* (1947). In 1949 appeared *Your Amiable Uncle*, letters to his nephews mostly about European travel and charmingly illustrated by Tarkington. In *Booth Tarkington: Gentleman from Indiana* (1955) James Woodress wrote a sympathetic account of Tarkington's contribution.

Tarzan.   A character in stories and novels by EDGAR RICE BURROUGHS. A hero of the jungle, Tarzan is the son of an English nobleman, abandoned in Africa in infancy. He is brought up by apes, becomes a man of prodigious strength and agility, learns the language of the apes, the elephants, and other jungle animals, and pursues an exciting series of incredible adventures. Tarzan first appeared in *Tarzan of the Apes* (1914); in the numerous sequels the hero marries, has a son and eventually a grandson. By the early 1940s, more than 25 million copies of the Tarzan books had been sold in fifty-six languages. In 1918, a film based on *Tarzan of the Apes*, with Elmo Lincoln as Tarzan, made a tremendous hit. In 1930, the same book became a sound film, and thereafter a long series of Tarzan movies appeared, the leading role passing among a succession of more than a dozen actors—the first was Johnny Weissmuller, a popular Olympic swimming champion. Since 1929 Tarzan has also been the central figure of a comic strip and radio and television broadcasts.

Tate, [John Orley] Allen (1899–1979),   poet, critic, novelist, teacher. A native of Clarke County, Kentucky, Tate studied at Vanderbilt University, where he—along with his teachers JOHN CROWE RANSOM and DONALD DAVIDSON—became a founding editor of *The Fugitive*, a little magazine of verse whose run from 1923–1925 signaled the literary renascence of the region. Tate participated with other so-called Fugitives in the Agrarian symposium *I'll Take My Stand* (1930) and later, with Herbert Agar, edited a sequel, *Who Owns America?* (1936).

In 1924 Tate married CAROLINE GORDON, who divorced him in 1959. They spent the 1920s and 1930s in New York City, where they shared a house with HART CRANE; in London, where Tate met T. S. ELIOT, whose poetry he had championed at Vanderbilt; in Paris, where he became friends with ERNEST HEMINGWAY and cemented friendships with Ford Madox Ford and JOHN PEALE BISHOP; and in Memphis, where he began at Southwestern a peripatetic career in teaching that saw him at Princeton from 1939 to 1942 and took him in 1951 to the University of Minnesota, from which he retired in 1968. Tate served as Southern editor for *Hound and Horn* (1932–34), consultant in poetry at the Library of Congress (1943–44), editor of the *Sewanee Review* (1944–45), and editor of belles-lettres for Henry Holt (1946–48). In 1950 Tate joined the Catholic Church, a move anticipated by his important poem "Seasons of the Soul" (1944). He received the Bollingen Prize in 1956. Tate spent his last years with his third wife and their young sons in Sewanee and Nashville, Tennessee.

The author of two biographies, *Stonewall Jackson: The Good Soldier* (1928) and *Jefferson Davis: His Rise and Fall* (1929), and of a distinguished novel of the Civil War, *The Fathers* (1938), Tate owes his renown to his poetry and criticism. These complement each other. A model of New Criticism, Tate's "Narcissus as Narcissus" explicates his own celebrated poem "Ode to the Confederate Dead." If his essays, as he confessed, "covertly" justify his own modernist verse, they are themselves remarkably varied in kind: his *Essays of Four Decades* (1969) includes reviews of his contemporaries, philosophical and sometimes polemical examinations of Southern culture, and incisive literary studies of writers with whom Tate felt an affinity: "Our Cousin, Mr. Poe" and "The Angelic Imagination" on EDGAR ALLAN POE, and "The Symbolic Imagination" on Dante.

Severe formality, a density of symbols, and allusions to classical and Christian myths characterize such eloquent, strenuously willed poems as "The Mediterranean," "Aeneas at Washington," "Sonnets at Christmas," "The Swimmers," and "The Buried Lake." Often more personal than they appear, Tate's poems—which have influenced ROBERT LOWELL and Geoffrey Hill—explore the predicament of modern man, estranged by science and abstraction from religious ritual and a tradition rooted in a place.

Collected Poems, 1919–1976 (1977) supersedes *The Swimmers and Other Selected Poems* (1971). Tate's work in prose includes *Memoirs and Opinions, 1926–1974* (1975), *The Poetry Reviews of Allen Tate, 1924–1944* (1983), and three volumes of letters: *The Literary Correspondence of Donald Davidson and Allen Tate* (1974), *The Republic of Letters in America: The Correspondence of John Peale Bishop and Allen Tate* (1981), and *The Lytle-Tate Letters* (1987). There is a literary biography by Radcliffe Squires (1971). Robert S. Dupree's *Allen Tate and the Augustinian Imagination* (1983) is a brilliant study of the poems. Thomas A. Underwood's *Allen Tate: Orphan of the South* (2001) treats the early life.

DAVID HAVIRD

Tate, James [Vincent] (1943–   ),   poet. Born in Kansas City, Tate was educated at the University of Missouri, Kansas State College (B.A., 1965), and the University of Iowa (M.F.A.). In 1967, he began a long career as a teaching poet at the University of Massachusetts. His first book, *The Lost Pilot*

(1967), won the praise of Robert Lowell, who noted its "estrangement, anger, and self-abasing humor," and Donald Justice, who observed its mixture of "despair" and "gaiety": qualities that have continued to mark his later work. Readers find bizarre and comic images clashing on a difficult and playful surface that frequently masks a substrata of peace and harmony. His *Selected Poems* (1992) won a Pulitzer Prize and *Company of Fletchers* (1994) a National Book Award. His many other verse titles include: *The Oblivion Ha-Ha* (1970), *Absences* (1972), *Viper Jazz* (1976), *Riven Doggeries* (1979), *Constant Defender* (1983), *Reckoner* (1986), *Shroud of Gnomes* (1997), and *Memoir of the Hawk* (2001). *The Route as Briefed* (1999) is a volume in the University of Michigan's Poets on Poetry series.

Taylor, [James] Bayard (1825–1878), journalist, lecturer, poet, translator, novelist, diplomat. As a boy in Kennett Square, Pennsylvania, Taylor was apprenticed to a printer, but left this work for a European walking tour. Some of his letters from Europe were printed in the New York *Tribune*, others in the *Saturday Evening Post*. They were published in book form as *Views Afoot; or, Europe Seen with Knapsack and Staff* (1846); the book was an immense success, the twentieth edition appearing in 1855. The *Tribune* sent Taylor to California to report on the 1849 gold rush, and these experiences were published as *Eldorado, or, Adventures in the Path of Empire* (1850). Taylor remained in journalism for the rest of his life, but held diplomatic posts in St. Petersburg and Berlin, served as historian on Commodore Perry's expedition to Japan, and professor of German literature at Cornell (1869–77).

In his Whittieresque *Home Pastorals* (1875) he dealt realistically with his own experience, but his verse mostly is hopelessly overromantic, as in *Poems of the Orient* (1855). His best-known poem is the BEDOUIN SONG. He wrote adroit parodies of *The Echo Club and Other Diversions* (1876). He also wrote several novels, with *The Story of Kennett* (1866) perhaps best. His competent translation of Goethe's *Faust* (1870–71) brought him academic recognition, as well as his appointment as minister to Germany (1878).

Taylor's works, in addition those already mentioned, include *Ximena* (1844); *Rhymes of Travel, Ballads, and Poems* (1849); *A Journey to Central Africa* (1854); *Hannah Thurston: A Story of American Life* (1863); *John Godfrey's Fortunes, Related by Himself: A Story of American Life* (1864); *The Picture of St. John* (1866); and *Studies in German Literature* (1879). Two collections were made in 1880: *The Dramatic Works of Bayard Taylor* and *The Poetical Works of Bayard Taylor*. Marie Hansen-Taylor and Horace E. Scudder wrote *Life and Letters of Bayard Taylor* (2 v. 1884). Richmond C. Beatty wrote *Bayard Taylor: Laureate of the Gilded Age* (1936). Richard Cary wrote *The Genteel Circle: Bayard Taylor and His New York Friends* (1952). John R. Schultz edited *The Unpublished Letters of Bayard Taylor in the Huntington Library* (1937).

Taylor, Edward (1642?–1729), Puritan minister, poet. Taylor, born in England and an ardent dissenter whose earliest poetry satirized "Popish" and Anglican worship, reputedly studied at Cambridge. He resisted the Act of Uniformity before his 1668 immigration to Boston, which is recounted in his *Diary* (1668–71, ed. by Francis Murphy, 1964). A roommate of SAMUEL SEWALL at Harvard, Taylor was graduated from Harvard and accepted the call to Westfield in 1671, where he formally established the town's first church, in 1679, and remained minister for fifty years until his death. In 1674, he married Elizabeth Fitch, who bore eight children, five dying in infancy, as he laments in "Upon Wedlock, & Death of Children"; his second wife, Ruth Wyllys, produced six children.

Taylor did not publish his writings, but his grandson, EZRA STILES, deposited some of the bound manuscripts in the Yale University library. The poems were discovered in 1937 and were edited by Thomas Johnson for *The Poetical Works of Edward Taylor* (1939). Numerous volumes of church records, sermons, and poems have been published since then. *Edward Taylor's Minor Poetry* (ed. Thomas Davis and Virginia Davis, 1981) collects the earliest religious satires, Harvard elegies and verse declamations, acrostics, love poems, occasional (1674–1683) and allegorical lyrics ("Huswifery"); the 1670–1700s metrical paraphrases of Psalms and Job; and his later elegies and 1720s valedictions anticipating death. Taylor defended the orthodox Calvinist theology and congregational polity against Northampton's SOLOMON STODDARD, who attempted to admit all believers to the Lord's Supper, a topic that preoccupies Taylor's sermons in *The Treatise Concerning the Lord's Supper* (1694, ed. by Norman Grabo, 1966) and collected prose writings, *Edward Taylor vs. Solomon Stoddard* (ed. by the Davises, 1981).

Celebrated today as colonial America's most prolific and inventive poet, Taylor is best known for *God's Determinations Touching His Elect* (c. 1680) and his *Preparatory Meditations* (1682–1725), published in *The Poems of Edward Taylor* (ed. by Donald Stanford, 1960). A thirty-five poem sequence, *God's Determination* recreates the providential history of Christ's warfare with Satan, reenacted in the "Elects Combat in their Conversion," as would-be saints seek church fellowship and eternal redemption. A frontier parson with a secret passion for confessional poetry, Taylor composed 217 meditations both as spiritual self-examinations of his readiness for God's grace and as disciplined preparations for administering the Lord's Supper. "Chiefly upon the Doctrine preached," as Taylor's subtitle indicates, these preparatory meditations correspond with sermon series, two of which have been recovered, *Edward Taylor's Christographia* (ed. by Grabo, 1966) and *Upon the Types of the Old Testament* (ed. by Charles Mignon, 1989).

Edward Taylor is considered a learned theologian and poet, an inheritor of the 17th-century English meditative tradition, yet a unique emergent American voice from the wilderness, remarkable for his imagistic versatility, affective religious passions, and colloquial vibrancy. The published body of his work also includes the 20,000-line *Metrical History of Christianity* (ed. by Stanford, 1962) and four-volume *Harmony of the Gospels* (ed. by the Davises, 1983). Major studies are John

Gatta, *Gracious Laughter* (1989); Norman Grabo, *Edward Taylor* (rev. ed. 1988); Karl Keller, *The Example of Edward Taylor* (1975); Karen Rowe, *Saint and Singer* (1986); and William Scheick, *The Will and the World* (1974).

KAREN E. ROWE

Taylor, Edward Thompson (1793–1871), clergyman. Taylor, born in England, went to sea as a orphaned boy of seven. He had no formal schooling, but was made a minister in the Methodist Church because of his fervor and eloquence. Preaching at the Seamen's Bethel in Boston, he was revered by sailors as "Father Taylor." Melville may have drawn on his sermons, which were heavily laced with metaphors of the sailor's life, for his characterization of Father Mapple in *Moby-Dick*. Richard Henry Dana refers to his fame among seafarers in *Two Years Before the Mast*. Harriet Martineau, Dickens, Emerson, and Whitman all wrote about him.

Taylor, Henry [Splawn] (1942–   ), poet. Born in Loudon County, Taylor grew up in rural Virginia and was educated at the University of Virginia (B.A., 1965) and Hollins College (M.A., 1966). In 1966 he began his academic career as a poet-teacher at Roanoke College and from the 1970s on has taught at American University in Washington, D.C. His first book, *The Horse Show at Midnight* (1966), contained parodies and other verse. In this, and in *An Afternoon of Pocket Billiards* (1975), which included the poems of the earlier *Breakings* (1971), he established a quiet, controlled, poetic voice, immersed in the pleasures of the country and of natural things and in the mastery of the traditional craft of poetry. His verse has earned him comparison with Robert Frost and placed him outside the mainstream of American poetic conventions since the 1960s, beside other formalist poets who have resisted the pull of free verse. The poems of *The Flying Change* (1985), with its title a term from horsemanship, present images of deer, a tractor, children, and cancer in a reminder of the traditional concern of poets for the passage of time, of continual change, and of the inevitability of loss. A more recent collection is *Understanding Fiction: Poems 1986–1996* (1996). *Brief Candles: 101 Clerihews* (2000) is a collection of light verse. *Compulsory Figures: Essays on Recent American Poets* appeared in 1992.

Taylor, John (1753–1824), statesman, agronomist. Taylor, born in Virginia, after two years at William and Mary and study for the law, was licensed to practice in 1774. He rose to major in the Continental Army, and lieutenant colonel in the Virginia militia. He was a member of the Virgina House of Delegates (1779–1782, 1796–1800) and served three Senate terms. An ardent believer in states rights and the independence of rural freeholders, he at first opposed the Constitution, but once convinced that the rights of individuals and states would be protected, supported it strongly. Much of his writing was devoted to championing Jefferson and attacking Hamiltonian federalism. His titles include *Definitions of Parties* (1794), *A Defense of the Measures of the Administration of Thomas Jefferson* (1804), *Inquiry into the Principles and Policy*

of the Government of the United States (1814), *Construction Construed and Constitutions Vindicated* (1820), *Tyranny Unmasked* (1822), and *New Views of the Constitution of the United States*. He also wrote *Arator . . . a Series of Agricultural Essays, Practical and Political* (1813). A collection of Taylor's *Letters* appears in the *John P. Branch Historical Papers of Randolph-Macon College* (Volume II, 1908).

Taylor, Peter [Hillsman] (1917–1994), short-story writer, novelist, playwright. Taylor was born in Tennessee to an illustrious family of statesmen and spent most of his life in the South. While attending school at Southwestern, Vanderbilt, Kenyon, and Louisiana State, he became a disciple of the poets and writers associated with the Southern literary renascence. Their agrarian philosophy had little impact on Taylor's subsequent fiction, but he was influenced by their preoccupation with poetic form. In 1943 he married the poet Eleanor Ross. His first collection of short stories, *A Long Fourth*, was published in 1948. Six more volumes were to follow as well as two novels—*A Woman of Means* (1950) and *A Summons to Memphis* (1986)—and several plays. In addition to being a prolific writer, Taylor was a lifelong teacher.

Peter Taylor had a distinguished writing career spanning more than four decades; however, he came to the attention of the general public as the recipient of the PEN/Faulkner Award for Fiction, the Pulitzer Prize, and the Ritz-Hemingway Award. Taylor believed that his preference for the short-story genre helped explain this delayed recognition: "Stories just don't get you the glory or the fame, or the readers either." Nevertheless, his fiction's frequent appearance in *The New Yorker* and other journals won him devoted followers. Because Taylor's work is devoid of linguistic pyrotechnics and controversial content, he has been labeled by some as an old-fashioned regionalist. Taylor would have been the last to deny his Southern roots, and the majority of his stories are set in Tennessee. Family, place, history, tradition, rootlessness, and dislocation form part of the Taylor canvas. Yet his most dominant hues are universal. The majority of the characters—normal, upwardly mobile, urban, middle-class professionals—though coming from small-town Southern backgrounds, face the same problems as any other citified population that must adjust to shifts in socioeconomic status, cope with geographical transplantation, and sustain troubled relationships shaped more by fundamental need than by environmental conditioning. Victimization and betrayal, a dominant motif in Taylor's finest stories, particularly define these relationships.

Whether his stories are cast in a "sort of broken line prose that looks like free verse," according to Taylor, or are written in his more typical digressional style, Taylor's central concern is that of narrative voice. With the appearance of his third collection, *Happy Families Are All Alike* (1959), the retrospective first-person voice, often an unreliable narrator, dominated his work, creating the ironic tension that characterizes his best fiction. Nowhere is this better demonstrated than in *In the Miro District and Other Stories* (1977), considered by many to be his most compelling and innovative work. In this collection and in many others, Peter Taylor clearly emerged as a man for all regions.

His other noteworthy volumes include *Miss Leonora When Last Seen and Fifteen Other Stories* (1963); *The Collected Stories of Peter Taylor* (1969); and *The Old Forest and Other Stories* (1985). Two critical books on Taylor are Albert J. Griffith's *Peter Taylor* (1970) and James Curry Robison's *The Short Stories of Peter Taylor* (1988). An annotated bibliography of commentary on Taylor appears in *Andrew Lytle, Walker Percy, Peter Taylor: A Reference Guide* by Victor A. Kramer, et al. (1983).

LINDA KANDEL KUEHL

Taylor, Robert Lewis (1912–1998), newspaperman, biographer, humorist. Taylor, born in Illinois, began as a newspaperman in St. Louis. From 1939 to 1948 he worked for *The New Yorker*, becoming one of its most adept writers of profiles. One collection of these profiles, *Doctor, Lawyer, Merchant, Chief* (1948), also includes four short stories and some war sketches. He wrote a number of biographies, among them *W. C. Fields: His Follies and Fortunes* (1949) and *Winston Churchill, An Informal Study in Greatness* (1958). His novels *Adrift in a Boneyard* (1947), *The Travels of Jamie McPheeters* (1958), and *A Journey to Matecumbe* (1961) are admired as examples of the modern use of picaresque technique.

Taylor, Samuel [Albert] (1913–), playwright, scriptwriter. Born in Chicago, Taylor attended the University of California, Berkeley, and served in the merchant marine during the early Depression, then wrote radio scripts for "The Aldrich Family" and other serial comedies. His fame rests largely on *Sabrina Fair*, a comedy of a rich man's love for his chauffeur's daughter that opened on Broadway in 1953. The play was filmed in 1954, with Humphrey Bogart and Audrey Hepburn, and again in 1995. Other plays include *The Happy Time* (1950), about a French-Canadian family in the 1920s; *The Pleasure of His Company* (1958), a comedy of manners; *No Strings* (1962), a musical written with RICHARD ROGERS, about an expatriate writer in Paris and his love for a black model; *Beekman Place* (1964); *Avanti!* (1968); *A Touch of Spring* (1975); *Flying Colors* (1985); and *Three by Three* (1988). Movie credits include work on Alfred Hitchcock's *Vertigo* (1958) and *Topaz* (1969).

Taylor, William (1821–1902), Methodist clergyman, evangelist. Taylor described his experiences during the gold rush in *Seven Years' Street Preaching in San Francisco* (1857) and *California Life Illustrated* (1858). *The Story of My Life* (1895) concerns his missionary work in other parts of the world.

Teach, Edward. See BLACKBEARD.

Teale, Edwin Way (1899–1980), teacher, editor, writer, naturalist. Teale, born in Illinois, taught public speaking for a while, became an editorial assistant to Dr. FRANK CRANE, from 1929 to 1941 worked for *Popular Science Monthly*, and in 1941 became a writer of popular books on nature and outdoor life. Among his books are *Grassroot Jungles* (1937, rev. 1944); *Boys' Book of Insects* (1939); *Byways to Adventure* (1942); *Dune Boy, The Early Years of a Naturalist* (1943); *Insect*

Life (1944); *The Lost Woods* (1945); *North with the Spring* (1951); *Circle of the Seasons* (1953); *The Wilderness World of John Muir* (1954); *Autumn Across America* (1956); and *Journey into Summer* (1960).

Teasdale, Sara (1884–1933), poet. Teasdale, born in St. Louis, was educated at home and in private schools. Although she traveled extensively and belonged to the literary group surrounding Harriet Monroe and POETRY magazine in Chicago—where she met JOHN HALL WHEELOCK and VACHEL LINDSAY—Teasdale continued to live at home until her marriage in 1914. Her first book, *Sonnets to Duse and Other Poems* (1907), was privately printed. *Helen of Troy and Other Poems* (1911) and *Rivers to the Sea* (1915) attracted wider attention. *Love Songs* (1917) went through five printings in a single year and won a special Pulitzer Prize. Her other titles are *Flame and Shadow* (1920), *Dark of the Moon* (1926), and *Strange Victory* (1933). *Collected Poems* (1937) was published after her death by suicide. Her anthologies for children are *Rainbow Gold* (1922) and *Stars Tonight* (1930).

Tecumseh (1768–1813), SHAWNEE chief, orator. Tecumseh took the position that the land was held in common by all Indians and no tribe could cede portions of it. To halt the westward movement of white settlement and rescind a 1795 treaty giving away more than half of what is now Ohio, he proposed a confederacy linking all the Indians of the Old Northwest, the South, and the eastern Mississippi Valley. He made recruiting trips to the tribes of the region, urging them to join in resisting the advance of settlement. In Tecumseh's absence, his twin brother Tenskwatawa, called "The Prophet," did battle with troops under WILLIAM HENRY HARRISON on Tippecanoe Creek in Indiana (November 7, 1811); the battle was indecisive, but Tecumseh knew that the unity he sought would be blighted by warfare. He gathered a large war party and marched to Fort Malden, where he joined the British forces in the War of 1812. Tecumseh was killed at the Battle of the Thames (October 5, 1813) by troops commanded by his old nemesis, Harrison. William Emmons treated Tecumseh in a pamphlet (1822) and a play, *Tecumseh, or the Battle of the Thames* (1836), and mentioned him in his epic poem *The Fredoniad* (1827). *Tecumseh, a Drama* (1886) by Charles Mair (1838–1927) was one of the first successful Canadian productions. Nonfiction about Tecumseh includes J. W. Oskison's *Tecumseh and His Times* (1938), Marion Campbell's *The Boyhood of Tecumseh* (1940), and Glenn Tucker's *Tecumseh, Vision of Glory* (1956). See SHAWNEE INDIANS.

Telling the Bees (1858, collected in *Home Ballads*, 1860), a poem by JOHN GREENLEAF WHITTIER. The title is derived from an old custom of telling the bees—that is, pinning a bit of black crape to the hives as a sign of mourning. A young man, coming to visit his beloved, sees the hired girl draping each hive "with a shred of black." He thinks his fiancée's grandfather has died, but then hears the hired girl singing to the bees: "Stay at home, pretty bees, fly not hence!/ Mistress Mary is dead and gone!"

Tell-Tale Heart, The (1843),   a story by EDGAR ALLAN POE. A homicidal maniac murders an old man and buries the dismembered body beneath the floor of the room in which he lives, replacing boards and removing bloodstains. The police come to make inquiries, and as they talk to the murderer he hears what he believes to be the beating of the dead man's heart. In a frenzy the murderer confesses his crime, thinking the police are mocking him in not hearing the beating of the heart. The story, one of Poe's best, has been called a forerunner of modern fictional treatments of the subconscious. It was contributed to the first issue of a magazine called THE PIONEER, edited by James Russell Lowell.

Tender Is the Night (1934),   a novel by F. SCOTT FITZGERALD.

Tennessee's Partner   (*Overland Monthly*, June 1869; in THE LUCK OF ROARING CAMP, 1870); a story by BRET HARTE. Tennessee runs off with his partner's wife but soon returns when she abandons him as well. When Tennessee is being tried for robbery, his partner silently strides into the courtroom and empties all his money on the table in payment for Tennessee's life. But Tennessee is hanged, and his partner dies a few months after burying him.

Tenney, Tabitha [Gilman] (1762–1837),   novelist, anthologist. Tenney's rearing was devout, bookish, and somewhat rural in her native New Hampshire. In 1788 she married Dr. Samuel Tenney, a surgeon in the Continental Army, and a congressman from 1800 to 1807. Her first book, *The Pleasing Instructor* (1799?), was an anthology of elevating selections from the poets and from classical authors. But she is chiefly known for her one novel, FEMALE QUIXOTISM: EXHIBITED IN THE ROMANTIC OPINIONS AND EXTRAVAGANT ADVENTURES OF DORCASINA SHELDON (1801). It is written in the picaresque tradition and pokes fun at popular sentimental novels.

Ten Nights in a Bar-Room and What I Saw There (1854),   a story by TIMOTHY SHAY ARTHUR. This melodramatic story held the attention of readers for more than twenty years and was a favorite with temperance lectures. It was dramatized in 1858 by William W. Pratt, and as a drama was more in demand than any other play except *Uncle Tom's Cabin*. It also led to passage of many temperance laws. During performances, when little Mary's plaintive song at the saloon door was sung, "Father, dear Father, come home with me now"—and she was accidentally killed by the saloonkeeper—there was rarely a dry eye in the house.

Tensas, Madison, M.D.,   pen name of Dr. Henry Clay Lewis (1825–1850). His humorous treatment of frontier life in Kentucky and Louisiana is called *Odd Leaves from the Life of a Louisiana Swamp Doctor* (1850).

Terhune, Albert Payson (1872–1942),   novelist. Terhune, born in New Jersey, was the son of Albert Payson Terhune, a clergyman, and MARY VIRGINIA TERHUNE (Marion Harland), a novelist. After his graduation from Columbia, Terhune traveled in Europe and the Far East, then returned to the United States and published *Syria From the Saddle* (1896). In 1900 he and his mother wrote the novel *Dr. Dale*. After he left

newspaper work, he devoted himself to writing and to raising collies. His kennels at Sunnybank, in Pompton, New Jersey, became widely known, and his pedigreed dogs were sold all over the world. After the success of *Lad: A Dog* (1919), he wrote almost exclusively of dogs, usually collies. There followed *Bruce* (1920); *Buff: A Collie* (1921); *Further Adventures of Lad* (1922); *His Dog* (1922); *Black Caesar's Clan* (1923); *The Heart of a Dog* (1925); *Treasure* (1926); *The Luck of the Laird* (1927); and *Lad of Sunnybank* (1928). His autobiography is *To the Best of My Memory* (1930).

Terhune, Mary Virginia [Hawes "Marion Harland"] (1830–1922),   novelist, home economist. Terhune, a native of Virginia, began to write at the age of nine; at fourteen, she was a regular contributor to Richmond newspapers. Two years later, under the name Marion Harland, she published the novel *Alone* (1854), the first of a long series of successes, among them *Sunnybank* (1866) and *A Gallant Fight* (1888). At the request of her publisher she produced *Common Sense in the Household* (1871), which was so successful that for many years she abandoned fiction for home economics. No Victorian kitchen was complete without her *National Cookbook* (1896). She wrote syndicated articles for newspapers and magazines on home management, edited the magazine *Babyhood*, and was for a time in charge of the children's department of *St. Nicholas*. *The Home of the Bible* (1895) was the result of a trip through the Holy Land with her son ALBERT PAYSON TERHUNE, who collaborated with her on the novel *Dr. Dale* (1900). She also wrote *Charlotte Brontë at Home* (1899), *Hannah More* (1900), *Everyday Etiquette* (1905), and *Marion Harland's Autobiography* (1910). She dictated her last novel, *The Carringtons of High Hall* (1919), when she was almost ninety and totally blind.

Terkel, Studs [Lewis] (1912–   ),   radio and television interviewer, commentator. Terkel turned his work for Chicago broadcasting stations into a valuable series of oral histories. They include: *Hard Times* (1970), on the Great Depression; *Working: People Talk About What They Do All Day* (1974); *American Dreams: Lost and Found* (1980); *The Good War: An Oral History of World War Two* (1984); *The Great Divide: Second Thoughts on the American Dream* (1988); *Race* (1982); *Coming of Age: The Story of Our Century by Those Who've Lived It* (1995); and *The Spectator: Talk About Movies and Plays by Those Who Made Them* (1999). *My American Century* (1997) is an anthology of selections from eight earlier books. Other titles include *Giants of Jazz* (1957); *Division Street: America* (1966); and *Amazing Grace* (1959), a play. *Talking to Myself: A Memoir of My Times* (1995) is autobiographical.

Territorial Enterprise.   A Nevada newspaper founded December 18, 1858, at Mormon Station. It was published in Carson City for a while and then, in 1860, settled down in Virginia City. Among those who contributed to it in early days were Mark Twain, Dan De Quille, and Joe Goodman. In 1952 Lucius Beebe became its publisher. He wrote *Comstock Commotion: The Story of the Territorial Enterprise* (1954).

Terry, Megan (1932–   ),   playwright. Terry began writing in her native Seattle. For the Off Broadway theaters of the 1960s, she wrote plays such as *Viet Rock* (1955), requiring the actors to change sex, age, or class and portray objects. *Approaching Simone* (1970) traces the life of Simone Weil. Most of her work after 1971 was written for the Omaha Magic Theater. Examples of these plays are *Hothouse* (1974), *Babes in the Bighouse* (1974), and *American Kings English for Queens* (1978).

Testut, Charles (1818?–1892),   physician, newspaperman, poet, novelist, biographer. Born in France, but a resident of New Orleans from an early age, Testut led a busy literary as well as medical life, writing many books and newspaper articles, and becoming a leader in the city's literary activities. Probably his most frequently consulted book is not his fiction or poetry but his *Portraits Littéraires de la Nouvelle-Orléans* (1850), sketches of fifty-two contemporary writers. He published two collections of poems, *Les Echos* (1849) and *Fleurs d' Eté* (1851). He wrote many novels, of which three received most attention: *Saint-Denis* (1845), *Calisto* (1849), and *Le Vieux Salomon* (1858, pub. 1877).

Thacher, James (1754–1844),   physician, historian. Thacher's *A Military Journal During the American Revolutionary War* (1823) is one of the best contemporary accounts of the Revolution. He was born on Cape Cod and after the war practiced and taught medicine in Plymouth, Massachusetts. His *The American Dispensatory* (1810) and *American Modern Practice* (1817) became standard medical texts, and his pioneer *American Medical Biography* (1828) is a valuable account of early American medicine and its practitioners. He also wrote *Essay on Demonology, Ghosts, and Apparitions* (1831).

Thanatopis,   a poem in blank verse by WILLIAM CULLEN BRYANT. This meditation on death reflects Bryant's reading of such English poets as Thomas Gray, Henry Kirke White, and Robert Southey, who are sometimes called the Graveyard School. Bryant, only seventeen when he wrote the first draft (1811), revised it both before and after its first publication (*North American Review*, September 1817). The most important change is the addition of the first and last stanzas, focusing on the personification of nature. The revised version appeared in Bryant's *Poems* (1821).

Thane, Elswyth [Mrs. William Beebe] (1900–1984), novelist. Thane, born in Iowa, published her first novel, *Riders of the Wind*, in 1925, and it was followed by many more. She is also the author of nonfiction works and several plays. Two summers' research in the British Museum (1928–29) resulted in a number of historical novels. Two of her plays were produced: *The Tudor Wench* (1934) and *Young Mr. Disraeli* (London 1935, New York 1937). Beginning with *Dawn's Early Light* (1943), she wrote seven historical novels that ended with *Homing* (1957), tracing an American family from 1774 to 1941, for the most part in Williamsburg, Virginia. *Washington's Lady* (1960) continued her novels of America. Her other titles include *Potomac Squire* (1963), *Mount Vernon Is Ours* (1966), *Mount Vernon: The Legacy* (1968), *Virginia Colony* (1969), and *The Fighting Quaker: Nathanael Greene* (1972).

England was an Island Once (1940), *The Bird Who Made Good* (1947), and *Reluctant Farmer* (1950) are memoirs, the latter two about her life in Vermont.

Thanet, Octave. See ALICE FRENCH.

Thatcher, Becky,   a character in MARK TWAIN's *Tom Sawyer*.

Thatcher, Benjamin Bussey (1809–1840),   lawyer, abolitionist, editor. Thatcher, born in Maine and an abolitionist favoring resettlement of freed slaves in Africa, clashed with WILLIAM LLOYD GARRISON over the Liberian colonization proposal and edited *Colonization and Journal of Freedom*. His edited version of the *Memoirs* of PHILLIS WHEATLEY (1834) was included in a collection of her verses. His interest in Native Americans is shown in *Indian Biography* (2 v. 1832) and *Indian Traits* (2 v. 1833). He also edited the anthology *Boston Book* (1837) and contributed poetry to periodicals.

Thaxter, Celia [Laighton] (1835–1894),   poet. Thaxter was born in Portsmouth, New Hampshire. She was educated by her father and a tutor—he later became a lawyer—whom she later married. Thaxter spent much of her life on Appledore Island off the New Hampshire coast, where her father ran a summer hotel. Her poetry and prose reflect her abiding interest in the sea. Her first published poem, "Land-Locked," appeared in the *Atlantic Monthly* in March 1861, and she began to contribute regularly to the magazine. *Poems* (1872) was followed by *Among the Isles of Shoals* (1873), a collection of sketches previously published in the *Atlantic*. She went on to write *Drift-Weed* (1879), *Poems for Children* (1884), *The Cruise of the Mystery* (1886), *Idyls and Pastorals* (1886), and *An Island Garden* (1894).

Thayer, Ernest Lawrence. See CASEY AT THE BAT.

Theatre Arts.   A magazine founded as a quarterly in 1916 and becoming a monthly in 1924. Sheldon Cheney was the first editor and was succeeded by Edith J.R. Isaacs and John D. MacArthur.

Theatre Guild.   The Theatre Guild, which asserted it existed "for drama, for beauty, for ideas," presented its first play, Jacinto Benevente's *Bonds of Interest*, on April 14, 1919. It opened the Guild Theater, April 13, 1925, with G.B. Shaw's *Caesar and Cleopatra*. Subscribers were the first to see new plays, after which the general public was welcome.

Their Eyes Were Watching God,   a 1937 novel by ZORA NEALE HURSTON, treats social problems from a racial and feminist perspective. Janie Crawford, raised by her grandmother in rural poverty, flees her old and dictatorial husband with Joe Starks, an ambitious man who becomes the mayor of Florida's first town run by African-Americans. When Joe dies, Janie falls in love with the younger Teacake and follows him to the truck farming area of the Florida swamps. In the floods following a hurricane, he is bitten by a rabid dog and, crazed, attacks Janie. She shoots him, is charged with murder, and finally exonerated. When she returns to the town she and Joe built, she tells her story to a friend.

Their Fathers' God (1931),   a novel by O.E. RÖLVAAG. This, the last volume of a trilogy including GIANTS IN THE EARTH (1927) and PEDER VICTORIOUS (1929), is set in the Dakotas during the late 19th century and treats the conflict between Peder Holm, a Norwegian farmer of Lutheran faith, and his Irish Catholic wife, Susie Doheny, over the rearing of their infant son Petie. It is a bleakly realistic study of antagonism.

Their Wedding Journey (1871),   a novel by WILLIAM DEAN HOWELLS. This first novel, describing Basil and Isabel March's honeymoon trip by boat and train to New York City, Rochester, Niagara Falls, and Canada, is largely autobiographical and treats with loving fidelity the people and scenes of everyday American life.

them,   a 1969 novel by JOYCE CAROL OATES, set in Detroit. In a foreword to the book, winner of the National Book Award, Oates recounts how the problems of Maureen, one of her night school students, overwhelmed her. The events, taking place between the Depression and the riots of 1967, focus on Maureen and her working-class family.

Theory of the Leisure Class, The (1899),   a treatise by THORSTEIN VEBLEN. Described in the subtitle as "An Economic Study of Institutions," this work was an early and exceedingly influential examination of the concept of status. Veblen held that the feudal subdivision of classes had continued into modern times, the lords employing themselves uselessly—as in killing animals—while the lower classes labored at industrial pursuits to support the whole of society. The leisure class, Veblen said, justifies itself solely by practicing "conspicuous leisure and conspicuous consumption"; he defined *waste* as any activity not contributing to material productivity. Veblen took a sternly economic view, refused to consider cultural values, though he himself was not an uncultivated man. Mainly his book was a passionate rejection of the economic system he saw flourishing in America during the late 19th century, before the great industrial baronies had been brought under control and before the day of meliorative labor legislation. *The Theory of the Leisure Class* was and is widely recognized as an American classic in economics and sociology. Veblen was attacked by various opponents, most famously by H. L. MENCKEN—no economist but an ardent believer in aristocratic values. In a piece called *Professor Veblen and the Cow*, first published in *Smart Set* (May 1919) and later included in *Prejudices I* (1919), Mencken ridiculed the theory of conspicuous waste.

theosophy.   The word means "divine wisdom," and its concepts go back to early idealistic philosophy, particularly to Plato, Plotinus, and the Christian gnostics. Theosophy also makes a deliberate attempt to include ideas from the world's great scriptures, especially of India, and of China and Egypt as well. It is mystical in tone, accepts the possibility of communication with another world, characterizes God as a causeless One Cause, and promulgates the doctrines of reincarnation. In modern times theosophy has been chiefly identified with the Theosophical Society, founded in 1875 by HELENA PETROVNA BLAVATSKY in New York City. Among Madame Blavatsky's chief followers were Annie Besant, president of the Society from 1907 to 1933, and William Butler Yeats. Blavatsky's *The Secret Doctrine* (2 v. 1888) is a fundamental document of the sect.

There Was a Child Went Forth   (1855, considerably revised in succeeding editions of *Leaves of Grass*), a poem by WALT WHITMAN. The poem, untitled in the first edition, was called *Poem of the Child That Went Forth, and Always Goes Forth, Forever and Forever* in 1860; the present title was given in 1871. It is obviously intended to be autobiographical, calls the months by the Quaker names with which Whitman was familiar in his childhood, and shows how he pantheistically identifies with the objects around him. There are sharply etched profiles of his mother and father.

Thériault, Yves (1915–1983),   novelist, short-story writer. Born in Quebec of Acadian and Montagnais Indian ancestry, Thériault wrote for radio, produced dime novels, and directed films. His early French Canadian fiction includes *Contes pour un homme seul* (1944), *La fille laide* (1950), *Le dompteur d'ours* (1951), and *Aaron* (1954). He first gained an international audience when *Agaguk* (1958) was translated into English in 1967. A love story of the Inuit of the Canadian north, it shows conflict with whites and the hostile environment. *Ashini* (1960, tr. 1972) deals with Montaignais Indians. *Si la bombe m'était contée* (1962) treats the atomic bomb. *Le ru d'Ikoué* (1963) describes the growth of an Algonquin boy. He produced six books in 1968, including *N'Tsuk* (tr. 1972). Among his later works are *Moi, Pierre Huneau* (1976), the life of a Gaspé fisherman; and story collections, *La femme Anna et autres contes* (1981) and *Valère et le grand canot* (1981). Thériault's output includes numerous novels, a thousand stories, a like number of radio and television scripts, plays, science fiction, and children's stories.

Theroux, Alexander [Louis] (1939–   ),   novelist. Born in Medford, Massachusetts, Theroux has taught at the University of Virginia, Harvard, and Phillips Academy. *Three Wogs* (1972) is a comic novel. *Darconville's Cat* (1981) is a flamboyant satire concerning Alaric Darconville, a young professor exiled in a Southern women's college. Rejected by a student, fired from his job, and unable to take revenge on his lover even with the advice of a reclusive expert on curses, Darconville leaves for Venice, where he dies. *An Adultery* (1987) deals with another amorous mismatch gone sour. *The Primary Colors* (1994) and *The Secondary Colors* (1996) include essays on colors in writers and artists. *The Lollipop Trollop* (1992) is a poetry collection.

Theroux, Paul (1941–   ),   novelist, short-story writer, travel writer. Brother of ALEXANDER THEROUX, Paul was educated at the University of Massachusetts (1963) and has traveled extensively, living in London and on Cape Cod. Among his more than two dozen books are accounts of long train trips from England to Japan, *The Great Railway Bazaar* (1975); train trips in Latin America, *The Old Patagonian Express* (1979); and train trips throughout China, *Riding the Iron Rooster* (1988). *The Kingdom by the Sea* (1983) recounts a hiking trip through Great Britain. *The Happy Isles of Oceania: Paddling the Pacific* (1992) recounts adventures in a kayak. *Fresh Air Fiend: Travel Writings* (2000) collects essays from a fifteen-year period. His fiction includes *Waldo* (1967); *Jungle Lovers* (1971); *Picture Palace* (1979); *World's End and Other Stories* (1980); *Mosquito Coast* (1982); *Half Moon Street* (1984), comprising two short novels; *Millroy the Magician*

(1994); *My Other Life* (1996); and *Kowloon Tong* (1997). *The Collected Stories* appeared in 1997. *Sir Vidia's Shadow: A Friendship Across Five Continents* (1998) is a sour portrayal of Theroux's relationship with his mentor, V. S. NAIPAUL, about whom he wrote an earlier study (1972).

These Thirteen (1931),   a collection of short stories by WILLIAM FAULKNER. This volume contains perhaps the most widely known of all of Faulkner's stories, "A Rose for Emily," which deals with an eccentric and aging Southern spinster. Miss Emily Grierson, after the death of her father, is courted by Homer Barron, a Yankee construction foreman, who mysteriously disappears. Many years later, after she has become a town legend, seldom seen but often speculated about, Emily dies and the townspeople find Barron's skeleton locked in an upstairs bedroom. The book also contains "Red Leaves" and "A Justice," two stories dealing with the Chickasaw Indians of Yoknapatawpha County in the days of early contact with the white man. The latter story is narrated to young Quentin Compson. See THE COMPSON FAMILY.

Thin Man, The (1934),   a novel by DASHIELL HAMMETT. Nick Charles, a former detective, solves a murder by discovering that the suspected killer, the thin man, had himself been slain many months earlier by the real murderer. A Pinkerton detective himself for eight years, Hammett originated in the novel a tough, hard-drinking hero who set a style in detective stories that has been widely imitated. The humor in the story was also a novelty. As a motion picture, *The Thin Man* (1936), with William Powell as Nick and Myrna Loy as his wife Nora, was very popular and had a series of sequels.

Thirteen Ways of Looking at a Blackbird,   a poem written by WALLACE STEVENS in 1917 and published in *Harmonium* (1923). As the title suggests, it comprises thirteen imagistic views.

This Side of Paradise (1920),   a novel by F. SCOTT FITZGERALD. Amory Blaine, a wealthy and snobbish young man from the Midwest, attends Princeton and acquires a refined sense of the proper social values. A series of flirtations with some predatory young women culminates in a genuine but ill-fated love for Rosaline Connage, who rejects Amory to marry a wealthier young man.

Thistlewood, Thomas (1721–1786),   plantation owner, diarist. Born in England, Thistlewood arrived in Jamaica in 1750 and lived there for the rest of his life, first as an overseer and later as a plantation owner. The thirty-odd volumes of his diaries, recording in minute detail the daily life of a plantation society, including relationships between masters and slaves, remained unpublished until the end of the 20th century. Douglas Hall edited a selection, *In Miserable Slavery: Thomas Thistlewood in Jamaica, 1750–86* (1990).

Thomas, A[lbert] E[llsworth] (1872–1947),   newspaperman, playwright. From 1895 to 1909 Thomas, who was born in Massachusetts, worked on newspapers in New York, including the *Times*, the *Sun*, the *Evening Post*, and the *Tribune*. But his deep interest was in the theater, and he wrote some lively plays, including *Thirty Days*, with Clayton Hamil-

ton (1910); *Her Husband's Wife* (1910); *What the Doctor Ordered* (1911); *The French Doll* (1922); *Our Nell*, with BRIAN HOOKER (1922); *White Magic* (1926); *The Big Pond*, with GEORGE MIDDLETON (1928); *Her Friend the King*, with Harrison Rhodes (1929); *No More Ladies* (1934); and *Merely Murder* (1937).

Thomas, Audrey (1935–   ),   novelist, short-story writer. Born in Binghamton, New York, and educated at Smith College, St. Andrews (Scotland), and the University of British Columbia, Thomas has spent most of her life in Canada since immigrating in 1959. Her first novel, *Songs My Mother Taught Me* (1973), deals with upstate New York, but her later fiction is set in Africa and Canada. *Ten Green Bottles* (1967), a story collection, and *Mrs. Blood* (1970), a novel, explore the author's experience as a hospital patient in Ghana, where Thomas lived from 1964 to 1966. *Coming Down from Wa* (1995) is a novel set in Ghana. *Munchmayer* and *Prospero on the Island* (1971) are two related novellas about writers and creativity. *Blown Figures* (1974) uses a collage style of narration. Her other titles are *Ladies and Escorts* (1977), *Latakia* (1979), *Real Mothers* (1981), and *Two in the Bush and Other Stories* (1981). *Goodbye Harold, Good Luck* (1986) and *The Wild Blue Yonder* (1990) are later story collections. Mothers and daughters from the core of the novels *Intertidal Life* (1984) and *Graven Images* (1993).

Thomas, Augustus (1857–1934),   actor, playwright. Thomas, born in St. Louis, was largely self-educated and wrote over sixty plays. His first two plays, *Alone* (1875) and *Editha's Burglar*, adapted from FRANCES HODGSON BURNETT, were produced by amateur theatrical clubs. He wrote and drew cartoons for the St. Louis *Post-Dispatch* and served as agent for an actress and a mind reader, before going to New York to expand his Burnett adaptation into the four-act *The Burglar* (1889), which ran for ten years. Among his other plays are *Alabama* (1891), *In Mizzoura* (1893), *Arizona* (1899), *The Witching Hour* (1907), *The Harvest Moon* (1909), *As a Man Thinks* (1911), *Rio Grande* (1916), *The Copperhead* (1918), and *Palmy Days* (1920). *The Print of My Remembrance* (1922) is an autobiography illustrated by the author's sketches.

Thomas, [Martha] Carey (1857–1935),   teacher, administrator, crusader. Thomas was graduated from Cornell (1877) in a day when women's higher education was frowned upon. She later studied at Johns Hopkins and abroad. All through her life she fought for women's rights, especially suffrage and higher education. She helped organize Bryn Mawr College (1884), became dean and professor of English there (1884–94), and then its president (1894–1922). Among her books are *The Higher Education of Women* (1900), *Should the Higher Education of Women Differ from That of Men?* (1901), and *The College* (1905).

Thomas, Edith Matilda (1854–1925),   poet. Born in Ohio, Thomas attended normal school, studied classics, and started to write poetry that reflected classical influences. In New York City she met HELEN HUNT JACKSON, who helped place her poems in leading magazines and newspapers. Among her books are *A New Year's Masque and Other Poems* (1885), *The*

Round Year (1886), *Lyrics and Sonnets* (1887), *The Dancers, and Other Legends and Lyrics* (1903), and *The Flower from the Ashes* (1915).

Thomas, Frederick William (1806–1866), novelist, lawyer, editor. Born in Rhode Island, Thomas lived in several regions and practiced various professions, as revealed in his fiction. This work includes *Clinton Bradshaw, or The Adventures of a Lawyer* (2 v. 1835), *East and West* (1836), *Howard Pinckney* (1840), and *John Randolph of Roanoke* (1853). He wrote a long poem, *The Emigrant* (1833), and a collection of essays, *Sketches of Character, and Tales Founded on Fact* (1849). Thomas is remembered as a close friend of EDGAR ALLEN POE.

Thomas, Isaiah (1749–1831), printer. Thomas, born in Boston, served a printing apprenticeship and then founded, with Zachariah Fowle, the *Massachusetts Spy* (1770), a patriotic paper that was still appearing as late as 1904. He fought at Lexington and Concord and later did printing work for the new government. After the war he became the leading printer in the country. His retirement gave him time to write *The History of Printing in America* (1810) and to found the American Antiquarian Society. Benjamin T. Hill edited *The Diary of Isaiah Thomas, 1805–1828* (1909) for the Society. Annie R. Marble wrote a biography, *From 'Prentice to Patron* (1935), and Clifford K. Shipton wrote *Isaiah Thomas: Printer, Patriot, and Philanthropist* (1948). See also CHAPBOOKS.

Thomas, Lowell [Jackson] (1892–1981), journalist, travel writer, lecturer, news commentator. Thomas worked as a gold miner, cook, reporter, professor of oratory, English instructor, historian, war correspondent, lecturer, magazine editor, and radio, television, and motion-picture news commentator. His many books of travel, adventure, and biography include *With Lawrence in Arabia* (1924), *The First World Flight* (1925), *Raiders of the Deep* (1928), *Out of This World* (1950), *History As You Heard It* (1957), *The Vital Spark* (1959), and *Sir Hubert Wilkins: His World of Adventure* (1961). He also made several travel films in the Far East. He is best known, however, for his news broadcasts.

Thomas, Norman [Mattoon] (1884–1968), clergyman, editor, writer. Thomas was educated at Princeton and was ordained as a Presbyterian minister. He founded *World Tomorrow* (1918), which he edited until 1921, was assistant editor of THE NATION (1921–22), and directed the League for Industrial Democracy (1922). Eventually, he resigned his ministerial duties to devote his time to writing and speaking for social reform and pacifism. As a Socialist Party candidate he ran unsuccessfully for many offices: governor of New York (1924), mayor of New York City (1925, 1929), congressman (1930), and president (1928–1948). His works include *The Challenge of War* (1925), *What Is Industrial Democracy?* (1927), *Socialism of Our Time* (1929), *The Conscientious Democracy* (1930), *The Choice Before Us* (1934), *War—No Profit, No Glory, No Need* (1935), *What Is Our Destiny?* (1944), *Appeal to the Nations* (1947), *A Socialist's Faith* (1951), *The Test of Freedom* (1954), *Prerequisites for Peace* (1959), and *The Great Dissenters* (1961).

Thomas, Robert Bailey. See THE OLD FARMER'S ALMANAC.

Thomason, John W[illiam], Jr. (1893–1944), soldier, author, artist. A native of Texas, Thomason had a career as an army officer and a literary career, and they were inextricably interwoven. He wrote *Fix Bayonets* (1926), a vivid first novel of fighting men in action during World War I, made even more graphic by his own illustrations. His other writings include *Red Pants and Other Stories* (1927) and *Jeb Stuart* (1930).

Thomes, William Henry (1824–1895), adventurer, novelist. Thomes lived at his boyhood home in Maine until he went to sea at age eighteen. He left his ship in California, where he took part in the fur trade. His adventures are recounted in *On Land and Sea* (1883) and *Lewey and I* (1884). After travels to the gold fields of California, the Pacific Islands, Australia, China, and Victoria, he returned to Boston in 1855, where he published and wrote for *The American Union*. Among his other books are *The Gold Hunters' Adventures, or, Life in Australia* (1864) and its sequel, *The Bushrangers* (1866), *The Whaleman's Adventures* (1872), *A Slaver's Adventures on Land and Sea* (1872), *Life in the East Indies* (1873), *Running the Blockade* (1875), and *The Ocean Rovers* (1896).

Thompson, Benjamin [Count Rumford] (1733–1814), scientist, public official. Born in Woburn, Massachusetts, Thompson fought with the Loyalists during the Revolution and fled to England, where he served in the Colonial Office; he was knighted after the war. In 1783 he joined the court of the Elector of Bavaria, where he filled several posts and was made a count of the Holy Roman Empire. Thompson chose the name Count Rumford after a region of New Hampshire. Back in England in 1795, he became a founder of the Royal Institution and gave money to award prizes for discoveries in light and heat to both the Royal Society and the American Academy of Arts and Sciences. His will provided for a Rumford professorship in science at Harvard. During this period he published his *Essays, Political, Economical and Philosophical* (4 v. 1796–1802).

He was among the first to demonstrate that heat was motion, and he experimented in military applications of science and moisture absorption. After 1802 he lived in France, where he married his second wife, the widow of French chemist Antoine Lavoisier. *The Complete Works of Count Rumford* were published (1870) by the American Academy of Arts and Sciences. His *Kleine Schriften* appeared in 1797. Among his other publications are *Proposals for Forming a Public Institution* (1799), *Philosophical Papers* (1802), and *On the Excellent Qualities of Coffee* (1812).

Thompson, Daniel Pierce (1795–1868), lawyer, historian, novelist. Thompson, born in Massachusetts and reared in frontier Vermont, was educated at Middlebury College. He practiced law, served as a probate judge, and compiled the *Laws of Vermont* (1834). *The Adventures of Timothy Peacock, Esquire* (1835) is a satire on the Masonic movement. From 1849 until the end of the Civil War, he edited the antislavery

Green Mountain Freeman. A founder of the Vermont Historical Society, Thompson is best known for his novels, patterned after those of Scott and Cooper and using Vermont history. *The Green Mountain Boys* (1839) was very popular, and *Locke Amsden; or, the Schoolmaster* (1847) details early 19th-century frontier life. His other works include *Lucy Hosmer, or, The Guardian and the Ghost* (1848); *The Rangers, or, the Tory's Daughter* (1851); *Gaut Gurley, or, the Trappers of Umbabog* (1857); and *The Doomed Chief* (1860). *The Shaker Lovers and Other Tales* (1847) and *Centeola and Other Tales* (1864) are collections. He also wrote *History of Vermont and the Northern Campaign of 1777* (1851) and *History of the Town of Montpelier* (1860). A novel, *The Honest Lawyer*, was left incomplete at his death.

Thompson, David (1770–1857), trader, explorer. Thompson came to Canada from England as an apprentice to the Hudson's Bay Company and spent the rest of his life in Canada. A trader and explorer in western Canada, Thompson kept careful journals of his various trips and made a map of the Canadian West. Because of his skill as a surveyor he was head of the British commission that fixed and marked the United States–Canadian boundary line (1816–26). Part of his journals was published as *David Thompson's Narrative of His Explorations in Western America* (1916).

Thompson, Denman (1833–1911), actor, playwright. Thompson was born in Pennsylvania. As a boy, he worked in a circus in Boston and then acted in the Royal Lyceum Company of Toronto. He turned to playwriting in 1875. His first attempt, written with George W. Ryer, was a two-scene character sketch of a Yankee farmer in which he acted the leading part. This was an immediate success at its premiere, in Pittsburgh. Thompson expanded it into a full-length play entitled *Joshua Whitcomb.* After two successful seasons in New York, Thompson wrote *The Old Homestead* (1886), still the same play but now grown to four acts. It proved so popular that most of Thompson's remaining life was devoted to playing it.

Thompson, Dorothy (1894–1961), journalist. Thompson, born in Lancaster, New York, became foreign correspondent in 1920 for the Philadelphia *Public Ledger* and the New York *Evening Post.* She remained in Vienna and Berlin until 1928. Later she started a column in the New York *Herald Tribune,* which in time was syndicated in 200 other papers. She also gave a weekly news program on the radio. From 1928 until 1942 she was married to SINCLAIR LEWIS. Among her books are *The New Russia* (1928), *I Saw Hitler* (1932), *Refugees* (1938), *Political Guide* (1938), *Let the Record Speak* (1939), *Listen, Hans* (1942), and *The Courage to Be Happy* (1957). A biographical study is Peter Kurth's *American Cassandra* (1990).

Thompson, Hunter S[tockton] (1939–), journalist. Born in Louisville, Kentucky, Thompson earned fame for his extension of NEW JOURNALISM into "Gonzo Journalism," outrageously subjective commentary on and involvement in the bizarre and crazy events of his time: "When the going gets weird, the Weird turn pro." In the late 1950s, after a teenage

stint in the Air Force, he moved to New York to become a writer, began and abandoned a novel, worked as a correspondent for the *National Observer,* and then spent a year with the motorcycle gang profiled in his *Hell's Angels: A Strange and Terrible Saga* (1966). *Fear and Loathing in Los Vegas: A Savage Journey to the Heart of the American Dream* (1971) solidified his reputation and remains his most celebrated book; a chronicle of the zany, drug-laden adventures of a sports journalist, Raoul Duke (pseudonym for Thompson) and Dr. Gonzo, a Samoan attorney modeled on OSCAR ZETA ACOSTA, it provided a central reference point for Gonzo Journalism, and led to the comic strip character Uncle Duke, who began his long life in Gary Trudeau's *Doonesbury* in 1974. It was followed by *Fear and Loathing: On the Campaign Trail '72* (1973), *The Great Shark Hunt: Strange Tales from a Strange Time* (1979), *Generation of Swine: Tales of Shame and Degradation in the '80s* (1988), *Songs of the Doomed: More Notes on the Death of the American Dream* (1990); *Better than Sex: Confessions of a Political Junkie* (1994), and *The Rum Diary: The Long Lost Novel* (1998). Two volumes of letters, edited by Douglas Brinkley, are in print: *The Proud Highway: Saga of a Desperate Southern Gentleman, 1955–1967* (1988) and *Fear and Loathing in America: The Brutal Odyssey of an Outlaw Journalist, 1968–1976* (2000). *Screwjack and Other Stories*, privately printed earlier, appeared in public in 2000.

Thompson, John R[euben] (1823–1873), editor, poet. Thompson, a native of Richmond, after graduating from the University of Virginia, practiced law for two years until his father purchased for him THE SOUTHERN LITERARY MESSENGER (1847), the foremost literary organ of the South, which EDGAR ALLAN POE had edited a decade earlier. As editor of the *Messenger,* Thompson published the writings of such eminent Southern authors as John Esten Cooke, Paul Hamilton Hayne, William Gilmore Simms, John Pendleton Kennedy, and Henry Timrod, and he encouraged many young writers. Later he was appointed literary editor of WILLIAM CULLEN BRYANT's New York *Evening Post.* Thompson's own poetry was popular in his day, especially his intensely patriotic war poems. In 1920, John S. Patton edited his *Poems*, with a memoir.

Thompson, [James] Maurice (1844–1901), poet, novelist, editor. The son of a Baptist minister who frequently moved from one small town to another, Thompson was born in Indiana and was educated by his mother. He enlisted in the Confederate Army at seventeen, served until the end of the war, and then took up civil engineering. He opened a law office in Crawfordsville, Indiana, and in his spare time wrote poetry and prose that was published in Southern magazines for some years before it was recognized in other parts of the country. *Hoosier Mosaics* (1875), a volume of sketches in dialect, was followed by a number of children's books and nature studies. His best-known work, ALICE OF OLD VINCENNES, appeared in 1900. A historical novel based on Clark's 1779 expedition, it became a best seller. From 1889 until his death he was literary editor of the *Independent.*

Thompson, Mortimer Neal. See MORTIMER NEAL THOMSON.

Thompson, Vance [Charles] (1863–1925), biographer, editor, poet, essayist, playwright, critic. Thompson is best remembered as the editor of the magazine M'LLE NEW YORK. He and JAMES HUNEKER, his fellow editor, introduced to American readers works written by many contemporary European authors. Thompson wrote several books, among them *French Portraits* (1900), *The Life and Letters of Ethelbert Nevin* (1913), *The Night Watchman and Other Poems* (1914), *Woman* (1917), *Take It from Me* (1919), *Strindberg and His Plays* (1921), and *Louisa* (1924).

Thompson, William Tappan (1812–1882), humorist, editor. Born in Ohio, Thompson worked as a printer's devil in Philadelphia, served as legal assistant to the secretary of the territory of Florida, and helped AUGUSTUS BALDWIN LONGSTREET on his newspaper in Augusta, Georgia. He edited several weekly literary journals and newspapers of his own (1838–82). It was in the last few issues of *Family Companion and Ladies' Mirror* (1843) and in his next weekly, *The Southern Miscellany* (1843–45), that his humorous letters of "Major Jones," one of the earliest representations of the Georgia cracker, appeared. The homely and amusing misadventures of this fictional farmer were collected in *Major Jones's Courtship* (1843), a book popular in both the North and the South. *Major Jones's Chronicles of Pineville* (1845) and *Major Jones's Sketches of Travel* (1848) continued the series. Thompson defended the institution of slavery in *The Slaveholder Abroad* (1860).

Thompson, Zadock (1796–1856), historian, naturalist. A native of Vermont, who worked his way through the University of Vermont by compiling almanacs, he became a tutor there (1825–33) and later taught for a time in two Canadian schools. His *History of the State of Vermont* (1833) was followed by *Geography and History of Lower Canada* (1835). Thompson's enduring work is the *History of Vermont, Natural, Civil, and Statistical* (1842), still useful. He became professor of chemistry and natural history at the University of Vermont and official Vermont naturalist.

Thomson, E[dward] W[illiam] (1849–1924), soldier, surveyor, newspaperman, editor, writer. Thomson was born near Toronto, entered business in Philadelphia, fought in the Union Army, practiced surveying in Canada, and worked for the Toronto *Globe*. For twelve years he was associate editor of the YOUTH'S COMPANION and in 1903 became Canadian correspondent of the Boston *Transcript*. Throughout his career he wrote short stories and poems. Among his books are *Old Man Savarin and Other Stories* (1895), *Smoky Days* (1901), *Between Earth and Sky* (verses, 1897), and *The Many-Mansioned House and Other Poems* (1909).

Thomson [or Thompson], Mortimer Neal ["Q. K. Philander Doesticks"] (1831–1875), humorist, newspaperman, editor. On the New York *Tribune* he did some serious work as a correspondent, reporting a slave auction in Savannah—his account became a tract translated into several languages—and serving at the front during the war. In 1854 he

began to use his pen name "Q.K.," standing for Queer Kritter. He wrote parodies on Longfellow, Scott, and others. In New York City, he edited magazines for several years. He wrote *Doesticks What He Says* (1855), comic sketches of New York society; *Plu-ri-bus-tah*, a parody of *Hiawatha* (1856); *Nothing to Say: A Slight Slap at Mobocratic Snobbery* (1857); *The History and Records of the Elephant Club* (1856); *The Witches of N.Y.* (1859); and *Lady of the Lake*, a parody of Scott (1860).

Thon, Melanie Rae (1957–), novelist, short-story writer. Born in Kalispell, Montana, Thon was educated at the University of Michigan (B.A., 1982) and Boston University (M.A., 1982). She has taught at Harvard, Syracuse, Ohio State, Utah, and other colleges while writing novels and stories about troubled people in extreme circumstances. In *Iona Moon* (1993), a novel, she depicts the anguish of a teen-age dropout whose mother dies of cancer and whose affair with a one-legged married man leads to her near starvation. The story "Xmas, Jamaica Plain," collected in *First, Body* (1996), begins "I'm your worst fear" and narrates a chilling tale of teenage homelessness, addiction, and housebreaking that stops just short of the abduction of a baby. *Girls in the Grass* (1993) is an earlier story collection; *Meteors in August* (1990) a first novel. A second novel, *Sweet Hearts* (2001), follows siblings Flint and Cecile to the Crow Reservation in Montana, where Flint's violent act puts the pair in jeopardy.

Thoreau, Henry David (1817–1862), essayist, travel and natural history writer, social critic. David Henry Thoreau—he would change the order of his first and middle names after college—was born in Concord, Massachusetts, the only one of the Transcendentalist writers who was a native to the village that became synonymous with their movement. Except for a few years spent in nearby Chelmsford and Boston during his early childhood and an unhappy six months spent in New York City in 1843, Thoreau lived his entire life in Concord. His family were shopkeepers and later successfully operated a small business manufacturing pencils and selling graphite for electroplating. Thoreau helped in the business from time to time, making numerous improvements in the machinery, but he regarded this work as a hindrance to his proper pursuits of writing and nature study. Choosing not to devote himself to the business, which might have made him prosperous, and thereby declining to participate in the burgeoning commercial enterprise of his age, was perhaps the single most characteristic gesture of Thoreau's life.

The family business was still quite modest in 1833, and it required considerable sacrifice to send him to Harvard. He had been an indifferent preparatory student at the Concord Academy, but he did well enough at Harvard—he stood as high as sixth in his class before illness caused him to lose some ground—to earn a place in commencement exercises in 1837. Like his classmates, Thoreau concentrated in the Greek and Latin curriculum that had been in place for generations and, despite his dislike of the rigidity of this system, developed a lifelong veneration of the classical writers, especially Homer, most notably reflected in the "Reading" chapter of *Walden*.

But Thoreau's life at Harvard was not all Greek and Latin recitation, for he was also influenced by the early stirrings of TRANSCENDENTALISM, especially EMERSON's seminal manifesto of the movement, NATURE (1836). Emerson also chanced to give the commencement speech at Thoreau's graduation, an address on THE AMERICAN SCHOLAR that outlined a hopeful future for the would-be man of letters in which a life of thought influenced by Nature, by "the mind of the past" (books), and by action would contribute to the gradual emancipation of American letters from the dominance of European models.

Especially significant among Emerson's predictions about American literature was his suggestion that familiar and indigenous things and events would constitute its material. In his devotion to the woods and streams of Concord, to New England natural history, to early European American and Native American history, Thoreau was to fashion a literary career that fulfilled, however idiosyncratically, Emerson's prophecy. As a recent graduate in 1837, however, he still had fairly conventional literary aspirations that took several years to outgrow. At first he taught school, briefly for the town of Concord and later, more successfully, with his older brother John from 1838 to 1841 as masters of the Concord Academy. Meanwhile, he launched a journal—probably at Emerson's suggestion—and began to submit poetry and essays to the Transcendentalists' short-lived (1840–1844) magazine, THE DIAL. These pieces chiefly reflected his college training in languages and literature, and his efforts to imitate his mentor Emerson in the hortatory essay. Necessarily derivative, they met with scant approval, even from the friendly editors of *The Dial*, MARGARET FULLER and Emerson, who frequently returned them for revision or even rejected them. Even less successful was his attempt in 1843 to break into the New York literary world by getting a job as tutor to one of Emerson's nephews on Staten Island, New York. He tried to write and sell essays to magazines, but found few willing to publish and fewer still willing to pay. By the end of the year he was back in Concord for good.

Thoreau also began to offer his services as a lecturer during the mid-1840s, and over the course of his career nearly all of his published works would begin as lectures. The New England lyceum circuit was one of the few paying outlets for aspiring writers, but like his attempts to write for periodicals and for basically the same reason Thoreau's lecturing met with limited success—he was unwilling to tailor his work to the popular taste. At various times he hoped to establish, like Emerson, courses of lectures in some of the large cities, but he generally had to content himself with the occasional performance in a village lyceum.

During the period of these setbacks to his literary aspirations, however, Thoreau was also beginning to find his true voice and metier as a writer. In 1842, Emerson commissioned him to review a recently published survey of the flora and fauna of Massachusetts for *The Dial*, recognizing that his protegé's knowledge of natural history and gifts as an observer of nature could be productively joined to his ambitions as a

writer. The result was "Natural History of Massachusetts," a rudimentary venture in a genre in which Thoreau was eventually to achieve distinction. He followed this with "A Walk to Wachusett" (1842) and "A Winter Walk" (1843), essays in which he began to develop the framework and structural device of the journey as emblematic of personal quest, and the close examination and careful description of the minute phenomena of nature that would be hallmarks of his mature work.

The Thoreau brothers' school closed in 1841 when John's health began to decline—he died in 1842. It was a loss that affected Thoreau deeply for the rest of his life. Until he took up surveying in 1849 Thoreau had no regular employment, supporting himself by tutoring, working in the family business, doing various types of manual labor, and doing two stints as live-in handyman at Emerson's house. Soon after John's death, Henry David began to plan his first book, which would celebrate his brother's memory through the retelling of a two-week boating trip they had taken on the Concord and Merrimack rivers in 1839. In part to reduce his expenses and thereby gain sufficient leisure to write this book, Thoreau moved on July 4, 1845, to a small cabin he built himself on the shores of nearby Walden Pond. He lived there for just over two years, returning to Concord village in the fall of 1847.

Beyond practical necessity, other factors helped generate this experiment in living deliberately. The 1840s were a decade swept by reform movements, and many of the movements sought to promote social change through the example of alternative modes of life in communities like the Transcendentalists' own BROOK FARM at nearby West Roxbury, Massachusetts. Thoreau declined to participate in this community, believing that all reform must begin with the individual, but he was nonetheless sensitive to the issues such experiments addressed, and his life at Walden Pond may be regarded as a kind of Transcendental community of one, based on the Emersonian virtue of self-reliance and the premise that one's life, through nature, could be actualized at a higher level than that sanctioned by conventional society. The same decade saw the first great wave of westward migration, culminating in the gold rush to California in 1849. Thoreau characteristically took pleasure in setting himself against this great tide by pioneering in his neighborhood woods and proclaiming, in the book that reported his experiment, that he had "travelled a good deal in Concord."

During his first year at the Pond, as he finished his cabin and raised his crop of beans, Thoreau worked on his first book and filled his journal with accounts of his experiences and observations at Walden. Thus, a second book was taking shape while the tribute to his brother was being written. By the time he left the cabin in 1847, Thoreau had completed a version of the first, entitled *A Week on the Concord and Merrimack Rivers*, as well as a first draft of his masterpiece, *Walden*.

The most notable event of his second summer at the Pond was his brief incarceration in the Concord jail for refusing to pay his poll tax as a protest against the Mexican War, widely regarded by abolitionists such as himself both as unjust and as a pretext for extending slavery. His protest and night in jail had little effect at the time, but it generated an essay, "Resistance to Civil Government" (1849), which under the title CIVIL DISOBEDIENCE would become widely known in the 20th century as a provocative and impassioned assertion of the rights of minorities and the claims of individual conscience over governmental authority. It also contained the germ of a theory of nonviolent resistance to unjust laws that would be developed into a powerful tool for social change by such charismatic leaders as Mahatma Gandhi and MARTIN LUTHER KING, JR.

After a number of rejections, Thoreau managed in 1848 to find a publisher for *A Week on the Concord and Merrimack Rivers*, and it was published in the next year. Although it received some praise from reviewers, in four years fewer than 300 copies were sold from an edition of one thousand. Thoreau was forced as a consequence to defer his hopes of making a modest living from his writing and also to postpone publication of his second book, *Walden*, for a number of years. *A Week* is a thoughtful but reticent book that relies on a discerning reader to penetrate its implicitness (Thoreau's brother John, for example, to whom it is an extended elegy, is never mentioned by name). Its intricate patterns of imagery, alternation of narrative with reflective essays on a variety of subjects (many condensed from his earlier *Dial* essays), and critique of Christianity virtually ensured its unpopularity in its own time, especially among a public accustomed to travel books based on adventures in the South Seas, Africa, and other exotic regions. However, its standing among American travel books and with critics has gradually risen along with Thoreau's overall reputation in the 20th century.

Although Thoreau is best known for celebrating his native environs and for his book about his experiment at Walden Pond, paradoxically much of what he wrote for publication is travel narrative, a form immensely popular in the mid-19th century and which gave him an opportunity to write for the new national literary magazines, such as *Putnam's Monthly* and *Atlantic Monthly*, that began during the 1850s. The form also enabled him to set his own principles and interests in a meaningful cultural context and to explore a number of the liveliest issues of his age. Beginning in 1846, while in residence at Walden, he made three trips to the Maine wilderness, then known to few white men besides loggers, and wrote extended essays on these excursions that were collected posthumously as THE MAINE WOODS (1864). In them Thoreau tested and sharpened his belief in the necessity of wilderness to the spiritual health and survival of civilization, explored the conflict between the wilderness as economic resource and as spiritual resource, described the lives of loggers and other inhabitants, studied the botany of the region, and wrote compellingly of his encounters with a series of Indian guides, to whom he looked for evidence of a relation between humans and nature that transcended his own culture's assumption that nature exists primarily to be exploited.

Thoreau's other favorite ground for exploration was Cape Cod, then an isolated and relatively undeveloped section of the New England coast, which he visited a number of times between 1849 and 1857. He began to publish a serial narrative of his excursions there in *Putnam's Monthly* in 1855, but it was broken off part way through—the reasons remain obscure—and not finally published in its entirety until a posthumous edition in 1865. The distinctive modes of life of the region's inhabitants, the ocean itself, and the history of the Cape as representative of the drama of the discovery and exploration of North America by Europeans make up the thematic threads of *Cape Cod*. It remains a valuable study of the region as well as a classic of travel and description.

Thoreau's chief work for publication during the 1850s, however, was WALDEN (1854). Forced to abandon his plans to publish it shortly after *A Week on the Concord and Merrimack Rivers* by the commercial failure of that work, Thoreau revised the manuscript extensively during the early 1850s, enriching and deepening both his prose and his conception of the experiment on which the book was based. The finished work is thus at the same time dramatic and retrospective, with passages recording his activities and observations at the time subjected to reflection and amplification as their significance gradually emerged over time.

The basic structure of the book is generated by its basic aims: the first chapters, in addition to describing the building of his cabin and mode of life at Walden, comprise an often vitriolic critique of the unexamined assumptions of mid-19th century American culture, particularly its emphasis on business, technology, and material success. Having reduced life to its essentials, and having disposed of what is merely received opinion about life, Thoreau proceeds in the later chapters to tell the story of his own experiment in living, describing his life and activities in the context of the seasonal cycle of the year, from spring to spring, emphasizing the awakening and renewal of life that are possible through elimination of superfluities and a saturation in the life of nature.

If *Walden* is the public expression of this vision, then Thoreau's journal constitutes its private enactment. Beginning about 1850, when it became evident that he was not destined for commercial success as a writer, Thoreau gradually converted his journal, which he had kept as a writer's workbook since 1837, into the primary imaginative work of his later career. His interest in nature became more professional and rigorous, and his attempts to make his observation of and interaction with it more sustained and cohesive, until the journal had grown at the time of his death in 1862 to some forty-seven manuscript volumes containing more than two million words.

Out of this intensified interest in nature and humanity's place in it, Thoreau developed a number of memorable lectures, such as "Walking," "Wild Apples," and "Autumnal Tints," which he revised for essay publication shortly before his death and which were collected along with other natural history pieces in the posthumous volume *Excursions* (1863). In addition, at the time of his death he was working on two large projects based on his natural history research, which were left incomplete in manuscript.

Like most other Americans during the late 1850s, Thoreau was becoming more and more preoccupied with the divisions within the country that finally resulted in the Civil War. Long a radical abolitionist, he personally helped fugitive slaves escape to Canada, and wrote a series of lectures and essays that attacked Northern complicity in slaveholding ("Slavery in Massachusetts") and defended John Brown and his abortive raid on Harper's Ferry in 1859 ("Martyrdom of John Brown"). The onset of his last illness coincided with the outbreak of war in 1861, and he died of tuberculosis before the tide of battle turned in favor of the North.

At the time of his death, Thoreau had a modest but secure reputation as a naturalist and as the author of *Walden*. This reputation grew gradually during the rest of the century as more of his works and selections from his journal came into print, culminating in the twenty-four volume Walden Edition published by Houghton Mifflin in 1906. His elevation to the status of major writer began in the 1920s and 1930s, when cultural and literary historians attempted to establish a canon of distinctly American literature, and coincides with the discovery or rediscovery of other relatively neglected 19th-century writers such as Emily Dickinson and Herman Melville. Today, Thoreau is securely established within the American culture that he helped to define, largely by opposition to its materialistic tendencies. In addition, he has had a lasting influence on the shape of 20th-century life itself through his natural history and polemical writings, which have strongly influenced both conservation and preservation movements and the struggles of oppressed peoples all over the world.

The most comprehensive edition of Thoreau's writings is currently in progress at Princeton University Press (1971–   ), superseding the Houghton Mifflin edition mentioned above. The standard biography is Walter Harding, *The Days of Henry Thoreau* (1965), to be supplemented by Robert D. Richardson, Jr., *Henry Thoreau: A Life of the Mind* (1986). Harding and Carl Bode edited *The Correspondence of Henry David Thoreau* (1958), and Bode edited the *Collected Poems* (rev. ed. 1964). Among the many critical books on Thoreau, comprehensive treatments include Sherman Paul, *The Shores of America* (1958); James McIntosh, *Thoreau as Romantic Naturalist* (1974); and William L. Howarth, *The Book of Concord* (1982). See A YANKEE IN CANADA.

ROBERT SATTLEMEYER

Thorpe, Rose Hartwick (1850–1939),   poet. Author of a dozen books of fiction and poetry, the Indiana-born Thorpe is best known for her popular ballad CURFEW MUST NOT RING TONIGHT! (1867). This melodramatic narrative poem relates how a girl, in order to prevent the execution of her lover at curfew time, clings to the clapper of the bell to silence it. The idea came from a short story called "Love and Loyalty," published anonymously in *Peterson's Magazine* (1865). Various ballads, lyrics, and inspirational poems are collected in *The Poetical Works of Rose Hartwick Thorpe* (1912).

Thorpe, Thomas B[angs] (1815–1878),   humorist, editor, painter. Born in Massachusetts, Thorpe was well known for his pictures of frontier scenes and for his portraits. He owned and edited several newspapers in Louisiana and coedited the popular humorous New York journal SPIRIT OF THE TIMES. From his experiences in the army during the Mexican War he wrote *Our Army on the Rio Grande* (1846), *Our Army at Monterey* (1847), and *The Taylor Anecdote Book* (1848). He was a colonel in the Civil War. From 1869 to his death he held a civil service post in the New York Custom House. His story "The Big Bear of Arkansas" (*Spirit of the Times*, 1841) is a classic of the humor of the old Southwest. His other sketches and tales were collected in *The Mysteries of the Backwoods* (1846) and *The Hive of the Bee Hunter* (1854). See also TOM OWEN, THE BEE HUNTER.

Three Black Pennys, The (1917),   a novel by JOSEPH HERGESHEIMER. This three-part romantic novel traces the decline of intemperate power and ruthless individualism through three generations of the Penny family, owners of a rich iron works in Pennsylvania.

Three Lives (1909),   three stories by GERTRUDE STEIN. Her first published book, *Three Lives* tells of the good Anna, a purposeful, subtly domineering German serving woman; Melanctha, an uneducated but sensitive and wise African American woman; and the gentle Lena, a feeble-minded young German maid.

Three Soldiers (1921),   a novel by JOHN DOS PASSOS. One of the finest of the pacifist novels to appear after World War I, *Three Soldiers* deals with John Andrews, a musician just graduated from Harvard who joins the army in expectation of finding comfort by contributing to a righteous cause. Instead he encounters tyranny, aimlessness, red tape, cruelty, and boredom. His two companions, an Italian American and a gentle farm boy, are likewise disillusioned. The farm boy, goaded beyond endurance, kills an officer; Andrews deserts with him and faces a long prison term.

Three Stories and Ten Poems (1923),   the first published volume by ERNEST HEMINGWAY. It was issued in Dijon, France, by Robert McAlmon's Contact Publishing Co. in a series devoted to the works of expatriates. Altogether 300 copies were printed. The three stories are "Up in Michigan," "Out of Season," and "My Old Man." Six of the poems had been first published in *Poetry* (January 1923).

Threnody (1847),   an elegy by RALPH WALDO EMERSON on the death of his five-year-old son Waldo. One of Emerson's most moving poems, "Threnody" begins with a lament for "The gracious boy, who did adorn / The world whereinto he was born." The opening 175 lines embody his lament; the rest is his attempt to find consolation in transcendental unity and in the belief that the individual, dying, is "Lost in God, in Godhead found."

Thurber, James [Grover] (1894–1961),   essayist, short-story writer, humorist, artist, playwright. Thurber was born and grew up in Columbus, Ohio, in a family which, by his own account, was addicted to absurdity. Some of his funniest pieces deal with events in his childhood home. As the result of an accident to one eye, the impairment of his vision began, ending in blindness. After spending 1917–18 as a code clerk in the State Department at Washington and in Paris, he returned to Ohio State University to complete his studies in 1919.

Until 1927 he worked as a newspaper reporter in Columbus, Paris, and New York. At a 1927 cocktail party in New York City he met E. B. WHITE, who became a lifelong friend and introduced him to Harold Ross, editor of the recently founded *The New Yorker*. Ross hired Thurber to be his managing editor, but Thurber apparently did not relish executive authority. He worked himself down to a position as staff writer and then left the organization altogether to become a contributor. During Thurber's time on the staff, however, *The New Yorker* won much popularity, and there is no doubt that he had a good deal to do with setting the tone and style of the magazine. Thurber wrote lucidly and straightforwardly, with an artist's understanding of American prose rhythms. His humor conveys a depth and consistency of thought and feeling that continue to make it eminently readable. His tender cynicism converts sex, for example, into a war, but a war from which may emerge an ultimate triumph of humility. He exposed the inevitable follies of humanity with an intelligence of heart that is seen in the end to be humanity's saving virtue. Thurber defined humor as "emotional chaos remembered in tranquility," and though the chaos is what provokes the immediate comic response, the power of ordered remembering is what remains as the permanent effect.

Thurber ranged widely in his work. He will always be known primarily as a comic writer, but many of his stories venture into fantasy and some go beyond, into the macabre. Thurber possessed an acute sensitivity to internal fears and bewilderments and used these human attributes skillfully in shaping the dramatic action of many pieces. "The Secret Life of Walter Mitty," for example, a favorite story among Thurber readers, describes the fantasies of an average little man who pictures himself doing heroic deeds.

Thurber deprecated his own drawings, but they make an apt complement to his writing. Using simple lines, he drew seals in the bedroom, dogs of indeterminable breed and implacable serenity, brawny women, and slight men. By the late 1940s Thurber's eyesight had become so poor that he was unable to continue his drawings. Yet, a fairly large body of work had been completed, enough to fix the patterns that other cartoonists, imitating Thurber, have turned into stereotypes of mid-century comic art.

Thurber's books include *Is Sex Necessary?* with E. B. White (1929); *The Owl in the Attic and Other Perplexities* (1931); *The Seal in the Bedroom and Other Predicaments* (1932); *My Life and Hard Times* (1933); *The Middle-Aged Man on the Flying Trapeze* (1935); *Let Your Mind Alone* (1937); *The Cream of Thurber* (1939); *The Male Animal*, a play with Elliot Nugent (1940); *Fables for Our Times* (1940, 1956); *My World—and Welcome to It* (1942); *Men, Women, and Dogs* (1943); *The White Deer*, a fantasy for children (1945); *The Thurber Carnival* (1945); *The Beast in Me and Other Animals* (1949); *The Thirteen Clocks*, a children's story (1950); *The Thurber Album*

(1952); *Thurber Country* (1953); *The Secret Dream of Stanley Caldwell* (1954); *Thurber's Dogs* (1955); *The Wonderful O*, a children's fantasy (1957); *Alarms and Diversions* (1957); and *The Years with Ross*, a memoir of Harold Ross (1959). His last book of essays, *Lanterns and Lances*, was published in 1961.

Thurman, Wallace [Henry] (1902–1934), novelist, playwright, editor. Born in Salt Lake City and educated at the University of Utah and the University of Southern California, Thurman settled in Harlem in 1925 and participated in the Harlem Renaissance. He edited the *Messenger*, publishing works by Langston Hughes and Zora Neale Hurston, and two short-lived magazines *Fire!!* (1926) and, two years later, *Harlem: A Forum of Negro Life*. His first play, *Harlem: A Melodrama of Negro Life in Harlem*, with William Jourdan Rapp, opened at the Apollo Theater in 1929. *Jeremiah, the Magnificent* (1930), based on the life of Marcus Garvey, was also a collaboration with Rapp. His first novel, *The Blacker the Berry* (1929), is a satire on prejudice against dark skin among African-Americans. *Infants of the Spring* (1932) is a satiric look at life in a Harlem boarding house inhabited by writers. *The Interne*, (1932), written with Abraham L. Furman, shows life in an urban hospital through the eyes of a young white doctor. After a brief period on West Coast as a screenwriter, Thurman died of tuberculosis in New York City.

Thurso's Landing (in *Thurso's Landing and Other Poems*, 1932), a narrative poem by ROBINSON JEFFERS. The characters in "Thurso's Landing" embody in varying degrees the death wish that Jeffers feels to be a characteristic of modern civilization. The poem deals with Helen Thurso's attitudes toward her husband, whom she alternately loves and hates, toward her crippled brother-in-law who loves her, and toward death itself, which simultaneously fascinates and repels her.

Thwaites, Reuben Gold (1853–1913), librarian, editor, historian. Born in Massachusetts, Thwaites in his youth worked as a Wisconsin farmer, teacher, and a reporter on the Oshkosh *Times*. After attending Yale, he became managing editor of the Wisconsin *State Journal* and later secretary of the Wisconsin Historical Society. With a group of assistants he collected and translated the seventy-three-volume *Jesuit Relations and Allied Documents* (1896–1901). He also edited *Early Western Travels, 1748–1846* (32 v. 1904–07), and *Original Journals of the Lewis and Clark Expedition* (8 v. 1904–05). Among his original writings were *Father Marquette* (1902) and *France in America* (1905).

Ticknor, Francis Orray (1822–1874), physician, poet. Ticknor studied medicine in Philadelphia and New York, then returned to his native Georgia to practice. He was in charge of war hospitals in and around Columbus, Georgia. He loved writing verse and composed many of his poems on prescription blanks while in the saddle on the way to see patients. His *Poems* were published in 1879; a later edition (1911), prepared by Michelle Cutliff Ticknor, included some theretofore unpublished poems.

Ticknor, George (1791–1871), educator, biographer, literary historian, scholar. Ticknor was born in Boston, studied

French, Spanish, Latin, and Greek as a boy, entered Dartmouth at age fourteen, and did graduate work at Göttingen, Germany. At age twenty-five Ticknor accepted the new Smith Professorship of French, Spanish, and Belles Lettres at Harvard. His *Syllabus of the Spanish Literature Course* (1823), the first of its kind in any language, systematically covered the materials in the best form of German historical criticism. He reorganized his department on lines patterned after Göttingen before resigning in 1835, when Longfellow succeeded him. In Boston he devoted himself to writing his great *History of Spanish Literature* (3 v. 1849, 1872), to charitable pursuits, to clubs, and to improving the Boston Public Library. He returned to Europe to search out books for the Library, to which he was to leave his collection of rare books on Spanish literature. In 1864 he published a biography of an old friend, *Life of William Hickling Prescott*. Ticknor also wrote a *Life of Lafayette* (1824). Anna Ticknor and George S. Hillard compiled *Life, Letters and Journals of George Ticknor* (2 v. 1876).

Ticknor, William Davis (1810–1864),   publisher. In 1832 Ticknor founded the firm, later known as Ticknor and Fields, that published the works of Emerson, Hawthorne, Holmes, Longfellow, Lowell, and Thoreau, as well as the *Atlantic Monthly* (1859) and the *North American Review* (1854–1864).

Tiernan, Mary Spear (1836–1891),   novelist. Born in Baltimore, Tiernan lived many years in Virginia. She described life there before the Civil War in such works as *Homoselle* (1881) and *Suzette* (1885).

Tietjens, Eunice [Strong] (1884–1944),   poet, novelist, editor, lecturer. Tietjens, born in Chicago, was active in the vigorous Chicago group of writers in the early 20th century. She published collections of poems, including *Profiles from China* (1917), *Body and Raiment* (1919), and *Leaves in Windy Weather* (1929). She also wrote novels, including *Jake* (1921), and juvenile fiction. She was a great traveler and wrote books on Japan (1924) and China (1930), prepared an anthology of *Poetry of the Orient* (1928), and lectured on the Far East at the University of Miami (1933–35). *The World at My Shoulder* (1938) is an autobiography. Among her greatest services was that of assisting HARRIET MONROE on the staff of *Poetry* from 1913 to her death.

Tiger-Lilies (1867),   a novel by Sidney Lanier. The hero, Philip Sterling—like Lanier himself—is taken prisoner by the Union Army. A Confederate deserter, Gorm Smallin, enraged against wealth, kills Philip's parents and burns down their home.

Tilbury Town.   The imaginary setting of many of EDWIN ARLINGTON ROBINSON's poems. Drawn partly from Robinson's home town of Gardiner, Maine, it is inhabited by materialistic, prudish, and smugly conventional people of the middle class. Richard Cory, Flammonde, Miniver Cheevy, old Eben Flood, and other protagonists of Robinson's poems are either rebels against or outcasts from the town. Lawrence Thompson edited a selection of 63 poems entitled *Tilbury Town* (1953).

Tillich, Paul (1886–1965),   philosopher, theologian. Tillich, who was born in Germany, was educated at the universities of Berlin, Tübingen, Halle, and Breslau. He served as chaplain in the German Army during World War I and later taught theology and philosophy at Berlin, Marburg, Dresden, and Frankfurt-am-Main. The rise of Nazism forced him to leave Germany. Coming to New York City, Tillich taught at the Union Theological Seminary from 1933 until 1955, becoming an American citizen in 1940. He was appointed University Professor at Harvard—an honor that permitted him freedom to work in any field he chose. His writings are concerned for the most part with the line dividing theology and philosophy and the relationship between religion and psychology. His theology was built on "the method of correlation between questions arising out of the human predicament and the answers given in the classical symbols of religion." Books by Tillich include *The Religious Situation* (1932), *The Interpretation of History* (1936), *The Protestant Era* (1948), *Systematic Theology, Volume I* (1951), *The Courage to Be* (1952), *Love, Power and Justice* (1954), *The New Being* (1955), *The Shaking of the Foundations* (1948), *Biblical Religion and the Search for Ultimate Reality* (1955), *Dynamics of Faith* (1957), *Systematic Theology, Volume II* (1959), and *Theology and Culture* (1959).

Tillinghast, Richard [Williford] (1940–),   poet. Born in Memphis, Tennessee, Tillinghast was educated at the University of the South (A.B., 1962) and Harvard University (A.M., 1963, Ph.D., 1970). A recipient of numerous fellowships and awards, he has taught at the University of Michigan since 1983. Verse is collected in *Sleep Watch* (1969); *The Knife and Other Poems* (1980); *Our Flag Was Still There* (1984), which includes the long poem "Sewanee in Ruins," a meditation on the history of his undergraduate college and the South it represents; and *The Stonecutter's Hand* (1994), containing more ruminations on the past. He is also the author of the brief study *Robert Lowell: Damaged Grandeur* (1995).

Tilton, Theodore (1835–1907),   editor. Tilton, born in New York City, is remembered chiefly for his suit against HENRY WARD BEECHER, in which he charged adultery with Mrs. Tilton. From 1883 on he lived abroad. He was the author of numerous stories and of *Sonnets Addressed to the Memory of Frederick Douglass* (1895).

Time of Your Life, The (1939),   a play by WILLIAM SAROYAN. One of the author's most successful fantasies, a blend of social consciousness and poetic symbolism, this play surprised its backers by becoming a Broadway hit. Set in a waterfront saloon, it takes as its themes the need to make the most of life, be compassionate toward the weak, and oppose the enemies of life, with force if necessary. A collection of lovable eccentrics represent the weak—a dreaming prostitute, a starving African-American musician, an ex-frontiersman, an Arab with a harmonica, and a young hopeful pouring nickels into a pinball machine during the entire play. The forces of evil are represented by Detective Blick of the Vice Squad, whom many critics identified with Hitler. The play won the New York

Drama Critics' Award and the Pulitzer Prize for 1940. Saroyan refused the Pulitzer Prize.

Timerman, Jacobo (1923–1999), journalist, human rights activist. Born in Bar, Ukraine, Timerman lived from age five in Argentina, became a citizen, had his citizenship revoked in 1979, lived in Israel, Manhattan, and Spain, then returned to Argentina after that country's return to a democratically elected government in 1983. Meanwhile, he had earned fame for *Preso sin nombre, celda sin numero*, translated as *Prisoner Without a Name, Cell Without a Number* (1981), an account of his thirty-month imprisonment, torture, and house arrest for his opposition to the ruling military junta of General Jorge Rafael Videla (his newspaper, *La Opinion*, published names of citizens who were among the 15,000 or more who "disappeared" and died). His other books are *The Longest War: Israel in Lebanon* (1982), in which he argued that all Israel's invasion and occupation was militarily unjustified and politically damaging, and *Chile: Death in the South* (1987), an account of suffering under the dictator Augusto Pinochet.

Timoleon (1891), a volume of poetry by HERMAN MELVILLE. Although it was the last of Melville's works published in his lifetime, much of it refers to his trip to the Mediterranean and the Near East in 1857.

Timrod, Henry (1828–1867), poet, essayist, war correspondent. Born and privately educated in Charleston, South Carolina, Timrod attended the University of Georgia until illness and lack of funds forced his withdrawal (1845–46). For two years he read law in Charleston. With the aim of obtaining a professorship, he was meanwhile continuing his classical studies on his own. Failing that, he worked as a tutor from 1850–61 on several plantations in the Carolinas.

Between 1850 and 1860 Timrod published several important literary essays in a Charleston periodical, *Russell's Magazine*. These included "Literature in the South" and "A Theory of Poetry," both of which disclosed Timrod's appreciation of Wordsworth and Tennyson. In 1859 Ticknor and Fields of Boston printed the only collection of Timrod's verse to appear during the poet's lifetime. His reputation, however, rests chiefly on his poems of the Civil War—he was called Laureate of the Confederacy. His best-known poems are "The Cotton Boll" and "Ethnogenesis," both written in 1861. Here he implies that it is economic well-being rather than idealism that must sustain the region's spirit of community.

Even though he had tuberculosis, Timrod served from February to December of 1862 as a regimental clerk in the Confederate Army and briefly reported on the war for the Charleston *Mercury*. His appointment as editor of the Columbia *South Carolinian* in 1864 enabled him to marry Kate S. Goodwin, to whom are dedicated his *Katie* poems, published together in 1884. The capture and burning of Columbia by Sherman's troops on February 17, 1865, completely ruined him, and the rest of his life was consumed in a series of ineffectual jobs, malnutrition, and despair.

Paul Hamilton Hayne's edition of *The Poems of Henry Timrod* (1873) includes a colorful memoir by the editor, a lifelong friend of Timrod. This collection and the Memorial Edition of 1899 have been superseded by *The Collected Poems of Henry Timrod: A Variorum Edition* (ed. Edd Winfield Parks and Aileen Wells Parks, 1965). Jay B. Hubbell's *The Last Years of Henry Timrod, 1864–1867* (1941) creates a poignant portrait of the poet from his own letters and the letters of others. The editor of *The Essays of Henry Timrod* (1942), Edd Winfield Parks, also published an authoritative critical biography (1964).

DAVID HAVIRD

Titan, The (1914), a novel by THEODORE DREISER. This sequel to THE FINANCIER (1912) continues the story of Frank Cowperwood, based on the life of the public utilities tycoon Charles Tyson Yerkes (1837–1905). After marrying Aileen Butler, his former mistress, Cowperwood moves from Philadelphia to Chicago, where he almost succeeds in establishing a monopoly of public utilities. Dissatisfaction with Aileen leads him to a series of affairs with other women; when the people of Chicago frustrate his financial schemes he departs for Europe with the daughter of the madam of a Louisiville brothel. Cowperwood, driven by a need for power, beautiful women, and social prestige, at last experiences "the pathos of the discovery that even giants are but pigmies, and that an ultimate balance must be struck." Dreiser wrote a sequel, *The Stoic*, which was published posthumously (1974), thus concluding "the trilogy of desire" with Cowperwood's life in England.

Titcomb, Timothy. Pen name of J.G. HODLAND.

To a Waterfowl (1815), a poem by WILLIAM CULLEN BRYANT. Written in the poet's twenty-first year, it was called by Matthew Arnold the best short poem in the language. In the winter of 1815 Bryant was journeying to Plainfield, Massachusetts, where he expected to make his living as a lawyer. He was "very forlorn and desolate indeed, not knowing what was to become of him in the big world," when he saw against the sunset a solitary bird making its way across the sky. The poem tells of the moral inspiration and belief in divine guidance that the bird's flight gave him.

Tobacco Road (1932), a novel by ERSKINE CALDWELL. Jeeter Lester, a Georgia farmer, lives in hopeless poverty on Tobacco Road with his starving old mother, his sickly wife Ada, and his two children, sixteen-year-old Dude and Ellie May. The hapless Lesters, at once comical and degenerate, became widely familiar to the public through Jack Kirkland's dramatization (1933), which ran for 3,182 performances on Broadway, and through a motion picture (1941).

Tocqueville, Alexis [Charles Maurice Henri Clérel] de (1805–1859), lawyer, sociologist, public official, writer. De Tocqueville, a Frenchman, is chiefly remembered for his *Democracy in America* (*De la Démocratic en Amérique*), which was published in two volumes (1835, 1840), and immediately translated into English for a British edition (1835, 1840).

Tocqueville began as a lawyer, took his final degree in 1826, and then began his travels in Italy and Sicily. While still in his twenties he was appointed an assistant magistrate. The French government sent him to the United States in 1831, along with his friend and fellow magistrate Gustave de Beaumont, to study the American prison system. From New York City they traveled as far east as Boston, as far west as Green Bay, as far north as Sault Ste. Marie and Quebec, and as far south as New Orleans. Back in France they wrote *Du Système Pénitentionaire aux États-Unis et de son Application en France* (1833), which appeared in the same year in the United States.

Meanwhile Tocqueville proceeded to write and publish his masterwork. He was elected to the French Academy in 1841 and was a member of the Chamber of Deputies until Louis Napoleon's coup d'état in 1851 forced him into retirement. With his new leisure he began a study of French history and democracy, publishing his *Histoire Philosophique de Règne de Louis XV* in 1846, his analysis of *L'Ancien Régime et la Révolution* in 1856. The first part of volume one of *Democracy in America* treats specific aspects of government and politics: the principle of sovereignty of the people, the nature of the states and local government, judicial power, the Constitution, political parties, freedom of the press, suffrage, the role of the majority and ways to mitigate its tyranny, and the present and possible future of the three races making up the population. The last section treats difficulties inhibiting the creation of an aristocracy and analyzes the causes of economic prosperity in the United States. The second volume describes American traits and tendencies. It examines the influence of democracy on manners, religion, science, literature, and art. Tocqueville's book is widely recognized as an important political treatise. Its implications and conclusions have been examined anew in each generation since it initally appeared.

The literature on Tocqueville is vast. Some books in English include M. C. M. Simpson's *Memoirs, Letters, and Remains of Alexis de Tocqueville* (2 v. 1861) and his *Correspondence and Conversations of Alexis de Tocqueville with Nassau William Senior from 1834 to 1859* (2 v. 1872); James Bryce's *The Predictions of Hamilton and Tocqueville* (1887); G. W. Pierson's *Tocqueville and Beaumont in America* (1938); Jacob P. Mayer's *Alexis de Tocqueville* (1940) and his edition of *The Recollections of Alexis de Tocqueville* (1949). Recent books include Andre Jardin, *Tocqueville: A Biography*, trans. Robert Hemenway (1998) and Michael Arthur Ledeen, *Tocqueville on American Character* (2000).

Todd, Mabel Loomis (1856–1932),   editor, author. Born in Cambridge, Massachusetts, Todd came to Amherst in 1879 when her husband was appointed a professor of astronomy at Amherst. She became acquainted with Emily Dickinson and the poet's family. After Emily's death in 1886, Todd was asked by Lavinia Dickinson to select and prepare for publication some of the nearly 2,000 poems found in packets among Dickinson's effects. With Thomas W. Higginson she edited *Poems, First Series*, containing 115 poems (1890), and *Poems, Second Series*, consisting of 166 poems (1891). Because Higginson was fearful that the public would not accept the poems as they were, the editors regularized rhymes and meters and used conventional punctuation. Todd was the sole editor of *Letters of Emily Dickinson* (1894, revised and enlarged 1931)

and *Poems*, third series (1896). *Bolts of Melody: New Poems of Emily Dickinson* (1945) was completed from Mabel Todd's transcriptions by her daughter, Millicent Todd Bingham. Other writings by Mabel L. Todd include a novelette, *Footprints* (1883), *Total Eclipses of the Sun* (1894), *A Cycle of Sonnets* (1896), and the travel books *Corona and Coronet* (1898) and *Tripoli, the Mysterious* (1912).

To Have and Have Not (1937),   a novel by ERNEST HEMINGWAY. Harry Morgan, a native of Key West, is forced by the Depression to turn to smuggling, bootlegging, and finally to helping four Cuban revolutionaries escape. Fatally wounded in a fight, Morgan is picked up by the Coast Guard and dies, gasping, "One man alone ain't got . . . no chance."

To Have and to Hold (1900),   a novel by MARY JOHNSTON. The Virginia colony of 1621 forms the background of this romantic tale. When adventurous Ralph Percy goes to Jamestown to choose a wife from a shipload of women sent over from England, he little suspects the noble birth of the beautiful woman who throws herself on his mercy. Jocelyn— fleeing the loathsome advances of Lord Carnal—at first despises her husband. But subsequent adventures on land and sea reveal her courage and devotion. Love finally blossoms. In the midst of all this derring-do *To Have and to Hold* presents an animated picture of primitive America as it must have looked to colonizers from a more civilized land.

To Helen.   The title of two poems by EDGAR ALLAN POE, one published in 1831 ("Helen, thy beauty is to me"), the other in 1848 ("I saw thee once—once only—years ago"). The first was inscribed to the memory of Mrs. Jane Stith Stanard of Richmond, Virginia, for whom Poe had cherished, in his own words, "the first purely ideal love of my soul." The second poem was addressed to Mrs. SARAH HELEN WHITMAN of Providence, Rhode Island, of whom he caught a glimpse one evening when he stayed overnight in Providence. Later he became acquainted with Mrs. Whitman and was betrothed to her. She reluctantly concluded that she could not marry him, but always remained his ardent defender.

Token, The (1827–1842),   a gift book (see ANNUALS AND GIFT BOOKS) published in Boston. Several Hawthorne stories were first published in *The Token*, including many later collected in *Twice Told Tales*. Longfellow, Harriet Beecher Stowe, Holmes, and Lowell were also contributors.

Toklas, Alice B[abette] (1877–1967),   memoirist, literary observer. Toklas, born in San Francisco, shared after 1907 with her longtime companion, Gertrude Stein, in the intellectual life of expatriate Americans in Paris. *The Autobiography of Alice B. Toklas* (1933), actually written by Stein, describes visitors to their salon. Toklas created a brief memoir, *What Is Remembered* (1963); *The Alice B. Toklas Cookbook* (1954), a combination of personal observation and recipes; *Aromas and Flavors of Past and Present* (1958), a French cookbook; and *Staying on Alone* (1973), a collection of letters written after Stein's death.

Tol'able David (1919),   a short story by JOSEPH HERGESHEIMER. This tale of a West Virginia mountain boy's triumph over great odds appeared in the collection *The Happy*

End (1919). David Kinemon, age 16, is forced into conflict with the Hatburns, a degenerate Kentucky family who cripple Allen, David's older brother. When he kills all three Hatburns after a savage battle, David recalls the story of Goliath and reflects that he is just a tol'able David.

Tolson, Melvin B[eaunorus] (1898?–1966),   poet, playwright, novelist. Tolson was the son of a Missouri minister and his schoolteacher wife. He was educated at Fisk University, Lincoln University, and Columbia. *Rendezvous with America*, his first collection celebrating the contributions of African-Americans to American culture, appeared in 1944. In 1947 he was named Poet Laureate of Liberia and responded with *Libretto for the Republic of Liberia* (1953), for which ALLEN TATE wrote the preface. Though Tate, JOHN CIARDI, and KARL SHAPIRO attempted to foster his work, and Shapiro wrote the introduction for *Harlem Gallery, Book One, The Curator* (1965), the work attracted little critical attention during Tolson's lifetime. *A Gallery of Harlem Portraits* was published posthumously in 1979. His novel *Beyond the Zaretto* and several dramatic adaptations of work by WALTER WHITE and RICHARD WRIGHT remain unpublished. Selections from his weekly column "Caviar and Cabbage" in the *Washington Tribune* (1937–1944) were collected in a book of the same title in 1982. Raymond Nelson edited *Harlem Gallery and Other Poems* (1999), with an introduction by Rita Dove and copious notes.

Tomlinson, E[verett] T[itsworth] (1859–1931), teacher, clergyman, writer of boys' books. Tomlinson was born in New Jersey and educated at Williams College. He became principal of the Auburn, New York, high school and in 1883 was appointed headmaster at Rutgers Preparatory School, New Brunswick, New Jersey. He became pastor in 1888 of New York City's Central Baptist Church, where he remained for twenty-three years. His earliest publications were Latin and Greek texts, but his great interest was in writing boys' books with historical backgrounds. During his lifetime more than 2 million copies of his books were sold. Some of the best known titles are *The Search for Andrew Field* (1894), *The Boy Soldiers of 1812* (1895), *The Colonial Boys* (1895), *Three Young Continentals* (1896), *Tecumseh's Young Braves* (1897), *Boys with Old Hickory* (1898), *The Rider of the Black Horse* (1904), *Light Horse Harry's Legion* (1910), *Champion of the Regiment* (1911), *Scouting with Daniel Boone* (1914), and *The Story of General Pershing* (1917).

Tom Owen, the Bee Hunter (1846),   a sketch by THOMAS BANGS THORPE. This account of "mighty Tom Owen" was printed in a collection entitled *The Mysteries of the Backwoods; or, Sketches of the Southwest, Including Character, Scenery, and Rural Sports* (1846). Equipped with an axe and a pair of buckets, the frontier hero scanned the distance for a bee, followed it with his keen eye to its hidden hive, and then chopped down the tree and harvested the honey. Tom also appears in Thorpe's *The Hive of the Bee-Hunter* (1854). Tom's statement that on a clear day he could see a bee over a mile away is typical of the author, a pioneer in the American tall tale, as exemplified in *The Big Bear of Arkansas* (1841).

Tompson, Benjamin (1642–1714),   schoolmaster, physician, poet. Tompson was born in Braintree, Massachusetts, and was educated at Harvard. In 1667 he became master of the Boston Latin School, then called the Free School, and later taught in Braintree and Roxbury, Massachusetts. Though trained for the ministry, he never had a pulpit, instead practicing medicine.

Tompson was much called on for memorial elegies and other verses for special occasions, but his reputation rests chiefly on his ambitious narrative poem on King Philip's War, NEW ENGLAND'S CRISIS (1676). This long narrative reflects the commonly held contemporary belief that wars were a celestial chastisement for the decline of piety. The poem is laced with enough irreverence to allow some question as to whether Tompson fully believed in the theory. The poem is also notable for its accurate use of Indian words and Indian English.

Tom Sawyer, The Adventures of (1876),   a novel by MARK TWAIN. The plot of *Tom Sawyer* is episodic, dealing in part with Tom's pranks in school and Sunday school, the respectable world of his Aunt Polly, and his adventures with Huck Finn, the outcast son of the local ne'er-do-well. Tom's shrewdness and ingenuity are revealed in his dealings with his peers, and his romantic love of adventure in the episodes involving Huck. While curing warts with a dead cat in the cemetery under a full moon, Tom and Huck witness a murder and, in terror of the murderer, Injun Joe, secretly flee to Jackson's Island. They are searched for and are finally mourned for dead. They return to town in time to attend their own funeral. Tom and his sweetheart, Becky Thatcher, get lost in a cave in which Injun Joe is hiding; Tom and Becky escape and Tom returns with Huck to find the treasure that Injun Joe has buried in the cave.

The story is set in Hannibal, Missouri, which Twain called St. Petersburg in the novel. Huck Finn was modeled on Tom Blankenship; Injun Joe, on a man who died in Hannibal in his nineties; Becky Thatcher, on Laura Hawkins, Twain's first sweetheart; Aunt Polly, on Twain's mother, but also bears a strong resemblance to B. P. Shillaber's MRS. PARTINGTON. *Tom Sawyer* was immensely popular with children and adults, appeared in English editions abroad, and was translated into many languages. Twain wrote a sequel, HUCKLEBERRY FINN (1884), his greatest book, and two sequels of lesser importance: TOM SAWYER ABROAD (1894) and TOM SAWYER, DETECTIVE (1896).

Tom Sawyer Abroad (1894),   a novel by MARK TWAIN. A sequel to *Huckleberry Finn*, this minor novel is a study of the provincial mind confronted with new and alien experiences. Tom Sawyer, Huck Finn, and Negro Jim sail in a balloon across the ocean to the Sahara Desert, Egypt, and Palestine. They encounter wild beasts, a desert caravan, and a mirage along the way. These adventures evoke lively and amusing discussions among the three adventurers.

Tom Sawyer, Detective (1896),   a novel by MARK TWAIN. Tom and Huck Finn revisit the Phelpses in Arkansas, the scene of the conclusion of *Huckleberry Finn*, and Tom saves Uncle Silas, mistakenly accused of murder, by unraveling a complicated plot of robbery, murder, and revenge. In a footnote Twain says that the incidents are based on "an old-time Swedish criminal trial," but also evident is the influence of Sherlock Holmes, whom Twain admired.

Tom Swift.   See SWIFT, TOM.

Tonty [or Tonti], Henry (c. 1650–1704),   explorer. Born in Italy, Tonty was the son of the Italian banker Lorenzo Tonti, who invented the tontine system of insurance. The son went into the service of the French, sailed for America, and helped explore various parts of the Mississippi Valley and Canada. He was with La Salle when the French explorer sailed down the Mississippi and claimed the adjoining territory for France (1678–83). His *Mémoires* cover two periods: 1678–1685 and 1687–1691. He also helped the Louisiana colony in its early days (1700–04) and died in Alabama.

Toole, John Kennedy (1937–1969),   novelist. Toole, born in New Orleans and educated at Tulane and Columbia, wrote the novel *A Confederacy of Dunces*, which was published posthumously. After his suicide, his mother convinced WALKER PERCY to read the manuscript of the satirical comedy, and with Percy's intervention, it was published and won the Pulitzer Prize in 1980. Nearly a decade later, a brief novel he had written as a teenager was published. *The Neon Bible* (1989) is a lyric and elegiac first person narrative of a young boy's life in a rural Southern town.

Toomer, Jean (1894–1967),   poet, fiction and nonfiction writer. Born Eugene Pinchback Toomer in Washington, D.C., he later changed his name to Nathan Jean Toomer. His parents divorced in 1896, his mother died in 1909, and until young adulthood Toomer lived mostly with her parents in that city. His grandfather, P.B.S. Pinchback, was a black politician of Louisiana Reconstruction fame. Toomer attended several colleges but earned no degrees. In 1919 he decided to write. His best-known work is *Cane* (1923), which incorporates poetry, fiction, and drama into an artistic vision of the black American experience: the internal dynamics of that community and the impact of racial oppression on it. For stylistic innovations and penetrating insights, *Cane*, widely acclaimed in 1923, is one of the most significant literary works of the Harlem Renaissance. Toomer, in search of internal harmony with the powers of the universe, rejected racial classification and did not identify with the Harlem movement. By 1924 he disavowed art in writing for the dogma of George Ivanovich Gurdjieff, who promised his disciples internal harmony. Toomer taught and wrote extensively of Gurdjieff's philosophy. Later, although he rejected Gurdjieff, he continued to search unsuccessfully for a system through which to achieve the goal of higher unity. Until the late 1940s he wrote profusely: poetry, short fiction, novels, and essays, but publishers found no literary merit in these writings, and little appeared in print. Still, *Cane* remains a work of genius, and Toomer an enigma. Scholars will continue to explore the life and writings of this man for many years to come. *Collected Poems* was published in 1988. See Nellie Y. McKay, *Jean Toomer, Artist: A Study of His Literary Life and Work* (1984), Rudolph P. Byrd, *Jean Toomer's Years with Gurdjieff* (1990), and Robert Jones, *Jean Toomer and the Prison-house of Thought* (1993).

NELLIE MCKAY/GP

Topper (1926),   a novel by THORNE SMITH. Cosmo Topper, a sober and respectable gentleman, is transformed by his adventures with two carefree young ghosts, George and Marion Kerby. Written during the era of prohibition, *Topper* and its sequel, *Topper Takes a Trip* (1932), dramatize the mood of rebellion against middle-class morality that was to form the staple of Smith's later novels. The book was made into a popular movie (1937) and a series of television shows (1953).

Torrence, [Frederic] Ridgely (1875–1950),   poet, playwright, editor, library official, critic. The Ohio-born Torrence served for several years on the staff of the New York Public Library, later on *The Critic* and *The Cosmopolitan*, then as poetry editor of the *New Republic*. At various times he was poet-in-residence at Antioch College and at Miami University. His first verse collection, *The House of a Hundred Lights*, appeared in 1900; *Hesperides*, in 1925; *Poems*, in 1941 and in enlarged form, posthumously in 1952. His collection *Plays for a Negro Theater* (1917) includes *Granny Maumee* (1914), perhaps the first serious drama about African-Americans by an American writer, and the first to be acted by an African-American cast (1917). *Story of John Hope* (1948) is a biography of the African-American educator.

Torrents of Spring, The (1926),   a novel by ERNEST HEMINGWAY. A burlesque of SHERWOOD ANDERSON and the Chicago school of authors, this comic novel tells of Yogi Johnson and Scripps O'Neil, workers in a pump factory in Petosky, Michigan; of Scripps' amours with two waitresses in Brown's Beanery; and of Yogi's adventures with the Indians.

Torrey, Bradford (1843–1912),   ornithologist, writer, teacher, editor. Born in Massachusetts, Torrey taught for two years, then earned a living as a businessman, but from his earliest years he made the study of birds his hobby. In 1886 he became a member of the staff of *Youth's Companion*. In his later years, suffering from ill health, he moved to a cabin near Santa Barbara, California, isolated from the world. He became a noted ornithologist. Mingled with his close observation was an almost mystical philosophy of nature, and he wrote in a style of marked literary grace. He published *Birds in the Bush* (1885), *A Rambler's Lease* (1889), *A Florida Sketch Book* (1894), *A World of Green Hills* (1898), *The Clerk of the Woods* (1903), *Field Days in California* (1913), and other volumes. He also edited the writings of Thoreau (14 v. 1906).

Torsvan, Berick Traven.   See B. TRAVEN.

Tortesa, or the Usurer (1839),   a play by NATHANIEL PARKER WILLIS. Written for James William Wallack, who played the lead, this romantic drama leans heavily on *Romeo and Juliet* and *A Winter's Tale* for its plot. The Florentine money-lender Tortesa desires the hand of Isabella, the Count's daughter, not for love, but as a symbol of rank and culture. In the end he gives her up to her true love, Angelo. Edgar Allan Poe declared *Tortesa* by far the best drama by an American author written up to that time.

Tortilla Flat (1935),   a novel by JOHN STEINBECK. This episodic tale concerns the poor but carefree *paisano* Danny and his friends Pillon, Pablo, Big Joe Portagee, Jesus Maria Corcoran, and the old Pirate, all of whom gather in Danny's house, which Steinbeck tells us "was not unlike the Round Table." The novel—accepted after nine publishers had turned it down—contrasts the complexities of modern civilization with the simple life of the *paisanos.*

Tourgée, Albion W[inegar] (1838–1905),   lawyer, consul, novelist. Born in Ohio and wounded during service in the Union army, in 1865 Tourgée moved to North Carolina and became active in Reconstruction measures. He finally grew tired of living in a hostile atmosphere and returned to the North. In A FOOL'S ERRAND (1879) he sought to combine romance and propaganda about Southern mistreatment of Northerners. The book was widely read and was followed by a sequel, BRICKS WITHOUT STRAW (1880). Tourgée was particularly distressed by the serious disabilities suffered by former slaves in the South. His books helped make the Southern theme a factor in American literature again. Writing in *The Forum* (December 1888), Tourgée stated his conviction that American literature had become "distinctly Confederate in sympathy." Among his other books are *Figs and Thistles* (1879), HOT PLOUGHSHARES (1883), *An Appeal to Caesar* (1884), *Button's Inn* (1887), and *Pactolus Prime* (1890).

Tour on the Prairies, A (1835),   a travel book by WASHINGTON IRVING. This rich narrative describes Irving's journey over the country west of Arkansas from Fort Gibson to the Cross Timbers, in what is now Oklahoma. It relates his experiences as a buffalo hunter, reveals his understanding of the Indians as individuals, and describes the vastness and loneliness of the prairies.

Toussaint L'Ouverture, Pierre François Dominique (1743–1803),   slave, soldier. Born a slave in Haiti, Toussaint was self-educated. Freed just prior to the black uprising in 1791, he joined the revolt and became its chief organizer, rapidly rising to power. In 1793 his forces were allied with the Spanish of Santo Domingo in a series of quick raids known as L'Ouverture (the opening), the term he incorporated into his name. His forces defeated the British and their Spanish allies (1798) and a revolt of mulattos (1799), and in 1801 conquered Santo Domingo and, thus, the entire island. When he petitioned Napoleon for approval of a constitutional form of government, a large force under General LeClerc was sent to subdue him. Toussaint was seized and sent to France, where he died ten months later in a dungeon at Fort-de-Joux. His career and tragic death made him a symbol for liberty and he was celebrated in a Wordsworth sonnet, a dramatic poem by Lamartine, verse by JOHN GREENLEAF WHITTIER, Harriet Martineau's historical novel *The Hour and the Man* (1840), and Ralph Korngold's biography *Citizen Toussaint* (1944, repr. 1965).

Tower Beyond Tragedy, The   (in *Tamar and Other Poems*, 1924), a play in verse by ROBINSON JEFFERS. Based on *Agamemnon* and *The Libation Bearers*, the first two plays of the Oresteian trilogy of Aeschylus, *The Tower Beyond Tragedy* departs from its Greek models primarily in enlarging the role of the Trojan prophetess Cassandra. It also gives less emphasis to the conflict between two equally compelling obligations than to the contrast between the incestuous desires of Electra, who begs Orestes to stay with her in the city and rule his people, and the desire of Orestes to break away from her and from whatever ties might bind him to humanity. The main characters are powerfully portrayed, and their speeches, which make up the body of the poem, reveal Jeffers to be a skilled dramatist as well as poet. *The Tower Beyond Tragedy* was produced on Broadway in 1950.

Town, The.   See THE HAMLET.

Town & Country.   A weekly magazine called *The National Press: A Home Journal* was first issued in New York City on February 14, 1846. With the November 21 issue it changed its name to *The Home Journal*, and in 1901 it became *Town & Country*. Its first editors were NATHANIEL PARKER WILLIS and GEORGE POPE MORRIS; for a time Edgar Allan Poe was their assistant. It was the announced goal of the editors to give "such a summary of news as will make our reader sure that he loses nothing worth knowing of the world's goings-on." But it early became a medium appealing particularly to the rich, whose "tastes and feelings" the editors planned to "instruct, refine, and amuse." Nevertheless, Willis and Morris took their missionary enterprise with some seriousness and included works of some of the leading British authors of the day as well as many contemporary American writers. When, in December 1946, the magazine published an impressive 348-page retrospective issue, it proved to be not so much a literary as a social composite. In 1925 the magazine was bought by WILLIAM RANDOLPH HEARST and placed under the editorship of the capable Harry Bull, who restored to it some of the ideals Willis and Morris had announced.

Townsend, Edward Waterman (1855–1942),   novelist, short-story writer. Townsend delineated life among the poor of New York City in stories first printed in newspapers and later collected in *Chimmie Fadden, Major Max, and Other Stories* (1895) and *Chimmie Fadden Explains* (1895). *A Daughter of the Tenements*, published in the same year, is a novel on the same topic.

Townsend, George Alfred (1841–1914),   journalist, novelist, playwright. Born in Delaware, Townsend was a correspondent for the New York *Herald* during the Civil War. His dispatches, published in 1866 as *Campaigns of a Non-Combatant* (repr. 1950), centered on the experiences of the common soldier and the sufferings of civilians. After the war he continued to write syndicated columns for over 100 newspapers under the pen name Gath. He wrote several books based on his newspaper work. Two biographies, *The Life and Battles of Garibaldi* and *The Real Life of Abraham Lincoln*, appeared in 1867. His best-known works are *The Entailed Hat*

(1884), a novel dealing with the kidnapping and selling of free blacks in Delaware and Maryland before the Civil War, and *Tales of the Chesapeake* (1880), local color stories. He also wrote *The Bohemians* (1861) and *President Cromwell* (1885), dramas; *Katy of Catocin* (1886) and *Mrs. Reynolds and Hamilton* (1890), novels; *Poems* (1870) and *Poems of Men and Events* (1899); and travel books.

Townsend, Mary Ashley [Van Voorhis "Mary Ashley Xariffa"] (1836–1901), essayist, poet, novelist. Mary Ashley, born in New York, married in 1853 and settled in New Orleans. Under the name Xariffa she contributed a series of essays called "Quillotypes" and "The Crossbone Papers" to the New Orleans *Delta*. As Mary Ashley she published articles in the *Crescent*. In 1881 the *Picayune* printed a group of her letters written on a trip to Mexico. *Xariffa's Poems* (1870) contained her well-known sentimental "Creed." *The Brother Clerks* (1857), a melodramatic novel in a New Orleans setting, was followed in 1874 by *The Captain's Story, and Other Verse*. Warmly praised by Oliver Wendell Holmes, the volume created a furor because it dealt with the then sensational theme of the discovery by a supposed white man that his mother was a mulatto. *Down the Bayou and Other Poems* (1882) and *Distaff and Spindle* (1895) followed.

Tragedy of Pudd'nhead Wilson, The. See PUDD'N-HEAD WILSON, THE TRAGEDY OF.

Tragic Muse, The (1890), a novel by HENRY JAMES. Nicholas Dormer, son of an eminent English statesman, gives up a brilliant career in Parliament, his godfather's promised fortune, and the hand of his beautiful and wealthy cousin, Julia Dallow, to become a portrait painter. He is inspired to do this partly by the example of his actress friend Miriam Rooth. The novel was originally published in *Atlantic Monthly* and was dramatized in 1927.

Traill, Catherine Parr [Strickland] (1802–1899), juvenile writer, novelist, naturalist. Born in Kent, England, Catherine Strickland had an early career there writing books for children. One of the books, *The Young Emigrants: or, Pictures of Life in Canada* (1826), presaged her own emigration in 1832. Accompanied by her husband, Thomas Traill, a soldier who owned land near Lakefield, Ontario; her sister, SUSANNA MOODIE; and her brother-in-law, she settled in frontier Canada. The two sisters wrote of the many trials and occasional rewards of frontier life with a frankness designed to disillusion the dupes of land agents. Mrs. Traill's *The Backwoods of Canada* (1836), a series of letters to her mother, is a good example of her candor and dry humor. Other books, such as *Lady Mary and Her Nurse* (1850) and *The Canadian Crusoes* (1852, republished 1855 as *Lost in the Backwoods; The Female Emigrants Guide*), appealed primarily to children. Canada's natural beauties are described in *Rambles in the Canadian Forest* (1859); *Plant Life in Canada, or Gleanings from Forest, Lake, and Plain* (1885); and *Pearls and Pebbles, or The Notes of an Old Naturalist* (1894).

Trail of the Lonesome Pine, The (1908), a novel by JOHN FOX. Fox combined many popular elements in this story of the Cumberland Mountains, and the book immediately became a best seller. A young engineer comes to the mountains in one of the early attempts to industrialize them, and finds himself in the midst of a mountain feud. He falls in love with a beautiful but uneducated girl who is prepared to marry her cousin, sends her east to be educated, and marries her. The novel was successfully made into a silent film (1922), but before that was made into a play (1912) by EUGENE WALTER and taken as the title of an appealing song (1913) by Ballard MacDonald and Harry Carroll.

Train, Arthur [Cheney] (1875–1945), lawyer, public official, writer. Train, born in Boston and educated at Harvard College and the Harvard Law School, was admitted to the bar in Massachusetts and New York. His first practice in New York City came as counsel for the New York Legal Aid Society, service that impressed him deeply and is reflected in his popular stories about Ephraim Tutt. His books became best sellers, and Train devoted more time to writing, finally giving up the law entirely.

Train first appeared in print when his short story "The Maximilian Diamond" was published in *Leslie's Magazine* (July 1904). His first book was *McAllister and His Double* (1905). But his Tutt stories, about a crafty old lawyer who uses his legal skill to help persons in trouble, won him his widest recognition. They appeared in the *Saturday Evening Post* and furnished material for more than a dozen books. Train wrote many other books, among them *The Prisoner at the Bar* (1906); *Confessions of Artemus Quibble* (1909); *The Earthquake* (1918); *On the Trail of the Bad Men* (1925); *Puritan's Progress* (1931), on America's Puritan tradition; *Mr. Tutt's Case Book* (1937); *My Day in Court* (1939), an autobiography; *From the District Attorney's Office* (1939), on the criminal justice system; and *Tassels on Her Boots* (1940).

Many readers believed Mr. Tutt was a real person whose pen name was Arthur Train. This belief became especially widespread after the appearance of *Yankee Lawyer: The Autobiography of Ephraim Tutt* (1943), a marvelously plausible narrative.

Tramp Abroad, A (1880), a travel book by MARK TWAIN. Based partly on a five-week walking tour Twain made with the Rev. JOSEPH TWICHELL (Mr. Harris in the book) through southern Germany and Switzerland in the summer of 1878, *A Tramp Abroad* is a discursive, occasionally humorous sequence of anecdotes, descriptive sketches of German scenes and customs, with comic illustrations, including a few by the author.

Transcendental Club. See TRANSCENDENTALISM.

transcendentalism. In America, a movement of philosophical idealism that reached its height in New England during the 1840s and inspired the work of EMERSON, BRONSON ALCOTT, THOREAU, MARGARET FULLER, and others. Rebelling against the coldness of 18th-century empiricism and its reliance on sense experience, the transcendentalists asserted the supremacy of mind over matter and defended intuition as a guide to truth.

The terms *transcendent* and *transcendental* were employed during the Middle Ages to designate concepts that overpass the finite. The Schoolmen had used them to describe universal truths that transcended the categories of Aristotle. Kant, who influenced the New England group, reserved the term *transcendent* for ideas that can in no way be experienced, using *transcendental* for *a priori* elements of thought—such as the concepts of space and time—which do not arise from sense experience but are manifested in and give meaning to sense experience.

New England transcendentalism was one of several aspects of the new romanticism, which stemmed from Germany and France. Its followers read widely in Kant, Hegel, Schelling, Fichte, Goethe, and Mme. de Staël, though many received their inspiration indirectly by way of Coleridge and Carlyle. Indeed, the transcendentalists often adopted the language of Coleridge in distinguishing between the old school of reason, which reached conclusions by observation and induction, and the new school of understanding, which used *a priori* pure reason to intuit an immediate perception of truth regardless of external evidence. They caught the contagion of Carlyle's moral fervor, sometimes echoing his jagged eloquence as well as his thoughts. When Thoreau writes, "We know but few men, a great many coats and breeches," one suspects he has been reading Carlyle's *Sartor Resartus*. However, both Thoreau and Emerson were genuinely inventive and original. Their chief debt to the European idealists was for an attitude of antiformalism and a philosophical sanction for their own independence of thought. To these ideas from Europe, they wedded a deep interest in Oriental mysticism, and they were influenced as well by American UNITARIANISM.

Emerson's *Nature* (1836) was the first significant statement of American transcendentalism. The beginning of his lecture "The Transcendentalist" (1842) summed up his position at that time: "What is popularly called Transcendentalism among us, is Idealism; Idealism as it appears in 1842. As thinkers, mankind have ever divided into two sects, Materialists and Idealists; the first class founding on experience, the second on consciousness; the first class beginning to think from the data of the senses, the second class perceive that the senses are not final, and say, 'The senses give us representations of things,' but what are the things themselves, they cannot tell. The materialist insists on facts, on history, on the force of circumstances and the animal wants of man; the idealist on the power of Thought and of Will, on inspiration, on miracle, on individual culture. These two modes of thinking are both natural, but the idealist contends that his way of thinking is in higher nature. He concedes all that the other affirms, admits the impressions of sense, admits their coherency, their use and beauty, and then asks the materialist for his grounds of assurance that things are as his senses represent them. But I, he says, affirm facts not affected by the illusions of sense, facts which are of the same nature as the faculty which reports them, and not liable to doubt; facts which in their first appearance to us assume a native superiority to material facts, degrading these into a language by which the first are to be spoken. . . ."

New England transcendentalism was not an organized movement, nor did it produce a philosophical system. Like its chief spokesman, Emerson, it stood for self-expression and so encouraged its followers to seek the light wherever their natures pointed it out. Three specific projects were closely related to the movement: the Transcendental Club, *The Dial*, and Brook Farm. The Transcendental Club was organized in 1836 at the home of the Rev. GEORGE RIPLEY for "exchange of thought among those interested in the new views in philosophy, theology, and literature." Early members were Ripley, Emerson, FREDERIC HENRY HEDGE, Convers Francis, JAMES FREEMAN CLARKE, and A. Bronson Alcott. Later they were joined by THEODORE PARKER, Margaret Fuller, ORESTES BROWNSON, ELIZABETH and SOPHIA PEABODY, WILLIAM ELLERY CHANNING, JONES VERY, CHRISTOPHER P. CRANCH, Charles T. Follen, and others. THE DIAL and BROOK FARM both had their roots in the discussions of the Transcendental Club. The *Dial* was issued quarterly under the editorship of Margaret Fuller until 1842, thereafter under Emerson until 1844, when it suspended. It published much material that could scarcely have found an outlet elsewhere in America, and in the case of Thoreau, at least, served to launch a career of great significance. Brook Farm was organized as a joint stock company in West Roxbury, Massachusetts, in 1841, and included among its members George Ripley, CHARLES A. DANA, JOHN S. DWIGHT, GEORGE P. BRADFORD, and HAWTHORNE. In 1844, influenced by ALBERT BRISBANE, Brook Farm became a Fourieristic phalanx, and in 1846 a fire destroyed much of the association's property. The group was dissolved in the following year. Hawthorne's picture of the community in THE BLITHEDALE ROMANCE (1852), though not to be accepted literally, undoubtedly reflects the attitude of one who knew the project intimately.

On the whole, however, the transcendentalists were slow to take group action. They regarded each man as a law unto himself and often looked on causes and charities with skepticism. They were somewhat slow to espouse active abolitionism, though their belief in freedom and individualism—together with their impatience with conventional ideas about property rights—made them sympathetic from the start. In the end many of them took action against the slave interests in one form or another, and both Emerson and Thoreau supported John Brown.

In addition to its effects on the lives and in the works of the central figures, New England transcendentalism had far-reaching secondary effects in bolstering American ideas of individualism, self-reliance, the worth of common humanity, the equality of races and sexes, and the interdependence of the natural world and its human inhabitants. These effects have continued, in some instances with increasing force, down to our own day.

Perry Miller compiled *The Transcendentalists: An Anthology* (1950). Studies include O. B. Frothingham, *Transcendentalism in New England* (1876), and Paul F. Boller, Jr., *American Transcendentalism, 1830–1860: An Intellectual Inquiry* (1974).

FREDERICK T. MCGILL, JR./GP

Traubel, Horace [Logo] (1858–1919),   editor, biographer. A native of Camden, New Jersey, and a friend of WALT WHITMAN, Traubel was deeply influenced by the poet. As a youth he worked as a newsboy, compositor, lithographer, bank clerk, and factory paymaster. In Philadelphia he founded and edited the monthly *Conservator* (1890–1919) and *The Artsman* (1903–1907). Traubel's political philosophy, a mixture of Marxist socialism and poetic mysticism, found expression in these periodicals and in his books: *Chants Communal* (1904), *Optimos* (1910), and *Collects* (1914). As one of Whitman's three literary executors, Traubel took part in the publication of several books by and about the poet. His own contribution was *With Walt Whitman in Camden* (3 v. 1906, 1908, 1914), part of a meticulously kept diary of daily conversations with Whitman. A fourth volume, edited by Sculley Bradley, appeared in 1953.

Traveler from Altruria, A (1894),   a novel by WILLIAM DEAN HOWELLS. America's social and economic shortcomings are revealed in a series of amusing conversations between Mr. Homos, a visitor from the utopian land of Altruria, and a popular novelist, a banker, a lawyer, a doctor, a professor, a minister, and a society woman. Mr. Homos expounds Howells' Christian socialist ideas in his account of the peaceful overthrow of "the Accumulation" (monopolies) in Altruria by the popular vote and the establishment of a truly democratic, humanitarian commonwealth. The account of Altruria is continued in a sequel, *Through the Eye of the Needle* (1907).

Traven, B. (?–1969),   novelist. The man who wrote under the name of B. Traven guarded the secret of his identity all his life. Although he is known to have lived his final years in Mexico, the details of his early life are shrouded in mystery. The two most common conjectures are that he was either born in Chicago in 1890 and named Berick Traven Torsvan or was born in Germany in 1882 and named Ret Marut. More fanciful interpretations identify him as everyone from JACK LONDON to the illegitimate son of Kaiser Wilhelm. It is not even known in what language Traven's novels were originally written. Whatever his identity, he left a legacy of hardboiled proletarian novels. The most enduring, *The Treasure of the Sierra Madre* (1935), is a brilliant psychological study of human greed, which became an outstanding movie. His major work was the *Caoba Cycle*, a series of six novels about the gruesome conditions that led to the Mexican Revolution of 1910.

Treatise of the New India, A (1553),   the first book about America published in England. The full title was *A Treatise of the New India, with Other New-Found Lands and Islands, as Well Eastward as Westward, as They Are Known and Found in These Our Days*. It was a translation by the Englishman Richard Eben of Sebastian Muenster's *Cosmographia Universalis* (1544). Eben's version discusses the Spanish explorations in the New World up to the year 1501, with references to such hazards as cannibals, Amazons, and poisoned arrows.

Treatise on the Gods, A (1930,   "corrected and rewritten" 1946), by H. L. MENCKEN. Mencken supported this analysis of world religion with a good deal of research and by

the time he finished regarded it as his masterpiece. In his 1946 revision Mencken left largely unchanged the first four sections, dealing with the nature and origin of religion, its evolution, its varieties, and its Christian form. But the fifth section—on the modern state of religion—was elaborately reworked to bring it up to date. Mencken regarded the book as forming one part of a trilogy with *Notes on Democracy* (1926) and *Treatise on Right and Wrong* (1934).

Trees (*Poetry*, August 1913; in *Trees and Other Poems*, 1914),   a poem by JOYCE KILMER. Kilmer's death in battle served to increase his popularity and that of the poem.

Tresselt, Alvin R. (1917–2000),   children's book author. Born in Passaic, New Jersey, Tresselt became a prolific author of children's books, an editor of *Humpty Dumpty's Magazine*, and an executive at Parent's Magazine Press. His books, which have sold in the millions, include these for younger children: *White Snow, Bright Snow* (1948), about the wonder of the first flakes falling, and *Sun Up* (1949), about one day on a family farm, both illustrated by Roger Duvoisin; and *The Dead Tree* (1972, reissued as *The Gift of the Tree*, 1992), about the cycle of life thriving around a tree that has died.

Trifles (1916),   a one-act play by SUSAN GLASPELL. Originally produced by the Provincetown Players, it immediately became a favorite of amateur companies. A woman in a New England community murders her husband—apparently without motivation. The quick observations of women neighbors are cleverly contrasted with the condescending obtuseness of their menfolk, and it becomes obvious that the husband had got what he had deserved. The play, a dramatization of Glaspell's short story "A Jury of Her Peers," was included in her collection of *Plays* (1920).

Trillin, Calvin (1935–   ),   journalist, humorous essayist, novelist, memoirist. Born in Kansas City and educated at Yale, Trillin has written for *Time* magazine, *The New Yorker*, and *The Nation*. His social and political commentary is gathered in books that include *An Education in Georgia* (1964), about the landmark integration of a southern university; *U.S. Journal* (1971); *Uncivil Liberties* (1982); *With All Disrespect* (1985); *If You Can't Say Something Nice* (1987); *Killings* (1984); *American Stories* (1991); and *Too Soon to Tell* (1995), short, comic essays on the world as it approaches the year 2000. His delight in good food is a major theme in *American Fried* (1974), *Alice, Let's Eat* (1978), and *Third Helpings* (1983), published together as *The Tummy Trilogy* (1994). Memoirs include *Travels with Alice* (1989), his wife; *Remembering Denny* (1993), a college friend of great promise who became a suicide at fifty-five; *Deadline Poet: Or My Life as a Doggerelist* (1994); *Messages from My Father* (1996); and *Family Man* (1998), essays, with observations on parenthood. His comic fiction includes *Barnett Frummer Is an Unbloomed Flower* (1969), stories; *Runestruck* (1977), about a New England town where Vikings are thought to have landed; and *Floater* (1980), a novel about writing for a news magazine.

Trilling, Diana Rubin (1905–1996),   writer. A native of New York City and a graduate of Radcliffe, Diana Trilling was the wife of the distinguished critic LIONEL TRILLING. She has edited and written the introductions for *The Portable D. H. Lawrence* (1947) and *The Selected Letters of D. H. Lawrence* (1958), in addition to contributing literary, political, and cultural essays to the *Partisan Review, The Nation,* and *The New Yorker. We Must March My Darlings* (1977) and *Reviewing the Forties* (1978) are collections of essays. *The Death of the Scarsdale Diet Doctor* (1981) is about a celebrated murder case and its implications for the treatment of women. *The Beginning of the Journey* (1993) is a memoir of her life with Lionel Trilling.

Trilling, Lionel (1905–1975),   teacher, critic, writer. Trilling, born in New York City, was educated at Columbia University. He taught at the University of Wisconsin and Hunter College before being appointed to the Columbia faculty in 1931, finally achieving the rank of professor of English. In his first published work, *Matthew Arnold* (1939), Trilling found new insights into Arnold's character and work by using the methods of modern psychology, anthropology, and political theory. In many other critical works he also employed these methods, among them *E. M. Forster* (1943), *The Liberal Imagination* (1950), *The Opposing Self* (1955), and *A Gathering of Fugitives* (1956). His interesting novel *The Middle of the Journey* (1947) is an effort in the exercise of what Trilling called the "moral imagination." Trilling's works include several excellent short stories. His highly influential essays in *The Nation, New Republic, The New York Times Book Review, Partisan Review,* and the *Kenyon Review* revived interest in many neglected works. As editorial adviser to *Partisan Review* and the *Kenyon Review* he inspired their consistent excellence. Among his other major works is *Freud and the Crisis of Our Culture* (1955). He also edited *The Portable Matthew Arnold* (1949) and the *Letters of John Keats* (1950). Leon Wieseltier edited *The Moral Obligation to Be Intelligent* (2000), a collection of thirty-two essays by Trilling.

Tripolitan War.   See BARBARY WARS.

Tristram (1927),   a narrative poem in blank verse by EDWIN ARLINGTON ROBINSON. *Tristram* is the third of Robinson's Arthurian poems; it was preceded by MERLIN (1917) and LANCELOT (1920). Tristram falls deeply in love with Isolt, his old uncle's beautiful wife, but he marries Isolt of Brittany, whose adoration he can never return. Her pitiable resignation begins and ends the poems. In between come the lovers' happiness and death, full of imagery of sea and stars. Robinson cunningly opposes the two Isolts: the longed-for unattainable and the neglected attainable.

Triumph of the Egg, The (1921),   "a book of impressions from American life in tales and poems," by SHERWOOD ANDERSON. In the title story an unsuccessful chicken farmer's life is dominated by eggs, and he comprehends his tragedy and frustration when he fails to perform a simple trick with an egg. Other stories in the book relate simple incidents in everyday lives that are given poignancy by Anderson's interpretations.

Triumphs of Love, The, or, Happy Reconciliation (1795),   a play by John Murdoch. This play introduced the first stage black to an American audience—using the name

Sambo, which became conventional thereafter. Quakers and the Whiskey Rebellion also enter into the plot.

Trollope, Anthony (1815–1882),   English novelist, editor. The novelist served the British Post Office from 1834 to 1867. In the course of his service he made trips abroad, including two to the United States. Perhaps because he remembered the harsh account of America given by his mother (*see next entry*), Trollope published a largely favorable account in his *North America* (1862) and wrote a novel called *The American Senator* (1877). He also wrote a travel book called *The West Indies and the Spanish Main* (1859).

Trollope, Frances [Milton] (1780–1863),   English novelist, author of travel books. Mrs. Trollope turned out more than fifty novels and travel books, but is remembered most for her *Domestic Manners of the Americans* (1832), written after a stay of twenty-five months in Cincinnati, then a frontier town, and sixteen months in the East. The failure of several of her schemes, including a plan to start a department store in Cincinnati, may have influenced her point of view toward things American, which ranged from mildly favorable to vicious condemnation. She found us so raw and proud that our "desire for approbation" and "delicate sensitiveness under censure" constituted "a weakness which amounts to imbecility." Two satirical replies to Mrs. Trollope were Asa Greene's *Travels in America by George Fibbleton* (1833) and Frederick William Shelton's *The Trollopiad, or, Traveling Gentlemen in America* (1837). More serious was Francis J. Grund's *The Americans in Their Moral, Social, and Political Relations* (1837). Mrs. Trollope also appears satirically as Mrs. Wollope in J. K. Paulding's play THE LION OF THE WEST (completed 1830, pub. 1954).

Tropic of Cancer (1934),   a book by HENRY MILLER. Miller's first published work, *Tropic of Cancer*, was published in Paris and was immediately banned by United States customs. In 1961 the first American edition became a best seller. The book is a history of Miller's life in Paris during the early thirties. Penniless and starving, he underwent complete physical and spiritual degradation.

Tropic of Capricorn (1939),   the companion volume to Henry Miller's *Tropic of Cancer*. It treats Miller's life in the United States, including his boyhood in Brooklyn. It was published in Paris in 1939 but was excluded from the United States by censors until 1962.

Troubetzkoy, Amélie Rives, Princess (1863–1945), novelist, playwright, poet. Born in Richmond, Virginia, Amélie Rives married J. A. Armstrong, whom she divorced in 1895, and then married (1896) a portrait painter, Prince Pierre Troubetzkoy of Russia, who died in 1936. She wrote some successful novels, including *The Quick, or the Dead?* (1889); *The World's End* (1914); and *Firedamp* (1930). She also wrote several books of verse, among them *Sélené* (1905) and *As the Wind Blew* (1922); and several plays, including *Herod and Mariamne* (1888), *Augustine the Man* (1906), *The Fear Market* (1916), *Allegiance* (1918), and, with Gilbert Emery, *Love-in-a-Mist* (1926). Her play *The Young Elizabeth* appeared in 1937.

Trowbridge, John Townsend ["Paul Creyton"] (1827–1916), author, editor. Trowbridge, born in Ogden, New York, was largely self-taught. His contributions of short stories to Mordecai M. Noah's *Dollar Magazine* won him that editor's friendship and help. Trowbridge began editing magazines in 1850. In 1865 he joined the staff of OUR YOUNG FOLKS and served as managing editor from 1870 to 1873; in October 1873 the magazine merged with *St. Nicholas*. In the meantime Trowbridge had been contributing verse to the *Atlantic* and writing books for boys. The books by which he is remembered are NEIGHBOR JACKWOOD (1857) and CUDJO'S CAVE (1864), both antislavery novels. In *Neighbor Jackwood* Camille Delisard, a fugitive slave of mixed ancestry, is protected by her Vermont neighbors. Like other authors of juveniles, Trowbridge did some books in series, especially the widely read Jack Hazard Series (1871–74). His *Poetical Works*, published in 1903, includes two pieces not yet forgotten: DARIUS GREEN AND HIS FLYING MACHINE and "The Vagabonds." *My Own Story* appeared in 1903. *Neighbor Jackwood* was dramatized in 1857.

True Relation of Virginia, A (1608), an account of the first American colony by JOHN SMITH. Largely written in a tent in the wilderness, this account was intended for the London stockholders who financed Smith's voyage, and is mostly concerned with early Indian troubles, the choice of a site for settlement, and civic organization in the colony.

True West (1980), a play by SAM SHEPARD dealing with intense rivalry between two brothers. Austin is a successful screenwriter, and Lee, the older brother, is a drifter.

Truman, Harry S (1884–1972), 33rd U.S. president. Truman was born in Lamar, Missouri. Unable to obtain a college education, he managed his father's farm and clerked in a bank for a while. He served overseas in the army during World War I, then started an unsuccessful business venture as a haberdasher. Through the influence of Thomas J. Pendergast, the political boss of Kansas City and the surrounding region, he won a series of public offices: county judge, presiding judge of the court, and U.S. senator. In the meantime he attended the Kansas City Law School for two years.

In 1944 Truman was elected vice-president under FRANKLIN D. ROOSEVELT. He took office in January and became president when Roosevelt died on April 12, 1945. Truman made many momentous decisions toward the end of World War II, the most portentous of which was to use two atomic bombs to end the war against Japan. He gave unwavering support to the newly formed United Nations. At first he sought to work with Russia, but soon realized that this was impractical and formulated the so-called Truman Doctrine of aid to the free peoples of the world "resisting attempted subjugation by armed minorities or outside pressures." In his domestic policies Truman generally followed Roosevelt's New Deal.

In the 1948 election Truman surprised most experts by defeating Thomas E. Dewey. In his full term he supplied aid and troops to the United Nations when North Korea, assisted by Russia and China, invaded South Korea (1950). To him must be credited the Marshall Plan, helping Europe recover from the effects of World War II. He refused to run for another term and retired to Independence, Missouri, where he devoted much of his time to preparing his memoirs and planning a memorial library.

He wrote *Years of Decision* (1955) and *Years of Trial and Hope* (1956)—his memoirs—as well as *Mr. Citizen* (1960).

Trumbo, Dalton (1905–1976), novelist, film writer. Born in Colorado, Trumbo wrote over forty screenplays. Among them are *A Man to Remember, Kitty Foyle, A Guy Named Joe, Thirty Seconds Over Tokyo*, and *Our Vines Have Tender Grapes*. He was a vigorous left-wing novelist, pamphleteer, and magazine writer during the 1930s. His fiction, essays, and verse appeared in numerous magazines. His most striking work is *Johnny Got His Gun* (1939), a vivid antiwar novel that won a National Booksellers Award. In it a mutilated victim of World War I wants to be displayed to people as an object lesson in the horrors of war, but the powers-that-be will not allow it. The book was published just six days after the German invasion of Poland. For a more than decade after World War II, Trumbo was blacklisted by the movie companies, who refused to hire him because of his political views and refusal to testify before the House Un-American Activities Committee. Writing under the pseudonym Robert Rich, he won an Oscar for *The Brave One* (1956). His other scripts include *Exodus* (1960) and *Spartacus* (1960), both written under his own name. In the early 1970s Trumbo was finally able to film his own *Johnny Got His Gun*, which won the Cannes Film Festival award. A collection of letters, *Additional Dialogue*, appeared in 1970.

Trumbull, Benjamin (1735–1820), clergyman, historian. Trumbell wrote *A Complete History of Connecticut* (1797, rev. 1818), portraying the state's early history. He projected a complete history of the United States, but only one volume, *General History of the Unites States* (1810), was published. *A Compendium of the Indian Wars in New England* (1924) was edited from his work.

Trumbull, John (1750–1831), poet. A child prodigy, Connecticut-born Trumbull passed the Yale entrance examination at the age of seven. As a student at Yale he criticized the academic curriculum and advocated a more liberal curriculum that would include the study of literature. This criticism forms the subject of *An Essay on the Uses and Advantages of the Fine Arts* (1770) as well as his long satirical poem THE PROGRESS OF DULNESS (1772–73), written after Trumbull had become a tutor at Yale (1772). He published a series of essays under the pen name The Correspondent in *The Connecticut Journal* (1770–73). Having passed the bar examination, he practiced law in the office of John Adams in Boston, and took part in the political agitation of the time. Later he was a representative in the legislature of Connecticut and a judge in the Supreme Court. The Revolution evoked the patriotic poem *An Elegy on the Times* (1774), and Trumbull's most popular poem, M'FINGAL (began 1775, completed 1782). After the Revolution Trumbull became leader of the HARTFORD WITS and a staunchly conservative Federalist. *The Poetical Works of John Trumbull* was published in two volumes (1820).

Truth, Sojourner [Isabella Van Wagener] (c. 1797–1883), abolitionist, orator. Born into slavery in Ulster County, New York, Sojourner Truth was called Isabella and, after fleeing to freedom in 1827, took the name of the Van Wagener family, who protected her. She became a domestic servant in New York City and set up a home for her youngest son and daughter about 1829—two older children had already been sold into slavery. Inspired by visions and voices, she renamed herself in 1843 and launched the speaking tours that made her widely known. Sojourner Truth was illiterate, but she dictated her story to Olive Gilbert and sold her autobiographical account *Narrative of Sojourner Truth* (1850) to her lecture audiences. Under the influence of ELIZABETH CADY STANTON, who recorded some of her speeches and printed transcripts in E. C. Stanton et al., *The History of Women's Suffrage* (1881–1886), Sojourner Truth also spoke for women's rights.

Tsukiyama, Gail (1950–), novelist. Born in San Francisco to a Chinese mother from Hong Kong and a father who was a Japanese-American from Hawaii, Tsukiyama graduated from San Francisco State University (B.A. and M.A.), with a master's thesis in poetry. Her first novel, *Women of the Silk* (1991) followed the success of AMY TAN's *The Joy Luck Club* at a time when, as Tsukiyama has observed, "publishing houses were suddenly opened to Asian women writers." It tells of the relative independence gained in China by women whose silk work supported them economically as no other work could. She based her second novel, *The Samurai's Garden* (1995), on the experience of a favorite uncle, a young Chinese man from Hong Kong sent to his family's vacation home in Japan to recover from tuberculosis, creating a fine novel of exile and illness, with parallels to life at the nearby leper colony and the societal sickness of war as Japan invades China. *Night of Many Dreams* (1998) chronicles the lives of sisters in Hong Kong who survive the Japanese occupation, one to become a film actress in Hong Kong, the other a student in San Francisco. *The Language of Threads* (1999), a sequel to *Women of the Silk*, brings the story to Hong Kong during the Japanese occupation.

Tubman, Harriet [Ross] (1821?–1913), emancipation leader. Tubman, born in Maryland, spent her early life as a field hand but escaped from that work about 1849. She returned to the South on the underground railroad and spent the next ten years leading more than 300 slaves to freedom. During the Civil War she worked as a cook and nurse for the Union Army, led scouting parties, and often spied behind Confederate lines. After the war she gave shelter to children and old people in her home in Auburn, New York. Sarah Hopkins Bradford wrote *Scenes in the Life of Harriet Tubman* (1869, re. as *Harriet the Moses of Her People*, 1886). Earl Conrad wrote *Harriet Tubman* (1943), a biography. Anne Parish's novel *Clouded Star* (1948) is centered on Tubman's work on the underground railroad. Ann Petry wrote *Harriet Tubman: Conductor on the Underground Railway* (1955).

Tucci, Niccolò (1908–1999), novelist, short-story writer. Born in Lugarno, Switzerland, in 1908, Tucci was raised in Florence, Italy, and studied in German universities and at Amherst College as an exchange student (1931–1932). Briefly a doctoral student at the University of California, Berkeley, he completed a Ph.D. in political science, with a defense of fascism, at the University of Florence and went to work for Mussolini's propaganda ministry. Disillusioned with fascism, he moved permanently to New York in 1938, and, after a court fight because of his background, became a citizen in 1953. His "pre-autobiography" provided the material for the novels *Before My Time* (1962), centered on his Russian grandmother, and *The Son and the Moon* (1977), about the courtship and marriage of his parents. *The Rain Came Last and Other Stories* (1990) draws on his childhood and that of his children. *Unfinished Funeral* (1964) is a novel about a European matriarch. *Il Segreto* (1956), *Gli Atlantici* (1968), and *Confessioni Involontarie* (1977) are autobiographical.

Tuchman, Barbara W[ertheim] (1912–1989), journalist, historian. Without an academic title or an advanced degree, Tuchman trained herself as a prize-winning writer of history. Her fourth book, *The Guns of August* (1962), about the background and beginnings of World War I, won a Pulitzer Prize and made her a celebrity. A second Pulitzer Prize winner is *Stilwell and The American Experience in China: 1911–45* (1971), about a major figure of World War II. She described mankind's penchant for war in *The March of Folly: From Troy to Vietnam* (1984) and discussed the American Revolution in *The First Salute* (1988). Her first books, *The Lost British Policy* (1938), *Bible and Sword* (1956), and *The Zimmerman Telegram* (1958), were published under her maiden name. Her other books include *The Proud Tower* (1965), on the period leading up to World War I; *Notes from China* (1972); *The Distant Mirror* (1978), on the parallels between the 14th century and the present; and *Practicing History* (1981), a collection of essays.

Tucker, George ["Joseph Atterley"] (1775–1861), public official, economist, teacher, writer. Tucker, a friend of Jefferson and Madison, wrote a life of Jefferson (2 v. 1837). He came to the United States from Bermuda in 1795, was graduated from the College of William and Mary (1797), studied law with his kinsman ST. GEORGE TUCKER, and began practice in Richmond. Along with his work in the law he did much writing—essays, letters for publication, and verse. Richmond's social activities demanded too much of his time, and he moved to southern Virginia. He continued to write and became increasingly interested in economics and philosophy. In 1815 he was elected to the Virginia House of Burgesses, in 1819 to the House of Representatives, and at the age of fifty was made professor of moral philosophy at the University of Virginia. He published books in economics, history, and philosophy, among them *The Laws of Wages, Profits, and Rent Investigated* (1837); *The Theory of Money and Banks Investigated* (1837); *The History of the United States* (4 v. 1856–57); *Political Economy for the People* (1859); and *Essays, Moral and Metaphysical* (1860). Tucker was also a novelist, but the only story still remembered is *A Voyage to the Moon* (1827), published under the pen name Joseph Atterley.

Tucker, Nathaniel Beverley (1784–1851), teacher, novelist. A Virginian, Tucker defended slavery and the Old South in his fiction and as professor of law at the College of William and Mary. His first novel, published anonymously, was *George Balcombe* (1836), a romantic tale of plantation life heavily indebted to Scott. Edgar Allan Poe praised the book as "*the best* American novel." Under the pen name Edward W. Sidney, Tucker wrote THE PARTISAN LEADER: A TALE OF THE FUTURE (1836), a novel that achieved notoriety by its prediction of secession and Civil War and its wholesale attack on Jackson, Van Buren, and northern democracy. Tucker's third novel, *Gertrude*, appeared serially in the *Southern Literary Messenger* (1844–45).

Tucker, St. George (1752–1827), lawyer, teacher, poet, editor. In the early 1770s Tucker left his home in Bermuda and came to Williamsburg, Virginia, to study law with George Wythe. Back in Bermuda, he furnished aid to the American patriots. He returned to Virginia in 1778, married Mrs. Frances Bland Randolph, mother of John Randolph of Roanoke, and served in the Virginia militia. After the war Tucker attained distinction as a lawyer, judge, and teacher of law at the College of William and Mary. In 1796 he published *A Dissertation on Slavery: With a Proposal for the Gradual Abolition of It in the State of Virginia*. He compiled an American edition of Blackstone's *Commentaries* (5 v. 1803), which became the standard authority in the South. Washington highly esteemed his *Liberty, a Poem on the Independence of America* (1788) and *Probationary Odes of Jonathan Pindar, Esq.* These political satires were in imitation of John Wolcot, who wrote in England under the pen name Peter Pindar. They appeared in part in Philip Freneau's *National Gazette* (1793) and then in book form (1796), and they have been erroneously ascribed to Freneau. The poems are anti-Federalist and satirize Alexander Hamilton and John Adams among others.

Tuckerman, Frederick Goddard (1821–1873), poet, lawyer, scientist. Tuckerman was born in Boston, admitted to the bar and practiced for a short time, but for the greater part of his life was a recluse living in Greenfield, Massachusetts. There he observed the skies and nature and made notes on eclipses and local fauna. In 1860 he published a slim book of *Poems*, all sonnets. He sent copies to some of the noted writers of the time; Tennyson regarded them highly. New American editions of his *Poems* appeared in 1864 and 1869, but his work dropped out of sight until the 20th century. In 1931 WITTER BYNNER prepared an edition of *The Sonnets of Frederick Goddard Tuckerman* with a long and enthusiastic introduction. N. Scott Momaday edited *The Complete Poems* (1965). In 1952 Samuel A. Golden prepared an informative account of *Frederick Goddard Tuckerman: An American Sonneteer*, which includes some theretofore unpublished poems and letters.

Tuckerman, Henry Theodore (1813–1871), critic, historian, writer. A man of great culture and sensitive appreciation, Boston-born Tuckerman was valued highly by his American contemporaries. Among his works are *Italian Sketch-Book* (1835); *Characteristics of Literature* (1840, 1851);

Rambles and Reveries (1841); *Thoughts of the Poets* (1846); *Artist Life* (1847); *Poems* (1851); *Essays Biographical and Critical* (1857); and *America and Her Commentators: With a Critical Sketch of Travel in the U.S.* (1864).

Tudor, William (1779–1830), merchant, editor, novelist. Tudor, born in Boston, was a founder of the Anthology Club. The club sponsored the *Monthly Anthology*, which published Tudor's travel accounts and essays. He was the first editor of *The North American Review*. His published works are *Letters on the Eastern States* (1820), *Miscellanies* (1821), and *Gebel Teir* (1829), a satirical novel published anonymously. Named American consul at Lima in 1823, he died of fever in South America.

Tuesday Club. [1] A club by this name flourished in Annapolis, Maryland, in the middle of the 18th century. It was a coffee-house affair, with ALEXANDER HAMILTON and Jonas Green as prominent members. [2] A similarly named club was active in Philadelphia in the early 19th century. It furnished contributions for the PORT FOLIO. [3] The Tuesday Evening Club of Boston had many brilliant, usually amateur, writers as members. Their work appeared in the earlier volumes of the *North American Review*.

Tulley, John (1639?–1701), almanac maker. Tulley was among the first to produce almanacs in America. He came to this country from England at a very early age and lived in Saybrook, Connecticut. He was also apparently the first to give his almanacs a humorous turn, a practice soon imitated. His almanacs were issued from 1687 to 1702 and became very popular. The 1689 issue contained a road guide to New England, the first of its kind.

Tully, Jim (1891–1947), hobo, farmer, prize fighter, writer, publicity man. Somehow in the course of his bitter, poverty-stricken youth in St. Mary's, Ohio, Tully learned to read. While hoboing he managed to get hold of many of the world's classics, and became what someone called "a literary burn." He haunted libraries during his pugilistic career and began writing, becoming one of the many writers whom H. L. Mencken discovered. Among his books are *Emmet Lawlor* (1922), BEGGARS OF LIFE (1924), *Jarnegan* (1926), *The Life of Charlie Chaplin* (1926), *Circus Parade* (1927), *Shanty Irish* (1928), *Close Ups* (1930), *Adventures in Interviewing* (1931), *Men in the Rough* (1933), *The Bruiser* (1936), and *A Dozen and One* (1943).

Tully, Richard Walton (1877–1945), playwright, producer. A native of Nevada City, California, and educated at the University of California, Tully won a prize there for a farce called *A Strenuous Life* (1900). He went on to write a large number of successful plays in which romance and picturesque backgrounds were emphasized. Perhaps the most noted of these was *The Bird of Paradise* (1912), a drama of Hawaii. The play was made into a musical comedy in 1930. Other plays by Tully include *Rose of the Rancho* (1906), *Omar the Tentmaker* (1914), *The Flame* (1916), and *Blossom Bride* (1927).

Turner, Frederick Jackson (1861–1932), historian. Turner was born in Portage, Wisconsin, and did his undergraduate work at the University of Wisconsin. While he was a graduate student at Johns Hopkins, he returned to Wisconsin as a member of the history faculty. In 1893 Turner read a short essay to the annual meeting of the American Historical Association in Philadelphia. It was "The Significance of the Frontier in American History," advocating the view that the frontier experience had played the greatest role in forming the American character. This idea, which held promise of a unique meaningfulness to American experience, was enthusiastically received by the profession and made Turner's career. At Wisconsin and Harvard, Turner taught and influenced a generation of American historians. His other writings include *The Rise of the West* (1906), *The Significance of Sections in American History* (1932), and *The United States, 1830–1850: The Nation and Its Sections* (1935). In 1938 a posthumous collection, *The Early Writings of Frederick Jackson Turner*, was compiled by E. F. Edwards. More recently, Ray Allen Billington edited *Frontier and Section: Selected Essays of Frederick Jackson Turner* (1961), and W. R. Jacobs compiled *Frederick Jackson Turner's Legacy: Unpublished Writings in American History* (1965) and *The Historical World of Frederick Jackson Turner* (1966). Turner's Ph.D. dissertation was published in 1977 as *The Character and Influence of the Indian Trade in Wisconsin*, ed. by D. H. Miller and W. W. Savage, Jr. The most important biography is Billington's *Frederick Jackson Turner* (1973). See FRONTIER IN AMERICAN HISTORY, THE.

DAVID HARRY MILLER

Turner, Nat (1800–1831),   slave leader. Turner, believing himself divinely appointed to bring his fellow slaves to freedom, led the revolt of approximately sixty slaves in the Southampton Insurrection (1831). In the short-lived revolt, fifty-five whites were killed; sixteen slaves were caught and hanged immediately. Turner escaped, but six months later was taken and hanged. The incident led to more rigorous slave laws in the South. The main character in Harriet Beecher Stowe's *Dred: a Tale of the Great Dismal Swamp* (1856) was modeled on Nat Turner. *Confessions of Nat Turner* (1967), a novel by William Styron, is a fictionalized first-person narrative account based on a pamphlet of the same name published in Virginia in 1832.

Turn of the Screw, The (1898),   a tale by HENRY JAMES. This framed first-person narrative is a study in ambiguity. A young governess put in sole charge of two small children, Miles and Flora, in a country house called Bly records her progressive discoveries that the children are not innocent but demonic, in communication with the ghosts of their deceased former governess, Miss Jessel, and a male servant, Peter Quint. The young governess fights for the souls of the two children against the pervasive influence of the evil dead. Criticism of the tale has been divided between the apparitionist position—this is a ghost tale of demonic horror—and the nonapparitionist, or psychoanalytic, position—the tale records the powerful hallucinations of an emotionally hungry governess. According to the second group of critics, the obsession of the governess with her employer or "Master," who is the children's

uncle, leads her to project the ghostly figures of Quint and Miss Jessel as the guilty doubles of her own fantasized romance. The nonapparitionist position, first advanced by Edna Kenton in *The Arts* (1924), received wider attention on publication of Edmund Wilson's essay "The Ambiguity of Henry James" (1934). Recent poststructuralist criticism has taken this undecidability as an allegory of textuality and reading, especially Shoshana Felman's "Turning the Screw of Interpretation," in *Literature and Psychoanalysis: The Question of Reading: Otherwise* (1982), which diagnoses the interpretive battle generated by the tale as a ghost effect akin to the hauntings within the tale itself.

JULIE RIVKIN

Turow, Scott (1949–   ),   novelist, memoirist. Born in Chicago and educated at New Trier High School, Amherst (B.A., 1970), Stanford (M.A., 1974), and Harvard (J.D., 1978). Intent on becoming a writer from his freshman year at college, Turow published short stories as an undergraduate and spent several years at the creative writing center at Stanford, before turning to the law, which became his ticket to book publication and best-sellerdom. *One L: An Inside Account of Life in the First Year at Harvard Law School* (1977), nonfiction, appeared before his graduation. As a lawyer, he worked as an assistant United States Attorney from 1978 to 1986, then entered a Chicago law firm as a partner, in his spare time writing his first novel, *Presumed Innocent* (1987). Combining the generic requirements of the suspense novel with his experience as a trial lawyer and his serious attention to the craft of writing, he produced a bestseller that was greeted enthusiastically by mass market readers and literary critics alike. Continuing his career as a lawyer, he has drawn on his profession for a series of later bestsellers that includes: *The Burden of Proof* (1990), with one of the characters from *Presumed Innocent* enmeshed in family intrigue after the suicide of his wife; *Pleading Guilty* (1993), about the disappearance of a lawyer and several million dollars of the firm's money; *The Laws of Our Fathers* (1996), with sixties radicals reunited in a case involving the shooting death of a state senator's wife; and *Personal Injuries* (1999), about an F.B.I. sting aimed at corrupt judges.

Tuscarora Indians.   A tribe of the Iroquoian linguistic stock formerly living in northwestern North Carolina. They were allied with the French and in 1711 attacked the white settlers. After a costly defeat they sued for peace in 1712, but again in 1713 they attacked and again were severely defeated. The remnants of the tribe fled to a region north of the Ohio River and in 1715 joined the Iroquois Confederacy, which then became the so-called Six Nations. Some descendants are found mingled with the Senecas in Ottawa County, Oklahoma.

James Fenimore Cooper introduces two prominent Tuscarora chieftains among his characters. One gives the title to his novel WYANDOTTÉ (1843); the other is Chief Arrowhead in THE PATHFINDER (1840). Chief Elias Johnson wrote *Legends, Traditions, and Laws of the Iroquois or Six Nations and History of the Tuscarora Indians* (1881). The tribe's conflict with New

York State officialdom is recounted in Edmund Wilson's *Apologies to the Iroquois* (1960).

Tutt, Ephraim.   See ARTHUR TRAIN.

Twain, Mark.   The pen name of Samuel Langhorne Clemens (1835–1910), humorist, novelist, journalist, lecturer, travel writer. He first adopted the pseudonym Mark Twain on February 3, 1863, in a contribution to the Virginia City *Territorial Enterprise*. The phrase, meaning two fathoms deep, was called in making soundings from Mississippi riverboats.

Born in Florida, Missouri, he was the son of a Virginian migrant who had married in Kentucky and all his life cultivated dreams of easy wealth on the frontier mingled with pride in Southern gentility. A claim to 20,000 acres of worthless Tennessee land continued to haunt the family, as did a nebulous claim to a British title. In 1839, when Sam was four, the Clemenses settled in Hannibal, Missouri. Its population had just risen to about a thousand. By 1847 the Hannibal *Gazette* reported the arrival of over a thousand steamboats annually—the packets were named out of Sir Walter Scott. It was in this busy port that Sam Clemens grew up and that was to serve as the setting for THE ADVENTURES OF TOM SAWYER and ADVENTURES OF HUCKLEBERRY FINN.

In 1847, when Sam was twelve, his father died and the boy was apprenticed to a printer. Soon he was writing for his brother Orion's newspaper. Roaming as a journeyman printer (1853–54), he planned to seek his fortune in South America, but in 1856 he pursued his boyhood ambition to become a steamboat pilot on the Mississippi. When the Civil War broke out, riverboats ceased operating. His older brother had turned Republican, but Sam vacillated, as he was to confess in his "Private History of a Campaign that Failed" (1865), but after three weeks' service as a Confederate volunteer, Sam deserted. Orion, newly appointed secretary to the Governor of the Nevada Territory by President Lincoln, had urged Sam to go to the West. The plan was "to wean Sam away from his rebel cause." It worked, and Sam went.

ROUGHING IT (1872) describes the trip West and his adventures as miner and journalist. Shortly after adopting the pseudonym "Mark Twain," he met ARTEMUS WARD, who encouraged his work, and collaborated with BRET HARTE in San Francisco, where Sam wrote THE CELEBRATED JUMPING FROG OF CALAVERAS COUNTY (1865). The folk tale, long in print in California, catapulted him to celebrity. Lecturing increased his popularity, and in 1867 his letters from the steamship *Quaker City* on a tour to Europe, Egypt, and the Holy Land were syndicated in the San Francisco *Alta California* and two New York papers. These letters, collected as THE INNOCENTS ABROAD (1869), established Mark Twain as America's leading humorist—more than humorist, a democratic buffoon who refused to be conned by high art, high culture, or the intolerable muddles of Mediterranean travel. This role of irreverent jester to the American people was to be maintained by Twain for the remainder of his life.

In 1870 he married Olivia Langdon, daughter of a coal-owning millionaire, whose brother he had met aboard the *Quaker City*. He remained devoted to her to the end, but her role in his life has roused much controversy. Genteel, often invalid, did she stifle her husband's taunting thrusts? Or was it to the loving security of their home that he owed his steady development as a master storyteller? After *Roughing It* Twain collaborated with CHARLES DUDLEY WARNER on THE GILDED AGE (1873), a satirical novel on the postwar boom. Its title became the eponym for the era. There followed—with digressions for a European walking tour, A TRAMP ABROAD (1880), and an English historical romance, THE PRINCE AND THE PAUPER (1882)— the three books for which Mark Twain will always be remembered. All three turn back to his frontier youth along the Mississippi: *The Adventures of Tom Sawyer* (1876), *Life on the Mississippi* (1883), and *Adventures of Huckleberry Finn* (1884–85). For tall tales and tall talk there had been nothing like this in American fiction. It was as if Twain, in the very current of the Mississippi, had discovered the uninterrupted energies of the American voice.

Meanwhile, Twain—always alert to speculations—had diversified. Already a partner of Charles L. Webster & Company, which had reaped a fortune from General Grant's *Personal Memoirs* and his own writings, he invested $200,000 in the as yet imperfect—it proved unperfectible—Paige automatic typesetting machine. As more and more money was poured in, Twain was eventually driven to bankruptcy in the same year that he published the last of his great Mississippi fictions, THE TRAGEDY OF PUDD'NHEAD WILSON (1894). To discharge his debts he made a lecture tour around the world, which he published as FOLLOWING THE EQUATOR (1897). However, much of the fizz had gone out of his style. Even more pedestrian were his efforts to cash in on the popularity of his Tom Sawyer saga. Could *Tom Sawyer* be transferred to the stage? Forced to draw on every scrap of literary capital, he dashed off TOM SAWYER ABROAD (1894) and TOM SAWYER, DETECTIVE (1896). The great matter of Tom and Huck continued to rumble around in his head, but Twain was no longer able to sustain or develop it.

By 1898 he had paid off all his debts, but the sly and once so cheekily vigorous pose now turned to a darker and permanently brooding pessimism in THE MAN THAT CORRUPTED HADLEYBURG (1900), WHAT IS MAN? (1906), THE MYSTERIOUS STRANGER (c. 1905, published posthumously in 1916), and *Letters from the Earth* (c. 1908, edited by Bernard De Voto, 1963). As Satan reports back to God in these *Letters*: "Human history in all its ages is red with blood, and bitter with hate, and stained with cruelties." Lynch law was only one aspect of that darkness exposed in "To the Person Sitting in Darkness" (1901), a Christian darkness conferring civilization on those assumed to be pagans. The address is as damning as the later attack on the Belgian reign of terror in the Congo exposed in "King Leopold's Soliloquy" (1906). Nor was America spared. As Pudd'nhead Wilson had recorded in his "Calendar," heading the final chapter of that novel: "October 12.—It was wonderful to find America, but it would have been more wonderful to miss it." In 1903 *Harper's* refused publication of Twain's assault on MARY BAKER EDDY (*Christian Science*, 1907), whom Twain called the "queen of frauds and hypocrites." By the time of his last writings—published posthumously as *Europe and Elsewhere* (1923)—America for Twain had become "the United States of Lyncherdom" whose "supreme trait" was moral cowardice.

His bitterness was deepened by the death of his wife and two daughters. He now felt, in Satan's words from *The Mysterious Stranger*, "but an empty thought, a useless thought, a homeless thought, wandering forlorn among empty eternities!" He had been engaged since 1906 in dictating his autobiography to his secretary, ALBERT BIGELOW PAINE—later the first literary editor of the Mark Twain Estate. The autobiography was issued in 1924, preceded by an authorized biography (3 v. 1912) and a collection of *Letters* (1917). The second editor, Bernard De Voto, edited further volumes from the vast remaining work, including *Letters from the Earth*. A third editor, Dixon Wecter, collected *The Love Letters of Mark Twain* (1949), and a fourth, Henry Nash Smith, has edited with William M. Gibson *Mark Twain-Howells Letters* (2 v. 1960). A scholarly edition of the complete *Works* began to be published by the University of California Press in 1972, which had also begun issuing in 1967 annotated editions of previously unpublished *Papers*, most of whose originals are now in the Bancroft Library at Berkeley.

Mark Twain was the laureate of the so-called Gilded Age. What had begun with the gold rush became the longest boom years the country had ever known. Fortunes were made and lost as unpredictably as the treasure found by Tom and Huck in the cave at the end of *The Adventures of Tom Sawyer*. The profits earned through publication of Grant's *Memoirs* were lost by Twain a few years later on the unfortunate Paige typesetting machine. One year Twain was a millionaire, the next year bankrupt, just as in his Nevada youth he had struck it rich one week and was out of pocket in the next. He married an heiress, built an extravagant steamboat of a mansion in Connecticut, and had to chase round the world on a lecture tour to recoup his finances. For about a sixth of his life he was more or less forced to live abroad. During the 1890s he was, in effect, an expatriate.

The idea of wealth stands at the center of his fictions. The man who corrupted Hadleyburg did so with wealth. Just the promise of wealth proves enough, as in "The $30,000 Bequest" or "The £1,000,000 Bank Note," two of his better late stories. The treasure found at the end of *Tom Sawyer* terrorizes Huck just as the gift of a moneyed life, made by the slave woman Roxy to her child in *The Tragedy of Pudd'nhead Wilson*, results in the child's destruction. Wealth for Twain is always something of a trap, a fraud, a hoax. It sends you up only to dump you with a bump, rather like Twain's own rhetorical style of humor. First inflation, then deflation or collapse. He perfected the excesses of the frontier, those swings from hyperbole, to bathos, which shape the world of humor and of dreams. Like another P. T. BARNUM, he fed the national greed for plugs and impostures. His very entrances and exits on and off the public stage were part of the performance: coming on with a sidelong, awkward stride or a funny little shuffle and often hippety-hopping off the stage. His verbal mannerism became

a trademark: impassive, diffident, drawling, even bumbling. He developed a deadpan style, punctured by mock perplexity at the laughter it evoked. He manipulated his audiences, as he manipulated his sales by means of door-to-door advance subscriptions. There was a ruthless aggression in all this.

His genial act, itself a parody of Victorian sincerity, was used for exposing sham and debunking humbug. In other words, he struck a phony posture to attack phony posturing. As he told a Yale audience in 1888, it was a humorist's calling to deride all shams and "nobilities and privileges and all kindred swindles." Twain was always the double man, the duplicit man, speaking with a dual voice. His *nom de plume*, whatever its origins, expressed this split personality. In this sense COLONEL SELLERS, of *The Gilded Age*, is Twain's first wholly fictional representative: verbal virtuoso, huckster, speculator, con man, whose very name is a pun on "salesman." All Twain's greatest characters, including down-to-earth Huck, are masters of masquerade. But Sellers, with his head buzz-full of promotions, is the very archetype of a capitalist dreamer: one who could see a city where others could just see featureless prairie and with street-lighting and a railway to connect it to Chicago.

In all this Twain was the man of his age. Born during the populist presidency of Andrew Jackson, coming of age during the war years of Abraham Lincoln, to die at the close of the imperial presidency of Theodore Roosevelt, Twain experienced American life from the humble frontier to its most plutocratic exhibitionism. In his own person he spanned the continent from West to Southwest to East. Missouri-born, he was both a Southerner—from the northernmost point of the South—and Midwesterner; migrating across the Rockies to California, he became a Westerner; settling finally in New England, he became, by adoption, an Easterner. To register something of this mix, which lies at the slippery source of his humor, consider *Life on the Mississippi*, in which a return to the river brings into play all the quixotic confusion of his emotions. But his heyday came during the presidencies of Ulysses S. Grant, Rutherford B. Hayes, and James A. Garfield. *Huckleberry Finn*, that is, was written not simply in the aftermath of the Civil War, during Federal Reconstruction, but in the aftermath of Reconstruction. It was begun the year after the passing of the Civil Rights Act, which assured equality of treatment for whites and blacks. It was finished in 1883, the year in which the Supreme Court declared the Civil Rights Act unconstitutional.

By then Twain had begun to detach himself from the Republican caucus. Through the summer of 1884, while *Huckleberry Finn* was going to press, he worked with the rebel Mugwumps, chairing rallies and canvassing. Dismissing James G. Blaine, the Republican presidential candidate, as "the filthy Blaine," Twain finally switched. He left the party of Lincoln for Grover Cleveland and the Democrats. It was a dramatic switch, even decisive, for Twain's political speeches were printed by both Republican and Democratic newspapers. Cleveland carried New York by only 1,149 votes, and it was the thirty-six electoral votes of New York State that won him the presidency.

Well before publication of *Huckleberry Finn*, then, Twain's name had become a household word. More than a household word, it was a brand-name guaranteeing the marketing of his coast-to-coast campaigns. His own image was his trademark: the bushy red (later white) hair and mustache; the black (later dazzling white) suits worn, as occasion offered, under a seal-skin coat or his honorary Oxford gown. He was his own best salesman, recognized from a thousand photographs and cartoons, another Colonel Sellers advertising his own literary speculations. Like the future Colonel Sanders, he offered—not Kentucky Fried Chicken—but his own inestimable range of products. If there was more than a hint of duplicity in all this, he openly confessed that he plotted "a little finely acted stumbling and stammering." He delighted in telling reporters about his ploys, aware that audiences would cheerfully cooperate in the masquerade.

As master of publicity, only Ernest Hemingway could equal him in our century. He was as much a tycoon of the mass market as were his contemporaries, JOSEPH PULITZER and WILLIAM RANDOLPH HEARST, who created the mass circulation newspapers of the 1880s and 1890s. Twain was the first coast-to-coast American bestseller. "The Celebrated Jumping Frog" hopped from state to state, reprint to reprint, across the land. What Charles Dickens, the Englishman, had achieved in sales and on lecture platforms, Twain was the first American to emulate successfully. If Dickens could "do the police in different voices," Twain could refine the Pike County dialect into at least six subgroups. Or he could outbid Dickens by writing a whole book in a single sustained, idiosyncratic voice. His very performances, like jumping frogs, were geared to bound from climax to climax, operating by bursts of energy rather than calculated overall control. As an entertainer, in the line of Artemus Ward and PETROLEUM V. NASBY, Twain was an improviser, an oral performer depending on an audience for his best effects.

He also kept up with the times. From decade to decade Twain watched shifts in literary fashion. He was early into the children's book market with *The Adventures of Tom Sawyer* and *The Prince and the Pauper*. Like the latter of these two books, A CONNECTICUT YANKEE IN KING ARTHUR'S COURT (1889) and *Personal Recollections of Joan of Arc* (1896) exploited the Victorian fondness for historical romance. Like CAPTAIN STORMFIELD'S VISIT TO HEAVEN (begun in 1868, published in 1907), *A Connecticut Yankee* also owed something to the new vogue for science fiction, just as *Pudd'nhead Wilson* had early picked up on the popularity of Arthur Conan Doyle's Sherlock Holmes. Twain's detective story even used the newly devised classification of fingerprints for his denouement. Like all Americans he adored JOEL CHANDLER HARRIS's collections of UNCLE REMUS tales (*His Songs and Sayings*, 1881, followed by *Nights with Uncle Remus*, 1883). Harris's use of authentic black and Southern dialect voices helped prompt and encourage his own virtuoso treatment in *Huckleberry Finn*.

In this, too, he was a man of his times. The postbellum decades produced the greatest flood of dialect literature that America has ever known. From HARRIET BEECHER STOWE's New England to Bret Harte's California poured stories that came collectively to be known as the LOCAL COLOR school. Nostalgia was much in vogue after the catastrophe of the Civil War, and Twain, like the rest, was quite capable of sustaining idyllic evocations of the past, of childhood, of rural America—in *Tom Sawyer*, for example, but not in *Huckleberry Finn*. However idyllic on the subject of nature, in a handful of pages, that book is consistently sardonic about society. Its multiplicity of dialect renderings can by no stretch of the imagination be called local color. Though even Huck is cleaned up, he too is idealized. His voice, too, is bowdlerized. Above all, as a poor white from the Missouri frontier, he is depoliticized. In subverting Huck's voice from within by his gentlemanly presence, Twain defused any hint of social radicalism and derailed the Southwestern tradition from its populist origins.

Little good did it do him. Was it a boys' book, he asked himself, or was it intended for adults? On its title page it was advertised as "(Tom Sawyer's Comrade)", as if it were just a companion volume to that bestseller. Yet, he allowed excerpts to be printed alongside adult fiction by HENRY JAMES and WILLIAM DEAN HOWELLS. Its status was to remain—and still remains—equivocal. In any case, it raised a howl of protest that has never wholly died down in the century since *Huck Finn* was published. Is it a vernacular masterpiece or mere humorous burlesque? Does it offer a reconciliation between black and white, or is it racist trash? Is Huck a new model hero from the West or just another amoral prankster and Western rogue? Is his narrative part of the tall tales and journalistic buffooneries of the frontier or to be read in that grandest of all picaresque traditions linking Homer's *Odyssey* to *Don Quixote* and *Tom Jones*? Twain would have enjoyed that. In his sly way he enjoyed offended vested interests. In the late 19th century the book offended the Northern bourgeoisie. By the early 20th century it offended the white South. By the mid-20th century it offended blacks everywhere, especially urban blacks. By the late-20th century it even offended urban whites. It must be said loud and clear that *Huckleberry Finn* is, at heart, a profoundly antiracist book, though the sense of betrayal evoked by the scenes at the Phelps farm has long provoked bitter arguments and disappointments. For Mark Twain fumbled forwards, seeking inspiration to continue. It was always momentum he was after, not destination. He was the last of the bards. If any text is an extempore performance, based wholly on the rhythm and tone of a speaking voice, that text is Huck's. A voice *has* no end—only pauses, slips, impersonations, quotations, digressions.

In this sense all of Twain's work is like a journey, if not, as in the case of *Huckleberry Finn*, the actual account of a journey. The seemingly formless form of Twain's most typical work is both that of storytelling and of travel; for like storytelling, travel is made up of episodic events and encounters. From *The Innocents Abroad*, through *A Tramp Abroad* and *Life on the Mississippi* to *Following the Equator*, Twain produced a series of travelogues. But travels can also be pilgrimages, read as allegories of life. Just as *Roughing It*, in its drive West, reveals its protagonist in a series of apprenticeships until he finds himself to be none other than the author in his achieved identity of Mark Twain, so *Huckleberry Finn*, in its drive South, reveals its protagonist in a series of initiations until he finds himself to be none other than . . . what? Huck's moral identity, alas, cannot be quite so securely claimed, since in his final masquerade he must be born again as the very buddy, Tom Sawyer, whom he had seemingly relinquished long ago. Such is the ambiguity of his tale. Of the journey itself, especially in its early stages, Twain was in no doubt at all. As a river pilot he knew every chute and snag, every island and towhead along its course. If he could steer a boat up and down river, he could also years later steer his imagination back to his boyhood. The writing of *Adventures of Huckleberry Finn* was intimately bound up with that earlier exercise in recall that resulted in the finest of all his autobiographical fragments, "Old Times on the Mississippi" (1875), which was later incorporated into *Life on the Mississippi*. Time travel could take him even further: to the Tudor court of *The Prince and the Pauper*, to the 15th-century France of *Personal Recollections of Joan of Arc*, to the 6th-century Camelot of *The Connecticut Yankee in King Arthur's Court*; and in such later stories as "The Man That Corrupted Hadleyburg" or "The Mysterious Stranger" the point of view abruptly shifts. It is no longer that of the innocent from abroad, but that of locals facing an outsider. For the first time, that is, Twain takes note of the disruptive effect these space invaders may have. Long before "King Leopold's Soliloquy," *The Connecticut Yankee* had detailed the horrors of technological imperialism.

There, a visit by an enlightened envoy from the progressive and scientific 19th century to a backward and superstitious kingdom ends in apocalyptic slaughter. At first it seems as if Hank Morgan (foreman of the Colt factory in Hartford, Connecticut) is merely the vehicle for a series of jokes to contrast the Dark (feudal) Ages and modern materialism. But an industrial revolution fails to transform the feudal structure of Camelot, except into a "colony" or "Factory" where only the fittest may survive. But who are the fittest? When Hank lobs a homemade bomb at the knights, it "resembled a steamboat explosion on the Mississippi; and during the next fifteen minutes we stood under a steady drizzle of microscopic fragments of knights and hardware and horseflesh." Civilization, it turns out, is just a matter of armaments versus an archaic religion and outdated elite. Nothing here could be less like a joke. The conflict ends with the Arthurian cavalry in full armor charging on to an electrified fence: "*There* was a groan you could hear! It voiced the death-pang of eleven thousand men." Thus ends Twain's devastating parable of underdevelopment and the mayhem implicit in trespassing across cultural frontiers. *A Connecticut Yankee*, like Conrad's *Heart of Darkness* published ten years later, can be read as a blueprint for our own arrogant and self-destructive age.

Mark Twain was not trained in a university. It was neither originality, nor invention, nor aesthetic formalism he valued; rather it was the merit put into stories "by the teller's *art.*" "Wherein lies a poet's claim to 'originality'?" he asked a correspondent. "That he invents his incidents? No. That he was present when the episodes had their birth? No. That he was the

first to report them? No. None of these things have any value; he confers upon them the only 'originality' that has any value, and that is his way of telling them." It is hardly helpful, therefore, to judge him by the standard of his contemporary, Henry James. Twain was a public performer. As a storyteller he must be judged by his own "How to Tell a Story" (1895), not James's "The Art of Fiction" (1884). For Twain storytelling was closer to the fine art of lying. The young Sam Clemens had been enthralled by fraud, by the card sharks and vagrant hucksters along the Mississippi. His very pen name was a fraud. Impostors crowd his fiction from "The Celebrated Frog of Calaveras County" to "King Leopold's Soliloquy." The comic radiance of fraud, double-crossed with treachery, was to become the hallmark of his fiction. The celebrated frog had been fraudulently filled with buck shot while his owner's attention was distracted. Those two con men in jeans, the king and duke of *Huckleberry Finn*, outwit the sleepy Mississippi riverside towns. It is loot they are after. They are out to plunder a passive world, just as Twain, on the platform, aims to outwit and con his passive audience. He too felt ultimately exiled from the very country that adulated him. In those final parables, "The $30,000 Bequest" and "The £1,000,000 Bank Note," he is setting the same psychological traps he had always set. Only in the end they became more unscrupulous, more satanic even, and as Satan became his favorite outsider, as metaphysical trickster and manipulator, more grimly paranoid.

Even as a youth of nineteen or twenty Twain had brooded over his own "ignorance, intolerance, egotism, self-assertion, opaque perception, dense and pitiful chuckleheadedness—and an almost pathetic unconsciousness of it all." The conscience, he knew, could be trained—"trained to approve any wild thing you *want* it to approve if you begin its education early & stick to it." Which left what? Only the heart, which "in a crucial moral emergency," he wrote in 1895, "is a safer guide than an ill-trained conscience." And what makes for a "sound heart"? That, for Twain, remained a mystery, an anarchic and attractively disruptive force, like laughter itself. See THE AMERICAN CLAIMANT, EVE'S DIARY, 1601.

The so-called Definitive Edition of *The Writings of Mark Twain* in 37 volumes (1929) is now being overtaken by two series from the University of California Press. The first consists of scholarly editions of Mark Twain's notebooks, journals, and other unpublished or abortive manuscripts (*The Mark Twain Papers*). The second consists of meticulously established texts of all previously published writings (*The Works of Mark Twain*). Biographical and critical sources include Justin Kaplan, *Mr Clemens and Mark Twain, A Biography* (1966); Kenneth S. Lynn, *Mark Twain and Southwestern Humor* (1966); and Harold Beaver, *Huckleberry Finn* (1987).

HAROLD BEAVER

'Twas the Night Before Christmas.   See A VISIT FROM ST. NICHOLAS.

Twenty Years at Hull House (1910),   an autobiographical narrative by JANE ADDAMS. One of the earliest of social workers and directors of settlement houses, Addams established the Hull House Settlement in Chicago in 1889.

Many social and educational activities were carried on under her capable direction. But her interests went far beyond the settlement house; she spoke and worked in connection with labor troubles and legislation and problems of immigration, and contributed to civic betterment as a member of the Chicago Board of Education. The book is a lively account of a remarkably fruitful social project and reveals a woman who was profoundly concerned with the welfare of humanity.

Twice a Year, a semiannual publication concerned with literature, the arts, and social issues. It was published from 1938 to 1948. The publication printed translations of Kafka, Lorca, and Proust and work by Henry Miller, Kenneth Patchen, Muriel Rukeyser, and William Saroyan.

Twice-Told Tales (1837, expanded 1842), a collection of tales and sketches by NATHANIEL HAWTHORNE. Some of the stories originally appeared in magazines and gift books. The name of the collection probably comes from the line in *King John*: "Life is as tedious as a twice-told tale." Particularly noteworthy are the picturesque historical sketches, such as *Howe's Masquerade* (see Sir WILLIAM HOWE), *The Grey Champion* (see WILLIAM GOFFE) THE GENTLE BOY, THE MAYPOLE OF MERRY MOUNT, and THE AMBITIOUS GUEST. Of the moral tales, *The Great Carbuncle* reveals Hawthorne's symbolism at its best. See THE MINISTER'S BLACK VEIL.

Twichell, Joseph [Hopkins] (1838–1918), clergyman, biographer, editor. For fifty years Twichell, who was born in Connecticut, served as a minister in Hartford and was an intimate member of MARK TWAIN's literary circle there. He also became Twain's closest friend, often went on trips with him, and is the Harris of A TRAMP ABROAD (1880). He had a decided literary gift of his own and wrote a biography of *John Winthrop* (1891); he also edited *Some Old Puritan Love-Letters: John and Margaret Winthrop, 1618–1638* (1893).

Two Admirals, The (1842), a novel by JAMES FENIMORE COOPER. Cooper, an expert in naval history, had long wanted to write a story based on "the teeming and glorious naval history" of England. He finally chose the period of the Young Pretender's attempt (1745) to regain his throne, an attempt abetted by the French navy. Two British admirals are the protagonists. Admiral Oakes is loyal to the Hanoverian occupants of the throne, and Admiral Bluewater believes that it belongs to the Stuarts. Oakes engages in battle with the French fleet and is near defeat when Bluewater decides to help his friend and his country. The French are defeated in a great engagement, which Cooper describes superbly. Cooper had a propagandistic motive in his discussion of fleet movements. He wanted to convince his countrymen and especially members of Congress that a fleet is a unit whose effectiveness is determined by its weakest member and that fleets at sea cannot be expected to obey orders from authorities on shore. He criticized, too, the lack of an American fleet. The novel is intimately related to his *History of the Navy of the U.S.* (1839); the one prepared for the writing of the other. He found additional details, however, in *The Public and Private Correspondence*

(1828) of Vice-Admiral Lord Collingwood, whose friendship for and collaboration with Lord Nelson resembled that of Bluewater for Oakes.

Two Lives (1922), a sonnet sequence by WILLIAM ELLERY LEONARD.

Two Years Before the Mast (1840), a narrative by RICHARD HENRY DANA, JR. To pass time while recovering his eyesight, impaired by a severe attack of measles, Dana shipped out of Boston in 1834 on the *Pilgrim* and sailed around the Horn to California on a hide-trading expedition. The book is based on the journal he kept during the voyage. Horrified by the brutal captain's mistreatment of the sailors, and shocked by their lack of legal redress, Dana wrote with a burning indignation that did much to rouse the public to the mariners' plight. The book went through many editions, was widely translated, and was adopted by the British Board of Admiralty for distribution to the British navy. Dana added a final chapter in 1859 in which he described a second trip to California and told what had happened to some of the men and ships mentioned earlier.

Tyler, Anne (1941–), novelist, short-story writer. Born in Minnesota, Tyler grew up in North Carolina and was educated at Duke. Since 1965 she has lived in Baltimore, and much of her work is set there. Her *Celestial Navigation* (1974) tells of an artist's attempt to fight off the comfortable isolation of his room and his art and make contact with others. *Dinner at the Homesick Restaurant* (1982) delineates the tension in an estranged family who try repeatedly to finish one family meal in harmony. *The Accidental Tourist* (1985) is the story of a travel writer who hates to leave home and his struggle to accept the death of his son. Maggie, the main character of *Breathing Lessons* (1988), fights to make her family life conform to her inner standard. In *Ladder of Years* (1995), a woman walks away from her family. In *A Patchwork Planet* (1998), a man redeems his own failure by helping the elderly and infirm. Her other titles include *If Morning Ever Comes* (1964), *The Tin Can Tree* (1965), *A Slipping Down Life* (1970), *Morgan's Passing* (1980), *Saint Maybe* (1991), and *Back When We Were Grownups* (2001).

Tyler, Moses Coit (1835–1900), minister, teacher, literary historian. Born in Connecticut, Tyler attended Yale College, Yale Divinity School, and the Andover Theological Seminary. He was ordained minister of the Owego, New York, Congregational Church and later was called to Poughkeepsie. When his health broke down he resigned his pastorate (1862). After a period in Europe, Tyler returned to the United States in 1867 and was appointed to the Chair of Rhetoric and English Literature at the University of Michigan. In 1881 he was called to Cornell to occupy the first chair of American history ever established in the United States. He was strongly influenced by H. T. Buckle's *History of Civilization in England* (1854, 1860), with its emphasis, as he explained in his *Journal*, on "a spirit of the age as ruling the evolution of the events of the age." With this thesis as a background he wrote his epical *History of American Literature During the Colonial Time, 1607–1765* (2 v. 1878;

1 v. 1950). His *Literary History of the American Revolution, 1763–1783* (2 v. 1897, repr. 1941) remains a basic study of American Revolutionary literature.

The long interval between his two masterpieces was devoted to efforts to establish the American Historical Association (1884), to sustained religious meditation that finally brought him into the Episcopal Church, to a biography of *Patrick Henry* (1887), and to his *Three Men of Letters* (1895), a discussion of Joel Barlow, Timothy Dwight, and Bishop Berkeley. *Moses Coit Tyler: Selections from His Letters and Diaries* (1911) was edited by J. T. Austen. Howard Mumford Jones wrote *The Life of Moses Coit Tyler* (1934).

Tyler, Royall (1757–1826),   lawyer, teacher, writer. Tyler was born in Boston and educated at Harvard. He studied law in the office of JOHN ADAMS [2], fell in love with Abigail Adams, daughter of the boss, and the boss promptly removed his daughter to France. In 1794 Tyler married Mary Palmer. During the Revolution he served as aide to General Sullivan in his attack on Newport. When Shays' Rebellion broke out, Tyler was serving on General Lincoln's staff. Then he began the practice of law in Guildford, Vermont. From 1807 to 1813 Tyler served as chief justice of the Supreme Court of Vermont and also served as professor of jurisprudence at the University of Vermont (1811–14).

In the meantime Tyler had been active in literary fields. He started the American drama on its course when his comedy THE CONTRAST was produced in New York City (1787). In this play, Yankees for the first time appear as characters in comic roles, speaking an authentic dialect. It is the first comedy written by a native American. In later years he and JOSEPH DENNIE operated under a dual pen name, Colon and Spondee, and became the first American columnists. Their contributions appeared in the *Farmer's Weekly Museum*, published at Walpole, New York, by Isaiah Thomas and David Carlisle, with Dennie as editor. Tyler showed remarkable skill in verse forms and a facile humor. In 1797 he wrote another comedy, *The Georgia Spec, or, Land in the Moon*, and his best-known novel, THE ALGERINE CAPTIVE. See YANKEE IN LONDON.

Typee: A Peep at Polynesian Life.   Herman Melville's first book (1846), about two American whalemen who, in reaction to harsh treatment by their captain, jump ship in the Marquesas Islands and are held in comfortable confinement by the Typee tribe. Melville's protagonist, called Tommo by the Typees, is a semiautobiographical character based on Melville's own experience on, and subsequent escape from, the *Acushnet* during his first whaling voyage. Throughout the book, Tommo, and for a while his companion Toby, attempt to decipher Polynesian culture. Tommo, especially after Toby's strange disappearance, is limited in his understanding of Typee life by his fears of the Typees, rumored widely to be cannibals, by the contradictory preconceptions about South Seas islanders derived from missionary and sailor narratives, and by their inscrutable system of taboos. As a result, while Tommo's experience of the simplicity and luxuriance of Typee culture generates scathing indictments of Western attempts to civilize them, the cultural presuppositions he brings to this peep at Polynesian life prevent him from becoming thoroughly sympathetic. Melville works through Tommo's perceptions and anxieties to dramatize and criticize Western cultural, political, and epistemological imperialism. Eventually, Tommo's fears are exacerbated by new evidence of cannibalism, and he makes a daring escape to a French ship.

Melville's contemporaries either valued the narrative for its vivid depiction of travel, adventure, and life among the supposedly savage Typees, or condemned it as gratuitously lewd in its representation of primitive culture and as too aggressive in its critique of Western hypocrisy. Criticism in the 20th century has revealed the depth of cultural and ideological implications embedded within this adventure book and has discovered anticipations of Melville's later philosophical explorations in *Mardi* and *Moby-Dick*.

RUSSELL J. REISING

U

Uchida, Yoshiko (1921–1972), writer of children's books, memoirist, novelist. Born in Almeda, California, Uchida had her education at the University of California, Berkeley (A.B., 1942) interrupted after the attack on Pearl Harbor when she was incarcerated with her family, first at Tenforan Racetrack and then at the internment camp constructed in the desert at Topaz, Utah. Released to accept a fellowship at Smith College, she received her M.Ed. in 1944. *The Dancing Kettle and Other Japanese Folk Tales* (1949) was the first of over twenty-five books for children, some self-illustrated, most presenting either the Japanese cultural heritage in the homeland or the process of acculturation for Japanese in America. Autobiographical works include *Journey to Topaz: A Story of the Japanese-American Evacuation* (1971); *Journey Home* (1978), a sequel to *Journey to Topaz*; and *Desert Exile: The Uprooting of a Japanese-American Family* (1982). *Picture Bride* (1987) is a novel on the subject also examined in the short story "Tears of Autumn," collected in *The Forbidden Stitch* (1989).

Ulalume (*American Whig Review*, December 1847), a poem by EDGAR ALLAN POE. It was written at the suggestion of Professor C. P. Bronson, an elocutionist who wanted "a poem suitable for recitation about the length and somewhat of the character of Collins' Ode to Passions." On Hallowe'en, when the dead have power, the speaker and his soul walk in the "misty-mid-region of Weir," "by the dark tarn of Auber" (the latter perhaps suggested by the name of the popular composer of the ballet *The Lake of the Fairies*). It is the land of imagination. They follow "Astarte's be-diamonded crescent," the planet Venus, but are stopped by the door of the forgotten tomb of the narrator's beloved. It had great influence on symbolist poetry in France and England.

Ullman, James Ramsey (1907–1971), mountaineer, novelist, playwright. Ullman, born in New York City, saw his Princeton thesis, *Mad Shelley*, published in 1930. After working as a journalist and writing and producing plays, he went to South America, where he traversed the Andes and followed the Amazon River, duplicating the route of the explorer Orellana. *The Other Side of the Mountain* (1938) describes this journey. Having climbed some of the most challenging mountains in the world, he wrote a history of mountain climbing, *High Conquest* (1941).

The White Tower (1945), a novel about mountain climbing, is perhaps the best of his books. Two years later he published an anthology of mountaineering stories, *Kingdom of Everest*. Ullman served as an ambulance driver with the British army in Africa as a member of the American Field Service (1942–43) and was decorated. His second novel, *River of the Sun* (1951), was based on his South American experiences. Among his later writings are *Windom's Way* (1952), *The Island of the Blue Macaws* (1953), *The Sands of Karakorum* (1953), *Banner in the Sky* (1954), and *The Age of Mountaineering* (1954). *The Day on Fire* (1958) is a novel based on the life of Rimbaud.

Ulloa, Antonio de (1716–1795), naval officer, scientist, public official. Governor of Louisiana from 1766–1768, Ulloa is best known for his travel books, *A Voyage to South America* (1758), *Secret Information Concerning America* (1826), and *Secret Expedition to Peru . . .* (1851), written with Jorge Juan y Santacilia.

Uncas. A young Indian chief, hero of THE LAST OF THE MOHICANS (1826) by James Fenimore Cooper. He dies heroically while trying to save Cora Munro from Magua, the Indian villain of the story. He has no connection with the historic character similarly named, who was a Pequot by birth.

Uncle Remus, His Songs and His Sayings (1880), a collection of thirty-four stories by JOEL CHANDLER HARRIS. Told to a small white boy by Uncle Remus, an aging black, these stories were based on African-American tales and legends Harris himself heard as a boy, and are among the finest examples of dialect and regional writing in America. The animal characters—Brer Rabbit, Brer Fox, Brer Wolf, and others—are cleverly drawn, and their adventures usually stress the contrast between strength and shrewdness and the conflict between characters of unequal size in which the smaller and more intelligent wins.

Uncle Sam. Originally a derogatory nickname for the Federal government used during the War of 1812 by New England opponents of its war policies, and now commonly accepted as the personification of the government. Uncle Sam may have been inspired by the nickname of a government inspector in Troy, New York, one Samuel Wilson, or it may represent an extension of the initials of the United States. *The*

Adventures of Uncle Sam (1816), by "Frederick Augustus Fidfaddy," seems to be the earliest use of the name in a book.

Uncle Tom's Cabin, or, Life among the Lowly (1852), a novel by HARRIET BEECHER STOWE. It is a controversial and important book. It has commanded one of the largest reading audiences in history; it tackled the issues of slavery and race at a time when white America hesitated to face them; and it is a brilliantly executed work of realist fiction. Serialized in an antislavery journal, *The National Era,* in 1851–52, *Uncle Tom* was immediately a bestseller in the United States and England. Translated into most of the world's languages, it has been admired and derided like no other novel.

Though filled with dozens of stories of slaves, *Uncle Tom's* plot centers on two people who triumph over slavery—one in this world, one in the next. Both heroes begin on the comfortable Shelby plantation in Kentucky, and each—betrayed by an irresponsible owner unable to afford keeping them—undertakes a journey. Eliza Harris, whose child is to be sold, escapes her beloved home and goes North, eluding the hired slave catchers in the scene where barefoot she crosses the broken ice on the Ohio River. Aided by the underground railroad, Quakers, and other Northerners morally opposed to the Fugitive Slave Act, Eliza and her son are eventually reunited in Canada with her husband, George, another escaped slave. They settle in the African state of Liberia, unwilling to remain in a nation that condones slavery.

As the Harrises move North toward freedom, "Uncle Tom" Shelby is sent "down the river" for sale. Too honorable to abuse his master's trust, too Christian to rebel, Tom wrenches himself from his family. Befriending a white child—Evangeline St. Clare—on the trip South, Tom is purchased by her father, Augustine, and taken to their opulent, decadent New Orleans home. There Tom's Christian faith grows under Eva's tutelage; when the angelic child dies—because the suffering of slaves hurts her "here," she says, striking her chest—her father resolves to free his slaves despite his selfish wife Marie's objections and his Vermont cousin Ophelia's reservations. Suddenly killed in an accident, St. Clare joins the ranks of those who mean well by slaves but never take action. Sold farther down river to Simon Legree's plantation, Tom finds his faith is tested by the most degrading servitude. Heroically and humbly defying Legree's attempts to subvert his Christianity, Tom endures a martyr's death under the whips of Legree's bestialized slaves. Through a surprising family connection, Tom's and Eliza's stories come together in the end, while Stowe's narrator demands of her readers whether slavery—an institution that breaks up families, brings about physical suffering, and undermines Christian teaching—can be tolerated.

Embraced at once by British and American abolitionists, reviled by slaveholders, *Uncle Tom* inspired anti-Tom novels purporting to show slavery's true, happy effect on blacks. Stowe published *A Key to Uncle Tom's Cabin* (1853) to document some of the anecdotes her novel reproduces. Adapted for the stage, *Uncle Tom* became an enormously popular melodrama, simplifying the characters into the stereotypes they

have become in the public imagination. Topsy, Eva's slave playmate, became an emblem of the wicked, fun-loving slave, averse to work; Eva herself evolved into Little Eva, a flat copy of Dickens' too-pure-to-live child heroines; and the martyred hero Uncle Tom came to signify a servile, cringing black who hypocritically acts to please whites. The stage adaptation originated much of what 20th-century commentators have found objectionable in *Uncle Tom.*

Readers who look at Stowe's text, rather than the mythology surrounding it, will find a novel strongly endorsing domestic family values for whites and blacks, while perpetuating prejudicial 19th-century assumptions about racial and cultural difference. Many critics have begun rereading and rehabilitating *Uncle Tom* as a great American novel, focusing on Stowe's portrayal of women's potential for positive influence and on the theological underpinnings of the novel's story and structure. The history of the novel's composition, impact, and reputation is admirably chronicled in Thomas Gossett's *"Uncle Tom's Cabin" and American Culture* (1985).
ROBYN R. WARHOL

Uncle Wiggily.   See BEDTIME STORY; HOWARD R. GARIS.

underground railroad, the.   The organized system for illegally transporting slaves to freedom before the Civil War. Slaves were frequently hidden on coastal vessels bound from the South Atlantic seaboard to New England, where they were helped farther north, sometimes to Canada. Others walked north by night, aided and hidden in the daytime by sympathetic whites. Many Quakers served as agents of the underground railroad, like the kindly Friends who aid the fleeing Eliza in UNCLE TOM'S CABIN. Prominent New England writers gave money and active support to fugitive slaves. The railroad appears in Neill C. Wilson's *The Freedom Song* (1955) and in many other novels of the antebellum period. See HARRIET TUBMAN.

Underhill, John (1597?–1672),   soldier, public official, memoirist. Underhill was a professional soldier who fought first in Holland, then in 1630 came to Boston to organize the militia. He helped the Connecticut colonists fight against the Pequot tribe, was for a time a deputy of the General Court, but got into trouble over religious controversies. He fought against the Dutch in the New Netherlands and wrote an account of the war, *News from America* (1638). It was reprinted in the *Collections* (1837) of the Massachusetts Historical Society. John Greenleaf Whittier greatly admired Underhill and wrote the poem "John Underhill" (in *Hazel Blossoms,* 1875).

Under the Gaslight   (produced in New York City in 1867, revised 1881), a melodrama by AUGUSTIN DALY. When Laura Courtlandt discovers that her father is a criminal, her lover deserts her and she suffers extreme poverty. In a famous scene, she rescues the hero, tied to a railroad track, by pulling the switch to divert the train. The New York scenes include famous realistic renditions of the Blue Room at Delmonico's and the New York pier. The characters are conventional, the plot implausible. The rescue scene was immediately duplicated in *After Dark,* by DION BOUCICAULT; Daly sued Boucicault successfully. Daly used the character of a one-armed soldier as a device for criticizing the United States government's treatment of wounded veterans. Carrie Meeber, of Dreiser's *Sister Carrie*, stars in the play. The play has been frequently and successfully revived.

Under the Volcano (1947),   a novel by MALCOLM LOWRY, the story of the murder of an alcoholic British consul in Mexico.

Union Magazine.   This magazine was founded in July 1847 with CAROLINE S. KIRKLAND as its editor for about eighteen months. Then John Sartain bought it and began publishing it as *Sartain's Union Magazine*. The magazine won attention for the excellence of its mezzotint reproductions. Edgar Allan Poe's second poem entitled *To Helen*, and *The Bells* and his *Poetic Principle*, were all published in the magazine; other contributors included Longfellow and James Russell Lowell. The magazine ceased publication in 1852.

Unitarianism,   a belief in the single person of God, as compared with a Trinitarian view. Although the idea dates to early movements, such as Arianism, modern Unitarianism dates from the Protestant Reformation. The movement in America began in the preaching of such liberal 18th-century ministers as Jonathan Mayhew, who rejected the harshness of orthodox New England Calvinist doctrine. The Anglicans of King's Chapel, Boston, founded the first Unitarian church on American soil when they eliminated the doctrine of the Trinity from their observances in 1785. The doctrine was spread by such English Unitarians as Joseph Priestley, who emigrated to the United States in 1794, and by prominent Americans, including Emerson. Unitarianism served as a basis for New England Transcendentalism. Joseph Ware, a Harvard professor of divinity (1805–1840) and founder of the Divinity School (1819), helped to promulgate the doctrine. William Ellery Channing articulated the characteristic mixture of rationalism with spirituality. Under the American Unitarian Association, founded in 1825, churches are organized by congregation, and neither members nor ministers are required to profess any particular creed.

United States Literary Gazette,   a semimonthly periodical published in Boston (1824–1826) under the editorship of Theophilus Parsons. In 1826 it was merged with the *New York Review and Athenaeum Magazine* and called *The United States Review and Literary Gazette*. Bryant, Dana, and Longfellow wrote for it.

United States Magazine,   a monthly edited by H. H. Brackenridge and published in Philadelphia during 1779. A later periodical of the same title was edited in New York by Seba Smith from 1854 to 1858.

United States Magazine and Democratic Review, a political and literary journal published monthly in Washington between 1837 and 1841. Hawthorne, Poe, Whitman, Whittier, and Bryant were published in it. The editorial offices were moved to New York City in 1841; after a merger with the *Boston Quarterly Review*, the publication became more markedly political.

Universalism,   a belief that it is God's intention that all souls be saved through divine grace revealed in Jesus Christ and that good overpowers evil. As an organized religious group in the United States, it springs from the teachings of John Murray, an English cleric who emigrated in 1770 and became pastor of the first Univeralist church at Gloucester, Massachusetts, in 1779. The group's doctrinal position was codified in the Winchester Profession, adopted in 1803. The church established Tufts University in 1852. In 1961 the movement merged with Unitarianism to form the Unitarian Universalist Association.

Unparalleled Adventures of One Hans Pfaal, The (*Southern Literary Messenger*, June 1835),   a tale by EDGAR ALLAN POE. One of the earliest specimens of science fiction in American literature, this tale describes a voyage to the moon, done with tongue-in-cheek verisimilitude. The conclusion reveals it as a hoax. Three weeks later there appeared in the New York *Sun* the first of a series of articles on certain lunar discoveries. These articles were supposedly reprinted from a nonexistent *Edinburgh Journal of Science* and described the discovery of life on the moon by Sir John Herschel, the eminent British astronomer. The articles made a sensation and were later revealed as the work of Richard Adams Locke. See BALLOON HOAX.

Untermeyer, Jean Starr (1886–1970),   singer, poet, critic, translator. Untermeyer, a native of Ohio, made her debut as a singer in Vienna and London in 1924, specializing in German songs. She translated numerous works from German, taught at Olivet and the New School for Social Research, and contributed critical articles to magazines. But her reputation is based mainly on her several collections of verse: *Growing Pains* (1918), *Dreams Out of Darkness* (1921), *Steep Ascent* (1927), *Winged Child* (1936), and *Love and Need: Collected Poems* (1940).

Untermeyer, Louis (1885–1977),   poet, translator, anthologist. Untermeyer was born in New York City. He did not complete high school and trained himself through reading. In 1923 he went to Europe to study for two years. He had already written *First Love* (1911), *Challenge* (1914), and several other volumes of poetry. His more mature poems are found in *Burning Bush* (1928) and *Food and Drink* (1932). His poem "Caliban" best expresses his social passion. He wrote some superb parodies, reissued in one volume as *Collected Parodies* (1926). He also wrote *American Poetry Since 1900* (1923); a novel, *Moses* (1928); *New Songs for New Voices* (with Clara and David Mannes, 1928); a biography of Heine (1937); an autobiography, *From Another World* (1939); and he translated Ernst Toller's *Masse Mensch* (1923). *Makers of the Modern World*, a series of compact biographies, appeared in 1955.

Untermeyer is best known, however, as an anthologist. His anthologies molded the taste of two generations of readers. These include *Modern American Poetry* (1919), *American Poetry from the Beginning to Whitman* (1931), *The Book of Living Verse* (1931), *New Modern American and British Poetry* (1950), *Magic Circle* (1952), *Modern American and British*

Poetry: Revised Shorter Edition (with Karl Shapiro and Richard Wilbur, 1955), *Treasury of Great Poems* (1955), *Treasury of Ribaldry* (1956), *Golden Treasury of Poetry* (1959), and *For You with Love* (1961).

Unvanquished, The (1934), a novel by WILLIAM FAULKNER. Set in the period of the Civil War, *The Unvanquished* deals with the Sartoris family, whose history Faulkner recounted in SARTORIS. Composed of seven stories that appeared first in the *Saturday Evening Post* and elsewhere, *The Unvanquished* centers primarily on the adventures of young Bayard Sartoris and his African-American companion Ringo. It is probable that Faulkner modeled COLONEL SARTORIS on William C. Falkner, his great-grandfather, who was also a colonel during the Civil War and was killed in 1889 by a former business partner under circumstances strikingly similar to those in which Colonel Sartoris was killed by Ben Redlaw.

Updike, John (1932–), novelist, short-story writer, poet, essayist. Updike grew up in Shillington, Pennsylvania, during the Great Depression as the only child in a relatively poor family, but his education was not ignored. His father was a school teacher, and his mother encouraged his interest in art and writing. In 1950 he won a scholarship to Harvard, where he studied literature and helped edit the *Harvard Lampoon*. After being graduated *summa cum laude* in 1954, he accepted a Knox Fellowship to study art at the Ruskin School of Drawing and Fine Art in Oxford, England. On his return to the United States in 1955, Updike, now married, joined the staff of *The New Yorker*, where he worked for two years. Although he left the magazine in 1957 and moved to Massachusetts to pursue his career as a writer, he has continued for nearly fifty years to publish stories, poems, reviews, and essays in *The New Yorker*. Elected to the National Institute of Arts and Letters in 1964 and to the American Academy of Arts and Letters in 1977, he now lives near Boston with his second wife.

Updike's initial professional publication was the short story "Friends from Philadelphia," which appeared in *The New Yorker* (October 30, 1954). In 1958 he published his first book, *The Carpentered Hen*, a collection of light verse that reflects the interest in technique and wit that he developed during his stint at the *Harvard Lampoon*. His breakthrough year was 1959, when he published a volume of short stories entitled *The Same Door*, and his first novel, *The Poorhouse Fair*, in which he wrote about an old man of faith in an era of unbelief. The religious underpinning of the novel is the theology of Karl Barth. Although Updike has in later years studied the writings of Kierkegaard and Tillich, Barth's thought has continued to inform much of his work.

A case in point is *Rabbit, Run* (1960), Updike's most celebrated novel and the first of the Rabbit chronicles, which include *Rabbit Redux* (1971), *Rabbit Is Rich* (1981), and *Rabbit at Rest* (1990). Updike collected them in *Rabbit Angstrom: A Tetralogy* (1995) and added a coda, Rabbit as seen by his grown-up children, in the novella "Rabbit Remembered," included with a dozen short stories in *Licks of Love* (2000).

Focusing on the common details of the daily routine and the unexceptional lives of ordinary people, Updike turns the story of Harry "Rabbit" Angstrom's bewilderment into an examination of the American dream of success. Harry causes grievous pain when he deserts his family, but for all his inarticulateness and intellectual incapacity, he intuitively accepts Karl Barth's elevation of faith over good works and is thus the only truly religious person in this disturbing novel. *Rabbit, Run* made Updike one of the most celebrated writers of his generation, and he solidified his reputation with the short stories in *Pigeon Feathers* (1962) and the novel *The Centaur* (1963). Nostalgia and loss direct the tales and the novel, and Updike develops a thematic relationship between such stories in *Pigeon Feathers* as "A Sense of Shelter" and *The Centaur*. Winner of the National Book Award, *The Centaur* pays homage to Updike's father, who sacrificed during the Depression to keep his family together. An epigraph from Karl Barth directs the reader to the religious mandate to believe, and Updike mythologizes the father by comparing his unacknowledged suffering to the agony of Chiron, the injured centaur of the Greek tale. Following his second gathering of poems, *Telephone Poles* (1963), and his first collection of essays, *Assorted Prose* (1965), which includes his famous essay about the baseball hero Ted Williams, Updike published *Of the Farm* (1965), a companion novel to *The Centaur*. A short, tense book about a strong-willed but old mother, *Of the Farm* is Updike's most penetrating examination of the psychological struggle between aging parents and grown children. The novel extends family considerations first examined in the short story "Flight" (*Pigeon Feathers*), and it illustrates again his commitment to the theology of Karl Barth.

Publication of the story collection *The Music School* (1966) signaled a change in the Updike canon that he developed in the novels *Couples* (1968) and *Marry Me* (1976). Rather than focus on childhood trauma and nostalgia, he turned to the sexual and spiritual tension in affluent suburban American families. The narrator of the story "The Music School" expresses the sentiment that directs Updike's marriage novels—"We are all pilgrims, faltering toward divorce"—and the implied theological perspective indicates Updike's concern for whether sexuality can replace the loss of certainty caused by the decline of religious faith. Two essays from *Assorted Prose*, "Faith in Search of Understanding" and "More Love in the Western World," elucidate his position on religion and romance and provide an indirect perspective on his novels of adultery.

Similar interests are considered in the poems of *Midpoint* (1969) and the stories of *Museums and Women* (1972); but following the publication of a play, *Buchanan Dying* (1974), and of a second collection of essays, *Picked-Up Pieces* (1975), Updike combined a comic tone with intellectually rigorous material as he extended his examination of theology and sexuality. Deliberately alluding to Nathaniel Hawthorne's *The Scarlet Letter*, the first great American novel of adultery, Updike published the intertextual trilogy *A Month of Sundays* (1975),

Roger's Version (1986), and *S.* (1988). The novels are set in the United States late in the 20th century, and each updates the crises of Hawthorne's three principal characters. *A Month of Sundays* reinvents Arthur Dimmesdale, *Roger's Version* rethinks Roger Chillingworth, and *S.* reprises Hester Prynne. Although comic, the trilogy is a serious, erudite consideration of the conflict between body and soul. The theological speculations of Barth, Kierkegaard, and Tillich shape much of the intellectual atmosphere of these novels, which both honor and rewrite Hawthorne's masterpiece. Updike's commitment to intertextuality, brilliantly and comically displayed in the Hawthorne trilogy, is delightfully extended in *Gertrude and Claudius* (2000), a witty prequel to *Hamlet.*

Updike's sense of existential fear, of inevitable loss and implacable mortality, is evident in the poems of *Tossing and Turning* (1977) and the stories of *Problems* (1979), but the comic mode first developed in *A Month of Sundays* is continued in *The Coup* (1978), a novel that grew out of his visits to Africa on behalf of the State Department. Ostensibly an exposé of the ineptness in Africa and the super-power meddling he observed, *The Coup* also investigates the unreliability of language. Like *A Month of Sundays*, the 1978 novel shows how linguistically nimble narrators become caught in a snare of words. The focus on language is a development of Updike's interest in literary technique, for an exceptionally graceful prose style has been a hallmark of his career since the publication of his earliest fiction.

That career was honored in 1981 when Updike won the Pulitzer Prize, American Book Award, and National Book Critics Circle Award for *Rabbit Is Rich*, and again in 1983, when he won the National Book Critics Circle Award for his third collection of essays, *Hugging the Shore* (1983). His lyrical style and exceptional eye for the small details of the quotidian are consistent characteristics in a canon that has moved from a concentration on domestic trauma to an interest in contemporary affairs, and thus one is not surprised that the political considerations of *The Coup* are continued in *The Witches of Eastwick* (1984). This comic satire of the feminist movement also suggests that the separation of the sexes by so-called gender politics violates nature. Updike's praise of natural processes is evident in *Witches* as well as in the seven odes in his collection of poems titled *Facing Nature* (1985). His *Collected Poems 1953–1993* (1993) extends his comic meditations on language, history, and myth. He showed his delight in metanarrative with *Memories of the Ford Administration* (1992) and *Brazil* (1994). As the twentieth century came to a close, he pondered the decline of religious surety in the United States in the thoughtful and poignant *In the Beauty of the Lilies* (1996) before speculating about the plight of a sensitive man in a depleted future America in *Toward the End of Time* (1997).

Updike is aware of the pitfalls inherent in his celebrity. While he is one of the most successful contemporary American authors, he nevertheless writes about the conflict between the need to create and the craving for applause. In *Bech: A Book* (1970), *Bech Is Back* (1982), and *Bech at Bay* (1998), he imagines Henry Bech as an alter ego who finds that the pressures of literary eminence push him toward silence. That fate is not likely to trap Updike. Since the mid-1950s, he has written in four genres, and although he has been interested in both the lyrical potential and the recalcitrance of language, he has not joined forces with the antirealist writers who influenced American fiction after 1950. Concerned primarily with the relationship between domestic matters and religious crises, Updike has become in recent years that rare species of literary artist: the man of letters.

At this writing there is no biography or collected edition of John Updike. Autobiographical sketches are gathered in *Self-Consciousness: Memoirs* (1989). The major collection of manuscripts is housed in the Houghton Library at Harvard. Significant critical studies include George Hunt, *John Updike and the Three Great Secret Things*, and Donald J. Greiner, *John Updike's Novels.*

DONALD J. GREINER

Up from Slavery (1900), an autobiography by BOOKER T. WASHINGTON. Washington here looks back over the long, hard pull that led from a poor Southern slave cabin to the presidency of Tuskegee Institute. In his struggles for an education at Hampton Institute, Washington recognized the need of emphasizing industrial education for African-Americans. He put this belief into practice when he helped found Tuskegee and rose to fame as its president.

Upham, Charles Wentworth (1802–1875), clergyman, public official, historian, biographer. Upham was born in New Brunswick and educated at Harvard. He became associate pastor of a Unitarian church. His sermon *The Scripture Doctrine of Regeneration* was printed in 1840. He also served in the Massachusetts legislature, was elected to Congress in 1853, and wrote a campaign biography of John C. Frémont. He wrote *Salem Witchcraft* (1867) and *Salem Witchcraft and Cotton Mather* (1869).

Upson, William Hazlett (1891–1975), novelist, short-story writer. After serving with the field artillery in France in World War I, Upson, a native of New Jersey, worked for a firm that sold tractors. His experiences in the war and in business served as material for groups of humorous stories later collected in books, and for novels. Particularly popular were the misadventures of a tractor salesman, Alexander Botts, who described his experiences in letters to his firm and to others. Among Upson's books are *The Piano Movers* (1927); *Me and Henry and the Artillery* (1928); *Alexander Botts—Earthworm Tractors* (1929); *Earthworm in Europe* (1931); *Botts in War, Botts in Peace* (1944); *How to Be Rich Like Me* (1947); *Earthworms Through the Ages* (1947); and *No Rest for Botts* (1951).

Uris, Leon M. (1924–   ), author, screenwriter. Uris achieved instantaneous success with his first novel, *Battle Cry* (1953), a long, vivid account of how the Marines were trained and fought in World War II. *Exodus* (1958) traces the history of European Jews from the close of the 19th century to the establishment of the state of Israel. The film versions of both novels also enjoyed tremendous popularity; Uris himself wrote the screenplay for *Battle Cry* in 1954. *Armageddon* (1967) describes Berlin life after World War II; *Topaz* (1967) is a spy novel; and *QB VII* concerns a libel trial in Queen's Benchcourt. *Trinity* (1976); *Redemption* (1995), a sequel to *Trinity*; and *Ireland: A Terrible Beauty* (1975), with photos by Uris's wife Jill, treat the tragic religious strife of that island. Uris's other books include *The Angry Hills* (1955), a novel; *Exodus Revisited* (1960), a collection of essays with photographs by D. Harissiadis; *Mila 18* (1961), a novel set in the uprising of the Warsaw ghetto during World War II; *The Haj* (1984), about violence in the Middle East; *Mitla Pass* (1988), about a writer caught up in the 1956 Sinai war; and *A God in Ruins* (1999), with the U.S. in a presidential election in 2008 between a computer billionaire and an ex-Marine.

U.S.A. (1938).   The title under which JOHN DOS PASSOS collected, in an omnibus volume, his trilogy of novels—THE 42ND PARALLEL (1930), *1919* (1932), and THE BIG MONEY (1936).

Ushant (1952),   an autobiographical novel by CONRAD AIKEN. The title comes from the name of an island off the coast of Brittany, called in French *Ile d'Ouessant*. On this island of rocks and reefs, Chateaubriand was wrecked on his return to France from America. The literati of the era appear—Aiken's associates in inaugurating the New Poetry in London—John Gould Fletcher, Harold Munro, Ezra Pound, and others. There are fairly affectionate but occasionally satiric references to T. S. Eliot, whom Aiken first knew when they were classmates at Harvard.

Usher, Roderick.   The leading character in Edgar Allan Poe's FALL OF THE HOUSE OF USHER (in *Tales of the Grotesque and the Arabesque*, 1840). Usher is a deeply melan-cholic character who slowly realizes that his twin sister Madeline has been buried alive. Then she appears at the door of his room, wounded and bleeding from her efforts to free herself, falls heavily upon him, and in her violent and now real death agonies carries him to the floor as a corpse.

Usigli, Rodolfo (1905–1979),   Mexican playwright. Usigli wrote historical drama and social and political satire. In *Tres comedias impoliticas* (1933–35), he questioned the pervading demagoguery of the Mexican political system. *El gesticulador* (1937), his best-known play, concerns the lack of authenticity in Mexican life. His antihero Cesar Rubio, a failed teacher, decides to impersonate General Cesar Rubio, a hero of the Mexican Revolution of 1910. Ironically the imposter comes to believe in the general's ideals and is murdered by the same assassin. In *Corona de luz* (1956, tr. *Two Plays: Crown of Light, One of These Days*, 1971), Usigli focuses on the birth of the cult of the Virgin of Guadalupe as a symbol of Mexican national consciousness. His other plays include *Corona de sombras* (1942, tr. *Crown of Shadows*, 1946), dealing with the empire of Carlotta and Maximilian; and *Buenos dìas, señor Presidente!* (1972). *Mexico in the Theater* (tr. 1976) is a collection of essays.

Uslar Pietri, Arturo (1906–2001),   Venezuelan novelist, essayist. Uslar Pietri's prose is rich in symbols and metaphors. His two most important historical novels are *El camino de El Dorado* (1948), a fictionalized biography of the conquistador Lope de Aguirre, and *Las lanzas coloradas* (1931, tr. *The Red Lances*, 1963). In both books Uslar Pietri depicts people who, failing to find meaningful points of contact in their lives, move irreversibly toward a tragic end. Later works include *33 Cuentos* (1986), *Paginas* (1992), essays, and *Mundo de homo y otros cuentos* (2000).

V

V., Thomas Pynchon's first novel, published in 1963, won the Faulkner Award and immediately established Pynchon as a major literary figure. The title initial refers to a mysterious woman who seems to turn up at key moments of chaos during the 20th century, and the chapters dealing with her appearances are stylistic tours de force, each written in a literary mode corresponding in some way to the nation and period in which the incident takes place: Egypt in the late 19th century, turn-of-the-century Florence, the German Southwest Protectorate in 1922, Malta in 1944, and Paris in 1913. Pervasive references to *The Education of Henry Adams* suggest that this V personifies a force analogous to the physical principle of entropy that destines Western civilization to a terminal rundown.

But all these manifestations of the elusive V are identified and put together only in retrospect, by the bumbling, questing protagonist Herbert Stencil, who is committed to finding V in order to give his own life some purpose. Stencil and the self-proclaimed schlemiel Benny Profane inhabit a postwar world—the fictional present of the novel is 1958—in which people and objects have come to resemble each other to the point where Stencil suspects that V has already done most of her work. Yet, the very existence of V is increasingly in doubt as the quest proceeds, and Stencil begins to wonder whether she may amount to nothing more than "the presence of an initial and a few dead objects." His need to locate a force or conspiracy that will explain his contemporary reality may have *created* that force or conspiracy, a characteristic Pynchon dilemma that the ending of the novel refuses to resolve.

MOLLY HITE

Valdez, Luis [Miguel] (1940–), dramatist. A graduate of San José State University, Valdez began his career as a member of the San Francisco Mime Troupe. In 1965 he founded Teatro Campesino, a cultural outgrowth of the farm worker's union organized by Cesar Chavez. As director of the company he helped foster the growth of Mexican-American literature. *No saco nada de la escuela* (I Don't Get Anything Out of School), first produced in 1969, shows how the American system of education fails Chicano and African-American students. It was published with eight other *actos*, or short plays, in a 1971 collection. Valdez has dramatized the type of popular Mexican-American ballad called the *corrido* and has written *mitos*, a form using fantastic elements of his Aztlán cultural heritage. *Pensamiento Serpentino: A Chicano Approach to the Theater of Reality* appeared in 1973. With Stan Steiner, he edited *Aztlán: An Anthology of Mexican American Literature* (1972). As a Hollywood writer and director, he has helped advance the Latino film cause with *Zoot Suit* (1980) and *La Bamba* (1987), the most successful Latino film to date. Books include *Early Works: Actos, Bernabe and Pensamiento Serpentino* (1990), and *Zoot Suit and Other Plays* (1992). Harry J. Elam, Jr. wrote *Taking It to the Streets: The Social Protest Theory of Luis Valdez and Amiri Baraka* (1997).

Valentine, Jean (1934–), poet, teacher. Valentine, born in Chicago, was educated at Radcliffe and since 1968 has taught creative writing at Barnard, Hunter, Sarah Lawrence, and New York University. The Yale Younger Poets Series published her first collection, *Dream Barker and Other Poems* (1965). These early poems present personal experiences in concrete images. Her later volumes, including *Pilgrims* (1969), *Ordinary Things* (1974), and *The Messenger* (1979), are less direct in their references. *Ordinary Things* includes translation from contemporary Dutch poetry. *Home, Deep, Blue: New and Selected Poems* was published in 1988. More recent collections are *The River at Wolf* (1992), *Growing Darkness, Growing Light* (1997), and *The Cradle of Real Life* (2000).

Valenzuela, Luisa (1938–), novelist. Valenzuela, born in Argentina, lived in the United States for a period after her works were blacklisted in Argentina in 1976. Both *Aquí pasa cosas raras* (1975, tr. *Strange Things Happen Here*, 1979) and *Cambio de armas* (1977, tr. *Other Weapons*, 1982) are set after the return of Juan Perón to Argentina in 1973. The novels deal with relations between men and women in a repressive political climate. Her most celebrated novel, *Cola de lagartija* (1983, tr. *The Lizard's Tail*, 1983), takes its name from an instrument of torture and centers on José Lopez Riga, self-styled minister of social welfare to the Peróns, who influenced their efforts to wipe out dissent and manipulate public opinion. In self-reflexive prose, Valenzuela muses about the possible roles of an exiled writer in her country's suffering. Her early writing, published in Spanish in the 1960s, was collected and translated as *Clara: Thirteen Short Stories and a Novel*

(1976). Later works, mixing politics, magical realism, and feminism, include the novels *He Who Searches* (tr. 1987): *Black Novel (with Argentines)* (tr. 1992), and *Bedside Manners* (tr. 1995), as well as the story collections *Open Door* (tr. 1988), *The Censors* (tr. 1992), and *Symmetries* (tr. 1998).

Vallejo, César (1892–1938),   poet, novelist. Born in northern Peru of Spanish and Indian heritage, Vallejo left his medical studies at the University of San Marcos to take a degree in literature from Trujillo University (1915). The influence of such modernist writers as RUBÉN DARÍO and Herrera y Reissig is apparent in his first collection, *Los Heraldos negros* (*The Dark Messengers*, 1918). In 1920, he was arrested on charges of sedition, and though apparently innocent, was imprisoned for a few months. Some of the best poems of his second collection were written during his imprisonment or make reference to it. He called this volume *Trilce* (1922, tr. 1971)—the title combines *tres* (three) and *dulce* (sweet), conveying the idea of three times sweet. The wordplay of the title signals the work's avant-garde structure. Influenced by the work of Mallarmé and others, Vallejo broke through convention and declared his poetic rebellion in verse free in syntax and logic as well as in rhyme and meter.

Embittered by his prison experience and the death of his mother, Vallejo left for Paris in 1923, never to return to Peru, although he continued to write about his country. He lived in poverty and ill health in France, supporting himself by writing mainly for the press. His leftist political sympathies, strengthened by trips to Russia in 1928 and 1929, led to his expulsion from France in 1930. He lived for a short time in Madrid, writing a number of left-wing plays and a novel, *El Tungsteno* (1931, tr. *Tungsten*, 1989), about a 1917 strike in Vallejo's home region. An example of social realism, it contains many details of Indian life and autobiographical references. His fiction is collected in *Novelas y cuentes completas* (1967).

During the Spanish Civil War, he worked with PABLO NERUDA to organize the Spanish American Group Committee for the defense of the Republic. During this period of intense political activity, Vallejo returned again to poetry, writing of anguish, pain, and hunger. The poems are uncompromising in their search for a new vocabulary and technique to express his deep feelings. He was already seriously ill and was to die without seeing any of the poems published. After his death in Paris, the poetry appeared in two separate volumes *Poemas humanos* (1939, tr. *Human Poems*, 1968) and *España, aparta de mi este cáliz* (*Spain, Take This Cup from Me*, 1940). *The Complete Posthumous Poetry*, an English edition, appeared in 1978.

Vallentine, Benjamin Bennaton (1843–1926), newspaperman, editor, playwright. Born in England, Vallentine lived in Australia for several years, then returned to England, and in 1871 came to the United States. He worked for a shipping firm, studied law, and became a civil service employee of New York City. He helped found PUCK in 1877, and for its first seven years was its managing editor. His letters written under the pen name Lord Fitz-Noodle satirized the British nobility. He was associated with other newspapers and magazines and also wrote several plays, including *Fadette* (1892) and *In Paradise* (1899).

Valley of Decision, The (1902),   a novel by EDITH WHARTON. This story depicts the clash in late 18th-century Italy between the new antireligious ideas of Rousseau and Voltaire and the old conservative beliefs. Despite its historical setting, the plot is actually another statement of Wharton's creed that breaks with convention are ultimately punished. Her chief character, Duke Odo, accepts the new ideas and seeks to alleviate the condition of his people. But by the time his subjects are ready to accept his ideas, he has become a conservative and is exiled. The plot also involves Fulvia, daughter of an exiled philosopher, whom Odo loves. He rescues her from a convent, but later she is killed by a bullet meant for him. (MARCIA DAVENPORT in 1942 wrote a novel bearing the same title.)

Valley of the Moon, The (1913),   a novel by JACK LONDON. In the fervor of his faith in socialism, London wrote this story of a strike in a California town, its consequences in the family life of Billy Roberts, a teamster and ex-prize fighter, and his final winning of happiness in the Valley of the Moon in Sonoma County. What London called the Valley of the Moon was Sonoma Valley; London lived on a ranch nearby and was buried there, on Little Hill.

Vance, Philo.   A detective in the stories of WILLARD HUNTINGTON WRIGHT, who published them under the pen name S. S. Van Dine.

Vancouver, George (1757–1798),   navigator, explorer. Born in England, Vancouver sailed on Captain James Cook's second and third voyages. In 1791 he set out to explore the northwest coast of North America. After rounding the Cape of Good Hope and exploring the coasts of Australia and New Zealand and visiting Tahiti and Hawaii, Vancouver reached his goal in 1792. For the next three years he explored and surveyed the area and circumnavigated the island that now bears his name. On his return to England he wrote an account of his voyage, left incomplete at his death. Vancouver's brother and his lieutenant, Peter Puget—also recalled in geography—readied the volume for publication. The three-volume work with accompanying atlas, *A Voyage of Discovery to the North Pacific Ocean and Round the World*, appeared in 1798 and was reprinted in 1968.

Van der Donck, Adriaen (1620–1655?),   colonist, historian. Van der Donck served from 1641 as an officer of the New Netherland government under PETER STUYVESANT and established a settlement along the Hudson on what is now the site of Yonkers, New York. He returned to Holland because of a disagreement with Stuyvesant and published his *Vertoogh van Nieu-Neder-Land* (*Representation of New Netherland*, 1650), which showed his strong prejudice against Stuyvesant. Later he returned to America. *Beschrijvinge van Nieuvv-Nederlant* (*Description of New Netherland*, 1655) was partly an expansion of his earlier book.

Van Dine, S. S.   Pen name of WILLARD HUNTINGTON WRIGHT.

Van Doren, Carl [Clinton] (1885–1950), editor, anthologist, critic, writer. Born in Illinois, Carl Van Doren, the brother of MARK VAN DOREN, served on the Columbia University faculty from 1911 to 1930, was headmaster of Brearley School (1916–18), managing editor of the CAMBRIDGE HISTORY OF AMERICAN LITERATURE (3 v. 1917, 1918, 1921), literary editor of THE NATION (1919–22), editor for the Literary Guild and The Living Library, and a member of the committee on management of the DICTIONARY OF AMERICAN BIOGRAPHY (1926–36). His *Benjamin Franklin* (1938) won a Pulitzer Prize for its presentation of Franklin's many-sided genius. *The Great Rehearsal* (1948) also treats the 18th century.

Other works by Carl Van Doren include *The Life of Thomas Love Peacock* (1911); *The American Novel* (1921, rev. 1940); *Contemporary Novelists* (1922); *Other Provinces* (short stories, 1925); *James Branch Cabell* (1925); *The Ninth Wave* (novel, 1926); *Swift* (1930); *Sinclair Lewis* (1933); *What Is American Literature?* (1935); *Three Worlds* (autobiography, 1936); *Secret History of the American Revolution* (1941); and *Jane Mecom, The Favorite Sister of Benjamin Franklin* (1950).

Van Doren, Mark (1894–1972), poet, critic, fiction writer, editor. Mark Van Doren, born in Illinois, was educated at the University of Illinois and Columbia University. He taught at Columbia, lectured, and wrote in various forms. He served as literary editor and film critic for THE NATION in the 1920s. In 1940 he won a Pulitzer Prize for his *Collected Poems* (1939).

Mark Van Doren's works include novels and many volumes of poetry, stories, and criticism. He brought poetic insight to such critical works and biographies as *Henry David Thoreau* (1916), *The Poetry of John Dryden* (1931), *Shakespeare* (1939), *Nathaniel Hawthorne* (1949), and *The Happy Critic* (1961). He also edited the *Anthology of World Poetry* (1928, 1936). A few of his books of poetry are *Spring Thunder and Other Poems* (1924), *A Winter Diary and Other Poems* (1935), *The Mayfield Deer* (1941), *Spring Birth* (1953), and *Morning Worship and Other Poems* (1960). *Tilda* (1943) is a novel, and *Nobody Say a Word, and Other Stories* (1953) contains some of his best short stories. He wrote one play, *Last Days of Lincoln* (1959), and an *Autobiography* (1958). His wife, Dorothy Graffe Van Doren—herself an editor, writer, and an editor on *The Nation*—wrote a biography of her husband, *The Professor and I* (1959).

Van Druten, John [William] (1901–1957), lawyer, teacher, dramatist, novelist, director. Born in England, Van Druten was teaching law in Wales when his first play, *Young Woodley* (1925), a study of adolescence, was banned by the British Censor. It was immediately produced in the United States and later opened peacefully in London. Van Druten accompanied the play to the United States and later became an American citizen.

His plays include *Old Acquaintance* (1940); *The Damask Cheek*, with Lloyd Morris (1942); *The Voice of the Turtle* (1943); *I Remember Mama*, based on sketches by KATHRYN FORBES (1944); *Bell, Book, and Candle* (1950); and *I Am a Camera*, based on sketches by Christopher Isherwood (1951). He directed several plays, both his own and the work of others; wrote several novels, including one based on *Young Woodley*; and dealt with his craft in *The Way to the Present* (1938) and *The Playwright at Work* (1953). Several of his plays were made into movies, and *The Voice of the Turtle* became the basis for a successful musical, *Cabaret*.

Van Duyn, Mona (1921–), poet. Van Duyn, born in Waterloo, Iowa, was educated at Iowa State Teachers' College and the University of Iowa. She taught mostly at Washington University. Many of her poems concern love, social situations, and everyday experiences. A meticulous user of poetic forms, Van Duyn has won many awards and served as poet laureate of the United States (1992–1993). She has written *Valentines to the Wide World* (1959); *To See, To Take* (1970); *Merciful Disguises* (1973); *Letters from a Father* (1982); *Near Changes* (1990); *If It Be Not I: Collected Poems, 1959–1982* (1994); and *Fireball* (1994).

Van Dyke, Henry (1852–1933), writer, educator, diplomat, preacher. Born in Pennsylvania and educated at Princeton, Van Dyke served as minister at the United Congregational Church of New Bedford, Rhode Island, and the Brick Presbyterian Church in New York City before becoming a professor of English at Princeton. President Woodrow Wilson appointed him minister to the Netherlands and Luxembourg (1913–1916), and he served as a navy chaplain in World War I.

Van Dyke's first book, *The Reality of Religion* (1884), presages his lifelong attempt to fuse religion and practical, everyday living in a keen personal enjoyment of life. His wide literary range is seen in such titles as *Little Rivers* (1895) and *Fisherman's Luck* (1899), nature essays; *The Story of the Other Wise Man* (1896); *The Builders* (1897) and *The White Bees* (1909), poetry; *The Poetry of Tennyson* (1899); *The Ruling Passion* (1901), short stories; *The Spirit of America* (1910), lectures delivered at the Sorbonne; and *The House of Rimmon* (1929), a play. *The Blue Flower* (1902) is a translation from Novalis. The Avalon edition of his collected works (17 v. 1920–22) was named for his home in Princeton.

Van Gelder, Robert (1904–1952), newspaperman, editor, writer. Van Gelder was born in Baltimore and worked for two Connecticut papers before joining the staff of the *New York Times*. He was editor of the *Times* Sunday book review from 1943 to 1946; some of his interviews with authors were collected in *Writers and Writing* (1946). At the suggestion of Somerset Maugham, he began writing fiction—*Important People*, a novel, appeared in 1948. He also wrote some juveniles—*Smash Picture* (1938), *Marjorie Fleming* (1940), and *The Enemy in the House* (1940). With his wife, Dorothy van Gelder, he edited an anthology, *American Legend: A Treasury of Our Country's Yesterdays* (1946).

Vanity Fair. [1] A comic weekly founded December 31, 1859, by three members of the Stephens family, Louis Henry, William Allan, and Henry Louis. CHARLES GODFREY LELAND was its managing editor in 1860–61, ARTEMUS WARD succeeded him (1861–62). This *Vanity Fair* expired on July 4, 1863. During its brief career it enlisted many contributors of note, among them Thomas Bailey Aldrich, R. H. Stoddard, William Winter, and William Dean Howells. The members of the staff and their contributors made the celebrated PFAFF'S CELLAR their meeting place. The *Vanity Fair* group appears in Albert Parry's *Garrets and Pretenders, A History of Bohemianism in America* (1933).

[2] A second magazine by the same name was founded as a monthly in New York City in 1868, but its beginnings are shadowy and it had various other names at first. It was edited by Frank Harris from 1907 to 1911. Condé Nast bought it in 1913, and under Frank Crowninshield, editor from 1914 to 1935, it became one of the sprightliest and most sophisticated magazines of its day. In 1935 it was absorbed by VOGUE, also owned by Nast. An elegant collection of pictures, articles, and fiction, *Vanity Fair: A Cavalcade of the Twenties*, edited by Cleveland Amory and Frederic Bradlee, appeared in 1960.

In 1983 and after, attempts were made to resurrect the magazine, giving it some of the verve of its heyday. By 1990 it had become a monthly, edited by Tina Brown, with a focus on film, style, finance, and other subjects of popular interest.

Van Loon, Hendrik Willem (1882–1944), journalist, historian. Van Loon left his birthplace, the Netherlands, to study at Cornell and Harvard, and then became a foreign correspondent. He earned a Ph.D. at Munich in 1911 and taught history at various American universities. In the meantime he had written *The Fall of the Dutch Republic* (1913) and *The Rise of the Dutch Kingdom* (1915), works of substantial scholarship. Much more popular were his *Ancient Man* (1920) and *The Story of Mankind* (1921). He became assistant editor of the Baltimore *Sun* (1924), and was a radio commentator for many years. He wrote children's books and biographies of Peter Stuyvesant and Rembrandt, and edited several songbooks. He is best known for surveys enlivened by his own drawings, such as *The Story of the Bible* (1923), *Man the Miracle Maker* (1928), *Van Loon's Geography* (1932), *Ships and How They Sailed the Seven Seas* (1935), *The Arts* (1937), *The Story of the Pacific* (1940), and *Van Loon's Lives* (1942).

van Paassen, Pierre [born Pieter Anthonie Laurusse van Paassen] (1895–1968), writer. After van Paassen completed his education in his native Holland, Canada, and France, he worked as a reporter on the Toronto *Globe* and the Atlanta *Constitution*, and as a columnist and foreign correspondent for the New York *Evening World* and the Toronto *Star*. A bitter foe of fascism, he was forced to leave Italy, France, and Germany in the 1930s.

Israel and the Vision of Humanity (1932), van Paassen's first book, reflects his identification of the fate of the Jewish people with the fate of all men. With J. W. Wise he edited *Nazism: An Assault on Civilization* (1934). *Days of Our Years* (1939), in which political history is interwoven with autobiographical reminiscences, was a best seller, as was *The Forgotten Ally* (1943), which deals with Jews during World War II. Van Passen's other books include *The Time Is Now!* (1941); *That Day Alone* (1941); *Who's on the Lord's Side? Who?* (1942); *Earth Could Be Fair* (1946); *The Tower of Terzel* (1948); *Why Jesus Died* (1949); *Jerusalem Calling* (1955); and *Crown of Fire* (1960).

Van Twiller, Wouter [or **Walter**] (1580?–1656?), public official. Van Twiller, born in Holland, was governor of New Netherland from 1633 to 1637. He is one of the chief characters in Washington Irving's HISTORY OF NEW YORK . . . BY DIEDRICH KNICKERBOCKER. Irving described him as "exactly five feet six inches in height and six feet five inches in circumference." He typifies the golden age of the Knickerbocker aristocrat, which Irving was satirizing in this work. Of Twiller, Irving goes on to say: "So invincible was his gravity that he was never known to laugh or even to smile through the whole course of a long and prosperous life. Nay, if a joke were uttered in his presence, that set light minded hearers in a roar, it was observed to throw him into a state of perplexity." Such irreverent descriptions incensed the old Dutch families, but delighted most of Irving's contemporaries. Irving's profile of Twiller was based on the memoirs of David Pieterszen de Vries, a sea captain and colonizer who had disliked Twiller intensely.

Van Vechten, Carl (1880–1964), novelist, music and dance critic, photographer. Van Vechten wrote seven novels; five books of music criticism, of which *Interpreters and Interpretations* (1917) is perhaps best known; numerous critical prefaces; and *The Tiger in the House* (1920), a charming book about cats. *Peter Whiffle* (1922), his first novel, is an imaginary autobiography of an aesthete and dilettante. *The Blind Bow-Boy* (1923) is a curious mixture of vulgarity and elegance. *The Tattooed Countess* (1924) depicts *fin-de-siècle* Iowa, Van Vechten's native state. NIGGER HEAVEN (1926) is a novel about Harlem. Van Vechten was one of the first white writers to take African American artists seriously. After writing *Parties* (1930), his last novel, he turned to a career in photography, but he wrote about himself in *Sacred and Profane Memories* (1932) and edited *Selected Works of Gertrude Stein* (1946) and *Last Operas and Plays by Gertrude Stein* (1949).

Van Vogt, A[lfred] E[lton] (1912–2000), science-fiction writer. Born in Manitoba, Canada, Van Vogt came to the U.S. in 1944 and became a citizen in 1952. A prolific writer of science fiction, he won recognition with two early novels. *Slan* (1946) concerns mutant humans who can read minds, and *The World of A* (1948, later *The World of Null-A*, 1953), deals with inhabitants of Venus who are conditioned semantically by the "null-A," or non-Aristotelian, doctrines of Alfred Korzybski. Van Vogt's later novels, generally less popular, include *The Battle of Forever* (1971), in which the last man alive cannot bring himself to use his superhuman powers against an enemy determined to exterminate humanity. Van Vogt's work has been collected in *The Far-Out Worlds of A. E. Van Vogt* (1968), *More Than Superhuman* (1971), and *The Best of A. E. Van Vogt* (1976).

Vargas Llosa, [Jorge] Mario [Pedro] (1936–   ), novelist. Along with the work of GABRIEL GARCIA MARQUEZ, the novels of Vargas Llosa, a Peruvian, are often acclaimed as exemplars of the remarkable riches of contemporary Latin-American fiction. Among his best-known novels are *La ciudad* *y los perros* (1962, tr. *The Time of the Hero*, 1966); *La casa verde* (1966, tr. *The Green House*, 1968); *Conversación en la Catedral* (1969, tr. *Conversation in the Cathedral*, 1975); *Pantaleón y las visitadoras* (1973, tr. *Captain Pantoja and the Special Service*, 1978); *La tía Julia y el escribidor* (1978, tr. *Aunt Julia and the Scriptwriter*, 1982); *La guerra del fin del mundo* (1981, tr. *The War of the End of the World*, 1984); *Historia de Mayta* (1984, tr. *The Real Life of Alejandro Mayta*, 1986); *El hablador* (1988, tr. *The Storyteller*, 1989); *Elogio de la Madrasta* (tr. *In Praise of the Stepmother*, 1990); *Lituma en los Andes* (1996, tr. *Death in the Andes*, 1996); and *Cuadernos de don Rigoberto* (1998, tr. *The Notebooks of Don Rigoberto*, 1998). A collection of stories is *Los cachorros* (1967, tr. *The Cubs*, 1980). His most notable nonfiction includes *The Perpetual Orgy* (1975, tr. 1986); a passionate appreciation of *Madame Bovary*; a study of Gabriel García Márquez (1971); *Pez en Agua* (1994, tr. *A Fish in the Water: A Memoir*, 1994). His most recent novel is *La Fiesta del Chivo* (2000).

Born in Arequipa, Peru, Vargas Llosa lived with his mother in Cochabamba, Bolivia, from 1937 to 1945, following his parents' separation. He returned to Peru in 1945, moving to Lima in 1946 when his parents reunited. In 1957 Vargas Llosa married his aunt, Julia Urquidi. His novel *Aunt Julia and the Scriptwriter* deftly plays with this experience, intertwining autobiographical material with comic variations on a character he called Pedro Camacho, who writes soap operas. *The War of the End of the World*, set in Brazil, recreates the life and legend of Antonio Conselheiro, visionary leader of the Canudos rebellion in Northwest Bahia at the turn of the century. Vargas Llosa's other fiction is usually set in Peru, often in Lima, a city he knows intimately. *The Green House*, set in Piura in northern Peru, where Vargas Llosa lived for a year with his mother in 1945, is a stylistically adventurous work that explores the movements of characters between two green houses—a brothel in Piura and the jungle. Although this novel, like *Conversations in the Cathedral*, has been acclaimed for its form, style, and experimentation—affirming popular North American conceptions of Latin-American fiction's distentions of realism—Vargas Llosa's fiction is also informed by a strong social conscience and vision. His first novel, *The Time of the Hero*, for example, is critical of the military academy Vargas Llosa attended in Lima, and the Peruvian military burned 1,000 copies of the novel when it was published in 1963. Vargas Llosa's novel *The Storyteller* (1989) returns to the Peruvian jungle to explore the fate of the Machiguenga Indians, a scattered tribe that survives its diaspora largely due to the agency of the *hablador*, the story-teller of the title, who walks from village to village preserving tribal memory and lore. The narrator gradually reveals how Mascarita, a childhood friend in Lima who had allegedly emigrated to Israel but who seems to have vanished, emerges as one of the Machiguenga storytellers, an unlikely contemporary preserver of Machiguenga culture. After becoming involved in Peruvian politics in the 1980s, Vargas Llosa lost the runoff election for president in June 1990.

NEIL BESNER

Varieties of Religious Experience, The (1902),   a work by WILLIAM JAMES. Based on material James had collected on the psychology and philosophy of religion for lectures at the University of Edinburgh in 1901 and 1902, *The Varieties of Religious Experience* contains numerous descriptions of religious states of consciousness, which James presented from a pragmatic point of view. He regarded the mystical experience in the light of his hypothesis of a subliminal self able to transcend the narrow limits of normal experience. The book has remained one of the most popular of James's works and is particularly important for the evidence it gives for religious experience as a unique phenomenon.

Variety.   In the language of show business at the beginning of the 20th century the word *variety* meant VAUDEVILLE. In 1905 Sime Silverman began publishing a weekly magazine named *Variety*. It became the chief trade journal of the theatrical business and one of the most successful periodicals in American history. At first it dealt mainly with vaudeville, but gradually it expanded to take in every branch of theater. In 1933 a separate edition began appearing in Hollywood as a daily. Abel Green succeeded Silverman as editor.

Variety is especially known for the outrageously appealing language it has been fabricating over the years, making the journal a great fertilizer of American slang. Abel Green collected some of *Variety's* neologisms, such as *big time, m.c., borscht circuit, eatery, vamp, angel*—someone who finances a Broadway production—and *pix*. The greatest neologist on the staff of *Variety* was Jack Conway, who is credited with the verb *click*—meaning succeed—and *high-hat, pushover, payoff, belly laugh, scram*, and many others. *Variety's* headline for the financial debacle of 1929 is still remembered: "Wall Street Lays an Egg."

David Stoddart told Silverman's story in *Lord Broadway* (1941). *The Spice of Variety* (1952), edited by Green, is an amusing collection of contributions from actors, critics, playwrights, and others.

Vashon, George (1820–1878),   poet. Sterling A. Brown, in *Negro Poetry and Drama* (1937), describes Vashon as a well-educated and ambitious writer who found inspiration in the abolitionist cause. He was the first African-American to write a narrative poem of any length. "Vincent Ogé," a chronicle of the Haitian revolutionary hero, appeared in a collection called *Autographs of Freedom* (1856).

Vassa, Gustavus.   See EQUIANO.

Vassall Morton (1856),   a novel by FRANCIS PARKMAN. In this narrative Parkman included some of his own experiences. It is the story of a Harvard graduate who studies races and peoples and who for a time is held captive by Indians.

Vaudeville.   A form of entertainment in the theater in which variety is the pattern. The origin of the word is obscure. *The Random House Dictionary of the English Language, Second Edition* (1987) states that it was derived from the Middle French village *chanson du vau de Vire*, song of the Vale of Vire, a valley of Calvados, France, noted for satirical folksongs. In

England a similar type of entertainment developed in the music halls, which originally were adjuncts to taverns. These music halls became popular in the early 18th century and provided programs of songs, dances, acrobatics, and pantomimes. Later, the links with taverns were broken. The English music hall undoubtedly influenced American vaudeville entertainments, except that pantomimes never became popular there.

Tony Pastor gave vaudeville its real start when on October 24, 1881, he opened his new 14th Street Theater in New York with a series of vaudeville acts. Competition was keen, and better theaters were built, stage properties were improved, and mechanical gadgets added wonderment to the acts. Theaters were open from eleven in the morning to eleven at night, offering two complete sets of performances. Some successful vaudeville producers were Oscar Hammerstein, Alexander Pantages, and Marcus Loew. The Palace Theater in New York City was once the principal home of vaudeville. For an astonishing number of performers, vaudeville became a training ground that led to stardom. From vaudeville came such performers as Eddie Cantor, the Marx brothers, WILL ROGERS, FRED ALLEN, W.C. Fields, Jimmy Durante, Fred and Adele Astaire, and Fannie Brice. Among the varieties of performers were acrobats, jugglers, ballad singers, magicians, midgets, monologists, animals, family teams, ventriloquists, sharpshooters, mind-readers, dancers, hypnotists, minstrels, contortionists, mimics, and female impersonators. Vaudeville flourished mightily during the 1920s, but suffered severely after the 1929 crash. Even worse, however, was the coming of the movies and radio. When television appeared after World War II, vaudeville experienced a minor revival that lasted only a short while.

Veblen, Thorstein B[unde] (1857–1929), economist, social philosopher. Veblen was born on the agricultural frontier in Wisconsin and reared in Minnesota among highly clannish Norwegian immigrants. Norwegian, not English, was his native language. His keen mind and biting tongue led to loneliness and unpopularity in his youth. Despite his dissent from the communal mores, however, Veblen shared deeply in the agrarian unrest of the 1870s and 1880s, in which pre-Marxian utopian socialist ingredients and real grievances combined to produce the later Populist outburst against the railroads and Eastern capitalists.

He was educated at Carleton College, Johns Hopkins, and Yale. Because academic posts in philosophy—Veblen's field of study—were then the private preserve of the clergy, Veblen returned to Minnesota, where he studied and translated from the Norse for seven years. In 1891 he went to Cornell for further study and began to teach in the economics department of the University of Chicago. Later he taught at Stanford University and the University of Missouri. It was at Missouri that he gave his best-known course, "Economic Factors in Civilization."

In 1918 he became an editor of THE DIAL in New York and a lecturer at the New School for Social Research. In 1925 he was offered the presidency of the American Economic Association, but rejected it because, as he said, "They didn't offer it to me when I needed it." Veblen's first published book, THE THEORY OF

THE LEISURE CLASS (1899), won him instant celebrity. His later books included *The Theory of Business Enterprise* (1904); *The Instinct of Workmanship* (1914), his most original and baffling effort; *Imperial Germany and the Industrial Revolution* (1915); *An Inquiry into the Nature of Peace* (1917); *The Higher Learning in America* (1918); *The Vested Interests and the State of the Industrial Arts* (1919); *The Place of Science in Modern Civilization* (1919); *The Engineers and the Price System* (1921); *The Laxdaela Saga* (translated from the Icelandic with an introduction, 1925); and *Essays in Our Changing Order* (ed. by Leon Ardzrooni, 1934). Max Lerner edited *The Portable Veblen* (1948).

Veblen's writings move constantly about what he defined as the two major contrasting human drives: the predatory and the productive. He distinguished sharply between business and industry; the latter was the endlessly fecund process of making goods to answer actual needs, the former a predatory scheme of parasites to make profits by interfering in the direct consumption of goods for use. Human nature, like human institutions, said Veblen, is not immutable; all aspects of culture, all moral standards, change with time and often with place. The development of the machine process is a free gift of evolution, and if left to the industrial factors and not to the business predators it would guarantee an abundant earthly peace for all.

Veblen is one of the historical figures treated in capsule biographies by JOHN DOS PASSOS in his trilogy U.S.A. (1938). Books about Veblen include Joseph Dorfman, *Thorstein Veblen and His America* (1934); David Riesman, *Thorstein Veblen, A Critical Interpretation* (1953); Douglas F. Dowd, *Thorstein Veblen* (1964); John Patrick Diggins, *Thorstein Veblen: Theorist of the Leisure Class* (1999); and Francisco Louca and Mark Perlman, eds., *Is Economics an Evolutionary Science: The Legacy of Thorstein Veblen* (2000).

Vedder, Elihu (1836–1923), painter, illustrator, writer. Vedder, born in New York City, painted some of the murals in the Library of Congress and was a well-known illustrator—his work included illustrations for the Edward FitzGerald translation of the *Rubáiyát of Omar Khayyám* (1884). Among his books are *Digressions of V* (1910), a humorous autobiography; *Miscellaneous Moods in Verse* (1914); and *Doubt and Other Things* (1922).

Veiller, Bayard (1869–1943), newspaperman, dramatist. Veiller, born in Brooklyn, New York, held jobs on Chicago and New York newspapers before beginning to write plays. He made a specialty of mystery dramas. Among his plays are *Within the Law* (1912); *The Thirteenth Chair* (1916), which used spiritualism as a theme; *The Trial of Mary Dugan* (1927), which included a meticulously arranged courtroom scene; *Damn Your Honor* (1929); and *That's the Woman* (1930). In his later days Veiller became a movie executive. He wrote an autobiography, *The Fun I've Had* (1941).

Vein of Iron (1935), a novel by ELLEN GLASGOW. It deals with the vein of iron in the character of a woman who meets all kinds of misfortune in the Virginia mountains, where she first lives and then later in Virginia towns. The period is the years before and during the depression of the 1930s.

Venable, William Henry (1836–1920), teacher, historian, writer. Venable, born in Waynesville, Ohio, for the greater part of his life taught English and science in the schools of Cincinnati. He wrote books of many kinds, among them one on pedagogy, *Let Him First Be a Man* (1893); several novels; and much miscellaneous verse. But he is chiefly remembered for his pioneering regional study *Beginnings of Literary Culture in the Ohio Valley* (1891). This book includes historical and biographical sketches, some of them offering material on early Western writers not mentioned elsewhere.

Venetian Glass Nephew, The (1925), a novel by ELINOR WYLIE. This fantasy tells how Rosalba, a woman of flesh and blood, falls in love with and marries Virginio, who is made of glass. To harmonize herself and her husband she is willingly transmogrified by fire into porcelain. The story has been interpreted as symbolizing the conflict between nature and art.

Venetian Life (1866), travel sketches by WILLIAM DEAN HOWELLS. See ITALIAN JOURNEYS.

Veríssimo, Érico [Lopes] (1905–1975), novelist. Veríssimo's novels are set in his native state of Rio Grande do Sul, Brazil, and in its capital city, Porto Alegre, and are rich in characterization and extensive in scope. His works include *Caminhos cruzados* (1935, tr. *Crossroads*, 1943), which describes five days in the lives of the inhabitants of a suburban street in Porto Alegre. *Olhai os lírios do campo* (1938, tr. *Consider the Lilies of the Field*, 1945) concerns a wealthy doctor who reviews his past at the deathbed of a former mistress. *O resto é silêncio* (1942, tr. *The Rest Is Silence*, 1946) studies the effect of a girl's suicide on seven people who witness the act. *O tempo e o vento* (1949, tr. *Time and the Wind*, 1951) is the title of a trilogy tracing the development of Rio Grande do Sul in the history of the Terra-Cambará family from the 18th through the 20th centuries.

Veritism. See GARLAND, HAMLIN.

Verplanck, G[ulian] C[rommelin] (1786–1870), politician, editor, author. Verplanck, born in New York City, is remembered chiefly for his hatred of Governor DeWitt Clinton and his friendship for WILLIAM CULLEN BRYANT. A decade-long feud with Clinton impelled Verplanck to write erudite satires in verse and prose, including *A Fable for Statesmen and Politicians* (1815), *The State Triumvirate* (1819), and *The Bucktail Bards* (1819). Charles King and Verplanck founded the New York *American*, in which many of his attacks on Clinton first appeared. With Bryant and R. C. SANDS, Verplanck edited an annual giftbook, THE TALISMAN (1828–30). One of the earliest of American Shakespearean scholars, Verplanck published *Shakespeare's Plays: With His Life* (3 v. 1847).

In addition to these literary enterprises, Verplanck served in the New York Assembly, in Congress, and as a state senator. His public addresses were collected in *Discourses and Addresses* (1833). Bryant wrote *A Discourse on the Life, Character and Writings of Gulian Crommelin Verplanck* (1870). Robert W.

July wrote a eulogistic account of *The Essential New Yorker* (1951) as an important voice of 19th-century American romanticism and nationalism. See KNICKERBOCKER SCHOOL.

Verrazzano, Giovanni da (c. 1485–1528), Italian navigator. Verrazzano discovered parts of North America while serving Francis I, of France. He gave the first description of the North American coast after actually viewing it. He found the mouth of the Hudson River in 1524 and prepared "Letter on My Voyages" (c. 1524), published in Hakluyt's *Voyages* (v. 8), the New York Historical Society's *Collections, Second Series* (v. 1, 1841), and the American Scenic and Historical Preservation Society's *Report* (appendix to v. 15, 1910).

Verrill, A[lpheus] Hyatt (1871–1954), naturalist, explorer, ethnologist, inventor, writer. Verrill, born in New Haven, Connecticut, made explorations mainly in the West Indies and Latin America and contributed ethnological and zoological information. He was also an expert photographer and produced a new process of color photography. He wrote more than a hundred books on natural history, Indians, and exploration, some of which were for boys. Among them are *In Morgan's Wake* (1915), *Book of the West Indies* (1917), *Panama Past and Present* (1921), *Boys' Book of Buccaneers* (1927), *Under Peruvian Skies* (1930), *Our Indians* (1935), *Along New England Shores* (1936), *My Jungle Trails* (1937), and *The Real Americans* (1954).

vers libre. See FREE VERSE.

Very, Jones (1813–1880), poet. Very, born in Salem, Massachusetts, taught at Fisk Latin School to earn money for tuition before studying at Harvard College and the Harvard Divinity School, where he served briefly as a tutor of Greek. Licensed as a Unitarian minister, he preached numerous sermons despite his shyness and otherworldliness. He lived a retired life in Salem with his sisters, occasionally contributing to the Salem *Gazette* and the *Christian Register* and writing sonnets and lyrics celebrating ecstatic religious visions and mysticism. At one time he was committed to McLean Asylum in Somerville, Massachusetts, but his friend Ralph Waldo Emerson insisted that Very was "profoundly sane." Very was associated with TRANSCENDENTALISM. His first book, *Essays and Poems* (1839), was edited and published by Emerson, and William Cullen Bryant and William Channing praised his sonnets highly. His work resembles that of Montaigne and the 17th-century English metaphysical poets. Two posthumously published collections are *Poems* (1883) and *Poems and Essays* (1886). Yvor Winters wrote a study of Very, *Maule's Curse* (1938).

Very, Lydia Louise Anne (1823–1901), poet. Though Lydia Very shared a Salem, Massachusetts, home with her brother, Jones Very, she was less influenced by the transcendentalists. Her work includes nature poetry and stories, personal anecdote, and romantic fiction. *Poems and Prose Writings* (1890) compiles earlier pieces. *Sayings and Doings Among the Insects and Flowers* (1897) and *An Old-Fashioned Garden and Walks and Musings Therein* (1900) are self-explanatory titles. Her novels include *The Better Path* (1898), *A Strange Disclosure* (1898), and *A Strange Recluse* (1899).

Vespucci, Amerigo [Latinized as **Americus**] (1454–1512), cosmographer, navigator, explorer. Vespucci was a clerk in the commercial office of the House of the Medici in Florence when word of Columbus's success in crossing the ocean reached Italy. It inspired Vespucci to set off for Spain immediately in search of a contract to furnish supplies for Columbus's second voyage. It is probable that Vespucci took part in fitting out that voyage, and he himself made four voyages to the New World. During Vespucci's third voyage he landed on the coast of Brazil—between May and October of 1502—but in a voyage of 1497 he mentions touching upon a coast "which we thought to be that of a continent." If he was right, the fact would give him priority over both John Cabot and Columbus in reaching the mainland of America.

In 1503 Vespucci wrote a short account of his third voyage that soon appeared in a Latin version, *Mundus Novus* (1504). It gives a vivid description of the country and its inhabitants. A copy came into the hands of a German geographer named Martin Waldseemüller, who remarked in a treatise entitled *Cosmographiae Introductio* (1507): "A fourth part of the earth has been discovered by Amerigo Vespucci. . . . I see no reason why anyone could justly object to naming this part *Amerige*, that is, the land of *Amerigo*, or *America*, after its discoverer."

Vestal, Stanley.   Pen name of WALTER S. CAMPBELL.

Victor, Frances [Fuller] (1826–1902),   journalist, poet, historian. In 1856 Frances Fuller of Oneida County, New York, married a naval engineer, Henry Clay Victor. Six years later her sister Metta Victoria (*see next entry*) married a New York editor, Orville James Victor, who was Frances's brother-in-law. Both sisters were protégées of RUFUS W. GRISWOLD, who edited a collection of verse they published jointly, *Poems of Sentiment and Imagination* (1851). Many years later, Frances published *Poems* (1900). Her husband died in a shipwreck, and her later years were full of hardship and poverty. She wrote a *History of Oregon* (2 v. 1886, 1888) and also wrote about other Northwestern states. Victor was a member of H. H. Bancroft's staff in the preparation of the *History of the Northwest Coast* (1884).

Victor, Metta Victoria [Fuller] (1831–1886),   poet, dime novelist, humorist. Metta's fame surpassed that of her sister Frances (*see above*). Together they wrote *Poems of Sentiment and Imagination* (1851). Then Metta began writing fiction and achieved celebrity with a temperance novel, *The Senator's Son* (1853). When she married Orville James Victor, who worked for ERASTUS F. BEADLE, she became a prolific writer of serials for the cheap magazines of her day. She wrote under her own name for the New York *Weekly* and for *Saturday Night*, but her contributions to Beadle's magazines and libraries appeared under various pen names. Typical of her books were *Alice Wilde, The Raftsman's Daughter* (1860); *The Backwoods Bride* (1861); MAUM GUINEA AND HER PLANTATION CHILDREN (1862); and *The Gold Hunters* (1874). Another of her books was *Lives of the Female Mormons* (1856). As the popu-

larity of the dime novel waned, she began writing humorous stories and sketches.

Victoria de Junín, La: Canto a Bolívar (1825),   an ode by José Joaquín Olmedo (1780–1847), the Ecuadorean poet and statesman. Dedicated to Simón Bolívar, the poem was inspired by the patriots' victories at Junín and Ayacucho, which virtually terminated the South American struggle for independence. In form and structure, the work reveals Olmedo's familiarity with the classics, and the opening lines closely imitate one of the odes of Horace. However, Olmedo's exuberance, imagination, and extravagant metaphors, which Bolívar himself satirized, make the poem one of the forerunners of the romantic movement in Latin America.

Vidal, Gore (1929–   ),   novelist, playwright, poet, essayist, historian. Vidal, whose given name came from his grandfather, Senator Gore of Oklahoma, was born at West Point, New York. His first book, *Williwaw* (1946), set in the Aleutian Islands, drew on his army experience during World War II. *The City and the Pillar* (1948) attracted some criticism for its portrayal of homosexuality.

Vidal often dramatizes historical figures in his fiction. *Julian* (1964) details the life of the Roman emperor (331?–363) called the Apostate for his battle against Christianity. *Creation* (1981) includes such persons as Confucius, Darius, and Xerxes. A series of novels constitutes a chronicle of American history. *Washington, D.C.* (1967) covers the New Deal and MCCARTHY-ISM. *Burr* (1973) details the incredible career of AARON BURR. *1876* (1976) centers on the election that was won in the popular vote by SAMUEL TILDEN but was awarded by the Electoral College to RUTHERFORD B. HAYES, the loser. *Lincoln* (1984) is a full treatment of the Great Emancipator. *Empire* (1987) portrays the Gilded Age. *Hollywood* (1990) is set in Washington and Hollywood in the 1920s. *The Golden Age* (2000) covers 1940 to the Korean War. Vidal's novelistic technique is to combine invented characters with historical figures, and fact with fiction.

A writer with a biting wit, Vidal has also written satires, including *Myra Breckenridge* (1968), *Myron* (1974), *Kalki* (1978), and *Duluth* (1983). *A Thirsty Evil* (1956) is a short-story collection. During the 1950s Vidal wrote detective novels under the name Edgar Box. His plays include *Visit to a Small Planet* (1956), first produced on television, and *The Best Man* (1960), detailing political intrigue at a nominating convention. His essays are collected in *The United States: Essays, 1952–1992* (1993) and *The Last Empire: Essays 1992–2000* (2001). Earlier collections include *Reflections Upon a Sinking Ship* (1969), *Homage to Daniel Shays* (1973), *Matters of Fact and Fiction* (1977), *The Second American Revolution* (1982), and *At Home* (1988). His other novels include *In a Yellow Wood* (1947), *The Season of Comfort* (1949), *A Search for the King* (1950), *Dark Green, Bright Red* (1950), *The Judgment of Paris* (1952), and *Messiah* (1954). *Palimpsest* (1995) is a memoir of his first 39 years. *Screening History* (1992) is a book on the movies. Fred Kaplan wrote a biography, *Gore Vidal* (1999), and edited *The Essential Gore Vidal* (1999).

Vielé, Herman Knickerbocker (1856–1908), novelist, playwright. Born in New York City, Vielé is best known for his novel *The Last of the Knickerbockers* (1901). His brother, Egbert Ludovicus Vielé (1863–1937), lived and wrote in France under the name Francis Vielé-Griffin and was regarded as one of the great French poets of his day.

Viereck, George Sylvester (1884–1962), novelist, essayist. Viereck left his native Germany and settled in New York City in 1895. He was associate editor of *Current Literature* (1906–15) and editor of *International* (1912–18) and *American Monthly* (1914–27). He championed the German cause during World War I. Among Viereck's numerous writings are *A Game at Love and Other Plays* (1906); *Nineveh, and Other Poems* (1907); *Roosevelt: A Study in Ambivalence* (1919); *My First Two Thousand Years*, a trilogy written with Paul Eldridge (1928–32); *The Temptation of Jonathan*, political essays (1938); *Gloria*, a novel (1952); and *Men into Beasts* (1952). During World War II, Viereck served as adviser to the German Library of Information, and was imprisoned from 1942 to 1947 for not declaring himself a German agent in the United States.

Viereck, Peter [Robert Edwin] (1916–), poet, scholar, teacher. A son of GEORGE SYLVESTER VIERECK, Peter Viereck was born in New York City and educated at Harvard. He has taught at Harvard and at Radcliffe, Smith, and Mount Holyoke. Viereck's political attitude of liberal conservatism found expression in *Metapolitics* (1941), a book he called "a psychoanalysis of Nazism"; most explicitly in *Conservatism Revisited* (1949); and also in *Shame and Glory of the Intellectuals* (1953), the brief *Dream and Responsibility* (1953), *Unadjusted Man: A New Hero for Americans* (1956), and *Metapolitics, the Roots of the Nazi Mind* (1961). *Conservatism Revisited* and *The New Conservatism—What Went Wrong* were published in a combined edition in 1962.

His novelette *Who Killed the Universe?* appeared in *New Directions* (1948). *Terror and Decorum*, his first book of poems, won the Tietjens Prize for poetry and a Pulitzer Prize (1948). It was followed by other collections: *Strike Through the Mask!* (1950), *The First Morning* (1952), *A Walk on Moss* (1956), *The Persimmon Tree* (1956), and *New and Selected Poems* (1967), *Archer in the Marrow: The Applewood Cycles, 1967–1986* (1987), and *Tide and Continuities: Last and First Poems, 1995–1938* (1995). *The Tree Witch* (1961) is a verse drama.

Vietnam War. The term "Vietnam War" denotes both an event in history and a cultural phenomenon. As a historical fact, the Vietnam War covers events that occurred during the period from entry of U.S. forces into Vietnam in 1954 to departure of those forces in 1973. As a cultural phenomenon, the Vietnam War describes a transformation that occurred in the U.S. during that period and some years afterward. John Hellman, in *American Myth and the Legacy of Vietnam*, characterizes this transformation as the nation's loss of a mythological rationale. Hellman said that combat soldiers in that war did not take possession of their experiences in the form of the "inner romance they projected upon it." Instead, according to

Hellman, they entered into a psychic landscape "that overwhelmed the American idea of frontier."

When televised on the evening news, incidents of that war could not become referents contributing to growth of the national myth, which cross-identifies discovery of the New World by Columbus with the colonists' successful revolution against the British. Unlike earlier sites where the American Revolution was successfully reenacted, Vietnam resisted such staging. Because the U.S. government could not provide acceptable justification for an American presence in Vietnam, combat soldiers lacked moral rationale for their actions, and in the absence of such a rationale lost the power to discriminate between what is just and what is unjust in a war.

Their collective difficulties changed the cultural image of the American soldier—from G.I. Joe, heroic adventurer, to the emotionally crippled Vietnam veteran. This transformation was accompanied by related changes in cultural representations of the scene of battle and the actions occurring there. In *Green Berets* (1965), Robin Moore tried to rehabilitate the myth of the cowboy who struggled with savages for ownership of a virgin land by superposing that myth on the Vietnam experience. But Robert Stone, in *Dog Soldiers* (1974), Michael Herr, in *Dispatches* (1977), and Tim O'Brien, in *Going After Cacciato* (1981), proved more faithful to the Vietnam veteran's war experience. In *Dog Soldiers,* Stone finds that war is the moral equivalent of an illicit drug transaction. Herr's *Dispatches* recounts his recognition of the will to violence in his own psyche. O'Brien describes the war experience as the soldiers' collective desire to escape from the country. This shift in cultural images of war was reflected in some movies. Not even John Wayne's cowboy-and-Indian *Green Berets* (1968) could persuade viewers of the Americanness of the war. In Francis Ford Coppola's *Apocalypse Now* (1979), the entire war is associated with the discovery by Kurtz, in *The Heart of Darkness*, of the horror at the core of imperialism.

Mounting opposition turned the domestic antiwar movement into a powerful constituency. Other opposition movements—Black Activists, the Student Counterculture, Women's Rights—depended on shared antiwar sentiment to develop a coalition politics directed against the ideological position that had displaced the Vietcong as the enemy in that war. Literature about the war referred simultaneously to events taking place in Nam and to events occurring at home. The antihero replaced the combat soldier as protagonist in such nonfiction works as Robert C. Mason, *Chickenhawk* (1981); Ron Kovic, *Born on the Fourth of July* (1976); and Wallace Terry, *Bloods: An Oral History of the Vietnam War by Black Veterans* (1982). These narratives referred to a quest for an escape from Vietnam and from a United States that had been reconstructed out of the images of what the narrators saw as a racist, imperialist war.

Because the war that soldiers in Vietnam had fought could not be justified within the ruling U.S. myth, they felt unable to return home until the myth met certain decisive moral criteria. In the Watergate scandal and subsequent trials began the work of historical revisionism, but the veterans had to await construction of the Vietnam War Memorial in the 1980s for the cultural understanding needed for their successful reintegration. The United States since then has undergone a transformation because it has come to grips with the experiences of the people who fought in that war.

The literature of the Vietnam War is vast. In addition to the books mentioned above, memoirs include Ronald J. Glasser, *365 Days* (1971), Tim O'Brien, *If I Die in a Combat Zone* (1973), Philip Caputo, *A Rumor of War* (1977), Frederick Downs, *The Killing Zone: My Life in the Vietnam War* (1978), and Harold G. Moore, *We Were Soldiers Once—and Young* (1992). Norman Mailer's *The Armies of the Night* (1968) is a personal report of the 1967 march on the Pentagon. Novels include Eugene Burdick and William Lederer, *The Ugly American* (1958); Peter Derrig, *The Pride of the Green Berets* (1966); Daniel Ford, *Incident at Muc Wa* (1967); Victor Kolpakoff, *The Prisoners of Quai Dong* (1967); Thomas Taylor, *A-18* (1967); John Briley, *The Traitors* (1969); James Crumley, *One to Count Cadence* (1969); WILLIAM EASTLAKE, *The Bamboo Bed* (1969); Asa Babar, *The Land of a Million Elephants* (1970); Josiah Bunting, *The Lionheads* (1972); William Pelfry, *The Big V* (1972); William Turner Huggett, *Body Count* (1973); Corrine Browne, *Body Shop* (1973); Tim O'Brien, *Northern Lights* (1974); Jonathan Rubin, *The Barking Deer* (1974); Robert Vaughn, *The Valkyrie Mandate* (1974); Stephen Phillip Smith, *American Boys* (1975); Charles Durden, *No Bugles, No Drums* (1976); Larry Heinemann, *Close Quarters* (1977) and *Paco's Story* (1986); James Webb, *Fields of Fire* (1978); John Cassidy, *A Station in the Delta* (1979); Thomas Fleming, *Officers' Wives* (1981); Bernard and Marvin Kalb, *The Last Ambassador* (1981); John Del Vecchio, *The Thirteenth Valley* (1982); Stephen Wright, *Meditations in Green* (1983); Robert Olden Butler, *On Distant Ground* (1985); BOBBIE ANN MASON, *In Country* (1985); Philip Caputo, *Indian Country* (1987); and Tim O'Brien, *The Things They Carried* (1990), *In the Lake of the Woods* (1994), and *Tomcat in Love* (1998).

Volumes of poetry include Dick Shea, *Vietnam Simply* (1967); John Balaban, *Vietnam Poems* (1970) and *After Our War* (1974); D.C. Berry, *Saigon Cemetery* (1972); C.K. Williams, *I Am a Bitter Name* (1972), and, as K. (a pseudonym), *The Sensuous President* (1972); W.D. Ehrhart, *A Generation of Peace* (1975), *The Outer Banks* (1978), and *To Those Who Have Gone Home Tired* (1984); Walter McDonald, *Caliban in Blue* (1976); and Bruce Weigl, *The Monkey Wars* (1985). Anthologies of poetry are E. D. Ehrhart, ed., *Carrying the Darkness* (1985), and Larry Rottmann et al., eds., *Winning Hearts and Minds* (1972).

Drama includes Barbara Garson, *MacBird* (1967); Megan Terry, *Viet Rock* (1967); DAVID RABE, *The Basic Training of Pavlo Hummel and Sticks and Bones: Two Plays* (1969) and *Streamers* (1970); Tom Cole, *Medal of Honor Rag* (1981); and Amil Gray, *How I Got That Story* (1981).

Histories include Frances FitzGerald, *Fire in the Lake: The Vietnamese and the Americans in Vietnam* (1972); Stanley Karnow, *Vietnam: A History* (1983; 2nd rev. ed. 1997); Neil Sheehan, *A Bright Shining Lie: John Paul Vann and America in* *Vietnam* (1988); Phillip P. Davidson, *Vietnam at War: The History, 1946–1975* (1988); and Larry H. Addington, *America's War in Vietnam: A Short Narrative History* (2000). The Library of America has published two compilations of reportage: *Reporting Vietnam: American Journalism 1959–1969* (1998) and *Reporting Vietnam: American Journalism 1969–1975* (1998).

DONALD PEASE/GP

vigilantes. The name is derived from the vigilance committees that undertook to maintain law and order through privately organized groups of civilians in the West of frontier days and in the South during the Civil War. Vigilantes in the South directed their activities mainly against Northern sympathizers and African-Americans. Those in the West administered a rough kind of justice in a lawless time. Lynching was a frequent penalty directed against robbers, outlaws, and horse and cattle thieves. In California the vigilantes were especially active during the gold rush that began in 1849. N. P. Langford wrote an account, *Vigilante Days and Ways* (1910). Four fictional stories of the vigilantes in California are Bret Harte's OUTCASTS OF POKER FLAT (1869), Frank Norris's THE OCTOPUS (1901), John Steinbeck's IN DUBIOUS BATTLE (1936), and Richard Summers' *Vigilante* (1949). One story of the shocking injustice the vigilantes sometimes perpetrated is Walter Van Tilburg Clark's THE OX-BOW INCIDENT (1940), which is set in Nevada and was made into an excellent film. Alan Valentine's *Vigilante Justice* (1956) is an account of early days in turbulent San Francisco.

Villa, Francisco [**Pancho Villa**, real name **Doroteo Arango**] (1877–1923), Mexican revolutionary leader. Originally a peon in the northern state of Chihuahua, Villa turned to cattle-rustling and became a romantic hero to the local peasantry. With the outbreak of the Mexican Revolution, Villa joined in the struggle against PORFIRIO DIAZ and Victoriano Huerta, and later vied with Venustiano Carranza for supreme power. He was defeated by Alvaro Obregon, Carranza's lieutenant, at the battle of Celaya in 1915. Hoping to embarrass the Carranza government, Villa led a raid on Columbus, New Mexico, in 1916, killing several Americans. President Wilson responded by dispatching a punitive force under JOHN J. PERSHING into Mexico, and the two nations came close to war. Villa eluded capture and subsequently retired to a hacienda given him after the successful revolt against Carranza in 1920. He was assassinated three years later. MARTÍN LUIS GUZMÁN draws an excellent portrait of him in *The Eagle and the Serpent* (1928).

Village Blacksmith, The (1839, in *Ballads and Other Poems*, 1841), a poem by HENRY WADSWORTH LONGFELLOW. The smithy described in this poem, one of the most popular and widely recited Longfellow ever wrote, was suggested by an actual smithy that stood on Brattle Street, Cambridge. The first stanza reads: "Under a spreading chestnut tree / The village smithy stands; / The smith, a mighty man is he, / With large and sinewy hands; / And the muscles of his brawny arms / Are as strong as iron bands."

Villagrá, Gaspar Peréz de (c. 1555–c. 1620), explorer, poet. Villagrá served as lieutenant to Juan de Oñate (fl. 1595–1614) in his 1598 expedition. The Spaniards claimed New Mexico for the Spanish king, and put down an Indian revolt at Acoma. In 1601 they explored areas that now are parts of Oklahoma and Kansas. In 1605 they sailed down the Colorado River to the Gulf of California, searching for a route to the South Sea. Villagrá described their travels in *Historia de la Neuva Mexico* (1610), an epic poem translated as *History of New Mexico* (1933).

Villard, Henry [original name **Ferdinand Heinrich Gustav Hilgard**] (1835–1900), financier, publisher, author. After emigration from his native Bavaria, Villard worked for the New York *Staatszeitung* (1858) and served as a Civil War correspondent for the New York *Herald* and the New York *Tribune*. He married the only daughter of WILLIAM LLOYD GARRISON (1866) and they had a son, OSWALD GARRISON VILLARD. An aggressive financier, Henry Villard controlled the Northern Pacific Railroad as president and chairman of the board of directors. In addition to his efforts to obtain a transportation monopoly in the Northwest, Villard gave financial aid to Thomas Edison, founded the Edison General Electric Company (1889), and became owner and editor of the New York *Evening Post* (1881). His earliest book was *The Past and Present of the Pike's Peak Gold Regions* (1860). *A Journey to Alaska* (1899) was published in the New York *Evening Post*, and his son published a posthumous edition of Villard's *The Early History of Transportation in Oregon* (1944). Two sources of biographical information are *Memoirs of Henry Villard* (2 v. 1904) and J. B. Hedges' *Henry Villard and the Railways of the Northwest* (1930).

Villard, Oswald Garrison (1872–1949), editor, author. Villard spent his long journalistic career championing such causes as pacifism, free trade, minority rights, and the moral responsibilities of the American press. Born in Germany and educated at Harvard, he worked on his father's paper, the New York *Evening Post* (1897–1918), eventually becoming editor and president. He was also manager and owner of THE NATION (1918–32) and a contributing editor until 1940. One of the founders of the National Association for the Advancement of Colored People (1910), he wrote *John Brown: A Biography Fifty Years Afterwards* (1910). Among his other books are *Germany Embattled* (1915); *Newspapers and Newspaper Men* (1923); *Prophets, True and False* (1927); *The German Phoenix* (1933); *Fighting Years: Memoirs of a Liberal Editor* (1939); *The Disappearing Daily* (1944); *Free Trade—Free World* (1947); and *How America Is Being Militarized* (1947).

Vinal, Harold (1891–1965), poet, editor, teacher. Vinal, born in Vinalhaven, Maine, is most successful in his poems that depict Maine scenery. Among his collections are *White April* (1922), *Voyage* (1923), *Nor Youth Nor Age* (1924), *A Stranger in Heaven* (1927), *Hymn to Chaos* (1931), *Hurricane* (1936), *Selected Poems* (1948), and *Hurricane and Other Poems* (1957). In 1921 he founded the quarterly magazine of poetry VOICES, which he also edited.

Vinland [also called **Wineland** and **Vineland**]. A region in the New World visited by Norsemen; so named because of the wild grapes they found there. It has been identified with Cape Cod and with many other localities from Labrador to New Jersey. It was visited by Norsemen from about 1000 A.D. on, and when Greenland became a bishopric Vinland was included in its boundaries. L'Anse aux Meadows, at the northern tip of Newfoundland, includes evidence of Norse settlements dating from about 1000 A.D. Vinland was perhaps south of there. WILLIAM T. VOLLMANN's *The Ice-Shirt* (1990) is a recent novel mixing history and speculation.

Viorst, Judith (1931–), light verse poet, juvenile author. Born Judith Stahl in Newark, New Jersey, she was educated at Rutgers and the Washington Psychoanalytic Institute. Her verse on family life, children, and personal experience has been collected in a dozen books, including *It's Hard to Be Hip over Thirty and Other Tragedies of Married Life* (1968), the best seller that launched her career. Follow-up collections of verse include *How Did I Get to Be Forty* (1976), *When Did I Stop Being Twenty* (1987), *Forever Fifty* (1989), and *Suddenly Sixty* (2000). Using her work in psychoanalysis, she wrote the well-received *Necessary Losses* (1986), a collection of theory, poetry, and anecdotes, and *Imperfect Control: Our Lifelong Struggle with Power and Control* (1998). Her juvenile fiction, often inspired by her three sons, includes *Alexander and the Terrible, Horrible, No Good, Very Bad Day* (1972), *My Mama Says There Aren't Any Zombies, Ghosts, Vampires, Creatures, Demons, Monsters, Friends, Goblins or Things* (1973), and *Absolutely Positively Alexander: The Complete Stories* (1997). She is married to the political writer MILTON VIORST.

Viorst, Milton (1930–), journalist. A native of Paterson, New Jersey, Viorst was educated Rutgers, Harvard, Columbia, and University of Lyons, in France. A reporter for newspapers in Washington and New York, he is a regular contributor to *The New Yorker*, *Harper's*, *Nation*, and other periodicals. His books include studies of liberalism (1963), the Republican Party (1968), the Peace Corps (1986), and Israel (1987). *Hostile Allies* (1965) treats the World War II relationship between FRANKLIN D. ROOSEVELT and Charles de Gaulle. *Fire in the Streets* (1980), an account of politics in the 1960s, includes profiles of ALLEN GINSBERG, Tom Hayden, Stokely Carmichael, Jerry Rubin—all of whom played activist roles in opposing the Vietnam War. *Sandcastles: The Arabs in Search of the Modern World* (1994) and *In the Shadow of the Prophet: the Struggle for the Soul of Islam* (1998) are recent studies illuminating the Mideast.

Virginia (1913), a novel by ELLEN GLASGOW. This story of a Southern woman is set in the years between 1884 and 1912. Her marriage is unhappy, she is unable to adapt herself to a new environment, loses the respect of her husband and daughters, but manages to retain the love of her son.

Virginia City Territorial Enterprise, The. See TERRITORIAL ENTERPRISE.

Virginia Comedians, The (1854), a novel by JOHN ESTEN COOKE. The principal character is a roué and cynic who abducts an actress and (as he supposes) kills the man who tries to rescue her. He flees to Europe, returning later to make a more suitable match with his cousin. The second part was published separately as *Captain Ralph*. A sequel to both works, HENRY ST. JOHN, GENTLEMAN (1859), is set in the Shenandoah Valley at the beginning of the Revolution.

Virginia Company. A joint-stock venture chartered in 1606 by King James I which authorized two companies: the Plymouth Company (meaning Plymouth, England) was to colonize northern sections of North America; the London Company was to be active in the southern territories claimed by England. In 1609, after the Plymouth branch had failed to show any activity, a new charter was obtained that made the London Company absolute. In the meantime energetic measures had been taken to colonize a region called Virginia. In 1612 the colony was made self-governing, and in 1619 the first legislature assembled. In 1623 the Privy Council investigated the colony and alleged misrule there. In 1624 the king annulled the charter of the London Company. Accounts of the company appear in H. L. Osgood, *American Colonies in the 17th Century* (3 v. 1904–07); S. M. Kingsbury, editor of the *Records of the Virginia Company of London* (4 v. 1906–35); T. J. Wertenbaker, *Planters of Colonial Virginia* (1932); and W. F. Craven, *Dissolution of the Virginia Company* (1932) and *Southern Colonies in the 17th Century* (1949).

Virginian, The (1902), a novel by OWEN WISTER. *The Virginian* has sometimes been described as the ancestor of the Western. The scene is Wyoming in pioneer days. The hero, never named, provokes the enmity of a local bad man named Trampas. In a poker game Trampas accuses the Virginian of cheating and impugns his ancestry. Instantly the Virginian's pistol is drawn and put on the table before him, and the Virginian launches into the famous retort: "When you call me that, smile." Trampas backs down. Later the Virginian rescues a New England schoolmistress from a stage coach that has been marooned in high water by a drunken driver. Eventually they get married. The novel's climax is a pistol duel between Trampas and the Virginian in which Trampas is vanquished, the scene constituting the first known walkdown in American literature.

Wister, a fanatical admirer of THEODORE ROOSEVELT, had followed Roosevelt's advice to go to Wyoming for his health and there began writing stories set in that locality. He dedicated *The Virginian* to Roosevelt, many of whose traits and ideals resemble those of Wister's hero. Everitt Cyril Johnson, once a fellow ranch hand with Wister, claimed to have been the original for the Virginian. But according to Wister himself, in a preface to the 16th edition of his book (1928), the hero was a combination of several persons he had known in Wyoming. Wister's book influenced writers of Western stories, plays, movies, and radio scripts, and the Virginian became the prototype of all cowboy heroes. The novel was dramatized in 1903 and was performed for ten years on the road and in New York, thereafter in stock. Several movie versions have also been made.

Virginia Quarterly Review. An influential critical magazine founded in 1925 and published at the University of

Virginia. Its many contributors have included such authors as Robert Frost, Sherwood Anderson, and Thomas Wolfe.

Virginians, The (1857–59), a novel by William Makepeace Thackeray. Thackeray made two visits to the United States, one in 1852–53, the other in 1855–56. The novel appeared in monthly installments over a period of two years. On one occasion he visited the home of the historian W. H. Prescott in Boston, where he saw two swords hung in a crossed position over the mantelpiece: one sword had belonged to Prescott's father's father, the other to his mother's father, and the two grandfathers had used the swords on opposite sides in the Revolution. It is said that this suggested to Thackeray the idea of a story about two brothers, one a loyalist and the other a rebel. He made the story into a sequel for *Henry Esmond* by placing the Esmond descendants on an estate in Virginia.

Vision of Sir Launfal, The (1848), a narrative poem by JAMES RUSSELL LOWELL. This story of the conversion of a proud medieval knight has no connection with Thomas Chester's 15th-century *Sir Launfal* or with the still earlier poem by Marie de France. The quest for the Grail comes from Malory, and Lowell may have been influenced by Tennyson's *Sir Galahad*. The poem opens with "What is so rare as a day in June" and goes on to tell how Sir Launfal, riding proudly forth in quest of the Grail, spurns a leper begging for alms but tosses him a piece of gold, which the leper refuses to lift from the dust. Many years later Launfal returns to his castle, weary and disappointed. Once more he encounters the leper, shares with him his last crust of bread, and offers him water from his wooden bowl. The leper thereupon is transformed into Christ, who tells Launfal that the bowl is the Grail—"Who gives himself with his alms feeds three: / Himself, his hungering neighbor, and me." Launfal accepts the lesson, and his future works show that one need not go abroad to find the Holy Grail.

Lowell was deeply pleased with his poem, saying, "I am the first poet who has endeavored to express the American Idea." By this he meant, according to H. E. Scudder, that just as Tennyson threw into his retelling of the Arthurian romance a moral sense, Lowell, also a moralist, made a parable of the tale and "in the broadest interpretation of democracy, sang of the leveling of all ranks in a common divine humanity." The poem is likewise an illustration of Lowell's great command of meter—he varies it constantly and skillfully in the 347 lines of the poem.

Visit from St. Nicholas, A (Troy, New York, *Sentinel*, December 23, 1823), a Christmas ballad by CLEMENT CLARKE MOORE. This famous poem was the work of a New York City scholar writing for his own family. It marked a dividing line between the old Puritan abhorrence for Christmas celebrations and a new attitude in which the Christmas spirit was embodied in the figure of Santa Claus, a Dutch and German creation.

Vizenor, Gerald (1934–), poet, novelist. Born in Minneapolis of Ojibway and French ancestry, Vizenor is an enrolled member of the White Earth Reservation Chippewa tribe. He was educated at the University of Minnesota and has taught American Indian Studies at the University of Minnesota and the University of California, Berkeley. His first collection of poetry, *Born in the Wind*, was privately printed in 1960. His other poetry titles include *Raising the Moon* (1964), *Seventeen Chirps* (1964), *Two Wings the Butterfly* (1967), and *Matushima: Haiku* (1984). *Darkness in Saint Louis Bearheart* (1978) is an ironic portrayal of life among contemporary Native Americans. *Bearheart: The Heirship Chronicles* appeared in 1990. *Griever: An American Monkey King in China* (1987) is the story of an exchange teacher's struggle with the Chinese bureaucracy. *Trickster of Liberty: Tribal Heirs to a Wild Baronage at Petronia* (1988) describes an ingenious and unconventional family. *Cross Bloods* (1990) is an essay collection. *The Heirs of Columbus* (1991) and *Hotline Healers* (1997) are comic fictions. *Chancers: A Novel* (2000) deals with the repatriation of native skeletal remains. *Interior Landscape* (1990) presents "Autobiographic Myths and Metaphors." *Shadow Distance* (1994) is a collection of memoirs, fiction, poetry, and essays. Vizenor has edited several collections of Native American writing, including *The Everlasting Sky: New Voices from the People Named the Chippewa* (1972); *Earthdivers: Tribal Narratives on Mixed Descent* (1981); *Summer in the Spring: Ojibwa Lyric Poems and Tribal Stories* (1981); and *The People Named the Chippewa: Narrative Histories* (1984).

Vogel, Paula (1951–   ),   playwright. Raised in Washington, D.C., Vogel attended Bryn Mawr and has taught at Cornell and Brown. She lost her brother to AIDS and is herself homosexual, but does not limit her dramatic concerns to gay issues. *The Oldest Profession* (1980), a play about geriatric prostitutes, was rejected by theaters throughout the country, but Vogel refused to give up. *And Baby Makes Seven* (1984; restaged 1993) has two lesbians cohabiting with a gay man who has fathered a child by one of them. The tension of impending birth causes the three adults to fantasize other children, much in the way that the older couple in EDWARD ALBEE's *Who's Afraid of Virginia Woolf* have a fantasy son. *The Baltimore Waltz* (1992, and in *The Baltimore Waltz and Other Plays*, 1996) brought national attention to Vogel's work. The main character of the surreal comedy, Anna, discovers she is afflicted with Acquired Toilet Disease while her brother is dying of AIDS. Between the beginning and ending in a Baltimore hospital, a fantasy European trip is shared by the two siblings. *Hot 'n' Throbbing* (1993) objects to Senator Jesse Helms's insistence that recipients of National Endowment for the Arts fellowships sign an anti-obscenity pledge. *The Mineola Twins* (1996) covers the period from Eisenhower to the elder George Bush. A parody morality play, it has the prudish Myrna and the promiscuous Myra portrayed by the same actress. Vogel's best-known play, the Pulitzer Prize–winning *How I Learned to Drive* (1997), dissects a sexual relationship between a young girl and her pedophilic uncle. The two plays were published together as *The Mammary Plays: How I Learned to Drive and The Mineola Twins* (1998).

Vogue.   A fashion magazine for women, founded as a weekly on December 17, 1892, in New York City by Arthur Turnure and Harry McVickar. In 1910 it became a semi-monthly. Condé Nast bought it in 1909, and it absorbed VANITY FAIR in 1935. Edna Woolman Chase (see ILKA CHASE) joined its staff in 1895, when it was a small weekly written by society for society, became its editor in 1914, and in 1919 was appointed editor-in-chief of the London, Paris, and New York editions. In 1952 she gave up her post as editor but continued as chairperson of the board. She was succeeded as editor by Jessica Daves. By 1960 the circulation was nearing 500,000 in America alone. In 1954 Chase, with the assistance of her daughter Ilka, published her autobiography, *Always in Vogue*, which describes her experiences in making the magazine an arbiter of taste.

The magazine has had many celebrated contributors. At one time Frank Crowninshield, Robert E. Sherwood, Dorothy Parker, and Robert Benchley were on the staff. Contributors included Marjorie Kinnan Rawlings, Rebecca West, James Hilton, Hemingway, Jules Romains, Hendrik Van Loon, Bemelmans, Katherine Anne Porter, Thomas Wolfe, Clare Boothe Luce, Maurois, Archibald MacLeish, Saroyan, Paul Gallico, Max Eastman, John Mason Brown, Mary Ellen Chase, and Ilka Chase.

Voices.   A magazine founded by HAROLD VINAL in 1921. It began as a bimonthly, later became a quarterly, and made itself a leading organ for new poets unable to secure an audience elsewhere. Among its contributors have been Allen Tate, Mark Van Doren, Robert Penn Warren, Kenneth Fearing, Genevieve Taggard, Donald Davidson, and Vinal himself.

Voices of the Night (1839),   a collection by HENRY WADSWORTH LONGFELLOW of poems previously published in magazines. Among them are A PSALM OF LIFE, HYMN TO THE NIGHT, and "The Beleaguered City." Edgar Allan Poe immediately accused Longfellow of plagiarism because of alleged similarities between "The Beleaguered City" and his own HAUNTED PALACE, but there is little resemblance in their moods. This book helped establish Longfellow as the country's most popular poet.

Vollmann, William T. (1959–   ),   novelist, short-story writer, journalist, memoirist. Born in Santa Monica, California, Vollmann attended Deep Springs College (1977–1979) before graduating with a degree in comparative literature from Cornell University (B.A., 1981) and undertaking a year of postgraduate study at the University of California, Berkeley (1982–1983). Among writers of his generation, he ranks near the forefront of those for whom a sense of belatedness (a fear that all good work may already have been done, all experiments tried, all worthwhile books written) appears to drive much of the creative effort. Influenced by postmodern pioneers of the fifties and sixties, especially Pynchon and Nabokov (Cornellians two decades before his own arrival on that campus), Vollmann writes encyclopedic metanarratives, linguistically fluent, charged with metaphor, overlaid with irony, and transformative of traditional genres. His most sustained and most celebrated effort began with the publication of *The Ice-Shirt: A Novel* (1990), announced as volume one of a cycle entitled *Seven Dreams: A Book of North American Landscapes*. In *The Ice-Shirt*, the narrator, "William the Blind," recounts Viking history especially as it relates to North America and the brief settlement at Vinland, drawing heavily on Icelandic Sagas, but interweaving his personal experiences as a twentieth-century visitor to the landscapes mentioned. In *Fathers and Crows* (1992), second in the series, William tells of the clashes between Jesuit priests and Native Americans during the discovery and settlement of French Canada. In *The Rifles* (1994), Vollmann skips to volume six of the seven projected, to focus on British explorer John Franklin's doomed search for a Northwest Passage to the Pacific Ocean, with William the Blind shape-shifting as Captain Subzero, a twentieth-century visitor to the frozen North in love with an Inuit woman. As in the earlier books, past and present mirror one another in exploratory aim, dire results, and theme (the degradation of native peoples by technologically superior outsiders).

Called novels, the volumes of *Seven Dreams* function as fiction, history, personal observation, and memoir. Others of Vollman's books share the same resistance to classification. They include: *You Bright and Risen Angels: A Cartoon* (1987), fantasy fiction in which computer-created humans and insects engage in war; *The Rainbow Stories* (1989), set in San Francisco slums; *Whores for Gloria* (1991), a "documentary novel" about a Vietnam veteran searching San Francisco for his prostitute lover; *Thirteen Stories and Thirteen Epitaphs* (1991), stories of drug addicts, prostitutes, and others of the marginalized rootless in unsavory environments from Afghanistan to Thailand to Guatamala and various points in the United States; *An Afghanistan Picture Show* (1992), a memoir of Vollmann's post-college days among Afghan guerrillas attempting to wrest their country from Russia; *Butterfly Stories: A Novel* (1993), about a journalist's worldwide search for love and prostitution; *The Atlas: People, Places, and Visions* (1966), generally autobiographical; and *The Royal Family* (2000), a massive exploration of the underworld of San Francisco, harrowing and encyclopedic, in which Vollmann's familiar themes and obsessions are strung on a story of a private investigator who mourns the loss through suicide of his true love—who happens to be his brother's wife—and searches for the legendary Queen of the Prostitutes.

Vollmer, Lulu (18?–1955), dramatist. Vollmer wrote dramas about the North Carolina mountain region where she lived. Her work includes *Sun-Up* (1923), *The Shame Woman* (1923), *The Dunce Boy* (1925), and *Trigger* (1927).

Voluntaries (1863), a poem by RALPH WALDO EMERSON. This dirge was written in honor of Col. Robert Gould Shaw, who was killed in the Civil War while storming Fort Wagner, July 18, 1863, at the head of the first enlisted black regiment, the 54th Massachusetts. Emerson's poem reflects the violent emotion of the era of disunion. He rejects the idea that preservation of the Union is superior to abolition of slavery and alludes scornfully to Daniel Webster. What saves the poem for later generations is the stirring third section, which begins, "In an age of fops and tops" and closes, "When Duty whispers low, *Thou must*, / The youth replies, *I can*."

Vonnegut, Kurt (1922–), novelist, short-story writer, playwright, essayist. Born in Indianapolis, Vonnegut

was educated at Cornell, Carnegie Institute, and the University of Chicago. During World War II, Vonnegut served in the U.S. infantry and witnessed the destruction of Dresden by firebombs. Between 1947 and 1951 Vonnegut worked in public relations for the General Electric Company. After his first stories were accepted for publication, he quit and devoted himself to writing and to teaching at the University of Iowa, Harvard, and City University of New York.

A successful story writer at first, Vonnegut fell into relative obscurity with the decline of the market for short stories in the 1950s. His first novels, *Player Piano* (1952) and *The Sirens of Titan* (1959), earned him the misleading label of science fiction writer, though both combine fantasy with realistic observation, describing an immediate future controlled by technological utopias and corporate bureaucracies such as those Vonnegut had observed. He reemerged as a major writer in the 1960s, when he published a series of formally innovative and thematically provocative novels, using fantasy as a defamiliarizing procedure. *Cat's Cradle* (1963) and *God Bless You, Mr. Rosewater* (1965) satirize contemporary mythologies—a populist religion in the former, the power of money in the latter—but also pit idealistic heroes with the capacity to "reinvent themselves and their universes" against these forms of collective manipulation. *Mother Night* (1962) and *Slaughterhouse Five* (1969) explore the self-denying postwar world that traps both resourceful villains like Howard W. Campbell, a superspy masquerading as Nazi propagandist, and baby-faced daydreamers like Billy Pilgrim. Vonnegut's fatalistic view of history is suggested by the ubiquitous imagery of the Dresden fire and the frequent recourse to a comic-fictitious planet, Tralfamadore, from which the fates of humans are arbitrarily controlled.

In 1972, after experimentation with other forms—nonfiction, drama, film—Vonnegut returned to the printed word as his medium. In *Breakfast of Champions* (1973), Vonnegut's most metafictional novel, the author vies for attention with his character Kilgore Trout, the science fiction writer responsible for creating Tralfamadore. *Slapstick* (1973), *Jailbird* (1979), and *Deadeye Dick* (1983) return to a darker, satirical tone, describing the effects of a post-apocalyptic, post-Watergate world on the lives of ordinary people. Critics found these novels somewhat anecdotal and disconnected, lacking the earnestness of Vonnegut's earlier work. That philosophic earnestness returns in *Galapagos* (1985), a rich historical parable that envisions the survival and subsequent mutation of humans into "fisherfolk . . . good at heart." *Bluebeard* (1987) is also concerned with history, tracing the personal and collective memories of an Armenian artist from the time of the Armenian genocide to his later association with the Abstract Expressionists. Both *Hocus Pocus* (1990), which is a first-person narrative by a Vietnam veteran stranded in a "thoroughly looted bankrupt" culture of the twenty-first century, and *Timequake* (1997), in which characters at the end of the millennium experience a "time wrinkle" which forces them to relive the 1990s, blend satire with reflection on the state of Western civilization at the end of the twentieth century. *Bagombo Snuff Box* (1999) brings together twenty-three previously uncollected stories from the 1950s and 1960s.

Critical studies include Stanley Schatt, *Kurt Vonnegut Jr.* (1976); James Lundquist, *Kurt Vonnegut* (1977); Leonard Mustazza, ed., *The Critical Response to Kurt Vonnegut* (1994); and Marc Leeds, *The Vonnegut Encyclopedia* (1995).

MARCEL CORNIS-POPE

Vorágine, La (1924, tr. *The Vortex*, 1935), the only novel by JOSÉ EUSTACIO RIVERA. Arturo Cova, a poet, flees his hometown with his lover, Alicia, and ventures into the cattle country of Colombia. For a variety of reasons he is drawn deeper and deeper into the jungle, only to discover how thin the veneer of civilization is in the face of the fierce and terrifying life of the Amazon basin. Ultimately, Cova and all his associates succumb to madness, leaving behind a feverish documentary of blood and death. The delirious lyricism of the tale is made credible through Cova's despair at not having lived to become a poet.

Vorse, Mary Heaton (1874–1966), novelist. Vorse lived most of her life in Provincetown, Massachusetts, where she was a sponsor of the Provincetown Players. Her novels include *The Prestons* (1918), *Second Cabin* (1928), and *Strike!* (1930). *Footnote to Folly* (1935) is her autobiography, and *Time and the Town* (1942) describes her home in Cape Cod.

Voyage dans la Haute Pennsylvanie et dans l'état de New York (3 v. 1801), a travel book of essays and stories by HECTOR ST. JOHN DE CRÈVECŒUR. This work was rescued from comparative oblivion in an article by Percy G. Adams in *American Literature* (May 1953). Adams later translated and published a selection of essays and stories from the *Voyage* under the title *Crèvecœur's Eighteenth-Century Travels in Pennsylvania and New York* (1961).

W

Wagoner, David (1926–), poet, novelist. Wagoner, born in Ohio, teaches at the University of Washington and was for nearly a decade a colleague of THEODORE ROETHKE. Wagoner's work reflects the landscape of the Northwest and his interest in the Indian heritage of the region. His poetry collections include *Dry Sun, Dry Wind* (1953), *A Place to Stand* (1958), *The Nesting Ground* (1963), *Staying Alive* (1966), *New and Selected Poems* (1969), *Working Against Time* (1970), *Riverbed* (1972), *Sleeping in the Woods* (1974), *Collected Poems* (1976), In *Broken Country* (1979), *Landfall* (1981), *Through the Forest* (1987), and *Walt Whitman Bathing* (1997). *Who Shall Be the Sun* (1978) is a collection of poetry derived from Native American myth. Wagoner's edition of Roethke's notebooks is entitled *Straw for the Fire* (1972). Among his novels are *The Man in the Middle* (1954), *Money Money Money* (1955), *Rock* (1958), *The Escape Artist* (1965), *Baby, Come on Inside* (1968), *Where Is My Wandering Boy Tonight?* (1970), *The Road to Many a Wonder* (1974), *Tracker* (1975), *Whole Hog* (1976), and *The Hanging Garden* (1980).

Waiting for Lefty (1935), a short play by CLIFFORD ODETS. This play, Odets' first, and one of the best of the proletarian plays of the 1930s, deals with a taxi drivers' strike. Using an impressionistic flashback technique, Odets presents six episodic scenes showing the lives of the people involved in the strike. At the climax, the news that Lefty, the committeeman, has been murdered rouses the men to decisive action.

Wakoski, Diane (1937–), poet. Born in Whittier, California, Wakoski was educated at the University of California, Berkeley. Since 1967 she has taught at Michigan State University. Her verse, usually written in the first person, deals with experiences of an unhappy childhood, painful relationships with others, and alienation. The tone of her poetry is spontaneous and the imagery fantastic. *Emerald Ice: Selected Poems 1962–87* appeared in 1990. Among her other titles are *The George Washington Poems* (1967), *The Motorcycle Betrayal Poems* (1971), *Cap of Darkness* (1980), *The Collected Greed, Parts 1–13* (1984), and *The Emerald City of Las Vegas* (1995). *Creating a Personal Mythology* (1975) is an essay collection.

Walam Olum [**Red Score**], a Leni-Lenape Indian document, the only surviving one that can be described as a book. It is something between a historical narrative and an epic, inscribed originally on birch bark in pictographs. It recounts a creation myth and a prehistoric migration from somewhere in the north and west to the Atlantic coast. The Leni-Lenapes were called Delawares by the whites and lived in the valley of the Delaware, mainly in New Jersey. Today the chief remnants of the tribe live in Oklahoma. See DELAWARE INDIANS.

The *Red Score* was discovered and translated by CONSTANTINE RAFINESQUE. The best account of it is given in Daniel G. Brinton's *The Lenape and Their Legends, With the Complete Text and Symbols of the Walam Olum* (1885).

Walcot, Charles Melton (1816–1868), architect, actor, singer, dramatist. Walcot came from England to the United States in 1837 as an architect, but became very successful in the theater because of his fine singing voice and ability as a comedian. He wrote a number of burlesques and comedies, among them *The Imp of the Elements* (1844), *Don Giovanni in Gotham* (1844), and *The Don Not Done* (1844). His son Charles Melton Walcot (1840–1921) also became an accomplished actor.

Walcott, Derek [Alton] (1930–), poet, playwright. Born of mixed racial and ethnic heritage on St. Lucia in the West Indies, Walcott grew up speaking a French and English patois. His education at St. Mary's College on his native island and the University of the West Indies in Kingston, Jamaica, was a traditional English one. His poetry blends English verse forms and Caribbean rhythms. He published three collections before his first major book, *In a Green Night: Poems, 1948–1960*, (1962), was published in England and brought him wide attention. *Selected Poems* came two years later and was followed by *The Castaway* (1965); *The Gulf* (1969); *Another Life* (1973), a long narrative poem; and *The Star Apple Kingdom* (1979), a collection of narrative verse based on Caribbean history and scenery.

Walcott worked as a journalist and taught in the West Indies, where he founded the Trinidad Theatre Workshop in 1959. Beginning in 1981 he taught at several U.S. universities including Columbia and Harvard, before joining the creative writing faculty at Boston University in 1985. His collection *The Fortunate Traveller* (1982) deals with experiences in the U.S. and elsewhere. *Midsummer* (1983) is a cycle of 54 verses recounting a year in the poet's life spent partly in the U.S. and in the islands. *Collected Poems 1948–1984* appeared in 1986 and *The Arkansas Testament* a year later. *Omeros* (1990) is a complex epic poem using the ocean as a central theme. *Tiepolo's Hound* (2000) reproduces 26 of Walcott's paintings along with new poems. Walcott has had a major role in promoting West Indian theater, including production of his own plays dealing with island subjects and utilizing Caribbean speech and folklore. Among them are *Henri Christophe* (1950), *Drums and Colours* (1958), *Dream on Monkey Mountain* (1970), *Ti-Jean and His Brothers* (1971), *The Jokes of Seville and O Babylon!* (both 1978), *Remembrance and Pantomime* (both 1980), *Three Plays* (1986) and *The Odyssey: A Stage Version* (1993). Walcott has been awarded a MacArthur Fellowship and the Nobel Prize for Literature (1992). *What the Twilight Says* (1999) is a collection of critical essays.

Walden.   A prose work by HENRY DAVID THOREAU, first published in 1854. *Walden* is a somewhat condensed and fictionalized journal of his stay at Walden Pond in Concord, Massachusetts, from 1845 to 1847, offering a rich mix of descriptive and narrative detail, self-examination and self-explanation, social commentary and criticism, and free-floating philosophical speculation.

Written in the epigrammatic, meditative, associative prose tradition of writers from Plutarch through Montaigne and Sir Thomas Browne, and practiced by Emerson, *Walden* is divided into 18 sections. The three longest are arranged strategically: the first, "Economy," states the basic themes; the ninth, "Ponds," represents the middle or still point around which the rest turns; and the seventeenth, "Spring," celebrates the rebirth of the seasons and his preparations for leaving. There is, thus, an overall chronological structure, and in between Thoreau reflects on what he observes around him, on his visitors, his reading, and the American mania for commerce and possessions and success—the whole forming something of an initiation, quest, purgation, rebirth pattern.

Thoreau stated his purpose clearly: "I went to the woods because I wished to live deliberately, to front only the essential facts of life . . ." Although there is something of the yogi ascetic or the Zen master in this, there is also the typically American project of finding some virgin territory beyond the frontier and starting life afresh with a clean slate. He did keep one foot firmly planted in the town, of course, and he omitted women and children and his darker moods from his list of essentials, but that we need fewer material goods, comforts, and distractions than we think we need in order to be fully alive is surely an authentic message. And it is supported mainly on the base of the Transcendental philosophy: the forms of the visible world embody the realities of things unseen. Thus, the emphasis is on direct experience of that visible world—especially of Nature—on the interplay between the ordinary and the miraculous (cf. William Blake), and on the experience of the reader.

"Shams and delusions are esteemed for soundest truths, while reality is fabulous," says Thoreau. "If men would stead-fastly observe realities only, and not allow themselves to be deluded, life to compare it with such things as we know, would be like a fairy tale and the Arabian Nights' Entertainments. God himself culminates in the present moment, and will never be more divine in the lapse of all the ages."

NORMAN FRIEDMAN

Walker, Alice (1944–   ),   novelist, short-story writer, essayist, poet. Born in Eatonton, Georgia, and educated at Spelman College and Sarah Lawrence, Walker is an African American feminist—her term is "womanist"—writer whose work explores issues of race, gender, liberation, and cultural tradition. Walker's early work draws on her Southern childhood, her civil rights activism in the 1960s, and her experiences in Africa. Her published work includes *The Third Life of Grange Copeland* (1970), a novel; *In Love and Trouble* (1973), stories; *Revolutionary Petunias* (1973), poems; *Meridian* (1976), a novel; and *You Can't Keep a Good Woman Down* (1981), stories. Her epistolary novel *The Color Purple* (1982), made into a movie in 1985, explores both the redemptive relations between women in a patriarchal black Southern family and the relations between African and African American culture. A contemporaneous collection of prose pieces—*In Search of Our Mother's Gardens* (1983)—considers Walker's relations to literal and figurative "foremothers," such as ZORA NEALE HURSTON. Walker had previously collected some of Hurston's work in an anthology, *I Love Myself When I Am Laughing* (1979). The three books that followed *In Search of Our Mother's Gardens*—*Horses Make a Landscape More Beautiful* (poems, 1984); *The Temple of My Familiar* (novel, 1988); and *Living by the Word* (prose pieces, 1989)—take a more mystical turn, and meditate on everything from Walker's multistranded racial identity to her commitment to animal rights and vegetarianism. Walker's work has generated controversy, particularly for a perceived negative representation of black men. It is also highly valued for its focus on the interaction of racism and sexism, its experimentation with form and dialect, its commitment to preserving an African American literary tradition, and its political vision. *Her Blue Body Everything We Know: Earthing Poems 1965–1990* appeared in 1991. *Possessing the Secret of Joy* (1992) and *Warrior Marks* (1993), with Pratibha Parmar, focus on the issue of female circumcision and other forms of sexual mutilation. *Anything We Love Can Be Saved: A Writer's Activism* (1997) is an essay collection. *By the Light of My Father's Smile* (1998) is a novel, and, *The Way Forward is with a Broken Heart* (2000) is a collection of memoirs and stories about marriage.

JULIE RIVKIN

Walker, David (1785–1830),   pamphleteer. Walker was born in Wilmington, North Carolina, the son of a free mother and a slave father. He was free because of his mother's status and traveled widely in the South observing the effects of slavery before settling in Boston, where he owned a second-hand clothing store on Brattle Street. He created a sensation with his 76-page octavo pamphlet entitled *Walker's Appeal . . .* (1829, rev. 1830), an eloquent and closely reasoned statement against slavery. The pamphlet was outlawed, and a price was put on his head in the South.

Walker, David Harry [Henry] (1911–1992), novelist. Walker was born in Scotland and received his education mostly in England. He was an army officer in the Black Watch from 1931 to 1947 and a prisoner of war for five years. After the war he went to India, and later retired to New Brunswick, Canada, where he began a prolific writing career. His works include *The Story and the Silence* (1949); *Geordie* (1950), which became the film *Wee Geordie; The Pillar* (1952); *Digby* (1953); *Harry Black* (1956), which also was filmed; *Sandy Was a Soldier's Boy; A Fable* (1957); *Where the High Winds Blow* (1960); *Come Back, Geordie* (1966); *Black Dougal* (1973), and *Pot of Gold* (1977). *Lean, Wind, Lean* (1984) is a memoir.

Walker, George F. (1947–), playwright. Born in Toronto, Canada, Walker was working as a taxi driver in that city when he submitted his first play, *Prince of Naples* (1971), to the Factory Theatre Lab, a company devoted to staging new Canadian plays. That production began a long association with the playhouse in which Walker has often directed his own work. His plays utilize popular culture images, dark humor, and dialogue noted for its sense of menace and colloquial usage. *Three Plays* (1978) collects *Bagdad Saloon* (prod. 1973), *Beyond Mozambique* (prod. 1975) and *Ramona and the White Slaves* (prod. 1976). *The Power Plays* (1984) collects three plays (*Gossip, Filthy Rich* and *The Art of War*) centered on the character of Tyrone M. Power, investigative reporter and private eye. Walker's third trilogy *The East End Plays* (1988), set in Walker's native working class neighborhood of East Toronto, contains his most popular work *Criminals in Love* (1984), the story of teenage lovers forced into a criminal conspiracy. *Better Living* (1986) and *Beautiful City* (1987) are also part of the collection. *Nothing Sacred* (1988), based on Turgenev's *Fathers and Sons, Love and Anger* (1989) and *Escape from Happiness* (1991) have all been produced in the United States. *Shared Anxiety* (1994) is a selection of eight plays. Walker also wrote plays for radio and television.

Walker, Joseph (1935–), playwright, actor. Born in Washington D.C., Walker was educated at Howard University, Catholic University, and New York University. He has taught at the Yale University School of Drama and City College of New York. His plays include *The Hiss, Old Judge Moses Is Dead, Themes of the Black Experience, The Harangues, Ododo, Yin Yang, Antigone Africanus, The Lion is a Soul Brother,* and *District Line*. His most successful play, *The River Niger* (1972), won an Obie Award. It parallels incidents in his own life as the only son of African American parents dedicated to education and culture. Walker narrated the CBS production of *In Black America* and has acted in television dramas, James Baldwin's *The Amen Corner* and Woody Allen's *Bananas*.

Walker, Margaret Abigail (1915–1998), poet, novelist. Born in Alabama, Walker was educated at Northwestern and the University of Iowa. Her *For My People* (1942), published by the Yale Series of Younger Poets, was a major event in African American literary history. Her other volumes of poetry include *Ballad of the Free* (1966), *Prophets for a New Day* (1970), *October Journey* (1973), and *This Is My Century: New and Collected Poems* (1990). Among her prose works are a novel, *Jubilee* (1965), the study *Richard Wright: Daemonic Genius* (1987), and *On Being Female, Black and Free* (1997), essays.

Walker, Mildred [Mrs. Ferdinand R. Schemm] (1905–1998). novelist, teacher. Walker, a native of Philadelphia, wrote much verse and fiction before her novel *Fireweed* (1934) won an Avery Hopwood Award. Her other books include *Light from Arcturus* (1935), *Dr. Norton's Wife* (1938), *The Brewers' Big Horses* (1940), *Unless the Wind Turns* (1941), *Winter Wheat* (1944), *The Quarry* (1947), about Vermont farm life, *Medical Meeting* (1949), domestic fiction centered on a doctor's wife, *Southwest Corner* (1951), *Curlew's Cry* (1955), *The Body of a Young Man* (1960), and *If a Lion Could Talk* (1970).

Walker, Stuart (1888–1941), actor, producer, playwright. Walker, born in Kentucky, worked at first with DAVID BELASCO in various capacities, then founded and directed repertory companies in Indianapolis and Cincinnati. Later he was a director and producer in Hollywood. He became especially celebrated for his Portmanteau Theatre, which began in New York City and then toured the country. It produced plays by Lord Dunsany and others, including many by Walker himself. Among the latter are *Six Who Pass While the Lentils Boil, Five Flights Up,* and *The King's Great Aunt Sits on the Floor,* which are included in Walker's collections *Portmanteau Plays* (1917) and *More Portmanteau Plays* (1919); and *The King's Great Aunt* (1923). He wrote *The Demi-Reds* (1936) with Gladys Unger.

Walker, William (1824–1860), adventurer. Walker, born in Tennessee, studied medicine and law, but became an extraordinary military leader. He first organized an expedition to turn Baja California and Sonora into a republic. When this failed, he invaded Nicaragua with an army of fifty-eight men, won some extraordinary successes, and was inaugurated president (1856). Financier Cornelius Vanderbilt organized a coalition of Central American powers to oust him (1857), and after several further attempts to conquer the country Walker was executed by a Honduran firing squad.

Walker wrote an account of *The War in Nicaragua* (1860). Richard Harding Davis wrote about him in *Real Soldiers of Fortune* (1906), Laurence Greene wrote *The Filibuster: The Career of William Walker* (1937), and Joaquin Miller composed a poem, "With Walker in Nicaragua." Bret Harte introduced Walker in disguise in two of his stories, and Walker appears in Darwin Teilhet's novel *The Lion's Skin* (1955). See WILLIAM VINCENT WELLS.

Wallace, Big-Foot. See BIG-FOOT WALLACE, THE ADVENTURES OF.

Wallace, David Foster (1962–), novelist, short-story writer, essayist. Born in Ithaca, New York, Wallace was educated at Amherst College and the University of Arizona. His first novel *The Broom of the System* (1987) was greeted with high praise for its sardonic humor and complex style. In a futuristic setting where Cleveland now rests on the edge of the Great Ohio Desert or G.O.D., the book has Lenore Beadsman searching for her great-grandmother of the same name who has disappeared from a nursing home—a search that becomes a test of her own identity. *Girl with Curious Hair* (1989) is a collection including a novella and short stories heavily referenced to popular culture, especially television. A nonfiction discussion of popular culture is *Signifying Rappers: Rap and Race in the Urban Present*, with Mark Costello (1990). Wallace's second novel was preceded by a huge publicity campaign, but its massive size—over 1,000 pages, with 900 footnotes—limited its readership. Set in the future when the United States has been taken into "The Organization of North American Nations," *Infinite Jest* (1996) features wheelchair-bound Quebecois terrorists, an assassinated right wing president, junkies, homosexuals, and the three Incandenza brothers in its large cast of characters. With no traditionally linear plot, it ends without resolution of the characters' crises. *A Supposedly Fun Thing I'll Never Do Again* (1997) collects nonfiction prose including musings on tennis, state fairs and television. *Brief Interviews with Hideous Men* (1999) is a collection of 23 essays and short stories.

Wallace, Dillon (1863–1939), author of adventure books. Wallace, born in Craigsville, New York, wrote books set for the most part in Labrador. Among them are *The Lure of the Labrador Wild* (1905) and *The Story of Grenfell of the Labrador* (1922), both of which were very popular.

Wallace, Lew[is] (1827–1905), lawyer, novelist, statesman, soldier. Wallace, born in Indiana, practiced law in Indianapolis, was elected to the Indiana state senate (1856), and rose to the rank of major-general during the Civil War. After the war he was appointed governor of New Mexico (1878–81) and minister to Turkey (1881–85). He also served as governor of Indiana. As early as 1843, under the influence of Prescott's *Conquest of Mexico*, he had begun to write a novel set in Mexico. It was finally published as THE FAIR GOD (1873). With BEN HUR: A TALE OF THE CHRIST (1880), Wallace achieved an almost incredible popularity. This dramatic, swiftly moving novel sold about 2 million copies and was translated into numerous languages. A stage version prepared by William Young (1899) was popular for several years, and two spectacular movies made from the book were very successful in 1925 and 1959. The chariot race in the novel was long a staple of Barnum & Bailey's Circus. Later books by Wallace were *The Life of Benjamin Harrison* (1888); *The Boyhood of Christ* (1888); THE PRINCE OF INDIA (1893); and *The Wooing of Malkatoon* (poem, 1898). In *Lew Wallace, An Autobiography* (2 v. 1906) he wrote of his life up to 1864—his wife completed the book. Irving McKee wrote an enthusiastic biography, *"Ben-Hur" Wallace* (1947).

Wallace, William Alexander Anderson. See BIG-FOOT WALLACE, THE ADVENTURES OF.

Wallace, William Ross (1819–1881), lawyer, poet. Wallace was born in Kentucky. In his time the poems of Wal-

lace were widely read. Today, only one is remembered, *What Rules the World* (c. 1865), and only for two lines: "The hand that rocks the cradle/Is the hand that rules the world." His verse was often intensely patriotic, and he was especially ardent in his advocacy of the North during the Civil War. In temperament and even in appearance he resembled Poe, whom he claimed to have known well. Among his other publications are *The Battle of Tippecanoe* (1837), *Alban the Pirate* (1848), *Meditations in America and Other Poems* (1851), and *The Liberty Bell* (1862).

Wallant, Edward Lewis (1926–1962), novelist. A native of New Haven, Connecticut, Wallant was educated at Pratt Institute and worked in advertising after serving in the navy during World War II. He began publishing short stories in 1955, and his first novel, *The Human Season*, appeared in 1960. It is the story of an immigrant Jew coping with his wife's death. His best-known work is *The Pawnbroker* (1961). Sol Nazerman, the sole survivor of a Polish Jewish family, relives the horror of the concentration camp in his Harlem pawnshop. Two of his works, *The Tenants of Moonbloom* (1963) and *The Children at the Gate* (1962), were published after his death.

Waller, Mary Ella (1855–1938), novelist, essayist. Waller was born in Boston and lived for many years in the White River Valley in Vermont. She wrote many books, of which one made an instantaneous hit—*The Wood-Carver of 'Lympus* (1904). She preached simplicity of living and goodwill to mankind.

Waller, Robert James (1939–), novelist, essay and short-story writer. Waller earned a Ph.D. in business at the University of Indiana and taught at the University of Northern Iowa before his first, widely sold novel, *The Bridges of Madison County* (1992), was published. The story centers on a brief and passionate love affair between Robert, who thinks of himself as "one of the last cowboys," and Francesca, an Italian war bride living on an isolated Iowa farm. They meet when Robert comes to photograph the neighborhood's covered bridges while Francesca's husband and two children are away at the state fair. Francesca leaves behind an account of the four-day romance when she dies. The novel was first promoted by independent booksellers, then taken up by major chains; the result was placement on best seller lists for over a year. Waller made a recording of *The Ballads of Madison County* (1993), singing songs he composed. *Slow Waltz in Cedar Bend* (1993), another bittersweet love tale, also sold well. *Border Music* (1995) features Jack, a cowboy who saves an exotic dancer from drunks and flees with her in his pick-up. His mental health affected by his Vietnam War experience, Jack is unable to form a lasting relationship. The melodramatic plot of *Puerta Vallarta Squeeze* (1996) has Luz, a kindly prostitute, aiding hit man Clayton Price in his escape from Mexican authorities. Story and essay collections include *Just Beyond the Firelight* (1988) and *One Good Road is Enough* (1990). *Images* (1994) is a collection of photographs.

Wall Street. A short, narrow street in the oldest section of New York City, between Broadway and the East River.

For more than a century Wall Street has been at the center of New York's financial district and has been the working address of some of the world's most powerful bankers and financiers. Originally, the street was the site of a wall built by the Dutch in New Amsterdam as a barricade against the Indians. When the English captured New York, the wall became a wagon road. Most of the official buildings of New York City clustered nearby. Federal Hall was the place where auctioneers sold stocks and bonds, and ultimately a group of stock brokers set up a room of their own at 40 Wall Street. This was the beginning of the New York Stock Exchange.

The tremendous influence of the Stock Exchange and of Wall Street generally was demonstrated in October 1929, when a crash of prices on this exchange tragically affected the whole world. Its history and the ramifications of finance are well described in Dorothy Sterling's *Wall Street* (1955). Novels about Wall Street and the financial world include R. B. Kimball, *Henry Powers, Banker* (1868); Charles Dudley Warner, *A Little Journey in the World* (1889), *The Golden House* (1894), and *That Fortune* (1899); Brander Matthews, *His Father's Son* (1896); John Dos Passos, THE BIG MONEY (1936); and Walter D. Edmonds, *Young Ames* (1942).

Waln, Robert ["Peter Atall"] (1794–1825), writer. Waln, born in Philadelphia, was a man of ample means who pursued literature at his leisure, writing articles of miscellaneous character, sometimes under the pen name of Peter Atall, Esq. It was under this pseudonym that he published a satire on fashionable Philadelphia, *The Hermit in America on a Visit to Philadelphia* (1819). He also produced several volumes of verse, among them *American Bards* (1820) and *Sisyphi Opus* (1820), as well as a biography of Lafayette and biographical sketches of the signers of the Declaration of Independence.

Walsh, Robert (1784–1859), journalist, editor, diplomat. Walsh, born in Baltimore, at first worked on magazines. For a time he practiced law and for several years taught school. From 1844 to 1851, he was consul-general at Paris and contributed articles to American magazines. Perhaps his most vigorous piece was a reply to the attacks by British travelers and editors on the United States, *An Appeal from the Judgments of Great Britain Respecting the U.S.* (1819). He engaged in controversy with Robert Goodloe Harper, who in 1813 delivered an address at Georgetown praising Russian military skill rather than the Russian winter for the victory over Napoleon. The address and Walsh's letters in opposition to it were published as *Correspondence with Robert Goodloe Harper Respecting Russia* (1813). Walsh pointed out the dangers of Russian ascendancy. He made a collection of his miscellaneous articles in *Didactics, Social, Literary, and Political* (2 v. 1837). J.C. Walsh wrote a biography of Robert Walsh in 1927.

Walter, Eugene (1874–1941), playwright. Walter began work as a reporter in Cleveland, his native city, and then worked in New York City, Cincinnati, and Seattle, where he was a business manager of public entertainments ranging from minstrel shows and circuses to symphony orchestras and grand opera companies. He also wrote more than two dozen plays, most of them melodramas that were realistic enough to become widely popular. Among them are *The Undertow* (1906), *Paid in Full* (1907), *The Easiest Way* (1908), *Fine Feathers* (1911), and dramatic adaptations of THE TRAIL OF THE LONESOME PINE (1911) and THE LITTLE SHEPHERD OF KINGDOM COME (1916). He collected a series of ten lectures in *How to Write a Play* (1925).

Walter, Thomas (1696–1725), clergyman, musician. Walter, a native of Roxbury, Massachusetts, and a nephew of Cotton Mather, was led away for a while from the strict Puritanical fold by John Checkley (1680–1753), who had studied in England and there had gone over to the Church of England. Back in Boston Checkley published two books defending the Congregational Church. The Mather family quickly took care of Walter by installing him as a minister at Roxbury. Walter later engaged in controversy with Checkley over the issue of inoculation for smallpox, which Checkley opposed. In *A Choice Dialogue between John Faustus a Conjurer and Jack Tory His Friend* (1720), an answer to Checkley's *A Modest Proof of the Order and Government in the Church*, Walter has a subordinate devil tell Checkley how much Satan liked his attempts, but accuses him of bungling the job. Walter is chiefly remembered for *The Grounds and Rules of Music Explained* (1721). He also wrote *The Sweet Psalmist of Israel* (1722).

Wampanoag Indians. An Algonquian tribe that occupied eastern Massachusetts when the Pilgrims landed there. They were also called Pokanokets. Their most prominent chieftains were MASSASOIT, who gave the English a friendly welcome, and King Philip, with whom the settlers fought what is called King Philip's War (1675–76)—the war that ended in almost complete extermination of the tribe. The Wampanoags figure in several dramas and poems, in some of which King Philip plays a role. See KING PHILIP.

Wapshot Chronicle, The (1957), a novel by John Cheever. Leander Wapshot and his cousin Honora are the oldest remnants of what once was a prominent family in the fishing village of St. Bodophs, Massachusetts. Leander, who keeps a journal, operates a ferry to an island tourist attraction until he swims out to sea and never returns. Honora, the actual owner of Leander's house and boat, fights with her cousin and his wife but loves their sons, Moses and Coverly. In a sequel, *The Wapshot Scandal* (1964), Honora is pursued to Italy by the Internal Revenue Service because she never opens her mail and therefore has not paid income taxes. Extradited back to St. Bodolphs, she starves herself to death. In the meantime, Moses and Coverly, miserable because of their marital failures, return to the home village.

War Between the States. See CIVIL WAR.

Ward, Artemus [pen name of **Charles Farrar Browne**] (1834–1867), newspaperman, editor, humorist, lecturer. Browne was born in Waterford, Maine. When he was thirteen his father died; he became a printer and worked for various New England newspapers. He sent his earliest writings to *The Carpet Bag* of Boston and began an itinerant life, settling finally in Ohio, where he worked on several newspapers.

A piece he wrote for the Toledo *Commercial* attracted the attention of editors at the Cleveland *Plain Dealer*, and he was asked to do a humorous column for that paper. He responded in 1858 with his first Artemus Ward letters. Ward, a shrewd and supposedly illiterate showman, wrote in what was represented as Yankee dialect and told of adventures and misadventures with his traveling museum of wax figures (also a few "snaiks and other critturs"). The letters were widely reprinted and gave Ward a national reputation. He became city editor of the *Plain Dealer*, but had some difficulties with his superiors and resigned in 1860. He and his character, drawn in part from SEBA SMITH's Jack Downing, were by that time merged, and Ward became better known by his pen name than by his own name.

From Cleveland, Ward went to New York City, where he wrote some of his best sketches for VANITY FAIR. They mostly took the form of interviews, and among them was a fictitious interview with Lincoln that delighted the President. At this time Ward published his first collection, *Artemus Ward, His Book* (1862), which quickly sold forty thousand copies. Ward also was a lecturer. He began in 1861 with an address called "Babes in the Woods," in which he never got around to discussing that subject. It was a great hit. Unlike many practitioners, Ward like to lecture. He made a point of seeming altogether solemn, affecting what Stephen Leacock called "an intense dullness of intelligence." He was a master of sudden and prolonged pauses that emphasized the incongruity of his remarks. In the course of his travels, he stayed in Virginia City, Nevada, for three weeks and had a hilarious time with MARK TWAIN and others in the newspaper crowd. In 1866 he left for England, where he won great success. He was made an editor of *Punch* and died in England of tuberculosis.

In Ward's lifetime he published only one more book, *Artemus Ward, His Travels* (1865). But there were posthumous works: *Artemus Ward in London* (1869), *Artemus Ward's Lectures* (1869), and *Artemus Ward: His Works Complete* (1875, 1890, 1910). Among his best-known articles and lectures are "High-Handed Outrage at Utica," "Among the Spirits," "The Showman's Courtship," "Wax Figures vs. Shakespeare," "Among the Free Lovers," "Artemus Ward in the Egyptian Hall," "The Tower of London," and "Artemus Ward Among the Mormons."

When one examines Ward's techniques it becomes obvious that some were already being widely used in his time, and that in general all of them are outstanding traits of American popular humor. Immediately prominent were his cacography, or humorous misspellings, and what he himself called "ingrammaticisms"—a parallel attack on grammatical conventions. Ward loved puns, burlesque, and anticlimax—delivered every time in solemn style.

Ward's other writings appear in *Letters of Artemus Ward to Charles E. Wilson, 1858–61* (1900); *Artemus Ward's Best Stories* (ed. by Clifton Johnson with an introduction by William Dean Howells, 1912); and *Selected Works of Artemus Ward* (ed. by A. J. Nock, 1924). E. P. Hingston wrote *Genial Showman* (1870) and Don C. Seitz wrote *Artemus Ward: A Biography and a Bibliography* (1926).

Ward, Christopher [Longstreth] (1868–1943), lawyer, humorist, historian. Ward, born in Delaware, practiced law and in 1920 became president of a business called the Corporation Service Co. He wrote well, often in a humorous vein, as in his best seller *The Triumph of the Nut* (1923) and in *Twisted Tales* (1924) and *Foolish Fiction* (1925), parodies of current novels. He also wrote historical works about his native state, among them *Sweden on the Delaware* (1938) and *The Delaware Continentals* (1941).

Ward, Elizabeth Stuart Phelps (1844–1911), novelist, poet. Daughter of ELIZABETH STUART PHELPS the religious novelist, Ward was born in Boston. As a young writer, she achieved immense success with THE GATES AJAR (1868), a religious novel with appeal to a society recovering from the Civil War. The young woman protagonist records in journal entries how she is comforted by her aunt and the child Faith and comes to believe she will be reunited with her dead soldier brother in the afterlife. The sequels *Beyond the Gates* (1883), *The Gates Between* (1887), and *Within the Gates* (1901) were less successful. These sentimental books are said to have been the inspiration for Mark Twain's burlesque CAPTAIN STORMFIELD'S VISIT TO HEAVEN (1909).

Elizabeth Ward also wrote several novels on the need for better treatment for women, including *Hedged In* (1870) on social hypocrisy. *The Silent Partner* (1871) dealt with the lives of New England mill workers. *The Story of Avis* (1877) tells of a woman trying to succeed as a painter. *Dr. Zay* (1882) concerns a woman physician. *The Madonna of the Tubs* (1886) and *Jack, the Fisherman* (1887) are short treatments of the lives of Gloucester fishermen. *A Singular Life* (1894) shows how a Christlike minister would be rejected by orthodox New England congregations. With her husband, Herbert Dickinson Ward (1861–1932), she wrote several romances centering on biblical figures. Her verse is collected in *Poetic Studies* (1875) and *Songs of the Silent World* (1885). *Chapters from a Life* (1896) is autobiographical.

Ward, Mary J[ane] [Mrs. Mary Jane Quayle] (1905–   ), author. A native of Indiana and a graduate of Northwestern, Ward wrote *The Tree Has Roots* (1937) and *The Wax Apple* (1938), before writing her best-known work; *The Snake Pit* (1946). It is the story of a young wife's years in a mental hospital and her struggle to regain sanity and freedom. Her later novels include *The Professor's Umbrella* (1948), *A Little Night Music* (1951), *It's Different for a Woman* (1952), and *The other Caroline* (1970), a fictional portrayal of paranoid Schizophrenia. *Counterclockwise* (1969) chronicles a relapse into mental illness that sends the author of a best-selling novel to a private hospital offering more effective therapy than the State institution depicted in *The Snake Pit*.

Ward, Nathaniel ["Theodore de la Guard"] (1587?–c. 1652), clergyman, lawyer, public official, writer. Ward, the son of an English clergyman, was educated at Cambridge, studied and practiced law, and traveled on the Continent. He became a minister and was known for wit and outspokenness in behalf of Puritan doctrine. In 1633 he was excommunicated by Archbishop Laud and took refuge in the

Massachusetts Bay Colony. From 1634 to 1636 he served as minister at Agawam (later Ipswich). He wrote a code restricting the autocracy of the magistrates, the so-called BODY OF LIBERTIES of 1641, which recognized fundamental human rights and therefore is ranked by some with the Magna Carta and the Bill of Rights, Ward's best-remembered work is THE SIMPLE COBLER OF AGGAWAM IN AMERICA. It was written in Massachusetts in 1645 and published in London in 1647 under the pen name Theodore de la Guard. The subtitle announces that the "simple cobler" is "willing to help 'mend his native country, lamentably tattered, both in the upper-leather and sole, with all the honest stitches he can take." The book, a denunciation of religious tolerance, of the strife between Parliament and King Charles, and of the frivolity of women, made a great stir and went through four editions. Ward returned to England in the winter of 1646–47, was called on to preach before the House of Commons, and did so with his usual uninhibited frankness. He ended his days as an active minister at Shenstone.

Moses Coit Tyler called the *Simple Cobler* "a tremendous partisan pamphlet, intensely vital . . . full of fire, wit, whim, eloquence, sarcasm, patriotism, bigotry." *The Simple Cobler* has appeared in several editions including a facsimile reprint prepared by Lawrence C. Wroth (1937). Two writings of Ward not reprinted are his *Religious Retreat Sounded to a Religious Army* (1647) and *A Word to Mr. Peters* (1647). *Body of Liberties* was edited for the *American History Leaflets* (1896). A biography of Ward was written by J. W. Dean (1868). See HUMOR IN THE U.S.

Ward, Ned [Edward] (?–1731), satirist. Although Ward claimed in *A Trip to New England With a Character of the Country and People, both English and Indians* (London, 1699) to have visited North America, he probably never left his native England. Instead he used secondary sources and his own fancy for his accounts of witchcraft and hypocrisy among the Puritans.

Ward, Samuel (1814–1884), poet, lobbyist, miner, memoirist. Ward, born in New York City, was the brother of JULIA WARD HOWE. He published a volume of verse, *Lyrical Recreations* (1865), and is believed to have been the original of Horace Bellingham in Marion Crawford's *Dr. Claudius* (1883). He became a representative of the banking interests in Washington and was known as the King of the Lobbyists. In mid-century Ward suffered a series of family deaths and financial reverses and went to California in the gold rush. He wrote a book about his experiences, calling himself "Midas Jr." In 1949 this book, rediscovered by Carvel Collins, was reprinted with some entertaining editorial information as *Sam Ward in the Gold Rush*. Meanwhile, entirely by coincidence, Frank Maloy Anderson was trying to discover the author of the anonymous DIARY OF A PUBLIC MAN (1879). In 1948 Anderson published a spectacular detective story to prove that Sam Ward was the author. Ward made a second fortune, traveled all over the world, remarried, and become a social figure. He appears in Louise Hall Tharp's *Three Saints and a Sinner* (1956).

Ward, Thomas ["Flaccus"] (1807–1873), physician, poet, musician, philanthropist. A man of wealth, Ward was born in Newark, New Jersey, took a medical degree, but worked as a physician for only a short time. He wrote much verse, collected in *Passaic, a Group of Poems Touching That River, with Other Musings* (1842). He used the pen name Flaccus. In later years he lived in New York City, where he built an impressive hall for charity performances of theatricals. He wrote an opera for such a performance, *Flora, or, The Gypsy's Frolic* (1858), and a group of *War Lyrics* (1865).

Warde, Frederick [Barkham] (1851–1935), actor, authority on Shakespeare, memoirist. Warde, born in England, acted in touring companies before coming to the U.S. in 1874. He starred in his own repertory company for several years but left the stage for the movies in 1919. His writing includes *Shakespeare's Fools* (1913), *Shakespearean Studies Simplified* (1925), and one of the best of stage autobiographies, *Fifty Years of Make-Believe* (1925).

Ware, Eugene Fitch ["Ironquill"] (1841–1911), army officer, lawyer, public official, poet, historian. Ware, born in Hartford, Connecticut, served throughout the Civil War and was mustered out as a captain of cavalry. He earned his living at first as a harnessmaker, but at his wife's urging studied law, was admitted to the bar, and became successful as a corporation lawyer. He also served in the Connecticut legislature and on several commissions. He was fond of history, wrote numerous papers, and prepared an account of *The Indian War of '64* (1892). He also wrote verse under the pen name Ironquill, collected in *The Rhymes of Ironquill* (1908), *From Court to Court* (1909), and other volumes.

Ware, Henry (1764–1845), clergyman, teacher, writer on religion. Ware, born in Massachusetts, held a pastorate at Hingham for eighteen years, then a professorship in the Harvard Divinity School, which he helped to organize. He also helped establish Unitarianism, taking an active part in the controversies with the Trinitarians. A volume of his lectures is called *An Inquiry into the Foundation, Evidences, and Truths of Religion* (1842). He married three times, and three of his nineteen children became well known. **Henry, Jr.** (1794–1843), a Unitarian minister who taught at Harvard, wrote many books and articles, and edited *The Christian Disciple* (1819–23). **John** (1795–1864), a physician who also taught at Harvard wrote lectures collected in *Discourses on Medical Education* (1847) and *Hints to Young Men* (1850). **William** (1797–1852), a Unitarian clergyman and novelist, wrote *Zenobia*, a very popular novel, originally called *Letters of Lucius M. Piso from Palmyra to His Friend Marcus Curtius at Rome* (1837); *Aurelian*, originally called *Probus* (1838); *Julian* (1841); and various travel sketches and biographies. William Ware also edited *American Unitarian Biography* (2 v. 1850, 1851).

Ware, John. See HENRY WARE.

Ware, Theron. See DAMNATION OF THERON WARE.

Ware, William. See HENRY WARE.

War Is Kind (1899), a collection of poems by STEPHEN CRANE. Most of the poems are cynical, for example, "A newspaper is a collection of half-injustices." A few are built by contrast of mood: hope and despair, illusion and reality. Some are syllogistic in form, and most are nonmetrical. Number XXI is a typical Crane parable poem, of a kind more frequently found in his BLACK RIDERS collection (1895): "A man said to the universe:/'Sir, I exist!'/ 'However,' replied the universe,/ 'The fact has not created in me/A sense of obligation.'" The title poem, "Do not weep, maiden, for war is kind," was scoffed at by the New York *World* as being "not poetry as Tennyson understood it."

Warman, Cy (1855–1914),   farmer, railroad worker, newspaperman, writer. Warman, born in Illinois, had a varied career that led to two kinds of celebrity. A facile verse writer, he wrote a song, "Sweet Marie" (music by Raymon Moore), which became an enormous success. He also wrote numerous convincing stories and books on railroaders, including *Tales of an Engineer* (1895), *The Express Messenger* (1897), *The Story of the Railroad* (1898), *Snow on the Headlight* (1899), and *The Last Spike* (1906). His poems were collected in *Mountain Melodies* (1892) and *Songs of Cy Warman* (1911).

Warner, Anna Bartlett ["Amy Lothrop"] (1827–1915),   novelist, author of juveniles and books on religion and gardening. Warner, born in New York City, and the sister of SUSAN B. WARNER, wrote fiction very much in her sister's style and sometimes collaborated with her. After the appearance of Susan's *The Wide, Wide World* (1851), Anna wrote *Dollars and Cents* (1852) under the pen name Amy Lothrop. The sisters collaborated on about fifteen novels, among them *Mr. Rutherford's Children* (2 v. 1853–55) and *Wych Hazel* (1876). Anna also wrote books on her own, among them *Stories of Vinegar Hill* (6 v. 1872); *The Fourth Watch*, a religious book (1872); and *Gardening by Myself* (1892). After Susan's death, Anna wrote a book about her (1909). Olivia E. P. Stokes wrote *Letters and Memories of Susan and Anna Bartlett Warner* (1925).

Warner, Charles Dudley (1829–1900),   essayist, editor, novelist. Warner is remembered today chiefly for his collaboration with MARK TWAIN ON THE GILDED AGE (1873), but in his lifetime he was a popular and prolific author in his own right. Warner was born in Massachusetts and worked as a railroad surveyor in Missouri and a lawyer in Chicago. He became editor of the Hartford *Evening Post* (1861), later the *Courant* (1867). His first book of essays, *My Summer in a Garden* (1871), was hailed as a worthy successor to Washington Irving's genial sketches and went through forty-four editions by 1895. Equally successful were the essays collected in *Backlog Studies* (1873), *Baddeck* (1874), and *Being a Boy* (1878). He also wrote travel books, among them *Saunterings* (1872), *My Winter on the Nile* (1876), and *In the Levant* (1877). His novel trilogy—*A Little Journey in the World* (1889), *The Golden House* (1895), and *That Fortune* (1899)—satirized the era to which *The Gilded Age* had given a popular name. He also published biographies of Washington Irving and Capt. John Smith for the AMERICAN MEN OF LETTERS SERIES, of which he was editor. He wrote literary criticism in *The Relation of Literature to Life* (1896) and *Fashions in Literature* (1902) and edited, with others, the multivolume *Library of the World's Best Literature*

(1896–97). He succeeded William Dean Howells in the "Editor's Study" of *Harper's* (1892), and was president of the American Social Science Association and the National Institute of Arts and Letters. A close friend of Twain, Howells, and Thomas Bailey Aldrich, Warner was in many respects a typical New England writer of the late-19th century.

Warner, Josiah (1798–1874),   musician, teacher, social reformer. A native of Boston, Warner for a time taught music and conducted an orchestra in Cincinnati. When Robert Owen founded his utopian colony at New Harmony, Indiana, Warner and his family joined him there. He soon found that he and Owen fundamentally differed, and Warner started what he called an "equity store" in Cincinnati. In 1850 Warner founded a colony called Modern Times on Long Island, New York, but gave it up in 1862 when it was clear that it attracted more than the usual proportion of fools and eccentrics. He wrote a series of books that are regarded as the basis of philosophical anarchism in the United States. Among them are *Equitable Commerce* (1846); *True Civilization* (1863, rev. 1875); and *Written Music Remodeled and Invested with the Simplicity of an Exact Science* (1860).

Warner belonged to the tribe of Yankee inventors. One of his devices was a lard-burning lamp. He also made several inventions for use in printing, including a cylinder self-inking press. William Bailie wrote *Josiah Warren, the First American Anarchist* (1906).

Warner, Susan Bogert ["Elizabeth Wetherell"] (1819–1885),   novelist, writer for children. Born into a prominent and well-to-do Manhattan family, Warner's life was severely affected by the death of her mother—when Susan was ten years old—and the loss of the family fortune. She was educated at home by her father and expected to make a marriage appropriate for her social class. When Mr. Warner lost his money in the financial crash of 1837, he and his two daughters were forced to move into a farmhouse on Constitution Island in the Hudson River opposite West Point which they had previously used as a summer retreat. There Susan and her sister, ANNA BARTLETT WARNER, engaged in the hard physical work of nineteenth century housekeepers—gardening, sewing, cooking and cleaning. When the family's poverty became so serious that creditors were threatening to take their furniture, the sisters decided to follow their aunt's suggestion to try writing novels to earn money. The copyright laws of the day did not adequately protect authors against piracy, and the sisters sold their manuscripts outright with no provision for royalties, so despite phenomenal sales for Susan's first novel *The Wide, Wide World* (1850), the Warner's financial problems continued. Like most of her work, *The Wide, Wide World*, published under the pen name Elizabeth Wetherell, is domestic fiction offering detailed looks at the mechanics of keeping house in the period. Ellen Montgomery, the heroine, is a preadolescent girl whose mother has died and whose family fortune has been lost. She has been left with a difficult and exploitive aunt who neither understands nor cares about her. Susan Warner's evangelical Presbyterianism is a strong theme in the novel, as Ellen makes her life decisions on a religious basis. Warner's second novel *Queechy* (1952) also concerns the spiritual development of a young girl. Other fictions including *Melbourne House* (1864), *Daisy* (1868), and *Daisy in the Field* (1869) embrace the abolitionist cause. Relief for women factory workers is the theme of *Wych Hazel* (1876) and *The Gold of Chickaree* (1876) written in collaboration with Anna. Warner continued to write novels and books for young people until the year of her death. Several children's books are the products of the sisters' joint effort, and Anna wrote a biography of her sister in 1909.

War of 1812 (1812–1814).   This was the second war between the United States and England. It was fought ostensibly to maintain American freedom of the seas, but was also directed toward the American annexation of Canada and Florida. The history of this war is mainly an account of disasters. Important for American literary history was the morning that followed a British attack on Fort McHenry. Francis Scott Key, seeing that "our flag was still there," wrote *The Star-Spangled Banner*, which later became the United States national anthem.

Among historical works on the War of 1812 are H. M. Brackenridge, *History of the Late War Between the U.S. and Great Britain* (1818); J. T. Headley, *Second War with England* (1853); D. D. Porter, *Memoir of Commodore David Porter* (1875); Theodore Roosevelt, *The Naval War of 1812* (1882); Henry Adams, *History of the U.S. During the Administrations of Jefferson and Madison* (9 v. 1885–91); A. T. Mahan, *Admiral Farragut* (1892) and *Sea Power in Its Relations to the War of 1812* (1905); K. C. Babcock, *Rise of American Nationality* (1906); S. E. Morison, *Letters of Harrison Gray Otis* (1913); C. K. Webster, *British Diplomacy, 1813–15* (1921); Fletcher Pratt, *The Heroic Years, 1801–15* (1934) and *Preble's Boys* (1950); Francis F. Beime, *The War of 1812* (1949); Glen Tucker, *Poltroons and Patriots* (2 v. 1954); and C. S. Forester, *The Age of Fighting Sail: The Story of the Naval War of 1812* (1956).

Novels on the war include J. K. Paulding, DIVERTING HISTORY OF JOHN BULL AND BROTHER JONATHAN (1812); Irving Bacheller, D'RI AND I (1901); Kenneth Roberts, *The Lively Lady* (1931) and *Captain Caution* (1934); F. Van Wyck Mason, *Captain Renegade* (1932, rewritten as *Wild Drums Beat*, 1954); James Street, *Oh, Promised Land* (1940); James Jennings, *Call the New World* (1941) and *The Salem Frigate* (1946); and Marguerite Allis, *To Keep Us Free* (1953). James Nelson Barker wrote a play called MARIMION, based on Sir Walter Scott's poem, which was produced in New York City on April 13, 1812. Its protests against tyranny echoed the feeling against England in those days, and it was received with great enthusiasm. Mordecai M. Noah's SHE WOULD BE A SOLDIER, OR, THE PLAINS OF CHIPPEWA (1819) and Richard Penn Smith's *The Triumph at Plattsburgh* (1830) were patriotic plays. William Emmons published what he called "a national drama," *Tecumseh, or, The Battle of the Thames* (1836). He had treated the same episode in a pamphlet published in 1822 and returned to it in one section of *The Fredoniad, or Freedom Preserved, an Epic Poem of the Late War of 1812*. Popular verse includes W.

Strickland's *Decatur's Victory*, Samuel Woodworth's *Erie and Champlain* and *The Hunters of Kentucky*, and Charles Miner's *James Bird*. The most famous poem about the war, aside from *The Star-Spangled Banner*, is Oliver Wendell Holmes' "Old Ironsides" (1830), dedicated to the preservation of the ship *Constitution*.

War of Independence.   See AMERICAN REVOLUTION.

Warren, Caroline Matilda [Thayer] (1787?–1844), novelist. Warren, sometimes known by her married name, Mrs. Thayer, wrote American history and religious books for children as well as sentimental novels, the best known being *The Gamesters: or, Ruins of Innocence*. (1805).

Warren, Mercy Otis (1728–1814),   poet, dramatist, historian. A sister of the patriot JAMES OTIS and wife of General James Warren, Mercy Otis Warren was born on Cape Cod. She devoted her literary talents to the service of the American republic. She corresponded with many prominent patriots, giving encouragement and respected advice in political matters. Her verse dramas, THE ADULATEUR: A TRAGEDY (1773) and THE GROUP (1775), were topical satires of the British and the American Tories. She also published the fervently republican *Poems Dramatic and Miscellaneous* (1790) and a *History of the Rise, Progress, and Termination of the American Revolution* (1805). Alice Brown wrote about her in *Mercy Warren* (1896). Katherine Anthony wrote *First Lady of the Revolution: Mercy Otis Warren* (1958). See also THE BLOCKADE.

Warren, Robert Penn (1905–1989),   novelist, poet, short-story writer, critic. The winner of Pulitzer Prizes for fiction (1947) and poetry (1958), Robert Penn Warren was probably the most versatile man of letters of his time. Over six decades, his fourteen volumes of poetry and ten novels were the most distinguished contributions of a career that also produced two plays, a volume of short stories, four volumes of historical meditations and political reflections, and a series of textbooks that revolutionized the teaching of poetry and fiction for generations of students.

Warren was born in Guthrie, Kentucky, where his father, Robert Warren, was a merchant and banker. His maternal grandfather, Gabriel Penn, had been a Confederate cavalryman under Nathan Bedford Forrest, and his war stories, along with Warren's own childhood interest in natural history, were major influences on Warren's later work. He was educated at public schools in Guthrie and in Clarksville, Tennessee. He was appointed to the Naval Academy but was prevented from enrolling by a hunting accident that blinded him in one eye. As a student at Vanderbilt, he joined an informal literary discussion group that included the poets JOHN CROWE RANSOM and DONALD DAVIDSON who were professors there, and the poet ALLEN TATE, who was Warren's college roommate. From 1922 to 1925 this group published *The Fugitive* under Warren's coeditorship, a magazine of short life and limited circulation that nevertheless published the work of many who would go on to distinguished literary careers and whose appearance is generally taken to mark the beginning of a new epoch in Southern letters.

During his graduate work at Berkeley and Yale, Warren wrote his first book, *John Brown: The Making of a Martyr* (1929). Its caustic analysis of Brown's life presaged much of Warren's later work on the dangers and attractiveness of political idealism. While a Rhodes Scholar at Oxford in 1929–30 he wrote the novella *Prime Leaf*, set during the turn of the century revolt of Tennessee and Kentucky tobacco growers against their subjection by tobacco buyers. Warren would return to this subject—the so-called Black Patch War—in his first published novel, *Night Rider* (1939). Also while at Oxford Warren wrote the essay "The Briar Patch," a defense of racial segregation included in *I'll Take My Stand*. This was a manifesto of Agrarianism written largely by Nashville friends from the days of *The Fugitive* and intended to defend the culture and economy of the South against the encroachment of Northern economic, religious, and political mores. Warren shortly afterward repudiated the essay, and his changing thoughts on race and the transformation of Southern culture are reflected in *Segregation: The Inner Conflict in the South* (1956) and *Who Speaks for the Negro?* (1965), as well as in such novels as *Band of Angels* (1955), *Wilderness* (1961), and *Flood* (1964).

On his return to the United States in 1930, Warren married Emma Brescia, of San Francisco, from whom he was divorced in 1950. After teaching briefly at Southwestern College in Memphis and at Vanderbilt, he taught at Louisiana State University, from 1934 to 1942. There he observed the political upheaval in Louisiana during and after the ascendancy of Huey Long. This is reflected in *All The King's Men* (1946), probably Warren's most enduring novel. At Louisiana State, Warren also founded, together with Cleanth Brooks and Charles Pipkin, *The Southern Review*, a distinguished periodical. In addition to writing his first two volumes of poems, *Thirty-Six Poems* (1935) and *Eleven Poems on the Same Theme* (1942), and his first two novels, *Night Rider* (1939) and *At Heaven's Gate* (1943), Warren at LSU also began, with Cleanth Brooks, to write a series of textbooks, including *Understanding Poetry* (1938) and *Understanding Fiction* (1943). These works introduced American students to the close-reading techniques now known as the NEW CRITICISM.

From 1942 to 1950 Warren was Professor of English at the University of Minnesota, also serving as Poetry Consultant to the Library of Congress in 1944–5. From 1950 to his retirement in 1975 he was Professor at Yale. Although he published his last six novels while at Yale, his artistic interests turned increasingly to poetry, first with a long narrative poem on the murder of a slave by Thomas Jefferson's nephews, *Brother to Dragons* (1953, rev. 1979). Then came a succession of volumes of lyric poetry commencing with *Promises* (1957) and including his most notable volumes: *Incarnations* (1968); the lyric sequence *Audubon: A Vision* (1969); *Or Else* (1974); *Can I See Arcturus from Where I Stand?* (1975, originally a section of *Selected Poems 1923–1975*, 1975); *Now and Then* (1978); and *Altitudes and Extensions* (1985, published as part of *New and Selected Poems, 1923–1985*, 1985).

In 1953 Warren married novelist ELEANOR CLARK. Their children are Rosanna Phelps Warren and Gabriel Penn Warren.

Warren's many awards include Guggenheim Fellowships in 1939 and 1947, Pulitzer Prizes in 1947 and 1958, National Book Awards in 1958 and 1978, Bollingen Prize in 1967, Jefferson Lectureship of the National Endowment of the Arts in 1974, and the MacArthur Foundation fellowship in 1981. In 1986 he was appointed first Poet Laureate of the United States.

Warren's literary career spanned six decades, his first poems appearing as Thomas Hardy's last poems were being published, and his last poems appearing in a poetic context several poetic generations removed from the one in which he first made his mark. Like Hardy, he distinguished himself equally in prose and in verse, and like Hardy his verse career followed a career in prose, although in both cases poetry represented the older and deeper commitment.

Warren's novels turn on a small number of related concerns. The strongest of his novels—*Night Rider* (1939), ALL THE KING'S MEN (1946), and WORLD ENOUGH AND TIME (1950)—as well as the long "Tale in Verse and Voices," *Brother to Dragons* (1953 and 1979), *Band of Angels* (1955), and *Wilderness* (1961)—concern the individual's moral experience in the context of political upheavals that require the making of commitments. Ultimately, the commitments betray the individual, and ultimately the individual betrays the commitments. Warren deals with the ironies and moral cruxes into which people are projected by political conflicts they can think about clearly but never fully understand. His characters are frequently swept up, sometimes through weakness and alienation, but just as frequently on account of their virtues, into political movements that undo them. His characters also are forced to confront the mixture of their own motives, to see how idealism and bloodthirstiness run together, for instance, or to see how pragmatism slides down easily into worship of expedience. Political upheaval and psychological confusion thus mirror each other in his works, and they portray the public world to which the characters are responsible and the private world of their moral experience as irredeemably fallen and self-betraying. The experience of history in these novels is the experience of guilt and sorrow, the experience of how the attempt to reestablish justice leads one almost inevitably into unanticipated sorts of corruption. These works are informed by a Calvinistic idea of human fallenness and an insight into the complexities of human motivations resembling those of Hawthorne. And like Hawthorne's novels, Warren's do not answer a Calvinist idea of human fallenness with a Calvinist view of redemption but choose instead to value the grim and rueful wisdom they provide as a kind of redemption in its own right.

Another strain of Warren's fiction, best represented by *At Heaven's Gate* (1943) and *Flood* (1965), as well as *A Place to Come to* (1977), *The Cave* (1959), and *Meet Me in the Green Glen* (1971), concerns the attempt of its principal characters to recover meaning, which the transformation of Southern culture has made unavailable to them. These novels stress the alienating and anonymous quality of cultures whose traditions have weakened under pressure of modernity and attempt to find ways, without turning one's back on modernity, to recover the integrity these traditions once made available.

Warren's poetic career falls into three phases. The first, starting from his *Fugitive* days and ending with his 1943 *Selected Poems* is characterized by highly formal verse and erudite diction. These early poems are marked by the enthusiasm for Renaissance lyric poetry encouraged by T. S. Eliot, and strongly show the influence of Marvell in particular. Their speakers are cool, ironic, and remote, although they brood on deep disquietes and give the impression of a poet mastering dark feelings with difficulty. The poems of the 1930s and early 1940s are increasingly haunted by a sense of primal guilt and by political bitterness. They end with the raucous and strange narrative "The Ballad of Billie Potts" (1943), which presages in plot and theme some of the great prose narratives to follow but which is followed by ten years of poetic silence.

Promises in 1958 signaled the beginning of a new poetic phase, marked first of all by the author's greater autobiographical presence in the poems, by a wider range of diction—some of it quite salty—with a more oral cast than the earlier poems, and by a looser style of verse generally. The books of this period, for example, *You, Emperors, and Others* (1960) and *Tale of Time* (included in *Selected Poems, New and Old, 1923–1966*, 1966), frequently turn on the poet's reflections on personal and family events or his reflections on stories told to him by his forebears, and they breathe a rueful sense of responsibility to private and public history.

The poems from *Incarnations* (1968) to *Altitudes and Extensions* (1985), although as a rule as dictionally and formally free as the poems of the 1950s and early 1960s, are fiercer and sharper generally, marked by a hard-bitten and gritty imaginative intensity and a poetic force that seem to originate not from the poet's psyche but from some deeper stratum of poetic power. They are as uncompromising visions of and confrontations with the transcendental forces of nature, of poetry, and of death as anything since the last poems of Hardy or Yeats.

Warren's other works include *The Circus in the Attic and Other Stories* (1947), *Selected Essays* (1958), *The Legacy of the Civil War* (1961), *Democracy and Poetry* (1975), *Jefferson Davis Gets His Citizenship Back* (1981), and *Chief Joseph of the Nez Perce* (1982). A biography is *Robert Penn Warren* (1997) by Joseph Blotner.

Washers of the Shroud, The (1861),   a poem by JAMES RUSSELL LOWELL. Lowell wrote the poem under pressure for publication in the *Atlantic* (November 1861). It was regarded as one of his most important poems. The verse expresses Lowell's strong reaction to the Civil War. In earlier days he had been something of a pacifist, but here he says that justice sometimes must resort to force and that democracy is more than easy words.

Washington, Booker T[aliaferro] (1856–1915), educator, author, lecturer. Born in rural Virginia, the son of a slave and a white man, Washington began work in the salt furnaces and coal mines of Malden, West Virginia, educating himself first at night school and later by working his way through Hampton Normal and Agricultural Institute (1872–75). After some years of teaching and advanced study, he returned to Hampton to take charge of an experimental group of Native American students and established a night school to aid especially needy aspirants. He was chosen to found Tuskegee Institute and built it up from humble beginnings to a large, influential organization. In addition he organized the National Negro Business League in Boston (1901) and gave many influential speeches. Among his many books are *Sowing and Reaping* (1900), UP FROM SLAVERY (1901), *Character Building* (1902), *Working with the Hands* (1904), *Tuskegee and Its People* (1905), *Frederick Douglass* (1907), *The Story of the Negro* (1909), *My Larger Education* (1911), and *The Man Farthest Down* (1912). Basil Matthews wrote *Booker T. Washington, Educator and Interracial Interpreter* (1948), and S. R. Spencer, Jr., wrote *Booker T. Washington and the Negro's Place in American Life* (1955).

Washington, George (1732–1799),   surveyor, soldier, statesman, first President. Born in Westmoreland County, Virginia, Washington had little formal education, but early showed an aptitude for mathematics and by age fifteen was a skilled surveyor. From 1753 to 1759 he was an officer in the French and Indian War, when the hardships under which he had to work and his difficulties with his superiors formed the beginnings of his antipathy for the British. He was elected to the Virginia House of Burgesses in 1758 and successively reelected until the House was dissolved by the colonial governor in 1774. During the decade before the outbreak of the Revolution, he became more and more dissatisfied with British rule, particularly with the commercial regulations that required him and other Virginia planters to trade exclusively with Britain under conditions he felt to be unfair to the colonists. After 1770 the increase in colonial taxation, in particular the Stamp Act and the British prohibition against colonial paper money, added to American grievances.

Washington was one of Virginia's delegates to the first and second Continental Congresses in 1774 and 1775, and was elected commander of the Continental Army in June 1775. He was faced with the problem of directing an untrained and inexperienced army, composed primarily of militiamen whose terms of enlistment were short. His task was further complicated by a lack of supplies and the hesitancy of Congress to establish the long-term enlistments necessary for a permanent army. In spite of these handicaps, his leadership and success in the field were remarkable.

The end of the war found the newly independent country in confusion. Under the ARTICLES OF CONFEDERATION, the central government could not provide a stable currency, raise taxes to pay debts, or adequately control the problems arising in the various states. Shays' Rebellion, in Massachusetts, added to Washington's growing feeling that a stronger, more centralized government was necessary. He was elected president of the Constitutional Convention that met in Philadelphia in 1787. The Constitution it adopted, which provided for a balance of powers in the federal government, and permitted the states to manage their local affairs, reflects many of Washington's ideas of government. He was unanimously elected U.S. President in 1789. During his administration he raised taxes by various tariff acts, made provisions for paying the war debts of the Union and the states, created a sound currency and a National Bank, and encouraged the growth of industries that would decrease American economic dependence on European products. Washington's tendency, particularly during his second term, to sympathize with Alexander Hamilton and the Federalists brought charges from the Republicans that he was creating too strong a central government and was, particularly in the Bank Act and the Excise Act, favoring business and industry at the expense of agriculture. He declined a third term and prepared, with the help of several friends, a FAREWELL ADDRESS. It was never actually delivered, but was published in *Claypoole's American Daily Advertiser* (September 17, 1796).

Washington was not primarily a writer. He sought help from his more articulate friends—Hamilton and Madison in particular—when it was necessary to prepare an important document, such as the "Farewell Address." He was, however, not without skill in the composition of a narrative, as in *The Journal of Major George Washington, Sent by the Hon. Robert Dinwiddie, Esq., His Majesty's Lieutenant-Governor and Commander-in-Chief of Virginia, to the Commandant of the French Forces on Ohio*, which was printed at Williamsburg in 1754. In later life Washington kept a journal, wrote many letters, prepared army orders, and composed numerous official documents.

The bicentenary edition of Washington's writings appeared in thirty-nine volumes (1931–44), with John C. Fitzpatrick as editor. Other editions of his works include A.B. Hulbert, *Washington and the West: Being George Washington's Diary of Sept. 1784* (1905, 1911); J.C. Fitzpatrick, *Calendar of the Correspondence of George Washington, Commander-in-Chief of the Continental Army* (5 v. 1905–15), *Diaries of George Washington, 1748–99* (4 v. 1925), and *George Washington, Colonial Traveler* (extracts from his papers, 1927); Philip S. Foner, *George Washington: Selections from His Writings* (1944), Saxe Commins, *Basic Writings of George Washington* (1948); and Saul K. Padover, *The Washington Papers: Basic Selections from the Public and Private Writings of George Washington* (1955).

Much mythology and adulation has grown up about Washington and his place in the nation's history. Jefferson said of him: "Never did nature and fortune combine more perfectly to make a man great." It is believed that General Harry Knox, Washington's close friend, was the first to refer to him as "The Father of his Country." (See FRANCIS BAILEY.) Another good friend, Colonel Henry ("Light-Horse Harry") Lee, offered resolutions in his memory (December 19, 1799) in which occurs the phrase "Washington, first in war, first in peace, and first in the hearts of his countrymen." The first of the myths was created by Mason Locke Weems, who wrote *A History of the Life and Death, Virtues, and Exploits, of General George Washington* (1800). His creation was the story that the child Washington admitted having cut down a cherry tree because he could not

tell a lie, and was immediately forgiven by his astonished father. Another widely repeated story showed Washington throwing stones—or silver dollars—across the Rappahannock River. John Marshall's *Life of Washington* (5 v. 1804–07) is adulatory and biased toward the Federalist side when discussing Washington's presidency. Jared Sparks, a professor of history at Harvard, produced a twelve-volume edition of Washington's writings (1834–37), the first volume of which is a life of Washington. The work must be used with caution, since Sparks altered the wording of documents in order to produce a picture of a flawless man. Washington Irving's *Life of George Washington* (5 v. 1855–59) relies on Sparks's work and is therefore not entirely accurate. More accurate biographies include Paul L. Ford, *The True George Washington* (1896, republished as *George Washington*, 1924); Henry C. Lodge, *George Washington* (2 v. 1898); Woodrow Wilson, *George Washington* (1903); J.C. Fitzpatrick, *George Washington Himself* (1933); Curtis P. Nettels, *George Washington and American Independence* (1951); William Alfred Bryan, *George Washington in American Literature, 1775–1865* (1952); Douglas Southall Freeman, a biography in seven volumes (1948–1957); and James Thomas Flexner, *Washington, The Indispensable Man* (1963).

Some of the works of fiction in which Washington appears directly or indirectly are H.H. Brackenridge, *Modern Chivalry* (1792–1815); Charles Brockden Brown, *Ormond* (1799); James Fenimore Cooper, *The Spy* (1821); Catharine Maria Sedgwick, *The Linwoods* (1835); J.K. Paulding. *The Old Continental* (1846); John Esten Cooke, *Fairfax, or, The Master of Greenway Court* (1868); Bret Harte, *Thankful Blossom* (1877); S. Weir Mitchell, *Hugh Wynne, Free Quaker* (1897) and *The Red City* (1907); Paul Leicester Ford, *Janice Meredith* (1899); Gertrude Atherton, *The Conqueror* (1902); Joseph Hergesheimer, *Balisand* (1924); Elizabeth Page, *The Tree of Liberty* (1939); Kenneth Roberts, *Oliver Wiswell* (1940); Howard Fast, *The Unvanquished* (1942); and Janet Whitney, *Judith* (1943). Two 20th-century plays that deal with Washington are of a quality far above that of plays about him produced earlier—Maxwell Anderson, *Valley Forge* (1934), and Sidney Kingsley, *The Patriots* (1945).

Among guides to the extensive manuscripts and printed material about Washington are W.S. Baker, *Bibliotheca Washingtoniana: A Descriptive List of the Biographies and Biographical Sketches of George Washington* (1889); A.P.C. Griffin, *Catalogue of the Washington Collection in the Boston Athenaeum* (1897); and the A.L.A. *Classified Washington Bibliography* (1931). To these may be added Gertrude R.B. Richards, *Select Critical Bibliography of Manuscript Sources*, and Geneva B. Snelling, *Selective Bibliography of Printed Sources*, both prepared for Volume VI of Freeman's biography (1954). See AMERICAN REVOLUTION IN U.S. LITERATURE.

Washington Square (1881),   a novel by HENRY JAMES. As a boy James lived on Washington Square in New York City, at that time the city's most fashionable residential district. The novel concerns Catherine Sloper, the shy and stolid daughter of wealthy, urbane, sardonic Dr. Austin Sloper. When young Morris Townsend, who is courting Catherine for her money, learns that her father will disinherit her if she marries him, he leaves her. Renewing his courtship after Dr. Sloper dies and leaves Catherine a small fortune, Morris is rejected sadly but firmly by Catherine, who lives on at Washington Square and is by then a spinster. Thus, Catherine, plain and unintelligent, nevertheless withstands the world's assaults. The novel was dramatized (1947) as THE HEIRESS and filmed in 1949.

Washington Square Players.   See LAWRENCE LANGNER.

Wasp, The.   A weekly founded in 1856. It gained reputation when AMBROSE BIERCE was its editor (1880–86); some of his scathing attacks appeared in its pages. Other contributors were Mark Twain and Bret Harte. It was later called *Wasp & News-Letter* and lasted into the 20th century.

Wasserstein, Wendy (1950–   ),   playwright. Born in Brooklyn and educated at Mount Holyoke, City University of New York and the Yale Drama School, Wasserstein had her first play produced Off Broadway when she was twenty-three. *Any Woman Can't* (1973) is a farce about a woman's attempt to succeed in a male-dominated world. *Uncommon Women*, written as a one-act play while she was at Yale, was lengthened to two acts and premiered at the Phoenix theater in 1977. The play centers on a group of undergraduates at Mount Holyoke threading their way between the desire for independence and the traditional goal of marriage. Wasserstein's alliance with the Off Off Broadway production group Playwrights Horizon gave rise to productions of *Isn't It Romantic* (1981), similar in theme to *Uncommon Women*, and *Miami* (1986), a musical comedy about a teenage boy on a Florida vacation with his parents. *The Heidi Chronicles* (1988) was Wasserstein's first play to be produced on Broadway and won the Pulitzer Prize for drama. In it a professor of art history confesses to a group of assembled women that she is successful, independent, and deeply unhappy. At the end, she adopts a baby with whom she poses against the backdrop of paintings by Georgia O'Keeffe. Other plays include *The Sisters Rosensweig* (1992), continuing the theme of feminine alienation, *An American Daughter* (1997), and *Old Money* (2000), a contemporary comedy with parallels to the late nineteenth-century world of Edith Wharton's novels. *Bachelor Girls* (1990) is a collection of comic essays. *Pamela's First Musical* (1996) is a children's book. Wasserstein has also written television screen plays and magazine articles.

Waste Land, The (1922),   a poem by T. S. ELIOT. A work of 434 lines in five sections, *The Waste Land* is undoubtedly the most influential poem written in English during the first half of the 20th century. Many of its symbols were drawn from Jesse L. Weston's *From Ritual to Romance*, a study of medieval themes and legends, and James G. Frazer's *Golden Bough*, a monumental work on anthropology and myth. *The Waste Land* is basically an examination of modern Western civilization in terms drawn from the Grail legend. The Fisher King is ill and impotent, and his kingdom is laid waste. Only

the arrival of the Grail knight, who will ask the three thaumaturgical questions, will destroy the spell and restore the kingdom to fertility. The poem, highly allusive and ironic, consists of a panoramic juxtaposition of episodes, historical sketches, imaginary landscapes, miniature dramas, and lyrical interludes.

The first section, "The Burial of the Dead," begins with April, "the cruellest month," in which the advent of spring only serves to reawaken the dull, sterile world to an awareness of its condition. Various protagonists and scenes are introduced that are allusively symptomatic of the living death of the 20th-century waste land. Section II, "A Game of Chess," deals primarily with lust and sterility. There is a sharp contrast between the two scenes—the one an opulently furnished bedroom, the other a London pub. The title of the section is taken from Thomas Middleton's play, *Women Beware Women*. In that work a woman is distracted by a game of chess while her daughter-in-law is being raped. In "The Fire Sermon" (III) the 20th-century world is merged with the past by means of the figures of the fisherman and of Tiresias, the ancient seer who had seen snakes coupling and had been changed, for a time, into a woman. The theme of boredom, barrenness, and shame in sexual encounters is reiterated in the scenes between the typist and the "young man carbuncular," Elizabeth and Leicester, and the three Thames maidens. Part IV, "Death by Water," refers back to the "drowned Phoenician sailor" of Part I and to the prophecy to "fear death by water." Part V, "What the Thunder Said," suggests the approach to the Chapel Perilous of medieval legend and, as Eliot's notes indicate, "the present decay of Eastern Europe." The thunder speaks the words of the Upanishad, "give, sympathize, control"; the final word, *shantih*, is the equivalent of the "peace that passes understanding."

Eliot has said that in its original form the poem was twice its present length and that the work of cutting it was entrusted to his friend EZRA POUND. Eliot acknowledges Pound's role in his dedication of the poem to Pound as *"il miglior fabbro."* The poem has been widely imitated by other poets, Eliot's contemporaries as well as younger writers. More has been written about *The Waste Land* than about any other work of modern poetry. No English or American critic has been able to feel that his work is complete without a consideration of the poem, which, because of its rich symbolical content, is susceptible to almost endless interpretations. A good elementary guide to the poem appears in George Williamson, *A Reader's Guide to T. S. Eliot.*

Watch on the Rhine, The (1941),   a play by LILLIAN HELLMAN. A German refugee in the United States whom Nazi agents want to intercept is recognized by a dissolute hanger-on at the German embassy, who demands a large bribe in return for keeping silent. The refugee kills him and in so doing helps awaken complacent Americans to the dangers of European tyrannies. The play was later made into a successful movie with a script by Dashiell Hammett.

Water Witch, The (1830),   a novel by JAMES FENIMORE COOPER. This novel, first published in Dresden, was written while Cooper was in Paris, far from the Sandy Hook region in which the action of the story occurs. The play is set in the time of Queen Anne's War (1702–13), and it seems to have been Cooper's intention to create a legendary history for his native New Jersey, as Washington Irving had done for New York. A phantom ship carries on illicit trade between freebooters and colonial New York, with a witch on board and a shrine in her honor in the cabin. Adventures of various kinds take place at sea, on the Atlantic highlands of New Jersey, and in a home on the Shrewsbury River. The novel was several times converted into successful plays.

Watkins, Tobias ["Pertinax Particular"] (1780–1855), physician, editor, historian. With JOHN NEAL. Watkins wrote *A History of the American Revolution* (2 v. 1819). He was one of the founders (1816) of the DELPHIAN CLUB in Baltimore and under his pen name edited *Tales of the Tripod; or, A Delphian Evening* (1821). He founded a magazine called *The Portico* (1816–18), to which members of the Delphian Club contributed.

Watson, John Whitaker.   See BEAUTIFUL SNOW.

Watson, Sheila (1909–1998), novelist, short-story writer. Sheila Doherty was born on the grounds of the Westminster, British Columbia, mental hospital where her father was superintendent. A teacher in the schools of her native province, she married the poet Wilfred Watson in 1941. Her novel *The Double Hook* (1959) details the struggles of inhabitants of a remote village similar to the area where she taught. The novel is elliptical, imagistic, and poetic. Her short fiction includes *Four Stories* (1979), *And the Four Animals* (1980), and *Five Stories* (1984). Watson completed her doctoral studies under Marshall McLuhan in 1965 and taught for a decade at the University of Alberta. With her husband and other writers, Watson edited the little magazine *White Pelican* (1971–78). The novel *Deep Hollow Creek* was written in the 30s but not published until 1992.

Watterson, Henry (1840–1921), newspaper editor, politician. Born in Washington, D.C., Watterson loved the South and fought in the Confederate cavalry during the Civil War. His father, a congressman from Tennessee, had also been a newspaper editor, and Watterson had considerable newspaper experience before he settled in Louisville. There he helped revive a dying paper, the *Journal*, and took over the *Courier* in 1868, presiding over the *Courier-Journal* until his death. His unabashedly rhetorical editorials became known all over the country. He was bitter against Theodore Roosevelt, supported Wilson in World War I, but opposed America's entry into the League of Nations. He received a Pulitzer Prize in 1918 for his editorials in support of American ideals during World War I. He published *Oddities of Southern Life and Character* (1882), *The Compromises of Life* (1903), and *"Marse Henry": An Autobiography* (1919). Two biographies have appeared: Isaac F. Marcosson's *"Marse Henry"* (1951) and J. F. Wall's *Henry Watterson: Reconstructed Rebel* (1956).

Watterston, George (1783–1854), lawyer, librarian, novelist, poet. Watterston, born on shipboard in New York Harbor, wrote some books that were published anonymously, including a novel called *The Lawyer; or, Man As He Ought Not to Be* (1808), a story of legal chicaneries. A story in the Gothic tradition was GLENCARN; OR, THE DISAPPOINTMENTS OF YOUTH (3 v. 1810). He was long a resident of Washington, D.C., edited the Washington City *Gazette* for a year, was Librarian of Congress from 1815 to 1829, and wrote several books under his name about the city. He also wrote verse, including *The Wanderer in Jamaica* (1810) and *The Scenes of Youth* (1813).

Watts, Alan (1915–1973), minister, teacher, philosopher. Watts was born in England, immigrated to the United States in 1938 and became a naturalized citizen in 1943. He was influential in popularizing Zen Buddhist philosophy, an influence on the Beat Generation. His works include *The Spirit of Zen* (1936), *Behold The Spirit* (1947), *The Way of Zen* (1957), *The Joyous Cosmology* (1962), *Beat Zen, Square Zen and Zen* (1967), *Beyond Theology* (1973), and his autobiography, *In My Own Way* (1973).

Watts, Mary S[tanbery] (1868–1958), novelist. Watts was a prolific and capable novelist whose best-known work is *Nathan Burke* (1910), a historical novel about her home state of Ohio. She made Thackeray and Defoe her models in an attempt to secure realism in dialogue and direct narrative. Among her other books are *The Legacy* (1911), *The Rudder* (1916), *Father and Son* (1919), *The Noon Mark* (1920), and *The Fabric of the Loom* (1924).

Wave, The.   See EVELYN SCOTT.

Way Down East (1898), a play by Lottie Blair Parker. This rural drama, replete with conventional rustic characters, jokes, and sentiments, ran for 361 performances in New York City and became a standard play for stock companies. It was also made into a movie (1920). In its most affecting scene the stern bucolic father orders the erring woman whom his son wants to marry out into the cold. The scene, always played straight, was a reliable tearjerker.

Wayside Inn, The.   See TALES OF A WAYSIDE INN.

Way West, The (1949), a novel by A. B GUTHRIE JR. This story of the great westward trek to Oregon won a Pulitzer Prize and is undoubtedly one of the best novels about the American migration to the Pacific Coast. The central figure is Lije Evans, strong, slow, and calm; his wife Rebecca is a proper mate for him, durable and uncomplaining. Her husband has to battle for leadership of the wagon train, and the conflict forms a main strand of the plot. The other chief strand is concerned with the love of two young people. Another impressive figure is the mountain guide, Dick Summers, a far from conventional backwoodsman who appeared also in an earlier Guthrie novel, THE BIG SKY (1947).

We Are Coming, Father Abraham, Three Hundred Thousand More (1862), a poem by James Sloan Gibbons (1810–1892), which first appeared anonymously in the New York *Evening Post*. It was at first attributed to the editor, William Cullen Bryant. Gibbons was an abolitionist, and the poem was written in response to Lincoln's call for 300,000 additional volunteers. Stephen Foster's musical setting of the poem became a great favorite in the North.

Weathers, W. T.   See WILLIAM BYRD.

Weaver, John V[an] A[lstyn] (1893–1938),   newspaperman, editor, writer. A student at Hamilton College and Harvard, newspaperman in Chicago and Brooklyn, and army officer in World War I, Weaver settled in New York City after leaving his native Charlotte, North Carolina. His verse attracted no attention until he adopted an H. L. Mencken suggestion that he write in slang. Several volumes of such verses were published, as well as some in conventional English: *In American* (1921), *Finders* (1923), *More in American* (1926), *To Youth* (1928), *Turning Point* (1930), and *Trial Balance* (1931)—the last an autobiography in verse. He also wrote three novels and then, in collaboration with George Abbott, a play based in part on some of his rhymed tales, *Love 'Em and Leave 'Em* (1926). His novel *Joy Girl* (1932) satirizes Hollywood.

Web and the Rock, The (1939),   a novel by THOMAS WOLFE. Here Wolfe follows his autobiographical hero, George Webber, to the enfabled rock that is New York City. There, in the midst of his youthful literary struggles, he meets the gifted scenic designer Mrs. Esther Jack—modeled on Aline Bernstein. During their turbulent love affair he is at first entranced by and then disillusioned with the magic of the city that is so much a part of Esther's personality. In passages of mingled satire and lyricism, Wolfe develops the cultural conflict of Christian and Jew, yokel and city dweller. At length George breaks from Esther's web of devotion and goes abroad to seek in an older culture the stability he could not find in the American city.

Webb, Charles Henry ["John Paul"] (1834–1905), whaler, newspaperman, inventor, humorist. Webb, born in Rouses Point, New York, read *Moby-Dick* and decided to be a whaler. He sailed the Arctic and the South Pacific for almost four years. Then he helped his brother in the family grain business in Illinois, wrote for New York papers as a columnist, and then migrated to San Francisco and joined the staff of the *Bulletin*. He founded and edited *The Californian* (1864) and established his chief claim on celebrity, friendship with and assistance to MARK TWAIN. Both Twain and Bret Harte contributed to Webb's magazine. In 1866 he settled in New York and was the publisher of Twain's first book, *The Celebrated Frog of Calaveras County and Other Sketches* (1867). For a while Webb was a Wall Street broker. In 1872 he began writing humorous sketches for the New York *Tribune* under the name of John Paul, compiled several volumes of sketches and verse, made various inventions, wrote plays, and traveled abroad. He parodied Charles Reade's *Griffith Gaunt* and Augusta Wilson's *St. Elmo* in his *Liffith Lank; or, Lunacy* (1866) and *St. Twel'mo* (1868). He also wrote *John Paul's Book* (1874); *Parodies, Prose and Verse* (1876); *Sea-Weed and What We Seed* (1876).

Webb, Phyllis (1927–   ),   poet. Born and educated in British Columbia, Webb moved first to Montreal and then to Toronto, where she was an executive producer for CBC radio. She returned to the west coast in the 1970s. Her early poetry, formal and rhetorical, is collected, along with the work of two other writers, in *Trio* (1954), *Even Your Right Eye* (1956), and *The Sea is Also a Garden* (1962). *Naked Poems* (1965) features spare minimalist pieces. Her other titles are

Selected Poems (1971), *Wilson's Bowl* (1980), *Sunday Water: Thirteen Antighazals* (1982), *The Vision Tree* (1982), *Water and Light: Ghazals and Antighazals* (1984), and *Hanging Fire* (1990). *Talking* (1982) is a collection of her essays, reviews and radio talks. *Nothing But Brush Strokes: Selected Prose* appeared in 1995.

Webb, Walter Prescott (1888–1963),   teacher, historian. In 1918 Webb, who was born in Texas, joined the faculty of the University of Texas as professor of history. He is chiefly known for his philosophy of American history as expressed in his most widely read work, *The Great Plains* (1931). He also wrote *The Growth of a Nation*, with collaborators (1928); *The Texas Rangers* (1935); *Divided We Stand: The Crisis of Frontierless Democracy* (1937); *The Great Frontier* (1952); *More Water for Texas* (1954); and *An Honest Preface* (1959).

Webber, Charles Wilkins (1819–1856),   Texas Ranger, newspaperman, explorer, naturalist, adventurer, writer of Westerns, historian. Webber was born in Kentucky. He studied medicine, then enrolled in the Princeton Theological Seminary. But at nineteen he joined the Texas Rangers, in 1849 led an expedition to the Colorado and Gila Rivers, and in 1854 organized a company to use camels as a means of crossing the western deserts. In the following year he became a member of WILLIAM WALKER's expedition to Nicaragua, where he was probably killed in battle.

All this time Webber was writing busily, usually tales of wild and improbable invention that he tried to dignify with a philosophy of primitivism. His best-known book is *Old Hicks, the Guide* (1848), the first seven chapters based on his journal of a trip to the headwaters of the Trinity River in Texas. He was a contributor to many newspapers and magazines, and for two years was editor and joint owner of the *American Review*, later the *American Whig Review*. He knew Audubon well and under his influence wrote *Wild Scenes and Song Birds* (1854). Among his other books are *The Gold Mines of the Gila* (1849); *The Hunter-Naturalist* (1851); *The Wild Girl of Nebraska* (1852); *Tales of the Southern Border* (1852); *The Prairie Scout, or, Agatone the Renegade* (1852); and *The Romance of Forest and Prairie Life* (1853). In his own day he was much praised by the critics.

Weber, Joseph ["Joe"] (1867–1942),   comedian. Weber, born in New York City, was the stage partner of LEWIS ("LEW") MAURICE FIELDS. They first appeared together in a juvenile skit satirizing German immigrants, which established their act for the rest of their lives. In 1885 they organized a company and gave their skits mainly in a New York City theater. Among their productions were *Twirly-Whirly, The Geezer, Whoop-Dee-Doo, Hoity-Toity*, and *Higgledy-Piggledy*. Then the team broke up and the men appeared separately, though neither was as successful alone as the two had been together. They were reunited in *Hokey-Pokey* (1912) and also appeared together in movies and on radio.

Webster, Daniel (1782–1852),   lawyer, public official, statesman, orator. Webster attended Dartmouth, taught school for a time, and then studied law. At first he practiced in his native New Hampshire and represented that state in the House of Representatives (1813–17). In 1816 he moved to Boston. He was representative from Massachusetts in 1823–27, senator in 1827–41. He gained wide renown as a statesman and lawyer, delivered many well-received orations and won many important cases. He served as Secretary of State (1841–43) and negotiated the Webster-Ashburton Treaty with Great Britain. From 1845–50 he was again senator from Massachusetts, and from 1850–52 again Secretary of State. He frequently sought the Presidential nomination, but unsuccessfully.

Webster represented a strong conservative tradition. He opposed the War of 1812, but was wholeheartedly against any action that would destroy the Union. By his willingness to compromise in order to avoid war, he incurred the distrust of both the radical Northern abolitionists and the Southern fire-eaters. After Webster's *Seventh of March Speech* (1850) John Greenleaf Whittier wrote a poem of denunciation ICHABOD. After the Civil War, Whittier repented his harsh indictment and in THE LOST OCCASION (1880) showed his tardy comprehension of Webster's motives. Oliver Wendell Holmes paralleled *Ichabod* in his poem *The Stateman's Secret* (1850); later he also repented and wrote sympathetically of Webster in *The Birthday of Daniel Webster*. Webster became the legal and political representative of big New England business, gained a lucrative practice before the Supreme Court, was careless about his own finances and usually in debt, and accepted from one of his best clients, the Bank of the United States, large sums of money while he was occupying offices of public trust.

Webster, a great orator, was also something of an actor. His appearance assisted him. Stephen Vincent Benét, in THE DEVIL AND DANIEL WEBSTER (1937), described him as having "a mouth like a mastiff, a voice like thunder, and eyes like burning anthracite." A report spread, according to Nathaniel Hawthorne's *The Great Stone Face* (1851), that "the likeness of the Great Stone Face had appeared upon the broad shoulders of a certain eminent statesman." When Webster delivered his *Eulogy of Adams and Jefferson* (1826) he said: "True eloquence does not consist in speech. . . . It must exist in the man, in the subject, in the occasion. . . . It comes, if it comes at all, like the outbreaking of a fountain from the earth, or the bursting forth of volcanic fires, with spontaneous, original, native force."

Webster's addresses may be classified as: (1) addresses made in Congress, such as his replies to Robert Y. Hayne and his *Seventh of March Speech*; (2) ceremonial addresses, such as the *Plymouth Oration* (1820) and the first *Bunker Hill Oration* (1825); and (3) addresses made before judges and juries, such as that in the *Dartmouth Case* (1818) and in the *White Murder Trial* (1830). He had a faculty for putting into glowing words the ideals that inspired men. The *Second Reply to Hayne* has the phrase "Liberty *and* Union, now and forever, one and inseparable." Other memorable statements are: "The people's government, made for the people, made by the people, and answerable to the people." "When my eyes shall be turned to behold for the last time the sun in heaven, may I not see him shining on the broken and dishonored fragments of a once glorious Union: on States dissevered, discordant, belligerent;

on a land rent with civil feuds, or drenched, it may be, in fraternal blood." "There is nothing so powerful as truth—and often nothing so strange." "Liberty exists in proportion to wholesome restraint."

Among books by and about Webster are S. L. Knapp, *Memoir of the Life of Daniel Webster* (1831); Edward Everett, ed., *The Works of Daniel Webster* (6 v. 1851); Charles Lamman, *Private Life of Daniel Webster* (1852); Fletcher Webster, ed., *The Private Correspondence of Daniel Webster* (2 v. 1857); H. C. Lodge, *Daniel Webster* (1883); C. H. Van Tyne, ed., *The Letters of Daniel Webster* (1902); J. W. McIntyre, ed., *The Writings and Speeches of Daniel Webster* (18 v. 1903); E. P. Wheeler, *Daniel Webster: The Expounder of the Constitution* (1905); F. A. Ogg, *Daniel Webster* (1916); R. L. Carey, *Daniel Webster as an Economist* (1929); S. H. Adams, *The Godlike Daniel* (1933); Claude M. Fuess, *Daniel Webster* (2 v. 1930); Gerald W. Johnson, *America's Silver Age* (1938); and Richard N. Current, *Daniel Webster and the Rise of National Conservatism* (1955). Webster appears as a character in Howard Breslin, *The Tamarack Tree* (1947).

Webster, H[arold] T[ucker] (1885–1952), cartoonist. Webster, born in West Virginia, studied art in Chicago and later worked for several newspapers, including the Denver *Republican*, the Chicago *Inter-Ocean*, the Cincinnati *Post*, and the New York *Tribune*. In 1925 he joined the New York *World*, but later appeared chiefly in the *Herald-Tribune*. The central figure in his cartoons, which in his last years were widely circulated, was often a middle-class professional man, the mild-mannered victim of modern civilization. The most noted was the "timid soul," CASPAR MILQUETOAST. Another series dealt with the vagaries of bridge players. "The Unseen Audience" poked fun at radio programs. Many collections of Webster's cartoons were made. The last, *The Best of H. T. Webster* (1953), was published after his death, with an introduction by Robert E. Sherwood and a biographical sketch by Philo Calhoun.

Webster, Henry Kitchell (1875–1932), teacher, novelist. A native of Illinois and a graduate of Hamilton College, Webster at first taught English, then began a long collaboration with SAMUEL MERVIN (1874–1936) on a series of novels, the best of which was a railroad story called *Calumet K* (1901). Among the Webster titles that became particular favorites were *The Whispering Man* (1908), *An American Family* (1918), and *Joseph Greer and His Daughter* (1922).

Webster, Jean (1876–1916), author of children's books. Webster was born Alice Jane Chandler Webster, in Fredonia, New York. The "Jean" was adopted in honor of Mark Twain's mother, who was Webster's aunt. Her father was the Webster who handled Twain's business affairs and was his partner as a publisher. Jean Webster, a kindly woman always deeply interested in the problems of down-trodden and handicapped people, wrote her well-known book *Daddy-Long-Legs* (1912) primarily to help the handicapped. *Dear Enemy* (1915) was a sequel. Among her other writings were two popular collections of stories for girls, *When Patty Went to College* (1903) and *Just Patty* (1911). *Daddy-Long-Legs* was successfully filmed in 1955.

Webster, Noah (1758–1843), lawyer, teacher, editor, author, lexicographer. Webster, a native of Connecticut, joined the Continental Army along with his father and was among those who marched against Burgoyne. After taking a degree at Yale (1778), he became a teacher at Hartford and Litchfield, taught in a singing school at Sharon, Connecticut, then in a classical school at Sharon, New York, and still later in a school in Philadelphia. He lectured and had a reputation as an orator of moderate ability. In the years following the Revolution, Webster's most intense interest was in the establishment of a strong central government. Admitted to the bar in 1781, he continued to teach and also practiced law. Irritated by the incompetence of the Confederation, he wrote pamphlets arguing for national union and for a stronger central establishment, among them *Sketches of American Policy* (1785). In 1787 he supported adoption of the Constitution. From 1793 to 1798 he worked as a journalist in supporting the policies of Washington and Adams. He edited a New York City daily called *The American Minerva* (founded December 9, 1793) and a semiweekly called *The Herald*, which consisted of articles selected from the daily.

By this time Webster's ruling passion had become what was later called Americanism. In his *Dissertation upon the English Language* (1789) he showed the exact direction his thought was taking: "As an independent nation, our honor requires us to have a system of our own, in language as well as government." His GRAMMATICAL INSTITUTE OF THE ENGLISH LANGUAGE demanded a purely American literature. This work appeared in three parts (1783, 1784, 1785). The first dealt with spelling, the second with grammar, the third with "the necessary rules of reading and speaking." The first part, when separately published, became the blue-back *Speller*, a best seller. Here, too, Webster demanded an American orthography. The *Speller* (see THE AMERICAN SPELLER was undoubtedly a great help in unifying the nation culturally and establishing a national language.

Meanwhile, Webster was hard at work on his monumental *Dictionary*. The multifariousness of his interests unquestionably assisted him when he began to define words of all sorts. He was a spelling reformer, a gardener, an experimental scientist. He wrote on literature, economics, and politics, edited Governor Winthrop's *Journal*, and wrote a revised version of the Bible. He served as committeeman of his Hartford school district and on the General Assembly of Connecticut and the General Court of Massachusetts; he was a councilman and alderman in New Haven and judge of the county court. In Amherst he was a selectman, president of the Amherst Academy, and helped found Amherst College. He was a director of the Hampshire Bible Society, a vice-president of the Hampshire and Hampden Agricultural Society, and a founder of the Connecticut Academy of Arts and Sciences. He took an active part in community affairs in New Haven, traveled widely in the United States, and studied in Paris, London, and Cambridge.

In 1825 he completed the work, and AN AMERICAN DICTIONARY OF THE ENGLISH LANGUAGE appeared in New Haven in 1828. He had an abridgment made a year later by JOSEPH EMERSON WORCESTER, who one day would produce a dictionary that became for a while a great rival of Webster's dictionary. In 1841 Webster brought out a revised form of the dictionary, and in 1843 the G & C. Merriam Co. took over all unsold copies and the right to produce further editions. From this firm have come many massive revisions and several abridgments of the dictionary, which has been acknowledged as supreme in its field.

Erwin C. Shoemaker wrote *Noah Webster, Pioneer of Learning* (1936). Harry R. Warfel, in addition to writing *Noah Webster, Schoolmaster to America* (1936), edited *Noah Webster's Poems* (1936), *Sketches of America* (1937), *Dissertations on the English Language* (1951), and *Letters* (1953). An exhaustive *Bibliography of the Writings of Noah Webster*, compiled by his granddaughter Emily Ford Skeel, was edited by Edwin H. Carpenter, Jr. (1958). See also WEBSTER'S DICTIONARY.

Webster, Pelatiah (1726–1795), political economist. A prolific pamphleteer of the Revolutionary period, Webster, who was born in Connecticut, wrote a series of letters on credit, free trade, and taxation for the Pennsylvania *Evening Post* (beginning October 5, 1776), later collected in *Political Essays* (1791). His *A Dissertation on the Political Union and Constitution of the Thirteen United States of North-America* (1783) advocated a stronger Federal union, and he supported adoption of the Constitution by Pennsylvania in *Remarks on the Address of Sixteen Members of the Assembly of Pennsylvania* (1787) and *The Weakness of Brutus Exposed* (1787). In *A Plea for the Poor Soldiers* (1790) Webster requested compensation for soldiers and creditors who had helped win the Revolution.

Webster's Dictionary. NOAH WEBSTER, after issuing a series of popular spelling books and a *Compendious Dictionary of the English Language* (1806), turned his attention to his *American Dictionary of the English Language* (1828), a great book in two volumes with definitions of 70,000 terms and emphasis on "the American way." It was not a financial success, since it sold at twenty dollars a copy. In 1840 Webster issued a corrected and enlarged second edition. When Webster died three years later, his book came onto the market, and the Merriam brothers, George and Charles, purchased the publishing rights. They took immediate steps to modernize the dictionary and make it accessible to a larger public. They engaged Chauncey A. Goodrich, Webster's son-in-law and literary heir, to revise the book. In 1847 they published a one-volume edition to sell at six dollars and won public favor immediately. The Massachusetts legislature proposed that a copy be placed in every schoolhouse in the state; New York State took similar action, and Congress made it a standard authority. In 1859 illustrations were made part of the text for the first time in any American dictionary, and lists of synonyms were introduced.

The *Unabridged Webster* was prepared under the editorship of NOAH PORTER, later president of Yale, and the 1847 book was withdrawn from the market. Yet half a century later this antiquated lexicon, no longer protected by copyright, was issued by some publishers as Webster's Dictionary, in which even the misprints were reproduced. In 1890 another complete revision was made, *Webster's International Dictionary*, with Porter again serving as editor. The next completely revised edition (1909) was called *Webster's New International Dictionary*, with William T. Harris, former U.S. Commissioner of Education, as editor; it contained twice as many entries as its immediate predecessor. In 1934 appeared *Webster's New International Dictionary, Second Edition*, under the editorship of William Allan Neilson, then president of Smith College, and Thomas A. Knott, a noted linguist. The *Third New International Dictionary* appeared in 1961 with Philip B. Gove as general editor. This edition generated considerable controversy chiefly because it accepted usage as the criterion for inclusion. The first edition of *Webster's Collegiate Dictionary* appeared in 1898.

Wechsberg, Joseph (1907–1983),   journalist. Wechsberg was born in Czechoslovakia; his lively career included working as a violinist on ocean liners, a lawyer, a soldier, and a writer. His first book, *Die Grosse Mauer* (1938), was a travel book. After coming to the United States to lecture and write for magazines (1938), he decided to remain and become a citizen. He won a Houghton Mifflin Literary Fellowship (1943), for which he wrote his first book in English, *Looking for a Bluebird* (1945). It was a collection of sketches that had appeared in *The New Yorker* and *Esquire*. During World War II he served in the army in Europe. *Homecoming* (1946) is the story of his return as an American soldier to Prague, his original home. The best of the sketches he wrote for American magazines after the war were published in *Sweet and Sour* (1948). *The Continental Touch* (1948), *The Self-Betrayed* (1955), and *Avalanche!* (1958) are novels. *Blue Trout and Black Truffles* (1953) recounts Wechsberg's culinary adventures, and *Melba and Her Times* (1961) tells of the famed operatic soprano Nellie Melba. Wechsberg's other writings include *The Best Things of Life* (1964), *The First Time Around* (1970), and books on the Strauss family (1973), Verdi (1974), Schubert (1978), East Germany (1964), Prague (1971), and Leningrad (1977).

Wecter, Dixon (1906–1950),   teacher, historian, biographer. Wecter was born in Houston, Texas, and studied at Baylor, Yale, and Oxford, returning to Yale for a Ph.D. He taught English at the University of Denver, the University of Colorado, and the University of California at Los Angeles; he taught American history at the University of Sydney; was appointed research fellow at the Huntington Library, and was made literary executor of the Mark Twain estate (1946). He was a writer and a scholar, with a keen eye for the significant facts. He wrote *The Saga of American Society* (1937), *Edmund Burke and His Kinsmen* (1939), *The Hero in America* (1941), *When Johnny Comes Marching Home* (1944), and *The Age of the Great Depression* (1948). He completed four projects relating to Mark Twain: editions of Twain's *Letters to Mrs. Fairbanks* (1949); *Report from Paradise*, a collection of Twain's "celestial" stories; *Love Letters of Mark Twain* (1950); and the opening volume of a projected definitive biography, *Sam Clemens of Hannibal* (posthumously pub., 1952).

Weed, Thurlow (1797–1882),   journalist, politician. Weed, born in Greene County, New York, was editor of the Rochester *Telegraph*, the *Anti-Masonic Enquirer*, the Albany *Evening Journal*, and the New York *Commercial Advertiser*. He was also a powerful leader of the Whig Party. He helped elect Presidents Adams, Harrison, Taylor, and Lincoln. His chief published writings are *Letters from Europe and the West Indies* (1886) and the posthumously issued autobiography *Life of Thurlow Weed* (1883–84).

Week on the Concord and Merrimack Rivers, A (1849),   a narrative by HENRY DAVID THOREAU. This book, Thoreau's first, describes a river voyage he made in August 1839 with his brother John. Each chapter covers a day of the week. Many passages of restrained but lyrical description made the book almost the equal of WALDEN, and there are bits of poetry, discourses on literature and history, and philosophical speculations.

Weems, Mason Locke (1759–1825),   biographer, bookseller, clergyman. "Parson" Weems, originator of the story of GEORGE WASHINGTON and the cherry tree, was an itinerant literary patriot and evangelist. Ordained a deacon in England, he served as a preacher in Maryland and then became a traveling book agent, distributing morally uplifting and entertaining books. His own writings were fervently moral: *Philanthropist* (1799), *True Patriot* (1802), *God's Revenge Against Murder* (1807), *The Drunkard's Looking Glass* (1812), and *The Bad Wife's Looking Glass* (1823). As a biographer Weems wrote with zest, imagination, and absolutely no regard for facts. His *History of the Life, Death, Virtues, and Exploits of George Washington* (1800) was vastly popular in its day; its original readers accepted it as semifictional, but later in the 19th century some of its exaggerations and inventions passed into the mythology of American childhood. Weems also wrote so-called biographies of Francis Marion (1809), Benjamin Franklin (1815), and William Penn (1822).

Weidman, Jerome (1913–1998),   novelist. Weidman, born in New York City and educated at the College of the City of New York and New York University, worked on the editorial staff of Simon and Schuster and served with the Office of War Information during World War II. His first novel, *I Can Get It for You Wholesale* (1937), depicted such repulsive Jewish characters that the publisher for a time ceased printing the book (1938). But the novel was so popular that Weidman wrote a sequel, *What's in It for Me?* (1938). His other novels are *I'll Never Go There Any More* (1941) and *The Price Is Right* (1949). *The Horse That Could Whistle "Dixie"* (1939) and *The Captain's Tiger* (1947) are short-story collections, and *Letter of Credit* (1940) describes a trip around the world. Weidman's wartime experiences furnished him with some of the material for *The Lights Around the Shore* (1943); *Too Early to Tell* (1946), a satire on war propaganda; and *The Third Angel* (1953). *After Your Daughter Iris* (1955), another novel, came *The Enemy Camp* (1958), a story of anti-Semitism, and *Before You Go* (1960). He also wrote Broadway plays, including *Fiorello!* (1959), which won a Pulitzer Prize, and *Tenderloin* (1961). His other novels include *The Sound of Bow Bells* (1962), *Word of Mouth* (1964), *Other People's Money* (1968), *The Center of the Action* (1969), *Fourth Street East* (1971), *Last*

Respects (1971), *Tiffany Street* (1974), *The Temple* (1975), and *A Family Fortune* (1978).

Weill, Kurt (1900–1950), composer. Born in Germany, Weill studied with Humperdinck and Busoni in Berlin. His *The Three-Penny Opera* (1927, New York production, 1933), with libretto by Bertolt Brecht, is a modern version of John Gay's *Beggar's Opera*. Brecht and Weill also collaborated on *The Rise and Fall of the City of Mahagonny* (1927). With his work denounced as decadent by the Nazis, Weill left Germany in 1933 and settled in the United States in 1935, becoming a U.S. citizen in 1943. His sophisticated musicals for the American theater include *Johnny Johnson* (1936); *Knickerbocker Holiday*, with MAXWELL ANDERSON (1938); *Lady in the Dark* (1941); and *One Touch of Venus*, with OGDEN NASH (1943). Among his serious later work for the theater was a musical play, *Street Scene*, from a 1929 play by ELMER RICE. LANGSTON HUGES wrote the lyrics for this 1947 production. *Down in the Valley* appeared in 1948, and his last production was *Lost in the Stars* (1949), with Maxwell Anderson from the book on South Africa by Alan Paton. Weill also wrote instrumental works and a cantata inspired by the flight made by Charles Lindbergh.

Weiman, Rita (1889–1954), dramatist, novelist, short-story writer. Weiman was born in Philadelphia, studied at the Art Students League in New York City, and worked for the New York *Herald* and the New York *Journal-American*, but her real love was the theater. *The Stage Door* (1920); *Footlights* (short stories, 1923); and *What Measure of Love?* (novel, 1935) reveal this interest. She also wrote another novel, *Playing the Game* (1910), and numerous plays.

Welch, James (1940–   ), poet, novelist. Welch, a Native American, was born in Montana, on his father's side a Blackfoot, on his mother's side Gros Ventre. He attended reservation schools and received a degree from the University of Montana. He has worked as a firefighter, prison official, and educational counselor and makes his home near Missoula. *Riding the Earthboy 40: Poems* (1971) is his first book. *Winter in the Blood* (1974) is a spare novel detailing the struggles of a young man trying to understand his heritage in the midst of the poverty and hardship of life on a reservation. *The Death of Jim Loney* (1979) contrasts the Midwestern urban experience with traditional Gros Ventre codes of living. *Fools Crow* (1986) is set in the Two Medicine territory of Montana in the 1870s, where the ancient customs of the Blackfeet clash with the westward rush of white settlement. Sylvester Yellow Calf, star basketball player, successful attorney, and candidate for Congress, is the protagonist of *The Indian Lawyer* (1990). *Killing Custer* (1994) is nonfiction prose. *The Heartsong of Charging Elk* (2000) centers on a young Oglala Sioux who witnessed the battle of Little Bighorn and then, to escape reservation life, became a member of the Buffalo Bill Cody Wild West Show troupe. When he becomes ill, Charging Elk is left behind in Marseille, France. He does not speak French or understand French culture, and both American and French official prove unable to help him; he must make his own new life.

Weld, Theodore Dwight (1803–1895), abolitionist. Weld, who was born in Connecticut, became a proselyte at Utica Academy, New York, of the revivalist Charles Grandison Finney and left school to become an itinerant preacher. By 1830 he had become an abolitionist, and he persuaded Arthur and Lewis Tappan to endow Lane Seminary in Cincinnati as an abolitionist school, with LYMAN BEECHER serving as president. There Weld converted Harriet and Henry Ward Beecher to abolitionism. He also helped found the American Anti-Slavery Society (1834), for which he trained missionaries and wrote numerous tracts: *The Bible Against Slavery* (1837); *The Power of Congress over the District of Columbia* (1837); a revision of *Emancipation in the West Indies* (1838); *American Slavery as It Is* (1839); and *Slavery and the Internal Slave Trade in the United States*, with J. A. Thome (1841). G. H. Barnes and D. L. Dumond edited *The Correspondence of Theodore Weld* (1934), and Benjamin P. Thomas wrote *Theodore Weld, Crusader for Freedom* (1950).

Weld, Thomas.   See BAY PSALM BOOK.

Welles, [George] Orson (1915–1985), actor, director, producer. Welles, a man of great originality and unpredictable temperament, was born in Wisconsin, began his career with the Gate Theater in Dublin, toured with Katharine Cornell, in 1934 directed the Woodstock Festival, and in 1935 played the lead in PANIC. His stage productions, especially after he founded the Mercury Theater, included an all-African American *Macbeth* and a provocative *Julius Caesar* performed in modern dress. Welles wrote and directed several radio and television programs, including one in the interest of hemispheric relations, *Hello, Americans* (1942–43). His radio dramatization of H. G. Wells' *War of the Worlds* (1938), done in the form of a newscast, convinced many listeners that Martians were invading North America and created a panic throughout the East. It is probably the most famous single radio broadcast ever made. He collaborated with Roger Hill in compiling *Everybody's Shakespeare* (1934) and the *Mercury Shakespeare* (1939). In Hollywood, Welles wrote, directed, and starred in *Citizen Kane* (1940), a story modeled on the life of William Randolph Hearst, and *The Magnificent Ambersons* (1941). He appeared as an actor in *Moby-Dick* (1956), *The Long Hot Summer* (1958), and *Compulsion* (1959), and as director and star of controversial productions of *Macbeth* (1948) and *Othello* (1955). In 1952 Welles staged *King Lear*, and due to an injury, played the part of Lear from a wheelchair.

Welles wrote the screenplay and directed *Touch of Evil* (1958). In later years he adapted several Shakespearean plays as *Chimes at Midnight/Falstaff* (1966) and acted in many films both in the United States and abroad. He was awarded a special Oscar in 1970 and received the American Film Institute Life Achievement Award in 1975.

Wellman, Paul I[selin] (1898–1966), newspaperman, writer. Wellman, born in Enid, Oklahoma, spent ten childhood years in West Africa with his family. After their return to the U.S., Wellman lived mainly in Utah and served in the army during World War I. For twenty-five years Wellman worked on the Wichita *Beacon*, the Wichita *Eagle*, and the Kansas City *Star*. He spent two years writing scripts in Hollywood and wrote four histories: *Death on the Prairie* (1934), *Death in the Desert* (1935), *The Trampling Herd* (1939), and *Glory, God and Gold* (1954). His historical fiction includes *Broncho Apache* (1936), *Jubal Troop* (1939), *Angel with Spurs* (1942), *The Bowl of Brass* (1944), *The Walls of Jericho* (1947), *The Chain* (1949), *The Iron Mistress* (1951), *The Comancheros* (1952), and *The Female* (1953). In 1950 his first two histories were issued in one volume as *Death on Horseback*. His later works include *Ride the Red Earth* (1958) and *Stuart Symington* (1959).

Wells, Carolyn (1869–1942), anthologist, author. Wells, born in New Jersey, was author of almost 170 books, ranging from detective stories to juvenile fiction, but she is known today by lovers of parody for her *A Nonsense Anthology* (1902). Her first book, *At the Sign of the Sphinx* (1896), was a collection of charades. Her other popular anthologies are *A Parody Anthology* (1904), *A Satire Anthology* (1905), and *A Whimsy Anthology* (1906). *The Patty Books* (1911) is one of a series of children's stories, and the *Fleming Stone Omnibus* (1933) is a good example of her work as a writer of detective stories. Wells was also a collector and editor of the writings of Walt Whitman and Edward Lear. Her autobiography is *The Rest of My Life* (1937).

Wells, [Grant] Carveth (1887–1957), lecturer, explorer, author. Wells was born in England and worked as a civil engineer in Canada and on the Malay Peninsula. After coming to America in 1918, he led expeditions to Uganda, Lapland, Panama, Mexico, Pakistan, the Caucasus, Kashmir, and Thailand for the American Museum of Natural History and the Geographic Society of Chicago. Except for his first book, *Field Engineer's Handbook* (1913), he wrote travel books, for example, *Six Years in the Malay Jungle* (1925), *In Coldest Africa* (1929), *Exploring the World* (1934), *The Road to Shalimar* (1951), and *Introducing Africa* (1953).

Wells, Helena (fl. 1798–1800), novelist. Little is known about Helena Wells. The frontispiece of her novel *The Stepmother* (1799) describes her as living in Charleston, South Carolina. She may also have spent some time as a governess in London. Her *Constantia Neville; or, The West Indian* was published in 1800.

Wells, William Vincent (1826–1876), sailor, government official, writer. Wells was born in Boston, spent his early years at sea, and was said to have been shipwrecked five times. He worked at various occupations in California—miner, farmer, engineer, businessman, newspaperman. In 1854 he visited Honduras, and in the following year returned as American consul. He sympathized with WILLIAM WALKER and wrote an account called *Walker's Expedition to Nicaragua* (1856). During the Civil War he was a clerk in the naval office in San Francisco. In 1856 he headed a propaganda agency for the Emperor Maximilian of Mexico. He based his *Explorations and Adventures in Honduras* (1857) on his personal diary and wrote a biography of his great-grandfather, Samuel Adams

(3 v. 1865). He also contributed to *Harper's Magazine* and other periodicals and acted as foreign correspondent for several newspapers while in Honduras.

Welty, Eudora [Alice] (1909–2001), short-story writer, novelist. Eudora Welty was born in Jackson, Mississippi, and educated at the Mississippi State College for Women and the University of Wisconsin. She studied advertising at the Columbia University School of Business in 1930–31 before returning to Jackson, her lifelong home. Mississippi is the characteristic locale for most of her fiction and provides the substance for it, though a handful of stories derive from trips to Europe during the 1950s. These are found in *The Bride of the Innisfallen* (1955). "Music from Spain" and some other stories reflect Welty's travel in the United States. After some work in journalism, a job doing publicity for the WPA during the Depression, and painting and photography as modes of aesthetic expression (see *Photographs*, 1989 and *Country Churchyards*, 2000), Welty devoted herself entirely to fiction. She began publishing in *The Southern Review* and in little magazines, among these *Manuscript*, in which her first story, "Death of a Traveling Salesman," appeared in 1936. Two early collections established Welty as a distinguished writer of short stories: *A Curtain of Green* (1941) and *The Wide Net* (1943). Three of these early stories received O. Henry Awards: "A Worn Path" (1941), "The Wide Net" (1942), and "Livvie [Is Back]" (1943). They were followed later by "The Burning" (1951) and "The Demonstrators" (1968). Altogether, Welty published four volumes of short stories.

Welty first tried longer forms in *The Robber Bridegroom* (1942), a mixed genre novella. *Delta Wedding* (1946), her first novel, was followed by *The Golden Apples* (1949), a complex cycle of interrelated stories novelistic in total effect, and by *The Ponder Heart* (1954), a comic novella. *Losing Battles* (1970), her longest novel, counterpoints memories and ongoing contemporary bustle in a conversational tour de force. In 1973 Welty won the Pulitzer Prize for her novella *The Optimist's Daughter* (1972), an inward flight of remembering and reinterpreting her parents' marriage by a young professional woman whose inquiring and detached stance may suggest Welty's own. Explicit autobiography is contained in *One Writer's Beginnings* (1984), comprising lectures Welty gave at Harvard in 1983. Modest but also illuminating as a critic of authors she admired and as a theorist, Welty published *The Eye of the Story: Selected Essays and Reviews* in 1977. Her views are elsewhere expressed in numerous interviews, inclusive volumes of these being *Conversations with Eudora Welty* (1984) and *More Conversations with Eudora Welty* (1996), ed. Peggy Whitman Prenshaw. Welty's honors and awards include the William Dean Howells Medal (1955), the Gold Medal for Fiction of the National Institute of Arts and Letters (1972), the National Medal for Literature (1980), Guggenheim Fellowships (1942, 1949), and honorary degrees from a dozen institutions including Smith, the University of the South at Sewanee, the University of Wisconsin, Mount Holyoke, Harvard, and Yale.

For Welty regional orientation is a vehicle and not an end, though her exact delineation of spatial and temporal space is a hallmark of her fiction. She was of the South—writing and in her dialogue listening with an insider's authority—and yet manifested a certain objective distance that was contingent, perhaps, on her first-generation status as a Southerner, her Midwestern father and Northern schooling, together with an omnivorous and eclectic reading experience to which she frequently testified. She was free of the burden of guilt and tortured remembrance that characterizes Faulkner's world, and touched only lightly on Gothic grotesquerie. African American characters are integral but secondary within her fictional landscape, though they are memorably and sympathetically rendered, for example, in "Powerhouse," "A Worn Path," and "Livvie." The antebellum South is excluded in favor of a contemporary vision encompassing the years between World War I and the present. A notable exception is "The Burning," and *The Robber Bridegroom* merges elements of Mississippi legend, folklore, and history pertaining to the Natchez Trace in the late 18th century with an adaptation of Grimm's fairy tales and of the classical myth of Cupid and Psyche.

Welty's fictions characteristically establish a public arena. Clusters of family members, neighbors, townspeople, or friends are brought together for a ceremonial event such as a wedding, funeral, or family reunion. *The Golden Apples* is the portrait of a town, Morgana, Mississippi, reminiscent of *Dubliners* or *Winesburg Ohio*. This drawing together of characters creates the opportunity for talk, and Welty was celebrated for her representation of Southern speech in its tones, patterns, cadences, and rhythms. Individual stories are developed as dramatic monologues. "Why I Live at the P.O.," "Shower of Gold," *The Ponder Heart*, and "Where Is the Voice Coming From?" are among the most remarkable. *Losing Battles* brilliantly orchestrates the talk of a throng of characters. In this publically oriented, communal aspect of her fiction, Welty was most obviously a comic realist. Her materials were drawn from the commonplace and the everyday, though in moments of hilarity she also exploited the farcical effects of Southwestern frontier humor. *The Robber Bridegroom, The Ponder Heart*, and part 2 of *Losing Battles* illustrate her exuberant sustained outbursts of fun and games.

Yet all things are double in Welty's complex vision, and the counterpart to the public arena is the solitary individual standing apart from the fray. Such figures may be commentators, scapegoats never fully accepted into the community, or persons whose inward vision isolates them in subjective attitudes of revulsion, reflection, or discovery. Peculiarities in individual point of view—feeble-mindedness, insanity, deafness, grief or despondency, extreme poverty—isolate others from the mainstream. When point of view is restricted to the inner vision of a central figure, the truths represented are those of the character and may take on the aspect of dream, fantasy, or hallucination. Welty employed a highly symbolic and poetic language and drew on such motifs as that of the journey, the plunge into water, or the flight of birds to repre-

sent these private visions. She most baffled and challenged her readers in such symbolist flights as those of Virgie Rainey at the end of "The Wanderers," that of the feeble-minded girl in "At the Landing," and that of Laura McKelva Hand in part III *of The Optimist's Daughter.*

The context of Southern Renaissance writers FAULKNER, ROBERT PENN WARREN, KATHERINE ANNE PORTER—highlights Welty's regionalist qualities and materials. Yet she is perhaps better placed beside authors she most admired: with Joyce, Virginia Woolf, and Elizabeth Bowen as regards technique, her rendering of subjective experience; and with both Joyce and Yeats in her poetic and visionary moments. Like Jane Austen, Welty invoked a comic, ironic voice; sustained narrative through self-revealing dialogue; and treated domestic bonds and daily experiences as themes. Juxtaposition with Chekov illuminates Welty's treatment of the short story both as a lyrical, liquid medium and as the fixing of the crucial moment. Her treatment of place as the revelation and exposition of character illustrates her fertile bond with WILLA CATHER. Welty was highly eclectic and yet altogether independent, an authentic, original voice and a superb stylist. It is for the qualities of nuanced voice, brilliant vital style, revealing dialogue and, as regards attitude, humane celebration of humble, even grotesque, characters that she will be most highly regarded, and also for her distinguishing merger of visionary experience and exuberant laughter. *The Collected Stories of Eudora Welty* appeared in 1980. Studies include *Eudora Welty: Critical Essays* (1979), ed. Peggy Whitman Prenshaw; *Understanding Eudora Welty* (1999) by Michael Kreyling; and Ruth Vande Kieft's *Eudora Welty* (1987), a critical biography.

JEAN FRANTZ BLACKALL

Wemyss, Francis Courtney (1797–1859), actor, stage manager, author. Wemyss, born in England, was a capable comedian who became a member of a Philadelphia stock company in 1822. He recorded his memories in *Twenty-Six Years of the Life of an Actor and Manager* (2 v. 1847, repr. as *A Theatrical Biography*, 1848) and wrote *A Chronology of the American Stage, from 1752 to 1852* (1852).

Wendell, Barrett (1855–1921), teacher, scholar, writer. Wendell, born in Boston, was educated at Harvard and taught there from 1880 to 1917. He gave the first course at Harvard in American literature. His first published books were two novels. He then went on to write scholarly books: *Cotton Mather, The Puritan Priest* (1891); *William Shakespeare* (1894); and *The Temper of the 17th Century in English Literature* (1894). He also wrote a textbook, *English Composition* (1891); essays, *Stelligeri and Other Essays Concerning America* (1893); and three short plays, *Raleigh in Guiana, Rosamund*, and *A Christmas Masque* (1902). His *The Traditions of European Literature* (1920) was based on a comparative literature course he gave at Harvard. His principal scholarly work was *A Literary History of America* (1900).

Wept of Wish-ton-Wish, The (1829), a novel by JAMES FENIMORE COOPER. This narrative is at once a story of

King Philip's War and an unfriendly study of Puritan theocracy in a small Connecticut community. The villain is the Rev. Meek Wolfe, who preaches the murder of Indian women and children as a religious duty and pries into everyone's private affairs. The hero is Conanchet, a "noble savage" of the Narragansett tribe. KING PHILIP of the Wampanoags is one of the chief characters, but the action centers around Conanchet, who for a while is captured by the whites and becomes a member of the Heathcote family. He later kidnaps the young daughter of the family. The daughter is the wept of the title. Wish-ton-Wish is the valley where the Heathcotes live. Later, in the course of the war, the Heathcotes are captured by the Indians, and Conanchet reveals to them that he has married their daughter. She has in the meantime become entirely Indian in viewpoint. James Grossman notes in his life of Cooper (1949) that Cooper makes both Conanchet and the Puritans derive their speech from the same model, the King James Bible. A short play based on the novel was performed in 1851.

Werner, M[orris] R[obert] (1897–1981), journalist. Morris wrote several books critical of well-known people and describing instances of political corruption, including *Barnum* (1923), *Brigham Young* (1925), *Tammany Hall* (1928), and *Teapot Dome* (1959). His memoir of World War I experiences is called *"Orderly!"* (1930).

Wescott, Glenway (1901–1989), poet, novelist. Wescott, born in Wisconsin, was educated at the University of Chicago. His first book, *The Bitterns* (1920), is a volume of poems, and for a time Wescott wrote reviews for *Poetry*. His first novel, *The Apple of the Eye* (1924), was originally published serially in the *Dial*. Although he lived abroad for many years, he turned to his native state for material and mood in *Goodbye Wisconsin* (1928), a collection of short stories. THE GRANDMOTHERS (1927), his best-known novel, and *The Babe's Bed* (1930) are also set in Wisconsin. *A Calendar of Saints for Unbelievers* and *Fear and Trembling* were published in 1932. *The Pilgrim Hawk* (1940) and *Apartment in Athens* (1945) are novels with European settings. *Images of Truth: Remembrances and Criticism* (1962) is a collection of essays.

West, Anthony [Panther] (1914–1987), novelist, critic. West, the son of Rebecca West and H. G. Wells, moved from England to the U.S., where he wrote *Heritage* (1955), a novel that explores the mind of a growing boy who, like West, is the son of two well-known people who are not married to each other. *The Trend Is Up* (1960) is a novel about how a nineteen-year-old ruthlessly reaches his goal of becoming a millionaire before the age of thirty. He also wrote a collection of semiautobiographical stories, *David Rees, Among Others* (1970). *Principles and Persuasions* (1957) is a collection of literary essays. His mother's treatment of him during his childhood, at a time when the existence of illegitimate offspring was usually concealed, led to lifelong bitterness and in 1984 to his writing *H. G. Wells: Aspects of a Life*, in which West attacks his mother and defends his father.

West, Benjamin (1730–1813), mathematician, astronomer, almanac publisher. Entirely self-taught, the Massachusetts-born West became learned enough in science to be elected a fellow of the American Academy of Arts and Sciences. In 1788 he became professor of mathematics and astronomy at Rhode Island College (later Brown University). He wrote *An Account of the Observation of Venus Upon the Sun the Third Day of June 1769* and reported an eclipse of the sun in 1781. He began issuing almanacs in 1763, using for some of them the pen name Isaac Bickerstaff. This was probably a reference to Jonathan Swift's fictitious astrologer and almanac maker of the same name. West's first issue was called simply *An Almanack*. In 1765 he issued *The New-England Almanack*, which continued to appear until 1781. *Bickerstaff's Boston Almanac* appeared in 1768, 1779, and 1783–93, and was the first illustrated almanac in Massachusetts. West also issued *The North-American Calendar, or Rhode Island Almanac* (1781–87) and *The Rhode Island Almanac* (1804–06).

West, Dorothy (1907–1998), novelist, short story writer. Born in Boston, she entered the elite Girls' Latin School at the age of ten and published her first writing in *The Boston Post* at 14. Her family was wealthy; her slave-born father was known as Boston's Black Banana King. West attended Boston University and Columbia, but encouraged by the success of her short story writing (at 17 she had tied with Zora Neale Hurston for a second place award), she moved to New York where she was given the nickname "The Kid" by Langston Hughes and other writers of the Harlem Renaissance. In 1932 she traveled to the Soviet Union with Hughes and others to make a film about American racism. It never was made, but she stayed for a year, returning only when her father died. She founded two literary magazines intended to feature young black writers: *Challenge* (1934) and *New Challenge* (1937). Richard Wright was her associate editor on the second venture. Though she worked as a Harlem welfare investigator and joined the Federal Writers Project, she continually wrote, submitting short pieces to newspapers, including *The New York Daily News*. In 1947 she moved to her family's summer cottage in Oak Bluffs on the island of Martha's Vineyard, Massachusetts. Her first novel *The Living Is Easy* appeared in 1948. Centered on a woman reminiscent of West's own strong-willed, light-skinned mother, the novel satirizes wealthy black Bostonians. Jackie Kennedy Onassis, the president's widow who also had a Vineyard home, visited West regularly, after 1992, to help her with the novel of Vineyard life she had been writing for years. Kennedy Onassis died shortly before *The Wedding* (1995) was published; the novel is dedicated to her memory. Set in Oak Bluffs, it concerns the hesitancies of beautiful, blonde Shelby Coles, a black woman engaged to a white musician, who finally decides that skin color is "a false distinction," but love is not. Oprah Winfrey used the novel as the basis for a television miniseries. A story collection *The Richer, The Poorer* also appeared in 1995.

West, Jessamyn (1902–1984), novelist, short-story writer. West, born in Indiana, lived in California after age six, and was educated at Whittier College and the University of California. She began to write while confined to a sanatorium with tuberculosis. Her first book, *The Friendly Persuasion*, was published in 1945 and was warmly praised by reviewers. It is a series of sketches of the life of a Quaker family in southern Indiana during the Civil War. Her subsequent books include *The Witch Diggers* (1951), a novel about life on an Indiana poor farm at the turn of the century; *Cress Delehanty* (1953), sketches about an adolescent girl; a collection of short stories, *Love, Death and the Ladies' Drill Team* (1959); and a novel set in Southern California, *South of the Angels* (1960). Almost without exception, they have also been praised. She is the author of *Mirror for the Sky* (1948), a script for an opera on the life of Audubon; *To See the Dream* (1957), an account of her experiences in Hollywood during the filming of *The Friendly Persuasion* (1956); and *Love Is Not What You Think* (1959). *Hide and Seek* (1973) details her childhood and youth; *The Woman Said Yes* (1976) describes West's bout with tuberculosis and the illness and suicide of her sister, material she had used in an earlier novel, *A Matter of Time* (1966). *The Secret Look* (1974) is a poetry collection, and *Double Discovery* (1980) is a travel diary. *Collected Stories* appeared in 1987.

West, Mae (1893?–1980), playwright, songwriter, actress. Born in Brooklyn and privately educated, West first appeared with a Brooklyn stock company about 1901; by 1907 she was performing on the vaudeville circuit in partnership with Frank Wallace, the man she married in 1911 and divorced after more than thirty years. She appeared on Broadway as a singer and acrobatic dancer in musical revues beginning in 1911. Soon she was writing her own material, beginning with *Sex* (1926), in which she played a prostitute. For that performance West was cited for "corrupting the morals of youth," sentenced to eight days in jail, and became nationally known. Her 1928 portrayal of the title character of *Diamond Lil* inaugurated a series of stage and screen productions she both wrote and starred in. Other plays include *The Pleasure Man* (1928), *The Constant Sinner* (1931), and *Catherine Was Great* (1944). Her first movie *Night After Night* (1932) had her depicting one of a series of women seemingly amused with their lives of easy sexuality. She wrote the screenplays for some of her most memorable performances: *She Done Him Wrong* (1933), an adaptation of *Diamond Lil*; *Klondike Annie* (1935); and with W. C. Fields, *My Little Chickadee* (1940). During World War II, Allied soldiers dubbed their inflatable life jackets "Mae Wests" in tribute to her magnificent proportions. Stage productions during and after the war often featured her surrounded by scantily-clad muscular young men. Her postwar film roles, including *Myra Breckenridge* (1970) and *Sextette* (1979) exploited her reputation as a sex symbol. Her autobiography is called *Goodness Had Nothing to Do with It* (1929), after one of her famous movie lines, a response to the observation "Goodness, what beautiful diamonds!" *The Fabulous Mae West* (1955) is an album of West singing some of her most popular songs. Claudia Shear's play *Dirty Blonde* (1999) is a tribute to West.

West, Nathanael [pen name of **Nathan Wallenstein Weinstein**] (1904–1940), novelist. *The Complete Works*

of *Nathaneal West* was published in 1957 with an introduction by Alan Ross. It contains just four short novels, yet it represents the work of a highly praised figure in American fiction. West's vision of the horror and emptiness of modern life is established most effectively in his two best works, MISS LONELYHEARTS (1933) and THE DAY OF THE LOCUST (1939). The former is about a newspaper writer who conducts an agony column and gradually succumbs to the real agony that underlies the absurd letters he receives daily. *The Day of the Locust* is about Hollywood as West saw it: a disturbingly surrealistic vision culminating in a riot at a movie premiere. Born in New York City, West had been living in Hollywood writing movie scripts for three years when he began to write his last novel. One of his films was *Advice to the Lovelorn*, an adaptation of *Miss Lonelyhearts*. In 1940, West and his wife, Eileen Mckenney, were killed in an automobile accident in California.

West, Paul (1930–), novelist, poet, essayist. West, educated at Oxford and Columbia, moved to the United States from his native England, becoming a U.S. citizen in 1971. His first three novels—*A Quality of Mercy* (1961), *Tenement of Clay* (1965), and *Alley Jaggers* (1966)—were published in London. Insisting on the primacy of imagination, West asserts that the realistic novel cannot adequately delineate contemporary experience. His other novels include *I'm Expecting to Live Quite Soon* (1970), *Caliban's Filibuster* (1971), *Bela Lugosi's White Christmas* (1972), *The Very Rich Hours of Count von Stauffenberg* (1980), and *Rat Man of Paris* (1986). West's fiction based on history includes war stories such as *Love's Mansion* (1992), set in Britain during World War I, and *Tent of Orange Mist* (1995), about the Sino-Japanese War. *Women of White Chapel and Jack the Ripper* (1992), on the famous serial killer, *Sporting with Amaryllis* (1996), centering on the poet John Milton, and *OK: the Corral, the Earps and Doc Holliday* (2000) also are based on real people and events. His poetry is collected in such volumes as *The Spellbound Horses* (1960) and *The Snow Leopard* (1965). He has also published essay collections and literary criticism.

Westcott, E[dward] N[oyes] (1846–1898), novelist. Westcott, born in Syracuse, New York, was an obscure New York banker, for a time secretary of the Syracuse Water Commission, and an amateur musician. When forced by ill health to retire from business, he began writing, chiefly for his own amusement, a humorous novel about a small-town banker named David Harum. By the time DAVID HARUM: A STORY OF AMERICAN LIFE finally appeared, in 1898, its author had died. Within a few months his novel become a great national favorite. It was later filmed with Will Rogers in the title role. A posthumously published story, *The Teller* (1901), is accompanied by some of Westcott's letters and a brief biographical sketch.

Western Messenger. A magazine issued from June 1835 to April 1841 in Cincinnati by a group of Unitarian ministers. R. L. Rusk called it "perhaps the highest point in the literary achievement of early western magazines," and it served as a western outlet for transcendentalists. Among its contributors were W. H. Channing, Elizabeth Peabody, Margaret Fuller, Jones Very, Francis Parkman, and Emerson.

Westerns.   A genre of American popular fiction. Early Westerns were often represented as true narratives of adventure in the West. Often they were built around historical characters, frontiersmen, Indian scouts, and the like. As the West was opened to cattle ranchers in the years after the Civil War, the cowboy became a frequent hero, and much was written about the Indian wars of the latter part of the 19th century.

Westerns were first popular in DIME NOVELS written, often under pseudonyms, by E. Z. C. JUDSON, PRENTISS INGRAHAM, EDWARD S. ELLIS, GEORGE CHARLES JENKS, EDWARD L. WHEELER, and others. At the turn of the century, OWEN WISTER, in his enormously popular THE VIRGINIAN (1902), established the pattern for much that followed, and FREDERIC REMINGTON, remembered later primarily as a painter and sculptor, also wrote fiction. EMERSON HOUGH was another Western writer of the same period. In the 20th century, in place of the dime novel the Western pulp magazine became for many years a major outlet for this kind of formula fiction. Among these—along with their dates of inception—were *Smith's Magazine* (1905), *Western Story Magazine* (1919), *Ranch Romances* (1924), *Wild West Weekly* (1927), *Ten Cent Story Western Magazine* (1932), *Ace-High Western Stories* (1933), *Star Western* (1943), and *Zane Grey's Western Magazine* (1947). Most writers in the first half of the century published in these magazines, often, like the dime novelists, under various pseudonyms, but many had huge sales from books as well. With *Riders of the Purple Sage* (1912) and subsequent books, ZANE GREY became one of the most prolific and widely read of all time. Others born before 1900 include WILLIAM MACLEOD RAINE; B. M. BOWER, who hid her gender behind initials; CLARENCE E. MULFORD, creator of Hopalong Cassidy; FREDERICK FAUST ("Max Brand"); and ERNEST HAYCOX. The tradition has continued in the work of such writers as HENRY W. ALLEN, OAKLEY HALL, and LOUIS L'AMOUR.

The Western as a genre has been often parodied, but its weaknesses have also been transcended, sometimes in the work of writers named above and sometimes in books by writers not primarily identified with the genre. Major examples among the latter include Walter van Tilburg Clark, THE OXBOW INCIDENT (1940); A. B. Guthrie, Jr., THE BIG SKY (1947) and THE WAY WEST (1949); and LARRY MCMURTRY, *Lonesome Dove* (1985). Studies include William W. Savage, Jr., *The Cowboy Hero* (1979), and John R. Milton, *The Novel of the American West* (1980).

West-Running Brook (1928),   by ROBERT FROST. This fifth book of Frost's poems is divided into six sections, the poem "West-Running Brook" standing alone as one of the sections.

Westward Ho! (1832),   a novel by J. K. PAULDING. This early best seller combines an account of pioneering in western Virginia and Kentucky with a love story.

Wetherald, [Agnes] Ethelwyn (1857–1940),   poet, periodical writer. Wetherald, born in Ontario, wrote for the

Toronto *Daily Globe* then went to Philadelphia to work for the *Ladies' Home Journal*. Her *Lyrics and Sonnets* appeared in 1931; most noteworthy are her bird songs and her poems for children, among them *The Last Robin* (1907) and *Tree Top Morning* (1921).

Wetherell, Elizabeth.   Pen name of SUSAN BOGERT WARNER.

Wetjen, Albert Richard (1900–1948),   sailor, newspaperman, writer. Wetjen, born in England, went to sea at age thirteen, fought in the British army during World War I, was twice shipwrecked, and went to Canada in 1920. In 1921 he went to the United States to live, although he continued to travel the world. He worked for Oregon newspapers and then began writing fiction. His experiences gave him material for many good stories of adventure. These were collected in *Captains All* (1924), *Way for a Sailor* (1928), *Beyond Justice* (1936), *In the Wake of the Shark* (1939), and *Outland Tales* (1940). He was cofounder and editor of *The Outlander* magazine (1933).

Wexley, John (1907–1985),   playwright. Wexley, born in New York City, treated social problems on the stage. His best-known play is *The Last Mile* (1930), a plea for prison reform. His other plays include *Steel* (1931); *They Shall Not Die*, built around the Scottsboro Trial (1934); and *Running Dogs* (1938). He also wrote for the movies. One of his movie scripts is *The Judgment of Julius and Ethel Rosenberg* (1955).

Whalen, Philip (1923–   ),   poet. Born in Oregon, Whalen lived for a time in Japan and was associated with Zen Buddhism and the Beats. His poetry, often printed with unusual typographical and visual effects, has been published in *Self-Portrait from Another Direction* (1959), *Memoirs of an Inter-Glacial Age* (1960), *Like I Say* (1960), *Monday in the Evening* (1964), *Every Day* (1965), *Highgrade* (1966), *On Bear's Head* (1969), *The Kindness of Strangers* (1976), *Enough Said* (1980), and *Heavy Breathing* (1983). *You Didn't Even Try* (1966) and *Speech for a Brazen Head* (1972) are novels.

Wharton, Edith [Newbold Jones] (1862–1937),   novelist, short-story writer, memoirist. Edith Newbold Jones was born in a house near Washington Square, in New York City, to a socially prominent family. She was early taken abroad and was educated at home by governesses. As a child she tried her hand at poetry, and published poems anonymously in the *Atlantic Monthly* in 1880. After her marriage to Edward Wharton she divided her time between foreign travel and her Newport, Rhode Island, home. Accustomed to the artistic glories of Europe, Edith Wharton despaired of improving the ugly exterior of the house, called Land's End, but she and the architect Ogden Codman decided to decorate the interior to express the owners' personalities, a new idea at the time. Their subsequent book, *The Decoration of Houses* (1897), sold widely. Bored with her stuffy social and cultural milieu and troubled by her husband's mental and physical ill health, Wharton had already turned to unfashionable intellectual pursuits. Now—with her family's full disapproval—she found herself launched on a career of distinguished prose writing.

She moved to Lenox, Massachusetts; finding happiness there in her work and her many literary friendships. In 1899 she published a volume of short stories, *The Greater Inclination*, followed by *The Touchstone* (1900), a novelette reflecting her admiration for Henry James and his interest in ethical values. Then came THE VALLEY OF DECISION (1902), a panoramic novel set in 18th-century Italy, and *Sanctuary* (1903). A keen and critical observer of the New York society she knew so well, Wharton found her chief literary problem in extracting human significance from this seemingly shallow soil. Out of this social milieu came Lily Bart, the heroine of her first major work, THE HOUSE OF MIRTH (1905), which dramatizes the dangers of departing from a set social pattern.

In 1907 Wharton moved to France. After writing *Madame de Treymes* and *The Fruit of the Tree* (both 1907) she turned to the "derelict mountain villages of New England" in her least typical but most single-mindedly tragic novel, ETHAN FROME (1911). Although contemporary sentimentalists disliked her grim picture of inarticulate farm people, *Ethan Frome* remains her most widely known work and a classic of its kind. From New England she turned to France with *The Reef* (1912). Set in a chateau, this is a study of the psychological effects of sexual promiscuity. Then she returned for setting to New York in THE CUSTOM OF THE COUNTRY (1913), a satire on the social climbing of the newly rich. Meanwhile, her longstanding difficulties with her marriage, largely the result of her husband's mental problems, culminated in divorce in 1913.

During World War I she remained in Paris, where her extensive relief work won her a cross of the Legion of Honor. She drew on her wartime experiences in two novels, *The Marne* (1918) and *A Son at the Front* (1923). Meantime she had returned to a simple New England scene in *Summer* (1917). In 1920 appeared THE AGE OF INNOCENCE, perhaps her best combination of the novel of manners and the ethical-psychological novel. This won a Pulitzer Prize. *The Glimpses of the Moon* (1922) is an international novel of manners. New York City in the 1840s to 1870s is depicted in the four novelettes collected in OLD NEW YORK (1924): *False Dawn*, THE OLD MAID, *The Spark*, and *New Year's Day*. The best of these is *The Old Maid*, dramatized by ZOE AKINS in 1935 and awarded a Pulitzer Prize. Family problems are treated in *The Mother's Recompense* (1925), *Twilight Sleep* (1927), and *The Children* (1928). *Hudson River Bracketed* (1929), another major work, and *The Gods Arrive* (1932), its sequel, contrast the cultural values of the Midwest, New York, England, and the Continent.

After *The Great Inclination*, Wharton continued to write short stories, collecting them regularly in volumes that include *Crucial Instances* (1901); *The Descent of Man* (1904), containing some of her most effective early work; *The Hermit and the Wild Woman* (1908); *Tales of Men and Ghosts* (1910); XINGU (1916); *Here and Beyond* (1926); *Certain People* (1930); *Human Nature* (1933); *The World Over* (1936), with her masterly "Roman Fever"; and *Ghosts* (1937). In these she displayed a special talent for social satire and comedy, which she varied occasionally with some finely drawn ghost tales.

In *The Writing of Fiction* (1925) Wharton acknowledged her debt to her great friend and literary mentor, Henry James. Like him, she took complex moral values to be the only proper background for fiction. Her psychological probings and keen sense of social gradations are reminiscent of James, though Wharton's writing is always more direct and often more conventional. In her evocative, urbane autobiography, *A Backward Glance* (1934), she attempted to analyze her creative processes.

The House of Mirth, The Reef, The Custom of the Country, and *The Age of Innocence* have been edited in one volume by R. W. B. Lewis (1988). Wayne Andrews has edited *Best Short Stories of Edith Wharton* (1958), and R. W. B. Lewis edited *The Collected Short Stories of Edith Wharton* in two volumes (1968). With Nancy Lewis he also edited *The Letters of Edith Wharton* (1988). A full biography is Lewis's *Edith Wharton* (1975). Cynthia Griffin Wolff's *A Feast of Words: The Triumph of Edith Wharton* (1977) is also excellent. Louis Auchincloss has written a brief life illustrated with well-chosen pictures in *Edith Wharton: A Woman in Her Time* (1971).

Wharton, William [pseudonym] (1925–   ), novelist. Born in Philadelphia and trained as a painter at the University of California, Los Angeles, Wharton depicts fantasy as an integral part of everyday life. His novels are written in the first person and the present tense. The title character of *Birdy* (1979) studies pigeons and canaries because he longs to fly. *Dad* (1981) deals with three male generations. *A Midnight Clear* (1982) is set in World War II. *Scumbler* (1984) concerns an American painter in Paris. *Pride* (1985) is set in the Depression. Wharton straddles the line between autobiography and fiction in such books as *Last Loves* (1991), *Wrongful Deaths* (1994) and *Houseboat on the Seine* (1996). *Ever After: A Father's True Story* (1995) describes the death of his daughter and her family in an Oregon automobile crash. Wharton also illustrated his novel *Frankie Furbo* (1989).

What Is Man? (1906),   a dialogue by MARK TWAIN. Written in 1898 and published anonymously, this dialogue between an Old Man and a Young Man embodies Twain's philosophy, a bleakly mechanistic determinism. Free will, genius, virtue, and vice are all dismissed as delusions of the human mind, which is the passive subject of inexorable natural laws. These ideas sprang in part from the intense personal despair and skepticism of Twain's old age and represent his attempt to free "the damned human race" from moral responsibility. In THE MYSTERIOUS STRANGER (1898) these ideas are transformed into literature far superior to *What Is Man?*

What Maisie Knew (1897),   a novel by HENRY JAMES. Always interested in the "small expanding consciousness" of a child, James deals in this novel with twelve-year-old Maisie Farange, whose parents were divorced when she was six; both subsequently remarried. Because custody of the child had been awarded to each of the parents for alternating periods of six months, Maisie presently learns that her stepfather and her stepmother are having an adulterous affair, just as she had become aware of her own parents' earlier infidelities. Instead of corrupting Maisie, this knowledge enables her to make the decision, based on psychological rather than moral maturity, to live with her old governess, Mrs. Wix, instead of with either of her parents.

What Makes Sammy Run? (1941), a novel by BUDD SCHULBERG. The protagonist, Sammy Glick, is a tough New York City youth who works his way into a position of power in the movie industry, where his harshness and crude manners are not out of place.

What Price Glory?, a pacifistic play by MAXWELL ANDERSON and LAURENCE STALLINGS produced in 1924 and published in 1926. It takes place in a World War I headquarters, where Captain Flagg and First Sergeant Quirt, professional soldiers, quarrel over a French girl. Their rivalry is interrupted by orders for the company to return to the front.

What's the Matter with Kansas? (Emporia *Gazette*, August 15, 1896), an editorial by WILLIAM ALLEN WHITE. An ardent but liberal Republican, White was outraged in the summer of 1896 by the arguments being presented by followers of WILLIAM JENNINGS BRYAN in the campaign for the presidency against WILLIAM MCKINLEY, and he composed his editorial as a reply. He answered the question of his title in a heavily ironic portrait of his state, condemning his fellow Kansans for their short-sighted lust for "money power." The editorial was reprinted all over the country and helped McKinley win, although Kansas went for Bryan.

What Was It? A Mystery (*Harper's Magazine*, March 1859), a short story by FITZ-JAMES O'BRIEN. This was perhaps O'Brien's most sensational tale. The setting is a boarding house in which the presence of an invisible but horrible something is felt. The story is included in O'Brien's *Poems and Stories* (1881).

Wheatley, Phillis (1753–1784), slave, first black American woman poet. Born in what is now Gambia, stolen from her home, and sold into slavery at age eight, Wheatley was bought by the Boston family of John Wheatley. There she served as personal maid to Susanna Wheatley, who taught her English and many classics of Western literature. Referred to as the "sable muse," Wheatley shocked the literary world with the publication of her *Poems on Various Subjects, Religious and Moral* (London 1773). Wheatley's works include numerous elegies, topical poems addressed to contemporary religious and political luminaries, and conventional odes in the neoclassical manner. Her poetry, long considered more as an issue for speculation on the intellectual capacity of blacks and on the sociology of literary production, has become central to Afro-American literary studies since the late 1960s. While Wheatley's life and work have been attacked by many critics who viewed her as a prime example of a black poet who absorbed the beliefs and values of her white owners and distanced herself from the oppression of slaves in colonial America, scholars in the 1980s began rejecting this reductive view in favor of a renewed interest in and appreciation of her work in aesthetic and racial/political terms. Critics have demonstrated that rather than being a competent but uninteresting imitator of Alexander Pope, as many early detractors believed, Wheatley in her verse style was largely innovative and not imitative of any isolable source. More politically interested critics have also argued for the boldness and originality of Wheatley's criticisms of slavery and oppression in many forms.

Wheatley died in relative poverty and obscurity, never having obtained a publisher for a second collection of her poems. Valuable primary and secondary sources include William H. Robinson's *Critical Essays on Phillis Wheatley* (1982), and John C. Shield's *The Collected Works of Phillis Wheatley* (1988).

RUSSELL J. REISING

Wheeler, Edward L. (fl. late 19th century), dime novelist. Little is known of Wheeler except that he wrote a great many dime novels and created three memorable characters, DEADWOOD DICK, Hurricane Nell, and CALAMITY JANE. Deadwood Dick was an exemplar of the American self-made man; he was married several times but fruitlessly courted Calamity Jane, who first appeared in stories about him. Hurricane Nell, a Wild West Amazon, appeared simultaneously with Deadwood Dick. Some of Wheeler's titles are *Nobby Dick of Nevada* (1880), *Sierra Sam* (1882), *Deadwood Dick in Leadville* (1885), *Corduroy Charlie* (1885), and *Colorado Charlie's Detective Dash* (1890).

Wheeler, Kate [Mahasi Sasana Yeiktha] (1955–), novelist, short-story writer. Born in Tulsa, Oklahoma and educated at Rice and Stanford, Wheeler was ordained a Buddhist nun in Rangoon, Burma in 1988. Her first story collection, *Not Where I Started From* (1993), earned her four major prizes and gained enthusiastic notice. The stories often center on American-born women traveling in search of spiritual meaning. *When Mountains Walked* (2000), her first novel, concerns a woman who has always felt herself to be an outsider trying to adjust to a new marriage and life in an isolated Peruvian village. Wheeler has translated the poetry of Spanish writer Enrique Marques and edited a collection of Buddhist writings.

Wheeler, Post (1869–1957), diplomat, editor, explorer, poet, memoirist. Wheeler, born in Oswego, New York, first was a newspaper reporter and then began serving in U.S. embassies abroad. He was the husband of the Kentucky novelist Hallie Erminie Rives. Among his books are *Love-in-a-Mist*, poems (1901); *Russian Wonder Tales* (1910); *Albanian Wonder Tales* (1936); *The Golden Legend of Ethiopia* (1936); *India Against the Storm* (1944); *Hawaiian Wonder Tales* (1946); and *The Sacred Scriptures of the Sun-Folk* (1948). In collaboration with his wife he wrote *Dome of Many-Colored Glass* (1955).

Wheelock, Eleazar (1711–1779), clergyman, educator. Wheelock founded a school for Indians in Lebanon, New Hampshire, in 1754; he described it in *Plain and Faithful Narrative of the . . . Indian Charity-School at Lebanon*. The school was merged into Dartmouth College, and Wheelock became the first president of the new institution (1769–1779).

Wheelock, John Hall (1886–1978), poet. Born in Far Rockaway, New York, and educated at Harvard, Göttingen, and Berlin, Wheelock became associated with Charles Scribner's Sons in 1911, serving as editor, director, and treasurer of the publishing house. With his friend and Harvard classmate VAN WYCK BROOKS, he published his first book, *Verses of Two Undergraduates* (1905). His other books of poetry are *The Human Fantasy* (1911), *The Beloved Adventure* (1912), *Love and Liberation* (1913), *Dust and Light* (1919), *The Black Pan-*

ther (1922), and *The Bright Doom* (1927). His *Collected Poems* (1936) won the Golden Rose Award of the New England Poetry Society (1937). His *Poems Old and New* appeared in 1956, and *The Gardener and Other Poems* in 1961. Wheelock's prose works include *Alan Seeger: Poet of the Foreign Legion* (1918); *A Bibliography of Theodore Roosevelt* (1920); *Editor to Author* (1950), a selection of the letters of Maxwell E. Perkins, and *Poets of Today* (v. 1–8, 1954–61).

Wheelwright, John (c. 1592–1679),   clergyman, religious writer. Wheelwright emigrated from England in 1636. In the controversy over ANTINOMIANISM he supported his sister-in-law ANNE HUTCHINSON and was banished from Massachusetts (1637). Wheelwright wrote his account of the controversy in *Mercurius Americanus* (1645). He later returned to a Congregational pastorate in Massachusetts.

Wheelwright, John Brooks (1897–1940),   poet. Wheelwright was a descendant of the early dissenter JOHN WHEELWRIGHT and of John Brooks, a 19th-century governor of Massachusetts. Educated at Harvard and the Massachusetts Institute of Technology, Wheelwright wrote poetry collected in *Rock and Shell* (1933), *Mirrors of Venus* (1938), and *Political Self-Portrait* (1940), all privately printed. Wheelwright was working on his poem "Dusk to Dusk" at the time of his death, in an automobile accident. It is included in the posthumous *Collected Poems of John Wheelwright* (1972).

When Johnny Comes Marching Home (1863),   an enduring marching song written by Patrick Sarsfield Gilmore (1829–1892), official bandmaster of the Union army. The song was used in later wars, and its tune is echoed in several serious compositions, notably Roy Harris's overture *When Johnny Comes Marching Home* (1934).

When Lilacs Last in the Dooryard Bloom'd (published in *Sequel to Drum-Taps*, 1865–66, and included in the 1867 edition of LEAVES OF GRASS), a poem by WALT WHITMAN. An elegy on the death of Abraham Lincoln, *Lilacs* is one of Whitman's finest poems and one of the great elegies of world literature. The first four sections constitute the first cycle, which voices the grief of the poet over the death of Lincoln and introduces the symbols of the lilac, with its blossoms and heartshaped leaves (love and rebirth), the western star (Lincoln, the beloved comrade), and the hermit thrush (the soul, the poet). The second cycle (sections five through nine) presents the journey of the coffin, first the coffin of Lincoln and then all coffins. Moving from the particular death to universal death, the poet covers the coffins with lilacs, placing the symbol of ever-returning spring over the symbol of death. The tension builds up between grief and the spiritual knowledge to be found in death, to be continued in cycle three (sections ten through thirteen). Cycle four (sections fourteen through the end) is a celebration of the mystery and glory of death, a reconciliation of the tension of cycle three, in which "lilac and star and bird [are] twined with the chant of [the poet's] soul."

When the Frost Is on the Punkin (1882),   a poem in Hoosier dialect by JAMES WHITCOMB RILEY.

Where the Blue Begins (1922),   a novel by CHRISTOPHER MORLEY. The fantastic plot concerns Gissing, a dog that acquires sufficient human personality to become a part of the business and social life of New York City. Gissing becomes a floorwalker in a large department store, and through the dog Morley preaches a satirical and philosophical lesson that home is, after all, the best place to be.

Whilomville Stories (1900),   short stories by STEPHEN CRANE. These thirteen stories, written during Crane's last years in England, have their setting in a town usually associated with Port Jervis, New York. Whilomville is any boy's town, and Jimmie Trescott is as much Tom Sawyer as he is Stephen Crane. The hair-cutting incident of "An Angel Child" and the comedy of "Lynx-Hunting," in which Jimmie shoots a cow, are based on Crane's childhood. The farmer in "Lynx-Hunting"—like the hero in "The Veteran"—is Henry Fleming of THE RED BADGE OF COURAGE, grown old, and Dr. Trescott is transposed from THE MONSTER. Although not Whilomville stories, Crane's baby sketches of 1893 belong in the same category, particularly "A Dark Brown Dog" and "An Ominous Baby." They deal with the cruelty of children, as do "Shame," "The Lover and the Telltale," and "The Flight." In "Shame" Crane speaks of "the jungles of childhood, where grown folk seldom penetrate." Crane's *Whilomville Stories* are only partly in the tradition of previous childhood literature, for they are less nostalgic and depict children as "little blood-fanged wolves." Realistic and unsentimental, they are akin to the writings of later authors like Hemingway, Sherwood Anderson, and J. D. Salinger.

Whipple, E[dwin] P[ercy] (1819–1886),   lecturer, essayist, critic. Whipple, a businessman born in Gloucester, Massachusetts, first attracted attention with his critical essay on Macaulay, published in the Boston *Miscellany* (1843). A critic by avocation, Whipple published many popular books, most of them based on his lectures. Among his titles are *Essays and Reviews* (2 v. 1848, 1849); *Literature of the Age of Elizabeth* (1869); *Recollections of Eminent Men* (1887); and *Outlooks on Society, Literature, and Politics* (1888). Whipple is described by Thomas Wentworth Higginson in *Short Studies of American Authors* (1906) and by William Dean Howells in *Literary Friends and Acquaintance* (1900).

Whistler, James [Abbott] McNeill (1834–1903), painter, etcher, writer. Whistler, born in Lowell, Massachusetts, went to Paris in 1855 and moved in 1860 to England, where his life turned into a series of battles in the cause of art against philistines, the bourgeoisie, and those who failed to recognize Whistler as a great genius. His picturesque appearance and bohemian way of life were excellent publicity for him. One celebrated literary and legal battle was with John Ruskin. In *Fors Clavigera* (1877), Ruskin sneered elaborately at Whistler's paintings. Whistler sued successfully for libel, but won only a farthing in damages. Immediately after the case closed, he published a vituperative pamphlet, *Whistler v. Ruskin; Art and Art Critics*. In 1890 he gave a fuller report of the case in *The Gentle Art of Making Enemies*, which is frequently inaccurate. When George du Maurier's *Trilby* was first serialized in *Harper's Magazine* (January–June 1894), Whistler appeared in caricature as Joe Sibley. The satire was mild, but Whistler protested furiously to *Harper's*, and du Maurier subsequently omitted the offending passages.

Whistler was one of the greatest and most influential artists of his generation. He followed the Impressionist movement in its earlier phases and greatly admired Japanese and Chinese art, pioneering in expressing that admiration. He was a master of haziness and mistiness in some of his celebrated drawings and despised those who claimed only to imitate nature, although his portraits, especially that of Carlyle, are extraordinary likenesses. He is known popularly for his painting *The Artist's Mother: Arrangement in Grey and Black.*

Elizabeth and Joseph Pennell, who wrote an authorized life of Whistler (2 v. 1908), were able to secure for their magnificent edition of *The Whistler Journal* (1921), with its numerous illustrations, the legal papers in the Whistler-Ruskin lawsuit.

Whitaker, Alexander (1585–1617?), clergyman, pamphleteer. Whitaker came to Virginia from England in 1611. The reprint of his sermon *Good News from Virginia* (1613) was used to exhort England to support the colonists more fully. The text includes detailed descriptions of the region and its indigenous peoples. Whitaker is remembered as the clergyman who converted Pocahantas.

Whitcher, Frances Miriam [Berry] (1814–1852), humorist. Whitcher, born in Whitesboro, New York, published a series of popular sketches called *The Widow Bedott's Table-Talk* in the *Saturday Gazette and Lady's Literary Museum* (1846–50). She also contributed *Aunt Magwire's Experiences* and *Letters from Timberville* to *Godey's Lady's Book*, illustrating many of the sketches herself. *The Widow Bedott Papers* (1856, frequently reissued) and *Widow Spriggins, Mary Elmer, and Other Sketches* (1868) are collections that reveal her skill at droll caricature, faithful reproduction of colloquial speech, and incisive satire of small-town life. Whitcher's sketches are the earliest extensive treatment of the humorous female character in American literature. Petroleum V. Nasby based his comedy *Widow Bedott, or, A Hunt for a Husband* (1879) on her sketches.

White, Andrew (1579–1656), Jesuit missionary. White was born in England, educated on the Continent, and taught for a while in Spain and Flanders. In 1633 he headed a mission of three Jesuit priests to Maryland, and in the same year published a *Declaration of the Lord Baltemore's Plantation*, in which he urged that missionary work be done among the natives and spoke enthusiastically of the resources of the country. L. C. Wroth's facsimile edition (1929) of the *Declaration* describes White as "a fervid, naive writer, gifted with an unconscious capacity for picturesque expression." Father White also kept a journal, it is suggested by Jarvis M. Morse in *American Beginnings* (1952), that formed the basis for his *Relatio Itineris in Marilandiam* (pub. in part in 1634 as *A Relation of the Successful Beginnings of the Lord Baltemore's Plantation in Maryland*). Again White gives much information about the natives and local products and praises the friendliness of the Virginia colonists. Yet, in the course of later disputes with some of the Virginians, Father White found himself in difficul-

ties, was imprisoned and sent to England (1645), where he was tried for treason and banished to the Low Countries. He is believed to have returned and died in London.

White, Andrew D[ickson] (1832–1918), educator, historian, diplomat. A leader in nonsectarian higher education, White was born in Homer, New York. He started his academic career as professor of history at the University of Michigan. His father's death left him with a comfortable private income, and when he was elected to the New York legislature (1864), he joined with his fellow senator Ezra Cornell to found Cornell University. White, who had planned a modern, liberal curriculum, became the school's first president (1868), attracting to the faculty as nonresident teachers James Russell Lowell, Louis Agassiz, G. W. Curtis, Bayard Taylor, and other prominent scholars. Attacks on Cornell as a godless institution evoked White's reply in *The Warfare of Science* (1876). Its liberal tenets were further developed in the *History of the Warfare of Science with Theology in Christendom* (2 v. 1896) and *Seven Great Statesmen in the Warfare of Humanity with Unreason* (1910). He revised another early work, *Paper-Money Inflation in France* (1876), reissued as *Fiat Money in France* (1896).

White helped found the American Historical Association (1884) and became its first president. Appointed minister to Germany (1878–81), he also served as minister to Russia (1892–94) and later as ambassador to Germany (1896–1902). He headed the American delegation to the Hague Conference (1899) and persuaded his friend Andrew Carnegie to build the Palace of Justice at the Hague. As a personal document, his *Autobiography of Andrew Dickson White* (2 v. 1905) is interesting, and a useful account of White's role as educator is found in W. P. Rogers' *Andrew D. White and the Modern University* (1942).

White, E[lwyn] B[rooks] (1899–1985), humorist, essayist. White, born in Mt. Vernon, New York, was educated at Cornell and then became a reporter for the Seattle *Times*. According to JAMES THURBER's classic account, White reported a husband identifying his wife's body in the municipal morgue as crying, "My God, it's her!" The city editor changed the quote to "My God, it is she," whereupon White resigned to become mess boy on a ship bound for Alaska.

As production assistant in a New York City advertising agency, White began sending manuscripts to *The New Yorker.* Editor Harold Ross spotted a new and rare talent and soon hired him. He had a finger in every *New Yorker* pie, including writing cartoon captions, but his chief contribution was writing the witty and urbane "Notes and Comment" column, which set the tone for the entire magazine. He married a *New Yorker* editor, Katharine Angell, in 1929, and later moved to North Brooklin, Maine. He remained a *New Yorker* staff member and continued his work for the magazine.

He conducted the "One Man's Meat" department for *Harper's* in 1938–43, and continued to contribute to *The New Yorker*, occasionally in "Talk of the Town" and in serious pieces dealing with national and international affairs. *The Lady Is Cold* (poetry) and *Is Sex Necessary?* (with James Thurber) both appeared in 1929 and were followed by *Alice Through the Cello-phane* (1933); *Every Day is Saturday* (1934); *The Fox of Peapack, and Other Poems* (1938); and *Quo Vadimus?* (1939). In 1941 the Whites compiled *A Subtreasury of American Humor.* Then came E. B. White's *One Man's Meat* (1942, enlarged ed. 1944); *The Wild Flag* (1946); *Here Is New York* (1949); and *The Second Tree from the Corner* (1953). In 1962 appeared *The Points of My Compass and Letters from the East, the West, the North, the South,* a collection of articles that originally appeared in *The New Yorker.* His revision of William Strunk, Jr.'s *The Elements of Style* (1959) became a best seller. He also wrote two highly acclaimed children's books, *Stuart Little* (1945) and *Charlotte's Web* (1952). White is recognized as one of America's most incisive and witty essayists.

White, Edmund (1940–), novelist. White is known particularly for *A Boy's Own Story* (1982), which treats an adolescent boy's awareness of his own homosexuality and his struggle to find a place in society, and *The Beautiful Room Is Empty* (1988), a treatment of the gay lifestyle. *The Farewell Symphony* (1997) is the third volume of his autobiography. His other books include *Forgetting Elena* (1973), *Nocturnes for the King of Naples* (1978), *States of Desire: Travels in Gay America* (1980), *Caracole* (1985), and *The Married Man* (2000).

White, Edward Lucas (1866–1934), author, teacher. White, born in New Jersey, was educated at Johns Hopkins and spent the rest of his life teaching Greek and Latin at secondary schools in or near Baltimore. His published works include *Narrative Lyrics* (1908); EL SUPREMO (1916); *The Unwilling Vestal* (1918); *The Song of the Sirens and Other Stories* (1919); *Andivius Hedulio* (1921); *Helen* (1925); *Lukundoo and Other Stories* (1927); *Why Rome Fell* (1927); and *Matrimony,* autobiography (1932). He is remembered today for *El Supremo,* which is an excellent novel, of a 19th-century Paraguayan dictator, and for *The Unwilling Vestal* and *Andivius Hedulio,* two lively novels of Roman life.

White, John (fl. 1585–1593), colonist, painter. White, a member of the Grenville expedition of 1585, agreed to collaborate with the naturalist THOMAS HARRIOT on an account of the Virginia colony, and his watercolors of plants, animals, and Native Americans were used to illustrate the second edition of Harriot's *Briefe and True Report of . . . Virginia* (1590). White, apparently back in England, was appointed to succeed Grenville as governor in 1587, but his rescue mission was delayed until 1590 when he returned to find no survivors of the Roanoke colony. Hakluyt printed White's letters and reports and his account of the 1590 voyage.

White, Nelia Gardner (1894–1957), novelist. The daughter of a Pennsylvania minister, White wrote her most successful novel, *No Trumpet Before Him* (1948), about a young clergyman. Also based in part on her own experiences was *The Fields of Gomorrah* (1935), the story of a minister's wife. *Daughter of Time* (1942) is a fictionalized biography of Katherine Mansfield. Among her other books are *David Strange* (1928), *Hathaway House* (1931), *Brook Willow* (1934), *The Pink House* (1950), and *The Thorn Tree* (1955).

White, Richard Grant (1821–1885), journalist, scholar. White, born in New York City, started his career as a lawyer and worked for some years in a customhouse. He was coeditor of the briefly published humorous paper *Yankee Doodle* (1846), wrote music, art, and literary criticism for the *Morning Courier* and *New-York Enquirer,* and contributed to numerous other magazines. Now remembered primarily as a Shakespearean scholar, he wrote *Shakespeare's Scholar* (1854) and *Studies in Shakespeare* (1886) and edited *The Works of William Shakespeare* (12 v. 1857–66, republished as *The Riverside Shakespeare,* 3 v. 1883).

White, Stewart Edward (1873–1946), novelist, writer on spiritualism. The author of more than fifty books, White was born in Grand Rapids, Michigan, and educated at the University of Michigan and Columbia Law School. When he prospected for gold in South Dakota during a summer vacation, he gained the background for his first novels, *The Westerners* (1901) and *The Claim Jumpers* (1901). An arduous winter in a Hudson Bay lumber camp led to *The Riverman* (1908). *The Pass* (1906) and *The Cabin* (1910) were based on camping and hunting trips he made in the West. In two visits to Africa, White obtained material for *The Land of Footprints* (1912), *African Camp Fires* (1913), and *Lions in the Path* (1926).

White also did extensive research for two series of historical novels. A trilogy entitled *The Story of California* (1927) consists of GOLD (1913), *The Grey Dawn* (1915), and *The Rose Dawn* (1920). Four novels set in the days of Daniel Boone are *The Long Rifle* (1932), *Ranchero* (1933), *Folded Hills* (1934), and *Stampede* (1942). *The Blazed Trail* (1902) is often considered his best novel. White and his wife Betty published *The Betty Book* in 1937, claiming it had been dictated by Mrs. White while in a trance. After her death, White wrote *The Unobstructed Universe* (1940), *The Road I Know* (1942), and *Job of Living* (1948)—claiming these books were dictated from beyond the grave.

White, Theodore H. (1915–1986), correspondent, author. White was born in Boston and educated at Harvard. He became chief of *Time's* China bureau from 1939 to 1945. He became editor of *The New Republic* in 1947, and shortly thereafter went to Europe as a correspondent during the postwar years. *Thunder Out of China* (1946), written with Annalee Jacoby, is an account of the war in China and the rise of Communist power there. *Fire in the Ashes: Europe in Mid-Century* (1953) was a widely acclaimed presentation of postwar Europe. *The Making of the President, 1960* (1961) records the events of President Kennedy's campaign for the Democratic nomination and his election to the presidency. It won the first Pulitzer Prize given for nonfiction (1962). White wrote successive volumes by the same title on the elections of 1964, 1968, and 1972. White's other books include *The Stillwell Papers* (1948), *The Mountain Road* (1958), *The View from the Fortieth Floor* (1960), *China: The Roots of Madness* (1968), *Breach of Faith; The Fall of Richard Nixon* (1975), and *In Search of History: A Personal Adventure* (1978).

White, Walter [Francis] (1893–1955),   novelist, memoirist. Born in Atlanta, White was long associated with the NAACP, first as an active member and later as executive secretary (1931). His first novel, *The Fire in the Flint* (1924), deals with a lynching in a Southern town. A second novel, *Flight* (1926), is a study of the middle-class African-American community of Atlanta. *Rope and Faggot—A Biography of Judge Lynch* (1929) is a nonfiction treatment of the subject of his first novel, and *A Rising Wind* (1945) is a report on the experiences of African-American soldiers in Europe during World War II. Perhaps the most popular of White's books was the autobiographical *A Man Called White* (1948). His wife, Poppy Cannon, wrote *A Gentle Knight: My Husband, Walter White* (1956). Though White was Caucasian in appearance, he emphasized his African-American heritage.

White, William Allen (1868–1944),   journalist, writer. White, born in Emporia, Kansas, became a newspaperman after attending, but never graduating from, two colleges. He worked for the Kansas City *Star* for a while and then bought the EMPORIA GAZETTE. He made himself and his newspaper with his scathing editorial WHAT'S THE MATTER WITH KANSAS? (August 15, 1896).

White tried writing poetry as a young man, but without success. His novels were moderately popular: *A Certain Rich Man* (1909), *In the Heart of a Fool* (1918), and *The Martial Adventures of Henry and Me* (1918). His short stories of life on the plains were collected in *The Court of Boyville* (1899) and *In Our Town* (1906). Some of his editorials and essays were collected in *The Old Order Changeth* (1910), *Politics: The Citizen's Business* (1924), and other volumes. Probably his most widely circulated piece of writing was his editorial tribute to his daughter Mary, who died as the result of a riding accident. Many papers reprinted the editorial, and it has often appeared in anthologies. White also wrote *Woodrow Wilson: The Man, The Times, and His Task* (1924); *Calvin Coolidge, the Man Who Is President* (1925); and *A Puritan in Babylon: The Story of Calvin Coolidge* (1938). Walter Johnson edited *Selected Letters of William Allen White* (1946). White's letters to an aspiring artist, Gil Wilson, were collected in *Letters of William Allen White and a Young Man* (1948).

White, William L[indsay] (1900–1973),   journalist, author. White was born in Emporia, Kansas. A graduate of Kansas State U. and Harvard, White—son of WILLIAM ALLEN WHITE—worked on his father's newspaper, went into politics briefly, made trips to Europe, served on the Washington *Post* and on *Fortune*, and was a war correspondent during World War II. One of his most popular books was *Journey for Margaret* (1941), the story of how he and his wife adopted a three-year-old war orphan. *They Were Expendable* (1942), an account of the heroism of a torpedo squadron in the Philippines, was a best seller. In 1944 he became publisher and editor of the Emporia *Gazette*. His other titles are *Lost Boundaries* (1948), *Land of Milk and Honey* (1949), *Bernard Baruch: Portrait of a Citizen* (1950), *Back Down the Ridge* (1953), and *The Captives of Korea* (1957).

White Buildings (1926),   a volume of poems by HART CRANE. Crane's first collection, which contains some of his finest poems, is perhaps most notable for the six-poem suite called "Voyages" and "For the Marriage of Faustus and Helen," both treating themes that recur in his major work, THE BRIDGE [2]. Many of the poems in *White Buildings* deal with the sea as a symbol of integration, with the division between imagination and reality, or with the artist as the isolated individual who can "still love the world" even though it rejects him. Crane's interest in the "logic of metaphor" and the "illogical impingements of the connotations of words" results in tight, multilevel poetry that often requires close reading.

White Fang (1905),   a novel by JACK LONDON. Written as a sequel to THE CALL OF THE WILD, which describes the reversion of a tame dog to a wild state, *White Fang* tells of a wild wolf-dog that is gradually domesticated. After being brutally treated by its first owner to improve its performance in dog fights, White Fang is rescued by Weedon Scott, a mining engineer, who tames the dog by applying patience and kindness. Scott takes White Fang from the Yukon to his home in California, where the dog defends its master's family from assault by an escaped convict.

Whitefield, George (1714–1770),   evangelist. While in school at Oxford, Whitefield met John and Charles Wesley. After the Wesley brothers left for America, Whitefield became the leader of the Methodists. He made seven visits to America, where he had a substantial influence on the GREAT AWAKENING and attracted supporters as diverse as Jonathan Edwards and Benjamin Franklin. *Works* (6 v. 1771–72) is a selection from his many pamphlets, sermons, and letters.

Whitehead, Alfred North (1861–1947),   mathematician, philosopher. A graduate of Trinity College, Cambridge, Whitehead lectured on mathematics there and taught applied mathematics and mechanics at University College, London, and at the Imperial College of Science and Technology. After moving to the United States (1924), he served as professor of philosophy at Harvard.

Whitehead approached philosophy through the medium of mathematics. His earliest writings were *A Treatise on Universal Algebra* (1898), *The Axioms of Projective Geometry* (1906), *The Axioms of Descriptive Geometry* (1907), and *An Introduction to Mathematics* (1911). With Bertrand Russell he wrote *Principia Mathematica* (3 v. 1910–13), a rigorous development of pure mathematics through formal logic. The evolution of Whitehead's philosophy can be traced through *The Organization of Thought* (1916), the popular *Science and the Modern World* (1925), *Religion in the Making* (1926), *Process and Reality* (1929), *The Function of Reason* (1929), *Adventures of Ideas* (1933), *Nature and Life* (1934), *Modes of Thought* (1938), and *Essays in Science and Philosophy* (1947). Whitehead's use of the technique of "extensive abstraction," the derivation of concepts from conscious perception, gave his writings what Victor Lowe in *Whitehead and the Modern World* (1950) calls his "unique combination of theory and concreteness." Whitehead was influenced by Henri Bergson. Like other modern philosophers, he rejected mechanical materialism for a subjective idealism and in his attempt to reconcile science and metaphysics viewed the universe as organic. *Dialogues of Alfred North Whitehead* was published in 1954.

White Jacket, or The World in a Man-of-War (1850), a novel by HERMAN MELVILLE. As in earlier volumes, Melville turned to his experiences in the Pacific to narrate with semiautobiographical accuracy his voyage from Hawaii to the Atlantic coast as a member of the U.S. Navy. Most of the book describes in realistic detail life on a man-of-war, and reveals Melville's abhorrence of brutality and inhumanity. The dramatic scenes of flogging, in addition to their artistic value, were also useful as propaganda and led eventually to abandonment of that practice. Melville, however, could not entirely constrain himself from symbolic composition. The subtitle suggests the theme of the ship as an analogue of the world, a theme Melville was to drive home in the final chapter. The description of the fall from the mast, the dramatic and stylistic high point of the book, may be regarded as the loss of innocence, and the jacket itself can be interpreted as a symbol of the innocence Melville finally succeeds in shedding. The most memorable character is Jack Chase, captain of the foretop, a tough-minded sailor with the soul of a poet. He is the one ideal figure in all of Melville's writings, a man equally of the head and the heart. Melville dedicated BILLY BUDD to Chase.

White Rose of Memphis, The (1882),   a novel by WILLIAM C. FALKNER,   the great-grandfather of WILLIAM FAULKNER, whose family spells the name both ways. His book was one of the most popular novels of the South after the Civil War.

Whitfield, James M. (1830–1870),   poet, abolitionist. Early in life Whitefield moved from Boston to Buffalo, then a center of abolitionist agitation, and earned a living for a while as a barber. When his collection *America and Other Poems* appeared in 1853, he gave up barbering and appears to have become a lecturer and writer. He joined Martin Delaney in believing that emigration was the solution of the African-American problem and urged Central America as a haven. His poetry shows the influence of Byron and Scott.

Whitlock, Brand (1869–1934),   reporter, lawyer, public official, writer. Whitlock, born in Urbana, Ohio, had a long and varied career, serving as reform mayor of Toledo, Ohio, and as minister and ambassador to Belgium. Under the influence of William Dean Howells's literary realism and the social criticism of the muckrakers, in his first novel, *The Thirteenth District* (1902), he dealt with the corruption of a Congressman. Among his novels are *The Turn of the Balance* (1907) and *J. Hardin & Son* (1923) Whitlock's experiences in Belgium during World War I are related in *Belgium: A Personal Narrative* (1919), but perhaps the most engaging of his nonfiction books is his autobiographical *Forty Years of It* (1914). Allan Nevins edited *The Letters and Journal of Brand Whitlock* (2 v. 1936).

Whitman, Albery A[llson] (1851–1901),   poet, clergyman. Born in Kentucky and a slave until age twelve, Whit-

man became an itinerant preacher for the African Methodist Episcopal Church and financial agent for Wilberforce College. His was the most ambitious poetry attempted by an African-American in the 19th century. *Not a Man and Yet a Man* (1877) is a long narrative poem; *The Rape of Florida* (1884, reissued with changes as *Twasinta's Seminoles*, 1893), is a poem in Spenserian stanzas. Other poems by Whitman are *Leelah Misled* (1873) and *The Octoroon* (1901).

Whitman, Sarah Helen [Power] (1803–1878), poet, critic. Whitman, born in Providence, Rhode Island, and early a widow, was one of the numerous sentimental women poets who became popular in the mid-19th century. She sometimes collaborated with her sister, Anna Power. In 1853 she published *Hours of Life and Other Poems*; a complete edition of her *Poems* appeared in 1879. One of her admirers was EDGAR ALLAN POE, whose work she praised warmly. He wrote in her honor his second poem entitled TO HELEN and wrote a series of letters to her. They were collected by James A. Harrison in *Last Letters of Edgar Allan Poe to Sarah Helen Whitman* (1909). Poe tried to persuade Mrs. Whitman to marry him, but her relatives and friends advised her against the match.

After Poe's death his alleged friend, the Rev. Rufus W. Griswold, made slanderous charges against him. His strictures finally led Mrs. Whitman to make a vigorous and effective reply, *Poe and His Critics* (1860).

Whitman, Walt[er] (1819–1892),   poet, journalist, essayist. Of Dutch and English ancestry, Walter Whitman was born in West Hills, New York, the second son of Louisa Van Velsor and Walter Whitman. To distinguish the son from the father, his family called him Walt, a nickname the poet later adopted for his literary name. The Whitmans had once owned five hundred acres of Long Island farmland, but the poet's father, a carpenter and occasional farmer, could not support his family on the small farm he inherited at West Hills, near Huntington. In 1823 he moved the family to Brooklyn, where he built and sold houses, but without financial success. Walt's mother was a genial person, adored by her children, though they disliked their father; but poverty and bearing nine children exhausted her. Her husband was a friend of the notorious Deist Tom Paine and the schismatic Quaker Elias Hicks, whom Mrs. Whitman also admired.

In Brooklyn Walt attended public school for five or six years, then studied the printing trade, which he practiced in Brooklyn and Manhattan. Unemployed in 1835 because of a great fire in New York, he returned to Long Island as a country schoolteacher. For a year (1838–39) he edited and printed a newspaper at Huntington, the *Long Islander*. From 1840 to 1845 he worked as a printer in New York City, edited newspapers for brief periods, and wrote sentimental poems and stories for popular magazines, such as the *Democratic Review*. Late in life he collected a few of these in an appendix to SPECIMEN DAYS AND COLLECT (1882). Emory Holloway salvaged these early poems, some of the fiction, and many essays and editorials, which he reprinted in several volumes. The most useful of these is *The Uncollected Poetry and Prose of Walt Whitman* (2 v.

1921), which also contains Whitman's temperance novel, FRANKLIN EVANS, OR, THE INEBRIATE (1842). Thomas Ollive Mabbott edited other short stories in *The Half-Breed and Other Stories* (1927). Copies of the New York *Aurora*, which Whitman edited for about two months in the spring of 1842, have survived, and J. J. Rubin and C. H. Brown edited a selection of his editorials and sketches in *Walt Whitman and the New York Aurora* (1950). These throw light on the personal, vindictive, and violent journalism of the times, but give no promise of the future poet.

In 1845 Whitman returned to Brooklyn as a reporter on the *Star*, for which he had earlier set type, but in March 1846 became editor of the Brooklyn *Daily Eagle*. Like the other papers he had edited—he was never editor of the Whig *Star*—the *Eagle* was Democratic. Early in 1848 he lost this position because his editorial support of the Free Soil movement offended the conservatives who dominated the Democratic Party in New York State. Thwarted in plans to found a Free Soil newspaper, Whitman took a job on the editorial staff of a paper soon to begin publication in New Orleans under the name of the *Crescent*. After an arduous trip by train, stage, and steamboat, he arrived in New Orleans on February 25, 1848, but stayed only until May 27 because of friction with the owners of the paper. He returned home by way of the Mississippi, the Great Lakes, and the Hudson River. Although there is no evidence at all for a love affair in New Orleans, which several biographers have hypothesized, the trip gave Whitman intimate knowledge of the expanding nation and a lifelong sympathy for the South. However, his opposition to the extension of slavery into the new Territories was unshaken, and he now carried out his earlier plan to found a Free Soil paper, which he called the *Freeman*. It was published from September 9, 1848, until September 11, 1849. Once more he was defeated by the conservative Democrats, who almost ended his journalistic career. After several years of odd jobs, including operating a printing office and building houses as a contractor and speculator, he edited one more paper, the Brooklyn *Times*, from 1857 to 1859.

Meanwhile, a major event in American literary history had occurred early in July 1855, when a thin quarto book called LEAVES OF GRASS, printed in Brooklyn at Whitman's expense, was placed on sale in Brooklyn and Manhattan. Whitman had been working on this collection of poems since the failure of the *Freeman*. The title was a multiple symbol—of fertility, universality, and cyclical life. The book contained twelve untitled poems, preceded by a preface (see LEAVES OF GRASS, PREFACE TO). It ultimately became as well known and influential as Wordsworth's Preface to *Lyrical Ballads*. The unconventional form of the verse, without rhyme or meter, the realistic—sometimes physiological—imagery, and the personal tone of the first poem, later called SONG OF MYSELF, shocked the few people who read the book. An exception was Ralph Waldo Emerson, who greeted the author "at the beginning of a great career." Despite the fact that the book did not sell, Whitman published an expanded edition in the following year, omitting the 1855 Preface but adding a long open letter to Emerson.

After the interlude as editor of the Brooklyn *Times*, Whitman returned to *Leaves of Grass* with renewed vigor, determined to make the growth of the book his lifework. This was also the period of his association with the Bohemian crowd at PFAFF'S CELLAR, a restaurant on lower Broadway. He was discouraged in autumn 1859, but an offer by Thayer and Eldridge in Boston to publish a new edition of *Leaves of Grass* revived his ambition. This third edition (1860) contained many new poems, notably three groups—"Chants Democratic," "Enfans d'Adam," and CALAMUS—representing the tripartite program of nationalism, sex, and love-friendship. In later editions Whitman broke up and redistributed the nationalistic poems, but he kept the CHILDREN OF ADAM (revised title) and "Calamus" groups with minor revisions.

At the outbreak of the Civil War Whitman wrote the recruiting poem "Beat! Beat! Drums!" and George, Walt's younger brother, enlisted. He himself continued to lead a Bohemian life, loafing at Pfaff's, riding the Broadway omnibuses with his friends the drivers, and hobnobbing with ferryboat pilots. Late in 1862, however, learning that George had been wounded in the battle near Fredericksburg, Walt rushed down to Virginia to nurse his brother. He found George not seriously hurt, but the sight of the other sick and wounded men so aroused his compassion that he volunteered his services in the military hospitals. The Army provided doctors and nurses, though not always in adequate numbers, but almost no provisions had been made for personal services and sympathetic attention. This was exactly the kind of service Whitman could best render, and he stayed on in Washington throughout the war, except for sick leave, in order to make his rounds of the hospital wards, distributing tobacco and reading matter, writing letters, cheering up the depressed, and sometimes assisting the physicians. The poem entitled THE WOUND DRESSER conveys the spirit of these experiences, though the wounds he dressed were mainly mental. The collection of poems published as DRUM-TAPS (1865) is not actually autobiographical, but gives vignettes of sights, sounds, and moods experienced by Whitman during the war years. A "Sequel" contained the great Lincoln elegy WHEN LILACS LAST IN THE DOORYARD BLOOM'D. Whitman also published his diary notes and sketches as *Memoranda During the War* (1875), later incorporated into the first part of *Specimen Days and Collect* (1882).

During 1863–64 Whitman supported himself by working part time in the Army Paymaster's Office, and at the beginning of 1865 he obtained a clerkship in the Department of the Interior. The new Secretary of the Interior, James Harlan, discharged him on June 30, apparently for being the author of *Leaves of Grass*, but friends obtained a similar position for him next day in the Attorney General's office. One of the poet's friends, WILLIAM DOUGLAS O'CONNOR wrote a vehement condemnation of Harlan and a vindication of Whitman in THE GOOD GRAY POET (1866). The first biography of Whitman was written by his friend JOHN BURROUGHS, and was called *Notes on Walt Whitman as Poet and Person* (1867, rev. 1871). One of Whitman's most intimate friends during this period was Peter

Doyle, a young ex-Confederate soldier, who worked in Washington as a streetcar conductor. His letters to Doyle were published under the title of *Calamus . . .* (1897) by Dr. R. M. BUCKE, who also edited *The Wound Dresser: A Series of Letters Written from the Hospitals in Washington During the War of the Rebellion by Walt Whitman* (1898).

In 1868 William Rossetti published a selected edition, *Poems of Walt Whitman*, which made Whitman known in England and gave rise to a reputation that was to grow steadily for several decades. One of the British readers was Mrs. Anne Gilchrist, who fell in love with the poet through his poems and proposed marriage, which was tactfully declined by Whitman. Thomas B. Harned edited *The Letters of Anne Gilchrist and Walt Whitman* (1918).

Still his own publisher of *Leaves of Grass*, Whitman issued a fifth edition in 1870–71, containing a major new poem, PASSAGE TO INDIA. Also in 1871 he published a philosophical essay on democracy called DEMOCRATIC VISTAS (rev. after serial publication in the *Galaxy* in 1867–68), which anticipated the PRAGMATISM of William James and John Dewey. Whitman regarded democracy less as a political system than as a training school for producing men and women of superior character.

A paralytic stroke on January 23, 1873, forced Whitman to leave Washington and go to live with his brother George in Camden, New Jersey. The death of his mother on May 23 severely depressed him and made 1873 the darkest year of his life. Three years later he began to recuperate on the Stafford farm near Camden, and he recovered sufficiently to give his first Lincoln lecture in New York City on April 14, 1879. He also could make a trip to Colorado in the following autumn, and could visit Dr. Bucke in Canada in 1880.

In 1881 James R. Osgood published a new edition of *Leaves of Grass* in Boston, but stopped distribution in 1882 when he was threatened with prosecution unless several poems were removed, which Whitman refused to do. Publication was resumed, however, by Rees Welsh in Philadelphia, who also published a volume of collected prose called *Specimen Days and Collect* (1882), subsequently and misleadingly entitled *Complete Prose* (1892). Later in 1882, David McKay, another Philadelphia publisher and a personal friend of Whitman's, took over both *Leaves of Grass* and *Specimen Days*. He was to remain the poet's publisher. The publicity resulting from the Boston suppression gave *Leaves of Grass* the best sale it had ever had, and the royalties enabled Whitman to buy a modest house on Mickle Street, Camden, where he lived at first alone and later with a motherly housekeeper, Mrs. Mary Oakes Davis, until his death.

In the Mickle Street house Whitman was visited by many prominent people, especially visitors from England. These included Oscar Wilde, Sir Edwin Arnold, Edmund Gosse, and Lord Houghton (Richard Monckton Milnes). Whitman was painted by Herbert Gilchrist, the son of Mrs. Anne Gilchrist, and by J. W. Alexander and Thomas Eakins. Sidney Morse sculpted Whitman. In 1890, angered by Symonds' belief that the "Calamus" poems had homosexual implications, Whitman claimed that he had fathered six unacknowledged children.

These children have never been identified, and most Whitman scholars doubt that they ever existed. Although gravely ill, Whitman managed—with help from HORACE TRAUBEL—to publish a final edition of *Leaves of Grass* in 1892. His friends called it the "deathbed edition." He died on March 26, 1892, and was buried in Harleigh Cemetery, Camden, N.J., in a tomb he had had constructed from his own design.

Whitman was already a legend when he died in 1892, and so many myths about him have flourished since his death that it is difficult to distinguish fact from fiction. More important, the legends and myths have interfered with the understanding and appreciation of his poems. And Whitman himself was the first myth-maker. Wishing to be a prophet, in the sense of moral and spiritual leader speaking through his poems, he acted the role of poet-prophet until perhaps at times he seemed even to himself to be superhuman. His rough clothes, shaggy beard, slouch hat, and affection for uneducated artisans symbolized his identification with the common people. And yet there was also a paradox, for his superdemocrat loved Italian opera, recited Shakespeare and Homer from memory, and spent many hours in New York City libraries and in the Egyptian Museum. In fact, he educated himself in the major works of world literature.

Critics for many years—even some of those most friendly to the poet—regarded *Leaves of Grass* as the spontaneous product of an untutored genius, and Whitman's own impatient remarks about artistry encouraged this opinion. The exact prosodic sources of Whitman's verse are still not definitely known, nor even that there were specific sources. The Bible has been suggested, and Whitman's parallelism does resemble the "thought rhythm" (repetition of statement) of Hebraic poetry, which survives in the English translations. Actually, whatever the means by which he achieved this feat, Whitman rediscovered poetic techniques as ancient as those of the old Babylonian-Chaldean epic *Gilgamesh* or the hymns of the Egyptian *Book of the Dead*.

In these ancient poems the line—or verse—is the unit, and much use is made of repeated phrases and clauses, which create both rhetorical and rhythmical patterns. Though Whitman is often regarded as one of the originators of FREE VERSE in the French *vers libre* and most of the later American attempts at free verse, the phrase, not the line, as in *Leaves of Grass*, is the rhythmical unit. But there is a similarity in the disregarding of meter and the production of variable musical effects. Whitman himself said that his rhythms were influenced by Italian opera, and many of his poems do contain passages resembling the aria (singing passage) and the recitative (speaking passage) of the Italian opera.

The themes of *Leaves of Grass* have also been interpreted in many ways, but some that he emphasized both in his prefaces and in his so-called program poems, such as "Inscriptions," STARTING FROM PAUMANOK, and BY BLUE ONTARIO'S SHORE are: (1) sacredness of self; (2) equality of all things and beings; (3) love and companionship as a force stronger than social compacts; (4) cosmic evolution; and (5) the beauty of death (a Lucretian theme), or death as part of the cycle of birth, life, death, and resurrection. Faith in the immortality of the soul runs throughout *Leaves of Grass*. In Whitman's own interpretations he usually regarded his poems either as preparing his nation for world leadership in spiritual democracy or as teaching the love of comrades. The former has enabled socialists and Communists to exploit his poetry and prose for political use, while love for comrades has led to homosexual interpretations. While there is no real evidence of homosexuality in Whitman's personal life, some of the "Calamus" poems do seem homoerotic, while others merely convey an exalted ideal of friendship. But the frequent sexual imagery in Whitman's poems more often symbolizes the fecundity of nature, cosmic energy, and the promise of rebirth in death. Thus, Whitman has become more important as a cosmic poet than as a national poet. He is a true poet when he images the concrete objects of nature, as in "Song of Myself," or symbolizes the cycles of life, death, and resurrection, as in OUT OF THE CRADLE ENDLESSLY ROCKING and the Lincoln elegy, "When Lilacs Last in the Dooryard Bloom'd."

The Complete Writings of Walt Whitman (10 v. 1902), edited by R. M. Bucke and others, is not complete. It is being superseded by *The Collected Writings of Walt Whitman*, a collaborative edition begun under the general editorship of Gay Wilson Allen and Sculley Bradley. There are many editions of *Leaves of Grass*, most relying for their texts on the 1891–1892 edition, the last authorized by Whitman. An excellent recent biography is Justin Kaplan, *Walt Whitman: A Life* (1980). Also excellent are Gay Wilson Allen, *The Solitary Singer: Walt Whitman* (1955, rev. 1967), and Roger Asselineau, *The Evolution of Walt Whitman* (2 v. 1960, 1962). Paul Zweig's *Walt Whitman: The Making of a Poet* (1984) is a study of the poet's literary genesis. David S. Reynolds's *Walt Whitman's America: A Cultural Biography* appeared in 1995.

GAY WILSON ALLEN/GP

Whitson, John Harvey ["Lieut. A. K. Sims"] (1854–1936),   dime novelist. Whitson, born in Indiana, wrote many Westerns under his pen name. No record of them is available, but among the titles were *Captain Cactus, Huckleberry the Foot Hills Detective, With Frémont the Pathfinder*, and *The Rainbow Chasers.*

Whittemore, [Edward] Reed [II] (1919–   ), poet. Whittemore, born in New Haven, Connecticut, became a witty, self-limited poet—sharp, cultivated, funny. His work is distinguished by hints of genuine lyric power and submerged, deeper feeling. Among his volumes are *Heroes and Heroines* (1946); *An American Takes a Walk* (1956); *The Self-Made Man* (1959); *The Boy from Iowa: Poems and Essays* (1962); *The Fascination of the Abomination* (1963); *Poems, New and Selected* (1967); *50 Poems 50* (1970); *The Mother's Breast and the Father's House* (1974); and *The Past, the Future, the Present: Poems Selected and New* (1990). *Six Literary Lives* (1993) is biography. A critical biography is *William Carlos Williams* (1975); *The Poet as Journalist* (1976) is a prose collection.

Whittier, John Greenleaf (1807–1892),   poet, abolitionist, journalist. Whittier was born on the farmstead along the Merrimack River near Haverhill, Massachusetts, that had been the family home in the generations since it was settled by his ancestor Thomas Whittier in 1648. The Whittiers were devout Quakers, and John was trained in the doctrine of simplicity, piety, frugality, and social consciousness central to that sect. As a boy he was apprenticed to a cobbler. Although his formal education was limited, he was an avid reader. The Bible, *Pilgrim's Progress*, and John Woolman's *Journal* were among the texts in the family library, and Joshua Coffin, Whittier's schoolmaster, lent him a copy of the poetry of Robert Burns. Burns's lyrical treatment of everyday life confirmed Whittier's natural inclination as a writer. At age nineteen, he had a poem accepted for publication by WILLIAM LLOYD GARRISON, at that time editor of the Newburyport *Press*. Garrison, soon to become editor of the abolitionist *Liberator*, became Whittier's lifelong friend and associate in the antislavery cause.

Garrison's encouragement led Whittier to leave the shoemaker's trade, and after a year at the Haverhill Academy, to teach school briefly, to edit *The American Manufacturer*, the Haverhill *Gazette*, and the *New England Weekly Review*, and to work for a Boston publisher while concentrating on his own writing. His first publication, *Legends of New England* (1831), in prose, was followed by the narrative poem *Moll Pitcher* in the following year. That work, like much of the poetry of this early period, Whittier excluded from his collected works.

Justice and Expediency (1833), an antislavery tract, was published in the same year that he was elected a delegate to the National Anti-Slavery Convention; two years later he was elected to a term in the Massachusetts legislature. He continued to devote most of his attention to the abolitionist movement. He and George Thompson, a British colleague, narrowly escaped being shot by a mob in 1835, while they were lecturing in Concord, New Hampshire. In 1836 he moved down the Merrimack River to Amesbury, leaving in the next year to edit the *Pennsylvania Freeman* (1837–1839) in Philadelphia. In 1840 he returned to Amesbury to a house he would live in for the rest of his life.

In the two decades before the Civil War, Whittier matured as a poet, demonstrating his firm and simple eloquence in *Ballads and Other Poems* (1844), *Voices of Freedom* (1846), SONGS OF LABOR (1850), *The Chapel of the Hermits and Other Poems* (1853), *The Panorama and Other Poems* (1856), and *Home Ballads and Poems* (1860). During this period, his talent was recognized by other New England literary figures, and he joined with Lowell, Holmes, and others in founding the *Atlantic Monthly* in 1857. A collected edition of his work was published in London in 1850, but it was not until the appearance of SNOW-BOUND in 1866 that Whittier was generally recognized as a major writer and his sales were sufficient to support him as an artist. The *Poetical Works* of 1869 was also a success and, in the remainder of his life, he enjoyed a modest prosperity.

Whittier had never married, but had devoted his resources to the support of his family. The death of his mother and two sisters between 1857 and 1864 proved traumatic, and his verse from this time shows an increasing religious fervor and meditation. His own health was increasingly poor and, though the end of the Civil War—celebrated in "Laus Deo"—brought profound relief, emancipation also brought an end to the crusade to which he had devoted his life. Continuing to write, he produced twelve volumes of poetry including *The Tent on the Beach* (1867), *Among the Hills* (1869), *The Pennsylvania Pilgrim* (1872), and *At Sundown* (1890), his last volume.

The *Atlantic Monthly* hosted a dinner for Whittier's 70th birthday that was attended by almost every living American author of note from the generation of William Cullen Bryant to the contemporaries of Mark Twain. His 80th birthday was marked by a national celebration in recognition of his successful expression of a vanishing era of American common life. Five years later, at Hampton Falls, New Hampshire, he died.

Though his contemporary satires and topical pieces have lost their interest, such elegant poems as "Telling the Bees" and "Abraham Davenport" combine impassioned simplicity with sharply etched description. *Snow-Bound* has a timeless appeal in its depiction of rural life. Many of his hymns, such as "Dear Lord and Father of Mankind," are still sung in churches. His other titles include *Lays of My Home and Other Poems* (1843), *Voices of Freedom* (1846), *Old Portraits and Modern Sketches* (1850), *In War Times and Other Poems* (1864), *Miriam and Other Poems* (1871), *Hazel-Blossoms* (1875), *The Vision of Echard and Other Poems* (1878), and *Saint Gregory's Guest and Recent Poems* (1886).

The standard edition is *The Writings of John Greenleaf Whittier* (Riverside Edition, 7 v. 1888–1889, rev. 1894). A one-volume edition is *The Complete Poetical Works of John Greenleaf Whittier* (1894). John B. Pickard edited *Letters of John Greenleaf Whittier* (3 v. 1975). There are biographies by Samuel T. Pickard (2 v. 1894); Thomas W. Higginson (1902); G. R. Carpenter (1903); Lewis Leary (1961); and Edward Wagenknecht (1967). Jayne K. Kribbs edited *Critical Essays on John Greenleaf Whittier* (1980). See BARBARA FRIETCHIE; THE BAREFOOT BOY; CASSANDRA SOUTHWICK; ICHABOD; LEAVES FROM MARGARET SMITH'S JOURNAL; MASSACHUSETTS TO VIRGINIA; A SABBATH SCENE.

Who's Afraid of Virginia Woolf? (1962),   a play by EDWARD ALBEE. Albee's first full-length work opened in New York City in October 1962 and ran for two years. A witty and intense play, it employs one set and four characters. George is a middle-aged professor at New Carthage—the name suggesting a place doomed to destruction. The others are his wife, Martha, and their guests of the evening, a young professor and his wife. George and Martha have failed in much of their lives, but they cling to one another in hatred, dependency, and perhaps love. They live mostly in their minds, which are keen and savagely playful. In the course of the three acts of the play, entitled "Fun and Games," "Walpurgisnacht," and "The Exorcism," which represent one long night of drinking and bitter talk, George and Martha draw their young guests into a series of ritual games. The games strip away drawing room demeanor and illusions and reveal the true condition of all

four characters: they are alienated, sterile, and frightened. In the climactic exorcism George puts to death the imaginary son he and Martha have mentioned all evening as though he were real, and whom they have considered real for the previous twenty-one years. This powerful and unsettling exorcism may express George's destructiveness and despair. But it could also portend deliverance for all four characters—a new determination to live, like Virginia Woolf, without illusions, no matter the consequences.

FRANK MCHUGH

Widdemer, Margaret (1890?–1978),   poet, teacher, novelist. Widdemer was born in Pennsylvania. Her first poem to win celebrity was *The Factories*, which denounces child labor; it was reprinted in *The Factories and Other Poems* (1915). She issued several other collections of verses, the best of which were gathered in *Collected Poems* (1928) and a second *Collected Poems* (1957). She wrote the Winona series of books for girls and numerous romantic and historical novels. Her first book, *The Rose-Garden Husband* (1915), the story of a young librarian, was a best seller. She also wrote a verse play, *The Singing Wood* (1926), and two manuals for beginning writers, *Do You Want to Write?* (1937) and *Basic Principles of Fiction Writing* (1953). *Red Cloak Flying* (1950) and *The Golden Wildcat* (1954) concern Sir William Johnson of colonial New York. *Buckskin Baronet* and *Stronger Woman's Son* both appeared in 1960.

Wide, Wide World, The (1850),   a novel by SUSAN BOGERT WARNER. It was published under the pseudonym Elizabeth Wetherell and immediately became a best seller in America and in England. Its emphasis on religion and its sentimentality appealed to the taste of the day.

Wide Awake.   A magazine for young people, founded July 1875, by Daniel Lothrop and absorbed by ST. NICHOLAS in 1893. In its day it published some prominent writers, among them James Whitcomb Riley, Edward Everett Hale, Sarah Orne Jewett, Charles Egbert Craddock and Louise Imogen Guiney. HARRIET MULFORD STONE LOTHROP wife of the publisher, contributed to the magazine under the pseudonym Margaret Sidney THE FIVE LITTLE PEPPERS AND HOW THEY GREW, which was published as a book in 1880.

Wideman, John Edgar (1941–   ),   novelist, short-story writer. Wideman was born in Washington, D.C. and educated at the University of Pennsylvania and New College, Oxford where he attended as a Rhodes Scholar. He has taught at Penn and the University of Wyoming and is presently on the faculty of the University of Massachusetts. He is best known for fiction set in Homewood, the African-American section of Pittsburgh where he grew up. His fiction includes *A Glance Away* (1967); *Damballah* (1981), a story collection; *Hiding Place* (1981), and *Sent for You Yesterday* (1983), winner of a P.E.N/Faulkner award. *Brothers and Keepers* (1984) is a nonfiction meditation on the different paths taken by the author and his younger brother, then serving a life sentence for murder. *Reuben* (1987), another novel describing the black urban life Wideman experienced as a child, centers on a legal aid worker.

Philadelphia Fire (1990) is a novel centered on the police bombing of a house in West Philadelphia in 1985. *Fever* (1989) is a collection of twelve stories emphasizing the commonality of human experience. *The Cattle Killing* (1996) is historical fiction, while *Two Cities* (1998) is a novel set in Pittsburgh and Philadelphia. *All Stories Are True* (1992) is a short fiction gathering, and *Father along: A Meditation on Fathers, Sons, Race and Society* (1994) collects essays. His other titles include *Hurry Home* (1970) and *The Lynchers* (1973).

Widow Bedott, The.   See FRANCES M. WHITCHER.

Wiebe, Rudy (1934–   ),   novelist, short-story writer. Born to a German-speaking Russian immigrant family in rural Saskatchewan, Wiebe was educated at the University of Alberta and the University of Tubingen, Germany. His family was Mennonite, and a strong religious sense is crucial to his fiction, which includes *Peace Shall Destroy Many* (1962), *First and Vital Candle* (1966), and *The Blue Mountains of China* (1970). His concern for Canadian Indians is voiced in *The Temptations of Big Bear* (1973). *The Scorched Wood People* (1977) and *The Mad Trapper* (1980) are set in the Canadian West. *My Lovely Enemy* (1983) describes a love affair of a professor and a graduate student. *The Angels of the Tar Sands* (1982) is a story collection; *Far as the Eye Can See* (1977) is a play. *Playing Dead: a Contemplation Concerning the Aretee* (1989) is a Series of essays on John Franklin's expedition of 1820–21. The novel *A Discovery of Strangers* (1994) won a Governor General's Award.

Wieland; or, The Transformation (1798),   a novel by CHARLES BROCKDEN BROWN. Set in Pennsylvania, the novel, Brown's first, deals with the baleful influence of a ventriloquist named Carwin on the Wielands, the family of a German mystic. The plot is based on the history of an actual religious fanatic of Tomhannock, New York, who murdered his wife and children at the command of imaginary voices. *Wieland* is the first American novel in the tradition of the Gothic romance, fusing melodramatic improbabilities with quasi-scientific phenomena and exploring the twilight regions of the human mind.

Wiener, Norbert (1894–1964),   teacher, mathematician. Wiener, born in Columbia, Missouri, was the son of noted philologist Leo Wiener (1862–1939). Norbert was an infant prodigy, early showing extraordinary linguistic and scientific ability. He entered Tufts College at age eleven and after graduation studied at Harvard, Cornell, Cambridge, Göttingen, and Columbia. In 1919 he began teaching mathematics at the Massachusetts Institute of Technology. His ideas brought him the title "the legitimate father of automation." Among Wiener's books are *Cybernetics* (1948), *The Human Use of Human Beings* (1950), *Ex-Prodigy* (1953), *I Am a Mathematician* (1956), and *Nonlinear Problems in Random theory* (1958).

Wiener coined the word "cybernetics," using the Greek word for the steersman of a ship as a basis, to designate the science of organizing information by means of devices such as computing machines.

Wieners, John (1934–   ),   poet, playwright. As a student at BLACK MOUNTAIN COLLEGE, Weiners was influenced by CHARLES OLSON and ROBERT DUNCAN. *A Memory* (1960) concerns that period. His small-press publication, *The Hotel Wentley Poems* (1958), deals with the Beat period in San Francisco. His plays include *Jive Shoelaces and Anklesox* (1967). His other titles are *Nerves* (1970) *Selected Poems* (1971), and *Selected Poems 1958–1984* (1986).

Wiese, Kurt (1887–1974),   author, illustrator. Wiese was born in Germany. His first book, *You Can Write Chinese* (1945), intended primarily for children, explained several of the Chinese characters entertainingly. His later books, also containing his illustrations, were for children up to the age of ten: *Fish in the Air* (1948); *Happy Easter* (1952); *The Fox, the Dog and the Fleas* (1953); *The Cunning Turtle* (1956); and *The Groundhog and His Shadow* (1959).

Wiesel, Elie (1928–   ),   novelist, historian, social activist, essayist, playwright. Wiesel, born in Romania, was sent in 1944 to the Auschwitz concentration camp with his father, mother, and younger sister. He was the only one of the four to survive the war. Wiesel was eventually reunited with his two older sisters. Wiesel sought refuge in Paris, where he was a student at the Sorbonne from 1948 to 1951. He supported himself as a journalist, traveling to Israel (1949) and the United States (1956). While reporting on the United Nations, he was struck by a taxicab and, during a long recuperation, was prevented from returning to France as required to renew his visa. He found himself a stateless person. Friends persuaded him to apply for U.S. citizenship, and he was naturalized in 1963.

Wiesel has dedicated himself to keeping the tragedy of the Holocaust before the memory of the world. "The only role I sought was that of witness. I believed that, having survived by chance, I was duty-bound to give meaning to my survival, to justify each moment of my life." Leader of the United States Holocaust Memorial Center, he has protested on behalf of oppressed people around the world. For these efforts he received the Nobel Peace Prize in 1986.

His first and best-known book is *Night*, first written in Yiddish as *Un di Velt Hot Geshvign*, an 800-page account of life in Auschwitz, later pared to 100 pages and translated first into French and then into English in 1960. *Dawn* (*L'Aube* 1960, tr. 1961) is a novella centering on Elisha, a young Holocaust survivor who struggles to make a new life in Palestine and goes from being a victim to being a persecutor. Eliezer, the survivor in *The Accident* (*Le Jour* 1961, tr. 1962) cannot escape the past. These three titles have been printed together as *The Night Trilogy* (1987). *Twilight* (1988) deals with the efforts of Raphael Lipkin, sole survivor of a Polish Jewish family and an authority on mysticism, to explore the boundaries between madness and prophecy. Raphael visits the Mountain Clinic in upstate New York to pursue his study and also to search for his friend Pedro, who has disappeared while attempting to rescue Raphael's brother from a Soviet prison. This background supports meditation on how human suffering can be reconciled with a belief in God.

Wiesel's other works, many translated from the French by Marion Wiesel, his wife, include *The Town Beyond the Wall* (1964); *The Gates of the Forest* (1966); *Legends of Our Time*

(1968); *The Jews of Silence: A Personal Report on Soviet Jewry* (1966); *Zalman, or the Madness of God* (1974), a play; *A Beggar in Jerusalem* (1970); *One Generation After* (1970); *Souls on Fire: Portraits and Legends of Hasidic Masters* (1972); *The Oath* (1973); Ani Maamin: *A Song Lost and Found Again* (1973); *Messengers of God: Biblical Portraits and Legends* (1976); *A Jew Today* (1978); *Four Hasidic Masters and Their Struggle Against Melancholy* (1978); *The Trial of God: A Play in Three Acts* (1979); *The Testament* (1981); *Five Biblical Portraits* (1981); *Somewhere a Master: Further Hasidic Portraits and Legends* (1982); *The Golem: The Story of a Legend* (1983); *The Fifth Son* (1985); *Against Silence: The Voice and Vision of Elie Wiesel* (3 v. 1985); and *From the Kingdom of Memory: Reminiscences* (1990). A two volume memoir is composed of *All Rivers Run to The Sea* (1969) and *And the Sea Is Never Full* (2000).

Wiggin, Kate Douglas (1856–1923),   teacher, writer for children. A lifelong student of child education, Wiggin was born in Philadelphia and organized in San Francisco the first free kindergarten in the West. She also joined her sister, NORA ARCHIBALD SMITH, in founding a kindergarten training school. To raise funds for her kindergarten she began writing children's books, the best-known being *The Birds' Christmas Carol* (1887), *The Story of Patsy* (1889), REBECCA OF SUNNYBROOK FARM (1903), and *Mother Carey's Chickens* (1911). Her understanding of children and her homespun humor show to best advantage in *Rebecca*. The delightfully precocious heroine is partly derived from Wiggin's own childhood.

Wiggin also published several adult semi-novels, the travel accounts of a heroine named Penelope, based on the author's travels in England. With her sister she wrote books on education—among them *Children's Rights* (1892) and *Froebel's Gifts* (1895)—and edited collections of children's poems and stories. Some of her novels were dramatized in the 1910s. Her autobiography, *My Garden of Memory*, was published in 1923.

Wigglesworth, Michael (1631–1705),   theologian, poet. Born in Yorkshire, England, Wigglesworth came to America with his family in 1638, settling in New Haven, Connecticut. He studied medicine and theology at Harvard and in 1656 took up a ministerial post in Malden, Massachusetts. He remained there for fifty years. Although long illnesses hampered his activities at times, he wrote, preached, served as a physician in Malden and neighboring communities, and found time for three marriages. His second marriage, to his "servant maid . . . not 20 years old," brought a protest from Increase Mather.

Wigglesworth's chief claim to fame, THE DAY OF DOOM (1662), sets forth the Puritan views of predestination, original sin, and God's grace and punishment. In 224 stanzas of eight lines each—each stanza combining two units of common meter, familiar to his readers from its use in hymns and folksongs—he taught his lessons in a plain style and a thumping beat embellished with many internal rhymes to complement those at line ends. The theology expressed is harsh in some respects—to children who died in infancy, for example, God allots "the easiest room in hell"—but it promises eternal bliss for the chosen. More important for later readers, the theology is correct for its time and place. In colonial America up until the time of Franklin, the book was surpassed in influence only by THE NEW ENGLAND PRIMER, which taught people to read, and by the Protestant Bible, the bedrock of the dominant religion. Children learned passages from *The Day of Doom* with their catechism, and many adults memorized it from beginning to end.

Apart from *The Day of Doom*, Wigglesworth's poetic output was limited. Reflecting on God's reasons for bringing on a serious drought in 1662, he produced a second long poem, *God's Controversy with New England*, in which he censured the people of his time for "those faults of thine/Which are notorious" and asked for help from the "many praying saints" still left among them. *God's Controversy* remained unpublished until late in the 19th century. A third long poem was titled in full, *Meat out of the Eater; or, Meditations Concerning the Necessity, End, and Usefulness of Afflictions unto God's Children, All Tending to Prepare Them for and Comfort Them under the Cross.* First published in 1669 and reprinted frequently thereafter, *Meat out of the Eater* was widely read for its message of Christian solace.

The Diary of Michael Wigglesworth (1951, repr. 1970) was edited by Edmund S. Morgan. Richard Crowder wrote *No Featherbed in Heaven: A Biography of Michael Wigglesworth* (1962).

Wigwam and Cabin (1845–46),   stories by W. G. SIMMS. These are mainly ingenious stories of horror and the grotesque. In his preface Simms wrote: "The material employed will be found to illustrate, in large degree, the border history of the South. The life of the planter, the squatter, the Indian, and the Negro—the bold and hardy pioneer and the vigorous yeoman—these are the subjects. In their delineations, I have mostly drawn from living portraits and, in frequent instances, from actual scenes and circumstances within the memories of men." Edgar Allan Poe reviewed the collection and praised it highly, one story in particular: " 'Murder Will Out . . . ' we have no hesitation in calling the best ghost story we have ever read. It is full of the richest and most vigorous imagination."

Wilbarger, John Wesley (fl. 1839–1889),   memoirist. Wilbarger's account of pioneer life in Texas, called *Indian Depredation in Texas* (1889), provides a primary source for study of early settlements in the region.

Wilbur, Homer.   See BIGLOW PAPERS.

Wilbur, Richard (1921–   ),   poet. Wilbur was born in New York City, graduated from Amherst in 1942, served overseas in the infantry, and returned to study at Harvard (M.A., 1947). He taught there for some years and then began teaching at Wesleyan University in 1957. Later, he served as poet in residence at Smith College. He was appointed Poet Laureate of the United States in 1987. His poetry, which owes something to Marianne Moore as well as to the metaphysical school, is formal, polished, yet lively, witty, and full of ingratiating detail. His collections are *The Beautiful Changes* (1947), *Ceremony and Other Poems* (1950), *Things of This World* (1956); *Poems* (1957), and *Advice to a Prophet and Other*

Poems (1961). He has translated Molière's *The Misanthrope* (1955) and written songs for the Broadway production of *Candide* (1957). His other titles include *The Poems of Richard Wilbur* (1963); *Walking to Sleep: New Poems and Translations* (1969); *Seed Leaves: Homage to R. F.* (1974); *The Mind Reader: New Poems* (1976); *Responses: Prose Pieces 1948–1976* (1976); and *Mayflies: New Poems and Translations* (2000).

Wilcox, Ella Wheeler (1850–1919),   poet, novelist. Wilcox, born in Wisconsin, wrote works that some consider to be rife with platitudes and sentimentality, but in her day was extremely popular. She wrote a sentimental novel when she was ten, and her first essay was published when she was fourteen, her first poem not long after. She tried college for a while, but didn't like it and turned to newspaper work. When her *Poems of Passion* (1876) appeared, it was an overnight success because it was considered daring. Whatever the reason, her reputation was made. Wilcox published more than forty volumes, from *Drops of Water* (1872) to *The Worlds and I* (1918). Most of these were verse, some fiction, two autobiographical. Who does not know the first lines of "Solitude": "Laugh and the world laughs with you, / Weep and you weep alone"? See THE EROTIC SCHOOL.

Wilde, Percival (1887–1953),   playwright, novelist. Wilde, born in New York City and educated at Columbia, was a skilled writer of one-act plays, many of which appeared in collections: *Dawn and Other One-Act Plays of Life Today* (1915), *Confessional and Other American Plays* (1916), and *Comrades in Arms and Other Plays for Little Theaters* (1935). He also wrote *The Craftmanship of the One-Act Play* (1923), which he later (1951) revised to include a discussion of radio and television plays. In his later years he wrote several mystery novels. One, called *Inquest* (1940), won special praise.

Wilde, Richard Henry (1789–1847),   lawyer, legislator, poet. Wilde, born in Ireland, became a lawyer in Georgia and was elected to Congress. In Italy (1835–1840) he wrote studies of Italian literature, including *Conjectures . . . Concerning . . . Tasso* (2 v. 1842) and translated from the Italian poets. He returned to Georgia to practice law and later became professor of constitutional law at the University of Louisiana. He wrote a long poem called *Hesperia*, which his son edited and published in 1867. The poem, never completed, obviously shows the influence of Byron. Wilde is remembered by some today for a single poem, MY LIFE IS LIKE THE SUMMER ROSE, which was part of *The Lament of the Captive*, a projected epic on the Seminole War.

Wilder, Billy (1906–   ),   film director, screenwriter, producer. Wilder was born in Vienna, where he studied law briefly before becoming a journalist. In Berlin he got his first movie experience, but because he was Jewish, he fled the Nazis in 1933. After a year in Paris, he arrived in the U.S. with little money and no knowledge of English. In 1938, he began a long and productive collaboration with screenwriter CHARLES BRACKETT. Together they wrote sophisticated comedies such as *Ninotchka* (1939) and dramas such as *The Lost Weekend* (1945) and *Sunset Boulevard* (1950). Other Wilder films include *Sta-*

lag 17 (1953), *Some Like It Hot* (1959), and *The Apartment* (1960).

Wilder, Laura Ingalls (1867–1957),   author. The author of The Little House Books for children, Wilder spent her life in the Wisconsin and Dakota country she wrote about. The Little House Books are autobiographical, and their popularity with children lies in their vivid portrayals of a family's life on the frontier. The books in the series are *Little House in the Big Woods* (1932), *Farmer Boy* (1933), *Little House on the Prairie* (1935), *On the Banks of Plum Creek* (1937), *By the Shores of Silver Lake* (1939), *The Long Winter* (1940), *Little Town on the Prairie* (1941), and *These Happy Golden Years* (1943).

Wilder, Thornton (1897–1975),   teacher, novelist, playwright. Born in Wisconsin and reared in China and the United States, Wilder was educated at Yale and Princeton. He also conducted archaeological studies in Rome and taught French at the Lawrenceville School, in New Jersey. In 1926 he wrote *The Cabala*, an ironic novel of decadent Italian nobility, and had his first play, *The Trumpet Shall Sound*, produced at a little theater. THE BRIDGE OF SAN LUIS REY (1927), a novel tracing the lives of a number of people killed in a South American bridge catastrophe, was his first popular success and won a Pulitzer Prize. *The Woman of Andros* (1930), a story based on Terence's *Andria*, was another success, enabling Wilder to give up teaching for a time and enjoy European travel.

From 1930 to 1936 Wilder taught creative writing and "The Classics in Translation" at the University of Chicago, where his students found him a stimulating lecturer. He also published collections of one-act plays in *The Angel That Troubled the Waters* (1928) and *The Long Christmas Dinner* (1931), and a comic novel, *Heaven's My Destination* (1934). Influenced by Gertrude Stein's ideas about America and universality, he wrote OUR TOWN (1938), a moving drama that won a Pulitzer Prize. A farcical play, *The Merchant of Yonkers*, also appeared in 1938; it was revived more successfully as *The Matchmaker* (1955) and provided the plot for the popular musical *Hello Dolly*. THE SKIN OF OUR TEETH, which *Time* magazine described as "a sort of Hellzapoppin with brains," was produced in 1942 and promptly won its author a third Pulitzer Prize. It made use of some unique theatrical techniques, as did *Our Town*.

Wilder served as an intelligence officer with the Air Force in Italy during World War II and wrote THE IDES OF MARCH (1948), a witty and learned epistolary novel about Julius Caesar. *Someone from Assisi, Infancy*, and *Childhood*, produced in New York City, under the collective title *Plays for Bleecker Street*, were intended as part of a 14-play cycle that he never completed. His novel *The Eighth Day* (1967, National Book Award) chronicles a Midwestern family. His other works are his novel *Theophilus North* (1973) and *American Characteristics*, an essay collection (1979). He was awarded the first National Medal for Literature in 1965.

Wilderness Road,   also known as **Boone's Trace**. This was the route followed by settlers going from eastern Virginia through the Cumberland Gap to Kentucky. Fiction set in the area includes WINSTON CHURCHILL's *The Crossing* (1904) and ELIZABETH MADOX ROBERTS's *The Great Meadow* (1930).

Wildfire, Colonel Nimrod.   A character in THE LION OF THE WEST (1830), a play by James K. Paulding. A congressman from Kentucky, Wildfire is regarded as the first uncouth frontiersman in American drama.

Wild Honey Suckle, The (1786),   a poem by PHILIP FRENEAU. This pleasant but conventional lyric may be the first that took as its theme an American flower.

Wild Palms, The (1939),   a novel by WILLIAM FAULKNER. *The Wild Palms* contains two narratives that alternate with each chapter—the title piece and a contrasting story later published separately in the *Viking Portable Faulkner* (ed. by Malcolm Cowley, 1954) under the title "Old Man." Each is a study of society versus nature, of order juxtaposed with chaos. *The Wild Palms* deals with a young intern who falls in love with a married woman; in their attempt to escape from the civilization that they fear will kill their love, they flee to different parts of the country, but are never able to remain anywhere for long. They seek refuge from the world in a mining camp in an isolated part of Utah, but even there they are confronted with the effects of commercial exploitation. Finally the woman dies as a result of the unsuccessful abortion performed on her by her lover, who is imprisoned for life.

"Old Man" begins in prison, from which a tall convict is sent to do rescue work during the Mississippi flood of 1927. Finding a pregnant woman stranded by the rising water, he takes her into his boat and attempts to deliver himself and his charge back to the authorities—a task which, because of the violence of the flood, takes him almost three months. His stoical, uncommunicative endurance in the face of the flood and his unquestioning sense of obligation to fulfill his mission and return to prison are implicitly contrasted with the fruitless and frantic efforts of the young intern to escape from the world.

Wilkins, Mary E[leanor].   See MARY E[LEANOR] WILKINS FREEMAN.

Wilkinson, Anne (1910–1961),   poet, novelist. Born Anne Gibbons, a member of the prominent Osler family of Ontario, Wilkinson spent her early life in London, Ontario. She and her husband raised three children in Toronto. Her first publications were poetry collections: *Counterpoint to Sleep* (1951) and *The Hangman Ties the Holly* (1956). *The Collected Poems of Anne Wilkinson* appeared in 1968. In her novel *Lions in the Way* (1956) she traced the story of her family, providing details of social life in the backwoods of Canada. An epilogue takes the story up to her own childhood, including descriptions of her grandfather's luxurious Toronto mansion. *Swann and Daphne* (1960) is a story for children.

Wilkinson, James (1757–1825),   soldier, public official, memoirist. Wilkinson, born in Maryland, abandoned medical studies to join Washington's army. He was promoted to brigadier general in 1777 and made secretary to the board of war, a position he was forced to relinquish because of his involvement with an abortive plan to remove Washington as commander-in-chief. Moving to Kentucky in 1784, he became

a key figure in a plan to form a separate nation allied to Spain. He reentered the army in 1791, serving under Anthony Wayne. As governor of the Louisiana Territory (1805–1806) he was allied with Aaron Burr. Fearing his involvement with Burr would be revealed, he informed President Jefferson of Burr's plans to disrupt the Union. He was a witness against Burr but escaped indictment. An official inquiry into his actions in the War of 1812 also left him untouched. His *Memoirs of My Own Times* (3 v. 1816) is an attempt to answer his critics. He spent his last years in Mexico. He appears as a character in E. E. HALE's *Philip Nolan's Friends* (1877) and Constance Skinner's *The White Leader* (1926).

Wilkinson, Marguerite (1883–1928),   poet, writer on poets and poetry. Wilkinson came to the United States from Canada when she was very young. She loved poetry and wrote profusely. Among her books are *In Vivid Gardens* (1911), *The Dingbat of Arcady* (1922), and *Citadels* (1928). In addition, she wrote *Contemporary Poetry* (1923) and compiled some anthologies.

Willard, Emma Hart (1787–1870),   teacher, writer. Willard, born and raised in Connecticut, taught herself many subjects that were barred from the curricula of the female seminaries. When in 1814 she opened a school for women in Vermont, she began introducing such subjects. In 1818 she sent Governor DeWitt Clinton of New York her *Proposing a Plan for Improving Female Education*. In 1821 she moved her school to Troy, New York, where it was called the Troy Female Seminary, later the Emma Willard School. She also founded the Willard Association for the Mutual Improvement of Female Teachers (1837). She wrote accounts of her travels, advanced a theory of blood circulation that later was generally accepted, and wrote verse. One of her poems became widely known—"Rocked in the Cradle of the Deep"—title poem of an 1830 collection. It was set to music by Joseph P. Knight.

Willard, Frances Elizabeth [Caroline] (1839–1898), temperance reformer, school administrator, writer. Willard was born near Rochester, New York. From 1871 to 1874, she presided over the Evanston College for Ladies, meanwhile lecturing successfully on trips she had made to Europe. In 1874 she started on a temperance crusade that made her a public figure, especially when in 1879 she became president of the Women's Christian Temperance Union. She wrote *Woman and Temperance* (1883) and *Glimpses of 50 Years* (1889).

Willard, Josiah Flynt ["Josiah Flynt"] (1869–1907), hobo, sociologist. Willard, born in Wisconsin and the nephew of temperance reformer FRANCES WILLARD, took to the road in the United States and Europe and not only acquired the special language of tramps but even adopted their philosophy. He refused to condemn the denizens of the underworld; they were, he believed, creations of a corrupt police system. In Europe he studied at the University of Berlin and met some noted authors, but preferred his friends at the bottom. Among his books are *Tramping with Tramps* (1899), *Notes of an Itinerant Policeman* (1900), *The World of Graft* (1901), *The Little Brother* (1902), and *My Life* (1908).

Willard, Samuel (1640–1707),   clergyman, educator. A graduate of Harvard, Willard preached in western Massachusetts before becoming pastor of Boston's Old South Church (1678–1707). He also served as a vice-president of Harvard from 1700 until his death. His sermons were collected in *Compleat Body of Divinity* (1726).

Williams, Ben Ames (1889–1953),   journalist, novelist. A graduate of Dartmouth (1910), the Mississippi-born writer worked for Boston newspapers until he published his first novel, *All the Brothers Were Valiant* (1919). Among his many popular titles are *The Silver Forest* (1926); *Money Musk* (1932); *Leave Her to Heaven* (1944); *House Divided* (1947), a Civil War saga; and *The Unconquered* (1953), dealing with post–Civil War New Orleans. He also edited MARY BOYKIN CHESTNUT's *Diary* (1949), dealing with life in the Confederacy. *Thrifty Stock* (1923) is a story collection.

Williams, Bert [Egbert Austin] (1875–1922), comedian, songwriter. While still a child Williams left the Bahamas for the United States and joined a minstrel troupe. In 1895 he and George Walker formed a popular vaudeville team. In 1902 he wrote and produced an all-African-American musical show, *In Dahomey*, in which he and his partner appeared with great success. He continued to write similar shows—*Abyssinia* (1906), *Bandanna Land* (1907), and others—until the death of Walker in 1909. In that year Williams joined the Ziegfeld Follies, for which he wrote his own songs and other material.

Williams, C[harles] K[enneth] (1936–   ),   poet, translater. Born in Newark, New Jersey, Williams studied at Bucknell University and the University of Pennsylvania. Williams's second wife is French, and they divide their time each year between Paris and the United States. His first publication, a long poem entitled *A Day for Anne Frank*, appeared in 1968; the same year Williams met ANNE SEXTON who recommended him to her publisher, Houghton Mifflin, the house that printed his *Lies* the following year. *I Am a Bitter Name* (1972) is a condemnation of the United States' involvement in the Vietnam War. Some of the most explicitly political verses from that book were republished in *The Sensuous President* (1972), edited under the pseudonym "K," a collection of drawings and verse attacking Richard Nixon. *With Ignorance* (1977) uses the long lines that have become a trademark of his style, and demonstrates an interest in the less-favored or outcasts of society. Other titles include *Tar* (1983), *Flesh and Blood* (1987), *A Dream of the Mind* (1992), the Pulitzer Prize–winning *Repair* (1989) and *My Father, My Mother, Myself* (2000). Williams has translated Sophocles's *Women of Trachis* (1978) and Euripedes's *Bacchae* (1990).

Williams, Eleazar (1789?–1858),   Indian scout, missionary, pretender to the French throne. Williams is thought to have been born in New York City. He claimed to be the son of Thomas Williams, who may have had an Oneida Indian father and a mother descended from Eunice Williams. She was a white woman taken captive in the Deerfield Raid of 1704. Eleazer Williams wrote a biography of his reputed father, *Life*

of Te-ho-ra-gwa-ne-gen, Alias Thomas Williams (1859). But in 1853 Williams also claimed to be the son of Louis XVI, and therefore the Dauphin and Louis XVII. J. H. Hanson wrote an article for *Putman's Magazine* (February 1853) entitled "Have We a Bourbon Among Us?" This roused much interest and controversy, and Hanson expanded his article into a book, *The Lost Prince* (1854). The controversy continued for close to a century. In 1934 Meade Minnegerode published *The Son of Marie Antoinette* on Williams' claim. Williams himself wrote *The Salvation of Sinners Through the Riches of Divine Grace* (1842) and is believed to have simplified the Mohawk alphabet by dropping several letters when he was translating the *Book of Common Prayer* for use by Indians. Williams is the subject of a romance, *Lazarre* (1910), by MARY HARTWELL CATHERWOOD.

Williams, Garth Montgomery (1912–1996),   illustrator, author of books for children, stage designer. Williams was born in New York City, attended the Royal College of Art in London, and worked in advertising and in stage design as well becoming a painter of murals and a sculptor. Among his many books are *The Tall Book of Make Believe* (1950), *The Adventures of Benjamin Pink* (1951), and *The Rabbit's Wedding* (1958). He also illustrated E. B. WHITE's *Charlotte's Web* and *Stuart Little*, as well as other classic books for the young.

Williams, Henry.   See IN THE SHADE OF THE OLD APPLE TREE.

Williams, Jesse Lynch (1871–1929),   newspaperman, short-story writer, novelist, playwright. Williams was born in Illinois. While at Princeton, he and Booth Tarkington founded the Triangle Club and helped write its musical revues. His first publication was *Princeton Stories* (1895), written while he was a reporter for the New York *Sun. The Stolen Story* (1899) is a collection based on his newspaper experiences. His novels include *The Married Life of the Frederic Carrolls* (1910), *And So They Were Married* (1914), *Not Wanted* (1923), *They Still Fall in Love* (1929), and *She Knew She Was Right* (1930). *The Day Dreamer* (1906) is a play derived from the plot of *The Stolen Story. Why Marry?* (1917), based on *And So They Were Married*, won a Pulitzer Prize, the first ever given. His later plays are *Why Not?* (1922) and *Lovely Lady* (1925).

Williams, John (1664–1729),   Congregational clergyman. After graduation from Harvard, Williams served as pastor in Deerfield, Massachusetts. During the Deerfield Massacre (1704), an Indian raid of the French and Indian War, he and his family were taken prisoner. His wife and two of their children were killed, and Williams and a son and daughter were marched to Quebec, where the captives were delivered to Jesuit priests who tried to convert them to Roman Catholicism. The three became separated and, in 1706, Williams was released from captivity and returned to Massachusetts where, at the urging of Cotton Mather, he wrote an account of his experiences published in 1707 as THE REDEEMED CAPTIVE RETURNED TO ZION. It included accounts of the raid, the march north, the proselytizing of the Jesuits, and letters Williams exchanged with his son. In some of the many printings, a Williams sermon is appended: "Reports of Divine Kindness, or Remarkable Mercies Should be Faithfully Published for the Praise of God the Giver." Williams's son was also set free and renounced his conversion to Catholicism. The youngest daughter, Eunice (see ELEAZAR WILLIAMS), refused to leave her Indian husband or renounce Catholicism.

Williams, John ["Anthony Pasquin"] (1761–1818), newspaper writer, satirist. Williams, born in England and an inveterate controversialist, first became a painter, then a translator, and then wrote for several Dublin newspapers. He also worked as a drama critic in England for a while, but soon became embroiled in various difficulties and decided to go to America. His pet aversion there was Alexander Hamilton, whom he attacked in a virulent verse satire. *The Hamiltoniad* (1804). He also wrote *The Children of Thespis* (1792) and *The Pin-Basket to the Children of Thespis* (1797).

Williams, John A[lfred] (1925–   ), novelist, poet. Williams was born in Mississippi and, after serving in the U.S. Navy during World War II, was educated at Syracuse University. He has worked for various New York publishers and advertising agencies. His first two novels, *The Angry Ones* (1960) and *Night Song* (1961), center on artists fighting against racial discrimination. Williams's strong assertion of African–American pride is evident in his biography of Richard Wright, *The Most Native of Sons* (1970), and in several of his politically militant novels. These include *Sissie* (1963), the story of an old African–American woman. *The Man Who Cried I Am* presents the recollections of a dying African–American author (1967). *Sons of Darkness, Sons of Light* (1969) concerns racial conflict in New York City. *Captain Blackman* (1972) details the experiences of an African–American soldier in Vietnam. His other novels include *Mothersill and the Foxes* (1975), *The Junior Bachelor Society* (1976), and *!Click Song* (1982). Williams has also written poetry and nonfiction, including *Africa: Her History, Lands and People* (1962); *This Is My Country, Too* (1965); and *The King God Didn't Save* (1970), a biography of Martin Luther King, Jr. Williams edited *Amistad I* (1970) and *Amistad II* (1971), essay collections on African–American history and culture.

Williams, John E[dward] (1922–1994), novelist, poet. Williams, born in Texas, served in World War II before attending the University of Denver, where he wrote his first novel, *Nothing But the Night* (1948). After earning a Ph.D. at the University of Missouri and studying at Oxford University, he worked as an editor and taught creative writing at several universities. His novels include *Butcher's Crossing* (1960), concerning the 19th-century frontier; *Stoner* (1965), about a college professor: and *Augustus* (1972), set in imperial Rome. His verse is collected in *The Broken Landscape* (1949) and *The Necessary Lie* (1965).

Williams, Joy (1944–   ), novelist, short-story writer. A native of Chelmsford, Massachusetts, Williams was educated at Marietta College and the University of Iowa. Key West, Florida, is the area she uses as a setting for much of her fiction. Her novels include *State of Grace* (1973), *The*

Changeling (1978), and *Breaking and Entering* (1988). *Taking Care* (1982) is a short-story collection; *The Florida Keys: A History and Guide* appeared in 1986. After more than a decade without a fiction publication, Williams brought out *The Quick and The Dead* (2000), concerning three teenage girls in the West.

Williams, Oscar (1900–1964),   poet, anthologist. Williams, born in New York City, was educated in Brooklyn public schools. For a number of years he was a successful advertising man, but abandoned advertising to write poetry, principally concerning the menace and disorder of urban life. His first two collections of poems, *The Golden Darkness* and *In Gossamer Grey*, were published in 1921. His next published work was *The Man Coming Toward You* (1940). It was followed by *That's All That Matters* (1945) and *Selected Poems* (1947). He was best known as an editor of poetry anthologies, among them *New Poems* (a series, 1940, 1942, 1943, 1944); *The War Poets* (1945); *A Little Treasury of Modern Poetry* (1946); *A Little Treasury of Great Poetry* (1947); *A Little Treasury of American Poetry* (1948); *A Little Treasury of British Poetry* (1951); *Immortal Poems of the English Language* (1952); Palgrave's *Golden Treasury* (ed., 1953); and *The Pocket Book of Modern Verse* (1954).

Williams, Roger (1603?–1683),   clergyman, colonist, writer. A highly educated man of deep religious and civic feeling, Williams at first was ordained in the Church of England. He then became a Puritan and emigrated to Massachusetts. He became pastor at Salem, moved to Plymouth, then returned to Salem. Because of his opposition to authoritarianism the Massachusetts General Court sentenced him to exile (1635). He sought refuge in what is now Rhode Island, where some of his followers joined him and founded the city of Providence. He established freedom for all creeds in his colony, treated the local Native Americans well, and in 1639 founded the first Baptist Church in America. Soon he became a seeker rather than a follower of any particular creed. He negotiated a charter for PROVIDENCE PLANTATIONS in 1644 and served as governor for several terms. His last years were clouded because of trouble with Indian tribes. During King Philip's War, Providence was razed.

Williams contributed enormously to the establishment of religious freedom as a fundamental doctrine. Passionately religious, as Perry Miller calls him in *Roger Williams: His Contribution to American Tradition* (with many selections from Williams, 1953), he was equally passionate in demanding that society respect sincerely held opinions. He was the first to welcome Jews to any American colony, though he opposed the Quakers.

Among the many writings of Roger Williams, the most remarkable is *A Key into the Language of America* (1643, repr. 1936), but Williams is known as a writer primarily for THE BLOUDY TENET OF PERSECUTION, FOR CAUSE OF CONSCIENCE, DISCUSSED (1644). His other works include *Mr. Cotton's Letter Lately Printed, Examined and Answered* (1644); *Queries of Highest Consideration* (1644); *The Bloudy Tenet Yet More*

Bloudy (1652); *The Hireling Ministry None of Christ's* (1652); *Experiments of Spiritual Life and Health* (1652); and *George Fox Digged Out of His Burrowes* (1676).

The Complete Writings of Roger Williams (6 v. 1866–1874) was reprinted with a seventh volume and an intepretive essay by Perry Miller in 1963. Perry Miller's *Roger Williams: His Contribution to the American Tradition* (1953) includes generous samples of Williams's writings. Recent studies include Henry Chupack, *Roger Williams* (1969); John Garrett, *Roger Williams: Witness Beyond Christendom* (1970); and W. Clark Gilpin, *The Millenarian Piety of Roger Williams* (1979). Williams appears as a fictional character in Daniel P. Thompson's *The Doomed Chief* (1860) and in W. D. Schofield's *Ashes in the Wilderness* (1942).

Williams, Tennessee [Thomas Lanier] (1911–1983), dramatist, fiction writer, poet. Thomas Lanier Williams III was born in Mississippi, the second of three children of Cornelius Coffin Williams, a traveling salesman, and Edwina Dakin Williams, a minister's daughter. As Williams would later remark, he was the heir of both Cavaliar and Calvinist strains in his ancestry. From early childhood he was emotionally close to his sister Rose, two years his elder. A sickly child, Williams read omnivorously and engaged in inventive play with his sister, affectionately supervised by Ozzie, an African-American servant. The family moved frequently, setting a pattern for Williams himself throughout his life. In 1918, when Edwina was pregnant with her third child, Cornelius moved his family away from his in-laws to St. Louis, to the disappointment of the children. When Edwina gave her son a typewriter for his eleventh birthday, the boy began to write—and he continued to write, with only intermittent lapses, for the rest of his life.

During three years at the University of Missouri, young Thomas Williams won prizes for verse and fiction, but he also read the plays of Strindberg whom he saw as a kindred spirit. Although Williams had seen little live theater, he wrote a few dramatic pieces. His father was intolerant of his son's writing, and, seizing upon his failure in ROTC at the height of the Depression, declined further support for his son. Back in St. Louis Williams first went to business school and then worked in a shoe warehouse. Performing routine tasks during the day—Williams later called it his "season in hell"—he continued to write at night, and the result in 1935 was an emotional breakdown, which not only incapacitated Williams for months but shook his sister's increasingly weak hold on sanity.

While recuperating at the home of his maternal grandparents in Memphis, Williams was strengthened in his determination to be a writer. Back in St. Louis he attended Washington University. In the mid-1930s, too, he first became aware of his homosexuality, and he discovered the poetry of HART CRANE, which appears to have been the major literary influence on Williams. After winning a Theater Guild contest—and failing in Greek—Williams transferred to the playwriting program at the University of Iowa, where he received his B.A. degree in 1938. In 1937, while Williams was at Iowa, a prefrontal lobtomy had been performed on his sister Rose, and she was institutionalized for the rest of her life.

During 1939 Williams was an itinerant writer in the South and the West, signing his works "Tennessee Williams." After winning a Group Theater award for some one-act plays, *American Blues*, he acquired Audrey Wood as an agent and moved temporarily to New York City. His hope for a New York production did not survive the 1940 Boston failure of his *Battle of Angels*, which he later would revise as *Orpheus Descending*. Rejected by the armed forces during World War II, Williams drifted through a variety of odd jobs to support his writing, but in 1945 *The Glass Menagerie* succeeded on Broadway, and Williams was never again in financial need—although he would often complain that he was. Between 1945 and 1961, when he won his fourth New York Drama Critics' Circle award, Williams was lionized on Broadway, where he opened a new play biannually.

The American theater scene changed radically during the 1960s. Serious drama was not popular on Broadway, and European Absurdists conquered the avant-garde. At the same time, the actor-centered work of The Living Theater and The Open Theater did not welcome the lyricism and violence of writers such as Williams. He nevertheless continued to write plays—as well as poems, fiction, and defensive essays—and he depended increasingly on alcohol and drugs, especially after the death in 1963 of his former lover, Frank Merlo. Although Williams called the 1960s his "stoned age," he nevertheless produced several plays. In 1969 he followed his younger brother, Dakin, into the Catholic Church. So distraught was Williams by the end of the year that Dakin had him committed to Barnes Hospital in St. Louis, where he underwent detoxification. He never forgave Dakin for what he had done and he soon returned to drugs.

Although Williams was haunted by death for all his adult life, his actual death, in a New York City hotel, was a wasteful accident. He choked on the plastic top of a nose spray, which he may have been using as a spoon for pills. Seventy-two years old, frail and unhappy, he had nevertheless experienced creative surges that are still not fully appreciated. In an interview that he recorded in his *Memoirs*, Williams explains his preoccupation with death: "Any artist dies two deaths . . . not only his own as a physical being but that of his creative power. . . ." In spite of a hostile press during the last two decades of his life, Tennessee Williams died only one death.

Tennessee Williams published two books of poems, two novels, four volumes of short fiction, a gathering of essays, an autobiography, and over sixty plays—about half of these providing a full evening in the theater. A compulsive reviser, Williams acknowledged: "My longer plays emerge out of earlier one-acters or short stories I may have written years before. I work over them again and again." Although revision does not always constitute improvement, it has burnished the dramas for which he is most acclaimed—THE GLASS MENAGERIE (1944) and A STREETCAR NAMED DESIRE (1947).

Lester Beaurline has traced the evolution of *Menagerie*. Before 1943 Williams wrote a short story, "Portrait of a Girl in Glass"; also before 1943 he adapted this story into a five-scene one-act play. In 1943, while working for MGM movie studios, he adapted the story and/or play into a film scenario, "The Gentleman Caller," which is no longer extant. Later in 1943 he enlarged the play to seven scenes, and this became the reading version of *The Glass Menagerie* that is found in most anthologies. During Chicago rehearsals he revised further, and in 1948 published the eight-scene acting version, available only through Dramatists' Play Service. It is unfortunate that this final version is not the one usually anthologized, since it is crisper and more concentrated.

Both the reading and the acting versions of *The Glass Menagerie* are so-called memory plays. The memorialist is Tom—Tennessee's real name. Tom looks back with compassion and some humor at the stifling St. Louis tenement apartment in which he lived with his nagging mother and lame sister. All four of the *Menagerie* characters retreat from the Depression in St. Louis to their individual fantasy worlds. Amanda, the mother, dwells on her past as a Southern belle. Jim, the gentleman caller, wavers between his glorious past in high school and his nebulous future in public speaking. Tom escapes to the movies or to his own writing. Laura flees from business school to her glass menagerie, which is led by a unicorn, a doubly imaginary animal. Too much has been written of the playwright's exploitation of his mother and sister for *Menagerie*. Although no other American playwright has portrayed female yearning with such sympathy, *The Glass Menagerie* endures because Williams was able to transmute autobiography into a work of mythic dimensions, where two women conjure a fading family structure and a failing society.

Williams may have seduced Broadway by the poetic stealth of *The Glass Menagerie*, but he stormed its ramparts with the daring of his 1947 drama, *A Streetcar Named Desire*. Williams, in the belief that he was dying, imbued the drama with a desperate intensity, and from then on the name Tennessee Williams would be triangulated into the South, sex, and violence. Elia Kazan was selected to direct this inflammatory blend, and he cast the play largely with members of the Actor's Studio. The impact of their performance was so strong that hard-hitting naturalism would become the dominant style on the American stage and especially on the screen. *Streetcar's* two-year run on Broadway spurred decades of critical debate, and no matter how explicit sexuality and violence have escalated since 1947, the drama retains its power to move audiences.

Although Blanche DuBois and Stanley Kowalski generate incandescence on the stage, Williams does not compel us to choose between them. The elegant South of Blanche's *Belle Rêve* has been displaced by Stanley's New Orleans populism, but both have a cruel streak. Stanley has provided a home for Stella and leadership for his friends, but he is violently sexist. Blanche boasts of her culture and compassion, but she has mortally wounded her young husband, indulged her desires in the face of death, and invaded the privacy of her sister's home. From a contemporary vantage, we can see that both Blanche and Stanley are emblematic of fading ways of life. In 1947, however, the two bold figures shocked audiences into a new

examination of American acting and American habits. Williams, sometimes called a scenewright rather than a playwright, indelibly etches our final view of Blanche, departing in dignity on the arm of a stranger and oblivious to the poker players who rise in respect—in spite of themselves.

Having gained notoriety as the creator of faded Southern belles, Williams flouted that formula in Maggie, the decidedly vigorous cat of CAT ON A HOT TIN ROOF (1955). Adapted from a short story, *Cat* dramatizes a woman's struggle to reclaim her husband from alcoholism and sexual indifference. Looming larger than the problematic marriage, however, is the husband's father, Big Daddy of insatiable appetites, who is dying of cancer. Although the old man appreciates Maggie the cat, he figures only minimally in the plot. The play's first director, Elia Kazan, perhaps smarting from the 1953 failure of *Camino Real*, persuaded Williams to compose a new third act, with a more optimistic ending and a valedictory appearance of Big Daddy. Williams complied, but he published the play with both endings. Dedicated to his agent, Audrey Wood, the original *Cat on a Hot Tin Roof* was the personal favorite of Williams among all his plays: "It comes closest to being both a work of art and a work of craft."

In 1961, at the age of 50, Williams was applauded on Broadway for the last time, winning his fourth New York Drama Critics' Circle award. *The Night of the Iguana* is set not in the South but in Mexico. Sexual potency is no longer a metaphor for creative vigor, and violence is subdued. The titular night witnesses not only the liberation of the iguana, but also the death of "a 97-year *young* poet," the continued nomadism of his granddaughter and, centrally, a libidinal haven for T. Lawrence Shannon, a defrocked Episcopalian minister given to alcohol and fornication. Although many Williams plays dwell on the past of their main characters, *Iguana* is the first to exude great weariness in the fabric of the present. Combined with the drunkenness and sexual profligacy, *Iguana* is almost a prophecy of its author's next decade.

Although revivals tend to support the awards given to *Glass Menagerie, Streetcar Named Desire, Cat on a Hot Tin Roof*, and *Night of the Iguana*, the full range of the playwright's exploration is rarely acknowledged. Consider the Dionysian farce of THE ROSE TATTOO (1948), the Expressionist quest of *Camino Real* (1953), the domestic comedy of *Period of Adjustment* (1958), and the cruel verbal duel of *Suddenly Last Summer* (1958), as well as many mood and memory plays. At the end of the 1960s, as though accepting his exile from Broadway, Williams built plays around the artist-protagonist and at the same time—with uneven results—he inaugurated his most radical stage experiments.

Almost universally castigated for his last plays, Williams deserves respect both for application and achievement. His *Slapstick Tragedy* (1966) embraces two contrasting representations of indomitable vigor in the face of the most grotesque cruelties. *In the Bar of a Tokyo Hotel* (1969) experiments with syntactical fragmentation to mirror the spiritual fragmentation of the painter who dies during the course of the drama.

Although *Vieux Carré* (1972) returns to a familiar New Orleans setting, the boardinghouse is newly peopled with artists—not only a writer, but a jazz clarinetist, a tubercular painter, and a dying fashion designer. By the end of the play, the first two depart, and the last two die, but the boardinghouse has been transformed into an art gallery. Though artists may be transient, art endures.

Less positive, *Clothes for a Summer Hotel* (1980) plays the effervescence of the American expatriate 1920s against the asylum in which Zelda Fitzgerald was confined until she died in a fire in 1947. The titular clothes are worn by Scott Fitzgerald, when he flies from Hollywood to visit his institutionalized wife, believing erroneously that her condition has improved. As in other plays by Williams, the protagonist Zelda is a suffering Southern woman, and the playwright makes inventive use of the Southern asylum setting—its ominous gates, howling wind, and intermittent lights that presage the final fire. As in earlier plays, the characters—especially Hemingway and the Fitzgeralds—explode in passion, but the personal crises of writers are transmuted into the fiction that is our cultural heritage.

The late Tennessee Williams plays have been too summarily dismissed, particularly *Out Cry*, which preoccupied the playwright between 1967 and 1975—the play was the putative cause of his break with his longtime friend and agent, Audrey Wood. Through the playwright's *Memoirs* runs the leitmotif of his yearning for an adequate production of *Out Cry*. He did not live to see the full potential of a drama that dynamically enfolds a prototypical old Williams plot into the mature awareness of his constant devotion to the art of theater. An actress and her playwright-actor brother, deserted by their theater company, perform in an unknown country at an uncertain time "The Two-Character Play." That play within the theater frame pivots on a brother and sister in their Southern home, where their astrologer father has shot their mother and then himself. As critics have refused to separate the life of Tennessee Williams from his drama, Williams refuses to separate the two characters of his inner and outer plays, weaving them instead into a shimmering tapestry. Through the familiar ingredients of South, sex, and violence, Williams probes the cannibalization of all life by all art.

The art of Tennessee Williams, an indefatigable writer for over half a century, still lacks appreciative analysis. Although Williams tried to accommodate himself to the prevalent realistic mode of American theater, he strained against the picture-frame stage, the crisp conflict, and the definite resolution. Coming late to the Southern literary renaissance, Williams shared his countrymen's taste for the grotesque, but he was neither nostalgic nor sentimental about his native region. At his worst—which too many critics seize upon gleefully—he sentimentalized the misfit. At his best, he invested his misfits with an undidactic dignity that implicitly condemns our materialistic society. Arthur Miller, his contemporary, has praised his accomplishment: "What was new in Tennessee Williams was his rhapsodic insistence that form serve his utterance rather than dominating and cramping it. In him the American theater found, perhaps for the first time, an eloquence and an amplitude of feeling."

In addition to his plays, Williams published two novels, *The Roman Spring of Mrs. Stone* (1950) and *Moise and the World of Reason* (1975). The stories from four earlier books were gathered in *Collected Stories* (1985). His volumes of verse are *In the Winter of Cities* (1956, rev. 1964) and *Androgyne, Mon Amour* (1977). Selected essays were edited by Christine R. Day and Bob Woods in *Where I Live* (1978).

Williams has been badly served by criticism—both his own and that of strangers. The seven volumes of *The Theatre of Tennessee Williams* (apparently chosen by him before his death) are quixotically edited, and they do not contain all his plays. The *Memoirs* (1975) and the biography by his brother Dakin Williams (1983) are both embarrassingly inadequate, failing to illuminate the work. (Williams asks in his autobiography: "Of course, I could have devoted this whole book to a discussion of the art of drama, but wouldn't that be a bore?" The answer is a resounding "No," not when we consider the bore he actually produced.) Only one full biography and one slim volume of criticism (aside from haphazard collections) have appeared since the death of Williams in 1983. Donald Spoto, in *The Kindness of Strangers* (1985), provides a plethora of detail, often correcting current legends, but he virtually reduces the plays and other works to autobiography. In spite of good insights Roger Boxill, *Tennessee Williams* (1987), tends to be too formulaic about the faded Southern belle and the male wanderer in the dramas of Williams. C. W. Bigsby's hundred-odd pages on Williams in Volume II of his *Critical Introduction to Twentieth-Century American Drama* is learned and intelligent but strays too far from the individual plays. Brenda Murphy's *Tennessee Williams and Elia Kazan: A Collaboration in the Theatre* appeared in 1992, and Ronald Hayman's *Tennessee Williams: Everyone Else Is an Audience* in 1994. *The Selected Letters of Tennessee Williams, Vol 1, 1920–1945* appeared in 2000. Williams awaits a critic worthy of what he has called in his *Memoirs* "the loveliest of all four-letter words"—Work!

RUBY COHN

Williams, William Carlos (1883–1963), poet, short-story writer, novelist, essayist, critic, playwright. Williams was born in Rutherford, New Jersey, the first planned commuter suburb to feed into the metropolis of New York City. Except for several extended stays in New York City and in Europe, Williams was to spend his eighty years rooted to this suburban town, for fifty of those years serving his community as a physician and later as a pediatrician.

His very name carries within it the two cultural strains that shaped his life and his poetry. His father, William George Williams, though he left England with his mother as a boy and spent his adult life selling cologne products in the West Indies and in Latin America, settling in Rutherford for the last thirty-six years of his life, died a British subject. Williams's mother, Helene Raquel, née Hoheb, a woman of Basque, French, and Jewish lineage, grew up in Mayaguez and St. Thomas and in her twenties spent several years in Paris studying art and paint-ing, before returning to Mayaguez when money ran out. Soon after, she married the father of the poet and moved to Ruther-ford, but she never let her son forget that she was a gifted artist whose career had been frustrated by financial circumstances. Ezra Pound was right to see Williams as an outsider in Amer-ica for, like millions of other immigrant families, English was the acquired language in a household where, in this instance, Spanish, French, and then British English were the languages spoken at home. This fact helps explain the intense interest of the poet in a distinctively American idiom, to which these, like so many other language strains, contributed.

In the late 1880s and 1890s Williams, together with his one sibling, Edgar, attended the Rutherford public schools. At the beginning of 1898, the two boys and their mother sailed to Europe. The boys were enrolled first at the Château de Lancy, outside Geneva, and then in the fall at the Lycée Condorcet, in Paris. On their return to Rutherford in the spring of 1899, the boys entered Horace Mann High School, in New York City. After Williams was graduated in 1902, he went on to the Uni-versity of Pennsylvania to study dentistry before switching to medicine. It was there that he met EZRA POUND, two years his junior. In spite of strains on the relationship, Pound was to remain one of Williams's closest friends for the rest of his life and provide him with literary guidance. At nearby Bryn Mawr, Williams met HILDA DOOLITTLE (H. D.), another lifelong literary friend, and, over a dish of prunes at the boarding house where he was living, the painter Charles Demuth.

After graduating from Penn in June 1906, Williams interned in New York City, first at French Hospital and then at Nursery and Children's Hospital in the Hell's Kitchen section of the city. Bright, idealistic, hardworking, Williams had expectations of eventually practicing medicine in Manhattan. But when he decided to write a letter detailing what he saw as a case of petty fraud at Children's, involving no less a figure than the power-ful financier J. P. Morgan, Williams resigned from the hospital and returned to his parents' home in 1909. That summer, he had *Poems*, his first book of poetry, privately printed in Rutherford and put on sale locally for 25 cents a copy. On its cover, in his brother's lettering, Williams garlanded his pam-phlet with quotations from Shakespeare and Keats—"Happy Melodist—Forever Piping Songs Forever New." When Pound, by this point self-exiled to London, read these flowery paeans to innocence and other abstractions, he bluntly informed Williams that he was twenty years out of date and that he had better get over to England as soon as possible and learn how to write.

That fall, after losing to his brother the woman to whom he had hoped to become engaged, and on impulse secretly becoming engaged to the woman's younger sister, Williams sailed not for London, but for Leipzig and a year of advanced work in pediatrics, financed by his parents. In the spring of 1910, he left Germany and traveled to London, where he saw Pound and met Yeats, and then went on to Italy, where his brother was studying architecture.

Back in Rutherford, Williams set up medical practice in his parents' house and, in December 1912, married his fiancée, Florence (Floss) Hermann, the woman who became his wife and friend for the rest of his life. In 1913, he and Floss moved into 9 Ridge Road, a Victorian house that was to remain their home. Williams practiced medicine out of the office attached to the house and over the next half century he wrote some forty-five books. The Williamses had two children, William Eric Williams, born in 1914, and Paul Williams, born in 1916. Paul became a businessman, and William Eric followed in his father's footsteps as a pediatrician and finally took over his father's practice when Williams became too infirm to practice any longer.

In September 1913, with the help of Pound and Pound's London publisher, Elkin Mathews, Williams published his sec-ond book of poems, *The Tempers*, a bolder volume laced with dramatic monologues that too clearly show Pound's influence. It was a transition volume. By the time he published his third book of poems, *Al Que Quiere!* (1917), Williams had found his own immediately recognizable poetic idiom. By then he had also made contact with a number of American poets in the vanguard of the Modernist movement, including Carl Sand-burg, Alfred Kreymborg, Wallace Stevens, and Marianne Moore, and was publishing *regularly in Poetry* (Chicago) and in the New York-based *Others*. If *Sour Grapes* (1921) contin-ued the work begun in *Al Que Quiere!*, Williams was attempt-ing in *Kora in Hell* (1918) to write a series of prose improvisations—brilliant but often opaque, and owing as much to the manifestos of Kandinsky as to Rimbaud—which the poet introduced with a long and important "Prologue" in 1920. Here he outlined the direction he hoped American poetry would follow, in the process taking some well-aimed shots not only at H. D. and Stevens, but especially at Pound's protégé and fellow-expatriate, T. S. Eliot, for his "Prufrock" and "Portrait of a Lady," an attack not lost on Eliot.

In the early 1920s Williams, with the help of ROBERT MCAL-MON, published five issues of an avant-garde magazine called *Contact*, which featured work by Marianne Moore, Wallace Stevens, and Williams, as well as other experimental writers such as Emmanuel Carnevalli. In 1923 Pound helped Williams get his experimental antinovella, *The Great American Novel*, printed in Paris, and in the same year McAlmon published Williams's most important book of poems to date, *Spring and All*. This volume, with its prose interspersed, is in fact a brilliant description, with examples, of what Williams meant by the modern imagination and what was distinctively modern about modern poetry. Unfortunately, only 300 copies were printed, most of which were never distributed, so the book's full impact was not felt until it became available again fifty years later.

The other seminal text Williams wrote in this decade was IN THE AMERICAN GRAIN (1925), his impressionistic study of American history from its beginnings (with Leif Ericson) up through Abraham Lincoln. The book also attempts to under-stand, without being chauvinistic, what is distinctively Ameri-can about the American literary experience, a question that preoccupied Williams all through his life. And while the book is subjective and certainly impassioned, the writing is always spirited and brilliant, and won high praise for its author from D. H. Lawrence, whose STUDIES IN CLASSIC AMERICAN LITERATURE (1923) had influenced Williams's own book. It remains an American classic prose text.

In the ten years after 1915, Williams became an increasingly vital part of the New York avant-garde, meeting not only many of the figures of the radical left, but especially such artists as Man Ray, Marcel Duchamp, Marsden Hartley, and Charles Scheeler—Hartley and Scheeler become his close friends—as well as Kenneth Burke, Walter Arensberg, Lola Ridge (at whose Greenwich Village apartment he met the Russian poet, Vladimir Mayakovsky), the novelist Evelyn Scott, the Baroness Elsa von Freytag Loringhoven, Hart Crane, and e. e. cummings.

Williams, at the beginning of 1924, halfway through the sabbatical he had promised himself when he reached forty, sailed to Europe with Floss and spent the next six months traveling around Europe. They started in Paris and moved on to southern France, Florence, Rome, Venice, and several months in Vienna, where Williams studied pediatrics. They went on to Switzerland and ended up once more in Paris. During the trip, Williams saw, among others, Joyce, Hemingway, Ford Madox Ford, McAlmon, H. D., Bryher, Djuna Barnes, Nancy Cunard, Mina Loy, Kay Boyle, Brancusi, Man Ray, Louis Aragon, and Valéry Larbaud, the critic-scholar who figures centrally in *In the American Grain*. While in Europe Williams worked on *In the American Grain*, his posthumously published *Rome Journal*, and had the experiences he transformed into his first true novel, *A Voyage to Pagany* (1928).

In the summer of 1927 he returned to Europe with his family to settle his sons in a Geneva school, where they might enjoy the experience Williams and his brother had had thirty-five years earlier. Sailing back to the U.S., he began writing "The Descent of Winter," a mixture of prose and poetry in the vein of *Spring and All,* though less successful than the earlier book. This was published the following year in Pound's *The Exile*. In 1929 Williams published his translation of Philippe Soupault's *Last Nights in Paris*, a novel about the life of a Paris prostitute, whose world Williams had glimpsed during his 1924 stay.

While continuing to practice pediatrics and delivering hundreds of babies, Williams continued to write during every spare moment he could find. In the early 1930s, besides editing another magazine with Nathanael West—this one also called *Contact*—Williams also published two additional volumes of prose. The first was *A Novelette and Other Prose* (1932), published by To Publishers in Toulon, France. It consisted of his novelette *January* and thirteen critical essays and stories. Later that year he published *The Knife of the Times and Other Stories* with the Dragon Press of Ithaca, New York. It was the first of his three collections of short stories and includes his brilliant cubist portrait, "Old Doc Rivers."

Then came three volumes of poetry in as many years. The first of these was *Collected Poems 1921–1931*, edited by Louis Zukofsky and published by *The Objectivist Press* (the old To

Press, with the backing of the OBJECTIVISTS, Zukofsky, George Oppen, and Carl Rakosi). Despite its title, the book was not published until 1934, with a preface by Wallace Stevens hailing Williams as the proponent of the antipoetic, a term Williams came to distrust. In the following year, 1935, Ronald Lane Latimer's Alcestis Press published Williams's *An Early Martyr and Other Poems* and in 1936 his *Adam & Eve & The City*, each in editions of less than 200.

Finally, in 1936, Williams found in JAMES LAUGHLIN, founder of New Directions and a disciple of Pound's, the publisher he had been looking for. Laughlin began by publishing Williams's novel *White Mule* in 1937, the first in a trilogy based on the Stecher family, a sharp and sympathetic imagining of the lives and fortunes of his in-laws as representative European immigrants coming to terms with American life, and including the imaginative re-creation of the birth of his wife and the first year of her life. In the following year Laughlin published Williams's second collection of short stories (nineteen in all), called *Life Along the Passaic River*, a volume that includes such anthology pieces as "The Use of Force," "The Girl with the Pimply Face," and "Jean Beicke." Late in the following year, he published Williams's *The Complete Collected Poems 1906–1938* in an edition of 1500 copies. In 1940 *In the Money*, the second volume of the Stecher trilogy, was published, and in 1941 a thin volume of Williams's new poems called *The Broken Span* in Laughlin's Poet of the Month series. But it was the last book to be published by New Directions for the next five years, Laughlin citing drastic paper shortages as a result of America's entry into World War II as the reason.

During the war, Williams continued to practice medicine at home, while his two sons served in the armed forces. It was then that Williams again began working on a project that had preoccupied him in one form or another since he had written "The Wanderer" in 1913. This was his autobiographical epic PATERSON, named for the manufacturing city just six miles from where he had grown up. Williams saw *Paterson* as his answer to Whitman's SONG OF MYSELF, Pound's CANTOS, Eliot's THE WASTE LAND, and Hart Crane's THE BRIDGE, all of which figure in Williams's poem.

Paterson is in four parts. *Paterson I*, published in 1946, deals with the elemental makeup of the city (the male) and its public park on Garrett Mountain (the female), together with the Passaic's still-majestic falls, despite their heavy pollution by the city's silk mills and other industries. The falls seem to represent the inherent possibilities of language itself, as well as the tawdry reality of that language as we hear it actually used. *Paterson II* (1948) deals more particularly with the poet's search for a language as he crosses and recrosses the depleted soil of the failed Eden the park has become and notes with despair what has happened to the people who work in Paterson's mills. *Paterson III* (1949) reenacts the threefold destruction of Paterson by flood, fire, and tornado in 1902–3, and the subsequent miracle of rebirth as the city—like the poem—rises from its ashes. *Paterson IV* (1951) celebrates the necessary replacement of the father (Williams himself as Van Winkle) by the children who must replace him: his biological son, William Eric, who would continue the tradition of caring for the bodies of Paterson's inhabitants, and Allen Ginsberg, whose poems, raw and vital, would carry on the struggle to make the poem new. In truth, the list of younger poets whom Williams has influenced reads like a roll call of contemporary American poety: Charles Olson, Theodore Roethke, Robert Lowell, David Ignatow, Denise Levertov, Robert Creeley, James Wright, Galway Kinnell, Philip Levine, and James Laughlin himself. Williams's home was always open to visitors, and hundreds of writers, from those well known to many still obscure, enjoyed the Williams hospitality. Williams tried always to make himself accessible, providing advice not only to figures like Pound and Lowell and Ginsberg, but to amateur writers and high school students who had been assigned to read his poems.

If much of the 1940s was taken up with the challenge of finding a viable form for Paterson, Williams still found time to publish two new groundbreaking books of poems with The Cummington Press of Massachusetts. The first was The Wedge, printed in 1944 in an edition of 380; the second The Clouds, printed in 1948 in an edition of 310. Then, in 1949, at age 65, Williams saw his first Selected Poems in print. The book was 140 pages long, had an intelligent introduction by Randall Jarrell, and was published in an initial run of 3600 copies, followed by another 4000 in the following year, another 6800 in 1963, and reprinted in batches of 10,000 copies from 1965 on.

After 1950, with the success of Paterson and the awards beginning at last to come his way, Williams had the wider audience he had spent the past forty years working for. In 1950 New Directions published his Collected Later Poems, the collected poems of the late 1930s and 1940s, followed in 1951 by The Collected Earlier Poems. Now his work could begin to be reassessed in the light of his more celebrated contemporaries, especially his bête noir, T. S. Eliot, whom Williams finally met in 1948, by which time, Williams believed, the battle for MODERNISM had already been fought. It would be left to the younger generation of poets, he told Lowell, to decide what would be salvaged for posterity.

Beginning in 1950, however, a rift arose between Williams and Laughlin. Williams, retired from medical practice and hoping to make more money than he had so far made with New Directions, began publishing with Random House. In 1950 Random House brought out his new and collected short stories, Make Light of It. In the following year they published his Autobiography, written under conditions that helped bring on the first of Williams's strokes and which, over the last decade of his life, left him more and more incapacitated, though they could not for long stop him from writing. In 1952 Williams published The Build-Up, the long-awaited third volume in his Stecher trilogy, again with Random House. He also returned to his poetry, searching all through the 1950s for a new poetry, which ranged from the medley of forms making up "The Desert Music," to the stately triadic step-down lines of "Asphodel, that Greeny Flower." In 1954 Random House published The Desert Music and in 1955 Journey to Love, both books of poetry. In 1954 they also published Selected Essays.

Knowing that time was running out for him, Williams published several other books with small presses, projects on which he had been working for years. In 1954 appeared his translation of Quevedo, The Dog & the Fever, on which he had worked with his mother since the 1920s, and in 1959 Yes, Mrs. Williams, his personal and loving record of his magisterial, bedridden, mysterious mother. In 1957 Selected Letters was published by McDowell-Obolensky, and in the following year a volume of spotty interviews of Williams talking about a lifetime of publishing was published by Beacon Press.

By the late 1950s Williams and Laughlin had managed to patch up their differences, and in 1958 New Directions published Paterson V, the slimmest of the poem's five books, written in part in the new line Williams had developed in Asphodel. By 1950, however, Williams knew that his epic would have to remain, like Pound's Cantos, an open-ended poem, to be closed only with the poet's death. By then also, Williams was willing to let the new addition to Paterson suggest the underlying universality of Paterson, as the poet now surveyed his teeming city from the vantage of the Cloisters, in New York City, the refuge which in his final years had become his own palace of the imagination.

Laughlin, unwilling to let his old friend slip away from him through any dereliction on his part, became in effect Williams's champion. In 1961 New Directions published Williams's collected short stories, The Farmers' Daughters, and his collected plays—"Many Loves," "A Dream of Love," "Tituba's Children," "The First President" (a fantasia centering on the life of Washington), and "The Cure"—under the collective title Many Loves. In 1962 New Directions published Pictures from Brueghel, which included not only the new poems Williams had written since 1955, but The Desert Music and Journey to Love as well. It was to be the last of Williams's books to pass through the poet's hands. In the spring of 1962, unable any longer to focus his eyes or control his barely functioning left hand, Williams ceased writing altogether. He died quietly at home in his sleep, six months short of his eightieth birthday, and was buried in the family plot about a mile south of his home.

As Braque, Picasso, and Juan Gris had demonstrated for art early in the century, and as Williams had early come to recognize, everything was subject matter for poetry. One did not have to go to Europe or to the museums or even to other texts to find subjects suitable for poetry. The subject was all around the poet. Only language and rhythms were necessary. So Williams's "No ideas but in things," was to become a shorthand manifesto for his disciples and critics. But this advice has too often been misunderstood and made the writing of poems look easier than it is. What Williams was calling for was what the Cubists had called for: the cleansing of the eye and the ear by first understanding what every major artist must understand, how the tradition works, and then how to make it new.

Like John Dewey, whose work he admired, Williams was an American pragmatist. We begin with the observed world and not with a theory, Williams insisted, and we generate our theories, manifestos, ideas, out of the world as we find it. Not symbolism, then, which gives a prior or rearranged meaning to the things of the world, but the sharply perceived image working on us and resonating outward from within. A world, then, of shimmering immanence, of continuing surprise, a world continually in the act of becoming.

For Williams, a good poem could carry no extraneous matter. In effect, what this meant was that everything—silences, line breaks, every descriptive modifier, every article—has to carry its share of the burden. Thousands of poems have been written in imitation of Williams, but few succeed. Moreover, the influence of Williams has been so pervasive that he has meant widely different things to different poets. For Olson, Williams was the poet of *Paterson*; for Charles Tomlinson, the English poet, as for John Berryman, it was the "late mysterious excellence" of such poems as "Asphodel" that mattered most; for Creeley as for Levertov, it was the shorter poems that acted as a revelation. Some see the essential Williams in a volume like *Spring and All*, others in *Paterson*. Others even find their Williams in the clear, lucid, unsentimental prose of his fiction. In truth, of course, Williams is to be found in all of these, as well as in his letters and in his best critical prose.

Williams's poems, exclusive of *Paterson* and his 1909 *Poems*—he asked Laughlin never to reprint the latter volume—have now been gathered and scrupulously edited by A. Walton Litz and Chistopher MacGowan into the two-volume *Collected Poems*, which together come to more than 1100 pages. Volume I covers the years 1909 to 1939; Volume II, 1939 to 1962. Fully a quarter of these poems, including the translations from Spanish, French, and Chinese, are here published in book form for the first time. A new edition of *Paterson*, edited by MacGowan appeared in 1992.

Williams also managed to write a great deal of seminal and intelligent criticism. This has been gathered into several volumes, including the *Selected Essays* (1954), the important *Imaginations* (1970), which made his early writings on the imagination generally available for the first time. These include *Kora in Hell, Spring and All, The Great American Novel, The Descent of Winter,* and *A Novelette and Other Prose.* Williams, always interested in avant-garde art, wrote extensively on art and its relationship to poetry, and these essays and reviews were edited by Bram Dijkstra and published as *A Recognizable Image* in 1978. Williams's essays, introductions, and reviews of younger poets, written between 1933 and 1962, have been edited by James E. Breslin and published as *Something to Say* in 1985. All these volumes are published by New Directions, as Laughlin continued to make Williams's name known to the world. A new *Selected Poems*, edited by Charles Tomlinson and superseding the Jarrell volume, was published in 1985.

There are as yet no collected letters, though Williams was a generous, vivid, and often brilliant letter writer. Thousands of these letters, some still restricted, others still in private hands, remain unpublished. The two main collections of letters to date are *The Selected Letters of William Carlos Williams*, edited by John Thirlwall (1957) and later reprinted—with corrections—by New Directions, and *William Carlos Williams and James Laughlin: Selected Letters*, edited by Hugh Wittemeyer (1989). *The Last Word: Letters between Marcia Nardi and William Carlos Williams*, edited by Elizabeth M. O'Neil, appeared in 1994. *Pound/Williams: Selected Letters*, edited by Hugh Witemeyer, in 1996. *The Letters of Denise Levertor and William Carlos Williams* in 1998.

Among the best commentaries on various aspects of Williams's work are James Breslin, *William Carlos Williams: An American Artist* (1970); Mike Weaver, *William Carlos Williams: The American Background* (1971); Christopher MacGowan, *William Carlos Williams' Early Poetry: The Visual Arts Background* (1984); Kerry Driscoll, *William Carlos Williams and the Maternal Muse* (1987); and David Frail, *The Early Politics and Poetics of William Carlos Williams* (1987). Two biographies are Reed Whittemore, *William Carlos Williams: Poet from Jersey* (1975); and Paul Mariani, *William Carlos Williams: A New World Naked* (1981).

PAUL MARIANI

Williamson, Jack [John Stewart] (1908–   ), science-fiction writer. Born in Bisbee in the Arizona Territory, Williamson grew up in New Mexico, was a journalist and magazine writer in the 1930s, served in the Air Force in World War II, and wrote for a newspaper comic strip, "Beyond Mars," after the war. Eventually he was graduated from Eastern New Mexico State University, where he began teaching in 1960. He received a Ph.D from the University of Colorado in 1964 with a dissertation on H. G. Wells. With the postwar boom in science fiction, he became a prolific writer in a genre that had interested him since age twenty, when he sold his first story to HUGO GERNSBACK's *Amazing Stories*. Of his more than forty novels, including some written with FREDERIK POHL, *The Humanoids* (1949), is known most widely. It is a story of robots that take over mankind's tasks, leaving people frustrated in purposeless lives. His Legion of Space series, originally a serial publication of the 1930s, involves aliens, Earth's treacherous leaders, and heroic defenders in *The Legion of Space* (1947), and *The Cometeers* and *One Against the Legion* (1950). *Darker Than You Think* (1948) is a werewolf tale. In *Bright New Universe* (1967) humans achieve first contact with much wiser aliens. *The Best of Jack Williamson* appeared in 1978. A memoir is *Wonder's Child: My life in Science Fiction* (1984).

William Wilson (*Burton's Gentleman's Magazine*, October 1839),   a short story by EDGAR ALLAN POE, that is included in *Tales of the Grotesque and Arabesque*. An allegory of the double personality, this story has been called one of Poe's best. An alter ego begins to haunt William Wilson at a boys' school not unlike one that Poe attended, and pursues Wilson like a conscience through all his adventures as a young man. Their conflict leads to a duel in which Wilson, who narrates the story, kills his alter ego. From the story Robert Louis Stevenson derived the idea for his *The Strange Case of Dr. Jekyll and Mr. Hyde* (1885).

Willingham, Calder (1922–1995), novelist, short-story writer. Willingham, born in Atlanta, hit it big with his first novel, *End as a Man* (1947), which was made into a play (1953) and a movie. It is a satirical treatment of life in a military academy very similar to the Citadel, which the author attended. Willingham's other novels include *Geraldine Bradshaw* (1950), *Reach to the Stars* (1951), *Natural Child* (1952), *To Eat a Peach* (1955), *Eternal Fire* (1963), *Providence Island* (1969), *Rambling Rose* (1972), and *The Big Nickel* (1975). *The Gates of Hell* (1951) is a collection of short stories. He wrote screenplays for *The Graduate* (1972) and *Rambling Rose* (1991), adapted from his novel of the same name.

Willis, Nathaniel Parker (1806–1867), editor, writer. Willis, born in Maine, won some celebrity while still at Yale, becoming known as a skillful writer of prose and verse. Soon after leaving Yale he began editing literary magazines, one of which, *The Token*, attained considerable success. As foreign correspondent for the New York *Mirror* he sent home lively sketches of travel abroad and interviewss with notable personages. On his return Willis took to writing plays in blank verse, one of which, TORTESA, OR, THE USURER (1839), was highly admired by Edgar Allan Poe. Willis encouraged Poe to write for the *Mirror* and also persuaded Thackeray to do columns for that paper. In 1846 he and GEORGE POPE MORRIS put out the HOME JOURNAL, which in 1901 became TOWN AND COUNTRY.

He was sometimes involved in the hot-tempered literary quarrels of the day. When Captain Frederick Marryat, then editor of the London *Metropolitan Magazine*, reviewed Willis's *Pencillings by the Way* (3 v. 1835) and made a personal attack on Willis, the latter challenged him to a duel and shots were exchanged.

Of all Willis's writings only one piece keeps some popularity, the moralistic poem called "Unseen Spirits." In 1840 Willis published a collection, called both *Romance of Travel: Comprising Tales of Five Lands* and *Loiterings of Travel*. In 1845 came *Dashes at Life with a Free Pencil*. He wrote one novel, *Paul Vane, or, Parts of a Life Else Untold* (1857). Among Willis's other books are *Poetical Scripture Sketches* (1827), *Fugitive Poetry* (1829), *Melanie and Other Poems* (1835), *A l'Abri* (1839), *Poems of Passion* (1843), *Lecture on Fashion* (1844), *Poems Sacred, Passionate, and Humorous* (1845), *People I Have Met* (1850), *Hurry-Graphs* (1851), *Famous Persons and Places* (1854), and *The Convalescent* (1859). During his lifetime he published *The Complete Works of N. P. Willis* (1846, reissued in 13 v. 1849–59). In London appeared *The Poetical Works of N. P. Willis* (1888). A selection of his *Prose Writings* was compiled (1885) by H. A. Beers, who also wrote his biography (1885). Willis's sister, SARA PAYSON WILLIS, drew an unflattering portrait of him in her novel *Ruth Hall* (1855). See KNICKERBOCKER SCHOOL; THE AMERICAN MAGAZINE; THE YOUTH'S COMPANION.

Willis, Sara Payson ["Fanny Fern"] (1811–1872), essayist, author of children's books. Fanny Fern, the sister of N. P. WILLIS, and like him born in Maine, led a varied literary career. She achieved her greatest success with *Fern Leaves from Fanny's Portfolio* (1853), which sold 70,000 copies within a year. A second series of *Leaves* appeared in 1854, *Fresh Leaves* in 1857. Fanny Fern had a gift for tart satire and by no means accepted the ideal of a meek and submissive womanhood. The only one of her novels to attract attention, *Ruth Hall* (1855), presumably depicts her own family, mostly in highly unflattering terms. She also wrote *A New Story Book for Children* (1864); *Folly as It Flies* (1868); *Ginger Snaps* (1870); and *Caper-Sauce: A Volume of Chit-Chat about Men, Women, and Things* (1872). A biography is Joyce Warren's Fanny Fern: *An Independent Woman* (1992). See ETHEL PARTON; JAMES PARTON.

Willkie, Wendell L[ewis] (1892–1944), lawyer, business administrator, Presidential candidate. Willkie's parents were both lawyers. Born in Indiana, Willkie took a B.A. and a law degree at Indiana University and then joined his parents' firm. He served in the army during World War I and then practiced law in Akron and in New York City. In 1929 he became counsel for an important utilities firm, the Commonwealth & Southern, and in 1933 became its president. As the New Deal policies toward public utilities developed, Willkie became an outspoken critic of FRANKLIN D. ROOSEVELT. Willkie's skill as a debater and critic attracted attention, and he won the 1940 Republican Presidential nomination.

After his defeat Willkie resumed the practice of law. In 1942 he was appointed as a special emissary by President Roosevelt and toured Europe and Asia, making shrewd observations that he reported in his widely read book *One World* (1943). Joseph Barnes wrote a biography, *Willkie* (1952), and Muriel Rukeyser wrote another, *One Life* (1957).

Will of Charles Lounsbury, The (1897). See WILLISTON FISH.

Will to Believe, The, and Other Essays in Popular Philosophy (1897), ten essays by WILLIAM JAMES. The title essay of the collection immediately aroused wide discussion and much vehement dissent, affecting theological and metaphysical circles, the latter less favorably than the former. It restated some of the ideas already expressed in his article "Reflex Action and Theism," published in the *Unitarian Review* (1881), in which James said: "The willing part of our nature . . . dominates both the conceiving department and the feeling department; in other words, perception and thinking are only there for behavior's sake." James was making his way toward his philosophy of PRAGMATISM.

Wilson, Alexander (1766–1813), ornithologist, teacher, editor, poet. Although Wilson had some schooling in his native Scotland, he was largely a self-taught man. He thought of himself first as a poet who admired Burns and followed in his footsteps. He published two volumes: *Watty and Meg* (1782) and *Poems, Humorous, Satirical, and Serious* (1789). He emigrated to America in 1793, worked for a while as a weaver, but gave himself enough education to become a teacher in New Jersey and Pennsylvania. His interest in nature was fostered by WILLIAM BARTRAM, who gave him the free use of his library. In 1806 Wilson became assistant editor of an encyclopedia. He interested his employer in the idea of a book on *American Ornithology*, of which the first volume appeared in 1808, the ninth and last in 1814. He made many tours of the country, during the first of which he met J. J. AUDUBON. The two naturalists thereafter engaged in a jealous and petty feud. In 1844 his *Poetical Works* appeared, but they are of minor importance. James S. Wilson wrote *Alexander Wilson, Poet-Naturalist* (1906).

Wilson, August (1945–   ),   playwright. Born in Pittsburgh, Wilson founded the Black Horizons Theater Company in St. Paul, Minnesota, in 1968. His first play, *Jitney*, is a realistic treatment of the African-American urban experience. It was produced on Broadway in a revised revision in 2000. *Ma Rainey's Black Bottom* imagines a recording session by the 1920s blues singer. It was produced on Broadway in 1984 and published the next year. *Fences* (first produced 1985, Broadway 1987, pub. 1986), winner of a Tony Award and Pulitzer Prize, treats the relationship between a former athlete and his son. *Joe Turner's Come and Gone* was first produced in 1986 and published in 1988. *The Piano Lesson* (1987, Broadway 1990), a second Pulitzer Prize winner, details the conflict between a brother and sister for an heirloom piano. Boy Willie wants to sell the instrument and buy the land on which their ancestors were slaves; Berenice wants to keep it for the family history carved on its surface and embedded in it. The play was inspired by a Romare Bearden painting called "The Piano Lesson." *Two Trains Running*, set in Pittsburgh in 1968, was produced by the Yale Repertory Theater in 1990. *Seven Guitars* (1995) and *King Hedley II*, set in 1985, complete the cycle of eighty years of African-American experience.

Wilson, Augusta.   See AUGUSTA JANE EVANS.

Wilson, Edmund (1895–1972),   critic, poet, novelist, short-story writer, playwright. Born in Red Bank, New Jersey, Wilson was one of the ablest intellects of his time and produced books in many fields. At Princeton he served as editor of the *Nassau Literary Magazine*, with JOHN PEALE BISHOP as his assistant and successor. In 1922 the two collaborated on a volume of prose and verse called *The Undertaker's Garland*. After graduation Wilson became a reporter on the New York Sun. In World War I he worked in a French hospital and then in the U.S. intelligence forces. On his return to New York City, he became managing editor of *Vanity Fair*. In 1926 he was on the staff of the *New Republic* as book review editor, later as associate editor, but resigned to do more writing. In 1944–48 he was regular book reviewer for *The New Yorker* and continued afterward to contribute long critical essays and other pieces to that magazine. He also applied his gift for scholarship to many other fields, as in his studies of Hebrew and Biblical manuscripts, and wrote on abstruse subjects with critical insight and reportorial skill. His *The Dead Sea Scrolls* (1955) is one of the best considerations of the scrolls.

Wilson's many works include criticism, travel books, novels, verse, and plays, and he edited a valuable anthology of criticism, THE SHOCK OF RECOGNITION (1943), and *The Crack-Up* (1945), a

volume of uncollected pieces of F. Scott Fitzgerald. *Memoirs of Hecate County* (1946), a collection of short stories, was banned after publication because of the candid treatment of sex in one of the stories. Other fiction includes *I Thought of Daisy* (1929) set in Greenwich Village; *The Higher Jazz*, published twenty-six years after his death, concerns businessman and aspiring composer Fritz Dietrich and features *roman á clef* portraits of such Twenties notables as Charles Ives, Robert Benchley, and Dorothy Parker. In reviewing *The Shores of Light* (1952), a collection of some of Wilson's literary essays, Alfred Kazin said: "Wilson is not like other critics: some critics are boring even when they are original; he fascinates even when he is wrong."

Wilson's critical interest always extended to the social and political implications of literature and a deep concern for moral values. His first critical works, AXEL'S CASTLE (1931), deals with symbolism as an international movement. *To the Finland Station* (1940) gives an authoritative account of the background of the Russian Revolution. His earliest travel book, *Travels in Two Democracies* (1936), relates experiences in Russia, where he enjoyed a greater opportunity than most visitors to move about freely. In 1956 he reprinted part of this book in *Red, Black, Blond, and Olive*, where "blond" refers to Russia, the other adjectives to the Zuñis, Haitians, and Israelis.

Wilson wrote several plays. One, *The Little Blue Light* (pub. 1950, prod. 1951), is a sardonic forecast of America in the "not-too-remote future." In 1937 Wilson collected three plays in book form, republished along with *Blue Light* and *Cyprian's Prayer as Five Plays* (1954). Among his other books are *Poets, Farewell* (verse, 1929); THE WOUND AND THE BOW (1931); *The American Jitters: A Year of the Slump* (1932); *Notebooks of Night* (prose and verse, 1942); *Europe Without Baedeker: Sketches Among the Ruins of Italy, Greece, and England* (1947); *Classics and Commercials* (1950); *A Piece of My Mind: Reflections at 60* (1956); *The American Earthquake* (1958); *Apologies to the Iroquois* (1960); *Night Thoughts* (1961); *Patriotic Gore* (1962); and *The Nabokov-Wilson Letters: Correspondence Between Vladimir Nabokov and Edmund Wilson, 1940–1971* (1979). At one time Wilson was married to MARY MCCARTHY. See F. SCOTT FITZGERALD.

Wilson, Ethel Davis [Bryant] (1888–1980),   novelist. Wilson was born in South Africa, educated in England and taught for several years in Vancouver before her marriage there to Dr. Wallace Wilson in 1920. She learned her craft by writing short stories for magazines. Her first novel, *Hetty Dorval*, did not appear until 1947. This began a series of sensitive, sophisticated novels: *The Innocent Traveler* (1949), based on the life of Topaz Edgeworth; *The Equations of Love* (1952), a group of three short novels; *Swamp Angel* (1954), generally regarded as her best; and *Love and Salt Water* (1956).

Wilson, [Robert] Forrest (1883–1942),   newspaperman, biographer, novelist. Wilson, born in Ohio, was a newspaperman in Cleveland and then a Washington correspondent. With Benedict Crowell, he wrote *How America Went to War* (6 v. 1921). For a time he worked in Paris and wrote *Paris on Parade* (1925), giving his impressions. His most important publication was a biography of HARRIET BEECHER STOWE, *Crusader in Crinoline* (1941), which won a Pulitzer Prize. He also wrote *Living Pageant of the Nile* (1924).

Wilson, Francis (1854–1935), actor, playwright, writer. Wilson, born in Philadelphia, took to the stage early, appearing in several musical plays, later in straight drama. In 1913 he became the first president of the Actors' Equity Association. His literary works mostly took the form of reminiscences. Among his books are *Recollections of a Player* (1897), *The Eugene Field I Knew* (1898), *Joseph Jefferson* (1906), *Francis Wilson's Life of Himself* (1924), and *John Wilkes Booth* (1929). His best-known play was *The Bachelor's Baby* (prod. 1909).

Wilson, Harriet (1808–c. 1870), novelist. Wilson, who lived in Milford, New Hampshire, was one of the first African-Americans to publish fiction. She wrote *Our Nig* (1859), a treatment of racism in the North before the Civil War. Her novel, subtitled "Sketches from the Life of a Free Black, in a Two-Story White House, North, Showing That Slavery's Shadows Fall Even There," is the story of Frado, a servant of mixed racial ancestry, who is abandoned by her white mother and abused by the family she works for. Although they are avowed abolitionists, they harbor racial bigotry. It was the first novel by an African-American to be published in the U.S.

Wilson, Harry Leon (1867–1939), humorist, novelist, playwright, short-story writer, editor. Born in Illinois, Wilson went west as a young man and lived in a mining camp, where he began writing humor for PUCK. His work was well liked, and in 1892 he was asked to join the staff. He succeeded H. C. Bunner as editor in 1896. After leaving the magazine in 1902, he began writing stories and novels. His first success was *The Boss of Little Arcady* (1905), which was followed by four best sellers: *Bunker Bean* (1912); RUGGLES OF RED GAP (1915); *Ma Pettingill* (1919); and MERTON OF THE MOVIES (1922). His last book, not a success, was *Two Black Sheep* (1931). Wilson and BOOTH TARKINGTON were fast friends and collaborated on a play, THE MAN FROM HOME (1907), which ran for nearly six years. Several of Wilson's books were made into popular movies, and he was one of the first authors to be paid handsomely for the movie rights to a book—*Merton of the Movies*. *Ruggles of Red Gap* is probably his most enduring work.

Wilson, James (1742–1798), lawyer, patriot. Wilson had a deep and lasting influence on the founding and early development of the American republic. Born in Scotland and educated there, he emigrated to America in 1765, studied law in Philadelphia, and was admitted to the bar in 1767. He took a leading role in the controversy with England, publishing in 1774 a widely read essay, *Considerations on the Nature and Extent of the Legislative Authority of the British Parliament*. He served as a delegate to the Continental Congress, signed the Declaration of Independence, served in the Continental Army, and after the war became one of the most persuasive members on the side of those who favored a strong central government. He helped draw up a conservative constitution for Pennsylvania. In 1789 Washington appointed Wilson to the Supreme Court, and he did much to guide its first steps.

Wilson's *Works* were edited by Bird Wilson (3 v. 1804) and again by James De W. Andrew (2 v. 1896). R. G. Adams compiled *Selected Political Essays of James Wilson* (1930). Charles Page Smith wrote a biography, *James Wilson, Founding Father* (1956).

Wilson, John (1591?–1667), Congregational minister, poet. Wilson entered the English ministry, emigrated to America because of his nonconformism, and was minister of a church in Boston for the rest of his life. Before leaving England he had published a long poem for children, *A Song or Story, for the Lasting Remembrance of Divers Famous Works Which God Hath Done in Our Time* (1626). A second edition, with a somewhat altered title, appeared in Boston in 1680. Cotton Mather wrote a life of Wilson in 1695, later incorporating it in *Magnalia Christi Americana* (1702).

Wilson, Lanford (1937–), playwright. Wilson, born in Missouri, has lived in the Ozarks and in Southern California. His career began at Caffe Cino in Greenwich Village and has been primarily fostered in the milieu of coffee house and Off-Broadway theater. His one-act plays include *So Long at the Fair* (1963), *Home Free* (1964), and *The Madness of Lady Bright* (1964). His longer works include *Balm in Gilead* (1964), *The Rimers of Eldritch* (1965), and *This Is the Rill Speaking* (1965). With *The Gingham Dog* (1968), a sensitive treatment of the breakup of an interracial marriage; *Lemon Sky* (1970), about a boy torn between his divorced parents; and *Serenading Louie* (1970) Wilson moved to more commercial productions with disappointing reception. In 1970 he joined the Circle Theater Company as playwright in residence. There, in 1973, *Hot l Baltimore* was staged. His other plays include *The Mound Builders* (1975); a trilogy concerning members of the Talley family: *Fifth of July* (1978), *Talley's Folly* (1979 Pulitzer Prize), and *A Tale Told* (1981). *Angels Fall* (1982), is set in an isolated New Mexico mission. *Burn This* appeared in 1987. *Redwood Curtain* (1993) deals with an adopted woman's search for her Vietnamese mother and G.I. father. Collections include *21 Short Plays* (1993), *Collected Plays 1965–70* (1996) and *Collected Plays 1987–1997* (1999). Wilson has worked in television and movies and wrote the libretto for an operatic version of *Summer and Smoke* (1971), a play by Tennessee Williams.

Wilson, Margaret (1882–1973), missionary, teacher, novelist. Wilson, born in Iowa, found missionary work in foreign lands disturbing because of the demands it made on her compassion. She returned to the United States to teach for a while and then began writing novels. Both *The Able McLaughlins* (1923), Pulitzer Prize 1924, and *Law and the McLaughlins* (1936), a sequel, deal with the life of Scottish pioneers in Iowa. Wilson wrote frankly from a woman's viewpoint for women readers. Among her other novels are *The Kenworthys* (1925), *Daughters of India* (1928), *One Came Out* (1932), *The Valiant Wife* (1933), and *Devon Treasury Mystery* (1939). In 1923 Wilson married G. D. Turner of Oxford, and moved to England.

Wilson, Mitchell (1913–1973), novelist. Trained as a research physicist, Wilson took up writing with detective stories and melodramatic family novels. His best work is found in

Live with Lightning (1949) and *Meeting at the Far Meridian* (1961), novels dealing with scientists who struggle with moral issues, particularly those posed by atomic weapons.

Wilson, Robert M. [Byrd Hoffman] (1944–   ), playwright, artist. Born in Waco, Texas, he has studied at the University of Texas and Pratt Institute and in Paris and Arizona. His work in the theater consists of marathon (3 1/2 hours to seven days) multimedia productions employing drama, ballet, scenic design, and primitive ritual. His titles include *The Life and Times of Joseph Stalin* (1973); *A Letter for Queen Victoria* (Italy 1974, New York 1975); *Einstein on the Beach*, in collaboration with Philip Glass (1976); *the civil wars: a tree is best measured when it is down*, staged in sections in various countries (1983–1984), and *The Black Rider* (1993).

Wilson, Sloan (1920–   ),   novelist. Wilson, born in Connecticut and educated at Harvard, served in the Coast Guard during World War II. Though he worked for newspapers and in public relations, his major professional focus has always been the novel. His main characters are typically men of Puritan ancestry, wealth, and education. Tom Rath is the suburban executive of *The Man in the Gray Flannel Suit* (1955), Wilson's best-known book. Wilson is a skilled depictor of the social milieu of the mid-20th century. *All the Best People* (1970) traces the effect of various national crises on a group of families with summer homes near Lake George, New York. World War II and the Vietnam War produce distant echoes in the lives of characters in *A Summer Place* (1958) and *Janus Island* (1967), but the major emphasis is on the personal tensions of everyday life. Among his other titles are *Voyage to Somewhere* (1947), *A Sense of Values* (1961), *Georgie Winthrop* (1963), *Small Town* (1978), *Ice Brothers* (1979), *The Greatest Crime* (1980), *Pacific Interlude* (1982), and *The Man in the Gray Flannel Suit II* (1984). *What Shall We Wear to This Party?* (1976) is autobiographical.

Wilson, [Thomas] Woodrow (1856–1924),   lawyer, teacher, university administrator, writer, public official, 27th president. Wilson was born in Virginia took his B.A. at Princeton, then studied law at the University of Virginia. He practiced law briefly, then went on to obtain a Ph.D. in history and political science at Johns Hopkins. After teaching there, at Bryn Mawr College, and at Wesleyan University, he accepted a professorship at Princeton. He was an excellent teacher, and in 1902 was unanimously chosen president of the university.

Always keenly interested in politics, Wilson left Princeton to run for Democratic governor of New Jersey in 1910. His outstanding oratorical ability, profound knowledge of American political aims and institutions, and genuine democratic feeling carried him to victory, and while governor he carried through some remarkable political and economic measures. At the Democratic Presidential convention in 1912 Wilson was nominated after WILLIAM JENNINGS BRYAN threw his support to him. The Republican Party was split by a political feud between THEODORE ROOSEVELT and WILLIAM H. TAFT, and Wilson was elected.

He supplied vigorous executive leadership to Congress and to his party, and fought privilege. But he was unable to com-

plete his projects for domestic reform because of the outbreak of war in Europe. U.S. entry into the war pushed the country into a position of leadership in international affairs. Wilson chose General J.J. PERSHING as United States military leader. Wilson's pronouncements aroused wide comment, such as his address to the Senate on January 22, 1917, in which he declared that the United States must seek "a peace without victory," and his address to Congress (April 2, 1917) asking for a declaration of war: "The world must be made safe for democracy." His program of "Fourteen Points" (January 8, 1918) had a tremendous influence on world opinion. In the midst of this turmoil he conducted a successful presidential campaign against Charles Evans Hughes.

With the end of the war Wilson began his last and greatest battle in favor of U.S. entry into the League of Nations. The Paris Peace Conference after World War I met in the Hall of Mirrors, in the royal chateau at Versailles in France; there on January 18, 1919, was signed the treaty of peace between the Allies and Germany, known as the Treaty of Versailles. It provided for a League of Nations, took away some German territory, limited Germany's armament, and included an acknowledgment of war guilt. But the United States refused to sign the treaty, ratification of which was defeated in the Senate because of the provision for a League of Nations. Wilson made a strenuous campaign to obtain ratification. The battle turned into a personal quarrel with Senator Henry Cabot Lodge of Massachusetts. Wilson was subjected to personal vituperation and controversy. He suffered a stroke, and the country remained outside the League. Wilson ended his days in physical breakdown and defeat.

As a writer, Wilson always knew how to turn a phrase, and his love of epigrams and a good story kept his style above the usual professional level. His *Congressional Government* (1885) was reprinted several times. *The State* (1889) was revised and rewritten in 1898 and again (by Edward Elliott) in 1918. *Division and Reunion* (1893) was brought up to date by Edward S. Corwin in 1924. Two collections of essays and lectures were *An Old Master and Other Political Essays* (1893) and *Mere Literature and Other Essays* (1896). Wilson's other titles are *George Washington* (1897) and *A History of the American People* (5 v. 1902). *Constitutional Government* (1908) and *The Public Papers of Woodrow Wilson* (6 v. 1925–27) were edited by Ray Stannard Baker and William E. Dodd. Biographies include RAY STANNARD BAKER, *Woodrow Wilson, His Life and Letters* (8 v. 1927–39); Arthur S. Link, a five-volume study published between 1947 and 1965 and *Woodrow Wilson: A Profile* (1968); James Kerney, *Political Education of Woodrow Wilson* (1926); Ruth Cranston, *The Story of Woodrow Wilson* (1945); David Loth, *Story of Woodrow Wilson* (1956); E. B. Alsop, ed., a symposium entitled *The Greatness of Wilson* (1956); Herbert Hoover, *The Ordeal of Woodrow Wilson* (1958); and Arthur Walworth, *Woodrow Wilson* (2 v. 1958).

In 1922 the Woodrow Wilson Foundation was established to further public understanding of international problems and the Wilsonian ideals of world cooperation. Howard Koch and John Huston based a play, *In Time to Come* (1942), on Wilson's life, and a movie biography with screenplay by Lamar Trotti was produced in 1944.

Winchevsky, Morris (1856–1932), poet, editor, translator. Winchevsky, born in Lithuania, was named Ben-Zion Novachovitch, and he also used the pen name Leopold Benedict. After leaving his native country and traveling in Denmark, Germany, France, and England, he came to New York City, where he was a radical in politics and wrote on proletarian themes. Winchevsky was best known for his poetry and was called "the Ghetto poet." In 1919 he collected his verse in *Lieder und Gedichte, 1871–1910*; in 1920 his *Gezamelte Schriftn* (3 v.) appeared. Some of his poems were translated into English. He himself was a skilled translator and rendered in Yiddish Hugo's *Les Misérables*, Ibsen's *Doll's House*, and Hood's *Song of the Shirt*.

Windham, Donald (1920–), novelist, playwright, short-story writer. Windham's schooling stopped at Boys High School in his native Atlanta. From then until he was able to concentrate on writing as a full-time job, Windham worked at a variety of jobs, ranging from laborer in a barrel factory to editor of *Dance Index* magazine. In 1947 he collaborated on a play with Tennessee Williams, *You Touched Me!*, which was based on the short story by D. H. Lawrence. His first book was *The Dog Star* (1950), a novel depicting the effect of a friend's suicide on a sensitive youth living on the seamy side of life. It was praised by E. M. Forster, André Gide, and Thomas Mann. His other books include *The Hero Continues* (1960), a novel, and *The Warm Country: Stories* (1960, with an introduction by E. M. Forster). His autobiography, *Emblems of Conduct*, appeared serially in *The New Yorker* (1961) and in book form in 1964. He also wrote *Lost Friendships: A Memoir of Truman Capote, Tennessee Williams, and Others* (1987).

Windy McPherson's Son (1916), a novel by SHERWOOD ANDERSON. The hero, Sam McPherson, grows up hating his squalid home in Caxton, Iowa, where his father, a drunken boaster, is a completely dominating force.

Winesburg, Ohio (1919), a book of twenty-three sketches by SHERWOOD ANDERSON. Anderson, in his best-known work, exhibits a typical Midwest town of narrow horizons and ingrown passions. This he does through the lives of various inhabitants—"grotesques," he calls them. A young reporter, George Willard, groping to find himself and achieve "the sadness of sophistication," forms the connecting link among these fragmentary lives. These straightforwardly realistic sketches were considered a radical venture in literature when they appeared. Winesburg was modeled in part on Clyde, Ohio, where Anderson lived as a youth.

Winfield, Arthur M. Pen name of EDWARD STRATEMEYER.

Winfrey, Oprah (1954–), actress, television talk show host, book club creator. Born in Kosciusko, Mississippi, and educated at Tennessee State University, Winfrey was a television news anchor at age 19. She moved from cohost of a Baltimore morning show to a similar role for a Chicago station. In 1985 that show was renamed *The Oprah Winfrey Show*; it became the highest-rated talk show on television and won

several Emmy awards. Her on-air book club, inaugurated in 1997, has been very influential in calling attention to writers and books; selections commonly appear on the best-seller lists. Winfrey has formed her own production company, Harpo Productions, and has appeared in such motion pictures as *The Color Purple* and *Beloved*. In 2000, she founded *O: The Oprah Magazine*, which had the most successful start in magazine history, with a circulation of two million after its first seven issues.

Wing-and-Wing (1842), a novel by JAMES FENIMORE COOPER. The complex plot is a mixture of sea story and historical novel, set in the period when England and France fought the Napoleonic Wars. In the novel appears an important historical character, Admiral Caraccioli, whom Lord Nelson executed. Cooper also presents an imaginary granddaughter, a devout Catholic who finds herself in love with a French privateer who is an atheist.

Wings of the Dove, The (1902), a novel by HENRY JAMES. *Wings*, is the second novel of James's late, so-called major phase. It treats characteristic themes: the confrontation of the naive American with sophisticated European societies, of innocence with experience, of moral sensibility with social expertise. Its heroine, Milly Theale, an orphaned New York heiress, journeys to Europe with Susan Stringham. Through Mrs. Stringham's connections, Milly meets Kate Croy and her unacknowledged fiancé, Merton Densher. Kate's betrothal is blocked by her Aunt Maud Lowder because Merton is not wealthy. Kate, learning that Milly Theale also favors Densher and that she has an undefined fatal illness, resolves to play a waiting game. She insidiously urges Densher to court Milly so that upon inheriting Milly's wealth he will subsequently become an acceptable suitor for Kate herself. Informed of the plot against her, Milly gives up her will to live. But her generosity in bequeathing Densher her fortune despite this betrayal affects his attitude, and he is unwilling to accept the money. Kate is unwilling to relinquish it, and so their relationship ends, ironically, in a split. Milly, the dove of the title, has enacted a high flight—a power play—that leaves her ascendant in death. In the subtle manipulation of point of view and of thematic metaphor *Wings* illustrates James's complex late manner, but structurally it is less perfectly realized than the other two novels of his major phase. James's placement of a dying woman at the center creates problems. Kate Croy, ruthless but vital, overshadows the fragile heroine, who yet must sustain the thematic statement.

JEAN FRANTZ BLACKALL

Winkle, Rip van. See RIP VAN WINKLE.

Winnebago Indians. A Sioux tribe, originally inhabitants of Wisconsin in the region south of Green Bay. Many are still found there, and others are found on a Nebraska reservation. The greatest authority on the tribe was Paul Radin, who discussed them in his report *The Winnebago Tribe* (1923), for the Bureau of American Ethnology, and also in *The World of Primitive Man* (1953). Radin showed that a Winnebago chieftain performed many other functions than those commonly assigned to him. His lodge was an asylum for wrongdoers, and he acted as intercessor between wrongdoers and their victims; in general, he was a symbol of peace rather than war. Radin also prepared an account of *Winnebago Hero Cycles* (1948).

Winnemucca, Sarah. See SARAH WINNEMUCCA HOPKINS.

Winner Take Nothing (1933), fourteen short stories and sketches by ERNEST HEMMINGWAY. Few of the stories in this volume have attracted much attention. Characteristic is "A Natural History of the Dead," a bitter attack on war that recalls a scene near Milan in World War I. Characters in other stories are prostitutes, neurotics, American tourists, and gamblers.

Winning of Barbara Worth, The (1911), a novel by HAROLD BELL WRIGHT. The scene is Rubio City, a recently founded town in Colorado. In a sandstorm nearby, many travelers die, including a beautiful woman near whom is found a girl still alive. The girl is adopted by Jefferson Worth and grows up an intelligent and beautiful young woman. She falls in love with Willard Holmes, a young engineer from New York City, but their marriage is opposed by his wealthy guardian. Of course the solution is inevitable. A casket is found with documents establishing Barbara's identity—she is the daughter of Willard's guardian's brother. The book's initial sales were tremendous and it remained Wright's most popular work.

Winning of the West, The (4 v. 1889–96), a historical study by THEODORE ROOSEVELT. Using original sources, Roosevelt gave a detailed account of the expansion of the U.S. after the Revolution. It also showed the immense significance of the westward expansion in determining the entire character of the country. Roosevelt was undoubtedly influenced in viewpoint and style by the writings of FRANCIS PARKMAN.

Winslow, Edward (1595–1655), government official, colonist author. Winslow came to New England on the MAYFLOWER, several times returned to England and then came back to the colonies, and was governor of Plymouth in 1633, 1636, and 1644. He was appointed by Oliver Cromwell as commissioner of an expedition to the West Indies (1655) that took Jamaica away from Spain. Winslow died at sea on the trip home. He was a skillful and vivid writer. Along with WILLIAM BRADFORD [1] he wrote the book, called in error *Mourt's Relation* (1622), which is the first account of the Plymouth settlement. On his own he wrote GOOD NEWS FROM NEW ENGLAND (1624), a lively account of personal experiences; *Hypocrisy Unmasked* (1646); *The Glorious Progress of the Gospel Amongst the Indians in New England* (1649); and *Platform of Church Discipline* (1653). See GEORGE MORTON.

Winslow, Thyra Samter (1893–1961), short-story writer, novelist, screenwriter. Winslow, an adept storyteller with a strong sense of character, set some of her stories in her native Arkansas; others are about the New York theater. Among her books are *Picture Frames* (1923); *Show Business* (1926); *People Round the Corner* (1927); *Blueberry Pie* (1932); *My Own, My Native Land* (short stories, 1939); *Window Panes* (short stories, 1946); *Divorcée* (1953); and *The Sex Without Sentiment* (short stories, 1954).

Winsor, Justin (1831–1897), historian, librarian, editor. This eminent scholar was born in Boston, studied abroad, then joined the staff of the Boston Public Library in 1866. He became superintendent in 1868 and instituted many reforms. In 1877 he became librarian of Harvard University. He was a founder of the American Library Association (1876) and served as president from 1876 to 1885. He was also a founder of the *Library Journal*. Winsor edited *The Narrative and Critical History of America* (8 v. 1884–89) and also published a *Reader's Handbook of the American Revolution* (1879); *Christopher Columbus* (1891); *Cartier to Frontenac* (1894); *The Mississippi Basin* (1895); and *The Westward Movement* (1897).

Winsor, Kathleen (1919–), novelist. Winsor, born in Wisconsin, set her first book, FOREVER AMBER (1944), in Restoration England. It centers on a country girl who goes to London and eventually becomes Charles II's mistress. The heroine's sexual activities attracted many readers, and the book was an enormous best seller. Her later, less successful, novels are *Star Money* (1950), *The Lovers* (1952), *America Without Love* (1957), *Wanderers Eastward, Wanderers West* (1965), *Calais* (1979), *Jacintha* (1985), and *Robert and Arabella* (1986).

Winter, William (1836–1917), drama critic, essayist, poet. Winter, born in Massachusetts studied at Harvard Law School and while there published his first book, *Poems* (1855). Encouraged by Longfellow to devote himself to literature, Winter never practiced law. He worked for a short while as reviewer for the Boston *Transcript* and then moved to New York City, where he joined the bohemians who met in PFAFF'S CELLAR on Broadway. He worked on the *Saturday Press* and then became drama critic for the New York *Albion* and the New York *Tribune*. Among Winter's many books are biographies of Henry Irving (1885) and Edward Booth (1893), *Shakespeare's England* (1886), *Gray Days and Gold* (1892), *Shadows of the Stage* (1892–95), and *Shakespeare on the Stage* (2 v. 1911–15). He continued to write verse: *My Witness* (1871), *Thistle-Down* (1878), *Wanderers* (1892), and *Poems* (a collected edition, 1909). *The Wallet of Time* (1913) is a collection of Tribune pieces. Volumes of reminiscence are *Other Days* (1908), *Old Friends* (1909), and *Vagrant Memories* (1915).

Winterich, John T[racy] (1891–1970), bibliophile. In *Another Day, Another Dollar* (1947), an autobiography, Winterich discusses the jobs he held in his youth—from reader of gas meters to trolley conductor and book peddler. Only the last led to his real vocation—the study of books. He became an authority on first editions and book collecting. A native of Connecticut and a graduate of Brown, Winterich taught English there in 1912–13, then worked on the Springfield (Massachusetts) *Republican* and later as editor for such magazines as *Stars and Stripes, Home Sector, American Legion Weekly, Colophon, New Colophon,* and *Saturday Review.* Among his books are *A Primer of Book Collecting* (1927), *Collector's Choice* (1928), *Books and the Man* (1929), *Early American Books and Printing* (1935), *Twenty-Three Books* (1938), *Three Lantern Slides* (1949), and *The Grolier Club* (1950).

Winters, [Arthur] Yvor (1900–1968), poet, critic, teacher. Winters was born in Chicago and educated at the University of Chicago and the University of Colorado. He taught

English at Stanford and was well known as a poet and critic. Although his work is often considered to be a part of the NEW CRITICISM, his critical theory is distinctly individual and often at variance with more popular opinions. He maintained that the critic should be concerned with the moral evaluation of a work of art, and that a poem should be a rational statement about human experience in which the poet is "seeking to state a true moral judgment." His books of criticism include *Primitivism and Decadence* (1937), *Maule's Curse* (1938), and *The Anatomy of Nonsense* (1943), all of which are collected in *In Defense of Reason* (1947); *Edwin Arlington Robinson* (1946); *The Function of Criticism: Problems and Exercises* (1957); *The Poetry of W. B. Yeats* (1960); and *The Poetry of J. V. Cunningham* (1961).

In his own poetry, which won a Bollingen Prize in 1960, Winters adhered to his critical theories on the necessity of balance between reason and emotion. His books of poetry include *The Immobile Wind* (1921), *The Magpie's Shadow* (1922), *The Bare Hills* (1927), *The Proof* (1930), *The Journey* (1931), *Before Disaster* (1934), *Poems* (1940), *The Giant Weapon* (1943), and *Collected Poems* (1952). *The Selected Poems of Yvor Williams*, based on his prize-winning *Collected Poems*, appeared in 1999. *The Selected Letters of Yvor Winters*, edited by R. L. Barth, was published in 2001. He edited and contributed to *Twelve Poets of the Pacific* (1937) and was married to JANET LEWIS.

Winterset (1935),   a tragedy in verse. See MAXWELL ANDERSON.

Winthrop, John (1588–1649),   colonial official. Winthrop attended Trinity College, Cambridge, and was admitted to the Inner Temple. A man of consequence and intensely religious, he was elected governor of the Massachusetts Bay Co., superintended the arrangements for departure, and arrived in Salem on June 12, 1630. For the greater part of his life thereafter, he was either governor or deputy governor of the colony and always recognized as its leading citizen. He did not believe in democracy and presented proof against it from the Bible, in that there was "no such government in Israel."

Winthrop's *A Model of Christian Charity* (1630) was first published in full (1838) by the Massachusetts Historical Society. He also wrote *A Short Story of the Antimomians* (1644). His *Journal* was first published, with James Savage as editor, as *History of New England, 1630–49* (2 v. 1825–1826, rev. 1853), and was reprinted, with J. K. Hosmer as editor, as *Winthrop's Journal* (2 v. 1908). A. B. Forbes edited his *Papers* (5 v. 1929–47), R. C. Winthrop's *Life and Letters* (2 v. 1869) gives other materials. Biographical and critical studies include Samuel Eliot Morison, *Builders of the Bay Colony* (1930); Edmund S. Morgan, *The Puritan Dilemma: The Story of John Winthrop* (1958); and D. B. Rutman, *Winthrop's Boston* (1965). Winthrop has appeared occasionally in fiction, for example, in Catherine M. Sedgwick's HOPE LESLIE (1827) and Irving Bacheller's *A Candle in the Wilderness* (1930). He is also portrayed in Hawthorne's *The Scarlet Letter* (1850).

Winthrop, Theodore (1828–1861),   poet, novelist, businessman. Winthrop, born in New Haven, Connecticut, was a descendant of both JOHN WINTHROP and JONATHAN EDWARDS. He traveled for his health in Europe, became acquainted with Panama in connection with his work for a steamship line, and toured extensively in the Northwest. For a time he practiced law, then determined to devote himself to writing. When the Civil War broke out, he enlisted and was killed while leading a charge at the Battle of Big Bethel, Virginia.

His books were all published posthumously, one of them, *Mr. Waddy's Return*, as late as 1904. For a time these books, mostly novels, won him wide acceptance as a writer. In 1884 his sister edited *The Life and Poems of Theodore Winthrop*. His three most important works were novels: *Cecil Dreeme* (1862), the story of a mysterious painter done in the style of Charles Brockden Brown and Hawthorne; *John Brent* (1862), one of the earliest novels of the West; and *Edwin Brothertoft* (1862), a romance of the American Revolution. *The Canoe and the Saddle* (1863) and *Life in the Open Air* (1863) are personal reminiscences.

Wirt, William (1772–1834),   essayist, lawyer. A native of Maryland and a Southern gentleman of the old school, Wirt combined polite literature with a legal career. He practiced law in Richmond, gaining fame as prosecutor in the trial of Aaron Burr. He was appointed attorney-general by President Monroe (1817–29). Wirt also practiced law in Baltimore and ran unsuccessfully as the Presidential candidate of the Anti-Masonic party against ANDREW JACKSON (1832). His earliest writing was a popular series of essays, THE LETTERS OF THE BRITISH SPY, printed anonymously in the Richmond *Argus* (1803). These were leisurely descriptions of Southern scenes in a style reminiscent of Addison. Wirt also published *The Rainbow* (1804) and *Sketches of the Life and Character of Patrick Henry* (1817).

Wise, Henry Augustus ["Harry Gringo"] (1819–1869),   naval officer, memoirist, novelist. Born in Brooklyn, New York, Wise became a midshipman at an early age. He served in the Mexican War and the Civil War. After the Civil War he served in the Bureau of Ordnance and became a captain. In the meantime he had traveled widely, publishing accounts of his war experiences in *Los Gringos, or, An Inside View of Mexico and California, with Wanderings in Peru, Chile, and Polynesia* (1849). Apparently, it was from the title of this book that Wise derived his pen name, under which he wrote some unimportant fiction. He also wrote *Tales for the Marines* (1855).

Wise, Isaac Mayer (1819–1900),   rabbi, editor, historian. Rabbi Wise was born in Bohemia and came to the United States in 1846, serving congregations in Albany, New York, and in Cincinnati. In the latter city he organized a new group, breaking away from strict orthodoxy, called Reform Judaism. He became editor of a magazine called *The American Israelite* in English and *Die Deborah* in German, in which he expounded his views. He also wrote numerous books, among them *History of the Israelitish Nation from Abraham to the Present Time* (1854), *The Cosmic God* (1876), and *Reminiscences* (1901). His *Selected Writings* appeared in 1900.

Wise, John (1652–1725),   Congregational clergyman, writer. This courageous, witty, and foresighted clergyman was born in Roxbury, Massachusetts, and was minister of various churches in Connecticut and Massachusetts—finally in lpswich, Massachusetts. He was also chaplain in two military expeditions, including one against Quebec. He was a leader in protests against arbitrary taxation and was tried for his protests on orders of Sir Edmund Andros, condemned, and imprisoned, but later restored as minister. He boldly presented a petition in behalf of the victims of the Salem witchcraft trials and defended government in church and state in *The Churches Quarrel Espoused* (1710).

Most influential of his writings was a continuation of the argument in the 1710 book in *A Vindication of the Government of New England Churches* (1717), in which he expounds, in direct opposition to the Calvinist doctrine of the so-called elect, ideas of human equality that undoubtedly influenced the writing of the Declaration of Independence. His book was reprinted in 1772 and widely read in the colonies. Wise had great literary gifts, including robust humor as a controversialist. George Allan Cook wrote a biography of Wise that included close analysis of his writing: *John Wise, Early American Democrat* (1952).

Wislizenus, Frederick Adolph (1810–1889), travel writer. A German-born physician, Wislizenus described his travels in the Far West in *A Journey to the Rocky Mountains in the Year 1839* (1840, tr. 1912) and an 1846 journey from St. Louis to Chihuahua in *Memoir of a Tour to Northern Mexico* (1848).

Wissler, Clark (1870–1947), anthropologist, psychologist, teacher, museum curator. Wissler, was born in Indiana was educated at Indiana State University and at Columbia, where he later taught psychology—he also taught at New York University and the Institute of Human Relations at Yale. He joined the staff of the American Museum of Natural History in 1902 and eventually became curator. His interest in psychological problems led Wissler into anthropological research and he conducted field studies among Indian tribes and made extensive ethnographical collections for the Museum. He made a systematic summary of Native American life in his classic volume *The American Indian: An Introduction to the Anthropology of the New World* (1917). Among his other books are *North American Indians of the Plains* (1912), *Man and Culture* (1922), *Social Anthropology* (1929), and *Indians of the United States* (1940).

Wister, Owen (1860–1938), novelist, short-story writer, essayist, biographer. Wister, grandson of the actress Fanny Kemble, was born in Philadelphia and attended St. Paul's School, in Concord, New Hampshire, where he made his first literary appearance in *Horae Scholasticae*. He also was a student at Harvard, where he and Theodore Roosevelt became friends for life. Wister at first studied music, then law, but when illness led him to the ranches of Wyoming he was so impressed with the West that he was inspired to write his Western stories, laid mainly in Wyoming. Wister's best-known story was THE VIRGINIAN (1902). The book was dedicated to Roosevelt and contained a number of portraits drawn from actual scenes he observed. The book sold more than 1,600,000 copies in English, many more in other languages.

Wister's *Philosophy Four* (1903) is a story of undergraduate life at Harvard. *U.S. Grant* (1900) and *The Seven Ages of Washington* (1907) are biographies. He also wrote *Red Men and White* (1895), LIN MCLEAN (1898), *Lady Baltimore* (1906), *The Pentecost of Calamity* (1915), *When West Was West* (1928), *Roosevelt: The Story of a Friendship* (1930), and other books. Because he was opposed to making war on Germany and because he shared Roosevelt's antipathy for Woodrow Wilson, he wrote a denunciatory sonnet on the latter president that aroused wide criticism.

Unquestionably, *The Virginian*, a pioneer in its field, gave great impetus to Western novels. Wister is sometimes criticized for the saccharinity of some of his work, but parts of *The Virginian* are in the tradition of the new realism; indeed, at the request of Roosevelt, Wister excised an eye-gouging episode as too offensive. *Owen Wister Out West: His Journals and Letters* (1958), edited by Fanny Kemble Wister, the novelist's daughter, contains some fine descriptions of scenery, travel, people, and the changing Western life.

Witherspoon, John (1723–1794), clergyman, teacher, college administrator. Witherspoon served as a minister in his native Scotland, became a follower of the exiled Stuarts, and engaged actively in theological controversy. His *Ecclesiastical Characteristics* (1753), directed against religious liberals, was a bitter satire and a best seller. Another satire, *History of a Corporation of Servants* (1765), was less successful. From 1756 to 1768 he published sermons and essays that were widely read. Witherspoon was elected president of the College of New Jersey at Princeton, and came to this country in 1768 to assume his duties. Besides his administrative work, he taught several courses and was considered a great teacher by such undergraduates as James Madison. He became an ardent patriot, was elected to the New Jersey Constitutional Convention, the Continental Congress (where in 1776 he signed the Declaration of Independence), and to numerous Congressional committees. He continued to act as president of the college until his death.

One of Witherspoon's later writings was *Considerations on the Nature and Extent of the Legislative Authority of the British Parliament* (1774). He was always interested in the linguistic peculiarities of the colonists, coined numerous words, and in an article published in the *Pennsylvania Journal and Weekly Advertiser* (May 9, 16, 23, and 30, 1781) he first used the term *Americanism*.

Wizard of Oz. See L. F. BAUM; WONDERFUL WIZARD OF OZ.

Wobblies. See I.W.W.

Wodehouse, Sir P[elham] G[renville] (1881–1975), novelist, short-story writer, musical comedy lyricist, screenwriter. One of the comic geniuses of the twentieth century, and one of its finest prose stylists, P. G. Wodehouse was born in Guilford, England, and educated at Dulwich College. He was naturalized as an American citizen in 1955 and knighted by Queen Elizabeth II a short time before his death. Because his father was a judge in Hong Kong, the young Wodehouse spent most of his childhood in the care of various aunts in England. He published the first of his hundred-plus novels in 1902 when he was a humor column writer for the *London Globe*. After 1909 he lived and worked for long periods in the United States and France. His first stories were about boys in British boarding schools, such as the cricket player Mike Jackson of *Mike at Wryken* and *Mike and Psmith* (printed together as *Mike* in 1909, later published as separate titles). In 1914, he sold a serial to THE SATURDAY EVENING POST; for the next quarter century most of his books were serialized there before book publication. With Jerome Kern and Guy Bolton, Wodehouse worked on musicals for the Princes Theatre in London, beginning in 1915. In subsequent years, he was involved in collaborations with Victor Herbert, George and Ira Gershwin, Sigmund Romberg, Rudolph Friml and others on both sides of the Atlantic. The story collection *The Man with Two Left Feet* (1917) introduced Bertram Wilberforce Wooster, "Bertie," and his valet Jeeves. In the first story about the pair, "Extricating Young Gussie," Jeeves had only two lines; Wodehouse later wrote, "I blush to think of the off-hand way I treated him at our first encounter." In later novels and stories, including *My Man Jeeves* (1919), *The Incredible Jeeves* (1923), *Carry On, Jeeves* (1925), *The Code of the Woosters* (1938), and *Joy in the Morning* (1946), the valet's ability to extricate his young and none-too-bright employer from brushes with authority and commitments to marriage became the chief plot turn. The human and porcine denizens of Blandings Castle form the nucleus of a series including *Something New* (1915), *Summer Lightning* (1929), *Heavy Weather* (1933), *Uncle Fred in the Springtime* (1939), *Full Moon* (1947), *Pigs Have Wings* (1952), and the posthumously published *Sunset at Blandings* (1977). In these novels Lord Emsworth, his censorious sisters, and his scheming younger brother Galahad contend with a succession of imposters, some of whom have designs on Lord Emsworth's prize winning pig, the Empress of Blandings. Other titles treat the Scottish Mr. Ukridge, the garrulous Mr. Mulliner, members of the Drones Club, assorted golfers, and American characters from New York or Hollywood. Many are set in the timeless Edwardian milieu of his youth that underscores Wodehouse's parodic vision of more modern times. In 1940, Wodehouse and his wife were captured by the Nazis at their French villa, Le Tourquet. They were kept in German custody throughout the war. In 1941 Wodehouse made five radio broadcasts to America; with humorous descriptions of their captivity, he intended them to reassure his American fans that the British prisoners were well and staying cheerful. When the recordings were broadcast to Britain—without the author's permission—as part of German propaganda minister Paul Goebbel's attempt to sap British morale, they cast an unwarranted shadow over Wodehouse's reputation in that country, although he was strongly defended by George Orwell and others. After the war he made his permanent home in the United States. The last decades of his life, spent on Long Island, produced some of his best writing, including *French Leave* (1956),

How Right You Are, Jeeves (1960), *Service With a Smile* (1961), *Jeeves and the Tie That Binds* (1971), and *The Cat-Nappers* (1974). Story collections include *The Heart of a Goof* (1926), *Meet Mr. Mulliner* (1927), *Eggs, Beans and Crumpets* (1940), *Selected Stories* (1958), *Plum Pie* (1966), and the posthumously published *Tales from the Drones Club* (1991) and *The Uncollected Wodehouse* (1991). Wodehouse collaborated with Ira Gershwin on the lyrics for *Rosalie* (1928), music by George Gershwin and Sigmund Romberg, and wrote the book, with Howard Lindsay, Russel Crouse and Guy Bolton, for *Anything Goes*, (1934), music and lyrics by Cole Porter. He wrote fourteen plays, some with collaborators, and worked on twenty-seven musicals. *America, I Like You* (1956), revised as *Seventy: An Autobiography with Digressions* (1957) is a collection of memories of a full and long life; *Wodehouse on Wodehouse* (1980) is also autobiographical. Several Wodehouse stories were dramatized by the British Broadcasting Company under the title *Wodehouse Playhouse*, and the series was later shown on American Public Television. Critical studies of his career include Robert A. Hall, Jr., *The Comic Style of P. G. Wodehouse* (1974) and Frances Donaldson, *P. G. Wodehouse* (1982).

Woiwode, Larry [Alfred] (1941–), novelist. Woiwode's novels are often set in North Dakota, his home state. *What I'm Going to Do, I Think* (1960) centers on a young married couple; *Indian Affairs* (1992) is a sequel. *Beyond the Bedroom Wall: A Family Album* (1975) involves several generations of the Neumiller family. *The Neumiller Stories* (1990) includes earlier material that formed the basis for the novel. *Poppa John* (1981) deals with a television actor. *Born Brothers* (1988) details the relationship of Charles and Jerome Neumiller, first introduced in *Beyond the Bedroom Wall*. *Even Tide* (1977) is a poetry collection. *Silent Passengers* (1993) is a collection of stories and *What I Think I Did* (2000) a memoir.

Wolcott, Roger (1679–1767), soldier, public official, poet. Wolcott, a man of many talents and interests, was deputy governor of his native state of Connecticut (1741–50), became a major general, and then served as governor of Connecticut (1751–54). His verse appeared in *Poetical Meditations* (1725).

Wolfe, Nero.   See REX STOUT.

Wolfe, Thomas [Clayton] (1900–1938), novelist, short-story writer, playwright. The youngest of eight children raised by the Julia Elizabeth Westall and William Oliver Wolfe, Thomas Wolfe was born in Asheville, a North Carolina mountain town caught in real estate fever and Yankee materialism. Like his fictional hero, Eugene Gant, Wolfe was the product of "two strong egotisms": his mother, ambitious and "inbrooding," owned a relatively successful boarding house in Asheville. His father, an extroverted and self-indulging Northerner, encouraged his son's literary interests and in 1912 sent him to Mr. and Mrs. J. M. Roberts's preparatory school. In 1916, at age fifteen, Wolfe enrolled at the University of North Carolina to attend Professor Koch's drama course, write and perform plays with the Carolina Playmakers, and edit a student paper. In 1920 he entered Harvard Graduate School to pursue his drama interests in George Pierce Baker's "47 Workshop," completing his M.A. in 1922.

After his play *Welcome to Our City* was turned down by the New York Theater Guild in 1923, Wolfe became an instructor at Washington Square College of New York University, teaching intermittently until 1930. In autumn 1924 he took his first voyage to Europe; on the return boat he met Mrs. Aline Bernstein (Esther Jack in his novels), a noted stage designer who was seventeen years his senior. Their intense relationship is recorded in Wolfe's *The Web and the Rock* and in Mrs. Bernstein's autobiographical novel *The Journey Down*.

Both Aline Bernstein and Scribner editor MAXWELL PERKINS were instrumental in disciplining Wolfe's prodigious narrative flow and getting his first novel, LOOK HOMEWARD ANGEL, published in 1929. This book of unusual lyrical intensity, reflecting Wolfe's childhood experiences but also his immersion in literature—from Milton to Joyce—was praised among others by Sinclair Lewis in his Nobel Prize acceptance speech. On The centenary of his birth, The University of South Caroline Press printed a version of the original manuscript of *Look Homeward Angel* with the materials excised under Perkin's direction restored. Edited by Matthew J. and Arlyn Bruccoli, it is retitled *O Lost: A Story of a Buried Life*. Wolfe resigned from New York University and after taking his fifth trip to Europe, on a Guggenheim Fellowship, spent the following three years in a Brooklyn apartment writing a novel of epic proportions entitled "October Fair." Part of this manuscript, reworked thoroughly at Perkins's suggestions, appeared in 1935 as OF TIME AND THE RIVER.

Though praised by Wolfe in his lecture-essay, *The Story of a Novel* (1936), Perkins is believed, in the editorial assistance he gave Wolfe, to have had certain negative effects on the novelist's creative process. Perkins strongly discouraged Wolfe's mythopoeic and sociological interests, forcing him to resume his earlier characters and the formula of the so-called apprenticeship novel. *Of Time and the River*, tracing Eugene Gant's experiences from the moment he leaves Altamont (Asheville) for Harvard, to his meeting with Esther Jack, lacks thematic-formal cohesion, excelling instead in larger-than-life portraits and a rhetorical-symbolic structure that became clearer after the appearance of Wolfe's last novels. Both *Of Time and the River* and *From Death to Morning* (1935), a collection of shorter narratives published previously in *Scribner's Magazine*, were judged severely by critics who missed their experimental intentions. Robert Penn Warren characteristically attributed to Wolfe an autobiographical naiveté and lack of formal concerns. Bernard DeVoto deplored Wolfe's amalgamation of fiction with documentary, "placental" matter.

These criticisms, as well as Wolfe's growing awareness that his ambitious plans to mythologize America were incompatible with Perkins, prompted his final break with Scribner's in 1937. Freed from supervision by Perkins, Wolfe embarked on a new epic project revolving around an "innocent man's discovery of life and the world." In May 1938 he delivered an eight-foot-high manuscript to Edward C. Aswell of Harper and Brothers, with the intention of returning to it for revision and restructuring. Following a trip to the Western states, Wolfe died unexpectedly from pneumonia and tuberculosis of the brain on September 15. He left the task of creative editing entirely to Aswell, who carved out of this manuscript two massive novels, THE WEB AND THE ROCK (1939) and YOU CAN'T GO HOME AGAIN (1940), and a collection of narrative fragments, *The Hills Beyond* (1941). The two novels follow the life story of George Webber, a character resembling Eugene Gant, but more mature and representative of a broader American experience. The episodes of George Webber's love affair in New York, as well as his visits to Nazi Germany and to his native Lybia Hill during the stock market crash, contain powerful sociological and psychological observation. The style of these books is also more economical and dramatically controlled.

As Wolfe confessed to Aswell, "I began to write with an intense and passionate concern with the designs and purposes of my own youth; and like many other men, that preoccupation has now changed to an intense and passionate concern with the designs and purposes of life." Various editorial constraints and Wolfe's premature death prevented him from completing this transition and realizing fully his intention. Wolfe's best work remains suspended between an unswerving desire to define America "with a poet's vision," and an intense focus on personal experience. His novels, encircling continuously "the strange and bitter miracle of life," are constructed around powerful oppositions: North-South, country-city, America-Europe, father-mother, web-rock. The concern with opposites reflects also in Wolfe's style, blending intense lyricism with panoramic narration, sensuous imagism with rhetoric. Structurally, Wolfe's work is also divided between self-contained, dramatically effective episodes and comic-exhortative passages that follow different principles of organization—associative and metaphoric rather than narrative. The variety of Wolfe's styles dramatizes the novelist's effort to articulate the symbolic purport of a scene, to move from autobiographical representation to mythic recreation.

Wolfe's mythopoeic imagination, "founded on exhorted fact . . . wrenched from the context of ten thousand days," has not been credited enough by criticism that often reads his works as autobiographical rhapsodies lost in "a waste of formlessness." It might help to see Wolfe not as a romantic writer, pursuing a spontaneous, organic form of art, but as a selfconscious and divided modern writer, fascinated with language and its rhetoric, experimenting with various narrative styles, allowing different types of discourse—including parodies of previous literature—to coexist in his work. Articulation, whether of personal or of national experience, was one of Wolfe's chief concerns. Conceiving his role as that of an epic-maker, he struggled to invent a "complete and whole articulation" that could do justice to the range and fluidity of American experience. Wolfe's existential themes are always linguistic themes as well, a matter of finding the "great forgotten language," the enabling door to meaning. These existential-mythic searches give Wolfe's work a poetic depth and dynamism, structuring it mostly through metaphor, rhetorical refrain, and symbolic motif—time, loneliness, memory, language.

Posthumous publications are *Mannerhouse* (1948), a play; *The Mountains* (1970), a play in two versions; *The Letters of Thomas Wolfe*, ed. Elizabeth Nowell (1956); *The Short Novels of Thomas Wolfe*, ed. C. Hugh Holman (1961); and *The Notebooks of Thomas Wolfe*, ed. Richard S. Kennedy and Paschal Reeves (1970). Studies and biographies include Louis D. Rubin, *Thomas Wolfe: the Weather of His Youth* (1955); Elizabeth Nowell, *Thomas Wolfe: A Biography* (1960); Richard S. Kennedy, *The Window of Memory: The Literary Career of Thomas Wolfe* (1962); Ladell Payne, *Thomas Wolfe* (1969); Paschal Reeves, *Thomas Wolfe's Albatross: Race and Nationality in America* (1970); Leo Gurko, *Thomas Wolfe: Beyond the Romantic Ego* (1975); and David Herbert Donald, *Look Homeward: A Life of Thomas Wolfe* (1987).

MARCEL CORNIS-POPE

Wolfe, Tom [Thomas Kennerly Wolfe, Jr.] (1931–   ), novelist, journalist, artist. After attending school in his native Virginia and earning a Ph.D. at Yale, Wolfe worked as a newspaper reporter in Washington and New York and as an editor for *New York Magazine* and *Esquire*. His writing, which combines objective detail with personal opinion, is an example of the so-called NEW JOURNALISM. *The Kandy-Kolored Tangerine-Flake Streamline Baby* (1965) satirizes pop heroes of the 1960s, including Muhammad Ali. *The Electric Kool-Aid Acid Test* (1968) details the escapades of novelist Ken Kesey and his group of Merry Pranksters. *Radical Chic and Mau Mauing the Flak Catchers* (1970), generated hostile reaction to its description of a fund-raising party for the Black Panthers at the home of LEONARD BERNSTEIN. The New York art world was incensed by *The Painted Word* (1975), written and illustrated by Wolfe, and *From Bauhaus to Our House* (1981), both derisive of art and architecture critics. *The Right Stuff* (1979), detailing the selection, training, and daily routines of the first seven U.S. astronauts, was made into a successful movie. *The Bonfire of the Vanities* (1987), also filmed, contrasts life on Park Avenue and in Bronx ghettoes. *A Man in Full* (1998) is a massive novel—set in the New South's Atlanta—where Charles Croker, who starred on the University of Georgia football team, is enmeshed in a breakdown of his marriage and his business empire. Wolfe's other works are *The Pump House Gang* (1968), *Mauve Gloves & Madmen, Clutter & Vine and Other Stories* (1976), *In Our Time* (1980), and *The Purple Decades: A Reader* (1982). *Hooking Up* (2000) is Wolfe's first collection of short pieces in two decades.

Wolfert's Roost (1855),   nineteen stories and sketches by WASHINGTON IRVING. These miscellaneous pieces, first published in the *Knickerbocker Magazine*, take their title from the "doughty and valorous little pile," first erected in 1656, that Irving bought and rebuilt as his beloved Sunnyside. Charming descriptions of scenes in and around Westchester County alternate with lighthearted fables of the American past and tongue-in-cheek Spanish romances.

Wolff, Geoffrey [Ansell] (1937–   ), novelist, biographer. Geoffrey Wolff, when his parents' marriage ended, went with his father, while his brother TOBIAS went with their mother. Geoffrey did not locate his mother and brother until his senior year at Princeton. He attended Cambridge as a Fulbright scholar and worked on *Newsweek* and the *Washington Post* before becoming a college teacher. His novels include *Bad Debts* (1969) and *Providence* (1986). *The Duke of Deception: Memories of My Father* (1979) describes Arthur Wolff, Geoffrey's father. *The Final Club* (1990) is an outsider's view of Princeton. *A Day at the Beach: Recollections* (1992) contains personal essays. *The Age of Consent* (1995) is a novel.

Wolff, Mary Evaline [Sister Mary Madeleva] (1887–1964),   teacher, poet, essayist, medievalist. Mary Evaline Wolff was born in Wisconsin. As Sister Mary Madeleva she became a member of the Order of the Sisters of the Holy Cross in 1908, and began a distinguished career as an English teacher, scholar, and poet. In 1934 she became president of St. Mary's College in Notre Dame, Indiana. She wrote many books, mainly in verse. Among them are *Knights Errant and Other Poems* (1923), *Gates and Other Poems* (1938), *Christmas Eve and Other Poems* (1938), *Selected Poems* (1939), and *Collected Poems* (1947). Among her prose writings are *Chaucer's Nuns and Other Essays* (1925), *The Pearl—A Study in Spiritual Dryness* (1925), and *The Lost Language and Other Essays on Chaucer* (1951).

Wolff, Tobias (1945–   ), novelist, short-story writer. Wolff lived with his divorced mother (see GEOFFREY WOLFF) in Connecticut, Florida, Utah, and Washington. His secondary education was interrupted but, after army service in Vietnam, a degree from Oxford, a job on the *Washington Post*, and study at Stanford, he became writer in residence at Syracuse University. His story collections are *In the Garden of the North American Martyrs* (1981) and *Back in the World* (1985). *The Barracks Thief*, a novella, won the 1985 PEN Faulkner Award. *This Boy's Life: A Memoir* (1989) is a painful reminiscence of growing up in his stepfather's home in the 1950s. *In Pharaoh's Army* (1994) is a Vietnam memoir. *The Night in Question* (1996) collects fifteen stories.

Wolfville (1897, 1923),   a collection of stories by ALFRED HENRY LEWIS (Dan Quin). These became so popular that they were followed by three other collections: *Wolfville Days* (1902), *Wolfville Nights* (1902), and *Wolfville Folks* (1908). Wolfville is supposedly a frontier town in Arizona, the inhabitants of which are miners and cattle raisers.

Woman's Home Companion.   A monthly magazine founded in 1873 in Cleveland as the *Ladies' Home Companion*, a magazine for children. It was bought by *Farm & Fireside* in 1884 and was moved to Springfield, Ohio. Like *Farm & Fireside* it became part of the Crowell-Collier chain, with editorial offices in New York. It published both fiction and nonfiction and for a time had a circulation above 4 million. It ceased publication in 1956.

Wonder-Book for Girls and Boys, A (1852),   a collection of Greek myths retold for children by NATHANIEL

HAWTHORNE. Here Hawthorne divested his mind of the moral conflict and dark fantasy he applied to so much of his adult fiction. Instead, he wrote simply, charmingly, and even a little naively. The myths are carefully purged of all elements Hawthorne thought unsuitable for children; the book was followed by a similar collection, TANGLEWOOD TALES, in 1853.

Wonderful One-Hoss Shay, The.   See THE DEACON'S MASTERPIECE.

Wonderful Wizard of Oz, The (1900),   a story for children by L. FRANK BAUM. It is a fairy tale that uses American materials. Dorothy and her dog Toto journey from Kansas to the imaginary realm of Oz, meeting on the way such marvelous creatures as the Scarecrow, the Tin Woodman, and the Cowardly Lion. In the end they return to Kansas. In 1902 the book became a successful musical. It was made into a silent film in 1925, broadcast as a radio drama in 1938, and turned into a Technicolor musical in 1939. Baum was much plagued by his publishers and admirers to produce sequels, and he wrote a number of them: *The New Wizard of Oz* (1903), *Ozma of Oz* (1907), *Dorothy and the Wizard of Oz* (1908), *The Road to Oz* (1909), *The Emerald City of Oz* (1910), and *The Patchwork Girl of Oz* (1913). After Baum's death the series was carried on by Ruth Plumly Thompson and others. Martin Gardner and Russel B. Nye wrote *The Wizard of Oz and Who He Was* (1957).

Wonders of the Invisible World, The (1693),   by COTTON MATHER. This tract is an account of witches and their alleged misdeeds, together with a general discussion of the supernatural. It contains an account of the SALEM WITCHCRAFT TRIALS. ROBERT CALEF replied to Mather in MORE WONDERS OF THE INVISIBLE WORLD, which was ready for publication in 1697. No Boston publisher dared to issue it until 1700. It greatly angered the Mathers, and Increase Mather had Calef's book burned in Harvard Yard.

Wonder-Working Providence of Sion's Saviour (1654),   a history of Massachusetts from 1628 to 1651 by EDWARD JOHNSON.

Wong, Jade Snow (1922–   ),   memoirist. Wong's idealized picture of life in San Francisco's Chinatown, *Fifth Chinese Daughter* (1945), includes recipes and describes family life among immigrants. She continues her autobiographical account in *No Chinese Stranger* (1975). She is also the author of *The Immigrant Experience* (1971).

Wood, Charles Erskine Scott (1852–1944),   soldier, lawyer, writer. A Pennsylvanian and a graduate of West Point, Wood helped explore Alaska and took part in several wars against Native Americans. But he was finally so outraged by injustices against them that he resigned from the army. While still in the army he had studied law, which he practiced in Oregon. Later he moved to California, the setting for much that he wrote. His second wife was the poet Sara Bard Field, who after his death edited, in collaboration with GENEVIEVE TAGGARD, his *Collected Poems* (1949). Wood's writings, marked by poetic sensitivity and a gift for phrase, show his keen, almost exacerbated sense of justice. His best-known book, *The Poet in the*

Desert (1915), was enlarged and rewritten in 1930. He also wrote *Maia* (1918), *Circe* (1919), *Poems from the Ranges* (1929), and *Sonnets to Sappho* (1940). His best-known prose writings are *Heavenly Discourse* (1927), a satire on war, injustice, and other social evils, and *Earthly Discourse* (1937). He also wrote *A Book of Tales, Being Myths of the North American Indians* (1901).

Wood, Sarah Sayward [Barrell] Keating (1759–1855), novelist. Probably the earliest of Maine's many writers of fiction, "Madam Wood" wrote *Julia and the Illuminated Baron* (1800); *Amelia, or, The Influence of Virtue* (1802); *Ferdinand and Elmira* (1804); and *Tales of the Night* (1827).

Wood, William (fl. 1629–1635),   poet, pamphleteer. Wood's *New England's Prospect* (1634), which was intended to encourage his fellow Englishmen to settle in the region, contains lyrics enumerating the plants and animals of the area. He apparently lived in Massachusetts from 1629 to 1633 and, in his writings, expressed his intention to return, but the details of his later life are unknown.

Woodberry, George E[dward] (1855–1930),   critic, poet, teacher. Woodberry was born in Beverly, Massachusetts. He was educated at Harvard, studying there under such eminent teachers as Henry Adams, James Russell Lowell, and C. E. Norton. After a brief period as professor of English at the University of Nebraska, he taught comparative literature at Columbia University. His poetry includes *The North Shore Watch* (1890), a traditional elegy; *Wild Eden* (1899); *Ideal Passion* (1917), a collection of sonnets; and *The Roamer, and Other Poems* (1920). Among Woodberry's critical works are *Makers of Literature* (1900), *America in Literature* (1903), *The Appreciation of Literature* (1907), *Great Writers* (1907), and *The Inspiration of Poetry* (1910). His biographies of Hawthorne (1902) and Emerson (1907) were followed by *The Life of Edgar Allan Poe* (2 v. 1909), an excellent study based on an earlier, shorter biography (1885) and on *The Works of Edgar Allan Poe* (10 v. 1894–95), edited by Woodberry and E. C. STEDMAN.

Woodcock, George (1912–1995),   poet, biographer, social commentator. Woodcock left his native Manitoba to study in England, where he joined the London literary world peopled by Dylan Thomas, Roy Campbell, and George Orwell among others. He declared himself a "literary anarchist" and, in addition to writing his own poetry collected in *The White Island* (1940) and *The Centre Cannot Hold* (1943), he studied earlier independent thinkers, producing such studies as *William Godwin: A Biographical Study* (1946) and *The Incomparable Aphra: A Life of Mrs. Aphra Behn* (1948). Returning to Canada after World War II service as a conscientious objector, Woodcock produced more than a dozen travel books, works on Canadian nationalism, and literary biographies. His later poetry collections include *Imagine the South* (1947); *Selected Poems* (1967); *Notes on Visitations: Poems, 1936–1975*; and *The Kestrel and Other Poems* (1978). *Two Plays* appeared in 1978. *Taking It to the Letter* (1982) is a selection of correspondence with other writers, and *Letter to the Past* (1983) is autobiography.

Woodhull, Victoria [Claflin] (1838–1927), reformer, lecturer. Woodhull, born in Ohio, began her lively career by giving spiritualist performances, telling fortunes, and selling patent medicines with her family. Twice married, she moved with her sister Tennessee Celeste Claflin to New York, where they were befriended by Cornelius Vanderbilt, Sr. The sisters founded *Woodhull and Claflin's Weekly* (1870–76), a periodical devoted to social and political reform in which they advocated women's rights and sexual freedom. Both the story of the notorious Beecher-Tilton affair (see HENRY WARD BEECHER) and the first English translation of the *Communist Manifesto* appeared in its pages (1872). The Equal Rights Party nominated Victoria for President (1872), with Frederick Douglass as her running mate. Moving to England, Victoria married the scion of a wealthy banking family, and her sister married a baronet. With her daughter Zulu Maud Woodhull, Victoria published a periodical entitled *Humanitarian* (1892–1901).

Among the articles and pamphlets she wrote are *Origin, Tendencies and Principles of Government* (1871); *Stirpiculture* (1888); *The Alchemy of Maternity* (1889); *The Human Body the Temple of God* (with Tennessee Claflin, 1890); and *And The Truth Shall Make You Free* (1894). The fullest biography is Emanie L. Sachs, *The Terrible Siren* (1928). Victoria and her sister are regarded as the models for Audacia Dangereyes in Harriet Beecher Stowe's novel *My Wife and I* (1871).

Woodman, Spare That Tree! (the opening line, now usually the title, of a poem called "The Oak," first printed in the New York *Mirror*, January 7, 1837, and later included in *The Deserted Bride and Other Poems*, 1838), a poem by GEORGE POPE MORRIS. It immediately became well known and has been used ever since as propaganda for the preservation of trees and forests.

Woodson, Carter Godwin (1875–1950), historian, editor. Woodson, born in Virginia, devoted himself to writing chronicles and providing material about members of his own African-American race. Among his books are *The Education of the Negro Prior to 1861* (1915), *History of The Negro Church* (1921), *The Negro in Our History* (1922), *Negro Orators and Their Orations* (1925), and *African Heroes and Heroines* (1939). He founded and edited the *Journal of Negro History* (1916).

Woodward, C. Vann (1908–1999), historian. A southerner himself, Woodward was considered one of the preeminent historians of the post-Civil War South. Born in Vanndale, Arkansas, Woodward was educated at Emory University (B.A., 1930), Columbia University (M.A., 1932) and the University of North Carolina (Ph.D., 1937). His early teaching career was varied, but he settled first at Johns Hopkins University (1946–61), then at Yale University from which he retired in 1977. Woodward's 1951 book, *Origins of the New South: 1877–1913* challenged the idea that political struggles in the South were between northern industrialists and southern landowners, but were rather conflicts between industrialists and landowners from the South. He further

demonstrated that economic recovery in the region was limited by extreme poverty. In 1955, with the publication of *The Strange Career of Jim Crow*, Woodward argued that racial segregation was a creation of the legal structure instituted in 1890 rather than a natural outgrowth of southern folkways, further inspiring the Civil Rights movement to eradicate segregation laws. Woodward won the Pulitzer Prize in 1982 for editing the diaries of Jefferson Davis's aide Mary Chesnut as *Mary Chesnut's Civil War*. He received the American Academy of Arts and Letters Gold Medal for History in 1990. His other works include *Tom Watson: Agrarian Rebel* (1938); *The Battle for Leyte Gulf* (1947); and *The Burden of Southern History* (1960).

SUZANNE PERKINS-HART

Woodward, William E. (1874–1950), editor, banker, writer. Woodward was born in South Carolina. In his autobiography, *The Gift of Life* (1947), Woodward zestfully described his long and varied career as a cotton picker, copyreader, editor of subscription books, advertising agent, newspaperman, banker, and writer in various fields. He wrote two debunking—a word he coined—biographies, *George Washington, The Image and the Man* (1926) and *Meet General Grant* (1928), as well as a more sympathetic one, *Tom Paine: America's Godfather* (1945), and several novels. *A New American History* (1936) and *The Way Our People Lived* (1944) give his own view of the way this country has developed.

Woodworth, Samuel (1784–1842), poet, editor, playwright. Woodworth, a native of Massachusetts, was a skillful miscellaneous writer who caught the popular fancy with one poem, THE OLD OAKEN BUCKET. His verses were collected in *Poems, Odes, Songs, and Other Metrical Effusions* (1818). His best-known play was THE FOREST ROSE (prod. 1825). He also wrote *The Widow's Son* (prod. 1825). *The Forest Rose*, one of the early Yankee plays, held the stage for forty years. F. A. Woodworth, his son, edited his *Poetical Works* (1861). See KNICKERBOCKER SCHOOL.

Woolf, Douglas (1922–1992), novelist. Woolf was born in New York City and studied at Harvard before serving in World War II. He furthered his education at the universities of New Mexico and Arizona. His novels, mostly set in the Southwest, include *The Hypocritic Days* (1955); *Fade Out* (1968), about an old man's attempt to save his dignity; *On Us* (1977); *HAD* (1977); and *The Timing Chain* (1985). *Ja! and John-Juan* (1971) and *A Douglas Woolf Notebook* (1972) both comprise two short pieces. His story collections include *Signs of a Migrant Worrier* (1965) and *Future Preconditional* (1978). Sandra Braman edited *Hypocritic Days and Other Tales* (1993).

Woollcott, Alexander [Humphreys] (1887–1943), newspaperman, drama critic, radio broadcaster, writer, anthologist. Woollcott was born in the Utopian colony called the NORTH AMERICAN PHALANX, in New Jersey, founded in 1843. His family lived in an eighty-five-room building, the last remnant of the colony. Woollcott was educated at Hamilton College and then became a bank clerk. He landed a job on the

New York *Times*, where he switched from straight reporting to drama reporting. After World War I he wrote for several New York papers and became a member of the ROUND TABLE group that assembled daily at the Algonquin Hotel. In 1929 he went on the air with a program called "The Town Crier." He also wrote for *The New Yorker*.

His comments on the New York literary world were often stinging, if witty, but Woollcott was also the butt of the wit of others. In his later years his appetite for rich foods grew unchecked until it was said of him that he was "all Woollcott and a yard wide." He was the acknowledged model for Sheridan Whiteside, a detestable egomaniac in THE MAN WHO CAME TO DINNER (1939), a play by George S. Kaufman and Moss Hart, but instead of taking offense accepted the characterization as a tribute and played the role himself in a touring company.

Woollcott's books include *Mrs. Fiske—Her Views on Acting, Actors, and the Problems of the Stage* (1917); *The Command Is Forward* (1919); *Shouts and Murmurs* (1923); *Enchanted Aisles* (1924); *The Story of Irving Berlin* (1925); *Going to Pieces* (1928); *Two Gentlemen and a Lady* (1928); *While Rome Burns* (1934); and such anthologies as *The Woollcott Reader* (1935) and *Woollcott's Second Reader* (1937). *The Portable Woollcott* (1946) was edited by Joseph Hennessy who, with Beatrice Kaufman, edited Woollcott's *Letters* (1944). *Long, Long Ago* (1943) is a posthumous collection of Woollcott's fugitive essays. Woollcott's stay at Neshobe Island is described in Charles Brackett's novel *Entirely Surrounded* (1934).

Woolman, John (1720–1772),   Quaker leader, abolitionist. The eldest son of Samuel and Elizabeth Burr Woolman, John Woolman was born in New Jersey, brought up in an atmosphere of earnest piety, and educated chiefly by his parents and through his own wide reading in the libraries of his father's friends. At age sixteen he experienced a mystical conversion during a severe illness, as a result of which he later testified: "I was early convinced in my mind that true religion consisted of an inward life. I found no narrowness respecting sects and opinions, but believed that sincere, upright-hearted people in every society, who truly love God, were accepted by him." This spirit of tolerance dominated the rest of Woolman's life as a leader among the Quakers.

Until he was twenty Woolman "wrought on the plantation" of his father, but he apparently did not take well to farming and in 1740 became apprentice to a shopkeeper and baker who also carried on a tailoring business. Woolman set himself to learn the trade of tailor, but during this period he became increasingly active in Friends' meetings and soon undertook his first independent preaching tour, a journey of six weeks through Pennsylvania and western Virginia. What he saw of slavery during this journey of 1756 prompted him to write an essay, *Some Considerations upon the Keeping of Negroes*, printed eight years later. "I saw in these Southern Provinces," he wrote, "so many Vices and Corruptions increased by this trade and this way of life, that it appeared to me as a dark gloominess hanging over the land." He spoke so pointedly of

the inevitable outcome of traffic in human lives that abolitionists a century later found in his words a forecast of the Civil War.

Meanwhile, Woolman set up his own tailoring and general merchandise shop in Mount Holly, New Jersey, and married a "well inclined" Quaker girl, Sarah Ellis. The remaining years of his life were filled with quiet but incessant activity. In 1752 he was made Clerk of the Burlington Quarterly Meeting of Ministers and Elders, a position he held for seventeen years, and became a regular and faithful representative of his district at yearly meetings of his fellow religionists at Philadelphia and elsewhere. For weeks at a time, year in and year out, he traveled among his Quaker friends, exhorting them and counseling with them, particularly attempting to arouse turgid consciences against "reaping the unrighteous profits of that iniquitous practice of dealing in Negroes." Many of his journeys were made on foot to New York and Connecticut, or to Newport and then by ship to Nantucket, slave ports where he felt his word was most greatly needed. In 1763 he held meetings among the Indians, whom he also accepted humbly as fellow aspirants toward the goodness of God. During the next several years he traveled often to the South and visited Friends in eastern New Jersey and Pennsylvania. In the intervals of his tours, while still carrying on his tailoring business, he conducted school in Mount Holly and prepared his own primers. The strain of all these activities, among which must be included the keeping of his *Journal* and his other writings, so told on him that he collapsed with pleurisy in 1770, and his life was despaired of. Nevertheless, in the next year he undertook a voyage to visit Friends in England with whom he had long corresponded. There he died of smallpox, contracted, it is supposed, while ministering among the poor of the manufacturing districts. He was buried in the Bishophill graveyard at York.

Woolman was a man of infinite humility and selflessness. He consistently "studied to be quiet" and to live according to the dictates of the inner light he sought in himself and recommended that all men seek. When, as was often the case, his principles brought him into opposition with the prevailing notions of his time, he governed himself by "passive obedience," which enabled him to follow the letter while disregarding the spirit of oppressive laws. "Woolman's saintliness," said John Greenleaf Whittier, a later Quaker, "was wholly unconscious. He seems never to have thought himself any nearer to the tender heart of God than the most miserable sinner for whom his compassion extended. As he did not live, so he did not die for himself. His prayer on his death bed was for others rather than for himself."

The life of John Woolman is best mirrored in the *Journal* (1774) that he began in his thirty-sixth year. Containing only a slender thread of personal history, introduced as necessary for a background, the *Journal* records Woolman's "inward life, wherein the Heart doth Love and Reverence God the Creator, and learn to Exercise true Justice and Goodness, not only toward all men, but also toward the Brute Creatures." The style of the *Journal* has been widely praised by many generations of critics for its sweetness and lucidity, yet the concreteness with which it reveals a mystical personality has commended it equally to other readers in search of realistic consolation. The *Journal* is, indeed, a classic of American spiritual experience.

Woolman's other writings were few, but they too have been often reprinted. The most important among them are *Considerations on Pure Wisdom and Human Policy* (1758), *A Plea for the Poor* (1763), and *Considerations on the True Harmony of Mankind* (1770). These and other writings were posthumously collected as *The Works of John Woolman* (2 v. 1774), of which the first volume contained the *Journal*. *The Journal and Major Essays of John Woolman* was edited by Phillips P. Moulton (1971). An earlier collection is *The Journal and Essays of John Woolman* (1922), edited with a biographical introduction by Amelia M. Gummere. Critical works include Edwin H. Cady, *John Woolman* (1965) and P. Rosenblatt, *John Woolman* (1969).

LEWIS LEARY/BP

Woolrich, Cornell [“George Hopley” and “William Irish”] (1903–1968),   writer. Woolrich was born in New York City. After his graduation from Columbia in 1925, Woolrich tried his hand at fiction with *Cover Charge* (1926) and was so successful that he continued writing at the rate of about one book a year. He is best known for *Rear Window* and for his own film adaptation of the story, which received a citation from the Screen Writers' Guild in 1954. In it a newspaper photographer confined to his Greenwich Village apartment with a broken leg, and thoroughly bored, watches his neighbors through his rear window—and gradually begins to suspect that a murder has been committed. The story demonstrates Woolrich's particular brand of mystery: suspenseful and neatly melodramatic. Among his books are *The Time of Her Life* (1931), *Rendezvous in Black* (1948), *Dead Man Blues* (1948), *Strangler's Serenade* (1951), *Eyes That Watch You* (1952), *Nightmare* (1956), and *Hotel Room* (1958).

Woolsey, Sarah Chauncey [“Susan Coolidge”] (1835–1905),   poet, author of books for girls, editor. Woolsey, born in Ohio, started out as a poet and went on to write popular books for girls, particularly the What Katy Did series. The series began in 1872 with *What Katy Did* and closed in 1886 with *What Katy Did Next*. Under her pen name, Susan Coolidge, Woolsey became known for her pleasant verse, her editions of the letters of several well-known women, and her *A Short History of Philadelphia* (1887).

Woolson, Constance Fenimore (1840–1894),   novelist, short-story writer. Woolson, whose great-uncle was James Fenimore Cooper, was born in New Hampshire, traveled a good deal in America, lived for a while in the South, and spent the remainder of her life in England and Europe. A sensitive analyst of human nature and a pioneer regionalist, Woolson was much impressed by Bret Harte's writings. She wrote *Two Women* (1862), a long narrative poem; *Castle Nowhere* (1875), a collection of stories about French settlers in the Great Lakes region; *Rodman the Keeper* (1880), sketches

about the South; *Anne* (1883), a novel about a Mackinac Island girl; *For the Major* (1883), *East Angels* (1886), *Jupiter Lights* (1889), and *Horace Chase* (1894), novels about the South; *The Front Yard* (1895) and *Dorothy* (1896), stories about Americans in Italy; and *Mentone, Cairo and Corfu* (1895), descriptive sketches. Much of her work, which was praised by Henry James, first appeared in *Atlantic Monthly, Harper's*, and *Century. Miss Grief and Other Stories*, which was edited as *Women Artists, Women Exiles: “Miss Grief” and Other Stories* by Joan Myers Weimer (1989), contains nine of Woolson's stories that were originally published between 1873 and 1894 as well as an 1888 essay on Woolson's writing by Henry James.

Worcester, Joseph Emerson (1784–1865),   lexicographer, geographer, historian. A native of New Hampshire and graduate of Yale, Joseph Worcester taught in Salem, Massachusetts. Hawthorne was one of his students for a short while. At Salem, Worcester wrote *A Geographical Dictionary, or Universal Gazetteer, Ancient and Modern* (1817). Similar works were his *Gazetteer of the United States* (1818), *Elements of Geography* (1819), *Sketches of the Earth and Its Inhabitants* (1823), and *Elements of History, Ancient and Modern* (1826).

With his edition of *Johnson's English Dictionary . . . with Walker's Pronouncing Dictionary, Combined* (1828), Worcester began his career as lexicographer. *A Comprehensive Pronouncing and Explanatory Dictionary of the English Language* (1830), the first of his own dictionaries, marked the beginning of a long and bitter rivalry between Worcester and NOAH WEBSTER. In reply to Webster's charge of plagiarism, Worcester published *A Gross Literary Fraud Exposed* (1853). His dictionaries, which were more conservative and closer to British usage than those of Webster, were preferred by the New England literati, especially his influential *Dictionary of the English Language* (1860), the first illustrated dictionary.

Work, Henry Clay (1832–1884),   songwriter. Work, born in Connecticut, was a printer by trade and a specialist in setting type for musical scores. He is known to have sometimes set type for his own songs as he composed them—without intervening manuscript or piano. Work's strong political interests favoring abolitionism, Unionism, and prohibition determined to some extent the content of his songs, among them MARCHING THROUGH GEORGIA (1865), which was preceded by other Civil War songs. One of his most successful songs was “Grandfather's Clock” (1876). He was also the author of the temperance song beginning, “Father, dear father, come home with me now.”

Workman, Fanny [Bullock] (1859–1925),   explorer, writer of travel books. Born in Worcester, Massachusetts, Fanny Workman was the wife of William Hunter Workman (1847–1937), with whom she explored many countries. She wrote accounts of their experiences in *Algerian Memories* (1895), *Sketches Awheel in Modern Iberia* (1897), *Peaks and Glaciers of Nun Kun* (1909), *Two Summers in the Ice Wilds of Eastern Karakoram* (1917), and other books.

Workshop 47.   See GEORGE PIERCE BAKER.

Works Progress Administration (WPA). At the height of the economic depression that began in 1929, the Roosevelt administration secured appropriation of huge sums of money and set up widespread measures designed to provide immediate relief of economic and social distress. The work was placed in May 1935 under a Works Progress (later Works Projects) Administration, with an initial appropriation of almost five billion dollars to be spent on many types of projects—highway building, lumber camps, rural rehabilitation, reforestation, electrification, health projects, and student aid. The WPA also took into its ranks writers, actors, musicians, and artists of all kinds, many of whom made notable achievements—especially in the Federal Theater. The WPA produced much literary material, notably the American Guide Series. Its volumes were produced with the collaboration of many local groups for all the states of the Union and outlying territories. See FEDERAL THEATER PROJECT; FEDERAL WRITERS' PROJECT.

The World According to Garp (1978), novel by JOHN IRVING. This, Irving's fourth novel, became an immediate best seller. It is a cautionary tale about the life and art of one T. S. Garp, an American writer who falls victim to his reading public's confusion of fiction with autobiography. Garp was conceived during a symbolically brief alliance between Jenny Fields, a strong-minded nurse who abhors male violence and lust, and a dying aerial gunner. Garp grows up with his mother, who writes a feminist autobiography that wins her instant celebrity, but eventually results in her assassination while running for political office. Garp's own writing, which is excerpted generously in the novel, begins as an exuberant, if mordant exercise of the imagination. His first and best story, for example, relates the exploits of a unicycling bear in Vienna. Garp's domestic life becomes increasingly troubled and finally is shattered by his struggles between lust and love. His fiction increasingly reflects this preoccupation. His later, luridly melodramatic fiction wins fame for Garp, but leads also to his murder at the hands of a childhood acquaintance who has turned radical feminist. Garp's imagination is most powerfully driven by his paradoxical celebration of energy and heightened awareness of mortality. But his life and fiction are shaped by social forces in contemporary America that obsess and destroy him. *The World According to Garp* is at once a compelling domestic tragicomedy and, for all its celebrated energy, a dark commentary on the relations between contemporary writers, their readers, and the fictions that consume us.

NEIL K. BESNER

World Enough and Time (1950), a novel by ROBERT PENN WARREN. The murder in Kentucky of Col. Solomon P. Sharp by Jeroboam O. Beauchamp, whose trial was the sensation of 1826, has been a popular theme for novelists ever since. Warren's version in this novel is based on *The Confession*, which Beauchamp published in 1826. Warren introduced many variations, however, and his quotations from documents are his own inventions. See also BEAUCHAMPE.

World War I. Long before Archduke Francis Ferdinand was assassinated in June 1914, the rise of nationalist movements in the Balkans had shaken the declining Austro-Hungarian Empire. Austrian retaliation for the incident at Sarajevo led to the collapse of a system of alliances that had developed since the Franco-Prussian war. Germany, having armed itself, declared war on France on August 3 and invaded Belgium on the same day, bringing England into the war to make good on a promise to protect Belgian neutrality. After initial fighting along the Marne, the Anglo-French line was established. The western front, a labyrinthine network of trenches and bunkers, stretched from Nieuport on the English Channel to the French fortresses at Verdun, and in no sector did it move more than a few miles between 1915 and the Armistice in November 1918.

Originally, American public opinion was strongly isolationist, and Woodrow Wilson won reelection in 1916 with the slogan "He Kept Us Out of War." John Dos Passos recalled that Wilson's declaration of war against the Central Powers was a bitter disappointment that caused him to despise Wilson. Dos Passos felt Wilson might have used the threat of American entry to force a negotiated settlement. Germany had strained American opinion by torpedoing neutral ships. When British intelligence passed on a telegram it had intercepted in which the German Secretary of Foreign Affairs, Alfred Zimmerman, proposed an alliance of Germany and Mexico, American public opinion tended to back Wilson. (Later, Wilson could not find enough support at home to get the Republican Congress to ratify the Treaty of Versailles, in which Wilson's chief contribution was the creation of the League of Nations.)

In *The Destructive Element* (1936), Stephen Spender argues that "the sufferings of Henry James's over-perceptive characters . . . found expression in the physical suffering of the war." Though James did not live long enough to write about the war, he did tell Edith Wharton that he considered the conflict "the crash of civilization." Indeed, the world appeared to pass beyond the power of a Jamesian sensibility to understand it, no matter how heroically one might have faced its horrors.

During the war, EDITH WHARTON stayed in Paris, organizing the American Hostels for Refugees and the Children of Flanders Rescue Committee and taking part in other relief activities. In 1915 she edited *The Book of the Homeless*, an anthology including writers as diverse as Rupert Brooke, Jean Cocteau, George Santayana, Thomas Hardy, and W. B. Yeats. The book raised fifteen thousand dollars for relief causes. But the aging novelist's energies could not ensure the artistic insight necessary to comprehend fully the experience of victims and soldiers. *The Marne* (1918), a short novel about an American ambulance driver, and *A Son at the Front* (1923) are novels in which Wharton is more successful at depicting generational conflicts than at understanding the war. Finally, the explanation of the war's causes and effects belonged to the next generation, especially modernists who sought to make a new order, and leftists who generally felt that the war had been fought by working men for bankers and industrialists.

T. S. ELIOT spent the war years in England as a noncombatant and in 1922 published the most important literary document of the time. THE WASTE LAND takes as its subject the collapse of civilization, beginning with the proclamation that "April is the cruellest month, breeding / Lilacs out of the dead land," lines recalling that early spring meant the resumption of heavy shelling along the western front. In its vision of devastation. *The Waste Land* echoes the sentiments of EZRA POUND'S HUGH SELWYN MAUBERLEY (1920), in which the speaker decides that the enormous human sacrifice of the war had been made "For an old bitch gone in the teeth, / For a botched civilization."

Gertrude Stein, in telling ERNEST HEMINGWAY that he and his friends comprised a LOST GENERATION, could not have guessed that they would go on to astonishing literary achievement. Notwithstanding, her label aptly describes the generation's concerns, for if Pound and Eliot were forcefully announcing the destruction of a culture and its symbols, novelists were investigating losses on a more personal level. In Hemingway's three World War I books, the protagonists are seriously wounded in a manner that emasculates and dehumanizes them. In OUR TIME (1925) reaches its climax with the wounding of Nick Adams. In THE SUN ALSO RISES (1926), Jake Barnes's war wound makes him incapable of love. In A FAREWELL TO ARMS (1929), Frederic Henry is healed by Catherine Barkley only to have her die trying to bring his child into the world. The message of all three seems to be that the partial body can only house a partial soul, and survivors take their places in the ranks of living dead who can know joy, love, and comfort only insufficiently and through nostalgia.

WILLA CATHER struck a similar theme in her war novel, ONE OF OURS (1922). In presenting Cather with the Pulitzer Prize for the novel, William Lyon Phelps called *One of Ours* Cather's "worst novel" but "better than everybody else's masterpiece." The story of a Nebraska farmer who dies in battle, the novel takes a rather naive view of combat and heroism. But in Cather's THE PROFESSOR'S HOUSE (1925), the war becomes a force of random and malignant energy, indiscriminately destructive of intelligence, courage, and youth. The death of Tom Outland registers as the symbolic death of the human principles of generosity and reverence for life and history.

Other writers found their experiences beyond imagination and wrote in an autobiographical manner that emphasized the difficulty the artist had in matching the horror of the war. Instead, a frequent theme is the persistence of common decency in the face of the savagery of battle, military ineptitude, and jingoism. E. E. CUMMINGS went to France as a volunteer in the Norton Harjes Ambulance Corps and through misadventure was imprisoned as a spy. THE ENORMOUS ROOM (1922) ironically parallels Bunyan's *Pilgrim's Progress* and, in spite of the circumstances it describes, it manages to celebrate the brotherhood of the prisoners. JOHN DOS PASSOS published two novels drawn directly from his experience. He too was a volunteer in the Norton Harjes Corps at Verdun and later served in Italy with the American Red Cross. *One Man's Initiation: 1917* recalls the time with the crisp verisimilitude characteristic of his major novels. Published in England in expurgated form in 1920, *One Man's Initiation* was overshadowed by THREE SOLDIERS (1921). A novel with a distinctly pacifist argument, it tells the story of John Andrews, a musician and Harvard graduate who fought along the western front. In

its critical look at army bureaucracy and the cruel absurdities of authoritarianism, *Three Soldiers* prefigures Joseph Heller's CATCH-22.

For some the war had a greater personal effect than direct artistic impact. ARCHIBALD MACLEISH enlisted as a private in 1917, was discharged as a captain of artillery and, after several unsatisfactory years practicing law in Boston, he took his family back to France, where he studied and wrote. EDMUND WILSON worked first as a volunteer in a French hospital and later as a U.S. intelligence agent. Others tried to get into the fight and could not. WILLIAM FAULKNER, for example, joined the Canadian Royal Flying Corps but never saw combat, though he did publish a war novel, *Soldier's Pay*, in 1926, and, years later, A FABLE (1954).

F. Scott Fitzgerald lived out the frustration of awaiting orders to go overseas and instead of seeing action in France found himself the chronicler of the Jazz Age. His was a view from a moderate distance, and in TENDER IS THE NIGHT (1933) the psychiatrist Dick Diver looks over a battlefield six years after the Armistice. He tells his party that the "western-front business couldn't be done again, not for a long time." According to Diver, the culture that could fight such a war had disappeared, for "this took religion and years of plenty and tremendous sureties and the exact relation that existed between the classes." It took, Diver says, "a whole-souled sentimental equipment going back further than you could remember."

Outside the boundaries of American letters, Erich Maria Remarque's *All Quiet on the Western Front* (1928) deserves mention for it shows the nightmare of the war from the German perspective. Humphrey Cobb, a naturalized Canadian born in Italy of American parents, published *Paths of Glory* in 1935; it is an unflinching and unsentimental look at the cruelties of false honor and military codes of justice. Among critical works, Paul Fussell's *The Great War and Modern Memory* (1975) stands above all the rest. Though primarily a study of British war poets, Fussell's book is an excellent general study of war literature. His thesis—the "one dominating form of modern understanding . . . is essentially ironic" and "it originates largely in the application of mind and memory to the events of the Great War"—is borne out as emphatically by the Americans as by the British.

MARK A. R. FACKNITZ

World War II.   The causes of World War II were intimately connected with those of World War I and with the unfavorable conditions remaining after the Treaty of Versailles. Economic distress, together with the unpopularity and weakness of the Weimar Republic in Germany, led the way to the growth of fascism and the rise of Adolf Hitler. The League of Nations, established to maintain peace and settle international disputes, was drastically weakened by the refusal of the United States to join. When the League did nothing but formally condemn Japan for its invasion of Manchuria in 1931–32, many countries felt the need to protect themselves by building up armaments. In 1935, the League failed to prevent Italy's invasion of Ethiopia. Under Hitler, Germany began to rearm and sent troops into the Rhineland (1936) in violation of the Treaty of Versailles. Germany seized Austria in 1938, and in August 1939 entered into a nonaggression pact with the USSR. The war began officially with the German invasion of Poland on September 1, 1939. Poland was crushed, Norway and Denmark were seized by the Nazis, the British army was driven off the Continent, and France fell.

On December 7, 1941, the Japanese bombed Pearl Harbor, in Hawaii, and destroyed the greater part of the United States fleet there. The United States immediately declared war not only on Japan but on Germany and Italy as well. Japan followed up the Pearl Harbor attack with others in the Pacific region, and the war from then on involved all the continents and all the oceans. The Japanese captured Wake, Guam, the Philippines, and other strategic islands before the Allied offensive, begun in the fall of 1942, began to dislodge them. However, it was not until President HARRY S. TRUMAN authorized the dropping of the first atomic bombs (on Hiroshima, August 6, 1945; on Nagasaki, three days later) that Japan was forced to surrender (September 2, 1945).

After an allied invasion of southern Italy the Italian army and navy surrendered (September 3, 1943), but German forces in Rome and to the north were not dislodged until the summer of 1944. On June 6, 1944, immense reinforcements of men and supplies, under the command of General Dwight D. Eisenhower, had landed in France and forced the Germans to retreat across the Rhine. Germany surrendered unconditionally on May 7, 1945.

Many of the novels published during or immediately after the war were examples of direct reportage. Norman Mailer's THE NAKED AND THE DEAD (1948), based on the author's experiences in battle on Pacific islands, traced the physical and psychological conflicts of a small group of enlisted men. John Horne Burns reported his own experience in North Africa and Italy in THE GALLERY (1947). JOHN HERSEY detailed the Allied occupation of Sicily in A Bell for Adano (1944) and later used the same documentary method to describe the 1943 Warsaw ghetto uprising in The Wall (1950). Gertrude Stein, who had to flee Paris for a country house, explored The War in two books: Wars I Have Seen (1945) and Brewsie and Willy (1946), a sympathetic look at the experiences of American enlisted men.

The experience of women working in the defense industry was realistically portrayed in HARRIETTE ARNOW's The Dollmaker (1947). JAMES GOULD COZZENS described U.S. Air Force units at home in Guard of Honor (1948). Irwin Shaw contrasted the careers of a Jew and a Gentile as U.S. soldiers in Germany in THE YOUNG LIONS (1948). JOHN HAWKES, who had left Harvard to drive an ambulance in Italy and Germany, returned to school and wrote The Cannibal (1949), a surrealistic view of the war's devastation seen from the German viewpoint. In addition to acting as a war correspondent, HEMINGWAY contributed Across the River and into the Trees (1950). His posthumous Islands in the Stream (1970) contains some passages on submarine hunting in the Caribbean. One of the most successful World War II novels was FROM HERE TO ETERNITY (1951) by James Jones. This novel examined the peacetime Army in Hawaii just before the attack on Pearl Harbor. In The Thin Red Line (1962), Jones covered the fighting on Guadalcanal in 1942 and 1943. The Whistle (1978) dealt with the adjustment of wounded veterans to civilian life.

THE CAINE MUTINY (1951), which Herman Wouk later turned into a play, The Caine Mutiny Court-Martial (1954), dealt with issues of authority and loyalty. Wouk's two lengthy novels The Winds of War (1971) and War and Remembrance (1978) treat the war in the Pacific and the Holocaust in Europe.

Some writers took a long time to deal with their war experiences in fiction. Joseph Heller, an Air Force veteran, brought out the madly comic CATCH-22 in 1961. Kurt Vonnegut, Jr., in SLAUGHTERHOUSE FIVE (1969), described the firebombing of Dresden, which he witnessed. MARGE PIERCY, who lived through the war as a child, detailed the experiences of combatants and workers on the home front in Gone to Soldiers (1987). Thomas Pynchon, also a child in wartime, created in GRAVITY'S RAINBOW (1973) a monumental account of the building of the V-2 rocket and the devastation of London.

American poets also wrote about the war. Before the United States declared war, Archibald MacLeish produced poetic radio plays about the European battles in THE FALL OF THE CITY (1937) and Air Raid (1938). T. S. ELLIOT's "Little Gidding" deals with the war and W. H. AUDEN described the deepening shadow of fascism. Younger poets who fought described their emotions. Notable examples are RANDALL JARRELL's Losses (1948); KARL SHAPIRO's V-Letter and Other Poems (1944); RICHARD EBERHART's "The Fury of Aerial Bombardment;" and work by JOHN CIARDI, LOUIS SIMPSON, JAMES DICKEY, and W. D. SNODGRASS. ROBERT LOWELL and WILLIAM EVERSON wrote from the perspective of conscientious objectors.

Playwrights attacking fascism included ROBERT E. SHERWOOD, in Idiot's Delight (1936) and There Shall Be No Night (1940). MAXWELL ANDERSON wrote Candle in the Wind (1941), The Eve of St. Mark (1942), and Storm Operation (1944). JOHN STEINBECK dramatized his novel about Norwegian resistance to the occupying Nazis, The Moon Is Down, in 1942. THOMAS HEGGEN's popular novel of heroics aboard ship, Mister Roberts (1946), was made into a play and a movie. Oscar Hammerstein II won a Pulitzer Prize for South Pacific (1949), which was also made into a successful movie. It was derived from JAMES MICHENER's TALES OF THE SOUTH PACIFIC (1947). ARTHUR MILLER's first successful stage play was All My Sons (1947), a study of moral responsibility in the defense industry. His Incident at Vichy (1965) treated similar issues in occupied France as Jews are rounded up by the Nazis.

Volumes of dispatches from such correspondents as ERNIE PYLE (Brave Men, 1944) and WILLIAM LINDSAY WHITE (They Were Expendable, 1942) were very popular, as were the wartime cartoons of BILL MAULDIN, collected in Up Front (1945). Established writers, such as Steinbeck, Hersey, and ERSKINE CALDWELL, in addition to Hemingway, served as correspondents. Women, including MARGARET BOURKE-WHITE and MARTHA GELLHORN, also covered troop action.

Wouk, Herman (1915–   ), novelist, playwright. Wouk was born in New York City and educated at Columbia. He first wrote radio scripts for comedian Fred Allen, but at the outbreak of World War II entered the Navy as a line officer and served for four years, winning four campaign stars. His first novel, *Aurora Dawn* (1947), was an ironic treatment of big business. *City Boy* (1948), an amusing story of youth, became a movie. His next novel, THE CAINE MUTINY (1951), a gripping account of Navy life during World War II, had a spectacular impact on the public, selling almost two million copies by 1953. It became a movie, and then part of it formed a play, *The Caine Mutiny Court-Martial.* MARJORIE MORNINGSTAR (1955) also became a best seller, despite sharply divided critical reaction. Among his other works are *The Traitor* (1949), a play; *Slattery's Hurricane* (1948), a movie script, in 1949 a novelette, and in 1956 a novel. He also has written *Nature's Way* (1958) and *This Is My God* (1959). At his best Wouk has an intelligent narrative style and an awareness of dramatic plot technique.

Wouk's most ambitious project, *The Winds of War* (1971) and *War and Remembrance* (1978), traces the life of naval officer Victor Henry through World War II and its aftermath. Both were produced for television. His other titles include *Youngblood Hawke* (1962), *Don't Stop the Carnival* (1965), *The Lomokome Papers* (1968), and *Inside, Outside* (1986). *The Hope* (1993) and *The Glory* (1994) deal with the history of Israel from the end of World War II to the War against the Arabs in 1967.

Wound and the Bow, The (1941),   a volume of literary criticism by EDMUND WILSON. The title is derived from Sophocles' play *Philoctetes*, in which a warrior exiled to an island because of his foul-smelling wound is yet sought out by his fellows, who need his magic bow to win the Trojan War. To Wilson this is a symbol of the modern artist, who pays for his creative abilities by his sickness. The same society that rejects him needs the restorative powers of his art. Using a psychological and mythological approach, Wilson explains the imagination of Dickens as the result of the psychic wounds induced by his father's imprisonment for debt. The volume includes similar essays on Rudyard Kipling, Edith Wharton, and Ernest Hemingway.

Wound Dresser, The (1898),   letters written by WALT WHITMAN to his mother from hospitals in Washington, D.C., during the Civil War. When his brother George was wounded in battle, Whitman set out to look for him, then took up residence in Washington and spent much of his time there in tending soldiers in army hospitals. In his letters he condemned the bad conditions in the hospitals, praised some of the doctors and nurses, and called himself a "self-appointed missionary" to the wounded.

Wounds in the Rain: A Collection of Stories Relating to the Spanish-American War of 1898 (1900), by STEPHEN CRANE. Of these short pieces *The Nation* said: "The manner in which these sketches and memories of the Spanish-American war are written is that of a clever and vivacious journalist, tempered by after-thought and softened by the desire to give literary effectiveness to descriptions of episodes in which the note of life is distressing or violent or brutal. The volume contains some of the best work that Mr. Crane has left behind him."

WPA and WPA Guides.   See WORKS PROGRESS ADMINISTRATION.

Wreck of the Hesperus, The (1841),   a ballad by HENRY WADSWORTH LONGFELLOW. In his *Journal* entry for December 17, 1839, Longfellow recorded his horror at reading an account of the wreck of a schooner named the *Hesperus* off Norman's Reef near Gloucester. Twenty bodies were washed ashore, one of them lashed to a piece of wreckage. On December 30 Longfellow sat smoking by the fire until midnight, when suddenly it came into his head to write "The Ballad of the Schooner Hesperus"—"It hardly cost me an effort." Lines in it echo the old Scottish ballad "Sir Patrick Spens."

Wright, Charles [Penzel] (1935–   ), poet. Wright, born in Tennessee, grew up and was educated in the rural South. After four years in the army, including three years in Italy, he enrolled in the University of Iowa writing program. He has taught at the University of California and the University of Virginia. His involvement with Italy has been reinforced by a Fulbright Fellowship and a Guggenheim award. His poetry shows the influence of Dante and Eugenio Montale, whose work he translated in *The Storm and Other Poems* (1978). His verse mixes names and places, real and surreal, in an ongoing private and spiritual autobiography. Selections from *The Grave of the Right Hand* (1970), *Hard Freight* (1973), *Bloodlines* (1975), and *China Trace* (1977) were brought together in *Selected Early Poems* (1982). His other titles, including *The Southern Cross* (1981), *The Other Side of the River* (1984), and *Xionia* (1990), provide the substance for *The World of Ten Thousand Things: Poems 1980–1990* (1991). *Negative Blue: Selected Later Poems* (2000) includes most of the contents of *Chicamauga* (1995), *Black Zodiac* (1997), and *Appalachia* (1998), together with some new poems.

Wright, Fanny [Frances] (1795–1852),   reformer, editor. Born in Scotland, Wright toured the United States several times and finally settled there in 1829. She was an outspoken freethinker in religion and a crusader for more equitable distribution of property as well as for women's rights, free public education, and the abolition of slavery. With the approval of Jefferson and Madison, she attempted to solve the slavery problem in the NASHOBA COMMUNITY. Her *Views of Society and Manners in America* (1821) was so enthusiastic about this country and so disparaging in its references to England that it was condemned roundly overseas. She also wrote *A Few Days in Athens* (1822), *A Course of Popular Lectures* (1829, Volume 2 1836), and a play about the fight for independence in Switzerland, *Altorf* (1819), which was produced and published in New York. Throughout her career she was associated with ROBERT DALE OWEN and his father's ideas. She edited with him the *New Harmony Gazette* and the *Free Enquirer*, the latter launched by her in 1829 in New York City. She is the subject of W. R. Waterman's *Frances Wright* (1924) and A. J. G. Perkins and Theresa Wolfson's *Frances Wright, Free Enquirer* (1939). Her views greatly influenced Walt Whitman.

Wright, Frank Lloyd (1869–1959),   architect. Wright studied civil engineering but quit before graduation to begin a career in architecture in Chicago. There he became assistant to Louis Sullivan, who was the most creative spirit in architecture in that city. After a disagreement with Sullivan, Wright left him and started his own practice, later moving back to his native Wisconsin, where he built his home and studio. He called it Taliesin, a Welsh word meaning "shining brow." Wright's buildings brought him fame as one of the giants of modern architecture and, despite few commissions from the late 1920s to the middle 1930s, when his buildings seemed to go out of style, at his death Wright was regarded as the greatest architect ever produced in America.

Never content to restrict himself to the drafting board, Wright wrote extensively about what he called organic architecture. His many books include *Experimenting with Human Lives* (1923); *Modern Architecture* (1931); *The Disappearing City* (1932); *An Autobiography* (1932, brought up to date in 1943); *On Architecture* (1941); *When Democracy Builds* (1945, drastically revised as *The Living City*, 1958); *Genius and the Mobocracy* (1949); *Testament* (1957); and *Drawings for a Living Architecture* (1959). Ayn Rand used Wright as a model for the protagonist in THE FOUNTAINHEAD (1943).

Some of his most notable buildings are the Imperial Hotel in Tokyo, successfully designed to withstand severe earthquakes; the Millard House in Pasadena, California, constructed of precast concrete blocks; the Johnson Wax Building, Racine, Wisconsin; Taliesin West, his winter home near Phoenix, Arizona; and the Solomon R. Guggenheim Museum in New York City. Hundreds of homes he built attest to his mastery of that form of architecture.

Wright, Harold Bell (1872–1944),   clergyman, novelist. Wright, a native of Rome, New York, was an extraordinarily successful writer despite the disesteem of literary critics. During most of his life he suffered from tuberculosis. He tried various trades, but while living in the Ozarks for his health he began to preach, and later spent ten years as a pastor in the Church of the Disciples, even though he never attended college or a seminary. He turned to writing novels and when he attained success with *The Shepherd of the Hills* (1907) he retired from the ministry, due to ill health. From then on he wrote a best seller about every two years. Among his books are *That Printer of Udell's* (1903), *The Calling of Dan Matthews* (1909), THE WINNING OF BARBARA WORTH (1911), *The eyes of the World* (1914), *When a Man's a Man* (1916), *The Mine with the Iron Door* (1923), *A Son of His Father* (1925), *Ma Cinderella* (1932), and *The Man Who Went Away* (1942). *To My Sons* (1934) is an autobiography.

Wright, James (Arlington) (1927–1980),   poet, translator. Wright, born in Martins Ferry, Ohio, was educated at Kenyon College, the University of Vienna, and the University of Washington. He taught at a number of colleges and universities, including the University of Minnesota and Hunter

College. One of the most prominent and affecting poets of the 1960s and 1970s, he was principally known for his association with the so-called deep image poets, of whom Robert Bly was the chief inspiration at that time. But his real asset was the conspicuous humanity that illuminated his continuing efforts at representing experience in poetic form. He won a wide reputation and received a number of prestigious honors, among them the Yale Series of Younger Poets Award (1957), Academy of American Poets Fellowship (1971), and the Pulitzer Prize (1972).

Wright's *Collected Poems* (1971) contains most of *The Green Wall* (1957) and all of *Saint Judas* (1959), *The Branch Will Not Break* (1963), and *Shall We Gather at the River* (1968), in addition to some translations and thirty-three new poems. Although it covers only 14 years of the poet's career, this volume reveals an authentic experimenter and enables us to discern three stages of development: the dense and formal poems of the early two volumes, the more open and economical work of *Branch*, and the even more open and painful later poems.

The Green Wall and *Saint Judas* are written in the formal style of the 1950s. The former is a youthful and lyrical celebration of the seasons, and the latter is a more dramatic presentation of love, loss, death, and crime in which Wright portrays the torment of separation and the uncertain search for love. *Branch*, as is characteristic of the apocalyptic 1960s, breaks through into open and direct lines, poems of varying lengths, and a more conversational diction and rhythm. Here Wright builds his poems on sharp images that are juxtaposed surrealistically without explanation or transition, leaving the reader to infer the meaning. There are many moments of ecstatic happiness, but there is an emotional—sometimes artistic—descent as we come to *River* and the new poems. Perhaps the title itself suggests the dead wandering by the Styx, and many of the poems support this dismal mood—"In Terror of Hospital Bills," "Listening to the Mourners," and others.

Two Citizens (1973), *Moments of the Italian Summer* (1976, 14 prose pieces), and *To a Blossoming Pear Tree* (1977, including work from *Moments*) presaged a fourth phase, somewhat less bitter and hopeless. Here the art and vision succeed in creating a sense of the complexity hidden beneath the surface of apparent simplicity. Confirmed now in his plain Ohio speech, as he proclaims, and free to resolve some painful conflicts, he writes of his travels to Europe, of his difficult childhood in Martins Ferry, of his love, and of nature, and at the same time he heightens the ordinary into the strange. In "Well, What Are You Going to Do?" for example, from *Citizens*, he depicts a childhood experience of assisting a cow that is giving birth to Marian, which became his calf. At first he feels confused in the face of "the problem; Of beautiful women." Then, after he helps Marian emerge, he wonders whether he belongs in the midst of such mystery. Then, in a shrugging gesture of acceptance, he concludes: "What are you going to do? Be kind? Kill? / Die?"

The same qualities are evident in his posthumous collections, *This Journey* (1982), *The Temple in Nimes* (1982), and

The Shape of Light (1986), where Wright came well past the agonies of *River* and rediscovered his genius for transforming the commonplace with a calm assurance that belies the approach of his premature demise. We read at the conclusion of "The Journey," for example, that we should not lose sleep over the dead, for they certainly "Will bury their own, don't worry." *Above the River: The Complete Poems* appeared in 1990. Wright was an authentically passionate and compassionate poet who did not withhold himself, and at his best he was among the most important poets of his time.

NORMAN FRIEDMAN

Wright, Jay (1935–   ),   poet, playwright. Born in Albuquerque, New Mexico, Wright briefly attended the University of New Mexico, but soon left for three years in the Army Medical Corps. Returning, he graduated from the University of California, Berkeley (B.A., 1961), spent a semester at Union Theological Seminary, and completed his formal education in 1967 with an M.A. in comparative Literature from Rutgers University. By the time of his first major poetry collection, *The Homecoming Singer* (1971), he had been awarded writing fellowships and written both poems and plays, some published. Living in Mexico from 1968 to 1971 and teaching in Scotland from 1971 to 1973, he was by this time confirmed in the seeking and questioning that runs as a major theme through his verse, constructing his poetic identity from widespread sources of experience and reading. In *Soothsayers and Omens* (1976) and *Dimensions of History* (1976) the allusive range is from present to past and from history to myth, with West African history and belief standing as a cultural touchstone for Afro-Americans living in a world as varied as California, New Jersey, Mexico, and Scotland. *The Double Invention of Komo* (1980) focuses on the initiation rites of the Bambara people of Africa, but as the poet enacts his own coming into the full consciousness of being, he turns also to Dante and St. Augustine, to the United States, Mexico, Italy, Germany, and France. *Boleros* (1991) continues Wright's multiculturalism of voice, place, and reference. Difficult and wide-ranging in his allusions—HART CRANE seems especially important to him, but his poetic references include also Goethe and Hugh MacDiarmid—he has merged his African-Americanness into an impresive personal statement of cultural inclusiveness. TRANSFIGURATIONS: COLLECTED POEMS (2000) contains all his work to date.

Wright, Louis B[ooker] (1899–1984),   journalist, scholar. Wright, born in South Carolina, wrote for several papers and taught at various universities before becoming director of the Folger Shakespeare library in 1948. In studies of the American frontier, such as *Atlantic Frontier* (1947) and *Culture on the Moving Frontier* (1955), Wright advanced the novel thesis that love of British culture was a strong force among settlers. His best-known work involves editing the papers of William Byrd (1674–1744). With Marion Tinling he coedited *The Secret Diary of William Byrd of Westover, 1709–1712* (1941); an abridged version of the same material entitled *The Great American Gentleman: William Byrd of West-*

over (1963); and *William Byrd of Virginia: The London Diary (1717–1721) and Other Writings* (1958). Wright also edited *The Prose Works of William Byrd of Westover* (1966) and wrote a biographical study, *The First Gentlemen of Virginia* (1940). Among his other publications are *The American Heritage History of the Thirteen Colonies*, with others (1967), and *Tradition and the Founding Fathers* (1975).

Wright, Orville.   See WILBUR WRIGHT.

Wright, Richard [Nathaniel] (1908–1960),   novelist, essayist. When *The New Caravan* in 1936 published the short story "Big Boy Leaves Home." Richard Wright contributed an author's note to the volume that in selectivity and emphasis makes for a striking self-portrayal. He was born in rural Mississippi, Wright says, to parents who dragged him through various towns in his native state, Arkansas, and Tennessee. At the age of fifteen, finished with school, he ran away from home, and "to make a living I washed dishes, swept streets, dug ditches, portered, waited on tables, bus-boyed, bell-boyed, carried messages, off-barred in brickyards, sold insurance and clerked in the United States Post Office. At present," the note concludes, "I'm busy with a novel."

The biographical facts in this note by the twenty-eight year old author can be readily fleshed out. He was born near Natchez, moved with his mother—after his father had deserted the family in 1914—among the homes of their extended family, and attended segregated schools until he completed ninth grade. Readers of the first volume of his autobiography, *Black Boy* (1945), will also recall detail about some of the menial jobs he took. Information to modify the author's note can be found as well. His mother's side of the family had some experience with middle-class life, and running away from home is an exaggerated way to describe the alienation he felt from his family's religion and the child-rearing practices he experienced.

Yet the importance of this early note lies in the implied formula it offers for the artist's portrait. In listing the names of towns and jobs, Wright stresses circumstances that appear unlikely to encourage culture and sensibility. Like many another African-American youngster, he was compelled by poverty and racism to shift restlessly about the South. But Wright sees himself breaking loose by an assertion of will: he ran away from home and "At present I'm busy with a novel." There lives in Richard Wright, he was telling readers, the ability to authenticate his experiences in literature and thereby to transcend the objective circumstances of oppression. Here is the psychological truth of the early self-portrait, and a measure of heroism besides.

In 1937, the year Wright moved from Chicago to New York City, he published a more analytic account of personal experience under the title "The Ethics of Living Jim Crow," which illustrates the way the caste system depends on terror. In addition, the essay tells us that terror is ineffective. Conflict is unavoidable between the agencies of racism and those African-Americans who reject white supremacy. Violence is its only resolution. The expository formula embodied in this essay informs Wright's first published book—the collection of short stories called *Uncle Tom's Children* (1938)—and when he expanded the volume in 1940, he added "The Ethics . . ." as a preface underlining the point that collectively the stories, including "Big Boy Leaves Home," record the development of a powerful response to racist terror by African American Southerners who reject the role of the popular Tom stereotype.

This earliest book won for Wright first prize in a contest open to new writers working for the WPA during the Great Depression. During this time of early recognition he was also working, of course, on a novel. Perhaps it was *Lawd Today*, the first work that extended his knowledge of racial mores to life in the migrant African-American communities of the North. This apprentice novel was not published until 1963, so it was the publication of NATIVE SON in 1940 that thrust him before a large audience. A Guggenheim Fellowship, selection of the novel by the Book-of-the-Month Club, and its consequent best-seller status verified the appearance of an important American author. The shocking account of Bigger Thomas ensures that *Native Son* will remain Wright's best-known work, but a little noted element of that shock, and certainly one source of its authenticity, is the kinship of author and protagonist. Though Bigger was impulsive where Wright was deliberate, Wright was articulate and imaginative where Bigger's perceptive expression was only nascent, they both are rebels whose defiance of assigned fate exposes the irrationality and violence beneath the ideology of racism. As if to enforce the point, Wright shortly after the appearance of *Native Son* set to work on the autobiography that would appear in two parts, BLACK BOY and *American Hunger* (1977).

The acclaim Wright received for *Native Son* and *Black Boy*, and his consequent elevation to the position of spokesperson for African-America, gained him a broad audience for lectures and incidental writings, but these changes did not alter the fact that racism nevertheless contravened his freedom. In 1946, therefore, he moved with his wife Ellen Poplar and their daughter to Paris. Taking up a self-determined physical exile did not mean that Wright abandoned the mission he set for himself as an artist, nor did it mean he was cut off from his American roots and practical education. Past experience and the strength of his conception of resourceful rebellion gave him material for two American novels. *The Outsider* (1953) casts the story of an antihero in the frame of a philosophical exploration of politics and freedom. *The Long Dream* (1958) reanimates the story of youth learning the reality of Jim Crow in Mississippi. The remaining fiction of his exile years consists of *Savage Holiday* (1954), a Freudian experiment with a raceless narrative, and short stories that eventually were published under the title *Eight Men* (1961).

The Paris years were not entirely a time of retrospection. Removal from America in fact provided Wright with an entirely new project—the application of his experience with one of the world's oldest social arrangements to developments of contemporary history. To grow in consciousness in the backwash of neoslavery, he believed, was paradoxically to be force-marched into the alienation of modern life. "The great majority of the human race," he wrote in the collection of essays entitled *White Man Listen!* (1957), "has undergone *experiences comparable to those which Negroes in America have* undergone for three centuries!" The writer who could express those experiences might become "the most representative voice of America and of oppressed people anywhere in the world today." Acting on that belief he traveled to the Gold Coast shortly before it achieved its independence as Ghana, recording his observations as an African-American in *Black Power* (1954). He journeyed to the Bandung Conference of nonaligned nations of the Third World to produce *The Color Curtain* (1956) and to complete the study of modernity he related in *Pagan Spain* (1957), his excursion into the nation he viewed as a museum of premodern culture.

An outsider by the accident of his birth as an African-American, Richard Wright displayed by his career the splendid resiliency and creativity of humanity. He was an important author when he died in Paris, and our growing understanding of his work since then enables us to accord him recognition as one of our most significantly representative literary voices of the 20th century. Studies include Constance Webb, *Richard Wright: A Biography* (1968); Edward Margolies, *The Art of Richard Wright* (1969); Michel Fabre, *The Unfinished Quest of Richard Wright* (1973); Joyce Ann Joyce, *Richard Wright's Art of Tragedy* (1986); and Hazel Rowley, *Richard Wright: The Life and Times* (2001).

JOHN M. REILLY

Wright, Wilbur (1867–1912), **Wright, Orville** (1871–1948), inventors. Wilbur Wright was born in Indiana, Orville in Ohio. These brothers were perhaps the most literate of American inventors since Morse. Orville became a printer, and Wilbur published a weekly newspaper. For a while the brothers manufactured bicycles but soon became interested in the problem of flight. They studied experiments being conducted in the United States and Europe, and then built gliders that were put into flight at Kill Devil Hill, a sandbar near Kitty Hawk, North Carolina. There, on December 17, 1903, they made the first successful heavier-than-air machine flights. Their first flights were made in a biplane powered by a four-cylinder motor and launched by a catapult. The Wrights were the first to supply the War Department with practical flying machines. In 1915, after they had endured a number of irritating patent suits, the Wright Company took over their patents, with Orville continuing to act as consultant.

F. C. Kelly, their authorized biographer, wrote *The Wright Brothers* (1943) and also edited and wrote an introduction and commentary for Orville Wright's *How We Invented the Airplane* (1953). An important collection of papers belonging to the brothers was placed in the Library of Congress and formed the basis for *The Papers of Wilbur and Orville Wright* (2 v. 1953). Wilbur Wright is one of the quartet treated in Gertrude Stein's *Four In America* (1947), in which Miss Stein tried to imagine what would have happened if Wilbur had become a painter.

Wright, Willard Huntington ["S. S. Van Dine"] (1888–1939), critic, editor, novelist. Wright, born in Virginia, began reporting for the *Los Angeles Times* and played an important role in art and drama criticism in the 1920s. He helped as editor (1912–1914) to make SMART SET a leading magazine and worked on the staffs of *Town Topics, The Forum, International Studio*, and other magazines. Under his own name he wrote *Songs of Youth* (1913), *The Creative Will* (1916) and *The Future of Painting* (1923), as well as a novel, *The Man of Promise* (1916). During an emotional breakdown in 1923 he read a great many detective stories and then, under an old family name, he began writing detective novels. His detective, PHILO VANCE, is a clever, learned, rather bored dilettante of great ingenuity and insight. *The Benson Murder Case* (1926) was an immediate hit, and *The "Canary" Murder Case* (1927) broke all records for sales of crime fiction at that time. Wright went on to even larger sales with many similarly entitled narratives, the last of which, *The Winter Murder Case* (1939), appeared posthumously.

Wurdemann, Audrey [May] [Mrs. Joseph Auslander] (1911–1960), poet, novelist. Wurdemann, born in Seattle, began writing verse at an early age. She published her first collection, *The House of Silk*, in 1926. Her second collection, *Bright Ambush* (1934), won a Pulitzer Prize—she was the youngest poet until that time to win the prize. Among her other collections are *The Seven Sins* (1935), *Splendor in the Grass* (1936), and *The Testament of Love* (1938). In collaboration with her husband she wrote two novels, *My Uncle Jan* (1948) and *The Islanders* (1951).

Wurlitzer, Rudolph (1938?–), novelist. A descendant of the family of musical instrument makers, Wurlitzer writes abstract minimalist fiction. *Nog* (1969) details the confused travels of a narrator, perhaps named Orin Carmele, with characters named Lockett and Meridith. *Flats* (1970) is peopled with characters named for cities. *Quake* (1972) is an apocalyptic fiction set in Los Angeles. *Slow Fade* (1984), more conventional than the earlier books, presents the lives of a film director and his children. *Hard Travel to Sacred Places* (1994) is a Southeast Asia travel book.

Wyandot Indians. See HURON INDIANS.

Wyandotté, or, The Hutted Knoll (1843), a novel by JAMES FENIMORE COOPER. In this story about New York State during the Revolution, Cooper again treats a favorite theme, a family rift in which one member favors England, another the colonies. In between them stands Captain Willoughby.

Wyckoff, Walter (1865–1908), teacher, economist, sociologist, writer. Wyckoff was born in India, where his American parents were working as missionaries. He studied in the United States, specializing in economics and sociology, and became professor of sociology at Princeton. He frequently went to live with workers and unemployed workers and recorded his experiences in *The Workers* (1897, 1898) and *A Day with a Tramp and Other Days* (1901).

Wyeth, Nathaniel Jarvis (1802–1856), ice dealer, explorer. Wyeth was an ice dealer in Cambridge, Massachu-

setts, who became fascinated by the fur trade in the Far West. In 1832 he led an expedition to the West Coast. One of the members of the company, a cousin named John Wyeth, wrote with the assistance of Dr. Benjamin Waterhouse a book about the trip called *Oregon, or, A Short History of a Long Journey* (1833). Wyeth once described it as a book of "little lies told for gain." Another member of the expedition, John Kirk Townsend, wrote an account entitled *Narrative of a Journey Across the Rocky Mountains to the Columbia River* (1839). The expedition did not fulfill Wyeth's hope of making a fortune, but he did establish a fur post at Fort Hall. His *Correspondence and Journals, 1831–36* was published by the Oregon Historical Society in *Sources of the History of Oregon* (Numbers 3–6, 1899). Wyeth plays a considerable role in Irving's ADVENTURES OF CAPTAIN BONNEVILLE (1837).

Wyeth, N[ewell] C[onvers] (1882–1945), artist, illustrator, editor. Wyeth, born in Needham, Massachusetts, was particularly noted for his illustrations for children's books. His only rival as an illustrator was his teacher, HOWARD PYLE. His son. **Andrew Wyeth** (1917–), is a realistic painter whose detailed canvases evoke somber or nostalgic moods.

Wylie, Elinor (1885–1928), poet, novelist, critic, editor. Wylie was born in Somerville, New Jersey. Her poetry is remarkable for its musicality, striking images, precision of thought, and mastery of language. In her happiest moments an amazing clarity and precision are joined to the most unyielding forms, as in her use of the Italian sonnet and of very short lines. Lines consisting of a scant three or four words unfailingly rhyme, and rhymes are often doubled as in slumber/number, internal rhymes appear, and assonance, consonance, and alliteration carry forward the musical design:

> A white well
> In a black cave:
> A bright shell
> In a dark wave . . .

Where other poets abandon metrics and fall back on half-rhyme or none at all in their desire for accuracy, Wylie masters the most complex forms with no sense of straining as she achieves the severe elegance and weightless movement of a ballerina. The comparison is apposite because Wylie had a preternatural beauty and grace, the essence of her being. However, this gracefulness was rudely attacked by multiple personal tragedies beginning early in her life so that her mature verse, begun at a high level of awareness in *Nets to Catch the Wind* (1921), took on increasing complexity of thought in *Black Armour* (1923) and *Trivial Breath* (1928), her second and third volumes, and ended in *Angels and Earthly Creatures* (1929) with the contemplation of ideal romantic love and the transcendent spiritual mysteries that had always flickered in and out of her verse.

Wylie was born to distinguished parentage. One forebear had been mayor of Philadelphia, another was governor of

Pennsylvania, and her father was solicitor general of the U.S. She was educated in private schools in Philadelphia and Washington and, after an unfortunate marriage and the birth of a son, abandoned husband and child to elope with Horace Wylie. They lived together in England in exile and double adultery. As a result, Wylie was permanently ostracized by her upper-class associates, a blow from which she suffered intensely and from which she never fully recovered. Wylie's real education began in England under the tutelage of her cultivated lover, thirteen years her senior. Wylie's mother paid for publication of her *Incidental Numbers* (1912), but her first serious effort, the poems contained in *Nets to Catch the Wind*, was not published until 1921, when Wylie was thirty-six years old. In the eight years that remained in her short life, she published short stories and criticism, served as editor for two magazines, did exhaustive research for four novels, and wrote three additional books of poetry along with numerous uncollected poems that were published posthumously.

Few authors have produced so much so quickly at such a high level of artistry. Though Wylie's novels are written in a somewhat artificial vein of fantasy and comedy, they have had many admirers. Her poems speak in natural and direct language and should be counted as a major achievement of American verse. As poet Wylie is a detached, forthright, and penetrating observer concerned with the themes of a willfully predatory nature. "Sea Lullaby" illuminates the contradiction between gentility and cruelty in human nature, as "Blood Feud" explores the human inclination to hate and destroy, and "A Crowded Trolley Car" explores the will to escape life's perturbations in an artificial world of art that is suffocating. On the positive side, Wylie shows the strength and self-reliance to be won from adversity in "Let No Charitable Hope," the spiritual home she found in the ineffable beauties of nature in

"Sunset on the Spire," and the refuge of Christian faith in "Letter to V" and "The Lion and the Lamb."

Most of Wylie's verse is contained in *Collected Poems* (1932) and *Last Poems* (1943). Her novels—JENNIFER LORN (1923), THE VENETIAN GLASS NEPHEW (1925), THE ORPHAN ANGEL (1926), and *Mr. Hodge and Mr. Hazard* (1928)—are gathered with stories and essays in *Collected Prose* (1933). A memoir by the poet's sister, Nancy Hoyt, is *Elinor Wylie: The Portrait of an Unknown Lady* (1935). Studies include Stanley Olson, *Elinor Wylie: A Life Apart* (1979), and Judith Farr, *The Life and Art of Elinor Wylie* (1983).
GLENN RICHARD RUIHLEY

Wylie, Philip [Gordon] (1902–1971), essayist, fiction writer. Wylie was born in Beverly, Massachusetts. His clever and penetrating surveys of American mores and behavior engaged him in various crusades. Best known is his attack on the American mother and what he terms "momism" in *Generation of Vipers* (1942). In the *Essay on Morals* (1947), Wylie makes an indignant attack on organized religion, as well as on American ethics. *Opus 21* (1949), a series of fictional dialogues between the author and various people, expresses his views of the problems of American society, with emphasis on its sexual ills. His fiction varies from excellent stories of fishing in Florida, *The Big Ones Get Away!* (1940), to gloomy predictions of the future, *Tomorrow!* (1954), in which he describes in detail the horrors of atomic war. Among his other science-fiction works, *When Worlds Collide* (1933) and *After Worlds Collide* (1934), both written with Edwin Balmer, are more optimistic about the possibility of cosmic disaster. Among his other books are *Heavy Laden* (1928), *Finnley Wren* (1934), *Night Unto Night* (1944), *Disappearance* (1951), *The Answer* (1956), *They Both Were Naked* (1965), and *The Spy Who Spoke Porpoise* (1969).

Wynne, Hugh.   See HUGH WYNNE, FREE QUAKER.

XYZ

X, Malcolm. See MALCOLM X.

Xingu (*Scribner's Magazine*, December 1911), a story by EDITH WHARTON. It is a satire on a snobbish and ignorant group of women in a luncheon club. To expose their stupidity one of the women, more intelligent than the rest, introduces Xingu for discussion. The others pretend to be well acquainted with the topic, only to discover later that it is the name of a Brazilian river.

Yaddo, a fifty-five room mansion at Saratoga Springs, New York, donated by Mrs. Katrina Nichols Trask Peabody as a haven for creative artists. Guests, twenty to thirty at a time, remain in residence for a month or two without charge. James T. Farrell, Katherine Anne Porter, Aaron Copland, John Cheever, and James Baldwin have been among the over five thousand beneficiaries of this art colony.

Yale Critics. A group of four critics—HAROLD BLOOM, PAUL DE MAN, Geoffrey Hartman, and J. Hillis Miller—active at Yale during the late 1970s and associated with the early practice of deconstruction in the United States. JACQUES DERRIDA is sometimes included among the Yale Critics. The Yale Critics reject the New Critical claim for the autonomous literary text that fully embodies its meaning in its language and its form. They are preoccupied with the noncoincidence of language and meaning, the particular status of literary texts in drawing attention to that noncoincidence, the epistemological status of figurative language, and the affiliations of literary and philosophical discourse. Each of the Yale Critics has explored different versions of this problematic. Bloom's "anxiety of influence" emphasizes a psychoanalytic version of intertextuality, with poems only readable—or misreadable—as acts of defense and rhetorical detour against earlier poems. De Man's "allegories of reading" explore the inability of interpretation to do anything but recapitulate the irresolvable aporias between rhetorical figures and meaning that characterize all texts. Hartman's analyses of "the fate of reading" and "criticism in the wilderness" are especially attentive to the position of the literary critic and questions of literary history. Miller's work on repetition pursues the particular implications of this nonmimeticism for the practice of narrative. See Harold Bloom et al., *Deconstruction and Criticism* (1979), and Jonathan Arac et al., ed. *The Yale Critics: Deconstruction in America* (1983).
JULIE RIVKIN

Yale Series of Younger Poets. This series, since inception, has been intended to encourage writers under age forty who have not yet had a volume published. The best manuscript received each year is published by the Yale University Press. These collections, restricted to a moderate size, have revealed some excellent poets to the public, among them Harold Vinal, Shirley Barker, Paul Engle, Adrienne Rich, Muriel Rukeyser, and John Ashbery. STEPHEN VINCENT BENÉT was series editor from 1918 to 1941. W. H. AUDEN and Archibald MacLeish served as consultants.

Yamamoto, Hisaye (1921–), short-story writer. Born to a Japanese immigrant family in Redondo Beach, California, she entered school speaking no English. When the federal government forced Japanese-Americans into internment camps, the Yamamoto family was sent to Poston, Arizona, an experience she described as "an episode of our collective life which wounded us more painfully than we realize." In the camp, she wrote a serialized mystery and short stories for the newspaper. Hisaye and two of her brothers left the camp to work for a short period in Massachusetts but returned when they learned that another brother had been killed in action in Italy. After the war she continued to write short fiction and essays, some of which are collected in *Seventeen Syllables and Other Stories* (Tokyo, 1985; enlarged New York, 1988) and *Yoneko's Earthquake: Collected Short Stories of Hisaye Yamamoto*. Her 50s correspondence with poet and scholar Yvor Winters is gathered in *Dear Miss Yamamoto: The Letters of Yvor Winters and Hisaye Yamamoto* (1999).

Yamasee [or **Yamasi** or **Yemasee**] **Indians.** A tribal group whose language is part of the Muskogean branch of the Hokan-Siouan linguistic family. They lived in south Georgia and northern Florida when the Spaniards arrived, late in the 16th century. They revolted and fled to South Carolina in 1687. Initially friendly to English settlement, they returned to Florida after raids against white villages in 1715 and became allies of the Spaniards. In the conflict between English and Spanish interests their village near St. Augustine was destroyed in 1727. They were eventually assimilated with the Seminole and Creek peoples. Their conflict with English settlements is the subject of William Gilmore Simm's THE YEMASSEE (1835).

Yañez, Agustín (1904–1980), novelist. One of the earliest Mexican writers to employ *nouveau roman* techniques. Yanez wrote lyrical prose enriched by personal memories of rural Mexico. The town in *Al filo del agua* (1947, tr. *The Edge of the Storm*, 1963), his tenth and most important novel, lives under the weight of a morbid, narrow, and collapsing religious order. The spontaneity of the young people is repressed by fear of gossip, and his characters agonize in a seesaw of guilt and eroticism that eventually explodes, fanned by the fresh winds of the Mexican Revolution of 1910. Yanez does not draw realistic characters. Like an impressionist painter, he creates a slow-moving, blurry atmosphere through which are discerned the feelings of a people on the verge of revolution. Among his other novels are *La creación* (1959), *La tierra pródiga* (1960), *Las tierras flacas* (1962, tr. *The Lean Lands*, 1968), and *Ojerosa y pintada* (1967).

Yank.   An army weekly that began publication in the summer of 1942 and continued till the end of World War II. With reporters in every part of the globe, *Yank* was uninhibited, served only the GI, and made a remarkable reputation. Its contents were miscellaneous and always interesting—stories, pictures, letters, poetry, and doggerel. The anthology *The Best from Yank* (1945) constitutes a vivid history of the war. Within its pages appear contributions from such well-known authors and cartoonists as Marion Hargrove, Irwin Shaw, Harry Brown, William Saroyan, and Dave Berger. Two noted characters made their initial appearance in *Yank*—the Sad Sack and ARTIE GREEN-GROIN.

Yankee,   a term used by Americans to denote a New Englander. In other parts of the world, particularly the British Commonwealth, the term denotes any American. Its origin is unknown. It may be derived from Dutch—it was used as early as 1683 among pirates of the Spanish Main as a nickname for sailors of Dutch lineage. By 1765 it was in use as a derisive term for New Englanders, but by the Revolutionary War, with the influence of the marching song "Yankee Doodle," it was a term of pride. In the Civil War, "Yankee" and "Yank" were used by Southern soldiers to disparage their Northern enemies, and it survived in this usage throughout Reconstruction. The shortened form was used to refer to American troops in World War I and II. In Latin America the term *Yanqui* is applied to U.S. citizens, often with a note of hostility.

Yankee Doodle.   Both the tune and several of the stanzas of "Yankee Doodle" were current early in colonial times, and the tune seems to have inspired innumerable verses. Both words in the title have significance. The derivation of "Yankee" has never been satisfactorily determined. A "doodle" is a colloquial word for "a trifler, a dolt," and the verb "doodle" is taken by many to mean "make a fool of, cheat." The song seems to have been used by the British to provoke American troops during the Revolutionary War. Like the wise fool suggested by "Yankee Doodle," however, the Americans adopted the song and may have deliberately created an image of an American rustic. The song was first printed in America as part of an instrumental medley, "The Federal Overture" (1795), arranged by Benjamin Carr. No one knows who wrote the words, although Edward Everett

Hale attributed them to Edward Bangs, a Harvard graduate of 1777.

Yankee in American language and literature. Out of the Yankee concept emerged many familiar figures of folklore and fiction, two in particular—Brother Jonathan and Uncle Sam. The homely and comic Jonathan was highly popular for a while, then was superseded by the more elderly figure whose initials represent the United States.

Commercial genius, dry humor, ingenuity, and reforming zeal also characterize the Yankee stereotype. Often his brashness concealed a heart of gold, and his wisdom hid behind tomfoolery. Often, too, he engaged in political and social satire. He was the first of the literary cracker-barrel philosophers. An outstanding trait of the Yankee, then and now, is his choice of words, his pronunciation, and the character of his voice. Best known and most ridiculed by irreverent persons living in other parts of the country is the English spoken in Boston or rural New England.

Walter Blair, in *Native American Humor* (1937), lists the chief exponents of Yankee humor in the early 19th century: SEBA SMITH, THOMAS C. HALIBURTON, J. R. LOWELL, FRANCES M. WHITCHER, and BENJAMIN P. SHILLABER. From 1830 to 1867 appeared a number of historically significant political caricatures of some literary merit. The greatest of these were the BIGLOW PAPERS of Lowell. JOSH BILLINGS and ARTEMUS WARD excelled in social caricatures.

Beginning in the 1830s, many novels with Yankee characters were published. Sometimes the novel, as was the fashion of the day, took the form of a sequence of letters, as in Ann Sophia Stephens's *High Life in New York* (1843). Possibly the most artistic work of Harriet Beecher Stowe may be found in her OLDTOWN FOLKS (1869) and other New England stories, written under the influence of her husband, Calvin Stowe. He was a skillful mimic who reproduced for his amused wife New England backgrounds, characters, and dialect. The best-known Yankee character was Ichabod Crane in Washington Irving's LEGEND OF SLEEPY HOLLOW (*The Sketch Book*, 1820). JAMES FENIMORE COOPER also had his Yankees, for example, in THE SPY (1821), THE PIONEERS (1823), and THE PILOT (1823). Of our writers of first rank, Mark Twain evoked the character in A CONNECTICUT YANKEE IN KING ARTHUR'S COURT (1889). The spilling over of Yankees into northern New York produced a magnificent portrait of a many-sided Yankee, Edward Noyes Westcott's DAVID HARUM (1898).

The Yankee legend was early fostered through a series of humorous courtin' poems, beginning with Thomas Green Fessenden's *The Country Lovers, or, Jonathan's Courtship* (1795). One of Lowell's best products in dialect was THE COURTIN' (1867). In modern poetry ROBERT P. TRISTRAM COFFIN was frequently the enlightened Yankee speaking. ROBERT FROST's poems are overflowingly rich in Yankee characterizations, the most celebrated and obdurate of which appears in MENDING WALL (1914).

The stage Yankee first appeared in Royal Tyler's THE CONTRAST (1787). Though the Yankee came into the act quite incidentally, he soon captured the center of the stage. Playing the character provided a marvelous opportunity for actors of the time who, even in connection with plays that had nothing to do with Yankees, would appear between acts to deliver monologues in Yankee dialect. On the stage the Yankee wasn't always a farmer. He might be a peddler, sailor, trader, Vermont wool dealer, or lawyer. He loved to make wisecracks, indulge in practical jokes, and boast about the United States. Usually he had a repertoire of songs, mostly variations on "Yankee Doodle." Among the numerous plays in which Yankee types appeared were David Humphreys's *The Yankee in England* (1805?); A. B. Lindsay's *Love and Friendship, or, Yankee Notions* (1809); Mordecai M. Noah's SHE WOULD BE A SOLDIER (1819); Samuel Woodworth's THE FOREST ROSE (1825); Joseph S. Jones's *Green Mountain Boy* (1833), SOLON SHINGLE, OR, THE PEOPLE'S LAWYER (1839), and *The Silver Spoon* (1852); James A. Herne's HEARTS OF OAK (1879); Denman Thompson's *The Old Homestead* (1885); Lottie Blair Parker's WAY DOWN EAST (1899); Owen Davis's ICEBOUND (1923); and Sidney Howard's *Ned McCobb's Daughter* (1926). The Yankee has been treated in numerous anthologies and nonfiction works, including B. A. Botkin's *Treasury of New England Folklore* (1947).

Yankee in Canada, A (published in part in *Putnam's Monthly Magazine*, 1853; in full posthumously, 1866, as part of *Anti-Slavery and Reform Papers*), a travel journal by HENRY DAVID THOREAU. The journey was made in 1850, in company with ELLERY CHANNING. "A Yankee in Canada" was intended originally as a lecture, although Thoreau was not a good platform performer.

Yankee [or **Yankey**] **in London** (1809), a series of letters by ROYAL TYLER. These letters supposedly came from London and deceived many readers of the day. Tyler joked about the American use of "I guess" and the invariable habit in New England of answering a question by asking another.

Yates, Elizabeth (1905–2001), novelist, author of children's books. Yates, born in Buffalo, New York, wrote books for adults, among them *Wind of Spring* (1945) and *Guardian Heart* (1950), but she is best known for her children's books. Among them are *Under the Little Fir* (1942), *Patterns on the Wall* (1943), *Mountain Born* (1943), *Nearby* (1947), *Amos Fortune, Free Man* (1950), *Rainbow Round the World* (1954) and *With Pipe, Paddle and Song: A Story of the French-Canadian Voyageurs* (1968; rev. ed. 1998). *Prudence Crandall* (1955) is a biography of a teacher who opened a racially integrated school for girls in 1833 in defiance of Connecticut law. *Pebble in a Pool* (1958) is a biography of Dorothy Canfield Fisher. Yates's autobiography appears in three installments: *My Diary—My World* (1981), *My Widening World* (1983), and *One Writer's Way* (1984).

Yates, Richard (1926–1992), novelist. Yates, born in Yonkers, New York, served in World War II. He has lectured at several universities and has written screenplays and political speeches. His realistic novels with middle-class characters and urban settings include *Revolutionary Road* (1961), a comic and masterful chronicle of 1950s suburban life; *A Special Providence* (1969); *Disturbing the Peace* (1975); *The Easter Parade* (1976); *A Good School* (1978); *Young Hearts Crying* (1984); and *Cold Spring Harbor* (1986) set on Long Island during

World War II. Yates collaborated on the screenplay for *The Bridge at Remagen* (1969), the story of a crucial battle in World War II. His story collections include *Eleven Kinds of Loneliness* (1964) and *Liars in Love* (1982). *The Collected Stories of Richard Yates* appeared in 2001.

Yau, John (1950–   ), poet, art critic, fiction writer. Born in Lynn, Massachusetts to parents who emigrated from China in 1949, Yau was educated at Bard College and Brooklyn College, studying with JOHN ASHBERY, whose work has been an important influence. Like Ashbery, Yau has immersed himself in the art world, writing art criticism and working as a Curatorial Fellow at the Museum of Contemporary Art in Los Angeles (1993–1996). Like Ashbery, he writes poems vivid in imagery, colloquial, and teasingly incomplete or alienated from the narratives that appear to haunt their opaque surfaces. In the 1980s a contributing editor to *Sulfur* (see CLAYTON ESHLEMAN), Yau has displayed obvious allegiances to that journal's avant garde and international agenda. Selections from his early verse appear in *Radiant Silhouette: New and Selected Work, 1974–1988* (1989). Later volumes of verse include *Edificio Sayonara* (1992), *Forbidden Entries* (1996), and *My Symptons* (1998). Volumes of art criticism include *In the Realm of Appearances: The Art of Andy Warhol* (1993) and *The United States of Jasper Johns* (1996). Stories of ethnicity and marginality are collected in *Hawaiian Cowboys* (1994).

Ybarra, Thomas R[ussell] (1880–?), newspaperman, author. Ybarra, whose father was a Venezuelan, was born in Boston, studied in the United States, Europe, and South America, reported for The New York *Times*, and later became Sunday editor. His first book was a collection of humorous verse, *Davy Jones's Yarns* (1908). As a correspondent for the *Times* and *Collier's*, Ybarra saw many parts of the world. He wrote lives of Bolivar, Hindenburg, Cervantes, Caruso, and Verdi, and a volume entitled *America Faces South* (1939). His best books are his accounts of his life in the United States and Venezuela: *Young Man of Caracas* (1941, 1956) and *Young Man of the World* (1942).

Yearling, The (1938), a novel by MARJORIE KINNAN RAWLINGS. Years after settling in the scrub country of northern Florida, Marjorie Kinnan Rawlings wrote her Pulitzer Prize novel, laid there. *The Yearling* recounts a year in the lives of a Florida backwoodsman, his wife, and their young son Jody. Lonely Jody adopts and cares for an orphaned fawn, finding in the animal the love and companionship he craves. When the fawn starts eating the Baxter family's precious crops, Jody must shoot him, because "love's got nothin' to do with corn." The tragedy lifts Jody out of his boyhood and into a more mature relationship with his hardworking parents. *The Yearling* reflects Rawlings' deep understanding of her neighbors, her sensitive ear for their speech, and her feeling for nature. The book was made into a movie in 1946.

Yemassee, The, an 1835 novel by WILLIAM GILMORE SIMMS, one of a series he called Border Romances. The war between the Yemassee, led by Chief Sanutee, and the English, captained by the mysterious Gabriel Harrison, serves as a backdrop to Harrison's pursuit of Bess Matthews, daughter of an aged Puritan parson. After several melodramatic scenes, including the killing of an Indian by his own mother to save him from being disowned by the tribe, the English are successful. Bess is rescued, and Harrison reveals himself to be the colonial governor in disguise. See YAMASEE INDIANS.

Yerby, Frank [Garvin] (1916–1992), novelist. Born in Georgia and educated at Paine College and Fisk University, Yerby received early recognition for his stories "Health Card" (1944) and "The Homecoming" (1946), concerned with racial bigotry. With the great success of *The Foxes of Harrow* (1947), a novel set in the antebellum South, Yerby turned to historical fiction. He wrote thirty-two historical novels that sold in the millions. The child of an interracial marriage, Yerby was sometimes criticized for neglecting the African-American experience. In the preface to *The Dahomean* (1971), his one book with a predominantly black cast, he stated his reason for writing the book as "to correct . . . the Anglo-Saxon reader's historical perspective. . . ." The novel centers on a chief's son sold into slavery by jealous relatives.

Yerby lived most of his life in Europe, and died in Madrid. Among his other novels are *The Vixens* (1947), *The Golden Hawk* (1948), *Pride's Castle* (1949), *A Women Called Fancy* (1951), *The Saracen Blade* (1952), *Judas My Brother* (1968), *Hail the Conquering Hero* (1977), and *McKenzie's Hundred* (1985).

Yezierska, Anzia (1885–1970), short-story writer. Yezierska, born in Russia, created something of a sensation with her honest and sympathetic stories of life on New York City's lower East Side, where her family came to live in the 1890s. The best known of her early books are *Hungry Hearts* (1920), stories of Jewish immigrants; *Salome of the Tenements* (1922); *Children of Loneliness* (1923); and *Bread Givers* (1925), an autobiographical novel. She spent some time in Hollywood, but found existence in the movie colony unpalatable. Her later works include another autobiographical novel, *All I Could Never Be* (1932), and *Red Ribbon on a White Horse* (1950), an autobiography. A selection of her work, some previously unpublished, is *The Open Cage* (1979).

Yglesias, Helen [Bassine] (1915–   ), novelist, editor. Yglesias, born in New York City, had an active editorial career and did not begin writing until she was over fifty. She described her career shift in an autobiographical work, *Starting: Early, Anew, Over, and Late* (1978). Her first novel, *How She Died* (1973), tells of a woman tending a dying friend whose husband she loves. *Family Feeling* (1977) is a semiautobiographical tale of life in a Jewish family. *Sweetsir* (1981) concerns a domestic battle. *The Girls* (1999) is a novel of aging in Miami as four sisters contend with cancer and nursing homes, sometimes comically.

Yglesias, Jose (1919–1995), novelist, translator. Born in Florida and educated at Black Mountain College, Yglesias served in the Navy in World War II. Married at one time to HELEN BASSINE YGLESIAS, he has drawn on his Cuban heritage and delineated the problem of straddling two cultures. *A Wake in Ybor City* (1963) is set in Tampa's Cuban community during the Castro revolution. His other novels include *An Orderly Life* (1968), *The Truth about Them* (1971), *Double, Double* (1974), *The Kill Price* (1976), and *Tristan and the Hispanics* (1989), about a famous Latin American writer. Yglesias has translated from Spanish and has written studies of Cuba and fascist Spain; these include *The Goodbye Land* (1967), about his father's native province in Spain; *In the Fist of the Revolution* (1968), about Castro's Cuba; and *The Franco Years* (1977). His son Rafael Yglesias is also a writer.

Yoknapatawpha. An imaginary county in Mississippi that is a setting for many stories by WILLIAM FAULKNER.

Yossarian. The protagonist caught in the absurdities of CATCH-22.

You Can't Go Home Again (pub. posthumously, 1940), a novel by THOMAS WOLFE. The sequel to THE WEB AND THE ROCK, this novel deals again with the experiences of George Webber, Wolfe's semiautobiographical hero, during the 1920s and 1930s. Webber, by now an author of some renown, revisits his hometown and is disillusioned both by what he sees and by the reception he receives. This episode parallels Wolfe's own experience in returning to Asheville, North Carolina, after publication of LOOK HOMEWARD, ANGEL. Webber stays for a while in New York City, where he is involved with Esther Jack (modeled on Mrs. Aline Bernstein), a talented stage designer, and then travels to Europe. Like the majority of Wolfe's work, the novel is uneven in quality, sometimes massive and overpowering, sometimes turgid. The section generally most admired is the one dealing with Esther Jack. Wolfe's description of Webber's meeting with the novelist Lloyd McHarg, for whom Sinclair Lewis was the prototype, was also highly praised. MAXWELL PERKINS, Wolfe's one-time mentor and the editor responsible for publication of Wolfe's first two novels, appears as Foxhall Edwards.

You Can't Take It With You (1936), a comedy by MOSS HART and GEORGE KAUFMAN. Grandpa Vanderhof, the hero of this 1937 Pulitzer Prize play, is the amiable autocrat of a bizarre but supremely happy family. Right in the middle of New York City the Vanderhofs make fireworks in the cellar, write plays, practice ballet, and print anarchistic leaflets "just for practice." Alice, the only conventional member of the family, becomes engaged to Tony Kirby, the son of her boss. The clash between the stuffy Kirby family and the flamboyant Vanderhofs nearly spoils the romance, but Grandpa puts all to rights.

You Know Me Al: A Busher's Letters (1916), the first collection of stories by RING LARDNER. Lardner wrote this series of baseball stories as a series of letters from a busher—a player doomed to play in the minor leagues—to his best friend. *You Know Me Al* captures perfectly the semiliterate Midwestern speech of its protagonist. Jack Keefe reveals himself as a conceited, irresponsible, stingy, gullible sorehead too dumb to resent an insult. He has a fantastic ability to pull the wool over his own eyes and eat his words without even realizing he is doing so. This character is an excellent example of Lardner's mixture of humor and misanthropy.

Youma (1890),   a novel by LAFCADIO HEARN. Hearn lived in Martinique from 1887 to 1889 and became familiar with some of the facts regarding the slave insurrection of 1848 on that island. His novel, based on an actual occurrence, describes the devotion of a black girl to the daughter of her deceased mistress, whom she had promised that she would never desert.

Young, Al[bert James] (1939–),   novelist, poet. Young's first novel, *Snakes* (1970), is the story of a jazz musician. *Who is Angelina?* (1975) delineates a young African-American woman's quest for self-realization. Young draws on his own experience as an African-American in such novels as *Sitting Pretty* (1976) and *Ask Me Now* (1980). His poetry is collected in *Dancing* (1969), *The Song Turning Back into Itself* (1971), *Geography of the Near Past* (1976), *The Blues Don't Change* (1982), and *Heaven: Collected Poems 1956–1990* (1992).

Young, Art[hur] (1866–1943),   cartoonist, writer. Young, born in Illinois, studied in New York and abroad and returned to the United States to work for Chicago newspapers, then for various weekly magazines, including one or two of radical trend. His cartoons were collected in *Trees at Night* (1927), *The Best of Art Young* (1936), and several other volumes. He wrote two autobiographical books, *On My Way* (1928) and *Art Young: His Life and Times* (1939). In 1918 Young was brought to court on the grounds that some of his pacifistic cartoons were subversive.

Young, Brigham (1801–1877),   Mormon leader. Young, born in Vermont, was in early life a carpenter and painter in Mendon, New York, not far from Palmyra. It was there that JOSEPH SMITH published *The Book of Mormon* (1830). In 1832, with his baptism, Young officially became converted to the Mormon creed, and soon became a preacher and leader of the group. When Smith was killed in 1844 at Carthage, Illinois, Young succeeded him as president of the Mormon Church and conducted the successful migration to Deseret (1847). President Fillmore made him governor of the Utah Territory in 1850. In 1852 Young announced the doctrine of polygamy and was removed from public office. In 1871 he was indicted for polygamy, but was never convicted. Young, skilled in diplomatic negotiations, prevented the complete suppression of Mormonism. He turned his church into a sound social and economic unit and Utah into a prosperous, self-reliant, conservative community. His *Journal of Discourses* was published in 1854–1886 (26 volumes).

Young, David (1781–1852),   astronomer, almanac maker, poet, teacher, lecturer. Young, born in New Jersey, turned his deep interest in astronomy into a vocation. He lectured on the subject and prepared almanacs that gave astronomical information. *The Citizens' & Farmers' Almanac* appeared in 1814. The *Family Almanac, Harper's U.S. Almanac, Knickerbocker's Almanac*, the *Methodist Almanac*, the *N.Y. Almanac, Paul Pry's Almanac*, and others followed. The *Farmers' Almanac* has continued to be published for more than a century after Young's death. He also wrote two poems on astronomy—*The Contrast* (1804) and *The Perusal* (1818).

He exposed a mining hoax in *The Wonderful History of the Morristown Ghost* (1826).

Young, Marguerite [Vivian] (1908–1995),   novelist, poet. Young was born in Indiana and educated at Butler University and the University of Chicago. She is best known for her massive novel *Miss MacIntosh, My Darling* (1965), which she worked on for nearly two decades. Catherine Cartwheel, the narrator, tells of her childhood in a small Midwest town and the characters of her memory: her nursemaid, Miss MacIntosh, her mysterious companion, Mr. Spitzer, and her dreamy mother. Young's verse is collected in *Prismatic Ground* (1937) and *Moderate Fable* (1944). Young also wrote a study of the New Harmony utopian community, *Angel in the Forest* (1945). *Harp Song for a Radical: The Life and Times of Eugene Victor Debs* (1999) was edited by Charles Ruas from a massive manuscript Young worked on in her last decades.

Young, Stark (1881–1963),   playwright, poet, novelist, essayist. Young was born in Como, Mississippi, and educated at the University of Mississippi. He described Mississippi as a rural and pleasant place. Until World War II, Young spent his summers traveling in Italy, his winters at teaching. While teaching English at the University of Mississippi, he published a book of poems (*The Blind Man*, 1906) and a verse drama (*Guenevere*, 1906). While teaching at the University of Texas, he published *Addio, Madretta and Other Plays* (1912). He was a professor at Amherst from 1915 to 1921 and published a series of plays in 1919. After this period he left teaching to write for *The New Republic*. He became its drama editor and also wrote dramatic criticism of enduring value during the 1920s for *Theatre Arts Monthly* and The New York *Times*. In 1923 he wrote *The Flower in Drama*, a series of essays on the theater.

In the 1920s also, Young saw two of his plays produced in New York City and in London, and he directed Eugene O'Neill's *Welded* for the THEATER GUILD. But the theater was not the only genre in which he worked. He wrote a series of novels: *Heaven Trees* (1926), *The Torches Flare* (1927), *River House* (1929), and his most important success, *So Red the Rose* (1934), a novel of life in Mississippi during the Civil War. Young was one of the twelve Southern writers who published in *The Fugitive* a manifesto citing the position of the new Southern agrarianism (see THE FUGITIVES). His essay in I'LL TAKE MY STAND (1930) was called "Not in Memoriam, but in Defense."

Young Goodman Brown (*New England Magazine*, 1835; in *Mosses from an Old Manse*, 1846),   a story by NATHANIEL HAWTHORNE. A young Puritan leaves his pretty wife and goes walking gloomily in the forest. He sees or dreams a Witches' Sabbath in which his wife Faith seems to be concerned; in his dream—or in reality—he sees a pink ribbon fluttering down from a treetop, a ribbon like those his wife wore in her hair. He returns home in the morning, and his wife hurries out to meet him, but he repulses her. For the rest of his life he lives in gloom and desperation, convinced there is no good on earth.

Young Lions, The (1948),   a novel by IRWIN SHAW. This first novel is one of the host of novels that attempted to find meaning in the experiences of World War II.

Young Lonigan (1932),   a novel by JAMES T. FARRELL. This opening book of the Lonigan trilogy is called in a subtitle "A Boyhood in Chicago." It is a story of the baneful effects of an urban environment on a boy living in the early 20th century. It was followed by *The Young Manhood of Studs Lonigan* (1934) and *Judgment Day* (1935).

Yourcenar, Marguerite [de Crayencour] (1903–1987), poet, novelist, critic, playwright. The first woman to be named to the *Académie Française* (1981) was born in Brussels to the wealthy de Crayencour family. Yourcenar, the name she assumed in the 1920s, is an imperfect anagram of her birth name. Yourcenar was an only child. Her mother died when Marguerite was a baby, and the child was educated by tutors in France. At age six she was reading the French classic dramatists, and in her teens had two books of her verse in print. An independently wealthy woman, she traveled widely. On a visit to the United States early in World War II, she elected to stay. She became an American citizen in 1947, but the French government later reinstated her French citizenship. She taught comparative literature for several years at Sarah Lawrence before settling in the home on Mount Desert Island off the Maine coast where she eventually died.

She wrote in French. Her best-known book, *Memoirs of Hadrian* (1951), was translated into English by a longtime companion, Grace Frick. An imaginary autobiography of the Roman emperor, written as a letter to his grandson Marcus Aurelius, it demonstrates the unique mix of classical studies and imagination typical of her work. She once said of her writing that she had "one foot in scholarship, the other in magic arts." Among her other books translated into English are *Coup de Grace* (1957); *The Abyss* (1976); *Fires* (1981); *A Coin in Nine Hands* (1982); *The Dark Brain of Piranesi and Other Essays* (1984); *Alexis* (1984); *Oriental Tales* (1985), a volume of fiction drawing on Japanese and other folktales; *Two Lives and a Dream* (1987), a collection of three short stories; *The Alms of Alcippe* (1982), poems; *A Blue Tale and Other Stories* (1995); and *Dreams and Destinies* (1999).

Her essay collections include *Sous Bénéfice d'Inventaire* (1978); *Le Temps, ce Grand Sculpteur* (1983, tr. *That Mighty Sculptor, Time*, 1988); and the posthumous *En Pèlerin et en Étranger* (1990). The first of her autobiographical volumes, *Souvenirs Pieux* (1974), deals with the maternal branch of her family. *Archives du Nord* (1977) concerns her paternal ancestors and her father. These have been translated as *Dear Departed* (1991) and *How Many Years* (1995). Yourcenar stated her intention of delineating her life from birth to World War II in the third volume, *Quoi? L'Eternité* (1990, edited by Yvon Bernier, tr. 1997). It was incomplete at the time of her death, but the manuscript actually has little by way of personal revelation, focusing instead on her father.

Yourcenar was a member of the American Academy and Institute of Arts and Letters and the Academy of the French Language and Literature of Belgium.

Youth and the Bright Medusa (1920),   eight short stories by WILLA CATHER. These brief narratives deal mainly with artists of all types and with sophisticates. The influence of

Henry James and Edith Wharton is obvious. "Paul's Case," a story of a neurotic boy, is in this collection. Part of the collection is a reprint of four of the seven stories from *The Troll Garden* (1905).

Youth's Companion, The.   A magazine for young people, founded in Boston, April 16, 1827, by NATHANIEL WILLIS and Asa Rand. It had at the beginning a circulation of several thousand, but the enterprise of later publishers pushed the list of subscribers up to half a million by 1899. In 1857 it became a magazine for adults as well as children and published the work of such distinguished contributors as Harriet Beecher Stowe, Tennyson, Whittier, William Dean Howells, Verne, and Jack London. In the 20th century the magazine began to encounter financial difficulties, merged with THE AMERICAN BOY in 1929, and passed out of existence in 1941. In 1954 four of its former editors—Lovell Thompson, M.A. DeWolfe Howe, Arthur Stanwood Pier, and Harford Powel—compiled an anthology, *Youth's Companion*.

Zara, Louis (1910–   ),   novelist. Born in New York City, Zara worked first in a law printshop in Chicago. He began writing at an early age, and had his first story accepted by H.L. Mencken for the *American Mercury*. Some of his early novels deal with the Jewish immigrant in the United States— among them *Blessed Is the Man* (1935) and *Give Us This Day* (1936). Later Zara turned to historical settings, and his best-known novel is *This Land Is Ours* (1940), which tells the story of the Old Northwest and the beginnings of Chicago. Among his other books are *Rebel Run* (1951), *Blessed Is the Land* (1954), and *Dark Rider* (1961).

Zaturenska, Marya (1902–1982),   poet, historian, biographer. Zaturenska came to the United States from Russia in 1909, was naturalized in 1912, and soon began writing. She married the poet and critic HORACE GREGORY. In 1924 she won the John Reed Memorial Award given by *Poetry*; in 1935, the Shelley Award; in 1936, *Poetry's* Guarantor's Prize; and in 1938 a Pulitzer Prize, for her collection *Cold Morning Sky* (1937). Her other volumes include *Threshold and Hearth* (1934), *The Listening Landscape* (1941), *The Golden Mirror* (1944), *Selected Poems* (1954), *Terraces of Light* (1960), *Collected Poems* (1965), and *The Hidden Waterfall* (1974). She wrote a life of Christina Rossetti (1949) and, with her husband, *A History of American Poetry, 1900–1940* (1946).

Zaza (1898),   a play adapted by DAVID BELASCO from a French play by Pierre Berton and Charles Simon. It portrays a love affair between a married man and a music hall entertainer. The play became the symbol for extreme naughtiness at the turn of the century. Ruggiero Leoncavallo made the play into an opera (premiere, 1900) in which Geraldine Farrar frequently sang the title role.

Zen and the Art of Motorcycle Maintenance.   See ROBERT PIRSIG.

Zenger, [John] Peter (1697–1746),   printer, newspaper publisher. Zenger came to this country from Germany at age thirteen, and at twenty-nine had a printing business of his own in New York City. In 1733 he began publishing the New

York *Weekly Journal*, which became the organ of a group opposed to the arbitrary rule of Governor William Cosby. In 1734 Zenger criticized the removal from office of Chief Justice Lewis Morris and was arrested for libel. He was defended by Andrew Hamilton and acquitted. The verdict was seen as a victory for freedom of the press, particularly after Zenger published *A Brief Narrative of the Case and Trial of John Peter Zenger* (1736), which had a wide circulation.

In his career as a printer Zenger published several tracts, some in Dutch, also the first arithmetic textbook in New York. He was made public printer for the colony of New York (1737) and of New Jersey (1738). Livingston Rutherford wrote his biography (1904). Vincent Buranelli wrote an account of his trial (1957). Kent Cooper wrote a novel, *Anna Zenger* (1946).

Zenith.   The imaginary midwestern town Sinclair Lewis used as a setting for his novel BABBITT (1922), and partially for DODSWORTH (1929).

Zenobia.   An exotic character in Nathaniel Hawthorne's THE BLITHEDALE ROMANCE (1852). She was modeled on MARGARET FULLER and FANNY KEMBLE.

Zenobia, or, The Fall of an Empire (1838),   a historical romance by William Ware. It dealt with the struggles of the early Christians and became a best seller. See HENRY WARE.

Zindel, Paul (1936–   ),   playwright, novelist for young people. Born and educated in New York City, Zindel taught high school for nearly a decade before success with *The Effect of Gamma Rays on Man-in-the-Moon Marigolds* (1965, produced in New York in 1970, Pulitzer Prize) enabled him to concentrate on writing. Tillie, the shy teenager in the play, prepares the experiment named in the title for her school science fair despite struggles with her neurotic mother and sister. Zindel's other plays include *And Miss Rearden Drinks a Little* (1967, produced in New York in 1971); and *Ladies at the Alamo* (1975). His fiction for young people includes *My Darling, My Hamburger* (1969) *Pardon Me, You're Stepping on My Eyeball!* (1976), *The Amazing and Death Defying Diary of Eugene Dingman* (1987), *David and Della* (1993), *The Doom Stone* (1995), *Loch* (1994), and *Rats* (2000).

Zinsser, Hans (1878–1940),   bacteriologist, author. Born in New York City, Zinsser taught at Stanford and Harvard medical schools and served in the medical corps in World War I. *His Rats, Lice and History* (1935) was widely read and admired for its prose style. His autobiography, related in the third person, is called *As I Remember Him* (1940).

Zitkala-Sa.   See GERTRUDE SIMMONS BONNIN.

Zubly, John Joachim (1724–1781),   clergyman, political commentator. Zubly was a Presbyterian clergyman of Swiss birth who became pastor of a church in Savannah. When the Stamp Act agitations began, he was firmly on the side of the colonists and published a sermon called *The Stamp-Act Repealed* (1766) and *An Humble Inquiry into the Nature of the Dependency of the American Colonies* (1769). Elected to the provincial congress of Georgia, he was a delegate to the Conti-

nental Congress in Philadelphia. He also was one of the representatives from Georgia to the Continental Congress at Philadelphia. However, he was unwilling to support what he felt to be radical demands for independence, and when accused of disloyalty, he returned to Georgia, but was banished in 1777.

Zuckerman, Nathan,   a semiautobiographical character in the fiction of PHILIP ROTH. Zuckerman first appeared in *My Life as a Man* (1974). Three later novels and a novella featuring the character were collected as *Zuckerman Bound* in 1985. He continues as a character in later novels, including the Trilogy *American Pastoral* (1997), *I Married a Communist* (1998), and *The Human Stain* (2000).

Zugsmith, Leane (1903–1969),   novelist. Born in Kentucky, Zugsmith was part of a group of leftist authors of the Depression period. *All Victories Are Alike* (1929) is the story of a journalist's loss of idealism. *The Reckoning* (1934) centers on a New York slum child. *A Time to Remember* (1936) deals with unionization, and *The Summer Soldier* (1938) with racism. Her other novels are *Goodbye and Tomorrow* (1931) and *Never Enough* (1932). *Home Is Where You Hang Your Childhood* (1937) and *Hard Times with Easy Payments* (1941) are story collections.

Zukofsky, Louis (1904–1978),   poet. Born of Russian immigrant parents in New York City, Zukofsky became known as a poet relatively late in life. His lyric poetry, which he began writing as a young man, was first printed solely in little magazines. He did not publish a collection until *All the Collected Short Poems, 1923–1958* appeared in 1965. *All the Collected Short Poems, 1956–1964* was published in 1966. Because he edited the 1931 so-called Objectivist number of *Poetry Magazine*, he is often called a leader of the Objectivist school.

Zukofsky began writing his celebrated poem A in 1928. It was printed in three installments (1–12 in 1959; 13–21 in 1969; and the complete version totaling 832 pages in 1979). The individual poems in A show Zukofsky's development over the years during which he worked on it. They may combine personal and historical themes and often comment on specific items with witty associations. Like William Carlos Williams, Zukofsky wanted to use everyday language and focus on common objects in order to deepen appreciation. "A 6," for example, describes a cross-country trip and the materialism and emptiness that the landscape reveals. "A 8" interweaves references to classical music and American history. "A 11" contains a message to the author's son. "A 15" focuses on the assassination of John F. Kennedy. "A 17" is a poem in memory of William Carlos Williams.

Zukofsky's critical work is collected in *Le Style Apollinaire* (Paris, 1934); *A Test of Poetry* (1948); *Bottom: On Shakespeare* (2 v. 1963); *Prepositions* (1967); and *The Gas Age* (1969). He and his wife Celia, a musician, translated Catullus (1969), and she wrote musical settings for some of his lyrics. Zukofsky's fiction includes *It Was* (1961), revised as *Ferdinand* (1968), and *Little; for Careenagers* (1970). Both works are printed together in *Collected Fiction* (1990). See OBJECTIVISM.

Zuñi Indians.   The largest unit of the group of pueblo dwellers. The Zuñi have lived in the area now located just east of the Arizona-New Mexico border for many centuries—the Spanish found them there in 1539. At that time they had a highly developed civilization. They made baskets and pottery, farmed, and lived in terraced buildings of stone and adobe several stories high. Analysis of wooden beams found in these buildings indicates that some were built as early as 919 A.D.

Apparently under Spanish control, the Zuñi preserved their culture and ceremonies covertly and, when Mexico revolted against Spain, they were declared selfgoverning. When the territory came under U.S. control in 1848, the government agreed to respect this right. Famous for their pottery and jew-elry, the Zuñi are among the most prosperous of modern tribal units.

Ruth Bunzel studied Zuñi ceremonials and poetry in several publications of the American Bureau of Ethnology. Three excellent books on the Zuñis are F. H. Cushing's *Outlines of Zuñi Creation Myths* (1896); *Zuñi Folk Tales* (1901, 1931); and *Zuñi Breadstuff* (1920).

Zury, The Meanest Man in Spring County (1887), a novel by JOSEPH KIRKLAND. In this story of Zury Prouder, a native of rural Illinois, and Anne Sparrow, a New England schoolteacher, three elements are combined: the tradition of the frontier, the faint foreshadowings of naturalism, and romance. *The McVeys* (1888) is a sequel.